ANNOTATED
GUIDE TO THE INSOLVENCY LEGIS

TWENTY-SECOND EDITION

VOLUME 2

ANNOTATED GUIDE TO THE INSOLVENCY LEGISLATION

Company Directors Disqualification Act 1986
EU Regulation on Insolvency Proceedings 2015
UNCITRAL Model Law on Cross-Border Insolvency
Cross-Border Insolvency Regulations 2006
Selected Statutes and Statutory Instruments
Practice Direction: Insolvency Proceedings
Other Appendices

Twenty-second Edition

Volume 2

Len Sealy MA LLM PhD, Barrister and Solicitor (NZ)
SJ Berwin Professor Emeritus of Corporate Law,
University of Cambridge

David Milman LLB PhD
Professor of Law
Law School
Lancaster University
Professorial Associate at Exchange Chambers

Peter Bailey LLM
In-House Author, Sweet & Maxwell

SWEET & MAXWELL  THOMSON REUTERS

Disclaimer

The publisher advises that any statutory or other materials issued by the Crown or other relevant bodies and reproduced or quoted in this publication are not the authorised official versions of those statutory or other materials. In their preparation, however, the greatest care has been taken to ensure exact conformity with the law as enacted or other material as issued.

While copyright in all statutory and other materials resides in the Crown or other relevant body, copyright in the remaining material in this publication is vested in the publisher.

Published in 2019 by Thomson Reuters, trading as Sweet & Maxwell.
Thomson Reuters is registered in England & Wales. Company No.1679046.
Registered Office and address for service: 5 Canada Square, Canary Wharf, London E14 5AQ.

For further information on our products and services, visit
http://www.sweetandmaxwell.co.uk

Typeset by Wright and Round Ltd, Gloucestershire
Printed and bound by CPI Group (UK) Ltd, Croydon, CR0 4YY

No natural forests were destroyed to make this product; only farmed timber was used and replanted.

A CIP catalogue record for this book is available from the British Library

ISBN 978-0-414-07068-4

© 1987, 1988, 1991, 1994, 1999 CCH Editions Limited (1st to 5th editions)
© 2001, 2002, 2004, 2005, 2006, 2007 Sweet & Maxwell Ltd (6th to 10th editions)
© 2008, 2010 Thomson Reuters (Legal) Limited (11th to 13th editions)
© 2011–2017 Thomson Reuters (Professional) UK Limited (14th to 20th editions)
© 2018 Thomson Reuters (21st edition)

PREFACE TO THE TWENTY-SECOND EDITION

For insolvency lawyers operating in England and Wales the past 12 months have seen only modest developments in terms of case law and legislative change. But (ignoring Brexit considerations for the moment) important reforms may be on the horizon, both in terms of the law relating to corporate rescue and personal insolvency. For example, we have had significant contributions from the Insolvency Service (26 August 2018) and HM Treasury (October 2018) as to the way forward. Moreover, tucked away in the November 2018 Budget, the Chancellor of the Exchequer announced that we will see the return of an old "favourite"—preferential claims for certain Crown debts. This is a significant volte face in government policy and it may be regarded by secured creditors as a betrayal of the carefully balanced arrangement made under the Enterprise Act 2002 in which they gave up certain economic and legal rights in return for the state agreeing to a diminution of preferential claims. HMRC consulted on the subject on 26 February 2019. Action on some of the Law Commission proposals outlined in "Consumer Prepayments on Retailer Insolvency" (2016) (LC 368, HC 543) on consumer prepayments also seems likely in view of the DBEIS statement issued on 27 December 2018.

Returning to actuality, and looking in particular at the position with regard to corporate insolvency, we see that liquidation remains the predominant regime. One of the more interesting questions concerns how the new creditor decision procedures ushered in by the Small Business, Enterprise and Employment Act 2015 are working in practice. This issue was tested in *Cash Generator Ltd v Fortune* [2018] EWHC 674 (Ch) and although the court came up with a pragmatic solution it indicated that the interaction between the Act and the new rules on decision-making by creditors was something that the Insolvency Rules Committee should look at. Specialists in construction liquidations, using adjudicators, will have been alarmed at the decision in *Michael J Lonsdale (Electrical) Ltd v Bresco Electrical Services Ltd (in liq.)* [2018] EWHC 2043 (TCC) although the recent ameliorating Court of Appeal decision ([2019] EWCA Civ 27) may somewhat have assuaged their fears.

Administration attracts a disproportionate amount of litigation when one considers its limited take up on the ground. There has been plenty of hostile litigation, much of which seeks to show that an administrator has acted unfairly. For the most part, the courts have rebuffed these allegations, but they have intervened in extreme cases. The proper procedure for the establishment of an administration out of court has come under the microscope once again. The saga of *Minmar* [2011] EWHC 1159 (Ch) has been revisited, albeit in a slightly different context. The comments of HHJ Klein in *Re NJM Clothing Ltd* [2018] EWHC 2388 (Ch) have caused concern, but these concerns have abated somewhat in view of the later decisions of HHJ Mathews in *Re Towcester Racecourse Co Ltd* [2018] EWHC 2902 (Ch) and Nugee J in *Re Spaces London Bridge Ltd* [2018] EWHC 3099 (Ch). One cannot help but think that this uncertainty would have been avoided had we retained standard forms in the Insolvency (England and Wales) Rules 2016.

CVAs have become very high profile with the travails on the High Street, but they remain statistically insignificant and generate little in the way of new law. What litigation there is often turns on matters of contractual interpretation, which admittedly can often be a complex question—see for instance *Heis v Financial Services Compensation Scheme Ltd* [2018] EWCA Civ 1327. An important authority is *Wright v Prudential Assurance Co Ltd* [2018] EWHC 402 (Ch) where in the CVA of the old High Street favourite BHS, the court stressed that, although CVAs are a form of statutory contract, it would be wrong to assume that every aspect of general contract law is made applicable.

Receiverships are in what appears to be terminal decline. But they are still just about utilised and cannot be ignored. We therefore note several important cases on the receiver's duty on sale of charged property. The relevant principles here can be extracted from analogous decisions on sales by mortgagees.

Moving away from a procedural/institutional focus we note some developments on director disqualification and also significant case law on misfeasance and wrongful trading. As a result of these decisions a strategically minded insolvency practitioner interested in undertaking effective recovery proceedings would be wise to opt for the former rather than wasting effort with the slim prospects of success on wrongful trading. This is a regrettable state of affairs.

On the personal insolvency front, there have been a number of decisions on what may be regarded as a "liquidated" debt (a prerequisite to presenting a statutory demand). A more fundamental debate concerns the question of when bankruptcy should be used to pursue a debt where it is clear that the debtor has no assets—the decision of HHJ Hodge QC in *Lock v Aylesbury Vale DC* [2018] EWHC 2015 (Ch) may usher in a period of self-doubt for creditors. There have been decisions on the scope of the estate over the years. Usually these take an expansive view so as to maximise potential dividends for creditors, but the curious case of *Gwinnutt v George* [2018] EWHC 2169 (Ch) is the exception that proves the rule.

We have noted a major case on s.340 preferences, namely *Re O'Shaughnessy; Abdulali v Finnegan* [2018] EWHC 1806 (Ch). This largely confirms the continuing importance of *Re MC Bacon Ltd* [1990] B.C.C. 78 and illustrates that an insolvency practitioner wishing to establish that a preference has occurred does not have an easy task because of the subjective mental element that must be established.

IVAs are, in terms of numbers, by far the most important of the personal insolvency procedures. Where IVA litigation occurs, we are reminded by the courts that contract is the order of the day. But good faith can intrude in the same way that it can be an issue in contract law. *Gertner v CFL Finance Ltd* [2018] EWCA Civ 1781 confirms the relevance of the exercise of good faith in the IVA procedure.

There is nothing to report in the way of legal change on debt relief orders. As they are being used extensively in practice that might indicate that this debt resolution tool is working well. Or it might suggest that there is no funding to litigate.

The Insolvency (England and Wales) Rules 2016 are bedding in and appear for the most part to be working effectively. The only significant problem with them has been the well-intentioned abolition of statutory forms. This has created some unexpected difficulties with regard to the appointment of administrators (see above).

Our friends in Scotland will have to undergo the trauma of getting to grips with the new secondary insolvency rules dealing with corporate insolvency, which take effect on 6 April 2019 to replace the Insolvency (Scotland) Rules 1986 (SI 1986/1915) and the Receivers (Scotland) Regulations 1986 (SI 1986/1917 (S.141)). The Insolvency (Scotland) (Company Voluntary Arrangements and Administration) Rules 2018 (SI 2018/1082 (S.4)) and the Insolvency (Scotland) (Receivership and Winding Up) Rules 2018 (SSI 2018/347) are to be found in Vol.2 in unannotated format.

Readers should note that a new version of the *Practice Direction: Insolvency Proceedings* was published in 2018 so as to take effect on 4 July 2018. See [2018] B.C.C. 421. It is reproduced as Appendix IV in Vol.2 and cross-referenced throughout our annotations.

Cross-border insolvency continues to be a litigation driver. There are a number of new authorities on the Cross-Border Insolvency Regulations 2006 (SI 2006/1030) to note. In any post-Brexit world, these Regulations will assume even greater significance.

We conclude this overview with our thoughts on the implications of Brexit which, if it occurs at all, could be deferred to as late as 31 October 2019. We can only go on the position as it stands in late April 2019 and, quite frankly, we have no firm idea of what the applicable legal regime will be for the upcoming 12 months. There are clearly identified possibilities covering the whole spectrum from remaining in the EU to a "hard Brexit", but no certainty as to which of these will prevail. Accordingly, we have decided to retain the EURIP 2015/848 in Vol.2 for this edition and have not changed the legislative text in the Insolvency Act 1986 and the Insolvency Rules in those many instances where the Regulation is referred to. A number of "no-deal" statutory instruments have been published, such as the Insolvency (Amendment) (EU Exit) Regulations 2018 (SI 2019/146) and the Scottish equivalent Insolvency (EU Exit) (Scotland) (Amendment) Regulations 2019 (SSI 2019/94). We hope that things will be clearer by the time we complete our 23rd edition but, if the legal situation changes suddenly and drastically, we would look to either accelerate the publication of the 23rd edition or potentially even produce a supplement to the 22nd edition that will deal with Brexit. There will also be updates to the Westlaw version of this book where relevant. In the meantime, we have reproduced the provisions relevant to England and Wales of the Insolvency (Amendment) (EU Exit) Regulations 2018 (SI 2019/146) in Vol.2 (beginning on p.1366) to assist readers in case of a no-deal Brexit (obviously we have not covered the putative amendments therein).

We would like to thank those readers who have contributed their thoughts. In particular, our gratitude is extended as always to Claire Patient who continues to mastermind the processing of each new edition, and to David Montague, Matt Seys-Llewellyn and Robin Waghorn at Thomson Reuters. Donna McKenzie Skene has provided expert oversight of the Scottish material. Len Sealy continues to oversee our work with a critical eye.

The law is described as it stood on 28 February 2019, although we have managed to update the text at proof stage with some case and legislative amendments (including by the Bankruptcy (Financial Services and Markets Act 2000) Rules 2001 and the Insurers (Winding Up) Rules 2001 (Amendment) Rules 2019 (SI 2019/754) and the Financial Services and Markets (Insolvency) (Amendment of Miscellaneous Enactments) Regulations 2019 (SI 2019/755), both in force from 23 April 2019).

We dedicate this edition to the memory of our friend, Professor Ian Fletcher. Ian was one of the founders of modern insolvency law scholarship in the UK. He typified the need for a clear understanding of how theory interacts with practice. A generation of insolvency law scholars have been influenced by his insights over some 40 years. This text has on a number of occasions been informed by his clear perceptions on particular matters. We all miss him.

Almost unbelievably it seems, Ian's friend and colleague in chambers—Gabriel Moss QC—died as we were finalising this edition. He was truly a titan of the insolvency legal world and the development of the jurisprudence in our subject will be much lessened by his untimely passing. Gabriel too will be sadly missed.

David Milman
Peter Bailey

18 April 2019

ABOUT THE AUTHORS

Len Sealy MA, LLM, PhD, Barrister and Solicitor (NZ) is SJ Berwin Professor Emeritus of Corporate Law at the University of Cambridge. He is an eminent commentator on company and commercial law, having written and lectured extensively in these areas and was for many years General Editor of *British Company Law and Practice*.

David Milman LLB, PhD is Professor of Law at Lancaster University. He is also Co-General Editor of *Insolvency Intelligence* and a Professorial Associate at Exchange Chambers.

Peter Bailey LLM is an In-House Author in Company Law and Insolvency Law at Sweet & Maxwell where he is the In-House Editor of *British Company Law and Practice*, *British Company Cases* and *Sweet & Maxwell's Company Law Newsletter*, and contributes to several other publications, including Totty & Moss, *Insolvency* and Lightman & Moss, *The Law of Administrators and Receivers of Companies* (6th edn).

ABBREVIATIONS

The following abbreviations are used in this work:

BA 1914	Bankruptcy Act 1914
B(A)A 1926	Bankruptcy (Amendment) Act 1926
BEIS	Department for Business, Energy and Industrial Strategy
BIS	Department for Business, Innovation and Skills
BR 1952	Bankruptcy Rules 1952
BRO	Bankruptcy restrictions order
BRU	Bankruptcy restrictions undertaking
CA	Companies Act (e.g. CA 2006 = Companies Act 2006)
CBIR	Cross-Border Insolvency Regulations 2006
CDDA 1986	Company Directors Disqualification Act 1986
CFCSA 1972	Companies (Floating Charges and Receivers) (Scotland) Act 1972
CDO	Competition Disqualification Order
CDU	Competition Disqualification Undertaking
CJA	Criminal Justice Act (e.g. CJA 1988 = Criminal Justice Act 1988)
CMA	Competition and Markets Authority
COMI	Centre of main interests
Cork Report	*Report of the Review Committee on Insolvency Law and Practice* (Cmnd.8558, 1982)
CPR	Civil Procedure Rules
CRAR	Commercial rent arrears recovery
CVA	Company voluntary arrangement
DA 2015	Deregulation Act 2015
DBEIS	Department for Business, Energy and Industrial Strategy
DBERR	Department for Business, Enterprise and Regulatory Reform
DBIS	Department for Business, Innovation and Skills
DRO	Debt relief order
DRRO	Debt relief restrictions order
DRRU	Debt relief restrictions undertaking
DTI	Department of Trade and Industry
EA 2002	Enterprise Act 2002
EC Regulation	EC Regulation on Insolvency Proceedings 2000 (also ECRIP)
ERRA 2013	Enterprise and Regulatory Reform Act 2013
EU Regulation	EU Regulation on Insolvency Proceedings 2015 (also EURIP)
FA	Finance Act (e.g. FA 1985 = Finance Act 1985)
FCA	Financial Conduct Authority
Finality Regulations	Financial Markets and Insolvency (Settlement Finality) Regulations 1999 (SI 1999/2979)
FSA	Financial Services Authority
FSA 1986	Financial Services Act 1986

FSA 2012	Financial Services Act 2012
FSMA 2000	Financial Services and Markets Act 2000
G to E	Model Law on Cross-Border Insolvency Guide to Enactment
HMRC	Her Majesty's Revenue & Customs
IA	Insolvency Act (e.g. IA 1986 = Insolvency Act 1986)
ICC	Insolvency and Companies Court
IPA	Income payments agreement
IPO	Income payments order
IR 1986	Insolvency Rules 1986
IR 2016	Insolvency (England and Wales) Rules 2016
I(A)R	Insolvency (Amendment) Rules (e.g. I(A)R 1993 = Insolvency Amendment Rules 1993)
IVA	Individual voluntary arrangement
Judgments Regulation	Council Regulation (EC) 44/2001 of December 22, 2000 on jurisdiction and the recognition and enforcement of judgments in civil and commercial matters (now recast as Judgments (Regulation 1215/2012)
LLP	Limited liability partnership
LLPA 2000	Limited Liability Partnerships Act 2000
LLPR 2001	Limited Liability Partnerships Regulations 2001 (SI 2001/1090)
LPA 1925	Law of Property Act 1925
LRO 2010	Legislative Reform (Insolvency) (Miscellaneous Amendments) Order 2010
OR	Official receiver
POCA 2002	Proceeds of Crime Act 2002
PRA	Prudential Regulation Authority
RSC	Rules of the Supreme Court
SBEEA 2015	Small Business, Enterprise and Employment Act 2015
TCEA 2007	Tribunals, Courts and Enforcement Act 2007
TLATA 1996	Trusts of Land and Appointment of Trustees Act 1996
TUPE Regulations	Transfer of Undertakings (Protection of Employment) Regulations 2006
White Paper	*A Revised Framework for Insolvency Law* (Cmnd.9175, 1984)

CONTENTS

Case Table

References within square brackets are located in Volume 2.

The following abbreviations are used in the tables to denote the location of entries in all tables:

[CBIR]	Cross-Border Insolvency Regulations 2006
[CDDA]	Company Directors Disqualification Act 1986
[ER]	EU Regulation on Insolvency Proceedings 2015
IA	Insolvency Act 1986
IR	Insolvency (England and Wales) Rules 2016
[UML]	UNCITRAL Model Law on Cross-Border Insolvency

	Provision
19 Entertainment Ltd, Re [2016] EWHC 1545 (Ch); [2017] B.C.C. 347	[CBIR Sch.1 arts 15, 17, 21]
1st Credit (Finance) Ltd v Bartram [2010] EWHC 2910 (Ch); [2011] B.P.I.R. 1	IA 269, 282(1)–(3), IR 10.5
3T Telecom Ltd, Re [2005] EWHC 275 (Ch); [2006] 2 B.C.L.C. 137	IA Sch.B1 para.111(1), (1A), (1B), [ER art.3(1)]
4 Eng Ltd v Harper; [2009] EWHC 2633 (Ch); [2010] B.C.C. 746; [2010] B.P.I.R. 1	IA 423(1)–(3), 425(1), 425(2), (3)
A Ltd, Petitioner [2016] SC Edin 77	IA 117
A/Wear UK (In admin.) Ltd, Re [2013] EWCA Civ 1626; [2014] 1 P. & C.R. DG15	IA Sch.B1 para.43(6)
A&BC Chewing Gum Ltd, Re [1975] 1 W.L.R. 579 Ch D	IA 123
A&C Group Services Ltd, Re [1993] B.C.L.C. 1297 Ch D	[CDDA 12C]
A&C Supplies Ltd, Re [1998] B.C.C. 708; [1998] B.P.I.R. 303 Ch D	IA 29(2), 45(1), (2), 172(1), (2)
A&J Fabrications (Batley) Ltd v Grant Thornton (A Firm) (No.1) [1999] B.C.C. 807 Ch D	IA 212(1)

	Provision
AA Mutual International Insurance Co Ltd, Re [2004] EWHC 2430 (Ch); [2005] 2 B.C.L.C. 8	IA 8, Sch.B1 paras 9, para.11
AA v BA [2015] IESC 102	IA 306
Aabar Block Sarl v Maud [2015] EWHC 3681 (Ch); [2016] B.P.I.R. 227	IA 266(3), (4), 271(3), IR 10.5
Aabar Block Sarl v Maud [2016] EWHC 1016 (Ch); [2016] B.P.I.R. 803	IA 266(3), (4), 271(3), IR 10.5
Aabar Block Sarl v Maud [2016] EWHC 2175 (Ch); [2016] Bus. L.R. 1243; [2016] B.P.I.R. 1486	IA 266(3), (4), IR 10.5
Aabar Block Sarl v Maud [2018] EWHC 1414 (Ch); [2019] Ch. 15; [2018] B.P.I.R. 1207	IA 271(3)
Aaron v Secretary of State for Business, Enterprise and Regulatory Reform [2008] EWCA Civ 1146; [2009] B.C.C. 375	[CDDA 7(1)]
AB Agri Ltd v Curtis [2016] B.P.I.R. 1297 Cty Ct	IA 262, IR 15.31
Abbey Forwarding Ltd (In liq.) v Revenue and Customs Commissioners [2015] EWHC 225 (Ch); [2015] Bus. L.R. 882	IA 135
Abbey Forwarding Ltd v Hone [2010] EWHC 1644 (Ch); [2010] B.P.I.R. 1053	IA 168(5)
Abbey Leisure Ltd, Re [1990] B.C.C. 60 CA (Civ Div)	IA 125(2)

Provision

Provision

Case Table

	Provision
Black v Sale Service and Maintenance Ltd [2018] EWHC 1344 (Ch); [2018] B.P.I.R. 1260 ... IA 127, IR 10.5
Blackburn v Alexander [2015] CSOH 179; 2016 G.W.D. 2–48 ... IA 242
Blackspur Group Plc (No.2), Re [1998] 1 W.L.R. 422; [1998] B.C.C. 11 CA (Civ Div) ... [CDDA 1, 7(1)]
Blackspur Group Plc (No.3), Re; sub nom. Secretary of State for Trade and Industry v Davies (No.3) [2001] EWCA Civ 1595; [2004] B.C.C. 839 [CDDA, 1A]
Blackspur Group Plc, Re; sub nom. Secretary of State for Trade and Industry v Eastaway [2003] B.C.C. 520 Ch D ... [CDDA, 7(1)]
Blair Carnegie Nimmo (as Liquidator of St Margaret's School Edinburgh Ltd), Re [2013] CSOH 4; [2013] B.P.I.R. 188 ... IA 135, IR 18.28
Blavo v Law Society [2018] EWCA Civ 2250; [2018] B.P.I.R. 1704 ... IA 267(1), (2)
Blemain Finance Ltd v Goulding [2013] EWCA Civ 1630; [2014] 1 P. & C.R. DG16 ... IA 283, 284(1)–(3), (6)
Blight v Brewster [2012] EWHC 165 (Ch); [2012] 1 W.L.R. 2841; [2012] B.P.I.R. 476 ... IA Pt III, 342A
Blights Builders Ltd, Re [2006] EWHC 3549 (Ch); [2007] 3 All E.R. 776; [2007] B.C.C. 712 ... IA Sch.B1 paras 25, 104, IR 1.2, 12.64
Block Transfer by Kaye, Re a [2010] EWHC 692 (Ch); [2010] B.P.I.R. 602 IA 263(4), IR Pt 12 Ch.6 sub-div.B
Bloom v Pensions Regulator. See Nortel Companies, Re
Blue Monkey Gaming Ltd v Hudson [2014] 4 All E.R. (D) 222 Ch D ... IA Sch.B1 para.67
BLV Realty Organisation Designs Ltd, Re [2010] EWHC 1791 (Ch) ... IA 123
BNY Corporate Trustee Services Ltd v Eurosail-UK 2007–3BL Plc [2013] UKSC 28; [2013] 1 W.L.R. 1408; [2013] B.C.C. 397 ... IA Pt IV, 123(1)
Bolsover DC v Ashfield Nominees Ltd [2010] EWCA Civ 1129; [2012] B.C.C. 803; [2011] B.P.I.R. 7 ... IA 123, Pt IX Ch.1, 267(1), (2)

	Provision
Bonney v Mirpuri [2013] B.P.I.R. 412 . IA 276(1), 376
Bonus Breaks Ltd, Re [1991] B.C.C. 546 Ch D (Companies Ct) ... IA 216(3)
Boorer v Boorer's Trustee in Bankruptcy [2002] B.P.I.R. 21 ... IA Pt IX
Border Counties Farmers Ltd, Re [2017] EWHC 2610 (Ch) ... IA 250
Borodzicz v Horton [2016] B.P.I.R. 24 Ch D ... IA 299(5), 304(2), IR 18.16, [App.IV]
Botleigh Grange Ltd v Revenue and Customs Commissioners [2016] EWHC 3081 (Ch) ... IA 123
Boulton v Queen Margaret's School, York Ltd [2018] EWHC 3729 (Ch) .. IA 271(3)
Bournemouth & Boscombe Athletic Football Club Co Ltd, Re [1998] B.P.I.R. 183 Ch D ... IA 6(3), IR 2.25–2.38
Bowe Watts Clargo Ltd [2017] EWHC 7879 (Ch) ... IR 14.25
Bowen Travel Ltd, Re [2012] EWHC 3405 (Ch); [2013] B.C.C. 182 ... IA Sch.B1 paras 3(1), (3), 13(1), (3)
Bower v Marris, 41 E.R. 525; (1841) Cr. & Ph. 351 Ch ... IR 14.23
Bowles v Trefilov unreported 29 April 2016 ... IA 279(3)–(5), 210
Bowman Power Systems (UK) Ltd, Re unreported 26 October 2004 Ch D .. IA 216(3)
Boyd & Hutchinson v Foenander [2003] EWCA Civ 1516; [2004] B.P.I.R. 20 ... IA 306
Boyden v Canty (No.2) [2007] EWCA Civ 241; [2007] B.P.I.R. 299 ... IA 311(1), 363(2), (4)
Boyden v Watson [2004] B.P.I.R. 1131 CC ... IA 310(1), (1A), (2)
BPE Solicitors v Gabriel [2015] UKSC 39; [2015] A.C. 1663 ... IA 306
BPR Ltd, Re [1998] B.C.C. 259 Ch D . [CDDA 22(5)]
Brabon, Re [2000] B.C.C. 1171; [2000] B.P.I.R. 537 Ch D ... IA 339(1)–(3), 423(1)–(3)
BRAC Rent-A-Car International Inc, Re [2003] EWHC 128 (Ch); [2003] 1 W.L.R. 1421; [2003] B.C.C. 248 ... [ER Preamble 25, art.3, 3(1)]
Bradburn v Kaye [2006] B.P.I.R. 605 Ch D ... IA 276(1)

Provision

Provision

Cooper v Fearnley [1997] B.P.I.R. 20 Ch D . . . . IA 255(1), (2)

Cooper v Official Receiver [2002] EWHC 1970 (Ch); [2003] B.P.I.R. 55 IA 276(1)

Cooper v PRG Powerhouse Ltd [2008] EWHC 498 (Ch); [2008] 2 All E.R. (Comm) 964; [2008] B.C.C. 588. . . . IA 107

Cooperative Bank Plc v Phillips [2014] EWHC 2862 (Ch); [2014] B.P.I.R. 1430. . . . . IA 42(1), Pt VIII

Co-operative Bank Plc v Phillips [2017] EWHC 1320 (Ch); [2017] B.P.I.R. 1156. . . . . IA Pt VIII

Copecrest Ltd, Re [1993] B.C.C. 844 CA (Civ Div). . . . . [CDDA 7(2)]

Copeland & Craddock Ltd, Re [1997] B.C.C. 294 CA (Civ Div) . . . . IA 125(2)

Corbenstoke Ltd (No.2), Re (1989) 5 B.C.C. 767 Ch D (Companies Ct) . . . IA 172(1), (2)

Cork v Gill [2004] EWHC 2536 (Ch); [2005] B.P.I.R. 272 . . . . IA 340(4), (5)

Cork v Rawlins [2001] EWCA Civ 202; [2001] Ch. 792; [2001] B.P.I.R. 222 . IA 283(2), (3), 306

Cornelius v Casson [2008] B.P.I.R. 504 Ch D . . . . IA 260(1), (2), (2A)

Cornercare Ltd, Re [2010] EWHC 893 (Ch); [2010] B.C.C. 592 . . . . IA Sch.B1 para.28

Cornhill Insurance Plc v Cornhill Financial Services Ltd [1992] B.C.C. 818. . . . . IR 12.59

Cornhill Insurance Plc v Improvement Services Ltd [1986] 1 W.L.R. 114; (1986) 2 B.C.C. 98942 Ch D . . . . IA 123(1)

Coroin Ltd (No.2), Re; sub nom. McKillen v Misland (Cyprus) Ltd [2013] EWCA Civ 781; [2014] B.C.C. 14. . . . . [CDDA 22(5)]

Corporate Jet Realisations Ltd (In liq.), Re [2015] EWHC 221 (Ch); [2015] B.C.C. 625. IA 234(1), (2), 236(3), (3A)

Corran v Butters [2017] EWHC 2294 (Ch) . . . . IA 307(2), (5), [CDDA 11]

Corvin Construction Ltd, Re unreported 21 December 2012 . . . . IA 124A

Cosco Bulk Carrier Co Ltd v Armada Shipping SA [2011] EWHC 216 (Ch); [2011] 2 All E.R. (Comm) 481; [2011] B.P.I.R. 626 . . . . IA 130(2),

[CBIR Sch.1 art.21.2]

Cosslett (Contractors) Ltd (In admin.) (No.2); sub nom. Re Smith (Administrator of Cosslett (Contractors) Ltd) v Bridgend CBC; Re [2001] UKHL 58; [2002] 1 A.C. 336; [2001] B.C.C. 740 . . . . IA 87(2), 234(1), (2), IR 14.25

Cosslett (Contractors) Ltd, Re [1998] Ch. 495; [1997] B.C.C. 724 CA (Civ Div). . . . . IA 234(1), (2)

Cosy Seal Insulation Ltd (In admin.), Re [2016] EWHC 1255 (Ch); [2016] 2 B.C.L.C. 319 . . . . IA 123(1), 239(6)

Cotswold Co Ltd, Re [2009] EWHC 1151 (Ch); [2010] B.C.C. 812 . . . . . . IA 4(3), 5(2)

Coulter v Chief Constable of Dorset [2004] EWCA Civ 1259; [2005] 1 W.L.R. 130; [2005] B.P.I.R. 62 . . . . . IA 267(1), (2), 10.5

Coulter v Chief Constable of Dorset [2005] EWCA Civ 1113; [2006] B.P.I.R. 10 . . . . IR 10.5

Country Farm Inns Ltd, Re [1997] B.C.C. 801 CA (Civ Div) . . . . [CDDA 6(1)]

County Bookshops Ltd v Grove [2002] EWHC 1160 (Ch); [2002] B.P.I.R. 772. . . . . IA 7(3)

County Leasing Management Ltd v Hawkes [2015] EWCA Civ 1251; [2016] B.C.C. 102 . . . . IA Pt IV Ch.IX

Courts Plc (In liq.), Re [2008] EWHC 2339 (Ch); [2009] 1 W.L.R. 1499; [2008] B.C.C. 917 . . . . IA 176A(3)–(5)

Courtwood Holdings SA v Woodley Properties Ltd [2018] EWHC 2163 (Ch) . . . . IA Pt III

Coutts & Co v Passey [2007] B.P.I.R. 323 Ch D . . . . IA 262

Coutts & Co v Stock [2000] 1 W.L.R. 906; [2000] B.C.C. 247 Ch D . . . . . IA 127

Cove (A Debtor), Re [1990] 1 W.L.R. 708; [1990] 1 All E.R. 949 Ch D . . . . IA 252(2), 256(5), 257(1), 262(4)–(7)

Cover Europe Ltd, Re [2002] EWHC 861 (Ch); [2002] B.P.I.R. 931 . . . . . . [ER Preamble 7, art.32]

Cowey v Insol Funding Ltd [2012] EWHC 2421 (Ch); [2012] B.P.I.R. 958. . . . . IA 306

Provision   **Provision**

Coyne v DRC Distribution Ltd [2008]
EWCA Civ 488; [2008] B.C.C. 612;
[2008] B.P.I.R. 1247 . . . .   IA Sch.B1
para.88

Cozens v Customs and Excise
Commissioners [2000] B.P.I.R. 252
CA (Civ Div) . . . .   IR 10.5

CQH1 Ltd and RTD1 Ltd, Re. *See*
Secretary of State for Business,
Energy and Industrial Strategy v
Steven

Craig v Humberclyde Industrial
Finance Group Ltd [1999] 1 W.L.R.
129; [1999] B.C.C. 378 . . . .   IA Sch.4 para.6

Craiglaw Developments Ltd v Gordon
Wilson & Co 1997 S.C. 356; [1998]
B.C.C. 530 CSIH (Ex Div) . . . .   IA 243

Crammer v West Bromwich Building
Society [2012] EWCA Civ 517;
[2012] B.P.I.R. 963 . . . .   IA 282(1), (3),
375(1)

Cranley Mansions Ltd, Re; sub nom.
Saigol v Goldstein [1994] 1 W.L.R.
1610; [1994] B.C.C. 576 Ch D . . . . .   IA 6, IR
2.25–2.38

Credit and Mercantile Plc v Kaymuu
Ltd [2014] EWHC 1746 (Ch); [2014]
B.P.I.R. 1127 . . . .   IA 283(2), (3)

Credit Lucky Ltd v National Crime
Agency [2014] EWHC 83 (Ch) . . . . .   IA 147(1),
12.59

Crestjoy Products Ltd, Re [1990]
B.C.C. 23 Ch D (Companies Ct) . . . .   [CDDA 7(2)]

Crigglestone Coal Co Ltd, Re [1906] 2
Ch. 327 CA . . . .   IA 125(1)

Croftbell Ltd, Re [1990] B.C.C. 781 Ch
D (Companies Ct) . . . .   IA Pt III, 29(2),
Sch.A1 para.45,
Sch.B1
para.14(2), (3)

Cross Construction Sussex Ltd v Tseliki
[2006] EWHC 1056 (Ch); [2006]
B.P.I.R. 888 . . . .   IA 265, [ER
art.3(1)]

Crossley-Cooke v Europanel (UK) Ltd
[2010] EWHC 124 (Ch); [2010]
B.P.I.R. 561 . . . .   IR 10.5

Crown Holdings (London) Ltd (In liq.),
Re; [2015] EWHC 1876 (Ch); [2015]
2 P. & C.R. DG20 . . . .   IA 107

Cruz City 1 Mauritius Holdings v
Unitech Ltd [2014] EWHC 3131
(Comm); [2015] 1 All E.R. (Comm)
336 . . . .   IA Pt III

Crystal Palace FC Ltd v Kavanagh
[2013] EWCA Civ 1410; [2014] 1
All E.R. 1033; [2014] B.C.C. 664 . . .   IA Sch.B1
para.3

CU Fittings Ltd, Re (1989) 5 B.C.C.
210 Ch D (Companies Ct) . . . .   [CDDA 12C]

Cubelock Ltd, Re [2001] B.C.C. 523 Ch
D . . . .   [CDDA 6(1),
12C]

Cuckmere Brick Co v Mutual Finance
[1971] Ch. 949; [1971] 2 W.L.R.
1207 . . . .   IA Pt III

Cullen Investments Ltd v Brown [2017]
EWHC 2793 (Ch) . . . .   IA 212(3)

Cullinane v Inland Revenue
Commissioners [2000] B.P.I.R. 996
Ch D . . . .   IA 268

Cumming's Trustee v Glenrinnes Farms
Ltd; sub nom. Taylor, Petitioner 1993
S.L.T. 904; [1993] B.C.C. 829 CSOH   IA 82(1), (2)

Cummings v Claremont Petroleum NL
[1998] B.P.I.R. 187 HC (Aus) . . . . . .   IA 306

Cupit, Re [1996] B.P.I.R. 560 (Note)
CA (Civ Div) . . . .   IA 253(1)–(3)

Customs and Excise Commissioners v
Allen [2003] B.P.I.R. 830 Ch D . . . .   IA 172(1), (2),
10.77

CVC/Opportunity Equity Partners Ltd v
Demarco Almeida [2002] UKPC 16;
[2002] B.C.C. 684 . . . .   IA 122(1),
125(2)

Cyona Distributors Ltd, Re [1967] Ch.
889 CA . . . .   IA 213(2)

D'Eye, Re [2016] B.P.I.R. 883   306

D'Jan of London Ltd, Re [1993] B.C.C.
646 Ch D (Companies Ct) . . . .   IA 212(1),
212(3), 214(4)

D/S Norden A/S v Samsun Logix Corp
[2009] EWHC 2304 (Ch); [2009]
B.P.I.R. 1367 . . . . [CBIR para.2(i)]

D&D Marketing (UK) Ltd, Re [2002]
EWHC 660 (Ch); [2003] B.P.I.R. 539   IA 123

D&D Wines International Ltd, Re
[2014] EWCA Civ 215; [2015] 1 All
E.R. (Comm) 36; [2014] B.P.I.R. 90 .   IA 107

Dadourian Group International Inc v
Simms [2008] EWHC 723 (Ch);
[2008] B.P.I.R. 508 . . . .   IA 282(1), (3),
285(3), (4),
287(1), (2), 306

Daewoo Motor Co Ltd v Stormglaze
UK Ltd [2005] EWHC 2799 (Ch);
[2006] B.P.I.R. 415 . . . .   IA 135

Case Table

	Provision

Dairy Farmers of Britain Ltd, Re [2009] EWHC 1389 (Ch); [2010] Ch. 63; [2010] B.C.C. 637 . . . . IA 29(2), 37(1), (2), Sch.B1, para.111(1), 111(1A), 111(1B)

Daisytek-ISA Ltd, Re [2003], B.C.C. 562; [2004] B.P.I.R. 30 Ch D . . . . . . [ER art.3(1)]

Dallhold Estates (UK) Pty Ltd, Re [1992] B.C.C. 394 Ch D (Companies Ct) . . . . IA 426(4), (5), (11)

Dalnyaya Step LLC (In liq.), Re; Cherkasov v Olegovich; Cherkasov v Nogotkov [2017] EWHC 756 (Ch); [2017] 1 W.L.R. 4264; [2019] B.C.C. 1 . . . . [CBIR, Sch.1 art.17]

Daltel Europe Ltd (In liq.) v Makki (No.1) [2004] EWHC 726 (Ch); [2005] 1 B.C.L.C. 594 . . . . IA 236

Dana (UK) Ltd, Re [1999] 2 B.C.L.C. 239 Ch D . . . . IA Sch.B1 para.53, 54, 68(2), (3)

Danka Business Systems Plc (In liq.), Re [2013] EWCA Civ 92; [2013] Ch. 506; [2013] B.C.C. 450 . . . . IR 14.14

DAP Holding NV, Re [2005] EWHC 2092 (Ch); [2006] B.C.C. 48 . . . . IA 220

Darbyshire v Turpin [2013] EWHC 954 (Ch); [2013] B.P.I.R. 558 . . . . IR 10.5, 10.18

Darjan Estate Co Plc v Hurley [2012] EWHC 189 (Ch); [2012] 1 W.L.R. 1782; [2012] B.P.I.R. 1021 . . . . IA 267(1), (2), IR 10.5

Darrell v Miller [2003] EWHC 2811 (Ch); [2004] B.P.I.R. 470 . . . . IA 172(1), (2)

Data Power Systems Ltd v Safehosts (London) Ltd [2013] EWHC 2479 (Ch); [2013] B.C.C. 721 . . . . IA Sch.B1 para.3(1), (3)

Davey v Money [2018] EWHC 766 (Ch); [2018] Bus. L.R. 1903 . . . . IA Pt III, Sch.B1 paras 3(1), (3), 49(2), 69, 75

Davidson v Stanley [2004] EWHC 2595 (Ch); [2005] B.P.I.R. 279 . . . . . IA 255(1), (2)

Davies (A Bankrupt), Re [1997] B.P.I.R. 619 Ch D . . . . IA 285(2)

Davies v Barnes Webster & Sons Ltd [2011] EWHC 2560 (Ch); [2012] B.P.I.R. 97 . . . . IR 10.5

	Provision

Davies v United Kingdom (42007/98) [2005] B.C.C. 401; (2002) 35 E.H.R.R. 29 ECHR . . . . [CDDA]

Davis v Jackson [2017] EWHC 698 (Ch); [2017] 1 W.L.R. 4005; [2017] B.P.I.R. 950 . . . . IA 335A

Davis v Martin-Sklan [1995] B.C.C. 1122; [1996] B.P.I.R. 160 Ch D (Bankruptcy) . . . . IA 263(5), (6)

Davis v Trustee in Bankruptcy of the Estate of Davis [1998] B.P.I.R. 572 Ch D . . . . IA 306

Davy v Pickering [2015] EWHC 380 (Ch); [2016] B.C.C. 50 . . . . IA Pt IV Ch.IX

Dawodu v American Express Bank [2001] B.P.I.R. 983 Ch D . . . . IR 10.24

Dawson Print Group Ltd, Re (1987) 3 B.C.C. 322 Ch D (Companies Ct) . . . [CDDA 12C]

Day v Haine; sub nom. Haine v Day [2008] EWCA Civ 626; [2008] B.C.C. 845; [2008] B.P.I.R. 1343 . . . IA Sch.B1 para.99(5)–(6), IR 7.108(1)–(4), 14.1, 14.2

Day v Refulgent Ltd [2016] EWHC 7 (Ch); [2016] B.P.I.R. 594 . . . . IA 271(3)

Day v Shaw [2014] EWHC 36 (Ch); [2014] 2 P. & C.R. DG1 . . . . IA 335A

Day v Tiuta International Ltd [2014] EWCA Civ 1246; [2015] 1 P. & C.R. DG10 . . . . IA Pt III

DC, HS, AD v United Kingdom (39031/97) [2000] B.C.C. 710 . . . . . [CDDA]

De Toucy v Bonhams 1793 Ltd [2011] EWHC 3809 (Ch); [2012] B.P.I.R. 793 . . . . IA 271(1), (2), (4), IR 12.24

Dean & Dean (A Firm) v Angel Airlines SA [2009] EWHC 447 (Ch); [2009] B.P.I.R. 409 . . . . IA 267(1), (2), 271(1), (2), (4)

Dean v Stout [2004] EWHC 3315 (Ch); [2006] 1 F.L.R. 725; [2005] B.P.I.R. 1113 . . . . IA 335A

Deansgate 123 LLP v Workman; Forrester v Workman [2019] EWHC 2 (Ch) . . . . IA 423, 425(1)

Dear v Reeves [2001] EWCA Civ 277; [2002] Ch. 1; [2001] B.P.I.R. 577 . . . IA 436

Debtor (No.400 of 1940), Re; sub nom. Debtor v Dodwell [1949] Ch. 236 Ch D . . . . IA 168(5), 303(1)

	Provision		Provision
Secretary of State for Business, Innovation and Skills v Chohan [2011] EWHC 1350 (Ch); [2012] 1 B.C.L.C. 138	[CDDA 6(1), 7(1)]	Secretary of State for Business, Innovation and Skills v PGMRS Ltd [2010] EWHC 2983 (Ch); [2011] B.C.C. 368	IA 124A
Secretary of State for Business, Innovation and Skills v Chohan, sub nom. Re UKLI Ltd [2013] EWHC 680 (Ch); [2013] Lloyd's Rep. F.C. 351	[CDDA 22(5)]	Secretary of State for Business, Innovation and Skills v Potiwal [2012] EWHC 3723 (Ch); [2013] Lloyd's Rep. F.C. 124	[CDDA 7(1)]
Secretary of State for Business, Innovation and Skills v Combined Maintenance Services Ltd unreported 6 November 2014	IA 124A, IR 7.4–7.12	Secretary of State for Business, Innovation and Skills v Rahman [2017] EWHC 2468 (Ch); [2018] B.C.C. 567	[CDDA 1(2), 2(1), (3), 6(4)]
Secretary of State for Business, Innovation and Skills v Coward [2011] B.C.C. 712 EAT	IA Pt IV	Secretary of State for Business, Innovation and Skills v Reza [2013] CSOH 86; 2013 G.W.D. 19–380	[CDDA 12C]
Secretary of State for Business, Innovation and Skills v Doffman [2010] EWHC 3175 (Ch); [2011] 2 B.C.L.C. 541	[CDDA 12C]	Secretary of State for Business, Innovation and Skills v Warry [2014] EWHC 1381 (Ch)	[CDDA 1(2)]
Secretary of State for Business, Innovation and Skills v Harriss [2016] EWHC 794 (Ch)	[CDDA 1(1)]	Secretary of State for Business, Innovation and Skills v Weston [2014] EWHC 2933 (Ch); [2014] B.C.C. 581	[CDDA 2(1), 4(1), 7]
Secretary of State for Business, Innovation and Skills v Hawkhurst Capital Plc [2013] EWHC 4219 (Ch); [2016] B.C.C. 125	IA 124A, 135	Secretary of State for Business, Innovation and Skills v World Future Ltd [2013] EWHC 723 (Ch)	IA 124A
Secretary of State for Business, Innovation and Skills v Jeromson [2013] ScotSC 26	[CDDA 12C]	Secretary of State for Trade and Industry v Arif [1996] B.C.C. 586 Ch D	[CDDA 1(1), 1(2)]
Secretary of State for Business, Innovation and Skills v KJK Investments Ltd; Secretary of State for Business, Innovation and Skills v G Loans Ltd [2015] EWHC 1589 (Ch)	IA 124A	Secretary of State for Trade and Industry v Arnold [2007] EWHC 1933 (Ch); [2008] B.C.C. 119	[CDDA 6(3)–(3C), 7(1)]
Secretary of State for Business, Innovation and Skills v Melaris (Re Waterfall Media Ltd) [2013] B.P.I.R. 1109	IA 279(3)–(5)	Secretary of State for Trade and Industry v Ashcroft (No.1) [1998] Ch. 71; [1997] B.C.C. 634 CA (Civ Div)	[CDDA 7(1)]
Secretary of State for Business, Innovation and Skills v New Horizon Energy Ltd [2015] EWHC 2961 (Ch); [2017] B.C.C. 629	IA 124A, 135	Secretary of State for Trade and Industry v Aurum Marketing Ltd [2002] B.C.C. 31 CA (Civ Div)	IA 124A
Secretary of State for Business, Innovation and Skills v PAG Management Services Ltd [2015] EWHC 2404 (Ch); [2015] B.C.C. 720; [2015] R.A. 519	IA 87(1), 91(1), 124A	Secretary of State for Trade and Industry v Bairstow [2003] EWCA Civ 321; [2004] Ch. 1; [2003] B.C.C. 682	[CDDA 7(1)]
Secretary of State for Business, Innovation and Skills v Pawson [2015] EWHC 2626 (Ch)	[CDDA 8(1)]	Secretary of State for Trade and Industry v Baker (No.2); sub nom. Barings Plc (No.2), Re [1998] Ch. 356; [1998] B.C.C. 888 Ch D (Companies Ct	[CDDA 1, 7(1)]
		Secretary of State for Trade and Industry v Baker (No.5) [2001] B.C.C. 273 CA (Civ Div)	[CDDA 6(1), 12C, 9A(5)–(8)]

Provision		Provision

Timothy, Re [2005] EWHC 1885 (Ch); [2006] B.P.I.R. 329 . . . . IA 262(1)–(3), (8)

Titan International Inc, Re [1998] 1 B.C.L.C. 102 CA (Civ Div) . . . . IA 124A

TLL Realisations Ltd, Re [2000] B.C.C. 998 Ch D . . . . [CDDA 1(1), 17]

TM Kingdom Ltd (In admin.), Re [2007] EWHC 3272 (Ch); [2007] B.C.C. 480 . . . . IA Sch.B1 paras 79(2), 83

Tobian Properties Ltd, Re [2012] EWCA Civ 998; [2013] B.C.C. 98 . . IA 124(2)–(4A)

Todd (Swanscombe), Re [1990] B.C.C. 125 Ch D (Companies Ct) . . . . IA 213(1)

Tomlinson v Bridging Finance Ltd [2010] B.P.I.R. 759 CC . . . . IA 284

Tony Rowse NMC Ltd, Re [1996] B.C.C. 196 Ch D . . . . IR 7.108(1)–(4), 18.23

Top Brands Ltd v Sharma [2015] EWCA Civ 1140; [2016] B.C.C. 1; [2016] B.P.I.R. 111 . . . . IA 212(1)

Top Marques Car Rental Ltd, Re [2006] EWHC 746 (Ch); [2006] B.P.I.R. 1328 . . . . IA Sch.B1 para.76

Toshoku Finance UK Plc (In liq.), Re; sub nom. Khan v Inland Revenue Commissioners [2002] UKHL 6; [2002] 1 W.L.R. 671; [2002] B.C.C. 110 HL . . . . IA 115, Sch.B1 para.99(3)–(4), IR 7.108(1)–(4), 14.1

Total Network SL v Revenue and Customs Commissioners [2008] UKHL 19; [2008] 1 A.C. 1174 [2008] B.P.I.R. 699 . . . . IA Pt IX Ch.1

Tottenham Hotspur Plc v Edennote Plc [1994] B.C.C. 681 Ch D . . . . IR 14.1

Tout and Finch Ltd, Re [1954] 1 W.L.R. 178 Ch D . . . . IA 283(2), (3)

Towcester Racecourse Co Ltd (in admin.), Re [2018] EWHC 2902 (Ch); [2019] B.C.C. 274 . . . . IA Sch.B1 para.29, 31, IR 3.23–3.26, 12–64

Townsend v Biscoe [2010] WL 3166608 Ch D . . . . IA Sch.B1 para.71

Towsey (t/a Towsey Plastering Contractors) v Highgrove Homes Ltd

[2013] B.L.R. 45 Ch D (Companies Ct) . . . . IA 123

TPS Investments (UK) Ltd; sub nom. Tailby v Hutchinson Telecom FZCO (in admin.), Re [2018] EWHC 360 (Ch); [2019] 1 B.C.L.C. 61 . . . . IA Sch.B1 para.43(6), IR 3.62–3.70

Tradegro (UK) Ltd v Wigmore Street Investments Ltd [2011] EWCA Civ 268; [2011] 2 B.C.L.C. 616 . . . . IA 107, 130(2)

Tradestar Ltd v Goldfarb [2018] EWHC 3595 (Ch) . . . . IA 213, 213(2)

Trading Partners Ltd, Re; Akers v Lomas [2002] B.P.I.R. 606 Ch D . . . IA 236, 236(2), 426(4), (5), (11)

Tradition (UK) Ltd v Ahmed [2008] EWHC 2946 (Ch); [2009] B.P.I.R. 626 . . . . IA 256(1), 262, IR 15.23

Trainfx Ltd, Re; sub nom. Hellenic Capital Investments Ltd v Trainfx Ltd [2015] EWHC 3713 (Ch); [2016] B.C.C. 493 . . . . IA Sch.B1 paras 11, 14, 35

Tramway Building & Construction Co Ltd, Re [1988] Ch. 293; (1987) 3 B.C.C. 443 Ch D . . . . IA 127

Transbus International Ltd (In liq.), Re [2004] EWHC 932 (Ch); [2004] 1 W.L.R. 2654; [2004] B.C.C. 401 . . . . IA Sch.B1, para.68(2), (3)

Transmetro Corp Ltd v Real Investments Pty Ltd (1999) 17 A.C.L.C. 1314 . . . . IA 178(3)

Transocean Equipment Manufacturing & Trading Ltd, Re [2005] EWHC 2603 (Ch); [2006] B.C.C. 184; [2006] B.P.I.R. 594 . . . . IA 212(1)

TransTec Automotive (Campsie) Ltd, Re [2001] B.C.C. 403 Ch D (Companies Ct) . . . . IA 37(1), (2)

TransTec Plc, Re [2005] EWHC 1723 (Ch); [2006] B.C.C. 295 . . . . [CDDA 1(4)]

TransTec Plc, Re [2006] EWHC 2110 (Ch); [2007] B.C.C. 313 . . . . [CDDA 12C]

Transworld Trading Ltd, Re [1999] B.P.I.R. 628 Ch D . . . . IA 239(6)

Travel Mondial (UK) Ltd, Re [1991] B.C.C. 224 Ch D (Companies Ct) . . . [CDDA 12C]

Treasury Solicitor v Doveton [2008] EWHC 2812 (Ch); [2009] B.P.I.R. 352 . . . . IA 423(1)–(3)

Provision | Provision

Provision

Welsby v Brelec Installations Ltd (In liq.) [2001] B.C.C. 421; [2001] B.P.I.R. 210 Ch D .... IA 7(4)

Welsh Development Agency v Export Finance Co Ltd [1992] B.C.C. 270 CA (Civ Div) .... IA 234(3), (4)

Welsh Ministers v Price [2017] EWCA Civ 1768; [2018] 1 W.L.R. 738; [2018] B.C.C. 93 .... IA Pt IV Ch.IX

Welsh v Bank of Ireland [2013] NIMaster 6 .... IR 10.5

Wentworth Sons Sub-Debt SARL v Lomas [2017] EWHC 3158 (Ch) ... IR 14.3–14.11

WeSellCNC.com Ltd, Re [2013] EWHC 4577 (Ch) .... IA 166(4), (5)

Wessex Computer Stationers Ltd, Re [1992] B.C.L.C. 366 Ch D .... IA 124(2)–(4A)

West Bromwich Building Society v Crammer [2002] EWHC 2618 (Ch); [2003] B.P.I.R. 783 .... IA 267(1), (2)

West Coast Gold Fields Ltd, Re [1906] 1 Ch. 1 CA.................... IR 14.25

West End Quay Estate Management Ltd, Re [2017] EWHC 958 (Ch); [2018] B.C.C. 1 .... IA 124, Sch.B1 para.79(4)

Westbrook Dolphin Square Ltd v Friends Life Ltd [2014] EWHC 2433 (Ch); [2014] L. & T.R. 28 .... IA 423(1)–(3)

Western Intelligence Ltd v KDO Label Printing Machines Ltd (In admin. rec.) [1998] B.C.C. 472 Ch D ...... IA 216

Western Welsh International System Buildings Ltd, Re (1988) 4 B.C.C. 449 Ch D (Companies Ct) .... [CDDA 12C]

Westlowe Storage & Distribution Ltd (In liq.), Re [2000] B.C.C. 851 Ch D ... IA 212(1)

Westmead Consultants Ltd (In liq.), Re [2002] 1 B.C.L.C. 384 Ch D .... IA 236

Westmid Packing Services Ltd (No.2), Re [1998] 2 All E.R. 124; [1998] B.C.C. 836 CA (Civ Div) .... [CDDA 1, 1(1), 1(2), 17]

Westminster City Council v Parkin [2001] B.P.I.R. 1156 Ch D .... IA 266(3), (4)

Westminster Property Management Ltd (No.1), Re; sub nom. Official Receiver v Stern (No.1) [2000] 1 W.L.R. 2230; [2001] B.C.C. 121 CA (Civ Div) .... IA 235, [CDDA]

Westminster Property Management Ltd (No.2), Re; sub nom. Official

Provision

Receiver v Stern (No.2) [2001] EWCA Civ 111; [2002] B.C.C. 937 . IA 220, [CDDA 1, 1(1)]

Westshield Ltd v Whitehouse [2013] EWHC 3576 (TCC); [2014] B.P.I.R. 317......................... IA Pt I

Westwood Shipping Lines Inc v Universal Schiffahrtsgesellschaft mbH [2012] EWHC 1394 (Comm); [2012] B.P.I.R. 1078 .... [ER arts 2(70, (8)]

WF Fearman Ltd, Re (No.2) (1988) 4 B.C.C. 141 Ch D (Companies Ct) ... IA 115, 135, 177, IR 7.108(1)–(4)

WGS v United Kingdom [2000] B.C.C. 719 ECHR .... [CDDA]

WH Smith Ltd v Wyndham Investments Ltd [1994] B.C.C. 699 Ch D .... IR 19.1–19.11

Wheatley v Wheatley [1999] 2 F.L.R. 205; [1999] B.P.I.R. 431 QBD ..... IA 264

Whig v Whig [2007] EWHC 1856 (Fam); [2008] 1 F.L.R. 453; [2007] B.P.I.R. 1418 .... IA 282(1), (3)

Whistlejacket Capital Ltd (In rec.), Re [2008] EWCA Civ 575; [2008] B.C.C. 826.................... IA Pt III

White v Davenham Trust Ltd [2011] EWCA Civ 747; [2012] 1 B.C.L.C. 123......................... IA 244(3), IR 10.5

Whitehouse & Co, Re (1878) 9 Ch. D. 595 Ch D .... IA 149(1)

Whitestar Management Ltd, Re; sub nom. Conn v Thompson [2018] EWHC 743 (Ch); [2018] B.P.I.R. 1524...................... IA 238(3)

Wicks v Russell [2008] EWHC 2713 (Ch); [2009] B.P.I.R. 194 .... IA 421A

Wiemer & Trachte GmbH v Tadzher (C-296/17) EU:C:2018:902; [2019] B.P.I.R. 252 .... [ER arts 3(1), 21, 22]

Wight v Eckhardt Marine GmbH [2003] UKPC 37; [2004] 1 A.C. 147; [2003] B.C.C. 702.................... IR 4.3–4.11

Wightman v Bennett [2005] B.P.I.R. 470 Ch D .... IA 212(5)

Wilcock v Duckworth [2005] B.P.I.R. 682 Ch D .... IA 282(1), (3)

Wilkinson v Inland Revenue Commissioners [1998] B.P.I.R. 418 Ch D .... IA 265

Statutes Table

cix

Provision

Provision

Statutory Instruments Table

Provision | **Provision**

European and Other Legislation Table

Company Directors Disqualification Act 1986

Introductory note to the Act

This Act brings together in consolidated form the whole of the law relating to the disqualification of company directors (and, in some circumstances, other persons), either by order of the court or by an undertaking accepted in lieu of a court order.

The title of the Act is somewhat misleading, in that it may be read as applying only to company directors. While it is true that some of its provisions (e.g. ss.6–8 and 9A) are restricted to persons who are or have been directors, most of the rest of the Act is not so limited; and its scope has been extended by supplementary legislation so as to include other categories of persons such as the members of insolvent partnerships.

There has been a power to make disqualification orders in the Companies Acts since 1947, and this power was extended in later Companies Acts, notably in CA 1976 and CA 1981; but little use was made of the sanction prior to 1985, mainly because the necessary resources were not committed to investigation and enforcement. With the enactment of the insolvency reforms of 1985, there was manifested a new resolve on the part of Government to make much greater use of the power to disqualify directors. Difficulties which had been experienced in the operation of the earlier law (e.g. as regards the heavy burden of proof required in some circumstances) were overcome by amending legislation and new grounds for disqualification introduced. These reforms were brought into force on 28 April 1986, several months ahead of the general implementation of IA 1985. The Department of Trade and Industry (now the Department for Business, Energy and Industrial Strategy) was authorised, in the name of the Secretary of State, to investigate cases of suspected breaches of the law and to institute proceedings for disqualification orders; and liquidators, administrators, receivers and other insolvency practitioners were required by law to make reports to the Department on the conduct of the directors in every case of corporate insolvency. A more recent innovation is the Disqualification Stakeholder Group, established by the Insolvency Service in 2012 as a forum for the Service, recognised professional bodies and insolvency practitioners' representatives to discuss issues relating to the duty of office-holders to report suspected cases of unfitness.

Under the legislation as originally enacted, a person could be disqualified only by order of the court, but the Insolvency Act 2000 introduced the alternative of a disqualification *undertaking*, which applies only to cases under CDDA 1986 ss.6–8, i.e. cases where the basis of the charge is that the director has shown by his conduct that he is unfit to be concerned in the management of a company. A person who is prepared to accept liability may give an undertaking to the Secretary of State that he will not be a director or otherwise concerned in the management of a company for an agreed period, with the same consequences as would follow if a court order had been made in the same terms. Since the change came into force, undertakings have displaced disqualification orders in the great majority (about 85 per cent) of cases.

The Act applies to "companies", an expression which (by s.22(2)) "includes any company which may be wound up under the Insolvency Act 1986". This means that it applies to "unregistered companies": see the note to IA 1986 s.220. As originally drafted, it did not apply to building societies or incorporated friendly societies, but it has since been extended so as to apply to the directors (or the members of the committee of management) and officers of both: see ss.22A and 22B, below. In 2004, the Act was extended to include the directors and officers (but not "shadow directors"—see below) of NHS Foundation Trusts: see s.22C. It applies also to EEIGs: see the European Economic Interest Grouping Regulations 1989 (SI 1989/638) reg.20. The Co-operative and Community Benefit Societies and Credit Unions Act 2010, when it was brought into force on 6 April 2014, extended the Act to registered co-operative and community benefit societies and credit unions by the insertion of s.22E. Section 22F, inserted by the Charitable Incorporated Organisations (Consequential Amendments) Order 2012 (SI 2012/3014) art.2, effective 2 January 2013, extends the Act to include the trustees of a charitable incorporated organisation. Extension to protected-cell companies was introduced by the Risk Transformation Regulations 2017 (SI 2017/1212) reg.190, Sch.4 para.3 as from 8 December 2017 by insertion of s.22H (which contains modifications in s.22H(4)). Its application to other bodies remains uncertain: see the note to s.22(2).

Where an insolvent partnership is wound up as an unregistered company under Pt V of IA 1986 (see the note to IA 1986 s.420), any member or former member of the partnership or any other person who has or has had control or management of the partnership business is treated in the same way as the director of a company, and ss.1, 1A, 6 to 10, 13 to 15, 17, 19(c) and 20 and Sch.1 of CDDA 1986 apply: see the Insolvent Partnerships Order 1994 (SI 1994/2421) art.16 (as amended).

The provisions of CDDA 1986 are made to apply to limited liability partnerships by the Limited Liability Partnerships Regulations 2001 (SI 2001/1090 reg.4(2)), subject to certain modifications set out in Sch.2 Pt II of the

Regulations. More particularly, references in the Act to a director or officer of a company are to be taken as including references to a member or officer of an LLP, and there is a new concept of "shadow member" corresponding to "shadow director".

For the purposes of the Act, "director" includes any person occupying the position of director, by whatever name called (s.22(3)), so that it is immaterial that, in the company in question, the members of the board may be called (e.g.) "trustees" or "governors". For the purposes of ss.6–9E, the term "director" includes a "shadow director", as defined in s.22(5). A de facto director has also been held to be within s.6: see the note to s.6(1) and, on the meaning of this term, the note to s.22(5).

All sections of CDDA 1986 apply to England and Wales and to Scotland, but not (except s.11) to Northern Ireland. However, equivalent legislation has been in force in that jurisdiction since 1986. Initially, this was brought about by the Companies (Northern Ireland) Order 1986 (SI 1986/1032 (NI 6)); but this has now been replaced by the Companies (Northern Ireland) Order 2002 (SI 2002/3150 (NI 4)). (See further the note to s.24(2).)

Generally speaking, the courts of England and Wales have no jurisdiction in matters of insolvency over companies registered in Scotland, and vice versa. Most sections of the CDDA 1986 also make it plain that this separation between the two jurisdictions applies also in relation to the present Act (frequently by reference to the "court having jurisdiction to wind up the company" in question). One notable exception is s.8 (below), where the language is ambiguous and arguably would allow the Secretary of State to choose to start proceedings concerning a Scottish company in either jurisdiction; but in *Re Helene plc* [2000] 2 B.C.L.C. 249 Blackburne J held that the distinction should be observed and it was competent only to make application to the court in Scotland. However, a disqualification order made (or an undertaking given) in either England and Wales or Scotland is operative in all parts of Britain (and, indeed, has unrestricted extraterritorial effect). And an amendment introduced by IA 2000 gives force throughout these jurisdictions to a Northern Ireland disqualification order or undertaking: see the note to s.12A, below.

In a number of cases relating to director disqualification an issue has arisen based on an allegation that there has been a violation of the European Convention for the Protection of Human Rights and Fundamental Freedoms (now largely embodied in UK domestic law following the enactment of the Human Rights Act 1998), and opinions have been expressed both by the courts in England and by the European Commission on Human Rights on the applicability of the Convention to disqualification proceedings.

In *EDC v United Kingdom (Application No.24433/94)* [1998] B.C.C. 370 the director concerned had been a respondent to an application for disqualification which had begun in August 1991 and was not finally disposed of until January 1996—nearly four and a half years from the start of the proceedings and seven years after the events had occurred on which the case was based. He alleged that there had been a violation of art.6(1) of the Convention, which states that "In the determination of his civil rights and obligations or of any criminal charge against him, everyone is entitled to a fair and public hearing within a reasonable time …". The Commission upheld his complaint, holding that the delay was in breach of the Convention (and accepting the view, incidentally, that the proceedings constituted a dispute over "civil rights and obligations").

In the later case of *DC, HS and AD v United Kingdom (Application No.39031/97)* [2000] B.C.C. 710 the European Court of Human Rights rejected an argument that disqualification proceedings constituted "criminal charges" within art.6(1): "the disqualification of directors is a matter which is regulatory rather than criminal". The applicants' main complaint was that it was unfair to base the disqualification proceedings on statements which had been obtained compulsorily under IA 1986 s.235, citing *Saunders v United Kingdom (Case 43/1994/490/572)* [1997] E.H.R.R. 313; [1997] B.C.C. 872. But this contention was rejected, one ground being that, unlike *Saunders*, this was not a criminal case. The court also ruled that the exclusion of evidence of the directors' good character was not incompatible with a fair hearing.

This ruling has been confirmed by the courts in this country. In *R. v Secretary of State for Trade and Industry Ex p. McCormick* [1998] B.C.C. 379, the Court of Appeal held that it was not unreasonable for the Secretary of State to continue to make use of compelled evidence in disqualification proceedings even though, in the light of the *Saunders* ruling, she had adopted a policy of not using compelled evidence in criminal cases. Again, in *Re Westminster Property Management Ltd, Official Receiver v Stern* [2000] 1 W.L.R. 2230; [2001] B.C.C. 121 the Court of Appeal, affirming Scott V.C. ruled that there had been no violation of the Convention on this ground, nor on the ground that an order would interfere with the freedom of establishment and freedom to provide services (arts 43, 49 of the Convention).

In *WGS and MSLS v United Kingdom (Application No.38172/97)* [2000] B.C.C. 719 the European Court of Human Rights held that director disqualification proceedings do not infringe art.8 of the Convention (respect for private life): in so far as the applicants' complaint was about press reporting of their case it was open to them to invoke the law of defamation. It was also ruled that no appeal could be made to the European Court until after the matter had been determined at a trial in the United Kingdom court and an order made.

It is normal practice for the Secretary of State to require that there should be attached to a disqualification undertaking a statement of the grounds on which the finding of unfitness against the director had been made: see the note to s.7. In *Re Blackspur Group plc (No.3), Secretary of State for Trade and Industry v Davies (No.2)* [2002] 2 B.C.L.C. 263 the court rejected a contention by the director that to impose such a requirement was a breach of his human rights. In another case concerning a different director of the same company, *Re Blackspur Group plc (No.3), Secretary of State for Trade and Industry v Eastaway* [2003] B.C.C. 520 a delay of over eight years was held not to have prevented the director from having a fair and public hearing of his case: the greater part of this delay was due to various unsuccessful actions taken by the applicant himself, trying to prevent the case from coming to trial. However, this issue was taken to the European Court of Human Rights (*Davies v UK* [2005] B.C.C. 401), where it was held that the Government was responsible for the greater part of the delay and was in breach of the Convention. On the strength of this ruling, the director applied to the domestic court to have the disqualification proceedings against him dismissed and his disqualification retrospectively set aside, but he was unsuccessful, both at first instance and on appeal: *Re Blackspur Group plc (No.4)* [2006] EWHC 299 (Ch); [2006] 2 B.C.L.C. 489; *Eastaway v Secretary of State for Trade and Industry* [2007] EWCA Civ 425; [2007] B.C.C. 550. See also, on the ECHR costs, *Eastaway v UK* [2006] 2 B.C.L.C. 361.

Although the Secretary of State may be compelled under IA 1986 to make disclosure of materials, this obligation is restricted to materials in his possession and does not extend to materials that could be in his possession: requirements of fairness under the Convention do not require him to interview or obtain documents from third parties (*Re Stakefield (Midlands) Ltd* [2010] EWHC 2518 (Ch)). Similarly, in *Secretary of State for Business, Innovation and Skills v Doffman* [2010] EWHC 2518 (Ch); [2011] 1 B.C.L.C. 597 it was held that neither the Convention nor his general duty to act fairly would normally extend to requiring the Secretary of State to obtain evidence or undertake investigations requested by the respondent.

Independently of the Human Rights legislation, a plea has been raised on occasion that it would be an infringement of the principle of "double jeopardy" to pursue disqualification proceedings against a defendant when he has been, or is concurrently being, faced with disciplinary proceedings by a professional body (e.g. the Financial Conduct Authority) in respect of the same charges. In *Re Barings plc (No.4)* [1999] B.C.C. 639; and *Re Migration Services International Ltd* [2000] B.C.C. 1,095 such an objection was not upheld, the court ruling that the issues in the two proceedings were materially different. An objection on the ground of "double jeopardy" was also not upheld in *Re Cedarwood Productions Ltd* [2001] EWCA Civ 1083; [2004] B.C.C. 65, where a disqualification order under CDDA 1986 s.2 had been made against the defendants as part of a criminal sentence and the Secretary of State wished to pursue civil proceedings for an order under s.6 which relied partly on the same facts. Although there was some overlap, the court in the latter proceedings would be looking at a wider picture. However, in the later case of *Secretary of State for Business, Innovation and Skills v Weston* [2014] EWHC 2933 (Ch), *Cedarwood* was distinguished and an application by the Secretary of State made after the criminal court had declined to make an order was refused: the facts in the two hearings would be identical and it would be unfair to expose the director to a second hearing on the same grounds. (See also *Re Denis Hilton Ltd* [2002] 1 B.C.L.C. 302.)

The present Act has its own definition section (s.22), but there is some cross-referencing between it and IA 1986, and also to the Companies Acts; and s.22(9) provides that any expression not specifically defined in this Act is to be interpreted by reference to the Companies Acts. The terms used in all of these Acts may therefore for the most part be taken to have the same meanings.

The Enterprise Act 2002 s.204, inserting new ss.9A–9E into CDDA 1986, introduced the regime of competition disqualification orders (CDOs) and competition disqualification undertakings (CDUs). This reform took effect from 20 June 2003: see the Enterprise Act 2002 (Commencement No.3, Transitional and Transitory Provisions and Savings) Order 2003 (SI 2003/1397 (C. 60)) arts 1, 2(1) and Sch.1. Under s.9A the court is empowered to make a disqualification order against a person who is or has been a director or shadow director of a company which has committed a breach of competition law where the court considers that his conduct as a director, taken together with his conduct in relation to one or more other undertakings, makes him unfit to be concerned in the management of a company. Responsibility under ss.9A–9E lies with the Competition and Markets Authority and a number of named regulators, and not with the Secretary of State. See further the notes to ss.9A–9E.

The Enterprise Act 2002 s.257 also introduced the system of bankruptcy restrictions orders and undertakings (see the comment to IA 1986 s.281A and Sch.4A). The law governing these orders and undertakings closely parallels that already established by the present Act for director disqualification, and the CDDA cases are likely to be relevant. This will be the case also with debt relief restrictions orders and undertakings, a regime introduced (as IA 1986 Pt 7A) by the Tribunals, Courts and Enforcement Act 2007.

The Companies Act 2006 Pt 40 introduced (from 1 October 2009) new provisions relating to persons who are subject to restrictions similar to those imposed by a director disqualification order (or equivalent undertaking) under the law of a country or territory outside the United Kingdom. The Secretary of State is empowered to make regulations which either (a) automatically disqualify such persons from acting as director, etc. of a UK company or (b) may be disqualified by order of the court on the application of the Secretary of State; and there may be provision also in the regulations for the Secretary of State to accept a disqualification undertaking in lieu of an order. No regulations have yet been made.

The Small Business, Enterprise and Employment Act 2015 has made a number of changes and introduced some new provisions relating to director disqualification, including:

- extending the power to disqualify a person convicted of a company-related offence abroad;

- restating the matters that the Secretary of State and the court are to take into account when considering whether a person should be disqualified;

- increasing the factors to be taken into account in determining a person's "unfitness" by including his conduct in regard to overseas companies;

- making a person who influences or instructs a person to engage in unfit conduct liable to disqualification;

- extending the time limit for instituting disqualification proceedings from two to three years;

- providing for a disqualified person to be ordered to pay compensation to either the company or a specified creditor (or creditors) who has suffered loss as a result of his improper conduct, with corresponding provision where a disqualification undertaking is accepted by the Secretary of State;

- extending the definition of "shadow director";

- introducing a streamlined system of reporting of director misconduct.

The majority of these changes were brought into force on 26 May or 1 October 2015, except for the new reporting regime, which took effect from 1 April 2016. Together with the Insolvent Companies (Reports on Conduct of Directors) (England and Wales) Rules 2016 (SI 2016/180), which from 6 April 2016, revoke and replace the Insolvent Companies (Reports on Conduct of Directors) Rules 1996/1909), the new provisions introduce a streamlined system for reporting of directors' conduct by insolvency office-holders using an online system, the Conduct Assessment Service, under which reports must be submitted within three months of the company's "insolvency date". The system is to be reviewed within five years.

The Deregulation Act 2015 has also made an amendment to the Act, extending the power of the Secretary of State to obtain information from third parties (s.7(4)).

Regulations relating to director disqualification were made under CA 1985 and replaced by new regulations in similar terms after the 1986 legislation became operative. Those currently in force are:

- the Insolvent Companies (Disqualification of Unfit Directors) Proceedings Rules 1987 (SI 1987/2023, as amended by SI 1999/1023, 2001/765, 2003/1367 and 2007/1906);

- the Insolvent Companies (Reports on Conduct of Directors) Rules (above);

- the Insolvent Companies (Reports on Conduct of Directors) (Scotland) Rules 2016 (SI 2016/185 (S.1));

- the Compensation Orders (Disqualified Directors) Proceedings (England and Wales) Rules 2016 (SI 2016/890);

- the Compensation Orders (Disqualified Directors) Proceedings (Scotland) Rules 2016 (SI 2016/895 (S.1));

- the Disqualified Directors Compensation Orders (Fees) (England and Wales) Order 2016 (SI 2016/1047); and

- the Disqualified Directors Compensation Orders (Fees) (Scotland) Order 2016 (SI 2016/1048).

Also of relevance are the Companies (Disqualification Orders) Regulations 2009 (SI 2009/2471, replacing SI 2001/967).

Comparable secondary legislation has been introduced in Northern Ireland. See the note to s.24(2).

The Insolvency Service has published Guidance Notes for the completion of statutory reports and returns under the Disqualification Act, which are available at *https://www.gov.uk/government/publications/company-directors-disqualification-act-1986-guidance-notes-completion-of-statutory-reports-and-returns*.

Attention should also be drawn to the *Practice Direction: Directors Disqualification Proceedings* [2015] B.C.C. 224 (reproduced as App.VI to this *Guide*).

Reference will be made at appropriate places in this section to Totty, Moss & Segal, *Insolvency* (Sweet & Maxwell, looseleaf), Ch.G1; and to Walters and Davis-White, *Directors' Disqualification & Insolvency Restrictions*, 3rd edn (Sweet & Maxwell, 2010).

Company Directors Disqualification Act 1986

(1986 Chapter 46)

ARRANGEMENT OF SECTIONS

An Act to consolidate certain enactments relating to the disqualification of persons from being directors of companies, and from being otherwise concerned with a company's affairs.

[25th July 1986]

Preliminary

1 Disqualification orders: general

1(1) [Disqualification order] In the circumstances specified below in this Act a court may, and under sections 6 and 9A shall, make against a person a disqualification order, that is to say an order that for a period specified in the order–

    (a) he shall not be a director of a company, act as receiver of a company's property or in any way, whether directly or indirectly, be concerned or take part in the promotion, formation or management of a company unless (in each case) he has the leave of the court, and

    (b) he shall not act as an insolvency practitioner.

1(2) [Maximum, minimum periods] In each section of this Act which gives to a court power or, as the case may be, imposes on it the duty to make a disqualification order there is specified the maximum (and, in sections 6 and 8ZA, the minimum) period of disqualification which may or (as the case may be) must be imposed by means of the order and, unless the court otherwise orders, the period of disqualification so imposed shall begin at the end of the period of 21 days beginning with the date of the order.

1(3) [Where two orders] Where a disqualification order is made against a person who is already subject to such an order or to a disqualification undertaking, the periods specified in those orders or, as the case may be, in the order and the undertaking shall run concurrently.

1(4) [Criminal grounds] A disqualification order may be made on grounds which are or include matters other than criminal convictions, notwithstanding that the person in respect of whom it is to be made may be criminally liable in respect of those matters.

General Note

This section brings forward from CA 1985 s.295 the provisions defining a disqualification order and describing its effect. The wording has been altered in a number of respects by IA 2000, as noted in the comments to subss.(1) to (3) below.

On the other hand, it has been stressed in a far greater number of cases (and particularly those brought under ss.6–9 and 11) that the court's primary concern is to ensure the protection of the public: see, e.g. *Re Lo-Line Electric Motors Ltd* [1988] Ch. 477 at 486; (1988) 4 B.C.C. 415 at 419; *Re Sevenoaks Stationers (Retail) Ltd* [1991] Ch. 164 at 176, [1990] B.C.C. 765 at 773; *Secretary of State for Trade & Industry v Langridge, Re Cedac Ltd* [1991] Ch. 402 at 413–414; [1991] B.C.C. 148 at 153–155; *R. v Secretary of State for Trade & Industry Ex p. Lonrho plc* [1992] B.C.C. 325 at 333, 335. However, even so, an order is clearly restrictive of the liberty of the person against whom it is made, and its contravention can have penal consequences under s.13 (above). It has also been observed that a disqualification order involves the termination of a civil right and obligation (*R. v Secretary of State for Trade &*

Differing views have been expressed regarding the nature and purpose of a disqualification order. On the one hand, it may be seen as a form of punishment for misconduct—a view that is reinforced by the fact that the courts have, on occasion, revised or lifted a disqualification order when a person has appealed against a criminal sentence: see, e.g. *R. v Young* [1990] B.C.C. 549, where the court said that a disqualification order was "unquestionably a punishment", and ruled that it was quite inappropriate to link such an order with a conditional discharge, and *R. v Millard* (1993) 15 Cr. App. R. (S) 445.

Industry Ex p. McCormick [1998] B.C.C. 379), that the objective of the legislation is to raise standards of responsibility (*Secretary of State for Trade & Industry v McTighe* [1997] B.C.C. 224) and that it is intended to have a real deterrent effect on others (*Re Blackspur Group plc* [1998] 1 W.L.R. 422; [1998] B.C.C. 11; *Secretary of State for Trade & Industry v Tjolle* [1998] B.C.C. 282). Of course, such remarks are often nothing more than observations made by a judge *en passant*; but in some cases the distinction has been squarely in issue before the court, and in these cases it has been emphasised that the jurisdiction is civil and not criminal in nature. For example the standard of proof is that of a balance of probabilities (*Re Living Images Ltd* [1996] B.C.C. 112)—although it is recognised that the more serious the allegations are, the more the court will require cogent evidence as proof (ibid., and see *Re Verby Print for Advertising Ltd* [1998] B.C.C. 652). Again, where dishonesty is alleged, evidence of good character has been ruled to be inadmissible, even though it would be relevant in criminal proceedings (*Secretary of State for Trade & Industry v Dawes* [1997] B.C.C. 121). However this is not always the approach: in *Secretary of State for Trade & Industry v Baker* [1998] Ch. 356 at 376, Scott V.C. said that disqualification proceedings "have, in many respects, much more in common with criminal proceedings than with civil litigation about private rights", and that it was appropriate for the Secretary of State to disclose to a respondent a report which in criminal proceedings would have to be disclosed. The Court of Appeal in *Re Westmid Packing Services Ltd; Secretary of State for Trade & Industry v Griffiths* [1998] B.C.C. 836, while stating that protection of the public is the primary purpose of disqualification, admitted that in truth the exercise engaged in is little different from any sentencing exercise. Lord Woolf said (at 843) "The period of disqualification must reflect the gravity of the offence. It must contain deterrent elements. That is what sentencing is all about". In *Re Liberty Holdings Unltd* [2017] B.C.C. 298 the applicant sought permission to act as a director when he had been disqualified pursuant to a conviction for an indictable offence. In granting leave subject to conditions, Chief Registrar Baister took into account the fact that he had served his sentence and the importance of the rehabilitation of offenders, distinguishing between the purposes of the criminal proceedings and those of the disqualification regime.

The view that disqualification proceedings are civil rather than criminal in nature has been endorsed in a number of cases where it has been claimed that the proceedings have involved, or would involve, a contravention of the European Convention for the Protection of Human Rights and Fundamental Freedoms (now incorporated into domestic legislation by the Human Rights Act 1998). See the Introductory note to CDDA 1986 at p.2 above.

In *R. v Holmes* [1991] B.C.C. 394 the Court of Appeal held that it was wrong in principle to make a criminal compensation order and at the same time to disqualify the person concerned from acting as a company director, since his ability to earn the means with which to pay the compensation would be significantly diminished. The compensation order which had been imposed by the trial court following his conviction for fraudulent trading was accordingly quashed.

On this topic, see further Walters and Davis-White, *Directors' Disqualification & Insolvency Restrictions*, Ch.2; and Totty, Moss & Segal, *Insolvency*, G1–03.

The legislation as enacted in 1986 made no provision for a disqualification order to be made by consent, or for a respondent to admit the case against him and plead guilty. Every application for a disqualification order had to be brought before a court and proved by evidence. The delay and expense (and, for respondents, the uncertainty and stress) involved was costly in every sense, and a large backlog of cases soon built up. It was not until the case of *Re Carecraft Construction Co Ltd* [1994] 1 W.L.R. 172; [1993] B.C.C. 336 that a first step was taken, by judicial ingenuity, to deal with the problem. The *Carecraft* procedure allowed the court to deal with uncontested cases in a summary way. In the ensuing years this summary procedure was regularly followed where the facts were agreed or, at least, not disputed and both the Secretary of State and the director were willing for the case to proceed on the basis of those facts. The *Practice Direction: Directors Disqualification Proceedings* [2015] B.C.C. 224 contains guidance as to the procedure to be followed where a *Carecraft* application for summary trial is made: see App.VI, para.12.

The introduction of the *Carecraft* procedure enabled the parties in many cases to avoid the delay, stress and expense involved in a full-scale hearing, but it still involved the participation of the court and a considerable amount of documentation had to be prepared in order that the court could be fully apprised of the facts of the case. The procedure has now been rendered obsolete by the Insolvency Act 2000, which introduced the disqualification undertaking as an alternative to a disqualification order and has made the involvement of the court no longer necessary in the great majority of cases: see the notes to s.1A, below.

The offence of acting as a director while disqualified under this section is probably an absolute offence, on analogy with the position of an undischarged bankrupt: there is no requirement of mens rea. See *R. v Brockley* [1994] B.C.C. 131, and the note to s.11 below; and compare *R. v Cole, Lees & Birch* [1998] B.C.C. 87 (a decision on IA 1986 s.216).

A person who is subject to a disqualification order or undertaking under this Act (or under the corresponding legislation for Northern Ireland) is disqualified from being a trustee of a charity: Charities Act 2011 s.178(1), or the Scottish equivalent (Law Reform (Miscellaneous Provisions) (Scotland) Act 1990 s.8(1)(d)), or the charity trustee of a charitable incorporated organisation (Charities Act 2011 s.178(1), Charitable Incorporated Organisations (General) Regulations 2012 (SI 2012/3012) reg.31(5)(b)). Other legislation imposes an equivalent ban from holding office (or provides that disqualification order or undertaking shall be a ground for the person's removal) as the trustee of a pension trust scheme (Pensions Act 1995 s.29(1)(f)), a member of a police authority (Police Act 1996; Sch.2 para.11(1)(c); Sch.2A para.7(1)(c)), a Police Commissioner or member of a Police Service Authority (Police Act 1997 s.91(7)(b)) and Sch.2 para.3(1)(c)), a registered social landlord (Housing Act 1996 Sch.1 para.4(2)(b)), or a school governor (Schools Standards and Framework Act 1998 Sch.11 and Education (Company Directors Disqualification Act 1986: Amendments to Disqualification Provisions) (England) Regulations 2004 (SI 2004/3264)). In some of these cases there is provision for the court or the relevant authority to give leave to act or to grant a waiver, but in others there appears to be no dispensing power at all; compare *Re Westminster Property Management Ltd, Official Receiver v Stern (No.2)* [2001] EWCA Civ 111; [2002] B.C.C. 937.

In the last-mentioned case the question arose whether a disqualification order would prevent the person concerned from acting as a director of an overseas company. This would appear to turn on whether a UK court would have jurisdiction to wind up the particular company under Pt V of the Act, which in turn would require it to be shown by proper evidence that it had a "sufficient connection" with the jurisdiction.

The Insolvent Partnerships Order 1994 (SI 1994/2421, as amended by SI 2001/767) applies the greater part of CDDA 1986 to the members or former members of insolvent partnerships: see the note to IA 1986 s.420. Sections 22A, 22B, 22C and 22F similarly extend this Act to building societies, incorporated friendly societies, NHS foundation trusts and charitable incorporated organisations: see the notes to those sections. The Co-operative and Community Benefit Societies and Credit Unions Act 2010 s.3 has extended the Act to registered co-operative and community benefit societies and credit unions, by introducing s.22E. The Act applies also to EEIGs: see the European Economic Interest Grouping Regulations 1989 (SI 1989/638) reg.20.

In the application of CDDA 1986 to LLPs, references in the former to a director or shadow director are to be construed as references to a member or shadow member of an LLP (LLPR 2001 reg.4(2)(f), (g)); and accordingly a person who is subject to a director disqualification order is prohibited from being a member or shadow member of an LLP, except with the leave of the court.

S.1(1)

The wording of this subsection was changed by IA 2000 s.5(1), with effect from 2 April 2001, but the only change of substance is that the ban on acting as an insolvency practitioner has been separated off so that the prohibition is in that respect absolute, and not subject to the power of the court to grant leave to act. The former wording "for a specified period *beginning with the date of the order*" was also changed (by dropping the italicised words) for the reasons described in the note to s.1(2), below.

A disqualification order may be made against a company or other corporate body, since the section uses the word "person" rather than "individual". This is confirmed by s.14, below.

The word "shall" reflects the fact that the court has no discretion; and ss.6 and 9A are expressed in similar imperative terms.

Section 1(1) states clearly that a disqualification order is an order that the person shall not, without the leave of the court, engage in the activities listed in paras (a) and (b). On occasion, orders have been made in which some only of these activities have been specified. It has been ruled that it is not competent for a court to make an order limited in this way. However, such an order is not a nullity but an error capable of being corrected under CPR r.40.12 (formerly RSC Ord.20 r.11) (the "slip rule"). (See *Re Gower Enterprises Ltd (No.2)* [1995] B.C.C. 1,081; *Re Seagull Manufacturing Co Ltd (No.3)* [1995] B.C.C. 1,088; *Re Brian Sheridan Cars Ltd* [1995] B.C.C. 1,035; and *Re Cannonquest Ltd* [1997] B.C.C. 644). On the same reasoning, it is not competent for a court to make an order limiting the disqualification to acting in relation to public companies: *R. v Ward* [2001] EWCA Crim 1648; [2002] B.C.C. 953.

"Management" for the purposes of para.(a) includes both the internal and external affairs of a company: *R. v Austen* (1985) 1 B.C.C. 99,528 (a case concerning the fraudulent raising of finance). In *R. v Campbell* [1984] B.C.L.C. 83, a management consultant who acted as adviser to the board of a company was held to have "been concerned in" and "taken part in" its management. It is not necessary that there should be any actual misconduct of the company's affairs: in *R. v Georgiou* (1988) 4 B.C.C. 322, a disqualification order was made against a person who had carried on an unauthorised insurance business through the medium of a limited company. In *R. v Creggy* [2008] EWCA Crim 364; [2008] 1 B.C.L.C. 625 the appellant, a solicitor, had allowed his client account to be used for money-laundering and had set up a company for the purpose: this was held to be an offence "in connection with the management" of the company. In the Australian case *Re Magna Alloys & Research Pty Ltd* (1975) C.L.C. para.40-227: (see: *British Company Law and Practice*, para.37-150), a former director who acted as marketing adviser, and in that capacity attended directors' meetings, was held not to have taken part in the management of the company. In another part of the same judgment the court expressed the view that a majority shareholder might so use his position on questions of management as to infringe a prohibition on "taking part in management"; but it was thought that he would be free to vote as a shareholder, "even on a management matter".

In another Australian case, *CCA v Brecht* (1989) 7 A.C.L.C. 40, the court considered that the concept of "management" required an involvement of some kind in the decision-making process of the company, and a degree of responsibility. It may not exonerate the person concerned simply to show that some other person has the final say in decision-making or signs all the cheques. Negotiating terms of credit facilities, for instance, may be a management activity, even though those terms have to be confirmed. Advice given to management, participation in the decision-making process, and execution of management's decisions which goes beyond the mere carrying out of directions is sufficient (ibid.). In contrast, in *Re Clasper Group Services Ltd* (1988) 4 B.C.C. 673 the respondent, who was the son of the controlling shareholder and director, was employed as a "management trainee"; he did not appear "to have risen much above the status of an office boy and messenger", but he did have authority to sign company cheques. Warner J held that his functions were too lowly to bring him within the phrase "is or has been concerned, or has taken part, in the ... management of the company" for the purposes of IA 1986 s.212(1)(c). In *Drew v Lord Advocate*, 1996 S.L.T. 1062 a person who purported to act only as an employee of a small company which he had himself set up was held to have taken part in its management. Further discussion of this topic can be found in *Re a Company* [1980] Ch. 138 at 144; and *Re Market Wizard Systems (UK) Ltd* [1998] 2 B.C.L.C. 282 at 298–301, where Carnwath J said (at 301): "Essentially it is a jury question. I would, however, agree with Ormiston J [in *CCA v Brecht*] in emphasising that 'ultimate control' in not a necessary element, and further in the emphasis that he gives to those functions which are relevant to 'the solvency or probity of the corporation's administration'."

A disqualification order need not impose a total prohibition on the activities of the person concerned, since the court has power under this subsection to give leave. The Act gives no guidance as to the exercise of the court's discretion in considering whether to grant leave: the discretion is wholly unfettered (*Shuttleworth v Secretary of State for Trade and Industry* [2000] B.C.C. 204). A balance has to be struck between the applicant's need to be able to act in the manner requested and the importance of protecting the public. In *Re Cargo Agency Ltd* [1992] B.C.C. 388 (where leave to act as a director was refused, but the respondent was allowed to act as a general manager of the subsidiary of a large public company) Harman J said, at 393: "It seems to me that ... applications for leave pursuant to s.1 should only be granted where there is a need for them to be granted, and should only be granted upon evidence of adequate protection from danger." The question of "need" has occasioned some debate. It has been described as a "practical" need (*Re Tech Textiles Ltd* [1998] 1 B.C.L.C. 259). The need is that of the companies concerned (and its employees and other stakeholders) rather than that of the individual applicant (*Re Verby Print for Advertising Ltd* [1998] B.C.C. 652; *Secretary of State for Trade and Industry v Rosenfield* [1999] B.C.C. 413). See also *Secretary of State for Business, Innovation and Skills v Harriss* [2016] EWHC 794 (Ch). An argument based on the need of the company carries little weight when the company is wholly or substantially owned by the applicant: *Secretary of State for Trade and Industry v Barnett* [1998] 2 B.C.L.C. 64; *Re Britannia Homes Centres Ltd* [2001] 2 B.C.L.C. 63. On the other hand, it is in the public interest that the applicant should be able to earn a living: *Shuttleworth v Secretary of State for Trade and Industry* [2000] B.C.C. 204. Somewhat exceptionally, in *Re Barings plc (No.5)* [1999] B.C.C. 960, where there had been no dishonesty and no abuse of the privilege of limited liability and the court was satisfied that the public would be adequately protected, leave was given despite the fact that "need" had not been demonstrated. In contrast, where there has been dishonesty or illegal conduct, considerations of public interest and the concern to protect the public will outweigh any argument based on "need": see, for instance *Re Amaron Ltd* [1998] B.C.C. 264; *Re Westminster Property Management Ltd, Official Receiver v Stern (No.2)* [2001] B.C.C 305 (on appeal [2001] EWCA Civ 111; [2002] B.C.C. 937). In *Re Portland Place (Historic House) Ltd* [2012] EWHC 4199 (Ch), leave was given to a disqualified director to instruct the company to defend possession proceedings brought against it by a mortgagee: there was no conceivable risk of harm to the public, he would not be dealing with the public and there was the added benefit of any confiscation order that might be made in relation to his assets. In *Haughey v Secretary of State for Business, Energy and Industrial Strategy* [2018] EWHC 3566 (Ch) although the "need" to be a director did not carry significant weight, the purposes of the disqualification were overcome as he had accepted the rigours of disqualification, shown remorse, offered stringent safeguards to protect the public and had worked hard to establish a new and successful business to the benefit of all involved and so leave was granted.

As regards protection of the public, "the public for this purpose includes all relevant interest groups, such as shareholders, employees, lenders, customers and other creditors" (*Re Tech Textiles Ltd* (above) at 268). "The public" is not confined to people within the jurisdiction: the effect of a disqualification order extends to foreign jurisdictions and the question whether disqualification could be imposed on the same facts by a foreign court is irrelevant (*Re Westminster Property Management (No.2)* (above), at 358–359). In the *Tech Textiles* case Arden J identified a number of key factors to be taken into account, including the grounds on which "unfitness" under s.6 was found (and in particular whether the applicant has misappropriated any assets or acted knowingly in breach of duty), the character of the applicant (and in particular his honesty, reliability and willingness to accept advice), the previous career of the applicant, and whether he had been disqualified previously. The court has also to consider the company or companies in relation to which he wishes to have leave to act: the nature of its business, its size and financial position, the number of directors, the risks involved in its business, and whether there is potential for the matters which were held to constitute unfitness to recur. See also *Re Hennelly's Utilities Ltd* [2004] EWHC 34 (Ch); [2005] B.C.C. 542; *Re Servaccomm Redhall Ltd* [2004] EWHC 760 (Ch); [2006] 1 B.C.L.C. 1.

The court may take into account for the purposes of an application for leave various factors which are treated as irrelevant when ruling on the question of a defendant's "unfitness". These factors include: the person's general good character; the fact that his management of other companies has been satisfactory; the likelihood that he will not offend again; and any period of de facto disqualification to which the applicant has been subject pending the hearing of his case.

The grant of leave is commonly made subject to conditions. Reported cases include: *Re Lo-Line Electric Motors Ltd* [1988] Ch. 477; (1988) 4 B.C.C. 415 (if another named person remained a director with voting control); *Re Majestic Recording Studios Ltd* (1988) 4 B.C.C. 519 (if a chartered accountant was willing to act as a co-director and audited accounts for the previous five years were produced and filed); *Re Chartmore Ltd* [1990] B.C.C. 673 (if monthly board meetings were held, attended by a representative of the auditors); *Re Godwin Warren Control Systems plc* [1992] B.C.C. 557 (if, in the case of two companies, the disqualification order and the reasons for making it were brought to the attention of the companies' boards of directors and, in regard to another, if similar disclosure was made to two outside shareholders); *Re Gibson Davies Ltd* [1995] B.C.C. 11 (a total of ten safeguards, including a ban on signing cheques without a countersignature and conditions that loans owed by the company to the applicant were not to be repaid and that the applicant should not take security over the company's assets); *Secretary of State for Trade and Industry v Arif* [1996] B.C.C. 960 (no loan to be made to associated company); *Secretary of State for Trade and Industry v Rosenfield* [1999] B.C.C. 413 (prompt settlement of inter-company debts; regular management accounts); *Re Barings plc* (above) (not undertaking executive duties or accepting fees); *Re TLL Realisations Ltd* [2000] B.C.C. 988 (that the person should perform only specified duties in a subordinate capacity). See also *Re Hennelly's Utilities Ltd* (above), where leave was granted (in a relatively serious case) subject to stringent conditions; *Re Clenaware Ltd*; *Harris v Secretary of State for Business, Innovation and Skills* [2013] EWHC 2514 (Ch); [2015] B.C.C. 283 (leave on detailed conditions granted in respect of one company but refused regarding two others). In *Haughey v Secretary of State for Business, Energy and Industrial Strategy* [2018] EWHC 3566 (Ch) the disqualified offered his own stringent conditions as safeguards (including appointment of two experienced directors one of whom was an accountant) which were accepted by the court for the grant of permission.

In *Re Brian Sheridan Cars Ltd* [1995] B.C.C. 1035 the applicant, who was already subject to a disqualification order, applied to the court to vary the order by removing the conditions on which he had been given leave to act, and to do so with retrospective effect. The court declined this request, which would have had the effect of decriminalising any past acts of his which were in breach of the conditions, and which would also have meant that third parties who might have had personal claims against him would have lost the right to sue him.

In *R. v Goodman* [1992] B.C.C. 625, it was held that there is no power under the Act to make an exception of a general kind, e.g. that the defendant be disqualified from being a director of a public company but given leave to be a director of any private company; compare *R. v Ward* [2001] EWCA Crim 1648; [2002] B.C.C. 953.

In *Re D J Matthews (Joinery Design) Ltd* (1988) 4 B.C.C. 513, there was a suggestion that the court might be more willing to consider granting a disqualified person leave to act as a director of a company if it was an unlimited company and he was prepared to assume unlimited personal liability. In *Shuttleworth v Secretary of State for Trade and Industry* [2000] B.C.C. 204 a director was allowed to act in relation to an unlimited company, so long as it did not convert to a limited company or have any limited subsidiaries. On similar reasoning, the courts have thought it appropriate that an applicant should act as a consultant (*Re Barings plc (No.5)* [1999] B.C.C. 960), or trade in partnership (*Re Amaron Ltd* [1998] B.C.C. 264), rather than be given leave to act as director of a limited company.

Leave to act under a disqualification order may be granted either at the time when the original order is made, or subsequently. The former course is desirable as "in everyone's interests" (*Re Dicetrade Ltd* [1994] B.C.C. 371 at 373). In the latter case application need not be made to the same court. See further s.17 below.

The Court of Appeal in *Re Westmid Packing Services Ltd Secretary of State for Trade and Industry v Griffiths* [1998] B.C.C. 836 gave guidance on what is relevant and admissible evidence in an application for leave under s.17.

Where the Secretary of State accepts a disqualification undertaking in lieu of applying to the court for a disqualification order, the person who has given the undertaking may apply to a court for leave to act notwithstanding the undertaking (s.1A(1)(a)). Section 17(3) and (4) gives guidance as to the appropriate court. The Secretary of State has no power to grant leave himself, or to accept an undertaking subject to conditions. This would be true also in the case of competition undertakings.

Neither the present Act nor any of the immediately relevant rules contain provisions dealing with appeals from a disqualification order, although *Practice Direction: Directors Disqualification Proceedings* [2015] B.C.C. 224 (see App.VI below) in para.32 contains some (now outdated) guidance. The current *Practice Direction: Insolvency Proceedings* [2018] B.C.C. 421, para.17.4 (see App.IV) provides guidance on appeals "in corporate insolvency matters" (undefined). By extension from the above *Practice Direction: Directors Disqualification Proceedings* [2015] B.C.C. 224, para.32, updated IR 2016 r.12.59 applies to disqualification proceedings under CDDA 1986 ss.6–8A or 9A, and applications for leave to act under s.17 from orders under ss.6–10. (Note that ss.8ZA–8ZE appear before s.8A but came into force after the 2015 *Practice Direction: Directors Disqualification Proceedings* was issued.) An appeal from a decision of a district judge in the county court on a corporate insolvency matter is to a High Court judge or an Insolvency and Companies Court Judge, depending on location in accordance with IR 2016 Sch.10. An appeal from a district judge sitting in a District Registry in a corporate insolvency matter is to a High Court judge (not a deputy, although a supervising judge in the Business and Property Courts (which includes the Companies Court or Bankruptcy Court of the Chancery Division) may by discretion allow the appeal to be handled by a circuit judge sitting as a High Court judge under s.9(1) of the Senior Courts Act 1981). An appeal from a decision by a recorder or circuit judge in a corporate insolvency matter is to a High Court judge (not a deputy). An appeal from a first-instance decision of an Insolvency and Companies Court Judge on a corporate insolvency matter is to a High Court judge (not a deputy). An appeal in a corporate insolvency matter from a decision of an Insolvency and Companies Court Judge on appeal from a district judge is to the Civil Division of the Court of Appeal. A first appeal is subject to the permission requirements of CPR r.52.3 (previously permission was not required of any court (*Secretary of State for Trade and Industry v Paulin* [2005] EWHC 888 (Ch); [2005] B.C.C. 927). A first appeal does not, however, include an appeal from a decision of a judge or Registrar of the High Court. See *Practice Direction: Insolvency Proceedings* [2018] B.C.C. 421, para.17.4(6)–(10) and for permission paras 18.1, 18.2.

An appeal from a decision of a judge of the High Court made on a first appeal lies to the Court of Appeal, but only with the permission of the Court of Appeal. Such permission will not be granted unless the Court of Appeal considers that (a) the appeal will raise an important point of principle or practice; or (b) there is some other compelling reason for the Court of Appeal to hear it (Access to Justice Act 1999 s.55). An appeal from a judge of the High Court which is not a decision on a first appeal lies to the Court of Appeal with the permission of either the judge or the Court of Appeal. The procedure and practice for an appeal from such a decision or from a first appeal are governed by IR 2016 r.12.59, which imports the procedure and practice of the Court of Appeal (CPR Pt 52).

Further guidance on these provisions governing appeals may be found in *Tanfern Ltd v Cameron-MacDonald* [2000] 2 All E.R. 801; and *Clark (Inspector of Taxes) v Perks* [2000] 4 All E.R. 1.

It was stated in *Re New Technology Systems Ltd* [1997] B.C.C. 810 that an application for leave to appeal should normally be made to the appeal court rather than the trial court, unless some point of law or principle is in issue which the lower court considers appropriate to be reviewed on appeal.

An appeal in disqualification proceedings is, at least in the normal case, a "true" appeal rather than a rehearing: the appellant has the burden of proving that the ruling below was wrong: *Secretary of State for Trade and Industry v Jones* [1999] B.C.C. 336. However, very exceptionally, the court will sometimes in its discretion proceed by way of rehearing (relying on CPR r.52.11): *Lewis v Secretary of State for Trade and Industry* [2001] 2 B.C.L.C. 597. However, where there is little or no dispute as to the primary facts, the appellate court is in as good a position as the trial judge to form a judgment as to the respondent's unfitness, so that it is free to draw its own conclusion and, where appropriate, reverse the judge's finding on the question: *Re Grayan Building Services Ltd* [1995] B.C.C. 554; *Re Structural Concrete Ltd* [2001] B.C.C. 588. Fresh evidence will not be admitted on an appeal unless it is shown (a) that it could not with reasonable diligence have been obtained for use at the trial; (b) the evidence, if given, would probably have an important influence on the result of the case; and (c) the evidence is apparently credible: *Re Barings plc (No.5)* [2000] 1 B.C.L.C. 534.

The court on appeal may extend or reduce the period of disqualification or discharge the order altogether: *Secretary of State for Trade & Industry v Bannister* [1996] 1 W.L.R. 118 at 122; [1995] B.C.C. 1,027 at 1,030. But it will interfere with the period fixed by the trial judge only if the latter has erred in principle (e.g. by not having regard to the threefold "bracketing" of periods recommended in the *Sevenoaks Stationers* case (see the note to s.1(2) below), or has taken wrong factors into account: *Secretary of State for Trade and Industry v McTighe* [1997] B.C.C. 224; *Secretary of State for Trade and Industry v Griffiths, Re Westmid Packing Services Ltd (No.3)* [1998] 2 All E.R. 124; [1998] B.C.C. 836; *Re Saver Ltd* [1999] B.C.C. 221; *Re TLL Realisations Ltd* [2000] B.C.C. 998. Where the appeal is from the refusal of the lower court to make a disqualification order and the appeal is successful, the appeal court may either determine the appropriate length of disqualification itself or remit the question to the court below (*Secretary of State for Trade and Industry v Deverell* [2001] Ch. 340; [2000] B.C.C. 1057). If a disqualification order has been made and the director has been granted leave to take part in the management of a company, and the Secretary of State considers that the court erred by giving leave, it is open to him to appeal against the decision to grant leave: *Secretary of State for Trade and Industry v Collins* [2000] B.C.C. 998. But an appeal court will interfere with the decision of the trial judge to grant or refuse leave only if he has misdirected himself about material considerations or come to a plainly erroneous conclusion (ibid.).

There is no express provision in the Act or the rules giving a court power to suspend the operation of a disqualification order pending the hearing of an appeal, but in *Bannister's* case (above) it was held that both the High Court and the Court of Appeal may do so in their inherent jurisdiction. The question whether the county court has such a power was left open. However, the question is probably academic because the court in *Bannister's* case also made it clear that normally the better procedure would be for the director to be given leave to act under s.17 in relation to specified companies pending the hearing of the appeal, and that the power to grant a stay should be invoked only in extreme cases "in which the court below went badly wrong and the very existence of the disqualification order causes irreparable harm to the person apparently disqualified". In such an extreme case, it is more appropriate that the question of a stay should be determined by the appeal court rather than the court below: *Re Continental Assurance Co of London plc* [1996] B.C.C. 888 at 899. See also *Secretary of State for Business, Innovation and Skills v Atkar* (unreported, 10 June 2016, Nugee J, following *Bannister*).

No specific provision is made in the Act for the variation of a disqualification order; but that there is power to do so is perhaps confirmed by the Companies (Disqualification Orders) Regulations 2009 (SI 2009/2471) reg.4(b) and the Insolvent Companies (Disqualification of Unfit Directors) Rules 1987 (SI 1987/2023) r.8(2). This is in any case something which the High Court, at least, could do in its inherent jurisdiction. The court in *Re Brian Sheridan Cars Ltd* [1995] B.C.C. 1035 made an order varying the terms of an original order, but this was pursuant to a power reserved in the earlier order. The Act makes special provision for the court to order the variation of a disqualification undertaking in s.8A.

The normal rule that costs are in the discretion of the court applies to proceedings in relation to disqualification orders. For a period it had come to be accepted that certain practices favourable to the Crown should displace this rule: (1) that costs should not be awarded against the Secretary of State in situations where a prima facie case of unfitness had been made out against a director which was subsequently rebutted by evidence (see, e.g. *Re Douglas Construction Services Ltd* (1988) 4 B.C.C. 553; *Re Cladrose Ltd* [1990] B.C.C. 11); and (2) that where costs were awarded against an unsuccessful respondent in favour of the Secretary of State or official receiver, it should be on an indemnity and not on the standard basis (see, e.g. *Re Brooks Transport (Purfleet) Ltd* [1993] B.C.C. 766 and the cases there cited). However the former practice was disapproved of in *Re Southbourne Sheet Metal Co Ltd* [1993] 1 W.L.R. 244; [1992] B.C.C. 797, where Nourse LJ made it clear that the ruling applied also where the applicant has discontinued the proceedings, and the latter practice was rejected by Chadwick J in *Re Godwin Warren Control Systems plc* [1992] B.C.C. 557 (a decision subsequently approved by the Court of Appeal in *Re Dicetrade Ltd, Secretary of State for Trade & Industry v Worth* [1994] B.C.C. 371). In the latter case it was said that it would not usually be appropriate to make a separate costs order in favour of the Secretary of State in regard to an application for leave to act when the application was made contemporaneously with the main hearing; but that the position would be otherwise if the application for leave was made at a later date. This distinction was endorsed by the Court of Appeal in *Re TLL Realisations Ltd* [2000] B.C.C. 998. In *Re Smart-Tel (UK) plc* [2007] B.C.C. 896 the claimant discontinued the proceedings after the defendant had filed and served his evidence in answer, following three hearings and more than a year after the commencement of the case. The court ordered that the defendant's costs should be discounted by 20 per cent because his conduct in failing to provide the claimant with full access to the company's books and records had contributed to the prolongation of the case.

Where the application is made by the official receiver, he is entitled to an award of costs on the basis that he is a litigant in person: *Official Receiver v Brunt* [1998] 4 All E.R. 500; [1999] B.C.C. 571.

In *Re Sykes (Butchers) Ltd* [1998] B.C.C. 484 one respondent was ordered to pay part of the costs of a second respondent against whom the Secretary of State's application had been dismissed.

Costs on an indemnity basis were awarded against the Secretary of State, when proceedings against a director (in which fraud had been alleged without justification) had been discontinued, in *Re City Truck Group Ltd* [2006] B.C.C. 384.

S.1(2)

Under the legislation as originally enacted, only s.6(4) contained provision for a minimum period of disqualification (two years), but it has now been joined by the new s.8ZA(4) (instructing director who has been disqualified on the ground of unfitness). (Although s.9A(1) makes it mandatory for the court to make an order if unfitness is found, no minimum period is fixed.) In *Re Bath Glass Ltd* (1988) 4 B.C.C. 130 at 133, Peter Gibson J expressed the view that the fact that the legislature had imposed this minimum disqualification period for "unfitness" was relevant to deciding whether a person should be classed as "unfit": only conduct which was sufficiently serious to warrant such a period of disqualification would justify a conclusion that a person was unfit. There is no power to make an order of indefinite duration.

In *Re Sevenoaks Stationers (Retail) Ltd* [1991] Ch. 164; [1990] B.C.C. 765 (the first reported director disqualification case decided by the Court of Appeal), Dillon LJ thought that it would be a helpful guide to the courts to divide the possible periods of disqualification under s.6 into three brackets. The top period of disqualification for periods of 10–15 years should be reserved for particularly serious cases. This might include cases where a director who had already been disqualified fell to be disqualified again. The minimum bracket of two to five years' disqualification should be applied where, although disqualification was mandatory, the case was relatively not very serious. The middle bracket of disqualification for from six to ten years should apply in serious cases which did not merit the top bracket. In *R. v Goodman* [1992] B.C.C. 625 at 628 the guidelines were not applied in criminal proceedings under s.2; but they were referred to in *R. v Millard* (1993) 15 Cr. App. R. (S) 445. In *Randhawa v Official Receiver* [2006] B.P.I.R. 1435 it was considered "helpful and appropriate" to adopt the same three brackets in the context of bankruptcy restrictions orders. (See also *Official Receiver v Pyman* [2007] EWHC 2002 (Ch); [2007] B.P.I.R. 1150.)

The Court of Appeal has since given further guidance in *Re Westmid Packing Services Ltd, Secretary of State for Trade and Industry v Griffiths* [1998] B.C.C. 836. In determining the appropriate period of disqualification the court should start with an assessment of the correct period to fit the gravity of the offence, bearing in mind that the period has to contain deterrent elements, and then allow for mitigating factors (such factors not being restricted to the facts of the offence). The power to grant leave under s.17 (and the fact that the court is minded to grant leave) is, however, not relevant at this stage. Relevant matters include the director's general reputation and conduct in discharge of the office of director, his age and state of health, the length of time he has been in jeopardy, whether he had admitted the offence, his general conduct before and after the offence and the periods of disqualification meted out to any of his co-directors.

In the same case Lord Woolf MR stated that in the great majority of cases it is unnecessary and inappropriate for the court to be taken through the facts of previous cases in order to guide it on the period of disqualification: this, he said, was a jurisdiction which the court should exercise in a summary manner, using a "broad brush" approach.

In *Re Smooth Financial Consultants Ltd* [2018] EWHC 2146 (Ch) the court stated that in determining disqualification periods it was important to take into account all the relevant circumstances, including the period of time for which each defendant had been culpable, their respective roles and knowledge of the company's financial position, the impact disqualification would have on their respective career prospects, and the extent to which each had been involved in the financial administration of the company.

In *Secretary of State for Business, Innovation and Skills v Warry* [2014] EWHC 1381 (Ch) the court gave guidance on the disqualification periods that should be imposed in cases of missing trader fraud: normally, in the top bracket (10–15 years).

In *Re Mea Corp Ltd* [2006] EWHC 1846 (Ch); [2007] B.C.C. 288 the disqualification period was increased from 7 to 11 years because the respondent was already subject to a disqualification order.

Chadwick J in *Secretary of State for Trade and Industry v Arif* [1996] B.C.C. 586 considered that the court cannot take into account in fixing the period of disqualification the fact that the person has been suspended from acting as a director or has voluntarily refrained from doing so pending the hearing, but he added that such de facto disqualification could be a relevant consideration on an application for leave to act under s.17. However, the Court of Appeal in *Re Westmid Packing Services Ltd, Secretary of State for Trade and Industry v Griffiths* [1998] B.C.C. 836 disagreed with that comment regarding the length of the disqualification period, and in the Scottish case *Secretary of State for Business, Innovation and Skills v Bloch* [2013] CSOH 57 the court took into account as a mitigating factor the fact that for several years the respondent had treated himself as de facto disqualified and had turned down a number of offers of directorships.

See *Secretary of State for Business, Innovation and Skills v Rahman* [2017] EWHC 2468 (Ch) for a useful review of disqualification period cases and in particular the correct disqualification period "bracket".

Section 1(2) (as amended by IA 2000) provides that the period of disqualification shall begin 21 days after the date of the order (unless the court orders otherwise). The defendant is thus given a breathing space to sort out his affairs before the order takes effect. The discretion given to the court to order otherwise will allow this period to be extended or curtailed in special circumstances—even, conceivably, to make the disqualification run from the end of a custodial sentence.

S.1(3)

This statutory prohibition on making cumulative disqualification orders has been amended to deal with the case where an order is sought against a respondent who is already subject to a disqualification undertaking. The counterpart situation, where an undertaking is given by a person who is already disqualified, is dealt with in ss.1A(3) and 9B(6).

The rule applies where an order is made as part of a criminal sentence and another in civil proceedings (*Re Living Images Ltd* [1996] B.C.C. 112 at 136).

S.1(4)

This makes it clear that disqualification proceedings may go ahead independently and without regard to the possibility that a criminal prosecution may be brought in respect of the same matter. In *Re TransTec plc* [2005] EWHC 1723 (Ch); [2006] B.C.C. 295 respondents to disqualification proceedings sought a stay, and more particularly a direction that they should not be required to prepare and serve their written evidence, before the commencement of criminal proceedings arising out of their conduct as directors. The application was refused, but some conditions were imposed relating to the disclosure of the evidence prior to the end of the criminal trial to persons other than the Secretary of State.

In *Re Cedarwood Productions Ltd, Secretary of State for Trade and Industry v Rayna* [2001] EWCA Civ 1083; [2004] B.C.C. 65 disqualification proceedings had been stayed pending the outcome of criminal proceedings against the respondents. On conviction, the trial judge disqualified them for two years under CDDA 1986 s.2. The Secretary of State then successfully applied for the disqualification proceedings to be restored, on the ground that factors which might justify a longer period of disqualification could be taken into account for that purpose which would not have been available to the criminal court. See also *Re Denis Hilton Ltd* [2002] B.C.L.C. 302, and the note to s.2(1).

In *Re Rex Williams Leisure plc* [1994] Ch. 350; [1994] B.C.C. 551 the respondent director sought a stay of disqualification proceedings which had been brought against him by the Secretary of State until civil litigation in which he was a defendant had been disposed of. The same matters were material to both sets of proceedings. The court refused to grant a stay. The Court of Appeal, affirming Nicholls V.C. [1994] Ch. 1; [1993] B.C.C. 79, stated that the public interest in having disqualification orders made against unfit directors of insolvent companies should not be subordinated to private litigation.

1A   Disqualification undertakings: general

1A(1)   [Power of Secretary of State] In the circumstances specified in sections 5A, 7, 8, 8ZC and 8ZE the Secretary of State may accept a disqualification undertaking, that is to say an undertaking by any person that, for a period specified in the undertaking, the person–

(a)   will not be a director of a company, act as receiver of a company's property or in any way, whether directly or indirectly, be concerned or take part in the promotion, formation or management of a company unless (in each case) he has the leave of a court, and

(b)   will not act as an insolvency practitioner.

1A(2)   [Maximum period] The maximum period which may be specified in a disqualification undertaking is 15 years; and the minimum period which may be specified in a disqualification undertaking under section 7 or 8ZC is two years.

1A(3)   [Undertakings, etc. to run concurrently] Where a disqualification undertaking by a person who is already subject to such an undertaking or to a disqualification order is accepted, the periods specified in those undertakings or (as the case may be) the undertaking and the order shall run concurrently.

1A(4)   [Matters other than criminal convictions] In determining whether to accept a disqualification undertaking by any person, the Secretary of State may take account of matters other than criminal convictions, notwithstanding that the person may be criminally liable in respect of those matters.

GENERAL NOTE

Section 1A contains one of the major reforms made by IA 2000: the introduction of disqualification undertakings as an alternative to disqualification orders made by a court. This regime applies only to disqualification cases under ss.7 and 8, i.e. to situations based on "unfitness", but there is also parallel provision for competition undertakings in s.9B. The Secretary of State is empowered to dispose of a case administratively, without any involvement by the court, if the person concerned is prepared to give an undertaking and the Secretary of State to accept it and they are agreed on the period for which the undertaking is to run. The *Carecraft* procedure (see the note to s.7(1), below) has, in consequence, now fallen into disuse, with a considerable saving of court time and expense. An undertaking has for all practical purposes the same effect as a disqualification order, and the consequences of a breach are also the same.

This may be contrasted with the handful of cases decided prior to 2000 in which, exceptionally, the court had been prepared to accept an undertaking from a respondent not to act as a director in lieu of making a disqualification order where, for example, he was not fit enough to face a full hearing (see, e.g. *Re Homes Assured Corp plc* [1993] B.C.C. 573). The undertaking in such a case was given to the court, and in the event of a breach would have been sanctioned by proceedings for contempt (which would have to be instituted by some interested party). Under s.1A, the civil consequences of a breach follow automatically under s.15 and criminal liability under ss.13–14 is strict, and the register of disqualification orders (s.18) now includes those who have given undertakings.

The Secretary of State is not obliged to accept an undertaking, even where the facts are admitted: he may (for instance) take a test case to the court, or consider that it is in the public interest that a full trial be held in a particular case. In *Re Blackspur Group plc (No.3), Secretary of State for Trade and Industry v Davies (No.2)* [2001] EWCA Civ 1595; [2002] 2 B.C.L.C. 363 the Court of Appeal, affirming Patten J, held that the Secretary of State was entitled to refuse to accept an undertaking unless the person giving the undertaking was prepared to sign a statement of agreed facts (which could be relied on, and would not be disputed, in any future proceedings).

If an undertaking is offered before proceedings have been issued, the Secretary of State will not usually seek to recover his costs, but if offered later, he normally will: see *Dear IP*, Ch.10(4).

If a person who has given an undertaking wishes to have leave to act, this must be sought from a court under s.17. The Secretary of State cannot give leave himself or accept an undertaking qualified by any concessions: *Re Morija plc* [2007] EWHC 3055 (Ch); [2008] 2 B.C.L.C. 313 at [7]. On an application to the court, the director cannot dispute the correctness of facts which he accepted when signing the disqualification undertaking (ibid.). The court also has power to vary an undertaking under s.8A, but only in limited respects: see the note to that section.

IR 2016 r.12.59 (appeals in insolvency proceedings) applies only to appeals from orders of the court, and has no application to disqualification undertakings: *Eastaway v Secretary of State for Trade and Industry* [2007] EWCA Civ 425; [2007] B.C.C. 550.

On disqualification undertakings, see Williams, *Disqualification Undertakings: Law, Policy and Practice* (Jordans, 2011).

S.1A(1), (2)
The detailed terms of an undertaking are identical with those of a disqualification order. The maximum period is 15 years under ss.7, 8 and 9B; there is a minimum of two years if the undertaking is given under s.7, but no minimum if it is under s.8 or 9B.

S.1A(3), (4)
These provisions correspond with s.1(3), (4). See the notes to those subsections.

Disqualification for general misconduct in connection with companies

2 Disqualification on conviction of indictable offence

2(1) **[Court's power]** The court may make a disqualification order against a person where he is convicted of an indictable offence (whether on indictment or summarily) in connection with the promotion, formation, management, liquidation or striking off of a company, with the receivership of a company's property or with his being an administrative receiver of a company.

2(1A) **[Overseas company included]** In subsection (1), "company" includes overseas company.

2(2) **["The court"]** "The court" for this purpose means–

  (a) any court having jurisdiction to wind up the company in relation to which the offence was committed, or

  (aa) in relation to an overseas company not falling within paragraph (a), the High Court or, in Scotland, the Court of Session, or

  (b) the court by or before which the person is convicted of the offence, or

  (c) in the case of a summary conviction in England and Wales, any other magistrates' court acting in the same local justice area;

and for the purposes of this section the definition of "indictable offence" in Schedule 1 to the Interpretation Act 1978 applies for Scotland as it does for England and Wales.

2(3) **[Maximum period]** The maximum period of disqualification under this section is–

(a) where the disqualification order is made by a court of summary jurisdiction, 5 years, and

(b) in any other case, 15 years.

GENERAL NOTE

Section 2(1A) and 2(2)(aa) inserted by SBEEA Sch.7 para.4 as from 1 October 2015. The Act now empowers the courts to make a disqualification order (and the Secretary of State to accept a disqualification undertaking) on the basis of a person's conduct in relation to an overseas company.

S.2(1)
A conviction for an indictable offence is a precondition for the operation of this section (although the proceedings need not have been on indictment). The disqualification order may be made by the court by which the offender is convicted or by the same or another court on an application made subsequently.

The scope of s.2 is not confined to offences which arise out of the management of the internal affairs of the company: it may extend to offences in relation to third parties, e.g. defrauding finance companies (*R. v Corbin* (1984) 6 Cr. App. R. (S) 17) or an insurance company (*R. v Appleyard* (1985) 81 Cr. App. R. 319). In *R. v Georgiou* (1988) 4 B.C.C. 322 there was no actual misconduct of the company's affairs, internal or external: the offence of which the respondent was convicted was the carrying on of an unauthorised insurance business through the medium of a limited liability company. In *R. v Goodman* [1992] B.C.C. 625 the defendant had been convicted of insider dealing under the Company Securities (Insider Dealing) Act 1985, and sentenced to a term of imprisonment. The Court of Appeal held that it was competent also to impose a disqualification order: it was sufficient that the accused had been convicted of an indictable offence which had some relevant factual connection with the management of a company.

See also *R. v Millard* (1993) 15 Cr. App. R. (S) 445.

It is not open to the Secretary of State to apply for a disqualification order after the court in criminal proceedings has been invited to disqualify the director and has declined to do so, unless his application is based on facts sufficiently different from those in the criminal case: *Secretary of State for Business, Innovation and Skills v Weston* [2014] EWHC 2933 (Ch); [2014] B.C.C. 581. The earlier decisions in *Re Cedarwood Productions Ltd* [2001] EWCA Civ 1083; [2004] B.C.C. 65 and *Re Denis Hilton Ltd* [2002] 1 B.C.L.C. 302 must be read in the light of this ruling. An alternative course which the Secretary of State might take is to initiate and then stay proceedings under s.6 pending the outcome of a criminal trial.

Although a disqualification order by the criminal court would normally be at the end of the criminal proceedings or (by the criminal or civil court) might be expected to follow shortly after the criminal proceedings, there appears no reason why it could not be made later (presumably subject to limitation principles). Following successful criminal proceedings in *Health and Safety Executive v Allen & Hunt Construction Engineers Ltd* (unreported, 22 November 2016) a disqualification undertaking was accepted 18 months later after the Insolvency Service intervened.

It is clear from the opening wording of s.2(1) ("The court may make a disqualification order") that the court's power is discretionary. It appears that in deciding whether to exercise the discretion to make a disqualification order under the section a civil court (but not the sentencing criminal court: s.12C(2)) must under s.12C(1)(b), (4)(a) have regard to the matters in paras 1–4 of Sch.1 (and see *Secretary of State for Business, Innovation and Skills v Rahman* [2017] EWHC 2468 (Ch); [2018] B.C.C. 567 at [52]–[54]), although for disqualification under s.2 the director does not need to be "unfit" (see s.12C(3), (4)(a)).

Applications for permission to act while disqualified under s.2 are extremely rare and carry a heavy burden of proof: *Re Liberty Holdings Unltd* [2017] B.C.C. 298, where in fact the court did grant leave.

In *R. v Chandler (Lloyd)* [2015] EWCA Crim 1825; [2016] B.C.C. 212 a director had been convicted of three regulatory offences (offences of strict liability) and, in addition to substantial fines, had been disqualified by the judge without prior warning or any opportunity to call witnesses or address issues relevant to the disqualification. The Court of Appeal quashed the disqualification order.

S.2(2)
The court having jurisdiction to wind up a company is defined by IA 1986 ss.117 et seq. (for England and Wales) and 120 et seq. (for Scotland). Where the application is made to such a court, the procedure is governed by s.16, below.

See also the note to s.6(3).

S.2(3)
In assessing the disqualification period the court will apply the three brackets from *Re Sevenoaks Stationers (Retail) Ltd* [1991] Ch. 164; [1990] B.C.C. 765 notwithstanding that the latter case was a civil court appeal: see *R. v Millard* (1994) 15 Cr. App. R. (S) 445 and *R. v Cadman* [2012] 2 Cr. App. R. (S) 88. See also *Secretary of State for Business,*

Innovation and Skills v Rahman [2017] EWHC 2468 (Ch); [2018] B.C.C. 567 for a discussion of the application of criminal court jurisprudence on disqualification periods under s.2 to civil proceedings.

3 Disqualification for persistent breaches of companies legislation

3(1) **[Court's power]** The court may make a disqualification order against a person where it appears to it that he has been persistently in default in relation to provisions of the companies legislation requiring any return, account or other document to be filed with, delivered or sent, or notice of any matter to be given, to the registrar of companies.

3(2) **[Conclusive proof of default]** On an application to the court for an order to be made under this section, the fact that a person has been persistently in default in relation to such provisions as are mentioned above may (without prejudice to its proof in any other manner) be conclusively proved by showing that in the 5 years ending with the date of the application he has been adjudged guilty (whether or not on the same occasion) of three or more defaults in relation to those provisions.

3(3) **[Guilty of default under s.3(2)]** A person is to be treated under subsection (2) as being adjudged guilty of a default in relation to any provision of that legislation if–

   (a)   he is convicted (whether on indictment or summarily) of an offence consisting in a contravention of or failure to comply with that provision (whether on his own part or on the part of any company), or

   (b)   a default order is made against him, that is to say an order under any of the following provisions–

       (i)   section 452 of the Companies Act 2006 (order requiring delivery of company accounts),

       (ia) section 456 of that Act (order requiring preparation of revised accounts),

       (ii) section 1113 of that Act (enforcement of company's filing obligations),

       (iii) section 41 of the Insolvency Act 1986 (enforcement of receiver's or manager's duty to make returns), or

       (iv) section 170 of that Act (corresponding provision for liquidator in winding up),

in respect of any such contravention of or failure to comply with that provision (whether on his own part or on the part of any company).

3(3A) **[Overseas company included]** In this section "company" includes overseas company.

3(4) **["The court"]** In this section "the court" means–

   (a)   any court having jurisdiction to wind up any of the companies in relation to which the offence or other default has been or is alleged to have been committed, or

   (b)   in relation to an overseas company not falling within paragraph (a), the High Court or, in Scotland, the Court of Session.

3(4A) **["The companies legislation" in s.3]** In this section "the companies legislation" means the Companies Acts and Parts 1 to 7 of the Insolvency Act 1986 (company insolvency and winding up).

3(5) **[Maximum period]** The maximum period of disqualification under this section is 5 years.

GENERAL NOTE

This section runs closely parallel with s.5, which empowers the court entering a summary conviction against a person for a company law offence to make a disqualification order if he has had two or more similar convictions in the preceding five years. Minor textual amendments were made and s.3(4A) inserted by the Companies Act 2006 (Consequential Amendments, Transitional Provisions and Savings) Order 2009 (SI 2009/1941) art.2(1) and Sch.1 para.85(2) as from 1 October 2009. Section 3(3A) and 3(4)(b) inserted by SBEEA Sch.7 para.5 as from 1 October

2015. The Act now empowers the courts to make a disqualification order (and the Secretary of State to accept a disqualification undertaking) on the basis of a person's conduct in relation to an overseas company.

S.3(1)
"Persistent default" in complying with the filing instructions of the companies legislation is made a ground for disqualification by this section. "Persistent default" may be established by invoking the presumptions contained in the following subsections.

In *Re Arctic Engineering Ltd* [1986] 1 W.L.R. 686; (1985) 1 B.C.C. 99, 563 it was held that the term "persistently" requires some degree of continuance or repetition. A person may persist in the same default, or persistently commit a series of defaults. However, it is not necessary to show that he or she has been culpable, in the sense of evincing a *deliberate* disregard of the statutory requirements, although such culpability can be taken into account in considering whether to make a disqualification order and, if so, for how long.

S.3(2)
The meaning of "adjudged guilty" is explained in s.3(3).

S.3(3)
Section 3(3)(b) was amended by the Companies Act 2006 (Consequential Amendments etc.) Order 2008 (SI 2008/948) art.3(1) and Sch.1 para.106(2), as from 6 April 2008.

The obligation to file documents with the registrar of companies is most often placed on the company itself rather than on any particular officer, but some duties (e.g. to deliver annual accounts) are specifically imposed on the directors, and others on the liquidator or some other office-holder. However, even where the duty lies with the company, it is ordinarily provided that the company and any "officer in default" shall be guilty of an offence—i.e. "any officer of the company who knowingly and wilfully authorises or permits the default ... or contravention" (CA 2006 s.1121(3)). A director can thus be guilty of an offence when his company is in breach of the Act, but for para.(a) of the present subsection to apply, it is the director who must have been convicted, and not merely the company.

The five statutory provisions mentioned in para.(b) empower the court to make an order directing a company and any officer of it to make good the default in question. This may be done on the application of the registrar of companies or any member (under IA 1986 s.170, any contributory) or creditor. Again, for para.(b) to apply, the default order must have been made against the person concerned and not merely his company.

S.3(4)
See the notes to ss.2(2) and 6(3) and, for the procedure, s.16.

4   Disqualification for fraud, etc., in winding up

4(1)   [Court's power] The court may make a disqualification order against a person if, in the course of the winding up of a company, it appears that he–

(a)   has been guilty of an offence for which he is liable (whether he has been convicted or not) under section 993 of the Companies Act 2006 (fraudulent trading), or

(b)   has otherwise been guilty, while an officer or liquidator of the company, receiver of the company's property or administrative receiver of the company, of any fraud in relation to the company or of any breach of his duty as such officer, liquidator, receiver or administrative receiver.

4(2)   [Definitions] In this section "the court" means any court having jurisdiction to wind up any of the companies in relation to which the offence or other default has been or is alleged to have been committed; and "officer" includes a shadow director.

4(3)   [Maximum period] The maximum period of disqualification under this section is 15 years.

S.4(1)
There is some overlap between this provision and s.2: the main points of distinction are that a conviction is a prerequisite for the operation of s.2, but not s.4, while a winding up is necessary for s.4, but not s.2. If the court has declined to make a disqualification order under s.2 following a conviction, an application for disqualification under s.4 may not be made on the same facts: *Secretary of State for Business, Innovation and Skills v Weston* [2014] EWHC 2933 (Ch).

The offence of fraudulent trading could formerly be committed only if the company ended up in liquidation, but this limitation was removed, so far as criminal proceedings are concerned, by CA 1981 s.96. However, the same limitation continues to apply in the present section, and so if a director is convicted under CA 2006 s.993 while his company is a going concern, any disqualification order must be sought under s.2 and not s.4.

There is also the possibility of an overlap between the present section and s.10, which allows a disqualification order to be made in the case where a person has had a declaration of liability made against him for fraudulent or wrongful trading.

Paragraph (b) does not appear to apply to an administrator or to the supervisor of a CVA.

For s.4(1)(b) to warrant the disqualification of an officer or office-holder, the "breach of duty" must be, if not fraudulent, at least very serious. The provision does not cover breaches of duty which are trivial or the result of a mistake: *Re Adbury Park Estates Ltd* [2003] B.C.C. 696; although, if serious misconduct is established, the court may take other less important breaches into account in deciding what order to make, and a number of relatively minor breaches might also, if taken together, be thought sufficiently serious to justify making an order (*Re Asegaai Consultants Ltd, Wood v Mistry* [2012] EWHC 1899 (Ch); [2013] 1 B.C.L.C. 389. In the *Adbury Park* case the court also held that only a person with a tangible interest in the order sought had standing to bring an application, but in *Asegaai Consultants* this was not held to be necessary where the applicant was a liquidator (or the Secretary of State or the official receiver), where the purpose of the disqualification was essentially the protection of the public.

Section 4(1)(a) was amended by the Companies Act 2006 (Commencement No.3, Consequential Amendments, Transitional Provisions and Savings) Order 2007 (SI 2007/2194 (C. 84)) art.9 and Sch.3 para.46 as from 1 October 2007.

S.4(2)

On the meaning of "the court", see the notes to ss.2(2) and 6(3).

The Companies Act definition of the term "officer" (CA 2006 s.1173) is incorporated into the present Act by s.22(9). For a discussion of this definition, see the note to IA 1986 s.206(3).

For the meaning of "shadow director", see s.22(5).

5   Disqualification on summary conviction

5(1)   [Relevant offences] An offence counting for the purposes of this section is one of which a person is convicted (either on indictment or summarily) in consequence of a contravention of, or failure to comply with, any provision of the companies legislation requiring a return, account or other document to be filed with, delivered or sent, or notice of any matter to be given, to the registrar of companies (whether the contravention or failure is on the person's own part or on the part of any company).

5(2)   [Court's power] Where a person is convicted of a summary offence counting for those purposes, the court by which he is convicted (or, in England and Wales, any other magistrates' court acting in the same local justice area) may make a disqualification order against him if the circumstances specified in the next subsection are present.

5(3)   [Circumstances in s.5(2)] Those circumstances are that, during the 5 years ending with the date of the conviction, the person has had made against him, or has been convicted of, in total not less than 3 default orders and offences counting for the purposes of this section; and those offences may include that of which he is convicted as mentioned in subsection (2) and any other offence of which he is convicted on the same occasion.

5(4)   [Definitions] For the purposes of this section–

(a)   the definition of "summary offence" in Schedule 1 to the Interpretation Act 1978 applies for Scotland as for England and Wales, and

(b)   "default order" means the same as in section 3(3)(b).

5(4A)   ["The companies legislation" in s.5] In this section "the companies legislation" means the Companies Acts and Parts 1 to 7 of the Insolvency Act 1986 (company insolvency and winding up).

5(4B)   [Overseas company included] In this section "company" includes overseas company.

5(5)   [Maximum period] The maximum period of disqualification under this section is 5 years.

GENERAL NOTE

Section 5(4A) was inserted by the Companies Act 2006 (Consequential Amendments, Transitional Provisions and Savings) Order 2009 (SI 2009/1941) art.2(1) and Sch.1 para.85(3) as from 1 October 2009. Section 5(4B) inserted by SBEEA Sch.7 para.6 as from 1 October 2015. The Act now empowers the courts to make a disqualification order (and the Secretary of State to accept a disqualification undertaking) on the basis of a person's conduct in relation to an overseas company.

This section and s.3 deal with very much the same situation, except that an order under s.3 may be made only by the court having jurisdiction to wind up one of the companies concerned, i.e. the High Court or in some cases the county court, and their Scottish counterparts. Prosecutions for failure to make company law returns will, however, invariably be brought summarily, and this section enables the court exercising summary jurisdiction in such a case itself to make a disqualification order for "persistent default".

For further discussion, see the note to s.3.

5A Disqualification for certain convictions abroad

5A(1) **[Application by Secretary of State]** If it appears to the Secretary of State that it is expedient in the public interest that a disqualification order under this section should be made against a person, the Secretary of State may apply to the court for such an order.

5A(2) **[Court's power to make disqualification order]** The court may, on an application under subsection (1), make a disqualification order against a person who has been convicted of a relevant foreign offence.

5A(3) **["Relevant foreign offence"]** A **"relevant foreign offence"** is an offence committed outside Great Britain–

(a) in connection with–

   (i) the promotion, formation, management, liquidation or striking off of a company (or any similar procedure),

   (ii) the receivership of a company's property (or any similar procedure), or

   (iii) a person being an administrative receiver of a company (or holding a similar position), and

(b) which corresponds to an indictable offence under the law of England and Wales or (as the case may be) an indictable offence under the law of Scotland.

5A(4) **[Secretary of State's acceptance of undertaking]** Where it appears to the Secretary of State that, in the case of a person who has offered to give a disqualification undertaking–

(a) the person has been convicted of a relevant foreign offence, and

(b) it is expedient in the public interest that the Secretary of State should accept the undertaking (instead of applying, or proceeding with an application, for a disqualification order),

the Secretary of State may accept the undertaking.

5A(5) **["Company", "the court"]** In this section–

"company" includes an overseas company;

"the court" means the High Court or, in Scotland, the Court of Session.

5A(6) **[Maximum disqualification period]** The maximum period of disqualification under an order under this section is 15 years.

GENERAL NOTE

Section 5A was inserted by SBEEA s.104(1) with effect from 1 October 2015. Section 5A applies in relation to a conviction of an offence which occurs on or after that date regardless of whether the act or omission which constituted the offence occurred before that day (s.104(2)). This provision broadly corresponds to s.2, but only the High Court and Court of Session have jurisdiction.

Disqualification for unfitness

6   Duty of court to disqualify unfit directors of insolvent companies

6(1)   [Court's duty] The court shall make a disqualification order against a person in any case where, on an application under this section, it is satisfied–

(a)   that he is or has been a director of a company which has at any time become insolvent (whether while he was a director or subsequently), and

(b)   that his conduct as a director of that company (either taken alone or taken together with his conduct as a director of one or more other companies or overseas companies) makes him unfit to be concerned in the management of a company.

6(1A)   [Conduct as director] In this section references to a person's conduct as a director of any company or overseas company include, where that company or overseas company has become insolvent, references to that person's conduct in relation to any matter connected with or arising out of the insolvency.

6(2)   [Interpretation] For the purposes of this section, a company becomes insolvent if–

(a)   the company goes into liquidation at a time when its assets are insufficient for the payment of its debts and other liabilities and the expenses of the winding up,

(b)   the company enters administration,

(c)   an administrative receiver of the company is appointed.

6(2A)   [When overseas company becomes insolvent] For the purposes of this section, an overseas company becomes insolvent if the company enters into insolvency proceedings of any description (including interim proceedings) in any jurisdiction.

6(3)   ["The court"] In this section and section 7(2), "the court" means–

(a)   where the company in question is being or has been wound up by the court, that court,

(b)   where the company in question is being or has been wound up voluntarily, any court which has or (as the case may be) had jurisdiction to wind it up,

(c)   where neither paragraph (a) nor (b) applies but an administrator or administrative receiver has at any time been appointed in respect of the company in question, any court which has jurisdiction to wind it up.

6(3A)   [Application of Insolvency Act 1986 ss.117 and 120] Sections 117 and 120 of the Insolvency Act 1986 (jurisdiction) shall apply for the purposes of subsection (3) as if the references in the definitions of "registered office" to the presentation of the petition for winding up were references–

(a)   in a case within paragraph (b) of that subsection, to the passing of the resolution for voluntary winding up,

(b)   in a case within paragraph (c) of that subsection, to the appointment of the administrator or (as the case may be) administrative receiver,

6(3B)   [Wrong court] Nothing in subsection (3) invalidates any proceedings by reason of their being taken in the wrong court; and proceedings–

(a)   for or in connection with a disqualification order under this section, or

(b)   in connection with a disqualification undertaking accepted under section 7,

may be retained in the court in which the proceedings were commenced, although it may not be the court in which they ought to have been commenced.

6(3C)   **["Director"]** In this section and section 7, "director" includes a shadow director.

6(4)   **[Minimum, maximum periods]** Under this section the minimum period of disqualification is 2 years, and the maximum period is 15 years.

GENERAL NOTE

This section is, without doubt, the "flagship" provision in the disqualification regime introduced by the 1985–86 reforms. Far more disqualification orders have been made under s.6 than under all the other sections put together; and it is only in relation to s.6 and the other "unfitness" section, s.8, that the alternative of a disqualification undertaking is available (although there are parallel provisions in ss.9A–9E as regards competition undertakings).

Only the Secretary of State (or the official receiver acting under directions from the Secretary of State) may institute proceedings under this section.

Section 6(1), (2) amended and s.6(1A), (2A) inserted by SBEEA s.106(2) with effect from 1 October 2015. These amendments are consequential on the extension of the scope of the Act to include conduct in relation to overseas companies as grounds for disqualification.

S.6(1)

Both the word "shall" and the use of the expression "duty" in the marginal note indicate that where unfitness is found the court is obliged to make a disqualification order. However, the court's discretion is not altogether excluded, since it is required to be "satisfied" that the director's conduct makes him "unfit to be concerned in the management of a company"; and a court which took the view that a director's conduct did not warrant the making of a disqualification order would be free to stop short of making such a finding. In *Re Bath Glass Ltd* (1988) 4 B.C.C. 133, Peter Gibson J reached such a conclusion: though the director's conduct had been imprudent and, in part, improper, it was not so serious as to justify a finding of unfitness warranting a two-year disqualification. See also *Secretary of State for Trade and Industry v Lewis* [2003] B.C.C. 611; and *Secretary of State for Trade and Industry v Walker* [2003] EWHC 175 (Ch); [2003] 1 B.C.L.C. 363, where no order was made because although incompetence was found it was not of a sufficiently high degree. In *Re Polly Peck International plc, Secretary of State for Trade & Industry v Ellis (No.2)* [1993] B.C.C. 890, Lindsay J took this factor into account in declining to grant the Secretary of State leave to issue proceedings out of time.

In *Re Polly Peck International plc, Secretary of State for Trade & Industry v Ellis (No.2)* (above) the court declined to qualify the wording of s.6(1)(b) by adding at the end the words "without the leave of the court": to do this would be to make the threshold which a claimant had to cross other than what parliament had by its language intended. In the same case it was held that "a company" in s.6(1)(b) meant "companies generally".

"Director" includes a shadow director: see ss.6(3C) and 22(4) and, for the meaning of the latter term, s.22(5). Former directors are also within the scope of the section. An order may also be made against a de facto director—i.e. a person who acts as a director without having been properly appointed, or whose appointment has expired: *Re Lo-Line Electric Motors Ltd* [1988] Ch. 477; (1988) 4 B.C.C. 415; *Re Cargo Agency Ltd* [1992] B.C.C. 388; *Re Hydrodan (Corby) Ltd* [1994] B.C.C. 161; *Re Moorgate Metals Ltd* [1995] B.C.C. 143; *Re Richborough Furniture Ltd* [1996] B.C.C. 155. For further discussion of this term and the distinction between it and "shadow director", see the note to s.22(5). In *Re Eurostem Maritime Ltd* [1987] B.C.C. 190 the court expressed the view, obiter, that it had power to disqualify a director in respect of a foreign company that was being wound up in England, and it held that in proceedings against the director of an English company his conduct in relation to foreign companies of which he was also a director could be taken into consideration. (See also *Re Dominion International Group plc (No.2)* [1996] 1 B.C.L.C. 572.)

Section 6 contains no territorial restriction. It may be applied to persons, whether British subjects or foreigners, who are out of the jurisdiction at the relevant time and in respect of conduct which occurred outside the jurisdiction. However, the court has a discretion not to order that the proceedings be served out of the jurisdiction, which it will exercise where it is not satisfied that there is a good arguable case on the requirements of s.6(1): *Re Seagull Manufacturing Co Ltd (No.2)* [1994] 1 W.L.R. 453; [1993] B.C.C. 833.

The one exception to the extraterritorial scope of the court's jurisdiction (above) is that the courts in England and Wales and those in Scotland have mutually exclusive jurisdictions and will not make disqualification orders based on a person's conduct in relation to a company incorporated in the other part of Great Britain: *Re Helene plc* [2000] 2 B.C.L.C. 249. But once jurisdiction is established, the person's conduct as a director of such companies may be taken into account in determining his "unfitness".

The phrase "has become insolvent" is explained in s.6(2).

There is no anterior time limit fixed by s.6(1)(a): the court may inquire right back into the defendant's history as a director of the company and any other companies, and also into his conduct after he has ceased to be a director, if it relates to a matter "connected with or arising out of the insolvency of that company" (s.6(2)). It should be noted that an application has to be made no later than three (previously two) years after the company "became insolvent": s.7(2).

The matters to be taken into account in determining the question of "unfitness" are dealt with by s.12C and Sch.1: see the note to s.12C.

For a discussion of the term "management", see the note to s.1(1).

The court may take into account a person's conduct in relation to other companies: it is not necessary that those companies should also have "become insolvent", but it is only his conduct as a director of those companies that is relevant. In the cases it has become customary to refer to the company with reference to which the disqualification proceedings are brought as the "lead company" and the other companies as "collateral companies". It is permissible to specify more than one lead company in an application (*Re Surrey Leisure Ltd* [1999] B.C.C. 847); and the court may, in its discretion, allow an amendment to add a further lead company, but this is not appropriate where to do so would alter the fundamental focus and nature of the complaint against the defendant (*Re Diamond Computer Systems Ltd* [1997] 1 B.C.L.C. 174). If there is no finding of unfitness in relation to the lead company, the court cannot proceed to consider the defendant's conduct as director of the other companies (*Secretary of State for Trade and Industry v Tillman* [1999] B.C.C. 703).

In *Re Country Farm Inns Ltd* [1997] B.C.C. 801 it was emphasised that it was not necessary that the director's conduct in relation to the collateral company should be the same as, similar to or explanatory or confirmatory of the conduct relied on in relation to the lead company, and that there was no need for a nexus of any kind between the two, over and above the fact that the respondent had been a director of both companies and that his conduct in each case tended to show unfitness. It was held, however, in *Re Bath Glass Ltd* (above), that the director's conduct in relation to other companies is to be looked at only "for the purpose of finding additional matters of complaint": in other words, it is not open to the director to adduce evidence that his conduct in relation to other companies has been impeccable in an endeavour to show that a disqualification order would be inappropriate. In determining the question of unfitness, the court will also disregard a plea that the respondent has mended his ways: the question for the court is whether disqualification is merited on the evidence relied on in the application, and not whether the future protection of the public might or might not merit a disqualification: *Re Grayan Building Services Ltd* [1995] B.C.C. 554. On similar reasoning, it was held in *Secretary of State for Trade & Industry v Dawes* [1997] B.C.C. 121 that evidence of the respondent's general good character was inadmissible (compare *Re Oakframe Construction Ltd* [1996] B.C.C. 67; and *Re Pinemoor Ltd* [1997] B.C.C. 708, where the court struck out as irrelevant evidence by accountants which purported to express expert opinions on the issue before the court). However, once unfitness has been established, evidence of a person's general conduct which relates specifically to discharging the office of director may be admitted in determining the appropriate length of the disqualification period; and it may also be relevant to the question whether the court should give leave to act under s.17: *Re Barings plc, Secretary of State for Trade & Industry v Baker* [1998] B.C.C. 583 at 590 (a point not raised on appeal, [2001] B.C.C. 273); *Secretary of State for Trade and Industry v Griffiths* [1998] B.C.C. 836.

Note also that, although matters subsequent to the initiation of disqualification proceedings are not normally relevant to the case, the conduct of the respondent in the proceedings themselves may be taken into account, as in *Secretary of State for Trade and Industry v Blunt* [2006] B.C.C. 112, where the defendant was given credit for admitting the allegations of misconduct; and in *Secretary of State for Trade and Industry v Reynard* [2002] B.C.C. 813, where the deceitful conduct of the director concerned in the witness box was held to justify a longer period of disqualification.

In *Secretary of State for Trade and Industry v Queen* [1998] B.C.C. 678 the court had regard to the fact that the respondent had been convicted of criminal offences as a director some years previously, even though these were now "spent" convictions under the Rehabilitation of Offenders Act 1974.

Procedural unfairness, such as not giving a respondent adequate notice of the charges that he has to face, may be a ground for refusing to make a disqualification order: *Re Cubelock Ltd* [2001] B.C.C. 523. (See further the note to s.7(1).) A defendant may seek clarification of the case against him by informal or formal requests or, in the last recourse, by application to the court: *Secretary of State for Business, Innovation and Skills v Chohan* [2011] EWHC 1350 (Ch); [2012] 1 B.C.L.C. 138. In *Official Receiver v Key* [2009] B.C.C. 11 the applicant had chosen to issue disqualification proceedings against only one of two directors, who in the opinion of the court could have been considered equally culpable, and had accepted without making proper inquiries the evidence of the other director: the court declined to make an order. See also *Department of Enterprise, Trade and Investment v Black* [2012] NI Master 1.

S.6(2), (2A)

Before the jurisdiction of s.6 can be invoked, the company must have "become insolvent", but this term is especially defined for the purposes of s.6 (and also s.7) by the present subsection. It should be distinguished, on the one hand, from the concept "unable to pay its debts" in IA 1986 s.123 and, on the other, from the term "insolvent" in IA 1986 Pt VI. The position is best discussed under four heads:

- Where the company is or has been in liquidation, an "assets-based" test applies. Of course, the company may not be insolvent at all by any definition (e.g. if it is in members' voluntary liquidation). If it has been ordered to be wound up on the just and equitable or public interest ground, proof of an assets deficit may be needed, unless it is conceded. Strictly speaking, this will be the case also if the winding-up petition was based purely on s.123(1), but it is unlikely that such a technical point would succeed without clear proof that the company was in fact solvent.

- Where the company is in administration or administrative receivership, the company is deemed to have "become insolvent" regardless of its actual financial position.

- For overseas companies, subs.(2A) applies. If the company is subject to any insolvency proceedings of any description (including interim proceedings) in any jurisdiction, it is deemed to be insolvent, regardless of its financial situation. There is no definition of "insolvency proceedings".

- Other insolvency procedures (e.g. a CVA) are irrelevant to this question.

It is no defence to disqualification proceedings under s.6 that the company's creditors have been, or could or might have been, paid in full (although this may be a factor in deciding whether unfitness is established): *Re Normanton Wells Properties Ltd* [2011] 1 B.C.L.C. 191.

It is not open to a respondent in disqualification proceedings to challenge the validity of the insolvency proceedings (liquidation, receivership, etc.) on the basis of which the company in question has "become insolvent": that issue must be resolved in other, appropriate, proceedings pending the determination of which the disqualification application may be adjourned or stayed (*Secretary of State for Trade & Industry v Jabble* [1998] B.C.C. 39).

In determining whether a company "becomes insolvent" within s.6(2)(a), "the expenses of the winding up" are to be brought into account. In *Official Receiver v Moore, Re Gower Enterprises Ltd* [1995] B.C.C. 293 Evans-Lombe J held that (1) the assets and liabilities are to be valued by reference to the date of the liquidation, and not what they subsequently realised; (2) interest accruing on the debts after liquidation, and statutory interest under IA 1986 s.189, should be disregarded; and (3) that "the expenses of the winding up" should read as meaning "the reasonable expenses of the winding up". He went on to suggest, as a "rule of thumb", that in ascertaining the "reasonable expenses" the liquidator's remuneration should prima facie be determined by applying the official receiver's scale fees under the Insolvency Fees Order 1986 [see now the Insolvency Proceedings (Fees) Order 2016] to the realisable assets of the winding up but added the qualification that, if the expenses actually incurred proved to be less than the sum so calculated, the figure for the actual expenses should be substituted. However in further proceedings (reported at 297 et seq.) Blackburne J held that where the expenses actually incurred included remuneration which has been properly fixed in accordance with the Rules (and, where applicable, the Insolvency Regulations) and had not been challenged, they should be regarded as reasonable whether the sum was higher or lower than the figure which would have been arrived at by these other methods.

The phrase "goes into liquidation" is also defined in IA 1986 s.247(2) and extended to this Act by s.22(3). A company "goes into liquidation" when it passes a resolution for voluntary winding up or when an order for its winding up is made by the court (unless it is then already in voluntary liquidation, when the time of the winding-up resolution will be the relevant time): see *Re Walter L Jacob & Co Ltd, Official Receiver v Jacob* [1993] B.C.C. 512.

S.6(3)–(3C)

On "the court having jurisdiction to wind up the company", see the note to s.2(2). Section 6(3) was recast, and s.6(3A)–(3C) added by IA 2000 (with effect from 2 April 2001) in order to resolve jurisdictional difficulties experienced under the former wording of the subsection, e.g. where the company in question had been dissolved (*Re Working Project Ltd* [1995] B.C.C. 197; *Official Receiver v Pafundo* [2000] B.C.C. 164) or had changed its registered office from the district of one county court to another (*Re Lichfield Freight Terminal Ltd* [1997] B.C.C. 11). (Note that this ruling will no longer be authoritative now that the single county court regime has come into operation.) The phrase "has jurisdiction" in s.6(3)(c) means "has at the time of that appointment": *Secretary of State for Trade and Industry v Arnold* [2007] EWHC 1933 (Ch); [2008] B.C.C. 119. Even if a proceeding is instituted in the wrong court, s.6(3B) should deter the defendant from making objection to its jurisdiction. In *Secretary of State for Trade and*

Industry v Arnold (above), HHJ Pelling Q.C. said that if proceedings against a dissolved company were held to be a nullity, so that an application to have the company reinstated was necessary, permission could be granted under s.7(2) to start disqualification proceedings out of time.

S.6(4)

The only other provision in the Act which fixes a minimum period of disqualification is the new s.8ZA (instructing director of an insolvent company who has been disqualified). In considering the appropriate period for disqualification under s.6, a civil court may apply disqualification decisions of the Court of Appeal Criminal Division under s.2 as guidance: *Secretary of State for Business, Innovation and Skills v Rahman* [2017] EWHC 2468 (Ch). (But contrast s.12C(1)(c) with s.12C(2).)

7　Disqualification orders under section 6: applications and acceptance of undertakings

7(1)　[Application by Secretary of State, official receiver] If it appears to the Secretary of State that it is expedient in the public interest that a disqualification order under section 6 should be made against any person, an application for the making of such an order against that person may be made–

(a)　by the Secretary of State, or

(b)　if the Secretary of State so directs in the case of a person who is or has been a director of a company which is being or has been wound up by the court in England and Wales, by the official receiver.

7(2)　[Time for application] Except with the leave of the court, an application for the making under that section of a disqualification order against any person shall not be made after the end of the period of 3 years beginning with the day on which the company of which that person is or has been a director became insolvent.

7(2A)　[Acceptance of undertaking where s.6(1) satisfied] If it appears to the Secretary of State that the conditions mentioned in section 6(1) are satisfied as respects any person who has offered to give him a disqualification undertaking, he may accept the undertaking if it appears to him that it is expedient in the public interest that he should do so (instead of applying, or proceeding with an application, for a disqualification order).

7(3)　[Deleted]

7(4)　[Extra information etc.] The Secretary of State or the official receiver may require any person–

(a)　to furnish him with such information with respect to that person's or another person's conduct as a director of a company which has at any time become insolvent (whether while the person was a director or subsequently), and

(b)　to produce and permit inspection of such books, papers and other records as are considered by the Secretary of State or (as the case may be) the official receiver to be relevant to that person's or another person's conduct as such a director,

as the Secretary of State or the official receiver may reasonably require for the purpose of determining whether to exercise, or of exercising, any function of his under this section.

7(5)　[Section 6(1A), (2) applies] Subsections (1A) and (2) of section 6 apply for the purposes of this section as they apply for the purposes of that section.

GENERAL NOTE

Section 7(5) inserted by SBEEA Sch.7 para.8 as from 26 May 2015. Section 7(4) amended by DA 2015 s.11 as from 1 October 2015. Heading substituted and s.7(3) deleted by SBEEA 2015 s.107(3), (4) as from 1 April 2016.

　This section deals (inter alia) with the procedure for making an application for a disqualification order under s.6. Responsibility lies with the Secretary of State (in practice, the Insolvency Service). If the director is also facing criminal proceedings, it may be appropriate for the Secretary of State to initiate and then stay the s.6 proceedings until the outcome of the criminal trial: see *Secretary of State for Business, Innovation and Skills v Weston* [2014] EWHC 2933 (Ch) and the note to s.2.

The House of Commons Business, Innovation and Skills Committee's Sixth Report of 2012–13, *The Insolvency Service*, published on 6 February 2013, expressed the Committee's concern that recent resource constraints had had an impact on the investigatory and enforcement regime and concluded that this area of activity remains under-resourced. In the view of the Committee, the levels of disqualification of errant directors should not be determined by an arbitrary level set in what the Insolvency Service regards as the public interest. The Committee believed that any dilution of enforcement activity would send entirely the wrong message to delinquent directors and recommended that the Department for Business, Innovation and Skills should provide the Insolvency Service with sufficient, and if necessary, additional funding to ensure that all directors who have been found guilty of misconduct are disqualified.

S.7(1)

The Secretary of State, or the official receiver acting at his direction, alone has standing to make an application. The procedure is prescribed in detail by the Insolvent Companies (Disqualification of Unfit Directors) Proceedings Rules 1987 (SI 1987/2023) and by the *Practice Direction: Directors Disqualification Proceedings* issued by the Vice-Chancellor following the introduction of the Civil Procedure Rules 1998 (SI 1998/3132: the "CPR") and reported (as amended) [2015] B.C.C. 224. The *Practice Direction* incorporates, where relevant, provisions from the 1987 Rules, and is reproduced in App.VI to this *Guide*. This procedure governs disqualification applications under ss.2(2)(a), 3, 4 and 8 as well as under the present section. An application is commenced by a claim form issued in the High Court, out of the office of the companies court registrar or a chancery district registry (or, in the county court, out of a county court office), in the form annexed to the *Practice Direction*. All disqualification proceedings are multi-track. The first hearing is before a registrar. Where the application is made under ss.7 or 8, the first hearing is on a summary basis and on that hearing a disqualification order of up to five years may be imposed; but if it appears that a longer period is justified on the evidence then before the court, the matter is adjourned to a later hearing. An adjournment may also be ordered if the registrar is of opinion that questions of law or fact arise which are not suitable for summary determination. The adjourned hearing may be before a registrar or a judge, as the registrar (or, at a later stage, the court) directs. Directions may also be given as to the subsequent management of the case, e.g. as to the filing and service of further evidence, a timetable for the steps to be taken prior to the hearing, etc. A pre-trial review may also be ordered. Special rules apply if the defendant does not intend to contest his liability and it is proposed to invite the court to adopt the *Carecraft* procedure (see below). The procedure set out in CPR Pt 8 applies, subject to any modification of that procedure under the *Practice Direction* or the Rules.

Evidence in disqualification applications is by affidavit (or, where the applicant is the official receiver, a written report, with or without affidavits by other persons, made by him (or his deputy: *Re Homes Assured Corp Ltd* [1993] B.C.C. 573); this, under the 1987 Rules, is prima facie evidence of any matter contained in it). (Note that the Legislative Reform (Insolvency) (Miscellaneous Provisions) Order 2010 (SI 2010/18) and the Insolvency (Amendment) Rules 2010 (SI 2010/686), which abolish the use of affidavits for many purposes in insolvency proceedings, do not extend to the CDDA 1986.) The same evidential status is accorded to any documents that are annexed to the report (*Re City Investments Ltd* [1992] B.C.L.C. 956). In practice, an affidavit from the insolvency practitioner concerned is invariably filed. (For a description of a typical affidavit and its contents, see D. S. Henry (1992) 5 Insolv. Int. 1.) Guidance on the drawing up of affidavits and the official receiver's report is to be found also in *Re Pamstock Ltd* [1994] B.C.C. 264 (avoidance of excessive detail); *Secretary of State for Trade and Industry v Hickling* [1996] B.C.C. 678 (significant available evidence in favour of a respondent should not be omitted); *Re Pinemoor Ltd* [1997] B.C.C. 708 (evidence of opinion as to respondent's fitness (unless expert opinion) must be excluded); *Re Park House Properties Ltd* [1998] B.C.C. 847 (distinction to be made between matters of fact, inferences which the court is invited to draw and matters said to amount to unfitness on the part of a defendant). The office-holder's report is a public document and, subject to any question of privilege, should be made available to the defendant (*Re Barings plc (No.2)* [1998] B.C.C. 888).

There is one exception to the requirement that evidence is to be by affidavit: where an application is made within the proceedings, it is made under CPR Pt 23, and is therefore supported by a witness statement.

The defendant has 28 days after service of the proceedings to file his own affidavit evidence in reply. Again, evidence of opinion must be excluded, unless that of an expert, as must evidence of good character (*Secretary of State for Trade and Industry v Dawes* [1997] B.C.C. 121). The *Practice Direction* states that, so far as possible, all evidence should be filed before the first hearing of the application.

Deponents may be cross-examined on their affidavit evidence (*Re Dominion International Group plc* [1995] B.C.C. 303). Disclosure (formerly discovery) may be ordered in the usual way, but an order for disclosure made against the Secretary of State will not extend to documents which are not held by him personally but by the insolvency practitioner on whose report the disqualification proceedings have been based: *Re Lombard Shipping and Forwarding Ltd* [1992] B.C.C. 700. (In practice, however, disclosure is always made available: *Re Thomas Christy Ltd* [1994] 2 B.C.L.C. 527 at 529.) Nor will it extend to internal departmental memoranda: *Re Astra Holdings plc* [1999] B.C.C. 121. Witness summonses (e.g. in a case prior to the introduction of the CPR, a *subpoena duces tecum*) may be issued, on general principles (*Re Global Information Ltd* [1999] 1 B.C.L.C. 74); but an order requiring the Secretary of State to file replies to interrogatories (under the CPR, further information) was refused (and doubts expressed whether such an order would ever be appropriate) in *Re Sutton Glassworks Ltd* [1996] B.C.C. 174.

In *Official Receiver v Stojevic* [2007] EWHC 1186 (Ch); [2008] Bus. L.R. 641 findings of fraud had been made against the defendant director in a claim based on deceit. It was held that the judgment could be adduced as prima facie evidence in disqualification proceedings subsequently brought against him. In *Secretary of State for Business, Innovation and Skills v Potiwal* [2012] EWHC 3723 (Ch) the sole director of a company had been found by the VAT Tribunal to have been involved in VAT evasion. Briggs J refused to allow him to re-litigate this finding in subsequent disqualification proceedings.

Where a report of inspectors appointed by the Secretary of State under Pt XIV of the Companies Act 1985 is to be put in evidence, s.441 of that Act provides that a certified copy of the inspectors' report shall be admissible in all legal proceedings. [These provisions are not consolidated within CA 2006.]

Rule 3(3) of the 1987 Rules requires that in the affidavit evidence (or, where appropriate, the official receiver's report) there shall be stated the matters by reference to which the defendant is alleged to be unfit to be concerned in the management of a company. In *Re Sevenoaks Stationers (Retail) Ltd* [1991] Ch. 164 at 177; [1990] B.C.C. 765 at 774 the Court of Appeal ruled that it was improper for matters not so stated to be taken into account by the court, either in determining the question of "unfitness" or in fixing the appropriate period of disqualification, unless the court had, in a proper exercise of its discretion, allowed the altered or new allegation to be relied on. This should be done only if there was no injustice to the accused director, and might call for the giving of prior notice or the granting of an adjournment, so that he would have an opportunity to put in new evidence if he wished, and generally a fair opportunity to answer the new allegations (*Re Jazzgold Ltd* [1992] B.C.C. 587 at 594). An amendment may be refused if its effect is to shift the fundamental focus of the complaint to the defendant's conduct in relation to a different company: *Re Diamond Computer Systems Ltd* [1997] 1 B.C.L.C. 174; *Secretary of State for Trade and Industry v Gill* [2004] EWHC 175 (Ch); [2005] B.C.C. 24. The cases of *Re Finelist Ltd* [2003] EWHC 1780 (Ch); [2004] B.C.C. 877, *Secretary of State for Trade and Industry v Gill* [2004] EWHC 175 (Ch); [2005] B.C.C. 24 and *Secretary of State for Business, Innovation and Skills v Chohan* [2011] EWHC 1350 (Ch); [2012] 1 B.C.L.C. 138 emphasise the need for a respondent to disqualification proceedings to have a clear statement of the charges and the evidence in support which are brought against him, and the desirability of offering the director an opportunity before the proceedings are begun to proffer explanations for his conduct. A defendant may seek clarification of the case against him by informal or formal requests or, in the last recourse, by application to the court: *Secretary of State for Business, Innovation and Skills v Chohan* (above). In *Kappler v Secretary of State for Trade and Industry* [2006] B.C.C. 845 the allegation against the director was that he had "caused" the use by the company of fraudulent invoices, whereas the case was conducted on the basis that he knew of the fraud and had not put a stop to it. On appeal, he argued that there should have been a formal amendment of the allegation from "caused" to "allowed", but it was ruled that the lack of an amendment had not prevented the trial from being conducted fairly.

The report of the official receiver and other evidence on the court file is confidential: it is punishable as a contempt of court to publish this information in a newspaper before the hearing of the application: *Dobson v Hastings* [1992] Ch. 394; [1992] 2 All E.R. 94.

In *Re Rex Williams Leisure plc* [1994] Ch. 350; [1994] B.C.C. 551 the respondent directors wished (a) to object to much of the evidence put forward on behalf of the Secretary of State on the ground that is was hearsay and inadmissible; (b) to file no affidavit evidence of their own before the hearing and give no evidence at all until they had had an opportunity of submitting that there was no case to answer; and (c) to have the disqualification proceedings stayed until a civil action brought against one of the respondents had been disposed of. They failed on all three counts. The court ruled (a) that evidence put forward by an examiner of the investigations division of the Department of Trade and Industry had to be treated analogously with the reports of inspectors appointed under the Companies Act 1985 s.431, and was accordingly admissible as evidence of the facts it contained, even though the examiner was reporting on matters of which he had little or no first-hand knowledge; (b) that the procedure as regards evidence on affidavit laid down in the 1987 Rules (above) should be followed as the norm; and (c) that disqualification proceedings, being a matter of public interest, should not be held up pending the outcome of parallel private litigation. Similarly, objection may not be taken to evidence in an affidavit or report by the official receiver or an officeholder (or a professional person, such as an accountant, employed to report on his behalf) on the ground that it is or contains hearsay: this may go to the weight to be attached to the evidence, but not to its admissibility (*Re Moonbeam Cards Ltd* [1993] B.C.L.C. 1,099; *Re Circle Holidays International plc* [1994] B.C.C. 226; *Secretary of State for Trade and Industry v Moffatt* [1997] 2 B.C.L.C. 16; *Secretary of State for Trade and Industry v Ashcroft* [1998] Ch. 71; [1997] B.C.C. 634; *Re Barings plc (No.3)* [1999] B.C.C. 146). The Court of Appeal considered the position more generally in *Aaron v Secretary of State for Business, etc.* [2008] EWCA Civ 1146; [2009] B.C.C. 375, where the defendant challenged the admissibility of a report by the Financial Services Authority [now the FCA] into complaints that had been made against the defendant's company, and also the decisions of the Financial Ombudsman Service in the same matter. It was held that in disqualification proceedings it was a well-established exception to the hearsay rule that material obtained under a statutory scheme for investigation was admissible as prima facie evidence and that it was a matter for the judge what weight should be given to it. Further, where the documents contained some inadmissible material (such as the recital of evidence given by complainants) this did not justify the exclusion of the documents as a whole and it would be for the judge to decide what weight should be attached to them.

Factual findings in an earlier civil case for breach of contract and wrongful dismissal are not admissible in later disqualification proceedings and the Secretary of State must make good his allegations afresh by legally admissible evidence (*Secretary of State for Trade and Industry v Bairstow* [2003] EWCA Civ 321; [2004] Ch. 1; [2003] B.C.C. 682; *Secretary of State for Trade and Industry v Arnold* [2007] EWHC 1933 (Ch); [2008] B.C.C. 119).

An order may be made in the absence of the defendant if he fails to appear. Where he has failed to file an acknowledgment of service and the time for doing so has expired, he may attend the hearing of the application but may not take part in the hearing unless the court gives permission (*Practical Direction: Directors Disqualification Proceedings* [2015] B.C.C. 224 (reproduced as App.VI to this *Guide*) para.7.3).

Disqualification proceedings are adversarial in nature. The court has no investigative function. It is up to the Secretary of State (or official receiver) to select the matters to be put to the court and if he decides, in the interest of saving time and costs, to weed out parts of the case which could possibly be advanced, he is justified in doing so (*Secretary of State for Trade and Industry v Tillman* [1999] B.C.C. 703). The judge has no power to open the case more widely than the applicant has chosen to present it (*Re SIG Security Services Ltd* [1998] B.C.C. 978). The burden of proof is on the applicant (*Re Verby Print for Advertising Ltd* [1998] B.C.C. 652).

As noted above (see the note to s.1), disqualification proceedings are essentially civil, but they differ from ordinary private law proceedings in many respects: "Significantly, the 1986 Act does not expressly equip the court with a discretion to deploy the armoury of common law and equitable remedies to restrain future misconduct (injunction or undertaking in lieu of injunction), to punish for disregard of restraints imposed by court order (contempt powers of imprisonment or fine), to compensate for past loss unlawfully inflicted (damages) or to restore benefits unjustly acquired (restitution)" (Lord Woolf MR in *Re Blackspur Group plc (No.2)* [1998] 1 W.L.R. 422 at 427D–E; [1998] B.C.C. 11 at 16B–C). However, there is no doubt that the court may, either under the Rules or in its inherent jurisdiction, exercise many powers which are not expressly conferred by the Act, e.g. to grant a stay or suspend an order pending an appeal (*Secretary of State for Trade and Industry v Bannister* [1996] 1 W.L.R. 118; [1995] B.C.C. 1,027; *Re Barings plc (No.4)* [1999] B.C.C. 639).

The legislation does not include any provision which expressly allows the court to make a disqualification order on the basis of a "plea of guilty" or an agreement reached between the Secretary of State or official receiver, on the one hand, and the respondent director, on the other. However, in practice this became possible as a result of the decision of Ferris J in *Re Carecraft Construction Co Ltd* [1994] 1 W.L.R. 172; [1993] B.C.C. 336. As a result, a very significant proportion of disqualification orders were made by this method in the years that followed. However, the power given to the Secretary of State by IA 2000 to accept an undertaking in lieu of making, or continuing with, an application to court provides an even more convenient way of dealing with an uncontested case (see the notes to s.1A, above), and there will be little reason to follow the *Carecraft* procedure in most instances. One exceptional situation might be where there is no dispute as to the facts, but disagreement on the appropriate length of disqualification.

The Secretary of State has a general power to delegate his functions to an official receiver under IA 1986 s.400, and accordingly he may direct an official receiver to make an application under s.7(1)(a) even where (because the company in question is not being wound up by the court) the case does not come within s.7(1)(b). In such a situation the proceedings should be brought in the name of the Secretary of State and not that of the official receiver; but if an error is made in this respect it can be cured by amendment: *Official Receiver v Pafundo* [2000] B.C.C. 164; not following *Re Probe Data Systems Ltd* (1989) 5 B.C.C. 384.

S.7(2)

Section 6 is the only provision in CDDA 1986 which imposes a time limit (increased from two years to three by SBEEA 2015). (Note that this is not a limitation provision conferring on the director immunity from suit, but merely a period after which proceedings can only be brought with permission: *Re Instant Access Properties Ltd* [2011] EWHC 3022 (Ch).) If the three-year limit expires on a day when the court office is closed, the time is extended until the next day when it is open (*Re Philipp & Lion Ltd* [1994] B.C.C. 261). An application for "making" an order is made when the application is brought, i.e. lodged in the court office: *Secretary of State for Trade and Industry v Vohora* [2007] EWHC 2656 (Ch); [2009] B.C.C. 369.

A company "becomes insolvent" for the purposes of s.7(2) on the happening of any of the events mentioned in s.6(2) (insolvent liquidation, administration, administrative receivership): see the note to that section (and note the special provision for overseas companies in s.6(2A)). In the case of a compulsory winding up, the relevant date is the date of the order and not that of the petition (*Re Walter L Jacob & Co Ltd, Official Receiver v Jacob* [1993] B.C.C. 512).

Where, on an application for the appointment of an administrator under the original regime, the court first makes an interim order under IA 1986 s.9(4) and later makes an administration order under s.8 of that Act, it is the date of the latter order from which time should be reckoned for the purposes of the present provision: *Secretary of State for Trade & Industry v Palmer* [1993] B.C.C. 650.

Where more than one of the events mentioned in s.7(2) happen in succession to the same company (e.g. the company is first put into administrative receivership and then into compulsory liquidation), the period of three years runs from the first of those events: *Re Tasbian Ltd* [1990] B.C.C. 318. However, if the company were to return to a state of solvency between the happening of the two events, it is arguable that a fresh three-year period would start when it "became insolvent" for the second time (ibid.).

The procedure to be followed by the Secretary of State or the official receiver in making application for an extension of time under s.7(2) is set out in Pt 3 of the *Practice Direction: Directors Disqualification Proceedings* [2015] B.C.C. 224. (See App.VI to this Guide.) Application is made by Application Notice under CPR Pt 23.

The section does not indicate the grounds upon which the court might see fit to extend the three-year time limit. It is for the Secretary of State or official receiver to show a good reason for the extension of time (*Re Crestjoy Products Ltd* [1990] B.C.C. 23 at 29; *Re Copecrest Ltd* [1993] B.C.C. 844 at 847, 852). The matters to be taken into account are: (1) the length of delay; (2) the reasons for the delay; (3) the strength of the case against the director; and (4) the degree of prejudice caused to the director by the delay (*Re Probe Data Systems Ltd (No.3), Secretary of State for Trade & Industry v Desai* [1992] B.C.C. 110 at 118). This list is not expressed to be exclusive but in most cases is likely to be so (*Re Polly Peck International plc, Secretary of State for Trade & Industry v Ellis (No.2)* [1993] B.C.C. 890 at 894). When each of these four matters has been looked at separately, there then needs to take place a balancing exercise; but even before this, the application for leave should be rejected if the applicant's case is so weak that it could not lead to a disqualification (ibid., and see also *Re Manlon Trading Ltd* [1996] Ch. 136; [1995] B.C.C. 579).

Other cases have elaborated upon the matters listed above. In *Re Copecrest Ltd* (above) Hoffmann LJ said that the three-year period under s.7(2) had to be treated as having built into it a contingency allowance for unexpected delays for which the applicant was not responsible, such as delays on the part of the liquidator or other office-holder; but on the other hand delays for which the respondent himself was to blame were a factor which it was proper to take into account. In *Re Crestjoy Products Ltd* (above) pressure of work and a shortage of staff in the Secretary of State's department was not considered a sufficient reason to grant leave out of time retrospectively, although the court indicated that an application made prior to the expiry of the statutory deadline would have been more favourably considered.

Notwithstanding the view expressed in the *Polly Peck* case (above) that the four factors mentioned will usually be sufficient, later cases have added to the list. These include: the director's own share of responsibility for the delay (*Secretary of State for Trade & Industry v McTighe* [1997] B.C.C. 224); the fact that the charges are particularly serious and that there is a public interest in having them determined (*Secretary of State for Trade & Industry v Davies* [1996] 4 All E.R. 289; [1997] B.C.C. 235); whether it is still possible to have a fair trial (*Secretary of State for Trade & Industry v Martin* [1998] B.C.C. 184). In *Re Instant Access Properties Ltd* [2011] EWHC 3022 (Ch); [2012] 1 B.C.L.C. 710 it was said that the gravity of the charge and the prospects of success could together measure the public interest in allowing the proceedings to continue. The mere fact that the delay after the three-year period is very short is not relevant (*Re Cedar Developments Ltd* [1995] B.C.C. 220); nor that the Secretary of State has a good reason for the delay: what must be shown is a good reason for being granted the extension of time (*Secretary of State for Trade & Industry v Davies* (above)).

Even though disqualification proceedings have been formally commenced in time, delay in bringing the case to a hearing may lead to the striking out or dismissal of the claim: *Secretary of State for Trade & Industry v Tjolle* [1998] B.C.C. 282. But where there has been no real prejudice to the defendant caused by the delay, or where his own acts have contributed to it, the courts will not readily take such a course: see, e.g. *Re Abermeadow Ltd* [2001] B.C.C. 724; *Re Rocksteady Service Ltd* [2001] B.C.C. 467; *Re Blackspur Group plc (No.3), Secretary of State for Trade and Industry v Eastaway* [2003] B.C.C. 520.

The European Commission of Human Rights has also ruled on the effects of delay, declaring in *EDC v United Kingdom (Application No.24433/94)* [1998] B.C.C. 370 that a stay of proceedings for seven years (pending the disposal of criminal proceedings against other parties) was excessive and breached the right of a respondent to have a hearing of the case within a reasonable time, as required by art.6(1) of the European Convention for the Protection of Human Rights and Fundamental Freedoms. In contrast, in the *Abermeadow* and *Blackspur* cases (above) a plea based on the ground that the Human Rights legislation had been infringed was unsuccessful.

Rule 3(1) of the Insolvent Companies (Disqualification of Directors) Proceedings Rules 1987 (SI 1987/2023) states that the evidence in support of an application for a disqualification order should be filed at the time when the summons is issued—although this provision is directory and not mandatory and failing to comply with it is an irregularity which the court may waive (*Re Jazzgold Ltd* [1992] B.C.C. 587; *Re Copecrest Ltd* [1993] B.C.C. 844 at 851). The evidence may take the form of, or include, a report by the official receiver (r.3(2)). The court may take into account evidence contained in a supplementary report filed after the expiry of the three-year limitation period (*Re Jazzgold Ltd* (above)). On the application for an extension of time, it is sufficient for the evidence to show that there is an arguable case (*Re Tasbian Ltd (No.3)* [1991] B.C.C. 435): the court will not, even where there is a conflict of evidence, virtually try the case (*Re Packaging Direct Ltd, Jones v Secretary of State for Trade & Industry* [1994] B.C.C. 213). It is not necessarily an obstacle to allowing the trial to proceed that the applicant's evidence has not been wholly accurate (*Re Tasbian Ltd (No.3)* (above)).

An application under s.7 may also be struck out for want of prosecution: *Re Noble Trees Ltd* [1993] B.C.C. 318; *Official Receiver v B Ltd* [1994] 2 B.C.L.C. 1.

S.7(2A)
On disqualification undertakings, see the note to s.1A. In *Gardiner v Secretary of State for Business, Enterprise and Regulatory Reform* [2009] B.C.C. 742 the applicant, who had given an undertaking after proceedings had been commenced against him, sought to have it rescinded or declared invalid on the grounds that the proceedings had been issued out of time. The court found that this was not so on the facts, but held that in any case an undertaking could be accepted by the Secretary of State even if the associated proceedings had not been commenced in time.

S.7(3)
This provision has been superseded by s.7A, below.

S.7(4)
The power of the Secretary of State to require the giving of information was formerly confined to office-holders such as liquidators and administrators, but the amendment made by DA 2015 has extended it to "any person", so that there is no longer any such limitation.

Documents in the custody of an administrative receiver or other office-holder were not "in the power of" the Secretary of State by virtue of this subsection so that he could be compelled to make discovery [disclosure] of them under RSC Ord.24 [CPR Pt 31]: *Re Lombard Shipping & Forwarding Ltd* [1992] B.C.C. 700.

In *Re Pantmaenog Timber Co Ltd, Official Receiver v Wadge Rapps & Hunt (a firm)* [2003] UKHL 49; [2004] 1 A.C. 158; [2003] B.C.C. 659 the official receiver was liquidator of the company, and (acting on behalf of the Secretary of State) had commenced disqualification proceedings against one of its directors. He sought an order of the court under IA 1986 s.236 requiring the company's solicitors and accountants to produce documents relating to the company for use as evidence in the disqualification proceedings. The House of Lords, overruling the Court of Appeal, held that the official receiver could seek disclosure of documents under s.236 for this purpose, and that he might do so even if he were not the liquidator of the company and even if this was his sole purpose. There is now, however, no need to resort to s.236, since the Insolvent Companies (Reports on Conduct of Directors) (England and Wales) Rules 2016 (SI 2016/180) r.3 and its Scottish counterpart expressly empower the court, on the application of the Secretary of State or the official receiver, to direct a person to comply with the requirements of the section.

It has also been held that it is not objectionable for a police officer to attend disqualification proceedings in order to gain information which may be useful in a proposed criminal prosecution (*Re Priority Stainless (UK) Ltd, Secretary of State for Trade and Industry v Crane* [2004] B.C.C. 825).

In appropriate circumstances, an order may also be made under CPR r.31.17(3) against a third party that he should disclose documents in his possession, if they are likely to be material to the case: *Re Howglen Ltd* [2001] B.C.C. 245 (company's banker); *Re Skyward Builders plc* [2002] 2 B.C.L.C. 750 (accountants).

S.7(5)
Section 6(2) and (2A) contain definitions of "becomes insolvent" for UK and overseas companies respectively.

7A   Office-holder's report on conduct of directors

7A(1) [Duty of office-holder to prepare conduct report] The office-holder in respect of a company which is insolvent must prepare a report (a "conduct report") about the conduct of each person who was a director of the company–

(a)   on the insolvency date, or

(b)   at any time during the period of 3 years ending with that date.

7A(2)   [When company insolvent] For the purposes of this section a company is insolvent if–

(a)   the company is in liquidation and at the time it went into liquidation its assets were insufficient for the payment of its debts and other liabilities and the expenses of the winding up,

(b)   the company has entered administration, or

(c)   an administrative receiver of the company has been appointed;

and subsection (1A) of section 6 applies for the purposes of this section as it applies for the purpose of that section.

7A(3)   [Conduct report] A conduct report must, in relation to each person, describe any conduct of the person which may assist the Secretary of State in deciding whether to exercise the power under section 7(1) or (2A) in relation to the person.

7A(4)   [Period to send report to Secretary of State] The office-holder must send the conduct report to the Secretary of State before the end of–

(a)   the period of 3 months beginning with the insolvency date, or

(b)   such other longer period as the Secretary of State considers appropriate in the particular circumstances.

7A(5)   [Duty to send new information] If new information comes to the attention of an office-holder, the office-holder must send that information to the Secretary of State as soon as reasonably practicable.

7A(6)   ["New information"] "New information" is information which an office-holder considers should have been included in a conduct report prepared in relation to the company, or would have been so included had it been available before the report was sent.

7A(7)   [Where more than one office-holder] If there is more than one office-holder in respect of a company at any particular time (because the company is insolvent by virtue of falling within more than one paragraph of subsection (2) at that time), subsection (1) applies only to the first of the office-holders to be appointed.

7A(8)   [Where company insolvent at different times] In the case of a company which is at different times insolvent by virtue of falling within one or more different paragraphs of subsection (2)–

(a)   the references in subsection (1) to the insolvency date are to be read as references to the first such date during the period in which the company is insolvent, and

(b)   subsection (1) does not apply to an office-holder if at any time during the period in which the company is insolvent a conduct report has already been prepared and sent to the Secretary of State.

7A(9)   [The "office-holder"] The "office-holder" in respect of a company which is insolvent is–

(a)   in the case of a company being wound up by the court in England and Wales, the official receiver;

(b)   in the case of a company being wound up otherwise, the liquidator;

(c)   in the case of a company in administration, the administrator;

(d)   in the case of a company of which there is an administrative receiver, the receiver.

7A(10)   [The "insolvency date"] The "insolvency date"–

(a)   in the case of a company being wound up by the court, means the date on which the court makes the winding-up order (see section 125 of the Insolvency Act 1986);

(b)   in the case of a company being wound up by way of a members' voluntary winding up, means the date on which the liquidator forms the opinion that the company will be unable to pay its debts in full (together with interest at the official rate) within the period stated in the directors' declaration of solvency under section 89 of the Insolvency Act 1986;

(c) in the case of a company being wound up by way of a creditors' voluntary winding up where no such declaration under section 89 of that Act has been made, means the date of the passing of the resolution for voluntary winding up;

(d) in the case of a company which has entered administration, means the date the company did so;

(e) in the case of a company in respect of which an administrative receiver has been appointed, means the date of that appointment.

7A(11)   [Replacement administrative receiver ignored for s.7A(10)(e)] For the purposes of subsection (10)(e), any appointment of an administrative receiver to replace an administrative receiver who has died or vacated office pursuant to section 45 of the Insolvency Act 1986 is to be ignored.

7A(12)   ["Court", "director"] In this section–

"court" has the same meaning as in section 6;

"director" includes a shadow director.

GENERAL NOTE

Section 7A was inserted by SBEEA 2015 s.107(2) and came into force on 6 April 2016.

This section replaces s.7(3). That provision imposed an obligation on the official receiver and every liquidator, administrator and administrative receiver of an insolvent company to submit a report to the Secretary of State on the conduct of any director if it appeared to that office-holder that such conduct made him unfit to be concerned in the management of a company. The new section goes further in that a conduct report must now be sent on every director (and every person who was a director within three years of the insolvency date), describing any conduct which may assist the Secretary of State in deciding whether it is in the public interest to apply for the making of a disqualification order. The report must be submitted within three months of the insolvency date. Any new information which comes to the attention of the office-holder subsequently must be submitted in a supplementary report (s.7A(5), (6)). However, there is no obligation to submit a report if a report has already been sent by another office-holder in the same or connected proceedings (s.7A(7), (8)).

Under the new regime, the procedure is streamlined. Instead of a requirement to submit a separate form in hard copy on each director, there is a single form covering all the directors, to be submitted online. As expected, these changes have been supplemented by subordinate legislation: the Insolvent Companies (Reports on Conduct of Directors) Rules 2016 (SI 2016/180 and SI 2016/185 (S.1) respectively for England and Wales and for Scotland). *Dear IP*, Ch.10 para.49 (introduced by Issue 82, November 2018) provides guidance for IPs on completion of the Director Conduct Reporting Service form.

For application of s.7A to building societies, see s.90E of the Building Societies Act 1986.

8   Disqualification of director on finding of unfitness

8(1)   [Application by Secretary of State] If it appears to the Secretary of State that it is expedient in the public interest that a disqualification order should be made against a person who is, or has been, a director or shadow director of a company, he may apply to the court for such an order.

8(1A)   [Deleted]

8(2)   [Court's power] The court may make a disqualification order against a person where, on an application under this section, it is satisfied that his conduct in relation to the company (either taken alone or taken together with his conduct as a director or shadow director of one or more other companies or overseas companies) makes him unfit to be concerned in the management of a company.

8(2A)   [Acceptance of undertaking] Where it appears to the Secretary of State that, in the case of a person who has offered to give him a disqualification undertaking–

(a) the conduct of the person in relation to a company of which the person is or has been a director or shadow director (either taken alone or taken together with his conduct as a director or shadow director of one or more other companies or overseas companies)makes him unfit to be concerned in the management of a company, and

(b) it is expedient in the public interest that he should accept the undertaking (instead of applying, or proceeding with an application, for a disqualification order),

he may accept the undertaking.

8(2B) [Application of s.6(1A) conduct as director] Subsection (1A) of section 6 applies for the purposes of this section as it applies for the purposes of that section.

8(3) ["The court"] In this section "the court" means the High Court or, in Scotland, the Court of Session.

8(4) [Maximum period] The maximum period of disqualification under this section is 15 years.

General Note

Section 8(1) was substituted and s.8(1A) inserted by the Financial Services and Markets Act 2000 (Consequential Amendments and Repeals) Order 2001 (SI 2001/3649) as from 1 December 2001. Section 8(2A) was inserted by IA 2000 s.6(1), (4) as from 2 April 2001. Section 8(1), (2A) amended, heading substituted and s.8(1A) deleted by SBEEA 2015 s.109 as from 1 October 2015; s.8(2), (2A)(a) amended and s.8(2B) inserted by SBEEA 2015 s.106(3) also from 1 October 2015.

S.8(1)

The present section gives the court power to make a disqualification order on the application of the Secretary of State, if it appears that it is expedient in the public interest that an order should be made against a director or former director (or shadow director) of any company. As with s.6, the person's conduct as a director or shadow director of other companies or overseas companies may be taken into account. Under the section as originally enacted, the Secretary of State could apply under this section only on the basis of information or documents obtained by him in the exercise of specified statutory powers of investigation, primarily powers conferred by CA 1985 and FSMA 2000. SBEEA 2015 has removed these restrictions, so that it is open to him to act on any information, however acquired. Although ss.6 and 8 are broadly based on the same criterion of "unfitness", there are some differences between the two. Under s.6, if unfitness is found, the court has no discretion to decline to make an order, and there is a minimum period of disqualification of two years. The official receiver has no standing to apply under s.8, and the county court has no jurisdiction. The Statutes of Limitation do not apply, and there is no requirement that any of the companies concerned should have been insolvent. (See *Re JA Chapman & Co Ltd* [2003] 2 B.C.L.C. 206.) In *Secretary of State for Trade and Industry v Hollier* [2006] EWHC 1804; [2007] B.C.C. 11 Etherton J expressed reservations on the question whether the principles and approach applicable to cases under s.6 should also apply under s.8, but did not pursue the matter. In *Secretary of State for Business, Enterprise and Regulatory Reform v Sullman* [2008] EWHC 3179 (Ch); [2009] B.C.C. 500 Norris J, while accepting that disqualification under s.8 was discretionary and not mandatory as under s.6 (see above) nevertheless felt that the protection of the public and the need to deter other directors justified a seven-year disqualification in the case before him.

Cases where orders have been made under s.8 include: *Re Samuel Sherman plc* [1991] 1 W.L.R. 1070; [1991] B.C.C. 699 (ultra vires use of public company's assets and failure to comply with statutory obligations: five-year disqualification); *Re Looe Fish Ltd* [1993] B.C.C. 348 (improper allotment of shares to manipulate voting: two and a half years); *Re Aldermanbury Trust plc* [1993] B.C.C. 598 (breaches of company law, City Code and fiduciary duty, "seriously flawed" commercial judgments: seven years); *Secretary of State for Business, Energy and Industrial Strategy v Gordon* (unreported, 18 April 2018) (allowing two companies which the director knew were actively trading to file dormant accounts involved serious breaches of directors' duty from which the public needed protection). In *Ghassemian v Secretary of State for Trade and Industry* [2006] EWHC 1715 (Ch); [2007] B.C.C. 229 the Secretary of State had written to the defendant saying that he was not satisfied that it was expedient that a disqualification order should be made against him but had then proceeded instead to petition for a winding-up order on public interest grounds. He later brought disqualification proceedings on the basis of investigative material procured for the winding-up application. The court held that the indication given to the defendant in the earlier letter did not stand in the way of the making of a disqualification order.

In *Secretary of State for Business, Innovation and Skills v Pawson* [2015] EWHC 2626 (Ch) the defendant had been the sole director of nine companies which had been wound up on public interest grounds. There was evidence of mismanagement (taking excessive remuneration, running an unsustainable business model) but, as the companies were solvent, proceedings could not be brought under s.6. The court made an order under s.8, disqualifying him for eight years.

In *Re TransTec plc (No.2)* [2006] EWHC 2110 (Ch); [2007] 2 B.C.L.C. 495 the respondent had been acquitted on charges of fraud but it was held competent for the Secretary of State to bring proceedings under s.8, and for the court to make a disqualification order, on the basis of the same facts, because there were significant differences between the two sets of proceedings and their underlying purpose and, in particular, the standard of proof was the less demanding civil standard.

In *Re Aldermanbury Trust plc* (above) it was held that the court could properly adopt the shortened form of procedure approved in *Re Carecraft Construction Co Ltd* (see the note to s.7(1) above), and avoid a full hearing. But there will be little cause to follow this course in the future, for (by virtue of the new s.8(2A)) the alternative of a disqualification undertaking in lieu of a court order is available in cases under s.8: see the notes to s.1A.

In *R. v Secretary of State for Trade & Industry Ex p. Lonrho plc* [1992] B.C.C. 325 an application for judicial review of the Secretary of State's decision not to seek a disqualification order under this section was unsuccessful. In *R. v Secretary of State for Trade & Industry Ex p. McCormick* [1998] B.C.C. 379 the Court of Appeal, affirming Rimer J, refused a similar application brought following the ruling of the European Court of Human Rights in *Saunders v UK* (1997) 23 E.H.R.R. 313; [1997] B.C.C. 872, where it had been held that the use in criminal proceedings of evidence obtained under compulsion was an infringement of the right against self-incrimination and accordingly rendered the trial unfair and in violation of art.6(1) of the European Convention for the Protection of Human Rights and Fundamental Freedoms. The director argued that the use of a report made by inspectors to the Secretary of State under CA 1985 s.437 and transcripts of the director's interviews with the inspectors should similarly not have been used in disqualification proceedings brought against him. However the court ruled that these proceedings were civil and not criminal in nature and that the report and transcripts were relevant, admissible and not privileged; and that their use was not unfair. (See further the Introductory note to CDDA 1986 at p.2 above.)

An application under s.8 was brought against the directors of Farepak Food & Gifts Ltd and European Home Retail plc following investigations under CA 1985 s.447, but the Secretary of State on 20 June 2012, discontinued the proceedings before getting to the judgment stage. Peter Smith J gave an extraordinary statement in open court (not a judgment, as the proceedings were discontinued) exonerating the directors and criticising the conduct of the proceedings and the companies' main creditor bank. Following this the Insolvency Service reviewed the proceedings and published the report of its review on 4 December 2012 (*Review of Disqualification Proceedings Taken in the Case of European Home Retail PLC and Farepak Food & Gifts Limited*, available on the Insolvency Service website at *http://www.bis.gov.uk/insolvency/news/news-stories/2012/Dec/Farepak%20final%20report*). The review acknowledges that certain of the Insolvency Service's procedures required to be revised in the light of this high-profile affair.

S.8(2)

The court must also be satisfied that the conduct of the director in relation to the company (and possibly other companies) makes him unfit to be concerned in the management of a company. But the phrase "conduct in relation to" the company is not to be construed narrowly. In *Secretary of State for Business, Enterprise and Regulatory Reform v Sullman* (above) it was argued unsuccessfully that it was necessary that the company should have been the victim of the conduct in question. Norris J held that it was sufficient that the person's conduct as a director had a bearing upon the company's business or affairs, whether that conduct occasioned prejudice to the company itself or its shareholders, customers, funders or anyone else with whom it had commercial relationships. The notes to ss.6(1) and 9 will be generally relevant in the present context.

The court's power here is discretionary rather than mandatory.

S.8(2A)

On disqualification undertakings, see the note to s.1A.

S.8(3)

The procedure before the High Court takes the same form as in an application under s.6. See the note to s.7(1) above.

S.8(4)

There is no minimum disqualification period under this section.

Persons instructing unfit directors

8ZA   Order disqualifying person instructing unfit director of insolvent company

8ZA(1)   [Court's power to make disqualification order] The court may make a disqualification order against a person ("P") if, on an application under section 8ZB, it is satisfied–

(a) either–

    (i) that a disqualification order under section 6 has been made against a person who is or has been a director (but not a shadow director) of a company, or

    (ii) that the Secretary of State has accepted a disqualification undertaking from such a person under section 7(2A), and

(b) that P exercised the requisite amount of influence over the person.

That person is referred to in this section as "the main transgressor".

8ZA(2) **[Requisite amount of influence]** For the purposes of this section, P exercised the requisite amount of influence over the main transgressor if any of the conduct–

(a) for which the main transgressor is subject to the order made under section 6, or

(b) in relation to which the undertaking was accepted from the main transgressor under section 7(2A),

was the result of the main transgressor acting in accordance with P's directions or instructions.

8ZA(3) **[No requisite amount of influence where professional advice]** But P does not exercise the requisite amount of influence over the main transgressor by reason only that the main transgressor acts on advice given by P in a professional capacity.

8ZA(4) **[Disqualification period]** Under this section the minimum period of disqualification is 2 years and the maximum period is 15 years.

8ZA(5) **["The court" in s.8ZA and 8ZB; s.6(3B) applies re wrong court]** In this section and section 8ZB "the court" has the same meaning as in section 6; and subsection (3B) of section 6 applies in relation to proceedings mentioned in subsection (6) below as it applies in relation to proceedings mentioned in section 6(3B)(a) and (b).

8ZA(6) **[Proceedings for disqualification order or undertaking]** The proceedings are proceedings–

(a) for or in connection with a disqualification order under this section, or

(b) in connection with a disqualification undertaking accepted under section 8ZC.

(See General Note after s.8ZE.)

8ZB   Application for order under section 8ZA

8ZB(1) **[Secretary of State's power to apply]** If it appears to the Secretary of State that it is expedient in the public interest that a disqualification order should be made against a person under section 8ZA, the Secretary of State may–

(a) make an application to the court for such an order, or

(b) in a case where an application for an order under section 6 against the main transgressor has been made by the official receiver, direct the official receiver to make such an application.

8ZB(2) **[Time for application]** Except with the leave of the court, an application for a disqualification order under section 8ZA must not be made after the end of the period of 3 years beginning with the day on which the company in question became insolvent (within the meaning given by section 6(2)).

8ZB(3) **[Application of s.7(4)]** Subsection (4) of section 7 applies for the purposes of this section as it applies for the purposes of that section.

(See General Note after s.8ZE.)

8ZC   Disqualification undertaking instead of an order under section 8ZA

8ZC(1)   [Secretary of State's power to accept undertaking] If it appears to the Secretary of State that it is expedient in the public interest to do so, the Secretary of State may accept a disqualification undertaking from a person ("P") if–

(a)   any of the following is the case–

    (i)   a disqualification order under section 6 has been made against a person who is or has been a director (but not a shadow director) of a company,

    (ii)   the Secretary of State has accepted a disqualification undertaking from such a person under section 7(2A), or

    (iii)   it appears to the Secretary of State that such an undertaking could be accepted from such a person (if one were offered), and

(b)   it appears to the Secretary of State that P exercised the requisite amount of influence over the person.

That person is referred to in this section as "the main transgressor".

8ZC(2)   [Requisite amount of influence] For the purposes of this section, P exercised the requisite amount of influence over the main transgressor if any of the conduct–

(a)   for which the main transgressor is subject to the disqualification order made under section 6,

(b)   in relation to which the disqualification undertaking was accepted from the main transgressor under section 7(2A), or

(c)   which led the Secretary of State to the conclusion set out in subsection (1)(a)(iii),

was the result of the main transgressor acting in accordance with P's directions or instructions.

8ZC(3)   [No requisite amount of influence where professional advice] But P does not exercise the requisite amount of influence over the main transgressor by reason only that the main transgressor acts on advice given by P in a professional capacity.

8ZC(4)   [Section 7(4) applies] Subsection (4) of section 7 applies for the purposes of this section as it applies for the purposes of that section.

(See General Note after s.8ZE.)

8ZD   Order disqualifying person instructing unfit director: other cases

8ZD(1)   [Court's power to make disqualification order] The court may make a disqualification order against a person ("P") if, on an application under this section, it is satisfied–

(a)   either–

    (i)   that a disqualification order under section 8 has been made against a person who is or has been a director (but not a shadow director) of a company, or

    (ii)   that the Secretary of State has accepted a disqualification undertaking from such a person under section 8(2A), and

(b)   that P exercised the requisite amount of influence over the person.

That person is referred to in this section as "the main transgressor".

8ZD(2)   [Secretary of State's power to apply] The Secretary of State may make an application to the court for a disqualification order against P under this section if it appears to the Secretary of State that it is expedient in the public interest for such an order to be made.

8ZD(3)   [Requisite amount of influence] For the purposes of this section, P exercised the requisite amount of influence over the main transgressor if any of the conduct–

(a)   for which the main transgressor is subject to the order made under section 8, or

(b)   in relation to which the undertaking was accepted from the main transgressor under section 8(2A),

was the result of the main transgressor acting in accordance with P's directions or instructions.

8ZD(4)   [No requisite amount of influence where professional advice] But P does not exercise the requisite amount of influence over the main transgressor by reason only that the main transgressor acts on advice given by P in a professional capacity.

8ZD(5)   [Maximum disqualification period] Under this section the maximum period of disqualification is 15 years.

8ZD(6)   ["The court"] In this section "the court" means the High Court or, in Scotland, the Court of Session.

(See General Note after s.8ZE.)

8ZE   Disqualification undertaking instead of an order under section 8ZD

8ZE(1)   [Secretary of State's power to accept undertaking] If it appears to the Secretary of State that it is expedient in the public interest to do so, the Secretary of State may accept a disqualification undertaking from a person ("P") if–

(a)   any of the following is the case–

(i)   a disqualification order under section 8 has been made against a person who is or has been a director (but not a shadow director) of a company,

(ii)   the Secretary of State has accepted a disqualification undertaking from such a person under section 8(2A), or

(iii)   it appears to the Secretary of State that such an undertaking could be accepted from such a person (if one were offered), and

(b)   it appears to the Secretary of State that P exercised the requisite amount of influence over the person.

That person is referred to in this section as "the main transgressor".

8ZE(2)   [Requisite amount of influence] For the purposes of this section, P exercised the requisite amount of influence over the main transgressor if any of the conduct–

(a)   for which the main transgressor is subject to the disqualification order made under section 8,

(b)   in relation to which the disqualification undertaking was accepted from the main transgressor under section 8(2A), or

(c)   which led the Secretary of State to the conclusion set out in subsection (1)(a)(iii),

was the result of the main transgressor acting in accordance with P's directions or instructions.

8ZE(3)   [No requisite amount of influence where professional advice] But P does not exercise the requisite amount of influence over the main transgressor by reason only that the main transgressor acts on advice given by P in a professional capacity.

GENERAL NOTE TO SS.8ZA–8ZE

These sections were inserted by SBEEA 2015 s.105 as from 1 October 2015. They introduce a new ground for the making of a disqualification order or the acceptance of a disqualification undertaking: directing or instructing a director who has been disqualified on the grounds of unfitness. This other person is referred to in the Act as "the main transgressor".

It has been established by the case-law that a shadow director (i.e. "a person on whose directions or instructions the directors of a company are accustomed to act" (s.22(5)) may be the subject of a disqualification order or undertaking, and plainly there is scope for some overlap between the new section and that case-law. Equally plainly, the present provision must have been intended to deal with situations which were not covered by that law. The main points of difference appear to be as follows.

- The main transgressor must already have been disqualified (and more particularly disqualified on the ground of unfitness under s.6, 7(2A), 8 or 8(2A)). It is not clear whether the main transgressor and the defendant can be dealt with at the same hearing (on the assumption that the former would be disqualified before the ruling in his case is given), but there could be difficulties in framing the case against him on the basis of facts which are in part conditional.

- It is sufficient that the influence has been exercised over a single person; a shadow director must exercise influence over the board of directors as a whole, or (probably) at least a majority.

- The exception for advice given in a professional capacity (ss.8ZA(3), 8ZC(3), 8ZD(4), 8ZE(3)) parallels that in s.22(5), but without the additional paragraphs (b) and (c) in the latter.

Other points to note are:

- Under s.6 (and s.9A) the court must make a disqualification order if unfitness is found: s.8ZA(1) and s.1(1), using the word "may", leave at least theoretically some room for discretion.

- Section 8ZA(4), like s.6, prescribes a minimum disqualification period.

- Both the main transgressor and the defendant are referred to as "persons", so either could be a corporate body.

- The main transgressor must be, or have been, a director (and not a shadow director), and presumably of a company in relation to which the finding of unfitness was made.

- The main transgressor may have been disqualified on either the general ground of unfitness or on public interest grounds.

Further provision about disqualification undertakings

8A   Variation etc. of disqualification undertaking

8A(1)   [Reduction, etc. of undertaking] The court may, on the application of a person who is subject to a disqualification undertaking–

(a)   reduce the period for which the undertaking is to be in force, or

(b)   provide for it to cease to be in force.

8A(2)   [Duty of Secretary of State to appear] On the hearing of an application under subsection (1), the Secretary of State shall appear and call the attention of the court to any matters which seem to him to be relevant, and may himself give evidence or call witnesses.

8A(2A)   [Non-application of s.8(2)] Subsection (2) does not apply to an application in the case of an undertaking given under section 9B, and in such a case on the hearing of the application whichever of the Competition and Markets Authority or a specified regulator (within the meaning of section 9E) accepted the undertaking–

(a)   must appear and call the attention of the court to any matters which appear to it or him (as the case may be) to be relevant;

(b)   may give evidence or call witnesses.

8A(3)   ["The court"] In this section "the court"–

(za)   in the case of an undertaking given under section 8ZC has the same meaning as in section 8ZA;

(zb) in the case of an undertaking given under section 8ZE means the High Court or, in Scotland, the Court of Session;

(a) in the case of an undertaking given under section 9B means the High Court or (in Scotland) the Court of Session;

(b) in any other case has the same meaning as in section 5A(5), 7(2) or 8 (as the case may be).

S.8A(1), (2)

Section 8A was introduced by IA 2000 as part of the new disqualification undertaking regime. It may be assumed that its purpose is to allay concerns that persons facing disqualification proceedings might be unfairly induced to give undertakings (e.g. as a result of undue pressure or without having had matters of mitigation taken fully into account); and that without some form of appeal or review by the courts, the new legislation could be held to contravene the Human Rights legislation. It is to be noted that the scope of the section is restricted in two ways. First, only the disqualified person may apply to the court; the Secretary of State has no standing to seek a variation (though he is required by s.8A(2) to appear and put his case). Secondly, the court may only vary the undertaking in the applicant's favour, or terminate it altogether: there is no power to increase the period. As an alternative, application may be made to the court under s.17 for leave to act notwithstanding the undertaking.

On procedure see the *Practice Direction* (reproduced as App.VI to the *Guide*).

In *Re I.N.S. Realisations Ltd* [2006] EWHC 135 (Ch); [2006] B.C.C. 307, Hart J examined the nature of the jurisdiction under this section. The court should treat the applicant's statement of agreed facts given at the time of the undertaking as prima facie binding on the applicant, subject to any factor which would be sufficient to discharge a private law contract or some ground of public interest. Nevertheless, the court's jurisdiction was unfettered; and on the special facts of the case (namely, that the Secretary of State had decided not to continue with disqualification proceedings against another director, the person principally concerned in the alleged misconduct) the applicant's undertaking should cease to be in force. However, there was no power under s.8A to annul the undertaking from the start. The latter case was applied in *Taylor v Secretary of State for Business, Innovation and Skills* [2016] EWHC 1953 (Ch); [2016] 2 B.C.L.C. 350 where in refusing an application to reduce the agreed period, Registrar Briggs stated that the applicant had to demonstrate special circumstances and in this case failure to take legal advice when invited to do so and failure to appreciate the consequential effects of the undertaking were not special circumstances.

S.8A(2A)

Subsection (2A) was inserted by the Enterprise Act 2002 s.204(1), (4) and SI 2003/1397 (C. 60) arts 1, 2(1) and Sch., as from 20 June 2003. On competition undertakings, see s.9B: the undertaking in these cases is given to the CMA or one of the regulators specified in s.9E(2), and not to the Secretary of State.

S.8A(3).

Subsection (3) was substituted by the Enterprise Act 2002 s.204(1), (5) and SI 2003/1397 (C. 60) arts 1, 2(1) and Sch., as from 20 June 2003, specifying in more detail the competent court for the present purpose. Section 8A(3)(za), (zb) inserted by SBEEA Sch.7 para.10 as from 1 October 2015.

9   Matters for determining unfitness of directors [Repealed]

[**Note:** Section 9 was repealed by SBEEA 2015 s.106(4) and has been replaced by s.12C as from 1 October 2015.]

Disqualification for competition infringements

9A   Competition disqualification order

9A(1)   [Court's power] The court must make a disqualification order against a person if the following two conditions are satisfied in relation to him.

9A(2)   [First condition] The first condition is that an undertaking which is a company of which he is a director commits a breach of competition law.

9A(3)   [Second condition] The second condition is that the court considers that his conduct as a director makes him unfit to be concerned in the management of a company.

9A(4)   [Breach of competition law] An undertaking commits a breach of competition law if it engages in conduct which infringes any of the following–

(a)   the Chapter 1 prohibition (within the meaning of the Competition Act 1998) (prohibition on agreements, etc. preventing, restricting or distorting competition);

(b)   the Chapter 2 prohibition (within the meaning of that Act) (prohibition on abuse of a dominant position);

(c)   Article 101 of the Treaty on the Functioning of the European Union (prohibition on agreements, etc. preventing, restricting or distorting competition);

(d)   Article 102 of that Treaty (prohibition on abuse of a dominant position).

9A(5)   [Decision as to unfitness] For the purpose of deciding under subsection (3) whether a person is unfit to be concerned in the management of a company the court–

(a)   must have regard to whether subsection (6) applies to him;

(b)   may have regard to his conduct as a director of a company in connection with any other breach of competition law;

(c)   must not have regard to the matters mentioned in Schedule 1.

9A(6)   [Application of s.9A(6)] This subsection applies to a person if as a director of the company–

(a)   his conduct contributed to the breach of competition law mentioned in subsection (2);

(b)   his conduct did not contribute to the breach but he had reasonable grounds to suspect that the conduct of the undertaking constituted the breach and he took no steps to prevent it;

(c)   he did not know but ought to have known that the conduct of the undertaking constituted the breach.

9A(7)   [Knowledge of breach immaterial] For the purposes of subsection (6)(a) it is immaterial whether the person knew that the conduct of the undertaking constituted the breach.

9A(8)   [Conduct of an undertaking] For the purposes of subsection (4)(a) or (c) references to the conduct of an undertaking are references to its conduct taken with the conduct of one or more other undertakings.

9A(9)   [Maximum disqualification period] The maximum period of disqualification under this section is 15 years.

9A(10)   [Who may make application] An application under this section for a disqualification order may be made by the Competition and Markets Authority or by a specified regulator.

9A(11)   [Application of Competition Act 1998 s.60] Section 60 of the Competition Act 1998 (c. 41) (consistent treatment of questions arising under United Kingdom and EU law) applies in relation to any question arising by virtue of subsection (4)(a) or (b) above as it applies in relation to any question arising under Part 1 of that Act.

GENERAL NOTE

Sections 9A–9E were inserted into CDDA 1986 by the Enterprise Act 2002 s.204, introducing the novel regime of competition disqualification orders (CDOs) and competition disqualification undertakings (CDUs). This reform took effect from 20 June 2003: see the Enterprise Act 2002 (Commencement No.3, Transitional and Transitory Provisions and Savings) Order 2003 (SI 2003/1397 (C. 60)) arts 1, 2(1) and Sch.1. Under s.9A the court is empowered to make a disqualification order against a person who is or has been a director or shadow director of a company which has committed a breach of competition law where the court considers that his conduct as a director, taken together with his conduct in relation to one or more other undertakings, makes him unfit to be concerned in the management of a company. In parallel with s.6 of the Act, if there is a finding of unfitness the obligation to make an order is mandatory, and the period of disqualification runs to a maximum of 15 years. However, in contrast with s.6, no minimum period is specified.

The body primarily responsible for the administration and enforcement of the competition disqualification regime when it was established in 2003 was the Office of Fair Trading (OFT). However, by ERRA 2013 ss.25–27, the Office of Fair Trading has been abolished and merged with the Competition Commission to become the Competition and Markets Authority (CMA), and the functions of the OFT have been transferred to the CMA. This amendment became operative with effect from 1 April 2014 by virtue of the Enterprise and Regulatory Reform Act 2013 (Competition) (Consequential, Transitional and Saving Provisions) Order 2014 (SI 2014/892) Sch.1 paras 52–54. Accordingly, in this and other sections of this Act where there was formerly a reference to the OFT, that name has been substituted by "the Competition and Markets Authority", without annotation.

Application to the court may be made by the Competition and Markets Authority or by a number of regulators who are specified in s.9E(2). Section 9B makes provision for the CMA or a specified regulator to accept a CDU instead of a CDO. Powers of investigation of suspected breaches of competition law are conferred on these authorities by s.9C. The court may give a disqualified person leave to act as with other disqualification orders and undertakings; and s.8A has been extended by the insertion of s.8A(2A) so as to give the court power to reduce the length of a CDU or discharge it altogether, as with an undertaking accepted under s.1A.

Guidance notes on this regime and its scope and procedure were published by the OFT and were republished in revised form on 29 June 2010.

Section 9A(4)(c), (d), (11) amended by the Treaty of Lisbon (Changes in Terminology or Numbering) Order 2012 (SI 2012/1809) Sch.1 para.1 as from 1 August 2012.

S.9A(1)–(3)

A CDO may be made only against a person who is or was at the time of the breach a director or shadow director (s.9E(5)). On analogy with orders made under s.6, the present section would probably be construed as applying also to a de facto director. But note that it is not necessary that the person should himself have committed a breach of competition law, still less have been convicted of one. What is relevant is whether his company (and possibly also other undertakings—see s.9A(8)) have committed such a breach. If that is so, and he is or was at the relevant time a director, the statutory conditions are satisfied.

"The court" for the purpose of the present provisions is the High Court or, in Scotland, the Court of Session (s.9E(3)). "Conduct" includes omission: see s.9E(4).

S.9A(4), (11)

The breaches of competition law which may lead to a CDO or CDU are specified in this subsection, and include both the domestic and EU competition regimes. The Competition Act 1998 did not deal with the law relating to mergers, but the competition aspects of this topic were later reformed by the Enterprise Act 2002 Pt 3. That Act does not include any measure making CDOs or CDUs available for breaches of Pt 3.

S.9A(5)–(8)

Although a finding of unfitness is at the heart of both ss.6–8 and s.9A, the criteria relevant in the two cases are different. In particular, no reference may be made to Sch.1 when considering a case for a competition order or undertaking, and the question of the company's solvency is of no concern. As with ss.6–8, the conduct of the person as a director of another company may be brought into account, but only in so far as it involves a breach of competition law. Section 9A(6) makes it plain that it may not be necessary to show any causal connection between the director's conduct and the breach: indeed, this and the succeeding subsections, together with s.9E(4), arguably go further in penalising ignorance and inaction than the common law has so far done, or in cases under s.6 such as *Re Barings plc (No.5)* [1999] 1 B.C.L.C. 433. Subsections (5)(b) and (8) extend the picture so that account may be taken of breaches of competition law committed by companies other than the "lead" company: the former deals with the individual's conduct as a director of those other companies, while in the latter case it is the conduct of the lead company taken together with the conduct of other undertakings (including, but not necessarily confined to, its subsidiaries) which is referred to. Where subs.(8) is invoked, the individual need not be a director of these other companies.

S.9A(9)

Although the court must make an order if unfitness is found, no minimum period is specified. This is confirmed by s.1(2).

S.9A(10)

For the specified regulators, see s.9E(2).

9B   Competition undertakings

9B(1)   [Application of s.9B] This section applies if–

(a)   the Competition and Markets Authority or a specified regulator thinks that in relation to any person an undertaking which is a company of which he is a director has committed or is committing a breach of competition law,

(b)   the Competition and Markets Authority or the specified regulator thinks that the conduct of the person as a director makes him unfit to be concerned in the management of a company, and

(c)   the person offers to give the Competition and Markets Authority or the specified regulator (as the case may be) a disqualification undertaking.

9B(2)   [Acceptance of undertaking] The Competition and Markets Authority or the specified regulator (as the case may be) may accept a disqualification undertaking from the person instead of applying for or proceeding with an application for a disqualification order.

9B(3)   [Disqualification undertaking] A disqualification undertaking is an undertaking by a person that for the period specified in the undertaking he will not–

(a)   be a director of a company;

(b)   act as receiver of a company's property;

(c)   in any way, whether directly or indirectly, be concerned or take part in the promotion, formation or management of a company;

(d)   act as an insolvency practitioner.

9B(4)   [Undertaking not apply where leave of court] But a disqualification undertaking may provide that a prohibition falling within subsection (3)(a) to (c) does not apply if the person obtains the leave of the court.

9B(5)   [Maximum disqualification period] The maximum period which may be specified in a disqualification undertaking is 15 years.

9B(6)   [Concurrent disqualification periods] If a disqualification undertaking is accepted from a person who is already subject to a disqualification undertaking under this Act or to a disqualification order the periods specified in those undertakings or the undertaking and the order (as the case may be) run concurrently.

9B(7)   [Application of s.9A(4)–(8)] Subsections (4) to (8) of section 9A apply for the purposes of this section as they apply for the purposes of that section but in the application of subsection (5) of that section the reference to the court must be construed as a reference to the Competition and Markets Authority or a specified regulator (as the case may be).

General Note

Both the Competition and Markets Authority and the regulators specified in s.9E(2) are empowered to accept competition undertakings in lieu of a disqualification order made by the court. Undertakings are to all intents and purposes the same as orders. As is the case under s.1A, the CMA or regulator is not required to accept the offer of an undertaking, but may take the matter to court. Undertakings are recorded on the public register kept under s.18. The notes to s.1A are generally applicable.

S.9B(4)
An application for leave is made under s.17. Note also that a person who has given an undertaking is entitled to apply to the court under s.8A to have the undertaking discharged or its period reduced, in which case s.8A(2A) applies. "The court" here means the High Court or, in Scotland, the Court of Session (s.8A(3)(a)).

S.9B(5)
There is no minimum period.

S.9B(6)
Compare ss.1(3) and 1A(3).

9C   Competition investigations

9C(1)   [Power to investigate] If the Competition and Markets Authority or a specified regulator has reasonable grounds for suspecting that a breach of competition law has occurred it or he (as the case may be) may carry out an investigation for the purpose of deciding whether to make an application under section 9A for a disqualification order.

9C(2)   [Application of Competition Act 1998 ss.26–30] For the purposes of such an investigation sections 26 to 30 of the Competition Act 1998 (c. 41) apply to the Competition and Markets Authority and the specified regulators as they apply to the Competition and Markets Authority for the purposes of an investigation under section 25 of that Act.

9C(3)   [Application of s.9C(4)] Subsection (4) applies if as a result of an investigation under this section the Competition and Markets Authority or a specified regulator proposes to apply under section 9A for a disqualification order.

9C(4)   [Duty to notify before application] Before making the application the Competition and Markets Authority or regulator (as the case may be) must–

(a)   give notice to the person likely to be affected by the application, and

(b)   give that person an opportunity to make representations.

GENERAL NOTE

Under the Competition Act 1998 the CMA has wide powers of investigation. This section makes it plain that comparable powers may be used for the purpose of deciding whether to make an application for a competition disqualification order or accept an undertaking in lieu, and also confers similar powers of investigation on a specified regulator.

S.9C(4)
The application referred to means the application to the court. There is no statutory obligation to give notice before carrying out the investigation.

9D   Co-ordination

9D(1)   [Power to make regulations] The Secretary of State may make regulations for the purpose of co-ordinating the performance of functions under sections 9A to 9C (relevant functions) which are exercisable concurrently by two or more persons.

9D(2)   [Application of Competition Act 1998 s.54(5)–(7)] Section 54(5) to (7) of the Competition Act 1998 (c. 41) applies to regulations made under this section as it applies to regulations made under that section and for that purpose in that section–

(a)   references to Part 1 functions must be read as references to relevant functions;

(b)   references to a regulator must be read as references to a specified regulator;

(ba)   the reference in subsection (6A)(b) to notice under section 31(1) of the Competition Act 1998 that the regulator proposes to make a decision within the meaning given by section 31(2) of that Act is to be read as notice under section 9C(4) that the specified regulator proposes to apply under section 9A for a disqualification order;

(c)   a competent person also includes any of the specified regulators.

9D(3) **[Procedure for regulations]** The power to make regulations under this section must be exercised by statutory instrument subject to annulment in pursuance of a resolution of either House of Parliament.

9D(4) **[Scope of regulations]** Such a statutory instrument may–

(a) contain such incidental, supplemental, consequential and transitional provision as the Secretary of State thinks appropriate;

(b) make different provision for different cases.

GENERAL NOTE

No regulations appear to have yet been made under this section.

History
Section 9D(2)(ba) inserted by the Enterprise and Regulatory Reform Act 2013 (Competition) (Consequential, Transitional and Saving Provisions) Order 2014 (SI 2014/892) Sch.1 para.54 as from 1 April 2014.

9E Interpretation

9E(1) **[Application of s.9E]** This section applies for the purposes of sections 9A to 9D.

9E(2) **[The specified regulators]** Each of the following is a specified regulator for the purposes of a breach of competition law in relation to a matter in respect of which he or it has a function–

(a) the Office of Communications;

(b) the Gas and Electricity Markets Authority;

(c) the Water Services Regulation Authority;

(d) the Office of Rail and Road;

(e) the Civil Aviation Authority;

(f) Monitor;

(g) the Payment Systems Regulator established under section 40 of the Financial Services (Banking Reform) Act 2013;

(h) the Financial Conduct Authority.

9E(3) **[The court]** The court is the High Court or (in Scotland) the Court of Session.

9E(4) **[Conduct]** Conduct includes omission.

9E(5) **[Shadow director]** Director includes shadow director.

GENERAL NOTE

The regulators specified for the purposes of ss.9A–9D are listed in s.9E(2).

Section 9E(2)(a) was amended by the Communications Act 2003 s.406(1) and Sch.17 para.83 as from 29 December 2003 (see the Office of Communications Act 2002 (Commencement No.3 and Communications Act 2003 (Commencement No.2) Order 2003 (SI 2003/3142) art.3(1) and Sch.1). The reference was formerly to the Director General of Telecommunications. Section 9E(2)(d) amended by the Office of Rail Regulation (Change of Name) Regulations 2015 (SI 2015/1682) Sch.1 para.4(h) as from 16 October 2015. Section 9E(2)(f) inserted by the Health and Social Care Act 2012 s.74(4) as from 1 April 2013. Section 9E(2)(g) inserted by the Financial Services (Banking Reform) Act 2013 s.67(1) as from 1 April 2015. Section 9E(2)(h) inserted by the Financial Services (Banking Reform) Act 2013 s.67 and Sch.8 para.8 as from 1 April 2015.

S.9E(3)
The county court has no jurisdiction in relation to competition orders and undertakings.

Other cases of disqualification

10 Participation in wrongful trading

10(1) [Court's power] Where the court makes a declaration under section 213 or 214 of the Insolvency Act 1986 that a person is liable to make a contribution to a company's assets, then, whether or not an application for such an order is made by any person, the court may, if it thinks fit, also make a disqualification order against the person to whom the declaration relates.

10(2) [Maximum period] The maximum period of disqualification under this section is 15 years.

10(3) [Overseas company included] In this section "company" includes overseas company.

GENERAL NOTE

Section 10(3) inserted by SBEEA Sch.7 para.11 as from 26 May 2015.

The sections referred to relate to fraudulent trading as well as wrongful trading. The court is empowered to make a disqualification order in addition to imposing personal liability on the person concerned (who, in the case of fraudulent trading, will not necessarily have been a director or shadow director). This it may do of its own motion, or on the application of any person. The section appears to assume that the disqualification order will be made in the same proceedings as the declaration of liability, but conceivably it could be the subject of a separate, later application.

According to a note in [1990] I.L. & P. 72 at 73, the respondent in *Re Purpoint Ltd* [1991] B.C.C. 121 was disqualified under this section for two years, as well as being ordered to pay compensation under s.214. See also *Re Brian D Pierson (Contractors) Ltd* [1999] B.C.C. 26 in which in an addendum to the judgment the respondents were disqualified under s.10 for five and two years respectively. In *Re Idessa (UK) Ltd* [2011] EWHC 804 (Ch) the judge did not deal with the disqualification issue but referred the matter to the Secretary of State.

In *Re Ralls Builders Ltd* [2016] EWHC 1812 (Ch) the defendant directors had in earlier proceedings ([2016] EWHC 243 (Ch)) been found guilty of wrongful trading but were not ordered to pay compensation because it was not clear that their conduct had caused the company's net deficiency. Snowden J held that the court could not make any disqualification order because the defendants had not had to make any contribution to the company, as s.10 stipulates.

11 Undischarged bankrupts

11(1) [Offence] It is an offence for a person to act as director of a company or directly or indirectly to take part in or be concerned in the promotion, formation or management of a company, without the leave of the court, at a time when any of the circumstances mentioned in subsection (2) apply to the person.

11(2) [Circumstances for offence] The circumstances are–

(a) the person is an undischarged bankrupt–

  (i) in England and Wales or Scotland, or

  (ii) in Northern Ireland,

(b) a bankruptcy restrictions order or undertaking is in force in respect of the person under–

  (i) the Bankruptcy (Scotland) Act 1985 or 2016 or the Insolvency Act 1986, or

  (ii) the Insolvency (Northern Ireland) Order 1989,

(c) a debt relief restrictions order or undertaking is in force in respect of the person under–

  (i) the Insolvency Act 1986, or

  (ii) the Insolvency (Northern Ireland) Order 1989,

(d) a moratorium period under a debt relief order applies in relation to the person under–

  (i) the Insolvency Act 1986, or

  (ii) the Insolvency (Northern Ireland) Order 1989.

11(2A) **["The court"]** In subsection (1) "the court" means–

(a) for the purposes of subsection (2)(a)(i)–

    (i) the court by which the bankruptcy order was made or (if the order was not made by a court) the court to which a debtor may appeal against a refusal to make a bankruptcy order, or

    (ii) in Scotland, the court by which sequestration of the person's estate was awarded or, if awarded other than by the court, the court which would have jurisdiction in respect of sequestration of the person's estate,

(b) for the purposes of subsection (2)(b)(i)–

    (i) the court which made the order,

    (ii) in Scotland, if the order has been made other than by the court, the court to which the person may appeal against the order, or

    (iii) the court to which the person may make an application for annulment of the undertaking,

(c) for the purposes of subsection (2)(c)(i)–

    (i) the court which made the order, or

    (ii) the court to which the person may make an application for annulment of the undertaking,

(d) for the purposes of subsection (2)(d)(i), the court to which the person would make an application under section 251M(1) of the Insolvency Act 1986 (if the person were dissatisfied as mentioned there),

(e) for the purposes of paragraphs (a)(ii), (b)(ii), (c)(ii) and (d)(ii) of subsection (2), the High Court of Northern Ireland.

11(3) **[Requirements for leave of court]** In England and Wales, the leave of the court shall not be given unless notice of intention to apply for it has been served on the official receiver; and it is the latter's duty, if he is of opinion that it is contrary to the public interest that the application should be granted, to attend on the hearing of the application and oppose it.

11(4) **["Company"]** In this section "company" includes a company incorporated outside Great Britain that has an established place of business in Great Britain.

GENERAL NOTE

The ban here imposed on an undischarged bankrupt (or person subject to a BRO or BRU) is analogous in many ways to a disqualification order. Some of the notes to s.1 are relevant to this section. See also IR 2016 rr.6.11.1 et seq., the Enterprise Act 2002 (Disqualification from Office: General) Order 2006 (SI 2006/1722) and the Education (Disqualification Provisions: Bankruptcy and Mental Health) (England) Regulations 2006 (SI 2006/2198).

Section 11(1) and (2) were substituted and s.11(2A) inserted by SBEEA 2015 s.113 as from 1 October 2015. The former provision applied only to a person who had been adjudged bankrupt (or the equivalent) in England and Wales or in Scotland. It has now been extended so as to apply to persons in Northern Ireland. Corresponding provision has simultaneously made by SBEEA 2015 s.114 so as to establish reciprocity as between all parts of the United Kingdom. Section 11(2A)(a)(i) substituted by the Enterprise and Regulatory Reform Act 2013 (Consequential Amendments) (Bankruptcy) and the Small Business, Enterprise and Employment Act 2015 (Consequential Amendments) Regulations 2016 (SI 2016/481) reg.2 and Sch.1 para.8 as from 6 April 2016. The reference to a bankruptcy restrictions order includes a bankruptcy restrictions undertaking (IA 1986 Sch.4A para.8). Section 11(1)(aa) was inserted, and s.11(1)(b) amended, by the Tribunals, Courts and Enforcement Act 2007 s.108(3) and Sch.20 para.16(1)–(3) as from 6 April 2009. Section 11(4) was inserted by the Companies Act 2006 (Consequential Amendments, Transitional Provisions and Savings) Order 2009 (SI 2009/1941) art.2(1) and Sch.1 para.85(7) as from 1 October 2009. Section 11(2) substituted by the Tribunals, Courts and Enforcement Act 2007 (Consequential Amendments) Order 2012 (SI 2012/2404) art.3(1) and Sch.1 para.1 as from 1 October 2012.

The offence of acting as a director while an undischarged bankrupt under this section is an absolute offence: there is no requirement of mens rea: *R. v Doring* [2002] EWCA Crim 1695; [2002] B.C.C. 838. It is no defence that the defendant genuinely believes that he has been discharged from his bankruptcy: *R. v Brockley* [1994] B.C.C. 131. A bankrupt who acts as a director in contravention of s.11 continues to be criminally liable even if the bankruptcy is later annulled (because his debts have been paid in full) or discharged: *Inland Revenue Commissioners v McEntaggart* [2004] EWHC 3431 (Ch); [2007] 1 B.C.C. 260.

A contract made by a company which is being unlawfully managed in breach of s.11 is not unenforceable on the grounds of illegality: *Hill v Secretary of State for the Environment, Food and Rural Affairs* [2005] EWHC 696 (Ch); [2006] 1 B.C.L.C. 601. The judgment in this case also contains a discussion of the expression "concerned in the management" of a company.

An undischarged bankrupt is also disqualified from acting as trustee of a charity and from serving on various other bodies, under provisions analogous to those which apply to a person subject to a disqualification order: see the note to s.1 above.

Being involved in the management of a company while an undischarged bankrupt would constitute unfairly prejudicial conduct (by both the person involved and a fellow director knowing that the company was being so managed) so as to found a petition under the Companies Act 2006 s.994: *Re C&MB Holdings Ltd; Hamilton v Brown* [2016] EWHC 191 (Ch); [2017] B.C.C. 457. However, in *Corran v Butters* [2017] EWHC 2294 (Ch) it was held that excluding a director who had failed to disclose that he was an undischarged bankrupt was admittedly prejudicial to him, but on a "clean heads" basis was not unfairly so for CA 2006 s.994 purposes.

For cases where a bankrupt sought the leave of the court under this, or an equivalent, provision see *Re McQuillan* (1989) 5 B.C.C. 137; *Re Altim Pty Ltd* [1968] 2 N.S.W.R. 762.

12   Failure to pay under county court administration order

12(1)   [Effect of s.12(2)] The following has effect where a court under section 429 of the Insolvency Act revokes an administration order under Part VI of the County Courts Act 1984.

12(2)   [Restriction on person] A person to whom that section applies by virtue of the order under section 429(2)(b) shall not, except with the leave of the court which made the order, act as director or liquidator of, or directly or indirectly take part or be concerned in the promotion, formation or management of, a company.

GENERAL NOTE

The "administration order" here referred to relates to an individual debtor and has no connection with an administration order made in respect of an insolvent company under IA 1985 s.8 or Sch.B1. The *Practice Direction: Directors Disqualification Proceedings* [2015] B.C.C. 224 (reproduced as App.VI to this *Guide*) applies to applications under s.12(2). Note prospective amendment by TCEA 2007 s.106 and Sch.16 para.5.

12A   Northern Irish disqualification orders

12A   A person subject to a disqualification order under the Company Directors Disqualification (Northern Ireland) Order 2002–

   (a)   shall not be a director of a company, act as receiver of a company's property or in any way, whether directly or indirectly, be concerned or take part in the promotion, formation or management of a company unless (in each case) he has the leave of the High Court of Northern Ireland, and

   (b)   shall not act as an insolvency practitioner.

GENERAL NOTE

This provision was inserted into CDDA 1986 by IA 2000 s.7(1), with effect from 2 April 2001. In consequence, a disqualification order made by a court in Northern Ireland will have the same effect as one made by a court in the rest of the United Kingdom, and a contravention of a Northern Ireland order will carry the same civil and criminal liabilities and penalties: see ss.13–15.

12B   Northern Irish disqualification undertakings

12B   A person subject to a disqualification undertaking under the Company Directors Disqualification (Northern Ireland) Order 2002–

(a) shall not be a director of a company, act as receiver of a company's property or in any way, whether directly or indirectly, be concerned or take part in the promotion, formation or management of a company unless (in each case) he has the leave of the High Court of Northern Ireland, and

(b) shall not act as an insolvency practitioner.

GENERAL NOTE

Section 7(2) and (3) of IA 2000 anticipated that legislation would be introduced for Northern Ireland allowing a person to give a disqualification undertaking in lieu of a disqualification order made by a court. This has been done by the Company Directors Disqualification (Northern Ireland) Order 2002 (SI 2002/3150 (NI 4)), and recognition of such undertakings throughout the UK is given effect by the present section, which was inserted into the Act by the Insolvency Act 2000 (Company Directors Disqualification Undertakings) Order 2004 (SI 2004/1941), operative from 1 September 2004. Other sections of the Act have been amended (but not retrospectively) to reflect this change in the law.

12C   Determining unfitness etc: matters to be taken into account

12C(1)   [Application of section] This section applies where a court must determine–

(a) whether a person's conduct as a director of one or more companies or overseas companies makes the person unfit to be concerned in the management of a company;

(b) whether to exercise any discretion it has to make a disqualification order under any of sections 2 to 4, 5A, 8 or 10;

(c) where the court has decided to make a disqualification order under any of those sections or is required to make an order under section 6, what the period of disqualification should be.

12C(2)   [Non-application of section] But this section does not apply where the court in question is one mentioned in section 2(2)(b) or (c).

12C(3)   [Further application of section] This section also applies where the Secretary of State must determine–

(a) whether a person's conduct as a director of one or more companies or overseas companies makes the person unfit to be concerned in the management of a company;

(b) whether to exercise any discretion the Secretary of State has to accept a disqualification undertaking under section 5A, 7 or 8.

12C(4)   [Matters court or Secretary of State to have regard to] In making any such determination in relation to a person, the court or the Secretary of State must–

(a) in every case, have regard in particular to the matters set out in paragraphs 1 to 4 of Schedule 1;

(b) in a case where the person concerned is or has been a director of a company or overseas company, also have regard in particular to the matters set out in paragraphs 5 to 7 of that Schedule.

12C(5)   [Shadow director included] In this section "director" includes a shadow director.

12C(6) [Section 6(1A) applies] Subsection (1A) of section 6 applies for the purposes of this section as it applies for the purposes of that section.

12C(7)   [Secretary of State power to modify Sch.1] The Secretary of State may by order modify Schedule 1; and such an order may contain such transitional provision as may appear to the Secretary of State to be necessary or expedient.

12C(8)   [Power exercisable by statutory instrument] The power to make an order under this section is exercisable by statutory instrument.

12C(9) **[Draft instrument to be laid and approved]** An order under this section may not be made unless a draft of the instrument containing it has been laid before, and approved by a resolution of, each House of Parliament.

GENERAL NOTE

Section 12C was inserted by SBEEA 2015 s.106(5) as from 1 October 2015. It replaces the original s.9, and brings with it a revised version of Sch.1. Strangely, it has not been enacted as a substitute s.9, but has been given a new number and placed uncomfortably under the heading "Other cases of disqualification", where it does not belong at all. In addition to taking full account of the extension of the disqualification regime to include conduct in relation to overseas companies, and making specific reference to disqualification undertakings, the section in conjunction with the more generally reworded schedule is designed to ensure that the concept of misconduct is not restricted by a narrow or technical approach to construction. Thus, "matters for determining unfitness" is replaced by "matters to be taken into account", and a long list of specific statutory provisions gives way to "any applicable legislative or other requirement". There is also a subtle difference of emphasis when the language is compared with that of the original schedule, with a specific mention of the frequency of any misconduct, and the nature and extent of any loss or harm caused.

Like its predecessor, the schedule is divided into two sections, but the grouping is based on different criteria. The first section lists "matters to be taken into account" (replacing "matters applicable") in all cases, but the content of the items grouped under these essentially similar wordings is quite different, reflecting the fact that the additional "matters to be taken into account" (or "matters applicable") which are grouped in the second section apply, under the former schedule, "where the company has become insolvent" but, in the new schedule, "where the person is or has been a director".

Despite these differences, it is probable that there will be little change in the interpretation and development of the concept of unfitness in practice. The discussion of the established case-law which follows necessarily relates to the earlier schedule, but it is likely that, at least in broad terms, it will hold good for the future. In *Secretary of State for Business, Innovation and Skills v Akbar* [2017] EWHC 2856 (Ch); [2018] B.C.C. 448 HHJ Davis-White QC commented (at [98]–[100]) that the new Sch.1 would make little real difference to the position applying under the previous version. See also the note to Sch.1.

Schedule 1 is not applicable in competition disqualification cases (s.9A(5)(c)).

In must be emphasised that the Act does not contain any definition of unfitness. The Schedule (unlike the former version) does not list specific instances of unfitness. But even when it did, these were treated only as guidelines for the court, which could treat any other conduct as evidencing unfitness (*Re Amaron Ltd* [1998] B.C.C. 264); and did not consider itself bound by statutory definitions (*Re Sykes (Butchers) Ltd* [1998] B.C.C. 484; *Re Migration Services International Ltd* [2000] B.C.C. 1,095).

In *Re Bath Glass Ltd* (1988) 4 B.C.C. 130 at 133, Peter Gibson J said: "To reach a finding of unfitness the court must be satisfied that the director has been guilty of a serious failure or serious failures, whether deliberately or through incompetence, to perform those duties of directors which are attendant on the privilege of trading through companies with limited liability. Any misconduct of the respondent qua director may be relevant, even if it does not fall within a specific section of the Companies Act or the Insolvency Act". In *Cathie v Secretary of State for Business, Innovation and Skills* [2012] EWCA Civ 739 it was held that in determining the question of unfitness the judge should consider the evidence as a whole, including any extenuating circumstances, and that in this context the use of the term "exceptional circumstances" was better avoided.

In *Re Lo-Line Electric Motors Ltd* [1988] Ch. 477 at 496; (1988) 4 B.C.C. 415 at 419; Browne-Wilkinson V.C. said: "Ordinary commercial misjudgment is in itself not sufficient to justify disqualification. In the normal case, the conduct complained of must display a lack of commercial probity although I have no doubt that in an extreme case of gross negligence or total incompetence disqualification could be appropriate". (It may be that under the reworded Sch.1 the court would now take a more severe view of cases of negligence.)

In *Re Polly Peck International plc, Secretary of State for Trade & Industry v Ellis (No.2)* [1993] B.C.C. 890 at 894, Lindsay J said that he would "pay regard to the clear thread derived from the authorities that whatever else is required of a respondent's conduct if he is to be disqualified, it must at least be 'serious'".

However, it should be borne in mind that in *Re Sevenoaks Stationers (Retail) Ltd* [1991] Ch. 164 at 176; [1990] B.C.C. 765 at 773 (the leading case on disqualification for "unfitness") Dillon LJ warned against treating such statements as "judicial paraphrases of the words of the statute, which fall to be construed as a matter of law in lieu of the words of the statute".

In *Re Landhurst Leasing plc* [1999] 1 B.C.L.C. 286 at 344, Park J observed that in disqualification cases the relevant standard of conduct "is more frequently described as a standard of 'probity' and 'competence' than stated in the traditional terms of care, skill and diligence". The standard may vary depending upon the nature and size of the company and the role which the defendant played in its affairs. Where it has been established that a defendant's conduct has fallen below the standard of probity and competence, a disqualification order must be made, even though this is not thought necessary in the public interest: *Re Grayan Building Services Ltd* [1995] Ch. 241; [1995] B.C.C. 554. The question for the court to determine is whether the director's conduct, *as shown by the evidence*, demonstrates unfitness—not whether, at the time of the hearing, the person is or continues to be unfit.

The fact that the director himself honestly believed that what he was doing was not wrong does not excuse him, if on an objective view his conduct justifies a finding of unfitness: *Goldberg v Secretary of State for Trade and Industry* [2003] EWHC 2843 (Ch); [2004] 1 B.C.L.C. 597.

In the leading Scottish case, *Secretary of State for Trade and Industry v Blackwood*, 2003 S.L.T. 120; [2005] B.C.C. 366 the court stressed that a failure to act reasonably (e.g. in deciding to continue to trade) did not necessarily lead to the conclusion that the person concerned was unfit to be a director. In such circumstances directors could not be expected to have wholly dispassionate minds, but might tend to cling to hope. In *Re Smooth Financial Consultants Ltd; Secretary of State for Business, Energy and Industrial Strategy v Broadstock* [2018] EWHC 2146 (Ch), after stressing that it was necessary to assess the conduct as a whole to determine if such made a director unfit, the court added that where a director remained in office while a company was involved in inappropriate activity, it was necessary to consider the merits of his explanation for doing so. If he was aware of such activity and did nothing, he was likely to be in breach of duty. If he remained in office with a view to bringing such activity to an end, however, and could be seen to have attempted to do so, a finding of unfitness by no means followed: it then became necessary to assess what he achieved and set out to achieve together with his explanation for doing so. Conversely, if he was entirely unaware of the relevant activity, it becomes necessary to ask why.

A number of reported cases have been concerned with a particular issue: the failure by a company and its directors to set aside sufficient funds to meet Crown debts for PAYE, NIC and VAT, in effect using this money as working capital as insolvency looms. The views expressed by different judges in these cases have ranged between treating such Crown debts as "quasi-trust moneys" (Harman J, *Re Wedgecraft Ltd* (unreported, 7 March 1986)), on the one hand, to a refusal to draw any distinction between these and other debts (Hoffmann J, in *Re Dawson Print Group Ltd* (1987) 3 B.C.C. 322), on the other. Prior to the ruling of the Court of Appeal in *Re Sevenoaks Stationers (Retail) Ltd* (above), a consensus had emerged among the judges in the Chancery Division which took a middle line between these extremes, holding that the failure to pay such moneys over to the Crown was, though not a breach of trust, "more serious" and "more culpable" than the non-payment of commercial debts (*Re Stanford Services Ltd* (1987) 3 B.C.C. 326; *Re Lo-Line Electric Motors Ltd* [1988] Ch. 477; (1988) 4 B.C.C. 415). However, in the *Sevenoaks Stationers* case passages from the judgment of Hoffmann J in *Dawson Print* were approved, and the ruling given that non-payment of a Crown debt cannot automatically be treated as evidence of unfitness; it is necessary to look more closely in each case to see what the significance, if any, of the non-payment of the Crown debt is. In more recent cases, emphasis has been put on another factor: that the company has pursued a policy of deliberately discriminating between creditors. This may be seen as evidence of unfitness regardless of the status of those who are discriminated against but, in the nature of things, it is very often the Crown which is disadvantaged by such a policy. (See *Secretary of State for Trade and Industry v McTighe* [1997] B.C.C. 224, and contrast *Official Receiver v Dhaliwall* [2006] 1 B.C.L.C. 285, where non-payment was held, in the circumstances, not to amount to unfitness.) Discriminating in not paying Crown debts together with non-validated payments by a director in breach of IA 1986 s.127 (especially payments to himself) was unfitness in *Re St John Law Ltd; Secretary of State for Business, Energy and Industrial Strategy v Murphy* [2019] EWHC 459 (Ch). The fact that there has been correspondence or negotiations with the Revenue authorities may count in the director's favour, and its absence weigh against him: *Re Funtime Ltd* [2000] 1 B.C.L.C. 247; *Re Structural Concrete Ltd* [2001] B.C.C. 578; *Re Amaron Ltd* [1998] B.C.C. 264; *Re Hopes (Heathrow) Ltd* [2001] 1 B.C.L.C. 575 at 581; *Cathie v Secretary of State for Business, Innovation and Skills* [2012] EWCA Civ 739. In the Scots case of *Bradley v Secretary of State for Business, Innovation and Skills* [2016] CSIH 80 divergent views were made on non-payment of Crown debts. In *Re CQH1 Ltd and RTD1 Ltd; Secretary of State for Business, Energy and Industrial Strategy v Steven* [2018] EWHC 1331 (Ch) the director's assertion that he believed business would improve sufficiently to clear the debts to HMRC were too speculative to deflect from the discriminatory treatment of HMRC, particularly given the prolonged trading period over which the discrimination had occurred, and he was disqualified for three years. See *Re Ixoyc Anesis (2014) Ltd; Secretary of State for Business, Energy and Industrial Strategy v Zannetou* [2018] EWHC 3190 (Ch) for a useful summary of cases on discriminating between creditors.

Other types of conduct which have been held to be evidence of "unfitness" include:

- failure to keep proper books of account and/or to make statutory returns (*Re Rolus Properties Ltd* (1988) 4 B.C.C. 446; *Re Western Welsh International System Buildings Ltd* (1988) 4 B.C.C. 449; *Re T & D Services (Timber Preservation & Damp Proofing Contractors) Ltd* [1990] B.C.C. 592; *Re Chartmore Ltd* [1990]

B.C.L.C. 673; *Re Carecraft Construction Co Ltd* [1994] 1 W.L.R. 172; [1993] B.C.C. 336; *Re Synthetic Technology Ltd, Secretary of State for Trade & Industry v Joiner* [1993] B.C.C. 549; *Re New Generation Engineers Ltd* [1993] B.C.L.C. 435; *Re A & C Group Services Ltd* [1993] B.C.L.C. 1297; *Re Pamstock Ltd* [1994] B.C.C. 264; *Re Firedart Ltd* [1994] 2 B.C.L.C. 340; *Re Park House Properties Ltd* [1998] B.C.C. 847; *Official Receiver v Stern (No.2)* [2001] EWCA Civ 1787; [2004] B.C.C. 581); *Secretary of State for Business, Innovation and Skills v Jeromson* [2013] ScotSC 26; *Re Artistic Investment Advisers Ltd* [2014] EWHC 2963 (Ch); *Carlson v Secretary of State for Business, Innovation and Skills* [2015] 1 B.C.L.C. 619;

- trading or continuing to draw remuneration while insolvent (*Re Western Welsh International System Buildings Ltd* (above)); *Re Ipcon Fashions Ltd* (1989) 5 B.C.C. 773; *Re Melcast (Wolverhampton) Ltd* [1991] B.C.L.C. 288; *Re Cargo Agency Ltd* [1992] B.C.C. 388; *Re City Investment Centres Ltd* [1992] B.C.L.C. 956; *Re Synthetic Technology Ltd, Secretary of State for Trade & Industry v Joiner* (above); *Re Firedart Ltd* (above); *Secretary of State for Trade & Industry v McTighe* [1997] B.C.C. 224; *Re Park House Properties Ltd* (above); *Re City Pram & Toy Co Ltd* (above); *Secretary of State for Trade & Industry v Van Hengel* [1995] B.C.C. 173; *Re Amaron Ltd* [1998] B.C.C. 264; *Official Receiver v Stern (No.2)* (above)); *Re Vintage Hallmark plc* [2006] EWHC 2761 (Ch); [2007] 1 B.C.L.C. 788;

- purportedly taking into his own hands the liquidation of the company, by-passing the statutory procedure and safeguards (*Re Ipcon Fashions Ltd* (above));

- misleading customers by high-pressure selling tactics (*Official Receiver v Wild* [2012] EWHC 4279 (Ch));

- inadequate capitalisation (*Re Chartmore Ltd* (above); *Re Austinsuite Furniture Ltd* [1992] B.C.L.C. 1047; *Re Pamstock Ltd* (above)); or trading (as a public company) in breach of the statutory minimum capital requirements (*Secretary of State for Trade and Industry v Hollier* [2006] EWHC 1804 (Ch); [2007] B.C.C. 11;

- trading with a succession of "phoenix" companies and/or using a prohibited company name (*Re Travel Mondial Ltd* [1991] B.C.C. 224; *Re Swift 736 Ltd* [1993] B.C.C. 312; *Re Linvale Ltd* [1993] B.C.L.C. 654; *Re Migration Services International Ltd* [2000] B.C.C. 1095);

- issuing false invoices or other financial statements: *Kappler v Secretary of State for Trade and Industry* [2006] B.C.C. 845; *Re Trans Tec plc (No.2)* [2006] EWHC 2110 (Ch); [2007] 2 B.C.L.C. 495;

- making misrepresentations to customers, suppliers of funds and others: *Secretary of State for Business, etc. v Sullman* [2008] EWHC 3179 (Ch); [2010] B.C.C. 500;

- generating fictitious funds by manipulating ("kiting") cheques (*Secretary of State for Trade and Industry v Swan (No.2)* [2005] EWHC 603 (Ch); [2005] B.C.C. 596); *Re City Truck Group Ltd (No.2)* [2007] EWHC 350 (Ch); [2008] B.C.C. 76;

- misapplication of company's funds or property (*Re Keypak Homecare Ltd (No.2)* [1990] B.C.C. 117; *Re Tansoft Ltd* [1991] B.C.L.C. 339; *Re City Investment Centres Ltd* (above); *Re Austinsuite Furniture Ltd* (above); *Re Synthetic Technology Ltd, Secretary of State for Trade & Industry v Joiner* (above); *Re Park House Properties Ltd* (above); *Secretary of State for Trade and Industry v Blunt* [2006] B.C.C. 112); *Re Mea Corp Ltd* [2006] EWHC 1846 (Ch); [2007] B.C.C. 288; *Secretary of State for Business, Innovation and Skills v Doffman* [2010] EWHC 3175 (Ch);

- irresponsible intra-group loans, etc. (*Re Continental Assurance Co of London plc* [1996] B.C.C. 888; *Re Dominion International Group plc (No.2)* [1996] 1 B.C.L.C. 572; *Official Receiver v Stern (No.2)* (above));

- drawing excessive remuneration (*Re Synthetic Technology Ltd, Secretary of State for Trade & Industry v Joiner* (above); *Re A & C Group Services Ltd* (above));

- irresponsible delegation (*Re Burnham Marketing Services Ltd, Secretary of State for Trade & Industry v Harper* [1993] B.C.C. 518; *Re RD Industries Ltd, Secretary of State for Business, Innovation and Skills v Dymond* [2014] EWHC 2844 (Ch));

- continuing to incur liabilities after trading had ceased (*Re McNulty's Interchange Ltd* (1988) 4 B.C.C. 533; *Re Ipcon Fashions Ltd* (above));

- dishonesty, deception and self-dealing (*Re Godwin Warren Control Systems plc* [1992] B.C.C. 557; *Official Receiver v Doshi* [2001] 2 B.C.L.C. 235; *Re Bunting Electric Manufacturing Co Ltd* [2005] EWHC 3345 (Ch); [2006] 1 B.C.L.C. 550; *Re City Truck Group Ltd* (above); it is immaterial whether the director's dishonesty has been towards the company itself or its clients or creditors: *Re JA Chapman & Co Ltd* [2003] EWHC 532 (Ch); [2003] 2 B.C.L.C. 206);

- breach of trust or fiduciary duty (*Secretary of State for Trade & Industry v Van Hengel* (above); *Re Dominion International Group plc (No.2)* (above));

- giving a preference to a particular creditor or paying creditors selectively (*Re Living Images Ltd* [1996] B.C.C. 112; *Secretary of State for Trade & Industry v McTighe* (above); *Re Funtime Ltd* [2000] 1 B.C.L.C. 247; *Re Structural Concrete Ltd* [2001] B.C.C. 578);

- failure to co-operate with the official receiver or the FSA [now the FCA], lack of frankness with the court, or dishonesty as a witness: *Re JA Chapman & Co Ltd* [2003] EWHC 532 (Ch); [2003] 2 B.C.L.C. 206 (*Re Tansoft Ltd* (above); *Re Godwin Warren Control Systems plc* (above); *Secretary of State for Trade & Industry v Reynard* [2002] B.C.C. 813); *Ghassemian v Secretary of State for Trade and Industry* [2006] EWHC 1715 (Ch); [2007] B.C.C. 229;

- entering into a transaction at an undervalue, contrary to s.238 or giving financial assistance, contrary to CA 2006: *Re Genosyis Technology Management Ltd* [2006] EWHC 989 (Ch); [2007] 1 B.C.L.C. 208; *Secretary of State for Business, Enterprise and Regulatory Reform v Poulter* [2009] B.C.C. 608;

- failure to ensure VAT returns were filed: *Re CQH1 Ltd and RTD1 Ltd; Secretary of State for Business, Energy and Industrial Strategy v Steven* [2018] EWHC 1331 (Ch);

- remaining in office whilst failing to protect client funds: *Re Smooth Financial Consultants Ltd; Secretary of State for Business Energy and Industrial Strategy v Broadstock* [2018] EWHC 2146 (Ch).

Of course, in many cases several of these features will have been present at the same time. Other considerations, such as the number of companies involved, their size, the extent of their losses, the position of the individual concerned in the managerial hierarchy and his experience (or lack of it), and whether there has been a lack of probity, may also go towards deciding whether unfitness has been established or determining the length of the order to be made.

Factors which have weighed with the court in deciding that a disqualification order should not be made, or that a reduced period of disqualification would be appropriate, have included the following:

- acting on professional advice (*Re Bath Glass Ltd* (1988) 4 B.C.C. 130; *Re McNulty's Interchange Ltd* (1988) 4 B.C.C. 533; *Re Douglas Construction Services Ltd* (1988) 4 B.C.C. 553; *Re C U Fittings Ltd* (1989) 5 B.C.C. 210; *Re Cladrose Ltd* [1990] B.C.C. 11; *Re Bradcrown Ltd* [2001] 1 B.C.L.C. 547);

- employing a qualified company secretary or finance director (*Re Rolus Properties Ltd* (1988) 4 B.C.C. 446; *Re Douglas Construction Services Ltd* (above));

- absence of dishonesty (*Re Bath Glass Ltd* (1988) 4 B.C.C. 130; *Re Lo-Line Electric Motors Ltd* [1988] Ch. 477; (1988) 4 B.C.C. 415; *Re D J Matthews (Joinery Design) Ltd* (1988) 4 B.C.C. 513; *Re Burnham Marketing Services Ltd* [1993] B.C.C. 518);

- readiness to make a personal financial commitment to the company or the fact that the respondent has sustained heavy personal loss (*Re Bath Glass Ltd* (above); *Re Douglas Construction Services Ltd* (above); *Re Swift 736 Ltd* [1993] B.C.C. 312);

- reliance on regular budgets and forecasts (even though subsequently shown to be inaccurate) (*Re Bath Glass Ltd* (above));

- the fact that events outside the director's control contributed to the company's misfortunes (*Re Bath Glass Ltd* (above); *Re Cladrose Ltd* (above));

- evidence that the same company or other companies have been successfully and properly run by the respondent (*Re D J Matthews (Joinery Design) Ltd* (above); *Re A & C Group Services Ltd* [1993] B.C.L.C. 1297; *Re Pamstock Ltd* [1994] B.C.C. 264);

- the fact that the business was kept going on assurances of help from others (*Re C U Fittings Ltd* (above));

- the respondent's relative youth and inexperience (*Re Chartmore Ltd* [1990] B.C.L.C. 673; *Re Austinsuite Furniture Ltd* [1992] B.C.L.C. 1047);

- the fact that the director was fully occupied as the company's production manager and had left board matters to others (ibid.);

- the fact that the proceedings have been a long time coming to a hearing and that the respondent has already been under a disqualification by reason of bankruptcy (*Re A & C Group Services Ltd* (above));

- the fact that the respondent has admitted his responsibility (*Re Carecraft Construction Co Ltd* [1994] 1 W.L.R. 172; [1993] B.C.C. 336; *Re Aldermanbury Trust plc* [1993] B.C.C. 598).

In *Re Melcast (Wolverhampton) Ltd* [1991] B.C.L.C. 288 the court held that a ten-year disqualification was merited, but reduced the term to seven years on account of the respondent's age (68). Where other directors have also been disqualified, the court may take into account the period of disqualification imposed on them for the purpose of comparison, but should not be over-influenced by this fact (*Re Swift 736 Ltd* (above)).

One or two cases have been reported in which the court has found that the defendant's conduct was not such as to warrant a finding of unfitness. These include *Re Stephenson Cobbold Ltd* [2001] B.C.C. 38; *Re Cubelock Ltd* [2001] B.C.C. 523; and *Secretary of State for Trade and Industry v Creegan* [2002] 1 B.C.L.C. 99.

The wording of Sch.1 appears to be directed primarily at those directors who have taken an active part in the company's affairs, rather than those whose role has been nominal or who have involved themselves only intermittently; but such passive conduct may also in itself justify a finding of unfitness. Even a non-executive director of a small family company is liable to disqualification if he merely stands by, or is content to remain in ignorance, while those who are actively managing the company run up losses or allow accounts, records and returns to fall into disarray: see *Re Peppermint Park Ltd* [1998] B.C.C. 23; *Re Park House Properties Ltd* [1998] B.C.C. 847; *Re Galeforce Pleating Ltd* [1999] 2 B.C.L.C. 704; *Official Receiver v Stern (No.2)* [2001] EWCA Civ 1787; [2001] 1 B.C.L.C. 119; *Re Bradcrown Ltd* [2002] B.C.C. 428; *Secretary of State for Trade and Industry v Thornbury* [2007] EWHC 3202 (Ch); [2008] 1 B.C.L.C. 139; *Re AG (Manchester) Ltd* [2008] EWHC 64 (Ch); [2008] 1 B.C.L.C. 321; *Secretary of State for Trade and Industry v Thornbury* [2007] EWHC 3202 (Ch); [2008] B.C.C. 768; *Secretary of State for Business, Innovation and Skills v Reza* [2013] CSOH 86. In *Re City Truck Group Ltd (No.2)* [2007] EWHC 350 (Ch); [2008] B.C.C. 76 a director who passively acquiesced in a fraud perpetrated by a co-director was disqualified for the same period as the principal offender (12 years). The courts in these cases have stressed that the title "director" is not to be accepted by any person without a corresponding assumption of responsibility—the more so if he is paid remuneration.

On the other hand, it has been a factor counting against a director that he held a high position in the company: the greater the status and its rewards, the higher the standard for measuring its responsibilities (*Re Barings plc, Secretary of State for Trade & Industry v Baker* [1998] B.C.C. 583; *Re Barings plc (No.5)* [1999] 1 B.C.L.C. 433 (affirmed on appeal [2001] B.C.C. 273); and see *Secretary of State for Trade and Industry v Swan (No.2)* [2005] EWHC 603 (Ch); [2005] B.C.C. 596). On similar reasoning individuals whose business consisted of acting as nominee directors of large numbers of "offshore" companies for remuneration have been severely dealt with: see *Re Kaytech International plc* [1999] B.C.C. 390; and *Official Receiver v Vass* [1999] B.C.C. 516. The fact that the respondent relied on his fellow-directors may be relevant, but only if it is shown that he was justified in doing so, and for this purpose evidence on his part of his perception of their reliability is material: *Secretary of State for Trade & Industry v Dawes* [1997] B.C.C. 121. In *Re Landhurst Leasing plc* [1999] 1 B.C.L.C. 286, relatively junior directors were held to have been justified in relying on their more experienced co-directors. The court held that a proper degree of delegation and division of responsibility by the board (not amounting to a total abrogation of responsibility by any individual director or directors) was permissible. An absentee director will not necessarily be excused: *Re Peppermint Park Ltd* [1998] B.C.C. 23. The position of a director who dissented from or opposed the course of conduct being followed by his colleagues as disaster loomed has brought a mixed reaction from the judges. Plainly, much depends on the circumstances. In *Re Peppermint Park Ltd* (above) it was said ([1996] B.C.C. 23 at 26) that the director in question should, at least, have resigned his directorship. However in *Secretary of State for Trade & Industry v Taylor, Re C S Holidays Ltd* [1997] 1 W.L.R. 407; [1997] B.C.C. 172 the fact that a director whose protests went unheeded did not resign was not held to be fatal.

On the topic of unfitness, see further Walters and Davis-White, *Directors' Disqualification & Insolvency Restrictions*, 3rd edn (Sweet & Maxwell, 2010), Ch.5; and Totty, Moss & Segal, *Insolvency*, G1–18 et seq.

S.12C(1)

Unlike the repealed s.9, which was concerned only with the question of determining whether the person was unfit to be a director (and therefore by implication only with cases under s.6), this provision applies also to cases under the provisions listed in para.(1)(b), and more generally when the length of the disqualification is being determined (para.(1)(c)). The wording of s.12C(1)(c) reflects the fact that if the director is found guilty of misconduct, the court is obliged to impose at least the minimum disqualification.

S.12C(2)

The reference is to the case where disqualification is imposed as part of a criminal sentence.

S.12C(3)

Similar considerations apply where the Secretary of State is determining whether to accept a disqualification undertaking.

S.12C(6)

Where a company has become insolvent, the conduct of a director in relation to any matter connected with or arising out of the insolvency is relevant, as well as any conduct as director.

Consequences of contravention

13   Criminal penalties

13   If a person acts in contravention of a disqualification order or disqualification undertaking or in contravention of section 12(2), 12A or 12B, or is guilty of an offence under section 11, he is liable–

(a)   on conviction on indictment, to imprisonment for not more than 2 years or a fine or both; and

(b)   on summary conviction, to imprisonment for not more than 6 months or a fine not exceeding the statutory maximum, or both.

GENERAL NOTE

The reference to s.12B was inserted by the Insolvency Act 2002 (Company Directors Disqualification Undertakings) Order 2004 (SI 2004/1941) art.2(2), as from 1 September 2004.

The breach of a disqualification order or of the analogous ban on an undischarged bankrupt is a criminal offence, as well as potentially attracting civil sanctions under s.15.

Reported prosecutions under this section include *R. v Theivendran* (1992) 13 Cr. App. R. (S) 601; *R. v Brockley* [1994] B.C.C. 131; *R. v Teece* (1994) 15 Cr. App. R. 302. Conviction may lead to a confiscation order, assessed by reference to the benefit that the offender has personally received: *R. v Seager & Blatch* [2009] EWCA Crim 1303; [2010] 1 W.L.R. 815; [2012] B.C.C. 124; *Hill v Department for Business, Innovation and Skills* [2011] EWHC 3436 (Admin); [2012] B.C.C. 151.

On the "statutory maximum", and penalties generally, see IA 1986 s.430 and Sch.10.

14   Offences by body corporate

14(1)   [Offence re officer] Where a body corporate is guilty of an offence of acting in contravention of a disqualification order or disqualification undertaking or in contravention of section 12A or 12B, and it is proved that the offence occurred with the consent or connivance of, or was attributable to any neglect on the part of any director, manager, secretary or other similar officer of the body corporate, or any person who was purporting to act in any such capacity he, as well as the body corporate, is guilty of the offence and liable to be proceeded against and punished accordingly.

14(2)   [Where managers are members] Where the affairs of a body corporate are managed by its members, subsection (1) applies in relation to the acts and defaults of a member in connection with his functions of management as if he were a director of the body corporate.

GENERAL NOTE

This is a standard provision, equivalent to IA 1986 s.432.

"Body corporate" and "officer" are defined in CA 2006 s.1173(1), and these definitions are incorporated into the present Act by s.22(6). A body corporate includes a company incorporated elsewhere than in Great Britain, but excludes a corporation sole and a Scottish firm. On the meaning of "officer", see the note to IA 1986 s.206(3).

15   Personal liability for company's debts where person acts while disqualified

15(1)   [Personal liability] A person is personally responsible for all the relevant debts of a company if at any time–

(a)   in contravention of a disqualification order or disqualification undertaking or in contravention of section 11, 12A or 12B of this Act he is involved in the management of the company, or

(b) as a person who is involved in the management of the company, he acts or is willing to act on instructions given without the leave of the court by a person whom he knows at that time–

    (i) to be the subject of a disqualification order made or disqualification undertaking accepted under this Act or under the Company Directors Disqualification (Northern Ireland) Order 2002, or

    (ii) to be an undischarged bankrupt.

15(2) **[Joint and several liability]** Where a person is personally responsible under this section for the relevant debts of a company, he is jointly and severally liable in respect of those debts with the company and any other person who, whether under this section or otherwise, is so liable.

15(3) **[Relevant debts of company]** For the purposes of this section the relevant debts of a company are–

(a) in relation to a person who is personally responsible under paragraph (a) of subsection (1), such debts and other liabilities of the company as are incurred at a time when that person was involved in the management of the company, and

(b) in relation to a person who is personally responsible under paragraph (b) of that subsection, such debts and other liabilities of the company as are incurred at a time when that person was acting or was willing to act on instructions given as mentioned in that paragraph.

15(4) **[Person involved in management]** For the purposes of this section, a person is involved in the management of a company if he is a director of the company or if he is concerned, whether directly or indirectly, or takes part, in the management of the company.

15(5) **[Presumption]** For the purposes of this section a person who, as a person involved in the management of a company, has at any time acted on instructions given without the leave of the court by a person whom he knew at that time–

(a) to be the subject of a disqualification order made or disqualification undertaking accepted under this Act or under the Company Directors Disqualification (Northern Ireland) Order 2002, or

(b) to be an undischarged bankrupt,

is presumed, unless the contrary is shown, to have been willing at any time thereafter to act on any instructions given by that person.

General Note

The references to s.12B in s.15(1) and to the 2002 Order in s.15(1) and (2) were inserted by the Insolvency Act 2002 (Company Directors Disqualification Undertakings) Order 2004 (SI 2004/1941) art.2(5), as from 1 September 2004. Section 15(1)(b) and (5) were substituted by the Companies Act 2006 (Consequential Amendments, Transitional Provisions and Savings) Order 2009 (SI 2009/1941) art.2(1) and Sch.1 para.85(9) as from 1 October 2009.

This section makes a person personally liable, without limit, for the debts of a company if he is involved in its management in breach of a disqualification order or undertaking or while he is an undischarged bankrupt or subject to a BRO or BRU. It is very closely analogous to IA 1986 s.217, which deals with the reuse of the name of a former insolvent company—indeed, the two sections are derived from the same source.

In *Re Prestige Grindings Ltd* [2006] B.C.C. 421 the liquidator sought a declaration that a director and former director of the company were in breach of a disqualification order and an order under s.15 that they should pay the relevant debts of the company. HHJ Norris Q.C. ruled (i) that the right conferred by s.15(1) was a right conferred on the creditors concerned and not on the liquidator, so that it was inappropriate to make an order under the CPR appointing him to represent those creditors, and (ii) that the company had a separate right of action (enforceable by her as liquidator) against the defendants for contribution arising out of their joint and several liability for the relevant debts under s.15(2).

For further comment, see the note to IA 1986 s.217.

In *Inland Revenue Commissioners v McEntaggart* [2004] EWHC 3431 (Ch); [2007] B.C.C. 260 liability under s.15(1)(a) and (b) was held to continue even after the bankruptcy in question had been annulled (because all the bankruptcy debts had been paid in full).

Compensation orders and undertakings

15A   Compensation orders and undertakings

15A(1)   **[Power of court to make compensation order]** The court may make a compensation order against a person on the application of the Secretary of State if it is satisfied that the conditions mentioned in subsection (3) are met.

15A(2)   **[Secretary of State's power to accept compensation undertaking]** If it appears to the Secretary of State that the conditions mentioned in subsection (3) are met in respect of a person who has offered to give the Secretary of State a compensation undertaking, the Secretary of State may accept the undertaking instead of applying, or proceeding with an application, for a compensation order.

15A(3)   **[Conditions for s.15A(1), (2)]** The conditions are that–

(a)   the person is subject to a disqualification order or disqualification undertaking under this Act, and

(b)   conduct for which the person is subject to the order or undertaking has caused loss to one or more creditors of an insolvent company of which the person has at any time been a director.

15A(4)   **["Insolvent company"]** An "insolvent company" is a company that is or has been insolvent and a company becomes insolvent if–

(a)   the company goes into liquidation at a time when its assets are insufficient for the payment of its debts and other liabilities and the expenses of the winding up,

(b)   the company enters administration, or

(c)   an administrative receiver of the company is appointed.

15A(5)   **[Time for application for compensation order]** The Secretary of State may apply for a compensation order at any time before the end of the period of two years beginning with the date on which the disqualification order referred to in paragraph (a) of subsection (3) was made, or the disqualification undertaking referred to in that paragraph was accepted.

15A(6)   **[Conduct in s.15A(3)(b)]** In the case of a person subject to a disqualification order under section 8ZA or 8ZD, or a disqualification undertaking under section 8ZC or 8ZE, the reference in subsection (3)(b) to conduct is a reference to the conduct of the main transgressor in relation to which the person has exercised the requisite amount of influence.

15A(7)   **["The court"]** In this section and sections 15B and 15C "the court" means–

(a)   in a case where a disqualification order has been made, the court that made the order,

(b)   in any other case, the High Court or, in Scotland, the Court of Session.

(See General Note after s.15C.)

15B   Amounts payable under compensation orders and undertakings

15B(1)   **[Compensation order]** A compensation order is an order requiring the person against whom it is made to pay an amount specified in the order–

(a)   to the Secretary of State for the benefit of–

(i)   a creditor or creditors specified in the order;

(ii)   a class or classes of creditor so specified;

(b)   as a contribution to the assets of a company so specified.

15B(2)   [Compensation undertaking] A compensation undertaking is an undertaking to pay an amount specified in the undertaking–

(a)   to the Secretary of State for the benefit of–

(i)   a creditor or creditors specified in the undertaking;

(ii)   a class or classes of creditor so specified;

(b)   as a contribution to the assets of a company so specified.

15B(3)   [Matters to be had regard to in specifying amount] When specifying an amount the court (in the case of an order) and the Secretary of State (in the case of an undertaking) must in particular have regard to–

(a)   the amount of the loss caused;

(b)   the nature of the conduct mentioned in section 15A(3)(b);

(c)   whether the person has made any other financial contribution in recompense for the conduct (whether under a statutory provision or otherwise).

15B(4)   [Compensation undertaking payable as if under court order] An amount payable by virtue of subsection (2) under a compensation undertaking is recoverable as if payable under a court order.

15B(5)   [Compensation order or undertaking provable as bankruptcy debt] An amount payable under a compensation order or compensation undertaking is provable as a bankruptcy debt.

(See General Note after s.15C.)

15C   Variation and revocation of compensation undertakings

15C(1)   [Power of court] The court may, on the application of a person who is subject to a compensation undertaking–

(a)   reduce the amount payable under the undertaking, or

(b)   provide for the undertaking not to have effect.

15C(2)   [Duty of Secretary of State in s.15C(1) application] On the hearing of an application under subsection (1), the Secretary of State must appear and call the attention of the court to any matters which the Secretary of State considers relevant, and may give evidence or call witnesses.

General Note to ss.15A–15C

Sections 15A–15C were inserted by SBEEA 2015 s.110 as from 1 October 2015.

Compensation orders and undertakings are a new development introduced by SBEEA 2015. The Secretary of State, in addition to seeking a disqualification order, is empowered to apply to the court for an order that the delinquent director should pay compensation for any loss which he has caused to one or more of the insolvent company's creditors, or alternatively to accept an undertaking to pay a corresponding amount to the Secretary of State. It would appear that there is no necessary link between the two procedures: a person who has been disqualified by court order may give a compensation undertaking, and conversely a person who has given a disqualification undertaking may be the subject of a compensation order.

The system remained dormant on the statute-book for a whole year, pending the enactment of supporting secondary legislation. A dedicated procedure for applications by the Secretary of State for a compensation order (under s.15A) or by a person who is subject to a compensation undertaking for variation or revocation thereof (under s.15C) is now provided by the Compensation Orders (Disqualified Directors) Proceedings (England and Wales) Rules 2016 (SI 2016/890) as from 1 October 2016. If compensation is paid in the first instance to the Secretary of State, provision is made for his remuneration for the onward distribution of the moneys by the Disqualified Directors Compensation Orders (Fees) (England and Wales) Order 2016 (SI 2016/1047). Comparable provision for Scotland is made by SI 2016/1048.

Only the Secretary of State has standing to make an application. The initiative cannot be taken by a creditor or an office-holder. The only other person who is given standing to make an application is a person already subject to a compensation undertaking, who seeks to have it varied or revoked (s.15C).

Perhaps strangely, there is no provision in these sections extending the definition of "company" to include an overseas company, and s.15A(4), unlike s.6, does not have any special definition of insolvency for an overseas company. It seems that we must necessarily infer that these sections do not have extra-territorial effect.

S.15A(3)(b)

The conduct in question is necessarily limited by the causation requirement to that which was relied on as grounds for the disqualification order or undertaking.

S.15A(4)

The wording is the same as in s.6(2). In the case of a liquidation, the company must have been insolvent on an "assets" basis. In an administration or administrative receivership, insolvency is presumed. If the disqualification order has been made under s.8, insolvency may have to be proved.

S.15A(5)

This provision fixes a time limit for making an application, but says nothing about how soon an application can be made. We find an answer in the Proceedings Rules (above), r.2(2)(b), which refers to "a case where proceedings for a disqualification order have or are being commenced". From this we may infer that an application for compensation under these provisions may be made contemporaneously with or at any time after the commencement of an application for disqualification. This would enable the hearings under the two claims to be heard together, or at least in succession, so avoiding the duplication of evidence. The liquidator would not have standing to support or object to the order sought or its quantification.

S.15A(6)

The reference is to persons disqualified on the ground of having instructed a director who has been found unfit.

S.15B

The order or undertaking may specify as beneficiaries either a particular creditor or creditors, or a class or classes of creditors, or simply a contribution to the general assets.

S.15C

This is modelled on s.8A, and the notes to that section are generally applicable.

Supplementary provisions

16 Application for disqualification order

16(1)   [Notice, appearance, etc.] A person intending to apply for the making of a disqualification order shall give not less than 10 days' notice of his intention to the person against whom the order is sought; and on the hearing of the application the last-mentioned person may appear and himself give evidence or call witnesses.

16(2)   [Applicants] An application to a court, other than a court mentioned in section 2(2)(b) or (c), for the making against any person of a disqualification order under any of sections 2 to 4 may be made by the Secretary of State or the official receiver, or by the liquidator or any past or present member or creditor of any company or overseas company in relation to which that person has committed or is alleged to have committed an offence or other default.

16(3)   [Appearance etc. of applicant] On the hearing of any application under this Act made by a person falling within subsection (4), the applicant shall appear and call the attention of the court to any matters which seem to him to be relevant, and may himself give evidence or call witnesses.

16(4)   [Applicant in s.16(3)] The following fall within this subsection–

  (a)   the Secretary of State;

  (b)   the official receiver;

  (c)   the Competition and Markets Authority;

(d)   the liquidator;

(e)   a specified regulator (within the meaning of section 9E).

GENERAL NOTE

The procedural provisions set out in s.16(1) apply only where application is made to the court having jurisdiction to wind up the company. They will not apply in those cases where the court is empowered of its own motion to make an order (see, e.g. ss.2, 10), "although doubtless the rules of natural justice will require that the person should be given some notice that the court is contemplating making a disqualification order": (*Secretary of State for Trade & Industry v Langridge, Re Cedac Ltd* [1991] Ch. 402 at 414; [1991] B.C.C. 148 at 155). Again, no notice has to be served (although again the rules of natural justice will have effect) where the proceedings are before a court other than that which has winding-up jurisdiction, e.g. in a case brought under s.5 (ibid.)

The requirement that an intended respondent should be given ten days' notice of the intention to apply for an order is directory rather than mandatory. Failure to give proper notice is a procedural irregularity which does not nullify the application (*Secretary of State for Trade & Industry v Langridge, Re Cedac Ltd*, above). This decision (by a majority) of the Court of Appeal effectively overrules the earlier decision of Harman J in *Re Jaymar Management Ltd* [1990] B.C.C. 303, but leaves undisturbed the ruling given in the latter case that "ten days' notice" means ten clear days, i.e. exclusive of both the date on which notice is given and that on which the proceedings are issued. See also *Secretary of State for Business, Enterprise and Regulatory Reform v Smith* [2009] B.C.C. 497.

There is no obligation to state in the notice the grounds upon which the application will be made (*Secretary of State for Trade and Industry v Langridge, Re Cedac Ltd* (above) at 414; 155) or to specify which is the "lead" company in relation to which it is made or which (if any) "collateral" companies will be included in the proceedings (*Re Surrey Leisure Ltd* [1999] B.C.C. 847 at 853). However, it is clear from cases such as *Re Finelist Ltd* [2003] EWHC 1780 (Ch); [2004] B.C.C. 877; and *Secretary of State for Trade and Industry v Gill* [2004] EWHC 175 (Ch); [2005] B.C.C. 24 that in the proceedings themselves the respondent must be given a clear statement of the charges which are brought against him and the evidence in support, and generally an opportunity before the proceedings are begun to proffer explanations for his conduct: see the note to s.7(1).

Although the second part of s.16(1) appears to suggest that the respondent may call oral evidence at the hearing, it is clear from the rules that (exceptional cases apart) evidence must be presented in the form of affidavits and in keeping with the time limits imposed by the rules (*Re Rex Williams Leisure plc* [1994] Ch. 1; [1993] B.C.C. 79 at 83; affirmed [1994] Ch. 350; [1994] B.C.C. 551). It follows that if he wishes to make a submission of no case to answer he must do so when he has seen and considered the applicant's affidavit evidence and that he cannot wait until after the close of the applicant's case at the hearing (ibid.).

Section 16(3) was amended and subs.(4) inserted by the Enterprise Act 2002 s.204(1), (6) and (7), as from 20 June 2003: see the Enterprise Act 2002 (Commencement No.3, Transitional and Transitory Provisions and Savings) Order 2003 (SI 2003/1397 (C. 60)) arts 1, 2(1) and Sch., in keeping with the introduction of competition disqualification orders and undertakings.

Section 16(1), (2) amended by SBEEA Sch.7 para.12 as from 1 October 2015.

17   Application for leave under an order or undertaking

17(1)   [Disqualification order by court with jurisdiction to wind up] Where a person is subject to a disqualification order made by a court having jurisdiction to wind up companies, any application for leave for the purposes of section 1(1)(a) shall be made to that court.

17(2)   [Disqualification orders made under s.2 or 5] Where–

(a)   a person is subject to a disqualification order made under section 2 by a court other than a court having jurisdiction to wind up companies, or

(b)   a person is subject to a disqualification order made under section 5,

any application for leave for the purposes of section 1(1)(a) shall be made to any court which, when the order was made, had jurisdiction to wind up the company (or, if there is more than one such company, any of the companies) to which the offence (or any of the offences) in question related.

17(3)   [Disqualification undertaking accepted under s.7 or 8] Where a person is subject to a disqualification undertaking accepted at any time under section 5A, 7 or 8, any application for leave for the purposes of section 1A(1)(a) shall be made to any court to which, if the Secretary of State had applied for a disqualification order under the section in question at that time, his application could have been made.

17(3ZA) **[Disqualification undertaking accepted under s.8ZC]** Where a person is subject to a disqualification undertaking accepted at any time under section 8ZC, any application for leave for the purposes of section 1A(1)(a) must be made to any court to which, if the Secretary of State had applied for a disqualification order under section 8ZA at that time, that application could have been made.

17(3ZB) **[Disqualification undertaking accepted under s.8ZE]** Where a person is subject to a disqualification undertaking accepted at any time under section 8ZE, any application for leave for the purposes of section 1A(1)(a) must be made to the High Court or, in Scotland, the Court of Session.

17(3A) **[Disqualification undertaking accepted under s.9B]** Where a person is subject to a disqualification undertaking accepted at any time under section 9B any application for leave for the purposes of section 9B(4) must be made to the High Court or (in Scotland) the Court of Session.

17(4) **[Persons subject to two or more disqualification orders]** But where a person is subject to two or more disqualification orders or undertakings (or to one or more disqualification orders and to one or more disqualification undertakings), any application for leave for the purposes of section 1(1)(a), 1A(1)(a) or 9B(4) shall be made to any court to which any such application relating to the latest order to be made, or undertaking to be accepted, could be made.

17(5) **[Duty of Secretary of State to appear]** On the hearing of an application for leave for the purposes of section 1(1)(a) or 1A(1)(a), the Secretary of State shall appear and call the attention of the court to any matters which seem to him to be relevant, and may himself give evidence or call witnesses.

17(6) **[Non-application of s.17(5)]** Subsection (5) does not apply to an application for leave for the purposes of section 1(1)(a) if the application for the disqualification order was made under section 9A.

17(7) **[Duty of CMA and specified regulator to appear etc.]** In such a case and in the case of an application for leave for the purposes of section 9B(4) on the hearing of the application whichever of the Competition and Markets Authority or a specified regulator (within the meaning of section 9E) applied for the order or accepted the undertaking (as the case may be)–

(a)   must appear and draw the attention of the court to any matters which appear to it or him (as the case may be) to be relevant;

(b)   may give evidence or call witnesses.

GENERAL NOTE

This section deals with the procedural aspects of an application to the court, by a person who is subject to a disqualification order, for leave to act in relation to the management, etc. of a company during the currency of the order. In consequence of amendments made by IA 2000, it also deals with applications for leave to act during the currency of a disqualification undertaking.

   Subsection (4) was amended and subss.(3A), (6) and (7) inserted by the Enterprise Act 2002 s.204(1), (8)–(10), as from 20 June 2003: see the Enterprise Act 2002 (Commencement No.3, Transitional and Transitory Provisions and Savings) Order 2003 (SI 2003/1397 (C. 60)) arts 1, 2(1) and Sch., in keeping with the introduction of competition disqualification orders and undertakings. Section 17(3) amended and s.17(3ZA), (3ZB) inserted by SBEEA Sch.7 para.13 as from 1 October 2015.

   On the substantive issues relating to the grant of leave, see the note to s.1(1) above, and see generally T. Clench (2008) 21 Insolv. Int. 113 and on certain problems of timing, S. Frieze (2009) 22 Insolv. Int. 179.

   The *Practice Direction: Directors Disqualification Proceedings* [2015] B.C.C. 224, Pt 4 (reproduced as App.VI to this *Guide*) applies to applications under s.17 and also to analogous applications (e.g. those made under s.12(2)). Subject to ss.12 and 17(2), applications may be made by Practice Form N. 208 under CPR Pt 8, or by application notice in an existing disqualification application. The claim form or application notice and all affidavits and other documents in the application must be served on the Secretary of State (or, in the case of a competition disqualification, the Competition and Markets Authority or appropriate regulator).

The Scottish court has confirmed in *Buckley v Secretary of State for Business, Energy and Industrial Strategy* [2017] CSOH 105 that "shall" in s.17(5) is mandatory rather than directory: there must be a hearing at which the Secretary of State must appear.

Evidence in support of an application is by affidavit. However, in relation to disqualification orders made following the *Carecraft* procedure (see the note to s.1 above), it was said in *Re TLL Realisations Ltd* [2000] B.C.C. 998 that the use of affidavit evidence going over matters included in the *Carecraft* statement would not normally be expected and that the parties should be confined to the facts recorded in the statement unless the court required them to be amplified or clarified. Similarly, on an application for leave to act notwithstanding a disqualification undertaking, the applicant may not seek to dispute the correctness of the facts accepted in the undertaking: *Re Morija plc* [2007] EWHC 3055 (Ch); [2008] 2 B.C.L.C. 313. The Court of Appeal in *Re Westmid Packing Services Ltd, Secretary of State for Trade and Industry v Griffiths* [1998] 2 All E.R. 124; [1998] B.C.C. 836 gave guidelines on what is relevant and admissible evidence for the purposes of an application under s.17.

It is normal for an application for leave to be made at the time of the original hearing when the order is made. In *Re Dicetrade Ltd, Secretary of State for Trade & Industry v Worth* [1994] B.C.C. 371 at 373, Dillon LJ said that this course was "desirable" and "in everyone's interests"; and in *Re TLL Realisations Ltd* (above) the Court of Appeal stated that it was highly desirable that a person who faced the possibility of disqualification and in that event might wish to seek leave to act should make application early enough so that the same judge would consider both the application for disqualification and the application for leave. Although some applicants might hope to derive a tactical advantage from isolating the two, since the former would inevitably highlight their misconduct while the latter would tend to focus on mitigation, the interests of justice overall were more likely to be served (and waste avoided) if both aspects of the case were investigated together; and where this tactic was adopted the judge at the second hearing would be entitled to view the evidence with "a proper degree of healthy scepticism".

If an application for leave to act notwithstanding disqualification is made at the same time as the hearing for the disqualification order and does not take up a substantial part of the time of that hearing, it is convenient not to make a separate order in respect of the costs of that application. However, where a separate application for leave is made some time later, it is to be regarded as free-standing for the purposes of costs. The Secretary of State may then be entitled to his costs on a standard basis: alternatively, if he simply intimates to the applicant (or to his solicitors) any particular points that are relied on so that they can be drawn to the attention of the court, but states that he does not oppose the grant of the relief sought, it may be appropriate to make no order as to costs (*Re Dicetrade Ltd* (above)). Despite this observation, in *Re TLL Realisations Ltd* (above) attention was drawn to the fact that the Secretary of State is placed in a special position by s.17(2) and that this can be attributed to the misconduct of the applicant; and so, it was said, it should be the ordinary consequence that he be allowed his costs.

An order granting leave to act may be made on an interim basis (e.g. pending the hearing of an appeal) and may also be made for a finite period—for instance, to enable the director to sort out matters pertinent to the company's business before the disqualification takes full effect (*Re Amaron Ltd* [1998] B.C.C. 264). In *Re Portland Place (Historic House) Ltd* [2012] EWHC 4199 (Ch) a director who had been refused leave to act was allowed to make a second application for leave on new grounds in the light of changed circumstances.

On s.17 applications, see S. Bristoll (2014) 27 Insol. Int. 49.

18   Register of disqualification orders and undertakings

18(1)   [Regulations re furnishing information] The Secretary of State may make regulations requiring officers of courts to furnish him with such particulars as the regulations may specify of cases in which–

(a)   a disqualification order is made, or

(b)   any action is taken by a court in consequence of which such an order or a disqualification undertaking is varied or ceases to be in force, or

(c)   leave is granted by a court for a person subject to such an order to do any thing which otherwise the order prohibits him from doing; or

(d)   leave is granted by a court for a person subject to such an undertaking to do anything which otherwise the undertaking prohibits him from doing;

and the regulations may specify the time within which, and the form and manner in which, such particulars are to be furnished.

18(2) **[Register of orders]** The Secretary of State shall, from the particulars so furnished, continue to maintain the register of orders, and of cases in which leave has been granted as mentioned in subsection (1)(c).

18(2A) **[Particulars to be included in register]** The Secretary of State must include in the register such particulars as he considers appropriate of–

(a) disqualification undertakings accepted by him under section 5A, 7, 8, 8ZC or 8ZE;

(b) disqualification undertakings accepted by the Competition and Markets Authority or a specified regulator under section 9B;

(c) cases in which leave has been granted as mentioned in subsection (1)(d).

18(3) **[Deletion of orders no longer in force]** When an order or undertaking of which entry is made in the register ceases to be in force, the Secretary of State shall delete the entry from the register and all particulars relating to it which have been furnished to him under this section or any previous corresponding provision and, in the case of a disqualification undertaking, any other particulars he has included in the register.

18(4) **[Inspection of register]** The register shall be open to inspection on payment of such fee as may be specified by the Secretary of State in regulations.

18(4A) **[Extension of s.18]** Regulations under this section may extend the preceding provisions of this section, to such extent and with such modifications as may be specified in the regulations, to disqualification orders or disqualification undertakings made under the Company Directors Disqualification (Northern Ireland) Order 2002.

18(5) **[Regulations by statutory instrument etc.]** Regulations under this section shall be made by statutory instrument subject to annulment in pursuance of a resolution of either House of Parliament.

General Note

Section 18(2), (4A) amended by the Companies Act 2006 (Consequential Amendments, Transitional Provisions and Savings) Order 2009 (SI 2009/1941) art.2(1) and Sch.1 para.85(10) as from 1 October 2009.

The Secretary of State, acting through the registrar of companies, has kept a register of disqualification orders since first being required to do so by CA 1976 s.29. The register, which also records cases where the court has given leave to act, is open to public inspection. It is possible to access without charge extracts from the register on the Companies House website at the internet address *http://wck2.companieshouse.gov.uk/dirsec* where names of individual directors can be keyed in to determine if they appear on the register. This section provides for the continuation of the register, and brings forward from the pre-consolidation Acts other rules relating to the register. The Insolvency Service also maintains a public register of disqualified directors in alphabetical order of names, accessible at *http://www.insolvencydirect.bis.gov.uk/IESdatabase/viewdirectorsummary-new.asp*.

This section has been extensively amended in order to accommodate the introduction of disqualification undertakings and competition disqualification orders and undertakings: see generally the notes to ss.1A, 7 and 9A–9E.

In *Cathie v Secretary of State for Business, Innovation and Skills* [2011] EWHC 2234 (Ch); [2011] B.C.C. 685 the court granted a stay (pending an appeal against a disqualification order) directing the registrar of companies to withhold recording the order where publication could give rise to irreversible reputational damage to the applicant.

Where a confidentiality order under CA 1985 ss.723B–723F is in force, prohibiting disclosure of a director's home address, the prohibition applies to this register: see the Companies (Disqualification Orders) (Amendment) Regulations 2002 (SI 2002/689, effective 2 April 2002). [CA 2006 has no equivalent to these sections.]

S.18(1)

The regulations currently in force are the Companies (Disqualification Orders) Regulations 2009 (SI 2009/2471), which prescribe forms on which the relevant officers of the courts are to make returns.

The Department of Trade and Industry (now the DBEIS) in January 1998 set up a rogue director telephone hotline intended to assist in catching directors and undischarged bankrupts who are acting in breach of the disqualification legislation. The number of the hotline, which is open 24 hours a day, is 0300 678 0017, email: intelligence.live@insolvency.gov.uk.

S.18(2A)

No forms are prescribed in which particulars of undertakings were to be recorded, corresponding to the forms on which court officers are to notify details of disqualification orders. Instead, it is left to the discretion of the Secretary of State to determine what particulars are appropriate.

Subsection (2A) was modified by the insertion of para.(b) by the Enterprise Act 2002 (Commencement No.3, etc.) Order 2003 (SI 2003/1397 (C. 60) arts 1, 2(1) and Sch., as from 20 June 2003.

S.18(4A)

Disqualification orders made by the courts in Northern Ireland were made effective throughout the rest of the United Kingdom from 2 April 2001 by s.12A: see the note to that section. This subsection allows for provision to be made to enable details of such disqualification orders to be recorded on the register. This was done by the Companies (Disqualification Orders) Regulations 2001 (SI 2001/967) reg.9, effective 6 April 2001, and has since been extended so as to include disqualification undertakings by an amendment made to s.18(4A) by the Insolvency Act 2000 (Company Directors Disqualification Undertakings) Order 2004 (SI 2004/1941) art.2(6), as from 1 September 2004.

19   Special savings from repealed enactments

19   Schedule 2 to this Act has effect–

  (a)   in connection with certain transitional cases arising under sections 93 and 94 of the Companies Act 1981, so as to limit the power to make a disqualification order, or to restrict the duration of an order, by reference to events occurring or things done before those sections came into force,

  (b)   to preserve orders made under section 28 of the Companies Act 1976 (repealed by the Act of 1981), and

  (c)   to preclude any applications for a disqualification order under section 6 or 8, where the relevant company went into liquidation before 28th April 1986.

GENERAL NOTE

This section, read in conjunction with Sch.2, makes transitional arrangements, preserving existing disqualification orders and making it clear that the new grounds of disqualification introduced by IA 1985 do not apply retrospectively to events before 28 April 1986, the date when the relevant provisions of that Act become operative.

Miscellaneous and general

20   Admissibility in evidence of statements

20(1)   **[General rule on admissibility of statements]** In any proceedings (whether or not under this Act), any statement made in pursuance of a requirement imposed by or under sections 5A, 6 to 10, 12C, 15 to 15C or 19(c) of, or Schedule 1 to, this Act, or by or under rules made for the purposes of this Act under the Insolvency Act 1986, may be used in evidence against any person making or concurring in making the statement.

20(2)   **[Limits on use of statement in criminal proceedings]** However, in criminal proceedings in which any such person is charged with an offence to which this subsection applies

  (a)   no evidence relating to the statement may be adduced, and

  (b)   no question relating to it may be asked,

by or on behalf of the prosecution, unless evidence relating to it is adduced, or a question relating to it is asked, in the proceedings by or on behalf of that person.

20(3)   **[Offences to which s.20(2) applies]** Subsection (2) applies to any offence other than–

  (a)   an offence which is–

    (i)   created by rules made for the purposes of this Act under the Insolvency Act 1986, and

    (ii)   designated for the purposes of this subsection by such rules or by regulations made by the Secretary of State;

  (b) an offence which is–

    (i)   created by regulations made under any such rules, and

    (ii)   designated for the purposes of this subsection by such regulations;

  (c) an offence under section 5 of the Perjury Act 1911 (false statements made otherwise than on oath); or

  (d) an offence under section 44(2) of the Criminal Law (Consolidation) (Scotland) Act 1995 (false statements made otherwise than on oath).

20(4)   [Procedure for making regulations] Regulations under subsection (3)(a)(ii) shall be made by statutory instrument and, after being made, shall be laid before each House of Parliament.

GENERAL NOTE

This section is similar to IA 1986 s.433, and is derived from the same source. Both sections were amended by the Youth Justice and Criminal Evidence Act 1999 s.59 and Sch.3 para.8, with effect from 14 April 2000, by adding new subss.(2) to (4). This was part of a general reform imposing restrictions on the use in criminal proceedings of statements given under compulsion, following rulings of the European Court of Human Rights. A similar amendment was made to IA 1986 s.219 by IA 2000 s.11. See the notes to IA 1986 ss.219 and 433. The enactment of s.20(2) should in most cases avoid the need to defer the hearing of disqualification applications until criminal proceedings based on the same facts have been disposed of: see *Secretary of State for Trade and Industry v Crane* [2001] 2 B.C.L.C. 222.

    Note that there is no similar restriction on the use of such statements in proceedings for disqualification orders: see the Introductory note to CDDA 1986 at p.1 above.

20A   Legal professional privilege

20A   In proceedings against a person for an offence under this Act nothing in this Act is to be taken to require any person to disclose any information that he is entitled to refuse to disclose on grounds of legal professional privilege (in Scotland, confidentiality of communications).

GENERAL NOTE

Section 20A was inserted by the Companies Act 2006 (Consequential Amendments etc.) Order 2008 (SI 2008/948) art.3(1) and Sch.1 para.106(3) as from 6 April 2008.

21   Interaction with Insolvency Act

21(1)   [Reference to official receiver] References in this Act to the official receiver, in relation to the winding up of a company or the bankruptcy of an individual, are to any person who, by virtue of section 399 of the Insolvency Act 1986, is authorised to act as the official receiver in relation to that winding up or bankruptcy; and, in accordance with section 401(2) of that Act, references in this Act to an official receiver includes a person appointed as his deputy.

21(2)   [Insolvency Act Pts I to VII] Sections 1A, 5A, 6 to 10, 12C to 15C, 19(c) and 20 of, and Schedule 1 to, this Act and sections 1 and 17 of this Act as they apply for the purposes of those provisions are deemed included in Parts I to VII of the Insolvency Act 1986 for the purposes of the following sections of that Act–

  section 411 (power to make insolvency rules);

  section 414 (fees orders);

  section 420 (orders extending provisions about insolvent companies to insolvent partnerships);

  section 422 (modification of such provisions in their application to recognised banks).

21(3)   [Application of Insolvency Act s.434] Section 434 of that Act (Crown application) applies to sections 1A, 5A, 6 to 10, 12C to 15C, 19(c) and 20 of, and Schedule 1 to, this Act and sections 1 and 17 of this Act as they apply for the purposes of those provisions as it does to the provisions of that Act which are there mentioned.

21(4)   [Summary proceedings in Scotland] For the purposes of summary proceedings in Scotland, section 431 of that Act applies to summary proceedings for an offence under section 11 or 13 of this Act as it applies to summary proceedings for an offence under Parts I to VII of that Act.

GENERAL NOTE

This section requires a reader of this Act to make extensive cross-references to IA 1986. Most of the matters referred to are administrative or procedural in nature, but the extension of the company director disqualification regime so that it applies to the former members of insolvent partnerships is both bold and surprising. The justification for the imposition of a director disqualification order is invariably stated to be that the delinquent director has abused the privilege of limited liability (see, e.g. the Cork Committee's *Report*, para.1807). To extend this penalty to partners, whose personal liability is necessarily unlimited, is anomalous.

The IR 2016, and in particular the review and appeal procedures prescribed by IR 2016 r.12.59, apply to orders made under this Act: *Re Tasbian Ltd (No.2)* [1992] B.C.C. 322; *Re Probe Data Systems Ltd (No.3)* [1992] B.C.C. 110.

Section 21(2) and (3) amended by the SBEEA 2015 s.111, Sch.7 para.16 as from 1 October 2015.

S.21(2)
In regard to the entry for s.411 see the Insolvent Companies (Reports on Conduct of Directors) Rules 1996 (SI 1996/1909, as amended by SI 2001/764 and 2003/2096) and the Insolvent Companies (Reports on Conduct of Directors) (Scotland) Rules 1996 (SI 1996/1910 (S 154), as amended by SI 2001/768).

In regard to the entry for s.420, reference should be made to the Insolvent Partnerships Order 1994 (SI 1994/2421, as amended).

Regulations relating to LLPs have been made under the LLP Act 2000 ss.14, 15: see the LLPR 2001 (SI 2001/1090) reg.4 (as amended).

S.21(3)
The Crown is not bound generally, but only in relation to matters specified in paras (a)–(e) of IA 1986 s.434. See the note to that section.

21A   Bank insolvency

21A   Section 121 of the Banking Act 2009 provides for this Act to apply in relation to bank insolvency as it applies in relation to liquidation.

GENERAL NOTE

Section 21A was inserted by the Banking Act 2009 (C. 1) s.121, as from 21 February 2009. This section applies in the case where a failing bank is the subject of government intervention. See Vol.1, p.6.

21B   Bank administration

21B   Section 155 of the Banking Act 2009 provides for this Act to apply in relation to bank administration as it applies in relation to liquidation.

GENERAL NOTE

Section 21B was inserted by the Banking Act 2009 (C. 1) s.155(4), as from 21 February 2009. This section applies in the case where a failing bank is the subject of government intervention. See Vol.1, p.6.

21C   Building society insolvency and special administration

21C   Section 90E of the Building Societies Act 1986 provides for this Act to apply in relation to building society insolvency and building society special administration as it applies in relation to liquidation.

GENERAL NOTE

Section 21C was inserted by the Building Societies (Insolvency and Special Administration) Order 2009 (SI 2009/805) art.12, as from 29 March 2009. It applies in the case where a failing building society is the subject of government intervention. See Vol.1, p.6.

22   Interpretation

22(1)   [Effect] This section has effect with respect to the meaning of expressions used in this Act, and applies unless the context otherwise requires.

22(2)   ["Company"] "Company" means–

(a) a company registered under the Companies Act 2006 in Great Britain, or

(b) a company that may be wound up under Part 5 of the Insolvency Act 1986 (unregistered companies).

22(2A)   ["Overseas company"] An "overseas company" is a company incorporated or formed outside Great Britain.

22(3)   [Application of Insolvency Act ss.247, 251] Section 247 in Part VII of the Insolvency Act 1986 (interpretation for the first Group of Parts of that Act) applies as regards references to a company's insolvency and to its going into liquidation; and "administrative receiver" has the meaning given by section 251 of that Act and references to acting as an insolvency practitioner are to be read in accordance with section 388 of that Act.

22(4)   ["Director"] "Director" includes any person occupying the position of director, by whatever name called.

22(5)   ["Shadow director"] "Shadow director", in relation to a company, means a person in accordance with whose directions or instructions the directors of the company are accustomed to act, but so that a person is not deemed a shadow director by reason only that the directors act–

(a) on advice given by that person in a professional capacity;

(b) in accordance with instructions, a direction, guidance or advice given by that person in the exercise of a function conferred by or under an enactment;

(c) in accordance with guidance or advice given by that person in that person's capacity as a Minister of the Crown (within the meaning of the Ministers of the Crown Act 1975).

22(6)   ["Body corporate" and "officer"] "Body corporate" and "officer" have the same meaning as in the Companies Acts (see section 1173(1) of the Companies Act 2006).

22(7)   ["The Companies Acts"] "The Companies Acts" has the meaning given by section 2(1) of the Companies Act 2006.

22(8)   [References to former legislation] Any reference to provisions, or a particular provision, of the Companies Acts or the Insolvency Act 1986 includes the corresponding provisions or provision of corresponding earlier legislation.

22(9)   [Application of Companies Acts] Subject to the provisions of this section, expressions that are defined for the purposes of the Companies Acts (see section 1174 of, and Schedule 8 to, the Companies Act 2006) have the same meaning in this Act.

22(10)   [References to acting as receiver] Any reference to acting as receiver–

(a) includes acting as manager or as both receiver and manager, but

(b) does not include acting as administrative receiver;

and "receivership" is to be read accordingly.

GENERAL NOTE

This section largely borrows or reproduces definitions from other Acts, notably CA 2006 and IA 1986.

Section 22(7), (8) and (9) were amended by the Companies Act 2006 (Consequential Amendments etc.) Order 2008 (SI 2008/948) art.3(1) and Sch.1 para.106(4), as from 6 April 2008. Section 22(2), (6), (7), (8) were substituted, and s.22(9) amended, by the Companies Act 2006 (Consequential Amendments, Transitional Provisions and Savings) Order 2009 (SI 2009/1941) art.2(1) and Sch.1 para.85(11) as from 1 October 2009. Section 22(2A) inserted by SBEEA Sch.7 para.17 as from 1 October 2015. Section 22(5) amended by SBEEA 2015 s.90(2) as from 26 May 2015 (in effect, by the insertion of paras (b) and (c)).

S.22(2)

On the term "unregistered company", see the note to IA 1986 s.220. But the question whether the Act applies to all such bodies is not free from doubt. That it applies to foreign companies has been settled by such cases as *Re Eurostem Maritime Ltd* [1987] P.C.C. 190; and *Official Receiver v Brady* [1999] B.C.C. 258. So far as concerns building societies, incorporated friendly societies, insolvent partnerships, NHS Foundation Trusts, EEIGs, charitable incorporated organisations, limited liability partnerships, co-operative and community benefit societies and protected cell companies the position is covered by specific legislation: see ss.22A–22H, IA 1986 s.420 and the Introductory note on p.1. It is in relation to other bodies not specifically dealt with by such legislation that the situation is unclear, e.g. unincorporated friendly societies. It could quite reasonably be argued (for example) that since the legislation has considered it necessary to make specific provision for *incorporated* friendly societies, unincorporated friendly societies are excluded.

S.22(4)

A provision to this effect is standard in companies legislation. The intention is to include the case where a corporate body uses such labels as "governor" or "trustee" for members of its board.

In addition to ss.6–9, some other sections of the Act extend to shadow directors (and de facto directors), e.g. s.10 (participation in wrongful trading).

S.22(5)

The definition of a shadow director is the same as that in IA 1986 s.251 and similar to that in CA 2006 s.251(1), (2): see the note to IA 1986 s.251. The term obviously covers the case where a puppet board is set up which acts on the dictates of a non-director who masterminds the company's activities from behind the scene. However, it could also apply to a holding company which exercises a degree of control over decision-making by the board of its subsidiary. In *Re Hydrodan (Corby) Ltd* [1994] B.C.C. 161 at 163 Millett J said:

> "What is needed is, first, a board of directors claiming and purporting to act as such; and, secondly, a pattern of behaviour in which the board did not exercise any discretion or judgment of its own, but acted in accordance with the directions of others."

A bank, also, might be caught within the definition if it had given "directions or instructions" to a client company (as distinct from giving professional advice, or merely imposing conditions upon which it was prepared to make or continue a loan) at a time when insolvency was threatening: *Re a Company (No.005009 of 1987)* (1988) 4 B.C.C. 424. In *Re Tasbian Ltd (No.3)* [1992] B.C.C. 358 the Court of Appeal held that there was an arguable case, sufficient to allow the issue to go to trial, that an accountant who had been brought in on the initiative of a debenture holder as a consultant and "company doctor" to advise and assist in the recovery of an ailing company was a shadow director, having allegedly gone further than merely acting as a watch-dog or adviser.

In *Secretary of State for Trade and Industry v Deverell* [2001] Ch. 340; [2000] B.C.C. 1,057 the law was summarised by Morritt LJ in a number of propositions, including the following:

(1) The term is to be construed in the normal way, and not more strictly because it may have penal consequences.

(2) It is not necessary that the person's influence should be exercised over the whole field of the company's activities.

(3) Whether any particular communication is to be construed as a direction or instruction is to be objectively ascertained by the court: the parties' own understanding or description of its nature may be relevant but cannot be conclusive.

(4) Non-professional advice may come within the statutory description: the concepts of "direction" and "instruction" do not exclude the concept of "advice".

(5)   It is not necessary (though probably sufficient) to show that the properly appointed directors or some of them cast themselves in a subservient role or surrendered their own discretions.

On this basis two so-called "consultants" were held to be shadow directors.

The judgment of Finn J in the Australian case *ASC v AS Nominees Ltd* (1995) 133 A.L.R. 1 at 51–53 examines the concept of "shadow director" in some detail. Here it was held that a person employed in a managerial role fell within the definition despite denials by directors that they acted on his directions or instructions, and even though the board did not always follow his advice. The evidence showed that this advice exceeded what would normally fall within the proper performance of his managerial duties.

In a later Australian case, *Buzzle Operations Pty Ltd (in liq.) v Apple Computer Australia Pty Ltd* [2011] NSWCA 109, the New South Wales Supreme Court considered that "in accordance" required a causal connection between the instruction or wishes and the action, and "accustomed" meant a pattern of compliance over a period of time. The instructions or wishes must be in relation to board activities and not just managerial decisions, the distinction being one of fact. However, they do not have to be in relation to every board activity and one must approach this subject with an eye to the ultimate question: who is effectively making board decisions? The following propositions were drawn from the leading authorities:

(1)   Not every person whose advice is in fact heeded as a general rule by the board is to be classed as a shadow (or de facto) director.

(2)   If a person has a genuine interest of his or her own in giving advice to the board (e.g. as a bank or mortgagee), the mere fact that the board will tend to take that advice to preserve it from the person's wrath will not make the person a shadow director.

(3)   The vital factor is that the shadow director has the potentiality of control: the fact that he or she does not seek to control every facet of the company or the fact that from time to time the board disregards the advice is of little moment.

(4)   Millett J's proposition (in *Hydrodan*) that the evidence must show "something more" than just being in a position of control must be shown. The whole of the facts of the case must be shown to see whether that power to control was put into practice.

(5)   Although there are problems with cases where the board of the company splits into a majority and minority faction, so long as the influence controls the real decision makers, the person providing the influence may be a shadow director.

In *Re UKLI Ltd, Secretary of State for Business, Innovation and Skills v Chohan* [2013] EWHC 680 (Ch) Hildyard J summarised the potential relevant factors under 12 headings.

In *Secretary of State for Trade and Industry v Becker* [2002] EWHC 2200 (Ch); [2003] 1 B.C.L.C. 555 it was alleged that the respondent was a shadow director of the company because its sole director had acted on his directions or instructions on one occasion. It was held that this was not sufficient: there had to be proof of a pattern of conduct. A person may be a shadow director even where he exercises influence over a limited range of the company's affairs: *Re Coroin Ltd (No.2), McKillen v Misland (Cyprus) Ltd* at first instance [2012] EWHC 2343 (Ch) per David Richards J (affirmed on appeal [2013] EWCA Civ 781; [2013] 2 B.C.L.C. 583, where this point was not in issue). The learned judge said (at [594]) that it is not necessary that all the directors should act in accordance with the person's directions; it is sufficient if a majority do so. But the instructions must be given to them so as to affect their decisions as directors.

Note the amendments made by SBEEA 2015, conferring specific exemption upon persons giving advice, etc. in the exercise of a statutory function or as a government Minister.

SBEEA 2015, inserting new ss.8ZA–8ZE, has introduced a new ground of disqualification: influencing or instructing the director of an insolvent company who has been disqualified. There is some overlap between the liability of a person to be disqualified as a shadow director and liability under these provisions. For discussion, see the note following s.8ZE.

A shadow director is to be distinguished from a de facto director. In *Re Hydrodan* (above), Millett J continued at 163:

"A de facto director is a person who assumes to act as a director. He is held out as a director by the company, and claims and purports to be a director, although never actually or validly appointed as such. To establish that a person was a de facto director of a company it is necessary to plead and prove that he undertook functions in relation to the company which could properly be discharged only by a director. It is not sufficient to show that he was concerned in the management of the company's affairs or undertook tasks in relation to its business which can properly be performed by a manager below board level."

This passage was cited by Lord Hope in *Holland v HM Revenue and Customs (Re Paycheck Services 3 Ltd)* [2010] UKSC 51; [2011] B.C.C. 1, where the concepts of "shadow director" and "de facto director" were considered for the first time by the Supreme Court.

In *Re Hydrodan* Millett J had expressed the view that the two terms "did not overlap" and "were mutually exclusive". However, Lewison J in *Re Mea Corp Ltd* [2006] EWHC 1846 (Ch); [2007] B.C.C. 288 expressed the view that there is no conceptual difficulty in concluding that a person could be both a shadow director and a de facto director simultaneously, and in *Re Paycheck Services 3 Ltd* Lord Hope agreed. It had already been held that it is not improper for the Secretary of State to allege as alternatives that a respondent was one or the other: *Re H Laing Demolition Building Contractors Ltd* [1998] B.C.C. 561. In *Re UKLI Ltd, Secretary of State for Business, Innovation and Skills v Chohan* [2013] EWHC 680 (Ch) Hildyard J said in relation to the two concepts that the one might shade into the other, and held that a person had been a de facto director in respect of certain of the company's activities and a shadow director in regard to others. He added that it may still be necessary to distinguish between the two categories in determining the extent of their culpability.

It had been said on more than one occasion that there is no single test of de facto directorship (*Secretary of State for Trade and Industry v Tjolle* [1998] B.C.C. 282 at 290; *Re Kaytech International plc* [1999] B.C.C. 390 at 402), and in *Re Paycheck Services 3 Ltd* this view was endorsed by all the members of the Supreme Court. Lord Collins in his judgment traced the development of the concept. Initially, the term was used in reference to a person who had been appointed as a director but whose appointment was defective, or to a person who had continued to act as a director after he had ceased to hold office. But in cases beginning with *Re Lo-Line Electric Motors Ltd* [1988] Ch. 477; (1988) B.C.C. 415 it was extended to persons who had never been appointed as directors but who took part in the management of the company.

In *Smithton Ltd v Naggar* [2014] EWCA Civ 939; [2014] B.C.C. 482 Arden LJ reviewed the cases and summarised the relevant points of general practical importance in determining whether someone is a de facto director as follows:

- The concepts of shadow director and de facto director are different but there is some overlap. As Lord Collins observed in *Re Paycheck Services 3 Ltd* ([2010] UKSC 51; [2011] B.C.C. 1 at [91]): "Once the concept of de facto director was divorced from the unlawful holding of office ... the distinction between de facto directors and shadow directors was eroded".

- A person may be de facto director even if there was no invalid appointment. The question is whether he has assumed responsibility to act as a director.

- To answer that question, the court may have to determine in what capacity the director was acting. (Cf. *Re Paycheck Services 3 Ltd*, above.)

- The court will in general also have to determine the corporate governance structure of the company so as to decide in relation to the company's business whether the defendant's acts were directorial in nature.

- The court is required to look at what the director actually did and not merely any job title given to him.

- The defendant does not avoid liability if he shows that he in good faith thought he was not acting as a director. The question whether or not he acted as a director is to be determined objectively and irrespective of the defendant's motivation or belief.

- The court must look at the cumulative effect of the activities relied on. A single act might lead to liability in an exceptional case.

- Relevant factors include (i) whether the company considered him to be a director and held him out as such; and (ii) whether third parties considered that he was a director.

- The fact that a person is consulted about directorial decisions or his approval sought does not in general make him a director, because he is not making the decision.

- Acts outside the period when he is said to have been a de facto director may throw light on whether he was a de facto director in the relevant period.

Arden LJ concluded by stating that in her judgment the question whether a person was a de facto director was a question of fact and degree.

In *Re Richborough Furniture Ltd* [1996] B.C.C. 155, the respondent's acts were consistent with directorship, but they were also tasks which could have been done by a professional or employee, or by someone performing consultancy services. He escaped liability, as did a person whose role was primarily that of accountant and company secretary in *Secretary of State for Trade and Industry v Hickling* [1996] B.C.C. 678; and a woman described as only "a manager and a compliant and dutiful wife" in *Re Red Label Fashions Ltd* [1999] B.C.C. 308; cf. *Re Paycheck Services 3 Ltd* [2009] B.C.C. 37 (wife performed clerical tasks and also signed cheques, but no "real influence" in corporate governance); *Gemma Ltd v Davies* [2008] EWHC 546 (Ch); [2008] 2 B.C.L.C. 281 (similar facts). In contrast, the respondent in *Secretary of State for Trade and Industry v Jones* [1999] B.C.C. 336, who had acted as management consultant to the company and was also a 50 per cent shareholder, and had (inter alia) signed cheques and dealt with a major customer, was held to have stepped over the borderline and become a de facto director. In several cases, a person who was an undischarged bankrupt or already subject to a disqualification order and who had run the company's business while using a "front man" as a nominee director has been held to have acted as a de facto director: see *Re Moorgate Metals Ltd* [1995] B.C.C. 143; *Re BPR Ltd* [1998] B.C.C. 259; *Re Kaytech International plc* [1999] B.C.C. 390; *Official Receiver v Vass* [1999] B.C.C. 516; *Re Snelling House Ltd* [2012] EWHC 440 (Ch). (For further discussion of the concept of de facto director, see the Australian case *ASC v AS Nominees Ltd* (1995) 133 A.L.R. 1; and A Dodsworth (1995) 11 I.L. & P. 176.) See also *Re Mea Corp Ltd* [2006] EWHC 1846 (Ch); [2007] B.C.C. 288; *Primlake Ltd v Matthews Associates* [2006] EWHC 1227 (Ch); [2007] 1 B.C.L.C. 666 (defendant allowed to perform all management functions apart from giving instructions to banks and signing cheques); *Shepherds Investments Ltd v Walters* [2006] EWHC 836 (Ch); [2007] 2 B.C.L.C. 202 (person held out by both the company and himself as a director); *Statek Corp v Alford* [2008] EWHC 32 (Ch); [2008] B.C.C. 266 (defendant told he would be appointed a director and acted as such, although did not receive accounts and minutes of directors' meetings); *Re Idessa (UK) Ltd* [2011] EWHC 804 (Ch); [2012] 1 B.C.L.C. 80 (defendant had "acted on an equal footing" with the company's sole de jure director and had "exercised real influence" over the company's affairs). If it is unclear whether a person's acts are referable to an assumed directorship or to some other capacity such as a consultant, he should be given the benefit of the doubt: *Elsworth Ethanol Co Ltd v Hartley* [2014] EWHC 99 (IPEC); [2015] 1 B.C.L.C. 221. In *Johnson v Arden* [2018] EWHC 1624 (Ch) on the facts there was no indication that a company secretary had held himself out as a director or had been viewed as such, and the fact that he had been involved with instructing and/or receiving advice from professionals was not sufficient to constitute him as a de facto director, nor was it relevant that he was a director of the company's subsidiaries.

A person who has resigned as a director or ceased to hold office may be held to be a de facto director if he continues to take management decisions: *Re Windows West Ltd* [2002] B.C.C. 760; cf. *Re Promwalk Services Ltd* [2002] EWHC 2688 (Ch); [2003] 2 B.C.L.C. 305 (where in fact the purported resignation was held to have been ineffective); and see *Re F Options Ltd* [2011] EWHC 3324 (Ch); [2012] B.P.I.R. 107. In *Secretary of State for Business, Enterprise and Regulatory Reform v Poulter* [2009] B.C.C. 608 Mrs Registrar Derrett said that, at least where the person concerned remained in management, the evidential burden in practice moved to him to show that his role and functions had changed, so that he was no longer acting as director.

The use by a person of the description director (e.g. as a courtesy title) does not necessarily mean that he or she is a de facto director or has been held out as such; *Secretary of State for Trade and Industry v Tjolle* [1998] B.C.C. 282.

Where one company is a director (whether de jure or de facto) of another, it does not follow that the directors of the former are shadow directors or de facto directors of the latter. The ruling of the Supreme Court in *Re Paycheck Services 3 Ltd* makes it very clear that to make such an allegation good it must be shown that they (or the individual director in question) became such by their (or his) own actions. In *Re Paycheck Services 3 Ltd* the defendant was the only active director of the principal company in a group and effectively the "directing mind and will" of all the group companies, one of which was the corporate director of the subject company. The majority held that, even in this extreme situation, the principle of the separate corporate personality should apply and that unless the defendant had played some direct part in the affairs of the subject company he was not a de facto director of it. (See also *Secretary of State for Trade and Industry v Laing* [1996] 2 B.C.L.C. 324.) Similarly, where a person was the sole director of a company which had set up a subsidiary to provide corporate directors for numerous subject companies, he was held to be neither a shadow director nor a de facto director of the subject companies. He had not played any part in their management at any stage or given instructions to its salaried directors, or taken any step which indicated that either he or his company had assumed the status and functions of a director. (*Secretary of State for Trade and Industry v Hall* [2006] EWHC 1995 (Ch); [2009] B.C.C. 190.) See also *Smithton Ltd v Naggar* (above) (major client and chairman of company's majority shareholder not without more a shadow director).

On the fiduciary duties of a shadow director, see *Re Vivendi SA, Centenary Holdings III Ltd v Richards* [2013] EWHC 3006 (Ch) and J. Morgan (2015) 28 Insolv. Int. 1. SBEEA 2015 s.89(1), effective 26 May 2015, has extended the statutory duties of directors (CA 2006 ss.170–177) to apply also to shadow directors, "where and to the extent that they are capable of so applying" (CA 2006 s.170(5)). Potential relief under s.1157 of the Companies Act 2006 from liability for breach of duty should also apply to shadow directors: *Instant Access Properties Ltd (in liq.) v Rosser* [2018] EWHC 756 (Ch); [2018] B.C.C. 751.

On this topic, see further Walters and Davis-White, *Directors' Disqualification & Insolvency Restrictions*, 3rd edn (Sweet & Maxwell, 2010), Ch.3 and S. Griffin (2011) 24 Insolv. Int. 44.

The Act also applies to shadow directors of building societies (see s.22A(3)), but not to shadow directors of incorporated friendly societies (s.22B(3)) or co-operative and community benefit societies (s.22E(4)(e)).

22A   Application of Act to building societies

22A(1)   [To building societies as to companies] This Act applies to building societies as it applies to companies.

22A(2)   [Interpretation] References in this Act to a company, or to a director or an officer of a company include, respectively, references to a building society within the meaning of the Building Societies Act 1986 or to a director or officer, within the meaning of that Act, of a building society.

22A(3)   ["Shadow director"] In relation to a building society the definition of "shadow director" in section 22(5) applies with the substitution of "building society" for "company".

22A(4)   [Deleted]

General Note

Section 22A(4) was deleted by SBEEA Sch.7 para.18 as from 1 October 2015.

22B   Application of Act to incorporated friendly societies

22B(1)   [Application as to companies] This Act applies to incorporated friendly societies as it applies to companies.

22B(2)   [Interpretation] References in this Act to a company, or to a director or an officer of a company include, respectively, references to an incorporated friendly society within the meaning of the Friendly Societies Act 1992 or to a member of the committee of management or officer, within the meaning of that Act, of an incorporated friendly society.

22B(3)   [Shadow directors] In relation to an incorporated friendly society every reference to a shadow director shall be omitted.

22B(3A)   [Non-application of ss.8ZA, 8ZE] In relation to an incorporated friendly society, this Act applies as if sections 8ZA to 8ZE were omitted.

22B(4)   [Deleted]

General Note

Section 22B(3A) inserted and s.22B(4) deleted by SBEEA Sch.7 para.19 as from 1 October 2015.

S.22B(3)
Contrast the position as regards shadow directors of building societies: see s.22A(3). In regard to unincorporated friendly societies, see the note to s.22(2).

S.22B(3A)
The sections referred to establish the new ground of disqualification: influencing or instructing a director who has been disqualified on the ground of unfitness.

22C   Application of Act to NHS foundation trusts

22C(1)   [Application of Act to NHS foundation trusts] This Act applies to NHS foundation trusts as it applies to companies within the meaning of this Act.

22C(2)   [References to company or director] References in this Act to a company, or to a director or officer of a company, include, respectively, references to an NHS foundation trust or to a director or officer of the trust; but references to shadow directors are omitted.

22C(3)   [Deleted]

GENERAL NOTE

This provision is inserted by the Health and Social Care (Community Health and Standards) Act 2003 s.34 and Sch.4 paras 67, 68, as from 1 April 2004. Section 22C(3) was amended by the National Health Service (Consequential Provisions) Act 2006 s.2 and Sch.1 para.92, as from 1 March 2007; and by the Companies Act 2006 (Consequential Amendments etc.) Order 2008 (SI 2008/948) art.3(1) and Sch.1 para.106(7), as from 6 April 2008. Section 22C(3) deleted by SBEEA Sch.7 para.20 as from 1 October 2015.

22D   Application of Act to open-ended investment companies [Deleted]

GENERAL NOTE

Section 22D inserted by the Companies Act 2006 (Consequential Amendments, Transitional Provisions and Savings) Order 2009 (SI 2009/1941) art.2(1) and Sch.1 para.85(13) as from 1 October 2009.
    Section 22D deleted by SBEEA Sch.7 para.21 as from 1 October 2015.

22E   Application of Act to registered societies

22E(1)   **["Registered society"]** In this section "registered society" has the same meaning as in the Co-operative and Community Benefit Societies Act 2014 ("the 2014 Act").

22E(2)   **[Application as to companies]** This Act applies to registered societies as it applies to companies.

22E(3)   **[References to company, director, officer, committee]** Accordingly, in this Act–

(a)   references to a company include a registered society, and

(b)   references to a director or an officer of a company include a member of the committee or an officer of a registered society.

In paragraph (b) "committee" and "officer" have the same meaning as in the 2014 Act: see section 149 of that Act.

22E(4)   **[Modifications in relation to registered societies]** As they apply in relation to registered societies, the provisions of this Act have effect with the following modifications–

(a)   in section 2(1) (disqualification on conviction of indictable offence), the reference to striking off includes cancellation of the registration of a society under the 2014 Act;

(b)   in section 3 (disqualification for persistent breaches) and section 5 (disqualification on summary conviction), references to the companies legislation shall be read as references to the legislation relating to registered societies;

(c)   [Deleted]

(d)   references to the registrar shall be read as references to the Financial Conduct Authority;

(e)   references to a shadow director shall be disregarded.

(f)   sections 8ZA to 8ZE are to be disregarded.

22E(5)   [Deleted]

22E(6)   **["The legislation relating to registered societies"]** "The legislation relating to registered societies" means the Credit Unions Act 1979 and the Co-operative and Community Benefit Societies Act 2014.

History
Section 22E inserted by the Co-operative and Community Benefit Societies and Credit Unions Act 2010 s.3 and SI 2014/183 art.2 as from 6 April 2014. Section 22E(4)(c)(ii) amended by the Co-operative and Community Benefit Societies and Credit Unions (Investigations) Regulations 2014 (SI 2014/574) reg.6 as from 6 April 2014. Heading substituted by the Co-operative and Community Benefit Societies and Credit Unions Act 2010 s.3 as from 6 April

2014 and s.22E(1), (3), (4), (6) amended by that Act Sch.4 para.38 as from 1 August 2014. Section 22E(4)(c) and 22E(5) deleted and s.22E(4)(f) inserted by SBEEA 2015 Sch.7 para.22(2) as from 1 October 2015.

S.22E(4)(f)
The sections referred to establish the new ground of disqualification: influencing or instructing a director who has been disqualified on the ground of unfitness.

22F   Application of Act to charitable incorporated organisations

22F(1)   [Application of Act to CIOs] This Act applies to charitable incorporated organisations ("CIOs") as it applies to companies.

22F(2) [References to company, director or officer, Insolvency Act 1986] Accordingly, in this Act–

(a)   references to a company are to be read as including references to a CIO;

(b)   references to a director or an officer of a company are to be read as including references to a charity trustee of a CIO; and

(c)   any reference to the Insolvency Act 1986 is to be read as including a reference to that Act as it applies to CIOs.

22F(3)   [Modifications to Act] As they apply in relation to CIOs, the provisions of this Act have effect with the following modifications–

(a)   in section 2(1), the reference to striking off is to be read as including a reference to dissolution;

(b)   in section 4(1)(a), the reference to an offence under section 993 of the Companies Act 2006 is to be read as including a reference to an offence under regulation 60 of the Charitable Incorporated Organisations (General) Regulations 2012 (fraudulent trading);

(c)   sections 9A to 9E are to be disregarded;

(d)   references to any of sections 9A to 9E are to be disregarded;

(e)   references to a shadow director are to be disregarded.

22F(4)   [Deleted]

22F(5)   ["Charity trustees"] In this section "charity trustees" has the meaning given by section 177 of the Charities Act 2011.

History
Section 22F inserted by the Charitable Incorporated Organisations (Consequential Amendments) Order 2012 (SI 2012/3014) art.2 as from 2 January 2013. Section 22F(4) deleted by SBEEA Sch.7 para.23 as from 1 October 2015.

22H   Application of Act to protected cell companies

22H(1)   ["Protected cell company" etc.] In this section–

(a)   "protected cell company" means a protected cell company incorporated under Part 4 of the Risk Transformation Regulations 2017 which has its registered office in England and Wales (or Wales) or Scotland; and

(b)   a reference to a part of a protected cell company is a reference to the core or a cell of the protected cell company (see regulations 42 and 43 of the Risk Transformation Regulations 2017).

22H(2)   [Application of Act] This Act applies to protected cell companies as it applies to companies.

22H(3)   [References to company] Accordingly, in this Act, references to a company are to be read as including references to a protected cell company.

22H(4)   [Modifications re protected cell companies] As they apply in relation to protected cell companies, the provisions of this Act have effect with the following modifications–

(a) references to the administration, insolvency, liquidation or winding up of a company are to be read as references to the administration, insolvency, liquidation or winding up of a part of a protected cell company;

(b) references to striking off are to be read as including references to dissolution;

(c) references to a director of a company which is or has been insolvent are to be read as references to the director of a protected cell company, a part of which is or has been insolvent;

(d) references to a director of a company which is being or has been wound up are to be read as references to the director of a protected cell company, a part of which is being or has been wound up;

(e) references to the court with jurisdiction to wind up a company are to be read as references to the court with jurisdiction to wind up the parts of a protected cell company;

(f) references to the companies legislation are to be read as references to Part 4 of, and Schedules 1 to 3 to, the Risk Transformation Regulations 2017;

(g) references to the Insolvency Act 1986 are to be read as references to that Act as applied by Part 4 of, and Schedules 1 to 3 to, the Risk Transformation Regulations 2017;

(h) references to section 452 and 456 of the Companies Act 2006 are to be read as references to those sections as applied by regulation 163 of the Risk Transformation Regulations 2017;

(i) references to the registrar of companies are to be read as references to the Financial Conduct Authority; and

(j) references to an overseas company include references to a protected cell company incorporated under the Risk Transformation Regulations 2017 which has its registered office in Northern Ireland.

22H(5)   **[Application of ss.6–7A, 8ZA–8ZC]** Where two or more parts of a protected cell company are or have been insolvent, then sections 6 to 7A and 8ZA to 8ZC apply in relation to each part separately.

22H(6)   **[Contributions under s.15A compensation orders/undertakings]** A contribution to the assets of a protected cell company given in accordance with a compensation order under section 15A(1) or a compensation undertaking under section 15A(2) is to be held by the protected cell company on behalf of the part of the protected cell company specified in the order or undertaking.

GENERAL NOTE

Section 22H was inserted by the Risk Transformation Regulations 2017 (SI 2017/1212) reg.190, Sch.4 para.3 as from 8 December 2017 to extend application of the Act as modified by s.22H(4) to protected cell companies.

23   Transitional provisions, savings, repeals

23(1)   **[Schedule 3]** The transitional provisions and savings in Schedule 3 to this Act have effect, and are without prejudice to anything in the Interpretation Act 1978 with regard to the effect of repeals.

23(2)   **[Schedule 4]** The enactments specified in the second column of Schedule 4 to this Act are repealed to the extent specified in the third column of that Schedule.

GENERAL NOTE

This section gives force to the repeals, transitional provisions and savings listed in the Schedules referred to.

    Nothing in Sch.4 is repealed that is not re-enacted in the consolidation, apart from the transitional provisions of IA 1985.

24 Extent

24(1) [England, Wales, Scotland] This Act extends to England and Wales and to Scotland.

24(2) [Extension to Northern Ireland] Subsections (1) to (2A) of section 11 also extend to Northern Ireland.

<small>GENERAL NOTE</small>

The disqualification regime in Northern Ireland is now contained in the Companies (Disqualification Orders) Regulations 2010 (SR 2010/184), consolidating all the previous legislation with effect from 18 June 2010.

S.24(2)

Although Northern Ireland has its own legislation relating to director disqualification, IA 2000 made changes to the present Act which give effect to orders of the Northern Ireland courts throughout the rest of the United Kingdom: see the notes to s.12A. Section 24(2) was substituted by SBEEA 2015 s.113(2) as from 1 October 2015. This means that the provisions mentioned (offence of acting as director while an undischarged bankrupt, etc.) now apply throughout the United Kingdom.

25 Commencement

25 This Act comes into force simultaneously with the Insolvency Act 1986.

<small>GENERAL NOTE</small>

The date of commencement was 29 December 1986: see IA 1986 s.443 and SI 1986/1924 (C. 71), but most of the reforms introduced by IA 1985 which were consolidated into the present Act were brought into force on 28 April 1986: see SI 1986/463 (C. 14).

26 Citation

26 This Act may be cited as the Company Directors Disqualification Act 1986.

SCHEDULES

SCHEDULE 1

DETERMINING UNFITNESS ETC: MATTERS TO BE TAKEN INTO ACCOUNT

Section 12C

Matters to be taken into account in all cases

1 The extent to which the person was responsible for the causes of any material contravention by a company or overseas company of any applicable legislative or other requirement.

2 Where applicable, the extent to which the person was responsible for the causes of a company or overseas company becoming insolvent.

3 The frequency of conduct of the person which falls within paragraph 1 or 2.

4 The nature and extent of any loss or harm caused, or any potential loss or harm which could have been caused, by the person's conduct in relation to a company or overseas company.

Additional matters to be taken into account where person is or has been a director

5 Any misfeasance or breach of any fiduciary duty by the director in relation to a company or overseas company.

6 Any material breach of any legislative or other obligation of the director which applies as a result of being a director of a company or overseas company.

7   The frequency of conduct of the director which falls within paragraph 5 or 6.

Interpretation

8   Subsections (1A) to (2A) of section 6 apply for the purposes of this Schedule as they apply for the purposes of that section.

9   In this Schedule "director" includes a shadow director.

GENERAL NOTE

Schedule 1 was substituted by SBEEA 2015 s.106(6) as from 1 October 2015.

A discussion of the case-law on the concept of unfitness is to be found in the note to s.12C. Of course, we must remember that the judgments in the pre-2015 cases are based on the former Sch.1 and, although the scope and purpose of the two versions of the Schedule are broadly the same (and see *Secretary of State for Business, Innovation and Skills v Akbar* [2017] EWHC 2856 (Ch); [2018] B.C.C. 448), it may be that in the future some differences between the two will become apparent.

The Schedule is divided into two parts: paras 1–4 apply in all cases and paras 5–7 apply in addition where the person is or has been a director (i.e. any relevant company and not just the "lead" company in the proceedings).

Some comments on the paragraphs of the new Schedule follow.

Para.1

It is not necessary that the person should have been convicted of the wrongdoing: indeed, if he has, s.5A may be applicable. The meaning of "requirement" is not elaborated. Note that causation must be shown.

Para.2

Again, causation must be shown.

Para.4

This reflects the introduction by SBEEA 2015 of new provisions (ss.15A–15C) empowering the court to make an order (or the Secretary of State to accept an undertaking) that a disqualified person should pay compensation for loss caused by his misconduct.

Paras 5, 6

There is some debate whether all of the duties of a director (and in particular the duty of care, skill and diligence) are correctly described as fiduciary, but since CA 2006 s.174 makes it a statutory duty any breach will come within para.6. Note that there is no mention of causation: a director may be disqualified even if his misconduct is not the cause of the insolvency or any loss: the younger defendant in *Re Simmon Box (Diamonds) Ltd* [2002] B.C.C. 82 was disqualified despite a finding that his negligence had not caused his company's loss.

Para.8

Where a company has become insolvent, the conduct of a director in relation to any matter connected with or arising out of the insolvency is relevant, as well as any conduct as director.

[Schedules 2, 3 and 4, which for practical purposes may be regarded as spent, are not reproduced.]

...

[**Note**: For reasons of space, the original Pt II of the Insolvency Act 1986 and the original Pt 2 of the Insolvency Rules 1986 (administration orders under the original regime) and extracts from the Insolvency Act 2000 and the Enterprise Act 2002 are no longer reproduced. Reference should be made to Vol.2 of the 19th edition of the *Guide*.]

EU Regulation on Insolvency Proceedings 2015

Regulation (EU) 2015/848

[**Special note:** The text which follows is the "recast" or replacement version of the Regulation, which came into force on 26 June 2017. Readers who wish to refer to the original EC Regulation are referred to the 19th edition of this work.]

Introductory note to the Regulation

The EU Regulation on Insolvency Proceedings 2015 was formally adopted by the European Parliament on 20 May 2015 and was published in the Official Journal on 5 June 2015 (OJ L141/19). It came into force on 26 June 2017 (arts 84, 92). It supersedes the EC Regulation on Insolvency Proceedings 2000 (Regulation (EC) 1346/2000), which had been operative since 31 May 2002. The 2015 Regulation will be referred to in this work as "the Regulation", or by the abbreviation "EURIP", and the 2000 Regulation (where it is necessary to distinguish between the two) as "ECRIP".

Notwithstanding the decision by the referendum on 23 June 2016 that the UK should withdraw from the EU, the Regulation will remain in force for all purposes in this country (including the right of appeal to the European Court) until the severance is formally effected. After that, it will remain operative as part of the domestic law of the UK unless and until it is repealed or superseded by UK legislation. From then on, questions of interpretation will be determined definitively by our own courts. Rulings of the European Court and of courts in other EU jurisdictions will be only of persuasive authority, and any amendments made by the EU to EURIP will have no effect in this country. Where an insolvency has a cross-border element as between this country and one or more EU Member States, recognition here of the insolvency proceedings and the office-holder(s) involved in those jurisdictions will be granted by recourse to the Cross-Border Insolvency Regulations 2006 and not the EU Regulation. In the converse situation, recognition of UK proceedings and office-holders will be accorded by other Member States only if they have enacted domestic legislation equivalent to the CBIR (and, to date, very few have done so), or possibly on the basis of comity.

Being a Regulation (as distinct from a Convention or Directive), EURIP has force throughout the EU (apart from Denmark, which has exercised its right to an opt-out), without the need for ratification or implementation by domestic legislation in the Member States. (References to the EU hereafter should not normally be taken as including Denmark.) The original Regulation became operative on 31 May 2002. On the same date, a number of statutory instruments were brought into force, amending the existing insolvency legislation, Rules and prescribed forms in order to facilitate the integration of the Regulation with our own law and practice. (These changes have been noted at the appropriate places in this *Guide*.) To the extent that insolvency is a devolved matter, it falls to the devolved administrations to make corresponding amendments.

The Regulation has introduced an ordered regime governing the administration of the affairs of an insolvent which extend beyond the jurisdiction of a Member State of the EU. It has made major advances in such areas as ensuring the recognition without further formality throughout the Union of a bankruptcy, liquidation or other insolvency proceeding, and defining the respective roles of the office-holders where more than one set of insolvency proceedings involving the same debtor have been instituted in different Member States.

The 2000 Regulation had a long and chequered history, having begun life initially in the 1960s as part of the proposals for reciprocal recognition and enforcement of foreign judgments which eventually became the Brussels Convention. But the two projects were severed at an early stage and the Draft Bankruptcy Convention (as it was then known) ran into considerable opposition, partly because its aims were over-ambitious and partly because it was over-complex and ineptly drafted. The project was quietly dropped in the 1980s. Meantime, a new initiative got under way under the aegis of the Council of Europe, which began with rather modest aims but as discussions progressed became more comprehensive and elaborate. In 1990 a final text was agreed, and the Convention was opened for signature in Istanbul in June of that year. The Istanbul Convention, as it is generally known, has been signed by a number of States (not including the UK), but has not attracted enough ratifications to come into force. So far as concerns the UK and its relationship with the rest of the EU, it is now a dead letter: art.44(k) of the EC Regulation provided that the Regulation should supersede the Istanbul Convention in this respect.

The real significance of the Istanbul Convention is that its success in reaching the stage of a final text agreed by all participants acted as a catalyst to get the negotiations for an EC Convention restarted. A fresh working party began to work on a revived project in May 1989, and by November 1995 a finalised text had been agreed and was opened for signature and, in the next few months, signed by all the EU Member States except the UK. Regrettably, the UK failed to do so (in the wake of the "beef ban") and the entire project ran out of time and the draft convention lapsed. However, all was not lost because the text, in virtually identical form, was revived (but in the form of a Regulation, and not a Convention) and following a joint initiative by Germany and Finland in 1999 was duly adopted by the Council of Ministers in the following May.

By virtue of art.46 of ECRIP, by 1 June 2012 (some 10 years after that Regulation came into force) the European Commission was required to present a report to the European Parliament, Council and the Economic and Social Committee on the application of ECRIP in practice. This requirement was effectively overtaken by events as on 30 March 2012, the Commission launched a public consultation exercise, *Consultation on the Future of European Insolvency Law*, which noted that after 10 years in operation, important developments in national insolvency law and considerable changes in the economic and political environment called for a fresh look at the Regulation. To that end comments to the consultation were sought by 21 June 2012. In response to the consultation exercise the Commission announced on 12 December 2012, that it had adopted a proposal for an amending Regulation. The main impetus of the amendments was to be a move toward a "rescue and recovery" culture to help companies and individuals in financial difficulties, particularly in light of the ongoing European austerity. The Commission considered that the existing Regulation was too much concerned with liquidation and thus wished to broaden its scope. The main proposals where reform of the Regulation was planned related to:

- widening its scope to extend the Regulation to include hybrid and pre-insolvency proceedings, debt discharge proceedings, etc.;

- clarifying the jurisdictional rules and improving the procedural framework for determining jurisdiction;

- widening its scope to extend the Regulation to include hybrid and pre-insolvency proceedings, debt discharge proceedings, etc.;

- clarifying the jurisdictional rules and improving the procedural framework for determining jurisdiction;

- making the administration of insolvency proceedings more efficient by enabling the court to refuse the opening of secondary proceedings which would be unnecessary to protect local creditors, abolishing the requirement that secondary proceedings should be only winding-up proceedings and improving the co-operation between main and secondary proceedings;

- improving the publicity of proceedings and lodging of claims by publishing the relevant court decisions in cross-border insolvency cases in a publicly accessible electronic register, providing for the interconnection of national insolvency registers and introducing standard forms for lodging claims; and

- improving the position for insolvent groups of companies in the cross-border context by co-ordinating insolvency proceedings concerning different members of the same group, obliging liquidators and courts in different proceedings to co-operate, and allowing liquidators to request a stay of the other proceedings and propose a rescue plan.

This proposal for a Regulation duly passed to the European Parliament and on 5 February 2014 it was backed by an overwhelming majority. In the event the Parliament finally approved and signed the text on 20 May 2015, and Regulation (EU) 2015/848 on insolvency proceedings was published in the Official Journal on 5 June 2015 at [2015] OJ L141/19 (see *http://eur-lex.europa.eu/legal-content/EN/TXT/?uri=uriserv:OJ.L_.2015.141.01.0019.01.ENG*) to enter into force 20 days after publication, i.e. on 26 June 2015. However, under art.84 the Regulation is to apply only after another two years, to insolvency proceedings opened on or after 26 June 2017 (except for art.86 (information on national and EU insolvency law: which applies from 26 June 2016), art.24(1) (establishment of insolvency registers: from 26 June 2018) and art.25 (interconnection of insolvency registers: from 26 June 2019)).

On the recast regulation, see G. McCormack (2015) 79 M.L.R. 121; I. Fletcher (2015) 28 Insol. Int. 97.

The emphasis in the recast Regulation is clearly shifting away from liquidation towards a "rescue and recovery" culture. Among the principal changes we may note:

- the extension of the scope of the Regulation to include various forms of voluntary arrangement and other pre-insolvency rescue proceedings, coupled with a repeal of the restriction of secondary proceedings to winding-up proceedings;

- increased court scrutiny in cases of "bankruptcy tourism";

- steps to permit and encourage the avoidance of multiple secondary proceedings, e.g. by the use of undertakings to respect creditors' priority rights in other jurisdictions;

- providing a better framework for group insolvencies;

- express exclusion of procedures which are primarily company-law based (e.g. Pt 26-type schemes of arrangement) from the scope of the Regulation. (However, in a separate initiative, the Commission is proposing that a reform be introduced to improve and harmonise the national laws on corporate restructuring, and on 3 March 2014 published a Recommendation to that end.)

One of the reform proposals listed above is for interconnection of national insolvency registers and this in part was brought about on 7 July 2014, when the Commission launched the linking up of databases from seven Member States—the Czech Republic, Germany, Estonia, Netherlands, Austria, Romania and Slovenia. The project is now well established and includes material from all the Member States, which is regularly updated. The Commission is required to authorise the linking of national databases on the "e-justice Portal": see *http://ec.europa.eu/justice/ criminal/european-e-justice/index_en.htm*.

On 23 March 2016 the Commission launched a public online consultation on insolvency frameworks in the EU. The consultation sought to identify changes which could be made to increase the effectiveness of insolvency structures in the different Member States, building on national regimes that work well, and in particular, to focus on rules that support businesses which are in temporary distress. The Commission on 22 November 2016 put forward a proposal for a Directive on preventive restructuring frameworks in the light of this consultation and on 24 September 2018 a general approach, including the then latest draft of a compromise for the proposed Directive *http:// data.consilium.europa.eu/doc/document/ST-12334-2018-INIT/en/pdf* was published. On 28 March 2019 the European Parliament finally approved the Directive on Restructuring and Insolvency, "on preventive restructuring frameworks, on discharge of debt and disqualifications, and on measures to increase the efficiency of procedures concerning restructuring, insolvency and discharge of debt, and amending Directive (EU) 2017/1132", reproduced at *http://www.europarl.europa.eu/sides/getDoc.do?pubRef=-//EP//NONSGML+TA+P8-TA-2019-0321+0+DOC+PDF +V0//EN*. The proposed Directive now merely requires final endorsement by the Council before being published in the *Official Journal*, probably by summer 2019. As a Directive it will require implementation into national law. Its main three aims are (i) a preventative restructuring framework to allow companies in financial difficulty to negotiate a restructuring plan with creditors, while maintaining their activity and preserving jobs; (ii) giving a second chance for honest insolvent or over-indebted entrepreneurs, through full debt discharge after a maximum period of three years, with safeguards against abuse; and (iii) targeted measures for Member States to increase efficiency of insolvency, restructuring and discharge procedures, in particular the expedient treatment of procedures. In addition, the final text also includes guarantees that workers' rights (e.g. collective bargaining and industrial action, right to information and consultation) will not be affected by restructuring procedures and also requirements on the duties of the company director in insolvency proceedings were introduced, including having regard to the interest of creditors, other stakeholders and equity holders, taking steps to avoid insolvency and avoiding deliberate or grossly negligent conduct that threatens the viability of the business.

As noted above, the Regulation has effect as primary legislation in its own right, and thus automatically repeals any existing legislation and supersedes any rule of law that is inconsistent with its provisions. The main area where this is likely to be seen is in relation to the wide jurisdiction which our courts have traditionally asserted over foreign nationals and companies to make bankruptcy and winding-up orders: in any case where the "centre of main interests" (COMI) of the individual or company concerned is in another Member State, this jurisdiction has been curtailed. In contrast, in some respects our courts are given wider powers under the Regulation than they have under the domestic legislation, e.g. to make administration orders in respect of foreign companies and other bodies which have their COMI within the UK: see the note to art.3.

For the purposes of the Regulation, the UK is regarded as one jurisdiction, and, until 1 November 2014, included Gibraltar. However, on that date, new insolvency legislation came into force in Gibraltar which provided, inter alia, that the EC Regulation should apply as if Gibraltar and the UK were separate Member States: see *Re Regent Centre Ltd* [2015] B.P.I.R. 730. This is, however, only effective as between these two jurisdictions: Gibraltar has not become a separate State vis-à-vis the other Member States and this has not led to any changes in the Annexes to the Regulation. The Regulation applies only where the debtor's COMI is situated in a Member State (other than Denmark). If the debtor is primarily based outside the EU, matters will continue to be governed by the existing domestic law, even as regards issues arising between EU jurisdictions *inter se*. Moreover, the Regulation has nothing to say about assets or creditors based outside the EU, or insolvency proceedings that have been instituted in a non-EU jurisdiction, even in a case where the debtor's COMI is in a Member State. And, of course, it applies only where the individual or company concerned is insolvent (or, in exceptional cases, in danger of insolvency).

While the Regulation aims for a substantial degree of "universality" (i.e. the recognition throughout the Union of proceedings that have been instituted in any Member State), it does not attempt to achieve "unity" (i.e. a regime which gives a single insolvency administration the sole and exclusive management of all the insolvent estate for the benefit of all the insolvent's creditors, in whatever parts of the EU it may be situated). The Regulation envisages a hierarchy of judicial competence, having one (and only one) "main" proceeding in one Member State (where the debtor's COMI is located), with the possibility of there being any number of "secondary" or "territorial" proceedings in any other jurisdictions where there are assets. (The term "territorial proceedings" refers to ancillary proceedings instituted *before* main proceedings have been opened, and "secondary proceedings" to those instituted subsequently.) A creditor based anywhere in the EU is free to prove in the main proceedings and also in any secondary or territorial proceedings (subject to safeguards to avoid his getting more than his share), and the proceedings in each State and the authority of its office-holder are to be automatically recognised with no special formalities throughout the Community. Recognition of the competence of main proceedings brings about a moratorium on the enforcement of claims applicable in all Member States, and there is provision for communication and co-operation between the officeholders in related insolvency proceedings. In principle, assets situated outside the jurisdiction of main proceedings can be removed from there to form part of the main estate; however, there is provision for a certain degree of ring-fencing so that the claims of local creditors, and particularly those entitled to preferential treatment, can be satisfied before anything is remitted to the main jurisdiction.

The Regulation does not seek to harmonise the substantive insolvency laws of the various Member States: by and large, it enshrines the general principle that the applicable law shall be that of the State in which the particular insolvency proceedings (whether main, secondary or territorial) are being conducted. However, it does deal with certain questions in the conflict of laws, declaring that a different law shall be applicable law in specified cases (so that, for instance, set-off shall be allowed even though it is not recognised by the law of the proceedings).

The Regulation applies to both individual and corporate insolvencies. (But it should be noted that it does not apply to *solvent* liquidations: cross-border issues in these proceedings are governed by Council Regulation EC 44/2001 of 22 December 2000 on jurisdiction and the recognition and enforcement of judgments in civil and commercial matters (the "Judgments Regulation", formerly the Brussels Convention).) In its scope it is capable of including insolvency procedures such as CVAs and administrations as well as bankruptcies and liquidations. But it does not extend to schemes of reconstruction and arrangement under CA 2006 Pt 26 (however, nothing in the Regulation restricts the jurisdiction of an English court to sanction such a scheme: *Re Rodenstock GmbH* [2011] EWHC 1104 (Ch); [2012] B.C.C. 459). It includes creditors' voluntary liquidations (after formal confirmation by the court), but not any form of receivership (that is, receiverships for the enforcement of a charge: on "interim receivers", see the note to Annex B). Although neither insolvent partnerships nor the estates of persons dying insolvent are specified as being within the Regulation, this has been assumed to be the case in the subordinate legislation accompanying ECRIP. Annexes A and B were amended by EU Regulation 2018/946.

There is a specific exclusion of insolvency proceedings concerning insurance undertakings, banks and other credit institutions, and collective and other investment undertakings, since these have their own special legislative or regulatory regimes. See the note to art.1(2).

The Regulation has its own special vocabulary, which calls for some mental adjustment by an English reader. In particular, it may be necessary to issue a warning in relation to terms such as the "opening" of insolvency proceedings (see the note to art.2(7)), and the terms "judgment" and "court", which by a mind-boggling feat are stretched so as to include the passing of a resolution for voluntary winding up by the shareholders at a general meeting!

One aspect of the Regulation which may be open to criticism is an underlying assumption that the debtor is (or has been) in business of some kind and that it is a creditor who will be the initiator of the insolvency proceedings. This can be seen, for instance, in art.3(2), where secondary proceedings can be opened only in a Member State if the debtor "*possesses* an establishment" within that State (present tense); and in art.3(4)(b), which restricts the right to open "territorial" proceedings to a creditor whose debt arises from the operation of that establishment. A non-trading individual (or a former trader who had ceased to carry on business) with an outstanding tax debt who wished to petition for his own bankruptcy in secondary or territorial proceedings could well have difficulty in surmounting the various hurdles imposed by these definitions. See further the notes to those provisions.

Mention should be made of the "Virgós-Schmit Report" (8 July 1996), a commentary on the text of the Convention which preceded the Regulation. Although this report does not refer directly to the Regulation and has never been officially adopted, it contains useful background material and has been referred to in a number of judgments in this country. The text is conveniently reproduced as an Appendix in Moss, Fletcher and Isaacs, *The EC Regulation on Insolvency Proceedings* (2nd edn, 2009); and in Goode, *Principles of Corporate Insolvency Law* (5th edn (ed., van Zwieten, Sweet & Maxwell, 2018); and is available online at *http://aei.pitt.edu/952*.

Note also the European Communication and Cooperation Guidelines for Cross-Border Insolvency (commonly known as the "Coco Guidelines") which were published in October 2007, establishing a non-binding set of standards for co-operation by insolvency practitioners in cross-border insolvency cases which are subject to the EC Regulation. The Guidelines are discussed by B. Wessels (2011) 24 Insolv. Int. 65.

The statutory instruments enacted to make the legislation and Rules compatible with ECRIP are as follows. All except the first came into force on 31 May 2002. Attention is drawn also to the Insolvency Service's Guidance Note, referred to in the General note to arts 53–56 below.

The Insolvency Act 1986 (Amendment) Regulations 2002 (SI 2002/1037, effective 3 May 2002)

The Insolvency Act 1986 (Amendment) (No.2) Regulations 2002 (SI 2002/1240)

The Insolvency (Amendment) Rules 2002 (SI 2002/1307)

The Insolvent Partnerships (Amendment) Order 2002 (SI 2002/1308)

The Administration of Insolvent Estates of Deceased Persons Order 2002 (SI 2002/1309)

By the Treaty of Accession of 16 April 2003 (see [2003] OJ L236/711), 10 new Member States were admitted to the European Community, and consequential amendments to ECRIP were made by EC Council Regulation 603/2005 (see [2005] OJ L100/1), as well as by the Treaty itself. Further changes were made by EC Council Regulation 694/2006 ([2006] OJ L121/1) as from 7 May 2006 and again by EC Council Regulation 681/2007 ([2007] OJ L159/1), in order to accommodate the expansion of EU membership so as to include Bulgaria and Romania and to incorporate amendments notified by other Member States. These changes took effect from 21 June 2007 and 1 January 2008). Croatia became a Member on 1 July 2013.

It was held in *ERSTE Bank Hungary Nyrt v Magyar Clllam* (C-527/10) [2012] I.L.Pr. 38 that if a Member State joins the EU, it immediately becomes bound by the Regulation and so is required to recognise pre-existing main proceedings in another EU jurisdiction.

On the national implementation of the EURIP across jurisdictions—see Madaus and Wessels [2018] 31 Insolv. Int. 105.

The EU Regulation is discussed in Totty, Moss & Segal, *Insolvency*, paras E2–01 et seq.

The Model Law on Cross-Border Insolvency, agreed by UNCITRAL in 1997, closely follows the scheme of the Regulation in many respects and uses some of the same terminology. It has been enacted for Britain by the Cross-Border Insolvency Regulations 2006 (SI 2006/1030), which are included, with annotation, later in this Volume. Article 3 of Sch.1 to the 2006 Regulations provides that to the extent that the Model Law conflicts with an obligation of the United Kingdom under the Regulation, the requirements of the latter shall prevail. It follows that where an insolvency concerns a debtor who has interests in more than one EU Member State and a COMI within the EU, cross-border issues concerning those interests will normally fall to be determined by the Regulation. However, there is not a complete overlap: in *Stocznia Gdynia SA v Bud-Bank Leasing sp z oo* [2010] B.C.C. 255 an application to the UK court concerning statutory compensation proceedings in a Polish insolvency was held to have been correctly brought under the CBIR rather than the Regulation because the compensation proceedings satisfied the requirements for recognition under the CBIR but not those of the Regulation.

In *Rubin v Eurofinance SA* and *New Cap Reinsurance Corp Ltd v Grant* [2012] UKSC 46; [2013] B.C.C. 1 the Supreme Court considered the various "gateways" through which a foreign insolvency appointment or judgment could be recognised or enforced in this jurisdiction, but did not consider the Regulation as the judgment debtors under consideration had their COMIs outside the EU. See the note to IA 1986 s.426.

This Regulation will cease to apply to the UK on Brexit. In the event of a "hard (i.e. no deal) Brexit" that cessation will be immediate, but if there is a negotiated withdrawal some transitional arrangement will operate.

Regulation (EU) 2015/848 of the European Parliament and of the Council of 20 May 2015 on insolvency proceedings

[Preamble]

THE EUROPEAN PARLIAMENT AND THE COUNCIL OF THE EUROPEAN UNION,

Having regard to the Treaty on the Functioning of the European Union, and in particular Article 81 thereof,

Having regard to the proposal from the European Commission,

After transmission of the draft legislative act to the national parliaments,

Having regard to the opinion of the European Economic and Social Committee,

Acting in accordance with the ordinary legislative procedure,

Whereas:

(1) On 12 December 2012, the Commission adopted a report on the application of Council Regulation (EC) No 1346/2000. The report concluded that the Regulation is functioning well in general but that it would be desirable to improve the application of certain of its provisions in order to enhance the effective administration of cross-border insolvency proceedings. Since that Regulation has been amended several times and further amendments are to be made, it should be recast in the interest of clarity.

(2) The Union has set the objective of establishing an area of freedom, security and justice.

(3) The proper functioning of the internal market requires that cross-border insolvency proceedings should operate efficiently and effectively. This Regulation needs to be adopted in order to achieve that objective, which falls within the scope of judicial cooperation in civil matters within the meaning of Article 81 of the Treaty.

(4) The activities of undertakings have more and more cross-border effects and are therefore increasingly being regulated by Union law. The insolvency of such undertakings also affects the proper functioning of the internal market, and there is a need for a Union act requiring coordination of the measures to be taken regarding an insolvent debtor's assets.

(5) It is necessary for the proper functioning of the internal market to avoid incentives for parties to transfer assets or judicial proceedings from one Member State to another, seeking to obtain a more favourable legal position to the detriment of the general body of creditors (forum shopping).

(6) This Regulation should include provisions governing jurisdiction for opening insolvency proceedings and actions which are directly derived from insolvency proceedings and are closely linked with them. This Regulation should also contain provisions regarding the recognition and enforcement of judgments issued in such proceedings, and provisions regarding the law applicable to insolvency proceedings. In addition, this Regulation should lay down rules on the coordination of insolvency proceedings which relate to the same debtor or to several members of the same group of companies.

(7) Bankruptcy, proceedings relating to the winding-up of insolvent companies or other legal persons, judicial arrangements, compositions and analogous proceedings and actions related to such proceedings are excluded from the scope of Regulation (EU) No 1215/2012 of the European Parliament and of the Council. Those proceedings should be covered by this Regulation. The interpretation of this Regulation should as much as possible avoid regulatory loopholes between the two instruments. However, the mere fact that a national procedure is not listed in Annex A to this Regulation should not imply that it is covered by Regulation (EU) No 1215/2012.

(8) In order to achieve the aim of improving the efficiency and effectiveness of insolvency proceedings having cross-border effects, it is necessary, and appropriate, that the provisions on jurisdiction, recognition and applicable law in this area should be contained in a Union measure which is binding and directly applicable in Member States.

(9) This Regulation should apply to insolvency proceedings which meet the conditions set out in it, irrespective of whether the debtor is a natural person or a legal person, a trader or an individual. Those insolvency proceedings are listed exhaustively in Annex A. In respect of the national procedures contained in Annex A, this Regulation should apply without any further examination by the courts of another Member State as to whether the conditions set out in this Regulation are met. National insolvency procedures not listed in Annex A should not be covered by this Regulation.

(10) The scope of this Regulation should extend to proceedings which promote the rescue of economically viable but distressed businesses and which give a second chance to entrepreneurs. It should, in particular, extend to proceedings which provide for restructuring of a debtor at a stage where there is only a likelihood of insolvency, and to proceedings which leave the debtor fully or partially in control of its assets and affairs. It should also extend to proceedings providing for a debt discharge or a debt adjustment in relation to consumers and self-employed persons, for

example by reducing the amount to be paid by the debtor or by extending the payment period granted to the debtor. Since such proceedings do not necessarily entail the appointment of an insolvency practitioner, they should be covered by this Regulation if they take place under the control or supervision of a court. In this context, the term 'control' should include situations where the court only intervenes on appeal by a creditor or other interested parties.

(11) This Regulation should also apply to procedures which grant a temporary stay on enforcement actions brought by individual creditors where such actions could adversely affect negotiations and hamper the prospects of a restructuring of the debtor's business. Such procedures should not be detrimental to the general body of creditors and, if no agreement on a restructuring plan can be reached, should be preliminary to other procedures covered by this Regulation.

(12) This Regulation should apply to proceedings the opening of which is subject to publicity in order to allow creditors to become aware of the proceedings and to lodge their claims, thereby ensuring the collective nature of the proceedings, and in order to give creditors the opportunity to challenge the jurisdiction of the court which has opened the proceedings.

(13) Accordingly, insolvency proceedings which are confidential should be excluded from the scope of this Regulation. While such proceedings may play an important role in some Member States, their confidential nature makes it impossible for a creditor or a court located in another Member State to know that such proceedings have been opened, thereby making it difficult to provide for the recognition of their effects throughout the Union.

(14) The collective proceedings which are covered by this Regulation should include all or a significant part of the creditors to whom a debtor owes all or a substantial proportion of the debtor's outstanding debts provided that the claims of those creditors who are not involved in such proceedings remain unaffected. Proceedings which involve only the financial creditors of a debtor should also be covered. Proceedings which do not include all the creditors of a debtor should be proceedings aimed at rescuing the debtor. Proceedings that lead to a definitive cessation of the debtor's activities or the liquidation of the debtor's assets should include all the debtor's creditors. Moreover, the fact that some insolvency proceedings for natural persons exclude specific categories of claims, such as maintenance claims, from the possibility of a debt-discharge should not mean that such proceedings are not collective.

(15) This Regulation should also apply to proceedings that, under the law of some Member States, are opened and conducted for a certain period of time on an interim or provisional basis before a court issues an order confirming the continuation of the proceedings on a non-interim basis. Although labelled as 'interim', such proceedings should meet all other requirements of this Regulation.

(16) This Regulation should apply to proceedings which are based on laws relating to insolvency. However, proceedings that are based on general company law not designed exclusively for insolvency situations should not be considered to be based on laws relating to insolvency. Similarly, the purpose of adjustment of debt should not include specific proceedings in which debts of a natural person of very low income and very low asset value are written off, provided that this type of proceedings never makes provision for payment to creditors.

(17) This Regulation's scope should extend to proceedings which are triggered by situations in which the debtor faces non-financial difficulties, provided that such difficulties give rise to a real and serious threat to the debtor's actual or future ability to pay its debts as they fall due. The time frame relevant for the determination of such threat may extend to a period of several months or even longer in order to account for cases in which the debtor is faced with non-financial difficulties threatening the status of its business as a going concern and, in the medium term, its liquidity. This may be the case, for example, where the debtor has lost a contract which is of key importance to it.

(18) This Regulation should be without prejudice to the rules on the recovery of State aid from insolvent companies as interpreted by the case-law of the Court of Justice of the European Union.

(19) Insolvency proceedings concerning insurance undertakings, credit institutions, investment firms and other firms, institutions or undertakings covered by Directive 2001/24/EC of the European Parliament and of the Council and collective investment undertakings should be excluded from the scope of this Regulation, as they are all subject to special arrangements and the national supervisory authorities have wide-ranging powers of intervention.

(20) Insolvency proceedings do not necessarily involve the intervention of a judicial authority. Therefore, the term 'court' in this Regulation should, in certain provisions, be given a broad meaning and include a person or body empowered by national law to open insolvency proceedings. In order for this Regulation to apply, proceedings (comprising acts and formalities set down in law) should not only have to comply with the provisions of this Regulation, but they should also be officially recognised and legally effective in the Member State in which the insolvency proceedings are opened.

(21) Insolvency practitioners are defined in this Regulation and listed in Annex B. Insolvency practitioners who are appointed without the involvement of a judicial body should, under national law, be appropriately regulated and authorised to act in insolvency proceedings. The national regulatory framework should provide for proper arrangements to deal with potential conflicts of interest.

(22) This Regulation acknowledges the fact that as a result of widely differing substantive laws it is not practical to introduce insolvency proceedings with universal scope throughout the Union. The application without exception of the law of the State of the opening of proceedings would, against this background, frequently lead to difficulties. This applies, for example, to the widely differing national laws on security interests to be found in the Member States. Furthermore, the preferential rights enjoyed by some creditors in insolvency proceedings are, in some cases, completely different. At the next review of this Regulation, it will be necessary to identify further measures in order to improve the preferential rights of employees at European level. This Regulation should take account of such differing national laws in two different ways. On the one hand, provision should be made for special rules on the applicable law in the case of particularly significant rights and legal relationships (e.g. rights in rem and contracts of employment). On the other hand, national proceedings covering only assets situated in the State of the opening of proceedings should also be allowed alongside main insolvency proceedings with universal scope.

(23) This Regulation enables the main insolvency proceedings to be opened in the Member State where the debtor has the centre of its main interests. Those proceedings have universal scope and are aimed at encompassing all the debtor's assets. To protect the diversity of interests, this Regulation permits secondary insolvency proceedings to be opened to run in parallel with the main insolvency proceedings. Secondary insolvency proceedings may be opened in the Member State where the debtor has an establishment. The effects of secondary insolvency proceedings are limited to the assets located in that State. Mandatory rules of coordination with the main insolvency proceedings satisfy the need for unity in the Union.

(24) Where main insolvency proceedings concerning a legal person or company have been opened in a Member State other than that of its registered office, it should be possible to open secondary insolvency proceedings in the Member State of the registered office, provided that the debtor is carrying out an economic activity with human means and assets in that State, in accordance with the case-law of the Court of Justice of the European Union.

(25) This Regulation applies only to proceedings in respect of a debtor whose centre of main interests is located in the Union.

(26) The rules of jurisdiction set out in this Regulation establish only international jurisdiction, that is to say, they designate the Member State the courts of which may open insolvency proceedings. Territorial jurisdiction within that Member State should be established by the national law of the Member State concerned.

(27) Before opening insolvency proceedings, the competent court should examine of its own motion whether the centre of the debtor's main interests or the debtor's establishment is actually located within its jurisdiction.

(28) When determining whether the centre of the debtor's main interests is ascertainable by third parties, special consideration should be given to the creditors and to their perception as to where a debtor conducts the administration of its interests. This may require, in the event of a shift of centre of main interests, informing creditors of the new location from which the debtor is carrying out its activities in due course, for example by drawing attention to the change of address in commercial correspondence, or by making the new location public through other appropriate means.

(29) This Regulation should contain a number of safeguards aimed at preventing fraudulent or abusive forum shopping.

(30) Accordingly, the presumptions that the registered office, the principal place of business and the habitual residence are the centre of main interests should be rebuttable, and the relevant court of a Member State should carefully assess whether the centre of the debtor's main interests is genuinely located in that Member State. In the case of a company, it should be possible to rebut this presumption where the company's central administration is located in a Member State other than that of its registered office, and where a comprehensive assessment of all the relevant factors establishes, in a manner that is ascertainable by third parties, that the company's actual centre of management and supervision and of the management of its interests is located in that other Member State. In the case of an individual not exercising an independent business or professional activity, it should be possible to rebut this presumption, for example where the major part of the debtor's assets is located outside the Member State of the debtor's habitual residence, or where it can be established that the principal reason for moving was to file for insolvency proceedings in the new jurisdiction and where such filing would materially impair the interests of creditors whose dealings with the debtor took place prior to the relocation.

(31) With the same objective of preventing fraudulent or abusive forum shopping, the presumption that the centre of main interests is at the place of the registered office, at the individual's principal place of business or at the individual's habitual residence should not apply where, respectively, in the case of a company, legal person or individual exercising an independent business or professional activity, the debtor has relocated its registered office or principal place of business to another Member State within the 3-month period prior to the request for opening insolvency proceedings, or, in the case of an individual not exercising an independent business or professional activity, the debtor has relocated his habitual residence to another Member State within the 6-month period prior to the request for opening insolvency proceedings.

(32) In all cases, where the circumstances of the matter give rise to doubts about the court's jurisdiction, the court should require the debtor to submit additional evidence to support its assertions and, where the law applicable to the insolvency proceedings so allows, give the debtor's creditors the opportunity to present their views on the question of jurisdiction.

(33) In the event that the court seised of the request to open insolvency proceedings finds that the centre of main interests is not located on its territory, it should not open main insolvency proceedings.

(34) In addition, any creditor of the debtor should have an effective remedy against the decision to open insolvency proceedings. The consequences of any challenge to the decision to open insolvency proceedings should be governed by national law.

(35) The courts of the Member State within the territory of which insolvency proceedings have been opened should also have jurisdiction for actions which derive directly from the insolvency proceedings and are closely linked with them. Such actions should include avoidance actions against defendants in other Member States and actions concerning obligations that arise in the

course of the insolvency proceedings, such as advance payment for costs of the proceedings. In contrast, actions for the performance of the obligations under a contract concluded by the debtor prior to the opening of proceedings do not derive directly from the proceedings. Where such an action is related to another action based on general civil and commercial law, the insolvency practitioner should be able to bring both actions in the courts of the defendant's domicile if he considers it more efficient to bring the action in that forum. This could, for example, be the case where the insolvency practitioner wishes to combine an action for director's liability on the basis of insolvency law with an action based on company law or general tort law.

(36) The court having jurisdiction to open the main insolvency proceedings should be able to order provisional and protective measures as from the time of the request to open proceedings. Preservation measures both prior to and after the commencement of the insolvency proceedings are important to guarantee the effectiveness of the insolvency proceedings. In that connection, this Regulation should provide for various possibilities. On the one hand, the court competent for the main insolvency proceedings should also be able to order provisional and protective measures covering assets situated in the territory of other Member States. On the other hand, an insolvency practitioner temporarily appointed prior to the opening of the main insolvency proceedings should be able, in the Member States in which an establishment belonging to the debtor is to be found, to apply for the preservation measures which are possible under the law of those Member States.

(37) Prior to the opening of the main insolvency proceedings, the right to request the opening of insolvency proceedings in the Member State where the debtor has an establishment should be limited to local creditors and public authorities, or to cases in which main insolvency proceedings cannot be opened under the law of the Member State where the debtor has the centre of its main interests. The reason for this restriction is that cases in which territorial insolvency proceedings are requested before the main insolvency proceedings are intended to be limited to what is absolutely necessary.

(38) Following the opening of the main insolvency proceedings, this Regulation does not restrict the right to request the opening of insolvency proceedings in a Member State where the debtor has an establishment. The insolvency practitioner in the main insolvency proceedings or any other person empowered under the national law of that Member State may request the opening of secondary insolvency proceedings.

(39) This Regulation should provide for rules to determine the location of the debtor's assets, which should apply when determining which assets belong to the main or secondary insolvency proceedings, or to situations involving third parties' rights in rem. In particular, this Regulation should provide that European patents with unitary effect, a Community trade mark or any other similar rights, such as Community plant variety rights or Community designs, should only be included in the main insolvency proceedings.

(40) Secondary insolvency proceedings can serve different purposes, besides the protection of local interests. Cases may arise in which the insolvency estate of the debtor is too complex to administer as a unit, or the differences in the legal systems concerned are so great that difficulties may arise from the extension of effects deriving from the law of the State of the opening of proceedings to the other Member States where the assets are located. For that reason, the insolvency practitioner in the main insolvency proceedings may request the opening of secondary insolvency proceedings where the efficient administration of the insolvency estate so requires.

(41) Secondary insolvency proceedings may also hamper the efficient administration of the insolvency estate. Therefore, this Regulation sets out two specific situations in which the court seised of a request to open secondary insolvency proceedings should be able, at the request of the insolvency practitioner in the main insolvency proceedings, to postpone or refuse the opening of such proceedings.

(42) First, this Regulation confers on the insolvency practitioner in main insolvency proceedings the possibility of giving an undertaking to local creditors that they will be treated as if secondary insolvency proceedings had been opened. That undertaking has to meet a number of conditions set out in this Regulation, in particular that it be approved by a qualified majority of local creditors. Where such an undertaking has been given, the court seised of a request to open secondary insolvency proceedings should be able to refuse that request if it is satisfied that the undertaking adequately protects the general interests of local creditors. When assessing those interests, the court should take into account the fact that the undertaking has been approved by a qualified majority of local creditors.

(43) For the purposes of giving an undertaking to local creditors, the assets and rights located in the Member State where the debtor has an establishment should form a sub-category of the insolvency estate, and, when distributing them or the proceeds resulting from their realisation, the insolvency practitioner in the main insolvency proceedings should respect the priority rights that creditors would have had if secondary insolvency proceedings had been opened in that Member State.

(44) National law should be applicable, as appropriate, in relation to the approval of an undertaking. In particular, where under national law the voting rules for adopting a restructuring plan require the prior approval of creditors' claims, those claims should be deemed to be approved for the purpose of voting on the undertaking. Where there are different procedures for the adoption of restructuring plans under national law, Member States should designate the specific procedure which should be relevant in this context.

(45) Second, this Regulation should provide for the possibility that the court temporarily stays the opening of secondary insolvency proceedings, when a temporary stay of individual enforcement proceedings has been granted in the main insolvency proceedings, in order to preserve the efficiency of the stay granted in the main insolvency proceedings. The court should be able to grant the temporary stay if it is satisfied that suitable measures are in place to protect the general interest of local creditors. In such a case, all creditors that could be affected by the outcome of the negotiations on a restructuring plan should be informed of the negotiations and be allowed to participate in them.

(46) In order to ensure effective protection of local interests, the insolvency practitioner in the main insolvency proceedings should not be able to realise or re-locate, in an abusive manner, assets situated in the Member State where an establishment is located, in particular, with the purpose of frustrating the possibility that such interests can be effectively satisfied if secondary insolvency proceedings are opened subsequently.

(47) This Regulation should not prevent the courts of a Member State in which secondary insolvency proceedings have been opened from sanctioning a debtor's directors for violation of their duties, provided that those courts have jurisdiction to address such disputes under their national law.

(48) Main insolvency proceedings and secondary insolvency proceedings can contribute to the efficient administration of the debtor's insolvency estate or to the effective realisation of the total assets if there is proper cooperation between the actors involved in all the concurrent proceedings. Proper cooperation implies the various insolvency practitioners and the courts involved cooperating closely, in particular by exchanging a sufficient amount of information. In order to ensure the dominant role of the main insolvency proceedings, the insolvency practitioner in such proceedings should be given several possibilities for intervening in secondary insolvency proceedings which are pending at the same time. In particular, the insolvency practitioner should be able to propose a restructuring plan or composition or apply for a suspension of the realisation of the assets in the secondary insolvency proceedings. When cooperating, insolvency practitioners and courts should take into account best practices for cooperation in cross-border insolvency cases, as set out in principles and guidelines on communication and cooperation adopted by

European and international organisations active in the area of insolvency law, and in particular the relevant guidelines prepared by the United Nations Commission on International Trade Law (Uncitral).

(49) In light of such cooperation, insolvency practitioners and courts should be able to enter into agreements and protocols for the purpose of facilitating cross-border cooperation of multiple insolvency proceedings in different Member States concerning the same debtor or members of the same group of companies, where this is compatible with the rules applicable to each of the proceedings. Such agreements and protocols may vary in form, in that they may be written or oral, and in scope, in that they may range from generic to specific, and may be entered into by different parties. Simple generic agreements may emphasise the need for close cooperation between the parties, without addressing specific issues, while more detailed, specific agreements may establish a framework of principles to govern multiple insolvency proceedings and may be approved by the courts involved, where the national law so requires. They may reflect an agreement between the parties to take, or to refrain from taking, certain steps or actions.

(50) Similarly, the courts of different Member States may cooperate by coordinating the appointment of insolvency practitioners. In that context, they may appoint a single insolvency practitioner for several insolvency proceedings concerning the same debtor or for different members of a group of companies, provided that this is compatible with the rules applicable to each of the proceedings, in particular with any requirements concerning the qualification and licensing of the insolvency practitioner.

(51) This Regulation should ensure the efficient administration of insolvency proceedings relating to different companies forming part of a group of companies.

(52) Where insolvency proceedings have been opened for several companies of the same group, there should be proper cooperation between the actors involved in those proceedings. The various insolvency practitioners and the courts involved should therefore be under a similar obligation to cooperate and communicate with each other as those involved in main and secondary insolvency proceedings relating to the same debtor. Cooperation between the insolvency practitioners should not run counter to the interests of the creditors in each of the proceedings, and such cooperation should be aimed at finding a solution that would leverage synergies across the group.

(53) The introduction of rules on the insolvency proceedings of groups of companies should not limit the possibility for a court to open insolvency proceedings for several companies belonging to the same group in a single jurisdiction if the court finds that the centre of main interests of those companies is located in a single Member State. In such cases, the court should also be able to appoint, if appropriate, the same insolvency practitioner in all proceedings concerned, provided that this is not incompatible with the rules applicable to them.

(54) With a view to further improving the coordination of the insolvency proceedings of members of a group of companies, and to allow for a coordinated restructuring of the group, this Regulation should introduce procedural rules on the coordination of the insolvency proceedings of members of a group of companies. Such coordination should strive to ensure the efficiency of the coordination, whilst at the same time respecting each group member's separate legal personality.

(55) An insolvency practitioner appointed in insolvency proceedings opened in relation to a member of a group of companies should be able to request the opening of group coordination proceedings. However, where the law applicable to the insolvency so requires, that insolvency practitioner should obtain the necessary authorisation before making such a request. The request should specify the essential elements of the coordination, in particular an outline of the coordination plan, a proposal as to whom should be appointed as coordinator and an outline of the estimated costs of the coordination.

(56) In order to ensure the voluntary nature of group coordination proceedings, the insolvency practitioners involved should be able to object to their participation in the proceedings within a

specified time period. In order to allow the insolvency practitioners involved to take an informed decision on participation in the group coordination proceedings, they should be informed at an early stage of the essential elements of the coordination. However, any insolvency practitioner who initially objects to inclusion in the group coordination proceedings should be able to subsequently request to participate in them. In such a case, the coordinator should take a decision on the admissibility of the request. All insolvency practitioners, including the requesting insolvency practitioner, should be informed of the coordinator's decision and should have the opportunity of challenging that decision before the court which has opened the group coordination proceedings.

(57) Group coordination proceedings should always strive to facilitate the effective administration of the insolvency proceedings of the group members, and to have a generally positive impact for the creditors. This Regulation should therefore ensure that the court with which a request for group coordination proceedings has been filed makes an assessment of those criteria prior to opening group coordination proceedings.

(58) The advantages of group coordination proceedings should not be outweighed by the costs of those proceedings. Therefore, it is necessary to ensure that the costs of the coordination, and the share of those costs that each group member will bear, are adequate, proportionate and reasonable, and are determined in accordance with the national law of the Member State in which group coordination proceedings have been opened. The insolvency practitioners involved should also have the possibility of controlling those costs from an early stage of the proceedings. Where the national law so requires, controlling costs from an early stage of proceedings could involve the insolvency practitioner seeking the approval of a court or creditors' committee.

(59) Where the coordinator considers that the fulfilment of his or her tasks requires a significant increase in costs compared to the initially estimated costs and, in any case, where the costs exceed 10 % of the estimated costs, the coordinator should be authorised by the court which has opened the group coordination proceedings to exceed such costs. Before taking its decision, the court which has opened the group coordination proceedings should give the possibility to the participating insolvency practitioners to be heard before it in order to allow them to communicate their observations on the appropriateness of the coordinator's request.

(60) For members of a group of companies which are not participating in group coordination proceedings, this Regulation should also provide for an alternative mechanism to achieve a coordinated restructuring of the group. An insolvency practitioner appointed in proceedings relating to a member of a group of companies should have standing to request a stay of any measure related to the realisation of the assets in the proceedings opened with respect to other members of the group which are not subject to group coordination proceedings. It should only be possible to request such a stay if a restructuring plan is presented for the members of the group concerned, if the plan is to the benefit of the creditors in the proceedings in respect of which the stay is requested, and if the stay is necessary to ensure that the plan can be properly implemented.

(61) This Regulation should not prevent Member States from establishing national rules which would supplement the rules on cooperation, communication and coordination with regard to the insolvency of members of groups of companies set out in this Regulation, provided that the scope of application of those national rules is limited to the national jurisdiction and that their application would not impair the efficiency of the rules laid down by this Regulation.

(62) The rules on cooperation, communication and coordination in the framework of the insolvency of members of a group of companies provided for in this Regulation should only apply to the extent that proceedings relating to different members of the same group of companies have been opened in more than one Member State.

(63) Any creditor which has its habitual residence, domicile or registered office in the Union should have the right to lodge its claims in each of the insolvency proceedings pending in the Union

relating to the debtor's assets. This should also apply to tax authorities and social insurance institutions. This Regulation should not prevent the insolvency practitioner from lodging claims on behalf of certain groups of creditors, for example employees, where the national law so provides. However, in order to ensure the equal treatment of creditors, the distribution of proceeds should be coordinated. Every creditor should be able to keep what it has received in the course of insolvency proceedings, but should be entitled only to participate in the distribution of total assets in other proceedings if creditors with the same standing have obtained the same proportion of their claims.

(64) It is essential that creditors which have their habitual residence, domicile or registered office in the Union be informed about the opening of insolvency proceedings relating to their debtor's assets. In order to ensure a swift transmission of information to creditors, Regulation (EC) No 1393/2007 of the European Parliament and of the Council should not apply where this Regulation refers to the obligation to inform creditors. The use of standard forms available in all official languages of the institutions of the Union should facilitate the task of creditors when lodging claims in proceedings opened in another Member State. The consequences of the incomplete filing of the standard forms should be a matter for national law.

(65) This Regulation should provide for the immediate recognition of judgments concerning the opening, conduct and closure of insolvency proceedings which fall within its scope, and of judgments handed down in direct connection with such insolvency proceedings. Automatic recognition should therefore mean that the effects attributed to the proceedings by the law of the Member State in which the proceedings were opened extend to all other Member States. The recognition of judgments delivered by the courts of the Member States should be based on the principle of mutual trust. To that end, grounds for non-recognition should be reduced to the minimum necessary. This is also the basis on which any dispute should be resolved where the courts of two Member States both claim competence to open the main insolvency proceedings. The decision of the first court to open proceedings should be recognised in the other Member States without those Member States having the power to scrutinise that court's decision.

(66) This Regulation should set out, for the matters covered by it, uniform rules on conflict of laws which replace, within their scope of application, national rules of private international law. Unless otherwise stated, the law of the Member State of the opening of proceedings should be applicable (lex concursus). This rule on conflict of laws should be valid both for the main insolvency proceedings and for local proceedings. The lex concursus determines all the effects of the insolvency proceedings, both procedural and substantive, on the persons and legal relations concerned. It governs all the conditions for the opening, conduct and closure of the insolvency proceedings.

(67) Automatic recognition of insolvency proceedings to which the law of the State of the opening of proceedings normally applies may interfere with the rules under which transactions are carried out in other Member States. To protect legitimate expectations and the certainty of transactions in Member States other than that in which proceedings are opened, provision should be made for a number of exceptions to the general rule.

(68) There is a particular need for a special reference diverging from the law of the opening State in the case of rights in rem, since such rights are of considerable importance for the granting of credit. The basis, validity and extent of rights in rem should therefore normally be determined according to the lex situs and not be affected by the opening of insolvency proceedings. The proprietor of a right in rem should therefore be able to continue to assert its right to segregation or separate settlement of the collateral security. Where assets are subject to rights in rem under the lex situs in one Member State but the main insolvency proceedings are being carried out in another Member State, the insolvency practitioner in the main insolvency proceedings should be able to request the opening of secondary insolvency proceedings in the jurisdiction where the rights in rem arise if the debtor has an establishment there. If secondary insolvency proceedings are not opened, any

surplus on the sale of an asset covered by rights in rem should be paid to the insolvency practitioner in the main insolvency proceedings.

(69) This Regulation lays down several provisions for a court to order a stay of opening proceedings or a stay of enforcement proceedings. Any such stay should not affect the rights in rem of creditors or third parties.

(70) If a set-off of claims is not permitted under the law of the State of the opening of proceedings, a creditor should nevertheless be entitled to the set-off if it is possible under the law applicable to the claim of the insolvent debtor. In this way, set-off would acquire a kind of guarantee function based on legal provisions on which the creditor concerned can rely at the time when the claim arises.

(71) There is also a need for special protection in the case of payment systems and financial markets, for example in relation to the position-closing agreements and netting agreements to be found in such systems, as well as the sale of securities and the guarantees provided for such transactions as governed in particular by Directive 98/26/EC of the European Parliament and of the Council. For such transactions, the only law which is relevant should be that applicable to the system or market concerned. That law is intended to prevent the possibility of mechanisms for the payment and settlement of transactions, and provided for in payment and set-off systems or on the regulated financial markets of the Member States, being altered in the case of insolvency of a business partner. Directive 98/26/EC contains special provisions which should take precedence over the general rules laid down in this Regulation.

(72) In order to protect employees and jobs, the effects of insolvency proceedings on the continuation or termination of employment and on the rights and obligations of all parties to such employment should be determined by the law applicable to the relevant employment agreement, in accordance with the general rules on conflict of laws. Moreover, in cases where the termination of employment contracts requires approval by a court or administrative authority, the Member State in which an establishment of the debtor is located should retain jurisdiction to grant such approval even if no insolvency proceedings have been opened in that Member State. Any other questions relating to the law of insolvency, such as whether the employees' claims are protected by preferential rights and the status such preferential rights may have, should be determined by the law of the Member State in which the insolvency proceedings (main or secondary) have been opened, except in cases where an undertaking to avoid secondary insolvency proceedings has been given in accordance with this Regulation.

(73) The law applicable to the effects of insolvency proceedings on any pending lawsuit or pending arbitral proceedings concerning an asset or right which forms part of the debtor's insolvency estate should be the law of the Member State where the lawsuit is pending or where the arbitration has its seat. However, this rule should not affect national rules on recognition and enforcement of arbitral awards.

(74) In order to take account of the specific procedural rules of court systems in certain Member States flexibility should be provided with regard to certain rules of this Regulation. Accordingly, references in this Regulation to notice being given by a judicial body of a Member State should include, where a Member State's procedural rules so require, an order by that judicial body directing that notice be given.

(75) For business considerations, the main content of the decision opening the proceedings should be published, at the request of the insolvency practitioner, in a Member State other than that of the court which delivered that decision. If there is an establishment in the Member State concerned, such publication should be mandatory. In neither case, however, should publication be a prior condition for recognition of the foreign proceedings.

(76) In order to improve the provision of information to relevant creditors and courts and to prevent the opening of parallel insolvency proceedings, Member States should be required to publish relevant

information in cross-border insolvency cases in a publicly accessible electronic register. In order to facilitate access to that information for creditors and courts domiciled or located in other Member States, this Regulation should provide for the interconnection of such insolvency registers via the European e-Justice Portal. Member States should be free to publish relevant information in several registers and it should be possible to interconnect more than one register per Member State.

(77) This Regulation should determine the minimum amount of information to be published in the insolvency registers. Member States should not be precluded from including additional information. Where the debtor is an individual, the insolvency registers should only have to indicate a registration number if the debtor is exercising an independent business or professional activity. That registration number should be understood to be the unique registration number of the debtor's independent business or professional activity published in the trade register, if any.

(78) Information on certain aspects of insolvency proceedings is essential for creditors, such as time limits for lodging claims or for challenging decisions. This Regulation should, however, not require Member States to calculate those time-limits on a case-by-case basis. Member States should be able to fulfil their obligations by adding hyperlinks to the European e-Justice Portal, where self-explanatory information on the criteria for calculating those time-limits is to be provided.

(79) In order to grant sufficient protection to information relating to individuals not exercising an independent business or professional activity, Member States should be able to make access to that information subject to supplementary search criteria such as the debtor's personal identification number, address, date of birth or the district of the competent court, or to make access conditional upon a request to a competent authority or upon the verification of a legitimate interest.

(80) Member States should also be able not to include in their insolvency registers information on individuals not exercising an independent business or professional activity. In such cases, Member States should ensure that the relevant information is given to the creditors by individual notice, and that claims of creditors who have not received the information are not affected by the proceedings.

(81) It may be the case that some of the persons concerned are not aware that insolvency proceedings have been opened, and act in good faith in a way that conflicts with the new circumstances. In order to protect such persons who, unaware that foreign proceedings have been opened, make a payment to the debtor instead of to the foreign insolvency practitioner, provision should be made for such a payment to have a debt-discharging effect.

(82) In order to ensure uniform conditions for the implementation of this Regulation, implementing powers should be conferred on the Commission. Those powers should be exercised in accordance with Regulation (EU) No 182/2011 of the European Parliament and of the Council.

(83) This Regulation respects the fundamental rights and observes the principles recognised in the Charter of Fundamental Rights of the European Union. In particular, this Regulation seeks to promote the application of Articles 8, 17 and 47 concerning, respectively, the protection of personal data, the right to property and the right to an effective remedy and to a fair trial.

(84) Directive 95/46/EC of the European Parliament and of the Council and Regulation (EC) No 45/2001 of the European Parliament and of the Council apply to the processing of personal data within the framework of this Regulation.

(85) This Regulation is without prejudice to Regulation (EEC, Euratom) No 1182/71 of the Council.

(86) Since the objective of this Regulation cannot be sufficiently achieved by the Member States but can rather, by reason of the creation of a legal framework for the proper administration of cross-

border insolvency proceedings, be better achieved at Union level, the Union may adopt measures in accordance with the principle of subsidiarity as set out in Article 5 of the Treaty on European Union. In accordance with the principle of proportionality, as set out in that Article, this Regulation does not go beyond what is necessary in order to achieve that objective.

(87) In accordance with Article 3 and Article 4a(1) of Protocol No 21 on the position of the United Kingdom and Ireland in respect of the area of freedom, security and justice, annexed to the Treaty on European Union and the Treaty on the Functioning of the European Union, the United Kingdom and Ireland have notified their wish to take part in the adoption and application of this Regulation.

(88) In accordance with Articles 1 and 2 of Protocol No 22 on the position of Denmark annexed to the Treaty on European Union and the Treaty on the Functioning of the European Union, Denmark is not taking part in the adoption of this Regulation and is not bound by it or subject to its application.

(89) The European Data Protection Supervisor was consulted and delivered an opinion on 27 March 2013,

HAVE ADOPTED THIS REGULATION:

GENERAL NOTE

This lengthy Preamble (typical of many pieces of EU legislation) gives rise to a number of problems, some of which are discussed by Professor Rajak in [2000] C.F.I.L.R. 180. It has been accepted by the European Court of Justice that a Preamble may be referred to where the text in the body of a Regulation is unclear or imprecise (*Schweizerische Lactina Panchaud AG (Bundesamt für Ernährung und Forstwirtschaft) v Germany (No.346/88)* [1991] 2 C.M.L.R. 283), and this approach reflects that of our own courts to recitals and similar "background" statements. But this Preamble, like many of its kind, goes much further: in some parts, it does simply set out the background, context and aims of the Regulation; in others, it does no more than duplicate substantive provisions in the various articles of the substantive text. However, there are other paragraphs which plainly have legislative effect (e.g. para.14: "This Regulation applies only to proceedings where the centre of the debtor's main interests is located in the Union"); and also many passages (characterised by the word "should") where it is unclear whether the intention is to go beyond the normal function of a Preamble and actually to formulate substantive rules which one would expect to find in the body of the legislation itself. So, e.g. para.9 states that the Regulation "should apply" to insolvency proceedings, "whether the debtor is a natural person or a legal person, a trader or an individual", without any corresponding provision in the articles which follow; and we find the statement that the Regulation applies exclusively to those proceedings listed in Annex A in para.9 of the Preamble, but not repeated in art.1, where one would expect to find it.

The Preamble is more than twice as long as its predecessor. In part, this is because new topics are covered, such as the paragraphs dealing with group insolvencies. In many places the text goes into more detail, sometimes giving legislative force to rulings given in leading cases under the previous legislation.

Consequential amendments were made to domestic law by the Insolvency Amendment (EU 2015/848) Regulations 2017 (SI 2017/702). These changes affect the Insolvency Act 1986, the Insolvency (England and Wales) Rules 2016 and specific provisions in both Scotland and Northern Ireland.

Note: Throughout the Regulation, the draftsman has had trouble with pronouns. The language of the text is not simply gender-neutral, in relation to the people who feature in the insolvencies in question; it has been decided that everyone should have no gender at all! So "he" and "she", "him" and "her" and "his" and "hers" have given way to "it" and "its" in all references to debtors, creditors and even insolvency practitioners! And "who" has yielded place to "which". It can be easy at times to draw the inference that a particular provision applies only to corporate bodies and not to individuals, but we should not fall into this trap: there is ample evidence, taking the Regulation as a whole, that natural as well as legal persons are included throughout the text.

Para.4

The term "activities" is not used in the body of the Regulation, but is found in other EC legislation, e.g. in Directive 80/987 of 20 October 1980 on the approximation of the laws of the Member States relating to the protection of employees in the insolvency of their employer. In this context it is not necessary that the undertaking concerned should have a branch or fixed establishment in the State concerned, so long as it has a "stable economic presence" there: *Sweden v Holmqvist* (C-310/07).

Para.6
This paragraph differs from its predecessor in stating what should be included, rather than being worded restrictively ("should be confined to"). There is an added reference to the co-ordination of proceedings in group insolvencies.

Para.7
ECRIP para.7 referred to the Brussels Convention of 1968. This Convention was replaced by EC Regulation 44/2001 on jurisdiction and the recognition and enforcement of judgments in civil and commercial matters ([2001] OJ L12/1, since recast as Regulation 1215/2012 ([2012] OJ L351/1) as from 10 January 2015), commonly known as the "Judgments Regulation" or "Jurisdiction and Judgments Regulation", and sometimes rather misleadingly as "Brussels 2". Insolvency matters are excluded from the scope of the Brussels Convention and the successor Regulation (see art.1(2)(b) of the latter Regulation). (But not winding-up proceedings as such; thus, matters arising in a members' voluntary winding up are within the Judgments Regulation: *Re Cover Europe Ltd* [2002] EWHC 861 (Ch); [2002] 2 B.C.L.C. 61 and see *Re ARM Asset Backed Securities SA* [2013] EWHC 3351 (Ch); [2014] B.C.C. 252; further proceedings [2014] EWHC 1097 (Ch); [2014] B.C.C. 260 (Insolvency Regulation held to give jurisdiction in relation to petition on the "just and equitable" ground where judge satisfied on the facts that company unable to pay its debts).) However, the Judgments Regulation is declared to apply to certain judgments handed down by a court in the course or "closure" of insolvency proceedings, and compositions approved by a court in such a context, by art.32 of the present Regulation: see the note to art.32, below.

Some rulings on the scope of the two Regulations and the boundary between their jurisdictions are discussed below. In *Byers v Yacht Bull Corp* [2010] EWHC 133 (Ch); [2010] B.C.C. 368 a claim brought by English liquidators as to the beneficial ownership of a yacht was held to fall under the general law and have no close connection with the winding up; accordingly the Judgments Regulation (which gave the French courts jurisdiction) applied. The mere fact that the claimants in the proceedings were insolvency office-holders was not sufficient to disapply that Regulation. See also *Citigate Dewe Rogerson Ltd v Artaban Public Affairs SPRL* [2009] EWHC 1689 (Ch); [2009] B.P.I.R. 1355; *Gibraltar Residential Properties Ltd v Gibralcon 2004 SA* [2010] EWHC 2595 (TCC); *Nickel & Goeldner Spedition GmbH v "Kintra" UAB* (C-157/13) (1 June 2013); *Tchenguiz v Grant Thornton UK LLP* [2015] EWHC 1864 (Comm), and contrast *Polymer Vision R&D Ltd v Van Dooren* [2011] EWHC 2951 (Comm); and see further the note to art.4 below. Neither the EC Regulation nor the Judgments Regulation restricts the jurisdiction of the courts in this country in relation to the sanctioning of schemes of arrangement. This is made clear in the present Regulation by paras 9 and 16 of the Preamble and the exclusion of any mention of reconstruction proceedings in Annex A. Previously, the same position had been established by rulings of the courts, at least in this country: see *Re Rodenstock GmbH* [2011] EWHC 1104 (Ch); [2012] B.C.C. 459; *Primacom Holdings GmbH v Credit Agricole* [2012] EWHC 164 (Ch); [2013] B.C.C. 201 and compare *Re Van Gansewinkel Groep BV* [2015] EWHC 2151 (Ch). See further the notes to paras 9 and 16 and art.6 and IA 1986 s.221.

The relationship between the Insolvency Regulation and EC Regulation 1393/2007 of 13 November 2007 on the service in Member States of judicial and extrajudicial documents in civil or commercial matters (the Service Regulation) is unclear (*Re Anderson Owen Ltd* [2009] EWHC 2837 (Ch); [2010] B.P.I.R. 37). However, it was held in *Re Baillies Ltd* [2012] EWHC 285 (Ch); [2012] B.C.C. 554 that the Service Regulation applies to insolvency proceedings and that compliance with it is mandatory, so that service on a person resident in France which had not been effected in accordance with French law (albeit in compliance with an order of the English court) was not valid.

"Judgment", for the purposes of the present Regulation, has an extended meaning: see the note to art.2(7).

Para.9
There is no counterpart to the first sentence of this paragraph in the body of the Regulation. This is of no significance so far as concerns debtors based in the UK, since our domestic legislation covers all the categories that are mentioned; but it could be material in some civil-law jurisdictions where traditionally bankruptcy has not been available to non-trading individuals.

There is a change from the ECRIP counterpart in that it is stated emphatically that the list of proceedings set out in Annex A is exhaustive. Previously the wording left this question in some doubt. As this edition goes to press, we have a problem as regards the administration of the insolvent estates of deceased persons, and possibly also the winding up, etc. of insolvent partnerships, since these procedures are not mentioned in Annex A. Nor were they listed in Annex A of ECRIP—a fact which was overlooked when supporting legislation was enacted in 2002 (see the Insolvent Partnerships (Amendment) Order 2002 (SI 2002/1308) and the Administration of the Estates of Deceased Persons (Amendment) Order 2002 (SI 2002/1309), both effective 31 May 2002). Unless steps are taken to have amendments made to Annex A before EURIP becomes effective, these two SIs will be left adrift.

The previous para.9 also declared that insolvency proceedings concerning insurers, credit institutions and investment undertakings should be excluded from the scope of the Regulation. This is now covered by art.1(2).

Paras 10–15

These paragraphs set out in some detail the scope of the recast Regulation. They should be read in conjunction with art.1, which defines the essential features of the proceedings concerned. They signify a major change not only in the range and types of procedure that are now included but also in the underlying basis of the legislation: whereas the main emphasis under ECRIP was on liquidation, it has now shifted to rescue and rehabilitation and the survival of the business. It is no longer a necessary feature of the procedure that the debtor should actually be or be deemed to be insolvent. Pre-insolvency restructuring procedures where there is only a likelihood of insolvency qualify for inclusion, as do proceedings of the "debtor in possession" type (if supervised by a court), and also various forms of debt discharge and debt adjustment (para.10). The Regulation also applies to procedures for the grant of a temporary stay of enforcement actions which threaten to hamper restructuring negotiations, and later proceedings continuing such stays (paras 11, 15). (However, it does not seem that there is any English procedure that matches any of the proceedings described in the text (and even if there were, it would have to be listed in Annex A), and so we can probably consider these procedures irrelevant so far as the UK is concerned.)

Para.11

See the notes to paras 20, 21 and art.1(1)(c).

Para.14

The phrase "collective proceedings" is defined in similar, but more detailed, terms in art.2(1).

Para.16

This paragraph, more particularly when read together with para.9, stresses that the Regulation only applies to procedures which are insolvency-based. There is no definition of "insolvency" anywhere in the Regulation. Where a definition is necessary in any particular case, it would fall to be determined by the domestic law of the relevant court. The exclusion of proceedings that are based on general company law supports the view that schemes of reconstruction under Part 26 of the Companies Act 2006 are not within the scope of the Regulation, as is also evidenced by their omission from Annex A. (If further confirmation were needed, we may note that the Commission has proposed that reform should be introduced to improve and harmonise the national laws in this area, and on 22 November 2016 published a proposal for a Directive on preventive restructuring frameworks with this end in view.) The final sentence makes it plain that debt relief orders are similarly excluded. See p.79 above.

Para.17

No such proceedings are recognised in UK law.

Para.19

See the note to art.1(2).

Para.20

The extended meaning of "court", and the provisions where the broader meaning is not applied, are discussed in the note to art.2(6).

Para.21

See the notes to art.2(5) and Annex B.

Para.22

As is explained in the Introductory note to the Regulation, the Regulation does not aim to harmonise the substantive insolvency laws of the Member States or to achieve an insolvency regime on the principle of "unity", where there would be only one proceeding in which the whole of the debtor's assets situated in all the Member States would be administered for the benefit of all the creditors in the Community. Instead, its principal object is to establish an ordered system of administration which allows for separate proceedings to be instituted in several Member States concurrently, with appropriate provisions for mutual recognition, co-operation and co-ordination designed to ensure that they do not compete with one another. Each of the separate proceedings is primarily to be governed by its national law (art.7), but this is subject to certain overriding rules dealing with security interests, contracts of employment, etc. (arts 8–18). In addition, the Regulation allows each separate jurisdiction a degree of ring-fencing, so that (for instance) the rights of creditors or particular classes of creditor in that jurisdiction are respected. The note that further measures relating to the preferential rights of employees should be considered at the next review (possibly inserted at a late stage) hints at unfinished business.

Paras 23, 24
On "main" and "secondary" proceedings, see the note to art.3, and for the definition of "establishment", art.2(10). The "centre of main interests" (COMI) is discussed in the note to para.25.

Paragraph 24 confirms the decision in *Burgo Group SpA* (C-327/13) [2015] B.C.C. 33.

Para.25
The entire focus is on the debtor's centre of main interests. There is no reference to the nationality, domicile, residence or physical presence of an individual debtor or to the place of incorporation of a company (except that these terms linked with the presumptions in art.3(1)). It is plain from this statement that the Regulation does not apply to a debtor whose centre of main interests is outside the EU: in that event, the courts of the UK may continue to assert their traditional wide jurisdiction (see the notes to IA 1986 ss.220 and 265); and in such a case the Regulation will not apply even where there are contemporaneous insolvency proceedings in more than one Member State. On the other hand, if the COMI is within the UK, the Regulation applies even where the debtor is a national of a non-EU country or a company incorporated in such a country (see *Re BRAC Rent-a-Car International Inc* [2003] EWHC 128 (Ch); [2003] B.C.C. 249, discussed in the note to art.3 below); while if the COMI is in another Member State, any proceedings instituted in the UK can only be "territorial" or "secondary" proceedings and the jurisdiction will be limited as prescribed by art.3(2)–(4).

The Regulation does not state, but rather takes it for granted, that the insolvency must have a cross-border element. This can readily be inferred from the title and para.3 of the Preamble.

Where the debtor has interests in more than one Member State and there is doubt or a dispute as to which is the centre of main interests, para.65 of the Preamble indicates that this should be settled on a "first seised" basis. The Irish High Court faced a conflict on this issue in *Re Eurofood IFSC Ltd* [2004] B.C.C. 383, in relation to the Irish subsidiary of the Italian Parmalat group of companies. After a provisional liquidator had been appointed to the subsidiary but before the hearing of the winding-up petition an Italian court made an order purporting to put it into "extraordinary administration", declaring that the subsidiary's COMI was in Italy. At the time when the provisional liquidator was appointed, all the evidence had pointed unquestionably to its COMI being in Ireland, but steps had since been taken by the holding company's administrator to appoint Italian directors in an attempt to move its COMI to Italy, and the Italian court was persuaded that this had been achieved. The Irish court nevertheless made a winding-up order, declaring that the appointment of the provisional liquidator constituted the "opening" of proceedings, which were main proceedings. The later purported decisions of the Italian court could not alter the fact that main proceedings (which under the Regulation were bound to be recognised throughout the EU) had already been opened. The Supreme Court of Ireland upheld this ruling [2004] IESC 45; [2005] B.C.C. 999, but primarily on the grounds that the Italian court had not followed fair procedures, with the consequence that its decision should not be recognised on public policy grounds.

The case was referred to the European Court of Justice (C-341/04), where the Advocate General's opinion is reported at [2005] B.C.C. 1,021 and the judgment of the Court at [2006] B.C.C. 397. In upholding the decisions of the Irish courts, the ECJ has firmly endorsed the "first seised" principle. It ruled not only that the Italian court was out of order in purporting to override the Irish court's finding that the COMI of Eurofoods was in Ireland and that in consequence its proceedings were "main" proceedings, but also that any challenge to this decision could only be brought before the Irish court itself and not in any other Member State. (Compare *Re Eurodis Electron plc* [2011] EWHC 1025 (Ch); [2012] B.C.C. 57, where a company whose COMI was in England had (it appeared wrongly) been wound up and dissolved in Belgium: the court in England had no power to declare that the Belgian court's winding-up order was invalid.)

In *McGuinness v McFeely* (unreported, 15 June 2012) Proudman J stated that the first court to open proceedings should be recognised by other Member States as having jurisdiction to decide the question of the location of the debtor's COMI, in accordance with the Preamble para.65: in this context the mere presentation of a bankruptcy petition did not amount to the "opening" of proceedings; rather, the term referred to the procedure (such as the making of a bankruptcy order) which resulted in the divesture of the debtor's powers of management.

The "first seised" principle also applies under the "Judgments Regulation" (the successor to the Brussels Convention of 1968: see the note to para.7 above). For a case under that Regulation, see *Kolden Holdens Ltd v Rodette Commerce Ltd* [2008] EWCA Civ 10; [2008] 1 B.C.L.C. 481.

Para.26
Once it is settled that the courts of a Member State have jurisdiction under the Regulation, it is still necessary to satisfy the requirements of the national law.

Para.27
See the note to art.4. The word "court" (which we must assume is used in its extended sense: see the note to art.2(6)) poses problems in many out-of-court appointments.

Paras 28–32

These paragraphs throw further light on the topics discussed in the note to art.3.

Para.33

The proceedings may, however, proceed as "territorial", if the requirements of art.3(4) are satisfied: see *Hans Brochier Holdings Ltd v Exner* [2006] EWHC 2594 (Ch); [2007] B.C.C. 127. The court may also, in an appropriate case, make a winding-up order under IA 1986 s.221(5)(a): *Re Eurodis Electron plc* [2011] EWHC 1025 (Ch); [2012] B.C.C. 57.

Para.34

This is confirmed by art.5.

Para.35

See the note to art.6.

Para.36

This paragraph contemplates the making of "provisional and protective measures" in rather convoluted language, which is fortunately clarified by the substantive provision in art.52. See the note to that article.

Para.37

This refers forward to the remarkably restrictive conditions laid down for the opening of insolvency proceedings, other than main proceedings, by art.3(2)–(4): see the note to that article.

Para.38

This paragraph, confirmed by art.37(1), is intended to ensure that the office-holder in "main" proceedings may himself institute secondary proceedings in any other Member State where the debtor has assets.

Para.39

This paragraph, supplemented in more detail by paras 10–15 and 66–72, looks forward to arts 7–18.

Paras 40–44

In authorising the use of undertakings, given by the office-holder in main proceedings, to avoid the formality and expense of opening secondary proceedings in other jurisdictions, the Regulation builds on a model which had already been used informally with success in some reported cases. The prescriptive approach laid down by the Regulation may detract somewhat from its appeal, but enables the consent of creditors to be secured by a majority vote. See the note to art.36.

Para.45

See the note to art.38, where this proposal is developed.

Paras 48–62

Paragraph 20 of the Preamble to the original Regulation urged the office-holders in concurrent insolvency proceedings involving the same debtor to cooperate closely, to coordinate the proceedings and to communicate information with each other. This was expressed in very general terms without going into any detail, apart from making it clear that the practitioner in the main proceedings should have the dominant role. We now have fifteen paragraphs (and 27 articles) devoted to these topics! The greater part of this new material focuses on a subject which was not addressed by ECRIP and had attracted considerable criticism on that account—namely, cross-border insolvencies involving companies in the same group. In the new Regulation, a very formal structured scheme is made available for the establishment of "group coordination proceedings", coupled with the appointment of a "coordinator", separate from the office-holders in the various proceedings, to oversee matters generally and make recommendations for a group coordination plan. This innovation, while welcome, may prove to be unattractive because of its formality and expense, when compared with the informal arrangements which have been used with considerable success up until now. It is also open to criticism because of the narrow definition of "group" in art.2(13). The relevant articles are arts 41–44 and 56–77.

Para.63

The Regulation distinguishes between at least three categories of creditor. A Venn diagram would be helpful! First, we have those creditors identified in this paragraph, which do not have a specific label. A sub-group of this category are defined as "foreign creditors" by art.2(12): these are those based in a Member State other than that of the opening of the particular proceedings (whether main, territorial or secondary). These may be contrasted with "local creditors", a term defined in art.2(11) and used to refer to those based in the State of the opening of the proceedings whose claim arose from or in connection with the operation of an establishment situated in a Member State other than that of the COMI. The term is used, we must presume in this sense, in para.45 of the Preamble and arts 38(2) and

51(1). This leaves a residual category, not mentioned anywhere in the Regulation, namely those based outside the EU and those resident or otherwise present within the EU who fall outside the habitual residence, etc. requirements (unless they come within the "operation of an establishment" test). Note that this category will not benefit from the statutory inclusion of revenue and social security authorities. It is not clear whether Denmark is to be regarded as a Member State in this context. See further the note to art.2(11), (12).

Para.64
Articles 54 and 55, which implement this requirement, are expressed to apply only to "foreign" creditors (as this term is defined in art.2(12), i.e. EU-based creditors other than those whose residence, etc. is within the jurisdiction of the proceedings in question). The right of other foreign-based creditors to prove and to be notified of their rights is left to be determined by the local law. The Regulation referred to is the "Service Regulation", which prescribes rather more formal requirements for the service of commercial documents as between different Member States.
    See the notes to arts 54, 55.

Para.65
The automatic recognition throughout the Community of the orders and judgments of the courts of a Member State and of the authority of the office-holder in any insolvency proceedings is one of the central principles of the Regulation. Articles 19, 20 and 22 carry this objective into effect.

Paras 66–72
The rules relating to the applicable law in insolvency proceedings which have a cross-border dimension within the Union are set out in arts 7 et seq. The basic rule is that the law of the State under which the proceedings have been instituted is prima facie to be applied, presumably including its own conflict of laws rules (art.7); but arts 8–18 contain a uniform set of rules prescribing exceptions to this general rule. A security interest (such as a mortgage), for instance, over an asset situated in another Member State is to be governed by the law of that State rather than that of the proceedings; and a debtor who is entitled to a right of set-off under the law applicable to his claim may assert that right even where such a right is not recognised by the law governing the insolvency proceedings. The Directive referred to in para.71 deals with settlement finality in payment and securities settlement systems. For more detailed comments, see the notes to arts 8–18.

Para.75
Article 28 gives substantive effect to these requirements.

Paras 76–80
The relevant articles are not yet in force. Article 24 (establishment of insolvency registers) is to be brought into force on 26 June 2018 and art.25 (interconnection of insolvency registers via the European e-Justice Portal) on 26 June 2019.

Paras 87–88
The UK (including Gibraltar) and Ireland have opted in to the Regulation, but Denmark has opted out, at least for the time being.

CHAPTER I—GENERAL PROVISIONS

Article 1

Scope

1. This Regulation shall apply to public collective proceedings, including interim proceedings, which are based on laws relating to insolvency and in which, for the purpose of rescue, adjustment of debt, reorganisation or liquidation:

(a) a debtor is totally or partially divested of its assets and an insolvency practitioner is appointed;

(b) the assets and affairs of a debtor are subject to control or supervision by a court; or

(c) a temporary stay of individual enforcement proceedings is granted by a court or by operation of law, in order to allow for negotiations between the debtor and its creditors, provided that the proceedings in which the stay is granted provide for suitable measures to protect the general body of creditors, and, where no agreement is reached, are preliminary to one of the proceedings referred to in point (a) or (b).

Where the proceedings referred to in this paragraph may be commenced in situations where there is only a likelihood of insolvency, their purpose shall be to avoid the debtor's insolvency or the cessation of the debtor's business activities.

The proceedings referred to in this paragraph are listed in Annex A.

2. This Regulation shall not apply to proceedings referred to in paragraph 1 that concern:

(a)   insurance undertakings;

(b)   credit institutions;

(c)   investment firms and other firms, institutions and undertakings to the extent that they are covered by Directive 2001/24/EC; or

(d)   collective investment undertakings.

GENERAL NOTE

The scope of the Regulation is defined by this article, as amplified by arts 2–3 and Annex A. So far as concerns UK insolvency procedures, it is clear that all forms of receivership are excluded, since receivership is not a "collective" procedure administered for the benefit of all concerned, or even all creditors. (On "interim receivers", see the note to Annex B.)

Winding up subject to the supervision of the court has, of course, been abolished in the UK.

The Regulation throughout makes the fundamental assumption that its application is confined to "insolvency" proceedings (or proceedings where there is a "likelihood" of insolvency); but there is nowhere any definition of "insolvency" or an equivalent term, and no guidance given as to how it is to be determined whether a debtor is insolvent. One area in which this issue may arise is where a company is the subject of proceedings on the "just and equitable" ground under IA 1986 s.122(1)(g). In *Re ARM Asset Backed Securities SA* [2013] EWHC 3351 (Ch); [2014] B.C.C. 252; further proceedings [2014] EWHC 1097 (Ch); [2014] B.C.C. 260 the judgment proceeded on the assumption that if the court was satisfied that the Luxembourg company in question was unable to pay its debts, the Regulation gave the English court jurisdiction under s.122(1)(g). However, if the petition is brought on public interest grounds under IA 1986 s.124A (or a corresponding provision in other legislation), the Regulation does not apply, even if the company concerned is insolvent: *Re Marann Brooks CSV Ltd* [2003] B.C.C. 239.

Art.1(1)
See the note to the Preamble, para.9: there is an increased emphasis on rescue and rehabilitation.

The word "court" is used in its judicial sense (art.2(6)(1)).

Although it is not stated here, the list of proceedings in Annex A is exhaustive (Preamble, para.9).

The exclusion of insurance undertakings, etc. is anticipated by the Preamble, para.19. These bodies have their own special legislative or regulatory regimes and are the subject of separate EU Directives and domestic legislation: see EC Directives 2001/17 (insurance undertakings) and 2001/24 (credit institutions). The former has been implemented by the Insurance (Reorganisation and Winding up) Regulations 2004 (SI 2004/353, replacing SI 2003/1102, effective 18 February 2004), and separately, for Lloyd's, by SI 2005/1998, as from 10 August 2005. The latter has been implemented by the Credit Institutions (Reorganisation and Winding up) Regulations 2004 (SI 2004/1045), effective 5 May 2004. The broad effect of the Insurance Regulations is that a UK court will not be able to make an administration or winding-up order or appoint a provisional liquidator to an insurance undertaking which is authorised in another EEA Member State, and such an insurer cannot enter into a voluntary arrangement under UK law. In the winding up of UK insurance undertakings, priority is now given to insurance claims over other debts. However, the focus of the relevant directive is primarily on direct insurance, rather than reinsurance, and the Regulations do not apply to undertakings engaged purely in reinsurance. Note that both the Insurance Regulations and the Credit Institutions Regulations apply throughout the EEA, in contrast with the EURIP which is restricted to the EU (excluding Denmark). The Credit Institutions Regulations were successfully invoked by the representative in Icelandic insolvency proceedings, applying Icelandic law to the exclusion of the rules applicable under IA 1986 in Scottish administration proceedings, in *Landsbanki Islands hf v Mills* [2010] CSOH 100; [2011] 2 B.C.L.C. 437. Accordingly, the extinguishment of a claim pursuant to the Icelandic proceedings debarred the claimant from initiating proceedings in Scotland to recover the debt. However, on appeal (*Heritable Bank plc v Winding-up Board of Landsbanki Islands HF* [2011] CSIH 61; [2012] 2 B.C.L.C. 21; affirmed by the Supreme Court [2013] UKSC 13; [2013] 1 B.C.L.C. 465) it was held that this ruling only prevented the claimant from taking *positive* action: it was still open to it to plead its claim by way of set-off in Scottish insolvency proceedings. See also *Rawlinson & Hunter Trustees SA v Kaupthing Bank HF* [2011] EWHC 566 (Comm); [2012] B.C.C. 441 (where it was held that the Regulations did not apply and that English law should apply to the proceedings); *Re Phoenix Kapitaldienst GmbH* [2012] EWHC 62 (Ch) and *Tchenguiz v Grant Thornton UK LLP* [2015] EWHC 1864 (Comm). (Note that in *Lornamead Acquisitions Ltd v Kaupthing Bank HF* [2011] EWHC 2611 (Comm) *Rawlinson* was followed in the interests of judicial comity, but doubts were expressed about the ruling in that case.) Other decisions on the Credit Institutions Regulations indicate that there is a close parallel with EURIP: in *LBI hf v Kepler Capita Markets SA* (C-85/12, 24 October 2013) the ECJ was required to consider whether a moratorium granted by an Icelandic court, which was later deemed by statute under the domestic law of that country to constitute winding-up proceedings, came within the scope of the Directive as "reorganisation and winding up measures taken by administrative or judicial authorities". The ruling illustrates a purposive approach giving effect to the objective of ensuring the recognition of proceedings across Member States. In *Isis Investments Ltd v Oscatello Investments Ltd* [2013] EWCA Civ 1493 the court relied on the Virgós-Schmit Report as an aid to the interpretation of the term "pending lawsuit" in the Credit Institutions Directive.

Article 2

Definitions

For the purposes of this Regulation:

(1) 'collective proceedings' means proceedings which include all or a significant part of a debtor's creditors, provided that, in the latter case, the proceedings do not affect the claims of creditors which are not involved in them;

(2) 'collective investment undertakings' means undertakings for collective investment in transferable securities (UCITS) as defined in Directive 2009/65/EC of the European Parliament and of the Council and alternative investment funds (AIFs) as defined in Directive 2011/61/EU of the European Parliament and of the Council;

(3) 'debtor in possession' means a debtor in respect of which insolvency proceedings have been opened which do not necessarily involve the appointment of an insolvency practitioner or the complete transfer of the rights and duties to administer the debtor's assets to an insolvency practitioner and where, therefore, the debtor remains totally or at least partially in control of its assets and affairs;

(4) 'insolvency proceedings' means the proceedings listed in Annex A;

(5) 'insolvency practitioner' means any person or body whose function, including on an interim basis, is to:

    (i) verify and admit claims submitted in insolvency proceedings;

    (ii) represent the collective interest of the creditors;

    (iii) administer, either in full or in part, assets of which the debtor has been divested;

    (iv) liquidate the assets referred to in point (iii); or

    (v) supervise the administration of the debtor's affairs.

The persons and bodies referred to in the first subparagraph are listed in Annex B;

(6) 'court' means:

    (i) in points (b) and (c) of Article 1(1), Article 4(2), Articles 5 and 6, Article 21(3), point (j) of Article 24(2), Articles 36 and 39, and Articles 61 to 77, the judicial body of a Member State;

    (ii) in all other articles, the judicial body or any other competent body of a Member State empowered to open insolvency proceedings, to confirm such opening or to take decisions in the course of such proceedings;

(7) 'judgment opening insolvency proceedings' includes:

   (i) the decision of any court to open insolvency proceedings or to confirm the opening of such proceedings; and

   (ii) the decision of a court to appoint an insolvency practitioner;

(8) 'the time of the opening of proceedings' means the time at which the judgment opening insolvency proceedings becomes effective, regardless of whether the judgment is final or not;

(9) 'the Member State in which assets are situated' means, in the case of:

   (i) registered shares in companies other than those referred to in point (ii), the Member State within the territory of which the company having issued the shares has its registered office;

   (ii) financial instruments, the title to which is evidenced by entries in a register or account maintained by or on behalf of an intermediary ('book entry securities'), the Member State in which the register or account in which the entries are made is maintained;

   (iii) cash held in accounts with a credit institution, the Member State indicated in the account's IBAN, or, for cash held in accounts with a credit institution which does not have an IBAN, the Member State in which the credit institution holding the account has its central administration or, where the account is held with a branch, agency or other establishment, the Member State in which the branch, agency or other establishment is located;

   (iv) property and rights, ownership of or entitlement to which is entered in a public register other than those referred to in point (i), the Member State under the authority of which the register is kept;

   (v) European patents, the Member State for which the European patent is granted;

   (vi) copyright and related rights, the Member State within the territory of which the owner of such rights has its habitual residence or registered office;

   (vii) tangible property, other than that referred to in points (i) to (iv), the Member State within the territory of which the property is situated;

   (viii) claims against third parties, other than those relating to assets referred to in point (iii), the Member State within the territory of which the third party required to meet the claims has the centre of its main interests, as determined in accordance with Article 3(1);

(10) 'establishment' means any place of operations where a debtor carries out or has carried out in the 3-month period prior to the request to open main insolvency proceedings a non-transitory economic activity with human means and assets;

(11) 'local creditor' means a creditor whose claims against a debtor arose from or in connection with the operation of an establishment situated in a Member State other than the Member State in which the centre of the debtor's main interests is located;

(12) 'foreign creditor' means a creditor which has its habitual residence, domicile or registered office in a Member State other than the State of the opening of proceedings, including the tax authorities and social security authorities of Member States;

(13) 'group of companies' means a parent undertaking and all its subsidiary undertakings;

(14) 'parent undertaking' means an undertaking which controls, either directly or indirectly, one or more subsidiary undertakings. An undertaking which prepares consolidated financial statements in accordance with Directive 2013/34/EU of the European Parliament and of the Council shall be deemed to be a parent undertaking.

GENERAL NOTE

This article contains the definitions of most of the terms that are used in a technical sense in the Regulation. One perhaps surprising omission is "Member State", which is defined in comparable Regulations (e.g. the Service Regulation) as meaning every EU Member except Denmark (art.1(3)). We may possibly infer that where the term is used in this Regulation, as in the definition of "foreign creditor" below, Denmark is not excluded.

Art.2(1)

See the notes to the Preamble, para.9 and art.1(1).

Art.2(2)
In *Byers v Yacht Bull Corp* [2010] EWHC 133 (Ch); [2010] B.C.C. 368 it was held that the exclusion for investment undertakings related not to such undertakings generally but only to undertakings which provided "services involving the holding of funds or securities for third parties".

Art.2(5)
The previous regulation unhelpfully used the term "liquidator" to refer to the office-holder in every type of insolvency proceeding—even a trustee in bankruptcy! The expression now chosen reflects the greater emphasis on rescue and rehabilitation in the new Regulation. There is no indication whether the list in Annex B is exhaustive, but it is likely to be so construed. The term "interim receiver", which did not appear in the corresponding Annex to ECRIP, must refer to a receiver appointed by the court incidentally to one of the procedures listed in Annex A, and has no connection with receivers appointed to enforce a security.

Art.2(6)
Curiously, the definition of "court" refers only to articles—there is no mention of the Preamble, although the word occurs there in a number of places.

Article 2(6)(ii) reflects the fact that insolvency proceedings do not necessarily involve the intervention of a judicial authority and, since in the definition of "judgment" the word "court" is to be understood in this extended sense, the language of the Regulation must be read with whatever modification is necessary to cover all of the extra-judicial procedures listed in the UK entry in Annex A.

Accordingly, a creditors' voluntary winding up is within the Regulation, and in that context "court" means the members in general meeting (for it is that body, and not the meeting of creditors, whose resolution is determinative); and "judgment" must be read as meaning the resolution.

Article 19 declares that a "judgment opening insolvency proceedings" shall be accorded recognition without further formality in all other Member States. Article 19 unhelpfully refers to such a judgment being "handed down by a court"; but any difficulty that this phrase might create is met by the requirement in Annex A that a creditors' voluntary winding up should be confirmed by the court (plainly, "court" is here to be understood in its normal sense). Provision is made for such confirmation by IR 2016 r.21.5. But the court's confirmation serves only an evidentiary purpose; it is the members' resolution that is the "judgment opening the insolvency proceedings".

On similar reasoning, the body which is to be taken as the "court" for the purposes of a CVA or IVA is the creditor's meeting: see IA 1986 ss.5(2)(a) and 260(2)(a), and the resolution as the "judgment": see *Re The Salvage Association* [2003] EWHC 1028 (Ch); [2003] B.C.C. 504, at 19 et seq. There is no mention in the Regulation of any need to have such a resolution confirmed by the court: presumably it is assumed that since the outcome of the creditors' meeting will have been reported to the court, it would be possible for a certificate sufficient to meet the purposes of the Regulation to be issued by the court without the formality of confirmation. It would have been helpful if some provision dealing with this point had been included in the Rules.

Similar comments apply to administration, where a company is put into administration by the holder of a floating charge or the company or its directors without a court order under IA 1986 Sch.B1 paras 14 or 22. The "court" will be the person or persons making the appointment, and the "judgment" will be the filing of the notice of appointment under paras 18 or 29, as the case may be: this will also determine the time of the opening of the insolvency proceedings (paras 19, 31). Again, there is no reference in the legislation to any need for confirmation by the court. Some disquiet has been expressed at the lack of clear legislative guidance on these points and in consequence it has been suggested that, in order to avoid uncertainty and misunderstanding in other EU jurisdictions (and a fortiori in foreign jurisdictions not covered by the Regulation), it may be prudent to have the administrator appointed by the court rather than under paras 14 or 22. However, so far as concerns other Member States, the specific mention in Annex A of out-of-court appointments should allay any doubts. Even so, it is likely to be helpful to foreign office-holders and creditors for the court to provide a supplementary order (as was done in *Re MG Rover España SA* [2006] B.C.C. 599), explaining the nature of the insolvency proceeding and the powers of the office-holder. (This case is important also for the view expressed that Sch.B1 para.66 can empower administrators to make payments to employees under the national laws of EU Member States over and above any entitlement they might have under English law, so possibly avoiding the need to open secondary proceedings in each national territory.) See also *Re Collins & Aikman Europe Ltd* [2006] EWHC 1343 (Ch); [2006] B.C.C. 861 and *Re Nortel Networks SA (No.2)* [2009] EWHC 1482 (Ch); [2010] B.C.C. 21.

Even when we have made all the necessary mental adjustments in order to accommodate our extra-judicial appointments to the wording of the Regulation, there is no escape from the fact that the draftsman has taken a judicial procedure as the norm and has not made allowance for many everyday situations in practice in this jurisdiction, such as the out-of-court appointment of an administrator by the holder of a floating charge or a pre-pack administration. There is an assumption in many places that the "judgment" will follow a hearing of some sort, with an opportunity to give notice to creditors, that the appointment of the office-holder will follow the hearing or the judgment, and so on, and that there will be rules providing for such procedures. We will be able to make the Regulation work in practice only by turning a blind eye to some of these niceties.

Art.2(7), (8)

These paragraphs throw light on the meaning of the expression "the opening of proceedings", which could well be a source of confusion. It is to be taken as referring to whatever step in the proceedings marks the effective beginning of the particular insolvency regime: liquidation, bankruptcy, administration, etc. Subject to the caveat below, it should not be confused with any earlier act, such as the filing in court of a petition for winding up or a bankruptcy or administration order, or with the "commencement" of a winding up as defined by IA 1986 ss.86, 129. It follows that the event which counts should be the court order or, in the case of a voluntary winding up, CVA or IVA, the resolution of the appropriate body. (Compare *McGuiness v McFeely* (unreported, 15 June 2012).) In an administration where the appointment is made out of court, it will be the time of the filing of the notice of appointment under IA 1986 Sch.B1 paras 18 or 29, as noted above. In *Re Eurofood IFSC Ltd* (C-341/04) [2006] Ch. 508; [2006] B.C.C. 397 the appointment of a provisional liquidator was held to constitute the "opening" of proceedings—confirmed by the phrase in art.2(f) "whether the judgment is final". Similarly, the appointment of a "preliminary liquidator" under German law was held to be the "opening" of insolvency proceedings in *Westwood Shipping Lines Inc v Universal Schiffahrts GmbH* [2012] EWHC 1394 (Comm). The one exceptional case would appear to be the insolvent estate of a deceased person, where the court's order is related back to the date of death (Administration of Insolvent Estates of Deceased Persons Order 1986 Sch.1 Pt II para.12).

However, the above interpretation of art.2(8) should be read subject to the caveat that in the opinion of the Advocate General in the *Eurofood* case ([2006] Ch. 508 at 511; [2005] B.C.C. 1,021) the time of the opening of proceedings might be taken to be the time filing of a winding-up petition because that is the key factor in the definition of the "commencement" of the winding up in IA 1986 s.129(2). (The ECJ found it unnecessary to rule on this point.) It is submitted that this is an unwarranted confusion and that the contention cannot be correct (see the note to IA 1986 s.129(2)), in view of the fact that the presentation of a petition does not of itself involve any divestment of the debtor company's assets, even retrospectively.

The concept of the "opening" of insolvency proceedings is critically examined by Gabriel Moss Q.C. in [2008] 21 Insolv. Int. 1.

See also the ruling of the Dutch court in *Re BenQ Mobile Holding BV* [2008] B.C.C. 489, noted by Paulus (2007) 20 Insolv. Int. 87.

There may be some significance in the use of the word "time", rather than "date": see the note to IA 1986 s.86. Contrast the use of "moment" in art.19.1.

Art.2(9)

This definition is much more detailed that that in ECRIP. Although the paragraph may not cover all possible forms of property (e.g. some non-registrable intangibles), it should avoid many conflict of laws questions that might otherwise arise. The concept is discussed by the CJEU in *Comité d'Entreprise de Nortel Networks SA v Rogeau* (C-649/13) [2015] B.C.C. 490. Where there are both main and secondary proceedings, the courts in both countries have concurrent jurisdiction to determine questions relating to assets situated in the State of the secondary proceedings.

Art.2(10)

This concept is the key factor in establishing jurisdiction to open territorial or secondary proceedings. See the note to art.3.

Art.2(11), (12)

It might be supposed that these terms, taken together, would constitute all the debtor's creditors, or all of the creditors in a particular insolvency proceeding. But this is not the case. Note the difference in wording: "local creditors", as defined, are linked with "the operation of an establishment", without any reference to habitual residence, etc. and vice versa as regards "foreign creditors". Note also that the definitions are worded by reference to the State of the opening of proceedings in the former case, and to the COMI in the second. There will be some creditors who fall within neither definition, and some within both—even in respect of the same debt! It is likely also that the phrase "local creditors" has been used at times in a general sense without regard to this more restricted definition. See further the note to para.63 of the Preamble.

Art.2(13), (14).

The recast regulation, in contrast with its predecessor, makes detailed provision in Ch.5 for cross-border insolvencies involving members of a corporate group. However, the scope of these provisions is limited by this rather narrow definition of a group.

Article 3

International jurisdiction

1. The courts of the Member State within the territory of which the centre of the debtor's main interests is situated shall have jurisdiction to open insolvency proceedings ('main insolvency proceedings'). The centre of main interests shall be the place where the debtor conducts the administration of its interests on a regular basis and which is ascertainable by third parties.

In the case of a company or legal person, the place of the registered office shall be presumed to be the centre of its main interests in the absence of proof to the contrary. That presumption shall only apply if the registered office has not been moved to another Member State within the 3-month period prior to the request for the opening of insolvency proceedings.

In the case of an individual exercising an independent business or professional activity, the centre of main interests shall be presumed to be that individual's principal place of business in the absence of proof to the contrary. That presumption shall only apply if the individual's principal place of business has not been moved to another Member State within the 3-month period prior to the request for the opening of insolvency proceedings.

In the case of any other individual, the centre of main interests shall be presumed to be the place of the individual's habitual residence in the absence of proof to the contrary. This presumption shall only apply if the habitual residence has not been moved to another Member State within the 6-month period prior to the request for the opening of insolvency proceedings.

2. Where the centre of the debtor's main interests is situated within the territory of a Member State, the courts of another Member State shall have jurisdiction to open insolvency proceedings against that debtor only if it possesses an establishment within the territory of that other Member State. The effects of those proceedings shall be restricted to the assets of the debtor situated in the territory of the latter Member State.

3. Where insolvency proceedings have been opened in accordance with paragraph 1, any proceedings opened subsequently in accordance with paragraph 2 shall be secondary insolvency proceedings.

4. The territorial insolvency proceedings referred to in paragraph 2 may only be opened prior to the opening of main insolvency proceedings in accordance with paragraph 1 where

   (a) insolvency proceedings under paragraph 1 cannot be opened because of the conditions laid down by the law of the Member State within the territory of which the centre of the debtor's main interests is situated; or

   (b) the opening of territorial insolvency proceedings is requested by:

      (i) a creditor whose claim arises from or is in connection with the operation of an establishment situated within the territory of the Member State where the opening of territorial proceedings is requested; or

      (ii) a public authority which, under the law of the Member State within the territory of which the establishment is situated, has the right to request the opening of insolvency proceedings.

When main insolvency proceedings are opened, the territorial insolvency proceedings shall become secondary insolvency proceedings.

GENERAL NOTE

The Regulation only applies where the centre of the debtor's main interests is located in the EU—although he (or it) need not be an EU national: see the Preamble para.25 and *Re BRAC Rent-A-Car Inc* [2003] EWHC 128 (Ch); [2003] B.C.C. 248 (followed in *Re Buccament Bay Ltd* [2014] EWHC 3130 (Ch)). It also applies only where the debtor has assets (and, usually, creditors) in more than one Member State. And it has nothing to say about assets situated outside the EU, or creditors resident or domiciled outside the Union. In any of the situations not covered by the Regulation, a Member State is free to apply its national law (including, in the case of the UK, the CBIR). It is not essential that the case should involve a cross-border element as between two or more Member States: in *Schmid v Hertel* (C-328/12); [2015] B.C.C. 25 it was confirmed that the Regulation applied where the defendant resided in a non-EU jurisdiction (Switzerland). Article 3 confers jurisdiction on the courts of the Member State of the opening of main proceedings, not only in matters of insolvency law *stricto sensu*, but also in regard to matters "directly derived from and closely related to" the insolvency proceedings: see the Preamble, para.35 and art.6 (confirming the rulings in *Seagon v Deko Marty Belgium NV* (C-339/07) [2009] 1 W.L.R. 2168; [2009] B.C.C. 347 and *Schmid v Hertel* (above); *H v HK* (C-295/13, 4 December 2014 CJEU)).

On whether the proceedings in question qualified as "insolvency proceedings" for the purposes of what is now art.3 see *Tunkers France* (C-641/16) EU:C:2017:847. The proceedings in question were concerned with an allegation of unfair competition made against the assignee of a business which was undergoing insolvency were found *not* to be insolvency proceedings and therefore could not be main proceedings for the purposes of the Regulation.

Article 3(1) deals with the jurisdiction to open "main" proceedings and art.3(2)–(4) with the jurisdiction for "secondary" and "territorial" proceedings. Non-main proceedings are "secondary" if they are opened after the opening of main proceedings, and "territorial" if they precede the opening of main proceedings. If main proceedings are opened at a time when any territorial proceedings are in existence, those proceedings "become" secondary proceedings (art.3(4)). Looking at the picture from another angle, there is no difference between territorial and secondary proceedings apart from the more stringent conditions imposed on the *opening* of territorial proceedings imposed by art.3(4). (Under the former Regulation, territorial proceedings could only be for winding up. This limitation is not continued.)

The reference in art.3(1) and (2) to "the courts of a Member State" could give rise to difficulties where it is sought to put a company into creditors' voluntary liquidation where the company is incorporated in one State but has its centre of main interests in another. The resolution would have to be passed by the company's shareholders in accordance with the law of the State of incorporation, but even assuming that the meeting was held in the "main" Member State it would call for some ingenuity to construe "the court of that other Member State" as meaning that meeting. Some of these questions arose in *Re TXU Europe German Finance BV* [2005] B.C.C. 90. Two companies registered respectively in Ireland and the Netherlands had their COMIs in England. Being satisfied that the law of both Ireland and the Netherlands made provision for a procedure equivalent to a special resolution and that the counterparts to the registrar of companies in each country were willing to recognise the winding up for the purposes of the dissolution of their companies, Mr Registrar Baister, in exercise of the discretion conferred by IR 1986 r.7.62(5) [IR 2016 r.21.5], made an order confirming resolutions which had been passed for a voluntary winding up of the two companies (which, in the circumstances, was a creditors' winding up). The court accepted that the liquidations would be conducted in accordance with English insolvency law, but did so only on the basis of assurances given by the liquidator that foreign creditors would be treated fairly.

Article 34 provides that the fact that main proceedings have been opened is to be taken as conclusive evidence of the debtor's insolvency in any later secondary proceedings.

On the primacy of art.3 see *Wiemer & Trachte GmbH v Tadzher* (C-296/17) EU:C:2018:902; [2019] B.P.I.R. 252. This case is discussed in the note to art.21 below.

Art.3(1)

This article differs from its predecessor in that the definition of the debtor's centre of main interests (COMI) is removed from the Preamble and set out in the body of the Regulation. It is also more detailed, in that it sets out the presumptions to be applied in the varying circumstances described in the later paragraphs and the different time limits applicable in each case.

These presumptions are, of course, rebuttable. Where the request for opening the proceedings falls within the particular time limit, the location of the COMI is to be ascertained purely on the basis of the evidence available, viewed objectively, without reference to any presumption. The time-limits do not impose a ban on the freedom of the debtor to move his COMI, as has sometimes been assumed. Unlike the definition of "establishment" in art.2(h), there is here no express reference to a business or "economic" activity.

The meaning of the term "centre of main interests" has been the subject of judicial consideration in a number of cases. (See the series of articles by Professor I.F. Fletcher in (2005) 18 Insolv. Int. 49, 68, 85, which include a discussion of some unreported cases, and the wide-ranging review by G. McCormack in [2009] Cambridge LJ 169.) Since the Regulation applies throughout the EU and should be interpreted consistently in all jurisdictions, the decisions of courts in other Member States may be relevant (*Interedil Srl v Fallimento Interedil Srl* (C-396/09) 20 October 2011, [2012] B.C.C. 851).

In *Skjevesland v Geveran Trading Co Ltd* [2002] EWHC 2898 (Ch); [2003] B.C.C. 391; affirming [2003] B.C.C. 209, the debtor was a banker domiciled in Switzerland who had homes in several European countries but had last lived in England over two years ago. He divided his time for business purposes between Switzerland and Spain and, although he spent more time in Spain, about 90 per cent of his economic activities were carried out in Switzerland. It was held that his centre of main interests was in Switzerland. The judge referred to the Virgós-Schmit Report (EC Council document 6500/DRS 8 (CFC)), a commentary on the draft EC Bankruptcy Convention (the forerunner of the EC Regulation), where the importance was emphasised of jurisdiction in international insolvency matters being based "on a place known to the debtor's potential creditors". The finding that the COMI was in Switzerland (and accordingly not within the EU) meant that the Regulation did not apply. A bankruptcy order could therefore be made under IA 1986 s.265(1)(c), based on his residence here within the past three years. On the same reasoning, if the COMI of a company is in Denmark, the English court will have jurisdiction to make a winding-up order, since Denmark has opted out of the Regulation: *Re The Arena Corp Ltd* [2003] EWHC 3032 (Ch); [2004] B.P.I.R. 375 (at first instance, a point not raised on appeal [2004] EWCA Civ 371; [2004] B.P.I.R. 415). In *Re Daisytek-ISA Ltd* [2003] B.C.C. 562 administration orders were made in respect of the English subsidiary of a US parent company (Daisytek) and its own subsidiaries incorporated respectively in England, Germany and France. Although the foreign subsidiaries had their registered offices and conducted their business abroad, they were managed to a large extent from Daisytek's head office in Bradford. In ruling that all of the European subsidiaries had their centre of main interests in England, the court had regard to various factors: the location of banking activities and the keeping of financial records, the degree of independence in making purchases (approval by the parent was required for purchases over €5000), policy in the recruitment of senior employees, the provision of services to customers, control of corporate identity and branding, and responsibility for corporate strategy. The scale and importance of the subsidiaries' interests carried out was greater in the UK than in the subsidiaries' own countries. Again, it was stressed that the most important "third parties" concerned with identifying the centre of main interests were the various companies' potential creditors—their financiers and trade suppliers. The evidence was that a large majority of these would have looked to Bradford in this regard. As a decision dealing with insolvency in a group-company context, this case is similar to *Re Aim Underwriting Agencies (Ireland) Ltd* (2 July 2004, noted (March 2005) Sweet & Maxwell's *Insolvency Bulletin* 10); but may be contrasted with *Re Eurofood IFSC Ltd* (C-341/04) [2006] B.C.C. 397, where none of these factors was present: the ECJ held that the mere fact of "parental control" was not sufficient to put the subsidiary's COMI into the jurisdiction of the holding company. (It should be noted that the reasoning of the ECJ is based not so much on an examination of the facts in isolation, but rather on whether they are sufficiently strong to displace the presumption that the subsidiary's COMI is that of its place of its registered office.) *Daisytek* was followed on finely-balanced facts in *Re Parkside Flexibles SA* [2006] B.C.C. 589. (The Court of Appeal of Versailles (4 September 2003, reported as *Klempka v ISA Daisytek SA* [2003] B.C.C. 984), in a robust judgment, subsequently endorsed this ruling, and their judgment has been affirmed by the Court of Cassation: *French Republic v Klempka* [2006] B.C.C. 841.) See also *Re MPOTEC GmbH* [2006] B.C.C. 681; *Re Lennox Holdings plc* [2009] B.C.C. 155; *Sparkasse Hilden Ratingen Velbert v Benk* [2012] EWHC 2432 (Ch); [2012] B.P.I.R. 1258; *Schrade v Sparkasse Lüdenscheid* [2013] B.P.I.R. 911 and the ruling of the Dutch court in *Re BenQ Mobile Holding BV* [2008] B.C.C. 489, noted by Paulus (2007) 20 Insolv. Int. 87. It appears from *Interedil Srl v Fallimento Interedil Srl* (C-396/09, 20 October 2011) that where a company had moved its registered office from one jurisdiction to another but had later ceased to have a registered office anywhere, the presumption is applied by reference to the last place where it was registered.

In *Shierson v Vlieland-Boddy* [2004] EWHC 2572 (Ch); [2005] B.C.C. 416, at first instance, the view was taken that the question of the location of the COMI should be decided as at the date of judgment and not at any earlier time. However, on appeal [2005] EWCA Civ 974; [2005] B.C.C. 949, it was held that this issue should be determined by reference to the time when the court is first required to decide whether to open the insolvency proceedings: this would normally be at the date of the hearing but occasionally at an earlier point, such as when an application had been made for leave to serve a bankruptcy petition out of the jurisdiction. This might also be appropriate in regard to any application for interim relief. It was conceded in this case that a debtor must be free to change his COMI from time to time, and even to do so when he is insolvent (although the court should "look critically" at the facts where this appears to have been done for the purpose of "forum-shopping") (para.[46]). These questions were explored further by the ECJ in *Re Staubitz-Schreiber* (C-1/04) [2006] B.C.C. 639; where the debtor had changed her COMI from Germany to Spain after her application to open insolvency proceedings had been filed but before the case had been heard. The Advocate General, in his opinion, which was endorsed by the European Court, stated that art.3(1) of the Regulation should be interpreted as meaning that the court of the Member State of the territory where the debtor's COMI is situated at the time when the request to open insolvency proceedings retains the jurisdiction to open those proceedings notwithstanding a subsequent move of the COMI by the debtor. As is pointed out by Petkovich (2006) 22 I.L. & P.76, this places the time for determination of the COMI even earlier than *Shierson v Vlieland-Boddy*, where it was the date of first hearing rather than the lodging of the request that was considered to be the relevant time. The ECJ in *Interedil Srl v Fallimento Interedil Srl* (C-396/09, 20 October 2011, [2012] B.C.C. 851 re-emphasised the statement in *Re Staubitz-Schreiber* that the relevant date for the purpose of locating the COMI is that "when the request to open the proceedings is made", without elaborating the meaning of "request". On the time for judging the question of the COMI for the purpose of Ch.17 of the US Bankruptcy Code see Moss (2013) 26 Insolv. Int. 122; and see also the decision of the US Bankruptcy Court (Southern District of New York) in *Re Kemsley* [2013] B.P.I.R. 822

(English bankruptcy proceedings not recognised by US court as neither COMI nor establishment in UK at the time of presentation of English petition).

For the purposes of the Regulation, a company must have a COMI, and only one: *Sparkasse Hilden Ratingen Velbert v Benk* [2012] EWHC 2432 (Ch); [2012] B.P.I.R. 1258. Its COMI may be moved from one jurisdiction to another, but it does not change simply because (e.g.) its principal director moves from one place to another. It will continue to have a COMI even after it has ceased trading (not necessarily the same as it had before): *Re Ci4net.com Inc* [2004] EWHC 1941 (Ch); [2005] B.C.C. 277.

An important concept in the law of a number of civil-law countries is the "seat" of a company. This is very similar to that of the COMI which is fundamental for the purposes of establishing jurisdiction under the EU Regulation, and in those countries the two will coincide. However, it is not possible as a matter of law in those countries for a company to move its seat from one jurisdiction to another without winding up in the place of origin and re-incorporating in the new one (*Cartesio Oktató és Szolgáltató bt* (C-210/06) [2009] B.C.C. 232). This is not a problem in other jurisdictions of the EU, so far as concerns the COMI: the location of the COMI is a matter of fact, and it can be moved from one country to another without any legal restriction.

Although it would appear to follow that there can only be one set of "main" proceedings in respect of the same debtor (as, indeed, is the view expressed in the Virgós-Schmit Report, para.73), it was held in *Re Ultra Motor Homes International Ltd* [2005] EWHC 872 (Ch); [2006] B.C.C. 57 at [34] that this is not the case where both sets of proceedings are in the same Member State—e.g. where a CVA and a liquidation involving the same company are current and subsisting at the same time.

A provision in the domestic law of a Member State which would deprive the courts of another Member State of jurisdiction to open main insolvency proceedings where the company concerned has its COMI is ineffective: *Rastelli David e C. Snc v Hidoux* (C-191/10, 15 December 2011); [2012] All E.R. (EC) 239. This important ECJ ruling confirms various other points: the mere fact that assets of company A have been intermingled with assets of company B which has its COMI within the jurisdiction does not mean that company A also has its COMI there; and a second company cannot be joined in main proceedings involving another company if its COMI is elsewhere.

Note that it is not necessary that the debtor should be domiciled (or, if a company, incorporated) within the EU. In *Re BRAC Rent-a-Car International Inc* [2003] EWHC 128 (Ch); [2003] 1 W.L.R. 1421; [2003] B.C.C. 248 an administration order was made in respect of a company incorporated in Delaware, on the basis of a finding that its centre of main interests was within the UK. Perhaps more controversially, in *Re 3T Telecom Ltd* [2005] EWHC 275 (Ch); [2006] 2 B.C.L.C. 137 it was held that an English court had jurisdiction to make an administration order in relation to a company incorporated in Northern Ireland on the basis that its COMI was in England, notwithstanding IA 1986 s.441(2). (The Regulation, in contrast with the CBIR reg.7, has no provision dealing with cross-border issues between the separate jurisdictions of the UK.)

The use of the present tense (*is* situated), if taken literally, would rule out the opening of insolvency proceedings in some cases where this plainly cannot have been intended—e.g. an insolvent deceased estate. The courts would surely give a purposive construction to the phrase in such a case (i.e. "the place where the debtor formerly had his centre of main interests is situated"). On the other hand, it must be understood literally where the debtor has moved his COMI from one Member State to another: only the latter will have jurisdiction.

In a number of cases the court has been concerned with a claim that a debtor's COMI has been effectively moved from one jurisdiction to another. Many corporate debtors originally based in other parts of the EU have sought at a late stage to relocate in this jurisdiction to take advantage of the more flexible business rescue models that may be available. The fact that this has been the underlying motivation will not necessarily be regarded as fatal: the court's primary concern in all cases has been to be satisfied that the change of COMI has been genuine, and effectively carried out so as to be, in the statutory wording, objectively "ascertainable by third parties". In *Re Hellas Telecommunications (Luxembourg) II SCA* [2009] EWHC 3199 (Ch); [2010] B.C.C. 295 the court was satisfied on the evidence that the company had moved its COMI from Luxembourg (where it was incorporated) to England some three months before the hearing, so giving the English court jurisdiction. See also *Shierson v Vlieland-Boddy* (above), and *Re European Directories (DH6) BV* [2010] EWHC 3472 (Ch); [2012] B.C.C. 46 (court satisfied that company's COMI had been successfully relocated from the Netherlands to England).

In these cases involving corporate debtors the objective may well be generally beneficial to creditors and other stakeholders. In contrast, in the case of an individual the motive is likely to be largely selfish and intended to evade obligations under the home State law, and the courts understandably view such "forum shopping" with caution. For example, see *Irish Bank Resolution Corp Ltd v Quinn* [2012] NICh 1; [2012] B.C.C. 608 (debtor failed to persuade court that COMI was in Northern Ireland rather than in Ireland, where he had his habitual residence); *Sparkasse Hilden Ratingen Velbert v Benk* [2012] EWHC 2432 (Ch) (unsuccessful attempt by German national to persuade court that his COMI was in England); *Die Sparkasse Bremen AG v Armutcu* [2012] EWHC 4026 (Ch) (a similar case where the debtor had also concealed material facts); contrast *O'Mahony v National Irish Bank* [2012] B.P.I.R. 1174 (move of COMI from Ireland to England held effective). The principles upon which legitimate and illegitimate forum shopping are to be distinguished are discussed in *JSC Bank of Moscow v Kekhman* [2014] B.P.I.R. 959 (a point which did not arise on appeal [2015] EWHC 396 (Ch)). Note also the many other cases noted under IA 1986 ss.272, 282 where an individual based abroad has (usually unsuccessfully) sought to establish that he has changed his COMI to England to take advantage of the more lenient bankruptcy regime in this country, and on "bankruptcy tourism" generally see Fannon (2013) 26 Insolv. Int. 85. In *Official Receiver v Eichler (No.2)* [2011] B.P.I.R. 1293 Chief Registrar Baister has confirmed the now-established procedural practice adopted in these cases of requiring additional evidence with supporting documents and giving notice of the hearing to creditors. (This practice now has the backing of the Regulation: see the Preamble, para.32.)

The cases discussed above were all decided under the original Regulation, which made no reference to the relocation of the COMI from one jurisdiction to another, or more particularly to the problems associated with forum shopping. The present Regulation in contrast, does address these matters in some detail, in terms which are broadly supported by the existing case-law. We have already mentioned (above) the non-application of the presumptions where the registered office, etc. has been moved shortly before the opening of proceedings (art.1(1)). Paragraphs 28–32 of the Preamble give some indication of the evidentiary factors which the court should take into account, and stress that fraudulent or abusive forum shopping will not be tolerated. There is, however, no specific mention of forum shopping in the body of the regulation.

The case-law on the COMI question continues to develop. Among recent decisions may be listed: *Re Parkside Flexibles SA* [2006] B.C.C. 589 (Polish subsidiary, member of English group, factors evenly balanced but regarded as decisive that creditors were having recourse to England, so COMI held to be in England); *Re Collins & Aikman Group Corp* [2005] EWHC 1754 (Ch); [2006] B.C.C. 606 (COMI of 24 European members of US group held to be in England and not in jurisdictions of their respective EU registered offices); *Re Sendo Ltd* [2005] EWHC 1604 (Ch); [2006] 1 B.C.L.C. 395 (wholly-owned Cayman Islands subsidiary of English company held to have COMI in England); *Cross Construction Sussex Ltd v Tseliki* [2006] EWHC 1056 (Ch); [2006] B.P.I.R. 888 (evidence insufficient to establish English COMI); *Energotech SARL* [2007] B.C.C. 123 (Polish-registered company held by French court to have COMI in France); *Re Lennox Holdings plc* [2009] B.C.C. 155 (all "head office functions" of Spanish subsidiaries located in England, where holding company was based: held that their COMI was in England); *Official Receiver v Mitterfellner* [2009] B.P.I.R. 1075 (insufficient evidence that COMI had been changed from Germany to England); *Re ARM Asset Backed Securities SA* [2013] EWHC 3351 (Ch); [2014] B.C.C. 252; further proceedings [2014] EWHC 1097 (Ch); [2014] B.C.C. 260 (presumption that COMI was in jurisdiction of incorporation successfully rebutted); *Re Northsea Base Investment Ltd* [2015] EWHC 121 (Ch); [2015] 1 B.C.L.C. 539 (operations and management devolved to agent in London: held sufficient evidence to rebut presumption). In *Hans Brochier Holdings Ltd v Exner* [2006] EWHC 2594 (Ch); [2007] B.C.C. 127 administrators were appointed out of court to a company registered in England in the belief, backed by credible evidence, that its COMI was in England. Later the same day a German court appointed a preliminary administrator on the basis that the COMI was in Germany, but this would not be formalised (and accordingly not "opened" for the purposes of the Regulation) until some time later. On further investigation, the administrators concluded that the COMI was in fact in Germany. Warren J held that the English appointment could not in the circumstances give rise to a main proceeding, although conceivably it could be effective as a territorial proceeding. In *Stojevic v Official Receiver* [2007] B.P.I.R. 141 the position was similar: the applicant had been made bankrupt by a court in Austria in January 2004, unaware of the fact that a bankruptcy order against him had been made in this country in March 2003. Investigation revealed that his COMI was in Austria. The Court granted an annulment of the English order. In *Re Eurodis Electron plc* [2011] EWHC 1025 (Ch); [2012] B.C.C. 57 a company incorporated in Belgium had its COMI in England. Notwithstanding this, it had been wound up and dissolved by a Belgian court, purportedly in main proceedings. It was ruled that the Regulation did not empower the courts in one country to determine that the orders of a court of another jurisdiction were invalid, so that the Belgian order had to stand. This did not prevent the English court from making a winding-up order under s.221(5)(a).

Decisions under the CBIR may also be relevant for the purposes of the Regulation, since both share the concept of the COMI. See, e.g. *Re Stanford International Bank Ltd* [2009] EWHC 1441; [2009] EWHC 1661; [2009] B.P.I.R. 1157; affirmed on appeal [2010] EWCA Civ 137; [2011] B.C.C. 211 (presumption that COMI was in jurisdiction of registered office supported by balance of evidence) and *Re Videology Ltd* [2018] EWHC 2186 (Ch); [2019] B.C.C. 195.

On the possibility that more than one Member State may claim the right to open main proceedings, see the note to the Preamble, para.25 and para.65.

Decisions in other EU jurisdictions on the COMI and related questions have been noted in English journals. These include *Parmalat Slovakia* (Hungary, 2004, (2004) 18 Insolv. Int. 31); *Stojevic* (Austria, 2003, (2005) 18 Insolv. Int. 141); and *Schefenacker*, *Deutsche Nickel* and *Hans Brochier* (Germany) 22 Insolv. Int. 25, 26; and see also the saga of the MG Rover subsidiaries recounted in (2005) 21 I.L. & P 91, 159 and the various cases discussed by Gabriel Moss QC (2012) 26 Insolv. Int. 14. Many cases are accessible on the database *http://www.eir-database.com.*

Note that the term "centre of main interests" is of no relevance to the determination of issues of jurisdiction within the UK.

Art.3(2)

The prerequisites for the opening of territorial proceedings in a particular Member State are:

- the debtor must possess an establishment within that Member State;

- there must be assets of the debtor situated within that Member State;

Art.3(2)–(4)

The Regulation distinguishes between "territorial" and "secondary" proceedings without any formal definition of these terms and, in art.3(2), confusing the reader by using the word "territorial" when in fact the paragraph refers to both. The distinction between the two is simple enough: proceedings opened in a Member State other than that where the debtor's COMI is situated are "territorial" if no main proceedings have yet been opened in the latter State, and "secondary" if they are opened when main proceedings have already been commenced. In both cases the requirements of art.3(2) must be satisfied: the debtor must possess an establishment within that other Member State, and there must be assets situated within that State.

The distinction between the two becomes apparent when we turn to art.3(4). If the proceedings are secondary, no further requirements need to be met. But if they are territorial, either para.4(a) or para.4(b) must also be satisfied.

In either case, the debtor must possess an "establishment" within the State of the opening of the proceedings—that is, "a place of operations where the debtor carries out or has carried out in the three-month period prior to the request to open main insolvency proceedings a non-transitory economic activity with human means and assets" (art.2(10)).

The words "or has carried out in the three-month period prior to the request to open main insolvency proceedings" are new, and are not easy to square with the use of the present tense ("possesses") in art.3(2). Under the former Regulation it was held in *Re Office Metro Ltd* [2012] EWHC 1191 (Ch); [2012] B.C.C. 829 that the relevant time to assess the question of "possessing" an establishment was by reference to the position when the request for the opening of the proceedings was lodged; and this must continue to be true where the proceedings are territorial (at least in the great majority of cases, where no step has been taken to initiate main proceedings). It was also held by the Supreme Court in *Re Olympic Airlines SA* [2015] UKSC 27; [2015] B.C.C. 404 that this was the relevant time when the application was for the opening of secondary proceedings (main proceedings having been commenced some nine months previously). Under the new Regulation, however, the focus in such a case will now shift to the time when the opening of main proceedings is requested, plus the three months before that. *Re Olympic Airlines SA* will no longer be authoritative on those facts.

Will the applicant for the opening of territorial proceedings ever be able to have the benefit of the three-month back-dating? If no request to open main proceedings has been made, the question will not arise. But if such a request has been made (and the applicant knows or becomes aware of the fact), he can presumably claim to be entitled to the extra three months—even if the proposed main proceedings never do get opened.

However, in many cases "possesses" will mean "currently possesses". This use of the present tense is disturbing, particularly when read in conjunction with art.3(4)(b)(i) (see below). It may well have been intended that if a debtor has ceased to possess an establishment in a particular jurisdiction, everything is to be administered in the main proceedings; but this would prevent any ring-fencing of the local assets for the benefit of local creditors and could cost preferential creditors their priority.

A company is not precluded from having an establishment in the Member State where it has its registered office (its COMI being in another Member State), and accordingly, where main proceedings have been opened in the latter, secondary proceedings may be opened in the former: *Burgo Group SpA* (C-327/13); [2015] B.C.C. 53 (now confirmed by the Preamble, para.24).

The liquidator in the main proceedings is given considerable powers to intervene in the administration of the secondary proceedings: see arts 45 et seq.

Art.3(3), (4)

Where no main proceedings have been opened in the Member State where the debtor has his COMI, "territorial" proceedings may be opened in another Member State. (In this case it was also held that the term "creditor" did not include a person or public body acting on behalf of the creditors as a group, but this has been reversed by the new art.3(4)(b)(ii).) The jurisdiction to open territorial proceedings is restricted not only by para.(2), which requires the debtor to possess an establishment within the jurisdiction and confines the effect of the proceedings to assets situated there, but also more severely by para.3(4) to the two situations set out in subparas (a) and (b). Subparagraph (4)(a) presupposes that the "main" Member State cannot exercise jurisdiction but that the "territorial" State can: this might be (e.g.) because the debtor is a non-trader or minor or foreign national who cannot be bankrupted under the law of the main State. Subparagraph (4)(b)(ii) requires the applicant to be a creditor based in the "territorial" Member State who seeks to have the debtor put into insolvency on the basis of a trading debt incurred by the debtor in running his establishment. For this reason the Court of Appeal of Paris held, in *EcoJet Ltd v Selafa MJA* [2005] B.C.C. 979, that it was not competent for a French court to open territorial proceedings of its own motion. In *Procurer-generaal bij het Hof van Bereoep te Antwerpen v Zaza Retail BV* (C-112/10, 20 November 2011); [2012] B.P.I.R. 438 the European Court of Justice ruled that the conditions for the opening of territorial proceedings must be interpreted strictly: the restrictions in art.3(4)(b) are to be construed objectively and do not depend on the circumstances of the individual applicant. These limitations would not only rule out an individual from petitioning for his own bankruptcy in a State other than that of his COMI, but also a resolution for the (creditors') voluntary winding up of a company incorporated here but having its COMI in another Member State, or an administration initiated by such a company or its directors; and it would appear to put obstacles in the way of setting up an IVA or CVA for a debtor who is a British national or UK-registered company with a COMI elsewhere in the Community.

The question whether a debtor has an establishment in the jurisdiction is to be determined objectively. The "economic activity" referred to in the definition must be a business or trading operation, viewed objectively, and merely dealing internally with matters incidental to the liquidation is insufficient: see *Re Olympic Airlines SA* (above). In *Interedil Srl v Fallimento Interedil Srl* (C-396/09, 20 October 2011, [2012] B.C.C. 851) the ECJ stated: "The term 'establishment'…must be interpreted as requiring the presence of a structure consisting of a minimum level of organisation and a degree of stability necessary for the purpose of pursuing an economic activity. The presence alone of goods in isolation or bank accounts does not, in principle, meet that definition". On these questions, see H. Rajak (2012) 322 Sweet & Maxwell's *Company Law Newsletter* 1.

If main proceedings are subsequently opened in the State where the COMI is situated, the liquidator in those proceedings has, by virtue of art.36, the extensive powers of intervention set out in arts 31–35, and also the right conferred by art.37 to request that the proceedings be converted into winding-up proceedings if they do not already take that form.

Territorial proceedings lose their distinctive label if main proceedings are subsequently opened. It follows that all references to secondary proceedings elsewhere in the Regulation will apply to them.

Article 4

Examination as to jurisdiction

1. A court seised of a request to open insolvency proceedings shall of its own motion examine whether it has jurisdiction pursuant to Article 3. The judgment opening insolvency proceedings shall specify the grounds on which the jurisdiction of the court is based, and, in particular, whether jurisdiction is based on Article 3(1) or (2).

2. Notwithstanding paragraph 1, where insolvency proceedings are opened in accordance with national law without a decision by a court, Member States may entrust the insolvency practitioner appointed in such proceedings to examine whether the Member State in which a request for the opening of proceedings is pending has jurisdiction pursuant to Article 3. Where this is the case, the insolvency practitioner shall specify in the decision opening the proceedings the grounds on which jurisdiction is based and, in particular, whether jurisdiction is based on Article 3(1) or (2).

GENERAL NOTE

This provision is new. "Court" obviously is used in the judicial sense, and art.4(1) poses no great problem. The second paragraph, however, sits very uncomfortably with many of the extra-judicial procedures which are standard practice in this country, e.g. a creditors' voluntary winding up, an administration resolved upon by the company or a pre-pack administration. In such cases there is no "request", and the "decision" opening the proceedings is not made by the insolvency practitioner appointed to act but by the general meeting, the directors or the secured creditor concerned. As the paragraph is not self-enforcing but depends on the enactment of implementing domestic legislation it will be interesting to see what sort of a fist is made of the challenge by our legislators and whether the legal requirements, once in place, are observed in practice.

Judicial review of the decision to open main insolvency proceedings

1. The debtor or any creditor may challenge before a court the decision opening main insolvency proceedings on grounds of international jurisdiction.

2. The decision opening main insolvency proceedings may be challenged by parties other than those referred to in paragraph 1 or on grounds other than a lack of international jurisdiction where national law so provides.

GENERAL NOTE

Article 5(1) is enabling: a debtor or creditor may challenge a ruling that the insolvent's COMI is or is not in a particular jurisdiction regardless of any limitation or doubt based on the national law. Whether such a challenge may be mounted on other grounds or by any other person (e.g. an insolvency practitioner purportedly appointed in another Member State) depends on the domestic law of the court which made the ruling (art.5(2)). In either case, the challenge must be brought in the jurisdiction which made the original ruling: a court in any other Member State is powerless to intervene: *Re Eurodis Electron plc* [2011] EWHC 1025 (Ch); [2012] B.C.C. 57.

The article is limited to main proceedings. The position in other proceedings would be governed by the law of the State of the opening of proceedings (art.7).

Article 6

Jurisdiction for actions deriving directly from insolvency proceedings and closely linked with them

1. The courts of the Member State within the territory of which insolvency proceedings have been opened in accordance with Article 3 shall have jurisdiction for any action which derives directly from the insolvency proceedings and is closely linked with them, such as avoidance actions.

2. Where an action referred to in paragraph 1 is related to an action in civil and commercial matters against the same defendant, the insolvency practitioner may bring both actions before the courts of the Member State within the territory of which the defendant is domiciled, or, where the action is brought against several defendants, before the courts of the Member State within the territory of which any of them is domiciled, provided that those courts have jurisdiction pursuant to Regulation (EU) No 1215/2012.

The first subparagraph shall apply to the debtor in possession, provided that national law allows the debtor in possession to bring actions on behalf of the insolvency estate.

3. For the purpose of paragraph 2, actions are deemed to be related where they are so closely connected that it is expedient to hear and determine them together to avoid the risk of irreconcilable judgments resulting from separate proceedings.

GENERAL NOTE

There was no equivalent enabling provision in the original Regulation, but some of the case-law decided on general principles may be relevant to the question whether an action "derives directly from" or "is closely linked with" an insolvency proceeding. In *Re Ultra Motorhomes International Ltd* [2005] EWHC 872 (Ch); [2006] B.C.C. 57 a dispute concerning the ownership of a motor vehicle was held not to be "closely connected" with liquidation proceedings so as to give the court of the liquidation jurisdiction; and see the similar ruling in *German Graphics v Alice van der Schee* (C-292/08, 10 September 2009). Contrast *SCT Industri AB v Alpenblume AB* (C-111/08, 2 July 2009), where the property had been sold by the liquidator under powers conferred on him by insolvency law. See further the notes to the Preamble paras 6, 7 and art.3(1).

Regulation (EU) 1215/2012 (the Judgments Regulation) does not normally accord jurisdiction to a court in a matter of insolvency, but art.6(2) allows such an action to be combined with another civil claim against the same defendant, so long as the court has jurisdiction under that Regulation.

Paragraph 3 is presumably explanatory rather than limiting.

Article 7

Applicable law

1. Save as otherwise provided in this Regulation, the law applicable to insolvency proceedings and their effects shall be that of the Member State within the territory of which such proceedings are opened (the 'State of the opening of proceedings').

2. The law of the State of the opening of proceedings shall determine the conditions for the opening of those proceedings, their conduct and their closure. In particular, it shall determine the following:

   (a)   the debtors against which insolvency proceedings may be brought on account of their capacity;

   (b)   the assets which form part of the insolvency estate and the treatment of assets acquired by or devolving on the debtor after the opening of the insolvency proceedings;

   (c)   the respective powers of the debtor and the insolvency practitioner;

   (d)   the conditions under which set-offs may be invoked;

   (e)   the effects of insolvency proceedings on current contracts to which the debtor is party;

   (f)   the effects of the insolvency proceedings on proceedings brought by individual creditors, with the exception of pending lawsuits;

   (g)   the claims which are to be lodged against the debtor's insolvency estate and the treatment of claims arising after the opening of insolvency proceedings;

   (h)   the rules governing the lodging, verification and admission of claims;

   (i)   the rules governing the distribution of proceeds from the realisation of assets, the ranking of claims and the rights of creditors who have obtained partial satisfaction after the opening of insolvency proceedings by virtue of a right *in rem* or through a set-off;

   (j)   the conditions for, and the effects of closure of, insolvency proceedings, in particular by composition;

   (k)   creditors' rights after the closure of insolvency proceedings;

   (l)   who is to bear the costs and expenses incurred in the insolvency proceedings;

   (m)   the rules relating to the voidness, voidability or unenforceability of legal acts detrimental to the general body of creditors.

GENERAL NOTE

This article is essentially the same as the former art.4. It applies to all forms of insolvency proceedings, whether main, secondary or territorial. Subject to arts 8 et seq., each jurisdiction is to apply its own laws and rules of procedure. To remove doubt, many of the respects to which this basic principle is to apply are spelt out in detail in subpara.(2). It follows that, once it is established that the UK has jurisdiction under art.3 (whether in main, territorial or secondary proceedings), the rules of law and practice and the powers of the office-holder will be the same as those in a domestic insolvency, and these will apply subject only to any limitations specifically set out elsewhere in the Regulation: see *Alitalia Linee Aeree Italiane SpA, Connock v Fantozzi* [2011] EWHC 15 (Ch); [2011] 1 W.L.R. 2049; [2011] B.C.C. 579, and compare *Re Hellas Telecommunications (Luxembourg) II SCA* [2013] B.P.I.R. 756; *Kornhaas v Dithmar* (C-594/14) [2016] B.C.C. 116 CJEU (German court could enforce payment by director of English company subject to insolvency proceedings in Germany).

    Article 7 is concerned only with enforcement or execution proceedings which have to be brought collectively in the jurisdiction where the insolvency has commenced; it is not intended to have any effect on lawsuits pending in other jurisdictions: *Fortress Value Recovery Fund I LLC v Blue Skye Special Opportunities Fund LP* [2013] EWHC 14 (Comm); [2013] 2 B.C.L.C. 351.

Article 7(1) is expressed in categorical terms. It is submitted that, even in the case where a certificate confirming a creditors' voluntary winding up is denied, the jurisdiction conferred on the local court by this article will apply: see the note to IR 2016 r.21.5.

Art.7(2)(e), (f)

An apparent inconsistency between the forerunners to paras (2)(e) and (2)(f) was discussed by Clarke J in *Elektrim SA v Vivendi Universal SA* [2008] EWHC 2155 (Comm); [2008] 2 Lloyd's Rep. 636. See the note to art.18.

Art.7(2)(j), (k)

These provisions would appear to put it beyond doubt that a discharge in bankruptcy or a composition which is effective under the law of any competent Member State will be recognised throughout the Community as extinguishing all the debts of the insolvent (or at least those comprehended by the composition), wherever incurred, but in territorial or secondary proceedings art.20(2) imposes a qualification, empowering creditors who have not consented to the discharge to pursue any assets of the debtor that are situated in another State. (See, however, the *Global* case, discussed in the note to art.28.) It is for the domestic law of the Member State in which proceedings have been opened to determine at which moment the closure of those proceedings occurs: *Bank Handlowy et Ryszard Adamiak v Christianapol sp z oo* (C-116/11, 22 November 2012).

Art.7(2)(m)

The law of the opening of the proceedings was applied by the Court of Appeal of Versailles in *Becheret Thierry v Industrie Guido Malvestio SpA* [2005] B.C.C. 974.

However, where the office-holder has assigned a right of action on such a ground to a third party, this has the effect of removing the claim from the insolvency exception under the Judgments Regulation, so that the Judgments Regulation applies to the exclusion of the EC Regulation and the court where the intended defendant is based alone has jurisdiction: *F-Tex SIA v Lietuvos-Anglijos UAB "Jadecloud"* (C-213/10, 19 April 2012); compare *SCT Industri AB v Alpenblume AB* (above).

Article 8

Third parties' rights in rem

1. The opening of insolvency proceedings shall not affect the rights in rem of creditors or third parties in respect of tangible or intangible, moveable or immoveable assets, both specific assets and collections of indefinite assets as a whole which change from time to time, belonging to the debtor which are situated within the territory of another Member State at the time of the opening of proceedings.

2. The rights referred to in paragraph 1 shall, in particular, mean:

   (a) the right to dispose of assets or have them disposed of and to obtain satisfaction from the proceeds of or income from those assets, in particular by virtue of a lien or a mortgage;

   (b) the exclusive right to have a claim met, in particular a right guaranteed by a lien in respect of the claim or by assignment of the claim by way of a guarantee;

   (c) the right to demand assets from, and/or to require restitution by, anyone having possession or use of them contrary to the wishes of the party so entitled;

   (d) a right in rem to the beneficial use of assets.

3. The right, recorded in a public register and enforceable against third parties, based on which a right in rem within the meaning of paragraph 1 may be obtained shall be considered to be a right in rem.

4. Paragraph 1 shall not preclude actions for voidness, voidability or unenforceability as referred to in point (m) of Article 7(2).

GENERAL NOTE

This is the first of the exceptions to the general rule that the administration of insolvency proceedings (whether main, secondary or territorial) in a particular Member State shall be governed by the law of those proceedings: all rights in rem (including security rights of a proprietary nature) in respect of assets situated outside the territory of that State are to be determined by reference to the law ordinarily applicable to such rights under conflict of laws rules. Lawyers in common-law jurisdictions (and Scotland) will be relieved to see that the security of a floating charge is specifically included.

Article 9

Set-off

1. The opening of insolvency proceedings shall not affect the right of creditors to demand the set-off of their claims against the claims of a debtor, where such a set-off is permitted by the law applicable to the insolvent debtor's claim.

2. Paragraph 1 shall not preclude actions for voidness, voidability or unenforceability as referred to in point (m) of Article 7(2).

GENERAL NOTE

The right of set-off referred to relates to the position between the debtor and a creditor whose claim arises in a jurisdiction other than that of the Member State in which the insolvency proceedings are being administered. This, as regards a claim governed by English law, will not be a right of set-off in insolvency under IA 1986 s.323 or IR 2016 r.14.25 but a right arising independently of the insolvency under the rules of common law or equity. See further the note to IR 2016 r.14.25.

Article 10

Reservation of title

1. The opening of insolvency proceedings against the purchaser of an asset shall not affect sellers' rights that are based on a reservation of title where at the time of the opening of proceedings the asset is situated within the territory of a Member State other than the State of the opening of proceedings.

2. The opening of insolvency proceedings against the seller of an asset, after delivery of the asset, shall not constitute grounds for rescinding or terminating the sale and shall not prevent the purchaser from acquiring title where at the time of the opening of proceedings the asset sold is situated within the territory of a Member State other than the State of the opening of proceedings.

3. Paragraphs 1 and 2 shall not preclude actions for voidness, voidability or unenforceability as referred to in point (m) of Article 7(2).

(See General Note after art.18.)

Article 11

Contracts relating to immoveable property

1. The effects of insolvency proceedings on a contract conferring the right to acquire or make use of immoveable property shall be governed solely by the law of the Member State within the territory of which the immoveable property is situated.

2. The court which opened main insolvency proceedings shall have jurisdiction to approve the termination or modification of the contracts referred to in this Article where:

    (a)   the law of the Member State applicable to those contracts requires that such a contract may only be terminated or modified with the approval of the court opening insolvency proceedings; and

    (b)   no insolvency proceedings have been opened in that Member State.

(See General Note after art.18.)

Article 12

Payment systems and financial markets

1. Without prejudice to Article 8, the effects of insolvency proceedings on the rights and obligations of the parties to a payment or settlement system or to a financial market shall be governed solely by the law of the Member State applicable to that system or market.

2. Paragraph 1 shall not preclude any action for voidness, voidability or unenforceability which may be taken to set aside payments or transactions under the law applicable to the relevant payment system or financial market.

(See General Note after art.18.)

Article 13

Contracts of employment

1. The effects of insolvency proceedings on employment contracts and relationships shall be governed solely by the law of the Member State applicable to the contract of employment.

2. The courts of the Member State in which secondary insolvency proceedings may be opened shall retain jurisdiction to approve the termination or modification of the contracts referred to in this Article even if no insolvency proceedings have been opened in that Member State.

   The first subparagraph shall also apply to an authority competent under national law to approve the termination or modification of the contracts referred to in this Article.

(See General Note after art.18.)

Article 14

Effects on rights subject to registration

The effects of insolvency proceedings on the rights of a debtor in immoveable property, a ship or an aircraft subject to registration in a public register shall be determined by the law of the Member State under the authority of which the register is kept.*(See General Note after art.18.)*

Article 15

European patents with unitary effect and Community trade marks

For the purposes of this Regulation, a European patent with unitary effect, a Community trade mark or any other similar right established by Union law may be included only in the proceedings referred to in Article 3(1).

(See General Note after art.18.)

Article 16

Detrimental acts

Point (m) of Article 7(2) shall not apply where the person who benefited from an act detrimental to all the creditors provides proof that:

   (a)   the act is subject to the law of a Member State other than that of the State of the opening of proceedings; and

(b) the law of that Member State does not allow any means of challenging that act in the relevant case.

(See General Note after art.18.)

Article 17

Protection of third-party purchasers

Where, by an act concluded after the opening of insolvency proceedings, a debtor disposes, for consideration, of:

(a) an immoveable asset;

(b) a ship or an aircraft subject to registration in a public register; or

(c) securities the existence of which requires registration in a register laid down by law;

the validity of that act shall be governed by the law of the State within the territory of which the immoveable asset is situated or under the authority of which the register is kept.*(See General Note after art.18.)*

Article 18

Effects of insolvency proceedings on pending lawsuits or arbitral proceedings

The effects of insolvency proceedings on a pending lawsuit or pending arbitral proceedings concerning an asset or a right which forms part of a debtor's insolvency estate shall be governed solely by the law of the Member State in which that lawsuit is pending or in which the arbitral tribunal has its seat.

GENERAL NOTE TO ARTS 13–18

Here are set out the remaining situations where the law of the State in which insolvency proceedings have been opened is to give way to the rules of the local law or those of some other jurisdiction. With the exception of the insertion of art.11(2) and the alterations made to art.18, noted below, these provisions are in all essential respects the same as ECRIP arts 7–15.

Art.11
Paragraph (2) has been added. It confers jurisdiction on the court which has opened main insolvency proceedings to terminate or modify a contract relating to immoveable property, in addition to the court of the State where the property is situated, provided that no *insolvency* proceedings have been opened in the latter court.

Art.12
Provision is made for the disapplication of the rules of insolvency law in payment and settlement systems and transactions on the financial markets by the Finality Directive and by CA 1989 Pt VII, respectively: see the notes at Vol.1 pp.1–3. This article ensures that a similar disapplication will apply where the insolvency proceedings have been opened in a Member State other than that whose law is applicable to the system or market in question.

Art.15
The effect of this article is that Community patents and trade marks cannot be dealt with at all in secondary or territorial proceedings, even (in the latter case) where no main proceedings have been opened.

Art.16
Article 7(2)(m) gives jurisdiction to the State of the opening of the proceedings in the application of "the rules relating to the voidness, voidability or unenforceability of legal acts detrimental to all the creditors" which would include provisions relating to preferences, transactions at an undervalue, etc. (For examples, see the judgment of the Court of Appeal of Versailles in *Becheret Thierry v Industrie Guido Malvestio SpA* [2005] B.C.C. 974; and *Seagon v Deko Marty Belgium NV* (C-339/07) [2009] 1 W.L.R. 2168; [2009] B.C.C. 347.) Article 16 disapplies this rule where (1) the person who benefited from the transaction in question shows that the proper law would, apart from art.7(2)(m), be that of another Member State; and (2) the transaction would not be open to challenge at all under that law. It would follow that the transaction cannot be avoided or held to be void or unenforceable in the court where

proceedings have been opened. Where, however, the transaction would be open to challenge under its proper law but the two laws differ in any respect, art.7(2)(m) will apply. Article 16 also displaces this rule where a payment is exercised in the enforcement of a pre-existing right in rem (e.g. a security interest), even though it is made after the opening of insolvency proceedings: *Lutz v Bäuerle* (C-557/13) [2015] B.C.C. 413. If the defendant to a clawback action alleges that a local law defence applies, the burden of proof is on him to show that the defence applies and is available: *Nike European Operations Netherlands BV v Sportland Oy* (C-310/14), 15 October 2015 CJEU). In *Nike European Operations Netherlands BV v Sportland Oy* (C-310/14) [2017] B.C.C. 446 the European Court of Justice stressed that what is now art.16 (detrimental acts) had to be interpreted in a narrow fashion as it was an exception to the basic rule. The case was concerned with the concept of legitimate expectations under art.16. Further discussion of what is now art.16 was provided by the European Court of Justice in *Vinyls Italia SpA v Mediterranea di Navigazione SpA* (C-54/16) [2018] 1 W.L.R. 543.

Art.18

Provision is now expressly made for pending arbitrations as well as lawsuits. The courts in this country had already held that the two should be treated as equivalent. In *Elektrim SA v Vivendi Universal SA* [2008] EWHC 2155 (Comm); [2008] 2 Lloyd's Rep. 636 an arbitration under English law between the parties had commenced in London but had not been heard when one of them was declared bankrupt by a Polish court. Polish insolvency law provided that in the event of bankruptcy any arbitration clause concluded by the bankrupt should lose its legal effect, and any pending arbitration proceedings should be discontinued. Clarke J held that under the former art.15 (now art.18). English law should prevail on the basis that the arbitration was a "lawsuit pending", with the consequence that the arbitration had not been annulled; and further that in so far as what is now art.7(2)(e) might be construed as nullifying the arbitration clause in a "current contract" and the ensuing proceedings it should give way to the clear intention of the legislator as expressed in art.15. This decision was affirmed by the Court of Appeal (sub nom. *Syska v Vivendi Universal SA*) [2009] EWCA Civ 677; [2009] 2 All E.R. (Comm) 891; [2010] B.C.C. 348. The position would be otherwise, however (and the general provisions of art.7 would prevail) where arbitration proceedings had not been begun before the date of commencement of the insolvency. On the meaning of the phrase "lawsuit pending", see *Fortress Value Recovery Fund 1 LLC v Blue Sky Special Opportunities Fund LP* [2013] EWHC 14 (Comm); [2013] 2 B.C.L.C. 351 (application to amend claim).

On the scope of art.18 (formerly ECRIP art.15) see *Tarrago da Silveira v Massa Insolvente da Espirito Santo Financial Group SA* (C-250/17) EU:C:2018:398; [2018] 1 W.L.R. 4148.

CHAPTER II

RECOGNITION OF INSOLVENCY PROCEEDINGS

Introductory note to Chapter II

"Recognition" in this chapter has two aspects: first, recognition of the "judgment" (i.e. the order of a national court or act of any other person or body which has effect as the "opening" of insolvency proceedings); and, secondly, recognition of the authority of the office-holder (the "insolvency practitioner") in such proceedings. In each case the validity of the judgment and the office-holder's authority is to be accepted without the need for a court order in the nature of an exequatur or any other formality in the other Member State. All that is needed is a certified copy of the office-holder's appointment (accompanied by a translation, where appropriate). The only additional requirement is that, in the case of a creditors' voluntary winding up, a certificate of confirmation must be obtained from a court in the host country.

Article 19

Principle

1. Any judgment opening insolvency proceedings handed down by a court of a Member State which has jurisdiction pursuant to Article 3 shall be recognised in all other Member States from the moment that it becomes effective in the State of the opening of proceedings

The rule laid down in the first subparagraph shall also apply where, on account of a debtor's capacity, insolvency proceedings cannot be brought against that debtor in other Member States.

2. Recognition of the proceedings referred to in Article 3(1) shall not preclude the opening of the proceedings referred to in Article 3(2) by a court in another Member State. The latter proceedings shall be secondary insolvency proceedings within the meaning of Chapter III.

(See General Note after art.20.)

Article 20

Effects of recognition

1. The judgment opening insolvency proceedings as referred to in Article 3(1) shall, with no further formalities, produce the same effects in any other Member State as under the law of the State of the opening of proceedings, unless this Regulation provides otherwise and as long as no proceedings referred to in Article 3(2) are opened in that other Member State.

2. The effects of the proceedings referred to in Article 3(2) may not be challenged in other Member States. Any restriction of creditors' rights, in particular a stay or discharge, shall produce effects vis-à-vis assets situated within the territory of another Member State only in the case of those creditors who have given their consent.

GENERAL NOTE TO ARTS 19, 20

These provisions mirror arts 16, 17 of ECRIP, the one change of possible significance being the substitution of "moment" for "time" in art.19(1)—so putting it beyond any doubt that in this context time will be reckoned in fractions of a day. Article 19 applies to all forms of insolvency proceedings, whether main proceedings under art.3(1), or secondary or territorial proceedings under art.3(2)–(4). "Court" and "judgment" have the wider meanings given by art.2(6), (7), so that (e.g.) "judgment" includes a resolution for creditors' voluntary winding up or the appointment of an administrator made out of court: see the notes to that article. A creditors' voluntary winding up requires to be confirmed by the court, following the procedure set out in IR 2016 r.21.4.

The concluding sentence of art.19(1) ensures that an insolvency proceeding opened in a Member State which has jurisdiction will be recognised in another Member State even where the debtor could not be the subject of insolvency proceedings in the latter—e.g. if its bankruptcy law does not extend to a debtor who is a minor.

The effect of art.20(1) is that once main proceedings have been opened in the State of the debtor's centre of main interests, its insolvency law is to apply automatically throughout the rest of the Community. So, in *MG Probud Gdynia sp z oo* (C-444/07) [2010] B.C.C. 453 the ECJ ruled that once main proceedings had been opened in Poland, the jurisdiction of the company's COMI, it was not competent for a creditor to attach assets in Germany, this being contrary to Polish law. In *Re ARM Asset Back Securities SA (No.2)* [2014] EWHC 1097 (Ch); [2014] B.C.C. 260 it was held that the appointment of provisional liquidators in England (the jurisdiction of the debtor's COMI) brought about an automatic stay of proceedings elsewhere in the EU.

Article 20(1) is subject to two exceptions: (i) if territorial proceedings have already been opened, or secondary proceedings are subsequently opened, in another State, the insolvency law of the latter will apply in that State; and (ii) where special provision is made elsewhere in the Regulation (as, e.g. under art.31), and in particular where arts 8–18 apply, the law of the insolvency proceedings in question will be displaced. Although art.20(2), which applies to territorial and secondary proceedings, also accords general recognition to such proceedings throughout the EU, it adds a caveat which reflects the limitation of the effects such proceedings may have on assets situated in the territory of the State concerned (art.3(2)). So, for instance, if territorial proceedings in the UK were to result in a compromise under which every creditor accepted a 50 per cent payment in full satisfaction of his debt, this would not prevent an individual creditor from pursuing a claim for the balance in another Member State where the debtor had assets, unless he had agreed otherwise.

Article 21

Powers of the insolvency practitioner

1. The insolvency practitioner appointed by a court which has jurisdiction pursuant to Article 3(1) may exercise all the powers conferred on it, by the law of the State of the opening of proceedings, in another Member State, as long as no other insolvency proceedings have been opened there and no preservation measure to the contrary has been taken there further to a request for the opening of insolvency

proceedings in that State. Subject to Articles 8 and 10, the insolvency practitioner may, in particular, remove the debtor's assets from the territory of the Member State in which they are situated.

2. The insolvency practitioner appointed by a court which has jurisdiction pursuant to Article 3(2) may in any other Member State claim through the courts or out of court that moveable property was removed from the territory of the State of the opening of proceedings to the territory of that other Member State after the opening of the insolvency proceedings. The insolvency practitioner may also bring any action to set aside which is in the interests of the creditors.

3. In exercising its powers, the insolvency practitioner shall comply with the law of the Member State within the territory of which it intends to take action, in particular with regard to procedures for the realisation of assets. Those powers may not include coercive measures, unless ordered by a court of that Member State, or the right to rule on legal proceedings or disputes.

(See General Note after art.22.)

Article 22

Proof of the insolvency practitioner's appointment

The insolvency practitioner's appointment shall be evidenced by a certified copy of the original decision appointing it or by any other certificate issued by the court which has jurisdiction.

A translation into the official language or one of the official languages of the Member State within the territory of which it intends to act may be required. No legalisation or other similar formality shall be required.

GENERAL NOTE TO ARTS 21, 22

Article 21: note the qualification "as long as no other insolvency proceedings have been opened there". In *Re Alitalia Linee Aeree Italiane SpA* [2011] EWHC 15 (Ch); [2011] B.C.C. 579 main proceedings had been opened in Italy and secondary proceedings in England. The Italian liquidator wished to make certain payments to employees out of funds in England which would have a preferential ranking under Italian law, but it was held that the funds had to be applied in accordance with English law under which the employees were unsecured creditors with no priority. The words "unless ordered by a court of that Member State" have been inserted into art.21(3), confirming the ruling which had been given in *Handelsveem BV v Hill* [2011] B.P.I.R. 1024.

In *Aria Inc v Credit Agricole Corporate and Investment Bank* [2014] EWHC 872 (Comm) a Greek liquidator was held to be entitled by art.21 to exercise in this country all the powers conferred on him by Greek insolvency law, including the right to take action to restrain payment under a guarantee, but the court held that English and not Greek law should apply to any procedural issues arising on the exercise of those powers in this jurisdiction.

In *Wiemer & Trachte GmbH v Tadzher* (C-296/17) EU:C:2018:902; [2019] B.P.I.R. 252 it was stressed that ECRIP art.3 (EURIP art.3) prevailed over ECRIP art.18 (EURIP art.21)—art.3 provided exclusive jurisdiction and therefore restricted the liquidator's flexibility as to the location where to sue. This is a regrettable ruling from the ECJ as it will tie the hands of those seeking to realise insolvent estates in the most efficient manner.

Article 22 ensures that the authority of an office-holder shall be recognised throughout the Community with the minimum of formality and with no additional requirement in any Member State apart from possibly a translation into the local language.

In main proceedings, the powers of the "insolvency practitioner" are extensive and, indeed, are restricted only if territorial or secondary proceedings have been opened in another Member State or if a moratorium or similar interim measure has come into operation there in anticipation of the opening of such proceedings. But whereas the office-holder in main proceedings has a general power to gather up assets that are situated in other Member States (art.21(1)), that of the insolvency practitioner in territorial or secondary proceedings is limited to repatriating assets that have been removed abroad after those proceedings have been opened—and in this regard it is submitted that "opened" in a winding up by the court refers to the court order (or possibly, some other event), but not the petition: see the note to IA 1986 s.129(2).

The local law and procedures must in all cases be respected (art.21(3)).

IR 2016 r.21.8 may apply.

Article 23

Return and imputation

1. A creditor which, after the opening of the proceedings referred to in Article 3(1), obtains by any means, in particular through enforcement, total or partial satisfaction of its claim on the assets belonging to a debtor situated within the territory of another Member State, shall return what it has obtained to the insolvency practitioner, subject to Articles 8 and 10.

2. In order to ensure the equal treatment of creditors, a creditor which has, in the course of insolvency proceedings, obtained a dividend on its claim shall share in distributions made in other proceedings only where creditors of the same ranking or category have, in those other proceedings, obtained an equivalent dividend.

GENERAL NOTE

Article 23(1) empowers the liquidator in main proceedings to require any creditor who has recovered part or all of his debt by proceeding against assets of the debtor situated in another Member State to disgorge what he has received. This would not normally be possible under UK national law unless the creditor sought to prove in the insolvency, in which case he would be required to surrender his gains under the principle of hotchpot. Article 23(2), in contrast, does not oblige a creditor who has been paid a dividend in other insolvency proceedings to part with what he has received: it is only if he chooses to prove in the second insolvency that he must bring that sum into account and participate on a pari passu basis.

Article 24

Establishment of insolvency registers

1. Member States shall establish and maintain in their territory one or several registers in which information concerning insolvency proceedings is published ('insolvency registers'). That information shall be published as soon as possible after the opening of such proceedings.

2. The information referred to in paragraph 1 shall be made publicly available, subject to the conditions laid down in Article 27, and shall include the following ('mandatory information'):

(a) the date of the opening of insolvency proceedings;

(b) the court opening insolvency proceedings and the case reference number, if any;

(c) the type of insolvency proceedings referred to in Annex A that were opened and, where applicable, any relevant subtype of such proceedings opened in accordance with national law;

(d) whether jurisdiction for opening proceedings is based on Article 3(1), 3(2) or 3(4);

(e) if the debtor is a company or a legal person, the debtor's name, registration number, registered office or, if different, postal address;

(f) if the debtor is an individual whether or not exercising an independent business or professional activity, the debtor's name, registration number, if any, and postal address or, where the address is protected, the debtor's place and date of birth;

(g) the name, postal address or e-mail address of the insolvency practitioner, if any, appointed in the proceedings;

(h) the time limit for lodging claims, if any, or a reference to the criteria for calculating that time limit;

(i) the date of closing main insolvency proceedings, if any;

(j)   the court before which and, where applicable, the time limit within which a challenge of the decision opening insolvency proceedings is to be lodged in accordance with Article 5, or a reference to the criteria for calculating that time limit.

3. Paragraph 2 shall not preclude Member States from including documents or additional information in their national insolvency registers, such as directors' disqualifications related to insolvency.

4. Member States shall not be obliged to include in the insolvency registers the information referred to in paragraph 1 of this Article in relation to individuals not exercising an independent business or professional activity, or to make such information publicly available through the system of inter-connection of those registers, provided that known foreign creditors are informed, pursuant to Article 54, of the elements referred to under point (j) of paragraph 2 of this Article.

Where a Member State makes use of the possibility referred to in the first subparagraph, the insolvency proceedings shall not affect the claims of foreign creditors who have not received the information referred to in the first subparagraph.

5. The publication of information in the registers under this Regulation shall not have any legal effects other than those set out in national law and in Article 55(6).

GENERAL NOTE

Article 24 is not to come into force until 26 June 2018.

Article 25

Interconnection of insolvency registers

1. The Commission shall establish a decentralised system for the interconnection of insolvency registers by means of implementing acts. That system shall be composed of the insolvency registers and the European e-Justice Portal, which shall serve as a central public electronic access point to information in the system. The system shall provide a search service in all the official languages of the institutions of the Union in order to make available the mandatory information and any other documents or information included in the insolvency registers which the Member States choose to make available through the European e-Justice Portal.

2. By means of implementing acts in accordance with the procedure referred to in Article 87, the Commission shall adopt the following by 26 June 2019:

(a)   the technical specification defining the methods of communication and information exchange by electronic means on the basis of the established interface specification for the system of interconnection of insolvency registers;

(b)   the technical measures ensuring the minimum information technology security standards for communication and distribution of information within the system of interconnection of insol-vency registers;

(c)   minimum criteria for the search service provided by the European e-Justice Portal based on the information set out in Article 24;

(d)   minimum criteria for the presentation of the results of such searches based on the information set out in Article 24;

(e)   the means and the technical conditions of availability of services provided by the system of interconnection; and

(f)   a glossary containing a basic explanation of the national insolvency proceedings listed in Annex A.

GENERAL NOTE

Article 25 is not to come into force until 26 June 2018.

Article 26

Costs of establishing and interconnecting insolvency registers

1. The establishment, maintenance and future development of the system of interconnection of insolvency registers shall be financed from the general budget of the Union.

2. Each Member State shall bear the costs of establishing and adjusting its national insolvency registers to make them interoperable with the European e-Justice Portal, as well as the costs of administering, operating and maintaining those registers. This shall be without prejudice to the possibility to apply for grants to support such activities under the Union's financial programmes.

(See General Note after art.27.)

Article 27

Conditions of access to information via the system of interconnection

1. Member States shall ensure that the mandatory information referred to in points (a) to (j) of Article 24(2) is available free of charge via the system of interconnection of insolvency registers.

2. This Regulation shall not preclude Member States from charging a reasonable fee for access to the documents or additional information referred to in Article 24(3) via the system of interconnection of insolvency registers.

3. Member States may make access to mandatory information concerning individuals who are not exercising an independent business or professional activity, and concerning individuals exercising an independent business or professional activity when the insolvency proceedings are not related to that activity, subject to supplementary search criteria relating to the debtor in addition to the minimum criteria referred to in point (c) of Article 25(2).

4. Member States may require that access to the information referred to in paragraph 3 be made conditional upon a request to the competent authority. Member States may make access conditional upon the verification of the existence of a legitimate interest for accessing such information. The requesting person shall be able to submit the request for information electronically by means of a standard form via the European e-Justice Portal. Where a legitimate interest is required, it shall be permissible for the requesting person to justify his request by electronic copies of relevant documents. The requesting person shall be provided with an answer by the competent authority within 3 working days.

The requesting person shall not be obliged to provide translations of the documents justifying his request, or to bear any costs of translation which the competent authority may incur.

GENERAL NOTE TO ARTS 26, 27

Although arts 24 and 25 are not to come into force until 26 June 2018 and 6 June 2019 respectively, these two articles will become operative along with the rest of the Regulation to provide back-up during the interim period.

Article 28

Publication in another Member State

1. The insolvency practitioner or the debtor in possession shall request that notice of the judgment opening insolvency proceedings and, where appropriate, the decision appointing the insolvency practitioner be published in any other Member State where an establishment of the debtor is located in accordance with the publication procedures provided for in that Member State. Such publication shall

specify, where appropriate, the insolvency practitioner appointed and whether the jurisdiction rule applied is that pursuant to Article 3(1) or (2).

2. The insolvency practitioner or the debtor in possession may request that the information referred to in paragraph 1 be published in any other Member State where the insolvency practitioner or the debtor in possession deems it necessary in accordance with the publication procedures provided for in that Member State.

(See General Note after art.30.)

Article 29

Registration in public registers of another Member State

1. Where the law of a Member State in which an establishment of the debtor is located and this establishment has been entered into a public register of that Member State, or the law of a Member State in which immovable property belonging to the debtor is located, requires information on the opening of insolvency proceedings referred to in Article 28 to be published in the land register, company register or any other public register, the insolvency practitioner or the debtor in possession shall take all the necessary measures to ensure such a registration.

2. The insolvency practitioner or the debtor in possession may request such registration in any other Member State, provided that the law of the Member State where the register is kept allows such registration.

(See General Note after art.30.)

Article 30

Costs

The costs of the publication and registration provided for in Articles 28 and 29 shall be regarded as costs and expenses incurred in the proceedings.

GENERAL NOTE TO ARTS 28–30

These articles are rather more directory than the corresponding provisions in ECRIP. Under the predecessor to art.28 it was left to the office-holder to decide whether to make the request for publication, *unless* the Member State where the debtor had an establishment had enacted legislation making publication mandatory. The position is now reversed. Member States are now by implication required to enact such legislation. In other circumstances the office-holder continues to have the option (art.28(2)). Article 29 shows a similar shift of emphasis: "the liquidator *may* request" has been replaced by "the insolvency practitioner *shall* take all the necessary measures".

No legislation has been enacted in this country requiring mandatory publication or registration under arts 8(1) or 9(1). However, Companies House maintains a register, the European Community Liquidation and Insolvency Register (ECLAIR), allowing the office holder of any company whose COMI is within the UK and which is in compulsory liquidation, creditors' voluntary liquidation or administration to request that certain information (namely, any notice that must be delivered to the Registrar of Companies) be placed on that register. Revised guidance on the use of ECLAIR was published in *Dear IP*, September 2013. Where this is requested by the liquidator, the ordinary procedures to be followed under IA 1986 and the Rules will be applicable. No special forms have been prescribed.

On the advantages of registration even though this is not mandatory, see the article by G. Flannery in [2005] 21 I.L. & P. 57.

Article 31

Honouring of an obligation to a debtor

1. Where an obligation has been honoured in a Member State for the benefit of a debtor who is subject to insolvency proceedings opened in another Member State, when it should have been honoured for the

benefit of the insolvency practitioner in those proceedings, the person honouring the obligation shall be deemed to have discharged it if he was unaware of the opening of the proceedings.

2. Where such an obligation is honoured before the publication provided for in Article 28 has been effected, the person honouring the obligation shall be presumed, in the absence of proof to the contrary, to have been unaware of the opening of insolvency proceedings. Where the obligation is honoured after such publication has been effected, the person honouring the obligation shall be presumed, in the absence of proof to the contrary, to have been aware of the opening of proceedings.

GENERAL NOTE

This article gives protection to a creditor, based in a Member State other than that in which the insolvency proceedings have been opened, who has paid a debt in ignorance of the existence of the proceedings. The liquidator will thus be unable to have the payment set aside as a preference or declared void under IA 1986 s.127, for instance. Note the different rules as to the onus of proof in art.31(2).

The European Court has ruled that the phrase "for the benefit of a debtor" in para.(1) cannot be construed so as to include the situation where an obligation is honoured on the order of a debtor for the benefit of a creditor: *Van Buggenhout and Van de Mierop (Liquidators of Grontimmo SA) v Banque Internationale a Luxembourg SA* (C-251/12).

Article 32

Recognition and enforceability of other judgments

1. Judgments handed down by a court whose judgment concerning the opening of proceedings is recognised in accordance with Article 19 and which concern the course and closure of insolvency proceedings, and compositions approved by that court, shall also be recognised with no further formalities. Such judgments shall be enforced in accordance with Articles 39 to 44 and 47 to 57 of Regulation (EU) No 1215/2012.

The first subparagraph shall also apply to judgments deriving directly from the insolvency proceedings and which are closely linked with them, even if they were handed down by another court.

The first subparagraph shall also apply to judgments relating to preservation measures taken after the request for the opening of insolvency proceedings or in connection with it.

2. The recognition and enforcement of judgments other than those referred to in paragraph 1 of this Article shall be governed by Regulation (EU) No 1215/2012 provided that that Regulation is applicable.

GENERAL NOTE

As noted in the Preamble para.7, insolvency proceedings are specifically excluded from the scope of the Judgments Regulation (formerly the Brussels Convention). However, this article brings back within its ambit the judgments and compositions referred to in para.(1), so as to make them enforceable in other Member States in the same way as other judgments of the courts. So, for instance, an order that a creditor return a payment on the ground that it was a preference under IA 1986 s.239 will be enforceable under the Judgments Regulation in another Member State. The object of para.2 was, presumably, to make it clear that nothing in the present Regulation was intended to qualify or restrict the operation of the Convention. The scope of this provision and the delimitation between it and the Judgments Regulation is the subject of a detailed article by B. Wessels, (2008) 21 Insolv. Int. 135.

An order made by the English court in bankruptcy proceedings requiring a Dutch company to disclose information was held enforceable under the provision in *Handelsveem v Hill* [2012] B.P.I.R. 1024.

A members' voluntary winding up, not being insolvency proceedings, was held to be within the Brussels Convention in *Re Cover Europe Ltd* [2002] EWHC 861 (Ch); [2002] 2 B.C.L.C. 61.

Article 32(1) would appear to make the discharge of a debt in another EU jurisdiction binding throughout the Community. This makes all the more anomalous the ruling in *Global Distressed Alpha Fund 1 LLP v PT Bakrie Investindo* [2011] EWHC 256 (Comm); [2011] B.P.I.R. 644 (not involving the EU Regulation) where it was held that a foreign discharge was not effective where the underlying contract is governed by English law. See further the note to IA 1986 s.426.

In the case *Rahman v GMAC Commercial Finance* [2012] EWCA Civ 1467 the relationship between this provision and art.28 of the Judgments Regulation was in issue, but was not conclusively resolved.

A third sub-paragraph, making an exception for judgments which might result in a limitation of personal freedom or postal secrecy, has been dropped.

See further the notes to the Preamble para.7 and arts 10–18.

Article 33

Public policy

Any Member State may refuse to recognise insolvency proceedings opened in another Member State or to enforce a judgment handed down in the context of such proceedings where the effects of such recognition or enforcement would be manifestly contrary to that State's public policy, in particular its fundamental principles or the constitutional rights and liberties of the individual.

GENERAL NOTE

No doubt the inclusion of this provision was considered an important safeguard when the representatives of the Member States agreed the final text.

One thing which is not spelt out is the way in which the objecting State is to declare its refusal—whether by an organ of government, a court, or an office-holder. In the Irish case *Re Eurofood IFSC Ltd* [2004] B.C.C. 383 the judge relied on public policy as one of the grounds for refusing to recognise a ruling of an Italian court that main proceedings had effectively been opened in Italy so as to oust his own jurisdiction, and this view was affirmed on appeal by the Irish Supreme Court [2004] IESC 47; [2005] B.C.C. 999, primarily because the Italian court had not given the provisional liquidator a fair opportunity to present his case. The ECJ (*Re Eurofood IFSC Ltd* (C-341/04) [2006] B.C.C. 397), whilst upholding this decision, stressed that recourse to the public policy clause should be reserved for exceptional cases (in keeping with existing ECJ case law on the Brussels Convention (now the Judgments Regulation), which it said was "transposable" to this provision in the Regulation). (See also *French Republic v Klempka* [2006] B.C.C. 841.)

Of interest also is the ruling of the Commercial Court of Nanterre in *Re SAS Rover France* (19 May 2005, unreported: see Haravon (2005) 18 Insolv. Int. 118 at 120), concerning a French subsidiary of the MG Rover Group Ltd which had been put into administration in England. The French Public Prosecutor claimed that the English decision should not be recognised on public policy grounds, in effect arguing that safeguards imposed by French employment and social security legislation might be jeopardised. The Commercial Court held that the English court order should be recognised under art.16 (now art.19) and accepted undertakings offered by the administrators that these safeguards would be respected. The Court of Appeal in Versailles upheld this ruling (see (2006) 19 Insolv. Int. 31).

However, one rule of public policy has been expressly abrogated by the Regulation. This is the widely accepted principle that the courts will not enforce the fiscal laws of another State. Article 39 explicitly includes the claims of the tax and social security authorities of Member States among the debts for which proofs may be lodged. But a State's penal laws are not accorded the same concession, and so it will be open to a liquidator to reject an attempt by the authorities of another State to prove for a fine imposed by a court in the latter.

CHAPTER III

SECONDARY INSOLVENCY PROCEEDINGS

Article 34

Opening of proceedings

Where main insolvency proceedings have been opened by a court of a Member State and recognised in another Member State, a court of that other Member State which has jurisdiction pursuant to Article 3(2) may open secondary insolvency proceedings in accordance with the provisions set out in this Chapter. Where the main insolvency proceedings required that the debtor be insolvent, the debtor's insolvency shall not be re-examined in the Member State in which secondary insolvency proceedings may be opened. The effects of secondary insolvency proceedings shall be restricted to the assets of the debtor situated within the territory of the Member State in which those proceedings have been opened.

(See General Note after art.40.)

Article 35

Applicable law

Save as otherwise provided in this Regulation, the law applicable to secondary proceedings shall be that of the Member State within the territory of which the secondary insolvency proceedings are opened.

(See General Note after art.40.)

Article 36

Right to give an undertaking in order to avoid secondary insolvency proceedings

1. In order to avoid the opening of secondary insolvency proceedings, the insolvency practitioner in the main insolvency proceedings may give a unilateral undertaking (the 'undertaking') in respect of the assets located in the Member State in which secondary insolvency proceedings could be opened, that when distributing those assets or the proceeds received as a result of their realisation, it will comply with the distribution and priority rights under national law that creditors would have if secondary insolvency proceedings were opened in that Member State. The undertaking shall specify the factual assumptions on which it is based, in particular in respect of the value of the assets located in the Member State concerned and the options available to realise such assets.

2. Where an undertaking has been given in accordance with this Article, the law applicable to the distribution of proceeds from the realisation of assets referred to in paragraph 1, to the ranking of creditors' claims, and to the rights of creditors in relation to the assets referred to in paragraph 1 shall be the law of the Member State in which secondary insolvency proceedings could have been opened. The relevant point in time for determining the assets referred to in paragraph 1 shall be the moment at which the undertaking is given.

3. The undertaking shall be made in the official language or one of the official languages of the Member State where secondary insolvency proceedings could have been opened, or, where there are several official languages in that Member State, the official language or one of the official languages of the place in which secondary insolvency proceedings could have been opened.

4. The undertaking shall be made in writing. It shall be subject to any other requirements relating to form and approval requirements as to distributions, if any, of the State of the opening of the main insolvency proceedings.

5. The undertaking shall be approved by the known local creditors. The rules on qualified majority and voting that apply to the adoption of restructuring plans under the law of the Member State where secondary insolvency proceedings could have been opened shall also apply to the approval of the undertaking. Creditors shall be able to participate in the vote by distance means of communication, where national law so permits. The insolvency practitioner shall inform the known local creditors of the undertaking, of the rules and procedures for its approval, and of the approval or rejection of the undertaking.

6. An undertaking given and approved in accordance with this Article shall be binding on the estate. If secondary insolvency proceedings are opened in accordance with Articles 37 and 38, the insolvency practitioner in the main insolvency proceedings shall transfer any assets which it removed from the territory of that Member State after the undertaking was given or, where those assets have already been realised, their proceeds, to the insolvency practitioner in the secondary insolvency proceedings.

7. Where the insolvency practitioner has given an undertaking, it shall inform local creditors about the intended distributions prior to distributing the assets and proceeds referred to in paragraph 1. If that information does not comply with the terms of the undertaking or the applicable law, any local creditor may challenge such distribution before the courts of the Member State in which main insolvency proceedings have been opened in order to obtain a distribution in accordance with the terms of the undertaking and the applicable law. In such cases, no distribution shall take place until the court has taken a decision on the challenge.

8. Local creditors may apply to the courts of the Member State in which main insolvency proceedings have been opened, in order to require the insolvency practitioner in the main insolvency proceedings to take any suitable measures necessary to ensure compliance with the terms of the undertaking available under the law of the State of the opening of main insolvency proceedings.

9. Local creditors may also apply to the courts of the Member State in which secondary insolvency proceedings could have been opened in order to require the court to take provisional or protective measures to ensure compliance by the insolvency practitioner with the terms of the undertaking.

10. The insolvency practitioner shall be liable for any damage caused to local creditors as a result of its non-compliance with the obligations and requirements set out in this Article.

11. For the purpose of this Article, an authority which is established in the Member State where secondary insolvency proceedings could have been opened and which is obliged under Directive 2008/94/EC of the European Parliament and of the Council to guarantee the payment of employees' outstanding claims resulting from contracts of employment or employment relationships shall be considered to be a local creditor, where the national law so provides.

(See General Note after art.40.)

Article 37

Right to request the opening of secondary insolvency proceedings

1. The opening of secondary insolvency proceedings may be requested by:

   (a)   the insolvency practitioner in the main insolvency proceedings;

   (b)   any other person or authority empowered to request the opening of insolvency proceedings under the law of the Member State within the territory of which the opening of secondary insolvency proceedings is requested.

2. Where an undertaking has become binding in accordance with Article 36, the request for opening secondary insolvency proceedings shall be lodged within 30 days of having received notice of the approval of the undertaking.

(See General Note after art.40.)

Article 38

Decision to open secondary insolvency proceedings

1. A court seised of a request to open secondary insolvency proceedings shall immediately give notice to the insolvency practitioner or the debtor in possession in the main insolvency proceedings and give it an opportunity to be heard on the request.

2. Where the insolvency practitioner in the main insolvency proceedings has given an undertaking in accordance with Article 36, the court referred to in paragraph 1 of this Article shall, at the request of the insolvency practitioner, not open secondary insolvency proceedings if it is satisfied that the undertaking adequately protects the general interests of local creditors.

3. Where a temporary stay of individual enforcement proceedings has been granted in order to allow for negotiations between the debtor and its creditors, the court, at the request of the insolvency practitioner or the debtor in possession, may stay the opening of secondary insolvency proceedings for a period not exceeding 3 months, provided that suitable measures are in place to protect the interests of local creditors.

The court referred to in paragraph 1 may order protective measures to protect the interests of local creditors by requiring the insolvency practitioner or the debtor in possession not to remove or dispose of any assets which are located in the Member State where its establishment is located unless this is done in the ordinary course of business. The court may also order other measures to protect the interest of local creditors during a stay, unless this is incompatible with the national rules on civil procedure.

The stay of the opening of secondary insolvency proceedings shall be lifted by the court of its own motion or at the request of any creditor if, during the stay, an agreement in the negotiations referred to in the first subparagraph has been concluded.

The stay may be lifted by the court of its own motion or at the request of any creditor if the continuation of the stay is detrimental to the creditor's rights, in particular if the negotiations have been disrupted or it has become evident that they are unlikely to be concluded, or if the insolvency practitioner or the debtor in possession has infringed the prohibition on disposal of its assets or on removal of them from the territory of the Member State where the establishment is located.

4. At the request of the insolvency practitioner in the main insolvency proceedings, the court referred to in paragraph 1 may open a type of insolvency proceedings as listed in Annex A other than the type initially requested, provided that the conditions for opening that type of proceedings under national law are fulfilled and that that type of proceedings is the most appropriate as regards the interests of the local creditors and coherence between the main and secondary insolvency proceedings. The second sentence of Article 34 shall apply.

(See General Note after art.40.)

Article 39

Judicial review of the decision to open secondary insolvency proceedings

The insolvency practitioner in the main insolvency proceedings may challenge the decision to open secondary insolvency proceedings before the courts of the Member State in which secondary insolvency proceedings have been opened on the ground that the court did not comply with the conditions and requirements of Article 38.

(See General Note after art.40.)

Article 40

Advance payment of costs and expenses

Where the law of the Member State in which the opening of secondary insolvency proceedings is requested requires that the debtor's assets be sufficient to cover in whole or in part the costs and expenses of the proceedings, the court may, when it receives such a request, require the applicant to make an advance payment of costs or to provide appropriate security.

GENERAL NOTE TO ARTS 34–40

These provisions are primarily concerned with secondary proceedings that are opened *after* the opening of main proceedings in the jurisdiction of the debtor's COMI. Equivalent proceeding opened *before* any main proceedings have been opened (which the Act refers to as "territorial" proceedings but does not define as such) are governed by art.3(2) and (4) and are subject to the conditions set out in art.3(4). In particular, the right to request the opening of territorial proceedings (art.3(4)) is more restrictive than that in secondary proceedings (art.37(1)(b)). However, if main proceedings are opened at a later date, art.3(4) states that any territorial proceedings already in existence "become" secondary proceedings: in other words, from that time onwards the provisions of arts 34–40 apply to such proceedings in all respects.

Secondary proceedings are subject to a number of limitations. In particular:

–   the debtor must possess an "establishment" within the State;

–   the effects of the proceedings are limited to assets within the State.

It is no longer a requirement that secondary proceedings must only be for the purpose of winding up. Consequently, the old Annex B which listed the permitted forms of secondary proceeding has been discontinued.

In addition, secondary proceedings are subject to the wide powers of intervention conferred on the liquidator in the main proceedings by arts 46 et seq. On the other hand, once secondary proceedings have been opened in another State, the powers of the "main" liquidator and the scope of the law of the "main" jurisdiction have to yield to those of the secondary proceedings: see *Alitalia Linee Aeree Italiane SpA, Connock v Fantozzi* [2011] EWHC 15 (Ch); [2011] B.C.C. 579 (law of secondary proceedings in England prevailed over Italian law, the jurisdiction of main proceedings). In *Comité d'Entreprise de Nortel Networks SA v Rogeau* (C-649/13) [2015] B.C.C. 490 the CJEU ruled that where there are both main and secondary proceedings, the courts in both countries have concurrent jurisdiction to determine questions relating to assets situated in the State of the secondary proceedings.

It is a matter for the national law of the Member State where it is sought to open secondary proceedings to determine the question of standing (provided that that law does not discriminate between local creditors and creditors domiciled in other Member States): *Burgo Group SpA* (C-327/13); [2014] B.C.C. 33.

Art.34

Note that the fact that main proceedings have been opened, if based on insolvency, is to be taken as proof of the debtor's insolvency in any secondary proceedings. This confirms the decision in *Bank Handlowy et Ryszard Adamiak v Christianapol sp z oo* (C-116/11, 22 November 2012). One situation where a proceeding is not necessarily "based on insolvency" is the appointment of an administrator by or on the application of the holder of a floating charge (IA 1986 Sch.B1 paras 14, 35).

Where the main proceedings have a "protective" purpose (e.g. the French *sauvegarde* proceedings), the court having jurisdiction to open secondary proceedings should have regard to the objectives of the main proceedings (and should not undermine those objectives), in keeping with the "principle of sincere co-operation": *Bank Handlowy et Ryszard Adamiak v Christianapol sp z oo* (above).

Art.36

This article gives statutory authority to a procedure which had received the blessing of the court in *Re SAS Rover France* (unreported, 19 May 2005, Commercial Court of Nanterre: see Haravon (2005) 8 Insolv. Int. 118 at 120).

In one or two cases decided under the original Regulation, the court gave its support to a proposal by which the office-holder in English main proceedings would treat employees or other creditors in another Member State on the same terms that would apply if secondary proceedings were opened in the latter jurisdiction: see, for example *Re MG Rover España SA* [2006] B.C.C. 599; *Re Collins & Aikman Europe SA* [2006] EWHC 1343 (Ch); [2006] B.C.C. 861; *Re MG Rover Belux SA NV* [2007] B.C.C. 446; *Re Nortel Networks SA (No.2)* [2009] EWHC 1482 (Ch); [2010] B.C.C. 21. In this way they averted the risk that secondary proceedings would be opened in the other jurisdiction, to the prejudice of the administration of the insolvency as a whole. In *Re Collins & Aikman Europe SA* the administrators had given oral assurances to the creditors concerned, so coming close to the formal undertakings which the article envisages. The creditors had refrained from opening secondary proceedings in their State in consequence.

This kind of arrangement has now been given statutory support by the present article, which adds clarification on various points of detail, but introduces a straitjacket of formality. It is restricted to Member States in which the debtor has an establishment. The undertaking (which is described as "unilateral" but is in effect an agreement with the local creditors) must relate to the distribution of assets located in the Member State in question, and evidence of valuation, etc. is required (art.36(1)). The local law of that jurisdiction is to apply, and the relevant time for determining the assets is the time of the undertaking (art.36(2)). Further directions are given regarding the form and language of the undertaking and the involvement and rights of local creditors (art.36(3)–(10)). An undertaking becomes binding when the local creditors have given their approval in accordance with art.36(5). (Note that this means all the local creditors, and not just those creditors directly affected by the undertaking.) "Local creditors" presumably has the special meaning defined by art.2(11).

If the creditors are few in number the office-holders will be able to give a commitment to each of them individually. There will be no need to resort to the Regulation. The statutory procedure under art.36, in contrast, provides a mechanism by which (at some cost in time, expense and formality) the consent of the creditors may be given by a majority vote, so binding dissentient and non-participating creditors. Presumably it will still be possible to avoid the formality in some other way if it is not anticipated that any creditor will object, e.g. by giving an undertaking to the court or having the terms of the proposal embodied in a court order, as was done in the *Collins & Aikman* case.

If, when an undertaking is in force, a request is made to open secondary proceedings in the non-main jurisdiction, art.38 applies: see the note to that provision. If such proceedings are in due course actually opened, any assets which have been removed from the territory of the secondary Member State to the State of main proceedings, or their proceeds if they been realised, must be returned or paid over (art.36(6)). An authority in the secondary State which is obliged under EU law to guarantee the rights of local employees is to be considered a creditor, where the local law so provides (art.36(11)).

Art.37
Article 37(1)(b) assumes that all insolvency proceedings are initiated by a "request", which does not sit easily with some procedures in this jurisdiction, such as a voluntary liquidation or an administration established out-of-court, still less a pre-pack. Paragraph (2) may cause problems in such a situation. Sub-paragraph (1)(b) allows secondary proceedings to be opened by any of the procedures, and any of the persons, recognised by the domestic law: contrast the restrictions imposed in relation to the opening of territorial proceedings by art.3(4).

Even where no secondary proceedings have been opened, it may be in the interests of the main proceedings for its office-holder to open secondary proceedings in another State, e.g. to take advantage of "claw-back" provisions in the law of the latter. Article 37(1)(a) gives him locus standi to set such proceedings in motion. IA 1986 s.124(1) has been amended to confirm this. The administrators in *Re Nortel Networks SA (No.2)* [2009] EWHC 1482 (Ch); [2010] B.C.C. 21 received the court's blessing to institute secondary proceedings in France in order to achieve savings in time and costs.

Art.38
Again, the language assumes a judicial or quasi-judicial procedure, which is well out of step with many of our forms of insolvency proceeding, even taking into account the extended definitions of "court", etc. in art.2. Take, for instance, the appointment of an administrator out of court by the holder of a floating charge. Who or what is the "court seised of a request"? And how is the office-holder in the main proceedings to be given an opportunity to be "heard on the request"? The appointment in such a case is instantaneous and final, not allowing time for any of the procedures set out in the ensuing paragraphs.

The phrase "individual enforcement proceedings" in paragraph (3) probably means "proceedings not brought by an office-holder on behalf of the insolvent estate", and has nothing to do with "individuals" as human beings.

Art.40
There is no reason to suppose that this provision would apply in the UK.

Article 41

Cooperation and communication between insolvency practitioners

1. The insolvency practitioner in the main insolvency proceedings and the insolvency practitioner or practitioners in secondary insolvency proceedings concerning the same debtor shall cooperate with each other to the extent such cooperation is not incompatible with the rules applicable to the respective proceedings. Such cooperation may take any form, including the conclusion of agreements or protocols.

2. In implementing the cooperation set out in paragraph 1, the insolvency practitioners shall:

 (a) as soon as possible communicate to each other any information which may be relevant to the other proceedings, in particular any progress made in lodging and verifying claims and all measures aimed at rescuing or restructuring the debtor, or at terminating the proceedings, provided appropriate arrangements are made to protect confidential information;

 (b) explore the possibility of restructuring the debtor and, where such a possibility exists, coordinate the elaboration and implementation of a restructuring plan;

 (c) coordinate the administration of the realisation or use of the debtor's assets and affairs; the insolvency practitioner in the secondary insolvency proceedings shall give the insolvency practitioner in the main insolvency proceedings an early opportunity to submit proposals on the realisation or use of the assets in the secondary insolvency proceedings.

3. Paragraphs 1 and 2 shall apply mutatis mutandis to situations where, in the main or in the secondary insolvency proceedings or in any territorial insolvency proceedings concerning the same debtor and open at the same time, the debtor remains in possession of its assets.

(See General Note after art.44.)

Article 42

Cooperation and communication between courts

1. In order to facilitate the coordination of main, territorial and secondary insolvency proceedings concerning the same debtor, a court before which a request to open insolvency proceedings is pending, or which has opened such proceedings, shall cooperate with any other court before which a request to open insolvency proceedings is pending, or which has opened such proceedings, to the extent that such cooperation is not incompatible with the rules applicable to each of the proceedings. For that purpose, the courts may, where appropriate, appoint an independent person or body acting on its instructions, provided that it is not incompatible with the rules applicable to them.

2. In implementing the cooperation set out in paragraph 1, the courts, or any appointed person or body acting on their behalf, as referred to in paragraph 1, may communicate directly with, or request information or assistance directly from, each other provided that such communication respects the procedural rights of the parties to the proceedings and the confidentiality of information.

3. The cooperation referred to in paragraph 1 may be implemented by any means that the court considers appropriate. It may, in particular, concern:

    (a)   coordination in the appointment of the insolvency practitioners;

    (b)   communication of information by any means considered appropriate by the court;

    (c)   coordination of the administration and supervision of the debtor's assets and affairs;

    (d)   coordination of the conduct of hearings;

    (e)   coordination in the approval of protocols, where necessary.

(See General Note after art.44.)

Article 43

Cooperation and communication between insolvency practitioners and courts

1. In order to facilitate the coordination of main, territorial and secondary insolvency proceedings opened in respect of the same debtor:

    (a)   an insolvency practitioner in main insolvency proceedings shall cooperate and communicate with any court before which a request to open secondary insolvency proceedings is pending or which has opened such proceedings;

    (b)   an insolvency practitioner in territorial or secondary insolvency proceedings shall cooperate and communicate with the court before which a request to open main insolvency proceedings is pending or which has opened such proceedings; and

    (c)   an insolvency practitioner in territorial or secondary insolvency proceedings shall cooperate and communicate with the court before which a request to open other territorial or secondary insolvency proceedings is pending or which has opened such proceedings;

to the extent that such cooperation and communication are not incompatible with the rules applicable to each of the proceedings and do not entail any conflict of interest.

2. The cooperation referred to in paragraph 1 may be implemented by any appropriate means, such as those set out in Article 42(3).

(See General Note after art.44.)

Article 44

Costs of cooperation and communication

The requirements laid down in Articles 42 and 43 shall not result in courts charging costs to each other for cooperation and communication.

GENERAL NOTE TO ARTS 41–44

These articles replace art.31 in the original Regulation, which directed the office-holders in all the proceedings (main and secondary, and secondary office-holders *inter se*) to communicate information to each other and to cooperate with each other in peremptory terms, but without going into any detail. We now have an abundance of detail, in quite prescriptive terms, compliance with which is bound to entail the incurring of (possibly unwanted) cost and delay.

"Court" throughout has the extended meaning given by art.2(6)(ii), including all out-of-court procedures. There is an assumption that there will be time for the cooperative measures to proceed at a leisurely pace, which may well be out of keeping with practical necessity: how, for example, can the administrator in a pre-pack give the office-holder in main proceedings "an early opportunity to submit proposals on the realisation or use of the debtor company's assets" (art.41(1)(c))?

Art.41(1)
Note that the incompatibility must be with the applicable *rules*, not with the actual proceedings.

Art.42
Article 41 above is concerned with cooperation and communication between the insolvency practitioners; in contrast, this article calls for cooperation and communication between the courts involved. Once again, "court" is to be understood in the extended sense (art.2(6)(ii)), but makes no concessions to suit the situation in out-of-court proceedings. If the option of appointing an independent person is chosen, it is not clear whether all the courts concerned must act jointly, both in making the appointment and in giving instructions. The attribution of "its" (singular) to "courts" (plural) does nothing to dispel the confusion. The independent person will be automatically authorised to act in this country without further formality by virtue of the dispensation in IA 1986 s.388(6).

Art.43
To complete the picture, the insolvency practitioners and the courts concerned in the various proceedings must cooperate and communicate with each other.

Article 45

Exercise of creditors' rights

1. Any creditor may lodge its claim in the main insolvency proceedings and in any secondary insolvency proceedings.

2. The insolvency practitioners in the main and any secondary insolvency proceedings shall lodge in other proceedings claims which have already been lodged in the proceedings for which they were appointed, provided that the interests of creditors in the latter proceedings are served by doing so, subject to the right of creditors to oppose such lodgement or to withdraw the lodgement of their claims where the law applicable so provides.

3. The insolvency practitioner in the main or secondary insolvency proceedings shall be entitled to participate in other proceedings on the same basis as a creditor, in particular by attending creditors' meetings.

There is an inconsistency here with the Preamble para.63, which states that "any creditor which has its habitual residence, domicile or registered office in the Union should have the right to lodge a claim in each of the insolvency proceedings pending in the Union relating to the debtor's assets". It might be argued that art.45 should be read subject to this restriction. If it were, it would be supplemented to some extent by art.53, which specifically empowers "any foreign creditor" to lodge claims, "foreign creditor" being defined by art.2(12) in terms which limit the definition of such a creditor to one based in another Member State. In any case, the point will not arise in UK proceedings, since our domestic law has always allowed foreign creditors to prove, wherever they are based. As regards foreign tax and social security claims, see the note to art.53.

The right of office-holders to participate in each other's proceedings on the same basis as a creditor, and in particular to prove claims on behalf of their own creditors and to withdraw a proof, is confirmed by the Rules: see IR 2016 r.21.8.

Article 46

Stay of the process of realisation of assets

1. The court which opened the secondary insolvency proceedings shall stay the process of realisation of assets in whole or in part on receipt of a request from the insolvency practitioner in the main insolvency proceedings. In such a case, it may require the insolvency practitioner in the main insolvency proceedings to take any suitable measure to guarantee the interests of the creditors in the secondary insolvency proceedings and of individual classes of creditors. Such a request from the insolvency practitioner may be rejected only if it is manifestly of no interest to the creditors in the main insolvency proceedings. Such a stay of the process of realisation of assets may be ordered for up to 3 months. It may be continued or renewed for similar periods.

2. The court referred to in paragraph 1 shall terminate the stay of the process of realisation of assets:

    (a)   at the request of the insolvency practitioner in the main insolvency proceedings;

    (b)   of its own motion, at the request of a creditor or at the request of the insolvency practitioner in the secondary insolvency proceedings if that measure no longer appears justified, in particular, by the interests of creditors in the main insolvency proceedings or in the secondary insolvency proceedings.

"The court" is again to be interpreted in its wider sense here, so we must take it that the article applies to all out-of-court proceedings, however mind-boggling the effort.

Although the article uses the word "shall", the court is in fact given a considerable amount of discretion in deciding whether or not to grant a stay, in particular to secure the position of local creditors.

In *Re Integrated Medical Solutions Ltd* [2012] B.C.C. 215 the office-holder in main proceedings in the insolvency of an Irish company successfully invoked this provision to have a winding-up petition which had been presented to a court in England dismissed.

Article 47

Power of the insolvency practitioner to propose restructuring plans

1. Where the law of the Member State where secondary insolvency proceedings have been opened allows for such proceedings to be closed without liquidation by a restructuring plan, a composition or a comparable measure, the insolvency practitioner in the main insolvency proceedings shall be empowered to propose such a measure in accordance with the procedure of that Member State.

2. Any restriction of creditors' rights arising from a measure referred to in paragraph 1 which is proposed in secondary insolvency proceedings, such as a stay of payment or discharge of debt, shall have no effect

in respect of assets of a debtor that are not covered by those proceedings, without the consent of all the creditors having an interest.

GENERAL NOTE

CA 2006 s.896(2) permits an application for a Pt 26 scheme of arrangement to be made by the company, any creditor or member, a liquidator or an administrator. We may now add the office-holder in main proceedings to this list. Presumably, if only by implication, he is also empowered to make an application for sanction under s.899 and to have standing to intervene for any other purpose where a scheme has been initiated by another applicant.

Article 48

Impact of closure of insolvency proceedings

1. Without prejudice to Article 49, the closure of insolvency proceedings shall not prevent the continuation of other insolvency proceedings concerning the same debtor which are still open at that point in time.

2. Where insolvency proceedings concerning a legal person or a company in the Member State of that person's or company's registered office would entail the dissolution of the legal person or of the company, that legal person or company shall not cease to exist until any other insolvency proceedings concerning the same debtor have been closed, or the insolvency practitioner or practitioners in such proceedings have given consent to the dissolution.

GENERAL NOTE

This is a new provision. Article 48(2) introduces a qualification to the provisions in IA 1986 regarding the dissolution of companies: if other insolvency proceedings are still open at the relevant time, the dissolution is suspended unless the local office-holder consents. An amendment of the Act or supplementary legislation, although not strictly necessary, may be thought desirable.

Article 49

Assets remaining in the secondary insolvency proceedings

If, by the liquidation of assets in the secondary insolvency proceedings, it is possible to meet all claims allowed under those proceedings, the insolvency practitioner appointed in those proceedings shall immediately transfer any assets remaining to the insolvency practitioner in the main insolvency proceedings.

(See General Note after art.52.)

Article 50

Subsequent opening of the main insolvency proceedings

Where the proceedings referred to in Article 3(1) are opened following the opening of the proceedings referred to in Article 3(2) in another Member State, Articles 41, 45, 46, 47 and 49 shall apply to those opened first, in so far as the progress of those proceedings so permits.

(See General Note after art.52.)

Article 51

Conversion of secondary insolvency proceedings

1. At the request of the insolvency practitioner in the main insolvency proceedings, the court of the Member State in which secondary insolvency proceedings have been opened may order the conversion of the secondary insolvency proceedings into another type of insolvency proceedings listed in Annex A,

provided that the conditions for opening that type of proceedings under national law are fulfilled and that that type of proceedings is the most appropriate as regards the interests of the local creditors and coherence between the main and secondary insolvency proceedings.

2. When considering the request referred to in paragraph 1, the court may seek information from the insolvency practitioners involved in both proceedings.

(See General Note after art.52.)

Article 52

Preservation measures

Where the court of a Member State which has jurisdiction pursuant to Article 3(1) appoints a temporary administrator in order to ensure the preservation of a debtor's assets, that temporary administrator shall be empowered to request any measures to secure and preserve any of the debtor's assets situated in another Member State, provided for under the law of that Member State, for the period between the request for the opening of insolvency proceedings and the judgment opening the proceedings.

GENERAL NOTE TO ARTS 49–52

Miscellaneous measures regarding secondary proceedings are set out here, which in the main are self-explanatory.

Art.52

There is no reason to suppose that "administrator" is used here in the formal sense of an administrator appointed under IA 1986 Sch.B1 (who would not in any sense be "temporary"). In UK law the equivalent would be a receiver appointed by the court pending the opening of insolvency proceedings—who is, in fact, listed in Annex B among the insolvency practitioners recognised by the Regulation.

CHAPTER IV

PROVISION OF INFORMATION FOR CREDITORS AND LODGEMENT OF THEIR CLAIMS

Article 53

Right to lodge claims

Any foreign creditor may lodge claims in insolvency proceedings by any means of communication, which are accepted by the law of the State of the opening of proceedings. Representation by a lawyer or another legal professional shall not be mandatory for the sole purpose of lodging of claims.

(See General Note after art.55.)

Article 54

Duty to inform creditors

1. As soon as insolvency proceedings are opened in a Member State, the court of that State having jurisdiction or the insolvency practitioner appointed by that court shall immediately inform the known foreign creditors.

2. The information referred to in paragraph 1, provided by an individual notice, shall in particular include time limits, the penalties laid down with regard to those time limits, the body or authority empowered to accept the lodgement of claims and any other measures laid down. Such notice shall also indicate whether creditors whose claims are preferential or secured in rem need to lodge their claims. The notice shall also include a copy of the standard form for lodging of claims referred to in Article 55 or information on where that form is available.

3. The information referred to in paragraphs 1 and 2 of this Article shall be provided using the standard notice form to be established in accordance with Article 88. The form shall be published in the European e-Justice Portal and shall bear the heading 'Notice of insolvency proceedings' in all the official languages of the institutions of the Union. It shall be transmitted in the official language of the State of the opening of proceedings or, if there are several official languages in that Member State, in the official language or one of the official languages of the place where insolvency proceedings have been opened, or in another language which that State has indicated it can accept, in accordance with Article 55(5), if it can be assumed that that language is easier to understand for the foreign creditors.

4. In insolvency proceedings relating to an individual not exercising a business or professional activity, the use of the standard form referred to in this Article shall not be obligatory if creditors are not required to lodge their claims in order to have their claims taken into account in the proceedings.

(See General Note after art.55.)

Article 55

Procedure for lodging claims

1. Any foreign creditor may lodge its claim using the standard claims form to be established in accordance with Article 88. The form shall bear the heading 'Lodgement of claims' in all the official languages of the institutions of the Union.

2. The standard claims form referred to in paragraph 1 shall include the following information:

    (a)   the name, postal address, e-mail address, if any, personal identification number, if any, and bank details of the foreign creditor referred to in paragraph 1;

    (b)   the amount of the claim, specifying the principal and, where applicable, interest and the date on which it arose and the date on which it became due, if different;

    (c)   if interest is claimed, the interest rate, whether the interest is of a legal or contractual nature, the period of time for which the interest is claimed and the capitalised amount of interest;

    (d)   if costs incurred in asserting the claim prior to the opening of proceedings are claimed, the amount and the details of those costs;

    (e)   the nature of the claim;

    (f)   whether any preferential creditor status is claimed and the basis of such a claim;

    (g)   whether security in rem or a reservation of title is alleged in respect of the claim and if so, what assets are covered by the security interest being invoked, the date on which the security was granted and, where the security has been registered, the registration number; and

    (h)   whether any set-off is claimed and, if so, the amounts of the mutual claims existing on the date when insolvency proceedings were opened, the date on which they arose and the amount net of set-off claimed.

The standard claims form shall be accompanied by copies of any supporting documents.

3. The standard claims form shall indicate that the provision of information concerning the bank details and the personal identification number of the creditor referred to in point (a) of paragraph 2 is not compulsory.

4. When a creditor lodges its claim by means other than the standard form referred to in paragraph 1, the claim shall contain the information referred to in paragraph 2.

5. Claims may be lodged in any official language of the institutions of the Union. The court, the insolvency practitioner or the debtor in possession may require the creditor to provide a translation in the

official language of the State of the opening of proceedings or, if there are several official languages in that Member State, in the official language or one of the official languages of the place where insolvency proceedings have been opened, or in another language which that Member State has indicated it can accept. Each Member State shall indicate whether it accepts any official language of the institutions of the Union other than its own for the purpose of the lodging of claims.

6. Claims shall be lodged within the period stipulated by the law of the State of the opening of proceedings. In the case of a foreign creditor, that period shall not be less than 30 days following the publication of the opening of insolvency proceedings in the insolvency register of the State of the opening of proceedings. Where a Member State relies on Article 24(4), that period shall not be less than 30 days following a creditor having been informed pursuant to Article 54.

7. Where the court, the insolvency practitioner or the debtor in possession has doubts in relation to a claim lodged in accordance with this Article, it shall give the creditor the opportunity to provide additional evidence on the existence and the amount of the claim.

GENERAL NOTE TO ARTS 53–55

These articles set out the requirements and procedure for the provision of information to creditors and the lodging of claims by them. They should be read in conjunction with art.88. They apply in all forms of insolvency proceedings, whether main, territorial or secondary.

Art.53

The term "foreign creditor" is defined in art.2(12) and is more restrictive (and, in one respect, wider) than might be supposed:

> "'foreign creditor' means a creditor which has its habitual residence, domicile or registered office in a Member State other than the State of the opening of proceedings, including the tax authorities and social security authorities of Member States".

In the absence of any definition of "Member State", it is unclear whether Denmark is included.

As noted in the comment to art.45(1), there is some inconsistency between these two articles. It would appear that a creditor must be based in the Community before he can assert any right specifically conferred by Regulation, but this would not rule out the right given to any other foreign creditor to prove in an insolvency under the domestic law of the particular proceedings (see art.7(2)(g)). The express inclusion of the tax and social security authorities among the permitted claimants is a remarkable change from the traditional position—although some other Crown debts, such as fines, will continue to be unenforceable abroad.

Art.54

The standard form of notice, accompanied by a standard claim form, must be used. At the time of going to press, neither form has yet been published. Note the (very limited) exception where the debtor has not been exercising a business or professional activity and creditors are not required to lodge claims. There does not appear to be any other situation where a similar dispensation may be obtained or special procedure made available.

Art.55

Note the provisions regarding the language(s) to be used, or permitted to be used, in paras 1 and 5. It was held in *R Jung GmbH v SIFA SA* [2006] B.C.C. 678 that these requirements must be strictly observed.

CHAPTER V

INSOLVENCY PROCEEDINGS OF MEMBERS OF A GROUP OF COMPANIES

GENERAL NOTE TO CHAPTER V

One of the major criticisms of the former Regulation was that it made no special provision for cross-border insolvencies involving the members of a corporate group. In consequence, the decided cases adhered quite strictly to the traditional approach, respecting the separate corporate personality of individual members of the group. It was left to the office-holders concerned to make such informal arrangements for cooperation as they could, sometimes with the support of the courts, but without any backing from the law.

The new Regulation has answered these criticisms with an elaborate array of provisions, setting up schemes for cooperation and coordination which are typically prescriptive in character with the accompanying disadvantages of formality, expense and delay.

There is also cause for some concern in the rather narrow definition of "group" (art.2(13), (14)):

"group of companies" means a parent undertaking and all its subsidiary undertakings;

"parent undertaking" means an undertaking which controls, either directly or indirectly, one or more subsidiary undertakings. An undertaking which prepares consolidated financial statements in accordance with Directive 2103/34/EU of the European Parliament and the Council shall be deemed to be a parent undertaking.

This definition is not, on the face of it, limited to subsidiaries which are incorporated in (or have their COMI or an establishment in or some other connection with) another Member State, but this must be the case for the purposes of the present chapter. Of course, the parent undertaking may well have subsidiaries outwith as well as within the EU, and there is no reason why the former should not be included in (say) a coordination scheme, but that would not in any way bring them within the scope of the Regulation.

There are, of course, a myriad of other structures by which an array of companies may be linked to form what would commonly be called a group, e.g. by cross-holdings of shares. Any scheme for cooperation between the members of such a group would need to be established informally, without reference to this Part of the Regulation.

SECTION 1

Cooperation and communication

Article 56

Cooperation and communication between insolvency practitioners

1. Where insolvency proceedings relate to two or more members of a group of companies, an insolvency practitioner appointed in proceedings concerning a member of the group shall cooperate with any insolvency practitioner appointed in proceedings concerning another member of the same group to the extent that such cooperation is appropriate to facilitate the effective administration of those proceedings, is not incompatible with the rules applicable to such proceedings and does not entail any conflict of interest. That cooperation may take any form, including the conclusion of agreements or protocols.

2. In implementing the cooperation set out in paragraph 1, insolvency practitioners shall:

  (a)   as soon as possible communicate to each other any information which may be relevant to the other proceedings, provided appropriate arrangements are made to protect confidential information;

  (b)   consider whether possibilities exist for coordinating the administration and supervision of the affairs of the group members which are subject to insolvency proceedings, and if so, coordinate such administration and supervision;

  (c)   consider whether possibilities exist for restructuring group members which are subject to insolvency proceedings and, if so, coordinate with regard to the proposal and negotiation of a coordinated restructuring plan.

For the purposes of points (b) and (c), all or some of the insolvency practitioners referred to in paragraph 1 may agree to grant additional powers to an insolvency practitioner appointed in one of the proceedings where such an agreement is permitted by the rules applicable to each of the proceedings. They may also agree on the allocation of certain tasks amongst them, where such allocation of tasks is permitted by the rules applicable to each of the proceedings.

(See General Note after art.60.)

Cooperation and communication between courts

1. Where insolvency proceedings relate to two or more members of a group of companies, a court which has opened such proceedings shall cooperate with any other court before which a request to open proceedings concerning another member of the same group is pending or which has opened such proceedings to the extent that such cooperation is appropriate to facilitate the effective administration of the proceedings, is not incompatible with the rules applicable to them and does not entail any conflict of interest. For that purpose, the courts may, where appropriate, appoint an independent person or body to act on its instructions, provided that this is not incompatible with the rules applicable to them.

2. In implementing the cooperation set out in paragraph 1, courts, or any appointed person or body acting on their behalf, as referred to in paragraph 1, may communicate directly with each other, or request information or assistance directly from each other, provided that such communication respects the procedural rights of the parties to the proceedings and the confidentiality of information.

3. The cooperation referred to in paragraph 1 may be implemented by any means that the court considers appropriate. It may, in particular, concern:

    (a)   coordination in the appointment of insolvency practitioners;

    (b)   communication of information by any means considered appropriate by the court;

    (c)   coordination of the administration and supervision of the assets and affairs of the members of the group;

    (d)   coordination of the conduct of hearings;

    (e)   coordination in the approval of protocols where necessary.

(See General Note after art.60.)

Article 58

Cooperation and communication between insolvency practitioners and courts

An insolvency practitioner appointed in insolvency proceedings concerning a member of a group of companies:

    (a)   shall cooperate and communicate with any court before which a request for the opening of proceedings in respect of another member of the same group of companies is pending or which has opened such proceedings; and

    (b)   may request information from that court concerning the proceedings regarding the other member of the group or request assistance concerning the proceedings in which he has been appointed;

to the extent that such cooperation and communication are appropriate to facilitate the effective administration of the proceedings, do not entail any conflict of interest and are not incompatible with the rules applicable to them.

(See General Note after art.60.)

Article 59

Costs of cooperation and communication in proceedings concerning members of a group of companies

The costs of the cooperation and communication provided for in Articles 56 to 60 incurred by an insolvency practitioner or a court shall be regarded as costs and expenses incurred in the respective proceedings.

(See General Note after art.60.)

Article 60

Powers of the insolvency practitioner in proceedings concerning members of a group of companies

1. An insolvency practitioner appointed in insolvency proceedings opened in respect of a member of a group of companies may, to the extent appropriate to facilitate the effective administration of the proceedings:

(a) be heard in any of the proceedings opened in respect of any other member of the same group;

(b) request a stay of any measure related to the realisation of the assets in the proceedings opened with respect to any other member of the same group, provided that:

    (i) a restructuring plan for all or some members of the group for which insolvency proceedings have been opened has been proposed under point (c) of Article 56(2) and presents a reasonable chance of success;

    (ii) such a stay is necessary in order to ensure the proper implementation of the restructuring plan;

    (iii) the restructuring plan would be to the benefit of the creditors in the proceedings for which the stay is requested; and

    (iv) neither the insolvency proceedings in which the insolvency practitioner referred to in paragraph 1 of this Article has been appointed nor the proceedings in respect of which the stay is requested are subject to coordination under Section 2 of this Chapter;

(c) apply for the opening of group coordination proceedings in accordance with Article 61.

2. The court having opened proceedings referred to in point (b) of paragraph 1 shall stay any measure related to the realisation of the assets in the proceedings in whole or in part if it is satisfied that the conditions referred to in point (b) of paragraph 1 are fulfilled.

Before ordering the stay, the court shall hear the insolvency practitioner appointed in the proceedings for which the stay is requested. Such a stay may be ordered for any period, not exceeding 3 months, which the court considers appropriate and which is compatible with the rules applicable to the proceedings.

The court ordering the stay may require the insolvency practitioner referred to in paragraph 1 to take any suitable measure available under national law to guarantee the interests of the creditors in the proceedings.

The court may extend the duration of the stay by such further period or periods as it considers appropriate and which are compatible with the rules applicable to the proceedings, provided that the conditions referred to in points (b)(ii) to (iv) of paragraph 1 continue to be fulfilled and that the total duration of the stay (the initial period together with any such extensions) does not exceed 6 months.

GENERAL NOTE TO ARTS 56–60

These articles follow closely arts 41–44, which provide for communication and cooperation where there are concurrently several insolvency proceedings involving the same debtor. Once again, "court" has its extended meaning and includes all out-of-court procedures.

SECTION 2

Coordination

<small>GENERAL NOTE TO SECTION 2</small>

This section, which is new, provides details of a formal scheme for coordination which may be set up between the insolvent members of a group and their respective office-holders. This includes the appointment of an independent qualified insolvency practitioner, separate from the existing office-holders, to act as "co-ordinator". Among the points which may be noted are:

- "Group" has the restricted meaning defined by art.2(13), (14).

- The participants must all be members of the group who are subject to EU insolvency proceedings, with an insolvency practitioner already in office. Other members of the group, whether solvent or insolvent, cannot be involved, still less any outsider such as a foreign parent or subsidiary or a creditor or shareholder.

- The court (which in this context has its traditional and not its extended meaning) has the limited function of making the formal appointment of the coordinator, and it must also be satisfied that the opening of proceedings is "appropriate", but its function is essentially one of rubber-stamping decisions made or agreed on by the parties: it does not appear to have any initiative or creative role or to be expected to adjudicate on any disputes.

- It is up to each individual group member and its office-holder to decide whether to participate in the scheme.

- The coordinator is required to propose a plan for the coordinated conduct of the proceedings, but the court is not involved in the formulation of the plan or required to approve it. There is no provision for the plan to be filed in court or for any report to be made on its implementation or conclusion. In effect, the court has no involvement once the coordinator has been appointed, apart from keeping some control of the costs (art.72(6)).

Subsection 1

Procedure

Article 61

Request to open group coordination proceedings

1. Group coordination proceedings may be requested before any court having jurisdiction over the insolvency proceedings of a member of the group, by an insolvency practitioner appointed in insolvency proceedings opened in relation to a member of the group.

2. The request referred to in paragraph 1 shall be made in accordance with the conditions provided for by the law applicable to the proceedings in which the insolvency practitioner has been appointed.

3. The request referred to in paragraph 1 shall be accompanied by:

(a) a proposal as to the person to be nominated as the group coordinator ('the coordinator'), details of his or her eligibility pursuant to Article 71, details of his or her qualifications and his or her written agreement to act as coordinator;

(b) an outline of the proposed group coordination, and in particular the reasons why the conditions set out in Article 63(1) are fulfilled;

(c) a list of the insolvency practitioners appointed in relation to the members of the group and, where relevant, the courts and competent authorities involved in the insolvency proceedings of the members of the group;

(d) an outline of the estimated costs of the proposed group coordination and the estimation of the share of those costs to be paid by each member of the group.

(See General Note after art.77.)

Article 62

Priority rule

Without prejudice to Article 66, where the opening of group coordination proceedings is requested before courts of different Member States, any court other than the court first seised shall decline jurisdiction in favour of that court.

(See General Note after art.77.)

Article 63

Notice by the court seised

1. The court seised of a request to open group coordination proceedings shall give notice as soon as possible of the request for the opening of group coordination proceedings and of the proposed coordinator to the insolvency practitioners appointed in relation to the members of the group as indicated in the request referred to in point (c) of Article 61(3), if it is satisfied that:

(a) the opening of such proceedings is appropriate to facilitate the effective administration of the insolvency proceedings relating to the different group members;

(b) no creditor of any group member expected to participate in the proceedings is likely to be financially disadvantaged by the inclusion of that member in such proceedings; and

(c) the proposed coordinator fulfils the requirements laid down in Article 71.

2. The notice referred to in paragraph 1 of this Article shall list the elements referred to in points (a) to (d) of Article 61(3).

3. The notice referred to in paragraph 1 shall be sent by registered letter, attested by an acknowledgment of receipt.

4. The court seised shall give the insolvency practitioners involved the opportunity to be heard.

(See General Note after art.77.)

Article 64

Objections by insolvency practitioners

1. An insolvency practitioner appointed in respect of any group member may object to:

(a) the inclusion within group coordination proceedings of the insolvency proceedings in respect of which it has been appointed; or

(b) the person proposed as a coordinator.

2. Objections pursuant to paragraph 1 of this Article shall be lodged with the court referred to in Article 63 within 30 days of receipt of notice of the request for the opening of group coordination proceedings by the insolvency practitioner referred to in paragraph 1 of this Article.

The objection may be made by means of the standard form established in accordance with Article 88.

3. Prior to taking the decision to participate or not to participate in the coordination in accordance with point (a) of paragraph 1, an insolvency practitioner shall obtain any approval which may be required under the law of the State of the opening of proceedings for which it has been appointed.

(See General Note after art.77.)

Article 65

Consequences of objection to the inclusion in group coordination

1. Where an insolvency practitioner has objected to the inclusion of the proceedings in respect of which it has been appointed in group coordination proceedings, those proceedings shall not be included in the group coordination proceedings.

2. The powers of the court referred to in Article 68 or of the coordinator arising from those proceedings shall have no effect as regards that member, and shall entail no costs for that member.

(See General Note after art.77.)

Article 66

Choice of court for group coordination proceedings

1. Where at least two-thirds of all insolvency practitioners appointed in insolvency proceedings of the members of the group have agreed that a court of another Member State having jurisdiction is the most appropriate court for the opening of group coordination proceedings, that court shall have exclusive jurisdiction.

2. The choice of court shall be made by joint agreement in writing or evidenced in writing. It may be made until such time as group coordination proceedings have been opened in accordance with Article 68.

3. Any court other than the court seised under paragraph 1 shall decline jurisdiction in favour of that court.

4. The request for the opening of group coordination proceedings shall be submitted to the court agreed in accordance with Article 61.

(See General Note after art.77.)

Article 67

Consequences of objections to the proposed coordinator

Where objections to the person proposed as coordinator have been received from an insolvency practitioner which does not also object to the inclusion in the group coordination proceedings of the member in respect of which it has been appointed, the court may refrain from appointing that person and invite the objecting insolvency practitioner to submit a new request in accordance with Article 61(3).

(See General Note after art.77.)

Article 68

Decision to open group coordination proceedings

1. After the period referred to in Article 64(2) has elapsed, the court may open group coordination proceedings where it is satisfied that the conditions of Article 63(1) are met. In such a case, the court shall:

  (a) appoint a coordinator;

(b)   decide on the outline of the coordination; and

(c)   decide on the estimation of costs and the share to be paid by the group members.

2. The decision opening group coordination proceedings shall be brought to the notice of the participating insolvency practitioners and of the coordinator.

(See General Note after art.77.)

Article 69

Subsequent opt-in by insolvency practitioners

1. In accordance with its national law, any insolvency practitioner may request, after the court decision referred to in Article 68, the inclusion of the proceedings in respect of which it has been appointed, where:

(a)   there has been an objection to the inclusion of the insolvency proceedings within the group coordination proceedings; or

(b)   insolvency proceedings with respect to a member of the group have been opened after the court has opened group coordination proceedings.

2. Without prejudice to paragraph 4, the coordinator may accede to such a request, after consulting the insolvency practitioners involved, where

(a)   he or she is satisfied that, taking into account the stage that the group coordination proceedings has reached at the time of the request, the criteria set out in points (a) and (b) of Article 63(1) are met; or

(b)   all insolvency practitioners involved agree, subject to the conditions in their national law.

3. The coordinator shall inform the court and the participating insolvency practitioners of his or her decision pursuant to paragraph 2 and of the reasons on which it is based.

4. Any participating insolvency practitioner or any insolvency practitioner whose request for inclusion in the group coordination proceedings has been rejected may challenge the decision referred to in paragraph 2 in accordance with the procedure set out under the law of the Member State in which the group coordination proceedings have been opened.

(See General Note after art.77.)

Article 70

Recommendations and group coordination plan

1. When conducting their insolvency proceedings, insolvency practitioners shall consider the recommendations of the coordinator and the content of the group coordination plan referred to in Article 72(1).

2. An insolvency practitioner shall not be obliged to follow in whole or in part the coordinator's recommendations or the group coordination plan.

If it does not follow the coordinator's recommendations or the group coordination plan, it shall give reasons for not doing so to the persons or bodies that it is to report to under its national law, and to the coordinator.

(See General Note after art.77.)

Subsection 2

General provisions

Article 71

The coordinator

1. The coordinator shall be a person eligible under the law of a Member State to act as an insolvency practitioner.

2. The coordinator shall not be one of the insolvency practitioners appointed to act in respect of any of the group members, and shall have no conflict of interest in respect of the group members, their creditors and the insolvency practitioners appointed in respect of any of the group members.

(See General Note after art.77.)

Article 72

Tasks and rights of the coordinator

1. The coordinator shall:

  (a) identify and outline recommendations for the coordinated conduct of the insolvency proceedings;

  (b) propose a group coordination plan that identifies, describes and recommends a comprehensive set of measures appropriate to an integrated approach to the resolution of the group members' insolvencies. In particular, the plan may contain proposals for:

    (i) the measures to be taken in order to re-establish the economic performance and the financial soundness of the group or any part of it;

    (ii) the settlement of intra-group disputes as regards intra-group transactions and avoidance actions;

    (iii) agreements between the insolvency practitioners of the insolvent group members.

2. The coordinator may also:

  (a) be heard and participate, in particular by attending creditors' meetings, in any of the proceedings opened in respect of any member of the group;

  (b) mediate any dispute arising between two or more insolvency practitioners of group members;

  (c) present and explain his or her group coordination plan to the persons or bodies that he or she is to report to under his or her national law;

  (d) request information from any insolvency practitioner in respect of any member of the group where that information is or might be of use when identifying and outlining strategies and measures in order to coordinate the proceedings; and

  (e) request a stay for a period of up to 6 months of the proceedings opened in respect of any member of the group, provided that such a stay is necessary in order to ensure the proper implementation of the plan and would be to the benefit of the creditors in the proceedings for which the stay is requested; or request the lifting of any existing stay. Such a request shall be made to the court that opened the proceedings for which a stay is requested.

3. The plan referred to in point (b) of paragraph 1 shall not include recommendations as to any consolidation of proceedings or insolvency estates.

4. The coordinator's tasks and rights as defined under this Article shall not extend to any member of the group not participating in group coordination proceedings.

5. The coordinator shall perform his or her duties impartially and with due care.

6. Where the coordinator considers that the fulfilment of his or her tasks requires a significant increase in the costs compared to the cost estimate referred to in point (d) of Article 61(3), and in any case, where the costs exceed 10 % of the estimated costs, the coordinator shall:

    (a)   inform without delay the participating insolvency practitioners; and

    (b)   seek the prior approval of the court opening group coordination proceedings.

(See General Note after art.77.)

Article 73

Languages

1. The coordinator shall communicate with the insolvency practitioner of a participating group member in the language agreed with the insolvency practitioner or, in the absence of an agreement, in the official language or one of the official languages of the institutions of the Union, and of the court which opened the proceedings in respect of that group member.

2. The coordinator shall communicate with a court in the official language applicable to that court.

(See General Note after art.77.)

Article 74

Cooperation between insolvency practitioners and the coordinator

1. Insolvency practitioners appointed in relation to members of a group and the coordinator shall cooperate with each other to the extent that such cooperation is not incompatible with the rules applicable to the respective proceedings.

2. In particular, insolvency practitioners shall communicate any information that is relevant for the coordinator to perform his or her tasks.

(See General Note after art.77.)

Article 75

Revocation of the appointment of the coordinator

The court shall revoke the appointment of the coordinator of its own motion or at the request of the insolvency practitioner of a participating group member where:

    (a)   the coordinator acts to the detriment of the creditors of a participating group member; or

    (b)   the coordinator fails to comply with his or her obligations under this Chapter.

(See General Note after art.77.)

Article 76

Debtor in possession

The provisions applicable, under this Chapter, to the insolvency practitioner shall also apply, where appropriate, to the debtor in possession.

(See General Note after art.77.)

Article 77

Costs and distribution

1. The remuneration for the coordinator shall be adequate, proportionate to the tasks fulfilled and reflect reasonable expenses.

2. On having completed his or her tasks, the coordinator shall establish the final statement of costs and the share to be paid by each member, and submit this statement to each participating insolvency practitioner and to the court opening coordination proceedings.

3. In the absence of objections by the insolvency practitioners within 30 days of receipt of the statement referred to in paragraph 2, the costs and the share to be paid by each member shall be deemed to be agreed. The statement shall be submitted to the court opening coordination proceedings for confirmation.

4. In the event of an objection, the court that opened the group coordination proceedings shall, upon the application of the coordinator or any participating insolvency practitioner, decide on the costs and the share to be paid by each member in accordance with the criteria set out in paragraph 1 of this Article, and taking into account the estimation of costs referred to in Article 68(1) and, where applicable, Article 72(6).

5. Any participating insolvency practitioner may challenge the decision referred to in paragraph 4 in accordance with the procedure set out under the law of the Member State where group coordination proceedings have been opened.

GENERAL NOTE TO ARTS 61–77

These articles set out the procedure to be followed in the appointment of the coordinator.

Art.61

It is not necessary that the applicant should be the office-holder in the insolvency proceedings of the member in that jurisdiction: it might be appropriate, for instance, for the liquidator of a subsidiary to make the application in the jurisdiction of the parent undertaking, or vice versa.

The court is not required to vet the credentials of the proposed coordinator in any depth or authorised to adjudicate between rival candidates for the post.

If the coordinator holds office in another Member State, he will be automatically authorised to act in this country without further formality by virtue of the dispensation in IA 1986 s.388(6).

It would not seem to be necessary that the "outline" of the proposed consolidation should go into any great detail. Nor that it would be binding on the coordinator when he produces his considered plan in accordance with art.72.

Arts 63–68

It is unclear what sort of a hearing (if any) is contemplated by the legislation, and what evidence the court would or should require before it makes its decision. An objecting office-holder clearly has standing to appear (art.63(4)) and he may object to the person proposed as co-ordinator (art.67)—but not, apparently, to the merits of the scheme. Is the court expected (or obliged) to go into the merits of the objection? He may object to the inclusion of his proceeding within the group coordination (art.64(1)(a)), but what can the court do about that? After all, the objecting office-holder is free to walk away from the exercise without giving any reason (art.65).

Art.69

It is not clear how the "objection" will have come about: who has made the objection, and to whom, and whether the proceedings in question have been thrown out of the scheme or have never been included. Has the decision to exclude been taken by the proposer, the other office-holders, or the court?

Art.70

In the absence of any statutory provision providing (e.g.) for decisions taken by majority vote being binding on dissentients, the success of a coordination plan plainly depends on an underlying consensus. This article gives scope for a degree of disagreement consistent with the continuation of that basic understanding.

Art.75
There is no provision in this Chapter dealing with the replacement of a coordinator in the normal course of affairs (e.g. on retirement, death or loss of qualification), and whether the new appointee should be notified to the court. Nor does this article mention the question of a new appointment: this is left to the participants.

Art.77
The article assumes that the coordination plan has come to a conclusion, successful or otherwise. Presumably a similar procedure will be applicable when a coordinator ceases to hold office for any other reason.

There is no requirement to report to the court on the outcome of the plan.

CHAPTER VI

DATA PROTECTION

Article 78

Data protection

1. National rules implementing Directive 95/46/EC shall apply to the processing of personal data carried out in the Member States pursuant to this Regulation, provided that processing operations referred to in Article 3(2) of Directive 95/46/EC are not concerned.

2. Regulation (EC) No 45/2001 shall apply to the processing of personal data carried out by the Commission pursuant to this Regulation.

(See General Note after art.83.)

Article 79

Responsibilities of Member States regarding the processing of personal data in national insolvency registers

1. Each Member State shall communicate to the Commission the name of the natural or legal person, public authority, agency or any other body designated by national law to exercise the functions of controller in accordance with point (d) of Article 2 of Directive 95/46/EC, with a view to its publication on the European e-Justice Portal.

2. Member States shall ensure that the technical measures for ensuring the security of personal data processed in their national insolvency registers referred to in Article 24 are implemented.

3. Member States shall be responsible for verifying that the controller, designated by national law in accordance with point (d) of Article 2 of Directive 95/46/EC, ensures compliance with the principles of data quality, in particular the accuracy and the updating of data stored in national insolvency registers.

4. Member States shall be responsible, in accordance with Directive 95/46/EC, for the collection and storage of data in national databases and for decisions taken to make such data available in the interconnected register that can be consulted via the European e-Justice Portal.

5. As part of the information that should be provided to data subjects to enable them to exercise their rights, and in particular the right to the erasure of data, Member States shall inform data subjects of the accessibility period set for personal data stored in insolvency registers.

(See General Note after art.83.)

Article 80

Responsibilities of the Commission in connection with the processing of personal data

1. The Commission shall exercise the responsibilities of controller pursuant to Article 2(d) of Regulation (EC) No 45/2001 in accordance with its respective responsibilities defined in this Article.

2. The Commission shall define the necessary policies and apply the necessary technical solutions to fulfil its responsibilities within the scope of the function of controller.

3. The Commission shall implement the technical measures required to ensure the security of personal data while in transit, in particular the confidentiality and integrity of any transmission to and from the European e-Justice Portal.

4. The obligations of the Commission shall not affect the responsibilities of the Member States and other bodies for the content and operation of the interconnected national databases run by them.

(See General Note after art.83.)

Article 81

Information obligations

Without prejudice to the information to be given to data subjects in accordance with Articles 11 and 12 of Regulation (EC) No 45/2001, the Commission shall inform data subjects, by means of publication through the European e-Justice Portal, about its role in the processing of data and the purposes for which those data will be processed.

(See General Note after art.83.)

Article 82

Storage of personal data

As regards information from interconnected national databases, no personal data relating to data subjects shall be stored in the European e-Justice Portal. All such data shall be stored in the national databases operated by the Member States or other bodies.

(See General Note after art.83.)

Article 83

Access to personal data via the European e-Justice Portal

Personal data stored in the national insolvency registers referred to in Article 24 shall be accessible via the European e-Justice Portal for as long as they remain accessible under national law.

GENERAL NOTE TO ARTS 78–83

The whole of this chapter is new. Its inclusion reflects the enlarged role of the e-Justice Portal (see arts 86–88) in consequence of which much personal data stored in national insolvency registers is now more widely available via the e-Justice Portal.

The EC Regulations referred to are the Regulations of the European Parliament and of the Council of (respectively) 24 October 1995 and 18 December 2000 on the protection of individuals with regard to the processing of personal data (a) generally and (b) by the Community institutions and bodies and on the free movement of such data ([1995] OJ L281/31 and [2001] OJ L8).

CHAPTER VII

TRANSITIONAL AND FINAL PROVISIONS

Article 84

Applicability in time

1. The provisions of this Regulation shall apply only to insolvency proceedings opened from 26 June 2017. Acts committed by a debtor before that date shall continue to be governed by the law which was applicable to them at the time they were committed.

2. Notwithstanding Article 91 of this Regulation, Regulation (EC) No 1346/2000 shall continue to apply to insolvency proceedings which fall within the scope of that Regulation and which have been opened before 26 June 2017.

GENERAL NOTE

Article 84 makes it clear that the Regulation is not retrospective, so as to apply to proceedings opened before 26 June 2017. However, it must be borne in mind that the term "opened" refers to the time when the proceedings take effect, and not (e.g.) to the time of presentation of a petition for a bankruptcy or winding-up order (see the note to art.2(8)). In *Re Ultra Motorhomes International Ltd* [2005] EWHC 872 (Ch); [2006] B.C.C. 57 the company had gone into a CVA and later into liquidation. The EC Regulation came into force between these events. The court was concerned with an application made by the supervisor of the CVA, to which the liquidator was not a party. It was held that the Regulation did not apply to these proceedings, which were purely a matter within the CVA.

By a Corrigendum note published on 16 October 2016 the words "from 26 June 2017" were substituted for "after 26 June 2017".

An amending Regulation ((EU) 2017/353) published on 15 February 2017 and effective 26 June 2017, made changes to the Polish entries in Annexes A and B. There was no alteration to the UK entries.

Article 85

Relationship to Conventions

1. This Regulation replaces, in respect of the matters referred to therein, and as regards relations between Member States, the Conventions concluded between two or more Member States, in particular:

[Not reproduced, except for:]

(i)   the Convention between the United Kingdom and the Kingdom of Belgium providing for the Reciprocal Enforcement of Judgments in Civil and Commercial Matters, with Protocol, signed at Brussels on 2 May 1934;

(k)   the European Convention on Certain International Aspects of Bankruptcy, signed at Istanbul on 5 June 1990;

2. The Conventions referred to in paragraph 1 shall continue to have effect with regard to proceedings opened before the entry into force of Regulation (EC) No 1346/2000.

3. This Regulation shall not apply:

(a)   in any Member State, to the extent that it is irreconcilable with the obligations arising in relation to bankruptcy from a convention concluded by that Member State with one or more third countries before the entry into force of Regulation (EC) No 1346/2000;

(b)   in the United Kingdom of Great Britain and Northern Ireland, to the extent that is irreconcilable with the obligations arising in relation to bankruptcy and the winding-up of insolvent companies from any arrangements with the Commonwealth existing at the time Regulation (EC) No 1346/2000 entered into force.

GENERAL NOTE

Few will be aware of the Convention referred to in para.1(i): it is not referred to in leading textbooks. Anyway, it is now spent!

The UK has not signed the Istanbul Convention (para.1(k)), which is in any event now superseded within the EU by the present Regulation.

The purpose of para.3(b) is obscure. Even if "with the Commonwealth" is to be read as "within the Commonwealth" or as "with other members of the Commonwealth", it has no obvious application, although it may perhaps to be taken as a clumsy and ill-informed allusion to the procedure under IA 1986 s.426.

Article 86

Information on national and Union insolvency law

1. The Member States shall provide, within the framework of the European Judicial Network in civil and commercial matters established by Council Decision 2001/470/EC, and with a view to making the information available to the public, a short description of their national legislation and procedures relating to insolvency, in particular relating to the matters listed in Article 7(2).

2. The Member States shall update the information referred to in paragraph 1 regularly.

3. The Commission shall make information concerning this Regulation available to the public.

GENERAL NOTE

This article has been in force since 26 June 2016.

Article 87

Establishment of the interconnection of registers

The Commission shall adopt implementing acts establishing the interconnection of insolvency registers as referred to in Article 25. Those implementing acts shall be adopted in accordance with the examination procedure referred to in Article 89(3).

Article 88

Establishment and subsequent amendment of standard forms

The Commission shall adopt implementing acts establishing and, where necessary, amending the forms referred to in Article 27(4), Articles 54 and 55 and Article 64(2). Those implementing acts shall be adopted in accordance with the advisory procedure referred to in Article 89(2).

Article 89

Committee procedure

1. The Commission shall be assisted by a committee. That committee shall be a committee within the meaning of Regulation (EU) No 182/2011.

2. Where reference is made to this paragraph, Article 4 of Regulation (EU) No 182/2011 shall apply.

3. Where reference is made to this paragraph, Article 5 of Regulation (EU) No 182/2011 shall apply.

Article 90

Review clause

1. No later than 27 June 2027, and every 5 years thereafter, the Commission shall present to the European Parliament, the Council and the European Economic and Social Committee a report on the application of

this Regulation. The report shall be accompanied where necessary by a proposal for adaptation of this Regulation.

2. No later than 27 June 2022, the Commission shall present to the European Parliament, the Council and the European Economic and Social Committee a report on the application of the group coordination proceedings. The report shall be accompanied where necessary by a proposal for adaptation of this Regulation.

3. No later than 1 January 2016, the Commission shall submit to the European Parliament, the Council and the European Economic and Social Committee a study on the cross-border issues in the area of directors' liability and disqualifications.

4. No later than 27 June 2020, the Commission shall submit to the European Parliament, the Council and the European Economic and Social Committee a study on the issue of abusive forum shopping.

Article 91

Repeal

Regulation (EC) No 1346/2000 is repealed.

References to the repealed Regulation shall be construed as references to this Regulation and shall be read in accordance with the correlation table set out in Annex D to this Regulation.

Article 92

Entry into force

This Regulation shall enter into force on the twentieth day following that of its publication in the Official Journal of the European Union.

It shall apply from 26 June 2017, with the exception of:

(a)　Article 86, which shall apply from 26 June 2016;

(b)　Article 24(1), which shall apply from 26 June 2018; and

(c)　Article 25, which shall apply from 26 June 2019.

This Regulation shall be binding in its entirety and directly applicable in the Member States in accordance with the Treaties.

Done at Strasbourg, 20 May 2015.

ANNEXES

GENERAL NOTE TO THE ANNEXES

Annexes A and B list (respectively), in each jurisdiction, the insolvency proceedings recognised for the purposes of the Regulation (arts 1(1), 2(4)) and the insolvency practitioners similarly recognised (art.2(5)(i)). In contrast with Annex A to ECRIP, Annex A is declared to be exhaustive, while Annex B is silent on this point. An amending Regulation ((EU) 2017/353) published on 15 February 2017 and effective 26 June 2017, made changes to the Polish entries in Annexes A and B. These have been incorporated in the text below, as have changes to the Belgian, Bulgarian, Croatian, Latvian and Portuguese entries in Annexes A and B made by amending Regulation ((EU) 2018/946), published on 6 July 2018 and effective on 26 July 2018. Note that Ireland has opted out of the application of Regulation 2018/946 (see para.5 of the Preamble).

The "United Kingdom", for the purposes of these Annexes, of course includes Gibraltar.

Annex C (which is not reproduced) lists the amendments made to the original Regulation during its lifetime, while Annex D conveniently provides a correlation table between ECRIP and the present Regulation.

Insolvency proceedings referred to in point (4) of Article 2

BELGIQUE/BELGIË

— Het faillissement/La faillite,

— De gerechtelijke reorganisatie door een collectief akkoord/La réorganisation judiciaire par accord collectif,

— De gerechtelijke reorganisatie door een minnelijk akkoord/La réorganisation judiciaire par accord amiable,

— De gerechtelijke reorganisatie door overdracht onder gerechtelijk gezag/La réorganisation judiciaire par transfert sous autorité de justice,

— De collectieve schuldenregeling/Le règlement collectif de dettes,

— De vrijwillige vereffening/La liquidation volontaire,

— De gerechtelijke vereffening/La liquidation judiciaire,

— De voorlopige ontneming van het beheer, als bedoeld in artikel XX.32 van het Wetboek van economisch recht/Le dessaisissement provisoire de la gestion, visé à l'article XX.32 du Code de droit économique,

БЪЛГАРИЯ

— Производство по несъстоятелност,

— Производство по стабилизация на търговеца,

ČESKÁ REPUBLIKA

— Konkurs,

— Reorganizace,

— Oddlužení,

DEUTSCHLAND

— Das Konkursverfahren,

— Das gerichtliche Vergleichsverfahren,

— Das Gesamtvollstreckungsverfahren,

— Das Insolvenzverfahren,

EESTI

— Pankrotimenetlus,

— Võlgade ümberkujundamise menetlus,

ÉIRE/IRELAND

— Compulsory winding up by the court,

— Bankruptcy,

— The administration in bankruptcy of the estate of persons dying insolvent,

— Winding-up in bankruptcy of partnerships,

— Creditors' voluntary winding up (with confirmation of a court),

— Arrangements under the control of the court which involve the vesting of all or part of the property of the debtor in the Official Assignee for realisation and distribution,

— Examinership,

— Debt Relief Notice,

— Debt Settlement Arrangement,

— Personal Insolvency Arrangement,

ΕΛΛΑΔΑ

— Η πτώχευση,

— Η ειδική εκκαθάριση εν λειτουργία,

— Σχέδιο αναδιοργάνωσης,

— Απλοποιημένη διαδικασία επί πτωχεύσεων μικρού αντικειμένου,

— Διαδικασία εξυγίανσης

ESPAÑA

— Concurso,

— Procedimiento de homologación de acuerdos de refinanciación,

— Procedimiento de acuerdos extrajudiciales de pago,

— Procedimiento de negociación pública para la consecución de acuerdos de refinanciación colectivos, acuerdos de refinanciación homologados y propuestas anticipadas de convenio,

FRANCE

— Sauvegarde,

— Sauvegarde accélérée,

— Sauvegarde financière accélérée,

— Redressement judiciaire,

— Liquidation judiciaire,

HRVATSKA

— Stečajni postupak,

— Predstečajni postupak,

— Postupak stečaja potrošača,

— Postupak izvanredne uprave u trgovačkim društvima od sistemskog značaja za Republiku Hrvatsku,

ITALIA

— Fallimento,

— Concordato preventivo,

— Liquidazione coatta amministrativa,

— Amministrazione straordinaria,

— Accordi di ristrutturazione,

— Procedure di composizione della crisi da sovraindebitamento del consumatore (accordo o piano),

— Liquidazione dei beni,

ΚΥΠΡΟΣ

— Υποχρεωτική εκκαθάριση από το Δικαστήριο,

— Εκούσια εκκαθάριση από μέλη,

— Εκούσια εκκαθάριση από πιστωτές,

— Εκκαθάριση με την εποπτεία του Δικαστηρίου,

— Διάταγμα παραλαβής και πτώχευσης κατόπιν Δικαστικού Διατάγματος,

— Διαχείριση της περιουσίας προσώπων που απεβίωσαν αφερέγγυα,

LATVIJA

— Tiesiskās aizsardzības process,

— Juridiskās personas maksātnespējas process,

— Fiziskās personas maksātnespējas process,

LIETUVA

— Įmonės restruktūrizavimo byla,

— Įmonės bankroto byla,

— Įmonės bankroto procesas ne teismo tvarka,

— Fizinio asmens bankroto procesas,

LUXEMBOURG

— Faillite,

— Gestion contrôlée,

— Concordat préventif de faillite (par abandon d'actif),

— Régime spécial de liquidation du notariat,

— Procédure de règlement collectif des dettes dans le cadre du surendettement,

MAGYARORSZÁG

— Csődeljárás,

— Felszámolási eljárás,

MALTA

— Xoljiment,

— Amministrazzjoni,

— Stralċ volontarju mill-membri jew mill-kredituri,

— Stralċ mill-Qorti,

— Falliment f'każ ta' kujjerċjant,

— Proċedura biex kumpanija tirkupra,

NEDERLAND

— Het faillissement,

— De surséance van betaling,

— De schuldsaneringsregeling natuurlijke personen,

ÖSTERREICH

— Das Konkursverfahren (Insolvenzverfahren),

— Das Sanierungsverfahren ohne Eigenverwaltung (Insolvenzverfahren),

— Das Sanierungsverfahren mit Eigenverwaltung (Insolvenzverfahren),

— Das Schuldenregulierungsverfahren,

— Das Abschöpfungsverfahren,

— Das Ausgleichsverfahren,

POLSKA

— Upadłość,

— Postępowanie o zatwierdzenie układu,

— Przyspieszone postępowanie układowe,

— Postępowanie układowe,

— Postępowanie sanacyjne,

PORTUGAL

— Processo de insolvência,

— Processo especial de revitalização,

— Processo especial para acordo de pagamento,

ROMÂNIA

— Procedura insolvenţei,

— Reorganizarea judiciară,

— Procedura falimentului,

— Concordatul preventiv,

SLOVENIJA

— Postopek preventivnega prestrukturiranja,

— Postopek prisilne poravnave,

— Postopek poenostavljene prisilne poravnave,

— Stečajni postopek: stečajni postopek nad pravno osebo, postopek osebnega stečaja in postopek stečaja zapuščine,

SLOVENSKO

— Konkurzné konanie,

— Reštrukturalizačné konanie,

— Oddlženie,

SUOMI/FINLAND

— Konkurssi/konkurs,

— Yrityssaneeraus/företagssanering,

— Yksityishenkilön velkajärjestely/ skuldsanering för privatpersoner,

SVERIGE

— Konkurs,

— Företagsrekonstruktion,

— Skuldsanering,

UNITED KINGDOM

— Winding up by or subject to the supervision of the court,

— Creditors' voluntary winding up (with confirmation by the court),

— Administration, including appointments made by filing prescribed documents with the court,

— Voluntary arrangements under insolvency legislation,

— Bankruptcy or sequestration.

Annex B

Insolvency practitioners referred to in point (5) of Article 2

BELGIQUE/BELGIË

— De curator/Le curateur,

— De gerechtsmandataris/Le mandataire de justice,

— De schuldbemiddelaar/Le médiateur de dettes,

— De vereffenaar/Le liquidateur,

— De voorlopige bewindvoerder/ L'administrateur provisoire,

БЪЛГАРИЯ

— Назначен предварително временен синдик,

— Временен синдик,

— (Постоянун) синдик,

— Служебен синдик,

— Доверено лице,

ČESKÁ REPUBLIKA

— Insolvenční správce,

— Předběžný insolvenční správce,

— Oddělený insolvenční správce,

— Zvláštní insolvenční správce,

— Zástupce insolvenční správce,

DEUTSCHLAND

— Konkursverwalter,

— Vergleichsverwalter,

— Sachwalter (nach der Vergleichsordnung),

— Verwalter,

— Insolvenzverwalter,

— Sachwalter (nach der Insolvenzordnung),

— Treuhänder,

— Vorläufiger Insolvenzverwalter,

— Vorläufiger Sachwalter,

EESTI

— Pankrotihaldur,

— Ajutine pankrotihaldur,

— Usaldusisik,

ÉIRE/IRELAND

— Liquidator,

— Official Assignee,

— Trustee in bankruptcy,

— Provisional Liquidator,

— Examiner,

— Personal Insolvency Practitioner,

— Insolvency Service,

ΕΛΛΑΔΑ

— Ο σύνδικος

— Ο εισηγητής

— Η επιτροπή των πιστωτών,

— Ο ειδικός εκκαθαριστής

ESPAÑA

— Administrador concursal,

— Mediador concursal,

FRANCE

— Mandataire judiciaire,

— Liquidateur,

— Administrateur judiciaire,

— Commissaire à l'exécution du plan,

HRVATSKA

— Stečajni upravitelj,

— Privremeni stečajni upravitelj,

— Stečajni povjerenik,

— Povjerenik,

— Izvanredni povjerenik,

ITALIA

— Curatore,

— Commissario giudiziale,

— Commissario straordinario,

— Commissario liquidatore,

— Liquidatore giudiziale,

— Professionista nominato dal Tribunale,

— Organismo di composizione della crisi nella procedura di composizione della crisi da sovraindebitamento del consumatore,

— Liquidatore,

ΚΥΠΡΟΣ

— Εκκαθαριστής και Προσωρινός Εκκαθαριστής

— Επίσημος Παραλήπτης

— Διαχειριστής της Πτώχευσης

LATVIJA

— Maksātnespējas procesa administrators,

— Tiesiskās aizardzības procesa uzraugošā persona,

LIETUVA

— Bankroto administratorius,

— Restruktūrizavimo administratorius,

LUXEMBOURG

— Le curateur,

— Le commissaire,

— Le liquidateur,

— Le conseil de gérance de la section d'assainissement du notariat,

— Le liquidateur dans le cadre du surendettement,

MAGYARORSZÁG

— Vagyonfelügyelő,

— Felszámoló,

MALTA

— Amministratur Proviżorju,

— Riċevitur Uffiċjali,

— Stralċjarju,

— Manager Speċjali,

— Kuraturi f'każ ta' proċeduri ta' falliment,

— Kontrollur Speċjali,

NEDERLAND

— De curator in het faillissement,

— De bewindvoerder in de surséance van betaling,

— De bewindvoerder in de schuldsaneringsregeling natuurlijke personen,

ÖSTERREICH

— Masseverwalter,

— Sanierungsverwalter,

— Ausgleichsverwalter,

— Besonderer Verwalter,

— Einstweiliger Verwalter,

— Sachwalter,

— Treuhänder,

— Insolvenzgericht,

— Konkursgericht,

POLSKA

— Syndyk,

— Nadzorca sądowy,

— Zarządca,

— Nadzorca układu,

— Tymczasowy nadzorca sądowy,

— Tymczasowy zarządca,

— Zarządca przymusowy,

PORTUGAL

— Administrador da insolvência,

— Administrador judicial provisório,

ROMÂNIA

— Practician în insolvenţă,

— Administrator concordatar,

— Administrator judiciar,

— Lichidator judiciar,

SLOVENIJA

— Upravitelj,

SLOVENSKO

— Predbežný správca,

— Správca,

SUOMI/FINLAND

— Pesänhoitaja/boförvaltare,

— Selvittäjä/utredare,

SVERIGE

— Förvaltare,

— Rekonstruktör,

UNITED KINGDOM

— Liquidator,

— Supervisor of a voluntary arrangement,

— Administrator,

— Official Receiver,

— Trustee,

— Provisional Liquidator,

— Interim Receiver,

— Judicial factor.

GENERAL NOTE

The UK entry "interim receiver" is new. This does not refer to a receiver appointed to enforce a floating or other charge but to a receiver appointed by the court to protect assets pending the opening of a formal insolvency proceeding. Interim receivers are recognised by statute in bankruptcy law (see IA 1986 s.286), but the court in its inherent jurisdiction could make a similar appointment in any other insolvency situation.

Annex C

Repealed Regulation with list of the successive amendments thereto

[Not reproduced]

Annex D

Correlation table

Regulation (EC) No 1346/2000	This Regulation
Article 1	Article 1
Article 2, introductory words	Article 2, introductory words
Article 2, point (a)	Article 2, point (4)
Article 2, point (b)	Article 2, point (5)
Article 2, point (c)	—
Article 2, point (d)	Article 2, point (6)
Article 2, point (e)	Article 2, point (7)
Article 2, point (f)	Article 2, point (8)
Article 2, point (g), introductory words	Article 2, point (9), introductory words
Article 2, point (g), first indent	Article 2, point (9)(vii)
Article 2, point (g), second indent	Article 2, point (9)(iv)
Article 2, point (g), third indent	Article 2, point (9)(viii)

Article 2, point (h)	Article 2, point 10
—	Article 2, points (1) to (3) and (11) to (13)
—	Article 2, point (9)(i) to (iii), (v), (vi)
Article 3	Article 3
—	Article 4
—	Article 5
—	Article 6
Article 4	Article 7
Article 5	Article 8
Article 6	Article 9
Article 7	Article 10
Article 8	Article 11(1)
—	Article 11(2)
Article 9	Article 12
Article 10	Article 13(1)
—	Article 13(2)
Article 11	Article 14
Article 12	Article 15
Article 13, first indent	Article 16, point (a)
Article 13, second indent	Article 16, point (b)
Article 14, first indent	Article 17, point (a)
Article 14, second indent	Article 17, point (b)
Article 14, third indent	Article 17, point (c)
Article 15	Article 18
Article 16	Article 19
Article 17	Article 20

Article 18	Article 21
Article 19	Article 22
Article 20	Article 23
—	Article 24
—	Article 25
—	Article 26
—	Article 27
Article 21(1)	Article 28(2)
Article 21(2)	Article 28(1)
Article 22	Article 29
Article 23	Article 30
Article 24	Article 31
Article 25	Article 32
Article 26	Article 33
Article 27	Article 34
Article 28	Article 35
—	Article 36
Article 29	Article 37(1)
—	Article 37(2)
—	Article 38
—	Article 39
Article 30	Article 40
Article 31	Article 41
—	Article 42
—	Article 43
—	Article 44

Article 32	Article 45
Article 33	Article 46
Article 34(1)	Article 47(1)
Article 34(2)	Article 47(2)
Article 34(3)	—
—	Article 48
Article 35	Article 49
Article 36	Article 50
Article 37	Article 51
Article 38	Article 52
Article 39	Article 53
Article 40	Article 54
Article 41	Article 55
Article 42	—
—	Article 56–83
Article 43	Article 84(1)
—	Article 84(2)
Article 44	Article 85
—	Article 86
Article 45	
—	Article 87
—	Article 88
—	Article 89
Article 46	Article 90(1)
—	Article 90(2) to (4)
—	Article 91

Article 47	Article 92
Annex A	Annex A
Annex B	—
Annex C	Annex B
—	Annex C
—	Annex D

UNCITRAL Model Law on Cross-Border Insolvency

Adopted by the UN Commission on International Trade Law (UNCITRAL) on 30 May 1997 and formally agreed by the UN General Assembly on 15 December 1997.

[**Note:** The text of the UNCITRAL Model Law, as formally agreed, is not reproduced here, since it is not part of the law of the UK but has been superseded for this purpose by Sch.1 to the Cross-Border Insolvency Regulations 2006 (below). However, since the Preamble to the Model Law has not been incorporated into Sch.1 and may be relevant for reference as an aid to interpretation of the Regulations, it is set out below.

The total number of jurisdictions which have enacted legislation based on the Model law is now 46 in 44 states. These are Australia, Benin, Burkina Faso, Cameroon, Canada, Central African Republic, Chad, Chile, Colombia, Comoros, Congo, Côte d'Ivoire, Democratic Republic of Congo, Dominican Republic, Equatorial Guinea, Gabon, Greece, Guinea, Guinea-Bissau, Israel, Japan, Kenya, Malawi, Mali, Mauritius, Mexico, Montenegro, New Zealand, Niger, Philippines, Poland, Republic of Korea, Romania, Senegal, Serbia, Seychelles, Singapore, Slovenia, South Africa, Togo, Uganda, United Kingdom of Great Britain and Northern Ireland (including the British Virgin Islands, Gibraltar, Great Britain), United States of America, and Vanuatu.

The Model Law is supplemented by Guide to Enactment and Interpretation of the UNCITRAL Model Law on Cross-Border Insolvency (2013).

On 2 July 2018 UNCITRAL approved and adopted the text of a new model law, the Model Law on the Recognition and Enforcement of Insolvency-Related Judgments, together with a guide to enactment thereto. The 2018 Model Law may be regarded as an attempt to supplement the existing 1997 UNCITRAL Model Law framework for cross-border insolvency cooperation, e.g. by cross-border recognition and enforcement of judgments in addition to the appointments of representatives etc. The 2018 Model Law was approved by resolution 73/200 of the UN General Assembly on 20 December 2018 (see *https://www.un.org/en/ga/search/view_doc.asp?symbol=A/ RES/73/200*). To be effective at national level it will need to be adopted into domestic legislation. See Moss [2019] 33 Insolv. Int. 21.

Preamble

The purpose of the present Law is to provide effective mechanisms for dealing with cases of cross-border insolvency so as to promote the objectives of:

(a) cooperation between the courts and other competent authorities of this State and foreign States involved in cases of cross-border insolvency;

(b) greater legal certainty for trade and investment;

(c) fair and efficient administration or cross-border insolvencies that protects the interests of all creditors and other interested persons, including the debtor;

(d) protection and maximization of the value of the debtor's assets;

(e) facilitation of the rescue of financially troubled businesses, thereby protecting investment and preserving employment.

Cross-Border Insolvency Regulations 2006

(SI 2006/1030)

Made on 3 April 2006 by the Secretary of State with the agreement of the Lord Chancellor and the Scottish Ministers. Operative from 4 April 2006.

Introductory note to the Regulations

These Regulations (the "CBIR") enact legislation for England and Wales and for Scotland based on the provisions of the Model Law on Cross-Border Insolvency which was adopted by the UN Commission on International Trade Law (UNCITRAL) on 30 May 1997 and later, on 15 December of that year, formally agreed by the UN General Assembly. The Preamble to the UNCITRAL Model Law is reproduced above. The original text of the Model Law is to be found in the Official Records of the General Assembly, 52nd Session, Supplement No.17. (For access to this text and related documents, see the note to reg.2.)

Comparable legislation has since been enacted for Northern Ireland: see the Cross-Border Insolvency Regulations (Northern Ireland) 2007 (SR 2007/115, effective 12 April 2007). These Regulations in Sch.1 provide a version of the Model Law as adapted for Northern Ireland.

The Model Law itself has no force either as legislation or as a treaty: instead, it is designed for use as a precedent by the legislative draftsman in any jurisdiction which is seeking to reform its law on cross-border insolvency. But it has the further objective of seeking to bring about the harmonisation of the laws of different countries, as they individually enact legislation based on the same model; and this will be enhanced as the courts in those jurisdictions have regard to judicial rulings and academic writings in other enacting States.

The principal objects of the Model Law are:

- to facilitate the recognition in one jurisdiction of insolvency proceedings which have been instituted in another, and similarly the recognition of the authority of the office-holder in such proceedings;

- to give foreign creditors access to local courts and allow them to participate in local insolvency proceedings;

- where insolvency proceedings have been, or are about to be, instituted in more than one jurisdiction, to establish an orderly regime to regulate the relationship between them;

- to encourage co-operation between the courts, office-holders and other competent authorities involved in cross-border insolvency proceedings.

Provision was made for the adoption of the Model Law in this country in the Insolvency Act 2000 s.14. Regulations with this in view were published in draft form by the Insolvency Service of the then DTI on 22 August 2005 as part of a consultation exercise, and revised in the light of responses to that consultation before being put before Parliament in March, 2006, and ultimately enacted as the CBIR on 3 April 2006. Regulation 2 provides that the UNCITRAL Model Law shall have the force of law in Great Britain "in the form set out in Schedule 1" to the Regulations, "which contains the UNCITRAL Model Law with certain modifications to adapt it for application in Great Britain". It is therefore the text of Sch.1 rather than that of the UNCITRAL Model Law that is the primary formulation of the law for this country; but reg.2(2) directs that the latter, together with other relevant UNCITRAL documents, may be considered in ascertaining the meaning or effect of any provision of the CBIR.

The CBIR apply to foreign insolvency proceedings anywhere in the world without any condition of reciprocity—i.e. it is not necessary that the particular foreign State should have enacted comparable legislation before recourse may be had to these Regulations. It follows that the office-holders in foreign proceedings may take full advantage of the CPIR in this country, whereas their counterparts here will be able to do so abroad only to the extent that there is enabling legislation in the relevant foreign country.

There is one limitation on the otherwise universal territorial scope of the Regulations: art.3 of Sch.1 provides that where there is any conflict with an obligation of the UK under the EU Regulation 2015/848, the requirements of the latter shall prevail. So to the extent that any cross-border issues arise between insolvency proceedings in a British jurisdiction and proceedings elsewhere in the EU (apart from Denmark), it is the EU Regulation that will apply. However, the definitions of "insolvency proceedings" for the purposes of the Regulations and the EU Regulation are not identical and in some circumstances the case may fall within the former and not the latter, so that the Regulations alone will apply: see *Re Stocznia Gdynia SA; Re v Bud-Bank Leasing sp z oo* [2010] B.C.C. 255, where statutory compensation proceedings under Polish law were held to be outside the jurisdiction of what is now the EU Regulation but within the Regulations. (Note that the EC Regulation 1346/2000 was superseded by the EU Regulation on Insolvency Proceedings 2015/848 from 26 June 2017.)

On the other hand, the Model Law is to have precedence if there is any conflict between it and UK domestic insolvency law (reg.3(2)). The CBIR do not apply to various utilities, building societies, insurers and credit institutions (Sch.1 art.1.2)).

In many respects, the Model Law has parallels in the EU Regulation, using some of the same concepts and definitions—e.g. those of "centre of main interests" (COMI), "main proceeding" and "establishment". Judicial rulings on those concepts and comments made in the notes to the EU Regulation in this *Guide* may be helpful in understanding parallel provisions in the CBIR. There, however, a number of important differences, including the following:

- The purpose of the CBIR is almost entirely enabling: there is very little in this legislation which restricts the jurisdiction of our own courts or limits their powers. In contrast, much more of the EU Regulation is prescriptive—for instance, where the COMI of the debtor is in another Member State, a British court's powers are limited in the orders which it may make, even if no main insolvency proceedings have been opened in the debtor's home State.

- It is only the UK courts which will have any role in interpreting the legislative text of the CBIR (although, no doubt, the judgments of foreign courts will be of persuasive authority): contrast the overriding powers of the European Court.

- The Regulations have been enacted unilaterally and independently by our own Parliament: there is no superior legislative authority which can countermand them. Even if UNCITRAL were to consider amending the Model Law, this would have no effect within the UK unless the changes were implemented by domestic legislation.

- No distinction is made by the CBIR between what are classified separately by the EU Regulation as "secondary" and "territorial" proceedings. Indeed, until "main" proceedings have been formally recognised in this country under the CBIR Ch.III, any form of insolvency proceeding available under IA 1986 may be commenced here without regard to issues such as whether the debtor's COMI may be in some other jurisdiction or whether main proceedings have been opened elsewhere.

The scope of the CBIR is broadly as follows:

- Chapter II provides for the recognition in this country of foreign office-holders with no special formalities (other than a translation, where needed), and gives them and foreign creditors direct access to courts in Great Britain.

- Chapter III similarly provides for the recognition of foreign insolvency proceedings. These include reorganisation and rescue proceedings as well as bankruptcies and liquidations, but receiverships are excluded by the CBIR for all purposes. The recognition of foreign proceedings as "main" proceedings brings about an automatic stay of proceedings and executions, etc. against the debtor in this country, but does not affect the right to institute the commencement of an insolvency proceeding or to file claims in such a proceeding. A stay or other appropriate relief may also be granted by the court as a matter of discretion following recognition of non-main proceedings. A foreign office-holder is empowered to intervene in proceedings here to which the debtor is a party.

- Chapter IV makes provision for co-operation and direct communication between a British court and foreign courts or office-holders. It should be noted that there is no repeal of IA 1986 s.426. The CBIR is not, like s.426, limited to "designated" countries and territories; and there may be some circumstances where recourse to that provision rather than the CBIR may be considered advantageous or necessary—e.g. where the debtor is an insurance company, or perhaps where it is a company in receivership in (say) Australia.

- Chapter V regulates the position where there are concurrent insolvency proceedings in this and one or more other jurisdictions. The provisions of this Chapter apply only after the foreign proceedings have been recognised under Chapter III. The rules are very similar to those of the EU Regulation. If the foreign proceeding has been recognised as a main proceeding, non-main proceedings may be commenced here only if the debtor has assets here, and are restricted in scope to assets within the jurisdiction. The rule of hotchpot applies where a creditor has received payment in another insolvency abroad.

The plan of the CBIR Sch.1 follows closely that of the UNCITRAL Model Law: in particular, the sequence and numbering of the articles correspond. But the paragraphs within each article sometimes vary considerably from the original model.

Evidence shows that the CBIR is proving useful in practice, although most appointments are uncontroversial and in the earlier years of its operation there were few reported cases but these have subsequently increased. Some earlier examples include *Re Phoenix Kapitaldienst GmbH* [2008] B.P.I.R. 1082 (German administrator); *Warner v Verfides*

[2008] EWHC 2609 (Ch); [2009] Bus. L.R. 500 (Australian trustee in bankruptcy); *Re Stanford International Bank Ltd* [2010] EWCA Civ 137; [2010] B.P.I.R. 679 (Antiguan liquidator); *Samsun Logix Corp v DEF* [2009] EWHC 576 (Ch); [2010] B.C.C. 556 (insolvency proceedings in Korean court); *Re SwissAir Schweizerische Luftverkehr-Aktiengesellschaft* [2009] EWHC 2099 (Ch); [2010] B.C.C. 667 (Swiss liquidation recognised as main proceeding and English liquidator ordered to remit assets to Swiss liquidator); *Williams v Simpson* [2011] B.P.I.R. 938 (HC, New Zealand, noted in (2011) 24 Insolv. Int. 14: interim relief in the form of a search and seizure order granted by New Zealand court pursuant to request by English trustee in bankruptcy). English courts have, of course, traditionally been well disposed to recognise foreign insolvency proceedings and their representatives, and these rulings at common law are commonly cited in cases under the CBIR. However, the scope of this jurisdiction has been curtailed by the ruling of the Supreme Court in *Rubin v Eurofinance SA* [2012] UKSC 46; [2013] B.C.C. 1, qualifying the wider view expressed in *Cambridge Gas Transport Corp v Navigator Holdings plc* [2006] UKPC 26; [2006] B.C.C. 962—see the note to IA 1986 s.426.

For valuable analysis of the CBIR and the UNCITRAL Model Law see the judgment of Rose J in *Re Dalnyaya Step LLC; Cherkasov v Olegovich* [2017] EWHC 756 (Ch); [2019] B.C.C. 1. See also Hildyard J in *Bakhshiyeva v Sberbank of Russia* [2018] EWHC 59 (Ch); [2018] B.C.C. 267 and the Court of Appeal in the same case: [2018] EWCA Civ 2802.

The text below incorporates amendments made by the Financial Services Act 2012 (Consequential Amendments and Transitional Provisions) Order 2013 (SI 2013/472), the Insolvency Amendment (EU 2015/848) Regulations 2017 (SI 2017/702), the Insolvency (England and Wales) and Insolvency (Scotland) (Miscellaneous and Consequential Amendments) Rules 2017 (SI 2017/1115) and by the Insolvency (Miscellaneous Amendments) Regulations 2017 (SI 2017/1119).

The CBIR have not been amended in relation to replacement of the Bankruptcy (Scotland) Act 1985 by the Bankruptcy (Scotland) Act 2016 and so still refer where relevant to the 1985 Act: presumably this is a legislative oversight.

1 Citation, commencement and interpretation

1(1) These Regulations may be cited as the Cross-Border Insolvency Regulations 2006 and shall come into force on the day after the day on which they are made.

1(2) In these Regulations "the UNCITRAL Model Law" means the Model Law on cross-border insolvency as adopted by the United Nations Commission on International Trade Law on 30th May 1997.

1(3) In these Regulations "overseas company" has the meaning given by section 1044 of the Companies Act 2006 and "establishment", in relation to such a company, has the same meaning as in the Overseas Companies Regulations 2009.

GENERAL NOTE

The effective date is 4 April 2006. Regulation 1(3) inserted by the Companies Act 2006 (Consequential Amendments, Transitional Provisions and Savings) Order 2009 (SI 2009/1941) art.2(1) and Sch.1 para.264, as from 1 October 2009.

2 UNCITRAL Model Law to have force of law

2(1) The UNCITRAL Model Law shall have the force of law in Great Britain in the form set out in Schedule 1 to these Regulations (which contains the UNCITRAL Model Law with certain modifications to adapt it for application in Great Britain).

2(2) Without prejudice to any practice of the courts as to the matters which may be considered apart from this paragraph, the following documents may be considered in ascertaining the meaning or effect of any provision of the UNCITRAL Model Law as set out in Schedule 1 to these Regulations–

  (a) the UNCITRAL Model Law;

  (b) any documents of the United Nations Commission on International Trade Law and its working group relating to the preparation of the UNCITRAL Model Law; and

  (c) the Guide to Enactment of the UNCITRAL Model Law (UNCITRAL document A/CN.9/442) prepared at the request of the United Nations Commission on International Trade Law made in May 1997.

GENERAL NOTE

The Model Law as adopted by UNCITRAL and agreed by the UN General Assembly has no legislative force: the source of law so far as concerns Great Britain is that set out in Sch.1, below. However, the Model Law and the other documents mentioned in reg.2(2) may be referred to for the purpose of interpreting Sch.1. The Model Law is supported by a Guide to Enactment, which was updated on 18 July 2013, to provide more information and guidance on the application and interpretation of key concepts of the Model Law relating to the characteristics of foreign proceedings susceptible of recognition under the Model Law and to the factors relevant to determining the debtor's centre of main interests for the purposes of recognition. On 14 January 2014, a revised and updated compendium version of the UNCITRAL *Model Law on Cross-Border Insolvency with Guide to Enactment and Interpretation* was published and is available at *http://www.uncitral.org/pdf/english/texts/insolven/1997-Model-Law-Insol-2013-Guide-Enactment-e.pdf*.

On 1 July 2009 UNCITRAL adopted the Practice Guide on Cross-Border Co-operation, a reference source for insolvency professionals and judges on the practical aspects of co-operation and communication in cross-border cases (discussed by L. Elliott and N. Griffiths [2010] C.R. & I. 12). (See further the note to art.27.) In 2011 a further text entitled "UNCITRAL Model Law on Cross-Border Insolvency: the judicial perspective" was published, offering general guidance to judges on how to approach applications for recognition and relief under the Model Law. This may be accessed under *http://www.uncitral.org.pdf/english/texts/insolven/pre-judicial-perspective.pdf*. UNCITRAL has also published, outside the Guide to Enactment of the Model Law, the UNCITRAL *Legislative Guide on Insolvency Law*, which may be accessed at *http://www.uncitral.org/uncitral/en/uncitral_texts/insolvency/2004 Guide.html*. This is in four parts, with Part 4: *Directors' obligations in the period approaching insolvency* issued in November 2013 and describing the obligations of directors, which are enforceable once insolvency proceedings commence, to protect the legitimate interests of creditors and other stakeholders and to provide incentives for timely action to minimise the effects of financial distress experienced by the enterprise.

The CBIR do not extend to Northern Ireland, but comparable legislation has now been enacted for that jurisdiction: see the Introductory note to the Regulations, preceding reg.1.

The Preamble to the Model Law is not reproduced in Sch.1, although, as noted above, it may be relevant for purposes of interpretation. For this reason the Preamble has been included in this *Guide*, immediately before the text of the CBIR.

The UNCITRAL Guide to Enactment is referred to in the present work by the abbreviation "G to E".

3   Modification of British insolvency law

3(1) British insolvency law (as defined in article 2 of the UNCITRAL Model Law as set out in Schedule 1 to these Regulations) and Part 3 of the Insolvency Act 1986 shall apply with such modifications as the context requires for the purpose of giving effect to the provisions of these Regulations.

3(2) In the case of any conflict between any provision of British insolvency law or of Part 3 of the Insolvency Act 1986 and the provisions of these Regulations, the latter shall prevail.

GENERAL NOTE

Regulation 3 confirms that British insolvency law is to be read subject to the CBIR, so that where there is any inconsistency the CBIR is to prevail. "British insolvency law" is defined in art.2 so as to exclude Pt 3 of IA 1986 (Receivership); but for the purposes of this one provision Pt 3 is, in effect, written back into the definition.

4   Procedural matters in England and Wales

4 Schedule 2 to these Regulations (which makes provision about procedural matters in England and Wales in connection with the application of the UNCITRAL Model Law as set out in Schedule 1 to these Regulations) shall have effect.

5   Procedural matters in Scotland

5 Schedule 3 to these Regulations (which makes provision about procedural matters in Scotland in connection with the application of the UNCITRAL Model Law as set out in Schedule 1 to these Regulations) shall have effect.

6   Notices delivered to the registrar of companies

6   Schedule 4 to these Regulations (which makes provision about notices delivered to the registrar of companies under these Regulations) shall have effect.

7   Co-operation between courts exercising jurisdiction in relation to cross-border insolvency

7(1)   An order made by a court in either part of Great Britain in the exercise of jurisdiction in relation to the subject matter of these Regulations shall be enforced in the other part of Great Britain as if it were made by a court exercising the corresponding jurisdiction in that other part.

7(2)   However, nothing in paragraph (1) requires a court in either part of Great Britain to enforce, in relation to property situated in that part, any order made by a court in the other part of Great Britain.

7(3)   The courts having jurisdiction in relation to the subject matter of these Regulations in either part of Great Britain shall assist the courts having the corresponding jurisdiction in the other part of Great Britain.

GENERAL NOTE

These provisions mirror IA 1986 s.426(1), (2) and (4). This avoids any supposition that the UNCITRAL regime should apply as between the two jurisdictions of England and Wales and Scotland in consequence of reg.3(2), above.

8   Disapplication of section 388 of the Insolvency Act 1986

8   Nothing in section 388 of the Insolvency Act 1986 applies to anything done by a foreign representative–

(a)   under or by virtue of these Regulations;

(b)   in relation to relief granted or cooperation or coordination provided under these Regulations.

GENERAL NOTE

IA 1986 s.388 defines the term "act as an insolvency practitioner". The effect of this disapplication is to ensure that an office-holder in foreign insolvency proceedings who is empowered to act under the CBIR is not required to be qualified under British law and will not commit an offence under s.389 (acting as an insolvency practitioner without qualification) when so acting. This may give rise to some practical difficulties (e.g. where the foreign proceedings do not involve the appointment of a "representative"): see D. Marks and G. Jones (2009) 22 Insolv. Int. 10.

SCHEDULE 1

Regulation 2(1)

UNCITRAL MODEL LAW ON CROSS-BORDER INSOLVENCY

CHAPTER I

GENERAL PROVISIONS

Article 1. Scope of Application

1   This Law applies where–

(a)   assistance is sought in Great Britain by a foreign court or a foreign representative in connection with a foreign proceeding; or

(b)   assistance is sought in a foreign State in connection with a proceeding under British insolvency law; or

(c)   a foreign proceeding and a proceeding under British insolvency law in respect of the same debtor are taking place concurrently; or

(d)   creditors or other interested persons in a foreign State have an interest in requesting the commencement of, or participating in, a proceeding under British insolvency law.

2   This Law does not apply to a proceeding concerning–

(a)   a company holding an appointment under Chapter 1 of Part 2 of the Water Industry Act 1991 (water and sewage undertakers) or a qualifying water supply licensee within the meaning of section 23(6) of that Act (meaning and effect of special administration order);

(b)   Scottish Water established under section 20 of the Water Industry (Scotland) Act 2002 (Scottish Water);

(c)   a protected railway company within the meaning of section 59 of the Railways Act 1993 (railway administration order) (including that section as it has effect by virtue of section 19 of the Channel Tunnel Rail Link Act 1996 (administration));

(d)   a licence company within the meaning of section 26 of the Transport Act 2000 (air traffic services);

(e)   a public private partnership company within the meaning of section 210 of the Greater London Authority Act 1999 (public-private partnership agreement);

(f)   a protected energy company within the meaning of section 154(5) of the Energy Act 2004 (energy administration orders);

(g)   a building society within the meaning of section 119 of the Building Societies Act 1986 (interpretation);

(h)   a UK credit institution or an EEA credit institution or any branch of either such institution as those expressions are defined by regulation 2 of the Credit Institutions (Reorganisation and Winding Up) Regulations 2004 (interpretation);

(i)   a third country credit institution within the meaning of regulation 36 of the Credit Institutions (Reorganisation and Winding Up) Regulations 2004 (interpretation of this Part);

(j)   a person who has permission under or by virtue of Parts 4 or 19 of the Financial Services and Markets Act 2000 to effect or carry out contracts of insurance;

(k)   an EEA insurer within the meaning of regulation 2 of the Insurers (Reorganisation and Winding Up) Regulations 2004 (interpretation);

(l)   a person (other than one included in paragraph 2(j)) pursuing the activity of reinsurance who has received authorisation for that activity from a competent authority within an EEA State; or

(m)   any of the Concessionaires within the meaning of section 1 of the Channel Tunnel Act 1987.

3   In paragraph 2 of this article–

(a)   in sub-paragraph (j) the reference to "contracts of insurance" must be construed in accordance with–

    (i)   section 22 of the Financial Services and Markets Act 2000 (classes of regulated activity and categories of investment);

    (ii)   any relevant order under that section; and

    (iii)   Schedule 2 to that Act (regulated activities);

(b)   in sub-paragraph (1) "EEA State" means a State, other than the United Kingdom, which is a contracting party to the agreement on the European Economic Area signed at Oporto on 2 May 1992.

4   The court shall not grant any relief, or modify any relief already granted, or provide any co-operation or coordination, under or by virtue of any of the provisions of this Law if and to the extent that such relief or modified relief or cooperation or coordination would–

(a)   be prohibited under or by virtue of–

    (i)   Part 7 of the Companies Act 1989;

    (ii)   Part 3 of the Financial Markets and Insolvency (Settlement Finality) Regulations 1999; or

    (iii)   Part 3 of the Financial Collateral Arrangements (No.2) Regulations 2003;

in the case of a proceeding under British insolvency law; or

(b)   interfere with or be inconsistent with any rights of a collateral taker under Part 4 of the Financial Collateral Arrangements (No.2) Regulations 2003 which could be exercised in the case of such a proceeding.

5   Where a foreign proceeding regarding a debtor who is an insured in accordance with the provisions of the Third Parties (Rights against Insurers) Act 2010 is recognised under this Law, any stay and suspension referred to in article 20(1) and any relief granted by the court under article 19 or 21 shall not apply to or affect–

(a)   any transfer of rights of the debtor under that Act; or

(b)   any claim, action, cause or proceeding by a third party against an insurer under or in respect of rights of the debtor transferred under that Act.

6   Any suspension under this Law of the right to transfer, encumber or otherwise dispose of any of the debtor's assets–

(a)   is subject to section 26 of the Land Registration Act 2002 where owner's powers are exercised in relation to a registered estate or registered charge;

(b)   is subject to section 52 of the Land Registration Act 2002, where the powers referred to in that section are exercised by the proprietor of a registered charge; and

(c)   in any other case, shall not bind a purchaser of a legal estate in good faith for money or money's worth unless the purchaser has express notice of the suspension.

7   In paragraph 6–

(a)   "owner's powers" means the powers described in section 23 of the Land Registration Act 2002 and "registered charge" and "registered estate" have the same meaning as in section 132(1) of that Act; and

(b)   "legal estate" and "purchaser" have the same meaning as in section 17 of the Land Charges Act 1972.

GENERAL NOTE

This article defines the circumstances in which the CBIR will come into play, and in arts 2.2 et seq. lists various bodies in regard to which the Regulations are excluded.

Art.1.1
The G to E conveniently uses the expressions "inward-bound" and "outward-bound" to describe the various purposes provided for by the Model Law: the former term where someone from abroad seeks to invoke the jurisdiction of a British court or seeks assistance from the office-holder in British insolvency proceedings; the latter where a similar request is made to a foreign court or office-holder for recognition or assistance in connection with an insolvency

proceeding in this country. Paragraphs (a) and (d) of art.1.1 are concerned with the "inward-bound" scope of the CBIR, and para.1.1(b) with their "outward-bound" aspects. Paragraph 1.1(c) refers to a third purpose: the co-ordination of matters where insolvency proceedings are taking place at the same time both here and in one or more foreign jurisdictions.

Art.1.2, 1.3

Although in principle the Model Law is formulated to apply generally to all insolvency proceedings, provision is made for the exception of "specially regulated insolvency proceedings", and in particular those concerning banks, insurance companies and public utilities. Those excluded from the application of the CBIR are listed here. It should be noted that there is no general exclusion of any particular category of company (e.g. banks), but each is specified by reference to the definition in a particular enactment or authorisation under it.

The DBIS (now the DBEIS) has intimated that it will consider the inclusion of credit institutions and insurance undertakings within the Model Law (under IA 2000 s.14) at a later stage. A suggestion that corporate bodies other than companies should be specifically excluded (see the note to IA 1986 s.1(4)–(6)) was rejected.

The Model Law allows an enacting State to make special provision for the insolvency of debtors who are non-traders or consumers. The UK, in keeping with its own domestic law, has not chosen to make any distinction in respect of these categories.

Art.1.4

There is an exclusion provision here for the various payment and settlement systems where parts of the domestic insolvency legislation is disapplied.

Art.1.5

The name of the Act was substituted for the previous Act of the same name (1930) by Sch.2 para.4 of the 2010 Act as from 1 August 2016. The rights of third parties under this Act are preserved by this provision, in the case where the insolvent is insured against liabilities to such parties.

Arts 1.6, 1.7

The sections referred to prevent the title of the disponee, registered proprietor or purchaser from being questioned.

Article 2. Definitions

For the purposes of this Law–

(a) "British insolvency law" means–

    (i) in relation to England and Wales, provision extending to England and Wales and made by or under the Insolvency Act 1986 (with the exception of Part 3 of that Act) or by or under that Act as extended or applied by or under any other enactment (excluding these Regulations); and

    (ii) in relation to Scotland, provision extending to Scotland and made by or under the Insolvency Act 1986 (with the exception of Part 3 of that Act), the Bankruptcy (Scotland) Act 1985 or by or under those Acts as extended or applied by or under any other enactment (excluding these Regulations);

GENERAL NOTE

IA 1986 Pt 3 deals with receivership (including administrative receivership) in England and Wales and in Scotland. The 1986 Act does not contain a comprehensive definition of receivership and there is room for doubt whether parts of it apply to particular types of receiver (e.g. court-appointed receivers, Law of Property Act receivers); but there can be no question that they also are outside the CBIR because such receiverships are not "collective" insolvency proceedings within the ambit of the Model Law.

(b) "British insolvency officeholder" means–

    (i) the official receiver within the meaning of section 399 of the Insolvency Act 1986 when acting as liquidator, provisional liquidator, trustee, interim receiver or nominee or supervisor of a voluntary arrangement;

    (ii) a person acting as an insolvency practitioner within the meaning of section 388 of that Act but shall not include a person acting as an administrative receiver; and

    (iii) the Accountant in Bankruptcy within the meaning of section 1 of the Bankruptcy (Scotland) Act 1985 when acting as interim or permanent trustee;

  (c) "the court" except as otherwise provided in articles 14(4) and 23(6)(b), means in relation to any matter the court which in accordance with the provisions of article 4 of this Law has jurisdiction in relation to that matter;

GENERAL NOTE

"Court" is here used in its normal sense, in contrast with the EU Regulation art.2(6), where it is given an extended definition which includes any body competent to open insolvency proceedings (such as a general meeting of shareholders resolving to put their company into liquidation).

  (d) "the EU Insolvency Regulation" means Regulation (EU) 2015/848 of the European Parliament and of the Council of 20 May 2015;

GENERAL NOTE

Sch.1 art.2(d) substituted by the Insolvency Amendment (EU 2015/848) Regulations 2017 (SI 2017/702) regs 1, 2(1), Sch. para.94(1), (2) in relation to proceedings opened on or after 26 June 2017 (see reg.3) when the Recast EU Regulation 2015/848 came into force.

  (e) "establishment" means any place of operations where the debtor carries out a non-transitory economic activity with human means and assets or services;

GENERAL NOTE

This definition was adopted from the former EC Regulation 1346/2000 art.2(h), with the substitution of the word "assets" for "goods" (in the context, a better translation, but EU Regulation 2015/848 art.2(10) from 26 June 2017 now refers to "assets" rather than "goods" (but does not mention "services")); art.2(10) of the Regulation also requires the operations to have been carried out in the three-month period prior to the request to open main insolvency proceedings). The definition is open to criticism in placing emphasis on the debtor's *economic* activity: as with the EU Regulation, an insolvent individual who is not (and perhaps never has been) in business but has assets and debts in the jurisdiction may be excluded from the scope of the CBIR.

  (f) "foreign court" means a judicial or other authority competent to control or supervise a foreign proceeding;

GENERAL NOTE

In contrast with the definition of "the court" in para.(c), this term is wider. The G to E, para.87 explains that a foreign proceeding which meets the requisites set out in para.(i) below "should receive the same treatment irrespective of whether it has been commenced or supervised by a judicial body or an administrative body. Therefore, the definition … includes also non-judicial authorities. [The paragraph] follows a similar definition contained in Article 2, subparagraph (d), of the European Convention on Insolvency Proceedings". (The Convention was the precursor to the former EC Regulation 1346/2000, now EU Regulation 2015/848.)

  (g) "foreign main proceeding" means a foreign proceeding taking place in the State where the debtor has the centre of its main interests;

  (h) "foreign non-main proceeding" means a foreign proceeding, other than a foreign main proceeding, taking place in a State where the debtor has an establishment within the meaning of sub-paragraph (e) of this article;

GENERAL NOTE

The terms "main proceeding" and "centre of main interests", like "establishment", have been adopted from the EC Convention on Insolvency Proceedings. The notes to the EU Regulation art.3, will therefore be relevant. The use of the word "its" (in the G to E (e.g. in para.71) is misleading: there is ample reference elsewhere to insolvencies of natural persons.

It should be noted also that the distinction made by the CBIR between "main" and "non-main" proceedings becomes relevant only after the foreign proceeding has been recognised by a British court under Chapter III. Prior to that time, it is of no concern to the court or any party to an insolvency proceeding before a British court to establish the location of the debtor's COMI or to determine whether that proceeding or any current proceeding in a foreign State is "main" or otherwise. (See, however, *Kemsley v Barclays Bank plc* [2013] EWHC 1274 (Ch) (application for anti-suit injunction refused pending decision of New York court as to COMI of debtor.) In *Re Videology Ltd* [2018] EWHC 2186 (Ch); [2019] B.C.C. 195 Snowden J refused to find, in relation to an English registered company with its registered office in England but which was a subsidiary of a US group, which group applied under Chapter 11 of the US Bankruptcy Code for protection from bankruptcy, that the US Chapter 11 proceedings in relation to the English company were foreign main proceedings. The COMI of companies within a group had to be separately assessed and the company had not displaced the presumption that its COMI was located in the place of its registered office in England, so that the US proceedings in relation to it were foreign non-main proceedings.

(i)   "foreign proceeding" means a collective judicial or administrative proceeding in a foreign State, including an interim proceeding, pursuant to a law relating to insolvency in which proceeding the assets and affairs of the debtor are subject to control or supervision by a foreign court, for the purpose of reorganisation or liquidation;

GENERAL NOTE

As noted above, the CBIR do not make a distinction between the categories which in the EU Regulation are termed "territorial" and "secondary" proceedings (see the note to the EU Regulation art.3). Nothing in the CBIR limits proceedings which would fall within the second category to winding-up proceedings, as the EC Regulation (although not EURIP 2015/848) did. In *Re Stanford International Bank Ltd* [2010] EWCA Civ 137; [2011] Ch. 33; [2011] B.C.C. 211 a receiver of an insolvent bank, appointed by a court in the United States, was held not to be entitled to recognition as he had not been appointed pursuant to a law relating to insolvency; but liquidators of the same bank appointed in Antigua (the jurisdiction of the bank's COMI) fulfilled this requirement and accordingly the liquidation proceedings were recognised as main proceedings and the liquidators as foreign representatives. In his judgment the Chancellor of the High Court examined in detail the definitions in art.2(g), ("foreign main proceeding"), 2(h) ("foreign non-main proceeding"), 2(i) ("foreign proceeding") and 2(j) ("foreign representative"). Note *Re Videology Ltd* [2018] EWHC 2186 (Ch); [2019] B.C.C. 195 (US Bankruptcy Code Chapter 11 proceedings in relation to UK-registered subsidiary whose COMI was in England were foreign non-main proceedings). See also *Re Stocznia Gdynia SA v Bud-Bank Leasing sp z oo* [2010] B.C.C. 255 (Polish administrator of statutory compensation scheme recognised as representative of insolvency proceedings); *Samsun Logix Corp v DEF* [2009] EWHC 576 (Ch); [2010] B.C.C. 556, further proceedings (sub nom. *D/S Norden A/S v Samsun Logix Corp*) [2009] EWHC 2304 (Ch); [2009] B.P.I.R. 1367. Note that "proceeding" is not confined to court proceedings. In *Re New Paragon Investments Ltd* [2012] B.C.C. 371 Mr Registrar Nicholls held that a creditors' voluntary winding up in Hong Kong was a "foreign proceeding" under the CBIR. In *Re Worldspreads Ltd* [2012] EWHC 1263 (Ch), where a court in this country made an order appointing special administrators under the Investment Bank Special Administration Regulations 2011 (SI 2011/245), a recital was added to the order stating that the special administrators were "foreign representatives" within art.2(d) in order to facilitate their being recognised in foreign jurisdictions.

As to whether Croatian administrative proceedings should be recognised as foreign proceedings under art.2(1) see *Re Agrokor DD* [2017] EWHC 2791 (Ch); [2018] B.C.C. 18, a decision of HHJ Paul Matthews. This case exemplifies a welcoming approach on the part of the English courts.

(j)   "foreign representative" means a person or body, including one appointed on an interim basis, authorised in a foreign proceeding to administer the reorganisation or the liquidation of the debtor's assets or affairs or to act as a representative of the foreign proceeding;

GENERAL NOTE

The term "representative" is a happier choice than the word "liquidator" that was used in the EC Regulation (replaced by "insolvency practitioner" in EU Regulation art.2(5)). This definition makes it plain that it includes office-holders in reorganisation as well as in winding-up and bankruptcy proceedings (i.e. IVAs, CVAs, administrations), and that interim liquidators, interim receivers (in bankruptcies) and interim trustees (in Scotland) also qualify. The concluding words appear also to contemplate that a foreign court might appoint a person other than the office-holder as the representative here of a foreign proceeding.

(k) "hire-purchase agreement" includes a conditional sale agreement, a chattel leasing agreement and a retention of title agreement;

GENERAL NOTE

This definition, added to the CBIR at a late stage, is adopted from IA 1986 Sch.A1 para.1 and Sch. B1 para.111(1).

(l) "section 426 request" means a request for assistance in accordance with section 426 of the Insolvency Act 1986 made to a court in any part of the United Kingdom;

(m) "secured creditor" in relation to a debtor, means a creditor of the debtor who holds in respect of his debt a security over property of the debtor;

(n) "security" means–

(i) in relation to England and Wales, any mortgage, charge, lien or other security; and

(ii) in relation to Scotland, any security (whether heritable or moveable), any floating charge and any right of lien or preference and any right of retention (other than a right of compensation or set off);

GENERAL NOTE

The definitions of this and the preceding expression make it plain that only securities over property are included (and not, e.g. a guarantee of the debt given by a third party); but the security may be proprietary or possessory. A "charge-back" over a sum held by a bank on deposit is arguably not within the definition.

(o) in the application of Articles 20 and 23 to Scotland, "an individual" means any debtor within the meaning of the Bankruptcy (Scotland) Act 1985;

(p) in the application of this Law to Scotland, references howsoever expressed to–

(i) "filing" an application or claim are to be construed as references to lodging an application or submitting a claim respectively;

(ii) "relief" and "standing" are to be construed as references to "remedy" and "title and interest" respectively; and

(iii) a "stay" are to be construed as references to restraint, except in relation to continuation of actions or proceedings when they shall be construed as a reference to sist; and

(q) references to the law of Great Britain include a reference to the law of either part of Great Britain (including its rules of private international law).

Article 3. International obligations of Great Britain under the EU Insolvency Regulation

To the extent that this Law conflicts with an obligation of the United Kingdom under the EU Insolvency Regulation, the requirements of the EU Insolvency Regulation prevail.

GENERAL NOTE

This article expresses "the supremacy of international obligations of the enacting State over internal law" (G to E, para.91). It may be that the CBIR are not entirely displaced by the EU Regulation: at the margins the scope of the CBIR may be slightly wider (e.g. the lists of excluded bodies differ in detail in some places).

The EU Regulation applies only in relation to cross-border insolvencies where the debtor's affairs extend into more than one jurisdiction and the debtor's COMI is in a Member State of the EU (other than Denmark) and it is not concerned with assets or creditors of the debtor based outside the EU, or insolvency proceedings that have been instituted in a non-EU jurisdiction. If the application of the EU Regulation is excluded on any of these grounds, the CBIR provides a complementary regime.

Title to and text of art.3 amended by the Insolvency (Miscellaneous Amendments) Regulations 2017 (SI 2017/1119) regs 1(1), (2), 2, Sch.5 paras 1(1), (2) as from 8 December 2017.

Article 4. Competent court

1 The functions referred to in this Law relating to recognition of foreign proceedings and cooperation with foreign courts shall be performed by the High Court and assigned to the Chancery Division, as regards England and Wales and the Court of Session as regards Scotland.

2 Subject to paragraph 1 of this article, the court in either part of Great Britain shall have jurisdiction in relation to the functions referred to in that paragraph if–

  (a) the debtor has–

   (i) a place of business; or

   (ii) in the case of an individual, a place of residence; or

   (iii) assets,

  situated in that part of Great Britain; or

  (b) the court in that part of Great Britain considers for any other reason that it is the appropriate forum to consider the question or provide the assistance requested.

3 In considering whether it is the appropriate forum to hear an application for recognition of a foreign proceeding in relation to a debtor, the court shall take into account the location of any court in which a proceeding under British insolvency law is taking place in relation to the debtor and the likely location of any future proceedings under British insolvency law in relation to the debtor.

GENERAL NOTE

Note that the conditions set out in art.4.2 apply only to determine the court's competence in relation to the recognition of foreign proceedings and co-operation with foreign courts. Competence in any other respect remains to be determined by IA 1986 or any other appropriate law.

Article 5. Authorisation of British insolvency officeholders to act in a foreign State

A British insolvency officeholder is authorised to act in a foreign State on behalf of a proceeding under British insolvency law, as permitted by the applicable foreign law.

GENERAL NOTE

This article provides "outward-bound" facilities for the office-holder in a British insolvency proceeding. Its concern is to ensure that his power to act in a foreign jurisdiction is not open to challenge for want of proper authorisation. It does not, of course, oblige the authorities in the foreign State to recognise him, or confer any particular powers on him: the scope of his powers will depend on the law of that State, but he will at least have the best possible evidence of his authorisation. It is not necessary that the foreign State should itself have enacted the Model Law or some similar legislation.

One further step which might with advantage be taken in some circumstances is illustrated by *Re MG Rover España SA* [2006] B.C.C. 599—to have the court make a supplementary order describing the nature of the proceeding (e.g. a CVA or administration) and the role and powers of the office-holder.

Article 6. Public policy exception

Nothing in this Law prevents the court from refusing to take an action governed by this Law if the action would be manifestly contrary to the public policy of Great Britain or any part of it.

GENERAL NOTE

A similar public policy exception is to be found in the EU Regulation art.33. This was a major factor in the judgment of the Irish Supreme Court in *Re Eurofood IFSC Ltd* [2004] I.E.S.C. 47; [2005] B.C.C. 999, in refusing to recognise the decision of the Italian court. (See also the ruling of the ECJ (*Re Eurofood IFSC Ltd* (C-341/04) [2006] B.C.C. 397

at paras 60–68.) No definition of public policy is given, but both provisions use the phrase "manifestly" contrary to public policy—an expression intended to invite a restrictive interpretation. The fact that foreign proceedings differ from those of this country, e.g. as regards creditors' rights and priorities, is not a ground to refuse recognition or relief: *Re Stocznia Gdynia SA v Bud-Bank Leasing sp z oo* [2010] B.C.C. 255.

Article 7. Additional assistance under other laws

Nothing in this Law limits the power of a court or a British insolvency officeholder to provide additional assistance to a foreign representative under other laws of Great Britain.

GENERAL NOTE

The most obvious "other law" is IA 1986 s.426; but there are also many known instances in which a judge in the UK has co-operated on an informal basis with a another judge administering a foreign insolvency, relying on the court's inherent jurisdiction or considerations of judicial comity, even where s.426 could not be invoked.

Article 8. Interpretation

In the interpretation of this Law, regard is to be had to its international origin and to the need to promote uniformity in its application and the observance of good faith.

GENERAL NOTE

A provision similar to this appears in a number of treaties and other Model Laws. The G to E, para.107, draws attention to the Case Law on International Texts (CLOUT) under which UNCITRAL publishes abstracts of judicial decisions, so facilitating a harmonised interpretation of the Model Law. The CLOUT system is available on the internet home page of UNCITRAL (*http://www.uncitral.org*), and also from the UNCITRAL Secretariat in hard copy.

CHAPTER II

ACCESS OF FOREIGN REPRESENTATIVES AND CREDITORS TO COURTS IN GREAT BRITAIN

Article 9. Right of direct access

A foreign representative is entitled to apply directly to a court in Great Britain.

GENERAL NOTE

This removes any doubt as to the representative's right of access. In practice the courts of the UK have normally been willing to allow such access, with rather less restriction or formality than many other countries.

Article 10. Limited jurisdiction

The sole fact that an application pursuant to this Law is made to a court in Great Britain by a foreign representative does not subject the foreign representative or the foreign assets and affairs of the debtor to the jurisdiction of the courts of Great Britain or any part of it for any purpose other than the application.

GENERAL NOTE

The G to E, para.109, explains that this provision constitutes a "safe conduct" rule aimed at ensuring that the court would not assume jurisdiction over all the assets of the debtor on the sole ground that the foreign representative had made an application for recognition of the foreign proceeding. It also makes it clear that the application alone is not a sufficient ground for the court to assert jurisdiction over the foreign representative in regard to matters unrelated to the insolvency. This does not rule out an assertion of jurisdiction that does not affect the assets of the debtor's estate—e.g. if a tort or misconduct is committed by the foreign representative the court would have grounds for jurisdiction to deal with the consequences of such misconduct. Note also that the court in granting relief under arts 19 et seq. may impose conditions, such as requiring the foreign representative to provide security or caution.

Article 11. Application by a foreign representative to commence a proceeding under British insolvency law

A foreign representative appointed in a foreign main proceeding or foreign non-main proceeding is entitled to apply to commence a proceeding under British insolvency law if the conditions for commencing such a proceeding are otherwise met.

GENERAL NOTE

This article gives the foreign representative procedural standing to commence a proceeding under British insolvency law. It makes it unnecessary for such an office-holder to be specifically listed in such provisions as IA 1986 s.124(1) (presentation of petition for winding up) or s.264(1) (presentation of bankruptcy petition). It is not a precondition for this purpose that the foreign proceeding should have been formally recognised under Chapter III, below. The conditions referred to are only those which would apply in any case (apart from the possible need to furnish a translation of documents under art.15.4): in contrast with art.19, the court is not given a discretion to impose other conditions.

Article 12. Participation of a foreign representative in a proceeding under British insolvency law

Upon recognition of a foreign proceeding, the foreign representative is entitled to participate in a proceeding regarding the debtor under British insolvency law.

GENERAL NOTE

This article gives the representative standing to participate in an insolvency proceeding concerning the debtor that is taking place in this country. It is limited to giving standing and does not vest the representative with any other rights or powers. Nor does it specify the kinds of application that he may make. In contrast with art.11, it is a prerequisite that the foreign proceeding has been recognised. Note that "proceeding" includes extra-judicial proceedings such as an administration or creditors' voluntary winding up.

The Model Law uses the term "participate" here and "intervene" in art.24, in the latter to refer to a case where the representative takes part in an "individual action" by or against the debtor as opposed to a collective insolvency proceeding (see G to E, para.117). It is not suggested that this differentiation is of significance.

Article 13. Access of foreign creditors to a proceeding under British insolvency law

1 Subject to paragraph 2 of this article, foreign creditors have the same rights regarding the commencement of, and participation in, a proceeding under British insolvency law as creditors in Great Britain.

2 Paragraph 1 of this article does not affect the ranking of claims in a proceeding under British insolvency law, except that the claim of a foreign creditor shall not be given a lower priority than that of general unsecured claims solely because the holder of such a claim is a foreign creditor.

3 A claim may not be challenged solely on the grounds that it is a claim by a foreign tax or social security authority but such a claim may be challenged–

(a) on the ground that it is in whole or in part a penalty, or

(b) on any other ground that a claim might be rejected in a proceeding under British insolvency law.

GENERAL NOTE

There has never been any discrimination against foreign creditors in UK insolvency law (apart from foreign revenue, etc. authorities: see the note to art.13.3 below).

Art.13.2
As well as giving them standing to file claims, this article establishes a minimum ranking for foreign creditors equal to that of the debtor's general unsecured creditors. Of course if they would have a lower priority here for some other reason (e.g. debts owed by a corporate debtor to its shareholders under IA 1986 s.74(2)(f)), the postponement is not affected by the present provision.

Art.13.3
Claims by foreign revenue, etc. authorities have traditionally not been provable debts in this country, but the reversal of this rule by art.13.3 mirrors that in the EU Regulation arts 2(12) and 53 (except that the concession in the Regulation is limited to the tax, etc. claims of Member States). Claims by a foreign State on other grounds (e.g. fines) are not affected by this provision.

Article 14. Notification to foreign creditors of a proceeding under British insolvency law

1   Whenever under British insolvency law notification is to be given to creditors in Great Britain, such notification shall also be given to the known creditors that do not have addresses in Great Britain. The court may order that appropriate steps be taken with a view to notifying any creditor whose address is not yet known.

2   Such notification shall be made to the foreign creditors individually, unless–

(a)   the court considers that under the circumstances some other form of notification would be more appropriate; or

(b)   the notification to creditors in Great Britain is to be by advertisement only, in which case the notification to the known foreign creditors may be by advertisement in such foreign newspapers as the British insolvency officeholder considers most appropriate for ensuring that the content of the notification comes to the notice of the known foreign creditors.

3   When notification of a right to file a claim is to be given to foreign creditors, the notification shall–

(a)   indicate a reasonable time period for filing claims and specify the place for their filing;

(b)   indicate whether secured creditors need to file their secured claims; and

(c)   contain any other information required to be included in such a notification to creditors pursuant to the law of Great Britain and the orders of the court.

4   In this article "the court" means the court which has jurisdiction in relation to the particular proceeding under British insolvency law under which notification is to be given to creditors.

GENERAL NOTE

See the G to E, paras 121 et seq. The main purpose of notifying foreign creditors is to inform them of the commencement of the insolvency proceeding and of the time-limit to file their claims. The concern of this article is that foreign creditors should be notified as expeditiously as possible and without the delay and expense which the use of letters rogatory and similar formalities would involve. Even where provision is made for the use of such formalities by another legal source, such as the Convention on the Service Abroad of Judicial and Extrajudicial Documents in Civil and Commercial Documents (1965), the G to E expresses the view that since art.14 is even more facilitative than the Convention there is no real conflict. In the last resort, reference could be made to art.3 to resolve any doubt.

Art.14.2
The object of the requirement for individual notification is to ensure that foreign creditors are not at a disadvantage in comparison with local creditors, e.g. where the law of the home jurisdiction allows notification to be made by advertisement in national newspapers, which foreign creditors would not usually see. But where, as is most likely, individual notification would be costly or impractical, subparas (a) and (b) give the court discretion to direct notification by other means.

CHAPTER III

RECOGNITION OF A FOREIGN PROCEEDING AND RELIEF

Article 15. Application for recognition of a foreign proceeding

1   A foreign representative may apply to the court for recognition of the foreign proceeding in which the foreign representative has been appointed.

2   An application for recognition shall be accompanied by–

(a)   a certified copy of the decision commencing the foreign proceeding and appointing the foreign representative; or

(b)   a certificate from the foreign court affirming the existence of the foreign proceeding and of the appointment of the foreign representative; or

(c)   in the absence of evidence referred to in sub-paragraphs (a) and (b), any other evidence acceptable to the court of the existence of the foreign proceeding and of the appointment of the foreign representative.

3   An application for recognition shall also be accompanied by a statement identifying all foreign proceedings, proceedings under British insolvency law and section 426 requests in respect of the debtor that are known to the foreign representative.

4   The foreign representative shall provide the court with a translation into English of documents supplied in support of the application for recognition.

GENERAL NOTE

Recognition of the foreign proceeding necessarily involves recognition of the foreign representative and the validity of his appointment. The Model Law aims to avoid the need for any formal "legalisation" of the foreign documents submitted as evidence—an aim endorsed by this article, stipulating for no other requirement than a translation where this is needed. The court is entitled to assume that the documents are authentic without further ado (art.16.2), but is not bound to do so. On the meaning of "foreign representative", see the note to art.2(j).

In *Re 19 Entertainment Ltd* [2016] EWHC 1545 (Ch); [2017] B.C.C. 347 the court accorded recognition to Chapter 11 proceedings in the United States which took the normal "debtor in possession" format, without any individual office-holder who could be recognised as the foreign representative. The court held that the company itself and each of its directors was the foreign representative.

On the procedure, see generally Sch.2 Pt 2, and on notice, Sch.2 paras 21 et seq. The G to E, para.135 points out that the Model Law does not make the issuance of any form of notice mandatory, but stresses the need for a recognition proceeding to be dealt with expeditiously. Mr Registrar Nicholls has issued a helpful note on various aspects of the procedure under arts 15 and 21, reported as *Re Rajapaske (Note)* [2007] B.P.I.R. 99.

Art.15.2
The Model Law uses the term "proceeding" to include insolvencies which are commenced extra-judicially, such as voluntary arrangements, creditors' voluntary liquidations and many administrations, as well as those effected by court order. In such cases, (or rather their foreign equivalents) an English court may be prepared to accept a certified copy of (e.g.) the resolutions of the company's general meeting and creditors by which the company was put into liquidation and the liquidator appointed (see, e.g. *Re New Paragon Investments Ltd* [2012] B.C.C. 371). If there is uncertainty, it may be thought preferable to obtain a certificate from the foreign court similar to that prescribed by IR 2016 rr.21.4, 21.5.

It will be recalled that interim foreign proceedings are within the definition (art.2(i)).

Art.15.3
The information prescribed by this provision will be needed by the court not so much for the grant of recognition itself but for any later decision granting relief: it is likely to be important to ensure that such relief is consistent with any other insolvency proceeding, wherever situated, involving the same debtor.

In *Nordic Trustee ASA v OGX Petroleo e Gas SA* [2016] EWHC 25 (Ch) Snowden J stressed that a foreign representative seeking recognition of a foreign proceeding must make full and frank disclosure to the court of the consequences that that recognition may have upon third parties who are not before the court (followed in *Cherkasov v Olegovich (the Official Receiver of Dalnyaya Step LLC) (No.2)* [2017] EWHC 3153 (Ch); [2019] B.C.C. 23).

See also art.8, on information that becomes known to the foreign representative after recognition, and art.30, on co-ordination of more than one foreign insolvency proceeding.

Art.15.4
The court is entitled, but not bound, to require a translation (G to E, para.134).

Article 16. Presumptions concerning recognition

1 If the decision or certificate referred to in paragraph 2 of article 15 indicates that the foreign proceeding is a proceeding within the meaning of sub-paragraph (i) of article 2 and that the foreign representative is a person or body within the meaning of sub-paragraph (j) of article 2, the court is entitled to so presume.

2 The court is entitled to presume that documents submitted in support of the application for recognition are authentic, whether or not they have been legalised.

3 In the absence of proof to the contrary, the debtor's registered office, or habitual residence in the case of an individual, is presumed to be the centre of the debtor's main interests.

GENERAL NOTE

These presumptions enable to court to expedite the evidentiary process.

Article 17. Decision to recognise a foreign proceeding

1 Subject to article 6, a foreign proceeding shall be recognised if–

   (a) it is a foreign proceeding within the meaning of sub-paragraph (i) of article 2;

   (b) the foreign representative applying for recognition is a person or body within the meaning of sub-paragraph (j) of article 2;

   (c) the application meets the requirements of paragraphs 2 and 3 of article 15; and

   (d) the application has been submitted to the court referred to in article 4.

2 The foreign proceeding shall be recognised–

   (a) as a foreign main proceeding if it is taking place in the State where the debtor has the centre of its main interests; or

   (b) as a foreign non-main proceeding if the debtor has an establishment within the meaning of sub-paragraph (e) of article 2 in the foreign State.

3 An application for recognition of a foreign proceeding shall be decided upon at the earliest possible time.

4 The provisions of articles 15 to 16, this article and article 18 do not prevent modification or termination of recognition if it is shown that the grounds for granting it were fully or partially lacking or have fully or partially ceased to exist and in such a case, the court may, on the application of the foreign representative or a person affected by recognition, or of its own motion, modify or terminate recognition, either altogether or for a limited time, on such terms and conditions as the court thinks fit.

GENERAL NOTE

The purpose of this article is to indicate that, if the application meets the requirements set out, recognition should be granted as a matter of course and without delay, so ensuring the effective protection of the debtor's assets. The decision to grant recognition should not involve an examination of the merits of the foreign court's decision or the foreign representative's suitability. The only exception is art.6 (public policy).

In *Global Maritime Investments Cyprus Ltd v OW Supply and Trading AS* [2015] EWHC 2690 (Comm) the question at issue was whether recognition of a foreign proceeding constituted a "real and present dispute" for the purposes of a jurisdiction clause. It was held that recognition in itself was not enough, until the office-holder in those proceedings took steps to obtain an order or judgment against the claimant.

On the question of determining COMI of an English registered company which operated in the USA see *Re 19 Entertainment Ltd* [2017] B.C.C. 347. Recognition was granted to the foreign representative pursuant to art.17 and relief in the form of a moratorium was made available under arts 20 and 21.

Re Dalnyaya Step LLC; Cherkasov v Olegovich [2017] EWHC 756 (Ch); [2019] B.C.C. 1 was concerned with recognition and security for costs (Rose J). An official receiver of a Russian company having been recognised for CBIR purposes was then ordered to provide security for costs in an application under of IA 1986 s.236. Rose J held that the art.6 exception on grounds of public policy came into play due to the difficulty of enforcing a costs order in Russia. For later proceedings see *Cherkasov v Olegovich (the Official Receiver of Dalnyaya Step LLC) (No.2)* [2017] EWHC 3153 (Ch); [2019] B.C.C. 23 where Vos C revoked the recognition order which had been granted under art.17 because there had been a lack of full and frank disclosure.

In *Re Videology Ltd* [2018] EWHC 2186 (Ch); [2019] B.C.C. 195 Snowden J refused to grant recognition under art.17 on the basis of the existence of foreign main proceedings. The US Chapter 11 insolvency proceedings related to the affairs of an English subsidiary of a US parent. In so deciding, he found that the COMI of the company was in the UK (where its registered office was located) and not in the USA. However, he granted recognition on the basis that the proceedings were foreign non-main proceedings and then he also granted relief under art.21(3). For comment see Hawthorn [2018] 11(5) C.R.I. 161.

Art.17.2

Recognition must categorise the foreign proceeding as "main" or "non-main". This is important because the former brings about an automatic stay of proceedings and the freezing of assets under art.20. If the proceeding is deemed to be non-main, the grant of a stay is in the discretion of the court.

It is not permitted to recognise a foreign proceeding as non-main if the debtor has assets but no establishment (as defined in art.2(e)) in the foreign jurisdiction. As noted in the comment to that article, the use of "it" is misleading: the CBIR apply to individual as well as corporate debtors. Non-recognition could not, of course, affect in any way the conduct of that proceeding in its home State; still less restrict the powers of the office-holder in the main proceedings (which could be British insolvency proceedings) from exercising any rights he may have in relation to those assets.

Art.17.4

Examples of the grounds which may justify the modification or termination of recognition include the emergence of new facts, or a change of circumstances such as the termination of the foreign proceeding or a change in its nature (reorganisation giving way to liquidation, or vice versa). Compare *Re Sanko Steamship Co Ltd* [2015] EWHC 1031 (Ch) (recognition by English court of termination of Japanese proceedings). The court may also be requested to re-examine whether in the decision-making process the requirements for recognition were observed. The G to E, para.166, stresses that the review of a decision should not involve an inquiry into the merits of the case, any more than the decision itself.

Procedural matters, including appeals, are not dealt with by the Model Law but left to the domestic law of the enacting State.

Article 18. Subsequent information

From the time of filing the application for recognition of the foreign proceeding, the foreign representative shall inform the court promptly of–

(a) any substantial change in the status of the recognised foreign proceeding or the status of the foreign representative's appointment; and

(b) any other foreign proceeding, proceeding under British insolvency law or section 426 request regarding the same debtor that becomes known to the foreign representative.

GENERAL NOTE

"Substantial" changes are to be distinguished from those which are merely technical. As well as the possibility that the foreign proceeding may change from reorganisation to liquidation, or vice versa, the court will wish to be informed if the recognition was of an interim proceeding or the appointment of the representative was on an interim basis and it has since been made permanent.

Art.18(b)

In the light of the new information the court may wish to consider whether the relief already granted should be modified so as to co-ordinate with the other proceeding or s.426 request.

Article 19. Relief that may be granted upon application for recognition of a foreign proceeding

1 From the time of filing an application for recognition until the application is decided upon, the court may, at the request of the foreign representative, where relief is urgently needed to protect the assets of the debtor or the interests of the creditors, grant relief of a provisional nature, including–

    (a)   staying execution against the debtor's assets;

    (b)   entrusting the administration or realisation of all or part of the debtor's assets located in Great Britain to the foreign representative or another person designated by the court, in order to protect and preserve the value of assets that, by their nature or because of other circumstances, are perishable, susceptible to devaluation or otherwise in jeopardy; and

    (c)   any relief mentioned in paragraph 1 (c), (d) or (g) of article 21.

2 Unless extended under paragraph 1(f) of article 21, the relief granted under this article terminates when the application for recognition is decided upon.

3 The court may refuse to grant relief under this article if such relief would interfere with the administration of a foreign main proceeding.

GENERAL NOTE

The provisional relief which may be granted under this provision is discretionary and the circumstances in which it may be granted under para.(b) would appear to be limited to those specified, but for the use of the word "including" in the opening sentence. Note that the power to refuse relief under para.(c) is also discretionary.

    It is stressed in the G to E, para.171 that the type of relief which the court is authorised to grant here is that which "is usually available only in collective insolvency proceedings", as opposed to the "individual" relief which may be granted under rules of civil procedure (i.e. measures covering specific assets identified by a creditor).

    The recognition of a foreign proceeding could not affect the substantive rights of any party. For instance, it could not give validity to the discharge of a foreign debt which would be regarded as ineffective under English law (as in *Global Distressed Alpha Fund 1 LLP v PT Bakrie Investindo* [2011] EWHC 256 (Comm); [2011] B.P.I.R. 645: see the note to IA 1986 s.426).

Article 20. Effects of recognition of a foreign main proceeding

1 Upon recognition of a foreign proceeding that is a foreign main proceeding, subject to paragraph 2 of this article–

    (a)   commencement or continuation of individual actions or individual proceedings concerning the debtor's assets, rights, obligations or liabilities is stayed;

    (b)   execution against the debtor's assets is stayed; and

    (c)   the right to transfer, encumber or otherwise dispose of any assets of the debtor is suspended.

2 The stay and suspension referred to in paragraph 1 of this article shall be–

    (a)   the same in scope and effect as if the debtor, in the case of an individual, had been adjudged bankrupt under the Insolvency Act 1986 or had his estate sequestrated under the Bankruptcy (Scotland) Act 1985, or, in the case of a debtor other than an individual, had been made the subject of a winding-up order under the Insolvency Act 1986; and

(b)   subject to the same powers of the court and the same prohibitions, limitations, exceptions and conditions as would apply under the law of Great Britain in such a case,

and the provisions of paragraph 1 of this article shall be interpreted accordingly.

3   Without prejudice to paragraph 2 of this article, the stay and suspension referred to in paragraph 1 of this article, in particular, does not affect any right–

(a)   to take any steps to enforce security over the debtor's property;

(b)   to take any steps to repossess goods in the debtor's possession under a hire-purchase agreement;

(c)   exercisable under or by virtue of or in connection with the provisions referred to in article 1(4); or

(d)   of a creditor to set off its claim against a claim of the debtor,

being a right which would have been exercisable if the debtor, in the case of an individual, had been adjudged bankrupt under the Insolvency Act 1986 or had his estate sequestrated under the Bankruptcy (Scotland) Act 1985, or, in the case of a debtor other than an individual, had been made the subject of a winding-up order under the Insolvency Act 1986.

4   Paragraph 1(a) of this article does not affect the right to–

(a)   commence individual actions or proceedings to the extent necessary to preserve a claim against the debtor; or

(b)   commence or continue any criminal proceedings or any action or proceedings by a person or body having regulatory, supervisory or investigative functions of a public nature, being an action or proceedings brought in the exercise of those functions.

5   Paragraph 1 of this article does not affect the right to request or otherwise initiate the commencement of a proceeding under British insolvency law or the right to file claims in such a proceeding.

6   In addition to and without prejudice to any powers of the court under or by virtue of paragraph 2 of this article, the court may, on the application of the foreign representative or a person affected by the stay and suspension referred to in paragraph 1 of this article, or of its own motion, modify or terminate such stay and suspension or any part of it, either altogether or for a limited time, on such terms and conditions as the court thinks fit.

GENERAL NOTE

The stay which comes into being under this article follows automatically from the recognition of a foreign proceeding as a main proceeding, and its extent is defined in the later paragraphs. No court order is necessary. Where the foreign law governing the main proceeding provides for a different (possibly less stringent) stay, the stay in this jurisdiction will be that defined by art.20.

Note that the automatic stay will apply even in the case of an "interim" foreign proceeding.

An application for recognition of a foreign main proceeding may be made without notice, but in that case the applicant must make full disclosure of any facts relative to the effect that recognition might have on third parties, which might justify the modification of the automatic stay which would follow from art.20: *Re OGX Petroleo e Gás SA* [2016] EWHC 25 (Ch) (also see *Cherkasov v Olegovich (the Official Receiver of Dalnyaya Step LLC) (No.2)* [2017] EWHC 3153 (Ch); [2019] B.C.C. 23).

The use of the phrase "or individual proceedings" is intended to include arbitrations, but it is conceded (G to E, para.145) that it may not always be possible, in practical terms, to implement a stay of arbitral proceedings—perhaps an international arbitration taking place under the law of a third jurisdiction. In any case, it may be thought in the interests of the debtor to allow such a proceeding to continue—a course which could be sanctioned by the court under arts 20.2 or 20.6.

The CBIR do not specify what sanctions might apply for breach of a stay.

Article 21 gives the court discretionary powers to grant a stay beyond the scope of art.20, e.g. because the foreign insolvency is a non-main proceeding, or where a wider stay is sought (see art.21.1(a)–(c)). Note the limitations imposed by arts 1.4–1.7.

In *Samsun Logix Corp v DEF* [2009] EWHC 576 (Ch); [2010] B.C.C. 556 the court ruled that a Korean receivership constituted foreign main proceedings, with the consequence that a stay under art.20 came into force.

Art.20.2

Under the Model Law, it is assumed that domestic law provisions such as those referred to may be invoked for the purpose of terminating the stay, for instance if a foreign interim proceeding is discontinued (G to E, para.179); but the CBIR make express provision for this in art.20.6.

Art.20.3

This reflects the general law principle that on the making of a winding-up order or equivalent in the domicile of a debtor his assets become subject to a statutory trust under the laws of that jurisdiction—that is, his foreign as well as his local assets (*Stichting Shell Pensioenfonds v Krys* [2014] UKPC 41; [2015] B.C.C. 205; but assets subject to a security interest or other right in rem are excluded. Rights of security, repossession and set-off (if they would be exercisable in an English insolvency) are not affected, as are the special regimes applicable to payment and settlement systems. "Hire-purchase agreement" has the extended meaning set out in art.2(k).

Arts 20.4, 20.5

Article 20.4(a) is restricted to the *commencing* of proceedings (e.g. to prevent a claim becoming statute-barred under the law of the proper law of the underlying contract). In any event, a foreign claimant might feel assured that by commencing local proceedings his claim would not be prejudiced.

Subparagraph (b), which is not so restricted, would include director disqualification proceedings.

Art.20.6

The court lifted a stay in *United Drug (UK) Holdings Ltd v Bilcare Singapore Pte Ltd* [2013] EWHC 4335 (Ch) to allow a local arbitration to proceed.

Article 21. Relief that may be granted upon recognition of a foreign proceeding

1 Upon recognition of a foreign proceeding, whether main or non-main, where necessary to protect the assets of the debtor or the interests of the creditors, the court may, at the request of the foreign representative, grant any appropriate relief, including–

(a) staying the commencement or continuation of individual actions or individual proceedings concerning the debtor's assets, rights, obligations or liabilities, to the extent they have not been stayed under paragraph 1(a) of article 20;

(b) staying execution against the debtor's assets to the extent it has not been stayed under paragraph 1(b) of article 20;

(c) suspending the right to transfer, encumber or otherwise dispose of any assets of the debtor to the extent this right has not been suspended under paragraph 1(c) of article 20;

(d) providing for the examination of witnesses, the taking of evidence or the delivery of information concerning the debtor's assets, affairs, rights, obligations or liabilities;

(e) entrusting the administration or realisation of all or part of the debtor's assets located in Great Britain to the foreign representative or another person designated by the court;

(f) extending relief granted under paragraph 1 of article 19; and

(g) granting any additional relief that may be available to a British insolvency officeholder under the law of Great Britain, including any relief provided under paragraph 43 of Schedule B1 to the Insolvency Act 1986.

2 Upon recognition of a foreign proceeding, whether main or non-main, the court may, at the request of the foreign representative, entrust the distribution of all or part of the debtor's assets located in Great Britain to the foreign representative or another person designated by the court, provided that the court is satisfied that the interests of creditors in Great Britain are adequately protected.

3 In granting relief under this article to a representative of a foreign non-main proceeding, the court must be satisfied that the relief relates to assets that, under the law of Great Britain, should be administered in the foreign non-main proceeding or concerns information required in that proceeding.

4 No stay under paragraph 1(a) of this article shall affect the right to commence or continue any criminal proceedings or any action or proceedings by a person or body having regulatory, supervisory or investigative functions of a public nature, being an action or proceedings brought in the exercise of those functions.

GENERAL NOTE

This article deals with "post-recognition" relief; for "pre-recognition" relief, see art.19.

As noted above, the grant of a stay under this provision is discretionary, and may be more extensive than that which comes into being automatically under art.20. But the relief available under this article is entirely general, and not restricted to a stay of proceedings: see paras 1(d)–(g) and (2).

In *Rubin v Eurofinance SA* [2012] UKSC 46; [2013] B.C.C. 1 Lord Collins said (at [143]) that this provision (and arts 25 and 27) are concerned with procedural matters, and could not be construed widely so as to extend to the recognition and enforcement of foreign judgments. See also *Re 19 Entertainment Ltd* [2017] B.C.C. 347.

Art.21.1

The relief available under art.21 is procedural only; it does not allow the court to grant relief by way of the application of a rule of foreign law: *Re Pan Ocean Co Ltd* [2014] EWHC 2124 (Ch). For examples of the court's exercise of discretion under this provision, see *Picard v FIM Advisers LLP* [2010] EWHC 1299 (Ch); [2011] 1 B.C.L.C. 129 (order granted for production of documents to US administrator of Madoff company); *Re Chesterfield United Inc* [2012] EWHC 244 (Ch); [2012] B.C.C. 786 (similar facts); *Larsen v Navios International Inc* [2011] EWHC 878 (Ch); [2012] B.C.C. 353 (contractual set-off which would infringe pari passu principle disallowed). In the *Larsen* case the court held that, while art.21 authorises relief to be given by the English court as from the date of recognition, the relevant date for identifying the rights in respect of which the relief is to be afforded is the date of the opening of the foreign proceedings. In *Re Pan Ocean Co Ltd* [2014] EWHC 2124 (Ch) it was held that art.21.2(a) did not empower the court to restrain a party to a contract from exercising its contractual right to terminate: this was something which the court could not do even in a domestic insolvency. In *Re Chesterfield United* (above) it was held that art.21.1(g) sets only minimum standards and that, if the local law (in this case IA 1986 s.236) provided for additional relief a foreign representative could seek that under art.21.1(g).

Where recognition is accorded to a foreign main proceeding which has as its purpose the restructuring of the debtor rather than its winding up, the English courts have been willing to use their powers under art.21.1 to replicate the moratorium against individual actions which is applicable in an administration, a point reiterated in *Re Videology Ltd* [2018] EWHC 2186 (Ch); [2019] B.C.C. 195 at [82] where the relief was granted in the court's discretion in foreign non-main proceedings in the US to facilitate sale of an English subsidiary's business and assets as part of a co-ordinated sale of the (US-owned) group in the US where it had sought protection from bankruptcy and the sale was likely to command a higher price.

Glasgow (Bankruptcy Trustee of Harlequin Property (SVG) Ltd) v ELS Law Ltd [2017] EWHC 3004 (Ch) involves an application for directions as a form of relief under art.21. Whilst giving directions the court noted that it has no power to apply the rule in *Ex p. James* (1874) L.R. 9 Ch. App. 609 to officers appointed by foreign courts.

In *Re Ex Ced Foods, ANZ National Bank v Sheahan* [2012] NZHC 3037; [2013] B.C.C. 321 an application was made to the court for an order authorising the liquidators of an Australian company to examine an officer of a connected New Zealand company, which was also in liquidation and to which the same individuals had been appointed liquidators. The court held that there was a fine balance in exercising its discretion whether to make the order, since information might be revealed which would not be available to the Australian liquidators under Australian law; and it also ruled that the liquidators had acted improperly in providing a transcript to themselves as Australian liquidators of an examination of the officer that had been held in the course of the New Zealand liquidation.

On the limits of relief under art.21 and the inability of the English courts to displace common law (in this case *Antony Gibbs & Sons v La Societe Industrielle et Commerciale des Metaux* (1890) 25 Q.B.D. 399) see *Bakhshiyeva v Sberbank of Russia* [2018] EWHC 59 (Ch). In so deciding, the High Court followed the views expressed by Morgan J in *Re Pan Ocean Co Ltd* [2014] EWHC 2124 (Ch). On the appeal in *Bakhshiyeva*, in *Re OJSC International Bank of Azerbaijan; Bakhshiyeva v Sberbank of Russia* [2018] EWCA Civ 2802 the Court of Appeal refused to extend a moratorium (which had earlier been granted under art.20 to facilitate a voluntary restructuring) after that restructuring had been completed. In so deciding it held that *Gibbs* (above) remained good authority in English law notwithstanding the advent of the Cross-Border Insolvency Regulations. The foreign restructuring could not defeat the rights of creditors whose debts were governed by English law. There was nothing in the Model Law to suggest that this rule of common law would be altered. An indefinite stay of proceedings under art.21 would therefore be inappropriate as this would defeat the rights of creditors under English law.

Art.21.2

The court's discretion extends to directing the "turnover" of assets to the foreign representative, or to some other person. A number of other provisions of the CBIR also provide safeguards intended to ensure the protection of local interests: see, e.g. arts 22.1, 22.2. In *Re SwissAir Schweizerische Luftverkehr-Aktiengesellschaft* [2009] EWHC 2099 (Ch); [2010] B.C.C. 667 an order was made for the remittal of assets to main proceedings in Switzerland, no conditions being held to be necessary. In *Re Sanko Steamship Co. Ltd* [2015] EWHC 1031 (Ch) the court felt unable to order a remittal of funds because the foreign proceedings (in Japan) had been terminated.

In *Cosco Bulk Carrier Shipping Co Ltd v Armada Shipping SA* [2011] EWHC 216 (Ch); [2011] B.P.I.R. 626 Briggs J exercised the discretion under art.21 to order the lifting of a stay in a case where the respondent company was in liquidation in Switzerland, on the ground that the issues involved questions of shipping law which could better be considered by expert arbitrators in this country. Compare *Re Pan Ocean Co Ltd* [2015] EWHC 1500 (Ch) (stay varied to allow arbitration proceedings to be heard in London). See also *Ronelp Marine Ltd v STX Offshore & Shipbuilding Co* [2016] EWHC 2228 (Ch) (stay lifted to allow case involving difficult issues of English law to continue).

Art.21.3

In contrast with the EU Regulation, which is a Community enactment effective in all the Member States (apart from Denmark) the authority of the Model Law cannot be imposed on a foreign jurisdiction by the CBIR or any other external source. It follows that the scope of a foreign non-main proceeding will not be limited to assets situated within its own jurisdiction unless such a restriction is imposed by the local law. Such a limitation can, however, be placed on the relief which the court may grant to a foreign non-main representative ("the law of Great Britain" including, of course, the CBIR). Moreover, if there are also insolvency proceedings current in another foreign State, the court can ensure that any relief granted will not interfere with the administration of those proceedings, in particular the main proceeding.

On art.21.3 see *Re Videology Ltd* [2018] EWHC 2186 (Ch); [2019] B.C.C. 195.

Article 22. Protection of creditors and other interested persons

1   In granting or denying relief under article 19 or 21, or in modifying or terminating relief under paragraph 3 of this article or paragraph 6 of article 20, the court must be satisfied that the interests of the creditors (including any secured creditors or parties to hire-purchase agreements) and other interested persons, including if appropriate the debtor, are adequately protected.

2   The court may subject relief granted under article 19 or 21 to conditions it considers appropriate, including the provision by the foreign representative of security or caution for the proper performance of his functions.

3   The court may, at the request of the foreign representative or a person affected by relief granted under article 19 or 21, or of its own motion, modify or terminate such relief.

GENERAL NOTE

It is to be noted that there is no reference here to "local" creditors, or indeed any definition of such a term in the CBIR. "The interests of the creditors" would, however, include the priority to which preferential creditors and those entitled to participate in the "prescribed part" under IA 1986 s.176A. Adequate protection may include the giving of notice to interested parties. This matter is left to be dealt with by the general law and the discretion of the court.

Article 23. Actions to avoid acts detrimental to creditors

1   Subject to paragraphs 6 and 9 of this article, upon recognition of a foreign proceeding, the foreign representative has standing to make an application to the court for an order under or in connection with sections 238, 239, 242, 243, 244, 245, 339, 340, 342A, 343, and 423 of the Insolvency Act 1986 and sections 34, 35, 36, 36A and 61 of the Bankruptcy (Scotland) Act 1985.

2 Where the foreign representative makes such an application ("an article 23 application"), the sections referred to in paragraph 1 of this article and sections 240, 241, 341, 342, 342B to 342F, 424 and 425 of the Insolvency Act 1986 and sections 36B and 36C of the Bankruptcy (Scotland) Act 1985 shall apply–

(a) whether or not the debtor, in the case of an individual, has been adjudged bankrupt or had his estate sequestrated, or, in the case of a debtor other than an individual, is being wound up or is in administration, under British insolvency law; and

(b) with the modifications set out in paragraph 3 of this article.

3 The modifications referred to in paragraph 2 of this article are as follows–

(a) for the purposes of sections 241(2A)(a) and 342(2A)(a) of the Insolvency Act 1986, a person has notice of the relevant proceedings if he has notice of the opening of the relevant foreign proceeding;

(b) for the purposes of sections 240(1) and 245(3) of that Act, the onset of insolvency shall be the date of the opening of the relevant foreign proceeding;

(c) the periods referred to in sections 244(2), 341(1)(a) to (c) and 343(2) of that Act shall be periods ending with the date of the opening of the relevant foreign proceeding;

(d) for the purposes of sections 242(3)(a), (3)(b) and 243(1) of that Act, the date on which the winding up of the company commences or it enters administration shall be the date of the opening of the relevant foreign proceeding; and

(e) for the purposes of sections 34(3)(a), (3)(b), 35(1)(c), 36(1)(a) and (1)(b) and 61(2) of the Bankruptcy (Scotland) Act 1985, the date of sequestration or granting of the trust deed shall be the date of the opening of the relevant foreign proceeding.

4 For the purposes of paragraph 3 of this article, the date of the opening of the foreign proceeding shall be determined in accordance with the law of the State in which the foreign proceeding is taking place, including any rule of law by virtue of which the foreign proceeding is deemed to have opened at an earlier time.

5 When the foreign proceeding is a foreign non-main proceeding, the court must be satisfied that the article 23 application relates to assets that, under the law of Great Britain, should be administered in the foreign non-main proceeding.

6 At any time when a proceeding under British insolvency law is taking place regarding the debtor–

(a) the foreign representative shall not make an article 23 application except with the permission of–

(i) in the case of a proceeding under British insolvency law taking place in England and Wales, the High Court; or

(ii) in the case of a proceeding under British insolvency law taking place in Scotland, the Court of Session; and

(b) references to "the court" in paragraphs 1, 5 and 7 of this article are references to the court in which that proceeding is taking place.

7 On making an order on an article 23 application, the court may give such directions regarding the distribution of any proceeds of the claim by the foreign representative, as it thinks fit to ensure that the interests of creditors in Great Britain are adequately protected.

8 Nothing in this article affects the right of a British insolvency officeholder to make an application under or in connection with any of the provisions referred to in paragraph 1 of this article.

9 Nothing in paragraph 1 of this article shall apply in respect of any preference given, floating charge created, alienation, assignment or relevant contributions (within the meaning of section 342A(5) of the Insolvency Act 1986) made or other transaction entered into before the date on which this Law comes into force.

GENERAL NOTE

This article empowers a foreign representative to make application to a British court for any of the forms of relief listed in para.1 (avoidance of preferences, transactions at an undervalue, etc.) even though the debtor is not the subject of an insolvency proceeding under British law, and where the foreign representative would not otherwise have standing to apply to the court. The article does not create any substantive right regarding the claims in question and is not concerned with any question that may arise under the conflict of laws.

In contrast with the EU Regulation, the foreign representative is not deemed to be a creditor or his position equated with that of a creditor for these or any other purposes under the CBIR.

Article 24. Intervention by a foreign representative in proceedings in Great Britain

Upon recognition of a foreign proceeding, the foreign representative may, provided the requirements of the law of Great Britain are met, intervene in any proceedings in which the debtor is a party.

GENERAL NOTE

Again, this article is concerned to ensure that the foreign representative is accorded standing, even in cases where the relevant legislation does not contemplate his intervention. It applies to representatives in both main and non-main proceedings, and includes extra-judicial proceedings as well as court actions. These will be proceedings between the debtor and a third party (as distinct from intervention or participation in the insolvency itself (on which see art.12)), and can only be those that have not been stayed under arts 20 or 21.

CHAPTER IV

COOPERATION WITH FOREIGN COURTS AND FOREIGN REPRESENTATIVES

Introductory note to Chapter IV
Chapter IV, on co-operation, is described as a "core element" of the Model Law (G to E, para.173). Its objective is to enable courts and insolvency administrators to be efficient and to achieve optimal results, whether in preventing the dissipation of assets, in maximising their value or in finding the best solutions for a reorganisation.

Note the use of the word "may", in contrast with "shall" in art.26. The Model Law itself also uses "shall" in art.25, but the substitution of "may" in the CBIR must be assumed to have been deliberate. Thus the court has a discretion, but an office-holder does not.

It is not a necessary condition for the application of Chapter IV that the foreign proceeding should have been recognised under Chapter III.

Article 25. Cooperation and direct communication between a court of Great Britain and foreign courts or foreign representatives

1 In matters referred to in paragraph 1 of article 1, the court may cooperate to the maximum extent possible with foreign courts or foreign representatives, either directly or through a British insolvency officeholder.

2 The court is entitled to communicate directly with, or to request information or assistance directly from, foreign courts or foreign representatives.

Art.25.1
The substitution of the word "may" (see above) sits oddly with retention of the phrase "to the maximum extent possible"! The extent to which the parties should be involved is a matter for the discretion of the court.

Art.25.2

The use of the word "directly" is intended to encourage the court to forgo the use of formalities, such as involving higher courts, or using letters rogatory or diplomatic or consular channels. See also the remarks of Lord Collins in *Rubin v Eurofinance SA* [2012] UKSC 46; [2013] B.C.C. 1 in the note to art.21.

Article 26. Cooperation and direct communication between the British insolvency officeholder and foreign courts or foreign representatives

1 In matters referred to in paragraph 1 of article 1, a British insolvency officeholder shall to the extent consistent with his other duties under the law of Great Britain, in the exercise of his functions and subject to the supervision of the court, cooperate to the maximum extent possible with foreign courts or foreign representatives.

2 The British insolvency officeholder is entitled, in the exercise of his functions and subject to the supervision of the court, to communicate directly with foreign courts or foreign representatives.

GENERAL NOTE

As noted above, this article is mandatory in its terms. The phrase "subject to the supervision of the court" is not intended to require the office-holder to seek approval of his acts on an ad hoc basis in situations where the court's supervisory role under the domestic law is largely nominal (e.g. a CVA or IVA): see G to E, para.180.

Article 27. Forms of cooperation

Cooperation referred to in articles 25 and 26 may be implemented by any appropriate means, including–

(a) appointment of a person to act at the direction of the court;

(b) communication of information by any means considered appropriate by the court;

(c) coordination of the administration and supervision of the debtor's assets and affairs;

(d) approval or implementation by courts of agreements concerning the coordination of proceedings;

(e) coordination of concurrent proceedings regarding the same debtor.

GENERAL NOTE

The list of options is not exhaustive. It would not rule out the suspension or termination of local insolvency proceedings, if appropriate. In *Rubin v Eurofinance SA* [2010] EWCA Civ 895; [2011] B.C.C. 649 Ward LJ (at [64]) expressed concern that the forms of co-operation specifically mentioned in art.27 did not include enforcement (and, indeed, that there was no mention of enforcement anywhere in the CBIR), but he did indicate that in his view co-operation "to the maximum extent possible" would include enforcement. (This point was not in issue on appeal [2012] UKSC 46; [2013] B.C.C. 1.)

In furtherance of art.27(d), on 1 July 2009, UNCITRAL adopted a *Practice Guide on Cross-Border Insolvency Cooperation* which was adopted by a resolution of the UN General Assembly on 16 December 2009, and published in 2010. The purpose of the *Practice Guide* is to "to provide information for practitioners and judges on practical aspects of cooperation and communication in cross-border insolvency cases, specifically in cases involving insolvency proceedings in multiple States where the insolvent debtor has assets and cases where some of the debtor's creditors are not from the State in which the insolvency proceedings have commenced". Although it might apply to individual debtors, it is typically aimed at enterprise groups with offices, business activities and assets in multiple States. The *Practice Guide* focuses on the use and negotiation of cross-border insolvency agreements, providing an analysis of a number of written agreements approved by courts and oral arrangements between parties to cross-border insolvency proceedings in the preceding 20 years. The *Practice Guide* is not intended to be prescriptive but to illustrate how resolution of issues and conflicts may be facilitated by the use of such agreements tailored to the specifics of each case and the requirements of applicable law. The *Practice Guide* is available on the Publications section of the UNCITRAL website.

CHAPTER V

CONCURRENT PROCEEDINGS

Article 28. Commencement of a proceeding under British insolvency law after recognition of a foreign main proceeding

After recognition of a foreign main proceeding, the effects of a proceeding under British insolvency law in relation to the same debtor shall, insofar as the assets of that debtor are concerned, be restricted to assets that are located in Great Britain and, to the extent necessary to implement cooperation and coordination under articles 25, 26 and 27, to other assets of the debtor that, under the law of Great Britain, should be administered in that proceeding.

GENERAL NOTE

This is another provision of the CBIR which is expressed in mandatory terms. It applies only after the foreign proceeding has been recognised, *and* recognised as a main proceeding. Before there has been any recognition, or if the foreign proceedings are recognised only as non-main, the law of the relevant British jurisdiction applies to the exclusion of the CBIR. So, for instance, the cases where the court assumed jurisdiction to make an order for the winding up of a foreign company under IA 1986 Pt V, even when the debtor company had no assets in the UK (e.g. *Re Eloc, etc. BV* [1982] Ch. 43: see IA 1986 s.220) will still be authoritative—unless, of course, the EU Regulation applies. But once a main foreign proceeding has been recognised, any domestic insolvency proceeding is restricted to dealing with local assets.

Does this restriction apply to a proceeding that has already commenced here before recognition? Far from making this clear, the draftsman has left us with an uncertainty. The heading to art.28 plainly confines its scope to the commencement of new proceedings, as does the Model Law ("a proceeding under [British] insolvency law may be commenced only if the debtor has assets in this State"). But the CBIR text alters this to "the effects of a proceeding under British insolvency law ... shall ... be restricted to assets that are located in Great Britain".

Article 28 does not require also (or instead) that the debtor should have an establishment in Britain: contrast art.17.2(b), dealing with the recognition of foreign non-main proceedings.

The concluding words (after "in Great Britain") are designed to cope with exceptional situations, such as where assets of the debtor have been fraudulently moved abroad, or where there is no foreign proceeding necessary or available in the State where the assets are situated; the G to E (para.187) suggests also "where it would be possible to sell the debtor's assets in the enacting State and the assets abroad as a 'going concern'". The words "to the extent necessary to implement co-operation and co-ordination under Articles 25, 26 and 27" limit the potential open-ended application of this provision.

Article 29. Coordination of a proceeding under British insolvency law and a foreign proceeding

Where a foreign proceeding and a proceeding under British insolvency law are taking place concurrently regarding the same debtor, the court may seek cooperation and coordination under articles 25, 26 and 27, and the following shall apply–

(a) when the proceeding in Great Britain is taking place at the time the application for recognition of the foreign proceeding is filed–

    (i) any relief granted under article 19 or 21 must be consistent with the proceeding in Great Britain; and

    (ii) if the foreign proceeding is recognised in Great Britain as a foreign main proceeding, article 20 does not apply;

(b) when the proceeding in Great Britain commences after the filing of the application for recognition of the foreign proceeding–

    (i) any relief in effect under article 19 or 21 shall be reviewed by the court and shall be modified or terminated if inconsistent with the proceeding in Great Britain;

(ii) if the foreign proceeding is a foreign main proceeding, the stay and suspension referred to in paragraph 1 of article 20 shall be modified or terminated pursuant to paragraph 6 of article 20, if inconsistent with the proceeding in Great Britain; and

(iii) any proceedings brought by the foreign representative by virtue of paragraph 1 of article 23 before the proceeding in Great Britain commenced shall be reviewed by the court and the court may give such directions as it thinks fit regarding the continuance of those proceedings; and

(c) in granting, extending or modifying relief granted to a representative of a foreign non-main proceeding, the court must be satisfied that the relief relates to assets that, under the law of Great Britain, should be administered in the foreign non-main proceeding or concerns information required in that proceeding.

GENERAL NOTE

Again, the words "shall apply" indicate that this provision is mandatory. The commencement of a local proceeding is not to prevent or terminate the recognition of a foreign proceeding, but the article maintains a pre-eminence of the local proceeding in various ways, e.g. by providing that:

- any relief granted to the foreign proceeding must be consistent with the local proceeding;

- any relief granted previously to the foreign proceeding must be reviewed and modified or terminated to ensure such consistency;

- if the foreign proceeding is a main proceeding, there must be a review of the effects of the automatic stay;

- where a local proceeding is pending at the time when a foreign proceeding is recognised as a main proceeding, no automatic stay ensues.

However, art.29 avoids establishing a rigid hierarchy between the different proceedings.

Art.29(c)
This provision incorporates the principle expressed also in arts 19.4, 21.3 and 30.

Article 30. Coordination of more than one foreign proceeding

In matters referred to in paragraph 1 of article 1, in respect of more than one foreign proceeding regarding the same debtor, the court may seek cooperation and coordination under articles 25, 26 and 27, and the following shall apply–

(a) any relief granted under article 19 or 21 to a representative of a foreign non-main proceeding after recognition of a foreign main proceeding must be consistent with the foreign main proceeding;

(b) if a foreign main proceeding is recognised after the filing of an application for recognition of a foreign non-main proceeding, any relief in effect under article 19 or 21 shall be reviewed by the court and shall be modified or terminated if inconsistent with the foreign main proceeding; and

(c) if, after recognition of a foreign non-main proceeding, another foreign non-main proceeding is recognised, the court shall grant, modify or terminate relief for the purpose of facilitating coordination of the proceedings.

GENERAL NOTE

This provision applies whether or not an insolvency proceeding is pending in Britain: but if it has already commenced, art.29 governs the position as between the home and any foreign proceeding. However, where there are proceedings here and also in two or more foreign jurisdictions, this article applies as between those foreign proceedings. If one of the latter is a main proceeding, this provision gives that proceeding primacy—unlike art.29, which gives the local proceeding priority. In other respects, it mirrors art.29.

Article 31. Presumption of insolvency based on recognition of a foreign main proceeding

In the absence of evidence to the contrary, recognition of a foreign main proceeding is, for the purpose of commencing a proceeding under British insolvency law, proof that the debtor is unable to pay its debts or, in relation to Scotland, is apparently insolvent within the meaning given to those expressions under British insolvency law.

GENERAL NOTE

The presumption created by this provision is rebuttable. It does not apply where the foreign proceeding is a non-main proceeding. Where applicable, it displaces the requirements of IA 1986 s.268 (proof of "inability to pay" in bankruptcy proceedings) and "apparently insolvent" in the Bankruptcy (Scotland) Act 1985 s.7.

Article 32. Rule of payment in concurrent proceedings

Without prejudice to secured claims or rights in rem, a creditor who has received part payment in respect of its claim in a proceeding pursuant to a law relating to insolvency in a foreign State may not receive a payment for the same claim in a proceeding under British insolvency law regarding the same debtor, so long as the payment to the other creditors of the same class is proportionately less than the payment the creditor has already received.

GENERAL NOTE

The principle of hotchpot applies in regard to the claims of unsecured creditors in concurrent insolvency proceedings.

SCHEDULE 2

Regulation 4

PROCEDURAL MATTERS IN ENGLAND AND WALES

Introductory note to Schedule 2
The notes to Sch.1 will generally be applicable. Schedule 3 contains corresponding provisions for Scotland. The text incorporates amendments made by the Financial Services Act 2012 (Consequential Amendments and Transitional Provisions) Order 2013 (SI 2013/472). Amendments of a cosmetic nature were made to Sch.2 para.1(1) by the Insolvency (England and Wales) and Insolvency (Scotland) (Miscellaneous and Consequential Amendments) Rules 2017 (SI 2017/1115) to reflect the arrival on the scene of the Insolvency (England and Wales) Rules 2016 (SI 2016/1024).

PART 1

INTRODUCTORY PROVISIONS

1 Interpretation

1(1) In this Schedule–

"the 1986 Act" means the Insolvency Act 1986;

"article 21 relief application" means an application to the court by a foreign representative under article 21(1) or (2) of the Model Law for relief;

"business day" means any day other than a Saturday, a Sunday, Christmas Day, Good Friday or a day which is a bank holiday in England and Wales under or by virtue of the Banking and Financial Dealings Act 1971;

"CPR" means the Civil Procedure Rules 1998 and "CPR" followed by a Part or rule by number means the Part or rule with that number in those Rules;

"enforcement officer" means an individual who is authorised to act as an enforcement officer under the Courts Act 2003;

"file in court" and "file with the court" means deliver to the court for filing;

"the Gazette" means the London Gazette;

"interim relief application" means an application to the court by a foreign representative under article 19 of the Model Law for interim relief;

"main proceedings" means proceedings opened in accordance with Article 3(1) of the EU Insolvency Regulation and falling within the definition of insolvency proceedings in Article 2(4) of the EU Insolvency Regulation;

"member State liquidator" means a person falling within the definition of "insolvency practitioner" in Article 2(5) of the EU Insolvency Regulation appointed in proceedings to which the Regulation applies in a member State other than the United Kingdom;

"the Model Law" means the UNCITRAL Model Law as set out in Schedule 1 to these Regulations;

"modification or termination order" means an order by the court pursuant to its powers under the Model Law modifying or terminating recognition of a foreign proceeding, the stay and suspension referred to in article 20(1) or any part of it or any relief granted under article 19 or 21 of the Model Law;

"originating application" means an application to the court which is not an application in pending proceedings before the court;

"ordinary application" means any application to the court other than an originating application;

"practice direction" means a direction as to the practice and procedure of any court within the scope of the CPR;

"recognition application" means an application to the court by a foreign representative in accordance with article 15 of the Model Law for an order recognising the foreign proceeding in which he has been appointed;

"recognition order" means an order by the court recognising a proceeding the subject of a recognition application as a foreign main proceeding or foreign non-main proceeding, as appropriate;

"relevant company" means a company that is–

    (a)   registered under the Companies Act 2006,

    (b)   subject to a requirement imposed by regulations under section 1043 of that Act 2006 (unregistered UK companies) to deliver any documents to the registrar of companies, or

    (c)   subject to a requirement imposed by regulations under section 1046 of that Act (overseas companies) to deliver any documents to the registrar of companies;

"review application" means an application to the court for a modification or termination order;

"the Rules" means the Insolvency (England and Wales) Rules 2016 and "Rule" followed by a number means the rule with that number in those Rules;

"secondary proceedings" means proceedings opened in accordance with Articles 3(2) and 3(3) of the EU Insolvency Regulation and falling within the definition of winding up proceedings in insolvency proceedings in Article 2(4) of the EU Insolvency Regulation;

"territorial proceedings" means proceedings opened in accordance with Articles 3(2) and 3(4) of the EU Insolvency Regulation and falling within the definition of insolvency proceedings in Article 2(4) of the EU Insolvency Regulation.

1(2)   Expressions defined in the Model Law have the same meaning when used in this Schedule.

1(3)   In proceedings under these Regulations, "Registrar" means–

(a)   an Insolvency and Companies Court Judge; and

(b)   where the proceedings are in a district registry, the district judge.

1(4)   References to the "venue" for any proceedings or attendance before the court, are to the time, date and place for the proceedings or attendance.

1(5)   References in this Schedule to ex parte hearings shall be construed as references to hearings without notice being served on any other party, and references to applications made ex parte as references to applications made without notice being served on any other party; and other references which include the expression "ex parte" shall be similarly construed.

1(6)   References in this Schedule to a debtor who is of interest to the Financial Conduct Authority are references to a debtor who–

(a)   is, or has been, an authorised person within the meaning of the Financial Services and Markets Act 2000;

(b)   is, or has been, an appointed representative within the meaning of section 39 of the Financial Services and Markets Act 2000; or

(c)   is carrying on, or has carried on, a regulated activity in contravention of the general prohibition.

1(6A)   References in this Schedule to a debtor who is of interest to the Prudential Regulation Authority are references to a debtor who–

(a)   is, or has been, a PRA-authorised person within the meaning of the Financial Services and Markets Act 2000; or

(b)   is carrying on, or has carried on, a PRA-regulated activity within the meaning of the Financial Services and Markets Act 2000 in contravention of the general prohibition.

1(7)   In sub-paragraphs (6) and (6A) "the general prohibition" has the meaning given by section 19 of the Financial Services and Markets Act 2000 and the reference to a "regulated activity" must be construed in accordance with–

(a)   section 22 of that Act (classes of regulated activity and categories of investment);

(b)   any relevant order under that section; and

(c)   Schedule 2 to that Act (regulated activities).

1(8)   References in this Schedule to a numbered form are to the form that bears that number in Schedule 5.

General Note

Definition of "relevant company" inserted into para.1(1) by the Companies Act 2006 (Consequential Amendments, Transitional Provisions and Savings) Order 2009 (SI 2009/1941) art.2(1) and Sch.1 para.264(3)(a) as from 1 October 2009. A company incorporated under an earlier Companies Act is deemed to be "registered under" CA 2006 by s.1(1) of that Act. Paragraph 1(6) substituted and para.1(6A) inserted by the Financial Services Act 2012

(Consequential Amendments and Transitional Provisions) Order 2013 (SI 2013/472) Sch.2 para.116(a)(i) as from 1 April 2013.

In para.1(1) the definition of "the Rules" substituted by Insolvency (England and Wales) Rules 2016 (Consequential Amendments and Savings) Rules 2017 (SI 2017/369) r.2(2), Sch.2 para.1 as from 6 April 2017.

In para.1(1) the definitions of "main proceedings" amended and "member State liquidator" substituted by the Insolvency Amendment (EU 2015/848) Regulations 2017 (SI 2017/702) regs 1, 2(1), Sch. para.94(1), (3) in relation to proceedings opened on or after 26 June 2017 (see reg.3) when the Recast EU Regulation 2015/848 came into force.

In para.1(1) the definition of "the Rules" amended by the Insolvency (England and Wales) and Insolvency (Scotland) (Miscellaneous and Consequential Amendments) Rules 2017 (SI 2017/1115) rr.1(1), (2), 20, 21 as from 8 December 2017.

In para.1(1) the definitions of "secondary proceedings" and "territorial proceedings" amended by the Insolvency (Miscellaneous Amendments) Regulations 2017 (SI 2017/1119) regs 1(1), (7), 2, Sch.5 paras 1(1), (3)(a), (b) as from 8 December 2017.

Paragraph 1(3)(a) amended by the Alteration of Judicial Titles (Registrar in Bankruptcy of the High Court) Order 2018 (SI 2018/130) arts 1, 3 Sch. para.12(d) as from 26 February 2018.

PART 2

APPLICATIONS TO COURT FOR RECOGNITION OF FOREIGN PROCEEDINGS

2 Affidavit in support of recognition application

2 A recognition application shall be in Form ML 1 and shall be supported by an affidavit sworn by the foreign representative complying with paragraph 4.

3 Form and content of application

3 The application shall state the following matters–

(a) the name of the applicant and his address for service within England and Wales;

(b) the name of the debtor in respect of which the foreign proceeding is taking place;

(c) the name or names in which the debtor carries on business in the country where the foreign proceeding is taking place and in this country, if other than the name given under sub-paragraph (b);

(d) the principal or last known place of business of the debtor in Great Britain (if any) and, in the case of an individual, his usual or last known place of residence in Great Britain (if any);

(e) any registered number allocated to the debtor under the Companies Act 2006;

(f) brief particulars of the foreign proceeding in respect of which recognition is applied for, including the country in which it is taking place and the nature of the proceeding;

(g) that the foreign proceeding is a proceeding within the meaning of article 2(i) of the Model Law;

(h) that the applicant is a foreign representative within the meaning of article 2(j) of the Model Law;

(i) the address of the debtor's centre of main interests and, if different, the address of its registered office or habitual residence, as appropriate; and

(j) if the debtor does not have its centre of main interests in the country where the foreign proceeding is taking place, whether the debtor has an establishment within the meaning of article 2(e) of the Model Law in that country, and if so, its address.

GENERAL NOTE

An application for recognition (using Form ML 1) must contain the matters listed in this paragraph, and must be supported by affidavit evidence complying with para.4.

Para.3(g), (h)

The foreign proceeding must be a collective proceeding (including an interim proceeding) but may be for reorganisation or rehabilitation as well as liquidation or bankruptcy. It appears that the representative need not necessarily be the office-holder in the foreign proceeding.

Para.3(i), (j)

Recognition involves classifying the foreign proceeding as "main" or "non-main", hence the need for this information. If the debtor does not have an establishment in the country concerned, recognition as a non-main proceeding is not possible.

4 Contents of affidavit in support

4(1) There shall be attached to the application an affidavit in support which shall contain or have exhibited to it–

(a) the evidence and statement required under article 15(2) and (3) respectively of the Model Law;

(b) any other evidence which in the opinion of the applicant will assist the court in deciding whether the proceeding the subject of the application is a foreign proceeding within the meaning of article 2(i) of the Model Law and whether the applicant is a foreign representative within the meaning of article 2(j) of the Model Law;

(c) evidence that the debtor has its centre of main interests or an establishment, as the case may be, within the country where the foreign proceeding is taking place; and

(d) any other matters which in the opinion of the applicant will assist the court in deciding whether to make a recognition order.

4(2) The affidavit shall state whether, in the opinion of the applicant, the EU Insolvency Regulation applies to any of the proceedings identified in accordance with article 15(3) of the Model Law and, if so, whether those proceedings are main proceedings, secondary proceedings or territorial proceedings.

4(3) The affidavit shall also have exhibited to it the translations required under article 15(4) of the Model Law and a translation in English of any other document exhibited to the affidavit which is in a language other than English.

4(4) All translations referred to in sub-paragraph (3) must be certified by the translator as a correct translation.

Para.4(2)

The reference is to proceedings other than that for which recognition is being sought: the court will wish to know of all insolvency proceedings relating to the same debtor, so as to have a complete picture.

Paragraph 4(2) amended by the Insolvency (Miscellaneous Amendments) Regulations 2017 (SI 2017/1119) regs 1(1), (7), 2, Sch.5 paras 1(1), (3)(c) as from 8 December 2017.

5 The hearing and powers of court

5(1) On hearing a recognition application the court may in addition to its powers under the Model Law to make a recognition order–

(a) dismiss the application;

(b) adjourn the hearing conditionally or unconditionally;

(c) make any other order which the court thinks appropriate.

5(2) If the court makes a recognition order, it shall be in Form ML 2.

6   Notification of subsequent information

6(1)   The foreign representative shall set out any subsequent information required to be given to the court under article 18 of the Model Law in a statement which he shall attach to Form ML 3 and file with the court.

6(2)   The statement shall include–

(a)   details of the information required to be given under article 18 of the Model Law; and

(b)   in the case of any proceedings required to be notified to the court under that article, a statement as to whether, in the opinion of the foreign representative, any of those proceedings are main proceedings, secondary proceedings or territorial proceedings under the EU Insolvency Regulation.

6(3)   The foreign representative shall send a copy of the Form ML 3 and attached statement filed with the court to the following–

(a)   the debtor; and

(b)   those persons referred to in paragraph 26(3).

GENERAL NOTE

Article 18 requires the court to be informed of any changes in the position occurring or becoming known after the application for recognition has been filed.

Paragraph 6(2)(b) amended by the Insolvency (Miscellaneous Amendments) Regulations 2017 (SI 2017/1119) regs 1(1), (7), 2, Sch.5 paras 1(1), (3)(d) as from 8 December 2017.

PART 3

APPLICATIONS FOR RELIEF UNDER THE MODEL LAW

7   Application for interim relief—affidavit in support

7(1)   An interim relief application must be supported by an affidavit sworn by the foreign representative stating–

(a)   the grounds on which it is proposed that the interim relief applied for should be granted;

(b)   details of any proceeding under British insolvency law taking place in relation to the debtor;

(c)   whether, to the foreign representative's knowledge, an administrative receiver or receiver or manager of the debtor's property is acting in relation to the debtor;

(d)   an estimate of the value of the assets of the debtor in England and Wales in respect of which relief is applied for;

(e)   whether, to the best of the knowledge and belief of the foreign representative, the interests of the debtor's creditors (including any secured creditors or parties to hire-purchase agreements) and any other interested parties, including if appropriate the debtor, will be adequately protected;

(f)   whether, to the best of the foreign representative's knowledge and belief, the grant of any of the relief applied for would interfere with the administration of a foreign main proceeding; and

(g)   all other matters that in the opinion of the foreign representative will assist the court in deciding whether or not it is appropriate to grant the relief applied for.

GENERAL NOTE

"Interim relief" is relief sought under art.19 while an application for recognition is pending; after recognition, art.21 applies. The applicant may be the representative of either main or non-main proceedings in the foreign jurisdiction.

8   Service of interim relief application not required

8   Unless the court otherwise directs, it shall not be necessary to serve the interim relief application on, or give notice of it to, any person.

9   The hearing and powers of court

9   On hearing an interim relief application the court may in addition to its powers under the Model Law to make an order granting interim relief under article 19 of the Model Law–

    (a)   dismiss the application;

    (b)   adjourn the hearing conditionally or unconditionally;

    (c)   make any other order which the court thinks appropriate.

10   Application for relief under article 21 of the Model Law—affidavit in support

10   An article 21 relief application must be supported by an affidavit sworn by the foreign representative stating–

    (a)   the grounds on which it is proposed that the relief applied for should be granted;

    (b)   an estimate of the value of the assets of the debtor in England and Wales in respect of which relief is applied for;

    (c)   in the case of an application by a foreign representative who is or believes that he is a representative of a foreign non-main proceeding, the reasons why the applicant believes that the relief relates to assets that, under the law of Great Britain, should be administered in the foreign non-main proceeding or concerns information required in that proceeding;

    (d)   whether, to the best of the knowledge and belief of the foreign representative, the interests of the debtor's creditors (including any secured creditors or parties to hire-purchase agreements) and any other interested parties, including if appropriate the debtor, will be adequately protected; and

    (e)   all other matters that in the opinion of the foreign representative will assist the court in deciding whether or not it is appropriate to grant the relief applied for.

GENERAL NOTE

Once again, the applicant may be the representative of either main or non-main proceedings, but in the former case he will already have the benefit of a general stay of proceedings. The types of relief available under art.21 range very widely, from the grant of a freezing injunction to an order for the examination of witnesses.

11   The hearing and powers of court

11   On hearing an article 21 relief application the court may in addition to its powers under the Model Law to make an order granting relief under article 21 of the Model Law–

    (a)   dismiss the application;

    (b)   adjourn the hearing conditionally or unconditionally;

    (c)   make any other order which the court thinks appropriate.

PART 4

REPLACEMENT OF FOREIGN REPRESENTATIVE

12   Application for confirmation of status of replacement foreign representative

12(1)   This paragraph applies where following the making of a recognition order the foreign representative dies or for any other reason ceases to be the foreign representative in the foreign proceeding in relation to the debtor.

12(2)   In this paragraph "the former foreign representative" shall mean the foreign representative referred to in sub-paragraph (1).

12(3)   If a person has succeeded the former foreign representative or is otherwise holding office as foreign representative in the foreign proceeding in relation to the debtor, that person may apply to the court for an order confirming his status as replacement foreign representative for the purpose of proceedings under these Regulations.

13   Contents of application and affidavit in support

13(1)   An application under paragraph 12(3) shall in addition to the matters required to be stated by paragraph 19(2) state the following matters–

- (a)   the name of the replacement foreign representative and his address for service within England and Wales;

- (b)   details of the circumstances in which the former foreign representative ceased to be foreign representative in the foreign proceeding in relation to the debtor (including the date on which he ceased to be the foreign representative);

- (c)   details of his own appointment as replacement foreign representative in the foreign proceeding (including the date of that appointment).

13(2)   The application shall be accompanied by an affidavit in support sworn by the applicant which shall contain or have attached to it–

- (a)   a certificate from the foreign court affirming–

  - (i)   the cessation of the appointment of the former foreign representative as foreign representative; and

  - (ii)   the appointment of the applicant as the foreign representative in the foreign proceeding; or

- (b)   in the absence of such a certificate, any other evidence acceptable to the court of the matters referred to in paragraph (a); and

- (c)   a translation in English of any document exhibited to the affidavit which is in a language other than English.

13(3)   All translations referred to in paragraph (c) must be certified by the translator as a correct translation.

14   The hearing and powers of court

14(1)   On hearing an application under paragraph 12(3) the court may–

- (a)   make an order confirming the status of the replacement foreign representative as foreign representative for the purpose of proceedings under these Regulations;

- (b)   dismiss the application;

(c) adjourn the hearing conditionally or unconditionally;

(d) make an interim order;

(e) make any other order which the court thinks appropriate, including in particular an order making such provision as the court thinks fit with respect to matters arising in connection with the replacement of the foreign representative.

14(2) If the court dismisses the application, it may also if it thinks fit make an order terminating recognition of the foreign proceeding and–

(a) such an order may include such provision as the court thinks fit with respect to matters arising in connection with the termination; and

(b) paragraph 15 shall not apply to such an order.

Part 5

Reviews of Court Orders

15 Reviews of court orders—where court makes order of its own motion

15(1) The court shall not of its own motion make a modification or termination order unless the foreign representative and the debtor have either–

(a) had an opportunity of being heard on the question; or

(b) consented in writing to such an order.

15(2) Where the foreign representative or the debtor desires to be heard on the question of such an order, the court shall give all relevant parties notice of a venue at which the question will be considered and may give directions as to the issues on which it requires evidence.

15(3) For the purposes of sub-paragraph (2), all relevant parties means the foreign representative, the debtor and any other person who appears to the court to have an interest justifying his being given notice of the hearing.

15(4) If the court makes a modification or termination order, the order may include such provision as the court thinks fit with respect to matters arising in connection with the modification or termination.

16 Review application—affidavit in support

16 A review application must be supported by an affidavit sworn by the applicant stating–

(a) the grounds on which it is proposed that the relief applied for should be granted;

(b) whether, to the best of the knowledge and belief of the applicant, the interests of the debtor's creditors (including any secured creditors or parties to hire-purchase agreements) and any other interested parties, including if appropriate the debtor, will be adequately protected; and

(c) all other matters that in the opinion of the applicant will assist the court in deciding whether or not it is appropriate to grant the relief applied for.

17 Hearing of review application and powers of the court

17 On hearing a review application, the court may in addition to its powers under the Model Law to make a modification or termination order–

(a) dismiss the application;

(b)   adjourn the hearing conditionally or unconditionally;

(c)   make an interim order;

(d)   make any other order which the court thinks appropriate, including an order making such provision as the court thinks fit with respect to matters arising in connection with the modification or termination.

PART 6

COURT PROCEDURE AND PRACTICE WITH REGARD TO PRINCIPAL APPLICATIONS AND ORDERS

18   Preliminary and interpretation

18(1)   This Part applies to–

(a)   any of the following applications made to the court under these Regulations–

(i)   a recognition application;

(ii)   an article 21 relief application;

(iii)   an application under paragraph 12(3) for an order confirming the status of a replacement foreign representative;

(iv)   a review application; and

(b)   any of the following orders made by the court under these Regulations–

(i)   a recognition order;

(ii)   an order granting interim relief under article 19 of the Model Law;

(iii)   an order granting relief under article 21 of the Model Law;

(iv)   an order confirming the status of a replacement foreign representative; and

(v)   a modification or termination order.

GENERAL NOTE

The procedure for an application for recognition is provided for separately in paras 2–6. The applicant will not necessarily be the foreign representative, e.g. under para.18(a)(iv) it could be another interested party.

19   Form and contents of application

19(1)   Subject to sub-paragraph (4) every application to which this Part applies shall be an ordinary application and shall be in Form ML 5.

19(2)   Each application shall be in writing and shall state–

(a)   the names of the parties;

(b)   the nature of the relief or order applied for or the directions sought from the court;

(c)   the names and addresses of the persons (if any) on whom it is intended to serve the application;

(d)   the names and addresses of all those persons on whom these Regulations require the application to be served (so far as known to the applicant); and

(e)   the applicant's address for service.

19(3)   The application must be signed by the applicant if he is acting in person, or, when he is not so acting, by or on behalf of his solicitor.

19(4)   This paragraph does not apply to a recognition application.

20   Filing of application

20(1)   The application (and all supporting documents) shall be filed with the court, with a sufficient number of copies for service and use as provided by paragraph 21(2).

20(2)   Each of the copies filed shall have applied to it the seal of the court and be issued to the applicant; and on each copy there shall be endorsed the date and time of filing.

20(3)   The court shall fix a venue for the hearing of the application and this also shall be endorsed on each copy of the application issued under sub-paragraph (2).

21   Service of the application

21(1)   In sub-paragraph (2), references to the application are to a sealed copy of the application issued by the court together with any affidavit in support of it and any documents exhibited to the affidavit.

21(2)   Unless the court otherwise directs, the application shall be served on the following persons, unless they are the applicant–

(a)   on the foreign representative;

(b)   on the debtor;

(c)   if a British insolvency officeholder is acting in relation to the debtor, on him;

(d)   if any person has been appointed an administrative receiver of the debtor or, to the knowledge of the foreign representative, as a receiver or manager of the property of the debtor in England and Wales, on him;

(e)   if a member State liquidator has been appointed in main proceedings in relation to the debtor, on him;

(f)   if to the knowledge of the foreign representative a foreign representative has been appointed in any other foreign proceeding regarding the debtor, on him;

(g)   if there is pending in England and Wales a petition for the winding up or bankruptcy of the debtor, on the petitioner;

(h)   on any person who to the knowledge of the foreign representative is or may be entitled to appoint an administrator of the debtor under paragraph 14 of Schedule B1 to the 1986 Act (appointment of administrator by holder of qualifying floating charge);

(i)   if the debtor is a debtor who is of interest to the Financial Conduct Authority, on that Authority; and

(j)   if the debtor is a debtor who is of interest to the Prudential Regulation Authority, on that Authority.

GENERAL NOTE

Paragraph 21(2)(i) substituted and para.21(2)(j) inserted by the Financial Services Act 2012 (Consequential Amendments and Transitional Provisions) Order 2013 (SI 2013/472) Sch.2 art.116(a)(ii) as from 1 April 2013.

22   Manner in which service to be effected

22(1)   Service of the application in accordance with paragraph 21(2) shall be effected by the applicant, or his solicitor, or by a person instructed by him or his solicitor, not less than 5 business days before the date fixed for the hearing.

22(2)   Service shall be effected by delivering the documents to a person's proper address or in such other manner as the court may direct.

22(3)   A person's proper address is any which he has previously notified as his address for service within England and Wales; but if he has not notified any such address or if for any reason service at such address is not practicable, service may be effected as follows–

  (a)   (subject to sub-paragraph (4)) in the case of a company incorporated in England and Wales, by delivery to its registered office;

  (b)   in the case of any other person, by delivery to his usual or last known address or principal place of business in Great Britain.

22(4)   If delivery to a company's registered office is not practicable, service may be effected by delivery to its last known principal place of business in Great Britain.

22(5)   Delivery of documents to any place or address may be made by leaving them there or sending them by first class post in accordance with the provisions of paragraphs 70 and 75(1).

23   Proof of service

23(1)   Service of the application shall be verified by an affidavit of service in Form ML 6, specifying the date on which, and the manner in which, service was effected.

23(2)   The affidavit of service, with a sealed copy of the application exhibited to it, shall be filed with the court as soon as reasonably practicable after service, and in any event not less than 1 business day before the hearing of the application.

24   In case of urgency

24   Where the case is one of urgency, the court may (without prejudice to its general power to extend or abridge time limits)–

  (a)   hear the application immediately, either with or without notice to, or the attendance of, other parties; or

  (b)   authorise a shorter period of service than that provided for by paragraph 22(1),

and any such application may be heard on terms providing for the filing or service of documents, or the carrying out of other formalities, as the court thinks fit.

25   The hearing

25(1)   At the hearing of the application, the applicant and any of the following persons (not being the applicant) may appear or be represented–

  (a)   the foreign representative;

  (b)   the debtor and, in the case of any debtor other than an individual, any one or more directors or other officers of the debtor, including–

    (i)   where applicable, any person specified in particulars registered under section 1046 of the Companies Act 2006 (overseas companies) as authorised to represent the debtor;

    (ii)   in the case of a debtor which is a partnership, any person who is an officer of the partnership within the meaning of article 2 of the Insolvent Partnerships Order 1994;

  (c)   if a British insolvency officeholder is acting in relation to the debtor, that person;

  (d)   if any person has been appointed an administrative receiver of the debtor or as a receiver or manager of the property of the debtor in England and Wales, that person;

(e)   if a member State liquidator has been appointed in main proceedings in relation to the debtor, that person;

(f)   if a foreign representative has been appointed in any other foreign proceeding regarding the debtor, that person;

(g)   any person who has presented a petition for the winding up or bankruptcy of the debtor in England and Wales;

(h)   any person who is or may be entitled to appoint an administrator of the debtor under paragraph 14 of Schedule B1 to the 1986 Act (appointment of administrator by holder of qualifying floating charge);

(i)   if the debtor is a debtor who is of interest to the Financial Conduct Authority, that Authority;

(ia) if the debtor is a debtor who is of interest to the Prudential Regulation Authority, that Authority; and

(j)   with the permission of the court, any other person who appears to have an interest justifying his appearance.

GENERAL NOTE

Paragraph 25(1)(b)(i) substituted by the Companies Act 2006 (Consequential Amendments, Transitional Provisions and Savings) Order 2009 (SI 2009/1941) art.2(1) and Sch.1 para.264(3)(c) as from 1 October 2009. Paragraph 25(1)(i) substituted and para.25(1)(ia) inserted by the Financial Services Act 2012 (Consequential Amendments and Transitional Provisions) Order 2013 (SI 2013/472) Sch.2 art.116(a)(iii) as from 1 April 2013.

26   Notification and advertisement of order

26(1)   If the court makes any of the orders referred to in paragraph 18(1)(b), it shall as soon as reasonably practicable send two sealed copies of the order to the foreign representative.

26(2)   The foreign representative shall send a sealed copy of the order as soon as reasonably practicable to the debtor.

26(3)   The foreign representative shall, as soon as reasonably practicable after the date of the order give notice of the making of the order–

(a)   if a British insolvency officeholder is acting in relation to the debtor, to him;

(b)   if any person has been appointed an administrative receiver of the debtor or, to the knowledge of the foreign representative, as a receiver or manager of the property of the debtor, to him;

(c)   if a member State liquidator has been appointed in main proceedings in relation to the debtor, to him;

(d)   if to his knowledge a foreign representative has been appointed in any other foreign proceeding regarding the debtor, that person;

(e)   if there is pending in England and Wales a petition for the winding up or bankruptcy of the debtor, to the petitioner;

(f)   to any person who to his knowledge is or may be entitled to appoint an administrator of the debtor under paragraph 14 of Schedule B1 to the 1986 Act (appointment of administrator by holder of qualifying floating charge);

(g)   if the debtor is a debtor who is of interest to the Financial Conduct Authority, to that Authority;

(ga) if the debtor is a debtor who is of interest to the Prudential Regulation Authority, to that Authority;

(h)   to such other persons as the court may direct.

26(4)   In the case of an order recognising a foreign proceeding in relation to the debtor as a foreign main proceeding, or an order under article 19 or 21 of the Model Law staying execution, distress or other legal process against the debtor's assets, the foreign representative shall also, as soon as reasonably practicable after the date of the order give notice of the making of the order–

(a)   to any enforcement officer or other officer who to his knowledge is charged with an execution or other legal process against the debtor or its property; and

(b)   to any person who to his knowledge is distraining against the debtor or its property.

26(5)   In the application of sub-paragraphs (3) and (4) the references to property shall be taken as references to property situated within England and Wales.

26(6)   Where the debtor is a relevant company, the foreign representative shall send notice of the making of the order to the registrar of companies before the end of the period of 5 business days beginning with the date of the order. The notice to the registrar of companies shall be in Form ML 7.

26(7)   The foreign representative shall advertise the making of the following orders once in the Gazette and once in such newspaper as he thinks most appropriate for ensuring that the making of the order comes to the notice of the debtor's creditors–

(a)   a recognition order;

(b)   an order confirming the status of a replacement foreign representative; and

(c)   a modification or termination order which modifies or terminates recognition of a foreign proceeding,

and the advertisement shall be in Form ML 8.

GENERAL NOTE

Paragraph 26(3)(g) substituted and para.26(3)(ga) inserted by the Financial Services Act 2012 (Consequential Amendments and Transitional Provisions) Order 2013 (SI 2013/472) Sch.2 art.116(a)(iv) as from 1 April 2013.

Para.26(6)
On notices to the registrar of companies, see Sch.4.

27   Adjournment of hearing; directions

27(1)   This paragraph applies in any case where the court exercises its power to adjourn the hearing of the application.

27(2)   The court may at any time give such directions as it thinks fit as to–

(a)   service or notice of the application on or to any person, whether in connection with the venue of a resumed hearing or for any other purpose;

(b)   the procedure on the application;

(c)   the manner in which any evidence is to be adduced at a resumed hearing and in particular as to–

(i)   the taking of evidence wholly or in part by affidavit or orally;

(ii)   the cross-examination on the hearing in court or in chambers, of any deponents to affidavits;

(d)   the matters to be dealt with in evidence.

28   Applications to Chief Land Registrar following court orders

28(1)   Where the court makes any order in proceedings under these Regulations which is capable of giving rise to an application or applications under the Land Registration Act 2002, the foreign representative shall, as soon as reasonably practicable after the making of the order or at the appropriate time, make the appropriate application or applications to the Chief Land Registrar.

28(2)   In sub-paragraph (1) an appropriate application is–

(a)   in any case where–

(i)   a recognition order in respect of a foreign main proceeding or an order suspending the right to transfer, encumber or otherwise dispose of any assets of the debtor is made, and

(ii)   the debtor is the registered proprietor of a registered estate or registered charge and holds it for his sole benefit,

an application under section 43 of the Land Registration Act 2002 for a restriction of the kind referred to in sub-paragraph (3) to be entered in the relevant registered title; and

(b)   in any other case, an application under the Land Registration Act 2002 for such an entry in the register as shall be necessary to reflect the effect of the court order under these Regulations.

28(3)   The restriction referred to in sub-paragraph (2)(a) is a restriction to the effect that no disposition of the registered estate or registered charge (as appropriate) by the registered proprietor of that estate or charge is to be completed by registration within the meaning of section 27 of the Land Registration Act 2002 except under a further order of the court.

GENERAL NOTE

See art.1.6.

PART 8

MISFEASANCE

29   Misfeasance by foreign representative

29(1)   The court may examine the conduct of a person who–

(a)   is or purports to be the foreign representative in relation to a debtor; or

(b)   has been or has purported to be the foreign representative in relation to a debtor.

29(2)   An examination under this paragraph may be held only on the application of–

(a)   a British insolvency officeholder acting in relation to the debtor;

(b)   a creditor of the debtor; or

(c)   with the permission of the court, any other person who appears to have an interest justifying an application.

29(3)   An application under sub-paragraph (2) must allege that the foreign representative–

(a)   has misapplied or retained money or other property of the debtor;

(b) has become accountable for money or other property of the debtor;

(c) has breached a fiduciary or other duty in relation to the debtor; or

(d) has been guilty of misfeasance.

29(4) On an examination under this paragraph into a person's conduct the court may order him–

(a) to repay, restore or account for money or property;

(b) to pay interest;

(c) to contribute a sum to the debtor's property by way of compensation for breach of duty or misfeasance.

29(5) In sub-paragraph (3) "foreign representative" includes a person who purports or has purported to be a foreign representative in relation to a debtor.

GENERAL NOTE

This provision corresponds with IA 1986 s.212 and Sch.B1 para.75.

PART 9

GENERAL PROVISION AS TO COURT PROCEDURE AND PRACTICE

30 Principal court rules and practice to apply with modifications

30(1) The CPR and the practice and procedure of the High Court (including any practice direction) shall apply to proceedings under these Regulations in the High Court with such modifications as may be necessary for the purpose of giving effect to the provisions of these Regulations and in the case of any conflict between any provision of the CPR and the provisions of these Regulations, the latter shall prevail.

30(2) All proceedings under these Regulations shall be allocated to the multi-track for which CPR Part 29 (the multi-track) makes provision, and accordingly those provisions of the CPR which provide for allocation questionnaires and track allocation shall not apply.

31 Applications other than the principal applications—preliminary

31 Paragraphs 32 to 37 of this Part apply to any application made to the court under these Regulations, except any of the applications referred to in paragraph 18(1)(a).

GENERAL NOTE

"Principal applications" refers to the applications specified in para.18(1)(a).

32 Form and contents of application

32(1) Every application shall be in the form appropriate to the application concerned. Forms ML 4 and ML 5 shall be used for an originating application and an ordinary application respectively under these Regulations.

32(2) Each application shall be in writing and shall state–

(a) the names of the parties;

(b) the nature of the relief or order applied for or the directions sought from the court;

(c) the names and addresses of the persons (if any) on whom it is intended to serve the application or that no person is intended to be served;

(d)   where these Regulations require that notice of the application is to be given to specified persons, the names and addresses of all those persons (so far as known to the applicant); and

(e)   the applicant's address for service.

32(3)   An originating application shall set out the grounds on which the applicant claims to be entitled to the relief or order sought.

32(4)   The application must be signed by the applicant if he is acting in person or, when he is not so acting, by or on behalf of his solicitor.

33   Filing and service of application

33(1)   The application shall be filed in court, accompanied by one copy and a number of additional copies equal to the number of persons who are to be served with the application.

33(2)   Subject as follows in this paragraph and in paragraph 34, or unless the court otherwise orders, upon the presentation of the documents mentioned in sub-paragraph (1), the court shall fix a venue for the application to be heard.

33(3)   Unless the court otherwise directs, the applicant shall serve a sealed copy of the application, endorsed with the venue of the hearing, on the respondent named in the application (or on each respondent if more than one).

33(4)   The court may give any of the following directions–

(a)   that the application be served upon persons other than those specified by the relevant provision of these Regulations;

(b)   that the giving of notice to any person may be dispensed with;

(c)   that notice be given in some way other than that specified in sub-paragraph (3).

33(5)   Subject to sub-paragraph (6), the application must be served at least 10 business days before the date fixed for the hearing.

33(6)   Where the case is one of urgency, the court may (without prejudice to its general power to extend or abridge time limits)–

(a)   hear the application immediately, either with or without notice to, or the attendance of, other parties; or

(b)   authorise a shorter period of service than that provided for by sub-paragraph (5);

and any such application may be heard on terms providing for the filing or service of documents, or the carrying out of other formalities, as the court thinks fit.

34   Other hearings *ex parte*

34(1)   Where the relevant provisions of these Regulations do not require service of the application on, or notice of it to be given to, any person, the court may hear the application *ex parte*.

34(2)   Where the application is properly made *ex parte*, the court may hear it forthwith, without fixing a venue as required by paragraph 33(2).

34(3)   Alternatively, the court may fix a venue for the application to be heard, in which case paragraph 33 applies (so far as relevant).

35   Use of affidavit evidence

35(1)   In any proceedings evidence may be given by affidavit unless the court otherwise directs; but the court may, on the application of any party, order the attendance for cross-examination of the person making the affidavit.

35(2) Where, after such an order has been made, the person in question does not attend, his affidavit shall not be used in evidence without the permission of the court.

36 Filing and service of affidavits

36(1) Unless the court otherwise allows–

(a) if the applicant intends to rely at the first hearing on affidavit evidence, he shall file the affidavit or affidavits (if more than one) in court and serve a copy or copies on the respondent, not less than 10 business days before the date fixed for the hearing; and

(b) where a respondent to an application intends to oppose it and to rely for that purpose on affidavit evidence, he shall file the affidavit or affidavits (if more than one) in court and serve a copy or copies on the applicant, not less than 5 business days before the date fixed for the hearing.

36(2) Any affidavit may be sworn by the applicant or by the respondent or by some other person possessing direct knowledge of the subject matter of the application.

37 Adjournment of hearings; directions

37 The court may adjourn the hearing of an application on such terms (if any) as it thinks fit and in the case of such an adjournment paragraph 27(2) shall apply.

38 Transfer of proceedings within the High Court

38(1) The High Court may, having regard to the criteria in CPR rule 30.3(2), order proceedings in the Royal Courts of Justice or a district registry, or any part of such proceedings (such as an application made in the proceedings), to be transferred–

(a) from the Royal Courts of Justice to a district registry; or

(b) from a district registry to the Royal Courts of Justice or to another district registry.

38(2) The High Court may order proceedings before a district registry for the detailed assessment of costs to be transferred to another district registry if it is satisfied that the proceedings could be more conveniently or fairly taken in that other district registry.

38(3) An application for an order under sub-paragraph (1) or (2) must, if the claim is proceeding in a district registry, be made to that registry.

38(4) A transfer of proceedings under this paragraph may be ordered–

(a) by the court of its own motion; or

(b) on the application of a person appearing to the court to have an interest in the proceedings.

38(5) Where the court orders proceedings to be transferred, the court from which they are to be transferred must give notice of the transfer to all the parties.

38(6) An order made before the transfer of the proceedings shall not be affected by the order to transfer.

39 Transfer of proceedings—actions to avoid acts detrimental to creditors

39(1) If–

(a) in accordance with article 23(6) of the Model Law, the court grants a foreign representative permission to make an application in accordance with paragraph 1 of that article; and

(b) the relevant proceedings under British insolvency law taking place regarding the debtor are taking place in the county court,

the court may also order those proceedings to be transferred to the High Court.

39(2)   Where the court makes an order transferring proceedings under sub-paragraph (1)–

(a) it shall send sealed copies of the order to the county court from which the proceedings are to be transferred, and to the official receivers attached to that court and the High Court respectively; and

(b) the county court shall send the file of the proceedings to the High Court.

39(3)   Following compliance with this paragraph, if the official receiver attached to the court to which the proceedings are transferred is not already, by virtue of directions given by the Secretary of State under section 399(6)(a) of the 1986 Act, the official receiver in relation to those proceedings, he becomes, in relation to those proceedings, the official receiver in place of the official receiver attached to the other court concerned.

GENERAL NOTE

General jurisdiction under the Regulations is conferred on the High Court (art.4). If a foreign representative wishes to participate in proceedings that are already current in the county court, it is likely to be thought appropriate that they be transferred to the High Court.

40   Shorthand writers

40(1)   The judge may in writing nominate one or more persons to be official shorthand writers to the court.

40(2)   The court may, at any time in the course of proceedings under these Regulations, appoint a shorthand writer to take down the evidence of a person examined in pursuance of a court order under article 19 or 21 of the Model Law.

40(3)   The remuneration of a shorthand writer appointed in proceedings under these Regulations shall be paid by the party at whose instance the appointment was made or otherwise as the court may direct.

40(4)   Any question arising as to the rates of remuneration payable under this paragraph shall be determined by the court in its discretion.

41   Enforcement procedures

41   In any proceedings under these Regulations, orders of the court may be enforced in the same manner as a judgment to the same effect.

42   Title of proceedings

42(1)   Every proceeding under these Regulations shall, with any necessary additions, be intituled "IN THE MATTER OF...(naming the debtor to which the proceedings relate) AND IN THE MATTER OF THE CROSS-BORDER INSOLVENCY REGULATIONS 2006".

42(2)   Sub-paragraph (1) shall not apply in respect of any form prescribed under these Regulations.

43   Court records

43   The court shall keep records of all proceedings under these Regulations, and shall cause to be entered in the records the taking of any step in the proceedings, and such decisions of the court in relation thereto, as the court thinks fit.

44   Inspection of records

44(1)   Subject as follows, the court's records of proceedings under these Regulations shall be open to inspection by any person.

44(2)   If in the case of a person applying to inspect the records the Registrar is not satisfied as to the propriety of the purpose for which inspection is required, he may refuse to allow it. That person may then apply forthwith and *ex parte* to the judge, who may refuse the inspection or allow it on such terms as he thinks fit.

44(3)   The decision of the judge under sub-paragraph (2) is final.

45   File of court proceedings

45(1)   In respect of all proceedings under these Regulations, the court shall open and maintain a file for each case; and (subject to directions of the Registrar) all documents relating to such proceedings shall be placed on the relevant file.

45(2)   No proceedings under these Regulations shall be filed in the Central Office of the High Court.

46   Right to inspect the file

46(1)   In the case of any proceedings under these Regulations, the following have the right, at all reasonable times, to inspect the court's file of the proceedings–

   (a)   the Secretary of State;

   (b)   the person who is the foreign representative in relation to the proceedings;

   (c)   if a foreign representative has been appointed in any other foreign proceeding regarding the debtor to which the proceedings under these Regulations relate, that person;

   (d)   if a British insolvency officeholder is acting in relation to the debtor to which the proceedings under these Regulations relate, that person;

   (e)   any person stating himself in writing to be a creditor of the debtor to which the proceedings under these Regulations relate;

   (f)   if a member State liquidator has been appointed in relation to the debtor to which the proceedings under these Regulations relate, that person; and

   (g)   the debtor to which the proceedings under these Regulations relate, or, if that debtor is a company, corporation or partnership, every person who is, or at any time has been–

      (i)   a director or officer of the debtor;

      (ii)   a member of the debtor; or

      (iii)   where applicable, any person specified in particulars registered under section 1046 of the Companies Act 2006 (overseas companies) as authorised to represent the debtor.

46(2)   The right of inspection conferred as above on any person may be exercised on his behalf by a person properly authorised by him.

46(3)   Any person may, by leave of the court, inspect the file.

46(4)   The right of inspection conferred by this paragraph is not exercisable in the case of documents, or parts of documents, as to which the court directs (either generally or specially) that they are not to be made open to inspection without the court's permission. An application for a direction of the court under this sub-paragraph may be made by the foreign representative or by any party appearing to the court to have an interest.

46(5)   If, for the purpose of powers conferred by the 1986 Act or the Rules, the Secretary of State or the official receiver wishes to inspect the file of any proceedings under these Regulations, and requests the transmission of the file, the court shall comply with such request (unless the file is for the time being in use for the court's purposes).

46(6)   Paragraph 44(2) and (3) apply in respect of the court's file of any proceedings under these Regulations as they apply in respect of court records.

46(7)   Where these Regulations confer a right for any person to inspect documents on the court's file of proceedings, the right includes that of taking copies of those documents on payment of the fee chargeable under any order made under section 92 of the Courts Act 2003.

GENERAL NOTE

Paragraph 46(1)(g)(iii) substituted by the Companies Act 2006 (Consequential Amendments, Transitional Provisions and Savings) Order 2009 (SI 2009/1941) art.2(1) and Sch.1 para.264(3)(d) as from 1 October 2009.

47   Copies of court orders

47(1)   In any proceedings under these Regulations, any person who under paragraph 46 has a right to inspect documents on the court file also has the right to require the foreign representative in relation to those proceedings to furnish him with a copy of any court order in the proceedings.

47(2)   Sub-paragraph (1) does not apply if a copy of the court order has been served on that person or notice of the making of the order has been given to that person under other provisions of these Regulations.

48   Filing of Gazette notices and advertisements

48(1)   In any court in which proceedings under these Regulations are pending, an officer of the court shall file a copy of every issue of the Gazette which contains an advertisement relating to those proceedings.

48(2)   Where there appears in a newspaper an advertisement relating to proceedings under these Regulations pending in any court, the person inserting the advertisement shall file a copy of it in that court.

The copy of the advertisement shall be accompanied by, or have endorsed on it, such particulars as are necessary to identify the proceedings and the date of the advertisement's appearance.

48(3)   An officer of any court in which proceedings under these Regulations are pending shall from time to time file a memorandum giving the dates of, and other particulars relating to, any notice published in the Gazette, and any newspaper advertisements, which relate to proceedings so pending.

The officer's memorandum is prima facie evidence that any notice or advertisement mentioned in it was duly inserted in the issue of the newspaper or the Gazette which is specified in the memorandum.

49   Persons incapable of managing their affairs—introductory

49(1)   Paragraphs 50 to 52 apply where in proceedings under these Regulations it appears to the court that a person affected by the proceedings is one who is incapable of managing and administering his property and affairs either–

(a)   by reason of mental disorder within the meaning of the Mental Health Act 1983; or

(b)   due to physical affliction or disability.

49(2)   The person concerned is referred to as "the incapacitated person".

GENERAL NOTE

Reference might also have been made to the Mental Capacity Act 2005 Pt I.

50   Appointment of another person to act

50(1)   The court may appoint such person as it thinks fit to appear for, represent or act for the incapacitated person.

50(2) The appointment may be made either generally or for the purpose of any particular application or proceeding, or for the exercise of particular rights or powers which the incapacitated person might have exercised but for his incapacity.

50(3) The court may make the appointment either of its own motion or on application by–

(a) a person who has been appointed by a court in the United Kingdom or elsewhere to manage the affairs of, or to represent, the incapacitated person; or

(b) any relative or friend of the incapacitated person who appears to the court to be a proper person to make the application; or

(c) in any case where the incapacitated person is the debtor, the foreign representative.

50(4) Application under sub-paragraph (3) may be made *ex parte*; but the court may require such notice of the application as it thinks necessary to be given to the person alleged to be incapacitated, or any other person, and may adjourn the hearing of the application to enable the notice to be given.

51 Affidavit in support of application

51 An application under paragraph 50(3) shall be supported by an affidavit of a registered medical practitioner as to the mental or physical condition of the incapacitated person.

52 Service of notices following appointment

52 Any notice served on, or sent to, a person appointed under paragraph 50 has the same effect as if it had been served on, or given to, the incapacitated person.

53 Rights of audience

53 Rights of audience in proceedings under these Regulations are the same as obtain in proceedings under British insolvency law.

54 Right of attendance

54(1) Subject as follows, in proceedings under these Regulations, any person stating himself in writing, in records kept by the court for that purpose, to be a creditor of the debtor to which the proceedings relate, is entitled at his own cost, to attend in court or in chambers at any stage of the proceedings.

54(2) Attendance may be by the person himself, or his solicitor.

54(3) A person so entitled may request the court in writing to give him notice of any step in the proceedings; and, subject to his paying the costs involved and keeping the court informed as to his address, the court shall comply with the request.

54(4) If the court is satisfied that the exercise by a person of his rights under this paragraph has given rise to costs for the estate of the debtor which would not otherwise have been incurred and ought not, in the circumstances, to fall on that estate, it may direct that the costs be paid by the person concerned, to an amount specified.

The rights of that person under this paragraph shall be in abeyance so long as those costs are not paid.

54(5) The court may appoint one or more persons to represent the creditors of the debtor to have the rights conferred by this paragraph, instead of the rights being exercised by any or all of them individually.

If two or more persons are appointed under this paragraph to represent the same interest, they must (if at all) instruct the same solicitor.

GENERAL NOTE

In keeping with the emphasis which the Model Law places generally on the need for speed and informality, a person claiming to be a creditor needs only to state the fact in writing to obtain standing. Note the provision in para.54(5) empowering all the creditors to act by a representative.

55   Right of attendance for member State liquidator

55   For the purposes of paragraph 54(1), a member State liquidator appointed in relation to a debtor subject to proceedings under these Regulations shall be deemed to be a creditor.

56   British insolvency officeholder's solicitor

56   Where in any proceedings the attendance of the British insolvency officeholder's solicitor is required, whether in court or in chambers, the British insolvency officeholder himself need not attend, unless directed by the court.

57   Formal defects

57   No proceedings under these Regulations shall be invalidated by any formal defect or by any irregularity, unless the court before which objection is made considers that substantial injustice has been caused by the defect or irregularity, and that the injustice cannot be remedied by any order of the court.

58   Restriction on concurrent proceedings and remedies

58   Where in proceedings under these Regulations the court makes an order staying any action, execution or other legal process against the property of a debtor, service of the order may be effected by sending a sealed copy of the order to whatever is the address for service of the claimant or other party having the carriage of the proceedings to be stayed.

59   Affidavits

59(1)   Where in proceedings under these Regulations, an affidavit is made by any British insolvency officeholder acting in relation to the debtor, he shall state the capacity in which he makes it, the position which he holds and the address at which he works.

59(2)   Any officer of the court duly authorised in that behalf, may take affidavits and declarations.

59(3)   Subject to sub-paragraph (4), where these Regulations provide for the use of an affidavit, a witness statement verified by a statement of truth may be used as an alternative.

59(4)   Sub-paragraph (3) does not apply to paragraphs 4 (affidavit in support of recognition application), 7 (affidavit in support of interim relief application), 10 (affidavit in support of article 21 relief application), 13 (affidavit in support of application regarding status of replacement foreign representative) and 16 (affidavit in support of review application).

GENERAL NOTE

A witness statement may be used as an alternative to an affidavit, except in the cases specified in para.59(4).

60   Security in court

60(1)   Where security has to be given to the court (otherwise than in relation to costs), it may be given by guarantee, bond or the payment of money into court.

60(2)   A person proposing to give a bond as security shall give notice to the party in whose favour the security is required, and to the court, naming those who are to be sureties to the bond.

60(3)   The court shall forthwith give notice to the parties concerned of a venue for the execution of the bond and the making of any objection to the sureties.

60(4)   The sureties shall make an affidavit of their sufficiency (unless dispensed with by the party in whose favour the security is required) and shall, if required by the court, attend the court to be cross-examined.

61 Further information and disclosure

61(1) Any party to proceedings under these Regulations may apply to the court for an order–

(a) that any other party–

(i) clarify any matter which is in dispute in the proceedings; or

(ii) give additional information in relation to any such matter,

in accordance with CPR Part 18 (further information); or

(b) to obtain disclosure from any other party in accordance with CPR Part 31 (disclosure and inspection of documents).

61(2) An application under this paragraph may be made without notice being served on any other party.

62 Office copies of documents

62(1) Any person who has under these Regulations the right to inspect the court file of proceedings may require the court to provide him with an office copy of any document from the file.

62(2) A person's right under this paragraph may be exercised on his behalf by his solicitor.

62(3) An office copy provided by the court under this paragraph shall be in such form as the Registrar thinks appropriate, and shall bear the court's seal.

63 "The court"

63(1) Anything to be done in proceedings under these Regulations by, to or before the court may be done by, to or before a judge of the High Court or a Registrar.

63(2) Where these Regulations require or permit the court to perform an act of a formal or administrative character, that act may be performed by a court officer.

PART 10

COSTS AND DETAILED ASSESSMENT

64 Requirement to assess costs by the detailed procedure

64 In any proceedings before the court, the court may order costs to be decided by detailed assessment.

65 Costs of officers charged with execution of writs or other process

65(1) Where by virtue of article 20 of the Model Law or a court order under article 19 or 21 of the Model Law an enforcement officer, or other officer, charged with execution of the writ or other process–

(a) is required to deliver up goods or money; or

(b) has deducted costs from the proceeds of an execution or money paid to him,

the foreign representative may require in writing that the amount of the enforcement officer's or other officer's bill of costs be decided by detailed assessment.

65(2) Where such a requirement is made, if the enforcement officer or other officer does not commence detailed assessment proceedings within 3 months of the requirement under sub-paragraph (1), or within such further time as the court, on application, may permit, any claim by the enforcement officer or other officer in respect of his costs is forfeited by such failure to commence proceedings.

65(3) Where, in the case of a deduction of costs by the enforcement officer or other officer, any amount deducted is disallowed at the conclusion of the detailed assessment proceedings, the enforcement officer or other officer shall forthwith pay a sum equal to that disallowed to the foreign representative for the benefit of the debtor.

66 Final costs certificate

66(1) A final costs certificate of the costs officer is final and conclusive as to all matters which have not been objected to in the manner provided for under the rules of the court.

66(2) Where it is proved to the satisfaction of a costs officer that a final costs certificate has been lost or destroyed, he may issue a duplicate.

PART 11

APPEALS IN PROCEEDINGS UNDER THESE REGULATIONS

67 Appeals from court orders

67(1) An appeal from a decision of a Registrar of the High Court in proceedings under these Regulations lies to a single judge of the High Court; and an appeal from a decision of that judge on such an appeal lies, with the permission of the Court of Appeal, to the Court of Appeal.

67(2) An appeal from a decision of a judge of the High Court in proceedings under these Regulations which is not a decision on an appeal made to him under sub-paragraph (1) lies, with the permission of that judge or the Court of Appeal, to the Court of Appeal.

GENERAL NOTE

These rules correspond to those applicable generally to decisions of the High Court in matters of insolvency. See IR 2016 rr.12.59 et seq. and the *Practice Direction: Insolvency Proceedings* [2018] B.C.C. 421 (reproduced as App.IV to this *Guide*), Pt 4.

68 Procedure on appeals

68(1) Subject as follows, CPR Part 52 (appeals to the Court of Appeal) and its practice direction apply to appeals in proceedings under these Regulations.

68(2) The provisions of Part 4 of the practice direction on Insolvency Proceedings supporting CPR Part 49 relating to first appeals (as defined in that Part) apply in relation to any appeal to a single judge of the High Court under paragraph 67, with any necessary modifications.

68(3) In proceedings under these Regulations, the procedure under CPR Part 52 is by ordinary application and not by appeal notice.

PART 12

GENERAL

69 Notices

69(1) All notices required or authorised by or under these Regulations to be given must be in writing, unless it is otherwise provided, or the court allows the notice to be given in some other way.

69(2) Where in proceedings under these Regulations a notice is required to be sent or given by any person, the sending or giving of it may be proved by means of a certificate by that person that he posted the notice, or instructed another person (naming him) to do so.

69(3) A certificate under this paragraph may be endorsed on a copy or specimen of the notice to which it relates.

70 "Give notice" etc.

70(1) A reference in these Regulations to giving notice, or to delivering, sending or serving any document, means that the notice or document may be sent by post.

70(2) Subject to paragraph 75, any form of post may be used.

70(3) Personal service of a document is permissible in all cases.

70(4) Notice of the venue fixed for an application may be given by service of the sealed copy of the application under paragraph 33(3).

71 Notice, etc. to solicitors

71 Where in proceedings under these Regulations a notice or other document is required or authorised to be given to a person, it may, if he has indicated that his solicitor is authorised to accept service on his behalf, be given instead to the solicitor.

72 Notice to joint British insolvency officeholders

72 Where two or more persons are acting jointly as the British insolvency officeholder in proceedings under British insolvency law, delivery of a document to one of them is to be treated as delivery to them all.

73 Forms for use in proceedings under these Regulations

73(1) The forms contained in Schedule 5 to these Regulations shall be used in, and in connection with, proceedings under these Regulations.

73(2) The forms shall be used with such variations, if any, as the circumstances may require.

74 Time limits

74(1) The provisions of CPR Rule 2.8 (time) apply, as regards computation of time, to anything required or authorised to be done by these Regulations.

74(2) The provisions of CPR rule 3.1(2)(a) (the court's general powers of management) apply so as to enable the court to extend or shorten the time for compliance with anything required or authorised to be done by these Regulations.

75 Service by post

75(1) For a document to be properly served by post, it must be contained in an envelope addressed to the person on whom service is to be effected, and pre-paid for first class post.

75(2) A document to be served by post may be sent to the last known address of the person to be served.

75(3) Where first class post is used, the document is treated as served on the second business day after the date of posting, unless the contrary is shown.

75(4) The date of posting is presumed, unless the contrary is shown, to be the date shown in the post-mark on the envelope in which the document is contained.

76 General provisions as to service and notice

76 Subject to paragraphs 22, 75 and 77, CPR Part 6 (service of documents) applies as regards any matter relating to the service of documents and the giving of notice in proceedings under these Regulations.

77 Service outside the jurisdiction

77(1)   Sections III and IV of CPR Part 6 (service out of the jurisdiction and service of process of foreign court) do not apply in proceedings under these Regulations.

77(2)   Where for the purposes of proceedings under these Regulations any process or order of the court, or other document, is required to be served on a person who is not in England and Wales, the court may order service to be effected within such time, on such person, at such place and in such manner as it thinks fit, and may also require such proof of service as it thinks fit.

77(3)   An application under this paragraph shall be supported by an affidavit stating–

(a)   the grounds on which the application is made; and

(b)   in what place or country the person to be served is, or probably may be found.

78 False claim of status as creditor

78(1)   Rule 12.18 (false claim of status as creditor, etc) shall apply with any necessary modifications in any case where a person falsely claims the status of a creditor of a debtor, with the intention of obtaining a sight of documents whether on the court's file or in the hands of the foreign representative or other person, which he has not under these Regulations any right to inspect.

78(2)   Rule 21.21 and Schedule 5 of the Rules shall apply to an offence under Rule 12.18 as applied by sub-paragraph (1) as they apply to an offence under Rule 12.18.

79 The Gazette

79(1)   A copy of the Gazette containing any notice required by these Regulations to be gazetted is evidence of any fact stated in the notice.

79(2)   In the case of an order of the court notice of which is required by these Regulations to be gazetted, a copy of the Gazette containing the notice may in any proceedings be produced as conclusive evidence that the order was made on the date specified in the notice.

SCHEDULE 3

Regulation 5

PROCEDURAL MATTERS IN SCOTLAND

Introductory note to Schedule 3
This Schedule is the counterpart for Scotland of Sch.2, but is less elaborate and detailed. General competence in matters under the Regulations is conferred on the Court of Session by art.4 of Sch.1. The text incorporates amendments made by the Financial Services Act 2012 (Consequential Amendments and Transitional Provisions) Order 2013 (SI 2013/472).

PART 1

INTERPRETATION

1 Interpretation

1(1)   In this Schedule–

"the 1986 Act" means the Insolvency Act 1986;

"article 21 remedy application" means an application to the court by a foreign representative under article 21(1) or (2) of the Model Law for remedy;

218

"business day" means any day other than a Saturday, a Sunday, Christmas Day, Good Friday or a day which is a bank holiday in Scotland under or by virtue of the Banking and Financial Dealings Act 1971;

"the Gazette" means the Edinburgh Gazette;

"main proceedings" means proceedings opened in accordance with Article 3(1) of the EU Insolvency Regulation and falling within the definition of insolvency proceedings in Article 2(4) of the EU Insolvency Regulation;

"member State liquidator" means a person falling within the definition of "insolvency practitioner" in Article 2(5) of the EU Insolvency Regulation appointed in proceedings to which the Regulation applies in a member State other than the United Kingdom;

"the Model Law" means the UNCITRAL Model Law as set out in Schedule 1 to these Regulations;

"modification or termination order" means an order by the court pursuant to its powers under the Model Law modifying or terminating recognition of a foreign proceeding, the sist, restraint or suspension referred to in article 20(1) or any part of it or any remedy granted under article 19 or 21 of the Model Law;

"recognition application" means an application to the court by a foreign representative in accordance with article 15 of the Model Law for an order recognising the foreign proceeding in which he has been appointed;

"recognition order" means an order by the court recognising a proceeding the subject of a recognition application as a foreign main proceeding or foreign non-main proceeding, as appropriate;

"relevant company" [Redefined by SI 2009/1941 in identical terms as for England and Wales.]

"review application" means an application to the court for a modification or termination order.

1(2)   Expressions defined in the Model Law have the same meaning when used in this Schedule.

1(3)   References in this Schedule to a debtor who is of interest to the Financial Conduct Authority are references to a debtor who–

(a)   is, or has been, an authorised person within the meaning of the Financial Services and Markets Act 2000;

(b)   is, or has been, an appointed representative within the meaning of section 39 of the Financial Services and Markets Act 2000; or

(c)   is carrying on, or has carried on, a regulated activity in contravention of the general prohibition.

1(3A)   References in this Schedule to a debtor who is of interest to the Prudential Regulation Authority are references to a debtor who–

(a)   is, or has been, a PRA-authorised person within the meaning of the Financial Services and Markets Act 2000; or

(b)   is carrying on, or has carried on, a PRA-regulated activity within the meaning of the Financial Services and Markets Act 2000 in contravention of the general prohibition.

1(4)   In sub-paragraphs (3) and (3A) "the general prohibition" has the meaning given by section 19 of the Financial Services and Markets Act 2000 and the reference to a "regulated activity" must be construed in accordance with–

(a)   section 22 of that Act (classes of regulated activity and categories of investment);

(b)   any relevant order under that section; and

(c)   Schedule 2 to that Act (regulated activities).

1(5) References in this Schedule to a numbered form are to the form that bears that number in Schedule 5.

GENERAL NOTE

Paragraph 1(3) substituted and para.1(3A) inserted by the Financial Services Act 2012 (Consequential Amendments and Transitional Provisions) Order 2013 (SI 2013/472) Sch.2 art.116(b)(i) as from 1 April 2013.

In para.1(1) the definitions of "main proceedings" amended and "member State liquidator" substituted by the Insolvency Amendment (EU 2015/848) Regulations 2017 (SI 2017/702) regs 1, 2(1), Sch. para.94(1), (4) in relation to proceedings opened on or after 26 June 2017 (see reg.3) when the Recast EU Regulation 2015/848 came into force.

PART 2

THE FOREIGN REPRESENTATIVE

2   Application for confirmation of status of replacement foreign representative

2(1) This paragraph applies where following the making of a recognition order the foreign representative dies or for any other reason ceases to be the foreign representative in the foreign proceedings in relation to the debtor.

2(2) In this paragraph "the former foreign representative" means the foreign representative referred to in sub-paragraph (1).

2(3) If a person has succeeded the former foreign representative or is otherwise holding office as foreign representative in the foreign proceeding in relation to the debtor, that person may apply to the court for an order confirming his status as replacement foreign representative for the purpose of proceedings under these Regulations.

2(4) If the court dismisses an application under sub-paragraph (3) then it may also, if it thinks fit, make an order terminating recognition of the foreign proceeding and–

(a) such an order may include such provision as the court thinks fit with respect to matters arising in connection with the termination; and

(b) paragraph 5 shall not apply to such an order.

3   Misfeasance by a foreign representative

3(1) The court may examine the conduct of a person who–

(a) is or purports to be the foreign representative in relation to a debtor, or

(b) has been or has purported to be the foreign representative in relation to a debtor.

3(2) An examination under this paragraph may be held only on the application of–

(a) a British insolvency officeholder acting in relation to the debtor,

(b) a creditor of the debtor, or

(c) with the permission of the court, any other person who appears to have an interest justifying an application.

3(3) An application under sub-paragraph (2) must allege that the foreign representative–

(a) has misapplied or retained money or other property of the debtor,

(b) has become accountable for money or other property of the debtor,

(c)   has breached a fiduciary duty or other duty in relation to the debtor, or

(d)   has been guilty of misfeasance.

3(4)   On an examination under this paragraph into a person's conduct the court may order him–

(a)   to repay, restore or account for money or property;

(b)   to pay interest;

(c)   to contribute a sum to the debtor's property by way of compensation for breach of duty or misfeasance.

3(5)   In sub-paragraph (3), "foreign representative" includes a person who purports or has purported to be a foreign representative in relation to a debtor.

PART 3

COURT PROCEDURE AND PRACTICE

4   Preliminary and interpretation

4(1)   This Part applies to–

(a)   any of the following applications made to the court under these Regulations–

    (i)   a recognition application;

    (ii)   an article 21 remedy application;

    (iii)   an application under paragraph 2(3) for an order confirming the status of a replacement foreign representative;

    (iv)   a review application; and

(b)   any of the following orders made by the court under these Regulations–

    (i)   a recognition order;

    (ii)   an order granting interim remedy under article 19 of the Model Law;

    (iii)   an order granting remedy under article 21 of the Model Law;

    (iv)   an order confirming the status of a replacement foreign representative; or

    (v)   a modification or termination order.

GENERAL NOTE

There is no separate provision in the Scottish procedural rules for recognition applications corresponding with Sch.2 paras 2–6.

5   Reviews of court orders—where court makes order of its own motion

5(1)   The court shall not of its own motion make a modification or termination order unless the foreign representative and the debtor have either–

(a)   had an opportunity of being heard on the question, or

(b)   consented in writing to such an order.

5(2)   If the court makes a modification or termination order, the order may include such provision as the court thinks fit with respect to matters arising in connection with the modification or termination.

6   The hearing

6(1)   At the hearing of the application, the applicant and any of the following persons (not being the applicant) may appear or be represented–

(a)   the foreign representative;

(b)   the debtor and, in the case of any debtor other than an individual, any one or more directors or other officers of the debtor, including–

    (i)   where applicable, any person specified in particulars registered under section 1046 of the Companies Act 2006 (overseas companies) as authorised to represent the debtor;

    (ii)   in the case of a debtor which is a partnership, any person who is a member of the partnership;

(c)   if a British insolvency officeholder is acting in relation to the debtor, that person;

(d)   if any person has been appointed an administrative receiver of the debtor or as a receiver or manager of the property of the debtor, that person;

(e)   if a member State liquidator has been appointed in main proceedings in relation to the debtor, that person;

(f)   if a foreign representative has been appointed in any other foreign proceeding regarding the debtor, that person;

(g)   any person who has presented a petition for the winding up or sequestration of the debtor in Scotland;

(h)   any person who is or may be entitled to appoint an administrator of the debtor under paragraph 14 of Schedule B1 to the 1986 Act (appointment of administrator by holder of qualifying floating charge);

(i)   if the debtor is a debtor who is of interest to the Financial Conduct Authority, that Authority;

(ia)   if the debtor is a debtor who is of interest to the Prudential Regulation Authority, that Authority; and

(j)   with the permission of the court, any other person who appears to have an interest justifying his appearance.

GENERAL NOTE

Paragraph 6(1)(b)(i) substituted by the Companies Act 2006 (Consequential Amendments, Transitional Provisions and Savings) Order 2009 (SI 2009/1941) art.2(1) and Sch.1 para.264(4)(b) as from 1 October 2009. Paragraph 6(1)(i) substituted and para.6(1)(ia) inserted by the Financial Services Act 2012 (Consequential Amendments and Transitional Provisions) Order 2013 (SI 2013/472) Sch.2 art.116(b)(ii) as from 1 April 2013.

7   Notification and advertisement of order

7(1)   This paragraph applies where the court makes any of the orders referred to in paragraph 4(1)(b).

7(2)   The foreign representative shall send a certified copy of the interlocutor as soon as reasonably practicable to the debtor.

7(3)   The foreign representative shall, as soon as reasonably practicable after the date of the order, give notice of the making of the order–

(a)   if a British insolvency officeholder is acting in relation to the debtor, to him;

(b)   if any person has been appointed an administrative receiver of the debtor or, to the knowledge of the foreign representative, as a receiver or manager of the property of the debtor, to him;

(c) if a member State liquidator has been appointed in main proceedings in relation to the debtor, to him;

(d) if to his knowledge a foreign representative has been appointed in any other foreign proceeding regarding the debtor, that person;

(e) if there is pending in Scotland a petition for the winding up or sequestration of the debtor, to the petitioner;

(f) to any person who to his knowledge is or may be entitled to appoint an administrator of the debtor under paragraph 14 of Schedule B1 to the 1986 Act (appointment of administrator by holder of qualifying floating charge);

(g) if the debtor is a debtor who is of interest to the Financial Conduct Authority, to that Authority;

(ga) if the debtor is a debtor who is of interest to the Prudential Regulation Authority, to that Authority; and

(h) to such persons as the court may direct.

7(4) Where the debtor is a relevant company, the foreign representative shall send notice of the making of the order to the registrar of companies before the end of the period of 5 business days beginning with the date of the order. The notice to the registrar of companies shall be in Form ML 7.

7(5) The foreign representative shall advertise the making of the following orders once in the Gazette and once in such newspaper as he thinks most appropriate for ensuring that the making of the order comes to the notice of the debtor's creditors–

(a) a recognition order,

(b) an order confirming the status of a replacement foreign representative, and

(c) a modification or termination order which modifies or terminates recognition of a foreign proceeding,

and the advertisement shall be in Form ML 8.

GENERAL NOTE

Paragraph 7(3)(g) substituted and para.7(3)(ga) inserted by the Financial Services Act 2012 (Consequential Amendments and Transitional Provisions) Order 2013 (SI 2013/472) Sch.2 art.116(b)(iii) as from 1 April 2013.

Para.7(4)
On notices to the registrar of companies, see Sch.4.

8 Registration of court order

8(1) Where the court makes a recognition order in respect of a foreign main proceeding or an order suspending the right to transfer, encumber or otherwise dispose of any assets of the debtor being heritable property, the clerk of the court shall send forthwith a certified copy of the order to the keeper of the register of inhibitions and adjudications for recording in that register.

8(2) Recording under sub-paragraph (1) or (3) shall have the effect as from the date of the order of an inhibition and of a citation in an adjudication of the debtor's heritable estate at the instance of the foreign representative.

8(3) Where the court makes a modification or termination order, the clerk of the court shall send forthwith a certified copy of the order to the keeper of the register of inhibitions and adjudications for recording in that register.

8(4) The effect mentioned in sub-paragraph (2) shall expire–

(a) on the recording of a modification or termination order under sub-paragraph (3); or

(b) subject to sub-paragraph (5), if the effect has not expired by virtue of paragraph (a), at the end of the period of 3 years beginning with the date of the order.

8(5) The foreign representative may, if recognition of the foreign proceeding has not been modified or terminated by the court pursuant to its powers under the Model Law, before the end of the period of 3 years mentioned in sub-paragraph (4)(b), send a memorandum in a form prescribed by the Court of Session by act of sederunt to the keeper of the register of inhibitions and adjudications for recording in that register, and such recording shall renew the effect mentioned in sub-paragraph (2); and thereafter the said effect shall continue to be preserved only if such memorandum is so recorded before the expiry of every subsequent period of 3 years.

9   Right to inspect court process

9(1) In the case of any proceedings under these Regulations, the following have the right, at all reasonable times, to inspect the court process of the proceedings–

(a) the Secretary of State;

(b) the person who is the foreign representative in relation to the proceedings;

(c) if a foreign representative has been appointed in any other foreign proceeding regarding the debtor, that person;

(d) if a British insolvency officeholder is acting in relation to the debtor, that person;

(e) any person stating himself in writing to be a creditor of the debtor to which the proceedings under these Regulations relate;

(f) if a member State liquidator has been appointed in relation to a debtor which is subject to proceedings under these Regulations, that person; and

(g) the debtor to which the proceedings under these Regulations relate, or, if that debtor is a company, corporation or partnership, every person who is, or at any time has been–

(i) a director or officer of the debtor,

(ii) a member of the debtor, or

(iii) where applicable, any person specified in particulars registered under section 1046 of the Companies Act 2006 (overseas companies) as authorised to represent the debtor.

9(2) The right of inspection conferred as above on any person may be exercised on his behalf by a person properly authorised by him.

General Note

Paragraph 9(1)(g)(iii) substituted by the Companies Act 2006 (Consequential Amendments, Transitional Provisions and Savings) Order 2009 (SI 2009/1941) art.2(1) and Sch.1 para.264(3)(c) as from 1 October 2009.

10   Copies of court orders

10(1) In any proceedings under these Regulations, any person who under paragraph 9 has a right to inspect documents in the court process also has the right to require the foreign representative in relation to those proceedings to furnish him with a copy of any court order in the proceedings.

10(2) Sub-paragraph (1) does not apply if a copy of the court order has been served on that person or notice of the making of the order has been given to that person under other provisions of these Regulations.

11   Transfer of proceedings—actions to avoid acts detrimental to creditors

11   If, in accordance with article 23(6) of the Model Law, the court grants a foreign representative permission to make an application in accordance with paragraph (1) of that article, it may also order the relevant proceedings under British insolvency law taking place regarding the debtor to be transferred to the Court of Session if those proceedings are taking place in Scotland and are not already in that court.

PART 3

GENERAL

12   Giving of notices, etc

12(1)   All notices required or authorised by or under these Regulations to be given, sent or delivered must be in writing, unless it is otherwise provided, or the court allows the notice to be sent or given in some other way.

12(2)   Any reference in these Regulations to giving, sending or delivering a notice or any such document means, without prejudice to any other way and unless it is otherwise provided, that the notice or document may be sent by post, and that, subject to paragraph 13, any form of post may be used. Personal service of the notice or document is permissible in all cases.

12(3)   Where under these Regulations a notice or other document is required or authorised to be given, sent or delivered by a person ("the sender") to another ("the recipient"), it may be given, sent or delivered by any person duly authorised by the sender to do so to any person duly authorised by the recipient to receive or accept it.

12(4)   Where two or more persons are acting jointly as the British insolvency officeholder in proceedings under British insolvency law, the giving, sending or delivering of a notice or document to one of them is to be treated as the giving, sending or delivering of a notice or document to each or all.

13   Sending by post

13(1)   For a document to be properly sent by post, it must be contained in an envelope addressed to the person to whom it is to be sent, and pre-paid for either first or second class post.

13(2)   Any document to be sent by post may be sent to the last known address of the person to whom the document is to be sent.

13(3)   Where first class post is used, the document is to be deemed to be received on the second business day after the date of posting, unless the contrary is shown.

13(4)   Where second class post is used, the document is to be deemed to be received on the fourth business day after the date of posting, unless the contrary is shown.

14   Certificate of giving notice, etc

14(1)   Where in any proceedings under these Regulations a notice or document is required to be given, sent or delivered by any person, the date of giving, sending or delivery of it may be proved by means of a certificate by that person that he gave, posted or otherwise sent or delivered the notice or document on the date stated in the certificate, or that he instructed another person (naming him) to do so.

14(2)   A certificate under this paragraph may be endorsed on a copy of the notice to which it relates.

14(3)   A certificate purporting to be signed by or on behalf of the person mentioned in sub-paragraph (1) shall be deemed, unless the contrary is shown, to be sufficient evidence of the matters stated therein.

15   Forms for use in proceedings under these Regulations

15(1)   Forms ML 7 and ML 8 contained in Schedule 5 to these Regulations shall be used in, and in connection with, proceedings under these Regulations.

15(2)   The forms shall be used with such variations, if any, as the circumstances may require.

SCHEDULE 4

Regulation 6

NOTICES DELIVERED TO THE REGISTRAR OF COMPANIES

1   Interpretation

1(1)   In this Schedule–

"electronic communication" means the same as in the Electronic Communications Act 2000;

"Model Law notice" means a notice delivered to the registrar of companies under paragraph 26(6) of Schedule 2 or paragraph 7(4) of Schedule 3.

1(2)   Expressions defined in the Model Law or Schedule 2 or 3, as appropriate, have the same meaning when used in this Schedule.

1(3)   References in this Schedule to delivering a notice include sending, forwarding, producing or giving it.

2   Functions of the registrar of companies

2(1)   Where a Model Law notice is delivered to the registrar of companies in respect of a relevant company, the registrar shall enter a note in the register relating to that company.

2(2)   The note referred to in sub-paragraph (1) shall contain the following particulars, in each case as stated in the notice delivered to the registrar–

(a)   brief details of the court order made;

(b)   the date of the court order; and

(c)   the name and address for service of the person who is the foreign representative in relation to the company.

3   Registrar of companies to whom notices to be delivered

3   [Omitted by the Companies Act 2006 (Consequential Amendments, Transitional Provisions and Savings) Order 2009 (SI 2009/1941) art.2(1) and Sch.1 para.264(5)(b) as from 1 October 2009.]

4   Delivery to registrar of notices

4(1)   Electronic communications may be used for the delivery of any Model Law notice, provided that such delivery is in such form and manner as is directed by the registrar.

4(2)   Where the Model Law notice is required to be signed, it shall instead be authenticated in such manner as is directed by the registrar.

4(3)   If a Model Law notice is delivered to the registrar which does not comply with the requirements of these Regulations, he may serve on the person by whom the notice was delivered (or, if there are two or more such persons, on any of them) a notice (a non-compliance notice) indicating the respect in which the Model Law notice does not comply.

4(4) Where the registrar serves a non-compliance notice, then, unless a replacement Model Law notice–

(a) is delivered to him within 14 days after the service of the non-compliance notice, and

(b) complies with the requirements of these Regulations or is not rejected by him for failure to comply with those requirements,

the original Model Law notice shall be deemed not to have been delivered to him.

5 Enforcement of foreign representative's duty to give notice to registrar

5(1) If a foreign representative, having made default in complying with paragraph 26(6) of Schedule 2 or paragraph 7(4) of Schedule 3 fails to make good the default within 14 days after the service of a notice on the foreign representative requiring him to do so, the court may, on an application made to it by any creditor, member, director or other officer of the debtor or by the registrar of companies, make an order directing the foreign representative to make good the default within such time as may be specified in the order.

5(2) The court's order may provide that all costs of and incidental to the application shall be borne by the foreign representative.

6 Rectification of the register under court order

6(1) The registrar shall remove from the register any note, or part of a note–

(a) that relates to or is derived from a court order that the court has declared to be invalid or ineffective, or

(b) that the court declares to be factually inaccurate or derived from something that is factually inaccurate or forged,

and that the court directs should be removed from the register.

6(2) The court order must specify what is to be removed from the register and indicate where on the register it is and the registrar shall carry out his duty under sub-paragraph (1) within a reasonable time of receipt by him of the relevant court order.

SCHEDULE 5

FORMS

[Not reproduced.]

Ancillary Statutes

Debtors Act 1869

(32 & 33 Vict. Chapter 62)

ARRANGEMENT OF SECTIONS

An Act for the Abolition of Imprisonment for Debt, for the punishment of fraudulent debtors, and for other purposes.

[*9th August 1869*]

[**Note**: Changes made by the Bankruptcy Act 1883, the Statute Law Revision (No.2) Act 1893, the Supreme Court of Judicature (Consolidation) Act 1925, the Theft Act 1968, the Civil Procedure (Modification of Enactments) Order 2002 (SI 2002/439), the Statute Law (Repeals) Act 2004 and the Crime and Courts Act 2013 have been incorporated into the text (in the case of pre-1996 legislation without annotation). See also the Debtors Act 1878, below.]

Preliminary

1 Short title

1 This Act may be cited for all purposes as "The Debtors Act 1869".

2 Extent of Act

2 This Act shall not extend to Scotland or Ireland.

3 Commencement and construction of Act

3 Words and expressions defined or explained in the Bankruptcy Act 1869 shall have the same meaning in this Act.

PART I

ABOLITION OF IMPRISONMENT FOR DEBT

4 Abolition of imprisonment for debt, with exceptions

4 With the exceptions herein-after mentioned, no person shall be arrested or imprisoned for making default in payment of a sum of money.

There shall be excepted from the operation of the above enactment:

(1) Default in payment of a penalty, or sum in the nature of a penalty, other than a penalty in respect of any contract:

(2) Default in payment of any sum recoverable summarily before a justice or justices of the peace:

(3) Default by a trustee or person acting in a fiduciary capacity and ordered to pay by a court of equity any sum in his possession or under his control:

(4) Default by a solicitor in payment of costs when ordered to pay costs for misconduct as such, or in payment of a sum of money when ordered to pay the same in his character of an officer of the court making the order:

(5) Default in payment for the benefit of creditors of any portion of a salary or other income in respect of the payment of which any court having jurisdiction in bankruptcy is authorized to make an order:

(6) Default in payment of sums in respect of the payment of which orders are in this Act authorized to be made:

Provided, first, that no person shall be imprisoned in any case excepted from the operation of this section for a longer period than one year; and, secondly, that nothing in this section shall alter the effect of any judgment or order of any court for payment of money except as regards the arrest and imprisonment of the person making default in paying such money.

5 Saving of power of committal for small debts

5 Subject to the provisions herein-after mentioned, and to the prescribed rules, any court may commit to prison for a term not exceeding six weeks, or until payment of the sum due, any person who makes default in payment of any debt or instalment of any debt due from him in pursuance of any order or judgment of that or any other competent court.

Provided–

(1) That the jurisdiction by this section given of committing a person to prison shall, in the case of the county court–

(a) Be exercised only by a judge of the court, and by an order made in open court and showing on its face the ground on which it is issued.

(b) [Repealed by the Bankruptcy Act 1883 s.169(1) and Sch.5.]

(c) [Repealed]

(2) That such jurisdiction shall only be exercised where it is proved to the satisfaction of the court that the person making default either has or has had since the date of the order or judgment the means to pay the sum in respect of which he has made default, and has refused or neglected, or refuses or neglects, to pay the same.

Proof of the means of the person making default may be given in such manner as the court thinks just.

For the purpose of considering whether to commit a debtor to prison under this section, the debtor may be summoned in accordance with the prescribed rules.

Any jurisdiction by this section given to the High Court or family court may be exercised by a judge sitting in chambers, or otherwise, in the prescribed manner.

Persons committed under this section by a High Court or family court may be committed to the prison in which they would have been confined if arrested on a writ of capias ad satisfaciendum, and every order of committal by any superior court shall, subject to the prescribed rules, be issued, obeyed, and executed in the like manner as such writ.

This section, so far as it relates to the county court, shall be deemed to be substituted for sections ninety-eight and ninety-nine of the County Courts Act 1846, and that Act and the Acts amending the same shall be construed accordingly, and shall extend to orders made by the county court with respect to sums due in pursuance of any order or judgment of any court other than the county court.

No imprisonment under this section shall operate as a satisfaction or extinguishment of any debt or demand or course of action, or deprive any person of any right to take out execution against the lands, goods, or chattels of the person imprisoned, in the same manner as if such imprisonment had not taken place.

Any person imprisoned under this section shall be discharged out of custody upon a certificate signed in the prescribed manner to the effect that he has satisfied the debt or instalment of a debt in respect of which he was imprisoned, together with the prescribed costs (if any).

Section 31E(1)(b) of the Matrimonial and Family Proceedings Act 1984 (family court has county court's powers) does not apply in relation to the powers given by this section to the county court.

History
Seventh (originally the fifth) paragraph of proviso (2) deleted by the Statute Law (Repeals) Act 2004 Sch.1 Pt 17, as from 22 July 2004. Proviso 1(c) repealed and various parts of Proviso 2 amended by the Crime and Courts Act 2013 Sch.9 para.78 and Sch.10 para.2(2) as from 22 April 2014.

6 Power under certain circumstances to arrest defendant about to quit England

6 Where the plaintiff in any action in the High Court in which, if brought before the commencement of this Act, the defendant would have been liable to arrest, proves at any time before final judgment by evidence on oath, to the satisfaction of a judge of the High Court, that the plaintiff has good cause of action against the defendant to the amount of fifty pounds or upwards, and that there is probable cause for believing that the defendant is about to quit England unless he be apprehended, and that the absence of the defendant from England will materially prejudice the plaintiff in the prosecution of his action such judge may in the prescribed manner order such defendant to be arrested and imprisoned for a period not exceeding six months, unless and until he has sooner given the prescribed security, not exceeding the amount claimed in the action, that he will not go out of England without the leave of the court.

Where the action is for a penalty or sum in the nature of a penalty other than a penalty in respect of any contract, it shall not be necessary to prove that the absence of the defendant from England will materially prejudice the plaintiff in the prosecution of his action, and the security given (instead of being that the defendant will not go out of England) shall be to the effect that any sum recovered against the defendant in the action shall be paid, or that the defendant shall be rendered to prison.

7 [Repealed by the Statute Law Revision Act 1883.]

8 Saving for sequestration against property

8 Sequestration against the property of a debtor may be issued by any court of equity in the same manner as if such debtor had been actually arrested.

9 [Repealed by the Statute Law Revision (No.2) Act 1893.]

10 Definition of "prescribed"

10 In this part of this Act–

"prescribed", where it appears other than as part of the expression "the prescribed rules", means prescribed by rules of court; and

"the prescribed rules" means rules of court.

Part II

Punishment of Fraudulent Debtors

11, 12 [Repealed by the Bankruptcy Act 1914 s.168 and Sch.6.]

13 Penalty on fraudulently obtaining credit, etc.

13 Any person shall in each of the cases following be deemed guilty of a misdemeanour, and on conviction thereof shall be liable to be imprisoned for any time not exceeding one year; that is to say,

(1) [Repealed by the Theft Act 1968 ss.33(3), 35 and Sch.3 Pt I.]

(2) If he has with intent to defraud his creditors, or any of them, made or caused to be made any gift, delivery, or transfer of or any charge on his property:

(3) If he has, with intent to defraud his creditors, concealed or removed any part of his property since or within two months before the date of any unsatisfied judgment or order for payment of money obtained against him.

Debtors Act 1878

(41 & 42 Vict. Chapter 54)

An Act to amend the Debtors Act 1869, and the Debtors Act (Ireland) 1872.

[13th August 1878]

1 Court or Judge to have discretion in cases within exceptions 3 and 4 in 32 & 33 Vict. c.62. s. 4, and 35 & 36 Vict. c.57. s. 5, respectively

1 In any case coming within the exceptions numbered three and four in the fourth section of the Debtors Act 1869, and in the fifth section of the Debtors Act (Ireland) 1872, respectively, or within either of those exceptions, any court or judge, making the order for payment, or having jurisdiction in the action or proceeding in which the order for payment is made, may inquire into the case, and (subject to the provisoes contained in the said sections respectively) may grant or refuse, either absolutely or upon terms, any process or order of arrest or imprisonment, and any application to stay the operation of any such process, or order, or for discharge from arrest or imprisonment thereunder.

History
Section 1 amended by the Statute Law (Repeals) Act 2004 Sch.1 Pt 17, as from 22 July 2004.

2 Short title and construction

2 This Act may be cited as the Debtors Act 1878, and shall be construed as one with the Debtors Act 1869, as regards England, and as one with the Debtors Act (Ireland) 1872, as regards Ireland; and the Debtors Act 1869, and this Act may be cited as the Debtors Acts 1869 and 1878; and the Debtors Act (Ireland) 1872, and this Act may be cited as the Debtors Acts (Ireland) 1872 and 1878.

Law of Property Act 1925

(15 &16 Geo. 5 Chapter 20)

ARRANGEMENT OF SECTIONS

An Act to consolidate the enactments relating to conveyancing and the law of property in England and Wales.

[9th April 1925]

[**Note**: Changes made by the Insolvency Act 1985, the Agricultural Tenancies Act 1995, the Trusts of Land and Appointment of Trustees Act 1996 and the Commonhold and Leasehold Reform Act 2002 have been incorporated into the text (without annotation).]

PART III

MORTGAGES, RENTCHARGES, AND POWERS OF ATTORNEY

Mortgages

98 Actions for possession by mortgagors

98(1) A mortgagor for the time being entitled to the possession or receipt of the rents and profits of any land, as to which the mortgagee has not given notice of his intention to take possession or to enter into the receipt of the rents and profits thereof, may sue for such possession, or for the recovery of such rents or profits, or to prevent or recover damages in respect of any trespass or other wrong relative thereto, in his own name only, unless the cause of action arises upon a lease or other contract made by him jointly with any other person.

98(2) This section does not prejudice the power of a mortgagor independently of this section to take proceedings in his own name only, either in right of any legal estate vested in him or otherwise.

98(3) This section applies whether the mortgage was made before or after the commencement of this Act.

99 Leasing powers of mortgagor and mortgagee in possession

99(1) A mortgagor of land while in possession shall, as against every incumbrancer, have power to make from time to time any such lease of the mortgaged land, or any part thereof, as is by this section authorised.

99(2) A mortgagee of land while in possession shall, as against all prior incumbrancers, if any, and as against the mortgagor, have power to make from time to time any such lease as aforesaid.

99(3)   The leases which this section authorises are–

(i)   agricultural or occupation leases for any term not exceeding twenty-one years, or, in the case of a mortgage made after the commencement of this Act, fifty years; and

(ii)   building leases for any term not exceeding ninety-nine years, or, in the case of a mortgage made after the commencement of this Act, nine hundred and ninety-nine years.

99(4)   Every person making a lease under this section may execute and do all assurances and things necessary or proper in that behalf.

99(5)   Every such lease shall be made to take effect in possession not later than twelve months after its date.

99(6)   Every such lease shall reserve the best rent that can reasonably be obtained, regard being had to the circumstances of the case, but without any fine being taken.

99(7)   Every such lease shall contain a covenant by the lessee for payment of the rent, and a condition of re-entry on the rent not being paid within a time therein specified not exceeding thirty days.

99(8)   A counterpart of every such lease shall be executed by the lessee and delivered to the lessor, of which execution and delivery the execution of the lease by the lessor shall, in favour of the lessee and all persons deriving title under him, be sufficient evidence.

99(9)   Every such building lease shall be made in consideration of the lessee, or some person by whose direction the lease is granted, having erected, or agreeing to erect within not more than five years from the date of the lease, buildings, new or additional, or having improved or repaired buildings, or agreeing to improve or repair buildings within that time, or having executed, or agreeing to execute within that time, on the land leased, an improvement for or in connexion with building purposes.

99(10)   In any such building lease a peppercorn rent, or a nominal or other rent less than the rent ultimately payable, may be made payable for the first five years, or any less part of the term.

99(11)   In case of a lease by the mortgagor, he shall, within one month after making the lease, deliver to the mortgagee, or, where there are more than one, to the mortgagee first in priority, a counterpart of the lease duly executed by the lessee, but the lessee shall not be concerned to see that this provision is complied with.

99(12)   A contract to make or accept a lease under this section may be enforced by or against every person on whom the lease if granted would be binding.

99(13)   Subject to subsection (13A) below, this section applies only if and as far as a contrary intention is not expressed by the mortgagor and mortgagee in the mortgage deed, or otherwise in writing, and has effect subject to the terms of the mortgage deed or of any such writing and to the provisions therein contained.

99(13A)   Subsection (13) of this section–

(a)   shall not enable the application of any provision of this section to be excluded or restricted in relation to any mortgage of agricultural land made after 1st March 1948 but before 1st September 1995, and

(b)   shall not enable the power to grant a lease of an agricultural holding to which, by virtue of section 4 of the Agricultural Tenancies Act 1995, the Agricultural Holdings Act 1986 will apply, to be excluded or restricted in relation to any mortgage of agricultural land made on or after 1st September 1995.

99(13B)   In subsection (13A) of this section–

"agricultural holding" has the same meaning as in the Agricultural Holdings Act 1986; and

"agricultural land" has the same meaning as in the Agriculture Act 1947.

99(14)   The mortgagor and mortgagee may, by agreement in writing, whether or not contained in the mortgage deed, reserve to or confer on the mortgagor or the mortgagee, or both, any further or other powers of leasing or having reference to leasing; and any further or other powers so reserved or conferred shall be exercisable, as far as may be, as if they were conferred by this Act, and with all the like incidents, effects, and consequences:

Provided that the powers so reserved or conferred shall not prejudicially affect the rights of any mortgagee interested under any other mortgage subsisting at the date of the agreement, unless that mortgagee joins in or adopts the agreement.

99(15)   Nothing in this Act shall be construed to enable a mortgagor or mortgagee to make a lease for any longer term or on any other conditions than such as could have been granted or imposed by the mortgagor, with the concurrence of all the incumbrancers, if this Act and the enactments replaced by this section had not been passed:

Provided that, in the case of a mortgage of leasehold land, a lease granted under this section shall reserve a reversion of not less than one day.

99(16)   Subject as aforesaid, this section applies to any mortgage made after the thirty-first day of December, eighteen hundred and eighty-one, but the provisions thereof, or any of them, may, by agreement in writing made after that date between mortgagor and mortgagee, be applied to a mortgage made before that date, so nevertheless that any such agreement shall not prejudicially affect any right or interest of any mortgagee not joining in or adopting the agreement.

99(17)   The provisions of this section referring to a lease shall be construed to extend and apply, as far as circumstances admit, to any letting, and to an agreement, whether in writing or not, for leasing or letting.

99(18)   For the purposes of this section "mortgagor" does not include an incumbrancer deriving title under the original mortgagor.

99(19)   The powers of leasing conferred by this section shall, after a receiver of the income of the mortgaged property or any part thereof has been appointed by a mortgagee under his statutory power, and so long as the receiver acts, be exercisable by such mortgagee instead of by the mortgagor, as respects any land affected by the receivership, in like manner as if such mortgagee were in possession of the land, and the mortgagee may, by writing, delegate any of such powers to the receiver.

100   Powers of mortgagor and mortgagee in possession to accept surrenders of leases

100(1)   For the purpose only of enabling a lease authorised under the last preceding section, or under any agreement made pursuant to that section, or by the mortgage deed (in this section referred to as an authorised lease) to be granted, a mortgagor of land while in possession shall, as against every incumbrancer, have, by virtue of this Act, power to accept from time to time a surrender of any lease of the mortgaged land or any part thereof comprised in the lease, with or without an exception of or in respect of all or any of the mines and minerals therein, and, on a surrender of the lease so far as it comprises part only of the land or mines and minerals leased, the rent may be apportioned.

100(2)   For the same purpose, a mortgagee of land while in possession shall, as against all prior or other incumbrancers, if any, and as against the mortgagor, have, by virtue of this Act, power to accept from time to time any such surrender as aforesaid.

100(3)   On a surrender of part only of the land or mines and minerals leased, the original lease may be varied, provided that the lease when varied would have been valid as an authorised lease if granted by the person accepting the surrender; and, on a surrender and the making of a new or other lease, whether for the same or for any extended or other term, and whether subject or not to the same or to any other covenants, provisions, or conditions, the value of the lessee's interest in the lease surrendered may, subject to the provisions of this section, be taken into account in the determination of the amount of the rent to be reserved, and of the nature of the covenants, provisions, and conditions to be inserted in the new or other lease.

100(4)   Where any consideration for the surrender, other than an agreement to accept an authorised lease, is given by or on behalf of the lessee to or on behalf of the person accepting the surrender, nothing in this section authorises a surrender to a mortgagor without the consent of the incumbrancers, or authorises a surrender to a second or subsequent incumbrancer without the consent of every prior incumbrancer.

100(5)   No surrender shall, by virtue of this section, be rendered valid unless–

(a)   An authorised lease is granted of the whole of the land or mines and minerals comprised in the surrender to take effect in possession immediately or within one month after the date of the surrender; and

(b)   The term certain or other interest granted by the new lease is not less in duration than the unexpired term or interest which would have been subsisting under the original lease if that lease had not been surrendered; and

(c)   Where the whole of the land mines and minerals originally leased has been surrendered, the rent reserved by the new lease is not less than the rent which would have been payable under the original lease if it had not been surrendered; or where part only of the land or mines and minerals has been surrendered, the aggregate rents respectively remaining payable or reserved under the original lease and new lease are not less than the rent which would have been payable under the original lease if no partial surrender had been accepted.

100(6)   A contract to make or accept a surrender under this section may be enforced by or against every person on whom the surrender, if completed, would be binding.

100(7)   This section applies only if and as far as a contrary intention is not expressed by the mortgagor and mortgagee in the mortgage deed, or otherwise in writing, and shall have effect subject to the terms of the mortgage deed or of any such writing and to the provisions therein contained.

100(8)   This section applies to a mortgage made after the thirty-first day of December, nineteen hundred and eleven, but the provisions of this section, or any of them, may, by agreement in writing made after that date, between mortgagor and mortgagee, be applied to a mortgage made before that date, so nevertheless that any such agreement shall not prejudicially affect any right or interest of any mortgagee not joining in or adopting the agreement.

100(9)   The provisions of this section referring to a lease shall be construed to extend and apply, as far as circumstances admit, to any letting, and to an agreement, whether in writing or not, for leasing or letting.

100(10) The mortgagor and mortgagee may, by agreement in writing, whether or not contained in the mortgage deed, reserve or confer on the mortgagor or mortgagee, or both, any further or other powers relating to the surrender of leases; and any further or other powers so conferred or reserved shall be exercisable, as far as may be, as if they were conferred by this Act, and with all the like incidents, effects and consequences:
   Provided that the powers so reserved or conferred shall not prejudicially affect the rights of any mortgagee interested under any other mortgage subsisting at the date of the agreement, unless that mortgagee joins in or adopts the agreement.

100(11)   Nothing in this section operates to enable a mortgagor or mortgagee to accept a surrender which could not have been accepted by the mortgagor with the concurrence of all the incumbrancers if this Act and the enactments replaced by this section had not been passed.

100(12)   For the purposes of this section "mortgagor" does not include an incumbrancer deriving title under the original mortgagor.

100(13)   The powers of accepting surrenders conferred by this section shall, after a receiver of the income of the mortgaged property or any part thereof has been appointed by the mortgagee, under the statutory power, and so long as the receiver acts, be exercisable by such mortgagee instead of by the mortgagor, as respects any land affected by the receivership, in like manner as if such mortgagee were in possession of the land; and the mortgagee may, by writing, delegate any of such powers to the receiver.

101   Powers incident to estate or interest of mortgagee

101(1)   A mortgagee, where the mortgage is made by deed, shall, by virtue of this Act, have the following powers, to the like extent as if they had been in terms conferred by the mortgage deed, but not further (namely):

(i)   A power, when the mortgage money has become due, to sell, or to concur with any other person in selling, the mortgaged property, or any part thereof, either subject to prior charges or not, and either together or in lots, by public auction or by private contract, subject to such conditions respecting title, or evidence of title, or other matter, as the mortgagee thinks fit, with power to vary any contract for sale, and to buy in at an auction, or to rescind any contract for sale, and to re-sell, without being answerable for any loss occasioned thereby; and

(ii)   A power, at any time after the date of the mortgage deed, to insure and keep insured against loss or damage by fire any building, or any effects or property of an insurable nature, whether affixed to the freehold or not, being or forming part of the property which or an estate or interest wherein is mortgaged, and the premiums paid for any such insurance shall be a charge on the mortgaged property or estate or interest, in addition to the mortgage money, and with the same priority, and with interest at the same rate, as the mortgage money; and

(iii)   A power, when the mortgage money has become due, to appoint a receiver of the income of the mortgaged property, or any part thereof; or, if the mortgaged property consists of an interest in income, or of a rentcharge or an annual or other periodical sum, a receiver of that property or any part thereof; and

(iv)   A power, while the mortgagee is in possession, to cut and sell timber and other trees ripe for cutting, and not planted or left standing for shelter or ornament, or to contract for any such cutting and sale, to be completed within any time not exceeding twelve months from the making of the contract.

101(1A)   Subsection (1)(i) is subject to section 21 of the Commonhold and Leasehold Reform Act 2002 (no disposition of part-units).

101(2)   Where the mortgage deed is executed after the thirty-first day of December, nineteen hundred and eleven, the power of sale aforesaid includes the following powers as incident thereto (namely)–

(i)   A power to impose or reserve or make binding, as far as the law permits, by covenant, condition, or otherwise, on the unsold part of the mortgaged property or any part thereof, or on the purchaser and any property sold, any restriction or reservation with respect to building on or other user of land, or with respect to mines and minerals, or for the purpose of the more beneficial working thereof, or with respect to any other thing:

(ii)   A power to sell the mortgaged property, or any part thereof, or all or any mines and minerals apart from the surface–

(a)   With or without a grant or reservation of rights of way, rights of water, easements, rights, and privileges for or connected with building or other purposes in relation to the property remaining in mortgage or any part thereof, or to any property sold: and

(b)   With or without an exception or reservation of all or any of the mines and minerals in or under the mortgaged property, and with or without a grant or reservation of powers of working, wayleaves, or rights of way, rights of water and drainage and other powers, easements, rights, and privileges for or connected with mining purposes in relation to the property remaining unsold or any part thereof, or to any property sold: and

(c)   With or without covenants by the purchaser to expend money on the land sold.

101(3)   The provisions of this Act relating to the foregoing powers, comprised either in this section, or in any other section regulating the exercise of those powers, may be varied or extended by the mortgage deed, and, as so varied or extended, shall, as far as may be, operate in the like manner and with all the like incidents, effects, and consequences, as if such variations or extensions were contained in this Act.

101(4)   This section applies only if and as far as a contrary intention is not expressed in the mortgage deed, and has effect subject to the terms of the mortgage deed and to the provisions therein contained.

101(5)   Save as otherwise provided, this section applies where the mortgage deed is executed after the thirty-first day of December, eighteen hundred and eighty-one.

101(6)   The power of sale conferred by this section includes such power of selling the estate in fee simple or any leasehold reversion as is conferred by the provisions of this Act relating to the realisation of mortgages.

102   Provision as to mortgages of undivided shares in land

102(1)   A person who was before the commencement of this Act a mortgagee of an undivided share in land shall have the same power to sell his interest under the trust to which the land is subject, as, independently of this Act, he would have had in regard to the share in the land; and shall also have a right to require the trustees in whom the land is vested to account to him for the income attributable to that share or to appoint a receiver to receive the same from such trustees corresponding to the right which, independently of this Act, he would have had to take possession or to appoint a receiver of the rents and profits attributable to the same share.

102(2)   The powers conferred by this section are exercisable by the persons deriving title under such mortgagee.

103   Regulation of exercise of power of sale

103   A mortgagee shall not exercise the power of sale conferred by this Act unless and until–

(i)   Notice requiring payment of the mortgage money has been served on the mortgagor or one of two or more mortgagors, and default has been made in payment of the mortgage money, or of part thereof, for three months after such service; or

(ii)   Some interest under the mortgage is in arrear and unpaid for two months after becoming due; or

(iii)   There has been a breach of some provision contained in the mortgage deed or in this Act, or in an enactment replaced by this Act, and on the part of the mortgagor, or of some person concurring in making the mortgage, to be observed or performed, other than and besides a covenant for payment of the mortgage money or interest thereon.

104   Conveyance on sale

104(1)   A mortgagee exercising the power of sale conferred by this Act shall have power, by deed, to convey the property sold, for such estate and interest therein as he is by this Act authorised to sell or convey or may be the subject of the mortgage, freed from all estates, interests, and rights to which the mortgage has priority, but subject to all estates, interests, and rights which have priority to the mortgage.

104(2)   Where a conveyance is made in exercise of the power of sale conferred by this Act, or any enactment replaced by this Act, the title of the purchaser shall not be impeachable on the ground–

(a)   that no case had arisen to authorise the sale; or

(b) that due notice was not given; or

(c) where the mortgage is made after the commencement of this Act, that leave of the court, when so required, was not obtained; or

(d) whether the mortgage was made before or after such commencement, that the power was otherwise improperly or irregularly exercised;

and a purchaser is not, either before or on conveyance, concerned to see or inquire whether a case has arisen to authorise the sale, or due notice has been given, or the power is otherwise properly and regularly exercised; but any person damnified by an unauthorised, or improper, or irregular exercise of the power shall have his remedy in damages against the person exercising the power.

104(3) A conveyance on sale by a mortgagee, made after the commencement of this Act, shall be deemed to have been made in exercise of the power of sale conferred by this Act unless a contrary intention appears.

105 Application of proceeds of sale

105 The money which is received by the mortgagee, arising from the sale, after discharge of prior incumbrances to which the sale is not made subject, if any, or after payment into court under this Act of a sum to meet any prior incumbrance, shall be held by him in trust to be applied by him, first, in payment of all costs, charges, and expenses properly incurred by him as incident to the sale or any attempted sale, or otherwise; and secondly, in discharge of the mortgage money, interest, and costs, and other money, if any, due under the mortgage; and the residue of the money so received shall be paid to the person entitled to the mortgaged property, or authorised to give receipts for the proceeds of the sale thereof.

106 Provisions as to exercise of power of sale

106(1) The power of sale conferred by this Act may be exercised by any person for the time being entitled to receive and give a discharge for the mortgage money.

106(2) The power of sale conferred by this Act does not affect the right of foreclosure.

106(3) The mortgagee shall not be answerable for any involuntary loss happening in or about the exercise or execution of the power of sale conferred by this Act, or of any trust connected therewith, or, where the mortgage is executed after the thirty-first day of December, nineteen hundred and eleven, of any power or provision contained in the mortgage deed.

106(4) At any time after the power of sale conferred by this Act has become exercisable, the person entitled to exercise the power may demand and recover from any person, other than a person having in the mortgaged property an estate, interest, or right in priority to the mortgage, all the deeds and documents relating to the property, or to the title thereto, which a purchaser under the power of sale would be entitled to demand and recover from him.

107 Mortgagee's receipts, discharges, etc.

107(1) The receipt in writing of a mortgagee shall be a sufficient discharge for any money arising under the power of sale conferred by this Act, or for any money or securities comprised in his mortgage, or arising thereunder; and a person paying or transferring the same to the mortgagee shall not be concerned to inquire whether any money remains due under the mortgage.

107(2) Money received by a mortgagee under his mortgage or from the proceeds of securities comprised in his mortgage shall be applied in like manner as in this Act directed respecting money received by him arising from a sale under the power of sale conferred by this Act, but with this variation, that the costs, charges, and expenses payable shall include the costs, charges, and expenses properly incurred of recovering and receiving the money or securities, and of conversion of securities into money, instead of those incident to sale.

108   Amount and application of insurance money

108(1)   The amount of an insurance effected by a mortgagee against loss or damage by fire under the power in that behalf conferred by this Act shall not exceed the amount specified in the mortgage deed, or, if no amount is therein specified, two third parts of the amount that would be required, in case of total destruction, to restore the property insured.

108(2)   An insurance shall not, under the power conferred by this Act, be effected by a mortgagee in any of the following cases (namely):

(i)   Where there is a declaration in the mortgage deed that no insurance is required:

(ii)   Where an insurance is kept up by or on behalf of the mortgagor in accordance with the mortgage deed:

(iii)   Where the mortgage deed contains no stipulation respecting insurance, and an insurance is kept up by or on behalf of the mortgagor with the consent of the mortgagee to the amount to which the mortgagee is by this Act authorised to insure.

108(3)   All money received on an insurance of mortgaged property against loss or damage by fire or otherwise effected under this Act, or any enactment replaced by this Act, or on an insurance for the maintenance of which the mortgagor is liable under the mortgage deed, shall, if the mortgagee so requires, be applied by the mortgagor in making good the loss or damage in respect of which the money is received.

108(4)   Without prejudice to any obligation to the contrary imposed by law, or by special contract, a mortgagee may require that all money received on an insurance of mortgaged property against loss or damage by fire or otherwise effected under this Act, or any enactment replaced by this Act, or on an insurance for the maintenance of which the mortgagor is liable under the mortgage deed, be applied in or towards the discharge of the mortgage money.

109   Appointment, powers, remuneration and duties of receiver

109(1)   A mortgagee entitled to appoint a receiver under the power in that behalf conferred by this Act shall not appoint a receiver until he has become entitled to exercise the power of sale conferred by this Act, but may then, by writing under his hand, appoint such person as he thinks fit to be receiver.

109(2)   A receiver appointed under the powers conferred by this Act, or any enactment replaced by this Act, shall be deemed to be the agent of the mortgagor; and the mortgagor shall be solely responsible for the receiver's acts or defaults unless the mortgage deed otherwise provides.

109(3)   The receiver shall have power to demand and recover all the income of which he is appointed receiver, by action, or under section 72(1) of the Tribunals, Courts and Enforcement Act 2007 (commercial rent arrears recovery), or otherwise, in the name either of the mortgagor or of the mortgagee, to the full extent of the estate or interest which the mortgagor could dispose of, and to give effectual receipts accordingly for the same, and to exercise any powers which may have been delegated to him by the mortgagee pursuant to this Act.

109(4)   A person paying money to the receiver shall not be concerned to inquire whether any case has happened to authorise the receiver to act.

109(5)   The receiver may be removed, and a new receiver may be appointed, from time to time by the mortgagee by writing under his hand.

109(6)   The receiver shall be entitled to retain out of any money received by him, for his remuneration, and in satisfaction of all costs, charges, and expenses incurred by him as receiver, a commission at such rate, not exceeding five per centum on the gross amount of all money received, as is specified in his appointment, and if no rate is so specified, then at the rate of five per centum on that gross amount, or at such other rate as the court thinks fit to allow, on application made by him for that purpose.

109(7)   The receiver shall, if so directed in writing by the mortgagee, insure to the extent, if any, to which the mortgagee might have insured and keep insured against loss or damage by fire, out of the money received by him, any building, effects, or property comprised in the mortgage, whether affixed to the freehold or not, being of an insurable nature.

109(8)   Subject to the provisions of this Act as to the application of insurance money, the receiver shall apply all money received by him as follows, namely:

(i)   In discharge of all rents, taxes, rates, and outgoings whatever affecting the mortgaged property; and

(ii)   In keeping down all annual sums or other payments, and the interest on all principal sums, having priority to the mortgage in right where of he is receiver; and

(iii)   In payment of his commission, and of the premiums on fire, life, or other insurances, if any, properly payable under the mortgage deed or under this Act, and the cost of executing necessary or proper repairs directed in writing by the mortgagee; and

(iv)   In payment of the interest accruing due in respect of any principal money due under the mortgage; and

(v)   In or towards discharge of the principal money if so directed in writing by the mortgagee;

and shall pay the residue, if any, of the money received by him to the person who, but for the possession of the receiver, would have been entitled to receive the income of which he is appointed receiver, or who is otherwise entitled to the mortgaged property.

History
Section 109(3) amended by the Tribunals, Courts and Enforcement Act 2007 s.86, Sch.14 para.22 as from 6 April 2014.

110   Effect of bankruptcy of the mortgagor on the power to sell or appoint a receiver

110(1)   Where the statutory or express power for a mortgagee either to sell or to appoint a receiver is made exercisable by reason of the mortgagor being adjudged a bankrupt, such power shall not be exercised only on account of the adjudication, without the leave of the court.

110(2)   This section applies only where the mortgage deed is executed after the commencement of this Act.

Administration of Justice Act 1970

(1970 Chapter 31)

An Act to make further provision about the courts (including assizes), their business, jurisdiction and procedure; to enable a High Court judge to accept appointment as arbitrator or umpire under an arbitration agreement; to amend the law respecting the enforcement of debt and other liabilities; to amend section 106 of the Rent Act 1968; and for miscellaneous purposes connected with the administration of justice.

[29th May 1970]

[**Note**: Changes made by the Social Security Act 1973, the Consumer Credit Act 1974, the Social Security Pensions Act 1975, the Social Security (Consequential Provisions) Acts 1975 and 1992, the Magistrates' Courts Act 1980, and the Pension Schemes Act 1993 have been incorporated into the text without annotation.]

PART II

ENFORCEMENT OF DEBT

Provisions restricting sanction of imprisonment

11   Restriction on power of committal under Debtors Act

11   The jurisdiction given by section 5 of the Debtors Act 1869 to commit to prison a person who makes default in payment of a debt, or instalment of a debt, due from him in pursuance of an order or judgment shall be exercisable only–

(a)   by the High Court in respect of a High Court maintenance order; and

(b)   by the county court in respect of a judgment or order which is enforceable by a court in England and Wales and is for the payment of any of the taxes, contributions or liabilities specified in Schedule 4 to this Act; and

(c)   by the family court in respect of a High Court or family court maintenance order.

[**Note**: A prospective amendment to be made by the Social Security Act 1973 s.100 and Sch.27 para.85 from a day to be appointed is now considered unlikely to be brought into force.]

PART IV

ACTIONS BY MORTGAGEES FOR POSSESSION

36   Additional powers of court in action by mortgagee for possession of dwelling-house

36(1)   Where the mortgagee under a mortgage of land which consists of or includes a dwelling-house brings an action in which he claims possession of the mortgaged property, not being an action for foreclosure in which a claim for possession of the mortgaged property is also made, the court may exercise any of the powers conferred on it by subsection (2) below if it appears to the court that in the event of its exercising the power the mortgagor is likely to be able within a reasonable period to pay any sums due under the mortgage or to remedy a default consisting of a breach of any other obligation arising under or by virtue of the mortgage.

36(2)   The court–

(a)   may adjourn the proceedings, or

(b)   on giving judgment, or making an order, for delivery of possession of the mortgaged property, or at any time before the execution of such judgment or order, may–

(i)   stay or suspend execution of the judgment or order, or

(ii)   postpone the date for delivery of possession,

for such period or periods as the court thinks reasonable.

36(3)   Any such adjournment, stay, suspension or postponement as is referred to in subsection (2) above may be made subject to such conditions with regard to payment by the mortgagor of any sum secured by the mortgage or the remedying of any default as the court thinks fit.

36(4)   The court may from time to time vary or revoke any condition imposed by virtue of this section.

36(5)   [Repealed by the Statute Law (Repeals) Act 2004 Sch.1 Pt 12, as from 22 July 2004.]

36(6)   In the application of this section to Northern Ireland, "the court" means a judge of the High Court in Northern Ireland, and in subsection (1) the words from "not being" to "made" shall be omitted.

37, 38   [Repealed by the County Courts Act 1984 s.148(3) and Sch.4.]

38A   This Part of this Act shall not apply to a mortgage securing an agreement which is a regulated agreement within the meaning of the Consumer Credit Act 1974.

39   Interpretation of Part IV

39(1)   In this Part of this Act–

"dwelling-house" includes any building or part thereof which is used as a dwelling;

"mortgage" includes a charge and "mortgagor" and "mortgagee" shall be construed accordingly;

"mortgagor" and "mortgagee" includes any person deriving title under the original mortgagor or mortgagee.

39(2)   The fact that part of the premises comprised in a dwelling-house is used as a shop or office or for business, trade or professional purposes shall not prevent the dwelling-house from being a dwelling-house for the purposes of this Part of this Act.

SCHEDULE 4

TAXES, SOCIAL INSURANCE CONTRIBUTIONS, ETC SUBJECT TO SPECIAL
ENFORCEMENT PROVISIONS IN PART II

Sections 11, 12, 14

1 Income tax or any other tax or liability recoverable under section 65, 66 or 68 of the Taxes Management Act 1970.

2 [Repealed by the Statute Law Repeals Act 1989.]

3 Contributions equivalent premiums under Part III of the Pension Schemes Act 1993.

3A Class 1, 2 and 4 contributions under Part I of the Social Security Contributions and Benefits Act 1992.

4 [Repealed by the Social Security Act 1973 s.100 and Sch.28 Pt I.]

Attachment of Earnings Act 1971

(1971 Chapter 32)

An Act to consolidate the enactments relating to the attachment of earnings as a means of enforcing the discharge of monetary obligations.

[12th May 1971]

[Note: Changes made by the Social Security Act 1973, the Social Security Pensions Act 1975, the Insolvency Act 1976, the Administration of Justice Act 1977, the Merchant Shipping Acts 1979 and 1995, the Magistrates' Courts Act 1980, the Contempt of Court Act 1981, the Criminal Justice Acts 1982 and 1991, the Administration of Justice Act 1982, the County Courts Act 1984, the Social Security Act 1985, the Courts and Legal Services Act 1990, the Maintenance Enforcement Act 1991, the Attachment of Earnings (Employer's Deduction) Order 1991 (SI 1991/356), the Transfer of Functions (Science) Order 1992 (SI 1992/1296), the Pension Schemes Act 1993, the Transfer of Functions (Science) Order 1995 (SI 1995/2985), the Reserve Forces Act 1998 (Consequential Provisions, etc.) Regulations 1998 (SI 1998/3086), the Access to Justice Act 1999, the Tax Credits Act 2002, the Civil Partnership Act 2004, the Criminal Defence Service Act 2006, the Collection of Fines (Final Scheme) Order 2006 (SI 2006/1737), the Civil Jurisdiction and Judgments (Maintenance) Regulations 2011 (SI 2011/1484), the Legal Aid, Sentencing and Punishment of Offenders Act 2012 Sch.5 para.6, the Crime and Courts Act 2013 and the Crime and Courts Act 2013 (Family Court: Consequential Provision) Order 2014 (SI 2014/605) have been incorporated into the text (in the case of pre-2003 legislation without annotation). Minor changes consequential upon the establishment of the single county court have been made without annotation. (See also history note to s.1). References to "justices' clerks" have been changed to "designated officers" (formerly "justices' chief executives") and other corresponding changes have been made pursuant to the Access to Justice Act 1999 s.90(1) and Sch.13 paras 64 et seq., as from 1 April 2001, and the Courts Act 2003 s.109(1) and Sch.8 paras 141 et seq., as from 1 September 2004. The government has announced that the prospective amendment of this Act to be effected by TCEA 2007 ss.91, 92 and Sch.15 will not now be brought into force.]

Cases in which attachment is available

1 Courts with power to attach earnings

1(1) The High Court may make an attachment of earnings order to secure payments under a High Court maintenance order.

1(1A) The family court may make an attachment of earnings order to secure payments under a High Court or family court maintenance order.

1(2) The county court may make an attachment of earnings order to secure–

(a) ...

(b) the payment of a judgment debt, other than a debt of less than £5 or such other sum as may be prescribed by rules of court; or

(c) payments under an administration order.

1(3) A magistrates' court may make an attachment of earnings order to secure–

(a) ...

(b) ...

(c) the payment of any sum required to be paid under regulations under section 23 or 24 of the Legal Aid, Sentencing and Punishment of Offenders Act 2012.

1(4) ...

1(5) Any power conferred by this Act to make an attachment of earnings order includes a power to make such an order to secure the discharge of liabilities arising before the coming into force of this Act.

History
Subsection (1)(3)(c) amended by the Criminal Defence Service Act 2006 s.4(1), as from 2 October 2006. Subsections (3)(b) and (4) omitted by the Collection of Fines (Final Scheme) Order 2006 (SI 2006/1737) arts 34, 35 as from 3 July 2006. Previously, these and other similar amendments to the Act (noted below) had been made by the Collection of Fines (Pilot Scheme) and Discharge of Fines by Unpaid Work (Pilot Schemes) (Amendment) Order 2006 (SI 2006/502) art.6, as from 27 March 2006 (one of several schemes for piloting the provisions of Sch.5 (collection of fines) to the Courts Act 2003). Section 1(3)(c) amended by the Legal Aid, Sentencing and Punishment of Offenders Act 2012 Sch.5 para.6 as from 1 April 2013. Section 1(2)(a), 1(3)(a) deleted and s.1(1A) inserted by the Crime and Courts Act 2013 Sch.10 para.21(2)–(4) as from 22 April 2014.

1A Orders to which this Act applies

1A The following provisions of this Act apply, except where otherwise stated, to attachment of earnings orders made, or to be made, by any court under this Act or under Schedule 5 to the Courts Act 2003, or by a fines officer under that Schedule.

2 Principal definitions

2 In this Act–

(a) "maintenance order" means any order, decision, settlement, arrangement or instrument specified in Schedule 1 to this Act and includes one which has been discharged or has otherwise ceased to operate if any arrears are recoverable thereunder;

(b) "High Court maintenance order" and "family court maintenance order" mean respectively a maintenance order enforceable by the High Court and the family court;

(c) "judgment debt" means a sum payable under–

    (i) a judgment or order enforceable by a court in England and Wales (not being a magistrates' court);

    (ii) an order of a magistrates' court for the payment of money recoverable summarily as a civil debt; or

    (iii) an order of any court which is enforceable as if it were for the payment of money so recoverable,

but does not include any sum payable under a maintenance order or an administration order;

(d) "the relevant adjudication", in relation to any payment secured or to be secured by an attachment of earnings order, means the conviction, judgment, order or other adjudication from which there arises the liability to make the payment; and

(e) "the debtor", in relation to an attachment of earnings order, or to proceedings in which a court has power to make an attachment of earnings order, or to proceedings arising out of such an order, means the person by whom payment is required by the relevant adjudication to be made.

History
Definition of "maintenance order" in subs.2(b) amended by the Civil Jurisdiction and Judgments (Maintenance) Regulations 2011 (SI 2011/1484) Sch.7 para.4(2) as from 18 June 2011 and by the International Recovery of Maintenance (Hague Convention 2007 etc.) Regulations 2012 (SI 2012/2814) Sch.4 para.3(1), (2) as from 1 August 2014. Section 2(b) amended by the Crime and Courts Act 2013 Sch.10 para.22 as from 22 April 2014.

3 Application for order and conditions of court's power to make it

3(A1) This section shall not apply to an attachment of earnings order to be made under Schedule 5 to the Courts Act 2003.

3(1) The following persons may apply for an attachment of earnings order–

(a) the person to whom payment under the relevant adjudication is required to be made (whether directly or through any court or an officer of any court);

(b) where the relevant adjudication is an administration order, any one of the creditors scheduled to the order;

(c) without prejudice to paragraph (a), an officer of the family court if the application is to the family court for an order to secure maintenance payments and there is in force an order that those payments be made to the court or an officer of the court;

(ca) without prejudice to paragraphs (a) and (c) above, an officer of the family court if the application is to the family court to secure payments under a maintenance order described in paragraphs 13, 14, 14A or 14B of Schedule 1 and those payments are to be made to the court;

(d) in the following cases the debtor–

    (i) where the application is to a magistrates' court; or

    (ii) where the application is to the High Court or the family court for an order to secure maintenance payments.

3(2) [Repealed by the Maintenance Enforcement Act 1991 s.11 and Sch.2 para.1 and Sch.3.]

3(3)   Subject to subsection (3A) below for an attachment of earnings order to be made on the application of any person other than the debtor it must appear to the court that the debtor has failed to make one or more payments required by the relevant adjudication.

3(3A)   Subsection (3) above shall not apply where the relevant adjudication is a maintenance order.

3(3B)   ...

3(3C)   ...

3(4)   Where proceedings are brought–

(a)   in the High Court or the family court for the enforcement of a maintenance order by committal under section 5 of the Debtors Act 1869;

(b)   ...

then the court may make an attachment of earnings order to secure payments under the maintenance order, instead of dealing with the case under section 5 of the said Act of 1869.

3(5)   [Repealed by the Maintenance Enforcement Act 1991 s.11 and Sch.2 para.1 and Sch.3.]

3(6)   Where proceedings are brought in the county court for an order of committal under section 5 of the Debtors Act 1869 in respect of a judgment debt for any of the taxes, contributions premiums or liabilities specified in Schedule 2 to this Act, the court may, in any circumstances in which it has power to make such an order, make instead an attachment of earnings order to secure the payment of the judgment debt.

3(7)   The county court shall not make an attachment of earnings order to secure the payment of a judgment debt if there is in force an order or warrant for the debtor's committal, under section 5 of the Debtors Act 1869, in respect of that debt; but in any such case the court may discharge the order or warrant with a view to making an attachment of earnings order instead.

History
Subsection (1)(ca) inserted by the International Recovery of Maintenance (Hague Convention 2007 etc.) Regulations 2012 (SI 2012/2814) Sch.4 para.3(1), (3) as from 1 August 2014. Subsection (A1) inserted, and subss.(3A) and (3B) omitted, by the Collection of Fines (Final Scheme) Order 2006 (SI 2006/1737) arts 34, 37, as from 3 July 2006. (See also History note to s.1.) Previously, subss.(3B) and (3C) inserted by the Criminal Procedure and Investigations Act 1996 s.33, as regards fines imposed and compensation orders made on convictions for offences committed on or after 1 October 1996; and s.3(3C)(a) modified by the Powers of Criminal Courts (Sentencing) Act 2000 s.165(1) and Sch.9 para.44 as from 25 August 2000. Section 3(1), (4) amended by the Crime and Courts Act 2013 Sch.10 para.23(2)–(5) as from 22 April 2014.
  Prospective amendment to subs.(6) made by the Social Security Act 1973 s.100 and Sch.27 Pt I para.88 is now considered unlikely to be brought into force.

Administration orders in the county court

4   Extension of power to make administration order

4(1)   Where, on an application to the county court for an attachment of earnings order to secure the payment of a judgment debt, it appears to the court that the debtor also has other debts, the court–

(a)   shall consider whether the case may be one in which all the debtor's liabilities should be dealt with together and that for that purpose an administration order should be made; and

(b)   if of opinion that it may be such a case, shall have power (whether or not it makes the attachment of earnings order applied for), with a view to making an administration order, to order the debtor to furnish to the court a list of all his creditors and the amounts which he owes to them respectively.

4(2)   If, on receipt of the list referred to in subsection (1)(b) above, it appears to the court that the debtor's whole indebtedness amounts to not more than the amount which for the time being is the county court limit for the purposes of section 112 of the County Courts Act 1984 (limit of total indebtedness governing county court's power to make administration order on application of debtor), the court may make such an order in respect of the debtor's estate.

4(2A) Subsection (2) above is subject to section 112(3) and (4) of the County Courts Act 1984 (which require that, before an administration order is made, notice is to be given to all the creditors and thereafter restricts the right of any creditor to institute bankruptcy proceedings).

4(3) [Repealed by the Insolvency Act 1976 ss.13(1), 14(4) and Sch.3.]

4(4) Nothing in this section is to be taken as prejudicing any right of a debtor to apply, under section 112 of the County Courts Act 1984 for an administration order.

5 Attachment of earnings to secure payments under administration order

5(1) Where the county court makes an administration order in respect of a debtor's estate, it may also make an attachment of earnings order to secure the payments required by the administration order.

5(2) At any time when an administration order is in force the county court may (with or without an application) make an attachment of earnings order to secure the payments required by the administration order, if it appears to the court that the debtor has failed to make any such payment.

5(3) The power of the county court under this section to make an attachment of earnings order to secure the payments required by an administration order shall, where the debtor is already subject to an attachment of earnings order to secure the payment of a judgment debt, include power to direct that the last-mentioned order shall take effect (with or without variation under section 9 of this Act) as an order to secure the payments required by the administration order.

Consequences of attachment order

6 Effect and contents of order

6(1) An attachment of earnings order shall be an order directed to a person who appears to the court, or as the case may be the fines officer, making the order to have the debtor in his employment and shall operate as an instruction to that person–

(a) to make periodical deductions from the debtor's earnings in accordance with Part I of Schedule 3 to this Act; and

(b) at such times as the order may require, or as the court, or where the order is made under Schedule 5 to the Courts Act 2003, as the court or the fines officer as the case may be, may allow, to pay the amounts deducted to the collecting officer of the court, as specified in the order.

6(2) For the purposes of this Act, the relationship of employer and employee shall be treated as subsisting between two persons if one of them as a principal and not as a servant or agent, pays to the other any sums defined as earnings by section 24 of this Act.

6(3) An attachment of earnings order shall contain prescribed particulars enabling the debtor to be identified by the employer.

6(4) Except where it is made to secure maintenance payments, the order shall specify the whole amount payable under the relevant adjudication (or so much of that amount as remains unpaid), including any relevant costs.

6(5) Subject to subsection (5A) below, the order shall specify–

(a) the normal deduction rate, that is to say, the rate (expressed as a sum of money per week, month or other period) at which the court thinks it reasonable for the debtor's earnings to be applied to meeting his liability under the relevant adjudication; and

   (b)   the protected earnings rate, that is to say the rate (so expressed) below which, having regard to the debtor's resources and needs, the court thinks it reasonable that the earnings actually paid to him should not be reduced.

6(5A)   If the order is made under Schedule 5 to the Courts Act 2003 then it shall specify the percentage deduction rate in accordance with fines collection regulations made under that Schedule.

6(6)   In the case of an order made to secure payments under a maintenance order (not being an order for the payment of a lump sum), the normal deduction rate–

   (a)   shall be determined after taking account of any right or liability of the debtor to deduct income tax when making the payments; and

   (b)   shall not exceed the rate which appears to the court necessary for the purpose of–

      (i)   securing payment of the sums falling due from time to time under the maintenance order, and

      (ii)   securing payment within a reasonable period of any sums already due and unpaid under the maintenance order.

6(7)   For the purposes of an attachment of earnings order, the collecting officer of the court shall be (subject to later variation of the order under section 9 of this Act)–

   (a)   in the case of an order made by the High Court, either–

      (i)   the proper officer of the High Court, or

      (ii)   the appropriate officer of the family court or the county court if the order so specifies;

   (aa)   in the case of an order made by the family court, the appropriate officer of that court;

   (b)   in the case of an order made by the county court, the appropriate officer of that court; and

   (c)   in the case of an order made by a magistrates' court, the designated officer for that court or for another magistrates' court specified in the order.

6(8)   In subsection (7) above "appropriate officer" means an officer designated by the Lord Chancellor.

History
Subsection (5A) inserted, and subss.(1) and (5) amended, by the Collection of Fines (Final Scheme) Order 2006 (SI 2006/1737) arts 34, 38, as from 3 July 2006. (See also history note to s.1.) Section 6(7)(a) amended and s.6(7)(aa) inserted by the Crime and Courts Act 2013 Sch.9 para.25(4) and Sch.10 para.24(b) as from 22 April 2014.
   Prospective amendment, inserting new s.6(9)–(12), by the Courts and Legal Services Act 1990 s.125(2) and Sch.17 para.5 from a day to be appointed, has not yet been brought into force.

7 Compliance with order by employer

7(1)   Where an attachment of earnings order has been made, the employer shall, if he has been served with the order, comply with it; but he shall be under no liability for non-compliance before seven days have elapsed since the service.

7(2)   Where a person is served with an attachment of earnings order directed to him and he has not the debtor in his employment, or the debtor subsequently ceases to be in his employment, he shall (in either case), within ten days from the date of service or, as the case may be, the cesser, give notice of that fact to the court.

7(3)   Part II of Schedule 3 to this Act shall have effect with respect to the priority to be accorded as between two or more attachment of earnings orders directed to a person in respect of the same debtor.

7(4)   On any occasion when the employer makes, in compliance with the order, a deduction from the debtor's earnings–

(a)   he shall be entitled to deduct, in addition, £1.00, or such other sum as may be prescribed by order made by the Lord Chancellor, towards his clerical and administrative costs; and

(b)   he shall give to the debtor a statement in writing of the total amount of the deduction.

7(5)   An order of the Lord Chancellor under subsection (4)(a) above–

(a)   may prescribe different sums in relation to different classes of cases;

(b)   may be varied or revoked by a subsequent order made under that paragraph; and

(c)   shall be made by statutory instrument subject to annulment by resolution of either House of Parliament.

8   Interrelation with alternative remedies open to creditor

8(1)   Where an attachment of earnings order has been made to secure maintenance payments, no order or warrant of commitment shall be issued in consequence of any proceedings for the enforcement of the related maintenance order begun before the making of the attachment of earnings order.

8(2)   Where the county court has made an attachment of earnings order to secure the payment of a judgment debt–

(a)   no order or warrant of commitment shall be issued in consequence of any proceedings for the enforcement of the debt begun before the making of the attachment of earnings order; and

(b)   so long as the order is in force, no execution for the recovery of the debt shall issue against any property of the debtor without the leave of the county court.

8(3)   An attachment of earnings order made to secure maintenance payments shall cease to have effect upon the making of an order of commitment or the issue of a warrant of commitment for the enforcement of the related maintenance order.

8(4)   An attachment of earnings order made to secure the payment of a judgment debt shall cease to have effect on the making of an order of commitment or the issue of a warrant of commitment for the enforcement of the debt.

8(5)   An attachment of earnings order made to secure–

(a)   any payment mentioned in section 1(3)(c) of this Act; or

(b)   the payment of any sum mentioned in paragraph 1 of Schedule 5 to the Courts Act 2003,

shall cease to have effect on the issue of a warrant committing the debtor to prison for default in making that payment.

History
Subsection (5) substituted by the Collection of Fines (Final Scheme) Order 2006 (SI 2006/1737) arts 34, 39, as from 3 July 2006. (See also history note to s.1.) Section 8(3) amended by the Crime and Courts Act 2013 Sch.10 para.25 as from 22 April 2014.

Subsequent proceedings

9   Variation, lapse and discharge of orders

9(1)   The court, or where an attachment of earnings order is made under Schedule 5 to the Courts Act 2003, the court or the fines officer as the case may be, may make an order discharging or varying an attachment of earnings order.

9(2)   Where an order is varied, the employer shall, if he has been served with notice of the variation, comply with the order as varied; but he shall be under no liability for non-compliance before seven days have elapsed since the service.

9(3)   Rules of court may make provision–

(a)   as to the circumstances in which an attachment of earnings order made under this Act may be varied or discharged by the court of its own motion;

(aa) as to the circumstances in which an attachment of earnings order made under Schedule 5 to the Courts Act 2003 may be varied or discharged by the court or the fines officer of its or his own motion;

(b)   in the case of an attachment of earnings order made by a magistrates' court, for enabling a single justice, on an application made by the debtor on the ground of a material change in his resources and needs since the order was made or last varied, to vary the order for a period of not more than four weeks by an increase of the protected earnings rate.

9(4)   Where an attachment of earnings order has been made and the person to whom it is directed ceases to have the debtor in his employment, the order shall lapse (except as respects deduction from earnings paid after the cesser and payment to the collecting officer of amounts deducted at any time) and be of no effect unless and until the court, or where the order was made under Schedule 5 to the Courts Act 2003, unless and until the court or the fines officer as the case may be, again directs it to a person (whether the same as before or another) who appears to the court or the fines officer (as the case may be) to have the debtor in his employment.

9(5)   The lapse of an order under subsection (4) above shall not prevent its being treated as remaining in force for other purposes.

History
Subparagraph (3)(ii)(aa) inserted, and subsections (1), (3) and (4) amended, by the Collection of Fines (Final Scheme) Order 2006 (SI 2006/1737) arts 34, 40, as from 3 July 2006. (See also history note to s.1.)

10   Normal deduction rate to be reduced in certain cases

10(1)   The following provisions shall have effect, in the case of an attachment of earnings order made to secure maintenance payments, where it appears to the collecting officer of the court that–

(a)   the aggregate of the payments made for the purposes of the related maintenance order by the debtor (whether under the attachment of earnings order or otherwise) exceeds the aggregate of the payments required up to that time by the maintenance order; and

(b)   the normal deduction rate specified by the attachment of earnings order (or, where two or more such orders are in force in relation to the maintenance order, the aggregate of the normal deduction rates specified by those orders) exceeds the rate of payments required by the maintenance order; and

(c)   no proceedings for the variation or discharge of the attachment of earnings order are pending.

10(2)   In the case of an order made by the High Court or the family court, the collecting officer shall give the prescribed notice to the person to whom he is required to pay sums received under the attachment of earnings order, and to the debtor; and the court shall make the appropriate variation order, unless the debtor requests it to discharge the attachment of earnings order, or to vary it in some other way, and the court thinks fit to comply with the request.

10(3)   ...

10(4)   In this section, "the appropriate variation order" means an order varying the attachment of earnings order in question by reducing the normal deduction rate specified thereby so as to secure that that rate (or, in the case mentioned in subsection (1)(b) above, the aggregate of the rates therein mentioned)–

(a)   is the same as the rate of payments required by the maintenance order; or

(b) is such lower rate as the court thinks fit having regard to the amount of the excess mentioned in subsection (1)(a).

History
Section 10(2) amended and s.10(3) omitted by the Crime and Courts Act 2013 Sch.10 para.26 as from 22 April 2014.

11 Attachment order in respect of maintenance payments to cease to have effect on the occurrence of certain events

11(1) An attachment of earnings order made to secure maintenance payments shall cease to have effect–

(a) upon the grant of an application for registration of the related maintenance order under section 2 of the Maintenance Orders Act 1958 (which provides for the registration in the family court of a High Court maintenance order);

(b) where the related maintenance order is registered under Part I of the said Act of 1958, upon the giving of notice with respect thereto under section 5 of that Act (notice with view to cancellation of registration);

(c) subject to subsection (3) below, upon the discharge of the related maintenance order while it is not registered under Part I of the said Act of 1958;

(d) upon the related maintenance order ceasing to be registered in a court in England or Wales, or becoming registered in a court in Scotland or Northern Ireland, under Part II of the Maintenance Orders Act 1950.

11(2) Subsection (1)(a) above shall have effect, in the case of an application for registration under section 2(1) of the said Act of 1958, notwithstanding that the grant of the application may subsequently become void under subsection (2) of that section.

11(3) Where the related maintenance order is discharged as mentioned in subsection (1)(c) above and it appears to the court discharging the order that arrears thereunder will remain to be recovered after the discharge, that court may, if it thinks fit, direct that subsection (1) shall not apply.

History
Section 11(1)(a) amended by the Crime and Courts Act 2013 Sch.10 para.27 as from 22 April 2014.

12 Termination of employer's liability to make deductions

12(1) Where an attachment of earnings order ceases to have effect under section 8 or 11 of this Act, the proper officer of the prescribed court shall give notice of the cesser to the person to whom the order was directed.

12(2) Where, in the case of an attachment of earnings order made otherwise than to secure maintenance payments, the whole amount payable under the relevant adjudication has been paid, and also any relevant costs, the court shall give notice to the employer that no further compliance with the order is required.

12(3) Where an attachment of earnings order–

(a) ceases to have effect under section 8 or 11 of this Act; or

(b) is discharged under section 9,

the person to whom the order has been directed shall be under no liability in consequence of his treating the order as still in force at any time before the expiration of seven days from the date on which the notice required by subsection (1) above or, as the case may be, a copy of the discharging order is served on him.

Administrative provisions

13   Application of sums received by collecting officer

13(1)   Subject to subsection (3) below, the collecting officer to whom a person makes payments in compliance with an attachment of earnings order shall, after deducting such court fees, if any, in respect of proceedings for or arising out of the order, as are deductible from those payments, deal with the sums paid in the same way as he would if they had been paid by the debtor to satisfy the relevant adjudication.

13(2)   Any sums paid to the collecting officer under an attachment of earnings order made to secure maintenance payments shall, when paid to the person entitled to receive those payments, be deemed to be payments made by the debtor (with such deductions, if any, in respect of income tax as the debtor is entitled or required to make) so as to discharge–

(a)   first, any sums for the time being due and unpaid under the related maintenance order (a sum due at an earlier date being discharged before a sum due at a later date); and

(b)   secondly, any costs incurred in proceedings relating to the related maintenance order which were payable by the debtor when the attachment of earnings order was made or last varied.

13(3)   Where the county court makes an attachment of earnings order to secure the payment of a judgment debt and also, under section 4(1) of this Act, orders the debtor to furnish to the court a list of all his creditors, sums paid to the collecting officer in compliance with the attachment of earnings order shall not be dealt with by him as mentioned in subsection (1) above, but shall be retained by him pending the decision of the court whether or not to make an administration order and shall then be dealt with by him as the court may direct.

14   Power of court to obtain statements of earnings etc.

14(1)   Where in any proceedings a court has power under this Act or under Schedule 5 to the Courts Act 2003, or a fines officer has power under that Schedule, to make an attachment of earnings order, the court or the fines officer, as the case may be, may–

(a)   order the debtor to give to the court or the fines officer, as the case may be, within a specified period, a statement signed by him of–

(i)   the name and address of any person by whom earnings are paid to him;

(ii)   specified particulars as to his earnings and anticipated earnings, and as to his resources and needs; and

(iii)   specified particulars for the purpose of enabling the debtor to be identified by any employer of his;

(b)   order any person appearing to the court or the fines officer, as the case may be, to have the debtor in his employment to give to the court, or the fines officer, as the case may be, within a specified period, a statement signed by him or on his behalf of specified particulars of the debtor's earnings and anticipated earnings.

14(2)   Where an attachment of earnings order has been made, the court or the fines officer, as the case may be, may at any time thereafter while the order is in force

(a)   make such an order as is described in subsection (1)(a) or (b) above; and

(b)   order the debtor to attend before the court on a day and at a time specified in the order to give the information described in subsection (1)(a) above.

14(3)   In the case of an application to a magistrates' court for an attachment of earnings order, or for the variation or discharge of such an order, the power to make an order under subsection (1) or (2) above shall be exercisable also, before the hearing of the application, by a single justice.

14(4)   Without prejudice to subsections (1) to (3) above, rules of court may provide that where notice of an application for an attachment of earnings order is served on the debtor, it shall include a requirement that he shall give to the court, within such period and in such manner as may be prescribed, a statement in writing of the matters specified in subsection (1)(a) above and of any other prescribed matters which are, or may be, relevant under section 6 of this Act to the determination of the normal deduction rate and the protected earnings rate to be specified in any order made on the application. This subsection does not apply to an attachment of earnings order to be made under Schedule 5 to the Courts Act 2003.

14(5)   In any proceedings in which a court has power under this Act or under Schedule 5 to the Courts Act 2003, or a fines officer has power under that Schedule, to make an attachment of earnings order, and in any proceedings for the making, variation or discharge of such an order, a document purporting to be a statement given to the court or the fines officer, as the case may be, in compliance with an order under subsection (1)(a) or (b) above, or with any such requirement of a notice of application for an attachment of earnings order as is mentioned in subsection (4) above, shall, in the absence of proof to the contrary, be deemed to be a statement so given and shall be evidence of the facts stated therein.

Note
Subsections (1), (2), (4), (5) amended by the Collection of Fines (Final Scheme) Order 2006 (SI 2006/1737) arts 34, 41, as from 3 July 2006. (See also history note to s.1.)

15   Obligation of debtor and his employers to notify changes of employment and earnings

15(1)   While an attachment of earnings order is in force–

(a)   the debtor shall from time to time notify the court in writing of every occasion on which he leaves any employment, or becomes employed or re-employed, not later (in each case) than seven days from the date on which he did so;

(b)   the debtor shall, on any occasion when he becomes employed or re-employed, include in his notification under paragraph (a) above particulars of his earnings and anticipated earnings from the relevant employment; and

(c)   any person who becomes the debtor's employer and knows that the order is in force and by, or (if the order was made by a fines officer) for, which court it was made shall, within seven days of his becoming the debtor's employer or of acquiring that knowledge (whichever is the later) notify that court in writing that he is the debtor's employer, and include in his notification a statement of the debtor's earnings and anticipated earnings.

15(2)   In the case of an attachment of earnings order made by a fines officer, the reference to "the court" in subsection (1)(a) above shall mean the court for which that order was made.

Note
Subsection (1) amended, and subsection (2) inserted, by the Collection of Fines (Final Scheme) Order 2006 (SI 2006/1737) arts 34, 42, as from 3 July 2006. (See also history note to s.1.)
   Note prospective insertion of ss.15A–15D by the Tribunals, Courts and Enforcement Act 2007 s.9(2), and prospective insertion of s.15D(2A) by the Crime and Courts Act 2013 Sch.10 para.28.

16   Power of court to determine whether particular payments are earnings

16(1)   Where an attachment of earnings order is in force, the court shall, on the application of a person specified in subsection (2) below, determine whether payments to the debtor of a particular class or description specified by the application are earnings for the purposes of the order; and the employer shall be entitled to give effect to any determination for the time being in force under this section.

16(2)   The persons referred to in subsection (1) above are–

(a)   the employer;

(b)   the debtor;

(c) the person to whom payment under the relevant adjudication is required to be made (whether directly or through an officer of any court); and

(d) without prejudice to paragraph (c) above, where the application is in respect of an attachment of earnings order made to secure payments under a family court maintenance order, the collecting officer.

16(3) Where an application under this section is made by the employer, he shall not incur any liability for non-compliance with the order as respects any payments of the class or description specified by the application which are made by him to the debtor while the application, or any appeal in consequence thereof, is pending; but this subsection shall not, unless the court otherwise orders, apply as respects such payments if the employer subsequently withdraws the application or, as the case may be, abandons the appeal.

History
Section 16(2)(d) amended by the Crime and Courts Act 2013 Sch.10 para.29 as from 22 April 2014.

17 Consolidated attachment orders

17(1) The powers of the county court under sections 1 and 3 of this Act shall include power to make an attachment of earnings order to secure the payment of any number of judgment debts; and the powers of a magistrates' court under those sections or under Schedule 5 to the Courts Act 2003, and the powers of a fines officer under that Schedule, shall include power to make an attachment of earnings order to secure the discharge of any number of such liabilities as are specified in section 1(3) of this Act and paragraph 1 of Schedule 5 to the Courts Act 2003.

17(2) An attachment of earnings order made by virtue of this section shall be known as a consolidated attachment order.

17(3) The power to make a consolidated attachment order shall be exercised subject to and in accordance with rules of court; and rules made for the purposes of this section may provide–

(a) for the transfer from one court to another or (where Schedule 5 to the Courts Act 2003 applies) from a court or a fines officer, as the case may be, acting in one local justice area, to a court or a fines officer, as the case may be, acting in another local justice area–

    (i) of an attachment of earnings order, or any proceedings for or arising out of such an order; and

    (ii) of functions relating to the enforcement of any liability capable of being secured by attachment of earnings;

(b) for enabling a court or a fines officer, as the case may be, to which or to whom any order, proceedings or functions have been transferred under the rules to vary or discharge an attachment of earnings order made by another court or fines officer and to replace it (if the court, or fines officer as the case may be, thinks fit) with a consolidated attachment order;

(c) for the cases in which any power exercisable under this section or the rules may be exercised by a court or a fines officer, as the case may be, of its or his own motion or on the application of a prescribed person;

(d) for requiring the officer of a court who receives payments made to him in compliance with an attachment of earnings order, instead of complying with section 13 of this Act, to deal with them as directed by the court or the rules; and

(e) for modifying or excluding provisions of this Act or Part III of the Magistrates' Courts Act 1980, but only so far as may be necessary or expedient for securing conformity with the operation of rules made by virtue of paragraphs (a) to (d) of this subsection.

History
Subparagraph (3)(d) substituted, and subss.(1), (3) amended, by the Collection of Fines (Final Scheme) Order 2006 (SI 2006/1737) arts 34, 43, as from 3 July 2006. (See also history note to s.1.)

Special provisions with respect to magistrates' courts

18   Certain action not to be taken by collecting officer except on request

18(1)   Where payments under a maintenance order are payable to the family court or an officer of the family court for transmission to a person, no officer of the family court is to–

(a)   apply for an attachment of earnings order to secure payments under the maintenance order; or

(b)   except as provided by section 10(3) of this Act, apply for an order discharging or varying such an attachment of earnings order; or

(c)   apply for a determination under section 16 of this Act,

unless he is requested in writing to do so by a person entitled to receive the payments through the family court or an officer of that court.

18(2)   Where an officer of the family court is so requested–

(a)   he shall comply with the request unless it appears to him unreasonable in the circumstances to do so; and

(b)   the person by whom the request was made shall have the same liabilities for all the costs properly incurred in or about any proceedings taken in pursuance of the request as if the proceedings had been taken by that person.

18(3)   ...

History
Section 18(1), (2) amended and s.18(3) omitted by the Crime and Courts Act 2013 Sch.10 para.30 as from 22 April 2014.

19   Procedure on applications

19(1)   Subject to rules of court made by virtue of the following subsection, an application to a magistrates' court for an attachment of earnings order, or an order discharging or varying an attachment of earnings order, shall be made by complaint.

19(2)   Rules of court may make provision excluding subsection (1) in the case of such an application as is referred to in section 9(3)(b) of this Act.

19(3)   An application to a magistrates' court for a determination under section 16 of this Act shall be made by complaint.

19(4)   For the purposes of section 51 of the Magistrates' Courts Act 1980 (which provides for the issue of a summons directed to the person against whom an order may be made in pursuance of a complaint)–

(a)   the power to make an order in pursuance of a complaint by the debtor for an attachment of earnings order, or the discharge or variation of such an order, shall be deemed to be a power to make an order against the person to whom payment under the relevant adjudication is required to be made (whether directly or through an officer of any court); and

(b)   the power to make an attachment of earnings order, or an order discharging or varying an attachment of earnings order, in pursuance of a complaint by any other person (including a complaint in proceedings to which section 3(4)(b) of this Act applies) shall be deemed to be a power to make an order against the debtor.

19(5) A complaint for an attachment of earnings order may be heard notwithstanding that it was not made within the six months allowed by section 127(1) of the Magistrates' Courts Act 1980.

20 Jurisdiction in respect of persons residing outside England and Wales

20(1) It is hereby declared that the family court has jurisdiction to hear an application by or against a person residing outside England and Wales for the discharge or variation of an attachment of earnings order made by a family court to secure maintenance payments; and where such an application is made, the following provisions shall have effect.

20(2) If the person resides in Scotland or Northern Ireland, section 15 of the Maintenance Orders Act 1950 (which relates to the service of process on persons residing in those countries) shall have effect in relation to the application as it has effect in relation to the proceedings therein mentioned.

20(3) Subject to the following subsection, if the person resides outside the United Kingdom and does not appear at the time and place appointed for the hearing of the application, the court may, if it thinks it reasonable in all the circumstances to do so, proceed to hear and determine the application at the time and place appointed for the hearing, or for any adjourned hearing, in like manner as if the person had then appeared.

20(4) Subsection (3) above shall apply only if it is proved to the satisfaction of the court, on oath or in such other manner as may be prescribed, that the applicant has taken such steps as may be prescribed to give to the said person notice of the application and of the time and place appointed for the hearing of it.

History
Section 20 amended by the Crime and Courts Act 2013 Sch.10 para.31 as from 22 April 2014.

21 Costs on application under s.16

21(1) On making a determination under section 16 of this Act, a magistrates' court may in its discretion make such order as it thinks just and reasonable for payment by any of the persons mentioned in subsection (2) of that section of the whole or any part of the costs of the determination.

21(2) Costs ordered to be paid under this section shall–

(a) in the case of costs to be paid by the debtor to the person in whose favour the attachment of earnings order in question was made, be deemed to be a sum due to the designated officer for the magistrates' court; and

(b) in any other case, be enforceable as a civil debt.

History
Section 21(1), (2)(a) amended by the Crime and Courts Act 2013 Sch.10 para.32 as from 22 April 2014.

Miscellaneous provisions

22 Persons employed under the Crown

22(1) The fact that an attachment of earnings order is made at the suit of the Crown shall not prevent its operation at any time when the debtor is in the employment of the Crown.

22(2) Where a debtor is in the employment of the Crown and an attachment of earnings order is made in respect of him, then for the purposes of this Act–

(a) the chief officer for the time being of the department, office or other body in which the debtor is employed shall be treated as having the debtor in his employment (any transfer of the debtor from one department, office or body to another being treated as a change of employment); and

(b) any earnings paid by the Crown or a Minister of the Crown, or out of the public revenue of the United Kingdom, shall be treated as paid by the said chief officer.

22(3) If any question arises, in proceedings for or arising out of an attachment of earnings order, as to what department, office or other body is concerned for the purposes of this section, or as to who for those purposes is the chief officer thereof, the question shall be referred to and determined by the Minister for the Civil Service; but that Minister shall not be under any obligation to consider a reference under this subsection unless it is made by the court.

22(4) A document purporting to set out a determination of the said Minister under subsection (3) above and to be signed by an official of the Office of Public Service shall, in any such proceedings as are mentioned in that subsection, be admissible in evidence and be deemed to contain an accurate statement of such a determination unless the contrary is shown.

22(5) This Act shall have effect notwithstanding any enactment passed before 29th May 1970 and preventing or avoiding the attachment or diversion of sums due to a person in respect of service under the Crown, whether by way of remuneration, pension or otherwise.

23 Enforcement provisions

23(1) If, after being served with notice of an application to the county court for an attachment of earnings order or for the variation of such an order or with an order made under section 14(2)(b) above, the debtor fails to attend on the day and at the time specified for any hearing of the application or specified in the order, the court may adjourn the hearing and order him to attend at a specified time on another day; and if the debtor–

(a) fails to attend at that time on that day; or

(b) attends, but refuses to be sworn or give evidence,

he may be ordered by the court to be imprisoned for not more than fourteen days.

23(1A) In any case where the court has power to make an order of imprisonment under subsection (1) for failure to attend, the court may, in lieu of or in addition to making that order, order the debtor to be arrested and brought before the court either forthwith or at such time as the court may direct.

23(2) Subject to this section, a person commits an offence if–

(a) being required by section 7(1) or 9(2) of this Act to comply with an attachment of earnings order, he fails to do so; or

(b) being required by section 7(2) of this Act to give a notice for the purposes of that subsection, he fails to give it, or fails to give it within the time required by that subsection; or

(c) he fails to comply with an order under section 14(1) of this Act or with any such requirement of a notice of application for an attachment of earnings order as is mentioned in section 14(4), or fails (in either case) to comply within the time required by the order or notice; or

(d) he fails to comply with section 15 of this Act; or

(e) he gives a notice for the purposes of section 7(2) of this Act, or a notification for the purposes of section 15, which he knows to be false in a material particular, or recklessly gives such a notice or notification which is false in a material particular; or

(f) in purported compliance with section 7(2) or 15 of this Act, or with an order under section 14(1), or with any such requirement of a notice of application for an attachment of earnings order as is mentioned in section 14(4), he makes any statement which he knows to be false in a material particular, or recklessly makes any statement which is false in a material particular.

23(3) Where a person commits an offence under subsection (2) above in relation to proceedings in, or to an attachment of earnings order made by, the High Court or the county court, he shall be liable on summary conviction to a fine of not more than level 2 on the standard scale or he may be ordered by a judge of the High Court or by the county court (as the case may be) to pay a fine of not more than £250 or, in the case of an offence specified in subsection (4) below, to be imprisoned for not more than fourteen days; and where a person commits an offence under subsection (2) otherwise than as mentioned above in this subsection, he shall be liable on summary conviction to a fine of not more than level 2 on the standard scale.

23(4)   The offences referred to above in the case of which a judge or court may impose imprisonment are–

(a)   an offence under subsection (2)(c) or (d), if committed by the debtor; and

(b)   an offence under subsection (2)(e) or (f), whether committed by the debtor or any other person.

23(5)   It shall be a defence–

(a)   for a person charged with an offence under subsection (2)(a) above to prove that he took all reasonable steps to comply with the attachment of earnings order in question;

(b)   for a person charged with an offence under subsection (2)(b) to prove that he did not know, and could not reasonably be expected to know, that the debtor was not in his employment, or (as the case may be) had ceased to be so, and that he gave the required notice as soon as reasonably practicable after the fact came to his knowledge.

23(6)   Where a person is convicted or dealt with for an offence under subsection (2)(a), the court may order him to pay, to whoever is the collecting officer of the court for the purposes of the attachment of earnings order in question, any sums deducted by that person from the debtor's earnings and not already paid to the collecting officer.

23(7)   Where under this section a person is ordered by a judge of the High Court or by the county court to be imprisoned, the judge or court may at any time revoke the order and, if the person is already in custody, order his discharge.

23(8)   Any fine imposed by a judge of the High Court under subsection (3) above and any sums ordered by the High Court to be paid under subsection (6) above shall be recoverable in the same way as a fine imposed by that court in the exercise of its jurisdiction to punish for contempt of court; section 129 of the County Courts Act 1984 (enforcement of fines) shall apply to payment of a fine imposed by the county court under subsection (3) and of any sums ordered by the county court to be paid under subsection (6); and any sum ordered by a magistrates' court to be paid under subsection (6) shall be recoverable as a sum adjudged to be paid on a conviction by that court.

23(9)   For the purposes of section 13 of the Administration of Justice Act 1960 (appeal in cases of contempt of court), subsection (3) above shall be treated as an enactment enabling the High Court or a county court to deal with an offence under subsection (2) above as if it were contempt of court.

23(10)   In this section references to proceedings in a court are to proceedings in which that court has power to make an attachment of earnings order or has made such an order.

23(10A)   This section applies in relation to the family court as it applies in relation to the county court, but as if the reference in subsection (8) to section 129 of the County Courts Act 1984 were a reference to section 31L(1) of the Matrimonial and Family Proceedings Act 1984.

23(11)   …

History
Section 23(1)–(8) amended and s.23(11) omitted, and new s.23(10A) inserted, by the Crime and Courts Act 2013 Sch.9 para.25(1), (5) and Sch.10 para.33 as from 22 April 2014.

24   Meaning of "earnings"

24(1)   For the purposes of this Act, but subject to the following subsection, "earnings" are any sums payable to a person–

(a) by way of wages or salary (including any fees, bonus, commission, overtime pay or other emoluments payable in addition to wages or salary or payable under a contract of service);

(b) by way of pension (including an annuity in respect of past services, whether or not rendered to the person paying the annuity, and including periodical payments by way of compensation for the loss, abolition or relinquishment, or diminution in the emoluments, of any office or employment);

(c) by way of statutory sick pay.

24(2) The following shall not be treated as earnings–

(a) sums payable by any public department of the Government of Northern Ireland or of a territory outside the United Kingdom;

(b) pay or allowances payable to the debtor as a member of Her Majesty's forces other than pay or allowances payable by his employer to him as a special member of a reserve force (within the meaning of the Reserve Forces Act 1996);

(ba) a tax credit (within the meaning of the Tax Credits Act 2002);

(c) pension, allowances or benefit payable under any enactment relating to social security;

(d) pension or allowances payable in respect of disablement or disability;

(e) except in relation to a maintenance order wages payable to a person as a seaman, other than wages payable to him as a seaman of a fishing boat.

(f) guaranteed minimum pension within the meaning of the Pension Schemes Act 1993.

24(3) In subsection (2)(e) above–

"fishing boat" means a vessel of whatever size, and in whatever way propelled, which is for the time being employed in sea fishing or in the sea-fishing service;

"seaman" includes every person (except masters and pilots) employed or engaged in any capacity on board any ship; and

"wages" includes emoluments.

25 General interpretation

25(1) In this Act, except where the context otherwise requires–

"administration order" means an order made under, and so referred to in, Part VI of the County Courts Act 1984;

"the court", in relation to an attachment of earnings order, means the court which made the order, subject to rules of court as to the venue for, and the transfer of, proceedings in the county court and magistrates' courts;

"debtor" and "relevant adjudication" have the meanings given by section 2 of this Act;

"the employer", in relation to an attachment of earnings order, means the person who is required by the order to make deductions from earnings paid by him to the debtor;

"the fines officer", in relation to a debtor who is subject to a collection order made under Schedule 5 to the Courts Act 2003, means any fines officer working at the fines office specified in that order;

"judgment debt" has the meaning given by section 2 of this Act;

"maintenance order" has the meaning given by section 2 of this Act;

"maintenance payments" means payments required under a maintenance order;

"prescribed" means prescribed by rules of court.

25(2) Any reference in this Act to sums payable under a judgment or order, or to the payment of such sums, includes a reference to costs and the payment of them; and the references in sections 6(4) and 12(2) to relevant costs are to any costs of the proceedings in which the attachment of earnings order in question was made, being costs which the debtor is liable to pay.

25(3) References in sections 6(5)(b), 9(3)(b) and 14(1)(a) of this Act to the debtor's needs include references to the needs of any person for whom he must, or reasonably may, provide.

25(4) [Repealed by the Dock Work Act 1989 s.7(1) and Sch. Pt I.]

25(5) Any power to make rules which is conferred by this Act is without prejudice to any other power to make rules of court.

25(6) This Act, so far as it relates to magistrates' courts, and Part III of the Magistrates' Courts Act 1980 shall be construed as if this Act were contained in that Part.

25(7) References in this Act to any enactment include references to that enactment as amended by or under any other enactment, including this Act.

History
Definition of "the fines officer" inserted by the Collection of Fines (Final Scheme) Order 2006 (SI 2006/1737) arts 34, 44, as from 3 July 2006. (See also history note to s.1.)
   Definition of "rules of court" in subs.(1) deleted by the Courts Act 2003 s.109(1), (3) and Sch.8 para.145 and Sch.10, as from 1 September 2004 (see SI 2004/2066 (C. 88) art.2(c)(vii), (d)(ii)).

General

26 Transitional provision

26(1) As from the appointed day, an attachment of earnings order made before that day under Part II of the Maintenance Orders Act 1958 (including an order made under that Part of that Act as applied by section 46 or 79 of the Criminal Justice Act 1967) shall take effect as an attachment of earnings order made under the corresponding power in this Act, and the provisions of this Act shall apply to it accordingly, so far as they are capable of doing so.

26(2) Rules of court may make such provision as the rule-making authority considers requisite–

  (a) for enabling an attachment of earnings order to which subsection (1) above applies to be varied so as to bring it into conformity, as from the appointed day, with the provisions of this Act, or to be replaced by an attachment of earnings order having effect as if made under the corresponding power in this Act;

  (b) to secure that anything required or authorised by this Act to be done in relation to an attachment of earnings order made thereunder is required or, as the case may be, authorised to be done in relation to an attachment of earnings order to which the said subsection (1) applies.

26(3) In this section, "the appointed day" means the day appointed under section 54 of the Administration of Justice Act 1970 for the coming into force of Part II of that Act.

[**Note**: The "appointed day" referred to was 2 August 1971.]

27 Consequential amendment of enactments

27(1) In consequence of the repeals effected by this Act, section 20 of the Maintenance Orders Act 1958 (which contains certain provisions about magistrates' courts and their procedure), except subsection (6) of that section (which amends section 52(3) of the Magistrates' Courts Act 1952), shall have effect as set out in Schedule 5 to this Act.

27(2) [Repealed by the Insolvency Act 1976 s.14(4) and Sch.3.]

27(3)   [Amended the Merchant Shipping Act 1970 s.95(4), now repealed.]

28   [Repealed by the Northern Ireland Constitution Act 1973 s.41(1) and Sch.6 Pt I.]

29   Citation, repeal, extent and commencement

29(1)   This Act may be cited as the Attachment of Earnings Act 1971.

29(2)   The enactments specified in Schedule 6 to this Act are hereby repealed to the extent specified in the third column of that Schedule.

29(3)   This Act, except section 20(2), does not extend to Scotland and, except section 20(2) does not extend to Northern Ireland.

29(4)   This Act shall come into force on the day appointed under section 54 of the Administration of Justice Act 1970 for the coming into force of Part II of that Act.

SCHEDULE 1

MAINTENANCE ORDERS TO WHICH THIS ACT APPLIES

Section 2

1   An order for alimony, maintenance or other payments made, or having effect as if made, under Part II of the Matrimonial Causes Act 1965 (ancillary relief in actions for divorce etc.).

2   An order for payments to or in respect of a child, being an order made, or having effect as if made, under Part III of the said Act of 1965 (maintenance of children following divorce, etc.).

3   An order for periodical or other payments made, or having effect as if made under Part II of the Matrimonial Causes Act 1973.

4   An order for maintenance or other payments to or in respect of a spouse or child, being an order made under Part I of the Domestic Proceedings and Magistrates' Courts Act 1978.

5   An order for periodical or other payments made or having effect as if made under Schedule 1 to the Children Act 1989.

6   [Repealed by the Family Law Reform Act 1987 s.33(1), (4) and Sch.2 para.44(b) and Sch.3 paras 1, 6 and Sch.4.]

7   An order under paragraph 23 of Schedule 2 to the Children Act 1989, paragraph 3 of Schedule 1 to the Social Services and Well-being (Wales) Act 2014, section 23 of the Ministry of Social Security Act 1966, section 18 of the Supplementary Benefits Act 1976 or section 106 of the Social Security Administration Act 1992 (various provisions for obtaining contributions from a person whose dependants are assisted or maintained out of public funds).

8   [Repealed by the Health and Social Care Act 2008 s.166 and Sch.15 Pt 5.]

9   An order to which section 16 of the Maintenance Orders Act 1950 applies by virtue of subsection (2)(b) or (c) of that section (that is to say an order made by a court in Scotland or Northern Ireland and corresponding to one of those specified in the foregoing paragraphs) and which has been registered in a court in England and Wales under Part II of that Act.

10   A maintenance order within the meaning of the Maintenance Orders (Facilities for Enforcement) Act 1920 (Commonwealth orders enforceable in the United Kingdom) registered in, or confirmed by, a court in England and Wales under that Act.

11   A maintenance order within the meaning of Part I of the Maintenance Orders (Reciprocal Enforcement) Act 1972 registered in the family court under the said Part I.

12   An order under section 34(1)(b) of the Children Act 1975 (payments of maintenance in respect of a child to his custodian).

13   A maintenance order within the meaning of Part I of the Civil Jurisdiction and Judgments Act 1982 which is registered in the family court under that Part.

14   A maintenance judgment within the meaning of Council Regulation (EC) No. 44/2001 of 22nd December 2000 on jurisdiction and the recognition and enforcement of judgments in civil and commercial matters, as amended from time to time and as applied by the Agreement made on 19th October 2005 between the European Community and the Kingdom of Denmark on jurisdiction and the recognition and enforcement of judgments in civil and commercial matters (OJ No.L 299 16.11.2005 at p.62), which is registered in a court in England and Wales under that Regulation.

14A(1)   A decision, court settlement or authentic instrument which falls to be enforced by the family court by virtue of the Maintenance Regulation and the Civil Jurisdiction and Judgments (Maintenance) Regulations 2011.

14A(2)   In this paragraph–

"the Maintenance Regulation" means Council Regulation (EC) No 4/2009 including as applied in relation to Denmark by virtue of the Agreement made on 19th October 2005 between the European Community and the Kingdom of Denmark;

"decision", "court settlement" and "authentic instrument" have the meanings given by Article 2 of that Regulation.

14B   A decision or maintenance arrangement which is registered in a magistrates' court under the Convention on the International Recovery of Child Support and other forms of Family Maintenance done at The Hague on 23rd November 2007.

15   An order made under Schedule 5 to the Civil Partnership Act 2004 (financial relief: provision corresponding to provision made by Part 2 of the Matrimonial Causes Act 1973), for periodical or other payments.

16   An order made under Schedule 6 to the 2004 Act (financial relief: provision corresponding to provision made by the Domestic Proceedings and Magistrates' Courts Act 1978), for maintenance or other payments to or in respect of a civil partner or child.

History
Paragraph 14 amended by the Civil Jurisdiction and Judgments Regulations 2007 (SI 2007/1655) reg.5 and Sch. para.7. Paragraph 14A added by Civil Jurisdiction and Judgments (Maintenance) Regulations 2011 (SI 2011/1484) Sch.7 para.4(3) as from 18 June 2011, and paras 15 and 16 added by the Civil Partnership Act 2004 Sch.27 para.35 as from 5 December 2005. Paras 11, 13–16 amended by the Crime and Courts Act 2013 (Family Court: Consequential Provision) Order 2014 (SI 2014/605) art.5 as from 22 April 2014. Paragraph 14B added by the International Recovery of Maintenance (Hague Convention 2007 etc.) Regulations 2012 (SI 2012/2814) Sch.4 para.3(1), (4) as from 1 August 2014.

SCHEDULE 2

TAXES, SOCIAL SECURITY CONTRIBUTIONS ETC. RELEVANT FOR PURPOSES OF SECTION 3(6)

Section 3

1   Income tax or any other tax or liability recoverable under section 65, 66 or 68 of the Taxes Management Act 1970.

2   [Repealed by Statute Law (Repeals) Act 1989.]

3   Contributions equivalent premiums under Part III of the Pension Schemes Act 1993.

3A   Class 1, 2 and 4 contributions under Part I of the Social Security Contributions and Benefits Act 1992.

4   [Repealed by Social Security Act 1973 s.100(2) and Sch.28 Pt I.]

SCHEDULE 3

DEDUCTIONS BY EMPLOYER UNDER ATTACHMENT OF EARNINGS ORDER

Sections 6 and 7

PART I

SCHEME OF DEDUCTIONS

Preliminary definitions

1   The following three paragraphs have effect for defining and explaining, for purposes of this Schedule, expressions used therein.

2   "Pay-day", in relation to earnings paid to a debtor, means an occasion on which they are paid.

3   "Attachable earnings", in relation to a pay-day, are the earnings which remain payable to the debtor on that day after deduction by the employer of–

   (a)   income tax;

   (b)   [Repealed by the Social Security Pensions Act 1975 s.65(3) and Sch.5.]

   (bb)   primary class 1 contributions under Part I of the Social Security Act 1975;

   (c)   amounts deductible under any enactment, or in pursuance of a request in writing by the debtor, for the purposes of a superannuation scheme, namely any enactment, rules, deed or other instrument providing for the payment of annuities or lump sums–

     (i)   to the persons with respect to whom the instrument has effect on their retirement at a specified age or on becoming incapacitated at some earlier age, or

     (ii)   to the personal representatives or the widows, relatives or dependants of such persons on their death or otherwise,

whether with or without any further or other benefits.

4(1)   On any pay-day–

   (a)   "the normal deduction" is arrived at by applying the normal deduction rate (as specified in the relevant attachment of earnings order) with respect to the relevant period; and

   (b)   "the protected earnings" are arrived at by applying the protected earnings rate (as so specified) with respect to the relevant period.

4(2)   For the purposes of this paragraph the relevant period in relation to any pay-day is the period beginning–

   (a)   if it is the first pay-day of the debtor's employment with the employer, with the first pay day of the employment; or

   (b)   if on the last pay-day earnings were paid in respect of a period falling wholly or partly after that pay-day, with the first day after the end of that period; or

   (c)   in any other case, with the first day after the last pay-day, and ending–

    (i)   where earnings are paid in respect of a period falling wholly or partly after the pay-day, with the last day of that period; or

    (ii)   in any other case, with the pay-day.

Employer's deduction (judgment debts and administration orders)

5   In the case of an attachment of earnings order made to secure the payment of a judgment debt or payments under an administration order, the employer shall on any pay-day–

    (a)   if the attachable earnings exceed the protected earnings, deduct from the attachable earnings the amount of the excess or the normal deduction, whichever is the less;

    (b)   make no deduction if the attachable earnings are equal to, or less than, the protected earnings.

Employer's deduction (other cases)

6(1)   The following provision shall have effect in the case of an attachment of earnings order to which paragraph 5 above and paragraph 6A below do not apply.

6(2)   If on a pay-day the attachable earnings exceed the sum of–

    (a)   the protected earnings; and

    (b)   so much of any amount by which the attachable earnings on any previous pay-day fell short of the protected earnings as has not been made good by virtue of this sub-paragraph on another previous pay-day,

then, in so far as the excess allows, the employer shall deduct from the attachable earnings the amount specified in the following sub-paragraph.

6(3)   The said amount is the sum of–

    (a)   the normal deduction; and

    (b)   so much of the normal deduction on any previous pay-day as was not deducted on that day and has not been paid by virtue of this sub-paragraph on any other previous pay-day.

6(4)   No deduction shall be made on any pay-day when the attachable earnings are equal to, or less than, the protected earnings.

6A   In the case of an attachment of earnings order made under Schedule 5 to the Courts Act 2003, the employer shall make deductions from the debtor's earnings in accordance with fines collection regulations made under that Schedule.

Note

Subparagraph (6A) inserted by the Collection of Fines (Final Scheme) Order 2006 (SI 2006/1737) arts 34, 45, as from 3 July 2006. (See also history note to s.1.)

PART II

PRIORITY AS BETWEEN ORDERS

7   Where the employer is required to comply with two or more attachment of earnings orders in respect of the same debtor, all or none of which orders are made to secure either the payment of judgment debts or payments under an administration order, then on any pay-day the employer shall, for the purpose of complying with Part I of this Schedule,–

    (a)   deal with the orders according to the respective dates on which they were made, disregarding any later order until an earlier one has been dealt with;

(b) deal with any later order as if the earnings to which it relates were the residue of the debtor's earnings after the making of any deduction to comply with any earlier order.

8 Where the employer is required to comply with two or more attachment of earnings orders, and one or more (but not all) of those orders are made to secure either the payment of judgment debts or payments under an administration order, then on any pay-day the employer shall, for the purpose of complying with Part I of this Schedule–

(a) deal first with any order which is not made to secure the payment of a judgment debt or payments under an administration order (complying with paragraph 7 above if there are two or more such orders); and

(b) deal thereafter with any order which is made to secure the payment of a judgment debt or payments under an administration order as if the earnings to which it relates were the residue of the debtor's earnings after the making of any deduction to comply with an order having priority by virtue of sub-paragraph (a) above; and

(c) if there are two or more orders to which sub-paragraph (b) above applies, comply with paragraph 7 above in respect of those orders.

Schedule 4

[Repealed by the Social Security Act 1986 s.86(2) and Sch.11.]

Schedule 5

Section 20 of Maintenance Orders Act 1958 as Having Effect In Consequence of this Act

Section 27

[Not reproduced.]

Schedule 6

Enactments Repealed

Section 29

[Not reproduced.]

Matrimonial Causes Act 1973

(1973 Chapter 18)

An Act to consolidate certain enactments relating to matrimonial proceedings, maintenance agreements, and declarations of legitimacy, validity of marriage and British nationality, with amendments to give effect to recommendations of the Law Commission.

[*23rd May 1973*]

[**Note:** Changes made by the Statute Law (Repeals) Act 1977 and the Insolvency Acts 1985 and 1986 have been incorporated, without annotation.]

39 Settlement, etc. made in compliance with a property adjustment order may be avoided on bankruptcy of settlor

39 The fact that a settlement or transfer of property had to be made in order to comply with a property adjustment order shall not prevent that settlement or transfer from being a transaction in respect of which an order may be made under section 339 or 340 of the Insolvency Act 1986 (transactions at an undervalue and preferences.)

55 Citation, commencement and extent

55(1) This Act may be cited as the Matrimonial Causes Act 1973.

55(2) This Act shall come into force on such day as the Lord Chancellor may appoint by order made by statutory instrument.

55(3) Subject to the provisions of paragraphs 3(2) of Schedule 2 below, this Act does not extend to Scotland or Northern Ireland.

[**Note:** the day appointed pursuant to s.45(2) was 1 January 1974: see the Matrimonial Causes Act 1973 (Commencement) Order 1973 (SI 1973/1972).]

Friendly Societies Act 1974

(1974 Chapter 46)

[*31st July 1974*]

87   Power of FCA and of PRA to apply for winding-up of registered friendly societies and branches

87(1)   If, on receiving the report on the state and conduct of the activities of a registered friendly society from a person appointed under section 65 of the 1992 Act, it appears to the FCA or the PRA that it is in the interests of the members of the society or of the public that the society should be wound up, then, unless the society is already being wound up by the court, the FCA, after consulting the PRA, or the PRA, after consulting the FCA, may present a petition to the High Court or, in Scotland, to the Court of Session for the society to be wound up by the court in accordance with the Insolvency Act 1986 or, as the case may be, the Insolvency (Northern Ireland) Order 1989 if the court thinks it just and equitable that this should be done.

87(2)   Subsection (1) above applies in relation to a registered branch of a registered friendly society as it applies in relation to such a society.

87(3)   Subsection (1) does not require the FCA to consult the PRA if the society in question is not a PRA-authorised person.

87(4)   The PRA may only present a petition under subsection (1) in respect of a society which is a PRA-authorised person.

History
Heading amended and s.87(3), (4) inserted by the Financial Services Act 2012 (Mutual Societies) Order 2013 (SI 2013/496) art.2(b) and Sch.5 para.13 as from 1 April 2013.

Administration of Justice Act 1977

(1977 Chapter 38)

[*29th July 1977*]

7 Extent of powers of receivers and managers in respect of companies

7(1) A receiver appointed under the law of any part of the United Kingdom in respect of the whole or part of any property or undertaking of a company and in consequence of the company having created a charge which, as created, was a floating charge may exercise his powers in any other part of the United Kingdom so far as their exercise is not inconsistent with the law applicable there.

7(2) In subsection (1) above "receiver" includes a manager and a person who is appointed both receiver and manager.

Credit Unions Act 1979

(1979 Chapter 34)

[*4th April 1979*]

[**Note**: Changes made by the Co-operative and Community Benefit Societies Act 2014 have been incorporated into the text.]

20 Cancellation or suspension of registration and petition for winding up

20(1) Section 5 of the 2014 Act (grounds for cancellation of registration) applies in relation to a credit union as if it were modified as specified in subsections (1ZA) to (1ZD).

20(1ZA) Subsection (1) applies as if for "any of conditions A to E" there were substituted "any of conditions A to F".

20(1ZB) Subsection (4)(b) (condition C) applies as if after "this Act" there were inserted "or the Credit Unions Act 1979".

20(1ZC) The section applies as if for subsection (5) (condition D) there were substituted–
"(5) Condition D is that it appears to the FCA that the credit union's rules provide for one or more common bonds involving a connection with a locality and the requirements of section 1B of the Credit Unions Act 1979 are no longer met."

20(1ZD) The section applies as if after subsection (6) there were inserted–
"(7) Condition F is that the credit union's permission under Part 4A of the Financial Services and Markets Act 2000 has been cancelled or the credit union has received a warning notice under section 55Z of that Act."

20(1B) The FCA must not cancel the registration of a credit union by virtue of condition F in section 5 of the 2014 Act unless the appropriate regulator (within the meaning of section 55A of the 2000 Act) has cancelled the credit union's permission under Part 4A of the 2000 Act and there is no possibility (or no further possibility) of that determination of the appropriate regulator being reversed or varied.

20(1C) Section 7 of the 2014 Act (cancellation of registration: additional procedure in certain cases) applies in relation to credit unions as if references to condition D included condition F.

20(1D) Section 9 of the 2014 Act (appeals) applies in relation to credit unions as if the reference to condition D included condition F (accordingly, no appeal may be made against a decision to cancel a credit union's registration on the ground that condition F is met).

20(1E) If the credit union is a PRA-authorised person, the FCA must consult the PRA before cancelling the registration of the credit union by virtue of condition F in section 5 of the 2014 Act.

20(2) A petition for the winding up of a credit union may be presented to the court by the FCA or the PRA if it appears to the FCA or the PRA that–

(a) the credit union is unable to pay sums due and payable to its members, or is able to pay such sums only by obtaining further subscriptions for shares or by defaulting in its obligations to creditors; or

(b) there has been, in relation to that credit union, a failure to comply with any provision of, or of any direction given under, this Act or the 2014 Act; or

(c) the rules of a credit union provide for one or more common bonds involving a connection with a locality and the requirements of section 1B are no longer met;

or in any other case where it appears to the FCA or the PRA that the winding up of the credit union is in the public interest or is just and equitable having regard to the interests of all the members of the credit union.

20(3) The FCA and the PRA must each consult the other before presenting a petition under subsection (2).

History
Section 20 substituted by the Co-operative and Community Benefit Societies Act 2014 Sch.4 para.10 as from 1 August 2014.

Charging Orders Act 1979

(1979 Chapter 53)

ARRANGEMENT OF SECTIONS

An Act to make provision for imposing charges to secure payment of money due, or to become due, under judgments or orders of court; to provide for restraining and prohibiting dealings with, and the making of payments in respect of, certain securities; and for connected purposes.

[6th December 1979]

[**Note**: Changes made by the Supreme Court Act 1981, the Administration of Justice Act 1982, the County Courts Act 1984, the Building Societies Act 1986, the Land Registration Act 2002, the Civil Procedure (Modification of Enactments) Order 2002 (SI 2002/439), the Tribunals, Courts and Enforcement Act 2007, the Crime and Courts Act 2013 and the Crime and Courts Act 2013 (Family Court: Consequential Provision) Order 2014 (SI 2014/605) have been incorporated into the text (in the case of pre-2003 legislation without annotation). Minor changes of wording consequential upon the conferring of jurisdiction on the family court have been made without annotation. The government has announced that the prospective amendment of this Act to be effected by TCEA 2007 ss.91, 92 and Sch.15 will not now be brought into force. See also the Charging Orders (Orders for Sale: Financial Thresholds) Regulations 2013 (SI 2013/491), below.]

Charging orders

1 Charging orders

1(1)   Where, under a judgment or order of the High Court or the family court or the county court, a person (the "debtor") is required to pay a sum of money to another person (the "creditor") then, for the purpose of enforcing that judgment or order, the appropriate court may make an order in accordance with the provisions of this Act imposing on any such property of the debtor as may be specified in the order a charge for securing the payment of any money due or to become due under the judgment or order.

1(2)   The appropriate court is–

(a)   in a case where the property to be charged is a fund in court, the court in which that fund is lodged;

(b)   in a case where paragraph (a) above does not apply and the order to be enforced is a maintenance order of the High Court or an order for costs made in family proceedings in the High Court, the High Court or the family court;

(ba)   in a case where paragraph (a) does not apply and the order to be enforced is an order of the family court, the family court;

(c)   in a case where none of paragraphs (a), (b) and (ba) above applies and the judgment or order to be enforced is a judgment or order of the High Court for a sum exceeding the county court limit, the High Court or the county court; and

(d)   in any other case, the county court.

In this section "county court limit" means the county court limit for the time being specified in an Order in Council under section 145 of the County Courts Act 1984 as the county court limit for the purposes of this section and "maintenance order" has the same meaning as in section 2(a) of the Attachment of Earnings Act 1971.

1(3)   An order under subsection (1) above is referred to in this Act as a "charging order".

1(4)   Where a person applies to the High Court for a charging order to enforce more than one judgment or order, that court shall be the appropriate court in relation to the application if it would be the appropriate court, apart from this subsection, on an application relating to one or more of the judgments or orders concerned.

1(5)   In deciding whether to make a charging order the court shall consider all the circumstances of the case and, in particular, any evidence before it as to–

(a)   the personal circumstances of the debtor, and

(b)   whether any other creditor of the debtor would be likely to be unduly prejudiced by the making of the order.

1(6)   Subsections (7) and (8) apply where, under a judgment or order of the High Court or the family court or the county court, a debtor is required to pay a sum of money by instalments.

1(7)   The fact that there has been no default in payment of the instalments does not prevent a charging order from being made in respect of that sum.

1(8)   But if there has been no default, the court must take that into account when considering the circumstances of the case under subsection (5).

1(9)   In this section "family proceedings" means proceedings in the Family Division of the High Court which are business assigned, by or under section 61 of (and Schedule 1 to) the Senior Courts Act 1981, to that Division of the High Court and no other.

History
Section 1(6)–(8) added by the Tribunals, Courts and Enforcement Act 2007 s.93(2) as from 1 October 2012. Section 1(2)(ba) inserted and s.1(2)(c) amended by the Crime and Courts Act 2013 Sch.10 para.38 as from 22 April 2014. Section 1(9) inserted and s.1(2)(b) amended by the Crime and Courts Act 2013 (Family Court: Consequential Provision) Order 2014 (SI 2014/605) arts 15, 16 as from 22 April 2014.

2   Property which may be charged

2(1)   Subject to subsection (3) below, a charge may be imposed by a charging order only on–

(a)   any interest held by the debtor beneficially–

(i)   in any asset of a kind mentioned in subsection (2) below, or

(ii)   under any trust; or

(b)   any interest held by a person as trustee of a trust ("the trust"), if the interest is in such an asset or is an interest under another trust and–

(i)   the judgment or order in respect of which a charge is to be imposed was made against that person as trustee of the trust, or

(ii)   the whole beneficial interest under the trust is held by the debtor unencumbered and for his own benefit, or

(iii) in a case where there are two or more debtors all of whom are liable to the creditor for the same debt, they together hold the whole beneficial interest under the trust unencumbered and for their own benefit.

2(2) The assets referred to in subsection (1) above are–

(a) land,

(b) securities of any of the following kinds–

(i) government stock,

(ii) stock of any body (other than a building society) incorporated within England and Wales,

(iii) stock of any body incorporated outside England and Wales or of any state or territory outside the United Kingdom, being stock registered in a register kept at any place within England and Wales,

(iv) units of any unit trust in respect of which a register of the unit holders is kept at any place within England and Wales, or

(c) funds in court.

2(3) In any case where a charge is imposed by a charging order on any interest in an asset of a kind mentioned in paragraph (b) or (c) of subsection (2) above, the court making the order may provide for the charge to extend to any interest or dividend payable in respect of the asset.

3 Provisions supplementing sections 1 and 2

3(1) A charging order may be made either absolutely or subject to conditions as to notifying the debtor or as to the time when the charge is to become enforceable, or as to other matters.

3(2) The Land Charges Act 1972 and the Land Registration Act 2002 shall apply in relation to charging orders as they apply in relation to other orders or writs issued or made for the purpose of enforcing judgments.

3(3) [Repealed]

3(4) Subject to the provisions of this Act, a charge imposed by a charging order shall have the like effect and shall be enforceable in the same courts and in the same manner as an equitable charge created by the debtor by writing under his hand.

3(4A) Subsections (4C) to (4E) apply where–

(a) a debtor is required to pay a sum of money in instalments under a judgment or order of the High Court or the family court or the county court (an "instalments order"), and

(b) a charge has been imposed by a charging order in respect of that sum.

3(4B) In subsections (4C) to (4E) references to the enforcement of a charge are to the making of an order for the enforcement of the charge.

3(4C) The charge may not be enforced unless there has been default in payment of an instalment under the instalments order.

3(4D) Rules of court may–

(a) provide that, if there has been default in payment of an instalment, the charge may be enforced only in prescribed cases, and

(b) limit the amounts for which, and the times at which, the charge may be enforced.

3(4E)   Except so far as otherwise provided by rules of court under subsection (4D)–

(a)   the charge may be enforced, if there has been default in payment of an instalment, for the whole of the sum of money secured by the charge and the costs then remaining unpaid, or for such part as the court may order, but

(b)   the charge may not be enforced unless, at the time of enforcement, the whole or part of an instalment which has become due under the instalments order remains unpaid.

3(5)   The court by which a charging order was made may at any time, on the application of the debtor or of any person interested in any property to which the order relates, make an order discharging or varying the charging order.

3(6)   Where a charging order has been protected by an entry registered under the Land Charges Act 1972 or the Land Registration Act 2002, an order under subsection (5) above discharging the charging order may direct that the entry be cancelled.

3(7)   The Lord Chancellor may by order made by statutory instrument amend section 2(2) of this Act by adding to, or removing from, the kinds of asset for the time being referred to there, any asset of a kind which in his opinion ought to be so added or removed.

3(8)   Any order under subsection (7) above shall be subject to annulment in pursuance of a resolution of either House of Parliament.

History
Section 3(4A)–(4E) added by the Tribunals, Courts and Enforcement Act 2007 s.93(3) as from 1 October 2012.

3A   Power to set financial thresholds

3A(1)   The Lord Chancellor may by regulations provide that a charge may not be imposed by a charging order for securing the payment of money of an amount below that determined in accordance with the regulations.

3A(2)   The Lord Chancellor may by regulations provide that a charge imposed by a charging order may not be enforced by way of order for sale to recover money of an amount below that determined in accordance with the regulations.

3A(3)   Regulations under this section may–

(a)   make different provision for different cases;

(b)   include such transitional provision as the Lord Chancellor thinks fit.

3A(4)   The power to make regulations under this section is exercisable by statutory instrument.

3A(5)   The Lord Chancellor may not make the first regulations under subsection (1) or (2) unless (in each case) a draft of the statutory instrument containing the regulations has been laid before, and approved by a resolution of, each House of Parliament.

3A(6)   A statutory instrument containing any subsequent regulations under those subsections is subject to annulment in pursuance of a resolution of either House of Parliament.

History
Section 3A added by the Tribunals, Courts and Enforcement Act 2007 s.94 as from 1 October 2012. See the Charging Orders (Orders for Sale: Financial Thresholds) Regulations 2013 (SI 2013/491), below, which sets a threshold of £1000 below which an order for sale of property charged under a "regulated agreement" (as defined by the Consumer Credit Act 1974) may not be made, as from 6 April 2013.

4   [Repealed by the Insolvency Act 1985 s.235 and Sch.10 Pt III.]

5 Stop orders and notices

5(1) In this section–

"stop order" means an order of the court prohibiting the taking, in respect of any of the securities specified in the order, of any of the steps mentioned in subsection (5) below;

"stop notice" means a notice requiring any person or body on whom it is duly served to refrain from taking, in respect of any of the securities specified in the notice, any of those steps without first notifying the person by whom, or on whose behalf, the notice was served; and

"prescribed securities" means securities (including funds in court) of a kind prescribed by rules of court made under this section.

5(2) The power to make rules of court under section 1 of, and Schedule 1 to, the Civil Procedure Act 1997 shall include power by any such rules to make provision–

(a) for the High Court to make a stop order on the application of any person claiming to be entitled to an interest in prescribed securities; and

(b) for the service of a stop notice by any person claiming to be entitled to an interest in prescribed securities.

5(3) [Repealed]

5(4) Rules of court made by virtue of subsection (2) above shall prescribe the person or body on whom a copy of any stop order or a stop notice is to be served.

5(5) The steps mentioned in subsection (1) above are–

(a) the registration of any transfer of the securities;

(b) in the case of funds in court, the transfer, sale, delivery out, payment or other dealing with the funds, or of the income thereon;

(c) the making of any payment by way of dividend, interest or otherwise in respect of the securities; and

(d) in the case of units of a unit trust, any acquisition of or other dealing with the units by any person or body exercising functions under the trust.

5(6) Any rules of court made by virtue of this section may include such incidental, supplemental and consequential provisions as the authority making them consider necessary or expedient, and may make different provision in relation to different cases or classes of case.

Supplemental

6 Interpretation

6(1) In this Act–

"building society" has the same meaning as in the Building Societies Act 1986;

"charging order" means an order made under section 1(1) of this Act;

"debtor" and "creditor" have the meanings given by section 1(1) of this Act;

"dividend" includes any distribution in respect of any unit of a unit trust;

"government stock" means any stock issued by Her Majesty's government in the United Kingdom or any funds of, or annuity granted by, that government;

"stock" includes shares, debentures and any securities of the body concerned, whether or not constituting a charge on the assets of that body;

"unit trust" means any trust established for the purpose, or having the effect, of providing, for persons having funds available for investment, facilities for the participation by them, as beneficiaries under the trust, in any profits or income arising from the acquisition, holding, management or disposal of any property whatsoever.

6(2)   For the purposes of sections 1 and 3 of this Act references to a judgment or order of the High Court or the family court or the county court shall be taken to include references to a judgment, order, decree or award (however called) of any court or arbitrator (including any foreign court or arbitrator) which is or has become enforceable (whether wholly or to a limited extent) as if it were a judgment or order of the High Court or the family court or the county court.

6(3)   References in section 2 of this Act to any securities include references to any such securities standing in the name of the Accountant General.

History
Section 6(2) amended by the Tribunals, Courts and Enforcement Act 2007 s.93(4) as from 1 October 2012.

7   Consequential amendment, repeals and transitional provisions

7(1)   [Repealed by the County Courts Act 1984 s.148(3) and Sch.4.]

7(2)   [Repealed by the Supreme Court Act 1981 s.152(4) and Sch.7, and the County Courts Act 1984 s.148(3) and Sch.4.]

7(3)   Any order made or notice given under any enactment repealed by this Act or under any rules of court revoked by rules of court made under this Act (the "new rules") shall, if still in force when the provisions of this Act or, as the case may be, the new rules come into force, continue to have effect as if made under this Act, or, as the case may be, under the new rules.

7(4)   [Repealed]

8   Short title, commencement and extent

8(1)   This Act may be cited as the Charging Orders Act 1979.

8(2)   This Act comes into force on such day as the Lord Chancellor may appoint by order made by statutory instrument.

8(3)   This Act does not extend to Scotland or Northern Ireland.

County Courts Act 1984

(1984 Chapter 28)

An Act to consolidate certain enactments relating to county courts.

[*26th June 1984*]

[**Note**: Changes made by the Insolvency Act 1985, the Civil Procedure Act 1997, the Tribunals, Courts and Enforcement Act 2007 and the Crime and Courts Act 2013 have been incorporated into the text (in the case of pre-2003 legislation without annotation). Prospective amendments made by the Courts and Legal Services Act 1990 s.13 as from a day to be appointed are now thought unlikely to be brought into force and have not been included. Note prospective amendment by TCEA 2007 s.106 and Sch.16.]

PART VI

ADMINISTRATION ORDERS

112 Power to make administration order

112(1) Where a debtor–

(a) is unable to pay forthwith the amount of a judgment obtained against him; and

(b) alleges that his whole indebtedness amounts to a sum not exceeding the county court limit, inclusive of the debt for which the judgment was obtained;

the county court may make an order providing for the administration of his estate.

112(2) In this Part of this Act–

"administration order" means an order under this section.

112(3) Before an administration order is made, the county court shall, in accordance with rules of court, send to every person whose name the debtor has notified to the county court as being a creditor of his, a notice that that person's name has been so notified.

112(4) So long as an administration order is in force, a creditor whose name is included in the schedule to the order shall not, without the leave of the county court, be entitled to present, or join in, a bankruptcy petition against the debtor unless–

(a) his name was so notified; and

(b) the debt by virtue of which he presents, or joins in, the petition, exceeds £1,500; and

(c) the notice given under subsection (3) was received by the creditor within 28 days immediately preceding the day on which the petition is presented.

112(5) An administration order shall not be invalid by reason only that the total amount of the debts is found at any time to exceed the county court limit, but in that case the court may, if it thinks fit, set aside the order.

112(6) An administration order may provide for the payment of the debts of the debtor by instalments or otherwise, and either in full or to such extent as appears practicable to the court under the circumstances of the case, and subject to any conditions as to his future earnings or income which the court may think just.

112(7) The Secretary of State may by regulations increase or reduce the sum for the time being specified in subsection (4)(b); but no such increase in the sum so specified shall affect any case in which the bankruptcy petition was presented before the coming into force of the increase.

112(8) The power to make regulations under subsection (7) shall be exercisable by statutory instrument; and no such regulations shall be made unless a draft of them has been approved by resolution of each House of Parliament.

Note
The "county court limit" is £5000: County Courts (Administration Order Jurisdiction) Order 1981 (SI 1981/1122) art.2.

History
Section 112(2) amended by the Crime and Courts Act 2013 Sch.9 para.10(51)(a) as from 22 April 2014.

113   Notice of order and proof of debts

113 Where an administration order has been made–

(a)   notice of the order–

    (i)   [Repealed by the Administration of Justice Act 1985 s.67(2) and Sch.8 Pt II as from 30 December 1985.]

    (ii)   shall be posted on an appropriate website, and

    (iii)   shall be sent to every person whose name the debtor has notified to the county court as being a creditor of his or who has proved;

(b)   any creditor of the debtor, on proof of his debt before the county court, shall be entitled to be scheduled as a creditor of the debtor for the amount of his proof;

(c)   any creditor may object in the prescribed manner to any debt scheduled, or to the manner in which payment is directed to be made by instalments;

(d)   any person who, after the date of the order, becomes a creditor of the debtor shall, on proof of his debt before the county court, be scheduled as a creditor of the debtor for the amount of his proof, but shall not be entitled to any dividend under the order until the creditors who are scheduled as having been creditors before the date of the order have been paid to the extent provided by the order.

History
Section 113 amended by the Crime and Courts Act 2013 Sch.9(1) para.10(51)(b)–(d) as from 22 April 2014.

114   Effect of administration order

114(1) Subject to sections 115 and 116, when an administration order is made, no creditor shall have any remedy against the person or property of the debtor in respect of any debt–

(a)   of which the debtor notified the county court before the administration order was made; or

(b)   which has been scheduled to the order,

except with the leave of the county court, and on such terms as that court may impose.

114(2)   Subject to subsection (3), when an administration order is made, the county court is to stay any proceedings in the county court which are pending against the debtor in respect of any debt so notified or scheduled, but may allow costs already incurred by the creditor, and such costs may, on application, be added to the debt.

114(3)   The requirement to stay proceedings shall not operate as a requirement to stay any proceedings in bankruptcy which are pending against the debtor.

History
Section 114 amended by the Crime and Courts Act 2013 Sch.9 para.10(51)(b), (e), (f) as from 22 April 2014.

115   Execution by registrar

115(1)   Where it appears to the county court at any time while an administration order is in force that property of the debtor exceeds in value the minimum amount, the court shall, at the request of any creditor, and without fee, issue execution against the debtor's goods.

115(1A)   In subsection (1) above "the minimum amount" means £50 or such other amount as the Lord Chancellor may by order specify instead of that amount or the amount for the time being specified in such an order; and an order under this subsection shall be made by statutory instrument subject to annulment in pursuance of a resolution of either House of Parliament.

115(2)   Section 89 applies on an execution under this section as it applies on an execution under Part V.

History
Section 115 amended by the Crime and Courts Act 2013 Sch.9 para.10(51)(b), (g) as from 22 April 2014.

116   [Repealed by the Tribunals, Courts and Enforcement Act 2007 Sch.23 para.1 as from 6 April 2014.]

117   Appropriation of money paid under order and discharge of order

117(1)   Money paid into court under an administration order shall be appropriated–

(a)   first in satisfaction of the costs of administration (which shall not exceed 10 pence in the pound on the total amount of the debts); and

(b)   then in liquidation of debts in accordance with the order.

117(2)   Where the amount received is sufficient to pay–

(a)   each creditor scheduled to the order to the extent provided by the order;

(b)   the costs of the plaintiff in the action in respect of which the order was made; and

(c)   the costs of the administration,

the order shall be superseded, and the debtor shall be discharged from his debts to the scheduled creditors.

Council Regulation (EEC No.2137/85) of 25 July 1985 on the European Economic Interest Grouping (EEIG)

[Relevant provisions of the Regulation (which has legislative force in the UK) are reproduced in Sch.1 to the European Economic Interest Grouping Regulations 1989 (SI 1989/638), below.]

Building Societies Act 1986

(1986 Chapter 53)

An Act to make fresh provision with respect to building societies and further provision with respect to conveyancing services.

[*25th July 1986*]

[**Note**: Changes made by the Companies Act 1989, the Insolvency (Northern Ireland) Order 1989 (SI 1989/2405), the Building Societies Act 1997, the Financial Services and Markets Act 2000 (Mutual Societies) Order 2001 (SI 2001/2617), the Financial Services and Markets Act 2000 (Consequential Amendments and Repeals) Order 2001 (SI 2001/3649), the Building Societies (Insolvency and Special Administration) Order 2009 (SI 2009/805), the Companies Act 2006 (Consequential Amendments, Transitional Provisions and Savings) Order 2009 (SI 2009/1941), the Financial Services Act 2012 (Mutual Societies) Order 2013 (SI 2013/496), the Building Societies (Funding) and Mutual Societies (Transfers) Act 2007, the Banks and Building Societies (Depositor Protection and Priorities) Order 2014 (SI 2014/3486) the Building Societies (Bail-in) Order 2014 (SI 2014/3344), the Building Societies (Floating Charges and Other Provisions) Order 2016 (SI 2016/679), the Deregulation Act 2015, the Small Business, Enterprise and Employment Act 2015 and the Insolvency (Amendment) Act (Northern Ireland) 2016 (Consequential Amendments and Transitional Provisions) Regulations 2017 (SI 2017/400) and the Small Business, Enterprise and Employment Act 2015 (Consequential Amendments, Savings and Transitional Provisions) Regulations 2018 (SI 2018/208) have been incorporated into the text (in the case of pre-2003 legislation without annotation).

Note that where a building society receives financial assistance from the Bank of England or has entered into an agreement for assistance or received an offer of such an agreement, these regulations are modified pursuant to the Banking (Special Provisions) Act 2008 s.11 and the Building Societies (Financial Assistance) Order 2010 (SI 2010/1188), effective 7 April 2010. The Act is also modified extensively by the Banking Act 2009 and the Building Societies (Insolvency and Special Administration) Order 2009 (SI 2009/805) to deal with the case where a failing building society is the subject of government intervention: see Vol.1.]

PART I

FUNCTIONS OF THE FINANCIAL CONDUCT AUTHORITY AND THE PRUDENTIAL REGULATION AUTHORITY

1   Functions of the Financial Conduct Authority and the Prudential Regulation Authority in relation to building societies

1(1)   The FCA has the following functions under this Act in relation to building societies–

(a)   [Omitted]

(b)   to administer the system of regulation of building societies provided for by or under this Act; and

(c)   to advise and make recommendations to the Treasury and other government departments on any matter relating to building societies.

1(1A)   The PRA has the following functions under this Act in relation to building societies–

(a)   to secure that the principal purpose of building societies remains that of making loans which are secured on residential property and are funded substantially by their members;

(b)   to administer the system of regulation of building societies provided by or under this Act, but only in so far as sections 5, 6, 7 and 9A confer functions on the PRA; and

(c)   to advise and make recommendations to the Treasury and other government departments on any matter relating to building societies.

1(2)   The FCA and the PRA also have, in relation to such societies, the other functions conferred on them respectively by or under this Act or any other enactment.

History
Heading to s.1 amended, s.1(1)(a) omitted and s.1(1A) inserted by the Financial Services Act 2012 (Mutual Societies) Order 2013 (SI 2013/496) art.2(b) and Sch.8 para.3 as from 1 April 2013. Section 1(1A)(b) amended by the Financial Services (Banking Reform) Act 2013 Sch.9 para.4(3)(a) as from 26 March 2015.

PART X

DISSOLUTION, WINDING UP, MERGERS AND TRANSFER OF BUSINESS

Dissolution and winding up

86   Modes of dissolution and winding up

86(1)   A building society–

(a)   may be dissolved by consent of the members, or

(b)   may be wound up voluntarily or by the court,

in accordance with this Part; and a building society may not, except where it is dissolved by virtue of section 93(5), 94(10) or 97(9), or following building society insolvency or building society special administration, be dissolved or wound up in any other manner.

86(2)   A building society which is in the course of dissolution by consent, or is being wound up voluntarily, may be wound up by the court.

History
Section 86 amended by the Building Societies (Insolvency and Special Administration) Order 2009 (SI 2009/805) art.7, as from 29 March 2009.

87 Dissolution by consent

87(1) A building society may be dissolved by an instrument of dissolution, with the consent (testified by their signature of that instrument) of three-quarters of the members of the society, holding not less than two-thirds of the number of shares in the society.

87(2) An instrument of dissolution under this section shall set out–

(a) the liabilities and assets of the society in detail;

(b) the number of members, and the amount standing to their credit in the accounting records of the society;

(c) the claims of depositors and other creditors, and the provision to be made for their payment;

(d) the intended appropriation or division of the funds and property of the society;

(e) the names of one or more persons to be appointed as trustees for the purposes of the dissolution, and their remuneration.

87(3) An instrument of dissolution made with consent given and testified as mentioned in subsection (1) above may be altered with the like consent, testified in the like manner.

87(4) The provisions of this Act shall continue to apply in relation to a building society as if the trustees appointed under the instrument of dissolution were the board of directors of the society.

87(5) The trustees, within 15 days of the necessary consent being given and testified (in accordance with subsection (1) above) to–

(a) an instrument of dissolution, or

(b) any alteration to such an instrument,

shall give notice to the FCA and, if the society is a PRA-authorised person, the PRA of the fact and, except in the case of an alteration to an instrument, of the date of commencement of the dissolution, enclosing a copy of the instrument or altered instrument, as the case may be; and if the trustees fail to comply with this subsection they shall each be liable on summary conviction to a fine not exceeding level 3 on the standard scale.

87(6) An instrument of dissolution under this section or an alteration to such an instrument, shall be binding on all members of the society as from the date on which the copy of the instrument or altered instrument, as the case may be, is placed in the public file of the society under subsection (10) below.

87(7) The trustees shall, within 28 days from the termination of the dissolution, give notice to the FCA and, if the society is a PRA-authorised person, the PRA of the fact and the date of the termination, enclosing an account and balance sheet signed and certified by them as correct, and showing the assets and liabilities of the society at the commencement of the dissolution, and the way in which those assets and liabilities have been applied and discharged; and, if they fail to do so they shall each be liable on summary conviction–

(a) to a fine not exceeding level 2 on the standard scale, and

(b) in the case of a continuing offence, to an additional fine not exceeding £10 for every day during which the offence continues.

87(8) Except with the consent of the appropriate authority, no instrument of dissolution, or alteration of such an instrument, shall be of any effect if the purpose of the proposed dissolution or alteration is to effect or facilitate the transfer of the society's engagements to any other society or the transfer of its business to a company.

87(9) Any provision in a resolution or document that members of a building society proposed to be dissolved shall accept investments in a company or another society (whether in shares, deposits or any other form) in or towards satisfaction of their rights in the dissolution shall be conclusive evidence of such a purpose as is mentioned in subsection (8) above.

87(10)   The FCA shall keep in the public file of the society any notice or other document received by it under subsection (5) or (7) above and shall record in that file the date on which the notice or document is placed in it.

88   Voluntary winding up

88(1)   A building society may be wound up voluntarily under the applicable winding up legislation if it resolves by special resolution that it be wound up voluntarily, but a resolution may not be passed if–

   (a)   the conditions in section 90D are not satisfied, or

   (b)   the society is in building society insolvency or building society special administration.

88(1A) A resolution under subsection (1) shall have no effect without the prior approval of the court.

88(2)   A copy of any special resolution passed for the voluntary winding up of a building society shall be sent by the society to the FCA and, if the society is a PRA-authorised person, the PRA within 15 days after it is passed; and the FCA must keep a copy in the public file of the society.

88(3)   A copy of any such resolution shall be annexed to every copy of the memorandum or of the rules issued after the passing of the resolution.

88(4)   If a building society fails to comply with subsection (2) or (3) above the society shall be liable on summary conviction to a fine not exceeding level 3 on the standard scale and so shall any officer who is also guilty of the offence.

88(5)   For the purposes of this section, a liquidator of the society shall be treated as an officer of it.

History
Section 88(1) modified by the Building Societies (Insolvency and Special Administration) Order 2009 (SI 2009/805) art.4, as from 29 March 2009.

89   Winding up by court: grounds and petitioners

89(1)   A building society may be wound up under the applicable winding up legislation by the court on any of the following grounds in addition to the grounds referred to or specified in section 37(1), that is to say, if–

   (a)   the society has by special resolution resolved that it be wound up by the court;

   (b)   the number of members is reduced below ten;

   (c)   the number of directors is reduced below two;

   (d)   being a society registered as a building society under this Act or the repealed enactments, the society has not been given permission under Part 4A of the Financial Services and Markets Act 2000 to accept deposits and more than three years has expired since it was so registered;

   (e)   the society's permission under Part 4A of the Financial Services and Markets Act 2000 to accept deposits has been cancelled (and no such permission has subsequently been given to it);

   (f)   the society exists for an illegal purpose;

   (g)   the society is unable to pay its debts; or

   (h)   the court is of the opinion that it is just and equitable that the society should be wound up.

89(2)   Except as provided by subsection (3) below, section 37 or the applicable winding up legislation, a petition for the winding up of a building society may be presented by–

(a)   the FCA, after consulting the PRA if the society is a PRA-authorised person,

(aa) if the society is a PRA-authorised person, the PRA, after consulting the FCA,

(b)   the building society or its directors,

(c)   any creditor or creditors (including any contingent or any prospective creditor), or

(d)   any contributory or contributories,

or by all or any of those parties, together or separately.

89(3)   A contributory may not present a petition unless either–

(a)   the number of members is reduced below ten, or

(b)   the share in respect of which he is a contributory has been held by him, or has devolved to him on the death of a former holder and between them been held, for at least six months before the commencement of the winding up.

89(4)   For the purposes of this section, in relation to a building society–

(a)   [Repealed by the Financial Services and Markets Act 2000 (Mutual Societies) Order (SI 2001/2617) art.13(2) and Sch.4 as from 1 December 2001.]

(b)   the reference to its existing for an illegal purpose includes a reference to its existing after it has ceased to comply with the requirement imposed by section 5(1)(a) (purpose or principal purpose).

89(5)   In this section, "contributory" has the same meaning as in paragraph 9(2) or, as the case may be, paragraph 37(2) of Schedule 15 to this Act.

History
Section 89(2)(a) substituted by the Financial Services Act 2012 (Mutual Societies) Order 2013 (SI 2013/496) art.2(b) and Sch.8 para.33(3) as from 1 April 2013.

89A   Building society insolvency as alternative order

89A(1)   On a petition for a winding up order or an application for an administration order in respect of a building society the court may, instead, make a building society insolvency order (under section 94 of the Banking Act 2009 as applied by section 90C below).

89A(2)   A building society insolvency order may be made under subsection (1) only–

(a)   on the application of the appropriate authority made with the consent of the Bank of England, or

(b)   on the application of the Bank of England.

History
Section 89A inserted by the Building Societies (Insolvency and Special Administration) Order 2009 (SI 2009/805) art.5, as from 29 March 2009.

90   Application of winding up legislation to building societies

90(1)   In this section "the companies winding up legislation" means the enactments applicable in relation to England and Wales, Scotland or Northern Ireland which are specified in paragraph 1 of Schedule 15 to this Act (including any enactment which creates an offence by any person arising out of acts or omissions occurring before the commencement of the winding up).

90(2)   In its application to the winding up of a building society, by virtue of section 88(1) or 89(1), the companies winding up legislation shall have effect with the modifications effected by Parts I to III of Schedule 15 to this Act; and the supplementary provisions of Part IV of that Schedule shall also have effect in relation to such a winding up.

90(3) In sections 37, 88, 89, and 103, "the applicable winding up legislation" means the companies winding up legislation as so modified.

90A Application of other companies insolvency legislation to building societies

90A For the purpose of–

(a) enabling voluntary arrangements to be approved in relation to building societies,

(b) enabling administration orders to be made in relation to building societies, and

(c) making provision with respect to persons appointed in England and Wales, Scotland or Northern Ireland as receivers and managers, or receivers, of building societies' property,

the enactments specified in paragraph 1(2) of Schedule 15A to this Act shall apply in relation to building societies with the modifications specified in that Schedule.

History
Section 90A(c) amended by the Building Societies (Floating Charges and Other Provisions) Order 2016 (SI 2016/679) art.3 as from 28 June 2016.

90B Power to alter priorities on dissolution and winding up

90B(1) The Treasury may by order make provision for the purpose of ensuring that, on the winding up, or dissolution by consent, of a building society, any assets available for satisfying the society's liabilities to creditors or to shareholders are applied in satisfying those liabilities pari passu.

90B(2) Liabilities to creditors do not include–

(a) liabilities in respect of subordinated deposits;

(b) liabilities in respect of preferential debts;

(c) any other category of liability which the Treasury specifies in the order for the purposes of this paragraph.

90B(3) Liabilities to shareholders do not include liabilities in respect of deferred shares.

90B(4) A preferential debt is a debt which constitutes a preferential debt for the purposes of any of the enactments specified in paragraph 1 of Schedule 15 to this Act (or which would constitute such a debt if the society were being wound up).

90B(5) An order under this section may–

(a) make amendments of this Act;

(b) make different provision for different purposes;

(c) make such consequential, supplementary, transitional and saving provision as appears to the Treasury to be necessary or expedient.

90B(6) The power to make an order under this section is exercisable by statutory instrument but no such order may be made unless a draft of it has been laid before and approved by a resolution of each House of Parliament.

History
Section 90B inserted by the Building Societies (Funding) and Mutual Societies (Transfers) Act 2007 s.2 and the Building Societies (Funding) and Mutual Societies (Transfers) Act 2007 (Commencement No.2) Order 2014 (SI 2014/2796) art.2 as from 20 November 2014.

90C   Application of bank insolvency and administration legislation to building societies

90C(1)   Parts 2 (Bank Insolvency) and 3 (Bank Administration) of the Banking Act 2009 shall apply in relation to building societies with any modifications specified in an order made under section 130 or 158 of that Act and with the modifications specified in subsection (2) below.

90C(2)   In the application of Parts 2 and 3 of that Act to building societies–

(a)   references to "bank" (except in the term "bridge bank" and the terms specified in paragraphs (b) and (c)) have effect as references to "building society";

(b)   references to "bank insolvency", "bank insolvency order", "bank liquidation" and "bank liquidator" have effect as references to "building society insolvency", "building society insolvency order", "building society liquidation" and "building society liquidator";

(c)   references to "bank administration", "bank administration order" and "bank administrator" have effect as references to "building society special administration", "building society special administration order" and "building society special administrator".

History
Section 90C inserted by the Building Societies (Insolvency and Special Administration) Order 2009 (SI 2009/805) art.2, as from 29 March 2009.

90D   Notice to the FCA and the PRA of preliminary steps

90D(1)   An application for an administration order in respect of a building society may not be determined unless the conditions below are satisfied.

90D(2)   A petition for a winding up order in respect of a building society may not be determined unless the conditions below are satisfied.

90D(3)   A resolution for voluntary winding up of a building society may not be passed unless the conditions below are satisfied.

90D(4)   An administrator of a building society may not be appointed unless the conditions below are satisfied.

90D(5)   Condition 1 is that the FCA, the Bank of England and, if the society is a PRA-authorised person, the PRA have been notified–

(a)   by the applicant for an administration order, that the application has been made,

(b)   by the petitioner for a winding up order, that the petition has been presented,

(c)   by the building society, that a resolution for voluntary winding up may be passed, or

(d)   by the person proposing to appoint an administrator, of the proposed appointment.

90D(6)   Condition 2 is that a copy of the notice complying with Condition 1 has been filed with the court (and made available for public inspection by the court).

90D(7)   Condition 3 is that–

(a)   the period of 7 days, beginning with the day on which the notice is received, has ended, or

(b)   both–

(i)   the Bank of England has informed the person who gave the notice that it does not intend to exercise a stabilisation power under Part 1 of the Banking Act 2009 in relation to the building society (and condition 5 has been met, if applicable), and

    (ii) each of the PRA and the Bank of England has informed the person who gave the notice that it does not intend to apply for a building society insolvency order (under section 95 of the Banking Act 2009 as applied by section 90C).

90D(8)   Condition 4 is that no application for a building society insolvency order is pending.

90D(8A)   Condition 5–

    (a) applies only if a resolution instrument has been made under section 12A of the Banking Act 2009 with respect to the building society in the three months ending with the date on which the Bank of England receives the notification under Condition 1, and

    (b) is that the Bank of England has informed the person who gave the notice that it consents to the insolvency procedure to which the notice relates going ahead.

90D(9)   Arranging for the giving of notice in order to satisfy Condition 1 can be a step with a view to minimising the potential loss to a building society's creditors for the purpose of section 214 of the Insolvency Act 1986 (wrongful trading) or Article 178 (wrongful trading) of the Insolvency (Northern Ireland) Order 1989 as applied in relation to building societies by section 90 of, and Schedule 15 to, this Act.

90D(10)   Where the society is a PRA-authorised person and notice has been given under Condition 1–

    (a) ...

    (b) the PRA shall inform the person who gave the notice, within the period in Condition 3(a), whether it intends to apply for a building society insolvency order,

    (c) if the Bank of England decides to apply for a building society insolvency order or to exercise a stabilisation power under Part 1 of the Banking Act 2009, the Bank shall inform the person who gave the notice, within the period in Condition 3(a); and

    (d) if Condition 5 applies, the Bank of England must, within the period in Condition 3(a), inform the person who gave the notice whether or not it consents to the insolvency procedure to which the notice relates going ahead.

90D(11)   Where the society is not a PRA-authorised person and notice has been received under Condition 1–

    (a) ...

    (b) if the Bank of England decides to apply for a building society insolvency order or to exercise a stabilisation power under Part 1 of the Banking Act 2009, the Bank shall inform the person who gave the notice, within the period in Condition 3(a); and

    (c) if Condition 5 applies, the Bank of England must, within the period in Condition 3(a), inform the person who gave the notice whether or not it consents to the insolvency procedure to which the notice relates going ahead.

90D(12)   References in this section to the insolvency procedure to which the notice relates are to the procedure for the determination, resolution or appointment in question (see subsections (1) to (4)).

History
Section 90D inserted by the Building Societies (Insolvency and Special Administration) Order 2009 (SI 2009/805) art.6, as from 29 March 2009.

    Heading to s.90D amended and s.90D(11) inserted by the Financial Services Act 2012 (Mutual Societies) Order 2013 (SI 2013/496) art 2(b) and Sch.8 para.35 as from 1 April 2013.

    Section 90D(10)(b), (11)(a) omitted, s.90D(7)(b) substituted, s.90D(8A), (12) inserted and s.90D(7)(a), (10), (11) amended by the Building Societies (Bail-in) Order 2014 (SI 2014/3344) s.4 as from 10 January 2015.

90E   Disqualification of directors

90E(1)   In this section "the Disqualification Act" means the Company Directors Disqualification Act 1986.

90E(2)   In the Disqualification Act–

(a)   a reference to liquidation includes a reference to building society insolvency and a reference to building society special administration,

(b)   a reference to winding up includes a reference to making or being subject to a building society insolvency order and a reference to making or being subject to a building society special administration order,

(c)   a reference to becoming insolvent includes a reference to becoming subject to a building society insolvency order and a reference to becoming subject to a building society special administration order, and

(d)   a reference to a liquidator includes a reference to a building society liquidator and a reference to a building society special administrator.

90E(3)   For the purposes of the application of section 7A of the Disqualification Act (office-holder's report on conduct of directors) to a building society which is subject to a building society insolvency order–

(a)   the "office-holder" is the building society liquidator,

(b)   the "insolvency date" means the date on which the building society insolvency order is made, and

(c)   subsections (9) to (11) are omitted.

90E(4)   For the purposes of the application of that section to a building society which is subject to a building society special administration order–

(a)   the "office-holder" is the building society special administrator,

(b)   the "insolvency date" means the date on which the building society special administration order is made, and

(c)   subsections (9) to (11) are omitted.

90E(5)   In the application of this section to Northern Ireland, references to the Disqualification Act are to the Company Directors Disqualification (Northern Ireland) Order 2002 and in subsections (3) and (4)–

(a)   the reference to section 7A of the Disqualification Act is a reference to Article 10A of that Order (office-holder's report on conduct of directors), and

(b)   the reference to subsections (9) to (11) of that section is a reference to paragraphs (9) to (11) of that Article.

History
Section 90E inserted by the Building Societies (Insolvency and Special Administration) Order 2009 (SI 2009/805) art.6, as from 29 March 2009. Section 90E(3), (4) substituted and subs.(5) amended by the Deregulation Act 2015, the Small Business, Enterprise and Employment Act 2015 and the Insolvency (Amendment) Act (Northern Ireland) 2016 (Consequential Amendments and Transitional Provisions) Regulations 2017 (SI 2017/400) regs 1, 2(1), (2) as from 6 April 2017.

91   Power of court to declare dissolution of building society void

91(1)   Where a building society has been dissolved under section 87 or following a winding up, building society insolvency or building society special administration, the High Court or, in relation to a society whose principal office was in Scotland, the Court of Session, may, at any time within 12 years after the date on which the society was dissolved, make an order under this section declaring the dissolution to have been void.

91(2)   An order under this section may be made, on such terms as the court thinks fit, on an application by the trustees under section 87 or the liquidator, building society liquidator or building society special administrator, as the case may be, or by any other person appearing to the Court to be interested.

91(3)   When an order under this section is made, such proceedings may be taken as might have been taken if the society had not been dissolved.

91(4)   The person on whose application the order is made shall, within seven days of its being so made, or such further time as the Court may allow, furnish the FCA and, if the society is a PRA-authorised person, the PRA with a copy of the order; and the FCA must keep a copy in the public file of the society.

91(5)   If a person fails to comply with subsection (4) above, he shall be liable on summary conviction–

    (a)   to a fine not exceeding level 3 on the standard scale, and

    (b)   in the case of a continuing offence, to an additional fine not exceeding £40 for every day during which the offence continues.

History
Section 91(1), (2) amended by the Building Societies (Insolvency and Special Administration) Order 2009 (SI 2009/805) art.8, as from 29 March 2009.

92   Supplementary

92   Where at any time a building society is being wound up or dissolved by consent, or is in building society insolvency or building society special administration, a borrowing member shall not be liable to pay any amount other than one which, at that time, is payable under the mortgage or other security by which his indebtedness to the society in respect of the loan is secured.

History
Section 92 amended by the Building Societies (Insolvency and Special Administration) Order 2009 (SI 2009/805) art.9, as from 29 March 2009.

PART XI

MISCELLANEOUS AND SUPPLEMENTARY AND CONVEYANCING SERVICES

119   Interpretation

119(1)   In this Act, except where the context otherwise requires–

[…]

"building society" means a building society incorporated (or deemed to be incorporated) under this Act;

"building society insolvency", "building society insolvency order" and "building society liquidator" shall be construed in accordance with Part 2 of the Banking Act 2009 as applied with modifications by section 90C above;

"building society special administration", "building society special administration order" and "building society special administrator" shall be construed in accordance with Part 3 of the Banking Act 2009 as applied with modifications by section 90C above;

"the Companies Acts" has the meaning given by section 2(1) of the Companies Act 2006;

[…]

History
Definition of "the Companies Acts" inserted by the Companies Act 2006 (Consequential Amendments, Transitional Provisions and Savings) Order 2009 (SI 2009/1941) Sch.1 para.87 as from 1 October 2009.

SCHEDULE 15

APPLICATION OF COMPANIES WINDING UP LEGISLATION TO BUILDING SOCIETIES

Section 90

PART I

GENERAL MODE OF APPLICATION

1   The enactments which comprise the companies winding up legislation (referred to in this Schedule as "the enactments") are the provisions of–

(a)   Parts IV, VI, VII and, XII and XIII of the Insolvency Act 1986, or

(b)   Articles 5 to 8 of Part I and Parts V, VII and XI of the Insolvency (Northern Ireland) Order 1989; or,

in so far as they relate to offences under any such enactment, sections 430 and 432 of, and Schedule 10 to, the Insolvency Act 1986 or Articles 2(6) and 373 of, and Schedule 7 to, the Insolvency (Northern Ireland) Order 1989.

1A   In this Schedule–
"deposit" means rights of the kind described in–

(a)   paragraph 22 of Schedule 2 to the Financial Services and Markets Act 2000 (deposits); or

(b)   section 1(2)(b) of the Dormant Bank and Building Society Accounts Act 2008 (balances transferred under that Act to authorised reclaim fund); and
"relevant deposit" means–

(a)   an "eligible deposit" within the meaning given by paragraph 15C(1) of Schedule 6 to the Insolvency Act 1986 (categories of preferential debts) or a deposit of the kind mentioned in paragraph 15BB of that Schedule; or

(b)   an "eligible deposit" within the meaning given by paragraph 21(1) of Schedule 4 to the Insolvency (Northern Ireland) Order 1989 (categories of preferential debts) or a deposit of the kind mentioned in paragraph 20 of that Schedule.

History
Paragraph 1A inserted by the Banks and Building Societies (Depositor Protection and Priorities) Order 2014 (SI 2014/3486) art.32(1), (2) as from 1 January 2015.

2   Subject to the following provisions of this Schedule, the enactments apply to the winding up of building societies as they apply to the winding up of companies limited by shares and registered under the Companies Act 2006 in England and Wales or Scotland or (as the case may be) in Northern Ireland.

3(1)   The enactments shall, in their application to building societies, have effect with the substitution–

(a)   for "company" of "building society" (except as otherwise specified in paragraphs 33B and 55G below);

(b)   for "the registrar of companies" or "the registrar" of "the Financial Conduct Authority";

(c)   for "the articles" of "the rules"; and

(d)   for "registered office" of "principal office".

3(2) In the application of the enactments to building societies–

(aa) every reference to a company registered in Scotland shall have effect as a reference to a building society whose principal office is situated in Scotland;

(ab) a reference to the debts of a company includes a reference to sums due to shareholding members of a building society in respect of deposits;

(a) every reference to the officers, or to a particular officer, of a company shall have effect as a reference to the officers, or to the corresponding officer, of the building society and as including a person holding himself out as such an officer; and

(b) every reference to an administrative receiver shall be omitted.

History
Paragraph 3(2)(ab) inserted by the Banks and Building Societies (Depositor Protection and Priorities) Order 2014 (SI 2014/3486) art.32(1), (3) as from 1 January 2015. Paragraph 3(1)(a) amendment by the Deregulation Act 2015, the Small Business, Enterprise and Employment Act 2015 and the Insolvency (Amendment) Act (Northern Ireland) 2016 (Consequential Amendments and Transitional Provisions) Regulations 2017 (SI 2017/400) regs 1, 2(1), (3)(a) as from 6 April 2017.

4(1) Where any of the enactments as applied to building societies requires a notice or other document to be sent to the FCA, it shall have effect as if it required the FCA to keep the notice or document in the public file of the society concerned and to record in that file the date on which the notice or document is placed in it.

4(2) Where any of the enactments, as so applied, refers to the registration, or to the date of registration, of such a notice or document, that enactment shall have effect as if it referred to the placing of the notice or document in the public file or (as the case may be) to the date on which it was placed there.

5 Any enactment which specifies a money sum altered by order under section 416 of the Insolvency Act 1986, or, as the case may be, Article 362 of the Insolvency (Northern Ireland) Order 1989, (powers to alter monetary limits) applies with the effect of the alteration.

PART II

MODIFIED APPLICATION OF INSOLVENCY ACT 1986 PARTS IV, 6, 7, 12 AND 13 AND SCHEDULE 10

History
Heading to Pt II amended by the Deregulation Act 2015, the Small Business, Enterprise and Employment Act 2015, the Insolvency (Amendment) Act (Northern Ireland) 2016 (Consequential Amendments and Transitional Provisions) Regulations 2017 (SI 2017/400) regs 1, 2(1), (3)(b) as from 6 April 2017 and the Small Business, Enterprise and Employment Act 2015 (Consequential Amendments, Savings and Transitional Provisions) Regulations 2018 (SI 2018/208) reg.2(2)(a) as from 13 March 2018.

Preliminary

6 In this Part of this Schedule, Part IV of the Insolvency Act 1986 is referred to as "Part IV"; and that Act is referred to as "the Act".

6ZA Parts 4, 6, 7 and 12 of, and Schedule 10 to, the Act, in their application to building societies, have effect without the amendments of those Parts and that Schedule made by–

(a) section 122 of the Small Business, Enterprise and Employment Act 2015 (abolition of requirements to hold meetings: company insolvency);

(b) section 124 of that Act (ability for creditors to opt not to receive certain notices: company insolvency); and

(c) Part 1 of Schedule 9 to that Act (sections 122 to 125: further amendments).

6A   In the following provisions of the Act a reference to the creditors, general creditors or unsecured creditors of a company includes a reference to every shareholding member of the building society to whom a sum due from the society in relation to the member's shareholding is due in respect of a deposit–

(a)   subsection (1) of section 143 (general functions of liquidator in winding up by the court);

(b)   subsection (3) of section 149 (debts due from contributory to company);

(c)   subsection (4) of section 168 (supplementary powers (England and Wales));

(d)   subsection (2)(b) of section 175 (preferential debts (general provision));

(e)   subsection (1) of section 176ZA (payment of expenses of winding up (England and Wales));

(f)   subsections (3)(b) and (5)(a) of section 176A (share of assets for unsecured creditors);

(g)   subsection (1)(e) of section 391O (direct sanctions orders);

(h)   subsection (5) of section 391Q (direct sanctions order: conditions); and

(i)   subsection (3)(e) of section 391R (direct sanctions direction instead of order).

History
Paragraph 6A inserted by the Banks and Building Societies (Depositor Protection and Priorities) Order 2014 (SI 2014/3486) art.33(2) as from 1 January 2015. Paragraph 6A(g)–(i) inserted by the Deregulation Act 2015, the Small Business, Enterprise and Employment Act 2015 and the Insolvency (Amendment) Act (Northern Ireland) 2016 (Consequential Amendments and Transitional Provisions) Regulations 2017 (SI 2017/400) regs 1, 2(1), (3)(c) as from 6 April 2017. Paragraph 6ZA was inserted by the Small Business, Enterprise and Employment Act 2015 (Consequential Amendments, Savings and Transitional Provisions) Regulations 2018 (SI 2018/208) reg.2(2)(b) with effect from 13 March 2018.

Members of a building society as contributories in winding up

7(1)   Section 74 (liability of members) of the Act is modified as follows.

7(2)   In subsection (1), the reference to any past member shall be omitted.

7(3)   Paragraphs (a) to (d) of subsection (2) shall be omitted; and so shall subsection (3).

7(3A)   In paragraph (f) of subsection (2) the reference to a sum due to a member of the company by way of dividends, profits or otherwise does not include a sum due to a shareholding member of a building society in respect of a deposit.

7(4)   The extent of the liability of a member of a building society in a winding up shall not exceed the extent of his liability under paragraph 6 of Schedule 2 to this Act.

History
Paragraph 7(3A) inserted by the Banks and Building Societies (Depositor Protection and Priorities) Order 2014 (SI 2014/3486) art.33(3) as from 1 January 2015.

8   Sections 75 to 78 and 83 in Chapter I of Part IV (miscellaneous provisions not relevant to building societies) do not apply.

9(1)   Section 79 (meaning of "contributory") of the Act does not apply.

9(2)   In the enactments as applied to a building society, "contributory"–

(a)   means every person liable to contribute to the assets of the society in the event of its being wound up, and

(b)   for the purposes of all proceedings for determining, and all proceedings prior to the determination of, the persons who are to be deemed contributories, includes any person alleged to be a contributory, and

(c) includes persons who are liable to pay or contribute to the payment of–

(i)   any debt or liability of the building society being wound up, or

(ii) any sum for the adjustment of rights of members among themselves, or

(iii) the expenses of the winding up;

but does not include persons liable to contribute by virtue of a declaration by the court under section 213 (imputed responsibility for fraudulent trading) or section 214 (wrongful trading) of the Act.

Voluntary winding up

10(1)   Section 84 of the Act does not apply.

10(2)   In the enactments as applied to a building society, the expression "resolution for voluntary winding up" means a resolution passed under section 88(1) of this Act.

11   In subsection (1) of section 101 (appointment of liquidation committee) of the Act, the reference to functions conferred on a liquidation committee by or under that Act shall have effect as a reference to its functions by or under that Act as applied to building societies.

12(1)   Section 107 (distribution of property) of the Act does not apply; and the following applies in its place.

12(2)   Subject to the provisions of Part IV relating to preferential payments, a building society's property in a voluntary winding up shall be applied in satisfaction of the society's liabilities to creditors *pari passu* and, subject to that application, in accordance with the rules of the society.

12(3)   In sub-paragraph (2) the reference to the society's liabilities to creditors includes a reference to the society's liabilities to shareholding members of the society in respect of deposits which are not relevant deposits.

History
Paragraph 12(3) inserted by the Banks and Building Societies (Depositor Protection and Priorities) Order 2014 (SI 2014/3486) art.33(4) as from 1 January 2015.

13   Sections 110 and 111 (liquidator accepting shares, etc. as consideration for sale of company property) of the Act do not apply.

14   Section 116 (saving for certain rights) of the Act shall also apply in relation to the dissolution by consent of a building society as it applies in relation to its voluntary winding up.

Winding up by the court

15   In sections 117 (High Court and county court jurisdiction) and 120 (Court of Session and sheriff court jurisdiction) of the Act, each reference to a company's share capital paid up or credited as paid up shall have effect as a reference to the amount standing to the credit of shares in a building society as shown by the latest balance sheet.

16(1)   Section 122 (circumstances in which company may be wound up by the court) of the Act does not apply in relation to a building society whose principal office is situated in England and Wales.

16(2)   Section 122 has effect in relation to a building society whose principal office is situated in Scotland as if subsection (1) were omitted.

History
Paragraph 16 substituted by the Building Societies (Floating Charges and Other Provisions) Order 2016 (SI 2016/679) art.2 as from 28 June 2016.

17 Section 124 (application for winding up) of the Act does not apply.

18(1) In section 125 (powers of court on hearing of petition) of the Act, subsection (1) applies with the omission of the words from "but the court" to the end of the subsection.

18(2) The conditions which the court may impose under section 125 of the Act include conditions for securing–

    (a) that the building society be dissolved by consent of its members under section 87, or

    (b) that the society amalgamates with, or transfers its engagements to, another building society under section 93 or 94, or

    (c) that the society transfers its business to a company under section 97,

and may also include conditions for securing that any default which occasioned the petition be made good and that the costs, or in Scotland the expenses, of the proceedings on that petition be defrayed by the person or persons responsible for the default.

19 Section 126 (power of court, between petition and winding-up order, to stay or restrain proceedings against company) of the Act has effect with the omission of subsection (2).

20 If, before the presentation of a petition for the winding up by the court of a building society, an instrument of dissolution under section 87 is placed in the society's public file, section 129(1) (commencement of winding up by the court) of the Act shall also apply in relation to the date on which the instrument is so placed and to any proceedings in the course of the dissolution as it applies to the commencement date for, and proceedings in, a voluntary winding up.

21(1) Section 130 of the Act (consequences of winding-up order) shall have effect with the following modifications.

21(2) Subsections (1) and (3) shall be omitted.

21(3) A building society shall, within 15 days of a winding-up order being made in respect of it, give notice of the order to the FCA and, if the society is a PRA-authorised person, the PRA; and the FCA must keep the notice in the public file of the society.

21(4) If a building society fails to comply with sub-paragraph (3) above, it shall be liable on summary conviction to a fine not exceeding level 3 on the standard scale; and so shall any officer who is also guilty of the offence.

22 Section 140 (appointment of liquidator by court in certain circumstances) of the Act does not apply.

23 In the application of sections 141(1) and 142(1) (liquidation committees), of the Act to building societies, the references to functions conferred on a liquidation committee by or under that Act shall have effect as references to its functions by or under that Act as so applied.

23A Section 143 (general functions of liquidator in winding up by the court) of the Act has effect as if after subsection (1) there were inserted–

    (1A) Subject to the provisions of Part 4 relating to preferential payments, a building society's property in the winding up shall be applied in satisfaction of the society's liabilities to creditors pari passu and, subject to that application, in accordance with the rules of the society.

    (1B) In subsection (1A) the reference to the society's liabilities to creditors includes a reference to the society's liabilities to shareholding members of the society in respect of deposits which are not relevant deposits.

History
Paragraph 23A inserted by the Banks and Building Societies (Depositor Protection and Priorities) Order 2014 (SI 2014/3486) art.3(1), (5) as from 1 January 2015.

24   The conditions which the court may impose under section 147 (power to stay or sist winding up) of the Act shall include those specified in paragraph 18(2) above.

25   Section 154 (adjustment of rights of contributories) of the Act shall have effect with the modification that any surplus is to be distributed in accordance with the rules of the society.

26   [Repealed by the Companies Act 2006 (Commencement No.3, Consequential Amendments, Transitional Provisions and Savings) Order 2007 SI 2007/2194 (C.84), art.10(1) and Sch.4 para.49(1), as from 1 October 2007.]

Winding up: general

27   Section 187 (power to make over assets to employees) of the Act does not apply.

28(1)   In section 201 (dissolution: voluntary winding up) of the Act, subsection (2) applies without the words from "and on the expiration" to the end of the subsection and, in subsection (3), the word "However" shall be omitted.

28(2)   Sections 202 to 204 (early dissolution) of the Act do not apply.

29   In section 205 (dissolution: winding up by the court) of the Act, subsection (2) applies with the omission of the words from "and, subject" to the end of the subsection; and in subsections (3) and (4) references to the Secretary of State shall have effect as references to the appropriate authority.

Penal provisions

30   Sections 216 and 217 of the Act (restriction on re-use of name) do not apply.

31(1)   Sections 218 and 219 (prosecution of delinquent officers) of the Act do not apply in relation to offences committed by members of a building society acting in that capacity.

31(2)   Sections 218(5) of the Act and subsections (1) and (2) of section 219 of the Act do not apply.

31(3)   The references in subsections (3) and (4) of section 219 of the Act to the Secretary of State shall have effect as references to the FCA; and the reference in subsection (3) to section 218 of the Act shall have effect as a reference to that section as supplemented by paragraph 32 below.

32(1)   Where a report is made to the prosecuting authority (within the meaning of section 218) under section 218(4) of the Act, in relation to an officer of a building society, he may, if he thinks fit, refer the matter to the FCA for further enquiry.

32(2)   On such a reference to it the FCA shall exercise its power under section 55(1) of this Act to appoint one or more investigators to investigate and report on the matter.

32(3)   An answer given by a person to a question put to him in exercise of the powers conferred by section 55 on a person so appointed may be used in evidence against the person giving it.

Preferential debts

33   Section 387 (meaning in Schedule 6 of "the relevant date") of the Act applies with the omission of subsections (2) and (4) to (6).

Insolvency practitioners: their qualification and regulation

33A   Section 390 of the Act (persons not qualified to act as insolvency practitioners) has effect as if for subsection (2) there were substituted–

"(2) A person is not qualified to act as an insolvency practitioner in relation to a building society at any time unless at that time the person is fully authorised to act as an insolvency practitioner or partially authorised to act as an insolvency practitioner only in relation to companies."

33B(1) In the following provisions of the Act, in a reference to authorisation or permission to act as an insolvency practitioner in relation to (or only in relation to) companies, the reference to companies has effect without the modification in paragraph 3(1)(a) above–

(a) sections 390A and 390B(1) and (3) (authorisation of insolvency practitioners); and

(b) sections 391O(1)(b) and 391R(3)(b) (court sanction of insolvency practitioners in public interest cases).

33B(2) In sections 391Q(2)(b) (direct sanctions order: conditions) and 391S(3)(e) (power for Secretary of State to obtain information) of the Act the reference to a company has effect without the modification in paragraph 3(1)(a) above.

History
Paragraphs 33A and 33B and heading thereto inserted by the Deregulation Act 2015, the Small Business, Enterprise and Employment Act 2015 and the Insolvency (Amendment) Act (Northern Ireland) 2016 (Consequential Amendments and Transitional Provisions) Regulations 2017 (SI 2017/400) regs 1, 2(1), (3)(d) as from 6 April 2017.

Part III

Modified Application of The Insolvency (Northern Ireland) Order 1989, Parts V, 11 and 12

[Not reproduced.]

Part IV

Dissolution of Building Society Wound up (England and Wales, Scotland and Northern Ireland)

56(1) Where a building society has been wound up voluntarily, it is dissolved as from 3 months from the date of the placing in the public file of the society of the return of the final meetings of the society and its creditors made by the liquidator under–

(a) section 94 or (as the case may be) 106 of the Insolvency Act 1986 (as applied to building societies), or on such other date as is determined in accordance with section 201 of that Act, or

(b) Article 80 or (as the case may be) 92 of the Insolvency (Northern Ireland) Order 1989 (as so applied), or on such other date as is determined in accordance with that Article,

as the case may be.

56(2) Where a building society has been wound up by the court, it is dissolved as from 3 months from the date of the placing in the public file of the society of–

(a) the liquidator's notice under section 172(8) of the Insolvency Act 1986 (as applied to building societies), or, as the case may be, Article 146(7) of the Insolvency (Northern Ireland) Order 1989 (as applied to building societies), or

(b) the notice of the completion of the winding up from the official receiver or the official receiver for Northern Ireland for company liquidations,

or on such other date as is determined in accordance with section 205 of that Act or Article 169 of that Order, as the case may be.

57(1) Sections 1012 to 1023 and 1034 of the Companies Act 2006 (property of dissolved company) apply in relation to the property of a dissolved building society (whether dissolved under section 87 or following its winding up) as they apply in relation to the property of a dissolved company.

57(2)   Paragraph 3(1) above shall apply to those sections for the purpose of their application to building societies.

57(3)   Any reference in those sections to restoration to the register shall be read as a reference to the effect of an order under section 91 of this Act.

57(4)   [Omitted]

History
Paragraph 57(1), (3) substituted and para.57(4) omitted by the Companies Act 2006 (Consequential Amendments, Transitional Provisions and Savings) Order 2009 (SI 2009/1941) art.2(1) and Sch.1 para.87(11)(b), (c) as from 1 October 2009.

Insolvency rules and fees: England and Wales and Scotland

58(1)   Rules may be made under section 411 of the Insolvency Act for the purpose of giving effect, in relation to building societies, to the provisions of the applicable winding up legislation.

58(2)   An order made by the competent authority under section 414 of the Insolvency Act 1986 may make provision for fees to be payable under that section in respect of proceedings under the applicable winding up legislation and the performance by the official receiver or the Secretary of State of functions under it.

Insolvency rules and fees: Northern Ireland

59(1)   Rules may be made under Article 359 the Insolvency (Northern Ireland) Order 1989 for the purpose of giving effect in relation to building societies, to the provisions of the applicable winding up legislation.

59(2)   An order made by the Department of Economic Development under Article 361 of the Insolvency (Northern Ireland) Order 1989 may make provision for fees to be payable under that Article in respect of proceedings under the applicable winding-up legislation and the performance by the official receiver for Northern Ireland or that Department of functions under it.

SCHEDULE 15A

APPLICATION OF OTHER COMPANIES INSOLVENCY LEGISLATION TO BUILDING SOCIETIES

Section 90A

PART I

GENERAL MODE OF APPLICATION

1(1)   Subject to the provisions of this Schedule, the enactments specified in sub-paragraph (2) below (referred to in this Schedule as "the enactments") apply in relation to building societies as they apply in relation to companies limited by shares and registered under the Companies Act 2006 in England and Wales or Scotland or (as the case may be) in Northern Ireland.

1(2)   The enactments referred to in sub-paragraph (1) above are–

   (a)   Parts I (except section 1A), II, and 3, section 176ZB (in Part 4), and VI, VII, XII and XIII, section 434 and Part XVIII of the Insolvency Act 1986, or

   (b)   Part I, Part II (except Article 14A), Parts III, IV, VII, XI and XII and Article 378 of the Insolvency (Northern Ireland) Order 1989, and, in so far as they relate to offences under any such enactment, sections 430 and 432 of, and Schedule 10 to, the Insolvency Act 1986 or Article 2(6) and 373 of, and Schedule 7 to, the Insolvency (Northern Ireland) Order 1989.

History

Paragraph 1(2)(a) amended by the Building Societies (Floating Charges and Other Provisions) Order 2016 (SI 2016/679) art.4(2)(a) as from 28 June 2016 and by the Deregulation Act 2015, the Small Business, Enterprise and Employment Act 2015 and the Insolvency (Amendment) Act (Northern Ireland) 2016 (Consequential Amendments and Transitional Provisions) Regulations 2017 (SI 2017/400) regs 1, 2(1), (4)(a) as from 6 April 2017.

2(1) The enactments shall, in their application to building societies, have effect with the substitution–

(a) for "company" of "building society" (except as otherwise specified in paragraphs 27H and 54 below);

(b) for "the registrar of companies" or "the registrar" of "the Financial Conduct Authority";

(c) for "the articles" of "the rules"; and

(d) for "registered office" of "principal office".

2(2) In the application of the enactments to building societies–

(aa) every reference to a company registered in Scotland shall have effect as a reference to a building society whose principal office is situated in Scotland;

(a) every reference to the officers, or to a particular officer, of a company shall have effect as a reference to the officers, or to the corresponding officer, of the building society and as including a person holding himself out as such an officer; and

(b) every reference to an administrative receiver, other than a reference in section 29(2), 72A or 251 of the Insolvency Act 1986 or in Article 5(1) or 59A of the Insolvency (Northern Ireland) Order 1989, shall be omitted.

History

Paragraph 2(2)(b) amended by the Building Societies (Floating Charges and Other Provisions) Order 2016 (SI 2016/679) art.4(2(b) as from 28 June 2016. Paragraph 2(1)(a) amended by the Deregulation Act 2015, the Small Business, Enterprise and Employment Act 2015 and the Insolvency (Amendment) Act (Northern Ireland) 2016 (Consequential Amendments and Transitional Provisions) Regulations 2017 (SI 2017/400) regs 1, 2(1), (4)(b) as from 6 April 2017.

3(1) Where any of the enactments as applied to building societies requires a notice or other document to be sent to the FCA, it shall have effect as if it required the FCA to keep the notice or document in the public file of the society concerned and to record in that file the date on which the notice or document is placed in it.

3(2) Where any of the enactments, as so applied, refers to the registration, or to the date of registration, of such a notice or document, that enactment shall have effect as if it referred to the placing of the notice or document in the public file or (as the case may be) to the date on which it was placed there.

3(3) Any reference in any of the enactments, as so applied, to the register shall have effect as a reference to the public file.

History

Paragraph 3(3) inserted by the Building Societies (Floating Charges and Other Provisions) Order 2016 (SI 2016/679) art.4(2)(c) as from 28 June 2016.

4(1) Rules may be made under section 411 of the Insolvency Act 1986 or, as the case may be, Article 359 of the Insolvency (Northern Ireland) Order 1989 for the purpose of giving effect, in relation to building societies, to the provisions of the enactments.

4(2) An order made by the competent authority under section 414 of the Insolvency Act 1986 may make provision for fees to be payable under that section in respect of proceedings under the enactments and the performance by the official receiver or the Secretary of State of functions under them.

4(3) An order made by the Department of Economic Development under Article 361 of the Insolvency (Northern Ireland) Order 1989 may make provision for fees to be payable under that Article in respect of proceedings under the enactments and the performance by the official receiver or that Department of functions under them.

5 Any enactment which specifies a money sum altered by order under section 416 of the Insolvency Act 1986, or, as the case may be, Article 362 of the Insolvency (Northern Ireland) Order 1989, (powers to alter monetary limits) applies with the effect of the alteration.

5A In this Schedule–

"deposit" and "relevant deposit" have the meaning given by paragraph 1A of Schedule 15; and

"scheme manager" has the same meaning as in the Financial Services and Markets Act 2000.

History
Paragraph 5A substituted by the Building Societies (Floating Charges and Other Provisions) Order 2016 (SI 2016/679) art.4(2)(d) as from 28 June 2016.

PART II

MODIFIED APPLICATION OF PARTS I TO III, 6, 7, 12 AND 13 OF INSOLVENCY ACT 1986

Preliminary

6 In this Part of this Schedule, the Insolvency Act 1986 is referred to as "the Act".

6A Parts 1, 3, 6, 7 and 12 of the Act, in their application to building societies, have effect without the amendments of those Parts made by–

(a) section 122 of the Small Business, Enterprise and Employment Act 2015 (abolition of requirements to hold meetings: company insolvency);

(b) section 124 of that Act (ability for creditors to opt not to receive certain notices: company insolvency); and

(c) Part 1 of Schedule 9 to that Act (sections 122 to 125: further amendments).

Voluntary arrangements

7 Section 1 of the Act (proposals for voluntary arrangements) has effect as if–

(a) it required any proposal under Part I of the Act to be so framed as to enable a building society to comply with the requirements of this Act; and

(b) any reference to debts included a reference to liabilities owed to the holders of shares in a building society.

8 In section 2 (procedure where nominee is not liquidator or administrator) and section 3 (summoning of meetings) of the Act as applied to a building society, any reference to a meeting of the society is a reference to–

(a) a meeting of both shareholding and borrowing members of the society; and

(b) a meeting of shareholding members alone,

and subsection (1) of section 2 shall have effect with the omission of the words from "and the directors" to the end.

8A In subsection (2) of section 4A of the Act (approval of arrangement) as applied to a building society, paragraph (b) and the word "or" immediately preceding that paragraph are omitted.

9   In section 6 of the Act (challenge of decisions) as applied to a building society, "contributory"–

(a)   means every person liable to contribute to the assets of the society in the event of its being wound up, and

(b)   for the purposes of all proceedings for determining, and all proceedings prior to the determination of, the persons who are to be deemed contributories, includes any person alleged to be a contributory, and

(c)   includes persons who are liable to pay or contribute to the payment of–

     (i)   any debt or liability of the building society being wound up, or

     (ii)   any sum for the adjustment of rights of members among themselves, or

     (iii)   the expenses of the winding up;

but does not include persons liable to contribute by virtue of a declaration by the court under section 213 (imputed responsibility for fraudulent trading) or section 214 (wrongful trading) of the Act.

9A   In section 7A of the Act (prosecution of delinquent officers) as applied to a building society–

(a)   in subsection (2), for paragraphs (i) and (ii) there is substituted "the FCA",

(b)   subsections (3) to (7) are omitted,

(c)   in subsection (8), for "Secretary of State" there is substituted "FCA".

Administration orders

10(1)   Section 8 of the Act (power of court to make administration order) has effect as if it included provision that, where–

(a)   an application for an administration order to be made in relation to a building society is made by the FCA or the PRA (with or without other parties); and

(b)   the society has defaulted in an obligation to pay any sum due and payable in respect of any deposit or share,

the society shall be deemed for the purposes of subsection (1) to be unable to pay its debts.

10(2)   In subsection (3) of that section, paragraph (c) and, in subsection (4) of that section, the words from "nor where" to the end are omitted.

11(1)   Subsection (1) of section 9 of the Act (application for administration order) as applied to a building society has effect as if–

(a)   it enabled an application to the court for an administration order to be by petition presented, with or without other parties, by the FCA or the PRA or by a shareholding member entitled under section 89(3) of this Act to petition for the winding up of the society; and

(b)   the words from "or by the clerk" to "on companies)" were omitted.

11(2)   In subsection (2)(a) of that section as so applied, the reference to any person who has appointed, or is or may be entitled to appoint, an administrative receiver of the society is a reference to the FCA or the PRA (unless it is a petitioner).

11(3)   Subsection (3) of that section, and in subsection (4) of that section, the words "Subject to subsection (3)," are omitted.

12   In section 10 of the Act (effect of application for administration order), the following are omitted, namely–

(a) in subsection (2), paragraphs (b) and (c); and

(b) subsection (3).

13 In section 11 of the Act (effect of administration order), the following are omitted, namely–

(a) in subsection (1), paragraph (b) and the word "and" immediately preceding that paragraph;

(b) in subsection (3), paragraph (b);

(c) in subsection (4), the words "an administrative receiver of the company has vacated office under subsection (1)(b), or"; and

(d) subsection (5).

14 In subsection (1) of section 12 of the Act (notification of administration order), the reference to every invoice, order for goods or business letter is a reference to every statement of account, order for goods or services, business letter or advertisement.

15 Subsection (3) of section 13 of the Act (appointment of administrator) has effect as if it enabled an application for an order under subsection (2) of that section to be made by the FCA or the PRA.

16(1) Subject to sub-paragraph (2) below, section 14 of the Act (general powers of administrator) has effect as if it required the administrator of a building society, in exercising his powers under that section–

(a) to ensure compliance with the provisions of this Act; and

(b) not to appoint to be a director any person who is not a fit and proper person to hold that position.

16(2) Sub-paragraph (1)(a) above does not apply in relation to section 5, 6 or 7 of this Act.

16(3) In subsection (4) of that section as applied to a building society, the reference to any power conferred by the Act or the Companies Acts or by the company's articles is a reference to any power conferred by this Act or by the society's memorandum or rules.

16(4) [Repealed]

17(1) Subject to sub-paragraph (3) below, paragraph 16 of Schedule 1 to the Act (powers of administrators) as applied to a building society has effect as if it conferred power to transfer liabilities in respect of deposits with or shares in the society.

17(2) No transfer under that paragraph shall be a transfer of engagements for the purposes of Part X of this Act.

17(3) No transfer under that paragraph which, apart from sub-paragraph (2) above, would be a transfer of engagements for the purposes of that Part shall be made unless it is approved by the court, or by meetings summoned under section 23(1) or 25(2) of the Act (as modified by paragraph 21 or 23 below).

18 In section 15 of the Act (power to deal with charged property etc.)–

(a) subsection (1) is omitted; and

(b) for subsections (3) and (4) there is substituted the following subsection–

"**(3)** Subsection (2) applies to any security other than one which, as created, was a floating charge."

19(1) Section 17 of the Act (general duties of administrator) has effect as if, instead of the requirement imposed by subsection (3), it required the administrator of a building society to summon a meeting of the society's creditors if–

(a) he is requested, in accordance with the rules, to do so by 500 of the society's creditors, or by one-tenth, in number or value, of those creditors, or

(b) he is directed to do so by the court.

19(2) That section also has effect as if it required the administrator of a building society to summon a meeting of the society's shareholding members if–

(a) he is requested, in accordance with the rules, to do so by 500 of the society's shareholding members, or by one-tenth, in number, of those members, or

(b) he is directed to do so by the court.

20 [Repealed]

21(1) Subsection (1) of section 23 of the Act (statement of proposals) as applied to a building society has effect as if–

(a) the reference to the Financial Conduct Authority included a reference to the scheme manager;

(b) the reference to all creditors included a reference to all holders of shares in the society; and

(c) the reference to a meeting of the society's creditors included a reference to a meeting of holders of shares in the society.

21(2) In subsection (2) of that section as so applied, references to members of the society do not include references to holders of shares in the society.

22 Section 24 of the Act (consideration of proposals by creditors' meeting) as applied to a building society has effect as if any reference to a meeting of creditors included a reference to a meeting of holders of shares in the society.

23(1) Section 25 of the Act (approval of substantial revisions) as applied to a building society has effect as if–

(a) subsection (2) required the administrator to send a statement in the prescribed form of his proposed revisions to the FCA, the PRA and to the scheme manager; and

(b) the reference in that subsection to a meeting of creditors included a reference to a meeting of holders of shares in the society.

23(2) In subsection (3) of that section as so applied, references to members of the society do not include references to holders of shares in the society.

24 Subsection (1) of section 27 of the Act (protection of interests of creditors and members) has effect–

(a) as if it enabled the FCA, the PRA or the scheme manager to apply to the court by petition for an order under that section; and

(b) in relation to an application by the FCA, the PRA or the scheme manager, as if the words "(including at least himself)" were omitted.

Receivers and managers

25 In section 38 of the Act (receivership accounts), "prescribed" means prescribed by regulations made by statutory instrument by the Treasury.

26 In subsection (1) of section 39 of the Act (notification that receiver or manager appointed), the reference to every invoice, order for goods or business letter is a reference to every statement of account, order for goods or services, business letter or advertisement.

27 Subsection (3) of section 40 of the Act (payment of debts out of assets subject to floating charge), as applied to a building society, has effect as if the reference to general creditors included a reference to shareholding members of the society in respect of deposits which are not relevant deposits.

27A Sections 42 to 49 of the Act (administrative receivers) are omitted.

27B   Subsection (1) of section 51 of the Act (power to appoint receiver), as applied to a building society, has effect as if for the words "an incorporated company (whether a company registered under the Companies Act 2006 or not)" there were substituted "a building society".

27C   Subsection (3) of section 59 of the Act (priority of debts), as applied to a building society, has effect as if the reference to ordinary creditors included a reference to shareholding members of the society in respect of deposits which are not relevant deposits.

27D   Subsection (1) of section 67 of the Act (report by receiver), as applied to a building society, has effect as if–

(a)   the reference to the Financial Conduct Authority included a reference to the scheme manager; and

(b)   in paragraph (d) the reference to other creditors included a reference to shareholding members of the society in respect of deposits which are not relevant deposits.

27E   Subsection (1) of section 70 of the Act (interpretation for Chapter 2), as applied to a building society, has effect as if–

(a)   in the definition of "company" for the words "an incorporated company (whether or not a company registered under the Companies Act 2006)" there were substituted "a building society"; and

(b)   the definition of "the register" were omitted.

27F   Chapter 4 of Part 3 of the Act (prohibition of appointment of administrative receiver), as applied to a building society, has effect as if–

(a)   in section 72A (floating charge holder not to appoint administrative receiver)–

  (i)   in subsections (1) and (2) the word "qualifying" and in subsection (3) the definition of "holder of a qualifying floating charge in respect of a company's property" were omitted; and

  (ii)   subsections (4)(a), (5) and (6) were omitted; and

(b)   sections 72B to 72H 6 (exceptions to prohibition) were omitted.

Insolvency practitioners: their qualification and regulation

27G   Section 390 of the Act (persons not qualified to act as insolvency practitioners) has effect as if for subsection (2) there were substituted–

"(2) A person is not qualified to act as an insolvency practitioner in relation to a building society at any time unless at that time the person is fully authorised to act as an insolvency practitioner or partially authorised to act as an insolvency practitioner only in relation to companies.".

27H(1)   In the following provisions of the Act, in a reference to authorisation or permission to act as an insolvency practitioner in relation to (or only in relation to) companies the reference to companies has effect without the modification in paragraph 2(1)(a) above–

(a)   sections 390A and 390B(1) and (3) (authorisation of insolvency practitioners); and

(b)   sections 391O(1)(b) and 391R(3)(b) (court sanction of insolvency practitioners in public interest cases).

27H(2)   In sections 391Q(2)(b) (direct sanctions order: conditions) and 391S(3)(e) (power for Secretary of State to obtain information) of the Act the reference to a company has effect without the modification in paragraph 2(1)(a) above.

27I In sections 391O, 391Q and 391R of the Act a reference to the creditors of a company includes a reference to every shareholding member of the building society to whom a sum due from the society in relation to the member's shareholding is due in respect of a deposit.

History

Paragraph 20 repealed by the Financial Services (Banking Reform) Act 2013 Sch.9 para.4(2)(b) as from 26 March 2015. Paragraph 27 substituted and paras 27A–27F inserted by the Building Societies (Floating Charges and Other Provisions) Order 2016 (SI 2016/679) art.4(3)(b) as from 28 June 2016. Paragraphs 27G–27I and the heading thereto inserted by the Deregulation Act 2015, the Small Business, Enterprise and Employment Act 2015 and the Insolvency (Amendment) Act (Northern Ireland) 2016 (Consequential Amendments and Transitional Provisions) Regulations 2017 (SI 2017/400) regs 1, 2(1), (4)(d) as from 6 April 2017. The heading was modified and para.6A was inserted by the Small Business, Enterprise and Employment Act 2015 (Consequential Amendments, Savings and Transitional Provisions) Regulations 2018 (SI 2018/208) reg.2(3)(a) and (b) with effect from 13 March 2018.

PART III

MODIFIED APPLICATION OF PARTS II, III, 4 AND 12 OF INSOLVENCY (NORTHERN IRELAND) ORDER 1989

[Applies to Northern Ireland only; not reproduced.]

Companies Act 1989

(1989 Chapter 40)

An Act to amend the law relating to company accounts; to make new provision with respect to the persons eligible for appointment as company auditors; to amend the Companies Act 1985 and certain other enactments with respect to investigations and powers to obtain information and to confer new powers exercisable to assist overseas regulatory authorities; to make new provision with respect to the registration of company charges and otherwise to amend the law relating to companies; to amend the Fair Trading Act 1973; to enable provision to be made for the payment of fees in connection with the exercise by the Secretary of State, the Director General of Fair Trading and the Monopolies and Mergers Commission of their functions under Part V of that Act; to make provision for safeguarding the operation of certain financial markets; to amend the Financial Services Act 1986; to enable provision to be made for the recording and transfer of title to securities without a written instrument; to amend the Company Directors Disqualification Act 1986, the Company Securities (Insider Dealing) Act 1985, the Policy-holders Protection Act 1975 and the law relating to building societies; and for connected purposes.

[16th November 1989]

[**Note**: Changes made by the Transfer of Functions (Financial Services) Order 1992 (SI 1992/1315), the Bank of England Act 1998, the Financial Markets and Insolvency Regulations 1998 (SI 1998/1748), the Financial Services and Markets Act 2000 (Consequential Amendments and Repeals) Order 2001 (SI 2001/3649), the Civil Jurisdiction and Judgments Regulations 2007 (SI 2007/1655), the Financial Services and Insolvency Regulations 2009 (SI 2009/853), the Enterprise Act 2002, the Tribunals, Courts and Enforcement Act 2007, the Financial Services Act 2012, the Financial Services and Markets Act 2000 (Over the Counter Derivatives, Central Counterparties and Trade Repositories) Regulations 2013 (SI 2013/504), the Financial Services and Markets Act 2000 (Over the Counter Derivatives, Central Counterparties and Trade Repositories) (No. 2) Regulations 2013 (SI 2013/1908), the Enterprise and Regulatory Reform Act 2013 (Consequential Amendments) (Bankruptcy) and the Small Business, Enterprise and Employment Act 2015 (Consequential Amendments) Regulations 2016 (SI 2016/481), the Bankruptcy (Scotland) Act 2016 (Consequential Provisions and Modifications) Order 2016 (SI 2016/1034), the Deregulation Act 2015 and Small Business, Enterprise and Employment Act 2015 (Consequential Amendments) (Savings) Regulations 2017 (SI 2017/540), the Central Securities Depositories Regulations 2017 (SI 2017/1064) and the Companies Act 1989 (Financial Markets and Insolvency) (Amendment) Regulations 2017 (SI 2017/1247) have been incorporated into the text (in the case of pre-2003 legislation without annotation). Note prospective amendment by TCEA 2007 s.62(3) and Sch.13.]

PART VII

FINANCIAL MARKETS AND INSOLVENCY

Introduction

154 Introduction

154 This Part has effect for the purposes of safeguarding the operation of certain financial markets by provisions with respect to–

(a) the insolvency, winding up or default of a person party to transactions in the market (sections 155 to 172),

(b) the effectiveness or enforcement of certain charges given to secure obligations in connection with such transactions (sections 173 to 176), and

(c) rights and remedies in relation to certain property provided as cover for margin in relation to such transactions or as default fund contribution, or subject to such a charge (sections 177 to 181).

History
Section 154(c) amended by the Financial Markets and Insolvency Regulations 2009 (SI 2009/853) reg.2(1), (2) as from 15 June 2009.

Recognised bodies

155 Market contracts

155(1) [**Definitions**] In this Part–

(a) "clearing member client contract" means a contract between a recognised central counterparty and one or more of the parties mentioned in subsection (1A) which is recorded in the accounts of the recognised central counterparty as a position held for the account of a client, an indirect client or a group of clients or indirect clients;

(b) "clearing member house contract" means a contract between a recognised central counterparty and a clearing member recorded in the accounts of the recognised central counterparty as a position held for the account of a clearing member;

(c) "client trade" means a contract between two or more of the parties mentioned in subsection (1A) which corresponds to a clearing member client contract;

(d) "market contracts" means the contracts to which this Part applies by virtue of subsections (2) to (3ZA).

155(1A) [Parties in s.155(a), (c)] The parties referred to in subsections (1)(a) and (c) are–

(a) a clearing member;

(b) a client; and

(c) an indirect client.

155(2) [Recognised investment exchange] Except as provided in subsection (2A), in relation to a recognised investment exchange this Part applies to–

(a) contracts entered into by a member or designated non-member of the exchange with a person other than the exchange which are either

    (i) contracts made on the exchange or on an exchange to whose undertaking the exchange has succeeded whether by amalgamation, merger or otherwise; or

    (ii) contracts in the making of which the member or designated non-member was subject to the rules of the exchange or of an exchange to whose undertaking the exchange has succeeded whether by amalgamation, merger or otherwise;

(b) contracts entered into by the exchange, in its capacity as such, with a member of the exchange or with a recognised clearing house or with a recognised CSD or with another recognised investment exchange for the purpose of enabling the rights and liabilities of that member or recognised body under a transaction to be settled; and

(c) contracts entered into by the exchange with a member of the exchange or with a recognised clearing house or with a recognised CSD or with another recognised investment exchange for the purpose of providing central counterparty clearing services to that member or recognised body.

A "designated non-member" means a person in respect of whom action may be taken under the default rules of the exchange but who is not a member of the exchange.

155(2A) [Recognised overseas investment exchange] Where the exchange in question is a recognised overseas investment exchange, this Part does not apply to a contract that falls within paragraph (a) of subsection (2) (unless it also falls within subsection (3)).

155(2B) [Application of Pt VII to transactions cleared through recognised central counterparty] In relation to transactions which are cleared through a recognised central counterparty, this Part applies to–

(a) clearing member house contracts;

(b) clearing member client contracts;

(c) client trades, other than client trades excluded by subsection (2C) or (2D); and

(d) contracts entered into by the recognised central counterparty with a recognised investment exchange or with a recognised CSD or a recognised clearing house for the purpose of providing central counterparty clearing services to that recognised body.

155(2C) [Client trade excluded from s.155(2B)(c)] A client trade is excluded by this subsection from subsection (2B)(c) if–

(a) the clearing member which is a party to the clearing member client contract corresponding to the client trade defaults; and

(b) the clearing member client contract is not transferred to another clearing member within the period specified for this purpose in the default rules of the recognised central counterparty.

155(2D) **[Client trade further excluded from s.155(2B)(c)]** A client trade is also excluded by this subsection from subsection (2B)(c) if–

  (a) the client trade was entered into by a client in the course of providing indirect clearing services to an indirect client;

  (b) the client defaults; and

  (c) the clearing member client contract corresponding to the client trade is not transferred within–

      (i) the period specified for this purpose in the default rules of the recognised central counterparty; or

      (ii) if no such period is specified in the default rules of the recognised central counterparty, a period of 14 days beginning with the day on which proceedings in respect of the client's insolvency are begun.

155(3) **[Recognised clearing house]** In relation to a recognised clearing house which is not a recognised central counterparty, this Part applies to–

  (a) contracts entered into by the clearing house, in its capacity as such, with a member of the clearing house or with a recognised investment exchange or with a recognised CSD or with another recognised clearing house for the purpose of enabling the rights and liabilities of that member or recognised body under a transaction to be settled; and

  (b) contracts entered into by the clearing house with a member of the clearing house or with a recognised investment exchange or with a recognised CSD or with another recognised clearing house for the purpose of providing central counterparty clearing services to that member or recognised body.

155(3ZA) **[Application of Part VII in relation to recognised CSD]** In relation to a recognised CSD, this Part applies to contracts entered into by the central securities depository with a member of the central securities depository or with a recognised investment exchange or with a recognised clearing house or with another recognised CSD for the purpose of providing authorised central securities depository services to that member or recognised body.

155(3A) **["Central counterparty clearing services"]** In this section "central counterparty clearing services" means–

  (a) the services provided by a recognised investment exchange or a recognised clearing house to the parties to a transaction in connection with contracts between each of the parties and the investment exchange or clearing house (in place of, or as an alternative to, a contract directly between the parties),

  (b) the services provided by a recognised clearing house to a recognised body in connection with contracts between them, or

  (c) the services provided by a recognised investment exchange to a recognised body in connection with contracts between them.

155(3B) **[Beginning of insolvency proceedings in s.155(2D)(c)(ii)]** The reference in subsection (2D)(c)(ii) to the beginning of insolvency proceedings is to–

  (a) the making of a bankruptcy application or the presentation of a bankruptcy petition or a petition for sequestration of a client's estate, or

  (b) the application for an administration order or the presentation of a winding-up petition or the passing of a resolution for voluntary winding up, or

  (c) the appointment of an administrative receiver.

155(3C) **[Reference to application for administration order in s.155(3B)(b)]** In subsection (3B)(b) the reference to an application for an administration order is to be taken to include a reference to–

(a) in a case where an administrator is appointed under paragraph 14 or 22 of Schedule B1 to the Insolvency Act 1986 (appointment by floating charge holder, company or directors) following filing with the court of a copy of a notice of intention to appoint under that paragraph, the filing of the copy of the notice, and

(b) in a case where an administrator is appointed under either of those paragraphs without a copy of a notice of intention to appoint having been filed with the court, the appointment of the administrator.

155(3D) **["Authorised central securities depository services"]** In this Part "authorised central securities depository services" means, in relation to a recognised CSD–

(a) the core services listed in Section A of the Annex to the CSD regulation which that central securities depository is authorised to provide pursuant to Article 16 or 19(1)(a) or (c) of the CSD regulation;

(b) the non-banking-type ancillary services listed in or permitted under Section B of that Annex which that central securities depository is authorised to provide, including services notified under Article 19 of the CSD regulation; and

(c) the banking-type ancillary services listed in or permitted under Section C of that Annex which that central securities depository is authorised to provide pursuant to Article 54(2)(a) of the CSD regulation.

155(4) **[Regulations]** The Secretary of State may by regulations make further provision as to the contracts to be treated as "market contracts", for the purposes of this Part, in relation to a recognised body.

155(5) **[Scope of regulations]** The regulations may add to, amend or repeal the provisions of subsections (2), (3), (3ZA) and (3D) above.

History
Section 155(2)(b), s.155(2A) and s.155(3) substituted and s.155(2)(c), s.155(3A) inserted by the Financial Markets and Insolvency Regulations 2009 (SI 2009/853) reg.2(1), (3) as from 15 June 2009. Section 155(1) substituted, s.155(1A), s.155(2B)–(2D) inserted and s.155(3) amended by the Financial Services and Markets Act 2000 (Over the Counter Derivatives, Central Counterparties and Trade Repositories) Regulations 2013 (SI 2013/504) reg.4(1), (2) as from 1 April 2013. Section 155(2D) and s.155(3B), (3C) inserted and s.155(2B)(c) amended by the Financial Services and Markets Act 2000 (Over the Counter Derivatives, Central Counterparties and Trade Repositories) (No.2) Regulations 2013 (SI 2013/1908) reg.2(1), (2) as from 26 August 2013. Section 155(3B) amended by the Enterprise and Regulatory Reform Act 2013 (Consequential Amendments) (Bankruptcy) and the Small Business, Enterprise and Employment Act 2015 (Consequential Amendments) Regulations 2016 (SI 2016/481) reg.2(1) and Sch.1 para.9(2) as from 6 April 2016.
Heading above s.155 and s.155(1), (2), (2B), (3), (3A), (4), (5) amended and subss.(3ZA), (3D) inserted by the Central Securities Depositories Regulations 2017 (SI 2017/1064) regs 1, 3(1)–(3) as from 28 November 2017.

155A   Qualifying collateral arrangements and qualifying property transfers

155A(1) **[Definitions]** In this Part–

(a) "qualifying collateral arrangements" means the contracts and contractual obligations to which this Part applies by virtue of subsection (2); and

(b) "qualifying property transfers" means the property transfers to which this Part applies by virtue of subsection (4).

155A(2) **[Application of Pt VII for provision of property as margin]** In relation to transactions which are cleared through a recognised central counterparty, this Part applies to any contracts or contractual obligations for, or arising out of, the provision of property as margin where–

(a) the margin is provided to a recognised central counterparty and is recorded in the accounts of the recognised central counterparty as an asset held for the account of a client, an indirect client, or a group of clients or indirect clients; or

(b) the margin is provided to a client or clearing member for the purpose of providing cover for exposures arising out of present or future client trades.

155A(3) **["Property" and provision of property as margin in s.155A(2)]** In subsection (2)–

(a) "property" has the meaning given by section 436(1) of the Insolvency Act 1986 and

(b) the reference to a contract or contractual obligation for, or arising out of, the provision of property as margin in circumstances falling within paragraph (a) or (b) of that subsection includes a reference to a contract or contractual obligation of that kind which has been amended to reflect the transfer of a clearing member client contract or client trade.

155A(4) **[Application of Pt VII to transactions cleared through recognised central counterparty]** In relation to transactions which are cleared through a recognised central counterparty, this Part applies to–

(a) transfers of property made in accordance with Article 48(7) of the EMIR Level 1 Regulation;

(aa) transfers of property made in accordance with Article 4(6) and (7) of the EMIR Level 2 Regulation or Article 4(6) and (7) of the MIFIR Level 2 Regulation;

(b) transfers of property to the extent that they–

    (i) are made by a recognised central counterparty to a non-defaulting clearing member instead of, or in place of, a defaulting clearing member;

    (ii) represent the termination or close out value of a clearing member client contract which is transferred from a defaulting clearing member to a non-defaulting clearing member; and

    (iii) are determined in accordance with the default rules of the recognised central counterparty.

(c) transfers of property to the extent that they–

    (i) are made by a clearing member to a non-defaulting client or another clearing member instead of, or in place of, a defaulting client;

    (ii) represent the termination or close out value of a client trade which is transferred from a defaulting client to another clearing member or a non-defaulting client; and

    (iii) do not exceed the termination or close out value of the clearing member client contract corresponding to that client trade, as determined in accordance with the default rules of the recognised central counterparty.

History

Section 155A inserted by the Financial Services and Markets Act 2000 (Over the Counter Derivatives, Central Counterparties and Trade Repositories) Regulations 2013 (SI 2013/504) reg.4(1), (3) as from 1 April 2013. Section 155A(4)(aa), 155A(4)(c) inserted by the Financial Services and Markets Act 2000 (Over the Counter Derivatives, Central Counterparties and Trade Repositories) (No.2) Regulations 2013 (SI 2013/1908) reg.2(1), (3) as from 26 August 2013.

Section 155A(4)(aa) substituted by the Companies Act 1989 (Financial Markets and Insolvency) (Amendment) Regulations 2017 (SI 2017/1247) regs 1, 2(1), (2) as from 3 January 2018.

156   Additional requirements for recognition: default rules, etc.

156   [Repealed by the Financial Services and Markets Act 2000 (Consequential Amendments and Repeals) Order 2001 (SI 2001/3649) arts 1, 75(e) as from 1 December 2001.]

157   Change in default rules

157(1)   [Notice of proposed amendment] A recognised body shall give the appropriate regulator at least three months' notice of any proposal to amend, revoke or add to its default rules; and the regulator may within three months from receipt of the notice direct the recognised body not to proceed with the proposal, in whole or in part.

157(1A)   [Shorter notice period] The appropriate regulator may, if it considers it appropriate to do so, agree a shorter period of notice and, in a case where it does so, any direction under this section must be given by it within that shorter period.

157(2)   [Direction] A direction under this section may be varied or revoked.

157(3)   [Breach of direction] Any amendment or revocation of, or addition to, the default rules of a recognised body in breach of a direction under this section is ineffective.

157(4)   ["The appropriate regulator"] "The appropriate regulator"–

    (a)   in relation to a recognised UK investment exchange, means the FCA, and

    (b)   in relation to a recognised clearing house or a recognised CSD, means the Bank of England.

History
Section 157(4) inserted by the Financial Services Act 2012 s.114(1) and Sch.18 para.65 as from 1 April 2013. Section 157(1A) inserted and s.157(1)(a), (4)(b) amended by the Financial Services and Markets Act 2000 (Over the Counter Derivatives, Central Counterparties and Trade Repositories) Regulations 2013 (SI 2013/504) reg.4(1), (4) as from 1 April 2013.
    Section 157(1), (3), (4) amended by the Central Securities Depositories Regulations 2017 (SI 2017/1064) regs 1, 3(1), (4) as from 28 November 2017.

158   Modifications of the law of insolvency

158(1)   [Effect of ss.159–165] The general law of insolvency has effect in relation to–

    (a)   market contracts,

    (b)   action taken under the rules of a recognised body other than a recognised central counterparty, with respect to market contracts,

    (c)   action taken under the rules of a recognised central counterparty to transfer clearing member client contracts, or settle clearing member client contracts or clearing member house contracts, in accordance with the default rules of the recognised central counterparty,

    (d)   where clearing member client contracts transferred in accordance with the default rules of a recognised central counterparty were entered into by the clearing member or client as a principal, action taken to transfer client trades, or groups of client trades, corresponding to those clearing member client contracts,

    (e)   action taken to transfer qualifying collateral arrangements in conjunction with a transfer of clearing member client contracts as mentioned in paragraph (c) or a transfer of client trades as mentioned in paragraph (d), and

    (f)   qualifying property transfers,

subject to the provisions of sections 159 to 165.

158(2)   [Relevant insolvency proceedings] So far as those provisions relate to insolvency proceedings in respect of a person other than a defaulter, they apply in relation to–

(a)   proceedings in respect of a recognised investment exchange or a member or designated non-member of a recognised investment exchange,

(aa)   proceedings in respect of a recognised clearing house or a member of a recognised clearing house,

(ab)   proceedings in respect of a recognised CSD or a member of a recognised CSD, and

(b)   proceedings in respect of a party to a market contract other than a client trade which are begun after a recognised body has taken action under its default rules in relation to a person party to the contract as principal,

but not in relation to any other insolvency proceedings, notwithstanding that rights or liabilities arising from market contracts fall to be dealt with in the proceedings.

158(3)   [Beginning of insolvency proceedings] The reference in subsection (2)(b) to the beginning of insolvency proceedings is to–

(a)   the making of a bankruptcy application or the presentation of a bankruptcy petition or a petition for sequestration of a person's estate, or

(b)   the application for an administration order or the presentation of a winding-up petition or the passing of a resolution for voluntary winding up, or

(c)   the appointment of an administrative receiver.

158(3A)   [Reference to an application for an administration order in s.158(3)(b)] In subsection (3)(b) the reference to an application for an administration order shall be taken to include a reference to–

(a)   in a case where an administrator is appointed under paragraph 14 or 22 of Schedule B1 to the Insolvency Act 1986 (appointment by floating charge holder, company or directors) following filing with the court of a copy of a notice of intention to appoint under that paragraph, the filing of the copy of the notice, and

(b)   in a case where an administrator is appointed under either of those paragraphs without a copy of a notice of intention to appoint having been filed with the court, the appointment of the administrator.

158(4)   [Regulations] The Secretary of State may make further provision by regulations modifying the law of insolvency in relation to the matters mentioned in paragraphs (a) to (d) of subsection (1).

158(5)   [Scope of regulations] The regulations may add to, amend or repeal the provisions mentioned in subsection (1), and any other provisions of this Part as it applies for the purposes of those provisions, or provide that those provisions have effect subject to such additions, exceptions or adaptations as are specified in the regulations.

History
Section 158(2)(a) substituted, and s.158(2)(aa) inserted, by the Financial Markets and Insolvency Regulations 2009 (SI 2009/853) reg.2(1), (4) as from 15 June 2009. Section 158(3)(b) substituted by the Enterprise Act 2002 s.248(3) Sch.17 paras 43, 44(a) as from 15 September 2003 (see the Enterprise Act 2002 (Commencement No.4 and Transitional Provisions and Savings) Order 2003 (SI 2003/2093 (C. 85)) art.2(1) Sch.1), subject to transitional provisions in SI 2003/2093 (C. 85) art.3. The amendment has no effect in relation to certain companies by virtue of the Enterprise Act 2002 s.249(1). Section 158(3A) inserted by the Enterprise Act 2002 s.248(3) Sch.17 paras 43, 44(b) as from 15 September 2003 (see the Enterprise Act 2002 (Commencement No.4 and Transitional Provisions and Savings) Order 2003 (SI 2003/2093 (C. 85)) art.2(1) Sch.1), subject to transitional provisions in SI 2003/2093 (C. 85) art.3. The amendment has no effect in relation to certain companies by virtue of the Enterprise Act 2002 s.249(1). Section 158(1) substituted and s.158(2)(b), (4) amended by the Financial Services and Markets Act 2000 (Over the Counter Derivatives, Central Counterparties and Trade Repositories) Regulations 2013 (SI 2013/504) reg.4(1), (2) as from 1 April 2013. Section 158(1)(d) amended by the Financial Services and Markets Act 2000 (Over

the Counter Derivatives, Central Counterparties and Trade Repositories) (No.2) Regulations 2013 (SI 2013/1908) reg.2(1), (4) as from 26 August 2013. Section 158(3) amended by the Enterprise and Regulatory Reform Act 2013 (Consequential Amendments) (Bankruptcy) and the Small Business, Enterprise and Employment Act 2015 (Consequential Amendments) Regulations 2016 (SI 2016/481) reg.2(1) and Sch.1 para.9(3) as from 6 April 2016. Section 158(1)(b), (2) amended by the Central Securities Depositories Regulations 2017 (SI 2017/1064) regs 1, 3(1), (5) as from 28 November 2017.

159 Proceedings of recognised bodies take precedence over insolvency procedures

159(1) **[Matters not invalidated on insolvency]** None of the following shall be regarded as to any extent invalid at law on the ground of inconsistency with the law relating to the distribution of the assets of a person on bankruptcy, winding up or sequestration, or in the administration of a company or other body or in the administration of an insolvent estate–

(a) a market contract,

(b) the default rules of a recognised body,

(c) the rules of a recognised body other than a recognised central counterparty as to the settlement of market contracts not dealt with under its default rules,

(d) the rules of a recognised central counterparty on which the recognised central counterparty relies to give effect to the transfer of a clearing member client contract, or the settlement of a clearing member client contract or clearing member house contract, in accordance with its default rules,

(e) a transfer of a clearing member client contract, or the settlement of a clearing member client contract or a clearing member house contract, in accordance with the default rules of a recognised central counterparty,

(f) where a clearing member client contract transferred in accordance with the default rules of a recognised central counterparty was entered into by the clearing member or client as principal, a transfer of a client trade or group of client trades corresponding to that clearing member client contract,

(g) a transfer of a qualifying collateral arrangement in conjunction with the transfer of clearing member client contract as mentioned in paragraph (e) or of a client trade as mentioned in paragraph (f), or

(h) a qualifying property transfer.

159(2) **[Office-holder's powers]** The powers of a relevant office-holder in his capacity as such, and the powers of the court under the Insolvency Act 1986, the Bankruptcy (Scotland) Act 2016, Part 10 of the Building Societies Act 1986, Parts 2 and 3 of the Banking Act 2009 or under regulations made under section 233 of that Act, shall not be exercised in such a way as to prevent or interfere with–

(a) the settlement in accordance with the rules of a recognised body other than a recognised central counterparty, of a market contract not dealt with under its default rules,

(b) any action taken under the default rules of a recognised body other than a recognised central counterparty,

(c) the transfer of a clearing member client contract, or the settlement of a clearing member client contract or a clearing member house contract, in accordance with the default rules of a recognised central counterparty,

(d) where a clearing member client contract transferred in accordance with the default rules of a recognised central counterparty was entered into by the clearing member or client as principal, the transfer of a client trade or group of client trades corresponding to that clearing member contract,

(e) the transfer of a qualifying collateral arrangement in conjunction with a transfer of a clearing member client contract as mentioned in paragraph (c), or a transfer of a client trade as mentioned in paragraph (d),

(f) any action taken to give effect to any of the matters mentioned in paragraphs (c) to (e), or

(g) any action taken to give effect to a qualifying property transfer.

This does not prevent a relevant office-holder from afterwards seeking to recover any amount under section 163(4) or 164(4) or prevent the court from afterwards making any such order or decree as is mentioned in section 165(1) or (2) (but subject to subsections (3) and (4) of that section).

159(3) **[Effect of following provisions]** Nothing in the following provisions of this Part shall be construed as affecting the generality of the above provisions.

159(4) **[Proof, set-off disallowed]** A debt or other liability arising out of a market contract which is the subject of default proceedings may not be proved in a winding up or bankruptcy or in the administration of a company or other body, or in Scotland claimed in a winding up or sequestration or in the administration of a company or other body, until the completion of the default proceedings.

A debt or other liability which by virtue of this subsection may not be proved or claimed shall not be taken into account for the purposes of any set-off until the completion of the default proceedings.

159(4A) **[Proof prior to completion of default proceedings]** However, prior to the completion of default proceedings–

(a) where it appears to the convener that a sum will be certified under section 162(1) to be payable, subsection (4) shall not prevent any proof or claim including or consisting of an estimate of that sum which has been lodged or, in Scotland, submitted, from being admitted or, in Scotland, accepted, for the purpose only of determining the entitlement of a creditor to vote in a decision procedure; and

(b) a creditor whose claim or proof has been lodged and admitted or, in Scotland, submitted and accepted, for the purpose of determining the entitlement of a creditor to vote in a decision procedure and which has not been subsequently wholly withdrawn, disallowed or rejected, is eligible as a creditor to be a member of a liquidation committee or, in bankruptcy proceedings in England and Wales or in the administration of a company or other body, a creditors' committee.

159(5) **[Completion of default proceedings]** For the purposes of subsections (4) and (4A) the default proceedings shall be taken to be completed in relation to a person when a report is made under section 162 stating the sum (if any) certified to be due to or from him.

History
Section 159(1), (4), (4A) amended by the Financial Markets and Insolvency Regulations 2009 (SI 2009/853) reg.2(1), (5) as from 15 June 2009. Section 159(1)(c), 159(2)(a), (b) amended and s.159(1)(d)–(h), (2)(c)–(g) inserted by the Financial Services and Markets Act 2000 (Over the Counter Derivatives, Central Counterparties and Trade Repositories) Regulations 2013 (SI 2013/504) reg.4(1), (6) as from 1 April 2013. Section 159(1)(f), (2)(d) amended by the Financial Services and Markets Act 2000 (Over the Counter Derivatives, Central Counterparties and Trade Repositories) (No.2) Regulations 2013 (SI 2013/1908) reg.2(1), (5) as from 26 August 2013. Section 159(4A) amended by the Deregulation Act 2015 and Small Business, Enterprise and Employment Act 2015 (Consequential Amendments) (Savings) Regulations 2017 (SI 2017/540) regs 1, 2, Sch.1 para.2(1), (2) as from 6 April 2017. Heading to s.159 and s.159(1)(b), (c), (2)(a), (b) amended by the Central Securities Depositories Regulations 2017 (SI 2017/1064) regs 1, 3(1), (6) as from 28 November 2017.

160   Duty to give assistance for purposes of default proceedings

160(1) **[Assistance reasonably required]** It is the duty of–

(a) any person who has or had control of any assets of a defaulter, and

(b) any person who has or had control of any documents of or relating to a defaulter, to give a recognised body such assistance as it may reasonably require for the purposes of its default proceedings.

This applies notwithstanding any duty of that person under the enactments relating to insolvency.

160(2) **[Legal professional privilege]** A person shall not under this section be required to provide any information or produce any document which he would be entitled to refuse to provide or produce on grounds of legal professional privilege in proceedings in the High Court or on grounds of confidentiality as between client and professional legal adviser in proceedings in the Court of Session.

160(3) **[Original documents]** Where original documents are supplied in pursuance of this section, the recognised body shall return them forthwith after the completion of the relevant default proceedings, and shall in the meantime allow reasonable access to them to the person by whom they were supplied and to any person who would be entitled to have access to them if they were still in the control of the person by whom they were supplied.

160(4) **[Office-holder's expenses]** The expenses of a relevant office-holder in giving assistance under this section are recoverable as part of the expenses incurred by him in the discharge of his duties; and he shall not be required under this section to take any action which involves expenses which cannot be so recovered, unless the recognised body undertakes to meet them.

There shall be treated as expenses of his such reasonable sums as he may determine in respect of time spent in giving the assistance and for the purpose of determining the priority in which his expenses are payable out of the assets, sums in respect of time spent shall be treated as his remuneration and other sums shall be treated as his disbursements or, in Scotland, outlays.

160(5) **[Regulations]** The Secretary of State may by regulations make further provision as to the duties of persons to give assistance to a recognised body for the purposes of its default proceedings, and the duties of the recognised body with respect to information supplied to it.

The regulations may add to, amend or repeal the provisions of subsections (1) to (4) above.

160(6) **["Document"]** In this section "document" includes information recorded in any form.

History
Section 160(1), (3)–(5) amended by the Central Securities Depositories Regulations 2017 (SI 2017/1064) regs 1, 3(1), (7) as from 28 November 2017.

161   Supplementary provisions as to default proceedings

161(1) **[Dissipation of assets]** If the court is satisfied on an application by a relevant office-holder that a party to a market contract with a defaulter intends to dissipate or apply his assets so as to prevent the office-holder recovering such sums as may become due upon the completion of the default proceedings, the court may grant such interlocutory relief (in Scotland, such interim order) as it thinks fit.

161(2) **[Reserve in respect of claims]** A liquidator, administrator or trustee of a defaulter or, in Scotland, a trustee in the sequestration of the estate of the defaulter shall not–

(a) declare or pay any dividend to the creditors, or

(b) return any capital to contributories,

unless he has retained what he reasonably considers to be an adequate reserve in respect of any claims arising as a result of the default proceedings of the recognised body concerned.

161(3) **[Court order]** The court may on an application by a relevant office-holder make such order as it thinks fit altering or dispensing from compliance with such of the duties of his office as are affected by the fact that default proceedings are pending or could be taken, or have been or could have been taken.

161(4) **[Disapplication of Insolvency Act 1986 provisions]** Nothing in section 126, 128, 130, 185 or 285 of, or paragraph 40, 41, 42 or 43 (including those paragraphs as applied by paragraph 44) of Schedule B1 to, the Insolvency Act 1986 (which restrict the taking of certain legal proceedings and other steps), and nothing in any rule of law in Scotland to the like effect as the said section 285, in the Bankruptcy (Scotland) Act 2016 or in the Debtors (Scotland) Act 1987 as to the effect of sequestration, shall affect any action taken by a recognised body for the purpose of its default proceedings.

History

Section 161(4) amended by the Enterprise Act 2002 s.248(3) and Sch.17 paras 43, 45 and further amended by the Financial Markets and Insolvency Regulations 2009 (SI 2009/853) reg.2(1), (6)(a), (b) as from 15 June 2009. The former amendment has no effect in relation to certain companies by virtue of the Enterprise Act 2002 s.249(1), and so the original wording of s.161(4) continues to apply to them, subject to a minor amendment made by reg.6(c); this now reads "Nothing in section 10, 11, 126, 128, 130, 185 or 285 of the Insolvency Act 1986 [etc.]".

Section 161(2), (4) amended by the Central Securities Depositories Regulations 2017 (SI 2017/1064) regs 1, 3(1), (8) as from 28 November 2017.

Note

See note after s.182.

162   Duty to report on completion of default proceedings

162(1)   **[Report to regulator]** Subject to subsection (1A), a recognised body shall, on the completion of proceedings under its default rules, report to the appropriate regulator on its proceedings stating in respect of each creditor or debtor the sum or sums certified by them to be payable from or to the defaulter or, as the case may be, the fact that no sum is payable.

162(1A)   **[When report not required]** A recognised overseas investment exchange or recognised overseas clearing house shall not be subject to the obligation under subsection (1) unless it has been notified by the appropriate regulator that a report is required for the purpose of insolvency proceedings in any part of the United Kingdom.

162(1B)   **[Report may exclude transferred clearing member client contract]** The report under subsection (1) need not deal with a clearing member client contract which has been transferred in accordance with the default rules of a recognised central counterparty.

162(2)   **[Report or reports]** The recognised body may make a single report or may make reports from time to time as proceedings are completed with respect to the transactions affecting particular persons.

162(3)   **[Copy report]** The recognised body shall supply a copy of every report under this section to the defaulter and to any relevant office-holder acting in relation to him or his estate.

162(4)   **[Publication]** When a report under this section is received by the appropriate regulator, it shall publish notice of that fact in such manner as it thinks appropriate for bringing the report to the attention of creditors and debtors of the defaulter.

162(5)   **[Inspection]** A recognised body shall make available for inspection by a creditor or debtor of the defaulter so much of any report by it under this section as relates to the sum (if any) certified to be due to or from him or to the method by which that sum was determined.

162(6)   **[Fee for copy]** Any such person may require the recognised body, on payment of such reasonable fee as the recognised body may determine, to provide him with a copy of any part of a report which he is entitled to inspect.

162(7)   **["The appropriate regulator"]** "The appropriate regulator"–

   (a)   in relation to a recognised investment exchange or a recognised overseas investment exchange, means the FCA, and

   (b)   in relation to a recognised CSD, a recognised clearing house or a recognised overseas clearing house, means the Bank of England.

History

Section 162(7) inserted by the Financial Services Act 2012 s.114(1) and Sch.18 para.66 as from 1 April 2013.

Section 162(1) amended and s.162(1A) inserted by the Financial Services and Markets Act 2000 (Over the Counter

Derivatives, Central Counterparties and Trade Repositories) Regulations 2013 (SI 2013/504) reg.4(1), (7) as from 1 April 2013. Section 162(1)–(3), (5)–(7) amended by the Central Securities Depositories Regulations 2017 (SI 2017/1064) regs 1, 3(1), (9) as from 28 November 2017.

163 Net sum payable on completion of default proceedings

163(1) [Application] The following provisions apply with respect to a net sum certified by a recognised body under its default rules to be payable by or to a defaulter.

163(2) [Debt in England and Wales] If, in England and Wales, a bankruptcy, winding-up or administration order has been made, or a resolution for voluntary winding up has been passed, the debt–

(a) is provable in the bankruptcy, winding up or administration or, as the case may be, is payable to the relevant office-holder, and

(b) shall be taken into account, where appropriate, under section 323 of the Insolvency Act 1986 (mutual dealings and set-off) or the corresponding provision applicable in the case of winding up or administration,

in the same way as a debt due before the commencement of the bankruptcy, the date on which the body corporate goes into liquidation (within the meaning of section 247 of the Insolvency Act 1986), or enters administration or, in the case of a partnership, the date of the winding-up order or the date on which the partnership enters administration.

163(3) [Scotland] If, in Scotland, an award of sequestration or a winding-up or administration order has been made, or a resolution for voluntary winding up has been passed, the debt–

(a) may be claimed in the sequestration, winding up or administration or, as the case may be, is payable to the relevant office-holder, and

(b) shall be taken into account for the purposes of any rule of law relating to set-off applicable in sequestration, winding up or administration,

in the same way as a debt due before the date of sequestration (within the meaning of section 22(7) of the Bankruptcy (Scotland) Act 2016) or the commencement of the winding up (within the meaning of section 129 of the Insolvency Act 1986) or the date on which the body corporate enters administration.

163(3A) [Making of an administration order in s.163(2), (3)] In subsections (2) and (3), a reference to the making of an administration order shall be taken to include a reference to the appointment of an administrator under–

(a) paragraph 14 of Schedule B1 to the Insolvency Act 1986 (appointment by holder of qualifying floating charge); or

(b) paragraph 22 of that Schedule (appointment by company or directors).

163(4) [Notice] However, where (or to the extent that) a sum is taken into account by virtue of subsection (2)(b) or (3)(b) which arises from a contract entered into at a time when the creditor had notice–

(a) that a bankruptcy application or a bankruptcy petition or, in Scotland, a petition for sequestration was pending,

(b) that a statement as to the affairs of the company had been made out and sent under section 99 of the Insolvency Act 1986 or that a winding-up petition was pending, or

(c) that an application for an administration order was pending or that any person had given notice of intention to appoint an administrator, the value of any profit to him arising from the sum being so taken into account (or being so taken into account to that extent) is recoverable from him by the relevant office-holder unless the court directs otherwise.

163(5) **[Non-application of s.163(4)]** Subsection (4) does not apply in relation to a sum arising from a contract effected under the default rules of a recognised body.

163(6) **[Priority]** Any sum recoverable by virtue of subsection (4) ranks for priority, in the event of the insolvency of the person from whom it is due, immediately before preferential or, in Scotland, preferred debts.

History
Section 163(2), (3) amended, and s.163(3A), (4)(c) inserted, by the Financial Markets and Insolvency Regulations 2009 (SI 2009/853) reg.2(1), (7) as from 15 June 2009. Section 163(1) substituted by the Financial Services and Markets Act 2000 (Over the Counter Derivatives, Central Counterparties and Trade Repositories) Regulations 2013 (SI 2013/504) reg.4(1), (8) as from 1 April 2013. Section 163(4)(a) amended by the Enterprise and Regulatory Reform Act 2013 (Consequential Amendments) (Bankruptcy) and the Small Business, Enterprise and Employment Act 2015 (Consequential Amendments) Regulations 2016 (SI 2016/481) reg.2(1) and Sch.1 para.9(4) as from 6 April 2016. Section 163(4)(b) amended by the Deregulation Act 2015 and Small Business, Enterprise and Employment Act 2015 (Consequential Amendments) (Savings) Regulations 2017 (SI 2017/540) regs 1, 2, Sch.1 para.2(1), (3) as from 6 April 2017. Section 163(1), (5) amended by the Central Securities Depositories Regulations 2017 (SI 2017/1064) regs 1, 3(1), (10) as from 28 November 2017.

Note
See note after s.182.

164 Disclaimer of property, rescission of contracts, etc.

164(1) **[Disapplication of Insolvency Act 1986 ss.178, 186, 315, 345]** Sections 178, 186, 315 and 345 of the Insolvency Act 1986 (power to disclaim onerous property and court's power to order rescission of contracts, etc.) do not apply in relation to–

(a) a market contract,

(aa) a qualifying collateral arrangement,

(ab) a transfer of a clearing member client contract, a client trade or a qualifying collateral arrangement, as mentioned in paragraphs (c) to (e) of section 158(1),

(ac) a qualifying property transfer, or

(b) a contract effected by the recognised body for the purpose of realising property provided as margin in relation to market contracts or as default fund contribution.

In the application of this subsection in Scotland, the reference to sections 178, 315 and 345 shall be construed as a reference to any rule of law having the like effect as those sections.

164(2) **[Scotland]** In Scotland, a trustee in the sequestration of the estate of a defaulter or a liquidator is bound by any market contract to which that defaulter is a party and by any contract as is mentioned in subsection (1)(b) above notwithstanding section 110 of the Bankruptcy (Scotland) Act 2016 or any rule of law to the like effect applying in liquidations.

164(3) **[Disapplication of Insolvency Act 1986 ss.127, 284]** Sections 127 and 284 of the Insolvency Act 1986 (avoidance of property dispositions effected after commencement of winding up, submission of bankruptcy application or presentation of bankruptcy petition), and section 87(4) of the Bankruptcy (Scotland) Act 2016 (effect of dealing with debtor relating to estate vested in trustee), do not apply to–

(a) a market contract, or any disposition of property in pursuance of such a contract,

(b) the provision of margin in relation to market contracts,

(ba) the provision of default fund contribution to the recognised body, (bb) a qualifying collateral arrangement,

(bc) a transfer of a clearing member client contract, a client trade or a qualifying collateral arrangement, as mentioned in paragraphs (c) to (e) of section 158(1),

(bd) a qualifying property transfer,

(c) a contract effected by the recognised body for the purpose of realising property provided as margin in relation to a market contract or as default fund contribution, or any disposition of property in pursuance of such a contract, or

(d) any disposition of property in accordance with the rules of the recognised body as to the application of property provided as margin or as default fund contribution.

164(4) [Notice] However, where–

(a) a market contract is entered into by a person who has notice that a bankruptcy application has been submitted or a petition has been presented for the winding up or bankruptcy or sequestration of the estate of the other party to the contract, or

(b) margin in relation to a market contract or default fund contribution is accepted by a person who has notice that such an application has been made or petition presented in relation to the person by whom or on whose behalf the margin or default fund contribution is provided,

the value of any profit to him arising from the contract or, as the case may be, the amount or value of the margin or default fund contribution is recoverable from him by the relevant office-holder unless the court directs otherwise.

164(5) [Non-application of s.164(4)] Subsection (4)(a) does not apply where the person entering into the contract is a recognised body acting in accordance with its rules, or where the contract is effected under the default rules of such a recognised body; but subsection (4)(b) applies in relation to the provision of–

(a) margin in relation to any such contract, unless the contract has been transferred in accordance with the default rules of the central counterparty, or

(b) default fund contribution.

164(6) [Priority] Any sum recoverable by virtue of subsection (4) ranks for priority, in the event of the insolvency of the person from whom it is due, immediately before preferential or, in Scotland, preferred debts.

History
Section 164(1), (3), (4), (5) amended by the Financial Markets and Insolvency Regulations 2009 (SI 2009/853) reg.2(1), (8) as from 15 June 2009. Section 164(3), (4)(a), (4)(b) amended by the Enterprise and Regulatory Reform Act 2013 (Consequential Amendments) (Bankruptcy) and the Small Business, Enterprise and Employment Act 2015 (Consequential Amendments) Regulations 2016 (SI 2016/481) reg.2(1) and Sch.1 para.9(5) as from 6 April 2016. Section 164(1), (3), (5) amended by the Central Securities Depositories Regulations 2017 (SI 2017/1064) regs 1, 3(1), (11) as from 28 November 2017.

Note
See note after s.182.

165 Adjustment of prior transactions

165(1) [Disapplication of Insolvency Act 1986 provisions] No order shall be made in relation to a transaction to which this section applies under–

(a) section 238 or 339 of the Insolvency Act 1986 (transactions at an under-value),

(b) section 239 or 340 of that Act (preferences), or

(c)   section 423 of that Act (transactions defrauding creditors).

165(2)   [Scotland] As respects Scotland, no decree shall be granted in relation to any such transaction–

(a)   under section 98 or 99 of the Bankruptcy (Scotland) Act 2016 or section 242 or 243 of the Insolvency Act 1986 (gratuitous alienations and unfair preferences), or

(b)   at common law on grounds of gratuitous alienations or fraudulent preferences.

165(3)   [Application] This section applies to–

(a)   a market contract to which a recognised body is a party or which is entered into under its default rules,

(ab)   a market contract to which this Part applies by virtue of section 155(2B), and

(b)   a disposition of property in pursuance of a market contract referred to in paragraph (a) or (ab).

165(4)   [Margin] Where margin is provided in relation to a market contract and (by virtue of subsection (3)(a), (3)(ab) or otherwise) no such order or decree as is mentioned in subsection (1) or (2) has been, or could be, made in relation to that contract, this section applies to–

(a)   the provision of the margin,

(ab)   a qualifying collateral arrangement,

(b)   any contract effected by the recognised body in question for the purpose of realising the property provided as margin, and

(c)   any disposition of property in accordance with the rules of the recognised body in question as to the application of property provided as margin.

165(5)   [Further application] This section also applies to–

(a)   the provision of default fund contribution to a recognised body,

(b)   any contract effected by a recognised body for the purpose of realising the property provided as default fund contribution,

(c)   any disposition of property in accordance with the rules of the recognised body as to the application of property provided as default fund contribution,

(d)   a transfer of a clearing member client contract, a client trade or a qualifying collateral arrangement as mentioned in paragraphs (c) to (e) of section 158(1), and

(e)   a qualifying property transfer.

History
Section 165(4)(c) amended, and s.165(5) inserted, by the Financial Markets and Insolvency Regulations 2009 (SI 2009/853) reg.2(1), (9) as from 15 June 2009. Section 165(3)(b) substituted, s.165(3)(a), 165(4), 165(5)(b) amended and s.165(4)(ab), 165(5)(d) inserted by the Financial Services and Markets Act 2000 (Over the Counter Derivatives, Central Counterparties and Trade Repositories) Regulations 2013 (SI 2013/504) reg.4(1), (10) as from 1 April 2013.
    Section 165(3)–(5) amended by the Central Securities Depositories Regulations 2017 (SI 2017/1064) regs 1, 3(1), (12) as from 28 November 2017.

166   Powers to give directions

166(1)   [Application] The powers conferred by this section are exercisable in relation to a recognised UK investment exchange or recognised clearing house or recognised CSD.

166(2)   [No action under default rules] Where in any case a recognised body has not taken action under its default rules–

(a)   if it appears to the appropriate regulator that it could take action, the regulator may direct it to do so, and

(b)   if it appears to the appropriate regulator that it is proposing to take or may take action, the regulator may direct it not to do so.

166(3)   **[Consultation]** Before giving such a direction the appropriate regulator shall consult the recognised body in question; and it shall not give a direction unless it is satisfied, in the light of that consultation–

(a)   in the case of a direction to take action, that failure to take action would involve undue risk to investors or other participants in the market,

(b)   in the case of a direction not to take action, that the taking of action would be premature or otherwise undesirable in the interests of investors or other participants in the market,

(c)   in either case, that the direction is necessary having regard to the public interest in the stability of the financial system of the United Kingdom, or

(d)   in either case, that the direction is necessary–

     (i)   to facilitate a proposed or possible use of a power under Part 1 of the Banking Act 2009 (special resolution regime), or

     (ii)   in connection with a particular exercise of a power under that Part.

166(3A)   **[Direction to office-holder]** The appropriate regulator may give a direction to a relevant office-holder appointed in respect of a defaulting clearing member to take any action, or refrain from taking any action, if the direction is given for the purposes of facilitating–

(a)   the transfer of a clearing member client contract, a client trade or a qualifying collateral arrangement, or

(b)   a qualifying property transfer.

166(3B)   **[Compliance by office-holder with s.166(3A) direction]** The relevant office-holder to whom a direction is given under subsection (3A)–

(a)   must comply with the direction notwithstanding any duty on the relevant office-holder under any enactment relating to insolvency, but

(b)   is not required to comply with the direction given if the value of the clearing member's estate is unlikely to be sufficient to meet the office-holder's reasonable expenses of complying.

166(3C)   **[Office-holder's expenses for compliance with s.166(3A) direction]** The expenses of the relevant office-holder in complying with a direction of the regulator under subsection (3A) are recoverable as part of the expenses incurred in the discharge of the office-holder's duties.

166(4)   **[Direction]** A direction shall specify the grounds on which it is given.

166(5)   **[Duration of direction]** A direction not to take action may be expressed to have effect until the giving of a further direction (which may be a direction to take action or simply revoking the earlier direction).

166(6)   **[Effect of insolvency]** No direction shall be given not to take action if, in relation to the person in question–

(a)   a bankruptcy order or an award of sequestration of his estate has been made, or an interim receiver or interim trustee has been appointed, or

(b)   a winding up order has been made, a resolution for voluntary winding up has been passed or an administrator, administrative receiver or provisional liquidator has been appointed;

and any previous direction not to take action shall cease to have effect on the making or passing of any such order, award or appointment.

166(7) [Action under default rules] Where a recognised body has taken or been directed to take action under its default rules, the appropriate regulator may direct it to do or not to do such things (being things which it has power to do under its default rules) as are specified in the direction.

166(7A) [Where direction under s.166(2)(a) by virtue of s.166(3)(a)] Where the recognised body is acting in accordance with a direction under subsection (2)(a) that was given only by virtue of paragraph (a) of subsection (3), the appropriate regulator shall not give a direction under subsection (7) unless it is satisfied that the direction under that subsection will not impede or frustrate the proper and efficient conduct of the default proceedings.

166(7B) [Conditions where action under default rules without direction] Where the recognised body has taken action under its default rules without being directed to do so, the appropriate regulator shall not give a direction under subsection (7) unless–

(a) it is satisfied that the direction under that subsection will not impede or frustrate the proper and efficient conduct of the default proceedings, or

(b) it is satisfied that the direction is necessary–

   (i) having regard to the public interest in the stability of the financial system of the United Kingdom,

   (ii) to facilitate a proposed or possible use of a power under Part 1 of the Banking Act 2009 (special resolution regime), or

   (iii) in connection with a particular exercise of a power under that Part.

166(8) [Enforcement] A direction under this section is enforceable, on the application of the regulator which gave the direction, by injunction or, in Scotland, by an order under section 45 of the Court of Session Act 1988; and where a recognised body or a relevant office-holder has not complied with a direction, the court may make such order as it thinks fit for restoring the position to what it would have been if the direction had been complied with.

166(9) ["The appropriate regulator"] "The appropriate regulator"–

(a) in relation to a recognised UK investment exchange, means the FCA, and

(b) in relation to a recognised CSD, a recognised clearing house or a defaulting clearing member, means the Bank of England.

History
Section 166(7A), (7B), (9) inserted by the Financial Services Act 2012 s.111 as from 1 April 2013. Section 166(3A)–(3C) inserted and s.166(1), 166(8), 166(9)(b) amended by the Financial Services and Markets Act 2000 (Over the Counter Derivatives, Central Counterparties and Trade Repositories) Regulations 2013 (SI 2013/504) reg.4(1), (11) as from 1 April 2013. Section 166(9)(b) amended by the Financial Services and Markets Act 2000 (Over the Counter Derivatives, Central Counterparties and Trade Repositories) (No.2) Regulations 2013 (SI 2013/1908) reg.2(1), (6) as from 26 August 2013.
    Section 166(1)–(3), (7)–(9) amended by the Central Securities Depositories Regulations 2017 (SI 2017/1064) regs 1, 3(1), (13) as from 28 November 2017.

Note
See note after s.167.

167 Application to determine whether default proceedings to be taken

167(1) [Application] This section applies where a relevant insolvency event has occurred in the case of–

(a) a recognised investment exchange or a member or designated non-member of a recognised investment exchange,

(b) a recognised clearing house or a member of a recognised clearing house,

(ba) a recognised CSD or a member of a recognised CSD, or

(c) a client which is providing indirect clearing services to an indirect client.

The person referred to in paragraphs (a) to (c) in whose case a relevant insolvency event has occurred is referred to below as "the person in default".

167(1A) ["Relevant insolvency event"] For the purposes of this section a "relevant insolvency event" occurs where–

(a) a bankruptcy order is made,

(b) an award of sequestration is made,

(c) an order appointing an interim receiver is made,

(d) an administration or winding up order is made,

(e) an administrator is appointed under paragraph 14 of Schedule B1 to the Insolvency Act 1986 (appointment by holder of qualifying floating charge) or under paragraph 22 of that Schedule (appointment by company or directors),

(f) a resolution for voluntary winding up is passed, or

(g) an order appointing a provisional liquidator is made.

167(1B) [Application by office-holder] Where in relation to a person in default a recognised body ("the responsible recognised body")–

(a) has power under its default rules to take action in consequence of the relevant insolvency event or the matters giving rise to it, but

(b) has not done so,

a relevant office-holder appointed in connection with or in consequence of the relevant insolvency event may apply to the appropriate regulator.

167(2) [Contents of application] The application shall specify the responsible recognised body and the grounds on which it is made.

167(3) [Regulator's duty] On receipt of the application the appropriate regulator shall notify the responsible recognised body, and unless within three business days after the day on which the notice is received the responsible recognised body–

(a) takes action under its default rules, or

(b) notifies the appropriate regulator that it proposes to do so forthwith,

then, subject as follows, the provisions of sections 158 to 165 above do not apply in relation to market contracts to which the person in default is a party or to anything done by the responsible recognised body for the purposes of, or in connection with, the settlement of any such contract.

For this purpose a "business day" means any day which is not a Saturday or Sunday, Christmas Day, Good Friday or a bank holiday in any part of the United Kingdom under the Banking and Financial Dealings Act 1971.

167(4) [Application of ss.158–165] The provisions of sections 158 to 165 are not disapplied if before the end of the period mentioned in subsection (3) the appropriate regulator gives the responsible recognised body a direction under section 166(2)(a) (direction to take action under default rules).

No such direction may be given after the end of that period.

167(5) **[Enforcement]** If the responsible recognised body notifies the appropriate regulator that it proposes to take action under its default rules forthwith, it shall do so; and that duty is enforceable, on the application of the appropriate regulator, by injunction or, in Scotland, by an order under section 45 of the Court of Session Act 1988.

167(6) **["The appropriate regulator"]** "The appropriate regulator"–

   (a)   in relation to a recognised investment exchange, means the FCA, and

   (b)   in relation to a recognised clearing house or recognised CSD, means the Bank of England.

History
Section 167(1A) inserted by the Enterprise Act 2002 s.248(3), Sch.17 paras 43, 46 as from 15 September 2003 subject to transitional provisions in SI 2003/2093 (C. 85) art.3. The amendment has no effect in relation to certain companies by virtue of the Enterprise Act 2002 s.249(1). Section 167(1), (1A) amended, and s.167(1B) inserted, by the Financial Markets and Insolvency Regulations 2009 (SI 2009/853) reg.2(1), (10)(a) as from 15 June 2009. Section 167(2)–(5) amended by the Financial Markets and Insolvency Regulations 2009 (SI 2009/853) reg.2(1), (10)(b)–(d) as from 15 June 2009. Section 167(6) inserted by the Financial Services Act 2012 s.114(1) and Sch.18 para.67 as from 1 April 2013. Section 167(1) amended by the Financial Services and Markets Act 2000 (Over the Counter Derivatives, Central Counterparties and Trade Repositories) (No.2) Regulations 2013 (SI 2013/1908) reg.2(1), (7) as from 26 August 2013.
    Section 167(1), (1B)–(6) amended by the Central Securities Depositories Regulations 2017 (SI 2017/1064) regs 1, 3(1), (14) as from 28 November 2017.

168   Delegation of functions to designated agency

168   [Repealed by the Financial Services and Markets Act 2000 (Consequential Amendments and Repeals) Order 2001 (SI 2001/3649) arts 1, 75(f) as from 1 December 2001.]

169   Supplementary provisions

169(1)   [Repealed by the Financial Services and Markets Act 2000 (Consequential Amendments and Repeals) Order 2001 (SI 2001/3649) arts 1, 75(g) as from 1 December 2001.]

169(2)   **[Application of ss.296, 297 of Financial Services and Markets Act 2000]** Sections 296 and 297 of the Financial Services and Markets Act 2000 apply in relation to a failure by a recognised investment exchange or recognised clearing house to comply with an obligation under this Part as to a failure to comply with an obligation under that Act.

169(2A)   **[Application of FSMA 2000 s.296]** Section 296 of the Financial Services and Markets Act 2000 applies in relation to a failure by a recognised CSD to comply with an obligation under this Part as to a failure to comply with an obligation under that Act.

169(3)   **[Revocation of recognition]** Where the recognition of an investment exchange, clearing house or central securities depository is revoked under the Financial Services and Markets Act 2000, the appropriate authority may, before or after the revocation order, give such directions as it thinks fit with respect to the continued application of the provisions of this Part, with such exceptions, additions and adaptations as may be specified in the direction, in relation to cases where a relevant event of any description specified in the directions occurred before the revocation order takes effect.

169(3A)   **["The appropriate authority"]** "The appropriate authority" means–

   (a)   in the case of an overseas investment exchange or clearing house, the Treasury;

   (b)   in the case of a UK investment exchange, the FCA,

   (c)   in the case of a UK clearing house, the Bank of England, and

   (d)   in the case of a central securities depository, the Bank of England.

169(4)   [Repealed by the Financial Services and Markets Act 2000 (Consequential Amendments and Repeals) Order 2001 (SI 2001/3649) arts 1, 75(g) as from 1 December 2001.]

169(5)   **[Application of s.414 regulations]** Regulations under section 414 of the Financial Services and Markets Act 2000 (service of notices) may make provision in relation to a notice, direction or other document required or authorised by or under this Part to be given to or served on any person other than the Treasury, the FCA or the Bank of England.

History
In s.169(2) the words "Sections 296 and 297 of the Financial Services and Markets Act 2000 apply" substituted by the Financial Services and Markets Act 2000 (Consequential Amendments and Repeals) Order 2001 (SI 2001/3649) arts 1, 83(1), (2) as from 1 December 2001.
     Section 169(3A)(b), (c) inserted by the Financial Services Act 2012 s.114(1) and Sch.18 para.68 as from 1 April 2013.
     Section 169(2A) and (3A)(d) inserted and subs.(3) amended by the Central Securities Depositories Regulations 2017 (SI 2017/1064) regs 1, 3(1), (15) as from 28 November 2017.

Other exchanges and clearing houses

170   Certain overseas exchanges and clearing houses

170(1)   **[Regulations]** The Secretary of State and the Treasury may by regulations provide that this Part applies in relation to contracts connected with an overseas investment exchange or overseas clearing house which–

   (a)   is not a recognised investment exchange or recognised clearing house, but

   (b)   is approved by the Treasury in accordance with such requirements as may be so specified,

as it applies in relation to contracts connected with a recognised investment exchange or recognised clearing house.

History
Section 170(1) substituted by the Financial Markets and Insolvency Regulations 2009 (SI 2009/853) reg.2(1), (11) as from 15 June 2009.

170(2)   **[Approval by Treasury]** The Treasury shall not approve an overseas investment exchange or clearing house unless they are satisfied–

   (a)   that the rules and practices of the body, together with the law of the country in which the body's head office is situated, provide adequate procedures for dealing with the default of persons party to contracts connected with the body, and

   (b)   that it is otherwise appropriate to approve the body.

170(3)   **[Section 170(2)(a) default]** The reference in subsection (2)(a) to default is to a person being unable to meet his obligations.

170(4)   **[Application of Financial Services and Markets Act]** The regulations may apply in relation to the approval of a body under this section such of the provisions of the Financial Services and Markets Act 2000 as the Secretary of State considers appropriate.

170(5)   **[Scope of regulations]** The Secretary of State may make regulations which, in relation to a body which is so approved–

   (a)   apply such of the provisions of the Financial Services and Markets Act 2000 as the Secretary of State considers appropriate, and

   (b)   provide that the provisions of this Part apply with such exceptions, additions and adaptations as appear to the Secretary of State to be necessary or expedient;

and different provision may be made with respect to different bodies or descriptions of body.

170(6) **[Modification of Financial Services Act 2000 provisions]** Where the regulations apply any provisions of the Financial Services and Markets Act 2000, they may provide that those provisions apply with such exceptions, additions and adaptations as appear to the Secretary of State to be necessary or expedient.

Note
Section 170 not in force with rest of Part.

170A   EEA central counterparties and third country central counterparties

170A(1) **[Definitions]** In this section and section 170B–

(a)   "assets" has the meaning given by Article 39(10) of the EMIR Level 1 Regulation;

(b)   "EBA" means the European Banking Authority established by Regulation 1093/2010/EU of 24 November 2010 establishing a European Supervisory Authority (European Banking Authority) 10;

(c)   "ESMA" means the European Securities and Markets Authority established by Regulation 1095/2010/EU of 24 November 2010 establishing a European Supervisory Authority (European Securities and Markets Authority) 11;

(d)   "overseas competent authority" means a competent authority responsible for the authorisation or supervision of clearing houses or central counterparties in a country or territory other than the United Kingdom;

(e)   "relevant provisions" means any provisions of the default rules of an EEA central counterparty or third country central counterparty which–

    (i)   provide for the transfer of the positions or assets of a defaulting clearing member;

    (ii)   are not necessary for the purposes of complying with the minimum requirements of Articles 48(5) and (6) of the EMIR Level 1 Regulation; and

    (iii)   may be relevant to a question falling to be determined in accordance with the law of a part of the United Kingdom;

(f)   "relevant requirements" means the requirements specified in paragraph 34(2) (portability of accounts: default rules going beyond requirements of EMIR) of Part 6 of the Schedule to the Financial Services and Markets Act 2000 (Recognition Requirements for Investment Exchanges, Clearing Houses and Central Securities Depositories) Regulations 2001;

(g)   "UK clearing member" means a clearing member to which the law of a part of the United Kingdom will apply for the purposes of an insolvent reorganisation or winding up, and

(h)   "UK client" means a client–

    (i)   which offers indirect clearing services, and

    (ii)   to which the law of a part of the United Kingdom will apply for the purposes of an insolvent re-organisation or winding up.

170A(2) **[Modifications of transactions through recognised central counterparty]** This Part applies to transactions cleared through an EEA central counterparty or a third country central counterparty by a UK clearing member or a UK client as it applies to transactions cleared through a recognised central counterparty, but subject to the modifications in subsections (3) to (5).

170A(3) **[Substitution of s.157]** For section 157 there is to be substituted–

    "**157 Change in default rules**

157(1) An EEA central counterparty or a third country central counterparty in respect of which an order under section 170B(4) has been made and not revoked must give the Bank of England at least three months' notice of any proposal to amend, revoke or add to its default rules.

157(2) The Bank of England may, if it considers it appropriate to do so, agree a shorter period of notice.

157(3) Where notice is given to the Bank of England under subsection (1) an EEA central counterparty or third country central counterparty must provide the Bank of England with such information, documents and reports as the Bank of England may require.

157(4) Information, documents and reports required under subsection (3) must be provided in English and be given at such times, in such form and at such place, and verified in such a manner, as the Bank of England may direct.".

170A(4) **[Condition for s.162 application]** Section 162 does not apply to an EEA central counterparty or a third country central counterparty unless it has been notified by the Bank of England that a report under that section is required for the purposes of insolvency proceedings in any part of the United Kingdom.

170A(5) **[References to "rules" or "default rules"]** In relation to an EEA central counterparty or third country central counterparty, references in this Part to the "rules" or "default rules" of the central counterparty are to be taken not to include references to any relevant provisions unless–

(a) the relevant provisions satisfy the relevant requirements; or

(b) the Bank of England has made an order under section 170B(4) recognising that the relevant provisions of its default rules satisfy the relevant requirements and the order has not been revoked.

History
Section 170A inserted by the Financial Services and Markets Act 2000 (Over the Counter Derivatives, Central Counterparties and Trade Repositories) Regulations 2013 (SI 2013/504) reg.4(1), (12) as from 1 April 2013. Section 170A((1)(h) inserted and s.170(2) amended by the Financial Services and Markets Act 2000 (Over the Counter Derivatives, Central Counterparties and Trade Repositories) (No.2) Regulations 2013 (SI 2013/1908) reg.2(1), (8) as from 26 August 2013.

Section 170A(1)(f) amended by the Central Securities Depositories Regulations 2017 (SI 2017/1064) regs 1, 3(1), (16) as from 28 November 2017.

170B   EEA central counterparties and third country central counterparties: procedure

170B(1) **[Application to Bank of England]** An EEA central counterparty or third country central counterparty may apply to the Bank of England for an order recognising that the relevant provisions of its default rules satisfy the relevant requirements.

170B(2) **[Bank of England may direct manner of application]** The application must be made in such manner, and must be accompanied by such information, documents and reports, as the Bank of England may direct.

170B(3) **[Provision and verification of information, documents and reports]** Information, documents and reports required under subsection (2) must be provided in English and be given at such times, in such form and at such place, and verified in such manner, as the Bank of England may direct.

170B(4) **[Recognition order by Bank]** The Bank of England may make an order recognising that the relevant provisions of the default rules satisfy the relevant requirements.

170B(5) **[Revocation of recognition order]** The Bank of England may by order revoke an order made under subsection (4) if–

(a) the EEA central counterparty or third country central counterparty consents;

(b) the EEA central counterparty or third country central counterparty has failed to pay a fee which is owing to the Bank of England under paragraph 36 of Schedule 17A to the Financial Services and Markets Act 2000;

(c) the EEA central counterparty or third country central counterparty is failing or has failed to comply with a requirement of or imposed under section 157 (as modified by section 170A(3)); or

(d) it appears to the Bank of England that the relevant provisions no longer satisfy the relevant requirements.

170B(6) [Time and date of s.170B(4), (5) orders] An order made under subsection (4) or (5) must state the time and date when it is to have effect.

170B(7) [Revocation order may contain transitional provision] An order made under subsection (5) may contain such transitional provision as the Bank of England considers appropriate.

170B(8) [Bank to maintain and publish register of s.170B(4) orders] The Bank of England must–

(a) maintain a register of orders made under subsection (4) which are in force; and

(b) publish the register in such manner as it appears to the Bank of England to be appropriate.

170B(9) [Application of FSMA 2000 s.298 subject to modifications] Section 298 of the Financial Services and Markets Act 2000 applies to a refusal to make an order under subsection (4) or the making of a revocation order under subsection (5)(b), (c) or (d) as it applies to the making of a revocation order under section 297(2) of the Financial Services and Markets Act 2000, but with the following modifications–

(a) for "appropriate regulator" substitute "the Bank of England";

(b) for "recognised body" substitute "EEA central counterparty or third country central counterparty"; and

(c) in subsection (7), for "give a direction under section 296" substitute "make an order under paragraph (b), (c) or (d) of section 170B(5) of the Companies Act 1989".

170B(10) [Reference to Upper Tribunal] If the Bank of England refuses to make an order under subsection (4) or makes an order under subsection (5)(b), (c) or (d), the EEA central counterparty or third country central counterparty may refer the matter to the Upper Tribunal.

170B(11) [Bank's reliance on information for s.170B(1), (5)(d)] The Bank of England may rely on information or advice from an overseas competent authority, the EBA or ESMA in its determination of an application under subsection (1) or the making of a revocation order under subsection (5)(d).

History
Section 170B inserted by the Financial Services and Markets Act 2000 (Over the Counter Derivatives, Central Counterparties and Trade Repositories) Regulations 2013 (SI 2013/504) reg.4(1), (12) as from 1 April 2013.

170C EEA CSDs and third country CSDs

170C(1) [Application of Pt VII] This Part applies to transactions settled through an EEA CSD or a third country CSD by a UK member of the central securities depository as it applies to transactions settled through a recognised CSD, but subject to subsections (2), (3) and (4).

170C(2) ["Authorised central securities depository services" in s.155(3D)] The definition of "authorised central securities depository services" in section 155(3D) applies to third country CSDs as if it read–

""authorised central securities depository services" means, in relation to a third country CSD, those services which that central securities depository is authorised to provide that are equivalent to the services listed in the Annex to the CSD regulation.".

170C(3)   [Non-application of s.157] Section 157 does not apply to an EEA CSD or a third country CSD.

170C(4)   [Non-application of s.162] Section 162 does not apply to an EEA CSD or a third country CSD unless it has been notified by the Bank of England that a report under that section is required for the purposes of insolvency proceedings in any part of the United Kingdom. Where an EEA CSD or a third country CSD has been so notified, the appropriate regulator for the purposes of section 162 shall be the Bank of England.

170C(5)   ["UK member"] In this section "UK member" means a member of an EEA CSD or a third country CSD to which the law of a part of the United Kingdom will apply for the purposes of an insolvent reorganisation or winding up.

History
Section 170C inserted by the Central Securities Depositories Regulations 2017 (SI 2017/1064) regs 1, 3(1), (17) as from 28 November 2017.

171   Certain money market institutions

171   [Repealed by the Financial Services and Markets Act 2000 (Consequential Amendments and Repeals) Order 2001 (SI 2001/3649) arts 1, 75(h) as from 1 December 2001.]

172   Settlement arrangements provided by the Bank of England

172(1)   [Regulations] The Secretary of State may by regulations provide that this Part applies to contracts of any specified description in relation to which settlement arrangements are provided by the Bank of England, as it applies to contracts connected with a recognised body.

172(2)   [Modification of provisions] Regulations under this section may provide that the provisions of this Part apply with such exceptions, additions and adaptations as appear to the Secretary of State to be necessary or expedient.

172(3)   [Consultation] Before making any regulations under this section, the Secretary of State and the Treasury shall consult the Bank of England.

Note
Section 172 not in force with rest of Part.
   Section 172(1) amended by the Central Securities Depositories Regulations 2017 (SI 2017/1064) regs 1, 3(1), (18) as from 28 November 2017.

Market charges

173   Market charges

173(1)   ["Market charge"] In this Part "market charge" means a charge, whether fixed or floating, granted–

(a)   in favour of a recognised investment exchange, for the purpose of securing debts or liabilities arising in connection with the settlement of market contracts;

(aa)   in favour of The Stock Exchange, for the purpose of securing debts or liabilities arising in connection with short term certificates;

(b)   in favour of a recognised clearing house, for the purpose of securing debts or liabilities arising in connection with their ensuring the performance of market contracts;

(ba)   in favour of a recognised CSD, for the purpose of securing debts or liabilities arising in connection with their ensuring the performance of market contracts, or

(c) in favour of a person who agrees to make payments as a result of the transfer or allotment of specified securities made through the medium of a computer-based system established by the Bank of England and The Stock Exchange, for the purpose of securing debts or liabilities of the transferee or allottee arising in connection therewith.

173(2)   [Specified purposes] Where a charge is granted partly for purposes specified in subsection (1)(a), (aa), (b), (ba) or (c) and partly for other purposes, it is a "market charge" so far as it has effect for the specified purposes.

173(3)   [Definitions] In subsection (1)–

"short term certificate" means an instrument issued by The Stock Exchange undertaking to procure the transfer of property of a value and description specified in the instrument to or to the order of the person to whom the instrument is issued or his endorsee or to a person acting on behalf of either of them and also undertaking to make appropriate payments in cash, in the event that the obligation to procure the transfer of property cannot be discharged in whole or in part;

"specified securities" means securities for the time being specified in the list in Schedule 1 to the Stock Transfer Act 1982, and includes any right to such securities; and

"transfer", in relation to any such securities or right, means a transfer of the beneficial interest.

173(4)   [Regulations] The Secretary of State may by regulations make further provision as to the charges granted in favour of any such person as is mentioned in subsection (1)(a), (b), (ba) or (c) which are to be treated as "market charges" for the purposes of this Part; and the regulations may add to, amend or repeal the provisions of subsections (1) to (3) above.

173(5)   [Scope of regulations] The regulations may provide that a charge shall or shall not be treated as a market charge if or to the extent that it secures obligations of a specified description, is a charge over property of a specified description or contains provisions of a specified description.

173(6)   [Consultation] Before making regulations under this section in relation to charges granted in favour of a person within subsection (1)(c), the Secretary of State and the Treasury shall consult the Bank of England.

History

Section 173(1)(ba) inserted and subss.(2) and (4) amended by the Central Securities Depositories Regulations 2017 (SI 2017/1064) regs 1, 3(1), (19) as from 28 November 2017.

174   Modifications of the law of insolvency

174(1)   [Application] The general law of insolvency has effect in relation to market charges and action taken in enforcing them subject to the provisions of section 175.

174(2)   [Regulations] The Secretary of State may by regulations make further provision modifying the law of insolvency in relation to the matters mentioned in subsection (1).

174(3)   [Scope of regulations] The regulations may add to, amend or repeal the provisions mentioned in subsection (1), and any other provision of this Part as it applies for the purposes of those provisions, or provide that those provisions have effect with such exceptions, additions or adaptations as are specified in the regulations.

174(4)   [Different provision for different cases] The regulations may make different provision for cases defined by reference to the nature of the charge, the nature of the property subject to it, the circumstances, nature or extent of the obligations secured by it or any other relevant factor.

174(5)   [Consultation] Before making regulations under this section in relation to charges granted in favour of a person within section 173(1)(c), the Secretary of State and the Treasury shall consult the Bank of England.

175   Administration orders, etc.

175(1)   **[Disapplication of Insolvency Act 1986 Sch.B1 paras 43(2), (3), 70–72]** The following provisions of Schedule B1 to the Insolvency Act 1986 (administration) do not apply in relation to a market charge–

  (a)   paragraph 43(2) and (3) (restriction on enforcement of security or repossession of goods) (including that provision as applied by paragraph 44 (interim moratorium)), and

  (b)   paragraphs 70, 71 and 72 (power of administrator to deal with charged or hire-purchase property).

175(1A)   **[Disapplication of Insolvency Act 1986 Sch.B1 para.41(2)]** Paragraph 41(2) of that Schedule (receiver to vacate office at request of administrator) does not apply to a receiver appointed under a market charge.

175(2)   **[Enforcing market charge]** However, where a market charge falls to be enforced after the occurrence of an event to which subsection (2A) applies, and there exists another charge over some or all of the same property ranking in priority to or *pari passu* with the market charge, on the application of any person interested the court may order that there shall be taken after enforcement of the market charge such steps as the court may direct for the purpose of ensuring that the chargee under the other charge is not prejudiced by the enforcement of the market charge.

175(2A)   **[Application of s.175(2A)]** This subsection applies to–

  (a)   making an administration application under paragraph 12 of Schedule B1 to the Insolvency Act 1986,

  (b)   appointing an administrator under paragraph 14 or 22 of that Schedule (appointment by floating charge holder, company or directors),

  (c)   filing with the court a copy of notice of intention to appoint an administrator under either of those paragraphs.

175(3)   **[Disapplication of Insolvency Act 1986 ss.43, 61]** The following provisions of the Insolvency Act 1986 (which relate to the powers of receivers) do not apply in relation to a market charge–

  (a)   section 43 (power of administrative receiver to dispose of charged property), and

  (b)   section 61 (power of receiver in Scotland to dispose of an interest in property).

175(4)   **[Disposition of property]** Sections 127 and 284 of the Insolvency Act 1986 (avoidance of property dispositions effected after commencement of winding up, making of bankruptcy application or presentation of bankruptcy petition), and section 87(4) of the Bankruptcy (Scotland) Act 2016 (effect of dealing with debtor relating to estate vested in trustee), do not apply to a disposition of property as a result of which the property becomes subject to a market charge or any transaction pursuant to which that disposition is made.

175(5)   **[Notice of petition for winding up, bankruptcy or sequestration of estate]** However, if a person who is party to a disposition mentioned in subsection (4) has notice at the time of the disposition that a bankruptcy application has been made or a petition has been presented for the winding up or bankruptcy or sequestration of the estate of the party making the disposition, the value of any profit to him arising from the disposition is recoverable from him by the relevant office-holder unless–

  (a)   the person is a chargee under the market charge,

  (b)   the disposition is made in accordance with the default rules of a recognised central counterparty for the purposes of transferring a position or asset of a clearing member in default, or

  (c)   the court directs otherwise.

175(5A)   **["Asset" in s.175(5)(b)]** In subsection (5)(b), "asset" has the meaning given by Article 39(10) of the EMIR Level 1 Regulation.

175(6)   **[Priority]** Any sum recoverable by virtue of subsection (5) ranks for priority, in the event of the insolvency of the person from whom it is due, immediately before preferential or, in Scotland, preferred debts.

175(7)   **[Application of s.164(4)]** In a case falling within both subsection (4) above (as a disposition of property as a result of which the property becomes subject to a market charge) and section 164(3) (as the provision of margin in relation to a market contract), section 164(4) applies with respect to the recovery of the amount or value of the margin and subsection (5) above does not apply.

History

Section 175(1), (1A) substituted, s.175(2) amended, and s.175(2A) inserted, by the Enterprise Act 2002 s.248(3) and Sch.17 paras 43, 47 as from 15 September 2003 (see the Enterprise Act 2002 (Commencement No.4 and Transitional and Savings) Order 2003 (SI 2003/2093 (C. 85) art.2(1) and Sch.1), subject to transitional provisions in SI 2003/2093 (C. 85) art.3. The amendments have no effect in relation to certain companies by virtue of the Enterprise Act 2002 s.249(1), and so the original wording of s.175 continues to apply to them (as amended, however, by the Financial Markets and Insolvency Regulations 2009 (SI 2009/853) reg.2(1), (12) as from 15 June 2009). Section 175(5) substituted and s.175(5A) inserted by the Financial Services and Markets Act 2000 (Over the Counter Derivatives, Central Counterparties and Trade Repositories) Regulations 2013 (SI 2013/504) reg.4(1), (13), (14) as from 1 April 2013. Section 175(4), (5) amended by the Enterprise and Regulatory Reform Act 2013 (Consequential Amendments) (Bankruptcy) and the Small Business, Enterprise and Employment Act 2015 (Consequential Amendments) Regulations 2016 (SI 2016/481) reg.2(1) and Sch.1 para.9(6) as from 6 April 2016.

See also note after s.182.

176   Power to make provision about certain other charges

176(1)   **[Regulations]** The Secretary of State may by regulations provide that the general law of insolvency has effect in relation to charges of such descriptions as may be specified in the regulations, and action taken in enforcing them, subject to such provisions as may be specified in the regulations.

176(2)   **[Kinds of charge]** The regulations may specify any description of charge granted in favour of–

(a)   a body approved under section 170 (certain overseas exchanges and clearing houses),

(aa) an EEA CSD or a third country CSD,

(b)   a person included in the list maintained by the Bank of England for the purposes of section 301 of the Financial Services and Markets Act 2000 (certain money market institutions),

(c)   the Bank of England,

(d)   a person who has permission under Part 4A of the Financial Services and Markets Act 2000 to carry on a relevant regulated activity, or

(e)   an international securities self-regulating organisation approved for the purposes of an order made under section 22 of the Financial Services and Markets Act 2000,

for the purpose of securing debts or liabilities arising in connection with or as a result of the settlement of contracts or the transfer of assets, rights or interests on a financial market.

176(3)   **[Other charges]** The regulations may specify any description of charge granted for that purpose in favour of any other person in connection with exchange facilities or clearing services or settlement arrangements provided by a recognised investment exchange or recognised clearing house or by any such body, person, authority or organisation as is mentioned in subsection (2), or in connection with authorised central securities depository services (see section 155(3D)) provided by a recognised CSD.

176(4)   **[Where charge granted partly for s.176(2) purpose]** Where a charge is granted partly for the purpose specified in subsection (2) and partly for other purposes, the power conferred by this section is exercisable in relation to the charge so far as it has effect for that purpose.

176(5)   [Scope of regulations] The regulations may–

(a)   make the same or similar provision in relation to the charges to which they apply as is made by or under sections 174 and 175 in relation to market charges, or

(b)   apply any of those provisions with such exceptions, additions or adaptations as are specified in the regulations.

176(6)   [Consultation] Before making regulations under this section relating to a description of charges defined by reference to their being granted in favour of a person included in the list maintained by the Bank of England for the purposes of section 301 of the Financial Services and Markets Act 2000, or in connection with exchange facilities or clearing services or settlement arrangements provided by a person included in that list, the Secretary of State and the Treasury shall consult the FCA and the Bank of England.

176(6A)   [Consultation] Before making regulations under this section relating to a description of charges defined by reference to their being granted in favour of the Bank of England, or in connection with settlement arrangements provided by the Bank, the Secretary of State and the Treasury shall consult the Bank.

176(7)   [Further provisions] Regulations under this section may provide that they apply or do not apply to a charge if or to the extent that it secures obligations of a specified description, is a charge over property of a specified description or contains provisions of a specified description.

176(8)   ["Relevant regulated activity" in s.176(2)(d)] For the purposes of subsection (2)(d), "relevant regulated activity" means–

(a)   dealing in investments as principal or as agent;

(b)   arranging deals in investments;

(ba)   operating a multilateral trading facility;

(bb)   operating an organised trading facility;

(c)   managing investments;

(d)   safeguarding and administering investments;

(e)   sending dematerialised instructions; or

(ea)   managing a UCITS;

(eb)   acting as trustee or depositary of a UCITS;

(ec)   managing an AIF;

(ed)   acting as trustee or depositary of an AIF; or

(f)   establishing etc. a collective investment scheme.

176(9)   [Provisions s.176(8) to be read with] Subsection (8) must be read with–

(a)   section 22 of the Financial Services and Markets Act 2000;

(b)   any relevant order under that section; and

(c)   Schedule 2 to that Act.

History
Section 176(8)(ea)–(ed) added by the Alternative Investment Fund Managers Regulations 2013 (SI 2013/1773) Sch.1 para.39 as from 22 July 2013. Section 176(2)(aa) inserted and subss.(3) and (6) amended by the Central Securities Depositories Regulations 2017 (SI 2017/1064) regs 1, 3(1), (20) as from 28 November 2017. Section 176(8)(bb) added by the Financial Services and Markets Act 2000 (Regulated Activities) (Amendment) Order 2017 (SI 2017/488) Sch.1 para.2 as from 3 January 2018.

177 Application of margin or default fund contribution not affected by certain other interests

177(1) **[Property held as margin or default fund contribution]** The following provisions have effect with respect to the application by a recognised body of property (other than land) held by the recognised body as margin in relation to a market contract or as default fund contribution.

177(2) **[Prior interest]** So far as necessary to enable the property to be applied in accordance with the rules of the recognised body, it may be so applied notwithstanding any prior equitable interest or right, or any right or remedy arising from a breach of fiduciary duty, unless the exchange or clearing house had notice of the interest, right or breach of duty at the time the property was provided as margin or as default fund contribution.

177(3) **[Subsequent right]** No right or remedy arising subsequently to the property being provided as margin or as default fund contribution may be enforced so as to prevent or interfere with the application of the property by the recognised body in accordance with its rules.

177(4) **[Disponee]** Where a recognised body has power by virtue of the above provisions to apply property notwithstanding an interest, right or remedy, a person to whom the recognised body disposes of the property in accordance with its rules takes free from that interest, right or remedy.

History

Section 177 amended by the Financial Markets and Insolvency Regulations 2009 (SI 2009/853) reg.2(1), (13) as from 15 June 2009.

Section 177 amended by the Central Securities Depositories Regulations 2017 (SI 2017/1064) regs 1, 3(1), (21) as from 28 November 2017.

178 Priority of floating market charge over subsequent charges

178(1) **[Regulations]** The Secretary of State may by regulations provide that a market charge which is a floating charge has priority over a charge subsequently created or arising, including a fixed charge.

178(2) **[Different provision for different cases]** The regulations may make different provision for cases defined, as regards the market charge or the subsequent charge, by reference to the description of charge, its terms, the circumstances in which it is created or arises, the nature of the charge, the person in favour of whom it is granted or arises or any other relevant factor.

Note

Section 178 not in force with rest of Part.

179 Priority of market charge over unpaid vendor's lien

179 Where property subject to an unpaid vendor's lien becomes subject to a market charge, the charge has priority over the lien unless the chargee had actual notice of the lien at the time the property became subject to the charge.

180 Proceedings against market property by unsecured creditors

180(1) **[No legal proceedings]** Where property (other than land) is held by a recognised body as margin in relation to market contracts or as default fund contribution, or is subject to a market charge, no execution or other legal process for the enforcement of a judgment or order may be commenced or continued, and no distress may be levied, and no power to use the procedure in Schedule 12 to the Tribunals, Courts and Enforcement Act 2007 (taking control of goods) may be exercised, against the property by a person not seeking to enforce any interest in or security over the property, except with the consent of–

   (a) in the case of property provided as cover for margin or as default fund contribution, the recognised body in question, or

(b) in the case of property subject to a market charge, the person in whose favour the charge was granted.

180(2) [Consent] Where consent is given the proceedings may be commenced or continued notwithstanding any provision of the Insolvency Act 1986 or the Bankruptcy (Scotland) Act 2016.

180(3) [Limit on ancillary relief] Where by virtue of this section a person would not be entitled to enforce a judgment or order against any property, any injunction or other remedy granted with a view to facilitating the enforcement of any such judgment or order shall not extend to that property.

180(4) [Scotland] In the application of this section to Scotland, the reference to execution being commenced or continued includes a reference to diligence being carried out or continued, and the reference to distress being levied shall be omitted.

History
Section 180(1) amended by the Financial Markets and Insolvency Regulations 2009 (SI 2009/853) reg.2(1), (14) as from 15 June 2009. Section 180(1) amended by the Tribunals, Courts and Enforcement Act 2007 s.62(3) and Sch.13 para.91 as from 6 April 2014.

Section 180(1) amended by the Central Securities Depositories Regulations 2017 (SI 2017/1064) regs 1, 3(1), (22) as from 28 November 2017.

181 Power to apply provisions to other cases

181(1) [Power to apply ss.177–180] A power to which this subsection applies includes the power to apply sections 177 to 180 to any description of property provided as cover for margin in relation to contracts in relation to which the power is exercised or, as the case may be, property subject to charges in relation to which the power is exercised.

181(2) [Modification of ss.177–180 by regulations] The regulations may provide that those sections apply with such exceptions, additions and adaptations as may be specified in the regulations.

181(3) [Application of s.181(1)] Subsection (1) applies to the powers of the Secretary of State and the Treasury to act jointly under–

(a) sections 170, 172 and 176 of this Act; and

(b) section 301 of the Financial Services and Markets Act 2000 (supervision of certain contracts).

History
In s.181(1) the words "A power to which this subsection applies includes the" substituted by the Financial Services and Markets Act 2000 (Consequential Amendments and Repeals) Order 2001 (SI 2001/3649) arts 1, 86(1), (2) as from 1 December 2001.

Supplementary provisions

182 Powers of court in relation to certain proceedings begun before commencement

182(1) [Relevant persons] The powers conferred by this section are exercisable by the court where insolvency proceedings in respect of–

(a) a member of a recognised investment exchange or a recognised clearing house, or

(b) a person by whom a market charge has been granted,

are begun on or after 22nd December 1988 and before the commencement of this section.

That person is referred to in this section as "the relevant person".

182(2) ["Insolvency proceedings"] For the purposes of this section "insolvency proceedings" means proceedings under Part II, IV, V or IX of the Insolvency Act 1986 (administration, winding up and bankruptcy) or under the Bankruptcy (Scotland) Act 2016; and references in this section to the beginning of such proceedings are to–

(za) the making of a bankruptcy application on which a bankruptcy order is made,

(a) the presentation of a petition on which an administration order, winding-up order, bankruptcy order or award of sequestration is made, or

(b) the passing of a resolution for voluntary winding up.

182(3)   [Insolvent estate of deceased person] This section applies in relation to–

(a) in England and Wales, the administration of the insolvent estate of a deceased person, and

(b) in Scotland, the administration by a judicial factor appointed under section 11A of the Judicial Factors (Scotland) Act 1889 of the insolvent estate of a deceased person,

as it applies in relation to insolvency proceedings.

In such a case references to the beginning of the proceedings shall be construed as references to the death of the relevant person.

182(4)   [Court order] The court may on an application made, within three months after the commencement of this section, by–

(a) a recognised investment exchange or recognised clearing house, or

(b) a person in whose favour a market charge has been granted,

make such order as it thinks fit for achieving, except so far as assets of the relevant person have been distributed before the making of the application, the same result as if the provisions of Schedule 22 had come into force on 22nd December 1988.

182(5)   [Schedule 22] The provisions of that Schedule ("the relevant provisions") reproduce the effect of certain provisions of this Part as they appeared in the Bill for this Act as introduced into the House of Lords and published on that date.

182(6)   [Court's powers] The court may in particular–

(a) require the relevant person or a relevant office-holder–

(i) to return property provided as cover for margin or which was subject to a market charge, or to pay to the applicant or any other person the proceeds of realisation of such property, or

(ii) to pay to the applicant or any other person such amount as the court estimates would have been payable to that person if the relevant provisions had come into force on 22nd December 1988 and market contracts had been settled in accordance with the rules of the recognised investment exchange or recognised clearing house, or a proportion of that amount if the property of the relevant person or relevant office-holder is not sufficient to meet the amount in full;

(b) provide that contracts, rules and dispositions shall be treated as not having been void;

(c) modify the functions of a relevant office-holder, or the duties of the applicant or any other person, in relation to the insolvency proceedings, or indemnify any such person in respect of acts or omissions which would have been proper if the relevant provisions had been in force;

(d) provide that conduct which constituted an offence be treated as not having done so;

(e) dismiss proceedings which could not have been brought if the relevant provisions had come into force on 22nd December 1988, and reverse the effect of any order of a court which could not, or would not, have been made if those provisions had come into force on that date.

182(7)   [Office-holder's remuneration] An order under this section shall not be made against a relevant office-holder if the effect would be that his remuneration, costs and expenses could not be met.

History

Section 182(2)(za) inserted by the Enterprise and Regulatory Reform Act 2013 (Consequential Amendments) (Bankruptcy) and the Small Business, Enterprise and Employment Act 2015 (Consequential Amendments) Regulations 2016 (SI 2016/481) reg.2(1) and Sch.1 para.9(7) as from 6 April 2016.

Note

For meaning of "the court" and description of insolvency applications in ss.161, 163, 164, 175 and 182 see the Financial Markets and Insolvency Regulations 1991 (SI 1991/880) reg.19.

182A   Recognised central counterparties: disapplication of provisions on mutual credit and set-off

182A(1)   **[What recognised central counterparty positions and assets may not be set off]** Nothing in the law of insolvency shall enable the setting off against each other of–

(a) positions and assets recorded in an account at a recognised central counterparty and held for the account of a client, an indirect client or a group of clients or indirect clients in accordance with Article 39 of the EMIR Level 1 Regulation or Article 3(1) of the EMIR Level 2 Regulation or Article 3(1) of the MIFIR Level 2 Regulation; and

(b) positions and assets recorded in any other account at the recognised central counterparty.

182A(2)   **[What clearing member positions and assets may not be set off]** Nothing in the law of insolvency shall enable the setting off against each other of–

(a) positions and assets recorded in an account at a clearing member and held for the account of an indirect client or a group of indirect clients in accordance with Article 4(2) of the EMIR Level 2 Regulation or Article 4(2) of the MIFIR Level 2 Regulation; and

(b) positions and assets recorded in any other account at the clearing member.

History

Section 182A inserted by the Financial Services and Markets Act 2000 (Over the Counter Derivatives, Central Counterparties and Trade Repositories) Regulations 2013 (SI 2013/504) reg.4(1), (15) as from 1 April 2013. Section 182A(2) inserted by the Financial Services and Markets Act 2000 (Over the Counter Derivatives, Central Counterparties and Trade Repositories) (No.2) Regulations 2013 (SI 2013/1908) reg.2(1), (9) as from 26 August 2013.

Section 182A(1)(a), (2)(a) amended by the Companies Act 1989 (Financial Markets and Insolvency) (Amendment) Regulations 2017 (SI 2017/1247) regs 1, 2(1), (3) as from 3 January 2018.

183   Insolvency proceedings in other jurisdictions

183(1)   **[Corresponding foreign law]** The references to insolvency law in section 426 of the Insolvency Act 1986 (co-operation with courts exercising insolvency jurisdiction in other jurisdictions) include, in relation to a part of the United Kingdom, the provisions made by or under this Part and, in relation to a relevant country or territory within the meaning of that section, so much of the law of that country or territory as corresponds to any provisions made by or under this Part.

183(2)   **[Where foreign order prohibited in UK]** A court shall not, in pursuance of that section or any other enactment or rule of law, recognise or give effect to–

(a) any order of a court exercising jurisdiction in relation to insolvency law in a country or territory outside the United Kingdom, or

(b) any act of a person appointed in such a country or territory to discharge any functions under insolvency law,

in so far as the making of the order or the doing of the act would be prohibited in the case of a court in the United Kingdom or a relevant office-holder by provisions made by or under this Part.

183(3)   **[Civil Jurisdiction and Judgments Act 1982]** Subsection (2) does not affect the recognition or enforcement of a judgment required to be recognised or enforced under or by virtue of the Civil

Jurisdiction and Judgments Act 1982 or Regulation (EU) No. 1215/2012 of the European Parliament and of the Council of 12 December 2012 on jurisdiction and the recognition and enforcement of judgments in civil and commercial matters (recast), as amended from time to time and as applied by virtue of the Agreement made on 19 October 2005 between the European Community and the Kingdom of Denmark on jurisdiction and the recognition and enforcement of judgments in civil and commercial matters (OJ No L 299, 16.11.2005, p62; OJ No L 79, 21.3.2013, p4).

History
Section 183(3) amended by the Civil Jurisdiction and Judgments Regulations 2007 (SI 2007/1655) reg.5 and Sch. para.15, as from 1 July 2007 and by the Civil Jurisdiction and Judgments (Amendment) Regulations 2014 (SI 2014/2947) Sch.4 para.2 as from 10 January 2015.

184 Indemnity for certain acts, etc.

184(1) **[Office-holder's negligence excepted]** Where a relevant office-holder takes any action in relation to property of a defaulter which is liable to be dealt with in accordance with the default rules of a recognised body, and believes and has reasonable grounds for believing that he is entitled to take that action, he is not liable to any person in respect of any loss or damage resulting from his action except in so far as the loss or damage is caused by the office-holder's own negligence.

184(2) **[Compliance with rules]** Any failure by a recognised body to comply with its own rules in respect of any matter shall not prevent that matter being treated for the purposes of this Part as done in accordance with those rules so long as the failure does not substantially affect the rights of any person entitled to require compliance with the rules.

184(3) **[Bad faith]** No recognised body, nor any officer or servant or member of the governing body of a recognised body, shall be liable in damages for anything done or omitted in the discharge or purported discharge of any functions to which this subsection applies unless the act or omission is shown to have been in bad faith.

184(4) **[Section 184(3) functions]** The functions to which subsection (3) applies are the functions of the recognised body so far as relating to, or to matters arising out of–

   (a)   its default rules, or

   (b)   any obligations to which it is subject by virtue of this Part.

184(5) **[Limit on liability in damages]** No person to whom the exercise of any function of a recognised body is delegated under its default rules, nor any officer or servant of such a person, shall be liable in damages for anything done or omitted in the discharge or purported discharge of those functions unless the act or omission is shown to have been in bad faith.

History
Section 184 amended by the Central Securities Depositories Regulations 2017 (SI 2017/1064) regs 1, 3(1), (23) as from 28 November 2017.

185 Power to make further provision by regulations

185(1) **[Regulations]** The Secretary of State may by regulations make such further provision as appears to him necessary or expedient for the purposes of this Part.

185(2) **[Particular provisions]** Provision may, in particular, be made–

   (a)   for integrating the provisions of this Part with the general law of insolvency, and

   (b)   for adapting the provisions of this Part in their application to overseas investment exchanges and clearing houses.

185(3)   **[Scope of regulations]** Regulations under this section may add to, amend or repeal any of the provisions of this Part or provide that those provisions have effect subject to such additions, exceptions or adaptations as are specified in the regulations.

185(4)   **[Section 301 of Financial Services and Markets Act]** References in this section to the provisions of this Part include any provision made under section 301 of the Financial Services and Markets Act 2000.

Note
See the Financial Markets and Insolvency Regulations 1991 (SI 1991/880) and the Financial Markets and Insolvency Regulations 1998 (SI 1998/1748).

186   Supplementary provisions as to regulations

186(1)   **[Different provision for cases]** Regulations under this Part may make different provision for different cases and may contain such incidental, transitional and other supplementary provisions as appear to the Secretary of State to be necessary or expedient.

186(2)   **[Regulations by statutory instrument]** Regulations under this Part shall be made by statutory instrument which shall be subject to annulment in pursuance of a resolution of either House of Parliament.

187   Construction of references to parties to market contracts

187(1)   **[Different capacities]** Where a person enters into market contracts in more than one capacity, the provisions of this Part apply (subject as follows) as if the contracts entered into in each different capacity were entered into by different persons.

187(2)   **[Agency]** References in this Part to a market contract to which a person is a party include (subject as follows, and unless the context otherwise requires) contracts to which he is party as agent.

187(2A)   **[Disapplication of s.187(1), (2)]** Subsections (1) and (2) do not apply to market contracts to which this Part applies by virtue of section 155(2B).

187(3)   **[Regulations]** The Secretary of State may by regulations–

  (a)   modify or exclude the operation of subsections (1) and (2), and

  (b)   make provision as to the circumstances in which a person is to be regarded for the purposes of those provisions as acting in different capacities.

History
Section 187(2A) inserted by the Financial Services and Markets Act 2000 (Over the Counter Derivatives, Central Counterparties and Trade Repositories) Regulations 2013 (SI 2013/504) reg.4(1), (16) as from 1 April 2013.

188   Meaning of "default rules" and related expressions

188(1)   **["Default rules"]** In this Part "default rules" means rules of a recognised body which provide for the taking of action in the event of a person (including another recognised body) appearing to be unable, or likely to become unable, to meet his obligations in respect of one or more market contracts connected with the recognised body.

188(1A)   **[Inclusion in default rules]** In the case of a recognised central counterparty, "default rules" includes–

  (a)   the default procedures referred to in Article 48 of the EMIR Level 1 Regulation; and

  (b)   any rules of the recognised central counterparty which provide for the taking of action in accordance with a request or instruction from a clearing member under the default procedures referred to in Article 4(6) and (7) of the EMIR Level 2 Regulation or Article 4(6) and (7) of the

MIFIR Level 2 Regulation in respect of assets or positions held by the recognised central counterparty for the account of an indirect client or group of indirect clients.

188(1B) **["Default rules"]** In the case of a recognised CSD, "default rules" includes the default rules and procedures referred to in Article 41 of the CSD regulation.

188(2) **["Defaulter"]** References in this Part to a "defaulter" are to a person in respect of whom action has been taken by a recognised body under its default rules, whether by declaring him to be a defaulter or otherwise; and references in this Part to "default", "defaulting" and "non-defaulting" shall be construed accordingly.

188(2A) **[Action under s.188(1A)(b) rules for s.188(2) purposes]** For the purposes of subsection (2), where a recognised central counterparty takes action under the rules referred to in subsection (1A)(b), the action is to be treated as taken in respect of the client providing the indirect clearing services.

188(3) **["Default proceedings"]** In this Part "default proceedings" means proceedings taken by a recognised body under its default rules.

188(3A) **[Default fund contribution]** In this Part "default fund contribution" means–

(a) contribution by a member or designated non-member of a recognised investment exchange to a fund which–

    (i) is maintained by that exchange for the purpose of covering losses arising in connection with defaults by any of the members of the exchange, or defaults by any of the members or designated non-members of the exchange, and

    (ii) may be applied for that purpose under the default rules of the exchange;

(b) contribution by a member of a recognised clearing house to a fund which–

    (i) is maintained by that clearing house for the purpose of covering losses arising in connection with defaults by any of the members of the clearing house, and

    (ii) may be applied for that purpose under the default rules of the clearing house;

(c) contribution by a recognised clearing house to a fund which–

    (i) is maintained by another recognised body (A) for the purpose of covering losses arising in connection with defaults by recognised bodies other than A or by any of their members, and

    (ii) may be applied for that purpose under A's default rules;

(d) contribution by a recognised investment exchange to a fund which–

    (i) is maintained by another recognised body (A) for the purpose of covering losses arising in connection with defaults by recognised bodies other than A or by any of their members, and

    (ii) may be applied for that purpose under A's default rules.

(e) contribution by a member of a recognised CSD to a fund which–

    (i) is maintained by that central securities depository for the purpose of covering losses arising in connection with defaults by any of the members of the central securities depository, and

    (ii) may be applied for that purpose under the default rules of the central securities depository; or

(f) contribution by a recognised CSD to a fund which–

    (i) is maintained by another recognised body (A) for the purpose of covering losses arising in connection with defaults by recognised bodies other than A or by any of their members, and

    (ii) may be applied for that purpose under A's default rules.

188(4)   **[Action under default rules]** If a recognised body takes action under its default rules in respect of a person, all subsequent proceedings under its rules for the purposes of or in connection with the settlement of market contracts to which the defaulter is a party shall be treated as done under its default rules.

History

Section 188(3A) inserted by the Financial Markets and Insolvency Regulations 2009 (SI 2009/853) reg.2(1), (15) as from 15 June 2009. Section 188(1), (2) amended by the Financial Services and Markets Act 2000 (Over the Counter Derivatives, Central Counterparties and Trade Repositories) Regulations 2013 (SI 2013/504) reg.4(1), (17) as from 1 April 2013. Section 188(1), (2) amended and s.188(1A), (2A) inserted by the Financial Services and Markets Act 2000 (Over the Counter Derivatives, Central Counterparties and Trade Repositories) (No.2) Regulations 2013 (SI 2013/1908) reg.2(1), (10) as from 26 August 2013.

Section 188(1B) and (3A)(e), (f) inserted and subss.(1), (2), (3A), (4) amended by the Central Securities Depositories Regulations 2017 (SI 2017/1064) regs 1, 3(1), (24) as from 28 November 2017.

Section 188(1A)(b) amended by the Companies Act 1989 (Financial Markets and Insolvency) (Amendment) Regulations 2017 (SI 2017/1247) regs 1, 2(1), (4) as from 3 January 2018.

189   Meaning of "relevant office-holder"

189(1)   **[Office-holders]** The following are relevant office-holders for the purposes of this Part–

  (a)   the official receiver,

  (b)   any person acting in relation to a company as its liquidator, provisional liquidator, administrator or administrative receiver,

  (c)   any person acting in relation to an individual (or, in Scotland, any debtor within the meaning of the Bankruptcy (Scotland) Act 2016) as his trustee in bankruptcy or interim receiver of his property or as trustee or interim trustee in the sequestration of his estate,

  (d)   any person acting as administrator of an insolvent estate of a deceased person.

189(2)   **["Company" in s.189(1)(b)]** In subsection (1)(b) "company" means any company, society, association, partnership or other body which may be wound up under the Insolvency Act 1986.

189A   Meaning of "transfer"

189A(1)   **[Reference re clearing member client contract, client trade, qualifying collateral arrangement]** In this Part, a reference to a transfer of a clearing member client contract, a client trade or a qualifying collateral arrangement shall be interpreted in accordance with this section.

189A(2)   **[What clearing member client contract or client trade to include]** A transfer of a clearing member client contract or client trade includes–

  (a)   an assignment;

  (b)   a novation; and

  (c)   terminating or closing out the clearing member client contract or client trade and establishing an equivalent position between different parties.

189A(3)   **[Position held for the account of indirect client or group]** Where a clearing member client contract is recorded in the accounts of a recognised central counterparty as a position held for the account of an indirect client or group of indirect clients, the clearing member client contract is to be treated as having been transferred if the position is transferred to a different account at the recognised central counterparty.

189A(4)   **[Reference to transfer of qualifying collateral arrangement]** A reference to a transfer of a qualifying collateral arrangement includes an assignment or a novation.

History
Section 189A inserted by the Financial Services and Markets Act 2000 (Over the Counter Derivatives, Central Counterparties and Trade Repositories) (No.2) Regulations 2013 (SI 2013/1908) reg.2(1), (11) as from 26 August 2013.

190 Minor definitions

190(1) [Definitions] In this Part–

"administrative receiver" has the meaning given by section 251 of the Insolvency Act 1986;

"charge" means any form of security, including a mortgage and, in Scotland, a heritable security;

"clearing member", in relation to a recognised central counterparty, has the meaning given by Article 2(14) of the EMIR Level 1 Regulation;

"client" has the meaning given by Article 2(15) of the EMIR Level 1 Regulation;

"CSD regulation" means Regulation (EU) No 909/2014 of the European Parliament and of the Council of 23 July 2014 on improving securities settlement in the European Union and on central securities depositories;

"EEA CSD", "recognised central counterparty", "recognised CSD", "recognised clearing house", "recognised investment exchange" and "third country CSD" have the same meaning as in the Financial Services and Markets Act 2000 (see section 285 of that Act);

"EMIR Level 1 Regulation" means Regulation (EU) No 648/2012 of the European Parliament and of the Council of 4 July 2012 on OTC derivatives, central counterparties and trade repositories;

"EMIR Level 2 Regulation" means Commission Delegated Regulation (EU) No 149/2013 of 19 December 2012 supplementing Regulation (EU) No 648/2012 of the European Parliament and of the Council of 4 July 2012 with regard to regulatory technical standards on indirect clearing arrangements, the clearing obligation, the public register, access to a trading venue, non-financial counterparties, risk mitigation for OTC derivatives contracts not cleared by a CCP as amended by Commission Delegated Regulation (EU) 2017/2155 of 22 September 2017;

"the FCA" means the Financial Conduct Authority;

"indirect clearing services" has the same meaning as in the EMIR Level 2 Regulation;

"indirect client" has the meaning given by Article 1(a) of the EMIR Level 2 Regulation;

"interim trustee" has the same meaning as in the Bankruptcy (Scotland) Act 2016;

"member", in relation to a central securities depository, means a participant of that central securities depository as defined in Article 2(1)(19) of the CSD regulation;

"member of a clearing house" includes a clearing member of a recognised central counterparty;

"MIFIR Level 2 Regulation" means Commission Delegated Regulation (EU) 2017/2154 of 22 September 2017 supplementing Regulation (EU) No 600/2014 of the European Parliament and of the Council with regard to regulatory technical standards on indirect clearing arrangements;

"overseas", in relation to an investment exchange or clearing house or central securities depository, means having its head office outside the United Kingdom;

"position" has the same meaning as in the EMIR Level 1 Regulation;

"the PRA" means the Prudential Regulation Authority;

"recognised body" has the same meaning as in section 313 of the Financial Services and Markets Act 2000;

"sequestration" means sequestration under the Bankruptcy (Scotland) Act 2016;

"set-off", in relation to Scotland, includes compensation;

"The Stock Exchange" means the London Stock Exchange Limited;

"UK", in relation to an investment exchange, means having its head office in the United Kingdom.

190(2)   [Settlement] References in this Part to settlement–

(a)   mean, in relation to a market contract, the discharge of the rights and liabilities of the parties to the contract, whether by performance, compromise or otherwise;

(b)   include, in relation to a clearing member client contract or a clearing member house contract, a reference to its liquidation for the purposes of Article 48 of the EMIR Level 1 Regulation.

190(3)   ["Margin", "cover for margin"] In this Part the expressions "margin" and "cover for margin" have the same meaning.

190(4)   [Repealed by the Financial Services and Markets Act 2000 (Consequential Amendments and Repeals) Order 2001 (SI 2001/3649) arts 1, 89(1), (6) as from 1 December 2001.]

190(5)   [Notice] For the purposes of this Part a person shall be taken to have notice of a matter if he deliberately failed to make enquiries as to that matter in circumstances in which a reasonable and honest person would have done so.

This does not apply for the purposes of a provision requiring "actual notice".

190(6)   [Insolvency law] References in this Part to the law of insolvency–

(a)   include references to every provision made by or under the Insolvency Act 1986 or the Bankruptcy (Scotland) Act 2016; and in relation to a building society references to insolvency law or to any provision of the Insolvency Act 1986 are to that law or provision as modified by the Building Societies Act 1986;

(b)   are also to be interpreted in accordance with the modifications made by the enactments mentioned in subsection (6B).

190(6A)   [References to administration, administrator, liquidator, winding up] For the avoidance of doubt, references in this Part to administration, administrator, liquidator and winding up are to be interpreted in accordance with the modifications made by the enactments mentioned in subsection (6B).

190(6B)   [Enactments in s.190(6)(b), (6A)] The enactments referred to in subsections (6)(b) and (6A) are–

(a)   article 3 of, and the Schedule to, the Banking Act 2009 (Parts 2 and 3 Consequential Amendments) Order 2009;

(b)   article 18 of, and paragraphs 1(a), (2) and (3) of Schedule 2 to, the Building Societies (Insolvency and Special Administration) Order 2009; and

(c)   regulation 27 of, and Schedule 6 to, the Investment Bank Special Administration Regulations 2011.

190(7)   [Scotland] In relation to Scotland, references in this Part–

(a)   to sequestration include references to the administration by a judicial factor of the insolvent estate of a deceased person, and

(b)   to an interim trustee or to a trustee in the sequestration of an estate include references to a judicial factor on the insolvent estate of a deceased person,

unless the context otherwise requires.

History
Definition of "the Authority" omitted and definitions of "the FCA" and "the PRA" inserted by the Financial Services Act 2012 s.114(1) and Sch.18 para.70 as from 1 April 2013. In s.190(1), definitions of "clearing member", "client",

"EMIR Level 1 Regulation", "EMIR Level 2 Regulation", "indirect client", "member of a clearing house", "position" "recognised central counterparty", "recognised clearing house", "recognised investment exchange" and "UK" inserted or substituted, s.190(2) substituted and s.190(3A) inserted by the Financial Services and Markets Act 2000 (Over the Counter Derivatives, Central Counterparties and Trade Repositories) Regulations 2013 (SI 2013/504) reg.4(1), (18) as from 1 April 2013. In s.190(1), definition of "indirect clearing services" inserted and s.190(3A) omitted by the Financial Services and Markets Act 2000 (Over the Counter Derivatives, Central Counterparties and Trade Repositories) (No.2) Regulations 2013 (SI 2013/1908) reg.2(1), (12) as from 26 August 2013. Definitions of "interim trustee" and "sequestration" respectively substituted and inserted by the Bankruptcy (Scotland) Act 2016 (Consequential Provisions and Modifications) Order 2016 (SI 2016/1034) art.7(1), Sch.1 para.6(1), (11) as from 30 November 2016. Definitions of "CSD regulation", "EEA CSD", "recognised central counterparty", "recognised CSD", "recognised clearing house", "recognised investment exchange", "third country CSD", "member" and "recognised body" inserted, and definition of "overseas" amended, by the Central Securities Depositories Regulations 2017 (SI 2017/1064) regs 1, 3(1), (25) as from 28 November 2017. Definition of "EMIR Level 2 Regulation" amended and definition of "MIFIR Level 2 Regulation" inserted by the Companies Act 1989 (Financial Markets and Insolvency) (Amendment) Regulations 2017 (SI 2017/1247) regs 1, 2(1), (5) as from 3 January 2018.

191   Index of defined expressions

191   The following Table shows provisions defining or otherwise explaining expressions used in this Part (other than provisions defining or explaining an expression used only in the same section or paragraph)–

Defined Expression	Section
administration	Sections 190(6A) and (6B)
administrator	Sections 190(6A) and (6B)
administrative receiver	Section 190(1)
authorised central securities depository services	Section 155(3D)
charge	Section 190(1)
clearing member	Section 190(1)
clearing member client contract	Section 155(1)(a)
clearing member house contract	Section 155(1)(b)
client	Section 190(1)
client trade	Section 155(1)(c)
cover for margin	Section 190(3)
CSD regulation	Section 190(1)
default fund contribution	Section 188(3A)
default rules (and related expressions)	Section 188
designated non-member	Section 155(2)
EEA CSD	Section 190(1)
EMIR Level 1 Regulation	Section 190(1)
EMIR Level 2 Regulation	Section 190(1)
the FCA	Section 190(1)
indirect clearing services	Section 190(1)
indirect client	Section 190(1)
insolvency law (and similar expressions)	Sections 190(6) and (6B)
interim trustee and trustee in the sequestration of an estate (in relation to Scotland)	Section 190(1) and (7)(b)
liquidator	Sections 190(6A) and (6B)
margin	Section 190(3)
market charge	Section 173
market contract	Section 155
member (in relation to a central securities depository)	Section 190(1)
member of a clearing house	Section 190(1)
MIFIR Level 2 Regulation	Section 190(1)

notice	Section 190(5)
overseas (in relation to investment exchanges, clearing houses and central securities depositories)	Section 190(1)
party (in relation to a market contract)	Section 187
the PRA	Section 190(1)
qualifying collateral arrangement	Section 155A(1)(a)
qualifying property transfers	Section 155A(1)(b)
recognised body	Section 190(1)
recognised central counterparty	Section 190(1)
recognised clearing house	Section 190(1)
recognised CSD	Section 190(1)
recognised investment exchange	Section 190(1)
relevant office-holder	Section 189
sequestration	Section 190(7)(a)
set off (in relation to Scotland)	Section 190(1)
settlement and related expressions (in relation to a market contract)	Section 190 (2)
The Stock Exchange	Section 190(1)
third country CSD	Section 190(1)
transfer	Section 189A
UK (in relation to investment exchanges)	Section 190(1)
winding up	Sections 190(6A) and (6B)

History
Table substituted by the Financial Services and Markets Act 2000 (Over the Counter Derivatives, Central Counterparties and Trade Repositories) Regulations 2013 (SI 2013/504) reg.4(1), (19) and Sch. as from 1 April 2013. Entries for "indirect clearing services" and "transfer" inserted by the Financial Services and Markets Act 2000 (Over the Counter Derivatives, Central Counterparties and Trade Repositories) (No.2) Regulations 2013 (SI 2013/1908) reg.2(1), (13) as from 26 August 2013. Entry for "permanent trustee" omitted and "interim trustee and trustee in the sequestration of an estate (in relation to Scotland)" substituted by the Bankruptcy (Scotland) Act 2016 (Consequential Provisions and Modifications) Order 2016 (SI 2016/1034) art.7(1), Sch.1 para.6(1), (12) as from 30 November 2016. Entries for "authorised central securities depository services", "CSD regulation", "EEA CSD", "member (in relation to a central securities depository)", "recognised body", "recognised CSD" and "third country CSD" inserted, and entry for "overseas" amended, by the Central Securities Depositories Regulations 2017 (SI 2017/1064) regs 1, 3(1), (26) as from 28 November 2017. Entry for "MIFIR Level 2 Regulation" inserted by the Companies Act 1989 (Financial Markets and Insolvency) (Amendment) Regulations 2017 (SI 2017/1247) regs 1, 2(1), (6) as from 3 January 2018.

Courts and Legal Services Act 1990

(1990 Chapter 41)

[**Note**: Changes made by the Access to Justice Act 1999, the Legal Aid, Sentencing and Punishment of Offenders Act 2012 and the Legal Aid, Sentencing and Punishment of Offenders Act 2012 (Commencement No.5 and Saving) Order 2013 (SI 2013/77) have been incorporated into the text.]

PART II

LEGAL SERVICES

Miscellaneous

58   Conditional fee agreements

58(1)   A conditional fee agreement which satisfies all of the conditions applicable to it by virtue of this section shall not be unenforceable by reason only of its being a conditional fee agreement; but (subject to subsection (5)) any other conditional fee agreement shall be unenforceable.

58(2)   For the purposes of this section and section 58A–

(a)   a conditional fee agreement is an agreement with a person providing advocacy or litigation services which provides for his fees and expenses, or any part of them, to be payable only in specified circumstances;

(b)   a conditional fee agreement provides for a success fee if it provides for the amount of any fees to which it applies to be increased, in specified circumstances, above the amount which would be payable if it were not payable only in specified circumstances; and

(c)   references to a success fee, in relation to a conditional fee agreement, are to the amount of the increase.

58(3)   The following conditions are applicable to every conditional fee agreement–

(a)   it must be in writing;

(b)   it must not relate to proceedings which cannot be the subject of an enforceable conditional fee agreement; and

(c)   it must comply with such requirements (if any) as may be prescribed by the Lord Chancellor.

58(4)   The following further conditions are applicable to a conditional fee agreement which provides for a success fee–

(a)   it must relate to proceedings of a description specified by order made by the Lord Chancellor;

(b)   it must state the percentage by which the amount of the fees which would be payable if it were not a conditional fee agreement is to be increased; and

(c)   that percentage must not exceed the percentage specified in relation to the description of proceedings to which the agreement relates by order made by the Lord Chancellor.

58(4A)   The additional conditions are applicable to a conditional fee agreement which–

(a)   provides for a success fee, and

(b) relates to proceedings of a description specified by order made by the Lord Chancellor for the purposes of this subsection.

58(4B)   The additional conditions are that–

(a) the agreement must provide that the success fee is subject to a maximum limit,

(b) the maximum limit must be expressed as a percentage of the descriptions of damages awarded in the proceedings that are specified in the agreement,

(c) that percentage must not exceed the percentage specified by order made by the Lord Chancellor in relation to the proceedings or calculated in a manner so specified, and

(d) those descriptions of damages may only include descriptions of damages specified by order made by the Lord Chancellor in relation to the proceedings.

58(5)   If a conditional fee agreement is an agreement to which section 57 of the Solicitors Act 1974 (non-contentious business agreements between solicitor and client) applies, subsection (1) shall not make it unenforceable.

History
Section 58(1) substituted by the Access to Justice Act 1999 s.27(1) as from 1 April 2000.
  Section 58(2)(a) amended and s.58(2)(c) inserted by the Legal Aid, Sentencing and Punishment of Offenders Act 2012 s.44(1), (b), (2) as from 1 April 2013, subject to savings as specified in SI 2013/77 (see note following s.58C below).

58A   Conditional fee agreements: supplementary

[Not reproduced.]

58AA   Damage-based agreements

[Not reproduced.]

58C   Recovery of insurance premiums by way of costs

58C(1)   A costs order made in favour of a party to proceedings who has taken out a costs insurance policy may not include provision requiring the payment of an amount in respect of all or part of the premium of the policy, unless such provision is permitted by regulations under subsection (2).

58C(2)   The Lord Chancellor may by regulations provide that a costs order may include provision requiring the payment of such an amount where–

(a) the order is made in favour of a party to clinical negligence proceedings of a prescribed description,

(b) the party has taken out a costs insurance policy insuring against the risk of incurring a liability to pay for one or more expert reports in respect of clinical negligence in connection with the proceedings (or against that risk and other risks),

(c) the policy is of a prescribed description,

(d) the policy states how much of the premium relates to the liability to pay for an expert report or reports in respect of clinical negligence ("the relevant part of the premium"), and

(e) the amount is to be paid in respect of the relevant part of the premium.

58C(3)   Regulations under subsection (2) may include provision about the amount that may be required to be paid by the costs order, including provision that the amount must not exceed a prescribed maximum amount.

58C(4)   The regulations may prescribe a maximum amount, in particular, by specifying–

(a)   a percentage of the relevant part of the premium;

(b)   an amount calculated in a prescribed manner.

58C(5)   In this section–

"clinical negligence" means breach of a duty of care or trespass to the person committed in the course of the provision of clinical or medical services (including dental or nursing services);

"clinical negligence proceedings" means proceedings which include a claim for damages in respect of clinical negligence;

"costs insurance policy", in relation to a party to proceedings, means a policy insuring against the risk of the party incurring a liability in those proceedings;

"expert report" means a report by a person qualified to give expert advice on all or most of the matters that are the subject of the report;

"proceedings" includes any sort of proceedings for resolving disputes (and not just proceedings in court), whether commenced or contemplated.

History
Section 58C inserted by the Legal Aid, Sentencing and Punishment of Offenders Act 2012 s.46(1) as from 1 April 2013, subject to savings as specified in SI 2013/77.

Note: Articles 2 and 3 of SI 2013/77 bring into force ss.44–47 of the 2012 Act (which, by amending the above sections, restrict the ability of a litigant to recover success fees and insurance premiums from the other side if the litigation is successful), but art.4(c)–(f) exempts the office-holder in specified forms of insolvency proceeding as follows:
    "[The relevant articles] do not apply to:

(c)   proceedings in England and Wales brought by a person acting in the capacity of–

(i)   a liquidator of a company which is being wound up in England and Wales or Scotland under Parts IV or V of the 1986 Act [IA 1986]; or

(ii)   a trustee of a bankrupt's estate under Part IX of the 1986 Act;

(d)   proceedings brought by a person acting in the capacity of an administrator appointed pursuant to the provisions of Part II of the 1986 Act;

(e)   proceedings in England and Wales brought by a company which is being wound up in England and Wales or Scotland under Parts IV or V of the 1986 Act; or

(f)   proceedings brought by a company which has entered administration under Part II of the 1986 Act."

This exemption will be withdrawn from 6 April 2016: see the Legal Aid, Sentencing and Punishment of Offenders Act 2012 (Commencement No.12) Order 2016 (SI 2016/345 (C. 19)) and the note to IA 1986 Sch.4 para.6.

Social Security Administration Act 1992

(1992 Chapter 5)

An Act to consolidate certain enactments relating to the administration of social security and related matters with amendments to give effect to recommendations of the Law Commission and the Scottish Law Commission.

[13th February 1992]

[**Note**: These two sections were inserted by the Social Security Act 1998 s.64. The text is shown as amended by the Social Security (Transfer of Functions, etc.) Act 1999 and the Transfer of Tribunal Functions, etc. Order 2009 (SI 2009/56). Changes made by the Finance Act 2009, Sections 101 and 102 (Interest on Late Payments and Repayments) (Consequential Amendments) Order 2014 (SI 2014/1283) have been incorporated into the text.]

PART VI

ENFORCEMENT

Unpaid contributions etc

121C   Liability of directors etc. for company's contributions

121C(1)   This section applies to contributions which a body corporate is liable to pay, where–

(a)   the body corporate has failed to pay the contributions at or within the time prescribed for the purpose; and

(b)   the failure appears to the Inland Revenue to be attributable to fraud or neglect on the part of one or more individuals who, at the time of the fraud or neglect, were officers of the body corporate ("culpable officers").

121C(2)   The Inland Revenue may issue and serve on any culpable officer a notice (a "personal liability notice")–

(a)   specifying the amount of the contributions to which this section applies ("the specified amount");

(b)   requiring the officer to pay to the Inland Revenue–

(i)   a specified sum in respect of that amount; and

(ii)   specified interest on that sum; and

(c)   where that sum is given by paragraph (b) of subsection (3) below, specifying the proportion applied by the Inland Revenue for the purposes of that paragraph.

121C(3)   The sum specified in the personal liability notice under subsection (2)(b)(i) above shall be–

(a)   in a case where there is, in the opinion of the Inland Revenue, no other culpable officer, the whole of the specified amount; and

(b)   in any other case, such proportion of the specified amount as, in the opinion of the Inland Revenue, the officer's culpability for the failure to pay that amount bears to that of all the culpable officers taken together.

121C(4)   In assessing an officer's culpability for the purposes of subsection (3)(b) above, the Inland Revenue may have regard both to the gravity of the officer's fraud or neglect and to the consequences of it.

121C(5)   The interest specified in the personal liability notice under subsection (2)(b)(ii) above shall be at the Class 1 rate on the Class 1 element of the specified sum, and otherwise at the prescribed rate, and shall run from the date on which the notice is issued.

121C(6)   An officer who is served with a personal liability notice shall be liable to pay to the Inland Revenue the sum and the interest specified in the notice under subsection (2)(b) above.

121C(7)   Where, after the issue of one or more personal liability notices, the amount of contributions to which this section applies is reduced by a payment made by the body corporate–

(a)   the amount that each officer who has been served with such a notice is liable to pay under this section shall be reduced accordingly;

(b)   the Inland Revenue shall serve on each such officer a notice to that effect; and

(c)   where the reduced liability of any such officer is less than the amount that he has already paid under this section, the difference shall be repaid to him together with interest on it at the Class 1 rate on the Class 1 element of it and otherwise at the prescribed rate.

121C(8)   Any amount paid under a personal liability notice shall be deducted from the liability of the body corporate in respect of the specified amount.

121C(8A)   The amount which an officer is liable to pay under this section is to be recovered in the same manner as a Class 1 contribution to which regulations under paragraph 6 of Schedule 1 to the Contributions and Benefits Act apply and for this purpose references in those regulations to Class 1 contributions are to be construed accordingly.

121C(9)   In this section–

"the Class 1 rate"–

(a)   in subsection (5) means the rate from time to time applicable under section 103(1) of the Finance Act 2009; and

(b)   in subsection (7)(c) means the rate from time to time applicable under section 103(2) of that Act;

"the Class 1 element", in relation to any amount, means so much of that amount as is calculated by–

(a)   multiplying that amount by so much of the specified amount as consists of Class 1 contributions; and

(b)   dividing the product of that multiplication by the specified amount;

"contributions" includes any interest or penalty in respect of contributions (and accordingly, in the definition of "the Class 1 element" given by this subsection, "Class 1 contributions" includes any interest or penalty in respect of Class 1 contributions);

"officer", in relation to a body corporate, means–

(a)   any director, manager, secretary or other similar officer of the body corporate, or any person purporting to act as such; and

(b)   in a case where the affairs of the body corporate are managed by its members, any member of the body corporate exercising functions of management with respect to it or purporting to do so;

"the prescribed rate" means the rate from time to time prescribed by regulations under section 178 of the Finance Act 1989 for the purposes of the corresponding provision of Schedule 1 to the Contributions and Benefits Act, that is to say–

(a)   in relation to subsection (5) above, paragraph 6(2)(a);

(b)   in relation to subsection (7) above, paragraph 6(2)(b).

History
Section 121C(8A) inserted by the National Insurance Contributions and Statutory Payments Act 2004 s.5(3). Section 121C(5), (7)(c), (9) amended, and definitions of "the Class 1 rate" and "the Class 1 element" inserted by the Finance Act 2009, Sections 101 and 102 (Interest on Late Payments and Repayments) (Consequential Amendments) Order 2014 (SI 2014/1283) Sch.1 para.2 as from 20 May 2014.

121D   Appeals in relation to personal liability notices

121D(1)   No appeal shall lie in relation to a personal liability notice except as provided by this section.

121D(2)   An individual who is served with a personal liability notice may appeal against the Inland Revenue's decision as to the issue and content of the notice on the ground that–

(a)   the whole or part of the amount specified under subsection (2)(a) of section 121C above (or the amount so specified as reduced under subsection (7) of that section) does not represent contributions to which that section applies;

(b)   the failure to pay that amount was not attributable to any fraud or neglect on the part of the individual in question;

(c)   the individual was not an officer of the body corporate at the time of the alleged fraud or neglect; or

(d)   the opinion formed by the Inland Revenue under subsection (3)(a) or (b) of that section was unreasonable.

121D(3)   The Inland Revenue shall give a copy of any notice of an appeal under this section, within 28 days of the giving of the notice, to each other individual who has been served with a personal liability notice.

121D(4)   On an appeal under this section, the burden of proof as to any matter raised by a ground of appeal shall be on the Inland Revenue.

121D(5)   Where an appeal under this section–

(a)   is brought on the basis of evidence not considered by the Inland Revenue, or on the ground mentioned in subsection (2)(d) above; and

(b)   is not allowed on some other basis or ground,

and is notified to the tribunal, the tribunal shall either dismiss the appeal or remit the case to the Inland Revenue, with any recommendations the tribunal sees fit to make, for the Inland Revenue to consider whether to vary their decision as to the issue and content of the personal liability notice.

121D(6)   In this section–

"officer", in relation to a body corporate, has the same meaning as in section 121C above;

"personal liability notice" has the meaning given by subsection (2) of that section;

"tribunal" means the First-tier Tribunal or, where determined under Tribunal Procedure Rules, the Upper Tribunal;

"vary" means vary under regulations made under section 10 of the Social Security Contributions (Transfer of Functions, etc.) Act 1999.

History
Section 121D(2), (5), (6) amended by the Transfer of Tribunal Functions, etc. Order 2009 (SI 2009/56) art.3(1) and Sch.1 paras 170, 171 as from 1 April 2009.

Friendly Societies Act 1992

(1992 Chapter 40)

An Act to make further provision for friendly societies; to provide for the cessation of registration under the Friendly Societies Act 1974; to make provision about disputes involving friendly societies or other bodies registered under the Friendly Societies Act 1974 and about the functions of the Chief Registrar of friendly societies; and for connected purposes.

[16th March 1992]

[**Note**: Changes made by the Financial Institutions (Prudential Supervision) Regulations 1996 (SI 1996/1669), the Financial Services and Markets Act 2000 (Mutual Societies) Order 2001 (SI 2001/2617), the Financial Services Act 2012 (Mutual Societies) Order 2013 (SI 2013/496), the Deregulation Act 2015, the Small Business, Enterprise and Employment Act 2015 and the Insolvency (Amendment) Act (Northern Ireland) 2016 (Consequential Amendments and Transitional Provisions) Regulations 2017 (SI 2017/400) and the Small Business, Enterprise and Employment Act 2015 (Consequential Amendments, Savings and Transitional Provisions) Regulations 2018 (SI 2018/208) have been incorporated into the text (in the case of pre-2003 legislation without annotation.)]

PART I

FUNCTIONS OF THE FINANCIAL CONDUCT AUTHORITY AND THE PRUDENTIAL REGULATION AUTHORITY

1 Functions of the Financial Conduct Authority and the Prudential Regulation Authority in relation to friendly societies

1(1) The Financial Conduct Authority ("the FCA") has the following functions under this Act and the 1974 Act in relation to friendly societies–

(a) to secure that the purposes of each friendly society are inconformity with this Act and any other enactment regulating the purposes of friendly societies;

(b) to administer the system of regulation of the activities of friendly societies provided for by or under this Act and the 1974 Act; and

(c) to advise and make recommendations to the Treasury and other government departments on any matter relating to friendly societies.

1(1A)   The function in subsection (1)(c) is also a function of the Prudential Regulation Authority ("the PRA").

1(2)   The FCA and the PRA also have, in relation to such societies, the other functions conferred on them respectively by or under this Act or any other enactment.

History
Heading to s.1 amended and s.1(1A) inserted by the Financial Services Act 2012 (Mutual Societies) Order 2013 (SI 2013/496) art 2(b) and Sch.9 para.3 as from 1 April 2013.

PART II

INCORPORATED FRIENDLY SOCIETIES

Dissolution and winding up

19   Modes of dissolution and winding up

19(1)   An incorporated friendly society–

(a)   may be dissolved by consent of the members; or

(b)   may be wound up voluntarily or by the court,

in accordance with this Part of this Act; and an incorporated friendly society may not, except where it is dissolved by virtue of section 85(4), 86(5) or 90(9) below, be dissolved or wound up in any other manner.

19(2)   An incorporated friendly society which is in the course of dissolution by consent, or is being wound up voluntarily, may be wound up by the court.

20   Dissolution by consent

20(1)   An incorporated friendly society may be dissolved by an instrument of dissolution.

20(2)   An instrument of dissolution shall only have effect if it is approved by special resolution.

20(3)   An instrument of dissolution shall set out–

(a)   the liabilities and assets of the society in detail;

(b)   the number of members, and the nature of their interests in the society;

(c)   the claims of creditors, and the provision to be made for their payment;

(d)   the intended appropriation or division of the funds and property of the society;

(e)   the names of one or more persons to be appointed as trustees for the purposes of the dissolution, and their remuneration.

20(4)   An instrument of dissolution may be altered, but the alteration shall only have effect if it is approved by special resolution.

20(5)   The provisions of this Act shall continue to apply in relation to an incorporated friendly society as if the trustees appointed under the instrument of dissolution were the committee of management of the society.

20(6)   The trustees shall–

(a)   within 15 days of the passing of a special resolution approving an instrument of dissolution, give notice to the FCA and, if the society is a PRA-authorised person, the PRA of the fact and the date of commencement of the dissolution, enclosing a copy of the instrument; and

(b)   within 15 days of the passing of a special resolution approving an alteration of such an instrument, give notice to the FCA and, if the society is a PRA-authorised person, the PRA of the fact, enclosing a copy of the altered instrument;

and if the trustees fail to comply with this subsection, they shall each be guilty of an offence and liable on summary conviction to a fine not exceeding level 3 on the standard scale.

20(7) An instrument of dissolution or an alteration to such an instrument shall be binding on all members of the society as from the date on which the copy of the instrument or altered instrument, as the case may be, is placed on the public file of the society under subsection (12) below.

20(8) The trustees shall, within 28 days from the termination of the dissolution, give notice to the FCA and, if the society is a PRA-authorised person, the PRA of the fact and the date of the termination, enclosing an account and balance sheet signed and certified by them as correct, and showing–

(a) the assets and liabilities of the society at the commencement of the dissolution; and

(b) the way in which those assets and liabilities have been applied and discharged.

20(9) If the trustees fail to comply with subsection (8) above they shall each be guilty of an offence and liable on summary conviction–

(a) to a fine not exceeding level 2 on the standard scale; and

(b) in the case of a continuing offence, to an additional fine not exceeding one-tenth of that level for every day during which the offence continues.

20(10) Except with the consent of the appropriate authority, no instrument of dissolution or alteration to such an instrument shall be of any effect if the purpose of the proposed dissolution or alteration is to effect or facilitate the transfer of the society's engagements to any other friendly society or to a company.

20(11) Any provision in a resolution or document that members of an incorporated friendly society proposed to be dissolved shall accept membership of some other body in or towards satisfaction of their rights in the dissolution shall be conclusive evidence of such purpose as is mentioned in subsection (10) above.

20(12) The FCA shall keep in the public file of the society any notice or other document received by it under subsection (6) or (8) above and shall record in that file the date on which the notice or document is placed in it.

21 Voluntary winding up

21(1) An incorporated friendly society may be wound up voluntarily under the applicable winding up legislation if it resolves by special resolution that it be wound up voluntarily.

21(2) A copy of any special resolution passed for the voluntary winding up of an incorporated friendly society shall be sent by the society to the FCA and, if the society is a PRA-authorised person, the PRA within 15 days after it is passed; and the FCA shall keep the copy in the public file of the society.

21(3) A copy of any such resolution shall be annexed to every copy of the memorandum or of the rules issued after the passing of the resolution.

21(4) If an incorporated friendly society fails to comply with subsection (2) or (3) above, the society shall be guilty of an offence and liable on summary conviction to a fine not exceeding level 3 on the standard scale.

21(5) For the purposes of this section, a liquidator of the society shall be treated as an officer of it.

22 Winding up by court: grounds and petitioners

22(1) An incorporated friendly society may be wound up under the applicable winding up legislation by the court on any of the following grounds, that is to say, if–

(a) the society has by special resolution resolved that it be wound up by the court;

(b) the number of members is reduced below 7;

(c) the number of members of the committee of management is reduced below 2;

(d) the society has not commenced business within a year from its incorporation or has suspended its business for a whole year;

(e) the society exists for an illegal purpose;

(f) the society is unable to pay its debts; or

(g) the court is of the opinion that it is just and equitable that the society should be wound up.

22(2) Except as provided by subsection (2A), (2B) or (3) or the applicable winding up legislation, a petition for the winding up of an incorporated friendly society may be presented by–

(a) the FCA;

(aa) the PRA;

(b) the society or its committee of management;

(c) any creditor or creditors (including any contingent or any prospective creditor); or

(d) any contributory or contributories,

or by all or any of those parties, together or separately.

22(2A) The FCA may only present a petition under subsection (2) in respect of a society which is a PRA-authorised person after consulting the PRA.

22(2B) The PRA may only present a petition under subsection (2)–

(a) in respect of a society which is a PRA-authorised person; and

(b) after consulting the FCA.

22(3) A contributory may not present a petition unless the number of members is reduced below 7 or he has been a contributory for at least six months before the winding up.

22(4) In this section "contributory" has the meaning assigned to it by paragraph 9 of Schedule 10 to this Act.

History
Section 22(2)(aa), (2A), (2B) inserted by the Financial Services Act 2012 (Mutual Societies) Order 2013 (SI 2013/496) art 2(b) and Sch.8 para.10(4), (5) as from 1 April 2013.

23 Application of winding up legislation to incorporated friendly societies

23(1) In this section "the companies winding up legislation" means the enactments applicable in relation to England and Wales, Scotland and Northern Ireland which are specified in paragraph 1 of Schedule 10 to this Act (including any enactment which creates an offence by any person arising out of acts or omissions occurring before the commencement of the winding up).

23(2) In its application to the winding up of an incorporated friendly society, by virtue of section 21(1) or 22(1) above, the companies winding up legislation shall have effect with the modifications effected by Parts I to III of Schedule 10 to this Act; and the supplementary provisions of Part IV of that Schedule also have effect in relation to such a winding up and in relation to a dissolution by consent.

23(3) In section 21 and 22 above "the applicable winding up legislation" means the companies winding up legislation as so modified.

24   Continuation of long term business

24(1)   This section has effect in relation to the winding up of an incorporated friendly society which carries on long term business (including any reinsurance business).

24(2)   The liquidator shall, unless the court otherwise orders, carry on the long term business of the society with a view to its being transferred as a going concern under this Act; and, in carrying on that business, the liquidator may agree to the variation of any contracts of insurance in existence when the winding up order is made but shall not effect any new contracts of insurance.

24(3)   If the liquidator is satisfied that the interests of the creditors in respect of liabilities of the society attributable to its long term business require the appointment of a special manager of the society's long term business, he may apply to the court, and the court may on such application appoint a special manager of that business to act during such time as the court may direct, with such powers (including any of the powers of a receiver or manager) as may be entrusted to him by the court.

24(4)   Section 177(5) of the Insolvency Act 1986 or, as the case may be, Article 151 of the Insolvency (Northern Ireland) Order 1989 shall apply to a special manager appointed under subsection (3) above as it applies to a special manager appointed under that section or that Article.

24(5)   The court may, if it thinks fit and subject to such conditions (if any) as it may determine, reduce the amount of the contracts made by the society in the course of carrying on its long term business.

24(6)   The court may, on the application of the liquidator, a special manager appointed under subsection (3) above or the FCA or the PRA appoint an independent actuary to investigate the long term business of the society and to report to the liquidator, the special manager or the FCA or the PRA, as the case may be, on the desirability or otherwise of that business being continued and on any reduction in the contracts made in the course of carrying on that business that may be necessary for its successful continuation.

25   Power of court to declare dissolution void

25(1)   Where an incorporated friendly society has been dissolved under section 20 above or following a winding up, the court may, at any time within 12 years after the date on which the society was dissolved, make an order under this section declaring the dissolution to have been void.

25(2)   An order under this section may be made, on such terms as the court thinks fit, on an application by the trustees under section 20 above or the liquidator, as the case may be, or by any other person appearing to the court to be interested.

25(3)   When an order under this section is made, such proceedings may be taken as might have been taken if the society had not been dissolved.

25(4)   The person on whose application the order is made shall, within 7 days of its being so made, or such further time as the court may allow, furnish the FCA and, if the society is a PRA-authorised person, the PRA with a copy of the order; and the FCA shall keep the copy in the public file of the society.

25(5)   If a person fails to comply with subsection (4) above, he shall be guilty of an offence and liable on summary conviction–

   (a)   to a fine not exceeding level 3 on the standard scale; and

   (b)   in the case of a continuing offence, to an additional fine not exceeding one-tenth of that level for every day during which the offence continues.

25(6)   In this section "the court" means–

   (a)   in relation to a society whose registered office is in England and Wales, the High Court;

   (b)   in relation to a society whose registered office is in Scotland, the Court of Session; and

(c) in relation to a society whose registered office is in Northern Ireland, the High Court in Northern Ireland.

26 Cancellation of registration

26(1) Where the FCA is satisfied that an incorporated friendly society has been dissolved under section 20 above or following a winding up, it shall cancel the society's registration under this Act.

26(2) Where the FCA is satisfied, with respect to an incorporated friendly society–

(a) that a certificate of incorporation has been obtained for the society by fraud or mistake; or

(b) that the society has ceased to exist; or

(c) in the case of a society to which section 37(2) or (3) below applies, that the principal place of business of the society is outside the United Kingdom,

it may cancel the registration of the society.

26(3) Without prejudice to subsection (2) above, the FCA may, if it thinks fit, cancel the registration of an incorporated friendly society at the request of the society, evidenced in such manner as the FCA may direct.

26(4) Before cancelling the registration of an incorporated friendly society under subsection (2) above, the FCA shall give to the society not less than two months' previous notice, specifying briefly the grounds of the proposed cancellation.

26(4A) The FCA must consult the PRA before cancelling under subsection (1), (2) or (3) the registration of a society which is a PRA-authorised person.

26(5) Where the registration of an incorporated friendly society is cancelled under subsection (2) above, the society may appeal–

(a) where the registered office of the society is situated in England and Wales, to the High Court;

(b) where that office is situated in Scotland, to the Court of Session; or

(c) where that office is situated in Northern Ireland, to the High Court in Northern Ireland;

and on any such appeal the court may, if it thinks it just to do so, set aside the cancellation.

26(6) Where the registration of a society is cancelled under subsection (2) or (3) above, then, subject to the right of appeal under subsection (5) above, the society, so far as it continues to exist, shall cease to be a society incorporated under this Act.

26(7) Subsection (6) above shall not affect any liability actually incurred by an incorporated friendly society; and any such liability may be enforced against the society as if the cancellation had not taken place.

26(8) Any cancellation of the registration of an incorporated friendly society under this section shall be effected by written notice given by the FCA to the society.

26(9) As soon as practicable after the cancellation of the registration of an incorporated friendly society under this section the FCA shall cause notice thereof to be published in the London Gazette, the Edinburgh Gazette or the Belfast Gazette according to the situation of the society's registered office, and if it thinks fit, in one or more newspapers.

History
Section 26(4A) inserted by the Financial Services Act 2012 (Mutual Societies) Order 2013 (SI 2013/496) art 2(b) and Sch.9 para.13(3) as from 1 April 2013.

SCHEDULE 10

APPLICATION OF COMPANIES WINDING UP LEGISLATION TO INCORPORATED FRIENDLY SOCIETIES

Section 23

PART I

GENERAL MODE OF APPLICATION

1   The enactments which comprise the companies winding up legislation (referred to in this Schedule as "the enactments") are the provisions of–

(a)   Parts IV, VI, VII, XII and XIII of the Insolvency Act 1986, or

(b)   Parts V, VI, XI and XII of the Insolvency (Northern Ireland) Order 1989,

and, in so far as they relate to offences under any such enactment, sections 430 and 432 of, and Schedule 10 to, that Act or Article 373 of, and Schedule 7 to, that Order.

2   Subject to the following provisions of this Schedule, the enactments apply to the winding up of incorporated friendly societies as they apply to the winding up of companies registered under the Companies Act 2006.

3(1)   Subject to the following provisions of this Schedule, the enactments shall, in their application to incorporated friendly societies, have effect with the substitution–

(a)   for "company" of "incorporated friendly society";

(b)   for "directors" of "committee of management";

(c)   for "the registrar of companies" or "the registrar" of "the Financial Conduct Authority"; and

(d)   for "the articles" of "the rules".

3(2)   Subject to the following provisions of this Schedule in the application of the enactments to incorporated friendly societies–

(aa)   every reference to a company registered in Scotland shall have effect as a reference to an incorporated friendly society whose registered office is situated in Scotland;

(a)   every reference to the officers, or to a particular officer, of a company shall have effect as a reference to the officers, or to the corresponding officer, of the incorporated friendly society and as including a person holding himself out as such an officer;

(b)   every reference to a director of a company shall be construed as a reference to a member of the committee of management; and

(c)   every reference to an administrator, an administration order, an administrative receiver, a shadow director or a voluntary arrangement shall be omitted.

4(1)   Where any of the enactments as applied to incorporated friendly societies requires a notice or other document to be sent to the FCA, it shall have effect as if it required the FCA to keep the notice or document in the public file of the society and to record in that file the date on which the notice or document is placed in it.

4(2)   Where any of the enactments, as so applied, refers to the registration, or to the date of registration, of such a notice or document, that enactment shall have effect as if it referred to the placing of the notice or document in the public file or (as the case may be) to the date on which it was placed there.

5 Any enactment which specifies a sum altered by order under section 416 of the Insolvency Act 1986 or Article 362 of the Insolvency (Northern Ireland) Order 1989 (powers to alter monetary limits) applies with the effect of the alteration.

PART II

MODIFIED APPLICATION OF INSOLVENCY ACT 1986 PARTS IV, 6, 7, 12 AND 13 AND SCHEDULE 10

Preliminary

6 In this Part of this Schedule, Part IV of the Insolvency Act 1986 is referred to as "Part IV"; and that Act is referred to as "the Act".

6A Parts 4, 6, 7 and 12 of, and Schedule 10 to, the Act, in their application to incorporated friendly societies, have effect without the amendments of those Parts and that Schedule made by–

  (a) section 122 of the Small Business, Enterprise and Employment Act 2015 (abolition of requirements to hold meetings: company insolvency);

  (b) section 124 of that Act (ability for creditors to opt not to receive certain notices: company insolvency); and

  (c) Part 1 of Schedule 9 to that Act (sections 122 to 125: further amendments).

Members of a friendly society as contributories in winding up

7(1) Section 74 (liability of members) of the Act is modified as follows.

7(2) In subsection (1), the reference to any past member shall be omitted.

7(3) Paragraphs (a) to (d) of subsection (2) shall be omitted; and so shall subsection (3).

7(4) The extent of the liability of a member of an incorporated friendly society in a winding up shall not exceed the extent of his liability under paragraph 8 of Schedule 3 to this Act.

8 Sections 75 to 78 and 83 in Chapter I of Part IV (miscellaneous provisions not relevant to incorporated friendly societies) do not apply.

9(1) Section 79 (meaning of "contributory") of the Act does not apply.

9(2) In the enactments as applied to an incorporated friendly society, "contributory"–

  (a) means every person liable to contribute to the assets of the society in the event of its being wound up; and

  (b) for the purposes of all proceedings for determining, and all proceedings prior to the determination of, the persons who are to be deemed contributories, includes any person alleged to be a contributory; and

  (c) includes persons who are liable to pay or contribute to the payment of–

     (i) any debt or liability of the incorporated friendly society being wound up; or

     (ii) any sum for the adjustment of rights of members among themselves; or

     (iii) the expenses of the winding up;

but does not include persons liable to contribute by virtue of a declaration by the court under section 213 (imputed responsibility for fraudulent trading) or section 214 (wrongful trading) of the Act.

Voluntary winding up

10(1)   Section 84 of the Act does not apply.

10(2)   In the enactments as applied to an incorporated friendly society, the expression "resolution for voluntary winding up" means a resolution passed under section 21(1) above.

11   Section 88 shall have effect with the omission of the words from the beginning to "and".

12(1)   Subsection (1) of section 89 shall have effect as if for the words from the beginning to "meeting" there were substituted the words–

> **"(1)** Where it is proposed to wind up an incorporated friendly society voluntarily, the committee of management (or, in the case of an incorporated friendly society whose committee of management has more than two members, the majority of them) may at a meeting of the committee".

12(2)   The reference to the directors in subsection (2) shall be construed as a reference to members of the committee of management.

13   Section 90 shall have effect as if for the words "directors statutory declaration under section 89" there were substituted the words "statutory declaration made under section 89 by members of the committee of management".

14   Sections 95(1) and 96 shall have effect as if the word "directors" were omitted from each of them.

15   In subsection (1) of section 101 (appointment of liquidation committee) of the Act, the reference to functions conferred on a liquidation committee by or under that Act shall have effect as a reference to its functions by or under that Act as applied to incorporated friendly societies.

16(1)   Section 107 (distribution of property) of the Act does not apply; and the following applies in its place.

16(2)   Subject to the provisions of Part IV relating to preferential payments, an incorporated friendly society's property in a voluntary winding up shall be applied in satisfaction of the society's liabilities to creditors pari passu and, subject to that application, in accordance with the rules of the society.

17   Sections 110 and 111 (liquidator accepting shares, etc. as consideration for sale of company property) of the Act do not apply.

Winding up by the court

18   In sections 117 (High Court and county court jurisdiction) and 120 (Court of Session and sheriff court jurisdiction) of the Act, each reference to a company's share capital paid up or credited as paid up shall have effect as a reference to the amount of the contribution or subscription income of an incorporated friendly society as shown by the latest balance sheet.

19   Section 122 (circumstances in which company may be wound up by the court) of the Act does not apply.

20   Section 124 (application for winding up) of the Act does not apply.

21(1)   In section 125 (powers of court on hearing of petition) of the Act, subsection (1) applies with the omission of the words from "but the court" to the end of the subsection.

21(2)   The conditions which the court may impose under section 125 of the Act include conditions for securing–

(a)   that the incorporated friendly society be dissolved by consent of its members under section 20 above; or

(b)   that the society amalgamates with, or transfers all or any of its engagements to, another friendly society under section 85 or 86 above, or

(c)   that the society converts itself into a company under section 91 above,

and may also include conditions for securing that any default which occasioned the petition be made good and that the costs, or in Scotland the expenses, of the proceedings on that petition be defrayed by the person or persons responsible for the default.

22   Section 126 (power of court, between petition and winding-up order, to stay or restrain proceedings against company) of the Act has effect with the omission of subsection (2).

23   If, before the presentation of a petition for the winding up by the court of an incorporated friendly society, an instrument of dissolution under section 20 above is placed in the society's public file, section 129(1) (commencement of winding up by the court) of the Act shall also apply in relation to the date on which the notice is so placed and to any proceedings in the course of the dissolution as it applies to the commencement date for, and proceedings in, a voluntary winding up.

24(1)   Section 130 of the Act (consequences of winding-up order) shall have effect with the following modifications.

24(2)   Subsections (1) and (3) shall be omitted.

24(3)   An incorporated friendly society shall, within 15 days of a winding-up order being made in respect of it, give notice of the order to the FCA and, if the society is a PRA-authorised person, the PRA; and the FCA, shall keep the notice in the public file of the society.

24(4)   If an incorporated friendly society fails to comply with sub-paragraph (3) above, it shall be guilty of an offence and liable on summary conviction to a fine not exceeding level 3 on the standard scale.

25   Section 140 (appointment of liquidator by court in certain circumstances) of the Act does not apply.

26   In the application of sections 141(1) and 142(1) to incorporated friendly societies, the references to functions conferred on a liquidation committee by or under that Act shall have effect as references to its functions by or under that Act as so applied.

27   The conditions which the court may impose under section 147 (power to stay or sist winding up) of the Act shall include those specified in paragraph 21(2) above.

28   Section 154 (adjustment of rights of contributories) of the Act shall have effect with the modification that any surplus is to be distributed in accordance with the rules of the society.

29   [Repealed by the Companies Act 2006 (Commencement No.3, Consequential Amendments, Transitional Provisions and Savings) Order 2007 (SI 2007/2194) Sch.5 para.71(1) as from 1 October 2007.]

Winding up: general

30   Section 187 (power to make over assets to employees) of the Act does not apply.

31(1)   In section 201 (dissolution: voluntary winding up) of the Act, subsection (2) applies without the words from "and on the expiration" to the end of the subsection and, in subsection (3), the word "However" shall be omitted.

31(2)   Sections 202 to 204 (early dissolution) of the Act do not apply.

32   In section 205 (dissolution: winding up by the court) of the Act, subsection (2) applies with the omission of the words from "and, subject" to the end of the subsection; and in subsections (3) and (4) references to the Secretary of State shall have effect as references to the FCA.

Penal provisions

33   Sections 216 and 217 of the Act (restriction on re-use of name) do not apply.

34(1)   Sections 218 and 219 (prosecution of delinquent officers) of the Act do not apply in relation to offences committed by members of an incorporated friendly society acting in that capacity.

34(2)   Sections 218(5) of the Act and subsections (1) and (2) of section 219 of the Act do not apply.

34(3)   The references in subsections (3) and (4) of section 219 of the Act to the Secretary of State shall have effect as references to the FCA; and the reference in subsection (3) to section 218 of the Act shall have effect as a reference to that section as supplemented by paragraph 35 below.

35(1)   Where a report is made to the prosecuting authority (within the meaning of section 218) under section 218(4) of the Act, in relation to an officer of an incorporated friendly society, he may, if he thinks fit, refer the matter to the FCA for further enquiry.

35(2)   On such a reference to it the FCA shall exercise its power under section 65(1) above to appoint one or more investigators to investigate and report on the matter.

35(3)   An answer given by a person to a question put to him, in exercise of the powers conferred by section 65 above on a person so appointed, may be used in evidence against the person giving it.

Preferential debts

36   Section 387 (meaning in Schedule 6 of "the relevant date") of the Act applies with the omission of subsections (2) and (4) to (6).

Insolvency practitioners: their qualification and regulation

36A   Section 390 of the Act (persons not qualified to act as insolvency practitioners) has effect as if for subsection (2) there were substituted–

> "**(2)** A person is not qualified to act as an insolvency practitioner in relation to an incorporated friendly society at any time unless at that time the person is fully authorised to act as an insolvency practitioner or partially authorised to act as an insolvency practitioner only in relation to companies.".

36B(1)   In the following provisions of the Act, in a reference to authorisation or permission to act as an insolvency practitioner in relation to (or only in relation to) companies the reference to companies has effect without the modification in paragraph 3(1)(a) above–

(a)   sections 390A and 390B(1) and (3) (authorisation of insolvency practitioners); and

(b)   sections 391O(1)(b) and 391R(3)(b) (court sanction of insolvency practitioners in public interest cases).

36B(2)   In sections 391Q(2)(b) (direct sanctions order: conditions) and 391S(3)(e) (power for Secretary of State to obtain information) of the Act the reference to a company has effect without the modification in paragraph 3(1)(a) above.

History

Paragraphs 36A, 36B and the heading thereto inserted by the Small Business, Enterprise and Employment Act 2015 and the Insolvency (Amendment) Act (Northern Ireland) 2016 (Consequential Amendments and Transitional Provisions) Regulations 2017 (SI 2017/400) regs 1, 3 as from 6 April 2017. The heading to Pt II was modified and para.6A was inserted by Small Business, Enterprise and Employment Act 2015 (Consequential Amendments, Savings and Transitional Provisions) Regulations 2018 (SI 2018/208) reg.3(a) and (b) with effect from 13 March 2018).

PART III

MODIFIED APPLICATION OF INSOLVENCY (NORTHERN IRELAND) ORDER 1989

[Applies to Northern Ireland only; not reproduced.]

PART IV

SUPPLEMENTARY

Dissolution of incorporated friendly society after winding up

67(1)   Where an incorporated friendly society has been wound up voluntarily, it is dissolved as from 3 months from the date of the placing in the public file of the society of the return of the final meetings of the society and its creditors made by the liquidator under–

(a)   section 94 or 106 of the Insolvency Act 1986 (as applied to incorporated friendly societies), or on such other date as is determined in accordance with section 201 of that Act; or

(b)   Article 80 or 92 of the Insolvency (Northern Ireland) Order 1989 (as so applied), or on such other date as is determined in accordance with Article 166 of that Order.

67(2)   Where an incorporated friendly society has been wound up by the court, it is dissolved as from 3 months from the date of the placing in the public file of the society of the liquidator's notice under–

(a)   section 172(8) of the Insolvency Act 1986 (as applied to incorporated friendly societies) or on such other date as is determined in accordance with section 205 of that Act; or

(b)   Article 146(7) of the Insolvency (Northern Ireland) Order 1989 (as so applied) or on such other date as is determined in accordance with Article 169 of that Order.

68(1)   Sections 1012 to 1023 and 1034 of the Companies Act 2006 (property of dissolved company) apply in relation to the property of a dissolved incorporated friendly society (whether dissolved under section 20 or following its winding up) as they apply in relation to the property of a dissolved company.

68(2)   Paragraph 3(1) above shall apply to those sections for the purpose of their application to incorporated friendly societies.

68(3)   Any reference in those sections to restoration to the register shall be read as a reference to the effect of an order under section 25 of this Act.

68(4)   [Deleted]

History
Paragraph 68(1), (3) substituted, and para.(4) deleted by the Companies Act 2006 (Consequential Amendments, Transitional Provisions and Savings) Order 2009 (SI 2009/1941) art.2(1) and Sch.1 para.133(7)(b) as from 1 October 2009.

Insolvency rules and fees

69(1)   Rules may be made under–

(a)   section 411 of the Insolvency Act 1986; or

(b)   Article 359 of the Insolvency (Northern Ireland) Order 1989,

for the purpose of giving effect, in relation to incorporated friendly societies, to the provisions of the applicable winding up legislation.

69(2)   An order made by the competent authority under section 414 of the Insolvency Act 1986 may make provision for fees to be payable under that section in respect of proceedings under the applicable winding-up legislation and the performance by the official receiver or the Secretary of State of functions under it.

69(3)   An order made by the competent authority under Article 361 of the Insolvency (Northern Ireland) Order 1989 may make provisions for fees to be payable under that section in respect of proceedings under the applicable winding-up legislation and the performance by the official receiver in Northern Ireland or the Department of Economic Development in Northern Ireland of functions under it.

Pension Schemes Act 1993

(1993 Chapter 48)

[5th November 1993]

[**Note:** Changes made by the Pensions Act 1995, the Employment Rights Act 1996, the Employment Rights (Dispute Resolution) Act 1998, the Welfare Reform and Pensions Act 1999, the Pensions Act 2004, the National Insurance Contributions Act 2008, the Pensions Act 2007, the Pensions Act 2014 and the Enterprise and Regulatory Reform Act 2013 (Consequential Amendments) (Bankruptcy), the Small Business, Enterprise and Employment Act 2015 (Consequential Amendments) Regulations 2016 (SI 2016/481) and the Employment Rights Act 1996 and Pension Schemes Act 1993 (Amendment) Regulations 2017 (SI 2017/1205) have been incorporated into the text (in the case of pre-2003 changes without annotation). References to administration orders, etc. have been altered appropriately throughout pursuant to changes made by the Enterprise Act 2002.]

PART VII

INSOLVENCY OF EMPLOYERS

CHAPTER II

PAYMENT BY SECRETARY OF STATE OF UNPAID SCHEME CONTRIBUTIONS

123   Interpretation of Chapter II

123(1)   [Insolvency of employer for purposes of Ch.II] For the purposes of this Chapter, an employer shall be taken to be insolvent if, but only if, in England and Wales–

(a)   he has been made bankrupt or has made a composition or arrangement with his creditors;

(b)   he has died and his estate falls to be administered in accordance with an order under section 421 of the Insolvency Act 1986;

(c)   where the employer is a company–

    (i)   a winding-up order is made or a resolution for voluntary winding up is passed with respect to it or the company enters administration,

    (ii)   a receiver or manager of its undertaking is duly appointed,

    (iii) possession is taken, by or on behalf of the holders of any debentures secured by a floating charge, of any property of the company comprised in or subject to the charge, or

    (iv) a voluntary arrangement proposed for the purpose of Part I of the Insolvency Act 1986 is approved under that Part, or

  (d) where subsection (2A) is satisfied.

123(2)   **[Insolvency of employer in Scotland for purposes of Ch.II]** For the purposes of this Chapter, an employer shall be taken to be insolvent if, but only if, in Scotland–

  (a) sequestration of his estate is awarded or he executes a trust deed for his creditors or enters into a composition contract;

  (b) he has died and a judicial factor appointed under section 11A of the Judicial Factors (Scotland) Act 1889 is required by that section to divide his insolvent estate among his creditors; or

  (c) where the employer is a company–

    (i) a winding-up order is made or a resolution for voluntary winding up is passed with respect to it or the company enters administration,

    (ii) a receiver of its undertaking is duly appointed, or

    (iii) a voluntary arrangement proposed for the purpose of Part I of the Insolvency Act 1986 is approved under that Part.

123(2A)   **[Conditions to be satisfied]** This subsection is satisfied if–

  (a) a request has been made for the first opening of collective proceedings–

    (i) based on the insolvency of the employer, as provided for under the laws, regulations and administrative provisions of a member State; and

    (ii) involving the partial or total divestment of the employer's assets and the appointment of a liquidator or a person performing a similar task; and

  (b) the competent authority has–

    (i) decided to open the proceedings; or

    (ii) established that the employer's undertaking or business has been definitively closed down and the available assets of the employer are insufficient to warrant the opening of the proceedings.

123(2B)   **["Liquidator or person performing a similar task", "competent authority" in s.123(2A)]** For the purposes of subsection (2A)–

  (a) "liquidator or person performing a similar task" includes the official receiver or an administrator, trustee in bankruptcy, judicial factor, supervisor of a voluntary arrangement, or person performing a similar task,

  (b) "competent authority" includes–

    (i) a court,

    (ii) a meeting of creditors,

    (iii) a creditors' committee,

    (iv) the creditors by a decision procedure, and

    (v) an authority of a member State empowered to open insolvency proceedings, to confirm the opening of such proceedings or to take decisions in the course of such proceedings.

123(2C)   [Application under s.124] An application under section 124 may only be made in respect of a worker who worked or habitually worked in Great Britain in that employment to which the application relates.

123(3)   [Definitions] In this Chapter–

"employer", "employment", "worker" and "worker's contract" and other expressions which are defined in the Employment Rights Act 1996 have the same meaning as in that Act (see further subsections (3A) and (3B));

"holiday pay" means–

(a)   pay in respect of holiday actually taken; or

(b)   any accrued holiday pay which under the worker's contract would in the ordinary course have become payable to him in respect of the period of a holiday if his employment with the employer had continued until he became entitled to a holiday.

123(3A)   [Application of Pensions Act 2008 s.89 re agency workers] Section 89 of the Pensions Act 2008 (agency workers) applies for the purposes of this Chapter as it applies for the purposes of Part 1 of that Act.

123(3B)   [References to a worker] References in this Chapter to a worker include references to an individual to whom Part 1 of the Pensions Act 2008 applies as if the individual were a worker because of regulations made under section 98 of that Act; and related expressions are to be read accordingly.

123(4)   [Repealed]

123(5)   [Resources of a scheme] Any reference in this Chapter to the resources of a scheme is a reference to the funds out of which the benefits provided by the scheme are from time to time payable.

History
Definition of "occupational pension scheme" and s.123(4) repealed by Pensions Act 2004 Sch.13 para.1 as from 22 September 2005. Definitions of "employer", etc. and s.123(3A), (3B) inserted and s.123(3) amended by the Pensions Act 2014 s.42 as from 11 September 2014.
    Section 123(1) amended and 123(2A)–(2C) inserted by the Employment Rights Act 1996 and Pension Schemes Act 1993 (Amendment) Regulations 2017 (SI 2017/1205) regs 1, 3 as from 26 December 2017.

124   Duty of Secretary of State to pay unpaid contributions to schemes

124(1)   [Duty of Secretary of State] If, on an application made to him in writing by the persons competent to act in respect of an occupational pension scheme or a personal pension scheme, the Secretary of State is satisfied–

(a)   that an employer has become insolvent; and

(b)   that at the time he did so there remained unpaid relevant contributions falling to be paid by him to the scheme,

then, subject to the provisions of this section and section 125, the Secretary of State shall pay into the resources of the scheme the sum which in his opinion is payable in respect of the unpaid relevant contributions.

124(2)   [Relevant contributions] In this section and section 125 "relevant contributions" means contributions falling to be paid by an employer to an occupational pension scheme or a personal pension scheme, either on his own account or on behalf of a worker; and for the purposes of this section a contribution shall not be treated as falling to be paid on behalf of a worker unless a sum equal to that amount has been deducted from the pay of the worker by way of a contribution from him.

124(3)   [Sum payable by employer re unpaid contributions] Subject to subsection (3A), the sum payable under this section in respect of unpaid contributions of an employer on his own account to an occupational pension scheme or a personal pension scheme shall be the least of the following amounts–

(a)   the balance of relevant contributions remaining unpaid on the date when he became insolvent and payable by the employer on his own account to the scheme in respect of the 12 months immediately preceding that date;

(b)   the amount certified by an actuary to be necessary for the purpose of meeting the liability of the scheme on dissolution to pay the benefits provided by the scheme to or in respect of the workers of the employer;

(c)   an amount equal to 10 per cent of the total amount of remuneration paid or payable to those workers in respect of the 12 months immediately preceding the date on which the employer became insolvent.

124(3A)   [Sum payable into money purchase scheme] Where the scheme in question is a money purchase scheme, the sum payable under this section by virtue of subsection (3) shall be the lesser of the amounts mentioned in paragraphs (a) and (c) of that subsection.

124(4)   [Remuneration] For the purposes of subsection (3)(c), "remuneration" includes holiday pay, statutory sick pay, statutory maternity pay under Part V of the Social Security Act 1986 or Part XII of the Social Security Contributions and Benefits Act 1992, and any payment such as is referred to in section 184(2) of the Employment Rights Act 1996.

124(5)   [Limit on payment of unpaid contributions] Any sum payable under this section in respect of unpaid contributions on behalf of a worker shall not exceed the amount deducted from the pay of the worker in respect of the worker's contributions to the scheme during the 12 months immediately preceding the date on which the employer became insolvent.

124(6)   ["On his own account"] In this section "on his own account", in relation to an employer, means on his own account but to fund benefits for, or in respect of, one or more workers.

History
Section 124(6) inserted by Pensions Act 2004 Sch.12 para.20 as from 22 September 2005.

125   Certification of amounts payable under section 124 by insolvency officers

125(1)   [Application of s.125(1)] This section applies where one of the officers mentioned in subsection (2) ("the relevant officer") has been or is required to be appointed in connection with an employer's insolvency.

125(2)   [Officers referred to in s.125(1)] The officers referred to in subsection (1) are–

(a)   a trustee in bankruptcy;

(b)   a liquidator;

(c)   an administrator;

(d)   a receiver or manager; or

(e)   a trustee under a composition or arrangement between the employer and his creditors or under a trust deed for his creditors executed by the employer;

and in this subsection "trustee", in relation to a composition or arrangement, includes the supervisor of a voluntary arrangement proposed for the purposes of and approved under Part I or VIII of the Insolvency Act 1986.

125(3)   [Payment under s.124 on receipt of statement by relevant officer] Subject to subsection (5), where this section applies the Secretary of State shall not make any payment under section 124 in respect of unpaid relevant contributions until he has received a statement from the relevant officer of the amount of relevant contributions which appear to have been unpaid on the date on which the employer became insolvent and to remain unpaid; and the relevant officer shall on request by the Secretary of State provide him as soon as reasonably practicable with such a statement.

125(4) **[Amount payable]** Subject to subsection (5), an amount shall be taken to be payable, paid or deducted as mentioned in subsection (3)(a) or (c) or (5) of section 124 only if it is so certified by the relevant officer.

125(5) **[Power of Secretary of State to make payment]** If the Secretary of State is satisfied–

(a) that he does not require a statement under subsection (3) in order to determine the amount of relevant contributions that was unpaid on the date on which the employer became insolvent and remains unpaid, or

(b) that he does not require a certificate under subsection (4) in order to determine the amounts payable, paid or deducted as mentioned in subsection (3)(a) or (c) or (5) of section 124,

he may make a payment under that section in respect of the contributions in question without having received such a statement or, as the case may be, such a certificate.

126 Complaint to employment tribunal

126(1) **[Persons acting re pension schemes]** Any persons who are competent to act in respect of an occupational pension scheme or a personal pension scheme and who have applied for a payment to be made under section 124 into the resources of the scheme may present a complaint to an employment tribunal that–

(a) the Secretary of State has failed to make any such payment; or

(b) any such payment made by him is less than the amount which should have been paid.

126(2) **[Entitlement to complaint]** Such a complaint must be presented within the period of three months beginning with the date on which the decision of the Secretary of State on that application was communicated to the persons presenting it or, if that is not reasonably practicable, within such further period as is reasonable.

126(3) **[Declaration of tribunal]** Where an employment tribunal finds that the Secretary of State ought to make a payment under section 124, it shall make a declaration to that effect and shall also declare the amount of any such payment which it finds that the Secretary of State ought to make.

127 Transfer to Secretary of State of rights and remedies

127(1) **[Where Secretary of State makes s.124 payment]** Where in pursuance of section 124 the Secretary of State makes any payment into the resources of an occupational pension scheme or a personal pension scheme in respect of any contributions to the scheme, any rights and remedies in respect of those contributions belonging to the persons competent to act in respect of the scheme shall, on the making of the payment, become rights and remedies of the Secretary of State.

127(2) **[Extent of rights and remedies re s.127(1)]** Where the Secretary of State makes any such payment as is mentioned in subsection (1) and the sum (or any part of the sum) falling to be paid by the employer on account of the contributions in respect of which the payment is made constitutes–

(a) a preferential debt within the meaning of the Insolvency Act 1986 for the purposes of any provision of that Act (including any such provision as applied by an order made under that Act) or any provision of the Companies Acts (as defined in section 2(1) of the Companies Act 2006); or

(b) a preferred debt within the meaning of the Bankruptcy (Scotland) Act 2016 for the purposes of any provision of that Act (including any such provision as applied by section 11A of the Judicial Factors (Scotland) Act 1889), then, without prejudice to the generality of subsection (1), there shall be included among the rights and remedies which become rights and remedies of the Secretary of State in accordance with that subsection any right arising under any such provision by reason of the status of that sum (or that part of it) as a preferential or preferred debt.

127(3)   **[Computation of claims in s.127(2)(a)]** In computing for the purposes of any provision referred to in subsection (2)(a) or (b) the aggregate amount payable in priority to other creditors of the employer in respect of–

(a)   any claim of the Secretary of State to be so paid by virtue of subsection (2); and

(b)   any claim by the persons competent to act in respect of the scheme, any claim falling within paragraph (a) shall be treated as if it were a claim of those persons; but the Secretary of State shall be entitled, as against those persons, to be so paid in respect of any such claim of his (up to the full amount of the claim) before any payment is made to them in respect of any claim falling within paragraph (b).

CHAPTER III

PRIORITY IN BANKRUPTCY

128   Priority in bankruptcy etc.

128   Schedule 4 shall have effect for the purposes of paragraph 8 of Schedule 6 to the Insolvency Act 1986 and paragraph 1 of Schedule 3 to the Bankruptcy (Scotland) Act 2016 (by virtue of which sums to which Schedule 4 to this Act applies are preferential or, as the case may be, preferred debts in cases of insolvency).

SCHEDULE 4

PRIORITY IN BANKRUPTCY ETC

Section 128

Earner's contributions to occupational pension scheme

1   This Schedule applies to any sum owed on account of an earner's contributions to an occupational pension scheme being contributions deducted from earnings paid in the period of four months immediately preceding the relevant date or otherwise due in respect of earnings paid or payable in that period.

Employer's contributions to occupational pension scheme

2(1)   This Schedule applies to any sum owed on account of an employer's contributions to a Northern Ireland salary related contracted-out scheme which were payable in the period of 12 months immediately preceding the relevant date.

2(1A)   The amount of the debt having priority by virtue of sub-paragraph (1) shall be taken to be an amount equal to the appropriate amount.

2(2)   [...]

2(3)   [...]

2(3A)   In sub-paragraph (1A) "the appropriate amount" means the aggregate of–

(a)   the percentage for non-contributing earners of the total reckonable earnings paid or payable, in the period of 12 months referred to in sub-paragraph (1), to or for the benefit of non-contributing earners; and

(b)   the percentage for contributing earners of the total reckonable earnings paid or payable, in that period, to or for the benefit of contributing earners.

History

Paragraph 2(2), (3) deleted and 2(3A) amended by the Pensions Act 2007 Sch.7 Pt 7 and the Pensions Act 2007 (Commencement No.4) Order 2011 (SI 2011/1267) art.2(c) as from 6 April 2012.

2(4)   For the purposes of sub-paragraph (3A)–

(a)   the earnings to be taken into account as reckonable earnings are those paid or payable to or for the benefit of earners in employment which is contracted-out by reference to the scheme in the whole or any part of the period of 12 months there mentioned; and

(b)   earners are to be identified as contributing or non-contributing in relation to service of theirs in employment which is contracted-out by reference to the scheme according to whether or not in the period in question they were liable under the terms of the scheme to contribute in respect of that service towards the provision of pensions under the scheme.

2(5)   In this paragraph–

"employer" shall be construed in accordance with regulations made under section 181(2); and

"Northern Ireland salary related contracted-out scheme" means a salary related contracted-out scheme within the meaning of the Pension Schemes (Northern Ireland) Act 1993 (and references to employment that is contracted-out by reference to a scheme are to be read accordingly);

"the percentage for contributing earners" means 3 per cent,

"the percentage for non-contributing earners" means 4.8 per cent,

"reckonable earnings", in relation to any employment, means the earner's earnings from that employment so far as those earnings–

(a)   were comprised in any payment of earnings made to him or for his benefit at a time when the employment was contracted-out employment; and

(b)   exceeded the current lower earnings limit but not the upper accrual point.

History

Definition of "reckonable earnings" amended by the National Insurance Contributions Act 2008 Sch.1 para.13(2). Definition of "appropriate flat-rate percentage" deleted and definitions of "the percentage for contributing earners" and "the percentage for non-contributing earners" amended by the Pensions Act 2007 Sch.7 Pt 7 and the Pensions Act 2007 (Commencement No.4) Order 2011 (SI 2011/1267) art.2(c) as from 6 April 2012.

State scheme premiums

3(1)   This Schedule applies to any sum owed on account of a Northern Ireland contributions equivalent premium payable at any time before, or in consequence of, a person going into liquidation or being made bankrupt, or in Scotland, the sequestration of a debtor's estate, or (in the case of a company not in liquidation)–

(a)   the appointment of a receiver as mentioned in section 40 of the Insolvency Act 1986 (debenture-holders secured by floating charge), or

(b)   the appointment of a receiver under section 53(6) or 54(5) of that Act (Scottish company with property subject to floating charge), or

(c) the taking of possession by debenture-holders (so secured) as mentioned in section 754 of the Companies Act 2006.

3(2)   Where any such premium is payable in respect of a period of service of more than 12 months (taking into account any previous linked qualifying service), the amount to be paid in priority by virtue of this paragraph shall be limited to the amount of the premium that would have been payable if the service had been confined to the last 12 months taken into account in fixing the actual amount of the premium.

3(3)   Where–

(a) by virtue of this paragraph the whole or part of a premium is required to be paid in priority to other debts of the debtor or his estate; and

(b) the person liable for the payment would be entitled to recover the whole or part of any sum paid on account of it from another person either under section 61 or under any provision made by the relevant scheme for the purposes of that section or otherwise,

then, subject to sub-paragraph (4), that other person shall be liable for any part of the premium for the time being unpaid.

3(4)   No person shall be liable by virtue of sub-paragraph (3) for an amount in excess of the sum which might be so recovered from him if the premium had been paid in full by the person liable for it, after deducting from that sum any amount which has been or may be recovered from him in respect of any part of that payment paid otherwise than under that sub-paragraph.

3(5)   The payment under sub-paragraph (3) of any amount in respect of a premium shall have the same effect on the rights and liabilities of the person making it (other than his liabilities under that sub-paragraph) as if it had been a payment of that amount on account of the sum recoverable from him in respect of a premium as mentioned in sub-paragraph (3)(b).

3(6)   In this paragraph "Northern Ireland contributions equivalent premium" means a contributions equivalent premium within the meaning of the Pension Schemes (Northern Ireland) Act 1993.

History
Paragraphs 3(1)(c) and 4(1)(a) amended by the Companies Act 2006 (Consequential Amendments etc.) Order 2008 (SI 2008/948) art.3(1) and Sch.1 para.194(3), as from 6 April 2008. Paragraphs 2–4 amended and para.4(2) deleted by the Pension Act 2014 Sch.13 para.47 as from 6 April 2016.

Interpretation

4(1)   In this Schedule–

(a) in its application in England and Wales, section 754(3) of the Companies Act 2006 and section 387 of the Insolvency Act 1986 apply as regards the meaning of the expression "the relevant date"; and

(b) in its application in Scotland, that expression has the same meaning as in Part 1 of Schedule 3 to the Bankruptcy (Scotland) Act 2016.

4(2)   [...]

History
See note after para.3.

Employment Rights Act 1996

(1996 Chapter 18)

ARRANGEMENT OF SECTIONS

[22nd May 1996]

[**Note:** Changes made by the Employment Rights (Dispute Resolution) Act 1998, the Employment Rights (Increase of Limits) Order 2012 (SI 2012/3007), the Enterprise Act 2002, the Tribunals, Courts and Enforcement Act 2007, the Charitable Incorporated Organisations (Consequential Amendments) Order 2012 (SI 2012/3014), the Enterprise and Regulatory Reform Act 2013 (Consequential Amendments) (Bankruptcy) and the Small Business, Enterprise and Employment Act 2015 (Consequential Amendments) Regulations 2016 (SI 2016/481) and the Employment Rights Act 1996 and Pension Schemes Act 1993 (Amendment) Regulations 2017 (SI 2017/1205) have been incorporated into the text. References to administration orders, etc. have been altered appropriately throughout, pursuant to changes made by the Enterprise Act 2002. References to "industrial tribunals" have been altered throughout to "employment tribunals" pursuant to the Employment Rights (Dispute Resolution) Act 1998.]

PART XI

REDUNDANCY PAYMENTS ETC.

CHAPTER VI

PAYMENTS BY SECRETARY OF STATE

166 Applications for payments

166(1) [Requirements for application] Where an employee claims that his employer is liable to pay to him an employer's payment and either–

(a) that the employee has taken all reasonable steps, other than legal proceedings, to recover the payment from the employer and the employer has refused or failed to pay it, or has paid part of it and has refused or failed to pay the balance, or

(b) that the employer is insolvent and the whole or part of the payment remains unpaid,

the employee may apply to the Secretary of State for a payment under this section.

375

166(2) **["Employer's payment"]** In this Part "employer's payment", in relation to an employee, means–

  (a)   a redundancy payment which his employer is liable to pay to him under this Part,

  (aa) a payment which his employer is liable to make to him under an agreement to refrain from instituting or continuing proceedings for a contravention or alleged contravention of section 135 which has effect by virtue of section 203(2)(e) or (f), or

  (b)   a payment which his employer is, under an agreement in respect of which an order is in force under section 157, liable to make to him on the termination of his contract of employment.

166(3) **[Part of redundancy payment]** In relation to any case where (in accordance with any provision of this Part) an employment tribunal determines that an employer is liable to pay part (but not the whole) of a redundancy payment the reference in subsection (2)(a) to a redundancy payment is to the part of the redundancy payment.

166(4) **["Legal proceedings"]** In subsection (1)(a) "legal proceedings"–

  (a)   does not include any proceedings before an employment tribunal, but

  (b)   includes any proceedings to enforce a decision or award of an employment tribunal.

166(5) **[Insolvency of employer]** An employer is insolvent for the purposes of subsection (1)(b)–

  (a)   where the employer is an individual, if (but only if) subsection (6) or (8A) is satisfied,

  (b)   where the employer is a company, if (but only if) subsection (7) or (8A) is satisfied,

  (c)   where the employer is a limited liability partnership, if (but only if) subsection (8) or (8A) is satisfied; and

  (d)   where the employer is not any of the above, if (but only if) subsection (8A) is satisfied.

166(6) **[Insolvency re individual]** This subsection is satisfied in the case of an employer who is an individual–

  (a)   in England and Wales if–

     (i)   he has been made bankrupt or has made a composition or arrangement with his creditors, or

     (ii) he has died and his estate falls to be administered in accordance with an order under section 421 of the Insolvency Act 1986, and

  (b)   in Scotland if–

     (i)   sequestration of his estate has been awarded or he has executed a trust deed for his creditors or has entered into a composition contract, or

     (ii) he has died and a judicial factor appointed under section 11A of the Judicial Factors (Scotland) Act 1889 is required by that section to divide his insolvent estate among his creditors.

166(7) **[Insolvency re company]** This subsection is satisfied in the case of an employer which is a company–

  (a)   if a winding up order has been made, or a resolution for voluntary winding up has been passed, with respect to the company,

  (aa) if the company is in administration for the purposes of the Insolvency Act 1986,

  (b)   if a receiver or (in England and Wales only) a manager of the company's undertaking has been duly appointed, or (in England and Wales only) possession has been taken, by or on behalf of the holders of any debentures secured by a floating charge, of any property of the company comprised in or subject to the charge, or

(c)   if a voluntary arrangement proposed in the case of the company for the purposes of Part I of the Insolvency Act 1986 has been approved under that Part of that Act.

166(8)   [Insolvency re limited liability partnership] This subsection is satisfied in the case of an employer which is a limited liability partnership–

(a)   if a winding-up order, an administration order or a determination for a voluntary winding-up has been made with respect to the limited liability partnership,

(b)   if a receiver or (in England and Wales only) a manager of the undertaking of the limited liability partnership has been duly appointed, or (in England and Wales only) possession has been taken, by or on behalf of the holders of any debentures secured by a floating charge, of any property of the limited liability partnership comprised in or subject to the charge, or

(c)   if a voluntary arrangement proposed in the case of the limited liability partnership for the purpose of Part I of the Insolvency Act 1986 has been approved under that Part of that Act.

166(8A)   [Conditions] This subsection is satisfied in the case of an employer if–

(a)   a request has been made for the first opening of collective proceedings–

(i)   based on the insolvency of the employer, as provided for under the laws, regulations and administrative provisions of a member State, and

(ii)   involving the partial or total divestment of the employer's assets and the appointment of a liquidator or a person performing a similar task, and

(b)   the competent authority has–

(i)   decided to open the proceedings, or

(ii)   established that the employer's undertaking or business has been definitively closed down and the available assets of the employer are insufficient to warrant the opening of the proceedings.

166(8B)   ["Liquidator or person performing a similar task", "competent authority" in s.166(8A)] For the purposes of subsection (8A)–

(a)   "liquidator or person performing a similar task" includes the official receiver or an administrator, trustee in bankruptcy, judicial factor, supervisor of a voluntary arrangement, or person performing a similar task,

(b)   "competent authority" includes–

(i)   a court,

(ii)   a meeting of creditors,

(iii)   a creditors' committee,

(iv)   the creditors by a decision procedure, and

(v)   an authority of a member State empowered to open insolvency proceedings, to confirm the opening of such proceedings or to take decisions in the course of such proceedings.

166(8C)   [Application under s.166] An employee may apply under this section only if he or she worked or habitually worked in Great Britain in that employment to which the application relates.

166(9)   [References to company, Insolvency Act 1986] In this section–

(a)   references to a company are to be read as including references to a charitable incorporated organisation, and

(b) any reference to the Insolvency Act 1986 in relation to a company is to be read as including a reference to that Act as it applies to charitable incorporated organisations.

History

Section 166(9) inserted by the Charitable Incorporated Organisations (Consequential Amendments) Order 2012 (SI 2012/3014) art.3 as from 2 January 2013.

Section 166(5)(a)–(c) amended and subss.(5)(d) and (8A)–(8C) inserted by the Employment Rights Act 1996 and Pension Schemes Act 1993 (Amendment) Regulations 2017 (SI 2017/1205) regs 1, 2(1), (2) as from 26 December 2017.

PART XII

INSOLVENCY OF EMPLOYERS

182   Employee's rights on insolvency of employer

182   If, on an application made to him in writing by an employee, the Secretary of State is satisfied that–

(a) the employee's employer has become insolvent,

(b) the employee's employment has been terminated, and

(c) on the appropriate date the employee was entitled to be paid the whole or part of any debt to which this Part applies,

the Secretary of State shall, subject to section 186, pay the employee out of the National Insurance Fund the amount to which, in the opinion of the Secretary of State, the employee is entitled in respect of the debt.

183   Insolvency

183(1)   [Insolvency of employer] An employer has become insolvent for the purposes of this Part–

(a) where the employer is an individual, if (but only if) subsection (2) or (4A) is satisfied,

(b) where the employer is a company, if (but only if) subsection (3) or (4A) is satisfied,

(c) where the employer is a limited liability partnership, if (but only if) subsection (4) or (4A) is satisfied; and

(d) where the employer is not any of the above, if (but only if) subsection (4A) is satisfied.

183(2)   [Insolvent individual employer] This subsection is satisfied in the case of an employer who is an individual–

(a) in England and Wales if–

(ai) a moratorium period under a debt relief order applies in relation to him,

(i) he has been made bankrupt or has made a composition or arrangement with his creditors, or

(ii) he has died and his estate falls to be administered in accordance with an order under section 421 of the Insolvency Act 1986, and

(b) in Scotland if–

(i) sequestration of his estate has been awarded or he has executed a trust deed for his creditors or has entered into a composition contract, or

(ii) he has died and a judicial factor appointed under section 11A of the Judicial Factors (Scotland) Act 1889 is required by that section to divide his insolvent estate among his creditors.

183(3)   [Insolvent company employer] This subsection is satisfied in the case of an employer which is a company–

(a) if a winding up order has been made, or a resolution for voluntary winding up has been passed, with respect to the company,

(aa) if the company is in administration for the purposes of the Insolvency Act 1986,

(b) if a receiver or (in England and Wales only) a manager of the company's undertaking has been duly appointed, or (in England and Wales only) possession has been taken, by or on behalf of the holders of any debentures secured by a floating charge, of any property of the company comprised in or subject to the charge, or

(c) if a voluntary arrangement proposed in the case of the company for the purposes of Part I of the Insolvency Act 1986 has been approved under that Part of that Act.

183(4)   [Insolvent limited liability partnership] This subsection is satisfied in the case of an employer which is a limited liability partnership–

(a) if a winding-up order, an administration order or a determination for a voluntary winding-up has been made with respect to the limited liability partnership,

(b) if a receiver or (in England and Wales only) a manager of the undertaking of the limited liability partnership has been duly appointed, or (in England and Wales only) possession has been taken, by or on behalf of the holders of any debentures secured by a floating charge, of any property of the limited liability partnership comprised in or subject to the charge, or

(c) if a voluntary arrangement proposed in the case of the limited liability partnership for the purposes of Part I of the Insolvency Act 1986 has been approved under that Part of that Act.

183(4A)   [Conditions to be satisfied] This subsection is satisfied in the case of an employer if–

(a) a request has been made for the first opening of collective proceedings–

  (i) based on the insolvency of the employer, as provided for under the laws, regulations and administrative provisions of a member State, and

  (ii) involving the partial or total divestment of the employer's assets and the appointment of a liquidator or a person performing a similar task, and

(b) the competent authority has–

  (i) decided to open the proceedings, or

  (ii) established that the employer's undertaking or business has been definitively closed down and the available assets of the employer are insufficient to warrant the opening of the proceedings.

183(4B)   ["Liquidator or person performing a similar task", "competent authority" in s.183((4A)] For the purposes of subsection (4A)–

(a) "liquidator or person performing a similar task" includes the official receiver or an administrator, trustee in bankruptcy, judicial factor, supervisor of a voluntary arrangement, or person performing a similar task,

(b) "competent authority" includes–

  (i) a court,

  (ii) a meeting of creditors,

  (iii) a creditors' committee,

    (iv) the creditors by a decision procedure, and

    (v) an authority of a member State empowered to open insolvency proceedings, to confirm the opening of such proceedings or to take decisions in the course of such proceedings.

183(4C)   **[Application under s.182]** An employee may apply under section 182 (employee's rights on insolvency of employer) only if he or she worked or habitually worked in England, Wales or Scotland in that employment to which the application relates.

183(5)   **[References to company, Insolvency Act 1986]** In this section–

    (a) references to a company are to be read as including references to a charitable incorporated organisation, and

    (b) any reference to the Insolvency Act 1986 in relation to a company is to be read as including a reference to that Act as it applies to charitable incorporated organisations.

History
Section 183(2)(ai) inserted by the Tribunals, Courts and Employment Act 2007 s.108(3) and Sch.20 para.17 as from 6 April 2009. Section 183(1)(c), (4) inserted by the Limited Liability Partnerships Regulations 2001 (SI 2001/1090) reg.5 and Sch.5 para.19(1), (3) as from 6 April 2001. Section 183(5) inserted by the Charitable Incorporated Organisations (Consequential Amendments) Order 2012 (SI 2012/3014) art.4 as from 2 January 2013. Section 183(1)(a)–(c) amended and subs.(1)(d) inserted, and s.183(4A)–(4C) inserted by the Employment Rights Act 1996 and Pension Schemes Act 1993 (Amendment) Regulations 2017 (SI 2017/1205) regs 1, 2 as from 26 December 2017.

184   Debts to which Part applies

184(1)   **[Application of Pt XII]** This Part applies to the following debts–

    (a) any arrears of pay in respect of one or more (but not more than eight) weeks,

    (b) any amount which the employer is liable to pay the employee for the period of notice required by section 86(1) or (2) or for any failure of the employer to give the period of notice required by section 86(1),

    (c) any holiday pay–

        (i) in respect of a period or periods of holiday not exceeding six weeks in all, and

        (ii) to which the employee became entitled during the twelve months ending with the appropriate date,

    (d) any basic award of compensation for unfair dismissal or so much of an award under a designated dismissal procedures agreement as does not exceed any basic award of compensation for unfair dismissal to which the employee would be entitled but for the agreement, and

    (e) any reasonable sum by way of reimbursement of the whole or part of any fee or premium paid by an apprentice or articled clerk.

184(2)   **[Arrears of pay for s.184(1)(a)]** For the purposes of subsection (1)(a) the following amounts shall be treated as arrears of pay–

    (a) a guarantee payment,

    (b) any payment for time off under Part VI of this Act or section 169 of the Trade Union and Labour Relations (Consolidation) Act 1992 (payment for time off for carrying out trade union duties etc.),

    (c) remuneration on suspension on medical grounds under section 64 of this Act and remuneration on suspension on maternity grounds under section 68 of this Act, and

    (d) remuneration under a protective award under section 189 of the Trade Union and Labour Relations (Consolidation) Act 1992.

184(3) **["Holiday pay" in s.184(1)(c)]** In subsection (1)(c) "holiday pay", in relation to an employee, means–

(a) pay in respect of a holiday actually taken by the employee, or

(b) any accrued holiday pay which, under the employee's contract of employment, would in the ordinary course have become payable to him in respect of the period of a holiday if his employment with the employer had continued until he became entitled to a holiday.

184(4) **[Reasonable sum under s.184(1)(e)]** A sum shall be taken to be reasonable for the purposes of subsection (1)(e) in a case where a trustee in bankruptcy, or (in Scotland) a trustee or interim trustee in the sequestration of an estate under the Bankruptcy (Scotland) Act 2016, or liquidator has been or is required to be appointed–

(a) as respects England and Wales, if it is admitted to be reasonable by the trustee in bankruptcy or liquidator under section 348 of the Insolvency Act 1986 (effect of bankruptcy on apprenticeships etc.), whether as originally enacted or as applied to the winding up of a company by rules under section 411 of that Act, and

(b) as respects Scotland, if it is accepted by the trustee or interim trustee or liquidator for the purposes of the sequestration or winding up.

185   The appropriate date

185   In this Part "the appropriate date"–

(a) in relation to arrears of pay (not being remuneration under a protective award made under section 189 of the Trade Union and Labour Relations (Consolidation) Act 1992) and to holiday pay, means the date on which the employer became insolvent,

(b) in relation to a basic award of compensation for unfair dismissal and to remuneration under a protective award so made, means whichever is the latest of–

(i)   the date on which the employer became insolvent,

(ii) the date of the termination of the employee's employment, and

(iii) the date on which the award was made, and

(c) in relation to any other debt to which this Part applies, means whichever is the later of–

(i)   the date on which the employer became insolvent, and

(ii) the date of the termination of the employee's employment.

186   Limit on amount payable under section 182

186(1)   **[Maximum amount for Pt XII]** The total amount payable to an employee in respect of any debt to which this Part applies, where the amount of the debt is referable to a period of time, shall not exceed–

(a) £525 in respect of any one week, or

(b) in respect of a shorter period, an amount bearing the same proportion to £525 as that shorter period bears to a week.

186(2)   [Repealed by Employment Relations Act 1999 ss.36(1)(a), 44 and Sch.9 Pt 10 with effect from 17 December 1999 (see Employment Relations Act 1999 (Commencement No.3 and Transitional Provision) Order 1999 (SI 1999/3374 (C. 90) art.2 and Sch.).]

History
In s.186(1), the figure "£525" substituted for the former figure "£508" by the Employment Rights (Increase of Limits) Order 2019 (SI 2019/324) arts 1, 3 and Sch. where the appropriate date falls on or after 6 April 2019.

Previously, the following substitutions took effect: "£508" for "£489" (SI 2018/194) as from 6 April 2018; £489 for £479 (SI 2017/175) from 6 April 2017; £479 for £475 (SI 2016/288) from 6 April 2016; £475 for £464 (SI 2015/226) from 6 April 2015; £464 for £450 (SI 2014/382) from 6 April 2014; £450 for £430 (SI 2012/3007) from 1 February 2013, £430 for £400 (SI 2011/3006), from 1 February 2012, £400 for £380 (SI 2010/2926), from 1 February 2011; £380 for £350 (SI 2009/1903), from 1 October 2009; £350 for £330 (SI 2008/3055), from 1 February 2009; £330 for £310 (SI 2007/3570, from 1 February 2008); £310 for £290 (SI 2006/3045, from 1 February 2007); £290 for £280 (SI 2005/3352, from 1 February 2006); £280 for £270 (SI 2004/3379, from 1 February 2005); £270 for £260 (SI 2003/3038, from 1 February 2004); £260 for £250 (SI 2002/2297, from 1 February 2003); £250 for £240 (SI 2002/10, from 1 February 2002); £240 for £230 (SI 2001/21, from 1 February 2001); £230 for £220 (SI 1999/3375, from 1 February 2000); £220 for £210 (SI 1998/924, from 1 April 1998).

Note
The figures in s.186(1)(a) and (b) may be varied by the Secretary of State (see Employment Relations Act 1999 s.34(1)(d)).

187 Role of relevant officer

187(1) [No payment until statement received] Where a relevant officer has been, or is required to be, appointed in connection with an employer's insolvency, the Secretary of State shall not make a payment under section 182 in respect of a debt until he has received a statement from the relevant officer of the amount of that debt which appears to have been owed to the employee on the appropriate date and to remain unpaid.

187(2) [Power of Secretary of State to make payment] If the Secretary of State is satisfied that he does not require a statement under subsection (1) in order to determine the amount of a debt which was owed to the employee on the appropriate date and remains unpaid, he may make a payment under section 182 in respect of the debt without having received such a statement.

187(3) [Duty of relevant officer to provide statement] A relevant officer shall, on request by the Secretary of State, provide him with a statement for the purposes of subsection (1) as soon as is reasonably practicable.

187(4) [Relevant officers for purposes of s.187] The following are relevant officers for the purposes of this section–

(a) a trustee in bankruptcy or a trustee or interim trustee (within the meaning of the Bankruptcy (Scotland) Act 2016),

(b) a liquidator,

(c) an administrator,

(d) a receiver or manager,

(e) a trustee under a composition or arrangement between the employer and his creditors, and

(f) a trustee under a trust deed for his creditors executed by the employer.

187(5) ["Trustee" in s.187(4)(e)] In subsection (4)(e) "trustee" includes the supervisor of a voluntary arrangement proposed for the purposes of, and approved under, Part I or VIII of the Insolvency Act 1986.

188 Complaints to employment tribunals

188(1) [Entitlement to present complaint] A person who has applied for a payment under section 182 may present a complaint to an employment tribunal–

(a) that the Secretary of State has failed to make any such payment, or

(b) that any such payment made by him is less than the amount which should have been paid.

188(2) [Time-limit for presentation of complaint] An employment tribunal shall not consider a complaint under subsection (1) unless it is presented–

(a) before the end of the period of three months beginning with the date on which the decision of the Secretary of State on the application was communicated to the applicant, or

(b) within such further period as the tribunal considers reasonable in a case where it is not reasonably practicable for the complaint to be presented before the end of that period of three months.

188(3) **[Declaration by tribunal]** Where an employment tribunal finds that the Secretary of State ought to make a payment under section 182, the tribunal shall–

(a) make a declaration to that effect, and

(b) declare the amount of any such payment which it finds the Secretary of State ought to make.

189   Transfer to Secretary of State of rights and remedies

189(1) **[Where s.182 payment made to employee]** Where, in pursuance of section 182, the Secretary of State makes a payment to an employee in respect of a debt to which this Part applies–

(a) on the making of the payment any rights and remedies of the employee in respect of the debt (or, if the Secretary of State has paid only part of it, in respect of that part) become rights and remedies of the Secretary of State, and

(b) any decision of an employment tribunal requiring an employer to pay that debt to the employee has the effect that the debt (or the part of it which the Secretary of State has paid) is to be paid to the Secretary of State.

189(2) **[Extent of rights and remedies re s.182]** Where a debt (or any part of a debt) in respect of which the Secretary of State has made a payment in pursuance of section 182 constitutes–

(a) a preferential debt within the meaning of the Insolvency Act 1986 for the purposes of any provision of that Act (including any such provision as applied by any order made under that Act) or any provision of the Companies Act 2006, or–

(b) a preferred debt within the meaning of the Bankruptcy (Scotland) Act 2016 for the purposes of any provision of that Act (including any such provision as applied by section 11A of the Judicial Factors (Scotland) Act 1889),

the rights which become rights of the Secretary of State in accordance with subsection (1) include any right arising under any such provision by reason of the status of the debt (or that part of it) as a preferential or preferred debt.

189(3) **[Computation of debts in s.189(2)]** In computing for the purposes of any provision mentioned in subsection (2)(a) or (b) the aggregate amount payable in priority to other creditors of the employer in respect of–

(a) any claim of the Secretary of State to be paid in priority to other creditors of the employer by virtue of subsection (2), and

(b) any claim by the employee to be so paid made in his own right,

any claim of the Secretary of State to be so paid by virtue of subsection (2) shall be treated as if it were a claim of the employee.

189(4) [Omitted and repealed by the Enterprise Act 2002 s.248(3) Sch.17 para.49(1), (4) and s.278(2) Sch.26 as from 15 September 2003 subject to transitional provisions.]

189(5) **[Sum recovered to be paid into National Insurance Fund]** Any sum recovered by the Secretary of State in exercising any right, or pursuing any remedy, which is his by virtue of this section shall be paid into the National Insurance Fund.

190 Power to obtain information

190(1) [Power of Secretary of State on application] Where an application is made to the Secretary of State under section 182 in respect of a debt owed by an employer, the Secretary of State may require–

    (a) the employer to provide him with such information as he may reasonably require for the purpose of determining whether the application is well-founded, and

    (b) any person having the custody or control of any relevant records or other documents to produce for examination on behalf of the Secretary of State any such document in that person's custody or under his control which is of such a description as the Secretary of State may require.

190(2) [Requirement by notice, etc.] Any such requirement–

    (a) shall be made by notice in writing given to the person on whom the requirement is imposed, and

    (b) may be varied or revoked by a subsequent notice so given.

190(3) [Penalty for refusal, etc.] If a person refuses or wilfully neglects to furnish any information or produce any document which he has been required to furnish or produce by a notice under this section he is guilty of an offence and liable on summary conviction to a fine not exceeding level 3 on the standard scale.

190(4) [Penalty for false statement] If a person, in purporting to comply with a requirement of a notice under this section, knowingly or recklessly makes any false statement he is guilty of an offence and liable on summary conviction to a fine not exceeding level 5 on the standard scale.

190(5) [Offence by body corporate and officers under s.190] Where an offence under this section committed by a body corporate is proved–

    (a) to have been committed with the consent or connivance of, or

    (b) to be attributable to any neglect on the part of,

any director, manager, secretary or other similar officer of the body corporate, or any person who was purporting to act in any such capacity, he (as well as the body corporate) is guilty of the offence and liable to be proceeded against and punished accordingly.

190(6) [Application of s.190(5)] Where the affairs of a body corporate are managed by its members, subsection (5) applies in relation to the acts and defaults of a member in connection with his functions of management as if he were a director of the body corporate.

Financial Services and Markets Act 2000

(2000 Chapter 8)

An Act to make provision about the regulation of financial services and markets; to provide for the transfer of certain statutory functions relating to building societies, friendly societies, industrial and provident societies and certain other mutual societies; and for connected purposes.

[14th June 2000]

[**Note**: Changes made by the Insolvency Act 2000, the Enterprise Act 2002, the Dormant Bank and Building Society Accounts Act 2008, the Banking Act 2009, the Financial Services Act 2010, the Companies Act 2006 (Consequential Amendments etc.) Order 2008 (SI 2008/948), the Building Societies (Insolvency and Special Administration) Order 2009 (SI 2009/805), the Undertakings for Collective Investment in Transferable Securities Regulations 2011 (SI 2011/1613), the Financial Services Act 2012, the Financial Services (Banking Reform) Act 2013, the Enterprise and Regulatory Reform Act 2013 (Consequential Amendments) (Bankruptcy) and the Small Business, Enterprise and Employment Act 2015 (Consequential Amendments) Regulations 2016 (SI 2016/481), the Deregulation Act 2015, the Small Business, Enterprise and Employment Act 2015 and the Insolvency (Amendment) Act (Northern Ireland) 2016 (Consequential Amendments and Transitional Provisions) Regulations 2017 (SI 2017/400), the Financial Services and Markets Act 2000 (Markets in Financial Instruments) Regulations 2017 (SI 2017/701) and the Small Business Enterprise and Employment Act 2015 (Consequential Amendments, Saving and Transitional Provisions) Regulations 2018 (SI 2018/208) have been incorporated into the text (in the case of pre-2003 legislation without annotation). References to administration orders, etc. have been altered appropriately throughout pursuant to changes made by the Enterprise Act 2002. References to "the Authority" have been altered to "the FCA", "the PRA", "the regulator" or equivalent and other minor verbal alterations made as appropriate without annotation. The provisions of this Act which apply to limited liability partnerships are noted at the appropriate places.]

PART XV

THE FINANCIAL SERVICES COMPENSATION SCHEME

The scheme manager

212   The scheme manager

212(1)   ["The scheme manager"] "The scheme manager" means the body corporate established by the Financial Services Authority under this section as originally enacted.

212(2)   [Regulators to ensure scheme manager capable of exercising functions] The regulators must take such steps as are necessary to ensure that the scheme manager is, at all times, capable of exercising the functions conferred on it by or under this Part or Part 15A.

212(3)   [Constitution] The constitution of the scheme manager must provide for it to have–

(a)   a chairman;

(aa)   a chief executive (who is to be the accounting officer); and

(b)   a board (which must include the chairman and chief executive) whose members are the scheme manager's directors.

212(4) **[Membership of board]** The chairman, chief executive and other members of the board must be persons appointed, and liable to removal from office, by the regulators (acting, in the case of the chairman and the chief executive, with the approval of the Treasury).

212(5) **[Independence of board members]** But the terms of their appointment (and in particular those governing removal from office) must be such as to secure their independence from the regulators in the operation of the compensation scheme.

212(6) **[Manager not exercising functions for Crown]** The scheme manager is not to be regarded as exercising functions on behalf of the Crown.

212(7) **[Manager's staff, etc. not Crown servants]** The scheme manager's officers and staff are not to be regarded as Crown servants.

History
Section 212(2) amended by the Financial Services Act 2010 Sch.2 para.21 as from 12 October 2010. Section 212(1), (2) substituted by the Financial Services Act 2012 s.38 and Sch.10 para.2(2) as from 1 April 2013. Section 212(3)(aa) inserted and s.212(4) amended by the Financial Services (Banking Reform) Act 2013 s.16 as from 1 April 2014.

The scheme

213 The compensation scheme

213(1) **[Establishment of scheme]** The regulators must by rules made in accordance with an order under subsection (1A) establish a scheme for compensating persons in cases where–

    (a) relevant persons are unable, or likely to be unable, to satisfy claims against them,

    (aa) relevant exchanges are unable, or likely to be unable, to satisfy claims made against them in connection with a regulated activity relating to a trading facility carried on by the exchange, or

    (b) persons who have assumed responsibility for liabilities arising from acts or omissions of relevant persons or relevant exchanges ("successors") are unable, or likely to be unable, to satisfy claims against the successors that are based on those acts or omissions.

213(1A) **[Treasury to specify cases for FCA and PRA rules]** The Treasury must by order specify–

    (a) the cases in which the FCA may, or may not, make rules under subsection (1), and

    (b) the cases in which the PRA may, or may not, make rules under that subsection.

213(2) **[The compensation scheme]** The rules (taken together) are to be known as the Financial Services Compensation Scheme (but are referred to in this Act as "the compensation scheme").

213(3) **[Provision for scheme manager to assess compensation, etc.]** The compensation scheme must, in particular, provide for the scheme manager–

    (a) to assess and pay compensation, in accordance with the scheme, to claimants in respect of claims made in connection with–

        (i) a regulated activity carried on (whether or not with permission) by relevant persons; and

        (ii) a regulated activity relating to a trading facility carried on (whether or not in accordance with any requirements relating to that activity resulting from section 286) by relevant exchanges; and

    (b) to have power to impose levies for the purpose of meeting its expenses (including in particular expenses incurred, or expected to be incurred, in paying compensation, borrowing or insuring risks)–

        (i) on authorised persons, or any class of authorised person;

    (ii)   on recognised investment exchanges carrying on a regulated activity relating to a trading facility, or any class of such exchanges; or

    (iii) on authorised persons and on recognised investment exchanges carrying on a regulated activity relating to a trading facility, or on any class of such persons and exchanges.

213(4)   **[Power of scheme manager to impose levies]** The compensation scheme may provide for the scheme manager to have power to impose levies–

    (a)   on authorised persons, or any class of authorised person;

    (b)   on recognised investment exchanges carrying on a regulated activity relating to a trading facility, or any class of such exchanges; or

    (c)   on authorised persons and on recognised investment exchanges carrying on a regulated activity relating to a trading facility, or on any class of such persons and exchanges,

for the purpose of recovering the cost (whenever incurred) of establishing the scheme.

213(5)   **[Duty of regulators re s.213(3)(b)]** In making any provision of the scheme by virtue of subsection (3)(b), the regulators must take account of the desirability of ensuring that the amount of the levies imposed on a particular–

    (a)   class of authorised person;

    (b)   class of recognised investment exchange carrying on a regulated activity relating to a trading facility; or

    (c)   class of authorised person and of recognised investment exchanges carrying on a regulated activity relating to a trading facility;

reflects, so far as is practicable, the amount of claims made, or likely to be made in respect of that class of person, exchange, or persons and exchanges.

213(6)   **[Recovery of levies as debts due]** An amount payable to the scheme manager as a result of any provision of the scheme made by virtue of subsection (3)(b) or (4) may be recovered as a debt due to the scheme manager.

213(7)   **[Application of ss.214–217]** Sections 214 to 217 make further provision about the scheme but are not to be taken as limiting the power conferred on the regulators by subsection (1).

213(8)   **["Specified"]** In those sections "specified" means specified in the scheme.

213(9)   **["Relevant person"]** In this Part (except in sections 219, 220 or 224) "relevant person" means a person who was–

    (a)   an authorised person at the time the act or omission giving rise to the claim against him, or against a successor falling within subsection (1)(b), took place; or

    (b)   an appointed representative at that time.

213(10)   **[Qualification for authorisation under Sch.3]** But a person who, at that time–

    (a)   qualified for authorisation under Schedule 3, and

    (b)   fell within a prescribed category in relation to any authorised activities,

is not to be regarded as a relevant person in relation to those activities, unless the person had elected to participate in the scheme in relation to those activities at that time.

213(11)   **["Authorised activities" in s.213(10)]** In subsection (10) "authorised activities", in relation to a person, means activities for which the person had, at the time mentioned in that subsection, permission as a result of any provision of, or made under, Schedule 3.

213(12) **["Relevant exchange" in Pt XV]** In this Part (except in sections 220 and 224) "relevant exchange" means a body corporate or unincorporated association which was a recognised investment exchange carrying on a regulated activity relating to a trading facility at the time the act or omission giving rise to the claim against it, or against a successor falling within subsection (1)(b), took place.

213(13) **["Regulated activity relating to a trading facility" in Pt XV]** In this Part "regulated activity relating to a trading facility" means–

    (a)   the regulated activity of operating a multilateral trading facility; or

    (b)   the regulated activity of operating an organised trading facility.

History
Section 213(10) substituted and s.213(11) inserted by the Undertakings for Collective Investment in Transferable Securities Regulations 2011 (SI 2011/1613) reg.2 from 1 July 2011. Section 213(1), (9) amended and s.212(1A) inserted by the Financial Services Act 2012 s.38 and Sch.10 para.3(3), (4), (6) as from 1 April 2013.
    Section 213(1), (3) amended, subss.(4) and (5) substituted and subss.(12) and (13) inserted by the Financial Services and Markets Act 2000 (Markets in Financial Instruments) Regulations 2017 (SI 2017/701) reg.50(1), Sch.2 para.23 as from 3 January 2018.

Note
See the Financial Services and Markets Act 2000 (Compensation Scheme: Electing Participants) Regulations 2001 (SI 2001/1783). See also the Deposit Guarantee Scheme Regulations 2015 (SI 2015/486). Note prospective amendment of ss.213(7), and 218(1), (2)(b) and insertion of new s.214A by the Banking Act 2009 s.170(2).

Provisions of the scheme

214   General

214(1) **[Provisions of the scheme]** The compensation scheme may, in particular, make provision–

    (a)   as to the circumstances in which a relevant person or relevant exchange is to be taken (for the purposes of the scheme) to be unable, or likely to be unable, to satisfy claims made against him or it;

   (aa)   as to the circumstances in which a successor falling within section 213(1)(b) is to be taken (for the purposes of the scheme) to be unable, or likely to be unable, to satisfy claims against the successor that are based on the acts or omissions of a relevant person or relevant exchange;

    (b)   for the establishment of different funds for meeting different kinds of claim;

    (c)   for the imposition of different levies in different cases;

    (d)   limiting the levy payable by a person in respect of a specified period;

    (e)   for repayment of the whole or part of a levy in specified circumstances;

    (f)   for a claim to be entertained only if it is made by a specified kind of claimant;

    (g)   for a claim to be entertained only if it falls within a specified kind of claim;

    (h)   as to the procedure to be followed in making a claim;

    (i)   for the making of interim payments before a claim is finally determined;

    (j)   limiting the amount payable on a claim to a specified maximum amount or a maximum amount calculated in a specified manner;

    (k)   for payment to be made, in specified circumstances, to a person other than the claimant.

Note
For the application of rules made under s.214(1) to credit unions, see the Financial Services and Markets Act 2000 (Consequential Amendments and Transitional Provisions) (Credit Unions) Order 2002 (SI 2002/1501).

214(1A)   **[Procedural rules in s.214(1)(h) allow for deemed claims]** Rules by virtue of subsection (1)(h) may, in particular, allow the scheme manager to treat persons who are or may be entitled to claim under the scheme as if they had done so.

214(1B)   **[Reference to enactment or instrument to include deemed claims]** A reference in any enactment or instrument to a claim or claimant under this Part includes a reference to a deemed claim or claimant in accordance with subsection (1A).

214(1C)   **[Power to settle claims subject to maximum in s.214(1)(j)]** Rules by virtue of subsection (1)(j) may, in particular, allow, or be subject to rules which allow, the scheme manager to settle a class of claim by payment of sums fixed without reference to, or by modification of, the normal rules for calculation of maximum entitlement for individual claims.

214(2)   **[Variability of provisions]** Different provision may be made with respect to different kinds of claim.

214(3)   **[Provision for manager to determine, etc. scheme matters]** The scheme may provide for the determination and regulation of matters relating to the scheme by the scheme manager.

214(4)   **[Scope of scheme]** The scheme, or particular provisions of the scheme, may be made so as to apply only in relation to–

    (a)   activities carried on,

    (b)   claimants,

    (c)   matters arising, or

    (d)   events occurring,

in specified territories, areas or localities.

214(5)   **[Persons qualified for authorisation under Sch.3]** The scheme may provide for a person who–

    (a)   qualifies for authorisation under Schedule 3, and

    (b)   falls within a prescribed category,

to elect to participate in the scheme in relation to some or all of the activities for which he has permission as a result of any provision of, or made under, that Schedule.

214(6)   **[Power of scheme manager where entitlement to payment under other scheme, etc.]** The scheme may provide for the scheme manager to have power–

    (a)   in specified circumstances,

    (b)   but only if the scheme manager is satisfied that the claimant is entitled to receive a payment in respect of his claim–

        (i)   under a scheme which is comparable to the compensation scheme, or

        (ii)   as the result of a guarantee given by a government or other authority,

to make a full payment of compensation to the claimant and recover the whole or part of the amount of that payment from the other scheme or under that guarantee.

History

In s.214 subss.(1A), (1B) and (1C) were inserted by Banking Act 2009 (C. 1) s.174, as from 21 February 2009. Section 214(1)(aa) inserted by the Financial Services Act 2012 s.38 and Sch.10 para.4 as from 1 April 2013.

    Section 214(1)(a), (aa) amended by the Financial Services and Markets Act 2000 (Markets in Financial Instruments) Regulations 2017 (SI 2017/701) reg.50(1), Sch.2 para.24 as from 3 January 2018.

Note
See the Financial Services and Markets Act 2000 (Compensation Scheme: Electing Participants) Regulations 2001 (SI 2001/1783).
Note prospective insertion of new s.214A by the Banking Act 2009 s.170(2).

214B　Contribution to costs of special resolution regime

214B(1)　[Application] This section applies if–

(a) a stabilisation power under Part 1 of the Banking Act 2009 has been exercised in respect of a bank, building society, credit union or investment firm within the meaning of that Part ("the institution"); and

(b) the Treasury think that the institution was or was likely to have been, or but for the exercise of the power would have become, unable to satisfy claims against it.

214B(2)　[Scheme manager to make payments for expenses] The Treasury may require the scheme manager to make payments (to the Treasury or any other person) in respect of expenses of a prescribed description incurred (by the Treasury or that person) in connection with the exercise of the power.

214B(3)　[Limit on s.216B(2) payments] Subsection (2) is subject to section 214C (limit on amount of special resolution regime payments).

214B(4)　["Expenses" in s.214B(2) includes interest] In subsection (2) "expenses" includes interest at a specified rate on the difference, at any time, between–

(a) the total amount of expenses (including interest) incurred at or before that time; and

(b) the total amount recovered, or received from the scheme manager, in respect of the institution, at or before that time, by–

(i) the Treasury; and

(ii) any other person who has incurred expenses in connection with the exercise of the power that are of a description prescribed under subsection (2).

214B(5)　[Treatment of s.214B payments] Any payment made by the scheme manager under subsection (2) is to be treated for the purposes of this Part as an expense under the compensation scheme.

214B(6)　["Specified rate" in ss.214B, 214C] In this section and section 214C "specified rate" means a rate specified by the Treasury.

214B(7)　[Different rates] Different rates may be specified under different provisions or for different periods.

214B(8)　[Setting of rate] A rate may be specified by reference to a rate set (from time to time) by any person.

214C　Limit on amount of special resolution regime payments

214C(1)　[Maximum amount] The total amount of special resolution regime payments required to be made in respect of a person ("the institution") may not exceed–

(a) notional net expenditure (see subsection (3)), minus

(b) actual net expenditure (see subsection (4)).

214C(2)　["Special resolution regime payment"] A "special resolution regime payment" is–

(a) a payment under section 214B(2); or

(b) a payment required to be made by the scheme manager by virtue of section 61 of the Banking Act 2009 (special resolution regime: compensation).

214C(3) **[Notional net expenditure]** Notional net expenditure is–

(a) the total amount of expenses that would have been incurred under the compensation scheme in respect of the institution if the stabilisation power had not been exercised and the institution had been unable to satisfy claims against it, minus

(b) the total amount that would have been likely, at the time when the power was exercised, to be recovered by the scheme manager in respect of the institution in those circumstances.

214C(4) **[Actual net expenditure]** Actual net expenditure is–

(a) the total amount of expenses (other than special resolution regime payments) actually incurred by the scheme manager in respect of the institution, minus

(b) the total amount actually recovered by the scheme manager in respect of the institution.

214C(5) **["Expenses" in s.214C(3)(a) includes interest]** In subsection (3)(a) "expenses" includes interest at a specified rate on the difference, at any time, between–

(a) the total amount of expenses (including interest) that would have been incurred as mentioned in subsection (3)(a) at or before that time; and

(b) the total amount that would have been likely to have been recovered as mentioned in subsection (3)(b) at or before that time.

214C(6) **["Expenses" in s.214C(4)(a) includes interest]** In subsection (4)(a) "expenses" includes interest at a specified rate on the difference, at any time, between–

(a) the total amount of expenses (including special resolution regime payments and interest) actually incurred by the scheme manager in respect of the institution at or before that time; and

(b) the total amount actually recovered by the scheme manager in respect of the institution at or before that time.

214C(7) **[Amounts recovered in s.214C(3)(b), (4)(b), (5b), (6)(b)]** In paragraph (b) of subsections (3) to (6) references to amounts recovered (or likely to have been recovered) by the scheme manager do not include any levy received (or likely to have been received) by it.

214D Contributions under section 214B: supplementary

214D(1) **[Scope]** This section supplements sections 214B and 214C.

214D(2) **[Scheme manager duty re s.214C(3)(a) expenses]** The scheme manager must determine–

(a) the amounts of expenses (other than interest) that would have been incurred as mentioned in section 214C(3)(a); and

(b) the time or times at which those amounts would have been likely to have been incurred.

214D(3) **[Appointment of valuer duty re s.214C(3)(b) amounts recoverable]** The Treasury, or a person designated by the Treasury, must in accordance with regulations appoint a person ("the valuer") to determine–

(a) the amounts that would have been likely, at the time when the stabilisation power was exercised, to be recovered as mentioned in section 214C(3)(b); and

(b) the time or times at which those amounts would have been likely to be recovered.

The person appointed under this subsection may be the person appointed as valuer under section 54 of the Banking Act 2009 in respect of the exercise of the stabilisation power.

214D(4) **[Regulations for principles re s.214D(2), (3)]** Regulations may enable the Treasury to specify principles to be applied by–

(a) the scheme manager when exercising functions under subsection (2); or

(b) the valuer when exercising functions under subsection (3).

214D(5)   [Particular matters in regulations] The regulations may in particular enable the Treasury to require the scheme manager or valuer–

(a) to use, or not to use, specified methods;

(b) to take specified matters into account in a specified manner; or

(c) not to take specified matters into account.

214D(6)   [Verification in regulations] Regulations–

(a) must provide for independent verification of expenses within section 214B(2);

(b) may provide for the independent verification of other matters; and

(c) may contain provision about the appointment and payment of an auditor.

214D(7)   [Regulations re valuer decision and payment] Regulations–

(a) must contain provision enabling the valuer to reconsider a decision;

(b) must provide a right of appeal to a court or tribunal against any decision of the valuer;

(c) may provide for payment of the valuer; and

(d) may apply (with or without modifications) or make provision corresponding to–

(i)   any provision of sections 54 to 56 of the Banking Act 2009; or

(ii) any provision made, or that could be made, by virtue of any of those sections.

214D(8)   [Provision for early payments under s.214B(2)] Regulations may make provision for payments under section 214B(2) to be made–

(a) before any verification required by the regulations is undertaken, and

(b) before the limit imposed by section 214C is calculated,

subject to any necessary later adjustment.

214D(9)   [No expectation for repayment after verification etc.] If they do so they must provide that the amount of any payment required by virtue of subsection (8) must not be such as to give rise to an expectation that an amount will be required to be repaid to the scheme manager (once any necessary verification has been undertaken and the limit imposed by section 214C has been calculated).

214D(10)   [Further provisions in regulations] Regulations may–

(a) make provision supplementing section 214B or 214C or this section;

(b) make further provision about the method by which amounts to be paid under section 214B(2) are to be determined;

(c) make provision about timing;

(d) make provision about procedures to be followed;

(e) provide for discretionary functions to be exercised by a specified body or by persons of a specified class; and

(f) make provision about the resolution of disputes (which may include provision conferring jurisdiction on a court or tribunal).

214D(11)   ["Regulations"] "Regulations" means regulations made by the Treasury.

214D(12)   [Source of s.214D payments by Treasury] Any payment made by the Treasury by virtue of this section is to be met out of money provided by Parliament.

214D(13)   [Compensation scheme provisions for s.214B(2) payments and levies] The compensation scheme may make provision about payments under section 214B(2) and levies in connection with such payments (except provision inconsistent with any provision made by or under section 214B or 214C or this section).

History
Section 214B substituted and s.214C, 214D inserted by the Financial Services Act 2010 s.16(1) as from 8 April 2010. Previously s.214B was inserted by Banking Act 2009 (C. 1) Pt 4 s.171, as from 21 February 2009.

For the relevant regulations, see the Financial Services and Markets Act 2000 (Contribution to Costs of Special Resolution Regime) Regulations 2009 (SI 2009/807).

215   Rights of the scheme in insolvency

215(1)   [Provisions of the scheme] The compensation scheme may make provision–

(a)   about the effect of a payment of compensation under the scheme on rights or obligations arising out of matters in connection with which the compensation was paid;

(b)   giving the scheme manager a right of recovery in respect of those rights or obligations.

215(2)   [Right of recovery in event of insolvency] Such a right of recovery conferred by the scheme does not, in the event of a person's insolvency, exceed such right (if any) as the claimant would have had in that event.

215(2A)   [Stabilisation payments under s.214B(2)] Any payment made by the scheme manager under section 214B(2) in connection with the exercise of a stabilisation power in respect of a bank, building society or credit union is to be treated as a debt due to the scheme manager from that bank, building society or (as the case may be) credit union.

215(2B)   ["Bank", "building society", "credit union" in s.215(2A)] In subsection (2)–

"bank" has the meaning given in section 2 of the Banking Act 2009;
"building society" has the meaning given in the Building Societies Act 1986;
"credit union" means a credit union within the meaning of–

    (a)   the Credit Unions Act 1979; or

    (b)   article 2 of the Credit Unions (Northern Ireland) Order 1985.

215(3)   [Manager's rights equivalent to regulators' under s.362] If a person other than the scheme manager makes an administration application under Schedule B1 to the 1986 Act or Schedule B1 to the 1989 Order in relation to a company–

(a)   a company or partnership which is a relevant person; or

(b)   a body corporate or unincorporated association which is a relevant exchange;

the scheme manager has the same rights as are conferred on the regulators by section 362.

215(3A)   [Making an administration application in s.215(3)] In subsection (3) the reference to making an administration application includes a reference to–

(a)   appointing an administrator under paragraph 14 or 22 of Schedule B1 to the 1986 Act or paragraph 15 or 23 of Schedule B1 to the 1989 Order, or

(b)   filing with the court a copy of notice of intention to appoint an administrator under any of those paragraphs.

215(4) **[Manager's rights equivalent to regulators' under s.371]** If a person other than the scheme manager presents a petition for the winding up of a body which is a relevant person or relevant exchange, the scheme manager has the same rights as are conferred on the regulators by section 371.

215(5) **[Manager's rights equivalent to regulators' under s.374]** If a person other than the scheme manager presents a bankruptcy petition to the court in relation to an individual who, or an entity which, is a relevant person, the scheme manager has the same rights as are conferred on the regulators by section 374.

215(6) **[Power to make insolvency rules]** Insolvency rules may be made for the purpose of integrating any procedure for which provision is made as a result of subsection (1) into the general procedure on the administration of a company or partnership or on a winding-up, bankruptcy or sequestration.

Note
Section 215(3), (4) and (6) apply to limited liability partnerships by virtue of the Limited Liability Partnerships Regulations 2001 (SI 2001/1090) regs 1, 6(1) as from 6 April 2001 subject to reg.6(2).

215(7) **["Bankruptcy petition"]** "Bankruptcy petition" means a petition to the court–

   (a)   under section 264 of the 1986 Act or Article 238 of the 1989 Order for a bankruptcy order to be made against an individual;

   (b)   under section 2 or 5 of the 2016 Act for the sequestration of the estate of an individual; or

   (c)   under section 6 of the 2016 Act for the sequestration of the estate belonging to or held for or jointly by the members of an entity mentioned in subsection (1) of that section.

215(8) **["Insolvency rules"]** "Insolvency rules" are–

   (a)   for England and Wales, rules made under sections 411 and 412 of the 1986 Act;

   (b)   for Scotland, rules made by order by the Treasury, after consultation with the Scottish Ministers, for the purposes of this section; and

   (c)   for Northern Ireland, rules made under Article 359 of the 1989 Order and section 55 of the Judicature (Northern Ireland) Act 1978.

215(9) **[Interpretation]** "The 1986 Act", "the 1989 Order", "the 2016 Act" and "court" have the same meaning as in Part XXIV.

History
Section 215(1) amended by the Banking Act 2009 s.175 as from 21 February 2009.
   Section 215(3), (4) amended by the Financial Services and Markets Act 2000 (Markets in Financial Instruments) Regulations 2017 (SI 2017/701) reg.50(1), Sch.2 para.25 as from 3 January 2018.

216 Continuity of long-term insurance policies

216(1) **[Duty of scheme manager]** The compensation scheme may, in particular, include provision requiring the scheme manager to make arrangements for securing continuity of insurance for policyholders, or policyholders of a specified class, of relevant long-term insurers.

216(2) **["Relevant long-term insurers"]** "Relevant long-term insurers" means relevant persons who–

   (a)   have permission to effect or carry out contracts of long-term insurance; and

   (b)   are unable, or likely to be unable, to satisfy claims made against them.

216(3) **[Transfer of policies to another authorised person, etc.]** The scheme may provide for the scheme manager to take such measures as appear to him to be appropriate–

   (a)   for securing or facilitating the transfer of a relevant long-term insurer's business so far as it consists of the carrying out of contracts of long-term insurance, or of any part of that business, to another authorised person;

(b)　for securing the issue by another authorised person to the policyholders concerned of policies in substitution for their existing policies.

216(4)　[Payments to policyholders] The scheme may also provide for the scheme manager to make payments to the policyholders concerned–

(a)　during any period while he is seeking to make arrangements mentioned in subsection (1);

(b)　if it appears to him that it is not reasonably practicable to make such arrangements.

216(5)　[Section 213(3)(b)–further powers] A provision of the scheme made by virtue of section 213(3)(b) may include power to impose levies for the purpose of meeting expenses of the scheme manager incurred in–

(a)　taking measures as a result of any provision of the scheme made by virtue of subsection (3);

(b)　making payments as a result of any such provision made by virtue of subsection (4).

217　Insurers in financial difficulties

217(1)　[Measures to safeguard policyholders] The compensation scheme may, in particular, include provision for the scheme manager to have power to take measures for safeguarding policyholders, or policyholders of a specified class, of relevant insurers.

217(2)　["Relevant insurers"] "Relevant insurers" means relevant persons who–

(a)　have permission to effect or carry out contracts of insurance; and

(b)　are in financial difficulties.

217(3)　[Measures to transfer insurance business, etc.] The measures may include such measures as the scheme manager considers appropriate for–

(a)　securing or facilitating the transfer of a relevant insurer's business so far as it consists of the carrying out of contracts of insurance, or of any part of that business, to another authorised person;

(b)　giving assistance to the relevant insurer to enable it to continue to effect or carry out contracts of insurance.

217(4)　[Further provisions re s.217(3) measures, etc.] The scheme may provide–

(a)　that if measures of a kind mentioned in subsection (3)(a) are to be taken, they should be on terms appearing to the scheme manager to be appropriate, including terms reducing, or deferring payment of, any of the things to which any of those who are eligible policyholders in relation to the relevant insurer are entitled in their capacity as such;

(b)　that if measures of a kind mentioned in subsection (3)(b) are to be taken, they should be conditional on the reduction of, or the deferment of the payment of, the things to which any of those who are eligible policyholders in relation to the relevant insurer are entitled in their capacity as such;

(c)　for ensuring that measures of a kind mentioned in subsection (3)(b) do not benefit to any material extent persons who were members of a relevant insurer when it began to be in financial difficulties or who had any responsibility for, or who may have profited from, the circumstances giving rise to its financial difficulties, except in specified circumstances;

(d)　for requiring the scheme manager to be satisfied that any measures he proposes to take are likely to cost less than it would cost to pay compensation under the scheme if the relevant insurer became unable, or likely to be unable, to satisfy claims made against him.

217(5)   [Provision for power of regulators] The scheme may provide for [the] either regulator or both regulators to have power–

(a)   to give such assistance to the scheme manager as it considers appropriate for assisting the scheme manager to determine what measures are practicable or desirable in the case of a particular relevant insurer;

(b)   to impose constraints on the taking of measures by the scheme manager in the case of a particular relevant insurer;

(c)   to require the scheme manager to provide it with information about any particular measures which the scheme manager is proposing to take.

217(6)   [Provision to make interim payments, etc.] The scheme may include provision for the scheme manager to have power–

(a)   to make interim payments in respect of eligible policyholders of a relevant insurer;

(b)   to indemnify any person making payments to eligible policyholders of a relevant insurer.

217(7)   [Imposition of levies to meet expenses] A provision of the scheme made by virtue of section 213(3)(b) may include power to impose levies for the purpose of meeting expenses of the scheme manager incurred in–

(a)   taking measures as a result of any provision of the scheme made by virtue of subsection (1);

(b)   making payments or giving indemnities as a result of any such provision made by virtue of subsection (6).

217(8)   [Interpretation] "Financial difficulties" and "eligible policyholders" have such meanings as may be specified.

Note
Note prospective amendment of s.217(3) by the Banking Act 2009 s.170(2).

Relationship with the regulators

217A   Co-operation

217A(1)   [Duty of co-operation in functions under Pt 15 and 15A] Each regulator and the scheme manager must take such steps as they consider appropriate to co-operate with each other in the exercise of their functions under this Part and Part 15A.

217A(2)   [Duty to maintain memorandum for co-operation] Each regulator and the scheme manager must prepare and maintain a memorandum describing how that regulator and the scheme manager intend to comply with subsection (1).

217A(3)   [Duty of scheme manager to publish memoranda] The scheme manager must ensure that the memoranda as currently in force are published in the way appearing to it to be best calculated to bring them to the attention of the public.

History
Section 217A inserted by the Financial Services Act 2012 s.38 and Sch.10 para.7 as from 1 April 2013.

Annual plan and report

217B   Annual plan

217B(1)   [Duty of scheme manager] The scheme manager must in respect of each of its financial years prepare an annual plan.

217B(2)   [When plan to be prepared] The plan must be prepared before the start of the financial year.

217B(3)   [Annual plan re use of resources] An annual plan in respect of a financial year must make provision about the use of the resources of the scheme manager.

217B(4)   [Plan for longer than financial year] The plan may include material relating to periods longer than the financial year in question.

217B(5)   [Duty of scheme manager to consult re plan] Before preparing an annual plan, the scheme manager must consult such persons (if any) as the scheme manager considers appropriate.

217B(6)   [Duty of scheme manager to publish plan] The scheme manager must publish each annual plan in the way it considers appropriate.

History
Section 217B inserted by the Financial Services Act 2012 s.38 and Sch.10 para.9 as from 1 April 2013.

218   Annual report

218(1)   [Duty of scheme manager] At least once a year, the scheme manager must make a report to the regulators on the discharge of its functions.

218(2)   [Content, etc. of report] The report must–

(a)   include a statement setting out the value of each of the funds established by the compensation scheme; and

(b)   comply with any requirements specified in rules made by the regulators.

218(3)   [Publication] The scheme manager must publish each report in the way it considers appropriate.

218(4)   [Requirement to comply with accounts audit] The Treasury may–

(a)   require the scheme manager to comply with any provisions of the Companies Act 2006 about accounts and their audit which would not otherwise apply to it, or

(b)   direct that any such provision of that Act is to apply to the scheme manager with such modifications as are specified in the direction.

218(5)   [Enforcement of s.218(4) requirement] Compliance with any requirement under subsection (4)(a) or (b) is enforceable by injunction or, in Scotland, an order for specific performance under section 45 of the Court of Session Act 1988.

218(6)   [Section 218(5) proceedings by Treasury] Proceedings under subsection (5) may be brought only by the Treasury.

History
Section 218(4), (5) and (6) inserted by the Financial Services Act 2012 s.38 and Sch.10 para.10 as from 1 April 2013.

Note
Note prospective amendment of s.218(1), (2)(b) by the Banking Act 2009 s.170(2).

218ZA   Audit of accounts

218ZA(1)   [Accounts to Comptroller and Auditor General and Treasury] The scheme manager must send a copy of its annual accounts to the Comptroller and Auditor General and the Treasury as soon as is reasonably practicable.

218ZA(2)   [Duty of Comptroller and Auditor General] The Comptroller and Auditor General must–

(a)   examine, certify and report on accounts received under this section, and

(b)   send a copy of the certified accounts and the report to the Treasury.

218ZA(3) **[Treasury to lay accounts and report before Parliament]** The Treasury must lay the copy of the certified accounts and the report before Parliament.

218ZA(4) **[Copy to regulators]** The scheme manager must send a copy of the certified accounts and the report to the regulators.

218ZA(5) **[Exemption from Companies Act audit]** Except as provided by section 218(4), the scheme manager is exempt from the requirements of Part 16 of the Companies Act 2006 (audit), and its balance sheet must contain a statement to that effect.

218ZA(6) **["Annual accounts"]** In this section "annual accounts" has the meaning given by section 471 of the Companies Act 2006.

History
Section 218ZA inserted by the Financial Services Act 2012 s.38 and Sch.10 para.11 as from 1 April 2013.

Information and documents

218A　Regulators' power to require information

218A(1) **[Rule-making power]** Each regulator may make rules enabling that regulator to require authorised persons or recognised investment exchanges carrying on a regulated activity relating to a trading facility to–

(a) provide information to the scheme manager on the request of that regulator or the scheme manager; or

(b) provide information to that regulator, which may then be made available to the scheme manager by that regulator.

218A(2) **[Required information to be of use to scheme manager]** A requirement may be imposed only if the regulator thinks the information is of a kind that may be of use to the scheme manager in connection with functions in respect of the scheme.

218A(3) **[Application of requirement]** A requirement under this section may apply–

(a) to authorised persons generally or only to specified persons or classes of person;

(aa) to recognised investment exchanges mentioned in subsection (1) generally or only to specified exchanges or classes of exchange;

(b) to the provision of information at specified periods, in connection with specified events or in other ways.

218A(4) **[Section 165 notice]** In addition to requirements under this section, a notice under section 165 may relate to information or documents which the regulator thinks are reasonably required by the scheme manager in connection with the performance of functions in respect of the scheme; and section 165(4) is subject to this subsection.

218A(5) **[Rules in s.218A(1)]** Rules under subsection (1) shall be prepared, made and treated in the same way as (and may be combined with) the regulator's general rules.

History
Section 218A inserted by Banking Act 2009 s.176(1), as from 21 February 2009.

Section 218A(1) amended by the Deposit Guarantee Scheme Regulations 2015 (SI 2015/486) reg.13(1), (4) as from 26 March 2015.

Section 218A(1), (3) amended by the Financial Services and Markets Act 2000 (Markets in Financial Instruments) Regulations 2017 (SI 2017/701) reg.50(1), Sch.2 para.26 as from 3 January 2018.

218B Treasury's power to require information from scheme manager

218B(1) [Notice in writing] The Treasury may by notice in writing require the scheme manager to provide specified information or information of a specified description that the Treasury reasonably require in connection with the duties of the Treasury under the Government Resources and Accounts Act 2000.

218B(2) [Period in which to be provided] Information required under this section must be provided before the end of such reasonable period as may be specified.

218B(3) ["Specified"] "Specified" means specified in the notice.

History
Section 218B inserted by the Financial Services (Banking Reform) Act 2013 s.15 as from 1 March 2014.

219 Scheme manager's power to require information

219(1) [Power of scheme manager] The scheme manager may, by notice in writing require a person–

(a) to provide specified information or information of a specified description; or

(b) to produce specified documents or documents of a specified description.

219(1A) [Persons who may be required to provide information etc.] A requirement may be imposed only–

(a) on a person (P) against whom a claim has been made under the scheme,

(b) on a person (P) who is unable or likely to be unable to satisfy claims under the scheme against P,

(c) on a person ("the Third Party") whom the scheme manager thinks was knowingly involved in matters giving rise to a claim against another person (P) under the scheme, or

(d) on a person ("the Third Party") whom the scheme manager thinks was knowingly involved in matters giving rise to the actual or likely inability of another person (P) to satisfy claims under the scheme.

219(1B) [Determination of P satisfying claims in s.219(1A)(b), (d)] For the purposes of subsection (1A)(b) and (d) whether P is unable or likely to be unable to satisfy claims shall be determined in accordance with provision to be made by the scheme (which may, in particular–

(a) apply or replicate, with or without modifications, a provision of an enactment;

(b) confer discretion on a specified person).

219(2) [Form, etc. of information] The information or documents must be provided or produced–

(a) before the end of such reasonable period as may be specified; and

(b) in the case of information, in such manner or form as may be specified.

219(3) [Application of section] This section applies only to information and documents the provision or production of which the scheme manager considers to be necessary (or likely to be necessary) for the fair determination of claims which have been or may be made against P.

219(3A) [Power to require information for determining s.214D(2) matters] Where a stabilisation power under Part 1 of the Banking Act 2009 has been exercised in respect of a bank, building society or credit union, the scheme manager may by notice in writing require the bank, building society or credit union, or the Bank of England to provide information that the scheme manager requires for the purpose of determining the matters mentioned in section 214D(2)(a) and (b) above.

219(4) [Power to take copies, etc. of documents] If a document is produced in response to a requirement imposed under this section, the scheme manager may–

(a)   take copies or extracts from the document; or

(b)   require the person producing the document to provide an explanation of the document.

219(5)   **[Failure to produce documents]** If a person who is required under this section to produce a document fails to do so, the scheme manager may require the person to state, to the best of his knowledge and belief, where the document is.

219(6)   **[Limitation of section in case of insolvency]** If P is insolvent, no requirement may be imposed under this section on a person to whom section 220 or 224 applies.

219(7)   **[Lien claimed]** If a person claims a lien on a document, its production under this Part does not affect the lien.

219(8)   […]

219(9)   **["Specified"]** "Specified" means specified in the notice given under subsection (1).

219(10)   […]

History
Subsections (1), (3) and (6) amended, subs.(3A) inserted and subs.(8) and (10) omitted by the Banking Act 2009 s.176, as from 21 February 2009. Subsection (3A) amended by the Financial Services Act 2010 s.21(8)(a), (b) and Sch.2 para.22 as from 8 April 2010.

220   Scheme manager's power to inspect information held by liquidator etc.

220(1)   **[Inspection of relevant documents]** For the purpose of assisting the scheme manager to discharge its functions in relation to a claim made in respect of an insolvent relevant person or insolvent relevant exchange, a person to whom this section applies must permit a person authorised by the scheme manager to inspect relevant documents.

220(2)   **[Extracts, etc. from documents]** A person inspecting a document under this section may take copies of, or extracts from, the document.

220(3)   **[Application to section]** This section applies to–

(a)   the administrative receiver, administrator, liquidator, bank liquidator, building society liquidator or trustee in bankruptcy of an insolvent relevant person or insolvent relevant exchange;

(b)   the trustee in the sequestration, under the Bankruptcy (Scotland) Act 2016, of the estate of an insolvent relevant person or insolvent relevant exchange.

220(4)   **[Scope of section]** This section does not apply to a liquidator, administrator or trustee in bankruptcy who is–

(a)   the Official Receiver;

(b)   the Official Receiver for Northern Ireland; or

(c)   the Accountant in Bankruptcy.

220(5)   **["Relevant person"]** "Relevant person" and "relevant exchange" have the same meaning as in section 224.

History
Section 220(3) amended by the Banking Act 2009 s.123(3) as from 21 February 2009 and by the Building Societies (Insolvency and Special Administration) Order 2009 (SI 2009/805) art.15 as from 29 March 2009.
    Section 220(1), (3) and (5) amended by the Financial Services and Markets Act 2000 (Markets in Financial Instruments) Regulations 2017 (SI 2017/701) reg.50(1), Sch.2 para.27 as from 3 January 2018.

221   Powers of court where information required

221(1)   [Power of court] If a person ("the defaulter")–

(a)   fails to comply with a requirement imposed under section 219, or

(b)   fails to permit documents to be inspected under section 220,

the scheme manager may certify that fact in writing to the court and the court may enquire into the case.

221(2)   [Penalty] If the court is satisfied that the defaulter failed without reasonable excuse to comply with the requirement (or to permit the documents to be inspected), it may deal with the defaulter (and, in the case of a body corporate, any director or other officer) as if he were in contempt; and "officer", in relation to a limited liability partnership, means a member of the limited liability partnership.

221(3)   ["Court"] "Court" means–

(a)   the High Court;

(b)   in Scotland, the Court of Session.

Miscellaneous

221A   Delegation of functions

221A(1)   [Delegation to scheme agent] The scheme manager may arrange for any of its functions to be discharged on its behalf by another person (a "scheme agent").

221A(2)   [Conditions re scheme agent] Before entering into arrangements the scheme manager must be satisfied that the scheme agent–

(a)   is competent to discharge the function, and

(b)   has been given sufficient directions to enable the agent to take any decisions required in the course of exercising the function in accordance with policy determined by the scheme manager.

221A(3)   [Payments to scheme agent] Arrangements may include provision for payments to be made by the scheme manager to the scheme agent (which payments are management expenses of the scheme manager except where the function in question is one under Part 15A).

History
Section 221A inserted by the Banking Act 2009 s.179(1), as from 21 February 2009. Section 221A(3) amended by the Financial Services Act 2010 Sch.2 para.23 as from 12 October 2010.

222   Statutory immunity

222(1)   [Immunity of scheme manager, etc.] Neither the scheme manager nor any person who is, or is acting as, its officer, scheme agent or member of staff is to be liable in damages for anything done or omitted in the discharge, or purported discharge, of the scheme manager's functions.

222(2)   [Non-application of s.222(1)] Subsection (1) does not apply–

(a)   if the act or omission is shown to have been in bad faith; or

(b)   so as to prevent an award of damages made in respect of an act or omission on the ground that the act or omission was unlawful as a result of section 6(1) of the Human Rights Act 1998.

History
Section 222(1) amended by the Banking Act 2009 s.179(2) as from 21 February 2009.

223   Management expenses

223(1)   [Limit on expenses] The amount which the scheme manager may recover, from the sums levied under the scheme, as management expenses attributable to a particular period may not exceed such amount as may be fixed by the scheme as the limit applicable to that period.

223(2)   [Calculation of levy] In calculating the amount of any levy to be imposed by the scheme manager, no amount may be included to reflect management expenses unless the limit mentioned in subsection (1) has been fixed by the scheme.

223(3)   ["Management expenses"] "Management expenses" means expenses incurred, or expected to be incurred, by the scheme manager in connection with its functions under this Act other than those incurred–

    (a)   in paying compensation;

    (b)   as a result of any provision of the scheme made by virtue of section 216(3) or (4) or 217(1) or (6);

    (c)   under section 214B or 214D;

    (d)   under Part 15A.

History

Section 222(3)(c) inserted by the Banking Act 2009 s.171(2) as from 21 February 2009. Section 223(3)(c) amended and s.223(3)(d) inserted by the Financial Services Act 2010 Sch.2 para.24(2), (3) as from 12 October 2010.
   Note prospective insertion of s.223A by the Banking Act 2009 s.172.

223B   Borrowing from National Loans Fund

223B(1)   [Scheme manager's power to borrow] The scheme manager may request a loan from the National Loans Fund for the purpose of funding expenses incurred or expected to be incurred under the scheme.

223B(2)   [Power of Treasury to arrange loan] The Treasury may arrange for money to be paid out of the National Loans Fund in pursuance of a request under subsection (1).

223B(3)   [Rate of interest and other terms] The Treasury shall determine–

    (a)   the rate of interest on a loan, and

    (b)   other terms and conditions.

223B(4)   [Power of Treasury to make regulations] The Treasury may make regulations–

    (a)   about the amounts that may be borrowed under this section;

    (b)   permitting the scheme manager to impose levies under section 213 for the purpose of meeting expenses in connection with loans under this section (and the regulations may have effect despite any provision of this Act);

    (c)   about the classes of person on whom those levies may be imposed;

    (d)   about the amounts and timing of those levies.

223B(5)   [Compensation scheme] The compensation scheme may include provision about borrowing under this section provided that it is not inconsistent with regulations under this section.

History

Section 223B inserted by Banking Act 2009 s.173, as from 21 February 2009.

223C   Payments in error

223C(1)   [Provision by levy in ss.213, 214A, 214B, 223B] Payments made by the scheme manager in error may be provided for in setting a levy by virtue of section 213, 214A, 214B or 223B.

223C(2)   [Non-application to payments in bad faith] This section does not apply to payments made in bad faith.

History
Section 223C inserted by Banking Act 2009 s.177, as from 21 February 2009.

224   Scheme manager's power to inspect documents held by Official Receiver etc.

224(1)   [Duty of Official Receiver, etc. re inspection of documents] If, as a result of the insolvency or bankruptcy of a relevant person or relevant exchange, or a successor falling within section 213(1)(b), any documents have come into the possession of a person to whom this section applies, he must permit any person authorised by the scheme manager to inspect the documents for the purpose of establishing–

(a)   the identity of persons to whom the scheme manager may be liable to make a payment in accordance with the compensation scheme; or

(b)   the amount of any payment which the scheme manager may be liable to make.

224(2)   [Extracts, etc. from documents] A person inspecting a document under this section may take copies or extracts from the document.

224(3)   ["Relevant person"] In this section "relevant person" means a person who was–

(a)   an authorised person at the time the act or omission which may give rise to the liability mentioned in subsection (1)(a) took place; or

(b)   an appointed representative at that time.

224(4)   [Persons qualified for authorisation under Sch.3] But a person who, at that time–

(a)   qualified for authorisation under Schedule 3, and

(b)   fell within a prescribed category,

is not to be regarded as a relevant person for the purposes of this section in relation to any activities for which he had permission as a result of any provision of, or made under, that Schedule unless he had elected to participate in the scheme in relation to those activities at that time.

Note
See the Financial Services and Markets Act 2000 (Compensation Scheme: Electing Participants) Regulations 2001 (SI 2001/1783).

224(4A)   ["Relevant exchange"] In this section "relevant exchange" means a body corporate or unincorporated association carrying on a regulated activity relating to a trading facility at the time the act or omission which may give rise to the liability mentioned in subsection (1)(a) took place.

224(5)   [Application of section] This section applies to–

(a)   the Official Receiver;

(b)   the Official Receiver for Northern Ireland; and

(c)   the Accountant in Bankruptcy.

History
Section 224(1) amended and subs.(4A) inserted by the Financial Services and Markets Act 2000 (Markets in Financial Instruments) Regulations 2017 (SI 2017/701) reg.50(1), Sch.2 para.28 as from 3 January 2018.

224ZA   Discharge of functions

224ZA(1)   [Duty of scheme manager] In discharging its functions the scheme manager must have regard to–

(a)   the need to ensure efficiency and effectiveness in the discharge of those functions, and

(b)   the need to minimise public expenditure attributable to loans made or other financial assistance given to the scheme manager for the purposes of the scheme.

224ZA(2)   ["Financial assistance"] In subsection (1)(b) "financial assistance" includes the giving of guarantees and indemnities and any other kind of financial assistance (actual or contingent).

History
Section 224ZA inserted by the Financial Services (Banking Reform) Act 2013 s.14 as from 1 March 2014.

224A   Functions under the Banking Act 2009

224A(1)   [Reference in Pt 15 to functions of scheme manager] A reference in this Part to functions of the scheme manager (including a reference to functions conferred by or under this Part) includes a reference to functions conferred by or under the Banking Act 2009.

224A(2)   [Special resolution regime compensation payments treated as expense] Any payment required to be made by the scheme manager by virtue of section 61 of that Act (special resolution regime: compensation) is to be treated for the purposes of this Part as an expense under the compensation scheme.

History
Section 224A inserted by Banking Act 2009 s.180, as from 21 February 2009 and s.224A(2) inserted by the Financial Services Act 2010 Sch.2 para.25 as from 12 October 2010.

Part XVA

Power to Require FSCS Manager to act in relation to Other Schemes

Introduction

224B   Meaning of "relevant scheme" etc

224B(1)   [Application for Pt XVA] The following provisions apply for the purposes of this Part.

224B(2)   ["Relevant scheme"] "Relevant scheme" means a scheme or arrangement (other than the FSCS) for the payment of compensation (in certain cases) to customers of persons who provide financial services or carry on a business connected with the provision of such services.

224B(3)   [References to manager] References to the manager of a relevant scheme are to the person who administers it or (if there is no such person) the person responsible for making payments under it.

224B(4)   ["The FSCS"] "The FSCS" means the Financial Services Compensation Scheme (see section 213(2)).

224B(5)   ["The FSCS manager"] "The FSCS manager" means the scheme manager as defined by section 212(1).

224B(6)   ["Expense"] "Expense" includes anything that, if incurred in relation to the FSCS, would amount to an expense for the purposes of the FSCS.

224B(7)   ["Notice"] "Notice" means a notice in writing.

224B(8)   ["Customers", "persons", provision of financial services in s.224B(2)] In subsection (2)–

(a)   "customers" includes customers outside the United Kingdom;

   (b)   "persons" includes persons outside the United Kingdom;

   (c)   references to the provision of financial services include the provision outside the United Kingdom of such services.

224B(9)   **[Application where manager is Treasury or Minister]** This Part applies to cases where the manager of the relevant scheme is the Treasury or any other Minister of the Crown as it applies to cases where that manager is any other person.

History
See note after s.224F

Power to require FSCS manager to act

224C   **Power to require FSCS manager to act on behalf of manager of relevant scheme**

224C(1)   **[Application of section]** This section applies if compensation is payable under a relevant scheme.

224C(2)   **[FSCS manager required to exercise specified functions]** The Treasury may by notice require the FSCS manager to exercise (on behalf of the manager of the relevant scheme) specified functions in respect of specified claims for compensation under the relevant scheme.

224C(3)   **[Notice requires scheme manager consent]** A notice may be given only with the consent of the manager of the relevant scheme.

224C(4)   **["Specified" in s.224C(2)]** In subsection (2) "specified" means specified, or of a description specified, in the notice.

224C(5)   **[Claims]** Claims or descriptions of claims may be specified by reference to the persons or description of persons whose claims they are.

History
See note after s.224F.

224D   **Cases where FSCS manager may decline to act**

224D(1)   **[Application of section]** This section applies where a notice under section 224C(2) (a "section 224C notice") has been given in respect of a relevant scheme.

224D(2)   **[Where no duty to comply with s.224C]** The FSCS manager is not under a duty to comply with the section 224C notice if, as soon as reasonably practicable after receiving it, the FSCS manager gives a notice to the Treasury stating that a ground set out in section 224E applies.

224D(3)   **[Recovery of expenses]** Where a notice under subsection (2) is given, the FSCS manager may recover from the manager of the relevant scheme an amount equal to the total expenses incurred by the FSCS manager in connection with the relevant scheme in the period–

   (a)   beginning with the giving of the section 224C notice; and

   (b)   ending with the giving of the notice under subsection (2).

224D(4)   **[Cessation of duty to comply with s.224C notice]** The duty to comply with the section 224C notice ceases if, after starting to comply with it, the FSCS manager gives a notice to the Treasury and the manager of the relevant scheme stating that a ground set out in section 224E applies.

224D(5)   **[FSCS manager to inform Treasury where s.224D(4) given]** Where a notice under subsection (4) is given, the FSCS manager must give the Treasury such information connected with the FSCS manager's exercise of functions in relation to the relevant scheme as the Treasury may reasonably require.

224D(6)   [Notice in s.224D] Any notice under this section–

(a)   may be given only if, before giving it, the FSCS manager has taken reasonable steps to deal with anything that is causing the ground or grounds in question to apply; and

(b)   must contain details of those steps.

History
See note after s.224F.

224E   Grounds for declining to act

224E(1)   [Grounds in s.224D(2), (4)] This section sets out the grounds referred to in section 224D(2) and (4).

224E(2)   [First ground: inability to obtain information] The first ground is that the FSCS manager is not satisfied that it will be able to obtain any information required in order to comply with the section 224C notice.

224E(3)   [Second ground: inability to obtain advice etc.] The second ground is that the FSCS manager is not satisfied that it will be able to obtain any advice or other assistance from the manager of the relevant scheme that is required in order to comply with the section 224C notice.

224E(4)   [Third ground: expenses not paid] The third ground is–

(a)   that the FSCS manager has not received an amount at least equal to the total expenses it expects to incur in connection with its relevant scheme functions; and

(b)   either–

(i)   that there are no arrangements for the provision of funds to the FSCS manager to enable it to exercise those functions and meet those expenses; or

(ii)   that the FSCS manager considers that any such arrangements are unsatisfactory.

224E(5)   [Fourth ground: s.224C notice compliance detrimental] The fourth ground is that the FSCS manager considers that complying with the section 224C notice would detrimentally affect the exercise of its functions under the FSCS.

224E(6)   [Fifth ground: no undertaking not to bring proceedings] The fifth ground is–

(a)   that there is no undertaking from the manager of the relevant scheme not to bring proceedings against the FSCS manager; or

(b)   that the FSCS manager considers that the terms of any such undertaking are unsatisfactory.

224E(7)   [Sixth ground: no reimbursement of expenses] The sixth ground is–

(a)   that there are no arrangements for the reimbursement of any expenses incurred by the FSCS manager in connection with any proceedings brought against it in respect of its relevant scheme functions (including expenses incurred in meeting any award of damages made against it); or

(b)   that the FSCS manager considers that any such arrangements are unsatisfactory.

224E(8)   [Undertaking in s.224E(6)] In subsection (6) references to an undertaking of the kind mentioned there are to an undertaking not to bring proceedings in respect of the FSCS manager's relevant scheme functions except proceedings in respect of an act or omission of the FSCS manager that is alleged to have been in bad faith.

224E(9)   ["Proceedings"] In this section "proceedings" includes proceedings outside the United Kingdom.

History
See note after s.224F.

Rules

224F   Rules about relevant schemes

224F(1) [Power of regulators to make rules] The regulators may by rules make provision in connection with the exercise by the FSCS manager of functions in respect of relevant schemes.

224F(2) [Corresponding provision in FSCS] The provision that may be made by the rules includes any provision corresponding to provision that could be contained in the FSCS; but this is subject to subsections (3) and (4).

224F(3) [Power to impose levies to meet management expenses] The rules may confer on the FSCS manager a power to impose levies on authorised persons (or any class of authorised persons) for the purpose of meeting its management expenses incurred in connection with its functions in respect of relevant schemes.

224F(4) [Reimbursement of expenses from scheme manager] But if the rules confer such a power they must provide that the power may be exercised in relation to expenses incurred in connection with a relevant scheme only if the FSCS manager has tried its best to obtain reimbursement of the expenses from the manager of the relevant scheme.

224F(5) [Rules may apply FSCS provisions] The rules may apply any provision of the FSCS, with or without modifications.

224F(6) [Management expenses recoverable as a debt] An amount payable to the FSCS manager as a result of any provision of the rules made by virtue of subsection (3) may be recovered as a debt due to the FSCS manager.

224F(7) ["Management expenses"] References to the FSCS manager's "management expenses" are to its expenses incurred otherwise than in paying compensation.

History
Sections 224B–224F inserted by the Financial Services Act 2010 s.17 as from 12 October 2010.

PART XXIV

INSOLVENCY

Interpretation

355   Interpretation of this Part

355(1) [Interpretation] In this Part–

"the 1986 Act" means the Insolvency Act 1986;

"the 1989 Order" means the Insolvency (Northern Ireland) Order 1989;

"the 2016 Act" means the Bankruptcy (Scotland) Act 2016;

"body" means a body of persons–

(a)   over which the court has jurisdiction under any provision of, or made under, the 1986 Act (or the 1989 Order); but

(b)   which is not a building society, a friendly society or a registered society; and

"court" means–

(a)   the court having jurisdiction for the purposes of the 1985 Act or the 1986 Act; or

(b)   in Northern Ireland, the High Court.

"creditors' decision procedure" has the meaning given by section 379ZA(11) of the 1986 Act;

"PRA-regulated person" means a person who–

(a)   is or has been a PRA-authorised person,

(b)   is or has been an appointed representative whose principal (or one of whose principals) is, or was, a PRA-authorised person, or

(c)   is carrying on or has carried on a PRA-regulated activity in contravention of the general prohibition.

"qualifying decision procedure" has the meaning given by section 246ZE(11) of the 1986 Act.

355(2)   ["Insurer"] In this Part "insurer" has such meaning as may be specified in an order made by the Treasury.

History
Definition of "PRA-registered person" inserted by the Financial Services Act 2012 s.44 and Sch.14 para.2 as from 1 April 2013.
  Definitions of "creditors' decision procedure" and "qualifying decision procedure" were inserted by the Small Business, Enterprise and Employment Act 2015 (Consequential Amendments, Saving and Transitional Provisions) Regulations 2018 (SI 2018/208) reg.4(2) with effect from 13 March 2018.

Note
For the definition of "insurer" for the purpose of Pt XXIV, see the Financial Services and Markets Act 2000 (Insolvency) (Definition of "Insurer") Order 2001 (SI 2001/2634) arts 1, 2 as from 1 December 2001 (as amended by the Financial Services and Markets Act 2000 (Administration Orders Relating to Insurers) Order 2002 (SI 2002/1242) arts 1, 2 as from 31 May 2002).

Voluntary arrangements

356   Powers of FCA and PRA to participate in proceedings: company voluntary arrangements

356(1)   [Application of the 1986 Act] Where a voluntary arrangement has effect under Part I of the 1986 Act in respect of a company or insolvent partnership which is an authorised person, or recognised investment exchange, the appropriate regulator may apply to the court under section 6 or 7 of that Act.

356(2)   [Application of the 1989 Order] Where a voluntary arrangement has been approved under Part II of the 1989 Order in respect of a company or insolvent partnership which is an authorised person, or recognised investment exchange, the appropriate regulator may apply to the court under Article 19 or 20 of that Order.

356(3)   [Regulator's right of audience] If a person other than a regulator makes an application to the court in relation to the company or insolvent partnership under any of those provisions, the appropriate regulator is entitled to be heard at any hearing relating to the application.

356(4)   ["The appropriate regulator"] "The appropriate regulator" means–

(a)   in the case of a PRA-authorised person–

  (i)   for the purposes of subsections (1) and (2), the FCA or the PRA, and

  (ii)   for the purposes of subsection (3), each of the FCA and the PRA;

(b)   in any other case, the FCA.

356(5)   [Right of other regulator on court application] If either regulator makes an application to the court under any of those provisions in relation to a PRA-authorised person, the other regulator is entitled to be heard at any hearing relating to the application.

History
Section 356(1), (2) substituted, and s.356(3) amended, by the Insolvency Act 2000 s.15(3)(c) as from 1 January 2003 (see the Insolvency Act 2000 (Commencement No.3 and Transitional Provisions) Order 2002 (SI 2002/2711 (C. 83)) arts 1, 2). Section 356(4), (5) inserted by the Financial Services Act 2012 s.44 and Sch.14 para.3(4) as from 1 April 2013.

Note
Section 356 applies to limited liability partnerships by virtue of the Limited Liability Partnerships Regulations 2001 (SI 2001/1090) regs 1, 6(1) as from 6 April 2001 subject to reg.6(2).

357   Powers of FCA and PRA to participate in proceedings: individual voluntary arrangements

357(1)   **[Regulator's right of audience]** The appropriate regulator is entitled to be heard on an application by an individual who is an authorised person under section 253 of the 1986 Act (or Article 227 of the 1989 Order).

357(2)   **[Application of s.357(3)–(6)]** Subsections (2A) to (6) apply if such an order is made on the application of such a person.

357(2A)   **[Entitlement to notice and participation]** Where under section 257 of the 1986 Act the individual's creditors are asked to decide whether to approve the proposed voluntary arrangement–

(a)   notice of the creditors' decision procedure must be given to the appropriate regulator; and

(b)   the appropriate regulator or a person appointed by the appropriate regulator is entitled to participate in (but not vote in) the creditors' decision procedure by which the decision is made.

357(2B)   **[Notice to be given by nominee]** Notice of the decision made by the creditors' decision procedure is to be given to the appropriate regulator by the nominee or the nominee's replacement under section 256(3) or 256A(4) of the 1986 Act.

357(3)   **[Meetings of creditors]** A person appointed for the purpose by the appropriate regulator is entitled to attend any meeting of creditors of the debtor summoned under Article 231 of the 1989 Order.

357(4)   **[Duty of chairman of meeting]** Notice of the result of a meeting so summoned is to be given to the appropriate regulator by the chairman of the meeting.

357(5)   **[Application to court]** The appropriate regulator may apply to the court–

(a)   under section 262 of the 1986 Act (or Article 236 of the 1989 Order); or

(b)   under section 263 of the 1986 Act (or Article 237 of the 1989 Order).

357(6)   **[Regulator's right of audience]** If a person other than a regulator makes an application to the court under any provision mentioned in subsection (5), the appropriate regulator is entitled to be heard at any hearing relating to the application.

357(7)   **["The appropriate regulator"]** "The appropriate regulator" means–

(a)   in the case of a PRA-authorised person, each of the FCA and the PRA, except that the references in subsections (2A)(b) and (3) to a person appointed by the appropriate regulator are to be read as references to a person appointed by either the FCA or the PRA;

(b)   in any other case, the FCA.

357(8)   **[Entitlement of other regulator to be heard on s.357(5) application]** If either regulator makes an application to the court under any of the provisions mentioned in subsection (5) in relation to a PRA-authorised person, the other regulator is entitled to be heard at any hearing relating to the application.

History
Section 357(7), (8) inserted by the Financial Services Act 2012 s.44 and Sch.14 para.4(4) as from 1 April 2013. Section 357(2), (3) and (7) were modified by, and s.357(2A) and (2B) were inserted by the Small Business,

Enterprise and Employment Act 2015 (Consequential Amendments, Savings and Transitional Provisions) Regulations 2018 (SI 2018/208) reg.4(3)(a)–(d) with effect from 13 March 2018.

358   Powers of FCA and PRA to participate in proceedings: trust deeds for creditors in Scotland

358(1)   **[Application of section]** This section applies where a trust deed has been granted by or on behalf of a debtor who is an authorised person or recognised investment exchange.

358(2)   **[Duty of trustee]** The trustee must, as soon as practicable after he becomes aware that the debtor is an authorised person or recognised investment exchange, send to the appropriate regulator–

(a)   in every case, a copy of the trust deed;

(b)   where any other document or information is sent to every creditor known to the trustee in pursuance of section 170 of the 2016 Act, a copy of such document or information.

358(3)   [Omitted]

358(4)   **[Notice to be given to appropriate regulator]** The appropriate regulator must be given the same notice as the creditors of any meeting of creditors held in relation to the trust deed.

358(5)   **[Regulator's right to attend, etc. meeting]** A person appointed for the purpose by the appropriate regulator is entitled to attend and participate in (but not to vote at) any such meeting of creditors as if that regulator were a creditor under the deed.

358(6)   **[Rights of a regulator as creditor unaffected]** This section does not affect any right a regulator has as a creditor of a debtor who is an authorised person or recognised investment exchange.

358(6A)   **["The appropriate regulator"]** "The appropriate regulator" means–

(a)   in the case of a PRA-authorised person–

    (i)   for the purposes of subsections (2) and (4), each of the FCA and the PRA, and

    (ii)   for the purposes of subsection (5), the FCA or the PRA;

(b)   in any other case, the FCA.

358(7)   **[Interpretation]** Expressions used in this section and in the 2016 Act have the same meaning in this section as in that Act.

History
Section 358(6A) inserted by the Financial Services Act 2012 s.44 and Sch.14 para.5(6) as from 1 April 2013.

Administration orders

359   Administration order

359(1)   **[Power to make administration application]** The FCA may make an administration application under Schedule B1 to the 1986 Act or Schedule B1 to the 1989 Order in relation to a company or insolvent partnership which–

(a)   is or has been an authorised person or recognised investment exchange,

(b)   is or has been an appointed representative, or

(c)   is carrying on or has carried on a regulated activity in contravention of the general prohibition.

359(1A)   **[Power of PRA to apply for administration order]** The PRA may make an administration application under Schedule B1 to the 1986 Act or Schedule B1 to the 1989 Order in relation to a company or insolvent partnership which is a PRA-regulated person.

359(2)   [Application of s.359(3)] Subsection (3) applies in relation to an administration application made (or a petition presented) by a regulator by virtue of this section.

359(3)   [Inability to pay debts] Any of the following shall be treated for the purpose of paragraph 11(a) of Schedule B1 to the 1986 Act or paragraph 12(a) of Schedule B1 to the 1989 Order as unable to pay its debts–

(a)   a company or partnership in default on an obligation to pay a sum due and payable under an agreement,

(b)   an authorised deposit taker in default on an obligation to pay a sum due and payable in respect of a relevant deposit, and

(c)   an authorised reclaim fund in default on an obligation to pay a sum payable as a result of a claim made by virtue of section 1(2)(b) or 2(2)(b) of the Dormant Bank and Building Society Accounts Act 2008.

359(4)   ["Agreement", "authorised deposit taker", "company ", "relevant deposit"] In this section–

"agreement" means an agreement the making or performance of which constitutes or is part of a regulated activity carried on by the company or partnership,

"authorised deposit taker" means a person with a Part 4A permission to accept deposits (but not a person who has a Part 4A permission to accept deposits only for the purpose of carrying on another regulated activity in accordance with that permission),

"authorised reclaim fund" means a reclaim fund within the meaning given by section 5(1) of the Dormant Bank and Building Society Accounts Act 2008 that is authorised for the purposes of this Act;

"company" means a company–

(a)   in respect of which an administrator may be appointed under Schedule B1 to the 1986 Act, or

(b)   in respect of which an administrator may be appointed under Schedule B1 to the 1989 Order, and

"relevant deposit" shall, ignoring any restriction on the meaning of deposit arising from the identity of the person making the deposit, be construed in accordance with–

(a)   section 22,

(b)   any relevant order under that section, and

(c)   Schedule 2.

359(5)   ["Authorised deposit taker" in s.359(4)] The definition of "authorised deposit taker" in subsection (4) shall be construed in accordance with–

(a)   section 22,

(b)   any relevant order under that section, and

(c)   Schedule 2.

History
See note after s.362A. Section 359(3)(c) inserted and s.359(4) amended by the Dormant Bank and Building Society Accounts Act 2008 Sch.2 para.6 as from 12 March 2009. Section 359(1A) inserted by the Financial Services Act 2012 s.44 and Sch.14 para.6(3) as from 1 April 2013.

Note
Section 359(1)–(4) applies to limited liability partnerships by virtue of the Limited Liability Partnerships Regulations 2001 (SI 2001/1090) regs 1, 6(1) as from 6 April 2001 subject to reg.6(2). See the Enterprise Act 2002 (Commencement No.4 and Transitional Provisions and Savings) Order 2003 (SI 2003/2093 (C. 85)) art.3(1), (3) for transitional saving.

360 Insurers

360(1) [Power of Treasury to make order] The Treasury may by order provide that such provisions of Part II of the 1986 Act (or Part III of the 1989 Order) as may be specified are to apply in relation to insurers with such modifications as may be specified.

360(2) [Provisions, etc. of s.360 order] An order under this section–

(a) may provide that such provisions of this Part as may be specified are to apply in relation to the administration of insurers in accordance with the order with such modifications as may be specified; and

(b) requires the consent of the Secretary of State.

360(3) ["Specified"] "Specified" means specified in the order.

Note
The definition of "insurer" for these purposes is that contained in the Financial Services and Markets Act 2000 (Insolvency) (Definition of "Insurer") Order 2001 (SI 2001/2634) art.2, as extended to apply to s.360 by virtue of the Financial Services and Markets Act 2000 (Administration Orders Relating to Insurers) Order 2002 (SI 2002/1242) arts 1(1), 2 as from 31 May 2002. The 2001 definition does not extend so as to include Lloyd's, but separate provision is now made for Lloyd's by the Insurers (Reorganisation and Winding Up) (Lloyd's) Regulations 2005 (SI 2005/1998) which, by reg.2(4), disapplies s.360. For Northern Ireland, see the Financial Services and Markets Act 2000 (Administration Orders Relating to Insurers) (Northern Ireland) Order 2007 (SI 2007/846), effective 6 April 2007.

361 Administrator's duty to report to FCA and PRA

361(1) [Application of s.361] This section applies where a company or partnership is–

(a) in administration within the meaning of Schedule B1 to the 1986 Act, or

(b) in administration within the meaning of Schedule B1 to the 1989 Order.

361(2) [Duty of administrator to report] If the administrator thinks that the company or partnership is carrying on, or has carried on–

(a) a regulated activity in contravention of the general prohibition, or

(b) a credit-related regulated activity in contravention of section 20,

the administrator must report the matter to the appropriate regulator without delay.

361(2A) ["The appropriate regulator"] "The appropriate regulator" means–

(a) where the regulated activity is a PRA-regulated activity, the FCA and the PRA;

(b) in any other case, the FCA.

361(3) [Non-application of s.361(2)] Subsection (2) does not apply where–

(a) the administration arises out of an administration order made on an application made or petition presented by a regulator, and

(b) the regulator's application or petition depended on a contravention by the company or partnership of the general prohibition.

History
See note after s.362A. Section 361(2), (3) substituted and s.361(2A) inserted by the Financial Services Act 2012 s.44 and Sch.14 para.7(2)–(4) as from 1 April 2013.

Note
Section 361 applies to limited liability partnerships by virtue of the Limited Liability Partnerships Regulations 2001 (SI 2001/1090) regs 1, 6(1) as from 6 April 2001 subject to reg.6(2). See the Enterprise Act 2002 (Commencement

No.4 and Transitional Provisions and Savings) Order 2003 (SI 2003/2093 (C. 85)) arts 3(1), (3) for transitional saving.

362   Powers of FCA and PRA to participate in proceedings

362(1)   [Application of section] This section applies if a person makes an administration application under Schedule B1 to the 1986 Act or Schedule B1 to the 1989 Order in relation to a company or partnership which–

(a)   is, or has been, an authorised person or recognised investment exchange;

(b)   is, or has been, an appointed representative; or

(c)   is carrying on, or has carried on, a regulated activity in contravention of the general prohibition.

362(1A)   [Further application of section] This section also applies in relation to–

(a)   the appointment under paragraph 14 or 22 of Schedule B1 to the 1986 Act or paragraph 15 or 23 of Schedule B1 to the 1989 Order of an administrator of a company of a kind described in subsection (1)(a) to (c), or

(b)   the filing with the court of a copy of notice of intention to appoint an administrator under any of those paragraphs.

362(1B)   [Application to appointment by company or directors] This section also applies in relation to–

(a)   the appointment under paragraph 22 of Schedule B1 to the 1986 Act (as applied by order under section 420 of the 1986 Act), or under paragraph 23 of Schedule B1 to the 1989 Order (as applied by order under Article 364 of the 1989 Order), of an administrator of a partnership of a kind described in subsection (1)(a) to (c), or

(b)   the filing with the court of a copy of notice of intention to appoint an administrator under either of those paragraphs (as so applied).

362(2)   [Regulator's right of audience] The appropriate regulator is entitled to be heard–

(a)   at the hearing of the administration application; and

(b)   at any other hearing of the court in relation to the company or partnership under Part II of the 1986 Act (or Part III of the 1989 Order).

362(3)   [Notices, etc.] Any notice or other document required to be sent to a creditor of the company or partnership must also be sent to the appropriate regulator.

362(4)   [Applications under Insolvency Act 1986 Sch.B1 para.74 etc.] The appropriate regulator may apply to the court under paragraph 74 of Schedule B1 to the 1986 Act or paragraph 75 of Schedule B1 to the 1989 Order.

362(4A)   [Application under s.362(4)] In respect of an application under subsection (4)–

(a)   paragraph 74(1)(a) and (b) shall have effect as if for the words "harm the interests of the applicant (whether alone or in common with some or all other members or creditors)" there were substituted the words "harm the interests of some or all members or creditors", and

(b)   paragraph 75(1)(a) and (b) of Schedule B1 to the 1989 Order shall have effect as if for the words "harm the interests of the applicant (whether alone or in common with some or all other members or creditors)" there were substituted the words "harm the interests of some or all members or creditors".

362(5)   [Attendance at meetings] A person appointed for the purpose by the appropriate regulator is entitled–

(a) to attend any meeting of creditors of the company or partnership summoned under any enactment;

(b) to attend any meeting of a committee established under paragraph 57 of Schedule B1 to the 1986 Act or paragraph 58 of Schedule B1 to the 1989 Order; and

(c) to make representations as to any matter for decision at such a meeting.

362(5A) [Entitlement to participate] The appropriate regulator or a person appointed by the appropriate regulator is entitled to participate in (but not vote in) a qualifying decision procedure by which a decision about any matter is sought from the creditors of the company or partnership.

362(6) [Applications under Companies Act 2006 Pt 26] If, during the course of the administration of a company, a compromise or arrangement is proposed between the company and its creditors, or any class of them, the appropriate regulator may apply to the court under section 896 or 899 of the Companies Act 2006.

362(7) ["The appropriate regulator"] "The appropriate regulator" means–

(a) where the company or partnership is a PRA-regulated person, each of the FCA and the PRA, except that the references in subsections (5) and (5A) to a person appointed by the appropriate regulator are to be read as references to a person appointed by either the FCA or the PRA;

(b) in any other case, the FCA.

362(8) ["The appropriate regulator" where application by regulator] But where the administration application was made by a regulator "the appropriate regulator" does not include that regulator.

History
See note after s.362A. Sections 362(6), 365(7) and 371(5) amended by the Companies Act 2006 (Consequential Amendments etc.) Order 2008 (SI 2008/948) art.3(1) and Sch.1 para.211 as from 6 April 2008. Section 362(1B), (7), (8) inserted by the Financial Services Act 2012 s.44 and Sch.14 para.(3), (5) as from 1 April 2013. Section 362(5A) was inserted by, and s.362(7) was modified by the Small Business, Enterprise and Employment Act 2015 (Consequential Amendments, Savings and Transitional Provisions) Regulations 2018 (SI 2018/208) reg.4(a) and (b) with effect from 13 March 2018.

Note
Section 362 applies to limited liability partnerships by virtue of the Limited Liability Partnerships Regulations 2001 (SI 2001/1090) regs 1, 6(1) as from 6 April 2001 subject to reg.6(2).

362A Administrator appointed by company or directors

362A(1) [Application of s.362A] This section applies in relation to a company or partnership of a kind described in section 362(1)(a) to (c).

362A(2) [Where consent of appropriate regulator needed] An administrator of the company or partnership may not be appointed under a provision specified in subsection (2A) without the consent of the appropriate regulator.

362A(2A) [Consent for appointment by company or directors] Those provisions are–

(a) paragraph 22 of Schedule B1 to the 1986 Act (including that paragraph as applied in relation to partnerships by order under section 420 of that Act);

(b) paragraph 23 of Schedule B1 to the 1989 Order (including that paragraph as applied in relation to partnerships by order under article 364 of that Order).

362A(2B) ["The appropriate regulator"] "The appropriate regulator" means–

(a) where the company or partnership is a PRA-regulated person, the PRA, and

(b) in any other case, the FCA.

362A(3)   [Form of consent] Consent under subsection (2)–

(a)   must be in writing, and

(b)   must be filed with the court along with the notice of intention to appoint under paragraph 27 of Schedule B1 to the 1986 Act or paragraph 28 of Schedule B1 to the 1989 Order.

362A(4)   [Where no notice of intention to appoint required] In a case where no notice of intention to appoint is required–

(a)   subsection (3)(b) shall not apply, but

(b)   consent under subsection (2) must accompany the notice of appointment filed under paragraph 29 of Schedule B1 to the 1986 Act or paragraph 30 of Schedule B1 to the 1989 Order.

History
Sections 359, 361 and 362(4), (4A) substituted, s.362(1), (2)(a), (5)(b) amended, and ss.362(1A), 362A inserted by the Enterprise Act 2002 s.248(3) Sch.17 paras 53, 55–58 as from 15 September 2003 (see the Enterprise Act 2002 (Commencement No.4 and Transitional Provisions and Savings) Order 2003 (SI 2003/2093 (C. 85)) art.2(1) Sch.1), subject to transitional provisions in SI 2003/2093 (C. 85) art.3. The amendments have no effect in relation to certain companies by virtue of the Enterprise Act 2002 s.249(1). Section 362A(2) substituted and s.362A(2A)–(2B) inserted by the Financial Services Act 2012 s.44 and Sch.14 para.9(3) as from 1 April 2013.

Receivership

363   Powers of FCA and PRA to participate in proceedings

363(1)   [Application of section] This section applies if a receiver has been appointed in relation to a company which–

(a)   is, or has been, an authorised person or recognised investment exchange;

(b)   is, or has been, an appointed representative; or

(c)   is carrying on, or has carried on, a regulated activity in contravention of the general prohibition.

363(2)   [Regulator's right of audience] The appropriate regulator is entitled to be heard on an application made under section 35 or 63 of the 1986 Act (or Article 45 of the 1989 Order).

363(3)   [Applications to court] The appropriate regulator is entitled to make an application under section 41(1)(a) or 69(1)(a) of the 1986 Act (or Article 51(1)(a) of the 1989 Order).

363(4)   [Reports] A report under section 48(1) or 67(1) of the 1986 Act (or Article 58(1) of the 1989 Order) must be sent by the person making it to the appropriate regulator.

363(5)   [Attendance at meetings] A person appointed for the purpose by the appropriate regulator is entitled–

(a)   to attend any meeting of creditors of the company summoned under any enactment;

(b)   to attend any meeting of a committee established under section 49 or 68 of the 1986 Act (or Article 59 of the 1989 Order); and

(c)   to make representations as to any matter for decision at such a meeting.

363(6)   ["The appropriate regulator"] "The appropriate regulator" means–

(a)   for the purposes of subsections (2) to (4)–

(i)   where the company is a PRA-regulated person, each of the FCA and the PRA, and

(ii)   in any other case, the FCA;

(b)   for the purposes of subsection (5)–

(i)   where the company is a PRA-regulated person, the FCA or the PRA, and

(ii)   in any other case, the FCA.

Note
Section 363 applies to limited liability partnerships by virtue of the Limited Liability Partnerships Regulations 2001 (SI 2001/1090) regs 1, 6(1) as from 6 April 2001 subject to reg.6(2). Section 363(6) inserted by the Financial Services Act 2012 s.44 and Sch.14 para.10(4) as from 1 April 2013.

364   Receiver's duty to report to FCA and PRA

364   If–

(a)   a receiver has been appointed in relation to a company, and

(b)   it appears to the receiver that the company is carrying on, or has carried on, a regulated activity in contravention of the general prohibition or a credit-related regulated activity in contravention of section 20,

the receiver must report the matter without delay to the FCA and, if the regulated activity concerned is a PRA-regulated activity, to the PRA.

Note
Section 364 applies to limited liability partnerships by virtue of the Limited Liability Partnerships Regulations 2001 (SI 2001/1090) regs 1, 6(1) as from 6 April 2001 subject to reg.6(2). Section 364(b) amended by the Financial Services Act 2012 s.44 and Sch.14 para.11(b) as from 1 April 2013.

Voluntary winding up

365   Powers of FCA and PRA to participate in proceedings

365(1)   [Application of section] This section applies in relation to a company which–

(a)   is being wound up voluntarily;

(b)   is an authorised person or recognised investment exchange; and

(c)   is not an insurer effecting or carrying out contracts of long-term insurance.

365(2)   [Applications to court under Insolvency Act 1986 s.112] The appropriate regulator may apply to the court under section 112 of the 1986 Act (or Article 98 of the 1989 Order) in respect of the company.

365(3)   [Regulator's right of audience] The appropriate regulator is entitled to be heard at any hearing of the court in relation to the voluntary winding up of the company.

365(4)   [Notices, etc.] Any notice or other document required to be sent to a creditor of the company must also be sent to the appropriate regulator.

365(5)   [Attendance at meetings] A person appointed for the purpose by the appropriate regulator is entitled–

(a)   to attend any meeting of creditors of the company summoned under any enactment;

(b)   to attend any meeting of a committee established under section 101 of the 1986 Act (or Article 87 of the 1989 Order); and

(c)   to make representations as to any matter for decision at such a meeting.

365(5A)   [Entitlement to participate] The appropriate regulator or a person appointed by the appropriate regulator is entitled to participate in (but not vote in) a qualifying decision procedure by which a decision about any matter is sought from the creditors of the company.

365(6) **[Voluntary winding-up of company]** The voluntary winding up of the company does not bar the right of the appropriate regulator to have it wound up by the court.

365(7) **[Applications under Companies Act 2006 Pt 26]** If, during the course of the winding up of the company, a compromise or arrangement is proposed between the company and its creditors, or any class of them, the appropriate regulator may apply to the court under section 896 or 899 of the Companies Act 2006.

365(8) **["The appropriate regulator"]** "The appropriate regulator" means–

(a) where the company is a PRA-authorised person, each of the FCA and the PRA, except that the references in subsections (5) and (5A) to a person appointed by the appropriate regulator are to be read as references to a person appointed by either the FCA or the PRA;

(b) in any other case, the FCA.

History
Section 365(8) inserted by the Financial Services Act 2012 s.44 and Sch.14 para.12(4) as from 1 April 2013. Section 365(5A) was inserted by, and s.365(8) was modified by the Small Business, Enterprise and Employment Act 2015 (Consequential Amendments, Savings and Transitional Provisions) Regulations 2018 (SI 2018/208) reg.4(5)(a) and (b) with effect from 13 March 2018.

Note
Section 365 applies to limited liability partnerships by virtue of the Limited Liability Partnerships Regulations 2001 (SI 2001/1090) regs 1, 6(1) as from 6 April 2001 subject to reg.6(2).

366 Insurers effecting or carrying out long-term contracts or insurance

366(1) **[Voluntary winding-up]** An insurer effecting or carrying out contracts of long-term insurance may not be wound up voluntarily without the consent of the PRA.

366(2) **[Notice of general meeting]** If notice of a general meeting of such an insurer is given, specifying the intention to propose a resolution for voluntary winding up of the insurer, a director of the insurer must notify the PRA as soon as practicable after he becomes aware of it.

366(3) **[Offence, penalty]** A person who fails to comply with subsection (2) is guilty of an offence and liable on summary conviction to a fine not exceeding level 5 on the standard scale.

366(4) **[No written resolution or by meeting at short notice]** A winding up resolution may not be passed–

(a) as a written resolution (in accordance with Chapter 2 of Part 13 of the Companies Act 2006), or

(b) at a meeting called in accordance with section 307(4) to (6) or 337(2) of that Act (agreement of members to calling of meeting at short notice).

366(5) **[Copies of winding-up resolutions]** A copy of a winding-up resolution forwarded to the registrar of companies in accordance with section 30 of the Companies Act 2006 must be accompanied by a certificate issued by the PRA stating that it consents to the voluntary winding up of the insurer.

366(6) **[Compliance with s.366(5)]** If subsection (5) is complied with, the voluntary winding up is to be treated as having commenced at the time the resolution was passed.

366(7) **[Non-compliance with s.366(5)]** If subsection (5) is not complied with, the resolution has no effect.

366(8) **["Winding-up resolution"]** "Winding-up resolution" means a resolution for voluntary winding up of an insurer effecting or carrying out contracts of long-term insurance.

366(9) **[Duty of PRA to consult FCA re consent]** Before giving or refusing consent under subsection (1), the PRA must consult the FCA.

366(10)   [Where long-term contracts not PRA-regulated] In the event that the activity of effecting or carrying out long-term contracts of insurance as principal is not to any extent a PRA-regulated activity–

(a)   references to the PRA in subsections (1), (2) and (5) are to be read as references to the FCA, and

(b)   subsection (9) does not apply.

History
Section 366(9), (10) inserted by the Financial Services Act 2012 s.44 and Sch.14 para.13(3) as from 1 April 2013.

Winding up by the court

367   Winding-up petitions

367(1)   [Power of FCA re petition for winding-up] The FCA may present a petition to the court for the winding up of a body which–

(a)   is, or has been, an authorised person or recognised investment exchange;

(b)   is, or has been, an appointed representative; or

(c)   is carrying on, or has carried on, a regulated activity in contravention of the general prohibition.

367(1A)   [Power of PRA to petition] The PRA may present a petition to the court for the winding up of a body which is a PRA-regulated person.

367(2)   ["Body"] In subsections (1) and (1A) "body" includes any partnership.

367(3)   [Power of court] On such a petition, the court may wind up the body if–

(za)   in the case of an insurance undertaking or reinsurance undertaking, the PRA has cancelled the body's Part 4A permission pursuant to section 55J(7C);

(a)   the body is unable to pay its debts within the meaning of section 123 or 221 of the 1986 Act (or Article 103 or 185 of the 1989 Order); or

(b)   the court is of the opinion that it is just and equitable that it should be wound up.

367(4)   [Body in default of obligation under agreement] If a body is in default on an obligation to pay a sum due and payable under an agreement, it is to be treated for the purpose of subsection (3)(a) as unable to pay its debts.

367(5)   ["Agreement"] "Agreement" means an agreement the making or performance of which constitutes or is part of a regulated activity carried on by the body concerned.

367(6)   [Application of s.367(7)] Subsection (7) applies if a petition is presented under subsection (1) or (1A) for the winding up of a partnership–

(a)   on the ground mentioned in subsection (3)(b); or

(b)   in Scotland, on a ground mentioned in subsection (3)(a) or (b).

367(7)   [Jurisdiction of court] The court has jurisdiction, and the 1986 Act (or the 1989 Order) has effect, as if the partnership were an unregistered company as defined by section 220 of that Act (or Article 184 of that Order).

History
Section 367(1A) inserted by the Financial Services Act 2012 s.44 and Sch.14 para.14(3) as from 1 April 2013.

Note
Section 367 applies to limited liability partnerships by virtue of the Limited Liability Partnerships Regulations 2001 (SI 2001/1090) regs 1, 6(1) as from 6 April 2001 subject to reg.6(2).

368   Winding-up petitions: EEA and Treaty firms

368(1)   [Condition for petition] A regulator may not present a petition to the court under section 367 for the winding up of–

(a)   an EEA firm which qualifies for authorisation under Schedule 3, or

(b)   a Treaty firm which qualifies for authorisation under Schedule 4,

unless it or the other regulator has been asked to do so by the home state regulator of the firm concerned.

368(2)   [Where home-state regulator requests petition] If a regulator receives from the home state regulator of a body falling within subsection (1)(a) or (b) a request to present a petition to the court under section 367 for the winding up of the body, it must–

(a)   notify the other regulator of the request, and

(b)   provide the other regulator with such information relating to the request as it thinks fit.

History
Section 368(2) inserted by the Financial Services Act 2012 s.44 and Sch.14 para.15(4) as from 1 April 2013.

369   Insurers: service of petition etc. on FCA and PRA

369(1)   [Petition for winding-up—persons other than regulator] If a person other than a regulator presents a petition for the winding up of an authorised person with permission to effect or carry out contracts of insurance, the petitioner must serve a copy of the petition on the appropriate regulator.

369(2)   [Appointment of liquidator—persons other than regulator] If a person other than a regulator applies to have a provisional liquidator appointed under section 135 of the 1986 Act (or Article 115 of the 1989 Order) in respect of an authorised person with permission to effect or carry out contracts of insurance, the applicant must serve a copy of the application on the appropriate regulator.

369(3)   ["The appropriate regulator"] "The appropriate regulator" means–

(a)   in relation to a PRA-authorised person, the FCA and the PRA, and

(b)   in any other case, the FCA.

369(4)   [Copy of petition or application to other regulator] If either regulator–

(a)   presents a petition for the winding up of a PRA-authorised person with permission to effect or carry out contracts of insurance, or

(b)   applies to have a provisional liquidator appointed under section 135 of the 1986 Act (or Article 115 of the 1989 Order) in respect of a PRA-authorised person with permission to effect or carry out contracts of insurance, that regulator must serve a copy of the petition or application (as the case requires) on the other regulator.

History
Section 369(3), (4) inserted by the Financial Services Act 2012 s.44 and Sch.14 para.16(4) as from 1 April 2013.

369A   Reclaim funds: service of petition etc on FCA and PRA

369A(1)   [Copy of winding-up petition on regulator] If a person other than a regulator presents a petition for the winding up of an authorised reclaim fund, the petitioner must serve a copy of the petition on the appropriate regulator.

369A(2)   [Copy of application for provisional liquidator on regulator] If a person other than a regulator applies to have a provisional liquidator appointed under section 135 of the 1986 Act (or Article 115 of the 1989 Order) in respect of an authorised reclaim fund, the applicant must serve a copy of the application on the appropriate regulator.

369A(3) **["Authorised reclaim fund"]** In this section "authorised reclaim fund" means a reclaim fund within the meaning given by section 5(1) of the Dormant Bank and Building Society Accounts Act 2008 that is authorised for the purposes of this Act.

369A(4) **["The appropriate regulator"]** "The appropriate regulator" means–

(a) in relation to an authorised reclaim fund that is a PRA-authorised person, the FCA and the PRA, and

(b) in relation to any other authorised reclaim fund, the FCA.

369A(5) **[Copy of petition or application to other regulator]** If either regulator–

(a) presents a petition for the winding up of an authorised reclaim fund that is a PRA-authorised person, or

(b) applies to have a provisional liquidator appointed under section 135 of the 1986 Act (or Article 115 of the 1989 Order) in respect of an authorised reclaim fund that is a PRA-authorised person,

that regulator must serve a copy of the petition or application (as the case requires) on the other regulator.

History
Section 369A inserted by the Dormant Bank and Building Society Accounts Act 2008 Sch.2 para.7 as from 12 March 2009. Section 369A(4), (5) inserted by the Financial Services Act 2012 s.44 and Sch.14 para.17(4) as from 1 April 2013.

370 Liquidator's duty to report to FCA and PRA

370(1) **[Duty of liquidator]** If–

(a) a company is being wound up voluntarily or a body is being wound up on a petition presented by any person, and

(b) it appears to the liquidator that the company or body is carrying on, or has carried on–

(i) a regulated activity in contravention of the general prohibition, or

(ii) a credit-related regulated activity in contravention of section 20,

the liquidator must report the matter without delay to the FCA and, if the regulated activity concerned is a PRA-regulated activity, to the PRA.

370(2) **[Non-application of s.370(1) duty]** Subsection (1) does not apply where–

(a) a body is being wound up on a petition presented by a regulator, and

(b) the regulator's petition depended on a contravention by the body of the general prohibition.

History
Section 370 substituted by the Financial Services Act 2012 s.44 and Sch.14 para.18 as from 1 April 2013.

Note
Section 370 applies to limited liability partnerships by virtue of the Limited Liability Partnerships Regulations 2001 (SI 2001/1090) regs 1, 6(1) as from 6 April 2001 subject to reg.6(2).

371 Powers of FCA and PRA to participate in proceedings

371(1) **[Application of section]** This section applies if a person presents a petition for the winding up of a body which–

(a) is, or has been, an authorised person or recognised investment exchange;

(b) is, or has been, an appointed representative; or

(c)　is carrying on, or has carried on, a regulated activity in contravention of the general prohibition.

371(2)　[Regulator's right of audience] The appropriate regulator is entitled to be heard–

(a)　at the hearing of the petition; and

(b)　at any other hearing of the court in relation to the body under or by virtue of Part IV or V of the 1986 Act (or Part V or VI of the 1989 Order).

371(3)　[Notice, etc.] Any notice or other document required to be sent to a creditor of the body must also be sent to the appropriate regulator.

371(4)　[Attendance at meetings] A person appointed for the purpose by the appropriate regulator is entitled–

(a)　to attend any meeting of creditors of the body;

(b)　to attend any meeting of a committee established for the purposes of Part IV or V of the 1986 Act under section 101 of that Act or under section 141 or 142 of that Act;

(c)　to attend any meeting of a committee established for the purposes of Part V or VI of the 1989 Order under Article 87 of that Order or under Article 120 of that Order; and

(d)　to make representations as to any matter for decision at such a meeting.

371(4A)　[Entitlement to participate] The appropriate regulator or a person appointed by the appropriate regulator is entitled to participate in (but not vote in) a qualifying decision procedure by which a decision about any matter is sought from the creditors of the body.

371(5)　[Applications under Companies Act 2006 Pt 26] If, during the course of the winding up of a company, a compromise or arrangement is proposed between the company and its creditors, or any class of them, the appropriate regulator may apply to the court under section 896 or 899 of the Companies Act 2006.

371(6)　["The appropriate regulator"] "The appropriate regulator" means–

(a)　where the body is a PRA-regulated person, each of the FCA and the PRA, except that the references in subsections (4) and (4A) to a person appointed by the appropriate regulator are to be read as references to a person appointed by either the FCA or the PRA;

(b)　in any other case, the FCA.

371(7)　[Non-application to presenting regulator] But where the petition was presented by a regulator "the appropriate regulator" does not include the regulator which presented the petition.

History
Section 371(6), (7) inserted by the Financial Services Act 2012 s.44 and Sch.14 para.19(4) as from 1 April 2013. Section 371(4A) was inserted by, and s.371(6) was modified by the Small Business, Enterprise and Employment Act 2015 (Consequential Amendments, Savings and Transitional Provisions) Regulations 2018 (SI 2018/208) reg.4(6)(a) and (b) with effect from 13 March 2018.

Note
Section 371 applies to limited liability partnerships by virtue of the Limited Liability Partnerships Regulations 2001 (SI 2001/1090) regs 1, 6(1) as from 6 April 2001 subject to reg.6(2).

Bankruptcy

372　Petitions

372(1)　[Power of FCA] The FCA may present a petition to the court–

(a)　under section 264 of the 1986 Act (or Article 238 of the 1989 Order) for a bankruptcy order to be made against an individual; or

(b)   under section 2 or 5 of the 2016 Act for the sequestration of the estate of an individual.

372(1A)   [Power of PRA to petition] The PRA may present a petition to the court–

(a)   under section 264 of the 1986 Act (or Article 238 of the 1989 Order) for a bankruptcy order to be made against an individual who is a PRA-regulated person;

(b)   under section 2 or 5 of the 2016 Act for the sequestration of the estate of an individual who is a PRA-regulated person.

372(2)   [Grounds for presentation of petition] But a petition may be presented by virtue of subsection (1) or (1A) only on the ground that–

(a)   the individual appears to be unable to pay a regulated activity debt; or

(b)   the individual appears to have no reasonable prospect of being able to pay a regulated activity debt.

372(3)   [Companies in default of obligation under agreement] An individual appears to be unable to pay a regulated activity debt if he is in default on an obligation to pay a sum due and payable under an agreement.

372(4)   [Ability to pay regulated activity debt] An individual appears to have no reasonable prospect of being able to pay a regulated activity debt if–

(a)   a regulator has served on him a demand requiring him to establish to the satisfaction of that regulator that there is a reasonable prospect that he will be able to pay a sum payable under an agreement when it falls due;

(b)   at least three weeks have elapsed since the demand was served; and

(c)   the demand has been neither complied with nor set aside in accordance with rules.

372(5)   [Demands made under s.372(4)(a)] A demand made under subsection (4)(a) is to be treated for the purposes of the 1986 Act (or the 1989 Order) as if it were a statutory demand under section 268 of that Act (or Article 242 of that Order).

372(6)   [Section 372(1)(b) or (1A)(b) petitions] For the purposes of a petition presented in accordance with subsection (1)(b) or (1A)(b)–

(a)   the regulator by which the petition is presented is to be treated as a qualified creditor; and

(b)   a ground mentioned in subsection (2) constitutes apparent insolvency.

372(7)   ["Individual"] "Individual" means an individual–

(a)   who is, or has been, an authorised person; or

(b)   who is carrying on, or has carried on, a regulated activity in contravention of the general prohibition.

372(8)   ["Agreement"] "Agreement" means an agreement the making or performance of which constitutes or is part of a regulated activity carried on by the individual concerned.

372(9)   ["Rules"] "Rules" means–

(a)   in England and Wales, rules made under section 412 of the 1986 Act;

(b)   in Scotland, rules made by order by the Treasury, after consultation with the Scottish Ministers, for the purposes of this section; and

(c)   in Northern Ireland, rules made under Article 359 of the 1989 Order.

History
Section 372(1A) inserted by the Financial Services Act 2012 s.44 and Sch.14 para.20(3) as from 1 April 2013.

373   Insolvency practitioner's duty to report to FCA and PRA

373(1)   [Duty of insolvency practitioner] If–

(a)   a bankruptcy order or sequestration award is in force in relation to an individual, and

(b)   it appears to the insolvency practitioner that the individual is carrying on, or has carried on–

   (i)   a regulated activity in contravention of the general prohibition, or

   (ii)   a credit-related regulated activity in contravention of section 20,

the insolvency practitioner must report the matter without delay to the FCA and, if the regulated activity concerned is a PRA-regulated activity, to the PRA.

373(1A)   [Non-application of s.373(1) duty] Subsection (1) does not apply where–

(a)   the bankruptcy order or sequestration award is in force by virtue of a petition presented by a regulator, and

(b)   the regulator's petition depended on a contravention by the individual of the general prohibition.

373(2)   ["Bankruptcy order"] "Bankruptcy order" means a bankruptcy order under Part IX of the 1986 Act (or Part IX of the 1989 Order).

373(3)   ["Sequestration award"] "Sequestration award" means an award of sequestration under section 22 of the 2016 Act.

373(4)   ["Individual"] "Individual" includes an entity mentioned in section 374(1)(c).

History
Section 373(1A) inserted and s.373(1) amended by the Financial Services Act 2012 s.44 and Sch.14 para.21(2), (3) as from 1 April 2013.

374   Powers of FCA or PRA to participate in proceedings

374(1)   [Application of section] This section applies if a person presents a petition to the court–

(a)   under section 264 of the 1986 Act (or Article 238 of the 1989 Order) for a bankruptcy order to be made against an individual;

(b)   under section 2 or 5 of the 2016 Act for the sequestration of the estate of an individual; or

(c)   under section 6 of the 2016 Act for the sequestration of the estate belonging to or held for or jointly by the members of an entity mentioned in subsection (1) of that section.

374(2)   [Regulator's right of audience] The appropriate regulator is entitled to be heard–

(a)   at the hearing of the petition; and

(b)   at any other hearing in relation to the individual or entity under–

   (i)   Part IX of the 1986 Act;

   (ii)   Part IX of the 1989 Order; or

   (iii) the 2016 Act.

374(3)   [Petition under Insolvency (Northern Ireland) Order 1989: copy report under art.248 to regulator] In the case of a petition presented under Article 238 of the 1989 Order, a copy of the report prepared under Article 248 of that Order must also be sent to the appropriate regulator.

374(4)   [Attendance at meetings] A person appointed for the purpose by the appropriate regulator is entitled–

(a)   to attend any meeting of creditors of the individual or entity;

(b)   to attend any meeting of a committee established under section 301 of the 1986 Act (or Article 274 of the 1989 Order);

(c)   to attend any meeting of commissioners held under paragraph 26 or 27 of Schedule 6 to the 2016 Act; and

(d)   to make representations as to any matter for decision at such a meeting.

374(4A)   [Entitlement to participate] The appropriate regulator or a person appointed by the appropriate regulator is entitled to participate in (but not vote in) a creditors' decision procedure by which a decision about any matter is sought from the creditors of the individual or entity.

374(5)   ["Individual"] "Individual" means an individual who–

(a)   is, or has been, an authorised person; or

(b)   is carrying on, or has carried on, a regulated activity in contravention of the general prohibition.

374(6)   ["Entity"] "Entity" means an entity which–

(a)   is, or has been, an authorised person; or

(b)   is carrying on, or has carried on, a regulated activity in contravention of the general prohibition.

374(7)   ["The appropriate regulator"] "The appropriate regulator" means–

(a)   where the individual or entity is a PRA-regulated person, each of the FCA and the PRA, except that the references in subsections (4) and (4A) to a person appointed by the appropriate regulator are to be read as references to a person appointed by either the FCA or the PRA;

(b)   in any other case, the FCA.

374(8)   [Non-application to presenting regulator] But where the petition was presented by a regulator "the appropriate regulator" does not include the regulator which presented the petition.

History
Section 374(7), (8) inserted by the Financial Services Act 2012 s.44 and Sch.14 para.22(4) as from 1 April 2013. Section 374(3) amended by the Enterprise and Regulatory Reform Act 2013 (Consequential Amendments) (Bankruptcy) and the Small Business, Enterprise and Employment Act 2015 (Consequential Amendments) Regulations 2016 (SI 2016/481) reg.2(1) and Sch.1 para.13 as from 6 April 2016. Section 374(4A) was inserted by, and s.374(7) was modified by the Small Business, Enterprise and Employment Act 2015 (Consequential Amendments, Savings and Transitional Provisions) Regulations 2018 (SI 2018/208) reg.4(7)(a) and (b) with effect from 13 March 2018.

Provisions against debt avoidance

375   Right of FCA and PRA to apply for an order

375(1)   [Insolvency Act 1986 s.423, etc.—application] The FCA may apply for an order under section 423 of the 1986 Act (or Article 367 of the 1989 Order) in relation to a debtor if–

(a)   at the time the transaction at an undervalue was entered into, the debtor was carrying on a regulated activity (whether or not in contravention of the general prohibition); and

(b)   a victim of the transaction is or was party to an agreement entered into with the debtor, the making or performance of which constituted or was part of a regulated activity carried on by the debtor.

375(1A)   [Power of PRA to apply for s.423 order] The PRA may apply for an order under section 423 of the 1986 Act (or Article 367 of the 1989 Order) in relation to a debtor if–

(a)   at the time the transaction at an undervalue was entered into, the debtor was carrying on a PRA-regulated activity (whether or not in contravention of the general prohibition); and

(b)   a victim of the transaction is or was party to an agreement entered into with the debtor, the making or performance of which constituted or was part of a PRA-regulated activity carried on by the debtor.

375(2)   [Treatment of s.375(1)(b) or 375(1A)(b) applications] An application made under this section is to be treated as made on behalf of every victim of the transaction to whom subsection (1)(b) or subsection (1A)(b) (as the case may be) applies.

375(3)   [Interpretation] Expressions which are given a meaning in Part XVI of the 1986 Act (or Article 367, 368 or 369 of the 1989 Order) have the same meaning when used in this section.

History
Section 375(1A) inserted by the Financial Services Act 2012 s.44 and Sch.14 para.23(3) as from 1 April 2013.

Supplemental provisions concerning insurers

376   Continuation of contracts of long-term insurance where insurer in liquidation

376(1)   [Application of section] This section applies in relation to the winding up of an insurer which effects or carries out contracts of long-term insurance.

376(2)   [Duty of liquidator] Unless the court otherwise orders, the liquidator must carry on the insurer's business so far as it consists of carrying out the insurer's contracts of long-term insurance with a view to its being transferred as a going concern to a person who may lawfully carry out those contracts.

376(3)   [Duty of liquidator—carrying on the business] In carrying on the business, the liquidator–

(a)   may agree to the variation of any contracts of insurance in existence when the winding up order is made; but

(b)   must not effect any new contracts of insurance.

376(4)   [Appointment of special manager] If the liquidator is satisfied that the interests of the creditors in respect of liabilities of the insurer attributable to contracts of long-term insurance effected by it require the appointment of a special manager, he may apply to the court.

376(5)   [Power of court] On such an application, the court may appoint a special manager to act during such time as the court may direct.

376(6)   [Powers of special manager] The special manager is to have such powers, including any of the powers of a receiver or manager, as the court may direct.

376(7)   [Application of Insolvency Act 1986 s.177(5), etc.] Section 177(5) of the 1986 Act (or Article 151(5) of the 1989 Order) applies to a special manager appointed under subsection (5) as it applies to a special manager appointed under section 177 of the 1986 Act (or Article 151 of the 1989 Order).

376(8)   [Company contracts—reduction of value] If the court thinks fit, it may reduce the value of one or more of the contracts of long-term insurance effected by the insurer.

376(9)   [Terms, etc. of reduction] Any reduction is to be on such terms and subject to such conditions (if any) as the court thinks fit.

376(10)   [Appointment of independent actuary] The court may, on the application of an official, appoint an independent actuary to investigate the insurer's business so far as it consists of carrying out its contracts of long-term insurance and to report to the official–

(a)   on the desirability or otherwise of that part of the insurer's business being continued; and

(b)   on any reduction in the contracts of long-term insurance effected by the insurer that may be necessary for successful continuation of that part of the insurer's business.

376(11) **["Official"]** "Official" means–

(a) the liquidator;

(b) a special manager appointed under subsection (5); or

(c) the PRA.

376(11A) **[Duty of PRA to consult and copy FCA]** The PRA must–

(a) consult the FCA before making an application under subsection (10), and

(b) provide the FCA with a copy of any actuary's report made to the PRA under that subsection.

376(11B) **[Where long-term contracts not PRA-regulated activity]** In the event that the activity of effecting or carrying out long-term contracts of insurance as principal is not to any extent a PRA-regulated activity–

(a) the reference in subsection (11)(c) to the PRA is to be read as a reference to the FCA, and

(b) subsection (11A) does not apply.

376(12) **[Applications by liquidator]** The liquidator may make an application in the name of the insurer and on its behalf under Part VII without obtaining the permission that would otherwise be required by Article 142 of, and Schedule 2 to, the 1989 Order.

History

Section 376(11A), (11B) inserted by the Financial Services Act 2012 s.44 and Sch.14 para.24(3) as from 1 April 2013.

Section 376(12) amended by Deregulation Act 2015, the Small Business, Enterprise and Employment Act 2015 and the Insolvency (Amendment) Act (Northern Ireland) 2016 (Consequential Amendments and Transitional Provisions) Regulations 2017 (SI 2017/400) regs 1, 4 as from 6 April 2017.

377 Reducing the value of contracts instead of winding up

377(1) **[Application of section]** This section applies in relation to an insurer which has been proved to be unable to pay its debts.

377(2) **[Power of court]** If the court thinks fit, it may reduce the value of one or more of the insurer's contracts instead of making a winding up order.

377(3) **[Terms, etc. of reduction]** Any reduction is to be on such terms and subject to such conditions (if any) as the court thinks fit.

378 Treatment of assets on winding up

378(1) **[Power of Treasury to make regulations]** The Treasury may by regulations provide for the treatment of the assets of an insurer on its winding up.

378(2) **[Content of regulations]** The regulations may, in particular, provide for–

(a) assets representing a particular part of the insurer's business to be available only for meeting liabilities attributable to that part of the insurer's business;

(b) separate general meetings of the creditors to be held in respect of liabilities attributable to a particular part of the insurer's business.

Note

See the Financial Services and Markets Act 2000 (Treatment of Assets of Insurers on Winding Up) Regulations 2001 (SI 2001/2968).

379   Winding-up rules

379(1)   [Content] Winding-up rules may include provision–

(a)   for determining the amount of the liabilities of an insurer to policyholders of any class or description for the purpose of proof in a winding up; and

(b)   generally for carrying into effect the provisions of this Part with respect to the winding up of insurers.

379(2)   [Further contents] Winding-up rules may, in particular, make provision for all or any of the following matters–

(a)   the identification of assets and liabilities;

(b)   the apportionment, between assets of different classes or descriptions, of–

(i)   the costs, charges and expenses of the winding up; and

(ii)   any debts of the insurer of a specified class or description;

(c)   the determination of the amount of liabilities of a specified description;

(d)   the application of assets for meeting liabilities of a specified description;

(e)   the application of assets representing any excess of a specified description.

379(3)   ["Specified"] "Specified" means specified in winding-up rules.

379(4)   ["Winding-up rules"] "Winding-up rules" means rules made under section 411 of the 1986 Act (or Article 359 of the 1989 Order).

379(5)   [Winding-up rules under Insolvency Act 1986, etc.] Nothing in this section affects the power to make winding-up rules under the 1986 Act or the 1989 Order.

Note
See the Insurers (Winding Up) Rules 2001 (SI 2001/3635).

Settlement finality

379A   Power to apply settlement finality regime to payment institutions

379A(1)   [Power of Treasury] The Treasury may by regulations made by statutory instrument provide for the application to payment institutions, as participants in payment or securities settlement systems, of provision in subordinate legislation–

(a)   modifying the law of insolvency or related law in relation to such systems, or

(b)   relating to the securing of rights and obligations.

379A(2)   ["Payment institution"] "Payment institution" means–

(a)   an authorised payment institution or small payment institution within the meaning of the Payment Services Regulations 2017, or

(b)   a person whose head office, registered office or place of residence, as the case may be, is outside the United Kingdom and whose functions correspond to those of an institution within paragraph (a).

379A(3)   ["Payment or securities settlement system"] "Payment or securities settlement system" means arrangements between a number of participants for or in connection with the clearing or execution of instructions by participants relating to any of the following–

(a)   the placing of money at the disposal of a recipient;

(b) the assumption or discharge of a payment obligation;

(c) the transfer of the title to, or an interest in, securities.

379A(4) ["Subordinate legislation" "Subordinate legislation" has the same meaning as in the Interpretation Act 1978.

379A(5) [Regulations] Regulations under this section may–

(a) make consequential, supplemental or transitional provision;

(b) amend subordinate legislation.

379A(6) [Statutory instrument subject to annulment] A statutory instrument containing regulations under this section is subject to annulment in pursuance of a resolution of either House of Parliament.

History

Section 379A added by the Digital Economy Act 2017 s.112 as from 27 April 2017. Subs.(2) amended by the Payment Services Regulations 2017 (SI 2017/752) Sch.8 para.2(6) as from 13 August 2017.

Limited Liability Partnerships Act 2000

(2000 Chapter 12)

An Act to make provision for limited liability partnerships.

[*20th July 2000*]

Regulations

14   Insolvency and winding up

14(1)   [Regulations to apply or incorporate Parts of Insolvency Act 1986] Regulations shall make provision about the insolvency and winding up of limited liability partnerships by applying or incorporating, with such modifications as appear appropriate–

  (a)   in relation to a limited liability partnership registered in Great Britain, Parts 1 to 4, 6 and 7 of the Insolvency Act 1986;

  (b)   in relation to a limited liability partnership registered in Northern Ireland, Parts 2 to 5 and 7 of the Insolvency (Northern Ireland) Order 1989, and so much of Part 1 of that Order as applies for the purposes of those Parts.

14(2)   [Other regulations] Regulations may make other provision about the insolvency and winding up of limited liability partnerships, and provision about the insolvency and winding up of oversea limited liability partnerships, by–

  (a)   applying or incorporating, with such modifications as appear appropriate, any law relating to the insolvency or winding up of companies or other corporations which would not otherwise have effect in relation to them, or

  (b)   providing for any law relating to the insolvency or winding up of companies or other corporations which would otherwise have effect in relation to them not to apply to them or to apply to them with such modifications as appear appropriate.

14(3)   ["Oversea limited liability partnership"] In this Act "oversea limited liability partnership" means a body incorporated or otherwise established outside the United Kingdom and having such connection with the United Kingdom, and such other features, as regulations may prescribe.

History
Section 14(1), (3) amended by the Limited Liability Partnerships (Application of Companies Act 2006) Regulations 2009 (SI 2009/1804) Sch.3 para.6 as from 1 October 2009.

15   Application of company law etc.

15   Regulations may make provision about limited liability partnerships and oversea limited liability partnerships (not being provision about insolvency or winding up) by–

  (a)   applying or incorporating, with such modifications as appear appropriate, any law relating to companies or other corporations which would not otherwise have effect in relation to them,

  (b)   providing for any law relating to companies or other corporations which would otherwise have effect in relation to them not to apply to them or to apply to them with such modifications as appear appropriate, or

  (c)   applying or incorporating, with such modifications as appear appropriate, any law relating to partnerships.

Note
See the Limited Liability Partnerships Regulations 2001 (SI 2001/1090), below.

Proceeds of Crime Act 2002

(2002 Chapter 29)

An Act to establish the Assets Recovery Agency and make provision about the appointment of its Director and his functions (including Revenue functions), to provide for confiscation orders in relation to persons who benefit from criminal conduct and for restraint orders to prohibit dealing with property, to allow the recovery of property which is or represents property obtained through unlawful conduct or which is intended to be used in unlawful conduct, to make provision about money laundering, to make provision about investigations relating to benefit from criminal conduct or to property which is or represents property obtained through unlawful conduct or to money laundering, to make provision to give effect to overseas requests and orders made where property is found or believed to be obtained through criminal conduct, and for connected purposes.

[24th July 2002]

[**Note**: Part 9 was brought into force by the Proceeds of Crime Act 2002 (Commencement No.5, Transitional Provisions, Savings and Amendment) Order 2003 (SI 2003/333) art.2 and Sch., as from 24 March 2003, subject to transitional provisions and savings. Changes made by the Serious Crime Act 2007, the Policing and Crime Act 2009 and the Enterprise and Regulatory Reform Act 2013 (Consequential Amendments) (Bankruptcy) and the Small Business, Enterprise and Employment Act 2015 (Consequential Amendments) Regulations 2016 (SI 2016/481) have been incorporated into the text. Note prospective amendment of the sections extracted below by the Policing and Crime Act 2009 Sch.7 paras 80 et seq. and Sch.8 Pt 4 from a date to be appointed.]

PART 9

INSOLVENCY ETC.

Bankruptcy in England and Wales

417 Modifications of the 1986 Act

417(1) This section applies if a person is made bankrupt in England and Wales.

417(2) The following property is excluded from the person's estate for the purposes of Part 9 of the 1986 Act–

(a) property for the time being subject to a restraint order which was made under section 41, 120 or 190 before the order adjudging the person bankrupt;

(b) property for the time being detained under or by virtue of section 44A, 47J, 47K, 47M, 47P, 122A, 127J, 127K, 127M, 127P, 193A, 195J, 195K, 195M or 195P;

(c) property in respect of which an order under section 50, 128(3) or 198 is in force;

(d) property in respect of which an order under section 67A, 131A or 215A is in force.

417(3) Subsection (2)(a) applies to heritable property in Scotland only if the restraint order is recorded in the General Register of Sasines or registered in the Land Register of Scotland before the order adjudging the person bankrupt.

417(4) If in the case of a debtor an interim receiver stands at any time appointed under section 286 of the 1986 Act and any property of the debtor is then subject to a restraint order made under section 41, 120 or 190 the powers conferred on the receiver by virtue of that Act do not apply to property then subject to the restraint order.

History
See note after s.430.

418 Restriction of powers

418(1) If a person is made bankrupt in England and Wales the powers referred to in subsection (2) must not be exercised in relation to the property referred to in subsection (3).

418(2) These are the powers–

(a) the powers conferred on a court by sections 41 to 67B, the powers conferred on an appropriate officer by section 47C and the powers of a receiver appointed under section 48 or 50;

(b) the powers conferred on a court by sections 120 to 136 and Schedule 3, the powers conferred on an appropriate officer by section 127C and the powers of an administrator appointed under section 125 or 128(3);

(c) the powers conferred on a court by sections 190 to 215B, the powers conferred on an appropriate officer by section 195C and the powers of a receiver appointed under section 196 or 198.

418(3) This is the property–

(a) property which is for the time being comprised in the bankrupt's estate for the purposes of Part 9 of the 1986 Act;

(b) property in respect of which his trustee in bankruptcy may (without leave of the court) serve a notice under section 307, 308 or 308A of the 1986 Act (after-acquired property, tools, tenancies etc);

(c) property which is to be applied for the benefit of creditors of the bankrupt by virtue of a condition imposed under section 280(2)(c) of the 1986 Act;

(d) in a case where a confiscation order has been made under section 6 or 156 of this Act, any sums remaining in the hands of a receiver appointed under section 50 or 198 of this Act after the amount required to be paid under the confiscation order has been fully paid;

(e) in a case where a confiscation order has been made under section 92 of this Act, any sums remaining in the hands of an administrator appointed under section 128 of this Act after the amount required to be paid under the confiscation order has been fully paid.

(f) in a case where a confiscation order has been made under section 6, 92 or 156 of this Act, any sums remaining in the hands of an appropriate officer after the amount required to be paid under the confiscation order has been fully paid under section 67D(2)(c), 131D(2)(c) or 215D(2)(c).

418(4) But nothing in the 1986 Act must be taken to restrict (or enable the restriction of) the powers referred to in subsection (2).

418(5)   In a case where a petition in bankruptcy was presented or a receiving order or adjudication in bankruptcy was made before 29 December 1986 (when the 1986 Act came into force) this section has effect with these modifications–

(a)   for the reference in subsection (3)(a) to the bankrupt's estate for the purposes of Part 9 of that Act substitute a reference to the property of the bankrupt for the purposes of the 1914 Act;

(b)   omit subsection (3)(b);

(c)   for the reference in subsection (3)(c) to section 280(2)(c) of the 1986 Act substitute a reference to section 26(2) of the 1914 Act;

(d)   for the reference in subsection (4) to the 1986 Act substitute a reference to the 1914 Act.

History
See note after s.430.

419   Tainted gifts

419(1)   This section applies if a person who is made bankrupt in England and Wales has made a tainted gift (whether directly or indirectly).

419(2)   No order may be made under section 339, 340 or 423 of the 1986 Act (avoidance of certain transactions) in respect of the making of the gift at any time when–

(a)   any property of the recipient of the tainted gift is subject to a restraint order under section 41, 120 or 190, or

(aa)   such property is detained under or by virtue of section 44A, 47J, 47K, 47M, 47P, 122A, 127J, 127K, 127M, 127P, 193A, 195J, 195K, 195M or 195P,

(b)   there is in force in respect of such property an order under section 50, 128(3) or 198, or

(c)   there is in force in respect of such property an order under section 67A, 131A or 215A.

419(3)   Any order made under section 339, 340 or 423 of the 1986 Act after an order mentioned in subsection (2)(a), (b) or (c) is discharged must take into account any realisation under Part 2, 3 or 4 of this Act of property held by the recipient of the tainted gift.

419(4)   A person makes a tainted gift for the purposes of this section if he makes a tainted gift within the meaning of Part 2, 3 or 4.

419(5)   In a case where a petition in bankruptcy was presented or a receiving order or adjudication in bankruptcy was made before 29 December 1986 (when the 1986 Act came into force) this section has effect with the substitution for a reference to section 339, 340 or 423 of the 1986 Act of a reference to section 27, 42 or 44 of the 1914 Act.

History
See note after s.430.

Winding up in England and Wales and Scotland

426   Winding up under the 1986 Act

426(1)   In this section "company" means any company which may be wound up under the 1986 Act.

426(2)   If an order for the winding up of a company is made or it passes a resolution for its voluntary winding up, the functions of the liquidator (or any provisional liquidator) are not exercisable in relation to the following property–

(a)   property for the time being subject to a restraint order which was made under section 41, 120 or 190 before the relevant time;

(b) property for the time being detained under or by virtue of section 44A, 47J, 47K, 47M, 47P, 122A, 127J, 127K, 127M, 127P, 193A, 195J, 195K, 195M or 195P;

(c) property in respect of which an order under section 50, 128(3) or 198 is in force;

(d) property in respect of which an order under section 67A, 131A or 215A is in force.

426(3) Subsection (2)(a) applies to heritable property in Scotland only if the restraint order is recorded in the General Register of Sasines or registered in the Land Register of Scotland before the relevant time.

426(4) If an order for the winding up of a company is made or it passes a resolution for its voluntary winding up the powers referred to in subsection (5) must not be exercised in the way mentioned in subsection (6) in relation to any property–

(a) which is held by the company, and

(b) in relation to which the functions of the liquidator are exercisable.

426(5) These are the powers–

(a) the powers conferred on a court by sections 41 to 67B, the powers conferred on an appropriate officer by section 47C and the powers of a receiver appointed under section 48 or 50;

(b) the powers conferred on a court by sections 120 to 136 and Schedule 3, the powers conferred on an appropriate officer by section 127C and the powers of an administrator appointed under section 125 or 128(3);

(c) the powers conferred on a court by sections 190 to 215B, the powers conferred on an appropriate officer by section 195C and the powers of a receiver appointed under section 196 or 198.

426(6) The powers must not be exercised–

(a) so as to inhibit the liquidator from exercising his functions for the purpose of distributing property to the company's creditors;

(b) so as to prevent the payment out of any property of expenses (including the remuneration of the liquidator or any provisional liquidator) properly incurred in the winding up in respect of the property.

426(7) But nothing in the 1986 Act must be taken to restrict (or enable the restriction of) the exercise of the powers referred to in subsection (5).

426(8) For the purposes of the application of Parts 4 and 5 of the 1986 Act (winding up) to a company which the Court of Session has jurisdiction to wind up, a person is not a creditor in so far as any sum due to him by the company is due in respect of a confiscation order made under section 6, 92 or 156.

426(9) The relevant time is–

(a) if no order for the winding up of the company has been made, the time of the passing of the resolution for voluntary winding up;

(b) if such an order has been made, but before the presentation of the petition for the winding up of the company by the court such a resolution has been passed by the company, the time of the passing of the resolution;

(c) if such an order has been made, but paragraph (b) does not apply, the time of the making of the order.

426(10) In a case where a winding up of a company commenced or is treated as having commenced before 29 December 1986, this section has effect with the following modifications–

(a) in subsections (1) and (7) for "the 1986 Act" substitute "the Companies Act 1985";

(b) in subsection (8) for "Parts 4 and 5 of the 1986 Act" substitute "Parts 20 and 21 of the Companies Act 1985".

History
See note after s.430.

427 Tainted gifts

427(1) In this section "company" means any company which may be wound up under the 1986 Act.

427(2) This section applies if–

(a) an order for the winding up of a company is made or it passes a resolution for its voluntary winding up, and

(b) it has made a tainted gift (whether directly or indirectly).

427(3) No order may be made under section 238, 239 or 423 of the 1986 Act (avoidance of certain transactions) and no decree may be granted under section 242 or 243 of that Act (gratuitous alienations and unfair preferences), or otherwise, in respect of the making of the gift at any time when–

(a) any property of the recipient of the tainted gift is subject to a restraint order under section 41, 120 or 190, or

(aa) such property is detained under or by virtue of section 44A, 47J, 47K, 47M, 47P, 122A, 127J, 127K, 127M, 127P, 193A, 195J, 195K, 195M or 195P,

(b) there is in force in respect of such property an order under section 50, 128(3) or 198, or

(c) there is in force in respect of such property an order under section 67A, 131A or 215A.

427(4) Any order made under section 238, 239 or 423 of the 1986 Act or decree granted under section 242 or 243 of that Act, or otherwise, after an order mentioned in subsection (3)(a), (b) or (c) is discharged must take into account any realisation under Part 2, 3 or 4 of this Act of property held by the recipient of the tainted gift.

427(5) A person makes a tainted gift for the purposes of this section if he makes a tainted gift within the meaning of Part 2, 3 or 4.

427(6) In a case where the winding up of a company commenced or is treated as having commenced before 29 December 1986 this section has effect with the substitution–

(a) for references to section 239 of the 1986 Act of references to section 615 of the Companies Act 1985 (c. 6);

(b) for references to section 242 of the 1986 Act of references to section 615A of the Companies Act 1985;

(c) for references to section 243 of the 1986 Act of references to section 615B of the Companies Act 1985.

History
See note after s.430.

Floating charges

430 Floating charges

430(1) In this section "company" means a company which may be wound up under–

(a) the 1986 Act, or

(b) the 1989 Order.

430(2)   If a company holds property which is subject to a floating charge, and a receiver has been appointed by or on the application of the holder of the charge, the functions of the receiver are not exercisable in relation to the following property–

(a)   property for the time being subject to a restraint order which was made under section 41, 120 or 190 before the relevant time;

(b)   property for the time being detained under or by virtue of section 44A, 47J, 47K, 47M, 47P, 122A, 127J, 127K, 127M, 127P, 193A, 195J, 195K, 195M or 195P;

(c)   property in respect of which an order under section 50, 128(3) or 198 is in force;

(d)   property in respect of which an order under section 67A, 131A or 215A is in force.

430(3)   Subsection (2)(a) applies to heritable property in Scotland only if the restraint order is recorded in the General Register of Sasines or registered in the Land Register of Scotland before the appointment of the receiver.

430(4)   If a company holds property which is subject to a floating charge, and a receiver has been appointed by or on the application of the holder of the charge, the powers referred to in subsection (5) must not be exercised in the way mentioned in subsection (6) in relation to any property–

(a)   which is held by the company, and

(b)   in relation to which the functions of the receiver are exercisable.

430(5)   These are the powers–

(a)   the powers conferred on a court by sections 41 to 67B, the powers conferred on an appropriate officer by section 47C and the powers of a receiver appointed under section 48 or 50;

(b)   the powers conferred on a court by sections 120 to 136 and Schedule 3, the powers conferred on an appropriate officer by section 127C and the powers of an administrator appointed under section 125 or 128(3);

(c)   the powers conferred on a court by sections 190 to 215B, the powers conferred on an appropriate officer by section 195C and the powers of a receiver appointed under section 196 or 198.

430(6)   The powers must not be exercised–

(a)   so as to inhibit the receiver from exercising his functions for the purpose of distributing property to the company's creditors;

(b)   so as to prevent the payment out of any property of expenses (including the remuneration of the receiver) properly incurred in the exercise of his functions in respect of the property.

430(7)   But nothing in the 1986 Act or the 1989 Order must be taken to restrict (or enable the restriction of) the exercise of the powers referred to in subsection (5).

430(8)   In this section "floating charge" includes a floating charge within the meaning of section 462 of the Companies Act 1985 (c. 6).

History
Sections 417, 418, 419, 426, and 427 amended (by the deletion of references to repealed sections) by the Serious Crime Act 2007 s.74(2) and Sch.8, as from 6 April 2008.

Limited liability partnerships

431   Limited liability partnerships

431(1)   In sections 426, 427 and 430 "company" includes a limited liability partnership which may be wound up under the 1986 Act.

431(2)   A reference in those sections to a company passing a resolution for its voluntary winding up is to be construed in relation to a limited liability partnership as a reference to the partnership making a determination for its voluntary winding up.

Insolvency practitioners

432   Insolvency practitioners

432(1)   Subsections (2) and (3) apply if a person acting as an insolvency practitioner seizes or disposes of any property in relation to which his functions are not exercisable because–

(a)   it is for the time being subject to a restraint order made under section 41, 120 or 190, or

(b)   it is for the time being subject to a property freezing order made under section 245A, an interim receiving order made under section 246, a prohibitory property order made under section 255A or an interim administration order made under section 256,

and at the time of the seizure or disposal he believes on reasonable grounds that he is entitled (whether in pursuance of an order of a court or otherwise) to seize or dispose of the property.

432(2)   He is not liable to any person in respect of any loss or damage resulting from the seizure or disposal, except so far as the loss or damage is caused by his negligence.

432(3)   He has a lien on the property or the proceeds of its sale–

(a)   for such of his expenses as were incurred in connection with the liquidation, bankruptcy, sequestration or other proceedings in relation to which he purported to make the seizure or disposal, and

(b)   for so much of his remuneration as may reasonably be assigned to his acting in connection with those proceedings.

432(4)   Subsection (2) does not prejudice the generality of any provision of the 1986 Act, the 1989 Order, the 2016 Act or any other Act or Order which confers protection from liability on him.

432(5)   Subsection (7) applies if–

(a)   property is subject to a restraint order made under section 41, 120 or 190,

(b)   a person acting as an insolvency practitioner incurs expenses in respect of property subject to the restraint order, and

(c)   he does not know (and has no reasonable grounds to believe) that the property is subject to the restraint order.

432(6)   Subsection (7) also applies if–

(a)   property is subject to a restraint order made under section 41, 120 or 190,

(b)   a person acting as an insolvency practitioner incurs expenses which are not ones in respect of property subject to the restraint order, and

(c)   the expenses are ones which (but for the effect of the restraint order) might have been met by taking possession of and realising property subject to it.

432(6A)   Subsection (7) also applies if–

(a)   property is detained under or by virtue of section 44A, 47J, 47K, 47M, 47P, 122A, 127J, 127K, 127M, 127P, 193A, 195J, 195K, 195M or 195P,

(b)   a person acting as an insolvency practitioner incurs expenses which are not ones in respect of the detained property, and

(c)   the expenses are ones which (but for the effect of the detention of the property) might have been met by taking possession of and realising the property.

432(7)   Whether or not the insolvency practitioner has seized or disposed of any property, the insolvency practitioner is entitled to payment of the expenses under–

(a)   section 54(2), 55(3) or 67D(2) if the restraint order was made under section 41 or (as the case may be) the property was detained under or by virtue of section 44A, 47J, 47K, 47M or 47P,

(b)   section 130(3), 131(3) or 131D(2) if the restraint order was made under section 120 or (as the case may be) the property was detained under or by virtue of section 122A, 127J, 127K, 127M or 127P, and

(c)   section 202(2), 203(3) or 215D(2) if the restraint order was made under section 190 or (as the case may be) the property was detained under or by virtue of section 193A, 195J, 195K, 195M or 195P.

432(8)   Subsection (10) applies if–

(a)   property is subject to a property freezing order made under section 245A, an interim receiving order made under section 246, a prohibitory property order made under section 255A or an interim administration order made under section 256,

(b)   a person acting as an insolvency practitioner incurs expenses in respect of property subject to the order, and

(c)   he does not know (and has no reasonable grounds to believe) that the property is subject to the order.

432(9)   Subsection (10) also applies if–

(a)   property is subject to a property freezing order made under section 245A, an interim receiving order made under section 246, a prohibitory property order made under section 255A or an interim administration order made under section 256,

(b)   a person acting as an insolvency practitioner incurs expenses which are not ones in respect of property subject to the order, and

(c)   the expenses are ones which (but for the effect of the order) might have been met by taking possession of and realising property subject to it.

432(10)   Whether or not he has seized or disposed of any property, he is entitled to payment of the expenses under section 280.

History
Section 432(1)(b), (8)(a) and (9)(a) amended by the Serious Organised Crime and Police Act 2005 s.109 and Sch.6 para.23 as from 1 January 2006. Section 432(7) amended (by the deletion of references to repealed sections) by the Serious Crime Act 2007 s.74(2) and Sch.8, as from 6 April 2008.

433   Meaning of insolvency practitioner

433(1)   This section applies for the purposes of section 432.

433(2)   A person acts as an insolvency practitioner if he so acts within the meaning given by section 388 of the 1986 Act or Article 3 of the 1989 Order; but this is subject to subsections (3) to (5).

433(3)   The expression "person acting as an insolvency practitioner" includes the official receiver acting as receiver or manager of the property concerned.

433(4)   In applying section 388 of the 1986 Act under subsection (2) above–

(a)   the reference in section 388(2)(a) to a permanent or interim trustee in sequestration must be taken to include a reference to a trustee in sequestration;

(b)   section 388(5) (which includes provision that nothing in the section applies to anything done by the official receiver or the Accountant in Bankruptcy) must be ignored.

433(5)   In applying Article 3 of the 1989 Order under subsection (2) above, paragraph (5) (which includes provision that nothing in the Article applies to anything done by the official receiver) must be ignored.

Interpretation

434   Interpretation

434(1)   The following paragraphs apply to references to Acts or Orders–

(a)   [...]

(b)   the 1914 Act is the Bankruptcy Act 1914 (c. 59);

(c)   [...]

(d)   the 1986 Act is the Insolvency Act 1986 (c. 45);

(e)   the 1989 Order is the Insolvency (Northern Ireland) Order 1989 (S.I. 1989/2405 (N.I. 19)).

(f)   the 2016 Act is the Bankruptcy (Scotland) Act 2016.

434(2)   An award of sequestration is made on the date of sequestration within the meaning of section 22(7) of the 2016 Act.

434(3)   This section applies for the purposes of this Part.

Companies (Audit, Investigations and Community Enterprise) Act 2004

(2004 Chapter 27)

[*28th October 2004*]

PART 2

COMMUNITY INTEREST COMPANIES

Requirements

31 Distribution of assets on winding up

31(1) [Distributions on winding up] Regulations may make provision for and in connection with the distribution, on the winding up of a community interest company, of any assets of the company which remain after satisfaction of the company's liabilities.

31(2) [Modification of enactments] The regulations may, in particular, amend or modify the operation of any enactment or instrument.

Supervision by Regulator

50 Petition for winding up

50(1) [Petition for winding up] The Regulator may present a petition for a community interest company to be wound up if the court is of the opinion that it is just and equitable that the company should be wound up.

50(2) [Non-application of s.50(1)] Subsection (1) does not apply if the company is already being wound up by the court.

50(3) [Insertion of s.124(4A) in 1986 Act] In section 124 of the Insolvency Act 1986 (c. 45) (application for winding up), after subsection (4) insert–

"**(4A)** A winding-up petition may be presented by the Regulator of Community Interest Companies in a case falling within section 50 of the Companies (Audit, Investigations and Community Enterprise) Act 2004."

51 Dissolution and striking off

51(1) [Restoration to the register] If a community interest company has been–

(a) dissolved, or

(b) struck off the register under section 1000 or 1001 of the Companies Act 2006, the Regulator may apply to the court under section 1029 of that Act for an order restoring the company's name to the register.

51(2)   [Omitted]

51(3)   [Copy of application for striking off to Regulator] If an application under section 1003 of the Companies Act 2006 (striking off on application by company) is made on behalf of a community interest company, section 1006 of the Companies Act 2006 (persons to be notified of application) is to be treated as also requiring a copy of the application to be given to the Regulator.

History

Section 51(3) amended by the Companies Act 2006 (Commencement No.2, Consequential Amendments, Transitional Provisions and Savings) Order 2007 (SI 2007/1093 (C. 49)) art.6(2) and Sch.4 para.17, as from 6 April 2007. Section 51(2) substituted, s.51(2) omitted and s.51(3) amended by the Companies Act 2006 (Consequential Amendments, Transitional Provisions and Savings) Order 2009 (SI 2009/1941) art.2(1) and Sch.1 para.234 as from 1 October 2009.

Pensions Act 2004

(2004 Chapter 35)

An Act to make provision relating to pensions and financial planning for retirement and provision relating to entitlement to bereavement payments, and for connected purposes.

[18th November 2004]

[**Note**: Changes made by the Enterprise and Regulatory Reform Act 2013 (Consequential Amendments) (Bankruptcy) and the Small Business, Enterprise and Employment Act 2015 (Consequential Amendments) Regulations 2016 (SI 2016/481) and the Deregulation Act 2015 and Small Business, Enterprise and Employment Act 2015 (Consequential Amendments) (Savings) Regulations 2017 (SI 2017/540) have been incorporated into the text. The provisions of Pt 2 of this Act are modified in their application to multi-employer pensions schemes by the Pension Protection Fund (Multi-employer Schemes) (Modification) Regulations 2005 (SI 2005/441), effective 6 April 2005.]

PART 2

THE BOARD OF THE PENSION PROTECTION FUND

CHAPTER 2

INFORMATION RELATING TO EMPLOYER'S INSOLVENCY ETC.

Insolvency events

120 Duty to notify insolvency events in respect of employers

120(1) This section applies where, in the case of an occupational pension scheme, an insolvency event occurs in relation to the employer.

120(2) The insolvency practitioner in relation to the employer must give a notice to that effect within the notification period to–

(a) the Board,

(b) the Regulator, and

(c) the trustees or managers of the scheme.

120(3) For the purposes of subsection (2) the "notification period" is the prescribed period beginning with the later of–

(a) the insolvency date, and

(b) the date the insolvency practitioner becomes aware of the existence of the scheme.

120(4) A notice under this section must be in such form and contain such information as may be prescribed.

121 Insolvency event, insolvency date and insolvency practitioner

121(1) In this Part each of the following expressions has the meaning given to it by this section–

"insolvency event"

"insolvency date"

"insolvency practitioner".

121(2) An insolvency event occurs in relation to an individual where–

(a) he is made bankrupt or sequestration of his estate has been awarded;

(b) the nominee in relation to a proposal for a voluntary arrangement under Part 8 of the Insolvency Act 1986 (c. 45) submits a report to the court under section 256(1) or 256A(3) of that Act which states that in his opinion the individual's creditors should consider the debtor's proposal;

(c) [...]

(d) he executes a trust deed for his creditors or enters into a composition contract;

(e) he has died and–

(i) an insolvency administration order is made in respect of his estate in accordance with an order under section 421 of the Insolvency Act 1986, or

(ii) a judicial factor appointed under section 11A of the Judicial Factors (Scotland) Act 1889 (c. 39) is required by that section to divide the individual's estate among his creditors.

121(3) An insolvency event occurs in relation to a company where–

(a) the nominee in relation to a proposal for a voluntary arrangement under Part 1 of the Insolvency Act 1986 submits a report to the court under section 2 of that Act (procedure where nominee is not the liquidator or administrator) which states that in his opinion the proposal should be considered by a meeting of the company and by the company's creditors;

(b) the directors of the company file (or in Scotland lodge) with the court documents and statements in accordance with paragraph 7(1) of Schedule A1 to that Act (moratorium where directors propose voluntary arrangement);

(c) an administrative receiver within the meaning of section 251 of that Act is appointed in relation to the company;

(d) the company enters administration within the meaning of paragraph 1(2)(b) of Schedule B1 to that Act;

(e) a resolution is passed for a voluntary winding up of the company without a declaration of solvency under section 89 of that Act;

(f) a winding up becomes a creditors' voluntary winding up under section 96 of that Act (conversion to creditors' voluntary winding up);

(g) an order for the winding up of the company is made by the court under Part 4 or 5 of that Act.

121(4)   An insolvency event occurs in relation to a partnership where–

(a)   an order for the winding up of the partnership is made by the court under any provision of the Insolvency Act 1986 (c. 45) (as applied by an order under section 420 of that Act (insolvent partnerships));

(b)   sequestration is awarded on the estate of the partnership under section 22 of the Bankruptcy (Scotland) Act 2016 or the partnership grants a trust deed for its creditors;

(c)   the nominee in relation to a proposal for a voluntary arrangement under Part 1 of the Insolvency Act 1986 (as applied by an order under section 420 of that Act) submits a report to the court under section 2 of that Act (procedure where nominee is not the liquidator or administrator) which states that in his opinion the proposal should be considered by a meeting of the members of the partnership and by the partnership's creditors;

(d)   the members of the partnership file with the court documents and statements in accordance with paragraph 7(1) of Schedule A1 to that Act (moratorium where directors propose voluntary arrangement) (as applied by an order under section 420 of that Act);

(e)   the partnership enters administration within the meaning of paragraph 1(2)(b) of Schedule B1 to that Act (as applied by an order under section 420 of that Act).

121(5)   An insolvency event also occurs in relation to a person where an event occurs which is a prescribed event in relation to such a person.

121(6)   Except as provided by subsections (2) to (5), for the purposes of this Part an event is not to be regarded as an insolvency event in relation to a person.

121(7)   The Secretary of State may by order amend subsection (4)(e) to make provision consequential upon any order under section 420 of the Insolvency Act 1986 (insolvent partnerships) applying the provisions of Part 2 of that Act (administration) as amended by the Enterprise Act 2002 (c. 40).

121(8)   "Insolvency date", in relation to an insolvency event, means the date on which the event occurs.

121(9)   "Insolvency practitioner", in relation to a person, means–

(a)   a person acting as an insolvency practitioner, in relation to that person, in accordance with section 388 of the Insolvency Act 1986;

(b)   in such circumstances as may be prescribed, a person of a prescribed description.

121(10)   In this section–

"company" means a company as defined in section 1(1) of the Companies Act 2006 or a company which may be wound up under Part 5 of the Insolvency Act 1986 (c. 45) (unregistered companies);

"person acting as an insolvency practitioner", in relation to a person, includes the official receiver acting as receiver or manager of any property of that person.

121(11)   In applying section 388 of the Insolvency Act 1986 under subsection (9) above–

(a)   [...]

(b)   section 388(5) (which includes provision that nothing in the section applies to anything done by the official receiver or the Accountant in Bankruptcy) must be ignored.

History
Section 121(4)(e) substituted by the Pension Protection Fund (Insolvent Partnerships) (Amendment of Insolvency Events) Order 2005 (SI 2005/2893) art.2, as from 10 November 2005. Section 121(2)(b), (3), (4)(c) amended and subs.(3)(f) substituted by the Deregulation Act 2015 and Small Business, Enterprise and Employment Act 2015 (Consequential Amendments) (Savings) Regulations 2017 (SI 2017/540) regs 1, 2, Sch.1 para.4 as from 6 April 2017.

122 Insolvency practitioner's duty to issue notices confirming status of scheme

122(1) This section applies where an insolvency event has occurred in relation to the employer in relation to an occupational pension scheme.

122(2) An insolvency practitioner in relation to the employer must–

(a) if he is able to confirm that a scheme rescue is not possible, issue a notice to that effect (a "scheme failure notice"), or

(b) if he is able to confirm that a scheme rescue has occurred, issue a notice to that effect (a "withdrawal notice").

122(3) Subsection (4) applies where–

(a) in prescribed circumstances, insolvency proceedings in relation to the employer are stayed or come to an end, or

(b) a prescribed event occurs.

122(4) If a person who was acting as an insolvency practitioner in relation to the employer immediately before this subsection applies has not been able to confirm in relation to the scheme–

(a) that a scheme rescue is not possible, or

(b) that a scheme rescue has occurred,

he must issue a notice to that effect.

122(5) For the purposes of this section–

(a) a person is able to confirm that a scheme rescue has occurred in relation to an occupational pension scheme if, and only if, he is able to confirm such matters as are prescribed for the purposes of this paragraph, and

(b) a person is able to confirm that a scheme rescue is not possible, in relation to such a scheme if, and only if, he is able to confirm such matters as are prescribed for the purposes of this paragraph.

122(6) Where an insolvency practitioner or former insolvency practitioner in relation to the employer issues a notice under this section, he must give a copy of that notice to–

(a) the Board,

(b) the Regulator, and

(c) the trustees or managers of the scheme.

122(7) A person must comply with an obligation imposed on him by subsection (2), (4) or (6) as soon as reasonably practicable.

122(8) Regulations may require notices issued under this section–

(a) to be in a prescribed form;

(b) to contain prescribed information.

123 Approval of notices issued under section 122

123(1) This section applies where the Board receives a notice under section 122(6) ("the section 122 notice").

123(2) The Board must determine whether to approve the section 122 notice.

123(3)   The Board must approve the section 122 notice if, and only if, it is satisfied–

(a)   that the insolvency practitioner or former insolvency practitioner who issued the notice was required to issue it under that section, and

(b)   that the notice complies with any requirements imposed by virtue of subsection (8) of that section.

123(4)   Where the Board makes a determination for the purposes of subsection (2), it must issue a determination notice and give a copy of that notice to–

(a)   the Regulator,

(b)   the trustees or managers of the scheme,

(c)   the insolvency practitioner or the former insolvency practitioner who issued the section 122 notice,

(d)   any insolvency practitioner in relation to the employer (who does not fall within paragraph (c)), and

(e)   if there is no insolvency practitioner in relation to the employer, the employer.

123(5)   In subsection (4) "determination notice" means a notice which is in the prescribed form and contains such information about the determination as may be prescribed.

Board's duties

124   Board's duty where there is a failure to comply with section 122

124(1)   This section applies where in relation to an occupational pension scheme–

(a)   the Board determines under section 123 not to approve a notice issued under section 122 by an insolvency practitioner or former insolvency practitioner in relation to the employer, or

(b)   an insolvency practitioner or former insolvency practitioner in relation to the employer fails to issue a notice under section 122 and the Board is satisfied that such a notice ought to have been issued under that section.

124(2)   The obligations on the insolvency practitioner or former insolvency practitioner imposed by subsections (2) and (4) of section 122 are to be treated as obligations imposed on the Board and the Board must accordingly issue a notice as required under that section.

124(3)   Subject to subsections (4) and (5), where a notice is issued under section 122 by the Board by virtue of this section, it has effect as if it were a notice issued under section 122 by an insolvency practitioner or, as the case may be, former insolvency practitioner in relation to the employer.

124(4)   Where a notice is issued under section 122 by virtue of this section, section 122(6) does not apply and the Board must, as soon as reasonably practicable, give a copy of the notice to–

(a)   the Regulator,

(b)   the trustees or managers of the scheme,

(c)   the insolvency practitioner or former insolvency practitioner mentioned in subsection (1),

(d)   any insolvency practitioner in relation to the employer (who does not fall within paragraph (c)), and

(e)   if there is no insolvency practitioner in relation to the employer, the employer.

124(5)   Where the Board–

(a)   is required to issue a notice under section 122 by virtue of this section, and

(b) is satisfied that the notice ought to have been issued at an earlier time,

it must specify that time in the notice and the notice is to have effect as if it had been issued at that time.

125 Binding notices confirming status of scheme

125(1) Subject to subsection (2), for the purposes of this Part, a notice issued under section 122 is not binding until–

(a) the Board issues a determination notice under section 123 approving the notice,

(b) the period within which the issue of the determination notice under that section may be reviewed by virtue of Chapter 6 has expired, and

(c) if the issue of the determination notice is so reviewed–

   (i)   the review and any reconsideration,

   (ii) any reference to the PPF Ombudsman in respect of the issue of the notice, and

   (iii) any appeal against his determination or directions,

has been finally disposed of and the determination notice has not been revoked, varied or substituted.

125(2) Where a notice is issued under section 122 by the Board by virtue of section 124, the notice is not binding until–

(a) the period within which the issue of the notice may be reviewed by virtue of Chapter 6 has expired, and

(b) if the issue of the notice is so reviewed–

   (i)   the review and any reconsideration,

   (ii) any reference to the PPF Ombudsman in respect of the issue of the notice, and

   (iii) any appeal against his determination or directions,

has been finally disposed of and the notice has not been revoked, varied or substituted.

125(3) Where a notice issued under section 122 becomes binding, the Board must as soon as reasonably practicable give a notice to that effect together with a copy of the binding notice to–

(a) the Regulator,

(b) the trustees or managers of the scheme,

(c) the insolvency practitioner or former insolvency practitioner who issued the notice under section 122 or, where that notice was issued by the Board by virtue of section 124, the insolvency practitioner or former insolvency practitioner mentioned in subsection (1) of that section,

(d) any insolvency practitioner in relation to the employer (who does not fall within paragraph (c)), and

(e) if there is no insolvency practitioner in relation to the employer, the employer.

125(4) A notice under subsection (3)–

(a) must be in the prescribed form and contain such information as may be prescribed, and

(b) where it is given in relation to a withdrawal notice issued under section 122(2)(b) which has become binding, must state the time from which the Board ceases to be involved with the scheme (see section 149).

Fraud Act 2006

(2006 Chapter 35)

An Act to make provision for, and in connection with, criminal liability for fraud and obtaining services dishonestly.

[8th November 2006]

[**Note**: Changes made by the Companies Act 2006 (Commencement No.3, Consequential Amendments, Transitional Provisions and Savings) Order 2007 (SI 2007/2194 (C. 84)) have been incorporated into the text.]

9   Participating in fraudulent business carried on by sole trader etc.

9(1)   A person is guilty of an offence if he is knowingly a party to the carrying on of a business to which this section applies.

9(2)   This section applies to a business which is carried on–

(a)   by a person who is outside the reach of section 993 of the Companies Act 2006 (offence of fraudulent trading), and

(b)   with intent to defraud creditors of any person or for any other fraudulent purpose.

9(3)   The following are within the reach of that section–

(a)   a company (as defined in section 1(1) of the Companies Act 2006);

(b)   a person to whom that section applies (with or without adaptations or modifications) as if the person were a company;

(c)   a person exempted from the application of that section.

9(4)   [Repealed]

9(5)   "Fraudulent purpose" has the same meaning as in that section.

9(6)   A person guilty of an offence under this section is liable–

(a)   on summary conviction, to imprisonment for a term not exceeding 12 months or to a fine not exceeding the statutory maximum (or to both);

(b)   on conviction on indictment, to imprisonment for a term not exceeding 10 years or to a fine (or to both).

9(7)   Subsection (6)(a) applies in relation to Northern Ireland as if the reference to 12 months were a reference to 6 months.

History
Section 9(2), (3), and (5) amended, and s.9(4) repealed, by the Companies Act 2006 (Commencement No.3, Consequential Amendments, Transitional Provisions and Savings) Order 2007 (SI 2007/2194 (C. 84)) art.10(1), (3) and Sch.4 para.111 and Sch.5, as from 1 October 2007.

Companies Act 2006

(2006 Chapter 46)

ARRANGEMENT OF SECTIONS

449

An Act to reform company law and restate the greater part of the enactments relating to companies; to make other provision relating to companies and other forms of business organisation; to make provision about directors' disqualification, business names, auditors and actuaries; to amend Part 9 of the Enterprise Act 2002; and for connected purposes.

[8th November 2006]

[Note: Changes made by the Companies (Mergers and Divisions of Public Companies) (Amendment) Regulations 2008 (SI 2008/690), by the Companies Act 2006 (Consequential Amendments etc.) Order 2008 (SI 2008/948), by the Companies Act 2006 (Consequential Amendments and Transitional Provisions) Order 2011 (SI 2011/1265), by the Companies (Reporting Requirements in Mergers and Divisions) Regulations 2011 (SI 2011/1606), by the Companies Act 2006 (Amendment of Part 25) Regulations 2013 (SI 2013/600), the Companies (Striking Off) (Electronic Communications) Order 2014 (SI 2014/1602) and SBEEA 2015 have been incorporated into the text. The following sections of CA 2006 apply to limited liability partnerships by virtue of the Limited Liability Partnerships (Application of Companies Act 2006) Regulations 2009 (SI 2009/1804) as from 1 October 2009 (subject to the modifications set out in those regulations and, in the case of ss.1012–1023, to the transitional provisions in the Companies Act 2006 and Limited Liability Partnerships (Transitional Provisions and Savings) (Amendment) Regulations 2009 (SI 2009/2476): ss.754, 860–892, 895–900, 993, 1000–1034.]

PART 10

A COMPANY'S DIRECTORS

CHAPTER 4

TRANSACTIONS WITH DIRECTORS REQUIRING APPROVAL OF MEMBERS

Substantial property transactions

190 Substantial property transactions: requirement of members' approval

190(1) [Requirement for members' approval] A company may not enter into an arrangement under which–

(a) a director of the company or of its holding company, or a person connected with such a director, acquires or is to acquire from the company (directly or indirectly) a substantial non-cash asset, or

(b) the company acquires or is to acquire a substantial non-cash asset (directly or indirectly) from such a director or a person so connected,

unless the arrangement has been approved by a resolution of the members of the company or is conditional on such approval being obtained.

For the meaning of "substantial non-cash asset" see section 191.

190(2) [Directors of company's holding company] If the director or connected person is a director of the company's holding company or a person connected with such a director, the arrangement must also have been approved by a resolution of the members of the holding company or be conditional on such approval being obtained.

190(3) [No liability for failure to obtain approval] A company shall not be subject to any liability by reason of a failure to obtain approval required by this section.

190(4) [Non-UK registered companies; wholly owned subsidiaries] No approval is required under this section on the part of the members of a body corporate that–

(a) is not a UK-registered company, or

(b) is a wholly-owned subsidiary of another body corporate.

190(5)   [Arrangements involving more than one non-cash asset] For the purposes of this section–

(a)   an arrangement involving more than one non-cash asset, or

(b)   an arrangement that is one of a series involving non-cash assets,

shall be treated as if they involved a non-cash asset of a value equal to the aggregate value of all the non-cash assets involved in the arrangement or, as the case may be, the series.

190(6)   [Disapplication of section] This section does not apply to a transaction so far as it relates–

(a)   to anything to which a director of a company is entitled under his service contract, or

(b)   to payment for loss of office as defined in section 215 (payments to which the requirements of Chapter 4 or 4A apply).

193   Exception in case of company in winding up or administration

193(1)   [Application of section] This section applies to a company–

(a)   that is being wound up (unless the winding up is a members' voluntary winding up), or

(b)   that is in administration within the meaning of Schedule B1 to the Insolvency Act 1986 (c. 45) or the Insolvency (Northern Ireland) Order 1989 (S.I. 1989/2405 (N.I. 19)).

193(2)   [Approval not required] Approval is not required under section 190 (requirement of members' approval for substantial property transactions)–

(a)   on the part of the members of a company to which this section applies, or

(b)   for an arrangement entered into by a company to which this section applies.

PART 19

DEBENTURES

Supplementary provisions

754   Priorities where debentures secured by floating charge

754(1)   [Application in England and Wales or Northern Ireland] This section applies where debentures of a company registered in England and Wales or Northern Ireland are secured by a charge that, as created, was a floating charge.

754(2)   [Priority of preferential creditors] If possession is taken, by or on behalf of the holders of the debentures, of any property comprised in or subject to the charge, and the company is not at that time in the course of being wound up, the company's preferential debts shall be paid out of assets coming to the hands of the persons taking possession in priority to any claims for principal or interest in respect of the debentures.

754(3)   ["Preferential debts", "the relevant date"] "Preferential debts" means the categories of debts listed in Schedule 6 to the Insolvency Act 1986 (c. 45) or Schedule 4 to the Insolvency (Northern Ireland) Order 1989 (S.I. 1989/2405 (N.I. 19)).

For the purposes of those Schedules "the relevant date" is the date of possession being taken as mentioned in subsection (2).

754(4)   [Recoupment of payment from company assets] Payments under this section shall be recouped, as far as may be, out of the assets of the company available for payment of general creditors.

PART 25

COMPANY CHARGES

[**Note**: the text which follows is that of the amended Pt 25, as inserted by the Companies Act 2006 (Amendment of Part 25) Regulations 2013 (SI 2013/600) reg.2 and Sch.1, as from 6 April 2013. The new Pt 25 regime for the registration of charges applies to limited liability partnerships in relation to charges created on or after 6 April 2013 (except that CA 2006 ss.859K, 859L and 859O apply also to charges created before that date): Limited Liability Partnerships (Application of Companies Act 2006) (Amendment) Regulations 2013 (SI 2013/618), amending SI 2009/1804.]

CHAPTER A1

REGISTRATION OF COMPANY CHARGES

Company charges

859A   Charges created by a company

859A(1)   [Application of s.859A] Subject to subsection (6), this section applies where a company creates a charge.

859A(2)   [Duty of registrar to register charge] The registrar must register the charge if, before the end of the period allowed for delivery, the company or any person interested in the charge delivers to the registrar for registration a section 859D statement of particulars.

859A(3)   [Where charge created or evidenced by an instrument] Where the charge is created or evidenced by an instrument, the registrar is required to register it only if a certified copy of the instrument is delivered to the registrar with the statement of particulars.

859A(4)   ["The period allowed for delivery"] "The period allowed for delivery" is 21 days beginning with the day after the date of creation of the charge (see section 859E), unless an order allowing an extended period is made under section 859F(3).

859A(5)   [Copy of order for extension of time] Where an order is made under section 859F(3) a copy of the order must be delivered to the registrar with the statement of particulars.

859A(6)   [Disapplication of s.859A] This section does not apply to–

(a)   a charge in favour of a landlord on a cash deposit given as a security in connection with the lease of land;

(b)   a charge created by a member of Lloyd's (within the meaning of the Lloyd's Act 1982) to secure its obligations in connection with its underwriting business at Lloyd's;

(c)   a charge excluded from the application of this section by or under any other Act.

859A(7)   ["Cash", "charge", "company"] In this Part–

"cash" includes foreign currency,

"charge" includes–

(a)   a mortgage;

(b)   a standard security, assignation in security, and any other right in security constituted under the law of Scotland, including any heritable security, but not including a pledge, and

"company" means a UK-registered company.

859B   Charge in series of debentures

859B(1)   [Application of s.859B] This section applies where–

  (a)   a company creates a series of debentures containing a charge, or giving a charge by reference to another instrument, and

  (b)   debenture holders of that series are entitled to the benefit of the charge pari passu.

859B(2)   [Duty of registrar to register charge] The registrar must register the charge if, before the end of the period allowed for delivery, the company or any person interested in the charge delivers to the registrar for registration, a section 859D statement of particulars which also contains the following–

  (a)   either–

     (i)   the name of each of the trustees for the debenture holders, or

     (ii)   where there are more than four such persons, the names of any four persons listed in the charge instrument as trustees for the debenture holders, and a statement that there are other such persons;

  (b)   the dates of the resolutions authorising the issue of the series;

  (c)   the date of the covering instrument (if any) by which the series is created or defined.

859B(3)   [Where charge created or evidenced by an instrument] Where the charge is created or evidenced by an instrument, the registrar is required to register it only if a certified copy of the instrument is delivered to the registrar with the statement of particulars.

859B(4)   [Where charge not created or evidenced by an instrument] Where the charge is not created or evidenced by an instrument, the registrar is required to register it only if a certified copy of one of the debentures in the series is delivered to the registrar with the statement of particulars.

859B(5)   [S.859D statement of particulars] For the purposes of this section a statement of particulars is taken to be a section 859D statement of particulars even if it does not contain the names of the debenture holders.

859B(6)   ["The period allowed for delivery"] "The period allowed for delivery" is–

  (a)   if there is a deed containing the charge, 21 days beginning with the day after the date on which the deed is executed;

  (b)   if there is no deed containing the charge, 21 days beginning with the day after the date on which the first debenture of the series is executed.

859B(7)   [Copy of order for extension of time] Where an order is made under section 859F(3) a copy of the order must be delivered to the registrar with the statement of particulars.

859B(8)   ["Deed"] In this section "deed" means–

  (a)   a deed governed by the law of England and Wales or Northern Ireland, or

  (b)   an instrument governed by a law other than the law of England and Wales or Northern Ireland which requires delivery under that law in order to take effect.

859C   Charges existing on property or undertaking acquired

859C(1)   [Application of s.859C] This section applies where a company acquires property or undertaking which is subject to a charge of a kind which would, if it had been created by the company after the acquisition of the property or undertaking, have been capable of being registered under section 859A.

859C(2) [Duty of registrar to register charge] The registrar must register the charge if the company or any person interested in the charge delivers to the registrar for registration a section 859D statement of particulars.

859C(3) [Where charge created or evidenced by an instrument] Where the charge is created or evidenced by an instrument, the registrar is required to register it only if a certified copy of the instrument is delivered to the registrar with the statement of particulars.

859D Particulars to be delivered to registrar

859D(1) ["Section 859D statement of particulars"] A statement of particulars relating to a charge created by a company is a "section 859D statement of particulars" if it contains the following particulars–

(a)   the registered name and number of the company;

(b)   the date of creation of the charge and (if the charge is one to which section 859C applies) the date of acquisition of the property or undertaking concerned;

(c)   where the charge is created or evidenced by an instrument, the particulars listed in subsection (2);

(d)   where the charge is not created or evidenced by an instrument, the particulars listed in subsection (3).

859D(2) [Particulars where charge created or evidenced by an instrument] The particulars referred to in subsection (1)(c) are–

(a)   any of the following–

(i)   the name of each of the persons in whose favour the charge has been created or of the security agents or trustees holding the charge for the benefit of one or more persons; or,

(ii)   where there are more than four such persons, security agents or trustees, the names of any four such persons, security agents or trustees listed in the charge instrument, and a statement that there are other such persons, security agents or trustees;

(b)   whether the instrument is expressed to contain a floating charge and, if so, whether it is expressed to cover all the property and undertaking of the company;

(c)   whether any of the terms of the charge prohibit or restrict the company from creating further security that will rank equally with or ahead of the charge;

(d)   whether (and if so, a short description of) any land, ship, aircraft or intellectual property that is registered or required to be registered in the United Kingdom, is subject to a charge (which is not a floating charge) or fixed security included in the instrument;

(e)   whether the instrument includes a charge (which is not a floating charge) or fixed security over–

(i)   any tangible or corporeal property, or

(ii)   any intangible or incorporeal property,

not described in paragraph (d).

859D(3) [Particulars where charge not created or evidenced by an instrument] The particulars referred to in subsection (1)(d) are–

(a)   a statement that there is no instrument creating or evidencing the charge;

(b)   the names of each of the persons in whose favour the charge has been created or the names of any security agents or trustees holding the charge for the benefit of one or more persons;

(c)   the nature of the charge;

(d)   a short description of the property or undertaking charged;

(e)   the obligations secured by the charge.

859D(4)   ["Fixed security"] In this section "fixed security" has the meaning given in section 486(1) of the Companies Act 1985.

859D(5)   ["Intellectual property"] In this section "intellectual property" includes–

(a)   any patent, trade mark, registered design, copyright or design right;

(b)   any licence under or in respect of any such right.

859E   Date of creation of charge

859E(1)   [Table for date of creation] For the purposes of this Part, a charge of the type described in column 1 of the Table below is taken to be created on the date given in relation to it in column 2 of that Table.

1. Type of charge	2. When charge created
Standard security	The date of its recording in the Register of Sasines or its registration in the Land Register of Scotland
Charge other than a standard security, where created or evidenced by an instrument	Where the instrument is a deed that has been executed and has immediate effect on execution and delivery, the date of delivery
	Where the instrument is a deed that has been executed and held in escrow, the date of delivery into escrow
	Where the instrument is a deed that has been executed and held as undelivered, the date of delivery
	Where the instrument is not a deed and has immediate effect on execution, the date of execution
	Where the instrument is not a deed and does not have immediate effect on execution, the date on which the instrument takes effect
Charge other than a standard security, where not created or evidenced by an instrument	The date on which the charge comes into effect.

859E(2)   [References in s.859E(1) Table to execution] Where a charge is created or evidenced by an instrument made between two or more parties, references in the Table in subsection (1) to execution are to execution by all the parties to the instrument whose execution is essential for the instrument to take effect as a charge.

859E(3) [Application of s.859E] This section applies for the purposes of this Chapter even if further forms, notices, registrations or other actions or proceedings are necessary to make the charge valid or effectual for any other purposes.

859E(4) [Date of creation of charge] For the purposes of this Chapter, the registrar is entitled without further enquiry to accept a charge as created on the date given as the date of creation of the charge in a section 859D statement of particulars.

859E(5) ["Deed"] In this section "deed" means–

(a) a deed governed by the law of England and Wales or Northern Ireland, or

(b) an instrument governed by a law other than the law of England and Wales or Northern Ireland which requires delivery under that law in order to take effect.

859E(6) [Delivery in relation to a deed] References in this section to delivery, in relation to a deed, include delivery as a deed where required.

859F Extension of period allowed for delivery

859F(1) [Satisfaction of court for extension] Subsection (3) applies if the court is satisfied that–

(a) neither the company nor any other person interested in the charge has delivered to the registrar the documents required under section 859A or (as the case may be) 859B before the end of the period allowed for delivery under the section concerned, and

(b) the requirement in subsection (2) is met.

859F(2) [Requirement for satisfaction of court] The requirement is–

(a) that the failure to deliver those documents–

  (i) was accidental or due to inadvertence or to some other sufficient cause, or

  (ii) is not of a nature to prejudice the position of creditors or shareholders of the company, or

(b) that on other grounds it is just and equitable to grant relief.

859F(3) [Power of court to extend period] The court may, on the application of the company or a person interested, and on such terms and conditions as seem to the court just and expedient, order that the period allowed for delivery be extended.

859G Personal information etc in certified copies

859G(1) [Information not required in certified copy] The following are not required to be included in a certified copy of an instrument or debenture delivered to the registrar for the purposes of any provision of this Chapter–

(a) personal information relating to an individual (other than the name of an individual);

(b) the number or other identifier of a bank or securities account of a company or individual;

(c) a signature.

859G(2) [Entitlement of registrar without enquiry] The registrar is entitled without further enquiry, to accept the certified copy of an instrument whether or not any of the information in subsection (1) is contained within the instrument.

Consequence of non-delivery

859H Consequence of failure to deliver charges

859H(1) [Application of s.859H] This section applies if–

(a) a company creates a charge to which section 859A or 859B applies, and

(b)   the documents required by section 859A or (as the case may be) 859B are not delivered to the registrar by the company or another person interested in the charge before the end of the relevant period allowed for delivery

859H(2)   ["The relevant period allowed for delivery"] "The relevant period allowed for delivery" is–

(a)   the period allowed for delivery under the section in question, or

(b)   if an order under section 859F(3) has been made, the period allowed by the order.

859H(3)   [Charge void against liquidator, administrator, creditor] Where this section applies, the charge is void (so far as any security on the company's property or undertaking is conferred by it) against–

(a)   a liquidator of the company,

(b)   an administrator of the company, and

(c)   a creditor of the company.

859H(4)   [Contract or obligation for repayment continues] Subsection (3) is without prejudice to any contract or obligation for repayment of the money secured by the charge; and when a charge becomes void under this section, the money secured by it immediately becomes payable.

The register

859I   Entries on the register

859I(1)   [Application of s.859I] This section applies where a charge is registered in accordance with a provision of this Chapter.

859I(2)   [Duty of registrar] The registrar must–

(a)   allocate to the charge a unique reference code and place a note in the register recording that reference code; and

(b)   include in the register any documents delivered under section 859A(3) or (5), 859B(3), (4) or (7), or 859C(3).

859I(3)   [Certificate of registration of charge] The registrar must give a certificate of the registration of the charge to the person who delivered to the registrar a section 859D statement of particulars relating to the charge.

859I(4)   [Contents of certificate] The certificate must state–

(a)   the registered name and number of the company in respect of which the charge was registered; and

(b)   the unique reference code allocated to the charge.

859I(5)   [Certificate to be signed or authenticated] The certificate must be signed by the registrar or authenticated by the registrar's official seal.

859I(6)   [Certificate conclusive evidence] In the case of registration under section 859A or 859B, the certificate is conclusive evidence that the documents required by the section concerned were delivered to the registrar before the end of the relevant period allowed for delivery.

859I(7)   ["The relevant period allowed for delivery"] "The relevant period allowed for delivery" is–

(a)   the period allowed for delivery under the section in question, or

(b)   if an order under section 859F(3) has been made, the period allowed by the order.

859J   **Company holding property or undertaking as trustee**

859J(1)   **[Statement to registrar]** Where a company is acting as trustee of property or undertaking which is the subject of a charge delivered for registration under this Chapter, the company or any person interested in the charge may deliver to the registrar a statement to that effect.

859J(2)   **[Contents of statement]** A statement delivered after the delivery for registration of the charge must include–

(a)   the registered name and number of the company; and

(b)   the unique reference code allocated to the charge.

859K   **Registration of enforcement of security**

859K(1)   **[Appointment of receiver or management]** Subsection (2) applies where a person–

(a)   obtains an order for the appointment of a receiver or manager of a company's property or undertaking, or

(b)   appoints such a receiver or manager under powers contained in an instrument.

859K(2)   **[Duty to give notice of appointment to registrar]** The person must, within 7 days of the order or of the appointment under those powers–

(a)   give notice to the registrar of that fact, and

(b)   if the order was obtained, or the appointment made, by virtue of a registered charge held by the person give the registrar a notice containing–

     (i)   in the case of a charge created before 6th April 2013, the information specified in subsection (4);

     (ii)   in the case of a charge created on or after 6th April 2013, the unique reference code allocated to the charge.

859K(3)   **[Duty to give notice of cessation of appointment to registrar]** Where a person appointed receiver or manager of a company's property or undertaking under powers contained in an instrument ceases to act as such a receiver or manager, the person must, on so ceasing–

(a)   give notice to the registrar of that fact, and

(b)   give the registrar a notice containing–

     (i)   in the case of a charge created before 6th April 2013, the information specified in subsection (4), or

     (ii)   in the case of a charge created on or after 6th April 2013, the unique reference code allocated to the charge.

859K(4)   **[Information in s.859K(2)(b)(i), (3)(b)(i) for charge created pre-6 April 2013]** The information referred to in subsections (2)(b)(i) and (3)(b)(i) is–

(a)   the date of the creation of the charge;

(b)   a description of the instrument (if any) creating or evidencing the charge;

(c)   short particulars of the property or undertaking charged

859K(5)   **[Notice in register]** The registrar must include in the register–

(a)   a fact of which notice is given under subsection (2)(a), and

(b)   a fact of which notice is given under subsection (3)(a).

859K(6) [Offence in default] A person who makes default in complying with the requirements of subsections (2) or (3) of this section commits an offence.

859K(7) [Penalty] A person guilty of an offence under this section is liable on summary conviction to a fine not exceeding level 3 on the standard scale and, for continued contravention, a daily default fine not exceeding one-tenth of level 3 on the standard scale.

859K(8)   [Application of s.859K] This section applies only to a receiver or manager appointed–

(a)   by a court in England and Wales or Northern Ireland, or

(b)   under an instrument governed by the law of England and Wales or Northern Ireland.

859K(9)   [Non-application to Scotland] This section does not apply to a receiver appointed under Chapter 2 of Part 3 of the Insolvency Act 1986 (receivers (Scotland)).

859L   Entries of satisfaction and release

859L(1)   [Application of s.859L(5)] Subsection (5) applies if the statement set out in subsection (2) and the particulars set out in subsection (4) are delivered to the registrar with respect to a registered charge.

859L(2)   [Statement] The statement referred to in subsection (1) is a statement to the effect that–

(a)   the debt for which the charge was given has been paid or satisfied in whole or in part, or

(b)   all or part of the property or undertaking charged–

    (i)   has been released from the charge, or

    (ii)   has ceased to form part of the company's property or undertaking.

859L(3)   [Statement in s.859L(2)(b)] Where a statement within subsection (2)(b) relates to part only of the property or undertaking charged, the statement must include a short description of that part.

859L(4)   [Required particulars in s.859L(1)] The particulars referred to in subsection (1) are–

(a)   the name and address of the person delivering the statement and an indication of their interest in the charge;

(b)   the registered name and number of the company that–

    (i)   created the charge (in a case within section 859A or 859B), or

    (ii)   acquired the property or undertaking subject to the charge (in a case within section 859C);

(c)   in respect of a charge created before 6th April 2013–

    (i)   the date of creation of the charge;

    (ii)   a description of the instrument (if any) by which the charge is created or evidenced;

    (iii)   short particulars of the property or undertaking charged;

(d)   in respect of a charge created on or after 6th April 2013, the unique reference code allocated to the charge.

859L(5)   [Statement in register] The registrar must include in the register–

(a)   a statement of satisfaction in whole or in part, or

(b)   a statement of the fact that all or part of the property or undertaking has been released from the charge or has ceased to form part of the company's property or undertaking (as the case may be).

859M   Rectification of register

859M(1)   [Application of s.859M(3)] Subsection (3) applies if the court is satisfied that–

   (a)   there has been an omission or mis-statement in any statement or notice delivered to the registrar in accordance with this Chapter, and

   (b)   the requirement in subsection (2) is met.

859M(2)   [Requirement to be satisfied] The requirement is that the court is satisfied–

   (a)   that the omission or mis-statement–

      (i)   was accidental or due to inadvertence or to some other sufficient cause, or

      (ii)   is not of a nature to prejudice the position of creditors or shareholders of the company, or

   (b)   that on other grounds it is just and equitable to grant relief.

859M(3)   [Court power of court to order rectification of register] The court may, on the application of the company or a person interested, and on such terms and conditions as seem to the court just and expedient, order that the omission or mis-statement be rectified.

859M(4)   [Copy of court order to be registered] A copy of the court's order must be sent by the applicant to the registrar for registration.

859N   Replacement of instrument or debenture

859N(1)   [Requirement for application of s.859N(2)] Subsection (2) applies if the court is satisfied that–

   (a)   a copy of an instrument or debenture delivered to the registrar under this Chapter contains material which could have been omitted under section 859G;

   (b)   the wrong instrument or debenture was delivered to the registrar; or

   (c)   the copy was defective.

859N(2)   [Court power to order replacement of copy] The court may, on the application of the company or a person interested, and on such terms and conditions as seem to the court just and expedient, order that the copy of the instrument or debenture be removed from the register and replaced.

859N(3)   [Copy of court order to be registered] A copy of the court's order must be sent by the applicant to the registrar for registration.

859O   Notification of addition to or amendment of charge

859O(1)   [Application of s.859O] This section applies where, after the creation of a charge, the charge is amended by adding or amending a term that–

   (a)   prohibits or restricts the creation of any fixed security or any other charge having priority over, or ranking pari passu with, the charge; or

   (b)   varies, or otherwise regulates the order of, the ranking of the charge in relation to any fixed security or any other charge.

859O(2)   [Delivery to registrar] Either the company that created the charge or the person taking the benefit of the charge (or another charge referred to in subsection (1)(b)) may deliver to the registrar for registration–

   (a)   a certified copy of the instrument effecting the amendment, variation or regulation, and

   (b)   a statement of the particulars set out in subsection (3).

859O(3) **[Required particulars in s.859O(2)(b) statement]** The particulars to be included in the statement are–

(a) the registered name and number of the company;

(b) in the case of a charge created before 6th April 2013–

(i) the date of creation of the charge;

(ii) a description of the instrument (if any) by which the charge was created or evidenced;

(iii) short particulars of the property or undertaking charged as set out when the charge was registered;

(c) in the case of a charge created on or after 6th April 2013, (where allocated) the unique reference code allocated to the charge.

859O(4) **[Application of Companies Act 1985 s.466]** Subsections (1) to (3) do not affect the continued application of section 466 of the Companies Act 1985.

859O(5) **["Fixed security"]** In this section "fixed security" has the meaning given in section 486(1) of the Companies Act 1985.

Companies' records and registers

859P **Companies to keep copies of instruments creating and amending charges**

859P(1) **[Duty of company]** A company must keep available for inspection a copy of every–

(a) instrument creating a charge capable of registration under this Chapter, and

(b) instrument effecting any variation or amendment of such a charge.

859P(2) **[Duty where series of debentures]** In the case of a charge contained in a series of uniform debentures, a copy of one of the debentures of the series is sufficient for the purposes of subsection (1)(a).

859P(3) **[Particulars to be available for inspection]** If the particulars referred to in section 859D(1) or the particulars of the property or undertaking charged are not contained in the instrument creating the charge, but are instead contained in other documents which are referred to in or otherwise incorporated into the instrument, then the company must also keep available for inspection a copy of those other documents.

859P(4) **[Copy of instrument creating charge]** It is sufficient for the purposes of subsection (1)(a) if the company keeps a copy of the instrument in the form delivered to the registrar under section 859A(3), 859B(3) or (4) or 859C(3).

859P(5) **[Translated copy available for inspection]** Where a translation has been delivered to the registrar in accordance with section 1105, the company must keep available for inspection a copy of the translation.

859Q **Instruments creating charges to be available for inspection**

859Q(1) **[Application of s.859Q]** This section applies to documents required to be kept available for inspection under section 859P (copies of instruments creating and amending charges).

859Q(2) **[Where documents to be available for inspection]** The documents must be kept available for inspection–

(a) at the company's registered office, or

(b) at a place specified in regulations under section 1136.

859Q(3) **[Notice to registrar]** The company must give notice to the registrar–

(a) of the place at which the documents are kept available for inspection, and

(b) of any change in that place,

unless they have at all times been kept at the company's registered office.

859Q(4) **[To whom inspection available]** The documents must be open to the inspection–

(a) of any creditor or member of the company, without charge, and

(b) of any other person, on payment of such fee as may be prescribed.

859Q(5) **[Default in compliance]** If default is made for 14 days in complying with subsection (3) or an inspection required under subsection (4) is refused, an offence is committed by–

(a) the company, and

(b) every officer of the company who is in default.

859Q(6) **[Penalty]** A person guilty of an offence under this section is liable on summary conviction to a fine not exceeding level 3 on the standard scale and, for continued contravention, a daily default fine not exceeding one-tenth of level 3 on the standard scale.

859Q(7) **[Where inspection refused]** If an inspection required under subsection (4) is refused the court may by order compel an immediate inspection.

859Q(8) **[Inspection by electronic means]** Where the company and a person wishing to carry out an inspection under subsection (4) agree, the inspection may be carried out by electronic means.

History
New Pt 25 Chs 1, 2 (ss.859A–859Q) inserted by the Companies Act 2006 (Amendment of Part 25) Regulations 2013 (SI 2003/600) reg.2 and Sch.1, as from 6 April 2013.

CHAPTER 3

POWERS OF THE SECRETARY OF STATE

893 Power to make provision for effect of registration in special register

893(1) **["Special register"]** In this section a "special register" means a register, other than the register, in which a charge to which Chapter A1 applies is required or authorised to be registered.

893(2) **[Power to make regulations for information-sharing arrangements]** The Secretary of State may by order make provision for facilitating the making of information-sharing arrangements between the person responsible for maintaining a special register ("the responsible person") and the registrar that meet the requirement in subsection (4).

"Information-sharing arrangements" are arrangements to share and make use of information held by the registrar or by the responsible person.

893(3) **[Power to make regulations for registration in special register]** If the Secretary of State is satisfied that appropriate information-sharing arrangements have been made, he may by order provide that–

(a) the registrar is authorised not to register a charge of a specified description under Chapter A1,

(b) a charge of a specified description that is registered in the special register within a specified period is to be treated as if it had been registered (and certified by the registrar as registered) in accordance with the requirements of Chapter A1, and

(c) the other provisions of Chapter A1 apply to a charge so treated with specified modifications.

893(4) **[Awareness of existence of charges in special register]** The information-sharing arrangements must ensure that persons inspecting the register–

(a) are made aware, in a manner appropriate to the inspection, of the existence of charges in the special register which are treated in accordance with provision so made, and

(b) are able to obtain information from the special register about any such charge.

893(5) **[Scope of regulations]** An order under this section may–

(a) modify any enactment or rule of law which would otherwise restrict or prevent the responsible person from entering into or giving effect to information-sharing arrangements,

(b) authorise the responsible person to require information to be provided to him for the purposes of the arrangements,

(c) make provision about–

(i) the charging by the responsible person of fees in connection with the arrangements and the destination of such fees (including provision modifying any enactment which would otherwise apply in relation to fees payable to the responsible person), and

(ii) the making of payments under the arrangements by the registrar to the responsible person,

(d) require the registrar to make copies of the arrangements available to the public (in hard copy or electronic form).

893(6) **["Specified"]** In this section "specified" means specified in an order under this section.

893(7) **[Description of charge]** A description of charge may be specified, in particular, by reference to one or more of the following–

(a) the type of company by which it is created,

(b) the form of charge which it is,

(c) the description of assets over which it is granted,

(d) the length of the period between the date of its registration in the special register and the date of its creation.

893(8) **[Registers maintained outside UK]** Provision may be made under this section relating to registers maintained under the law of a country or territory outside the United Kingdom.

893(9) **[Negative resolution procedure]** An order under this section is subject to negative resolution procedure.

History
Section 893(1), (3) and (4) amended by the Companies Act 2006 (Amendment of Part 25) Regulations 2013 (SI 2013/600) reg.2 and Sch.2 para.3 as from 6 April 2013.

894 General power to make amendments to this Part

894(1) **[Power to amend provisions]** The Secretary of State may by regulations under this section–

(a) amend this Part by altering, adding or repealing provisions,

(b) make consequential amendments or repeals in this Act or any other enactment (whether passed or made before or after this Act).

894(2)   [Affirmative resolution procedure] Regulations under this section are subject to affirmative resolution procedure.

PART 26

ARRANGEMENTS AND RECONSTRUCTIONS

Application of this Part

895   Application of this Part

895(1)   [Proposed compromise or arrangement between creditors or members] The provisions of this Part apply where a compromise or arrangement is proposed between a company and–

(a)   its creditors, or any class of them, or

(b)   its members, or any class of them.

895(2)   ["Arrangement", "company"] In this Part–

"arrangement" includes a reorganisation of the company's share capital by the consolidation of shares of different classes or by the division of shares into shares of different classes, or by both of those methods; and

"company"–

(a)   in section 900 (powers of court to facilitate reconstruction or amalgamation) means a company within the meaning of this Act, and

(b)   elsewhere in this Part means any company liable to be wound up under the Insolvency Act 1986 (c. 45) or the Insolvency (Northern Ireland) Order 1989 (S.I. 1989/2405 (N.I. 19)).

895(3)   [Part 26 subject to application of Pt 27] The provisions of this Part have effect subject to Part 27 (mergers and divisions of public companies) where that Part applies (see sections 902 and 903).

Meeting of creditors or members

896   Court order for holding of meeting

896(1)   [Power of court to order meeting on application] The court may, on an application under this section, order a meeting of the creditors or class of creditors, or of the members of the company or class of members (as the case may be), to be summoned in such manner as the court directs.

896(2)   [Who may make application] An application under this section may be made by–

(a)   the company,

(b)   any creditor or member of the company,

(c)   if the company is being wound up, the liquidator, or

(d)   if the company is in administration, the administrator.

896(3)   [Application of s.323 re corporate representation] Section 323 (representation of corporations at meetings) applies to a meeting of creditors under this section as to a meeting of the company (references to a member of the company being read as references to a creditor).

History
Section 896(2)(c) substituted and s.896(2)(d) and (3) inserted by the Companies Act 2006 (Consequential Amendments etc.) Order 2008 (SI 2008/948) Sch.1 para.249 as from 6 April 2008.

897 Statement to be circulated or made available

897(1)   [Explanatory statement with notice summoning meeting] Where a meeting is summoned under section 896–

(a)   every notice summoning the meeting that is sent to a creditor or member must be accompanied by a statement complying with this section, and

(b)   every notice summoning the meeting that is given by advertisement must either–

  (i)   include such a statement, or

  (ii)   state where and how creditors or members entitled to attend the meeting may obtain copies of such a statement.

897(2)   [Contents of statement] The statement must–

(a)   explain the effect of the compromise or arrangement, and

(b)   in particular, state–

  (i)   any material interests of the directors of the company (whether as directors or as members or as creditors of the company or otherwise), and

  (ii)   the effect on those interests of the compromise or arrangement, in so far as it is different from the effect on the like interests of other persons.

897(3)   [Where compromise or arrangement affects debenture holder rights] Where the compromise or arrangement affects the rights of debenture holders of the company, the statement must give the like explanation as respects the trustees of any deed for securing the issue of the debentures as it is required to give as respects the company's directors.

897(4)   [Explanatory statement free of charge] Where a notice given by advertisement states that copies of an explanatory statement can be obtained by creditors or members entitled to attend the meeting, every such creditor or member is entitled, on making application in the manner indicated by the notice, to be provided by the company with a copy of the statement free of charge.

897(5)   [Offence] If a company makes default in complying with any requirement of this section, an offence is committed by–

(a)   the company, and

(b)   every officer of the company who is in default.

This is subject to subsection (7) below.

897(6)   [Officers of the company re offence] For this purpose the following are treated as officers of the company–

(a)   a liquidator or administrator of the company, and

(b)   a trustee of a deed for securing the issue of debentures of the company.

897(7)   [Defence] A person is not guilty of an offence under this section if he shows that the default was due to the refusal of a director or trustee for debenture holders to supply the necessary particulars of his interests.

897(8) **[Penalty]** A person guilty of an offence under this section is liable–

(a) on conviction on indictment, to a fine;

(b) on summary conviction, to a fine not exceeding the statutory maximum.

898 Duty of directors and trustees to provide information

898(1) **[Notice of director or trustee re explanatory statement]** It is the duty of–

(a) any director of the company, and

(b) any trustee for its debenture holders,

to give notice to the company of such matters relating to himself as may be necessary for the purposes of section 897 (explanatory statement to be circulated or made available).

898(2) **[Offence]** Any person who makes default in complying with this section commits an offence.

898(3) **[Penalty]** A person guilty of an offence under this section is liable on summary conviction to a fine not exceeding level 3 on the standard scale.

Court sanction for compromise or arrangement

899 Court sanction for compromise or arrangement

899(1) [Majority required before sanction] If a majority in number representing 75% in value of the creditors or class of creditors or members or class of members (as the case may be), present and voting either in person or by proxy at the meeting summoned under section 896, agree a compromise or arrangement, the court may, on an application under this section, sanction the compromise or arrangement.

899(2) **[Who may apply to court for sanction]** An application under this section may be made by–

(a) the company,

(b) any creditor or member of the company,

(c) if the company is being wound up, the liquidator, or

(d) if the company is in administration, the administrator.

899(3) **[Who sanction binding on]** A compromise or arrangement sanctioned by the court is binding on–

(a) all creditors or the class of creditors or on the members or class of members (as the case may be), and

(b) the company or, in the case of a company in the course of being wound up, the liquidator and contributories of the company.

899(4) **[Court order to registrar]** The court's order has no effect until a copy of it has been delivered to the registrar.

899(5) **[Application of s.323 re corporate representation]** Section 323 (representation of corporations at meetings) applies to a meeting of creditors under this section as to a meeting of the company (references to a member of the company being read as references to a creditor).

History

Section 899(2)(c) substituted and s.899(2)(d) and (5) inserted by the Companies Act 2006 (Consequential Amendments etc.) Order 2008 (SI 2008/948) Sch.1 para.250 as from 6 April 2008. Section 899(3) amended by the Companies Act 2006 (Consequential Amendments and Transitional Provisions) Order 2011 (SI 2011/1265) art.28(3) as from 12 May 2011.

Reconstructions and amalgamations

900　Powers of court to facilitate reconstruction or amalgamation

900(1)　[Application to court] This section applies where application is made to the court under section 899 to sanction a compromise or arrangement and it is shown that–

(a)　the compromise or arrangement is proposed for the purposes of, or in connection with, a scheme for the reconstruction of any company or companies, or the amalgamation of any two or more companies, and

(b)　under the scheme the whole or any part of the undertaking or the property of any company concerned in the scheme ("a transferor company") is to be transferred to another company ("the transferee company").

900(2)　[Provision in court order] The court may, either by the order sanctioning the compromise or arrangement or by a subsequent order, make provision for all or any of the following matters–

(a)　the transfer to the transferee company of the whole or any part of the undertaking and of the property or liabilities of any transferor company;

(b)　the allotting or appropriation by the transferee company of any shares, debentures, policies or other like interests in that company which under the compromise or arrangement are to be allotted or appropriated by that company to or for any person;

(c)　the continuation by or against the transferee company of any legal proceedings pending by or against any transferor company;

(d)　the dissolution, without winding up, of any transferor company;

(e)　the provision to be made for any persons who, within such time and in such manner as the court directs, dissent from the compromise or arrangement;

(f)　such incidental, consequential and supplemental matters as are necessary to secure that the reconstruction or amalgamation is fully and effectively carried out.

900(3)　[Order for transfer of property or liabilities] If an order under this section provides for the transfer of property or liabilities–

(a)　the property is by virtue of the order transferred to, and vests in, the transferee company, and

(b)　the liabilities are, by virtue of the order, transferred to and become liabilities of that company.

900(4)　[Property to vest free of any charge] The property (if the order so directs) vests freed from any charge that is by virtue of the compromise or arrangement to cease to have effect.

900(5)　["Property", "liabilities"] In this section–

"property" includes property, rights and powers of every description; and

"liabilities" includes duties.

900(6)   [Copy of order to registrar] Every company in relation to which an order is made under this section must cause a copy of the order to be delivered to the registrar within seven days after its making.

900(7)   [Offence] If default is made in complying with subsection (6) an offence is committed by–

(a)   the company, and

(b)   every officer of the company who is in default.

900(8) [Penalty] A person guilty of an offence under subsection (7) is liable on summary conviction to a fine not exceeding level 3 on the standard scale and, for continued contravention, a daily default fine not exceeding one-tenth of level 3 on the standard scale.

Obligations of company with respect to articles etc

901   Obligations of company with respect to articles etc

901(1)   [Application of s.901] This section applies–

(a)   to any order under section 899 (order sanctioning compromise or arrangement), and

(b)   to any order under section 900 (order facilitating reconstruction or amalgamation) that alters the company's constitution.

901(2)   [Copy of amended articles or resolution to registrar] If the order amends–

(a)   the company's articles, or

(b)   any resolution or agreement to which Chapter 3 of Part 3 applies (resolution or agreement affecting a company's constitution),

the copy of the order delivered to the registrar by the company under section 899(4) or section 900(6) must be accompanied by a copy of the company's articles, or the resolution or agreement in question, as amended.

901(3)   [Subsequent issue of articles accompanied by order] Every copy of the company's articles issued by the company after the order is made must be accompanied by a copy of the order, unless the effect of the order has been incorporated into the articles by amendment.

901(4)   [References to effect or order, articles] In this section–

(a)   references to the effect of the order include the effect of the compromise or arrangement to which the order relates; and

(b)   in the case of a company not having articles, references to its articles shall be read as references to the instrument constituting the company or defining its constitution.

901(5)   [Offence] If a company makes default in complying with this section an offence is committed by–

(a)   the company, and

(b)   every officer of the company who is in default.

901(6)   [Penalty] A person guilty of an offence under this section is liable on summary conviction to a fine not exceeding level 3 on the standard scale.

PART 27

MERGERS AND DIVISIONS OF PUBLIC COMPANIES

CHAPTER 1

INTRODUCTORY

902   Application of this Part

902(1)   **[Compromise for reconstruction involving merger or division]** This Part applies where–

(a) a compromise or arrangement is proposed between a public company and–

    (i) its creditors or any class of them, or

    (ii) its members or any class of them,

for the purposes of, or in connection with, a scheme for the reconstruction of any company or companies or the amalgamation of any two or more companies,

(b) the scheme involves–

    (i) a merger (as defined in section 904), or

    (ii) a division (as defined in section 919), and

(c) the consideration for the transfer (or each of the transfers) envisaged is to be shares in the transferee company (or one or more of the transferee companies) receivable by members of the transferor company (or transferor companies), with or without any cash payment to members.

902(2)   **["New company", "existing company"]** In this Part–

(a) a "new company" means a company formed for the purposes of, or in connection with, the scheme, and

(b) an "existing company" means a company other than one formed for the purposes of, or in connection with, the scheme.

902(3)   **[No application of Pt 27 in winding up]** This Part does not apply where the company in respect of which the compromise or arrangement is proposed is being wound up.

903   Relationship of this Part to Part 26

903(1)   **[No sanction under Pt 26 unless Pt 27 complied with]** The court must not sanction the compromise or arrangement under Part 26 (arrangements and reconstructions) unless the relevant requirements of this Part have been complied with.

903(2)   **[Requirements applicable to merger]** The requirements applicable to a merger are specified in sections 905 to 914.

Certain of those requirements, and certain general requirements of Part 26, are modified or excluded by the provisions of sections 915 to 918A.

903(3)   **[Requirements applicable to decision]** The requirements applicable to a division are specified in sections 920 to 930.

Certain of those requirements, and certain general requirements of Part 26, are modified or excluded by the provisions of sections 931 to 934.

History

Section 903(2) amended by the Companies (Reporting Requirements in Mergers and Divisions) Regulations 2011 (SI 2011/1606) reg.4 as from 1 August 2011.

CHAPTER 2

MERGER

Introductory

904   Mergers and merging companies

904(1)   [Requirements under the scheme] The scheme involves a merger where under the scheme–

   (a)   the undertaking, property and liabilities of one or more public companies, including the company in respect of which the compromise or arrangement is proposed, are to be transferred to another existing public company (a "merger by absorption"), or

   (b)   the undertaking, property and liabilities of two or more public companies, including the company in respect of which the compromise or arrangement is proposed, are to be transferred to a new company, whether or not a public company, (a "merger by formation of a new company").

904(2)   ["The merging companies"] References in this Part to "the merging companies" are–

   (a)   in relation to a merger by absorption, to the transferor and transferee companies;

   (b)   in relation to a merger by formation of a new company, to the transferor companies.

Requirements applicable to merger

905   Draft terms of scheme (merger)

905(1)   [Draft adopted by directors of merging companies] A draft of the proposed terms of the scheme must be drawn up and adopted by the directors of the merging companies.

905(2)   [Particulars of draft terms] The draft terms must give particulars of at least the following matters–

   (a)   in respect of each transferor company and the transferee company–

      (i)   its name,

      (ii)   the address of its registered office, and

      (iii)   whether it is a company limited by shares or a company limited by guarantee and having a share capital;

   (b)   the number of shares in the transferee company to be allotted to members of a transferor company for a given number of their shares (the "share exchange ratio") and the amount of any cash payment;

   (c)   the terms relating to the allotment of shares in the transferee company;

   (d)   the date from which the holding of shares in the transferee company will entitle the holders to participate in profits, and any special conditions affecting that entitlement;

   (e)   the date from which the transactions of a transferor company are to be treated for accounting purposes as being those of the transferee company;

(f) any rights or restrictions attaching to shares or other securities in the transferee company to be allotted under the scheme to the holders of shares or other securities in a transferor company to which any special rights or restrictions attach, or the measures proposed concerning them;

(g) any amount of benefit paid or given or intended to be paid or given–

(i) to any of the experts referred to in section 909 (expert's report), or

(ii) to any director of a merging company,

and the consideration for the payment of benefit.

905(3) **[Requirements in s.905(2)(b), (c), (d) not required under s.915]** The requirements in subsection (2)(b), (c) and (d) are subject to section 915 (circumstances in which certain particulars not required).

906 Publication of draft terms by registrar (merger)

906(1) **[Copy draft terms to registrar]** The directors of each of the merging companies must deliver a copy of the draft terms to the registrar.

906(2) **[Registrar to publish receipt in Gazette]** The registrar must publish in the Gazette notice of receipt by him from that company of a copy of the draft terms.

906(3) **[Time limit for publication in Gazette]** That notice must be published at least one month before the date of any meeting of that company summoned for the purpose of approving the scheme.

906(4) **[Requirements subject to s.906A]** The requirements in this section are subject to section 906A (publication of draft terms on company website).

History
Heading amended and s.906(4) inserted by the Companies (Reporting Requirements in Mergers and Divisions) Regulations 2011 (SI 2011/1606) reg.5 as from 1 August 2011.

906A Publication of draft terms on company website (merger)

906A(1) **[When s.906 not applicable]** Section 906 does not apply in respect of a company if the conditions in subsections (2) to (6) are met.

906A(2) **[First condition: draft terms on website]** The first condition is that the draft terms are made available on a website which–

(a) is maintained by or on behalf of the company, and

(b) identifies the company.

906A(3) **[Second condition: availability free]** The second condition is that neither access to the draft terms on the website nor the supply of a hard copy of them from the website is conditional on payment of a fee or otherwise restricted.

906A(4) **[Third condition: notice to registrar of website]** The third condition is that the directors of the company deliver to the registrar a notice giving details of the website.

906A(5) **[Fourth condition: gazetting]** The fourth condition is that the registrar publishes the notice in the Gazette at least one month before the date of any meeting of the company summoned for the purpose of approving the scheme.

906A(6) **[Fifth condition: minimum period on website]** The fifth condition is that the draft terms remain available on the website throughout the period beginning one month before, and ending on, the date of any such meeting.

History
Section 906A inserted by the Companies (Reporting Requirements in Mergers and Divisions) Regulations 2011 (SI 2011/1606) reg.6 as from 1 August 2011.

907   Approval of members of merging companies

907(1)   **[Requisite majority]** The scheme must be approved by a majority in number, representing 75% in value, of each class of members of each of the merging companies, present and voting either in person or by proxy at a meeting.

907(2)   **[Approval subject to ss.916, 917, 918]** This requirement is subject to sections 916, 917 and 918 (circumstances in which meetings of members not required).

908   Directors' explanatory report (merger)

908(1)   **[Duty of directors]** The directors of each of the merging companies must draw up and adopt a report.

908(2)   **[Contents of report]** The report must consist of–

(a)   the statement required by section 897 (statement explaining effect of compromise or arrangement), and

(b)   insofar as that statement does not deal with the following matters, a further statement–

     (i)   setting out the legal and economic grounds for the draft terms, and in particular for the share exchange ratio, and

     (ii)   specifying any special valuation difficulties.

908(3)   **[Requirement subject to ss.915, 915A, 918A]** The requirement in this section is subject to section 915 (circumstances in which reports not required), section 915A (other circumstances in which reports and inspection not required) and section 918A (agreement to dispense with reports etc).

History
Section 908(3) amended by the Companies (Reporting Requirements in Mergers and Divisions) Regulations 2011 (SI 2011/1606) reg.7 as from 1 August 2011.

909   Expert's report (merger)

909(1)   **[Requirement for expert's report]** An expert's report must be drawn up on behalf of each of the merging companies.

909(2)   **[Report on draft terms]** The report required is a written report on the draft terms to the members of the company.

909(3)   **[Single report by joint expert]** The court may on the joint application of all the merging companies approve the appointment of a joint expert to draw up a single report on behalf of all those companies.

If no such appointment is made, there must be a separate expert's report to the members of each merging company drawn up by a separate expert appointed on behalf of that company.

909(4)   **[The expert]** The expert must be a person who–

(a)   is eligible for appointment as a statutory auditor (see section 1212), and

(b)   meets the independence requirement in section 936.

909(5)   **[Contents of expert's report]** The expert's report must–

(a)   indicate the method or methods used to arrive at the share exchange ratio;

(b) give an opinion as to whether the method or methods used are reasonable in all the circumstances of the case, indicate the values arrived at using each such method and (if there is more than one method) give an opinion on the relative importance attributed to such methods in arriving at the value decided on;

(c) describe any special valuation difficulties that have arisen;

(d) state whether in the expert's opinion the share exchange ratio is reasonable; and

(e) in the case of a valuation made by a person other than himself (see section 935), state that it appeared to him reasonable to arrange for it to be so made or to accept a valuation so made.

909(6) **[Rights of expert to documents and information]** The expert (or each of them) has–

(a) the right of access to all such documents of all the merging companies, and

(b) the right to require from the companies' officers all such information,

as he thinks necessary for the purposes of making his report.

909(7) **[Requirement for report subject to ss.915, 915A, 918A]** The requirement in this section is subject to section 915 (circumstances in which reports not required), section 915A (other circumstances in which reports and inspection not required) and section 918A (agreement to dispense with expert's report).

History
Section 909(7) amended by the Companies (Mergers and Divisions of Public Companies) (Amendment) Regulations 2008 (SI 2008/690) reg.2 as from 6 April 2008 and further amended by the Companies (Reporting Requirements in Mergers and Divisions) Regulations 2011 (SI 2011/1606) reg.8 as from 1 August 2011.

910 Supplementary accounting statement (merger)

910(1) **[Application of section]** This section applies if the last annual accounts of any of the merging companies relate to a financial year ending before–

(a) the date seven months before the first meeting of the company summoned for the purposes of approving the scheme, or

(b) if no meeting of the company is required (by virtue of any of sections 916 to 918), the date six months before the directors of the company adopt the draft terms of the scheme.

910(1A) **[Half-yearly financial report not made public]** If the company has not made public a half-yearly financial report relating to a period ending on or after the date mentioned in subsection (1), the directors of the company must prepare a supplementary accounting statement.

910(2) **[Statement to consist of balance sheet]** That statement must consist of–

(a) a balance sheet dealing with the state of affairs of the company as at a date not more than three months before the draft terms were adopted by the directors, and

(b) where the company would be required under section 399 to prepare group accounts if that date were the last day of a financial year, a consolidated balance sheet dealing with the state of affairs of the company and the undertakings that would be included in such a consolidation.

910(3) **[Requirements as to balance sheet]** The requirements of this Act (and where relevant Article 4 of the IAS Regulation) as to the balance sheet forming part of a company's annual accounts, and the matters to be included in notes to it, apply to the balance sheet required for an accounting statement under this section, with such modifications as are necessary by reason of its being prepared otherwise than as at the last day of a financial year.

910(4)   **[Signing and approval of balance sheet]** The provisions of section 414 as to the approval and signing of accounts apply to the balance sheet required for an accounting statement under this section.

910(5)   **["Half-yearly financial report"]** In this section "half-yearly financial report" means a report of that description required to be made public by rules under section 89A of the Financial Services and Markets Act 2000 (transparency rules).

910(6)   **[Section 910 requirement subject to ss.915A, 918A]** The requirement in this section is subject to section 915A (other circumstances in which reports and inspection not required) and section 918A (agreement to dispense with reports etc).

History
Section 910(1) amended and s.910(1A), (5), (6) inserted by the Companies (Reporting Requirements in Mergers and Divisions) Regulations 2011 (SI 2011/1606) reg.9 as from 1 August 2011.

911   Inspection of documents (merger)

911(1)   **[Rights of members]** The members of each of the merging companies must be able, during the period specified below–

   (a)   to inspect at the registered office of that company copies of the documents listed below relating to that company and every other merging company, and

   (b)   to obtain copies of those documents or any part of them on request free of charge.

911(2)   **[Specified period]** The period referred to above is the period–

   (a)   beginning one month before, and

   (b)   ending on the date of,

the first meeting of the members, or any class of members, of the company for the purposes of approving the scheme.

911(3)   **[Kind of documents]** The documents referred to above are–

   (a)   the draft terms;

   (b)   the directors' explanatory report;

   (c)   the expert's report;

   (d)   the company's annual accounts and reports for the last three financial years ending on or before the first meeting of the members, or any class of members, of the company summoned for the purposes of approving the scheme;

   (e)   any supplementary accounting statement required by section 910; and

   (f)   if no statement is required by section 910 because the company has made public a recent half-yearly financial report (see subsection (1A) of that section), that report.

911(3A)   **[Inspection at registered office subject to s.911A(1)]** The requirement in subsection (1)(a) is subject to section 911A(1) (publication of documents on company website).

911(4)   **[Requirements of s.311(3)(b), (c) subject to s.915]** The requirements of subsection (3)(b) and (c) are subject to section 915 (circumstances in which reports not required) and section 918A (agreement to dispense with reports etc).

911(5)   **[No right to free hard copy under s.1145]** Section 1145 (right to hard copy) does not apply to a document sent or supplied in accordance with subsection (1)(b) to a member who has consented to information being sent or supplied by the company by electronic means and has not revoked that consent.

911(6) **[Website communications not applicable re s.911(1)(b)]** Part 4 of Schedule 5 (communications by means of a website) does not apply for the purposes of subsection (1)(b) (but see section 911A(5)).

911(7) **[Inspection requirements subject to s.915A]** The requirements in this section are subject to section 915A (other circumstances in which reports and inspection not required).

History

Section 911(3), (4) amended and s.911(3A), (5)–(7) inserted by the Companies (Reporting Requirements in Mergers and Divisions) Regulations 2011 (SI 2011/1606) reg.10 as from 1 August 2011.

911A **Publication of documents on company website (merger)**

911A(1) **[When inspection of documents at registered office not applicable]** Section 911(1)(a) does not apply to a document if the conditions in subsections (2) to (4) are met in relation to that document.

This is subject to subsection (6).

911A(2) **[First condition: availability on website]** The first condition is that the document is made available on a website which–

(a) is maintained by or on behalf of the company, and

(b) identifies the company.

911A(3) **[Second condition: no fee]** The second condition is that access to the document on the website is not conditional on payment of a fee or otherwise restricted.

911A(4) **[Third condition: minimum period of availability]** The third condition is that the document remains available on the website throughout the period beginning one month before, and ending on, the date of any meeting of the company summoned for the purpose of approving the scheme.

911A(5) **[Obtaining copy of documents under s.911A(2)–(4) conditions]** A person is able to obtain a copy of a document as required by section 911(1)(b) if–

(a) the conditions in subsections (2) and (3) are met in relation to that document, and

(b) the person is able, throughout the period specified in subsection (4)–

(i) to retain a copy of the document as made available on the website, and

(ii) to produce a hard copy of it.

911A(6) **[Continuing right of inspection]** Where members of a company are able to obtain copies of a document only as mentioned in subsection (5), section 911(1)(a) applies to that document even if the conditions in subsections (2) to (4) are met.

History

Section 911A inserted by the Companies (Reporting Requirements in Mergers and Divisions) Regulations 2011 (SI 2011/1606) reg.11 as from 1 August 2011.

911B **Report on material changes of assets of merging companies**

911B(1) **[Duty of merging companies' directors to report]** The directors of each of the merging companies must report–

(a) to every meeting of the members, or any class of members, of that company summoned for the purpose of agreeing to the scheme, and

(b) to the directors of every other merging company,

any material changes in the property and liabilities of that company between the date when the draft terms were adopted and the date of the meeting in question.

911B(2) **[Duty of other merging companies' directors to report]** The directors of each of the other merging companies must in turn–

  (a)   report those matters to every meeting of the members, or any class of members, of that company summoned for the purpose of agreeing to the scheme, or

  (b)   send a report of those matters to every member entitled to receive notice of such a meeting.

911B(3) **[Duty subject to ss.915A and 918A]** The requirement in this section is subject to section 915A (other circumstances in which reports and inspection not required) and section 918A (agreement to dispense with reports etc).

History
Section 911B inserted by the Companies (Reporting Requirements in Mergers and Divisions) Regulations 2011 (SI 2011/1606) reg.12 as from 1 August 2011.

912   Approval of articles of new transferee company (merger)

912   In the case of a merger by formation of a new company, the articles of the transferee company, or a draft of them, must be approved by ordinary resolution of each of the transferor companies.

History
Section 912 amended by the Companies (Reporting Requirements in Mergers and Divisions) Regulations 2011 (SI 2011/1606) reg.13 as from 1 August 2011.

913   Protection of holders of securities to which special rights attached (merger)

913(1) **[Scheme to provide]** The scheme must provide that where any securities of a transferor company (other than shares) to which special rights are attached are held by a person otherwise than as a member or creditor of the company, that person is to receive rights in the transferee company of equivalent value.

913(2) **[Non-application of s.913(1)]** Subsection (1) does not apply if–

  (a)   the holder has agreed otherwise, or

  (b)   the holder is, or under the scheme is to be, entitled to have the securities purchased by the transferee company on terms that the court considers reasonable.

914   No allotment of shares to transferor company or transferee company (merger)

914   The scheme must not provide for any shares in the transferee company to be allotted to–

  (a)   a transferor company (or its nominee) in respect of shares in the transferor company held by the transferor company itself (or its nominee); or

  (b)   the transferee company (or its nominee) in respect of shares in a transferor company held by the transferee company (or its nominee).

History
Section 914 substituted by the Companies (Cross-Border Mergers and Divisions of Public Companies) (Amendment) Regulations 2008 (SI 2008/690) reg.3 as from 6 April 2008.

Exceptions where shares of transferor company held by transferee company

915   Circumstances in which certain particulars and reports not required (merger)

915(1) [Application of s.915] This section applies in the case of a merger by absorption where all of the relevant securities of the transferor company (or, if there is more than one transferor company, of each of them) are held by or on behalf of the transferee company.

915(2) [Draft terms] The draft terms of the scheme need not give the particulars mentioned in section 905(2)(b), (c) or (d) (particulars relating to allotment of shares to members of transferor company).

915(3) [Circulation of explanatory statement] Section 897 (explanatory statement to be circulated or made available) does not apply.

915(4) [Directors' explanatory report, expert's report] The requirements of the following sections do not apply–

section 908 (directors' explanatory report),

section 909 (expert's report).

915(5) [Inspection of certain reports subject to ss.915 and 918A] The requirements of section 911 (inspection of documents) so far as relating to any document required to be drawn up under the provisions mentioned in subsection (4) above do not apply.

915(6) ["Relevant securities"] In this section "relevant securities", in relation to a company, means shares or other securities carrying the right to vote at general meetings of the company.

History
Section 915(5) amended by the Companies Act 2006 (Consequential Amendments and Transitional Provisions) Order 2011 (SI 2011/1265) art.28(4) as from 12 May 2011.

915A   Other circumstances in which reports and inspection not required (merger)

915A(1) [Applicability of s.915A in merger by absorption] This section applies in the case of a merger by absorption where 90% or more (but not all) of the relevant securities of the transferor company (or, if there is more than one transferor company, of each of them) are held by or on behalf of the transferee company.

915A(2) [Disapplication of ss.908, 909, 910, 911, 911B requirements] If the conditions in subsections (3) and (4) are met, the requirements of the following sections do not apply–

(a)   section 908 (directors' explanatory report),

(b)   section 909 (expert's report),

(c)   section 910 (supplementary accounting statement),

(d)   section 911 (inspection of documents), and

(e)   section 911B (report on material changes of assets of merging company).

915A(3) [First condition: right to require acquisition of securities] The first condition is that the scheme provides that every other holder of relevant securities has the right to require the transferee company to acquire those securities.

915A(4) [Second condition: consideration to be fair and reasonable] The second condition is that, if a holder of securities exercises that right, the consideration to be given for those securities is fair and reasonable.

915A(5) [Power of court to determine consideration for securities] The powers of the court under section 900(2) (power to facilitate reconstruction or amalgamation) include the power to determine, or make provision for the determination of, the consideration to be given for securities acquired under this section.

915A(6) ["Other holder", "relevant securities"] In this section–

"other holder" means a person who holds securities of the transferor company otherwise than on behalf of the transferee company (and does not include the transferee company itself);

"relevant securities", in relation to a company, means shares or other securities carrying the right to vote at general meetings of the company.

History

Section 915A inserted by the Companies (Reporting Requirements in Mergers and Divisions) Regulations 2011 (SI 2011/1606) reg.14 as from 1 August 2011.

916   Circumstances in which meeting of members of transferee company not required (merger)

916(1)   [Application of s.916] This section applies in the case of a merger by absorption where 90% or more (but not all) of the relevant securities of the transferor company (or, if there is more than one transferor company, of each of them) are held by or on behalf of the transferee company.

916(2)   [Court satisfied conditions complied with] It is not necessary for the scheme to be approved at a meeting of the members, or any class of members, of the transferee company if the court is satisfied that the following conditions have been complied with.

916(3)   First condition: s.916(3A), (3B) satisfied] The first condition is that either subsection (3A) or subsection (3B) is satisfied.

916(3A)   [Registrar's publication of notice of receipt of draft terms] This subsection is satisfied if publication of notice of receipt of the draft terms by the registrar took place in respect of the transferee company at least one month before the date of the first meeting of members, or any class of members, of the transferor company summoned for the purpose of agreeing to the scheme.

916(3B)   [Publication of draft terms on website etc.] This subsection is satisfied if–

(a)   the conditions in section 906A(2) to (4) are met in respect of the transferee company,

(b)   the registrar published the notice mentioned in subsection (4) of that section in the Gazette at least one month before the date of the first meeting of members, or any class of members, of the transferor company summoned for the purpose of agreeing to the scheme, and

(c)   the draft terms remained available on the website throughout the period beginning one month before, and ending on, that date.

916(4)   [Second condition: s.916(4A), (4B) satisfied] The second condition is that subsection (4A) or (4B) is satisfied for each of the documents listed in the applicable paragraphs of section 911(3)(a) to (f) relating to the transferee company and the transferor company (or, if there is more than one transferor company, each of them).

916(4A)   [Inspection of document at transferee's registered office] This subsection is satisfied for a document if the members of the transferee company were able during the period beginning one month before, and ending on, the date mentioned in subsection (3A) to inspect that document at the registered office of that company.

916(4B)   [Document available on website free of charge] This subsection is satisfied for a document if–

(a)   the document is made available on a website which is maintained by or on behalf of the transferee company and identifies the company,

(b)   access to the document on the website is not conditional on the payment of a fee or otherwise restricted, and

(c)   the document remains available on the website throughout the period beginning one month before, and ending on, the date mentioned in subsection (3A).

916(4C)   [Third condition: minimum period of free availability] The third condition is that the members of the transferee company were able to obtain copies of the documents mentioned in subsection

(4), or any part of those documents, on request and free of charge, throughout the period beginning one month before, and ending on, the date mentioned in subsection (3A).

916(4D)   **[Application of s.911A(5) on website for s.916(4C)]** For the purposes of subsection (4C)–

  (a)   section 911A(5) applies as it applies for the purposes of section 911(1)(b), and

  (b)   Part 4 of Schedule 5 (communications by means of a website) does not apply.

916(5)   **[Fourth condition: no minority requisition of meeting]** The fourth condition is that–

  (a)   one or more members of the transferee company, who together held not less than 5% of the paid-up capital of the company which carried the right to vote at general meetings of the company (excluding any shares in the company held as treasury shares) would have been able, during that period, to require a meeting of each class of members to be called for the purpose of deciding whether or not to agree to the scheme, and

  (b)   no such requirement was made.

916(6)   **["Relevant securities"]** In this section "relevant securities", in relation to a company, means shares or other securities carrying the right to vote at general meetings of the company.

History
Section 916(3)–(4D) substituted and s.916(5) amended by the Companies (Reporting Requirements in Mergers and Divisions) Regulations 2011 (SI 2011/1606) reg.15 as from 1 August 2011.

917   Circumstances in which no meetings required (merger)

917(1)   **[Application of s.917]** This section applies in the case of a merger by absorption where all of the relevant securities of the transferor company (or, if there is more than one transferor company, of each of them) are held by or on behalf of the transferee company.

917(2)   **[Court satisfied conditions complied with]** It is not necessary for the scheme to be approved at a meeting of the members, or any class of members, of any of the merging companies if the court is satisfied that the following conditions have been complied with.

917(3)   **[First condition: s.917(3A), (3B) satisfied]** The first condition is that either subsection (3A) or subsection (3B) is satisfied.

917(3A)   **[Registrar's publication of notice of receipt of draft terms]** This subsection is satisfied if publication of notice of receipt of the draft terms by the registrar took place in respect of all the merging companies at least one month before the date of the court's order.

917(3B)   **[Publication of draft terms on website etc.]** This subsection is satisfied if–

  (a)   the conditions in section 906A(2) to (4) are met in respect of each of the merging companies,

  (b)   in each case, the registrar published the notice mentioned in subsection (4) of that section in the Gazette at least one month before the date of the court's order, and

  (c)   the draft terms remained available on the website throughout the period beginning one month before, and ending on, that date.

917(4)   **[Second condition: s.917(4A), (4B) satisfied]** The second condition is that subsection (4A) or (4B) is satisfied for each of the documents listed in the applicable paragraphs of section 911(3)(a) to (f) relating to the transferee company and the transferor company (or, if there is more than one transferor company, each of them).

917(4A)   **[Inspection of document at transferee's registered office]** This subsection is satisfied for a document if the members of the transferee company were able during the period beginning one month before, and ending on, the date mentioned in subsection (3A) to inspect that document at the registered office of that company.

917(4B) **[Document available on website free of charge]** This subsection is satisfied for a document if–

(a) the document is made available on a website which is maintained by or on behalf of the transferee company and identifies the company,

(b) access to the document on the website is not conditional on the payment of a fee or otherwise restricted, and

(c) the document remains available on the website throughout the period beginning one month before, and ending on, the date mentioned in subsection (3A).

917(4C) **[Third condition: minimum period of free copies]** The third condition is that the members of the transferee company were able to obtain copies of the documents mentioned in subsection (4), or any part of those documents, on request and free of charge, throughout the period beginning one month before, and ending on, the date mentioned in subsection (3A).

917(4D) **[Application of s.911A(5) on website for s.917(4C)]** For the purposes of subsection (4C)–

(a) section 911A(5) applies as it applies for the purposes of section 911(1)(b), and

(b) Part 4 of Schedule 5 (communications by means of a website) does not apply.

917(5) **[Fourth condition: no minority requisition of meeting]** The fourth condition is that–

(a) one or more members of the transferee company, who together held not less than 5% of the paid-up capital of the company which carried the right to vote at general meetings of the company (excluding any shares in the company held as treasury shares) would have been able, during that period, to require a meeting of each class of members to be called for the purpose of deciding whether or not to agree to the scheme, and

(b) no such requirement was made.

917(6) **["Relevant securities"]** In this section "relevant securities", in relation to a company, means shares or other securities carrying the right to vote at general meetings of the company.

History
Section 917(3)–(4D) substituted and s.917(5) amended by the Companies (Reporting Requirements in Mergers and Divisions) Regulations 2011 (SI 2011/1606) reg.16 as from 1 August 2011.

Other exceptions

918 Other circumstances in which meeting of members of transferee company not required (merger)

918(1) **[Court satisfied conditions complied with]** In the case of any merger by absorption, it is not necessary for the scheme to be approved by the members of the transferee company if the court is satisfied that the following conditions have been complied with.

918(2) **[First condition: s.918(2A), (2B) satisfied]** The first condition is that either subsection (2A) or subsection (2B) is satisfied.

918(2A) **[Registrar's publication of notice of receipt of draft terms]** This subsection is satisfied if publication of notice of receipt of the draft terms by the registrar took place in respect of the transferee company at least one month before the date of the first meeting of members, or any class of members, of the transferor company (or, if there is more than one transferor company, any of them) summoned for the purposes of agreeing to the scheme.

918(2B)   **[Publication of draft terms on website etc.]** This subsection is satisfied if–

(a)   the conditions in section 906A(2) to (4) are met in respect of the transferee company,

(b)   the registrar published the notice mentioned in subsection (4) of that section in the Gazette at least one month before the date of the first meeting of members, or any class of members, of the transferor company (or, if there is more than one transferor company, any of them) summoned for the purposes of agreeing to the scheme, and

(c)   the draft terms remained available on the website throughout the period beginning one month before, and ending on, that date.

918(3)   **[Second condition: s.918(3A), (3B) satisfied]** The second condition is that subsection (3A) or (3B) is satisfied for each of the documents listed in the applicable paragraphs of section 911(3) relating to the transferee company and the transferor company (or, if there is more than one transferor company, each of them).

918(3A)   **[Inspection of document at transferee's registered office]** This subsection is satisfied for a document if the members of the transferee company were able during the period beginning one month before, and ending on, the date of any such meeting as is mentioned in subsection (2A) to inspect that document at the registered office of that company.

918(3B)   **[Document available on website free of charge]** This subsection is satisfied for a document if–

(a)   the document is made available on a website which is maintained by or on behalf of the transferee company and identifies the company,

(b)   access to the document on the website is not conditional on the payment of a fee or otherwise restricted, and

(c)   the document remains available on the website throughout the period beginning one month before, and ending on, the date of any such meeting as is mentioned in subsection (2A).

918(3C)   **[Third condition: minimum period of free copies]** The third condition is that the members of the transferee company were able to obtain copies of the documents mentioned in subsection (3), or any part of those documents, on request and free of charge, throughout the period beginning one month before, and ending on, the date of any such meeting as is mentioned in subsection (2A).

918(3D)   **[Application of s.911A(5) on website for s.918(3C)]** For the purposes of subsection (3C)–

(a)   section 911A(5) applies as it applies for the purposes of section 911(1)(b), and

(b)   Part 4 of Schedule 5 (communications by means of a website) does not apply.

918(4)   **[Fourth condition: no minority requisition of meeting]** The fourth condition is that–

(a)   one or more members of that company, who together held not less than 5% of the paid-up capital of the company which carried the right to vote at general meetings of the company (excluding any shares in the company held as treasury shares) would have been able, during that period, to require a meeting of each class of members to be called for the purpose of deciding whether or not to agree to the scheme, and

(b)   no such requirement was made.

History

Section 918(2)–(3D) substituted and s.918(4) amended by the Companies (Reporting Requirements in Mergers and Divisions) Regulations 2011 (SI 2011/1606) reg.17 as from 1 August 2011.

918A   Agreement to dispense with reports etc (merger)

918A(1)   [Agreement of members of merging companies] If all members holding shares in, and all persons holding other securities of, the merging companies, being shares or securities that carry a right to vote in general meetings of the company in question, so agree, the following requirements do not apply.

918A(1A)   [Dispensation of ss.908, 909, 910, 911, 911B requirements] The requirements that may be dispensed with under this section are–

(a)   the requirements of–

     (i)   section 908 (directors' explanatory report),

     (ii)   section 909 (expert's report),

     (iii)   section 910 (supplementary accounting statement), and

     (iv)   section 911B (report on material changes of assets of merging company); and

(b)   the requirements of section 911 (inspection of documents) so far as relating to any document required to be drawn up under sections 908, 909 or 910.

918A(2)   [Date for determining members etc. and voting rights] For the purposes of this section–

(a)   the members, or holders of other securities, of a company, and

(b)   whether shares or other securities carry a right to vote in general meetings of the company,

are determined as at the date of the application to the court under section 896.

History
Section 918A inserted by the Companies (Cross-Border Mergers and Divisions of Public Companies) (Amendment) Regulations 2008 (SI 2008/690) reg.2(2) as from 6 April 2008. Section 918A(1) and the heading amended and s.918A(1A) inserted by the Companies (Reporting Requirements in Mergers and Divisions) Regulations 2011 (SI 2011/1606) reg.18 as from 1 August 2011.

CHAPTER 3

DIVISION

Introductory

919   Divisions and companies involved in a division

919(1)   [Requirements under the scheme] The scheme involves a division where under the scheme the undertaking, property and liabilities of the company in respect of which the compromise or arrangement is proposed are to be divided among and transferred to two or more companies each of which is either–

(a)   an existing public company, or

(b)   a new company (whether or not a public company).

919(2)   [Companies involved in the division] References in this Part to the companies involved in the division are to the transferor company and any existing transferee companies.

Requirements to be complied with in case of division

920   Draft terms of scheme (division)

920(1)   [Draft adopted by directors of companies involved] A draft of the proposed terms of the scheme must be drawn up and adopted by the directors of each of the companies involved in the division.

920(2) **[Contents of draft terms]** The draft terms must give particulars of at least the following matters–

(a) in respect of the transferor company and each transferee company–

    (i) its name,

    (ii) the address of its registered office, and

    (iii) whether it is a company limited by shares or a company limited by guarantee and having a share capital;

(b) the number of shares in a transferee company to be allotted to members of the transferor company for a given number of their shares (the "share exchange ratio") and the amount of any cash payment;

(c) the terms relating to the allotment of shares in a transferee company;

(d) the date from which the holding of shares in a transferee company will entitle the holders to participate in profits, and any special conditions affecting that entitlement;

(e) the date from which the transactions of the transferor company are to be treated for accounting purposes as being those of a transferee company;

(f) any rights or restrictions attaching to shares or other securities in a transferee company to be allotted under the scheme to the holders of shares or other securities in the transferor company to which any special rights or restrictions attach, or the measures proposed concerning them;

(g) any amount of benefit paid or given or intended to be paid or given–

    (i) to any of the experts referred to in section 924 (expert's report), or

    (ii) to any director of a company involved in the division,

and the consideration for the payment of benefit.

920(3) **[Further contents]** The draft terms must also–

(a) give particulars of the property and liabilities to be transferred (to the extent that these are known to the transferor company) and their allocation among the transferee companies;

(b) make provision for the allocation among and transfer to the transferee companies of any other property and liabilities that the transferor company has acquired or may subsequently acquire; and

(c) specify the allocation to members of the transferor company of shares in the transferee companies and the criteria upon which that allocation is based.

921 Publication of draft terms by registrar (division)

921(1) **[Duty of directors to deliver copy to registrar]** The directors of each company involved in the division must deliver a copy of the draft terms to the registrar.

921(2) **[Registrar to publish receipt in the Gazette]** The registrar must publish in the Gazette notice of receipt by him from that company of a copy of the draft terms.

921(3) **[Time limit for publication of notice]** That notice must be published at least one month before the date of any meeting of that company summoned for the purposes of approving the scheme.

921(4) **[Publication requirements subject to ss.921A, 934]** The requirements in this section are subject to section 921A (publication of draft terms on company website) and section 934 (power of court to exclude certain requirements).

History
Section 921(4) and the heading amended by the Companies (Reporting Requirements in Mergers and Divisions) Regulations 2011 (SI 2011/1606) reg.19 as from 1 August 2011.

921A   Publication of draft terms on company website (division)

921A(1)   [Non-application of s.921A subject to conditions] Section 921 does not apply in respect of a company if the conditions in subsections (2) to (6) are met.

921A(2)   [First condition: draft terms on website] The first condition is that the draft terms are made available on a website which–

    (a)   is maintained by or on behalf of the company, and

    (b)   identifies the company.

921A(3)   [Second condition: availability free] The second condition is that neither access to the draft terms on the website nor the supply of a hard copy of them from the website is conditional on payment of a fee or otherwise restricted.

921A(4)   [Third condition: notice to registrar of website] The third condition is that the directors of the company deliver to the registrar a notice giving details of the website.

921A(5)   [Fourth condition: gazetting] The fourth condition is that the registrar publishes the notice in the Gazette at least one month before the date of any meeting of the company summoned for the purpose of approving the scheme.

921A(6)   [Fifth condition: minimum period available on website] The fifth condition is that the draft terms remain available on the website throughout the period beginning one month before, and ending on, the date of any such meeting.

History
Section 921A inserted by the Companies (Reporting Requirements in Mergers and Divisions) Regulations 2011 (SI 2011/1606) reg.20 as from 1 August 2011.

922   Approval of members of companies involved in the division

922(1)   [Requisite majority for approval] The compromise or arrangement must be approved by a majority in number, representing 75% in value, of each class of members of each of the companies involved in the division, present and voting either in person or by proxy at a meeting.

922(2)   [Approval subject to ss.931, 932] This requirement is subject to sections 931 and 932 (circumstances in which meeting of members not required).

923   Directors' explanatory report (division)

923(1)   [Duty of directors to adopt report] The directors of the transferor and each existing transferee company must draw up and adopt a report.

923(2)   [Contents of report] The report must consist of–

    (a)   the statement required by section 897 (statement explaining effect of compromise or arrangement), and

    (b)   insofar as that statement does not deal with the following matters, a further statement–

        (i)   setting out the legal and economic grounds for the draft terms, and in particular for the share exchange ratio and for the criteria on which the allocation to the members of the transferor company of shares in the transferee companies was based, and

        (ii)   specifying any special valuation difficulties.

923(3)   [Valuation of non-cash consideration for shares] The report must also state–

(a)   whether a report has been made to any transferee company under section 593 (valuation of non-cash consideration for shares), and

(b)   if so, whether that report has been delivered to the registrar of companies.

923(4)   [Dispensing with report] The requirement in this section is subject to section 933 (agreement to dispense with reports etc) and section 933A (certain requirements excluded where shareholders given proportional rights).

History

Section 923(4) amended by the Companies (Reporting Requirements in Mergers and Divisions) Regulations 2011 (SI 2011/1606) reg.21 as from 1 August 2011.

924   Expert's report (division)

924(1)   [Requirement for expert's report] An expert's report must be drawn up on behalf of each company involved in the division.

924(2)   [Report on draft terms] The report required is a written report on the draft terms to the members of the company.

924(3)   [Single report by joint expert] The court may on the joint application of the companies involved in the division approve the appointment of a joint expert to draw up a single report on behalf of all those companies.

If no such appointment is made, there must be a separate expert's report to the members of each company involved in the division drawn up by a separate expert appointed on behalf of that company.

924(4)   [The expert] The expert must be a person who–

(a)   is eligible for appointment as a statutory auditor (see section 1212), and

(b)   meets the independence requirement in section 936.

924(5)   [Content of expert's report] The expert's report must–

(a)   indicate the method or methods used to arrive at the share exchange ratio;

(b)   give an opinion as to whether the method or methods used are reasonable in all the circumstances of the case, indicate the values arrived at using each such method and (if there is more than one method) give an opinion on the relative importance attributed to such methods in arriving at the value decided on;

(c)   describe any special valuation difficulties that have arisen;

(d)   state whether in the expert's opinion the share exchange ratio is reasonable; and

(e)   in the case of a valuation made by a person other than himself (see section 935), state that it appeared to him reasonable to arrange for it to be so made or to accept a valuation so made.

924(6)   [Rights of expert to documents and information] The expert (or each of them) has–

(a)   the right of access to all such documents of the companies involved in the division, and

(b)   the right to require from the companies' officers all such information,

as he thinks necessary for the purposes of making his report.

924(7)   [Agreement to dispense with report] The requirement in this section is subject to section 933 (agreement to dispense with reports etc) and section 933A (certain requirements excluded where shareholders given proportional rights).

History
Section 924(7) amended by the Companies (Reporting Requirements in Mergers and Divisions) Regulations 2011 (SI 2011/1606) reg.22 as from 1 August 2011.

925 Supplementary accounting statement (division)

925(1) [Application of s.925] This section applies if the last annual accounts of a company involved in the division relate to a financial year ending before–

(a) the date seven months before the first meeting of the company summoned for the purposes of approving the scheme, or

(b) if no meeting of the company is required (by virtue of section 931 or 932), the date six months before the directors of the company adopt the draft terms of the scheme.

925(1A) [Statement if half-yearly financial report not made] If the company has not made public a half-yearly financial report relating to a period ending on or after the date mentioned in subsection (1), the directors of the company must prepare a supplementary accounting statement.

925(2) [Statement to consist of balance sheet] That statement must consist of–

(a) a balance sheet dealing with the state of affairs of the company as at a date not more than three months before the draft terms were adopted by the directors, and

(b) where the company would be required under section 399 to prepare group accounts if that date were the last day of a financial year, a consolidated balance sheet dealing with the state of affairs of the company and the undertakings that would be included in such a consolidation.

925(3) [Requirements as to balance sheet] The requirements of this Act (and where relevant Article 4 of the IAS Regulation) as to the balance sheet forming part of a company's annual accounts, and the matters to be included in notes to it, apply to the balance sheet required for an accounting statement under this section, with such modifications as are necessary by reason of its being prepared otherwise than as at the last day of a financial year.

925(4) [Signing and approval of balance sheet] The provisions of section 414 as to the approval and signing of accounts apply to the balance sheet required for an accounting statement under this section.

925(4A) ["Half-yearly financial report"] In this section "half-yearly financial report" means a report of that description required to be made public by rules under section 89A of the Financial Services and Markets Act 2000 (transparency rules).

925(5) [Agreement to dispense with report] The requirement in this section is subject to section 933 (agreement to dispense with reports etc) and section 933A (certain requirements excluded where shareholders given proportional rights).

History
Section 925(1) substituted, s.925(5) amended and s.925(1A), (4A) inserted by the Companies (Reporting Requirements in Mergers and Divisions) Regulations 2011 (SI 2011/1606) reg.23 as from 1 August 2011.

926 Inspection of documents (division)

926(1) [Rights of members] The members of each company involved in the division must be able, during the period specified below–

(a) to inspect at the registered office of that company copies of the documents listed below relating to that company and every other company involved in the division, and

(b) to obtain copies of those documents or any part of them on request free of charge.

926(2)   [Specified period] The period referred to above is the period–

(a)   beginning one month before, and

(b)   ending on the date of,

the first meeting of the members, or any class of members, of the company for the purposes of approving the scheme.

926(3)   [Kind of documents] The documents referred to above are–

(a)   the draft terms;

(b)   the directors' explanatory report;

(c)   the expert's report;

(d)   the company's annual accounts and reports for the last three financial years ending on or before the first meeting of the members, or any class of members, of the company summoned for the purposes of approving the scheme;

(e)   any supplementary accounting statement required by section 925; and

(f)   if no statement is required by section 925 because the company has made public a recent half-yearly financial report (see subsection (1A) of that section), that report.

926(3A)   [Rights of inspection/copies subject to website availability] The requirement in subsection (1)(a) is subject to section 926A(1) (publication of documents on company website).

926(4)   [Requirements of s.927(3)(b), (c), (e) subject to ss.933, 933A, 934] The requirements in subsection (3)(b), (c) and (e) are subject to section 933 (agreement to dispense with reports etc), section 933A (certain requirements excluded where shareholders given proportional rights) and section 934 (power of court to exclude certain requirements).

926(5)   [No right to free hard copy under s.1145] Section 1145 (right to hard copy) does not apply to a document sent or supplied in accordance with subsection (1)(b) to a member who has consented to information being sent or supplied by the company by electronic means and has not revoked that consent.

926(6)   [Website communications not applicable re s.926(1)(b)] Part 4 of Schedule 5 (communications by means of a website) does not apply for the purposes of subsection (1)(b) (but see section 926A(5)).

History
Section 926(3)(e), (4) amended and s.926((3)(f), (3A), (5), (6) inserted by the Companies (Reporting Requirements in Mergers and Divisions) Regulations 2011 (SI 2011/1606) reg.24 as from 1 August 2011.

926A   Publication of documents on company website (division)

926A(1)   [No inspection of documents subject to conditions] Section 926(1)(a) does not apply to a document if the conditions in subsections (2) to (4) are met in relation to that document.
This is subject to subsection (6).

926A(2)   [First condition: document available on website] The first condition is that the document is made available on a website which–

(a)   is maintained by or on behalf of the company, and

(b)   identifies the company.

926A(3)   [Second condition: availability free] The second condition is that access to the document on the website is not conditional on payment of a fee or otherwise restricted.

926A(4)   **[Third condition: minimum period on website]** The third condition is that the document remains available on the website throughout the period beginning one month before, and ending on, the date of any meeting of the company summoned for the purpose of approving the scheme.

926A(5)   **[Ability to obtain copy]** A person is able to obtain a copy of a document as required by section 926(1)(b) if–

(a)   the conditions in subsections (2) and (3) are met in relation to that document, and

(b)   the person is able, throughout the period specified in subsection (4)–

    (i)   to retain a copy of the document as made available on the website, and

    (ii)   to produce a hard copy of it.

926A(6)   **[Inspection where ability to obtain copy under s.926A(5)]** Where members of a company are able to obtain copies of a document only as mentioned in subsection (5), section 926(1)(a) applies to that document even if the conditions in subsections (2) to (4) are met.

History
Section 926A inserted by the Companies (Reporting Requirements in Mergers and Divisions) Regulations 2011 (SI 2011/1606) reg.25 as from 1 August 2011.

927   Report on material changes of assets of transferor company (division)

927(1)   **[Duty of directors of transferor company]** The directors of the transferor company must report–

(a)   to every meeting of the members, or any class of members, of that company summoned for the purpose of agreeing to the scheme, and

(b)   to the directors of each existing transferee company,

any material changes in the property and liabilities of the transferor company between the date when the draft terms were adopted and the date of the meeting in question.

927(2)   **[Duty of directors of each transferee company]** The directors of each existing transferee company must in turn–

(a)   report those matters to every meeting of the members, or any class of members, of that company summoned for the purpose of agreeing to the scheme, or

(b)   send a report of those matters to every member entitled to receive notice of such a meeting.

927(3)   **[Agreement to dispense with report]** The requirement in this section is subject to section 933 (agreement to dispense with reports etc) and section 933A (certain requirements excluded where shareholders given proportional rights).

History
Section 927(3) amended by the Companies (Reporting Requirements in Mergers and Divisions) Regulations 2011 (SI 2011/1606) reg.26 as from 1 August 2011.

928   Approval of articles of new transferee company (division)

928   The articles of every new transferee company, or a draft of them, must be approved by ordinary resolution of the transferor company.

929   Protection of holders of securities to which special rights attached (division)

929(1)   **[Scheme to provide]** The scheme must provide that where any securities of the transferor company (other than shares) to which special rights are attached are held by a person otherwise than as a member or creditor of the company, that person is to receive rights in a transferee company of equivalent value.

929(2)   [Non-application of s.929(1)] Subsection (1) does not apply if–

(a)   the holder has agreed otherwise, or

(b)   the holder is, or under the scheme is to be, entitled to have the securities purchased by a transferee company on terms that the court considers reasonable.

930   No allotment of shares to transferor company or to transferee company (division)

930   The scheme must not provide for any shares in a transferee company to be allotted to–

(a)   the transferor company (or its nominee) in respect of shares in the transferor company held by the transferor company itself (or its nominee); or

(b)   a transferee company (or its nominee) in respect of shares in the transferor company held by the transferee company (or its nominee).

History

Section 930 substituted by the Companies (Cross-Border Mergers and Divisions of Public Companies) (Amendment) Regulations 2008 (SI 2008/690) reg.4 as from 6 April 2008.

Exceptions where shares of transferor company held by transferee company

931   Circumstances in which meeting of members of transferor company not required (division)

931(1)   [Application of s.931] This section applies in the case of a division where all of the shares or other securities of the transferor company carrying the right to vote at general meetings of the company are held by or on behalf of one or more existing transferee companies.

931(2)   [Court satisfied conditions complied with] It is not necessary for the scheme to be approved by a meeting of the members, or any class of members, of the transferor company if the court is satisfied that the following conditions have been complied with.

931(3)   [First condition: s.931(3A), (3B) satisfied] The first condition is that either subsection (3A) or subsection (3B) is satisfied.

931(3A)   [Registrar's publication of notice of receipt of draft terms] This subsection is satisfied if publication of notice of receipt of the draft terms by the registrar took place in respect of all the companies involved in the division at least one month before the date of the court's order.

931(3B)   [Availability on website etc.] This subsection is satisfied if–

(a)   the conditions in section 921A(2) to (4) are met in respect of each of the companies involved in the division,

(b)   in each case, the registrar published the notice mentioned in subsection (4) of that section in the Gazette at least one month before the date of the court's order, and

(c)   the draft terms remained available on the website throughout the period beginning one month before, and ending on, that date.

931(4)   [Second condition: s.931(4A), (4B) satisfied] The second condition is that subsection (4A) or (4B) is satisfied for each of the documents listed in the applicable paragraphs of section 926(3) relating to every company involved in the division.

931(4A)   [Inspection by members at registered office] This subsection is satisfied for a document if the members of every company involved in the division were able during the period beginning one month before, and ending on, the date of the court's order to inspect that document at the registered office of their company.

931(4B) **[Document available on website free of charge]** This subsection is satisfied for a document if–

(a) the document is made available on a website which is maintained by or on behalf of the company to which it relates and identifies the company,

(b) access to the document on the website is not conditional on payment of a fee or otherwise restricted, and

(c) the document remains available on the website throughout the period beginning one month before, and ending on, the date of the court's order.

931(4C) **[Third condition: minimum period of free copies]** The third condition is that the members of every company involved in the division were able to obtain copies of the documents mentioned in subsection (4), or any part of those documents, on request and free of charge, throughout the period beginning one month before, and ending on, the date of the court's order.

931(4D) **[Application of s.926A(5) on website for s.931(4C)]** For the purposes of subsection (4C)–

(a) section 926A(5) applies as it applies for the purposes of section 926(1)(b), and

(b) Part 4 of Schedule 5 (communications by means of a website) does not apply.

931(5) [Omitted]

931(6) **[Fourth condition]** The fourth condition is that the directors of the transferor company have sent–

(a) to every member who would have been entitled to receive notice of a meeting to agree to the scheme (had any such meeting been called), and

(b) to the directors of every existing transferee company,

a report of any material change in the property and liabilities of the transferor company between the date when the terms were adopted by the directors and the date one month before the date of the court's order.

History
Section 931(3), (4) substituted, s.931(4A)–(4D) inserted and s.931(5) omitted by the Companies (Reporting Requirements in Mergers and Divisions) Regulations 2011 (SI 2011/1606) reg.27 as from 1 August 2011.

Other exceptions

932 Circumstances in which meeting of members of transferee company not required (division)

932(1) **[Court satisfied conditions complied with]** In the case of a division, it is not necessary for the scheme to be approved by the members of a transferee company if the court is satisfied that the following conditions have been complied with in relation to that company.

932(2) **[First condition: s.932(2A), (2B) satisfied]** The first condition is that either subsection (2A) or subsection (2B) is satisfied.

932(2A) **[Registrar's publication of notice of receipt of draft terms]** This subsection is satisfied if publication of notice of receipt of the draft terms by the registrar took place in respect of the transferee company at least one month before the date of the first meeting of members of the transferor company summoned for the purposes of agreeing to the scheme.

932(2B) **[Availability on website etc.]** This subsection is satisfied if–

(a) the conditions in section 921A(2) to (4) are met in respect of the transferee company,

(b) the registrar published the notice mentioned in subsection (4) of that section in the Gazette at least one month before the date of the first meeting of members of the transferor company summoned for the purposes of agreeing to the scheme, and

(c) the draft terms remained available on the website throughout the period beginning one month before, and ending on, that date.

932(3) **[Second condition: s.932(3A), (3B) satisfied]** The second condition is that subsection (3A) or (3B) is satisfied for each of the documents listed in the applicable paragraphs of section 926(3) relating to the transferee company and every other company involved in the division.

932(3A) **[Inspection by transferee's members at registered office]** This subsection is satisfied for a document if the members of the transferee company were able during the period beginning one month before, and ending on, the date mentioned in subsection (2A) to inspect that document at the registered office of that company.

932(3B) **[Availability on website free of charge etc.]** This subsection is satisfied for a document if–

(a) the document is made available on a website which is maintained by or on behalf of the transferee company and identifies the company,

(b) access to the document on the website is not conditional on payment of a fee or otherwise restricted, and

(c) the document remains available on the website throughout the period beginning one month before, and ending on, the date mentioned in subsection (2A).

932(3C) **[Third condition: minimum period of free copies]** The third condition is that the members of the transferee company were able to obtain copies of the documents mentioned in subsection (3), or any part of those documents, on request and free of charge, throughout the period beginning one month before, and ending on, the date mentioned in subsection (2A).

932(3D) **[Application of s.926A(5) on website for s.932(3C)]** For the purposes of subsection (3C)–

(a) section 926A(5) applies as it applies for the purposes of section 926(1)(b), and

(b) Part 4 of Schedule 5 (communications by means of a website) does not apply.

932(4) **[Fourth condition: no minority requisition of meeting]** The fourth condition is that–

(a) one or more members of that company, who together held not less than 5% of the paid-up capital of the company which carried the right to vote at general meetings of the company (excluding any shares in the company held as treasury shares) would have been able, during that period, to require a meeting of each class of members to be called for the purpose of deciding whether or not to agree to the scheme, and

(b) no such requirement was made.

932(5) **[Exclusion of first, second and third conditions]** The first, second and third conditions above are subject to section 934 (power of court to exclude certain requirements).

History
Section 932(2), (3) substituted and s.932(4), (5) amended by the Companies (Reporting Requirements in Mergers and Divisions) Regulations 2011 (SI 2011/1606) reg.28 as from 1 August 2011.

933 Agreement to dispense with reports etc (division)

933(1) **[Agreements of all members and holders of securities]** If all members holding shares in, and all persons holding other securities of, the companies involved in the division, being shares or securities that carry a right to vote in general meetings of the company in question, so agree, the following requirements do not apply.

933(2)   [Requirements to be dispensed with] The requirements that may be dispensed with under this section are–

(a)   the requirements of–

    (i)   section 923 (directors' explanatory report),

    (ii)   section 924 (expert's report),

    (iii) section 925 (supplementary accounting statement), and

    (iv)   section 927 (report on material changes in assets of transferor company); and

(b)   the requirements of section 926 (inspection of documents) so far as relating to any document required to be drawn up under the provisions mentioned in paragraph (a)(i), (ii) or (iii) above.

933(3)   [Date for determination of members and security holders] For the purposes of this section–

(a)   the members, or holders of other securities, of a company, and

(b)   whether shares or other securities carry a right to vote in general meetings of the company,

are determined as at the date of the application to the court under section 896.

933A   Certain requirements excluded where shareholders given proportional rights (division)

933A(1) [Application where each transferee a new company] This section applies in the case of a division where each of the transferee companies is a new company.

933A(2) [Where proportional allotment rights] If all the shares in each of the transferee companies are to be allotted to the members of the transferor company in proportion to their rights in the allotted share capital of the transferor company, the following requirements do not apply.

933A(3) [Disapplication of ss.923, 924, 925, 926, 927] The requirements which do not apply are–

(a)   the requirements of–

    (i)   section 923 (directors' explanatory report),

    (ii)   section 924 (expert's report),

    (iii) section 925 (supplementary accounting statement), and

    (iv)   section 927 (report on material changes in assets of transferor company); and

(b)   the requirements of section 926 (inspection of documents) so far as relating to any document required to be drawn up under the provisions mentioned in paragraph (a)(i), (ii) or (iii) above.

History
Section 933A inserted by the Companies (Reporting Requirements in Mergers and Divisions) Regulations 2011 (SI 2011/1606) reg.29 as from 1 August 2011.

934   Power of court to exclude certain requirements (division)

934(1)   [Court satisfied condition complied with] In the case of a division, the court may by order direct that–

(a)   in relation to any company involved in the division, the requirements of–

    (i)   section 921 (publication of draft terms), and

    (ii)   section 926 (inspection of documents),

  do not apply, and

(b) in relation to an existing transferee company, section 932 (circumstances in which meeting of members of transferee company not required) has effect with the omission of the first, second and third conditions specified in that section,

if the court is satisfied that the following conditions will be fulfilled in relation to that company.

934(2) **[First condition: members' free copies within time period]** The first condition is that the members of that company will have received, or will have been able to obtain free of charge, copies of the documents listed in section 926–

(a) in time to examine them before the date of the first meeting of the members, or any class of members, of that company summoned for the purposes of agreeing to the scheme, or

(b) in the case of an existing transferee company where in the circumstances described in section 932 no meeting is held, in time to require a meeting as mentioned in subsection (4) of that section.

934(3) **[Second condition: creditors' free copies within time period]** The second condition is that the creditors of that company will have received or will have been able to obtain free of charge copies of the draft terms in time to examine them–

(a) before the date of the first meeting of the members, or any class of members, of the company summoned for the purposes of agreeing to the scheme, or

(b) in the circumstances mentioned in subsection (2)(b) above, at the same time as the members of the company.

934(4) **[Third condition: order not to prejudice to any members or creditors]** The third condition is that no prejudice would be caused to the members or creditors of the transferor company or any transferee company by making the order in question.

History

Section 934(1)(b) amended by the Companies (Reporting Requirements in Mergers and Divisions) Regulations 2011 (SI 2011/1606) reg.30 as from 1 August 2011.

CHAPTER 4

SUPPLEMENTARY PROVISIONS

Expert's report and related matters

935   Expert's report: valuation by another person

935(1) **[Power of expert to delegate valuation]** Where it appears to an expert–

(a) that a valuation is reasonably necessary to enable him to draw up his report, and

(b) that it is reasonable for that valuation, or part of it, to be made by (or for him to accept a valuation made by) another person who–

    (i) appears to him to have the requisite knowledge and experience to make the valuation or that part of it, and

    (ii) meets the independence requirement in section 936,

he may arrange for or accept such a valuation, together with a report which will enable him to make his own report under section 909 or 924.

935(2) **[Disclosure in expert's report]** Where any valuation is made by a person other than the expert himself, the latter's report must state that fact and must also–

(a) state the former's name and what knowledge and experience he has to carry out the valuation, and

(b) describe so much of the undertaking, property and liabilities as was valued by the other person, and the method used to value them, and specify the date of the valuation.

936 Experts and valuers: independence requirement

936(1) [Requirement for independence] A person meets the independence requirement for the purposes of section 909 or 924 (expert's report) or section 935 (valuation by another person) only if–

(a) he is not–

(i) an officer or employee of any of the companies concerned in the scheme, or

(ii) a partner or employee of such a person, or a partnership of which such a person is a partner;

(b) he is not–

(i) an officer or employee of an associated undertaking of any of the companies concerned in the scheme, or

(ii) a partner or employee of such a person, or a partnership of which such a person is a partner; and

(c) there does not exist between–

(i) the person or an associate of his, and

(ii) any of the companies concerned in the scheme or an associated undertaking of such a company,

a connection of any such description as may be specified by regulations made by the Secretary of State.

936(2) [Auditor not officer or employee of company] An auditor of a company is not regarded as an officer or employee of the company for this purpose.

936(3) [Definitions] For the purposes of this section–

(a) the "companies concerned in the scheme" means every transferor and existing transferee company;

(b) "associated undertaking", in relation to a company, means–

(i) a parent undertaking or subsidiary undertaking of the company, or

(ii) a subsidiary undertaking of a parent undertaking of the company; and

(c) "associate" has the meaning given by section 937.

936(4) [Regulations subject to negative resolution procedure] Regulations under this section are subject to negative resolution procedure.

937 Experts and valuers: meaning of "associate"

937(1) [Definition of associate] This section defines "associate" for the purposes of section 936 (experts and valuers: independence requirement).

937(2) ["Associate" re individual] In relation to an individual, "associate" means–

(a) that individual's spouse or civil partner or minor child or step-child,

  (b) any body corporate of which that individual is a director, and

  (c) any employee or partner of that individual.

937(3)   **["Associate" re body corporate]** In relation to a body corporate, "associate" means–

  (a) any body corporate of which that body is a director,

  (b) any body corporate in the same group as that body, and

  (c) any employee or partner of that body or of any body corporate in the same group.

937(4)   **["Associate" re partnership that is a legal person]** In relation to a partnership that is a legal person under the law by which it is governed, "associate" means–

  (a) any body corporate of which that partnership is a director,

  (b) any employee of or partner in that partnership, and

  (c) any person who is an associate of a partner in that partnership.

937(5)   **["Associate" re partnership that is not a legal person]** In relation to a partnership that is not a legal person under the law by which it is governed, "associate" means any person who is an associate of any of the partners.

937(6)   **[Meanings for limited liability partnership]** In this section, in relation to a limited liability partnership, for "director" read "member".

Powers of the court

938   Power of court to summon meeting of members or creditors of existing transferee company

938(1)   **[Power of court]** The court may order a meeting of–

  (a) the members of an existing transferee company, or any class of them, or

  (b) the creditors of an existing transferee company, or any class of them,

to be summoned in such manner as the court directs.

938(2)   **[Who may make application to court]** An application for such an order may be made by–

  (a) the company concerned,

  (b) a member or creditor of the company, or

  (c) if the company is being wound up, the liquidator, or

  (d) if the company is in administration, the administrator.

938(3)   **[Creditors' meeting covered by s.323]** Section 323 (representation of corporations at meetings) applies to a meeting of creditors under this section as to a meeting of the company (references to a member being read as references to a creditor).

History

Section 938(3) inserted by the Companies Act 2006 (Consequential Amendments, etc.) Order 2008 (SI 2008/948) arts 2(1), (2), 3(1) and Sch.1 Pt 2 para.251 as from 6 April 2008. Section 938(c), (d) inserted by the Companies Act 2006 (Consequential Amendments, Transitional Provisions and Savings) Order 2009 (SI 2009/1941) Sch.1 para.260(5) as from 1 October 2009.

939   Court to fix date for transfer of undertaking etc of transferor company

939(1)   [Duty of court] Where the court sanctions the compromise or arrangement, it must–

  (a)   in the order sanctioning the compromise or arrangement, or

  (b)   in a subsequent order under section 900 (powers of court to facilitate reconstruction or amalgamation),

fix a date on which the transfer (or transfers) to the transferee company (or transferee companies) of the undertaking, property and liabilities of the transferor company is (or are) to take place.

939(2)   [Where order provides for dissolution of transferor company] Any such order that provides for the dissolution of the transferor company must fix the same date for the dissolution.

939(3)   [Where transferor company to take steps re transfer] If it is necessary for the transferor company to take steps to ensure that the undertaking, property and liabilities are fully transferred, the court must fix a date, not later than six months after the date fixed under subsection (1), by which such steps must be taken.

939(4)   [Power of court to postpone dissolution] In that case, the court may postpone the dissolution of the transferor company until that date.

939(5)   [Postponement when transferor company to take steps] The court may postpone or further postpone the date fixed under subsection (3) if it is satisfied that the steps mentioned cannot be completed by the date (or latest date) fixed under that subsection.

Liability of transferee companies

940   Liability of transferee companies for each other's defaults

940(1)   [Joint and several liability] In the case of a division, each transferee company is jointly and severally liable for any liability transferred to any other transferee company under the scheme to the extent that the other company has made default in satisfying that liability.
This is subject to the following provisions.

940(2)   [Non-application of s.940(1) re liability to creditors] If a majority in number representing 75% in value of the creditors or any class of creditors of the transferor company, present and voting either in person or by proxy at a meeting summoned for the purposes of agreeing to the scheme, so agree, subsection (1) does not apply in relation to the liabilities owed to the creditors or that class of creditors.

940(3)   [Maximum liability of transferee] A transferee company is not liable under this section for an amount greater than the net value transferred to it under the scheme. The "net value transferred" is the value at the time of the transfer of the property transferred to it under the scheme less the amount at that date of the liabilities so transferred.

Disruption of websites

940A   Disregard of website failures beyond control of company

940A(1)   [Conditions for not making information available under s.940A(2)] A failure to make information or a document available on the website throughout a period specified in any of the provisions mentioned in subsection (2) is to be disregarded if–

  (a)   it is made available on the website for part of that period, and

  (b)   the failure to make it available throughout that period is wholly attributable to circumstances that it would not be reasonable to have expected the company to prevent or avoid.

940A(2)   [Provisions referred to in s.940A(1)] The provisions referred to above are–

(a)   section 906A(6),

(b)   section 911A(4),

(c)   section 916(3B) and (4B)

(d)   section 917(3B) and (4B),

(e)   section 918(2B) and (3B),

(f)   section 921A(6),

(g)   section 926A(4),

(h)   section 931(3B) and (4B), and

(i)   section 932(2B) and (3B).

History

Section 940A inserted by the Companies (Reporting Requirements in Mergers and Divisions) Regulations 2011 (SI 2011/1606) reg.31 as from 1 August 2011.

Interpretation

941   Meaning of "liabilities" and "property"

941   In this Part–

"liabilities" includes duties;

"property" includes property, rights and powers of every description.

PART 29

FRAUDULENT TRADING

993   Offence of fraudulent trading

993(1)   [Offence] If any business of a company is carried on with intent to defraud creditors of the company or creditors of any other person, or for any fraudulent purpose, every person who is knowingly a party to the carrying on of the business in that manner commits an offence.

993(2)   [Whether or not company in winding up] This applies whether or not the company has been, or is in the course of being, wound up.

993(3)   [Penalty] A person guilty of an offence under this section is liable–

(a)   on conviction on indictment, to imprisonment for a term not exceeding ten years or a fine (or both);

(b)   on summary conviction–

(i)   in England and Wales, to imprisonment for a term not exceeding twelve months or a fine not exceeding the statutory maximum (or both);

(ii)   in Scotland or Northern Ireland, to imprisonment for a term not exceeding six months or a fine not exceeding the statutory maximum (or both).

Registrar's power to strike off defunct company

[**Note:** The provisions of this Chapter apply also (with modifications) to LLPs: see the Limited Liability Partnerships (Application of Companies Act 2006) Regulations 2009 (SI 2009/1804) reg.50.]

1000 Power to strike off company not carrying on business or in operation

1000(1) [Inquiry as to whether company carrying on business] If the registrar has reasonable cause to believe that a company is not carrying on business or in operation, the registrar may send to the company a communication inquiring whether the company is carrying on business or in operation.

1000(2) Failure to respond to inquiry] If the registrar does not within 14 days of sending the communication receive any answer to it, the registrar must within 14 days after the expiration of that period send to the company a second communication referring to the first communication, and stating–

(a)   that no answer to it has been received, and

(b)   that if an answer is not received to the second communication within 14 days from its date,

a notice will be published in the Gazette with a view to striking the company's name off the register.

1000(3) [Publication on notice of striking off and dissolution] If the registrar–

(a)   receives an answer to the effect that the company is not carrying on business or in operation, or

(b)   does not within 14 days after sending the second communication receive any answer,

the registrar may publish in the Gazette, and send to the company, a notice that at the expiration of 2 months from the date of the notice the name of the company mentioned in it will, unless cause is shown to the contrary, be struck off the register and the company will be dissolved.

1000(4) [Power to strike name off register] At the expiration of the time mentioned in the notice the registrar may, unless cause to the contrary is previously shown by the company, strike its name off the register.

1000(5) [Notice in Gazette] The registrar must publish notice in the Gazette of the company's name having been struck off the register.

1000(6) [Dissolution] On the publication of the notice in the Gazette the company is dissolved.

1000(7) [Directors' liabilities; Court power to wind-up] However–

(a)   the liability (if any) of every director, managing officer and member of the company continues and may be enforced as if the company had not been dissolved, and

(b)   nothing in this section affects the power of the court to wind up a company the name of which has been struck off the register.

History
Section 1000(1)–(3) amended and s.1000(4) inserted by the Companies (Striking Off) (Electronic Communications) Order 2014 (SI 2014/1602) art.2(1), (2) as from 11 July 2014. Section 1000(1)–(3) amended by SBEEA 2015 s.103(1), (2) as from 10 October 2015.

1001 Duty to act in case of company being wound up

1001(1) **[Extent of duty]** If, in a case where a company is being wound up–

(a) the registrar has reasonable cause to believe–

    (i) that no liquidator is acting, or

    (ii) that the affairs of the company are fully wound up, and

(b) the returns required to be made by the liquidator have not been made for a period of six consecutive months,

the registrar must publish in the Gazette and send to the company or the liquidator (if any) a notice that at the expiration of 2 months from the date of the notice the name of the company mentioned in it will, unless cause is shown to the contrary, be struck off the register and the company will be dissolved.

1001(2) **[Power to strike name off register]** At the expiration of the time mentioned in the notice the registrar may, unless cause to the contrary is previously shown by the company, strike its name off the register.

1001(3) **[Publication of notice in Gazette]** The registrar must publish notice in the Gazette of the company's name having been struck off the register.

1001(4) **[Dissolution of company]** On the publication of the notice in the Gazette the company is dissolved.

1001(5) **[Directors' liabilities; Court power to wind-up]** However–

(a) the liability (if any) of every director, managing officer and member of the company continues and may be enforced as if the company had not been dissolved, and

(b) nothing in this section affects the power of the court to wind up a company the name of which has been struck off the register.

1002 Supplementary provisions as to service of communication or notice

1002(1) **[Where notice or communication to company not possible]** If the registrar is not able to send a communication or notice under section 1000 or 1001 to a company in accordance with Schedule 4, the communication may be sent to an officer of the company at an address for that officer that has been notified to the registrar by the company.

1002(2) **[Service where officer's details are not known]** If there is no officer of the company whose name and address are known to the registrar, the communication or notice may be sent to each of the persons who subscribed the memorandum (if their addresses are known to the registrar).

1002(3) **[Notice to liquidator]** A notice to be sent to a liquidator under section 1001 may be sent to the address of the liquidator's last known place of business or to an address specified by the liquidator to the registrar for the purpose of receiving notices, or notices of that kind.

1002(4) **["Address" in s.1002]** In this section "address" has the same meaning as in section 1148(1).

History
Section 1002(1)–(3) amended and s.1002(4) inserted by the Companies (Striking Off) (Electronic Communications) Order 2014 (SI 2014/1602) art.2(1), (3) as from 11 July 2014. Section 1001(1) amended by SBEEA 2015 s.103(1), (3) as from 10 October 2015.

1003 Striking off on application by company

1003(1) **[Power to strike off]** On application by a company, the registrar of companies may strike the company's name off the register.

1003(2) **[Requirements for application]** The application–

(a) must be made on the company's behalf by its directors or by a majority of them, and

(b) must contain the prescribed information.

1003(3) **[Timing of striking off]** The registrar may not strike a company off under this section until after the expiration of 2 months from the publication by the registrar in the Gazette of a notice–

(a) stating that the registrar may exercise the power under this section in relation to the company, and

(b) inviting any person to show cause why that should not be done.

1003(4) **[Publication of notice in Gazette]** The registrar must publish notice in the Gazette of the company's name having been struck off.

1003(5) **[Dissolution of company]** On the publication of the notice in the Gazette the company is dissolved.

1003(6) **[Directors' liabilities; Court power to wind-up]** However–

(a) the liability (if any) of every director, managing officer and member of the company continues and may be enforced as if the company had not been dissolved, and

(b) nothing in this section affects the power of the court to wind up a company the name of which has been struck off the register.

History
Section 1003(3) amended by SBEEA 2015 s.103(1), (4) as from 10 October 2015.

1004 Circumstances in which application not to be made: activities of company

1004(1) **[Activities restricting applications]** An application under section 1003 (application for voluntary striking off) on behalf of a company must not be made if, at any time in the previous three months, the company has–

(a) changed its name,

(b) traded or otherwise carried on business,

(c) made a disposal for value of property or rights that, immediately before ceasing to trade or otherwise carry on business, it held for the purpose of disposal for gain in the normal course of trading or otherwise carrying on business, or

(d) engaged in any other activity, except one which is–

(i) necessary or expedient for the purpose of making an application under that section, or deciding whether to do so,

(ii) necessary or expedient for the purpose of concluding the affairs of the company,

(iii) necessary or expedient for the purpose of complying with any statutory requirement, or

(iv) specified by the Secretary of State by order for the purposes of this sub-paragraph.

1004(2) **[Trading or carrying on business]** For the purposes of this section, a company is not to be treated as trading or otherwise carrying on business by virtue only of the fact that it makes a payment in respect of a liability incurred in the course of trading or otherwise carrying on business.

1004(3) **[Amendment of subs.(1) by order]** The Secretary of State may by order amend subsection (1) for the purpose of altering the period in relation to which the doing of the things mentioned in paragraphs (a) to (d) of that subsection is relevant.

1004(4) **[Negative resolution procedure]** An order under this section is subject to negative resolution procedure.

1004(5) **[Offence]** It is an offence for a person to make an application in contravention of this section.

1004(6) **[Defence]** In proceedings for such an offence it is a defence for the accused to prove that he did not know, and could not reasonably have known, of the existence of the facts that led to the contravention.

1004(7) **[Penalty]** A person guilty of an offence under this section is liable–

   (a) on conviction on indictment, to a fine;

   (b) on summary conviction, to a fine not exceeding the statutory maximum.

1005 **Circumstances in which application not to be made: other proceedings not concluded**

1005(1) **[Circumstances where application not to be made]** An application under section 1003 (application for voluntary striking off) on behalf of a company must not be made at a time when–

   (a) an application to the court under Part 26 has been made on behalf of the company for the sanctioning of a compromise or arrangement and the matter has not been finally concluded;

   (b) a voluntary arrangement in relation to the company has been proposed under Part 1 of the Insolvency Act 1986 (c. 45) or Part 2 of the Insolvency (Northern Ireland) Order 1989 (S.I. 1989/2405 (N.I. 19)) and the matter has not been finally concluded;

   (c) the company is in administration under Part 2 of that Act or Part 3 of that Order;

   (d) paragraph 44 of Schedule B1 to that Act or paragraph 45 of Schedule B1 to that Order applies (interim moratorium on proceedings where application to the court for an administration order has been made or notice of intention to appoint administrator has been filed);

   (e) the company is being wound up under Part 4 of that Act or Part 5 of that Order, whether voluntarily or by the court, or a petition under that Part for winding up of the company by the court has been presented and not finally dealt with or withdrawn;

   (f) there is a receiver or manager of the company's property;

   (g) the company's estate is being administered by a judicial factor.

1005(2) **[Matters considered concluded: subs.(1)(a)]** For the purposes of subsection (1)(a), the matter is finally concluded if–

   (a) the application has been withdrawn,

   (b) the application has been finally dealt with without a compromise or arrangement being sanctioned by the court, or

   (c) a compromise or arrangement has been sanctioned by the court and has, together with anything required to be done under any provision made in relation to the matter by order of the court, been fully carried out.

1005(3) **[Matters considered concluded: subs.(1)(b)]** For the purposes of subsection (1)(b), the matter is finally concluded if–

   (a) no meetings are to be summoned under section 3 of the Insolvency Act 1986 (c. 45) or Article 16 of the Insolvency (Northern Ireland) Order 1989,

(b)   meetings summoned under that section or Article fail to approve the arrangement with no, or the same, modifications,

(c)   an arrangement approved by meetings summoned under that section, or in consequence of a direction under section 6(4)(b) of that Act or Article 19(4)(b) of that Order, has been fully implemented, or

(d)   the court makes an order under section 6(5) of that Act or Article 19(5) of that Order revoking approval given at previous meetings and, if the court gives any directions under section 6(6) of that Act or Article 19(6) of that Order, the company has done whatever it is required to do under those directions.

1005(4)   [Offence] It is an offence for a person to make an application in contravention of this section.

1005(5)   [Defence] In proceedings for such an offence it is a defence for the accused to prove that he did not know, and could not reasonably have known, of the existence of the facts that led to the contravention.

1005(6)   [Penalty] A person guilty of an offence under this section is liable–

(a)   on conviction on indictment, to a fine;

(b)   on summary conviction, to a fine not exceeding the statutory maximum.

1006   Copy of application to be given to members, employees, etc

1006(1)   [Duty to provide copies] A person who makes an application under section 1003 (application for voluntary striking off) on behalf of a company must secure that, within seven days from the day on which the application is made, a copy of it is given to every person who at any time on that day is–

(a)   a member of the company,

(b)   an employee of the company,

(c)   a creditor of the company,

(d)   a director of the company,

(e)   a manager or trustee of any pension fund established for the benefit of employees of the company, or

(f)   a person of a description specified for the purposes of this paragraph by regulations made by the Secretary of State.

Regulations under paragraph (f) are subject to negative resolution procedure.

1006(2)   [Director who is party to application] Subsection (1) does not require a copy of the application to be given to a director who is a party to the application.

1006(3)   [Withdrawn applications] The duty imposed by this section ceases to apply if the application is withdrawn before the end of the period for giving the copy application.

1006(4)   [Offence] A person who fails to perform the duty imposed on him by this section commits an offence.

If he does so with the intention of concealing the making of the application from the person concerned, he commits an aggravated offence.

1006(5)   [Defence] In proceedings for an offence under this section it is a defence for the accused to prove that he took all reasonable steps to perform the duty.

1006(6)   [Penalty] A person guilty of an offence under this section (other than an aggravated offence) is liable–

(a)   on conviction on indictment, to a fine;

(b)   on summary conviction, to a fine not exceeding the statutory maximum.

1006(7)   [Penalty: aggravated offence] A person guilty of an aggravated offence under this section is liable–

(a)   on conviction on indictment, to imprisonment for a term not exceeding seven years or a fine (or both);

(b)   on summary conviction–

   (i)   in England and Wales, to imprisonment for a term not exceeding twelve months or to a fine not exceeding the statutory maximum (or both);

   (ii)   in Scotland or Northern Ireland, to imprisonment for a term not exceeding six months, or to a fine not exceeding the statutory maximum (or both).

1007   Copy of application to be given to new members, employees, etc

1007(1)   [Application of section] This section applies in relation to any time after the day on which a company makes an application under section 1003 (application for voluntary striking off) and before the day on which the application is finally dealt with or withdrawn.

1007(2)   [Duty to supply copy of application] A person who is a director of the company at the end of a day on which a person (other than himself) becomes–

(a)   a member of the company,

(b)   an employee of the company,

(c)   a creditor of the company,

(d)   a director of the company,

(e)   a manager or trustee of any pension fund established for the benefit of employees of the company, or

(f)   a person of a description specified for the purposes of this paragraph by regulations made by the Secretary of State,

must secure that a copy of the application is given to that person within seven days from that day.

Regulations under paragraph (f) are subject to negative resolution procedure.

1007(3)   [Withdrawn application] The duty imposed by this section ceases to apply if the application is finally dealt with or withdrawn before the end of the period for giving the copy application.

1007(4)   [Offence] A person who fails to perform the duty imposed on him by this section commits an offence.

If he does so with the intention of concealing the making of the application from the person concerned, he commits an aggravated offence.

1007(5)   [Defence] In proceedings for an offence under this section it is a defence for the accused to prove–

(a)   that at the time of the failure he was not aware of the fact that the company had made an application under section 1003, or

(b)   that he took all reasonable steps to perform the duty.

1007(6)   [Penalty] A person guilty of an offence under this section (other than an aggravated offence) is liable–

(a)   on conviction on indictment, to a fine;

(b)   on summary conviction, to a fine not exceeding the statutory maximum.

1007(7)   [Penalty: aggravated offence] A person guilty of an aggravated offence under this section is liable–

(a)   on conviction on indictment, to imprisonment for a term not exceeding seven years or a fine (or both);

(b)   on summary conviction–

    (i)   in England and Wales, to imprisonment for a term not exceeding twelve months or to a fine not exceeding the statutory maximum (or both);

    (ii)   in Scotland or Northern Ireland, to imprisonment for a term not exceeding six months, or to a fine not exceeding the statutory maximum (or both).

1008   Copy of application: provisions as to service of documents

1008(1)   [Effect of provisions] The following provisions have effect for the purposes of–

section 1006 (copy of application to be given to members, employees, etc), and

section 1007 (copy of application to be given to new members, employees, etc).

1008(2)   [Service of documents] A document is treated as given to a person if it is–

(a)   delivered to him, or

(b)   left at his proper address, or

(c)   sent by post to him at that address.

1008(3)   [Proper address] For the purposes of subsection (2) and section 7 of the Interpretation Act 1978 (c. 30) (service of documents by post) as it applies in relation to that subsection, the proper address of a person is–

(a)   in the case of a firm incorporated or formed in the United Kingdom, its registered or principal office;

(b)   in the case of a firm incorporated or formed outside the United Kingdom–

    (i)   if it has a place of business in the United Kingdom, its principal office in the United Kingdom, or

    (ii)   if it does not have a place of business in the United Kingdom, its registered or principal office;

(c)   in the case of an individual, his last known address.

1008(4)   [Creditors] In the case of a creditor of the company a document is treated as given to him if it is left or sent by post to him–

(a)   at the place of business of his with which the company has had dealings by virtue of which he is a creditor of the company, or

(b)   if there is more than one such place of business, at each of them.

1009   Circumstances in which application to be withdrawn

1009(1)   [Application of section] This section applies where, at any time on or after the day on which a company makes an application under section 1003 (application for voluntary striking off) and before the day on which the application is finally dealt with or withdrawn–

(a) the company–

    (i) changes its name,

    (ii) trades or otherwise carries on business,

    (iii) makes a disposal for value of any property or rights other than those which it was necessary or expedient for it to hold for the purpose of making, or proceeding with, an application under that section, or

    (iv) engages in any activity, except one to which subsection (4) applies;

(b) an application is made to the court under Part 26 on behalf of the company for the sanctioning of a compromise or arrangement;

(c) a voluntary arrangement in relation to the company is proposed under Part 1 of the Insolvency Act 1986 (c. 45) or Part 2 of the Insolvency (Northern Ireland) Order 1989 (S.I. 1989/2405 (N.I. 19));

(d) an application to the court for an administration order in respect of the company is made under paragraph 12 of Schedule B1 to that Act or paragraph 13 of Schedule B1 to that Order;

(e) an administrator is appointed in respect of the company under paragraph 14 or 22 of Schedule B1 to that Act or paragraph 15 or 23 of Schedule B1 to that Order, or a copy of notice of intention to appoint an administrator of the company under any of those provisions is filed with the court;

(f) there arise any of the circumstances in which, under section 84(1) of that Act or Article 70 of that Order, the company may be voluntarily wound up;

(g) a petition is presented for the winding up of the company by the court under Part 4 of that Act or Part 5 of that Order;

(h) a receiver or manager of the company's property is appointed; or

(i) a judicial factor is appointed to administer the company's estate.

1009(2) **[Director's duty to withdraw application]** A person who, at the end of a day on which any of the events mentioned in subsection (1) occurs, is a director of the company must secure that the company's application is withdrawn forthwith.

1009(3) **[Company not treated as trading]** For the purposes of subsection (1)(a), a company is not treated as trading or otherwise carrying on business by virtue only of the fact that it makes a payment in respect of a liability incurred in the course of trading or otherwise carrying on business.

1009(4) **[Excepted activities]** The excepted activities referred to in subsection (1)(a)(iv) are–

(a) any activity necessary or expedient for the purposes of–

    (i) making, or proceeding with, an application under section 1003 (application for voluntary striking off),

    (ii) concluding affairs of the company that are outstanding because of what has been necessary or expedient for the purpose of making, or proceeding with, such an application, or

    (iii) complying with any statutory requirement;

(b) any activity specified by the Secretary of State by order for the purposes of this subsection.

An order under paragraph (b) is subject to negative resolution procedure.

1009(5) **[Offence]** A person who fails to perform the duty imposed on him by this section commits an offence.

1009(6) **[Defence]** In proceedings for an offence under this section it is a defence for the accused to prove–

   (a) that at the time of the failure he was not aware of the fact that the company had made an application under section 1003, or

   (b) that he took all reasonable steps to perform the duty.

1009(7)   **[Penalty]** A person guilty of an offence under this section is liable–

   (a) on conviction on indictment, to a fine;

   (b) on summary conviction, to a fine not exceeding the statutory maximum.

1010   Withdrawal of application

1010   An application under section 1003 is withdrawn by notice to the registrar.

1011   Meaning of "creditor"

1011   In this Chapter "creditor" includes a contingent or prospective creditor.

CHAPTER 2

PROPERTY OF DISSOLVED COMPANY

Property vesting as bona vacantia

1012   Property of dissolved company to be bona vacantia

1012(1)   **[Property and rights deemed bona vacantia]** When a company is dissolved, all property and rights whatsoever vested in or held on trust for the company immediately before its dissolution (including leasehold property, but not including property held by the company on trust for another person) are deemed to be *bona vacantia* and–

   (a) accordingly belong to the Crown, or to the Duchy of Lancaster or to the Duke of Cornwall for the time being (as the case may be), and

   (b) vest and may be dealt with in the same manner as other *bona vacantia* accruing to the Crown, to the Duchy of Lancaster or to the Duke of Cornwall.

1012(2)   **[Restoration to register]** Subsection (1) has effect subject to the possible restoration of the company to the register under Chapter 3 (see section 1034).

1013   Crown disclaimer of property vesting as bona vacantia

1013(1)   **[Crown disclaimer of property]** Where property vests in the Crown under section 1012, the Crown's title to it under that section may be disclaimed by a notice signed by the Crown representative, that is to say the Treasury Solicitor, or, in relation to property in Scotland, the Queen's and Lord Treasurer's Remembrancer.

1013(2)   **[Right to execute notice of disclaimer]** The right to execute a notice of disclaimer under this section may be waived by or on behalf of the Crown either expressly or by taking possession.

1013(3)   **[Time limit for execution]** A notice of disclaimer must be executed within three years after–

   (a) the date on which the fact that the property may have vested in the Crown under section 1012 first comes to the notice of the Crown representative, or

   (b) if ownership of the property is not established at that date, the end of the period reasonably necessary for the Crown representative to establish the ownership of the property.

1013(4) **[Time limit for execution where application for decision made]** If an application in writing is made to the Crown representative by a person interested in the property requiring him to decide whether he will or will not disclaim, any notice of disclaimer must be executed within twelve months after the making of the application or such further period as may be allowed by the court.

1013(5) **[Execution outside time limit]** A notice of disclaimer under this section is of no effect if it is shown to have been executed after the end of the period specified by subsection (3) or (4).

1013(6) **[Delivery of notice to registrar]** A notice of disclaimer under this section must be delivered to the registrar and retained and registered by him.

1013(7) **[Publication of copy in Gazette]** Copies of it must be published in the Gazette and sent to any persons who have given the Crown representative notice that they claim to be interested in the property.

1013(8) **[Application of section]** This section applies to property vested in the Duchy of Lancaster or the Duke of Cornwall under section 1012 as if for references to the Crown and the Crown representative there were respectively substituted references to the Duchy of Lancaster and to the Solicitor to that Duchy, or to the Duke of Cornwall and to the Solicitor to the Duchy of Cornwall, as the case may be.

1014 Effect of Crown disclaimer

1014(1) **[Effect of notice of disclaimer]** Where notice of disclaimer is executed under section 1013 as respects any property, that property is deemed not to have vested in the Crown under section 1012.

1014(2) **[Application of other sections to Crown disclaimer]** The following sections contain provisions as to the effect of the Crown disclaimer–

> sections 1015 to 1019 apply in relation to property in England and Wales or Northern Ireland;

> sections 1020 to 1022 apply in relation to property in Scotland.

Effect of Crown disclaimer: England and Wales and Northern Ireland

1015 General effect of disclaimer

1015(1) **[General effect of disclaimer]** The Crown's disclaimer operates so as to terminate, as from the date of the disclaimer, the rights, interests and liabilities of the company in or in respect of the property disclaimed.

1015(2) **[Exemption]** It does not, except so far as is necessary for the purpose of releasing the company from any liability, affect the rights or liabilities of any other person.

1016 Disclaimer of leaseholds

1016(1) **[Effect of disclaimer of leaseholds]** The disclaimer of any property of a leasehold character does not take effect unless a copy of the disclaimer has been served (so far as the Crown representative is aware of their addresses) on every person claiming under the company as underlessee or mortgagee, and either–

(a) no application under section 1017 (power of court to make vesting order) is made with respect to that property before the end of the period of 14 days beginning with the day on which the last notice under this paragraph was served, or

(b) where such an application has been made, the court directs that the disclaimer shall take effect.

1016(2) **[Fixtures, tenant's improvements, etc.]** Where the court gives a direction under subsection (1)(b) it may also, instead of or in addition to any order it makes under section 1017, make such order as it thinks fit with respect to fixtures, tenant's improvements and other matters arising out of the lease.

1016(3) [**"Crown representative"**] In this section the "Crown representative" means–

(a) in relation to property vested in the Duchy of Lancaster, the Solicitor to that Duchy;

(b) in relation to property vested in the Duke of Cornwall, the Solicitor to the Duchy of Cornwall;

(c) in relation to property in Scotland, the Queen's and Lord Treasurer's Remembrancer;

(d) in relation to other property, the Treasury Solicitor.

1017 Power of court to make vesting order

1017(1) [Power to make order] The court may on application by a person who–

(a) claims an interest in the disclaimed property, or

(b) is under a liability in respect of the disclaimed property that is not discharged by the disclaimer,

make an order under this section in respect of the property.

1017(2) [Nature of order] An order under this section is an order for the vesting of the disclaimed property in, or its delivery to–

(a) a person entitled to it (or a trustee for such a person), or

(b) a person subject to such a liability as is mentioned in subsection (1)(b) (or a trustee for such a person).

1017(3) [Justification for making order] An order under subsection (2)(b) may only be made where it appears to the court that it would be just to do so for the purpose of compensating the person subject to the liability in respect of the disclaimer.

1017(4) [Terms of order] An order under this section may be made on such terms as the court thinks fit.

1017(5) [Effect of order] On a vesting order being made under this section, the property comprised in it vests in the person named in that behalf in the order without conveyance, assignment or transfer.

1018 Protection of persons holding under a lease

1018(1) [Requirement for terms] The court must not make an order under section 1017 vesting property of a leasehold nature in a person claiming under the company as underlessee or mortgagee except on terms making that person–

(a) subject to the same liabilities and obligations as those to which the company was subject under the lease, or

(b) if the court thinks fit, subject to the same liabilities and obligations as if the lease had been assigned to him.

1018(2) [Orders relating to part of property] Where the order relates to only part of the property comprised in the lease, subsection (1) applies as if the lease had comprised only the property comprised in the vesting order.

1018(3) [Declination of order on terms set] A person claiming under the company as underlessee or mortgagee who declines to accept a vesting order on such terms is excluded from all interest in the property.

1018(4) [Acceptance of order on terms set] If there is no person claiming under the company who is willing to accept an order on such terms, the court has power to vest the company's estate and interest in the property in any person who is liable (whether personally or in a representative character, and whether alone or jointly with the company) to perform the lessee's covenants in the lease.

1018(5) **[Vesting in person freed from estates, etc.]** The court may vest that estate and interest in such a person freed and discharged from all estates, incumbrances and interests created by the company.

1019 Land subject to rentcharge

1019 Where in consequence of the disclaimer land that is subject to a rentcharge vests in any person, neither he nor his successors in title are subject to any personal liability in respect of sums becoming due under the rentcharge, except sums becoming due after he, or some person claiming under or through him, has taken possession or control of the land or has entered into occupation of it.

Effect of Crown disclaimer: Scotland

1020 General effect of disclaimer

1020(1) **[General effect of disclaimer]** The Crown's disclaimer operates to determine, as from the date of the disclaimer, the rights, interests and liabilities of the company, and the property of the company, in or in respect of the property disclaimed.

1020(2) **[Exception]** It does not (except so far as is necessary for the purpose of releasing the company and its property from liability) affect the rights or liabilities of any other person.

1021 Power of court to make vesting order

1021(1) **[Extent of power]** The court may–

(a) on application by a person who either claims an interest in disclaimed property or is under a liability not discharged by this Act in respect of disclaimed property, and

(b) on hearing such persons as it thinks fit,

make an order for the vesting of the property in or its delivery to any persons entitled to it, or to whom it may seem just that the property should be delivered by way of compensation for such liability, or a trustee for him.

1021(2) **[Terms of order]** The order may be made on such terms as the court thinks fit.

1021(3) **[Vesting of property]** On a vesting order being made under this section, the property comprised in it vests accordingly in the person named in that behalf in the order, without conveyance or assignation for that purpose.

1022 Protection of persons holding under a lease

1022(1) **[Requirement for terms]** Where the property disclaimed is held under a lease the court must not make a vesting order in favour of a person claiming under the company, whether–

(a) as sub-lessee, or

(b) as creditor in a duly registered or (as the case may be) recorded heritable security over a lease,

except on the following terms.

1022(2) **[Terms]** The person must by the order be made subject–

(a) to the same liabilities and obligations as those to which the company was subject under the lease in respect of the property, or

(b) if the court thinks fit, only to the same liabilities and obligations as if the lease had been assigned to him.

In either event (if the case so requires) the liabilities and obligations must be as if the lease had comprised only the property comprised in the vesting order.

1022(3)   **[Declination of order on terms set]** A sub-lessee or creditor declining to accept a vesting order on such terms is excluded from all interest in and security over the property.

1022(4)   **[Acceptance of order on terms set]** If there is no person claiming under the company who is willing to accept an order on such terms, the court has power to vest the company's estate and interest in the property in any person liable (either personally or in a representative character, and either alone or jointly with the company) to perform the lessee's obligations under the lease.

1022(5)   **[Vesting in person freed from estates, etc.]** The court may vest that estate and interest in such a person freed and discharged from all interests, rights and obligations created by the company in the lease or in relation to the lease.

1022(6)   **[Heritable securities]** For the purposes of this section a heritable security–

    (a)   is duly recorded if it is recorded in the Register of Sasines, and

    (b)   is duly registered if registered in accordance with the Land Registration etc. (Scotland) Act 2012 (asp 5).

Supplementary provisions

1023   Liability for rentcharge on company's land after dissolution

1023(1)   **[Application of section]** This section applies where on the dissolution of a company land in England and Wales or Northern Ireland that is subject to a rentcharge vests by operation of law in the Crown or any other person ("the proprietor").

1023(2)   **[Personal liability of proprietor]** Neither the proprietor nor his successors in title are subject to any personal liability in respect of sums becoming due under the rentcharge, except sums becoming due after the proprietor, or some person claiming under or through him, has taken possession or control of the land or has entered into occupation of it.

1023(3)   **[Body corporate]** In this section "company" includes any body corporate.

CHAPTER 3

RESTORATION TO THE REGISTER

Administrative restoration to the register

1024   Application for administrative restoration to the register

1024(1)   **[Right to apply]** An application may be made to the registrar to restore to the register a company that has been struck off the register under section 1000 or 1001 (power of registrar to strike off defunct company).

1024(2)   **[Dissolved companies]** An application under this section may be made whether or not the company has in consequence been dissolved.

1024(3)   **[Former directors or members]** An application under this section may only be made by a former director or former member of the company.

1024(4)   **[Time limit]** An application under this section may not be made after the end of the period of six years from the date of the dissolution of the company.

    For this purpose an application is made when it is received by the registrar.

1025 Requirements for administrative restoration

1025(1) [Requirement for conditions to be met] On an application under section 1024 the registrar shall restore the company to the register if, and only if, the following conditions are met.

1025(2) [Carrying on business] The first condition is that the company was carrying on business or in operation at the time of its striking off.

1025(3) [Bona vacantia property] The second condition is that, if any property or right previously vested in or held on trust for the company has vested as *bona vacantia*, the Crown representative has signified to the registrar in writing consent to the company's restoration to the register.

1025(4) [Consent of Crown representative] It is the applicant's responsibility to obtain that consent and to pay any costs (in Scotland, expenses) of the Crown representative–

(a) in dealing with the property during the period of dissolution, or

(b) in connection with the proceedings on the application,

that may be demanded as a condition of giving consent.

1025(5) [Delivery of documents; payment of penalties] The third condition is that the applicant has–

(a) delivered to the registrar such documents relating to the company as are necessary to bring up to date the records kept by the registrar, and

(b) paid any penalties under section 453 or corresponding earlier provisions (civil penalty for failure to deliver accounts) that were outstanding at the date of dissolution or striking off.

1025(6) ["Crown representative"] In this section the "Crown representative" means–

(a) in relation to property vested in the Duchy of Lancaster, the Solicitor to that Duchy;

(b) in relation to property vested in the Duke of Cornwall, the Solicitor to the Duchy of Cornwall;

(c) in relation to property in Scotland, the Queen's and Lord Treasurer's Remembrancer;

(d) in relation to other property, the Treasury Solicitor.

1026 Application to be accompanied by statement of compliance

1026(1) [Requirement for statement of compliance] An application under section 1024 (application for administrative restoration to the register) must be accompanied by a statement of compliance.

1026(2) [Nature of statement] The statement of compliance required is a statement–

(a) that the person making the application has standing to apply (see subsection (3) of that section), and

(b) that the requirements for administrative restoration (see section 1025) are met.

1026(3) [Evidence of contents] The registrar may accept the statement of compliance as sufficient evidence of those matters.

1027 Registrar's decision on application for administrative restoration

1027(1) [Duty to give notice] The registrar must give notice to the applicant of the decision on an application under section 1024 (application for administrative restoration to the register).

1027(2) [Restoration to register] If the decision is that the company should be restored to the register, the restoration takes effect as from the date that notice is sent.

1027(3)   **[Publication of entry in Gazette]** In the case of such a decision, the registrar must–

(a) enter on the register a note of the date as from which the company's restoration to the register takes effect, and

(b) cause notice of the restoration to be published in the Gazette.

1027(4)   **[Content of notice]** The notice under subsection (3)(b) must state–

(a) the name of the company or, if the company is restored to the register under a different name (see section 1033), that name and its former name,

(b) the company's registered number, and

(c) the date as from which the restoration of the company to the register takes effect.

1028   Effect of administrative restoration

1028(1)   **[General effect]** The general effect of administrative restoration to the register is that the company is deemed to have continued in existence as if it had not been dissolved or struck off the register.

1028(2)   **[Penalties under s.453]** The company is not liable to a penalty under section 453 or any corresponding earlier provision (civil penalty for failure to deliver accounts) for a financial year in relation to which the period for filing accounts and reports ended–

(a) after the date of dissolution or striking off, and

(b) before the restoration of the company to the register.

1028(3)   **[Court directions]** The court may give such directions and make such provision as seems just for placing the company and all other persons in the same position (as nearly as may be) as if the company had not been dissolved or struck off the register.

1028(4)   **[Timing of application for court directions]** An application to the court for such directions or provision may be made any time within three years after the date of restoration of the company to the register.

1028A   Administrative restoration of company with share warrants

1028A(1)   This section applies in relation to a company which has been struck off the register under section 1000 or 1001 and which, at the time it was struck off, had any share warrant in issue.

1028A(2)   If the registrar restores the company to the register under section 1025, the share warrant and the shares specified in it are cancelled with effect from the date the restoration takes effect.

1028A(3)   If as a result of subsection (2) the company has no issued share capital, the company must, before the end of the period of one month beginning with the date the restoration takes effect, allot at least one share in the company; and section 549(1) does not apply to such an allotment.

1028A(4)   The company must, before the end of the period of 15 days beginning with the date the restoration takes effect, deliver a statement of capital to the registrar.

1028A(5)   Subsection (4) does not apply in a case where the company is required under subsection (3) to make an allotment (because in such a case section 555 will apply).

1028A(6)   The statement of capital must state with respect to the company's share capital as reduced by the cancellation of the share warrant and the shares specified in it–

(a) the total number of shares of the company,

(b) the aggregate nominal value of those shares,

(c)   the aggregate amount (if any) unpaid on those shares (whether on account of their nominal value or by way of premium), and

(d)   for each class of shares–

(i)   prescribed particulars of the rights attached to the shares,

(ii)   the total number of shares of that class, and

(iii)   the aggregate nominal value of shares of that class.

(e)   [...]

1028A(7)   Where a share warrant is cancelled in accordance with subsection (2), the company must, as soon as reasonably practicable–

(a)   enter the date the cancellation takes effect in its register of members,

(b)   where an election is in force under section 128B of the Companies Act 2006 (option to keep membership information on central register) in respect of the company, deliver that information to the registrar as if it were information required to be delivered under section 128E of that Act.

1028A(8)   Subsection (9) applies where–

(a)   any property or right previously vested in or held on trust for the company in respect of any share specified in a share warrant has vested as *bona vacantia* (see section 1012), and

(b)   the warrant and the share are cancelled on the restoration of the company in accordance with this section.

1028A(9)   On restoration of the company, that property or right–

(a)   may not be returned to the company, and

(b)   accordingly, remains vested as bona vacantia.

1028A(10)   If default is made in complying with subsection (3) or (4), an offence is committed by–

(a)   the company, and

(b)   every officer of the company who is in default.

For this purpose a shadow director is treated as an officer of the company.

1028A(11)   A person guilty of an offence under this section is liable–

(a)   on conviction on indictment, to a fine;

(b)   on summary conviction–

(i)   in England and Wales, to a fine;

(ii)   in Scotland or Northern Ireland, to a fine not exceeding the statutory maximum.

History
Section 1028A inserted by SBEEA 2015 Sch.4 para.27(1) as from 26 May 2015 and subsequently modified by the same Act Sch.4 para.27(2), (3) as from 30 June 2016.

Restoration to the register by the court

1029   Application to court for restoration to the register

1029(1)   [Scope of application] An application may be made to the court to restore to the register a company–

(a) that has been dissolved under Chapter 9 of Part 4 of the Insolvency Act 1986 (c. 45) or Chapter 9 of Part 5 of the Insolvency (Northern Ireland) Order 1989 (S.I. 1989/2405 (N.I. 19)) (dissolution of company after winding up),

(b) that is deemed to have been dissolved under paragraph 84(6) of Schedule B1 to that Act or paragraph 85(6) of Schedule B1 to that Order (dissolution of company following administration), or

(c) that has been struck off the register–

    (i) under section 1000 or 1001 (power of registrar to strike off defunct company), or

    (ii) under section 1003 (voluntary striking off),

whether or not the company has in consequence been dissolved.

1029(2) **[Entitlement to make application]** An application under this section may be made by–

(a) the Secretary of State,

(b) any former director of the company,

(c) any person having an interest in land in which the company had a superior or derivative interest,

(d) any person having an interest in land or other property–

    (i) that was subject to rights vested in the company, or

    (ii) that was benefited by obligations owed by the company,

(e) any person who but for the company's dissolution would have been in a contractual relationship with it,

(f) any person with a potential legal claim against the company,

(g) any manager or trustee of a pension fund established for the benefit of employees of the company,

(h) any former member of the company (or the personal representatives of such a person),

(i) any person who was a creditor of the company at the time of its striking off or dissolution,

(j) any former liquidator of the company,

(k) where the company was struck off the register under section 1003 (voluntary striking off), any person of a description specified by regulations under section 1006(1)(f) or 1007(2)(f) (persons entitled to notice of application for voluntary striking off),

or by any other person appearing to the court to have an interest in the matter.

1030   When application to the court may be made

1030(1)   [Timing of application] An application to the court for restoration of a company to the register may be made at any time for the purpose of–

(a) bringing proceedings against the company for damages for personal injury;

(b) an insurer (within the meaning of the Third Parties (Rights Against Insurers) Act 2010) bringing proceedings against a third party in the name of that company in respect of that company's liability for damages for personal injury.

1030(2)   [Limitation provisions of other enactments] No order shall be made on such an application if it appears to the court that the proceedings would fail by virtue of any enactment as to the time within which proceedings must be brought.

1030(3)   [Power to disregard time periods] In making that decision the court must have regard to its power under section 1032(3) (power to give consequential directions etc) to direct that the period between the dissolution (or striking off) of the company and the making of the order is not to count for the purposes of any such enactment.

1030(4)   [Six-year limit] In any other case an application to the court for restoration of a company to the register may not be made after the end of the period of six years from the date of the dissolution of the company, subject as follows.

1030(5)   [Timing following refusal of administrative restoration to register] In a case where–

(a)   the company has been struck off the register under section 1000 or 1001 (power of registrar to strike off defunct company),

(b)   an application to the registrar has been made under section 1024 (application for administrative restoration to the register) within the time allowed for making such an application, and

(c)   the registrar has refused the application,

an application to the court under this section may be made within 28 days of notice of the registrar's decision being issued by the registrar, even if the period of six years mentioned in subsection (4) above has expired.

1030(6)   [Interpretation] For the purposes of this section–

(a)   "personal injury" includes any disease and any impairment of a person's physical or mental condition; and

(b)   references to damages for personal injury include–

(i)   any sum claimed by virtue of section 1(2)(c) of the Law Reform (Miscellaneous Provisions) Act 1934 (c. 41) or section 14(2)(c) of the Law Reform (Miscellaneous Provisions) Act (Northern Ireland) 1937 (1937 c. 9 (N.I.)) (funeral expenses)), and

(ii)   damages under the Fatal Accidents Act 1976 (c. 30), the Damages (Scotland) Act 2011 (asp 7) or the Fatal Accidents (Northern Ireland) Order 1977 (S.I. 1977/1251 (N.I. 18)).

History

Section 1030(6)(b)(ii) amended by the Damages (Scotland) Act 2011 Sch.1 para.9 as from 7 July 2011.

Section 1030(1) amended by the Third Parties (Rights Against Insurers) Act 2010 (Consequential Amendment of Companies Act 2006) Regulations 2018 (SI 2018/1162) regs 1, 2 as from 23 November 2018.

1031   Decision on application for restoration by the court

1031(1)   [Power to order restoration to register[On an application under section 1029 the court may order the restoration of the company to the register–

(a)   if the company was struck off the register under section 1000 or 1001 (power of registrar to strike off defunct companies) and the company was, at the time of the striking off, carrying on business or in operation;

(b)   if the company was struck off the register under section 1003 (voluntary striking off) and any of the requirements of sections 1004 to 1009 was not complied with;

(c)   if in any other case the court considers it just to do so.

1031(2)   [Effect of court order] If the court orders restoration of the company to the register, the restoration takes effect on a copy of the court's order being delivered to the registrar.

1031(3)   [Publication of notice in Gazette] The registrar must cause to be published in the Gazette notice of the restoration of the company to the register.

1031(4)   [Content of notice] The notice must state–

(a)   the name of the company or, if the company is restored to the register under a different name (see section 1033), that name and its former name,

(b)   the company's registered number, and

(c)   the date on which the restoration took effect.

1032   Effect of court order for restoration to the register

1032(1)   [General effect] The general effect of an order by the court for restoration to the register is that the company is deemed to have continued in existence as if it had not been dissolved or struck off the register.

1032(2)   [Penalties under s.453] The company is not liable to a penalty under section 453 or any corresponding earlier provision (civil penalty for failure to deliver accounts) for a financial year in relation to which the period for filing accounts and reports ended–

(a)   after the date of dissolution or striking off, and

(b)   before the restoration of the company to the register.

1032(3)   [Power of court to give directions] The court may give such directions and make such provision as seems just for placing the company and all other persons in the same position (as nearly as may be) as if the company had not been dissolved or struck off the register.

1032(4)   [Scope of directions] The court may also give directions as to–

(a)   the delivery to the registrar of such documents relating to the company as are necessary to bring up to date the records kept by the registrar,

(b)   the payment of the costs (in Scotland, expenses) of the registrar in connection with the proceedings for the restoration of the company to the register,

(c)   where any property or right previously vested in or held on trust for the company has vested as *bona vacantia*, the payment of the costs (in Scotland, expenses) of the Crown representative–

(i)   in dealing with the property during the period of dissolution, or

(ii)   in connection with the proceedings on the application.

1032(5)   ["Crown representative"] In this section the "Crown representative" means–

(a)   in relation to property vested in the Duchy of Lancaster, the Solicitor to that Duchy;

(b)   in relation to property vested in the Duke of Cornwall, the Solicitor to the Duchy of Cornwall;

(c)   in relation to property in Scotland, the Queen's and Lord Treasurer's Remembrancer;

(d)   in relation to other property, the Treasury Solicitor.

1032A   Restoration by court of company with share warrants

1032A(1)   This section applies in relation to a company falling within section 1029(1) if, at the time it was dissolved, deemed to be dissolved or (as the case may be) struck off, it had any share warrant in issue.

1032A(2)   If the court orders the restoration of the company to the register, the order must also cancel the share warrant and the shares specified in it with effect from the date the restoration takes effect.

1032A(3)   If as a result of subsection (2) the company has no issued share capital, the company must, before the end of the period of one month beginning with the date the restoration takes effect, allot at least one share in the company; and section 549(1) does not apply to such an allotment.

1032A(4) Subsection (6) applies in a case where–

(a) the application under section 1029 was made by a person mentioned in subsection (2)(b) or (h) of that section, or

(b) the court order specifies that it applies.

1032A(5) But subsection (6) does not apply in any case where the company is required under subsection (3) to make an allotment (because in such a case section 555 will apply).

1032A(6) In a case where this subsection applies, the company must, before the end of the period of 15 days beginning with the date the restoration takes effect, deliver a statement of capital to the registrar.

1032A(7) The statement of capital must state with respect to the company's share capital as reduced by the cancellation of the share warrant and the shares specified in it–

(a) the total number of shares of the company,

(b) the aggregate nominal value of those shares,

(c) the aggregate amount (if any) unpaid on those shares (whether on account of their nominal value or by way of premium), and

(d) for each class of shares–

    (i) prescribed particulars of the rights attached to the shares,

    (ii) the total number of shares of that class, and

    (iii) the aggregate nominal value of shares of that class.

(e) [...]

1032A(8) Where a share warrant is cancelled by an order as mentioned in subsection (2), the company must, as soon as reasonably practicable–

(a) enter the date the cancellation takes effect in its register of members, or

(b) where an election is in force under section 128B of the Companies Act 2006 (option to keep membership information on central register) in respect of the company, deliver that information to the registrar as if it were information to be delivered under section 128E of that Act.

1032A(9) Subsection (10) applies where–

(a) any property or right previously vested in or held on trust for the company in respect of any share specified in a share warrant has vested as bona vacantia (see section 1012), and

(b) the warrant and the share are cancelled on the restoration of the company in accordance with this section.

1032A(10) On restoration of the company, that property or right–

(a) may not be returned to the company, and

(b) accordingly, remains vested as bona vacantia.

1032A(11) If default is made in complying with subsection (3) or (6), an offence is committed by–

(a) the company, and

(b) every officer of the company who is in default.

For this purpose a shadow director is treated as an officer of the company.

1032A(12) A person guilty of an offence under this section is liable–

(a) on conviction on indictment, to a fine;

(b) on summary conviction–

    (i) in England and Wales, to a fine;

    (ii) in Scotland or Northern Ireland, to a fine not exceeding the statutory maximum.

History
Section 1032A inserted by SBEEA 2015 Sch.4 para.28(1) as from 26 May 2015 and subsequently modified by the same Act Sch.4 para.28(2), (3) as from 30 June 2016.

Supplementary provisions

1033 Company's name on restoration

1033(1) [Name on restoration] A company is restored to the register with the name it had before it was dissolved or struck off the register, subject to the following provisions.

1033(2) [Name where previous name not permitted] If at the date of restoration the company could not be registered under its former name without contravening section 66 (name not to be the same as another in the registrar's index of company names), it must be restored to the register–

(a) under another name specified–

    (i) in the case of administrative restoration, in the application to the registrar, or

    (ii) in the case of restoration under a court order, in the court's order, or

(b) as if its registered number was also its name.

References to a company's being registered in a name, and to registration in that context, shall be read as including the company's being restored to the register.

1033(3) [Restoration under name specified in application] If a company is restored to the register under a name specified in the application to the registrar, the provisions of–

    section 80 (change of name: registration and issue of new certificate of incorporation), and

    section 81 (change of name: effect),

apply as if the application to the registrar were notice of a change of name.

1033(4) [Restoration under name specified in court order] If a company is restored to the register under a name specified in the court's order, the provisions of–

    section 80 (change of name: registration and issue of new certificate of incorporation), and

    section 81 (change of name: effect),

apply as if the copy of the court order delivered to the registrar were notice of a change a name.

1033(5) [Restoration under registered number] If the company is restored to the register as if its registered number was also its name–

(a) the company must change its name within 14 days after the date of the restoration,

(b) the change may be made by resolution of the directors (without prejudice to any other method of changing the company's name),

(c) the company must give notice to the registrar of the change, and

(d) sections 80 and 81 apply as regards the registration and effect of the change.

1033(6) **[Offence]** If the company fails to comply with subsection (5)(a) or (c) an offence is committed by–

    (a) the company, and

    (b) every officer of the company who is in default.

1033(7) **[Penalty]** A person guilty of an offence under subsection (6) is liable on summary conviction to a fine not exceeding level 5 on the standard scale and, for continued contravention, a daily default fine not exceeding one-tenth of the greater of £5,000 or level 4 on the standard scale.

1034   Effect of restoration to the register where property has vested as bona vacantia

1034(1) **[Right to dispose property]** The person in whom any property or right is vested by section 1012 (property of dissolved company to be *bona vacantia*) may dispose of, or of an interest in, that property or right despite the fact that the company may be restored to the register under this Chapter.

1034(2) **[Effect of restoration on disposition]** If the company is restored to the register–

    (a) the restoration does not affect the disposition (but without prejudice to its effect in relation to any other property or right previously vested in or held on trust for the company), and

    (b) the Crown or, as the case may be, the Duke of Cornwall shall pay to the company an amount equal to–

        (i) the amount of any consideration received for the property or right or, as the case may be, the interest in it, or

        (ii) the value of any such consideration at the time of the disposition,

or, if no consideration was received an amount equal to the value of the property, right or interest disposed of, as at the date of the disposition

1034(3) **[Crown representative's costs]** There may be deducted from the amount payable under subsection (2)(b) the reasonable costs of the Crown representative in connection with the disposition (to the extent that they have not been paid as a condition of administrative restoration or pursuant to a court order for restoration).

1034(4) **[Duchy of Lancaster]** Where a liability accrues under subsection (2) in respect of any property or right which before the restoration of the company to the register had accrued as *bona vacantia* to the Duchy of Lancaster, the Attorney General of that Duchy shall represent Her Majesty in any proceedings arising in connection with that liability.

1034(5) **[Duchy of Cornwall]** Where a liability accrues under subsection (2) in respect of any property or right which before the restoration of the company to the register had accrued as *bona vacantia* to the Duchy of Cornwall, such persons as the Duke of Cornwall (or other possessor for the time being of the Duchy) may appoint shall represent the Duke (or other possessor) in any proceedings arising out of that liability.

1034(6) **["Crown representative"]** In this section the "Crown representative" means–

    (a) in relation to property vested in the Duchy of Lancaster, the Solicitor to that Duchy;

    (b) in relation to property vested in the Duke of Cornwall, the Solicitor to the Duchy of Cornwall;

    (c) in relation to property in Scotland, the Queen's and Lord Treasurer's Remembrancer;

    (d) in relation to other property, the Treasury Solicitor.

PART 34

OVERSEAS COMPANIES

Other requirements

1052 Company charges

1052(1) [Power to make regulations] The Secretary of State may by regulations make provision about the registration of specified charges over property in the United Kingdom of a registered overseas company.

1052(2) [Scope of power] The power in subsection (1) includes power to make provision about–

(a) a registered overseas company that–

    (i) has particulars registered in more than one part of the United Kingdom;

    (ii) has property in more than one part of the United Kingdom;

(b) the circumstances in which property is to be regarded, for the purposes of the regulations, as being, or not being, in the United Kingdom or in a particular part of the United Kingdom;

(c) the keeping by a registered overseas company of records and registers about specified charges and their inspection;

(d) the consequences of a failure to register a charge in accordance with the regulations;

(e) the circumstances in which a registered overseas company ceases to be subject to the regulations.

1052(3) [Company charges] The regulations may for this purpose apply, with or without modifications, any of the provisions of Part 25 (company charges).

1052(4) [Modification of Pt 25] The regulations may modify any reference in an enactment to Part 25, or to a particular provision of that Part, so as to include a reference to the regulations or to a specified provision of the regulations.

1052(5) [Negative resolution procedure] Regulations under this section are subject to negative resolution procedure.

1052(6) [Interpretation] In this section–

"registered overseas company" means an overseas company that has registered particulars under section 1046(1), and

"specified" means specified in the regulations.

PART 40

COMPANY DIRECTORS: FOREIGN DISQUALIFICATION ETC

Introductory

1182 Persons subject to foreign restrictions

1182(1) [Scope of section] This section defines what is meant by references in this Part to a person being subject to foreign restrictions.

1182(2) [Persons subject to foreign restrictions] A person is subject to foreign restrictions if under the law of a country or territory outside the United Kingdom–

(a) he is, by reason of misconduct or unfitness, disqualified to any extent from acting in connection with the affairs of a company,

(b) he is, by reason of misconduct or unfitness, required–

    (i) to obtain permission from a court or other authority, or

    (ii) to meet any other condition,

before acting in connection with the affairs of a company, or

(c) he has, by reason of misconduct or unfitness, given undertakings to a court or other authority of a country or territory outside the United Kingdom–

    (i) not to act in connection with the affairs of a company, or

    (ii) restricting the extent to which, or the way in which, he may do so.

1182(3)   [Actions in connection with company's affairs] The references in subsection (2) to acting in connection with the affairs of a company are to doing any of the following–

(a) being a director of a company,

(b) acting as receiver of a company's property, or

(c) being concerned or taking part in the promotion, formation or management of a company.

1182(4)   [Interpretation] In this section–

(a) "company" means a company incorporated or formed under the law of the country or territory in question, and

(b) in relation to such a company–

"director" means the holder of an office corresponding to that of director of a UK company; and

"receiver" includes any corresponding officer under the law of that country or territory.

1183   Meaning of "the court" and "UK company"

1183   In this Part–

"the court" means–

(a) in England and Wales, the High Court or the county court;

(b) in Scotland, the Court of Session or the sheriff court;

(c) in Northern Ireland, the High Court;

"UK company" means a company registered under this Act.

Power to disqualify

1184   Disqualification of persons subject to foreign restrictions

1184(1)   [Power to make regulations] The Secretary of State may make provision by regulations disqualifying a person subject to foreign restrictions from–

(a) being a director of a UK company,

(b) acting as receiver of a UK company's property, or

(c) in any way, whether directly or indirectly, being concerned or taking part in the promotion, formation or management of a UK company.

1184(2)   [Scope of regulations] The regulations may provide that a person subject to foreign restrictions–

(a)   is disqualified automatically by virtue of the regulations, or

(b)   may be disqualified by order of the court on the application of the Secretary of State.

1184(3)   [Power of Secretary of State to accept undertakings] The regulations may provide that the Secretary of State may accept an undertaking (a "disqualification undertaking") from a person subject to foreign restrictions that he will not do anything which would be in breach of a disqualification under subsection (1).

1184(4)   ["Person disqualified under this Part"] In this Part–

(a)   a "person disqualified under this Part" is a person–

   (i)   disqualified as mentioned in subsection (2)(a) or (b), or

   (ii)   who has given and is subject to a disqualification undertaking;

(b)   references to a breach of a disqualification include a breach of a disqualification undertaking.

1184(5)   [Applications to court for permission to act] The regulations may provide for applications to the court by persons disqualified under this Part for permission to act in a way which would otherwise be in breach of the disqualification.

1184(6)   [Cessation of disqualification] The regulations must provide that a person ceases to be disqualified under this Part on his ceasing to be subject to foreign restrictions.

1184(7)   [Affirmative resolution procedure] Regulations under this section are subject to affirmative resolution procedure.

1185   Disqualification regulations: supplementary

1185(1)   [Scope of regulation under s.1184] Regulations under section 1184 may make different provision for different cases and may in particular distinguish between cases by reference to–

(a)   the conduct on the basis of which the person became subject to foreign restrictions;

(b)   the nature of the foreign restrictions;

(c)   the country or territory under whose law the foreign restrictions were imposed.

1185(2)   [Scope of regulations under s.1184(2)(b)] Regulations under section 1184(2)(b) or (5) (provision for applications to the court)–

(a)   must specify the grounds on which an application may be made;

(b)   may specify factors to which the court shall have regard in determining an application.

1185(3)   [Factors to be taken into consideration] The regulations may, in particular, require the court to have regard to the following factors–

(a)   whether the conduct on the basis of which the person became subject to foreign restrictions would, if done in relation to a UK company, have led a court to make a disqualification order on an application under the Company Directors Disqualification Act 1986 (c. 46) or the Company Directors Disqualification (Northern Ireland) Order 2002 (S.I. 2002/3150 (N.I. 4));

(b)   in a case in which the conduct on the basis of which the person became subject to foreign restrictions would not be unlawful if done in relation to a UK company, the fact that the person acted unlawfully under foreign law;

(c)   whether the person's activities in relation to UK companies began after he became subject to foreign restrictions;

(d) whether the person's activities (or proposed activities) in relation to UK companies are undertaken (or are proposed to be undertaken) outside the United Kingdom.

1185(4) **[Scope of regulations under s.1184(3)]** Regulations under section 1184(3) (provision as to undertakings given to the Secretary of State) may include provision allowing the Secretary of State, in determining whether to accept an undertaking, to take into account matters other than criminal convictions notwithstanding that the person may be criminally liable in respect of those matters.

1185(5) **[Scope of regulations under s.1184(5)]** Regulations under section 1184(5) (provision for application to court for permission to act) may include provision–

(a) entitling the Secretary of State to be represented at the hearing of the application, and

(b) as to the giving of evidence or the calling of witnesses by the Secretary of State at the hearing of the application.

1186 Offence of breach of disqualification

1186(1) **[Offence]** Regulations under section 1184 may provide that a person disqualified under this Part who acts in breach of the disqualification commits an offence.

1186(2) **[Penalty]** The regulations may provide that a person guilty of such an offence is liable–

(a) on conviction on indictment, to imprisonment for a term not exceeding two years or a fine (or both);

(b) on summary conviction–

    (i) in England and Wales, to imprisonment for a term not exceeding twelve months or to a fine not exceeding the statutory maximum (or both);

    (ii) in Scotland or Northern Ireland, to imprisonment for a term not exceeding six months, or to a fine not exceeding the statutory maximum (or both).

1186(3) **[Offences committed before commencement of s.154(1) of 2003 Act]** In relation to an offence committed before the commencement of section 154(1) of the Criminal Justice Act 2003 (c. 44), for "twelve months" in subsection (2)(b)(i) substitute "six months".

Power to make persons liable for company's debts

1187 Personal liability for debts of company

1187(1) **[Persons subject to foreign restrictions]** The Secretary of State may provide by regulations that a person who, at a time when he is subject to foreign restrictions–

(a) is a director of a UK company, or

(b) is involved in the management of a UK company,

is personally responsible for all debts and other liabilities of the company incurred during that time.

1187(2) **[Joint and several liability]** A person who is personally responsible by virtue of this section for debts and other liabilities of a company is jointly and severally liable in respect of those debts and liabilities with–

(a) the company, and

(b) any other person who (whether by virtue of this section or otherwise) is so liable.

1187(3) **[Persons involved in management of company]** For the purposes of this section a person is involved in the management of a company if he is concerned, whether directly or indirectly, or takes part, in the management of the company.

1187(4) **[Different provisions for different cases]** The regulations may make different provision for different cases and may in particular distinguish between cases by reference to–

(a) the conduct on the basis of which the person became subject to foreign restrictions;

(b) the nature of the foreign restrictions;

(c) the country or territory under whose law the foreign restrictions were imposed.

1187(5) **[Affirmative resolution procedure]** Regulations under this section are subject to affirmative resolution procedure.

Power to require statements to be sent to the registrar of companies

1188   Statements from persons subject to foreign restrictions

1188(1) **[Power to make regulations]** The Secretary of State may make provision by regulations requiring a person who–

(a) is subject to foreign restrictions, and

(b) is not disqualified under this Part,

to send a statement to the registrar if he does anything that, if done by a person disqualified under this Part, would be in breach of the disqualification.

1188(2) **[Contents of statement]** The statement must include such information as may be specified in the regulations relating to–

(a) the person's activities in relation to UK companies, and

(b) the foreign restrictions to which the person is subject.

1188(3) **[Specification of time limit]** The statement must be sent to the registrar within such period as may be specified in the regulations.

1188(4) **[Different provisions for different cases]** The regulations may make different provision for different cases and may in particular distinguish between cases by reference to–

(a) the conduct on the basis of which the person became subject to foreign restrictions;

(b) the nature of the foreign restrictions;

(c) the country or territory under whose law the foreign restrictions were imposed.

1188(5) **[Affirmative resolution procedure]** Regulations under this section are subject to affirmative resolution procedure.

1189   Statements from persons disqualified

1189(1) **[Power to make regulations]** The Secretary of State may make provision by regulations requiring a statement or notice sent to the registrar of companies under any of the provisions listed below that relates (wholly or partly) to a person who–

(a) is a person disqualified under this Part, or

(b) is subject to a disqualification order or disqualification undertaking under the Company Directors Disqualification Act 1986 (c. 46) or the Company Directors Disqualification (Northern Ireland) Order 2002 (S.I. 2002/3150 (N.I. 4)),

to be accompanied by an additional statement.

1189(2) **[Specified provisions]** The provisions referred to above are–

(a)   section 12 (statement of a company's proposed officers),

(b)   section 167(2) (notice of person having become director), and

(c)   section 276 (notice of a person having become secretary or one of joint secretaries).

1189(3) **[Additional statement]** The additional statement is a statement that the person has obtained permission from a court, on an application under section 1184(5) or (as the case may be) for the purposes of section 1(1)(a) of the Company Directors Disqualification Act 1986 (c. 46) or Article 3(1) of the Company Directors Disqualification (Northern Ireland) Order 2002 (S.I. 2002/3150 (N.I. 4)), to act in the capacity in question.

1189(4) **[Affirmative resolution procedure]** Regulations under this section are subject to affirmative resolution procedure.

1190   Statements: whether to be made public

1190(1) **[Regulations may require statement to be public]** Regulations under section 1188 or 1189 (statements required to be sent to registrar) may provide that a statement sent to the registrar of companies under the regulations is to be treated as a record relating to a company for the purposes of section 1080 (the companies register).

1190(2) **[Provision for withholding from public inspection]** The regulations may make provision as to the circumstances in which such a statement is to be, or may be–

(a)   withheld from public inspection, or

(b)   removed from the register.

1190(3) **[Conditions for withholding from public inspection]** The regulations may, in particular, provide that a statement is not to be withheld from public inspection or removed from the register unless the person to whom it relates provides such information, and satisfies such other conditions, as may be specified.

1190(4) **[Disapplication of s.1081]** The regulations may provide that section 1081 (note of removal of material from the register) does not apply, or applies with such modifications as may be specified, in the case of material removed from the register under the regulations.

1190(5) **["Specified"]** In this section "specified" means specified in the regulations.

1191   Offences

1191(1) **[Offence]** Regulations under section 1188 or 1189 may provide that it is an offence for a person–

(a)   to fail to comply with a requirement under the regulations to send a statement to the registrar;

(b)   knowingly or recklessly to send a statement under the regulations to the registrar that is misleading, false or deceptive in a material particular.

1191(2) **[Penalty]** The regulations may provide that a person guilty of such an offence is liable–

(a)   on conviction on indictment, to imprisonment for a term not exceeding two years or a fine (or both);

(b)   on summary conviction–

(i)   in England and Wales, to imprisonment for a term not exceeding twelve months or to a fine not exceeding the statutory maximum (or both);

(ii)   in Scotland or Northern Ireland, to imprisonment for a term not exceeding six months, or to a fine not exceeding the statutory maximum (or both).

1191(3)   [Offences committed before commencement of s.154(1) of 2003 Act] In relation to an offence committed before the commencement of section 154(1) of the Criminal Justice Act 2003 (c. 44), for "twelve months" in subsection (2)(b)(i) substitute "six months".

Third Parties (Rights against Insurers) Act 2010

(2010 Chapter 10)

An Act to make provision about the rights of third parties against insurers of liabilities to third parties in the case where the insured is insolvent, and in certain other cases.

[25th March 2010]

[**Note:** Changes made by the Insurance Act 2015 and the Third Parties (Rights against Insurers) Regulations 2016 (SI 2016/570) have been incorporated into the text.]

Transfer of rights to third parties

1 Rights against insurer of insolvent person etc

1(1) This section applies if–

(a) a relevant person incurs a liability against which that person is insured under a contract of insurance, or

(b) a person who is subject to such a liability becomes a relevant person.

1(2) The rights of the relevant person under the contract against the insurer in respect of the liability are transferred to and vest in the person to whom the liability is or was incurred (the "third party").

1(3) The third party may bring proceedings to enforce the rights against the insurer without having established the relevant person's liability; but the third party may not enforce those rights without having established that liability.

1(4) For the purposes of this Act, a liability is established only if its existence and amount are established; and, for that purpose, "establish" means establish–

(a) by virtue of a declaration under section 2 or a declarator under section 3,

(b) by a judgment or decree,

(c) by an award in arbitral proceedings or by an arbitration, or

(d) by an enforceable agreement.

1(5) In this Act–

(a) references to an "insured" are to a person who incurs or who is subject to a liability to a third party against which that person is insured under a contract of insurance;

(b) references to a "relevant person" are to a person within sections 4 to 7 (and see also paragraph 1A of Schedule 3);

(c) references to a "third party" are to be construed in accordance with subsection (2);

(d) references to "transferred rights" are to rights under a contract of insurance which are transferred under this section.

History
Section 1(5)(b) amended by the Insurance Act 2015 s.20 and Sch.2 para.4 from 1 August 2016.

2 Establishing liability in England and Wales and Northern Ireland

2(1) This section applies where a person (P)–

(a) claims to have rights under a contract of insurance by virtue of a transfer under section 1, but

(b) has not yet established the insured's liability which is insured under that contract.

2(2) P may bring proceedings against the insurer for either or both of the following–

(a) a declaration as to the insured's liability to P;

(b) a declaration as to the insurer's potential liability to P.

2(3) In such proceedings P is entitled, subject to any defence on which the insurer may rely, to a declaration under subsection (2)(a) or (b) on proof of the insured's liability to P or (as the case may be) the insurer's potential liability to P.

2(4) Where proceedings are brought under subsection (2)(a) the insurer may rely on any defence on which the insured could rely if those proceedings were proceedings brought against the insured in respect of the insured's liability to P.

2(5) Subsection (4) is subject to section 12(1).

2(6) Where the court makes a declaration under this section, the effect of which is that the insurer is liable to P, the court may give the appropriate judgment against the insurer.

2(7) Where a person applying for a declaration under subsection (2)(b) is entitled or required, by virtue of the contract of insurance, to do so in arbitral proceedings, that person may also apply in the same proceedings for a declaration under subsection (2)(a).

2(8) In the application of this section to arbitral proceedings, subsection (6) is to be read as if "tribunal" were substituted for "court" and "make the appropriate award" for "give the appropriate judgment".

2(9) When bringing proceedings under subsection (2)(a), P may also make the insured a defendant to those proceedings.

2(10) If (but only if) the insured is a defendant to proceedings under this section (whether by virtue of subsection (9) or otherwise), a declaration under subsection (2) binds the insured as well as the insurer.

2(11)   In this section, references to the insurer's potential liability to P are references to the insurer's liability in respect of the insured's liability to P, if established.

3   Establishing liability in Scotland

3(1)   This section applies where a person (P)–

(a)   claims to have rights under a contract of insurance by virtue of a transfer under section 1, but

(b)   has not yet established the insured's liability which is insured under that contract.

3(2)   P may bring proceedings against the insurer for either or both of the following–

(a)   a declarator as to the insured's liability to P;

(b)   a declarator as to the insurer's potential liability to P.

3(3)   Where proceedings are brought under subsection (2)(a) the insurer may rely on any defence on which the insured could rely if those proceedings were proceedings brought against the insured in respect of the insured's liability to P.

3(4)   Subsection (3) is subject to section 12(1).

3(5)   Where the court grants a declarator under this section, the effect of which is that the insurer is liable to P, the court may grant the appropriate decree against the insurer.

3(6)   Where a person applying for a declarator under subsection (2)(b) is entitled or required, by virtue of the contract of insurance, to do so in an arbitration, that person may also apply in the same arbitration for a declarator under subsection (2)(a).

3(7)   In the application of this section to an arbitration, subsection (5) is to be read as if "tribunal" were substituted for "court" and "make the appropriate award" for "grant the appropriate decree".

3(8)   When bringing proceedings under subsection (2)(a), P may also make the insured a defender to those proceedings.

3(9)   If (but only if) the insured is a defender to proceedings under this section (whether by virtue of subsection (8) or otherwise), a declarator under subsection (2) binds the insured as well as the insurer.

3(10)   In this section, the reference to the insurer's potential liability to P is a reference to the insurer's liability in respect of the insured's liability to P, if established.

Relevant persons

4   Individuals

4(1)   An individual is a relevant person if any of the following is in force in respect of that individual in England and Wales–

(a)   [Repealed]

(b)   an administration order made under Part 6 of the County Courts Act 1984,

(c)   an enforcement restriction order made under Part 6A of that Act,

(d)   subject to subsection (4), a debt relief order made under Part 7A of the Insolvency Act 1986,

(e)   a voluntary arrangement approved in accordance with Part 8 of that Act, or

(f)   a bankruptcy order made under Part 9 of that Act.

4(2)   An individual is a relevant person if either of the following is in force in respect of the individual's estate in Scotland–

(a) an award of sequestration made by virtue of section 2 or 5 of the Bankruptcy (Scotland) Act 2016, or

(b) a protected trust deed within the meaning of that Act.

4(3) An individual is a relevant person if any of the following is in force in respect of that individual in Northern Ireland–

(a) an administration order made under Part 6 of the Judgments Enforcement (Northern Ireland) Order 1981 (S.I. 1981/226 (N.I. 6)),

(b) a deed of arrangement registered in accordance with Chapter 1 of Part 8 of the Insolvency (Northern Ireland) Order 1989 (S.I. 1989/2405 (N.I. 19)),

(ba) subject to subsection (4), a debt relief order made under Part 7A of that Order,

(c) a voluntary arrangement approved under Chapter 2 of Part 8 of that Order, or

(d) a bankruptcy order made under Part 9 of that Order.

4(4) If an individual is a relevant person by virtue of subsection (1)(d) or (3)(ba), that person is a relevant person for the purposes of section 1(1)(b) only.

4(5) Where an award of sequestration made by virtue of section 2 or 5 of the Bankruptcy (Scotland) Act 2016 is recalled or reduced, any rights which were transferred under section 1 as a result of that award are re-transferred to and vest in the person who became a relevant person as a result of the award.

History
Section 4(3)(ba) inserted and s.4(4) amended by the Insurance Act 2015 s.20 and Sch.2 para.2 from 1 August 2016. Section 4(1)(a) repealed by the Deregulation Act 2015 Sch.6 para.2(22) as from 1 August 2016.

5 Individuals who die insolvent

5(1) An individual who dies insolvent is a relevant person for the purposes of section 1(1)(b) only.

5(2) For the purposes of this section an individual (D) is to be regarded as having died insolvent if, following D's death–

(a) D's estate falls to be administered in accordance with an order under section 421 of the Insolvency Act 1986 or Article 365 of the Insolvency (Northern Ireland) Order 1989 (S.I. 1989/2405 (N. I. 19)),

(b) an award of sequestration is made by virtue of section 2 or 5 of the Bankruptcy (Scotland) Act 2016 in respect of D's estate and the award is not recalled or reduced, or

(c) a judicial factor is appointed under section 11A of the Judicial Factors (Scotland) Act 1889 in respect of D's estate and the judicial factor certifies that the estate is absolutely insolvent within the meaning of the Bankruptcy (Scotland) Act 2016.

5(3) Where a transfer of rights under section 1 takes place as a result of an insured person being a relevant person by virtue of this section, references in this Act to an insured are, where the context so requires, to be read as references to the insured's estate.

6 Corporate bodies etc

6(1) A body corporate or unincorporated body is a relevant person if a compromise or arrangement between the body and its creditors (or a class of them) is in force, having been sanctioned in accordance with section 899 of the Companies Act 2006.

6(2) A body corporate or an unincorporated body is a relevant person if, in England and Wales or Scotland–

(a) a voluntary arrangement approved in accordance with Part 1 of the Insolvency Act 1986 is in force in respect of it,

(b) the body is in administration under Schedule B1 to that Act,

(c) there is a person appointed in accordance with Part 3 of that Act who is acting as receiver or manager of the body's property (or there would be such a person so acting but for a temporary vacancy),

(d) the body is, or is being, wound up voluntarily in accordance with Chapter 2 of Part 4 of that Act,

(e) there is a person appointed under section 135 of that Act who is acting as provisional liquidator in respect of the body (or there would be such a person so acting but for a temporary vacancy), or

(f) the body is, or is being, wound up by the court following the making of a winding-up order under Chapter 6 of Part 4 of that Act or Part 5 of that Act.

6(3) A body corporate or an unincorporated body is a relevant person if, in Scotland–

(a) an award of sequestration has been made by virtue of section 6 of the Bankruptcy (Scotland) Act 2016 in respect of the body's estate, and the body has not been discharged under that Act,

(b) the body has been dissolved and an award of sequestration has been made by virtue of that section in respect of its estate, or

(c) a protected trust deed within the meaning of the Bankruptcy (Scotland) Act 2016 is in force in respect of the body's estate.

6(4) A body corporate or an unincorporated body is a relevant person if, in Northern Ireland–

(a) a voluntary arrangement approved in accordance with Part 2 of the Insolvency (Northern Ireland) Order 1989 (S.I. 1989/2405 (N. I. 19)) is in force in respect of the body,

(b) the body is in administration under Schedule B1 to that Order,

(c) there is a person appointed in accordance with Part 4 of that Order who is acting as receiver or manager of the body's property (or there would be such a person so acting but for a temporary vacancy),

(d) the body is, or is being, wound up voluntarily in accordance with Chapter 2 of Part 5 of that Order,

(e) there is a person appointed under Article 115 of that Order who is acting as provisional liquidator in respect of the body (or there would be such a person so acting but for a temporary vacancy), or

(f) the body is, or is being, wound up by the court following the making of a winding-up order under Chapter 6 of Part 5 of that Order or Part 6 of that Order.

6(4A) A body corporate or unincorporated body is a relevant person if it is in insolvency under Part 2 of the Banking Act 2009.

6(4B) A body corporate or unincorporated body is a relevant person if it is in administration under relevant sectoral legislation as defined in Schedule A1.

6(5) A body within subsection (1) is not a relevant person in relation to a liability that is transferred to another body by the order sanctioning the compromise or arrangement.

6(6) Where a body is a relevant person by virtue of subsection (1), section 1 has effect to transfer rights only to a person on whom the compromise or arrangement is binding.

6(7) Where an award of sequestration made by virtue of section 6 of the Bankruptcy (Scotland) Act 2016 is recalled or reduced, any rights which were transferred under section 1 as a result of that award are re-transferred to and vest in the person who became a relevant person as a result of the award.

6(8)   [Omitted]

6(9)   In this section–

(a)   a reference to a person appointed in accordance with Part 3 of the Insolvency Act 1986 includes a reference to a person appointed under section 101 of the Law of Property Act 1925;

(b)   a reference to a receiver or manager of a body's property includes a reference to a receiver or manager of part only of the property and to a receiver only of the income arising from the property or from part of it;

(c)   for the purposes of subsection (3) "body corporate or unincorporated body" includes any entity, other than a trust, the estate of which may be sequestrated by virtue of section 6 of the Bankruptcy (Scotland) Act 2016;

(d)   a reference to a person appointed in accordance with Part 4 of the Insolvency (Northern Ireland) Order 1989 (S.I. 1989/2405 (N. I. 19)) includes a reference to a person appointed under section 19 of the Conveyancing Act 1881.

History
Section 6(2)(b), (4)(b) substituted by the Insurance Act 2015 s.20 and Sch.2 para.3 from 1 August 2016. Section 6(4A), (4B) inserted and s.6(1) amended by the Third Parties (Rights against Insurers) Regulations 2016 (SI 2016/570) reg.3(1), 5(2) as from 1 August 2016.

6A   Corporate bodies etc that are dissolved

6A(1)   A body corporate or unincorporated body is a relevant person if the body has been dissolved, subject to the exceptions in subsections (2) and (3).

6A(2)   The body is not a relevant person by virtue of subsection (1) if, since it was dissolved (or, if it has been dissolved more than once, since it was last dissolved), something has happened which has the effect that the body is treated as not having been dissolved or as no longer being dissolved.

6A(3)   Subsection (1) applies to a partnership only if it is a body corporate.

6A(4)   For the purposes of this section, "dissolved" means dissolved under the law of England and Wales, Scotland or Northern Ireland (whether or not by a process referred to as dissolution).

History
Section 6A inserted by the Third Parties (Rights against Insurers) Regulations 2016 (SI 2016/570) reg.4 as from 1 August 2016.

7   Scottish trusts

7(1)   A trustee of a Scottish trust is, in respect of a liability of that trustee that falls to be met out of the trust estate, a relevant person if–

(a)   an award of sequestration has been made by virtue of section 6 of the Bankruptcy (Scotland) Act 2016 in respect of the trust estate, and the trust has not been discharged under that Act, or

(b)   a protected trust deed within the meaning of that Act is in force in respect of the trust estate.

(c)   [Omitted]

7(2)   Where an award of sequestration made by virtue of section 6 of the Bankruptcy (Scotland) Act 2016 is recalled or reduced any rights which were transferred under section 1 as a result of that award are re-transferred to and vest in the person who became a relevant person as a result of the award.

7(3)   [Omitted]

7(4)   In this section "Scottish trust" means a trust the estate of which may be sequestrated by virtue of section 6 of the Bankruptcy (Scotland) Act 2016.

Transferred rights: supplemental

8   Limit on rights transferred

8   Where the liability of an insured to a third party is less than the liability of the insurer to the insured (ignoring the effect of section 1), no rights are transferred under that section in respect of the difference.

9   Conditions affecting transferred rights

9(1)   This section applies where transferred rights are subject to a condition (whether under the contract of insurance from which the transferred rights are derived or otherwise) that the insured has to fulfil.

9(2)   Anything done by the third party which, if done by the insured, would have amounted to or contributed to fulfilment of the condition is to be treated as if done by the insured.

9(3)   The transferred rights are not subject to a condition requiring the insured to provide information or assistance to the insurer if that condition cannot be fulfilled because the insured is–

  (a)   an individual who has died,

  (b)   a body corporate that has been dissolved, or

  (c)   an unincorporated body, other than a partnership, that has been dissolved.

9(4)   A condition requiring the insured to provide information or assistance to the insurer does not include a condition requiring the insured to notify the insurer of the existence of a claim under the contract of insurance.

9(5)   The transferred rights are not subject to a condition requiring the prior discharge by the insured of the insured's liability to the third party.

9(6)   In the case of a contract of marine insurance, subsection (5) applies only to the extent that the liability of the insured is a liability in respect of death or personal injury.

9(7)   In this section–

"contract of marine insurance" has the meaning given by section 1 of the Marine Insurance Act 1906;

"personal injury" includes any disease and any impairment of a person's physical or mental condition.

9(8)   For the purposes of this section–

  (a)   "dissolved" means dissolved under the law of England and Wales, Scotland or Northern Ireland (whether or not by a process referred to as dissolution), and

  (b)   a body has been dissolved even if, since it was dissolved, something has happened which has the effect that (but for this paragraph) the body is treated as not having been dissolved or as no longer being dissolved.

History
Section 9(7) omitted and s.9(3)(c), (8) inserted by the Third Parties (Rights against Insurers) Regulations 2016 (SI 2016/570) reg.5(3) as from 1 August 2016.

10   Insurer's right of set off

10(1)   This section applies if–

  (a)   rights of an insured under a contract of insurance have been transferred to a third party under section 1,

  (b)   the insured is under a liability to the insurer under the contract ("the insured's liability"), and

(c) if there had been no transfer, the insurer would have been entitled to set off the amount of the insured's liability against the amount of the insurer's own liability to the insured.

10(2) The insurer is entitled to set off the amount of the insured's liability against the amount of the insurer's own liability to the third party in relation to the transferred rights.

Provision of information etc

11 Information and disclosure for third parties

11 Schedule 1 (information and disclosure for third parties) has effect.

Enforcement of transferred rights

12 Limitation and prescription

12(1) Subsection (2) applies where a person brings proceedings for a declaration under section 2(2)(a), or for a declarator under section 3(2)(a), and the proceedings are started or, in Scotland, commenced–

(a) after the expiry of a period of limitation applicable to an action against the insured to enforce the insured's liability, or of a period of prescription applicable to that liability, but

(b) while such an action is in progress.

12(2) The insurer may not rely on the expiry of that period as a defence unless the insured is able to rely on it in the action against the insured.

12(3) For the purposes of subsection (1), an action is to be treated as no longer in progress if it has been concluded by a judgment or decree, or by an award, even if there is an appeal or a right of appeal.

12(4) Where a person who has already established an insured's liability to that person brings proceedings under this Act against the insurer, nothing in this Act is to be read as meaning–

(a) that, for the purposes of the law of limitation in England and Wales, that person's cause of action against the insurer arose otherwise than at the time when that person established the liability of the insured,

(b) that, for the purposes of the law of prescription in Scotland, the obligation in respect of which the proceedings are brought became enforceable against the insurer otherwise than at that time, or

(c) that, for the purposes of the law of limitation in Northern Ireland, that person's cause of action against the insurer arose otherwise than at the time when that person established the liability of the insured.

13 Jurisdiction within the United Kingdom

13(1) Where a person (P) domiciled in a part of the United Kingdom is entitled to bring proceedings under this Act against an insurer domiciled in another part, P may do so in the part where P is domiciled or in the part where the insurer is domiciled (whatever the contract of insurance may stipulate as to where proceedings are to be brought).

13(2) The following provisions of the Civil Jurisdiction and Judgments Act 1982 (relating to determination of domicile) apply for the purposes of subsection (1)–

(a) section 41(2), (3), (5) and (6) (individuals);

(b) section 42(1), (3), (4) and (8) (corporations and associations);

(c) section 45(2) and (3) (trusts);

(d) section 46(1), (3) and (7) (the Crown).

13(3)   In Schedule 5 to that Act (proceedings excluded from general provisions as to allocation of jurisdiction within the United Kingdom) at the end add–

  "Proceedings by third parties against insurers

  11   Proceedings under the Third Parties (Rights against Insurers) Act 2010.*"*

Enforcement of insured's liability

14   Effect of transfer on insured's liability

14(1)   Where rights in respect of an insured's liability to a third party are transferred under section 1, the third party may enforce that liability against the insured only to the extent (if any) that it exceeds the amount recoverable from the insurer by virtue of the transfer.

14(2)   Subsection (3) applies if a transfer of rights under section 1 occurs because the insured person is a relevant person by virtue of–

  (a)   section 4(1)(a) or (e), (2)(b) or (3)(b) or (c),

  (b)   section 6(1), (2)(a), (3)(c) or (4)(a), or

  (c)   section 7(1)(b).

14(3)   If the liability is subject to the arrangement, trust deed or compromise by virtue of which the insured is a relevant person, the liability is to be treated as subject to that arrangement, trust deed or compromise only to the extent that the liability exceeds the amount recoverable from the insurer by virtue of the transfer.

14(4)   [Omitted]

14(5)   [Omitted]

14(6)   For the purposes of this section the amount recoverable from the insurer does not include any amount that the third party is unable to recover as a result of–

  (a)   a shortage of assets on the insurer's part, in a case where the insurer is a relevant person, or

  (b)   a limit set by the contract of insurance on the fund available to meet claims in respect of a particular description of liability of the insured.

14(7)   Where a third party is eligible to make a claim in respect of the insurer's liability under or by virtue of rules made under Part 15 of the Financial Services and Markets Act 2000 (the Financial Services Compensation Scheme)–

  (a)   subsection (6)(a) applies only if the third party has made such a claim, and

  (b)   the third party is to be treated as being able to recover from the insurer any amount paid to, or due to, the third party as a result of the claim.

Application of Act

15   Reinsurance

15   This Act does not apply to a case where the liability referred to in section 1(1) is itself a liability incurred by an insurer under a contract of insurance.

16   Voluntarily-incurred liabilities

16   It is irrelevant for the purposes of section 1 whether or not the liability of the insured is or was incurred voluntarily.

17   Avoidance

17(1)   A contract of insurance to which this section applies is of no effect in so far as it purports, whether directly or indirectly, to avoid or terminate the contract or alter the rights of the parties under it in the event of the insured–

    (a)   becoming a relevant person, or

    (b)   dying insolvent (within the meaning given by section 5(2)).

17(2)   A contract of insurance is one to which this section applies if the insured's rights under it are capable of being transferred under section 1.

18   Cases with a foreign element

18   Except as expressly provided, the application of this Act does not depend on whether there is a connection with a part of the United Kingdom; and in particular it does not depend on–

    (a)   whether or not the liability (or the alleged liability) of the insured to the third party was incurred in, or under the law of, England and Wales, Scotland or Northern Ireland;

    (b)   the place of residence or domicile of any of the parties;

    (c)   whether or not the contract of insurance (or a part of it) is governed by the law of England and Wales, Scotland or Northern Ireland;

    (d)   the place where sums due under the contract of insurance are payable.

Supplemental

19   Power to change the meaning of "relevant person"

19(1)   The Secretary of State may by regulations make provision adding or removing circumstances in which a person is a "relevant person" for the purposes of this Act, subject to subsection (2).

19(2)   Regulations under this section may add circumstances only if, in the Secretary of State's opinion, the additional circumstances–

    (a)   involve actual or anticipated dissolution of a body corporate or an unincorporated body,

    (b)   involve actual or anticipated insolvency or other financial difficulties for an individual, a body corporate or an unincorporated body, or

    (c)   are similar to circumstances for the time being described in sections 4 to 7.

19(3)   Regulations under this section may make provision about–

    (a)   the persons to whom, and the extent to which, rights are transferred under section 1 in the circumstances added or removed by the regulations (the "affected circumstances"),

    (b)   the re-transfer of rights transferred under section 1 where the affected circumstances change, and

    (c)   the effect of a transfer of rights under section 1 on the liability of the insured in the affected circumstances.

19(4)   Regulations under this section which add or remove circumstances involving actual or anticipated dissolution of a body corporate or unincorporated body may change the cases in which the following provisions apply so that they include or exclude cases involving that type of dissolution or any other type of dissolution of a body–

    (a)   section 9(3) (cases in which transferred rights are not subject to a condition requiring the insured to provide information or assistance to the insurer), and

(b)   paragraph 3 of Schedule 1 (notices requiring disclosure).

19(5)   Regulations under this section which add circumstances may provide that section 1 of this Act applies in cases involving those circumstances in which either or both of the following occurred in relation to a person before the day on which the regulations come into force–

(a)   the circumstances arose in relation to the person;

(b)   a liability against which the person was insured under an insurance contract was incurred.

19(6)   Regulations under this section which–

(a)   add circumstances, and

(b)   provide that section 1 of this Act applies in a case involving those circumstances in which both of the events mentioned in subsection (5)(a) and (b) occurred in relation to a person before the day on which the regulations come into force,

must provide that, in such a case, the person is to be treated for the purposes of this Act as not having become a relevant person until that day or a later day specified in the regulations.

19(7)   Regulations under this section which remove circumstances may provide that section 1 of this Act does not apply in cases involving those circumstances in which one of the events mentioned in subsection (5)(a) and (b) (but not both) occurred in relation to a person before the day on which the regulations come into force.

19(8)   Regulations under this section may–

(a)   include consequential, incidental, supplementary, transitional, transitory or saving provision,

(b)   make different provision for different purposes, and

(c)   make provision by reference to an enactment as amended, extended or applied from time to time,

(and subsections (3) to (7) are without prejudice to the generality of this subsection).

19(9)   Regulations under this section may amend an enactment, whenever passed or made, including this Act.

19(10)   Regulations under this section are to be made by statutory instrument.

19(11)   Regulations under this section may not be made unless a draft of the statutory instrument containing the regulations has been laid before, and approved by a resolution of, each House of Parliament.

History
Section 19 substituted by the Insurance Act 2015 s.19 as from 12 April 2015.

19A   Interpretation

19A(1)   The references to enactments in sections 4 to 7, Schedule A1 and paragraph 3(2)(b), (4) and (5) of Schedule 1 are to be treated as including references to those enactments as amended, extended or applied by another enactment, whenever passed or made, unless the contrary intention appears.

19A(2)   In this Act, "enactment" means an enactment contained in, or in an instrument made under, any of the following–

(a)   an Act;

(b)   an Act or Measure of the National Assembly for Wales;

(c)   an Act of the Scottish Parliament;

(d)   Northern Ireland legislation.

History
Section 19A inserted by the Insurance Act 2015 s.20 and Sch.2 para.6 as from 1 August 2016.

20 Amendments, transitionals, repeals, etc

20(1)   Schedule 2 (amendments) has effect.

20(2)   Schedule 3 (transitory, transitional and saving provisions) has effect.

20(3)   Schedule 4 (repeals and revocations) has effect.

21 Short title, commencement and extent

21(1)   This Act may be cited as the Third Parties (Rights against Insurers) Act 2010.

21(2)   This Act comes into force on such day as the Secretary of State may by order made by statutory instrument appoint.

21(3)   This Act extends to England and Wales, Scotland and Northern Ireland, subject as follows.

21(4)   Section 2 and paragraphs 3 and 4 of Schedule 1 do not extend to Scotland.

21(5)   Section 3 extends to Scotland only.

21(6)   Any amendment, repeal or revocation made by this Act has the same extent as the provision to which it relates.

SCHEDULE A1

ADMINISTRATION UNDER RELEVANT SECTORAL LEGISLATION

For the purposes of section 6(4B)–

(a)   a body is in administration under relevant sectoral legislation if the appointment of an administrator of the body under an enactment listed below has effect, and

(b)   the body does not cease to be in administration merely because an administrator vacates office (by reason of resignation, death or otherwise) or is removed from office.

LIST OF ENACTMENTS

[List not reproduced]

History
Schedule A1 was inserted by the Third Parties (Rights against Insurers) Regulations 2016 (SI 2016/570) reg.3(2) as from 1 August 2016.

SCHEDULE 1

INFORMATION AND DISCLOSURE FOR THIRD PARTIES

Notices requesting information

1(1)   If a person (A) reasonably believes that–

(a)   another person (B) has incurred a liability to A, and

(b)   B is a relevant person,

A may, by notice in writing, request from B such information falling within sub-paragraph (3) as the notice specifies.

1(2) If a person (A) reasonably believes that–

(a)   a liability has been incurred to A,

(b)   the person who incurred the liability is insured against it under a contract of insurance,

(c)   rights of that person under the contract have been transferred to A under section 1, and

(d)   there is a person (C) who is able to provide information falling within sub-paragraph (3),

A may, by notice in writing, request from C such information falling within that sub-paragraph as the notice specifies.

1(3) The following is the information that falls within this sub-paragraph–

(a)   whether there is a contract of insurance that covers the supposed liability or might reasonably be regarded as covering it;

(b)   if there is such a contract–

(i)   who the insurer is;

(ii)   what the terms of the contract are;

(iii)   whether the insured has been informed that the insurer has claimed not to be liable under the contract in respect of the supposed liability;

(iv)   whether there are or have been any proceedings between the insurer and the insured in respect of the supposed liability and, if so, relevant details of those proceedings;

(v)   in a case where the contract sets a limit on the fund available to meet claims in respect of the supposed liability and other liabilities, how much of it (if any) has been paid out in respect of other liabilities;

(vi)   whether there is a fixed charge to which any sums paid out under the contract in respect of the supposed liability would be subject.

1(4) For the purpose of sub-paragraph (3)(b)(iv), relevant details of proceedings are–

(a)   in the case of court proceedings–

(i)   the name of the court;

(ii)   the case number;

(iii)   the contents of all documents served in the proceedings in accordance with rules of court or orders made in the proceedings, and the contents of any such orders;

(b)   in the case of arbitral proceedings or, in Scotland, an arbitration–

(i)   the name of the arbitrator;

(ii)   information corresponding with that mentioned in paragraph (a)(iii).

1(5) In sub-paragraph (3)(b)(vi), in its application to Scotland, "fixed charge" means a fixed security within the meaning given by section 47(1) of the Bankruptcy and Diligence etc (Scotland) Act 2007 (asp 3).

1(6) A notice given by a person under this paragraph must include particulars of the facts on which that person relies as entitlement to give the notice.

Provision of information where notice given under paragraph 1

2(1) A person (R) who receives a notice under paragraph 1 must, within the period of 28 days beginning with the day of receipt of the notice–

(a) provide to the person who gave the notice any information specified in it that R is able to provide;

(b) in relation to any such information that R is not able to provide, notify that person why R is not able to provide it.

2(2) Where–

(a) a person (R) receives a notice under paragraph 1,

(b) there is information specified in the notice that R is not able to provide because it is contained in a document that is not in R's control,

(c) the document was at one time in R's control, and

(d) R knows or believes that it is now in another person's control,

R must, within the period of 28 days beginning with the day of receipt of the notice, provide the person who gave the notice with whatever particulars R can as to the nature of the information and the identity of that other person.

2(3) If R fails to comply with a duty imposed on R by this paragraph, the person who gave R the notice may apply to court for an order requiring R to comply with the duty.

2(4) No duty arises by virtue of this paragraph in respect of information as to which a claim to legal professional privilege or, in Scotland, to confidentiality as between client and professional legal adviser could be maintained in legal proceedings.

Notices requiring disclosure: bodies that have been dissolved

3(1) If–

(a) a person (P) has started proceedings under this Act against an insurer in respect of a liability

(b) P claims the liability has been incurred to P by–

(i) a body corporate, or

(ii) an unincorporated body other than a partnership, and

(c) the body has been dissolved,

P may by notice in writing require a person to whom sub-paragraph (2) applies to disclose to P any documents that are relevant to that liability.

3(2) This sub-paragraph applies to a person if–

(a) immediately before the time of the alleged transfer under section 1, that person was an officer or employee of the body, or

(b) immediately before the body was dissolved (or, if it has been dissolved more than once, immediately before it was last dissolved), that person was–

(i) acting as an insolvency practitioner in relation to the body (within the meaning given by section 388(1) of the Insolvency Act 1986 or Article 3 of the Insolvency (Northern Ireland) Order 1989 (S.I. 1989/2405 N.I. 19)), or

(ii) acting as the official receiver in relation to the winding up of the body.

3(3) A notice under this paragraph must be accompanied by–

(a) a copy of the particulars of claim required to be served in connection with the proceedings mentioned in sub-paragraph (1), or

(b) where those proceedings are arbitral proceedings, the particulars of claim that would be required to be so served if they were court proceedings.

3(4) [Omitted]

3(5) [Omitted]

3(6) For the purposes of this paragraph–

(a) "dissolved" means dissolved under the law of England and Wales, Scotland or Northern Ireland (whether or not by a process referred to as dissolution), and

(b) a body has been dissolved even if, since it was dissolved, something has happened which has the effect that (but for this paragraph) the body is treated as not having been dissolved or as no longer being dissolved.

History
Heading of para.3 and para.3(1) amended, para.3(4), (5) omitted, and para.3(6) inserted by the Third Parties (Rights against Insurers) Regulations 2016 (SI 2016/570) Sch.1 as from 1 August 2016.

Disclosure and inspection where notice given under paragraph 3

4(1) Subject to the provisions of this paragraph and to any necessary modifications–

(a) the duties of disclosure of a person who receives a notice under paragraph 3, and

(b) the rights of inspection of the person giving the notice,

are the same as the corresponding duties and rights under Civil Procedure Rules of parties to court proceedings in which an order for standard disclosure has been made.

4(2) In sub-paragraph (1), in its application to Northern Ireland–

(a) the reference to Civil Procedure Rules is–

(i) in the case of proceedings in the High Court, to be read as a reference to the Rules of the Court of Judicature (Northern Ireland) 1980 (S.R. 1980 No. 346), and

(ii) in the case of proceedings in the county court, to be read as a reference to the County Court Rules (Northern Ireland) 1981 (S.R. 1981 No. 225), and

(b) the reference to an order for standard disclosure is to be read as a reference to an order for discovery.

4(3) A person who by virtue of sub-paragraph (1) or (2) has to serve a list of documents must do so within the period of 28 days beginning with the day of receipt of the notice.

4(4) A person who has received a notice under paragraph 3 and has served a list of documents in response to it is not under a duty of disclosure by reason of that notice in relation to documents that the person did not have when the list was served.

Avoidance

5 A contract of insurance is of no effect in so far as it purports, whether directly or indirectly–

(a) to avoid or terminate the contract or alter the rights of the parties under it in the event of a person providing information, or giving disclosure, that the person is required to provide or give by virtue of a notice under paragraph 1 or 3, or

(b) otherwise to prohibit, prevent or restrict a person from providing such information or giving such disclosure.

Other rights to information etc

6   Rights to information, or to inspection of documents, that a person has by virtue of paragraph 1 or 3 are in addition to any such rights as the person has apart from that paragraph.

Interpretation

7   For the purposes of this Schedule–

    (a)   a person is able to provide information only if–

        (i)   that person can obtain it without undue difficulty from a document that is in that person's control, or

        (ii)   where that person is an individual, the information is within that person's knowledge;

    (b)   a document is in a person's control if it is in that person's possession or if that person has a right to possession of it or to inspect or take copies of it.

[Schedules 2–4 not reproduced.]

Charities Act 2011

(2011 Chapter 25)

[14th March 2012]

PART 6

CY-PRÈS POWERS AND ASSISTANCE AND SUPERVISION OF CHARITIES BY COURT AND COMMISSION

Legal proceedings relating to charities

113 Petitions for winding up charities under Insolvency Act

113(1)   This section applies where a charity may be wound up by the High Court under the Insolvency Act 1986.

113(2)   A petition for the charity to be wound up under the 1986 Act by any court in England or Wales having jurisdiction may be presented by the Attorney General, as well as by any person authorised by that Act.

113(3)   Such a petition may also be presented by the Commission if, at any time after it has instituted an inquiry under section 46 with respect to the charity, it is satisfied either as mentioned in section 76(1)(a) (misconduct or mismanagement etc.) or as mentioned in section 76(1)(b) (need to protect property etc.).

113(4)   The power exercisable by the Commission by virtue of this section is exercisable–

(a)   by the Commission of its own motion, but

(b)   only with the agreement of the Attorney General on each occasion.

PART 11

CHARITABLE INCORPORATED ORGANISATIONS (CIOs)

CHAPTER 5

SUPPLEMENTARY

245 Regulations about winding up, insolvency and dissolution

245(1)   CIO regulations may make provision about–

(a)   the winding up of CIOs,

(b)   their insolvency,

(c)   their dissolution, and

(d)   their revival and restoration to the register following dissolution.

245(2)   The regulations may, in particular, make provision–

(a)   about the transfer on the dissolution of a CIO of its property and rights (including property and rights held on trust for the CIO) to the official custodian or another person or body;

(b)   requiring any person in whose name any stocks, funds or securities are standing in trust for a CIO to transfer them into the name of the official custodian or another person or body;

(c) about the disclaiming, by the official custodian or other transferee of a CIO's property, of title to any of that property;

(d) about the application of a CIO's property cy-près;

(e) about circumstances in which charity trustees may be personally liable for contributions to the assets of a CIO or for its debts;

(f) about the reversal on a CIO's revival of anything done on its dissolution.

245(3) The regulations may–

(a) apply any enactment which would not otherwise apply, either without modification or with modifications specified in the regulations,

(b) disapply, or modify (in ways specified in the regulations) the application of, any enactment which would otherwise apply.

245(4) In subsection (3), "enactment" includes a provision of subordinate legislation within the meaning of the Interpretation Act 1978.

[**Note:** see the Charitable Incorporated Organisations (Insolvency and Dissolution) Regulations 2012 (SI 2012/3013), effective 2 January 2013.]

Co-operative and Community Benefit Societies Act 2014

(2014 Chapter 14)

[*14 May 2014*]

PART 1

REGISTRATION

Introduction

1 Meaning of "registered society"

1(1) In this Act "registered society" means a society registered under this Act, that is–

(a) a society registered under this Act on or after 1 August 2014 (the day this Act comes into force), or

(b) (by virtue of section 150(1)) a society that immediately before that date was registered or treated as registered under the 1965 Act.

1(2) In this Act "the 1965 Act" means the Industrial and Provident Societies Act 1965.

547

2   Societies that may be registered

2(1)   A society for carrying on any industry, business or trade (including dealings of any kind with land) which meets the conditions in subsection (2) may be registered under this Act as–

(a)   a co-operative society, or

(b)   a community benefit society.

2(2)   The conditions are–

(a)   that it is shown to the satisfaction of the FCA–

    (i)   in the case of registration as a co-operative society, that the society is a bona fide co-operative society, or

    (ii)   in the case of registration as a community benefit society, that the business of the society is being, or is intended to be, conducted for the benefit of the community,

(b)   that–

    (i)   the society has at least 3 members, or

    (ii)   the society has 2 members both of which are registered societies,

(c)   that the society's rules contain provision in respect of the matters mentioned in section 14, and

(d)   that the place that under those rules is to be the society's registered office is in Great Britain or the Channel Islands.

2(3)   For the purposes of subsection (2)(a)(i) "co-operative society" does not include a society that carries on, or intends to carry on, business with the object of making profits mainly for the payment of interest, dividends or bonuses on money invested or deposited with, or lent to, the society or any other person.

2(4)   For registration under this Act as a credit union, see the Credit Unions Act 1979.

3   Registration

3(1)   An application for the registration of a society under this Act is made by
sending the following to the FCA–

(a)   an application for registration, signed by–

    (i)   the society's secretary and 3 of its members, or

    (ii)   where both or all of its members are registered societies, the secretaries of 2 of those registered societies, and

(b)   2 copies of the society's rules or, if the application is made by electronic means, 1 copy of those rules.

3(2)   If the FCA is satisfied that the society has complied with the requirements under this Act as to registration, it must–

(a)   register the society, and

(b)   give the society an acknowledgment of registration bearing the FCA's seal.

3(3) A registered society is by virtue of its registration a body corporate by its registered name, with limited liability.

3(4) The society may sue and be sued by its registered name.

3(5) Registration vests in the society all property for the time being vested in any person in trust for the society.

3(6) Any legal proceedings pending by or against the trustees of the society may (once the society is registered) be brought or continued by or against the society.

3(7) The acknowledgement of registration also constitutes an acknowledgment of, and is conclusive evidence of, the registration under this Act of the rules of the society in force at the date of the society's registration.

Cancellation of registration

5 Cancellation of registration: conditions for cancellation

5(1) The FCA may, in writing, cancel the registration of a registered society if any of conditions A to E is met.

5(2) Condition A is that–

    (a) the society has requested the cancellation of its registration,

    (b) the request is evidenced in such way as the FCA from time to time directs, and

    (c) the FCA considers it appropriate to cancel the registration.

5(3) Condition B is that any of the following is proved to the FCA's satisfaction–

    (a) that an acknowledgment of registration has been obtained by fraud or mistake;

    (b) that the society has less than 3 members (and does not have 2 members both of which are registered societies);

    (c) that the society has ceased to exist.

5(4) Condition C is that it is proved to the FCA's satisfaction–

    (a) that the society exists for an illegal purpose, or

    (b) that the society has wilfully and after notice from the FCA violated any of the provisions of this Act.

5(5) Condition D is that it appears to the FCA–

    (a) in the case of a society registered as a co-operative society, that the condition in section 2(2)(a)(i) is not met;

    (b) in the case of a society registered as a community benefit society, that the condition in section 2(2)(a)(ii) is not met;

    (c) in the case of a pre-commencement society, that neither of the conditions in section 2(2)(a) is met.

5(6) Condition E is that–

    (a) the society's registered rules contain provision of a kind authorised by section 22 (rules of agricultural, horticultural or forestry society), and

    (b) it appears to the FCA that–

    (i)   the society no longer consists mainly of members of a kind mentioned in that section, or

    (ii) the activities carried on by the society do not mainly consist in making advances to its members for the purposes mentioned there.

6   Cancellation of registration: procedure and effect

6(1)   The FCA must give a registered society at least 2 months' notice in writing of the proposed cancellation of its registration, specifying briefly the ground of the proposed cancellation.

6(2)   Subsection (1) does not apply to any cancellation–

    (a)   made by virtue of condition A in section 5 (cancellation at society's request),

    (b)   made by virtue of section 112(2) (cancellation following conversion into a company etc), or

    (c)   made after a relevant certificate within the meaning of section 126 (certificate that society's property has been transferred to persons entitled to it) has been lodged with the FCA.

6(3)   If the society appeals under section 9 before the end of the period of notice, its registration may not be cancelled before the date the appeal is determined or abandoned.

For the FCA's power to suspend the society's registration in these circumstances, see section 8(3).

6(4)   For the right of the society to make representations and to be heard by the FCA in a case where condition D in section 5 is relied on, see section 7.

6(5)   The FCA must consult the PRA before cancelling the registration of a registered society that is a PRA-authorised person.

6(6)   The FCA must ensure that, as soon as practicable after a society's registration is cancelled, notice of the cancellation is published in–

    (a)   the Gazette, and

    (b)   a local newspaper circulating in or about the locality in which the society's registered office is situated.

6(7)   As from the date of publication of the notice in the Gazette, the society ceases to be entitled to any of the privileges of this Act as a registered society.

This does not affect any liability incurred by the society (which may be enforced against it as if the cancellation had not occurred).

7   Cancellation of registration: additional procedure in cases involving condition D

7(1)   This section applies where the FCA gives a registered society a notice under section 6 (notice of proposed cancellation of registration) specifying a ground set out in condition D in section 5.

7(2)   The FCA must consider any representations about the proposed cancellation that the society makes to it in the period of notice.

7(3)   If the society requests, the FCA must give the society an opportunity of being heard by the FCA before its registration is cancelled.

7(4)   If, at any time after the end of one month from the date the notice is given, it appears to the FCA that there have not been taken the steps which by that time could reasonably have been taken for the purpose of–

    (a)   converting the society into a company, amalgamating it with a company, or transferring its engagements to a company, in accordance with section 112, or

    (b)   dissolving the society under section 119 or 123,

the FCA may give such directions as it considers appropriate for securing that the society's affairs are wound up before its registration is cancelled.

7(5)   The FCA must consult the PRA before giving directions under subsection (4) to a registered society that is a PRA-authorised person.

7(6)   A person who contravenes or fails to comply with a direction under subsection (4) commits an offence.

7(7)   A person guilty of an offence under this section is liable on summary conviction–

(a)   in England and Wales, to a fine not exceeding level 3 on the standard scale;

(b)   in Scotland, to a fine not exceeding level 3 on the standard scale or imprisonment for a term not exceeding 3 months (or both).

Suspension of registration

8   Suspension of registration

8(1)   If any of conditions C to E in section 5 is met in relation to a society, the FCA may by notice in writing–

(a)   suspend the society's registration for a term not exceeding 3 months, and

(b)   from time to time renew any suspension for a term not exceeding 3 months.

8(2)   The FCA must give a registered society at least 2 months' notice in writing of the proposed suspension of its registration under subsection (1)(a), specifying briefly the ground of the proposed suspension.

8(3)   Where–

(a)   a notice of proposed cancellation of a society's registration is given under section 6, and

(b)   before the end of the period of notice, the society appeals under section 9 against the proposed cancellation,

the FCA may by notice in writing suspend the society's registration from the end of that period until the date the appeal is determined or abandoned.

8(4)   The FCA must consult the PRA before suspending, or renewing the suspension of, the registration of a registered society that is a PRA-authorised person.

8(5)   The FCA must ensure that, as soon as practicable after the suspension or renewal of suspension of a society's registration, notice of the suspension or renewal is published in–

(a)   the Gazette, and

(b)   a local newspaper circulating in or about the locality in which the society's registered office is situated.

8(6)   From the date of publication of the notice in the Gazette until the end of the period for which the society's registration is suspended, the society is not entitled to any of the privileges of this Act as a registered society.

This does not affect any liability incurred by the society (which may be enforced against it as if the suspension had not occurred).

PART 9

AMALGAMATIONS, CONVERSIONS, DISSOLUTION ETC

Voluntary arrangements and administration

118   Power to apply provisions about company arrangements and administration

118(1)   The Treasury may with the concurrence of the Secretary of State by order provide for a company arrangement or administration provision to apply (with or without modifications) in relation to registered societies.

118(2)   "Company arrangement or administration provision" means–

(a)   a provision of Part 1 of the Insolvency Act 1986 (company voluntary arrangements);

(b)   a provision of Part 2 of that Act (administration);

(c)   Part 26 of the Companies Act 2006 (compromise or arrangement with creditors).

118(3)   The order may not provide for a company arrangement or administration provision to apply in relation to a society that is–

(a)   a private registered provider of social housing, or

(b)   registered as a social landlord under Part 1 of the Housing Act 1996 or Part 2 of the Housing (Scotland) Act 2010 (asp 17).

118(4)   The order may–

(a)   make provision generally or for a specified purpose only;

(b)   make different provision for different purposes;

(c)   make transitional, consequential or incidental provision.

118(5)   Provision made by virtue of subsection (4)(c) may, in particular–

(a)   apply an enactment (with or without modifications);

(b)   amend an enactment (including any provision of this Act except this section).

118(6)   Section 277 of the Enterprise Act 2002 (power of Secretary of State to make supplementary, consequential or incidental provision) has effect as if this section were part of that Act.

Dissolution by an instrument of dissolution

119   Dissolution of society by an instrument of dissolution

119(1)   A registered society may be dissolved by an instrument of dissolution that–

(a)   complies with subsection (2), and

(b)   is approved in a way mentioned in subsection (3).

119(2)   The instrument must set out–

(a)   the society's assets and liabilities in detail;

(b)   the number of members and the nature of their interests in the society;

(c)   any creditors' claims, and the provision to be made for their payment;

(d) the intended appropriation or division of the society's funds and property (unless the instrument states that this is to be left to the award of the FCA or PRA).

119(3) The ways in which the instrument may be approved are as follows–

(a) by at least 75% of the society's members consenting to it, that consent being testified by their signatures to the instrument;

(b) in the case of a dormant society that is not a credit union, by a special resolution of the society;

(c) in the case of a credit union, by a special resolution of the society that is confirmed by the appropriate authority.

119(4) An alteration in an instrument of dissolution may be made–

(a) by the consent of at least 75% of the society's members, testified by their signatures to the alteration, or

(b) if the instrument was approved by a special resolution of the society, by a further special resolution.

119(5) Section 120 contains provisions about special resolutions under this section.

119(6) In subsection (3)(b) "dormant society" means a society–

(a) whose accounts for the current year of account and the two years of account preceding it show no accounting transactions except–

(i) fees paid to the FCA;

(ii) fees paid to the PRA;

(iii) payments of dividends;

(iv) payments of interest; and

(b) that has notified the FCA that it is dormant.

119(7) For the purposes of subsection (3)(c) the appropriate authority is treated as confirming a special resolution unless it notifies the society in writing to the contrary within 21 days of the society sending a copy of the resolution to it.

120 Special resolutions under section 119

120(1) This section supplements section 119.

120(2) A resolution is a "special resolution" if–

(a) the resolution is passed at a general meeting by at least two-thirds of the eligible members who vote,

(b) notice of this meeting ("the first meeting"), specifying the intention to propose the resolution, is duly given in accordance with the society's rules,

(c) the resolution is confirmed at a subsequent general meeting by over half of the eligible members who vote,

(d) notice of this meeting ("the second meeting") is duly given, and

(e) the second meeting is held at least 14 days, and no more than one month, from the day of the first meeting.

120(3)   In this section–

(a)   "eligible member" means a member entitled under the society's rules to vote;

(b)   references to voting are to voting in person or, where the rules allow proxies, by proxy.

121   Instruments of dissolution: notification to FCA etc

121(1)   This section applies in relation to an instrument of dissolution within section 119(1).

121(2)   The instrument must be sent to the FCA (and, if the society is a PRA-authorised person, the PRA), accompanied by a statutory declaration that all relevant provisions of this Act have been complied with.

121(3)   The statutory declaration must be made by the society's secretary and–

(a)   3 members, or

(b)   both members (if the society consists solely of 2 registered societies).

121(4)   A copy of any special resolution under section 119–

(a)   signed by the chair of the second meeting, and

(b)   countersigned by the society's secretary,

must be sent to the FCA (and, if the society is a PRA-authorised person, the PRA) within the period of 14 days beginning with the day of the second meeting.

121(5)   The FCA must register the instrument of dissolution (and any alterations to it) in the same way as an amendment of the society's rules.

But it must not register it until it has received the society's annual return for its last year of account (see section 77(8) or 78(7)).

121(6)   The FCA must register a copy special resolution received under subsection (4) at the same time as it registers the instrument of dissolution (and any alterations to it).

121(7)   The instrument of dissolution (and any alterations to it) are binding on the society's members.

121(8)   In this section "the second meeting" has the same meaning as in section 120.

122   Instruments of dissolution: advertisement, dissolution etc

122(1)   Where the FCA receives an instrument of dissolution of a society under section 121, it must ensure that notice of the dissolution is advertised in–

(a)   the Gazette, and

(b)   a newspaper circulating in or about the locality in which the society's registered office is situated.

122(2)   Subject to subsection (3), the society is dissolved from–

(a)   the date of the advertisement, or

(b)   if later, the date the certificate under section 126 is lodged with the FCA;

and the requisite consents to, or approval of, the instrument of dissolution are treated as duly obtained without proof of the signatures to it or of the special resolution (as the case may be).

122(3)   Subsection (2) does not apply if–

(a)   within the period of 3 months from the date of the Gazette in which the advertisement appears, a member of the society or a person interested in or having a claim on its funds commences proceedings in the appropriate court to set aside the dissolution of the society, and

(b)   the dissolution is accordingly set aside.

122(4)   The "appropriate court" means–

(a)   the county court, or

(b)   in Scotland, the sheriff having jurisdiction in the locality in which the society's registered office is situated.

122(5)   A person who takes proceedings to set aside the dissolution of a society must send the FCA (and, if the society is a PRA-authorised person, the PRA) notice of the proceedings–

(a)   within 7 days after the commencement of proceedings, or

(b)   if earlier, by the end of the period mentioned in subsection (3)(a).

122(6)   If an order setting aside the dissolution of a society is made, the society must send the FCA (and, if the society is a PRA-authorised person, the PRA) notice of the order within 7 days after the making of the order.

Dissolution on winding up

123   Dissolution of society on winding up

123(1)   A registered society may be dissolved on its being wound up in pursuance of an order or resolution made as is directed in the case of companies.

123(2)   The provisions relating to the winding up of companies have effect in relation to a registered society as if the society were a company, subject to the following modifications–

(a)   a reference to the registrar of companies is to be read as the FCA;

(b)   a reference to a company registered in Scotland is to be read as a registered society whose registered office is in Scotland;

(c)   if the society is wound up in Scotland, the court having jurisdiction is the sheriff court whose jurisdiction contains the society's registered office.

123(3)   Where a resolution for the voluntary winding up of a registered society is passed–

(a)   the society must send a copy of it to the FCA (and, if the society is a PRA-authorised person, the PRA) within 15 days after it is passed, and

(b)   a copy of it must be annexed to every copy of the society's registered rules issued after it is passed.

123(4)   In this section "company" means a company registered under the Companies Acts.

123(5)   This section is subject to section 126 (dissolution to occur only after society's property has been dealt with).

124   Liability of existing and former members in winding up

124(1)   This section applies where a registered society is wound up by virtue of section 123.

124(2)   The liability of an existing or former member to contribute for payment of the society's debts and liabilities, the expenses of winding up, and the adjustment of the rights of contributories amongst themselves, is qualified as follows–

(a)   a former member whose membership ceased at least one year before the beginning of the winding up is not liable to contribute;

(b) a former member is not liable to contribute in respect of a debt or liability contracted after the person's membership ceased;

(c) a former member is not liable to contribute unless it appears to the court that the contributions of the existing members are insufficient to satisfy the just demands on the society;

(d) the maximum contribution that a person may be required to make is the amount (if any) unpaid on the shares in respect of which the person is liable as an existing or former member;

(e) in the case of a withdrawable share that has been withdrawn, a person is treated as ceasing to be a member in respect of that share as from the date of the notice or application for withdrawal.

Dissolution following administration

125   Dissolution following administration

125(1)   A relevant society may also be dissolved under paragraph 84 of Schedule B1 to the 1986 Act as applied in relation to a relevant society by an order under section 118.

125(2)   In this section "relevant society" means a registered society which is not–

(a) a private registered provider of social housing, or

(b) registered as a social landlord under Part 1 of the Housing Act 1996 or under Part 2 of the Housing (Scotland) Act 2010.

Restriction on dissolution etc

126   Dissolution etc to occur only after society's property dealt with

126(1)   This section applies where–

(a) a registered society's engagements are transferred under section 110 or 112, or

(b) a registered society is to be dissolved in accordance with section 119 or 123.

126(2)   The society must not be dissolved, and its registration must not be cancelled, until a relevant certificate has been lodged with the FCA.

126(3)   "Relevant certificate" means a certificate certifying that all property vested in the society has been duly conveyed or transferred by the society to the persons entitled, signed by–

(a) the liquidator, or

(b) the secretary or some other officer of the society approved by the FCA.

Small Business, Enterprise and Employment Act 2015

(2015 Chapter 26)

[26th March 2015]

PART 10

INSOLVENCY

Power to establish single regulator of insolvency practitioners

144 Power to establish single regulator of insolvency practitioners

144(1) **[Secretary of State's power]** The Secretary of State may by regulations designate a body for the purposes of–

(a) authorising persons to act as insolvency practitioners, and

(b) regulating persons acting as such.

144(2) **[Designated body]** The designated body may be either–

(a) a body corporate established by the regulations, or

(b) a body (whether a body corporate or an unincorporated association) already in existence when the regulations are made (an "existing body").

144(3) **[Functions of designated body]** The regulations may, in particular, confer the following functions on the designated body–

(a) establishing criteria for determining whether a person is a fit and proper person to act as an insolvency practitioner;

(b) establishing the requirements as to education, practical training and experience which a person must meet in order to act as an insolvency practitioner;

(c) establishing and maintaining a system for providing full authorisation or partial authorisation to persons who meet those criteria and requirements;

(d) imposing technical standards for persons so authorised and enforcing compliance with those standards;

(e) imposing professional and ethical standards for persons so authorised and enforcing compliance with those standards;

(f) monitoring the performance and conduct of persons so authorised;

(g) investigating complaints made against, and other matters concerning the performance or conduct of, persons so authorised.

144(4) **[Requirements of designated body]** The regulations may require the designated body, in discharging regulatory functions, so far as is reasonably practicable, to act in a way–

(a) which is compatible with the regulatory objectives, and

(b) which the body considers most appropriate for the purpose of meeting those objectives.

144(5) **[Enforcement of technical, professional and ethical standards]** Provision made under subsection (3)(d) or (3)(e) for the enforcement of the standards concerned may include provision enabling

557

the designated body to impose a financial penalty on a person who is or has been authorised to act as an insolvency practitioner.

144(6)　[Treatment of insolvency practitioners authorised before regulations in force] The regulations may, in particular, include provision for the purpose of treating a person authorised to act as an insolvency practitioner by virtue of being a member of a professional body recognised under section 391 of the Insolvency Act 1986 immediately before the regulations come into force as authorised to act as an insolvency practitioner by the body designated by the regulations after that time.

144(7)　[Application of defined expressions in Insolvency Act 1986 Pt 13] Expressions used in this section which are defined for the purposes of Part 13 of the Insolvency Act 1986 have the same meaning in this section as in that Part.

144(8)　[Further provision about regulations in s.145] Section 145 makes further provision about regulations under this section which designate an existing body.

144(9)　[Schedule 11 supplementary provision by regulations] Schedule 11 makes supplementary provision in relation to the designation of a body by regulations under this section.

145　Regulations under section 144: designation of existing body

145(1)　[Secretary of State's power] The Secretary of State may make regulations under section 144 designating an existing body only if it appears to the Secretary of State that–

(a)　the body is able and willing to exercise the functions that would be conferred by the regulations, and

(b)　the body has arrangements in place relating to the exercise of those functions which are such as to be likely to ensure that the conditions in subsection (2) are met.

145(2)　[Conditions] The conditions are–

(a)　that the functions in question will be exercised effectively, and

(b)　where the regulations are to contain any requirements or other provisions prescribed under subsection (3), that those functions will be exercised in accordance with any such requirements or provisions.

145(3)　[Requirements or other provisions as to designated body's functions] Regulations which designate an existing body may contain such requirements or other provisions relating to the exercise of the functions by the designated body as appear to the Secretary of State to be appropriate.

146　Regulations under section 144: timing and supplementary

146(1)　[Expiry of at end of relevant period] Section 144 and, accordingly, section 145 and subsections (3) and (4) below expire at the end of the relevant period unless the power conferred by subsection (1) of section 144 is exercised before the end of that period.

146(2)　["Relevant period"] The "relevant period" is the period of 7 years beginning with the day on which section 144 comes into force.

146(3)　[Affirmative resolution procedure] Regulations under section 144 are subject to affirmative resolution procedure.

146(4)　[Draft instrument to proceed not as hybrid instrument] If a draft of a statutory instrument containing regulations under section 144 would, apart from this subsection, be treated for the purposes of the Standing Orders of either House of Parliament as a hybrid instrument, it is to proceed in that House as if it were not a hybrid instrument.

SCHEDULE 11

SINGLE REGULATOR OF INSOLVENCY PRACTITIONERS: SUPPLEMENTARY PROVISION

1 Operation of this Schedule

1(1) This Schedule has effect in relation to regulations under section 144 designating a body (referred to in this Schedule as "the Regulations") as follows–

(a) paragraphs 2 to 13 have effect where the Regulations establish the body;

(b) paragraphs 6, 7 and 9 to 13 have effect where the Regulations designate an existing body (see section 144(2)(b));

(c) paragraph 14 also has effect where the Regulations designate an existing body that is an unincorporated association.

1(2) Provision made in the Regulations by virtue of paragraph 6 or 12, where that paragraph has effect as mentioned in sub-paragraph (1)(b), may only apply in relation to–

(a) things done by or in relation to the body in or in connection with the exercise of functions conferred on it by the Regulations, and

(b) functions of the body which are functions so conferred.

2 Name, members and chair

2(1) The Regulations must prescribe the name by which the body is to be known.

2(2) The Regulations must provide that the members of the body must be appointed by the Secretary of State after such consultation as the Secretary of State thinks appropriate.

2(3) The Regulations must provide that the Secretary of State must appoint one of the members as the chair of the body.

2(4) The Regulations may include provision about–

(a) the terms on which the members of the body hold and vacate office;

(b) the terms on which the person appointed as the chair holds and vacates that office.

3 Remuneration etc.

3(1) The Regulations must provide that the body must pay to its chair and members such remuneration and allowances in respect of expenses properly incurred by them in the exercise of their functions as the Secretary of State may determine.

3(2) The Regulations must provide that, as regards any member (including the chair) in whose case the Secretary of State so determines, the body must pay or make provision for the payment of–

(a) such pension, allowance or gratuity to or in respect of that person on retirement or death as the Secretary of State may determine, or

(b) such contributions or other payment towards the provision of such a pension, allowance or gratuity as the Secretary of State may determine.

3(3) The Regulations must provide that where–

(a) a person ceases to be a member of the body otherwise than on the expiry of the term of office, and

(b) it appears to the Secretary of State that there are special circumstances which make it right for that person to be compensated, the body must make a payment to the person by way of compensation of such amount as the Secretary of State may determine.

4   Staff

4   The Regulations must provide that–

(a)   the body may appoint such persons to be its employees as the body considers appropriate, and

(b)   the employees are to be appointed on such terms and conditions as the body may determine.

5   Proceedings

5(1)   The Regulations may make provision about the proceedings of the body.

5(2)   The Regulations may, in particular–

(a)   authorise the body to exercise any function by means of committees consisting wholly or partly of members of the body;

(b)   provide that the validity of proceedings of the body, or of any such committee, is not affected by any vacancy among the members or any defect in the appointment of a member.

6   Fees

6(1)   The Regulations may make provision–

(a)   about the setting and charging of fees by the body in connection with the exercise of its functions;

(b)   for the retention by the body of any such fees payable to it;

(c)   about the application by the body of such fees.

6(2)   The Regulations may, in particular, make provision–

(a)   for the body to be able to set such fees as appear to it to be sufficient to defray the expenses of the body exercising its functions, taking one year with another;

(b)   for the setting of fees by the body to be subject to the approval of the Secretary of State.

6(3)   The expenses referred to in sub-paragraph (2)(a) include any expenses incurred by the body on such staff, accommodation, services and other facilities as appear to it to be necessary or expedient for the proper exercise of its functions.

7   Consultation

7   The Regulations may make provision as to the circumstances and manner in which the body must consult others before exercising any function conferred on it by the Regulations.

8   Training and other services

8(1)   The Regulations may make provision authorising the body to provide training or other services to any person.

8(2)   The Regulations may make provision authorising the body–

(a)   to charge for the provision of any such training or other services, and

(b)   to calculate any such charge on the basis that it considers to be the appropriate commercial basis.

9   Report and accounts

9(1)   The Regulations must require the body, at least once in each 12 month period, to report to the Secretary of State on–

(a)   the exercise of the functions conferred on it by the Regulations, and

(b)   such other matters as may be prescribed in the Regulations.

9(2)   The Regulations must require the Secretary of State to lay before Parliament a copy of each report received under this paragraph.

9(3)   Unless section 394 of the Companies Act 2006 applies to the body (duty on every company to prepare individual accounts), the Regulations must provide that the Secretary of State may give directions to the body with respect to the preparation of its accounts.

9(4)   Unless the body falls within sub-paragraph (5), the Regulations must provide that the Secretary of State may give directions to the body with respect to the audit of its accounts.

9(5)   The body falls within this sub-paragraph if it is a company whose accounts–

(a)   are required to be audited in accordance with Part 16 of the Companies Act 2006 (see section 475 of that Act), or

(b)   are exempt from the requirements of that Part under section 482 of that Act (non-profit making companies subject to public sector audit).

9(6)   The Regulations may provide that, whether or not section 394 of the Companies Act 2006 applies to the body, the Secretary of State may direct that any provisions of that Act specified in the directions are to apply to the body with or without modifications.

10   Funding

10   The Regulations may provide that the Secretary of State may make grants to the body.

11   Financial penalties

11(1)   This paragraph applies where the Regulations include provision enabling the body to impose a financial penalty on a person who is, or has been, authorised to act as an insolvency practitioner (see section 144(5)).

11(2)   The Regulations–

(a)   must include provision about how the body is to determine the amount of a penalty, and

(b)   may, in particular, prescribe a minimum or maximum amount.

11(3)   The Regulations must provide that, unless the Secretary of State (with the consent of the Treasury) otherwise directs, income from penalties imposed by the body is to be paid into the Consolidated Fund.

11(4)   The Regulations may also, in particular–

12   Status etc.

12   The Regulations must provide that–

(a)   the body is not to be regarded as acting on behalf of the Crown, and

(b)   its members, officers and employees are not to be regarded as Crown servants.

13   Transfer schemes

13(1)   This paragraph applies if the Regulations make provision designating a body (whether one established by the Regulations or one already in existence) in place of a body designated by earlier regulations under section 144; and those bodies are referred to as the "new body" and the "former body" respectively.

13(2)   The Regulations may make provision authorising the Secretary of State to make a scheme (a "transfer scheme") for the transfer of property, rights and liabilities from the former body to the new body.

13(3)   The Regulations may provide that a transfer scheme may include provision–

(a)   about the transfer of property, rights and liabilities that could not otherwise be transferred;

(b)   about the transfer of property acquired, and rights and liabilities arising, after the making of the scheme.

13(4)   The Regulations may provide that a transfer scheme may make consequential, supplementary, incidental or transitional provision and may in particular–

(a)   create rights, or impose liabilities, in relation to property or rights transferred;

(b)   make provision about the continuing effect of things done by the former body in respect of anything transferred;

(c)   make provision about the continuation of things (including legal proceedings) in the process of being done by, on behalf of or in relation to the former body in respect of anything transferred;

(d)   make provision for references to the former body in an instrument or other document in respect of anything transferred to be treated as references to the new body;

(e)   make provision for the shared ownership or use of property;

(f)   if the TUPE regulations do not apply to in relation to the transfer, make provision which is the same or similar.

13(5)   The Regulations must provide that, where the former body is an existing body, a transfer scheme may only make provision in relation to–

(a)   things done by or in relation to the former body in or in connection with the exercise of functions conferred on it by previous regulations under section 144, and

(b)   functions of the body which are functions so conferred.

13(6)   In sub-paragraph (4)(f), "TUPE regulations" means the Transfer of Undertakings (Protection of Employment) Regulations 2006 (S.I. 2006/246).

13(7)   In this paragraph–

(a)   references to rights and liabilities include rights and liabilities relating to a contract of employment;

(b)   references to the transfer of property include the grant of a lease.

14   Additional provision where body is unincorporated association

14(1)   This paragraph applies where the body is an unincorporated association.

14(2)   The Regulations must provide that any relevant proceedings may be brought by or against the body in the name of any body corporate whose constitution provides for the establishment of the body.

14(3)   In sub-paragraph (2) "relevant proceedings" means proceedings brought in or in connection with the exercise of any function conferred on the body by the Regulations.

EC Regulation 2157/2001

Council Regulation (EC) No 2157/2001 of 8 October 2001 on the Statute for a European company (SE)

[Preamble]

THE COUNCIL OF THE EUROPEAN UNION,

Having regard to the Treaty establishing the European Community, and in particular Article 308 thereof,

Having regard to the proposal from the Commission,

Having regard to the opinion of the European Parliament,

Having regard to the opinion of the Economic and Social Committee,

Whereas:

(20) This Regulation does not cover other areas of law such as taxation, competition, intellectual property or insolvency. The provisions of the Member States' law and of Community law are therefore applicable in the above areas and in other areas not covered by this Regulation.

TITLE I

GENERAL PROVISIONS

Article 7

7   [Registered office] The registered office of an SE shall be located within the Community, in the same Member State as its head office. A Member State may in addition impose on SEs registered in its territory the obligation of locating their head office and their registered office in the same place.

Article 10

10   [Treatment of SE as public limited-liability company] Subject to this Regulation, an SE shall be treated in every Member State as if it were a public limited-liability company formed in accordance with the law of the Member State in which it has its registered office.

TITLE V

WINDING UP, LIQUIDATION, INSOLVENCY AND CESSATION OF PAYMENTS

Article 63

63   [Applicable law] As regards winding up, liquidation, insolvency, cessation of payments and similar procedures, an SE shall be governed by the legal provisions which would apply to a public limited-liability company formed in accordance with the law of the Member State in which its registered office is situated, including provisions relating to decision-making by the general meeting.

Article 64

64(1)   [Infringement by SE of art.7] When an SE no longer complies with the requirement laid down in Article 7, the Member State in which the SE's registered office is situated shall take appropriate measures to oblige the SE to regularise its position within a specified period either:

(a)   by re-establishing its head office in the Member State in which its registered office is situated or

(b)   by transferring the registered office by means of the procedure laid down in Article 8.

64(2) **[Liquidation for failure to rectify infringement]** The Member State in which the SE's registered office is situated shall put in place the measures necessary to ensure that an SE which fails to regularise its position in accordance with paragraph 1 is liquidated.

64(3) **[Judicial remedy for infringement]** The Member State in which the SE's registered office is situated shall set up a judicial remedy with regard to any established infringement of Article 7. That remedy shall have a suspensory effect on the procedures laid down in paragraphs 1 and 2.

64(4) **[Notification of infringement]** Where it is established on the initiative of either the authorities or any interested party that an SE has its head office within the territory of a Member State in breach of Article 7, the authorities of that Member State shall immediately inform the Member State in which the SE's registered office is situated.

Article 65

65 **[Publication of insolvency proceedings]** Without prejudice to provisions of national law requiring additional publication, the initiation and termination of winding up, liquidation, insolvency or cessation of payment procedures and any decision to continue operating shall be publicised in accordance with Article 13.

Note

Article 13 refers to Directive 68/151, which has been implemented for this purpose in the UK by CA 1985 s.711 [now CA 2006 ss.1064, 1077 et seq.].

Article 66

66(1) **[Conversion to public limited-liability company]** An SE may be converted into a public limited-liability company governed by the law of the Member State in which its registered office is situated. No decision on conversion may be taken before two years have elapsed since its registration or before the first two sets of annual accounts have been approved.

66(2) **[Legal implications of conversion]** The conversion of an SE into a public limited-liability company shall not result in the winding up of the company or in the creation of a new legal person.

66(3) **[Draft terms of conversion]** The management or administrative organ of the SE shall draw up draft terms of conversion and a report explaining and justifying the legal and economic aspects of the conversion and indicating the implications of the adoption of the public limited-liability company for the shareholders and for the employees.

66(4) **[Publication of draft terms]** The draft terms of conversion shall be publicised in the manner laid down in each Member State's law in accordance with Article 3 of Directive 68/151/EEC at least one month before the general meeting called to decide thereon.

66(5) **[Expert examination of draft terms]** Before the general meeting referred to in paragraph 6, one or more independent experts appointed or approved, in accordance with the national provisions adopted in implementation of Article 10 of Directive 78/855/EEC, by a judicial or administrative authority in the Member State to which the SE being converted into a public limited-liability company is subject shall certify that the company has assets at least equivalent to its capital.

66(6) **[Approval of draft terms by general meeting]** The general meeting of the SE shall approve the draft terms of conversion together with the statutes of the public limited-liability company. The decision of the general meeting shall be passed as laid down in the provisions of national law adopted in implementation of Article 7 of Directive 78/855/EEC.

Ancillary Statutory Instruments

Insolvency Proceedings (Monetary Limits) Order 1986

(SI 1986/1996)

Made on 20 November 1986 by the Secretary of State, by ss.416 and 418 of, and paras 9 and 12 of Sch.6 to, the Insolvency Act 1986. Operative from 29 December 1986.

[**Note:** Changes made by the Insolvency Proceedings (Monetary Limits) (Amendment) Order 2004 (SI 2004/547), the Insolvency Proceedings (Monetary Limits) (Amendment) Order 2009 (SI 2009/465) and the Insolvency Proceedings (Monetary Limits) (Amendment) Order 2015 (SI 2015/26) have been incorporated into the text.]

1(1) This Order may be cited as the Insolvency Proceedings (Monetary Limits) Order 1986 and shall come into force on 29th December 1986.

1(2) In this Order "the Act" means the Insolvency Act 1986.

2(1) The provisions in the first Group of Parts of the Act (companies winding up) set out in column 1 of Part 1 of the Schedule to this Order (shortly described in column 2) are hereby amended by substituting for the amounts specified in column 3 in relation to those provisions the amounts specified in column 4.

2(2) The sum specified in column 4 of Part I of the Schedule in relation to section 184(3) of the Act is not to affect any case where the goods are sold or payment to avoid sale is made, before the coming into force of the increase.

3 The amounts prescribed for the purposes of the provisions in the second Group of Parts of the Act (bankruptcy and debt relief orders) set out in column 1 of Part II of the Schedule to this Order (shortly described in column 2) are the amounts specified in column 3 in relation to those provisions.

4 The amount prescribed for the purposes of paragraphs 9 and 12 of Schedule 6 to the Act (maximum amount for preferential status of employees' claims for remuneration and under the Reserve Forces (Safeguard of Employment) Act 1985 is £800.

5 The court shall, in determining the value of the bankrupt's interest for the purposes of section 313A(2), disregard that part of the value of the property in which the bankrupt's interest subsists which is equal to the value of:

(a)   any loans secured by mortgage or other charge against the property;

(b)   any other third party interest; and

(c)   the reasonable costs of sale.

History
Article 3 amended by the Insolvency Proceedings (Monetary Limits) (Amendment) Order 2009 (SI 2009/465) art.2 as from 6 April 2009. Article 5 inserted as from 1 April 2004 by the Insolvency Proceedings (Monetary Limits) (Amendment) Order (SI 2004/547) art.3.

SCHEDULE

PART I

INCREASES OF MONETARY AMOUNTS IN FIRST GROUP OF PARTS OF INSOLVENCY ACT 1986

Section of the Act (1)	Short Description (2)	Present Amount (3)	New Amount (4)
184(3)	Minimum value of judgment, affecting sheriff's duties on levying execution	£250	£500
206(1)(a) and (b)	Minimum value of company property concealed or fraudulently removed, affecting criminal liability of officer of company in liquidation	£120	£500

PART II

MONETARY AMOUNTS FOR PURPOSES OF SECOND GROUP OF PARTS OF INSOLVENCY ACT 1986

Section of the Act (1)	Short Description (2)	Monetary Amount (3)
251S(4)	Maximum amount of credit which a person in respect of whom a debt relief order is made may obtain without disclosure of his status	£500
273(1)(a)	Maximum level of unsecured bankruptcy debts on debtor's petition for case to be referred to insolvency practitioner to assess possibility of voluntary arrangement with creditors.	£40,000
273(1)(b)	Minimum potential value of bankrupt's estate for case to be referred as described above.	£4,000
313A(2)	Minimum value of interests in a dwelling-house for application by trustee for order for sale, possession or an order under section 313.	£1,000
346(3)	Minimum amount of judgment, determining whether amount recovered on sale of debtor's goods is to be treated as part of his estate in bankruptcy.	£1,000
354(1) and (2)	Minimum amount of concealed debt, or value of property concealed or removed, determining criminal liability under the section.	£1,000
358	Minimum value of property taken by a bankrupt out of England and Wales, determining his criminal liability.	£1,000
360(1)	Maximum amount of credit which bankrupt may obtain without disclosure of his status.	£500
364(2)(d)	Minimum value of goods removed by the bankrupt, determining his liability to arrest.	£1,000

Section of the Act (1)	Short Description (2)	Monetary Amount (3)
Schedule 4ZA–	Monetary conditions which must be satisfied for a debt relief order to be made–	
(a) paragraph 6(1)	(a) maximum amount of a person's debts:	£20,000
(b) paragraph 7(1)	(b) maximum amount of monthly surplus income:	£50
(c) paragraph 8(1)	(c) maximum total value of property:	£1,000

History

Part II substituted as from 1 April 2004 by the Insolvency Proceedings (Monetary Limits) (Amendment) Order (SI 2004/547) art.3, Sch. Part II amended by the Insolvency Proceedings (Monetary Limits) (Amendment) Order 2009 (SI 2009/465) art.3 as from 6 April 2009 and by the Insolvency Proceedings (Monetary Limits) (Amendment) Order 2015 (SI 2015/26) art.2 as from 1 October 2015.

Administration of Insolvent Estates of Deceased Persons Order 1986

(SI 1986/1999)

Made on 21 November 1986 by the Lord Chancellor under s.421 of the Insolvency Act 1986. Operative from 29 December 1986.

[**Note:** Changes made by the Enterprise and Regulatory Reform Act 2013 (Consequential Amendments) (Bankruptcy) and the Small Business, Enterprise and Employment Act 2015 (Consequential Amendments) Regulations 2016 (SI 2016/481), the Deregulation Act 2015 and Small Business, Enterprise and Employment Act 2015 (Consequential Amendments) (Savings) Regulations 2017 (SI 2017/540) and the Insolvency (Miscellaneous Amendments) Regulations 2017 (SI 2017/1119) have been incorporated into the text.]

1   This Order may be cited as the Administration of Insolvent Estates of Deceased Persons Order 1986 and shall come into force on 29th December 1986.

2   In this Order–

"the Act" means the Insolvency Act 1986;

"insolvency administration order" means an order for the administration in bankruptcy of the insolvent estate of a deceased debtor (being an individual at the date of his death);

"insolvency administration petition" means a petition for an insolvency administration order; and

"the Rules" means the Insolvency (England and Wales) Rules 2016.

History
In art.2 the definition of "the Rules" amended by the Insolvency (Miscellaneous Amendments) Regulations 2017 (SI 2017/1119) regs 1(1), (6), 2, Sch.3 para.1(1), (2) as from 8 December 2017.

3(1)   The provisions of the Act specified in Parts II and III of Schedule 1 to this Order shall apply to the administration in bankruptcy of the insolvent estates of deceased persons dying before the making of a bankruptcy application or presentation of a bankruptcy petition with the modifications specified in those Parts and with any further such modifications as may be necessary to render them applicable to the estate of a deceased person and in particular with the modifications specified in Part I of that Schedule, and the provisions of the Rules, the Insolvency Regulations 1986 and any order made under section 415 of the Act (fees and deposits) shall apply accordingly.

3(2)   In the case of any conflict between any provision of the Rules and any provision of this Order, the latter provision shall prevail.

History
Article 3(1) amended by the Enterprise and Regulatory Reform Act 2013 (Consequential Amendments) (Bankruptcy) and the Small Business, Enterprise and Employment Act 2015 (Consequential Amendments) Regulations 2016 (SI 2016/481) reg.2(2) and Sch.2 para.2(2) as from 6 April 2016.

4(1)   Where the estate of a deceased person is insolvent and is being administered otherwise than in bankruptcy, subject to paragraphs (2) and (3) below, the same provisions as may be in force for the time being under the law of bankruptcy with respect to the assets of individuals made bankrupt shall apply to the administration of the estate with respect to the respective rights of secured and unsecured creditors, to debts and liabilities provable, to the valuation of future and contingent liabilities and to the priorities of debts and other payments.

4(2)   The reasonable funeral, testamentary and administration expenses have priority over the preferential debts listed in Schedule 6 to the Act.

4(3)   Section 292(2) of the Act shall not apply.

5(A1)   If a debtor dies after making a bankruptcy application, the proceedings will continue as if the deceased debtor were alive, with the modifications specified in Schedule 2 to this Order.

5(1)   If a debtor against whom a bankruptcy petition has been presented dies, the proceedings in the matter shall, unless the court otherwise orders, be continued as if he were alive, with the modifications specified in Schedule 2 to this Order.

5(2)   The reasonable funeral and testamentary expenses have priority over the preferential debts listed in Schedule 6 to the Act.

5(3)   If a debtor dies after presentation of a bankruptcy petition but before service, the court may order service to be effected on his personal representative or such other person as it thinks fit.

History

Article 5(A1) inserted and art.5(1) amended by the Enterprise and Regulatory Reform Act 2013 (Consequential Amendments) (Bankruptcy) and the Small Business, Enterprise and Employment Act 2015 (Consequential Amendments) Regulations 2016 (SI 2016/481) reg.2(2) and Sch.2 para.2(4) as from 6 April 2016.

6   The definitions in Article 2 of this Order other than the first definition shall be added to those in section 385 of the Act.

SCHEDULE 1

PROVISIONS OF THE ACT APPLYING WITH RELEVANT MODIFICATIONS TO THE ADMINISTRATION IN BANKRUPTCY OF INSOLVENT ESTATES OF DECEASED PERSONS DYING BEFORE MAKING OF A BANKRUPTCY APPLICATION OR PRESENTATION OF A BANKRUPTCY PETITION

Article 3

PART I

GENERAL MODIFICATIONS OF PROVISIONS OF THE ACT

Except in so far as the context otherwise requires, for any such reference as is specified in column 1 of the Table set out below there shall be substituted the reference specified in column 2.

Table

Reference in provision of the Act specified in Part II of this Schedule (1)	*Substituted references* (2)
the bankrupt; the debtor.	the deceased debtor or his personal representative (or if there is no personal representative such person as the court may order) as the case may require.
the bankrupt's estate.	the deceased debtor's estate.
the commencement of the bankruptcy.	the date of the insolvency administration order.
a bankruptcy order.	an insolvency administration order.
an individual being made bankrupt.	an insolvency administration order being made.
a bankruptcy application.	a petition by the personal representative of a deceased debtor for an insolvency administration order.

Part II

Provisions of the Act not included in Part III of this Schedule

The following provisions of the Act shall apply:–

1 Section 264 with the following modifications:–

(a) the words "against an individual" shall be omitted;

(b) at the end of paragraph 1(a) there shall be added the words "in Form 1 set out in Schedule 3 to the Administration of Insolvent Estates of Deceased Persons Order 1986";

(ba) after subsection (1)(a) there shall be added–

"(aa) by the personal representative of the deceased debtor,"

(c) [Omitted]

(ca) at the end of paragraph 1(ba) there shall be added the words "in Form 1, with such variations as the case requires (if any), set out in Schedule 3 to the Administration of Insolvent Estates of Deceased Persons Order 1986";

(cb) at the end of paragraph 1(bb) there shall be added the words "in Form 1, with such variations as the case requires (if any), set out in Schedule 3 to the Administration of Insolvent Estates of Deceased Persons Order 1986";

(d) in paragraph 1(c) after the words "Part VIII" there shall be added the words "in Form 2 set out in the said Schedule 3";

(e) at the end of paragraph 1(d) there shall be added the words "in Form 3 set out in the said Schedule 3 in any case where a creditor could present such a petition under paragraph (a) above"; and

(f) at the end of subsection (2) there shall be added the words "in Form 4 set out in the said Schedule 3".

1A Section 265 with the modification that after subsection (4) there shall be inserted–

"**(5)** A petition by the personal representative of a deceased debtor for an insolvency administration order in Form 6 set out in Schedule 3 to the Administration of Insolvent Estates of Deceased Persons Order 1986 may be presented to the court only on the grounds that the estate of a deceased debtor is insolvent.

(6) A petition under subsection (5) must be accompanied by a statement of the deceased debtor's affairs containing–

(a) such particulars of the debtor's creditors and of his debts and other liabilities and of his assets as may be prescribed; and

(b) such other information as is required by Form 7 set out in Schedule 3 to the Administration of Insolvent Estates of Deceased Persons Order 1986."

2 Section 266 with the following modifications:–

(a) for subsection (1) there shall be substituted the following:–

"**(1)** An insolvency administration petition shall–

(a) if a liquidator (within the meaning of Article 2(b) of the EC Regulation) has been appointed in proceedings by virtue of Article 3(1) of the EC Regulation in relation to the deceased debtor, be served on him;

(b) unless the court directs otherwise, be served on the personal representative; and

(c) be served on such other persons as the court may direct."; and".

(b) in subsection (3) for the words "bankruptcy petition" there shall be substituted the words "petition to the court for an insolvency administration order with or without costs".

3   Section 267 with the following modifications to subsection (2):–

(a)   before the words "at the time" there shall be inserted the words "had the debtor been alive"; and

(b)   for paragraphs (a) to (d) there shall be substituted the following:–

"(a)   the amount of the debt, or the aggregate amount of the debts, owed by the debtor would have been equal to or exceeded the bankruptcy level, or

(b)   the debt, or each of the debts, owed by the debtor would have been for a liquidated sum payable to the petitioning creditor, or one or more of the petitioning creditors, either immediately or at some certain future time, and would have been unsecured.".

4   Section 269 with the modification that in subsection (2) for the words "sections 267 to 270" there shall be substituted the words "section 267 and this section".

5   Section 271 as if for that section there were substituted the following:–

"**271(1)**   The court may make an insolvency administration order on a petition for such an order under section 264(1) if it is satisfied–

(a)   that the debt, or one of the debts, in respect of which the petition was presented is a debt which,

(i)   having been payable at the date of the petition or having since become payable, has neither been paid nor secured or compounded for; or

(ii)   has no reasonable prospect of being able to be paid when it falls due; and

(b)   that there is a reasonable probability that the estate will be insolvent.

271(2)   A petition for an insolvency administration order shall not be presented to the court after proceedings have been commenced in any court of justice for the administration of the deceased debtor's estate.

271(3)   Where proceedings have been commenced in any such court for the administration of the deceased debtor's estate, that court may, if satisfied that the estate is insolvent, transfer the proceedings to the court exercising jurisdiction for the purposes of the Parts in the second Group of Parts.

271(4)   Where proceedings have been transferred to the court exercising jurisdiction for the purposes of the Parts in the second Group of Parts, that court may make an insolvency administration order in Form 5 set out in Schedule 3 to the Administration of Insolvent Estates of Deceased Persons Order 1986 as if a petition for such an order had been presented under section 264.

271(5)   Nothing in sections 264, 266, 267, 269 or 271 to 273 shall invalidate any payment made or any act or thing done in good faith by the personal representative before the date of the insolvency administration order.

271(6)   The court must make an insolvency administration order in Form 4 set out in Schedule 3 to the Administration of Insolvent Estates of Deceased Persons Order 1986 on the hearing of a petition presented under section 265(5) if it is satisfied that the deceased debtor's estate is insolvent.".

6   [Omitted]

7   [Omitted]

8   Section 276(2).

9   Section 277.

10   Section 278 except paragraph (b) as if for paragraph (a) there were substituted the following:–

"(a)   commences with the day on which the insolvency administration order is made;".

11   Section 282(1) and (4).

12   Sections 283 to 285 with the modification that they shall have effect as if the petition had been presented and the insolvency administration order had been made on the date of death of the deceased debtor, and with the following modifications to section 283:–

(a) in subsection (2)(b), for the words "bankrupt and his family" there shall be substituted the words "family of the deceased debtor"; and

(b) after subsection (4) there shall be added the following subsection:–

> "**(4A)** References in any of this Group of Parts to property, in relation to a deceased debtor, include the capacity to exercise and take proceedings for exercising all such powers over or in respect of property as might have been exercised by his personal representative for the benefit of the estate on the date of the insolvency administration order and as are specified in subsection (4) above.".

13 Section 286(1) and (3) to (8).

14 Section 287.

15 Section 288 with the modification that for subsections (1) to (3) there shall be substituted the following–

> "**288(1)** Where an insolvency administration order has been made, the official receiver may at any time require the personal representative, or if there is no personal representative such person as the court may on the application of the official receiver direct, to submit to the official receiver a statement of the deceased debtor's affairs.
>
> **288(2)** The statement of affairs must contain–
>
> (a) particulars of the assets and liabilities of the estate as at the date of the insolvency administration order, and
>
> (b) other particulars of the affairs of the deceased debtor in Form 7 set out in Schedule 3 to the Administration of Insolvent Estates of Deceased Persons Order 1986, or as the official receiver may require.
>
> **288(3)** Where the personal representative or such person as the court may direct is required under subsection (1) to submit a statement of affairs to the official receiver, the statement must be submitted before the end of the period of 56 days beginning with the date on which notice of the requirement under subsection (1) is given by the official receiver, or such longer period as he or the court may allow.".

16 Section 289 as if for that section there were substituted the following:–

> "**289** The official receiver is not under any duty to investigate the conduct and affairs of the deceased debtor unless he thinks fit but may make such report (if any) to the court as he thinks fit.".

17 Section 291.

17A Section 291A.

18 Sections 292 to 302.

19 Sections 303 and 304.

20 Section 305 with the modification that after subsection (4) there shall be added the following subsection:–

> "**(5)** In the exercise of his functions under this section where an insolvency administration order has been made, the trustee shall have regard to any claim by the personal representative to payment of reasonable funeral, testamentary and administration expenses incurred by him in respect of the deceased debtor's estate or, if there is no such personal representative, to any claim by any other person to payment of any such expenses incurred by him in respect of the estate provided that the trustee has sufficient funds in hand for the purpose, and such claims shall have priority over the preferential debts listed in Schedule 6 to this Act.".

21 Section 306.

22 Section 307 with the modification that in subsection (1) for the words "commencement of the bankruptcy" there shall be substituted the words "date of death of the deceased debtor".

23 Sections 308 to 327.

24   Sections 328 and 329 with the modification that for the words "commencement of the bankruptcy", wherever they occur, there shall be substituted the words "date of death of the deceased debtor".

25   Section 330 with the following modifications–

   (a)   in subsection (5) for the words "the bankrupt is entitled to the surplus" there shall be substituted the words "the surplus shall be paid to the personal representative unless the court otherwise orders", and

   (b)   after subsection (5) there shall be added:–

> "**(6)** Subsection (5) is subject to Article 35 of the EC Regulation (surplus in secondary proceedings to be transferred to main proceedings)."

26   Sections 331 to 340.

27   Section 341 with the modification that in subsection (1)(a) for the words from "day of the making" to "made bankrupt" there shall be substituted the words "date of death of the deceased debtor".

28   Sections 342 to 349, 350(1), (2) and (4) to (6).

29   Section 359 with the following modifications:–

   (a)   subsection (1), and the reference to that subsection in subsection (3), shall be omitted; and

   (b)   in subsection (2), for the words from "the making" to "initial period" there shall be substituted the words "the date of death of the deceased debtor".

30   Sections 363 and 365 to 381.

31   Section 382 with the modification that in the definition of "bankruptcy debt" for the words "commencement of the bankruptcy", wherever they occur, there shall be substituted the words "date of death of the deceased debtor".

32   Sections 383 to 384.

33   Section 385 with the modification that at the end of the definition of "the court" there shall be added the words "and subject thereto "the court" means the court within the jurisdiction of which the debtor resided or carried on business for the greater part of the six months immediately prior to his death".

34   Section 386.

35   Section 387(1), (5) and (6) with the modification that in subsection (6)(a) and (b) for the reference to the making of the bankruptcy order there shall be substituted a reference to the date of death of the deceased debtor.

36   Sections 388 to 410, 412, 413, 415, 418 to 420, 423 to 426, 428, 430 to 436 and 437 so far as it relates to Parts II, except paragraph 13, IV and V of Schedule 11 to the Act.

Part III

Provisions of Part VIII of the Act relating to Individual Voluntary Arrangements

The following provisions of the Act shall apply where the court has made an interim order under section 252 of the Act in respect of an individual who subsequently dies:–

1   Section 256 with the modification that where the individual dies before he has submitted the document and statement referred to in subsection (2), after subsection (1) there shall be added the following subsections:–

> "**(1A)** The nominee shall after the death of the individual comes to his knowledge give notice to the court that the individual has died.
>
> **(1B)** After receiving such a notice the court shall discharge the order mentioned in subsection (1) above.".

2   Section 257 with the modification that where the individual dies before the individual's creditors have decided whether to approve the proposed voluntary arrangement, the creditors must not approve the proposal and, if the individual was at the date of his death an undischarged bankrupt, the personal representative shall give notice of the death to the deceased debtor's creditors, the trustee of his estate and the official receiver.

3   Section 258.

3A   Section 259 with the modification that after subsection (1) there shall be added–

"**259(1A)** Where the individual's creditors considered the debtor's proposal pursuant to a report to the court under section 256(1)(aa) but the individual has died before the creditors have decided whether to approve the proposed voluntary arrangement–

(a)   the creditors must not approve the proposal;

(b)   the personal representative must report to the court that the proposal has not been approved; and

(c)   if the individual was at the date of his death an undischarged bankrupt, the personal representative must give notice of the death to the deceased debtor's creditors, the trustee of his estate and the official receiver."

4   Sections 260 to 262 with the modification that they shall cease to apply on or after the death of the individual.

5   Section 263 with the modification that where the individual dies after a voluntary arrangement has been approved, then–

(a)   in subsection (3), for the words "debtor, any of his" there shall be substituted the words "personal representative of the deceased debtor, any of the deceased debtor's"; and

(b)   the supervisor shall give notice to the court that the individual has died.

History
Part II para.1(c) omitted, paras 6, 27, 29(b) substituted and para.18 amended by the Enterprise and Regulatory Reform Act 2013 (Consequential Amendments) (Bankruptcy) and the Small Business, Enterprise and Employment Act 2015 (Consequential Amendments) Regulations 2016 (SI 2016/481) reg.2(2) and Sch.2 para.2(7) as from 6 April 2016. Part II para.17A inserted, paras 15, 18 and 28 substituted and Pt III paras 2 and 3 substituted by the Deregulation Act 2015 and Small Business, Enterprise and Employment Act 2015 (Consequential Amendments) (Savings) Regulations 2017 (SI 2017/540) regs 1, 3, Sch.2 para.1 as from 6 April 2017. In Pt II paras 1(ba), 1A, 5(6) inserted and paras 6 and 7 omitted by the Insolvency (Miscellaneous Amendments) Regulations 2017 (SI 2017/1119) regs 1(1), (6), 2, Sch.3 para.1(1), (3) as from 8 December 2017 subject to transitional and saving provisions in para.3.

SCHEDULE 2

DEATH OF DEBTOR AFTER MAKING OF A BANKRUPTCY APPLICATION OR PRESENTATION OF A BANKRUPTCY PETITION

Article 5

1   Modifications

1   For subsections (1) and (2) of section 288 of the Act there shall be substituted the following:–

"**(1)** Where a bankruptcy order has been made otherwise than on a bankruptcy application and the debtor has subsequently died without submitting a statement of his affairs to the official receiver, the personal representative or such other person as the court, on the application of the official receiver, may direct shall submit to the official receiver a statement of the deceased debtor's affairs containing particulars of the assets and liabilities of the estate as at the date of the order together with other particulars of the affairs of the deceased debtor in Form 7 set out in Schedule 3 to the Administration of Insolvent Estates of Deceased Persons

Order 1986 or as the official receiver may require, and the Rules shall apply to such a statement as they apply to an ordinary statement of affairs of a debtor.

(2) The statement shall be submitted before the end of the period of fifty-six days beginning with the date of a request by the official receiver for the statement or such longer period as he or the court may allow.".

2   At the end of section 330(4)(b) of the Act there shall be added the words "and of the personal representative of a debtor dying after the making of a bankruptcy application, or (as the case may be) the presentation of a bankruptcy petition in respect of reasonable funeral and testamentary expenses of which notice has not already been given to the trustee".

History

Paragraphs 1(1), 2 and heading amended by the Enterprise and Regulatory Reform Act 2013 (Consequential Amendments) (Bankruptcy) and the Small Business, Enterprise and Employment Act 2015 (Consequential Amendments) Regulations 2016 (SI 2016/481) reg.2(2) and Sch.2 para.2(8) as from 6 April 2016.

Schedule 3

Forms Relating to Administration in Bankruptcy of Insolvent Estates of Deceased Debtors

Part II of Schedule 1, paragraphs 1, 5 to 7 and 15, Schedule 2, paragraph 1

[Not reproduced.]

Act of Sederunt (Company Directors Disqualification) 1986

(SI 1986/2296 (S.168))

Made on 19 December 1986 by the Lords of Council and Session under s.32 of the Sheriff Courts (Scotland) Act 1971. Operative from 29 December 1986.

1 Citation, commencement and interpretation

1(1) This Act of Sederunt may be cited as the Act of Sederunt (Company Directors Disqualification) 1986 and shall come into operation on 29th December 1986.

1(2) This Act of Sederunt shall be inserted in the Books of Sederunt.

1(3) In this Act of Sederunt–

"disqualification order" shall have the meaning assigned to it by section 1(1) of the Company Directors Disqualification Act 1986.

2 Revocation

2 The Act of Sederunt (Disqualification of Directors etc.) 1986 is hereby revoked.

3 Applications for disqualification orders

3(1) An application to the sheriff for a disqualification order or for leave of the court under the Company Directors Disqualification Act 1986 shall be made by summary application.

3(2) In an application under sub-paragraph (1) which proceeds as unopposed, evidence submitted by way of affidavit shall be admissible in place of parole evidence.

3(3) For the purposes of this paragraph–

(a) "affidavit" includes affirmation and statutory declaration; and

(b) an affidavit shall be treated as admissible if it is duly emitted before a notary public or any other competent authority.

4 Orders to furnish information or for inspection

4(1) Subject to sub-paragraph (2), an application for an order of the court under rule 3(2) of the Insolvent Companies (Reports on Conduct of Directors) (Scotland) Rules 2016 (application for order directing compliance with requirements to furnish information etc.) shall be made by summary application.

4(2) Where an application has been made under the Company Directors Disqualification Act 1986 for a disqualification order, an application under this paragraph may be made by minute in the proceedings in which the disqualification order is sought.

Act of Sederunt (Sheriff Court Company Insolvency Rules) 1986

(SI 1986/2297 (S.169))

Made on 19 December 1986 by the Lords of Council and Session under s.32 of the Sheriff Courts (Scotland) Act 1971. Operative from 29 December 1986.

[**Note:** Changes made by the Act of Sederunt (Sheriff Court Company Insolvency Rules 1986) Amendment 2003 (SI 2003/388), the Act of Sederunt (Sheriff Court Company Insolvency Rules 1986) Amendment (UNCITRAL Model Law on Cross-Border Insolvency) 2006 (SI 2006/200), the Act of Sederunt (Sheriff Court Company Insolvency Rules 1986) Amendment (Vulnerable Witnesses (Scotland) Act 2004) 2007 (SSI 2007/464), the Act of Sederunt (Sheriff Court Rules) (Miscellaneous Amendments) 2008 (SSI 2008/223), the Act of Sederunt (Sheriff Court Rules) (Miscellaneous Amendments) (No.3) 2013 (SSI 2013/171) and the Act of Sederunt (Rules of the Court of Session and Sheriff Court Company Insolvency Rules Amendment) (Miscellaneous) (SSI 2014/119) have been incorporated into the text. References to administration petitions, orders, etc. have been adapted throughout, following the introduction of the new administration regime, pursuant to r.4 and Sch. paras 1 et seq. of the 2003 rules, as from 15 September 2003. Any references to a "messenger-at-arms", a "sheriff officer" and an "officer of court" are to be construed as references to a judicial officer: see the Bankruptcy and Diligence etc. (Scotland) Act 2007 s.60.]

1 Citation and commencement

1(1) This Act of Sederunt may be cited as the Act of Sederunt (Sheriff Court Company Insolvency Rules) 1986 and shall come into operation on 29th December 1986.

1(2) This Act of Sederunt shall be inserted in the Books of Sederunt.

2 Revocation and transitional provision

2(1) The Act of Sederunt (Sheriff Court Liquidations) 1930 is hereby revoked.

2(2) Notwithstanding paragraph (1), the Act of Sederunt (Sheriff Court Liquidations) 1930 shall continue to have effect in relation to proceedings commenced before the coming into operation of this Act of Sederunt.

3 Interpretation

3(1) In these rules–

"the Act of 1986" means the Insolvency Act 1986;

"the Act of 2004" means the Energy Act 2004;

"the Act of 2011" means the Energy Act 2011;

"administration" shall include an energy administration under the Act of 2004 or the Energy Administration Rules and an energy supply company administration under the Act of 2011 or the Energy Supply Company Administration Rules and "administration order" and "administrator" shall be construed accordingly;

"the Council Regulation" means Regulation (EU) 2015/848 of the European Parliament and of the Council of 20th May 2015 on insolvency proceedings, as amended from time to time;

"the Energy Administration Rules" means the Energy Administration (Scotland) Rules 2006;

"the Energy Supply Company Administration Rules" means the Energy Supply Company Administration (Scotland) Rules 2013;

"the Insolvency Rules" means the Insolvency (Scotland) Rules 1986;

"the Model Law" means the Model Law on Cross-Border Insolvency as set out in Schedule 1 to the Cross-Border Insolvency Regulations 2006;

"non GB company" for the purposes of an energy administration shall have the meaning assigned in section 171 of the Act of 2004 and for the purposes of an energy supply company administration shall have the meaning assigned in section 102 of the 2011 Act;

"registered office" means–

(a) the place specified, in the statement of the company delivered to the registrar of companies under section 10 of the Companies Act 1985, as the intended place of its registered office on incorporation; or

(b) where notice has been given by the company to the registrar of companies under section 287 of the Companies Act 1985 of a change of registered office, the place specified in the last such notice;

"sheriff-clerk" has the meaning assigned to it in section 3(f) of the Sheriff Courts (Scotland) Act 1907.

3(2)   Unless the context otherwise requires, words and expressions used in these rules which are also used in the Act of 1986, the Act of 2004, the Act of 2011, the Energy Administration Rules, the Energy Supply Company Administration Rules or the Insolvency Rules have the same meaning as in those Acts or those Rules.

History
See also note after r.31B.
   Rule 3 amended by the Act of Sederunt (Sheriff Court Rules) (Miscellaneous Amendments) 2008 (SSI 2008/223) r.10(2) as from 1 July 2008. Definitions of "the Act of 2004", "the Act of 2011", "administration", "the Energy Administration Rules", "the Energy Supply Company Administration Rules" and "non GB company" inserted in r.3(1), and r.3(2) amended, by the Act of Sederunt (Sheriff Court Rules) (Miscellaneous Amendments) (No.3) (SSI 2013/171) r.3(1), (2) as from 7 June 2013.

3A   Representation

3A(1)   A party may be represented by any person authorised under any enactment to conduct proceedings in the sheriff court in accordance with the terms of that enactment.

3A(2)   The person referred to in paragraph (1) may do everything for the preparation and conduct of the proceedings as may have been done by an individual conducting his own action.

3A(3)   For the purposes of this rule, "enactment" includes an enactment comprised in, or in an instrument made under, an Act of the Scottish Parliament.

3B   Expenses

3B   A party who–

(a) is or has been represented by a person authorised under any enactment to conduct proceedings in the sheriff court; and

(b) would have been found entitled to expenses if he had been represented by a solicitor or an advocate,

may be awarded expenses or outlays to which a party litigant may be found entitled under the Litigants in Person (Cost and Expenses) Act 1975 or under any enactment under that Act.

History
Rules 3A, 3B inserted by the Act of Sederunt (Sheriff Court Rules) (Miscellaneous Amendments) 2008 (SSI 2008/223) r.12, as from 1 July 2008.

PART I

COMPANY VOLUNTARY ARRANGEMENTS

4　Lodging of nominee's report (Part 1, Chapter 2 of the Insolvency Rules)

4(1)　This rule applies where the company is not being wound up, is not in liquidation and is not in administration.

4(2)　A report of a nominee, sent to the court under section 2(2) of the Act of 1986, shall be accompanied by a covering letter, lodged in the offices of the court and marked by the sheriff-clerk with the date on which it is received.

4(3)　The report shall be placed before the sheriff for consideration of any direction which he may make under section 3(1) of the Act of 1986.

4(4)　An application by a nominee to extend the time within which he may lodge his report under section 2(2) of the Act of 1986 shall be made by letter addressed to the sheriff-clerk, who shall place the matter before the sheriff for determination.

4(5)　The letter of application under paragraph (4) and a copy of the reply by the court shall be placed by the sheriff-clerk with the nominee's report when it is subsequently lodged.

4(6)　A person who states in writing that he is a creditor, member or director of the company may, by himself or his agent, on payment of the appropriate fee, inspect the nominee's report lodged under paragraph (2).

5　Lodging of nominee's report (Part 1, Chapter 4 of the Insolvency Rules)

5(1)　This rule applies where the company is being wound up, is in liquidation or is in administration.

5(2)　Where a report of a nominee is sent to the court under section 2(2) of the Act of 1986, it shall be lodged in the process of the petition to wind up the company or any petition in respect of an administration which is in force in respect of it, as the case may be.

5(3)　Where the nominee is not the liquidator or administrator, the report shall be placed before the sheriff for consideration of any direction which he may make under section 3(1) of the Act of 1986.

5(4)　An application by a nominee to extend the time within which he may lodge his report under section 2(2) of the Act of 1986 shall be made by letter addressed to the sheriff-clerk, who shall place the matter before the sheriff for determination.

5(5)　The letter of application under paragraph (4) and a copy of the reply by the court shall be placed by the sheriff-clerk in the process of the petition to wind up the company or any petition in respect of an administration which is in force in respect of it, as the case may be.

5(6)　A person who states in writing that he is a creditor, member or director of the company may, by himself or his agent, on payment of the appropriate fee, inspect the nominee's report lodged under paragraph (2).

6　Applications to replace nominee

6　An application under section 2(4) of the Act of 1986 to replace a nominee who has failed to lodge a report under section 2(2) of the Act of 1986, shall be made–

(a)　by petition where the company is not being wound up, is not in liquidation and there is no order in respect of an administration; or

(b)　by note in the process of the petition to wind up the company or the petition in respect of an administration which is in force in respect of it, as the case may be,

and shall be intimated and served as the court shall direct.

7   Report of meetings to approve arrangement

7   The report of the result of a meeting to be sent to the court under section 4(6) of the Act of 1986 shall be sent to the sheriff-clerk who shall cause it to be lodged–

(a)   in a case to which rule 4 applies, with the nominee's report lodged under that rule; or

(b)   in a case to which rule 5 applies, in the process of the petition to wind up the company or the petition for an order in respect of an administration which is in force in respect of it, as the case may be.

8   Abstracts of supervisor's receipts and payments and notices of completion of arrangement

8   An abstract of receipts and payments prepared by a supervisor to be sent to the court under rule 1.21(2) of the Insolvency Rules or a notice of completion of the arrangement (together with a copy of the supervisor's report) to be sent to the court under rule 1.23(3) of those Rules shall be sent to the sheriff-clerk, who shall cause it to be lodged–

(a)   in a case to which rule 4 applies, with the nominee's report lodged under that rule; or

(b)   in a case to which rule 5 applies, in the process of the petition to wind up the company or the petition for an order in respect of an administration which is in force in respect of it, as the case may be.

9   Form of certain applications

9(1)   This rule applies to applications under any of the following provisions of the Act of 1986 and the Insolvency Rules:–

(a)   section 6 (to challenge a decision in relation to an arrangement);

(b)   section 7(3) (to challenge actings of a supervisor);

(c)   section 7(4)(a) (by supervisor for directions);

(d)   section 7(5) (to appoint a supervisor);

(e)   rule 1.21(5) (to dispense with sending abstracts or reports or to vary dates on which obligation to send abstracts or reports arises);

(f)   rule 1.23(4) (by supervisor to extend period for sending notice of implementation of arrangement); and

(g)   any other provision relating to company voluntary arrangements not specifically mentioned in this Part.

9(2)   An application shall be made–

(a)   in a case to which rule 4 applies, by petition; or

(b)   in a case to which rule 5 applies, by note in the process of the petition to wind up the company or the petition for an order in respect of an administration which is in force in respect of it, as the case may be.

PART II

ADMINISTRATION PROCEDURE

10   Petitions for administration orders

10(1)   A petition for an administration order or any other order in an administration shall include averments in relation to–

(a)   the petitioner and the capacity in which he presents the petition, if other than the company;

(b)   whether it is believed that the company is, or is likely to become, unable to pay its debts and the grounds of that belief;

(c)   in the case of a petition under the Act of 1986, how the making of that order will achieve–

(i)   any of the purposes specified in section 8(3) of the Act of 1986; or

(ii)   an objective specified in paragraph 3 of Schedule B1 to the Act of 1986;

(d)   the company's financial position, specifying (so far as known) assets and liabilities, including contingent and prospective liabilities;

(e)   any security known or believed to be held by creditors of the company, whether in any case the security confers power on the holder to appoint a receiver, and whether a receiver has been appointed;

(f)   so far as known to the petitioner, whether any steps have been taken for the winding up of the company, giving details of them;

(g)   other matters which, in the opinion of the petitioner, will assist the court in deciding whether to grant that order;

(h)   in the case of a petition under the Act of 1986, jurisdiction under the Council Regulation, in particular stating, so far as known to the petitioner–

(i)   where the centre of main interests of the company is and whether the company has any other establishments in another member State;

(ii)   whether there are insolvency proceedings elsewhere in respect of the company and whether those proceedings are main or territorial proceedings;

(i)   the name and address of the person proposed to be appointed, and his or her qualification to act, as administrator;

(j)   whether the Secretary of State has certified the case as one in which he or she considers it would be appropriate for him or her to petition under section 124A of the Act of 1986 (petition for winding up on grounds of public interest);

(k)   so far as is known to the petitioner in a petition for an energy administration order or an energy supply company administration order, whether any steps have been taken for an administration order under Schedule B1 to the Act of 1986; and

(l)   whether a protected energy company in a petition for an energy administration order, or an energy supply company in a petition for an energy supply company administration order, is a non GB company.

History

In Pt II in the heading the words "PROCEDURE" substituted for the former words "ORDERS" and in r.10(1) the words "or any other order in an administration" inserted by the Act of Sederunt (Sheriff Court Company Insolvency Rules 1986) Amendment 2003 (SI 2003/388) r.2 as from 15 September 2003.

Paragraph 1(h) substituted by the Act of Sederunt (Sheriff Court Rules) (Miscellaneous Amendments) 2008 (SSI 2008/223) r.10(3) as from 1 July 2008. Rule 10(1)(c), (h) amended, r.10(1)(i) substituted and r.10(1)(j)–(l) inserted by the Act of Sederunt (Sheriff Court Rules) (Miscellaneous Amendments) (No.3) (SSI 2013/171) r.3(1), (4) as from 7 June 2013.

10(2)   There shall be produced with the petition–

(a)   any document instructing the facts relied on, or otherwise founded on, by the petitioner; and

(b)   [Omitted by the Act of Sederunt (Sheriff Court Company Insolvency Rules 1986) Amendment (SI 2003/388) r.2 as from 15 September 2003.]

11 Notice of petition

11 Notice of the petition on the persons to whom notice is to be given under rule 2.3 of the Insolvency Rules, section 156(2)(a) to (c) of the 2004 Act, rule 5(1) of the Energy Administration Rules or rule 6(1) of the Energy Supply Company Administration Rules, shall be made in such manner as the court shall direct.

History
In r.11 "2.3" substituted for the former "2.2" by Act of Sederunt (Sheriff Court Company Insolvency Rules 1986) Amendment 2003 (SI 2003/388) r.2 as from 15 September 2003. Rule 11 amended by the Act of Sederunt (Sheriff Court Rules) (Miscellaneous Amendments) (No.3) (SSI 2013/171) r.3(1), (5) as from 7 June 2013.

12 Applications during an administration

12 An application or appeal under any provision of the Act of 1986, the Insolvency Rules, the Act of 2004, the Energy Administration Rules, the Act of 2011, or an application to participate under article 12 of the Model Law in an administration during an administration shall be–

(a) where no previous application or appeal has been made, by petition; or

(b) where a petition for an order in respect of an administration has been made, by note in the process of that petition.

History
Rule 12 substituted by the Act of Sederunt (Sheriff Court Company Insolvency Rules 1986) Amendment 2003 (SI 2003/388) r.2 as from 15 September 2003. Rule 12 amended by the Act of Sederunt (Sheriff Court Rules) (Miscellaneous Amendments) (No.3) (SSI 2013/171) r.3(1), (6) as from 7 June 2013. See also note after r.31B.

13 Report of administrator's proposals

13(1) A report of the meeting to approve the administrator's proposals to be sent to the court under section 24(4) of the Act of 1986 shall be sent to the sheriff-clerk, who shall cause it to be lodged in the process of the petition.

13(2) Where the report lodged under paragraph (1) discloses that the meeting has declined to approve the administrator's proposals, the court shall appoint a special diet for determination by the sheriff of any order he may make under section 24(5) of the Act of 1986.

14 Report of administrator's proposals: Schedule B1 to the Act of 1986

14(1) Paragraph (2) shall apply where a report under paragraphs 53(2) or 54(6) of Schedule B1 to the Act of 1986 discloses a failure to approve, or to approve a revision of, an administrator's proposals.

14(2) The sheriff clerk shall appoint a hearing for determination by the sheriff of any order that may be made under paragraph 55(2) of Schedule B1 to the Act of 1986.

14A Time and date of lodging in an administration

14A(1) The time and date of lodging of a notice or document relating to an administration shall be noted by the sheriff clerk upon the notice or document.

14A(2) Subject to any provision of the Insolvency Rules–

(a) where the time of lodging of a notice or document cannot be ascertained by the sheriff clerk, the notice or document shall be deemed to be lodged at 10 a.m. on the date of lodging; and

(b) where a notice or document under paragraph (1) is delivered on any day other than a business day, the date of lodging shall be the first business day after such delivery.

History
Rule 14 substituted and r.14A inserted by the Act of Sederunt (Sheriff Court Company Insolvency Rules 1986) Amendment 2003 (SI 2003/388) r.2 as from 15 September 2003. Rule 14A amended by the Act of Sederunt (Sheriff Court Rules) (Miscellaneous Amendments) (No.3) (SSI 2013/171) r.3(1), (7) as from 7 June 2013.

PART III

RECEIVERS

15 Petitions to appoint receivers

15(1) A petition to appoint a receiver for a company shall include averments in relation to–

(a) any floating charge and the property over which it is secured;

(b) so far as known to the petitioner whether any petition for an order in respect of an administration has been made, or an administrator has been appointed, in respect of the company, giving details of it;

(c) other matters which, in the opinion of the petitioner, will assist the court in deciding whether to appoint a receiver; and

(d) the person proposed to be appointed as receiver, giving his name and address and that he is qualified to act as a receiver.

15(2) There shall be produced with the petition any document instructing the facts relied on, or otherwise founded on, by the petitioner.

16 Intimation, service and advertisement

16(1) Intimation, service and advertisement of the petition shall be made in accordance with the following provisions of this rule unless the court otherwise directs.

16(2) There shall be included in the order for service, a requirement to serve–

(a) upon the company;

(b) where a petition for an order in respect of an administration has been presented, on that petitioner and any respondent to that petition; and

(c) upon an administrator.

16(3) Subject to paragraph (5), service of a petition on the company shall be effected at its registered office–

(a) by registered or recorded delivery post addressed to the company; or

(b) by sheriff officer–

    (i) leaving the citation in the hands of a person who, after due inquiry, he has reasonable grounds for believing to be a director, other officer or responsible employee of the company or authorised to accept service on behalf of the company; or

    (ii) if there is no such person as is mentioned in head (i) present, depositing it in the registered office in such a way that it is likely to come to the attention of such a person attending at that office.

16(4) Where service is effected in accordance with paragraph (3)(b)(ii), the sheriff officer thereafter shall send a copy of the petition and citation by ordinary first class post to the registered office of the company.

16(5)   Where service cannot be effected at the registered office of the company or the company has no registered office–

(a) service may be effected at the last known principal place of business of the company in Scotland or at some place in Scotland at which the company carries on business, by leaving the citation in the hands of such a person as is mentioned in paragraph (3)(b)(i) or by depositing it as specified in paragraph (3)(b)(ii); and

(b) where the citation is deposited as is specified in paragraph (3)(b)(ii), the sheriff officer thereafter shall send a copy of the petition and citation by ordinary first class post to such place mentioned in sub-paragraph (a) of this paragraph in which the citation was deposited.

16(6)   The petition shall be advertised forthwith–

(a) once in the Edinburgh Gazette; and

(b) once in one or more newspapers as the court shall direct for ensuring that it comes to the notice of the creditors of the company.

16(7)   The advertisement under paragraph (6) shall state–

(a) the name and address of the petitioner;

(b) the name and address of the solicitor for the petitioner;

(c) the date on which the petition was presented;

(d) the precise order sought;

(e) the period of notice; and

(f) that any person who intends to appear in the petition must lodge answers to the petition within the period of notice.

16(8)   The period of notice within which answers to the petition may be lodged and after which further consideration of the petition may proceed shall be 8 days after such intimation, service and advertisement as the court may have ordered.

17   Form of certain applications where receiver appointed

17(1)   An application under any of the following sections of the Act of 1986 shall be made by petition or, where the receiver was appointed by the court, by note in the process of the petition for appointment of a receiver:–

(a) section 61(1) (by receiver for authority to dispose of interest in property);

(b) section 62 (for removal or resignation of receiver);

(c) section 63(1) (by receiver for directions);

(d) section 69(1) (to enforce receiver to make returns, etc.); and

(e) any other section relating to receivers not specifically mentioned in this Part.

17(2)   An application under any of the following provisions of the Act of 1986 or the Insolvency Rules shall be made by motion in the process of the petition–

(a) section 67(1) or (2) (by receiver to extend time for sending report); and

(b) rule 3.9(2) (by receiver to extend time for sending abstract of receipts and payments).

WINDING UP BY THE COURT OF COMPANIES REGISTERED UNDER THE COMPANIES ACTS AND OF UNREGISTERED COMPANIES

18   Petitions to wind up a company

18(1)   A petition to wind up a company under the Act of 1986 shall include–

  (a)   particulars of the petitioner, if other than the company;

  (aa)   averments in relation to jurisdiction under the Council Regulation, in particular stating, so far as known to the petitioner:–

  (i)   where the centre of main interests of the company is and whether the company has any other establishments in another member State;

  (ii)   whether there are insolvency proceedings elsewhere in respect of the company and whether those proceedings are main or territorial proceedings;

  (b)   in respect of the company–

  (i)   the registered name;

  (ii)   the address of the registered office and any change of that address within the last 6 months so far as known to the petitioner;

  (iii)   a statement of the nature and objects, the amount of its capital (nominal and issued) and indicating what part is called up, paid up or credited as paid, and the amount of the assets of the company so far as known to the petitioner;

  (c)   a narrative of the facts on which the petitioner relies and any particulars required to instruct the title of the petitioner to present the petition;

  (d)   the name and address of the person to be appointed as interim liquidator and a statement that he is qualified to act as an insolvency practitioner in relation to the company; and

  (e)   a crave setting out the orders applied for, including any intimation, service and advertisement and any appointment of an interim liquidator.

18(2)   There shall be lodged with the petition any document–

  (a)   instructing the title of the petitioner; and

  (b)   instructing the facts relied on, or otherwise founded on, by the petitioner.

History
Rule 18(1)(aa) inserted by the Act of Sederunt (Sheriff Court Rules) (Miscellaneous Amendments) 2008 (SSI 2008/223) r.10(4) as from 1 July 2008.

19   Intimation, service and advertisement

19(1)   Intimation, service and advertisement shall be in accordance with the following provisions of this rule unless the court–

  (a)   summarily dismisses the petition; or

  (b)   otherwise directs.

19(2)   There shall be included in the order for intimation and service, a requirement–

  (a)   to intimate on the walls of the court;

  (b)   where the petitioner is other than the company, to serve upon the company;

(c) where the company is being wound up voluntarily and a liquidator has been appointed, to serve upon the liquidator;

(d) where a receiver has been appointed for the company, to serve upon the receiver;

(dd) where a company is in administration, to serve upon the administrator;

(e) where the company is–

    (i)   a recognised bank or licensed institution within the meaning of the Banking Act 1979; or

    (ii) an institution to which sections 16 and 18 of that Act apply as if it were licensed,

and the petitioner is not the Bank of England, to serve upon the Bank of England.

History
In r.19(2) para.(dd) inserted by the Act of Sederunt (Sheriff Court Company Insolvency Rules 1986) Amendment 2003 (SI 2003/388) r.4, Sch. paras 1, 10 as from 15 September 2003.

19(3)   Subject to paragraph (5), service of a petition on the company shall be executed at its registered office–

(a) by registered or recorded delivery post addressed to the company; or

(b) by sheriff officer–

    (i)   leaving the citation in the hands of a person who, after due inquiry, he has reasonable grounds for believing to be a director, other officer or responsible employee of the company or authorised to accept service on behalf of the company; or

    (ii) if there is no such person as is mentioned in head (i) present, depositing it in the registered office in such a way that it is likely to come to the attention of such a person attending at that office.

19(4)   Where service is effected in accordance with paragraph (3)(b)(ii), the sheriff officer thereafter shall send a copy of the petition and citation by ordinary first class post to the registered office of the company.

19(5)   Where service cannot be effected at the registered office or the company has no registered office–

(a) service may be effected at the last known principal place of business of the company in Scotland or at some place in Scotland at which the company carries on business, by leaving the citation in the hands of such a person as is mentioned in paragraph (3)(b)(i) or by depositing it as specified in paragraph (3)(b)(ii); and

(b) where the citation is deposited as is specified in paragraph (3)(b)(ii), the sheriff officer thereafter shall send a copy of the petition and the citation by ordinary first class post to such place mentioned in sub-paragraph (a) of this paragraph in which the citation was deposited.

19(6)   The petition shall be advertised forthwith–

(a) once in the Edinburgh Gazette; and

(b) once in one or more newspapers as the court shall direct for ensuring that it comes to the notice of the creditors of the company.

19(7)   The advertisement under paragraph (6) shall state–

(a) the name and address of the petitioner and, where the petitioner is the company, the registered office;

(b) the name and address of the solicitor for the petitioner;

(c) the date on which the petition was presented;

(d)   the precise order sought;

(e)   where a provisional liquidator has been appointed, his name, address and the date of his appointment;

(f)   the period of notice; and

(g)   that any person who intends to appear in the petition must lodge answers to the petition within the period of notice.

19(8)   The period of notice within which answers to the petition may be lodged and after which further consideration of the petition may proceed shall be 8 days after such intimation, service and advertisement as the court may have ordered.

20   [Omitted by the Act of Sederunt (Sheriff Court Caveat Rules) 2006 (SI 2006/198) as from 28 April 2006.]

21   Substitution of creditor or contributory for petitioner

21(1)   This rule applies where a petitioner–

(a)   is subsequently found not entitled to present the petition;

(b)   fails to make intimation, service and advertisement as directed by the court;

(c)   consents to withdraw the petition or to allow it to be dismissed or refused;

(d)   fails to appear when the petition is called for hearing; or

(e)   appears, but does not move for an order in terms of the prayer of the petition.

21(2)   The court may, on such terms as it considers just, sist as petitioner in room of the original petitioner any creditor or contributory who, in the opinion of the court, is entitled to present a petition.

21(3)   An application by a creditor or contributory to be sisted under paragraph (2)–

(a)   may be made at any time before the petition is dismissed or refused; and

(b)   shall be made by note in the process of the petition, and if necessary the court may continue the cause for a specified period to allow a note to be presented.

22   Advertisement of appointment of liquidator

22   Where a liquidator is appointed by the court, the court may order that the liquidator shall advertise his appointment once in one or more newspapers as the court shall direct for ensuring that it comes to the notice of creditors of the company.

23   Provisional liquidators

23(1)   An application to appoint a provisional liquidator under section 135 of the Act of 1986 may be made–

(a)   by the petitioner, in the crave of the petition or subsequently by note in the process of the petition; or

(b)   by a creditor or contributory of the company, the company, Secretary of State or a person entitled under any enactment to present a petition to wind up the company, in a note in the process of the petition.

23(2)   The petition or note, as the case may be, shall include averments in relation to–

(a)   the grounds on which it is proposed that a provisional liquidator should be appointed;

(b) the name and address of the person to be appointed as provisional liquidator and that he is qualified to act as an insolvency practitioner in relation to the company; and

(c) whether, to the knowledge of the applicant, there is a receiver or administrator for the company or a liquidator has been appointed for the voluntary winding up of the company.

History
In r.23(2)(c) the words "or administrator" inserted by the Act of Sederunt (Sheriff Court Company Insolvency Rules 1986) Amendment 2003 (SI 2003/388) r.4, Sch. paras 1, 11 as from 15 September 2003.

23(3)   Where the court is satisfied that sufficient grounds exist for the appointment of a provisional liquidator, it shall, on making the appointment, specify the functions to be carried out by him in relation to the affairs of the company.

23(4)   The applicant shall send a certified copy of the interlocutor appointing a provisional liquidator forthwith to the person appointed.

23(5)   On receiving a certified copy of his appointment on an application by note, the provisional liquidator shall intimate his appointment forthwith–

(a) once in the Edinburgh Gazette; and

(b) once in one or more newspapers as the court shall direct for ensuring that it comes to the notice of creditors of the company.

23(6)   An application for discharge of a provisional liquidator shall be by note in the process of the petition.

24   Applications and appeals in relation to a statement of affairs

24(1)   An application under section 131(5) of the Act of 1986 for–

(a) release from an obligation imposed under section 131(1) or (2) of the Act of 1986; or

(b) an extension of time for the submission of a statement of affairs,

shall be made by note in the process of the petition.

24(2)   A note under paragraph (1) shall be served on the liquidator or provisional liquidator, as the case may be.

24(3)   The liquidator or provisional liquidator may lodge answers to the note or lodge a report of any matters which he considers should be drawn to the attention of the court.

24(4)   Where the liquidator or provisional liquidator lodges a report under paragraph (3), he shall send a copy of it to the noter forthwith.

24(5)   Where the liquidator or provisional liquidator does not appear, a certified copy of the interlocutor pronounced by the court disposing of the note shall be sent by the noter forthwith to him.

24(6)   An appeal under rule 4.9(6) of the Insolvency Rules against a refusal by the liquidator of an allowance towards the expense of preparing a statement of affairs shall be made by note in the process of the petition.

25   Appeals against adjudication of claims

25(1)   An appeal under rule 4.16B(6) of the Insolvency Rules (adjudication of claims) by a creditor or any member or contributory of the company against a decision of the liquidator shall be made by note in the process of the petition.

25(2)   A note under paragraph (1) shall be served on the liquidator.

25(3)   On receipt of the note served on him under this rule, the liquidator forthwith shall send to the court the claim in question and a copy of his adjudication for lodging in process.

25(4)   After the note has been disposed of, the court shall return the claim and the adjudication to the liquidator together with a copy of the interlocutor.

History
Rule 25(1) substituted by the Act of Sederunt (Rules of the Court of Session and Sheriff Court Company Insolvency Rules Amendment) (Miscellaneous) (SSI 2014/119) r.3(1), (2) as from 30 May 2014.

26   Appointment of liquidator by the court

26(1)   An application to appoint a liquidator under section 139(4) of the Act of 1986 shall be made by note in the process of the petition.

26(2)   Where the court appoints a liquidator under section 138(5) of the Act of 1986, the sheriff-clerk shall send a certified copy of the interlocutor pronounced by the court to the liquidator forthwith.

27   Removal of liquidator

27   An application by a creditor of the company for removal of a liquidator or provisional liquidator from office under section 172 of the Act of 1986 or for an order under section 171(3) of the Act of 1986 directing a liquidator to summon a meeting of creditors for the purpose of removing him shall be made by note in the process of the petition.

28   Applications in relation to remuneration of liquidator

28(1)   An application by a liquidator under rule 4.34 of the Insolvency Rules shall be made by note in the process of the petition.

28(2)   An application by a creditor of the company under rule 4.35 of the Insolvency Rules shall be made by note in the process of the petition.

28(3)   A note under paragraph (2) shall be served on the liquidator.

29   Application to appoint a special manager

29(1)   An application under section 177 of the Act of 1986 by a liquidator or provisional liquidator for the appointment of a special manager shall be made by note in the process of the petition.

29(2)   The cautioner, for the caution to be found by the special manager within such time as the court shall direct, may be–

   (a)   a private person, if approved by the court; or

   (b)   a guarantee company, chosen from a list of such companies prepared for this purpose annually by the Accountant of Court and approved by the Lord President of the Court of Session.

29(3)   A bond of caution certified by the noter under rule 4.70(4) of the Insolvency Rules shall be delivered to the sheriff-clerk by the noter, marked as received by him and transmitted forthwith by him to the Accountant of Court.

29(4)   On receipt of the bond of caution, the sheriff-clerk shall issue forthwith to the person appointed to be special manager a certified copy of the interlocutor appointing him.

29(5)   An application by a special manager to extend the time within which to find caution shall be made by motion.

30   Other applications

30   An application under the Act of 1986 or rules made under that Act in relation to a winding up by the court not specifically mentioned in this Part or an application to participate under article 12 of the Model Law in a winding up by the court shall be made by note in the process of the petition.

History
See note after r.31B.

Part V

General Provisions

31   Application

31   This Part applies to Parts I to IV of these rules.

31A   Applications under section 176A of the Act of 1986

31A(1)   An application by a liquidator, administrator or receiver under section 176A of the Act of 1986 shall be–

  (a)   where there is no existing process in relation to any liquidation, administration or receivership, by petition; or

  (b)   where a process exists in relation to any liquidation, administration or receivership, by note in that process.

31A(2)   The sheriff clerk shall–

  (a)   after lodging of any petition or note fix a hearing for the sheriff to consider an application under paragraph (1); and

  (b)   give notice of the hearing fixed under paragraph (2)(a) to the petitioner or noter.

31A(3)   The petitioner or noter shall not be required to give notice to any person of the hearing fixed under paragraph (2)(a), unless the sheriff directs otherwise.

History
Rule 31A inserted by the Act of Sederunt (Sheriff Court Company Insolvency Rules 1986) Amendment 2003 (SI 2003/388) r.3 as from 15 September 2003.

31AA   Limited disclosure of statement of affairs

31AA   Any application under rules 1.50, 2.22, 3.2A or 4.8A of the Insolvency Rules (orders of limited disclosure etc.) shall be made–

  (a)   where there is no existing process in relation to any liquidation, administration or receivership, by petition; or

  (b)   where a process exists in relation to any liquidation, administration or receivership, by note in that process.

History
Rule 31AA inserted by the Act of Sederunt (Rules of the Court of Session and Sheriff Court Company Insolvency Rules Amendment) (Miscellaneous) (SSI 2014/119) r.3(1), (3) as from 30 May 2014.

31B   UNCITRAL Model Law on Cross-Border Insolvency

31B   On receipt of a certified copy interlocutor of a Lord Ordinary ordering proceedings under these rules to be transferred to the Court of Session under paragraph 11 of Schedule 3 to the Cross-Border

590

Insolvency Regulations 2006, the sheriff clerk shall within four days transmit the process to the deputy principal clerk of session.

History

Rules 3, 12 and 30 were amended and r.31B inserted by the Act of Sederunt (Sheriff Court Company Insolvency Rules 1986) Amendment (UNCITRAL Model Law on Cross-Border Insolvency) 2006 (SI 2006/200, effective 6 April 2006), to take account of the adoption by the UK of the UNCITRAL Model Law.

32   Intimation, service and advertisement of notes and appeals

32   An application by note, or an appeal, to the court under these rules shall be intimated, served and, if necessary, advertised as the court shall direct.

33   Affidavits

33   The court may accept as evidence an affidavit lodged in support of a petition or note.

34   Notices, reports and other documents sent to the court

34   Where, under the Act of 1986 or rules made under that Act–

(a)   notice of a fact is to be given to the court;

(b)   a report is to be made, or sent, to the court; or

(c)   some other document is to be sent to the court;

it shall be sent or delivered to the sheriff-clerk of the court, who shall cause it to be lodged in the appropriate process.

35   Failure to comply with rules

35(1)   The court may, in its discretion, relieve a party from the consequences of any failure to comply with the provisions of a rule shown to be due to mistake, oversight or other cause, which is not wilful non-observance of the rule, on such terms and conditions as the court considers just.

35(2)   Where the court relieves a party from the consequences of failure to comply with a rule under paragraph 1, the court may pronounce such interlocutor as may be just so as to enable the cause to proceed as if the failure to comply with the rule had not occurred.

35A   Vulnerable witnesses

35A(1)   At any hearing on an application under these rules the sheriff shall ascertain whether there is or is likely to be a vulnerable witness who is to give evidence at or for the purposes of any proof or hearing, consider any child witness notice or vulnerable witness application that has been lodged where no order has been made under section 12(1) or (6) of the Vulnerable Witnesses (Scotland) Act 2004 and consider whether any order under section 12(1) of that Act requires to be made.

35A(2)   Except where the sheriff otherwise directs, where a vulnerable witness is to give evidence at or for the purposes of any proof or hearing in an application under these rules, any application in relation to the vulnerable witness or special measure that may be ordered shall be dealt with in accordance with the rules within Chapter 45 of the Ordinary Cause Rules in the First Schedule to the Sheriff Courts (Scotland) Act 1907.

35A(3)   In this rule, "vulnerable witness" means a witness within the meaning of section 11(1) of the Vulnerable Witnesses (Scotland) Act 2004.

History

Rule 35A inserted by the Act of Sederunt (Sheriff Court Company Insolvency Rules 1986) Amendment (Vulnerable Witnesses (Scotland) Act 2004) 2007 (SSI 2007/464) r.2, as from 1 November 2007.

PART VI

APPEALS

36 Appeals to the Court of Session

36(1) Where an appeal to the Court of Session is competent, it shall be taken by note of appeal which shall–

   (a) be written by the appellant or his solicitor on–

      (i)   the interlocutor sheet or other written record containing the interlocutor appealed against; or

      (ii) a separate document lodged with the sheriff-clerk;

   (b) be as nearly as may be in the following terms:– "The (*petitioner, noter, respondent or other party*) appeals to [the Court of Session]"; and

   (c) be signed by the appellant or his solicitor and bear the date on which it is signed.

36(2) Such an appeal shall be marked within 14 days of the date of the interlocutor appealed against.

36(3) The note of appeal shall specify the name and address of the solicitor in Edinburgh who will be acting for the appellant.

36(4) On an appeal being taken, the sheriff-clerk shall within 4 days–

   (a) transmit the process to the Deputy Principal Clerk of Session; and

   (b) send written notice of the appeal to any other party to the cause and certify in the interlocutor sheet, or other written record containing the interlocutor appealed against, that he has done so.

36(5) Failure of the sheriff-clerk to give notice under paragraph 4(b) shall not invalidate the appeal.

36A Appeals to the Sheriff Appeal Court

36A Where an appeal to the Sheriff Appeal Court is competent, it is to be made in accordance with Chapter 6 of the Act of Sederunt (Sheriff Appeal Court Rules) 2015.

Insolvent Companies (Disqualification of Unfit Directors) Proceedings Rules 1987

(SI 1987/2023)

Made on 25 November 1987 by the Lord Chancellor, under ss.411 and 413 of the Insolvency Act 1986 and s.21 of the Company Directors Disqualification Act 1986. Operative from 11 January 1988.

[**Note:** These Regulations apply (with modifications) to limited liability partnerships by virtue of the Limited Liability Partnerships Regulations 2001 (SI 2001/1090) regs 1, 10(1) and Sch.6 Pt III para.3 as from 6 April 2001. Amendments to these Rules by the Insolvent Companies (Disqualification of Unfit Directors) Proceedings (Amendment) Rules 1999 (SI 1999/1023), the Insolvent Companies (Disqualification of Unfit Directors) Proceedings (Amendment) Rules 2003 (SI 2003/1367), the Insolvent Companies (Disqualification of Unfit Directors) Proceedings (Amendment) Rules 2007 (SI 2007/1906), the Deregulation Act 2015 (Insolvency) (Consequential Amendments and Transitional and Savings Provisions) Order 2015 (SI 2015/1641) and the Small Business, Enterprise and Employment Act 2015 (Consequential Amendments) (Insolvency and Company Directors Disqualification) Regulations 2015 (SI 2015/1651) have been incorporated into the text (in the case of pre-2003 legislation without annotation).]

1   Citation, commencement and interpretation

1(1)   These Rules may be cited as the Insolvent Companies (Disqualification of Unfit Directors) Proceedings Rules 1987 and shall come into force on 11th January 1988.

1(2)   In these Rules–

(a)   "the Companies Act" means the Companies Act 1985,

(b)   "the Company Directors Disqualification Act" means the Company Directors Disqualification Act 1986,

(c)   "CPR" followed by a Part or rule by number means that Part or rule with that number in the Civil Procedure Rules 1998,

(d)   "practice direction" means a direction as to the practice and procedure of any court within the scope of the Civil Procedure Rules,

(e)   "registrar" has the same meaning as in rule 1.2(2) of the Insolvency (England and Wales) Rules 2016, and

(f)   "file in court" means deliver to the court for filing.

1(3)   These Rules apply to an application made under the Company Directors Disqualification Act on or after 6th August 2007–

(a)   for leave to commence proceedings for a disqualification order after the end of the period mentioned in section 7(2) of that Act;

(b)   to enforce any duty arising under section 7(4) of that Act;

(c)   for a disqualification order where made–

(i)   by the Secretary of State or the official receiver under section 7(1) of that Act (disqualification of unfit directors of insolvent companies);

(ii)   by the Secretary of State under section 5A (disqualification for certain convictions abroad), 8 (disqualification of director on finding of unfitness), 8ZB (Application for order under section 8ZA) or 8ZD (order disqualifying person instructing unfit director: other cases) of that Act; or

      (iii) by the Competition and Markets Authority or a specified regulator under section 9A of that Act (competition disqualification order);

(d) under section 8A of that Act (variation etc. of disqualification undertaking); or–

(e) for leave to act under–

      (i) section 1A(1) or 9B(4) of that Act (and section 17 of that Act as it applies for the purposes of either of those sections); or

      (ii) sections 1 and 17 as they apply for the purposes of section 5A, 6, 7(1), 8, 8ZA, 8ZC, 8ZD, 8ZE, 9A or 10 of that Act.

History
Rule 1(3) replaced by the Insolvent Companies (Disqualification of Unfit Directors) Proceedings (Amendment) Rules 2007 (SI 2007/1906) r.2 as from 6 August 2007. Rule 1(3)(c)(ii) substituted by the Small Business, Enterprise and Employment Act 2015 (Consequential Amendments) (Insolvency and Company Directors Disqualification) Regulations 2015 (SI 2015/1651) reg.2(1), (2) as from 1 October 2015. Rule 1(3)(e) substituted by the Insolvency (England and Wales) Rules 2016 (Consequential Amendments and Savings) Rules 2017 (SI 2017/369) r.2(2), Sch.2 para.3(1), (2) as from 6 April 2017.

2   Form and conduct of applications

2(1)   The Civil Procedure Rules 1998, and any relevant practice direction, apply in respect of any application to which these Rules apply, except where these Rules make provision to inconsistent effect.

2(2)   Subject to paragraph (5), an application shall be made either–

(a) by claim form as provided by the relevant practice direction and the claimant must use the CPR Part 8 (alternative procedure for claims) procedure, or

(b) by application notice as provided for by the relevant practice direction.

2(3)   CPR rule 8.1(3) (power of the court to order the claim to continue as if the claimant had not used the Part 8 procedure), CPR rule 8.2 (contents of the claim form) and CPR rule 8.7 (Part 20 claims) do not apply.

2(4)   Rule 12.59 (appeals and reviews of court orders in corporate insolvency) and rule 12.62 (procedure on appeal) of the Insolvency (England and Wales) Rules 2016 apply.

2(5)   The Insolvency (England and Wales) Rules 2016 shall apply to an application to enforce any duty arising under section 7(4) of the Company Directors Disqualification Act.

History
Rule 2(2) replaced, and r.2(5) inserted, by the Insolvent Companies (Disqualification of Unfit Directors) Proceedings (Amendment) Rules 2007 (SI 2007/1906) r.3 as from 6 August 2007. Rule 2(5) amended by the Deregulation Act 2015 (Insolvency) (Consequential Amendments and Transitional and Savings Provisions) Order 2015 (SI 2015/1641) art.6 and Sch.3 para.4 as from 1 October 2015. Rule 2(4) substituted and r.2(5) amended by the Insolvency (England and Wales) Rules 2016 (Consequential Amendments and Savings) Rules 2017 (SI 2017/369) r.2(2), Sch.2 para.3(1), (3) as from 6 April 2017.

2A   Application of Rules 3 to 8

2A   Rules 3 to 8 only apply to the types of application referred to in Rule 1(3)(c).

History
Rule 2A inserted by the Insolvent Companies (Disqualification of Unfit Directors) Proceedings (Amendment) Rules 2007 (SI 2007/1906) r.4 as from 6 August 2007.

3   The case against the defendant

3(1)   There shall, at the time when the claim form is issued, be filed in court evidence in support of the application for a disqualification order; and copies of the evidence shall be served with the claim form on the defendant.

3(2)   The evidence shall be by one or more affidavits, except where the claimant is the official receiver, in which case it may be in the form of a written report (with or without affidavits by other persons) which shall be treated as if it had been verified by affidavit by him and shall be prima facie evidence of any matter contained in it.

3(3)   There shall in the affidavit or affidavits or (as the case may be) the official receiver's report be included a statement of the matters by reference to which the defendant is alleged to be unfit to be concerned in the management of a company.

4   Endorsement on claim form

4   There shall on the claim form be endorsed information to the defendant as follows–

   (a)   that the application is made in accordance with these Rules;

   (b)   that, in accordance with the relevant enactments, the court has power to impose disqualifications as follows–

      (i)   where the application is under section 7 or 8ZB of the Company Directors Disqualification Act, for a period of not less than 2, and up to 15, years; and

      (ii)   where the application is under section 5A, 8, 8ZD, or 9A of that Act, for a period of up to 15 years;

   (c)   that the application for a disqualification order may, in accordance with these Rules, be heard and determined summarily, without further or other notice to the defendant, and that, if it is so heard and determined, the court may impose disqualification for a period of up to 5 years;

   (d)   that if at the hearing of the application the court, on the evidence then before it, is minded to impose, in the defendant's case, disqualification for any period longer than 5 years, it will not make a disqualification order on that occasion but will adjourn the application to be heard (with further evidence, if any) at a later date to be notified; and

   (e)   that any evidence which the defendant wishes to be taken into consideration by the court must be filed in court in accordance with the time limits imposed under Rule 6 (the provisions of which shall be set out on the claim form).

History
In r.4(b)(ii) the words "under section 8 or 9A of that Act" substituted for the former words "under section 8 of that Act" by the Insolvent Companies (Disqualification of Unfit Directors) Proceedings (Amendment) Rules 2003 (SI 2003/1367) rr.1, 3, Sch. para.2(1), (2) as from 20 June 2003.

5   Service and acknowledgement

5(1)   The claim form shall be served on the defendant by sending it by first class post to his last known address; and the date of service shall, unless the contrary is shown, be deemed to be the 7th day next following that on which the claim form was posted.

5(2)   Where any process or order of the court or other document is required under proceedings subject to these Rules to be served on any person who is not in England and Wales, the court may order service on him of that process or order or other document to be effected within such time and in such manner as it thinks fit, and may also require such proof of service as it thinks fit.

5(3)   The claim form served on the defendant shall be accompanied by an acknowledgment of service as provided for by practice direction and CPR rule 8.3(2) (dealing with the contents of an acknowledgment of service) does not apply.

5(4)   The acknowledgement of service shall state that the defendant should indicate–

(a)   whether he contests the application on the grounds that, in the case of any particular company–

   (i)   he was not a director or shadow director of the company at a time when conduct of his, or of other persons, in relation to that company is in question, or

   (ii)   his conduct as director or shadow director of that company was not as alleged in support of the application for a disqualification order,

(b)   whether, in the case of any conduct of his, he disputes the allegation that such conduct makes him unfit to be concerned in the management of a company, and

(c)   whether he, while not resisting the application for a disqualification order, intends to adduce mitigating factors with a view to justifying only a short period of disqualification.

6   Evidence

6(1)   The defendant shall, within 28 days from the date of service of the claim form, file in court any affidavit evidence in opposition to the application he wishes the court to take into consideration and shall forthwith serve upon the claimant a copy of such evidence.

6(2)   The claimant shall, within 14 days from receiving the copy of the defendant's evidence, file in court any further evidence in reply he wishes the court to take into consideration and shall forthwith serve a copy of that evidence upon the defendant.

6(3)   CPR rules 8.5 (filing and serving written evidence) and 8.6(1) (requirements where written evidence is to be relied on) do not apply.

7   The hearing of the application

7(1)   When the claim form is issued, the court will fix a date for the first hearing of the claim which shall not be less than 8 weeks from the date of issue of the claim form.

7(2)   The hearing shall in the first instance be before the registrar in open court.

7(3)   The registrar shall either determine the case on the date fixed or adjourn it.

7(4)   The registrar shall adjourn the case for further consideration if–

(a)   he forms the provisional opinion that a disqualification order ought to be made, and that a period of disqualification longer than 5 years is appropriate, or

(b)   he is of opinion that questions of law or fact arise which are not suitable for summary determination.

7(5)   If the registrar adjourns the case for further consideration he shall–

(a)   direct whether the case is to be heard by a registrar or, if he thinks it appropriate, by the judge, for determination by him;

(b)   state the reasons for the adjournment; and

(c)   give directions as to the following matters–

   (i)   the manner in which and the time within which notice of the adjournment and the reasons for it are to be given to the defendant,

   (ii)   the filing in court and the service of further evidence (if any) by the parties,

   (iii) such other matters as the registrar thinks necessary or expedient with a view to an expeditious disposal of the application, and

   (iv) the time and place of the adjourned hearing.

7(6) Where a case is adjourned other than to the judge, it may be heard by the registrar who originally dealt with the case or by another registrar.

8 Making and setting aside of disqualification order

8(1) The court may make a disqualification order against the defendant, whether or not the latter appears, and whether or not he has completed and returned the acknowledgement of service of the claim form, or filed evidence in accordance with Rule 6.

8(2) Any disqualification order made in the absence of the defendant may be set aside or varied by the court on such terms as it thinks just.

9 Commencement of disqualification order

9 [Revoked by Insolvent Companies (Disqualification of Unfit Directors) Proceedings (Amendment) Rules 2001 (SI 2001/765) rr.1, 2 as from 2 April 2001.]

10 Right of audience

10 Official receivers and deputy official receivers have right of audience in any proceedings to which these Rules apply, whether the application is made by the Secretary of State or by the official receiver at his direction, and whether made in the High Court or a county court.

11 Revocation and saving

11(1) The Insolvent Companies (Disqualification of Unfit Directors) Proceedings Rules 1986 ("the former Rules") are hereby revoked.

11(2) Notwithstanding paragraph (1) the former Rules shall continue to apply and have effect in relation to any application described in paragraph 3(a) or (b) of Rule 1 of these Rules made before the date on which these Rules come into force.

Insolvency (ECSC Levy Debts) Regulations 1987

(SI 1987/2093)

Made on 1 December 1987 by the Secretary of State for Trade and Industry, for the purposes of s.2(2) of the European Communities Act 1972. Operative from 1 January 1988.

1 Citation and commencement

These Regulations, which extend to Great Britain, may be cited as the Insolvency (ECSC Levy Debts) Regulations 1987 and shall come into force on 1st January 1988.

2 Amendment of Insolvency Act 1986

2(1) Schedule 6 to the Insolvency Act 1986 is hereby amended by the insertion after paragraph 15 of the following paragraph–

[Insertion of para.15A—not reproduced here.]

2(2) Accordingly in section 386(1) of that Act (construction of references to preferential debts) after "remuneration etc. of employees" there shall be inserted ": levies on coal and steel production".

2(3) The amendment made by paragraph (1) above shall have effect in relation to a debtor whether the relevant date referred to in that amendment is a date falling before or after the commencement of these Regulations, but shall not affect any declaration or payment of a dividend made before that commencement.

3 Amendment of Bankruptcy (Scotland) Act 1985 [Revoked]

4 Preferential treatment under former law

4(1) Where the payment of preferential or preferred debts falls to be regulated by the law in force at any time before 29th December 1986, there shall be treated as included among those debts any sums due from the debtor at the relevant date in respect of–

(a) the levies on the production of coal and steel referred to in Articles 49 and 50 of the E.C.S.C. Treaty, or

(b) any surcharge for delay provided for in Article 50(3) of that Treaty and Article 6 of Decision 3/52 of the High Authority of the Coal and Steel Community.

4(2) In paragraph (1) above "the relevant date" means the date by reference to which the debtor's preferential or preferred debts fall to be ascertained in accordance with the law referred to in that paragraph.

Department of Trade and Industry (Fees) Order 1988

(SI 1988/93)

Made on 21 January 1988 by the Secretary of State for Trade and Industry under s.102(5) of the Finance (No.2) Act 1987. Operative from 22 January 1988.

[**Note:** Only those parts of this Order relevant to companies and insolvency have been reproduced—also relevant amendment by the Financial Services and Markets Act 2000 (Consequential Amendments and Repeals) Order 2001 (SI 2001/3649) (operative from 1 December 2001) included, without annotation.]

1   Citation and commencement

1(1)   This Order may be cited as the Department of Trade and Industry (Fees) Order 1988, and shall come into force on the day after the day on which it is made.

2   Interpretation

2   In this Order–

(a)   "the Act" means the Finance (No. 2) Act 1987;

"the 1938 Act" means the Trade Marks Act 1938;

"the 1949 Act" means the Registered Designs Act 1949;

"the 1977 Act" means the Patents Act 1977;

"the 1985 Act" means the Companies Act 1985;

"the 1986 Act" means the Insolvency Act 1986;

"wireless telegraphy", "wireless telegraphy apparatus" and "interference" have the meanings given to them in section 19 of the Wireless Telegraphy Act 1949;

(b)   any reference to any provision of the 1985 Act includes any corresponding provision of any enactment repealed and re-enacted, with or without modification, by the 1985 Act.

3(1)   In relation to the power of the Secretary of State under section 708 of the 1985 Act by regulations made by statutory instrument to require the payment to the registrar of companies of such fees as may be specified in the regulations in respect of–

(a)   the performance by the registrar of such functions under the 1985 Act or the 1986 Act as may be so specified, including the receipt by him of any notice or other document which under either of those Acts is required to be given, delivered, sent or forwarded to him,

(b)   the inspection of documents or other material kept by him under either of those Acts,

the functions specified for the purpose of section 102(3) of the Act shall be those specified in Part I of Schedule 1 hereto.

3(2)   In relation to the power of the Secretary of State specified in paragraph (1) above, the matters specified for the purposes of section 102(4) of the Act shall be those specified in Part I of Schedule 2 hereto.

4(1)   In relation to the power of the Secretary of State to fix fees under sections 53(5), 54(4) and 71(2) of the 1986 Act, the functions specified for the purposes of section 102(3) of the Act shall be those specified in Part I of Schedule 1 hereto.

4(2)   In relation to the power of the Secretary of State specified in paragraph (1) above, the matters specified for the purposes of section 102(4) of the Act shall be those specified in Part I of Schedule 2 hereto.

9(1) In relation to the power of the Lord Chancellor to fix fees under section 133(1) of the Bankruptcy Act 1914, section 663(4) of the 1985 Act and sections 414 and 415 of the 1986 Act and in relation to the power of the Secretary of State to fix fees under sections 4 and 10 of the Insolvency Act 1985 and sections 392, 414 and 419 of the 1986 Act, the functions specified for the purposes of section 102(3) of the Act shall be those specified in Part VI of Schedule 1 hereto.

SCHEDULE 1

PART I

1 Functions of the Secretary of State and the registrar of companies by virtue of the 1985 Act.

2 Functions of the registrar of companies by virtue of the 1986 Act.

3 Functions of inspectors appointed under Part XIV of the 1985 Act and of officers authorised under section 447 of that Act.

4 Functions of the Secretary of State in relation to anything done by the European Union or any of their institutions with respect to company law, and the maintenance of relations with authorities and other persons both within the United Kingdom and abroad in respect of matters relating to company law.

5 Any other functions of the Secretary of State and the registrar of companies in relation to companies, including, without prejudice to the generality of the foregoing:–

 (a) prosecution of offences under the 1985 Act and the taking of action with a view to ensuring compliance with any obligation arising under the 1985 Act;

 (b) investigation of complaints relating to the conduct of the affairs of companies and consideration of requests for advice on questions of company law;

 (c) review of the functioning of company law and consideration and development of proposals for legislation relating to companies;

 (d) consideration, including in international fora, of accounting standards and auditing practices in relation to accounts of companies;

 (e) the conduct of civil proceedings in relation to any of the functions specified in this part of this Schedule.

PART VI

16 Functions of official receivers as provisional liquidators, interim receivers of a debtor's property, receivers and managers of a bankrupt's estate, liquidators, trustees in bankruptcy and in their capacity as official receivers, under the Companies Act 1948, the 1985 Act, the Bankruptcy Acts 1914 and 1926, the Powers of Criminal Courts Act 1973, the Insolvency Act 1976, the Insolvency Act 1985, the 1986 Act and the Company Directors Disqualification Act 1986 and subordinate legislation made under those enactments.

17 Functions of the Secretary of State, the Board of Trade and the Insolvency Practitioners Tribunal under Part V of the Companies Act 1948, Parts IX and XX of the 1985 Act, the Deeds of Arrangement Act 1914, the Bankruptcy Acts 1914 and 1926, the Insolvency Services (Accounting and Investment) Act 1970, the Insolvency Act 1976, the Insolvency Act 1985, the 1986 Act and the Company Directors Disqualification Act 1986 and subordinate legislation made under those enactments.

18 Functions of official receivers, the Secretary of State and the Board of Trade in relation to the investigation and prosecution of fraud or other malpractice in respect of the affairs of bankrupts and bodies in liquidation.

19 Functions of the Secretary of State in relation to the supervision of the operation of all the insolvency and related procedures set out in the Insolvency Act 1986, the Bankruptcy (Scotland) Act 1985, the other enactments set out in paragraphs 16 and 17 above and the Bankruptcy (Scotland) Act 1913, including the development and implementation of proposals for the modification or improvement of those procedures by primary or subordinate legislation and the consideration of and contribution to proposals for other United Kingdom legislation having an impact on those procedures.

20 Functions of the Secretary of State in relation to anything done by the European Union or any of their institutions, or any international instruments, in relation to insolvency and the maintenance of relations with authorities and other persons both within the United Kingdom and abroad in respect of insolvency matters.

European Economic Interest Grouping Regulations 1989

(SI 1989/638)

Made on 10 April 1989 by the Secretary of State for Trade and Industry under s.2(2) of the European Communities Act 1972. Operative from 1 July 1989.

[**Note:** Changes made by the Companies Act 2006 (Consequential Amendments etc.) Order 2008 (SI 2008/948), the European Economic Interest Grouping (Amendment) Regulations 2009 (SI 2009/2399) and the European Economic Interest Grouping and European Public Limited-Liability Company (Amendment) Regulations 2014 (SI 2014/2382) have been incorporated into the text.]

PART I

GENERAL

1 Citation, commencement and extent

1 These Regulations, which extend to the whole of the United Kingdom, may be cited as the European Economic Interest Grouping Regulations 1989 and shall come into force on 1st July 1989.

2 Interpretation

2(1) In these Regulations–

"the 1985 Act" means the Companies Act 1985;

"the 2006 Act" means the Companies Act 2006;

"the Companies Acts" has the meaning given by section 2 of the 2006 Act;

"the contract" means the contract for the formation of an EEIG;

"the EC Regulation" means Council Regulation (EEC) No. 2137/85 set out in Schedule 1 to these Regulations;

"EEIG" means a European Economic Interest Grouping being a grouping formed in pursuance of article 1 of the EC Regulation;

"officer", in relation to an EEIG, includes a manager, or any other person provided for in the contract as an organ of the EEIG; and

"the registrar" has the same meaning as in the Companies Acts (see section 1060 of the 2006 Act);

and other expressions used in these Regulations and defined for the purposes of the Companies Acts or in relation to insolvency and winding up by the Insolvency Act 1986 or, as regards Northern Ireland, by the Insolvency (Northern Ireland) Order 1989 have the meanings assigned to them by those provisions as if any reference to a company in any such definition were a reference to an EEIG.

2(2) [Repealed by the European Economic Interest Grouping and European Public Limited-Liability Company (Amendment) Regulations 2014 (SI 2014/2382) reg.3 as from 1 October 2014.]

2(3) In these Regulations, "certified translation" means a translation certified to be a correct translation–

(a) if the translation was made in the United Kingdom, by

   (i) a notary public in any part of the United Kingdom;

   (ii) a solicitor (if the translation was made in Scotland), a solicitor of the Supreme Court of Judicature of England and Wales (if it was made in England or Wales), or a solicitor of the Supreme Court of Judicature of Northern Ireland (if it was made in Northern Ireland); or

  (iii) a person certified by a person mentioned above to be known to him to be competent to translate the document into English; or

 (b) if the translation was made outside the United Kingdom, by–

  (i) a notary public;

  (ii) a person authorised in the place where the translation was made to administer an oath;

  (iii) any of the British officials mentioned in section 6 of the Commissioners for Oaths Act 1889;

  (iv) a person certified by a person mentioned in sub-paragraph (i), (ii) or (iii) of this paragraph to be known to him to be competent to translate the document into English.

History

Regulation 2(1) amended by the Companies Act 2006 (Consequential Amendments etc.) Order 2008 (SI 2008/948) art.161 as from 6 April 2008. Regulation 2(1), (2) amended by the European Economic Interest Grouping (Amendment) Regulations 2009 (SI 2009/2399) reg.5 as from 1 October 2009.

PART II

PROVISIONS RELATING TO ARTICLES 1–38 OF THE EC REGULATION

[Regulations 3–5 not reproduced.]

6 Cessation of membership (Article 28(1) of the EC Regulation)

6 For the purposes of national law on liquidation, winding up, insolvency or cessation of payments, a member of an EEIG registered under these Regulations shall cease to be a member if–

 (a) in the case of an individual–

  (i) a bankruptcy order has been made against him in England and Wales or Northern Ireland; or

  (ii) sequestration of his estate has been awarded by the court in Scotland under the Bankruptcy (Scotland) Act 1985;

 (b) in the case of a partnership–

  (i) a winding up order has been made against the partnership in England and Wales or Northern Ireland;

  (ii) a bankruptcy order has been made against each of the partnership's members in England and Wales on a bankruptcy petition presented under Article 11(1) of the Insolvent Partnerships Order 1994;

  (iia) a bankruptcy order has been made against each of the partnership's members in Northern Ireland on a bankruptcy petition presented under Article 11(1) of the Insolvent Partnerships Order (Northern Ireland) 1995; or

  (iii) sequestration of the estate of the partnership has been awarded by the court in Scotland under the Bankruptcy (Scotland) Act 1985;

 (c) in the case of a company, the company goes into liquidation in the United Kingdom; or

 (d) in the case of any legal person or partnership, it is otherwise wound up or otherwise ceases to exist after the conclusion of winding up or insolvency.

History

Regulation 6(b)(ii) substituted and reg.6(b)(iia) inserted by the European Economic Interest Grouping (Amendment) Regulations 2009 (SI 2009/2399) reg.9 as from 1 October 2009.

7 Competent authority (Articles 32(1) and (3) and 38 of the EC Regulation)

7(1) The competent authority for the purposes of making an application to the court under Article 32(1) of the EC Regulation (winding up of EEIG in certain circumstances) shall be–

(a) in the case of an EEIG whose official address is in Northern Ireland, the Department of Enterprise, Trade and Investment in Northern Ireland;

(b) in any other case, the Secretary of State.

7(2) The court may, on an application by the appropriate authority, order the winding up of an EEIG which has its official address in the United Kingdom, if the EEIG acts contrary to the public interest and it is expedient in the public interest that the EEIG should be wound up and the court is of the opinion that it is just and equitable for it to be so.

7(2A) In paragraph (2) above "the appropriate authority" means–

(a) in the case of an EEIG whose official address is in Great Britain, the Secretary of State;

(b) in the case of an EEIG whose official address is in Northern Ireland, the Department of Enterprise, Trade and Investment in Northern Ireland.

7(3) The court, on an application by the appropriate authority, shall be the competent authority for the purposes of prohibiting under article 38 of the EC Regulation any activity carried on in the United Kingdom by an EEIG where such an activity is in contravention of the public interest there.

7(4) In paragraph (3) above "the appropriate authority" means–

(a) in the case of any activity carried on in Great Britain, the Secretary of State;

(b) in the case of any activity carried on in Northern Ireland, the Department of Enterprise, Trade and Investment in Northern Ireland.

History
Regulation 7(1)–(3) amended and reg.7(4) inserted by the European Economic Interest Grouping (Amendment) Regulations 2009 (SI 2009/2399) reg.10 as from 1 October 2009.

8 Winding up and conclusion of liquidation (Articles 35 and 36 of the EC Regulation)

8(1) Where an EEIG is wound up as an unregistered company under Part V of the Insolvency Act 1986, the provisions of Part V shall apply in relation to the EEIG as if any reference in that Act to a director or past director of a company included a reference to a manager of the EEIG and any other person who has or has had control or management of the EEIG's business and with the modification that in section 221(1) after the words "all the provisions" there shall be added the words "of Council Regulation (EEC) No. 2137/85 and".

8(1A) Where an EEIG is wound up as an unregistered company under Part 6 of the Insolvency (Northern Ireland) Order 1989, the provisions of Part 6 shall apply in relation to the EEIG as if–

(a) any reference in that Order to a director or past director of a company included a reference to a manager of the EEIG and any other person who has or has had control or management of the EEIG's business; and

(b) in Article 185(1) after "all the provisions" there were inserted "of Council Regulation (EEC) No 2137/85 and".

8(2) At the end of the period of three months beginning with the day of receipt by the registrar of a notice of the conclusion of the liquidation of an EEIG, the EEIG shall be dissolved.

History
Regulation 8 amended by the Companies Act 2006 (Consequential Amendments etc.) Order 2008 (SI 2008/948) art.162 as from 6 April 2008. Regulation 8(1A) inserted by the European Economic Interest Grouping (Amendment) Regulations 2009 (SI 2009/2399) reg.11 as from 1 October 2009.

PART III

REGISTRATION ETC. (ARTICLE 39 OF THE EC REGULATION)

[Regulations 9–16 not reproduced.]

PART IV

SUPPLEMENTAL PROVISIONS

17 Application of the Business Names Act 1985

17 [Omitted by the European Economic Interest Grouping (Amendment) Regulations 2009 (SI 2009/2399) reg.18 as from 1 October 2009.]

18 Application of provisions of the Companies Acts

18(1) The provisions of the Companies Acts specified in Schedule 4 to these Regulations apply to EEIGs, and their establishments, registered or in the process of being registered under these Regulations, as if they were companies formed and registered or in the process of being registered under the 2006 Act.

18(2) The provisions applied have effect with the following adaptations–

(a) any reference to the 1985 Act, the 2006 Act or the Companies Acts includes a reference to these Regulations;

(b) any reference to a registered office includes a reference to an official address;

(ba) any reference to the register is to be read as a reference to the EEIG register;

(bb) any reference to an officer of a company is to be read as a reference to an officer of an EEIG, within the meaning of these Regulations;

(c) any reference to a daily default fine shall be omitted.

18(3) The provisions applied also have effect subject to any limitations mentioned in relation to those provisions in that Schedule.

18(4) In this regulation "the EEIG register" means–

(a) the documents and particulars required to be kept by the registrar under these Regulations; and

(b) the records falling within section 1080(1) of the 2006 Act which relate to EEIGs or their establishments.

18(5) This regulation does not affect the application of provisions of the Companies Acts to EEIGs or their establishments otherwise than by virtue of this regulation.

History
Regulation 18 substituted by the Companies Act 2006 (Consequential Amendments etc.) Order 2008 (SI 2008/948) art.163 as from 6 April 2008. Regulation 18(1), (2) amended and reg.18(4), (5) inserted by the European Economic Interest Grouping (Amendment) Regulations 2009 (SI 2009/2399) reg.19 as from 1 October 2009.

19 Application of insolvency legislation

19(1) Part III of the Insolvency Act 1986 shall apply to EEIGs, and their establishments, registered under these Regulations in England and Wales or Scotland, as if they were companies registered under the 2006 Act.

19(1A) Part 4 of the Insolvency (Northern Ireland) Order 1989 shall apply to EEIGs, and their establishments, registered under these Regulations in Northern Ireland, as if they were companies registered under the 2006 Act.

19(2)   Section 120 of the Insolvency Act 1986 shall apply to an EEIGs and its establishments, registered under these Regulations in Scotland, as if it were a company registered in Scotland the paid-up or credited as paid-up share capital of which did not exceed £120,000 and as if in that section any reference to the Company's registered office were a reference to the official address of the EEIG.

History
Regulation 19(1) and the heading amended and reg.19(1A) inserted by the European Economic Interest Grouping (Amendment) Regulations 2009 (SI 2009/2399) reg.20 as from 1 October 2009.

20   Application of legislation relating to disqualification of directors

20(1)   Where an EEIG is wound up as an unregistered company under Part V of the Insolvency Act 1986, the provisions of sections 1, 2, 4 to 7, 8, 9, 10, 11, 12(2), 15 to 17, 20 and 22 of, and Schedule 1 to, the Company Directors Disqualification Act 1986 shall apply in relation to the EEIG as if any reference to a director or past director of a company included a reference to a manager of the EEIG and any other person who has or has had control or management of the EEIG's business and the EEIG were a company as defined by section 22(2)(b) of that Act.

20(2)   Where an EEIG is wound up as an unregistered company under Part 6 of the Insolvency (Northern Ireland) Order 1989 the provisions of Articles 2(2) to (6), 3, 5, 7 to 11, 13, 14, 15, 16(2), 19 to 21 and 23 of, and Schedule 1 to, the Company Directors Disqualification (Northern Ireland) Order 2002 shall apply in relation to the EEIG as if–

(a)   any reference to a director or past director of a company included a reference to a manager of the EEIG and any other person who has or has had control or management of the EEIG's business; and

(b)   the EEIG were a company as defined by Article 2(2) of that Order.

History
Regulation 20(1) and the heading amended and reg.20(2) inserted by the European Economic Interest Grouping (Amendment) Regulations 2009 (SI 2009/2399) reg.21 as from 1 October 2009.

21   Penalties

21   Nothing in these Regulations shall create any new criminal offence punishable to a greater extent than is permitted under paragraph 1(1)(d) of Schedule 2 to the European Communities Act 1972.

Schedule 1

Council Regulation (EEC) No. 2137/85 of 25th July 1985 on the European Economic Interest Grouping (EEIG)

Regulation 2(1)

THE COUNCIL OF THE EUROPEAN COMMUNITIES

Having regard to the Treaty establishing the European Economic Community, and in particular Article 235 thereof,
   Having regard to the proposal from the Commission,
   Having regard to the opinion of the European Parliament,
   Having regard to the opinion of the Economic and Social Committee,
   Whereas a harmonious development of economic activities and a continuous and balanced expansion throughout the Community depend on the establishment and smooth functioning of a common market offering conditions analogous to those of a national market; whereas to bring about this single market and

to increase its unity a legal framework which facilitates the adaptation of their activities to the economic conditions of the Community should be created for natural persons, companies, firms and other legal bodies in particular; whereas to that end it is necessary that those natural persons, companies, firms and other legal bodies should be able to co-operate effectively across frontiers;

Whereas co-operation of this nature can encounter legal, fiscal or psychological difficulties; whereas the creation of an appropriate Community legal instrument in the form of a European Economic Interest Grouping would contribute to the achievement of the abovementioned objectives and therefore proves necessary;

Whereas the Treaty does not provide the necessary powers for the creation of such a legal instrument;

Whereas a grouping's ability to adapt to economic conditions must be guaranteed by the considerable freedom for its members in their contractual relations and the internal organisation of the grouping;

Whereas a grouping differs from a firm or company principally in its purpose, which is only to facilitate or develop the economic activities of its members to enable them to improve their own results, whereas, by reason of that ancillary nature, a grouping's activities must be related to the economic activities of its members but not replace them so that, to that extent, for example, a grouping may not itself, with regard to third parties, practise a profession, the concept of economic activities being interpreted in the widest sense;

Whereas access to grouping form must be made as widely available as possible to natural persons, companies, firms and other legal bodies, in keeping with the aims of this Regulation; whereas this Regulation shall not, however, prejudice the application at national level of legal rules and/or ethical codes concerning the conditions for the pursuit of business and professional activities;

Whereas this Regulation does not itself confer on any person the right to participate in a grouping, even where the conditions it lays down are fulfilled;

Whereas the power provided by this Regulation to prohibit or restrict participation in a grouping on grounds of public interest is without prejudice to the laws of Member States which govern the pursuit of activities and which may provide further prohibitions or restrictions or otherwise control or supervise participation in a grouping by any natural person, company, firm or other legal body or any class of them;

Whereas, to enable a grouping to achieve its purpose, it should be endowed with legal capacity and provision should be made for it to be represented *vis-à-vis* third parties by an organ legally separate from its membership;

Whereas the protection of third parties requires widespread publicity; whereas the members of a grouping have unlimited joint and several liability for the grouping's debts and other liabilities including those relating to tax or social security, without, however, that principle's affecting the freedom to exclude or restrict the liability of one or more of its members in respect of a particular debt or other liability by means of a specific contract between the grouping and a third party;

Whereas matters relating to the status or capacity of natural persons and to the capacity of legal persons are governed by national law;

Whereas the grounds for winding up which are peculiar to the grouping should be specific while referring to national law for its liquidation and the conclusion thereof;

Whereas groupings are subject to national laws relating to insolvency and cessation of payments; whereas such laws may provide other grounds for the winding up of groupings;

Whereas this Regulation provides that the profits or losses resulting from the activities of a grouping shall be taxable only in the hands of its members; whereas it is understood that otherwise national tax laws apply, particularly as regards the apportionment of profits, tax procedures and any obligations imposed by national tax law;

Whereas in matters not covered by this Regulation the laws of the Member States and EU law are applicable, for example with regard to:

(a)   social and labour laws,

(b)   competition law,

(c)   intellectual property law;

Whereas the activities of groupings are subject to the provisions of Member States' laws on the pursuit and supervision of activities; whereas in the event of abuse or circumvention of the laws of a Member State by a grouping or its members that Member State may impose appropriate sanctions;

Whereas the Member States are free to apply or to adopt any laws, regulations or administrative measures which do not conflict with the scope or objectives of this Regulation;

Whereas this Regulation must enter into force immediately in its entirety; whereas the implementation of some provisions must nevertheless be deferred in order to allow the Member States first to set up the necessary machinery for the registration of groupings in their territories and the disclosure of certain matters relating to groupings; whereas, with effect from the date of implementation of this Regulation, groupings set up may operate without territorial restrictions,

HAS ADOPTED THIS REGULATION:

[Articles 1–14 not reproduced.]

Article 15

15(1)   Where the law applicable to a grouping by virtue of Article 2 provides for the nullity of that grouping, such nullity must be established or declared by judicial decision. However, the court to which the matter is referred must, where it is possible for the affairs of the grouping to be put in order, allow time to permit that to be done.

15(2)   The nullity of a grouping shall entail its liquidation in accordance with the conditions laid down in Article 35.

15(3)   A decision establishing or declaring the nullity of a grouping may be relied on as against third parties in accordance with the conditions laid down in Article 9(1).

Such a decision shall not of itself affect the validity of liabilities, owed by or to a grouping, which originated before it could be relied on as against third parties in accordance with the conditions laid down in the previous subparagraph.

[Articles 16–23 not reproduced.]

Article 24

24(1)   The members of a grouping shall have unlimited joint and several liability for its debts and other liabilities of whatever nature. National law shall determine the consequences of such liability.

24(2)   Creditors may not proceed against a member for payment in respect of debts and other liabilities, in accordance with the conditions laid down in paragraph 1, before the liquidation of a grouping is concluded, unless they have first requested the grouping to pay and payment has not been made within an appropriate period.

[Articles 25–27 not reproduced.]

Article 28

28(1)   A member of a grouping shall cease to belong to it on death or when he no longer complies with the conditions laid down in Article 4(1).

In addition, a Member State may provide, for the purposes of its liquidation, winding up, insolvency or cessation of payments laws, that a member shall cease to be a member of any grouping at the moment determined by those laws.

28(2)   In the event of the death of a natural person who is a member of a grouping, no person may become a member in his place except under the conditions laid down in the contract for the formation of the grouping or, failing that, with the unanimous agreement of the remaining members.

[Article 29 not reproduced.]

Article 30

30   Except where the contract for the formation of a grouping provides otherwise and without prejudice to the rights acquired by a person under Articles 22(1) or 28(2), a grouping shall continue to exist for the remaining members after a member has ceased to belong to it, in accordance with the conditions laid down in the contract for the formation of the grouping or determined by unanimous decision of the members in question.

Article 31

31(1)   grouping may be wound up by a decision of its members ordering its winding up. Such a decision shall be taken unanimously, unless otherwise laid down in the contract for the formation of the grouping.

31(2)   A grouping must be wound up by a decision of its members:

(a)   noting the expiry of the period fixed in the contract for the formation of the grouping or the existence of any other cause for winding up provided for in the contract, or

(b)   noting the accomplishment of the grouping's purpose or the impossibility of pursuing it further.

Where, three months after one of the situations referred to in the first subparagraph has occurred, a members' decision establishing the winding up of the grouping has not been taken, any member may petition the court to order winding up.

31(3)   A grouping must also be wound up by a decision of its members or of the remaining member when the conditions laid down in Article 4(2) are no longer fulfilled.

31(4)   After a grouping has been wound up by decision of its members, the manager or managers must take the steps required as listed in Articles 7 and 8. In addition, any person concerned may take those steps.

Article 32

32(1)   On application by any person concerned or by a competent authority, in the event of the infringement of Articles 3, 12 or 31(3), the court must order a grouping to be wound up, unless its affairs can be and are put in order before the court has delivered a substantive ruling.

32(2)   On application by a member, the court may order a grouping to be wound up on just and proper grounds.

32(3)   A Member State may provide that the court may, on application by a competent authority, order the winding up of a grouping which has its official address in the State to which that authority belongs, wherever the grouping acts in contravention of that State's public interest, if the law of that State provides for such a possibility in respect of registered companies or other legal bodies subject to it.

Article 33

33   When a member ceases to belong to a grouping for any reason other than the assignment of his rights in accordance with the conditions laid down in Article 22(1), the value of his rights and obligations shall be determined taking into account the assets and liabilities of the grouping as they stand when he ceases to belong to it.

The value of the rights and obligations of a departing member may not be fixed in advance.

Article 34

34 Without prejudice to Article 37(1), any member who ceases to belong to a grouping shall remain answerable, in accordance with the conditions laid down in Article 24, for the debts and other liabilities arising out of the grouping's activities before he ceased to be a member.

Article 35

35(1) The winding up of a grouping shall entail its liquidation.

35(2) The liquidation of a grouping and the conclusion of its liquidation shall be governed by national law.

35(3) A grouping shall retain its capacity, within the meaning of Article 1(2), until its liquidation is concluded.

35(4) The liquidator or liquidators shall take the steps required as listed in Articles 7 and 8.

Article 36

36 Groupings shall be subject to national laws governing insolvency and cessation of payments. The commencement of proceedings against a grouping on grounds of its insolvency or cessation of payments shall not by itself cause the commencement of such proceedings against its members.

Article 37

37(1) A period of limitation of five years after the publication, pursuant to Article 8, of notice of a member's ceasing to belong to a grouping shall be substituted for any longer period which may be laid down by the relevant national law for actions against that member in connection with debts and other liabilities arising out of the grouping's activities before he ceased to be a member.

37(2) A period of limitation of five years after the publication, pursuant to Article 8, of notice of the conclusion of the liquidation of a grouping shall be substituted for any longer period which may be laid down by the relevant national law for actions against a member of the grouping in connection with debts and other liabilities arising out of the grouping's activities.

[Articles 38 and 39 not reproduced.]

Article 40

40 The profits or losses resulting from the activities of a grouping shall be taxable only in the hands of its members.

[Articles 41 and 42 not reproduced.]

Article 43

43 This Regulation shall enter into force on the third day following its publication in the *Official Journal of the European Communities*.

It shall apply from 1 July 1989, with the exception of Articles 39, 41 and 42 which shall apply as from the entry into force of the Regulation.

This Regulation shall be binding in its entirety and directly applicable in all Member States.

SCHEDULE 2

FORMS RELATING TO EEIGS

[Revoked by SI 2014/2382 regs 2, 10 as from 1 October 2014.]

SCHEDULE 3

AUTHORISED EQUIVALENTS IN OTHER COMMUNITY OFFICIAL LANGUAGES OF "EUROPEAN ECONOMIC INTEREST GROUPING" AND "EEIG"

[Not reproduced.]

SCHEDULE 4

PROVISIONS OF COMPANIES ACTS APPLYING TO EEIGS AND THEIR ESTABLISHMENTS

Regulation 18

PART I

PROVISIONS OF COMPANIES ACT 1985

13　Part XVIII relating to floating charges and receivers (Scotland).

PART 2

PROVISIONS OF COMPANIES ACT 2006

…

26　Part 25 (company charges).

27　Section 993 (offence of fraudulent trading).

…

31　Section 1084 (records relating to companies that have been dissolved etc), as if subsection (4) were omitted.

…

37　Section 1112 (general false statement offence).

History
Schedule 4 amended by the Companies Act 2006 (Consequential Amendments etc.) Order 2008 (SI 2008/948) art.164 as from 6 April 2008. Schedule 4 amended by the European Economic Interest Grouping (Amendment) Regulations 2009 (SI 2009/2399) reg.23 as from 1 October 2009.

Insolvency Act 1986 (Guernsey) Order 1989

(SI 1989/2409)

Made on 19 December 1989 under s.442 of the Insolvency Act 1986. Operative from 1 February 1990.

1   This Order may be cited as the Insolvency Act 1986 (Guernsey) Order 1989 and shall come into force on 1st February 1990.

2   Subsections (4), (5), (10) and (11) of section 426 of the Insolvency Act 1986 shall extend to the Bailiwick of Guernsey with the modifications specified in the Schedule to this Order.

SCHEDULE

MODIFICATIONS IN THE EXTENSION OF PROVISIONS OF THE INSOLVENCY ACT 1986 TO THE BAILIWICK OF GUERNSEY

Article 2

1   Any reference to any provision of section 426 of the Insolvency Act 1986 shall be construed as a reference to that provision as it has effect in the Bailiwick of Guernsey.

2   In subsections (4) and (5), for "United Kingdom" there shall be substituted "Bailiwick of Guernsey."

3 · For paragraphs (a), (b) and (c) of subsection (10) there shall be substituted the following paragraphs:

"(a)   in relation to Guernsey:

   (i)   Titres II to V of the Law entitled "Loi ayant rapport aux Débiteurs et à la Renonciation" of 1929;

   (ii)   the Ordinance entitled "Ordonnance relative à la Renonciation" of 1929;

   (iii)   articles LXXI to LXXXI of the Law entitled "Loi relative aux Sociétés Anonymes ou à Responsabilité Limitée" of 1908;

   (iv)   sections 1, 3(3) and 4(2) of the Law of Property (Miscellaneous Provisions) (Guernsey) Law 1979;

   (v)   the Preferred Debts (Guernsey) Law 1983;

   (vi)   sections 12 and 32 to 39 of the Insurance Business (Guernsey) Law 1986;

   (vii)   the rules of the customary law of Guernsey concerning persons who are unable to pay their judgment debts;

   (viii) any enactment for the time being in force in Guernsey which amends, modifies, supplements or replaces any of those rules or provisions;

(b)   in relation to Alderney:

   (i)   Part I of the Companies (Amendment) (Alderney) Law 1962;

   (ii)   the Preferred Debts (Guernsey) Law 1983;

   (iii)   sections 12, 32 to 39, 68(2) and 68(5) of the Insurance Business (Guernsey) Law 1986;

   (iv)   the rules of the customary law of Alderney concerning persons who are unable to pay their judgment debts;

   (v)   any enactment for the time being in force in Alderney which amends, modifies, supplements or replaces any of those rules or provisions;

(c)   in relation to Sark:

   (i)   the rules of the customary law of Sark concerning persons who are unable to pay their judgment debts;

(ii)   any enactment for the time being in force in Sark which amends, modifies, supplements or replaces any of those rules;".

4   For paragraphs (a) and (b) of subsection (11) there shall be substituted "the United Kingdom, the Bailiwick of Jersey or the Isle of Man".

Act of Sederunt (Applications Under Part VII of the Companies Act 1989) 1991

(SI 1991/145 (S.10))

Made on 30 January 1991 by the Lords of Council and Session under ss.32 and 34 of the Sheriff Courts (Scotland) Act 1971. Operative from 25 February 1991.

1 Citation and commencement

1(1) This Act of Sederunt may be cited as the Act of Sederunt (Applications under Part VII of the Companies Act 1989) 1991 and shall come into force on 25th February 1991.

1(2) This Act of Sederunt shall be inserted in the Books of Sederunt.

1(3) In this Act of Sederunt, "insolvency proceedings" means proceedings commenced by a petition in accordance with rules 10 (administration orders), 15 (appointment of receiver) or 18 (winding up of a company) of the Act of Sederunt (Sheriff Court Company Insolvency Rules) 1986, a petition for sequestration under section 2, 5 or 6 of the Bankruptcy (Scotland) Act 2016 or a summary petition under section 11A of the Judicial Factors (Scotland) Act 1889.

2 Applications under Part VII of the Companies Act 1989

2(1) An application for an order or direction under the provisions of the Companies Act 1989 ("the Act") specified in sub-paragraph (2) below shall be made:

  (a) where there are before the sheriff insolvency proceedings to which the application relates, by note in the process of those proceedings; or

  (b) where there are no such proceedings before the sheriff, by summary application.

2(2) The provisions of the Act referred to in sub-paragraph (1) above are–

  (a) section 161(1) (interim order in relation to party to market contract dissipating or applying assets to prevent recovery by relevant office-holder);

  (b) section 161(3) (order altering or dispensing from compliance with duties of relevant office-holder);

  (c) section 163(4) (direction that profit arising from a sum is not recoverable by relevant office-holder);

  (d) section 164(4) (direction that profit from a market contract or the amount or value of a margin is not recoverable by relevant office-holder);

  (e) section 175(2) (order to ensure that charge under a prior or *pari passu* ranked charge is not prejudiced by enforcement of market charge);

  (f) section 175(5) (direction that profit from a property disposition is not recoverable by relevant office-holder); and

  (g) section 182(4) (order to achieve same result as if provisions of Schedule 22 to the Act had been in force).

3 Intimation

3 Without prejudice to any other order in respect of intimation which the sheriff may make, he shall not make an order under section 175(2) of the Act unless intimation has been made to such persons having an interest as he considers necessary and any such person has had an opportunity to be heard.

Financial Markets and Insolvency Regulations 1991

(SI 1991/880)

Made on 27 March 1991 by the Secretary of State under ss.155(4), (5); 158(4), (5); 160(5); 173(4), (5); 174(2)–(4); 185; 186 and 187(3) of the Companies Act 1989. Operative from 25 April 1991.

[**Note:** Changes made by the Financial Markets and Insolvency (Amendment) Regulations 1992 (SI 1992/716), the Financial Services and Markets Act 2000 (Consequential Amendments and Repeals) Order 2001 (SI 2001/3649), the Enterprise Act 2002 (Insolvency) Order 2003 (SI 2003/2096), the Financial Markets and Insolvency Regulations 2009 (SI 2009/853), the Financial Services Act 2012 (Consequential Amendments and Transitional Provisions) Order 2013 (SI 2013/472), the Financial Services and Markets Act 2000 (Over the Counter Derivatives, Central Counterparties and Trade Repositories) Regulations 2013 (SI 2013/504) and the Central Securities Depositories Regulations 2017 (SI 2017/1064) have been incorporated into the text (in the case of pre-2003 legislation without annotation). References to administration petitions, orders, etc. have been adapted throughout, following the introduction of the new administration regime, pursuant to the Enterprise Act 2002 (Insolvency) Order 2003 (SI 2003/2096), as from 15 September 2003.]

ARRANGEMENT OF REGULATIONS

PART I

GENERAL

1   Citation and commencement

1   These Regulations may be cited as the Financial Markets and Insolvency Regulations 1991 and shall come into force on 25th April 1991.

2   Interpretation: general

2(1)   In these Regulations "the Act" means the Companies Act 1989.

2(1A)   In these Regulations "the Recognition Requirements Regulations" means the Financial Services and Markets Act 2000 (Recognition Requirements for Investment Exchanges, Clearing Houses and Central Securities Depositories) Regulations 2001.

2(2)   A reference in any of these Regulations to a numbered regulation shall be construed as a reference to the regulation bearing that number in these Regulations.

2(3)   A reference in any of these Regulations to a numbered paragraph shall, unless the reference is to a paragraph of a specified regulation, be construed as a reference to the paragraph bearing that number in the regulation in which the reference is made.

History
Regulation 2(1A) inserted by the Financial Markets and Insolvency Regulations 2009 (SI 2009/853) reg.3(1), (2) as from 15 June 2009.
   Regulation 2(1A) amended by the Central Securities Depositories Regulations 2017 (SI 2017/1064) regs 1, 10 and Sch. para.20(1), (2) as from 28 November 2017.

PART II

FURTHER PROVISION AS TO MARKET CONTRACTS

3   Further provision as to market contracts

3   [Substitution of s.155(2) of the Act not reproduced here.]

PART III

INSOLVENCY PROCEEDINGS

4   Voting at meetings of creditors

4   [Insertion of s.159(4A) and amendment of s.159(5) of the Act not reproduced here.]

5   Ranking of expenses of relevant office-holder

5   [Amendment of s.160(4) of the Act not reproduced here.]

PART IV

REPORTS BY RECOGNISED OVERSEAS INVESTMENT EXCHANGE OR CLEARING HOUSE

6   Duty of recognised overseas investment exchange or clearing house to report on completion of default proceedings

6   [Amendment of s.162(1) and insertion of s.162(1A) of the Act not reproduced here.]

PART V

MARKET CHARGES

7   Interpretation of Part V

7   In this Part of these Regulations, unless the context otherwise requires–

"the Bank" means the Bank of England;

"business day" has the same meaning as in section 167(3) of the Act;

"CGO Service" means the computer-based system established by the Bank and The Stock Exchange to facilitate the transfer of specified securities;

"CGO Service charge" means a charge of the kind described in section 173(1)(c) of the Act;

"CGO Service member" means a person who is entitled by contract with CRESTCo Limited (which is now responsible for operating the CGO Service) to use the CGO Service;

"clearing member" has the same meaning as in section 190(1) of the Act;

"client" has the same meaning as in section 190(1) of the Act;

"default fund contribution" has the same meaning as in section 188(3A) of the Act;

"EEA CSD" has the same meaning as in section 190(1) of the Act;

"former CGO Service member" means a person whose entitlement to use the CGO Service has been terminated or suspended;

"indirect client" has the same meaning as in section 190(1) of the Act;

"market charge" means a charge which is a market charge for the purposes of Part VII of the Act;

"recognised body" has the same meaning as in section 190(1) of the Act;

"recognised central counterparty" has the same meaning as in section 190(1) of the Act;

"recognised CSD" has the same meaning as in section 190(1) of the Act;

"settlement bank" means a person who has agreed under a contract with CRESTCo Limited (which is now responsible for operating the CGO Service) to make payments of the kind mentioned in section 173(1)(c) of the Act;

"specified securities" has the meaning given in section 173(3) of the Act;

"Talisman" means The Stock Exchange settlement system known as Talisman;

"Talisman charge" means a charge granted in favour of The Stock Exchange over property credited to an account within Talisman maintained in the name of the chargor in respect of certain property beneficially owned by the chargor;

"third country CSD" has the same meaning as in section 190(1) of the Act; and

"transfer" when used in relation to specified securities has the meaning given in section 173(3) of the Act.

History

The entry for "default fund contribution" inserted by the Financial Markets and Insolvency Regulations 2009 (SI 2009/853) reg.3(1), (3) as from 15 June 2009. Definitions of "clearing member", "client", "indirect client" and "recognised central counterparty" inserted by the Financial Services and Markets Act (Over the Counter Derivatives, Central Counterparties and Trade Repositories) Regulations 2013 (SI 2013/504) reg.30(1), (2) as from 1 April 2013.

The entries for "EEA CSD", "recognised body", "recognised CSD" and "third country CSD" inserted by the Central Securities Depositories Regulations 2017 (SI 2017/1064) regs 1, 10 and Sch. para.20(1), (3) as from 28 November 2017.

8 Charges on land or any interest in land not to be treated as market charges

8(1)   No charge, whether fixed or floating, shall be treated as a market charge to the extent that it is a charge on land or any interest in land.

8(2)   For the purposes of paragraph (1), a charge on a debenture forming part of an issue or series shall not be treated as a charge on land or any interest in land by reason of the fact that the debenture is secured by a charge on land or any interest in land.

9 Amendments to section 173 of Act concerning certain charges granted in favour of The Stock Exchange and certain charges securing debts and liabilities arising in connection with allotment of specified securities

9   [Amendments of s.173(1)–(3) of the Act not reproduced here.]

10 Extent to which charge granted in favour of recognised investment exchange to be treated as market charge

10(1)   A charge granted in favour of a recognised investment exchange other than The Stock Exchange shall be treated as a market charge only to the extent that–

(a)   it is a charge over property provided as margin in respect of market contracts entered into by the exchange for the purposes of or in connection with the provision of clearing services or over property provided as a default fund contribution to the exchange;

(b)   in the case of a recognised UK investment exchange, it secures the obligation to pay to the exchange any sum due to the exchange from a member or designated non-member of the exchange or from a recognised clearing house or from a recognised CSD or from another recognised investment exchange in respect of unsettled market contracts to which the member, designated non-member or recognised body is a party under the rules referred to in paragraph 12 of the Schedule to the Recognition Requirements Regulations in paragraph 9(2)(a) of Schedule 21 of the Act as it applies by virtue of paragraph 1(4) of that Schedule; and

(c)   in the case of a recognised overseas investment exchange, it secures the obligation to reimburse the cost (other than fees and other incidental expenses) incurred by the exchange in settling unsettled market contracts in respect of which the charged property is provided as margin.

10(2)   A charge granted in favour of The Stock Exchange shall be treated as a market charge only to the extent that–

(a)   it is a charge of the kind described in paragraph (1); or

(b)   it is a Talisman charge and secures an obligation of either or both of the kinds mentioned in paragraph (3).

10(3)   The obligations mentioned in this paragraph are–

(a)   the obligation of the chargor to reimburse The Stock Exchange for payments (including stamp duty and taxes but excluding Stock Exchange fees and incidental expenses arising from the operation by The Stock Exchange of settlement arrangements) made by The Stock Exchange in settling, through Talisman, market contracts entered into by the chargor; and

(b)   the obligation of the chargor to reimburse The Stock Exchange the amount of any payment it has made pursuant to a short term certificate.

10(4)   In paragraph (3), "short term certificate" means an instrument issued by The Stock Exchange undertaking to procure the transfer of property of a value and description specified in the instrument to or to the order of the person to whom the instrument is issued or his endorsee or to a person acting on behalf of either of them and also undertaking to make appropriate payments in cash, in the event that the obligation to procure the transfer of property cannot be discharged in whole or in part.

History

Regulation 10(1)(a), (b) amended by the Financial Markets and Insolvency Regulations 2009 (SI 2009/853) reg.3(1), (4) as from 15 June 2009.

Regulation 10(1)(b) amended by the Central Securities Depositories Regulations 2017 (SI 2017/1064) regs 1, 10 and Sch. para.20(1), (4) as from 28 November 2017.

11   Extent to which charge granted in favour of recognised clearing house to be treated as market charge

11   A charge granted in favour of a recognised clearing house shall be treated as a market charge only to the extent that–

(a)   it is a charge over property provided as margin in respect of market contracts entered into by the clearing house or over property provided as a default fund contribution to the clearing house;

(aa)   in the case of a recognised central counterparty, it secures the obligation to pay to the recognised central counterparty any sum due to it from a clearing member, a client, an indirect client, a recognised investment exchange, a recognised CSD or recognised clearing house in respect of unsettled market contracts to which the clearing member, client, indirect client or recognised body is a party;

(b)   in the case of a recognised clearing house which is not a recognised central counterparty, it secures the obligation to pay to the clearing house any sum due to the clearing house from a member of the clearing house or from a recognised investment exchange or from a recognised CSD or from another recognised clearing house in respect of unsettled market contracts to which the member or recognised body is a party under the rules referred to in paragraph 25 of the Schedule to the Recognition Requirements Regulations; and

(c)   in the case of a recognised overseas clearing house, it secures the obligation to reimburse the cost (other than fees or other incidental expenses) incurred by the clearing house in settling unsettled market contracts in respect of which the charged property is provided as margin.

History

Regulation 11 amended by the Financial Markets and Insolvency Regulations 2009 (SI 2009/853) reg.3(1), (5) as from 15 June 2009. Regulation 11(aa) inserted and reg.11(b) amended by the Financial Services and Markets Act (Over the Counter Derivatives, Central Counterparties and Trade Repositories) Regulations 2013 (SI 2013/504) reg.30(1), (3) as from 1 April 2013.

Regulation 11(aa), (b) amended by the Central Securities Depositories Regulations 2017 (SI 2017/1064) regs 1, 10 and Sch. para.20(1), (5) as from 28 November 2017.

11A   Extent to which charge granted in favour of recognised CSD to be treated as market charge

11A(1)   A charge granted in favour of a recognised CSD shall be treated as a market charge only to the extent that–

(a)   it is a charge over property provided as margin in respect of market contracts entered into by the recognised CSD or over property provided as a default fund contribution to the recognised CSD; and

(b)   it secures the obligation to pay to the recognised CSD any sum due to it from a member of the recognised CSD or from a recognised clearing house or from a recognised investment exchange or from another recognised CSD in respect of unsettled market contracts to which the member or recognised body is a party.

11A(2) A charge granted in favour of an EEA CSD or third country CSD shall be treated as a market charge only to the extent that–

(a) it is a charge over property provided as margin in respect of market contracts entered into by the EEA CSD or third country CSD or over property provided as a default fund contribution to the EEA CSD or third country CSD; and

(b) it secures the obligation to reimburse the cost (other than fees or other incidental expenses) incurred by the EEA CSD or third country CSD in settling unsettled market contracts in respect of which the charged property is provided as margin.

History
Regulation 11A inserted by the Central Securities Depositories Regulations 2017 (SI 2017/1064) regs 1, 10 and Sch. para.20(1), (6) as from 28 November 2017.

12 Circumstances in which CGO Service charge to be treated as market charge

12 A CGO Service charge shall be treated as a market charge only if–

(a) it is granted to a settlement bank by a person for the purpose of securing debts or liabilities of the kind mentioned in section 173(1)(c) of the Act incurred by that person through his use of the CGO Service as a CGO Service member; and

(b) it contains provisions which refer expressly to the CGO Service.

13 Extent to which CGO Service charge to be treated as market charge

13 A CGO Service charge shall be treated as a market charge only to the extent that–

(a) it is a charge over any one or more of the following–

(i) specified securities held within the CGO Service to the account of a CGO Service member or a former CGO Service member;

(ii) specified securities which were held as mentioned in sub-paragraph (i) above immediately prior to their being removed from the CGO Service consequent upon the person in question becoming a former CGO Service member;

(iii) sums receivable by a CGO Service member or former CGO Service member representing interest accrued on specified securities held within the CGO Service to his account or which were so held immediately prior to their being removed from the CGO Service consequent upon his becoming a former CGO Service member;

(iv) sums receivable by a CGO Service member or former CGO Service member in respect of the redemption or conversion of specified securities which were held within the CGO Service to his account at the time that the relevant securities were redeemed or converted or which were so held immediately prior to their being removed from the CGO Service consequent upon his becoming a former CGO Service member; and

(v) sums receivable by a CGO Service member or former CGO Service member in respect of the transfer by him of specified securities through the medium of the CGO Service; and

(b) it secures the obligation of a CGO Service member or former CGO Service member to reimburse a settlement bank for the amount due from him to the settlement bank as a result of the settlement bank having discharged or become obliged to discharge payment obligations in respect of transfers or allotments of specified securities made to him through the medium of the CGO Service.

14 Limitation on disapplication of moratorium on certain legal processes under Schedule B1 to the Insolvency Act 1986 (administration) in relation to CGO Service charges

History

Heading to reg.14 substituted by the Enterprise Act 2002 (Insolvency) Order 2003 (SI 2003/2096) art.5, Sch. Pt 2 paras 47, 48(a) as from 15 September 2003 subject to transitional provision in art.6.

14(1) In this regulation "qualifying period" means the period beginning with the fifth business day before the day on which an application for the making of an administration order in relation to the relevant CGO Service member or former CGO Service member is presented and ending with the second business day after the day on which an administration order is made in relation to the relevant CGO Service member or former CGO service member pursuant to the petition.

14(1A) A reference in paragraph (1) to an application for an administration order shall be treated as including a reference to–

(a) appointing an administrator under paragraph 14 or 22 of Schedule B1 to the Insolvency Act 1986, or

(b) filing with the court a notice of intention to appoint an administrator under either of those paragraphs,

and a reference to "an administration order" shall include the appointment of an administrator under paragraph 14 or 22 of Schedule B1 to the Insolvency Act 1986.

14(2) The disapplication of paragraph 43(2) of Schedule B1 to the Insolvency Act 1986 (including that provisions as applied by paragraph 44 of that Schedule) by section 175(1)(a) of the Act shall be limited in respect of a CGO Service charge so that it has effect only to the extent necessary to enable there to be realised, whether through the sale of specified securities or otherwise, a sum equal to whichever is less of the following–

(a) the total amount of payment obligations discharged by the settlement bank in respect of transfers and allotments of specified securities made during the qualifying period to the relevant CGO Service member or former CGO Service member through the medium of the CGO Service less the total amount of payment obligations discharged to the settlement bank in respect of transfers of specified securities made during the qualifying period by the relevant CGO Service member or former CGO Service member through the medium of the CGO Service; and

(b) the amount (if any) described in regulation 13(b) due to the settlement bank from the relevant CGO Service member or former CGO Service member.

History

Regulation 14(2) amended by the Enterprise Act 2002 (Insolvency) Order 2003 (SI 2003/2096) art.5, Sch. Pt 2 paras 47, 48(d) as from 15 September 2003 subject to transitional provision in art.6.

15 Ability of administrator or receiver to recover assets in case of property subject to CGO Service charge or Talisman charge

15(1) The disapplication–

(a) by section 175(1)(b) of the Act, of paragraphs 70, 71 and 72 of Schedule B1 to the Insolvency Act 1986, and

(b) by section 175(3) of the Act, of sections 43 and 61 of the 1986 Act,

shall cease to have effect in respect of a charge which is either a CGO Service charge or a Talisman charge after the end of the second business day after the day on which an administration order is made or, as the case may be, an administrative receiver or a receiver is appointed, in relation to the grantor of the charge, in relation to property subject to it which–

(a) in the case of a CGO Service charge, is not, on the basis of a valuation in accordance with paragraph (2), required for the realisation of whichever is the less of the sum referred to in regulation 14(2)(a) and the amount referred to in regulation 14(2)(b) due to the settlement bank at the close of business on the second business day referred to above; and

(b) in the case of a Talisman charge is not, on the basis of a valuation in accordance with paragraph (2), required to enable The Stock Exchange to reimburse itself for any payment it has made of the kind referred to in regulation 10(3).

History
Regulation 15(1) amended by the Enterprise Act 2002 (Insolvency) Order 2003 (SI 2003/2096) art.5, Sch. Pt 2 paras 47, 49(a) as from 15 September 2003 subject to transitional provision in art.6.

15(1A)   A reference in paragraph (1) to "an administration order" shall include the appointment of an administrator under paragraph 14 or 22 of Schedule B1 to the Insolvency Act 1986.

15(2)   For the purposes of paragraph (1) the value of property shall, except in a case falling within paragraph (3), be such as may be agreed between whichever is relevant of the administrator, administrative receiver or receiver on the one hand and the settlement bank or The Stock Exchange on the other.

15(3)   For the purposes of paragraph (1), the value of any investment for which a price for the second business day referred to above is quoted in the Daily Official List of The Stock Exchange shall–

(a) in a case in which two prices are so quoted, be an amount equal to the average of those two prices, adjusted where appropriate to take account of any accrued interest; and

(b) in a case in which one price is so quoted, be an amount equal to that price, adjusted where appropriate to take account of any accrued interest.

Part VI

Construction of References to Parties to Market Contracts

16   Circumstances in which member or designated non-member dealing as principal to be treated as acting in different capacities

16(1)   In this regulation "relevant transaction" means–

(a) a market contract, effected as principal by a member or designated non-member of a recognised investment exchange or a member of a recognised clearing house or a member of a recognised CSD, in relation to which money received by the member or designated non-member is–

(i) clients' money for the purposes of rules relating to clients' money, or

(ii) would be clients' money for the purposes of those rules were it not money which, in accordance with those rules, may be regarded as immediately due and payable to the member or designated non-member for its own account; and

(b) a market contract which would be regarded as a relevant transaction by virtue of sub-paragraph (a) above were it not for the fact that no money is received by the member or designated non-member in relation to the contract.

16(1A)   In addition "relevant transaction" means a market contract entered into by a recognised clearing house effected as principal in relation to which money is received by the recognised clearing house from a recognised investment exchange or from a recognised CSD or from another recognised clearing house.

16(1B)   In addition "relevant transaction" means a market contract entered into by a recognised investment exchange effected as principal in relation to which money is received by the recognised investment exchange from a recognised clearing house or from a recognised CSD or from another recognised investment exchange.

16(1BA)   In addition "relevant transaction" means a market contract entered into by a recognised CSD effected as principal in relation to which money is received by the recognised CSD from a recognised clearing house or from a recognised investment exchange or from another recognised CSD.

16(1C)   Where paragraph (1A), (1B) or (1BA) applies, paragraph (1) applies to the recognised clearing house, recognised investment exchange or recognised CSD as it does to a member of the recognised clearing house, recognised investment exchange or recognised CSD, and as if the recognised clearing house, recognised investment exchange or recognised CSD were subject to the rules referred to in paragraph (1)(a)(i).

16(1D)   In paragraph (1), "rules relating to clients' money" are rules made by the Financial Conduct Authority under sections 137A and 137B of the Financial Services and Markets Act 2000.

16(2)   For the purposes of section 187(1) of the Act (construction of references to parties to market contracts)–

(a)   a recognised investment exchange or a member or designated non-member of a recognised investment exchange,

(b)   a recognised clearing house or a member of a recognised clearing house, or

(c)   a recognised CSD or a member of a recognised CSD.

shall be treated as effecting relevant transactions in a different capacity from other market contracts it has effected as principal.

History
Regulation 16(1)(a) substituted, and reg.16(1A)–(1D) inserted, by the Financial Markets and Insolvency Regulations 2009 (SI 2009/853) reg.3(1), (6)(a)–(b) as from 15 June 2009. Regulation 16(1D) amended by the Financial Services Act 2012 (Consequential Amendments and Transitional Provisions) Order 2013 (SI 2013/472) art.3 and Sch.2 para.9 as from 1 April 2013.
   Regulation 16(2) substituted, and former reg.16(3), (4) omitted, by the Financial Markets and Insolvency Regulations 2009 (SI 2009/853) reg.3(1), (6)(c)–(d) as from 15 June 2009.
   Regulation 16(1)(a), (1A), (1B), (2) amended, (1BA) inserted and (1C) substituted by the Central Securities Depositories Regulations 2017 (SI 2017/1064) regs 1, 10 and Sch. para.20(1), (7) as from 28 November 2017.

PART VII

ADDITIONAL REQUIREMENTS FOR RECOGNITION

17   Restriction of paragraph 2 of Schedule 21 to Act

17   [Addition of Sch.21 para.2(4) to the Act not reproduced here.]

PART VIII

LEGAL PROCEEDINGS

18   Applications for order under section 175(2) of Act

18   [Amendment of s.175(2) of the Act not reproduced here.]

19   Court having jurisdiction in respect of proceedings under Part VII of Act

19(1)   For the purposes of sections 161, 163, 164, 175(5) and 182 of the Act (various legal proceedings under Part VII of Act) "the court" shall be the court which has last heard an application in the proceedings under the Insolvency Act 1986 or the Bankruptcy (Scotland) Act 1985 in which the relevant office-holder is acting or, as the case may be, any court having jurisdiction to hear applications in those proceedings.

19(2)   For the purposes of subsection (2) and (2A) of section 175 of the Act (administration orders etc.), "the court" shall be the court which has made the administration order or, as the case may be, to which the application for an administration order has been presented or the notice of intention to appoint has been filed.

19(3)   The rules regulating the practice and procedure of the court in relation to applications to the court in England and Wales under sections 161, 163, 164, 175 and 182 of the Act shall be the rules applying in relation to applications to that court under the Insolvency Act 1986.

Act of Sederunt (Rules of the Court of Session 1994) 1994

(SI 1994/1443)

Made on 31 May 1994 by the Lords of Council and Session under s.5 of the Court of Session Act 1988 and other provisions specified in Sch.1 to this Act of Sederunt. Operative from 5 September 1994.

[**Note**: Changes made by the Act of Sederunt (Rules of the Court of Session Amendment No.5) (Insolvency Proceedings) 2003 (SSI 2003/385), the Act of Sederunt (Rules of the Court of Session Amendment No.6) (Miscellaneous) 2004 (SSI 2004/514), the Act of Sederunt (Rules of the Court of Session Amendment No.7) (Miscellaneous) 2005 (SSI 2005/268), the Act of Sederunt (Rules of the Court of Session Amendment) (Miscellaneous) 2006 (SSI 2006/83), the Act of Sederunt (Rules of the Court of Session Amendment No.2) (UNCITRAL Model Law on Cross-Border Insolvency) 2006 (SSI 2006/199), the Act of Sederunt (Rules of the Court of Session Amendment No.8) (Miscellaneous) 2007 (SSI 2007/449), the Act of Sederunt (Rules of the Court of Session Amendment No.9) (Miscellaneous) 2009 (SSI 2009/450), the Financial Services Act 2012 (Consequential Amendments and Transitional Provisions) Order 2013 (SI 2013/472), the Act of Sederunt (Rules of the Court of Session and Sheriff Court Company Insolvency Rules Amendment) (Miscellaneous) (SSI 2014/119) and the Act of Sederunt (Rules of the Court of Session 1994 and Sheriff Court Rules Amendment) (Regulation (EU) 2015/848) 2017 (SSI 2017/202) have been incorporated into the text. References to administration petitions, orders, etc. have been adapted throughout, following the introduction of the new administration regime, pursuant to the Enterprise Act 2002 (Insolvency) Order 2003 (SSI 2003/2096), as from 15 September 2003. Amendments dealing with the special administration regime for insolvent banks and building societies have been omitted.]

SCHEDULE 2

THE RULES OF THE COURT OF SESSION 1994

Paragraph 2

PRELIMINARY

CHAPTER 1

CITATION, APPLICATION, ETC.

1.1 Citation

1.1 These Rules may be cited as the Rules of the Court of Session 1994.

1.2 Application

1.2 These Rules apply to any cause whether initiated before or after the coming into force of these Rules.

1.3 Interpretation etc.

1.3(1) In these Rules, unless the context otherwise requires–

"the Act of 1988" means the Court of Session Act 1988;

"the Act of 2014" means the Courts Reform (Scotland) Act 2014;

"act" means an order of the court which is extractable, other than a decree;

"agent", except in rule 16.2(2)(e) (service furth of United Kingdom by party's authorised agent) and rule 16.14(1) (arrestment of cargo), means a solicitor or person having a right to conduct the litigation:

"the Auditor" means the Auditor of the Court of Session;

"cause" means any proceedings;

"clerk of court" means the clerk of session acting as such;

"clerk of session" means a depute clerk of session or an assistant clerk of session, as the case may be;

"counsel" means a practising member of the Faculty of Advocates;

"depute clerk of session" means a depute clerk of session and justiciary;

"Deputy Principal Clerk" means the Deputy Principal Clerk of Session;

"document" has the meaning assigned to it in section 9 of the Civil Evidence (Scotland) Act 1988;

"the Extractor" means the Extractor of the Court of Session or the Extractor of the acts and decrees of the Teind Court, as the case may be;

"Keeper of the Records" means the Keeper of the Records of Scotland;

"Keeper of the Registers" means the Keeper of the Registers of Scotland;

"other person having a right of audience" means a person having a right of audience before the court by virtue of Part II of the Law Reform (Miscellaneous Provisions) (Scotland) Act 1990 (legal services) in respect of the category and nature of the cause in question;

"party" means a person who has entered appearance in an action or lodged a writ in the process of a cause (other than a minuter seeking leave to be sisted to a cause); and "parties" shall be construed accordingly;

"period of notice" means–

(a) in relation to service, or intimation on a warrant for intimation before calling, of a summons, the period determined in accordance with rule 13.4 (period of notice in summonses); and

(b) in relation to service of any other writ, intimation of a writ other than intimation referred to in sub-paragraph (a), or the period for lodging answers to a writ, the period determined in accordance with rule 14.6 (period of notice for lodging answers);

"person having a right to conduct the litigation" means a person having a right to conduct litigation by virtue of Part II of the Law Reform (Miscellaneous Provisions) (Scotland) Act 1990 in respect of the category and nature of the cause in question;

"Principal Clerk" means the Principal Clerk of Session and Justiciary;

"principal writ" means the writ by which a cause is initiated before the court;

"proof" includes proof before answer;

"rolls" means the lists of the business of the court issued from time to time by the Keeper of the Rolls;

"send" includes deliver; and "sent" shall be construed accordingly;

"simple procedure case" has the meaning given by section 72(9) of the Courts Reform (Scotland) Act 2014;

"step of process" means a document lodged in process other than a production;

"summons" includes the condescendence and pleas-in-law annexed to it;

"vacation judge" means a judge of the court sitting as such in vacation;

"writ" means summons, petition, note, application, appeal, minute, defences, answers, counterclaim, issue or counter-issue, as the case may be.

1.3(2)   for the purpose of these Rules–

(a) "affidavit" includes an affirmation and a statutory or other declaration; and

(b)   an affidavit shall be sworn or affirmed before a notary public or any other competent authority.

1.3(3)   Where a power is conferred in these Rules on the Lord President to make directions, the power may be exercised in his absence by the Lord Justice-Clerk.

1.3(4)   Where a provision in these Rules imposes an obligation on a principal officer, the obligation may be performed by a clerk of session authorised by him or by another principal officer; and in this paragraph "principal officer" means the Principal Clerk, Deputy Principal Clerk, Deputy Principal Clerk (Administration), Keeper of the Rolls or Principal Extractor.

1.3(5)   Unless the context otherwise requires, where a provision in these Rules requires a party to intimate, give written intimation, or send a document, to another party, it shall be sufficient compliance with that provision if intimation is given or the document is sent, as the case may be, to the agent acting in the cause for that party.

1.3(6)   Unless the context otherwise requires, anything done or required to be done by a party under a provision in these Rules may be done by the agent for that party acting on his behalf.

1.3(7)   Where a provision in these Rules requires a document to be lodged in an office or department of the Office of Court within or not later than a specified period and the last day of that period is a day on which that office or department is closed, the period shall be extended to include the next day on which that office or department, as the case may be, is open or on such other day as may be specified in a notice published in the rolls.

1.3(8)   Unless the context otherwise requires, a reference to a specified Chapter, Part, rule or form is a reference to the Chapter, Part, rule, or the form in the appendix, so specified in these Rules; and a reference to a specified paragraph, sub-paragraph or head is a reference to that paragraph of the rule or form, that sub-paragraph of the paragraph or that head of the sub-paragraph, in which the reference occurs.

1.4   Forms

1.4   Where there is a reference to the use of a form in these Rules, that form in the appendix to these Rules, or a form substantially to the same effect, shall be used with such variation as circumstances may require.

1.5   Direction relating to Advocate General

1.5   The Lord President may, by direction, specify such arrangements as he considers necessary for, or in connection with, the appearance in court of the Advocate General for Scotland.

OTHER PROCEEDINGS IN RELATION TO STATUTORY APPLICATIONS

PART XIII

UNCITRAL MODEL LAW ON CROSS-BORDER INSOLVENCY

62.90   Application and interpretation of this Part

62.90(1)   This Part applies to applications under the Model Law and applications under the Scottish Provisions.

62.90(2)   In this Part–

"application for an interim remedy" means an application under article 19 of the Model Law for an interim remedy by a foreign representative;

"former representative" means a foreign representative who has died or who for any other reason has ceased to be the foreign representative in the foreign proceeding in relation to the debtor;

"main proceeding" means proceedings opened in accordance with Article 3(1) of the EC Insolvency Regulation and falling within the definition of insolvency proceedings in Article 2(a) of the EC Insolvency Regulation;

"the Model Law" means the UNCITRAL Model Law on Cross-Border Insolvency as set out in Schedule 1 to the Cross-Border Insolvency Regulations 2006;

"modification or termination order" means an order by the court pursuant to its powers under the Model Law modifying or terminating recognition of a foreign proceeding, the restraint, sist and suspension referred to in article 20(1) of the Model Law or any part of it or any remedy granted under article 19 or 21 of the Model Law;

"recognition application" means an application by a foreign representative in accordance with article 15 of the Model Law for an order recognising the foreign proceeding in which he has been appointed;

"recognition order" means an order by the court recognising a proceeding as a foreign main proceeding or a foreign non-main proceeding, as appropriate;

"review application" means an application to the court for a modification or termination order;

"the Scottish Provisions" are the provisions of Schedule 3 to the Cross-Border Insolvency Regulations 2006; and

words and phrases defined in the Model Law have the same meaning when used in this Part.

62.90(3)   References in this Part to a debtor who is of interest to the Financial Conduct Authority or the Prudential Regulation Authority are references to a debtor who–

(a)   is, or has been, an authorised person within the meaning of section 31 of the Financial Services and Markets Act 2000 (authorised persons);

(b)   is, or has been, an appointed representative within the meaning of section 39 (exemption of appointed representatives) of that Act; or

(c)   is carrying on, or has carried on, a regulated activity in contravention of the general prohibition.

62.90(4)   In paragraph (3) "the general prohibition" has the meaning given by section 19 of the Financial Services and Markets Act 2000 and the reference to "regulated activity" shall be construed in accordance with–

(a)   section 22 of that Act (classes of regulated activity and categories of investment);

(b)   any relevant order under that section; and

(c)   Schedule 2 to that Act (regulated activities).

History
See note after r.62.96.

62.91   General

62.91(1)   Rule 62.1 (disapplication of certain rules to Chapter 62) shall not apply to an application to which this Part relates.

62.91(2)   Unless otherwise specified in this Part, an application under the Model Law or the Scottish Provisions shall be made by petition.

62.91(3)   For the purposes of the application of rule 14.5(1) (first order for intimation, service and advertisement) to a petition under this Part, where necessary, the petitioner shall seek an order for service of the petition on:–

(a)   the foreign representative;

(b) the debtor;

(c) any British insolvency officeholder acting in relation to the debtor;

(d) any person appointed an administrative receiver of the debtor or as a receiver or manager of the property of the debtor in Scotland;

(e) any member State insolvency practitioner who has been appointed in main proceedings in relation to the debtor;

(f) any foreign representative who has been appointed in any other foreign proceeding regarding the debtor;

(g) if there is pending in Scotland a petition for the winding up or sequestration of the debtor, the petitioner in those proceedings;

(h) any person who is or may be entitled to appoint an administrator of the debtor under paragraph 14 of Schedule B1 to the Insolvency Act 1986 (appointment of administrator by holder of qualifying floating charge); and

(i) the Financial Conduct Authority or the Prudential Regulation Authority if the debtor is a debtor who is of interest to that Authority.

62.91(4)   On the making of–

(a) a recognition order;

(b) an order granting an interim remedy under article 19 of the Model Law;

(c) an order granting a remedy under article 21 of the Model Law;

(d) an order confirming the status of a replacement foreign representative; or

(e) a modification or termination order,

the Deputy Principal Clerk shall send a certified copy of the interlocutor to the foreign representative.

History
See note after r.62.96.

62.92   Recognition application

62.92(1)   A petition containing a recognition application shall include averments as to–

(a) the name of the applicant and his address for service in Scotland;

(b) the name of the debtor in respect of which the foreign proceeding is taking place;

(c) the name or names in which the debtor carries on business in the country where the foreign proceeding is taking place and in this country, if other than the name given under sub-paragraph (b);

(d) the principal or last known place of business of the debtor in Great Britain (if any) and, in the case of an individual, his last known place of residence in Great Britain, (if any);

(e) any registered number allocated to the debtor under the Companies Act 2006;

(f) the foreign proceeding in respect of which recognition is applied for, including the country in which it is taking place and the nature of the proceeding;

(g) whether the foreign proceeding is a proceeding within the meaning of article 2(i) of the Model Law;

(h) whether the applicant is a foreign representative within the meaning of article 2(j) of the Model Law;

   (i)   the address of the debtor's centre of main interests and, if different, the address of its registered office or habitual residence as appropriate;

   (j)   if the debtor does not have its centre of main interests in the country where the foreign proceeding is taking place, whether the debtor has an establishment within the meaning of article 2(e) of the Model Law in that country, and if so, its address.

62.92(3)   There shall be lodged with the petition–

   (a)   an affidavit sworn by the foreign representative as to the matters averred under paragraph (2);

   (b)   the evidence and statement required under article 15(2) and (3) respectively of the Model Law;

   (c)   any other evidence which in the opinion of the applicant will assist the court in deciding whether the proceeding in respect of which the application is made is a foreign proceeding within the meaning of article 2(i) of the Model Law and whether the applicant is a foreign representative within the meaning of article 2(j) of the Model Law; and

   (d)   evidence that the debtor has its centre of main interests or an establishment, as the case may be, within the country where the foreign proceeding is taking place.

62.92(4)   The affidavit to be lodged under paragraph (3)(a) shall state whether, in the opinion of the applicant, the EC Insolvency Regulation applies to any of the proceedings identified in accordance with article 15(3) of the Model Law and, if so, whether those proceedings are main proceedings, secondary proceedings or territorial proceedings.

62.92(5)   Any subsequent information required to be given to the court by the foreign representative under article 18 of the Model Law shall be given by amendment of the petition.

History
See note after r.62.96. There appears to be no para.2. The reference to para.(2) in para.(3) should obviously to para.(1).

62.93   Application for interim remedy

62.93(1)   An application for an interim remedy shall be made by note in process.

62.93(2)   There shall be lodged with the note an affidavit sworn by the foreign representative stating–

   (a)   the grounds on which it is proposed that the interim remedy applied for should be granted;

   (b)   the details of any proceeding under British insolvency law taking place in relation to the debtor;

   (c)   whether to the foreign representative's knowledge, an administrative receiver or receiver or manager of the debtor's property is acting in relation to the debtor;

   (d)   an estimate of the assets of the debtor in Scotland in respect of which the remedy is applied for;

   (e)   all other matters that would in the opinion of the foreign representative assist the court in deciding whether or not to grant the remedy applied for, including whether, to the best of the knowledge and belief of the foreign representative, the interests of the debtor's creditors (including any secured creditors or parties to hire-purchase agreements) and any other interested parties, including if appropriate the debtor, are adequately protected; and

   (f)   whether to the best of the foreign representative's knowledge and belief, the grant of any of the remedy applied for would interfere with the administration of the foreign main proceeding.

History
See note after r.62.96.

62.94   Application for remedy

62.94(1)   An application under article 21 of the Model Law for a remedy shall be made by note in process.

62.94(2)   There shall be lodged with the note an affidavit sworn by the foreign representative stating–

(a) the grounds on which it is proposed that the remedy applied for should be granted;

(b) an estimate of the value of the assets of the debtor in Scotland in respect of which the remedy is requested;

(c) in the case of an application by a foreign representative who is or believes that he is a representative of a foreign non-main proceeding, the reasons why the applicant believes that the remedy relates to assets that, under the law of Great Britain, should be administered in the foreign non-main proceeding or concerns information required in that proceeding; and

(d) all other matters that would in the opinion of the foreign representative assist the court in deciding whether or not it is appropriate to grant the remedy requested, including whether, to the best of the knowledge and belief of the foreign representative, the interests of the debtor's creditors (including any secured creditors or parties to hire-purchase agreements) and any other interested parties, including if appropriate the debtor, are adequately protected.

History
See note after r.62.96.

62.95   Application for confirmation of status of replacement foreign representative

62.95(1)   An application under paragraph 2(3) of the Scottish Provisions for an order confirming the status of a replacement foreign representative shall be made by note in process.

62.95(2)   The note shall include averments as to–

(a) the name of the replacement foreign representative and his address for service within Scotland;

(b) the circumstances in which the former foreign representative ceased to be foreign representative in the foreign proceeding in relation to the debtor (including the date on which he ceased to be the foreign representative);

(c) his own appointment as replacement foreign representative in the foreign proceeding (including the date of that appointment).

62.95(3)   There shall be lodged with the note–

(a) an affidavit sworn by the foreign representative as to the matters averred under paragraph (2);

(b) a certificate from the foreign court affirming–

(i)   the cessation of the appointment of the former foreign representative as foreign representative, and

(ii) the appointment of the applicant as the foreign representative in the foreign proceeding, or

(c) in the absence of such a certificate, any other evidence acceptable to the court of the matters referred to in sub-paragraph (a).

History
See note after r.62.96.

62.96 Review application

62.96(1) A review application shall be made by note in process.

62.96(2) There shall be lodged with the note an affidavit sworn by the applicant as to–

  (a) the grounds on which it is proposed that the remedy applied for should be granted; and

  (b) all other matters that would in the opinion of the applicant assist the court in deciding whether or not it is appropriate to grant the remedy requested, including whether, to the best of the knowledge and belief of the applicant, the interests of the debtor's creditors (including any secured creditors or parties to hire-purchase agreements) and any other interested parties, including if appropriate the debtor, are adequately protected.

History
Rules 62.90 to 62.96 inserted by the Act of Sederunt ((Rules of the Court of Session Amendment No.2) (UNCITRAL Model Law on Cross-Border Insolvency) 2006 (SSI 2006/199, effective 6 April 2006), to take account of the adoption by the UK of the UNCITRAL Model Law.

CHAPTER 74

COMPANIES

PART I

GENERAL PROVISIONS

74.1 Application and interpretation of this Chapter

74.1(1) This Chapter applies to causes under–

  (a) the Insolvency Act 1986; and

  (b) the Company Directors Disqualification Act 1986; and

  (c) Chapter 3 of Part 3 of the Energy Act 2004;

  (d) Parts 2 or 3 of the Banking Act 2009;

  (e) Chapter 5 of Part 2 of the Energy Act 2011; and

  (f) Part 4 of the Postal Services Act 2011.

74.1(2) In this Chapter–

"the Act of 1986" means the Insolvency Act 1986;

"the Act of 2004" means the Energy Act 2004;

"the Act of 2009" means the Banking Act 2009;

"the Act of 2011" means the Energy Act 2011;

"the Bank Administration Rules" means the Bank Administration (Scotland) Rules 2009;

"the Bank Insolvency Rules" means the Bank Insolvency (Scotland) Rules 2009;

"the Insolvency Rules" means the Insolvency (Scotland) Rules 1986;

"the Investment Bank Regulations" means the Investment Bank Special Administration Regulations 2011;

"the Investment Bank Rules" means the Investment Bank Special Administration (Scotland) Rules 2011;

"the Energy Administration Rules" means the Energy Administration (Scotland) Rules 2006;

"the 2013 Rules" means the Energy Supply Company Administration (Scotland) Rules 2013;

"the Council Regulation" means Regulation (EU) 2015/848 of the European Parliament and of the Council of 20th May 2015 on insolvency proceedings, as amended from time to time;

"centre of main interests" has the same meaning as in the Council Regulation;

"establishment" has the same meaning as in Article 2(10) of the Council Regulation;

"main proceedings" means proceedings opened in accordance with Article 3(1) of the Council Regulation and falling within the definition of insolvency proceedings in Article 2(4) of the Council Regulation and–

(a)   in relation to England and Wales and Scotland, set out in Annex A to the Council Regulation under the heading "United Kingdom"; and

(b)   in relation to another Member State, set out in Annex A to the Council Regulation under the heading relating to that Member State;

"Member State" means a Member State of the European Community that has adopted the Council Regulation;

"non GB company" shall have the meaning assigned in section 171 of the Act of 2004;

"the Postal Act" means the Postal Services Act 2011;

"the Postal Administration Rules" means the Postal Administration (Scotland) Rules 2016;

"registered office" means–

(i)   the place specified in the statement of the company delivered to the register of companies under section 9 of the Companies Act 2006 as the intended place of its registered office on incorporation, or

(ii)   where notice has been given by the company to the registrar of companies under section 87 of the Companies Act 2006 of a change of registered office, the place specified in the last such notice;

"territorial proceedings" means proceedings opened in accordance with Article 3(2) and 3(4) of the Council Regulation and falling within the definition of insolvency proceedings in Article 2(a) of the Council Regulation and–

(a)   in relation to England and Wales and Scotland, set out in Annex A to the Council Regulation under the heading "United Kingdom"; and

(b)   in relation to another Member State, set out in Annex A to the Council Regulation under the heading relating to that Member State.

74.1(3)   Unless the context otherwise requires, words and expressions used in this Chapter which are also used in the Act of 1986, Chapter 3 of Part 3 of the Act of 2004, Parts 2 or 3 of the Act of 2009, Chapter 5 of Part 2 of the Act of 2011, Part 4 of the Postal Act, the Insolvency Rules, the Bank Insolvency Rules, the Bank Administration Rules, the Energy Administration Rules, the 2013 Rules or the Postal Administration Rules have the same meaning as in those Acts or Rules, as the case may be.

History

Rule 74.1(1)(c) and the definitions of "the Act of 2004", "the Energy Administration Rules" and "non GB company" inserted, and r.74.1(3) substituted, by the Act of Sederunt (Rules of the Court of Session Amendment) (Miscellaneous) 2006 (SSI 2006/83) r.2(9), as from 17 March 2006.

The definitions from "the Council Regulation" to "Member State" and of "territorial proceedings" inserted by the Act of Sederunt (Rules of the Court of Session Amendment No.8) (Miscellaneous) 2007 (SSI 2007/449) r.8 as from 25 October 2007.

74.2 Proceedings before insolvency judge

74.2 All proceedings in the Outer House in a cause under or by virtue of the Act of 1986, the Company Directors Disqualification Act 1986, Chapter 3 of Part 3 of the Act of 2004, Parts 2 or 3 of the Act of 2009, or Part 4 of the Postal Act shall be brought before a judge of the court nominated by the Lord President as the insolvency judge or, where the insolvency judge is not available, any other judge of the court (including the vacation judge): and "insolvency judge" shall be construed accordingly.

74.3 Notices and reports, etc., sent to the court

74.3 Where, under the Act of 1986, the Act of 2004, the Act of 2009, the Act of 2011, the Postal Act, the Insolvency Rules, the Bank Insolvency Rules, the Bank Administration Rules, the Energy Administration Rules, the 2013 Rules or the Postal Administration Rules–

(a) notice of a fact is to be given to the court,

(b) a report is to be made, or sent, to the court, or

(c) any other document is to be sent to the court,

it shall be sent to the Deputy Principal Clerk who shall cause it to be lodged in the process to which it relates.

History
Rules 74.2, 74.3 substituted by the Act of Sederunt (Rules of the Court of Session Amendment) (Miscellaneous) 2006 (SSI 2006/83) r.2(9), as from 17 March 2006.

PART II

COMPANY VOLUNTARY ARRANGEMENTS

74.4 Lodging of nominee's report (company not in liquidation etc.)

74.4(1) This rule applies where the company is not being wound up by the court and is not in administration.

74.4(2) A report of a nominee submitted to the court under section 2(2) of the Act of 1986 (procedure where nominee is not the liquidator or administrator) shall be–

(a) lodged, with a covering letter, in the Petition Department;

(b) marked by the clerk of session receiving it with the date on which it is received; and

(c) placed before the insolvency judge for consideration of any direction which he may make under section 3(1) of that Act (which relates to the summoning of meetings).

74.4(3) An application by a nominee to extend the time within which he may submit his report under section 2(2) of the Act of 1986 shall be made by letter addressed to the Deputy Principal Clerk who shall–

(a) place the letter before the insolvency judge for determination:

(b) intimate that determination by a written reply; and

(c) attach the letter, and a copy of the reply, to the nominee's report when it is subsequently lodged.

74.5 Lodging of nominee's report (company in liquidation etc.)

74.5(1) This rule applies where the company is being wound up by the court or is in administration.

74.5(2) In this rule, "process" means the process of the petition under section 9 (petition for administration order), or section 124 (petition to wind up a company), of the Act of 1986, as the case may be.

74.5(3)   A report of a nominee submitted to the court under section 2(2) of the Act of 1986 (procedure where nominee is not the liquidator or administrator) shall be–

(a)   lodged in process; and

(b)   placed before the insolvency judge for consideration of any direction which he may make under section 3(1) of that Act.

74.5(4)   An application by a nominee to extend the time within which he may submit his report under section 2(2) of the Act of 1986 shall be made by letter addressed to the Deputy Principal Clerk who shall–

(a)   place the letter before the insolvency judge for determination;

(b)   intimate that determination by a written reply; and

(c)   lodge the letter, and a copy of the reply, in the process of the petition to which it relates.

74.6   Inspection of nominee's report

74.6   A person who states in a letter addressed to the Deputy Principal Clerk that he is a creditor, member or director of the company or his agent, may, on payment of the appropriate fee, inspect the nominee's report lodged under rule 74.4(2) (company not in liquidation etc.) 74.5(3) (company in liquidation etc.), as the case may be.

74.7   Report of meetings to approve arrangement

74.7   The report of the result of a meeting to be sent to the court under section 4(6) of the Act of 1986 shall be sent to the Deputy Principal Clerk who shall lodge it–

(a)   in a case to which rule 74.4 (lodging of nominee's report (company not in liquidation etc.)) applies, with the nominee's report lodged under that rule; or

(b)   in a case to which rule 74.5 (lodging of nominee's report (company in liquidation etc.)) applies, in process as defined by paragraph (2) of that rule.

74.8   Abstracts of supervisor's receipts and payments and notices of completion of arrangement

74.8   An abstract of receipts and payments prepared by a supervisor and sent to the court under rule 1.21(2) of the Insolvency Rules or a notice of completion of the arrangement (and a copy of the supervisor's report) to be sent to the court under rule 1.23(3) of those Rules shall be sent to the Deputy Principal Clerk who shall cause it to be lodged–

(a)   in a case to which rule 74.4 (lodging of nominee's report (company not in liquidation etc.)) applies, with the nominee's report lodged under that rule; or

(b)   in a case to which rule 74.5 (lodging of nominee's report (company in liquidation etc.)) applies, in process as defined by paragraph (2) of that rule.

74.9   Form of other applications

74.9(1)   An application to which this rule applies shall be made–

(a)   where the company is not being wound up by the court and is not in administration, by petition; or

(b)   where the company is being wound up by the court or is in administration, by note in the process to which it relates.

74.9(1A)   In the case of a bank, an application to which this rule applies shall be made–

(a)   where the bank is not subject to a bank insolvency order and is not in bank administration, by petition; or

(b)   where the bank is subject to a bank insolvency order by the court or is in bank administration, by note in the process to which it relates.

74.9(2)   This rule applies to an application under–

(a)   section 2(4) of the Act of 1986 (for the replacement of a nominee);

(b)   section 6 of that Act (to challenge a decision made in relation to an arrangement);

(c)   section 7(3) of that Act (to challenge the actings of a supervisor);

(d)   section 7(4)(a) of that Act (by a supervisor for directions);

(e)   section 7(5) of that Act (for the appointment of a supervisor);

(f)   rule 1.21(5) of the Insolvency Rules (to dispense with sending abstracts or reports or to vary the dates on which the obligation to send abstracts or reports arises);

(g)   rule 1.23(4) of those Rules (to extend the period for sending a notice of implementation of arrangement or report);

(h)   any other provision in the Act of 1986 or the Insolvency Rules relating to company voluntary arrangements not mentioned in this Part; or

(i)   any provision in the Act of 1986, as applied by the Act of 2009, relating to voluntary arrangements.

PART III

ADMINISTRATION PROCEDURE

74.10   Form of petition in administration procedure

74.10(1)   In this Part, "the petition" means a petition under section 9 of, or section 8 of and Schedule B1 to, the Act of 1986 (petition for administration order), or section 156 of the Act of 2004 (petition for energy administration order), or section 70 of the Postal Act (applications for postal administration orders).

74.10(2)   The petition shall include averments in relation to–

(a)   the petitioner and the capacity in which he presents the petition, if other than the company;

(b)   whether it is believed that the company is, or is likely to become, unable to pay its debts and the grounds of that belief;

(c)   in the case of a petition under the Act of 1986, how the making of that order will achieve–

     (i)   any of the purposes specified in section 8(3) of the Act of 1986; or

     (ii)   an objective specified in paragraph 3 of Schedule B1 to the Act of 1986;

(d)   the company's financial position specifying, so far as known, assets and liabilities, including contingent and prospective liabilities;

(e)   any security known or believed to be held by creditors of the company, whether in any case the security confers power on the holder to appoint a receiver or an administrator, and whether a receiver or an administrator, as the case may be, has been appointed;

(f)   so far as known to the petitioner, whether any steps have been taken for the winding up of the company;

(g)   other matters which, in the opinion of the petitioner, will assist the court in deciding whether to grant an order in respect of an administration or an energy administration or a postal administration, as the case may be;

636

(h)   [Omitted]

(i)   the name and address of the person proposed to be appointed, and his qualification to act, as administrator or energy administrator or postal administrator, as the case may be; and

(j)   in the case of a petition under the Act of 1986, jurisdiction under the Council Regulation, in particular stating, so far as known to the petitioner–

  (i)   where the centre of main interests of the company is and whether the company has any other establishments in another Member State; and

  (ii)   whether there are insolvency proceedings elsewhere in respect of the company and whether those proceedings are main or territorial proceedings;

(k)   whether the Secretary of State has certified the case as one in which he considers it would be appropriate for him to petition under section 124A of the Act of 1986 (petition for winding up on grounds of public interest);

(l)   so far as known to the petitioner in a petition for an energy administration order or a postal administration order, as the case may be, whether any steps have been taken for an administration order under Schedule B1 to the Act of 1986;

(m)   whether a protected energy company in a petition for an energy administration order is a non GB company.

(n)   whether a universal service provider (within the meaning of section 65(1) of the Postal Act) in a petition for a postal administration order is a foreign company.

74.10(3)   [Omitted]

History
Rule 74.10(1)(c) substituted by the Act of Sederunt (Rules of the Court of Session Amendment No.5) (Insolvency Proceedings) 2003 (SSI 2003/385) rr.2(1), (7)(b)(i) as from 15 September 2003.
   Rule 74.10(1) substituted r.74.10(2)(c), (e), (g), (i), (j) amended, r.74.10(2)(h) and 74.10(3) omitted, and r.74.10(2)k)–(m) inserted, by the Act of Sederunt (Rules of the Court of Session Amendment) (Miscellaneous) 2006 (SSI 2006/83) r.2(9), as from 17 March 2006.
   Rule 74.10(2)(j) substituted by the Act of Sederunt (Rules of the Court of Session Amendment No.8) (Miscellaneous) 2007 (SSI 2007/449) r.9 as from 25 October 2007.

74.10A   Interim orders

74.10A(1)   On making an interim order under paragraph 13(1)(d) of Schedule B1 to the Act of 1986 or section 157(1)(d) of the Act of 2004 or section 71(1)(d) of the Postal Act, the Lord Ordinary shall fix a hearing on the By Order Roll for a date after the expiry of the period of notice mentioned in rule 14.6 (period of notice for lodging answers).

74.10A(2)   At the hearing under paragraph (1) the Lord Ordinary shall make such order as to further procedure as he thinks fit.

History
Rule 74.10A inserted by the Act of Sederunt (Rules of the Court of Session Amendment No.7) (Miscellaneous) 2005 (SSI 2005/268) r.2(1), (9) as from 7 June 2005.
   Rule 74.10A(1) amended by the Act of Sederunt (Rules of the Court of Session Amendment) (Miscellaneous) 2006 (SSI 2006/83) r.2(9), as from 17 March 2006.

74.11   Notice of petition

74.11   Where–

(a)   the petition is to be served on a person mentioned in rule 2.3 of the Insolvency Rules, and

(b)   by virtue of paragraph (2) of that rule, notice requires to be given to that person, or,

(c)   the petition and a notice are to be served on a person mentioned in section 156(2)(a) to (c) of the Act of 2004 (notice of application for energy administration order) rule 5(1) of the Energy Administration Rules or rule 6(1) of the 2013 Rules, or

(d)   the petition and a notice are to be served on a person mentioned in section 70(2)(a) to (c) of the Postal Act (applications for postal administration orders) or Rule 7 of the Postal Administration (Scotland) Rules,

it shall be sufficient for the petitioner, where such notice and service is to be executed by post, to enclose the statutory notice and a copy of the petition in one envelope and to certify the giving of such notice and the execution of such service by one certificate.

History
In r.74.11(a) the words "rule 2.3" substituted for the former words "rule 2.2" by the Act of Sederunt (Rules of the Court of Session Amendment No.5) (Insolvency Proceedings) 2003 (SSI 2003/385) r.2(1), (8) as from 15 September 2003.
Rule 74.11(c) inserted by the Act of Sederunt (Rules of the Court of Session Amendment) (Miscellaneous) 2006 (SSI 2006/83) r.2(9), as from 17 March 2006.

74.12   Report of proposals of administrator

74.12(1)   A report of the meeting to approve the proposals of the administrator to be sent to the court under section 24(4) of the Act of 1986 shall be sent to the Deputy Principal Clerk of Session, who shall–

(a)   cause it to be lodged in the process of the petition to which it relates; and

(b)   give written intimation to the parties of the receipt and lodging of the report.

74.12(2)   Where a report under section 24(4) of the Act of 1986 discloses that the meeting has declined to approve the proposals of the administrator, the Keeper of the Rolls shall put the cause out on the By Order Roll for determination by the insolvency judge for any order he may make under section 24(5) of that Act.

74.13   Report of administrator's proposals: Schedule B1 to the Act of 1986

74.13(1)   Paragraph (2) shall apply where a report under paragraphs 53(2) or 54(6) of Schedule B1 to the Act of 1986 discloses a failure to approve, or to approve a revision of, an administrator's proposals.

74.13(2)   The Deputy Principal Clerk shall fix a hearing for determination by the insolvency judge of any order that may be made under paragraph 55(2) of Schedule B1 to the Act of 1986.

History
Rule 74.13 substituted by the Act of Sederunt (Rules of the Court of Session Amendment No.5) (Insolvency Proceedings) 2003 (SSI 2003/385) r.2(1), (9) as from 15 September 2003.

74.14   Time and date of lodging in administration, energy administration or postal administration

74.14(1)   The time and date of lodging of a notice or document relating to an administration under the Act of 1986 or the Insolvency Rules, or an energy administration under the Act of 2004 or the Energy Administration Rules or a postal administration under the Postal Act or the Postal Administration Rules, shall be noted by the Deputy Principal Clerk upon the notice or document.

74.14(2)   Subject to any provision in the Insolvency Rules or the Energy Administration Rules or the Postal Administration Rules, as the case may be–

(a)   where the time of lodging of a notice or document cannot be ascertained by the Deputy Principal Clerk, the notice or document shall be deemed to be lodged at 10 a.m. on the date of lodging; and

(b)   where a notice or document under paragraph (1) is delivered on any day other than a business day, the date of lodging shall be the first business day after such delivery.

History
Rule 74.14 substituted by the Act of Sederunt (Rules of the Court of Session Amendment) (Miscellaneous) 2006 (SSI 2006/83) r.2(9), as from 17 March 2006.

74.15   Applications during an administration, energy administration or postal administration

74.15   An application or appeal under any provision of the Act of 1986, the Insolvency Rules, the Act of 2004, the Postal Act or the Energy Administration Rules or the Postal Administration Rules during an administration, energy administration or postal administration, as the case may be, shall be–

   (a)   where no previous application or appeal has been made, by petition; or

   (b)   where a petition for an order in respect of an administration, or energy administration or postal administration, as the case may be, has been lodged, by note in the process of that petition.

History
Rule 74.15 substituted by the Act of Sederunt (Rules of the Court of Session Amendment) (Miscellaneous) 2006 (SSI 2006/83) r.2(9), as from 17 March 2006.

74.15A   Application for administration by a bank liquidator

74.15A   An application by a bank liquidator for an administration order under section 114 of the Act of 2009 shall be made by note in the existing process of the bank insolvency petition.

PART IV

RECEIVERS

74.16   Interpretation of this Part

74.16   In this Part, "the petition" means a petition under section 54(1) of the Act of 1986 (petition to appoint a receiver).

74.17   Petition to appoint a receiver

74.17   The petition shall include averments in relation to–

   (a)   any floating charge and the property over which it is secured;

   (b)   so far as known to the petitioner, whether any application for an order in respect of an administration has been made, or an administrator has been appointed, in respect of the company;

   (c)   other matters which, in the opinion of the petitioner, will assist the court in deciding whether to appoint a receiver; and

   (d)   the name and address of the person proposed to be appointed, and his qualification to act, as receiver.

74.18   Intimation, service and advertisement under this Part

74.18(1)   Unless the court otherwise directs, the order under rule 14.5 (first order in petitions) for intimation, service and advertisement of the petition shall include a requirement–

   (a)   to serve the petition–

      (i)   on the company; and

      (ii)   where an application for an administration order has been presented, on that applicant and any respondent to that application; and

   (b)   to advertise the petition forthwith–

    (i)   once in the Edinburgh Gazette; and

    (ii)   once in one or more of such newspapers as the court shall direct.

74.18(2)   Subject to rule 14.6(2) (application to shorten or extend the period of notice), the period of notice for lodging answers to the petition shall be 8 days.

74.18(3)   An advertisement under paragraph (1) shall include–

    (a)   the name and address of the petitioner;

    (b)   the name and address of the agent for the petitioner;

    (c)   the date on which the petition was presented;

    (d)   the nature of the order sought;

    (e)   the period of notice for lodging answers; and

    (f)   a statement that any person who intends to appear in the petition must lodge answers within the period of notice.

74.19   Form of other applications and appeals

74.19(1)   An application under–

    (a)   section 61(1) of the Act of 1986 (by a receiver for authority to dispose of property or an interest in property),

    (b)   section 62 of that Act (for removal of a receiver),

    (c)   section 63(1) of that Act (by a receiver for directions),

    (d)   section 69(1) of that Act (to enforce the receiver's duty to make returns etc.), or

    (e)   any other provision of the Act of 1986 or the Insolvency Rules relating to receivers not mentioned in this Part,

shall, where the court has appointed the receiver, be made by note or, in any other case, by petition.

74.19(2)   An appeal against a decision of a receiver as to expenses of submitting a statement of affairs under rule 3.3(2) of the Insolvency Rules shall, where the receiver was appointed by the court, be made by note or, in any other case, by petition.

74.19(3)   An application by a receiver–

    (a)   under section 67(1) or (2) of the Act of 1986 (to extend the time for sending a report),

    (b)   under rule 3.9(2) of the Insolvency Rules (to extend the time for sending an abstract of his receipts and payments),

shall, where the court has appointed the receiver, be made by motion or, in any other case, by petition.

Part V

Winding up of Companies

74.20   Interpretation of this Part

74.20   In this Part, "the petition" means a petition under section 124 of the Act of 1986 (petition to wind up a company).

74.21   Petition to wind up a company

74.21(1)   The petition shall include averments in relation to–

(a)   the petitioner, if other than the company, and his title to present the petition;

(b)   in respect of the company–

    (i)   its current and any previous registered name;

    (ii)   the address of its registered office, and any previous such address within 6 months immediately before the presentation of the petition so far as known to the petitioner;

    (iii)   a statement of the nature of its business and objects, the amount of its capital (nominal and issued) indicating what part is called up, paid up or credited as paid up, and the amount of the assets of the company so far as known to the petitioner;

    (iv)   where the centre of main interests of the company is and whether the company has any other establishments in another Member State;

(c)   whether, to the knowledge of the petitioner, a receiver has been appointed in respect of any part of the property of the company or a liquidator has been appointed for the voluntary winding up of the company;

(d)   the grounds on which the petition proceeds;

(e)   the name and address of the person proposed to be appointed, and his qualification to act, as interim liquidator; and

(f)   whether there are insolvency proceedings elsewhere in respect of the company and whether those proceedings are main or territorial proceedings.

History

Rule 74.21(b)(iv) and (f) inserted by the Act of Sederunt (Rules of the Court of Session Amendment No.8) (Miscellaneous) 2007 (SSI 2007/449) r.10 as from 25 October 2007.

74.22   Intimation, service and advertisement under this Part

74.22(1)   Unless the court otherwise directs, the order under rule 14.5 (first order in petitions) for intimation, service and advertisement of the petition shall include a requirement–

(a)   to serve the petition–

    (i)   where the petitioner is not the company, on the company;

    (ii)   where the company is being wound up voluntarily and a liquidator has been appointed, on the liquidator; and

    (iii)   where a receiver or administrator has been appointed, on the receiver or administrator, as the case may be;

(b)   where the company is an authorised institution or former authorised institution within the meaning assigned in section 106(1) of the Banking Act 1987 and the petitioner is not the Bank of England, to serve the petition on the Bank of England; and

(c)   to advertise the petition forthwith–

    (i)   once in the Edinburgh Gazette; and

    (ii)   once in one or more of such newspapers as the court shall direct.

74.22(2)   Subject to rule 14.6(2) (application to shorten or extend the period of notice), the period of notice for lodging answers to the petition shall be 8 days.

74.22(3)   An advertisement under paragraph (1) shall include–

(a)   the name and address of the petitioner and, where the petitioner is the company, its registered office;

(b)   the name and address of the agent for the petitioner;

(c)   the date on which the petition was presented;

(d)   the nature of the order sought;

(e)   where a provisional liquidator has been appointed by the court, his name, address and the date of his appointment;

(f)   the period of notice for lodging answers; and

(g)   a statement that any person who intends to appear in the petition must lodge answers within the period of notice.

74.23   Remits from one court to another

74.23(1)   An application under section 120(3)(a)(i) of the Act of 1986 (application for remit of petition to a sheriff court) shall be made by motion.

74.23(2)   An application under–

(a)   section 120(3)(a)(ii) of the Act of 1986 (application for remit of petition from a sheriff court to the court), or

(b)   section 120(3)(b) of that Act (application for remit of petition from one sheriff court to another),

shall be made by petition.

74.24   Substitution of creditor or contributory for petitioner

74.24(1)   Where a petitioner in the petition–

(a)   is subsequently found not entitled to present the petition,

(b)   fails to make intimation, service and advertisement as directed by the court,

(c)   moves or consents to withdraw the petition or to allow it to be dismissed or refused,

(d)   fails to appear when the petition is called for hearing, or

(e)   appears, but does not move for an order in terms of the prayer of the petition,

the court may, on such terms as it thinks fit, sist as petitioner in place of the original petitioner any creditor or contributory who, in the opinion of the court, is entitled to present the petition.

74.24(1A)   Where a member State insolvency practitioner has been appointed in main proceedings in relation to the company, without prejudice to paragraph (1) the court may, on such terms as it thinks fit, substitute the member State liquidator as petitioner, where he is desirous of prosecuting the petition.

74.24(2)   An application by a creditor or a contributory to be sisted under paragraph (1)–

(a)   may be made at any time before the petition is dismissed or refused, and

(b)   shall be made by note;

and, if necessary, the court may continue the petition for a specified period to allow a note to be presented.

History
Rule 74.24(1A) inserted by the Act of Sederunt (Rules of the Court of Session Amendment No.5) (Insolvency Proceedings) 2003 (SSI 2003/385) r.2(1), (11) as from 15 September 2003.

74.25 Provisional liquidator

74.25(1) An application to appoint a provisional liquidator under section 135 of the Act of 1986 may be made–

  (a) by the petitioner, in the prayer of the petition or, if made after the petition has been presented, by note; or

  (b) by a creditor or contributory of the company, the company, the Secretary of State, a member State insolvency practitioner appointed in main proceedings or a person entitled under any enactment to present a petition, by note.

74.25(2) The application mentioned in paragraph (1) shall include averments in relation to–

  (a) the grounds for the appointment of the provisional liquidator;

  (b) the name and address of the person proposed to be appointed, and his qualification to act, as provisional liquidator; and

  (c) whether, to the knowledge of the applicant, an administrator has been appointed to the company or a receiver has been appointed in respect of any part of its property or a liquidator has been appointed voluntarily to wind it up.

74.25(3) Where the court decides to appoint a provisional liquidator–

  (a) it shall pronounce an interlocutor making the appointment and specifying the functions to be carried out by him in relation to the affairs of the company; and

  (b) the applicant shall forthwith send a certified copy of such interlocutor to the person appointed.

74.25(4) On receiving a certified copy of an interlocutor pronounced under paragraph (3), the provisional liquidator shall intimate his appointment forthwith–

  (a) once in the Edinburgh Gazette; and

  (b) once in one or more of such newspapers as the court has directed.

74.25(5) An application for the discharge of a provisional liquidator shall be made by note.

History
In r.74.25(1)(b) the words ", a member State liquidator appointed in main proceedings" inserted by the Act of Sederunt (Rules of the Court of Session Amendment No.5) (Insolvency Proceedings) 2003 (SSI 2003/385) r.2(1), (12) as from 15 September 2003. In r.74.25(1)(b) the word "liquidator" substituted by the Act of Sederunt (Rules of the Court of Session 1994 and Sheriff Court Rules Amendment) (Regulation (EU) 2015/848) 2017 (SSI 2017/202) rr.1, 3(5) as from 16 June 2017, subject to savings in r.6.

74.26 Appointment of a liquidator

74.26(1) Where the court pronounces an interlocutor appointing a liquidator–

  (a) the Deputy Principal Clerk shall send a certified copy of that interlocutor to the liquidator;

  (b) the court may, for the purposes of rule 4.18(4) of the Insolvency Rules (liquidator to give notice of appointment), give such direction as it thinks fit as to advertisement of such appointment.

74.26(2) An application to appoint a liquidator under section 139(4) of the Act of 1986 shall be made by note.

74.27 Applications and appeals in relation to a statement of affairs

74.27(1) An application under section 131(5) of the Act of 1986 for–

  (a) release from an obligation imposed under section 131(1) or (2) of that Act, or

  (b) an extension of time for the submission of a statement of affairs, shall be made by note.

74.27(2) A note under paragraph (1) shall be served on the liquidator or provisional liquidator, as the case may be, who may lodge–

(a) answers to the note; or

(b) a report on any matters which he considers should be drawn to the attention of the court.

74.27(3) Where the liquidator or provisional liquidator lodges a report under paragraph (2), he shall forthwith send a copy of it to the noter.

74.27(4) Where the liquidator or the provisional liquidator does not appear at any hearing on the note, a certified copy of the interlocutor disposing of the note shall be sent to him forthwith by the noter.

74.27(5) An appeal under rule 4.9(6) of the Insolvency Rules (appeal against refusal by liquidator of allowance towards expenses of preparing statement of affairs) shall be made by note.

74.28 Appeals against adjudication of claims

74.28(1) An appeal under rule 4.16B(6) of the Insolvency Rules (adjudication of claims) by a creditor or any member or contributory of the company against a decision of the liquidator shall be made by note in process.

74.28(2) A note under paragraph (1) shall be served on the liquidator.

74.28(3) On such a note being served on him, the liquidator shall send the claim in question, and a copy of his adjudication, forthwith to the Deputy Principal Clerk who shall cause them to be lodged in process.

74.28(4) After the note has been disposed of, the Deputy Principal Clerk shall return the claim and the adjudication to the liquidator with a copy of the interlocutor disposing of the note.

History
Rule 74.28(1) substituted by the Act of Sederunt (Rules of the Court of Session and Sheriff Court Company Insolvency Rules Amendment) (Miscellaneous) (SSI 2014/119) r.2(1), (2) as from 30 May 2014.

74.29 Removal of liquidator

74.29 An application by a creditor of the company for an order–

(a) under section 171(3) of the Act of 1986 (order directing a liquidator to summon a meeting of creditors for the purpose of removing him), or

(b) under section 172 of that Act (order for removal of a liquidator),

shall be made by note.

74.30 Application in relation to remuneration of liquidator

74.30(1) An application–

(a) by a liquidator under rule 4.34 of the Insolvency Rules (application to increase remuneration), or

(b) by a creditor of the company under rule 4.35 of those Rules (application to reduce liquidator's remuneration),

shall be made by note.

74.30(2) A note under paragraph (1)(b) shall be served on the liquidator.

74.30A Applications under section 176A of the Act of 1986

74.30A(1) An application by a liquidator, administrator or receiver under section 176A of the Act of 1986 shall be–

(a) where there is no existing process in relation to any liquidation, administration or receivership, by petition; or

(b) where a process exists in relation to any liquidation, administration or receivership, by note in that process.

74.30A(2)   The Deputy Principal Clerk shall–

(a) after the lodging of any petition or note fix a hearing for the insolvency judge to consider an application under paragraph (1); and

(b) give notice of the hearing fixed under paragraph (2)(a) to the petitioner or noter.

74.30A(3)   The petitioner or noter shall not be required to give notice to any person of the hearing fixed under paragraph (2)(a), unless the insolvency judge directs otherwise.

History
Rule 74.30A inserted by the Act of Sederunt (Rules of the Court of Session Amendment No.5) (Insolvency Proceedings) 2003 (SSI 2003/385) r.2(1), (13) as from 15 September 2003.

74.31   Application to appoint a special manager

74.31(1)   An application under section 177 of the Act of 1986 (application for the appointment of a special manager) shall be made by note.

74.31(2)   A bond of caution certified by the noter under rule 4.70(4) of the Insolvency Rules shall be sent to the Petition Department by the noter.

74.31(3)   After the Deputy Principal Clerk has satisfied himself as to the sufficiency of caution under rule 33.7(1) of these Rules, the clerk of session shall issue to the person appointed to be special manager a certified copy of the interlocutor appointing him.

74.31(4)   A special manager may, before the expiry of the period for finding caution, apply to the insolvency judge for an extension of that period.

74.32   Other applications

74.32(1)   An application under the Act of 1986 or any subordinate legislation made under that Act, or Part VII of the Companies Act 1989, in relation to a winding up by the court not mentioned in this Part shall–

(a) if made by a party to the petition, be made by motion; or

(b) in any other case, be made by note.

74.32(2)   At the hearing of a motion under paragraph (1)(a), the court may order that the application be made by note; and, in such a case, shall make an order for the lodging of answers to the note in process within such period as it thinks fit.

74.32A   Replacement liquidators: block transfer orders

74.32A(1)   This rule applies to an application under rule 4.26B(1) of the Insolvency Rules (application for block transfer order).

74.32A(2)   An application mentioned in paragraph (1) shall be made by petition.

74.32A(3)   Paragraph (4) applies where an application includes the name of one or more sheriff court petition.

74.32A(4)   The Deputy Principal Clerk shall notify the sheriff clerk of every sheriff court listed in the application that an application has been made.

74.32A(5)   Where the court grants an application, it may order the replacement liquidator to be appointed in any or all of the cases listed in the application.

74.32A(6)   Where the court pronounces an interlocutor granting a block transfer order–

(a)   the Deputy Principal Clerk shall send a certified copy of that interlocutor to the replacement liquidator;

(b)   the court may direct that a copy of the interlocutor is–

   (i)   to be put in the process of every Court of Session petition where the replacement liquidator has been appointed;

   (ii)   to be sent to the sheriff clerk to be put in the process of every sheriff court petition where the replacement liquidator has been appointed; and

(c)   the court may make such orders as it thinks fit for the intimation and advertisement of the appointment of the replacement liquidator.

History
Rule 74.32A substituted by the Act of Sederunt (Rules of the Court of Session and Sheriff Court Company Insolvency Rules Amendment) (Miscellaneous) (SSI 2014/119) r.2(1), (3) as from 30 May 2014.

74.32B   Approval of the voluntary winding up of a bank or building society

74.32B(1)   An application for the prior approval of a resolution for voluntary winding up of a bank under section 84 of the Act of 1986 or voluntary winding up of a building society under section 88 of the Building Societies Act 1986 shall be made to the Deputy Principal Clerk by letter.

74.32B(2)   An application under paragraph (1) shall be marked as having been made on the date on which the letter is received by the court.

74.32B(3)   The letter shall be placed before the insolvency judge forthwith for consideration.

74.32B(4)   The court shall approve such a resolution by pronouncing an interlocutor to that effect.

History
Rule 74.32B inserted by the Act of Sederunt (Rules of the Court of Session Amendment) (Miscellaneous) 2009 (SSI 2009/63) r.3(8) as from 25 February 2009. Heading substituted and r.74.32B(1) amended by the Act of Sederunt (Rules of the Court of Session Amendment No.6) (Building Society Special Administration etc.) 2009 (SSI 2009/135) r.2(2), (3) as from 29 March 2009.

PART VI

DISQUALIFICATION OF COMPANY DIRECTORS

74.33   Applications in relation to disqualification orders or undertakings

74.33   An application–

(a)   under section 3(2) of the Company Directors Disqualification Act 1986 (for disqualification for persistent breaches of companies legislation);

(aa)   under section 5A of that Act (for disqualification for certain convictions abroad);

(b)   under section 6(1) of that Act (to disqualify unfit directors of insolvent companies);

(c)   under section 8 of that Act (for disqualification of unfit director after investigation of a company);

(ca)   under section 8A of that Act (variation or cessation of disqualification undertaking);

(cb)   under section 8ZB of that Act (for disqualification of person instructing unfit director of insolvent company);

(cc) under section 8ZD of that Act (for order disqualifying person instructing unfit director: other cases);

(d) under section 11(1) of that Act (for leave by an undischarged bankrupt to be concerned in a company),

(da) under section 15A of that Act (for compensation orders);

(db) under section 15C of that Act (for variation and revocation of compensation undertakings);

(e) for leave under that Act; or

(f) by the Secretary of State under rule 3(2) of the Insolvent Companies (Reports on Conduct of Directors) (Scotland) Rules 2016 (application for order directing compliance with requirements to furnish information etc.),

shall be made by petition.

History
See history note after r.74.34.

74.34   Intimation, service and advertisement under this Part

74.34(1)   Rule 74.22, except paragraphs (1)(c) and (2) of that rule, shall apply to the intimation, service and advertisement of a petition referred to in rule 74.33 (applications in relation to disqualification orders) as it applies to a petition under that rule.

74.34(2)   A petition presented under rule 74.33 shall be intimated–

(a) to the Secretary of State for Business, Enterprise and Regulatory Reform; or

(b) where a petition is presented under rule 74.33(ca) and the disqualification undertaking was given under section 9B of the Company Directors Disqualification Act 1986 (competition undertaking), to the Office of Fair Trading or any specified regulator which has accepted the undertaking, as the case may be;

unless the petition is presented by that person or body.

History
Rule 7.33(ca) inserted, and r.7.34(2) substituted, by the Act of Sederunt (Rules of the Court of Session Amendment No.8) (Miscellaneous) 2005 (SSI 2005/521) r.2(2), as from 21 October 2005.

APPENDIX

Rule 1.4
[Forms: not reproduced.]

Insolvent Partnerships Order 1994

(SI 1994/2421)

Made on 13 September 1994 by the Secretary of State for Trade and Industry under s.420(1), (2) of the Insolvency Act 1986 and s.21(2) of the Company Directors Disqualification Act 1986. Operative from 1 December 1994.

[**Note:** Changes made by the Financial Services and Markets Act 2000 (Consequential Amendments and Repeals) Order 2001 (SI 2001/3649), the Insolvent Partnerships (Amendment) Order 2001 (SI 2001/767), the Insolvent Partnerships (Amendment) Order 2002 (SI 2002/1308), the Insolvent Partnerships (Amendment) (No.2) Order 2002 (SI 2002/2708), the Civil Partnership Act 2004 (Amendments to Subordinate Legislation) Order 2005 (SI 2005/2114), the Insolvent Partnerships (Amendment) Order 2005 (SI 2005/1516), the Insolvent Partnerships (Amendment) Order 2006 (SI 2006/622), the Lord Chancellor (Transfer of Functions and Supplementary Provisions) Order 2006 (SI 2006/680), the Financial Services Act 2012 (Consequential Amendments and Transitional Provisions) Order 2013 (SI 2013/472), the Banks and Building Societies (Depositor Preference and Priorities) Order 2014 (SI 2014/3486), the Insolvency (Protection of Essential Supplies) Order 2015 (SI 2015/989), the Deregulation Act 2015 (Insolvency) (Consequential Amendments and Transitional and Savings Provisions) Order 2015 (SI 2015/1641), the Enterprise and Regulatory Reform Act 2013 (Consequential Amendments) (Bankruptcy), the Small Business, Enterprise and Employment Act 2015 (Consequential Amendments) Regulations 2016 (SI 2016/481), the Deregulation Act 2015 and Small Business, Enterprise and Employment Act 2015 (Consequential Amendments) (Savings) Regulations 2017 (SI 2017/540), the Insolvency (Miscellaneous Amendments) Regulations 2017 (SI 2017/1119) and the Banks and Building Societies (Priorities on Insolvency) Order 2018 (SI 2018/1244) have been incorporated into the text (in the case of pre-2003 legislation without annotation). References to administration petitions, orders, etc. have been adapted throughout, following the introduction of the new administration regime, pursuant to the 2005 Order.]

ARRANGEMENT OF ARTICLES

PART I

GENERAL

1 Citation, commencement and extent

1(1) This Order may be cited as the Insolvent Partnerships Order 1994 and shall come into force on 1st December 1994.

1(2) This Order–

(a) in the case of insolvency proceedings in relation to companies and partnerships, relates to companies and partnerships which the courts in England and Wales have jurisdiction to wind up; and

(b) in the case of insolvency proceedings in relation to individuals, extends to England and Wales only.

1(3) In paragraph (2) the term "insolvency proceedings" has the meaning ascribed to it by article 2 below.

2 Interpretation: definitions

2(1) In this Order, except in so far as the context otherwise requires–

"the Act" means the Insolvency Act 1986;

"agricultural charge" has the same meaning as in the Agricultural Credits Act 1928;

"agricultural receiver" means a receiver appointed under an agricultural charge;

"corporate member" means an insolvent member which is a company;

"the court", in relation to an insolvent partnership, means the court which has jurisdiction to wind up the partnership;

"individual member" means an insolvent member who is an individual;

"insolvency order" means–

(a)   in the case of an insolvent partnership or a corporate member, a winding-up order; and

(b)   in the case of an individual member, a bankruptcy order;

"insolvency petition" means, in the case of a petition presented to the court–

(a)   against a corporate member, a petition for its winding up by the court;

(b)   against an individual member, a petition for a bankruptcy order to be made against that individual,

where the petition is presented in conjunction with a petition for the winding up of the partnership by the court as an unregistered company under the Act;

"insolvency proceedings" means any proceedings under the Act, this Order or the Insolvency (England and Wales) Rules 2016;

"insolvent member" means a member of an insolvent partnership, against whom an insolvency petition is being or has been presented;

"joint bankruptcy petition" means a petition by virtue of article 11 of this Order;

"joint debt" means a debt of an insolvent partnership in respect of which an order is made by virtue of Part IV or V of this Order;

"joint estate" means the partnership property of an insolvent partnership in respect of which an order is made by virtue of Part IV or V of this Order;

"joint expenses" means expenses incurred in the winding up of an insolvent partnership or in the winding up of the business of an insolvent partnership and the administration of its property;

"limited partner" has the same meaning as in the Limited Partnerships Act 1907;

"member" means a member of a partnership and any person who is liable as a partner within the meaning of section 14 of the Partnership Act 1890;

"officer", in relation to an insolvent partnership, means–

(a)   a member; or

(b)   a person who has management or control of the partnership business;

"partnership property" has the same meaning as in the Partnership Act 1890;

"postponed debt" means a debt the payment of which is postponed by or under any provision of the Act or of any other enactment;

"responsible insolvency practitioner" means–

(a)   in winding up, the liquidator of an insolvent partnership or corporate member; and

(b)   in bankruptcy, the trustee of the estate of an individual member,

and in either case includes the official receiver when so acting;

"separate debt" means a debt for which a member of a partnership is liable, other than a joint debt;

"separate estate" means the property of an insolvent member against whom an insolvency order has been made;

"separate expenses" means expenses incurred in the winding up of a corporate member, or in the bankruptcy of an individual member; and

"trustee of the partnership" means a person authorised by order made by virtue of article 11 of this Order to wind up the business of an insolvent partnership and to administer its property.

2(2) The definitions in paragraph (1), other than the first definition, shall be added to those in section 436 of the Act.

2(3) References in provisions of the Act applied by this Order to any provision of the Act so applied shall, unless the context otherwise requires, be construed as references to the provision as so applied.

2(4) Where, in any Schedule to this Order, all or any of the provisions of two or more sections of the Act are expressed to be modified by a single paragraph of the Schedule, the modification includes the combination of the provisions of those sections into the one or more sections set out in that paragraph.

History

In art.2(1) the definition of "insolvency proceedings" amended by the Insolvency (Miscellaneous Amendments) Regulations 2017 (SI 1017/1119) regs 1(1), (3), 2, Sch.2 paras 1, 2 as from 8 December 2017 subject to transitional and savings provision in para.10.

3 Interpretation: expressions appropriate to companies

3(1) This article applies for the interpretation in relation to insolvent partnerships of expressions appropriate to companies in provisions of the Act and of the Company Directors Disqualification Act 1986 applied by this Order, unless the contrary intention appears.

3(2) References to companies shall be construed as references to insolvent partnerships and all references to the registrar of companies shall be omitted.

3(3) References to shares of a company shall be construed–

(a) in relation to an insolvent partnership with capital, as references to rights to share in that capital; and

(b) in relation to an insolvent partnership without capital, as references to interests–

    (i) conferring any right to share in the profits or liability to contribute to the losses of the partnership, or

    (ii) giving rise to an obligation to contribute to the debts or expenses of the partnership in the event of a winding up.

3(4) Other expressions appropriate to companies shall be construed, in relation to an insolvent partnership, as references to the corresponding persons, officers, documents or organs (as the case may be) appropriate to a partnership.

PART II

VOLUNTARY ARRANGEMENTS

4 Voluntary arrangement of insolvent partnership

4(1) The provisions of Part I of, and Schedule A1 to, the Act shall apply in relation to an insolvent partnership, certain of those provisions being modified in such manner that, after modification, they are as set out in Schedule 1 to this Order.

History

Article 4(1) substituted by the Insolvent Partnerships (Amendment) (No.2) Order 2002 (SI 2002/2708) arts 1, 4 as from 1 January 2003 subject to transitional provisions contained in art.11(1), (3).

4(2) For the purposes of the provisions of the Act applied by paragraph (1), the provisions of the Act specified in paragraph (3) below, insofar as they relate to company voluntary arrangements, shall also apply in relation to insolvent partnerships.

4(3) The provisions referred to in paragraph (2) are–

(za) section 176AZA in Part IV,

(a) section 233 and section 233A in Part VI,

(b) Part VII, with the exception of section 250,

(c) Part XII,

(d) Part XIII,

(e) sections 411, 413, 414 and 419 in Part XV, and

(f) Parts XVI to XIX.

History
Article 4(3)(za) inserted by the Banks and Building Societies (Priorities on Insolvency) Order 2018 (SI 2018/1244) arts 1, 3, 15, 16 as from 19 December 2018 in relation to insolvency proceedings commenced on or after that date.

5 Voluntary arrangements of members of insolvent partnership

5(1) Where insolvency orders are made against an insolvent partnership and an insolvent member of that partnership in his capacity as such, Part I of the Act shall apply to corporate members and Part VIII to individual members of that partnership, with the modification that any reference to the creditors of the company or of the debtor, as the case may be, includes a reference to the creditors of the partnership.

5(2) Paragraph (1) is not to be construed as preventing the application of Part I or (as the case may be) Part VIII of the Act to any person who is a member of an insolvent partnership (whether or not a winding-up order has been made against that partnership) and against whom an insolvency order has not been made under this Order or under the Act.

PART III

ADMINISTRATION

6 Administration in relation to insolvent partnership

6(1) The provisions of Part II of, and Schedule B1 to, the Act shall apply in relation to an insolvent partnership, certain of those provisions being modified in such manner that, after modification, they are as set out in Schedule 2 to this Order.

6(2) In its application to insolvent partnerships, Part II of, and Schedule B1 to, the Act (as modified as set out in Schedule 2 to this Order) shall be read subject to paragraph (3).

6(3) For every reference to–

(a) "administrative receiver" there shall be substituted "agricultural receiver"; and

(b) "floating charge" there shall be substituted "agricultural floating charge".

6(4) For the purposes of the provisions of the Act applied by paragraph (1), the provisions of the Act specified in paragraph (5) below, insofar as they relate to the appointment of an administrator, shall also apply in relation to insolvent partnerships.

6(5) The provisions referred to in paragraph (4) are–

(za) section 176AZA in Part IV,

    (a)   Part VI,

    (b)   Part VII (with the exception of section 250),

    (c)   Part XII,

    (d)   Part XIII,

    (e)   sections 411, 413, 414 and 419 in Part XV, and

    (f)   Parts XVI to XIX.

6(6) For the purposes of this Article and the provisions of the Act applied by paragraph (1), "agricultural floating charge" shall be construed as a reference to a floating charge created under section 5 of the Agricultural Credits Act 1928.

History
Part III (art.6) substituted by the Insolvent Partnerships (Amendment) Order 2005 (SI 2005/1516) art.3 as from 1 July 2005 subject to transitional provisions contained in art.2 of that Order.
    Article 6(5)(za) inserted by the Banks and Building Societies (Priorities on Insolvency) Order 2018 (SI 2018/1244) arts 1, 3, 15, 17 as from 19 December 2018 in relation to insolvency proceedings commenced on or after that date.

PART IV

CREDITORS' ETC. WINDING-UP PETITIONS

7   Winding up of insolvent partnership as unregistered company on petition of creditor etc. where no concurrent petition presented against member

7(1) Subject to paragraph (2) below, the provisions of Part V of the Act shall apply in relation to the winding up of an insolvent partnership as an unregistered company on the petition of a creditor, of a liquidator (within the meaning of Article 2(b) of the EC Regulation) appointed in proceedings by virtue of Article 3(1) of the EC Regulation, of a temporary administrator (within the meaning of Article 38 of the EC Regulation), of a responsible insolvency practitioner, of the Secretary of State or of any other person other than a member, where no insolvency petition is presented by the petitioner against a member or former member of that partnership in his capacity as such.

7(2) Certain of the provisions referred to in paragraph (1) are modified in their application in relation to insolvent partnerships which are being wound up by virtue of that paragraph in such manner that, after modification, they are as set out in Part I of Schedule 3 to this Order.

7(3) The provisions of the Act specified in Part II of Schedule 3 to this Order shall apply as set out in that Part for the purposes of section 221(5) of the Act, as modified by Part I of that Schedule.

8   Winding up of insolvent partnership as unregistered company on the petition of creditor etc. where concurrent petitions presented against one or more members

8(1) Subject to paragraph (2) below, the provisions of Part V of the Act (other than sections 223 and 224), shall apply in relation to the winding up of an insolvent partnership as an unregistered company on the petition of a creditor, of a liquidator (within the meaning of Article 2(b) of the EC Regulation) appointed in proceedings by virtue of Article 3(1) of the EC Regulation, or of a temporary administrator (within the meaning of Article 38 of the EC Regulation) where insolvency petitions are presented by the petitioner against the partnership and against one or more members or former members of the partnership in their capacity as such.

8(2) Certain of the provisions referred to in paragraph (1) are modified in their application in relation to insolvent partnerships which are being wound up by virtue of that paragraph in such manner that, after modification, they are as set out in Part I of Schedule 4 to this Order.

8(3)   The provisions of the Act specified in Part II of Schedule 4 to this Order shall apply as set out in that Part for the purposes of section 221(5) of the Act, as modified by Part I of that Schedule.

8(4)   The provisions of the Act specified in paragraph (5) below, insofar as they relate to winding up of companies by the court in England and Wales on a creditor's petition, shall apply in relation to the winding up of a corporate member or former corporate member (in its capacity as such) of an insolvent partnership which is being wound up by virtue of paragraph (1).

8(5)   The provisions referred to in paragraph (4) are–

    (a)   Part IV,

    (b)   Part VI,

    (c)   Part VII, and

    (d)   Parts XII to XIX.

History
In art.8(5)(a) the words "(other than section 176A)" inserted by the Insolvent Partnerships (Amendment) Order 2005 (SI 2005/1516) art.4 as from 1 July 2005, and subsequently deleted by SI 2006/622 art.3.

8(6)   The provisions of the Act specified in paragraph (7) below, insofar as they relate to the bankruptcy of individuals in England and Wales on a petition presented by a creditor, shall apply in relation to the bankruptcy of an individual member or former individual member (in his capacity as such) of an insolvent partnership which is being wound up by virtue of paragraph (1).

8(7)   The provisions referred to in paragraph (6) are–

    (a)   Part IX (other than sections 269, 270, 287 and 297), and

    (b)   Parts X to XIX.

8(8)   Certain of the provisions referred to in paragraphs (4) and (6) are modified in their application in relation to the corporate or individual members or former corporate or individual members of insolvent partnerships in such manner that, after modification, they are as set out in Part II of Schedule 4 to this Order.

8(9)   The provisions of the Act applied by this Article shall further be modified so that references to a corporate or individual member include any former such member against whom an insolvency petition is being or has been presented by virtue of this Article.

PART V

MEMBERS' PETITIONS

9   Winding up of insolvent partnership as unregistered company on member's petition where no concurrent petition presented against member

9   The following provisions of the Act shall apply in relation to the winding up of an insolvent partnership as an unregistered company on the petition of a member where no insolvency petition is presented by the petitioner against a member of that partnership in his capacity as such–

    (a)   sections 117 and 221, modified in such manner that, after modification, they are as set out in Schedule 5 to this Order; and

    (b)   the other provisions of Part V of the Act, certain of those provisions being modified in such manner that, after modification, they are as set out in Part I of Schedule 3 to this Order.

10   Winding up of insolvent partnership as unregistered company on member's petition where concurrent petitions presented against all members

10(1)   The following provisions of the Act shall apply in relation to the winding up of an insolvent partnership as an unregistered company on a member's petition where insolvency petitions are presented by the petitioner against the partnership and against all its members in their capacity as such–

(a)   sections 117, 124, 125, 221, 264, 265 and 271 of the Act, modified in such manner that, after modification, they are as set out in Schedule 6 to this Order; and

(b)   sections 220, 225 and 227 to 229 in Part V of the Act, section 220 being modified in such manner that, after modification, it is as set out in Part I of Schedule 4 to this Order.

10(2)   The provisions of the Act specified in paragraph (3) below, insofar as they relate to winding up of companies by the court in England and Wales on a member's petition, shall apply in relation to the winding up of a corporate member (in its capacity as such) of an insolvent partnership which is wound up by virtue of paragraph (1).

10(3)   The provisions referred to in paragraph (2) are–

(a)   Part IV,

(b)   Part VI,

(c)   Part VII, and

(d)   Parts XII to XIX.

10(4)   The provisions of the Act specified in paragraph (5) below, insofar as they relate to the bankruptcy of individuals in England and Wales where a bankruptcy application is made by a debtor, shall apply in relation to the bankruptcy of an individual member (in his capacity as such) of an insolvent partnership which is being wound up by virtue of paragraph (1).

10(5)   The provisions referred to in paragraph (4) are–

(a)   Part IX (other than sections 287 and 297), and

(b)   Parts X to XIX.

10(6)   Certain of the provisions referred to in paragraphs (2) and (4) are modified in their application in relation to the corporate or individual members of insolvent partnerships in such manner that, after modification, they are as set out in Part II of Schedule 4 to this Order.

History
Article 10(6) substituted by the Insolvent Partnerships (Amendment) Order 2005 (SI 2005/1516) art.5(b) as from 1 July 2005.

   Article 10(1)(a) amended by the Insolvency (Miscellaneous Amendments) Regulations 2017 (SI 2017/1119) regs 1(1), (6), 2, Sch.2 paras 1, 3 as from 8 December 2017 subject to transitional and savings provision in para.10.

11   Insolvency proceedings not involving winding up of insolvent partnership as unregistered company where individual members present joint bankruptcy petition

11(1)   The provisions of the Act specified in paragraph (2) below shall apply in relation to the bankruptcy of the individual members of an insolvent partnership where those members jointly present a petition to the court for orders to be made for the bankruptcy of each of them in his capacity as a member of the partnership, and the winding up of the partnership business and administration of its property, without the partnership being wound up as an unregistered company under Part V of the Act.

11(2)   The provisions referred to in paragraph (1) are–

(a)   Part IX (other than section 287), and

(b)   Parts X to XIX,

insofar as they relate to the insolvency of individuals in England and Wales where a bankruptcy application is made by a debtor.

11(3)   Certain of the provisions referred to in paragraph (1) are modified in their application in relation to the individual members of insolvent partnerships in such manner that, after modification, they are as set out in Schedule 7 to this Order.

PART VI

PROVISIONS APPLYING IN INSOLVENCY PROCEEDINGS IN RELATION TO INSOLVENT PARTNERSHIPS

11A   Decision procedure in insolvency proceedings in relation to insolvent partnerships

11A   Sections 246ZE, 246ZF, 379ZA and 379ZB of the Act apply in insolvency proceedings in relation to insolvent partnerships with the modifications set out in Schedule 7A to this Order.

History
Article 11A inserted by the Deregulation Act 2015 and Small Business, Enterprise and Employment Act 2015 (Consequential Amendments) (Savings) Regulations 2017 (SI 2017/540) regs 1, 3, Sch.2 paras 2, 3 as from 6 April 2017.

12   Winding up of unregistered company which is a member of insolvent partnership being wound up by virtue of this Order

12   Where an insolvent partnership or other body which may be wound up under Part V of the Act as an unregistered company is itself a member of an insolvent partnership being so wound up, articles 8 and 10 above shall apply in relation to the latter insolvent partnership as though the former body were a corporate member of that partnership.

13   Deposit on petitions

13(1)   Where an order under section 414(4) or 415(3) of the Act (security for fees) provides for any sum to be deposited on presentation of a winding-up or bankruptcy petition, that sum shall, in the case of petitions presented by virtue of articles 8 and 10 above, only be required to be deposited in respect of the petition for winding up the partnership, but shall be treated as a deposit in respect of all those petitions.

13(2)   Production of evidence as to the sum deposited on presentation of the petition for winding up the partnership shall suffice for the filing in court of an insolvency petition against an insolvent member.

14   Supplemental powers of court

14(1)   [Amends IA 1986 s.168.]

14(2)   [Amends IA 1986 s.303.]

15   Meaning of "act as insolvency practitioner"

15(1)   [Amends IA 1986 s.388.]

PART VII

DISQUALIFICATION

16   Application of Company Directors Disqualification Act 1986

16   Where an insolvent partnership is wound up as an unregistered company under Part V of the Act, the provisions of sections 1, 1A, 5A, 6 to 10, 12C, 13 to 15C, 17, 19(c) and 20 of, and Schedule 1 to, the Company Directors Disqualification Act 1986 shall apply, certain of those provisions being modified in such manner that, after modification, they are as set out in Schedule 8 to this Order.

History
Article 16 amended by the Insolvency (Miscellaneous Amendments) Regulations 2017 (SI 2017/1119) regs 1(1), (6), 2, Sch.2 paras 1, 4 as from 8 December 2017 subject to transitional and savings provision in para.10.

PART VIII

MISCELLANEOUS

17 Forms

17(1) The forms contained in Schedule 9 to this Order shall be used in and in connection with proceedings by virtue of this Order, whether in the High Court or a county court.

17(2) The forms shall be used with such variations, if any, as the circumstances may require.

18 Application of subordinate legislation

18(1) The subordinate legislation specified in Schedule 10 to this Order shall apply as from time to time in force and with such modifications as the context requires for the purpose of giving effect to the provisions of the Act and of the Company Directors Disqualification Act 1986 which are applied by this Order.

18(2) In the case of any conflict between any provision of the subordinate legislation applied by paragraph (1) and any provision of this Order, the latter provision shall prevail.

19 Supplemental and transitional provisions

19(1) This Order does not apply in relation to any case in which a winding-up or a bankruptcy order was made under the Insolvent Partnerships Order 1986 in relation to a partnership or an insolvent member of a partnership, and where this Order does not apply the law in force immediately before this Order came into force continues to have effect.

19(2) Where winding-up or bankruptcy proceedings commenced under the provisions of the Insolvent Partnerships Order 1986 were pending in relation to a partnership or an insolvent member of a partnership immediately before this Order came into force, either–

(a) those proceedings shall be continued, after the coming into force of this Order, in accordance with the provisions of this Order, or

(b) if the court so directs, they shall be continued under the provisions of the 1986 Order, in which case the law in force immediately before this Order came into force continues to have effect.

19(3) For the purpose of paragraph (2) above, winding-up or bankruptcy proceedings are pending if a statutory or written demand has been served or a winding-up or bankruptcy petition has been presented.

19(4) Nothing in this Order is to be taken as preventing a petition being presented against an insolvent partnership under section 367 of the Financial Services and Markets Act 2000, or any other enactment except where paragraph 12 of Schedule A1 to the Act, as applied by this Order, has the effect of preventing a petition being so presented.

History
In art.19(4) the words "except where paragraph 12 of Schedule A1 to the Act, as applied by this Order, has the effect of preventing a petition being so presented" inserted by the Insolvent Partnerships (Amendment) (No.2) Order 2002 (SI 2002/2708) arts 1, 5 as from 1 January 2003 subject to transitional provisions contained in arts 11(1), (3).

19(5) Nothing in this Order is to be taken as preventing any creditor or creditors owed one or more debts by an insolvent partnership from presenting a petition under the Act against one or more members of the partnership liable for that debt or those debts (as the case may be) without including the others and without presenting a petition for the winding up of the partnership as an unregistered company.

19(6)   Bankruptcy proceedings may be consolidated by virtue of article 14(2) above irrespective of whether they were commenced under the Bankruptcy Act 1914 or the Insolvency Act 1986 or by virtue of the Insolvent Partnerships Order 1986 or this Order, and the court shall, in the case of proceedings commenced under or by virtue of different enactments, make provision for the manner in which the consolidated proceedings are to be conducted.

20   Revocation

20   The Insolvent Partnerships Order 1986 is hereby revoked.

SCHEDULE 1

MODIFIED PROVISIONS OF PART I OF, AND SCHEDULE A1 TO, THE ACT (COMPANY VOLUNTARY ARRANGEMENTS) AS APPLIED BY ARTICLE 4

Article 4

PART I

MODIFIED PROVISIONS OF SECTIONS 1 TO 7B OF THE ACT

For sections 1 to 7B of the Act there shall be substituted:–

"PART I

PARTNERSHIP VOLUNTARY ARRANGEMENTS

The proposal

1   Those who may propose an arrangement

1(1)   The members of an insolvent partnership (other than one which is in administration, or which is being wound up as an unregistered company, or in respect of which an order has been made by virtue of article 11 of the Insolvent Partnerships Order 1994) may make a proposal under this Part to the partnership's creditors for a composition in satisfaction of the debts of the partnership or a scheme of arrangement of its affairs (from here on referred to, in either case, as a "voluntary arrangement").

1(2)   A proposal under this Part is one which provides for some person ("the nominee") to act in relation to the voluntary arrangement either as trustee or otherwise for the purpose of supervising its implementation; and the nominee must be a person who is qualified to act as an insolvency practitioner, in relation to the voluntary arrangement.

1(3)   Such a proposal may also be made–

(a)   where the partnership is in administration, by the administrator,

(b)   where the partnership is being wound up as an unregistered company, by the liquidator, and

(c)   where an order has been made by virtue of article 11 of the Insolvent Partnerships Order 1994, by the trustee of the partnership.

1(4)   (Omitted by the Insolvent Partnerships (Amendment) Order 2005 (SI 2005/1516) art.6(1), (2)(c) as from 1 July 2005.)

1A   Moratorium

1A(1)   Where the members of an eligible insolvent partnership intend to make a proposal for a voluntary arrangement, they may take steps to obtain a moratorium for the insolvent partnership.

1A(2)   Subject to subsections (3), (4), (5), (6) and (7), the provisions of Schedule A1 to this Act have effect with respect to–

(a)   insolvent partnerships eligible for a moratorium under this section,

(b)   the procedure for obtaining such a moratorium,

(c)   the effects of such a moratorium, and

(d)   the procedure applicable (in place of sections 2 to 6 and 7) in relation to the approval and implementation of a voluntary arrangement where such a moratorium is or has been in force.

1A(3)   Certain of the provisions applied in relation to insolvent partnerships by virtue of subsection (2) are modified in their application in relation to insolvent partnerships in such manner that, after modification, they are as set out in Part II of Schedule 1 to the Insolvent Partnerships Order 1994.

1A(4)   Paragraphs 4A, 4B, 4C, 4D, 4E, 4F, 4G, 4H, 4I, 4J, 4K, 5, 7(4), 8(8), 32(7), 34(2), 41(5) and 45 of Schedule A1 to this Act shall not apply.

1A(5)   An insolvent partnership is not liable to a fine under paragraphs 16(2), 17(3), 18(3), 19(3), 22 or 23(1) of Schedule A1 to the Act.

1A(6)   Notwithstanding subsection (5) an officer of an insolvent partnership may be liable to imprisonment or a fine under the paragraphs referred to in that subsection in the same manner as an officer of a company.

1A(7)   In the application of Schedule A1, and the application of the entries in Schedule 10 relating to offences under Schedule A1, to insolvent partnerships–

(a)   references to the directors or members of a company shall be construed as references to the members of an insolvent partnership,

(b)   references to officers of a company shall be construed as references to the officers of an insolvent partnership,

(c)   references to a meeting of a company shall be construed as references to a meeting of the members of an insolvent partnership, and

(d)   references to a floating charge shall be construed as references to a floating charge created under section 5 of the Agricultural Credits Act 1928.

2   Procedure where nominee is not the liquidator, administrator or trustee

2(1)   This section applies where the nominee under section 1 is not the liquidator, administrator or trustee of the insolvent partnership and the members of the partnership do not propose to take steps to obtain a moratorium under section 1A for the insolvent partnership.

2(2)   The nominee shall, within 28 days (or such longer period as the court may allow) after he is given notice of the proposal for a voluntary arrangement, submit a report to the court stating–

(a)   whether, in his opinion, the proposed voluntary arrangement has a reasonable prospect of being approved and implemented,

(b)   whether, in his opinion, the proposal should be considered by a meeting of the members of the partnership and by the partnership's creditors, and

(c)   if in his opinion it should, the date on which, and time and place at which, he proposes a meeting should be held.

2(3)   The nominee shall also state in his report whether there are in existence any insolvency proceedings in respect of the insolvent partnership or any of its members.

2(4)   For the purposes of enabling the nominee to prepare his report, the person intending to make the proposal shall submit to the nominee–

(a)   a document setting out the terms of the proposed voluntary arrangement, and

(b)   a statement of the partnership's affairs containing–

(i)   such particulars of the partnership's creditors and of the partnership's debts and other liabilities and of the partnership property as may be prescribed, and

(ii)   such other information as may be prescribed.

2(5)   The court may–

(a)   on an application made by the person intending to make the proposal, in a case where the nominee has failed to submit the report required by this section or has died, or

(b)   on an application made by that person or the nominee, in a case where it is impracticable or inappropriate for the nominee to continue to act as such,

direct that the nominee be replaced as such by another person qualified to act as an insolvency practitioner in relation to the voluntary arrangement.

History
Substituted s.2(2)(b), (c) substituted by the Deregulation Act 2015 and Small Business, Enterprise and Employment Act 2015 (Consequential Amendments) (Savings) Regulations 2017 (SI 2017/540) regs 1, 3, Sch.2 para.4(1), (2) as from 6 April 2017.

3   Summoning of meetings

3(1)   Where the nominee under section 1 is not the liquidator, administrator or trustee of the insolvent partnership, and it has been reported to the court under section 2(2) that the proposal should be considered by a meeting of the members of the partnership and by the partnership's creditors, the person making the report shall (unless the court otherwise directs)–

(a)   summon a meeting of the members of the partnership to consider the proposal for the time, date and place proposed in the report, and

(b)   seek a decision from the partnership's creditors as to whether they approve the proposal.

3(2)   Where the nominee is the liquidator, administrator or trustee of the insolvent partnership, he must–

(a)   summon a meeting of the members of the partnership to consider the proposal for such time, date and place as he thinks fit, and

(b)   seek a decision from the partnership's creditors as to whether they approve the proposal.

3(3)   A decision of the partnership's creditors as to whether they approve the proposal is to be made by a qualifying decision procedure.

3(4)   Notice of the qualifying decision procedure must be given to every creditor of the partnership of whose claim and address the person summoning the meeting is aware.

History
Substituted s.3 amended by the Deregulation Act 2015 and Small Business, Enterprise and Employment Act 2015 (Consequential Amendments) (Savings) Regulations 2017 (SI 2017/540) regs 1, 3, Sch.2 paras 2, 4(1), (3) as from 6 April 2017.

Consideration and implementation of proposal

4   Decisions of the members of the partnership and its creditors

4(1)   This section applies where, under section 3–

(a)   a meeting of the members of the partnership is summoned to consider the proposed voluntary arrangement, and

(b)   the partnership's creditors are asked to decide whether to approve the proposed voluntary arrangement.

4(1A)   The members of the partnership and its creditors may approve the proposed voluntary arrangement with or without modifications.

4(2)   The modifications may include one conferring the functions proposed to be conferred on the nominee on another person qualified to act as an insolvency practitioner in relation to the voluntary arrangement.

But they shall not include any modification by virtue of which the proposal ceases to be a proposal such as is mentioned in section 1.

4(3) Neither the members of the partnership nor its creditors may approve any proposal or modification which affects the right of a secured creditor of the partnership to enforce his security, except with the concurrence of the creditor concerned.

4(4) Subject as follows, neither the members of the partnership nor its creditors may approve any proposal or modification under which–

(a) any preferential debt of the partnership is to be paid otherwise than in priority to such of its debts as are not preferential debts,

(aa) any ordinary preferential debt of the partnership is to be paid otherwise than in priority to any secondary preferential debts that it may have,

(b) a preferential creditor of the partnership is to be paid an amount in respect of an ordinary preferential debt that bears to that debt a smaller proportion than is borne to another ordinary preferential debt by the amount that is to be paid in respect of that other debt,

(c) a preferential creditor of the partnership is to be paid an amount in respect of a secondary preferential debt that bears to that debt a smaller proportion than is borne to another secondary preferential debt by the amount that is to be paid in respect of that other debt, or

(d) in the case of a company which is a relevant financial institution (see section 387A), any non-preferential debt is to be paid otherwise than in accordance with the rules in section 176AZA(2) or (3).

However, such a proposal or modification may be approved with the concurrence of the creditor concerned.

4(5) Subject as above, the meeting of the members of the partnership and the qualifying decision procedure shall be conducted in accordance with the rules.

4(6) After the conclusion of the meeting of the members of the partnership in accordance with the rules, the chairman of the meeting shall report the result of the meeting to the court, and, immediately after reporting to the court, shall give notice of the result of the meeting to all those who were sent notice of the meeting in accordance with the rules.

4(6A) After the partnership's creditors have decided whether to approve the proposed voluntary arrangement the person who sought the decision must–

(a) report the creditors' decision to the court, and

(b) immediately after reporting to the court, give notice of the creditors' decision to everyone who was invited to consider the proposal or to whom notice of a decision procedure or meeting was delivered.

4(7) References in this section to preferential debts, ordinary preferential debts, secondary preferential debts and preferential creditors are to be read in accordance with section 386 in Part XII of this Act.

History
Substituted s.4(4)(a), (b), 4(7) amended and s.4(4)(aa), (c) inserted by the Banks and Building Societies (Depositor Preference and Priorities) Order 2014 (SI 2014/3486) art.12(1), (2) as from 1 January 2015. Substituted s.4 amended by the Deregulation Act 2015 and Small Business, Enterprise and Employment Act 2015 (Consequential Amendments) (Savings) Regulations 2017 (SI 2017/540) regs 1, 3, Sch.2 paras 2, 4(1), (4) as from 6 April 2017.

Modified para.4(4)(d) inserted and following words amended by the Banks and Building Societies (Priorities on Insolvency) Order 2018 (SI 2018/1244) arts 1, 3, 15, 18 as from 19 December 2018 in relation to insolvency proceedings commenced on or after that date.

Approval of arrangement

4A(1) This section applies to a decision, under section 4, with respect to the approval of a proposed voluntary arrangement.

4A(2) The decision has effect if, in accordance with the rules–

(a) it has been taken by the meeting of the members of the partnership summoned under section 3 and by the partnership's creditors pursuant to that section, or

(b) (subject to any order made under subsection (6)) it has been taken by the partnership's creditors pursuant to that section.

4A(3) If the decision taken by the partnership's creditors differs from that taken by the meeting of the members of the partnership, a member of the partnership may apply to court.

4A(4) An application under subsection (3) shall not be made after the end of the period of 28 days beginning with–

(a) the day on which the decision was taken by the partnership's creditors, or

(b) where the decision of the meeting of the members of the partnership was taken on a later day, that day.

4A(5) Where a member of an insolvent partnership which is regulated applies to the court under subsection (3), the appropriate regulator is entitled to be heard on the application.

4A(5A) "The appropriate regulator" means–

(a) where the partnership is a PRA-regulated partnership, the Prudential Regulation Authority and the Financial Conduct Authority;

(b) in any other case the Financial Conduct Authority.

4A(5B) For the purposes of subsection (5A), a "PRA-regulated partnership" means a partnership which–

(a) is or has been, a PRA-authorised person (within the meaning of the Financial Services and Markets Act 2000),

(b) is, or has been, an appointed representative within the meaning given by section 39 of that Act, whose principal (or one of whose principals) is, or was, a PRA-authorised person, or

(c) is carrying on, or has carried on, a PRA-regulated activity (within the meaning of that Act) in contravention of the general prohibition under section 19 of that Act.

4A(6) On an application under subsection (3), the court may–

(a) order the decision of the meeting of the members of the partnership to have effect instead of the decision of the partnership's creditors, or

(b) make such other order as it thinks fit.

4A(7) In this section "regulated" in relation to an insolvent partnership means a person who–

(a) is, or has been, an authorised person within the meaning given by section 31 of the Financial Services and Markets Act 2000,

(b) is, or has been, an appointed representative within the meaning given by section 39 of that Act, or

(c) is carrying on, or has carried on, a regulated activity, within the meaning given by section 22 of that Act, in contravention of the general prohibition within the meaning given by section 19 of that Act.

History
Substituted s.4A(5) substituted and s.4A(5A), (5B) inserted by the Financial Services Act 2012 (Consequential Amendments and Transitional Provisions) Order 2013 (SI 2013/472) art.3 and Sch.2 para.11(a) as from 1 April 2013. Substituted s.4A(2), (3), (4)(a), (6)(a) amended by the Deregulation Act 2015 and Small Business, Enterprise and Employment Act 2015 (Consequential Amendments) (Savings) Regulations 2017 (SI 2017/540) regs 1, 3, Sch.2 paras 2, 4(1), (5) as from 6 April 2017.

5 Effect of approval

5(1) This section applies where a decision approving a voluntary arrangement has effect under section 4A.

5(2) The voluntary arrangement–

(a) takes effect as if made by the members of the partnership at the time the creditors decided to approve the voluntary arrangement, and

(b) binds every person who in accordance with the rules–

(i) was entitled to vote in the qualifying decision procedure by which the creditors' decision to approve the voluntary arrangement was made, or

(ii)   would have been so entitled if he had had notice of the procedure,

as if he were a party to the voluntary arrangement.

5(2A)   If–

(a)   when the arrangement ceases to have effect any amount payable under the arrangement to a person bound by virtue of subsection 2(b)(ii) has not been paid, and

(b)   the arrangement did not come to an end prematurely,

the insolvent partnership shall at that time become liable to pay to that person the amount payable under the arrangement.

5(3)   Subject as follows, if the partnership is being wound up as an unregistered company, or is in administration or an order by virtue of article 11 of the Insolvent Partnerships Order 1994 is in force, the court may do one or both of the following, namely–

(a)   by order–

(i)   stay all proceedings in the winding up or in the proceedings under the order made by virtue of the said article 11 (as the case may be), including any related insolvency proceedings of a member of the partnership in his capacity as such, or

(ii)   provide for the appointment of the administrator to cease to have effect;

(b)   give such directions as it thinks appropriate for facilitating the implementation of the voluntary arrangement with respect to–

(i)   the conduct of the winding up, the proceedings by virtue of the said article 11 or the administration (as the case may be), and

(ii)   the conduct of any related insolvency proceedings as referred to in paragraph (a)(i) above.

5(4)   The court shall not make an order under subsection (3)(a)–

(a)   at any time before the end of the period of 28 days beginning with the first day on which each of the reports required by section 4(6) and (6A) has been made to the court, or

(b)   at any time when an application under the next section or an appeal in respect of such an application is pending, or at any time in the period within which such an appeal may be brought.

History

Substituted s.5(2), (4) amended by the Deregulation Act 2015 and Small Business, Enterprise and Employment Act 2015 (Consequential Amendments) (Savings) Regulations 2017 (SI 2017/540) regs 1, 3, Sch.2 paras 2, 4(1), (6) as from 6 April 2017.

6   Challenge of decisions

6(1)   Subject to this section, an application to the court may be made, by any of the persons specified below, on one or both of the following grounds, namely–

(a)   that a voluntary arrangement which has effect under section 4A unfairly prejudices the interests of a creditor, member or contributory of the partnership;

(b)   that there has been some material irregularity at or in relation to the meeting of the members of the partnership or in the relevant qualifying decision procedure.

6(2)   The persons who may apply under this section are–

(a)   a person entitled, in accordance with the rules, to vote at the meeting of the members of the partnership or in the relevant qualifying decision procedure;

(b)   a person who would have been entitled, in accordance with the rules, to vote in the relevant qualifying decision procedure if he had had notice of it;

(c)   the nominee or any person who has replaced him under section 2(5) or 4(2); and

    (d)   if the partnership is being wound up as an unregistered company or is in administration or an order by virtue of article 11 of the Insolvent Partnerships Order 1994 is in force, the liquidator, administrator or trustee of the partnership.

6(3)   An application under this section shall not be made–

    (a)   after the end of the period of 28 days beginning with the first day on which each of the reports required by section 4(6) and (6A) has been made to the court, or

    (b)   in the case of a person who was not given notice of the relevant qualifying decision procedure, after the end of the period of 28 days beginning with the day on which he became aware that the relevant qualifying decision procedure had taken place,

but (subject to that) an application made by a person within subsection (2)(b) on the ground that the voluntary arrangement prejudices his interests may be made after the voluntary arrangement has ceased to have effect, unless it came to an end prematurely.

6(4)   Where on such an application the court is satisfied as to either of the grounds mentioned in subsection (1), it may do any of the following, namely–

    (a)   revoke or suspend any decision approving the voluntary arrangement which has effect under section 4A or, in a case falling within subsection (1)(b), any decision taken by the meeting of the members of the partnership, or in the relevant qualifying decision procedure, which has effect under that section;

    (b)   give a direction to any person for the summoning of a further meeting of the members of the partnership to consider any revised proposal the person who made the original proposal may make or, in a case falling within subsection (1)(b) and relating to the meeting of the members of the partnership, a further meeting of the members of the partnership to reconsider the original proposal;

    (c)   direct any person–

        (i)   to seek a decision from the partnership's creditors (using a qualifying decision procedure) as to whether they approve any revised proposal the person who made the original proposal may make, or

        (ii)   in a case falling within subsection (1)(b) and relating to the relevant qualifying decision procedure, to seek a decision from the partnership's creditors (using a qualifying decision procedure) as to whether they approve the original proposal.

6(5)   Where at any time after giving a direction under subsection (4)(b) or (c) in relation to a revised proposal the court is satisfied that the person who made the original proposal does not intend to submit a revised proposal, the court shall revoke the direction and revoke or suspend any decision approving the voluntary arrangement which has effect under section 4A.

6(6)   In a case where the court, on an application under this section with respect to any meeting or relevant qualifying decision procedure–

    (a)   gives a direction under subsection (4)(b) or (c), or

    (b)   revokes or suspends an approval under subsection (4)(a) or (5),

the court may give such supplemental directions as it thinks fit, and, in particular, directions with respect to things done under the voluntary arrangement since it took effect.

6(7)   Except in pursuance of the preceding provisions of this section,

    (a)   a decision taken at a meeting of the members of the partnership summoned under section 3 is not invalidated by any irregularity at or in relation to the meeting, and

    (b)   a decision of the creditors of the partnership made in the relevant qualifying decision procedure is not invalidated by any irregularity in relation to the relevant qualifying decision procedure.

History
Substituted s.6 amended by the Deregulation Act 2015 and Small Business, Enterprise and Employment Act 2015 (Consequential Amendments) (Savings) Regulations 2017 (SI 2017/540) regs 1, 3, Sch.2 paras 2, 4(1), (7) as from 6 April 2017.

6A   False representations, etc.

6A(1)   If, for the purpose of obtaining the approval of the members or creditors of an insolvent partnership or of the members or creditors of any of its members to a proposal for a voluntary arrangement in relation to the partnership or any of its members, a person who is an officer of the partnership or an officer (which for this purpose includes a shadow director) of a corporate member in relation to which a voluntary arrangement is proposed–

(a)   makes a false representation, or

(b)   fraudulently does, or omits to do, anything,

he commits an offence.

6A(2)   Subsection (1) applies even if the proposal is not approved.

6A(3)   A person guilty of an offence under this section is liable to imprisonment or a fine, or both.

7   Implementation of proposal

7(1)   This section applies where a voluntary arrangement has effect under section 4A.

7(2)   The person who is for the time being carrying out in relation to the voluntary arrangement the functions conferred–

(a)   on the nominee by virtue of the approval of the voluntary arrangement by the members of the partnership or its creditors (or both) pursuant to section 3, or

(b)   by virtue of section 2(5) or 4(2) on a person other than the nominee,

shall be known as the supervisor of the voluntary arrangement.

7(3)   If any of the partnership's creditors or any other person is dissatisfied by any act, omission or decision of the supervisor, he may apply to the court; and on the application the court may–

(a)   confirm, reverse or modify any act or decision of the supervisor,

(b)   give him directions, or

(c)   make such other order as it thinks fit.

7(4)   The supervisor–

(a)   may apply to the court for directions in relation to any particular matter arising under the voluntary arrangement, and

(b)   is included among the persons who may apply to the court for the winding up of the partnership as an unregistered company or for an administration order to be made in relation to it.

7(5)   The court may, whenever–

(a)   it is expedient to appoint a person to carry out the functions of the supervisor, and

(b)   it is inexpedient, difficult or impracticable for an appointment to be made without the assistance of the court,

make an order appointing a person who is qualified to act as an insolvency practitioner in relation to the voluntary arrangement, either in substitution for the existing supervisor or to fill a vacancy.

7(6)   The power conferred by subsection (5) is exercisable so as to increase the number of persons exercising the functions of supervisor or, where there is more than one person exercising those functions, so as to replace one or more of those persons.

History

Substituted s.7(2)(a) amended by the Deregulation Act 2015 and Small Business, Enterprise and Employment Act 2015 (Consequential Amendments) (Savings) Regulations 2017 (SI 2017/540) regs 1, 3, Sch.2 paras 2, 4(1), (8) as from 6 April 2017.

7A   Prosecution of delinquent officers of partnership

7A(1)   This section applies where a moratorium under section 1A has been obtained for an insolvent partnership or the approval of a voluntary arrangement in relation to an insolvent partnership has taken effect under section 4A or paragraph 36 of Schedule A1.

7A(2)   If it appears to the nominee or supervisor that any past or present officer of the insolvent partnership has been guilty of any offence in connection with the moratorium or, as the case may be, voluntary arrangement for which such officer is criminally liable, the nominee or supervisor shall forthwith–

(a)   report the matter to the Secretary of State, and

(b)   provide the Secretary of State with such information and give him such access to and facilities for inspecting and taking copies of documents (being information or documents in the possession or under the control of the nominee or supervisor and relating to the matter in question) as the Secretary of State requires.

7A(3)   Where a prosecuting authority institutes criminal proceedings following any report under subsection (2), the nominee or supervisor, and every officer and agent of the insolvent partnership past or present (other than the defendant), shall give the authority all assistance in connection with the prosecution which he is reasonably able to give.

For this purpose–

"agent" includes any banker or solicitor of the insolvent partnership and any person employed by the insolvent partnership as auditor, whether that person is or is not an officer of the insolvent partnership,

"prosecuting authority" means the Director of Public Prosecutions or the Secretary of State.

7A(4)   The court may, on the application of the prosecuting authority, direct any person referred to in subsection (3) to comply with that subsection if he has failed to do so.

7B   Arrangements coming to an end prematurely

7B   For the purposes of this Part, a voluntary arrangement the approval of which has taken effect under section 4A or paragraph 36 of Schedule A1 comes to an end prematurely if, when it ceases to have effect, it has not been fully implemented in respect of all persons bound by the arrangement by virtue of section 5(2)(b)(i) or, as the case may be, paragraph 37(2)(b)(i) of Schedule A1."

PART II

MODIFIED PROVISIONS OF SCHEDULE A1 TO THE ACT

The following provisions of Schedule A1 to the Act are modified so as to read as follows:

"**3(1)**   An insolvent partnership meets the requirements of this paragraph if the qualifying conditions are met–

(a)   in the year ending with the date of filing, or

(b)   in the tax year of the insolvent partnership which ended last before that date.

3(2)   For the purposes of sub-paragraph (1) the qualifying conditions are met by an insolvent partnership in a period if, in that period, it satisfies two or more of the requirements set out in sub-paragraph (3).

3(3)   The qualifying conditions referred to in this paragraph are–

(a)   turnover of not more than £5.6 million,

(b)   assets of not more than £2.8 million, and

(c)   no more than 50 employees.

3(4)   For the purposes of sub-paragraph (3)–

(a)   the total of turnover is the amount which is or would be, as the case may be, entered as turnover in the partnership's tax return,

(b)   the total of assets is the amount which–

    (i)   in the case of the period referred to in paragraph 3(1)(a), is entered in the partnership's statement of affairs which must be filed with the court under paragraph 7(1)(b), or

    (ii)   in the case of the period referred to in paragraph 3(1)(b), would be entered in the partnership's statement of affairs had it prepared such a statement on the last day of the period to which the amount for turnover is calculated for the purposes of paragraph 3(4)(a),

  (c)   the number of employees is the average number of persons employed by the insolvent partnership–

    (i)   in the case of the period referred to in paragraph 3(1)(a), in the period ending with the date of filing,

    (ii)   in the case of the period referred to in paragraph 3(1)(b), in the period to which the amount for turnover is calculated for the purposes of paragraph 3(4)(a).

3(5)   Where the period covered by the qualifying conditions in respect of the insolvent partnership is not a year the total of turnover referred to in paragraph 3(3)(a) shall be proportionately adjusted.

3(6)   The average number of persons employed by the insolvent partnership shall be calculated as follows–

  (a)   by ascertaining the number of persons employed by it under contracts of service for each month of the year (whether throughout the month or not),

  (b)   by adding those figures together, and

  (c)   by dividing the resulting figure by the number of months during which persons were so employed by it during the year.

3(7)   In this paragraph–

"tax return" means a return under section 12AA of the Taxes Management Act 1970,

"tax year" means the 12 months beginning with 6th April in any year.

4(1)   An insolvent partnership is excluded from being eligible for a moratorium if, on the date of filing–

  (a)   the partnership is in administration,

  (b)   the insolvent partnership is being wound up as an unregistered company,

  (c)   there is an agricultural receiver of the insolvent partnership,

  (d)   a voluntary arrangement has effect in relation to the insolvent partnership,

  (e)   there is a provisional liquidator of the insolvent partnership,

  (f)   a moratorium has been in force for the insolvent partnership at any time during the period of 12 months ending with the date of filing and–

    (i)   no voluntary arrangement had effect at the time at which the moratorium came to an end, or

    (ii)   a voluntary arrangement which had effect at any time in that period has come to an end prematurely,

  (g)   a voluntary arrangement in relation to the insolvent partnership which had effect in pursuance of a proposal under section 1(3) has come to an end prematurely and, during the period of 12 months ending with the date of filing, an order under section 5(3)(a) has been made, or

  (h)   an order has been made by virtue of article 11 of the Insolvent Partnerships Order 1994.

4(2)   Sub-paragraph (1)(b) does not apply to an insolvent partnership which, by reason of a winding-up order made after the date of filing, is treated as being wound up on that date.

12   Effect on creditors, etc.

12(1)   During the period for which a moratorium is in force for an insolvent partnership–

  (a)   no petition may be presented for the winding-up of the insolvent partnership as an unregistered company,

  (b)   no meeting of the members of the partnership may be called or requisitioned except with the consent of the nominee or the leave of the court and subject (where the court gives leave) to such terms as the court may impose,

(c)   no order may be made for the winding-up of the insolvent partnership as an unregistered company,

(d)   no administration application may be made in respect of the partnership,

(da) no administrator of the partnership may be appointed under paragraph 14 or 22 of Schedule B1,

(e)   no agricultural receiver of the partnership may be appointed except with the leave of the court and subject to such terms as the court may impose,

(f)   no landlord or other person to whom rent is payable may exercise any rights of forfeiture by peaceable re-entry in relation to premises forming part of the partnership property or let to one or more officers of the partnership in their capacity as such in respect of a failure by the partnership or one or more officers of the partnership to comply with any term or condition of the tenancy of such premises, except with the leave of the court and subject to such terms as the court may impose,

(g)   no other steps may be taken to enforce any security over the partnership property, or to repossess goods in the possession, under any hire-purchase agreement, of one or more officers of the partnership in their capacity as such, except with the leave of the court and subject to such terms as the court may impose,

(h)   no other proceedings and no execution or other legal process may be commenced or continued, and no distress may be levied, against the insolvent partnership or the partnership property except with the leave of the court and subject to such terms as the court may impose,

(i)   no petition may be presented, and no order may be made, by virtue of article 11 of the Insolvent Partnerships Order 1994, and

(j)   no application or order may be made under section 35 of the Partnership Act 1890 in respect of the insolvent partnership.

12(2)   Where a petition, other than an excepted petition, for the winding-up of the insolvent partnership has been presented before the beginning of the moratorium, section 127 shall not apply in relation to any disposition of partnership property, any transfer of an interest in the insolvent partnership or alteration in status of a member of the partnership made during the moratorium or at a time mentioned in paragraph 37(5)(a).

12(3)   Paragraph (a) of sub-paragraph (1) does not apply to an excepted petition and, where such a petition has been presented before the beginning of the moratorium or is presented during the moratorium, paragraphs (b) and (c) of that sub-paragraph do not apply in relation to proceedings on the petition.

12(4)   For the purposes of this paragraph, "excepted petition" means a petition under–

(a)   article 7(1) of the Insolvent Partnerships Order 1994 presented by the Secretary of State on the grounds mentioned in subsections (b), (c) and (d) of section 124A of this Act,

(b)   section 72 of the Financial Services Act 1986 on the ground mentioned in subsection (1)(b) of that section,

(c)   section 92 of the Banking Act 1987 on the ground mentioned in subsection (1)(b) of that section, or

(d)   section 367 of the Financial Services and Markets Act 2000 on the ground mentioned in subsection (3)(b) of that section.

20   Disposal of charged property, etc

20(1)   This paragraph applies where–

(a)   any partnership property of the insolvent partnership is subject to a security, or

(b)   any goods are in possession of one or more officers of the partnership in their capacity as such under a hire-purchase agreement.

20(2)   If the holder of the security consents, or the court gives leave, the insolvent partnership may dispose of the property as if it were not subject to the security.

20(3)   If the owner of the goods consents, or the court gives leave, the insolvent partnership may dispose of the goods as if all rights of the owner under the hire-purchase agreement were vested in the members of the partnership.

20(4) Where property subject to a security which, as created, was a floating charge is disposed of under sub-paragraph (2), the holder of the security has the same priority in respect of any partnership property directly or indirectly representing the property disposed of as he would have had in respect of the property subject to the security.

20(5) Sub-paragraph (6) applies to the disposal under sub-paragraph (2) or (as the case may be) sub-paragraph (3) of–

(a)   any property subject to a security other than a security which, as created, was a floating charge, or

(b)   any goods in the possession of one or more officers of the partnership in their capacity as such under a hire-purchase agreement.

20(6) It shall be a condition of any consent or leave under sub-paragraph (2) or (as the case may be) sub-paragraph (3) that–

(a)   the net proceeds of the disposal, and

(b)   where those proceeds are less than such amount as may be agreed, or determined by the court, to be the net amount which would be realised on a sale of the property or goods in the open market by a willing vendor, such sums as may be required to make good the deficiency,

shall be applied towards discharging the sums secured by the security or payable under the hire-purchase agreement.

20(7) Where a condition imposed in pursuance of sub-paragraph (6) relates to two or more securities, that condition requires–

(a)   the net proceeds of the disposal, and

(b)   where paragraph (b) of sub-paragraph (6) applies, the sums mentioned in that paragraph,

to be applied towards discharging the sums secured by those securities in the order of their priorities.

20(8) In this paragraph "floating charge" means a floating charge created under section 5 of the Agricultural Credits Act 1928.

37   Effect of approval of voluntary arrangement

37(1) This paragraph applies where a decision approving a voluntary arrangement has effect under paragraph 36.

37(2) The approved voluntary arrangement–

(a)   takes effect as if made by the members of the partnership at the time the creditors decided to approve the voluntary arrangement, and

(b)   binds every person who in accordance with the rules–

(i)   was entitled to vote in the qualifying decision procedure by which the creditors' decision to approve the voluntary arrangement was made, or

(ii)   would have been so entitled if he had had notice of the procedure,

as if he were a party to the voluntary arrangement.

37(3) If–

(a)   when the arrangement ceases to have effect any amount payable under the arrangement to a person bound by virtue of sub-paragraph (2)(b)(ii) has not been paid, and

(b)   the arrangement did not come to an end prematurely,

the insolvent partnership shall at that time become liable to pay to that person the amount payable under the arrangement.

37(4) Where a petition for the winding-up of the insolvent partnership as an unregistered company or a petition by virtue of article 11 of the Insolvent Partnerships Order 1994, other than an excepted petition within the meaning of paragraph 12, was presented before the beginning of the moratorium, the court shall dismiss the petition.

37(5)   The court shall not dismiss a petition under sub-paragraph (4)–

(a)   at any time before the end of the period of 28 days beginning with the first day on which each of the reports required by paragraph 30(3) and (4) has been made to the court, or

(b)   at any time when an application under paragraph 38 or an appeal in respect of such an application is pending, or at any time in the period within which such an appeal may be brought.

40   Challenge of actions of officers of insolvent partnership

40(1)   This paragraph applies in relation to acts or omissions of the officers of a partnership during a moratorium.

40(2)   A creditor or member of the insolvent partnership may apply to the court for an order under this paragraph on the ground–

(a)   that the partnership's affairs and business and partnership property are being or have been managed by the officers of the partnership in a manner which is unfairly prejudicial to the interests of its creditors or members generally, or of some part of its creditors or members (including at least the petitioner), or

(b)   that any actual or proposed act or omission of the officers of the partnership is or would be so prejudicial.

40(3)   An application for an order under this paragraph may be made during or after the moratorium.

40(4)   On an application for an order under this paragraph the court may–

(a)   make such order as it thinks fit for giving relief in respect of the matters complained of,

(b)   adjourn the hearing conditionally or unconditionally, or

(c)   make an interim order or any other order that it thinks fit.

40(5)   An order under this paragraph may in particular–

(a)   regulate the management by the officers of the partnership of the partnership's affairs and business and partnership property during the remainder of the moratorium,

(b)   require the officers of the partnership to refrain from doing or continuing an act complained of by the petitioner, or to do an act which the petitioner has complained they have omitted to do,

(c)   require the summoning of a meeting of members of the partnership for the purpose of considering such matters as the court may direct,

(ca)   require a decision of the partnership's creditors to be sought (using a qualifying decision procedure) on such matters as the court may direct,

(d)   bring the moratorium to an end and make such consequential provision as the court thinks fit.

40(6)   In making an order under this paragraph the court shall have regard to the need to safeguard the interests of persons who have dealt with the insolvent partnership in good faith and for value.

40(7)   Sub-paragraph (8) applies where–

(a)   the appointment of an administrator has effect in relation to the insolvent partnership and the appointment took effect before the moratorium came into force, or

(b)   the insolvent partnership is being wound up as an unregistered company or an order by virtue of article 11 of the Insolvent Partnerships Order 1994 has been made, in pursuance of a petition presented before the moratorium came into force.

40(8)   No application for an order under this paragraph may be made by a creditor or member of the insolvent partnership; but such an application may be made instead by the administrator (or as the case may be) the liquidator.

42(1)   If, for the purpose of obtaining a moratorium, or an extension of a moratorium, for an insolvent partnership or any of its members (a moratorium meaning in the case of an individual the effect of an application for, or the making of, an interim order under Part VIII of the Act), a person who is an officer of an insolvent partnership or an officer (which for this purpose includes a shadow director) of a corporate member in relation to which a voluntary arrangement is proposed–

(a) makes any false representation, or

(b) fraudulently does, or omits to do, anything,

he commits an offence.

42(2) Sub-paragraph (1) applies even if no moratorium or extension is obtained.

42(3) A person guilty of an offence under this paragraph is liable to imprisonment or a fine, or both."

History
In Pt 2 of Sch.1, modified para.37(2) and (5) and para.40(5) amended by the Deregulation Act 2015 and Small Business, Enterprise and Employment Act 2015 (Consequential Amendments) (Savings) Regulations 2017 (SI 2017/540) regs 1, 3, Sch.2 paras 2, 5 as from 6 April 2017.

Schedule 1 previously amended by the Insolvent Partnerships (Amendment) Order 2005 (SI 2005/1516) art.6 as from 1 July 2005 in keeping with the new administration regime, and also as follows:

(1) Modified s.1(4) omitted.

(2) In modified para.3(3)(a) of Sch.A1 "£5.6" substituted for "£2.8" and in para.3(3)(b) "£2.8" substituted for "£1.4".

(3) Modified para.12(1)(d) and (da) of Sch.A1 substituted for the former para.12(1)(d).

(4) Modified para.40(7) and (8) of Sch.A1 substituted for the former para.40(7).

Previously Sch.1 substituted by the Insolvent Partnerships (Amendment) (No.2) Order 2002 (SI 2002/2708) arts 1, 6 Sch.1 as from 1 January 2003 subject to transitional provisions contained in art.11(1), (3).

SCHEDULE 2

MODIFIED PROVISIONS OF PART II OF, AND SCHEDULE B1 TO, THE ACT (ADMINISTRATION) AS APPLIED BY ARTICLE 6

1 The following provisions of Schedule B1 and Schedule 1 to the Act are modified as follows.

2 Paragraph 2 is modified so as to read as follows–

"**2.** A person may be appointed as administrator of a partnership–

(a) by administration order of the court under paragraph 10,

(b) by the holder of an agricultural floating charge under paragraph 14, or

(c) by the members of the insolvent partnership in their capacity as such under paragraph 22."

3 Paragraph 7 is modified so as to read as follows–

"**7.** A person may not be appointed as administrator of a partnership which is in administration (subject to the provisions of paragraphs 90 to 93, 95 to 97, and 100 to 103 about replacement and additional administrators)."

4 Paragraph 8 is modified so as to read as follows–

"**8(1)** A person may not be appointed as administrator of a partnership after–

(a) an order has been made in relation to it by virtue of Article 11 of the Insolvent Partnerships Order 1994; or

(b) an order has been made for it to be wound up by the court as an unregistered company.

8(2) Sub-paragraph (1)(a) is subject to paragraph 38.

8(3) Sub-paragraph (1)(b) is subject to paragraphs 37 and 38."

5 Paragraph 11 is modified so as to read as follows–

"**11.** The court may make an administration order in relation to a partnership only if satisfied–

    (a) that the partnership is unable to pay its debts, and

    (b) that the administration order is reasonably likely to achieve the purpose of administration."

6 Paragraph 12 is modified so as to read as follows–

"**12(1)** An application to the court for an administration order in respect of a partnership ("an administration application") shall be by application in Form 1 in Schedule 9 to the Insolvent Partnerships Order 1994 and may be made only by–

    (a) the members of the insolvent partnership in their capacity as such;

    (b) one or more creditors of the partnership; or

    (c) a combination of persons listed in paragraphs (a) and (b).

12(2) As soon as is reasonably practicable after the making of an administration application the applicant shall notify–

    (a) any person who has appointed an agricultural receiver of the partnership;

    (b) any person who is or may be entitled to appoint an agricultural receiver of the partnership;

    (c) any person who is or may be entitled to appoint an administrator of the partnership under paragraph 14; and

    (d) such other persons as may be prescribed.

12(3) An administration application may not be withdrawn without the permission of the court.

12(4) In sub-paragraph (1) "creditor" includes a contingent creditor and a prospective creditor.

12(5) Sub-paragraph (1) is without prejudice to section 7(4)(b)."

7 Paragraph 14 is modified so as to read as follows–

"**14(1)** The holder of a qualifying agricultural floating charge in respect of partnership property may appoint an administrator of the partnership.

14(2) For the purposes of sub-paragraph (1) an agricultural floating charge qualifies if created by an instrument which–

    (a) states that this paragraph applies to the agricultural floating charge,

    (b) purports to empower the holder of the agricultural floating charge to appoint an administrator of the partnership, or

    (c) purports to empower the holder of the agricultural floating charge to make an appointment which would be the appointment of an agricultural receiver.

14(3) For the purposes of sub-paragraph (1) a person is the holder of a qualifying agricultural floating charge in respect of partnership property if he holds one or more charges of the partnership secured–

    (a) by a qualifying agricultural floating charge which relates to the whole or substantially the whole of the partnership property,

    (b) by a number of qualifying agricultural floating charges which together relate to the whole or substantially the whole of the partnership property, or

    (c) by charges and other forms of security which together relate to the whole or substantially the whole of the partnership property and at least one of which is a qualifying agricultural floating charge."

History
Paragraph 7 amended by the Insolvent Partnerships (Amendment) Order 2006 (SI 2006/622) art.5(2)(a), as from 6 April 2006.

8   Paragraph 15 is modified so as to read as follows–

"**15(1)**   A person may not appoint an administrator under paragraph 14 unless–

(a)   he has given at least two business days' written notice to the holder of any prior agricultural floating charge which satisfies paragraph 14(2); or

(b)   the holder of any prior agricultural floating charge which satisfies paragraph 14(2) has consented in writing to the making of the appointment.

15(2)   For the purposes of this paragraph, one agricultural floating charge is prior to another in accordance with the provisions of section 8(2) of the Agricultural Credits Act 1928."

History
Paragraph 8 amended by the Insolvent Partnerships (Amendment) Order 2006 (SI 2006/622) art.5(2)(b), as from 6 April 2006.

9   Paragraph 22 is modified so as to read as follows–

"**22.**   The members of the insolvent partnership may appoint an administrator."

10   Paragraph 23 is modified so as to read as follows–

"**23(1)**   This paragraph applies where an administrator of a partnership is appointed–

(a)   under paragraph 22, or

(b)   on an administration application made by the members of the partnership.

23(2)   An administrator of the partnership may not be appointed under paragraph 22 during the period of 12 months beginning with the date on which the appointment referred to in sub-paragraph (1) ceases to have effect."

11   Paragraph 26 is modified so as to read as follows–

"**26(1)**   A person who proposes to make an appointment under paragraph 22 shall give at least five business days' written notice to–

(a)   any person who is or may be entitled to appoint an agricultural receiver of the partnership, and

(b)   any person who is or may be entitled to appoint an administrator of the partnership under paragraph 14.

26(2)   A person who proposes to make an appointment under paragraph 22 shall also give such notice as may be prescribed to such other persons as may be prescribed.

26(3)   A notice under this paragraph must–

(a)   identify the proposed administrator, and

(b)   be in Form 1A in Schedule 9 to the Insolvent Partnerships Order 1994."

12   Paragraph 27 is modified so as to read as follows–

"**27(1)**   A person who gives notice of intention to appoint under paragraph 26 shall file with the court as soon as is reasonably practicable a copy of–

(a)   the notice, and

(b)   any document accompanying it.

27(2)   The copy filed under sub-paragraph (1) must be accompanied by a statutory declaration made by or on behalf of the person who proposes to make the appointment–

(a)   that the partnership is unable to pay its debts,

(b)   that the partnership is not in liquidation, and

(c)   that, so far as the person making the statement is able to ascertain, the appointment is not prevented by paragraphs 23 to 25, and

(d)   to such additional effect, and giving such information, as may be prescribed.

27(3) A statutory declaration under sub-paragraph (2) must–

(a) be in the prescribed form, and

(b) be made during the prescribed period.

27(4) A person commits an offence if in a statutory declaration under sub-paragraph (2) he makes a statement–

(a) which is false, and

(b) which he does not reasonably believe to be true."

13 Paragraph 29 is modified so as to read as follows–

"**29(1)** A person who appoints an administrator of a partnership under paragraph 22 shall file with the court–

(a) a notice of appointment, and

(b) such other documents as may be prescribed

29(2) The notice of appointment must include a statutory declaration by or on behalf of the person who makes the appointment–

(a) that the person is entitled to make an appointment under paragraph 22,

(b) that the appointment is in accordance with this Schedule, and

(c) that, so far as the person making the statement is able to ascertain, the statements made, and information given in the statutory declaration filed with the notice of intention to appoint remain accurate.

29(3) The notice of appointment must identify the administrator and must be accompanied by a statement by the administrator–

(a) that he consents to the appointment,

(b) that in his opinion the purpose of administration is reasonably likely to be achieved, and

(c) giving such other information and opinions as may be prescribed.

29(4) For the purpose of a statement under sub-paragraph (3) an administrator may rely on information supplied by members of the partnership (unless he has reason to doubt its accuracy).

29(5) The notice of appointment must be in Form 1B in Schedule 9 to the Insolvent Partnerships Order 1994 and any document accompanying it must be in the prescribed form.

29(6) A statutory declaration under sub-paragraph (2) must be made during the prescribed period.

29(7) A person commits an offence if in a statutory declaration under sub-paragraph (2) he makes a statement–

(a) which is false, and

(b) which he does not reasonably believe to be true."

14 Paragraph 35 is modified so as to read as follows–

"**35(1)** This paragraph applies where an administration application in respect of a partnership–

(a) is made by the holder of a qualifying agricultural floating charge in respect of the partnership property, and

(b) includes a statement that the application is made in reliance on this paragraph.

35(2) The court may make an administration order–

(a) whether or not satisfied that the partnership is unable to pay its debts; but

(b) only if satisfied that the applicant could appoint an administrator under paragraph 14."

15 Paragraph 39 is modified so as to read as follows–

"**39(1)** Where there is an agricultural receiver of a partnership the court must dismiss an administration application in respect of the partnership unless–

(a) the person by or on behalf of whom the agricultural receiver was appointed consents to the making of the administration order,

(b) the court thinks that the security by virtue of which the agricultural receiver was appointed would be liable to be released or discharged under sections 238 to 240 (transaction at undervalue and preference) if an administration order were made, or

(c) the court thinks that the security by virtue of which the agricultural receiver was appointed would be avoided under section 245 (avoidance of floating charge) if an administration order were made.

39(2) Sub-paragraph (1) applies whether the agricultural receiver is appointed before or after the making of the administration application."

16 Paragraph 41 is modified so as to read as follows–

"**41(1)** When an administration order takes effect in respect of a partnership any agricultural receiver of the partnership shall vacate office.

41(2) Where a partnership is in administration, any receiver of part of the partnership property shall vacate office if the administrator requires him to.

41(3) Where an agricultural receiver vacates office under sub-paragraph (1) or (2), his remuneration shall be charged on and paid out of any partnership property which was in his custody or under his control immediately before he vacated office.

41(4) In the application of sub-paragraph (3)–

(a) "remuneration" includes expenses properly incurred and any indemnity to which the agricultural receiver is entitled out of the partnership property,

(b) the charge imposed takes priority over security held by the person by whom or on whose behalf the agricultural receiver was appointed, and

(c) the provision for payment is subject to paragraph 43."

17 Paragraph 42 is modified so as to read as follows–

"**42(1)** This paragraph applies to a partnership in administration.

42(2) No order may be made for the winding up of the partnership.

42(3) No order may be made by virtue of Article 11 of the Insolvent Partnerships Order 1994 in respect of the partnership.

42(4) No order may be made under section 35 of the Partnership Act 1890 in respect of the partnership.

42(5) Sub-paragraph (2) does not apply to an order made on a petition presented under–

(a) section 124A (public interest); or

(b) section 367 of the Financial Services and Markets Act 2000 (c.8) (winding-up petitions).

42(6) If a petition presented under a provision referred to in sub-paragraph (5) comes to the attention of the administrator, he shall apply to the court for directions under paragraph 63."

18 Paragraph 43 is modified so as to read as follows–

"**43(1)** This paragraph applies to a partnership in administration.

43(2) No step may be taken to enforce security over the partnership property except–

(a) with the consent of the administrator, or

(b) with the permission of the court.

43(3)   No step may be taken to repossess goods in the partnership's possession under a hire-purchase agreement except–

   (a)   with the consent of the administrator, or

   (b)   with the permission of the court.

43(4)   A landlord may not exercise a right of forfeiture by peaceable re-entry in relation to premises forming part of the partnership property or let to one or more officers of the partnership in their capacity as such except–

   (a)   with the consent of the administrator, or

   (b)   with the permission of the court.

43(5)   No legal process (including legal proceedings, execution, distress and diligence) may be instituted or continued against the partnership or partnership property except–

   (a)   with the consent of the administrator, or

   (b)   with the permission of the court.

43(6)   An agricultural receiver of the partnership may not be appointed.

43(7)   Where the court gives permission for a transaction under this paragraph it may impose a condition on or a requirement in connection with the transaction.

43(8)   In this paragraph "landlord" includes a person to whom rent is payable."

19   Paragraph 47 is modified so as to read as follows–

"**47(1)**   As soon as is reasonably practicable after appointment the administrator of a partnership shall by notice in the prescribed form require one or more relevant persons to provide the administrator with a statement of the affairs of the partnership.

47(2)   The statement must–

   (a)   be verified by a statement of truth in accordance with Civil Procedure Rules,

   (b)   be in the prescribed form,

   (c)   give particulars of the partnership property, debts and liabilities,

   (d)   give the names and addresses of the creditors of the partnership,

   (e)   specify the security held by each creditor,

   (f)   give the date on which each security was granted, and

   (g)   contain such other information as may be prescribed.

47(3)   In sub-paragraph (1) "relevant person" means–

   (a)   a person who is or has been an officer of the partnership,

   (b)   a person who took part in the formation of the partnership during the period of one year ending with the date on which the partnership enters administration,

   (c)   a person employed by the partnership during that period, and

   (d)   a person who is or has been during that period an officer or employee of a partnership which is or has been during that year an officer of the partnership.

47(4)   For the purpose of sub-paragraph (3) a reference to employment is a reference to employment through a contract of employment or a contract for services."

20   Paragraph 49 is modified so as to read as follows–

"**49(1)**   The administrator of a partnership shall make a statement setting out proposals for achieving the purpose of administration.

49(2) A statement under sub-paragraph (1) must, in particular–

(a) deal with such matters as may be prescribed, and

(b) where applicable, explain why the administrator thinks that the objective mentioned in paragraph 3(1)(a) or (b) cannot be achieved.

49(3) Proposals under this paragraph may include a proposal for a voluntary arrangement under Part I of this Act (although this paragraph is without prejudice to section 4(3)).

49(4) The administrator shall send a copy of the statement of his proposals–

(a) to the court,

(b) to every creditor of the partnership, other than an opted-out creditor, of whose claim and address he is aware, and

(c) to every member of the partnership of whose address he is aware.

49(5) The administrator shall comply with sub-paragraph (4)–

(a) as soon as is reasonably practicable after the partnership enters administration, and

(b) in any event, before the end of the period of eight weeks beginning with the day on which the partnership enters administration.

49(6) The administrator shall be taken to comply with sub-paragraph (4)(c) if he publishes in the prescribed manner a notice undertaking to provide a copy of the statement of proposals free of charge to any member of the partnership who applies in writing to a specified address.

49(7) An administrator commits an offence if he fails without reasonable excuse to comply with sub-paragraph (5).

49(8) A period specified in this paragraph may be varied in accordance with paragraph 107."

History
In para.20 modified para.49(4) amended by the Deregulation Act 2015 and Small Business, Enterprise and Employment Act 2015 (Consequential Amendments) (Savings) Regulations 2017 (SI 2017/540) regs 1, 3, Sch.2 paras 2, 6(1), (2) as from 6 April 2017.

21 Paragraph 52 is modified so as to read as follows–

"**52(1)** Paragraph 51(1) shall not apply where the statement of proposals states that the administrator thinks–

(a) that the partnership has sufficient property to enable each creditor of the partnership to be paid in full,

(b) that the partnership has insufficient property to enable a distribution to be made to unsecured creditors, or

(c) that neither of the objectives specified in paragraph 3(1)(a) and (b) can be achieved.

52(2) But the administrator shall seek a decision from the partnership's creditors as to whether they approve the proposals set out in the statement made under paragraph 49(1) if requested to do so–

(a) by creditors of the partnership whose debts amount to at least 10 per cent of the total debts of the partnership,

(b) in the prescribed manner, and

(c) in the prescribed period.

52(3) Where a decision is sought by virtue of sub-paragraph (2) the initial decision date (as defined in paragraph 51(3)) must be within the prescribed period.

52(4) The period prescribed under sub-paragraph (3) may be varied in accordance with paragraph 107."

History
In para.21 modified para.52(2) amended and para.52(3) substituted by the Deregulation Act 2015 and Small Business, Enterprise and Employment Act 2015 (Consequential Amendments) (Savings) Regulations 2017 (SI 2017/540) regs 1, 3, Sch.2 paras 2, 6(12), (3) as from 6 April 2017.

22   Paragraph 61 is modified so as to read as follows–

"**61**   The administrator of a partnership–

    (a)   may prevent any person from taking part in the management of the partnership business, and

    (b)   may appoint any person to be a manager of that business."

23   Paragraph 65 is modified so as to read as follows–

"**65(1)**   The administrator of a partnership may make a distribution to a creditor of the partnership.

65(2)   Section 175(1), (1A), (1B), and (3) and section 176AZA shall apply in relation to a distribution under this paragraph as it applies in relation to a winding up.

65(3)   A payment may not be made by way of distribution under this paragraph to a creditor of the partnership who is neither secured nor preferential unless the court gives permission."

History
Modified para.65(2) amended by the Banks and Building Societies (Priorities on Insolvency) Order 2018 (SI 2018/1244) arts 1, 3, 15, 19(1), (2) as from 19 December 2018 in relation to insolvency proceedings commenced on or after that date.

24   Paragraph 69 is modified so as to read as follows–

"**69(1)**   Subject to sub-paragraph (2) below, in exercising his function under this Schedule the administrator of a partnership acts as the agent of the members of the partnership in their capacity as such.

69(2)   An officer of the partnership shall not, unless he otherwise consents, be personally liable for the debts and obligations of the partnership incurred during the period when the partnership is in administration."

25   Paragraph 73 is modified so as to read as follows–

"**73(1)**   An administrator's statement of proposals under paragraph 49 may not include any action which–

    (a)   affects the right of a secured creditor of the partnership to enforce his security,

    (b)   would result in a preferential debt of the partnership being paid otherwise than in priority to its non-preferential debts,

   (bb)   would result in an ordinary preferential debt of the partnership being paid otherwise than in priority to any secondary preferential debts that it may have,

    (c)   would result in one preferential creditor of the partnership being paid a smaller proportion of an ordinary preferential debt than another,

    (d)   would result in one preferential creditor of the partnership being paid a smaller proportion of a secondary preferential debt than another, or

    (e)   if the company is a relevant financial institution (see section 387A), any non-preferential debt is to be paid otherwise than in accordance with the rules in section 176AZA(2) or (3).

73(2)   Sub-paragraph (1) does not apply to–

    (a)   action to which the relevant creditor consents, or

    (b)   a proposal for a voluntary arrangement under Part I of this Act (although this sub-paragraph is without prejudice to section 4(3)).

73(3)   The reference to a statement of proposals in sub-paragraph (1) includes a reference to a statement as revised or modified."

History
Paragraph 73(1)(c) amended and para.73(1)(bb), (d) inserted by the Banks and Building Societies (Depositor Preference and Priorities) Order 2014 (SI 2014/3486) art.13(1), (2) as from 1 January 2015.

    Modified para.73(1)(e) inserted by the Banks and Building Societies (Priorities on Insolvency) Order 2018 (SI 2018/1244) arts 1, 3, 15, 19(1), (3) as from 19 December 2018 in relation to insolvency proceedings commenced on or after that date.

26   Paragraph 74 is modified so as to read as follows–

"**74(1)**   A creditor or member of a partnership in administration may apply to the court claiming that–

(a)   the administrator is acting or has acted so as unfairly to harm the interests of the applicant (whether alone or in common with some or all other members or creditors), or

(b)   the administrator proposes to act in a way which would unfairly harm the interests of the applicant (whether alone or in common with some or all other members or creditors).

74(2)   A creditor or member of a partnership in administration may apply to the court claiming that the administrator is not performing his functions as quickly or as efficiently as is reasonably practicable.

74(3)   The court may–

(a)   grant relief;

(b)   dismiss the application;

(c)   adjourn the hearing conditionally or unconditionally;

(d)   make an interim order;

(e)   make any other order it thinks appropriate.

74(4)   In particular, an order under this paragraph may–

(a)   regulate the administrator's exercise of his functions;

(b)   require the administrator to do or not do a specified thing;

(c)   require a decision of the partnership's creditors to be sought on a matter;

(d)   provide for the appointment of an administrator to cease to have effect;

(e)   make consequential provision.

74(5)   An order may be made on a claim under sub-paragraph (1) whether or not the action complained of–

(a)   is within the administrator's powers under that Schedule;

(b)   was taken in reliance on an order under paragraph 71 or 72.

74(6)   An order may not be made under this paragraph if it would impede or prevent the implementation of–

(a)   a voluntary arrangement approved under Part I, or

(b)   proposals or a revision approved under paragraph 53 or 54 more than 28 days before the day on which the application for the order under this paragraph is made."

History

In para.26 modified para.74(4)(c) substituted by the Deregulation Act 2015 and Small Business, Enterprise and Employment Act 2015 (Consequential Amendments) (Savings) Regulations 2017 (SI 2017/540) regs 1, 3, Sch.2 paras 2, 6(1), (4) as from 6 April 2017.

27   Omit paragraph 83.

28   Paragraph 84 is modified so as to read as follows–

"**84(1)**   If the administrator of a partnership thinks that the partnership has no property which might permit a distribution to its creditors, he shall file a notice to that effect with the court.

84(2)   The court may on the application of the administrator of a partnership disapply sub-paragraph (1) in respect of the partnership.

84(3)   On the filing of a notice in respect of a partnership under sub-paragraph (1) the appointment of an administrator of the partnership shall cease to have effect.

84(4)   If an administrator files a notice under sub-paragraph (1) he shall as soon as is reasonably practicable send a copy of the notice to each creditor of whose claim and address he is aware.

84(5) At the end of the period of three months beginning with the date of filing of a notice in respect of a partnership under sub-paragraph (1) the partnership is deemed to be dissolved.

84(6) On an application in respect of a partnership by the administrator or another interested person the court may–

(a) extend the period specified in sub-paragraph (5);

(b) suspend that period; or

(c) disapply sub-paragraph (5).

84(7) An administrator commits an offence if he fails without reasonable excuse to comply with sub-paragraph (4).".

29 Paragraph 87 is modified to read as follows–

"**87(1)** An administrator may resign only in prescribed circumstances.

87(2) Where an administrator may resign he may do so only–

(a) in the case of an administrator appointed by administration order, by notice in writing to the court,

(b) in the case of an administrator appointed under paragraph 14, by notice in writing to the holder of the agricultural floating charge by virtue of which the appointment was made, or

(c) in the case of an administrator appointed under paragraph 22, by notice in writing to the members of the insolvent partnership."

30 Paragraph 89 is modified so as to read as follows–

"**89(1)** The administrator of a partnership shall vacate office if he ceases to be qualified to act as an insolvency practitioner in relation to the partnership.

89(2) Where an administrator vacates office by virtue of sub-paragraph (1) he shall give notice in writing–

(a) in the case of an administrator appointed by administration order, to the court,

(b) in the case of an administrator appointed under paragraph 14, to the holder of the agricultural floating charge by virtue of which the appointment was made, or

(c) in the case of an administrator appointed under paragraph 22, to the members of the insolvent partnership.

89(3) An administrator who fails without reasonable excuse to comply with sub-paragraph (2) commits an offence."

31 Paragraph 90 is modified so as to read as follows–

"**90.** Paragraphs 91 to 93 and 95 apply where an administrator–

(a) dies

(b) resigns

(c) is removed from office under paragraph 88, or

(d) vacates office under paragraph 89."

32 Paragraph 91 is modified so as to read as follows–

"**91(1)** Where the administrator was appointed by administration order, the court may replace the administrator on an application under this sub-paragraph made by–

(a) a creditors' committee of the partnership,

(b) the members of the partnership,

(c) one or more creditors of the partnership, or

(d) where more than one person was appointed to act jointly or concurrently as the administrator, any of those persons who remains in office.

91(2) But an application may be made in reliance on sub-paragraph (1)(b) and (c) only where–

(a) there is no creditors' committee of the partnership,

(b) the court is satisfied that the creditors' committee or a remaining administrator is not taking reasonable steps to make a replacement, or

(c) the court is satisfied that for another reason it is right for the application to be made."

33 Paragraph 93 is modified so as to read as follows–

"**93(1)** Where the administrator was appointed under paragraph 22 by the members of the partnership they may replace the administrator.

93(2) A replacement under this paragraph may be made only–

(a) with the consent of each person who is the holder of a qualifying agricultural floating charge in respect of the partnership property, or

(b) where consent is withheld, with the permission of the court."

34 Omit paragraph 94.

35 Paragraph 95 is modified so as to read as follows–

"**95.** The court may replace an administrator on the application of a person listed in paragraph 91(1) if the court–

(a) is satisfied that a person who is entitled to replace the administrator under any of paragraphs 92 and 93 is not taking reasonable steps to make a replacement, or

(b) that for another reason it is right for the court to make the replacement."

36 Paragraph 96 is modified so as to read as follows–

"**96(1)** This paragraph applies where an administrator of a partnership is appointed under paragraph 14 by the holder of a qualifying agricultural floating charge in respect of the partnership property.

96(2) The holder of a prior qualifying agricultural floating charge in respect of the partnership property may apply to the court for the administrator to be replaced by an administrator nominated by the holder of the prior agricultural floating charge.

96(3) One agricultural floating charge is prior to another for the purposes of this paragraph if–

(a) it was created first, or

(b) it is to be treated as having priority in accordance with an agreement to which the holder of each agricultural floating charge was party."

37 Paragraph 97 is modified so as to read as follows–

"**97(1)** This paragraph applies where–

(a) an administrator of a partnership is appointed by the members of the partnership under paragraph 22, and

(b) there is no holder of a qualifying agricultural floating charge in respect of the partnership property.

97(2) The administrator may be replaced by a decision of the creditors made by a qualifying decision procedure.

97(3) The decision has effect only if, before the decision is made, the new administrator has consented to act in writing.

History
In para.37 modified para.97(2), (3) substituted by the Deregulation Act 2015 and Small Business, Enterprise and Employment Act 2015 (Consequential Amendments) (Savings) Regulations 2017 (SI 2017/540) regs 1, 3, Sch.2 paras 2, 6(1), (5) as from 6 April 2017.

38   Paragraph 103 is modified so as to read as follows–

"**103(1)**   Where a partnership is in administration, a person may be appointed to act as administrator jointly or concurrently with the person or persons acting as the administrator of the partnership.

103(2)   Where a partnership entered administration by administration order, an appointment under sub-paragraph (1) must be made by the court on the application of–

    (a)   a person or group listed in paragraph 12(1)(a) to (c), or

    (b)   the person or persons acting as the administrator of the partnership.

103(3)   Where a partnership entered administration by virtue of an appointment under paragraph 14, an appointment under sub-paragraph (1) must be made by–

    (a)   the holder of the agricultural floating charge by virtue of which the appointment was made, or

    (b)   the court on the application of the person or persons acting as the administrator of the partnership.

103(4)   Where a partnership entered administration by virtue of an appointment under paragraph 22, an appointment under sub-paragraph (1) above must be made either by the court on the application of the person or persons acting as the administrator of the partnership or–

    (a)   by the members of the partnership, and

    (b)   with the consent of each person who is the holder of a qualifying agricultural floating charge in respect of the partnership property or, where consent is withheld, with the permission of the court.

103(5)   An appointment under sub-paragraph (1) may be made only with the consent of the person or persons acting as the administrator of the partnership."

39   Omit paragraph 105.

40   Paragraph 106 is modified so as to read as follows–

"**106(1)**   A person who is guilty of an offence under this Schedule is liable to a fine (in accordance with section 430 and Schedule 10).

106(2)   A person who is guilty of an offence under any of the following paragraphs of this Schedule is liable to a daily default fine (in accordance with section 430 and Schedule 10)–

    (a)   paragraph 20,

    (b)   paragraph 32,

    (c)   paragraph 46,

    (d)   paragraph 48,

    (e)   paragraph 49,

    (f)   paragraph 51,

    (g)   paragraph 53,

    (h)   paragraph 54,

    (i)   paragraph 56,

    (j)   paragraph 78,

    (k)   paragraph 80,

    (l)   paragraph 84, and

    (m)   paragraph 89."

41   Paragraph 111 is modified so as to read as follows–

"**111(1)**   In this Schedule–

"administrator" has the meaning given by paragraph 1 and, where the context requires, includes a reference to a former administrator

"agricultural floating charge" means a charge which is an agricultural floating charge on its creation,

"enters administration" has the meaning given by paragraph 1,

"in administration" has the meaning given by paragraph 1,

"hire-purchase agreement" includes a conditional sale agreement, a chattel leasing agreement and a retention of title agreement,

"holder of a qualifying agricultural floating charge" in respect of partnership property has the meaning given by paragraph 14,

"market value" means the amount which would be realised on a sale of property in the open market by a willing vendor,

"the purpose of administration" means an objective specified in paragraph 3, and

"unable to pay its debts" has the meaning given by sections 222, 223, and 224.

111(2)   A reference in this Schedule to a thing in writing includes a reference to a thing in electronic form.

111(3)   In this Schedule a reference to action includes a reference to inaction."

History
In para.41 modified para.111(1) amended by the Deregulation Act 2015 and Small Business, Enterprise and Employment Act 2015 (Consequential Amendments) (Savings) Regulations 2017 (SI 2017/540) regs 1, 3, Sch.2 paras 2, 6(1), (6) as from 6 April 2017.

42   Omit paragraphs 112–116.

43   Schedule 1 is modified to read as follows:–

"SCHEDULE 1

POWERS OF ADMINISTRATOR

Paragraph 60 of Schedule B1

1.   Power to take possession of, collect and get in the partnership property and, for that purpose, to take such proceedings as may seem to him expedient.

2.   Power to sell or otherwise dispose of the partnership property by public auction or private auction or private contract or, in Scotland, to sell, feu, hire out or otherwise dispose of the partnership property by public roup or private bargain.

3.   Power to raise or borrow money and grant security therefor over the partnership property.

4.   Power to appoint a solicitor or accountant or other professionally qualified person to assist him in the performance of his functions.

5.   Power to bring or defend any action or other legal proceedings in the name and on behalf of any member of the partnership in his capacity as such or of the partnership.

6.   Power to refer to arbitration any question affecting the partnership.

7.   Power to effect and maintain insurances in respect of the partnership business and property.

8.   Power to do all acts and execute, in the name and on behalf of the partnership or of any member of the partnership in his capacity as such, any deed, receipt or other document.

9.   Power to draw, accept, make and endorse any bill of exchange or promissory note in the name and on behalf of any member of the partnership in his capacity as such or of the partnership.

10.   Power to appoint any agent to do any business which he is unable to do himself or which can more conveniently be done by an agent and power to employ and dismiss employees.

11.   Power to do all such things (including the carrying out of works) as may be necessary for the realisation of the partnership property.

12. Power to make any payment which is necessary or incidental to the performance of his functions.

13. Power to carry on the business of the partnership.

14. Power to establish subsidiary undertakings of the partnership.

15. Power to transfer to subsidiary undertakings of the partnership the whole or any part of the business of the partnership or of the partnership property.

16. Power to grant or accept a surrender of a lease or tenancy of any of the partnership property, and to take a lease or tenancy of any property required or convenient for the business of the partnership.

17. Power to make any arrangement or compromise on behalf of the partnership or of its members in their capacity as such.

18. Power to rank and claim in the bankruptcy, insolvency, sequestration or liquidation of any person indebted to the partnership and to receive dividends, and to accede to trust deeds for the creditors of any such person.

19. Power to present or defend a petition for the winding up of the partnership under the Insolvent Partnerships Order 1994.

20. Power to do all other things incidental to the exercise of the foregoing powers."

History
Schedule 2 substituted by the Insolvent Partnerships (Amendment) Order 2005 (SI 2005/1516) art.7 and Sch.1 as from 1 July 2005 subject to the transitional provisions set out in art.2 of that Order.

SCHEDULE 3

PROVISIONS OF THE ACT WHICH APPLY WITH MODIFICATIONS FOR THE PURPOSES OF ARTICLE 7 TO WINDING UP OF INSOLVENT PARTNERSHIP ON PETITION OF CREDITOR ETC. WHERE NO CONCURRENT PETITION PRESENTED AGAINST MEMBER

Article 7

PART I

MODIFIED PROVISIONS OF PART V OF THE ACT

1 Sections 220 to 223 of the Act are set out as modified in Part I of this Schedule, and sections 117, 131, 133, 234 and Schedule 4 are set out as modified in Part II.

2 Section 220: Meaning of "unregistered company"

2 Section 220 is modified so as to read as follows:–

"**220** For the purposes of this Part, the expression "unregistered company" includes any insolvent partnership."

3 Section 221: Winding up of unregistered companies

3 Section 221 is modified so as to read as follows:–

"**221(1)** Subject to subsections (2) and (3) below and to the provisions of this Part, any insolvent partnership may be wound up under this Act if it has, or at any time had, in England and Wales either–

(a) a principal place of business, or

(b) a place of business at which business is or has been carried on in the course of which the debt (or part of the debt) arose which forms the basis of the petition for winding up the partnership.

221(2) Subject to subsection (3) below, an insolvent partnership shall not be wound up under this Act if the business of the partnership has not been carried on in England and Wales at any time in the period of 3 years ending with the day on which the winding-up petition is presented.

221(3)   If an insolvent partnership has a principal place of business situated in Scotland or in Northern Ireland, the court shall not have jurisdiction to wind up the partnership unless it had a principal place of business in England and Wales–

(a)   in the case of a partnership with a principal place of business in Scotland, at any time in the period of 1 year, or

(b)   in the case of a partnership with a principal place of business in Northern Ireland, at any time in the period of 3 years,

ending with the day on which the winding-up petition is presented.

221(3A)   The preceding subsections are subject to Article 3 of the EC Regulation (jurisdiction under the EC Regulation).

221(4)   No insolvent partnership shall be wound up under this Act voluntarily.

221(5)   To the extent that they are applicable to the winding up of a company by the court in England and Wales on the petition of a creditor or of the Secretary of State, all the provisions of this Act and the Companies Act about winding up apply to the winding up of an insolvent partnership as an unregistered company–

(a)   with the exceptions and additions mentioned in the following subsections of this section and in section 221A, and

(b)   with the modifications specified in Part II of Schedule 3 to the Insolvent Partnerships Order 1994.

221(6)   Sections 73(1), 74(2)(a) to (d) and (3), 75 to 78, 83, 122, 123, 176A, 202, 203, 205 and 250 shall not apply.

History
Modified s.221(6) amended by the Insolvent Partnerships (Amendment) Order 2006 (SI 2006/622) art.6, as from 6 April 2006.

221(7)   The circumstances in which an insolvent partnership may be wound up as an unregistered company are as follows–

(a)   if the partnership is dissolved, or has ceased to carry on business, or is carrying on business only for the purpose of winding up its affairs;

(b)   if the partnership is unable to pay its debts;

(c)   if the court is of the opinion that it is just and equitable that the partnership should be wound up;

(d)   at the time at which a moratorium for the insolvent partnership under section 1A comes to an end, no voluntary arrangement approved under Part I of this Act has effect in relation to the insolvent partnership.

221(7A)   A winding-up petition on the ground set out in section 221(7)(d) may only be presented by one or more creditors.

History
Modified ss.221(7)(d) and (7A) inserted by the Insolvent Partnerships (Amendment) (No.2) Order 2002 (SI 2002/2708) arts 1, 8 as from 1 January 2003 subject to transitional provisions contained in art.11(1), (3).

221(8)   Every petition for the winding up of an insolvent partnership under Part V of this Act shall be verified by affidavit in Form 2 in Schedule 9 to the Insolvent Partnerships Order 1994.

221A   Petition by liquidator, administrator, trustee or supervisor to wind up insolvent partnership as unregistered company

221A(1)   A petition in Form 3 in Schedule 9 to the Insolvent Partnerships Order 1994 for winding up an insolvent partnership may be presented by–

(a)   the liquidator or administrator of a corporate member or of a former corporate member, or

(b)   the administrator of the partnership, or

(c)   the trustee of an individual member's, or of a former individual member's, estate, or

(d)   the supervisor of a voluntary arrangement approved under Part I of this Act in relation to a corporate member or the partnership, or under Part VIII of this Act in relation to an individual member,

if the ground of the petition is one of the circumstances set out in section 221(7).

221A(2)   In this section "petitioning insolvency practitioner" means a person who has presented a petition under subsection (1).

221A(3)   If the ground of the petition presented under subsection (1) is that the partnership is unable to pay its debts and the petitioning insolvency practitioner is able to satisfy the court that an insolvency order has been made against the member whose liquidator or trustee he is because of that member's inability to pay a joint debt, that order shall, unless it is proved otherwise to the satisfaction of the court, be proof for the purposes of section 221(7) that the partnership is unable to pay its debts.

221A(4)   Where a winding-up petition is presented under subsection (1), the court may appoint the petitioning insolvency practitioner as provisional liquidator of the partnership under section 135 (appointment and powers of provisional liquidator).

221A(5)   Where a winding-up order is made against an insolvent partnership after the presentation of a petition under subsection (1), the court may appoint the petitioning insolvency practitioner as liquidator of the partnership; and where the court makes an appointment under this subsection, section 140(3) (official receiver not to become liquidator) applies as if an appointment had been made under that section.

221A(6)   Where a winding-up petition is presented under subsection (1), in the event of the partnership property being insufficient to satisfy the costs of the petitioning insolvency practitioner the costs may be paid out of the assets of the corporate or individual member, as the case may be, as part of the expenses of the liquidation, administration, bankruptcy or voluntary arrangement of that member, in the same order of priority as expenses properly chargeable or incurred by the practitioner in getting in any of the assets of the member."

4   Section 222: Inability to pay debts: unpaid creditor for £750 or more

4   Section 222 is modified so as to read as follows:–

"**222(1)**   An insolvent partnership is deemed (for the purposes of section 221) unable to pay its debts if there is a creditor, by assignment or otherwise, to whom the partnership is indebted in a sum exceeding £750 then due and–

(a)   the creditor has served on the partnership, in the manner specified in subsection (2) below, a written demand in the prescribed form requiring the partnership to pay the sum so due, and

(b)   the partnership has for 3 weeks after the service of the demand neglected to pay the sum or to secure or compound for it to the creditor's satisfaction.

222(2)   Service of the demand referred to in subsection (1)(a) shall be effected–

(a)   by leaving it at a principal place of business of the partnership in England and Wales, or

(b)   by leaving it at a place of business of the partnership in England and Wales at which business is carried on in the course of which the debt (or part of the debt) referred to in subsection (1) arose, or

(c)   by delivering it to an officer of the partnership, or

(d)   by otherwise serving it in such manner as the court may approve or direct.

222(3)   The money sum for the time being specified in subsection (1) is subject to increase or reduction by regulations under section 417 in Part XV; but no increase in the sum so specified affects any case in which the winding-up petition was presented before the coming into force of the increase."

5   Section 223: Inability to pay debts: debt remaining unsatisfied after action brought

5   Section 223 is modified so as to read as follows:–

"**223(1)**   An insolvent partnership is deemed (for the purposes of section 221) unable to pay its debts if an action or other proceeding has been instituted against any member for any debt or demand due, or claimed to be due, from the partnership, or from him in his character of member, and–

(a) notice in writing of the institution of the action or proceeding has been served on the partnership in the manner specified in subsection (2) below, and

(b) the partnership has not within 3 weeks after service of the notice paid, secured or compounded for the debt or demand, or procured the action or proceeding to be stayed or sisted, or indemnified the defendant or defender to his reasonable satisfaction against the action or proceeding, and against all costs, damages and expenses to be incurred by him because of it.

223(2) Service of the notice referred to in subsection (1)(a) shall be effected–

(a) by leaving it at a principal place of business of the partnership in England and Wales, or

(b) by leaving it at a place of business of the partnership in England and Wales at which business is carried on in the course of which the debt or demand (or part of the debt or demand) referred to in subsection (1) arose, or

(c) by delivering it to an officer of the partnership, or

(d) by otherwise serving it in such manner as the court may approve or direct."

PART II

OTHER MODIFIED PROVISIONS OF THE ACT ABOUT WINDING UP BY THE COURT

6 Section 117: High Court and county court jurisdiction

6 Section 117 is modified so as to read as follows:–

"**117(1)** Subject to subsections (3) and (4) below, the High Court has jurisdiction to wind up any insolvent partnership as an unregistered company by virtue of article 7 of the Insolvent Partnerships Order 1994 if the partnership has, or at any time had, in England and Wales either–

(a) a principal place of business, or

(b) a place of business at which business is or has been carried on in the course of which the debt (or part of the debt) arose which forms the basis of the petition for winding up the partnership.

117(2) Subject to subsections (3) and (4) below, a petition for the winding up of an insolvent partnership by virtue of the said article 7 may be presented to a county court in England and Wales if the partnership has, or at any time had, within the insolvency district of that court either–

(a) a principal place of business, or

(b) a place of business at which business is or has been carried on in the course of which the debt (or part of the debt) arose which forms the basis of the winding-up petition.

117(3) Subject to subsection (4) below, the court only has jurisdiction to wind up an insolvent partnership if the business of the partnership has been carried on in England and Wales at any time in the period of 3 years ending with the day on which the petition for winding it up is presented.

117(4) If an insolvent partnership has a principal place of business situated in Scotland or in Northern Ireland, the court shall not have jurisdiction to wind up the partnership unless it had a principal place of business in England and Wales–

(a) in the case of a partnership with a principal place of business in Scotland, at any time in the period of 1 year, or

(b) in the case of a partnership with a principal place of business in Northern Ireland, at any time in the period of 3 years,

ending with the day on which the petition for winding it up is presented.

117(5) The Lord Chancellor may, with the concurrence of the Lord Chief Justice, by order in a statutory instrument exclude a county court from having winding-up jurisdiction, and for the purposes of that jurisdiction may attach its district, or any part thereof, to any other county court, and may by statutory instrument revoke or vary any such order.

In exercising the powers of this section, the Lord Chancellor shall provide that a county court is not to have winding-up jurisdiction unless it has for the time being jurisdiction for the purposes of Parts VIII to XI of this Act (individual insolvency).

117(6)   Every court in England and Wales having winding-up jurisdiction has for the purposes of that jurisdiction all the powers of the High Court; and every prescribed officer of the court shall perform any duties which an officer of the High Court may discharge by order of a judge of that court or otherwise in relation to winding up.

117(7)   This section is subject to Article 3 of the EC Regulation (jurisdiction under the EC Regulation).

117(8)   The Lord Chief Justice may nominate a judicial office holder (as defined in section 109(4) of the Constitutional Reform Act 2005) to exercise his functions under this section."

History
Modified s.117(5) amended, and s.117(8) inserted by the Lord Chancellor (Transfer of Functions and Supplementary Provisions) Order 2006 (SI 2006/680) Sch.2 paras 5, 6 as from 3 April 2006.

7   Section 131: Statement of affairs of insolvent partnership

7   Section 131 is modified so as to read as follows:–

"**131(1)**   Where the court has, by virtue of article 7 of the Insolvent Partnerships Order 1994, made a winding-up order or appointed a provisional liquidator in respect of an insolvent partnership, the official receiver may require some or all of the persons mentioned in subsection (3) below to make out and submit to him a statement in the prescribed form as to the affairs of the partnership.

131(2)   The statement shall be verified by affidavit by the persons required to submit it and shall show–

(a)   particulars of the debts and liabilities of the partnership and of the partnership property;

(b)   the names and addresses of the partnership's creditors;

(c)   the securities held by them respectively;

(d)   the dates when the securities were respectively given; and

(e)   such further or other information as may be prescribed or as the official receiver may require.

131(3)   The persons referred to in subsection (1) are–

(a)   those who are or have been officers of the partnership;

(b)   those who have taken part in the formation of the partnership at any time within one year before the relevant date;

(c)   those who are in the employment of the partnership, or have been in its employment within that year, and are in the official receiver's opinion capable of giving the information required;

(d)   those who are or have been within that year officers of, or in the employment of, a company which is, or within that year was, an officer of the partnership.

131(4)   Where any persons are required under this section to submit a statement of affairs to the official receiver, they shall do so (subject to the next subsection) before the end of the period of 21 days beginning with the day after that on which the prescribed notice of the requirement is given to them by the official receiver.

131(5)   The official receiver, if he thinks fit, may–

(a)   at any time release a person from an obligation imposed on him under subsection (1) or (2) above; or

(b)   either when giving the notice mentioned in subsection (4) or subsequently, extend the period so mentioned;

and where the official receiver has refused to exercise a power conferred by this subsection, the court, if it thinks fit, may exercise it.

131(6) In this section–

"employment" includes employment under a contract for services; and

"the relevant date" means–

(a) in a case where a provisional liquidator is appointed, the date of his appointment; and

(b) in a case where no such appointment is made, the date of the winding-up order.

131(7) If a person without reasonable excuse fails to comply with any obligation imposed under this section, he is liable to a fine and, for continued contravention, to a daily default fine."

8 Section 133: Public examination of officers of insolvent partnerships

8 Section 133 is modified so as to read as follows:–

"**133(1)** Where an insolvent partnership is being wound up by virtue of article 7 of the Insolvent Partnerships Order 1994, the official receiver may at any time before the winding up is complete apply to the court for the public examination of any person who–

(a) is or has been an officer of the partnership; or

(b) has acted as liquidator or administrator of the partnership or as receiver or manager or, in Scotland, receiver of its property; or

(c) not being a person falling within paragraph (a) or (b), is or has been concerned, or has taken part, in the formation of the partnership.

133(2) Unless the court otherwise orders, the official receiver shall make an application under subsection (1) if he is requested in accordance with the rules to do so by one-half, in value, of the creditors of the partnership.

133(3) On an application under subsection (1), the court shall direct that a public examination of the person to whom the application relates shall be held on a day appointed by the court; and that person shall attend on that day and be publicly examined as to the formation or management of the partnership or as to the conduct of its business and affairs, or his conduct or dealings in relation to the partnership.

133(4) The following may take part in the public examination of a person under this section and may question that person concerning the matters mentioned in subsection (3), namely–

(a) the official receiver;

(b) the liquidator of the partnership;

(c) any person who has been appointed as special manager of the partnership's property or business;

(d) any creditor of the partnership who has tendered a proof in the winding up."

8A Sections 165 and 167

8A(1) Section 165(2) has effect as if for "Parts 1 to 3" there were substituted "Parts 1 and 2".

8A(2) Section 167(1) has effect as if for "Parts 1 to 3" there were substituted "Parts 1 and 2".

History
Paragraph 8A inserted by the Deregulation Act 2015 and Small Business, Enterprise and Employment Act 2015 (Consequential Amendments) (Savings) Regulations 2017 (SI 2017/540) regs 1, 3, Sch.2 paras 2, 7(1), (2) as from 6 April 2017.

9 Section 234: Getting in the partnership property

9 Section 234 is modified so as to read as follows:–

"**234(1)** This section applies where, by virtue of article 7 of the Insolvent Partnerships Order 1994–

(a) an insolvent partnership is being wound up, or

(b)   a provisional liquidator of an insolvent partnership is appointed;

and "the office-holder" means the liquidator or the provisional liquidator, as the case may be.

234(2)   Any person who is or has been an officer of the partnership, or who is an executor or administrator of the estate of a deceased officer of the partnership, shall deliver up to the office-holder, for the purposes of the exercise of the office-holder's functions under this Act and (where applicable) the Company Directors Disqualification Act 1986, possession of any partnership property which he holds for the purposes of the partnership.

234(3)   Where any person has in his possession or control any property, books, papers or records to which the partnership appears to be entitled, the court may require that person forthwith (or within such period as the court may direct) to pay, deliver, convey, surrender or transfer the property, books, papers or records to the office-holder or as the court may direct.

234(4)   Where the office-holder–

(a)   seizes or disposes of any property which is not partnership property, and

(b)   at the time of seizure or disposal believes, and has reasonable grounds for believing, that he is entitled (whether in pursuance of an order of the court or otherwise) to seize or dispose of that property,

the next subsection has effect.

234(5)   In that case the office-holder–

(a)   is not liable to any person in respect of any loss or damage resulting from the seizure or disposal except in so far as that loss or damage is caused by the office-holder's own negligence, and

(b)   has a lien on the property, or the proceeds of its sale, for such expenses as were incurred in connection with the seizure or disposal."

10   Schedule 4 is modified so as to read as follows:–

"SCHEDULE 4

POWERS OF LIQUIDATOR IN A WINDING UP

Section 167

PART I

1   Power to pay any class of creditors in full.

2   Power to make any compromise or arrangement with creditors or persons claiming to be creditors, or having or alleging themselves to have any claim (present or future, certain or contingent, ascertained or sounding only in damages) against the partnership, or whereby the partnership may be rendered liable.

3   Power to compromise, on such terms as may be agreed–

(a)   all debts and liabilities capable of resulting in debts, and all claims (present or future, certain or contingent, ascertained or sounding only in damages) subsisting or supposed to subsist between the partnership and a contributory or alleged contributory or other debtor or person apprehending liability to the partnership, and

(b)   all questions in any way relating to or affecting the partnership property or the winding up of the partnership,

and take any security for the discharge of any such debt, liability or claim and give a complete discharge in respect of it.

3A   Power to bring legal proceedings under section 213, 214, 238, 239 or 423.

4   Power to bring or defend any action or other legal proceeding in the name and on behalf of any member of the partnership in his capacity as such or of the partnership.

5   Power to carry on the business of the partnership so far as may be necessary for its beneficial winding up.

PART II

6 Power to sell any of the partnership property by public auction or private contract, with power to transfer the whole of it to any person or to sell the same in parcels.

7 Power to do all acts and execute, in the name and on behalf of the partnership or of any member of the partnership in his capacity as such, all deeds, receipts and other documents.

8 Power to prove, rank and claim in the bankruptcy, insolvency or sequestration of any contributory for any balance against his estate, and to receive dividends in the bankruptcy, insolvency or sequestration in respect of that balance, as a separate debt due from the bankrupt or insolvent, and rateably with the other separate creditors.

9 Power to draw, accept, make and endorse any bill of exchange or promissory note in the name and on behalf of any member of the partnership in his capacity as such or of the partnership, with the same effect with respect to the liability of the partnership or of any member of the partnership in his capacity as such as if the bill or note had been drawn, accepted, made or endorsed in the course of the partnership's business.

10 Power to raise on the security of the partnership property any money requisite.

11 Power to take out in his official name letters of administration to any deceased contributory, and to do in his official name any other act necessary for obtaining payment of any money due from a contributory or his estate which cannot conveniently be done in the name of the partnership.

In all such cases the money due is deemed, for the purpose of enabling the liquidator to take out the letters of administration or recover the money, to be due to the liquidator himself.

12 Power to appoint an agent to do any business which the liquidator is unable to do himself.

13 Power to do all such other things as may be necessary for winding up the partnership's affairs and distributing its property."

History
In para.10 (modified Sch.4) para.3A inserted by the Insolvent Partnerships (Amendment) Order 2005 (SI 2005/1516) art.8 as from 1 July 2005.
  Headings to Pt I and Pt II amended by the Deregulation Act 2015 and Small Business, Enterprise and Employment Act 2015 (Consequential Amendments) (Savings) Regulations 2017 (SI 2017/540) regs 1, 3, Sch.2 paras 2, 7(1), (3), (4) as from 6 April 2017.

SCHEDULE 4

PROVISIONS OF THE ACT WHICH APPLY WITH MODIFICATIONS FOR THE PURPOSES OF ARTICLE 8 TO WINDING UP OF INSOLVENT PARTNERSHIP ON CREDITOR'S PETITION WHERE CONCURRENT PETITIONS ARE PRESENTED AGAINST ONE OR MORE MEMBERS

Article 8

PART I

MODIFIED PROVISIONS OF PART V OF THE ACT

1(1) Sections 220 to 222 of the Act are set out as modified in Part I of this Schedule, and the provisions of the Act specified in sub-paragraph (2) below are set out as modified in Part II.

1(2) The provisions referred to in sub-paragraph (1) are sections 117, 122 to 125, 131, 133, 136, 137, 139 to 141, 143, 146, 147, 168, 172, 174, 175, 189, 211, 230, 231, 234, 264, 265, 267, 268, 271, 283, 283A, 284, 288, 292 to 296, 298 to 303, 305, 313A, 314, 328, 331 and 356, and Schedule 4.

History
In para.1(2) "283A" and "313A" inserted by the Insolvent Partnerships (Amendment) Order 2005 (SI 2005/1516) art.9(1), (2) as from 1 July 2005.

2   Section 220: Meaning of "unregistered company"

2   Section 220 is modified so as to read as follows:–

"**220**   For the purposes of this Part, the expression "unregistered company" includes any insolvent partnership."

3   Section 221: Winding up of unregistered companies

3   Section 221 is modified so as to read as follows:–

"**221(1)**   Subject to subsections (2) and (3) below and to the provisions of this Part, any insolvent partnership may be wound up under this Act if it has, or at any time had, in England and Wales either–

(a)   a principal place of business, or

(b)   a place of business at which business is or has been carried on in the course of which the debt (or part of the debt) arose which forms the basis of the petition for winding up the partnership.

221(2)   Subject to subsection (3) below, an insolvent partnership shall not be wound up under this Act if the business of the partnership has not been carried on in England and Wales at any time in the period of 3 years ending with the day on which the winding-up petition is presented.

221(3)   If an insolvent partnership has a principal place of business situated in Scotland or in Northern Ireland, the court shall not have jurisdiction to wind up the partnership unless it had a principal place of business in England and Wales–

(a)   in the case of a partnership with a principal place of business in Scotland, at any time in the period of 1 year, or

(b)   in the case of a partnership with a principal place of business in Northern Ireland, at any time in the period of 3 years,

ending with the day on which the winding-up petition is presented.

221(3A)   The preceding subsections are subject to Article 3 of the EC Regulation (jurisdiction under the EC Regulation).

221(4)   No insolvent partnership shall be wound up under this Act voluntarily.

221(5)   To the extent that they are applicable to the winding up of a company by the court in England and Wales on a creditor's petition, all the provisions of this Act and the Companies Act about winding up apply to the winding up of an insolvent partnership as an unregistered company–

(a)   with the exceptions and additions mentioned in the following subsections of this section, and

(b)   with the modifications specified in Part II of Schedule 4 to the Insolvent Partnerships Order 1994.

221(6)   Sections 73(1), 74(2)(a) to (d) and (3), 75 to 78, 83, 154, 176A, 202, 203, 205 and 250 shall not apply.

History
Modified s.221(6) amended by the Insolvent Partnerships (Amendment) Order 2006 (SI 2006/622) art.7, as from 6 April 2006.

221(7)   Unless the contrary intention appears, a member of a partnership against whom an insolvency order has been made by virtue of article 8 of the Insolvent Partnerships Order 1994 shall not be treated as a contributory for the purposes of this Act.

221(8)   The circumstances in which an insolvent partnership may be wound up as an unregistered company are as follows–

(a)   the partnership is unable to pay its debts,

(b)   at the time at which a moratorium for the insolvent partnership under section 1A comes to an end, no voluntary arrangement approved under Part I of this Act has effect in relation to the insolvent partnership.

History
Modified s.221(8) substituted by the Insolvent Partnerships (Amendment) (No.2) Order 2002 (SI 2002/2708) arts 1, 9(1), (2) as from 1 January 2003 subject to transitional provisions contained in arts 11(1), (3).

221(9) Every petition for the winding up of an insolvent partnership under Part V of this Act shall be verified by affidavit in Form 2 in Schedule 9 to the Insolvent Partnerships Order 1994."

4 Section 222: Inability to pay debts: unpaid creditor for £750 or more

4 Section 222 is modified so as to read as follows:–

"**222(1)** An insolvent partnership is deemed (for the purposes of section 221) unable to pay its debts if there is a creditor, by assignment or otherwise, to whom the partnership is indebted in a sum exceeding £750 then due and–

(a) the creditor has served on the partnership, in the manner specified in subsection (2) below, a written demand in Form 4 in Schedule 9 to the Insolvent Partnerships Order 1994 requiring the partnership to pay the sum so due,

(b) the creditor has also served on any one or more members or former members of the partnership liable to pay the sum due (in the case of a corporate member by leaving it at its registered office and in the case of an individual member by serving it in accordance with the rules) a demand in Form 4 in Schedule 9 to that Order, requiring that member or those members to pay the sum so due, and

(c) the partnership and its members have for 3 weeks after the service of the demands, or the service of the last of them if served at different times, neglected to pay the sum or to secure or compound for it to the creditor's satisfaction.

222(2) Service of the demand referred to in subsection (1)(a) shall be effected–

(a) by leaving it at a principal place of business of the partnership in England and Wales, or

(b) by leaving it at a place of business of the partnership in England and Wales at which business is carried on in the course of which the debt (or part of the debt) referred to in subsection (1) arose, or

(c) by delivering it to an officer of the partnership, or

(d) by otherwise serving it in such manner as the court may approve or direct.

222(3) The money sum for the time being specified in subsection (1) is subject to increase or reduction by regulations under section 417 in Part XV; but no increase in the sum so specified affects any case in which the winding-up petition was presented before the coming into force of the increase."

PART II

OTHER MODIFIED PROVISIONS OF THE ACT ABOUT WINDING UP BY THE COURT AND BANKRUPTCY OF INDIVIDUALS

5 Sections 117 and 265: High Court and county court jurisdiction

5 Sections 117 and 265 are modified so as to read as follows:–

"**117(1)** Subject to the provisions of this section, the High Court has jurisdiction to wind up any insolvent partnership as an unregistered company by virtue of article 8 of the Insolvent Partnerships Order 1994 if the partnership has, or at any time had, in England and Wales either–

(a) a principal place of business, or

(b) a place of business at which business is or has been carried on in the course of which the debt (or part of the debt) arose which forms the basis of the petition for winding up the partnership.

117(2) Subject to subsections (3) and (4) below, a petition for the winding up of an insolvent partnership by virtue of the said article 8 may be presented to a county court in England and Wales if the partnership has, or at any time had, within the insolvency district of that court either–

(a) a principal place of business, or

(b) a place of business at which business is or has been carried on in the course of which the debt (or part of the debt) arose which forms the basis of the winding-up petition.

117(3)   Subject to subsection (4) below, the court only has jurisdiction to wind up an insolvent partnership if the business of the partnership has been carried on in England and Wales at any time in the period of 3 years ending with the day on which the petition for winding it up is presented.

117(4)   If an insolvent partnership has a principal place of business situated in Scotland or in Northern Ireland, the court shall not have jurisdiction to wind up the partnership unless it had a principal place of business in England and Wales–

(a)   in the case of a partnership with a principal place of business in Scotland, at any time in the period of 1 year, or

(b)   in the case of a partnership with a principal place of business in Northern Ireland, at any time in the period of 3 years,

ending with the day on which the petition for winding it up is presented.

117(5)   Subject to subsection (6) below, the court has jurisdiction to wind up a corporate member or former corporate member, or make a bankruptcy order against an individual member or former individual member, of a partnership against which a petition has been presented by virtue of article 8 of the Insolvent Partnerships Order 1994 if it has jurisdiction in respect of the partnership.

117(6)   Petitions by virtue of the said article 8 for the winding up of an insolvent partnership and the bankruptcy of one or more members or former members of that partnership may not be presented to a district registry of the High Court.

117(7)   The Lord Chancellor may, with the concurrence of the Lord Chief Justice, by order in a statutory instrument exclude a county court from having winding-up jurisdiction, and for the purposes of that jurisdiction may attach its district, or any part thereof, to any other county court, and may by statutory instrument revoke or vary any such order.

In exercising the powers of this section, the Lord Chancellor shall provide that a county court is not to have winding-up jurisdiction unless it has for the time being jurisdiction for the purposes of Parts VIII to XI of this Act (individual insolvency).

117(8)   Every court in England and Wales having winding-up jurisdiction has for the purposes of that jurisdiction all the powers of the High Court; and every prescribed officer of the court shall perform any duties which an officer of the High Court may discharge by order of a judge of that court or otherwise in relation to winding up.

117(9)   This section is subject to Article 3 of the EC Regulation (jurisdiction under the EC Regulation).

117(10)   The Lord Chief Justice may nominate a judicial office holder (as defined in section 109(4) of the Constitutional Reform Act 2005) to exercise his functions under this section."

History
Modified s.117(7) amended, and s.117(10) inserted, by the Lord Chancellor (Transfer of Functions and Supplementary Provisions) Order 2006 (SI 2006/680) Sch.2 paras 5, 7, as from 3 April 2006.

6   Circumstances in which members of insolvent partnerships may be wound up or made bankrupt by the court: Section 122—corporate member; Section 267—individual member

6(a)   Section 122 is modified so as to read as follows:–

"**122**   A corporate member or former corporate member of an insolvent partnership may be wound up by the court if–

(a)   it is unable to pay its debts,

(b)   there is a creditor, by assignment or otherwise, to whom the insolvent partnership is indebted and the corporate member or former corporate member is liable in relation to that debt and at the time at which a moratorium for the insolvent partnership under section 1A comes to an end, no voluntary arrangement approved under Part I of this Act has effect in relation to the insolvent partnership."

6(b)   Section 267 is modified so as to read as follows:–

"**267(1)**   Where a petition for the winding up of an insolvent partnership has been presented to the court by virtue of article 8 of the Insolvent Partnerships Order 1994, a creditor's petition against any individual member or former individual member of that partnership by virtue of that article must be in respect of one or more joint debts owed by the insolvent partnership, and the petitioning creditor or each of the petitioning creditors must be a person to whom the debt or (as the case may be) at least one of the debts is owed.

267(2)   Subject to subsection (2A) below and section 268, a creditor's petition may be presented to the court in respect of a joint debt or debts only if, at the time the petition is presented–

(a)   the amount of the debt, or the aggregate amount of the debts, is equal to or exceeds the bankruptcy level,

(b)   the debt, or each of the debts, is for a liquidated sum payable to the petitioning creditor, or one or more of the petitioning creditors, immediately, and is unsecured,

(c)   the debt, or each of the debts, is a debt for which the individual member or former member is liable and which he appears to be unable to pay, and

(d)   there is no outstanding application to set aside a statutory demand served (under section 268 below) in respect of the debt or any of the debts.

267(2A)   A creditor's petition may be presented to the court in respect of a joint debt or debts if at the time at which a moratorium for the insolvent partnership under section 1A comes to an end, no voluntary arrangement approved under Part I of this Act has effect in relation to the insolvent partnership.

267(3)   "The bankruptcy level" is £5,000; but the Secretary of State may by order in a statutory instrument substitute any amount specified in the order for that amount or (as the case may be) for the amount which by virtue of such an order is for the time being the amount of the bankruptcy level.

267(4)   An order shall not be made under subsection (3) unless a draft of it has been laid before, and approved by a resolution of, each House of Parliament."

History
In para.6(a) modified s.122 substituted by the Insolvent Partnerships (Amendment) (No.2) Order 2002 (SI 2002/2708) arts 1, 9(1), (3) as from 1 January 2003 subject to transitional provisions contained in arts 11(1), (3).
   In para.6(b) modified s.267(2) amended and modified s.267(2A) inserted by the Insolvent Partnerships (Amendment) (No.2) Order 2002 (SI 2002/2708) arts 1, 9(1), (4)(a), (b) as from 1 January 2003 subject to transitional provisions contained in art.11(1), (3). Modified s.267(3) amended by the Insolvency (Miscellaneous Amendments) Regulations 2017 (SI 2017/1119) regs 1(1), (6), 2, Sch.2 paras 1, 5(1), (2) as from 8 December 2017 subject to transitional and savings provision in para.10.

7   Definition of inability to pay debts: Section 123—corporate member; Section 268—individual member

7(a)   Section 123 is modified so as to read as follows:–

"**123(1)**   A corporate member or former member is deemed unable to pay its debts if there is a creditor, by assignment or otherwise, to whom the partnership is indebted in a sum exceeding £750 then due for which the member or former member is liable and–

(a)   the creditor has served on that member or former member and the partnership, in the manner specified in subsection (2) below, a written demand in Form 4 in Schedule 9 to the Insolvent Partnerships Order 1994 requiring that member or former member and the partnership to pay the sum so due, and

(b)   the corporate member or former member and the partnership have for 3 weeks after the service of the demands, or the service of the last of them if served at different times, neglected to pay the sum or to secure or compound for it to the creditor's satisfaction.

123(2)   Service of the demand referred to in subsection (1)(a) shall be effected, in the case of the corporate member or former corporate member, by leaving it at its registered office, and, in the case of the partnership–

(a)   by leaving it at a principal place of business of the partnership in England and Wales, or

(b)   by leaving it at a place of business of the partnership in England and Wales at which business is carried on in the course of which the debt (or part of the debt) referred to in subsection (1) arose, or

    (c)   by delivering it to an officer of the partnership, or

    (d)   by otherwise serving it in such manner as the court may approve or direct.

123(3)   The money sum for the time being specified in subsection (1) is subject to increase or reduction by order under section 416 in Part XV."

7(b)   Section 268 is modified so as to read as follows:–

"**268(1)**   For the purposes of section 267(2)(c), an individual member or former individual member appears to be unable to pay a joint debt for which he is liable if the debt is payable immediately and the petitioning creditor to whom the insolvent partnership owes the joint debt has served–

    (a)   on the individual member or former individual member in accordance with the rules a demand (known as "the statutory demand"), in Form 4 in Schedule 9 to the Insolvent Partnerships Order 1994, and

    (b)   on the partnership in the manner specified in subsection (2) below a demand (known as "the written demand") in the same form,

requiring the member or former member and the partnership to pay the debt or to secure or compound for it to the creditor's satisfaction, and at least 3 weeks have elapsed since the service of the demands, or the service of the last of them if served at different times, and neither demand has been complied with nor the demand against the member set aside in accordance with the rules.

268(2)   Service of the demand referred to in subsection (1)(b) shall be effected–

    (a)   by leaving it at a principal place of business of the partnership in England and Wales, or

    (b)   by leaving it at a place of business of the partnership in England and Wales at which business is carried on in the course of which the debt (or part of the debt) referred to in subsection (1) arose, or

    (c)   by delivering it to an officer of the partnership, or

    (d)   by otherwise serving it in such manner as the court may approve or direct."

8   Sections 124 and 264: Applications to wind up insolvent partnership and to wind up or bankrupt insolvent member

8   Sections 124 and 264 are modified so as to read as follows:–

"**124(1)**   An application to the court by virtue of article 8 of the Insolvent Partnerships Order 1994 for the winding up of an insolvent partnership as an unregistered company and the winding up or bankruptcy (as the case may be) of at least one of its members or former members shall–

    (a)   in the case of the partnership, be by petition in Form 5 in Schedule 9 to that Order,

    (b)   in the case of a corporate member or former corporate member, be by petition in Form 6 in that Schedule, and

    (c)   in the case of an individual member or former individual member, be by petition in Form 7 in that Schedule.

124(2)   Each of the petitions mentioned in subsection (1) may be presented by a liquidator (within the meaning of Article 2(b) of the EC Regulation) appointed in proceedings by virtue of Article 3(1) of the EC Regulation, a temporary administrator (within the meaning of Article 38 of the EC Regulation) or any creditor or creditors to whom the partnership and the member or former member in question is indebted in respect of a liquidated sum payable immediately.

124(3)   The petitions mentioned in subsection (1)–

    (a)   shall all be presented to the same court and, except as the court otherwise permits or directs, on the same day, and

    (b)   except in the case of the petition mentioned in subsection (1),

    (c)   shall be advertised in Form 8 in the said Schedule 9.

124(4)   At any time after presentation of a petition under this section the petitioner may, with the leave of the court obtained on application and on such terms as it thinks just, add other members or former members of the partnership as parties to the proceedings in relation to the insolvent partnership.

124(5)   Each petition presented under this section shall contain particulars of other petitions being presented in relation to the partnership, identifying the partnership and members concerned.

124(6)   The hearing of the petition against the partnership fixed by the court shall be in advance of the hearing of any petition against an insolvent member.

124(7)   On the day appointed for the hearing of the petition against the partnership, the petitioner shall, before the commencement of the hearing, hand to the court Form 9 in Schedule 9 to the Insolvent Partnerships Order 1994, duly completed.

124(8)   Any member of the partnership or any person against whom a winding-up or bankruptcy petition has been presented in relation to the insolvent partnership is entitled to appear and to be heard on any petition for the winding up of the partnership.

124(9)   A petitioner under this section may at the hearing withdraw a petition if–

(a)   subject to subsection (10) below, he withdraws at the same time every other petition which he has presented under this section; and

(b)   he gives notice to the court at least 3 days before the date appointed for the hearing of the relevant petition of his intention to withdraw the petition.

124(10)   A petitioner need not comply with the provisions of subsection (9)(a) in the case of a petition against an insolvent member if the court is satisfied on application made to it by the petitioner that, because of difficulties in serving the petition or for any other reason, the continuance of that petition would be likely to prejudice or delay the proceedings on the petition which he has presented against the partnership or on any petition which he has presented against any other insolvent member.

124(11)   Where notice is given under subsection (9)(b), the court may, on such terms as it thinks just, substitute as petitioner, both in respect of the partnership and in respect of each insolvent member against whom a petition has been presented, any creditor of the partnership who in its opinion would have a right to present the petitions, and if the court makes such a substitution the petitions in question will not be withdrawn.

124(12)   Reference in subsection (11) to substitution of a petitioner includes reference to change of carriage of the petition in accordance with the rules."

9   Sections 125 and 271: Powers of court on hearing of petitions against insolvent partnership and members

9   Sections 125 and 271 are modified so as to read as follows:–

"**125(1)**   Subject to the provisions of section 125A, on hearing a petition under section 124 against an insolvent partnership or any of its insolvent members, the court may dismiss it, or adjourn the hearing conditionally or unconditionally or make any other order that it thinks fit; but the court shall not refuse to make a winding-up order against the partnership or a corporate member on the ground only that the partnership property or (as the case may be) the member's assets have been mortgaged to an amount equal to or in excess of that property or those assets, or that the partnership has no property or the member no assets.

125(2)   An order under subsection (1) in respect of an insolvent partnership may contain directions as to the future conduct of any insolvency proceedings in existence against any insolvent member in respect of whom an insolvency order has been made.

125A   Hearing of petitions against members

125A(1)   On the hearing of a petition against an insolvent member the petitioner shall draw the court's attention to the result of the hearing of the winding-up petition against the partnership and the following subsections of this section shall apply.

125A(2)   If the court has neither made a winding-up order, nor dismissed the winding-up petition, against the partnership the court may adjourn the hearing of the petition against the member until either event has occurred.

125A(3)   Subject to subsection (4) below, if a winding-up order has been made against the partnership, the court may make a winding-up order against the corporate member in respect of which, or (as the case may be) a bankruptcy order against the individual member in respect of whom, the insolvency petition was presented.

125A(4)   If no insolvency order is made under subsection (3) against any member within 28 days of the making of the winding-up order against the partnership, the proceedings against the partnership shall be conducted as if the winding-up petition against the partnership had been presented by virtue of article 7 of the Insolvent Partnerships Order 1994 and the proceedings against any member shall be conducted under this Act without the modifications made by that Order (other than the modifications made to sections 168 and 303 by article 14).

125A(5)   If the court has dismissed the winding-up petition against the partnership, the court may dismiss the winding-up petition against the corporate member or (as the case may be) the bankruptcy petition against the individual member. However, if an insolvency order is made against a member, the proceedings against that member shall be conducted under this Act without the modifications made by the Insolvent Partnerships Order 1994 (other than the modifications made to sections 168 and 303 of this Act by article 14 of that Order).

125A(6)   The court may dismiss a petition against an insolvent member if it considers it just to do so because of a change in circumstances since the making of the winding-up order against the partnership.

125A(7)   The court may dismiss a petition against an insolvent member who is a limited partner, if–

(a)   the member lodges in court for the benefit of the creditors of the partnership sufficient money or security to the court's satisfaction to meet his liability for the debts and obligations of the partnership; or

(b)   the member satisfies the court that he is no longer under any liability in respect of the debts and obligations of the partnership.

125A(8)   Nothing in sections 125 and 125A or in sections 267 and 268 prejudices the power of the court, in accordance with the rules, to authorise a creditor's petition to be amended by the omission of any creditor or debt and to be proceeded with as if things done for the purposes of those sections had been done only by or in relation to the remaining creditors or debts."

10   Sections 131 and 288: Statements of affairs—insolvent partnerships; corporate members; individual members

10   Sections 131 and 288 are modified so as to read as follows:–

"**131(1)**   This section applies where the court has, by virtue of article 8 of the Insolvent Partnerships Order 1994–

(a)   made a winding-up order or appointed a provisional liquidator in respect of an insolvent partnership, or

(b)   made a winding-up order or appointed a provisional liquidator in respect of any corporate member of that partnership, or

(c)   made a bankruptcy order in respect of any individual member of that partnership.

131(2)   The official receiver may require some or all of the persons mentioned in subsection (4) below to make out and submit to him a statement as to the affairs of the partnership or member in the prescribed form.

131(3)   The statement shall be verified by affidavit by the persons required to submit it and shall show–

(a)   particulars of the debts and liabilities of the partnership or of the member (as the case may be), and of the partnership property and member's assets;

(b)   the names and addresses of the creditors of the partnership or of the member (as the case may be);

(c)   the securities held by them respectively;

(d)   the dates when the securities were respectively given; and

(e)   such further or other information as may be prescribed or as the official receiver may require.

131(4)   The persons referred to in subsection (2) are–

(a)   those who are or have been officers of the partnership;

(b)   those who are or have been officers of the corporate member;

(c)   those who have taken part in the formation of the partnership or of the corporate member at any time within one year before the relevant date;

(d)   those who are in the employment of the partnership or of the corporate member, or have been in such employment within that year, and are in the official receiver's opinion capable of giving the information required;

(e)   those who are or have been within that year officers of, or in the employment of, a company which is, or within that year was, an officer of the partnership or an officer of the corporate member.

131(5)   Where any persons are required under this section to submit a statement of affairs to the official receiver, they shall do so (subject to the next subsection) before the end of the period of 21 days beginning with the day after that on which the prescribed notice of the requirement is given to them by the official receiver.

131(6)   The official receiver, if he thinks fit, may–

(a)   at any time release a person from an obligation imposed on him under subsection (2) or (3) above; or

(b)   either when giving the notice mentioned in subsection (5) or subsequently, extend the period so mentioned;

and where the official receiver has refused to exercise a power conferred by this subsection, the court, if it thinks fit, may exercise it.

131(7)   In this section–

"employment" includes employment under a contract for services; and

"the relevant date" means–

(a)   in a case where a provisional liquidator is appointed, the date of his appointment; and

(b)   in a case where no such appointment is made, the date of the winding-up order.

131(8)   Any person who without reasonable excuse fails to comply with any obligation imposed under this section (other than, in the case of an individual member, an obligation in respect of his own statement of affairs), is liable to a fine and, for continued contravention, to a daily default fine.

131(9)   An individual member who without reasonable excuse fails to comply with any obligation imposed under this section in respect of his own statement of affairs, is guilty of a contempt of court and liable to be punished accordingly (in addition to any other punishment to which he may be subject)."

11   Section 133: Public examination of officers of insolvent partnerships

11   Section 133 is modified so far as insolvent partnerships are concerned so as to read as follows:–

"**133(1)**   Where an insolvent partnership is being wound up by virtue of article 8 of the Insolvent Partnerships Order 1994, the official receiver may at any time before the winding up is complete apply to the court for the public examination of any person who–

(a)   is or has been an officer of the partnership; or

(b)   has acted as liquidator or administrator of the partnership or as receiver or manager or, in Scotland, receiver of its property;

(c)   not being a person falling within paragraph (a) or (b), is or has been concerned, or has taken part, in the formation of the partnership.

133(2)   Unless the court otherwise orders, the official receiver shall make an application under subsection (1) if he is requested in accordance with the rules to do so by one-half, in value, of the creditors of the partnership.

133(3)   On an application under subsection (1), the court shall direct that a public examination of the person to whom the application relates shall be held on a day appointed by the court; and that person shall attend on that day and be publicly examined as to the formation or management of the partnership or as to the conduct of its business and affairs, or his conduct or dealings in relation to the partnership.

133(4)   The following may take part in the public examination of a person under this section and may question that person concerning the matters mentioned in subsection (3), namely–

    (a)   the official receiver;

    (b)   the liquidator of the partnership;

    (c)   any person who has been appointed as special manager of the partnership's property or business;

    (d)   any creditor of the partnership who has tendered a proof in the winding up.

133(5)   On an application under subsection (1), the court may direct that the public examination of any person under this section in relation to the affairs of an insolvent partnership be combined with the public examination of any person under this Act in relation to the affairs of a corporate member of that partnership against which, or an individual member of the partnership against whom, an insolvency order has been made."

12   Sections 136, 293 and 294: Functions of official receiver in relation to office of responsible insolvency practitioner

12   Sections 136, 293 and 294 are modified so as to read as follows:–

"**136(1)**   The following provisions of this section have effect, subject to section 140 below, where insolvency orders are made in respect of an insolvent partnership and one or more of its insolvent members by virtue of article 8 of the Insolvent Partnerships Order 1994.

136(2)   The official receiver, by virtue of his office, becomes the responsible insolvency practitioner of the partnership and of any insolvent member and continues in office until another person becomes responsible insolvency practitioner under the provisions of this Part.

136(3)   The official receiver is, by virtue of his office, the responsible insolvency practitioner of the partnership and of any insolvent member during any vacancy.

136(4)   At any time when he is the responsible insolvency practitioner of the insolvent partnership and of any insolvent member, the official receiver may in accordance with the rules seek nominations from the creditors of the partnership and the creditors of such member, for the purpose of choosing a person to be responsible insolvency practitioner in place of the official receiver.

136(5)   It is the duty of the official receiver–

    (a)   as soon as practicable in the period of 12 weeks beginning with the day on which the insolvency order was made, to decide whether to exercise his power under subsection (4), and

    (b)   if in pursuance of paragraph (a) he decides not to exercise that power, to give notice of his decision, before the end of that period, to the court and to the creditors of the partnership and of the creditors of any insolvent member against whom an insolvency order has been made, and

    (c)   (whether or not he has decided to exercise that power) to exercise his power under subsection (4) if he is at any time requested, in accordance with the rules, to do so by one-quarter, in value, of either–

        (i)   the partnership's creditors, or

        (ii) the creditors of any insolvent member against whom an insolvency order has been made,

and accordingly, where the duty imposed by paragraph (c) arises before the official receiver has performed a duty imposed by paragraph (a) or (b), he is not required to perform the latter duty.

136(6)   A notice given under subsection (5)(b) to the creditors must contain an explanation of the creditors' power under subsection (5)(c) to require the official receiver to seek nominations from the creditors of the partnership and of any insolvent member.".

136A [Omitted]

History

In para.12 modified s.136(1), (4) amended, s.136(5), (6) inserted and s.136A omitted by the Deregulation Act 2015 and Small Business, Enterprise and Employment Act 2015 (Consequential Amendments) (Savings) Regulations 2017 (SI 2017/540) regs 1, 3, Sch.2 paras 2, 8(1), (2) as from 6 April 2017.

13 Sections 137, 295, 296 and 300: Appointment of responsible insolvency practitioner by Secretary of State

13 Sections 137, 295, 296 and 300 are modified so as to read as follows:–

"**137(1)** This section and the next apply where the court has made insolvency orders in respect of an insolvent partnership and one or more of its insolvent members by virtue of article 8 of the Insolvent Partnerships Order 1994.

137(2) The official receiver may, at any time when he is the responsible insolvency practitioner of the partnership and of any insolvent member, apply to the Secretary of State for the appointment of a person as responsible insolvency practitioner of both the partnership and of such member in his place.

137(3) If a nomination is sought from the creditors of the partnership and of any insolvent member, but no person is chosen to be responsible insolvency practitioner by the creditors, it is the duty of the official receiver to decide whether to refer the need for an appointment to the Secretary of State.

History

In para.13 modified s.137(3) amended by the Deregulation Act 2015 and Small Business, Enterprise and Employment Act 2015 (Consequential Amendments) (Savings) Regulations 2017 (SI 2017/540) regs 1, 3, Sch.2 paras 2, 8(1), (3)(a) as from 6 April 2017.

137A Consequences of section 137 application

137A(1) On an application under section 137(2), or a reference made in pursuance of a decision under section 137(3), the Secretary of State shall either make an appointment or decline to make one.

137A(2) If on an application under section 137(2), or a reference made in pursuance of a decision under section 137(3), no appointment is made, the official receiver shall continue to be responsible insolvency practitioner of the partnership and its insolvent member or members, but without prejudice to his power to make a further application or reference.

137A(3) Where a responsible insolvency practitioner has been appointed by the Secretary of State under subsection (1) of this section, and an insolvency order is subsequently made against a further insolvent member by virtue of article 8 of the Insolvent Partnerships Order 1994, then the practitioner so appointed shall also be the responsible insolvency practitioner of the member against whom the subsequent order is made.

137A(4) Where a responsible insolvency practitioner has been appointed by the Secretary of State under subsection (1), or has become responsible insolvency practitioner of a further insolvent member under subsection (3), that practitioner shall give notice of his appointment or further appointment (as the case may be) to the creditors of the insolvent partnership and the creditors of the insolvent member or members against whom insolvency orders have been made or, if the court so allows, shall advertise his appointment in accordance with the directions of the court.

137A(5) Subject to subsection (6) below, in that notice or advertisement the responsible insolvency practitioner must explain the procedure for establishing a liquidation committee under section 141.

137A(6) In a case where subsection (3) applies, in the notice or advertisement the responsible insolvency practitioner must–

(a) if a liquidation committee has already been established under section 141, state whether he proposes to appoint additional members of the committee under section 141A(3); or

(b) if such a committee has not been established, explain the procedure for establishing a liquidation committee under section 141."

History
In para.13 modified s.137A(5) amended, s.137A(6) substituted by the Deregulation Act 2015 and Small Business, Enterprise and Employment Act 2015 (Consequential Amendments) (Savings) Regulations 2017 (SI 2017/540) regs 1, 3, Sch.2 paras 2, 8(1), (3)(b), (c) as from 6 April 2017.

14 Section 139: Rules applicable to decision making

14 Section 139 is modified so as to read as follows:–

"**139(1)** This section applies where the court has made insolvency orders against an insolvent partnership and one or more of its insolvent members by virtue of article 8 of the Insolvent Partnerships Order 1994.

139(2) Subject to subsection (4) below, the rules relating to decision making on the winding up of a company are to apply (with the necessary modifications) to decisions sought from creditors of the partnership, of any corporate members against which an insolvency order has been made or of any insolvent member, where the decision is one to be made with creditors of the partnership.

139(3) Subject to subsection (4) below, the rules relating to decision making on the bankruptcy of an individual are to apply (with the necessary modifications) to decisions sought from creditors of any individual member against whom an insolvency order has been made.

139(4) Any decision to be made by the creditors of the partnership and of the insolvent member or members must be conducted as if there were a single set of creditors."

History
The heading to para.14 amended and modified s.139(2)–(4) substituted by the Deregulation Act 2015 and Small Business, Enterprise and Employment Act 2015 (Consequential Amendments) (Savings) Regulations 2017 (SI 2017/540) regs 1, 3, Sch.2 paras 2, 8(1), (4) as from 6 April 2017.

15 Section 140: Appointment by the court following administration or voluntary arrangement

15 Section 140 is modified so as to read as follows:–

"**140(1)** This section applies where insolvency orders are made in respect of an insolvent partnership and one or more of its insolvent members by virtue of article 8 of the Insolvent Partnerships Order 1994.

140(2) Where the orders referred to in subsection (1) are made immediately upon the appointment of an administrator in respect of the partnership ceasing to have effect, the court may appoint as responsible insolvency practitioner the person whose appointment as administrator has ceased to have effect.

140(3) Where the orders referred to in subsection (1) are made at a time when there is a supervisor of a voluntary arrangement approved in relation to the partnership under Part I, the court may appoint as responsible insolvency practitioner the person who is the supervisor at the time when the winding-up order against the partnership is made.

140(4) Where the court makes an appointment under this section, the official receiver does not become the responsible insolvency practitioner as otherwise provided by section 136(2), and section 136(5)(a) and (b) does not apply."

History
In para.15 modified s.140(4) amended by the Deregulation Act 2015 and Small Business, Enterprise and Employment Act 2015 (Consequential Amendments) (Savings) Regulations 2017 (SI 2017/540) regs 1, 3, Sch.2 paras 2, 8(1), (5) as from 6 April 2017.

16 Sections 141, 301 and 302: Creditors' Committee: insolvent partnership and members

16 Sections 141, 301 and 302 are modified so as to read as follows:–

"**141(1)** This section applies where insolvency orders are made in respect of an insolvent partnership and one or more of its insolvent members by virtue of article 8 of the Insolvent Partnerships Order 1994.

141(2) If both the creditors of the partnership and the creditors of any insolvent members decide that a liquidation committee should be established, a liquidation committee is to be established in accordance with the rules.

141(3) A "liquidation committee" is a committee having such functions as are conferred on it by or under this Act.

141(4) The responsible insolvency practitioner must seek a decision from the creditors of the partnership and of any insolvent members as to whether a liquidation committee should be established if requested, in accordance with the rules, to do so by one-tenth in value of the creditors.

141A Functions and membership of creditors' committee

141A(1) The committee established under section 141 shall act as liquidation committee for the partnership and for any corporate member against which an insolvency order has been made, and as creditors' committee for any individual member against whom an insolvency order has been made, and shall as appropriate exercise the functions conferred on liquidation and creditors' committees in a winding up or bankruptcy by or under this Act.

141A(2) The rules relating to liquidation committees are to apply (with the necessary modifications and with the exclusion of all references to contributories) to a committee established under section 141.

141A(3) Where the appointment of the responsible insolvency practitioner also takes effect in relation to a further insolvent member under section 136A(5) or 137A(3), the practitioner may appoint any creditor of that member (being qualified under the rules to be a member of the committee) to be an additional member of any creditors' committee already established under section 141, provided that the creditor concerned consents to act.

141A(4) The court may at any time, on application by a creditor of the partnership or of any insolvent member against whom an insolvency order has been made, appoint additional members of the creditors' committee.

141A(5) If additional members of the creditors' committee are appointed under subsection (3) or (4), the limit on the maximum number of members of the committee specified in the rules shall be increased by the number of additional members so appointed.

141A(6) The creditors' committee is not to be able or required to carry out its functions at any time when the official receiver is responsible insolvency practitioner of the partnership and of its insolvent member or members; but at any such time its functions are vested in the Secretary of State except to the extent that the rules otherwise provide.

141A(7) Where there is for the time being no creditors' committee, and the responsible insolvency practitioner is a person other than the official receiver, the functions of such a committee are vested in the Secretary of State except to the extent that the rules otherwise provide."

History
In para.16 modified s.141 substituted by the Deregulation Act 2015 and Small Business, Enterprise and Employment Act 2015 (Consequential Amendments) (Savings) Regulations 2017 (SI 2017/540) regs 1, 3, Sch.2 paras 2, 8(1), (6) as from 6 April 2017.

17 Sections 143, 168(4) and 305: General functions of responsible insolvency practitioner

17 Sections 143, 168(4) and 305 are modified so as to read as follows:–

"**143(1)** The functions of the responsible insolvency practitioner of an insolvent partnership and of its insolvent member or members against whom insolvency orders have been made by virtue of article 8 of the Insolvent Partnerships Order 1994, are to secure that the partnership property and the assets of any such corporate member, and the estate of any such individual member, are got in, realised and distributed to their respective creditors and, if there is a surplus of such property or assets or in such estate, to the persons entitled to it.

143(2) In the carrying out of those functions, and in the management of the partnership property and of the assets of any corporate member and of the estate of any individual member, the responsible insolvency practitioner is entitled, subject to the provisions of this Act, to use his own discretion.

143(3) It is the duty of the responsible insolvency practitioner, if he is not the official receiver–

   (a)   to furnish the official receiver with such information,

   (b)   to produce to the official receiver, and permit inspection by the official receiver of, such books, papers and other records, and

   (c)   to give the official receiver such other assistance,

as the official receiver may reasonably require for the purposes of carrying out his functions in relation to the winding up of the partnership and any corporate member or the bankruptcy of any individual member.

143(4)   The official name of the responsible insolvency practitioner in his capacity as trustee of an individual member shall be "the trustee of the estate of………..., a bankrupt" (inserting the name of the individual member); but he may be referred to as "the trustee in bankruptcy" of the particular member."

18   Sections 146 and 331: Duty to summon final meeting of creditors

18   Sections 146 and 331 are modified so as to read as follows:–

"146   Final Account

146(1)   This section applies if it appears to the responsible insolvency practitioner of an insolvent partnership which is being wound up by virtue of article 8 of the Insolvent Partnerships Order 1994 and of its insolvent member or members that the winding up of the partnership or of any corporate member, or the administration of any individual member's estate is for practical purposes complete and the practitioner is not the official receiver.

146(2)   The responsible insolvency practitioner must make up an account of the winding up or administration, showing how it has been conducted and the property disposed of.

146(3)   The responsible insolvency practitioner must–

(a)   send a copy of the account to the creditors of the partnership (other than opted-out creditors), and

(b)   give the partnership's creditors (other than opted-out creditors) a notice explaining the effect of section 174(4)(d) and how they may object to the liquidator's release.

146(4)   The liquidator must during the relevant period send to the court and, in the case of a corporate member, send to the registrar of companies–

(a)   a copy of the account, and

(b)   a statement of whether any of the partnership's creditors objected to the liquidator's release.

146(5)   The relevant period is the period of 7 days beginning with the day after the last day of the period prescribed by the rules as the period within which the creditors may object to the responsible insolvency practitioner's release."

History
In para.18 modified s.146 substituted by the Deregulation Act 2015 and Small Business, Enterprise and Employment Act 2015 (Consequential Amendments) (Savings) Regulations 2017 (SI 2017/540) regs 1, 3, Sch.2 paras 2, 8(1), (7) as from 6 April 2017.

19   Section 147: Power of court to stay proceedings

19   Section 147 is modified, so far as insolvent partnerships are concerned, so as to read as follows:–

"**147(1)**   The court may, at any time after an order has been made by virtue of article 8 of the Insolvent Partnerships Order 1994 for winding up an insolvent partnership, on the application either of the responsible insolvency practitioner or the official receiver or any creditor or contributory, and on proof to the satisfaction of the court that all proceedings in the winding up of the partnership ought to be stayed, make an order staying the proceedings, either altogether or for a limited time, on such terms and conditions as the court thinks fit.

147(2)   If, in the course of hearing an insolvency petition presented against a member of an insolvent partnership, the court is satisfied that an application has been or will be made under subsection (1) in respect of a winding-up order made against the partnership, the court may adjourn the petition against the insolvent member, either conditionally or unconditionally.

147(3)   Where the court makes an order under subsection (1) staying all proceedings on the order for winding up an insolvent partnership–

(a)   the court may, on hearing any insolvency petition presented against an insolvent member of the partnership, dismiss that petition; and

(b) if any insolvency order has already been made by virtue of article 8 of the Insolvent Partnerships Order 1994 in relation to an insolvent member of the partnership, the court may make an order annulling or rescinding that insolvency order, or may make any other order that it thinks fit.

147(4) The court may, before making any order under this section, require the official receiver to furnish to it a report with respect to any facts or matters which are in his opinion relevant to the application."

19A Sections 165 and 167

19A(1) Section 165(2) has effect as if for "Parts 1 to 3" there were substituted "Parts 1 and 2".

19A(2) Section 167(1) has effect as if for "Parts 1 to 3" there were substituted "Parts 1 and 2".

History
Paragraph 19A inserted by the Deregulation Act 2015 and Small Business, Enterprise and Employment Act 2015 (Consequential Amendments) (Savings) Regulations 2017 (SI 2017/540) regs 1, 3, Sch.2 paras 2, 8(1), (8) as from 6 April 2017.

20 Sections 168, 303 and 314(7): Supplementary powers of responsible insolvency practitioner

20 Sections 168(1) to (3) and (5), 303 and 314(7) are modified so as to read as follows:–

"**168(1)** This section applies where the court has made insolvency orders in respect of an insolvent partnership and one or more of its insolvent members by virtue of article 8 of the Insolvent Partnerships Order 1994.

168(2) The responsible insolvency practitioner may seek a decision on any matter from the creditors of the partnership or of any insolvent member; and must seek a decision on a matter if requested to do so by one-tenth in value of the creditors.

168(3) [Omitted]

168(4) The responsible insolvency practitioner may apply to the court (in the prescribed manner) for directions in relation to any particular matter arising in the winding up of the insolvent partnership or in the winding up or bankruptcy of an insolvent member.

168(5) If any person is aggrieved by an act or decision of the responsible insolvency practitioner, that person may apply to the court; and the court may confirm, reverse or modify the act or decision complained of, and make such order in the case as it thinks just."

History
In para.20 modified s.168(2) amended and s.168(3) omitted by the Deregulation Act 2015 and Small Business, Enterprise and Employment Act 2015 (Consequential Amendments) (Savings) Regulations 2017 (SI 2017/540) regs 1, 3, Sch.2 paras 2, 8(1), (9) as from 6 April 2017.

21 Sections 172 and 298: Removal etc. of responsible insolvency practitioner or of provisional liquidator

21 Sections 172 and 298 are modified so as to read as follows:–

"**172(1)** This section applies with respect to the removal from office and vacation of office of–

(a) the responsible insolvency practitioner of an insolvent partnership which is being wound up by virtue of article 8 of the Insolvent Partnerships Order 1994 and of its insolvent member or members against whom insolvency orders have been made, or

(b) a provisional liquidator of an insolvent partnership, and of any corporate member of that partnership, against which a winding-up petition is presented by virtue of that article,

and, subject to subsections (6) and (7) below, any removal from or vacation of office under this section relates to all offices held in the proceedings relating to the partnership.

172(2) Subject as follows, the responsible insolvency practitioner or provisional liquidator may be removed from office only by an order of the court.

172(3) If appointed by the Secretary of State, the responsible insolvency practitioner may be removed from office by a direction of the Secretary of State.

172(4) A responsible insolvency practitioner or provisional liquidator, not being the official receiver, shall vacate office if he ceases to be a person who is qualified to act as an insolvency practitioner in relation to the insolvent partnership or any insolvent member of it against whom an insolvency order has been made.

172(5) The responsible insolvency practitioner may, with the leave of the court (or, if appointed by the Secretary of State, with the leave of the court or the Secretary of State), resign his office by giving notice of his resignation to the court.

172(6) A responsible insolvency practitioner who has produced an account of the winding up or administration under section 146 must vacate office immediately upon complying with the requirements of section 146(3).

172(7) The responsible insolvency practitioner shall vacate office as trustee of the estate of an individual member if the insolvency order against that member is annulled."

History
In para.21 modified s.172(6) substituted by the Deregulation Act 2015 and Small Business, Enterprise and Employment Act 2015 (Consequential Amendments) (Savings) Regulations 2017 (SI 2017/540) regs 1, 3, Sch.2 paras 2, 8(1), (10) as from 6 April 2017.

22 Sections 174 and 299: Release of responsible insolvency practitioner or of provisional liquidator

22 Sections 174 and 299 are modified so as to read as follows:–

"**174(1)** This section applies with respect to the release of–

(a) the responsible insolvency practitioner of an insolvent partnership which is being wound up by virtue of article 8 of the Insolvent Partnerships Order 1994 and of its insolvent member or members against whom insolvency orders have been made, or

(b) a provisional liquidator of an insolvent partnership, and of any corporate member of that partnership, against which a winding-up petition is presented by virtue of that article.

174(2) Where the official receiver has ceased to be the responsible insolvency practitioner and a person is appointed in his stead, the official receiver has his release with effect from the following time, that is to say–

(a) in a case where that person was nominated by the creditors of the partnership and of any insolvent member or members, or was appointed by the Secretary of State, the time at which the official receiver gives notice to the court that he has been replaced;

(b) in a case where that person is appointed by the court, such time as the court may determine.

174(3) If the official receiver while he is a responsible insolvency practitioner gives notice to the Secretary of State that the winding up of the partnership or of any corporate member or the administration of the estate of any individual member is for practical purposes complete, he has his release as liquidator or trustee (as the case may be) with effect from such time as the Secretary of State may determine.

174(4) A person other than the official receiver who has ceased to be a responsible insolvency practitioner has his release with effect from the following time, that is to say–

(a) in the case of a person who has died, the time at which notice is given to the court in accordance with the rules that person has ceased to hold office;

(b) in the case of a person who has been removed from office by the court or by the Secretary of State, or who has vacated office under section 172(4), such time as the Secretary of State may, on an application by that person, determine;

(c) in the case of a person who has resigned, such time as may be directed by the court (or, if he was appointed by the Secretary of State, such time as may be directed by the court or as the Secretary of State may, on an application by that person, determine);

(d) in the case of a person who has vacated office under section 172(6)–

(i)   if any of the creditors of the partnership or of any insolvent member objected to the person's release before the end of the period for so objecting prescribed by the rules, such time as the Secretary of State may, on an application by that person, determine, and

(ii)   otherwise, the time at which the person vacated office.

174(5)   A person who has ceased to hold office as a provisional liquidator has his release with effect from such time as the court may, on an application by him, determine.

174(6)   Where a bankruptcy order in respect of an individual member is annulled, the responsible insolvency practitioner at the time of the annulment has his release with effect from such time as the court may determine.

174(7)   Where the responsible insolvency practitioner or provisional liquidator (including in both cases the official receiver when so acting) has his release under this section, he is, with effect from the time specified in the preceding provisions of this section, discharged from all liability both in respect of acts or omissions of his in the winding up of the insolvent partnership or any corporate member or the administration of the estate of any individual member (as the case may be) and otherwise in relation to his conduct as responsible insolvency practitioner or provisional liquidator.

But nothing in this section prevents the exercise, in relation to a person who has had his release under this section, of the court's powers under section 212 (summary remedy against delinquent directors, liquidators, etc.) or section 304 (liability of trustee)."

History
In para.22 modified s.174(2)(a) amended and s.174(4)(d) substituted by the Deregulation Act 2015 and Small Business, Enterprise and Employment Act 2015 (Consequential Amendments) (Savings) Regulations 2017 (SI 2017/540) regs 1, 3, Sch.2 paras 2, 8(1), (11) as from 6 April 2017.

23   Sections 175, 176AZA and 328: Priority of expenses and debts

23   Sections 175, 176AZA and 328(1) to (3) and (6) are modified so as to read as follows:–

"175   Priority of expenses

175(1)   The provisions of this section shall apply in a case where article 8 of the Insolvent Partnerships Order 1994 applies, as regards priority of expenses incurred by a responsible insolvency practitioner of an insolvent partnership, and of any insolvent member of that partnership against whom an insolvency order has been made.

175(2)   The joint estate of the partnership shall be applicable in the first instance in payment of the joint expenses and the separate estate of each insolvent member shall be applicable in the first instance in payment of the separate expenses relating to that member.

175(3)   Where the joint estate is insufficient for the payment in full of the joint expenses, the unpaid balance shall be apportioned equally between the separate estates of the insolvent members against whom insolvency orders have been made and shall form part of the expenses to be paid out of those estates.

175(4)   Where any separate estate of an insolvent member is insufficient for the payment in full of the separate expenses to be paid out of that estate, the unpaid balance shall form part of the expenses to be paid out of the joint estate.

175(5)   Where after the transfer of any unpaid balance in accordance with subsection (3) or (4) any estate is insufficient for the payment in full of the expenses to be paid out of that estate, the balance then remaining unpaid shall be apportioned equally between the other estates.

175(6)   Where after an apportionment under subsection (5) one or more estates are insufficient for the payment in full of the expenses to be paid out of those estates, the total of the unpaid balances of the expenses to be paid out of those estates shall continue to be apportioned equally between the other estates until provision is made for the payment in full of the expenses or there is no estate available for the payment of the balance finally remaining unpaid, in which case it abates in equal proportions between all the estates.

175(7)   Without prejudice to subsections (3) to (6) above, the responsible insolvency practitioner may, with the sanction of any creditors' committee established under section 141 or with the leave of the court obtained on application–

(a)   pay out of the joint estate as part of the expenses to be paid out of that estate any expenses incurred for any separate estate of an insolvent member; or

(b)   pay out of any separate estate of an insolvent member any part of the expenses incurred for the joint estate which affects that separate estate.

175A   Priority of debts in joint estate

175A(1)   The provisions of this section and the next (which are subject to the provisions of section 9 of the Partnership Act 1890 as respects the liability of the estate of a deceased member) shall apply as regards priority of debts in a case where article 8 of the Insolvent Partnerships Order 1994 applies.

175A(2)   After payment of expenses in accordance with section 175 and subject to section 175C(2), the joint debts of the partnership shall be paid out of its joint estate in the following order of priority–

(a)   the ordinary preferential debts;

(aa)   the secondary preferential debts;

(b)   the ordinary non-preferential debts;

(ba)   the secondary non-preferential debts;

(bb)   the tertiary non-preferential debts;

(c)   interest under section 189 on the joint debts (other than postponed debts);

(d)   the postponed debts;

(e)   interest under section 189 on the postponed debts.

175A(3)   The responsible insolvency practitioner shall adjust the rights among themselves of the members of the partnership as contributories and shall distribute any surplus to the members or, where applicable, to the separate estates of the members, according to their respective rights and interests in it.

175A(4)   The debts referred to in each of paragraphs (a) to (ba) of subsection (2) rank equally between themselves, and in each case if the joint estate is insufficient for meeting them, they abate in equal proportions between themselves.

175A(5)   Where the joint estate is not sufficient for the payment of the joint debts in accordance with paragraphs (a), (aa) and (b) of subsection (2), the responsible insolvency practitioner shall aggregate the value of those debts to the extent that they have not been satisfied or are not capable of being satisfied, and that aggregate amount shall be a claim against the separate estate of each member of the partnership against whom an insolvency order has been made which–

(a)   shall be a debt provable by the responsible insolvency practitioner in each such estate, and

(b)   shall rank equally with the debts of the member referred to in section 175B(1)(b) below.

175A(5A)   Where the joint estate is not sufficient for the payment of the secondary non-preferential debts in accordance with paragraph (ba) of subsection (2), the responsible insolvency practitioner shall aggregate the value of those debts to the extent that they have not been satisfied or are not capable of being satisfied, and that aggregate amount shall be a claim against the separate estate of each member of the partnership against whom an insolvency order has been made which–

(a)   shall be a debt provable by the responsible insolvency practitioner in each such estate, and

(b)   shall rank equally with the debts of the member referred to in section 175B(1)(ba) below.

175A(5B)   Where the joint estate is not sufficient for the payment of the tertiary non-preferential debts in accordance with paragraph (bb) of subsection (2), the responsible insolvency practitioner shall aggregate the value of those debts to the extent that they have not been satisfied or are not capable of being satisfied, and that aggregate amount shall be a claim against the separate estate of each member of the partnership against whom an insolvency order has been made which–

(a)   shall be a debt provable by the responsible insolvency practitioner in each such estate, and

(b)   shall rank as a debt of the member in accordance with section 175B(1)(bc) below.

175A(6)   Where the joint estate is sufficient for the payment of the joint debts in accordance with paragraphs (a) to (bb) of subsection (2) but not for the payment of interest under paragraph (c) of that subsection, the responsible insolvency practitioner shall aggregate the value of that interest to the extent that it has not been satisfied or is not capable of being satisfied, and that aggregate amount shall be a claim against the separate estate of each member of the partnership against whom an insolvency order has been made which–

(a)   shall be a debt provable by the responsible insolvency practitioner in each such estate, and

(b)   shall rank equally with the interest on the separate debts referred to in section 175B(1)(c) below.

175A(7)   Where the joint estate is not sufficient for the payment of the postponed joint debts in accordance with paragraph (d) of subsection (2), the responsible insolvency practitioner shall aggregate the value of those debts to the extent that they have not been satisfied or are not capable of being satisfied, and that aggregate amount shall be a claim against the separate estate of each member of the partnership against whom an insolvency order has been made which–

(a)   shall be a debt provable by the responsible insolvency practitioner in each such estate, and

(b)   shall rank equally with the postponed debts of the member referred to in section 175B(1)(d) below.

175A(8)   Where the joint estate is sufficient for the payment of the postponed joint debts in accordance with paragraph (d) of subsection (2) but not for the payment of interest under paragraph (e) of that subsection, the responsible insolvency practitioner shall aggregate the value of that interest to the extent that it has not been satisfied or is not capable of being satisfied, and that aggregate amount shall be a claim against the separate estate of each member of the partnership against whom an insolvency order has been made which–

(a)   shall be a debt provable by the responsible insolvency practitioner in each such estate, and

(b)   shall rank equally with the interest on the postponed debts referred to in section 175B(1)(e) below.

175A(9)   Where the responsible insolvency practitioner receives any distribution from the separate estate of a member in respect of a debt referred to in paragraph (a) of subsection (5), (5A), (5B), (6), (7) or (8) above, that distribution shall become part of the joint estate and shall be distributed in accordance with the order of priority set out in subsection (2) above.

175B   Priority of debts in separate estate

175B(1)   The separate estate of each member of the partnership against whom an insolvency order has been made shall be applicable, after payment of expenses in accordance with section 175 and subject to section 175C(2) below, in payment of the separate debts of that member in the following order of priority–

(a)   the ordinary preferential debts;

(aa)   the secondary preferential debts;

(b)   the ordinary non-preferential debts (including any debt referred to in section 175A(5)(a));

(ba)   the secondary non-preferential debts (including any debt referred to in section 175A(5A)(a));

(bb)   the tertiary non-preferential debts;

(bc)   the debt referred to in section 175A(5B)(a);

(c)   interest under section 189 on the separate debts and under section 175A(6);

(d)   the postponed debts of the member (including any debt referred to in section 175A(7)(a));

(e)   interest under section 189 on the postponed debts of the member and under section 175A(8).

175B(2)   The debts referred to in each of paragraphs (a) to (ba) of subsection (1) rank equally between themselves, and in each case if the separate estate is insufficient for meeting them, they abate in equal proportions between themselves.

175B(3)   Where the responsible insolvency practitioner receives any distribution from the joint estate or from the separate estate of another member of the partnership against whom an insolvency order has been made, that distribution shall become part of the separate estate and shall be distributed in accordance with the order of priority set out in subsection (1) of this section.

175C   Provisions generally applicable in distribution of joint and separate estates

175C(1)   Distinct accounts shall be kept of the joint estate of the partnership and of the separate estate of each member of that partnership against whom an insolvency order is made.

175C(2)   No member of the partnership shall prove for a joint or separate debt in competition with the joint creditors, unless the debt has arisen–

   (a)   as a result of fraud, or

   (b)   in the ordinary course of a business carried on separately from the partnership business.

175C(3)   For the purpose of establishing the value of any debt referred to in section 175A(5)(a), (5A)(a), (5B)(a) or (7)(a), that value may be estimated by the responsible insolvency practitioner in accordance with section 322 or (as the case may be) in accordance with the rules.

175C(4)   Interest under section 189 on preferential debts ranks equally with interest on ordinary non-preferential debts, secondary non-preferential debts and tertiary non-preferential debts.

175C(5)   Sections 175A and 175B are without prejudice to any provision of this Act or of any other enactment concerning the ranking between themselves of postponed debts and interest thereon, but in the absence of any such provision postponed debts and interest thereon rank equally between themselves.

175C(6)   If any two or more members of an insolvent partnership constitute a separate partnership, the creditors of such separate partnership shall be deemed to be a separate set of creditors and subject to the same statutory provisions as the separate creditors of any member of the insolvent partnership.

175C(7)   Where any surplus remains after the administration of the estate of a separate partnership, the surplus shall be distributed to the members or, where applicable, to the separate estates of the members of that partnership according to their respective rights and interests in it.

175C(8)   Neither the official receiver, the Secretary of State nor a responsible insolvency practitioner shall be entitled to remuneration or fees under the Insolvency (England and Wales) Rules 2016, the Insolvency Regulations 1986 or the Insolvency Fees Order 1986 for his services in connection with–

   (a)   the transfer of a surplus from the joint estate to a separate estate under section 175A(3),

   (b)   a distribution from a separate estate to the joint estate in respect of a claim referred to in section 175A(5), (5A), (5B), (6), (7) or (8), or

   (c)   a distribution from the estate of a separate partnership to the separate estates of the members of that partnership under subsection (7) above."

History
In para.23, modified s.175A(4)–(6) amended, s.175A(2)(aa) inserted, s.175B(2) amended and s.175B(1)(aa) inserted by the Banks and Building Societies (Depositor Preference and Priorities) Order 2014 (SI 2014/3486) art.14(1)–(4) as from 1 January 2015.
  Modified s.175C(8) amended by the Insolvency (Miscellaneous Amendments) Regulations 2017 (SI 2017/1119) regs 1(1), (6), 2, Sch.2 paras 1, 5(1), (3) as from December 2017 subject to transitional and savings provision in para.10.
  Modified s.175A(2), (4), amended, s.175A(5A), (5B) inserted, ss.175A(6), (9), 175B(1), (2) and 175C(3), (4), (8) amended by the Banks and Building Societies (Priorities on Insolvency) Order 2018 (SI 2018/1244) arts 1, 3, 15, 20 as from 19 December 2018 in relation to insolvency proceedings commenced on or after that date.

24   Sections 189 and 328: Interest on debts

24   Sections 189 and 328(4) and (5) are modified so as to read as follows:–

   "**189(1)**   In the winding up of an insolvent partnership or the winding up or bankruptcy (as the case may be) of any of its insolvent members interest is payable in accordance with this section, in the order of priority laid down by sections 175A and 175B, on any debt proved in the winding up or bankruptcy, including so much of any such debt as represents interest on the remainder.

189(2)　Interest under this section is payable on the debts in question in respect of the periods during which they have been outstanding since the winding-up order was made against the partnership or any corporate member (as the case may be) or the bankruptcy order was made against any individual member.

189(3)　The rate of interest payable under this section in respect of any debt ("the official rate" for the purposes of any provision of this Act in which that expression is used) is whichever is the greater of–

(a)　the rate specified in section 17 of the Judgments Act 1838 on the day on which the winding-up or bankruptcy order (as the case may be) was made, and

(b)　the rate applicable to that debt apart from the winding up or bankruptcy."

25　Sections 211 and 356: False representations to creditors

25　Sections 211 and 356(2)(d) are modified so as to read as follows:–

"**211(1)**　This section applies where insolvency orders are made against an insolvent partnership and any insolvent member or members of it by virtue of article 8 of the Insolvent Partnerships Order 1994.

211(2)　Any person, being a past or present officer of the partnership or a past or present officer (which for these purposes includes a shadow director) of a corporate member against which an insolvency order has been made–

(a)　commits an offence if he makes any false representation or commits any other fraud for the purpose of obtaining the consent of the creditors of the partnership (or any of them) or of the creditors of any of its members (or any of such creditors) to an agreement with reference to the affairs of the partnership or of any of its members or to the winding up of the partnership or of a corporate member, or the bankruptcy of an individual member, and

(b)　is deemed to have committed that offence if, prior to the winding up or bankruptcy (as the case may be), he has made any false representation, or committed any other fraud, for that purpose.

211(3)　A person guilty of an offence under this section is liable to imprisonment or a fine, or both."

26　Sections 230, 231 and 292: Appointment to office of responsible insolvency practitioner or provisional liquidator

26　Sections 230, 231 and 292 are modified so as to read as follows:–

"**230(1)**　This section applies with respect to the appointment of–

(a)　the responsible insolvency practitioner of an insolvent partnership which is being wound up by virtue of article 8 of the Insolvent Partnerships Order 1994 and of one or more of its insolvent members, or

(b)　a provisional liquidator of an insolvent partnership, or of any of its corporate members, against which a winding-up petition is presented by virtue of that article,

but is without prejudice to any enactment under which the official receiver is to be, or may be, responsible insolvency practitioner or provisional liquidator.

230(2)　No person may be appointed as responsible insolvency practitioner unless he is, at the time of the appointment, qualified to act as an insolvency practitioner both in relation to the insolvent partnership and to the insolvent member or members.

230(3)　No person may be appointed as provisional liquidator unless he is, at the time of the appointment, qualified to act as an insolvency practitioner both in relation to the insolvent partnership and to any corporate member in respect of which he is appointed.

230(4)　If the appointment or nomination of any person to the office of responsible insolvency practitioner or provisional liquidator relates to more than one person, or has the effect that the office is to be held by more than one person, then subsection (5) below applies.

230(5)　The appointment or nomination shall declare whether any act required or authorised under any enactment to be done by the responsible insolvency practitioner or by the provisional liquidator is to be done by all or any one or more of the persons for the time being holding the office in question.

230(6) The appointment of any person as responsible insolvency practitioner takes effect only if that person accepts the appointment in accordance with the rules. Subject to this, the appointment of any person as responsible insolvency practitioner takes effect at the time specified in his certificate of appointment.

230A Conflicts of interest

230A(1) If the responsible insolvency practitioner of an insolvent partnership being wound up by virtue of article 8 of the Insolvent Partnerships Order 1994 and of one or more of its insolvent members is of the opinion at any time that there is a conflict of interest between his functions as liquidator of the partnership and his functions as responsible insolvency practitioner of any insolvent member, or between his functions as responsible insolvency practitioner of two or more insolvent members, he may apply to the court for directions.

230A(2) On an application under subsection (1), the court may, without prejudice to the generality of its power to give directions, appoint one or more insolvency practitioners either in place of the applicant to act as responsible insolvency practitioner of both the partnership and its insolvent member or members or to act as joint responsible insolvency practitioner with the applicant."

27   Section 234: Getting in the partnership property

27   Section 234 is modified, so far as insolvent partnerships are concerned, so as to read as follows:–

"**234(1)** This section applies where–

(a) insolvency orders are made by virtue of article 8 of the Insolvent Partnerships Order 1994 in respect of an insolvent partnership and its insolvent member or members, or

(b) a provisional liquidator of an insolvent partnership and any of its corporate members is appointed by virtue of that article;

and "the office-holder" means the liquidator or the provisional liquidator, as the case may be.

234(2) Any person who is or has been an officer of the partnership, or who is an executor or administrator of the estate of a deceased officer of the partnership, shall deliver up to the office-holder, for the purposes of the exercise of the office-holder's functions under this Act and (where applicable) the Company Directors Disqualification Act 1986, possession of any partnership property which he holds for the purposes of the partnership.

234(3) Where any person has in his possession or control any property, books, papers or records to which the partnership appears to be entitled, the court may require that person forthwith (or within such period as the court may direct) to pay, deliver, convey, surrender or transfer the property, books, papers or records to the office-holder or as the court may direct.

234(4) Where the office-holder–

(a) seizes or disposes of any property which is not partnership property, and

(b) at the time of seizure or disposal believes, and has reasonable grounds for believing, that he is entitled (whether in pursuance of an order of the court or otherwise) to seize or dispose of that property,

the next subsection has effect.

234(5) In that case the office-holder–

(a) is not liable to any person in respect of any loss or damage resulting from the seizure or disposal except in so far as that loss or damage is caused by the office-holder's own negligence, and

(b) has a lien on the property, or the proceeds of its sale, for such expenses as were incurred in connection with the seizure or disposal."

28   Section 283: Definition of individual member's estate

28   Section 283 is modified so as to read as follows:–

"**283(1)** Subject as follows, the estate of an individual member for the purposes of this Act comprises–

(a) all property belonging to or vested in the individual member at the commencement of the bankruptcy, and

(b)   any property which by virtue of any of the provisions of this Act is comprised in that estate or is treated as falling within the preceding paragraph.

283(2)   Subsection (1) does not apply to–

(a)   such tools, books, vehicles and other items of equipment as are not partnership property and as are necessary to the individual member for use personally by him in his employment, business or vocation;

(b)   such clothing, bedding, furniture, household equipment and provisions as are not partnership property and as are necessary for satisfying the basic domestic needs of the individual member and his family.

This subsection is subject to section 308 in Chapter IV (certain excluded property reclaimable by trustee).

283(3)   Subsection (1) does not apply to–

(a)   property held by the individual member on trust for any other person, or

(b)   the right of nomination to a vacant ecclesiastical benefice.

283(4)   References in any provision of this Act to property, in relation to an individual member, include references to any power exercisable by him over or in respect of property except in so far as the power is exercisable over or in respect of property not for the time being comprised in the estate of the individual member and–

(a)   is so exercisable at a time after either the official receiver has had his release in respect of that estate under section 174(3) or the trustee of that estate has vacated office under section 298(6), or

(b)   cannot be so exercised for the benefit of the individual member;

and a power exercisable over or in respect of property is deemed for the purposes of any provision of this Act to vest in the person entitled to exercise it at the time of the transaction or event by virtue of which it is exercisable by that person (whether or not it becomes so exercisable at that time).

283(5)   For the purposes of any such provision of this Act, property comprised in an individual member's estate is so comprised subject to the rights of any person other than the individual member (whether as a secured creditor of the individual member or otherwise) in relation thereto, but disregarding any rights which have been given up in accordance with the rules.

283(6)   This section has effect subject to the provisions of any enactment not contained in this Act under which any property is to be excluded from a bankrupt's estate."

History

In para.28 modified s.283(4)(a) amended by the Deregulation Act 2015 and Small Business, Enterprise and Employment Act 2015 (Consequential Amendments) (Savings) Regulations 2017 (SI 2017/540) regs 1, 3, Sch.2 paras 2, 8(1), (12) as from 6 April 2017.

28A   Section 283A: Individual member's home ceasing to form part of estate

28A   Section 283A is modified so as to read as follows:–

"**283A(1)**   This section applies where property comprised in the estate of an individual member consists of an interest in a dwelling-house which at the date of the bankruptcy was the sole or principal residence of–

(a)   the individual member;

(b)   the individual member's spouse or civil partner, or

(c)   a former spouse or former civil partner of the individual member.

283A(2)   At the end of the period of three years beginning with the date of the bankruptcy the interest mentioned in subsection (1) shall–

(a)   cease to be comprised in the individual member's estate, and

(b)   vest in the individual member (without conveyance, assignment or transfer).

283A(3)   Subsection (2) shall not apply if during the period mentioned in that subsection–

(a)   the trustee realises the interest mentioned in subsection (1),

(b)   the trustee applies for an order for sale in respect of the dwelling-house,

(c)   the trustee applies for an order for possession of the dwelling-house,

(d)   the trustee applies for an order under section 313 in Chapter IV in respect of that interest, or

(e)   the trustee and the individual member agree that the individual member shall incur a specified liability to his estate (with or without the addition of interest from the date of the agreement) in consideration of which the interest mentioned in subsection (1) shall cease to form part of the estate.

283A(4)   Where an application of a kind described in subsection (3)(b) to (d) is made during the period mentioned in subsection (2) and is dismissed, unless the court orders otherwise the interest to which the application relates shall on the dismissal of the application–

(a)   cease to be comprised in the individual member's estate, and

(b)   vest in the individual member (without conveyance, assignment or transfer).

283A(5)   If the individual member does not inform the trustee or the official receiver of his interest in a property before the end of the period of three months beginning with the date of the bankruptcy, the period of three years mentioned in subsection (2)–

(a)   shall not begin with the date of the bankruptcy, but

(b)   shall begin with the date on which the trustee or official receiver becomes aware of the individual member's interest.

283A(6)   The court may substitute for the period of three years mentioned in subsection (2) a longer period–

(a)   in prescribed circumstances, and

(b)   in such other circumstances as the court thinks appropriate.

283A(7)   The rules may make provision for this section to have effect with the substitution of a shorter period for the period of three years mentioned in subsection (2) in specified circumstances (which may be described by reference to action to be taken by a trustee in bankruptcy).

283A(8)   The rules may also, in particular, make provision–

(a)   requiring or enabling the trustee of an individual member's estate to give notice that this section applies or does not apply;

(b)   about the effect of a notice under paragraph (a);

(c)   requiring the trustee of an individual member's estate to make an application to the Chief Land Registrar.

283A(9)   Rules under subsection (8)(b) may, in particular–

(a)   disapply this section;

(b)   enable a court to disapply this section;

(c)   make provision in consequence of a disapplication of this section;

(d)   enable a court to make provision in consequence of a disapplication of this section;

(e)   make provision (which may include provision conferring jurisdiction on a court or tribunal) about compensation."

History
Paragraph 28A inserted by the Insolvent Partnerships (Amendment) Order 2005 (SI 2005/1516) art.9(1), (4) as from 1 July 2005.

29   Section 284: Individual member: Restrictions on dispositions of property

29   Section 284 is modified so as to read as follows:–

"**284(1)**   Where an individual member is adjudged bankrupt by virtue of article 8 of the Insolvent Partnerships Order 1994, any disposition of property made by that member in the period to which this section applies is void except to the extent that it is or was made with the consent of the court, or is or was subsequently ratified by the court.

284(2)   Subsection (1) applies to a payment (whether in cash or otherwise) as it applies to a disposition of property and, accordingly, where any payment is void by virtue of that subsection, the person paid shall hold the sum paid for the individual member as part of his estate.

284(3)   This section applies to the period beginning with the day of the presentation of the petition for the bankruptcy order and ending with the vesting, under Chapter IV of this Part, of the individual member's estate in a trustee.

284(4)   The preceding provisions of this section do not give a remedy against any person–

(a)   in respect of any property or payment which he received before the commencement of the bankruptcy in good faith, for value and without notice that the petition had been presented, or

(b)   in respect of any interest in property which derives from an interest in respect of which there is, by virtue of this subsection, no remedy.

284(5)   Where after the commencement of his bankruptcy the individual member has incurred a debt to a banker or other person by reason of the making of a payment which is void under this section, that debt is deemed for the purposes of any provision of this Act to have been incurred before the commencement of the bankruptcy unless–

(a)   that banker or person had notice of the bankruptcy before the debt was incurred, or

(b)   it is not reasonably practicable for the amount of the payment to be recovered from the person to whom it was made.

284(6)   A disposition of property is void under this section notwithstanding that the property is not or, as the case may be, would not be comprised in the individual member's estate; but nothing in this section affects any disposition made by a person of property held by him on trust for any other person other than a disposition made by an individual member of property held by him on trust for the partnership."

29A   Section 313A: Low value home: Application for sale, possession or charge

29A   Section 313A is modified so as to read as follows:–

"**313A(1)**   This section applies where-

(a)   property comprised in the individual member's estate consists of an interest in a dwelling-house which at the date of the bankruptcy was the sole or principal residence of–

(i)   the individual member,

(ii)   the individual member's spouse or civil partner, or

(iii)   a former spouse or former civil partner of the individual member, and

(b)   the trustee applies for an order for the sale of the property, for an order for possession of the property or for an order under section 313 in respect of the property.

313A(2)   The court shall dismiss the application if the value of the interest is below the amount prescribed for the purposes of this subsection.

313A(3)   In determining the value of an interest for the purposes of this section the court shall disregard any matter which it is required to disregard by the order which prescribes the amount for the purposes of subsection (2)."

History

Paragraph 29A inserted by the Insolvent Partnerships (Amendment) Order 2005 (SI 2005/1516) art.9(1), (5) as from 1 July 2005, and modified by the Civil Partnership Act 2004 (Amendments to Subordinate Legislation) Order 2005 (SI 2005/2114) Sch.18 Pt I para.2(1), (3), as from 5 December 2005.

30   Schedule 4 is modified so as to read as follows:–

"SCHEDULE 4

POWERS OF LIQUIDATOR IN A WINDING UP

Section 167

PART I

1   Power to pay any class of creditors in full.

2   Power to make any compromise or arrangement with creditors or persons claiming to be creditors, or having or alleging themselves to have any claim (present or future, certain or contingent, ascertained or sounding only in damages) against the partnership, or whereby the partnership may be rendered liable.

3   Power to compromise, on such terms as may be agreed–

    (a)   all debts and liabilities capable of resulting in debts, and all claims (present or future, certain or contingent, ascertained or sounding only in damages) subsisting or supposed to subsist between the partnership and a contributory or alleged contributory or other debtor or person apprehending liability to the partnership, and

    (b)   all questions in any way relating to or affecting the partnership property or the winding up of the partnership,

and take any security for the discharge of any such debt, liability or claim and give a complete discharge in respect of it.

3A   Power to bring legal proceedings under section 213, 214, 238, 239 or 423.

4   Power to bring or defend any action or other legal proceeding in the name and on behalf of any member of the partnership in his capacity as such or of the partnership.

5   Power to carry on the business of the partnership so far as may be necessary for its beneficial winding up.

PART II

6   Power to sell any of the partnership property by public auction or private contract, with power to transfer the whole of it to any person or to sell the same in parcels.

7   Power to do all acts and execute, in the name and on behalf of the partnership or of any member of the partnership in his capacity as such, all deeds, receipts and other documents.

8   Power to prove, rank and claim in the bankruptcy, insolvency or sequestration of any contributory for any balance against his estate, and to receive dividends in the bankruptcy, insolvency or sequestration in respect of that balance, as a separate debt due from the bankrupt or insolvent, and rateably with the other separate creditors.

9   Power to draw, accept, make and endorse any bill of exchange or promissory note in the name and on behalf of any member of the partnership in his capacity as such or of the partnership, with the same effect with respect to the liability of the partnership or of any member of the partnership in his capacity as such as if the bill or note had been drawn, accepted, made or endorsed in the course of the partnership's business.

10   Power to raise on the security of the partnership property any money requisite.

11   Power to take out in his official name letters of administration to any deceased contributory, and to do in his official name any other act necessary for obtaining payment of any money due from a contributory or his estate which cannot conveniently be done in the name of the partnership.

In all such cases the money due is deemed, for the purpose of enabling the liquidator to take out the letters of administration or recover the money, to be due to the liquidator himself.

12   Power to appoint an agent to do any business which the liquidator is unable to do himself.

13   Power to do all such other things as may be necessary for winding up the partnership's affairs and distributing its property."

History
In Sch.4 the heading to Pt I and Pt II omitted by the Deregulation Act 2015 and Small Business, Enterprise and Employment Act 2015 (Consequential Amendments) (Savings) Regulations 2017 (SI 2017/540) regs 1, 3, Sch.2 paras 2, 8(1), (13), (14) as from 6 April 2017.
In para.30 (modified Sch.4) para.3A inserted by the Insolvent Partnerships (Amendment) Order 2005 (SI 2005/1516) art.9(1), (6) as from 1 July 2005.

SCHEDULE 5

PROVISIONS OF THE ACT WHICH APPLY WITH MODIFICATIONS FOR THE PURPOSES OF ARTICLE 9 TO WINDING UP OF INSOLVENT PARTNERSHIP ON MEMBER'S PETITION WHERE NO CONCURRENT PETITION PRESENTED AGAINST MEMBER

Article 9

1 Section 117: High Court and county court jurisdiction

1 Section 117 is modified so as to read as follows:–

"**117(1)** Subject to subsections (3) and (4) below, the High Court has jurisdiction to wind up any insolvent partnership as an unregistered company by virtue of article 9 of the Insolvent Partnerships Order 1994 if the partnership has, or at any time had, a principal place of business in England and Wales.

117(2) Subject to subsections (3) and (4) below, a petition for the winding up of an insolvent partnership by virtue of the said article 9 may be presented to a county court in England and Wales if the partnership has, or at any time had, a principal place of business within the insolvency district of that court.

117(3) Subject to subsection (4) below, the court only has jurisdiction to wind up an insolvent partnership if the business of the partnership has been carried on in England and Wales at any time in the period of 3 years ending with the day on which the petition for winding it up is presented.

117(4) If an insolvent partnership has a principal place of business situated in Scotland or in Northern Ireland, the court shall not have jurisdiction to wind up the partnership unless it had a principal place of business in England and Wales–

    (a)   in the case of a partnership with a principal place of business in Scotland, at any time in the period of 1 year, or

    (b)   in the case of a partnership with a principal place of business in Northern Ireland, at any time in the period of 3 years,

ending with the day on which the petition for winding it up is presented.

117(5) The Lord Chancellor may, with the concurrence of the Lord Chief Justice, by order in a statutory instrument exclude a county court from having winding-up jurisdiction, and for the purposes of that jurisdiction may attach its district, or any part thereof, to any other county court, and may by statutory instrument revoke or vary any such order.

In exercising the powers of this section, the Lord Chancellor shall provide that a county court is not to have winding-up jurisdiction unless it has for the time being jurisdiction for the purposes of Parts VIII to XI of this Act (individual insolvency).

117(6) Every court in England and Wales having winding-up jurisdiction has for the purposes of that jurisdiction all the powers of the High Court; and every prescribed officer of the court shall perform any duties which an officer of the High Court may discharge by order of a judge of that court or otherwise in relation to winding up.

117(7) This section is subject to Article 3 of the EC Regulation (jurisdiction under the EC Regulation).

117(8) The Lord Chief Justice may nominate a judicial office holder (as defined in section 109(4) of the Constitutional Reform Act 2005) to exercise his functions under this section."

History
Modified s.117(5) amended, and s.117(8) inserted, by the Lord Chancellor (Transfer of Functions and Supplementary Provisions) Order 2006 (SI 2006/680) Sch.2 paras 5, 6, as from 3 April 2006.

2   Section 221: Winding up of unregistered companies

2   Section 221 is modified so as to read as follows:–

"**221(1)**   Subject to subsections (2) and (3) below and to the provisions of this Part, any insolvent partnership which has, or at any time had, a principal place of business in England and Wales may be wound up under this Act.

221(2)   Subject to subsection (3) below an insolvent partnership shall not be wound up under this Act if the business of the partnership has not been carried on in England and Wales at any time in the period of 3 years ending with the day on which the winding-up petition is presented.

221(3)   If an insolvent partnership has a principal place of business situated in Scotland or in Northern Ireland, the court shall not have jurisdiction to wind up the partnership unless it had a principal place of business in England and Wales–

  (a)   in the case of a partnership with a principal place of business in Scotland, at any time in the period of 1 year, or

  (b)   in the case of a partnership with a principal place of business in Northern Ireland, at any time in the period of 3 years,

ending with the day on which the winding-up petition is presented.

221(3A)   The preceding subsections are subject to Article 3 of the EC Regulation (jurisdiction under the EC Regulation).

221(4)   No insolvent partnership shall be wound up under this Act voluntarily.

221(5)   To the extent that they are applicable to the winding up of a company by the court in England and Wales on a member's petition or on a petition by the company, all the provisions of this Act and the Companies Act about winding up apply to the winding up of an insolvent partnership as an unregistered company–

  (a)   with the exceptions and additions mentioned in the following subsections of this section and in section 221A, and

  (b)   with the modifications specified in Part II of Schedule 3 to the Insolvent Partnerships Order 1994.

221(6)   Sections 73(1), 74(2)(a) to (d) and (3), 75 to 78, 83, 122, 123, 124(2) and (3), 176A, 202, 203, 205 and 250 shall not apply.

History
Modified s.221(6) amended by the Insolvent Partnerships (Amendment) Order 2006 (SI 2006/622) art.8 as from 6 April 2006.

221(7)   The circumstances in which an insolvent partnership may be wound up as an unregistered company are as follows–

  (a)   if the partnership is dissolved, or has ceased to carry on business, or is carrying on business only for the purpose of winding up its affairs;

  (b)   if the partnership is unable to pay its debts;

  (c)   if the court is of the opinion that it is just and equitable that the partnership should be wound up.

221(8)   Every petition for the winding up of an insolvent partnership under Part V of this Act shall be verified by affidavit in Form 2 in Schedule 9 to the Insolvent Partnerships Order 1994.

221A   Who may present petition

221A(1)   A petition for winding up an insolvent partnership may be presented by any member of the partnership if the partnership consists of not less than 8 members.

221A(2) A petition for winding up an insolvent partnership may also be presented by any member of it with the leave of the court (obtained on his application) if the court is satisfied that–

   (a) the member has served on the partnership, by leaving at a principal place of business of the partnership in England and Wales, or by delivering to an officer of the partnership, or by otherwise serving in such manner as the court may approve or direct, a written demand in Form 10 in Schedule 9 to the Insolvent Partnerships Order 1994 in respect of a joint debt or debts exceeding £750 then due from the partnership but paid by the member, other than out of partnership property;

   (b) the partnership has for 3 weeks after the service of the demand neglected to pay the sum or to secure or compound for it to the member's satisfaction; and

   (c) the member has obtained a judgment, decree or order of any court against the partnership for reimbursement to him of the amount of the joint debt or debts so paid and all reasonable steps (other than insolvency proceedings) have been taken by the member to enforce that judgment, decree or order.

221A(3) Subsection (2)(a) above is deemed included in the list of provisions specified in subsection (1) of section 416 of this Act for the purposes of the Secretary of State's order-making power under that section."

SCHEDULE 6

PROVISIONS OF THE ACT WHICH APPLY WITH MODIFICATIONS FOR THE PURPOSES OF ARTICLE 10 TO WINDING UP OF INSOLVENT PARTNERSHIP ON MEMBER'S PETITION WHERE CONCURRENT PETITIONS ARE PRESENTED AGAINST ALL THE MEMBERS

Article 10

1   Sections 117 and 265: High Court and county court jurisdiction

1 Sections 117 and 265 are modified so as to read as follows:–

"**117(1)** Subject to the provisions of this section, the High Court has jurisdiction to wind up any insolvent partnership as an unregistered company by virtue of article 10 of the Insolvent Partnerships Order 1994 if the partnership has, or at any time had, a principal place of business in England and Wales.

117(2) Subject to the provisions of this section, a petition for the winding up of an insolvent partnership by virtue of the said article 10 may be presented to a county court in England and Wales if the partnership has, or at any time had, a principal place of business within the insolvency district of that court.

117(3) Subject to subsection (4) below, the court only has jurisdiction to wind up an insolvent partnership if the business of the partnership has been carried on in England and Wales at any time in the period of 3 years ending with the day on which the petition for winding it up is presented.

117(4) If an insolvent partnership has a principal place of business situated in Scotland or in Northern Ireland, the court shall not have jurisdiction to wind up the partnership unless it had a principal place of business in England and Wales–

   (a) in the case of a partnership with a principal place of business in Scotland, at any time in the period of 1 year, or

   (b) in the case of a partnership with a principal place of business in Northern Ireland, at any time in the period of 3 years,

ending with the day on which the petition for winding it up is presented.

117(5) Subject to subsection (6) below, the court has jurisdiction to wind up a corporate member, or make a bankruptcy order against an individual member, of a partnership against which a petition has been presented by virtue of article 10 of the Insolvent Partnerships Order 1994 if it has jurisdiction in respect of the partnership.

117(6) Petitions by virtue of the said article 10 for the winding up of an insolvent partnership and the bankruptcy of one or more members of that partnership may not be presented to a district registry of the High Court.

117(7)   The Lord Chancellor may, with the concurrence of the Lord Chief Justice, by order in a statutory instrument exclude a county court from having winding-up jurisdiction, and for the purposes of that jurisdiction may attach its district, or any part thereof, to any other county court, and may by statutory instrument revoke or vary any such order.

In exercising the powers of this section, the Lord Chancellor shall provide that a county court is not to have winding-up jurisdiction unless it has for the time being jurisdiction for the purposes of Parts VIII to XI of this Act (individual insolvency).

117(8)   Every court in England and Wales having winding-up jurisdiction has for the purposes of that jurisdiction all the powers of the High Court; and every prescribed officer of the court shall perform any duties which an officer of the High Court may discharge by order of a judge of that court or otherwise in relation to winding up.

117(9)   This section is subject to Article 3 of the EC Regulation (jurisdiction under the EC Regulation).

117(10)   The Lord Chief Justice may nominate a judicial office holder (as defined in section 109(4) of the Constitutional Reform Act 2005) to exercise his functions under this section."

History
Modified s.117(7) amended, and s.117(10) inserted, by the Lord Chancellor (Transfer of Functions and Supplementary Provisions) Order 2006 (SI 2006/680) Sch.2 paras 5, 7, as from 3 April 2006.

2   Sections 124 and 264: Applications to wind up insolvent partnership and to wind up or bankrupt insolvent members

2   Sections 124 and 264 are modified so as to read as follows:–

"**124(1)**   An application to the court by a member of an insolvent partnership by virtue of article 10 of the Insolvent Partnerships Order 1994 for the winding up of the partnership as an unregistered company and the winding up or bankruptcy (as the case may be) of all its members shall–

(a)   in the case of the partnership, be by petition in Form 11 in Schedule 9 to that Order,

(b)   in the case of a corporate member, be by petition in Form 12 in that Schedule, and

(c)   in the case of an individual member, be by petition in Form 13 in that Schedule.

124(2)   Subject to subsection (3) below, a petition under subsection (1)(a) may only be presented by a member of the partnership on the grounds that the partnership is unable to pay its debts and if–

(a)   petitions are at the same time presented by that member for insolvency orders against every member of the partnership (including himself or itself); and

(b)   each member is willing for an insolvency order to be made against him or it and the petition against him or it contains a statement to this effect.

124(3)   If the court is satisfied, on application by any member of an insolvent partnership, that presentation of petitions under subsection (1) against the partnership and every member of it would be impracticable, the court may direct that petitions be presented against the partnership and such member or members of it as are specified by the court.

124(4)   The petitions mentioned in subsection (1)–

(a)   shall all be presented to the same court and, except as the court otherwise permits or directs, on the same day, and

(b)   except in the case of the petition mentioned in subsection (1)(c) shall be advertised in Form 8 in the said Schedule 9.

124(5)   Each petition presented under this section shall contain particulars of the other petitions being presented in relation to the partnership, identifying the partnership and members concerned.

124(6)   The hearing of the petition against the partnership fixed by the court shall be in advance of the hearing of the petitions against the insolvent members.

124(7) On the day appointed for the hearing of the petition against the partnership, the petitioner shall, before the commencement of the hearing, hand to the court Form 9 in Schedule 9 to the Insolvent Partnerships Order 1994, duly completed.

124(8) Any person against whom a winding-up or bankruptcy petition has been presented in relation to the insolvent partnership is entitled to appear and to be heard on any petition for the winding up of the partnership.

124(9) A petitioner under this section may at the hearing withdraw the petition if–

(a) subject to subsection (10) below, he withdraws at the same time every other petition which he has presented under this section; and

(b) he gives notice to the court at least 3 days before the date appointed for the hearing of the relevant petition of his intention to withdraw the petition.

124(10) A petitioner need not comply with the provisions of subsection (9)(a) in the case of a petition against a member, if the court is satisfied on application made to it by the petitioner that, because of difficulties in serving the petition or for any other reason, the continuance of that petition would be likely to prejudice or delay the proceedings on the petition which he has presented against the partnership or on any petition which he has presented against any other insolvent member."

History

Paragraph 2 amended by the Insolvency (Miscellaneous Amendments) Regulations 2017 (SI 2017/1119) regs 1(1), (6), 2, Sch.2 paras 1, 6 as from 8 December 2017 subject to transitional and savings provision in para.10.

3 Sections 125 and 271: Powers of court on hearing of petitions against insolvent partnership and members

3 Sections 125 and 271 are modified so as to read as follows:–

"**125(1)** Subject to the provisions of section 125A, on hearing a petition under section 124 against an insolvent partnership or any of its insolvent members, the court may dismiss it, or adjourn the hearing conditionally or unconditionally or make any other order that it thinks fit; but the court shall not refuse to make a winding-up order against the partnership or a corporate member on the ground only that the partnership property or (as the case may be) the member's assets have been mortgaged to an amount equal to or in excess of that property or those assets, or that the partnership has no property or the member no assets.

125(2) An order under subsection (1) in respect of an insolvent partnership may contain directions as to the future conduct of any insolvency proceedings in existence against any insolvent member in respect of whom an insolvency order has been made.

125A Hearing of petitions against members

125A(1) On the hearing of a petition against an insolvent member the petitioner shall draw the court's attention to the result of the hearing of the winding-up petition against the partnership and the following subsections of this section shall apply.

125A(2) If the court has neither made a winding-up order, nor dismissed the winding-up petition, against the partnership the court may adjourn the hearing of the petition against the member until either event has occurred.

125A(3) Subject to subsection (4) below, if a winding-up order has been made against the partnership, the court may make a winding-up order against the corporate member in respect of which, or (as the case may be) a bankruptcy order against the individual member in respect of whom, the insolvency petition was presented.

125A(4) If no insolvency order is made under subsection (3) against any member within 28 days of the making of the winding-up order against the partnership, the proceedings against the partnership shall be conducted as if the winding-up petition against the partnership had been presented by virtue of article 7 of the Insolvent Partnerships Order 1994, and the proceedings against any member shall be conducted under this Act without the modifications made by that Order (other than the modifications made to sections 168 and 303 by article 14).

125A(5) If the court has dismissed the winding-up petition against the partnership, the court may dismiss the winding-up petition against the corporate member or (as the case may be) the bankruptcy petition against the individual member. However, if an insolvency order is made against a member, the proceedings against that member shall be conducted under this Act without the modifications made by the Insolvent Partnerships Order 1994 (other than the modifications made to sections 168 and 303 of this Act by article 14 of that Order).

125A(6)   The court may dismiss a petition against an insolvent member if it considers it just to do so because of a change in circumstances since the making of the winding-up order against the partnership.

125A(7)   The court may dismiss a petition against an insolvent member who is a limited partner, if–

   (a)   the member lodges in court for the benefit of the creditors of the partnership sufficient money or security to the court's satisfaction to meet his liability for the debts and obligations of the partnership; or

   (b)   the member satisfies the court that he is no longer under any liability in respect of the debts and obligations of the partnership."

4   Section 221: Winding up of unregistered companies

4   Section 221 is modified so as to read as follows:–

"**221(1)**   Subject to subsections (2) and (3) below and to the provisions of this Part, any insolvent partnership which has, or at any time had, a principal place of business in England and Wales may be wound up under this Act.

221(2)   Subject to subsection (3) below, an insolvent partnership shall not be wound up under this Act if the business of the partnership has not been carried on in England and Wales at any time in the period of 3 years ending with the day on which the winding-up petition is presented.

221(3)   If an insolvent partnership has a principal place of business situated in Scotland or in Northern Ireland, the court shall not have jurisdiction to wind up the partnership unless it had a principal place of business in England and Wales–

   (a)   in the case of a partnership with a principal place of business in Scotland, at any time in the period of 1 year, or

   (b)   in the case of a partnership with a principal place of business in Northern Ireland, at any time in the period of 3 years,

ending with the day on which the winding-up petition is presented.

221(3A)   The preceding subsections are subject to Article 3 of the EC Regulation (jurisdiction under the EC Regulation).

221(4)   No insolvent partnership shall be wound up under this Act voluntarily.

221(5)   To the extent that they are applicable to the winding up of a company by the court in England and Wales on a member's petition, all the provisions of this Act and the Companies Act about winding up apply to the winding up of an insolvent partnership as an unregistered company–

   (a)   with the exceptions and additions mentioned in the following subsections of this section, and

   (b)   with the modifications specified in Part II of Schedule 4 to the Insolvent Partnerships Order 1994.

221(6)   Sections 73(1), 74(2)(a) to (d) and (3), 75 to 78, 83, 124(2) and (3), 154, 176A, 202, 203, 205 and 250 shall not apply.

221(7)   Unless the contrary intention appears, the members of the partnership against whom insolvency orders are made by virtue of article 10 of the Insolvent Partnerships Order 1994 shall not be treated as contributories for the purposes of this Act.

221(8)   The circumstances in which an insolvent partnership may be wound up as an unregistered company are that the partnership is unable to pay its debts.

221(9)   Every petition for the winding up of an insolvent partnership under Part V of this Act shall be verified by affidavit in Form 2 in Schedule 9 to the Insolvent Partnerships Order 1994."

History
Modified s.221(6) amended by the Insolvent Partnerships (Amendment) Order 2006 (SI 2006/622) art.9, as from 6 April 2006.

SCHEDULE 7

PROVISIONS OF THE ACT WHICH APPLY WITH MODIFICATIONS FOR THE PURPOSES OF ARTICLE 11 WHERE JOINT BANKRUPTCY PETITION PRESENTED BY INDIVIDUAL MEMBERS WITHOUT WINDING UP PARTNERSHIP AS UNREGISTERED COMPANY

Article 11

1(1) The provisions of the Act specified in sub-paragraph (2) below, are set out as modified in this Schedule.

1(2) The provisions referred to in sub-paragraph (1) above are sections 264 to 266, 283, 284, 290, 292 to 301, 305, 312, 328, 331 and 387.

History

In para.1(2) the reference to s.275 omitted by the Insolvent Partnerships (Amendment) Order 2005 (SI 2005/1516) art.10(1), (2) as from 1 July 2005.

The reference to s.272 was omitted by the Insolvency (Miscellaneous Amendments) Regulations 2017 (SI 2017/1119) regs 1(1), (6), 2, Sch.2 paras 1, 7(1), (2) as from 8 December 2017 subject to transitional and savings provision in para.10.

2 Section 264: Presentation of joint bankruptcy petition

2 Section 264 is modified so as to read as follows:–

"**264(1)** Subject to section 266(1) below, a joint bankruptcy petition may be presented to the court by virtue of article 11 of the Insolvent Partnerships Order 1994 by all the members of an insolvent partnership in their capacity as such provided that all the members are individuals and none of them is a limited partner.

264(2) A petition may not be presented under paragraph (1) by the members of an insolvent partnership if the partnership–

(a) has permission under Part 4A of the Financial Services and Markets Act 2000 to accept deposits, other than such a permission only for the purpose of carrying on another regulated activity in accordance with that permission, or

(b) continues to have a liability in respect of a deposit which was held by it in accordance with the Banking Act 1979 or the Banking Act 1987.

264(2A) Subsection (2)(a) must be read with–

(a) section 22 of the Financial Services and Markets Act 2000;

(b) any relevant order under that section; and

(c) Schedule 2 to that Act.

264(3) The petition–

(a) shall be in Form 14 in Schedule 9 to the Insolvent Partnerships Order 1994; and

(b) shall contain a request that the trustee shall wind up the partnership business and administer the partnership property without the partnership being wound up as an unregistered company under Part V of this Act.

264(4) The petition shall either–

(a) be accompanied by an affidavit in Form 15 in Schedule 9 to the Insolvent Partnerships Order 1994 made by the member who signs the petition, showing that all the members are individual members (and that none of them is a limited partner) and concur in the presentation of the petition, or

(b) contain a statement that all the members are individual members and be signed by all the members.

264(5) On presentation of a petition under this section, the court may make orders in Form 16 in Schedule 9 to the Insolvent Partnerships Order 1994 for the bankruptcy of the members and the winding up of the partnership business and administration of its property."

3   Section 265: Conditions to be satisfied in respect of members

3   Section 265 is modified so as to read as follows:–

"**265(1)**   Subject to the provisions of this section, a joint bankruptcy petition by virtue of article 11 of the Insolvent Partnerships Order 1994 may be presented–

    (a)   to the High Court (other than to a district registry of that Court) if the partnership has, or at any time had, a principal place of business in England and Wales, or

    (b)   to a county court in England and Wales if the partnership has, or at any time had, a principal place of business within the insolvency district of that court.

265(2)   A joint bankruptcy petition shall not be presented to the court by virtue of article 11 unless the business of the partnership has been carried on in England and Wales at any time in the period of 3 years ending with the day on which the joint bankruptcy petition is presented."

265(3)   A joint bankruptcy petition may be presented to the court by the members of a partnership only on the grounds that the partnership is unable to pay its debts.

265(4)   A petition under subsection (3) must be accompanied by–

    (a)   a statement of each member's affairs in Form 17 in Schedule 9 to the Insolvent Partnerships Order 1994, and

    (b)   a statement of the affairs of the partnership in Form 18 in that Schedule, sworn by one or more members of the partnership.

265(5)   The statements of affairs required by subsection (4) must contain–

    (a)   particulars of the member's or (as the case may be) partnership's creditors, debts and other liabilities and of their assets, and

    (b)   such other information as is required by the relevant form."

History
In para.3 modified s.265(3)–(5) inserted by the Deregulation Act 2015 and Small Business, Enterprise and Employment Act 2015 (Consequential Amendments) (Savings) Regulations 2017 (SI 2017/540) regs 1, 3, Sch.2 paras 2, 9(1), (2) as from 6 April 2017.

4   Section 266: Other preliminary conditions

4   Section 266 is modified so as to read as follows:–

"**266(1)**   If the court is satisfied, on application by any member of an insolvent partnership, that the presentation of the petition under section 264(1) by all the members of the partnership would be impracticable, the court may direct that the petition be presented by such member or members as are specified by the court.

266(2)   A joint bankruptcy petition shall not be withdrawn without the leave of the court.

266(3)   The court has a general power, if it appears to it appropriate to do so on the grounds that there has been a contravention of the rules or for any other reason, to dismiss a joint bankruptcy petition or to stay proceedings on such a petition; and, where it stays proceedings on a petition, it may do so on such terms and conditions as it thinks fit."

5   Section 272: Grounds of joint bankruptcy petition

5   [Omitted by the Deregulation Act 2015 and Small, Enterprise and Employment Act 2015 (Consequential Amendments) (Savings) Regulations 2017 (SI 2017/540) regs 1, 3, Sch.2 paras 2, 9(1), (3) as from 6 April 2017.]

6   Section 275: Summary administration

6   [Omitted by the Insolvent Partnerships (Amendment) Order 2005 (SI 2005/1516) art.10(1), (3) as from 1 July 2005.]

7   Section 283: Definition of member's estate

7   Section 283 is modified so as to read as follows:–

"**283(1)**   Subject as follows, a member's estate for the purposes of this Act comprises–

(a)   all property belonging to or vested in the member at the commencement of the bankruptcy, and

(b)   any property which by virtue of any of the provisions of this Act is comprised in that estate or is treated as falling within the preceding paragraph.

283(2)   Subsection (1) does not apply to–

(a)   such tools, books, vehicles and other items of equipment as are not partnership property and as are necessary to the member for use personally by him in his employment, business or vocation;

(b)   such clothing, bedding, furniture, household equipment and provisions as are not partnership property and as are necessary for satisfying the basic domestic needs of the member and his family.

This subsection is subject to section 308 in Chapter IV (certain excluded property reclaimable by trustee).

283(3)   Subsection (1) does not apply to–

(a)   property held by the member on trust for any other person, or

(b)   the right of nomination to a vacant ecclesiastical benefice.

283(4)   References in any provision of this Act to property, in relation to a member, include references to any power exercisable by him over or in respect of property except insofar as the power is exercisable over or in respect of property not for the time being comprised in the member's estate and–

(a)   is so exercisable at a time after either the official receiver has had his release in respect of that estate under section 299(2) in Chapter III or the trustee of that estate has vacated office under section 298(6), or

(b)   cannot be so exercised for the benefit of the member;

and a power exercisable over or in respect of property is deemed for the purposes of any provision of this Act to vest in the person entitled to exercise it at the time of the transaction or event by virtue of which it is exercisable by that person (whether or not it becomes so exercisable at that time).

283(5)   For the purposes of any such provision of this Act, property comprised in a member's estate is so comprised subject to the rights of any person other than the member (whether as a secured creditor of the member or otherwise) in relation thereto, but disregarding any rights which have been given up in accordance with the rules.

283(6)   This section has effect subject to the provisions of any enactment not contained in this Act under which any property is to be excluded from a bankrupt's estate."

History
In para.7 modified s.283(4) amended by the Deregulation Act 2015 and Small Business, Enterprise and Employment Act 2015 (Consequential Amendments) (Savings) Regulations 2017 (SI 2017/540) regs 1, 3, Sch.2 paras 2, 9(1), (4) as from 6 April 2017.

7A   Section 283A: Bankrupt's home ceasing to form part of estate

7A   Section 283A is modified so as to read as follows:–

"**283A(1)**   This section applies where property comprised in the estate of an individual member consists of an interest in a dwelling-house which at the date of the bankruptcy was the sole or principal residence of–

(a)   the individual member;

(b)   the individual member's spouse or civil partner, or

(c)   a former spouse or former civil partner of the individual member.

283A(2)   At the end of the period of three years beginning with the date of the bankruptcy the interest mentioned in subsection (1) shall–

   (a)   cease to be comprised in the individual member's estate, and

   (b)   vest in the individual member (without conveyance, assignment or transfer).

283A(3)   Subsection (2) shall not apply if during the period mentioned in that subsection–

   (a)   the trustee realises the interest mentioned in subsection (1),

   (b)   the trustee applies for an order for sale in respect of the dwelling-house,

   (c)   the trustee applies for an order for possession of the dwelling-house,

   (d)   the trustee applies for an order under section 313 in Chapter IV in respect of that interest, or

   (e)   the trustee and the individual member agree that the individual member shall incur a specified liability to his estate (with or without the addition of interest from the date of the agreement) in consideration of which the interest mentioned in subsection (1) shall cease to form part of the estate.

283A(4)   Where an application of a kind described in subsection (3)(b) to (d) is made during the period mentioned in subsection (2) and is dismissed, unless the court orders otherwise the interest to which the application relates shall on the dismissal of the application–

   (a)   cease to be comprised in the individual member's estate, and

   (b)   vest in the individual member (without conveyance, assignment or transfer).

283A(5)   If the individual member does not inform the trustee or the official receiver of his interest in a property before the end of the period of three months beginning with the date of the bankruptcy, the period of three years mentioned in subsection (2)–

   (a)   shall not begin with the date of the bankruptcy, but

   (b)   shall begin with the date on which the trustee or official receiver becomes aware of the individual member's interest.

283A(6)   The court may substitute for the period of three years mentioned in subsection (2) a longer period–

   (a)   in prescribed circumstances, and

   (b)   in such other circumstances as the court thinks appropriate.

283A(7)   The rules may make provision for this section to have effect with the substitution of a shorter period for the period of three years mentioned in subsection (2) in specified circumstances (which may be described by reference to action to be taken by a trustee in bankruptcy).

283A(8)   The rules may also, in particular, make provision–

   (a)   requiring or enabling the trustee of an individual member's estate to give notice that this section applies or does not apply;

   (b)   about the effect of a notice under paragraph (a);

   (c)   requiring the trustee of an individual member's estate to make an application to the Chief Land Registrar.

283A(9)   Rules under subsection (8)(b) may, in particular–

   (a)   disapply this section;

   (b)   enable a court to disapply this section;

   (c)   make provision in consequence of a disapplication of this section;

   (d)   enable a court to make provision in consequence of a disapplication of this section;

   (e)   make provision (which may include provision conferring jurisdiction on a court or tribunal) about compensation."

History
Paragraph 7A inserted by the Insolvent Partnerships (Amendment) Order 2005 (SI 2005/1516) art.10(1), (4) as from 1 July 2005.

8   Section 284: Restrictions on dispositions of property

8   Section 284 is modified so as to read as follows:–

"**284(1)**   Where a member is adjudged bankrupt on a joint bankruptcy petition, any disposition of property made by that member in the period to which this section applies is void except to the extent that it is or was made with the consent of the court, or is or was subsequently ratified by the court.

284(2)   Subsection (1) applies to a payment (whether in cash or otherwise) as it applies to a disposition of property and, accordingly, where any payment is void by virtue of that subsection, the person paid shall hold the sum paid for the member as part of his estate.

284(3)   This section applies to the period beginning with the day of the presentation of the joint bankruptcy petition and ending with the vesting, under Chapter IV of this Part, of the member's estate in a trustee.

284(4)   The preceding provisions of this section do not give a remedy against any person–

(a)   in respect of any property or payment which he received before the commencement of the bankruptcy in good faith, for value, and without notice that the petition had been presented, or

(b)   in respect of any interest in property which derives from an interest in respect of which there is, by virtue of this subsection, no remedy.

284(5)   Where after the commencement of his bankruptcy the member has incurred a debt to a banker or other person by reason of the making of a payment which is void under this section, that debt is deemed for the purposes of any provision of this Act to have been incurred before the commencement of the bankruptcy unless–

(a)   that banker or person had notice of the bankruptcy before the debt was incurred, or

(b)   it is not reasonably practicable for the amount of the payment to be recovered from the person to whom it was made.

284(6)   A disposition of property is void under this section notwithstanding that the property is not or, as the case may be, would not be comprised in the member's estate; but nothing in this section affects any disposition made by a person of property held by him on trust for any other person other than a disposition made by a member of property held by him on trust for the partnership."

9   Section 290: Public examination of member

9   Section 290 is modified so as to read as follows:–

"**290(1)**   Where orders have been made against the members of an insolvent partnership on a joint bankruptcy petition, the official receiver may at any time before the discharge of any such member apply to the court for the public examination of that member.

290(2)   Unless the court otherwise orders, the official receiver shall make an application under subsection (1) if notice requiring him to do so is given to him, in accordance with the rules, by one of the creditors of the member concerned with the concurrence of not less than one-half, in value, of those creditors (including the creditor giving notice).

290(3)   On an application under subsection (1), the court shall direct that a public examination of the member shall be held on a day appointed by the court; and the member shall attend on that day and be publicly examined as to his affairs, dealings and property and as to those of the partnership.

290(4)   The following may take part in the public examination of the member and may question him concerning the matters mentioned in subsection (3), namely–

(a)   the official receiver,

(b)   the trustee of the member's estate, if his appointment has taken effect,

(c)   any person who has been appointed as special manager of the member's estate or business or of the partnership property or business,

(d)   any creditor of the member who has tendered a proof in the bankruptcy.

290(5)   On an application under subsection (1), the court may direct that the public examination of a member under this section be combined with the public examination of any other person.

290(6)   If a member without reasonable excuse fails at any time to attend his public examination under this section he is guilty of a contempt of court and liable to be punished accordingly (in addition to any other punishment to which he may be subject)."

10   Section 292: Power to appoint trustee

10   Section 292 is modified so as to read as follows:–

"**292(1)**   This section applies to any appointment of a person (other than the official receiver) as trustee of a bankrupt's estate.

292(2)   No person may be appointed as trustee of the members' estates and as trustee of the partnership unless he is, at the time of the appointment, qualified to act as an insolvency practitioner both in relation to the insolvent partnership and to each of the members.

292(3)   Any power to appoint a person as trustee of the members' estates and of the partnership includes power to appoint two or more persons as joint trustees; but such an appointment must make provision as to the circumstances in which the trustees must act together and the circumstances in which one or more of them may act for the others.

292(4)   The appointment of any person as trustee of the members' estates and of the partnership takes effect only if that person accepts the appointment in accordance with the rules. Subject to this, the appointment of any person as trustee takes effect at the time specified in his certificate of appointment.

292(5)   [Omitted]

292A   Conflicts of interest

292A(1)   If the trustee of the members' estates and of the partnership is of the opinion at any time that there is a conflict of interest between his functions as trustee of the members' estates and his functions as trustee of the partnership, or between his functions as trustee of the estates of two or more members, he may apply to the court for directions.

292A(2)   On an application under subsection (1), the court may, without prejudice to the generality of its power to give directions, appoint one or more insolvency practitioners either in place of the applicant to act both as trustee of the members' estates and as trustee of the partnership, or to act as joint trustee with the applicant."

History
In para.10 modified s.292(1) substituted and s.292(5) omitted by the Deregulation Act 2015 and Small Business, Enterprise and Employment Act 2015 (Consequential Amendments) (Savings) Regulations 2017 (SI 2017/540) regs 1, 3, Sch.2 paras 2, 9(1), (5) as from 6 April 2017.

11   Sections 293 and 294: Summoning of meeting to appoint trustee

11   [Omitted by the Deregulation Act 2015 and Small Business, Enterprise and Employment Act 2015 (Consequential Amendments) (Savings) Regulations 2017 (SI 2017/540) regs 1, 3, Sch.2 paras 2, 9(1), (6) as from 6 April 2017.]

12   Section 295: Failure of meeting to appoint trustee

12   [Omitted by the Deregulation Act 2015 and Small Business, Enterprise and Employment Act 2015 (Consequential Amendments) (Savings) Regulations 2017 (SI 2017/540) regs 1, 3, Sch.2 paras 2, 9(1), (6) as from 6 April 2017.]

13   Section 296: Appointment of trustee by Secretary of State

13   Section 296 is modified so as to read as follows:–

"**296(1)**   At any time when the official receiver is the trustee of the members' estates and of the partnership by virtue of any provision of this Chapter he may apply to the Secretary of State for the appointment of a person as trustee instead of the official receiver.

296(2)   On an application under subsection (1) the Secretary of State shall either make an appointment or decline to make one.

296(3)   Such an application may be made notwithstanding that the Secretary of State has declined to make an appointment either on a previous application under subsection (1) or on a reference under section 295 or under section 300(2) below.

296(4)   Where a trustee has been appointed by the Secretary of State under subsection (2) of this section, and an insolvency order is subsequently made against a further insolvent member by virtue of article 11 of the Insolvent Partnerships Order 1994, then the trustee so appointed shall also be the trustee of the member against whom the subsequent order is made.

296(5)   Where the trustee of the members' estates and of the partnership has been appointed by the Secretary of State (whether under this section or otherwise) or has become trustee of a further insolvent member under subsection (4), the trustee shall give notice of his appointment or further appointment (as the case may be) to the creditors of the members and the creditors of the partnership or, if the court so allows, shall advertise his appointment in accordance with the court's directions.

296(6)   In that notice or advertisement the trustee must explain the procedure for establishing a creditors' committee under section 301, except in a case where such a committee has already been formed, in which case the trustee must state whether he proposes to appoint additional members of the committee under section 301A(3)."

History
In para.13 modified s.296(6) and (7) substituted as s.296(6) by the Deregulation Act 2015 and Small Business, Enterprise and Employment Act 2015 (Consequential Amendments) (Savings) Regulations 2017 (SI 2017/540) regs 1, 3, Sch.2 paras 2, 9(1), (7) as from 6 April 2017.

14   Section 297: Rules applicable to meetings of creditors

14   [Omitted by the Deregulation Act 2015 and Small Business, Enterprise and Employment Act 2015 (Consequential Amendments) (Savings) Regulations 2017 (SI 2017/540) regs 1, 3, Sch.2 paras 2, 9(1), (8) as from 6 April 2017.]

15   Section 298: Removal of trustee; vacation of office

15   Section 298 is modified so as to read as follows:–

"**298(1)**   Subject as follows, the trustee of the estates of the members and of the partnership may be removed from office only by an order of the court or by a decision of the creditors of the members and the partnership made by a creditors' decision procedure instigated specially for that purpose in accordance with the rules.

298(1A)   Where the official receiver is trustee or a trustee is appointed by the Secretary of State or by the court, a creditors' decision procedure may be instigated for the purpose of removing the trustee only if–

(a)   the trustee thinks fit;

(b)   the court so directs; or

(c)   one of the creditors of the members or the partnership so requests, with the concurrence of not less than one-quarter, in value, of the creditors (including the creditor making the request).

298(1B)   Where the creditors of the members and the partnership decide to remove a trustee, they may in accordance with the rules appoint another person as trustee in his place.

298(1C)   Where the decision to remove a trustee is made under subsection (1A), the decision does not take effect until the creditors of the members and the partnership appoint another person as trustee in his place.

298(2)   If the trustee was appointed by the Secretary of State, he may be removed by a direction of the Secretary of State.

298(3)   The trustee (not being the official receiver) shall vacate office if he ceases to be a person who is for the time being qualified to act as an insolvency practitioner in relation to any member or to the partnership.

298(4)   The trustee may, with the leave of the court (or, if appointed by the Secretary of State, with the leave of the court or the Secretary of State), resign his office by giving notice of his resignation to the court.

298(5)   Subject to subsection (7), any removal from or vacation of office under this section relates to all offices held in the proceedings by virtue of article 11 of the Insolvent Partnerships Order 1994.

298(6)   A trustee who has produced an account of the winding up or administration under section 331 vacates office immediately upon complying with the requirements of section 331(3).

298(7)   The trustee must vacate office as trustee of a member if the order made by virtue of article 11 of the Insolvent Partnerships Order 1994 in relation to that member is annulled."

History

In para.15 former modified s.298(6) substituted by the Deregulation Act 2015 and Small Business, Enterprise and Employment Act 2015 (Consequential Amendments) (Savings) Regulations 2017 (SI 2017/540) regs 1, 3, Sch.2 paras 2, 9(1), (9) as from 6 April 2017.

Modified s.298 substituted by the Insolvency (Miscellaneous Amendments) Regulations 2017 (SI 2017/1119) regs 1(1), (6), 2, Sch.2 paras 1, 7(1), (3) as from 8 December 2017 subject to transitional and savings provision in para.10.

16   Section 299: Release of trustee

16   Section 299 is modified so as to read as follows:–

"**299(1)**   Where the official receiver has ceased to be the trustee of the members' estates and of the partnership and a person is appointed in his stead, the official receiver shall have his release with effect from the following time, that is to say–

  (a)   where that person is appointed by the creditors of the members and of the partnership or by the Secretary of State, the time at which the official receiver gives notice under this paragraph to the prescribed person that he has been replaced, and

  (b)   where that person is appointed by the court, such time as the court may determine.

299(2)   If the official receiver while he is the trustee gives notice to the Secretary of State that the administration of the estate of any member, or the winding up of the partnership business and administration of its affairs, is for practical purposes complete, he shall have his release as trustee of any member or as trustee of the partnership (as the case may be) with effect from such time as the Secretary of State may determine.

299(3)   A person other than the official receiver who has ceased to be the trustee of the estate of any member or of the partnership shall have his release with effect from the following time, that is to say–

  (a)   in the case of a person who has died, the time at which notice is given to the court in accordance with the rules that that person has ceased to hold office;

  (b)   in the case of a person who has been removed from office by the court or by the Secretary of State, or who has vacated office under section 298(3), such time as the Secretary of State may, on an application by that person, determine;

  (c)   in the case of a person who has resigned, such time as may be directed by the court (or, if he was appointed by the Secretary of State, such time as may be directed by the court or as the Secretary of State may, on an application by that person, determine);

  (d)   in the case of a person who has vacated office under section 298(6)–

     (i)   if any of the creditors of the members and of the partnership objected to the person's release before the end of the period for so objecting prescribed by the rules, such time as the Secretary of State may, on an application by that person, determine, and

     (ii)   otherwise, the time at which the person vacated office.

299(4)   Where an order by virtue of article 11 of the Insolvent Partnerships Order 1994 is annulled in so far as it relates to any member, the trustee at the time of the annulment has his release in respect of that member with effect from such time as the court may determine.

299(5)   Where the trustee (including the official receiver when so acting) has his release under this section, he shall, with effect from the time specified in the preceding provisions of this section, be discharged from all liability both in respect of acts or omissions of his in the administration of the estates of the members and in the winding up of the partnership business and administration of its affairs and otherwise in relation to his conduct as trustee.

But nothing in this section prevents the exercise, in relation to a person who has had his release under this section, of the court's powers under section 304 (liability of trustee)."

History
In para.16 modified s.299(1)(a) amended and (3)(d) substituted by the Deregulation Act 2015 and Small Business, Enterprise and Employment Act 2015 (Consequential Amendments) (Savings) Regulations 2017 (SI 2017/540) regs 1, 3, Sch.2 paras 2, 9(1), (10) as from 6 April 2017.

17   Section 300: Vacancy in office of trustee

17   Section 300 is modified so as to read as follows:–

"**300(1)**   This section applies where the appointment of any person as trustee of the members' estates and of the partnership fails to take effect or, such an appointment having taken effect, there is otherwise a vacancy in the office of trustee.

300(2)   The official receiver may refer the need for an appointment to the Secretary of State and shall be trustee until the vacancy is filled.

300(3)   On a reference to the Secretary of State under subsection (2) the Secretary of State shall either make an appointment or decline to make one.

300(4)   If on a reference under subsection (2) no appointment is made, the official receiver shall continue to be trustee, but without prejudice to his power to make a further reference.

300(5)   References in this section to a vacancy include a case where it is necessary, in relation to any property which is or may be comprised in a member's estate, to revive the trusteeship of that estate after the vacation of office by the trustee under section 298(6) or the giving by the official receiver of notice under section 299(2)."

History
In para.17 modified para.300(5) amended by the Deregulation Act 2015 and Small Business, Enterprise and Employment Act 2015 (Consequential Amendments) (Savings) Regulations 2017 (SI 2017/540) regs 1, 3, Sch.2 paras 2, 9(1), (11) as from 6 April 2017.

18   Section 301: Creditors' committee

18   Section 301 is modified so as to read as follows:–

"**301(1)**   Subject as follows, the creditors of the members and of the partnership may establish a committee (known as "the creditors' committee") to exercise the functions conferred on it by or under this Act.

301(2)   The creditors of the members and of the partnership shall not establish such a committee, or confer any functions on such a committee, at any time when the official receiver is the trustee, except in connection with the appointment of a person to be trustee instead of the official receiver.

301A   Functions and membership of creditors' committee

301A(1)   The committee established under section 301 shall act as creditors' committee for each member and as liquidation committee for the partnership, and shall as appropriate exercise the functions conferred on creditors' and liquidation committees in a bankruptcy or winding up by or under this Act.

301A(2)   The rules relating to liquidation committees are to apply (with the necessary modifications and with the exclusion of all references to contributories) to a committee established under section 301.

301A(3)   Where the appointment of the trustee also takes effect in relation to a further insolvent member under section 293(8) or 296(4), the trustee may appoint any creditor of that member (being qualified under the rules to be a member of the committee) to be an additional member of any creditors' committee already established under section 301, provided that the creditor concerned consents to act.

301A(4)   The court may at any time, on application by a creditor of any member or of the partnership, appoint additional members of the creditors' committee.

301A(5)   If additional members of the creditors' committee are appointed under subsection (3) or (4), the limit on the maximum number of members of the committee specified in the rules shall be increased by the number of additional members so appointed."

History
In para.18 modified s.301 amended by the Deregulation Act 2015 and Small Business, Enterprise and Employment Act 2015 (Consequential Amendments) (Savings) Regulations 2017 (SI 2017/540) regs 1, 3, Sch.2 paras 2, 9(1), (12) as from 6 April 2017.

19   Section 305: General functions and powers of trustee

19   Section 305 is modified so as to read as follows:

"**305(1)**   The function of the trustee of the estates of the members and of the partnership is to get in, realise and distribute the estates of the members and the partnership property in accordance with the following provisions of this Chapter.

305(2)   The trustee shall have all the functions and powers in relation to the partnership and the partnership property that he has in relation to the members and their estates.

305(3)   In the carrying out of his functions and in the management of the members' estates and the partnership property the trustee is entitled, subject to the following provisions of this Chapter, to use his own discretion.

305(4)   It is the duty of the trustee, if he is not the official receiver–

(a)   to furnish the official receiver with such information,

(b)   to produce to the official receiver, and permit inspection by the official receiver of, such books, papers and other records, and

(c)   to give the official receiver such other assistance,

as the official receiver may reasonably require for the purpose of enabling him to carry out his functions in relation to the bankruptcy of the members and the winding up of the partnership business and administration of its property."

305(5)   The official name of the trustee in his capacity as trustee of a member shall be "the trustee of the estate of............, a bankrupt" (inserting the name of the member concerned); but he may be referred to as "the trustee in bankruptcy" of the particular member.

305(6)   The official name of the trustee in his capacity as trustee of the partnership shall be "the trustee of............, a partnership" (inserting the name of the partnership concerned)."

20   Section 312: Obligation to surrender control to trustee

20   Section 312 is modified so as to read as follows:–

"**312(1)**   This section applies where orders are made by virtue of article 11 of the Insolvent Partnerships Order 1994 and a trustee is appointed.

312(2)   Any person who is or has been an officer of the partnership in question, or who is an executor or administrator of the estate of a deceased officer of the partnership, shall deliver up to the trustee of the partnership, for the purposes of the exercise of the trustee's functions under this Act, possession of any partnership property which he holds for the purposes of the partnership.

312(3)   Each member shall deliver up to the trustee possession of any property, books, papers or other records of which he has possession or control and of which the trustee is required to take possession.
   This is without prejudice to the general duties of the members as bankrupts under section 333 in this Chapter.

312(4)   If any of the following is in possession of any property, books, papers or other records of which the trustee is required to take possession, namely–

(a)   the official receiver,

(b)   a person who has ceased to be trustee of a member's estate,

(c)   a person who has been the administrator of the partnership or supervisor of a voluntary arrangement approved in relation to the partnership under Part I,

(d)   a person who has been the supervisor of a voluntary arrangement approved in relation to a member under Part VIII,

the official receiver or, as the case may be, that person shall deliver up possession of the property, books, papers or records to the trustee.

312(5)   Any banker or agent of a member or of the partnership, or any other person who holds any property to the account of, or for, a member or the partnership shall pay or deliver to the trustee all property in his possession or under his control which forms part of the member's estate or which is partnership property and which he is not by law entitled to retain as against the member, the partnership or the trustee.

312(6)   If any person without reasonable excuse fails to comply with any obligation imposed by this section, he is guilty of a contempt of court and liable to be punished accordingly (in addition to any other punishment to which he may be subject)."

20A   Section 313A: Low value home: application for sale, possession or charge

20A   Section 313A is modified so as to read as follows:–

"**313A(1)**   This section applies where–

(a)   property comprised in the individual member's estate consists of an interest in a dwelling-house which at the date of the bankruptcy was the sole or principal residence of–

(i)   the individual member,

(ii)   the individual member's spouse or civil partner, or

(iii)   a former spouse or former civil partner of the individual member, and

(b)   the trustee applies for an order for the sale of the property, for an order for possession of the property or for an order under section 313 in respect of the property.

313A(2)   The court shall dismiss the application if the value of the interest is below the amount prescribed for the purposes of this subsection.

313A(3)   In determining the value of an interest for the purposes of this section the court shall disregard any matter which it is required to disregard by the order which prescribes the amount for the purposes of subsection (2)."

History
Paragraph 20A inserted by the Insolvent Partnerships (Amendment) Order 2005 (SI 2005/1516) art.10(1), (5) as from 1 July 2005.

21   Section 328: Priority of expenses and debts

21   Section 328 is modified so as to read as follows:–

"**328   Priority of expenses**

328(1)   The provisions of this section shall apply in a case where article 11 of the Insolvent Partnerships Order 1994 applies, as regards priority of expenses incurred by a person acting as trustee of the estates of the members of an insolvent partnership and as trustee of that partnership.

328(2)   The joint estate of the partnership shall be applicable in the first instance in payment of the joint expenses and the separate estate of each insolvent member shall be applicable in the first instance in payment of the separate expenses relating to that member.

328(3)   Where the joint estate is insufficient for the payment in full of the joint expenses, the unpaid balance shall be apportioned equally between the separate estates of the insolvent members against whom insolvency orders have been made and shall form part of the expenses to be paid out of those estates.

328(4)   Where any separate estate of an insolvent member is insufficient for the payment in full of the separate expenses to be paid out of that estate, the unpaid balance shall form part of the expenses to be paid out of the joint estate.

328(5)   Where after the transfer of any unpaid balance in accordance with subsection (3) or (4) any estate is insufficient for the payment in full of the expenses to be paid out of that estate, the balance then remaining unpaid shall be apportioned equally between the other estates.

328(6)   Where after an apportionment under subsection (5) one or more estates are insufficient for the payment in full of the expenses to be paid out of those estates, the total of the unpaid balances of the expenses to be paid out of those estates shall continue to be apportioned equally between the other estates until provision is made for the payment in full of the expenses or there is no estate available for the payment of the balance finally remaining unpaid, in which case it abates in equal proportions between all the estates.

328(7)   Without prejudice to subsections (3) to (6) above, the trustee may, with the sanction of any creditors' committee established under section 301 or with the leave of the court obtained on application–

    (a)   pay out of the joint estate as part of the expenses to be paid out of that estate any expenses incurred for any separate estate of an insolvent member; or

    (b)   pay out of any separate estate of an insolvent member any part of the expenses incurred for the joint estate which affects that separate estate.

328A   Priority of debts in joint estate

328A(1)   The provisions of this section and the next (which are subject to the provisions of section 9 of the Partnership Act 1890 as respects the liability of the estate of a deceased member) shall apply as regards priority of debts in a case where article 11 of the Insolvent Partnerships Order 1994 applies.

328A(2)   After payment of expenses in accordance with section 328 and subject to section 328C(2), the joint debts of the partnership shall be paid out of its joint estate in the following order of priority–

    (a)   the ordinary preferential debts;

    (aa)   the secondary preferential debts;

    (b)   the ordinary non-preferential debts;

    (ba)   the secondary non-preferential debts;

    (bb)   the tertiary non-preferential debts;

    (c)   interest under section 328D on the joint debts (other than postponed debts);

    (d)   the postponed debts;

    (e)   interest under section 328D on the postponed debts.

328A(3)   The responsible insolvency practitioner shall adjust the rights among themselves of the members of the partnership as contributories and shall distribute any surplus to the members or, where applicable, to the separate estates of the members, according to their respective rights and interests in it.

328A(4)   The debts referred to in each of paragraphs (a) to (ba) of subsection (2) rank equally between themselves, and in each case if the joint estate is insufficient for meeting them, they abate in equal proportions between themselves.

328A(5)   Where the joint estate is not sufficient for the payment of the joint debts in accordance with paragraphs (a), (aa) and (b) of subsection (2), the responsible insolvency practitioner shall aggregate the value of those debts to the extent that they have not been satisfied or are not capable of being satisfied, and that aggregate amount shall be a claim against the separate estate of each member of the partnership against whom an insolvency order has been made which–

    (a)   shall be a debt provable by the responsible insolvency practitioner in each such estate, and

(b)   shall rank equally with the debts of the member referred to in section 328B(1)(b) below.

328A(5A)   Where the joint estate is not sufficient for the payment of the secondary non-preferential debts in accordance with paragraph (ba) of subsection (2), the responsible insolvency practitioner shall aggregate the value of those debts to the extent that they have not been satisfied or are not capable of being satisfied, and that aggregate amount shall be a claim against the separate estate of each member of the partnership against whom an insolvency order has been made which–

(a)   shall be a debt provable by the responsible insolvency practitioner in each such estate, and

(b)   shall rank equally with the debts of the member referred to in section 328B(1)(ba) below.

328A(5B)   Where the joint estate is not sufficient for the payment of the tertiary non-preferential debts in accordance with paragraph (bb) of subsection (2), the responsible insolvency practitioner shall aggregate the value of those debts to the extent that they have not been satisfied or are not capable of being satisfied, and that aggregate amount shall be a claim against the separate estate of each member of the partnership against whom an insolvency order has been made which–

(a)   shall be a debt provable by the responsible insolvency practitioner in each such estate, and

(b)   shall rank as a debt of the member in accordance with section 328B(1)(bc) below.

328A(6)   Where the joint estate is sufficient for the payment of the joint debts in accordance with paragraphs (a) to (bb) of subsection (2) but not for the payment of interest under paragraph (c) of that subsection, the responsible insolvency practitioner shall aggregate the value of that interest to the extent that it has not been satisfied or is not capable of being satisfied, and that aggregate amount shall be a claim against the separate estate of each member of the partnership against whom an insolvency order has been made which–

(a)   shall be a debt provable by the responsible insolvency practitioner in each such estate, and

(b)   shall rank equally with the interest on the separate debts referred to in section 328B(1)(c) below.

328A(7)   Where the joint estate is not sufficient for the payment of the postponed joint debts in accordance with paragraph (d) of subsection (2), the responsible insolvency practitioner shall aggregate the value of those debts to the extent that they have not been satisfied or are not capable of being satisfied, and that aggregate amount shall be a claim against the separate estate of each member of the partnership against whom an insolvency order has been made which–

(a)   shall be a debt provable by the responsible insolvency practitioner in each such estate, and

(b)   shall rank equally with the postponed debts of the member referred to in section 328B(1)(d) below.

328A(8)   Where the joint estate is sufficient for the payment of the postponed joint debts in accordance with paragraph (d) of subsection (2) but not for the payment of interest under paragraph (e) of that subsection, the responsible insolvency practitioner shall aggregate the value of that interest to the extent that it has not been satisfied or is not capable of being satisfied, and that aggregate amount shall be a claim against the separate estate of each member of the partnership against whom an insolvency order has been made which–

(a)   shall be a debt provable by the responsible insolvency practitioner in each such estate, and

(b)   shall rank equally with the interest on the postponed debts referred to in section 328B(1)(e) below.

328A(9)   Where the responsible insolvency practitioner receives any distribution from the separate estate of a member in respect of a debt referred to in paragraph (a) of subsection (5), (5A). (5B), (6), (7) or (8) above, that distribution shall become part of the joint estate and shall be distributed in accordance with the order of priority set out in subsection (2) above.

328B   Priority of debts in separate estate

328B(1)   The separate estate of each member of the partnership against whom an insolvency order has been made shall be applicable, after payment of expenses in accordance with section 328 and subject to section 328C(2) below, in payment of the separate debts of that member in the following order of priority–

(a)   the ordinary preferential debts;

(aa)   the secondary preferential debts;

(b)   the ordinary non-preferential debts (including any debt referred to in section 328A(5)(a));

(ba) the secondary non-preferential debts (including any debt referred to in section 328A(5A)(a));

(bb) the tertiary non-preferential debts;

(bc) the debt referred to in section 175A(5B)(a);

(c)   interest under section 328D on the separate debts and under section 328A(6);

(d)   the postponed debts of the member (including any debt referred to in section 328A(7)(a));

(e)   interest under section 328D on the postponed debts of the member and under section 328A(8).

328B(2)   The debts referred to in each of paragraphs (a) to (ba) of subsection (1) rank equally between themselves, and in each case if the separate estate is insufficient for meeting them, they abate in equal proportions between themselves.

328B(3)   Where the responsible insolvency practitioner receives any distribution from the joint estate or from the separate estate of another member of the partnership against whom an insolvency order has been made, that distribution shall become part of the separate estate and shall be distributed in accordance with the order of priority set out in subsection (1) of this section.

328C   Provisions generally applicable in distribution of joint and separate estates

328C(1)   Distinct accounts shall be kept of the joint estate of the partnership and of the separate estate of each member of that partnership against whom an insolvency order is made.

328C(2)   No member of the partnership shall prove for a joint or separate debt in competition with the joint creditors, unless the debt has arisen–

(a)   as a result of fraud, or

(b)   in the ordinary course of a business carried on separately from the partnership business.

328C(3)   For the purpose of establishing the value of any debt referred to in section 328A(5)(a), (5A)(a), (5B)(a) or (7)(a), that value may be estimated by the responsible insolvency practitioner in accordance with section 322.

328C(4)   Interest under section 328D on preferential debts ranks equally with interest on ordinary non-preferential debts, secondary non-preferential debts and tertiary non-preferential debts.

328C(5)   Sections 328A and 328B are without prejudice to any provision of this Act or of any other enactment concerning the ranking between themselves of postponed debts and interest thereon, but in the absence of any such provision postponed debts and interest thereon rank equally between themselves.

328C(6)   If any two or more members of an insolvent partnership constitute a separate partnership, the creditors of such separate partnership shall be deemed to be a separate set of creditors and subject to the same statutory provisions as the separate creditors of any member of the insolvent partnership.

328C(7)   Where any surplus remains after the administration of the estate of a separate partnership, the surplus shall be distributed to the members or, where applicable, to the separate estates of the members of that partnership according to their respective rights and interests in it.

328C(8)   Neither the official receiver, the Secretary of State nor a responsible insolvency practitioner shall be entitled to remuneration or fees under the Insolvency (England and Wales) Rules 2016, the Insolvency Regulations 1986 or the Insolvency Fees Order 1986 for his services in connection with–

(a)   the transfer of a surplus from the joint estate to a separate estate under section 328A(3),

(b)   a distribution from a separate estate to the joint estate in respect of a claim referred to in section 328A(5), (5A), (5B), (6), (7) or (8), or

(c)   a distribution from the estate of a separate partnership to the separate estates of the members of that partnership under subsection (7) above.

328D   Interest on debts

328D(1)   In the bankruptcy of each of the members of an insolvent partnership and in the winding up of that partnership's business and administration of its property, interest is payable in accordance with this section, in the order of priority laid down by sections 328A and 328B, on any debt proved in the bankruptcy including so much of any such debt as represents interest on the remainder.

328D(2) Interest under this section is payable on the debts in question in respect of the periods during which they have been outstanding since the relevant order was made by virtue of article 11 of the Insolvent Partnerships Order 1994.

328D(3) The rate of interest payable under this section in respect of any debt ("the official rate" for the purposes of any provision of this Act in which that expression is used) is whichever is the greater of–

(a) the rate specified in section 17 of the Judgments Act 1838 on the day on which the relevant order was made, and

(b) the rate applicable to that debt apart from the bankruptcy or winding up."

History
In para.21, modified s.328A(4)–(6) amended, s.328A(2)(aa) inserted, s.328B(2) amended and s.328B(1)(aa) inserted by the Banks and Building Societies (Depositor Preference and Priorities) Order 2014 (SI 2014/3486) art.15(1)–(4) as from 1 January 2015.
   Modified s.328C(8) amended by the Insolvency (Miscellaneous Amendments) Regulations 2017 (SI 2017/1119) regs 1(1), (6), 2, Sch.2 paras 1, 7(1), (4) as from 8 December 2017 subject to transitional and savings provision in para.10.
   Modified s.328A(2), (4) amended, s.382A(5A), (5B) inserted and ss.382A(6), (9), 382B(1), (2) and 382C(3), (4), (8) amended by the Banks and Building Societies (Priorities on Insolvency) Order 2018 (SI 2018/1244) arts 1, 3, 15, 21 as from 19 December 2018 in relation to insolvency proceedings commenced on or after that date.

22   Section 331: Final Account

22 Section 331 is modified to read as follows–

"**331(1)** Subject as follows in this section and the next, this section applies where–

(a) it appears to the trustee of the estates of the members and of the partnership that the administration of any member's estate or the winding up of the partnership business and administration of the partnership property is for practical purposes complete, and

(b) the trustee is not the official receiver.

331(2) The trustee must–

(a) give the creditors of the members and of the partnership (other than opted-out creditors) notice that it appears to the trustee that the administration of the member's estate or the winding up of the partnership business and administration of the partnership property is for practical purposes complete,

(b) make up an account of the administration or winding up, showing how it has been conducted and the property disposed of.

(c) send a copy of the account to the creditors of the members and of the partnership (other than opted-out creditors), and

(d) give the creditors of the members and of the partnership (other than opted-out creditors) a notice explaining the effect of section 299(3)(d) and how they may object to the trustee's release.

331(3) The trustee must during the relevant period send to the court and, in the case of a corporate member, send to the registrar of companies–

(a) a copy of the account, and

(b) a statement of whether any of the creditors of the members and of the partnership objected to the trustee's release.

331(4) The relevant period is the period of 7 days beginning with the day after the last day of the period prescribed by the rules as the period within which the creditors may object to the trustee's release."

History

Paragraph 22 substituted by the Deregulation Act 2015 and Small Business, Enterprise and Employment Act 2015 (Consequential Amendments) (Savings) Regulations 2017 (SI 2017/540) regs 1, 3, Sch.2 paras 2, 9(1), (13) as from 6 April 2017.

23   Section 387: The "relevant date"

23   Section 387 is modified so as to read as follows:–

"**387**   Where an order has been made in respect of an insolvent partnership by virtue of article 11 of the Insolvent Partnerships Order 1994, references in Schedule 6 to this Act to the relevant date (being the date which determines the existence and amount of a preferential debt) are to the date on which the said order was made."

Schedule 7A

Decisions of Creditors of the Partnership and of the Members of the Partnership

Article 11A

1   Sections 246ZE, 246ZF, 379ZA and 379ZB of the Act are set out as modified in this Schedule.

2   Sections 246ZE and 246ZF are modified so as to read as follows–

"**246ZE Creditors' decisions: general**

246ZE(1)   This section applies where, for the purposes of this Group of Parts, a person ("P") seeks a decision about any matter from the creditors of the partnership and the creditors of any insolvent members.

246ZE(2)   The decision may be made by any qualifying decision procedure P thinks fit, except that it may not be made by a meeting of the creditors of the partnership and the creditors of any insolvent members unless subsection (3) applies.

246ZE(3)   This subsection applies if at least the minimum number of creditors make a request to P in writing that the decision be made by a meeting.

246ZE(4)   If subsection (3) applies P must summon a meeting of the creditors of the partnership and the creditors of any insolvent members.

246ZE(5)   Subsection (2) is subject to any provision of this Act, the rules or any other legislation, or any order of the court–

   (a)   requiring a decision to be made, or prohibiting a decision from being made, by a particular qualifying decision procedure (other than a meeting);

   (b)   permitting or requiring a decision to be made by a meeting.

246ZE(6)   Section 246ZF provides that in certain cases the deemed consent procedure may be used instead of a qualifying decision procedure.

246ZE(7)   For the purposes of subsection (3) the "minimum number" of creditors is any of the following–

   (a)   10% in value of the creditors;

   (b)   10% in number of the creditors;

   (c)   10 creditors.

246ZE(8)   The references in subsection (7) to creditors are to creditors of any class, even where a decision is sought only from creditors of a particular class.

246ZE(9)   In this section references to a meeting are to a meeting where the creditors are invited to be present together at the same place (whether or not it is possible to attend the meeting without being present at that place).

246ZE(10)   Except as provided by subsection (8), references in this section to creditors include creditors of a particular class.

246ZE(11)   In this Group of Parts "qualifying decision procedure" means a procedure prescribed or authorised under paragraph 8A of Schedule 8.

246ZF   Deemed consent procedure

246ZF(1)   The deemed consent procedure may be used instead of a qualifying decision procedure where the creditors of the partnership and the creditors of any insolvent members are to make a decision about any matter, unless–

(a)   a decision about the matter is required by virtue of this Act, the rules, or any other legislation to be made by a qualifying decision procedure, or

(b)   the court orders that a decision about the matter is to be made by a qualifying decision procedure.

246ZF(2)   If the rules provide for the creditors of the partnership and the creditors of any insolvent members to make a decision about the remuneration of any person, they must provide that the decision is to be made by a qualifying decision procedure.

246ZF(3)   The deemed consent procedure is that the relevant creditors (other than opted-out creditors) are given notice of–

(a)   the matter about which they are to make a decision,

(b)   the decision that the person giving the notice proposes should be made (the "proposed decision"),

(c)   the effect of subsections (4) and (5), and

(d)   the procedure for objecting to the proposed decision.

246ZF(4)   If less than the appropriate number of relevant creditors object to the proposed decision in accordance with the procedure set out in the notice, the creditors are to be treated as having made the proposed decision.

246ZF(5)   Otherwise–

(a)   the creditors are to be treated as not having made a decision about the matter in question, and

(b)   if a decision about that matter is again sought from the creditors it must be sought using a qualifying decision procedure.

246ZF(6)   For the purposes of subsection (4) the "appropriate number" of relevant creditors or is 10% in value of those creditors.

246ZF(7)   "Relevant creditors" means the creditors who, if the decision were to be made by a qualifying decision procedure, would be entitled to vote in the procedure.

246ZF(8)   In this section references to creditors include creditors of a particular class."

3   Sections 379ZA and 379ZB are modified so as to read as follows–

"379ZA   Creditors' decisions: general

379ZA(1)   This section applies where, for the purposes of this Group of Parts, a person ("P") seeks a decision from the creditors of the partnership and the creditors of any insolvent members about any matter.

379ZA(2)   The decision may be made by any creditors' decision procedure P thinks fit, except that it may not be made by a meeting of the creditors of the partnership and the creditors of any insolvent members unless subsection (3) applies.

379ZA(3)   This subsection applies if at least the minimum number of creditors request in writing that the decision be made by a creditors' meeting.

379ZA(4)   If subsection (3) applies, P must summon a meeting of the creditors of the partnership and the creditors of any insolvent member.

379ZA(5)   Subsection (2) is subject to any provision of this Act, the rules or any other legislation, or any order of the court–

(a)   requiring a decision to be made, or prohibiting a decision from being made, by a particular creditors' decision procedure (other than a meeting);

(b)   permitting or requiring a decision to be made by a meeting.

379ZA(6)   Section 379ZB provides that in certain cases the deemed consent procedure may be used instead of a creditors' decision procedure.

379ZA(7)   For the purposes of subsection (3) the "minimum number" of creditors is any of the following–

(a)   10% in value of the creditors;

(b)   10% in number of the creditors;

(c)   10 creditors.

379ZA(8)   The references in subsection (7) to creditors are to creditors of any class, even where a decision is sought only from creditors of a particular class.

379ZA(9)   In this section references to a meeting are to a meeting where the creditors are invited to be present together at the same place (whether or not it is possible to attend the meeting without being present at that place).

379ZA(10)   Except as provided by subsection (8), references in this section to creditors include creditors of a particular class.

379ZA(11)   In this Group of Parts "creditors' decision procedure" means a procedure prescribed or authorised under paragraph 11A of Schedule 9.

379ZB   Deemed consent procedure

379ZB(1)   The deemed consent procedure may be used instead of a creditors' decision procedure where the creditors of the partnership and the creditors of any insolvent members are to make a decision about any matter, unless–

(a)   a decision about the matter is required by virtue of this Act, the rules or any other legislation to be made by a creditors' decision procedure, or

(b)   the court orders that a decision about the matter is to be made by a creditors' decision procedure.

379ZB(2)   If the rules provide for the creditors of the partnership and the creditors of any insolvent members to make a decision about the remuneration of any person, they must provide that the decision is to be made by a creditors' decision procedure.

379ZB(3)   The deemed consent procedure is that the relevant creditors (other than opted-out creditors) are given notice of–

(a)   the matter about which the creditors are to make a decision,

(b)   the decision the person giving the notice proposes should be made (the "proposed decision"),

(c)   the effect of subsections (4) and (5), and

(d)   the procedure for objecting to the proposed decision.

379ZB(4)   If less than the appropriate number of relevant creditors object to the proposed decision in accordance with the procedure set out in the notice, the creditors are to be treated as having made the proposed decision.

379ZB(5)   Otherwise–

(a)   the creditors are to be treated as not having made a decision about the matter in question, and

(b)   if a decision about that matter is again sought from the creditors, it must be sought using a creditors' decision procedure.

379ZB(6)   For the purposes of subsection (4) the "appropriate number" of relevant creditors is 10% in value of those creditors.

379ZB(7)   "Relevant creditors" means the creditors who, if the decision were to be made by a creditors' decision procedure, would be entitled to vote in the procedure.

379ZB(8)   In this section references to creditors include creditors of a particular class.

379ZB(9)   The rules may make further provision about the deemed consent procedure."

History
Schedule 7A inserted by the Deregulation Act 2015 and Small Business, Enterprise and Employment Act 2015 (Consequential Amendments) (Savings) Regulations 2017 (SI 2017/540) regs 1, 3, Sch.2 paras 2, 10 as from 6 April 2017.

Schedule 8

Modified Provisions of Company Directors Disqualification Act 1986 for the Purposes of Article 16

Article 16

The following provisions of the Company Directors Disqualification Act 1986 are modified so as to read as follows:–

Section 5A: Disqualification for certain convictions abroad

5A(1)   If it appears to the Secretary of State that it is expedient in the public interest that a disqualification order under this section should be made against a person, the Secretary of State may apply to the court for such an order.

5A(2)   The court may, on an application under subsection (1), make a disqualification order against a person who has been convicted of a relevant foreign offence.

5A(3)   A "relevant foreign offence" is an offence committed outside Great Britain in connection with the promotion, formation, management or liquidation of a partnership (or any similar procedure) which corresponds to an indictable offence under the law of England and Wales.

5A(4)   Where it appears to the Secretary of State that, in the case of a person who has offered to give a disqualification undertaking–

(a)   the person has been convicted of a relevant foreign offence; and

(b)   it is expedient in the public interest that the Secretary of State should accept the undertaking (instead of applying, or proceeding with an application, for a disqualification order),

the Secretary of State may accept the undertaking.

5A(5)   In this section–

"partnership" includes an overseas partnership;

"the court" means the High Court.

5A(6)   The maximum period of disqualification under an order under this section is 15 years."

History
See note after s.12C.

Section 6: Duty of court to disqualify unfit officers of certain partnerships

6(1)   The court shall make a disqualification order against a person in any case where, on an application under this section, it is satisfied–

(a)   that he is or has been an officer of a partnership which has at any time become insolvent (whether while he was an officer or subsequently); and

(b)   that his conduct as an officer of that partnership (either taken alone or taken together with his conduct as an officer of one or more other partnerships or overseas partnerships, or as a director of one or more companies or overseas companies) makes him unfit to be concerned in the management of a company.

6(1A)   In this section references to a person's conduct as an officer of any partnership or overseas partnership, or as a director of any company or overseas company include, where that partnership or overseas partnership, or company or overseas company, has become insolvent, references to that person's conduct in relation to any matter connected with or arising out of the insolvency.

6(2)   For the purposes of this section–

   (a)   a partnership becomes insolvent if–

      (i)   the court makes an order for it to be wound up as an unregistered company at a time when its assets are insufficient for the payment of its debts and other liabilities and the expenses of the winding up; or

      (ii)   the partnership enters administration; and

   (b)   a company becomes insolvent if–

      (i)   the company goes into liquidation at a time when its assets are insufficient for the payment of its debts and other liabilities and the expenses of the winding up;

      (ii)   the company enters administration; or

      (iii)   an administrative receiver of the company is appointed.

6(2A)   For the purposes of this section, an overseas company or partnership becomes insolvent if the company or partnership enters into insolvency proceedings of any description (including interim proceedings) in any jurisdiction.

6(3)   In this section and section 7(2), "the court" means–

   (a)   where the partnership in question is being or has been wound up as an unregistered company by the court, that court;

   (b)   where paragraph (a) does not apply but an administrator has at any time been appointed in relation to the partnership in question, any court which has jurisdiction to wind it up.

6(3A)   Section 117 of the Insolvency Act 1986 (High Court and county court jurisdiction), as modified and set out in Schedule 5 to the 1994 Order, shall apply for the purposes of subsection (3) as if in a case within paragraph (b) of that subsection the references to the presentation of the petition for winding up in sections 117(3) and 117(4) of the Insolvency Act 1986, as modified and set out in that Schedule, were references to the making of the administration order.

6(3B)   Nothing in subsection (3) invalidates any proceedings by reason of their being taken in the wrong court; and proceedings–

   (a)   for or in connection with a disqualification order under this section; or

   (b)   in connection with a disqualification undertaking accepted under section 7,

may be retained in the court in which the proceedings were commenced, although it may not be the court in which they ought to have been commenced.

6(3C)   In this section and section 7, "director" includes a shadow director.

6(4)   Under this section the minimum period of disqualification is 2 years, and the maximum period is 15 years.

History
See note after s.12C.

Section 7: Disqualification order or undertaking; applications and acceptance of undertakings

7(1)   If it appears to the Secretary of State that it is expedient in the public interest that a disqualification order under section 6 should be made against any person, an application for the making of such an order against that person may be made–

   (a)   by the Secretary of State; or

   (b)   if the Secretary of State so directs in the case of a person who is or has been an officer of a partnership which is being or has been wound up by the court as an unregistered company, by the official receiver.

7(2)   Except with the leave of the court, an application for the making under that section of a disqualification order against any person shall not be made after the end of the period of 3 years beginning with the day on which the partnership of which that person is or has been an officer became insolvent.

7(2A) If it appears to the Secretary of State that the conditions mentioned in section 6(1) are satisfied as respects any person who has offered to give him a disqualification undertaking, he may accept the undertaking if it appears to him that it is expedient in the public interest that he should do so (instead of applying, or proceeding with an application, for a disqualification order).

7(4) The Secretary of State or the official receiver may require any person–

(a) to furnish him with such information with respect to that person's or another person's conduct as an officer of a partnership, or as a director of a company which has at any time become insolvent (whether while the person was an officer or director or subsequently); and

(b) to produce and permit inspection of such books, papers and other records as are considered by the Secretary of State or (as the case may be) the official receiver to be relevant to that person's or another person's conduct as such an officer or director, as the Secretary of State or the official receiver may reasonably require for the purpose of determining whether to exercise, or of exercising, any function of his under this section.

7(5) Subsections (1A) and (2) of section 6 apply for the purposes of this section as they apply for the purposes of that section.

History
See note after s.12C.

Section 7A: Office-holder's report on conduct of officers of the partnership

7A(1) The office-holder in respect of a partnership which is insolvent must prepare a report (a "conduct report") about the conduct of each person who was an officer of the partnership–

(a) on the insolvency date; or

(b) at any time during the period of 3 years ending with that date.

7A(2) For the purposes of this section a partnership is insolvent if–

(a) the partnership is in liquidation and at the time it went into liquidation its assets were insufficient for the payment of its debts and other liabilities and the expenses of the winding up; or

(b) the partnership enters administration,

and subsection (1A) of section 6 applies for the purposes of this section as it applies for the purpose of that section.

7A(3) A conduct report must, in relation to each person, describe any conduct of the person which may assist the Secretary of State in deciding whether to exercise the power under section 7(1) or (2A) in relation to the person.

7A(4) The office-holder must send the conduct report to the Secretary of State before the end of–

(a) the period of 3 months beginning with the insolvency date; or

(b) such other longer period as the Secretary of State considers appropriate in the particular circumstances.

7A(5) If new information comes to the attention of an office-holder, the office-holder must send that information to the Secretary of State as soon as reasonably practicable.

7A(6) "New information" is information which an office-holder considers should have been included in a conduct report prepared in relation to the partnership, or would have been so included had it been available before the report was sent.

7A(7) If there is more than one office-holder in respect of a partnership at any particular time, subsection (1) applies only to the first of the office-holders to be appointed.

7A(9) The "office-holder" in respect of a partnership which is insolvent is–

(a) in the case of a partnership being wound up by the court in England and Wales, the official receiver;

(b) in the case of a partnership being wound up otherwise, the liquidator;

(c) in the case of a partnership in administration, the administrator.

7A(10)   The "insolvency date"–

    (a)   in the case of a partnership being wound up by the court, means the date on which the court makes the winding-up order (see section 125 of the Insolvency Act 1986);

    (b)   in the case of a partnership being wound up by way of a members' voluntary winding up, means the date on which the liquidator forms the opinion that the partnership will be unable to pay its debts in full (together with interest at the official rate) within the period stated in the declaration of solvency under section 89 of the Insolvency Act 1986;

    (c)   in the case of a partnership being wound up by way of a creditors' voluntary winding up where no such declaration under section 89 of that Act has been made, means the date of the passing of the resolution for voluntary winding up;

    (d)   in the case of a company which has entered administration, means the date the company did so.

7A(12)   In this section "court" has the same meaning as in section 6.

History
See note after s.12C.

Section 8: Disqualification of officer on finding of unfitness

8(1)   If it appears to the Secretary of State that it is expedient in the public interest that a disqualification order should be made against a person who is or has been an officer of an insolvent partnership, he may apply to the court for such an order.

8(2)   The court may make a disqualification order against a person where, on an application under this section, it is satisfied that his conduct in relation to the partnership (either taken alone or taken together with his conduct as an officer of one or more other partnerships or overseas partnerships, or as a director of one or more companies or overseas companies) makes him unfit to be concerned in the management of a company.

8(2A)   Where it appears to the Secretary of State that, in the case of a person who has offered to give him a disqualification undertaking–

    (a)   the conduct of the person in relation to an insolvent partnership of which the person is or has been an officer (either taken alone or taken together with his conduct as an officer of one or more other partnerships or overseas partnerships, or as a director of one or more companies or overseas companies) makes him unfit to be concerned in the management of a company; and

    (b)   it is expedient in the public interest that he should accept the undertaking (instead of applying, or proceeding with an application, for a disqualification order),

he may accept the undertaking.

8(2B)   Subsection (1A) of section 6 applies for the purposes of this section as it applies for the purposes of that section.

8(3)   In this section "the court" means the High Court.

8(4)   The maximum period of disqualification under this section is 15 years.

History
See note after s.12C.

Section 8ZA: Persons instructing unfit officers

8ZA(1)   The court may make a disqualification order against a person ("P") if, on an application under section 8ZB, it is satisfied–

    (a)   either–

        (i)   that a disqualification order under section 6 has been made against a person who is or has been an officer of a partnership; or

        (ii)   that the Secretary of State has accepted a disqualification undertaking from such a person under section 7(2A); and

    (b)   that P exercised the requisite amount of influence over the person.

That person is referred to in this section as "the main transgressor".

8ZA(2) For the purposes of this section, P exercised the requisite amount of influence over the main transgressor if any of the conduct–

(a)   for which the main transgressor is subject to the order made under section 6; or

(b)   in relation to which the undertaking was accepted from the main transgressor under section 7(2A),

was the result of the main transgressor acting in accordance with P's directions or instructions.

8ZA(3) But P does not exercise the requisite amount of influence over the main transgressor by reason only that the main transgressor acts on advice given by P in a professional capacity.

8ZA(4) Under this section the minimum period of disqualification is 2 years and the maximum period is 15 years.

8ZA(5) In this section and section 8ZB"the court" has the same meaning as in section 6; and subsection (3B) of section 6 applies in relation to proceedings mentioned in subsection (6) below as it applies in relation to proceedings mentioned in section 6(3B)(a) and (b).

8ZA(6) The proceedings are proceedings–

(a)   for or in connection with a disqualification order under this section; or

(b)   in connection with a disqualification undertaking accepted under section 8ZC.

History
See note after s.12C.

Section 8ZB: Application for order under section 8ZA

8ZB(1) If it appears to the Secretary of State that it is expedient in the public interest that a disqualification order should be made against a person under section 8ZA, the Secretary of State may–

(a)   make an application to the court for such an order; or

(b)   in a case where an application for an order under section 6 against the main transgressor has been made by the official receiver, direct the official receiver to make such an application.

8ZB(2) Except with the leave of the court, an application for a disqualification order under section 8ZA must not be made after the end of the period of 3 years beginning with the day on which the partnership in question became insolvent (within the meaning given by section 6(2)).

8ZB(3) Subsection (4) of section 7 applies for the purposes of this section as it applies for the purposes of that section.

History
See note after s.12C.

Section 8ZC: Disqualification undertaking instead of an order under section 8ZA

8ZC(1) If it appears to the Secretary of State that it is expedient in the public interest to do so, the Secretary of State may accept a disqualification undertaking from a person ("P") if–

(a)   any of the following is the case–

    (i)   a disqualification order under section 6 has been made against a person who is or has been an officer of a partnership;

    (ii)   the Secretary of State has accepted a disqualification undertaking from such a person under section 7(2A); or

    (iii)   it appears to the Secretary of State that such an undertaking could be accepted from such a person (if one were offered); and

(b)   it appears to the Secretary of State that P exercised the requisite amount of influence over the person.

That person is referred to in this section as "the main transgressor".

8ZC(2) For the purposes of this section, P exercised the requisite amount of influence over the main transgressor if any of the conduct–

(a) for which the main transgressor is subject to the disqualification order made under section 6;

(b) in relation to which the disqualification undertaking was accepted from the main transgressor under section 7(2A); or

(c) which led the Secretary of State to the conclusion set out in subsection (1)(a)(iii),

was the result of the main transgressor acting in accordance with P's directions or instructions.

8ZC(3) But P does not exercise the requisite amount of influence over the main transgressor by reason only that the main transgressor acts on advice given by P in a professional capacity.

8ZC(4) Subsection (4) of section 7 applies for the purposes of this section as it applies for the purposes of that section.

History
See note after s.12C.

Section 8ZD: Order disqualifying person instructing unfit director; other cases

8ZD(1) The court may make a disqualification order against a person ("P") if, on an application under this section, it is satisfied–

(a) either–

(i) that a disqualification order under section 8 has been made against a person who is or has been an officer of a partnership; or

(ii) that the Secretary of State has accepted a disqualification undertaking from such a person under section 8(2A); and

(b) that P exercised the requisite amount of influence over the person.

That person is referred to in this section as "the main transgressor".

8ZD(2) The Secretary of State may make an application to the court for a disqualification order against P under this section if it appears to the Secretary of State that it is expedient in the public interest for such an order to be made.

8ZD(3) For the purposes of this section, P exercised the requisite amount of influence over the main transgressor if any of the conduct–

(a) for which the main transgressor is subject to the order made under section 8; or

(b) in relation to which the undertaking was accepted from the main transgressor under section 8(2A),

was the result of the main transgressor acting in accordance with P's directions or instructions.

8ZD(4) But P does not exercise the requisite amount of influence over the main transgressor by reason only that the main transgressor acts on advice given by P in a professional capacity.

8ZD(5) Under this section the maximum period of disqualification is 15 years.

8ZD(6) In this section "the court" means the High Court.

History
See note after s.12C.

Section 8ZE: Disqualification undertaking instead of an order under section 8ZD

8ZE(1) If it appears to the Secretary of State that it is expedient in the public interest to do so, the Secretary of State may accept a disqualification undertaking from a person ("P") if–

(a) any of the following is the case–

(i) a disqualification order under section 8 has been made against a person who is or has been an officer of a partnership;

(ii) the Secretary of State has accepted a disqualification undertaking from such a person under section 8(2A); or

(iii) it appears to the Secretary of State that such an undertaking could be accepted from such a person (if one were offered); and

(b) it appears to the Secretary of State that P exercised the requisite amount of influence over the person.

That person is referred to in this section as "the main transgressor".

8ZE(2) For the purposes of this section, P exercised the requisite amount of influence over the main transgressor if any of the conduct–

(a) for which the main transgressor is subject to the disqualification order made under section 8;

(b) in relation to which the disqualification undertaking was accepted from the main transgressor under section 8(2A); or

(c) which led the Secretary of State to the conclusion set out in subsection (1)(a)(iii),

was the result of the main transgressor acting in accordance with P's directions or instructions.

8ZE(3) But P does not exercise the requisite amount of influence over the main transgressor by reason only that the main transgressor acts on advice given by P in a professional capacity."

History
See note after s.12C.

12C   Section 12C: Determining unfitness etc.: matters to be taken into account

12C(1) This section applies where a court must determine–

(a) whether a person's conduct as an officer of a partnership (either taken alone or taken together with his conduct as an officer of one or more other partnerships or overseas partnerships, or as a director of one or more companies or overseas companies) makes the person unfit to be concerned in the management of a company;

(b) whether to exercise any discretion it has to make a disqualification order under any of sections 5A or 8;

(c) where the court has decided to make a disqualification order under any of those sections or is required to make an order under section 6, what the period of disqualification should be.

12C(3) This section also applies where the Secretary of State must determine–

(a) whether a person's conduct as an officer of a partnership (either taken alone or taken together with his conduct as an officer of one or more other partnerships or overseas partnerships, or as a director of one or more companies or overseas companies) makes the person unfit to be concerned in the management of a company;

(b) whether to exercise any discretion the Secretary of State has to accept a disqualification undertaking under section 5A, 7 or 8.

12C(4) In making any such determination in relation to a person, the court or the Secretary of State must–

(a) in every case, have regard in particular to the matters set out in paragraphs 1 to 4 of Schedule 1;

(b) in a case where the person concerned is or has been an officer of a partnership or overseas partnership, or director of a company or overseas company, also have regard in particular to the matters set out in paragraphs 5 to 7 of that Schedule.

12C(6) Subsection (1A) of section 6 applies for the purposes of this section as it applies for the purposes of that section.

History
Substitute s.5A, 7A and 8ZA–8ZE, 12C inserted, substitute ss.6, 7 and 8 substituted and substitute s.9 omitted by the Insolvency (Miscellaneous Amendments) Regulations 2017 (SI 2017/1119) regs 1(1), (6), 2, Sch.2 paras 1, 8(1)–(8) as from 8 December 2017 subject to transitional and savings provision in para.10.

Section 13: Criminal penalties

13 If a person acts in contravention of a disqualification order or disqualification undertaking he is liable–

    (a) on conviction on indictment, to imprisonment for not more than 2 years or a fine or both; and

    (b) on summary conviction, to imprisonment for not more than 6 months or a fine not exceeding the statutory maximum, or both.

Section 14: Offences by body corporate

14(1) Where a body corporate is guilty of an offence of acting in contravention of a disqualification order or disqualification undertaking and it is proved that the offence occurred with the consent or connivance of, or was attributable to any neglect on the part of any director, manager, secretary or other similar officer of the body corporate, or any person who was purporting to act in any such capacity he, as well as the body corporate, is guilty of the offence and liable to be proceeded against and punished accordingly.

14(2) Where the affairs of a body corporate are managed by its members, subsection (1) applies in relation to the acts and defaults of a member in connection with his functions of management as if he were a director of the body corporate.

Section 15: Personal liability for company's debts where person acts while disqualified

15(1) A person is personally responsible for all the relevant debts of a company if at any time–

    (a) in contravention of a disqualification order or disqualification undertaking he is involved in the management of the company, or

    (b) as a person who is involved in the management of the company, he acts or is willing to act on instructions given without the leave of the court by a person whom he knows at that time to be the subject of a disqualification order or disqualification undertaking or a disqualification order under Part II of the Companies (Northern Ireland) Order 1989 or to be an undischarged bankrupt.

15(2) Where a person is personally responsible under this section for the relevant debts of a company, he is jointly and severally liable in respect of those debts with the company and any other person who, whether under this section or otherwise, is so liable.

15(3) For the purposes of this section the relevant debts of a company are–

    (a) in relation to a person who is personally responsible under paragraph (a) of subsection (1), such debts and other liabilities of the company as are incurred at a time when that person was involved in the management of the company, and

    (b) in relation to a person who is personally responsible under paragraph (b) of that subsection, such debts and other liabilities of the company as are incurred at a time when that person was acting or was willing to act on instructions given as mentioned in that paragraph.

15(4) For the purposes of this section, a person is involved in the management of a company if he is a director of the company or if he is concerned, whether directly or indirectly, or takes part, in the management of the company.

15(5) For the purposes of this section a person who, as a person involved in the management of a company, has at any time acted on instructions given without the leave of the court by a person whom he knew at that time to be the subject of a disqualification order or disqualification undertaking or a disqualification order under Part II of the Companies (Northern Ireland) Order 1989 or to be an undischarged bankrupt is presumed, unless the contrary is shown, to have been willing at any time thereafter to act on any instructions given by that person.

Section 15A: Compensation orders and undertakings

15A(1) The court may make a compensation order against a person on the application of the Secretary of State if it is satisfied that the conditions mentioned in subsection (3) are met.

15A(2) If it appears to the Secretary of State that the conditions mentioned in subsection (3) are met in respect of a person who has offered to give the Secretary of State a compensation undertaking, the Secretary of State may accept the undertaking instead of applying, or proceeding with an application, for a compensation order.

15A(3)   The conditions are that–

(a)   the person is subject to a disqualification order or disqualification undertaking under this Act; and

(b)   conduct for which the person is subject to the order or undertaking has caused loss to one or more creditors of an insolvent partnership of which the person has at any time been an officer.

15A(4)   An "insolvent partnership" is a partnership that is or has been insolvent and a partnership becomes insolvent if the partnership goes into liquidation at a time when its assets are insufficient for the payment of its debts and other liabilities and the expenses of the winding up.

15A(5)   The Secretary of State may apply for a compensation order at any time before the end of the period of two years beginning with the date on which the disqualification order referred to in paragraph (a) of subsection (3) was made, or the disqualification undertaking referred to in that paragraph was accepted.

15A(6)   In the case of a person subject to a disqualification order under section 8ZA or 8ZD, or a disqualification undertaking under section 8ZC or 8ZE, the reference in subsection (3)(b) to conduct is a reference to the conduct of the main transgressor in relation to which the person has exercised the requisite amount of influence.

15A(7)   In this section and sections 15B and 15C "the court" means–

(a)   in a case where a disqualification order has been made, the court that made the order;

(b)   in any other case, the High Court.

Section 15B: Amounts payable under compensation orders and undertakings

15B(1)   A compensation order is an order requiring the person against whom it is made to pay an amount specified in the order–

(a)   to the Secretary of State for the benefit of–

    (i)   a creditor or creditors specified in the order;

    (ii)   a class or classes of creditor so specified;

(b)   as a contribution to the assets of a partnership so specified.

15B(2)   A compensation undertaking is an undertaking to pay an amount specified in the undertaking–

(a)   to the Secretary of State for the benefit of–

    (i)   a creditor or creditors specified in the undertaking;

    (ii)   a class or classes of creditor so specified;

(b)   as a contribution to the assets of a partnership so specified.

15B(3)   When specifying an amount the court (in the case of an order) and the Secretary of State (in the case of an undertaking) must in particular have regard to–

(a)   the amount of the loss caused;

(b)   the nature of the conduct mentioned in section 15A(3)(b);

(c)   whether the person has made any other financial contribution in recompense for the conduct (whether under a statutory provision or otherwise).

15B(4)   An amount payable by virtue of subsection (2) under a compensation undertaking is recoverable as if payable under a court order.

15B(5)   An amount payable under a compensation order or compensation undertaking is provable as a bankruptcy debt."

History

Substitute ss.15A, 15B inserted by the Insolvency (Miscellaneous Amendments) Regulations 2017 (SI 2017/1119) regs 1(1), (6), 2, Sch.2 paras 1, 8(1), (9) as from 8 December 2017 subject to transitional and savings provision in para.10.

Section 17: Application for leave under an order or undertaking

17(1) Where a person is subject to a disqualification order made by a court having jurisdiction to wind up partnerships, any application for leave for the purposes of section 1(1)(a) shall be made to that court.

17(3) Where a person is subject to a disqualification undertaking accepted at any time under section 5A, 7 or 8, any application for leave for the purposes of section 1A(1)(a) shall be made to any court to which, if the Secretary of State had applied for a disqualification order under the section in question at that time, his application could have been made.

17(3ZA) Where a person is subject to a disqualification undertaking accepted at any time under section 8ZC, any application for leave for the purposes of section 1A(1)(a) must be made to any court to which, if the Secretary of State had applied for a disqualification order under section 8ZA at that time, that application could have been made.

17(3ZB) Where a person is subject to a disqualification undertaking accepted at any time under section 8ZE, any application for leave for the purposes of section 1A(1)(a) must be made to the High Court.

17(3A) Where a person is subject to a disqualification undertaking accepted at any time under section 9B any application for leave for the purposes of section 9B(4) must be made to the High Court.

17(4) But where a person is subject to two or more disqualification orders or undertakings (or to one or more disqualification orders and to one or more disqualification undertakings), any application for leave for the purposes of sections 1(1)(a) or 1A(1)(a) shall be made to any court to which any such application relating to the latest order to be made, or undertaking to be accepted, could be made.

17(5) On the hearing of an application for leave for the purposes of section 1(1)(a) or 1A(1)(a), the Secretary of State shall appear and call the attention of the court to any matters which seem to him to be relevant, and may himself give evidence or call witnesses.

History
Substitute s.17 substituted by the Insolvency (Miscellaneous Amendments) Regulations 2017 (SI 2017/1119) regs 1(1), (6), 2, Sch.2 paras 1, 8(1), (10) as from 8 December 2017 subject to transitional and savings provision in para.10.

SCHEDULE 1

DETERMINING UNFITNESS ETC.: MATTERS TO BE TAKEN INTO ACCOUNT

Section 12C

MATTERS TO BE TAKEN INTO ACCOUNT IN ALL CASES

1 The extent to which the person was responsible for the causes of any material contravention by a partnership or overseas partnership, or a company or overseas company, of any applicable legislative or other requirement.

2 Where applicable, the extent to which the person was responsible for the causes of a partnership or overseas partnership, or company or overseas company, becoming insolvent.

3 The frequency of conduct of the person which falls within paragraph 1 or 2.

4 The nature and extent of any loss or harm caused, or any potential loss or harm which could have been caused, by the person's conduct as an officer of any partnership or overseas partnership or as a director of any company or overseas company.

ADDITIONAL MATTERS TO BE TAKEN INTO ACCOUNT WHERE PERSON IS OR HAS BEEN AN OFFICER OF A PARTNERSHIP OR A DIRECTOR

5 Any misfeasance or breach of any fiduciary or other duty by the person in relation to a partnership or overseas partnership or a company or overseas company.

6 Any material breach of any legislative or other obligation of the person which applies as a result of being–

    (a) an officer of a partnership or overseas partnership; or

(b) a director of a company or overseas company.

7 The frequency of conduct of the person which falls within paragraph 5 or 6.

INTERPRETATION

8 Subsections (1A) to (2A) of section 6 apply for the purposes of this Schedule as they apply for the purposes of that section.

9 In this Schedule "director" includes a shadow director.".

History
Substitute Sch.1 substituted by the Insolvency (Miscellaneous Amendments) Regulations 2017 (SI 2017/1119) regs 1(1), (6), 2, Sch.2 paras 1, 8(1), (11) as from 8 December 2017 subject to transitional and savings provision in para.10.
  Previously, modified Sch.1 para.10 omitted and para.11(c) amended by the Deregulation Act 2015 and Small Business, Enterprise and Employment Act 2015 (Consequential Amendments) (Savings) Regulations 2017 (SI 2017/540) regs 1, 3, Sch.2 paras 2, 11 as from 6 April 2017. Previous to that modified Sch.1 para.12(a) amended by the Insolvent Partnerships (Amendment) Order 2005 (SI 2005/1516) art.11(1), (4), as from 1 July 2005.

SCHEDULE 9

FORMS

Article 17

[Not reproduced.]

SCHEDULE 10

SUBORDINATE LEGISLATION APPLIED

Article 18

The Insolvency Practitioners Tribunal (Conduct of Investigations) Rules 1986

The Insolvency Practitioners (Recognised Professional Bodies) Order 1986

The Insolvency (England and Wales) Rules 2016

The Insolvency Proceedings (Monetary Limits) Order 1986

The Administration of Insolvent Estates of Deceased Persons Order 1986

The Insolvency (Amendment of Subordinate Legislation) Order 1986

The Co-operation of Insolvency Courts (Designation of Relevant Countries and Territories) Order 1986

The Insolvent Companies (Disqualification of Unfit Directors) Proceedings Rules 1987

The Insolvency Regulations 1994

The Insolvent Companies (Reports on Conduct of Directors) Rules 1996

The Companies (Disqualification Orders) Regulations 2001

The Insolvency Practitioners and Insolvency Services Accounts (Fees) Order 2003

The Insolvency Proceedings (Fees) Order 2004

The Insolvency Practitioners Regulations 2005

History
In Sch.10 "The Insolvency (England and Wales) Rules 2016" substituted for "The Insolvency Rules 1986" by the Insolvency (Miscellaneous Amendments) Regulations 2017 (SI 2017/1119) regs 1(1), (6), 2, Sch.2 paras 1, 9 as from 8 December 2017 subject to transitional and savings provision in para.10.

Insolvency Regulations 1994

(SI 1994/2507)

Made on 26 September 1994 by the Secretary of State for Trade and Industry under r.12.1 of the Insolvency Rules 1986 and ss.411, 412 of and para.27 of Sch.8 and para.30 of Sch.9 to the Insolvency Act 1986. Operative from 24 October 1994.

[**Note:** These Regulations apply (with modifications) to limited liability partnerships by virtue of the Limited Liability Partnerships Regulations 2001 (SI 2001/1090) regs 1, 10(1) and Sch.6 Pt II para.10 as from 6 April 2001. Changes made by the Insolvency (Amendment) Regulations 2000 (SI 2000/485), the Insolvency (Amendment) Regulations 2001 (SI 2001/762), the Financial Services and Markets Act 2000 (Consequential Amendments and Repeals) Order 2001 (SI 2001/3649), the Insolvency (Amendment) Regulations 2004 (SI 2004/472), the Insolvency (Amendment) Regulations 2005 (SI 2005/512), the Insolvency (Amendment) Regulations 2008 (SI 2008/670), the Insolvency (Amendment) Regulations 2009 (SI 2009/482), the Insolvency (Amendment) Regulations 2011 (SI 2011/2203) and the Insolvency (England and Wales) and Insolvency (Scotland) (Miscellaneous and Consequential Amendments) Rules 2017 (SI 2017/1115) have been incorporated into the text (in the case of pre-2003 legislation without annotation).]

Part 1

General

1 Citation and commencement

1   These Regulations may be cited as the Insolvency Regulations 1994 and shall come into force on 24th October 1994.

2 Revocations

2   Subject to regulation 37 below, the Regulations listed in Schedule 1 to these Regulations are hereby revoked.

3 Interpretation and application

3(1)   In these Regulations, except where the context otherwise requires–

"bank" means–

(a)   a person who has permission under Part 4A of the Financial Services and Markets Act 2000 to accept deposits, or

(b)   an EEA firm of the kind mentioned in paragraph 5(b) of Schedule 3 to that Act, which has permission under paragraph 15 of that Schedule (as a result of qualifying for authorisation under paragraph 12(1) of that Schedule) to accept deposits;

"bankrupt" means the bankrupt or his estate;

"company" means the company which is being wound up;

"creditors' committee" means any committee established under section 301;

"electronic transfer" means transmission by any electronic means;

"liquidation committee" means, in the case of a winding up by the court, any committee established under section 141 and, in the case of a creditors' voluntary winding up, any committee established under section 101;

"liquidator" includes, in the case of a company being wound up by the court, the official receiver when so acting;

"local bank" means any bank in, or in the neighbourhood of, the insolvency district, or the district in respect of which the court has winding-up jurisdiction, in which the proceedings are taken, or in the locality in which any business of the company or, as the case may be, the bankrupt is carried on;

"local bank account" means, in the case of a winding up by the court, a current account opened with a local bank under regulation 6(2) below and, in the case of a bankruptcy, a current account opened with a local bank under regulation 21(1) below;

"payment instrument" means a cheque or payable order;

"the Rules" means the Insolvency (England and Wales) Rules 2016; and

"trustee", subject to regulation 19(2) below, means trustee of a bankrupt's estate including the official receiver when so acting;

and other expressions used in these Regulations and defined by the Rules have the meanings which they bear in the Rules.

3(2) A Rule referred to in these Regulations by number means the Rule so numbered in the Rules.

3(3) Any application to be made to the Secretary of State or to the Department or anything required to be sent to the Secretary of State or to the Department under these Regulations shall be addressed to the Department for Business, Energy and Industrial Strategy, The Insolvency Service, PO Box 3690, Birmingham B2 4UY.

3(4) Where a regulation makes provision for the use of a form obtainable from the Department, the Department may provide different forms for different cases arising under that regulation.

3(5) Subject to regulation 37 below, these Regulations (except for regulations 3A and 36A) apply–

(a) to winding-up proceedings commenced on or after 29th December 1986; and

(b) to bankruptcy proceedings where the bankruptcy petition is or was presented on or after that day.

3(6) Regulation 3A applies in any case where a company entered into administration on or after 15th September 2003 other than a case where the company entered into administration by virtue of a petition presented before that date.

3(7) Regulation 36A applies in any case where an insolvency practitioner is appointed on or after 1st April 2005.

History
In reg.3(1) the definition of "the Rules" substituted by the Insolvency (England and Wales) Rules 2016 (Consequential Amendments and Savings) Rules 2017 (SI 2017/369) r.2(2), Sch.2 para.4(1), (2) as from 6 April 2017.

In reg.3(5) the words in round brackets inserted by the Insolvency (Amendment) Regulations 2005 (SI 2005/512) reg.5(1), (2) as from 1 April 2005.

Regulation 3(6) inserted by the Insolvency (Amendment) Regulations 2005 (SI 2005/512) reg.5(1), (3) as from 1 April 2005.

Regulation 3(7) inserted by the Insolvency (Amendment) Regulations 2005 (SI 2005/512) reg.5(1), (3) as from 1 April 2005.

Part 1A

Administration

3A   Disposal of company's records and provision of information to the Secretary of State

3A(1) The person who was the last administrator of a company which has been dissolved may, at any time after the expiration of a period of one year from the date of dissolution, destroy or otherwise dispose of the books, papers and other records of the company.

3A(2)   An administrator or former administrator shall within 14 days of a request by the Secretary of State give the Secretary of State particulars of any money in his hands or under his control representing unclaimed or undistributed assets of the company or dividends or other sums due to any person as a member or former member of the company.

History
Regulation 3A inserted by the Insolvency (Amendment) Regulations 2005 (SI 2005/512) reg.6 as from 1 April 2005.

3B   Payment of unclaimed dividends or other money

3B(1)   This regulation applies to monies which–

(a)   are held by the former administrator of a dissolved company, and

(b)   represent either or both of the following–

    (i)   unclaimed dividends due to creditors, or

    (ii)   sums held by the company in trust in respect of dividends or other sums due to any person as a member or former member of the company.

3B(2)   Any monies to which this regulation applies may be paid into the Insolvency Services Account.

3B(3)   Where under this regulation the former administrator pays any sums into the Insolvency Services Account, he shall at the same time give notice to the Secretary of State of–

(a)   the name of the company,

(b)   the name and address of the person to whom the dividend or other sum is payable,

(c)   the amount of the dividend or other sum, and

(d)   the date on which it was paid.

3B(4)   Where a dividend or other sum is paid to a person by way of a payment instrument, any payment into the Insolvency Services Account in respect of that dividend or sum pursuant to paragraph (2) may not be made earlier than on or after the expiry of 6 months from the date of the payment instrument.

PART 1B

ADMINISTRATIVE RECEIVERSHIP

3C   Payment of unclaimed dividends or other money

3C(1) This regulation applies to monies which–

(a)   are held by the former administrative receiver of a dissolved company, and

(b)   represent either or both of the following–

    (i)   unclaimed dividends due to creditors, or

    (ii)   sums held by the company in trust in respect of dividends or other sums due to any person as a member or former member of the company.

3C(2)   Any monies to which this regulation applies may be paid into the Insolvency Services Account.

3C(3)   Where under this regulation the former administrative receiver pays any sums into the Insolvency Services Account, he shall at the same time give notice to the Secretary of State of–

(a)   the name of the company,

(b)   the name and address of the person to whom the dividend or other sum is payable,

(c)   the amount of the dividend or other sum, and

(d)   the date on which it was paid.

3C(3)   Where a dividend or other sum is paid to a person by way of a payment instrument, any payment in respect of that dividend or sum into the Insolvency Services Account pursuant to paragraph (2) may not be made earlier than on or after the expiry of 6 months from the date of the payment instrument.

History
Regulations 3B, 3C inserted by the Insolvency (Amendment) Regulations 2008 (SI 2008/670) reg.3(1), (2) as from 6 April 2008.

PART 2

WINDING UP

4 Introductory

4   This Part of these Regulations relates to–

(a)   voluntary winding up and

(b)   winding up by the court

of companies which the courts in England and Wales have jurisdiction to wind up.

Payments into and out of the Insolvency Services Account

5 Payments into the Insolvency Services Account

5(1)   In the case of a winding up by the court, subject to regulation 6 below, the liquidator shall pay all money received by him in the course of carrying out his functions as such without any deduction into the Insolvency Services Account kept by the Secretary of State with the Bank of England to the credit of the company once every 14 days or forthwith if £5,000 or more has been received.

5(2)   [Omitted by the Insolvency (Amendment) Regulations 2011 (SI 2011/2203) Sch. para.1 as from 1 October 2011.]

5(3)   Every payment of money into the Insolvency Services Account under this regulation shall be–

(a)   made through the Bank Giro system; or

(b)   sent direct to the Bank of England, Threadneedle Street, London EC2R 8AH by cheque drawn in favour of the "Insolvency Services Account" and crossed "A/c payee only" "Bank of England"; or

(c)   made by electronic transfer,

and the liquidator shall on request be given by the Department a receipt for the money so paid.

5(4)   Every payment of money made under sub-paragraph (a) or (b) of paragraph (3) above shall be accompanied by a form obtainable from the Department for that purpose or by a form that is substantially similar. Every payment of money made under sub-paragraph (c) of paragraph (3) above shall specify the name of the liquidator making the payment and the name of the company to whose credit such payment is made.

5(5)   Where in a voluntary winding up a liquidator pays any unclaimed dividend into the Insolvency Services Account, he shall at the same time give notice to the Secretary of State, on a form obtainable from the Department or on one that is substantially similar, of the name and address of the person to whom the dividend is payable and the amount of the dividend.

6 Local bank account and handling of funds not belonging to the company

6(1) This regulation does not apply in the case of a voluntary winding up.

6(2) Where the liquidator intends to exercise his power to carry on the business of the company, he may apply to the Secretary of State for authorisation to open a local bank account, and the Secretary of State may authorise him to make his payments into and out of a specified bank, subject to a limit, instead of into and out of the Insolvency Services Account if satisfied that an administrative advantage will be derived from having such an account.

6(3) Money received by the liquidator relating to the purpose for which the account was opened may be paid into the local bank account to the credit of the company to which the account relates.

6(4) Where the liquidator opens a local bank account pursuant to an authorisation granted under paragraph (2) above, he shall open and maintain the account in the name of the company.

6(5) Where money which is not an asset of the company is provided to the liquidator for a specific purpose, it shall be clearly identifiable in a separate account.

6(6) The liquidator shall keep proper records, including documentary evidence of all money paid into and out of every local bank account opened and maintained under this regulation.

6(7) The liquidator shall pay without deduction any surplus over any limit imposed by an authorisation granted under paragraph (2) above into the Insolvency Services Account in accordance with regulation 5 above as that regulation applies in the case of a winding up by the court.

6(8) As soon as the liquidator ceases to carry on the business of the company or vacates office or an authorisation given in pursuance of an application under paragraph (2) above is withdrawn, he shall close the account and pay any balance into the Insolvency Services Account in accordance with regulation 5 above as that regulation applies in the case of a winding up by the court.

7 Payment of disbursements etc. out of the Insolvency Services Account

7(A1) Paragraphs (1) and (2) of this regulation are subject to paragraph (3A).

7(1) In the case of a winding up by the court, on application to the Department, the liquidator shall be repaid all necessary disbursements made by him, and expenses properly incurred by him, in the course of his administration to the date of his vacation of office out of any money standing to the credit of the company in the Insolvency Services Account.

7(2) In the case of a winding up by the court, the liquidator shall on application to the Department obtain payment instruments to the order of the payee for sums which become payable on account of the company for delivery by the liquidator to the persons to whom the payments are to be made.

7(3) [Omitted]

7(3A) In respect of an application made by the liquidator under paragraph (1) or (2) above, the Secretary of State, if requested to do so by the liquidator, may, at his discretion,

(a) make the payment which is the subject of the application to the liquidator by electronic transfer; or

(b) as an alternative to the issue of payment instruments, make payment by electronic transfer to the persons to whom the liquidator would otherwise deliver payment instruments.

7(4) Any application under this regulation shall be made by the liquidator on a form obtainable from the Department for the purpose or on a form that is substantially similar.

7(5) In the case of a winding up by the court, on the liquidator vacating office, he shall be repaid by any succeeding liquidator out of any funds available for the purpose any necessary disbursements made by him and any expenses properly incurred by him but not repaid before he vacates office.

History
Regulation 7(A1), 7(3A) amended and reg.7(3) omitted by the Insolvency (Amendment) Regulations 2011 (SI 2011/2203) regs 2–4 as from 1 October 2011.

Dividends to creditors and returns of capital to contributories of a company

8 Payment

8(A1) Paragraphs (1) and (2) of this regulation are subject to paragraph (3A).

8(1) In the case of a winding up by the court, the liquidator shall pay every dividend by payment instruments which shall be prepared by the Department on the application of the liquidator and transmitted to him for distribution amongst the creditors.

8(2) In the case of a winding up by the court, the liquidator shall pay every return of capital to contributories by payment instruments which shall be prepared by the Department on application.

8(3) [Omitted]

8(3A) In respect of an application made by the liquidator under paragraph (1) or (2) above, the Secretary of State, if requested to do so by the liquidator, may, at his discretion,

(a) as an alternative to the issue of payment instruments, make payment by electronic transfer to the persons to whom the liquidator would otherwise deliver payment instruments; or

(b) make the payment which is the subject of the application to the liquidator by electronic transfer.

8(4) Any application under this regulation for a payment instrument or payment by electronic transfer shall be made by the liquidator on a form obtainable from the Department for the purpose or on a form which is substantially similar.

8(5) In the case of a winding up by the court, the liquidator shall enter the total amount of every dividend and of every return to contributories that he desires to pay under this regulation in the records to be kept under regulation 10 below in one sum.

8(6) On the liquidator vacating office, he shall send to the Department any valid unclaimed or undelivered payment instruments for dividends or returns to contributories after endorsing them with the word "cancelled".

History
Regulation 8(A1) inserted by the Insolvency (Amendment) Regulations 2000 (SI 2000/485) regs 1, 3 and Sch. para.6 as from 31 March 2000. Regulation 8(A1), 8(3A) amended and reg.8(3) omitted by the Insolvency (Amendment) Regulations 2011 (SI 2011/2203) regs 5–7 as from 1 October 2011.

9 Investment or otherwise handling of funds in winding up of companies and payment of interest

9(1) When the cash balance standing to the credit of the company in the account in respect of that company kept by the Secretary of State is in excess of the amount which, in the opinion of the liquidator, is required for the immediate purposes of the winding up and should be invested, he may request the Secretary of State to invest the amount not so required in Government securities, to be placed to the credit of that account for the company's benefit.

9(2) When any of the money so invested is, in the opinion of the liquidator, required for the immediate purposes of the winding up, he may request the Secretary of State to raise such sum as may be required by the sale of such of those securities as may be necessary.

9(3) In cases where investments have been made at the request of the liquidator in pursuance of paragraph (1) above and additional sums to the amounts so invested, including money received under paragraph (7) below, are paid into the Insolvency Services Account to the credit of the company, a request shall be made to the Secretary of State by the liquidator if it is desired that these additional sums should be invested.

9(4)   Any request relating to the investment in, or sale of, as the case may be, Treasury Bills made under paragraphs (1), (2) or (3) above shall be made on a form obtainable from the Department or on one that is substantially similar and any request relating to the purchase or sale, as the case may be, of any other type of Government security made under the provisions of those paragraphs shall be made in writing.

9(5)   Any request made under paragraphs (1), (2) or (3) above shall be sufficient authority to the Secretary of State for the investment or sale as the case may be.

9(6)   Subject to paragraphs (6A) and (6B), at any time after 1st April 2004 whenever there are any monies standing to the credit of the company in the Insolvency Services Account the company shall be entitled to interest on those monies at the rate of 4.25 per cent per annum.

9(6A)   Interest shall cease to accrue pursuant to paragraph (6) from the date of receipt by the Secretary of State of a notice in writing from the liquidator that in the opinion of the liquidator it is necessary or expedient in order to facilitate the conclusion of the winding up that interest should cease to accrue but interest shall start to accrue again pursuant to paragraph (6) where the liquidator gives a further notice in writing to the Secretary of State requesting that interest should start to accrue again.

9(6B)   The Secretary of State may by notice published in the London Gazette vary the rate of interest prescribed by paragraph (6) and such variation shall have effect from the day after the date of publication of the notice in the London Gazette or such later date as may be specified in the notice.

9(7)   All money received in respect of investments and interest earned under this regulation shall be paid into the Insolvency Services Account to the credit of the company.

9(8)   [Omitted]

History
Regulation 9(6) substituted and reg.9(6A), (6B) inserted by the Insolvency (Amendment) Regulations 2004 (SI 2004/472) reg.2 and Sch. para.2 as from 1 April 2004. Regulation 9(8) omitted by the Insolvency (Amendment) Regulations 2011 (SI 2011/2203) reg.9 as from 1 October 2011.

Records to be maintained by liquidators and the provision of information

10   Financial records

10(1)   This regulation does not apply in the case of a members' voluntary winding up.

10(2)   The liquidator shall prepare and keep–

(a)   separate financial records in respect of each company; and

(b)   such other financial records as are required to explain the receipts and payments entered in the records described in sub-paragraph (a) above or regulation 12(2) below, including an explanation of the source of any receipts and the destination of any payments;

and shall, subject to regulation 12(2) below as to trading accounts, from day to day enter in those records all the receipts and payments made by him.

10(3)   In the case of a winding up by the court, the liquidator shall obtain and keep bank statements relating to any local bank account in the name of the company.

10(4)   The liquidator shall submit financial records to the liquidation committee when required for inspection.

10(5)   In the case of a winding up by the court, if the liquidation committee is not satisfied with the contents of the financial records submitted under paragraph (4) above it may so inform the Secretary of

State, giving the reasons for its dissatisfaction, and the Secretary of State may take such action as he thinks fit.

History
Regulation 10(2) amended by the Insolvency (Amendment) Regulations 2011 (SI 2011/2203) reg.9 as from 1 October 2011.

11   Provision of information by liquidator

11(1)   In the case of a winding up by the court, the liquidator shall, within 14 days of the receipt of a request for a statement of his receipts and payments as liquidator from any creditor, contributory or director of the company, supply free of charge to the person making the request, a statement of his receipts and payments as liquidator during the period of one year ending on the most recent anniversary of his becoming liquidator which preceded the request.

11(2)   In the case of a voluntary winding up, the liquidator shall, on request from any creditor, contributory or director of the company for a copy of a statement for any period, including future periods, sent to the registrar of companies under section 192, send such copy free of charge to the person making the request and the copy of the statement shall be sent within 14 days of the liquidator sending the statement to the registrar or the receipt of the request whichever is the later.

12   Liquidator carrying on business

12(1)   This regulation does not apply in the case of a members' voluntary winding up.

12(2)   Where the liquidator carries on any business of the company, he shall–

(a)   keep a separate and distinct account of the trading, including, where appropriate, in the case of a winding up by the court, particulars of all local bank account transactions; and

(b)   incorporate in the financial records required to be kept under regulation 10 above the total weekly amounts of the receipts and payments made by him in relation to the account kept under sub-paragraph (a) above.

13   Retention and delivery of records

13(1)   All records kept by the liquidator under regulations 10 and 12(2) and any such records received by him from a predecessor in that office shall be retained by him for a period of 6 years following–

(a)   his vacation of office, or

(b)   in the case of the official receiver, his release as liquidator under section 174,

unless he delivers them to another liquidator who succeeds him in office.

13(2)   Where the liquidator is succeeded in office by another liquidator, the records referred to in paragraph (1) above shall be delivered to that successor forthwith, unless, in the case of a winding up by the court, the winding up is for practical purposes complete and the successor is the official receiver, in which case the records are only to be delivered to the official receiver if the latter so requests.

14   Provision of accounts by liquidator and audit of accounts

14(1)   The liquidator shall, if required by the Secretary of State at any time, send to the Secretary of State an account in relation to the company of the liquidator's receipts and payments covering such period as the Secretary of State may direct and such account shall, if so required by the Secretary of State, be certified by the liquidator.

14(2)   Where the liquidator in a winding up by the court vacates office prior to sending the final account to creditors under section 146, he shall within 14 days of vacating office send to the Secretary of State an account of his receipts and payments as liquidator for any period not covered by an account previously so sent by him or if no such account has been sent, an account of his receipts and payments in respect of the whole period of his office.

14(3)　In the case of a winding up by the court, where an account has been sent pursuant to section 146(3)(a), the liquidator shall, within 14 days of sending the account, send to the Secretary of State an account of his receipts and payments as liquidator which are not covered by any previous account so sent by him, or if no such account has been sent an account of his receipts and payments in respect of the whole period of his office.

14(4)　In the case of a winding up by the court, where a statement of affairs has been submitted under the Act, any account sent under this regulation shall be accompanied by a summary of that statement of affairs and shall show the amount of any assets realised and explain the reasons for any non-realisation of any assets not realised.

14(5)　In the case of a winding up by the court, where a statement of affairs has not been submitted under the Act, any account sent under this regulation shall be accompanied by a summary of all known assets and their estimated values and shall show the amounts actually realised and explain the reasons for any non-realisation of any assets not realised.

14(6)　Any account sent to the Secretary of State shall, if he so requires, be audited, but whether or not the Secretary of State requires the account to be audited, the liquidator shall send to the Secretary of State on demand any documents (including vouchers and bank statements) and any information relating to the account.

History
In reg.14(3) the words "rules 7.69 and 7.70" substituted for the former words "Rule 4.125(5)" in each place by the Insolvency (England and Wales) Rules 2016 (Consequential Amendments and Savings) Rules 2017 (SI 2017/369) r.2(2), Sch.2 para.4(1), (2) as from 6 April 2017.
　Regulation 14(2) amended and reg.14(3) substituted by the Insolvency (England and Wales) and Insolvency (Scotland) (Miscellaneous and Consequential Amendments) Rules 2017 (SI 2017/1115) rr.1(1), (2), 15, 16 as from 8 December 2017.

15　Production and inspection of records

15(1)　The liquidator shall produce on demand to the Secretary of State, and allow him to inspect, any accounts, books and other records kept by him (including any passed to him by a predecessor in office), and this duty to produce and allow inspection shall extend–

(a)　to producing and allowing inspection at the premises of the liquidator; and

(b)　to producing and allowing inspection of any financial records of the kind described in regulation 10(2)(b) above prepared by the liquidator (or any predecessor in office of his) before 24th October 1994 and kept by the liquidator;

and any such demand may–

(i)　require the liquidator to produce any such accounts, books or other records to the Secretary of State, and allow him to inspect them–

(A)　at the same time as any account is sent to the Secretary of State under regulation 14 above; or

(B)　at any time after such account is sent to the Secretary of State;

whether or not the Secretary of State requires the account to be audited; or

(ii)　where it is made for the purpose of ascertaining whether the provisions of these Regulations relating to the handling of money received by the liquidator in the course of carrying out his functions have been or are likely to be complied with, be made at any time, whether or not an account has been sent or should have been sent to the Secretary of State under regulation 14 above and whether or not the Secretary of State has required any account to be audited.

15(2)   The liquidator shall allow the Secretary of State on demand to remove and take copies of any accounts, books and other records kept by the liquidator (including any passed to him by a predecessor in office), whether or not they are kept at the premises of the liquidator.

16   Disposal of company's books, papers and other records

16(1)   The liquidator in a winding up by the court, on the authorisation of the official receiver, during his tenure of office or on vacating office, or the official receiver while acting as liquidator, may at any time sell, destroy or otherwise dispose of the books, papers and other records of the company.

16(2)   In the case of a voluntary winding up, the person who was the last liquidator of a company which has been dissolved may, at any time after the expiration of a period of one year from the date of dissolution, destroy or otherwise dispose of the books, papers and other records of the company.

17   Voluntary liquidator to provide information to Secretary of State

17(1)   In the case of a voluntary winding up, a liquidator or former liquidator, shall, within 14 days of a request by the Secretary of State, give the Secretary of State particulars of any money in his hands or under his control representing unclaimed or undistributed assets of the company or dividends or other sums due to any person as a member or former member of the company.

17(2)   [Omitted]

History
Regulation 17(1) amended and reg.17(2) omitted by the Insolvency (Amendment) Regulations 2011 (SI 2011/2203) regs 10–11 as from 1 October 2011. Regulation 17(1) further amended by the Insolvency (England and Wales) Rules 2016 (Consequential Amendments and Savings) Rules 2017 (SI 2017/369) r.2(2), Sch.2 para.4(1), (4) as from 6 April 2017.

18   Payment of unclaimed dividends or other money

18(1)   This regulation applies to monies which–

(a)   are held by the former liquidator of a dissolved company, and

(b)   represent either or both of the following–

  (i)   unclaimed dividends due to creditors, or

  (ii)   sums held by the company in trust in respect of dividends or other sums due to any person as a member or former member of the company.

18(2)   Monies to which this regulation applies–

(a)   may in the case of a voluntary winding up,

(b)   must in the case of a winding up by the court,

be paid into the Insolvency Services Account.

18(3)   Where the former liquidator pays any sums into the Insolvency Services Account pursuant to paragraph (2), he shall at the same time give notice to the Secretary of State of–

(a)   the name of the company,

(b)   the name and address of the person to whom the dividend or other sum is payable,

(c)   the amount of the dividend, and

(d)   the date on which it was paid.

18(4)   Where a dividend or other sum is paid to a person by way of a payment instrument, any payment into the Insolvency Services Account in respect of that dividend or sum pursuant to paragraph (2) may not be made earlier than on or after the expiry of 6 months from the date of the payment instrument.

History
Regulation 18 substituted by the Insolvency (Amendment) Regulations 2008 (SI 2008/670) reg.3(1), (3) as from 6 April 2008.

PART 3

BANKRUPTCY

19   Introductory

19(1)   This Part of these Regulations relates to bankruptcy and extends to England and Wales only.

19(2)   In addition to the application of the provisions of this Part to the official receiver when acting as trustee, the provisions of this Part (other than regulations 30 and 31) shall also apply to him when acting as receiver or manager under section 287 and the term "trustee" shall be construed accordingly.

Payments into and out of the Insolvency Services Account

20   Payments into the Insolvency Services Account

20(1)   Subject to regulation 21 below, the trustee shall pay all money received by him in the course of carrying out his functions as such without any deduction into the Insolvency Services Account kept by the Secretary of State with the Bank of England to the credit of the bankrupt once every 14 days or forthwith if £5,000 or more has been received.

20(2)   Every payment of money into the Insolvency Services Account under this regulation shall be–

(a)   made through the Bank Giro system; or

(b)   sent direct to the Bank of England, Threadneedle Street, London EC2R 8AH by cheque drawn in favour of the "Insolvency Services Account" and crossed "A/c payee only" "Bank of England"; or

(c)   made by electronic transfer,

and the trustee shall on request be given by the Department a receipt for the money so paid.

20(3)   Every payment of money made under sub-paragraph (a) or (b) of paragraph (2) above shall be accompanied by a form obtainable from the Department for that purpose or by a form that is substantially similar. Every payment of money made under sub-paragraph (c) of paragraph (2) above shall specify the name of the trustee making the payment and the name of the bankrupt to whose credit such payment is made.

21   Local bank account and handling of funds not forming part of the bankrupt's estate

21(1)   Where the trustee intends to exercise his power to carry on the business of the bankrupt, he may apply to the Secretary of State for authorisation to open a local bank account, and the Secretary of State may authorise him to make his payments into and out of a specified bank, subject to a limit, instead of into and out of the Insolvency Services Account if satisfied that an administrative advantage will be derived from having such an account.

21(2)   Money received by the trustee relating to the purpose for which the account was opened may be paid into the local bank account to the credit of the bankrupt to whom the account relates.

21(3) Where the trustee opens a local bank account pursuant to an authorisation granted under paragraph (1) above he shall open and maintain the account in the name of the bankrupt.

21(4) Where money which does not form part of the bankrupt's estate is provided to the trustee for a specific purpose it shall be clearly identifiable in a separate account.

21(5) The trustee shall keep proper records, including documentary evidence of all money paid into and out of every local bank account opened and maintained under this regulation.

21(6) The trustee shall pay without deduction any surplus over any limit imposed by an authorisation granted under paragraph (1) above into the Insolvency Services Account in accordance with regulation 20(1) above.

21(7) As soon as the trustee ceases to carry on the business of the bankrupt or vacates office or an authorisation given in pursuance of an application under paragraph (1) above is withdrawn, he shall close the account and pay any balance into the Insolvency Services Account in accordance with regulation 20(1) above.

22 Payment of disbursements etc. out of the Insolvency Services Account

22(A1) Paragraphs (1) and (2) of this regulation are subject to paragraph (2A).

History
Regulation 22(A1) inserted by the Insolvency (Amendment) Regulations 2000 (SI 2000/485) regs 1, 3 and Sch. para.11 as from 31 March 2000.

22(1) On application to the Department, the trustee shall be repaid all necessary disbursements made by him, and expenses properly incurred by him, in the course of his administration to the date of his vacation of office out of any money standing to the credit of the bankrupt in the Insolvency Services Account.

22(2) The trustee shall on application to the Department obtain payment instruments to the order of the payee for sums which become payable on account of the bankrupt for delivery by the trustee to the persons to whom the payments are to be made.

22(2A) In respect of an application made by the trustee under paragraph (1) or (2) above, the Secretary of State, if requested to do so by the trustee, may, at his discretion,

(a) make the payment which is the subject of the application to the trustee by electronic transfer; or

(b) as an alternative to the issue of payment instruments, make payment by electronic transfer to the persons to whom the trustee would otherwise deliver payment instruments.

22(3) Any application under this regulation shall be made on a form obtainable from the Department or on one that is substantially similar.

22(4) On the trustee vacating office, he shall be repaid by any succeeding trustee out of any funds available for the purpose any necessary disbursements made by him and any expenses properly incurred by him but not repaid before he vacates office.

Dividends to creditors

23 Payment

23(1) Subject to paragraph (1A), the trustee shall pay every dividend by payment instruments which shall be prepared by the Department on the application of the trustee and transmitted to him for distribution amongst the creditors.

23(1A) In respect of an application made by the trustee under paragraph (1) above, the Secretary of State, if requested to do so by the trustee, may, at his discretion, as an alternative to the issue of payment instruments, make payment by electronic transfer to the persons to whom the trustee would otherwise deliver payment instruments.

23(2) Any application under this regulation for a payment instrument or payment by electronic transfer shall be made by the trustee on a form obtainable from the Department for the purpose or on a form which is substantially similar.

23(3) The trustee shall enter the total amount of every dividend that he desires to pay under this regulation in the records to be kept under regulation 24 below in one sum.

23(4) On the trustee vacating office, he shall send to the Department any valid unclaimed or undelivered payment instruments for dividends after endorsing them with the word "cancelled".

Investment or otherwise handling of funds in bankruptcy and payment of interest

23A(1) When the cash balance standing to the credit of the bankrupt in the account in respect of that bankrupt kept by the Secretary of State is in excess of the amount which, in the opinion of the trustee, is required for the immediate purposes of the bankruptcy and should be invested, he may request the Secretary of State to invest the amount not so required in Government securities, to be placed to the credit of that account for the benefit of the bankrupt.

23A(2) When any of the money so invested is, in the opinion of the trustee, required for the immediate purposes of the bankruptcy, he may request the Secretary of State to raise such sum as may be required by the sale of such of those securities as may be necessary.

23A(3) In cases where investments have been made at the request of the trustee in pursuance of paragraph (1) above and additional sums to the amounts so invested, including money received under paragraph (7) below, are paid into the Insolvency Services Account to the credit of the bankrupt, a request shall be made to the Secretary of State by the trustee if it is desired that these additional funds should be invested.

23A(4) Any request relating to the investment in, or sale of, as the case may be, Treasury Bills under paragraphs (1), (2) or (3) above shall be made on a form obtainable from the Department or on one that is substantially similar and any request relating to the purchase or sale, as the case may be, of any other type of Government security made under the provisions of those paragraphs shall be made in writing.

23A(5) Any request made under paragraphs (1), (2) or (3) above shall be sufficient authority to the Secretary of State for the investment or sale as the case may be.

23A(6) Subject to paragraphs (6A) and (6B), at any time after 1st April 2004 whenever there are any monies standing to the credit of the estate of the bankrupt in the Insolvency Services Account the estate shall be entitled to interest on those monies at the rate of 4.25 per cent per annum.

23A(6A) Interest shall cease to accrue pursuant to paragraph (6) from the date of receipt by the Secretary of State of a notice in writing from the trustee that in the opinion of the trustee it is necessary or expedient in order to facilitate the conclusion of the bankruptcy that interest should cease to accrue but interest shall start to accrue again pursuant to paragraph (6) where the trustee gives a further notice in writing to the Secretary of State requesting that interest should start to accrue again.

23A(6B) The Secretary of State may by notice published in the London Gazette vary the rate of interest prescribed by paragraph (6) and such variation shall have effect from the day after the date of publication of the notice in the London Gazette or such later date as may be specified in the notice.

23A(7) All money received in respect of investments and interest earned under this regulation shall be paid into the Insolvency Services Account to the credit of the bankrupt.

History
Regulation 23A(6) substituted and reg.23A(6A) and (6B) added by the Insolvency (Amendment) Regulations 2004
(SI 2004/472) reg.2, Sch. para.3 as from 1 April 2004.

Records to be maintained by trustees and the provision of information

24   Financial records

24(1)   The trustee shall prepare and keep–

(a)   separate financial records in respect of each bankrupt; and

(b)   such other financial records as are required to explain the receipts and payments entered in the records described in sub-paragraph (a) above or regulation 26 below, including an explanation of the source of any receipts and the destination of any payments;

and shall, subject to regulation 26 below as to trading accounts, from day to day enter in those records all the receipts and payments made by him.

24(2)   The trustee shall obtain and keep bank statements relating to any local bank account in the name of the bankrupt.

24(3)   The trustee shall submit financial records to the creditors' committee when required for inspection.

24(4)   If the creditors' committee is not satisfied with the contents of the financial records submitted under paragraph (3) above it may so inform the Secretary of State, giving the reasons for its dissatisfaction and the Secretary of State may take such action as he thinks fit.

25   Provision of information by trustee

25   The trustee shall, within 14 days of the receipt of a request from any creditor or the bankrupt for a statement of his receipts and payments as trustee, supply free of charge to the person making the request, a statement of his receipts and payments as trustee during the period of one year ending on the most recent anniversary of his becoming trustee which preceded the request.

26   Trustee carrying on business

26   Subject to paragraph (2) below, where the trustee carries on any business of the bankrupt, he shall–

(a)   keep a separate and distinct account of the trading, including, where appropriate, particulars of all local bank account transactions; and

(b)   incorporate in the financial records required to be kept under regulation 24 above the total weekly amounts of the receipts and payments made by him in relation to the account kept under paragraph (a) above.

27   Retention and delivery of records

27(1)   All records kept by the trustee under regulations 24 and 26 and any such records received by him from a predecessor in that office shall be retained by him for a period of 6 years following–

(a)   his vacation of office, or

(b)   in the case of the official receiver, his release as trustee under section 299,

unless he delivers them to another trustee who succeeds him in office.

27(2)   Where the trustee is succeeded in office by another trustee, the records referred to in paragraph (1) above shall be delivered to that successor forthwith, unless the bankruptcy is for practical purposes complete and the successor is the official receiver, in which case the records are only to be delivered to the official receiver if the latter so requests.

28   Provision of accounts by trustee and audit of accounts

28(1)   The trustee shall, if required by the Secretary of State at any time, send to the Secretary of State an account of his receipts and payments as trustee of the bankrupt covering such period as the Secretary of State may direct and such account shall, if so required by the Secretary of State, be certified by the trustee.

28(2)   Where the trustee vacates office prior to sending the final report to creditors under section 331, he shall within 14 days of vacating office send to the Secretary of State an account of his receipts and payments as trustee for any period not covered by an account previously so sent by him, or if no such account has been sent, an account of his receipts and payments in respect of the whole period of his office.

28(3)   Where a report has been sent pursuant to section 331(2A)(a), the trustee shall, within 14 days of sending the report, send to the Secretary of State an account of his receipts and payments as trustee which are not covered by any previous account so sent by him, or if no such account has been sent, an account of his receipts and payments in respect of the whole period of his office.

28(4)   Where a statement of affairs has been submitted under the Act, any account sent under this regulation shall be accompanied by a summary of that statement of affairs and shall show the amount of any assets realised and explain the reasons for any non-realisation of any assets not realised.

28(5)   Where a statement of affairs has not been submitted under the Act, any account sent under this regulation shall be accompanied by a summary of all known assets and their estimated values and shall show the amounts actually realised and explain the reasons for any non-realisation of any assets not realised.

28(6)   Any account sent to the Secretary of State shall, if he so requires, be audited, but whether or not the Secretary of State requires the account to be audited, the trustee shall send to the Secretary of State on demand any documents (including vouchers and bank statements) and any information relating to the account.

History
In reg.28(3) "rule 10.87(7)" substituted for the former "6.137(5)" by the Insolvency (England and Wales) Rules 2016 (Consequential Amendments and Savings) Rules 2017 (SI 2017/369) r.2(2), Sch.2 para.4(1), (5) as from 6 April 2017.
    Regulation 28(2) amended and reg.28(3) substituted by the Insolvency (England and Wales) and Insolvency (Scotland) (Miscellaneous and Consequential Amendments) Rules 2017 (SI 2017/1115) rr.1(1), (2), 15, 17 as from 8 December 2017.

29   Production and inspection of records

29(1)   The trustee shall produce on demand to the Secretary of State, and allow him to inspect, any accounts, books and other records kept by him (including any passed to him by a predecessor in office), and this duty to produce and allow inspection shall extend–

(a)   to producing and allowing inspection at the premises of the trustee; and

(b)   to producing and allowing inspection of any financial records of the kind described in regulation 24(1)(b) above prepared by the trustee before 24th October 1994 and kept by him;

and any such demand may–

(i) require the trustee to produce any such accounts, books or other records to the Secretary of State, and allow him to inspect them–

(A) at the same time as any account is sent to the Secretary of State under regulation 28 above; or

(B) at any time after such account is sent to the Secretary of State;

whether or not the Secretary of State requires the account to be audited; or

(ii) where it is made for the purpose of ascertaining whether the provisions of these Regulations relating to the handling of money received by the trustee in the course of carrying out his functions have been or are likely to be complied with, be made at any time, whether or not an account has been sent or should have been sent to the Secretary of State under regulation 28 above and whether or not the Secretary of State has required any account to be audited.

29(2) The trustee shall allow the Secretary of State on demand to remove and take copies of any accounts, books and other records kept by the trustee (including any passed to him by a predecessor in office), whether or not they are kept at the premises of the trustee.

30 Disposal of bankrupt's books, papers and other records

30 The trustee, on the authorisation of the official receiver, during his tenure of office or on vacating office, or the official receiver while acting as trustee, may at any time sell, destroy or otherwise dispose of the books, papers and other records of the bankrupt.

31 Payment of unclaimed or undistributed assets, dividends or other money

31 Notwithstanding anything in these Regulations, any money–

(a) in the hands of the trustee at the date of his vacation of office, or

(b) which comes into the hands of any former trustee at any time after his vacation of office,

representing, in either case, unclaimed or undistributed assets of the bankrupt or dividends, shall forthwith be paid by him into the Insolvency Services Account.

PART 4

CLAIMING MONEY PAID INTO THE INSOLVENCY SERVICES ACCOUNT

32(1) Any person claiming to be entitled to any money paid into the Insolvency Services Account may apply to the Secretary of State for payment and shall provide such evidence of his claim as the Secretary of State may require.

32(2) Any person dissatisfied with the decision of the Secretary of State in respect of his claim made under this regulation may appeal to the court.

PART 5

REMUNERATION OF OFFICIAL RECEIVER

33 Official receiver's remuneration while acting as liquidator or trustee calculated as a percentage of the value of assets realised or distributed

33 [Revoked by the Insolvency (Amendment) Regulations 2004 (SI 2004/472) reg.2, Sch. para.4 as from 1 April 2004.]

34   Limits on official receiver's remuneration as trustee

34   [Revoked by the Insolvency (Amendment) Regulations 2004 (SI 2004/472) reg.2, Sch. para.4 as from 1 April 2004.]

35   Official receiver's general remuneration while acting as interim receiver, provisional liquidator, liquidator or trustee

35(1)   The official receiver shall be entitled to remuneration calculated in accordance with the applicable hourly rates set out in paragraph (2) for services provided by him (or any of his officers) in relation to–

(a)   a distribution made by him when acting as liquidator or trustee to creditors (including preferential or secured creditors or both such classes of creditor);

(b)   the realisation of assets on behalf of the holder of a fixed or floating charge or both types of those charges;

(c)   the supervision of a special manager;

(d)   the performance by him of any functions where he acts as provisional liquidator; or

(e)   the performance by him of any functions where he acts as an interim receiver.

35(2)   The applicable hourly rates referred to in paragraph (1) are–

(a)   in relation to the official receiver of the London insolvency district, those set out in Table 2 in Schedule 2; and

(b)   in relation to any other official receiver, those set out in Table 3 in Schedule 2.

History
Regulation 35 substituted by the Insolvency (Amendment) Regulations 2005 (SI 2005/512) reg.7 as from 1 April 2005 subject to transitional provisions contained in reg.3 of those Regulations.

36   Official receiver's remuneration while acting as liquidator or provisional liquidator in respect of the realisation of property charged

36   [Revoked by the Insolvency (Amendment) Regulations 2004 (SI 2004/472) reg.2, Sch. para.4 as from 1 April 2004.]

PART 5A

INFORMATION ABOUT TIME SPENT ON A CASE TO BE PROVIDED BY INSOLVENCY PRACTITIONER TO CREDITORS ETC.

36A(1)   Subject as set out in this regulation, in respect of any case in which he acts, an insolvency practitioner shall on request in writing made by any person mentioned in paragraph (2), supply free of charge to that person a statement of the kind described in paragraph (3).

36A(2)   The persons referred to in paragraph (1) are–

(a)   any creditor in the case;

(b)   where the case relates to a company, any director or contributory of that company; and

(c)   where the case relates to an individual, that individual.

36A(3)   The statement referred to in paragraph (1) shall comprise in relation to the period beginning with the date of the insolvency practitioner's appointment and ending with the relevant date the following details–

(a) the total number of hours spent on the case by the insolvency practitioner and any staff assigned to the case during that period;

(b) for each grade of individual so engaged, the average hourly rate at which any work carried out by individuals in that grade is charged; and

(c) the number of hours spent by each grade of staff during that period.

36A(4) In relation to paragraph (3) the "relevant date" means the date next before the date of the making of the request on which the insolvency practitioner has completed any period in office which is a multiple of six months or, where the insolvency practitioner has vacated office, the date that he vacated office.

36A(5) Where an insolvency practitioner has vacated office, an obligation to provide information under this regulation shall only arise in relation to a request that is made within 2 years of the date he vacates office.

36A(6) Any statement required to be provided to any person under this regulation shall be supplied within 28 days of the date of the receipt of the request by the insolvency practitioner.

36A(7) In this regulation the expression "insolvency practitioner" shall be construed in accordance with section 388 of the Insolvency Act 1986.

History
Regulation 36A inserted by the Insolvency (Amendment) Regulations 2005 (SI 2005/512) reg.8 as from 1 April 2005.

PART 6

TRANSITIONAL AND SAVING PROVISIONS

37 The Regulations shall have effect subject to the transitional and saving provisions set out in Schedule 3 to these Regulations.

SCHEDULE 1

Regulation 2

The Insolvency Regulations 1986

The Insolvency (Amendment) Regulations 1987

The Insolvency (Amendment) Regulations 1988

The Insolvency (Amendment) Regulations 1991

SCHEDULE 2

Regulations 33 to 36

Table 1

[Omitted by the Insolvency (Amendment) Regulations 2004 (SI 2004/472) reg.2, Sch. para.6 as from 1 April 2004.]

Table 2—London Rates

Grade according to the Insolvency Service grading structure/Status of Official	Total hourly rate £
D2/Official Receiver	75
C2/Deputy or Assistant Official Receiver	63
C1/Senior Examiner	58
L3/Examiner	46
L2/Examiner	42
B2/Administrator	46
L1/Examiner	40
B1/Administrator	46
A2/Administrator	40
A1/Administrator	35

Table 3—Provincial Rates

Grade according to the Insolvency Service grading structure/Status of Official	Total hourly rate £
D2/Official Receiver	69
C2/Deputy or Assistant Official Receiver	58
C1/Senior Examiner	52
L3/Examiner	46
L2/Examiner	40
B2/Administrator	43
L1/Examiner	38
B1/Administrator	42
A2/Administrator	36
A1/Administrator	31

History
Table 2 and Table 3 substituted by the Insolvency (Amendment) Regulations 2004 (SI 2004/472) reg.2, Sch. para.7 as from 1 April 2004, and further substituted by the Insolvency (Amendment) Regulations 2009 (SI 2009/482) reg.2 as from 6 April 2009.

SCHEDULE 3

Regulation 37

1   Interpretation

1   In this Schedule the expression "the former Regulations" means the Insolvency Regulations 1986 as amended by the Insolvency (Amendment) Regulations 1987, the Insolvency (Amendment) Regulations 1988 and the Insolvency (Amendment) Regulations 1991.

2   Requests pursuant to regulation 13(1) of the former Regulations

2   Any request made pursuant to regulation 13(1) of the former Regulations which has not been complied with prior to 24th October 1994 shall be treated, in the case of a company that is being wound up by the court, as a request made pursuant to regulation 11(1) of these Regulations and, in the case of a bankruptcy, as a request made pursuant to regulation 25 of these Regulations and in each case the request shall be treated as if it had been made on 24th October 1994.

3 Things done under the provisions of the former Regulations

3 So far as anything done under, or for the purposes of, any provision of the former Regulations could have been done under, or for the purposes of, the corresponding provision of these Regulations, it is not invalidated by the revocation of that provision but has effect as if done under, or for the purposes of, the corresponding provision.

4 Time periods

4 Where any period of time specified in a provision of the former Regulations is current immediately before 24th October 1994, these Regulations have effect as if the corresponding provision of these Regulations had been in force when the period began to run; and (without prejudice to the foregoing) any period of time so specified and current is deemed for the purposes of these Regulations–

    (a)   to run from the date or event from which it was running immediately before 24th October 1994, and

    (b)   to expire whenever it would have expired if these Regulations had not been made;

and any rights, obligations, requirements, powers or duties dependent on the beginning, duration or end of such period as above-mentioned shall be under these Regulations as they were or would have been under the former Regulations.

5 References to other provisions

5 Where in any provision of these Regulations there is reference to another provision of these Regulations, and the first-mentioned provision operates, or is capable of operating, in relation to things done or omitted, or events occurring or not occurring, in the past (including in particular past acts of compliance with the former Regulations), the reference to that other provision is to be read as including a reference to the corresponding provision of the former Regulations.

6 Provisions of Schedule to be without prejudice to the operation of sections 16 and 17 of the Interpretation Act 1978

6 The provisions of this Schedule are to be without prejudice to the operation of sections 16 and 17 of the Interpretation Act 1978 (saving from, and effect of, repeals) as they are applied by section 23 of that Act.

7 Meaning of "corresponding provision"

7(1) A provision in the former Regulations, except regulation 13(1) of those Regulations, is to be regarded as the corresponding provision of a provision in these Regulations notwithstanding any modifications made to the provision as it appears in these Regulations.

7(2) Without prejudice to the generality of the term "corresponding provision" the following table shall, subject to sub-paragraph (3) below, have effect in the interpretation of that expression with a provision of these Regulations listed in the left hand column being regarded as the corresponding provision of a provision of the former Regulations listed opposite it in the right hand column and that latter provision being regarded as the corresponding provision of the first-mentioned provision:

TABLE

Provision in these Regulations	*Provision in the former Regulations*
5(1), 5(3), 5(4)	4
5(2), 5(3), 5(4)	24
6	6
7(1), 7(2), 7(4), 7(5)	5
7(3), 7(4)	25
8(1), 8(2), 8(4), 8(5), 8(6)	15
8(3), 8(4)	25
9	18, 34
10	9, 27
11(2)	31
12	10, 28
13	10A, 28A
15	12A, 30A
16(1)	14
16(2)	32
17	35
18	16, 33
20	4
21	6
22	5
23	15
24	9
26	10
27	10A
29	12A
30	14
31	16A
32	17, 33
33, Table 1 in Schedule 2	19
35, Tables 2 and 3 in Schedule 2	20
36, Table 1 in Schedule 2	22

7(3)   Where a provision of the former Regulations is expressed in the Table in sub-paragraph (2) above to be the corresponding provision of a provision in these Regulations and the provision in the former Regulations was capable of applying to other proceedings in addition to those to which the provision in these Regulations is capable of applying, the provision in the former Regulations shall be construed as the corresponding provision of the provision in these Regulations only to the extent that they are both capable of applying to the same type of proceedings.

Financial Markets and Insolvency Regulations 1996

(SI 1996/1469)

Made on 5 June 1996 by the Treasury and the Secretary of State for Trade and Industry under ss.185 and 186 of the Companies Act 1989. Operative from 15 July 1996.

[**Note:** Changes made by the Uncertificated Securities Regulations 2001 (SI 2001/3755) and the Enterprise Act 2002 (Insolvency) Order 2003 (SI 2003/2096) have been incorporated into the text (in the case of pre-2003 legislation without annotation). Where references to administration petitions, orders, etc. and to the original IA 1986 Pt II have been altered by the Enterprise Act 2002 (Insolvency) Order 2003 (SI 2003/2096) art.5 and Sch. Pt 2 as from 15 September 2003 (subject to transitional provision in art.6), following the introduction of the new administration regime, history notes have been omitted.]

PART I

GENERAL

1 Citation and commencement

1 These Regulations may be cited as the Financial Markets and Insolvency Regulations 1996 and shall come into force on 15th July 1996.

2 Interpretation

2(1) In these Regulations–

"the Act" means the Companies Act 1989;

"business day" means any day which is not a Saturday or Sunday, Christmas Day, Good Friday or a bank holiday in any part of the United Kingdom under the Banking and Financial Dealings Act 1971;

"issue", in relation to an uncertificated unit of a security, means to confer on a person title to a new unit;

"register of securities"–

(a) in relation to shares, means a register of members; and

(b) in relation to units of a security other than shares, means a register, whether maintained by virtue of the Uncertificated Securities Regulations 2001 or otherwise, of persons holding the units;

"relevant nominee" means a system-member who is a subsidiary undertaking of the Operator designated by him as such in accordance with such rules and practices as are mentioned in paragraph 25(f) of Schedule 1 to the Uncertificated Securities Regulations 2001;

"settlement bank" means a person who has contracted with an Operator to make payments in connection with transfers, by means of a relevant system, of title to uncertificated units of a security and of interests of system-beneficiaries in relation to such units;

"system-beneficiary" means a person on whose behalf a system-member or former system-member holds or held uncertificated units of a security;

"system-charge" means a charge of a kind to which regulation 3(2) applies;

"system-member" means a person who is permitted by an Operator to transfer by means of a relevant system title to uncertificated units of a security held by him; and "former system-member" means a person whose participation in the relevant system is terminated or suspended;

"transfer", in relation to title to uncertificated units of a security, means the registration of a transfer of title to those units in the relevant Operator register of securities; and in relation to an interest of a system-beneficiary in relation to uncertificated units of a security, means the transfer of the interest to another system-beneficiary by means of a relevant system; and

other expressions used in these Regulations which are also used in the Uncertificated Securities Regulations 2001 have the same meanings as in those Regulations.

2(2)   For the purposes of these Regulations, a person holds a unit of a security if–

(a)   in the case of an uncertificated unit, he is entered on a register of securities in relation to the unit in accordance with regulation 20, 21 or 22 of the Uncertificated Securities Regulations 2001; and

(b)   in the case of a certificated unit, he has title to the unit.

2(3)   A reference in any of these Regulations to a numbered regulation shall be construed as a reference to the regulation bearing that number in these Regulations.

2(4)   A reference in any of these Regulations to a numbered paragraph shall, unless the reference is to a paragraph of a specified regulation, be construed as a reference to the paragraph bearing that number in the regulation in which the reference is made.

PART II

SYSTEM-CHARGES

3   Application of Part VII of the Act in relation to system-charges

3(1)   Subject to the provisions of these Regulations, Part VII of the Act shall apply in relation to–

(a)   a charge to which paragraph (2) applies ("a system-charge") and any action taken to enforce such a charge; and

(b)   any property subject to a system-charge,

in the same way as it applies in relation to a market charge, any action taken to enforce a market charge and any property subject to a market charge.

3(2)   This paragraph applies in relation to a charge granted in favour of a settlement bank for the purpose of securing debts or liabilities arising in connection with any of the following–

(a)   a transfer of uncertificated units of a security to a system-member by means of a relevant system whether the system-member is acting for himself or on behalf of a system-beneficiary;

(b)   a transfer, by one system-beneficiary to another and by means of a relevant system, of his interests in relation to uncertificated units of a security held by a relevant nominee where the relevant nominee will continue to hold the units;

(c)   an agreement to make a transfer of the kind specified in paragraph (a);

(d)   an agreement to make a transfer of the kind specified in paragraph (b); and

(e)   an issue of uncertificated units of a security to a system-member by means of a relevant system whether the system-member is acting for himself or on behalf of a system-beneficiary.

3(3)   In its application, by virtue of these Regulations, in relation to a system-charge, section 173(2) of the Act shall have effect as if the references to "purposes specified" and "specified purposes" were references to any one or more of the purposes specified in paragraph (2).

4   Circumstances in which Part VII applies in relation to system-charge

4(1)   Part VII of the Act shall apply in relation to a system-charge granted by a system-member and in relation to property subject to such a charge only if–

(a) it is granted to a settlement bank by a system-member for the purpose of securing debts or liabilities arising in connection with any of the transactions specified in regulation 3(2), being debts or liabilities incurred by that system-member or by a system-beneficiary on whose behalf he holds uncertificated units of a security; and

(b) it contains provisions which refer expressly to the relevant system in relation to which the grantor is a system-member.

4(2) Part VII of the Act shall apply in relation to a system-charge granted by a system-beneficiary and in relation to property subject to such a charge only if–

(a) it is granted to a settlement bank by a system-beneficiary for the purpose of securing debts or liabilities arising in connection with any of the transactions specified in regulation 3(2), incurred by that system-beneficiary or by a system-member who holds uncertificated units of a security on his behalf; and

(b) it contains provisions which refer expressly to the relevant system in relation to which the system-member who holds the uncertificated units of a security in relation to which the system-beneficiary has the interest is a system-member.

5   Extent to which Part VII applies to a system-charge

5 Part VII of the Act shall apply in relation to a system-charge only to the extent that–

(a) it is a charge over any one or more of the following–

    (i)   uncertificated units of a security held by a system-member or a former system-member;

    (ii)   interests of a kind specified in regulation 31(2)(b) or 31(4)(b) of the Uncertificated Securities Regulations 2001 in uncertificated units of a security in favour of a system-member or a former system-member;

    (iii) interests of a system-beneficiary in relation to uncertificated units of a security;

    (iv)   units of a security which are no longer in uncertificated form because the person holding the units has become a former system-member;

    (v)   sums or other benefits receivable by a system-member or former system-member by reason of his holding uncertificated units of a security, or units which are no longer in uncertificated form because the person holding the units has become a former system-member;

    (vi)   sums or other benefits receivable by a system-beneficiary by reason of his having an interest in relation to uncertificated units of a security or in relation to units which are no longer in uncertificated form because the person holding the units has become a former system-member;

    (vii) sums or other benefits receivable by a system-member or former system-member by way of repayment, bonus, preference, redemption, conversion or accruing or offered in respect of uncertificated units of a security, or units which are no longer in uncertificated form because the person holding the units has become a former system-member;

    (viii) sums or other benefits receivable by a system-beneficiary by way of repayment, bonus, preference, redemption, conversion or accruing or offered in respect of uncertificated units of a security in relation to which he has an interest or in respect of units in relation to which the system-beneficiary has an interest and which are no longer in uncertificated form because the person holding the units has become a former system-member;

(ix)   sums or other benefits receivable by a system-member or former system-member in respect of the transfer of uncertificated units of a security by or to him by means of a relevant system;

(x)   sums or other benefits receivable by a system-member or former system-member in respect of an agreement to transfer uncertificated units of a security by or to him by means of a relevant system;

(xi)   sums or other benefits receivable by a system-beneficiary in respect of the transfer of the interest of a system-beneficiary in relation to uncertificated units of a security by or to him by means of a relevant system or in respect of the transfer of uncertificated units of a security by or to a system-member acting on his behalf by means of a relevant system;

(xii)   sums or other benefits receivable by a system-beneficiary in respect of an agreement to transfer the interest of a system-beneficiary in relation to uncertificated units of a security by or to him by means of a relevant system, or in respect of an agreement to transfer uncertificated units of a security by or to a system-member acting on his behalf by means of a relevant system; and

(b) it secures–

(i)   the obligation of a system-member or former system-member to reimburse a settlement bank, being an obligation which arises in connection with any of the transactions specified in regulation 3(2) and whether the obligation was incurred by the system-member when acting for himself or when acting on behalf of a system-beneficiary; or

(ii)   the obligation of a system-beneficiary to reimburse a settlement bank, being an obligation which arises in connection with any of the transactions specified in regulation 3(2) and whether the obligation was incurred by the system-beneficiary when acting for himself or by reason of a system-member acting on his behalf.

6   Limitation on disapplication of moratorium on certain legal processes under Schedule B1 to the Insolvency Act 1986 (administration) in relation to system-charges

History
Heading to reg.6 substituted by the Enterprise Act 2002 (Insolvency) Order 2003 art.5, Sch. Pt 2 paras 61, 62(a) as from 15 September 2003 subject to transitional provision in art.6.

6(1)   This regulation applies where an administration order is made in relation to a system-member or former system-member.

6(1A)   A reference in paragraph (1) to "an administration order" shall include the appointment of an administrator under paragraph 14 or 22 of Schedule B1 to the Insolvency Act 1986.

History
Regulation 6(1A) inserted by the Enterprise Act 2002 (Insolvency) Order 2003 art.5, Sch. Pt 2 paras 61, 62(b) as from 15 September 2003 subject to transitional provision in art.6.

6(2)   The disapplication of paragraph 43(2) of Schedule B1 to the Insolvency Act 1986 (including that provision as applied by paragraph 44 of that Schedule) by section 175(1)(a) of the Act shall have effect, in relation to a system-charge granted by a system-member or former system-member, only to the extent necessary to enable there to be realised, whether through the sale of uncertificated units of a security or otherwise, the lesser of the two sums specified in paragraphs (3) and (4).

6(3)   The first sum of the two sums referred to in paragraph (2) is the net sum of–

(a) all payment obligations discharged by the settlement bank in connection with–

    (i)   transfers of uncertificated units of a security by means of a relevant system made during the qualifying period to or by the relevant system-member or former system-member, whether acting for himself or on behalf of a system-beneficiary;

   (ii)   agreements made during the qualifying period to transfer uncertificated units of a security by means of a relevant system to or from the relevant system-member or former system-member, whether acting for himself or on behalf of a system-beneficiary; and

   (iii)   issues of uncertificated units of a security by means of a relevant system made during the qualifying period to the relevant system-member or former system-member, whether acting for himself or on behalf of a system-beneficiary; less

  (b)   all payment obligations discharged to the settlement bank in connection with transactions of any kind described in paragraph (3)(a)(i) and (ii).

6(4)   The second of the two sums referred to in paragraph (2) is the sum (if any) due to the settlement bank from the relevant system-member or former system-member by reason of an obligation of the kind described in regulation 5(b)(i).

6(5)   In this regulation and regulation 7, "qualifying period" means the period–

  (a)   beginning with the fifth business day before the day on which an application for the making of the administration order was presented; and

  (b)   ending with the second business day after the day on which the administration order is made.

6(5A)   A reference in paragraph (5) to an application for an administration order shall be treated as including a reference to–

  (a)   appointing an administrator under paragraph 14 or 22 of Schedule B1 to the Insolvency Act 1986, or

  (b)   filing with the court a notice of intention to appoint an administrator under either of those paragraphs,

and a reference to "an administration order" shall include the appointment of an administrator under paragraph 14 or 22 of Schedule B1 to the Insolvency Act 1986.

7   Limitation on disapplication of moratorium on certain legal processes under Schedule B1 to the Insolvency Act 1986 (administration) in relation to system-charges granted by a system-beneficiary

7(1)   This regulation applies where an administration order is made in relation to a system-beneficiary.

    A reference in paragraph (1) to "an administration order" shall include the appointment of an administrator under paragraph 14 or 22 of Schedule B1 to the Insolvency Act 1986.

7(2)   The disapplication of paragraph 43(2) of Schedule B1 to the Insolvency Act 1986 (including that provision as applied by paragraph 44 of that Schedule) by section 175(1)(a) of the Act shall have effect, in relation to a system-charge granted by a system-beneficiary, only to the extent necessary to enable there to be realised, whether through the sale of interests of a system-beneficiary in relation to uncertificated units of a security or otherwise, the lesser of the two sums specified in paragraphs (3) and (4).

7(3)   The first of the two sums referred to in paragraph (2) is the net sum of–

  (a)   all payment obligations discharged by the settlement bank in connection with–

    (i)   transfers, to or by the relevant system-beneficiary by means of a relevant system made during the qualifying period, of interests of the system- beneficiary in relation to uncertificated units of a security held by a relevant nominee, where the relevant nominee has continued to hold the units;

(ii) agreements made during the qualifying period to transfer, to or from the relevant system-beneficiary by means of a relevant system, interests of the system-beneficiary in relation to uncertificated units of a security held by a relevant nominee, where the relevant nominee will continue to hold the units;

(iii) transfers, during the qualifying period and by means of a relevant system, of uncertificated units of a security, being transfers made to or by a system-member acting on behalf of the relevant system-beneficiary;

(iv) agreements made during the qualifying period to transfer uncertificated units of a security by means of a relevant system to or from a system-member acting on behalf of the relevant system-beneficiary; and

(v) issues of uncertificated units of a security made during the qualifying period and by means of a relevant system, being issues to a system-member acting on behalf of the relevant system-beneficiary; less

(b) all payment obligations discharged to the settlement bank in connection with transactions of any kind described in paragraph (3)(a)(i) to (iv).

7(4) The second of the two sums referred to in paragraph (2) is the sum (if any) due to the settlement bank from the relevant system-beneficiary by reason of an obligation of the kind described in regulation 5(b)(ii).

8 Ability of administrator or receiver to recover assets in case of property subject to system-charge

8(1) This regulation applies where an administration order is made or an administrator or an administrative receiver or a receiver is appointed, in relation to a system-member, former system-member or system-beneficiary.

8(1A) A reference in paragraph (1) to "an administration order" shall include the appointment of an administrator under paragraph 14 or 22 of Schedule B1 to the Insolvency Act 1986.

8(2) The disapplication–

(a) by section 175(1)(b) of the Act, of paragraphs 70, 71 and 72 of Schedule B1 to the Insolvency Act 1986, and

(b) by section 175(3) of the Act, of sections 43 and 61 of the 1986 Act,

shall cease to have effect after the end of the relevant day in respect of any property which is subject to a system-charge granted by the system-member, former system-member or system-beneficiary if on the basis of a valuation in accordance with paragraph (3), the charge is not required for the realisation of the sum specified in paragraph (4) or (5).

8(3) For the purposes of paragraph (2), the value of property shall, except in a case falling within paragraph (6), be such as may be agreed between the administrator, administrative receiver or receiver on the one hand and the settlement bank on the other.

8(4) Where the system-charge has been granted by a system-member or former system-member, the sum referred to in paragraph (2) is whichever is the lesser of–

(a) the sum referred to in regulation 6(3);

(b) the sum referred to in regulation 6(4) due to the settlement bank at the close of business on the relevant day.

8(5) Where the system-charge has been granted by a system-beneficiary, the sum referred to in paragraph (2) is whichever is the lesser of–

(a)   the sum referred to in regulation 7(3);

(b)   the sum referred to in regulation 7(4) due to the settlement bank at the close of business on the relevant day.

8(6)   For the purposes of paragraph (2), the value of any property for which a price for the relevant day is quoted in the Daily Official List of The London Stock Exchange Limited shall–

(a)   in a case in which two prices are so quoted, be an amount equal to the average of those two prices, adjusted where appropriate to take account of any accrued dividend or interest; and

(b)   in a case in which one price is so quoted, be an amount equal to that price, adjusted where appropriate to take account of any accrued dividend or interest.

8(7)   In this regulation "the relevant day" means the second business day after the day on which the company enters administration, or the administrative receiver or receiver is appointed.

PART III

MARKET CONTRACTS

9   **Amendments to section 156 of the Act**

9   [Insertion of s.156(3A) into the Act.]

Civil Procedure Rules 1998

(SI 1998/3132)

Made on 10 December 1998. Operative from 26 April 1999.

[**Note**: The text which follows includes all updates to 29 February 2016, without detailed annotation. Note prospective introduction (from 1 April 2016) of PD 51P (Pilot for insolvency express trials).]

PART 2

APPLICATION AND INTERPRETATION OF THE RULES

2.1 Application of the Rules

2.1(1) Subject to paragraph (2), these Rules apply to all proceedings in–

(a) the County Court;

(b) the High Court; and

(c) the Civil Division of the Court of Appeal.

2.1(2) These Rules do not apply to proceedings of the kinds specified in the first column of the following table (proceedings for which rules may be made under the enactments specified in the second column) except to the extent that they are applied to those proceedings by another enactment–

PROCEEDINGS	ENACTMENTS
1. Insolvency proceedings	Insolvency Act 1986, ss. 411 and 412

Note
IA 1986 ss.411 and 412 are, of course, the provisions under which the Insolvency Rules are made; and IR 2016 r.12 provides for the application generally of the CPR to insolvency proceedings in the High Court and county court.

PART 6

SERVICE OF DOCUMENTS

I   Scope of this part and interpretation

6.1 Part 6 rules about service apply generally

6.1 This Part applies to the service of documents, except where–

(a) another Part, any other enactment or a practice direction makes different provision; or

(b) the court orders otherwise.

(Other Parts, for example, Part 54 (Judicial Review) and Part 55 (Possession Claims) contain specific provisions about service.)

6.2 Interpretation

6.2 In this Part–

(a) "bank holiday" means a bank holiday under the Banking and Financial Dealings Act 1971 in the part of the United Kingdom where service is to take place;

(b) "business day" means any day except Saturday, Sunday, a bank holiday, Good Friday or Christmas Day;

(c) "claim" includes petition and any application made before action or to commence proceedings and "claim form", "claimant" and "defendant" are to be construed accordingly;

(d) "solicitor" includes any other person who, for the purposes of the Legal Services Act 2007, is an authorised person in relation to an activity which constitutes the conduct of litigation (within the meaning of that Act); and

(e) "European Lawyer" has the meaning set out in article 2 of the European Communities (Services of Lawyers) Order 1978 (S. I. 1978/1910).

(The European Communities (Services of Lawyers) Order 1978 is annexed to Practice Direction 6A.)

III   Service of documents other than the claim form in the United Kingdom or in specified circumstances within the EEA

6.20   Methods of service

6.20(1)   Subject to Section IV of this Part and the rules in this Section relating to service out of the jurisdiction on solicitors, European Lawyers and parties, a document may be served by any of the following methods–

(a) personal service, in accordance with rule 6.22;

(b) first class post, document exchange or other service which provides for delivery on the next business day, in accordance with Practice Direction 6A;

(c) leaving it at a place specified in rule 6.23;

(d) fax or other means of electronic communication in accordance with Practice Direction 6A; or

(e) any method authorised by the court under rule 6.27.

6.20(2)   A company may be served–

(a) by any method permitted under this Part; or

(b) by any of the methods of service permitted under the Companies Act 2006.

6.20(3)   A limited liability partnership may be served–

(a) by any method permitted under this Part; or

(b) by any of the methods of service permitted under the Companies Act 2006 as applied with modification by regulations made under the Limited Liability Partnerships Act 2000.

6.21   Who is to serve

6.21(1)   Subject to Section IV of this Part and the rules in this Section relating to service out of the jurisdiction on solicitors, European Lawyers and parties, a party to proceedings will serve a document which that party has prepared except where–

(a) a rule or practice direction provides that the court will serve the document; or

(b) the court orders otherwise.

6.21(2)   The court will serve a document which it has prepared except where–

(a) a rule or practice direction provides that a party must serve the document;

(b) the party on whose behalf the document is to be served notifies the court that the party wishes to serve it; or

(c) the court orders otherwise.

6.21(3) Where the court is to serve a document, it is for the court to decide which method of service is to be used.

6.21(4) Where the court is to serve a document prepared by a party, that party must provide a copy for the court and for each party to be served.

6.22 Personal service

6.22(1) Where required by another Part, any other enactment, a practice direction or a court order, a document must be served personally.

6.22(2) In other cases, a document may be served personally except–

(a) where the party to be served has given an address for service under rule 6.23; or

(b) in any proceedings by or against the Crown.

6.22(3) A document may be served personally as if the document were a claim form in accordance with rule 6.5(3).

(For service out of the jurisdiction see rules 6.40 to 6.47.)

6.23 Address for service to be given after proceedings are started

6.23(1) A party to proceedings must give an address at which that party may be served with documents relating to those proceedings. The address must include a full postcode or its equivalent in any EEA state (if applicable) unless the court orders otherwise.

(Paragraph 2.4 of Practice Direction 16 contains provisions about postcodes.)

6.23(2) Except where any other rule or practice direction makes different provision, a party's address for service must be–

(a) the business address either within the United Kingdom or any other EEA state of a solicitor acting for the party to be served; or

(b) the business address in any EEA state of a European Lawyer nominated to accept service of documents; or

(c) where there is no solicitor acting for the party or no European Lawyer nominated to accept service of documents–

    (i) an address within the United Kingdom at which the party resides or carries on business; or

    (ii) an address within any other EEA state at which the party resides or carries on business.

(For Production Centre Claims see paragraph 2.3(7) and (7A) of Practice Direction 7C; for Money Claims Online see paragraph 4(3A) and (6) of Practice Direction 7E; and for Possession Claims Online see paragraph 5.1(3A) and (4) of Practice Direction 55B.)

6.23(3) Where none of sub-paragraphs (2)(a), (b) or (c) applies, the party must give an address for service within the United Kingdom. (Part 42 contains provisions about change of solicitor. Rule 42.1 provides that where a party gives the business address of a solicitor as that party's address for service, that solicitor will be considered to be acting for the party until the provisions of Part 42 are complied with.)

6.23(4) Subject to the provisions of Section IV of this Part (where applicable), any document to be served in proceedings must be sent or transmitted to, or left at, the party's address for service under paragraph (2) or (3) unless it is to be served personally or the court orders otherwise.

6.23(5) Where, in accordance with Practice Direction 6A, a party indicates or is deemed to have indicated that they will accept service by fax, the fax number given by that party must be at the address for service.

6.23(6) Where a party indicates in accordance with Practice Direction 6A that they will accept service by electronic means other than fax, the e-mail address or electronic identification given by that party will be deemed to be at the address for service.

6.23(7) In proceedings by or against the Crown, service of any document in the proceedings on the Crown must be effected in the same manner prescribed in rule 6.10 as if the document were a claim form.

6.23(8) This rule does not apply where an order made by the court under rule 6.27 (service by an alternative method or at an alternative place) specifies where a document may be served.

(For service out of the jurisdiction see rules 6.40 to 6.47.)

6.24 Change of address for service

6.24 Where the address for service of a party changes, that party must give notice in writing of the change as soon as it has taken place to the court and every other party.

6.25 Service on children and protected parties

6.25(1) An application for an order appointing a litigation friend where a child or protected party has no litigation friend must be served in accordance with rule 21.8(1) and (2).

6.25(2) Any other document which would otherwise be served on a child or a protected party must be served on the litigation friend conducting the proceedings on behalf of the child or protected party.

6.25(3) The court may make an order permitting a document to be served on the child or protected party or on some person other than the person specified in rule 21.8 or paragraph (2).

6.25(4) An application for an order under paragraph (3) may be made without notice.

6.25(5) The court may order that, although a document has been sent or given to someone other than the person specified in rule 21.8 or paragraph (2), the document is to be treated as if it had been properly served.

6.25(6) This rule does not apply where the court has made an order under rule 21.2(3) allowing a child to conduct proceedings without a litigation friend.

6.26 Deemed Service

6.26 A document, other than a claim form, served within the United Kingdom in accordance with these Rules or any relevant practice direction is deemed to be served on the day shown in the following table–

Method of service	*Deemed date of service*
1. First class post (or other service which provides for delivery on the next business day)	The second day after it was posted, left with, delivered to or collected by the relevant service provider provided that day is a business day; or if not, the next business day after that day.
2. Document exchange	The second day after it was left with, delivered to or collected by the relevant service provider provided that day is a business day; or if not, the next business day after that day.
3. Delivering the document to or leaving it at a permitted address	If it is delivered to or left at the permitted address on a business day before 4.30p.m., on that day;

	or in any other case, on the next business day after that day.
4. Fax	If the transmission of the fax is completed on a business day before 4.30p.m., on that day;
	or in any other case, on the next business day after the day on which it was transmitted.
5. Other electronic method	If the e-mail or other electronic transmission is sent on a business day before 4.30p.m., on that day;
	or in any other case, on the next business day after the day on which it was sent.
6. Personal service	If the document is served personally before 4.30p.m. on a business day, on that day;
	or in any other case, on the next business day after that day.

(Paragraphs 10.1 to 10.7 of Practice Direction 6A contain examples of how the date of deemed service is calculated.)

6.27 Service by an alternative method or at an alternative place

6.27   Rule 6.15 applies to any document in the proceedings as it applies to a claim form and reference to the defendant in that rule is modified accordingly.

6.28 Power to dispense with service

6.28(1)   The court may dispense with service of any document which is to be served in the proceedings.

6.28(2)   An application for an order to dispense with service must be supported by evidence and may be made without notice.

6.29 Certificate of service

6.29   Where a rule, practice direction or court order requires a certificate of service, the certificate must state the details required by the following table–

Method of Service	*Details to be certified*
1. Personal service	Date and time of personal service.
2. First class post, document exchange or other service which provides for delivery on the next business day	Date of posting, or leaving with, delivering to or collection by the relevant service provider.
3. Delivery of document to or leaving it at a permitted place	Date and time of when the document was delivered to or left at the permitted place.
4. Fax	Date and time of completion of the transmission.
5. Other electronic method	Date and time of sending the e-mail or other electronic transmission.
6. Alternative method or place permitted by the court	As required by the court.

IV   Service of the claim form and other documents out of the jurisdiction

[Not reproduced.]

PART 49

SPECIALIST PROCEEDINGS

49   These Rules apply to proceedings under–

(a)   the Companies Act 1985;

(b)   the Companies Act 2006; and

(c)   other legislation relating to companies and limited liability partnerships,

subject to the provision of the relevant practice direction which applies to those proceedings.

[**Note**: Part 49 is supplemented by *Practice Direction 49A—Applications under the Companies Acts and Related Legislation*. The *Practice Direction* applies (para.2) to proceedings under:

(a)   CA 1985;

(b)   CA 2006 (except proceedings under Chapter 1 of Pt 11 or Pt 30);

(c)   Criminal Justice and Police Act 2001 s.59;

(d)   Articles 22, 25 and 26 of the EC Regulation;

(e)   FSMA 2000 Pt VII;

(f)   the Companies (Cross-Border Mergers) Regulations 2007 (SI 2007/2974).

Part 49 is further supplemented by *Practice Direction 49B—Order under section 127 of the Insolvency Act 1986* (reproduced in App.V, below).]

Financial Markets and Insolvency (Settlement Finality) Regulations 1999

(SI 1999/2979)

Made on 2 November 1999 by the Treasury under s.2(2) of the European Communities Act 1972. Operative from 11 December 1999.

[**Note**: Changes made by the Financial Services and Markets Act 2000 (Consequential Amendments) Order 2000 (SI 2000/1555), the Banking Consolidation Directive (Consequential Amendments) Regulations 2000 (SI 2000/2952), the Civil Jurisdiction and Judgments Regulations 2001 (SI 2001/3929), the Electronic Money (Miscellaneous Amendments) Regulations 2002 (SI 2002/765), the Enterprise Act (Insolvency) Order 2003 (SI 2003/2096), the Financial Markets and Insolvency (Settlement Finality) (Amendment) Regulations 2006 (SI 2006/50), the Capital Requirements Regulations 2006 (SI 2006/3221), the Financial Services and Insolvency (Settlement Finality) (Amendment) Regulations 2007 (SI 2007/832), the Financial Services (EEA State) Regulations 2007 (SI 2007/108), the Civil Jurisdiction and Judgments Regulations 2007 (SI 2007/1655), the Financial Markets and Insolvency (Settlement Finality) (Amendment) Regulations 2009 (SI 2009/1972), the Financial Markets and Insolvency (Settlement Finality and Financial Collateral Arrangements) (Amendment) Regulations 2010 (SI 2010/2993), the Electronic Money Regulations 2011 (SI 2011/99), the Financial Services and Markets Act 2000 (Over the Counter Derivatives, Central Counterparties and Trade Repositories) Regulations 2013 (SI 2013/504), the Financial Services Act 2012 (Consequential Amendments and Transitional Provisions) Order 2013 (SI 2013/472), the Capital Requirements Regulations 2013 (SI 2013/3115), the Bank Recovery and Resolution (No.2) Order 2014 (SI 2014/3348), the Financial Services and Insolvency (Settlement Finality) (Amendment) Regulations 2015 (SI 2015/347), the Financial Services and Markets (Disclosure of Information to the European Securities and Markets Authority etc. and Other Provisions) Regulations 2016 (SI 2016/1095), the Financial Services and Markets Act 2000 (Markets in Financial Instruments) Regulations 2017 (SI 2017/701), the Central Securities Depositories Regulations 2017 (SI 2017/1064) and the Financial Services and Markets (Insolvency) (Amendment of Miscellaneous Enactments) Regulations 2019 (SI 2019/755) have been incorporated into the text (in the case of pre-2003 legislation without annotation). Where references to administration petitions, orders, etc. and to the original IA 1986 Pt II have been altered by the Enterprise Act 2002 (Insolvency) Order 2003 (SI 2003/2096) art.5 and Sch. Pt 2 as from 15 September 2003 (subject to transitional provision in art.6), following the introduction of the new administration regime, history notes have been omitted. The text has been amended throughout (without detailed annotation) to reflect the extension of the Regulations to Northern Ireland, pursuant to the Financial Markets and Insolvency (Settlement Finality) (Amendment) Regulations 2006 (SI 2006/50), effective 2 February 2006.]

PART I

GENERAL

1   Citation, commencement and extent

1(1)   These Regulations may be cited as the Financial Markets and Insolvency (Settlement Finality) Regulations 1999 and shall come into force on 11th December 1999.

1(2)   [Deleted: the Regulations now extend to Northern Ireland.]

2   Interpretation

2(1)   In these Regulations

"the 2000 Act" means the Financial Services and Markets Act 2000;

"administration" and "administrator" shall be interpreted in accordance with the modifications made by the enactments mentioned in paragraph (5);

"business day" shall cover both day and night-time settlements and shall encompass all events happening during the business cycle of a system;

"central bank" means a central bank of an EEA State or the European Central Bank;

"central counterparty" means a body corporate or unincorporated association interposed between the institutions in a system and which acts as the exclusive counterparty of those institutions with regard to transfer orders;

"charge" means any form of security, including a mortgage and, in Scotland, a heritable security;

"clearing house" means a body corporate or unincorporated association which is responsible for the calculation of the net positions of institutions and any central counterparty or settlement agent in a system;

"collateral security" means any realisable assets provided under a charge or a repurchase or similar agreement, or otherwise (including credit claims and money provided under a charge)–

(a) for the purpose of securing rights and obligations potentially arising in connection with a system ("collateral security in connection with participation in a system"); or

(b) to a central bank for the purpose of securing rights and obligations in connection with its operations in carrying out its functions as a central bank ("collateral security in connection with the functions of a central bank");

"collateral security charge" means, where collateral security consists of realisable assets (including money) provided under a charge, that charge;

"credit claims" means pecuniary claims arising out of an agreement whereby a credit institution grants credit in the form of a loan;

"credit institution" means a credit institution as defined in Article 4(1)(1) of Regulation (EU) No. 575/2013 of the European Parliament and of the Council of 26 June 2013 on prudential requirements for credit institutions and investment firms and amending Regulation (EU) No. 648/2012;

"creditors' voluntary winding-up resolution" means a resolution for voluntary winding up (within the meaning of the Insolvency Act 1986 or the Insolvency (Northern Ireland) Order 1989) where the winding up is a creditors' winding up (within the meaning of that Act or that Order);

"default arrangements" means the arrangements put in place by a designated system or by a system which is an interoperable system in relation to that system to limit systemic and other types of risk which arise in the event of a participant or a system operator of an interoperable system appearing to be unable, or likely to become unable, to meet its obligations in respect of a transfer order, including, for example, any default rules within the meaning of Part VII or Part V or any other arrangements for–

(a) netting,

(b) the closing out of open positions,

(c) the application or transfer of collateral security; or

(d) the transfer of assets or positions on the default of a participant in the system;

"defaulter" means a person in respect of whom action has been taken by a designated system under its default arrangements;

"designated system" means a system which is declared by a designation order for the time being in force to be a designated system for the purposes of these Regulations;

"designating authority" means–

(a) in the case of a system which is, or the operator of which is, a recognised investment exchange for the purposes of the 2000 Act, the FCA;

(b) in any other case, the Bank of England;

"designation order" has the meaning given by regulation 4;

"EEA State" has the meaning given by Schedule 1 to the Interpretation Act 1978;

"ESMA" means the European Securities and Markets Authority established by Regulation (EU) No. 1095/2010 of the European Parliament and of the Council of 24th November 2010 establishing a European Supervisory Authority (European Securities and Markets Authority);

"the FCA" means the Financial Conduct Authority;

"guidance", in relation to a designated system, means guidance issued or any recommendation made by it which is intended to have continuing effect and is issued in writing or other legible form to all or any class of its participants or users or persons seeking to participate in the system or to use its facilities and which would, if it were a rule, come within the definition of a rule;

"indirect participant" means an institution, central counterparty, settlement agent, clearing house or system operator–

(a) which has a contractual relationship with a participant in a designated system that enables the indirect participant to effect transfer orders through that system, and

(b) the identity of which is known to the system operator;

"institution" means–

(a) a credit institution;

(aa) an electronic money institution within the meaning of Article 2.1 of Directive 2009/110/EC of the European Parliament and of the Council of 16 September 2009 on the taking up, pursuit and prudential supervision of the business of electronic money institutions amending Directives 2005/60/EC and 2006/48/EC and repealing Directive 2000/46/EC;

(ab) an authorised payment institution or small payment institution as defined in regulation 2(1) of the Payment Services Regulations 2017, or a person whose head office, registered office or place of residence, as the case may be, is outside the United Kingdom and whose functions correspond to those of such an institution;

(b) an investment firm as defined in Article 4.1.1 of Directive 2014/65/EU of the European Parliament and of the Council of 15 May 2014 on markets in financial instruments, other than a person to whom Article 2 applies;

(c) a public authority or publicly guaranteed undertaking;

(d) any undertaking whose head office is outside the European Union and whose functions correspond to those of a credit institution or investment firm as defined in (a) and (b) above; or

(e) any undertaking which is treated by the designating authority as an institution in accordance with regulation 8(1),

which participates in a system and which is responsible for discharging the financial obligations arising from transfer orders which are effected through the system;

"interoperable system" in relation to a system ("the first system"), means a second system whose system operator has entered into an arrangement with the system operator of the first system that involves cross-system execution of transfer orders;

"netting" means the conversion into one net claim or obligation of different claims or obligations between participants resulting from the issue and receipt of transfer orders between them, whether on a bilateral or multilateral basis and whether through the interposition of a clearing house, central counterparty or settlement agent or otherwise;

"Part V" means Part V of the Companies (No. 2) (Northern Ireland) Order 1990;

"Part VII" means Part VII of the Companies Act 1989;

"participant" means–

(a) an institution,

(aa) a system operator;

(b) a body corporate or unincorporated association which carries out any combination of the functions of a central counterparty, a settlement agent or a clearing house, with respect to a system, or

(c) an indirect participant which is treated as a participant, or is a member of a class of indirect participants which are treated as participants, in accordance with regulation 9;

"the PRA" means the Prudential Regulation Authority;

"protected trust deed" and

"trust deed" shall be construed in accordance with section 73(1) of the Bankruptcy (Scotland) Act 1985 (interpretation);

"relevant office-holder" means–

(a) the official receiver;

(b) any person acting in relation to a company as its liquidator, provisional liquidator, or administrator;

(c) any person acting in relation to an individual (or, in Scotland, any debtor within the meaning of the Bankruptcy (Scotland) Act 1985) as his trustee in bankruptcy or interim receiver of his property or as permanent or interim trustee in the sequestration of his estate or as his trustee under a protected trust deed;

(d) any person acting as administrator of an insolvent estate of a deceased person; or

(e) any person appointed pursuant to insolvency proceedings of a country or territory outside the United Kingdom;

and in sub-paragraph (b), "company" means any company, society, association, partnership or other body which may be wound up under the Insolvency Act 1986 or the Insolvency (Northern Ireland) Order 1989;

"rules", in relation to a designated system, means rules or conditions governing the system with respect to the matters dealt with in these Regulations;

"securities" means (except for the purposes of the definition of "charge") any instruments referred to in C of Annex I to Directive 2014/65/EU of the European Parliament and of the Council of 15 May 2014 on markets in financial instruments;

"settlement account" means an account at a central bank, a settlement agent or a central counterparty used to hold funds or securities (or both) and to settle transactions between participants in a system;

"settlement agent" means a body corporate or unincorporated association providing settlement accounts to the institutions and any central counterparty in a system for the settlement of transfer orders within the system and, as the case may be, for extending credit to such institutions and any such central counterparty for settlement purposes;

"the Settlement Finality Directive" means Directive 98/26/EC of the European Parliament and of the Council of 19th May 1998 on settlement finality in payment and securities settlement systems, as last amended by Regulation (EU) No 909/2014 of the European Parliament and of the Council of 23rd July 2014 on improving securities settlement in the European Union and on central securities depositories;

"system operator" means the entity or entities legally responsible for the operation of a system. A system operator may also act as a settlement agent, central counterparty or clearing house;

"transfer order" means–

(a) an instruction by a participant to place at the disposal of a recipient an amount of money by means of a book entry on the accounts of a credit institution, a central bank, a central counterparty or a settlement agent, or an instruction which results in the assumption or discharge of a payment obligation as defined by the rules of a designated system ("a payment transfer order"); or

(b) an instruction by a participant to transfer the title to, or interest in, securities by means of a book entry on a register, or otherwise ("a securities transfer order");

"winding up" means–

(a) winding up by the court or creditors' voluntary winding up within the meaning of the Insolvency Act 1986 or the Insolvency (Northern Ireland) Order 1989 (but does not include members' voluntary winding up within the meaning of that Act or that Order);

(b) sequestration of a Scottish partnership under the Bankruptcy (Scotland) Act 1985;

and shall be interpreted in accordance with the modifications made by the enactments mentioned in paragraph (5); and "liquidator" shall be construed accordingly.

2(2) In these Regulations–

(za) references to the Bank of England do not include the Bank acting in its capacity as the Prudential Regulation Authority;

(a) references to the law of insolvency–

(i) include references to every provision made by or under the Bankruptcy (Scotland) Act 1985, Part 10 of the Building Societies Act 1986, the Insolvency Act 1986, the Insolvency (Northern Ireland) Order 1989 and in relation to a building society references to insolvency law or to any provision of the Insolvency Act 1986 or the Insolvency (Northern Ireland) Order 1989 are to that law or provision as modified by the Building Societies Act 1986;

(ii) shall also be interpreted in accordance with the modifications made by the enactments mentioned in paragraph (5);

(b) in relation to Scotland, references to–

(i) sequestration include references to the administration by a judicial factor of the insolvent estate of a deceased person,

(ii) an interim or permanent trustee include references to a judicial factor on the insolvent estate of a deceased person, and

(iii) "set off" include compensation.

2(2A) For the purposes of these regulations, references to insolvency proceedings do not include crisis prevention measures or crisis management measures taken in relation to an undertaking under the recovery and resolution directive unless–

(a) express provision is made in a contract to which that undertaking is a party that crisis prevention measures or crisis management measures taken in relation to the undertaking are to be treated as insolvency proceedings; and

(b the substantive obligations provided for in the contract containing that provision (including payment and delivery obligations and provision of collateral) are no longer being performed.

2(2B) For the purposes of paragraph (2A)–

(a) "crisis prevention measure" and "crisis management measure" have the meaning given in section 48Z of the Banking Act 2009; and

(b) "recovery and resolution directive" means Directive 2014/59/EU of the European Parliament and of the Council of 15th May 2014 establishing a framework for the recovery and resolution of credit institutions and investment firms.

2(3)   Subject to paragraph (1), expressions used in these Regulations which are also used in the Settlement Finality Directive have the same meaning in these Regulations as they have in the Settlement Finality Directive.

2(4)   References in these Regulations to things done, or required to be done, by or in relation to a designated system shall, in the case of a designated system which is neither a body corporate nor an unincorporated association, be treated as references to things done, or required to be done, by or in relation to the operator of that system.

2(5)   The enactments referred to in the definitions of "administration", "administrator", "liquidator" and "winding up" in paragraph (1), and in paragraph (2)(a)(ii), are–

(a)   article 3 of, and the Schedule to, the Banking Act 2009 (Parts 2 and 3 Consequential Amendments) Order 2009;

(b)   article 18 of, and paragraphs (1)(a), (2) and (3) of Schedule 2 to, the Building Societies (Insolvency and Special Administration) Order 2009;

(c)   regulation 27 of, and Schedule 6 to, the Investment Bank Special Administration Regulations 2011.

History
Definition of "credit institution" amended by the Capital Requirements Regulations 2006 (SI 2006/3221) reg.29(4) and Sch.6 para.3 as from 1 January 2007, by the Electronic Money Regulations 2011 (SI 2011/99) reg.79 and Sch.4 para.8 as from 30 April 2011 and by the Capital Requirements Regulations 2013 (SI 2013/3115) reg.46 and Sch.2 para.48 as from 1 January 2014. Definition of "EEA State" substituted by the Financial Services (EEA State) Regulations 2007 (SI 2007/108) reg.5 as from 13 February 2007. The definition was inserted into the 1978 Act by the Legislative and Regulatory Reform Act 2006. Definitions of "business day", "credit claims", "interoperable system" and "system operator" inserted and reg.2(1)–(3) extensively amended by the Financial Markets and Insolvency (Settlement Finality and Financial Collateral Arrangements) (Amendment) Regulations 2010 (SI 2010/2993) reg.2(1), (2) as from 6 April 2011. Definition of "designating authority" amended and definitions of "the FCA" and "the PRA" inserted by the Financial Services Act 2012 (Consequential Amendments and Transitional Provisions) Order 2013 (SI 2013/472) art.3 and Sch.2 para.27(a) as from 1 April 2013. Definitions of "administration" and "administrator" inserted, definitions of "default arrangements" and "winding up" amended, reg.2(2)(a) substituted, and reg.2(5) inserted by the Financial Services and Markets Act 2000 (Over the Counter Derivatives, Central Counterparties and Trade Repositories) Regulations 2013 (SI 2013/504) reg.32(1), (2) as from 1 April 2013. Regulation 2(2A), (2B) inserted by the Bank Recovery and Resolution (No.2) Order 2014 (SI 2014/3348) Sch.3 para.7 as from 10 January 2015. Definition of "the Settlement Finality Directive" amended by the Financial Services and Insolvency (Settlement Finality) (Amendment) Regulations 2015 (SI 2015/347) reg.2(1), (2) as from 18 March 2015. Definition of "ESMA" inserted by the Financial Services and Markets (Disclosure of Information to the European Securities and Markets Authority etc. and Other Provisions) Regulations 2016 (SI 2016/1095) reg.2(2) as from 8 December 2016. Definitions of "institution" and "securities" amended by the Financial Services and Markets Act 2000 (Markets in Financial Instruments) Regulations 2017 (SI 2017/701) reg.50(4), Sch.5 para.2 as from 3 January 2018. Definition of "institution" further amended by Payment Systems and Services and Electronic Money (Miscellaneous Amendments) Regulations 2017 (SI 2017/1173) reg.2 as from 13 January 2018.

PART II

DESIGNATED SYSTEMS

3   Application for designation

3(1)   Any body corporate or unincorporated association may apply to the designating authority for an order declaring it, or any system of which it is the operator, to be a designated system for the purposes of these Regulations.

3(2)   Any such application–

(a)   shall be made in such manner as the designating authority may direct; and

(b)   shall be accompanied by such information as the designating authority may reasonably require for the purpose of determining the application.

3(3)   At any time after receiving an application and before determining it, the designating authority may require the applicant to furnish additional information.

3(4)   The directions and requirements given or imposed under paragraphs (2) and (3) may differ as between different applications.

3(5)   Any information to be furnished to the designating authority under this regulation shall be in such form or verified in such manner as it may specify.

3(6)   Every application shall be accompanied by copies of the rules of the system to which the application relates and any guidance relating to that system.

4   Grant and refusal of designation

4(1)   Where–

(a)   an application has been duly made under regulation 3;

(b)   the applicant has paid any fee charged by virtue of regulation 5(1); and

(c)   the designating authority is satisfied that the requirements of the Schedule are satisfied with respect to the system to which the application relates;

the designating authority may make an order (a "designation order") declaring the system to be a designated system and identifying the system operator of that system for the purposes of these Regulations.

4(2)   In determining whether to make a designation order, the designating authority shall have regard to systemic risks.

4(3)   Where an application has been made to the FCA under regulation 3 in relation to a system through which both securities transfer orders and payment transfer orders are effected, the Authority shall consult the Bank of England before deciding whether to make a designation order.

4(4)   A designation order shall state the date on which it takes effect.

4(5)   Where the designating authority refuses an application for a designation order it shall give the applicant a written notice to that effect stating the reasons for the refusal.

4(6)   The designating authority must notify ESMA of a designation order made by it.

History
Regulation 4 amended by the Financial Markets and Insolvency (Settlement Finality and Financial Collateral Arrangements) (Amendment) Regulations 2010 (SI 2010/2993) reg.2(3) as from 6 April 2011. Regulation 4(6) inserted by the Financial Services and Insolvency (Settlement Finality) (Amendment) Regulations 2015 (SI 2015/347) reg.2(1), (3) as from 18 March 2015. Regulation 4(6) substituted by the Financial Services and Markets (Disclosure of Information to the European Securities and Markets Authority etc. and Other Provisions) Regulations 2016 (SI 2016/1095) reg.2(3) as from 8 December 2016.

5   Fees

5(1)   The designating authority may charge a fee to an applicant for a designation order.

5(2)   The designating authority may charge the system operator of a designated system a periodical fee.

5(3)   Fees chargeable by the designating authority under this regulation shall not exceed an amount which reasonably represents the amount of costs incurred or likely to be incurred–

(a)   in the case of a fee charged to an applicant for a designation order, in determining whether the designation order should be made; and

(b) in the case of a periodical fee, in satisfying itself that the designated system and its system operator continue to meet the requirements of the Schedule and are complying with any obligations to which they are subject by virtue of these Regulations.

History

Regulation 5 amended by the Financial Markets and Insolvency (Settlement Finality and Financial Collateral Arrangements) (Amendment) Regulations 2010 (SI 2010/2993) reg.2(4) as from 6 April 2011.

6   Certain bodies deemed to satisfy requirements for designation

6(1)   Subject to paragraph (2), a recognised body, an EEA central counterparty, a third country central counterparty, an EEA CSD and a third country CSD shall be deemed to satisfy the requirements in paragraphs 2 and 3 of the Schedule.

6(2)   Paragraph (1) does not apply to overseas investment exchanges or overseas clearing houses within the meaning of the 2000 Act.

6(3)   "EEA central counterparty", "third country central counterparty", "EEA CSD" and "third country CSD" have the meanings given by section 285 of the 2000 Act.

6(4)   "Recognised body" has the meaning given by section 313 of the 2000 Act.

History

Regulation 6(1) amended and reg.6(3) inserted by the Financial Services and Markets Act 2000 (Over the Counter Derivatives, Central Counterparties and Trade Repositories) Regulations 2013 (SI 2013/504) reg.32(1), (3) as from 1 April 2013.

Regulation 6(1) and (3) substituted and reg.6(4) inserted by the Central Securities Depositories Regulations 2017 (SI 2017/1064) regs 1, 10 and Sch. para.22(1), (2) as from 28 November 2017 subject to transitional provision in reg.9.

7   Revocation of designation

7(1)   A designation order may be revoked by a further order made by the designating authority if at any time it appears to the designating authority–

(a) that any requirement of the Schedule is not satisfied in the case of the system to which the designation order relates; or

(b) that the system or the system operator of that system has failed to comply with any obligation to which they are subject by virtue of these Regulations.

7(2)   Subsections (1) to (6) of section 298 of the 2000 Act shall apply in relation to the revocation of a designation order under paragraph (1) as they apply in relation to the revocation of a recognition order section 297(2) of that Act; and in those subsections as they so apply–

(a) any reference to a recognised body shall be taken to be a reference to a designated system;

(b) any reference to members of a recognised body shall be taken to be a reference to participants in a designated system;

(ba) any reference to the appropriate regulator shall be taken to be a reference to the designating authority;

(c) [Omitted]

(d) subsection (4) has effect as if the period for making representations specified in the notice must be at least three months.

7(3)   An order revoking a designation order–

(a) shall state the date on which it takes effect, being no earlier than three months after the day on which the revocation order is made; and

(b) may contain such transitional provisions as the designating authority thinks necessary or expedient.

7(4) A designation order may be revoked at the request or with the consent of the system operator of the designated system, and any such revocation shall not be subject to the restriction imposed by paragraph (3)(a), or to the requirements imposed by subsections (1) to (6) of section 298 of the 2000 Act.

History
Regulation 7 amended by the Financial Markets and Insolvency (Settlement Finality and Financial Collateral Arrangements) (Amendment) Regulations 2010 (SI 2010/2993) reg.2(5) as from 6 April 2011. Regulation 7(2)(c) omitted and reg.7(2)(d) inserted by the Financial Services Act 2012 (Consequential Amendments and Transitional Provisions) Order 2013 (SI 2013/472) art.3 and Sch.2 para.27(c) as from 1 April 2013. Note transitional provision in Sch.2 para.28: the Bank of England may exercise the power of revocation in respect of pre-1 April 2013 designating orders.
Regulation 7(2) amended by the Central Securities Depositories Regulations 2017 (SI 2017/1064) regs 1, 10 and Sch. para.22(1), (3) as from 28 November 2017 subject to transitional provision in reg.9.

8 Undertakings treated as institutions

8(1) A designating authority may treat as an institution any undertaking which participates in a designated system and which is responsible for discharging financial obligations arising from transfer orders effected through that system, provided that–

(a) the designating authority considers such treatment to be required on grounds of systemic risk, and

(b) the designated system is one in which at least three institutions (other than any undertaking treated as an institution by virtue of this paragraph) participate and through which securities transfer orders are effected.

8(2) Where a designating authority decides to treat an undertaking as an institution in accordance with paragraph (1), it shall give written notice of that decision to the designated system in which the undertaking is to be treated as a participant and to the system operator of that system.

History
Regulation 8 amended by the Financial Markets and Insolvency (Settlement Finality and Financial Collateral Arrangements) (Amendment) Regulations 2010 (SI 2010/2993) reg.2(7) as from 6 April 2011.

9 Indirect participants treated as participants

9(1) A designating authority may treat–

(a) an indirect participant as a participant in a designated system, or

(b) a class of indirect participants as participants in a designated system, where it considers this to be required on grounds of systemic risk, and shall give written notice of any decision to that effect to the designated system and to the system operator of that system.

9(2) Where a designating authority, in accordance with paragraph (1), treats an indirect participant as a participant in a designated system, the liability of the participant through which that indirect participant passes transfer orders to the designated system is not affected.

History
Regulation 9 amended by the Financial Markets and Insolvency (Settlement Finality and Financial Collateral Arrangements) (Amendment) Regulations 2010 (SI 2010/2993) reg.2(8) as from 6 April 2011.

10 Provision of information by designated systems

10(1) The system operator of a designated system shall, when that system is declared to be a designated system, provide to the designating authority in writing a list of the participants (including the indirect participants) in the designated system and shall give written notice to the designating authority of any amendment to the list within seven days of such amendment.

10(2)   The designating authority may, in writing, require the system operator of a designated system to furnish to it such other information relating to that designated system as it reasonably requires for the exercise of its functions under these Regulations, within such time, in such form, at such intervals and verified in such manner as the designating authority may specify.

10(3)   When the system operator of a designated system amends, revokes or adds to its rules or its guidance, it shall within fourteen days give written notice to the designating authority of the amendment, revocation or addition.

10(4)   The system operator of a designated system shall give the designating authority at least three months' written notice of any proposal to amend, revoke or add to its default arrangements.

10(4A)   The designating authority may, if it considers it appropriate, agree a shorter period of notice.

10(5)   Nothing in this regulation shall require the system operator of a designated system to give any notice or furnish any information to the FCA or the Bank of England where the notice or information has already been given or furnished to the FCA or the Bank of England (as the case may be) pursuant to any requirement imposed by or under section 293 of the 2000 Act (notification requirements) or any other enactment.

History
Regulation 10 amended by the Financial Markets and Insolvency (Settlement Finality and Financial Collateral Arrangements) (Amendment) Regulations 2010 (SI 2010/2993) reg.2(9) as from 6 April 2011. Regulation 10(5) amended by the Financial Services Act 2012 (Consequential Amendments and Transitional Provisions) Order 2013 (SI 2013/472) art.3 and Sch.2 para.27(d) as from 1 April 2013. Regulation 10(4) amended and reg.10(4A) inserted by the Financial Services and Markets Act 2000 (Over the Counter Derivatives, Central Counterparties and Trade Repositories) Regulations 2013 (SI 2013/504) reg.32(1), (4) as from 1 April 2013.

11   Exemption from liability in damages

11(1)   Neither the designating authority nor any person who is, or is acting as, a member, officer or member of staff of the designating authority shall be liable in damages for anything done or omitted in the discharge, or purported discharge, of the designating authority's functions under these Regulations.

11(2)   Paragraph (1) does not apply–

(a)   if the act or omission is shown to have been in bad faith; or

(b)   so as to prevent an award of damages made in respect of an act or omission on the ground that the act or omission was unlawful as a result of section 6(1) of the Human Rights Act 1998 (acts of public authorities).

12   Publication of information and advice

12   A designating authority may publish information or give advice, or arrange for the publication of information or the giving of advice, in such form and manner as it considers appropriate with respect to any matter dealt with in these Regulations.

PART III

TRANSFER ORDERS EFFECTED THROUGH A DESIGNATED SYSTEM AND COLLATERAL SECURITY

13   Modifications of the law of insolvency

13(1)   The general law of insolvency has effect in relation to–

(a)   transfer orders effected through a designated system and action taken under the rules of a designated system with respect to such orders; and

(b)   collateral security,

subject to the provisions of this Part.

13(2)   Those provisions apply in relation to—

(a)   insolvency proceedings in respect of a participant in a designated system, or of a participant in a system which is an interoperable system in relation to that designated system;

(b)   insolvency proceedings in respect of a provider of collateral security in connection with the functions of a central bank, in so far as the proceedings affect the rights of the central bank to the collateral security; and

(c)   insolvency proceedings in respect of a system operator of a designated system or of a system which is an interoperable system in relation to that designated system;

but not in relation to any other insolvency proceedings, notwithstanding that rights or liabilities arising from transfer orders or collateral security fall to be dealt with in the proceedings.

13(3)   Subject to regulation 21, nothing in this Part shall have the effect of disapplying Part VII or Part V.

13(4)   References in this Part to "insolvency proceedings" shall include winding up and administration.

History
Regulation 13(3) amended by the Financial Markets and Insolvency (Settlement Finality) (Amendment) Regulations 2006 (SI 2006/50) reg.2(1), (5) as from 2 February 2006 and by the Financial Markets and Insolvency (Settlement Finality and Financial Collateral Arrangements) (Amendment) Regulations 2010 (SI 2010/2993) reg.2(10) as from 6 April 2011. Regulation 13(4) amended by the Financial Services and Markets Act 2000 (Over the Counter Derivatives, Central Counterparties and Trade Repositories) Regulations 2013 (SI 2013/504) reg.32(1), (5) as from 1 April 2013.

14   Proceedings of designated system take precedence over insolvency proceedings

14(1)   None of the following shall be regarded as to any extent invalid at law on the ground of inconsistency with the law relating to the distribution of the assets of a person on bankruptcy, winding up, administration, sequestration or under a protected trust deed, or in the administration of an insolvent estate or with the law relating to other insolvency proceedings of a country or territory outside the United Kingdom—

(a)   a transfer order;

(b)   the default arrangements of a designated system;

(c)   the rules of a designated system as to the settlement of transfer orders not dealt with under its default arrangements;

(d)   a contract for the purpose of realising collateral security in connection with participation in a designated system or in a system which is an interoperable system in relation to that designated system otherwise than pursuant to its default arrangements; or

(e)   a contract for the purpose of realising collateral security in connection with the functions of a central bank.

14(2)   The powers of a relevant office-holder in his capacity as such, and the powers of the court under the Insolvency Act 1986, the Insolvency (Northern Ireland) Order 1989 or the Bankruptcy (Scotland) Act 1985, shall not be exercised in such a way as to prevent or interfere with—

(a)   the settlement in accordance with the rules of a designated system of a transfer order not dealt with under its default arrangements;

(b)   any action taken under the default arrangements of a designated system;

(c) any action taken to realise collateral security in connection with participation in a designated system or in a system which is an interoperable system in relation to that designated system otherwise than pursuant to its default arrangements; or

(d) any action taken to realise collateral security in connection with the functions of a central bank.

14(3) Nothing in the following provisions of this Part shall be construed as affecting the generality of the above provisions.

14(4) A debt or other liability arising out of a transfer order which is the subject of action taken under default arrangements may not be proved in a winding up, bankruptcy, or administration, or in Scotland claimed in a winding up, sequestration or under a protected trust deed, until the completion of the action taken under default arrangements.

A debt or other liability which by virtue of this paragraph may not be proved or claimed shall not be taken into account for the purposes of any set-off until the completion of the action taken under default arrangements.

14(5) Paragraph (1) has the effect that the following provisions (which relate to preferential debts and the payment of expenses etc) apply subject to paragraph (6), namely–

(a) in the case of collateral security provided by a company (within the meaning of section 1 of the Companies Act 2006) or by a building society (within the meaning of section 119 of the Building Societies Act 1986)–

   (i)   sections 175, 176ZA and 176A of, and paragraph 65(2) of Schedule B1 to, the Insolvency Act 1986 or Articles 149, 150ZA, and 150A of, and paragraph 66(2) of Schedule B1 to, the Insolvency (Northern Ireland) Order 1989;

   (ii) Rules 6.42(2)(b) and 7.38(3) of the Insolvency (England and Wales) Rules 2016, Rules 4.033(3) and 4.228(2)(b) of the Insolvency Rules (Northern Ireland) 1991 and rule 5.9(4) of the Insolvency (Scotland) (Receivership and Winding up) Rules 2018;

   (iii) section 40 (or in Scotland, section 59 and 60(1)(e)) of the Insolvency Act 1986, paragraph 99(3) of Schedule B1 to that Act and section 19(4) of that Act as that section has effect by virtue of section 249(1) of the Enterprise Act 2002;

   (iv) paragraph 100(3) of Schedule B1 to the Insolvency (Northern Ireland) Order 1989, Article 31(4) of that Order, as it has effect by virtue of Article 4(1) of the Insolvency (Northern Ireland) Order 2005, and Article 50 of the Insolvency (Northern Ireland) Order 1989; and

   (v)   section 754 of the Companies Act 2006 (including that section as applied or modified by any enactment made under the Banking Act 2009); and

(b) in the case of collateral security provided by an individual, section 328(1) and (2) of the Insolvency Act 1986 or, in Northern Ireland, Article 300(1) and (2) of the Insolvency (Northern Ireland) Order 1989 or, in Scotland, in the case of collateral security provided by an individual or a partnership, section 51 of the Bankruptcy (Scotland) Act 1985 and any like provision or rule of law affecting a protected trust deed.

14(6) The claim of a participant, system operator or central bank to collateral security shall be paid in priority to–

(a) the expenses of the winding up mentioned in sections 115 and 156 of the Insolvency Act 1986 or Articles 100 and 134 of the Insolvency (Northern Ireland) Order 1989, the expenses of the bankruptcy within the meaning of that Act or that Order or, as the case may be, the remuneration and expenses of the administrator mentioned in paragraph 99(3) of Schedule B1 to that Act and in section 19(4) of that Act as that section has effect by virtue of section 249(1) of the Enterprise Act 2002 or in paragraph 100(3) to Schedule B1 to that Order and Article 31(4) of that Order, as that Article has effect by virtue of Article 4(1) of the Insolvency (Northern Ireland) Order 2005, and

(b)   the preferential debts of the company or the individual (as the case may be) within the meaning given by section 386 of that Act or Article 346 of that Order, and

(c)   the debts or liabilities arising or incurred under contracts mentioned in–

    (i)   paragraph 99(4) of Schedule B1 to the Insolvency Act 1986 and section 19(5) of that Act, as that section has effect by virtue of section 249(1) of the Enterprise Act 2002, or

    (ii)   paragraph 100(4) of Schedule B1 to, the Insolvency (Northern Ireland) Order 1989 and Article 31(5) of that Order as that article has effect by virtue of Article 4(1) of the Insolvency (Northern Ireland) Order 2005,

unless the terms on which the collateral security was provided expressly provide that such expenses, remuneration or preferential debts are to have priority.

14(7)   As respects Scotland–

(a)   the reference in paragraph (6)(a) to the expenses of bankruptcy shall be taken to be a reference to the matters mentioned in paragraphs (a) to (d) of section 51(1) of the Bankruptcy (Scotland) Act 1985, or any like provision or rule of law affecting a protected trust deed; and

(b)   the reference in paragraph (6)(b) to the preferential debts of the individual shall be taken to be a reference to the preferred debts of the debtor within the meaning of the Bankruptcy (Scotland) Act 1985, or any like definition applying with respect to a protected trust deed by virtue of any provision or rule of law affecting it.

History
Regulation 14(5)(a)(ii) and 14(6)(a) amended by the Financial Markets and Insolvency (Settlement Finality) (Amendment) Regulations 2007 (SI 2007/832) reg.2(1)–(3), as from 6 April 2007. Regulation 14(1), (2), (4)–(7) amended by the Financial Markets and Insolvency (Settlement Finality) (Amendment) Regulations 2009 (SI 2009/1972) reg.4 as from 1 October 2009. Regulation 14 further amended by the Financial Markets and Insolvency (Settlement Finality and Financial Collateral Arrangements) (Amendment) Regulations 2010 (SI 2010/2993) reg.2(11) as from 6 April 2011. Regulation 14(5)(a)(ii) amended by the Financial Services and Markets (Insolvency) (Amendment of Miscellaneous Enactments) Regulations 2019 (SI 2019/755) regs 1, 2(1), (2) as from 23 April 2019.
   Regulation 14 modified in relation to building societies which receive financial assistance from the Bank of England by the Building Societies (Financial Assistance) Order 2008 (SI 2008/1427) art.12 from 5 June 2008.

15   Net sum payable on completion of action taken under default arrangements

15(1)   The following provisions apply with respect to any sum which is owed on completion of action taken under default arrangements of a designated system by or to a defaulter but do not apply to any sum which (or to the extent that it) arises from a transfer order which is also a market contract within the meaning of Part VII or Part V, in which case sections 162 and 163 of the Companies Act 1989 or Articles 85 and 86 of the Companies (No. 2) (Northern Ireland) Order 1990 apply subject to the modification made by regulation 21.

15(2)   If, in England and Wales or Northern Ireland, a bankruptcy, winding-up or administration order has been made or a creditors' voluntary winding-up resolution has been passed, the debt–

(a)   is provable in the bankruptcy, winding-up or administration or, as the case may be, is payable to the relevant office-holder; and

(b)   shall be taken into account, where appropriate, under section 323 of the Insolvency Act 1986 or Article 296 of the Insolvency (Northern Ireland) Order 1989 or rule 14.24 of the Insolvency (England and Wales) Rules 2016 or Rule 2.086 of the Insolvency Rules (Northern Ireland) 1991 (mutual dealings and set-off) or the corresponding provision applicable in the case of winding-up or administration;

in the same way as a debt due before the commencement of bankruptcy, the date on which the body corporate goes into liquidation (within the meaning of section 247 of the Insolvency Act 1986 or Article 6 of the Insolvency (Northern Ireland) Order 1989) or enters into administration (within the meaning of paragraph 1 of Schedule B1 to the Insolvency Act 1986 or paragraph 2 of Schedule B1 to the Insolvency (Northern Ireland) Order 1989) or, in the case of a partnership, the date of the winding-up order.

15(3) If, in Scotland, an award of sequestration or a winding-up order has been made, or a creditors' voluntary winding-up resolution has been passed, or a trust deed has been granted and it has become a protected trust deed, the debt–

(a) may be claimed in the sequestration or winding up or under the protected trust deed or, as the case may be, is payable to the relevant office-holder; and

(b) shall be taken into account for the purposes of any rule of law relating to set-off applicable in sequestration, winding up or in respect of a protected trust deed;

in the same way as a debt due before the date of sequestration (within the meaning of section 73(1) of the Bankruptcy (Scotland) Act 1985) or the commencement of the winding up (within the meaning of section 129 of the Insolvency Act 1986) or the grant of the trust deed.

15(4) A reference in this regulation to "administration order" shall include–

(a) the appointment of an administrator under paragraph 14 or 22 of Schedule B1 to the Insolvency Act 1986 or under paragraph 15 or 23 of Schedule B1 to the Insolvency (Northern Ireland) Order 1989;

(b) the making of an order under section 8 of that Act as it has effect by virtue of section 249(1) of the Enterprise Act 2002; and

(c) the making of an order under Article 21 of that Order as it has effect by virtue of Article 4(1) of the Insolvency (Northern Ireland) Order 2005;

and "administration" shall be construed accordingly.

History
Regulation 15(2) amended and reg.15(4) inserted by the Financial Markets and Insolvency (Settlement Finality) (Amendment) Regulations 2009 (SI 2009/1972) reg.5 as from 1 October 2009. Regulation 15(1) amended by the Financial Markets and Insolvency (Settlement Finality and Financial Collateral Arrangements) (Amendment) Regulations 2010 (SI 2010/2993) reg.2(12) as from 6 April 2011. Regulation 15(2)(b) amended by the Financial Services and Markets (Insolvency) (Amendment of Miscellaneous Enactments) Regulations 2019 (SI 2019/755) regs 1, 2(1), (3) as from 23 April 2019.

16 Disclaimer of property, rescission of contracts, &c

16(1) Sections 178, 186, 315 and 345 of the Insolvency Act 1986 or Articles 152, 157, 288 and 318 of the Insolvency (Northern Ireland) Order 1989 (power to disclaim onerous property and court's power to order rescission of contracts, &c) do not apply in relation to–

(a) a transfer order; or

(b) a contract for the purpose of realising collateral security.

In the application of this paragraph in Scotland, the reference to sections 178, 315 and 345 shall be construed as a reference to any rule of law having the like effect as those sections.

16(2) In Scotland, a permanent trustee on the sequestrated estate of a defaulter or a liquidator or a trustee under a protected trust deed granted by a defaulter is bound by any transfer order given by that defaulter and by any such contract as is mentioned in paragraph (1)(b) notwithstanding section 42 of the Bankruptcy (Scotland) Act 1985 or any rule of law having the like effect applying in liquidations or any like provision or rule of law affecting the protected trust deed.

16(3) Sections 88, 127, 245 and 284 of the Insolvency Act 1986 or Articles 74, 107, 207 and 257 of the Insolvency (Northern Ireland) Order 1989 (avoidance of property dispositions effected after commencement of winding up or presentation of bankruptcy petition), section 32(8) of the Bankruptcy (Scotland) Act 1985 (effect of dealing with debtor relating to estate vested in permanent trustee) and any like provision or rule of law affecting a protected trust deed, do not apply to–

(a)   a transfer order, or any disposition of property in pursuance of such an order;

(b)   the provision of collateral security;

(c)   a contract for the purpose of realising collateral security or any disposition of property in pursuance of such a contract; or

(d)   any disposition of property in accordance with the rules of a designated system as to the application of collateral security.

History
Regulation 16(3) amended by the Financial Markets and Insolvency (Settlement Finality) (Amendment) Regulations 2009 (SI 2009/1972) reg.6 as from 1 October 2009.

17   Adjustment of prior transactions

17(1) No order shall be made in relation to a transaction to which this regulation applies under–

(a)   section 238 or 339 of the Insolvency Act 1986 or Article 202 or 312 of the Insolvency (Northern Ireland) Order 1989 (transactions at an undervalue);

(b)   section 239 or 340 of that Act or Article 203 or 313 of that Order (preferences); or

(c)   section 423 of that Act or Article 367 of that Order (transactions defrauding creditors).

17(2) As respects Scotland, no decree shall be granted in relation to any such transaction–

(a)   under section 34 or 36 of the Bankruptcy (Scotland) Act 1985 or section 242 or 243 of the Insolvency Act 1986 (gratuitous alienations and unfair preferences); or

(b)   at common law on grounds of gratuitous alienations or fraudulent preferences.

17(3) This regulation applies to–

(a)   a transfer order, or any disposition of property in pursuance of such an order;

(b)   the provision of collateral security;

(c)   a contract for the purpose of realising collateral security or any disposition of property in pursuance of such a contract; or

(d)   any disposition of property in accordance with the rules of a designated system as to the application of collateral security.

Collateral security charges

18   Modifications of the law of insolvency

18 The general law of insolvency has effect in relation to a collateral security charge and the action taken to enforce such a charge, subject to the provisions of regulation 19.

19   Administration orders, &c

19(1) The following provisions of Schedule B1 to the Insolvency Act 1986 (which relate to administration orders and administrators) do not apply in relation to a collateral security charge–

(a)   paragraph 43(2) including that provision as applied by paragraph 44; and

(b)   paragraphs 70, 71 and 72 of that Schedule;

and paragraph 41(2) of that Schedule (receiver to vacate office when so required by administrator) does not apply to a receiver appointed under such a charge.

19(1ZA)   The following provisions of the Insolvency Act 1986 (which relate to administration orders and administrators), as they have effect by virtue of section 249(1) of the Enterprise Act 2002, do not apply in relation to a collateral security charge–

(a)   sections 10(1)(b) and 11(3)(c) (restriction on enforcement of security while petition for administration order pending or order in force); and

(b)   sections 15(1) and (2) (power of administrator to deal with charged property);

and section 11(2) (receiver to vacate office when so required by administrator) does not apply to a receiver appointed under such a charge.

19(1A)   The following provisions of Schedule B1 to the Insolvency (Northern Ireland) Order 1989 (which relate to administration orders and administrators) do not apply in relation to a collateral security charge–

(a)   paragraph 44(2), including that provision as applied by paragraph 45 (restrictions on enforcement of security where company in administration or where administration application has been made); and

(b)   paragraphs 71, 72 and 73 (charged and hire purchase property);

and paragraph 42(2) (receiver to vacate office when so required by administrator) does not apply to a receiver appointed under such a charge.

19(1B)   The following provisions of the Insolvency (Northern Ireland) Order 1989 (administration), as they have effect by virtue of Article 4(1) of the Insolvency (Northern Ireland) Order 2005, do not apply in relation to a collateral security charge–

(a)   Article 23(1)(b) and Article 24(3)(c) (restriction on enforcement of security while petition for administration order pending or order in force); and

(b)   Article 28(1) and (2) (power of administrator to deal with charged property);

and Article 24(2) of that Order (receiver to vacate office at request of administrator) shall not apply to a receiver appointed under such a charge.

19(2)   However, where a collateral security charge falls to be enforced after an administration order has been made or a petition for an administration order has been presented, and there exists another charge over some or all of the same property ranking in priority to or *pari passu* with the collateral security charge, on the application of any person interested, the court may order that there shall be taken after enforcement of the collateral security charge such steps as the court may direct for the purpose of ensuring that the chargee under the other charge is not prejudiced by the enforcement of the collateral security charge.

19(2A)   A reference in paragraph (2) to "an administration order" shall include the appointment of an administrator under paragraph 14 or 22 of Schedule B1 to the Insolvency Act 1986 or under paragraph 15 or 23 of Schedule B1 to the Insolvency (Northern Ireland) Order 1989.

19(3)   Sections 127 and 284 of the Insolvency Act 1986 or Articles 107 and 257 of the Insolvency (Northern Ireland) Order 1989 (avoidance of property dispositions effected after commencement of winding up or presentation of bankruptcy petition), section 32(8) of the Bankruptcy (Scotland) Act 1985 (effect of dealing with debtor relating to estate vested in permanent trustee) and any like provision or rule of law affecting a protected trust deed, do not apply to a disposition of property as a result of which the property becomes subject to a collateral security charge or any transactions pursuant to which that disposition is made.

19(4) Paragraph 20 and paragraph 12(1)(g) of Schedule A1 to the Insolvency Act 1986, and paragraph 31 and paragraph 23(1)(g) of Schedule A1 to the Insolvency (Northern Ireland) Order 1989 (effect of moratorium on creditors) shall not apply (if they would otherwise do so) to any collateral security charge.

History
Regulation 19(1A), (2A) amended by the Financial Markets and Insolvency (Settlement Finality) (Amendment) Regulations 2007 (SI 2007/832) reg.2(1), (4), (5), as from 6 April 2007. Regulation 19(1ZA), (1B), (4) inserted by the Financial Markets and Insolvency (Settlement Finality) (Amendment) Regulations 2009 (SI 2009/1972) reg.7 as from 1 October 2009.

General

20 Transfer order entered into designated system following insolvency

20(1) This Part does not apply in relation to any transfer order given by a participant which is entered into a designated system after–

(a) a court has made an order of a type referred to in regulation 22 in respect of–

   (i) that participant;

   (ii) a participant in a system which is an interoperable system in relation to the designated system; or

   (iii) a system operator which is not a participant in the designated system, or

(b) that participant, a participant in a system which is an interoperable system in relation to the designated system or a system operator of that designated system has passed a creditors' voluntary winding-up resolution, or

(c) a trust deed granted by that participant, a participant in a system which is an interoperable system in relation to the designated system or a system operator of that designated system has become a protected trust deed,

unless the conditions mentioned in either paragraph (2) or paragraph (4) are satisfied.

20(2) The conditions referred to in this paragraph are that–

(a) the transfer order is carried out on the same business day of the designated system that the event specified in paragraph (1)(a), (b) or (c) occurs, and

(b) the system operator can show that it did not have notice of that event at the time the transfer order became irrevocable.

20(3) For the purposes of paragraph (2)(b), the relevant system operator shall be taken to have notice of an event specified in paragraph (1)(a), (b) or (c) if it deliberately failed to make enquiries as to that matter in circumstances in which a reasonable and honest person would have done so.

20(4) The conditions referred to in this paragraph are that–

(a) a recognised central counterparty, EEA central counterparty or third country central counterparty is the system operator;

(b) a clearing member of that central counterparty has defaulted; and

(c) the transfer order has been entered into the system pursuant to the provisions of the default rules of the central counterparty that provide for the transfer of the positions or assets of a clearing member on its default.

20(5) In paragraph (4)–

(a) "recognised central counterparty", "EEA central counterparty" and "third country central counterparty" have the meanings given by section 285 of the 2000 Act; and

(b) "clearing member" has the meaning given by section 190(1) of the Companies Act 1989.

History
Regulation 20 amended by the Financial Markets and Insolvency (Settlement Finality and Financial Collateral Arrangements) (Amendment) Regulations 2010 (SI 2010/2993) reg.2(13) as from 6 April 2011. Regulation 20(1), (2) amended and reg.20(4), (5) inserted by the Financial Services and Markets Act 2000 (Over the Counter Derivatives, Central Counterparties and Trade Repositories) Regulations 2013 (SI 2013/504) reg.32(1), (6) as from 1 April 2013.

21 Disapplication of certain provisions of Part VII and Part V

21(1) The provisions of the Companies Act 1989 or the Companies (No. 2) (Northern Ireland) Order 1990 mentioned in paragraph (2) do not apply in relation to–

(a) a market contract which is also a transfer order effected through a designated system; or

(b) a market charge which is also a collateral security charge.

21(2) The provisions referred to in paragraph (1) are as follows–

(a) section 163(4) to (6) and Article 86(3) to (5) (net sum payable on completion of default proceedings);

(b) section 164(4) to (6) and Article 87(3) to (5) (disclaimer of property, rescission of contracts, &c); and

(c) section 175(5) and (6) and Article 97(5) and (6) (administration orders, &c).

22 Notification of insolvency order or passing of resolution for creditors' voluntary winding up

22(1) Upon the making of an order for bankruptcy, sequestration, administration or winding up in respect of a participant in a designated system, the court shall forthwith notify both the system operator of that designated system and the designating authority that such an order has been made.

22(2) Following receipt of–

(a) such notification from the court, or

(b) notification from a participant of the passing of a creditors' voluntary winding-up resolution or of a trust deed becoming a protected trust deed, pursuant to paragraph 5(4) of the Schedule,

the designating authority shall forthwith inform the Treasury, the Board, ESMA and other EEA States of the notification.

22(3) In paragraph (2) "the Board" means the European Systemic Risk Board established by Regulation (EU) No. 1092/2010 of the European Parliament and of the Council of 24th November 2010 on European Union macro-prudential oversight of the financial system and establishing a European Systemic Risk Board.

History
Regulation 22(1) amended by the Financial Markets and Insolvency (Settlement Finality and Financial Collateral Arrangements) (Amendment) Regulations 2010 (SI 2010/2993) reg.2(14) as from 6 April 2011. Regulation 22(2) amended and reg.22(3) inserted by the Financial Services and Markets (Disclosure of Information to the European Securities and Markets Authority etc. and Other Provisions) Regulations 2016 (SI 2016/1095) reg.2(4) as from 8 December 2016.

23 Applicable law relating to securities held as collateral security

23 Where–

(a) securities (including rights in securities) are provided as collateral security to a participant, a system operator or a central bank (including any nominee, agent or third party acting on behalf of the participant, the system operator or the central bank), and

(b) a register, account or centralised deposit system located in an EEA State legally records the entitlement of that person to the collateral security,

the rights of that person as a holder of collateral security in relation to those securities shall be governed by the law of the EEA State or, where appropriate, the law of the part of the EEA State, where the register, account, or centralised deposit system is located.

History
Regulation 23 amended by the Financial Markets and Insolvency (Settlement Finality and Financial Collateral Arrangements) (Amendment) Regulations 2010 (SI 2010/2993) reg.2(15) as from 6 April 2011.

24 Applicable law where insolvency proceedings are brought

24 Where insolvency proceedings are brought in any jurisdiction against a person who participates, or has participated, in a system designated for the purposes of the Settlement Finality Directive, any question relating to the rights and obligations arising from, or in connection with, that participation and falling to be determined by a court in England and Wales, the High Court in Northern Ireland or in Scotland shall (subject to regulation 23) be determined in accordance with the law governing that system.

25 Insolvency proceedings in other jurisdictions

25(1) The references to insolvency law in section 426 of the Insolvency Act 1986 (co-operation between courts exercising jurisdiction in relation to insolvency) include, in relation to a part of the United Kingdom, this Part and, in relation to a relevant country or territory within the meaning of that section, so much of the law of that country or territory as corresponds to this Part.

25(2) A court shall not, in pursuance of that section or any other enactment or rule of law, recognise or give effect to–

(a) any order of a court exercising jurisdiction in relation to insolvency law in a country or territory outside the United Kingdom, or

(b) any act of a person appointed in such a country or territory to discharge any functions under insolvency law,

in so far as the making of the order or the doing of the act would be prohibited in the case of a court in England and Wales or Scotland, the High Court in Northern Ireland or a relevant office-holder by this Part.

25(3) Paragraph (2) does not affect the recognition or enforcement of a judgment required to be recognised or enforced under or by virtue of the Civil Jurisdiction and Judgments Act 1982 or Regulation (EU) No. 1215/2012 of the European Parliament and of the Council of 12 December 2012 on jurisdiction and the recognition and enforcement of judgments in civil and commercial matters (recast), as amended from time to time and as applied by virtue of the Agreement made on 19 October 2005 between the European Community and the Kingdom of Denmark on jurisdiction and the recognition and enforcement of judgments in civil and commercial matters (OJ No L 299, 16.11.2005, p62; OJ No L79, 21.3.2013, p4).

History
Paragraph (3) amended by the Civil Jurisdiction and Judgments Regulations 2007 (SI 2007/1655) reg.5 and Sch. para.32 as from 1 July 2007 and the Civil Jurisdiction and Judgments (Amendment) Regulations 2014 (SI 2014/2947) reg.5, Sch.4 para.5 as from 10 January 2015.

26 Systems designated in other EEA States and Gibraltar

26(1) Where an equivalent overseas order or equivalent overseas security is subject to the insolvency law of England and Wales or Scotland or Northern Ireland, this Part shall apply–

(a) in relation to the equivalent overseas order as it applies in relation to a transfer order; and

(b)   in relation to the equivalent overseas security as it applies in relation to collateral security.

26(2)   In paragraph (1)–

(a)   "equivalent overseas order" means an order having the like effect as a transfer order which is effected through a system designated for the purposes of the Settlement Finality Directive in another EEA State or Gibraltar; and

(b)   "equivalent overseas security" means any realisable assets provided under a charge or a repurchase or similar agreement, or otherwise (including credit claims and money provided under a charge)–

(i)   for the purpose of securing rights and obligations potentially arising in connection with such a system, or

(ii)   to a central bank for the purpose of securing rights and obligations in connection with its operations in carrying out its functions as a central bank.

History
Regulation 26 amended by the Financial Markets and Insolvency (Settlement Finality and Financial Collateral Arrangements) (Amendment) Regulations 2010 (SI 2010/2993) reg.2(16) as from 6 April 2011.

SCHEDULE

REQUIREMENTS FOR DESIGNATION OF SYSTEM

Regulation 4(1)

1   Establishment, participation and governing law

1(1)   The head office of at least one of the participants in the system must be in the United Kingdom and the law of England and Wales, Northern Ireland or Scotland must be the governing law of the system.

1(2)   There must be not less than three institutions participating in the system, unless otherwise determined by the designating authority in any case where–

(a)   there are two institutions participating in a system; and

(b)   the designating authority considers that designation is required on the grounds of systemic risk.

1(3)   The system must be a system through which transfer orders are effected.

1(4)   Where orders relating to financial instruments other than securities are effected through the system–

(a)   the system must primarily be a system through which securities transfer orders are effected; and

(b)   the designating authority must consider that designation is required on grounds of systemic risk.

1(5)   An arrangement entered into between interoperable systems shall not constitute a system.

2   Arrangements and resources

2   The system must have adequate arrangements and resources for the effective monitoring and enforcement of compliance with its rules or, as respects monitoring, arrangements providing for that function to be performed on its behalf (and without affecting its responsibility) by another body or person who is able and willing to perform it.

3 Financial resources

3 The system operator must have financial resources sufficient for the proper performance of its functions as a system operator.

4 Co-operation with other authorities

4 The system operator must be able and willing to co-operate, by the sharing of information and otherwise, with–

(a) the FCA,

(b) the Bank of England,

(ba) the PRA,

(c) any relevant office-holder, and

(d) any authority, body or person having responsibility for any matter arising out of, or connected with, the default of a participant.

5 Specific provision in the rules

5(1) The rules of the system must–

(a) specify the point at which a transfer order takes effect as having been entered into the system,

(b) specify the point after which a transfer order may not be revoked by a participant or any other party, and

(c) prohibit the revocation by a participant or any other party of a transfer order from the point specified in accordance with paragraph (b).

5(1A) Where the system has one or more interoperable systems, the rules required under paragraph (1)(a) and (b) shall, as far as possible, be co-ordinated with the rules of those interoperable systems.

5(1B) The rules of the system which are referred to in paragraph (1)(a) and (b) shall not be affected by any rules of that system's interoperable systems in the absence of express provision in the rules of the system and all of those interoperable systems.

5(2) The rules of the system must require each institution which participates in the system to provide upon payment of a reasonable charge the information mentioned in sub-paragraph (3) to any person who requests it, save where the request is frivolous or vexatious. The rules must require the information to be provided within fourteen days of the request being made.

5(3) The information referred to in sub-paragraph (2) is as follows–

(a) details of the systems which are designated for the purposes of the Settlement Finality Directive in which the institution participates, and

(b) information about the main rules governing the functioning of those systems.

5(4) The rules of the system must require each participant upon–

(a) the passing of a creditors' voluntary winding up resolution, or

(b) a trust deed granted by him becoming a protected trust deed,

to notify forthwith both the system and the designating authority that such a resolution has been passed, or, as the case may be, that such a trust deed has become a protected trust deed.

6 Default arrangements

6 The system must have default arrangements which are appropriate for that system in all the circumstances.

History

Paragraphs 1, 3–5 amended by the Financial Markets and Insolvency (Settlement Finality and Financial Collateral Arrangements) (Amendment) Regulations 2010 (SI 2010/2993) reg.2(17) as from 6 April 2011.

Limited Liability Partnerships (Scotland) Regulations 2001

(Scottish SI 2001/128)

Made on 28 March 2001 by the Scottish Ministers under ss.14(1) and (2), 15, 16 and 17(1) and (3) of the Limited Liability Partnerships Act 2000. Operative from 6 April 2001.

[**Note**: Changes made by the Limited Liability Partnerships (Scotland) Amendment Regulations 2009 (SSI 2009/310) and the Insolvency (Protection of Essential Supplies) Order 2015 (SI 2015/989) have been incorporated into the text.]

PART I

CITATION, COMMENCEMENT, EXTENT AND INTERPRETATION

1 Citation, commencement and extent

1(1) These Regulations may be cited as the Limited Liability Partnerships (Scotland) Regulations 2001 and shall come into force on 6th April 2001.

1(2) These Regulations extend to Scotland only.

2 Interpretation

2 In these Regulations–

"the 1985 Act" means the Companies Act 1985;

"the 1986 Act" means the Insolvency Act 1986;

"limited liability partnership agreement", in relation to a limited liability partnership, means any agreement, express or implied, made between the members of the limited liability partnership or between the limited liability partnership and the members of the limited liability partnership which determines the mutual rights and duties of the members, and their rights and duties in relation to the limited liability partnership;

"the principal Act" means the Limited Liability Partnerships Act 2000; and

"shadow member", in relation to a limited liability partnership, means a person in accordance with whose directions or instructions the members of the limited liability partnership are accustomed to act (but so that a person is not deemed a shadow member by reason only that the members of the limited liability partnership act on advice given by that person in a professional capacity).

PART II

COMPANIES ACT

3 Application of the 1985 Act to limited liability partnerships

3 The provisions of the 1985 Act specified in the first column of Schedule 1 to these Regulations shall apply to limited liability partnerships, with the following modifications–

(a) references to a company shall include references to a limited liability partnership;

(b) references to the Companies Acts shall include references to the principal Act and any regulations made thereunder;

(c) references to the 1986 Act shall include references to that Act as it applies to limited liability partnerships by virtue of Part III of these Regulations;

(d)   references in a provision of the 1985 Act to other provisions of that Act shall include references to those other provisions as they apply to limited liability partnerships by virtue of these Regulations; and

(e)   the modifications, if any, specified in the second column of Schedule 1 of the provision specified opposite them in the first column.

Part III

Winding Up and Insolvency

4   Application of the 1986 Act to limited liability partnerships

4(1)   Subject to paragraph (2), the provisions of the 1986 Act listed in Schedule 2 shall apply in relation to limited liability partnerships as they apply in relation to companies.

4(2)   The provisions of the 1986 Act referred to in paragraph (1) shall so apply, with the following modifications–

(a)   references to a company shall include references to a limited liability partnership;

(b)   references to a director or to an officer of a company shall include references to a member of a limited liability partnership;

(c)   references to a shadow director shall include references to a shadow member;

(d)   references to the 1985 Act, the Company Directors Disqualification Act 1986, the Companies Act 1989 or to any provisions of those Acts or to any provisions of the 1986 Act shall include references to those Acts or provisions as they apply to limited liability partnerships by virtue of the principal Act or these Regulations; and

(e)   the modifications set out in Schedule 3 to these Regulations.

Part IV

Miscellaneous

5   General and consequential amendments

5   The enactments referred to in Schedule 4 shall have effect subject to the amendments specified in that Schedule.

6   Application of subordinate legislation

6(1)   The Insolvency (Scotland) Rules 1986 shall apply to limited liability partnerships with such modifications as the context requires for the purpose of giving effect to the provisions of the Insolvency Act 1986 which are applied by these Regulations.

6(2)   In the case of any conflict between any provision of the subordinate legislation applied by paragraph (1) and any provision of these Regulations, the latter shall prevail.

Schedule 1

Modifications to Provisions of the 1985 Act

Regulation 3

Formalities of Carrying on Business	
36B (execution of documents by companies)	
Floating Charges and Receivers (Scotland)	
462 (power of incorporated company to create floating charge)	In subsection (1), for the words "an incorporated company (whether a company within the meaning of this Act or not)," substitute "a limited liability partnership", and the words "(including uncalled capital)" are omitted.
463 (effect of floating charge on winding up)	
466 (alteration of floating charges) Subsections (1), (2), (3) and (6)	
486 (interpretation for Part XVIII generally)	For the definition of "company" substitute ""company" means a limited liability partnership;"
487 (extent of Part XVIII)	

Schedule 2

Provisions of the 1986 Act

Regulation 4(1)

The relevant provisions of the 1986 Act are as follows:

Sections 50 to 52;

Section 53(1) and (2), to the extent that those subsections do not relate to the requirement for a copy of the instrument and notice being delivered to the registrar of companies;

Section 53(4), (6) and (7);

Section 54(1), (2), (3) (to the extent that that subsection does not relate to the requirement for a copy of the interlocutor to be delivered to the registrar of companies), and subsections (5), (6) and (7);

Sections 55 to 58;

Section 60, other than subsection (1);

Section 61, including subsections (6) and (7) to the extent that those subsections do not relate to anything to be done or which may be sent to the registrar of companies;

Section 62, including subsection (5) to the extent that that subsection does not relate to anything to be done or which may be sent to the registrar of companies;

Sections 63 to 66;

Section 67, including subsections (1) and (8) to the extent that those subsections do not relate to anything to be sent to the registrar of companies;

Section 68;

Section 69, including subsections (1) and (2) to the extent that those subsections do not relate to anything to be done or which may be done by the registrar of companies;

Sections 70 and 71;

Subsection 84(3) to the extent that it does not concern the copy of the resolution being forwarded to the registrar of companies within 15 days;

Sections 91 to 93;

Section 94, including subsections (3) and (4) to the extent that those subsections do not relate to the liquidator being required to send to the registrar of companies a copy of the account and a return of the final meeting;

Section 95;

Section 97;

Sections 100 to 102;

Sections 104 to 105;

Section 106, including subsections (3) to (7) to the extent that those subsections do not relate to the liquidator being required to send to the registrar of companies a copy of the account of winding up and a return of the final meeting/quorum or a statement about a member State liquidator;

Sections 109 to 111;

Section 112, including subsection (3) to the extent that that subsection does not relate to the liquidator being required to send to the registrar of companies a copy of the order made by the court;

Sections 113 to 115;

Sections 126 to 128;

Section 130(1) to the extent that that subsection does not relate to a copy of the order being forwarded by the court to the registrar of companies;

Section 131;

Sections 133 to 135;

Sections 138 to 140;

Sections 142 to 146;

Section 147, including subsection (3) to the extent that that subsection does not relate to a copy of the order being forwarded by the company to the registrar of companies;

Section 162 to the extent that the section concerns the matters set out in Section C.2 of Schedule 5 to the Scotland Act 1998 as being exceptions to the reservation of insolvency;

Sections 163 to 167;

Section 169;

Section 170, including subsection (2) to the extent that that subsection does not relate to an application being made by the registrar to make good the default;

Section 171;

Section 172, including subsections (8) to (10) to the extent that those subsections do not relate to the liquidator being required to give notice to the registrar of companies or a statement about a member State liquidator;

Sections 173 and 174;

Section 177;

Sections 185 to 189;

Sections 191 to 194;

Section 196;

Section 199;

Section 200;

Sections 206 to 215;

Section 218 subsections (1), (2), (4) and (6);

Sections 231 to 232 to the extent that the sections apply to administrative receivers, liquidators and provisional liquidators;

Section 233 to the extent that that section applies in the case of the appointment of an administrative receiver, of a voluntary arrangement taking effect, of a company going into liquidation or where a provisional liquidator is appointed;

Section 233A to the extent that that section applies in the case of a voluntary arrangement taking effect;

Section 234 to the extent that that section applies to situations other than those where an administration has been entered into;

Section 235 to the extent that that section applies to situations other than those where an administration has been entered into;

Sections 236 to 237 to the extent that those sections apply to situations other than administrations entered into and winding up;

Sections 242 to 243;

Section 244 to the extent that that section applies in circumstances other than a company which has entered into administration;

Section 245;

Section 251;

Section 416(1) and (4) to the extent that those subsections apply to section 206(1)(a) and (b) in connection with the offence provision relating to the winding up of a limited liability partnership;

Section 430;

Section 436;

Schedule 2;

Schedule 3;

Schedule 4;

Schedule 8 to the extent that that Schedule does not apply to voluntary arrangements or administrations within the meaning of Parts I and II of the 1986 Act;

Schedule 10 to the extent that it refers to any of the sections referred to above.

History
Entry for s.233A inserted by the Insolvency (Protection of Essential Supplies) Order 2015 (SI 2015/989) Sch.1 para.3 as from 1 October 2015.
   Entries in relation to ss.106 and 172 amended by the Insolvency (Miscellaneous Amendments) Regulations 2017 (SI 2017/1119) regs 1(1), (3), 2, Sch.1 para.57 as from 8 December 2017 subject to transitional and savings provision in para.10.

SCHEDULE 3

MODIFICATIONS TO PROVISIONS OF THE 1986 ACT

Regulation 4(2)

Provisions	Modifications
Section 84 (circumstances in which company may be wound up voluntarily)	
Subsection (3)	For subsection (3) substitute the following— "(3) Within 15 days after a limited liability partnership has determined that it be wound up there shall be forwarded to the registrar of companies either a printed copy or a copy in some other form approved by the registrar of the determination." After subsection (3) insert a new subsection—
Subsection (3A)	"(3A) If a limited liability partnership fails to comply with this regulation the limited liability partnership and every designated member of it who is in default is liable on summary conviction to a fine not exceeding level 3 on the standard scale."
Section 91 (appointment of liquidator)	
Subsection (1)	Delete "in general meeting".
Subsection (2)	For subsection (2) substitute the following— "(2) On the appointment of a liquidator the powers of the members of the limited liability partnership shall cease except to the extent that a meeting of the members of the limited liability partnership summoned for the purpose or the liquidator sanctions their continuance." After subsection (2) insert— "(3) Subsections (3) and (4) of section 92 shall apply for the purposes of this section as they apply for the purposes of that section."
Section 92 (power to fill vacancy in office of liquidator)	
Subsection (1)	For "the company in general meeting" substitute "a meeting of the members of the limited liability partnership summoned for the purpose".
Subsection (2)	For "a general meeting" substitute "a meeting of the members of the limited liability partnership".
Subsection (3)	In subsection (3), for "articles" substitute "limited liability partnership agreement".
new subsection (4)	Add a new subsection (4) as follows— "(4) The quorum required for a meeting of the members of the limited liability partnership shall be any quorum required by the limited liability partnership agreement for meetings of the members of the limited liability partnership and if no requirement for a quorum has been agreed upon the quorum shall be 2 members."
Section 93 (general company meeting at each year's end)	
subsection (1)	For "a general meeting of the company" substitute "a meeting of the members of the limited liability partnership".

Provisions	Modifications
new subsection (4)	Add a new subsection (4) as follows— "(4) Subsections (3) and (4) of section 92 shall apply for the purposes of this section as they apply for the purposes of that section."
Section 94 (final meeting prior to dissolution)	
subsection (1)	For "a general meeting of the company" substitute "a meeting of the members of the limited liability partnership".
new subsection 5(A)	Add a new subsection (5A) as follows— "(5A) Subsections (3) and (4) of section 92 shall apply for the purposes of this section as they apply for the purposes of that section."
subsection (6)	For "a general meeting of the company" substitute "a meeting of the members of the limited liability partnership".
Section 95 (effect of company's insolvency)	
subsection (1)	For "directors'" substitute "designated members'".
subsection (7)	For subsection (7) substitute the following— "(7) In this section 'the relevant period' means the period of 6 months immediately preceding the date on which the limited liability partnership determined that it be wound up voluntarily."
Section 100 (appointment of liquidator)	
subsection (1)	For "The creditors and the company at their respective meetings mentioned in section 98" substitute "The creditors at their meeting mentioned in section 98 and the limited liability partnership".
subsection (3)	Delete "director,".
Section 101 (appointment of liquidation committee)	
subsection (2)	For subsection (2) substitute the following— "(2) If such a committee is appointed, the limited liability partnership may, when it determines that it be wound up voluntarily or at any time thereafter, appoint such number of persons as they think fit to act as members of the committee, not exceeding 5."
Section 105 (meetings of company and creditors at each year's end)	
subsection (1)	For "a general meeting of the company" substitute "a meeting of the members of the limited liability partnership".
new subsection (5)	Add a new subsection (5) as follows— "(5) Subsections (3) and (4) of section 92 shall apply for the purposes of this section as they apply for the purposes of that section."
Section 106 (final meeting prior to dissolution)	
subsection (1)	For "a general meeting of the company" substitute "a meeting of the members of the limited liability partnership".
new subsection (5A)	After subsection (5) insert a new subsection (5A) as follows— "(5A) Subsections (3) and (4) of section 92 shall apply for the purposes of this section as they apply for the purposes of that section."
subsection (6)	For "a general meeting of the company" substitute "a meeting of the members of the limited liability partnership".

Provisions	Modifications
Section 110 (acceptance of shares, etc, as consideration for sale of company property)	
	For the existing section substitute the following:
	"(1) This section applies, in the case of a limited liability partnership proposed to be, or being, wound up voluntarily, where the whole or part of the limited liability partnership's business or property is proposed to be transferred or sold to another company whether or not it is a company within the meaning of the Companies Act ("the transferee company") or to a limited liability partnership ("the transferee limited liability partnership").
	(2) With the requisite sanction, the liquidator of the limited liability partnership being, or proposed to be, wound up ("the transferor limited liability partnership") may receive, in compensation or part compensation for the transfer or sale, shares, policies or other like interests in the transferee company or the transferee limited liability partnership for distribution among the members of the transferor limited liability partnership.
	(3) The sanction required under subsection (2) is—
	(a) in the case of a members' voluntary winding up, that of a determination of the limited liability partnership at a meeting of the members of the limited liability partnership conferring either a general authority on the liquidator or an authority in respect of any particular arrangement, (subsections (3) and (4) of section 92 to apply for this purpose as they apply for the purposes of that section), and
	(b) in the case of a creditor's voluntary winding up, that of either court or the liquidation committee.
	(4) Alternatively to subsection (2), the liquidator may (with the sanction) enter into any other arrangement whereby the members of the transferor limited liability partnership may, in lieu of receiving cash, shares, policies or other like interests (or in addition thereto), participate in the profits, or receive any other benefit from the transferee company or the transferee limited liability partnership.
	(5) A sale or arrangement in pursuance of this section is binding on members of the transferor limited liability partnership.
	(6) A determination by the limited liability partnership is not invalid for the purposes of this section by reason that it is made before or concurrently with a determination by the limited liability partnership that it be wound up voluntarily or for appointing liquidators; but, if an order is made within a year for winding up the limited liability partnership by the court, the determination by the limited liability partnership is not valid unless sanctioned by the court."
Section 111 (dissent from arrangement under section 110)	
subsections (1)–(3)	For subsections (1)–(3) substitute the following—
	"(1) This section applies in the case of a voluntary winding up where, for the purposes of section 110(2) or (4), a determination of the limited liability partnership has provided the sanction requisite for the liquidator under that section.

Provisions	Modifications
	(2) If a member of the transferor limited liability partnership who did not vote in favour of providing the sanction required for the liquidator under section 110 expresses his dissent from it in writing addressed to the liquidator and left at the registered office of the limited liability partnership within 7 days after the date on which that sanction was given, he may require the liquidator either to abstain from carrying the arrangement so sanctioned into effect or to purchase his interest at a price to be determined by agreement or arbitration under this section. (3) If the liquidator elects to purchase the member's interest, the purchase money must be paid before the limited liability partnership is dissolved and be raised by the liquidator in such manner as may be determined by the limited liability partnership."
subsection (4)	Omit subsection (4).
Section 126 (power to stay or restrain proceedings against company)	
subsection (2)	Delete subsection (2).
Section 127 (avoidance of property dispositions, etc)	
	For "any transfer of shares" substitute "any transfer by a member of the limited liability partnership of his interest in the property of the limited liability partnership".
Section 165 (voluntary winding up)	
subsection (2)	In paragraph (a) for "an extraordinary resolution of the company" substitute "a determination by a meeting of the members of the limited liability partnership".
subsection (4)	For paragraph (c) substitute the following— "(c) summon meetings of the members of the limited liability partnership for the purpose of obtaining their sanction or for any other purpose he may think fit."
new subsection (4A)	Insert a new subsection (4A) as follows— "(4A) Subsections (3) and (4) of section 92 shall apply for the purposes of this section as they apply for the purposes of that section."
Section 166 (creditors' voluntary winding up)	
subsection (5)	In paragraph (b) for "directors" substitute "designated members".
Section 171 (removal, etc (voluntary winding up))	
subsection (2)	For paragraph (a) substitute the following— "(a) in the case of a members' voluntary winding up, by a meeting of the members of the limited liability partnership summoned specially for that purpose, or".
subsection (6)	In paragraph (a) for "final meeting of the company" substitute "final meeting of the members of the limited liability partnership" and in paragraph (b) for "final meetings of the company" substitute "final meetings of the members of the limited liability partnership".
new subsection (7)	Insert a new subsection (7) as follows— "(7) Subsections (3) and (4) of section 92 apply for the purposes of this section as they apply for the purposes of that section."

Provisions	Modifications
Section 173 (release (voluntary winding up))	
subsection (2)	In paragraph (a) for "a general meeting of the company" substitute "a meeting of the members of the limited liability partnership".
Section 187 (power to make over assets to employees)	
	Delete section 187
Section 194 (resolutions passed at adjourned meetings)	
	After "contributories" insert "or of the members of a limited liability partnership".
Section 206 (fraud, etc in anticipation of winding up)	
subsection (1)	For "passes a resolution for voluntary winding up" substitute "makes a determination that it be wound up voluntarily".
Section 207 (transactions in fraud of creditors)	
subsection (1)	For "passes a resolution for voluntary winding up" substitute "makes a determination that it be wound up voluntarily".
Section 210 (material omissions from statement relating to company's affairs)	
subsection (2)	For "passed a resolution for voluntary winding up" substitute "made a determination that it be wound up voluntarily".
Section 214 (wrongful trading)	
subsection (2)	Delete from "but the court shall not" to the end of the subsection.
After section 214	Insert the following new section 214A "Adjustment of withdrawals 214A(1) This section has effect in relation to a person who is or has been a member of a limited liability partnership where, in the course of the winding up of that limited liability partnership, it appears that subsection (2) of this section applies in relation to that person. (2) This subsection applies in relation to a person if— (a) within the period of two years ending with the commencement of the winding up, he was a member of the limited liability partnership who withdrew property of the limited liability partnership, whether in the form of a share of profits, salary, repayment of or payment of interest on a loan to the limited liability partnership or any other withdrawal of property, and (b) it is proved by the liquidator to the satisfaction of the court that at the time of the withdrawal he knew or had reasonable grounds for believing that the limited liability partnership— (i) was at the time of the withdrawal unable to pay its debts within the meaning of section 123 of the Act, or (ii) would become so unable to pay its debts after the assets of the limited liability partnership had been depleted by that withdrawal taken together with all other withdrawals (if any) made by any members contemporaneously with that withdrawal or in contemplation when that withdrawal was made.

Provisions	Modifications
	(3) Where this section has effect in relation to any person the court, on the application of the liquidator, may declare that that person is to be liable to make such contribution (if any) to the limited liability partnership's assets as the court thinks proper. (4) The court shall not make a declaration in relation to any person the amount of which exceeds the aggregate of the amounts or values of all the withdrawals referred to in subsection (2) made by that person within the period of 2 years referred to in that subsection.
	(5) The court shall not make a declaration under this section with respect to any person unless that person knew or ought to have concluded that after each withdrawal referred to in subsection (2) there was no reasonable prospect that the limited liability partnership would avoid going into insolvent liquidation.

	(6) For the purposes of subsection (5) the facts which a member ought to know or ascertain, the conclusions which he ought to reach and the steps which he ought to have taken are those which would be known or ascertained, or reached or taken, by a reasonably diligent person having both:
	
	    (a) the general knowledge, skill and experience that may reasonably be expected of a person carrying out the same functions as are carried out by that member in relation to the limited liability partnership, and
	
	    (b) the general knowledge, skill and experience that that member has.
	
	(7) For the purposes of this section a limited liability partnership goes into insolvent liquidation if it goes into liquidation at a time when its assets are insufficient for the payment of its debts and other liabilities and the expenses of the winding up.
	
	(8) In this section "member" includes a shadow member.
	
	(9) This section is without prejudice to section 214."

Section 215 (proceedings under ss 213, 214)	
subsection (1)	Omit the word "or" between the words "213" and "214" and insert after "214" "or 214A".
subsection (2)	For "either section" substitute "any of those sections".
subsection (4)	For "either section" substitute "any of those sections".
subsection (5)	For "Sections 213 and 214" substitute "Sections 213, 214 or 214A".
Section 218 (prosecution of delinquent officers and members of company)	
subsection (1)	For "officer, or any member, of the company" substitute "member of the limited liability partnership"
subsections (4) and (6)	For "officer of the company, or any member of it," substitute "officer or member of the limited liability partnership".
Section 251 (expressions used generally)	
	Delete the word "and" appearing after the definition of "the rules" and insert the word "and" after the definition of "shadow director".

Provisions	Modifications
	After the definition of "shadow director" insert the following— " "shadow member", in relation to a limited liability partnership, means a person in accordance with whose directions or instructions the members of the limited liability partnership are accustomed to act (but so that a person is not deemed a shadow member by reason only that the members of the limited liability partnership act on advice given by him in a professional capacity);"
Section 416 (monetary limits (companies winding up))	
subsection (1)	In subsection (1), omit the words "section 117(2) (amount of company's share capital determining whether county court has jurisdiction to wind it up);" and the words "section 120(3) (the equivalent as respects sheriff court jurisdiction in Scotland);".
Section 436 (expressions used generally)	
	The following expressions and definitions shall be added to the section— "designated member" has the same meaning as it has in the Limited Liability Partnerships Act 2000; "limited liability partnership" means a limited liability partnership formed and registered under the Limited Liability Partnership Act 2000; "limited liability partnership agreement", in relation to a limited liability partnership, means any agreement, express or implied, made between the members of the limited liability partnership or between the limited liability partnership and the members of the limited liability partnership which determines the mutual rights and duties of the members, and their rights and duties in relation to the limited liability partnership.
Schedule 2	
Paragraph 17	For paragraph 17 substitute the following— "**17.** Power to enforce any rights the limited liability partnership has against the members under the terms of the limited liability partnership agreement"
Schedule 10	
Section 93(3)	In the entry relating to section 93(3) for "general meeting of the company" substitute "meeting of members of the limited liability partnership".
Section 105(3)	In the entry relating to section 105(3) for "company general meeting" substitute "meeting of the members of the limited liability partnership".
Section 106(6)	In the entry relating to section 106(6) for "company" substitute "the members of the limited liability partnership"

History
The entry relating to s.84 amended and that to s.233 omitted by the Limited Liability Partnerships (Scotland) Amendment Regulations 2009 (SSI 2009/310) reg.4 and Sch.2 as from 1 October 2009.

SCHEDULE 4

GENERAL AND CONSEQUENTIAL AMENDMENTS IN OTHER LEGISLATION

Regulation 5

[Not reproduced.]

Limited Liability Partnerships Regulations 2001

(SI 2001/1090)

Made on 19 March 2001 by the Secretary of State under ss.14, 15, 16 and 17 of the Limited Liability Partnerships Act 2000. Operative from 6 April 2001.

[**Note:** Changes made by the Financial Services and Markets Act 2000 (Consequential Amendments) Order 2004 (SI 2004/355), the Limited Liability Partnerships (Amendment) Regulations 2005 (SI 2005/1989) (in this latter case, minor amendments to Sch.3 have been made without annotation), the Limited Liability Partnerships (Amendment) Regulations 2007 (SI 2007/2073), the Limited Liability Partnerships (Accounts and Audit) (Application of Companies Act 2006) Regulations 2008 (SI 2008/1911), the Limited Liability Partnerships (Application of Companies Act 2006) Regulations 2009 (SI 2009/1804), the Companies Act 2006 (Consequential Amendments, Transitional Provisions and Savings) Order 2009 (SI 2009/1941), the Insolvency (Protection of Essential Supplies) Order 2015 (SI 2015/989), the Deregulation Act 2015 (Insolvency) (Consequential Amendments and Transitional and Savings Provisions) Order 2015 (SI 2015/1641), the Enterprise and Regulatory Reform Act 2013 (Consequential Amendments) (Bankruptcy) and the Small Business, Enterprise and Employment Act 2015 (Consequential Amendments) Regulations 2016 (SI 2016/481) and the Insolvency (Miscellaneous Amendments) Regulations 2017 SI 2017/1119) have been incorporated into the text (in the case of pre-2003 legislation without annotation). On the registration of charges by LLPs, see the note to the Companies Act 2006 Pt 25.]

PART I

CITATION, COMMENCEMENT AND INTERPRETATION

1 Citation and commencement

1 These Regulations may be cited as the Limited Liability Partnerships Regulations 2001 and shall come into force on 6th April 2001.

2 Interpretation

2 In these Regulations–

"the 1985 Act" means the Companies Act 1985;

"the 1986 Act" means the Insolvency Act 1986;

"the 2000 Act" means the Financial Services and Markets Act 2000;

"devolved", in relation to the provisions of the 1986 Act, means the provisions of the 1986 Act which are listed in Schedule 4 and, in their application to Scotland, concern wholly or partly, matters which are set out in Section C.2 of Schedule 5 to the Scotland Act 1998 as being exceptions to the reservations made in that Act in the field of insolvency;

"limited liability partnership agreement", in relation to a limited liability partnership, means any agreement express or implied between the members of the limited liability partnership or between the limited liability partnership and the members of the limited liability partnership which determines the mutual rights and duties of the members, and their rights and duties in relation to the limited liability partnership;

"the principal Act" means the Limited Liability Partnerships Act 2000; and

"shadow member", in relation to limited liability partnerships, means a person in accordance with whose directions or instructions the members of the limited liability partnership are accustomed to act (but so that a person is not deemed a shadow member by reason only that the members of the limited partnership act on advice given by him in a professional capacity).

2A Application of provisions

2A(1) The provisions of these Regulations applying–

  (a) the Company Directors Disqualification Act 1986, or

  (b) provisions of the Insolvency Act 1986,

have effect only in relation to limited liability partnerships registered in Great Britain.

2A(2) The other provisions of these Regulations have effect in relation to limited liability partnerships registered in any part of the United Kingdom.

History

Regulation 2A inserted by the Limited Liability Partnerships (Application of Companies Act 2006) Regulations 2009 (SI 2009/1804) Sch.3 Pt 2 para.13(1), (2) as from 1 October 2009.

PART II

ACCOUNTS AND AUDIT

3 Application of the accounts and audit provisions of the 1985 Act to limited liability partnerships

3 [Revoked by the Limited Liability Partnerships (Accounts and Audit) (Application of Companies Act 2006) Regulations 2008 (SI 2008/1911) reg.58 as from 1 October 2008.]

PART III

COMPANIES ACT 1985 AND COMPANY DIRECTORS DISQUALIFICATION ACT 1986

4 Application of certain provisions of the 1985 Act and of the provisions of the Company Directors Disqualification Act 1986 to limited liability partnerships

4(1) The provisions of the 1985 Act specified in the first column of Part I of Schedule 2 to these Regulations shall apply to limited liability partnerships, except where the context otherwise requires, with the following modifications–

  (a) references to a company shall include references to a limited liability partnership;

  (b) [Omitted]

  (c) references to the Insolvency Act 1986 shall include references to that Act as it applies to limited liability partnerships by virtue of Part IV of these Regulations;

  (d) references in a provision of the 1985 Act to–

    (i) other provisions of that Act, or

    (ii) provisions of the Companies Act 2006,

  shall include references to those provisions as they apply to limited liability partnerships;

  (e), (f) [Omitted]

  (g) references to a director of a company or to an officer of a company shall include references to a member of a limited liability partnership;

  (h) the modifications, if any, specified in the second column of Part I of Schedule 2 opposite the provision specified in the first column; and

  (i) such further modifications as the context requires for the purpose of giving effect to that legislation as applied by these Regulations.

4(2)   The provisions of the Company Directors Disqualification Act 1986 shall apply to limited liability partnerships, except where the context otherwise requires, with the following modifications–

(a)   references to a company shall include references to a limited liability partnership;

(b)   references to the Companies Acts shall include references to the principal Act and regulations made thereunder and references to the companies legislation shall include references to the principal Act, regulations made thereunder and to any enactment applied by regulations to limited liability partnerships;

(d)   references to the Insolvency Act 1986 shall include references to that Act as it applies to limited liability partnerships by virtue of Part IV of these Regulations;

(e)   [Omitted by the Companies Act 2006 (Consequential Amendments, Transitional Provisions and Savings) Order 2009 (SI 2009/1941) art.2(1) and Sch.1 para.192(2), as from 1 October 2009.]

(f)   references to a shadow director shall include references to a shadow member;

(g)   references to a director of a company or to an officer of a company shall include references to a member of a limited liability partnership;

(h)   the modifications, if any, specified in the second column of Part II of Schedule 2 opposite the provision specified in the first column; and

(i)   such further modifications as the context requires for the purpose of giving effect to that legislation as applied by these Regulations.

History
Regulation 4 (heading) amended, reg.4(1)(b), (e), (f) omitted and reg.4(1)(d) substituted by the Limited Liability Partnerships (Application of Companies Act 2006) Regulations 2009 (SI 2009/1804) Sch.3 Pt 2 para.13(3) and the Companies Act 2006 (Consequential Amendments, Transitional Provisions and Savings) Order 2009 (SI 2009/1941) Sch.1 para.192(2) as from 1 October 2009.

PART IV

WINDING UP AND INSOLVENCY

5   Application of the 1986 Act to limited liability partnerships

5(1)   Subject to paragraphs (2) and (3), the following provisions of the 1986 Act, shall apply to limited liability partnerships–

(a)   Parts I, II, III, IV, VI and VII of the First Group of Parts (company insolvency; companies winding up),

(b)   the Third Group of Parts (miscellaneous matters bearing on both company and individual insolvency; general interpretation; final provisions).

5(2)   The provisions of the 1986 Act referred to in paragraph (1) shall apply to limited liability partnerships, except where the context otherwise requires, with the following modifications–

(a)   references to a company shall include references to a limited liability partnership;

(b)   references to a director or to an officer of a company shall include references to a member of a limited liability partnership;

(c)   references to a shadow director shall include references to a shadow member;

(d)   references to the Companies Acts, the Company Directors Disqualification Act 1986, the Companies Act 1989 or to any provisions of those Acts or to any provisions of the 1986 Act shall include references to those Acts or provisions as they apply to limited liability partnerships by virtue of the principal Act;

(e)   references to the articles of association of a company shall include references to the limited liability partnership agreement of a limited liability partnership;

(f)   the modifications set out in Schedule 3 to these Regulations; and

(g)   such further modifications as the context requires for the purpose of giving effect to that legislation as applied by these Regulations.

5(3)   In the application of this regulation to Scotland, the provisions of the 1986 Act referred to in paragraph (1) shall not include the provisions listed in Schedule 4 to the extent specified in that Schedule.

PART V

FINANCIAL SERVICES AND MARKETS

6   Application of provisions contained in Parts XV and XXIV of the 2000 Act to limited liability partnerships

6(1)   Subject to paragraph (2), sections 215(3),(4) and (6), 356, 359(1) to (4), 361 to 365, 367, 370 and 371 of the 2000 Act shall apply to limited liability partnerships.

6(2)   The provisions of the 2000 Act referred to in paragraph (1) shall apply to limited liability partnerships, except where the context otherwise requires, with the following modifications–

(a)   references to a company shall include references to a limited liability partnership;

(b)   references to body shall include references to a limited liability partnership; and

(c)   references to the 1985 Act, the 1986 Act or to any of the provisions of those Acts shall include references to those Acts or provisions as they apply to limited liability partnerships by virtue of the principal Act.

PART VI

DEFAULT PROVISION

7   Default provision for limited liability partnerships

7   The mutual rights and duties of the members and the mutual rights and duties of the limited liability partnership and the members shall be determined, subject to the provisions of the general law and to the terms of any limited liability partnership agreement, by the following rules:

7(1)   All the members of a limited liability partnership are entitled to share equally in the capital and profits of the limited liability partnership.

7(2)   The limited liability partnership must indemnify each member in respect of payments made and personal liabilities incurred by him–

(a)   in the ordinary and proper conduct of the business of the limited liability partnership; or

(b)   in or about anything necessarily done for the preservation of the business or property of the limited liability partnership.

7(3)   Every member may take part in the management of the limited liability partnership.

7(4)   No member shall be entitled to remuneration for acting in the business or management of the limited liability partnership.

7(5)   No person may be introduced as a member or voluntarily assign an interest in a limited liability partnership without the consent of all existing members.

7(6)   Any difference arising as to ordinary matters connected with the business of the limited liability partnership may be decided by a majority of the members, but no change may be made in the nature of the business of the limited liability partnership without the consent of all the members.

7(7)   The books and records of the limited liability partnership are to be made available for inspection at the registered office of the limited liability partnership or at such other place as the members think fit and every member of the limited liability partnership may when he thinks fit have access to and inspect and copy any of them.

7(8)   Each member shall render true accounts and full information of all things affecting the limited liability partnership to any member or his legal representatives.

7(9)   If a member, without the consent of the limited liability partnership, carries on any business of the same nature as and competing with the limited liability partnership, he must account for and pay over to the limited liability partnership all profits made by him in that business.

7(10)   Every member must account to the limited liability partnership for any benefit derived by him without the consent of the limited liability partnership from any transaction concerning the limited liability partnership, or from any use by him of the property of the limited liability partnership, name or business connection.

8   Expulsion

8   No majority of the members can expel any member unless a power to do so has been conferred by express agreement between the members.

PART VII

MISCELLANEOUS

9   General and consequential amendments

9(1)   Subject to paragraph (2), the enactments mentioned in Schedule 5 shall have effect subject to the amendments specified in that Schedule.

9(2)   In the application of this regulation to Scotland–

(a)   paragraph 15 of Schedule 5 which amends section 110 of the 1986 Act shall not extend to Scotland; and

(b)   paragraph 22 of Schedule 5 which applies to limited liability partnerships the culpable officer provisions in existing primary legislation shall not extend to Scotland insofar as it relates to matters which have not been reserved by Schedule 5 to the Scotland Act 1998.

10   Application of subordinate legislation

10(1)   The subordinate legislation specified in Schedule 6 shall apply as from time to time in force to limited liability partnerships and–

(a)   in the case of the subordinate legislation listed in Part I of that Schedule with such modifications as the context requires for the purpose of giving effect to the provisions of the Companies Act 1985 which are applied by these Regulations;

(b)   in the case of the subordinate legislation listed in Part II of that Schedule with such modifications as the context requires for the purpose of giving effect to the provisions of the Insolvency Act 1986 which are applied by these Regulations; and

(c)   in the case of the subordinate legislation listed in Part III of that Schedule with such modifications as the context requires for the purpose of giving effect to the provisions of the Company Directors Disqualification Act 1986 which are applied by these Regulations.

10(2)   In the case of any conflict between any provision of the subordinate legislation applied by paragraph (1) and any provision of these Regulations, the latter shall prevail.

History
Regulation 10(1)(c) amended by the Limited Liability Partnerships (Application of Companies Act 2006) Regulations 2009 (SI 2009/1804) as from 1 October 2009.

SCHEDULE 1

MODIFICATIONS TO PROVISIONS OF PART VII OF THE 1985 ACT APPLIED BY THESE REGULATIONS

[Revoked by the Limited Liability Partnerships (Accounts and Audit) (Application of Companies Act 2006) Regulations 2008 (SI 2008/1911) reg.58 as from 1 October 2008.]

SCHEDULE 2

Regulation 4

PART I

MODIFICATIONS TO PROVISIONS OF THE 1985 ACT APPLIED TO LIMITED LIABILITY PARTNERSHIPS

Provisions	*Modifications*
Investigation of companies and their affairs: Requisition of documents	
431 (investigation of a company on its own application or that of its members)	For subsection (2) substitute the following: "(2)—The appointment may be made on the application of the limited liability partnership or on the application of not less than one-fifth in number of those who appear from notifications made to the registrar of companies to be currently members of the limited liability partnership."
432 (other company investigations)	
subsection (4)	For the words "but to whom shares in the company have been transferred or transmitted by operation of law" substitute "but to whom a member's share in the limited liability partnership has been transferred or transmitted by operation of law."
433 (inspectors' powers during investigation)	
434 (production of documents and evidence to inspectors)	

Provisions	Modifications
436 (obstruction of inspectors treated as contempt of court)	
437 (inspectors' reports)	
439 (expenses of investigating a company's affairs)	
subsection (5)	Omit paragraph (b) together with the word "or" at the end of paragraph (a).
441 (inspectors' report to be evidence)	
section 446A (general powers to give directions)	
section 446B (direction to terminate investigation)	
section 446C (resignation and revocation of appointment)	
section 446D (appointment of replacement inspectors)	
section 446E (obtaining information from former inspectors etc)	
447 (Secretary of State's power to require production of documents)	
447A (information provided: evidence)	
448 (entry and search of premises)	
448A (protection in relation to certain disclosures: information provided to Secretary of State)	
449 (provision for security of information obtained)	
450 (punishment for destroying, mutilating etc. company documents)	Omit subsection (1A).
451 (punishment for furnishing false information)	

Provisions	Modifications
451A (disclosure of information by Secretary of State or inspector)	In subsection (1), for the words "sections 434 to 446E" substitute "sections 434 to 441 and 446E". Omit subsection (5).
452 (privileged information)	In subsection (1), for the words "sections 431 to 446E" substitute "sections 431 to 441 and 446E". In subsection (1A), for the words "sections 434, 443 or 446" substitute "section 434".
453A (power to enter and remain on premises)	In subsection (7), for the words "section 431, 432 or 442" substitute "section 431 or 432.
453B (power to enter and remain on premises: procedural)	
453C (failure to comply with certain requirements)	
Fraudulent Trading	
458 (punishment for fraudulent trading)	
Floating Charges and Receivers (Scotland)	
464 (ranking of floating charges)	In subsection (1), for the words "section 462" substitute "the law of Scotland".
466 (alteration of floating charges)	Omit subsections (1), (2), (3) and (6).
486 (interpretation for Part XVIII generally)	For the current definition of "company" substitute " "company" means a limited liability partnership;" Omit the definition of "Register of Sasines"
487 (extent of Part XVIII)	
Schedule 15C (security of information obtained: specified persons)	
Schedule 15D (security of information obtained: specified disclosures)	

History
Entries for ss.447A, 448A and 453A–453C inserted by the Limited Liability Partnerships (Amendment) Regulations 2007 (SI 2007/2073) reg.2 as from 1 October 2007. The modification to s.450 substituted as from 4 March 2004 by the Financial Services and Markets Act 2000 (Consequential Amendments) Order 2004 (SI 2004/355). Schedule 2 Pt 1 extensively amended by the Limited Liability Partnerships (Application of Companies Act 2006) Regulations 2009 (SI 2009/1804) Sch.3 Pt 2 para.13(5) as from 1 October 2009.

Part II

Modifications to the Company Directors Disqualification Act 1986

[Omitted]

History
Schedule 2 Pt II omitted by the Insolvency (Miscellaneous Amendments) Regulations 2017 (SI 2017/1119) regs 1(1), (2), 2, Sch.1 paras 4, 5 as from 8 December 2017.

Schedule 3

Modifications to the 1986 Act

Regulation 5

Provisions	Modifications
Section 1 (those who may propose an arrangement)	
subsection (1)	For "The directors of a company" substitute "A limited liability partnership" and delete "to the company and".
subsection (3)	At the end add "but where a proposal is so made it must also be made to the limited liability partnership".
Section 1A (moratorium)	
subsection (1)	For "the directors of an eligible company intend" substitute "an eligible limited liability partnership intends". For "they" substitute "it".
The following modifications to sections 2 to 7 apply where a proposal under section 1 has been made by the limited liability partnership.	
Section 2 (procedure where the nominee is not the liquidator or administrator)	
subsection (1)	For "the directors do" substitute "the limited liability partnership does".
subsection (2)	In paragraph (b) omit "a meeting of the company and by". Omit paragraph (c).

Provisions	Modifications
subsection (3)	For "the person intending to make the proposal" substitute "the designated members of the limited liability partnership".
subsection (4)	In paragraph (a) for "the person intending to make the proposal" substitute "the designated members of the limited liability partnership". In paragraph (b) for "that person" substitute "those designated members".
Section 3 (summoning of meetings)	
subsection (1)	For subsection (1) substitute– "(1) Where the nominee under section 1 is not the liquidator or administrator, and it has been reported to the court under section 2(2) that the proposal should be considered by the creditors of the limited liability partnership, the person making the report shall (unless the court otherwise directs) seek a decision from the creditors of the limited liability partnership as to whether they approve the proposal.".
subsection (2)	Omit paragraph (a).
Section 4 (decisions of meetings)	
subsection (1)	Omit paragraph (a).
subsection (1A)	For "The company and its creditors" substitute "The creditors of the limited liability partnership".
subsection (3)	For "Neither the company nor its creditors" substitute "The creditors of the limited liability partnership may not".
subsection (4)	For "Neither the company nor its creditors" substitute "The creditors of the limited liability partnership may not".
subsection (5)	Omit "the meeting of the company and".
new subsection (5A)	Insert a new subsection (5A) as follows– "(5A) If modifications to the proposal are proposed by creditors, the nominee under section 1(2) must, before the date on which the creditors are to be asked whether to approve the proposed voluntary

Provisions	Modifications
	arrangement, ascertain from the limited liability partnership whether or not it agrees to the proposed modifications; and if at that date the limited liability partnership has failed to respond to a proposed modification, it shall be presumed not to have agreed to it."
subsection (6)	Omit.
subsection (6A)	In paragraph (a) after "creditors' decision" insert "(including, where modifications to the proposal were proposed, the response of the limited liability partnership)". In paragraph (b) after "be prescribed" insert "and to the limited liability partnership".
Section 4A (approval of arrangement)	
subsection (2)	In paragraph (a) for "meeting of the company summoned under section 3 and by the company's creditors pursuant to that section, or", substitute "the creditors of the limited liability partnership pursuant to section 3"; Omit paragraph (b).
subsection (3)	Omit.
subsection (4)	Omit.
subsection (5)	Omit.
subsection (5A)	Omit.
subsection (6)	Omit.
Section 5 (effect of approval)	
subsection (4)	In paragraph (a) for "each of the reports required by section 4(6) and (6A)" substitute "the report required by section 4(6A)".
Section 6 (challenge of decisions)	
subsection (1)	In paragraph (b) omit "the meeting of the company, or in relation to".

Provisions	Modifications
subsection (2)	In paragraph (a) omit "at the meeting of the company or". After paragraph (aa) insert a new paragraph as follows– "(ab) any member of the limited liability partnership; and". Omit the word "and" at the end of paragraph (b). Omit paragraph (c).
subsection (3)	In paragraph (a) for "each for the reports required by section 4(6) and (6A)" substitute "the report required by section 4(6A)".
subsection (4)	For subsection (4) substitute the following– "(4) Where on such an application the court is satisfied as to either of the grounds mentioned in subsection (1), it may do either of the following, namely– (a) revoke or suspend any decision approving the voluntary arrangement which has effect under section 4A or, in a case falling within subsection (1)(b) any decision taken in the relevant qualifying decision procedure which has effect under that section; (b) direct any person– (i) to seek a decision from the creditors of the limited liability partnership, using a qualifying decision procedure, as to whether they approve any revised proposal the person who made the original proposal may make; or (ii) in a case falling within subsection (1)(b) and relating to the relevant qualifying decision procedure, to seek a decision from the creditors of the limited liability partnership, using a qualifying decision procedure, as to whether they approve the original proposal."
subsection (5)	Omit "or (c)".
subsection (7)	Omit paragraph (a).

Provisions	Modifications
Section 6A (false representations, etc)	
subsection (1)	Omit "members or".
Section 7 (implementation of proposal)	
subsection (2)	In paragraph (a) for "company or its creditors (or both)" substitute "creditors of the limited liability partnership".
The following modifications to sections 2 and 3 apply where a proposal under section 1 has been made, where the limited liability partnership is in administration, by the administrator or, where the limited liability partnership is being wound up, by the liquidator.	
Section 2 (procedure where the nominee is not the liquidator or administrator)	
subsection (2)	In paragraph (a) for "the company" substitute "members of the limited liability partnership".
Section 3 (summoning of meetings)	
subsection (2)	In paragraph (a) for "the company" substitute "members of the limited liability partnership".
[Item relating to s.73(1) omitted]	
Section 74 (liability as contributories of present and past members)	
For section 74 there shall be substituted the following–	"**74** When a limited liability partnership is wound up every present and past member of the limited liability partnership who has agreed with the other members or with the limited liability partnership that he will, in circumstances which have arisen, be liable to contribute to the assets of the limited liability partnership in the event that the limited liability partnership goes into liquidation is liable, to the extent that he has so agreed, to contribute to its assets to any amount sufficient for payment of its debts and liabilities, and the expenses of the winding up, and for the adjustment of the rights of the contributories among themselves. However, a past member shall only be liable if the obligation arising from such agreement survived his ceasing to be a member of the limited liability partnership."

Provisions	Modifications
Section 75 to 78	Delete sections 75 to 78.
Section 79 (meaning of "contributory")	
subsection (1)	In subsection (1) for "every person" substitute "(a) every present member of the limited liability partnership and (b) every past member of the limited liability partnership".
subsection (2)	After "section 214 (wrongful trading)" insert "or 214A (adjustment of withdrawals)".
subsection (3)	Delete subsection (3).
Section 83 (companies registered under Companies Act, Part XXII, Chapter II)	Delete Section 83.
Section 84 (circumstances in which company may be wound up voluntarily)	
subsection (1)	For subsection (1) substitute the following– "(1) A limited liability partnership may be wound up voluntarily when it determines that it is to be wound up voluntarily."
subsection (2)	Omit subsection (2).
subsection (2A)	For "company passes a resolution for voluntary winding up" substitute "limited liability partnership determines that it is to be wound up voluntarily" and for "resolution" where it appears for the second time substitute "determination".
subsection (2B)	For "resolution for voluntary winding up may be passed only" substitute "determination to wind up voluntarily may only be made" and in sub-paragraph (b), for "passing of the resolution" substitute "making of the determination".
subsection (3)	For subsection (3) substitute the following– "(3) Within 15 days after a limited liability partnership has determined that it be wound up there shall be forwarded to the registrar of companies either a printed copy or else a copy in some other form approved by the registrar of the determination."

Provisions	**Modifications**
subsection (4)	After subsection (4) insert a new subsection (5)– "(5) If a limited liability partnership fails to comply with this regulation the limited liability partnership and every designated member of it who is in default is liable on summary conviction to a fine not exceeding level 3 on the standard scale."
Section 85 (notice of resolution to wind up)	
subsection (1)	For subsection (1) substitute the following– "(1) When a limited liability partnership has determined that it shall be would up voluntarily, it shall within 14 days after the making of the determination give notice of the determination by advertisement in the Gazette."
Section 86 (commencement of winding up)	
	Substitute the following new section– "**86.** A voluntary winding up is deemed to commence at the time when the limited liability partnership determines that it be wound up voluntarily.".
Section 87 (effect on business and status of company)	
subsection (2)	In subsection (2), for "articles" substitute "limited liability partnership agreement".
Section 88 (avoidance of share transfers, etc. after winding-up resolution)	
	For "shares" substitute "the interest of any member in the property of the limited liability partnership".
Section 89 (statutory declaration of solvency)	
	For "director(s)" wherever it appears in section 89 substitute "designated member(s)";

Provisions	Modifications
subsection (2)	For paragraph (a) substitute the following– "(a) it is made within the 5 weeks immediately preceding the date when the limited liability partnership determined that it be wound up voluntarily or on that date but before the making of the determination, and".
subsection (3)	For "the resolution for winding up is passed" substitute "the limited liability partnership determined that it be wound up voluntarily".
subsection (5)	For "in pursuance of a resolution passed" substitute "voluntarily".
Section 90 (distinction between "members" and "creditors" voluntary winding up)	
	For "directors" substitute "designated members".
Section 91 (appointment of liquidator)	
subsection (1)	Delete "in general meeting".
subsection (2)	For the existing wording substitute "(2) On the appointment of a liquidator the powers of the members of the limited liability partnership shall cease except to the extent that a meeting of the members of the limited liability partnership summoned for the purpose or the liquidator sanctions their continuance."
	After subsection (2) insert– "(3) Subsections (3) and (4) of section 92 shall apply for the purposes of this section as they apply for the purposes of that section."
Section 92 (power to fill vacancy in office of liquidator)	
subsection (1)	For "the company in general meeting" substitute "a meeting of the members of the limited liability partnership summoned for the purpose".
subsection (2)	For "a general meeting" substitute "a meeting of the members of the limited liability partnership".

Provisions	Modifications
subsection (3)	In subsection (3), for "articles" substitute "limited liability partnership agreement".
new subsection (4)	Add a new subsection (4) as follows– "(4) The quorum required for a meeting of the members of the limited liability partnership shall be any quorum required by the limited liability partnership agreement for meetings of the members of the limited liability partnership and if no requirement for a quorum has been agreed upon the quorum shall be 2 members."
[Items relating to s.94(1), (5A), (6) omitted]	
Section 95 (effect of company's insolvency)	
subsection (1)	For "directors'" substitute "designated members'".
subsection (7)	[Omitted]
Section 96 (conversion to creditors' voluntary winding up)	
subsection (2)	For "directors'" substitute "designated members'".
[Items relating to s.98(1), (2) omitted]	
Section 99 (directors to lay statement of affairs before creditors)	
subsection (1)	For "directors of the company" substitute "designated members".
subsection (2A)	For "directors" substitute "designated members".
subsection (3)	For "directors" substitute "designated members".
Section 100 (appointment of liquidator)	
subsection (1)	For subsection (1) substitute the following– "(1) The members of the limited liability partnership may nominate a person to be liquidator at the meeting at which the resolution for voluntary winding up is passed."

Provisions	Modifications
subsection (1B)	For "directors of the company" substitute "designed members".
subsection (3)	Delete "director,".
Section 101 (appointment of liquidation committee)	
subsection (2)	For subsection (2) substitute the following– "(2) If such a committee is appointed, the limited liability partnership may, when it determines that it be wound up voluntarily or at any time thereafter, appoint such number of persons as they think fit to act as members of the committee, not exceeding 5."
Section 106 (final meeting prior to dissolution)	
subsection (1)	[Omitted]
new subsection (5A)	After subsection (5) insert a new subsection (5A) as follows– "(5A) Subsections (3) and (4) of section 92 shall apply for the purposes of this section as they apply for the purposes of that section."
subsection (6)	For "a general meeting of the company" substitute "a meeting of the members of the limited liability partnership".
Section 110 (acceptance of shares, etc., as consideration for sale of company property)	
	For the existing section substitute the following: "(1) This section applies, in the case of a limited liability partnership proposed to be, or being, wound up voluntarily, where the whole or part of the limited liability partnership's business or property is proposed to be transferred or sold to another company whether or not it is a company within the meaning of the Companies Act ("the transferee company") or to a limited liability partnership ("the transferee limited liability partnership").

Provisions	Modifications
	(2) With the requisite sanction, the liquidator of the limited liability partnership being, or proposed to be, wound up ("the transferor limited liability partnership") may receive, in compensation or part compensation for the transfer or sale, shares, policies or other like interests in the transferee company or the transferee limited liability partnership for distribution among the members of the transferor limited liability partnership.
	(3) The sanction required under subsection (2) is–
	(a) in the case of a members' voluntary winding up, that of a determination of the limited liability partnership at a meeting of the members of the limited liability partnership conferring either a general authority on the liquidator or an authority in respect of any particular arrangement, (subsections (3) and (4) of section 92 to apply for this purpose as they apply for the purposes of that section), and
	(b) in the case of a creditor's voluntary winding up, that of either court or the liquidation committee.
	(4) Alternatively to subsection (2), the liquidator may (with the sanction) enter into any other arrangement whereby the members of the transferor limited liability partnership may, in lieu of receiving cash, shares, policies or other like interests (or in addition thereto), participate in the profits, or receive any other benefit from the transferee company or the transferee limited liability partnership.
	(5) A sale or arrangement in pursuance of this section is binding on members of the transferor limited liability partnership.
	(6) A determination by the limited liability partnership is not invalid for the purposes of this section by reason that it is made before or concurrently with a determination by the limited liability partnership that it be wound up voluntarily or for appointing liquidators; but, if an order is made within a year for winding up the limited liability partnership by the court, the determination by the limited liability partnership is not valid unless sanctioned by the court."

Provisions	Modifications
Section 111 (dissent from arrangement under section 110)	
subsections (1)–(3)	For subsections (1)–(3) substitute the following– "(1) This section applies in the case of a voluntary winding up where, for the purposes of section 110(2) or (4), a determination of the limited liability partnership has provided the sanction requisite for the liquidator under that section. (2) If a member of the transferor limited liability partnership who did not vote in favour of providing the sanction required for the liquidator under section 110 expresses his dissent from it in writing addressed to the liquidator and left at the registered office of the limited liability partnership within 7 days after the date on which that sanction was given, he may require the liquidator either to abstain from carrying the arrangement so sanctioned into effect or to purchase his interest at a price to be determined by agreement or arbitration under this section. (3) If the liquidator elects to purchase the member's interest, the purchase money must be paid before the limited liability partnership is dissolved and be raised by the liquidator in such manner as may be determined by the limited liability partnership."
subsection (4)	Omit subsection (4).
Section 117 (high court and county court jurisdiction)	
subsection (2)	Delete "Where the amount of a company's share capital paid up or credited as paid up does not exceed £120,000, then (subject to this section)".
subsection (3)	Delete subsection (3).
Section 120 (court of session and sheriff court jurisdiction)	
subsection (3)	Delete "Where the amount of a company's share capital paid up or credited as paid up does not exceed £120,000,".

Provisions	Modifications
subsection (5)	Delete subsection (5).
Section 122 (circumstances in which company may be wound up by the court)	
subsection (1)	For subsection (1) substitute the following– "(1) A limited liability partnership may be wound up by the court if– (a) the limited liability partnership has determined that the limited liability partnership be wound up by the court, (b) the limited liability partnership does not commence its business within a year from its incorporation or suspends its business for a whole year, (c) the number of members is reduced below two, (d) the limited liability partnership is unable to pay its debts, (da) at the time at which a moratorium for the limited liability partnership under section 1A comes to an end, no voluntary arrangement approved under Part I has effect in relation to the limited liability partnership, (e) the court is of the opinion that it is just and equitable that the limited liability partnership should be wound up."
Section 124 (application for winding up)	
subsections (2), (3) and (4)(a)	Delete these subsections.
subsection (3A)	For "122(1)(fa)" substitute "122(1)(da)".
Section 124A (petition for winding-up on grounds of public interest)	
subsection (1)	Omit paragraphs (b) and (bb).
Section 126 (power to stay or restrain proceedings against company)	
subsection (2)	Delete subsection (2).

Provisions	Modifications
Section 127 (avoidance of property dispositions, etc.)	
subsection (1)	For "any transfer of shares" substitute "any transfer by a member of the limited liability partnership of his interest in the property of the limited liability partnership".
Section 129 (commencement of winding up by the court)	
subsection (1)	For "a resolution has been passed by the company" substitute "a determination has been made" and for "at the time of the passing of the resolution" substitute "at the time of that determination".
Section 130 (consequences of winding-up order)	
subsection (3)	Delete subsection (3).
Section 148 (settlement of list of contributories and application of assets)	
subsection (1)	Delete ", with power to rectify the register of members in all cases where rectification is required in pursuance of the Companies Act or this Act,".
Section 149 (debts due from contributory to company)	
subsection (1)	Delete "the Companies Act or".
subsection (2)	Delete subsection (2).
subsection (3)	Delete ", whether limited or unlimited,".
Section 160 (delegation of powers to liquidator (England and Wales))	
subsection (1)	In subsection (1)(b) delete "and the rectifying of the register of members".
subsection (2)	For subsection (2) substitute the following– "(2) But the liquidator shall not make any call without the special leave of the court or the sanction of the liquidation committee."

Provisions	Modifications
Section 165 (voluntary winding up)	
subsection (2)	[Omitted]
subsection (4)	For paragraph (c) substitute the following– "(c) summon meetings of the members of the limited liability partnership for the purpose of obtaining their sanction or for any other purpose he may think fit."
new subsection (4A)	Insert a new subsection (4A) as follows– "(4A) Subsections (3) and (4) of section 92 shall apply for the purposes of this section as they apply for the purposes of that section."
Section 166 (creditors' voluntary winding up)	
subsection (5)	For "directors" substitute "designated members".
Section 171 (removal, etc. (voluntary winding up))	
subsection (2)	For paragraph (a) substitute the following– "(a) in the case of a members' voluntary winding up, by a meeting of the members of the limited liability partnership summoned specially for that purpose, or"
new subsection (8)	Insert a new subsection (8) as follows– "(8) subsections (3) and (4) of section 92 are to apply for the purposes of this section as they apply for the purposes of that section."
Section 173 (release (voluntary winding up))	
subsection (2)	In paragraph (a)(i) for "a general meeting of the company" substitute "a meeting of the members of the limited liability partnership".
Section 183 (effect of execution or attachment (England and Wales))	
subsection (2)	Delete paragraph (a).

Provisions	Modifications
Section 184 (duties of sheriff (England and Wales))	
subsection (1)	For "a resolution for voluntary winding up has been passed" substitute "the limited liability partnership has determined that it be wound up voluntarily".
subsection (4)	Delete "or of a meeting having been called at which there is to be proposed a resolution for voluntary winding up," and "or a resolution is passed (as the case may be)".
Section 187 (power to make over assets to employees)	
	Delete section 187.
[Item relating to s.194 omitted]	
Section 195 (meetings to ascertain wishes of creditors or contributories)	
subsection (3)	Delete "the Companies Act or".
Section 206 (fraud, etc. in anticipation of winding up)	
subsection (1)	For "passes a resolution for voluntary winding up" substitute "makes a determination that it be wound up voluntarily".
Section 207 (transactions in fraud of creditors)	
subsection (1)	For "passes a resolution for voluntary winding up" substitute "makes a determination that it be wound up voluntarily".
Section 210 (material omissions from statement relating to company's affairs)	
subsection (2)	For "passes a resolution for voluntary winding up" substitute "made a determination that it be wound up voluntarily".
Section 214 (wrongful trading)	
subsection (2)	Delete from "but the court shall not" to the end of the subsection.

Provisions	**Modifications**
After section 214	
	Insert the following new section 214A
	"214A Adjustment of withdrawals
	(1) This section has effect in relation to a person who is or has been a member of a limited liability partnership where, in the course of the winding up of that limited liability partnership, it appears that subsection (2) of this section applies in relation to that person.
	(2) This subsection applies in relation to a person if–
	(a) within the period of two years ending with the commencement of the winding up, he was a member of the limited liability partnership who withdrew property of the limited liability partnership, whether in the form of a share of profits, salary, repayment of or payment of interest on a loan to the limited liability partnership or any other withdrawal of property, and
	(b) it is proved by the liquidator to the satisfaction of the court that at the time of the withdrawal he knew or had reasonable ground for believing that the limited liability partnership–
	(i) was at the time of the withdrawal unable to pay its debts within the meaning of section 123, or
	(ii) would become so unable to pay its debts after the assets of the limited liability partnership had been depleted by that withdrawal taken together with all other withdrawals (if any) made by any members contemporaneously with that withdrawal or in contemplation when that withdrawal was made.
	(3) Where this section has effect in relation to any person the court, on the application of the liquidator, may declare that that person is to be liable to make such contribution (if any) to the limited liability partnership's assets as the court thinks proper.

Provisions	Modifications
	(4) The court shall not make a declaration in relation to any person the amount of which exceeds the aggregate of the amounts or values of all the withdrawals referred to in subsection (2) made by that person within the period of two years referred to in that subsection.
	(5) The court shall not make a declaration under this section with respect to any person unless that person knew or ought to have concluded that after each withdrawal referred to in subsection (2) there was no reasonable prospect that the limited liability partnership would avoid going into insolvent liquidation.
	(6) For the purposes of subsection (5) the facts which a member ought to know or ascertain and the conclusions which he ought to reach are those which would be known, ascertained, or reached by a reasonably diligent person having both:
	(a) the general knowledge, skill and experience that may reasonably be expected of a person carrying out the same functions as are carried out by that member in relation to the limited liability partnership, and
	(b) the general knowledge, skill and experience that that member has.
	(7) For the purposes of this section a limited liability partnership goes into insolvent liquidation if it goes into liquidation at a time when its assets are insufficient for the payment of its debts and other liabilities and the expenses of the winding up.
	(8) In this section "member" includes a shadow member.
	(9) This section is without prejudice to section 214."
Section 215 (proceedings under ss 213, 214)	
subsection (1)	Omit the word "or" between the words "213" and "214" and insert after "214" or "214A".
subsection (2)	For "either section" substitute "any of those sections".

Provisions	Modifications
subsection (4)	For "either section" substitute "any of those sections".
subsection (5)	For "Sections 213 and 214" substitute "Sections 213, 214 or 214A".
Section 218 (prosecution of delinquent officers and members of company)	
subsection (1)	For "officer, or any member, of the company" substitute "member of the limited liability partnership".
subsections (3), (4) and (6)	For "officer of the company, or any member of it," substitute "officer or member of the limited liability partnership".
Section 247 ("insolvency" and "go into liquidation")	
subsection (2)	For "passes a resolution for voluntary winding up" substitute "makes a determination that it be wound up voluntarily" and for "passing such a resolution" substitute "making such a determination".
subsection (3)	For "resolution for voluntary winding up" substitute "determination to wind up voluntarily".
Section 249 ("connected with a company")	For the existing words substitute– "For the purposes of any provision in this Group of Parts, a person is connected with a company (including a limited liability partnership) if– (a) he is a director or shadow director of a company or an associate of such a director or shadow director (including a member or a shadow member of a limited liability partnership or an associate of such a member or shadow member); or (b) he is an associate of the company or of the limited liability partnership."
Section 250 ("member" of a company)	
	Delete section 250.

Provisions	Modifications
Section 251 (expressions used generally)	
	Delete the word "and" appearing after the definition of "the rules" and insert the word "and" after the definition of "shadow director".
	After the definition of "shadow director" insert the following–
	" 'shadow member', in relation to a limited liability partnership, means a person in accordance with whose directions or instructions the members of the limited liability partnership are accustomed to act (but so that a person is not deemed a shadow member by reason only that the members of the limited liability partnership act on advice given by him in a professional capacity);".
Section 386 (categories of preferential debts)	
subsection (1)	In subsection (1), omit the words "or an individual".
subsection (2)	In subsection (2), omit the words "or the individual".
Section 387 ("the relevant date")	
subsection (3)	In paragraph (ab) for "passed a resolution for voluntary winding up" substitute "made a determination that it be wound up voluntarily".
	In paragraph (c) for "passing of the resolution for the winding up of the company" substitute "making of the determination by the limited liability partnership that it be wound up voluntarily".
subsection (5)	Omit subsection (5).
subsection (6)	Omit subsection (6).
Section 388 (meaning of "act as insolvency practitioner")	
subsection (2)	Omit subsection (2).
subsection (3)	Omit subsection (3).

Provisions	Modifications
subsection (4)	Delete " "company" means a company within the meaning given by section 735(1) of the Companies Act or a company which may be wound up under Part V of this Act (unregistered companies);" and delete " "interim trustee" and "permanent trustee" mean the same as the Bankruptcy (Scotland) Act 1985".
Section 389 (acting without qualification an offence)	
subsection (1)	Omit the words "or an individual".
Section 402 (official petitioner)	Delete section 402.
Section 412 (individual insolvency rules (England and Wales))	Delete section 412.
Section 415 (Fees orders (individual insolvency proceedings in England and Wales))	Delete section 415.
Section 416 (monetary limits (companies winding up))	
subsection (1)	In subsection (1), omit the words "section 117(2) (amount of company's share capital determining whether county court has jurisdiction to wind it up);" and the words "section 120(3) (the equivalent as respects sheriff court jurisdiction in Scotland),".
subsection (3)	In subsection (3), omit the words "117(2), 120(3) or".
Section 418 (monetary limits (bankruptcy))	Delete section 418.
Section 420 (insolvent partnerships)	
	Delete section 420.
Section 421 (insolvent estates of deceased persons)	
	Delete section 421.
Section 422 (recognised banks, etc.)	
	Delete section 422.

Provisions	Modifications
Section 426A (disqualification from Parliament (England and Wales))	Omit.
Section 426B (devolution)	Omit.
Section 426C (irrelevance of privilege)	Omit.
Section 427 (parliamentary disqualification)	Delete section 427.
Section 429 (disabilities on revocation or administration order against an individual)	
	Delete section 429.
Section 432 (offences by bodies corporate)	
subsection (2)	Delete "secretary or".
Section 435 (meaning of "associate")	
new subsection (3A)	Insert a new subsection (3A) as follows– "(3A) A member of a limited liability partnership is an associate of that limited liability partnership and of every other member of that limited liability partnership and of the husband or wife or civil partner or relative of every other member of that limited liability partnership.".
subsection (11)	For subsection (11) there shall be substituted "(11) In this section "company" includes any body corporate (whether incorporated in Great Britain or elsewhere); and references to directors and other officers of a company and to voting power at any general meeting of a company have effect with any necessary modifications."
Section 436 (expressions used generally)	
	The following expressions and definitions shall be added to the section– "designated member" has the same meaning as it has in the Limited Liability Partnerships Act 2000; "limited liability partnership" means a limited liability partnership formed and registered under the Limited Liability Partnerships Act 2000;

Provisions	Modifications
	"limited liability partnership agreement", in relation to a limited liability partnership, means any agreement, express or implied, made between the members of the limited liability partnership or between the limited liability partnership and the members of the limited liability partnership which determines the mutual rights and duties of the members, and their rights and duties in relation to the limited liability partnership.
Section 437 (transitional provisions, and savings)	Delete section 437.
Section 440 (extent (Scotland))	
subsection (2)	In subsection (2), omit paragraph (b).
Section 441 (extent (Northern Ireland))	
	Delete section 441.
Section 442 (extent (other territories))	
	Delete section 442.
Schedule A1	
Paragraph 6	
sub-paragraph (1)	For "directors of a company wish" substitute "limited liability partnership wishes". For "they" substitute "the designated members of the limited liability partnership".
sub-paragraph (2)	For "directors" substitute "designated members of the limited liability partnership". In sub-paragraph (c), for "company and by the company's creditors" substitute "creditors of the limited liability partnership".
Paragraph 7	
sub-paragraph (1)	For "directors of a company" substitute "designated members of the limited liability partnership".

Provisions	Modifications
	In sub-paragraph (e)(iii) for "company and by the company's creditors" substitute "creditors of the limited liability partnership".
Paragraph 8	
sub-paragraph (2)(a)	Omit.
sub-paragraph (3A)	Omit.
sub-paragraph (4)(a)	Omit.
sub-paragraph (6)(c)(i)	Omit.
Paragraph 9	
sub-paragraph (1)	For "directors" substitute "designated members of the limited liability partnership".
sub-paragraph (2)	For "directors" substitute "designated members of the limited liability partnership".
Paragraph 12	
sub-paragraph (1)(b)	Omit.
sub-paragraph (1)(c)	For "resolution may be passed" substitute "determination that it may be wound up may be made".
sub-paragraph (2)	For "transfer of shares" substitute "any transfer by a member of the limited liability partnership of his interest in the property of the limited liability partnership".
Paragraph 20	
sub-paragraph (8)	For "directors" substitute "designated members of the limited liability partnership".
sub-paragraph (9)	For "directors" substitute "designated members of the limited liability partnership".
Paragraph 24	
sub-paragraph (2)	For "directors" substitute "designated members of the limited liability partnership".

Provisions	*Modifications*
Paragraph 25	
sub-paragraph (2)(c)	For "directors" substitute "designated members of the limited liability partnership".
Paragraph 26	
sub-paragraph (1)	Omit ", director".
Paragraph 29	
sub-paragraph (1)(a)	Omit.
Paragraph 30	
sub-paragraph (1)	Omit "the company meeting summoned under paragraph 29 and". For "that paragraph" substitute "paragraph 29".
new sub-paragraph (1A)	"If modifications to the proposal are proposed by creditors, the nominee must, before the date on which the creditors are to be asked whether to approve the proposed voluntary arrangement, ascertain from the limited liability partnership whether or not it agrees to the proposed modifications; and if at that date the limited liability partnership has failed to respond to a proposed modification, it shall be presumed not to have agreed to it."
sub-paragraph (2)	Omit.
new sub-paragraph (2A)	[Omitted]
sub-paragraph (3)	Omit.
Paragraph 31	
sub-paragraph (1)(a)	Omit.
sub-paragraph (1A)	For "The company and its creditors" substitute "The creditors of the limited liability partnership".
sub-paragraph (4)	For "Neither the company nor its creditors may" substitute "The creditors of the limited liability partnership may not".

Provisions	Modifications
sub-paragraph (5)	For "neither the company nor its creditors may" substitute "the creditors of the limited liability partnership may not".
sub-paragraph (7)	For sub-paragraph (7) substitute the following– "(7) The designated members of the limited liability partnership may, before the beginning of the relevant period, give notice to the nominee of any modifications of the proposal for which the designated members intend to seek the approval of the creditors.".
sub-paragraph (7A)(a)	Omit.
Paragraph 32	
sub-paragraph (1)	Omit.
sub-paragraph (3)	Omit "the meeting of the company or (as the case may be) inform".
sub-paragraph (4)	For sub-paragraph (4) substitute– "(4) Where, in accordance with sub-paragraph (3)(b) the nominee informs the creditors of the limited liability partnership, of the expected cost of his intended actions, the creditors by a qualifying decision procedure shall decide whether or not to approve that expected cost.".
sub-paragraph (6)	For "A meeting of the company may resolve, and the creditors by a qualifying decision procedure may decide," substitute "The creditors by a qualifying decision procedure may decide".
Paragraph 35	
sub-paragraph (1)	Omit "a meeting of the company resolves, or".
sub-paragraph (1A)	Omit "meeting may resolve, and the". Omit "by the meeting or (as the case may be)".
sub-paragraph (2)	Omit.

Provisions	Modifications
Paragraph 36	
sub-paragraph (2)	For sub-paragraph (2) substitute– "(2) The decision has effect if, in accordance with the rules, it has been taken by the creditors' meeting summoned under paragraph 29.".
sub-paragraph (3)	Omit.
sub-paragraph (4)	Omit.
sub-paragraph (5)	Omit.
[Item relating to para.37 omitted]	
Paragraph 38	
sub-paragraph (1)(b)	Omit "at or in relation to the meeting of the company summoned under paragraph 29, or".
sub-paragraph (2)(a)	Omit "at the meeting of the company or".
sub-paragraph (3)(a)	For "30(3) and (4)" substitute "30(4)".
sub-paragraph (4)(a)(ii)	Omit "by the meeting of the company, or".
sub-paragraph (4)(b)	Omit.
sub-paragraph (5)	Omit "(b)(i) or ".
sub-paragraph (6)	For "(4)(b) or (c)" substitute "(4)(c)".
sub-paragraph (7)(a)	Omit "(b) or ".
Paragraph 39	
sub-paragraph (1)	[Omitted]
Schedule B1	
Paragraph 2	
sub-paragraph (c)	For "company or its directors" substitute "limited liability partnership".

Provisions	Modifications
Paragraph 8	
sub-paragraph (1)(a)	For "resolution for voluntary winding up" substitute "determination to wind up voluntarily".
Paragraph 9	Omit.
Paragraph 12	
sub-paragraph (1)(b)	Omit.
Paragraph 22	For sub-paragraph (1) substitute– "(1) A limited liability partnership may appoint an administrator.". Omit sub-paragraph (2).
Paragraph 23	
sub-paragraph (1)(b)	Omit "or its directors".
Paragraph 42	
sub-paragraph (2)	For "resolution may be passed for the winding up of" substitute "determination to wind up voluntarily may be made by".
Paragraph 60A	
sub-paragraph (3)(b)	For "a company connected with the company." substitute "a company or limited liability partnership connected with the limited liability partnership."
Paragraph 61	For paragraph 61 substitute– "**61.** The administrator has power to prevent any person from taking part in the management of the business of the limited liability partnership and to appoint any person to be a manager of that business.".
Paragraph 62	At the end add the following– Subsections (3) and (4) of section 92 shall apply for the purposes of this paragraph as they apply for the purposes of that section.

Provisions	Modifications
Paragraph 83	
sub-paragraph (6)(b)	For "resolution for voluntary winding up" substitute "determination to wind up voluntarily".
sub-paragraph (8)(b)	For "passing of the resolution for voluntary winding up" substitute "determination to wind up voluntarily".
sub-paragraph (8)(e)	For "passing of the resolution for voluntary winding up" substitute "determination to wind up voluntarily".
Paragraph 87	
sub-paragraph (2)(b)	Insert at the end "or".
sub-paragraph (2)(c)	Omit ", or".
sub-paragraph (2)(d)	Omit the words from "(d)" to "company".
Paragraph 89	
sub-paragraph (2)(b)	Insert at the end "or".
sub-paragraph (2)(c)	Omit ", or".
sub-paragraph (2)(d)	Omit the words from "(d)" to "company".
Paragraph 91	
sub-paragraph (1)(c)	Omit.
Paragraph 94	Omit.
Paragraph 95	For "to 94" substitute "and 93".
Paragraph 97	
sub-paragraph (1)(a)	Omit "or directors".
Paragraph 103	
sub-paragraph (5)	Omit.
Paragraph 105	Omit.

Provisions	Modifications
Schedule 1	
Paragraph 19	For paragraph 19 substitute the following– "**19.** Power to enforce any rights the limited liability partnership has against the members under the terms of the limited liability partnership agreement."
Schedule 10	
Section 6A(1)	In the entry relating to section 6A omit "members' or".
Section 85(2)	In the entry relating to section 85(2) for "resolution for voluntary winding up" substitute "making of determination for voluntary winding up".
Section 89(4)	In the entry relating to section 89(4) for "Director" substitute "Designated member".
Section 93(3)	In the entry relating to section 93(3) for "general meeting of the company" substitute "meeting of members of the limited liability partnership".
Section 99(3)	In the entries relating to section 99(3) for "director" and "directors" where they appear substitute "designated member" or "designated members" as appropriate.
Section 105(3)	In the entry relating to section 105(3) for "company general meeting" substitute "meeting of the members of the limited liability partnership".
Section 106(6)	[Omitted]
Sections 353(1) to 362	Delete the entries relating to sections 353(1) to 362 inclusive.
Section 429(5)	Delete the entry relating to section 429(5).
Schedule A1, paragraph 9(2)	For "Directors" substitute "Designated Members".
Schedule A1, paragraph 20(9)	For "Directors" substitute "Designated Members".
Schedule B1, paragraph 27(4)	Omit "or directors".

Provisions	**Modifications**
Schedule B1, paragraph 29(7)	Omit "or directors".
Schedule B1, paragraph 32	Omit "or directors".

History

The modification to s.8(1A) was revoked and the modification to s.8(5), (6) inserted as from 4 March 2004 by the Financial Services and Markets Act 2000 (Consequential Amendments) Order 2004 (SI 2004/355) art.10(2).

The modification to s.124A(1) substituted as from 4 March 2004 by the Financial Services and Markets Act 2000 (Consequential Amendments) Order 2004 (SI 2004/355) art.10(3).

Numerous minor amendments made to Sch.3 by the Limited Liability Partnerships (Amendment) Regulations 2005 (SI 2005/1989), as from 1 October 2005.

Numerous amendments made to Sch.3 by the Insolvency (Miscellaneous Amendments) Regulations 2017 (SI 2017/1119) regs 1(1)–(3), 2, Sch.1 paras 4, 6–53 as from 8 December 2017.

SCHEDULE 4

APPLICATION OF PROVISIONS TO SCOTLAND

Regulation 5(3)

The provisions listed in this Schedule are not applied to Scotland to the extent specified below:

Sections 50 to 52;

Section 53(1) and (2), to the extent that those subsections do not relate to the requirement for a copy of the instrument and notice being forwarded to the registrar of companies;

Section 53(4), (6) and (7);

Section 54(1), (2), (3) (to the extent that that subsection does not relate to the requirement for a copy of the interlocutor to be sent to the registrar of companies), and subsections (5), (6) and (7);

Sections 55 to 58;

Section 60, other than subsection (1);

Section 61, including subsections (6) and (7) to the extent that those subsections do not relate to anything to be done or which may be done to or by the registrar of companies;

Section 62, including subsection (5) to the extent that that subsection does not relate to anything to be done or which may be done to or by the registrar of companies;

Sections 63 to 66;

Section 67, including subsections (1) and (8) to the extent that those subsections do not relate to anything to be done or which may be done to the registrar of companies;

Section 68;

Section 69, including subsections (1) and (2) to the extent that those subsections do not relate to anything to be done or which may be done by the registrar of companies;

Sections 70 and 71;

Subsection 84(3), to the extent that it does not concern the copy of the resolution being forwarded to the registrar of companies within 15 days;

Sections 91 to 92A;

Section 94, including subsections (3) and (4) to the extent that those subsections do not relate to the liquidator being required to send to the registrar of companies a copy of the account and a return of the final meeting;

Section 95;

Section 97;

Sections 100 to 102;

Sections 104 to 104A;

Section 106, including subsections (3) to (7) to the extent that those subsections do not relate to the liquidator being required to send to the registrar of companies a copy of the account of winding up and a return of the final meeting/quorum or a statement about a member State liquidator;

Sections 109 to 111;

Section 112, including subsection (3) to the extent that that subsection does not relate to the liquidator being required to send to the registrar a copy of the order made by the court;

Sections 113 to 115;

Sections 126 to 128;

Section 130(1) to the extent that that subsection does not relate to a copy of the order being forwarded by the court to the registrar;

Section 131;

Sections 133 to 135;

Sections 138 to 140;

Sections 142 to 146;

Section 147, including subsection (3) to the extent that that subsection does not relate to a copy of the order being forwarded by the company to the registrar;

Section 162 to the extent that that section concerns the matters set out in Section C.2 of Schedule 5 to the Scotland Act 1998 as being exceptions to the insolvency reservation;

Sections 163 to 167;

Section 169;

Section 170, including subsection (2) to the extent that that subsection does not relate to an application being made by the registrar to make good the default;

Section 171;

Section 172, including subsections (8) to (10) to the extent that those subsections do not relate to the liquidator being required to give notice to the registrar or a statement about a member State liquidator;

Sections 173 and 174;

Section 177;

Sections 185 to 189;

Sections 191 to 194;

Section 196 to the extent that that section applies to the specified devolved functions of Part IV of the Insolvency Act 1986;

Section 199;

Section 200 to the extent that it applies to the specified devolved functions of Part IV of the First Group of Parts of the 1986 Act;

Sections 206 to 215;

Section 218 subsections (1), (2), (4) and (6);

Section 231 to 232 to the extent that the sections apply to administrative receivers, liquidators and provisional liquidators;

Section 233, to the extent that that section applies in the case of the appointment of an administrative receiver, of a voluntary arrangement taking effect, of a company going into liquidation or where a provisional liquidator is appointed;

Section 233A to the extent that that section applies in the case of a voluntary arrangement taking effect;

Section 234 to the extent that that section applies to situations other than those where an administration order applies;

Section 235 to the extent that that section applies to situations other than those where an administration order applies;

Sections 236 to 237 to the extent that those sections apply to situations other than administration orders and winding up;

Sections 242 to 243;

Section 244 to the extent that that section applies in circumstances other than a company which is subject to an administration order;

Section 245;

Section 251, to the extent that that section contains definitions which apply only to devolved matters;

Section 416(1) and (4), to the extent that those subsections apply to section 206(1)(a) and (b) in connection with the offence provision relating to the winding up of a limited liability partnership;

Schedule 2;

Schedule 3;

Schedule 4;

Schedule 8, to the extent that that Schedule does not apply to voluntary arrangements or administrations within the meaning of Parts I and II of the 1986 Act.

In addition, Schedule 10, which concerns punishment of offences under the Insolvency Act 1986, lists various sections of the Insolvency Act 1986 which create an offence. The following sections, which are listed in Schedule 10, are devolved in their application to Scotland:

Section 51(4);

Section 51(5);

Sections 53(2) to 62(5) to the extent that those subsections relate to matters other than delivery to the registrar of companies;

Section 64(2);

Section 65(4);

Section 66(6);

Section 67(8) to the extent that that subsection relates to matters other than delivery to the registrar of companies;

Section 93(3);

Section 94(4) to the extent that that subsection relates to matters other than delivery to the registrar of companies;

Section 94(6);

Section 95(8);

Section 105(3);

Section 106(4) to the extent that that subsection relates to matters other than delivery to the registrar of companies;

Section 106(6);

Section 109(2);

Section 114(4);

Section 131(7);

Section 164;

Section 166(7);

Section 188(2);

Section 192(2);

Sections 206 to 211; and

Section 235(5) to the extent that it relates to matters other than administration orders.

History
Entry for s.233A inserted by the Insolvency (Protection of Essential Supplies) Order 2015 (SI 2015/989) Sch.1 para.2 as from 1 October 2015.
  Entries in relation to ss.106 and 172 amended by the Insolvency (Miscellaneous Amendments) Regulations 2017 (SI 2017/1119) regs 1(1), (3), 2, Sch.1 paras 4, 56 as from 8 December 2017.

SCHEDULE 5

GENERAL AND CONSEQUENTIAL AMENDMENTS IN OTHER LEGISLATION

Regulation 9

[Not reproduced but noted where relevant elsewhere in this *Guide*.]

SCHEDULE 6

APPLICATION OF SUBORDINATE LEGISLATION

Regulation 10

PART I

REGULATIONS MADE UNDER THE 1985 ACT

1–3 [Revoked]

4 [Omitted]

5 [Omitted]

6   [Revoked]

7   The Companies Act 1985 (Power to Enter and Remain on Premises: Procedural) Regulations 2005

History
Paragraph 7 inserted by the Limited Liability Partnerships (Amendment) Regulations 2007 (SI 2007/2073) reg.3 as from 1 October 2007.
   Paragraphs 1–3 and 6 revoked by the Limited Liability Partnerships (Accounts and Audit) (Application of Companies Act 2006) Regulations 2008 (SI 2008/1911) reg.58 as from 1 October 2008.
   Paragraphs 4 and 5 omitted by the Limited Liability Partnerships (Application of Companies Act 2006) Regulations 2009 (SI 2009/1804) Sch.3 Pt 2 para.13(7) as from 1 October 2009.

PART II

REGULATIONS MADE UNDER THE 1986 ACT

1   Insolvency Practitioners Regulations 1990

2   The Insolvency Practitioners (Recognised Professional Bodies) Order 1986

3   The Insolvency (England and Wales) Rules 2016 and the Insolvency (Scotland) Rules 1986 (except in so far as they relate to the exceptions to the reserved matters specified in section C.2 of Part II of Schedule 5 to the Scotland Act 1998)

4   The Insolvency Fees Order 1986

5   The Co-operation of Insolvency Courts (Designation of Relevant Countries and Territories) Order 1986

6   The Co-operation of Insolvency Courts (Designation of Relevant Countries and Territories) Order 1996

7   The Co-operation of Insolvency Courts (Designation of Relevant Country) Order 1998

8   Insolvency Proceedings (Monetary Limits) Order 1986

9   [Omitted]

10   Insolvency Regulations 1994

11   Insolvency (Amendment) Regulations 2000

PART III

REGULATIONS MADE UNDER OTHER LEGISLATION

1   [Omitted by the Limited Liability Partnerships (Application of Companies Act 2006) Regulations 2009 (SI 2009/1804) Sch.3 Pt 2 para.13(7)(b) as from 1 October 2009.]

2   The Companies (Disqualification Orders) Regulations 1986

3   The Insolvent Companies (Disqualification of Unfit Directors) Proceedings Rules 1987

4   The Contracting Out (Functions of the Official Receiver) Order 1995

5   The Uncertificated Securities Regulations 1995

6   The Insolvent Companies (Reports on Conduct of Directors) (England and Wales) Rules 2016

7   The Insolvent Companies (Reports on Conduct of Directors) (Scotland) Rules 2016

History
In Pt III paras 6, 7 amended by the Enterprise and Regulatory Reform Act 2013 (Consequential Amendments) (Bankruptcy) and the Small Business, Enterprise and Employment Act 2015 (Consequential Amendments) Regulations 2016 (SI 2016/481) reg.2(2) and Sch.2 para.4 as from 6 April 2016.
In Pt II para.3 amended by the Insolvency (Miscellaneous Amendments) Regulations 2017 (SI 2017/1119) regs 1(1), (2), 2, Sch.1 para.1 as from 8 December 2017.

SCHEDULE 7

TRANSITIONAL AND SAVINGS PROVISIONS

1   Interpretation

1   In this Schedule–

"the 1986 Act" means the Insolvency Act 1986, as applied to limited liability partnerships;

"the 1986 Rules" means the Insolvency Rules 1986 as they had effect immediately before the 6th April 2017 in their application to limited liability partnerships;

"the 2016 Rules" means the Insolvency (England and Wales) Rules 2016, as applied to limited liability partnerships; and

"the commencement date" means the date this Schedule comes into force.

2   Amendments to the 2016 Rules made by the Insolvency Amendment (EU 2015/848) Regulations 2017 do not apply where proceedings opened before commencement date

2(1)   The amendments made by the Insolvency Amendment (EU 2015/848) Regulations 2017 to the 2016 Rules do not apply where proceedings in relation to a limited liability partnership opened before the commencement date.

2(2)   The time at which proceedings are opened is to be determined for the purpose of this paragraph in accordance with Article 2(8) of Regulation (EU) 2015/848 of the European Parliament and of the Council of 20th May 2015.

3   Requirement for office-holder to provide information to creditors on opting out

3(1)   Rule 1.39 of the 2016 Rules (which requires an office-holder to inform a creditor in the first communication that the creditor may elect to opt out of receiving further documents relating to the proceedings) does not apply to an office-holder in relation to a limited liability partnership who delivers the first communication before the commencement date.

3(2)   However, if such an office-holder informs a creditor in a communication that the creditor may elect to opt out as mentioned in sub-paragraph (1), the communication must contain the information required by rule 1.39(2) of the 2016 Rules.

4   Electronic communication

4(1)   Where proceedings in relation to a limited liability partnership commence before the commencement date, Rule 1.45(4) of the 2016 Rules does not apply.

4(2)   For the purposes of this paragraph proceedings "commence" on–

(a)   the delivery of a proposal for a voluntary arrangement to the intended nominee;

(b)   the appointment of an administrator under paragraph 14 or 22 of Schedule B1 to the 1986 Act;

(c)   the making of an administration order;

(d)   the appointment of an administrative receiver;

(e)   the passing or deemed passing of a resolution to wind up a limited liability partnership; or

(f)   the making of a winding-up order.

5   Statements of affairs

5(1)   Where proceedings in relation to a limited liability partnership commence before the commencement date and a person is required to provide a statement of affairs, the provisions of the 2016 Rules relating to statements of affairs in administration, administrative receivership and winding up do not apply and the following rules in the 1986 Rules continue to apply–

(a)   rules 2.28 to 2.32 (administration);

(b)   rules 3.3 to 3.8 (administrative receivership); and

(c)   rules 4.32 to 4.42 (winding up).

5(2)   For the purposes of this paragraph proceedings "commence" on–

(a)   the appointment of an administrator under paragraph 14 or 22 of Schedule B1;

(b)   the making of an administration order;

(c)   the appointment of an administrative receiver

(d)   the passing or deemed passing of a resolution to wind up a limited liability partnership; or

(e)   the making of a winding-up order.

6   Savings in respect of meetings taking place on or after the commencement date and resolutions by correspondence

6(1)   This paragraph applies where in relation to a limited liability partnership on or after the commencement date–

(a)   a creditors' or contributories' meeting is to be held as a result of a notice issued before that date in relation to a meeting for which provision is made by the 1986 Rules or the 1986 Act;

(b)   a meeting is to be held as a result of a requisition by a creditor or contributory made before that date;

(c)   a meeting is to be held as a result of a statement made under paragraph 52(1)(b) of Schedule B1 to the 1986 Act and a request is made before that date which obliges the administrator to summon an initial creditors' meeting; or

(d)   a meeting is required by sections 93 or 105 of the 1986 Act in the winding up of a limited liability partnership where the resolution to wind up was passed before 6th April 2010.

6(2)   Where a meeting referred to in sub-paragraph (1)(a) to (d) is held in relation to a limited liability partnership, Part 15 of the 2016 Rules does not apply and the provisions of the 1986 Rules relating to the following continue to apply–

(a)   the requirement to hold the meeting;

(b)   notice and advertisement of the meeting;

(c)   governance of the meeting;

(d)   recording and taking minutes of the meeting;

(e)   the report or return of the meeting;

(f)   membership and formalities of establishment of liquidation and creditors' committees where a resolution to form the committee is passed at the meeting;

(g)   the office-holder's resignation or removal at the meeting;

(h)   the office-holder's release;

(i)   fixing the office-holder's remuneration;

(j)   hand-over of assets to a supervisor of a voluntary arrangement where the proposal is approved at the meeting;

(k)   the notice of the appointment of a supervisor of a voluntary arrangement where the appointment is made at the meeting;

(l)   claims that remuneration is or that other expenses are excessive; and

(m)   complaints about exclusion at the meeting.

6(3)   Where in relation to a limited liability partnership, before the commencement date, the office-holder seeks to obtain the passing of a resolution by correspondence under rule 2.48, 4.63A or 6.88A of the 1986 Rules–

(a)   the relevant provisions of the 2016 Rules do not apply;

(b)   the provisions of the 1986 Rules relating to resolutions by correspondence continue to apply; and

(c)   the provisions of the 1986 Rules referred to in sub-paragraph (2) of this paragraph apply in relation to any meeting that those provisions require the office-holder to summon.

6(4)   However, any application to the court in respect of a meeting or vote to which this paragraph applies is to be made in accordance with Part 12 of the 2016 Rules.

7   Savings in respect of final meetings taking place on or after the commencement date

7(1)   This paragraph applies where–

(a)   before the commencement date–

(i)   a final report to creditors is sent under rule 4.49D of the 1986 Rules (final report to creditors in liquidation),

(ii)   a final report to creditors and bankrupt is sent under rule 6.78B of the 1986 Rules (final report to creditors and bankrupt), or

(iii)   a meeting is called under sections 94, 106, 146 or 331 of the 1986 Act (final meeting); and

(b)   a meeting under section 94, 106, 146 or 331 of the 1986 Act is held on or after the commencement date.

7(2)   Where this paragraph applies, Part 15 of the 2016 Rules does not apply and the provisions of the 1986 Rules relating to the following continue to apply–

(a)   the requirement to hold the meeting;

(b)   notice and advertisement of the meeting;

(c)   governance of the meeting;

(d)   recording and taking minutes of the meeting;

(e)   the form and content of the final report;

(f)   the office-holder's resignation or removal;

(g)   the office-holder's release;

   (h)   fixing the office-holder's remuneration;

   (i)   requests for further information from creditors;

   (j)   claims that remuneration is or other expenses are excessive; and

   (k)   complaints about exclusion at the meeting.

7(3) However, any application to the court in respect of such a meeting is to be made in accordance with Part 12 of the 2016 Rules.

8   Progress reports and statements to the registrar of companies

8(1) Where in relation to a limited liability partnership an obligation to prepare a progress report arises but is not fulfilled before the commencement date the following provisions of the 1986 Rules continue to apply–

   (a)   rule 2.47 (reports to creditors in administration); and

   (b)   rules 4.49B and 4.49C (progress reports—winding up).

8(2) Where before the commencement date, a notice under paragraph 83(3) of Schedule B1 to the 1986 Act is sent to the registrar of companies, rule 2.117A(1) of the 1986 Rules continues to apply.

8(3) The provisions of the 2016 Rules relating to progress reporting do not apply in the case of the winding up of a limited liability partnership, where the winding-up order was made on a petition presented before 6th April 2010.

8(4) Where the voluntary winding up of a limited liability partnership commenced before 6th April 2010, rule 4.223–CVL of the 1986 Rules as it had effect immediately before that date in its application to limited liability partnerships, continues to apply

8(5) Where, in relation to a limited liability partnership, before the commencement date an office-holder ceases to act, or an administrator sends a progress report to creditors in support of a request for their consent to an extension of the administration, resulting in a change in reporting period under rule 2.47(3A), 2.47(3B), 4.49B(5), 4.49C(3), or 6.78A(4) of the 1986 Rules, the period for which reports must be made is the period for which reports were required to be made under the 1986 Rules immediately before the commencement date.

9   Foreign currency

9(1) Where, in relation to a limited liability partnership, before the commencement date an amount stated in a foreign currency on an application, claim or proof of debt is converted into sterling by the office-holder under rules 2.86, 4.91, 5A.3 or 6.111 of the 1986 Rules, the office-holder and any successor to the office-holder must continue to use the same exchange rate for subsequent conversions of that currency into sterling for the purpose of distributing any assets of the limited liability partnership.

9(2) However when, in relation to a limited liability partnership, an office-holder, convener, appointed person or chair uses an exchange rate to convert an application, claim or proof in a foreign currency into sterling solely for voting purposes before the commencement date, sub-paragraph (1) does not prevent the office-holder from using an alternative rate for subsequent conversions.

10   CVA moratoria

10 Where, before the commencement date, the designated members of a limited liability partnership submit to the nominee the document, statement and information required under paragraph 6(1) of Schedule A1 to the 1986 Act, the provisions of the 1986 Rules relating to moratoria continue to apply to the proposed voluntary arrangement.

11 Priority of expenses of voluntary arrangements

11 Rule 4.21A of the 1986 Rules (expenses of voluntary arrangement) continues to apply in relation to a limited liability partnership where a winding up petition is presented before the commencement date.

12 General powers of liquidator

12 Rule 4.184 of the 1986 Rules (general powers of liquidator) continues to apply in relation to a limited liability partnership as regards a person dealing in good faith and for value with a liquidator and in respect of the power of the court or the liquidation committee to ratify anything done by the liquidator without permission before the commencement date.

13 Applications before the court

13(1) Where, in relation to a limited liability partnership, an application to court is filed or a petition for winding up is presented under the 1986 Act or under the 1986 Rules before the commencement date and the court remains seised of that application or petition on the commencement date, the 1986 Rules continue to apply to that application or petition.

13(2) For the purpose of sub-paragraph (1), the court is no longer seised of an application or petition for winding up when–

   (a) in relation to an application, it makes an order having the effect of determining of the application; or

   (b) in relation to a petition for winding up–

      (i) the court makes a winding up order,

      (ii) the court dismisses the petition, or

      (iii) the petition is withdrawn.

14 Forms

14 A form contained in Schedule 4 to the 1986 Rules may be used in relation to a limited liability partnership on or after the commencement date if–

   (a) the form is used to provide a statement of affairs in proceedings where pursuant to paragraph 5 of this Schedule the provisions of the 1986 Rules set out in that paragraph continue to apply;

   (b) the form relates to a meeting held under the 1986 Rules as described in paragraph 6(1) of this Schedule;

   (c) the form is required because before the commencement date, the office-holder seeks to obtain the passing of a resolution by correspondence; or

   (d) the form relates to any application to the court or petition for winding up presented before the commencement date.

15 Administrations commenced before 15th September 2003

15 The 1986 Rules continue to apply to administrations of limited liability partnerships where the petition for an administration order was presented before 15th September 2003.

16 Set-off in insolvency proceedings commenced before 1st April 2005

16 Where before 1st April 2005 a limited liability partnership entered administration or went into liquidation, the office-holder calculating any set-off must apply the 1986 Rules as they had effect in their application to limited liability partnerships immediately before 1st April 2005.

17   Calculating the value of future debts in insolvency proceedings commenced before 1st April 2005

17   Where before 1st April 2005 a limited liability partnership entered administration or went into liquidation the office-holder calculating the value of a future debt for the purpose of dividend (and no other purpose) must apply the 1986 Rules as they had effect in their application to limited liability partnerships immediately before 1st April 2005.

18   Insolvency practitioner fees and expenses estimates

18(1)   Rules 18.4(1)(e), 18.16(4) to (10), and 18.30 of the 2016 Rules do not apply in relation to limited liability partnerships where before 1st October 2015–

(a)   the appointment of an administrator took effect;

(b)   a liquidator was nominated under section 100(2), or 139(3) of the 1986 Act;

(c)   a liquidator was appointed under section 139(4) or 140 of the 1986 Act;

(d)   a person was directed by the court or appointed to be a liquidator under section 100(3) of the 1986 Act; or

(e)   a liquidator was nominated or the administrator became the liquidator under paragraph 83(7) of Schedule B1 to the 1986 Act.

18(2)   Rule 18.20(4) and (5) of the 2016 Rules do not apply in relation to a limited liability partnership where an administrator was appointed before 1st October 2015 and–

(a)   the limited liability partnership is wound up under paragraph 83 of Schedule B1 to the 1986 Act on or after the commencement date and the administrator becomes the liquidator; or

(b)   a winding-up order is made upon the appointment of an administrator ceasing to have effect on or after the commencement date and the court under section 140(1) of the 1986 Act appoints as liquidator the person whose appointment as administrator has ceased to have effect.

19   Transitional provision for limited liability partnerships entering administration before 6th April 2010 and moving to voluntary liquidation between 6th April 2010 and commencement (inclusive of those dates)

19   Where–

(a)   a limited liability partnership went into administration before 6th April 2010, and

(b)   the limited liability partnership goes into voluntary liquidation under paragraph 83 of Schedule B1 between 6th April 2010 and commencement (inclusive of those dates),

the 1986 Rules as amended by the Insolvency (Amendment) Rules 2010 apply to the extent necessary to give effect to section 104A of the Act notwithstanding that by virtue of paragraph 1(6)(a) or (b) of Schedule 4 to the Insolvency (Amendment) Rules 2010 those amendments to the Insolvency Rules 1986 would otherwise not apply.

History
Schedule 7 inserted by the Insolvency (Miscellaneous Amendments) Regulations 2017 (SI 2017/1119) regs 1(1), (2), 2, Sch.1 paras 4, 55 as from 8 December 2017.

Financial Services and Markets Act 2000 (Insolvency) (Definition of Insurer) Order 2001

(SI 2001/2634)

Made on 20 July 2001 by the Treasury under ss.355(2) and 428(3) of the Financial Services and Markets Act 2000. Operative from 1 December 2001.

1(1) This Order may be cited as the Financial Services and Markets Act 2000 (Insolvency) (Definition of "Insurer") Order 2001 and comes into force on the day on which section 19 of the Act comes into force.

1(2) In this Order, the "Regulated Activities Order" means the Financial Services and Markets Act 2000 (Regulated Activities) Order 2001.

2 In Part XXIV of the Act (insolvency), "insurer" means any person who is carrying on a regulated activity of the kind specified by article 10(1) or (2) of the Regulated Activities Order (effecting and carrying out contracts of insurance) but who is not–

(a) exempt from the general prohibition in respect of that regulated activity;

(b) a friendly society; or

(c) a person who effects or carries out contracts of insurance all of which fall within paragraphs 14 to 18 of Part I of Schedule 1 to the Regulated Activities Order in the course of, or for the purposes of, a banking business.

History
In art.2 the words "except section 360 (administration orders in relation to insurers)," omitted by the Financial Services and Markets Act 2000 (Administration Orders Relating to Insurers) Order 2002 (SI 2002/1242) arts 1, 2 as from 31 May 2002.

Bankruptcy (Financial Services and Markets Act 2000) Rules 2001

(SI 2001/3634)

Made on 9 November 2001 by the Lord Chancellor, in the exercise of his powers under s.412 of the Insolvency Act 1986 with the concurrence of the Secretary of State, and after consulting the committee existing for that purpose under s.413 of that Act. Operative from 1 December 2001.

1 Citation and commencement

1 These Rules may be cited as the Bankruptcy (Financial Services and Markets Act 2000) Rules 2001 and come into force on 1st December 2001.

2 Interpretation

2 In these Rules–

"the Act" means the Financial Services and Markets Act 2000;

"the Authority" in relation to an individual means–

    (a) if the individual is a PRA-authorised person or was carrying on a PRA-regulated activity in contravention of the general prohibition, the FCA or the PRA,

    (b) in any other case, the FCA,

and terms used in this definition which are defined in the Act have the meaning given in the Act;

"debt" means the sum referred to in section 372(4)(a) of the Act;

"demand" means a demand made under section 372(4)(a) of the Act;

"individual" has the meaning given by section 372(7) of the Act;

"person" excludes a body of persons corporate or unincorporate.

History
Rule 2 amended by the Bankruptcy (Financial Services and Markets Act 2000) Rules 2001 and the Insurers (Winding Up) Rules 2001 (Amendment) Rules 2019 (SI 2019/754) rr.1, 2(1), (2) as from 23 April 2019.

3 Modification of the Insolvency (England and Wales) Rules 2016

3 The Insolvency (England and Wales) Rules 2016 apply in relation to a demand with the following modifications.

History
Rule 3 amended by the Bankruptcy (Financial Services and Markets Act 2000) Rules 2001 and the Insurers (Winding Up) Rules 2001 (Amendment) Rules 2019 (SI 2019/754) rr.1, 2(1), (3) as from 23 April 2019.

4 Rule 10.1

4(1) Rule 10.1 (the statutory demand (section 268)) is disapplied.

4(2) A demand must be dated and signed by a member of the Authority's staff authorised by it for that purpose.

4(3) A demand must specify that it is made under section 372(4)(a) of the Act.

4(4) A demand must state the amount of the debt, to whom it is owed and the consideration for it or, if there is no consideration, the way in which it arises; but if the person to whom the debt is owed holds any security in respect of the debt of which the Authority is aware–

(a)   the demand must specify the nature of the security and the value which the Authority puts upon it as at the date of the demand; and

(b)   the amount of which payment is claimed by the demand must be the full amount of the debt less the amount specified as the value of the security.

4(5)   A demand must state the grounds on which it is alleged that the individual appears to have no reasonable prospect of paying the debt.

4(6)   A demand must include an explanation to the individual of the following matters–

(a)   the purpose of the demand and the fact that, if the individual does not comply with the demand, bankruptcy proceedings may be commenced against the individual;

(b)   the time within which the demand must be complied with, if that consequence is to be avoided; (c) the methods of compliance which are open to the individual; and (d) the individual's right to apply to the court for the demand to be set aside.

4(7)   A demand must specify the name and address (and telephone number, if any) of one or more persons with whom the individual may, if the individual wishes, enter into communication with a view to establishing to the Authority's satisfaction that there is a reasonable prospect that the debt will be paid when it falls due or (as the case may be) that the debt will be secured or compounded.

History
Heading to r.4 and r.4(1) amended and r.4(6), (7) inserted by the Bankruptcy (Financial Services and Markets Act 2000) Rules 2001 and the Insurers (Winding Up) Rules 2001 (Amendment) Rules 2019 (SI 2019/754) rr.1, 2(1), (4) as from 23 April 2019.

5   Rule 10.2

[Omitted by the Bankruptcy (Financial Services and Markets Act 2000) Rules 2001 and the Insurers (Winding Up) Rules 2001 (Amendment) Rules 2019 (SI 2019/754) rr.1, 2(1), (5) as from 23 April 2019.]

6   Rules 10.2, 10.3, 10.5 and 10.24

6(1)   Rules 10.2 (service of statutory demand), 10.3 (proof of service of statutory demand), 10.5 (hearing of application to set aside), and 10.24 (decision on the hearing) apply as if–

(a)   references to the debtor were references to an individual;

(b)   references (other than in Rule 10.5(3) and (5)(c)) to the creditor were references to the Authority; and

(c)   references to the creditor in Rule 10.5(3) and (5)(c) were references to the person to whom the debt is owed.

6(2)   Rule 10.5(3) applies as if the reference to the creditor also included a reference to the Authority.

6(3)   Rule 10.5(7) is disapplied and there is substituted the following–

"Where the person to whom the debt is owed holds some security in respect of his debt, and rule 4(4) of the Bankruptcy (Financial Services and Markets Act 2000) Rules 2001 is complied with in respect of it but the court is satisfied that the security is undervalued in the demand, the Authority may be required to amend the demand accordingly (but without prejudice to its right to present a bankruptcy by reference to the original demand)."

History
Heading to r.6 and r.6(2) and (3) amended and r.6(1) substituted by the Bankruptcy (Financial Services and Markets Act 2000) Rules 2001 and the Insurers (Winding Up) Rules 2001 (Amendment) Rules 2019 (SI 2019/754) rr.1, 2(1), (6) as from 23 April 2019.

7 Rule 10.4

7 Rule 10.4 (application to set aside statutory demand) applies as if–

(a) references to the debtor were references to an individual; and

(b) in paragraph (4)(b)–

  (i) in paragraph (i) for "a Minister of the Crown or a Government Department" there were substituted "the Authority"; and

  (ii) in paragraph (iii)(bb) for "creditor's" substitute "Authority's".

History
Rule 7 substituted by the Bankruptcy (Financial Services and Markets Act 2000) Rules 2001 and the Insurers (Winding Up) Rules 2001 (Amendment) Rules 2019 (SI 2019/754) rr.1, 2(1), (7) as from 23 April 2019.

8 Rule 12.5

8 Rule 12.5 (allocation of proceedings to the London Insolvency District) applies as if in paragraph (b) for "a Minister of the Crown or a Government Department" there were substituted "the Authority".

History
Rule 8 substituted by the Bankruptcy (Financial Services and Markets Act 2000) Rules 2001 and the Insurers (Winding Up) Rules 2001 (Amendment) Rules 2019 (SI 2019/754) rr.1, 2(1), (8) as from 23 April 2019.

Insurers (Winding Up) Rules 2001

(SI 2001/3635)

Made on 9 November 2001 by the Lord Chancellor, in exercise of the powers conferred on him by s.411 of the Insolvency Act 1986 and s.379 of the Financial Services and Markets Act 2000, with the concurrence of the Secretary of State, and after consulting the committee existing for that purpose under s.413 of the 1986 Act. Operative from 1 December 2001.

[**Note**: Changes made by the Insurers (Reorganisation and Winding Up) Regulations 2003 (SI 2003/1102), the Insurers (Reorganisation and Winding Up) Regulations 2004 (SI 2004/353), the Insurers (Reorganisation and Winding Up) (Amendment) Regulations 2004 (SI 2004/546), the Financial Services Act 2012 (Consequential Amendments and Transitional Provisions) Order 2013 (SI 2013/472), the Small Business Enterprise and Employment Act 2015 (Consequential Amendments, Saving and Transitional Provisions) Regulations 2018 (SI 2018/208) and the Bankruptcy (Financial Services and Markets Act 2000) Rules 2001 and the Insurers (Winding Up) Rules 2001 (Amendment) Rules 2019 (SI 2019/754) have been incorporated into the text.]

1 Citation, commencement and revocation

1(1) These Rules may be cited as the Insurers (Winding Up) Rules 2001 and come into force on 1st December 2001.

1(2) The Insurance Companies (Winding Up) Rules 1985 are revoked.

2 Interpretation

2(1) In these Rules, unless the context otherwise requires–

"the 1923 Act" means the Industrial Assurance Act 1923;

"the 1985 Act" means the Companies Act 1985;

"the 1986 Act" means the Insolvency Act 1986;

"the 2000 Act" means the Financial Services and Markets Act 2000;

"the Authority" means the Financial Conduct Authority or the Prudential Regulation Authority;

"company" means an insurer which is being wound up;

"contract of general insurance" and "contract of long-term insurance" have the meaning given by article 3(1) of the Financial Services and Markets Act 2000 (Regulated Activities) Order 2001;

"excess of the long-term business assets" means the amount, if any, by which the value of the assets representing the fund or funds maintained by the company in respect of its long-term business as at the liquidation date exceeds the value as at that date of the liabilities of the company attributable to that business;

"excess of the other business assets" means the amount, if any, by which the value of the assets of the company which do not represent the fund or funds maintained by the company in respect of its long-term business as at the liquidation date exceeds the value as at that date of the liabilities of the company (other than liabilities in respect of share capital) which are not attributable to that business;

"Financial Services Compensation Scheme" means the scheme established under section 213 of the 2000 Act;

"general business" means the business of effecting or carrying out a contract of general insurance;

"the general regulations" means the Insolvency Regulations 1994;

"the Industrial Assurance Acts" means the 1923 Act and the Industrial Assurance and Friendly Societies Act 1948;

"insurer" has the meaning given by article 2 of the Financial Services and Markets Act 2000 (Insolvency) (Definition of "Insurer") Order 2001;

"linked liability" means any liability under a policy the effecting of which constitutes the carrying on of long-term business the amount of which is determined by reference to–

(a)   the value of property of any description (whether or not specified in the policy),

(b)   fluctuations in the value of such property,

(c)   income from any such property, or

(d)   fluctuations in an index of the value of such property;

"linked policy" means a policy which provides for linked liabilities and a policy which when made provided for linked liabilities is deemed to be a linked policy even if the policy holder has elected to convert his rights under the policy so that at the liquidation date there are no longer linked liabilities under the policy;

"liquidation date" means the date of the winding-up order or the date on which a resolution for the winding up of the company is passed by the members of the company (or the policyholders in the case of a mutual insurance company) and, if both a winding-up order and winding-up resolution have been made, the earlier date;

"long-term business" means the business of effecting or carrying out any contract of long-term insurance;

"non-linked policy" means a policy which is not a linked policy;

"other business", in relation to a company carrying on long-term business, means such of the business of the company as is not long-term business;

"the principal rules" means the Insolvency (England and Wales) Rules 2016;

"qualifying decision procedure" has the meaning given by section 246ZE(11) of the 1986 Act;

"stop order", in relation to a company, means an order of the court, made under section 376(2) of the 2000 Act, ordering the liquidator to stop carrying on the long-term business of the company;

"unit" in relation to a policy means any unit (whether or not described as a unit in the policy) by reference to the numbers and value of which the amount of the liabilities under the policy at any time is measured.

2(2)   Unless the context otherwise requires, words or expressions contained in these Rules bear the same meaning as in the principal rules, the general regulations, the 1986 Act, the 2000 Act or any statutory modification thereof respectively.

History
In r.2(1) in the definition of "the principal rules" the words "the Insolvency (England and Wales) Rules 2016" substituted for the former words "the Insolvency Rules 1986" by the Insolvency (England and Wales) Rules 2016 (Consequential Amendments and Savings) Rules 2017 (SI 2017/369) r.2(2), Sch.2 para.6(1), (2) as from 6 April 2017. The definition of "qualifying decision procedure" was inserted by the Small Business, Enterprise and Employment Act 2015 (Consequential Amendments, Savings and Transitional Provisions) Regulations 2018 (SI 2018/208) reg.7(2) with effect from 13 March 2018.

3 Application

3(1)   These Rules apply to proceedings for the winding up of an insurer which commence on or after the date on which these Rules come into force.

3(2)   These Rules supplement the principal rules and the general regulations which continue to apply to the proceedings in the winding up of an insurer under the 1986 Act as they apply to proceedings in the winding up of any company under that Act; but in the event of a conflict between these Rules and the principal rules or the general regulations these Rules prevail.

[**Note:** the courts in Scotland have corresponding jurisdiction if the insurer is capable of being wound up there. See the Insurers (Winding Up) (Scotland) Rules 2001(SI 2001/4040 (S.21)) (not reproduced in this volume).]

4 Appointment of liquidator

4 Where the court is considering whether to appoint a liquidator under–

(a) section 139(4) of the 1986 Act (appointment of liquidator where conflict between creditors and contributories), or

(b) section 140 of the 1986 Act (appointment of liquidator following administration or voluntary arrangement),

the manager of the Financial Services Compensation Scheme may appear and make representations to the court as to the person to be appointed.

5 Maintenance of separate financial records for long-term and other business in winding up

5(1) This rule applies in the case of a company carrying on long-term business in whose case no stop order has been made.

5(2) The liquidator shall prepare and keep separate financial records in respect of the long-term business and the other business of the company.

5(3) Paragraphs (4) and (5) apply in the case of a company to which this rule applies which also carries on permitted general business ("a hybrid insurer").

5(4) Where, before the liquidation date, a hybrid insurer has, or should properly have, apportioned the assets and liabilities attributable to its permitted general business to its long term business for the purposes of any accounts, those assets and liabilities must be apportioned to its long term business for the purposes of complying with paragraph (2) of this rule.

5(5) Where, before the liquidation date, a hybrid insurer has, or should properly have, apportioned the assets and liabilities attributable to its permitted general business other than to its long term business for the purposes of any accounts, those assets and liabilities must be apportioned to its other business for the purposes of complying with paragraph (2) of this rule.

5(6) Regulation 10 of the general regulations (financial records) applies only in relation to the company's other business.

5(7) In relation to the long-term business, the liquidator shall, with a view to the long-term business of the company being transferred to another insurer, maintain such accounting, valuation and other records as will enable such other insurer upon the transfer being effected to comply with the requirements of any rules made by the Authority under Part 9A of the 2000 Act relating to accounts and statements of insurers.

5(8) In paragraphs (4) and (5)–

(a) "accounts" means any accounts or statements maintained by the company in compliance with a requirement under the Companies Act 1985 or any rules made by the Authority under Part 9A of the 2000 Act;

(b) "permitted general business" means the business of effecting or carrying out a contract of general insurance where the risk insured against relates to either accident or sickness.

History
Rule 5 revoked and replaced by the Insurers (Reorganisation and Winding Up) Regulations 2003 (SI 2003/1102) regs 1, 52, 53(1) as from 20 April 2003.

6 Valuation of general business policies

6 Except in relation to amounts which have fallen due for payment before the liquidation date and liabilities referred to in paragraph 2(1)(b) of Schedule 1, the holder of a general business policy shall be admitted as a creditor in relation to his policy without proof for an amount equal to the value of the policy and for this purpose the value of a policy shall be determined in accordance with Schedule 1.

7 Valuation of long-term policies

7(1) This rule applies in relation to a company's long-term business where no stop order has been made.

7(2) In relation to a claim under a policy which has fallen due for payment before the liquidation date, a policy holder shall be admitted as a creditor without proof for such amount as appears from the records of the company to be due in respect of that claim.

7(3) In all other respects a policy holder shall be admitted as a creditor in relation to his policy without proof for an amount equal to the value of the policy and for this purpose the value of a policy of any class shall be determined in the manner applicable to policies of that class provided by Schedules 2, 3 and 4.

7(4) This rule applies in relation to a person entitled to apply for a free paid-up policy under section 24 of the 1923 Act (provisions as to forfeited policies) and to whom no such policy has been issued before the liquidation date (whether or not it was applied for) as if such a policy had been issued immediately before the liquidation date–

(a) for the minimum amount determined in accordance with section 24(2) of the 1923 Act, or

(b) if the liquidator is satisfied that it was the practice of the company during the five years immediately before the liquidation date to issue policies under that section in excess of the minimum amounts so determined, for the amount determined in accordance with that practice.

8(1) This rule applies in relation to a company's long-term business where a stop order has been made.

8(2) In relation to a claim under a policy which has fallen due for payment on or after the liquidation date and before the date of the stop order, a policy holder shall be admitted as a creditor without proof for such amount as appears from the records of the company and of the liquidator to be due in respect of that claim.

8(3) In all other respects a policy holder shall be admitted as a creditor in relation to his policy without proof for an amount equal to the value of the policy and for this purpose the value of a policy of any class shall be determined in the manner applicable to policies of that class provided by Schedule 5.

8(4) Paragraph (4) of rule 7 applies for the purposes of this rule as if references to the liquidation date (other than that in sub-paragraph (b) of that paragraph) were references to the date of the stop order.

9 Attribution of liabilities to company's long-term business

9(1) This rule applies in the case of a company carrying on long-term business if at the liquidation date there are liabilities of the company in respect of which it is not clear from the accounting and other records of the company whether they are or are not attributable to the company's long-term business.

9(2) The liquidator shall, in such manner and according to such accounting principles as he shall determine, identify the liabilities referred to in paragraph (1) as attributable or not attributable to a company's long-term business and those liabilities shall for the purposes of the winding-up be deemed as at the liquidation date to be attributable or not as the case may be.

9(3) For the purposes of paragraph (2) the liquidator may–

(a) determine that some liabilities are attributable to the company's long-term business and that others are not (the first method); or

(b) determine that a part of a liability shall be attributable to the company's long-term business and that the remainder of the liability is not (the second method),

and he may use the first method for some of the liabilities and the second method for the remainder of them.

9(4) Notwithstanding anything in the preceding paragraphs of this rule, the court may order that the determination of which (if any) of the liabilities referred to in paragraph (1) are attributable to the company's long-term business and which (if any) are not shall be made in such manner and by such methods as the court may direct or the court may itself make the determination.

10   Attribution of assets to company's long-term business

10(1) This rule applies in the case of a company carrying on long-term business if at the liquidation date there are assets of the company in respect of which–

(a) it is not clear from the accounting and other records of the company whether they do or do not represent the fund or funds maintained by the company in respect of its long-term business, and

(b) it cannot be inferred from the source of the income out of which those assets were provided whether they do or do not represent those funds.

10(2) Subject to paragraph (6) the liquidator shall determine which (if any) of the assets referred to in paragraph (1) are attributable to those funds and which (if any) are not and those assets shall, for the purposes of the winding up, be deemed as at the liquidation date to represent those funds or not in accordance with the liquidator's determination.

10(3) For the purposes of paragraph (2) the liquidator may–

(a) determine that some of those assets shall be attributable to those funds and that others of them shall not (the first method); or

(b) determine that a part of the value of one of those assets shall be attributable to those funds and that the remainder of that value shall not (the second method),

and he may use the first method for some of those assets and the second method for others of them.

10(4)

(a) In making the attribution the liquidator's objective shall in the first instance be so far as possible to reduce any deficit that may exist, at the liquidation date and before any attribution is made, either in the company's long-term business or in its other business.

(b) If there is a deficit in both the company's long-term business and its other business the attribution shall be in the ratio that the amount of the one deficit bears to the amount of the other until the deficits are eliminated.

(c) Thereafter the attribution shall be in the ratio which the aggregate amount of the liabilities attributable to the company's long-term business bears to the aggregate amount of the liabilities not so attributable.

10(5) For the purposes of paragraph (4) the value of a liability of the company shall, if it falls to be valued under rule 6 or 7, have the same value as it has under that rule but otherwise it shall have such value as would have been included in relation to it in a balance sheet of the company prepared in accordance with the 1985 Act as at the liquidation date; and, for the purpose of determining the ratio referred to in paragraph (4) but not for the purpose of determining the amount of any deficit therein referred to, the net balance of shareholders' funds shall be included in the liabilities not attributable to the company's long-term business.

10(6) Notwithstanding anything in the preceding paragraphs of this rule, the court may order that the determination of which (if any) of the assets referred to in paragraph (1) are attributable to the fund or funds maintained by the company in respect of its long-term business and which (if any) are not shall be made in such manner and by such methods as the court may direct or the court may itself make the determination.

11   Excess of long-term business assets

11(1)   Where the company is one carrying on long-term business and in whose case no stop order has been made, for the purpose of determining the amount, if any, of the excess of the long-term business assets, there shall be included amongst the liabilities of the company attributable to its long-term business an amount determined by the liquidator in respect of liabilities and expenses likely to be incurred in connection with the transfer of the company's long-term business as a going concern to another insurance company being liabilities not included in the valuation of the long-term policies made in pursuance of rule 7.

History
In r.11(1) the words "and in whose case no stop order has been made" inserted by the Insurers (Reorganisation and Winding Up) Regulations 2003 (SI 2003/1102) regs 1, 52, 54 as from 20 April 2003.

11(2)   Where the liquidator is carrying on the long-term business of an insurer with a view to that business being transferred as a going concern to a person or persons ("transferee") who may lawfully carry out those contracts (or substitute policies being issued by another insurer), the liquidator may, in addition to any amounts paid by the Financial Services Compensation Scheme for the benefit of the transferee to secure such a transfer or to procure substitute policies being issued, pay to the transferee or other insurer all or part of such funds or assets as are attributable to the long-term business being transferred or substituted.

12   Actuarial advice

12(1)   Before doing any of the following, that is to say–

(a)   determining the value of a policy in accordance with Schedules 1 to 5 (other than paragraph 3 of Schedule 1);

(b)   identifying long-term liabilities and assets in accordance with rules 9 and 10;

(c)   determining the amount (if any) of the excess of the long-term business assets in accordance with rule 11;

(d)   determining the terms on which he will accept payment of overdue premiums under rule 21(1) or the amount and nature of any compensation under rule 21(2);

the liquidator shall obtain and consider advice thereon (including an estimate of any value or amount required to be determined) from an actuary.

12(2)   Before seeking, for the purpose of valuing a policy, the direction of the court as to the assumption of a particular rate of interest or the employment of any rates of mortality or disability, the liquidator shall obtain and consider advice thereon from an actuary.

13   Utilisation of excess of assets

13(1)   Except at the direction of the court, no distribution may be made out of and no transfer to another insurer may be made of–

(a)   any part of the excess of the long-term business assets which has been transferred to the other business; or

(b)   any part of the excess of the other business assets, which has been transferred to the long-term business.

13(2) Before giving a direction under paragraph (1) the court may require the liquidator to advertise the proposal to make a distribution or a transfer in such manner as the court shall direct.

14 In the case of a company carrying on long-term business in whose case no stop order has been made, regulation 5 of the general regulations (payments into the Insolvency Services Account) applies only in relation to the company's other business.

15 Custody of assets

15(1) The Secretary of State may, in the case of a company carrying on long-term business in whose case no stop order has been made, require that the whole or a specified proportion of the assets representing the fund or funds maintained by the company in respect of its long-term business shall be held by a person approved by him for the purpose as trustee for the company.

15(2) No assets held by a person as trustee for a company in compliance with a requirement imposed under this rule shall, so long as the requirement is in force, be released except with the consent of the Secretary of State but they may be transposed by the trustee into other assets by any transaction or series of transactions on the written instructions of the liquidator.

15(3) The liquidator may not grant any mortgage or charge of assets which are held by a person as trustee for the company in compliance with a requirement imposed under this rule except with the consent of the Secretary of State.

16 Maintenance of accounting, valuation and other records

16(1) In the case of a company carrying on long-term business in whose case no stop order has been made, regulation 10 of the general regulations (financial records) applies only in relation to the company's other business.

16(2) The liquidator of such company shall, with a view to the long-term business of the company being transferred to another insurer, maintain such accounting, valuation and other records as will enable such other insurer upon the transfer being effected to comply with the requirements of any rules made by the Authority under Part 9A of the 2000 Act relating to accounts and statements of insurers.

17 Additional powers in relation to long-term business

17(1) In the case of a company carrying on long-term business in whose case no stop order has been made, regulation 9 of the general regulations (investment or otherwise handling of funds in winding up of companies and payment of interest) applies only in relation to the company's other business.

17(2) The liquidator of a company carrying on long-term business shall, so long as no stop order has been made, have power to do all such things as may be necessary to the performance of his duties under section 376(2) of the 2000 Act (continuation of contracts of long-term insurance where insurer in liquidation) but the Secretary of State may require him–

  (a) not to make investments of a specified class or description,

  (b) to realise, before the expiration of a specified period, the whole or a specified proportion of investments of a specified class or description held by the liquidator.

18 Accounts and audit

18(1) In the case of a company carrying on long-term business in whose case no stop order has been made, regulation 12 of the general regulations (liquidator carrying on business) applies only in relation to the company's other business.

18(2) The liquidator of such a company shall supply the Secretary of State, at such times or intervals as he may specify, with such accounts as he may specify and audited in such manner as he may require and with such information about specified matters and verified in such specified manner as he may require.

18(3)   The liquidator of such a company shall, if required to do so by the Secretary of State, instruct at actuary to investigate the financial condition of the company's long-term business and to report thereon in such manner as the Secretary of State may specify.

19   Security by the liquidator and special manager

19   In the case of a company carrying on long-term business in whose case no stop order has been made, rules 5.18 (security by the liquidator and special manager in a members' voluntary winding up), 6.38 (security in a creditors' voluntary winding up) and 7.94 (winding up by the court) of the principal rules apply separately to the company's long-term business and to its other business.

History
In r.19 the words "rules 5.18" to "of the principal rules apply" substituted for the former words "rule 4.207 of the principal rules (security) applies" by the Insolvency (England and Wales) Rules 2016 (Consequential Amendments and Savings) Rules 2017 (SI 2017/369) r.2(2), Sch.2 para.6(1), (3) as from 6 April 2017.

20   Proof of debts

20(1)   This rule applies in the case of a company carrying on long-term business in whose case no stop order has been made.

History
In r.20(1) the words "and in whose case no stop order has been made" inserted by the Insurers (Reorganisation and Winding Up) Regulations 2003 (SI 2003/1102) regs 1, 52, 55 as from 20 April 2003.

20(2)   The liquidator may in relation to the company's long-term business and to its other business fix different days on or before which the creditors of the company who are required to prove their debts or claims are to prove their debts or claims and he may fix one of those days without at the same time fixing the other.

20(3)   In submitting a proof of any debt a creditor may claim the whole or any part of such debt as attributable to the company's long-term business or to its other business or he may make no such attribution.

20(4)   When he admits any debt, in whole or in part, the liquidator shall state in writing how much of what he admits is attributable to the company's long-term business and how much to the company's other business.

21   Failure to pay premiums

21(1)   The liquidator may in the course of carrying on the company's long-term business and on such terms as he thinks fit accept payment of a premium even though the payment is tendered after the date on which under the terms of the policy it was finally due to be paid.

21(2)   The liquidator may in the course of carrying on the company's long-term business, and having regard to the general practice of insurers, compensate a policy holder whose policy has lapsed in consequence of a failure to pay any premium by issuing a free paid-up policy for reduced benefits or otherwise as the liquidator thinks fit.

22   Notice of valuation of policy

22(1)   Before paying a dividend respect of claims other than under contracts of long-term insurance, the liquidator shall give notice of the value of each general business policy, as determined by him in accordance with rule 6, to the persons appearing from the records of the company or otherwise to be entitled to an interest in that policy and he shall do so in such manner as the court may direct.

22(2)   Before paying a dividend in respect of claims under contracts of long-term insurance and where a stop order has not been made in relation to the company, the liquidator shall give notice to the persons appearing from the records of the company or otherwise to be entitled to a payment under or to an interest in a long-term policy of the amount of that payment or the value of that policy as determined by him in accordance with rule 7(2) or (3), as the case may be.

22(3) If a stop order is made in relation to the company, the liquidator shall give notice to all the persons appearing from the records of the company or otherwise to be entitled to a payment under or to an interest in a long-term policy of the amount of that payment or the value of that policy as determined by him in accordance with rule 8(2) or (3), as the case may be, and he shall give that notice in such manner as the court may direct.

22(4) Any person to whom notice is so given shall be bound by the value so determined unless and until the court otherwise orders.

22(5) Paragraphs (2) and (3) of this rule have effect as though references therein to persons appearing to be entitled to an interest in a long-term policy and to the value of that policy included, respectively, references to persons appearing to be entitled to apply for a free paid-up policy under section 24 of the 1923 Act and to the value of that entitlement under rule 7 (in the case of paragraph (2) of this rule) or under rule 8 (in the case of paragraph (3) of this rule).

22(6) Where the liquidator seeks a decision of creditors in respect of liabilities of the company attributable to either or both its long-term business or other business, he may adopt any valuation carried out in accordance with rules 6, 7 or 8 as the case may be or, if no such valuation has been carried out before the date on which the liquidator seeks the decision, the liquidator may for the purposes of the qualifying decision procedure use such estimates of the value of policies as he thinks fit.

History
In r.22(6) the words "attributable to either or both" substituted for the former words "attributable either to" by the Insurers (Reorganisation and Winding Up) Regulations 2003 (SI 2003/1102) regs 1, 52, 56 as from 20 April 2003. Rule 22(6) was modified by the Small Business, Enterprise and Employment Act 2015 (Consequential Amendments, Savings and Transitional Provisions) Regulations 2018 (SI 2018/208) reg.7(3)(a) and (b) with effect from 13 March 2018.

23 Dividends to creditors

23(1) This rule applies in the case of a company carrying on long-term business.

23(2) Chapter 3 of Part 14 of the principal rules (distribution to creditors in winding up) applies as though–

(a) the assets of the company which are available for meeting the liabilities of the company attributable to its long-term business and those liabilities, and

(b) the assets of the company which are available for meeting the liabilities of the company attributable to its other business and those liabilities,

were the assets and liabilities of separate companies.

23(3) The court may, at any time before the making of a stop order, permit a dividend to be declared and paid on such terms as thinks fit in respect only of debts which fell due to payment before the liquidation date or, in the case of claims under long-term policies, which have fallen due for payment on or after the liquidation date.

History
Rule 23(2) substituted by the Bankruptcy (Financial Services and Markets Act 2000) Rules 2001 and the Insurers (Winding Up) Rules 2001 (Amendment) Rules 2019 (SI 2019/754) rr.1, 3 as from 23 April 2019. Previously, in r.23(2) the words "Part III" substituted for the former words "Part II" by the Insolvency (England and Wales) Rules 2016 (Consequential Amendments and Savings) Rules 2017 (SI 2017/369) r.2(2), Sch.2 para.6(1), (4) as from 6 April 2017. Rule 23(2) was modified by the Small Business, Enterprise and Employment 2015 (Consequential Amendments, Savings and Transitional Provisions) Regulations 2018 (SI 2018/208) reg.7(4) with effect from 13 March 2018.

24 Creditors' decisions

24(1) In the case of a company carrying on long-term business in whose case no stop order has been made, the creditors entitled to participate in a qualifying decision procedure may be–

(a) in relation to the long-term business assets of the company, only those who are creditors in respect of liabilities attributable to the long-term business of the company; and

(b) in relation to the other business assets of the company, only those who are creditors in respect of liabilities attributable to the other business of the company.

24(1A) For the purposes of any such separate qualifying decision procedure, rule 15.34 of the principal rules (requisite majorities) applies with the modification in paragraph (2).

24(2) For the purpose of calculating the proportion (in value) of creditors voting who have voted in favour of the proposed decision, the value to be attributed to a creditor who is not, by virtue of rule 6, 7 or 8 above, required to prove for the amount of a debt or claim, is the value most recently notified to the creditor under rule 22 above, or, if the court has determined a different value in accordance with rule 22(4), that different value.

24(3) In paragraph (1)–

"long-term business assets" means the assets representing the fund or funds maintained by the company in respect of its long-term business;

"other business assets" means any assets of the company which are not long-term business assets.

History
In r.24(1A), the words "regulation 29 Insurers (Reorganisation and Winding Up) (No.2) Regulations 2004" substituted for the former words "regulation 29 Insurers (Reorganisation and Winding Up) Regulations 2003" as from 18 February 2004 by the Insurers (Reorganisation and Winding Up) (No.2) Regulations 2004 (SI 2004/353) regs 51(1), (2). The amendment was later corrected by deleting the erroneous words "(No. 2)" by the Insurers (Reorganisation and Winding Up) (Amendment) Regulations 2004 (SI 2004/546) reg.2(6), as from 3 March 2004.
    Previously r.24(1), (1A) substituted for the former r.24(1) by the Insurers (Reorganisation and Winding Up) Regulations 2003 (SI 2003/1102) regs 1, 52, 57(1), (2) as from 20 April 2003. The heading and r.24(1), (2) were modified and r.24(1A) was replaced again by the Small Business, Enterprise and Employment Act 2015 (Consequential Amendments, Savings and Transitional Provisions) Regulations 2018 (SI 2018/208) reg.7(5)(a)–(c) with effect from 13 March 2018.
    Rule 24(3) inserted by the Insurers (Reorganisation and Winding Up) Regulations 2003 (SI 2003/1102) regs 1, 52, 57(1), (3) as from 20 April 2003.

25 Remuneration of liquidator carrying on long-term business

25(1) So long as no stop order has been made in relation to a company carrying on long-term business, the liquidator is entitled to receive remuneration for his services as such in relation to the carrying on of that business provided for in this rule.

25(2) The remuneration shall be fixed by the liquidation committee by reference to the time properly given by the liquidator and his staff in attending to matters arising in the winding up.

25(3) If there is no liquidation committee or the committee does not make the requisite determination, the liquidator's remuneration may be fixed (in accordance with paragraph (2)) by decision of the creditors made by a qualifying decision procedure.

25(4) If not fixed as above, the liquidator's remuneration shall be in accordance with the scale laid down for the Official Receiver by the general regulations.

25(5) If the liquidator's remuneration has been fixed by the liquidation committee, and the liquidator considers the amount to be insufficient, he may request that it be increased by resolution of the creditors.

History
Rule 25(3) was modified by the Small Business, Enterprise and Employment Act 2015 (Consequential Amendments, Savings and Transitional Provisions) Regulations 2018 (SI 2018/208) reg.7(6) with effect from 13 March 2018.

26   Apportionment of costs payable out of the assets

26(1)   Where no stop order has been made in relation to a company, rules 6.42 (general rule as to priority in a creditors' winding up) and 7.108 (general rule as to priority in a winding up by the court) of the principal rules apply separately to the assets of the company's long-term business and to the assets of the company's other business.

26(2)   But where any fee, expense, cost, charge, disbursement or remuneration does not relate exclusively to the assets of the company's long-term business or to the assets of the company's other business, the liquidator shall apportion it amongst those assets in such manner as he shall determine.

History
In r.26(1) the words "rules 6.42 (general rule as to priority in a creditors' winding up) and 7.108 (general rule as to priority in a winding up by the court) of the principal rules apply" substituted for the former words "rule 4.218 of the principal rules (general rule as to priority) applies" by the Insolvency (England and Wales) Rules 2016 (Consequential Amendments and Savings) Rules 2017 (SI 2017/369) r.2(2), Sch.2 para.6(1), (5) as from 6 April 2017.
    Previously in r.26(1) the words "Where no stop order has been made in relation to a company, rule 4.218" substituted for the former words "Rule 4.218" by the Insurers (Reorganisation and Winding Up) Regulations 2003 (SI 2003/1102) regs 1, 52, 58(1) as from 20 April 2003.

27   Notice of stop order

27(1)   When a stop order has been made in relation to the company, the court shall, on the same day send to the Official Receiver a notice informing him that the stop order has been made.

27(2)   The notice shall be in Form No 1 set out in Schedule 6 with such variation as circumstances may require.

27(3)   Three copies of the stop order sealed with the seal of the court shall forthwith be sent by the court to the Official Receiver.

27(4)   The Official Receiver shall cause a sealed copy of the order to be served upon the liquidator by prepaid letter or upon such other person or persons, or in such other manner as the court may direct, and shall forward a copy of the order to the registrar of companies.

27(5)   The liquidator shall forthwith on receipt of a sealed copy of the order–

   (a)   cause notice of the order in Form 2 set out in Schedule 6 to be gazetted, and

   (b)   advertise the making of the order in the newspaper in which the liquidation date was advertised, by notice in Form No 3 set out in Schedule 6.

SCHEDULE 1

RULES FOR VALUING GENERAL BUSINESS POLICIES

Rule 6

1(1)   This paragraph applies in relation to periodic payments under a general business policy which fall due for payment after the liquidation date where the event giving rise to the liability to make the payments occurred before the liquidation date.

1(2)   The value to be attributed to such periodic payments shall be determined on such actuarial principles and assumptions in regard to all relevant factors as the court shall direct.

2(1) This paragraph applies in relation to liabilities under a general business policy which arise from events which occurred before the liquidation date but which have not–

   (a) fallen due for payment before the liquidation date; or

   (b) been notified to the company before the liquidation date.

2(2) The value to be attributed to such liabilities shall be determined on such actuarial principles and assumptions in regard to all relevant factors as the court shall direct.

3(1) This paragraph applies in relation to liabilities under a general business policy not dealt with by paragraphs 1 or 2.

3(2) The value to be attributed to those liabilities shall–

   (a) if the terms of the policy provide for a repayment of premium upon the early termination of the policy or the policy is expressed to run from one definite date to another or the policy may be terminated by any of the parties with effect from a definite date, be the greater of the following two amounts:

      (i) the amount (if any) which under the terms of the policy would have been repayable on early termination of the policy had the policy terminated on the liquidation date, and

      (ii) where the policy is expressed to run from one definite date to another or may be terminated by any of the parties with effect from a definite date, such proportion of the last premium paid as is proportionate to the unexpired portion of the period in respect of which that premium was paid; and

   (b) in any other case, be a just estimate of that value.

SCHEDULE 2

RULES FOR VALUING NON-LINKED LIFE POLICIES, NON-LINKED DEFERRED ANNUITY POLICIES, NON-LINKED ANNUITIES IN PAYMENT, UNITISED NON-LINKED POLICIES AND CAPITAL REDEMPTION POLICIES

Rule 7

1 General

1 In valuing a policy–

   (a) where it is necessary to calculate the present value of future payments by or to the company, interest shall be assumed at such fair and reasonable rate or rates as the court may direct;

   (b) where relevant, the rates of mortality and the rates of disability to be employed shall be such rates as the court considers appropriate after taking into account:

      (i) relevant published tables of rates of mortality and rates of disability, and

      (ii) the rates of mortality and the rates of disability experienced in connection with similar policies issued by the company;

   (c) there shall be determined:

      (i) the present value of the ordinary benefits,

      (ii) the present value of additional benefits;

      (iii) the present value of options, and

      (iv) if further premiums fall to be paid under the policy on or after the liquidation date, the present value of the premiums;

and for the purposes of this Schedule if the ordinary benefits only take into account premiums paid to date, the present value of future premiums shall be taken as nil.

2 Present value of the ordinary benefits

2(1) Ordinary benefits are the benefits which will become payable to the policy holder on or after the liquidation date without his having to exercise any option under the policy (including any bonus or addition to the sum assured or the amount of annuity declared before the liquidation date) and for this purpose "option" includes a right to surrender the policy.

2(2) Subject to sub-paragraph (3), the present value of the ordinary benefits shall be the value at the liquidation date of the reversion in the ordinary benefits according to the contingency upon which those benefits are payable calculated on the basis of the rates of interest, mortality and disability referred to in paragraph 1.

2(3) For accumulating with profits policies–

(a) where the benefits are not expressed in the form of units in a with-profits fund, the value of the ordinary benefits is the amount that would have been payable, excluding any discretionary additions, if the policyholder had been able to exercise a right to terminate the policy at the liquidation date; and

(b) where the benefits are expressed in the form of units in a with-profits fund, the value of the ordinary benefits is the number of units held by the policy holder at the liquidation date valued at the unit price in force at that time or, if that price is not calculated on a daily basis, such price as the court may determine having regard to the last published unit price and any change in the value of assets attributable to the fund since the date of the last published unit price.

2(4) Where–

(a) sub-paragraph (3) applies, and

(b) paragraph 3(1) of Schedule 3 applies to the calculation of the unit price (or as the case may be) the fund value,

the value shall be adjusted on the basis set out in paragraph 3(3) to (5) of Schedule 3.

2(5) Where sub-paragraph (3) applies, the value may be further adjusted by reference to the value of the assets underlying the unit price (or as the case may be) the value of the fund, if the liquidator considers such an adjustment to be necessary.

3 Present value of additional benefits

3(1) Where under the terms of the policy or on the basis of the company's established practice the policy holder has a right to receive or an expectation of receiving benefits additional to the minimum benefits guaranteed under those terms, the court shall determine rates of interest, bonus (whether reversionary, terminal or any other type of bonus used by the company), mortality and disability to provide for the present value (if any) of that right or expectation.

3(2) In determining what (if any) value to attribute to any such expectations the court shall have regard to the premium payable in relation to the minimum guaranteed benefits and the amount (if any) an insurer is required to provide in respect of those expectations in any rules made by the Authority under Part 9A of the 2000 Act.

4 Present value of options

4 The amount of the present value of options shall be the amount which, in the opinion of the liquidator, is necessary to be provided at the liquidation date (in addition to the amount of the present value of the ordinary benefits) to cover the additional liabilities likely to arise upon the exercise on or after that date by the policy holder of any option conferred upon him by the terms of the policy or, in the case of an industrial assurance policy, by the Industrial Assurance Acts other than an option whereby the policy holder can secure a guaranteed cash payment within the period of 12 months beginning with that date.

5 Present value of premiums

5 The present value of the premiums shall be the value at the liquidation date of the premiums which fall due to be paid by the policy holder after the liquidation date calculated on the basis of the rates of interest, mortality and disability referred to in paragraph 1.

6 Value of the policy

6(1) Subject to sub-paragraph (2)–

  (a) if no further premiums fall due to be paid under the policy on or after the liquidation date, the value of the policy shall be the aggregate of:

    (i) the present value of the ordinary benefits;

    (ii) the present value of options; and

    (iii) the present value of additional benefits;

  (b) if further premiums fall due to be so paid and the aggregate value referred to in sub-paragraph (a) exceeds the present value of the premiums, the value of the policy shall be the amount of that excess; and

  (c) if further premiums fall due to be so paid and that aggregate does not exceed the present value of the premiums, the policy shall have no value.

6(2) Where the policy holder has a right conferred upon him by the terms of the policy or by the Industrial Assurance Acts whereby the policy holder can secure a guaranteed cash payment within the period of 12 months beginning with the liquidation date, the liquidator shall determine the amount which in his opinion it is necessary to provide at that date to cover the liabilities which will accrue when that option is exercised (on the assumption that it will be exercised) and the value of the policy shall be that amount if it exceeds the value of the policy (if any) determined in accordance with sub-paragraph (1).

SCHEDULE 3

RULES FOR VALUING LIFE POLICIES AND DEFERRED ANNUITY POLICIES WHICH ARE LINKED POLICIES

Rule 7

1(1) Subject to sub-paragraph (2) the value of the policy shall be the aggregate of the value of the linked liabilities (calculated in accordance with paragraphs 2 or 4) and the value of other than linked liabilities (calculated in accordance with paragraph 5) except where that aggregate is a negative amount it which case the policy shall have no value.

1(2) Where the terms of the policy include a right whereby the policy holder can secure a guaranteed cash payment within the period of 12 months beginning with the liquidation date then, if the amount which in the opinion of the liquidator is necessary to be provided at that date to cover any liabilities which will accrue when that option is exercised (on the assumption that it will be exercised) is greater than the value determined under sub-paragraph (1) of this paragraph, the value of the policy shall be that greater amount.

2(1) Where the linked liabilities are expressed in terms of units the value of those liabilities shall, subject to paragraph 3, be the amount arrived at by taking the product of the number of units of each class of units allocated to the policy on the liquidation date and the value of each such unit on that date and then adding those products.

886

2(2)   For the purposes of sub-paragraph (1)–

(a)   where under the terms of the policy the value of a unit at any time falls to be determined by reference to the value at that time of the assets of a particular fund maintained by the company in relation to that and other policies, the value of a unit on the liquidation date shall be determined by reference to the net realisable value of the assets credited to that fund on that date (after taking account of disposal costs, any tax liabilities resulting from the disposal of assets insofar as they have not already been provided for by the company and any other amounts which under the terms of those policies are chargeable to the fund), and

(b)   in any other case, the value of a unit on the liquidation date shall be the value which would have been ascribed to each unit credited to the policy holder, after any deductions which may be made under the terms of the policy, for the purpose of determining the benefits payable under the policy on the liquidation date had the policy matured on that date.

3(1)   This paragraph applies where–

(a)   paragraph 2(2)(a) applies and the company has a right under the terms of the policy either to make periodic withdrawals from the fund referred to in that paragraph or to retain any part of the income accruing in respect of the assets of that fund,

(b)   paragraph 2(2)(b) applies and the company has a right under the terms of the policy to receive the whole or any part of any distributions made in respect of the units referred to in that paragraph, or

(c)   paragraph 2(2)(a) or paragraph 2(2)(b) applies and the company has a right under the terms of the policy to make periodic cancellations of a proportion of the number of units credited to the policy.

3(2)   Where this paragraph applies, the value of the linked liabilities calculated in accordance with paragraph 2(1) shall be reduced by an amount calculated in accordance with sub-paragraph (3) of this paragraph.

3(3)   The said amount is–

(a)   where this paragraph applies by virtue of head (a) or (b) of sub-paragraph (1), the value as at the liquidation date, calculated on actuarial principles, of the future income of the company in respect of the units in question arising from the rights referred to in head (a) or (b) of sub-paragraph (1) as the case may be, or

(b)   where this paragraph applies by virtue of head (c) of sub-paragraph (1), the value as at the liquidation date, calculated on actuarial principles, of the liabilities of the company in respect of the units which fall to be cancelled in the future under the right referred to in head (c) of sub-paragraph (1).

3(4)   In calculating any amount in accordance with sub-paragraph (3) there shall be disregarded–

(a)   such part of the rights referred to in the relevant head of sub-paragraph (1) which in the opinion of the liquidator constitutes appropriate provision for future expenses and mortality risks, and

(b)   such part of those rights (if any) which the court considers to constitute appropriate provision for any right or expectation of the policy holder to receive benefits additional to the benefits guaranteed under the terms of the policy.

3(5)   In determining the said amount–

(a)   interest shall be assumed at such rate or rates as the court may direct, and

(b)   where relevant, the rates of mortality and the rates of disability to be employed shall be such rates as the court considers appropriate after taking into account:

(i)   relevant published tables of rates of mortality and rates of disability, and

    (ii) the rates of mortality and the rates of disability experienced in connection with similar policies issued by the company.

4 Where the linked liabilities are not expressed in terms of units the value of those liabilities shall be the value (subject to adjustment for any amounts which would have been deducted for taxation) which would have been ascribed to those liabilities had the policy matured on the liquidation date.

5(1) The value of any liabilities other than linked liabilities including reserves for future expenses, options and guarantees shall be determined on actuarial principles and appropriate assumptions in regard to all relevant factors including the assumption of such rate or rates of interest, mortality and disability as the court may direct.

5(2) In valuing liabilities under this paragraph credit shall be taken for those parts of future premiums which do not fall to be applied in the allocation of further units to the policy and for any rights of the company which have been disregarded under paragraph 3(4)(a) in valuing the linked liabilities.

SCHEDULE 4

RULES FOR VALUING LONG-TERM POLICIES WHICH ARE NOT DEALT WITH IN SCHEDULES 2 OR 3

Rule 7

The value of a long-term policy not covered by Schedule 2 or 3 shall be the value of the benefits due to the policy holder determined on such actuarial principles and assumptions in regard to all relevant factors as the court shall determine.

SCHEDULE 5

RULES FOR VALUING LONG-TERM POLICIES WHERE A STOP ORDER HAS BEEN MADE

Rule 8

1 Subject to paragraphs 2 and 3, in valuing a policy Schedules 2, 3 or 4 shall apply according to the class of that policy as if those Schedules were herein repeated but with a view to a fresh valuation of each policy on appropriate assumptions in regard to all relevant factors and subject to the following modifications–

    (a) references to the stop order shall be substituted for references to the liquidation date,

    (b) in paragraph 4 of Schedule 2 for the words "whereby the policy holder can secure a guaranteed cash payment within the period of 12 months beginning with that date" there shall be substituted the words "to surrender the policy which can be exercised on that date",

    (c) paragraph 6(2) of Schedule 2 shall be deleted, and

    (d) paragraph 1(2) of Schedule 3 shall be deleted.

2(1) This paragraph applies where the policy holder has a right conferred upon him under the terms of the policy or by the Industrial Assurance Acts to surrender the policy and that right is exercisable on the date of the stop order.

2(2) Where this paragraph applies and the amount required at the date of the stop order to provide for the benefits payable upon surrender of the policy (on the assumption that the policy is surrendered on the date of the stop order) is greater than the value of the policy determined in accordance with paragraph 1, the value of the policy shall, subject to paragraph 3, be the said amount so required.

2(3) Where any part of the surrender value is payable after the date of the stop order, sub-paragraph (2) shall apply but the value therein referred to shall be discounted at such a rate of interest as the court may direct.

3(1)   This paragraph applies in the case of a linked policy where–

(a)   the terms of the policy include a guarantee that the amount assured will on maturity of the policy be worth a minimum amount calculable in money terms, or

(b)   the terms of the policy include a right on the part of the policy holder to surrender the policy and a guarantee that the payment on surrender will be worth a minimum amount calculable in money terms and that right is exercisable on or after the date of the stop order.

3(2)   Where this paragraph applies the value of the policy shall be the greater of the following two amounts–

(a)   the value the policy would have had at the date of the stop order had the policy been a non-linked policy, that is to say, had the linked liabilities provided by the policy not been so provided but the policy had otherwise been on the same terms, and

(b)   the value the policy would have had at the date of the stop order had the policy not included any guarantees of payments on maturity or surrender worth a minimum amount calculable in money terms.

SCHEDULE 6

FORMS

Rule 27

[Not reproduced.]

Land Registration Rules 2003

(SI 2003/1417)

Made on 19 May 2003 by the Lord Chancellor in exercise of the powers conferred on him by the Land Registration Act 2002 and other legislation. Operative from 13 October 2003.

[**Note**: Changes made by the Enterprise and Regulatory Reform Act 2013 (Consequential Amendments) (Bankruptcy), the Small Business, Enterprise and Employment Act 2015 (Consequential Amendments) Regulations 2016 (SI 2016/481) and the Insolvency of Registered Providers of Social Housing Regulations 2018 (SI 2018/728) have been incorporated into the text.]

PART 14

MISCELLANEOUS AND SPECIAL CASES

Bankruptcy of proprietor

165 Bankruptcy notice

165(1) The bankruptcy notice in relation to a registered estate must be entered in the proprietorship register and the bankruptcy notice in relation to a registered charge must be entered in the charges register.

165(1A) The bankruptcy notice on registration of a petition in bankruptcy must be in the following form–

"BANKRUPTCY NOTICE entered under section 86(2) of the Land Registration Act 2002 in respect of a pending action, as the title of the [proprietor of the registered estate] *or* [the proprietor of the charge dated.....referred to above] appears to be affected by a petition in bankruptcy against [*name of debtor*], presented in the [*name*] Court (Court Reference Number......) (Land Charges Reference Number PA......)."

165(1B) The bankruptcy notice on registration of a bankruptcy application must be in the following form–

"BANKRUPTCY NOTICE entered under section 86(2) of the Land Registration Act 2002 in respect of a pending action, as the title of [the proprietor of the registered estate] or [the proprietor of the charge dated.....referred to above] appears to be affected by a bankruptcy application made by [name of debtor] (reference.....) (Land Charges Reference Number PA.....)."

165(2)   The registrar must give notice of the entry of a bankruptcy notice to the proprietor of the registered estate or registered charge to which it relates.

165(3)   In this rule, "bankruptcy notice" means the notice which the registrar must enter in the register under section 86(2) of the Act.

History
(See History Note after r.167.)

166   Bankruptcy restriction

166(1)   The bankruptcy restriction in relation to a registered estate must be entered in the proprietorship register and the bankruptcy restriction in relation to a registered charge must be entered in the charges register.

166(1A)   The bankruptcy restriction on registration of a bankruptcy order made by the court must be in the following form–

"BANKRUPTCY RESTRICTION entered under section 86(4) of the Land Registration Act 2002, as the title of [the proprietor of the registered estate] or [the proprietor of the charge dated......referred to above] appears to be affected by a bankruptcy order made by the [name] Court (Court Reference Number......) against [name of debtor] (Land Charges Reference Number WO........).

[No disposition of the registered estate] or [No disposition of the charge] is to be registered until the trustee in bankruptcy of the property of the bankrupt is registered as proprietor of the [registered estate] or [charge].".

166(1B)   The bankruptcy restriction on registration of a bankruptcy order made by the adjudicator must be in the following form–

"BANKRUPTCY RESTRICTION entered under section 86(4) of the Land Registration Act 2002 as the title of [the proprietor of the registered estate] or [the proprietor of the charge dated.....referred to above] appears to be affected by a bankruptcy order made by the adjudicator (reference.....) against [name of debtor] (Land Charges Reference Number WO.....).

[No disposition of the registered estate] or [No disposition of the charge] is to be registered until the trustee in bankruptcy of the property of the bankrupt is registered as proprietor of the [registered estate] or [charge]."

166(2)   The registrar must give notice of the entry of a bankruptcy restriction to the proprietor of the registered estate or registered charge to which it relates.

166(3)   In this rule, "bankruptcy restriction" means the restriction which the registrar must enter in the register under section 86(4) of the Act.

History
(See History Note after r.167.)

167   Action of the registrar in relation to bankruptcy entries

167(1)   Where the registrar is satisfied that–

(a)   the bankruptcy order has been annulled, or

(ab)   the adjudicator has refused to make a bankruptcy order, or

(b)   the bankruptcy petition has been dismissed or withdrawn with the court's permission, or

(c)   the bankruptcy proceedings do not affect or have ceased to affect the registered estate or registered charge in relation to which a bankruptcy notice or bankruptcy restriction has been entered on the register, he must as soon as practicable cancel any bankruptcy notice or bankruptcy restriction which relates to that bankruptcy application, to that bankruptcy order, to that bankruptcy petition or to those proceedings from the register.

167(2)   Where it appears to the registrar that there is doubt as to whether the debtor or bankrupt is the same person as the proprietor of the registered estate or registered charge in relation to which a bankruptcy notice or bankruptcy restriction has been entered, he must as soon as practicable take such action as he considers necessary to resolve the doubt.

167(3)   In this rule–

"bankruptcy notice" means the notice which the registrar must enter in the register under section 86(2) of the Act, and

"bankruptcy restriction" means the restriction which the registrar must enter in the register under section 86(4) of the Act.

History
Rules 165(1A), (1B), 166(1A), (1B) and 167(1)(ab) added and minor amendments made by the Enterprise and Regulatory Reform Act 2013 (Consequential Amendments) (Bankruptcy) and the Small Business, Enterprise and Employment Act 2015 (Consequential Amendments) Regulations 2016 (SI 2016/481) as from 6 April 2016.

168   Registration of trustee in bankruptcy

168(1)   Where–

(a)   a proprietor has had a bankruptcy order made against him, or

(b)   an insolvency administration order has been made in respect of a deceased proprietor, and the bankrupt's or deceased's registered estate or registered charge has vested in the trustee in bankruptcy, the trustee may apply for the alteration of the register by registering himself in place of the bankrupt or deceased proprietor.

168(2)   The application must be supported by, as appropriate–

(a)   the bankruptcy order relating to the bankrupt or the insolvency administration order relating to the deceased's estate, and

(b)   a certificate signed by the trustee that the registered estate or registered charge is comprised in the bankrupt's estate or deceased's estate, and

(c)   where the official receiver is the trustee, a certificate by him to that effect, and, where the trustee is another person, the evidence referred to in paragraph (3).

168(3)   The evidence referred to at paragraph (2)(c) is–

(a)   his certificate of appointment as trustee by the meeting of the bankrupt's or deceased debtor's creditors, or

(b)   his certificate of appointment as trustee by the Secretary of State, or

(c)   the order of the court appointing him trustee.

168(4)   In this rule, "insolvency administration order" has the same meaning as in section 385(1) of the Insolvency Act 1986.

169   Trustee in bankruptcy vacating office

169(1)   This rule applies where–

(a)   a trustee in bankruptcy, who has been registered as proprietor, vacates his office, and

(b) the official receiver or some other person has been appointed the trustee of the relevant bankrupt's estate, and

(c) the official receiver or that person applies to be registered as proprietor in place of the former trustee.

169(2) The application referred to in paragraph (1)(c) must be supported by the evidence required by rule 168(2)(c).

170 Description of trustee in register

170 Where the official receiver or another trustee in bankruptcy is registered as proprietor, the words "Official Receiver and trustee in bankruptcy of [name]" or "Trustee in bankruptcy of [name]" must be added to the register, as appropriate.

Overseas insolvency proceedings

171 Proceedings under the EU Regulation on insolvency proceedings

171(1) A relevant person may apply for a note of a judgment opening insolvency proceedings to be entered in the register.

171(2) An application under paragraph (1) must be accompanied by such evidence as the registrar may reasonably require.

171(3) Following an application under paragraph (1) if the registrar is satisfied that the judgment opening insolvency proceedings has been made he may enter a note of the judgment in the register.

171(4) In this rule–

"judgment opening insolvency proceedings" means a judgment opening proceedings within the meaning of article 3(1) of the Regulation,

"Regulation" means Regulation (EU) 2015/848 of the European Parliament and of the Council,

"relevant person" means any person authorised under the provisions of Article 29 of the Regulation to request or require an entry to be made in the register in respect of the judgment opening insolvency proceedings the subject of the application.

History
Heading to r.171 and r.171(4) amended by the Insolvency Amendment (EU 2015/848) Regulations 2017 (SI 2017/702) regs 1, 2(1), Sch. para.53 in relation to proceedings opened on or after 26 June 2017 (see reg.3) when the Recast EU Regulation 2015/848 came force.

Companies and other corporations

184 Administration orders and liquidation of a company

184(1) Paragraph (2) applies where a company which is the registered proprietor of a registered estate or registered charge enters administration under the Insolvency Act 1986.

184(2) Upon the application of the company's administrator, supported by the order or the notice of appointment, the registrar must make an entry in the individual register of the relevant registered title as to the making of the order or the notice of appointment and the appointment of the administrator.

184(3) Paragraphs (4) and (5) apply where a company which is the registered proprietor of a registered estate or registered charge is in liquidation.

184(4) Upon the application of the company's liquidator, the registrar must make an entry in the individual register of the relevant registered title as to the appointment of the liquidator.

184(5) The application under paragraph (4) must be supported by the order, appointment by the Secretary of State or resolution under which the liquidator was appointed and such other evidence as the registrar may require.

184A Housing administration orders

184A(1) Paragraph (2) applies where a housing administration order is made under the Housing and Planning Act 2016 in relation to a registered provider which is the registered proprietor of a registered estate or a registered charge.

184A(2) Upon the application of the registered provider's housing administrator, supported by the order, the registrar must make an entry in the individual register of the relevant registered title as to the making of the order and the appointment of the housing administrator.

184A(3) In this rule "housing administration order", "housing administrator" and "registered provider" have the meanings set out in Chapter 5 of Part 4 of the Housing and Planning Act 2016.

History
Rule 184A inserted by the Insolvency of Registered Providers of Social Housing Regulations 2018 (SI 2018/728) regs 1, 4 as from 4 July 2018.

185 Note of dissolution of a corporation

185 Where a corporation shown in an individual register as the proprietor of the registered estate or of a registered charge has been dissolved, the registrar may enter a note of that fact in the proprietorship register or in the charges register, as appropriate.

Insolvency Act 1986 (Prescribed Part) Order 2003

(SI 2003/2097)

Made on 8 August 2002 by the Secretary of State for Trade and Industry under s.176A of the Insolvency Act 1986. Operative from 15 September 2003.

1 Citation, Commencement and Interpretation

1(1) This Order may be cited as the Insolvency Act 1986 (Prescribed Part) Order 2003 and shall come into force on 15th September 2003.

1(2) In this Order "the 1986 Act" means the Insolvency Act 1986.

2 Minimum value of the company's net property

2 For the purposes of section 176A(3)(a) of the 1986 Act the minimum value of the company's net property is £10,000.

3 Calculation of prescribed part

3(1) The prescribed part of the company's net property to be made available for the satisfaction of unsecured debts of the company pursuant to section 176A of the 1986 Act shall be calculated as follows–

(a) where the company's net property does not exceed £10,000 in value, 50% of that property;

(b) subject to paragraph (2), where the company's net property exceeds £10,000 in value the sum of–

(i) 50% of the first £10,000 in value; and

(ii) 20% of that part of the company's net property which exceeds £10,000 in value.

3(2) The value of the prescribed part of the company's net property to be made available for the satisfaction of unsecured debts of the company pursuant to section 176A shall not exceed £600,000.

Financial Collateral Arrangements (No.2) Regulations 2003

(SI 2003/3226)

Made on 10 December 2003 by the Treasury, being a government department designated for the purposes of s.2(2) of the European Communities Act 1972 in relation to collateral security, in exercise of the powers conferred on them by that section. Operative from 26 December 2003.

[**Note**: Changes made by the Financial Collateral Arrangements (No.2) Regulations 2003 (Amendment) Regulations 2009 (SI 2009/2462), the Financial Markets and Insolvency (Settlement Finality and Financial Collateral Arrangements) (Amendment) Regulations 2010 (SI 2010/2993), the Companies Act 2006 (Amendment of Part 25) Regulations 2013 (SI 2013/600), the Capital Requirements Regulations 2013 (SI 2013/3115), the Bank Recovery and Resolution (No.2) Order 2014 (SI 2014/3348), the Small Business Enterprise and Employment Act 2015 (Consequential Amendments, Saving and Transitional Provisions) Regulations 2018 (SI 2018/208) and the Financial Services and Markets (Insolvency) (Amendment of Miscellaneous Enactments) Regulations 2019 (SI 2019/755) have been incorporated into the text.]

PART 1

GENERAL

1 Citation and commencement

1(1) These Regulations may be cited as the Financial Collateral Arrangements (No. 2) Regulations 2003.

1(2) Regulation 2 shall come into force on 11th December 2003 and all other Regulations thereof shall come into force on 26th December 2003.

2 Revocation

2 The Financial Collateral Arrangements Regulations 2003 are hereby revoked.

[**Note:** These Regulations were never brought into force.]

3 Interpretation

3(1) In these Regulations–

"book entry securities collateral" means financial collateral subject to a financial collateral arrangement which consists of financial instruments, title to which is evidenced by entries in a register or account maintained by or on behalf of an intermediary;

"cash" means money in any currency, credited to an account, or a similar claim for repayment of money and includes money market deposits and sums due or payable to, or received between the parties in connection with the operation of a financial collateral arrangement or a close-out netting provision;

"close-out netting provision" means a term of a financial collateral arrangement, or of an arrangement of which a financial collateral arrangement forms part, or any legislative provision under which on the occurrence of an enforcement event, whether through the operation of netting or set-off or otherwise–

(a) the obligations of the parties are accelerated to become immediately due and expressed as an obligation to pay an amount representing the original obligation's estimated current value or replacement cost, or are terminated and replaced by an obligation to pay such an amount; or

(b) an account is taken of what is due from each party to the other in respect of such obligations and a net sum equal to the balance of the account is payable by the party from whom the larger amount is due to the other party;

"credit claims" means pecuniary claims which arise out of an agreement whereby a credit institution, as defined in Article 4(1)(1) of Regulation (EU) 575/2013 of the European Parliament and of the Council of 26 June 2013, and including the institutions listed in Article 2(5)(2) to (23) of Directive 2013/36/EU of the European Parliament and of the Council of 26 June 2013, grants credit in the form of a loan;

"equivalent financial collateral" means–

(a) in relation to cash, a payment of the same amount and in the same currency;

(b) in relation to financial instruments, financial instruments of the same issuer or debtor, forming part of the same issue or class and of the same nominal amount, currency and description or, where the financial collateral arrangement provides for the transfer of other assets following the occurrence of any event relating to or affecting any financial instruments provided as financial collateral, those other assets;

and includes the original financial collateral provided under the arrangement;

"financial collateral arrangement" means a title transfer financial collateral arrangement or a security financial collateral arrangement, whether or not these are covered by a master agreement or general terms and conditions;

"financial collateral" means either cash, financial instruments or credit claims;

"financial instruments" means–

(a) shares in companies and other securities equivalent to shares in companies;

(b) bonds and other forms of instruments giving rise to or acknowledging indebtedness if these are tradeable on the capital market; and

(c) any other securities which are normally dealt in and which give the right to acquire any such shares, bonds, instruments or other securities by subscription, purchase or exchange or which give rise to a cash settlement (excluding instruments of payment);

and includes units of a collective investment scheme within the meaning of the Financial Services and Markets Act 2000, eligible debt securities within the meaning of the Uncertificated Securities Regulations 2001, money market instruments, claims relating to or rights in or in respect of any of the financial instruments included in this definition and any rights, privileges or benefits attached to or arising from any such financial instruments;

"intermediary" means a person that maintains registers or accounts to which financial instruments may be credited or debited, for others or both for others and for its own account but does not include–

(a) a person who acts as a registrar or transfer agent for the issuer of financial instruments; or

(b) a person who maintains registers or accounts in the capacity of operator of a system for the holding and transfer of financial instruments on records of the issuer or other records which constitute the primary record of entitlement to financial instruments as against the issuer;

"non-natural person" means any corporate body, unincorporated firm, partnership or body with legal personality except an individual, including any such entity constituted under the law of a country or territory outside the United Kingdom or any such entity constituted under international law;

"recovery and resolution directive" means Directive 2014/59/EU of the European Parliament and of the Council of 15th May 2014 establishing a framework for the recovery and resolution of credit institutions and investment firms;

"relevant account" means, in relation to book entry securities collateral which is subject to a financial collateral arrangement, the register or account, which may be maintained by the collateral-taker, in which entries are made, by which that book entry securities collateral is transferred or designated so as to be in the possession or under the control of the collateral-taker or a person acting on its behalf;

"relevant financial obligations" means the obligations which are secured or otherwise covered by a financial collateral arrangement, and such obligations may consist of or include–

(a) present or future, actual or contingent or prospective obligations (including such obligations arising under a master agreement or similar arrangement);

(b) obligations owed to the collateral-taker by a person other than the collateral-provider;

(c) obligations of a specified class or kind arising from time to time;

"reorganisation measures" means–

(a) administration within the meaning of the Insolvency Act 1986 or the Insolvency (Northern Ireland) Order 1989;

(b) a company voluntary arrangement within the meaning of that Act or that Order;

(c) administration of a partnership within the meaning of that Act or that Order or, in the case of a Scottish partnership, a protected trust deed within the meaning of the Bankruptcy (Scotland) Act 1985;

(d) a partnership voluntary arrangement within the meaning of the Insolvency Act 1986 or the Insolvency (Northern Ireland) Order 1989 or, in the case of a Scottish partnership, a protected trust deed within the meaning of the Bankruptcy (Scotland) Act 1985; and

(e) the making of an interim order on an administration application;

"security financial collateral arrangement" means an agreement or arrangement, evidenced in writing, where–

(a) the purpose of the agreement or arrangement is to secure the relevant financial obligations owed to the collateral-taker;

(b) the collateral-provider creates or there arises a security interest in financial collateral to secure those obligations;

(c) the financial collateral is delivered, transferred, held, registered or otherwise designated so as to be in the possession or under the control of the collateral-taker or a person acting on its behalf; any right of the collateral-provider to substitute financial collateral of the same or greater value or withdraw excess financial collateral or to collect the proceeds of credit claims until further notice shall not prevent the financial collateral being in the possession or under the control of the collateral-taker; and

(d) the collateral-provider and the collateral-taker are both non-natural persons;

"security interest" means any legal or equitable interest or any right in security, other than a title transfer financial collateral arrangement, created or otherwise arising by way of security including–

(a) a pledge;

(b) a mortgage;

(c) a fixed charge;

(d) a charge created as a floating charge where the financial collateral charged is delivered, transferred, held, registered or otherwise designated so as to be in the possession or under the control of the collateral-taker or a person acting on its behalf; any right of the collateral-provider to substitute financial collateral of the same or greater value or withdraw excess financial collateral or to collect the proceeds of credit claims until further notice shall not prevent the financial collateral being in the possession or under the control of the collateral-taker; or

(e) a lien;

"title transfer financial collateral arrangement" means an agreement or arrangement, including a repurchase agreement, evidenced in writing, where–

(a) the purpose of the agreement or arrangement is to secure or otherwise cover the relevant financial obligations owed to the collateral-taker;

(b) the collateral-provider transfers legal and beneficial ownership in financial collateral to a collateral-taker on terms that when the relevant financial obligations are discharged the collateral-taker must transfer legal and beneficial ownership of equivalent financial collateral to the collateral-provider; and

(c) the collateral-provider and the collateral-taker are both non-natural persons;

"winding-up proceedings" means–

(a) winding up by the court or voluntary winding up within the meaning of the Insolvency Act 1986 or the Insolvency (Northern Ireland) Order 1989;

(b) sequestration of a Scottish partnership under the Bankruptcy (Scotland) Act 1985;

(c) bank insolvency within the meaning of the Banking Act 2009.

3(1A) For the purpose of these Regulations–

(a) "enforcement event" means an event of default, or (subject to sub-paragraph (b)) any similar event as agreed between the parties, on the occurrence of which, under the terms of a financial collateral agreement or by operation of law, the collateral taker is entitled to realise or appropriate financial collateral or a close-out netting provision comes into effect;

(b) a crisis management measure or crisis prevention measure taken in relation to an entity under the recovery and resolution directive shall not be considered to be an enforcement event pursuant to an agreement between the parties if the substantive obligations provided for in that agreement (including payment and delivery obligations and provision of collateral) continue to be performed; and

(c) for the purposes of sub-paragraph (b) "crisis prevention measure" and "crisis management measure" have the meaning given in section 48Z of the Banking Act 2009.

3(2) For the purposes of these Regulations "possession" of financial collateral in the form of cash or financial instruments includes the case where financial collateral has been credited to an account in the name of the collateral-taker or a person acting on his behalf (whether or not the collateral-taker, or person acting on his behalf, has credited the financial collateral to an account in the name of the collateral-provider on his, or that person's, books) provided that any rights the collateral-provider may have in relation to that financial collateral are limited to the right to substitute financial collateral of the same or greater value or to withdraw excess financial collateral.

History
Definitions of "financial collateral", "reorganisation measures", "security financial collateral arrangement", "security interest" and "winding up proceedings" amended and definition of "credit claims" and reg.3(1) inserted by the Financial Markets and Insolvency (Settlement Finality and Financial Collateral Arrangements) (Amendment) Regulations 2010 (SI 2010/2993) reg.4(2) as from 6 April 2011. Definition of "credit claims" amended by the Capital Requirements Regulations 2013 (SI 2013/3115) reg.46 and Sch.2 para.61 as from 1 January 2014. Definition of "enforcement event" deleted and definition of "recovery and resolution directive" and reg.3(1A) inserted by the Bank Recovery and Resolution (No.2) Order 2014 (SI 2014/3348) Sch.3 para.9(1), (2) as from 10 January 2015.

PART 2

MODIFICATION OF LAW REQUIRING FORMALITIES

4   Certain legislation requiring formalities not to apply to financial collateral arrangements

4(1)   Section 4 of the Statute of Frauds 1677 (no action on a third party's promise unless in writing and signed) shall not apply (if it would otherwise do so) in relation to a financial collateral arrangement.

4(2)   Section 53(1)(c) of the Law of Property Act 1925 (disposition of equitable interest to be in writing and signed) shall not apply (if it would otherwise do so) in relation to a financial collateral arrangement.

4(3)   Section 136 of the Law of Property Act 1925 (legal assignments of things in action) shall not apply (if it would otherwise do so) in relation to a financial collateral arrangement, to the extent that the section requires an assignment to be signed by the assignor or a person authorised on its behalf, in order to be effectual in law.

4(4)   Sections 859A (charges created by a company) and 859H (consequence of failure to register charges created by a company) of the Companies Act 2006 shall not apply (if they would otherwise do so) in relation to a security financial collateral arrangement or any charge created or otherwise arising under a security financial collateral arrangement or, in Scotland, to relation to any charge created or arising under a financial collateral arrangement.

4(5)   Section 4 of the Industrial and Provident Societies Act 1967 (filing of information relating to charges) shall not apply (if it would otherwise do so) in relation to a financial collateral arrangement or any charge created or otherwise arising under a financial collateral arrangement.

(See history note after reg.7.)

5   Certain legislation affecting Scottish companies not to apply to financial collateral arrangements [Omitted]

(See history note after reg.7.)

6   No additional formalities required for creation of a right in security over book entry securities collateral in Scotland

6(1)   Where under the law of Scotland an act is required as a condition for transferring, creating or enforcing a right in security over any book entry securities collateral, that requirement shall not apply (if it would otherwise do so).

6(2)   For the purposes of paragraph (1) an "act"–

   (a)   is any act other than an entry on a register or account maintained by or on behalf of an intermediary which evidences title to the book entry securities collateral;

   (b)   includes the entering of the collateral-taker's name in a company's register of members.

(See history note after reg.7.)

6A   Certain legislation affecting overseas companies not to apply to financial collateral arrangements

6A   Any provision about registration of charges made by regulations under section 1052 of the Companies Act 2006 (overseas companies) does not apply (if it would otherwise do so) in relation to a security financial collateral arrangement or any charge created or otherwise arising under a security financial collateral arrangement or, in Scotland, to any charge created or arising under a financial collateral arrangement.

(See history note after reg.7.)

7   Certain legislation affecting Northern Ireland companies and requiring formalities not to apply to financial collateral arrangements [Omitted]

History
Regulations 4, 5 amended, reg.6A inserted and reg.7 omitted by the Financial Collateral Arrangements (No.2) Regulations 2003 (Amendment) Regulations 2009 (SI 2009/2462) reg.2(1)–(5) as from 1 October 2009. Regulations 4, 5, 6A amended by the Financial Markets and Insolvency (Settlement Finality and Financial Collateral Arrangements) (Amendment) Regulations 2010 (SI 2010/2993) reg.4(3)–(5) as from 6 April 2011. Regulation 4(4) amended and reg.5 omitted by the Companies Act 2006 (Amendment of Part 25) Regulations 2013 (SI 2013/600) reg.5, 6(1) and Sch.2 para.4 as from 6 April 2013, in relation to charges created on or after that date.

PART 3

MODIFICATION OF INSOLVENCY LAW

8   Certain legislation restricting enforcement of security not to apply to financial collateral arrangements

8(1)   The following provisions of Schedule B1 to the Insolvency Act 1986 (administration) shall not apply to any security interest created or otherwise arising under a financial collateral arrangement–

(a)   paragraph 43(2) (restriction on enforcement of security or repossession of goods) including that provision as applied by paragraph 44 (interim moratorium);

(aa)   paragraph 65(2) (distribution);

(b)   paragraphs 70 and 71 (power of administrator to deal with charged property); and

(c)   paragraph 99(3) and (4) (administrator's remuneration, expenses and liabilities).

8(2)   Paragraph 41(2) of Schedule B1 to the Insolvency Act 1986 (receiver to vacate office when so required by administrator) shall not apply to a receiver appointed under a charge created or otherwise arising under a financial collateral arrangement.

8(3)   The following provisions of the Insolvency Act 1986 (administration) shall not apply in relation to any security interest created or otherwise arising under a financial collateral arrangement–

(a)   sections 10(1)(b) and 11(3)(c) (restriction on enforcement of security while petition for administration order pending or order in force); and

(b)   section 15(1) and 15(2) (power of administrator to deal with charged property); and

(c)   section 19(4) and 19(5) (administrator's remuneration, expenses and liabilities).

8(4)   Section 11(2) of the Insolvency Act 1986 (receiver to vacate office when so required by administrator) shall not apply to a receiver appointed under a charge created or otherwise arising under a financial collateral arrangement.

8(5)   Paragraph 20 and sub-paragraph 12(1)(g) of Schedule A1 to the Insolvency Act 1986 (Effect of moratorium on creditors) shall not apply (if it would otherwise do so) to any security interest created or otherwise arising under a financial collateral arrangement.

History
Regulation 8 amended by the Financial Markets and Insolvency (Settlement Finality and Financial Collateral Arrangements) (Amendment) Regulations 2010 (SI 2010/2993) reg.4(6) as from 6 April 2011.

9   Certain Northern Ireland legislation restricting enforcement of security not to apply to financial collateral arrangements

9(1)   The following provisions of the Insolvency (Northern Ireland) Order 1989 (administration) shall not apply to any security interest created or otherwise arising under a financial collateral arrangement–

(a)   Article 23(1)(b) and Article 24(3)(c) (restriction on enforcement of security while petition for administration order pending or order in force);

(b)   Article 28(1) and (2) (power of administrator to deal with charged property);

(c)   Article 31(4) and (5) (administrator's remuneration, expenses and liabilities); and

(d)   Paragraphs 44(2), 45 (restriction on enforcement of security), 66(2) (distribution), 71, 72 (power of administrator to deal with charged property), 100(3) and (4) (administrator's remuneration, expenses and liabilities) of Schedule B1 to the Order.

9(2)   Article 24(2) of that Order (receiver to vacate office at request of administrator) shall not apply to a receiver appointed under a charge created or otherwise arising under a financial collateral arrangement.

(See history note after reg.11.)

10   Certain insolvency legislation on avoidance of contracts and floating charges not to apply to financial collateral arrangements

10(1)   In relation to winding-up proceedings of a collateral-taker or collateral-provider, section 127 of the Insolvency Act 1986 (avoidance of property dispositions, etc) shall not apply (if it would otherwise do so)–

(a)   to any property or security interest subject to a disposition or created or otherwise arising under a financial collateral arrangement; or

(b)   to prevent a close-out netting provision taking effect in accordance with its terms.

10(2)   Section 88 of the Insolvency Act 1986 (avoidance of share transfers, etc after winding-up resolution) shall not apply (if it would otherwise do so) to any transfer of shares under a financial collateral arrangement.

10(2A)   Sections 40 (or in Scotland, sections 59, 60(1)(e)) and 175 of the Insolvency Act 1986 (preferential debts) shall not apply to any debt which is secured by a charge created or otherwise arising under a financial collateral arrangement.

10(2B)   Section 176ZA of the Insolvency Act 1986 (expenses of winding up) shall not apply in relation to any claim to any property which is subject to a disposition or created or otherwise arising under a financial collateral arrangement.

10(3)   Section 176A of the Insolvency Act 1986 (share of assets for unsecured creditors) shall not apply (if it would otherwise do so) to any charge created or otherwise arising under a financial collateral arrangement.

10(4)   Section 178 of the Insolvency Act 1986 (power to disclaim onerous property) or, in Scotland, any rule of law having the same effect as that section, shall not apply where the collateral-provider or collateral-taker under the arrangement is subject to winding-up proceedings, to any financial collateral arrangement.

10(5)   Section 245 of the Insolvency Act 1986 (avoidance of certain floating charges) shall not apply (if it would otherwise do so) to any charge created or otherwise arising under a security financial collateral arrangement.

10(6)   Section 754 of the Companies Act 2006 (priorities where debentures secured by floating charge) (including that section as applied or modified by any enactment made under the Banking Act 2009) shall not apply (if it would otherwise do so) to any charge created or otherwise arising under a financial collateral arrangement.

(See history note after reg.11.)

11 Certain Northern Ireland insolvency legislation on avoidance of contracts and floating charges not to apply to financial collateral arrangements

11(1) In relation to winding-up proceedings of a collateral-provider or collateral-taker, Article 107 of the Insolvency (Northern Ireland) Order 1989 (avoidance of property dispositions effected after commencement of winding up) shall not apply (if it would otherwise do so)–

(a) to any property or security interest subject to a disposition or created or otherwise arising under a financial collateral arrangement; or

(b) to prevent a close-out netting provision taking effect in accordance with its terms.

11(1A) Article 50 of that Order (payment of debts out of assets subject to floating charge) shall not apply (if it would otherwise do so), to any charge created or otherwise arising under a financial collateral arrangement.

11(2) Article 74 of that Order (avoidance of share transfers, etc after winding-up resolution) shall not apply (if it would otherwise do so) to any transfer of shares under a financial collateral arrangement.

11(2A) Articles 149 of that Order (preferential debts) and 150ZA (expenses of winding up) shall not apply (if they would otherwise do so) to any charge created or otherwise arising under a financial collateral arrangement.

11(3) Article 152 of that Order (power to disclaim onerous property) shall not apply where the collateral-provider or collateral-taker under the arrangement is being wound-up, to any financial collateral arrangement.

11(4) Article 207 of that Order (avoidance of certain floating charges) shall not apply (if it would otherwise do so) to any charge created or otherwise arising under a security financial collateral arrangement.

11(5) [Omitted]

History
Regulation 10(6) amended and reg.11(5) omitted by the Financial Collateral Arrangements (No.2) Regulations 2003 (Amendment) Regulations 2009 (SI 2009/2462) reg.2(6), (7) as from 1 October 2009. Regulations 9–11 amended by the Financial Markets and Insolvency (Settlement Finality and Financial Collateral Arrangements) (Amendment) Regulations 2010 (SI 2010/2993) reg.4(7)–(9) as from 6 April 2011.

12 Close-out netting provisions to take effect in accordance with their terms

12(1) A close-out netting provision shall, subject to paragraph (2), take effect in accordance with its terms notwithstanding that the collateral-provider or collateral-taker under the arrangement is subject to winding-up proceedings or reorganisation measures.

12(2) Paragraph (1) shall not apply if at the time that a party to a financial collateral arrangement entered into such an arrangement or that the relevant financial obligations came into existence–

(a) that party was aware or should have been aware that winding up proceedings or re-organisation measures had commenced in relation to the other party;

(aa) in Scotland, that party had notice that a meeting of creditors of the other party had been summoned under section 98 of the Insolvency Act 1986;

(ab) in England and Wales, that party had notice that a statement as to the affairs of the other party had been sent to the other party's creditors under section 99(1) of that Act;

(ac) that party had notice that a meeting of creditors of the other party had been summoned under Article 84 of the Insolvency (Northern Ireland) Order 1989;

(b) that party had notice that a petition for the winding-up of or, in Scotland, a petition for winding-up proceedings in relation to the other party was pending;

(c) that party had notice that an application for an administration order was pending or that any person had given notice of an intention to appoint an administrator; or

(d) that party had notice that an application for an administration order was pending or that any person had given notice of an intention to appoint an administrator and liquidation of the other party to the financial collateral arrangement was immediately preceded by an administration of that party.

12(3) For the purposes of paragraph (2)–

(a) winding-up proceedings commence on the making of a winding-up order or, in the case of a Scottish partnership, the award of sequestration by the court; and

(b) reorganisation measures commence on the appointment of an administrator, whether by a court or otherwise or, in the case of a Scottish partnership, when a protected trust deed is entered into.

12(4) The following provisions of the Insolvency (England and Wales) Rules 2016, or, in Scotland, any rule of law with the same or similar effect to the effect of these Rules, do not apply to a close-out netting provision unless paragraph (2)(a) applies–

(a) in rule 14.24 (administration: mutual dealings and set-off), in paragraph (6), in the definition of "mutual dealings", paragraphs (a) and (d); and

(b) in rule 14.25 (winding up: mutual dealings and set-off), in paragraph (6), in the definition of "mutual dealings", paragraph (c).

12(4A) Rules 2.086(2)(a) and (d) and 4.096(2)(c) of the Insolvency Rules (Northern Ireland) 1991 (mutual credits and set off) do not apply to a close-out netting provision unless paragraph (2)(a) applies.

12(5) Nothing in this regulation prevents the Bank of England imposing a restriction on the effect of a close out netting provision in the exercise of its powers under Part 1 of the Banking Act 2009.

[**Note**: the references in reg.12(4) are to provisions which were in force when these Regulations were made. They correspond approximately to the present r.2.85(2)(a) and (d) and r.4.90(2)(c).]

History
Regulation 12 amended by the Financial Markets and Insolvency (Settlement Finality and Financial Collateral Arrangements) (Amendment) Regulations 2010 (SI 2010/2993) reg.4(10) as from 6 April 2011. Regulation 12(5) inserted by the Bank Recovery and Resolution (No.2) Order 2014 (SI 2014/3348) Sch.3 para.9(1), (3) as from 10 January 2015. Regulation 12(2)(aa)–(ac) were inserted by, and reg.12(2)(b) was modified by the Small Business, Enterprise and Employment Act 2015 (Consequential Amendments, Savings and Transitional Provisions) Regulations 2018 (SI 2018/208) reg.8(a) and (b) with effect from 13 March 2018.
　　Regulation 12(4), (4A) substituted by the Financial Services and Markets (Insolvency) (Amendment of Miscellaneous Enactments) Regulations 2019 (SI 2019/755) regs 1, 3(1), (2) as from 23 April 2019.

13　Financial collateral arrangements to be enforceable where collateral-taker not aware of commencement of winding-up proceedings or reorganisation measures

13(1) Where any of the events specified in paragraph (2) occur on the day of, but after the moment of commencement of, winding-up proceedings or reorganisation measures those events, arrangements and obligations shall be legally enforceable and binding on third parties if the collateral-taker can show that he was not aware, nor should have been aware, of the commencement of such proceedings or measures.

13(2) The events referred to in paragraph (1) are–

(a) a financial collateral arrangement coming into existence;

(b) a relevant financial obligation secured by a financial collateral arrangement coming into existence; or

(c)   the delivery, transfer, holding, registering or other designation of financial collateral so as to be in the possession or under the control of the collateral-taker.

13(3)   For the purposes of paragraph (1)–

(a)   the commencement of winding-up proceedings means the making of a winding-up order or, in the case of a Scottish partnership, the award of sequestration by the court; and

(b)   commencement of reorganisation measures means the appointment of an administrator, whether by a court or otherwise or, in the case of a Scottish partnership, the date of registration of a protected trust deed.

History
Regulation 13 amended by the Financial Markets and Insolvency (Settlement Finality and Financial Collateral Arrangements) (Amendment) Regulations 2010 (SI 2010/2993) reg.4(11) as from 6 April 2011.

14   Modification of the Insolvency (England and Wales) Rules 2016 and the Insolvency Rules (Northern Ireland) 1991

14   Where the collateral-provider or the collateral-taker under a financial collateral arrangement goes into liquidation or administration and the arrangement or a close out netting provision provides for, or the mechanism provided under the arrangement permits, either–

(a)   the debt owed by the party in liquidation or administration under the arrangement, to be assessed or paid in a currency other than sterling; or

(b)   the debt to be converted into sterling at a rate other than the official exchange rate prevailing on the date when that party went into liquidation or administration;

then rule 14.21 of the Insolvency (England and Wales) Rules 2016 (debts in foreign currency), or rule 4.097 of the Insolvency Rules (Northern Ireland) 1991 (liquidation, debt in foreign currency), as appropriate, shall not apply unless the arrangement provides for an unreasonable exchange rate or the collateral-taker uses the mechanism provided under the arrangement to impose an unreasonable exchange rate in which case the appropriate rule shall apply.

History
Heading to and reg.14 amended by the Financial Services and Markets (Insolvency) (Amendment of Miscellaneous Enactments) Regulations 2019 (SI 2019/755) regs 1, 3(1), (3) as from 23 April 2019.

15   Modification of the Insolvency (Scotland) (Receivership and Winding up) Rules 2018 and the Insolvency (Scotland) (Company Voluntary Arrangements and Administration) Rules 2018

15   Where the collateral-provider or the collateral-taker under a financial collateral arrangement goes into liquidation or administration or, in the case of a partnership, sequestration and the arrangement provides for, or the mechanism provided under the arrangement permits, either–

(a)   the debt owed by the party in liquidation or sequestration under the arrangement, to be assessed or paid in a currency other than sterling; or

(b)   the debt to be converted into sterling at a rate other than the official exchange rate prevailing on the date when that party went into liquidation or sequestration;

then rule 7.25 of the Insolvency (Scotland) (Receivership and Winding up) Rules 2018 and rule 3.114 of the Insolvency (Scotland) Company Voluntary Arrangements and Administration Rules 2018, as appropriate, shall not apply unless the arrangement provides for an unreasonable exchange rate or the collateral-taker uses the mechanism provided under the arrangement to impose an unreasonable exchange rate in which case the appropriate rule shall apply.

History
Regulation 15 amended by the Financial Markets and Insolvency (Settlement Finality and Financial Collateral Arrangements) (Amendment) Regulations 2010 (SI 2010/2993) reg.4(12) as from 6 April 2011. Heading to and

reg.15 amended the Financial Services and Markets (Insolvency) (Amendment of Miscellaneous Enactments) Regulations 2019 (SI 2019/755) regs 1, 3(1), (4) as from 23 April 2019.

15A   Insolvency proceedings in other jurisdictions

15A(1)   The references to insolvency law in section 426 of the Insolvency Act 1986 (co-operation between courts exercising jurisdiction in relation to insolvency) include, in relation to a part of the United Kingdom, this Part of these Regulations and, in relation to a relevant country or territory within the meaning of that section, so much of the law of that country or territory as corresponds to this Part

15A(2)   A court shall not, in pursuance of that section or any other enactment or rule of law, recognise or give effect to–

(a)   any order of a court exercising jurisdiction in relation to insolvency law in a country or territory outside the United Kingdom, or

(b)   any act of a person appointed in such a country or territory to discharge any functions under insolvency law,

in so far as the making of the order or the doing of the act would be prohibited by this Part in the case of a court in England and Wales or Scotland, the High Court in Northern Ireland or a relevant office holder.

15A(3)   Paragraph (2) does not affect the recognition of a judgment required to be recognised or enforced under or by virtue of the Civil Jurisdiction and Judgments Act 1982 or Council Regulation (EC) No 44/2001 of 22nd December 2000 on jurisdiction and the recognition and enforcement of judgments in civil and commercial matters, as amended from time to time and as applied by the Agreement made on 19th October 2005 between the European Community and the Kingdom of Denmark on jurisdiction and the recognition and enforcement of judgments in civil and commercial matters.

History
Regulation 15A inserted by the Financial Markets and Insolvency (Settlement Finality and Financial Collateral Arrangements) (Amendment) Regulations 2010 (SI 2010/2993) reg.4(13) as from 6 April 2011.

PART 4

RIGHT OF USE AND APPROPRIATION

16   Right of use under a security financial collateral arrangement

16(1)   If a security financial collateral arrangement provides for the collateral-taker to use and dispose of any financial collateral provided under the arrangement, as if it were the owner of it, the collateral-taker may do so in accordance with the terms of the arrangement.

16(2)   If a collateral-taker exercises such a right of use, it is obliged to replace the original financial collateral by transferring equivalent financial collateral on or before the due date for the performance of the relevant financial obligations covered by the arrangement or, if the arrangement so provides, it may set off the value of the equivalent financial collateral against or apply it in discharge of the relevant financial obligations in accordance with the terms of the arrangement.

16(3)   The equivalent financial collateral which is transferred in discharge of an obligation as described in paragraph (2), shall be subject to the same terms of the security financial collateral arrangement as the original financial collateral was subject to and shall be treated as having been provided under the security financial collateral arrangement at the same time as the original financial collateral was first provided.

16(3A)   In Scotland, paragraphs (1) and (3) apply to title transfer financial collateral arrangements as they apply to security financial collateral arrangements.

906

16(4)   If a collateral-taker has an outstanding obligation to replace the original financial collateral with equivalent financial collateral when an enforcement event occurs, that obligation may be the subject of a close-out netting provision.

16(5)   This regulation does not apply in relation to credit claims.

History
Regulation 16 amended by the Financial Markets and Insolvency (Settlement Finality and Financial Collateral Arrangements) (Amendment) Regulations 2010 (SI 2010/2993) reg.4(14) as from 6 April 2011.

17   Appropriation of financial collateral under a security financial collateral arrangement

17(1)   Where a security interest is created or arises under a security financial collateral arrangement on terms that include a power for the collateral-taker to appropriate the financial collateral, the collateral-taker may exercise that power in accordance with the terms of the security financial collateral arrangement, without any order for foreclosure from the courts (and whether or not the remedy of foreclosure would be available).

17(2)   Upon the exercise by the collateral-taker of the power to appropriate the financial collateral, the equity of redemption of the collateral-provider shall be extinguished and all legal and beneficial interest of the collateral-provider in the financial collateral shall vest in the collateral taker.

History
Regulation 17 substituted by the Financial Markets and Insolvency (Settlement Finality and Financial Collateral Arrangements) (Amendment) Regulations 2010 (SI 2010/2993) reg.4(15) as from 6 April 2011.

18   Duty to value collateral and account for any difference in value on appropriation

18(1)   Where a collateral-taker exercises a power contained in a security financial collateral arrangement to appropriate the financial collateral the collateral-taker must value the financial collateral in accordance with the terms of the arrangement and in any event in a commercially reasonable manner.

18(2)   Where a collateral-taker exercises such a power and the value of the financial collateral appropriated differs from the amount of the relevant financial obligations, then as the case may be, either–

(a)   the collateral-taker must account to the collateral-provider for the amount by which the value of the financial collateral exceeds the relevant financial obligations; or

(b)   the collateral-provider will remain liable to the collateral-taker for any amount whereby the value of the financial collateral is less than the relevant financial obligations.

18A   Restrictions on enforcement of financial collateral arrangements, etc.

18A(1)   Nothing in regulations 16 and 17 prevents the Bank of England imposing a restriction–

(a)   on the enforcement of financial collateral arrangements, or

(b)   on the effect of a security financial collateral arrangement, close out netting provision or set-off arrangement,

in the exercise of its powers under Part 1 of the Banking Act 2009.

18A(2)   For the purpose of paragraph (1) "set-off arrangement" has the meaning given in Article 2.1(99) of the recovery and resolution directive.

History
Regulation 18A inserted by the Bank Recovery and Resolution (No.2) Order 2014 (SI 2014/3348) Sch.3 para.9(1), (4) as from 10 January 2015.

PART 5

CONFLICT OF LAWS

19   Standard test regarding the applicable law to book entry securities financial collateral arrangements

19(1)   This regulation applies to financial collateral arrangements where book entry securities collateral is used as collateral under the arrangement and are held through one or more intermediaries.

19(2)   Any question relating to the matters specified in paragraph (4) of this regulation which arises in relation to book entry securities collateral which is provided under a financial collateral arrangement shall be governed by the domestic law of the country in which the relevant account is maintained.

19(3)   For the purposes of paragraph (2) "domestic law" excludes any rule under which, in deciding the relevant question, reference should be made to the law of another country.

19(4)   The matters referred to in paragraph (2) are–

(a)   the legal nature and proprietary effects of book entry securities collateral;

(b)   the requirements for perfecting a financial collateral arrangement relating to book entry securities collateral and the transfer or passing of control or possession of book entry securities collateral under such an arrangement;

(c)   the requirements for rendering a financial collateral arrangement which relates to book entry securities collateral effective against third parties;

(d)   whether a person's title to or interest in such book entry securities collateral is overridden by or subordinated to a competing title or interest; and

(e)   the steps required for the realisation of book entry securities collateral following the occurrence of any enforcement event.

Insolvency Practitioners and Insolvency Services Account (Fees) Order 2003

(SI 2003/3363)

Made on 30 December 2003 by the Secretary of State under s.415A of the Insolvency Act 1986. Operative from 1 April 2004.

[**Note**: Changes made by the Insolvency Practitioners and Insolvency Services Account (Fees) Order 2004 (SI 2004/476), the Insolvency Practitioners and Insolvency Services Account (Fees) (Amendment) Order 2005 (SI 2005/523), the Insolvency Practitioners and Insolvency Services Account (Fees) (Amendment) (No.2) Order 2005 (SI 2005/3524), the Insolvency Practitioners and Insolvency Services Account (Fees) (Amendment) Order 2007 (SI 2007/133), the Insolvency Practitioners and Insolvency Services Account (Fees) (Amendment) Order 2008 (SI 2008/3), the Insolvency Practitioners and Insolvency Services Account (Fees) (Amendment) (No.2) Order 2008 (SI 2008/672), the Insolvency Practitioners and Insolvency Services Account (Fees) (Amendment) Order (SI 2009/487), the Provision of Services (Insolvency Practitioners) Regulations 2009 (SI 2009/3081), the Insolvency Practitioners and Insolvency Services Account (Fees) (Amendment) Order 2012 (SI 2012/2264), the Deregulation Act 2015 (Insolvency) (Consequential Amendments and Transitional and Savings Provisions) Order 2015 (SI 2015/1641) and the Insolvency Practitioners and Insolvency Services Account (Fees) (Amendment) Order 2015 (SI 2015/1977) have been incorporated into the text.]

1 Citation, commencement, interpretation and extent

1(1) This Order may be cited as the Insolvency Practitioners and Insolvency Services Account (Fees) Order 2003 and shall come into force on 1st April 2004 ("the principal commencement date") except for Article 2(3) which shall come into force on 30th January 2004.

1(2) In this Order any reference to a numbered section is to the section so numbered in the Insolvency Act 1986.

1(3) All the provisions of this Order except Article 5 and the Schedule to this Order extend to England and Wales and Scotland and Article 5 and the Schedule to this Order extend only to England and Wales.

2 Fees payable in connection with the recognition of professional bodies pursuant to section 391

2(1) Every application by a body for recognition pursuant to section 391 shall be accompanied by a fee of £12,000.

2(2) On or before 6th April 2009 and on or before 6th April in each subsequent year, there shall be paid to the Secretary of State by each body recognised pursuant to section 391 in respect of the maintenance of that body's recognition pursuant to that section, a fee calculated by multiplying £360 by the number of persons who as at the 1st January in that year were authorised to act as insolvency practitioners by virtue of membership of that body.

2(3) Each body recognised pursuant to section 391 shall on or before 31st January in each year submit to the Secretary of State a list of its members who as at 1st January in that year were authorised to act as insolvency practitioners by virtue of membership of that body.

History
Article 2 substituted, and former art.2(2A), 2(2B) deleted, by the Insolvency Practitioners and Insolvency Services Account (Fees) (Amendment) Order 2008 (SI 2008/3) art.3 as from 30 January 2008, subject to transitional provisions in art.4. Article 2(2) further substituted by the Insolvency Practitioners and Insolvency Services Account (Fees) (Amendment) Order 2009 (SI 2009/487) arts 2, 3 as from 6 April 2009, subject to transitional provisions in art.4. Article 2 amended by the Insolvency Practitioners and Insolvency Services Account (Fees) (Amendment) Order 2015 (SI 2015/1977) art.2 as from 31 December 2015.

3   Fees payable in connection with authorisations by the Secretary of State under section 393

[Omitted]

History
The figure "£2100" substituted for "£2000" in art.3(2) by the Insolvency Practitioners and Insolvency Services Account (Fees) (Amendment) (No.2) Order 2005 (SI 2005/3524) art.3(2), as from 1 April 2006. Article 3(3), (4), (5) amended, and art.3(3A) inserted, by the Provision of Services (Insolvency Practitioners) Regulations 2009 (SI 2009/3081) reg.3, 5 as from 28 December 2009.

4   Transitional cases early applications for authorisation [Omitted]

5   Fees payable in connection with the operation of the Insolvency Services Account

5   There shall be payable in connection with the operation of the Insolvency Services Account fees as provided for in the Schedule to this Order.

6   Value added tax

6   Where Value Added Tax is chargeable in respect of the provision of a service for which a fee is prescribed by any provision of this Order, there shall be payable in addition to that fee the amount of the Value Added Tax.

History
Articles 3, 4 omitted by the Deregulation Act 2015 (Insolvency) (Consequential Amendments and Transitional and Savings Provisions) Order 2015 (SI 2015/1641) Sch.1 para.4 as from 1 October 2015.

SCHEDULE

FEES PAYABLE IN CONNECTION WITH THE OPERATION OF THE INSOLVENCY SERVICES ACCOUNT

Article 5

1   Interpretation for the purposes of the Schedule

1(1)   In this Schedule a reference to a numbered regulation is to the regulation so numbered in the Insolvency Regulations 1994

1(2)   In this Schedule "payment date" means any of the following dates in any year–

    (a)   1st January;

    (b)   1st April;

    (c)   1st July; and

    (d)   1st October.

1(2A)   In this Schedule "working day" means any day other than a Saturday, a Sunday, Good Friday, Christmas Day or a Bank Holiday in England and Wales in accordance with the Banking and Financial Dealings Act 1971.

History
Paragraph 1(2A) inserted by the Insolvency Practitioners and Insolvency Services Account (Fees) (Amendment) Order 2005 (SI 2005/523) art.2(2) as from 1 April 2005.

1(3)   Subject to paragraphs (4) and (5), for the purposes of this Schedule an account is "maintained with the Secretary of State in respect of monies which may from time to time be paid into the Insolvency Services Account" where–

    (a)   in a winding up by the court or a bankruptcy the Secretary of State creates a record in relation to the winding up or, as the case may be, the bankruptcy for the purpose of recording payments into and out of the Insolvency Services Account relating to the winding up or, as the case may be, the bankruptcy; and

(b) in a voluntary winding up on the request of the liquidator the Secretary of State creates a record in relation to the winding up for the purposes of recording payments into and out of the Insolvency Services Account relating to the winding up.

1(4) An account ceases to be maintained with the Secretary of State in the case of a winding up by the court or a bankruptcy where–

(a) the liquidator or the trustee has filed a receipts and payments account with the Secretary of State pursuant to regulation 14 or regulation 28;

(b) the account contains, or is accompanied by, a statement that it is a final receipts and payments account; and

(c) four working days have elapsed since the requirements of paragraphs (a) and (b) have been met,

but an account is revived in the circumstances mentioned in paragraph (5).

1(4A) An account ceases to be maintained with the Secretary of State in the case of a voluntary winding up where–

(a) no monies to which that account relates are held in the Insolvency Services Account (other than any unclaimed dividends or any amount that it is impracticable to distribute to creditors or is required for the payment of fees that are or will become payable while the account is maintained); and

(b) notice in writing has been given to the Secretary of State that the account is no longer required and four working days have elapsed since the receipt of that notice by the Secretary of State,

but an account is revived in the circumstances mentioned in paragraph (5).

History
Paragraph 1(4), (4A) substituted for the original para.1(4) by the Insolvency Practitioners and Insolvency Services Account (Fees) (Amendment) Order 2005 (SI 2005/523) art.2(3) as from 1 April 2005.

1(5) The circumstances referred to in paragraphs (4) and (4A) are–

(a) the receipt by the Secretary of State of notice in writing given by the trustee or liquidator for the revival of the account; or

(b) the payment into the Insolvency Services Account of any sums to the credit of the company or, as the case may be, the estate of the bankrupt,

and on the occurrence of either of the circumstances mentioned above, an account is "maintained with the Secretary of State in respect of monies which may from time to time be paid into the Insolvency Services Account".

History
In para.1(5) the words "paragraphs (4) and (4A)" substituted for the former words "paragraph (4)" by the Insolvency Practitioners and Insolvency Services Account (Fees) (Amendment) Order 2005 (SI 2005/523) art.2(4) as from 1 April 2005.

1(6) References to a bankruptcy include a bankruptcy under the Bankruptcy Act 1914 and references to a winding up include a winding up under the provisions of the Companies Act 1985.

2   Fees payable in connection with the operation of the Insolvency Services Account

2 Fees shall be payable in relation to the operation of the Insolvency Services Account (including payments into and out of that account) in the circumstances set out in the table below–

No. of fee	*Description of fee and circumstances in which it is payable*	*Amount*
1.	**Banking fee; winding up by the court and bankruptcy** Where in any bankruptcy or winding up by the court an account is maintained with the Secretary of State in respect of monies which may from time to time be paid into the Insolvency Services Account, there shall be payable out of the estate of the bankrupt or, as the case may be, the assets of the company on each payment date where the liquidator or the trustee is not the official receiver, a fee of–	£22
2.	**Banking fee; voluntary winding up** Where in a voluntary winding up an account is maintained with the Secretary of State in respect of monies which may from time to time be paid into the Insolvency Services Account there shall be payable out of the assets of the company on each payment date a fee of–	£25
2A.	**Payment of unclaimed dividends or other money—administration** Where any money is paid into the Insolvency Services Account pursuant to regulation 3B, that payment shall be accompanied by a fee in respect of each company to which it relates of–	£25.75
2B.	**Payment of unclaimed dividends or other money—administrative receivership** Where any money is paid into the Insolvency Services Account pursuant to regulation 3C, that payment shall be accompanied by a fee in respect of each company to which it relates of–	£25.75
2C.	**Payment of unclaimed dividends or other money—voluntary winding up** Where any money is paid into the Insolvency Services Account pursuant to regulation 18(2)(a), that payment shall be accompanied by a fee in respect of each company to which it relates of–	£25.75
3.	**Cheque etc. issue fee** Where a cheque, money order or payable order in respect of monies in the Insolvency Services Account is issued or reissued on the application of–	

(a) a liquidator pursuant to regulations 7 or 8;

(b) a trustee pursuant to regulations 22 or 23; or

(c) any person claiming any monies in that account pursuant to regulation 32,

there shall be payable out of the assets of the company, the estate of the bankrupt or, as the case may be, by the claimant–

	(i) where the application is made before principal commencement date, a fee in respect of that cheque, money order or payable order of–	£0.65
	(ii) where the application is made on or after the principal commencement date, a fee in respect of that cheque, money order or payable order of–	£1.10
4.	**Electronic funds systems (CHAPs and BACs etc.) fees** On the making or remaking of a transfer in respect of funds held in the Insolvency Services Account on an application made by–	

(a) a liquidator pursuant to regulations 7 or 8;

(b) a trustee pursuant to regulations 22 or 23; or

(c) any person claiming pursuant to regulation 32 any monies held in the Insolvency Services Account,

there shall be payable out of the assets of the company, the estate of the bankrupt or, as the case may be, by the claimant, a fee in respect of that transfer as follows:

(i) where it is made through the Clearing House Automated Payments System (CHAPs), a fee of–   £10.30

(ii) where it is made through the Bankers' Clearing System (BACs) or any electronic funds transfer system other than CHAPs, a fee of–   £0.15

History
Paragraphs 2A, 2B inserted by the Insolvency Practitioners and Insolvency Services Account (Fees) (Amendment) (No.2) Order 2008 (SI 2008/672) art.4 as from 6 April 2008. Paragraph 4 substituted by the Insolvency Practitioners and Insolvency Services Account (Fees) (Amendment) Order 2007 (SI 2007/133) art.4 as from 1 April 2007. Paragraph 2C inserted and paras 1, 2A, 3(ii) amended by the Insolvency Practitioners and Insolvency Services Account (Fees) (Amendment) Order 2009 (SI 2009/487) arts 2, 6 as from 6 April 2009. Schedule further amended by the Insolvency Practitioners and Insolvency Services Account (Fees) (Amendment) Order 2012 (SI 2012/2264) art.2 as from 1 October 2012.

Insurers (Reorganisation and Winding Up) Regulations 2004

(SI 2004/353)

*Made on 12 February 2004 by the Treasury under s.2(2) of the European Communities Act 1972.
Operative from 18 February 2004.*

[**Note:** Changes made by the Insurers (Reorganisation and Winding Up) (Amendment) Regulations 2004 (SI 2004/546), the Insurers (Reorganisation and Winding Up) (Lloyd's) Regulations 2005 (SI 2005/1998), the Financial Services (EEA State) Regulations 2007 (SI 2007/108), the Financial Services and Markets Act 2000 (Markets in Financial Instruments) Regulations 2007 (SI 2007/126), the Insurers (Reorganisation and Winding Up) (Amendment) Regulations 2007 (SI 2007/851), the Companies Act 2006 (Consequential Amendments and Transitional Provisions) Order 2011 (SI 2011/1265), the Financial Services Act 2012 (Consequential Amendments and Transitional Provisions) Order 2013 (SI 2013/472), the Co-operative and Community Benefit Societies and Credit Unions Act 2010 (Consequential Amendments) Regulations 2014 (SI 2014/1815), the Solvency 2 Regulations 2015 (SI 2015/575), the Financial Services and Markets Act 2000 (Markets in Financial Instruments) Regulations 2017 (SI 2017/701), the Small Business Enterprise and Employment Act 2015 (Consequential Amendments, Saving and Transitional Provisions) Regulations 2018 (SI 2018/208) and the Financial Services and Markets (Insolvency) (Amendment of Miscellaneous Enactments) Regulations 2019 (SI 2019/755) have been incorporated into the text. Where the 2007 Regulations simply add references to paragraphs of Sch.B1 to the Insolvency (Northern Ireland) Order 1989 corresponding to those of Sch.B1 to IA 1986, annotations have been omitted.]

PART I

GENERAL

1 Citation and commencement

1   These Regulations may be cited as the Insurers (Reorganisation and Winding Up) Regulations 2004, and come into force on 18th February 2004.

2 Interpretation

2(1)   In these Regulations–

"the 1986 Act" means the Insolvency Act 1986;

"the 2000 Act" means the Financial Services and Markets Act 2000;

"the 2006 Act" means the Companies Act 2006;

"the 1989 Order" means the Insolvency (Northern Ireland) Order 1989;

"administrator" has the meaning given by paragraph 13 of Schedule B1, or by paragraph 14 of Schedule B1 to the 1989 Order;

"branch", in relation to an EEA or UK insurer has the meaning given by Article 268(1)(b) of the Solvency 2 Directive;

"claim" means a claim submitted by a creditor of a UK insurer in the course of–

(a)   a winding up,

(b)   an administration, or

(c)   a voluntary arrangement,

with a view to recovering his debt in whole or in part, and includes a proof within the meaning given in rule 1.2 of the Insolvency Rules, a proof of debt within the meaning given in Rule 4.079(4) of the Insolvency Rules (Northern Ireland) or in Scotland a claim made in accordance with rule 7.16 of the

Insolvency (Scotland) (Receivership and Winding up) Rules 2018 (in relation to a winding up) or rule 3.105 of the Insolvency (Scotland) (Company Voluntary Arrangements and Administration) Rules 2018 (in relation to an administration);

"creditors' voluntary winding up" has the meaning given by section 90 of the 1986 Act or Article 76 of the 1989 Order;

"debt"–

(a)   in England and Wales and Northern Ireland–

    (i)   in relation to a winding up or administration of a UK insurer, has the meaning given by rule 14.1(3) of the Insolvency Rules or Article 5 of the 1989 Order, and

    (ii)   in a case where a voluntary arrangement has effect in relation to a UK insurer, means a debt which would constitute a debt in relation to the winding up (not immediately preceded by an administration) of that insurer, except that in paragraph (c) of the definition of "relevant date" in rule 14.1(3) of the Insolvency Rules and in paragraph (1A) of Article 5 of the 1989 Order the reference to the date on which the company went into liquidation has effect as a reference to the date on which the voluntary arrangement had effect;

(b)   in Scotland–

    (i)   in relation to a winding up of a UK insurer, shall be interpreted in accordance with rule 7.22 of the Insolvency (Scotland) (Receivership and Winding up) Rules 2018, and, in relation to an administration of a UK insurer, has the meaning given in rule 1.2 of the Insolvency (Scotland) (Company Voluntary Arrangements and Administration) Rules 2018,

    (ii)   in a case where a voluntary arrangement has effect in relation to a UK insurer, means a debt which would constitute a debt in relation to the winding up (not immediately preceded by an administration) of that insurer, except that references in rule 7.22 of the Insolvency (Scotland) (Receivership and Winding up) Rules 2018 to the date on which the company went into liquidation have effect as a reference to the date on which the voluntary arrangement had effect;

"directive reorganisation measure" means a reorganisation measure as defined in Article 268(1)(c) of the Solvency 2 Directive which was adopted or imposed on or after 20th April 2003;

"directive winding up proceedings" means winding up proceedings as defined in Article 268(1)(d) of the Solvency 2 Directive which were opened on or after 20th April 2003;

"EEA creditor" means a creditor of a UK insurer who–

(a)   in the case of an individual, is ordinarily resident in an EEA State, and

(b)   in the case of a body corporate or unincorporated association of persons, has its head office in an EEA State;

"EEA insurer" means an insurance undertaking, other than a UK insurer, pursuing the activity of direct insurance (within the meaning of the Solvency 2 Directive) which has received authorisation under Article 14 or Article 162 of the Solvency 2 Directive from its home state regulator;

"EEA regulator" means a supervisory authority (within the meaning of Article 13(10) of the Solvency 2 Directive) of an EEA State;

"EEA State" has the meaning given by Schedule 1 to the Interpretation Act 1978;

"the FCA" means the Financial Conduct Authority;

"home state regulator", in relation to an EEA insurer, means the EEA regulator–

(a)   in the EEA State in which its head office is located; or

(b)   if it is a branch of a third-country insurance undertaking (within the meaning of Article 13(3) of the Solvency 2 Directive), the EEA State in which the branch was granted authorisation in accordance with Articles 145 to 149 of the Solvency 2 Directive;

"the Insolvency Rules" means the Insolvency (England and Wales) Rules 2016;

"the Insolvency Rules (Northern Ireland)" means the Insolvency Rules (Northern Ireland) 1991;

"insurance claim" means any claim in relation to an insurance debt;

"insurance creditor" means a person who has an insurance claim against a UK insurer (whether or not he has claims other than insurance claims against that insurer);

"insurance debt" means a debt to which a UK insurer is, or may become liable, pursuant to a contract of insurance, to a policyholder or to any person who has a direct right of action against that insurer, and includes any premium paid in connection with a contract of insurance (whether or not that contract was concluded) which the insurer is liable to refund;

"officer", in relation to a company, has the meaning given by section 1173(1) of the Companies Act 2006;

"official language" means a language specified in Article 1 of Council Regulation No 1 of 15th April 1958 determining the languages to be used by the European Economic Community (Regulation 1/58/EEC), most recently amended by paragraph (a) of Part XVIII of Annex I to the Act of Accession 1994 (194 N);

"policyholder" has the meaning given by the Financial Services and Markets Act 2000 (Meaning of "Policy" and "Policyholder") Order 2001;

"the PRA" means the Prudential Regulation Authority;

"PRA-authorised person" has the meaning given in section 2B of the 2000 Act;

"registered society" means a society, other than a society registered as a credit union, which is–

(a)   a registered society within the meaning given by section 1(1) of the Co-operative and Community Benefit Societies Act 2014; or

(b)   a society registered or deemed to be registered under the Industrial and Provident Societies Act (Northern Ireland) 1969;

"Schedule B1" means Schedule B1 to the 1986 Act as inserted by section 248 of the Enterprise Act 2002, unless specified otherwise;

"section 899 compromise or arrangement" means a compromise or arrangement sanctioned by the court in relation to a UK insurer under section 899 of the 2006 Act but does not include a compromise or arrangement falling within section 900 (powers of court to facilitate reconstruction or amalgamation) or Part 27 (mergers and divisions of public companies) of that Act;

"the Solvency 2 Directive" means Directive 2009/138/EC of the European Parliament and of the Council of 25 November 2009 on the taking-up and pursuit of the business of Insurance and Reinsurance (Solvency II);

"supervisor" has the meaning given by section 7 of the 1986 Act or Article 20 of the 1989 Order;

"UK insurer" means a person who has permission under Part 4A of the 2000 Act to effect or carry out contracts of insurance, but does not include a person who, in accordance with that permission, carries on that activity exclusively in relation to reinsurance contracts;

"voluntary arrangement" means a voluntary arrangement which has effect in relation to a UK insurer in accordance with section 4A of the 1986 Act or Article 17A of the 1989 Order; and

"winding up" means–

(a) winding up by the court, or

(b) a creditors' voluntary winding up.

2(2) In paragraph (1)–

(a) for the purposes of the definition of "directive reorganisation measure", a reorganisation measure is adopted or imposed at the time when it is treated as adopted or imposed by the law of the relevant EEA State; and

(b) for the purposes of the definition of "directive winding up proceedings", winding up proceedings are opened at the time when they are treated as opened by the law of the relevant EEA State,

and in this paragraph "relevant EEA State" means the EEA State under the law of which the reorganisation is adopted or imposed, or the winding up proceedings are opened, as the case may be.

2(3) In these Regulations, references to the general law of insolvency of the United Kingdom include references to every provision made by or under the 1986 Act or the 1989 Order; and in relation to friendly societies or to registered societies references to the law of insolvency or to any provision of the 1986 Act or the 1989 Order are to that law as modified by the Friendly Societies Act 1992 or by the Co-operative and Community Benefit Societies Act 2014 or the Industrial and Provident Societies Act (Northern Ireland) 1969 (as the case may be).

2(4) References in these Regulations to a "contract of insurance" must be read with–

(a) section 22 of the 2000 Act;

(b) any relevant order made under that section; and

(c) Schedule 2 to that Act,

but for the purposes of these Regulations a contract of insurance does not include a reinsurance contract.

2(5) Functions imposed or falling on the FCA or the PRA by or under these Regulations shall be deemed to be functions under the 2000 Act.

History
Definition of "Schedule B1" amended by the Insurers (Reorganisation and Winding Up) (Amendment) Regulations 2007 (SI 2007/851) reg.2(1), (2)(b), as from 6 April 2007. Definition of "EEA State" substituted by the Financial Services (EEA State) Regulations 2007 (SI 2007/108) reg.8 as from 13 February 2007. The definition was inserted into the 1978 Act by the Legislative and Regulatory Reform Act 2006. Definition of "officer" amended, definitions of "the 2006 Act" and of "section 899 compromise or arrangement" inserted and various definitions deleted by the Companies Act 2006 (Consequential Amendments and Transitional Provisions) Order 2011 (SI 2011/1265) art.23(2) as from 12 May 2011. Definition of "the Authority" omitted and definitions of "the FCA", "the PRA" and "PRA-authorised person" inserted by the Financial Services Act 2012 (Consequential Amendments and Transitional Provisions) Order 2013 (SI 2013/472) art.3 and Sch.2 para.88(a) as from 1 April 2013. Definition of "registered society" inserted by the Co-operative and Community Benefit Societies and Credit Unions Act 2010 (Consequential Amendments) Regulations 2014 (SI 2014/1815) Sch.1 para.12(2)(a) as from 1 August 2014. Definitions of "the first non-life insurance directive", "life insurance directive", "the reorganisation and winding-up directive" and "the third non-life directive" omitted, definition of "the Solvency 2 Directive" inserted, definitions of "branch", "directive reorganisation measure" and "directive winding-up proceedings" amended and definitions of "EEA insurer", "EEA regulator" and "home state regulator" substituted by the Solvency 2 Regulations 2015 (SI 2015/575) reg.17(2) as from 1 January 2016. Definitions of "claim", "debt" and "the Insolvency Rules" amended and former definition of "Insolvency (Scotland) Rules" omitted by the Financial Services and Markets (Insolvency) (Amendment of Miscellaneous Enactments) Regulations 2019 (SI 2019/755) regs 1, 4(1), (2) as from 23 April 2019.

3 Scope

3 For the purposes of these Regulations, neither the Society of Lloyd's nor the persons specified in section 316(1) of the 2000 Act are UK insurers.

History

Regulation 2(3) amended by the Co-operative and Community Benefit Societies and Credit Unions Act 2010 (Consequential Amendments) Regulations 2014 (SI 2014/1815) Sch.1 para.12(2)(b) as from 1 August 2014.

Note

In regard to Lloyd's, see now the Insurers (Reorganisation and Winding Up) (Lloyd's) Regulations 2005 (SI 2005/1998), effective 10 August 2005.

PART II

INSOLVENCY MEASURES AND PROCEEDINGS: JURISDICTION IN RELATION TO INSURERS

4   Prohibition against winding up etc. EEA insurers in the United Kingdom

4(1)   On or after the relevant date a court in the United Kingdom may not, in relation to an EEA insurer or any branch of an EEA insurer–

(a)   make a winding up order pursuant to section 221 of the 1986 Act or Article 185 of the 1989 Order;

(b)   appoint a provisional liquidator;

(c)   make an administration order.

4(2)   Paragraph (1)(a) does not prevent–

(a)   the court from making a winding up order after the relevant date in relation to an EEA insurer if–

(i)   a provisional liquidator was appointed in relation to that insurer before the relevant date, and

(ii)   that appointment continues in force until immediately before that winding up order is made;

(b)   the winding up of an EEA insurer after the relevant date pursuant to a winding up order which was made, and has not been discharged, before that date.

4(3)   Paragraph (1)(b) does not prevent a provisional liquidator of an EEA insurer appointed before the relevant date from acting in relation to that insurer after that date.

4(4)   Paragraph (1)(c) does not prevent an administrator appointed before the relevant date from acting after that date in a case in which the administration order under which he or his predecessor was appointed remains in force after that date.

4(5)   An administrator may not, in relation to an EEA insurer, be appointed under paragraphs 14 or 22 of Schedule B1 or paragraph 15 or 23 of Schedule B1 to the 1989 Order.

4(6)   A proposed voluntary arrangement shall not have effect in relation to an EEA insurer if a decision, under section 4 of the 1986 Act or Article 17 of the 1989 Order, with respect to the approval of that arrangement was made after the relevant date.

4(7)   Section 377 of the 2000 Act (reducing the value of contracts instead of winding up) does not apply in relation to an EEA insurer.

4(8)   An order under section 254 of the Enterprise Act 2002 (application of insolvency law to a foreign company) or under Article 9 of the Insolvency (Northern Ireland) Order 2005 (application of insolvency law to company incorporated outside Northern Ireland) may not provide for any of the following provisions of the 1986 Act or of the 1989 Order to apply in relation to an EEA insurer–

(a)   Part I of the 1986 Act or Part II of the 1989 Order (company voluntary arrangements);

(b)   Part II of the 1986 Act or Part III of the 1989 Order (administration);

(c)   Chapter VI of Part IV of the 1986 Act (winding up by the Court) or Chapter VI of Part V of the 1989 Order (winding up by the High Court).

4(9)   In this regulation and regulation 5, "relevant date" means 20th April 2003.

History
Regulation 4(8) substituted by the Insurers (Reorganisation and Winding Up) (Amendment) Regulations 2007 (SI 2007/851) reg.2(1), (4), as from 6 April 2007.

5   Schemes of arrangement: EEA insurers

5(1)   For the purposes of section 895(2)(b) of the 2006 Act, an EEA insurer or a branch of an EEA insurer is to be treated as a company liable to be wound up under the 1986 Act or the 1989 Order if it would be liable to be wound up under that Act or Order but for the prohibition in regulation 4(1)(a).

5(2)   But a court may not make a relevant order under section 899 of the 2006 Act in relation to an EEA insurer which is subject to a directive reorganisation measure or directive winding up proceedings, or a branch of an EEA insurer which is subject to such a measure or proceedings unless the conditions set out in paragraph (3) are satisfied.

5(3)   Those conditions are–

(a)   the person proposing the section 899 compromise or arrangement ("the proposal") has given–

(i)   the administrator or liquidator, and

(ii)   the relevant competent authority,

reasonable notice of the details of that proposal; and

(b)   no person notified in accordance with sub-paragraph (a) has objected to the proposal.

5(4)   Nothing in this regulation invalidates a compromise or arrangement which was sanctioned by the court by an order made before the relevant date.

5(5)   For the purposes of paragraph (2), a relevant order means an order sanctioning a section 899 compromise or arrangement which–

(a)   is intended to enable the insurer, and the whole or any part of its undertaking, to survive as a going concern and which affects the rights of persons other than the insurer or its contributories; or

(b)   includes among its purposes a realisation of some or all of the assets of the EEA insurer to which the order relates and the distribution of the proceeds to creditors, with a view to terminating the whole or any part of the business of that insurer.

5(6)   For the purposes of this regulation–

(a)   "administrator" means an administrator, as defined by Article 268(1)(e) of the Solvency 2 Directive, who is appointed in relation to the EEA insurer in relation to which the proposal is made;

(b)   "liquidator" means a liquidator, as defined by Article 268(1)(f) of the Solvency 2 Directive, who is appointed in relation to the EEA insurer in relation to which the proposal is made;

(c)   "competent authority" means the competent authority, as defined by Article 268(1)(a) of the Solvency 2 Directive, which is competent for the purposes of the directive reorganisation measure or directive winding up proceedings mentioned in paragraph (2).

History
Regulation 5(1), 5(2), 5(3) and 5(5) amended by the Companies Act 2006 (Consequential Amendments and Transitional Provisions) Order 2011 (SI 2011/1265) art.23(3) as from 12 May 2011. Regulation 5(6) amended by the Solvency 2 Regulations (SI 2015/575) reg.17(3) as from 1 January 2016.

6   Reorganisation measures and winding up proceedings in respect of EEA insurers effective in the United Kingdom

6(1)   An EEA insolvency measure has effect in the United Kingdom in relation to–

(a)   any branch of an EEA insurer,

(b)   any property or other assets of that insurer,

(c)   any debt or liability of that insurer

as if it were part of the general law of insolvency of the United Kingdom.

6(2)   Subject to paragraph (4)–

(a)   a competent officer who satisfies the condition mentioned in paragraph (3); or

(b)   a qualifying agent appointed by a competent officer who satisfies the condition mentioned in paragraph (3),

may exercise in the United Kingdom, in relation to the EEA insurer which is subject to an EEA insolvency measure, any function which, pursuant to that measure, he is entitled to exercise in relation to that insurer in the relevant EEA State.

6(3)   The condition mentioned in paragraph (2) is that the appointment of the competent officer is evidenced–

(a)   by a certified copy of the order or decision by a judicial or administrative authority in the relevant EEA State by or under which the competent officer was appointed; or

(b)   by any other certificate issued by the judicial or administrative authority which has jurisdiction in relation to the EEA insolvency measure,

and accompanied by a certified translation of that order, decision or certificate (as the case may be).

6(4)   In exercising functions of the kind mentioned in paragraph (2), the competent officer or qualifying agent–

(a)   may not take any action which would constitute an unlawful use of force in the part of the United Kingdom in which he is exercising those functions;

(b)   may not rule on any dispute arising from a matter falling within Part V of these Regulations which is justiciable by a court in the part of the United Kingdom in which he is exercising those functions; and

(c)   notwithstanding the way in which functions may be exercised in the relevant EEA State, must act in accordance with relevant laws or rules as to procedure which have effect in the part of the United Kingdom in which he is exercising those functions.

6(5)   For the purposes of paragraph (4)(c), "relevant laws or rules as to procedure" mean–

(a)   requirements as to consultation with or notification of employees of an EEA insurer;

(b)   law and procedures relevant to the realisation of assets;

(c)   where the competent officer is bringing or defending legal proceedings in the name of, or on behalf of, an EEA insurer, the relevant rules of court.

6(6)   In this regulation–

"competent officer" means a person appointed under or in connection with an EEA insolvency measure for the purpose of administering that measure;

"qualifying agent" means an agent validly appointed (whether in the United Kingdom or elsewhere) by a competent officer in accordance with the relevant law in the relevant EEA State;

"EEA insolvency measure" means, as the case may be, a directive reorganisation measure or directive winding up proceedings which has effect in relation to an EEA insurer by virtue of the law of the relevant EEA State;

"relevant EEA State", in relation to an EEA insurer, means the EEA State in which that insurer has been authorised in accordance with Article 14 or Article 162 of the Solvency 2 Directive.

History
Definition of "relevant EEA State" in reg.5(6) amended by the Solvency 2 Regulations (SI 2015/575) reg.17(4) as from 1 January 2016.

7 Confirmation by the court of a creditors' voluntary winding up

7(1)   Rule 21.4 of the Insolvency Rules or Rule 7.56 of the Insolvency Rules (Northern Ireland) applies in relation to a UK insurer with the modification specified in paragraph (2) or (3).

7(2)   For the purposes of this regulation, rule 21.4 of the Insolvency Rules has effect as if after paragraph (2) there were inserted–

"**(2A)** Where the company is a UK insurer (within the meaning given in regulation 2(1) of the Insurers (Reorganisation and Winding Up) Regulations 2004), paragraph (2) does not apply, but the liquidator may apply to court for an order confirming the winding up as a creditors' voluntary winding up for the purposes of Articles 274 and 280 of the Solvency 2 Directive.".

7(3)   For the purposes of this regulation, rule 7.56 of the Insolvency Rules (Northern Ireland) has effect as if for paragraph (1) there were substituted–

"**(1)** Where a UK insurer (within the meaning given in regulation 2(1) of the Insurers (Reorganisation and Winding Up) Regulations 2004) has passed a resolution for voluntary winding up and no declaration under Article 75 has been made, the liquidator may apply to the court for an order confirming the winding up as a creditors' voluntary winding up for the purposes of Articles 274 and 280 of the Solvency 2 Directive.".

History
Regulation 7(1) amended and reg.(2) substituted by the Financial Services and Markets (Insolvency) (Amendment of Miscellaneous Enactments) Regulations 2019 (SI 2019/755) regs 1, 4(1), (3) as from 23 April 2019.

PART III

MODIFICATIONS OF THE LAW OF INSOLVENCY: NOTIFICATION AND PUBLICATION

8 Modifications of the law of insolvency

8   The general law of insolvency has effect in relation to UK insurers subject to the provisions of this Part.

9 Notification of relevant decision to the FCA and, if the insurer is a PRA-authorised person, the PRA

9(1)   Where on or after 3rd March 2004 the court makes a decision, order or appointment of any of the following kinds–

    (a)   an administration order under paragraph 13 of Schedule B1, or paragraph 14 of Schedule B1 to the 1989 Order;

    (b)   a winding up order under section 125 of the 1986 Act or Article 105 of the 1989 Order;

(c)   the appointment of a provisional liquidator under section 135(1) of the 1986 Act or Article 115(1) of the 1989 Order;

(d)   an interim order under paragraph 13(1)(d) of Schedule B1 or paragraph 14(1)(d) of Schedule B1 to the 1989 Order;

(e)   a decision to reduce the value of one or more of the insurer's contracts, in accordance with section 377 of the 2000 Act,

it must immediately inform the FCA and, if the insurer is a PRA-authorised person, the PRA, or cause the FCA and, if the insurer is a PRA-authorised person, the PRA to be informed of the decision, order or appointment which has been made.

9(2)   Where a decision with respect to the approval of a voluntary arrangement has effect, and the arrangement which is the subject of that decision is a qualifying arrangement, the supervisor must forthwith inform the FCA and, if the insurer is a PRA-authorised person, the PRA of the arrangement.

9(3)   Where a liquidator is appointed as mentioned in section 100 of the 1986 Act, paragraph 83 of Schedule B1, paragraph 84 of Schedule B1 to the 1989 Order or Article 86 of the 1989 Order (appointment of liquidator in a creditors' voluntary winding up), the liquidator must inform the FCA and, if the insurer is a PRA-authorised person, the PRA forthwith of his appointment.

9(4)   Where in the case of a members' voluntary winding up, section 95 of the 1986 Act (effect of company's insolvency) or Article 81 of the 1989 Order applies, the liquidator must inform the FCA and, if the insurer is a PRA-authorised person, the PRA forthwith that he is of that opinion.

Note
There does not appear to be a reg.9(5).

9(6)   Paragraphs (1), (2) and (3) do not require the FCA to be informed in any case where the FCA was represented at all hearings in connection with the application in relation to which the decision, order or appointment is made.

9(6A)   Paragraphs (1), (2) and (3) do not require the PRA to be informed in any case where the PRA was represented at all hearings in connection with the application in relation to which the decision, order or appointment is made.

9(7)   For the purposes of paragraph (2), a "qualifying arrangement" means a voluntary arrangement which–

(a)   varies the rights of creditors as against the insurer and is intended to enable the insurer, and the whole or any part of its undertaking, to survive as a going concern; or

(b)   includes a realisation of some or all of the assets of the insurer and distribution of the proceeds to creditors, with a view to terminating the whole or any part of the business of that insurer.

9(8)   An administrator, supervisor or liquidator who fails without reasonable excuse to comply with paragraph (2), (3), or (4) (as the case may be) commits an offence and is liable on summary conviction to a fine not exceeding level 3 on the standard scale.

History
In reg.9(1) the date "3rd March 2004" substituted for "[_] February 2004" (or, in some printed versions "18th February 2004") by the Insurers (Reorganisation and Winding Up) (Amendment) Regulations 2004 (SI 2004/546) reg.2(2), as from 3 March 2004.

  Heading to reg.9 amended, reg.9(6) substituted and reg.9(6A) inserted by the Financial Services Act 2012 (Consequential Amendments and Transitional Provisions) Order 2013 (SI 2013/472) art.3 and Sch.2 para.88(c), (d) as from 1 April 2013.

10   Notification of relevant decision to EEA regulators

10(1)   Where the FCA or the PRA is informed of a decision, order or appointment in accordance with regulation 9, that Authority must as soon as is practicable inform the EEA regulators in every EEA State–

(a) that the decision, order or appointment has been made; and

(b) in general terms, of the possible effect of a decision, order or appointment of that kind on–

    (i)   the business of an insurer, and

    (ii) the rights of policyholders under contracts of insurance effected and carried out by an insurer.

10(2) Where the FCA or the PRA has been represented at all hearings in connection with the application in relation to which the decision, order or appointment has been made, that Authority must inform the EEA regulators in every EEA State of the matters mentioned in paragraph (1) as soon as is practicable after that decision, order or appointment has been made.

11 Publication of voluntary arrangement, administration order, winding up order or scheme of arrangement

11(1) This regulation applies where a qualifying decision has effect, or a qualifying order or qualifying appointment is made, in relation to a UK insurer on or after 20th April 2003.

11(2) For the purposes of this regulation–

(a) a qualifying decision means a decision with respect to the approval of a proposed voluntary arrangement, in accordance with section 4A of the 1986 Act or Article 17A of the 1989 Order;

(b) a qualifying order means–

    (i)   an administration order under paragraph 13 of Schedule B1 or under paragraph 14 of Schedule B1 to the 1989 Order,

    (ii) an order appointing a provisional liquidator in accordance with section 135 of the 1986 Act or Article 115 of the 1989 Order, or

    (iii) a winding up order made by the court under Part IV of the 1986 Act or Part V of the 1989 Order.

(c) a qualifying appointment means the appointment of a liquidator as mentioned in section 100 of the 1986 Act or Article 86 of the 1989 Order (appointment of liquidator in a creditors' voluntary winding up).

11(3) Subject to paragraph (8), as soon as is reasonably practicable after a qualifying decision has effect, or a qualifying order or a qualifying appointment has been made, the relevant officer must publish, or cause to be published, in the Official Journal of the European Union the information mentioned in paragraph (4) and (if applicable) paragraphs (5), (6) or (7).

11(4) That information is–

(a) a summary of the terms of the qualifying decision or qualifying appointment or the provisions of the qualifying order (as the case may be);

(b) the identity of the relevant officer; and

(c) the statutory provisions in accordance with which the qualifying decision has effect or the qualifying order or appointment has been made or takes effect.

11(5) In the case of a qualifying appointment falling within paragraph (2)(c), that information includes the court to which an application under section 112 of the 1986 Act (reference of questions to the court) or Article 98 of the 1989 Order (reference of questions to the High Court) may be made.

11(6) In the case of a qualifying decision, that information includes the court to which an application under section 6 of the 1986 Act or Article 19 of the 1989 Order (challenge of decisions) may be made.

11(7)   Paragraph (3) does not apply where a qualifying decision or qualifying order falling within paragraph (2)(b)(i) affects the interests only of the members, or any class of members, or employees of the insurer (in their capacity as members or employees).

11(8)   This regulation is without prejudice to any requirement to publish information imposed upon a relevant officer under any provision of the general law of insolvency.

11(9)   A relevant officer who fails to comply with paragraph (3) of this regulation commits an offence and is liable on summary conviction to a fine not exceeding level 3 on the standard scale.

11(10)   A qualifying decision, qualifying order or qualifying appointment is not invalid or ineffective if the relevant official fails to comply with paragraph (3) of this regulation.

11(11)   In this regulation, "relevant officer" means–

(a)   in the case of a voluntary arrangement, the supervisor;

(b)   in the case of an administration order or the appointment of an administrator, the administrator;

(c)   in the case of a creditors' voluntary winding up, the liquidator;

(d)   in the case of winding up order, the liquidator;

(e)   in the case of an order appointing a provisional liquidator, the provisional liquidator.

12   Notification to creditors: winding up proceedings

12(1)   When a relevant order or appointment is made, or a relevant decision is taken, in relation to a UK insurer on or after 20th April 2003, the appointed officer must as soon as is reasonably practicable–

(a)   notify all known creditors of that insurer in writing of–

(i)   the matters mentioned in paragraph (4), and

(ii)   the matters mentioned in paragraph (5); and

(b)   notify all known insurance creditors of that insurer in writing of the matters mentioned in paragraph 6,

in any case.

12(2)   The appointed officer may comply with the requirement in paragraph (1)(a)(i) and the requirement in paragraph (1)(a)(ii) by separate notifications.

12(3)   For the purposes of this regulation–

(a)   "relevant order" means–

(i)   an administration order made under section 8 of the 1986 Act before 15th September 2003, or made on or after that date under paragraph 13 of Schedule B1 in the prescribed circumstances or under paragraph 14 of Schedule B1 to the 1989 Order in the prescribed circumstances,

(ii)   a winding up order under section 125 of the 1986 Act (powers of the court on hearing a petition) or Article 105 of the 1989 Order (powers of High Court on hearing of petition),

(iii)   the appointment of a liquidator in accordance with section 138 of the 1986 Act (appointment of a liquidator in Scotland), and

(iv)   an order appointing a provisional liquidator in accordance with section 135 of that Act or Article 115 of the 1989 Order;

(b)   "relevant appointment" means the appointment of a liquidator as mentioned in section 100 of the 1986 Act or Article 86 of the 1989 Order (appointment of liquidator in a creditors' voluntary winding up); and

(c)   "relevant decision" means a decision as a result of which a qualifying voluntary arrangement has effect.

12(4)   The matters which must be notified to all known creditors in accordance with paragraph (1)(a)(i) are as follows–

(a)   that a relevant order or appointment has been made, or a relevant decision taken, in relation to the UK insurer; and

(b)   the date from which that order, appointment or decision has effect.

12(5)   The matters which must be notified to all known creditors in accordance with paragraph (1)(a)(ii) are as follows–

(a)   if applicable, the date by which a creditor must submit his claim in writing;

(b)   the matters which must be stated in a creditor's claim;

(c)   details of any category of debt in relation to which a claim is not required;

(d)   the person to whom any such claim or any observations on a claim must be submitted; and

(e)   the consequences of any failure to submit a claim by any specified deadline.

12(6)   The matters which must be notified to all known insurance creditors, in accordance with paragraph (1)(b), are as follows–

(a)   the effect which the relevant order, appointment or decision will, or is likely, to have on the kind of contract of insurance under, or in connection with, which that creditor's insurance claim against the insurer is founded; and

(b)   the date from which any variation (resulting from the relevant order or relevant decision) to the risks covered by, or the sums recoverable under, that contract has effect.

12(7)   Subject to paragraph (8), where a creditor is notified in accordance with paragraph (1)(a)(ii), the notification must be headed with the words "Invitation to lodge a claim: time limits to be observed", and that heading must be given in–

(a)   the official language, or one of the official languages, of the EEA State in which that creditor is ordinarily resident; or

(b)   every official language.

12(8)   Where a creditor notified in accordance with paragraph (1) is–

(a)   an insurance creditor; and

(b)   ordinarily resident in an EEA State,

the notification must be given in the official language, or one of the official languages, of that EEA State.

12(9)   The obligation under paragraph (1)(a)(ii) may be discharged by sending a form of proof in accordance with Rule 4.080 of the Insolvency Rules (Northern Ireland) in cases where those rules apply, provided that the form of proof complies with paragraph (7) or (8) (whichever is applicable).

12(10)   The prescribed circumstances are where the administrator includes in the statement required under rule 3.3 of the Insolvency Rules or under Rule 2.003 of the Insolvency Rules (Northern Ireland) a statement to the effect that the objective set out in paragraph 3(1)(a) of Schedule B1 or in paragraph 4(1)(a) of Schedule B1 to the 1989 Order is not reasonably likely to be achieved.

12(11)   Where, after the appointment of an administrator, the administrator concludes that it is not reasonably practicable to achieve the objective specified in paragraph 3(1)(a) of Schedule B1 or in paragraph 4(1)(a) of Schedule B1 to the 1989 Order, he shall inform the court the FCA and, if the insurer is a PRA-authorised person, the PRA in writing of that conclusion and upon so doing the order by which he was appointed shall be a relevant order for the purposes of this regulation and the obligation under paragraph (1) shall apply as from the date on which he so informs the court, the FCA and, if the insurer is a PRA-authorised person, the PRA.

12(12) An appointed officer commits an offence if he fails without reasonable excuse to comply with an applicable requirement under this regulation, and is liable on summary conviction to a fine not exceeding level 3 on the standard scale.

12(13) For the purposes of this regulation–

(a) "appointed officer" means–

    (i) in the case of a relevant order falling within paragraph (3)(a)(i) or a relevant appointment falling within paragraph (3)(b)(i), the administrator,

    (ii) in the case of a relevant order falling within paragraph (3)(a)(ii) or (iii) or a relevant appointment falling within paragraph (3)(b)(ii), the liquidator,

    (iii) in the case of a relevant order falling within paragraph (3)(a)(iv), the provisional liquidator, or

    (iv) in the case of a relevant decision, the supervisor; and

(b) a creditor is a "known" creditor if the appointed officer is aware, or should reasonably be aware of–

    (i) his identity,

    (ii) his claim or potential claim, and

    (iii) a recent address where he is likely to receive a communication.

12(14) For the purposes of paragraph (3), and of regulations 13 and 14, a voluntary arrangement is a qualifying voluntary arrangement if its purposes include a realisation of some or all of the assets of the UK insurer to which the order relates and a distribution of the proceeds to creditors, with a view to terminating the whole or any part of the business of that insurer.

History
Regulation 12(10) substituted by the Insurers (Reorganisation and Winding Up) (Amendment) Regulations 2007 (SI 2007/851) reg.2(1), (9), as from 6 April 2007. Regulation 12(9), (10) amended by the Financial Services and Markets (Insolvency) (Amendment of Miscellaneous Enactments) Regulations 2019 (SI 2019/755) regs 1, 4(1), (4) as from 23 April 2019.

13 Submission of claims by EEA creditors

13(1) An EEA creditor who on or after 20th April 2003 submits a claim or observations relating to his claim in any relevant proceedings (irrespective of when those proceedings were commenced or had effect) may do so in his domestic language, provided that the requirements in paragraphs (3) and (4) are complied with.

13(2) For the purposes of this regulation, "relevant proceedings" means–

(a) a winding up;

(b) a qualifying voluntary arrangement;

(c) administration.

13(3) Where an EEA creditor submits a claim in his domestic language, the document must be headed with the words "Lodgement of claim" (in English).

13(4)   Where an EEA creditor submits observations on his claim (otherwise than in the document by which he submits his claim), the observations must be headed with the words "Submission of observations relating to claims" (in English).

13(5)   Paragraph (3) does not apply where an EEA creditor submits his claim using–

(a)   in the case of a winding up, a form of proof supplied by the liquidator in accordance with Rule 4.080 of the Insolvency Rules (Northern Ireland);

(b)   in the case of a qualifying voluntary arrangement, a form approved by the court for that purpose.

13(6)   In this regulation–

(a)   "domestic language", in relation to an EEA creditor, means the official language, or one of the official languages, of the EEA State in which he is ordinarily resident or, if the creditor is not an individual, in which the creditor's head office is located; and

(b)   "qualifying voluntary arrangement" has the meaning given by regulation 12(12).

History
Regulation 13(5)(a) amended by the Financial Services and Markets (Insolvency) (Amendment of Miscellaneous Enactments) Regulations 2019 (SI 2019/755) regs 1, 4(1), (5) as from 23 April 2019.

14   Reports to creditors

14(1)   This regulation applies where, on or after 20th April 2003–

(a)   a liquidator is appointed in accordance with section 100 of the 1986 Act or Article 86 of the 1989 Order (creditors' voluntary winding up: appointment of liquidator) or, on or after 15th September 2003, paragraph 83 of Schedule B1 or paragraph 84 of Schedule B1 to the 1989 Order (moving from administration to creditors' voluntary liquidation);

(b)   a winding up order is made by the court;

(c)   a provisional liquidator is appointed; or

(d)   an administrator is appointed under paragraph 13 of Schedule B1 or under paragraph 14 of Schedule B1 to the 1989 Order.

14(2)   The liquidator or provisional liquidator (as the case may be) must send to every known creditor a report once in every 12 months beginning with the date when his appointment has effect.

14(3)   The requirement in paragraph (2) does not apply where a liquidator or provisional liquidator is required by order of the court to send a report to creditors at intervals which are more frequent than those required by this regulation.

14(4)   This regulation is without prejudice to any requirement to send a report to creditors, imposed by the court on the liquidator or provisional liquidator, which is supplementary to the requirements of this regulation.

14(5)   A liquidator or provisional liquidator commits an offence if he fails without reasonable excuse to comply with an applicable requirement under this regulation, and is liable on summary conviction to a fine not exceeding level 3 on the standard scale.

14(6)   For the purposes of this regulation–

(a)   "known creditor" means–

(i)   a creditor who is known to the liquidator or provisional liquidator, and

(ii)   in a case falling within paragraph (1)(b) or (c), a creditor who is specified in the insurer's statement of affairs (within the meaning of section 131 of the 1986 Act or Article 111 of the 1989 Order); and

(b) "report" means a written report setting out the position generally as regards the progress of the winding up or provisional liquidation (as the case may be).

History
In reg.14(1) the words "an administrator is appointed under paragraph 13 of Schedule B1" substituted for the word "administration" by the Insurers (Reorganisation and Winding Up) (Amendment) Regulations 2004 (SI 2004/546) reg.2(3), as from 3 March 2004.

15 Service of notices and documents

15(1) This regulation applies to any notification, report or other document which is required to be sent to a creditor of a UK insurer by a provision of this Part ("a relevant notification").

15(2) A relevant notification may be sent to a creditor by either of the following methods–

(a) posting it to the proper address of the creditor;

(b) transmitting it electronically, in accordance with paragraph (4).

15(3) For the purposes of paragraph (2)(a), the proper address of a creditor is any current address provided by that creditor as an address for service of a relevant notification or, if no such address is provided–

(a) the last known address of that creditor (whether his residence or a place where he carries on business);

(b) in the case of a body corporate, the address of its registered or principal office; or

(c) in the case of an unincorporated association, the address of its principal office.

15(4) A relevant notification may be transmitted electronically only if it is sent to–

(a) an electronic address notified to the relevant officer by the creditor for this purpose; or

(b) if no such address has been notified, an electronic address at which the relevant officer reasonably believes the creditor will receive the notification.

15(5) Any requirement in this part to send a relevant notification to a creditor shall also be treated as satisfied if–

(a) the creditor has agreed with–

   (i) the UK insurer which is liable under the creditor's claim, or

   (ii) the relevant officer,

that information which is required to be sent to him (whether pursuant to a statutory or contractual obligation, or otherwise) may instead be accessed by him on a web site;

(b) the agreement applies to the relevant notification in question;

(c) the creditor is notified of–

   (i) the publication of the relevant notification on a web site,

   (ii) the address of that web site,

   (iii) the place on that web site where the relevant notification may be accessed, and how it may be accessed; and

(d) the relevant notification is published on that web site throughout a period of at least one month beginning with the date on which the creditor is notified in accordance with sub-paragraph (c).

15(6) Where, in a case in which paragraph (5) is relied on for compliance with a requirement of regulation 12 or 14–

(a) a relevant notification is published for a part, but not all, of the period mentioned in paragraph (5)(d); but

(b) the failure to publish it throughout that period is wholly attributable to circumstances which it would not be reasonable to have expected the relevant officer to prevent or avoid,

no offence is committed under regulation 12(10) or regulation 14(5) (as the case may be) by reason of that failure.

15(7)   In this regulation–

(a) "electronic address" includes any number or address used for the purposes of receiving electronic communications;

(b) "electronic communication" means an electronic communication within the meaning of the Electronic Communications Act 2000 the processing of which on receipt is intended to produce writing; and

(c) "relevant officer" means (as the case may be) an administrator, liquidator, provisional liquidator or supervisor who is required to send a relevant notification to a creditor by a provision of this Part.

16   Disclosure of confidential information received from an EEA regulator

16(1)   This regulation applies to information ("insolvency information") which–

(a) relates to the business or affairs of any other person; and

(b) is supplied to the FCA or the PRA by an EEA regulator acting in accordance with Articles 5, 8 or 30 of the reorganisation and winding up directive.

16(2)   Subject to paragraphs (3) and (4), sections 348, 349 and 352 of the 2000 Act apply in relation to insolvency information in the same way as they apply in relation to confidential information within the meaning of section 348(2) of the 2000 Act.

16(3)   Insolvency information is not subject to the restrictions on disclosure imposed by section 348(1) of the 2000 Act (as it applies by virtue of paragraph (2)) if it satisfies any of the criteria set out in section 348(4) of the 2000 Act.

16(4)   The Disclosure Regulations apply in relation to insolvency information as they apply in relation to single market directive information (within the meaning of those Regulations).

16(5)   In this regulation, "the Disclosure Regulations" means the Financial Services and Markets Act 2000 (Disclosure of Confidential Information) Regulations 2001.

PART IV

PRIORITY OF PAYMENT OF INSURANCE CLAIMS IN WINDING UP ETC.

17   Interpretation of this Part

17(1)   For the purposes of this Part–

"composite insurer" means a UK insurer who is authorised to carry on both general business and long term business, in accordance with Article 73(2) of the Solvency 2 Directive;

"floating charge" has the meaning given by section 251 of the 1986 Act or paragraph (1) of Article 5 of the 1989 Order;

"general business" means the business of effecting or carrying out a contract of general insurance;

"general business assets" means the assets of a composite insurer which are, or should properly be, apportioned to that insurer's general business, in accordance with the requirements of Article 73(5) of the Solvency 2 Directive (separate management of long term and general business of a composite insurer);

"general business liabilities" means the debts of a composite insurer which are attributable to the general business carried on by that insurer;

"general insurer" means a UK insurer who carries on exclusively general business;

"long term business" means the business of effecting or carrying out a contract of long term insurance;

"long term business assets" means the assets of a composite insurer which are, or should properly be, apportioned to that insurer's long term business, in accordance with the requirements of Article 73(5) of the Solvency 2 Directive (separate management of long term and general business of a composite insurer);

"long term business liabilities" means the debts of a composite insurer which are attributable to the long term business carried on by that insurer;

"long term insurer" means a UK insurer who–

(a)   carries on long term business exclusively, or

(b)   carries on long term business and permitted general business;

"non-transferring composite insurer" means a composite insurer the long term business of which has not been, and is not to be, transferred as a going concern to a person who may lawfully carry out those contracts, in accordance with section 376(2) of the 2000 Act;

"other assets" means any assets of a composite insurer which are not long term business assets or general business assets;

"other business", in relation to a composite insurer, means such of the business (if any) of the insurer as is not long term business or general business;

"permitted general business" means the business of effecting or carrying out a contract of general insurance where the risk insured against relates to either accident or sickness;

"preferential debt" means a debt falling into any of categories 4 or 5 of the debts listed in Schedule 6 to the 1986 Act or Schedule 4 to the 1989 Order, that is–

(a)   contributions to occupational pension schemes, etc., and

(b)   remuneration etc. of employees;

"society" means–

(a)   a friendly society incorporated under the Friendly Societies Act 1992;

(b)   a society which is a friendly society within the meaning of section 7(1)(a) of the Friendly Societies Act 1974, and registered within the meaning of that Act, or

(c)   a registered society.

17(2)   In this Part, references to assets include a reference to proceeds where an asset has been realised, and any other sums representing assets.

17(3)   References in paragraph (1) to a contract of long term or of general insurance must be read with–

(a)   section 22 of the 2000 Act;

(b)   any relevant order made under that section; and

(c)   Schedule 2 to that Act.

History
Regulation 17(1)(c) amended by the Co-operative and Community Benefit Societies and Credit Unions Act 2010 (Consequential Amendments) Regulations 2014 (SI 2014/1815) Sch.1 para.12(3) as from 1 August 2014. Definitions of "composite insurer", "general business assets" and "long term business assets" in reg.17(1) amended by the Solvency 2 Regulations (SI 2015/575) reg.17(5) as from 1 January 2016.

18   Application of regulations 19 to 27

18(1)   Subject to paragraph (2), regulations 19 to 27 apply in the winding up of a UK insurer where–

(a)   in the case of a winding up by the court, the winding up order is made on or after 20th April 2003; or

(b)   in the case of a creditors' voluntary winding up, the liquidator is appointed, as mentioned in section 100 of the 1986 Act, paragraph 83 of Schedule B1, paragraph 84 of Schedule B1 to the 1989 Order or Article 86 of the 1989 Order, on or after 20th April 2003.

18(2)   Where a relevant compromise or arrangement is in place,

(a)   no winding up proceedings may be opened without the permission of the court, and

(b)   the permission of the court is to be granted only if required by the exceptional circumstances of the case.

18(3)   For the purposes of paragraph (2), winding up proceedings include proceedings for a winding up order or for a creditors' voluntary liquidation with confirmation by the court.

18(4)   Regulations 20 to 27 do not apply to a winding up falling within paragraph (1) where, in relation to a UK insurer–

(a)   an administration order was made before 20th April 2003, and that order is not discharged until the commencement date; or

(b)   a provisional liquidator was appointed before 20th April 2003, and that appointment is not discharged until the commencement date.

18(5)   For purposes of this regulation, "the commencement date" means the date when a UK insurer goes into liquidation within the meaning given by section 247(2) of the 1986 Act or Article 6(2) of the 1989 Order.

18(6)   In paragraph (2) "relevant compromise or arrangement" means–

(a)   a section 899 compromise or arrangement, or

(b)   a compromise or arrangement sanctioned by the court in relation to a UK insurer before 6th April 2008 under–

(i)   section 425 of the Companies Act 1985 (excluding a compromise or arrangement falling within section 427 or 427A of that Act), or

(ii)   Article 418 of the Companies (Northern Ireland) Order 1986 (excluding a compromise or arrangement falling within Article 420 or 420A of that Order).

History
Regulation 18(2) amended and reg.18(6) inserted by the Companies Act 2006 (Consequential Amendments and Transitional Provisions) Order 2011 (SI 2011/1265) art.23(4) as from 12 May 2011.

19   Application of this Part: certain assets excluded from insolvent estate of UK insurer

19(1)   For the purposes of this Part, the insolvent estate of a UK insurer shall not include any assets which at the commencement date are subject to a relevant compromise or arrangement.

19(2)   In this regulation–

(a)   "assets" has the same meaning as "property" in section 436 of the 1986 Act or Article 2(2) of the 1989 Order;

(b)   "commencement date" has the meaning given in regulation 18(5);

(c)   "insolvent estate"–

    (i)   in England, Wales and Northern Ireland has the meaning given by rule 1.2 of the Insolvency Rules or Rule 0.2 of the Insolvency Rules (Northern Ireland), and

    (ii)   in Scotland means the company's assets;

(d)   "relevant compromise or arrangement" means–

    (i)   a compromise or arrangement sanctioned by the court in relation to a UK insurer before 20th April 2003 under–

        (aa) section 425 of the Companies Act 1985 (excluding a compromise or arrangement falling within section 427 or 427A of that Act), or

        (bb) Article 418 of the Companies (Northern Ireland) Order 1986 (excluding a compromise or arrangement falling within Article 420 or 420A of that Order); or

    (ii)   any subsequent compromise or arrangement sanctioned by the court to amend or replace a compromise or arrangement of a kind mentioned in paragraph (i) which is–

        (aa) itself of a kind mentioned in sub-paragraph (aa) or (bb) of paragraph (i) (whether sanctioned before, on or after 20th April 2003), or

        (bb) a section 899 compromise or arrangement.

History

In reg.19(2)(b), "18(5)" substituted for "18(4)" by the Insurers (Reorganisation and Winding Up) (Lloyd's) Regulations 2005 (SI 2005/1998) art.49, as from 10 August 2005. Heading and reg.19(1) amended and reg.19(2)(d) substituted by the Companies Act 2006 (Consequential Amendments and Transitional Provisions) Order 2011 (SI 2011/1265) art.23(5), (6) as from 12 May 2011. Regulation 19(2)(c)(i) amended by the Financial Services and Markets (Insolvency) (Amendment of Miscellaneous Enactments) Regulations 2019 (SI 2019/755) regs 1, 4(1), (6) as from 23 April 2019.

20   Preferential debts: disapplication of section 175 of the 1986 Act or article 149 of the 1989 Order

20   Except to the extent that they are applied by regulation 27, section 175 of the 1986 Act or Article 149 of the 1989 Order (preferential debts (general provision)) does not apply in the case of a winding up of a UK insurer, and instead the provisions of regulations 21 to 26 have effect.

21   Preferential debts: long term insurers and general insurers

21(1)   This regulation applies in the case of a winding up of–

(a)   a long term insurer;

(b)   a general insurer;

(c)   a composite insurer, where the long term business of that insurer has been or is to be transferred as a going concern to a person who may lawfully carry out the contracts in that long term business in accordance with section 376(2) of the 2000 Act.

21(2)   Subject to paragraph (3), the debts of the insurer must be paid in the following order of priority–

(a)   preferential debts;

    (b)   insurance debts;

    (c)   all other debts.

21(3)   Preferential debts rank equally among themselves after the expenses of the winding up and must be paid in full, unless the assets are insufficient to meet them, in which case they abate in equal proportions.

21(4)   Insurance debts rank equally among themselves and must be paid in full, unless the assets available after the payment of preferential debts are insufficient to meet them, in which case they abate in equal proportions.

21(5)   Subject to paragraph (6), so far as the assets of the insurer available for the payment of unsecured creditors are insufficient to meet the preferential debts, those debts (and only those debts) have priority over the claims of holders of debentures secured by, or holders of, any floating charge created by the insurer, and must be paid accordingly out of any property comprised in or subject to that charge.

21(6)   The order of priority specified in paragraph (2)(a) and (b) applies for the purposes of any payment made in accordance with paragraph (5).

21(7)   Section 176A of the 1986 Act and Article 150A of the 1989 Order have effect with regard to an insurer so that insurance debts must be paid out of the prescribed part in priority to all other unsecured debts.

History

In reg.21(3) the words "after the expenses of the winding up" inserted by the Insurers (Reorganisation and Winding Up) (Amendment) Regulations 2004 (SI 2004/546) reg.2(4), as from 3 March 2004.

22   Composite insurers: preferential debts attributable to long term and general business

22(1)   This regulation applies in the case of the winding up of a non-transferring composite insurer.

22(2)   Subject to the payment of costs in accordance with regulation 30, the long term business assets and the general business assets must be applied separately in accordance with paragraphs (3) and (4).

22(3)   Subject to paragraph (6), the long term business assets must be applied in discharge of the long term business preferential debts in the order of priority specified in regulation 23(1).

22(4)   Subject to paragraph (8), the general business assets must be applied in discharge of the general business preferential debts in the order of priority specified in regulation 24(1).

22(5)   Paragraph (6) applies where the value of the long term business assets exceeds the long term business preferential debts and the general business assets are insufficient to meet the general business preferential debts.

22(6)   Those long term business assets which represent the excess must be applied in discharge of the outstanding general business preferential debts of the insurer, in accordance with the order of priority specified in regulation 24(1).

22(7)   Paragraph (8) applies where the value of the general business assets exceeds the general business preferential debts, and the long term business assets are insufficient to meet the long term business preferential debts.

22(8)   Those general business assets which represent the excess must be applied in discharge of the outstanding long term business preferential debts of the insurer, in accordance with the order of priority specified in regulation 23(1).

22(9)   For the purposes of this regulation and regulations 23 and 24–

   "long term business preferential debts" means those debts mentioned in regulation 23(1) and, unless the court orders otherwise, any expenses of the winding up which are apportioned to the long term business assets in accordance with regulation 30;

"general business preferential debts" means those debts mentioned in regulation 24(1) and, unless the court orders otherwise, any expenses of the winding up which are apportioned to the general business assets in accordance with regulation 30.

22(10)   For the purposes of paragraphs (6) and (8)–

"outstanding long term business preferential debts" means those long term business preferential debts, if any, which remain unpaid, either in whole or in part, after the application of the long term business assets, in accordance with paragraph (3);

"outstanding general business preferential debts" means those general business preferential debts, if any, which remain unpaid, either in whole or in part, after the application of the general business assets, in accordance with paragraph (3).

23   Preferential debts: long term business of a non-transferring composite insurer

23(1)   For the purpose of compliance with the requirement in regulation 22(3), the long term business assets of a non-transferring composite insurer must be applied in discharge of the following debts and in the following order of priority–

(a)   relevant preferential debts;

(b)   long term insurance debts.

23(2)   Relevant preferential debts rank equally among themselves, unless the long term business assets, any available general business assets and other assets (if any) applied in accordance with regulation 24 are insufficient to meet them, in which case they abate in equal proportions.

23(3)   Long term insurance debts rank equally among themselves, unless the long term business assets available after the payment of relevant preferential debts and any available general business assets and other assets (if any) applied in accordance with regulation 25 are insufficient to meet them, in which case they abate in equal proportions.

23(4)   So far as the long term business assets, and any available general business assets, which are available for the payment of unsecured creditors are insufficient to meet the relevant preferential debts, those debts (and only those debts) have priority over the claims of holders of debentures secured by, or holders of, any floating charge created by the insurer over any of its long term business assets, and must be paid accordingly out of any property comprised in or subject to that charge.

23(5)   The order of priority specified in paragraph (1) applies for the purposes of any payment made in accordance with paragraph (4).

23(6)   For the purposes of this regulation–

"available general business assets" means those general business assets which must be applied in discharge of the insurer's outstanding long term business preferential debts, in accordance with regulation 22(8);

"long term insurance debt" means an insurance debt which is attributable to the long term business of the insurer;

"relevant preferential debt" means a preferential debt which is attributable to the long term business of the insurer.

24   Preferential debts: general business of a composite insurer

24(1)   For the purpose of compliance with the requirement in regulation 22(4), the long term business assets of a non-transferring composite insurer must be applied in discharge of the following debts and in the following order of priority–

(a) relevant preferential debts;

(b) general insurance debts.

24(2) Relevant preferential debts rank equally among themselves, unless the general business assets, any available long term business assets, and other assets (if any) applied in accordance with regulation 25 are insufficient to meet them, in which case they abate in equal proportions.

24(3) General insurance debts rank equally among themselves, unless the general business assets available after the payment of relevant preferential debts, any available long term business assets, and other assets (if any) applied in accordance with regulation 26 are insufficient to meet them, in which case they abate in equal proportions.

24(4) So far as the other business assets and available long term assets of the insurer which are available for the payment of unsecured creditors are insufficient to meet relevant preferential debts, those debts (and only those debts) have priority over the claims of holders of debentures secured by, or holders of, any floating charge created by the insurer, and must be paid accordingly out of any property comprised in or subject to that charge.

24(5) The order of priority specified in paragraph (1) applies for the purposes of any payment made in accordance with paragraph (4).

24(6) For the purposes of this regulation–

"available long term business assets" means those long term business assets which must be applied in discharge of the insurer's outstanding general business preferential debts, in accordance with regulation 22(6);

"general insurance debt" means an insurance debt which is attributable to the general business of the insurer;

"relevant preferential debt" means a preferential debt which is attributable to the general business of the insurer.

25   Insufficiency of long term business assets and general business assets

25(1) This regulation applies in the case of the winding up of a non-transferring composite insurer where the long term business assets and the general business assets, applied in accordance with regulation 22, are insufficient to meet in full the preferential debts and insurance debts.

25(2) In a case in which this regulation applies, the other assets (if any) of the insurer must be applied in the following order of priority–

(a) outstanding preferential debts;

(b) unattributed preferential debts;

(c) outstanding insurance debts;

(d) all other debts.

25(3) So far as the long term business assets, and any available general business assets, which are available for the payment of unsecured creditors are insufficient to meet the outstanding preferential debts and the unattributed preferential debts, those debts (and only those debts) have priority over the claims of holders of debentures secured by, or holders of, any floating charge created by the insurer over any of its other assets, and must be paid accordingly out of any property comprised in or subject to that charge.

25(4) For the purposes of this regulation–

"outstanding insurance debt" means any insurance debt, or any part of an insurance debt, which was not discharged by the application of the long term business assets and the general business assets in accordance with regulation 22;

"outstanding preferential debt" means any preferential debt attributable either to the long term business or the general business of the insurer which was not discharged by the application of the long term business assets and the general business assets in accordance with regulation 23;

"unattributed preferential debt" means a preferential debt which is not attributable to either the long term business or the general business of the insurer.

26   Composite insurers: excess of long term business assets and general business assets

26(1)   This regulation applies in the case of the winding up of a non-transferring composite insurer where the value of the long term business assets and the general business assets, applied in accordance with regulation 22, exceeds the value of the sum of the long term business preferential debts and the general business preferential debts.

26(2)   In a case to which this regulation applies, long term business assets or general business assets which have not been applied in discharge of long term business preferential debts or general business preferential debts must be applied in accordance with regulation 27.

26(3)   In this regulation, "long term business preferential debts" and "general business preferential debts" have the same meaning as in regulation 22.

27   Composite insurers: application of other assets

27(1)   This regulation applies in the case of the winding up of a non-transferring composite insurer where regulation 25 does not apply.

27(2)   The other assets of the insurer, together with any outstanding business assets, must be paid in discharge of the following debts in accordance with section 175 of the 1986 Act or Article 149 of the 1989 Order–

(a)   unattributed preferential debts;

(b)   all other debts.

27(3)   In this regulation–

"unattributed preferential debt" has the same meaning as in regulation 25;

"outstanding business assets" means assets of the kind mentioned in regulation 26(2).

28   Composite insurers: proof of debts

28(1)   This regulation applies in the case of the winding up of a non-transferring composite insurer in compliance with the requirement in regulation 23(2).

28(2)   The liquidator may in relation to the insurer's long term business assets and its general business assets fix different days on or before which the creditors of the company who are required to prove their debts or claims are to prove their debts or claims, and he may fix one of those days without at the same time fixing the other.

28(3)   In submitting a proof of any debt a creditor may claim the whole or any part of such debt as is attributable to the company's long term business or to its general business, or he may make no such attribution.

28(4)   When he admits any debt, in whole or in part, the liquidator must state in writing how much of what he admits is attributable to the company's long term business, how much is attributable to the company's general business, and how much is attributable to its other business (if any).

28(5)   Paragraph (2) does not apply in Scotland.

28A   Composite insurers: seeking decisions from creditors

28A(1) This regulation applies in the same circumstances as regulation 28, but only if the non-transferring composite insurer is–

(a) a company registered in England and Wales;

(b) a registered society within the meaning given by section 1(1) of the Co-operative and Community Benefit Societies Act 2014 which the courts in England and Wales have jurisdiction to wind up; or

(c) a friendly society within the meaning of section 7(1)(a) of the Friendly Societies Act 1974, which is registered within the meaning of that Act and is being wound up by the High Court under the Insolvency Act 1986.

28A(2) The creditors from whom the liquidator is to seek a decision about any matter in relation to the winding up are to be–

(a) in relation to the long term business assets of that insurer, only those who are creditors in respect of long term business liabilities, and

(b) in relation to the general business assets of that insurer, only those who are creditors in respect of general business liabilities.

History

Regulation 28A was inserted by the Small Business, Enterprise and Employment Act 2015 (Consequential Amendments, Savings and Transitional Provisions) Regulations 2018 (SI 2018/208) reg.9(2) with effect from 13 March 2018.

29   Composite insurers: general meetings of creditors

29(1) This regulation applies in the same circumstances as regulation 28, but only if the non-transferring composite insurer is a company registered in Scotland or Northern Ireland or a society other than a society of a kind to which regulation 28A applies.

29(2) The creditors mentioned in section 168(2) of the 1986 Act (as applied in relation to such a society), Article 143(2) of the 1989 Order or rule 4.13 of the Insolvency (Scotland) Rules 1986 (power of liquidator to summon general meetings of creditors) are to be–

(a) in relation to the long term business assets of that insurer, only those who are creditors in respect of long term business liabilities; and

(b) in relation to the general business assets of that insurer, only those who are creditors in respect of general business liabilities,

and, accordingly, any general meetings of creditors summoned for the purposes of that section, Article or rule are to be separate general meetings of creditors in respect of long term business liabilities and general business liabilities.

History

Regulation 29(1) and (2) were modified by the Small Business, Enterprise and Employment Act 2015 (Consequential Amendments, Savings and Transitional Provisions) Regulations 2018 (SI 2018/208) reg.9(3)(a) and (b) with effect from 13 March 2018. Regulation 29(2) amended by the Financial Services and Markets (Insolvency) (Amendment of Miscellaneous Enactments) Regulations 2019 (SI 2019/755) regs 1, 4(1), (7) as from 23 April 2019.

30   Composite insurers: apportionment of costs payable out of the assets

30(1) In the case of the winding up of a non-transferring composite insurer, rule 6.42 (general rule as to priority in creditors' voluntary winding up) or 7.108 (general rule as to priority in winding up by the court) of the Insolvency Rules or Rule 4.228 of the Insolvency Rules (Northern Ireland) (general rules as to priority) or rule 7.28 of the Insolvency (Scotland) (Receivership and Winding up) Rules 2018 applies separately to long-term business assets and to the general business assets of that insurer.

30(2)   But where any fee, expense, cost, charge, or remuneration does not relate exclusively to the long-term business assets or to the general business assets of that insurer, the liquidator must apportion it amongst those assets in such manner as he shall determine.

History
Regulation 30(1) amended by the Financial Services and Markets (Insolvency) (Amendment of Miscellaneous Enactments) Regulations 2019 (SI 2019/755) regs 1, 4(1), (8) as from 23 April 2019.

31   Summary remedy against liquidators

31   Section 212 of the 1986 Act or Article 176 of the 1989 Order (summary remedy against delinquent directors, liquidators etc.) applies in relation to a liquidator who is required to comply with regulations 21 to 27, as it applies in relation to a liquidator who is required to comply with section 175 of the 1986 Act or Article 149 of the 1989 Order.

32   Priority of subrogated claims by the Financial Services Compensation Scheme

32(1)   This regulation applies where an insurance creditor has assigned a relevant right to the scheme manager ("a relevant assignment").

32(2)   For the purposes of regulations 21, 23 and 24, where the scheme manager proves for an insurance debt in the winding up of a UK insurer pursuant to a relevant assignment, that debt must be paid to the scheme manager in the same order of priority as any other insurance debt.

32(3)   In this regulation–

"relevant right" means any direct right of action against a UK insurer under a contract of insurance, including the right to prove for a debt under that contract in a winding up of that insurer;

"scheme manager" has the meaning given by section 212(1) of the 2000 Act.

33   Voluntary arrangements: treatment of insurance debts

33(1)   The modifications made by paragraph (2) apply where a voluntary arrangement is proposed under section 1 of the 1986 Act or Article 14 of the 1989 Order in relation to a UK insurer, and that arrangement includes–

   (a)   a composition in satisfaction of any insurance debts; and

   (b)   a distribution to creditors of some or all of the assets of that insurer in the course of, or with a view to, terminating the whole or any part of the business of that insurer.

33(2)   Section 4 of the 1986 Act (decisions of meetings) has effect as if–

   (a)   after subsection (4) there were inserted

   "**(4ZA)** In relation to a company registered in England and Wales, neither the company nor its creditors may approve any proposal or modification under which any insurance debt of the company is to be paid otherwise than in priority to such of its debts as are not insurance debts or preferential debts.

   (4A) In relation to a company registered in Scotland, a meeting summoned under section 3 and taking place on or after 20th April 2003 shall not approve any proposal or modification under which any insurance debt of the company is to be paid otherwise than in priority to such of its debts as are not insurance debts or preferential debts.

   (4B) Paragraph (4A) does not apply where–

   (a)   a winding up order made before 20th April 2003 is in force; or

   (b)   a relevant insolvency appointment made before 20th April 2003 has effect,

   in relation to the company.";

(b)   for subsection (7) there were substituted

"**(7)** References in this section to preferential debts mean debts falling into any of categories 4 and 5 of the debts listed in Schedule 6 to this Act; and references to preferential creditors are to be construed accordingly."; and

(c)   after subsection (7) as so substituted there were inserted–

"**(8)** For the purposes of this section–

(a)   'insurance debt' has the meaning it has in the Insurers (Reorganisation and Winding up) Regulations 2004; and

(b)   'relevant insolvency measure' means–

(i)   the appointment of a provisional liquidator, or

(ii)   the appointment of an administrator,

where an effect of the appointment will be, or is intended to be, a realisation of some or all of the assets of the insurer and the distribution of the proceeds to creditors, with a view to terminating the whole or any part of the business of that insurer.".

33(3)   Article 17 of the 1989 Order (decisions of meetings) has effect as if–

(a)   after paragraph (4) there were inserted–

"**(4A)** A meeting so summoned and taking place on or after 20th April 2003 shall not approve any proposal or modification under which any insurance debt of the company is to be paid otherwise than in priority to such of its debts as are not insurance debts or preferential debts.

(4B) Paragraph (4A) does not apply where–

(a)   a winding up order made before 20th April 2003 is in force; or

(b)   a relevant insolvency appointment made before 20th April 2003 has effect, in relation to the company.";

(b)   for paragraph (7) there were substituted–

"**(7)** References in this Article to preferential debts mean debts falling into any of categories 4 and 5 of the debts listed in Schedule 4 to this Order, and references to preferential creditors are to be construed accordingly."; and

(c)   after paragraph (7) as so substituted there were inserted–

"**(8)** For the purposes of this section–

(a)   'insurance debt' has the meaning it has in the Insurers (Reorganisation and Winding Up) Regulations 2004 and

(b)   'relevant insolvency measure' means–

(i)   the appointment of a provisional liquidator, or

(ii)   the appointment of an administrator,

where an effect of the appointment will be, or is intended to be, a realisation of some or all of the assets of the insurer and the distribution of the proceeds to creditors, with a view to terminating the whole or any part of the business of that insurer.".

History
The date "2003", originally omitted in two places after "20th April" in reg.32(2), (3) inserted by the Insurers (Reorganisation and Winding Up) (Amendment) Regulations 2004 (SI 2004/546) reg.2(5), as from 3 March 2004. Regulation 33(2)(a) was modified by the Small Business, Enterprise and Employment Act 2015 (Consequential Amendments, Savings and Transitional Provisions) Regulations 2018 (SI 2018/208) reg.9(4)(a) and (b) with effect from 13 March 2018.

PART V

REORGANISATION OR WINDING UP OF UK INSURERS: RECOGNITION OF EEA RIGHTS

34   Application of this Part

34(1)   This Part applies–

(a)   where a decision with respect to the approval of a proposed voluntary arrangement having a qualifying purpose is made under section 4A of the 1986 Act or Article 17A of the 1989 Order on or after 20th April 2003 in relation to a UK insurer;

(b)   where an administration order made under section 8 of the 1986 Act on or after 20th April 2003 or, on or after 15th September 2003, made under paragraph 13 of Schedule B1 or under paragraph 14 of Schedule B1 to the 1989 Order is in force in relation to a UK insurer;

(c)   where on or after 20th April 2003 the court reduces the value of one or more of the contracts of a UK insurer under section 377 of the 2000 Act or section 24(5) of the Friendly Societies Act 1992;

(d)   where a UK insurer is subject to a relevant winding up;

(e)   where a provisional liquidator is appointed in relation to a UK insurer on or after 20th April 2003.

34(2)   For the purposes of paragraph (1)(a), a voluntary arrangement has a qualifying purpose if it–

(a)   varies the rights of the creditors as against the insurer and is intended to enable the insurer, and the whole or any part of its undertaking, to survive as a going concern; or

(b)   includes a realisation of some or all of the assets of the insurer to which it relates and the distribution of the proceeds to creditors, with a view to terminating the whole or any part of the business of that insurer.

34(3)   For the purposes of paragraph (1)(d), a winding up is a relevant winding up if–

(a)   in the case of a winding up by the court, the winding up order is made on or after 20th April 2003; or

(b)   in the case of a creditors' voluntary winding up, the liquidator is appointed in accordance with section 100 of the 1986 Act, paragraph 83 of Schedule B1, paragraph 84 of Schedule B1 to the 1989 Order or Article 86 of the 1989 Order on or after 20th April 2003.

35   Application of this Part: certain assets excluded from insolvent estate of UK insurer

35(1)   For the purposes of this Part, the insolvent estate of a UK insurer shall not include any assets which at the commencement date are subject to a relevant compromise or arrangement.

35(2)   In this regulation–

(a)   "assets" has the same meaning as "property" in section 436 of the 1986 Act or Article 2(2) of the 1989 Order;

(b)   "commencement date" has the meaning given in regulation 18(4);

(c)   "insolvent estate" in England and Wales and Northern Ireland has the meaning given by rule 1.2 of the Insolvency Rules or Rule 0.2 of the Insolvency Rules (Northern Ireland) and in Scotland means the company's assets;

(d)   "relevant compromise or arrangement" means–

(i)   a compromise or arrangement sanctioned by the court in relation to a UK insurer before 20th April 2003 under–

(aa) section 425 of the Companies Act 1985 (excluding a compromise or arrangement falling within section 427 or 427A of that Act), or

(bb) Article 418 of the Companies (Northern Ireland) Order 1986 (excluding a compromise or arrangement falling within Article 420 or 420A of that Order); or

(ii) any subsequent compromise or arrangement sanctioned by the court to amend or replace a compromise or arrangement of a kind mentioned in paragraph (i) which is–

(aa) itself of a kind mentioned in sub-paragraph (aa) or (bb) of paragraph (i) (whether sanctioned before, on or after 20th April 2003), or

(bb) a section 899 compromise or arrangement.)

History
Heading and reg.35(1) amended and reg.35(2)(d) substituted by the Companies Act 2006 (Consequential Amendments and Transitional Provisions) Order 2011 (SI 2011/1265) art.23(7), (8) as from 12 May 2011. Regulation 35(2)(c) amended by the Financial Services and Markets (Insolvency) (Amendment of Miscellaneous Enactments) Regulations 2019 (SI 2019/755) regs 1, 4(1), (9) as from 23 April 2019.

36 Interpretation of this Part

36(1) For the purposes of this Part–

(a) "affected insurer" means a UK insurer which is the subject of a relevant reorganisation or a relevant winding up;

(b) "relevant reorganisation or a relevant winding up" means any voluntary arrangement, administration order, winding up, or order referred to in regulation 34(1)(d) to which this Part applies; and

(c) "relevant time" means the date of the opening of a relevant reorganisation or a relevant winding up.

36(2) In this Part, references to the opening of a relevant reorganisation or a relevant winding up mean–

(a) in the case of winding up proceedings–

(i) in the case of a winding up by the court, the date on which the winding up order is made, or

(ii) in the case of a creditors' voluntary winding up, the date on which the liquidator is appointed in accordance with section 100 of the 1986 Act, paragraph 83 of Schedule B1 or Article 86 of the 1989 Order or paragraph 84 of Schedule B1 to the 1989 Order;

(b) in the case of a voluntary arrangement, the date when a decision with respect to that voluntary arrangement has effect in accordance with section 4A(2) of the 1986 Act or Article 17A(2) of the 1989 Order;

(c) in a case where an administration order under paragraph 13 of Schedule B1 or under paragraph 14 of Schedule B1 to the 1989 Order is in force, the date of the making of that order;

(d) in a case where an administrator is appointed under paragraphs 14 or 22 of Schedule B1 or under paragraph 15 or 23 of Schedule B1 to the 1989 Order, the date on which that appointment takes effect;

(e) in a case where the court reduces the value of one or more of the contracts of a UK insurer under section 377 of the 2000 Act or section 24(5) of the Friendly Societies Act 1992, the date the court exercises that power; and

(f) in a case where a provisional liquidator has been appointed, the date of that appointment, and references to the time of an opening must be construed accordingly.

37   EEA rights: applicable law in the winding up of a UK insurer

37(1)   This regulation is subject to the provisions of regulations 38 to 47.

37(2)   In a relevant winding up, the matters mentioned in paragraph (3) in particular are to be determined in accordance with the general law of insolvency of the United Kingdom.

37(3)   Those matters are–

(a)   the assets which form part of the estate of the affected insurer;

(b)   the treatment of assets acquired by, or devolving on, the affected insurer after the opening of the relevant winding up;

(c)   the respective powers of the affected insurer and the liquidator or provisional liquidator;

(d)   the conditions under which set-off may be revoked;

(e)   the effects of the relevant winding up on current contracts to which the affected insurer is a party;

(f)   the effects of the relevant winding up on proceedings brought by creditors;

(g)   the claims which are to be lodged against the estate of the affected insurer;

(h)   the treatment of claims against the affected insurer arising after the opening of the relevant winding up;

(i)   the rules governing–

  (i)   the lodging, verification and admission of claims,

  (ii)   the distribution of proceeds from the realisation of assets,

  (iii)   the ranking of claims,

  (iv)   the rights of creditors who have obtained partial satisfaction after the opening of the relevant winding up by virtue of a right in rem or through set-off;

(j)   the conditions for and the effects of the closure of the relevant winding up, in particular by composition;

(k)   the rights of creditors after the closure of the relevant winding up;

(l)   who is to bear the cost and expenses incurred in the relevant winding up;

(m)   the rules relating to the voidness, voidability or unenforceability of legal acts detrimental to all the creditors.

37(4)   In this regulation, "relevant winding up" has the meaning given by regulation 34(3).

38   Employment contracts and relationships

38(1)   The effects of a relevant reorganisation or a relevant winding up on any EEA employment contract and any EEA employment relationship are to be determined in accordance with the law of the EEA State to which that contract or that relationship is subject.

38(2)   In this regulation, an employment contract is an EEA employment contract, and an employment relationship is an EEA employment relationship, if it is subject to the law of an EEA State.

39   Contracts in connection with immovable property

39   The effects of a relevant reorganisation or a relevant winding up on a contract conferring the right to make use of or acquire immovable property situated within the territory of an EEA State are to be determined in accordance with the law of that State.

40   Registrable rights

40   The effects of a relevant reorganisation or a relevant winding up on rights of the affected insurer with respect to–

(a)   immovable property,

(b)   a ship, or

(c)   an aircraft

which is subject to registration in a public register kept under the authority of an EEA State are to be determined in accordance with the law of that State.

41   Third parties' rights in rem

41(1)   A relevant reorganisation or a relevant winding up shall not affect the rights in rem of creditors or third parties in respect of tangible or intangible, movable or immovable assets (including both specific assets and collections of indefinite assets as a whole which change from time to time) belonging to the affected insurer which are situated within the territory of an EEA State at the relevant time.

41(2)   The rights in rem referred to in paragraph (1) shall in particular include–

(a)   the right to dispose of the assets in question or have them disposed of and to obtain satisfaction from the proceeds of or the income from those assets, in particular by virtue of a lien or a mortgage;

(b)   the exclusive right to have a claim met out of the assets in question, in particular a right guaranteed by a lien in respect of the claim or by assignment of the claim by way of guarantee;

(c)   the right to demand the assets in question from, or to require restitution by, any person having possession or use of them contrary to the wishes of the party otherwise entitled to the assets;

(d)   a right in rem to the beneficial use of assets.

41(3)   A right, recorded in a public register and enforceable against third parties, under which a right in rem within the meaning of paragraph (1) may be obtained, is also to be treated as a right in rem for the purposes of this regulation.

41(4)   Paragraph (1) does not preclude actions for voidness, voidability or unenforceability of legal acts detrimental to creditors under the general law of insolvency of the United Kingdom, as referred to in regulation 37(3)(m).

42   Reservation of title agreements etc.

42(1)   The opening of a relevant reorganisation or a relevant winding up in relation to an insurer purchasing an asset shall not affect the seller's rights based on a reservation of title where at the time of that opening the asset is situated within the territory of an EEA State.

42(2)   The opening of a relevant reorganisation or a relevant winding up in relation to an insurer selling an asset, after delivery of the asset, shall not constitute grounds for rescinding or terminating the sale and shall not prevent the purchaser from acquiring title where at the time of that opening the asset sold is situated within the territory of an EEA State.

42(3)   Paragraphs (1) and (2) do not preclude actions for voidness, voidability or unenforceability of legal acts detrimental to creditors under the general law of insolvency of the United Kingdom, as referred to in regulation 37(3)(m).

43   Creditors' rights to set off

43(1)   A relevant reorganisation or a relevant winding up shall not affect the right of creditors to demand the set-off of their claims against the claims of the affected insurer, where such a set-off is permitted by the applicable EEA law.

43(2)   In paragraph (1), "applicable EEA law" means the law of the EEA State which is applicable to the claim of the affected insurer.

43(3)   Paragraph (1) does not preclude actions for voidness, voidability or unenforceability of legal acts detrimental to creditors under the general law of insolvency of the United Kingdom, as referred to in regulation 37(3)(m).

44   Regulated markets

44(1)   Without prejudice to regulation 40, the effects of a relevant reorganisation measure or winding up on the rights and obligations of the parties to a regulated market operating in an EEA State must be determined in accordance with the law applicable to that market.

44(2)   Paragraph (1) does not preclude actions for voidness, voidability or unenforceability of legal acts detrimental to creditors under the general law of insolvency of the United Kingdom, as referred to in regulation 37(3)(m).

44(3)   For the purposes of this regulation, "regulated market" has the meaning given by Article 4.1.21 of Directive 2014/65/EU of the European Parliament and of the Council of 15 May 2014 on markets in financial instruments.

History
Regulation 44 amended by the Financial Services and Markets Act 2000 (Markets in Financial Instruments) Regulations 2007 (SI 2007/126) reg.6 and Sch.6 para.17, as from 1 April 2007 for the purposes specified in reg.1(2) and from 1 November 2007 for all other purposes.
  Regulation 44(3) amended by the Financial Services and Markets Act 2000 (Markets in Financial Instruments) Regulations 2017 (SI 2017/701) reg.50(4), Sch.5 para.4 as from 3 January 2018.

45   Detrimental acts pursuant to the law of an EEA State

45(1)   In a relevant reorganisation or a relevant winding up, the rules relating to detrimental transactions shall not apply where a person who has benefited from a legal act detrimental to all the creditors provides proof that–

(a)   the said act is subject to the law of an EEA State; and

(b)   that law does not allow any means of challenging that act in the relevant case.

45(2)   For the purposes of paragraph (1), "the rules relating to detrimental transactions" means any provisions of the general law of insolvency relating to the voidness, voidability or unenforceability of legal acts detrimental to all the creditors, as referred to in regulation 37(3)(m).

46   Protection of third party purchasers

46(1)   This regulation applies where, by an act concluded after the opening of a relevant reorganisation or a relevant winding up, an affected insurer disposes for a consideration of–

(a)   an immovable asset situated within the territory of an EEA State;

(b)   a ship or an aircraft subject to registration in a public register kept under the authority of an EEA State; or

(c)   securities whose existence or transfer presupposes entry into a register or account laid down by the law of an EEA State or which are placed in a central deposit system governed by the law of an EEA State.

46(2)   The validity of that act is to be determined in accordance with the law of the EEA State within whose territory the immovable asset is situated or under whose authority the register, account or system is kept, as the case may be.

47   Lawsuits pending

47(1)   The effects of a relevant reorganisation or a relevant winding up on a relevant lawsuit pending in an EEA State shall be determined solely in accordance with the law of that EEA State.

47(2)   In paragraph (1), "relevant lawsuit" means a lawsuit concerning an asset or right of which the affected insurer has been divested.

PART VI

THIRD COUNTRY INSURERS

48   Interpretation of this Part

48(1)   In this Part–

(a)   "relevant measure", in relation to a third country insurer, means

    (i)   a winding up;

    (ii)   an administration order made under paragraph 13 of Schedule B1 or under paragraph 14 of Schedule B1 to the 1989 Order; or

    (iii)   a decision of the court to reduce the value of one or more of the insurer's contracts, in accordance with section 377 of the 2000 Act;

(b)   "third country insurer" means a person–

    (i)   who has permission under the 2000 Act to effect or carry out contracts of insurance; and

    (ii)   whose head office is not in the United Kingdom or an EEA State.

48(2)   In paragraph (1), the definition of "third country insurer" must be read with–

(a)   section 22 of the 2000 Act;

(b)   any relevant order made under that section; and

(c)   Schedule 2 to that Act.

49   Application of these Regulations to a third country insurer

49   Parts III, IV and V of these Regulations apply where a third country insurer is subject to a relevant measure, as if references in those Parts to a UK insurer included a reference to a third country insurer.

50   Disclosure of confidential information: third country insurers

50(1)   This regulation applies to information ("insolvency practitioner information") which–

(a)   relates to the business or other affairs of any person; and

(b)   is information of a kind mentioned in paragraph (2).

50(2)   Information falls within paragraph (1)(b) if it is supplied to–

(a)   the FCA or the PRA by an EEA regulator; or

(b)   an insolvency practitioner by an EEA administrator or liquidator,

in accordance with or pursuant to Article 296 of the Solvency 2 Directive.

945

50(3)   Subject to paragraphs (4), (5) and (6), sections 348, 349 and 352 of the 2000 Act apply in relation to insolvency practitioner information in the same way as they apply in relation to confidential information within the meaning of section 348(2) of that Act.

50(4)   For the purposes of this regulation, sections 348, 349 and 352 of the 2000 Act and the Disclosure Regulations have effect as if the primary recipients specified in subsection (5) of section 348 of the 2000 Act included an insolvency practitioner.

50(5)   Insolvency practitioner information is not subject to the restrictions on disclosure imposed by section 348(1) of the 2000 Act (as it applies by virtue of paragraph (3)) if it satisfies any of the criteria set out in section 348(4) of the 2000 Act.

50(6)   The Disclosure Regulations apply in relation to insolvency practitioner information as they apply in relation to single market directive information (within the meaning of those Regulations).

50(7)   In this regulation–

"the Disclosure Regulations" means the Financial Services and Markets Act 2000 (Disclosure of Confidential Information) Regulations 2001;

"EEA administrator" and "EEA liquidator" mean respectively an administrator or liquidator within the meaning of Title IV of the Solvency 2 Directive;

"insolvency practitioner" means an insolvency practitioner, within the meaning of section 388 of the 1986 Act or Article 3 of the 1989 Order, who is appointed or acts in relation to a third country insurer.

History
Regulation 50(2), (7) amended by the Solvency 2 Regulations (SI 2015/575) reg.17(6) as from 1 January 2016.

PART VII

REVOCATION AND AMENDMENTS

51   Amendment of the Insurers (Winding Up) Rules 2001 and the Insurers (Winding Up) (Scotland) Rules 2001

51   [Amends reg.29 of each of the above.]

52   Financial Services and Markets Act 2000 (Administration Orders Relating to Insurers) Order 2002

52   [Revoked by the Financial Services and Markets Act 2000 (Administration Orders Relating to Insurers) Order 2010 (SI 2010/3023) art.5(c) as from 1 February 2011.]

53   Revocation and transitional

53(1)   Except as provided in this regulation, the Insurers (Reorganisation and Winding Up) Regulations 2003 are revoked.

53(2)   Subject to (3), the provisions of Parts III and IV shall continue in force in respect of decisions orders or appointments referred to therein and made before the coming into force of these Regulations.

53(3)   Where an administrator has been appointed in respect of a UK insurer on or after 15th September 2003, he shall be treated as being so appointed on the date these regulations come into force.

Credit Institutions (Reorganisation and Winding Up) Regulations 2004

(SI 2004/1045)

Made on 1 April 2004 by the Treasury under s.2(2) of the European Communities Act 1972. Operative from 5 May 2004.

PART 1

GENERAL

[**Note:** Changes made by the Capital Requirement Regulations 2006 (SI 2006/3221), the Financial Services (EEA State) Regulations 2007 (SI 2007/108), the Financial Services and Markets Act 2000 (Markets in Financial Instruments) Regulations 2007 (SI 2007/126), the Credit Institutions (Reorganisation and Winding Up) (Amendment) Regulations 2007 (SI 2007/830), the Electronic Money Regulations 2011 (SI 2011/99), the Companies Act 2006 (Consequential Amendments and Transitional Provisions) Order 2011 (SI 2011/1265), the Financial Services Act 2012 (Consequential Amendments and Transitional Provisions) Order 2013 (SI 2013/472), the Capital Requirements Regulations 2013 (SI 2013/3115), the Bank Recovery and Resolution (No.2) Order 2014 (SI 2014/3348), the Financial Services and Markets Act 2000 (Markets in Financial Instruments) Regulations 2017 (SI 2017/701) and the Financial Services and Markets (Insolvency) (Amendment of Miscellaneous Enactments) Regulations 2019 (SI 2019/755) have been incorporated into the text. Where the 2007 Regulations simply add references to articles and paragraphs of Sch.B1 to the Insolvency (Northern Ireland) Order 1989 corresponding to sections and paragraphs of Sch.B1 to IA 1986, annotations have been omitted.]

1 Citation and commencement

1 These Regulations may be cited as the Credit Institutions (Reorganisation and Winding up) Regulations 2004, and come into force on 5th May 2004.

2 Interpretation

2(1) In these Regulations–

"the 1986 Act" means the Insolvency Act 1986;

"the 2000 Act" means the Financial Services and Markets Act 2000;

"the 2006 Act" means the Companies Act 2006;

"the 1989 Order" means the Insolvency (Northern Ireland) Order 1989;

"administrator" has the meaning given by paragraph 13 of Schedule B1 to the 1986 Act, paragraph 14 of Schedule B1 to the 1989 Order, section 8(2) of the 1986 Act, or Article 21(2) of the 1989 Order as the case may be;

"branch", in relation to an EEA or UK credit institution has the meaning given by Article 4(1)(17) of the capital requirements regulation;

"capital requirements directive" means Directive 2013/36/EU of the European Parliament and of the Council of 26 June 2013 relating to the activity of credit institutions and the prudential supervision of credit institutions and investment firms, amending Directive 2002/87/EC and repealing Directives 2006/48/EC and 2006/49/EC;

"capital requirements regulation" means Regulation (EU) No. 575/2013 of the European Parliament and of the Council of 26 June 2013 on prudential requirements for credit institutions and investment firms and amending Regulation (EU) No. 648/2012;

"claim" means a claim submitted by a creditor of a UK credit institution in the course of–

    (a)   a winding up,

    (b)   an administration, or

    (c)   a voluntary arrangement,

with a view to recovering his debt in whole or in part, and includes a proof within the meaning given in rule 1.2 of the Insolvency Rules, a proof of debt within the meaning given in Rule 4.079(4) of the Insolvency Rules (Northern Ireland) or in Scotland a claim made in accordance with rule 7.16 of the Insolvency (Scotland) (Receivership and Winding up) Rules 2018 (in relation to a winding up) or rule 3.105 of the Insolvency (Scotland) (Company Voluntary Arrangements and Administration) Rules 2018 (in relation to an administration);

"creditors' voluntary winding up" has the meaning given by section 90 of the 1986 Act or Article 76 of the 1989 Order as the case may be;

"debt"–

    (a)   in relation to a winding up or administration of a UK credit institution, has the meaning given by rule 14.1(3) of the Insolvency Rules or Article 5(1) of the 1989 Order except that where the credit institution is not a company, references in rule 14.1(3) or Article 5(1) to a company are to be read as references to the credit institution, and

    (b)   in a case where a voluntary arrangement has effect in relation to a UK credit institution, means a debt which would constitute a debt in relation to the winding up (not immediately preceded by an administration) of that credit institution, except that in paragraph (c) of the definition of "relevant date" in rule 14.1(3) of the Insolvency Rules and in paragraph (1A) of Article 5 of the 1989 Order the reference to the date on which the company went into liquidation has effect as a reference to the date on which the voluntary arrangement had effect;

    (c)   in Scotland–

        (i)   in relation to a winding up of a UK credit institution, shall be interpreted in accordance with rule 7.22 of the Insolvency (Scotland) (Receivership and Winding up) Rules 2018, and, in relation to an administration of a UK credit institution, has the meaning given in rule 1.2 of the Insolvency (Scotland) (Company Voluntary Arrangements and Administration) Rules 2018; and

        (ii)   in a case where a voluntary arrangement has effect in relation to a UK credit institution, means a debt which would constitute a debt in relation to the winding up (not immediately preceded by an administration) of that insurer, except that references in rule 7.22 of the Insolvency (Scotland) (Receivership and Winding up) Rules 2018 to the date on which the company went into liquidation has effect as a reference to the date on which the voluntary arrangement had effect;

"directive reorganisation measure" means a reorganisation measure as defined in Article 2 of the reorganisation and winding up directive which was adopted or imposed on or after the 5th May 2004, or any other measure to be given effect in or under the law of the United Kingdom pursuant to Article 66 of the recovery and resolution directive;

"directive winding-up proceedings" means winding-up proceedings as defined in Article 2 of the reorganisation and winding up directive which were opened on or after the 5th May 2004;

"Disclosure Regulations" means the Financial Services and Markets Act 2000 (Disclosure of Confidential Information) Regulations 2001;

"EEA credit institution" means an EEA undertaking, other than a UK credit institution, of the kind mentioned in Article 4(1)(1) and 4(1)(17) of the capital requirements regulation and subject to the exclusion of the undertakings referred to in Article 2(5)(2) to (23) of the capital requirements directive;

"EEA creditor" means a creditor of a UK credit institution who–

(a)   in the case of an individual, is ordinarily resident in an EEA State; and

(b)   in the case of a body corporate or unincorporated association of persons, has its head office in an EEA State;

"EEA regulator" means–

(a)   a competent authority (within the meaning given by point (40) of Article 4(1) of the capital requirements regulation) established in an EEA State; or

(b)   the resolution authority (within the meaning given by point (18) of Article 2(1) of the recovery and resolution directive) established in an EEA State;

"EEA State" has the meaning given by Schedule 1 to the Interpretation Act 1978;

"the FCA" means the Financial Conduct Authority;

"home state regulator", in relation to an EEA credit institution, means the relevant EEA regulator in the EEA State where its head office is located;

"the Insolvency Rules" means the Insolvency (England and Wales) Rules 2016;

"the Insolvency Rules (Northern Ireland)" means the Insolvency Rules (Northern Ireland) 1991;

"liquidator", except for the purposes of regulation 4, includes any person or body appointed by the administrative or judicial authorities whose task is to administer winding-up proceedings in respect of a UK credit institution which is not a body corporate;

"officer", in relation to a company, has the meaning given by section 1173(1) of the Companies Act 2006;

"official language" means a language specified in Article 1 of Council Regulation No 1 of 15 April 1958 determining the languages to be used by the European Economic Community (Regulation 1/58/EEC), most recently amended by paragraph (a) of Part XVIII of Annex I to the Act of Accession 1994 (194 N);

"the PRA" means the Prudential Regulation Authority;

"PRA-authorised person" has the meaning given in section 2B of the 2000 Act;

"recovery and resolution directive" means Directive 2014/59/EU of the European Parliament and of the Council of 15th May 2014 establishing a framework for the recovery and resolution of credit institutions and investment firms;

"the reorganisation and winding up directive" means Directive 2001/24/EC of the European Parliament and of the Council of 4th April 2001 on the reorganisation and winding up of credit institutions as amended by Article 117 of the recovery and resolution directive;

"section 899 compromise or arrangement" means a compromise or arrangement sanctioned by the court in relation to a UK credit institution under section 899 of the 2006 Act but does not include a compromise or arrangement falling within section 900 (powers of court to facilitate reconstruction or amalgamation) or Part 27 (mergers and divisions of public companies) of that Act;

"stabilisation instrument" means any of the following–

(a)   a "mandatory reduction instrument" made under section 6B of the Banking Act 2009;

(b)   a "resolution instrument" made under section 12A of the Banking Act 2009;

(c)   a "share transfer instrument" as defined in section 15 of the Banking Act 2009;

(d)   a "share transfer order" as defined in section 16 of the Banking Act 2009;

(e) a "property transfer instrument" as defined in section 33 of the Banking Act 2009; or

(f) a "third country instrument" made under section 89H of the Banking Act 2009;

"supervisor" has the meaning given by section 7 of the 1986 Act or Article 20 of the 1989 Order as the case may be;

"UK credit institution" means an undertaking whose head office is in the United Kingdom with permission under Part 4A of the 2000 Act to accept deposits or to issue electronic money as the case may be but does not include–

(a) an undertaking which also has permission under Part 4A of the 2000 Act to effect or carry out contracts of insurance; or

(b) a credit union within the meaning of section 1 of the Credit Unions Act 1979;

"voluntary arrangement" means a voluntary arrangement which has effect in relation to a UK credit institution in accordance with section 4A of the 1986 Act or Article 17A of the 1989 Order as the case may be; and

"winding up" means–

(a) winding up by the court, or

(b) a creditors' voluntary winding up.

2(2)   In paragraph (1)–

(a) for the purposes of the definition of "directive reorganisation measure", a reorganisation measure is adopted at the time when it is treated as adopted or imposed by the law of the relevant EEA State; and

(b) for the purposes of the definition of "directive winding-up proceedings", winding-up proceedings are opened at the time when they are treated as opened by the law of the relevant EEA State,

and in this paragraph "relevant EEA State" means the EEA State under the law of which the reorganisation is adopted or imposed, or the winding-up proceedings are opened, as the case may be.

2(3)   In these Regulations, references to the law of insolvency of the United Kingdom include references to every provision made by or under the 1986 Act or the 1989 Order as the case may be; and in relation to partnerships, limited liability partnerships or building societies, references to the law of insolvency or to any provision of the 1986 Act or the 1989 Order are to that law as modified by the Insolvent Partnerships Order 1994, the Insolvent Partnerships Order (Northern Ireland) 1995, the Limited Liability Partnerships Regulations 2001, the Limited Liability Partnerships Regulations (Northern Ireland) 2004 or the Building Societies Act 1986 (as the case may be).

2(4)   References in these Regulations to "accepting deposits" and a "contract of insurance" must be read with–

(a) section 22 of the 2000 Act;

(b) any relevant order made under that section; and

(c) Schedule 2 to that Act.

2(5)   For the purposes of the 2000 Act, functions imposed or falling on the FCA or the PRA under these Regulations shall be deemed to be functions under the 2000 Act.

History
In reg.2(1) definition of "banking consolidation directive" substituted, and definitions of "branch", "EEA credit institution" and "EEA regulator" amended, by the Capital Requirements Regulations 2006 (SI 2006/3221) reg.29(4) and Sch.6 para.17(1), (2) as from 1 January 2007. Definition of "banking consolidation directive" further amended by the Electronic Money Regulations 2011 (SI 2011/99) reg.79 and Sch.4 para.16 as from 30 April 2011. Definition of

"EEA State" substituted by the Financial Services (EEA State) Regulations 2007 (SI 2007/108) reg.9 as from 13 February 2007. This definition was inserted into the 1978 Act by the Legislative and Regulatory Reform Act 2006. Definitions of "the 2006 Act" and "officer" amended, definitions of "the 2006 Act" and "section 899 compromise or arrangement" inserted and various other definitions deleted by the Companies Act 2006 (Consequential Amendments and Transitional Provisions) Order 2011 (SI 2011/1265) art.24(2) as from 12 May 2011. Definition of "the Authority" omitted and definitions of "the FCA", "the PRA" and "PRA-authorised person" inserted by the Financial Services Act 2012 (Consequential Amendments and Transitional Provisions) Order 2013 (SI 2013/472) art.3 and Sch.2 para.91(a) as from 1 April 2013. Definition of "banking consolidation directive" omitted, definitions of "capital requirements directive" and "capital requirements regulation" inserted and definitions of "branch", "EEA credit institution" and "EEA regulator" amended by the Capital Requirements Regulations 2013 (SI 2013/3115) reg.46 and Sch.2 para.63 as from 1 January 2014. Definitions of "directive reorganisation measure", "EEA regulator" and "the reorganisation and winding up directive" substituted and definitions of "recovery and resolution directive" and "stabilisation instrument" inserted by the Bank Recovery and Resolution (No.2) Order 2014 (SI 2014/3348) Sch.3 para.10(1), (2) as from 10 January 2015.

Definitions of "claim", "debt" and "the Insolvency Rules" amended and former definition of "Insolvency (Scotland) Rules" omitted by the Financial Services and Markets (Insolvency) (Amendment of Miscellaneous Enactments) Regulations 2019 (SI 2019/755) regs 1, 5(1), (2) as from 23 April 2019.

Regulation 2(3) amended by the Credit Institutions (Reorganisation and Winding Up) (Amendment) Regulations 2007 (SI 2007/830) reg.2(1), (3) as from 6 April 2007.

PART 2

INSOLVENCY MEASURES AND PROCEEDINGS: JURISDICTION IN RELATION TO CREDIT INSTITUTIONS

3 Prohibition against winding up etc. EEA credit institutions in the United Kingdom

3(1) On or after the relevant date a court in the United Kingdom may not, in relation to an EEA credit institution or any branch of an EEA credit institution–

(a) make a winding-up order pursuant to section 221 of the 1986 Act or Article 185 of the 1989 Order;

(b) appoint a provisional liquidator;

(c) make an administration order.

3(2) Paragraph (1)(a) does not prevent–

(a) the court from making a winding-up order on or after the relevant date in relation to an EEA credit institution if–

(i) a provisional liquidator was appointed in relation to that credit institution before the relevant date, and

(ii) that appointment continues in force until immediately before that winding-up order is made;

(b) the winding up of an EEA credit institution on or after the relevant date pursuant to a winding-up order which was made, and has not been discharged, before that date.

3(3) Paragraph (1)(b) does not prevent a provisional liquidator of an EEA credit institution appointed before the relevant date from acting in relation to that credit institution on or after that date.

3(4) Paragraph (1)(c) does not prevent an administrator appointed before the relevant date from acting on or after that date in a case in which the administration order under which he or his predecessor was appointed remains in force after that date.

3(5) On or after the relevant date, an administrator may not, in relation to an EEA credit institution, be appointed under paragraphs 14 or 22 of Schedule B1 to the 1986 Act or paragraphs 15 or 23 of Schedule B1 to the 1989 Order.

3(6)   A proposed voluntary arrangement shall not have effect in relation to an EEA credit institution if a decision under section 4 of the 1986 Act or Article 17 of the 1989 Order with respect to the approval of that arrangement was taken on or after the relevant date.

3(7)   An order under section 254 of the Enterprise Act 2002 (application of insolvency law to a foreign company) or under Article 9 of the Insolvency (Northern Ireland) Order 2005 (application of insolvency law to company incorporated outside Northern Ireland) may not provide for any of the following provisions of the 1986 Act or of the 1989 Order to apply in relation to an incorporated EEA credit institution–

   (a)   Part 1 of the 1986 Act or Part 2 of the 1989 Order (company voluntary arrangements);

   (b)   Part 2 of the 1986 Act or Part 3 of the 1989 Order (administration);

   (c)   Chapter 4 of Part 4 of the 1986 Act or chapter 4 of Part 5 of the 1989 Order (creditors' voluntary winding up);

   (d)   Chapter 6 of Part 4 of the 1986 Act (winding up by the Court).

3(7A)   A stabilisation instrument shall not be made in respect of an EEA credit institution.

3(8)   In this regulation and regulation 4, "relevant date" means the 5th May 2004.

History
Regulation 3(7) substituted by the Credit Institutions (Reorganisation and Winding Up) (Amendment) Regulations 2007 (SI 2007/830) reg.2(1), (5) as from 6 April 2007. Regulation 3(7A) inserted by the Bank Recovery and Resolution (No.2) Order 2014 (SI 2014/3348) Sch.3 para.10(1), (3) as from 10 January 2015.

4   Schemes of arrangement

4(1)   For the purposes of section 895(2)(b) of the 2006 Act, an EEA credit institution or a branch of an EEA credit institution is to be treated as a company liable to be wound up under the 1986 Act or the 1989 Order if it would be liable to be wound up under that Act or Order but for the prohibition in regulation 3(1)(a).

4(2)   But a court may not make a relevant order under section 899 of the 2006 Act in relation to an EEA credit institution which is subject to a directive reorganisation measure or directive winding-up proceedings, or a branch of an EEA credit institution which is subject to such a measure or proceedings, unless the conditions set out in paragraph (3) are satisfied.

4(3)   Those conditions are–

   (a)   the person proposing the section 899 compromise or arrangement ("the proposal") has given–

      (i)   the administrator or liquidator, and

      (ii)   the relevant administrative or judicial authority,
            reasonable notice of the details of that proposal; and

   (b)   no person notified in accordance with sub-paragraph (a) has objected to the proposal.

4(4)   Nothing in this regulation invalidates a compromise or arrangement which was sanctioned by the court by an order made before the relevant date.

4(5)   For the purposes of paragraph (2), a relevant order means an order sanctioning a section 899 compromise or arrangement which–

   (a)   is intended to enable the credit institution, and the whole or any part of its undertaking, to survive as a going concern and which affects the rights of persons other than the credit institution or its contributories; or

(b) includes among its purposes a realisation of some or all of the assets of the EEA credit institution to which the order relates and the distribution of the proceeds to creditors, with a view to terminating the whole or any part of the business of that credit institution.

4(6) For the purposes of this regulation–

(a) "administrator" means an administrator, as defined by Article 2 of the reorganisation and winding up directive, who is appointed in relation to the EEA credit institution in relation to which the proposal is made;

(b) "liquidator" means a liquidator, as defined by Article 2 of the reorganisation and winding up directive, who is appointed in relation to the EEA credit institution in relation to which the proposal is made;

(c) "administrative or judicial authority" means the administrative or judicial authority, as defined by Article 2 of the reorganisation and winding up directive, which is competent for the purposes of the directive reorganisation measure or directive winding-up proceedings mentioned in paragraph (2).

History
Regulation 4(1)–(3) and 4(5) amended by the Companies Act 2006 (Consequential Amendments and Transitional Provisions) Order 2011 (SI 2011/1265) art.24(3) as from 12 May 2011.

5   Reorganisation measures and winding-up proceedings in respect of EEA credit institutions effective in the United Kingdom

5(1) An EEA insolvency measure has effect in the United Kingdom in relation to–

(a) any branch of an EEA credit institution,

(b) any property or other assets of that credit institution,

(c) any debt or liability of that credit institution,

as if it were part of the general law of insolvency of the United Kingdom.

5(2) Subject to paragraph (4)–

(a) a competent officer who satisfies the condition mentioned in paragraph (3); or

(b) a qualifying agent appointed by a competent officer who satisfies the condition mentioned in paragraph (3),

may exercise in the United Kingdom, in relation to the EEA credit institution which is subject to an EEA insolvency measure, any function which, pursuant to that measure, he is entitled to exercise in relation to that credit institution in the relevant EEA State.

5(3) The condition mentioned in paragraph (2) is that the appointment of the competent officer is evidenced–

(a) by a certified copy of the order or decision by a judicial or administrative authority in the relevant EEA State by or under which the competent officer was appointed; or

(b) by any other certificate issued by the judicial or administrative authority which has jurisdiction in relation to the EEA insolvency measure,

and accompanied by a certified translation of that order, decision or certificate (as the case may be).

5(4) In exercising the functions of the kind mentioned in paragraph (2), the competent officer or qualifying agent–

(a) may not take any action which would constitute an unlawful use of force in the part of the United Kingdom in which he is exercising those functions;

(b)   may not rule on any dispute arising from a matter falling within Part 4 of these Regulations which is justiciable by a court in the part of the United Kingdom in which he is exercising those functions; and

(c)   notwithstanding the way in which functions may be exercised in the relevant EEA State, must act in accordance with relevant laws or rules as to procedure which have effect in the part of the United Kingdom in which he is exercising those functions.

5(5)   For the purposes of paragraph (4)(c), "relevant laws or rules as to procedure" means–

(a)   requirements as to consultation with or notification of employees of an EEA credit institution;

(b)   law and procedures relevant to the realisation of assets;

(c)   where the competent officer is bringing or defending legal proceedings in the name of, or on behalf of an EEA credit institution, the relevant rules of court.

5(6)   In this regulation–

"competent officer" means a person appointed under or in connection with an EEA insolvency measure for the purpose of administering that measure;

"qualifying agent" means an agent validly appointed (whether in the United Kingdom or elsewhere) by a competent officer in accordance with the relevant law in the relevant EEA State;

"EEA insolvency measure" means, as the case may be, a directive reorganisation measure or directive winding-up proceedings which have effect in relation to an EEA credit institution by virtue of the law of the relevant EEA State;

"relevant EEA State", in relation to an EEA credit institution, means the EEA State in which that credit institution has been authorised in accordance with Article 8 of the capital requirements directive.

History
Definition of "relevant EEA State" amended by the Capital Requirements Regulations 2006 (SI 2006/3221) reg.29(4) and Sch.6 para.17(1), (3) as from 1 January 2007. Definition of "relevant EEA state" amended by the Capital Requirements Regulations 2013 (SI 2013/3115) reg.46 and Sch.2 para.63(3) as from 1 January 2014.

6   Confirmation by the court of a creditors' voluntary winding up

6(1)   Rule 21.4 of the Insolvency Rules or Rule 7.56 of the Insolvency Rules (Northern Ireland) applies in relation to a UK credit institution with the modification specified in paragraph (2) or (3).

6(2)   For the purposes of this regulation, rule 21.4 of the Insolvency Rules has effect as if after paragraph (2) there were inserted–

"**(2A)** Where the company is a UK credit institution (within the meaning given in regulation 2(1) of the Credit Institutions (Reorganisation and Winding up) Regulations 2004), paragraph (2) does not apply, but the liquidator may apply to court for an order confirming the winding up as a creditors' voluntary winding up for the purposes of Articles 10 and 28 of directive 2001/24/EC of the European Parliament and of the Council of 4th April 2001 on the reorganisation and winding up of credit institutions."

6(3)   For the purposes of this regulation, Rule 7.56 of the Insolvency Rules (Northern Ireland) has effect as if there were substituted for paragraph (1)–

"**(1)** Where a UK credit institution (within the meaning of the Credit Institutions (Reorganisation and Winding up) Regulations 2004) has passed a resolution for voluntary winding up, and no declaration under Article 75 has been made, the liquidator may apply to court for an order confirming the creditors' voluntary winding up for the purposes of Articles 10 and 28 of directive 2001/24/EC of the European Parliament and of the Council of 4 April 2001 on the reorganisation and winding up of credit institutions.".

History
Regulation 6(1) amended and reg.6(2) substituted by the Financial Services and Markets (Insolvency) (Amendment of Miscellaneous Enactments) Regulations 2019 (SI 2019/755) regs 1, 5(1), (3) as from 23 April 2019.

PART 3

MODIFICATIONS OF THE LAW OF INSOLVENCY: NOTIFICATION AND PUBLICATION

7 Modifications of the law of insolvency

7 The general law of insolvency has effect in relation to UK credit institutions subject to the provisions of this Part.

8 Consultation of the FCA and, if the institution is a PRA-authorised person, the PRA prior to a voluntary winding up

8(1) Where, on or after 5th May 2004, a UK credit institution ("the institution") intends to pass a resolution to wind up the institution under paragraph (b) or (c) of section 84(1) of the 1986 Act or sub-paragraph (b) or (c) of Article 70(1) of the 1989 Order, the institution must give written notice of the resolution to the FCA and, if the institution is a PRA-authorised person, the PRA before it passes the resolution.

8(2) Where notice is given under paragraph (1), the resolution may be passed only after the end of the period of five business days beginning with the day on which the notice was given.

[Note: see the Financial Services Act 2012 (Consequential Amendments and Transitional Provisions) Order 2013 (SI 2013/472) art.3 and Sch.2 para.92 for transitional provision where notice was given to the FSA before 1 April 2013.]

9 Notification of relevant decision to the FCA and, if the institution is a PRA-authorised person, the PRA

9(1) Where on or after 5th May 2004 the court makes a decision, order or appointment of any of the following kinds–

(a) an administration order under paragraph 13 of Schedule B1 to the 1986 Act, paragraph 14 of Schedule B1 to the 1989 Order, section 8(1) of the 1986 Act or Article 21(1) of the 1989 Order;

(b) a winding-up order under section 125 of the 1986 Act or Article 105 of the 1989 Order;

(c) the appointment of a provisional liquidator under section 135(1) of the 1986 Act or Article 115(1) of the 1989 Order;

(d) the appointment of an administrator in an interim order under paragraph 13(1)(d) of Schedule B1 to the 1986 Act, paragraph 14(1)(d) of Schedule B1 to the 1989 Order, section 9(4) of the 1986 Act or Article 22(4) of the 1989 Order,

it must immediately inform the FCA and, if the institution is a PRA-authorised person, the PRA, or cause the FCA and, if the institution is a PRA-authorised person, the PRA to be informed, of the order or appointment which has been made.

9(2) Where a decision with respect to the approval of a voluntary arrangement has effect, and the arrangement which is the subject of that decision is a qualifying arrangement, the supervisor must forthwith inform the FCA and, if the institution is a PRA-authorised person, the PRA of the arrangement which has been approved.

9(3) Where a liquidator is appointed as mentioned in section 100 of the 1986 Act, paragraph 83 of Schedule B1 to the 1986 Act, paragraph 84 of Schedule B1 to the 1989 Order or Article 86 of the 1989 Order (appointment of liquidator in a creditors' voluntary winding up), the liquidator must inform the FCA and, if the institution is a PRA-authorised person, the PRA forthwith of his appointment.

9(4) Where in the case of a members' voluntary winding up, section 95 of the 1986 Act (effect of company's insolvency) or Article 81 of the 1989 Order applies, the liquidator must inform the FCA and, if the institution is a PRA-authorised person, the PRA forthwith that he is of that opinion.

9(5)   Paragraphs (1), (2) and (3) do not require the FCA to be informed in any case where the FCA was represented at all hearings in connection with the application in relation to which the decision, order or appointment is made.

9(5A)   Paragraphs (1), (2) and (3) do not require the PRA to be informed in any case where the PRA was represented at all hearings in connection with the application in relation to which the decision, order or appointment is made.

9(6)   For the purposes of paragraph (2), a "qualifying arrangement" means a voluntary arrangement which–

(a)   varies the rights of creditors as against the credit institution and is intended to enable the credit institution, and the whole or any part of its undertaking, to survive as a going concern; or

(b)   includes a realisation of some or all of the assets of the credit institution, with a view to terminating the whole or any part of the business of that credit institution.

9(7)   A supervisor, administrator or liquidator who fails without reasonable excuse to comply with paragraph (2), (3), or (4) (as the case may be) commits an offence and is liable on summary conviction to a fine not exceeding level 3 on the standard scale.

History
Heading to reg.9 amended, reg.9(5) substituted and reg.9(5A) inserted by the Financial Services Act 2012 (Consequential Amendments and Transitional Provisions) Order 2013 (SI 2013/472) art.3 and Sch.2 para.91(d), (e) as from 1 April 2013.

10   Notification to EEA regulators

10(1)   Where the FCA or the PRA is informed of a decision, order or appointment in accordance with regulation 9, that Authority must as soon as is practicable inform the relevant person–

(a)   that the decision, order or appointment has been made; and

(b)   in general terms, of the possible effect of a decision, order or appointment of that kind on the business of a credit institution.

10(2)   Where the FCA or the PRA has been represented at all hearings in connection with the application in relation to which the decision, order or appointment has been made, that authority must inform the relevant person of the matters mentioned in paragraph (1) as soon as is practicable after that decision, order or appointment has been made.

10(3)   Where, on or after 5th May 2004, it appears to the Bank of England, the FCA or the PRA that a directive reorganisation measure should be adopted in relation to or imposed on an EEA credit institution which has a branch in the United Kingdom, it will inform the home state regulator as soon as is practicable.

10(4)   In this regulation, the "relevant person" means the EEA regulator of any EEA State in which the UK credit institution has a branch.

History
Regulation 10(3) amended by the Bank Recovery and Resolution (No.2) Order 2014 (SI 2014/3348) Sch.3 para.10(4) as from 10 January 2015.

11   Withdrawal of authorisation

11(1)   For the purposes of this regulation–

(a)   a qualifying decision means a decision with respect to the approval of a voluntary arrangement where the voluntary arrangement includes a realisation of some or all of the assets of the credit institution with a view to terminating the whole or any part of the business of that credit institution;

(b)   a qualifying order means–

    (i)   a winding-up order under section 125 of the 1986 Act or Article 105 of the 1989 Order; or

    (ii)   an administration order under paragraph 13 of Schedule B1 to the 1986 Act or paragraph 14 of Schedule B1 to the 1989 Order in the prescribed circumstances;

(c)   a qualifying appointment means–

    (i)   the appointment of a provisional liquidator under section 135(1) of the 1986 Act or Article 115(1) of the 1989 Order; or

    (ii)   the appointment of a liquidator as mentioned in section 100 of the 1986 Act, Article 86 of the 1989 Order (appointment of liquidator in a creditors' voluntary winding up) or paragraph 83 of Schedule B1 to the 1986 Act or paragraph 84 of Schedule B1 to the 1989 Order (moving from administration to creditors' voluntary liquidation).

11(2)   The prescribed circumstances are where, after the appointment of an administrator, the administrator concludes that it is not reasonably practicable to achieve the objective specified in paragraph 3(1)(a) of Schedule B1 to the 1986 Act or paragraph 4(1)(a) of Schedule B1 to the 1989 Order.

11(3)   When the FCA or the PRA is informed of a qualifying decision, qualifying order or qualifying appointment, that authority will as soon as reasonably practicable exercise its power under section 55J of the 2000 Act to vary or to cancel the UK credit institution's permission under Part 4A of that Act to accept deposits or to issue electronic money as the case may be.

12   Publication of voluntary arrangement, administration order, winding-up order or scheme of arrangement

12(1)   This regulation applies where a qualifying decision is approved, or a qualifying order or qualifying appointment is made, in relation to a UK credit institution on or after 5th May 2004.

12(2)   For the purposes of this regulation–

(a)   a qualifying decision means a decision with respect to the approval of a proposed voluntary arrangement, in accordance with section 4A of the 1986 Act or Article 17A of the 1989 Order;

(b)   a qualifying order means–

    (i)   an administration order under paragraph 13 of Schedule B1 to the 1986 Act, paragraph 14 of Schedule B1 to the 1989 Order, section 8(1) of the 1986 Act or Article 21(1) of the 1989 Order,

    (ii)   an order appointing a provisional liquidator in accordance with section 135 of that Act or Article 115 of that Order, or

    (iii)   a winding-up order made by the court under Part 4 of that Act or Part V of the 1989 Order;

(c)   a qualifying appointment means the appointment of a liquidator as mentioned in section 100 of the 1986 Act or Article 86 of the 1989 Order (appointment of liquidator in a creditors' voluntary winding up).

12(3)   Subject to paragraph (7), as soon as is reasonably practicable after a qualifying decision has effect or a qualifying order or a qualifying appointment has been made, the relevant officer must publish, or cause to be published, in the Official Journal of the European Union and in 2 national newspapers in each EEA State in which the UK credit institution has a branch the information mentioned in paragraph (4) and (if applicable) paragraphs (5) or (6).

12(4)   That information is–

(a)   a summary of the terms of the qualifying decision, qualifying appointment or the provisions of the qualifying order (as the case may be);

(b) the identity of the relevant officer;

(c) the statutory provisions in accordance with which the qualifying decision has effect or the qualifying order or appointment has been made or takes effect.

12(5) In the case of a qualifying appointment, that information includes the court to which an application under section 112 of the 1986 Act (reference of questions to the court) or Article 98 of the 1989 Order (reference of questions to the High Court) may be made.

12(6) In the case of a qualifying decision, that information includes the court to which an application under section 6 of the 1986 Act or Article 19 of the 1989 Order (challenge of decisions) may be made.

12(7) Paragraph (3) does not apply where a qualifying decision or qualifying order falling within paragraph (2)(b)(i) affects the interests only of the members, or any class of members, or employees of the credit institution (in their capacity as members or employees).

12(8) This regulation is without prejudice to any requirement to publish information imposed upon a relevant officer under any provision of the general law of insolvency.

12(9) A relevant officer who fails to comply with paragraph (3) of this regulation commits an offence and is liable on summary conviction to a fine not exceeding level 3 on the standard scale.

12(10) A qualifying decision, qualifying order or qualifying appointment is not invalid or ineffective if the relevant official fails to comply with paragraph (3) of this regulation.

12(11) In this regulation, "relevant officer" means–

(a) in the case of a voluntary arrangement, the supervisor;

(b) in the case of an administration order, the administrator;

(c) in the case of a creditors' voluntary winding up, the liquidator;

(d) in the case of winding-up order, the liquidator; or

(e) in the case of an order appointing a provisional liquidator, the provisional liquidator.

12(12) The information to be published in accordance with paragraph (3) of this regulation shall be–

(a) in the case of the Official Journal of the European Union, in the official language or languages of each EEA State in which the UK credit institution has a branch;

(b) in the case of the national newspapers of each EEA State in which the UK credit institution has a branch, in the official language or languages of that EEA State.

History
Regulation 12(5) amended by the Credit Institutions (Reorganisation and Winding Up) (Amendment) Regulations 2007 (SI 2007/830) reg.2(1), (11) as from 6 April 2007.

13 Honouring of certain obligations

13(1) This regulation applies where, on or after 5th May 2004, a relevant obligation has been honoured for the benefit of a relevant credit institution by a relevant person.

13(2) Where a person has honoured a relevant obligation for the benefit of a relevant credit institution, he shall be deemed to have discharged that obligation if he was unaware of the winding up of that credit institution.

13(3) For the purposes of this regulation–

(a) a relevant obligation is an obligation which, after the commencement of the winding up of a relevant credit institution, should have been honoured for the benefit of the liquidator of that credit institution;

(b) a relevant credit institution is a UK credit institution which–

   (i)   is not a body corporate; and

   (ii) is the subject of a winding up;

(c) a relevant person is a person who at the time the obligation is honoured–

   (i)   is in the territory of an EEA State; and

   (ii) is unaware of the winding up of the relevant credit institution.

13(4)   For the purposes of paragraph (3)(c)(ii) of this regulation–

(a) a relevant person shall be presumed, in the absence of evidence to the contrary, to have been unaware of the winding up of a relevant credit institution where the relevant obligation was honoured before date of the publication provided for in regulation 12 in relation to that winding up;

(b) a relevant person shall be presumed, in the absence of evidence to the contrary, to have been aware of the winding up of the relevant credit institution where the relevant obligation was honoured on or after the date of the publication provided for in regulation 12 in relation to that winding up.

14   Notification to creditors: winding-up proceedings

14(1)   When a relevant order or appointment is made, or a relevant decision is taken, in relation to a UK credit institution on or after 5th May 2004, the appointed officer must, as soon as is reasonably practicable, notify in writing all known creditors of that credit institution–

(a) of the matters mentioned in paragraph (4); and

(b) of the matters mentioned in paragraph (5).

14(2)   The appointed officer may comply with the requirement in paragraphs (1)(a) and the requirement in paragraph (1)(b) by separate notifications.

14(3)   For the purposes of this regulation–

(a) "relevant order" means–

   (i)   an administration order under paragraph 13 of Schedule B1 to the 1986 Act or paragraph 14 of Schedule B1 to the 1989 Order in the prescribed circumstances or an administration order made for the purposes set out in section 8(3)(b) or (d) of the 1986 Act or Article 21(3)(b) or (d) of the 1989 Order, as the case may be,

   (ii) a winding-up order under section 125 of the 1986 Act (powers of the court on hearing a petition) or Article 105 of the 1989 Order (powers of High Court on hearing of petition),

   (iii) the appointment of a liquidator in accordance with section 138 of the 1986 Act (appointment of a liquidator in Scotland), or

   (iv) an order appointing a provisional liquidator in accordance with section 135 of that Act or Article 115 of the 1989 Order;

(b) a "relevant appointment" means the appointment of a liquidator as mentioned in section 100 of the 1986 Act or Article 86 of the 1989 Order (appointment of liquidator in a creditors' voluntary winding up); and

(c) a "relevant decision" means a decision as a result of which a qualifying voluntary arrangement has effect.

14(4)   The matters which must be notified to all known creditors in accordance with paragraph (1)(a) are as follows–

    (a)   that a relevant order or appointment has been made, or a relevant decision taken, in relation to the UK credit institution; and

    (b)   the date from which that order, appointment or decision has effect.

14(5)   The matters which must be notified to all known creditors in accordance with paragraph (1)(b) are as follows–

    (a)   if applicable, the date by which a creditor must submit his claim in writing;

    (b)   the matters which must be stated in a creditor's claim;

    (c)   details of any category of debt in relation to which a claim is not required;

    (d)   the person to whom any such claim or any observations on a claim must be submitted; and

    (e)   the consequences of any failure to submit a claim by any specified deadline.

14(6)   Where a creditor is notified in accordance with paragraph (1)(b), the notification must be headed with the words "Invitation to lodge a claim. Time limits to be observed", and that heading must be given in every official language.

14(7)   The obligation under paragraph (1)(b) may be discharged by sending a form of proof in accordance with Rule 4.080 of the Insolvency Rules (Northern Ireland) in cases where those rules apply, provided that the form of proof complies with paragraph (6).

14(8)   The prescribed circumstances are where the administrator includes in the statement required under rule 3.3 of the Insolvency Rules or under Rule 2.003 of the Insolvency Rules (Northern Ireland) a statement to the effect that the objective set out in paragraph 3(1)(a) of Schedule B1 to the 1986 Act or in paragraph 4(1)(a) of Schedule B1 to the 1989 Order is not reasonably likely to be achieved.

14(9)   Where, after the appointment of an administrator, the administrator concludes that it is not reasonably practicable to achieve the objective specified in paragraph 3(1)(a) of Schedule B1 to the 1986 Act or paragraph 4(1)(a) of Schedule B1 to the 1989 Order, he shall inform the court, the FCA and, if the institution is a PRA-authorised person, the PRA in writing of that conclusion and upon so doing the order by which he was appointed shall be a relevant order for the purposes of this regulation and the obligation under paragraph (1) shall apply as from the date on which he so informs the court, the FCA and, if the institution is a PRA-authorised person, the PRA.

14(10)   An appointed officer commits an offence if he fails without reasonable excuse to comply with a requirement under paragraph (1) of this regulation, and is liable on summary conviction to a fine not exceeding level 3 on the standard scale.

14(11)   For the purposes of this regulation–

    (a)   "appointed officer" means–

        (i)   in the case of a relevant order falling within paragraph (3)(a)(i), the administrator,

        (ii)   in the case of a relevant order falling within paragraph (3)(a)(ii) or (iii) or a relevant appointment falling within paragraph (3)(b), the liquidator,

        (iii)   in the case of a relevant order falling within paragraph (3)(a)(iv), the provisional liquidator, or

        (iv)   in the case of a relevant decision, the supervisor; and

    (b)   a creditor is a "known" creditor if the appointed officer is aware of–

        (i)   his identity,

        (ii)   his claim or potential claim, and

        (iii)   a recent address where he is likely to receive a communication.

14(12) For the purposes of paragraph (3), a voluntary arrangement is a qualifying voluntary arrangement if its purposes include a realisation of some or all of the assets of the UK credit institution to which the order relates with a view to terminating the whole or any part of the business of that credit institution.

History
Regulation 14(8) substituted by the Credit Institutions (Reorganisation and Winding Up) (Amendment) Regulations 2007 (SI 2007/830) reg.2(1), (12) as from 6 April 2007.
   Regulation 14(7), (8) amended by the Financial Services and Markets (Insolvency) (Amendment of Miscellaneous Enactments) Regulations 2019 (SI 2019/755) regs 1, 5(1), (4) as from 23 April 2019.

15   Submission of claims by EEA creditors

15(1)   An EEA creditor who, on or after 5th May 2004, submits a claim or observations relating to his claim in any relevant proceedings (irrespective of when those proceedings were commenced or had effect) may do so in his domestic language, provided that the requirements in paragraphs (3) and (4) are complied with.

15(2)   For the purposes of this regulation, "relevant proceedings" means–

   (a)   a winding up;

   (b)   a qualifying voluntary arrangement; or

   (c)   administration.

15(3)   Where an EEA creditor submits a claim in his domestic language, the document must be headed with the words "Lodgement of claim" (in English).

15(4)   Where an EEA creditor submits observations on his claim (otherwise than in the document by which he submits his claim), the observations must be headed with the words "Submission of observations relating to claims" (in English).

15(5)   Paragraph (3) does not apply where an EEA creditor submits his claim using–

   (a)   in the case of a winding up, a form of proof supplied by the liquidator in accordance with Rule 4.080 of the Insolvency Rules (Northern Ireland);

   (b)   in the case of a qualifying voluntary arrangement, a form approved by the court for that purpose.

15(6)   In this regulation–

   (a)   "domestic language", in relation to an EEA creditor, means the official language, or one of the official languages, of the EEA State in which he is ordinarily resident or, if the creditor is not an individual, in which the creditor's head office is located; and

   (b)   "qualifying voluntary arrangement" means a voluntary arrangement whose purposes include a realisation of some or all of the assets of the UK credit institution to which the order relates with a view to terminating the whole or any part of the business of that credit institution.

History
Regulation 15(5)(a) amended by the Financial Services and Markets (Insolvency) (Amendment of Miscellaneous Enactments) Regulations 2019 (SI 2019/755) regs 1, 5(1), (5) as from 23 April 2019.

16   Reports to creditors

16(1)   This regulation applies where, on or after 5th May 2004–

   (a)   a liquidator is appointed in accordance with section 100 of the 1986 Act, Article 86 of the 1989 Order (creditors' voluntary winding up: appointment of liquidator) or paragraph 83 of Schedule B1 to the 1986 Act or paragraph 84 of Schedule B1 to the 1989 Order (moving from administration to creditors' voluntary liquidation);

(b)   a winding-up order is made by the court;

(c)   a provisional liquidator is appointed; or

(d)   an administrator is appointed under paragraph 13 of Schedule B1 to the 1986 Act or paragraph 14 of Schedule B1 to the 1989 Order.

16(2)   The liquidator, provisional liquidator or administrator (as the case may be) must send a report to every known creditor once in every 12 months beginning with the date when his appointment has effect.

16(3)   The requirement in paragraph (2) does not apply where a liquidator, provisional liquidator or administrator is required by order of the court to send a report to creditors at intervals which are more frequent than those required by this regulation.

16(4)   This regulation is without prejudice to any requirement to send a report to creditors, imposed by the court on the liquidator, provisional liquidator or administrator, which is supplementary to the requirements of this regulation.

16(5)   A liquidator, provisional liquidator or administrator commits an offence if he fails without reasonable excuse to comply with an applicable requirement under this regulation, and is liable on summary conviction to a fine not exceeding level 3 on the standard scale.

16(6)   For the purposes of this regulation–

(a)   "known creditor" means–

(i)   a creditor who is known to the liquidator, provisional liquidator or administrator, and

(ii)   in a case falling within paragraph (1)(b) or (c), a creditor who is specified in the credit institution's statement of affairs (within the meaning of section 131 of the 1986 Act or Article 111 of the 1989 Order);

(b)   "report" means a written report setting out the position generally as regards the progress of the winding up, provisional liquidation or administration (as the case may be).

History
Regulation 16(1)(d) substituted by the Credit Institutions (Reorganisation and Winding Up) (Amendment) Regulations 2007 (SI 2007/830) reg.2(1), (13) as from 6 April 2007.

17   Service of notices and documents

17(1)   This regulation applies to any notification, report or other document which is required to be sent to a creditor of a UK credit institution by a provision of this Part ("a relevant notification").

17(2)   A relevant notification may be sent to a creditor by one of the following methods–

(a)   by posting it to the proper address of the creditor;

(b)   by transmitting it electronically, in accordance with paragraph (4).

17(3)   For the purposes of paragraph (2)(a), the proper address of a creditor is any current address provided by that person as an address for service of a relevant notification and, if no such address is provided–

(a)   the last known address of that creditor (whether his residence or a place where he carries on business);

(b)   in the case of a body corporate, the address of its registered or principal office; or

(c)   in the case of an unincorporated association, the address of its principal office.

17(4)   A relevant notification may be transmitted electronically only if it is sent to–

(a)   an electronic address notified to the relevant officer by the creditor for this purpose; or

(b)   if no such address has been notified, to an electronic address at which the relevant officer reasonably believes the creditor will receive the notification.

17(5)   Any requirement in this Part to send a relevant notification to a creditor shall also be treated as satisfied if the conditions set out in paragraph (6) are satisfied.

17(6)   The conditions of this paragraph are satisfied in the case of a relevant notification if–

(a)   the creditor has agreed with–

(i)   the UK credit institution which is liable under the creditor's claim, or

(ii)   the relevant officer,

that information which is required to be sent to him (whether pursuant to a statutory or contractual obligation, or otherwise) may instead be accessed by him on a web site;

(b)   the agreement applies to the relevant notification in question;

(c)   the creditor is notified of–

(i)   the publication of the relevant notification on a web site,

(ii)   the address of that web site,

(iii)   the place on that web site where the relevant notification may be accessed, and how it may be accessed; and

(d)   the relevant notification is published on that web site throughout a period of at least one month beginning with the date on which the creditor is notified in accordance with sub-paragraph (c).

17(7)   Where, in a case in which paragraph (5) is relied on for compliance with a requirement of regulation 14 or 16–

(a)   a relevant notification is published for a part, but not all, of the period mentioned in paragraph (6)(d) but

(b)   the failure to publish it throughout that period is wholly attributable to circumstances which it would not be reasonable to have expected the relevant officer to prevent or avoid,

no offence is committed under regulation 14(10) or regulation 16(5) (as the case may be) by reason of that failure.

17(8)   In this regulation–

(a)   "electronic address" includes any number or address used for the purposes of receiving electronic communications which are sent electronically;

(b)   "electronic communication" means an electronic communication within the meaning of the Electronic Communications Act 2000 the processing of which on receipt is intended to produce writing; and

(c)   "relevant officer" means (as the case may be) an administrator, liquidator, provisional liquidator or supervisor who is required to send a relevant notification to a creditor by a provision of this Part.

18   Disclosure of confidential information received from an EEA regulator

18(1)   This regulation applies to information ("insolvency information") which–

(a)   relates to the business or affairs of any other person; and

(b)   is supplied to the FCA or the PRA by an EEA regulator acting in accordance with Articles 4, 5, 9, or 11 of the reorganisation and winding up directive.

18(2)   Subject to paragraphs (3), (4) and (5), sections 348, 349 and 352 of the 2000 Act apply in relation to insolvency information as they apply in relation to confidential information within the meaning of section 348(2) of the 2000 Act.

18(3)   Insolvency information is not subject to the restrictions on disclosure imposed by section 348(1) of the 2000 Act (as it applies by virtue of paragraph (2)) if it satisfies any of the criteria set out in section 348(4) of the 2000 Act.

18(4)   The Disclosure Regulations apply in relation to insolvency information as they apply in relation to single market information (within the meaning of those Regulations).

18(5)   The sections of the 2000 Act specified in paragraph (2) apply with the modifications set out in section 89L of the Banking Act 2009 where that section applies.

History
Regulation 18(2), (4) amended and reg.18(5) inserted by the Bank Recovery and Resolution (No.2) Order 2014 (SI 2014/3348) Sch.3 para.10(5) as from 10 January 2015.

Part 4

Reorganisation or Winding up of UK Credit Institutions: Recognition of EEA Rights

19   Application of this Part

19(1)   This Part applies as follows–

(a)   where a decision with respect to the approval of a proposed voluntary arrangement having a qualifying purpose is made under section 4A of the 1986 Act or Article 17A of the 1989 Order on or after 5th May 2004 in relation to a UK credit institution;

(b)   where an administration order made under paragraph 13 of Schedule B1 to the 1986 Act, paragraph 14 of Schedule B1 to the 1989 Order, section 8(1) of the 1986 Act or Article 21(1) of the 1989 Order on or after 5th May 2004 is in force in relation to a UK credit institution;

(c)   where a UK credit institution is subject to a relevant winding up;

(d)   where a provisional liquidator is appointed in relation to a UK credit institution on or after 5th May 2004; or

(e)   where a stabilisation instrument is made in respect of a UK credit institution.

19(2)   For the purposes of paragraph (1)(a), a voluntary arrangement has a qualifying purpose if it–

(a)   varies the rights of the creditors as against the credit institution and is intended to enable the credit institution, and the whole or any part of its undertaking, to survive as a going concern; or

(b)   includes a realisation of some or all of the assets of the credit institution to which the compromise or arrangement relates, with a view to terminating the whole or any part of the business of that credit institution.

19(3)   For the purposes of paragraph (1)(c), a winding up is a relevant winding up if–

(a)   in the case of a winding up by the court, the winding-up order is made on or after 5th May 2004; or

(b)   in the case of a creditors' voluntary winding up, the liquidator is appointed in accordance with section 100 of the 1986 Act, Article 86 of the 1989 Order or paragraph 83 of Schedule B1 to the 1986 Act or paragraph 84 of Schedule B1 to the 1989 Order on or after 5th May 2004.

History
Regulation 19(1)(e) inserted by the Bank Recovery and Resolution (No.2) Order 2014 (SI 2014/3348) Sch.3 para.10(6) as from 10 January 2015.

20   Application of this Part: certain assets excluded from insolvent estate of UK credit institution

20(1)   For the purposes of this Part, the insolvent estate of a UK credit institution shall not include any assets which at the commencement date are subject to a relevant compromise or arrangement.

20(2)   In this regulation–

(a)   "assets" has the same meaning as "property" in section 436 of the 1986 Act or Article 2(2) of the 1989 Order;

(b)   "commencement date" means the date when a UK credit institution goes into liquidation within the meaning given by section 247(2) of the 1986 Act or Article 6(2) of the 1989 Order;

(c)   "insolvent estate" has the meaning given by rule 1.2 of the Insolvency Rules or Rule 0.2 of the Insolvency Rules (Northern Ireland) and in Scotland means the company's assets;

(d)   "relevant compromise or arrangement" means–

(i)   a compromise or arrangement sanctioned by the court before 5th May 2004 under–

(aa)   section 425 of the Companies Act 1985 (excluding a compromise or arrangement falling within section 427 or 427A of that Act), or

(bb)   Article 418 of the Companies (Northern Ireland) Order 1986 (excluding a compromise or arrangement falling within Article 420 or 420A of that Order); or

(ii)   any subsequent compromise or arrangement sanctioned by the court to amend or replace a compromise or arrangement of a kind mentioned in paragraph (i) which is–

(aa)   itself of a kind mentioned in sub-paragraph (aa) or (bb) of paragraph (i) (whether sanctioned before, on or after 5th May 2004), or

(bb)   a section 899 compromise or arrangement.

History
Heading of reg.20 and reg.20(1) amended and reg.20(2)(d) substituted by the Companies Act 2006 (Consequential Amendments and Transitional Provisions) Order 2011 (SI 2011/1265) art.24(4), (5) as from 12 May 2011. Regulation 20(2)(c) amended by the Financial Services and Markets (Insolvency) (Amendment of Miscellaneous Enactments) Regulations 2019 (SI 2019/755) regs 1, 5(1), (6) as from 23 April 2019.

21   Interpretation of this Part

21(1)   For the purposes of this Part–

(a)   "affected credit institution" means a UK credit institution which is the subject of a relevant reorganisation or winding up;

(b)   "relevant reorganisation" or "relevant winding up" means any voluntary arrangement, administration, winding up, making of a stabilisation instrument or order referred to in regulation 19(1) to which this Part applies; and

(c)   "relevant time" means the date of the opening of a relevant reorganisation or a relevant winding up.

21(2)   In this Part, references to the opening of a relevant reorganisation or a relevant winding up mean–

(a)   in the case of winding-up proceedings–

(i)   in the case of a winding up by the court, the date on which the winding-up order is made, or

(ii)   in the case of a creditors' voluntary winding up, the date on which the liquidator is appointed in accordance with section 100 of the 1986 Act, Article 86 of the 1989 Order or paragraph 83 of Schedule B1 to the 1986 Act or paragraph 84 of Schedule B1 to the 1989 Order;

(b) in the case of a voluntary arrangement, the date when a decision with respect to the approval of that voluntary arrangement has effect in accordance with section 4A(2) of the 1986 Act or Article 17A(2) of the 1989 Order;

(c) in a case where an administration order under paragraph 13 of Schedule B1 to the 1986 Act, paragraph 14 of Schedule B1 to the 1989 Order, section 8(1) of the 1986 Act or Article 21(1) of the 1989 Order is in force, the date of the making of that order;

(d) in a case where a provisional liquidator has been appointed, the date of that appointment, and

(e) in a case where a stabilisation instrument is made, the date on which that instrument is made,

and references to the time of an opening must be construed accordingly.

History
Regulation 21(1)(b) amended and reg.21(2)(e) inserted by the Bank Recovery and Resolution (No.2) Order 2014 (SI 2014/3348) Sch.3 para.10(7) as from 10 January 2015.

22   EEA rights: applicable law in the winding up of a UK credit institution

22(1)   This regulation is subject to the provisions of regulations 23 to 35.

22(2)   In a relevant winding up, the matters mentioned in paragraph (3) are to be determined in accordance with the general law of insolvency of the United Kingdom.

22(3)   Those matters are–

(a) the assets which form part of the estate of the affected credit institution;

(b) the treatment of assets acquired by the affected credit institution after the opening of the relevant winding up;

(c) the respective powers of the affected credit institution and the liquidator or provisional liquidator;

(d) the conditions under which set-off may be invoked;

(e) the effects of the relevant winding up on current contracts to which the affected credit institution is a party;

(f) the effects of the relevant winding up on proceedings brought by creditors;

(g) the claims which are to be lodged against the estate of the affected credit institution;

(h) the treatment of claims against the affected credit institution arising after the opening of the relevant winding up;

(i) the rules governing–

   (i) the lodging, verification and admission of claims,

   (ii) the distribution of proceeds from the realisation of assets,

   (iii) the ranking of claims,

   (iv) the rights of creditors who have obtained partial satisfaction after the opening of the relevant winding up by virtue of a right in rem or through set-off;

(j) the conditions for and the effects of the closure of the relevant winding up, in particular by composition;

(k) the rights of creditors after the closure of the relevant winding up;

(l) who is to bear the cost and expenses incurred in the relevant winding up;

(m) the rules relating to the voidness, voidability or unenforceability of legal acts detrimental to all the creditors.

23   Employment contracts and relationships

23(1)   The effects of a relevant reorganisation or a relevant winding up on EEA employment contracts and EEA employment relationships are to be determined in accordance with the law of the EEA State to which that contract or that relationship is subject.

23(2)   In this regulation, an employment contract is an EEA employment contract, and an employment relationship is an EEA employment relationship if it is subject to the law of an EEA State.

24   Contracts in connection with immovable property

24(1)   The effects of a relevant reorganisation or a relevant winding up on a contract conferring the right to make use of or acquire immovable property situated within the territory of an EEA State shall be determined in accordance with the law of that State.

24(2)   The law of the EEA State in whose territory the property is situated shall determine whether the property is movable or immovable.

25   Registrable rights

25   The effects of a relevant reorganisation or a relevant winding up on rights of the affected UK credit institution with respect to–

   (a)   immovable property,

   (b)   a ship, or

   (c)   an aircraft

which is subject to registration in a public register kept under the authority of an EEA State are to be determined in accordance with the law of that State.

26   Third parties' rights in rem

26(1)   A relevant reorganisation or a relevant winding up shall not affect the rights in rem of creditors or third parties in respect of tangible or intangible, movable or immovable assets (including both specific assets and collections of indefinite assets as a whole which change from time to time) belonging to the affected credit institution which are situated within the territory of an EEA State at the relevant time.

26(2)   The rights in rem referred to in paragraph (1) shall mean–

   (a)   the right to dispose of assets or have them disposed of and to obtain satisfaction from the proceeds of or the income from those assets, in particular by virtue of a lien or a mortgage;

   (b)   the exclusive right to have a claim met, in particular a right guaranteed by a lien in respect of the claim or by assignment of the claim by way of guarantee;

   (c)   the right to demand the assets from, or to require restitution by, any person having possession or use of them contrary to the wishes of the party so entitled;

   (d)   a right in rem to the beneficial use of assets.

26(3)   A right, recorded in a public register and enforceable against third parties, under which a right in rem within the meaning of paragraph (1) may be obtained, is also to be treated as a right in rem for the purposes of this regulation.

26(4)   Paragraph (1) does not preclude actions for voidness, voidability or unenforceability of legal acts detrimental to creditors under the general law of insolvency of the United Kingdom.

27   Reservation of title agreements etc.

27(1)   The adoption of a relevant reorganisation or opening of a relevant winding up in relation to a credit institution purchasing an asset shall not affect the seller's rights based on a reservation of title where at the time of that adoption or opening the asset is situated within the territory of an EEA State.

27(2)   The adoption of a relevant reorganisation or opening of a relevant winding up in relation to a credit institution selling an asset, after delivery of the asset, shall not constitute grounds for rescinding or terminating the sale and shall not prevent the purchaser from acquiring title where at the time of that adoption or opening the asset sold is situated within the territory of an EEA State.

27(3)   Paragraphs (1) and (2) do not preclude actions for voidness, voidability or unenforceability of legal acts detrimental to creditors under the general law of insolvency of the United Kingdom.

28   Creditors' rights to set off

28(1)   A relevant reorganisation or a relevant winding up shall not affect the right of creditors to demand the set-off of their claims against the claims of the affected credit institution, where such a set-off is permitted by the law applicable to the affected credit institution's claim.

28(2)   Paragraph (1) does not preclude actions for voidness, voidability or unenforceability of legal acts detrimental to creditors under the general law of insolvency of the United Kingdom.

29   Regulated markets

29(1)   Subject to regulation 33, the effects of a relevant reorganisation or winding up on transactions carried out in the context of a regulated market operating in an EEA State must be determined in accordance with the law applicable to those transactions.

29(2)   For the purposes of this regulation "regulated market" has the meaning given by point (21) of Article 4(1) of Directive 2014/65/EU of the European Parliament and of the Council on markets in financial instruments.

History
Regulation 29(2) substituted by the Bank Recovery and Resolution (No.2) Order 2014 (SI 2014/3348) Sch.3 para.10(8) as from 10 January 2015. See also note after reg.31.

30   Detrimental acts pursuant to the law of an EEA State

30(1)   In a relevant reorganisation or a relevant winding up, the rules relating to detrimental transactions shall not apply where a person who has benefited from a legal act detrimental to all the creditors provides proof that–

   (a)   the said act is subject to the law of an EEA State; and

   (b)   that law does not allow any means of challenging that act in the relevant case.

30(2)   For the purposes of paragraph (1), "the rules relating to detrimental transactions" means any provision of the general law of insolvency relating to the voidness, voidability or unenforceability of legal acts detrimental to all the creditors.

31   Protection of third party purchasers

31(1)   This regulation applies where, by an act concluded after the adoption of a relevant reorganisation or opening of a relevant winding up, an affected credit institution disposes for a consideration of–

   (a)   an immovable asset situated within the territory of an EEA State;

   (b)   a ship or an aircraft subject to registration in a public register kept under the authority of an EEA State;

(c) relevant instruments or rights in relevant instruments whose existence or transfer presupposes entry into a register or account laid down by the law of an EEA State or which are placed in a central deposit system governed by the law of an EEA State.

31(2) The validity of that act is to be determined in accordance with the law of the EEA State within whose territory the immoveable asset is situated or under whose authority the register, account or system is kept, as the case may be.

31(3) In this regulation, "relevant instruments" means the instruments referred to in Section C of Annex I to Directive 2014/65/EU of the European Parliament and of the Council of 15 May 2014 on markets in financial instruments.

History
Regulations 29(2) and 31(3) amended by the Financial Services and Markets Act 2000 (Markets in Financial Instruments) Regulations 2007 (SI 2007/126) reg.6 and Sch.6 paras 17, 18 as from 1 April 2007 for the purposes specified in reg.1(2) and from 1 November 2007 for all other purposes.
   Regulation 31(3) amended by the Financial Services and Markets Act 2000 (Markets in Financial Instruments) Regulations 2017/701) reg.50(4), Sch.5 para.5 as from 3 January 2018.

32 Lawsuits pending

32(1) The effects of a relevant reorganisation or a relevant winding up on a relevant lawsuit pending in an EEA State shall be determined solely in accordance with the law of that EEA State.

32(2) In paragraph (1), "relevant lawsuit" means a lawsuit concerning an asset or right of which the affected credit institution has been divested.

33 Lex rei sitae

33(1) The effects of a relevant reorganisation or a relevant winding up on the enforcement of a relevant proprietary right shall be determined by the law of the relevant EEA State.

33(2) In this regulation–

"relevant proprietary right" means proprietary rights in relevant instruments or other rights in relevant instruments the existence or transfer of which is recorded in a register, an account or a centralised deposit system held or located in an EEA state;

"relevant EEA State" means the Member State where the register, account or centralised deposit system in which the relevant proprietary right is recorded is held or located;

"relevant instrument" has the meaning given by regulation 31(3).

34 Netting agreements

34(1) The effects of a relevant reorganisation or a relevant winding up on a netting agreement shall be determined in accordance with the law applicable to that agreement.

34(2) Nothing in paragraph (1) affects the application of–

(a) section 48Z of the Banking Act 2009;

(b) section 70C of the Banking Act 2009;

(c) Articles 68 and 71 of the recovery and resolution directive or the law of any EEA State (other than the United Kingdom) transposing these provisions; or

(d) any instrument made under the provisions referred to in sub-paragraph (a) or (b).

History
Regulation 34 substituted by the Bank Recovery and Resolution (No.2) Order 2014 (SI 2014/3348) Sch.3 para.10(9) as from 10 January 2015.

35   Repurchase agreements

35(1)   Subject to regulation 33, the effects of a relevant reorganisation or a relevant winding up on a repurchase agreement shall be determined in accordance with the law applicable to that agreement.

35(2)   Nothing in paragraph (1) affects the application of–

    (a)   section 48Z of the Banking Act 2009;

    (b)   section 70C of the Banking Act 2009;

    (c)   Articles 68 and 71 of the recovery and resolution directive or the law of any EEA State (other than the United Kingdom) transposing these provisions; or

    (d)   any instrument made under the provisions referred to in sub-paragraph (a) or (b).

History
Regulation 35 substituted by the Bank Recovery and Resolution (No.2) Order 2014 (SI 2014/3348) Sch.3 para.10(10) as from 10 January 2015.

PART 5

THIRD COUNTRY CREDIT INSTITUTIONS

36   Interpretation of this Part

36(1)   In this Part–

    (a)   "relevant measure", in relation to a third country credit institution, means–

       (i)   a winding up;

       (ii)   a provisional liquidation;

       (iii)   an administration order made under paragraph 13 of Schedule B1 to the 1986 Act, paragraph 14 of Schedule B1 to the 1989 Order, section 8(1) of the 1986 Act or Article 21(1) of the 1989 Order as the case may be; or

       (iv)   the making of a stabilisation instrument.

    (b)   "third country credit institution" means a person–

       (i)   who has permission under the 2000 Act to accept deposits or to issue electronic money as the case may be; and

       (ii)   whose head office is not in the United Kingdom or an EEA State.

36(2)   In paragraph (1), the definition of "third country credit institution" must be read with–

    (a)   section 22 of the 2000 Act;

    (b)   any relevant order made under that section; and

    (c)   Schedule 2 to that Act.

History
Regulation 36(1)(a)(iv) inserted by the Bank Recovery and Resolution (No.2) Order 2014 (SI 2014/3348) Sch.3 para.10(11) as from 10 January 2015.

37   Application of these Regulations to a third country credit institution

37   Regulations 9 and 10 apply where a third country credit institution is subject to a relevant measure, as if references in those regulations to a UK credit institution included a reference to a third country credit institution.

38   Disclosure of confidential information: third country credit institution

38(1)   This regulation applies to information ("insolvency practitioner information") which–

(a)   relates to the business or other affairs of any person; and

(b)   is information of a kind mentioned in paragraph (2).

38(2)   Information falls within paragraph (1)(b) if it is supplied to–

(a)   the FCA or the PRA by an EEA regulator; or

(b)   an insolvency practitioner by an EEA administrator or liquidator,

in accordance with or pursuant to Articles 8 or 19 of the reorganisation and winding up directive.

38(3)   Subject to paragraphs (4), (5), (6) and (8), sections 348, 349 and 352 of the 2000 Act apply in relation to insolvency practitioner information in the same way as they apply in relation to confidential information within the meaning of section 348(2) of that Act.

38(4)   For the purposes of this regulation, sections 348, 349 and 352 of the 2000 Act and the Disclosure Regulations have effect as if the primary recipients specified in subsection (5) of section 348 of the 2000 Act included an insolvency practitioner.

38(5)   Insolvency practitioner information is not subject to the restrictions on disclosure imposed by section 348(1) of the 2000 Act (as it applies by virtue of paragraph (2)) if it satisfies any of the criteria set out in section 348(4) of the 2000 Act.

38(6)   The Disclosure Regulations apply in relation to insolvency practitioner information as they apply in relation to single market information (within the meaning of those Regulations).

38(7)   In this regulation–

"EEA administrator" and "EEA liquidator" mean an administrator or liquidator of a third country credit institution as the case may be within the meaning of the reorganisation and winding up directive;

"insolvency practitioner" means an insolvency practitioner, within the meaning of section 388 of the 1986 Act or Article 3 of the 1989 Order, who is appointed or acts in relation to a third country credit institution.

38(8)   The sections of the 2000 Act specified in paragraph (3) apply with the additional modifications set out in section 89L of the Banking Act 2009 where that section applies

History
Regulation 38(3), (6) amended and reg.38(8) inserted by the Bank Recovery and Resolution (No.2) Order 2014 (SI 2014/3348) Sch.3 para.10(12) as from 10 January 2015.

PART 6

APPLICATION TO INVESTMENT FIRMS

39   Interpretation of this Part

39   In this Part–

(a)   "EEA investment firm" means an investment firm as defined in point (2) of Article 4(1) of the capital requirements regulation whose head office is in an EEA State other than the United Kingdom; and

(b)   "UK investment firm" means an investment firm as defined in subsections (1) and (2)(a) of section 258A of the Banking Act 2009.

40   Application to UK investment firms

40   These Regulations apply to UK investment firms as if such firms were UK credit institutions, subject to the modifications set out in this Part.

41   Application to EEA investment firms

41   These Regulations apply to EEA investment firms as if such firms were EEA credit institutions, subject to the modifications set out in this Part.

42   Withdrawal of authorisation

42   Paragraph (3) of regulation 11 (withdrawal of authorisation) applies to UK investment firms as if the reference in that paragraph to section 55J of the 2000 Act included a reference to any other power of the FCA or PRA under that Act to vary or cancel any permission of a body or firm.

43   Reorganisation measures and winding-up proceedings in respect of EEA investment firms effective in the United Kingdom

43   Regulation 5 (reorganisation measures and winding-up proceedings in respect of EEA credit institutions effective in the United Kingdom) applies to EEA investment firms as if, in paragraph (6), the phrase "relevant EEA State" meant the EEA State under the law of which the reorganisation is adopted or imposed, or the winding-up proceedings are opened, as the case may be.

PART 7

APPLICATION TO GROUP COMPANIES

44   Interpretation of this Part

44   In this Part–

(a)   "EEA group company" means–

(i)   a financial institution as defined in point (26) of Article 4(1) of the capital requirements regulation,

(ii)   a parent undertaking as defined in point (15)(a) of Article 4(1) of the capital requirements regulation, or

(iii) any other firm within the scope of Article 1(1) of the recovery and resolution directive,

the head office of which is in an EEA State other than the United Kingdom and which is not otherwise subject to these Regulations; and

(b)   "UK group company" means–

(i)   a financial institution as defined in point (26) of Article 4(1) of the capital requirements regulation that is authorised by the PRA or FCA,

(ii)   a parent undertaking as defined in Article 4(1)(15)(a) of the capital requirements regulation, or

(iii) any other firm within the scope of Article 1(1) of the recovery and resolution directive,

the head office of which is in the United Kingdom and which is not otherwise subject to these Regulations.

45   Application to UK group companies

45   These Regulations apply to UK group companies with respect to which a stabilisation instrument has been made, as if they were UK credit institutions.

46 Application to EEA group companies

46 These Regulations apply to EEA group companies with respect to which one or more of the resolution tools or resolution powers provided for in the recovery and resolution directive have been applied, as if they were EEA credit institutions, subject to the modifications set out in this Part.

47 Reorganisation measures and winding-up proceedings in respect of EEA group companies effective in the United Kingdom

47 Regulation 5 (reorganisation measures and winding-up proceedings in respect of EEA group companies effective in the United Kingdom) applies to EEA group companies as if, in paragraph (6), the phrase "relevant EEA State" meant the EEA State under the law of which the reorganisation is adopted or imposed, or the winding-up proceedings are opened, as the case may be.

PART 8

APPLICATION TO THIRD COUNTRY INVESTMENT FIRMS

48 Interpretation of this Part

48 In this Part "third country investment firm" means an investment firm as defined in point (2) of Article 4(1) of the capital requirements regulation whose head office is not in an EEA State.

49 Application to third country investment firms

49 Part 5 of these Regulations applies to third country investment firms as if such firms were third country credit institutions (within the meaning given by regulation 36(1)(b) (interpretation of Part 5)).

History
Regulations 39–49 inserted by the Bank Recovery and Resolution (No.2) Order 2014 (SI 2014/3348) Sch.3 para.10(13) as from 10 January 2015.

Insolvency Practitioners Regulations 2005

(SI 2005/524)

Made on 8 March 2005 by the Secretary of State under ss.390, 392, 393 and 419 of the Insolvency Act 1986. Operative from 1 April 2005.

[**Note**: Changes made by the Provision of Services (Insolvency Practitioners) Regulations 2009 (SI 2009/3081), the Insolvency Practitioners (Amendment) Regulations 2015 (SI 2015/391) and the Deregulation Act 2015 (Insolvency) (Consequential Amendments and Transitional and Savings Provisions) Order 2015 (SI 2015/1641) have been incorporated into the text.]

PART 1

INTRODUCTORY

1 Citation and commencement

1 These Regulations may be cited as the Insolvency Practitioners Regulations 2005 and shall come into force on 1st April 2005.

2 Interpretation: General

2(1) In these Regulations–

"the Act" means the Insolvency Act 1986;

"commencement date" means the date on which these Regulations come into force;

"initial capacity" shall be construed in accordance with regulation 3;

"insolvency practitioner" means a person who is authorised to act as an insolvency practitioner under section 390A of the Act;

"insolvent" means a person in respect of whom an insolvency practitioner is acting;

"interim trustee", "permanent trustee" and "trust deed for creditors" have the same meanings as in the Bankruptcy (Scotland) Act 1985;

"subsequent capacity" shall be construed in accordance with regulation 3.

2(2) In these Regulations a reference to the date of release or discharge of an insolvency practitioner includes–

(a) where the insolvency practitioner acts as nominee in relation to proposals for a voluntary arrangement under Part I or VIII of the Act, whichever is the earlier of the date on which–

    (i) the proposals are rejected by creditors;

    (ii) he is replaced as nominee by another insolvency practitioner; or

    (iii) the arrangement takes effect without his becoming supervisor in relation to it; and

(b) where an insolvency practitioner acts as supervisor of a voluntary arrangement, whichever is the earlier of the date on which–

    (i) the arrangement is completed or terminated; or

    (ii) the insolvency practitioner otherwise ceases to act as supervisor in relation to the arrangement.

History
Definition of "insolvency practitioner" in reg.2(1) amended by the Deregulation Act 2015 (Insolvency) (Consequential Amendments and Transitional and Savings Provisions) Order 2015 (SI 2015/1641) art.5(2) as from 1 October 2015.

3 Interpretation—meaning of initial and subsequent capacity

3(1) In these Regulations an insolvency practitioner holds office in relation to an insolvent in a "subsequent capacity" where he holds office in relation to that insolvent in one of the capacities referred to in paragraph (3) and immediately prior to his holding office in that capacity, he held office in relation to that insolvent in another of the capacities referred to in that paragraph.

3(2) The first office held by the insolvency practitioner in the circumstances referred to in paragraph (1) is referred to in these Regulations as the "initial capacity".

3(3) The capacities referred to in paragraph (1) are, nominee in relation to proposals for a voluntary arrangement under Part I of the Act, supervisor of a voluntary arrangement under Part I of the Act, administrator, provisional liquidator, liquidator, nominee in relation to proposals for a voluntary arrangement under Part VIII of the Act, supervisor of a voluntary arrangement under Part VIII of the Act, trustee, interim trustee and permanent trustee.

4 Revocations and transitional and saving provisions

4(1) Subject to paragraphs (2), (3) and (4), the Regulations listed in Schedule 1 are revoked.

4(2) [Revoked]

4(3) Parts I, III and IV of the Insolvency Practitioners Regulations 1990 shall continue to apply in relation to any case in respect of which an insolvency practitioner is appointed–

(a) before the commencement date; or

(b) in a subsequent capacity and he was appointed in an initial capacity in that case before the commencement date.

4(4) Only regulations 16 and 17 of these Regulations shall apply in relation to the cases mentioned in paragraph (3).

History
Regulation 4(2) revoked by the Deregulation Act 2015 (Insolvency) (Consequential Amendments and Transitional and Savings Provisions) Order 2015 (SI 2015/1641) art.5(3) as from 1 October 2015.

Part 2

Authorisation of Insolvency Practitioners by Competent Authorities

5–9 [Revoked]

History
Regulations 5–9 revoked by the Deregulation Act 2015 (Insolvency) (Consequential Amendments and Transitional and Savings Provisions) Order 2015 (SI 2015/1641) art.5(4) as from 1 October 2015.

10 Maximum period of authorisation

10 [Revoked by the Provision of Services (Insolvency Practitioners) Regulations 2009 (SI 2009/3081) reg.4 and Sch. para.5 as from 28 December 2009.]

11   Returns by insolvency practitioners authorised by the Secretary of State [Revoked]

History
Regulation 11 revoked by the Deregulation Act 2015 (Insolvency) (Consequential Amendments and Transitional and Savings Provisions) Order 2015 (SI 2015/1641) art.5(5) as from 1 October 2015.

PART 3

THE REQUIREMENTS FOR SECURITY AND CAUTION FOR THE PROPER PERFORMANCE OF THE FUNCTIONS OF AN INSOLVENCY PRACTITIONER ETC.

12(1)   Schedule 2 shall have effect in respect of the requirements prescribed for the purposes of section 390(3)(b) in relation to security or caution for the proper performance of the functions of an insolvency practitioner and for related matters.

12(2)   Where two or more persons are appointed jointly to act as insolvency practitioners in relation to any person, the provisions of this regulation shall apply to each of them individually.

12(3)   Where, in accordance with sections 390(2) and 390A(2)(b) of the Act a person is qualified to act as an insolvency practitioner by virtue of an authorisation granted by the Department of Enterprise, Trade and Investment for Northern Ireland under Article 352 of the Insolvency (Northern Ireland) Order 1989, this Part applies in relation to that person as if that authorisation had been granted pursuant to section 393 of the Act immediately before 1st October 2015.

History
Regulation 12(3) inserted by the Provision of Services (Insolvency Practitioners) Regulations 2009 (SI 2009/3081) reg.4 and Sch. para.7 as from 28 December 2009. Regulation 12(3) substituted by the Deregulation Act 2015 (Insolvency) (Consequential Amendments and Transitional and Savings Provisions) Order 2015 (SI 2015/1641) art.5(6) as from 1 October 2015.

PART 4

RECORDS TO BE MAINTAINED BY INSOLVENCY PRACTITIONERS—INSPECTION OF RECORDS

13   Records to be maintained by insolvency practitioners

13(1)   In respect of each case in which an insolvency practitioner acts, the insolvency practitioner shall maintain records containing information sufficient to show and explain–

(a)   the administration of that case by the insolvency practitioner and the insolvency practitioner's staff; and

(b)   any decisions made by the insolvency practitioner which materially affect that case.

13(2)   Where at any time the records referred to in paragraph (1) do not contain all the information referred to in paragraph (1), the insolvency practitioner shall forthwith make such changes to the records as are necessary to ensure that the records contains all such information.

13(3)   [Revoked]

13(4)   [Revoked]

13(5)   Any records created in relation to a case pursuant to this regulation shall be preserved by the insolvency practitioner until whichever is the later of–

(a)   the sixth anniversary of the date of the grant to the insolvency practitioner of his release or discharge in that case; or

(b) the sixth anniversary of the date on which any security or caution maintained in that case expires or otherwise ceases to have effect.

History
Regulation 13(1) substituted, reg.13(2) amended and reg.13(3), (4) revoked by the Insolvency Practitioners (Amendment) Regulations 2015 (SI 2015/391) reg.3 as from 1 October 2015.

14 Notification of whereabouts of records [Revoked]

History
Regulation 14 revoked by the Deregulation Act 2015 (Insolvency) (Consequential Amendments and Transitional and Savings Provisions) Order 2015 (SI 2015/1641) art.5(7) as from 1 October 2015.

15 Inspection of records

15(1) Any records maintained by an insolvency practitioner pursuant to this Part shall on the giving of reasonable notice be made available by him for inspection by–

(a) any professional body recognised under section 391 of the Act of which he is a member and the rules of membership of which entitle him to act as an insolvency practitioner;

(b) [Revoked]

(c) the Secretary of State.

15(2) Any person who is entitled to inspect any record pursuant to paragraph (1) shall also be entitled to take a copy of those records.

History
Regulation 15(1)(b) revoked by the Deregulation Act 2015 (Insolvency) (Consequential Amendments and Transitional and Savings Provisions) Order 2015 (SI 2015/1641) art.5(8) as from 1 October 2015.

16 Inspection of practice records [Revoked]

History
Regulation 16 revoked by the Deregulation Act 2015 (Insolvency) (Consequential Amendments and Transitional and Savings Provisions) Order 2015 (SI 2015/1641) art.5(9) as from 1 October 2015.

17 Inspection of records in administration and administrative receiverships

17 On the giving of reasonable notice to the insolvency practitioner, the Secretary of State shall be entitled to inspect and take copies of any records in the possession or control of that insolvency practitioner which–

(a) were required to be created by or under any provision of the Act (or any provision made under the Act); and

(b) relate to an administration or an administrative receivership.

SCHEDULE 1

REGULATIONS REVOKED

Regulation 4

The Insolvency Practitioners Regulations 1990

The Insolvency Practitioners (Amendment) Regulations 1993

The Insolvency Practitioners (Amendment) Regulations 2002

The Insolvency Practitioners (Amendment) (No 2) Regulations 2002

The Insolvency Practitioners (Amendment) Regulations 2004

SCHEDULE 2

REQUIREMENTS FOR SECURITY OR CAUTION AND RELATED MATTERS

Regulation 12

PART 1

INTERPRETATION

1   Interpretation

1   In this Schedule–

"cover schedule" means the schedule referred to in paragraph 3(2)(c);

"the insolvent" means the individual or company in relation to which an insolvency practitioner is acting;

"general penalty sum" shall be construed in accordance with paragraph 3(2)(b);

"insolvent's assets" means all assets comprised in the insolvent's estate together with any monies provided by a third party for the payment of the insolvent's debts or the costs and expenses of administering the insolvent's estate;

"professional liability insurance" means insurance taken out by the insolvency practitioner in respect of potential liabilities to the insolvent and third parties arising out of acting as an insolvency practitioner;

"specific penalty sum" shall be construed in accordance with paragraph 3(2)(a).

History
Definition of "professional liability insurance" amended by the Provision of Services (Insolvency Practitioners) Regulations 2009 (SI 2009/3081) reg.4 and Sch. para.8(1), (2) as from 28 December 2009.

PART 2

REQUIREMENTS RELATING TO SECURITY AND CAUTION

2   Requirements in respect of security or caution

2   The requirements in respect of security or caution for the proper performance of the duties of insolvency practitioners prescribed for the purposes of section 390(3)(b) shall be as set out in this Part.

2A   Requirement for bond or professional liability insurance

2A   Where an insolvency practitioner is appointed to act in respect of an insolvent there must be in force–

(a)   a bond in a form approved by the Secretary of State which complies with paragraph 3.

(b) where the insolvency practitioner is already established in another EEA state and is already covered in that state by professional liability insurance or a guarantee, professional liability insurance or a guarantee which complies with paragraph 8A.

History
Paragraph 2A inserted by the Provision of Services (Insolvency Practitioners) Regulations 2009 (SI 2009/3081) reg.4 and Sch. para.8(1), (3) as from 28 December 2009.

3   Terms of the bond

3(1) The bond must–

(a) be in writing or in electronic form;

(b) contain provision whereby a surety or cautioner undertakes to be jointly and severally liable for losses in relation to the insolvent caused by–

(i) the fraud or dishonesty of the insolvency practitioner whether acting alone or in collusion with one or more persons; or

(ii) the fraud or dishonesty of any person committed with the connivance of the insolvency practitioner; and

(c) otherwise conform to the requirements of this paragraph and paragraphs 4 to 8.

3(2) The terms of the bond shall provide–

(a) for the payment, in respect of each case where the insolvency practitioner acts, of claims in respect of liabilities for losses of the kind mentioned in sub-paragraph (1) up to an aggregate maximum sum in respect of that case ("the specific penalty sum") calculated in accordance with the provisions of this Schedule;

(b) in the event that any amounts payable under (a) are insufficient to meet all claims arising out of any case, for a further sum of £250,000 ("the general penalty sum") out of which any such claims are to be met;

(c) for a schedule containing the name of the insolvent and the value of the insolvent's assets to be submitted to the surety or cautioner within such period as may be specified in the bond;

(d) that where at any time before the insolvency practitioner obtains his release or discharge in respect of his acting in relation to an insolvent, he forms the opinion that the value of that insolvent's assets is greater than the current specific penalty sum, a revised specific penalty sum shall be applicable on the submission within such time as may be specified in the bond of a cover schedule containing a revised value of the insolvent's assets;

(e) for the payment of losses of the kind mentioned in sub-paragraph (1), whether they arise during the period in which the insolvency practitioner holds office in the capacity in which he was initially appointed or a subsequent period where he holds office in a subsequent capacity;

3(3) The terms of the bond may provide–

(a) that total claims in respect of the acts of the insolvency practitioner under all bonds relating to him are to be limited to a maximum aggregate sum (which shall not be less than £25,000,000); and

(b) for a time limit within which claims must be made.

History
Title of para.3 amended and para.(1) substituted by the Provision of Services (Insolvency Practitioners) Regulations 2009 (SI 2009/3081) reg.4 and Sch. para.8(4) as from 28 December 2009.

4   Subject to paragraphs 5, 6 and 7, the amount of the specific penalty in respect of a case in which the insolvency practitioner acts, shall equal at least the value of the insolvent's assets as estimated by the insolvency practitioner as at the date of his appointment but ignoring the value of any assets–

(a)   charged to a third party to the extent of any amount which would be payable to that third party; or

(b)   held on trust by the insolvent to the extent that any beneficial interest in those assets does not belong to the insolvent.

5   In a case where an insolvency practitioner acts as a nominee or supervisor of a voluntary arrangement under Part I or Part VIII of the Act, the amount of the specific penalty shall be equal to at least the value of those assets subject to the terms of the arrangement (whether or not those assets are in his possession) including, where under the terms of the arrangement the debtor or a third party is to make payments, the aggregate of any payments to be made.

6   Where the value of the insolvent's assets is less than £5,000, the specific penalty sum shall be £5,000.

7   Where the value of the insolvent's assets is more than £5,000,000 the specific penalty sum shall be £5,000,000.

8   In estimating the value of an insolvent's assets, unless he has reason to doubt their accuracy, the insolvency practitioner may rely upon–

(a)   any statement of affairs produced in relation to that insolvent pursuant to any provision of the Act; and

(b)   in the case of a sequestration–

(i)   the debtor's list of assets and liabilities under section 19 of the Bankruptcy (Scotland) Act 1985;

(ii)   the preliminary statement under that Act; or

(iii)   the final statement of the debtor's affairs by the interim trustee under section 23 of the Bankruptcy (Scotland) Act 1985.

8A   Compliance of professional liability insurance cover in another EEA state

8A   Where paragraph 2A(b) applies to an insolvency practitioner, the professional liability insurance or guarantee complies with this paragraph if the Secretary of State determines that it is equivalent or essentially comparable to the bond referred to in paragraph 3 as regards–

(a)   its purpose, and

(b)   the cover it provides in terms of–

(i)   the risk covered,

(ii)   the amount covered, and

(iii)   exclusions from the cover.

8B   Procedure for determining compliance of professional liability insurance or guarantee

8B(1)   Where an insolvency practitioner seeks a determination under paragraph 8A, the insolvency practitioner must send to the Secretary of State–

(a)   a copy of the document providing the professional liability insurance or guarantee cover in the EEA state in which the insolvency practitioner is established;

(b)   where the document in sub-paragraph (a) is not in English, a translation of it into English; and

(c)   a notice–

    (i)   where the insolvency practitioner intends to act in respect of an insolvent, specifying–

        (aa) the name of the insolvent; and

        (bb) the time and date when the insolvency practitioner intends to consent to be appointed to act; or

    (ii)   that the insolvency practitioner seeks a determination without reference to a specific appointment.

8B(2)   Where there is a notice sent under sub-paragraph (1)(c)(i), the documents sent under sub-paragraph (1) must be sent to the Secretary of State such that the Secretary of State receives them no later than 5 business days before the date in the notice.

8B(3)   Where the Secretary of State receives the documents sent under sub-paragraph (1), the Secretary of State must–

(a)   as soon as is reasonably practicable, notify the insolvency practitioner whether they were received in accordance with sub-paragraph (2);

(b)   consider them; and

(c)   determine whether the document sent under sub-paragraph (1)(a) complies with paragraph 8A.

8B(4)   Where the Secretary of State determines that the document sent under sub-paragraph (1)(a) complies with paragraph 8A, the Secretary of State must–

(a)   notify the insolvency practitioner that it complies with paragraph 8A; and

(b)   determine whether it contains a term equivalent or essentially comparable to a requirement to provide–

    (i)   a specific penalty sum; or

    (ii)   a cover schedule.

8B(5)   Where the Secretary of State determines under sub-paragraph (4)(b) that the document sent under sub-paragraph (1)(a)–

(a)   contains a term equivalent or essentially comparable to a requirement to provide a specific penalty sum or a cover schedule, the notice sent under paragraph (4)(a) must specify–

    (i)   the term equivalent or essentially comparable to a requirement to provide a specific penalty sum or a cover schedule; and

    (ii)   the thing in the term in sub-paragraph (i) which is equivalent or essentially comparable to a specific penalty sum or a cover schedule; or

(b)   does not contain a term equivalent or essentially comparable to a requirement to provide a specific penalty sum or a cover schedule, the notice sent under paragraph (4)(a) must state that determination.

8B(6)   Where the Secretary of State determines that the document sent under sub-paragraph (1)(a) does not comply with paragraph 8A, the Secretary of State must notify the insolvency practitioner and–

(a)   give reasons for the determination; and

(b)   specify any terms which, if included in a supplementary guarantee, will cause the Secretary of State to make a determination in accordance with paragraph 8A.

8B(7)   In this paragraph a "business day" means any day other than a Saturday, a Sunday, Christmas Day, Good Friday or a day which is a bank holiday in England and Wales under or by virtue of the Banking and Financial Dealings Act 1971.

8B(8)   Any documents in this paragraph or paragraph 8C or 8D may be sent electronically.

8C   Procedure for determining compliance of supplementary guarantee

8C(1)   Where the Secretary of State has made a determination under paragraph 8B(6), the insolvency practitioner may send to the Secretary of State–

(a)   a supplementary guarantee purporting to provide for the matters specified in paragraph 8B(6)(b); and

(b)   where the supplementary guarantee is not in English, a translation of it into English.

8C(2)   Where the Secretary of State receives the documents sent under sub-paragraph (1), the Secretary of State must–

(a)   as soon as is reasonably practicable, notify the insolvency practitioner of the date and time of their receipt;

(b)   consider them; and

(c)   determine whether the document sent under sub-paragraph (1)(a) provides for the matters specified in paragraph 8B(6)(b).

8C(3)   Where the Secretary of State determines that the document sent under sub-paragraph (1)(a)–

(a)   provides for the matters in specified in paragraph 8B(6)(b); and

(b)   together with the document in paragraph 8B(1)(a) complies with paragraph 8A, the Secretary of State must notify the insolvency practitioner that the documents sent under sub-paragraph (1)(a) and paragraph 8B(1)(a) together comply with paragraph 8A.

8C(4)   Where the Secretary of State determines in accordance with sub-paragraph (3), the Secretary of State must also determine whether the document sent under sub-paragraph (1)(a) or paragraph 8B(1)(a) contains a term equivalent or essentially comparable to a requirement to provide–

(a)   a specific penalty sum; or

(b)   a cover schedule.

8C(5)   Where the Secretary of State determines under sub-paragraph (4) that the document sent under sub-paragraph (1)(a) or paragraph 8B(1)(a)–

(a)   contains a term equivalent or essentially comparable to a requirement to provide a specific penalty sum or a cover schedule, the notice sent under sub-paragraph (3) must specify–

    (i)   the term equivalent or essentially comparable to a requirement to provide a specific penalty sum or a cover schedule;

    (ii)   the thing in the term in sub-paragraph (i) which is equivalent or essentially comparable to a requirement to a specific penalty sum or a cover schedule; and

    (iii)   the document in which the term in sub-paragraph (i) and the thing in sub-paragraph (ii) are to be found; or

(b)   does not contain a term equivalent or essentially comparable to a requirement to provide a specific penalty sum or a cover schedule, the notice sent under sub-paragraph (3) must state that determination.

8C(6)   Where the Secretary of State determines that the document sent under sub-paragraph (1)(a)–

(a)   does not provide for the matters specified in paragraph 8B(6)(b), or

(b)   together with the document sent under paragraph 8B(1)(a) does not comply with paragraph 8A, the Secretary of State must notify the insolvency practitioner that the documents sent under sub-paragraphs (1)(a) and paragraph 8B(1)(a) together do not comply with paragraph 8A.

8D Time for notification of determinations

8D(1) The Secretary of State must notify the insolvency practitioner of the determinations under paragraph 8B or 8C in the periods set out in this paragraph.

8D(2) The Secretary of State must notify the insolvency practitioner–

(a) where a notice under paragraph 8B(1)(c)(i) is received by the Secretary of State in accordance with paragraph 8B(2) and the determination is under–

    (i) paragraph 8B(4), (5) or (6), such that the insolvency practitioner receives the notice sent under paragraph 8B(4) or (6) or before the time and date in the notice sent under paragraph 8B(1)(c)(i); or

    (ii) paragraph 8C(4), (5) or (6), as soon as is reasonably practicable after receipt of the documents sent under paragraph 8C(1);

(b) where a notice sent under paragraph 8B(1)(c)(i) is received by the Secretary of State but not in accordance with paragraph 8B(2), and the determination is under–

    (i) paragraph 8B(4), (5) or (6), as soon as is reasonably practicable after receipt of the documents sent under paragraph 8B(1); or

    (ii) paragraph 8C(3), (5) or (6), as soon as is reasonably practicable after receipt of the documents sent under paragraph 8C(1); or

(c) where the notice is sent under paragraph 8B(1)(c)(ii), and the determination is under–

    (i) paragraph 8B(4), (5) or (6), within 28 days of receipt of the documents sent under paragraph 8B(1); or

    (ii) paragraph 8C(3), (5) or (6), within 14 days of receipt of the documents sent under paragraph 8C(1).

8E Notification of determination out of time

8E(1) This paragraph applies where the insolvency practitioner–

(a) sends a notice under paragraph 8B(1)(c)(i);

(b) receives notification sent under paragraph 8B(3)(a) that the Secretary of State received the documents in paragraph 8B(1) in accordance with paragraph 8B(2); and

(c) does not receive the notifications in the time in paragraph 8D(2)(a)(i).

8E(2) The insolvency practitioner is qualified to act as an insolvency practitioner in respect of the insolvent specified in the notice under paragraph 8B(1)(c)(i) until the Secretary of State notifies the insolvency practitioner of the determination under paragraph 8B or 8C.

8E(3) Subject to sub-paragraph (4), where the Secretary of State notifies the insolvency practitioner of the determination under paragraph 8B or 8C–

(a) the determination applies; and

(b) the insolvency practitioner ceases to be qualified to act as an insolvency practitioner under sub-paragraph (2).

8E(4) Where–

(a) the Secretary of State gives notice under paragraph 8B(6); and

(b) the insolvency practitioner sends the documents in paragraph 8C(1), the insolvency practitioner is qualified to act as an insolvency practitioner under sub-paragraph (2) until the Secretary of State determines in accordance with paragraph 8C(4) or (6).

History
Paragraphs 8A–8E inserted by the Provision of Services (Insolvency Practitioners) Regulations 2009 (SI 2009/3081) reg.4 and Sch. para.8(5) as from 28 December 2009.

PART 3

RECORDS RELATING TO BONDING AND CONNECTED MATTERS

9   Record of specific penalty sums to be maintained by insolvency practitioner

9(1)   An insolvency practitioner shall maintain a record of all specific penalty sums that are applicable in relation to any case where he is acting and such record shall contain the name of each person to whom the specific penalty sum relates and the amount of each penalty sum that is in force.

9(2)   Any record maintained by an insolvency practitioner pursuant to this paragraph shall, on the giving of reasonable notice, be made available for inspection by–

(a)   any professional body recognised under section 391 of the Act of which he is or was a member and the rules of membership of which entitle or entitled him to act as an insolvency practitioner;

(b)   [Revoked]

(c)   the Secretary of State.

9(3)   Subject to sub-paragraph (4), where the Secretary of State has notified the insolvency practitioner in accordance with paragraph 8B(5)(a) or 8C(5)(a) in relation to a specific penalty sum, the thing notified under paragraph 8B(5)(a)(ii) or 8C(5)(a)(ii) is construed as a specific penalty sum for the purposes of this paragraph.

9(4)   Where the Secretary of State has notified the insolvency practitioner in accordance with paragraph 8B(5)(b) or 8C(5)(b) in relation to a specific penalty sum, this paragraph does not apply.

History
Paragraphs 9(3), (4) inserted by the Provision of Services (Insolvency Practitioners) Regulations 2009 (SI 2009/3081) reg.4 and Sch. para.8(6) as from 28 December 2009. Paragraph 9(2)(b) revoked by the Deregulation Act 2015 (Insolvency) (Consequential Amendments and Transitional and Savings Provisions) Order 2015 (SI 2015/1641) art.5(10) as from 1 October 2015.

10   Retention of bond by recognised professional body or competent authority

10(1)   The documents in sub-paragraph (2) or a copy must be sent by the insolvency practitioner to–

(a)   any professional body recognised under section 391 of the Act of which he is a member and the rules of membership of which entitle him to act as an insolvency practitioner; or

(b)   [Revoked]

10(2)   The documents in this sub-paragraph are–

(a)   the bond referred to in paragraph 3;

(b)   where the Secretary of State has determined under paragraph 8B(4)–

  (i)   the document in paragraph 8B(1)(a) and (b); and

  (ii)   the notice under paragraph 8B(4);

(c)   where the Secretary of State has determined under paragraph 8C(4)–

  (i)   the documents in paragraphs 8B(1)(a) and (b) and 8C(1)(a) and (b); and

  (ii)   the notice under paragraph 8C(3).

10(3) The documents in sub-paragraph (2) or a copy of it may be sent electronically.

History

Paragraph 10 amended and renumbered as para.10(1) and paras 10(2), (3) inserted by the Provision of Services (Insolvency Practitioners) Regulations 2009 (SI 2009/3081) reg.4 and Sch. para.8(7) as from 28 December 2009. Paragraph 10(1)(b) revoked by the Deregulation Act 2015 (Insolvency) (Consequential Amendments and Transitional and Savings Provisions) Order 2015 (SI 2015/1641) art.5(11) as from 1 October 2015.

11 Inspection and retention requirements relating to cover schedule—England and Wales

11(1) This regulation applies to an insolvency practitioner appointed in insolvency proceedings under the Act to act–

(a) in relation to a company which the courts in England and Wales have jurisdiction to wind up; or

(b) in respect of an individual.

11(2) The insolvency practitioner shall retain a copy of the cover schedule submitted by him in respect of his acting in relation to the company or, as the case may be, individual until the second anniversary of the date on which he is granted his release or discharge in relation to that company or, as the case may be, that individual.

11(3) The copy of a schedule kept by an insolvency practitioner in pursuance of sub-paragraph (2) shall be produced by him on demand for inspection by–

(a) any creditor of the person to whom the schedule relates;

(b) where the schedule relates to an insolvent who is an individual, that individual;

(c) where the schedule relates to an insolvent which is a company, any contributory or director or other officer of the company; and

(d) the Secretary of State.

11(4) Subject to sub-paragraph (5), where the Secretary of State has notified the insolvency practitioner in accordance with paragraph 8B(5)(a) or 8C(5)(a) in relation to a cover schedule, the thing notified under paragraph 8B(5)(a)(ii) or 8C(5)(a)(ii) is construed as a cover schedule for the purposes of this paragraph, paragraph 12 and paragraph 13.

11(5) Where the Secretary of State has notified the insolvency practitioner in accordance with paragraph 8B(5)(b) or 8C(5)(b) in relation to a cover schedule, this paragraph, paragraph 12 and paragraph 13 do not apply.

History

Paragraph 11(4), (5) inserted by the Provision of Services (Insolvency Practitioners) Regulations 2009 (SI 2009/3081) reg.4 and Sch. para.8(8) as from 28 December 2009. Paragraph 11(4) amended by the Insolvency Practitioners (Amendment) Regulations 2015 (SI 2015/391) reg.6 as from 1 October 2015.

12 Inspection and retention requirements relating to the cover schedule—Scotland

12(1) Where an insolvency practitioner is appointed to act in relation to a company which the courts in Scotland have jurisdiction to wind up, he shall retain in the sederunt book kept under rule 7.33 of the Insolvency (Scotland) Rules 1986, the principal copy of any cover schedule containing entries in relation to his so acting.

12(2) Where an insolvency practitioner is appointed to act as interim trustee or permanent trustee or as a trustee under a trust deed for creditors, he shall retain in the sederunt book kept for those proceedings, the principal copy of any cover schedule containing entries in relation to his so acting.

13   Requirements to submit cover schedule to authorising body

13(1)   Every insolvency practitioner shall submit to his authorising body not later than 20 days after the end of each month during which he holds office in a case–

(a)   the information submitted to a surety or cautioner in any cover schedule related to that month;

(b)   where no cover schedule is submitted in relation to the month, a statement either that there are no relevant particulars to be supplied or, as the case may be, that it is not practicable to supply particulars in relation to any appointments taken in that month; and

(c)   a statement identifying any case in respect of which he has been granted his release or discharge.

13(2)   In this regulation "authorising body" means in relation to an insolvency practitioner–

(a)   any professional body recognised under section 391 of the Act of which he is a member and the rules of membership of which entitle him to act as an insolvency practitioner; or

(b)   [Revoked]

History
Paragraph 13(2)(b) revoked by the Deregulation Act 2015 (Insolvency) (Consequential Amendments and Transitional and Savings Provisions) Order 2015 (SI 2015/1641) art.5(12) as from 1 October 2015.

SCHEDULE 3

RECORDS TO BE MAINTAINED—MINIMUM REQUIREMENTS

[Revoked]

Schedule 3 revoked by the Insolvency Practitioners (Amendment) Regulations 2015 (SI 2015/391) reg.7 as from 1 October 2015.

Community Interest Company Regulations 2005

(SI 2005/1788)

Made on 30 June 2005 by the Secretary of State for Trade and Industry under ss.30(1) to (4), 30(7), 31, 32(3), (4) and (6), 34(3), 35(4) to (6), 36(2), 37(7), 47(12) and (13), 57(1) and (2), 58, 59(1) and 62(2) and (3) of and para.4 of Sch.4 to the Companies (Audit, Investigations and Community Enterprise) Act 2004. Operative from 1 July 2005.

[**Note**: Changes made by the Companies Act 2006 (Commencement No.2, Consequential Amendments, Transitional Provisions and Savings) Order 2007 and the Housing and Regeneration Act 2008 (Consequential Provisions) (No.2) Order 2010 (SI 2010/671) have been incorporated into the text.]

PART 6
RESTRICTIONS ON DISTRIBUTIONS AND INTEREST

23 Distribution of assets on a winding up

23(1) This regulation applies where–

(a) a community interest company is wound up under the Insolvency Act 1986 or the Insolvency (Northern Ireland) Order 1989; and

(b) some property of the company (the "residual assets") remains after satisfaction of the company's liabilities.

23(2) Subject to paragraph (3), the residual assets shall be distributed to those members of the community interest company (if any) who are entitled to share in any distribution of assets on the winding up of the company according to their rights and interests in the company.

23(3) No member shall receive under paragraph (2) an amount which exceeds the paid up value of the shares which he holds in the company.

23(4) If any residual assets remain after any distribution to members under paragraph (2) (the "remaining residual assets"), they shall be distributed in accordance with paragraphs (5) and (6).

23(5) If the articles of the company specify an asset-locked body to which any remaining residual assets of the company should be distributed, then, unless either of the conditions specified in sub-paragraphs (b) and (c) of paragraph (6) is satisfied, the remaining residual assets shall be distributed to that asset-locked body in such proportions or amounts as the Regulator shall direct.

23(6) If–

(a) the articles of the company do not specify an asset-locked body to which any remaining residual assets of the company should be distributed;

(b) the Regulator is aware that the asset-locked body to which the articles of the company specify that the remaining residual assets of the company should be distributed is itself in the process of being wound up; or

(c) the Regulator–

(i) has received representations from a member or director of the company stating, with reasons, that the asset-locked body to which the articles of the company specify that the remaining residual assets of the company should be distributed is not an appropriate recipient of the company's remaining residual assets; and

(ii) has agreed with those representations,

then the remaining residual assets shall be distributed to such asset-locked bodies, and in such proportions or amounts, as the Regulator shall direct.

23(7)   In considering any direction to be made under this regulation, the Regulator must–

(a)   consult the directors and members of the company, to the extent that he considers it practicable and appropriate to do so; and

(b)   have regard to the desirability of distributing assets in accordance with any relevant provisions of the company's articles.

23(8)   The Regulator must give notice of any direction under this regulation to the company and the liquidator.

23(9)   This regulation has effect notwithstanding anything in the Insolvency Act 1986 or the Insolvency (Northern Ireland) Order 1989.

23(10)   This regulation has effect subject to the provisions of the Housing Act 1996, Part 2 of the Housing and Regeneration Act 2008 and the Housing (Scotland) Act 2001.

23(11)   Any member or director of the company may appeal to the Appeal Officer against a direction of the Regulator made under this regulation.

Note
"Asset-locked body" is defined in reg.2 as follows:

"'asset-locked body' means–

(a)   a community interest company, charity or Scottish charity; or

(b)   a body established outside Great Britain that is equivalent to any of those persons."

History
Paragraph 23(1)(a), (9) amended by the Companies Act 2006 (Commencement No.2, Consequential Amendments, Transitional Provisions and Savings) Order 2007 (SI 2007/1093 (C. 49) art.6(2) and Sch.4 para.36, as from 6 April 2007. Paragraph 23(10) amended by the Housing and Regeneration Act 2008 (Consequential Provisions) (No.2) Order 2010 (SI 2010/671) art.4 and Sch.1 para.42 as from 1 April 2010.

Transfer of Undertakings (Protection of Employment) Regulations 2006

(SI 2006/246)

Made on 6 February 2006 by the Secretary of State under the European Communities Act 1972 s.2(2) and the Employment Relations Act 1999 s.38. Operative from 6 April 2006

[**Note:** Changes made by the Transfer of Undertakings (Protection of Employment) (Amendment) Regulations 2009 (SI 2009/592), the Agency Workers Regulations 2010 (SI 2010/93), the Collective Redundancies and Transfer of Undertakings (Protection of Employment) (Amendment) Regulations 2014 (SI 2014/16), the Enterprise and Regulatory Reform Act 2013 (Consequential Amendments) (Employment) Order 2014 (SI 2014/386) and the Enterprise and Regulatory Reform Act 2013 (Consequential Amendments) (Employment) (No.2) Order 2014 (SI 2014/853) have been incorporated into the text.]

1 Citation, commencement and extent

1(1) These Regulations may be cited as the Transfer of Undertakings (Protection of Employment) Regulations 2006.

1(2) These Regulations shall come into force on 6 April 2006.

1(3) These Regulations shall extend to Northern Ireland, except where otherwise provided.

2 Interpretation

2(1) In these Regulations–

"assigned" means assigned other than on a temporary basis;

"collective agreement", "collective bargaining" and "trade union" have the same meanings respectively as in the 1992 Act;

"contract of employment" means any agreement between an employee and his employer determining the terms and conditions of his employment;

references to "contractor" in regulation 3 shall include a sub-contractor;

"employee" means any individual who works for another person whether under a contract of service or apprenticeship or otherwise but does not include anyone who provides services under a contract for services and references to a person's employer shall be construed accordingly;

"insolvency practitioner" has the meaning given to the expression by Part XIII of the Insolvency Act 1986;

references to "organised grouping of employees" shall include a single employee;

"recognised" has the meaning given to the expression by section 178(3) of the 1992 Act;

"relevant transfer" means a transfer or a service provision change to which these Regulations apply in accordance with regulation 3 and "transferor" and "transferee" shall be construed accordingly and in the case of a service provision change falling within regulation 3(1)(b), "the transferor" means the person who carried out the activities prior to the service provision change and "the transferee" means the person who carries out the activities as a result of the service provision change;

"the 1992 Act" means the Trade Union and Labour Relations (Consolidation) Act 1992;

"the 1996 Act" means the Employment Rights Act 1996;

"the 1996 Tribunals Act" means the Employment Tribunals Act 1996;

"the 1981 Regulations" means the Transfer of Undertakings (Protection of Employment) Regulations 1981.

2(2)   For the purposes of these Regulations the representative of a trade union recognised by an employer is an official or other person authorised to carry on collective bargaining with that employer by that trade union.

2(3)   In the application of these Regulations to Northern Ireland the Regulations shall have effect as set out in Schedule 1.

3   A relevant transfer

3(1)   These Regulations apply to–

(a)   a transfer of an undertaking, business or part of an undertaking or business situated immediately before the transfer in the United Kingdom to another person where there is a transfer of an economic entity which retains its identity;

(b)   a service provision change, that is a situation in which–

    (i)   activities cease to be carried out by a person ("a client") on his own behalf and are carried out instead by another person on the client's behalf ("a contractor");

    (ii)   activities cease to be carried out by a contractor on a client's behalf (whether or not those activities had previously been carried out by the client on his own behalf) and are carried out instead by another person ("a subsequent contractor") on the client's behalf; or

    (iii)   activities cease to be carried out by a contractor or a subsequent contractor on a client's behalf (whether or not those activities had previously been carried out by the client on his own behalf) and are carried out instead by the client on his own behalf,

and in which the conditions set out in paragraph (3) are satisfied.

3(2)   In this regulation "economic entity" means an organised grouping of resources which has the objective of pursuing an economic activity, whether or not that activity is central or ancillary.

3(2A)   References in paragraph (1)(b) to activities being carried out instead by another person (including the client) are to activities which are fundamentally the same as the activities carried out by the person who has ceased to carry them out.

3(3)   The conditions referred to in paragraph (1)(b) are that–

(a)   immediately before the service provision change–

    (i)   there is an organised grouping of employees situated in Great Britain which has as its principal purpose the carrying out of the activities concerned on behalf of the client;

    (ii)   the client intends that the activities will, following the service provision change, be carried out by the transferee other than in connection with a single specific event or task of short-term duration; and

(b)   the activities concerned do not consist wholly or mainly of the supply of goods for the client's use.

3(4)   Subject to paragraph (1), these Regulations apply to–

(a)   public and private undertakings engaged in economic activities whether or not they are operating for gain;

(b)   a transfer or service provision change howsoever effected notwithstanding–

    (i)   that the transfer of an undertaking, business or part of an undertaking or business is governed or effected by the law of a country or territory outside the United Kingdom or that the service provision change is governed or effected by the law of a country or territory outside Great Britain;

    (ii)   that the employment of persons employed in the undertaking, business or part transferred or, in the case of a service provision change, persons employed in the organised grouping of employees, is governed by any such law;

(c)   a transfer of an undertaking, business or part of an undertaking or business (which may also be a service provision change) where persons employed in the undertaking, business or part transferred ordinarily work outside the United Kingdom.

3(5)   An administrative reorganisation of public administrative authorities or the transfer of administrative functions between public administrative authorities is not a relevant transfer.

3(6)   A relevant transfer–

(a)   may be effected by a series of two or more transactions; and

(b)   may take place whether or not any property is transferred to the transferee by the transferor.

3(7)   Where, in consequence (whether directly or indirectly) of the transfer of an undertaking, business or part of an undertaking or business which was situated immediately before the transfer in the United Kingdom, a ship within the meaning of the Merchant Shipping Act 1995 registered in the United Kingdom ceases to be so registered, these Regulations shall not affect the right conferred by section 29 of that Act (right of seamen to be discharged when ship ceases to be registered in the United Kingdom) on a seaman employed in the ship.

History
Regulation 3(2A) inserted by the Collective Redundancies and Transfer of Undertakings (Protection of Employment) (Amendment) Regulations 2014 (SI 2014/16) reg.5. This amendment applies in relation to a TUPE transfer which takes place on or after 31 January 2014.

4   Effect of relevant transfer on contracts of employment

4(1)   Except where objection is made under paragraph (7), a relevant transfer shall not operate so as to terminate the contract of employment of any person employed by the transferor and assigned to the organised grouping of resources or employees that is subject to the relevant transfer, which would otherwise be terminated by the transfer, but any such contract shall have effect after the transfer as if originally made between the person so employed and the transferee.

4(2)   Without prejudice to paragraph (1), but subject to paragraph (6), and regulations 8 and 15(9), on the completion of a relevant transfer–

(a)   all the transferor's rights, powers, duties and liabilities under or in connection with any such contract shall be transferred by virtue of this regulation to the transferee; and

(b)   any act or omission before the transfer is completed, of or in relation to the transferor in respect of that contract or a person assigned to that organised grouping of resources or employees, shall be deemed to have been an act or omission of or in relation to the transferee.

4(3)   Any reference in paragraph (1) to a person employed by the transferor and assigned to the organised grouping of resources or employees that is subject to a relevant transfer, is a reference to a person so employed immediately before the transfer, or who would have been so employed if he had not been dismissed in the circumstances described in regulation 7(1), including, where the transfer is effected by a series of two or more transactions, a person so employed and assigned or who would have been so employed and assigned immediately before any of those transactions.

4(4)   Subject to regulation 9, any purported variation of a contract of employment that is, or will be, transferred by paragraph (1), is void if the sole or principal reason for the variation is the transfer.

4(5)   Paragraph (4) does not prevent a variation of the contract of employment if–

(a)   the sole or principal reason for the variation is an economic, technical, or organisational reason entailing changes in the workforce, provided that the employer and employee agree that variation; or

(b)   the terms of that contract permit the employer to make such a variation.

4(5A)   In paragraph (5), the expression "changes in the workforce" includes a change to the place where employees are employed by the employer to carry on the business of the employer or to carry out work of a particular kind for the employer (and the reference to such a place has the same meaning as in section 139 of the 1996 Act).

4(5B)   Paragraph (4) does not apply in respect of a variation of the contract of employment in so far as it varies a term or condition incorporated from a collective agreement, provided that–

(a)   the variation of the contract takes effect on a date more than one year after the date of the transfer; and

(b)   following that variation, the rights and obligations in the employee's contract, when considered together, are no less favourable to the employee than those which applied immediately before the variation.

4(5C)   Paragraphs (5) and (5B) do not affect any rule of law as to whether a contract of employment is effectively varied.

4(6)   Paragraph (2) shall not transfer or otherwise affect the liability of any person to be prosecuted for, convicted of and sentenced for any offence.

4(7)   Paragraphs (1) and (2) shall not operate to transfer the contract of employment and the rights, powers, duties and liabilities under or in connection with it of an employee who informs the transferor or the transferee that he objects to becoming employed by the transferee.

4(8)   Subject to paragraphs (9) and (11), where an employee so objects, the relevant transfer shall operate so as to terminate his contract of employment with the transferor but he shall not be treated, for any purpose, as having been dismissed by the transferor.

4(9)   Subject to regulation 9, where a relevant transfer involves or would involve a substantial change in working conditions to the material detriment of a person whose contract of employment is or would be transferred under paragraph (1), such an employee may treat the contract of employment as having been terminated, and the employee shall be treated for any purpose as having been dismissed by the employer.

4(10)   No damages shall be payable by an employer as a result of a dismissal falling within paragraph (9) in respect of any failure by the employer to pay wages to an employee in respect of a notice period which the employee has failed to work.

4(11)   Paragraphs (1), (7), (8) and (9) are without prejudice to any right of an employee arising apart from these Regulations to terminate his contract of employment without notice in acceptance of a repudiatory breach of contract by his employer.

History
Regulation 4(4), (5) substituted and reg.4(5A)–(5C) inserted by the Collective Redundancies and Transfer of Undertakings (Protection of Employment) (Amendment) Regulations 2014 (SI 2014/16) reg.6. This amendment applies in relation to any purported variation of a contract of employment that is transferred by a TUPE transfer if (a) the TUPE transfer takes place on or after 31 January 2014 and (b) that purported variation is agreed on or after 31 January 2014, or, in a case where the variation is not agreed, it starts to have effect on or after that date.

4A   Effect of relevant transfer on contracts of employment which incorporate provisions of collective agreements

4A(1)   Where a contract of employment, which is transferred by regulation 4(1), incorporates provisions of collective agreements as may be agreed from time to time, regulation 4(2) does not transfer any rights, powers, duties and liabilities in relation to any provision of a collective agreement if the following conditions are met–

(a)   the provision of the collective agreement is agreed after the date of the transfer; and

(b)   the transferee is not a participant in the collective bargaining for that provision.

4A(2)   For the purposes of regulation 4(1), the contract of employment has effect after the transfer as if it does not incorporate provisions of a collective agreement which meet the conditions in paragraph (1).

History
Regulation 4A inserted by the Collective Redundancies and Transfer of Undertakings (Protection of Employment) (Amendment) Regulations 2014 (SI 2014/16) reg.7. This amendment applies in relation to a TUPE transfer which takes place on or after 31 January 2014.

5   Effect of relevant transfer on collective agreements

5   Where at the time of a relevant transfer there exists a collective agreement made by or on behalf of the transferor with a trade union recognised by the transferor in respect of any employee whose contract of employment is preserved by regulation 4(1) above, then–

(a)   without prejudice to sections 179 and 180 of the 1992 Act (collective agreements presumed to be unenforceable in specified circumstances) that agreement, in its application in relation to the employee, shall, after the transfer, have effect as if made by or on behalf of the transferee with that trade union, and accordingly anything done under or in connection with it, in its application in relation to the employee, by or in relation to the transferor before the transfer, shall, after the transfer, be deemed to have been done by or in relation to the transferee; and

(b)   any order made in respect of that agreement, in its application in relation to the employee, shall, after the transfer, have effect as if the transferee were a party to the agreement.

6   Effect of relevant transfer on trade union recognition

6(1)   This regulation applies where after a relevant transfer the transferred organised grouping of resources or employees maintains an identity distinct from the remainder of the transferee's undertaking.

6(2)   Where before such a transfer an independent trade union is recognised to any extent by the transferor in respect of employees of any description who in consequence of the transfer become employees of the transferee, then, after the transfer–

(a)   the trade union shall be deemed to have been recognised by the transferee to the same extent in respect of employees of that description so employed; and

(b)   any agreement for recognition may be varied or rescinded accordingly.

7   Dismissal of employee because of relevant transfer

7(1)   Where either before or after a relevant transfer, any employee of the transferor or transferee is dismissed, that employee is to be treated for the purposes of Part 10 of the 1996 Act (unfair dismissal) as unfairly dismissed if the sole or principal reason for the dismissal is the transfer.

7(2)   This paragraph applies where the sole or principal reason for the dismissal is an economic, technical or organisational reason entailing changes in the workforce of either the transferor or the transferee before or after a relevant transfer.

7(3)   Where paragraph (2) applies–

(a)   paragraph (1) does not apply;

(b)   without prejudice to the application of section 98(4) of the 1996 Act (test of fair dismissal), for the purposes of sections 98(1) and 135 of that Act (reason for dismissal)–

(i)   the dismissal is regarded as having been for redundancy where section 98(2)(c) of that Act applies; or

(ii)   in any other case, the dismissal is regarded as having been for a substantial reason of a kind such as to justify the dismissal of an employee holding the position which that employee held.

7(3A)   In paragraph (2), the expression "changes in the workforce" includes a change to the place where employees are employed by the employer to carry on the business of the employer or to carry out work of a particular kind for the employer (and the reference to such a place has the same meaning as in section 139 of the 1996 Act).

7(4)   The provisions of this regulation apply irrespective of whether the employee in question is assigned to the organised grouping of resources or employees that is, or will be, transferred.

7(5)   Paragraph (1) shall not apply in relation to the dismissal of any employee which was required by reason of the application of section 5 of the Aliens Restriction (Amendment) Act 1919 to his employment.

7(6)   Paragraph (1) shall not apply in relation to a dismissal of an employee if the application of section 94 of the 1996 Act to the dismissal of the employee is excluded by or under any provision of the 1996 Act, the 1996 Tribunals Act or the 1992 Act.

History
Regulation 7(1)–(3) substituted and reg.7(3A) inserted by the Collective Redundancies and Transfer of Undertakings (Protection of Employment) (Amendment) Regulations 2014 (SI 2014/16) reg.8. This amendment applies in relation to any case where (a) the TUPE transfer takes place on or after 31 January 2014 and (b) the date when any notice of termination is given by an employer or an employee in respect of any dismissal is 31 January 2014 or later, or, in a case where no notice is given, the date on which the termination takes effect is 31 January 2014 or later.

8   Insolvency

8(1)   If at the time of a relevant transfer the transferor is subject to relevant insolvency proceedings paragraphs (2) to (6) apply.

8(2)   In this regulation "relevant employee" means an employee of the transferor–

(a)   whose contract of employment transfers to the transferee by virtue of the operation of these Regulations; or

(b)   whose employment with the transferor is terminated before the time of the relevant transfer in the circumstances described in regulation 7(1).

8(3)   The relevant statutory scheme specified in paragraph (4)(b) (including that sub-paragraph as applied by paragraph 5 of Schedule 1) shall apply in the case of a relevant employee irrespective of the fact that the qualifying requirement that the employee's employment has been terminated is not met and for those purposes the date of the transfer shall be treated as the date of the termination and the transferor shall be treated as the employer.

8(4)   In this regulation the "relevant statutory schemes" are–

(a)   Chapter VI of Part XI of the 1996 Act;

(b)   Part XII of the 1996 Act.

8(5) Regulation 4 shall not operate to transfer liability for the sums payable to the relevant employee under the relevant statutory schemes.

8(6) In this regulation "relevant insolvency proceedings" means insolvency proceedings which have been opened in relation to the transferor not with a view to the liquidation of the assets of the transferor and which are under the supervision of an insolvency practitioner.

8(7) Regulations 4 and 7 do not apply to any relevant transfer where the transferor is the subject of bankruptcy proceedings or any analogous insolvency proceedings which have been instituted with a view to the liquidation of the assets of the transferor and are under the supervision of an insolvency practitioner.

9   Variations of contract where transferors are subject to relevant insolvency proceedings

9(1) If at the time of a relevant transfer the transferor is subject to relevant insolvency proceedings these Regulations shall not prevent the transferor or transferee (or an insolvency practitioner) and appropriate representatives of assigned employees agreeing to permitted variations.

9(2) For the purposes of this regulation "appropriate representatives" are–

   (a) if the employees are of a description in respect of which an independent trade union is recognised by their employer, representatives of the trade union; or

   (b) in any other case, whichever of the following employee representatives the employer chooses–

      (i) employee representatives appointed or elected by the assigned employees (whether they make the appointment or election alone or with others) otherwise than for the purposes of this regulation, who (having regard to the purposes for, and the method by which they were appointed or elected) have authority from those employees to agree permitted variations to contracts of employment on their behalf;

      (ii) employee representatives elected by assigned employees (whether they make the appointment or election alone or with others) for these particular purposes, in an election satisfying requirements identical to those contained in regulation 14 except those in regulation 14(1)(d).

9(3) An individual may be an appropriate representative for the purposes of both this regulation and regulation 13 provided that where the representative is not a trade union representative he is either elected by or has authority from assigned employees (within the meaning of this regulation) and affected employees (as described in regulation 13(1)).

9(4) In section 168 of the 1992 Act (time off for carrying out trade union duties) in subsection (1), after paragraph (c) there is inserted–

   " , or

   (d) negotiations with a view to entering into an agreement under regulation 9 of the Transfer of Undertakings (Protection of Employment) Regulations 2006 that applies to employees of the employer, or

   (e) the performance on behalf of employees of the employer of functions related to or connected with the making of an agreement under that regulation.".

9(5) Where assigned employees are represented by non-trade union representatives–

   (a) the agreement recording a permitted variation must be in writing and signed by each of the representatives who have made it or, where that is not reasonably practicable, by a duly authorised agent of that representative; and

   (b) the employer must, before the agreement is made available for signature, provide all employees to whom it is intended to apply on the date on which it is to come into effect with copies of the text of the agreement and such guidance as those employees might reasonably require in order to understand it fully.

9(6)   A permitted variation shall take effect as a term or condition of the assigned employee's contract of employment in place, where relevant, of any term or condition which it varies.

9(7)   In this regulation–

"assigned employees" means those employees assigned to the organised grouping of resources or employees that is the subject of a relevant transfer;

"permitted variation" is a variation to the contract of employment of an assigned employee where–

(a)   the sole or principal reason for the variation is the transfer and not a reason referred to in regulation 4(5)(a); and

(b)   it is designed to safeguard employment opportunities by ensuring the survival of the undertaking, business or part of the undertaking or business that is the subject of the relevant transfer;

"relevant insolvency proceedings" has the meaning given to the expression by regulation 8(6).

History
Regulation 9(7)(a) substituted by the Collective Redundancies and Transfer of Undertakings (Protection of Employment) (Amendment) Regulations 2014 (SI 2014/16) reg.9. This amendment applies in relation to any case where (a) the TUPE transfer takes place on or after 31 January 2014 and (b) the permitted variation is agreed on or after 31 January 2014.

10   Pensions

10(1)   Regulations 4 and 5 shall not apply–

(a)   to so much of a contract of employment or collective agreement as relates to an occupational pension scheme within the meaning of the Pension Schemes Act 1993; or

(b)   to any rights, powers, duties or liabilities under or in connection with any such contract or subsisting by virtue of any such agreement and relating to such a scheme or otherwise arising in connection with that person's employment and relating to such a scheme.

10(2)   For the purposes of paragraphs (1) and (3), any provisions of an occupational pension scheme which do not relate to benefits for old age, invalidity or survivors shall not be treated as being part of the scheme.

10(3)   An employee whose contract of employment is transferred in the circumstances described in regulation 4(1) shall not be entitled to bring a claim against the transferor for–

(a)   breach of contract; or

(b)   constructive unfair dismissal under section 95(1)(c) of the 1996 Act,

arising out of a loss or reduction in his rights under an occupational pension scheme in consequence of the transfer, save insofar as the alleged breach of contract or dismissal (as the case may be) occurred prior to the date on which these Regulations took effect.

11   Notification of employee liability information

11(1)   The transferor shall notify to the transferee the employee liability information of any person employed by him who is assigned to the organised grouping of resources or employees that is the subject of a relevant transfer–

(a)   in writing; or

(b)   by making it available to him in a readily accessible form.

11(2)   In this regulation and in regulation 12 "employee liability information" means–

(a)   the identity and age of the employee;

(b)   those particulars of employment that an employer is obliged to give to an employee pursuant to section 1 of the 1996 Act;

(c)   information of any–

    (i)   disciplinary procedure taken against an employee;

    (ii)   grievance procedure taken by an employee,

    within the previous two years, in circumstances where a Code of Practice issued under Part IV of the Trade Union and Labour Relations (Consolidation) Act 1992 which relates exclusively or primarily to the resolution of disputes applies;

(d)   information of any court or tribunal case, claim or action–

    (i)   brought by an employee against the transferor, within the previous two years;

    (ii)   that the transferor has reasonable grounds to believe that an employee may bring against the transferee, arising out of the employee's employment with the transferor; and

(e)   information of any collective agreement which will have effect after the transfer, in its application in relation to the employee, pursuant to regulation 5(a).

History
Regulation 11(2)(c) amended by the Transfer of Undertakings (Protection of Employment) (Amendment) Regulations 2009 (SI 2009/592) reg.2(1), (2) as from 6 April 2009.

11(3)   Employee liability information shall contain information as at a specified date not more than fourteen days before the date on which the information is notified to the transferee.

11(4)   The duty to provide employee liability information in paragraph (1) shall include a duty to provide employee liability information of any person who would have been employed by the transferor and assigned to the organised grouping of resources or employees that is the subject of a relevant transfer immediately before the transfer if he had not been dismissed in the circumstances described in regulation 7(1), including, where the transfer is effected by a series of two or more transactions, a person so employed and assigned or who would have been so employed and assigned immediately before any of those transactions.

11(5)   Following notification of the employee liability information in accordance with this regulation, the transferor shall notify the transferee in writing of any change in the employee liability information.

11(6)   A notification under this regulation shall be given not less than 28 days before the relevant transfer or, if special circumstances make this not reasonably practicable, as soon as reasonably practicable thereafter.

11(7)   A notification under this regulation may be given–

(a)   in more than one instalment;

(b)   indirectly, through a third party.

History
Regulation 11(6) amended by the Collective Redundancies and Transfer of Undertakings (Protection of Employment) (Amendment) Regulations 2014 (SI 2014/16) reg.10. This amendment applies in relation to a TUPE transfer which takes place on or after 1 May 2014.

12   Remedy for failure to notify employee liability information

12(1)   On or after a relevant transfer, the transferee may present a complaint to an employment tribunal that the transferor has failed to comply with any provision of regulation 11.

12(2)   An employment tribunal shall not consider a complaint under this regulation unless it is presented–

(a)   before the end of the period of three months beginning with the date of the relevant transfer;

(b)   within such further period as the tribunal considers reasonable in a case where it is satisfied that it was not reasonably practicable for the complaint to be presented before the end of that period of three months.

12(2A)   Regulation 16A (extension of time limits to facilitate conciliation before institution of proceedings) applies for the purposes of paragraph (2).

12(3)   Where an employment tribunal finds a complaint under paragraph (1) well-founded, the tribunal–

(a)   shall make a declaration to that effect; and

(b)   may make an award of compensation to be paid by the transferor to the transferee.

12(4)   The amount of the compensation shall be such as the tribunal considers just and equitable in all the circumstances, subject to paragraph (5), having particular regard to–

(a)   any loss sustained by the transferee which is attributable to the matters complained of; and

(b)   the terms of any contract between the transferor and the transferee relating to the transfer under which the transferor may be liable to pay any sum to the transferee in respect of a failure to notify the transferee of employee liability information.

12(5)   Subject to paragraph (6), the amount of compensation awarded under paragraph (3) shall be not less than £500 per employee in respect of whom the transferor has failed to comply with a provision of regulation 11, unless the tribunal considers it just and equitable, in all the circumstances, to award a lesser sum.

12(6)   In ascertaining the loss referred to in paragraph (4)(a) the tribunal shall apply the same rule concerning the duty of a person to mitigate his loss as applies to any damages recoverable under the common law of England and Wales, Northern Ireland or Scotland, as applicable.

12(7)   Sections 18A to 18C of the 1996 Tribunals Act (conciliation) shall apply to the right conferred by this regulation and to proceedings under this regulation as it applies to the rights conferred by that Act and the employment tribunal proceedings mentioned in that Act.

History
Regulation 12(7) amended by the Enterprise and Regulatory Reform Act 2013 (Consequential Amendments) (Employment) Order 2014 (SI 2014/386) art.2 and Sch. paras 36, 37 as from 6 April 2014. Regulation 12((2A) inserted by the Enterprise and Regulatory Reform Act 2013 (Consequential Amendments) (Employment) (No.2) Order 2014 (SI 2014/853) art.2(1), (2) as from 20 April 2014. This amendment applies in any case where the worker concerned complies with the requirement in the Employment Tribunals Act 1996 s.18A(1) on or after 20 April 2014.

13   Duty to inform and consult representatives

13(1)   In this regulation and regulations 13A, 14 and 15 references to affected employees, in relation to a relevant transfer, are to any employees of the transferor or the transferee (whether or not assigned to the organised grouping of resources or employees that is the subject of a relevant transfer) who may be affected by the transfer or may be affected by measures taken in connection with it; and references to the employer shall be construed accordingly.

13(2)   Long enough before a relevant transfer to enable the employer of any affected employees to consult the appropriate representatives of any affected employees, the employer shall inform those representatives of–

(a)   the fact that the transfer is to take place, the date or proposed date of the transfer and the reasons for it;

(b)   the legal, economic and social implications of the transfer for any affected employees;

(c)   the measures which he envisages he will, in connection with the transfer, take in relation to any affected employees or, if he envisages that no measures will be so taken, that fact; and

(d)   if the employer is the transferor, the measures, in connection with the transfer, which he envisages the transferee will take in relation to any affected employees who will become employees of the transferee after the transfer by virtue of regulation 4 or, if he envisages that no measures will be so taken, that fact.

13(2A)   Where information is to be supplied under paragraph (2) by an employer–

(a)   this must include suitable information relating to the use of agency workers (if any) by that employer; and

(b)   "suitable information relating to the use of agency workers" means–

(i)   the number of agency workers working temporarily for and under the supervision and direction of the employer;

(ii)   the parts of the employer's undertaking in which those agency workers are working; and

(iii)   the type of work those agency workers are carrying out.

13(3)   For the purposes of this regulation the appropriate representatives of any affected employees are–

(a)   if the employees are of a description in respect of which an independent trade union is recognised by their employer, representatives of the trade union; or

(b)   in any other case, whichever of the following employee representatives the employer chooses–

(i)   employee representatives appointed or elected by the affected employees otherwise than for the purposes of this regulation, who (having regard to the purposes for, and the method by which they were appointed or elected) have authority from those employees to receive information and to be consulted about the transfer on their behalf;

(ii)   employee representatives elected by any affected employees, for the purposes of this regulation, in an election satisfying the requirements of regulation 14(1).

13(4)   The transferee shall give the transferor such information at such a time as will enable the transferor to perform the duty imposed on him by virtue of paragraph (2)(d).

13(5)   The information which is to be given to the appropriate representatives shall be given to each of them by being delivered to them, or sent by post to an address notified by them to the employer, or (in the case of representatives of a trade union) sent by post to the trade union at the address of its head or main office.

13(6)   An employer of an affected employee who envisages that he will take measures in relation to an affected employee, in connection with the relevant transfer, shall consult the appropriate representatives of that employee with a view to seeking their agreement to the intended measures.

13(7)   In the course of those consultations the employer shall–

(a)   consider any representations made by the appropriate representatives; and

(b)   reply to those representations and, if he rejects any of those representations, state his reasons.

13(8) The employer shall allow the appropriate representatives access to any affected employees and shall afford to those representatives such accommodation and other facilities as may be appropriate.

13(9) If in any case there are special circumstances which render it not reasonably practicable for an employer to perform a duty imposed on him by any of paragraphs (2) to (7), he shall take all such steps towards performing that duty as are reasonably practicable in the circumstances.

13(10) Where–

(a) the employer has invited any of the affected employee to elect employee representatives; and

(b) the invitation was issued long enough before the time when the employer is required to give information under paragraph (2) to allow them to elect representatives by that time,

the employer shall be treated as complying with the requirements of this regulation in relation to those employees if he complies with those requirements as soon as is reasonably practicable after the election of the representatives.

13(11) If, after the employer has invited any affected employees to elect representatives, they fail to do so within a reasonable time, he shall give to any affected employees the information set out in paragraph (2).

13(12) The duties imposed on an employer by this regulation shall apply irrespective of whether the decision resulting in the relevant transfer is taken by the employer or a person controlling the employer.

History
Regulation 13(2A) inserted by the Agency Workers Regulations 2010 (SI 2010/93) reg.2 and Sch.2(2) para.29 as from 1 October 2011. Regulation 13(1) amended by the Collective Redundancies and Transfer of Undertakings (Protection of Employment) (Amendment) Regulations 2014 (SI 2014/16) reg.11(1). This amendment applies in relation to a TUPE transfer which takes place on or after 31 July 2014.

13A Micro-business's duty to inform and consult where no appropriate representatives

13A(1) This regulation applies if, at the time when the employer is required to give information under regulation 13(2)–

(a) the employer employs fewer than 10 employees;

(b) there are no appropriate representatives within the meaning of regulation 13(3); and

(c) the employer has not invited any of the affected employees to elect employee representatives.

13A(2) The employer may comply with regulation 13 by performing any duty which relates to appropriate representatives as if each of the affected employees were an appropriate representative.

History
Regulation 13A inserted by the Collective Redundancies and Transfer of Undertakings (Protection of Employment) (Amendment) Regulations 2014 (SI 2014/16) reg.11(2). This amendment applies in relation to a TUPE transfer which takes place on or after 31 July 2014.

14 Election of employee representatives

14(1) The requirements for the election of employee representatives under regulation 13(3) are that–

(a) the employer shall make such arrangements as are reasonably practicable to ensure that the election is fair;

(b) the employer shall determine the number of representatives to be elected so that there are sufficient representatives to represent the interests of all affected employees having regard to the number and classes of those employees;

(c)   the employer shall determine whether the affected employees should be represented either by representatives of all the affected employees or by representatives of particular classes of those employees;

(d)   before the election the employer shall determine the term of office as employee representatives so that it is of sufficient length to enable information to be given and consultations under regulation 13 to be completed;

(e)   the candidates for election as employee representatives are affected employees on the date of the election;

(f)   no affected employee is unreasonably excluded from standing for election;

(g)   all affected employees on the date of the election are entitled to vote for employee representatives;

(h)   the employees entitled to vote may vote for as many candidates as there are representatives to be elected to represent them or, if there are to be representatives for particular classes of employees, may vote for as many candidates as there are representatives to be elected to represent their particular class of employee;

(i)   the election is conducted so as to secure that–

  (i)   so far as is reasonably practicable, those voting do so in secret; and

  (ii) the votes given at the election are accurately counted.

14(2)   Where, after an election of employee representatives satisfying the requirements of paragraph (1) has been held, one of those elected ceases to act as an employee representative and as a result any affected employees are no longer represented, those employees shall elect another representative by an election satisfying the requirements of paragraph (1)(a), (e), (f) and (i).

15   Failure to inform or consult

15(1)   Where an employer has failed to comply with a requirement of regulation 13 or regulation 14, a complaint may be presented to an employment tribunal on that ground–

(a)   in the case of a failure relating to the election of employee representatives, by any of his employees who are affected employees;

(b)   in the case of any other failure relating to employee representatives, by any of the employee representatives to whom the failure related;

(c)   in the case of failure relating to representatives of a trade union, by the trade union; and

(d)   in any other case, by any of his employees who are affected employees.

15(2)   If on a complaint under paragraph (1) a question arises whether or not it was reasonably practicable for an employer to perform a particular duty or as to what steps he took towards performing it, it shall be for him to show–

(a)   that there were special circumstances which rendered it not reasonably practicable for him to perform the duty; and

(b)   that he took all such steps towards its performance as were reasonably practicable in those circumstances.

15(3)   If on a complaint under paragraph (1) a question arises as to whether or not an employee representative was an appropriate representative for the purposes of regulation 13, it shall be for the employer to show that the employee representative had the necessary authority to represent the affected employees except where the question is whether or not regulation 13A applied.

15(3A) If on a complaint under paragraph (1), a question arises as to whether or not regulation 13A applied, it is for the employer to show that the conditions in sub-paragraphs (a) and (b) of regulation 13A(1) applied at the time referred to in regulation 13A(1).

15(4) On a complaint under paragraph (1)(a) it shall be for the employer to show that the requirements in regulation 14 have been satisfied.

15(5) On a complaint against a transferor that he had failed to perform the duty imposed upon him by virtue of regulation 13(2)(d) or, so far as relating thereto, regulation 13(9), he may not show that it was not reasonably practicable for him to perform the duty in question for the reason that the transferee had failed to give him the requisite information at the requisite time in accordance with regulation 13(4) unless he gives the transferee notice of his intention to show that fact; and the giving of the notice shall make the transferee a party to the proceedings.

15(6) In relation to any complaint under paragraph (1), a failure on the part of a person controlling (directly or indirectly) the employer to provide information to the employer shall not constitute special circumstances rendering it not reasonably practicable for the employer to comply with such a requirement.

15(7) Where the tribunal finds a complaint against a transferee under paragraph (1) well-founded it shall make a declaration to that effect and may order the transferee to pay appropriate compensation to such descriptions of affected employees as may be specified in the award.

15(8) Where the tribunal finds a complaint against a transferor under paragraph (1) well-founded it shall make a declaration to that effect and may–

(a) order the transferor, subject to paragraph (9), to pay appropriate compensation to such descriptions of affected employees as may be specified in the award; or

(b) if the complaint is that the transferor did not perform the duty mentioned in paragraph (5) and the transferor (after giving due notice) shows the facts so mentioned, order the transferee to pay appropriate compensation to such descriptions of affected employees as may be specified in the award.

15(9) The transferee shall be jointly and severally liable with the transferor in respect of compensation payable under sub-paragraph (8)(a) or paragraph (11).

15(10) An employee may present a complaint to an employment tribunal on the ground that he is an employee of a description to which an order under paragraph (7) or (8) relates and that–

(a) in respect of an order under paragraph (7), the transferee has failed, wholly or in part, to pay him compensation in pursuance of the order;

(b) in respect of an order under paragraph (8), the transferor or transferee, as applicable, has failed, wholly or in part, to pay him compensation in pursuance of the order.

15(11) Where the tribunal finds a complaint under paragraph (10) well-founded it shall order the transferor or transferee as applicable to pay the complainant the amount of compensation which it finds is due to him.

15(12) An employment tribunal shall not consider a complaint under paragraph (1) or (10) unless it is presented to the tribunal before the end of the period of three months beginning with–

(a) in respect of a complaint under paragraph (1), the date on which the relevant transfer is completed; or

(b) in respect of a complaint under paragraph (10), the date of the tribunal's order under paragraph (7) or (8),

or within such further period as the tribunal considers reasonable in a case where it is satisfied that it was not reasonably practicable for the complaint to be presented before the end of the period of three months.

15(13) Regulation 16A (extension of time limits to facilitate conciliation before institution of proceedings) applies for the purposes of paragraph (12).

History
Regulation 15(3) amended and reg.15(3A) inserted by the Collective Redundancies and Transfer of Undertakings (Protection of Employment) (Amendment) Regulations 2014 (SI 2014/16) reg.11(3), (4). This amendment applies in relation to a TUPE transfer which takes place on or after 31 July 2014. Regulation 15(13) inserted by the Enterprise and Regulatory Reform Act 2013 (Consequential Amendments) (Employment) (No.2) Order 2014 (SI 2014/853) art.2(1), (3) as from 20 April 2014. This amendment applies in any case where the worker concerned complies with the requirement in the Employment Tribunals Act 1996 s.18A(1) on or after 20 April 2014.

16   Failure to inform or consult: supplemental

16(1) Section 205(1) of the 1996 Act (complaint to be sole remedy for breach of relevant rights) and sections 18A to 18C of the 1996 Tribunals Act (conciliation) shall apply to the rights conferred by regulation 15 and to proceedings under this regulation as they apply to the rights conferred by those Acts and the employment tribunal proceedings mentioned in those Acts.

16(2) An appeal shall lie and shall lie only to the Employment Appeal Tribunal on a question of law arising from any decision of, or arising in any proceedings before, an employment tribunal under or by virtue of these Regulations; and section 11(1) of the Tribunals and Inquiries Act 1992 (appeals from certain tribunals to the High Court) shall not apply in relation to any such proceedings.

16(3) "Appropriate compensation" in regulation 15 means such sum not exceeding thirteen weeks' pay for the employee in question as the tribunal considers just and equitable having regard to the seriousness of the failure of the employer to comply with his duty.

16(4) Sections 220 to 228 of the 1996 Act shall apply for calculating the amount of a week's pay for any employee for the purposes of paragraph (3) and, for the purposes of that calculation, the calculation date shall be–

(a) in the case of an employee who is dismissed by reason of redundancy (within the meaning of sections 139 and 155 of the 1996 Act) the date which is the calculation date for the purposes of any entitlement of his to a redundancy payment (within the meaning of those sections) or which would be that calculation date if he were so entitled;

(b) in the case of an employee who is dismissed for any other reason, the effective date of termination (within the meaning of sections 95(1) and (2) and 97 of the 1996 Act) of his contract of employment;

(c) in any other case, the date of the relevant transfer.

History
Regulation 16(1) amended by the Enterprise and Regulatory Reform Act 2013 (Consequential Amendments) (Employment) Order 2014 (SI 2014/386) art.2 and Sch. paras 32, 38 as from 6 April 2014.

16A   Extension of time limit to facilitate conciliation before institution of proceedings

16A(1) This regulation applies where these Regulations provide for it to apply for the purposes of a provision in these Regulations ("a relevant provision").

16A(2) In this regulation–

(a) Day A is the day on which the worker concerned complies with the requirement in subsection (1) of section 18A of the Employment Tribunals Act 1996 (requirement to contact ACAS before instituting proceedings) in relation to the matter in respect of which the proceedings are brought, and

(b)   Day B is the day on which the worker concerned receives or, if earlier, is treated as receiving (by virtue of regulations made under subsection (11) of that section) the certificate issued under subsection (4) of that section.

16A(3)   In working out when the time limit set by a relevant provision expires the period beginning with the day after Day A and ending with Day B is not to be counted.

16A(4)   If the time limit set by a relevant provision would (if not extended by this paragraph) expire during the period beginning with Day A and ending one month after Day B, the time limit expires instead at the end of that period.

16A(5)   Where an employment tribunal has power under these Regulations to extend the time limit set by a relevant provision, the power is exercisable in relation to that time limit as extended by this regulation.

History
Regulation 16A inserted by the Enterprise and Regulatory Reform Act 2013 (Consequential Amendments) (Employment) (No.2) Order 2014 (SI 2014/853) art.2(1), (4) as from 20 April 2014. This amendment applies in any case where the worker concerned complies with the requirement in the Employment Tribunals Act 1996 s.18A(1) on or after 20 April 2014.

17   Employers' Liability Compulsory Insurance

17(1)   Paragraph (2) applies where–

(a)   by virtue of section 3(1)(a) or (b) of the Employers' Liability (Compulsory Insurance) Act 1969 ("the 1969 Act"), the transferor is not required by that Act to effect any insurance; or

(b)   by virtue of section 3(1)(c) of the 1969 Act, the transferor is exempted from the requirement of that Act to effect insurance.

17(2)   Where this paragraph applies, on completion of a relevant transfer the transferor and the transferee shall be jointly and severally liable in respect of any liability referred to in section 1(1) of the 1969 Act, in so far as such liability relates to the employee's employment with the transferor.

18   Restriction on contracting out

18   Section 203 of the 1996 Act (restrictions on contracting out) shall apply in relation to these Regulations as if they were contained in that Act, save for that section shall not apply in so far as these Regulations provide for an agreement (whether a contract of employment or not) to exclude or limit the operation of these Regulations.

19   Amendment to the 1996 Act

19   In section 104 of the 1996 Act (assertion of statutory right) in subsection (4)–

(a)   the word "and" at the end of paragraph (c) is omitted; and

(b)   after paragraph (d), there is inserted–

", and

(e)   the rights conferred by the Transfer of Undertakings (Protection of Employment) Regulations 2006.".

20   Repeals, revocations and amendments

20(1)   Subject to regulation 21, the 1981 Regulations are revoked.

20(2)   Section 33 of, and paragraph 4 of Schedule 9 to, the Trade Union Reform and Employment Rights Act 1993 are repealed.

20(3)   Schedule 2 (consequential amendments) shall have effect.

21   Transitional provisions and savings

21(1)   These Regulations shall apply in relation to–

(a)   a relevant transfer that takes place on or after 6 April 2006;

(b)   a transfer or service provision change, not falling within sub-paragraph (a), that takes place on or after 6 April 2006 and is regarded by virtue of any enactment as a relevant transfer.

21(2)   The 1981 Regulations shall continue to apply in relation to–

(a)   a relevant transfer (within the meaning of the 1981 Regulations) that took place before 6 April 2006;

(b)   a transfer, not falling within sub-paragraph (a), that took place before 6 April 2006 and is regarded by virtue of any enactment as a relevant transfer (within the meaning of the 1981 Regulations).

21(3)   In respect of a relevant transfer that takes place on or after 6 April 2006, any action taken by a transferor or transferee to discharge a duty that applied to them under regulation 10 or 10A of the 1981 Regulations shall be deemed to satisfy the corresponding obligation imposed by regulations 13 and 14 of these Regulations, insofar as that action would have discharged those obligations had the action taken place on or after 6 April 2006.

21(4)   The duty on a transferor to provide a transferee with employee liability information shall not apply in the case of a relevant transfer that takes place on or before 19 April 2006.

21(5)   Regulations 13, 14, 15 and 16 shall not apply in the case of a service provision change that is not also a transfer of an undertaking, business or part of an undertaking or business that takes place on or before 4 May 2006.

21(6)   The repeal of paragraph 4 of Schedule 9 to the Trade Union Reform and Employment Rights Act 1993 does not affect the continued operation of that paragraph so far as it remains capable of having effect.

SCHEDULE 1

APPLICATION OF THE REGULATION TO NORTHERN IRELAND

[Not reproduced.]

SCHEDULE 2

CONSEQUENTIAL AMENDMENTS

[Not reproduced.]

Banks (Former Authorised Institutions) (Insolvency) Order 2006

(SI 2006/3107)

Made on 20 November 2006 by the Secretary of State under the Insolvency Act 1986 s.422, having consulted the Financial Services Authority in accordance with s.422(1). Operative from 15 December 2006.

[**Note**: Changes made by the Financial Services Act 2012 (Consequential Amendments and Transitional Provisions) Order 2013 (SI 2013/472) and the Small Business Enterprise and Employment Act 2015 (Consequential Amendments, Saving and Transitional Provisions) Regulations 2018 (SI 2018/208) have been incorporated into the text.]

1 Citation and commencement

1(1) This Order may be cited as the Banks (Former Authorised Institutions) (Insolvency) Order 2006 and shall come into force on 15th December 2006 ("the commencement date").

1(2) In this Order, "the 1986 Act" means the Insolvency Act 1986.

2 Revocation of the Banks (Administration Proceedings) Order 1989

2(1) Subject to paragraph (2), the Banks (Administration Proceedings) Order 1989 ("the 1989 Order") is revoked.

2(2) The 1989 Order shall continue in effect for the purposes of any proceedings begun before the commencement date under the first Group of Parts of the 1986 Act in relation to a former authorised institution within the meaning of Article 1A of that Order.

3 Modification of first Group of Parts of the Insolvency Act 1986 in their application to companies that are former authorised institutions

3(1) This article applies to a person of the kind mentioned in section 422(1) of the 1986 Act that is a company within the meaning of section 735(1) of the Companies Act 1985.

3(2) The first Group of Parts of the 1986 Act shall apply in relation to a person to which this article applies with the modifications set out in the Schedule to this Order.

SCHEDULE

MODIFICATIONS OF PART 2 OF THE INSOLVENCY ACT IN ITS APPLICATION TO COMPANIES THAT ARE FORMER AUTHORISED INSTITUTIONS

Article 3

1 References to a numbered paragraph in this Schedule are references to the paragraph so numbered in Schedule B1 to the Insolvency Act 1986.

2 In their application to a person falling within article 3(1), section 8 of, and Schedule B1 to, the 1986 Act shall apply subject to the modifications set out below.

3 Paragraph 9 shall apply with the omission of sub-paragraph (1).

4 For paragraph 12(1) there is substituted–

"**12.**—(1) An application to the court for an administration order in respect of a company ("an administration application") may be made only by–

(a)   the company,

(b)   the directors of the company,

(c)   one or more creditors of the company,

(d)   the Financial Conduct Authority,

(da)   the Prudential Regulation Authority,

(e)   the designated officer for a magistrates' court in exercise of the power conferred by section 87A of the Magistrates' Courts Act 1980 (c.43) (fine imposed on company), or

(f)   a combination of persons listed in paragraphs (a) to (e).

(1A) Where an administration application is made to which the Financial Conduct Authority is not a party, the applicant shall, as soon as is reasonably practicable after the making of the application, give notice of the making of the application to the Financial Conduct Authority.

(1B) Where an administration application is made to which the Prudential Regulation Authority is not a party, the applicant shall, as soon as is reasonably practicable after the making of the application, give notice of the making of the application to the Prudential Regulation Authority."

History
Paragraph 12(1) amended and para.12(1B) inserted by the Financial Services Act 2012 (Consequential Amendments and Transitional Provisions) Order 2013 (SI 2013/472) art.3 Sch.2 para.117(1)(a) as from 1 April 2013.

5   For paragraph 22 there is substituted–

"**22.**—(1) Subject as set out in this paragraph–

(a)   a company may appoint an administrator; and

(b)   the directors of a company may appoint an administrator.

(2) An administrator may not be appointed under this paragraph without the consent in writing of the Financial Conduct Authority and the Prudential Regulation Authority.

(3) The written consent under paragraph (2) must be filed in court–

(a)   at the same time that any notice of intention to appoint under paragraph 26 is filed in court pursuant to paragraph 27; or,

(b)   where no such notice of intention to appoint is required to be given, at the same time that notice of appointment is filed under paragraph 29.".

6   After paragraph 91 there is inserted–

"**91A.** Where the administrator was appointed by administration order, the court may replace the administrator on an application under this paragraph made by the Financial Conduct Authority or the Prudential Regulation Authority.

91B. Where the administrator was appointed otherwise than by administration order any replacement administrator may only be appointed with the consent of the Financial Conduct Authority or the Prudential Regulation Authority.".

7   After paragraph 116 there is inserted–

Miscellaneous—Powers of the Financial Conduct Authority and Prudential Regulation Authority

"**117.**—(1) [Omitted]

(2) The Financial Conduct Authority and the Prudential Regulation Authority is entitled to be heard at the hearing of an administration application or at any other court hearing in relation to the company pursuant to any provision of Schedule B1.

(3) Any notice or other document required to be sent to a creditor of the company must also be sent to the Financial Conduct Authority and the Prudential Regulation Authority.

(4) The Financial Conduct Authority or the Prudential Regulation Authority may apply to the court under paragraph 74 and in such a case paragraphs 74(1)(a) and 74(1)(b) shall have effect as if for the words "harm the interests of the applicant (whether alone or in common with some or all other members or creditors)" there were substituted the words "harm the interests of some or all members or creditors".

(4A) The Financial Conduct Authority and the Prudential Regulation Authority are entitled to participate (but not vote) in a qualifying decision procedure by which a decision about any matter is sought from the creditors of the company.

(5) A person appointed for the purpose by the Financial Conduct Authority or the Prudential Regulation Authority is entitled–

  (a)   to attend any meeting of creditors of the company summoned under this Act;

  (b)   to attend any meeting of a committee established under paragraph 57; and

  (c)   to make representations as to any matter for decision at such a meeting."

History
Paragraph 117(1) omitted and heading and para.117(2)–(5) amended by the Financial Services Act 2012 (Consequential Amendments and Transitional Provisions) Order 2013 (SI 2013/472) art.3 Sch.2 para.117(1)(d) as from 1 April 2013. Paragraph 117(4A) was inserted by the Small Business, Enterprise and Employment Act 2015 (Consequential Amendments, Savings and Transitional Provisions) Regulations 2018 (SI 2018/208) reg.11(a) with effect from 13 March 2018.

8   Where this Schedule applies in relation to the administration in Scotland of a person referred to in article 3(1), paragraph 117 of Schedule B1 (treated as inserted by paragraph 7) has effect as if sub-paragraph (4A) were omitted.

History
Paragraph 8 was inserted by the Small Business, Enterprise and Employment Act 2015 (Consequential Amendments, Savings and Transitional Provisions) Regulations 2018 (SI 2018/208) reg.11(b) with effect from 13 March 2018.

Non-Domestic Rating (Unoccupied Property) (England) Regulations 2008

(SI 2008/386)

Made on 18 February 2008 by the Secretary of State under the Local Government Finance Act 1988 ss.45(1)(d), (9) and (10), 143(2) and 146(6). Effective 1 April 2008.

[**Note**: Changes made by the Non-Domestic Rating (Unoccupied Property) (England) (Amendment) Regulations 2010 (SI 2010/408) and the Deregulation Act 2015 (Insolvency) (Consequential Amendments and Transitional and Savings Provisions) Order 2015 (SI 2015/1641) have been incorporated into the text.

Comparable legislation for Scotland is to be found in the Non-domestic Rating (Unoccupied Property) (Scotland) Regulations 1994 (SI 1994/3200) (as amended by SSI 2008/83 and SSI 2014/31) which, for reasons of space, are not reproduced in this work. For Wales, see below, p.1183.]

1 Citation, application and commencement

1 These Regulations, which apply in relation to England only, may be cited as the Non-Domestic Rating (Unoccupied Property) (England) Regulations 2008 and shall come into force on 1st April 2008.

2 Interpretation

2 In these Regulations–

"qualifying industrial hereditament" means any hereditament other than a retail hereditament in relation to which all buildings comprised in the hereditament are–

(a) constructed or adapted for use in the course of a trade or business; and

(b) constructed or adapted for use for one or more of the following purposes, or one or more such purposes and one or more purposes ancillary thereto–

    (i) the manufacture, repair or adaptation of goods or materials, or the subjection of goods or materials to any process;

    (ii) storage (including the storage or handling of goods in the course of their distribution);

    (iii) the working or processing of minerals; and

    (iv) the generation of electricity;

"relevant non-domestic hereditament" means any non-domestic hereditament consisting of, or of part of, any building, together with any land ordinarily used or intended for use for the purposes of the building or part;

"retail hereditament" means any hereditament where any building or part of a building comprised in the hereditament is constructed or adapted for the purpose of the retail provision of–

(a) goods, or

(b) services, other than storage for distribution services, where the services are to be provided on or from the hereditament; and

"the Act" means the Local Government Finance Act 1988.

3 Hereditaments prescribed for the purposes of section 45(1)(d) of the Act

3 The class of non-domestic hereditaments prescribed for the purposes of section 45(1)(d) of the Act consists of all relevant non-domestic hereditaments other than those described in regulation 4.

4   Hereditaments not prescribed for the purposes of section 45(1)(d) of the Act

4   The relevant non-domestic hereditaments described in this regulation are any hereditament–

(a)   which, subject to regulation 5, has been unoccupied for a continuous period not exceeding three months;

(b)   which is a qualifying industrial hereditament that, subject to regulation 5, has been unoccupied for a continuous period not exceeding six months;

(c)   whose owner is prohibited by law from occupying it or allowing it to be occupied;

(d)   which is kept vacant by reason of action taken by or on behalf of the Crown or any local or public authority with a view to prohibiting the occupation of the hereditament or to acquiring it;

(e)   which is the subject of a building preservation notice within the meaning of the Planning (Listed Buildings and Conservation Areas) Act 1990 or is included in a list compiled under section 1 of that Act;

(f)   which is included in the Schedule of monuments compiled under section 1 of the Ancient Monuments and Archaeological Areas Act 1979;

(g)   whose rateable value is less than £2,600 [but see note below];

(h)   whose owner is entitled to possession only in his capacity as the personal representative of a deceased person;

(i)   where, in respect of the owner's estate, there subsists a bankruptcy order within the meaning of section 381(2) of the Insolvency Act 1986;

(j)   [Revoked]

(k)   whose owner is a company which is subject to a winding-up order made under the Insolvency Act 1986 or which is being wound up voluntarily under that Act;

(l)   whose owner is a company in administration within the meaning of paragraph 1 of Schedule B1 to the Insolvency Act 1986 or is subject to an administration order made under the former administration provisions within the meaning of article 3 of the Enterprise Act 2002 (Commencement No. 4 and Transitional Provisions and Savings) Order 2003;

(m)   whose owner is entitled to possession of the hereditament in his capacity as liquidator by virtue of an order made under section 112 or section 145 of the Insolvency Act 1986.

History
Regulation 4(g) amended by the Non-Domestic Rating (Unoccupied Property) (England) (Amendment) Regulations 2010 (SI 2010/408) reg.2(2)(a) as from 1 April 2010. Note however that in relation to the financial year beginning on 1 April 2010 the figure "£18,000" is substituted for "£2,600" (reg.2(2)(b)). Regulation 4(j) revoked by the Deregulation Act 2015 (Insolvency) (Consequential Amendments and Transitional and Savings Provisions) Order 2015 (SI 2015/1641) Sch.3 para.3(8) as from 1 October 2015.

5   Continuous occupation

5   A hereditament which has been unoccupied and becomes occupied on any day shall be treated as having been continuously unoccupied for the purposes of regulation 4(a) and (b) if it becomes unoccupied again on the expiration of a period of less than six weeks beginning with that day.

6   Hereditaments not previously occupied

6   For the purposes of regulation 4(a) and (b), a hereditament which has not previously been occupied shall be treated as becoming unoccupied–

(a)   on the day determined under paragraph 8 of Schedule 1 to the General Rate Act 1967, or on the day determined under Schedule 4A to the Act, whichever day first occurs; or

(b)   where paragraph (a) does not apply, on the day for which the hereditament is first shown in a local rating list.

7   Revocation and saving

7(1)   Subject to paragraph (2), the Non-Domestic Rating (Unoccupied Property) Regulations 1989 are revoked in their application to England.

7(2)   Those Regulations shall continue to apply for the purposes of calculating liability for rates in respect of financial years beginning before 1st April 2008.

Civil Proceedings Fees Order 2008

(SI 2008/1053 (L.5))

Made on 7 April 2008 by the Lord Chancellor, with the consent and sanction of the Treasury under the Courts Act 2003 s.92 and the Insolvency Act 1986 ss.414 and 415. Operative from 1 May 2008.

[**Note**: Changes made by the Civil Proceedings Fees (Amendment) Order 2008 (SI 2008/2853 (L.19)), the Civil Proceedings Fees (Amendment) Order 2009 (SI 2009/1498 (L.15)), the Civil Proceedings Fees (Amendment) Order 2011 (SI 2011/586 (L.2)), the Courts and Tribunals Fees (Miscellaneous Amendments) Order 2014 (SI 2014/590), and the Civil Proceedings Fees (Amendment) Order 2014 (SI 2014/874 (L.17)), the Civil Proceedings, First-tier Tribunal, Upper Tribunal and Employment Tribunals Fees (Amendment) Order 2016 (SI 2016/807), the Insolvency Amendment (EU 2015/848) Regulations 2017 (SI 2017/702) and the Court of Protection, Civil Proceedings and Magistrates' Courts Fees (Amendment) Order 2018 (SI 2018/812) have been incorporated into the text.]

1 Citation and commencement

1(1) This Order may be cited as the Civil Proceedings Fees Order 2008 and shall come into force on 1st May 2008.

1(2) In this Order–

(a) "CCBC" means County Court Business Centre;

(b) "the CPR" means the Civil Procedure Rules 1998;

(c) "LSC" means the Legal Services Commission established under section 1 of the Access to Justice Act 1999;

(d) expressions also used in the CPR have the same meaning as in those Rules.

2 Fees payable

2 The fees set out in column 2 of Schedule 1 are payable in the Senior Courts of England and Wales and in the County Court in respect of the items described in column 1 in accordance with and subject to the directions specified in that column.

SCHEDULE 1

Article 2

FEES TO BE TAKEN

Column 1	Column 2
Number and description of fee	Amount of fee
3 Companies Act 1985, Companies Act 2006 and Insolvency Act 1986 (High Court and County Court)	
3.1 On entering a bankruptcy petition:	
(a) if presented by a debtor or the personal representative of a deceased debtor;	£180
(b) if presented by a creditor or other person.	£280

1012

Column 1	Column 2
Number and description of fee	Amount of fee
3.2 On entering a petition for an administration order.	£280
3.3 On entering any other petition.	£280
One fee only is payable where more than one petition is presented in relation to a partnership.	
3.4(a) On a request for a certificate of discharge from bankruptcy;	£70
3.4(b) after the first certificate, for each copy.	£10
3.5 On an application under the Companies Act 1985, the Companies Act 2006 or the Insolvency Act 1986 other than one brought by petition and where no other fee is specified.	£280
Fee 3.5 is not payable where the application is made in existing proceedings.	
3.6 On the conversion of insolvency proceedings into a different type of insolvency proceedings under Article 51 of Regulation (EU) 2015/848 of the European Parliament and of the Council	£160
3.7 On an application, for the purposes of Regulation (EU) 2015/848 of the European Parliament and of the Council, for an order confirming creditors' voluntary winding up (where the company has passed a resolution for voluntary winding up, and no declaration under section 89 of the Insolvency Act 1986 has been made).	£50
3.8 On filing:	£50
• a notice of intention to appoint an administrator under paragraph 14 of Schedule B1 to the Insolvency Act 1986 or in accordance with paragraph 27 of that Schedule; or	
• a notice of appointment of an administrator in accordance with paragraphs 18 or 29 of that Schedule.	
Where a person pays fee 3.8 on filing a notice of intention to appoint an administrator, no fee is payable on that same person filing a notice of appointment of that administrator.	
3.9 On submitting a nominee's report under section 2(2) of the Insolvency Act 1986.	£50
3.10 On filing documents in accordance with paragraph 7(1) of Schedule A1 to the Insolvency Act 1986.	£50

Column 1	*Column 2*
Number and description of fee	Amount of fee
3.11 On an application by consent or without notice within existing proceedings where no other fee is specified.	£25
3.12 On an application with notice within existing proceedings where no other fee is specified.	£95
3.13 On a search in person of the bankruptcy and companies records, in the County Court.	£45
Requests and applications with no fee:	
No fee is payable on a request or on an application to the Court by the Official Receiver when applying only in the capacity of Official Receiver to the case (and not as trustee or liquidator), or on an application to set aside a statutory demand.	
7 Enforcement in the High Court	
7.1. On sealing a writ of control/possession/delivery.	£66
Where the recovery of a sum of money is sought in addition to a writ of possession and delivery, no further fee is payable.	
7.2 On an application for an order requiring a judgment debtor or other person to attend court to provide information in connection with enforcement of a judgment or order.	£55
7.3(a) On an application for a third party debt order or the appointment of a receiver by way of equitable execution.	£110
Fee 7.3(a) is payable in respect of each third party against whom the order is sought.	
7.3(b) On an application for a charging order.	£110
Fee 7.3(b) is payable in respect of each charging order applied for.	
7.4 On an application for a judgment summons.	£110
7.5 On a request or application to register a judgment or order, or for permission to enforce an arbitration award, or for a certificate or a certified copy of a judgment or order for use abroad.	£66

Column 1	Column 2
Number and description of fee	Amount of fee
8 Enforcement in the County Court	
8.1 On an application for or in relation to enforcement of a judgment or order of the County Court or through the County Court, by the issue of a warrant of control against goods except a warrant to enforce payment of a fine:	
(a) in CCBC cases or cases in which a warrant of control is requested in accordance with paragraph 11.2 of Practice Direction 7E to the Civil Procedure Rules (Money Claim OnLine cases);	£77
(b) in any other case.	£110
8.2 On a request for a further attempt at execution of a warrant at a new address following a notice of the reason for non-execution (except a further attempt following suspension and CCBC cases brought by Centre users).	£33
8.3 On an application for an order requiring a judgment debtor or other person to attend court to provide information in connection with enforcement of a judgment or order.	£55
8.4(a) On an application for a third party debt order or the appointment of a receiver by way of equitable execution.	£110
Fee 8.4(a) is payable in respect of each third party against whom the order is sought.	
8.4(b) On an application for a charging order.	£110
Fee 8.4(b) is payable in respect of each charging order applied for.	
8.5 On an application for a judgment summons.	£110
8.6 On the issue of a warrant of possession or a warrant of delivery.	£121
Where the recovery of a sum of money is sought in addition, no further fee is payable.	
8.7 On an application for an attachment of earnings order (other than a consolidated attachment of earnings order) to secure payment of a judgment debt.	£110
Fee 8.7 is payable for each defendant against whom an order is sought.	
Fee 8.7 is not payable where the attachment of earnings order is made on the hearing of a judgment summons.	

Column 1	Column 2
Number and description of fee	Amount of fee
8.8 On a consolidated attachment of earnings order or on an administration order.	For every £1 or part of a £1 of the money paid into court in respect of debts due to creditors—10p

Fee 8.8 is calculated on any money paid into court under any order at the rate in force at the time when the order was made (or, where the order has been amended, at the time of the last amendment before the date of payment).

FEES PAYABLE IN HIGH COURT ONLY

10 Miscellaneous proceedings or matters

Searches

10.3 On a search in person of the court's records, including inspection, for each 15 minutes or part of 15 minutes.	£11

History

Amendments made in respect of fees 7.3(b), 8.1 and 8.4(b) by the Civil Proceedings Fees (Amendment) Order 2008 (SI 2008/2853 (L.19)) arts 2–5, as from 26 November 2008. Amendments made in respect of fees 8.1, 8.3–8.5, 8.7 by the Civil Proceedings Fees (Amendment) Order 2009 (SI 2009/1498 (L.15)) art.11–16 as from 13 July 2009. Amendments made in respect of fees 3.1–3.13, 7.1, 7.5, 8.2, 8.6, 10.3 by the Civil Proceedings Fees (Amendment) Order 2011 (SI 2011/586 (L.2)) Sch. as from 4 April 2011. Amendments made to arts 1 and 2 and in respect of fees 3.3, 3.4(b), 3.5–3.13, 7.1, 8.1, 10.3 by the Civil Proceedings Fees (Amendment) Order 2014 (SI 2014/874 (L.17)) art.2(5) and Sch. as from 22 April 2014. Amendments made in respect of fees 7.1 and 8.1 by the Courts and Tribunals Fees (Miscellaneous Amendments) Order 2014 (SI 2014/590) art.4(1), (2) as from 6 April 2014. Amendments made in respect of fee 3.5 by the Civil Proceedings Fees (Amendment No.2) Order 2014 (SI 2014/1834 (L.27)) art.3(a) as from 4 August 2014. Amendments made in respect of fee 8.1 by the Civil Proceedings Fees (Amendment No.3) Order 2014 (SI 2014/2059) art.2 as from 4 August 2014. Amendments made in respect of fees 8.1–8.7 and 10.3 by the Civil Proceedings, First-tier Tribunal, Upper Tribunal and Employment Tribunals Fees (Amendment) Order 2016 (SI 2016/807) art.3(9), (11) as from 25 July 2016. Amendments made in respect of fees 3.6 and 3.7 by the Insolvency Amendment (EU 2015/848) Regulations 2017 (SI 2017/702) regs 1, 2(1), Sch. para.54 in relation to proceedings opened on or after 26 June 2017 (see reg.3) when the Recast EU Regulation 2015/848 came into force. Amendments made in respect of fees 3.11 and 3.12 by the Court of Protection, Civil Proceedings and Magistrates' Courts Fees (Amendment) Order 2018 (SI 2018/812) regs 1, 3(1)–(3) as from 25 July 2018.

Non-Domestic Rating (Unoccupied Property) (Wales) Regulations 2008

SI 2008/2499 (W.217)

Made on 20 September 2008 by the Welsh Ministers in exercise of the powers conferred on the Secretary of State by the Local Government Finance Act 1988 and now vested in them. Effective 1 November 2008.

[**Note**: changes made by the Non-Domestic Rating (Unoccupied Property) (Wales) (Amendment) Regulations 2009 (SI 2009/272) and Non-Domestic Rating (Unoccupied Property) (Wales) (Amendment) Regulations 2011 (SI 2011/197) and the Deregulation Act 2015 (Insolvency) (Consequential Amendments and Transitional and Savings Provisions) Order 2015 (SI 2015/1641) have been incorporated into the text.]

1   Title, application and commencement

1(1)   The title of these Regulations is The Non-Domestic Rating (Unoccupied Property) (Wales) Regulations 2008 and they come into force on 1 November 2008.

1(2)   These Regulations apply in relation to Wales.

2   Interpretation

2   In these Regulations–

"the Act" ("*y Ddeddf*") means the Local Government Finance Act 1988;

"qualifying industrial hereditament" ("*hereditament diwydiannol cymwys*") means any hereditament, other than a retail hereditament, in relation to which all buildings comprised in the hereditament are–

(a)   constructed or adapted for use in the course of a trade or business; and

(b)   constructed or adapted for use for one or more of the following purposes, or one or more such purposes and one or more purposes ancillary thereto–

  (i)   the manufacture, repair or adaptation of goods or materials, or the subjection of goods or materials to any process;

  (ii)   storage (including the storage or handling of goods in the course of their distribution);

  (iii)   the working or processing of minerals; and

  (iv)   the generation of electricity;

"relevant non-domestic hereditament" ("*hereditament annomestig perthnasol*") means any non-domestic hereditament consisting of, or of part of, any building, together with any land ordinarily used or intended for use for the purposes of the building or part; and

"retail hereditament" ("*hereditament masnachol*") means any hereditament where any building or part of a building comprised in the hereditament is constructed or adapted for the purpose of the retail provision of–

(a)   goods, or

(b)   services, other than storage for distribution services, where the services are to be provided on or from the hereditament.

3   Hereditaments prescribed for the purposes of section 45(1)(d) of the Act

3   The class of non-domestic hereditaments prescribed for the purposes of section 45(1)(d) of the Act consists of all relevant non-domestic hereditaments other than those described in regulation 4.

4   Hereditaments not prescribed for the purposes of section 45(1)(d) of the Act

4   The relevant non-domestic hereditaments described in this regulation are any hereditament–

(a)   the whole of which, subject to regulation 5, has been unoccupied for a continuous period not exceeding three months;

(b)   which is a qualifying industrial hereditament and the whole of which, subject to regulation 5, has been unoccupied for a continuous period not exceeding six months;

(c)   whose owner is prohibited by law from occupying it or allowing it to be occupied;

(d)   which is kept vacant by reason of action taken by or on behalf of the Crown or any local or public authority with a view to prohibiting the occupation of the hereditament or to acquiring it;

(e)   which is the subject of a building preservation notice within the meaning of the Planning (Listed Buildings and Conservation Areas) Act 1990 or is included in a list compiled under section 1 of that Act;

(f)   which is included in the Schedule of monuments compiled under section 1 of the Ancient Monuments and Archaeological Areas Act 1979;

(g)   whose rateable value is less than–

    (i)   in relation to the financial year beginning on 1st April 2008, £2,200;

    (ii)   in relation to the financial year beginning on 1st April 2009, £15,000;

    (iii)   in relation to the financial year beginning on 1st April 2010, £18,000;

    (iv)   in relation to the financial years beginning on 1st April 2011, 1st April 2012, 1st April 2013, 1st April 2014, 1st April 2015 and 1st April 2016, £2,600;

    (v)   in relation to financial years beginning on or after 1st April 2017, £2,900;

(h)   whose owner is entitled to possession only in his or her capacity as the personal representative of a deceased person;

(i)   where, in respect of the owner's estate, there subsists a bankruptcy order within the meaning of section 381(2) of the Insolvency Act 1986;

(j)   [Revoked]

(k)   whose owner is a company which is subject to a winding-up order made under the Insolvency Act 1986 or which is being wound up voluntarily under that Act;

(l)   whose owner is a company in administration within the meaning of paragraph 1 of Schedule B1 to the Insolvency Act 1986 or is subject to an administration order made under the former administration provisions within the meaning of article 3 of the Enterprise Act 2002 (Commencement No. 4 and Transitional Provisions and Savings) Order 2003;

(m)   whose owner is entitled to possession in his or her capacity as liquidator by virtue of an order made under section 112 or section 145 of the Insolvency Act 1986.

History
Regulation 4(g) amended (in relation to the financial year beginning with 1 April 2010) by the Non-Domestic Rating (Unoccupied Property) (Wales) (Amendment) Regulations 2009 (SI 2009/272 (W.27)) reg.2 as from 7 March 2009. The figure "£2,600" substituted for £18,000" by the Non-Domestic Rating (Unoccupied Property) (Wales) (Amendment) Regulations 2011 (SI 2011/197) reg.2 as from 1 April 2011. Regulation 4(j) revoked by the Deregulation Act 2015 (Insolvency) (Consequential Amendments and Transitional and Savings Provisions) Order 2015 (SI 2015/1641) Sch.3 para.3(9) as from 1 October 2015.

    Regulation 4(g) substituted by the Non-Domestic Rating (Reliefs, Thresholds and Amendment) (England) Order 2017 (SI 2017/102) art.4(2) as from 3 March 2017.

5 Continuous occupation

5 A hereditament which has been unoccupied and becomes occupied on any day is to be treated as having been continuously unoccupied for the purposes of regulation 4(a) and (b) if it becomes unoccupied again on the expiration of a period of less than six weeks beginning with that day.

6 Hereditaments not previously occupied

6 For the purposes of regulation 4(a) and (b), a hereditament which has not previously been occupied is to be treated as becoming unoccupied–

  (a) on the day determined under paragraph 8 of Schedule 1 to the General Rate Act 1967, or on the day determined under Schedule 4A to the Act, whichever day first occurs; or

  (b) where paragraph (a) does not apply, on the day for which the hereditament is first shown in a local rating list.

7 Revocation and saving

7(1) Subject to paragraph (2), the Non-Domestic Rating (Unoccupied Property) Regulations 1989 are revoked in their application to Wales.

7(2) Those Regulations continue to apply for the purposes of calculating liability for rates in respect of any day before 1 November 2008.

Overseas Companies Regulations 2009

(SI 2009/1801)

Made on 8 July 2009 by the Secretary of State in exercise of the powers conferred by various sections of the Companies Act 2006. Operative from 1 October 2009.

68   Application of Part

68   This Part applies to an overseas company that has one or more UK establishments.

69   Return in case of winding up

69(1)   Where a company to which this Part applies is being wound up, it must deliver to the registrar a return containing the following particulars–

(a)   the company's name;

(b)   whether the company is being wound up by an order of a court and if so, the name and address of the court and the date of the order;

(c)   if the company is not being so wound up, as a result of what action the winding up has commenced;

(d)   whether the winding up has been instigated by–

    (i)   the company's members,

    (ii)   the company's creditors, or

    (iii)   some other person (stating the person's identity); and

(e)   the date on which the winding up became or will become effective.

69(2)   The return must be delivered not later than–

(a)   if the winding up began before the company had a UK establishment, one month after the company first opens a UK establishment;

(b)   if the winding up begins when the company has a UK establishment, 14 days after the date on which the winding up begins.

69(3)   Where the company has more than one UK establishment the obligation to deliver a return under this regulation applies in respect of each of them, but a return giving the registered numbers of more than one UK establishment is regarded as a return in respect of each establishment whose number is given.

69(4)   No return is required under this regulation in respect of winding up under the Insolvency Act 1986 or the Insolvency (Northern Ireland) Order 1989.

70   Returns to be made by liquidator

70(1)   A person appointed to be the liquidator of a company to which this Part applies must deliver to the registrar a return containing the following particulars–

(a)   their name and address,

(b)   date of the appointment, and

(c)   a description of such of the person's powers, if any, as are derived otherwise than from the general law or the company's constitution.

70(2)   The period allowed for delivery of the return required by paragraph (1) is–

(a)   if the liquidator was appointed before the company had a UK establishment (and continues in office at the date of the opening), one month after the company first opens a UK establishment;

(b)   if the liquidator is appointed when the company has a UK establishment, 14 days after the date of the appointment.

70(3)   The liquidator of a company to which this Part applies must–

(a)   on the termination of the winding up of the company, deliver a return to the registrar stating the name of the company and the date on which the winding up terminated;

(b)   on the company ceasing to be registered in circumstances where ceasing to be registered is an event of legal significance, deliver a return to the registrar stating the name of the company and the date on which it ceased to be registered.

70(4)   The period allowed for delivery of the return required by paragraph (3)(a) or (b) is 14 days from the date of the event.

70(5)   Where the company has more than one UK establishment the obligation to deliver a return under this regulation applies in respect of each of them, but a return giving the registered numbers of more than one UK establishment is regarded as a return in respect of each establishment whose number is given.

70(6)   No return is required under this regulation in respect of a liquidator appointed under the Insolvency Act 1986 or the Insolvency (Northern Ireland) Order 1989.

71   Return in case of insolvency proceedings etc (other than winding up)

71(1)   Where a company to which this Part applies becomes subject to insolvency proceedings or an arrangement or composition or any analogous proceedings (other than proceedings for winding up of the company), it must deliver to the registrar a return containing the following particulars–

(a)   the company's name;

(b)   whether the proceedings are by an order of a court and if so, the name and address of the court and the date of the order;

(c)   if the proceedings are not by an order of a court, as a result of what action the proceedings have been commenced;

(d)   whether the proceedings have been commenced by–

(i)   the company's members,

(ii)   the company's creditors, or

(iii)   some other person (giving the person's identity);

(e)   the date on which the proceedings became or will become effective.

71(2)   The period allowed for delivery of the return required by paragraph (1) is–

(a)   if the company became subject to the proceedings before it had a UK establishment, one month after the company first opens a UK establishment;

(b)   if the company becomes subject to the proceedings when it has a UK establishment,

14 days from the date on which it becomes subject to the proceedings.

71(3)   Where a company to which this Part applies ceases to be subject to any of the proceedings referred to in paragraph (1) it must deliver to the registrar a return stating–

(a)   the company's name, and

(b)   the date on which it ceased to be subject to the proceedings.

71(4)   The period allowed for delivery of the return required by paragraph (3) is 14 days from the date on which it ceases to be subject to the proceedings.

71(5)   Where the company has more than one UK establishment the obligation to deliver a return under this regulation applies in respect of each of them, but a return giving the registered numbers of more than one UK establishment is regarded as a return in respect of each establishment whose number is given.

71(6)   No return is required under this regulation in respect of–

(a)   a company's becoming or ceasing to be subject to a voluntary arrangement under Part 1 of the Insolvency Act 1986 or Part 2 of the Insolvency (Northern Ireland) Order 1989, or

(b)   a company's entering administration under Part 2 and Schedule B1 of that Act or becoming or ceasing to be subject to an administration order under Part 3 of that Order.

72   Penalties for non-compliance

72(1)   If a company fails to comply with regulation 69(1) or 71(1) or (3) within the period allowed for compliance, an offence is committed by–

(a)   the company, and

(b)   every person who immediately before the end of that period was a director of the company.

72(2)   A liquidator who fails to comply with regulation 70(1) or (3)(a) or (b) within the period allowed for compliance commits an offence.

72(3)   A person who takes all reasonable steps to secure compliance with the requirements concerned does not commit an offence under this regulation.

72(4)   A person guilty of an offence under this regulation is liable–

(a)   on conviction on indictment, to a fine;

(b)   on summary conviction to a fine not exceeding the statutory maximum and, for continued contravention, a daily default fine not exceeding one-fiftieth of the statutory maximum.

73   Notice of appointment of judicial factor

73(1)   Notice must be given to the registrar of the appointment in relation to a company to which this Part applies of a judicial factor (in Scotland).

73(2)   The notice must be given by the judicial factor.

73(3)   The notice must specify an address at which service of documents (including legal process) may be effected on the judicial factor.

73(4)   Notice of a change in the address for service may be given to the registrar by the judicial factor.

73(5)   A judicial factor who has notified the registrar of the appointment must also notify the registrar of the termination of the appointment.

74 Offence of failure to give notice

74(1) A judicial factor who fails to give notice of the appointment in accordance with regulation 73 within the period of 14 days after the appointment commits an offence.

74(2) A person guilty of an offence under this regulation is liable on summary conviction to–

(a) a fine not exceeding level 5 on the standard scale, and

(b) for continued contravention, a daily default fine not exceeding one-tenth of level 5 on the standard scale.

Debt Relief Orders (Designation of Competent Authorities) Regulations 2009

(SI 2009/457)

Made on 2 March 2009 by the Secretary of State in exercise of the powers conferred by the Insolvency Act 1986 s.251U(4). Effective 6 April 2009.

[**Note:** Changes made by the Debt Relief Orders (Designation of Competent Authorities) (Amendment) Regulations 2009 (SI 2009/1553) have been incorporated into the text.]

1 Citation, commencement and interpretation

These Regulations may be cited as the Debt Relief Orders (Designation of Competent Authorities) Regulations and come into force on 6th April 2009.

2 "The Act" means the Insolvency Act 1986.

PART I

COMPETENT AUTHORITIES

3 Designated competent authorities

3(1) The Secretary of State may designate a body which appears to him to fall within paragraph (2) to be a competent authority for the purposes of granting approvals under section 251U of the Act.

3(2) A body may be designated by the Secretary of State if–

(a) it makes an application to the Secretary of State to be designated as a competent authority in accordance with the Act and these Regulations;

(b) it provides or ensures–

    (i) the provision of debt management or debt counselling services through intermediaries, and

    (ii) the provision to those intermediaries of education, training and development (including continuing education, training and development) in debt management or debt counselling services, and

(c) it appears to the Secretary of State that it is a fit and proper body to approve individuals to act as intermediaries between a person wishing to make an application for a debt relief order and the official receiver.

4 Application for designation as a competent authority

4(1) An application by a body ("the applicant body") for designation as a competent authority for the purposes of granting approvals under section 251U of the Act ("the application") shall be made to the Secretary of State in writing and contain–

(a) the applicant body's full name;

(b) the address of its registered office or, if it has no registered office, the address of its centre of administration or principal place of business;

(c) its registered number (if any);

(d)   if registered outside the United Kingdom, the state in which it is registered and the place where the register is maintained;

(e)   if not registered, the nature of the applicant body;

(f)   a copy of its constitution;

(g)   if a charitable body, the objects or purposes of the charity (if not set out in the constitution) and–

   (i)   if registered as a charity, its registered number as such and (if registered outside the United Kingdom) the state in which it is registered and the place where the register is maintained, or,

   (ii)   if not registered as a charity, reasons why it is not so registered;

(h)   a description of the applicant body's current occupation or activities;

(i)   reasons why the applicant body should be considered for designation;

(j)   a copy of its most recent–

   (i)   audited accounts and balance sheet, and

   (ii)   other statutorily required report, if any;

(k)   a statement of the sources of the applicant body's income over the past 24 months and of its assets and liabilities not earlier than 12 months before the day on which the application is made;

(l)   details of the nature of the applicant body's connection with the provision of debt management or debt counselling services to the public;

(m)   details of existing or proposed education, training and development programmes which are, or which are to be, made available to individuals who are to be approved as, or who are acting as, approved intermediaries;

(n)   a description and explanation of–

   (i)   the procedure which the applicant body proposes to adopt for the approval of individuals to act as intermediaries;

   (ii)   the manner in which the applicant body will ensure that individuals meet the conditions set out in these Regulations subject to compliance with which an intermediary may be approved;

   (iii)   any additional criteria which the applicant body proposes to adopt against which it will assess the competence of individuals to act as intermediaries;

(o)   an undertaking on the part of the applicant body that–

   (i)   it will not grant approval to individuals to act as intermediaries except as provided in these Regulations;

   (ii)   it will withdraw approvals of individuals to act as intermediaries as provided in these Regulations; and

   (iii)   it will adopt an accessible, effective, fair and transparent procedure for dealing with complaints about its functions as a competent authority, including complaints about–

      (aa)   any intermediary approved by it, or

      (bb)   the activities of any such intermediary;

(p)   details of the procedures referred to in subparagraph (o)(iii) and how and to what extent they are or will be published;

(q) a statement that such procedures will include the giving of notice to any complainant to the applicant body under subparagraph (o)(iii) that, if dissatisfied with the applicant body's response to the complaint, the complainant may refer the complaint and the response to the Secretary of State;

(r) details of any consumer credit licence and public liability or indemnity insurance which the applicant body holds;

(s) if the applicant body holds a consumer credit licence, whether it provides cover for persons approved by it to act as, and in the course of acting as such intermediaries.

4(2) The application may be accompanied by further information in support of the application;

and the Secretary of State may request the applicant body to supply further information or evidence.

5   Fit and proper body

5(1) A body may not be designated a competent authority unless it is a fit and proper body to act as such.

5(2) Without prejudice to the generality of paragraph (1), a body is not a fit and proper body qualified to act as a competent authority if it–

(a) has committed any offence under any enactment contained in insolvency legislation;

(b) has engaged in any deceitful or oppressive or otherwise unfair or improper practices, whether unlawful or not, or any practices which otherwise cast doubt upon the probity of the body; or

(c) has not carried on its activities with integrity and the skills appropriate to the proper performance of the duties of–

(i) a body which purports to ensure the provision of, or to provide, debt management or debt counselling services to the public, or

(ii) a competent authority; or

(d) has entered into a company voluntary arrangement under Part 1 of the Act.

6   Extent of designation

6 The Secretary of State shall designate a competent authority by sending to the applicant body a letter of designation which shall contain–

(a) a statement that the applicant body as competent authority is designated to approve persons of any description ("unlimited designation"), or

(b) a statement that the applicant body as competent authority is designated to approve persons only of a particular description ("limited designation") and the description of person to which the designation is limited.

7   Withdrawal of designation as competent authority

7(1) The Secretary of State may at any time–

(a) modify or withdraw an existing designation where a competent authority so requests or with its consent, or

(b) withdraw an existing designation where it appears to the Secretary of State that a body–

(i) is not or is no longer a fit and proper body to act as a competent authority;

(ii) has failed to comply with any provision of Part 7A of the Act or any rules, regulations or order made under it, including any failure to approve an intermediary, or failure to withdraw approval of an intermediary, in accordance with these regulations;

(iii) has furnished the Secretary of State with any false, inaccurate or misleading information.

7(2) The Secretary of State may from time to time request a competent authority to supply such information or evidence about–

(a) itself and its activities as a competent authority, or

(b) any intermediary appointed by it or the activities of any such intermediary,

as may be required by him or her for the purpose of ensuring that the requirements of these regulations are being met.

PART II

APPROVAL OF INTERMEDIARIES

8 Approval by competent authority

8(1) A competent authority may approve an individual to act as an intermediary between a person wishing to make an application for a debt relief order and the official receiver subject as follows.

8(2) An individual may be approved–

(a) if the individual makes an application to a competent authority to be approved as an intermediary in accordance with the Act and these regulations; and

(b) it appears to the competent authority that the individual is a fit and proper person to act as intermediary between a person wishing to make an application for a debt relief order and the official receiver.

9 Ineligibility

9 Individuals of any of the following descriptions are ineligible to be approved by a competent authority to act as intermediaries–

(a) individuals convicted of any offence involving fraud or other dishonesty or violence whose convictions are not spent;

(b) individuals who have committed any offence in any enactment contained in insolvency legislation;

(c) individuals who, in the course of carrying on any trade, profession or vocation or in the course of the discharge of any functions relating to any office or employment have engaged in any deceitful or oppressive or otherwise unfair or improper practices, whether unlawful or not, or which otherwise cast doubt upon their probity;

(d) individuals who have no experience, education or other training in the provision of debt management or debt counselling services;

(e) individuals who have not acted with the independence, integrity and the skills appropriate to the proper performance of the duties of a provider of debt management or debt counselling services or of an approved intermediary;

(f) undischarged bankrupts;

(g) individuals in respect of whom there is or has been in force a bankruptcy restrictions order or undertaking or an interim bankruptcy restrictions order or undertaking or any bankruptcy

1027

restrictions order or undertaking made under the Insolvency (Northern Ireland) Order 1989 or the Bankruptcy (Scotland) Act 1985

(h)   individuals to whom a moratorium period applies or in respect of whom a debt relief order or application for a debt relief order, has been made;

(i)   individuals in respect of whom there is or has been in force a debt relief restrictions order or undertaking or an interim debt relief restrictions order or undertaking;

(j)   individuals who are or have been subject to a disqualification order or undertaking accepted under the Company Directors Disqualification Act 1986 or to a disqualification order made under Part 11 of the Companies (Northern Ireland) Order 1989 or to a disqualification undertaking accepted under the Company Directors Disqualification (Northern Ireland) Order 2002;

(k)   individuals who are patients within meaning of section 329(1) of the Mental Health (Care and Treatment) (Scotland) Act 2003 or have had a guardian appointed to them under the Adults with Incapacity (Scotland) Act 2000;

(l)   individuals who lack capacity within the meaning of the Mental Health Capacity Act 2005 to act as intermediaries between a person wishing to make an application for a debt relief order and the official receiver;

(m)   individuals who, subject to any exemption from the requirement to possess or be covered by a relevant consumer credit licence which would otherwise apply to or in relation to them, neither possess nor are validly covered by such a licence; and

(n)   individuals who are not covered, either individually or by way of a group policy, by public liability or personal indemnity insurance.

10   Applications to a competent authority for approval to act as intermediary

10(1)   Applications to a competent authority by an individual for approval to act as an intermediary shall be in writing and contain–

(a)   the individual's full name and address, date of birth and gender;

(b)   any name or names used by the applicant for any purpose, if different from the above;

(c)   a description of the individual's current occupation or activities;

(d)   a description giving reasons why the individual should be considered suitable for approval;

(e)   whether the individual is a member of a relevant body and if so which;

(f)   the individual's educational and professional qualifications;

(g)   the source of the individual's income and the individual's current financial status;

(h)   details of the individual's expertise in the provision of debt management or debt counselling services including details of any education, training and development which the individual has undergone and any qualifications the individual has acquired in connection with the provision of debt management or debt counselling services;

(i)   details of any consumer credit licence which the individual has in place or of any exemption claimed by him or her from the requirement to possess or be covered by such a licence (as the case may be), or, if none, how the individual proposes to secure that he or she has in place, or is validly covered by, a consumer credit licence;

(j)   details of any public liability or personal indemnity insurance which the individual has in place, or, if none, how the individual proposes to secure that he or she has in place, or is validly covered by, appropriate public liability or personal indemnity insurance;

(k)   copies of–

  (i)   documents confirming the individual's name, address and date of birth;

  (ii)   material relating to the educational, training and development experience referred to in sub-paragraph (h);

  (iii)   material relating to the individual's professional or other qualifications.

10(2)   In this regulation, "relevant body" means a body concerned with the regulation of persons who provide or ensure the provision of debt management or debt counselling services.

10(3)   The application may be accompanied by further information in support of the application; and the competent authority may request the individual to supply further information or evidence.

History
Regulation 10(3) amended by the Debt Relief Orders (Designation of Competent Authorities) (Amendment) Regulations 2009 (SI 2009/1553) reg.2 as from 20 July 2009.

11   Procedure for withdrawal of approval to act as intermediary

11   A competent authority shall withdraw an approval to act as intermediary from any individual–

  (a)   where the individual so requests or with the individual's consent;

  (b)   where it becomes clear to the competent authority after approval that the individual–

    (i)   was ineligible at the time of approval, or

    (ii)   has become ineligible for approval;

    (iii)   is at any time not or no longer a fit and proper person to act as intermediary;

    (iv)   has failed to comply with any provision of Part 7A of the Act or any rule, regulations or orders made under it, including these regulations;

    (v)   has furnished the competent authority with any false, inaccurate or misleading information.

11(2)   The competent authority may from time to time request an approved intermediary to supply such information or evidence about that intermediary or his or her activities as may be required by that authority for the purpose of ensuring that the requirements of these Regulations are being met.

Companies (Disqualification Orders) Regulations 2009

(SI 2009/2471)

Made on 8 September 2009 by the Secretary of State in exercise of the powers conferred by the Company Directors Disqualification Act 1986 s.18. Effective 1 October 2009.

[**Note**: Changes made by the Small Business, Enterprise and Employment Act 2015 (Consequential Amendments) (Insolvency and Company Directors Disqualification) Regulations 2015 (SI 2015/1651) have been incorporated into the text.]

1 Citation and commencement

1 These Regulations may be cited as the Companies (Disqualification Orders) Regulations 2009 and come into force on 1st October 2009.

2 Definitions

2(1) In these Regulations–

"the Act" means the Company Directors Disqualification Act 1986;

"disqualification order" means an order of the court under any of sections 2 to 5, 5A, 6, 8, 8ZA, 8ZD, 9A and 10 of the Act;

"disqualification undertaking" means an undertaking accepted by the Secretary of State under section 5A, 7, 8, 8ZC, 8ZE or 9B of the Act;

"grant of leave" means a grant by the court of leave under section 17 of the Act to any person in relation to a disqualification order or a disqualification undertaking.

2(2) For the purposes of regulations 5 and 9, "leave granted"–

(a) in relation to a disqualification order granted under Part 2 of the Companies (Northern Ireland) Order 1989 means leave granted by a court for a person subject to such an order to do anything which otherwise the order prohibits that person from doing; and

(b) in relation to a disqualification undertaking accepted under the Company Directors Disqualification (Northern Ireland) Order 2002 means leave granted by a court for a person subject to such an undertaking to do anything which otherwise the undertaking prohibits that person from doing.

History
Definitions of "disqualification order" and "disqualification undertaking" substituted by the Small Business, Enterprise and Employment Act 2015 (Consequential Amendments) (Insolvency and Company Directors Disqualification) Regulations 2015 (SI 2015/1651) reg.4(2)(a), (b) as from 1 October 2015.

3 Revocations

3 The following instruments are revoked–

(a) the Companies (Disqualification Orders) Regulations 2001;

(b) the Companies (Disqualification Orders) (Amendment No. 2) Regulations 2002; and

(c) the Companies (Disqualification Orders) (Amendment) Regulations 2004.

4 Transitional provisions

4 Other than regulation 9, these Regulations apply–

(a) in relation to a disqualification order made after the coming into force of these Regulations; and

    (b) in relation to–

        (i) a grant of leave made after the coming into force of these Regulations; or

        (ii) any action taken by a court after the coming into force of these Regulations in consequence of which a disqualification order or a disqualification undertaking is varied or ceases to be in force,

whether the disqualification order or disqualification undertaking to which the grant of leave or the action relates was made by the court or accepted by the Secretary of State before or after the coming into force of these Regulations.

5   Regulation 9 applies to–

    (a) particulars of disqualification orders made and leave granted under Part 2 of the Companies (Northern Ireland) Order 1989 received by the Secretary of State on or after 1st October 2009 other than particulars of disqualification orders made and leave granted under that Order which relate to disqualification orders made by the courts of Northern Ireland before 2nd April 2001; and

    (b) particulars of undertakings accepted under the Company Directors Disqualification (Northern Ireland) Order 2002 on or after 1st October 2009, and to leave granted under that Order in relation to such undertakings.

6   Particulars to be furnished by officers of the court

6(1)   The following officers of the court must furnish to the Secretary of State the particulars specified in regulation 7(a) to (c) in the form and manner there specified–

    (a) where a disqualification order is made by the Crown Court, the Court Manager;

    (b) where a disqualification order or grant of leave is made by the High Court, the Court Manager;

    (c) where a disqualification order or grant of leave is made by a County Court, the Court Manager;

    (d) where a disqualification order is made by a Magistrates' Court, the designated officer for a Magistrates' Court;

    (e) where a disqualification order is made by the High Court of Justiciary, the Deputy Principal Clerk of Justiciary;

    (f) where a disqualification order or grant of leave is made by a Sheriff Court, the Sheriff Clerk;

    (g) where a disqualification order or grant of leave is made by the Court of Session, the Deputy Principal Clerk of Session;

    (h) where a disqualification order or grant of leave is made by the Court of Appeal, the Court Manager; and

    (i) where a disqualification order or grant of leave is made by the Supreme Court, the Registrar of the Supreme Court.

6(2)   Where–

    (a) a disqualification order has been made by any of the courts mentioned in paragraph (1), or

    (b) a disqualification undertaking has been accepted by the Secretary of State,

and subsequently any action is taken by a court in consequence of which that order or that undertaking is varied or ceases to be in force, the officer specified in paragraph (1) of the court which takes such action must furnish to the Secretary of State the particulars specified in regulation 7(d) in the form and manner there specified.

7   The form in which the particulars are to be furnished is–

(a)   that set out in Schedule 1 to these Regulations with such variations as circumstances require when the person against whom the disqualification order is made is an individual, and the particulars contained therein are the particulars specified for that purpose;

(b)   that set out in Schedule 2 to these Regulations with such variations as circumstances require when the person against whom the disqualification order is made is a body corporate, and the particulars contained therein are the particulars specified for that purpose;

(c)   that set out in Schedule 3 to these Regulations with such variations as circumstances require when a grant of leave is made by the court in relation to a disqualification order or a disqualification undertaking, and the particulars contained therein are the particulars specified for that purpose;

(d)   that set out in Schedule 4 to these Regulations with such variations as circumstances require when any action is taken by a court in consequence of which a disqualification order or a disqualification undertaking is varied or ceases to be in force, and the particulars contained therein are the particulars specified for that purpose.

8   The time within which the officer specified in regulation 6(1) is to furnish the Secretary of State with the said particulars is the period of 14 days beginning with the day on which the disqualification order or grant of leave is made or on which action is taken by a court in consequence of which the disqualification order or disqualification undertaking is varied or ceases to be in force.

9   Extension of certain of the provisions of section 18 of the Act to orders made, undertakings accepted and leave granted in Northern Ireland

9(1)   Section 18(2) of the Act is extended to the particulars furnished to the Secretary of State of disqualification orders made and leave granted under Part 2 of the Companies (Northern Ireland) Order 1989.

9(2)   Section 18(2A) of the Act is extended to the particulars of disqualification undertakings accepted under and leave granted in relation to disqualification undertakings under the Company Directors Disqualification (Northern Ireland) Order 2002.

9(3)   Section 18(3) of the Act is extended to all entries in the register and particulars relating to them furnished to the Secretary of State in respect of orders made under Part 2 of the Companies (Northern Ireland) Order 1989 or disqualification undertakings accepted under the Company Directors Disqualification (Northern Ireland) Order 2002.

[Schedules 1–4 not reproduced]

Financial Services and Markets Act 2000 (Administration Orders Relating to Insurers) Order 2010

(SI 2010/3023)

Made on 20 December 2010 in exercise of the powers conferred on them by ss.360, 426(1) and 428(3) of the Financial Services and Markets Act 2000 by the Treasury with the consent of the Secretary of State for Business, Innovation and Skills. Operative from 1 February 2011.

[**Note**: Changes made by the Financial Services Act 2012 (Consequential Amendments and Transitional Provisions) Order 2013 (SI 2013/472), the Small Business Enterprise and Employment Act 2015 (Consequential Amendments, Saving and Transitional Provisions) Regulations 2018 (SI 2018/208) and the Financial Services and Markets (Insolvency) (Amendment of Miscellaneous Enactments) Regulations 2019 (SI 2019/755) have been incorporated into the text.]

1 Citation, commencement and interpretation

1(1) This Order may be cited as the Financial Services and Markets Act 2000 (Administration Orders Relating to Insurers) Order 2010 and comes into force on 1st February 2011.

1(2) In this Order–

"the 1986 Act" means the Insolvency Act 1986;

"Schedule B1" means Schedule B1 to the 1986 Act.

2 Application and modification of Part 2 of the 1986 Act in relation to insurers

2(1) Part 2 of the 1986 Act (administration), other than paragraph 14 of Schedule B1 (power of holder of floating charge to appoint administrator) and paragraph 22 of Schedule B1 (power of company or directors to appoint administrator), applies in relation to insurers with the modifications specified in the Schedule to this Order.

2(2) Accordingly paragraph 9(2) of Schedule B1 does not preclude the making of an administration order in relation to an insurer.

3 Application and modification of the Insolvency (England and Wales) Rules 2016 in relation to insurers

3 The Insolvency (England and Wales) Rules 2016, so far as they give effect to Part 2 of the 1986 Act, have effect in relation to insurers with the following modifications–

(a) in Rule 3.12(1) (the hearing) after sub-paragraph (a) insert–

"(aa) the Financial Conduct Authority and, where the person is a PRA-authorised person within the meaning of the Financial Services and Markets Act 2000, the Prudential Regulation Authority;

(ab) the scheme manager of the Financial Services Compensation Scheme;".

History
Heading to and reg.3 amended by the Financial Services and Markets (Insolvency) (Amendment of Miscellaneous Enactments) Regulations 2019 (SI 2019/755) regs 1, 8(1), (2) as from 23 April 2019.

4 Application and modification of the Insolvency (Scotland) (Company Voluntary Arrangements and Administration) Rules 2018 in relation to insurers

4 The Insolvency (Scotland) (Company Voluntary Arrangements and Administration) Rules 2018, so far as they give effect to Part 2 of the 1986 Act, have effect in relation to insurers with the following modifications–

(a)   in Rule 3.6 (application) after subparagraph (a) insert–

"(aa) the Financial Conduct Authority and, where the person is a PRA-authorised person within the meaning of the Financial Services and Markets Act 2000, the Prudential Regulation   Authority;"

(ab) the scheme manager of the Financial Services Compensation Scheme;".

History
Heading to and reg.4 amended by the Financial Services and Markets (Insolvency) (Amendment of Miscellaneous Enactments) Regulations 2019 (SI 2019/755) regs 1, 8(1), (3) as from 23 April 2019.

5   Revocation

5   The following are revoked–

(a)   the Financial Services and Markets Act 2000 (Administration Orders Relating to Insurers) Order 2002;

(b)   articles 2 to 8 of the Financial Services and Markets Act 2000 (Administration Orders Relating to Insurers) (Amendment) Order 2003;

(c)   regulation 52 of the Insurers (Reorganisation and Winding Up) Regulations 2004.

6   Saving

6   Nothing in articles 2 to 5 applies in relation to any case where the appointment of an administrator takes effect before the coming into force of this Order.

SCHEDULE

MODIFICATIONS OF PART 2 OF THE INSOLVENCY ACT 1986 IN RELATION TO INSURERS

Article 2

1(1)   In paragraph 3 of Schedule B1 (purpose of administration)–

(a)   at the beginning of sub-paragraph (1) insert "Subject to sub-paragraph (1A)";

(b)   after sub-paragraph (1) insert–

"(1A)   The administrator of an insurer which effects or carries out contracts of insurance shall, at the request of the scheme manager of the Financial Services Compensation Scheme, provide any assistance identified by the scheme manager as being necessary–

(a)   to enable the scheme manager to administer the compensation scheme in relation to contracts of insurance, and

(b)   to enable the scheme manager to secure continuity of insurance in relation to contracts of long-term insurance.

(1B) For the purposes of this Schedule–

(a)   "compensation scheme" has the same meaning as in section 213 of the Financial Services and Markets Act 2000;

(b)   "contracts of insurance" and "contracts of long-term insurance" have the same meaning as in article 3 of the Financial Services and Markets Act 2000 (Regulated Activities) Order 2001;

(c)   "scheme manager" means the body corporate established by the Financial Services Authority under section 212 of the Financial Services and Markets Act 2000.".

1(2)   In sub-paragraph (2), for "sub-paragraph (4)," substitute "sub-paragraphs (1A) and (4) and to paragraph 3A".

2(1) After paragraph 3 of Schedule B1, insert–

"3A.–

(1) This paragraph applies in relation to the administration of an insurer which effects or carries out contracts of long-term insurance.

(2) Unless the court orders otherwise, the administrator must carry on the insurer's business so far as that business consists of carrying out the insurer's contracts of long-term insurance ("the long-term insurance business") with a view to the business being transferred as a going concern to a person who may lawfully carry out those contracts.

(3) In carrying on the long-term insurance business, the administrator–

    (a) may agree to the variation of any contracts of insurance in existence when the administration order is made; but

    (b) must not effect any new contracts of insurance without the approval of the Prudential Regulation Authority and, if the insurer is not a PRA-authorised person within the meaning of the Financial Services and Markets Act 2000, the Financial Conduct Authority.

(4) If the administrator is satisfied that the interests of the creditors in respect of liabilities of the insurer attributable to contracts of long-term insurance effected by it require the appointment of a special manager, the administrator may apply to the court.

(5) On such an application, the court may appoint a special manager to act during such time, and to have such powers (including powers of a receiver or manager) as the court may direct.

(6) Section 177(5) of this Act (duties of special manager) applies to a special manager appointed under sub-paragraph (5) as it applies to a special manager appointed under section 177.

(7) If the court thinks fit, it may reduce the value of one or more of the contracts of long-term insurance effected by the insurer.

(8) Any reduction is to be on such terms and subject to such conditions (if any) as the court thinks fit.

(9) The court may, on the application of an official, appoint an independent actuary to investigate the insurer's long-term insurance business and to report to the official–

    (a) on the desirability or otherwise of the insurer's long-term insurance business being continued; and

    (b) on any reduction in the contracts of long-term insurance effected by the insurer that may be necessary for successful continuation of the insurer's long-term insurance business.

(10) "Official" means–

    (a) the administrator;

    (b) a special manager appointed under sub-paragraph (5); or

    (c) the Financial Conduct Authority or the Prudential Regulation Authority.".

3 In paragraph 49(4) of Schedule B1 (administrator's proposals), omit "and" at the end of paragraph (b) and at the end of paragraph (c) add–

"(d) to the Financial Conduct Authority and the Prudential Regulation Authority, and

(e) to the scheme manager of the Financial Services Compensation Scheme."

3A(1) For the purposes of paragraph 51 of Schedule B1 a decision of the insurer's creditors as to whether they approve the proposals set out in the administrator's statement made under paragraph 49(1) of Schedule B1 is required to be made by a qualifying decision procedure.

3A(2) At the time of seeking that decision the administrator must also seek a decision from the insurer's creditors as to whether they consent to the exercise by the administrator of the powers specified in Schedule 1 to the 1986 Act.

3A(3)   That decision is also required to be made by a qualifying decision procedure.

4   In paragraph 53(2) of Schedule B1 (creditors' decision), omit "and" at the end of paragraph (b) and at the end of paragraph (c), add–

> "(d) the Financial Conduct Authority and the Prudential Regulation Authority, and

> (e) to the scheme manager of the Financial Services Compensation Scheme."

5   In paragraph 54(2)(b) of Schedule B1 (revision of administrator's proposals), after "opted-out creditor" insert ", to the Financial Conduct Authority and the Prudential Regulation Authority and to the scheme manager of the Financial Services Compensation Scheme.".

6   In paragraph 76(1) of Schedule B1 (automatic end of administration), for "one year" substitute "30 months".

7   [Omitted]

8   In paragraph 79(1) of Schedule B1 (court ending administration on application of administrator), after the first reference to "company" insert "or the Financial Conduct Authority or the Prudential Regulation Authority".

9   In paragraph 91(1) of Schedule B1 (supplying vacancy in office of administrator)–

(a)   at the end of sub-paragraph (d), omit "or";

(b)   at the end of sub-paragraph (e), insert "or";

(c)   after sub-paragraph (e), insert

> "(f) the Financial Conduct Authority or the Prudential Regulation Authority".

10(1)   The powers of the administrator specified in Schedule 1 to the 1986 Act (powers of administrator or administrative receiver) include the power to make–

(a)   any payments due to a creditor; or

(b)   any payments on account of any sum which may become due to a creditor.

10(2)   Any payments to a creditor made pursuant to sub-paragraph (1) must not exceed, in aggregate, the amount which the administrator reasonably considers that the creditor would be entitled to receive on a distribution of the insurer's assets in a winding up.

10(3)   The powers conferred by sub-paragraph (1) may be exercised until the initial decision date for the decision referred to in paragraph 51(1), but may only be exercised after that date–

(a)   if–

(i)   the administrator, when seeking the decision referred to in paragraph 3A(2), gave the creditors a statement containing the information specified in sub-paragraph (4); and

(ii)   a majority in number representing three-fourths in value of the creditors has consented to the exercise by the administrator of those powers; or

(b)   with the consent of the court.

10(4)   The information referred to in sub-paragraph (3)(a)(i) is an estimate of the aggregate amount of–

(a)   the insurer's assets and liabilities (whether actual, contingent or prospective); and

(b)   all payments which the administrator proposes to make to creditors pursuant to subparagraph (1);

including any assumptions which the administrator has made in calculating that estimate.

10(5)   [Omitted]

11   Where this Schedule applies in relation to the administration of an insurer in Scotland, it is to be read with the following modifications–

(a)   ignore paragraph 3A;

(b)   in paragraph 4 for "(creditors' decision)" read "(business and result of initial creditors' meeting)";

(c)   in paragraph 5 for ""opted-out creditor"" read ""creditor""; and

(d)   read paragraph 10 as if–

   (i)   for sub-paragraph (3) there were substituted–

   "(3) The powers conferred by sub-paragraph (1) may be exercised until an initial creditors' meeting, but may only be exercised thereafter–

   (a)   if the following conditions are met–

      (i)   the administrator has laid before that meeting or any subsequent creditors' meeting ("the relevant meeting") a statement containing the information specified in sub-paragraph (4); and

      (ii)   the powers are exercised with the consent of a majority in number representing three-fourths in value of the creditors present and voting either in person or by proxy at the relevant meeting; or

   (b)   with the consent of the court.";

   (ii)   there were added at the end–

   "(5) In this paragraph "initial creditors' meeting" has the meaning given in paragraph 51(1) of Schedule B1.".

History

Paragraph 7 omitted by the Small Business, Enterprise and Employment Act 2015 and the Insolvency (Amendment) Act (Northern Ireland) 2016 (Consequential Amendments and Transitional Provisions) Regulations 2017 (SI 2017/400) regs 1, 9 as from 6 April 2017. Paragraphs 3A and 11 were inserted, para.10(3) was modified and para.10(5) was omitted by the Small Business, Enterprise and Employment Act 2015 (Consequential Amendments, Savings and Transitional Provisions) Regulations 2018 (SI 2018/208) reg.12 with effect from 13 March 2018.

Charging Orders (Orders for Sale: Financial Thresholds) Regulations 2013

(SI 2013/491)

Made on 5 March 2013 by the Lord Chancellor under the Charging Orders Act 1979 s.3A(2), (3). Operative from 6 April 2013.

2   Cases in which these Regulations apply

2(1)   These Regulations apply where a charging order has been made for securing the payment of money due under a judgment or order made for the purpose of enforcing payment under a regulated agreement.

2(2)   "Regulated agreement" has the meaning given to it by section 189(1) of the Consumer Credit Act 1974.

3   Financial threshold

3   Where these Regulations apply, the charge imposed by the charging order may not be enforced by way of order for sale to recover an amount which is less than £1,000.

4   Transitional provision

4   These Regulations do not have effect to prevent a charge imposed by a charging order being enforced by way of an order for sale to recover an amount which is less than £1,000 if the application for the order for sale was made before the date on which these Regulations come into force.

London Insolvency District (County Court at Central London) Order 2014

(SI 2014/818)

Made on 31 March 2014 by the Lord Chancellor in exercise of the powers conferred on him by s.374 of the Insolvency Act 1986 and with the concurrence of the Chancellor of the High Court nominated by the Lord Chief Justice under s.374(5). Operative from 22 April 2014

1 Citation and commencement

1 This Order may be cited as the London Insolvency District (County Court at Central London) Order 2014 and comes into force on 22nd April 2014.

2 Revocations and savings

2 The London Insolvency District (Central London County Court) Order 2011 is revoked.

3 Insolvency Districts

3 The London insolvency district comprises the areas served by the following hearing centres of the county court–

(a) Barnet,

(b) Bow,

(c) Brentford,

(d) The County Court at Central London,

(e) Clerkenwell and Shoreditch,

(f) Edmonton,

(g) Lambeth,

(h) Mayor's and City of London Court,

(i) Wandsworth,

(j) West London, and

(k) Willesden.

Company, Limited Liability Partnership and Business (Names and Trading Disclosures) Regulations 2015

(SI 2015/17)

Made on 7 January 2015 by the Secretary of State in exercise of the powers conferred on him by specified sections of the Companies Act 2006 and that Act as applied to limited liability partnerships by regulations 8 and 81 of the Limited Liability Partnerships (Application of Companies Act 2006) Regulations 2009. Operative from 31 January 2015.

21 Requirement to display registered name at registered office and inspection place

21(1) A company shall display its registered name at–

(a) its registered office; and

(b) any inspection place.

21(2) But paragraph (1) does not apply to any company which has at all times since its incorporation been dormant.

21(3) Paragraph (1) shall also not apply to the registered office or an inspection place of a company where–

(a) in respect of that company, a liquidator, administrator or administrative receiver has been appointed; and

(b) the registered office or inspection place is also a place of business of that liquidator, administrator or administrative receiver.

22 Requirement to display registered name at other business locations

22(1) This regulation applies to a location other than a company's registered office or any inspection place.

22(2) A company shall display its registered name at any such location at which it carries on business.

22(3) But paragraph (2) shall not apply to a location which is primarily used for living accommodation.

22(4) Paragraph (2) shall also not apply to any location at which business is carried on by a company where–

(a) in respect of that company, a liquidator, administrator or administrative receiver has been appointed; and

(b) the location is also a place of business of that liquidator, administrator or administrative receiver.

22(5) Paragraph (2) shall also not apply to any location at which business is carried on by a company of which every director who is an individual is a relevant director.

22(6) In this regulation–

(a) "administrative receiver" has the meaning given–

(i) in England and Wales or Scotland, by section 251 of the Insolvency Act 1986, and

(ii) in Northern Ireland, by Article 5 of the Insolvency (Northern Ireland) Order 1989

(b) "credit reference agency" has the meaning given in section 243(7) of the Act;

(c) "protected information" has the meaning given in section 240 of the Act; and

(d) "relevant director" means an individual in respect of whom the registrar is required by regulations made pursuant to section 243(4) of the Act to refrain from disclosing protected information to a credit reference agency.

23 Manner of display of registered name

23(1) This regulation applies where a company is required to display its registered name at any office, place or location.

23(2) Where that office, place or location is shared by no more than five companies, the registered name–

(a) shall be so positioned that it may be easily seen by any visitor to that office, place or location; and

(b) shall be displayed continuously.

23(3) Where any such office, place or location is shared by six or more companies, each such company must ensure that either–

(a) its registered name is displayed for at least fifteen continuous seconds at least once every three minutes; or

(b) its registered name is available for inspection on a register by any visitor to that office, place or location.

24 Registered name to appear in communications

24(1) Every company shall disclose its registered name on–

(a) its business letters, notices and other official publications;

(b) its bills of exchange, promissory notes, endorsements and order forms;

(c) cheques purporting to be signed by or on behalf of the company;

(d) orders for money, goods or services purporting to be signed by or on behalf of the company;

(e) its bills of parcels, invoices and other demands for payment, receipts and letters of credit;

(f) its applications for licences to carry on a trade or activity; and

(g) all other forms of its business correspondence and documentation.

24(2) Every company shall disclose its registered name on its websites.

25 Further particulars to appear in business letters, order forms and websites

25(1) Every company shall disclose the particulars set out in paragraph (2) on–

(a) its business letters;

(b) its order forms; and

(c) its websites.

25(2)   The particulars are–

(a)   the part of the United Kingdom in which the company is registered;

(b)   the company's registered number;

(c)   the address of the company's registered office;

(d)   in the case of a limited company exempt from the obligation to use the word "limited" as part of its registered name under section 60 of the Act, the fact that it is a limited company;

(e)   in the case of a community interest company which is not a public company, the fact that it is a limited company; and

(f)   in the case of an investment company within the meaning of section 833 of the Act, the fact that it is such a company.

25(3)   If, in the case of a company having a share capital, there is a disclosure as to the amount of share capital on–

(a)   its business letters;

(b)   its order forms; or

(c)   its websites,

that disclosure must be as to paid up share capital.

29   Interpretation

29   In this Part–

(a)   "company record" means–

   (i)   any register, index, accounting records, agreement, memorandum, minutes or other document required by the Companies Acts to be kept by a company; and

   (ii)   any register kept by a company of its debenture holders;

(b)   "inspection place" means any location, other than a company's registered office, at which a company keeps available for inspection any company record which it is required under the Companies Acts to keep available for inspection;

(c)   a reference to any type of document is a reference to a document of that type in hard copy, electronic or any other form; and

(d)   in relation to a company, a reference to "its websites" includes a reference to any part of a website relating to that company which that company has caused or authorised to appear.

European Grouping of Territorial Cooperation Regulations 2015

(SI 2015/1493)

Made on 8 July 2015 by the Secretary of State under the European Communities Act 1972. Operative from 31 July 2015.

GENERAL

2 Interpretation

2(1) In these Regulations–

"the 2006 Act" means the Companies Act 2006;

"the 1986 Act" means the Insolvency Act 1986;

"the 1989 Order" means the Insolvency (Northern Ireland) Order 1989;

"the EU Regulation" means Regulation (EC) No 1082/2006 of the European Parliament and of the Council as amended by Regulation (EU) 1302/2013 of the European Parliament and of the Council;

"EGTC" means a European grouping of territorial cooperation formed under the EC Regulation;

"the Insolvency Rules" means–

in the case of a UK EGTC with its registered office in England and Wales, the Insolvency (England and Wales) Rules 2016;

in the case of a UK ECTG with its registered office in Scotland, the Insolvency (Scotland) Rules 1986;

in the case of a UK EGTC with its registered office in Northern Ireland, the Insolvency Rules (Northern Ireland) 1991; and

"UK EGTC" means an EGTC which has a registered office in the United Kingdom.

History
In the definition of "the Insolvency Rules" the definition in relation to England and Wales substituted by the Insolvency (England and Wales) Rules 2016 (Consequential Amendments and Savings) Rules 2017 (SI 2017/369) r.2(2), Sch.2 para.1 as from 6 April 2017.

PART 2

PROVISIONS RELATING TO THE ESTABLISHMENT OF AN EGTC

6 Proceedings in relation to the winding-up of a UK EGTC (Article 14(1) of the EU Regulation)

6(1) The High Court is the competent court for the purpose of ordering the winding-up of a UK EGTC which has its registered office in England and Wales or in Northern Ireland.

6(2) The Court of Session will be the competent court for the purposes of ordering the winding-up of a UK EGTC which has its registered office in Scotland.

8   Insolvency and winding up (Article 12(1) of the EU Regulation)

8(1)   A UK EGTC will be wound-up as an unregistered company–

(a)   if its registered office is in England and Wales or in Scotland, under Part 5 of the 1986 Act; or

(b)   if its registered office is in Northern Ireland, under Part 6 of the 1989 Order.

8(2) The provisions of the 1986 Act or the 1989 Order and the Insolvency Rules apply to a UK EGTC that is being wound up in accordance with paragraph (1), with the modifications set out in Parts 2 and 3 of the Schedule to The European Grouping of Territorial Cooperation Regulations 2007.

PART 4

SUPPLEMENTAL PROVISIONS RELATING TO THE EFFECTIVE APPLICATION OF THE EU REGULATION

10   Application of the Company Directors Disqualification Act 1986

10   Where a UK EGTC is wound-up under regulation 9(1)(a) or 9(1)(b) of these regulations, the Company Directors Disqualification Act 1986 or the Company Directors Disqualification (Northern Ireland) Order 2002, as appropriate, applies to the UK EGTC and does so as if the EGTC were a company as defined by section 22(2)(b) of that Act or by article 2(2) of that Order.

Insolvent Companies (Reports on Conduct of Directors) (England and Wales) Rules 2016

(SI 2016/180)

Made on 11 February 2016 by the Lord Chancellor under s.411(1)(a) of the Insolvency Act 1986 and s.21(2) of the Company Directors Disqualification Act 1986, with the concurrence of the Secretary of State. Effective 6 April 2016

1 Citation, extent, commencement and interpretation

1(1) These Rules may be cited as the Insolvent Companies (Reports on Conduct of Directors) (England and Wales) Rules 2016, and extend to England and Wales only.

1(2) These Rules come into force on 6th April 2016.

1(3) In these Rules–

"by electronic means" means sent initially and received at its destination by means of electronic equipment for the processing (which expression includes digital compression) or storage of data, and entirely transmitted, conveyed and received by wire, by radio, by optical means or by other electromagnetic means;

"the Act" means the Company Directors Disqualification Act 1986;

"the former Rules" means the Insolvent Companies (Reports on Conduct of Directors) Rules 1996; and

"the portal" means a digital service provided by the Secretary of State for the functions of both the sending and acknowledgement of receipt, by electronic means, of reports, applications, information and notifications in accordance with these Rules.

2 Revocations

2 Subject to rule 10, the following are revoked–

(a) the former Rules;

(b) the Insolvent Companies (Reports on Conduct of Directors) (Amendment) Rules 2001; and

(c) the Enterprise Act 2002 (Insolvency) Order 2003, paragraphs 68 to 70 of the Schedule.

3 Enforcement of section 7(4) of the Act

3(1) This rule applies where, for the purpose of determining whether to exercise any function under section 7 of the Act (disqualification orders under section 6: applications and acceptance of undertakings), the Secretary of State or the official receiver requires or has required a person to–

(a) furnish the Secretary of State or (as the case may be) the official receiver with information under section 7(4)(a), or

(b) produce and permit inspection of books, papers and other records in accordance with section 7(4)(b).

3(2) On the application of the Secretary of State or (as the case may be) the official receiver, the court may make an order directing compliance within such period as may be specified.

3(3) The court's order may provide that all costs of and incidental to the application are to be borne by the person to whom the order is directed.

4   Conduct reports required to be sent under section 7A(4) of the Act

4(1)   This rule is subject to rule 7.

4(2)   A conduct report required to be sent under section 7A(4) of the Act must be sent by the office-holder to the Secretary of State by electronic means via the portal.

4(3)   The Secretary of State must as soon as reasonably practicable acknowledge receipt, by electronic means via the portal, of a conduct report sent in accordance with this rule.

5   Applications for a longer period under section 7A(4)(b) of the Act

5(1)   This rule is subject to rule 7.

5(2)   This rule applies where the particular circumstances of a case may require a period longer than that provided for by section 7A(4)(a) of the Act for the sending of a conduct report to the Secretary of State.

5(3)   The office-holder may apply to the Secretary of State for a longer period in which to send the report.

5(4)   The application must be sent by electronic means via the portal before the expiry of the period specified in section 7A(4)(a) of the Act.

5(5)   The application must explain the particular circumstances for the making of the application.

5(6)   The Secretary of State must as soon as reasonably practicable acknowledge receipt, by electronic means via the portal, of an application sent in accordance with this rule.

5(7)   The Secretary of State must, as soon as is reasonably practicable, notify the office-holder, by electronic means via the portal,–

   (a)   of the outcome of the application; and

   (b)   if the application is successful, of the longer period considered appropriate in the particular circumstances for the sending of the report to the Secretary of State under section 7A(4)(b) of the Act.

6   New information required to be sent under section 7A(5) of the Act

6(1)   This rule is subject to rule 7.

6(2)   New information required to be sent under section 7A(5) of the Act must be sent by the office-holder to the Secretary of State by electronic means via the portal.

6(3)   The Secretary of State must as soon as reasonably practicable acknowledge receipt, by electronic means via the portal, of new information sent in accordance with this rule.

7   Unavailability of the portal

7(1)   The Secretary of State–

   (a)   may at any time when the portal is unable to carry out one or more of its functions, and

   (b)   must, where the portal has been unable to carry out one or more of its functions for a period of 7 business days,

provide alternative means for complying with a requirement under rules 4, 5 or 6.

7(2)   The Secretary of State must give notice to office-holders specifying the means provided for the purposes of paragraph (1) and the period of time for which those means are made available.

7(3) The Secretary of State may by notice vary the means provided under paragraph (1) or the period of time for which those means are made available.

7(4) A notice under paragraph (3) must give office-holders at least 1 business day's notice before any variation takes effect.

7(5) The time within which an office-holder must comply with rules 4, 5 or 6 does not include any day the whole or part of which forms part of a suspension period.

7(6) For the purpose of paragraph (5) a suspension period is a period of time during which–

(a) the portal is unable to receive reports, applications or information;

(b) no notice under paragraph (2) or (3) is in force; and

(c) the office-holder has attempted to and been prevented from sending a report, application or information at least once during that period on the basis of sub-paragraph (a).

7(7) In this rule, *"business day"* means any day other than a Saturday, a Sunday, Christmas Day, Good Friday or a day which is a bank holiday in any part of Great Britain.

8 Enforcement of rules 4 to 6

8(1) An office-holder who without reasonable excuse fails to comply with any of the obligations imposed by section 7A(4) or 7A(5) of the Act is guilty of an offence and–

(a) on summary conviction of the offence, is liable to a fine not exceeding level 3 on the standard scale, and

(b) for continued contravention, is liable to a daily default fine; that is to say, the office-holder is liable on a second or subsequent summary conviction of the offence to a fine not exceeding one-tenth of level 3 on the standard scale for each day on which the contravention is continued (instead of the penalty specified in sub-paragraph (a)).

8(2) Section 431 of the Insolvency Act 1986 (summary proceedings), as it applies to England and Wales, has effect in relation to an offence under this rule as to offences under Parts 1 to 7 of that Act.

9 Review

9(1) The Secretary of State must from time to time–

(a) carry out a review of these Rules,

(b) set out the conclusions of the review in a report, and

(c) publish the report.

9(2) The report must in particular–

(a) set out the objectives intended to be achieved by the regulatory system established by these Rules,

(b) assess the extent to which those objectives are achieved, and

(c) assess whether those objectives remain appropriate and, if so, the extent to which they could be achieved with a system that imposes less regulation.

9(3) The first report under this rule must be published before the end of the period of 5 years beginning on 6th April 2016.

9(4) Reports under this rule are afterwards to be published at intervals not exceeding 5 years.

10   Transitional and savings provisions

10(1)   Rule 6 of the former Rules continues to apply when a period referred to in rule 6(2) of the former Rules has not expired by 6th April 2016.

10(2)   Until 6th October 2016 rules 3 to 5 of the former Rules continue to apply as if the former Rules had not been revoked when the relevant date for the purposes of rule 4 of the former Rules occurred before 6th April 2016.

10(3)   Until 6th October 2016 the forms contained in the Schedule to the former Rules must be used for the purpose of complying with rules 3 to 5 of the former Rules.

Insolvent Companies (Reports on Conduct of Directors) (Scotland) Rules 2016

(SI 2016/185 (S.1))

Made on 7 February 2016 by the Lord Chancellor under s.411(1)(b) of the Insolvency Act 1986 and s.21(2) of the Company Directors Disqualification Act 1986. Effective 6 April 2016.

1   Citation, extent commencement and interpretation

1(1)   These Rules may be cited as the Insolvent Companies (Reports on Conduct of Directors) (Scotland) Rules 2016, and extend to Scotland only.

1(2)   These Rules come into force on 6th April 2016.

1(3)   In these Rules–

"by electronic means" means sent initially and received at its destination by means of electronic equipment for the processing (which expression includes digital compression) or storage of data, and entirely transmitted, conveyed and received by wire, by radio, by optical means or by other electromagnetic means;

"the Act" means the Company Directors Disqualification Act 1986;

"the former Rules" means the Insolvent Companies (Reports on Conduct of Directors) (Scotland) Rules 1996; and

"the portal" means a digital service provided by the Secretary of State for the functions of both the sending and acknowledgement of receipt, by electronic means, of reports, applications, information and notifications in accordance with these Rules.

2   Revocation

2   Subject to rule 10 the following are revoked–

(a)   the former Rules,

(b)   the Insolvent Companies (Reports on Conduct of Directors) (Scotland) (Amendment) Rules 2001

3   Enforcement of section 7(4) of the Act

3(1)   This rule applies where, for the purpose of determining whether to exercise any function under section 7 of the Act (disqualification orders under section 6: applications and acceptance of undertakings), the Secretary of State requires or has required a person to–

(a)   furnish the Secretary of State with information under section 7(4)(a), or

(b)   produce and permit inspection of books, papers and other records in accordance with section 7(4)(b).

3(2)   On the application of the Secretary of State the court may make an order directing compliance within such period as may be specified.

3(3)   The court's order may provide that all expenses of and incidental to the application are to be borne by the person to whom the order is directed.

4 Conduct reports required to be sent under section 7A(4) of the Act

4(1)   This rule is subject to rule 7.

4(2)   A conduct report required to be sent under section 7A(4) of the Act must be sent by the office-holder to the Secretary of State by electronic means via the portal.

4(3)   The Secretary of State must as soon as reasonably practicable acknowledge receipt, by electronic means via the portal, of a conduct report sent in accordance with this rule.

5 Applications for a longer period under section 7A(4)(b) of the Act

5(1)   This rule is subject to rule 7.

5(2)   This rule applies where the particular circumstances of a case may require a period longer than that provided for by section 7A(4)(a) of the Act for the sending of a conduct report to the Secretary of State.

5(3)   The office-holder may apply to the Secretary of State for a longer period in which to send the report.

5(4)   The application must be sent by electronic means via the portal before the expiry of the period specified in section 7A(4)(a) of the Act.

5(5)   The application must explain the particular circumstances for the making of the application.

5(6)   The Secretary of State must as soon as reasonably practicable acknowledge receipt, by electronic means via the portal, of an application sent in accordance with this rule.

5(7)   The Secretary of State must, as soon as is reasonably practicable, notify the office-holder, by electronic means via the portal,–

(a)   of the outcome of the application; and

(b)   if the application is successful, of the longer period considered appropriate in the particular circumstances for the sending of the report to the Secretary of State under section 7A(4)(b) of the Act.

6 New information required to be sent under section 7A(5) of the Act

6(1)   This rule is subject to rule 7.

6(2)   New information required to be sent under section 7A(5) of the Act must be sent by the office-holder to the Secretary of State by electronic means via the portal.

6(3)   The Secretary of State must as soon as reasonably practicable acknowledge receipt, by electronic means via the portal, of new information sent in accordance with this rule.

7 Unavailability of the portal

7(1)   The Secretary of State–

(a)   may at any time when the portal is unable to carry out one or more of its functions, and

(b)   must, where the portal has been unable to carry out one or more of its functions for a period of 7 business days,

provide alternative means for complying with a requirement under rules 4, 5 or 6.

7(2)   The Secretary of State must give notice to office-holders specifying the means provided for the purposes of paragraph (1) and the period of time for which those means are made available.

7(3)   The Secretary of State may by notice vary the means provided under paragraph (1) or the period of time for which those means are made available.

7(4)   A notice under paragraph (3) must give office-holders at least 1 business day's notice before any variation takes effect.

7(5)   The time within which an office-holder must comply with rules 4, 5 or 6 does not include any day the whole or part of which forms part of a suspension period.

7(6)   For the purpose of paragraph (5) a suspension period is a period of time during which–

(a)   the portal is unable to receive reports, applications or information;

(b)   no notice under paragraph (2) or (3) is in force; and

(c)   the office-holder has attempted to and been prevented from sending a report, application or information at least once during that period on the basis of sub-paragraph (a).

7(7)   In this rule *"business day"* means any day other than a Saturday, a Sunday, Christmas Day, Good Friday or a day which is a bank holiday in any part of Great Britain.

8   Enforcement of rules 4 to 6

8(1)   An office-holder who without reasonable excuse fails to comply with any of the obligations imposed by section 7A(4) or 7A(5) of the Act is guilty of an offence and–

(a)   on summary conviction of the offence, is liable to a fine not exceeding level 3 on the standard scale, and

(b)   for continued contravention, is liable to a daily default fine; that is to say, the office-holder is liable on a second or subsequent summary conviction of the offence to a fine not exceeding one-tenth of level 3 on the standard scale for each day on which the contravention is continued (instead of the penalty specified in sub-paragraph (a)).

8(2)   Section 431 of the Insolvency Act 1986 (summary proceedings), as it applies to Scotland, has effect in relation to an offence under this rule as to offences under Parts 1 to 7 of that Act.

9   Review

9(1)   The Secretary of State must from time to time–

(a)   carry out a review of these Rules,

(b)   set out the conclusions of the review in a report, and

(c)   publish the report.

9(2)   The report must in particular–

(a)   set out the objectives intended to be achieved by the regulatory system established by these Rules,

(b)   assess the extent to which those objectives are achieved, and

(c)   assess whether those objectives remain appropriate and, if so, the extent to which they could be achieved with a system that imposes less regulation.

9(3)   The first report under this rule must be published before the end of the period of 5 years beginning on 6th April 2016.

9(4)   Reports under this rule are afterwards to be published at intervals not exceeding 5 years.

10 Transitional and savings provisions

10(1)   Rule 6 of the former Rules continues to apply when a period referred to in rule 6(2) of the former Rules has not expired by 6th April 2016.

10(2)   Until 6th October 2016 rules 3 to 5 of the former Rules continue to apply as if the former Rules had not been revoked when the relevant date for the purposes of rule 4 of the former Rules occurred before 6th April 2016.

10(3)   Until 6th October 2016 the forms contained in the Schedule to the former Rules must be used for the purpose of complying with rules 3 to 5 of the former Rules.

Insolvency Proceedings (Fees) Order 2016

(SI 2016/692)

Made on 29 June 2016 by the Lord Chancellor in exercise of the powers conferred by the Insolvency Act 1986 ss.414 and 415, and with the sanction of the Treasury. Operative from 30 June 2016.

1 Citation and commencement

1 This Order may be cited as the Insolvency Proceedings (Fees) Order 2016 and comes into force twenty-one days after the day on which it is laid.

2 Interpretation

2 In this Order–

"the Act" means the Insolvency Act 1986;

"chargeable receipts" means the sums which are paid into the Insolvency Services Account after deducting any amounts which are paid out to secured creditors or paid out in carrying on the business of the bankrupt or the company;

"the commencement date" means the date this Order comes into force;

"deposit" means–

(a) on the making of a bankruptcy application, the sum of £550,

(b) on the presentation of a bankruptcy petition, the sum of £990,

(c) on the presentation of a winding up petition, other than a petition presented under section 124A of the Act, the sum of £1,600,

(d) on the presentation of a winding-up petition under section 124A of the Act, the sum of £5,000;

"official receiver's administration fee" means the fee payable to the official receiver on the making of a bankruptcy or winding up order out of the chargeable receipts of the estate of the bankrupt or, as the case may be, the assets of the insolvent company for the performance of the official receiver's functions under the Act.

3 Fees payable in connection with individual voluntary arrangements, debt relief orders and bankruptcy and winding up

3 The fees payable to the Secretary of State in respect of the matters specified in column 1 of the Table of Fees in Schedule 1 (Fees payable in insolvency proceedings) are the fees specified in column 2 to that Table.

4 Deposit

4(1) On the making of a bankruptcy application, the debtor will pay a deposit to the adjudicator as security for the payment of the official receiver's administration fee.

4(2) On the presentation of a bankruptcy petition or a winding-up petition, the petitioner will pay a deposit to the court as security for the payment of the official receiver's administration fee.

4(3) Where a deposit is paid to the court, the court will transmit the deposit paid to the official receiver attached to the court.

4(4)   The deposit will be used to discharge the official receiver's administration fee to the extent that the assets comprised in the estate of the bankrupt or, as the case may be, the assets of the company are insufficient to discharge the official receiver's administration fee.

4(5)   Where a bankruptcy order or a winding up order is made (including any case where a bankruptcy order or a winding up is subsequently annulled, rescinded or recalled), the deposit will be returned to the person who paid it save to the extent that the assets comprised in the estate of the bankrupt or, as the case may be, the assets of the company are insufficient to discharge the official receiver's administration fee.

4(6)   The deposit will be repaid to the debtor where–

(a)   the adjudicator has refused to make a bankruptcy order,

(b)   14 days have elapsed from the date of delivery of the notice of refusal, and

(c)   the debtor has not made a request to the adjudicator to review the decision.

4(7)   Where the debtor has made a request to the adjudicator to review the decision to refuse to make a bankruptcy order the deposit will be repaid to the debtor where–

(a)   the adjudicator has confirmed the refusal to make a bankruptcy order,

(b)   28 days have elapsed from the date of delivery of the confirmation of the notice of refusal, and

(c)   the debtor has not appealed to the court against the refusal to make a bankruptcy order.

4(8)   Where the debtor has appealed to the court against the refusal to make a bankruptcy order the deposit will be repaid to the debtor where the appeal is dismissed or withdrawn.

4(9)   Where–

(a)   a deposit was paid by the petitioner to the court, and

(b)   the petition is withdrawn or dismissed by the court

that deposit, less an administration fee of £50, will be repaid to the petitioner.

5   Value Added Tax

5   Where Value Added Tax is chargeable in respect of the provision of a service for which a fee is payable by virtue of any provision of this Order, Value Added Tax must be paid on that fee.

6   Revocation

6   The enactments listed in Schedule 2 are revoked.

7   Transitional and saving provisions

7(1)   This Order has no effect in respect of any fees payable in respect of–

(a)   the preparation and submission of a report under section 274 (action on report of insolvency practitioner) of the Act; and

(b)   bankruptcy orders and winding-up orders made following the making of a bankruptcy application or presentation of a petition before the commencement date.

7(2)   This Order has no effect in respect of any deposit paid on the making of a bankruptcy application or the presentation of a petition for bankruptcy or winding up before the commencement date.

SCHEDULE 1

FEES PAYABLE IN INSOLVENCY PROCEEDINGS

Article 3

Table of Fees

Description of fee and circumstances in which it is charged	*Amount of fee or applicable %*
Individual voluntary arrangement registration fee	£15
On the registration by the Secretary of State of an individual voluntary arrangement made under Part 8 of the Act, the fee of–	
Application for a debt relief order – official receiver's administration fee and costs of persons acting as approved intermediaries	£90
On the application for a debt relief order, for the performance of the official receiver's functions and for the payment of an amount not exceeding £10 in respect of the costs of persons acting as approved intermediaries under Part 7A of the Act, the fee of–	
Application for a bankruptcy order – adjudicator's administration fee	£130
On the application to the adjudicator for a bankruptcy order, for the performance of the adjudicator functions, the fee of–	
Bankruptcy – official receiver's administration fee following debtor's application	£1,990
On the making of a bankruptcy order on a debtor's application, for the performance of the official receiver's duties as official receiver the fee of–	
Bankruptcy – official receiver's administration fee following creditor's petition	£2,775
On the making of a bankruptcy order on a creditor's petition, for the performance of the official receiver's duties as official receiver the fee of–	
Bankruptcy – trustee in bankruptcy fee	15%
For the performance of the official receiver's duties while acting as trustee in bankruptcy of the bankrupt's estate a fee calculated as a percentage of chargeable receipts realised by the official receiver in the capacity of trustee in bankruptcy at the rate of–	
Bankruptcy – income payments agreement fee	£150
On entering into an income payments agreement with the official receiver under section 310A of the Act, the fee of–	
Bankruptcy – income payments order fee	£150
On the making of an income payments order by the court under section 310 of the Act, the fee of–	
Winding up by the court other than a winding up on a petition presented under section 124A – official receiver's administration fee	£5,000
On the making of a winding-up order, other than on a petition presented under section 124A, for the performance of the official receiver's duties as official receiver, including the duty to investigate and report on the affairs of bodies in liquidation, the fee of–	

Winding up by the court on a petition presented under section 124A – official receiver's administration fee   £7,500

On the making of a winding-up order on a petition presented under section 124A, for the performance of the official receiver's duties as official receiver, including the duty to investigate and report on the affairs of bodies in liquidation, the fee of–

Winding up – liquidator fee   15%

For the performance of the official receiver's duties while acting as liquidator of the insolvent estate a fee calculated as a percentage of chargeable receipts realised by the official receiver in the capacity of liquidator at the rate of–

Official receiver's general fee   £6,000

On the making of a bankruptcy order or the making of a winding up order by the court for the costs not recovered out of the official receiver's administration fee of administering–

(a) bankruptcy orders,

(b) winding up orders made by the court the fee of–

SCHEDULE 2

REVOCATIONS

[Not reproduced]

Compensation Orders (Disqualified Directors) Proceedings (England and Wales) Rules 2016

(SI 2016/890)

Made on 7 September 2016 by the Lord Chancellor, with the concurrence of the Secretary of State and Chancellor of the High Court, in exercise of the power conferred by the Insolvency Act 2016 s.411, read in conjunction with the Company Directors Disqualification Act 1986 s.21(2). Operative from 1 October 2016.

[**Note**: Comparable legislation has been enacted for Scotland by the Compensation Orders (Disqualified Directors) Proceedings (Scotland) Rules 2016 (SI 2016/895 (S.1)).]

1 Citation, commencement and interpretation

1(1) These Rules may be cited as the Compensation Orders (Disqualified Directors) Proceedings (England and Wales) Rules 2016.

1(2) These Rules come into force on 1st October 2016.

1(3) In these Rules–

"the Act" means the Company Directors Disqualification Act 1986 and a reference to a numbered section is to that section of that Act;

"CPR" followed by a Part or rule by number means that Part or rule with that number in the Civil Procedure Rules 1998;

"practice direction" means a direction as to the practice and procedure of any court within the scope of the Civil Procedure Rules 1998;

"registrar" has the same meaning as in rule 1.2(2) of the Insolvency (England and Wales) Rules 2016; and

"relevant party" means–

(a) the defendant (in the case of an application under section 15A(1)); or

(b) the Secretary of State (in the case of an application under section 15C(1)).

History
In r.1(3) the entry for "registrar" substituted by the Insolvency (England and Wales) Rules 2016 (Consequential Amendments and Savings) Rules 2017 (SI 2017/369) r.2(2), Sch.2 para.12(1), (2) as from 6 April 2017.

2 Application

2(1) Subject to paragraph (2), these Rules apply to an application under the Act made on or after 1st October 2016–

(a) by the Secretary of State for a compensation order against a person under section 15A(1); and

(b) by a person who is subject to a compensation undertaking under section 15A(2) for variation or revocation of that undertaking under section 15C(1).

2(2) These Rules apply to applications where the courts in England and Wales–

(a) have made a disqualification order against the person;

(b) have jurisdiction to make a disqualification order against the person (in a case where proceedings for a disqualification order have or are being commenced); or

(c)   would have had jurisdiction to make a disqualification order against the person (in a case where the person is subject to disqualification undertaking).

3   Form and conduct of applications

3(1)   The Civil Procedure Rules 1998, and any relevant practice direction, apply in respect of applications under these Rules, except where these Rules make different provision.

3(2)   An application must be made by claim form and the claimant must use the CPR Part 8 (alternative procedure for claims) procedure.

3(3)   In the case of an application under section 15C(1), the Secretary of State is the defendant for the purposes of the Civil Procedure Rules 1998.

3(4)   CPR rule 8.1(3) (power of the court to order the claim to continue as if the claimant had not used the Part 8 procedure), CPR rule 8.2 (contents of the claim form) and CPR rule 8.7 (Part 20 claims) do not apply to applications under these Rules.

3(5)   Rule 12.49 (appeals and reviews of court orders in corporate insolvency) and rule 12.61 (procedure on appeal) of the Insolvency (England and Wales) Rules 2016 apply to applications under these rules.

History
Rule 3(5) substituted by the Insolvency (England and Wales) Rules 2016 (Consequential Amendments and Savings) Rules 2017 (SI 2017/369) r.2(2), Sch.2 para.12(1), (3) as from 6 April 2017.

4   The claimant's case

4(1)   The claimant must, at the time when the claim form is issued, file in court evidence in support of the application.

4(2)   The claimant must serve on the relevant party with the claim form copies of the evidence under paragraph (1).

4(3)   The evidence must be by one or more affidavits or witness statements, which must include–

(a)   in the case of an application under section 15A(1), a statement–

(i)   of the disqualification order or undertaking in respect of which the application is being brought, or of the proceedings for a disqualification order either commenced or being commenced alongside the application;

(ii)   of the loss it is alleged has been caused by the conduct in respect of which–

(aa) the defendant is subject to the disqualification order or undertaking, or

(bb) proceedings for a disqualification order have been or are being commenced;

(iii)   identifying the creditor or creditors to whom it is alleged loss has been caused;

(iv)   identifying particulars of the order the claimant is seeking under section 15B(1); and

(v)   of any other matters considered to be of relevance to the application; and

(b)   in the case of an application under section 15C(1), the compensation undertaking (or a copy).

4(4)   In the case of an application under section 15A(1), where the insolvent company as referred to in section 15A(3)(b) is in administration or liquidation, or there is an administrative receiver of that company, the claimant must also give notice of the claim to the administrator, liquidator or administrative receiver within 14 days of the claim form being issued.

4(5)   The notice under paragraph (4) must identify particulars of the order the claimant is seeking under section 15B(1).

5 Endorsements etc. on claim form

5(1) The following information must be endorsed on the claim form–

(a) that the application is made in accordance with these Rules;

(b) in the case of an application under section 15A(1), that the court has the power to make such an order in respect of loss it is alleged has been caused by the defendant's conduct;

(c) in the case of an application under 15C(1), that the court has the power to reduce the amount of a compensation undertaking offered and accepted under section 15A(2) or to provide that such an undertaking is not to have effect; and

(d) that any evidence which the relevant party wishes the court to take into consideration must be filed in court in accordance with the time limit under rule 7(1).

5(2) The time limit referred to in paragraph (1)(d) must be set out in the claim form.

6 Acknowledgment of service

6(1) The claim form served on the relevant party must be accompanied by an acknowledgment of service and CPR rule 8.3(2) (dealing with the contents of an acknowledgment of service) does not apply.

6(2) In the case of an application under section 15A(1), the acknowledgment of service must state that the defendant should indicate–

(a) whether the defendant is contesting the disqualification on which the application is based by–

(i) contesting the making of a disqualification order (either before it has been made or by way of an appeal), or

(ii) applying for a disqualification undertaking to cease to be in force;

(b) whether the defendant disputes that the conduct on which the application is based caused the loss alleged in the application; or

(c) whether the defendant, while not resisting the application, intends to adduce mitigating factors with a view to justifying a reduced level of compensation.

6(3) In the case of an application under section 15C(1)–

(a) the acknowledgment of service must state whether or not the Secretary of State intends to file any evidence relating to the application; and

(b) CPR rule 8.4 (consequence of not filing an acknowledgment of service) does not apply.

7 Evidence

7(1) The relevant party must, within 28 days from the date of service of the claim form, file in court any evidence relating to the application which the relevant party wishes the court to take into consideration.

7(2) The relevant party must, at the same time, serve on the claimant a copy of any such evidence.

7(3) The claimant must, within 14 days of receiving the copy of the relevant party's evidence, file in court any further evidence in reply which the claimant wishes the court to take into consideration.

7(4) The claimant must, at the same time, serve a copy of any such further evidence on the relevant party.

7(5) Any evidence filed and served under this rule must be by either affidavit or witness statement.

7(6) CPR rules 8.5 (filing and serving written evidence) and 8.6(1) (requirements where written evidence is to be relied on) do not apply.

8 The hearing of the application

8(1) When the claim form is issued, the court must fix a date for the first hearing of the claim for a date not less than 8 weeks from the date of issue of the claim form.

8(2) The hearing must in the first instance be before the registrar in open court.

8(3) Without prejudice to the Secretary of State's rights and obligations under sections 15C(2) and 16(3) on the hearing of an application, subject to the direction of the court, any of the parties may give evidence, call and cross-examine witnesses at the hearing.

8(4) The registrar must either determine the case on the date fixed or adjourn it.

8(5) If the registrar adjourns the case for further consideration the registrar must–

   (a) direct whether the case is to be heard by a registrar or, if the registrar thinks it appropriate, for determination by the judge;

   (b) state the reasons for the adjournment; and

   (c) give directions as to the following matters–

      (i) the manner in which and the time within which notice of the adjournment and the reasons for it are to be given to the relevant party,

      (ii) any order for the provision of further information or for disclosure by the parties,

      (iii) the filing in court and the service of further evidence (if any) by the parties,

      (iv) such other matters as the registrar thinks necessary or expedient with a view to an expeditious disposal of the application, and

      (v) the time and place of the adjourned hearing.

8(6) Where a case is adjourned other than to the judge, it may be heard by the registrar who originally dealt with the case or by another registrar.

9 Compensation orders: making and setting aside of an order

9(1) The court may make a compensation order under section 15A(1) against the defendant whether or not the defendant–

   (a) appears,

   (b) has completed and returned the acknowledgment of service of the claim form, or

   (c) has filed evidence in accordance with rule 7.

9(2) Any compensation order made in the absence of the defendant may be set aside or varied by the court on such terms as it thinks just.

Disqualified Directors Compensation Orders (Fees) (England and Wales) Order 2016

(SI 2016/1047)

Made on 31 October 2016 by the Lord Chancellor, with the sanction of the Treasury, in exercise of the power conferred by the Insolvency Act 2016 s.414(1)(b), read in conjunction with the Company Directors Disqualification Act 1986 s.21(2). Operative from 30 November 2016.

[**Note**: comparable legislation has been enacted for Scotland by the Disqualified Directors (Compensation Orders) (Fees) (Scotland) Order 2016 (SI 2016/1048).]

1 Citation, commencement and interpretation

1(1) This Order may be cited as the Disqualified Directors Compensation Orders (Fees) (England and Wales) Order 2016 and comes into force on 30th November 2016.

1(2) In this Order–

"compensation order" means a court order under section 15A(1) of the Company Directors Disqualification Act 1986; and

"compensation undertaking" means an undertaking accepted by the Secretary of State under section 15A(2) of the Company Directors Disqualification Act 1986.

2 Application

2 This Order applies in relation to–

(a) compensation orders made by the courts in England and Wales; and

(b) compensation undertakings accepted in cases where the courts in England and Wales would have had jurisdiction to make a compensation order.

3 Fees payable in connection with compensation orders and compensation undertakings

3(1) The Secretary of State is to be paid a fee for performing the function of distributing to a creditor an amount received by the Secretary of State in respect of a compensation order or a compensation undertaking to which this Order applies.

3(2) The fee is to be paid out of the amount received before such a distribution is made to a creditor.

3(3) The fee means the aggregate of–

(a) the time spent by the appropriate officials carrying out the Secretary of State's function under paragraph (1) in relation to all creditors specified in a compensation order or a compensation undertaking, multiplied by the hourly rate in accordance with the table in the Schedule; and

(b) any necessary disbursements or expenses properly incurred in carrying out that function,

divided equally between the total number of creditors specified in the compensation order or the compensation undertaking.

4 Value Added Tax

4 Where Value Added Tax is chargeable in respect of the provision of a service for which a fee is payable by virtue of this Order, the amount of the Value Added Tax must be paid in addition to the fee.

SCHEDULE

Article 3

Hourly rates for Secretary of State's fee

Grade according to the Insolvency Service grading structure	Total hourly rate £
D2/Section Head	69
C2/Deputy Section Head	58
C1/Senior Examiner	52
L3/Examiner	46
L2/Examiner	40
B2/Administrator	43
L1/Examiner	38
B1/Administrator	42
A2/Administrator	36
A1/Administrator	31

Insolvency (England and Wales) Rules 2016 (Consequential Amendments and Savings) Rules 2017

(SI 2017/369)

Made on 9 March 2017 by the Lord Chancellor under the Insolvency Act 1986 ss.411 and 412 after consultation with the Insolvency Rules Committee under the Insolvency Act 1986 s.413 and with the concurrence of the Secretary of State. Operative from 6 April 2017.

1 Citation and commencement

1 These Rules may be cited as the Insolvency (England and Wales) Rules 2016 (Consequential Amendments and Savings) Rules 2017 and come into force on 6th April 2017.

2 Amendments consequential on the Insolvency (England and Wales) Rules 2016

2(1) Schedule 1, which amends Acts of Parliament, has effect.

2(2) Schedule 2, which amends subordinate legislation, has effect.

3 Savings in relation to special insolvency rules

3 The Insolvency Rules 1986, as they had effect immediately before 6th April 2017, insofar as they apply to proceedings under the following instruments, continue to have effect for the purposes of the application of–

(a)   the Railway Administration Order 2001;

(b)   [Omitted]

(c)   the Energy Act 2004;

(d)   the Energy Administration Rules 2005;

(e)   the PPP Administration Order Rules 2007;

(f)   the Water Industry (Special Administration) Rules 2009;

(g)   the Energy Act 2011;

(h)   the Charitable Incorporated Organisations (Insolvency and Dissolution) Regulations 2012;

(i)   the Energy Supply Company Administration Rules 2013; and

(j)   the Postal Administration Rules 2013.

History
Rule 3(b) omitted by the Insolvency (Miscellaneous Amendments) Regulations 2017 (SI 2017/1119) regs 1(1), (2), 2, Sch.1 para.2 as from 8 December 2017.

SCHEDULE 1

Rule 2(1)

CONSEQUENTIAL AMENDMENTS TO ACTS OF PARLIAMENT

1 Solicitors Act 1974

1 In section 16(2A)(a) of the Solicitors Act 1974 (duration of suspension of practising certificates), for "Rule 5A.16 of the Insolvency Rules 1986" substitute "Rule 9.18 of the Insolvency (England and Wales) Rules 2016".

2 Administration of Justice Act 1985

2 In section 18(2ZA) of the Administration of Justice Act 1985 (suspension or termination of licences), for "Rule 5A.16 of the Insolvency Rules 1986" substitute "Rule 9.18 of the Insolvency (England and Wales) Rules 2016".

3 Insolvency Act 1986

3 [Not reproduced]

SCHEDULE 2

Rule 2(2)

CONSEQUENTIAL AMENDMENTS TO SUBORDINATE LEGISLATION

1 References to "Insolvency Rules 1986"

1 In each of the following provisions, for "Insolvency Rules 1986", in each place it occurs, substitute "Insolvency (England and Wales) Rules 2016".

Subordinate legislation	References	Provision
Enterprise Act 2002 (Part 9 Restrictions on Disclosure of Information (Amendment and Specification) Order 2003	2003/1400	Schedule 4
Cross-Border Insolvency Regulations 2006	2006/1030	Regulation 1(1)
European Grouping of Territorial Cooperation Regulations 2015	2015/1493	Regulation 2(1)

2 Solicitors' Recognised Bodies Order 1991

2 In Schedule 1 to the Solicitor's Recognised Bodies Order 1991, in the table headed "Statutory instruments which apply to recognised bodies"–

(a) omit the entry for the Insolvency Rules 1986; and

(b) insert in the relevant place–

"S.I. 2016/1024	Insolvency (England and Wales) Rules 2016	The whole instrument except rules 7.7, 7.30, 7.106, 10.11, 10.103 and 12.19".

3   Insolvent Companies (Disqualification of Unfit Directors) Proceedings Rules 1987

3   [Not reproduced]

4   Insolvency Regulations 1994

4   [Not reproduced]

5   Contracting Out (Functions of the Official Receiver) Order 1995

5(1)   The Contracting Out (Functions of the Official Receiver) Order 1995 is amended as follows.

5(2)   In rule 2(1) (interpretation)–

(a)   In the definition of "the insolvency legislation", for "rule 12.1" substitute "Introductory Rule 5".

(b)   For the definition of "the Rules" substitute ""the Rules" means the Insolvency (England and Wales) Rules 2016".

5(3)   In the Schedule–

(a)   Omit paragraph 3.

(b)   For paragraph 8, substitute–

"**8.** The functions of the official receiver–

(a)   exercisable under rule 17.28(2) (functions of committee in winding up by court or

bankruptcy exercisable by official receiver); or

(b)   in relation to the hearing of an application made under–

(i)   section 280 (discharge by order of the court);

(ii)   rule 7.44(2) (application to court for a release or extension of time in respect of statement of affairs in a winding up by the court); or

(iii)   rule 10.58(2) (application to court by bankrupt for a release or extension of time in respect of statement of affairs)."

5(4)   Omit paragraph 11.

5(5)   In paragraph 14–

(a)   In sub-paragraph (d), for "rule 4.36(5)" substitute "rule 7.44(6)(a)";

(b)   In sub-paragraph (e), for "rule 6.62(5)" substitute "rule 10.58(6)(a)"; and

(c)   In sub-paragraph (f), for "rule 6.215(2)" substitute "rule 10.142(2)".

5(6)   Omit paragraph 21.

6   Insurers (Winding Up) Rules 2001

6   [Not reproduced]

7   Pension Protection Fund (Entry Rules) Regulations 2005

7(1)   The Pension Protection Fund (Entry Rules) Regulations 2005 are amended as follows.

7(2)   In regulation 1 (citation, commencement and interpretation), paragraph 3, omit the definition of "the Insolvency Rules".

7(3) In regulation 5(1)(a)(iii) (prescribed insolvency events), for "Rule 2.132 of the Insolvency Rules (conversion of administration to winding up – power of court)" substitute "rule 21.3 of the Insolvency (England and Wales) Rules 2016 (conversion into winding up proceedings or bankruptcy: court order)".

7(4) In regulation 5(1)(aa)(i) (prescribed insolvency events), for "Insolvency Rules" substitute "Insolvency Rules 1986".

7(5) In regulation 6(1)(a)(iii) (circumstances in which insolvency proceedings in relation to the employer are stayed or come to an end), for "Rule 2.132 of the Insolvency Rules (conversion of administration to winding up – power of court)" substitute "rule 21.3 of the Insolvency (England and Wales) Rules 2016 (conversion into winding up proceedings or bankruptcy: court order)".

7(6) In regulation 6(1)(c)(iii)(bb), for "the Insolvency Rules" substitute "the Insolvency Rules 1986".

8 Civil Partnership (Treatment of Overseas Relationships) Order 2005

8 For article 2(e)(ii) (overseas relationships dissolved etc. before commencement treated as civil partnerships) of the Civil Partnership (Treatment of Overseas Relationships) Order 2005, substitute–

"(ii) (rules 10.167 (bankrupt's home: property falling within section 283A), 10.168 (application in relation to the vesting of an interest in a dwelling-house (registered land), 10.169 (vesting of bankrupt's interest (unregistered land)) and 10.171 (charging order) of the Insolvency (England and Wales) Rules 2016."

9 Legal Services Act 2007 (Designation of a Licensing Authority) (No. 2) Order 2011

9(1) The Legal Services Act 2007 (Designation as a Licensing Authority) (No. 2) Order 2011 is amended as follows.

9(2) In the table in Schedule 2–

(a) omit the entry for the Insolvency Rules 1986; and

(b) insert in the relevant place–

"Insolvency (England and Wales) Rules 2016 (S.I. 2016/1024)	The whole instrument except rules 7.6, 7.105, 10.10, 10.103 and 12.20".

10 Assets of Community Value (England) Regulations 2012

10 In Schedule 3 (relevant disposals to which section 95(1) of the Act does not apply) of the Assets of Community Value (England) Regulations 2012, for paragraph 7 substitute–

"**7.** A disposal pursuant to insolvency proceedings defined as proceedings under the Insolvency Act 1986 or the Insolvency (England and Wales) Rules 2016."

11 Care and Support (Cross-border Placements) (Business Failure Duties of Scottish Local Authorities) Regulations 2014

11 In regulation 4(1)(j) of the Care and Support (Cross-border Placements) (Business Failure Duties of Scottish Local Authorities) Regulations 2014, for "rule 2.12 (conversion of administration to winding up – power of court) of the Insolvency Rules 1986" substitute "rule 21.3 (conversion into winding up proceedings or bankruptcy: court order) of the Insolvency (England and Wales) Rules 2016."

12 Compensation Orders (Disqualified Directors) Proceedings (England and Wales) Rules 2016

12 [Not reproduced]

Deregulation Act 2015 and Small Business, Enterprise and Employment Act 2015 (Consequential Amendments) (Savings) Regulations 2017

(SI 2017/540)

Made on April 2017 by the Secretary of State for Business, Energy and Industrial Strategy makes these Regulations in exercise of the powers conferred by s.112(1) and (2) of the Deregulation Act 2015 and s.159(1) and (2) of the Small Business, Enterprise and Employment Act 2015. Operative from 6 April 2017.

1 Citation and commencement

1 These Regulations may be cited as the Deregulation Act 2015 and Small Business, Enterprise and Employment Act 2015 (Consequential Amendments) (Savings) Regulations 2017 and come into force on 6th April 2017.

2 Consequential amendments to primary legislation

2 Schedule 1 has effect.

3 Consequential amendments to subordinate legislation

3 Schedule 2 has effect.

4 Savings for certain insolvency rules

4(1) In this regulation, "the relevant amendments" means the amendments made by–

(a) paragraphs 12, 13(1), 14 and 15 of Schedule 6 to, the Deregulation Act 2015; and

(b) sections 122, 123, 124 and 125 of, and Schedule 9 to, the Small Business, Enterprise and Employment Act 2015.

4(2) The Insolvency Act 1986, insofar as it applies to proceedings under the following instruments, continues to have effect without the relevant amendments for the purposes of the application of those instruments–

(a) the Railway Administration Order 2001;

(b) [Omitted]

(c) the Energy Act 2004;

(d) the Energy Administration Rules 2005;

(e) the PPP Administration Order Rules 2007;

(f) the Water Industry (Special Administration) Rules 2009;

(g) the Energy Act 2011;

(h) the Charitable Incorporated Organisations (Insolvency and Dissolution) Regulations 2012;

(i) the Energy Supply Company Administration Rules 2013; and

(j) the Postal Administration Rules 2013.

History
Regulation 4(2)(b) omitted by the Insolvency (Miscellaneous Amendments) Regulations 2017 (SI 2017/1119) regs 1, 2, Sch.1 para.3 as from 8 December 2017.

SCHEDULE 1

Regulation 2

CONSEQUENTIAL AMENDMENTS TO PRIMARY LEGISLATION

[Not reproduced.]

SCHEDULE 2

Regulation 3

CONSEQUENTIAL AMENDMENTS TO SUBORDINATE LEGISLATION

[Not reproduced.]

Insolvency (Scotland) (Company Voluntary Arrangements and Administration) Rules 2018

Introduction to the Scottish legislation

Like the Insolvency (England and Wales) Rules 2016 (hereafter "the 2016 Rules"), the Insolvency (Scotland) (Company Voluntary Arrangements and Administration) Rules 2018 (SI 2018/1082 (S.4)) and the Insolvency (Scotland) (Receivership and Winding Up) Rules 2018 (SSI 2018/347) (hereafter collectively "the Scottish corporate insolvency rules") had a protracted gestation period, not least because of the stated policy intention that they be modelled as closely as possible on what are now the 2016 Rules (see further below). This resulted in a further time lag between the introduction of the 2016 Rules and the introduction of the Scottish corporate insolvency rules. It may be noted that unlike the 2016 Rules, the Scottish corporate insolvency rules relate only to corporate insolvency: non-corporate insolvency in Scotland is the subject of separate bankruptcy legislation.

The fact that the Scottish corporate insolvency rules are contained in two separate statutory instruments rather than one is an unfortunate consequence of devolution. As is explained in more detail in the Explanatory Memorandum which accompanies the Insolvency (Scotland) (Company Voluntary Arrangements and Administration) Rules 2018 and the Policy Note which accompanies the Insolvency (Scotland) (Receivership and Winding Up) Rules 2018, competence in respect of corporate insolvency in Scotland is split between the UK and Scottish Parliaments: in broad terms, company voluntary arrangements ("CVAs") and administration are reserved, receivership is devolved, and winding up is partly reserved and partly devolved (see Scotland Act 1998 Sch.5 Section C2). The rule-making power in s.411 of the Insolvency Act 1986 is similarly split: the power to make rules relating to receivership and the devolved aspects of winding up was transferred to the Scottish Ministers by virtue of s.53 of the Scotland Act 1998, while the power to make rules in relation to reserved matters remained with the Secretary of State. This gave rise to a particular complication with regard to winding up, and in light of the fact that there has been debate about exactly which aspects of winding up are reserved and which are devolved, and in order to avoid the rules on winding up being split between two different statutory instruments, the Scotland Act 1998 (Insolvency Functions) Order 2018 (SI 2018/174) made provision for the mutual transfer of the rule-making power in s.411 in relation to winding up, thus enabling the making of all of the rules relating to winding up by *either* the Scottish Ministers *or* the Secretary of State with the consent of the other where relevant. As a matter of policy, it was then agreed that the rules relating to winding up would be made by the Scottish Ministers with the consent of the Secretary of State (see the Policy Note which accompanies the Insolvency (Scotland) (Receivership and Winding Up) Rules 2018). Thus, although having the Scottish corporate insolvency rules in two statutory instruments rather than one cannot be regarded as satisfactory, the position could have been worse: the rules on winding up could have been split between the two statutory instruments. As it is, this at least has been avoided, and one must no doubt be grateful for such small mercies.

Except in relation to limited liability partnerships, special administration regimes and other special insolvency regimes, the Scottish corporate insolvency rules replace the Insolvency (Scotland) Rules 1986 (SI 1986/1915) and the Receivers (Scotland) Regulations 1986 (SI 1986/1917) which, like their counterparts in England and Wales, had been amended on numerous occasions (see Sch.1 to the Insolvency (Scotland) (Company Voluntary Arrangements and Administration) Rules 2018 and Sch.1 to the Insolvency (Scotland) (Receivership and Winding Up) Rules 2018 for details of the relevant amending instruments thereby revoked). Like the 2016 Rules, therefore, the Scottish corporate insolvency rules represent a fresh start up to a point. Like the 2016 Rules, they embody the reforms flowing from the Small Business, Enterprise and Insolvency Act 2015 brought into force in Scotland contemporaneously with them. In addition, they also embody certain reforms to devolved areas of corporate insolvency law which mirror reforms previously introduced to corporate insolvency law in England and Wales and to reserved areas of corporate insolvency law in Scotland by the Legislative Reform (Insolvency) (Miscellaneous Provisions) Order 2010 (SI 2010/18). These reforms had not previously been extended to the devolved areas of corporate insolvency law as a result of an inexplicable delay in bringing the necessary legislation before the Scottish Parliament, a situation which was finally remedied by the Public Service Reform (Insolvency) (Scotland) Order 2016 (SSI 2016/141) and the Public Service Reform (Corporate Insolvency and Bankruptcy) (Scotland) Order 2017 (SSI 2017/209). Like the 2016 Rules, the Scottish corporate insolvency rules seek to modernise the rules in terms of their structure, language and style and, as previously referred to, they also seek to provide as much consistency as possible with the 2016 Rules. Like the 2016 Rules, however, they are largely a consolidation of the previous, amended, Scottish rules, albeit intended to better meet the needs of users including the judiciary, insolvency office-holders, creditors and public officials. The UK Insolvency Service has published a table of derivations and destinations prepared in conjunction with the Accountant in Bankruptcy (who has responsibility for the devolved areas of corporate insolvency law) which can be found on the Insolvency Service website at *https://www.gov.uk/government/news/insolvency-scotland-rules-table-of-destinations-now-available* and on the Accountant in Bankruptcy's website at *https://www.aib.gov.uk/sites/default/files/2018_ci_rules_-_collated_derivation_and_destination_tables.pdf*.

The Scottish corporate insolvency rules were not the subject of formal consultation as such, although there were public consultations prior to the enactment of the Public Service Reform (Insolvency) (Scotland) Order 2016 and the Public Service Reform (Corporate Insolvency and Bankruptcy) (Scotland) Order 2017 which encompassed the possible modernisation of the Scottish corporate insolvency rules. A working group including representation from the insolvency profession was established and considered the content of both statutory instruments in draft and the final impact assessment which accompanies the Insolvency (Scotland) (Receivership and Winding Up) Rules 2018 gives further details of other consultation and discussion which took place during the development of the Scottish corporate insolvency rules, including with the UK Insolvency Service, the Scottish Courts and Tribunals Service, the Scottish Civil Justice Council, Companies House and other stakeholders.

Like the 2016 Rules, the Scottish corporate insolvency rules have introduced "common parts", which are repeated in each of the statutory instruments, and the comments made in relation to this approach in the 2016 Rules apply equally to the Scottish corporate insolvency rules. Similarly, the Scottish corporate insolvency rules eschew the use of prescribed forms and instead set out details of required information. In the final impact assessment which accompanies the Insolvency (Scotland) (Receivership and Winding Up) Rules 2018, however, it is stated that the Accountant in Bankruptcy will produce non-statutory template forms containing the prescribed information which will be made available on their website for the use of all stakeholders, although at the time of writing, these were not yet available. As in England and Wales, however, the break with statutory forms will remain incomplete due to the continuing use of such forms in other areas.

The Scottish corporate insolvency rules came into force on 6 April 2019, subject to the transitional and savings provisions set out in Sch.2 to each statutory instrument. Both instruments were subject to negative parliamentary procedure. The Joint Committee on Statutory Instruments reported the Insolvency (Scotland) (Company Voluntary Arrangements and Administration) Rules 2018 for defective drafting in two respects (see their 38th Report of Session 2017–19), but noted that the Department for Business, Energy and Industrial Strategy had provided clarification on both points and had undertaken to make appropriate clarificatory amendments at the first opportunity. The Economy, Energy and Fair Work Committee made no comments on the Insolvency (Scotland) (Receivership and Winding Up) Rules 2018 (see Scottish Parliament Official Report, Economy, Energy and Fair Work Committee, Tuesday 11 December 2018, Session 5, pp.26–27). Anecdotal evidence suggests that some problematic issues have already been identified, including some which flow through from the 2016 Rules. It is therefore to be expected that some amendments might be made to the Scottish corporate insolvency rules in due course.

As referred to above, an Explanatory Memorandum accompanies the Insolvency (Scotland) (Company Voluntary Arrangements and Administration) Rules 2018 and a Policy Note and final impact assessment accompany the Insolvency (Scotland) (Receivership and Winding Up) Rules 2018. These documents contain helpful summaries of the policy background and the main changes brought about by the Scottish corporate insolvency rules. The final impact assessment also states that the Accountant in Bankruptcy will, where appropriate, prepare and publish on their website guidance to support stakeholders in implementing the new Scottish corporate insolvency rules, although at the time of writing, no such guidance was yet available. Like the 2016 Rules, the Scottish corporate insolvency rules themselves also contain non-legislative notes to assist users.

Like the 2016 Rules, the Insolvency (Scotland) (Company Voluntary Arrangements and Administration) Rules 2018 contain provision for their periodic review with the first report to be published before the end of the period of five years after they come into force. Oddly, the Insolvency (Scotland) (Receivership and Winding Up) Rules 2018 contain no such specific provision, but the accompanying final impact assessment states that the Accountant in Bankruptcy will carry out continuous monitoring of the provisions post-commencement.

Insolvency (Scotland) (Company Voluntary Arrangements and Administration) Rules 2018

(SI 2018/1082 (S.4))

Made on 11 October 2018 by the Secretary of State for Business, Energy and Industrial Strategy in exercise of the power conferred by s.411(1)(b), (2) and (2A) of the Insolvency Act 1986; the Scottish Ministers have consented to these Rules in accordance with art.5(2) of the Scotland Act 1998 (Insolvency Functions) Order 2018 (SI 2018/174). Operative from 6 April 2019

[**Note**: These Rules from 6 April 2019 revoke and replace the Insolvency (Scotland) Rules 1986 (SI 1986/1915 (S.139)) Pt 1 and 2 and rr.0.1–0.3 and Pt 7 (and Schs 3–5) insofar as they apply to company voluntary arrangements and administration, subject to transitional and savings provisions in Sch.2 to these Rules. The Insolvency (Scotland) Rules 1986 are reproduced in the 21st edition of this *Guide*.]

CONTENTS

INTRODUCTORY RULES

1 Citation and commencement

1 These Rules may be cited as the Insolvency (Scotland) (Company Voluntary Arrangements and Administration) Rules 2018 and come into force on 6th April 2019.

2 Revocations

2 The enactments listed in the first column of the table in Schedule 1 are revoked to the extent specified in the third column of that table.

3 Extent and application

3(1) These Rules extend to Scotland only.

3(2) These Rules, as they relate to company voluntary arrangements under Part 1 of the Act and administration under Part 2 of the Act, apply in relation to companies which the courts in Scotland have jurisdiction to wind up.

4 Transitional and savings provisions

4 The transitional and savings provisions set out in Schedule 2 have effect.

5 Punishment of offences

5 Schedule 3 sets out the maximum penalties for offences under these Rules.

6 Review

6(1) The Secretary of State must from time to time–

(a) carry out a review of the regulatory provision contained in these Rules; and

(b) publish a report setting out the conclusions of the review.

6(2) The first report must be published before the end of the period of five years beginning with the day on which these Rules come into force.

6(3) Subsequent reports must be published at intervals not exceeding five years.

6(4) Section 30(4) of the Small Business, Enterprise and Employment Act 2015 requires that a report published under this rule must, in particular–

(a) set out the objectives intended to be achieved by the regulatory provision referred to in paragraph (1)(a);

(b) assess the extent to which those objectives are achieved;

(c) assess whether those objectives remain appropriate; and

(d) if those objectives remain appropriate, assess the extent to which they could be achieved in another way which involves less onerous regulatory provision.

6(5) In this rule, "regulatory provision" has the same meaning as in sections 28 to 32 of the Small Business, Enterprise and Employment Act 2015 (see section 32 of that Act).

PART 1

SCOPE, INTERPRETATION, TIME AND RULES ABOUT DOCUMENTS

CHAPTER 1

SCOPE OF THESE RULES

1.1   Scope

1.1(1)   These Rules are made to give effect, in Scotland, in relation to company voluntary arrangements and administration, to–

(a)   Parts 1 and 2 of the Insolvency Act 1986; and

(b)   the EU Regulation.

1.1(2)   Consequently, references to insolvency proceedings and requirements relating to such proceedings are, unless the context requires otherwise, limited to insolvency proceedings in respect of Parts 1 and 2 of the Act and the EU Regulation (whether or not court proceedings).

CHAPTER 2

INTERPRETATION

[Note: the terms which are defined in rule 1.2 include some terms defined in the Act for limited purposes which are applied generally by these Rules. Such terms have the meaning given by the Act for those limited purposes.]

1.2   Defined terms

1.2(1)   In these Rules, unless the context otherwise requires–

"the Act" means the Insolvency Act 1986, and–

(a)   a reference to a numbered section without mention of another Act is to that section of the Act; and

(b)   a reference to Schedule A1 or B1 is to that Schedule to the Act;

"the Companies Act" means the Companies Act 2006;

"appointed person" means a person who meets the requirements in paragraph (2) and who is appointed by an office-holder;

"Article 1.2 undertaking" means one of the following within the meaning of Article 1.2 of the EU Regulation–

(a)   an insurance undertaking;

(b)   a credit institution;

(c)   an investment undertaking which provides services involving the holding of funds or securities for third parties;

(d)   a collective investment undertaking;

[Note: "associate" is defined in section 435];

"attendance" and "attend"–

> a person attends a meeting by being present, by attending remotely in accordance with section 246A or rule 5.6, or by participating in a virtual meeting; and a person may attend a meeting in person, by proxy or by corporate representative (in accordance with section 434B of the Act or section 323 of the Companies Act, as applicable);

"authenticate" means to authenticate in accordance with rule 1.6;

"blank proxy" is to be interpreted in accordance with rule 6.3

[Note: "business day" is defined in section 251]

"centre of main interests" has the same meaning as in the EU Regulation;

[Note: "connected" used of a person in relation to a company is defined in section 249 of the Act];

"consumer" means an individual acting for purposes that are wholly or mainly outside that individual's trade, business, craft or profession;

"convener" means an office-holder or other person who seeks a decision in accordance with Part 5 of these Rules;

[Note: "the court" is defined in section 251];

"CVA" means a voluntary arrangement in relation to a company made under Part 1 of the Act;

"debt" as it relates to administration, means any of the following–

(a) any debt or liability to which the company is subject at the relevant date;

(b) any debt or liability to which the company may become subject after the relevant date by reason of any obligation incurred before that date;

(c) any interest provable as mentioned in rule 3.111;

and for the purposes of the definition of debt, "relevant date" means–

(a) in the case of an administration which was not immediately preceded by a winding up, the date on which the company entered administration; and

(b) in the case of an administration which was immediately preceded by a winding up, the date on which the company went into liquidation.

"decision date" and "decision procedure" are to be interpreted in accordance with rule 5.2;

[Note: "deemed consent procedure" is defined in section 246ZF];

"deliver" and "delivery" are to be interpreted in accordance with Chapter 9 of Part 1 of these Rules;

"deliver to the creditors" and similar expressions in these Rules and the Act are to be interpreted in accordance with rule 1.33;

"document" includes a written notice or statement or anything else in writing capable of being delivered to a recipient;

[Note: "the EU Regulation" is defined in section 436 as "Regulation (EU) 2015/848 of the European Parliament and of the Council of 20 May 2015 on insolvency proceedings"];

[Note: "the Gazette" has the meaning given in section 251];

"Gazette notice" means a notice which is, has been, or is to be gazetted;

"to gazette" means to advertise in the Gazette, whether electronically or otherwise;

[Note: "hire-purchase agreement" is defined in section 436(1); and is supplemented by paragraph 1 of Schedule A1 (company voluntary arrangements) for the purposes of that Schedule and by paragraph 111(1) of Schedule B1 (administration) for the purposes of that Schedule];

"identification details" and similar references to information identifying persons, insolvency proceedings etc. are to be interpreted in accordance with rule 1.7;

"insolvent estate" means the company's assets;

"IP number" means the number assigned to an office-holder as an insolvency practitioner by the Secretary of State;

"local creditor" has the same meaning as in Article 2 of the EU Regulation;

"main proceedings" means proceedings opened in accordance with Article 3(1) of the EU Regulation and falling within the definition of insolvency proceedings in Article 2(4) of the EU Regulation and which–

    (a)   in relation to Scotland, are set out in Annex A to that Regulation under the heading "United Kingdom"; and

    (b)   in relation to another member State, are set out in Annex A under the heading relating to that member State;

"meeting" in relation to a company's creditors means either a "physical meeting" or a "virtual meeting";

"member State liquidator" means a person falling within the definition of "insolvency practitioner" in Article 2(5) of the EU Regulation appointed in proceedings to which the EU Regulation applies in a member State other than the United Kingdom;

[Note: "nominee" is defined in section 1(2) in relation to company voluntary arrangements];

"non-EU proceedings" means insolvency proceedings which are not main, secondary or territorial proceedings;

"office-holder" means a person who under the Act or these Rules holds an office in relation to insolvency proceedings and includes a nominee;

"official rate" is the rate of interest on a sheriff court decree or extract under section 9 of the Sheriff Courts (Scotland) Extracts Act 1892 (as it may be amended by section 4 of the Administration of Justice (Scotland) Act 1972);

"physical meeting" has the meaning given by rule 5.2;

"prescribed part" has the same meaning as in section 176A(2)(a) and the Insolvency Act 1986 (Prescribed Part) Order 2003;

"progress report" means a report which complies with rules 3.93 and 3.94;

[Note: "property" is defined in section 436(1)];

"proxy" and "proxy-holder" are to be interpreted in accordance with rule 6.2;

"qualified to act as an insolvency practitioner", in relation to a company, is to be interpreted in accordance with Part 13 of the Act;

[Note: "records" are defined in section 436(1)];

"secondary proceedings" means proceedings opened in accordance with Article 3(2) and (3) of the EU Regulation and falling within the definition of insolvency proceedings in Article 2(4) of the EU Regulation and which–

(a) in relation to Scotland, are set out in Annex A to that Regulation under the heading "United Kingdom"; and

(b) in relation to another member State are set out in Annex A under the heading relating to that member State;

"serve" and "service" are to be interpreted in respect of a particular document by reference to the Rules of Court;

"standard contents" means–

(a) for a Gazette notice, the standard contents set out in Chapter 5 of Part 1;

(b) for a notice to be advertised other than in the Gazette, the standard contents set out in Chapter 6 of Part 1;

(c) for a document to be delivered to the registrar of companies, the standard contents set out in Chapter 7 of Part 1; and

(d) for notices to be delivered to other persons, the standard contents set out in Chapter 8 of Part 1;

"standard fee for copies" means 15 pence per A4 or A5 page or 30 pence per A3 page;

"statement of claim" is to be interpreted in accordance with rule 3.105;

"statement of proposals" means a statement made by an administrator under paragraph 49 of Schedule B1 setting out proposals for achieving the purpose of an administration;

"territorial proceedings" means proceedings opened in accordance with Article 3(2) and (4) of the EU Regulation and falling within the definition of insolvency proceedings in Article 2(4) of that Regulation and which–

(a) in relation to Scotland, are set out in Annex A to the EU Regulation under the heading "United Kingdom"; and

(b) in relation to another member State, are set out in Annex A under the heading relating to that member State;

"venue" in relation to any proceedings, attendance before the court, decision procedure or meeting means the time, date and place or platform for the proceedings, attendance, decision procedure or meeting;

"virtual meeting" has the meaning given by rule 5.2;

[Note: "writing" is to be construed in accordance with section 436B];

"written resolution" in respect of a private company means a written resolution passed in accordance with Chapter 2 of Part 13 of the Companies Act.

1.2(2)   An appointed person in relation to a company must be–

(a) qualified to act as an insolvency practitioner in relation to that company, or

(b) a person experienced in insolvency matters who is–

(i) a member or employee of the office-holder's firm, or

(ii) an employee of the office-holder.

1.2(3)   A fee or remuneration is chargeable when the work to which it relates is done.

CHAPTER 3

CALCULATION OF TIME PERIODS

1.3 Periods of time expressed in days

1.3(1)   This rule applies to the calculation of a period of time expressed in days.

1.3(2)   A period of time expressed as a number of days is to be computed as clear days.

1.3(3)   In this rule, "clear days" means that in computing the number of days–

(a)   the day on which the period begins; and

(b)   if the end of the period is defined by reference to an event, the day on which that event occurs,

are not included.

1.4 Periods of time expressed in months

1.4(1)   This rule applies to the calculation of a period of time expressed in months.

1.4(2)   The beginning and the end of a period expressed in months are to be determined as follows–

(a)   if the beginning of the period is specified–

  (i)   the month in which the period ends is the specified number of months after the month in which it begins; and

  (ii)   the date in the month on which the period ends is–

    (aa) the day before the date corresponding to the date in the month on which it begins, or

    (bb) if there is no such date in the month in which it ends, the last day of that month;

(b)   if the end of the period is specified–

  (i)   the month in which the period begins is the specified number of months before the month in which it ends; and

  (ii)   the date in the month on which the period begins is–

    (aa) the day after the date corresponding to the date in the month on which it ends, or

    (bb) if there is no such date in the month in which it begins, the last day of that month.

CHAPTER 4

FORM AND CONTENT OF DOCUMENTS

1.5 Requirement for writing and form of documents

1.5(1)   A notice or statement must be in writing unless the Act or these Rules provide otherwise.

1.5(2)   A document in electronic form must be capable of being–

(a)   read by the recipient in electronic form; and

(b)   reproduced by the recipient in hard-copy form.

1.6   Authentication

1.6(1)   A document in electronic form is authenticated–

(a)   if the identity of the sender is confirmed in a manner specified by the recipient; or

(b)   where the recipient has not so specified, if the communication contains or is accompanied by a statement of the identity of the sender and the recipient has no reason to doubt the truth of that statement.

1.6(2)   A document in hard copy form is authenticated if it is signed.

1.6(3)   If a document is authenticated by the signature of an individual on behalf of–

(a)   a body of persons, the document must also state the position of that individual in relation to the body;

(b)   a body corporate of which the individual is the sole member, the document must also state that fact.

1.7   Information required to identify persons and insolvency proceedings etc.

1.7(1)   Where the Act or these Rules require a document to identify, or to contain identification details in respect of, a person or insolvency proceedings, or to provide contact details for an office-holder, the information set out in the table must be given.

1.7(2)   Where a requirement relates to a proposed office-holder, the information set out in the table in respect of an office-holder must be given with any necessary adaptations.

Company where it is the subject of the insolvency proceedings	In the case of a registered company–
	(a) the registered name;
	(b) for a company incorporated in Scotland under the Companies Act or a previous Companies Act, its registered number;
	(c) for a company incorporated outside the United Kingdom–
	    (i) the country or territory in which it is incorporated,
	    (ii) the number, if any, under which it is registered, and
	    (iii) the number, if any, under which it is registered as an overseas company under Part 34 of the Companies Act.
	In the case of an unregistered company–
	    (d) its name; and
	    (e) the postal address of any principal place of business.

Company other than one which is the subject of the insolvency proceedings	In the case of a registered company–
	(f) the registered name;
	(g) for a company incorporated in any part of the United Kingdom under the Companies Act or a previous Companies Act, its registered number;
	(h) for a company incorporated outside the United Kingdom–
	    (i) the country or territory in which it is incorporated;
	    (ii) the number, if any, under which it is registered; and
	    (iii) the number, if any, under which it is registered as an overseas company under Part 34 of the Companies Act;

	In the case of an unregistered company– (i) its name; and (j) the postal address of any principal place of business
Office-holder	(k) the name of the office-holder; and (l) the nature of the appointment held by the office-holder.
Contact details for an officeholder	(m) a postal address for the office-holder; and (n) either an email address, or a telephone number, through which the office-holder may be contacted.

Insolvency proceedings	(o) information identifying the company to which the insolvency proceedings relate;
	 (p) if the insolvency proceedings are, or are to be, conducted in a court–
	      (i) the full name of the court and, if applicable;
	      (ii) any number assigned to those insolvency proceedings by the court.

1.8   Reasons for stating that insolvency proceedings are or will be main, secondary etc. under the EU Regulation

1.8   Where these Rules require reasons to be given for a statement that proceedings are or will be main, secondary, territorial or non-EU insolvency proceedings, the reasons must include–

(a)   the company's centre of main interests,

(b)   the place of the company's registered office within the meaning of Article 3(1) of the EU Regulation and where appropriate an explanation why this is not the same as the centre of main interests, or

(c)   a statement that there is no registered office if that is the case in non-EU proceedings.

1.9   Prescribed format of documents

1.9(1)   Where a rule sets out the required contents of a document any title required by the rule must appear at the beginning of the document.

1.9(2)   Any other contents required by the rule (or rules where more than one apply to a particular document) must be provided in the order listed in the rule (or rules) or in another order which the maker of the document considers would be more convenient for the intended recipient.

1.10   Variations from prescribed contents

1.10   Where a rule sets out the required contents of a document, the document may depart from the required contents if–

(a)   the circumstances require such a departure (including where the requirement is not applicable in the particular case); or

(b)   the departure (whether or not intentional) is immaterial.

CHAPTER 5

STANDARD CONTENTS OF GAZETTE NOTICES AND THE GAZETTE AS EVIDENCE ETC.

[Note: the requirements in Chapter 5 must be read with rule 1.7 which sets out the information required to identify an office-holder, a company etc.]

1.11   Contents of notices to be gazetted under the Act or Rules

1.11(1)   Where, in accordance with the Act or these Rules, a notice is to be gazetted, the notice must contain the standard contents set out in this Chapter (in addition to any content specifically required by the Act or any other provision of these Rules).

1.11(2)   Information which this Chapter requires to be included in a Gazette notice may be omitted if it is not reasonably practicable to obtain it.

1.12   Standard contents of Gazette notices

1.12(1)   A Gazette notice must identify the insolvency proceedings and, if it is relevant to the particular notice, identify the office-holder and state–

(a)   the office-holder's contact details;

(b)   the office-holder's IP number;

(c)   the name of any person other than the office-holder who may be contacted about the insolvency proceedings; and

(d)   the date of the office-holder's appointment.

1.12(2)   A Gazette notice relating to a registered company must also state–

(a)   its registered office;

(b)   any principal trading address if this is different from its registered office;

(c)   any name under which it was registered in the period of 12 months before the date of the commencement of the insolvency proceedings which are the subject of the Gazette notice; and

(d)   any other name or style (not being a registered name)–

(i)   under which the company carried on business, and

(ii)   in which any debt owed to a creditor was incurred.

1.12(3)   A Gazette notice relating to an unregistered company must also identify the company and specify any name or style–

(a)   under which the company carried on business, and

(b)   in which any debt owed to a creditor was incurred.

1.13   The Gazette: evidence, variations, errors and timing

1.13(1)   Where a notice is gazetted under the Act or these Rules a copy of the Gazette containing the notice is evidence of any facts stated in the notice.

1.13(2)   Where the Act or these Rules require an order of the court to be gazetted, a copy of the Gazette containing the notice of the order may be produced in any proceedings as conclusive evidence that the order was made on the date specified in the Gazette notice.

1.13(3)   Where an order of the court which is gazetted has been varied, or any matter has been erroneously or inaccurately gazetted, the person whose responsibility it was to gazette the order or other matter must, as soon as reasonably practicable, cause the variation to be gazetted or a further entry to be made in the Gazette for the purpose of correcting the error or inaccuracy.

1.13(4)   A Gazette notice, variation or correction is taken to be gazetted or published on the date it first appears in either electronic or hard copy form.

CHAPTER 6

STANDARD CONTENTS OF NOTICES ADVERTISED OTHERWISE THAN IN THE GAZETTE

[Note: the requirements in Chapter 6 must be read with rule 1.7 which sets out the information required to identify an office-holder, a company etc.]

1.14   Standard contents of notices advertised otherwise than in the Gazette

1.14(1)   Where, in accordance with the Act or these Rules, a notice is to be advertised otherwise than in the Gazette, the notice must contain the standard contents set out in this rule (in addition to any content specifically required by the Act or any other provision of these Rules).

1.14(2)   A notice relating to a company must also identify the insolvency proceedings and state–

(a)   the company's principal trading address;

(b)   any name under which the company was registered in the 12 months before the date of the commencement of the insolvency proceedings which are the subject of the notice; and

(c)   any name or style (not being a registered name)–

　　(i)   under which the company carried on business, and

　　(ii)   in which any debt owed to a creditor was incurred.

1.14(3)   A notice must, if it is relevant to the particular notice, identify the office-holder and specify the office-holder's contact details.

1.14(4)   Information which this rule requires to be included in a notice may be omitted if it is not reasonably practicable to obtain it.

1.15   Non-Gazette notices: clear and comprehensible

1.15   Information which this Chapter requires to be stated in a notice must be so stated in a way that is clear and comprehensible.

CHAPTER 7

STANDARD CONTENTS OF DOCUMENTS TO BE DELIVERED TO THE REGISTRAR OF COMPANIES

[Note: the requirements in Chapter 7 must be read with rule 1.7 which sets out the information required to identify an office-holder, a company etc.]

1.16   Standard contents of documents delivered to the registrar of companies

1.16(1)   Where the Act or these Rules require a document to be delivered to the registrar of companies the document must contain the standard contents set out in this Chapter (in addition to any content specifically required by the Act or any other provision of these Rules).

1.16(2)   A document of more than one type must satisfy the requirements which apply to each.

1.17   Registrar of companies: covering notices

1.17(1)   This rule applies where the Act or these Rules require an office-holder to deliver any of the following documents to the registrar of companies–

(a)   an account or a summary of receipts and payments;

(b)   a court order;

   (c)   a statement of administrator's proposals or a statement of revised proposals;

   (d)   a statement of affairs;

   (e)   a statement of concurrence;

   (f)   a notice of an administrator's resignation under paragraph 87(2) of Schedule B1;

   (g)   any report including–

      (i)   a final report,

      (ii)   a progress report (including a final progress report),

      (iii)   a report of a creditors' decision under paragraph 53(2) or 54(6) of Schedule B1, and

      (iv)   a report of a decision approving a CVA under section 4(6) and 4(6A) or paragraph 30(3) and (4) of Schedule A1;

   (h)   a copy of the notice that a CVA has been fully implemented or terminated that the supervisor is required to deliver under rule 2.44(3);

   (i)   an undertaking given under Article 36 of the EU Regulation.

1.17(2)   The office-holder must deliver to the registrar of companies with a document mentioned in paragraph (1) a notice containing the standard contents required by this Part.

1.17(3)   Such a notice may relate to more than one document where those documents relate to the same insolvency proceedings and are delivered together to the registrar of companies.

1.18   Standard contents of all documents

1.18(1)   A document to be delivered to the registrar of companies must–

   (a)   identify the company;

   (b)   state–

      (i)   the nature of the document,

      (ii)   the section (or paragraph) of the Act, or the rule under which the document is delivered,

      (iii)   the date of the document,

      (iv)   the name and address of the person delivering the document, and

      (v)   the capacity in which that person is acting in relation to the company; and

   (c)   be authenticated by the person delivering the document.

1.18(2)   Where the person delivering the document is the office-holder, the address may be omitted if it has previously been notified to the registrar of companies in the insolvency proceedings and is unchanged.

1.19   Standard contents of documents relating to the office of office-holders

1.19(1)   A document relating to the office of the office-holder must also identify the officeholder and state–

   (a)   the date of the event of which notice is delivered or of the notice (as applicable);

   (b)   where the document relates to an appointment, the person, body or court making the appointment;

   (c)   where the document relates to the termination of an appointment, the reason for that termination; and

(d)   the contact details for the office-holder.

1.19(2)   Where the person delivering the document is the office-holder, the address may be omitted if it has previously been notified to the registrar of companies in the insolvency proceedings and is unchanged.

1.20   Standard contents of documents relating to other documents

1.20   A document relating to another document must also state–

(a)   the nature of the other document;

(b)   the date of the other document; and

(c)   where the other document relates to a period of time, the period of time to which it relates.

1.21   Standard contents of documents relating to court orders

1.21   A document relating to a court order must also specify–

(a)   the nature of the order;

(b)   the name of the court; and

(c)   the date of the order.

1.22   Standard contents of returns or reports of decisions

1.22   A return or report of a decision procedure, deemed consent procedure or meeting must also state–

(a)   the purpose of the procedure or meeting;

(b)   a description of the procedure or meeting used;

(c)   in the case of a decision procedure or meeting, the venue;

(d)   in the case of a deemed consent procedure, the date the decision was deemed to have been made;

(e)   whether, in the case of a meeting, the required quorum was in place; and

(f)   the outcome (including any decisions made or resolutions passed).

1.23   Standard contents of returns or reports of matters considered by company members by written resolution

1.23   A return or report of a matter, consideration of which has been sought from the members of a company by written resolution, must also state–

(a)   the purpose of the consideration; and

(b)   the outcome of the consideration (including any resolutions passed).

1.24   Standard contents of documents relating to other events

1.24   A document relating to any other event must also state–

(a)   the nature of the event, including the section (or paragraph) of the Act or the rule in relation to which it took place; and

(b)   the date on which the event occurred.

CHAPTER 8

STANDARD CONTENTS OF NOTICES FOR DELIVERY TO OTHER PERSONS ETC.

[Note: the requirements in Chapter 8 must be read with rule 1.7 which sets out the information required to identify an office-holder, a company etc.]

1.25   Standard contents of notices to be delivered to persons other than the registrar of companies

1.25(1)   Where the Act or these Rules require a notice to be delivered to a person other than the registrar of companies in respect of insolvency proceedings under Parts 1 and 2 of the Act or the EU Regulation, the notice must contain the standard contents set out in this Chapter (in addition to any content specifically required by the Act or another provision of these Rules).

1.25(2)   A notice of more than one type must satisfy the requirements which apply to each.

1.25(3)   The requirements in respect of a document which is to be delivered to another person at the same time as the registrar of companies may be satisfied by delivering to that other person a copy of the document delivered to the registrar.

1.26   Standard contents of all notices

1.26   A notice must–

(a)   state the nature of the notice;

(b)   identify the insolvency proceedings;

(c)   state the section (or paragraph) of the Act or the rule under which the notice is given; and

(d)   in the case of a notice delivered by the office-holder, state the contact details for the office-holder.

1.27   Standard contents of notices relating to the office of office-holders

1.27   A notice relating to the office of the office-holder must also identify the office-holder and state–

(a)   the date of the event of which notice is delivered;

(b)   where the notice relates to an appointment, the person, body or court making the appointment; and

(c)   where the notice relates to the termination of an appointment, the reason for that termination.

1.28   Standard contents of notices relating to documents

1.28   A notice relating to a document must also state–

(a)   the nature of the document;

(b)   the date of the document; and

(c)   where the document relates to a period of time the period of time to which the document relates.

1.29   Standard contents of notices relating to court proceedings or orders

1.29   A notice relating to court proceedings must also identify those proceedings and if the notice relates to a court order state–

(a)   the nature of the order; and

(b)   the date of the order.

1.30   Standard contents of notices of the results of decisions

1.30   A notice of the result of a decision procedure, deemed consent procedure or meeting must also state–

(a)   the purpose of the procedure or meeting;

(b)   a description of the procedure or meeting used;

(c)   in the case of a decision procedure or meeting, the venue;

(d)   in the case of a deemed consent procedure, the date the decision was deemed to have been made;

(e)   whether, in the case of a meeting, the required quorum was in place; and

(f)   the outcome (including any decisions made or resolutions passed).

1.31   Standard contents of returns or reports of matters considered by company members by written resolution

1.31   A return or report of a matter, consideration of which has been sought from the members of a company by written resolution, must also specify–

(a)   the purpose of the consideration; and

(b)   the outcome of the consideration (including any resolutions passed).

CHAPTER 9

DELIVERY OF DOCUMENTS AND OPTING OUT (SECTIONS 246C AND 248A)

1.32   Application of Chapter

[Note: the registrar's rules include provision for the electronic delivery of documents.]

1.32(1)   Subject to paragraph (2) this Chapter applies where a document is required under the Act or these Rules to be delivered, lodged, forwarded, furnished, given, sent, or submitted in respect of insolvency proceedings under Parts 1 and 2 of the Act or the EU Regulation unless the Act, a rule or an order of the court makes different provision.

1.32(2)   Rules 1.41 and 1.43 to 1.46 do not apply to–

(a)   the lodging of any petition or application or other document with the court;

(b)   the service of any application or other document lodged with the court;

(c)   the service of any order of the court; or

(d)   the delivery of a document to the registrar of companies, except in accordance with paragraph 3.

1.32(3)   In respect of delivery of a document to the registrar of companies–

(a)   subject to sub-paragraph (b) only the following rules in this Chapter apply: rules 1.38 (postal delivery of documents), 1.39 (delivery by document exchange), 1.40 (personal delivery) and 1.47 (proof of delivery of documents);

(b)   requirements imposed under section 1068 and rules made under section 1117 of the Companies Act apply to determine the date when any document is received by the registrar of companies.

1.32(4)   Where a document is required or permitted to be served at a company's registered office service may be effected at a previous registered office in accordance with section 87(2) of the Companies Act.

1.32(5)   In the case of an overseas company service may be effected in any manner provided for by section 1139(2) of the Companies Act.

1.33   Delivery to the creditors and opting out

1.33(1)   Where the Act or a rule requires an office-holder to deliver a document to the creditors, or the creditors in a class, the requirement is satisfied by the delivery of the document to all such creditors of whose address the office-holder is aware other than opted-out creditors unless the opt out does not apply.

1.33(2)   Where a creditor has opted out from receiving documents, the opt out does not apply to–

(a)   a notice which the Act requires to be delivered to all creditors without expressly excluding opted-out creditors;

(b)   a notice of a change in the office-holder or the contact details for the office-holder;

(c)   a notice as provided for by section 246C(2) (notices of distributions, intended distributions and notices required to be given by court order); or

(d)   a document which these Rules require to accompany a notice within sub-paragraphs (a) to (c).

1.33(3)   The office-holder must begin to treat a creditor as an opted-out creditor as soon as reasonably practicable after delivery of the creditor's election to opt out.

1.33(4)   An office-holder in any consecutive insolvency proceedings of a different kind under Parts 1, 2, 4 or 5 of the Act in respect of the same company who is aware that a creditor was an opted-out creditor in the earlier insolvency proceedings must treat the creditor as an opted-out creditor in the consecutive insolvency proceedings.

1.34   Creditor's election to opt out

1.34(1)   A creditor may at any time elect to be an opted-out creditor.

1.34(2)   The creditor's election to opt out must be by a notice in writing authenticated and dated by the creditor.

1.34(3)   The creditor must deliver the notice to the office-holder.

1.34(4)   A creditor becomes an opted-out creditor when the notice is delivered to the office-holder.

1.34(5)   An opted-out creditor–

(a)   will remain an opted-out creditor for the duration of the insolvency proceedings unless the opt out is revoked; and

(b)   is deemed to be an opted-out creditor in respect of any consecutive insolvency proceedings under Parts 1, 2, 4 or 5 of the Act of a different kind relating to the same company.

1.34(6)   The creditor may at any time revoke the election to opt out by a further notice in writing, authenticated and dated by the creditor and delivered to the office-holder.

1.34(7)   The creditor ceases to be an opted-out creditor from the date the notice is delivered to the office-holder.

1.35   Office-holder to provide information to creditors on opting out

1.35(1)   The office-holder must, in the first communication with a creditor, inform the creditor in writing that the creditor may elect to opt out of receiving further documents relating to the insolvency proceedings.

1.35(2)   The communication must contain–

(a)   identification and contact details for the office-holder;

(b) a statement that the creditor has the right to elect to opt out of receiving further documents about the insolvency proceedings unless–

  (i)   the Act requires a document to be delivered to all creditors without expressly excluding opted-out creditors;

  (ii) the document is a notice relating to a change in the office-holder or the office-holder's contact details;

  (iii) the document is a notice of a dividend or proposed dividend; or

  (iv) the document is a notice which the court orders to be sent to all creditors or all creditors of a particular category to which the creditor belongs;

(c) a statement that opting out will not affect the creditor's entitlement to receive dividends should any be paid to creditors;

(d) a statement that unless these Rules provide to the contrary opting out will not affect any right the creditor may have to vote in a decision procedure or to participate in a deemed consent procedure in the insolvency proceedings although the creditor will not receive notice of it;

(e) a statement that a creditor who opts out will be treated as having opted out in respect of any consecutive insolvency proceedings of a different kind in respect of the same company; and

(f) information about how the creditor may elect to be or cease to be an opted-out creditor.

1.36 Delivery of documents to authorised recipients

1.36 Where under the Act or these Rules a document is to be delivered to a person (other than by being served on that person), it may be delivered instead to any other person authorised in writing to accept delivery on behalf of the first-mentioned person.

1.37 Delivery of documents to joint office-holders

1.37 Where there are joint office-holders in insolvency proceedings, delivery of a document to one of them is to be treated as delivery to all of them.

1.38 Postal delivery of documents

1.38(1) A document is delivered if it is sent by post in accordance with the provisions of this rule.

1.38(2) A document delivered by post may be delivered to the last known address of a person.

1.38(3) First class or second class post may be used to deliver a document.

1.38(4) Unless the contrary is shown–

(a) a document sent by first class post is to be treated as delivered on the second business day after the day on which it is posted;

(b) a document sent by second class post is to be treated as delivered on the fourth business day after the day on which it is posted;

(c) where a post-mark appears on the envelope in which a document was posted, the date of that post-mark is to be treated as the date on which the document was posted.

1.38(5) In this rule "post-mark" means a mark applied by a postal operator which records the date on which a letter entered the postal system of the postal operator.

1.39 Delivery by document exchange

1.39(1) A document is delivered to a member of a document exchange if it is delivered to that document exchange.

1.39(2)   Unless the contrary is shown, a document is to be treated as delivered–

(a)   one business day after the day it is delivered to the document exchange where the sender and the intended recipient are members of the same document exchange; or

(b)   two business days after the day it is delivered to the departure facility of the sender's document exchange where the sender and the intended recipient are members of different document exchanges.

1.40   Personal delivery of documents

1.40(1)   A document is delivered if it is personally delivered in accordance with this rule.

1.40(2)   In the case of an individual, a document is personally delivered if it is left with that individual.

1.40(3)   In the case of a legal person, a document is personally delivered if it is left with an individual at the registered office, official address or place of business of that legal person.

1.41   Electronic delivery of documents

1.41(1)   A document is delivered if it is sent by electronic means and the following conditions apply.

1.41(2)   The conditions are that the intended recipient of the document has–

(a)   given actual or deemed consent for the electronic delivery of the document;

(b)   not revoked that consent before the document is sent; and

(c)   provided an electronic address for the delivery of the document.

1.41(3)   Consent may relate to a specific case or generally.

1.41(4)   For the purposes of paragraph (2)(a) an intended recipient is deemed to have consented to the electronic delivery of a document where the intended recipient and the company who is the subject of the insolvency proceedings had customarily communicated with each other by electronic means before the insolvency proceedings commenced.

1.41(5)   Unless the contrary is shown, a document is to be treated as delivered by electronic means to an electronic address where the sender can produce a copy of the electronic communication which–

(a)   contains the document; and

(b)   shows the time and date the communication was sent and the electronic address to which it was sent.

1.41(6)   Unless the contrary is shown, a document sent electronically is treated as delivered to the electronic address to which it is sent at 9.00 a.m. on the next business day after it was sent.

1.42   Electronic delivery of documents to the court

1.42(1)   A document may not be delivered to a court by electronic means unless this is expressly permitted by Rules of Court.

1.42(2)   A document delivered by electronic means is to be treated as delivered to the court at the time it is recorded by the court as having been received or otherwise as the Rules of Court provide.

1.43   Electronic delivery by office-holders

1.43(1)   Where an office-holder delivers a document by electronic means, the document must contain, or be accompanied by, a statement that the recipient may request a hard copy of the document and a telephone number, email address and postal address that may be used to make that request.

1.43(2)   An office-holder who receives such a request must deliver a hard copy of the document to the recipient free of charge within five business days of receipt of the request.

1.44   Use of website by office-holder to deliver a particular document (section 246B)

[Note: rule 3.54(3) allows notice of an extension to an administration to be given on a website and rule 2.25(6) does likewise in respect of notice of the result of the consideration of a proposal for a CVA]

1.44(1)   This rule applies for the purposes of section 246B.

1.44(2)   An office-holder who proposes to satisfy the requirement to deliver a document to any person by making it available on a website in accordance with section 246B(1) must deliver a notice to that person which contains–

(a)   a statement that the document is available for viewing and downloading on a website;

(b)   the website's address and any password necessary to view and download the document; and

(c)   a statement that that person may request a hard copy of the document together with a telephone number, email address and postal address which may be used to make that request.

1.44(3)   An office-holder who receives such a request must deliver a hard copy of the document to the person who made the request free of charge within five business days of receipt of the request.

1.44(4)   A document to which a notice under paragraph (2) relates must–

(a)   remain available on the website for the period required by rule 1.46; and

(b)   be in a format that enables it to be downloaded within a reasonable time of an electronic request being made for it to be downloaded.

1.44(5)   A document which is delivered to a person by means of a website in accordance with this rule is deemed to have been delivered–

(a)   when it is first made available on the website; or

(b)   when the notice under paragraph (2) is delivered to that person, if that is later.

1.44(6)   Section 246B(1) does not apply to a notice delivered under paragraph (2).

1.44(7)   In this rule "document" includes any notice or information in any other form.

1.45   General use of website to deliver documents

1.45(1)   The office-holder may deliver a notice to each person to whom a document will be required to be delivered in the insolvency proceedings which contains–

(a)   a statement that future documents in the insolvency proceedings other than those mentioned in paragraph (2) will be made available for viewing and downloading on a website without notice to the recipient and that the office-holder will not be obliged to deliver any such documents to the recipient of the notice unless it is requested by that person;

(b)   a telephone number, email address and postal address which may be used to make a request for a hard copy of a document;

(c)   a statement that the recipient of the notice may at any time request a hard copy of–

(i)   any document available for viewing on the website,

(ii)   any document which may be made available there in the future; and

(d)   the address of the website and any password required to view and download a relevant document from that site.

1.45(2)   A statement under paragraph (1)(a) does not apply to the following documents–

(a)   a document for which personal delivery is required; and

(b)   a document which is not delivered generally.

1.45(3)   A document is delivered generally if it is delivered to some or all of the following classes of persons–

(a)   members,

(b)   creditors,

(c)   any class of members or creditors.

1.45(4)   An office-holder who has delivered a notice under paragraph (1) is under no obligation–

(a)   to notify a person to whom the notice has been delivered when a document to which the notice applies has been made available on the website; or

(b)   to deliver a hard copy of such a document unless a request for a hard copy is received under paragraph (1)(c).

1.45(5)   An office-holder who receives a request under paragraph (1)(c)–

(a)   in respect of a document which is already available on the website must deliver a hard copy of the document to the recipient free of charge within five business days of receipt of the request; and

(b)   in respect of all future documents must deliver each such document in accordance with the requirements for delivery of such a document in the Act and these Rules.

1.45(6)   A document to which a statement under paragraph (1)(a) applies must–

(a)   remain available on the website for the period required by rule 1.46; and

(b)   be in such a format as to enable it to be downloaded within a reasonable time of an electronic request being made for it to be downloaded.

1.45(7)   A document which is delivered to a person by means of a website in accordance with this rule, is deemed to have been delivered–

(a)   when the relevant document was first made available on the website; or

(b)   when the notice under paragraph (1) is delivered to that person, if that is later.

1.45(8)   Paragraph (7) does not apply in respect of a person who has made a request under paragraph (1)(c)(ii) for hard copies of all future documents.

1.46   Retention period for documents made available on websites

1.46(1)   This rule applies to a document which is made available on a website under rules 1.44, 1.45, 2.24(7) and 3.54(3).

1.46(2)   Such a document must continue to be made available on the website until two months after the end of the particular insolvency proceedings or the release of the last person to hold office as the office-holder in those insolvency proceedings, whichever is later.

1.47   Proof of delivery of documents

1.47(1)   A certificate complying with this rule is proof that a document has been duly delivered to the recipient in accordance with this Chapter unless the contrary is shown.

1.47(2)   A certificate must state the method of delivery and the date of the sending, posting or delivery (as the case may be).

1.47(3)   In the case of an office-holder the certificate must be given by–

(a)   the office-holder;

(b)   the office-holder's solicitor; or

(c)   a partner or an employee of either of them.

1.47(4)   In the case of a person other than an office-holder the certificate must be given by that person and must state–

(a)   that the document was delivered by that person; or–

(b)   that another person (named in the certificate) was instructed to deliver it.

1.47(5)   A certificate under this rule may be endorsed on a copy of the document to which it relates.

1.48   Delivery of statements of claim and documentary evidence of debt

1.48(1)   Once a statement of claim or documentary evidence of debt has been delivered to an office-holder in accordance with these Rules it need not be delivered again.

1.48(2)   Accordingly, where these Rules require such delivery by a certain time, that requirement is satisfied if that statement or evidence has already been delivered.

1.48(3)   This rule also applies where a creditor in an administration is deemed to have submitted a statement of claim and documentary evidence of a debt in winding up proceedings which immediately preceded the administration.

1.48(4)   In a CVA, where a creditor has given written notification of a debt in accordance with rule 5.9(1)(b)(i), it need not be given again.

CHAPTER 10

INSPECTION OF DOCUMENTS, COPIES AND PROVISION OF INFORMATION

1.49   Right to copies of documents

1.49   Where the Act, in relation to proceedings under Parts 1 and 2, or these Rules, gives a person the right to inspect documents, that person has a right to be supplied on request with copies of those documents on payment of the standard fee for copies.

1.50   Charges for copies of documents provided by the office-holder

1.50   Except where prohibited by these Rules, an office-holder is entitled to require the payment of the standard fee for copies of documents requested by a creditor, member or member of a creditors' committee.

1.51   Offence in relation to inspection of documents

1.51(1)   It is an offence for a person who does not have a right under these Rules to inspect a relevant document falsely to claim to be a creditor or a member of a company with the intention of gaining sight of the document.

1.51(2)   A relevant document is one which is on the court file or held by the office-holder or any other person and which a creditor or a member of a company has the right to inspect under these Rules.

1.52 Right to list of creditors

1.52(1) In an administration, a creditor has the right to require the administrator to provide a list of the names and addresses of the creditors and the amounts of their respective debts.

1.52(2) The administrator, on being required to provide such a list–

(a) must deliver it to the person requiring the list as soon as reasonably practicable; and

(b) may charge the standard fee for copies for a hard copy.

1.52(3) The administrator may omit the name and address of a creditor if the administrator thinks its disclosure would be prejudicial to the conduct of the insolvency proceedings or might reasonably be expected to lead to violence against any person.

1.52(4) In such a case the list must include–

(a) the amount of that creditor's debt; and

(b) a statement that the name and address of the creditor has been omitted for that debt.

1.53 Confidentiality of documents: grounds for refusing inspection

1.53(1) Where an office-holder considers that a document forming part of the records of the insolvency proceedings–

(a) should be treated as confidential; or

(b) is of such a nature that its disclosure would be prejudicial to the conduct of the insolvency proceedings or might reasonably be expected to lead to violence against any person,

the office-holder may decline to allow it to be inspected by a person who would otherwise be entitled to inspect it.

1.53(2) The persons to whom the office-holder may refuse inspection include members of a creditors' committee.

1.53(3) Where the office-holder refuses inspection of a document, the person wishing to inspect it may apply to the court which may reconsider the office-holder's decision.

1.53(4) The court's decision may be subject to such conditions (if any) as it thinks just.

1.54 Sederunt book

1.54(1) The office-holder must maintain a sederunt book during the office-holder's term of office for the purpose of providing an accurate record of the insolvency proceedings.

1.54(2) The office-holder must include in the sederunt book–

(a) the information listed in Schedule 4; and

(b) a copy of anything else required to be recorded in it by any provision of the Act or these Rules.

1.54(3) The office-holder must make the sederunt book available for inspection at all reasonable hours by any interested person.

1.54(4) Any entry in the sederunt book is sufficient evidence of the facts stated in it, except where it is relied upon by the office-holder in the office-holder's own interest.

1.54(5) The office-holder must retain, or make arrangements for the retention of, the sederunt book for the period specified in regulation 13(5) of the Insolvency Practitioners Regulations 2005.

1.54(6) Where the sederunt book is maintained in electronic form, it must be capable of reproduction in hard copy form.

1.55   Transfer and disposal of company's books, papers and other records

1.55(1)   Where an administration has terminated and other insolvency proceedings under Parts 2 to 5 of the Act have commenced in relation to the same company, the administrator must, before the expiry of the earlier of–

  (a)   the period of 30 days beginning with the date the office-holder in the subsequent insolvency proceedings makes a request to the administrator to do so; or

  (b)   the period of six months beginning with the date the administration ends,

deliver to the office-holder appointed in the subsequent proceedings the books, papers and other records of the company.

1.55(2)   Where an administration has terminated and no subsequent insolvency proceedings under Parts 2 to 5 of the Act have commenced in relation to the same company, the administrator must dispose of the books, papers and records of the company in accordance with the directions of–

  (a)   the creditors' committee (if there is one); or

  (b)   where there is no creditors' committee, the court.

1.55(3)   If no directions under paragraph (2) have been given by the expiry of the period of 12 months after the date of dissolution of the company, the administrator may dispose of the company's books, papers and records in such a way as the administrator considers appropriate.

CHAPTER 11

FORMAL DEFECTS

1.56   Power to cure defects in procedure

1.56(1)   The court may, on the application of any person having an interest–

  (a)   if there has been a failure to comply with any requirement of the Act or the Rules, make an order waiving any such failure and, so far as practicable, restoring any person prejudiced by the failure to the position that person would have been in but for the failure;

  (b)   if for any reason anything required or authorised to be done in, or in connection with, the insolvency proceedings cannot be done, make such order as may be necessary to enable that thing to be done.

1.56(2)   The court, in an order under paragraph (1), may impose such conditions, including conditions as to expenses, as the court thinks fit and may in particular–

  (a)   authorise or dispense with the performance of any act in the insolvency proceedings;

  (b)   appoint as office-holder in the insolvency proceedings any person who would be eligible to act in that capacity, whether or not in place of an existing office-holder;

  (c)   extend or waive any time limit specified in or under the Act or the Rules.

1.56(3)   An application under paragraph (1) which is made to the sheriff–

  (a)   may at any time be remitted by the sheriff to the Court of Session;

  (b)   must be so remitted if the Court of Session so directs on an application by any person;

if the sheriff or the Court of Session, as the case may be, considers that the remit is desirable because of the importance or complexity of the matters raised by the application.

1.57   Formal defects

1.57   No insolvency proceedings are invalidated by any formal defect or irregularity unless the court before which objection is made considers that substantial injustice has been caused by the defect or irregularity and that the injustice cannot be remedied by any order of the court.

PART 2

COMPANY VOLUNTARY ARRANGEMENTS

CHAPTER 1

PRELIMINARY

2.1   Interpretation

2.1   In this part–

"nominee" and "supervisor" include the proposed nominee or supervisor in relation to a proposal; and

"proposal" means a proposal for a CVA.

CHAPTER 2

THE PROPOSAL FOR A CVA (SECTION 1)

[Notes:

(1) Section 1 sets out who may propose a CVA.

(2) A document required by the Act or these Rules must also contain the standard contents set out in Part 1.]

2.2   Proposal for a CVA: general principles and amendment

2.2(1)   A proposal must–

(a)   contain identification details for the company;

(b)   explain why the proposer thinks a CVA is desirable;

(c)   explain why the creditors are expected to agree to a CVA; and

(d)   be authenticated and dated by the proposer.

2.2(2)   The proposal may be amended with the nominee's agreement in writing in the following cases.

2.2(3)   The first case is where–

(a)   no steps have been taken to obtain a moratorium;

(b)   the nominee is not the liquidator or administrator of the company; and

(c)   the nominee's report has not been lodged with the court under section 2(2).

2.2(4)   The second case is where–

(a)   the proposal is made with a view to obtaining a moratorium; and

(b)   the nominee's statement under paragraph 6(2) of Schedule A1 (nominee's opinion on prospects of CVA being approved etc.) has not yet been submitted to the directors.

2.3   Proposal: contents

2.3(1)   The proposal must set out the following so far as known to the proposer–

Assets	(a) the company's assets, with an estimate of their respective values;
	(b) which assets are subject to any security in favour of creditors and the extent of any such security;
	(c) which assets are to be excluded from the CVA;
	(d) particulars of any property to be included in the CVA which is not owned by the company, including details of who owns such property, and the terms on which it will be available for inclusion;
Liabilities	(a) the nature and amount of the company's liabilities;
	(b) how the company's liabilities will be met, modified, postponed or otherwise dealt with by means of the CVA and, in particular–
	(i) how preferential creditors and creditors who are, or claim to be, secured will be dealt with,
	(ii) how creditors who are connected with the company will be dealt with,
	(iii) if the company is not in administration or liquidation whether, if the company did go into administration or liquidation, there are circumstances which might give rise to claims under section 242 (gratuitous alienations) section 243 (unfair preferences), section 244 (extortionate credit transactions) or section 245 (floating charges invalid) and
	(iv) where there are circumstances that might give rise to such claims, whether, and if so what, provision will be made to indemnify the company in respect of them;
Nominee's fees and expenses	the amount proposed to be paid to the nominee by way of fees and expenses;
Supervisor	(a) identification and contact details for the supervisor;
	(b) confirmation that the supervisor is qualified to act as an insolvency practitioner in relation to the company and the name of the relevant recognised professional body which is the source of the supervisor's authorisation;
	(c) how the fees and expenses of the supervisor will be determined and paid;
	(d) the functions to be performed by the supervisor;
	(e) where it is proposed that two or more supervisors be appointed a statement whether acts done in connection with the CVA may be done by any one or more of them or must be done by all of them;
Cautionary obligations and proposed cautionary obligations	(a) whether any, and if so what, cautionary obligations (including guarantees) have been given in respect of the company's debts, specifying which of the guarantors are persons connected with the company;
	(b) whether any, and if so what, cautionary obligations (including guarantees) are proposed to be offered for the purposes of the CVA and, if so, by whom and whether security is to be given or sought;

Timing	(a) the proposed duration of the CVA;
	(b) the proposed dates of distributions to creditors, with estimates of their amounts;
Type of insolvency proceedings	whether the insolvency proceedings will be main, secondary, territorial or non-EU insolvency proceedings with reasons;
Conduct of the business	how the business of the company will be conducted during the CVA;
Further credit facilities	details of any further proposed credit facilities for the company, and how the debts so arising are to be paid;
Handling of funds arising	(a) the manner in which funds held for the purposes of the CVA are to be banked, invested or otherwise dealt with pending distribution to creditors;
	(b) how funds held for the purpose of payment to creditors, and not so paid on the termination of the CVA, will be dealt with;
	(c) how the claim of any person bound by the CVA by virtue of section 5(2)(b)(ii) or paragraph 37(2)(b)(ii) of Schedule A1 will be dealt with;
Address (where moratorium proposed)	where the proposal is made in relation to a company that is eligible for a moratorium (in accordance with paragraphs 2 and 3 of Schedule A1) with a view to obtaining a moratorium under Schedule A1, the address to which the documents referred to in paragraph 6(1) of that Schedule must be delivered; and
Other matters	any other matters which the proposer considers appropriate to enable members and creditors to reach an informed decision on the proposal.

2.3(2)   Where the proposal is made by the directors, it must contain an estimate so far as known to them of–

(a)   the value of the prescribed part if the proposal for the CVA is not accepted and the company goes into liquidation (whether or not the liquidator might be required under section 176A to make the prescribed part available for the satisfaction of unsecured debts); and

(b)   the value of the company's net property (as defined in section 176A(6)) on the date that the estimate is made.

2.3(3)   Where the proposal is made by the administrator or liquidator, it must contain the following so far as known to the office-holder–

(a)   an estimate of–

(i)   the value of the prescribed part (whether or not the administrator or liquidator might be required under section 176A to make the prescribed part available for the satisfaction of unsecured debts) and

(ii)   the value of the company's net property (as defined in section 176A(6));

(b)   a statement as to whether the administrator or liquidator proposes to make an application to the court under section 176A(5) and if so the reasons for the application; and

(c)   details of the nature and amount of the company's preferential creditors.

2.3(4)   Information may be excluded from an estimate under paragraph (2) or (3)(a) if the inclusion of the information could seriously prejudice the commercial interests of the company.

2.3(5)   If the exclusion of such information affects the calculation of the estimate, the proposal must include a statement to that effect.

Chapter 3

Procedure for a CVA without a moratorium

[Note: A document required by the Act or these Rules must also contain the standard contents set out in Part 1.]

2.4   Procedure for proposal where the nominee is not the liquidator or the administrator (section 2)

2.4(1)   This rule applies where the nominee is not the same person as the liquidator or the administrator.

2.4(2)   A nominee who consents to act must deliver a notice of that consent to the proposer as soon as reasonably practicable after the proposal has been submitted to the nominee under section 2(3).

2.4(3)   The notice must state the date the nominee received the proposal.

2.4(4)   The period of 28 days in which the nominee must submit a report to the court under section 2(2) begins on the date the nominee received the proposal as stated in the notice.

2.5   Statement of affairs (section 2(3))

2.5(1)   The statement of the company's affairs required by section 2(3) must contain the following information–

(a)   a list of the company's assets, divided into such categories as are appropriate for easy identification, and with each category given an estimated value;

(b)   in the case of any property on which a claim against the company is wholly or partly secured, particulars of the claim, and of how and when the security was created;

(c)   the names and addresses of the preferential creditors, with the amounts of their respective claims;

(d)   the names and addresses of the unsecured creditors with the amounts of their respective claims;

(e)   particulars of any debts owed by the company to persons connected with it;

(f)   particulars of any debts owed to the company by persons connected with it;

(g)   the names and addresses of the company's members, with details of their respective shareholdings; and

(h)   any other particulars that the nominee in writing requires to be provided for the purposes of making the nominee's report on the proposal to the court.

2.5(2)   The statement must be made up to a date not earlier than two weeks before the date of the proposal.

2.5(3)   However the nominee may allow the statement to be made up to an earlier date (but not more than two months before the proposal) where that is more practicable.

2.5(4)   Where the statement is made up to an earlier date, the nominee's report to the court on the proposal must explain why.

2.5(5)   The statement of affairs must include a declaration that the information provided in it is, to the best of the proposer's knowledge and belief, accurate and complete.

2.5(6)   Where the proposal is made by the directors, only one director need make a declaration in accordance with paragraph (5).

2.6   Application to omit information from statement of affairs delivered to creditors

2.6   The nominee, the directors or any person appearing to the court to have an interest, may apply to the court for a direction that specified information be omitted from the statement of affairs, as delivered to the creditors, where disclosure of that information would be likely to prejudice the conduct of the CVA, or might reasonably be expected to lead to violence against any person.

2.7   Additional disclosure for assistance of nominee where nominee is not the liquidator or administrator

2.7(1)   This rule applies where the nominee is not the administrator or the liquidator of the company.

2.7(2)   If it appears to the nominee that the nominee's report to the court cannot properly be prepared on the basis of information in the proposal and statement of affairs, the nominee may require the proposer to provide–

(a)   more information about the circumstances in which, and the reasons why, a CVA is being proposed;

(b)   particulars of any previous proposals which have been made in relation to the company under Part 1 of the Act; and

(c)   any further information relating to the company's affairs which the nominee thinks necessary for the purposes of the report.

2.7(3)   The nominee may require the proposer to inform the nominee whether, and if so in what circumstances, any person referred to in paragraph (4) has–

(a)   been concerned in the affairs of any other company (whether or not incorporated in Scotland) or limited liability partnership which has been the subject of insolvency proceedings;

(b)   been made bankrupt or had his or her estate sequestrated;

(c)   been the subject of a debt relief order;

(d)   granted a trust deed; or

(e)   entered into an arrangement with creditors.

2.7(4)   The persons referred to for the purposes of paragraph (3) are–

(a)   a director or officer of the company; and

(b)   a person who has been a director or officer of the company at any time in the period of two years ending with the date the nominee received the proposal.

2.7(5)   The proposer must give the nominee such access to the company's accounts and records as the nominee may require to enable the nominee to consider the proposal and prepare the nominee's report.

2.8   Nominee's report on proposal where the nominee is not the liquidator or administrator (section 2(2))

2.8(1)   The nominee's report must be lodged with the court under section 2(2) accompanied by–

(a)   a copy of the report;

(b)   a copy of the proposal (as amended under rule 2.2(2) if that is the case); and

(c)   a copy of the statement of the company's affairs or a summary of it.

2.8(2)   The report must state–

(a)   why the nominee considers the proposal does or does not have a reasonable prospect of being implemented; and

(b) why the members and the creditors should or should not be invited to consider the proposal.

2.8(3) The court must endorse the nominee's report and the copy of it with the date of lodging and deliver the copy to the nominee.

2.8(4) The nominee must deliver a copy of the report to the company.

2.9   Replacement of nominee (section 2(4))

2.9(1) A person (other than the nominee) who intends to apply to the court under section 2(4) for the nominee to be replaced must deliver a notice that such an application is intended to be made to the nominee at least five business days before lodging the application with the court.

2.9(2) A nominee who intends to apply under that section to be replaced must deliver a notice that such an application is intended to be made to the person intending to make the proposal at least five business days before lodging the application with the court.

2.9(3) The court must not appoint a replacement nominee unless a statement by the replacement nominee has been lodged with the court confirming that person–

(a) consents to act; and

(b) is qualified to act as an insolvency practitioner in relation to the company.

CHAPTER 4

PROCEDURE FOR A CVA WITH A MORATORIUM

[Note: A document required by the Act or these Rules must also contain the standard contents set out in Part 1.]

2.10   Statement of affairs (paragraph 6(1)(b) of Schedule A1)

2.10(1) The statement of affairs required by paragraph 6(1)(b) of Schedule A1 must contain the same information as is required by rule 2.5.

2.10(2) The statement must be made up to a date not earlier than two weeks before the date of the proposal.

2.10(3) However the nominee may allow the statement to be made up to an earlier date (but no more than two months before the date of the proposal) where that is more practicable.

2.10(4) Where the statement is made up to an earlier date, the nominee's statement to the directors on the proposal must explain why.

2.10(5) The statement of affairs must include a declaration that the information provided in it is, to the best of the knowledge and belief of at least one of the directors, accurate and complete.

2.11   Application to omit information from a statement of affairs

2.11 The nominee, the directors or any person appearing to the court to have an interest, may apply to the court for a direction that specified information be omitted from the statement of affairs, as delivered to the creditors, where disclosure of that information would be likely to prejudice the conduct of the CVA, or might reasonably be expected to lead to violence against any person.

2.12   The nominee's statement (paragraph 6(2) of Schedule A1)

2.12(1) The nominee must submit to the directors the statement required by paragraph 6(2) of Schedule A1 within 28 days of the submission to the nominee of the proposal.

2.12(2)   The statement must–

(a)   include the name and address of the nominee; and

(b)   be authenticated and dated by the nominee.

2.12(3)   A statement which contains an opinion on all the matters referred to in paragraph 6(2) must–

(a)   explain why the nominee has formed that opinion; and

(b)   if the nominee is willing to act, be accompanied by a statement of the nominee's consent to act in relation to the proposed CVA.

2.12(4)   The statement of the nominee's consent must–

(a)   include the name and address of the nominee;

(b)   state that the nominee is qualified to act as an insolvency practitioner in relation to the company; and

(c)   be authenticated and dated by the nominee.

2.13   Documents lodged with court to obtain moratorium (paragraph 7(1) of Schedule A1)

2.13(1)   The statement of the company's affairs which the directors lodge with the court under paragraph 7(1)(b) of Schedule A1 must be the same as the statement they submit to the nominee under paragraph 6(1)(b) of that Schedule.

2.13(2)   The statement required by paragraph 7(1)(c) of that Schedule that the company is eligible for a moratorium must–

(a)   be made by the directors;

(b)   state that the company meets the requirements of paragraph 3 of Schedule A1 and is not a company which falls within paragraph 2(2) of that Schedule; and

(c)   be authenticated and dated by the directors.

2.13(3)   The statement required by paragraph 7(1)(d) of Schedule A1 that the nominee has consented to act must be in the same terms as the statement referred to in rule 2.12(3)(b).

2.13(4)   The statement of the nominee's opinion required by paragraph 7(1)(e) of that Schedule–

(a)   must be the same as the statement of opinion required by paragraph 6(2) of that Schedule; and

(b)   must be lodged with the court not later than ten business days after it was submitted to directors.

2.13(5)   A statement from the nominee whether the proceedings will be main, secondary, territorial or non-EU proceedings with reasons for so stating must also be lodged with the court.

2.13(6)   The documents lodged with the court under paragraph 7(1) of Schedule A1, together with the statement required by paragraph (5) of this rule, must be accompanied by four copies of a schedule, authenticated and dated by the directors, identifying the company and listing all the documents lodged.

2.13(7)   The court must endorse the copies of the schedule with the date on which the documents were lodged and deliver three copies of the endorsed schedule to the directors.

2.14   Notice and advertisement of beginning of moratorium

2.14(1)   The directors must, as soon as reasonably practicable, after delivery to them of the endorsed copies of the schedule deliver two copies of the schedule referred to in rule 2.13(6) to the nominee and one to the company.

2.14(2)   After delivery of the copies of the schedule, the nominee–

(a) must, as soon as reasonably practicable, gazette a notice of the coming into force of the moratorium; and

(b) may advertise the notice in such other manner as the nominee thinks fit.

2.14(3)   The notice must specify–

(a) the nature of the business of the company;

(b) that a moratorium under section 1A has come into force; and

(c) the date on which it came into force.

2.14(4)   The nominee must, as soon as reasonably practicable, deliver a notice of the coming into force of the moratorium to–

(a) the registrar of companies;

(b) the company; and

(c) any petitioning creditor of whose address the nominee is aware.

2.14(5)   The notice must specify–

(a) the date on which the moratorium came into force; and

(b) the court with which the documents to obtain the moratorium were lodged.

2.14(6)   The nominee must deliver a notice of the coming into force of the moratorium and the date on which it came into force to–

(a) any messenger-at-arms or sheriff officer who to the knowledge of the nominee is charged with executing diligence against the company or its property; and

(b) the Keeper of the Register of Inhibitions and Adjudications.

2.15 Notice of continuation of moratorium where physical meeting of creditors is summoned (paragraph 8(3B) of Schedule A1)

2.15(1)   This rule applies where under paragraph 8(3B)(b) and (3C) of Schedule A1 the moratorium continues after the initial period of 28 days referred to in paragraph 8(3) of that Schedule because a physical meeting of the company's creditors is first summoned to take place after the end of that period.

2.15(2)   The nominee must lodge with the court and deliver to the registrar of companies a notice of the continuation as soon as reasonably practicable after summoning such a meeting of the company's creditors.

2.15(3)   The notice must–

(a) identify the company;

(b) give the name and address of the nominee;

(c) state the date on which the notice of the meeting was sent to the creditors under rule 5.6;

(d) state the date for which the meeting is summoned;

(e) state that under paragraph 8(3B)(b) and (3C) of Schedule A1 the moratorium will be continued to that date; and

(f) be authenticated and dated by the nominee.

2.16   Notice of decision extending or further extending a moratorium (paragraph 36 of Schedule A1)

2.16(1)   This rule applies where the moratorium is extended, or further extended, by a decision which takes effect under paragraph 36 of Schedule A1.

2.16(2)   The nominee must, as soon as reasonably practicable, lodge with the court and deliver to the registrar of companies a notice of the decision.

2.16(3)   The notice must–

   (a)   identify the company;

   (b)   give the name and address of the nominee;

   (c)   state the date on which the moratorium was extended or further extended;

   (d)   state the new expiry date of the moratorium; and

   (e)   be authenticated and dated by the nominee.

2.17   Notice of court order extending, further extending, renewing or continuing a moratorium (paragraph 34(2) of Schedule A1)

2.17   Where the court makes an order extending, further extending, renewing or continuing a moratorium, the nominee must, as soon as reasonably practicable, deliver to the registrar of companies a notice stating the new expiry date of the moratorium.

2.18   Advertisement of end of a moratorium (paragraph 11(1) of Schedule A1)

2.18(1)   After the moratorium ends, the nominee–

   (a)   must, as soon as reasonably practicable, gazette a notice of its coming to an end; and

   (b)   may advertise the notice in such other manner as the nominee thinks fit.

2.18(2)   The notice must specify–

   (a)   the nature of the company's business;

   (b)   that a moratorium under section 1A has ended; and

   (c)   the date on which it came to an end.

2.18(3)   The nominee must, as soon as reasonably practicable,–

   (a)   lodge with the court a notice specifying the date on which the moratorium ended; and

   (b)   deliver such a notice to–

      (i)   the registrar of companies,

      (ii)   the company,

      (iii)   all the creditors, and

      (iv)   the Keeper of the Register of Inhibitions and Adjudications.

2.19   Disposal of secured property etc. during a moratorium

2.19(1)   This rule applies where the company applies to the court under paragraph 20 of Schedule A1 for permission to dispose of–

   (a)   property subject to a security, or

(b)   goods under a hire-purchase agreement.

2.19(2)   The court must fix a venue for hearing the application.

2.19(3)   The company must, as soon as reasonably practicable, deliver a notice of the venue to the holder of the security or the owner of the goods under the agreement.

2.19(4)   If an order is made, the court must deliver two copies of the order certified by the court to the company and the company must, as soon as reasonably practicable, deliver one of them to the holder or owner.

2.20   Withdrawal of nominee's consent to act (paragraph 25(5) of Schedule A1)

2.20(1)   A nominee who withdraws consent to act must lodge with the court and deliver a notice under paragraph 25(5) of Schedule A1 as soon as reasonably practicable.

2.20(2)   The notice must–

(a)   identify the company;

(b)   give the name and address of the nominee;

(c)   specify the date on which the nominee withdrew consent;

(d)   state, with reference to the circumstances mentioned in paragraph 25(2) of that Schedule, why the nominee withdrew consent; and

(e)   be authenticated and dated by the nominee.

2.21   Application to the court to replace the nominee (paragraph 28 of Schedule A1)

2.21(1)   Directors who intend to make an application under paragraph 28 of Schedule A1 for the nominee to be replaced must deliver a notice of the intention to make the application to the nominee at least five business days before lodging the application with the court.

2.21(2)   A nominee who intends to make an application under that paragraph to be replaced must deliver notice of the intention to make the application to the directors at least five business days before lodging the application with the court.

2.21(3)   The court must not appoint a replacement nominee unless a statement by the replacement nominee has been lodged with the court confirming that that person–

(a)   consents to act, and

(b)   is qualified to act as an insolvency practitioner in relation to the company.

2.22   Notice of appointment of replacement nominee

2.22(1)   A person appointed as a replacement nominee must as soon as reasonably practicable–

(a)   deliver a notice of the appointment to the registrar of companies and the former nominee; and

(b)   where the appointment is not by the court, lodge a notice of the appointment with the court.

2.22(2)   The notice of the appointment must–

(a)   identify the company;

(b)   give the name and address of the replacement nominee;

(c)   specify the date on which the replacement nominee was appointed to act; and

(d)   be authenticated and dated by the replacement nominee.

2.23 Applications to court to challenge nominee's actions etc. (paragraphs 26 and 27 of Schedule A1)

2.23   A person intending to make an application to the court under paragraph 26 or 27 of Schedule A1 must deliver a notice of the intention to make the application to the nominee at least five business days before lodging the application with the court.

CHAPTER 5

CONSIDERATION OF THE PROPOSAL BY THE COMPANY MEMBERS AND CREDITORS

[Note: A document required by the Act or these Rules must also contain the standard contents set out in Part 1.]

2.24 Consideration of proposal: common requirements (section 3)

2.24(1)   The nominee must invite the members of the company to consider a proposal by summoning a meeting of the company as required by section 3.

2.24(2)   The nominee must invite the creditors to consider the proposal by way of a decision procedure.

2.24(3)   The nominee must examine whether there is jurisdiction to open the proceedings and must specify in the nominee's comments on the proposal required by paragraphs (4)(d)(iii) and (6)(a)(iii) whether the proceedings will be main, secondary, territorial or non-EU proceedings with the reasons for so stating.

2.24(4)   In the case of the members, the nominee must deliver to every person whom the nominee believes to be a member a notice which must–

(a)   identify the insolvency proceedings;

(b)   state the purpose of, and venue for, the meeting;

(c)   state the effect of the following–

    (i)   rule 2.34 about members' voting rights,

    (ii)   rule 2.35 about the requisite majority of members for passing resolutions, and

    (iii)   rule 5.32 about rights of appeal; and

(d)   be accompanied by–

    (i)   a copy of the proposal,

    (ii)   a copy of the statement of affairs, or if the nominee thinks fit, a summary including a list of creditors with the amounts of their debts,

    (iii)   the nominee's comments on the proposal, unless the nominee is the administrator or liquidator,

    (iv)   details of each resolution to be voted on and

    (v)   a blank proxy.

2.24(5)   In the case of the creditors, the nominee must deliver to each creditor a notice which complies with rule 5.8 so far as is relevant.

2.24(6)   The notice delivered under paragraph (5) must also–

(a)   be accompanied by–

    (i)   a copy of the proposal,

    (ii) a copy of the statement of affairs or, if the nominee thinks fit, a summary including a list of creditors with the amounts of their debts, and

    (iii) the nominee's comments on the proposal, unless the nominee is the administrator or liquidator; and

  (b) state how a creditor may propose a modification to the proposal, and how the nominee will deal with such a proposal for a modification.

2.24(7)   A notice delivered under paragraph (4) or (5) may also state that the results of the consideration of the proposal will be made available for viewing and downloading on a website and that no other notice will be delivered to the creditors or members (as the case may be).

2.24(8)   Where the results of the consideration of the proposal are to be made available for viewing and downloading on a website the nominee must comply with the requirements for use of a website to deliver a document set out in rule 1.44(2)(a) to (c), (3) and (4) with any necessary adaptations and rule 1.44(5)(a) applies to determine the time of delivery of the results of the consideration of the proposal.

2.25   Members' consideration at a meeting

2.25(1)   The nominee must have regard to the convenience of those invited to attend when fixing the venue for a meeting (including the resumption of an adjourned meeting).

2.25(2)   The date of the meeting (except where the nominee is the administrator or liquidator of the company) must not be more than 28 days from the date on which–

  (a) the nominee's report was lodged with the court under rule 2.8; or

  (b) the moratorium came into force.

2.26   Creditors' consideration by a decision procedure

2.26   Where the nominee is inviting the creditors to consider the proposal by a decision procedure, the decision date must be not less than 14 days from the date of delivery of the notice and not more than 28 days from the date on which–

  (a) the nominee's report is lodged with the court under rule 2.8; or

  (b) the moratorium came into force.

2.27   Timing of decisions on proposal

2.27(1)   The decision date for the creditors' decision procedure may be on the same day as, or on a different day to, the meeting of the company.

2.27(2)   The creditors' decision on the proposal must be made before the members' decision.

2.27(3)   The members' decision must be made not later than five business days after the creditors' decision.

2.27(4)   For the purpose of this rule, the timing of the members' decision is either the date and time of the meeting of the company or, where the members are using the written resolution procedure, the deadline for receipt of members' votes.

2.28   Creditors' approval of modified proposal

2.28(1)   This rule applies where a decision is sought from the creditors following notice to the nominee of proposed modifications to the proposal from the company's directors under paragraph 31(7) of Schedule A1.

2.28(2)   The decision must be sought by a decision procedure with a decision date within 14 days of the date on which the directors gave notice to the nominee of the modifications.

2.28(3)   The creditors must be given at least seven days' notice of the decision date.

2.29   Notice of members' meeting and attendance of officers

2.29(1)   A notice under rule 2.24(4) summoning a meeting of the company must be delivered at least 14 days before the day fixed for the meeting to all the members and to–

   (a)   every officer or former officer of the company whose presence the nominee thinks is required; and

   (b)   all other directors of the company.

2.29(2)   Every officer or former officer who receives such a notice stating that the nominee thinks that person's attendance is required, is required to attend the meeting.

2.30   Requisition of physical meeting by creditors

2.30(1)   This rule applies where the creditors requisition a physical meeting to consider a proposal (with or without modifications) in accordance with section 246ZE and rule 5.6.

2.30(2)   The meeting must take place within 14 days of the date on which one of the thresholds under section 246ZE(7) has been met or surpassed.

2.30(3)   A notice summoning a meeting of the creditors must be delivered to the creditors at least seven days before the day fixed for the meeting.

2.31   Non-receipt of notice by members

2.31   Where in accordance with the Act or these Rules the members are invited to consider a proposal, the consideration is presumed to have taken place even if not everyone to whom the notice is to be delivered receives it.

2.32   Proposal for alternative supervisor

2.32(1)   If, in response to a notice inviting the creditors to consider the proposal other than at a meeting, a creditor proposes that a person other than the nominee be appointed as supervisor, that person's consent to act and confirmation that that person is qualified to act as an insolvency practitioner in relation to the company must be delivered to the nominee by the decision date.

2.32(2)   Where the members of the company are using the written resolution procedure and a member proposes that a person other than the nominee be appointed as supervisor, that person's consent to act and confirmation that that person is qualified to act as an insolvency practitioner in relation to the company must be delivered to the nominee by the deadline for receipt of members' votes.

2.32(3)   If, at either a meeting of the company or the creditors to consider the proposal, a resolution is moved for the appointment of a person other than the nominee to be supervisor, the person moving the resolution must produce to the chair at or before the meeting–

   (a)   confirmation that the person proposed as supervisor is qualified to act as an insolvency practitioner in relation to the company; and

   (b)   that person's written consent to act (unless that person is present at the meeting and there signifies consent to act).

2.33   Chair at meetings

2.33   The chair of a meeting under this Part must be the nominee or an appointed person.

2.34 Members' voting rights

2.34(1) A member is entitled to vote according to the rights attaching to the member's shares in accordance with the articles of the company.

2.34(2) A member's shares include any other interest that person may have as a member of the company.

2.34(3) The value of a member for the purposes of voting is determined by reference to the number of votes conferred on that member by the company's articles.

2.35 Requisite majorities of members

2.35(1) A resolution is passed by members by the written resolution procedure or at a meeting of the company when a majority (in value) of those voting have voted in favour of it.

2.35(2) This is subject to any express provision to the contrary in the company's articles.

2.35(3) A resolution is not passed by written resolution unless at least one member has voted in favour of it.

2.36 Notice of order made under section 4A(6) or paragraph 36(5) of Schedule A1

2.36(1) This rule applies where the court makes an order under section 4A(6) or paragraph 36(5) of Schedule A1.

2.36(2) The member who applied for the order must deliver a copy of it certified by the court to–

   (a) the proposer; and

   (b) the supervisor (if different).

2.36(3) If the directors are the proposer a single certified copy may be delivered to the company at its registered office.

2.36(4) The supervisor, or the proposer where there is no supervisor, must as soon as reasonably practicable deliver a notice that the order has been made to every person who had received a notice to vote on the matter or who is affected by the order.

2.36(5) The member who applied for the order must, within five business days of the date the order is made, deliver a copy of the certified copy to the registrar of companies.

2.37 Report of consideration of proposal under section 4(6) and (6A) or paragraph 30(3) and (4) of Schedule A1

2.37(1) A report, or reports as the case may be, must be prepared of the consideration of a proposal under section 4(6) and (6A) or paragraph 30(3) and (4) of Schedule A1 by the convener or, in the case of a meeting, the chair.

2.37(2) The report must–

   (a) state whether the proposal was approved or rejected and whether by the creditors alone or by both the creditors and members and, in either case, whether any approval was met with any modifications;

   (b) list the creditors and members who voted or attended or who were represented at a meeting or decision procedure (as applicable) used to consider the proposal, setting out (with their respective values) how they voted on each resolution or whether they abstained;

   (c) identify which of those creditors were considered to be connected with the company;

(d) if the proposal was approved, state with reasons whether the proceedings are main, secondary, territorial or non-EU proceedings; and

(e) include such further information as the nominee or the chair thinks it appropriate to make known to the court.

2.37(3) A copy of the report must be lodged with the court within four business days of the date of the company meeting.

2.37(4) The court must endorse the copy of the report with the date of lodging.

2.37(5) The chair (in the case of a company meeting) or otherwise the convener must give notice of the result of the consideration of the proposal to everyone who was invited to consider the proposal or to whom notice of a decision procedure or meeting was delivered as soon as reasonably practicable after a copy of the report is lodged with the court.

2.37(6) Where the decision approving the CVA has effect under section 4A or paragraph 36 of Schedule A1 with or without modifications, the supervisor must as soon as reasonably practicable deliver a copy of the convener's report or, in the case of a meeting, the chair's report, to the registrar of companies.

CHAPTER 6

ADDITIONAL MATTERS CONCERNING AND FOLLOWING APPROVAL OF CVA

[Note: A document required by the Act or these Rules must also contain the standard contents set out in Part 1.]

2.38 Handover of property etc. to supervisor

2.38(1) Where the decision approving a CVA has effect under section 4A or paragraph 36 of Schedule A1, and the supervisor is not the same person as the proposer, the proposer must, as soon as reasonably practicable, do all that is required to put the supervisor in possession of the assets included in the CVA.

2.38(2) Where the company is in administration or liquidation and the supervisor is not the same person as the administrator or liquidator, the supervisor must–

(a) before taking possession of the assets included in the CVA, deliver to the administrator or liquidator an undertaking to discharge the balance referred to in paragraph (3) out of the first realisation of assets; or

(b) upon taking possession of the assets included in the CVA, discharge such balance.

2.38(3) The balance is any balance due to the administrator or liquidator–

(a) by way of fees or expenses properly incurred and payable under the Act or any rules made under section 411 which apply to Scotland; and

(b) on account of any advances made in respect of the company together with interest on such advances at the official rate at the date on which the company entered administration or went into liquidation.

2.38(4) The administrator or liquidator has a security over the assets included in the CVA in respect of any sums comprising the balance referred to in paragraph (3), subject to deduction from any realisations by the supervisor of the proper costs and expenses of such realisations.

2.38(5) The supervisor must from time to time out of the realisation of assets–

(a) discharge all cautionary obligations (including guarantees) properly given by the administrator or liquidator for the benefit of the company; and

(b) pay all the expenses of the administrator or liquidator.

2.39   Revocation or suspension of CVA

2.39(1) This rule applies where the court makes an order of revocation or suspension under section 6 or paragraph 38 of Schedule A1.

2.39(2) The applicant for the order must deliver a copy of it certified by the court to–

     (a) the proposer; and

     (b) the supervisor (if different).

2.39(3) If the directors are the proposer, a single certified copy of the order may be delivered to the company at its registered office.

2.39(4) If the order includes a direction by the court under section 6(4)(b) or (c) or under paragraph 38(4)(b) or (c) of Schedule A1 for action to be taken, the applicant for the order must deliver a notice that the order has been made to the person who is directed to take such action.

2.39(5) The proposer must–

     (a) as soon as reasonably practicable deliver a notice that the order has been made to all of those persons to whom a notice to consider the matter was delivered or who appear to be affected by the order;

     (b) within five business days of delivery of a copy of the order (or within such longer period as the court may allow), deliver (if applicable) a notice to the court advising that it is intended to make a revised proposal to the company and its creditors, or to invite reconsideration of the original proposal.

2.39(6) The applicant for the order must deliver a copy of the certified copy to the registrar of companies within five business days of the making of the order with a notice which must contain the date on which the CVA took effect.

2.40   Supervisor's accounts and reports

2.40(1) The supervisor must keep accounts and records where the CVA authorises or requires the supervisor–

     (a) to carry on the business of the company;

     (b) to realise assets of the company; or

     (c) otherwise to administer or dispose of any of its funds.

2.40(2) The accounts and records which must be kept are of the supervisor's acts and dealings in, and in connection with, the CVA, including in particular records of all receipts and payments of money.

2.40(3) The supervisor must preserve any such accounts and records which were kept by any other person who has acted as supervisor of the CVA and are in the supervisor's possession.

2.40(4) The supervisor must deliver reports on the progress and prospects for the full implementation of the CVA to–

     (a) the registrar of companies;

     (b) the company;

     (c) the creditors bound by the CVA;

     (d) subject to paragraph (10) below, the members; and

(e)   if the company is not in liquidation, the company's auditors (if any) for the time being.

2.40(5)   The report delivered to the registrar of companies must be accompanied by a notice which must contain the date on which the CVA took effect.

2.40(6)   The first report must cover the period of 12 months commencing on the date on which the CVA was approved and a further report must be made for each subsequent period of 12 months.

2.40(7)   Each report must be delivered within the period of two months after the end of the 12 month period.

2.40(8)   Such a report is not required if the obligation to deliver a final report under rule 2.43 arises in the two month period.

2.40(9)   Where the supervisor is authorised or required to do any of the things mentioned in paragraph (1), the report must–

(a)   include or be accompanied by a summary of receipts and payments required to be recorded by virtue of paragraph (2); or

(b)   state that there have been no such receipts and payments.

2.40(10)   The court may, on application by the supervisor, dispense with the delivery of such reports or summaries to members, either altogether or on the basis that the availability of the report to members is to be advertised by the supervisor in a specified manner.

2.41   Production of accounts and records to Secretary of State

2.41(1)   The Secretary of State may, during the CVA, or after its full implementation or termination, require the supervisor to produce for inspection (either at the premises of the supervisor or elsewhere)–

(a)   the supervisor's accounts and records in relation to the CVA; and

(b)   copies of reports and summaries prepared in compliance with rule 2.40.

2.41(2)   The Secretary of State may require the supervisor's accounts and records to be audited and, if so, the supervisor must provide such further information and assistance as the Secretary of State requires for the purposes of audit.

2.42   Fees and expenses

2.42   The fees and expenses that may be incurred for the purposes of the CVA are–

(a)   fees for the nominee's services agreed with the company (or, as the case may be, the administrator or liquidator) and disbursements made by the nominee before the decision approving the CVA takes effect under section 4A or paragraph 36 of Schedule A1;

(b)   fees or expenses which–

(i)   are sanctioned by the terms of the CVA, or

(ii)   where they are not sanctioned by the terms of the CVA would be payable, or correspond to those which would be payable, in an administration or winding up.

2.43   Termination or full implementation of CVA

2.43(1)   Not more than 28 days after the termination or full implementation of the CVA the supervisor must deliver a notice that the CVA has been terminated or fully implemented to all the members and those creditors who are bound by the arrangement.

2.43(2)   The notice must state the date the CVA took effect, and must be accompanied by a copy of a report by the supervisor which–

(a)   summarises all receipts and payments in relation to the CVA;

(b)   explains any departure from the terms of the CVA as it originally had effect;

(c)   if the CVA has terminated, sets out the reasons why; and

(d)   states (if applicable) the amount paid to any unsecured creditors by virtue of section 176A.

2.43(3)   The supervisor must, within the period of 28 days mentioned in paragraph (1) send to the registrar of companies and lodge with the court a copy of the notice to creditors and of the supervisor's report.

2.43(4)   The supervisor must not vacate office until after the copies of the notice and report have been delivered to the registrar of companies and lodged with the court.

CHAPTER 7

TIME RECORDING INFORMATION

[Note: A document required by the Act or these Rules must also contain the standard contents set out in Part 1.]

2.44   Provision of information

2.44(1)   This rule applies where the remuneration of the nominee or the supervisor has been fixed on the basis of the time spent.

2.44(2)   A person who is acting, or has acted within the previous two years, as–

(a)   the nominee in relation to a proposal; or

(b)   the supervisor in relation to a CVA,

must, within 28 days of receipt of a request from a person mentioned in paragraph (3), deliver free of charge to that person a statement complying with paragraphs (4) and (5).

2.44(3)   The persons are–

(a)   any director of the company; and

(b)   where the proposal has been approved, any creditor or member.

2.44(4)   The statement must cover the period which–

(a)   in the case of a person who has ceased to act as nominee or supervisor in relation to a company, begins with the date of appointment as nominee or supervisor and ends with the date of ceasing to act; and

(b)   in any other case, consists of one or more complete periods of six months beginning with the date of appointment and ending most nearly before the date of receiving the request.

2.44(5)   The statement must set out–

(a)   the total number of hours spent on the matter during that period by the nominee or supervisor, and any staff;

(b)   for each grade of staff engaged on the matter, the average hourly rate at which work carried out by staff in that grade is charged; and

(c)   the number of hours spent on the matter by each grade of staff during that period.

PART 3

ADMINISTRATION

CHAPTER 1

INTERPRETATION FOR THIS PART

[Note: a document required by the Act or these Rules must also contain the standard contents set out in Part 1.]

3.1   Interpretation for Part 3

3.1   In this Part–

"pre-administration costs" means fees charged, and expenses incurred, by the administrator or another person qualified to act as an insolvency practitioner in relation to the company, before the company entered administration but with a view to it doing so; and

"unpaid pre-administration costs" means pre-administration costs which had not been paid when the company entered administration.

3.2   Proposed administrator's statement and consent to act

3.2(1)   References in this Part to a consent to act are to a statement by a proposed administrator headed "Proposed administrator's statement and consent to act" which contains the following–

(a)   identification details for the company immediately below the heading;

(b)   a certificate that the proposed administrator is qualified to act as an insolvency practitioner in relation to the company;

(c)   the proposed administrator's IP number;

(d)   the name of the relevant recognised professional body which is the source of the proposed administrator's authorisation to act;

(e)   a statement that the proposed administrator consents to act as administrator of the company;

(f)   a statement whether or not the proposed administrator has had any prior professional relationship with the company and, if so, a short summary of the relationship;

(g)   the name of the person by whom the appointment is to be made or the applicant in the case of an application to the court for an appointment; and

(h)   a statement that the proposed administrator is of the opinion that the purpose of the administration is reasonably likely to be achieved in the particular case.

3.2(2)   The consent to act must be authenticated and dated by the proposed administrator.

3.2(3)   Where a number of persons are proposed to be appointed to act jointly or concurrently as the administrator of a company, each must make a separate consent to act.

CHAPTER 2

APPOINTMENT OF ADMINISTRATOR BY COURT

[Note: A document required by the Act or these Rules must also contain the standard contents set out in Part 1.]

3.3 Administration application (paragraph 12 of Schedule B1)

3.3 An application made by way of petition for an administration order ("administration application") must be lodged with the court together with a proposed administrator's consent to act.

3.4 Administration application made by the directors

3.4 Where an administration application is made by the directors, it is to be treated as if it were an application by the company.

3.5 Administration application by the supervisor of a CVA

3.5 Where notice of an administration application by the supervisor of a CVA in respect of the company has been given to the company in accordance with rule 3.6(e) it is to be treated as if it were an application by the company.

3.6 Application

3.6 The applicant must give notice of the administration application to the following (in addition to notifying the persons referred to in paragraph 12(2)(a) to (c) of Schedule B1)–

    (a)   any administrative receiver;

    (b)   if there is a petition pending for the winding up of the company–

        (i)   the petitioner, and

        (ii) any provisional liquidator;

    (c)   any member State liquidator appointed in main proceedings in relation to the company;

    (d)   the Keeper of the Register of Inhibitions and Adjudications;

    (e)   the company, if the application is made by anyone other than the company or its directors;

    (f)   any supervisor of a CVA in relation to the company;

    (g)   the proposed administrator; and

    (h)   any other person on whom the court orders that the application be served.

3.7 Notice to messengers-at-arms or sheriff officers

3.7 The applicant must as soon as reasonably practicable after lodging the administration application deliver a notice of its being made to–

    (a)   any messenger-at-arms or sheriff officer who to the knowledge of the applicant is charged with executing diligence or other legal process against the company or its property; and

    (b)   any person who to the knowledge of the applicant has executed diligence against the company or its property.

3.8 Notice of other insolvency proceedings

3.8 After the administration application has been lodged and until an order is made, it is the duty of the applicant to lodge with the court notice of the existence of any insolvency proceedings in relation to the company, as soon as the applicant becomes aware of them–

    (a)   anywhere in the world, in the case of a company registered under the Companies Acts in Scotland;

    (b)   in any EEA State (including the United Kingdom), in the case of a company incorporated in an EEA State other than the United Kingdom; or

(c)   in any member State other than Denmark, in the case of a company not incorporated in an EEA State.

3.9   Intervention by holder of a qualifying floating charge (paragraph 36(1)(b) of Schedule B1)

3.9(1)   Where the holder of a qualifying floating charge applies to the court under paragraph 36(1)(b) of Schedule B1 to have a specified person appointed as administrator, the holder must produce to the court–

(a)   the written consent of the holder of any prior qualifying floating charge;

(b)   the proposed administrator's consent to act; and

(c)   sufficient evidence to satisfy the court that the holder is entitled to appoint an administrator under paragraph 14 of Schedule B1.

3.9(2)   If an administration order is made appointing the specified person, the expenses of the person who made the administration application and of the applicant under paragraph 36(1)(b) of Schedule B1 are, unless the court orders otherwise, to be paid as an expense of the administration.

3.10   The hearing

3.10   At the hearing of the administration application, any of the following may appear or be represented–

(a)   the applicant;

(b)   the company;

(c)   one or more of the directors;

(d)   any administrative receiver;

(e)   any person who has presented a petition for the winding up of the company;

(f)   the proposed administrator;

(g)   any member State liquidator appointed in main proceedings in relation to the company;

(h)   the holder of any qualifying floating charge;

(i)   any supervisor of a CVA;

(j)   with the permission of the court, any other person who appears to have an interest which justifies appearance.

3.11   The order

3.11(1)   Where the court makes an administration order the court's order must be headed "Administration order" and must contain the following–

(a)   identification details for the insolvency proceedings;

(b)   the address for service of the applicant;

(c)   details of any other parties (including the company) appearing and by whom represented;

(d)   an order that during the period the administration order is in force the affairs, business and property of the company are to be managed by the administrator;

(e)   the name of the person appointed as administrator;

(f)   an order that that person is appointed as administrator of the company;

(g)   a statement that the court is satisfied either that the EU Regulation does not apply or that it does;

(h)   where the EU Regulation does apply, a statement whether the proceedings are main, secondary, or territorial proceedings;

(i)   the date of the order (and, if the court so orders, the time); and

(j)   such other provisions, if any, as the court thinks just.

3.11(2)   Where two or more administrators are appointed, the order must also specify, in terms of paragraph 100(2) of Schedule B1–

(a)   which functions, if any, are to be exercised by those persons appointed acting jointly; and

(b)   which functions, if any, are to be exercised by any or all of the persons appointed.

3.12   Order on an application under paragraph 37 or 38 of Schedule B1

3.12   Where the court makes an administration order in relation to a company on an application under paragraph 37 or 38 of Schedule B1, the court must also include in the order–

(a)   in the case of a liquidator appointed in a voluntary winding up, the removal of that liquidator from office;

(b)   provision for payment of the expenses of the winding up;

(c)   such provision as the court thinks just relating to–

(i)   any indemnity given to the liquidator,

(ii)   the release of the liquidator,

(iii) the handling or realisation of any of the company's assets in the hands of, or under the control of the liquidator, and

(iv)   other matters arising in connection with the winding up; and

(d)   such other provisions, if any, as the court thinks just.

3.13   Notice of administration order

3.13(1)   If the court makes an administration order, it must as soon as reasonably practicable deliver two copies of the order certified by the court to the applicant.

3.13(2)   The applicant must, as soon as reasonably practicable, deliver a certified copy of the order to the person appointed as administrator.

3.13(3)   If the court makes an order under sub-paragraph (d) or (f) of paragraph 13(1) of Schedule B1, it must give directions as to the persons to whom, and how, notice of that order is to be delivered.

3.14   Notice of dismissal of application for an administration order

3.14   If the court dismisses the administration application under paragraph 13(1)(b) of Schedule B 1, the applicant must as soon as reasonably practicable send notice of the court's order dismissing the application to all those to whom the application was notified under rule 3.6.

3.15   Expenses allowed by the court

3.15   If the court makes an administration order, the expenses of the applicant, and of any other party whose expenses are allowed by the court, are to be regarded as expenses of the administration.

CHAPTER 3

APPOINTMENT OF ADMINISTRATOR BY HOLDER OF FLOATING CHARGE

[Note: a document required by the Act or these Rules must also contain the standard contents set out in Part 1.]

3.16   Notice of intention to appoint

3.16(1)   This rule applies where the holder of a qualifying floating charge ("the appointer") gives notice under paragraph 15(1)(a) of Schedule B1 of intention to appoint an administrator under paragraph 14 of that Schedule and lodges a copy of the notice with the court under paragraph 44(2) of that Schedule.

3.16(2)   The notice lodged with the court must be headed "Notice of intention to appoint an administrator by holder of qualifying floating charge" and must contain the following–

(a)   identification details for the insolvency proceedings;

(b)   the name and address of the appointer;

(c)   a statement that the appointer intends to appoint an administrator of the company;

(d)   the name and address of the proposed administrator;

(e)   a statement that the appointer is the holder of the qualifying floating charge in question and that it is now enforceable;

(f)   details of the charge including the date the charge was created, the date the charge was registered and the maximum amount, if any, secured by the charge;

(g)   a statement that the notice is being given in accordance with paragraph 15(1)(a) of Schedule B1 to the holder of every prior floating charge which satisfies paragraph 14(2) of that Schedule;

(h)   the names and addresses of the holders of such prior floating charges and details of the charges;

(i)   a statement whether the company is or is not subject to insolvency proceedings at the date of the notice, and details of the proceedings if it is;

(j)   a statement whether the company is an Article 1.2 undertaking; and

(k)   a statement whether the proceedings flowing from the appointment will be main, secondary, territorial or non-EU proceedings with reasons for the statement.

3.16(3)   The notice must be authenticated by the appointer or the appointer's solicitor and dated.

3.16(4)   The lodging of the copy with the court under paragraph 44(2) of Schedule B1 must be done at the same time as notice is given in accordance with paragraph 15(1)(a).

3.17   Notice of appointment

3.17(1)   Notice of an appointment under paragraph 14 of Schedule B1 must be headed "Notice of appointment of an administrator by holder of a qualifying floating charge" and must contain–

(a)   identification details for the insolvency proceedings;

(b)   the name and address of the appointer;

(c)   a statement that the appointer has appointed the person named as administrator of the company;

(d)   the name and address of the person appointed as administrator;

(e)   a statement that a copy of the administrator's consent to act accompanies the notice;

(f) a statement that the appointer is the holder of the qualifying floating charge in question and that it is now enforceable;

(g) details of the charge including the date of the charge, the date on which it was registered and the maximum amount if any secured by the charge;

(h) one of the following statements–

  (i) that notice has been given in accordance with paragraph 15(1)(a) of Schedule B1 to the holder of every prior floating charge which qualifies as such in terms of paragraph 14(2) of that Schedule, that two business days have elapsed from the date the last such notice was given (if more than one), and–

   (aa) that a copy of every such notice was lodged with the court under paragraph 44(2) of Schedule B1, and the date of that lodging (or the latest date of lodging if more than one), or

   (bb) that a copy of every such notice accompanies the notice of appointment but was not lodged with the court under paragraph 44(2) of Schedule B1,

  (ii) that the holder of every such floating charge to whom notice was given has consented in writing to the making of the appointment and that a copy of every consent accompanies the notice of appointment,

  (iii) that the holder of every such floating charge has consented in writing to the making of the appointment without notice having been given to all and that a copy of every consent accompanies the notice of appointment, or

  (iv) that there is no such floating charge;

(i) a statement whether the company is or is not subject to insolvency proceedings at the date of the notice, and details of the insolvency proceedings if it is;

(j) a statement whether the company is an Article 1.2 undertaking;

(k) a statement whether the insolvency proceedings flowing from the appointment will be main, secondary, territorial or non-EU proceedings and the reasons for so stating; and

(l) a statement that the appointment is in accordance with Schedule B1.

3.17(2) Where two or more administrators are appointed the notice must also specify, in terms of paragraph 100(2) of Schedule B1–

(a) which functions, if any, are to be exercised by those persons acting jointly; and

(b) which functions, if any, are to be exercised by any or all of those persons.

3.17(3) The statutory declaration included in the notice in accordance with paragraph 18(2) of Schedule B1 must be made not more than five business days before the notice is lodged with the court.

3.18 Lodging of notice with the court

3.18(1) Three copies of the notice of appointment must be lodged with the court, accompanied by–

(a) the administrator's consent to act; and

(b) either–

  (i) evidence that the appointer has given notice as required by paragraph 15(1)(a) of Schedule B1, or

  (ii) copies of the written consent of all those required to give consent in accordance with paragraph 15(1)(b) of Schedule B1.

3.18(2) The court must certify the copies of the notice, endorse them with the date and time of lodging and deliver two of the certified copies to the appointer.

3.18(3) The appointer must as soon as reasonably practicable deliver one of the certified copies to the administrator.

3.18(4) This rule is subject to rules 3.20 and 3.21.

3.19 Appointment by floating charge holder after administration application made

3.19(1) This rule applies where the holder of a qualifying floating charge, after receiving notice that an administration application has been made, appoints an administrator under paragraph 14 of Schedule B1.

3.19(2) The holder must as soon as reasonably practicable deliver a copy of the notice of appointment to–

   (a) the person making the administration application; and

   (b) the court in which the application has been made.

3.20 Appointment taking place out of court business hours: procedure

3.20(1) When (but only when) the court is not open for public business, the holder of a qualifying floating charge may lodge a notice of appointment in court in accordance with this rule.

3.20(2) The person making the appointment must lodge the notice with the court by–

   (a) faxing it to the court; or

   (b) where rule 1.42 applies, by electronic means.

3.20(3) Where the notice under paragraph (2) is faxed to the court the person making the appointment must–

   (a) ensure that a fax transmission report is produced by the sending machine which records the date and time of sending; and

   (b) send to the administrator, as soon as reasonably practicable, a copy of the notice of appointment and, where paragraph (2)(a) applies, a copy of the fax transmission report.

3.20(4) The person making the appointment must lodge in court, on the next occasion that the court is open for public business, the original notice of appointment together with the documents required by rule 3.21 and–

   (a) the fax transmission report showing the date and time when the notice was sent; and

   (b) a statement of the full reasons for the out of hours lodging of the notice of appointment, including why it would have been damaging to the company or its creditors not to have so acted.

3.21 Appointment taking place out of court business hours: content of notice

3.21(1) A notice of appointment lodged in accordance with rule 3.20 must be headed "Notice of appointment of an administrator by holder of qualifying floating charge pursuant to paragraphs 14 and 18 of Schedule B1 to the Insolvency Act 1986 and Rule 3.20 of the Insolvency (Scotland) (Company Voluntary Arrangements and Administration) Rules 2018" and must contain–

   (a) identification details for the insolvency proceedings;

   (b) the name and address of the appointer;

   (c) a statement that the appointer has appointed the person named as administrator of the company;

   (d) the name and address of the person appointed as administrator;

(e)   a statement that a copy of the administrator's consent to act accompanies the notice;

(f)   a statement that the appointer is the holder of the qualifying floating charge in question and that it is now enforceable;

(g)   details of the charge including the date of the charge, the date on which it was registered and the maximum amount, if any, secured by the charge;

(h)   one of the following statements–

     (i)   that notice has been given in accordance with paragraph 15(1)(a) of Schedule B1 to the holder of every prior floating charge which satisfied paragraph 14(2) of that Schedule, that two business days have elapsed from the date the last such notice was given (if more than one) and–

         (aa)   that a copy of every such notice was lodged with the court under paragraph 44(2) of Schedule B1, and the date of that lodging (or the latest date of lodging if more than one), or

         (bb)   that a copy of every such notice accompanies the notice of appointment but was not lodged with the court under paragraph 44(2) of Schedule B1,

     (ii)   that the holder of every such floating charge to whom notice was given has consented in writing to the making of the appointment and that a copy of every consent accompanies the notice of appointment,

     (iii)   that the holder of every such floating charge has consented in writing to the making of the appointment without notice having been given to all and that a copy of every consent accompanies the notice of appointment, or

     (iv)   that there is no such floating charge;

(i)   a statement whether the company is or is not subject to insolvency proceedings at the date of the notice, and details of the proceedings if it is;

(j)   a statement whether the company is an Article 1.2 undertaking;

(k)   a statement whether the proceedings flowing from the appointment will be main, secondary, territorial or non-EU proceedings and the reasons for so stating and that a copy of the statement accompanies the notice of appointment;

(l)   a statement that the appointment is in accordance with Schedule B1; and

(m)   an undertaking that the following will be delivered to the court on the next occasion on which the court is open for public business–

     (i)   any document referred to in the notice in accordance with rule 3.20 as accompanying the notice,

     (ii)   the fax transmission report, and

     (iii)   a statement of reasons for the lodging of the notice out of court business hours.

3.21(2)   Where two or more administrators are appointed the notice must also specify, in terms of paragraph 100(2) of Schedule B1–

(a)   which functions, if any, are to be exercised by those persons acting jointly; and

(b)   which functions, if any, are to be exercised by any or all of those persons.

3.21(3)   The statutory declaration included in the notice in accordance with paragraph 18(2) of Schedule B1 must be made not more than five business days before notice is lodged with the court.

3.22   Appointment taking place out of court business hours: legal effect

3.22(1)   The lodging of a notice in accordance with rule 3.20 has the same effect for all purposes as the lodging of a notice of appointment in accordance with rule 3.18.

3.22(2)   The appointment–

(a)   takes effect either–

    (i)   from the date and time of the fax transmission, or

    (ii)   in accordance with rule 1.42(2)

but ceases to have effect if the requirements of rule 3.20(4) are not completed on the next occasion the court is open for public business.

3.22(3)   Where any question arises in relation to the date and time that the appointment was lodged with the court, it is a presumption capable of rebuttal that the date and time shown on the appointer's fax transmission report is the date and time at which the notice was lodged.

CHAPTER 4

APPOINTMENT OF ADMINISTRATOR BY COMPANY OR DIRECTORS

[Note: A document required by the Act or these Rules must also contain the standard contents set out in Part 1.]

3.23   Notice of intention to appoint

3.23(1)   A notice required by paragraph 26(1) of Schedule B1 must be headed "Notice of intention to appoint an administrator by company or directors" and must contain the following–

(a)   identification details for the insolvency proceedings;

(b)   a statement that the company or the directors, as the case may be, intend to appoint an administrator of the company;

(c)   the name and address of the proposed administrator;

(d)   the names and addresses of the persons to whom notice is being given in accordance with paragraph 26(1) of Schedule B1;

(e)   a statement that each of those persons is or may be entitled to appoint–

    (i)   an administrative receiver of the company, or

    (ii)   an administrator of the company under paragraph 14 of Schedule B1;

(f)   a statement that the company has not within the preceding 12 months been–

    (i)   in administration,

    (ii)   the subject of a moratorium under Schedule A1 which ended on a date when no CVA was in force, or

    (iii)   the subject of a CVA which was made during a moratorium under Schedule A1 and which ended prematurely within the meaning of section 7B;

(g)   a statement that in relation to the company there is no–

    (i)   petition for winding up which has been presented but not yet disposed of,

1125

  (ii) administration application which has not yet been disposed of, or

  (iii) administrative receiver in office;

(h) a statement whether the company is an Article 1.2 undertaking;

(i) a statement whether the proceedings flowing from the appointment will be main, secondary, territorial or non-EU proceedings and the reasons for so stating;

(j) a statement that the notice is accompanied (as appropriate) by either–

  (i) a copy of the resolution of the company to appoint an administrator, or

  (ii) a record of the decision of the directors to appoint an administrator; and

(k) a statement that if a recipient of the notice who is named in terms of paragraph (e) wishes to consent in writing to the appointment that person may do so but that after five business days have expired from delivery of the notice the appointer may make the appointment although such a recipient has not replied.

3.23(2) The notice must be accompanied by–

(a) a copy of the resolution of the company to appoint an administrator, where the company intends to make the appointment; or

(b) a record of the decision of the directors, where the directors intend to make the appointment.

3.23(3) If notice of intention to appoint is given under paragraph 26(1) of Schedule B1, a copy of that notice must be sent at the same time to–

(a) any messenger-at-arms or sheriff officer who, to the knowledge of the person giving the notice, is instructed to execute diligence or other legal process against the company;

(b) any person who, to the knowledge of the person giving the notice, has executed diligence against the company or its property;

(c) any supervisor of a CVA; and

(d) the company, if the company is not intending to make the appointment.

3.23(4) The statutory declaration accompanying the notice in accordance with paragraph 27(2) of Schedule B1 must–

(a) if it is not made by the person making the appointment, indicate the capacity in which the person making the declaration does so; and

(b) be made not more than five business days before the notice is lodged with the court.

3.24 Notice of appointment after notice of intention to appoint

3.24(1) Notice of an appointment under paragraph 22 of Schedule B1 (when notice of intention to appoint has been given under paragraph 26) must be headed "Notice of appointment of an administrator by a company (where a notice of intention to appoint has been given)" or "Notice of appointment of an administrator by the directors of a company (where a notice of intention to appoint has been given)" and must contain–

(a) identification details for the company immediately below the heading;

(b) a statement that the company has, or the directors have, as the case may be, appointed the person named as administrator of the company;

(c) the name and address of the person appointed as administrator;

(d) a statement that a copy of the administrator's consent to act accompanies the notice;

(e)   a statement that the company is, or the directors are, as the case may be, entitled to make an appointment under paragraph 22 of Schedule B1;

(f)   a statement that the appointment is in accordance with Schedule B1;

(g)   a statement whether the company is an Article 1.2 undertaking;

(h)   a statement whether the proceedings flowing from the appointment will be main, secondary, territorial, or non-EU proceedings and the reasons for so stating;

(i)   a statement that the company has, or the directors have, as the case may be, given notice of their intention to appoint in accordance with paragraph 26(1) of Schedule B1, that a copy of the notice was lodged with the court, the date of that lodging and either–

  (i)   that five business days have elapsed since notice was given under paragraph 26(1) of Schedule B1, or

  (ii)   that each person to whom the notice was given has consented to the appointment; and

(j)   the date and time of the appointment by the company or its directors.

3.24(2)   Where two or more administrators are appointed, the notice must also specify in terms of paragraph 100(2) of Schedule B1–

(a)   which functions, if any, are to be exercised by those persons acting jointly; and

(b)   which functions, if any, are to be exercised by any or all of those persons.

3.24(3)   The statutory declaration included in the notice in accordance with paragraph 29(2) of Schedule B1 must be made not more than five business days before the notice is lodged with the court.

3.24(4)   If the statutory declaration is not made by the person making the appointment it must indicate the capacity in which the person making the declaration does so.

3.25   Notice of appointment without prior notice of intention to appoint

3.25(1)   Notice of an appointment under paragraph 22 of Schedule B1 (when notice of intention to appoint has not been given under paragraph 26) must be headed "Notice of appointment of an administrator by a company (where a notice of intention to appoint has not been given)" or "Notice of appointment of an administrator by the directors of a company (where a notice of intention to appoint has not been given)" and must identify the company immediately below the heading.

3.25(2)   The notice must state the following–

(a)   that the company has, or the directors have, as the case may be, appointed the person specified under sub-paragraph (b) as administrator of the company;

(b)   the name and address of the person appointed as administrator;

(c)   that a copy of the administrator's consent to act accompanies the notice;

(d)   that the company is or the directors are, as the case may be, entitled to make an appointment under paragraph 22 of Schedule B1;

(e)   that the appointment is in accordance with Schedule B1;

(f)   that the company has not within the preceding 12 months been–

  (i)   in administration,

  (ii)   the subject of a moratorium under Schedule A1 which ended on a date when no CVA was in force, or

      (iii) the subject of a CVA which was made during a moratorium under Schedule A1 and which ended prematurely within the meaning of section 7B;

(g) that in relation to the company there is no–

      (i)   petition for winding up which has been presented but not yet disposed of,

      (ii) administration application which has not yet been disposed of, or

      (iii) administrative receiver in office;

(h) whether the company is an Article 1.2 undertaking;

(i) whether the proceedings flowing from the appointment will be main, secondary, territorial or non-EU proceedings and the reasons for so stating;

(j) that the notice is accompanied by–

      (i)   a copy of the resolution of the company to appoint an administrator, or

      (ii) a record of the decision of the directors to appoint an administrator; and

(k) the date and time of the appointment.

3.25(3)   Where two or more administrators are appointed the notice must also specify in terms of paragraph 100(2) of Schedule B1–

(a) which functions (if any) are to be exercised by those persons acting jointly; and

(b) which functions (if any) are to be exercised by any or all of those persons.

3.25(4)   The statutory declaration included in the notice in accordance with paragraph 29(2) and 30 of Schedule B1 must–

(a) if the declaration is made on behalf of the person making the appointment, indicate the capacity in which the person making the declaration does so; and

(b) be made not more than five business days before the notice is lodged with the court.

3.26 Notice of appointment: lodging with the court

3.26(1)   Three copies of the notice of appointment in accordance with rule 3.24 or 3.25 must be lodged with the court, accompanied by–

(a) the administrator's consent to act; and

(b) the written consent of all those persons to whom notice was given in accordance with paragraph 26(1) of Schedule B1 unless the period of notice set out in paragraph 26(1) has expired.

3.26(2)   Where a notice of intention to appoint an administrator has not been given, the copies of the notice of appointment must also be accompanied by–

(a) a copy of the resolution of the company to appoint an administrator, where the company is making the appointment; or

(b) a record of the decision of the directors, where the directors are making the appointment.

3.26(3)   The court must certify the copies, endorse them with the date and time of lodging and deliver two of the certified copies to the appointer.

3.26(4)   The appointer must as soon as reasonably practicable deliver one of the certified copies to the administrator.

CHAPTER 5

NOTICE OF ADMINISTRATOR'S APPOINTMENT

[Note: a document required by the Act or these Rules must also contain the standard contents set out in Part 1.]

3.27 Publication of administrator's appointment

3.27(1) The notice of appointment, to be published by the administrator as soon as reasonably practicable after appointment under paragraph 46(2)(b) of Schedule B1, must be gazetted and may be advertised in such other manner as the administrator thinks fit.

3.27(2) The notice of appointment must state the following–

(a) that an administrator has been appointed;

(b) the date of the appointment; and

(c) the nature of the business of the company.

3.27(3) The administrator must, as soon as reasonably practicable after the date specified in paragraph 46(6) of Schedule B1, deliver a notice of the appointment–

(a) if a receiver has been appointed, to that receiver;

(b) if there is pending a petition for the winding up of the company, to the petitioner (and also to the provisional liquidator, if any);

(c) to any messenger-at-arms or sheriff officer who, to the administrator's knowledge, is instructed to execute diligence or other legal process against the company or its property;

(d) to any person who, to the administrator's knowledge, has executed diligence against the company or its property;

(e) to the Keeper of the Register of Inhibitions and Adjudications; and

(f) to any supervisor of a CVA.

3.27(4) Where, under Schedule B1 or these Rules, the administrator is required to deliver a notice of the appointment to the registrar of companies or any other person, it must be headed "Notice of administrator's appointment" and must contain–

(a) the administrator's name and address and IP number;

(b) identification details for the insolvency proceedings; and

(c) a statement that the administrator has been appointed as administrator of the company.

3.27(5) The notice under paragraph (4) must be authenticated and dated by the administrator.

CHAPTER 6

STATEMENT OF AFFAIRS

[Note: A document required by the Act or these Rules must also contain the standard contents set out in Part 1.]

3.28 Interpretation

3.28 In this Chapter–

"nominated person" means a relevant person who has been required by the administrator to make out and deliver to the administrator a statement of affairs;

"relevant person" means a person mentioned in paragraph 47(3) of Schedule B1; and

"fixed security", in relation to any property of a company, means any security, other than a floating charge or a charge having the nature of a floating charge, which on the winding up of the company in Scotland would be treated as an effective security over that property, and (without prejudice to that generality) includes a security over that property, being a heritable security within the meaning of section 9(8) of the Conveyancing and Feudal Reform (Scotland) Act 1970.

3.29 Statement of affairs: notice requiring and delivery to the administrator (paragraph 47(1) of Schedule B1)

[Note: see section 234(1) and 235(1) for the application of section 235 to administrators.]

3.29(1)   A notice under paragraph 47(1) of Schedule B1 must be delivered to each person required to provide a statement of affairs of the company ("statement of affairs").

3.29(2)   The notice must be headed "Notice requiring statement of affairs" and must–

(a) require each nominated person to whom the notice is delivered to prepare and submit to the administrator a statement of affairs of the company;

(b) inform each nominated person of–

    (i)   the names and addresses of all others (if any) to whom the same notice has been delivered,

    (ii) the requirement to deliver the statement of affairs to the administrator not later than 11 days after receipt of the notice requiring the statement of affairs, and

    (iii) the effect of paragraph 48(4) of Schedule B1 (penalty for non-compliance) and section 235 (duty to co-operate with the office-holder).

3.29(3)   The administrator must inform each nominated person to whom notice is delivered that a document for the preparation of the statement of affairs capable of completion in compliance with rule 3.30 will be supplied if requested.

3.29(4)   The nominated person (or one of them, if more than one) must deliver the statement of affairs to the administrator together with a copy of the statement.

3.30 Statement of affairs: content (paragraph 47 of Schedule B1)

3.30(1)   The statement of affairs must be headed "Statement of affairs" and must–

(a) identify the company immediately below the heading; and

(b) state that it is a statement of the affairs of the company on a specified date, being the date on which it entered administration.

3.30(2)   The statement of affairs must contain (in addition to the matters required by paragraph 47(2) of Schedule B1)–

(a) a summary of the assets of the company, setting out the book value and the estimated realisable value of–

    (i)   any assets subject to a fixed security,

    (ii) any assets subject to a floating charge,

    (iii) any uncharged assets, and

    (iv) the total assets available for preferential creditors;

(b) a summary of the liabilities of the company, setting out–

    (i)   the amount of preferential debts,

    (ii) an estimate of the deficiency with respect to preferential debts or the surplus available after paying the preferential debts,

    (iii) an estimate of the prescribed part, if applicable,

    (iv) an estimate of the total assets available to pay debts secured by floating charges,

    (v) the amount of debts secured by floating charges,

    (vi) an estimate of the deficiency with respect to debts secured by floating charges or the surplus available after paying the debts secured by fixed security or floating charges,

    (vii) the amount of unsecured debts (excluding preferential debts),

    (viii) an estimate of the deficiency with respect to unsecured debts or the surplus available after paying unsecured debts,

    (ix) any issued and called-up capital, and

    (x) an estimate of the deficiency with respect to, or surplus available to, members of the company;

(c)   a list of the company's creditors with the further particulars required by paragraph (3) indicating–

    (i)   any creditors under hire-purchase, conditional sale and hiring agreements,

    (ii) any creditors claiming retention of title over property in the company's possession; and

(d)   the name and address of each member of the company and the number, nominal value and other details of the shares held by each member.

3.30(3)   The list of creditors required by paragraph 47(2) of Schedule B1 and paragraph (2)(c) of this rule must contain the particulars mentioned in paragraph (4) except where paragraphs (5) and (6) apply.

3.30(4)   The particulars required by paragraph (3) are as follows–

(a)   the name and postal address of the creditor;

(b)   the amount of the debt owed to the creditor;

(c)   details of any security held by the creditor;

(d)   the date on which the security was given; and

(e)   the value of any such security.

3.30(5)   Paragraph (6) applies where the particulars mentioned in paragraph (4) relate to creditors who are either–

(a)   employees or former employees of the company; or

(b)   consumers claiming amounts paid in advance for the supply of goods or services.

3.30(6)   Where this paragraph applies–

(a)   the statement of affairs itself must state separately for each of paragraph (5)(a) and (b) the number of such creditors and the total of the debts owed to them; and

(b)   the particulars required by paragraph (4) must be set out in separate schedules to the statement of affairs for each of paragraphs (5)(a) and (b).

3.31 Statement of affairs: statement of concurrence

3.31(1)   The administrator may require a relevant person to deliver to the administrator a statement of concurrence.

3.31(2) A statement of concurrence is a statement that that person concurs in the statement of affairs submitted by a nominated person.

3.31(3) The administrator must inform the nominated person who has been required to submit a statement of affairs that the relevant person has been required to deliver a statement of concurrence.

3.31(4) The nominated person must deliver a copy of the statement of affairs to every relevant person who has been required to deliver a statement of concurrence.

3.31(5) A statement of concurrence–

(a) must identify the company; and

(b) may be qualified in relation to matters dealt with in the statement of affairs where the relevant person–

    (i) is not in agreement with the statement of affairs,

    (ii) considers the statement of affairs to be erroneous or misleading, or

    (iii) is without the direct knowledge necessary for concurring with it.

3.31(6) A statement of concurrence must be a statutory declaration made in accordance with the Statutory Declarations Act 1835.

3.31(7) The relevant person must deliver the required statement of concurrence together with a copy to the administrator before the end of the period of five business days (or such other period as the administrator may agree) beginning with the day on which the relevant person receives the statement of affairs.

3.32 Statement of affairs: registrar of companies

3.32(1) The administrator must as soon as reasonably practicable deliver to the registrar of companies a copy of–

(a) the statement of affairs; and

(b) any statement of concurrence.

3.32(2) The administrator must not deliver to the registrar of companies with the statement of affairs any schedule required by rule 3.30(6)(b).

3.32(3) The requirement to deliver the statement of affairs is subject to any order of the court made under rule 3.45 that the statement of affairs or a specified part must not be delivered to the registrar of companies.

3.33 Statement of affairs: release from requirement and extension of time

3.33(1) The power of the administrator under paragraph 48(2) of Schedule B1 to revoke a requirement to provide a statement of affairs or to extend the period within which it must be submitted may be exercised upon the administrator's own initiative or at the request of a nominated person who has been required to provide it.

3.33(2) The nominated person may apply to the court if the administrator refuses that person's request for a revocation or extension.

3.33(3) On receipt of an application, the court may, if it is satisfied that no sufficient cause is shown for it, dismiss it without giving notice to any party other than the applicant.

3.33(4) The applicant must, at least 14 days before any hearing, deliver to the administrator a notice stating the venue with a copy of the application and of any evidence on which the applicant intends to rely.

3.33(5)   The administrator may do either or both of the following–

(a) lodge a report of any matters which the administrator thinks ought to be drawn to the court's attention; or

(b) appear and be heard on the application.

3.33(6)   If a report is lodged, the administrator must deliver a copy of it to the applicant not later than five business days before the hearing.

3.33(7)   Copies of any order made on the application must be certified by the court and delivered by the court to the applicant and the administrator.

3.33(8)   The expenses of an application under this rule must be paid by the applicant in any event, but the court may order that an allowance of all or part of them be payable as an expense of the administration.

3.34   Statement of affairs: expenses

3.34(1)   The administrator must pay as an expense of the administration any expenses which the administrator considers to have been reasonably incurred by–

(a) a nominated person in making a statement of affairs and a statutory declaration; or

(b) a relevant person in making a statement of concurrence.

3.34(2)   Any decision by the administrator under this rule is subject to appeal to the court.

CHAPTER 7

ADMINISTRATOR'S PROPOSALS

[Note: A document required by the Act or these Rules must also contain the standard contents set out in Part 1.]

3.35   Administrator's proposals: additional content

3.35(1)   The administrator's statement of proposals (which is required by paragraph 49(4) to be sent to the registrar of companies, creditors and members) must identify the insolvency proceedings and, in addition to the matters set out in paragraph 49, contain–

(a) any other trading names of the company;

(b) details of the administrator's appointment, including–

(i) the date of the appointment,

(ii) the person making the application or appointment, and

(iii) where a number of persons have been appointed as administrators, details of the matters set out in paragraph 100(2) of Schedule B1 relating to the exercise of their functions;

(c) the names of the directors and secretary of the company and details of any shareholdings in the company which they may have;

(d) an account of the circumstances giving rise to the appointment of the administrator;

(e) the date the proposals were sent to the creditors;

(f) if a statement of the company's affairs has been submitted–

    (i)   a copy or summary of it, except so far as an order under rule 3.44 or 3.45 limits disclosure of it, and excluding any schedule referred to in rule 3.30(6)(b), or the particulars relating to individual creditors contained in any such schedule,

    (ii)   details of who provided the statement of affairs, and

    (iii) any comments which the administrator may have upon the statement of affairs;

  (g) if an order under rule 3.45 or 3.46 has been made–

    (i)   a statement of that fact, and

    (ii)   the date of the order;

  (h) if no statement of affairs has been submitted–

    (i)   the details of the financial position of the company at the latest practicable date (which must, unless the court orders otherwise, be a date not earlier than that on which the company entered administration), and

    (ii)   an explanation as to why there is no statement of affairs;

  (i)   a full list of the company's creditors in accordance with paragraph (2) if either–

    (i)   no statement of affairs has been submitted, or

    (ii)   a statement of affairs has been submitted but it does not include such a list, or the administrator believes the list included is less than full;

  (j)   a statement of–

    (i)   how it is envisaged the purpose of the administration will be achieved, and

    (ii)   how it is proposed that the administration will end, including, where it is proposed that the administration will end by the company moving to a creditors' voluntary winding up–

       (aa) details of the proposed liquidator,

       (bb) where applicable, the declaration required by section 231, and

       (cc) a statement that the creditors may, before the proposals are approved, nominate a different person as liquidator in accordance with paragraph 83(7)(a) of Schedule B1 and rule 3.60(6)(b);

  (k) a statement of either–

    (i)   the method by which the administrator has decided to seek a decision by creditors as to whether they approve the proposals, or

    (ii)   the administrator's reasons for not seeking a decision by creditors;

  (l)   the manner in which the affairs and business of the company–

    (i)   have, since the date of the administrator's appointment, been managed and financed, including, where any assets have been disposed of, the reasons for the disposals and the terms upon which the disposals were made, and

    (ii)   will, if the administrator's proposals are approved, continue to be managed and financed;

  (m) a statement whether the proceedings are main, secondary, territorial or non-EU proceedings; and

  (n) any other information that the administrator thinks necessary to enable creditors to decide whether or not to approve the proposals.

3.35(2)   The list of creditors required by paragraph (1)(i) must contain the details required by paragraph (3) except where paragraphs (4) and (5) apply.

3.35(3)   The particulars required by paragraph (2) are as follows and must be given in this order–

(a)   the name and postal address of the creditor;

(b)   the amount of the debt owed to the creditor;

(c)   details of any security held by the creditor;

(d)   the date on which any such security was given; and

(e)   the value of any such security;

3.35(4)   This paragraph applies where the particulars required by paragraph (3) relate to creditors who are either–

(a)   employees or former employees of the company; or

(b)   consumers claiming amounts paid in advance for the supply of goods and services.

3.35(5)   Where paragraph (4) applies–

(a)   the list of creditors required by paragraph (1)(i) must state separately for each of paragraphs (4)(a) and (b) the number of the creditors and the total debts owed to them;

(b)   the particulars required by paragraph (3) in respect of such creditors must be set out in separate schedules to the list of creditors for each of paragraphs (4)(a) and (b); and

(c)   the administrator must not deliver any such schedule to the registrar of companies with the statement of proposals.

3.35(6)   Except where the administrator proposes a CVA in relation to the company, the statement made by the administrator under paragraph 49 of Schedule B1 must also include–

(a)   to the best of the administrator's knowledge and belief, an estimate of the value of–

(i)   the prescribed part (whether or not the administrator might be required under section 176A to make the prescribed part available for the satisfaction of unsecured debts), and

(ii)   the company's net property (as defined in section 176A(6)); and

(b)   a statement whether the administrator proposes to make an application to the court under section 176A(5) and if so the reason for the application.

3.35(7)   The administrator may exclude from an estimate under paragraph (6)(a) information the disclosure of which could seriously prejudice the commercial interests of the company.

3.35(8)   If the exclusion of such information affects the calculation of an estimate, the report must say so.

3.35(9)   The document containing the statement of proposals must include a statement of the basis on which it is proposed that the administrator's remuneration should be fixed by a decision in accordance with Chapter 14 of Part 3 of these Rules.

3.35(10)   Where applicable, the document containing the statement of proposals must include–

(a)   a statement of any pre-administration costs charged or incurred by the administrator or, to the administrator's knowledge, by any other person qualified to act as an insolvency practitioner in relation to the company;

(b)   a statement that the payment of any unpaid pre-administration costs as an expense of the administration is–

(i)   subject to approval under rule 3.52, and

(ii)   not part of the proposals subject to approval under paragraph 53 of Schedule B1.

3.36   Administrator's proposals: statement of pre-administration costs

3.36   A statement of pre-administration costs under rule 3.35(10)(a) must include–

(a)   details of any agreement under which the fees were charged and expenses incurred, including the parties to the agreement and the date on which the agreement was made;

(b)   details of the work done for which the fees were charged and expenses incurred;

(c)   an explanation of why the work was done before the company entered administration and how it had been intended to further the achievement of an objective in paragraph 3(1) of Schedule B1 in accordance with sub-paragraphs (2) to (4) of that paragraph;

(d)   a statement of the amount of the pre-administration costs, setting out separately–

    (i)   the fees charged by the administrator,

    (ii)   the expenses incurred by the administrator,

    (iii) the fees charged (to the administrator's knowledge) by any other person qualified to act as an insolvency practitioner in relation to the company (and, if more than one, by each separately), and

    (iv)   the expenses incurred (to the administrator's knowledge) by any other person qualified to act as an insolvency practitioner in relation to the company (and, if more than one, by each separately);

(e)   a statement of the amounts of pre-administration costs which have already been paid (set out separately as under sub-paragraph (d));

(f)   the identity of the person who made the payment or, if more than one person made the payment, the identity of each such person and of the amounts paid by each such person set out separately as under sub-paragraph (d);

(g)   a statement of the amounts of unpaid pre-administrations costs (set out separately as under sub-paragraph (d)); and

(h)   a statement that the payment of unpaid pre-administration costs as an expense of the administration is–

    (i)   subject to approval under rule 3.52, and

    (ii)   not part of the proposals subject to approval under paragraph 53 of Schedule B1.

3.37   Advertising administrator's proposals and notices of extension of time for delivery of proposals (paragraph 49 of Schedule B1)

3.37(1)   A notice published by the administrator under paragraph 49(6) of Schedule B1 must–

(a)   identify the insolvency proceedings and contain the registered office of the company;

(b)   be advertised in such manner as the administrator thinks fit; and

(c)   be published as soon as reasonably practicable after the administrator has delivered the statement of proposals to the company's creditors but not later than eight weeks (or such other period as may be agreed by the creditors or as the court may order) from the date on which the company entered administration.

3.37(2)   Where the court orders, on an application by the administrator under paragraph 107 of Schedule B1, an extension of the period in paragraph 49(5) of Schedule B1 for delivering copies of the statement of proposals, the administrator must as soon as reasonably practicable after the making of the order deliver a notice of the extension to–

(a)   the creditors of the company;

(b)   the members of the company of whose address the administrator is aware; and

(c)   the registrar of companies.

3.37(3)   The notice must–

(a)   identify the insolvency proceedings;

(b)   state the date to which the court has ordered an extension; and

(c)   contain the registered office of the company.

3.37(4)   The administrator is taken to comply with paragraph (2)(b) if the administrator publishes a notice complying with paragraph (5).

3.37(5)   The notice must–

(a)   contain the information required by paragraph (3);

(b)   be advertised in such manner as the administrator thinks fit;

(c)   state that members may request in writing a notice of the extension, and state the address to which to write; and

(d)   be published as soon as reasonably practicable after the administrator has delivered the notice of the extension to the company's creditors.

3.38   Seeking approval of the administrator's proposals

3.38(1)   This rule applies where the administrator is required by paragraph 51 of Schedule B1 to seek approval from the company's creditors of the statement of proposals.

3.38(2)   The statement of proposals delivered under paragraph 49(4) of Schedule B1 must be accompanied by a notice to the creditors of the decision procedure in accordance with rule 5.8.

3.38(3)   The administrator may seek approval from the creditors using the deemed consent procedure in which case the statement of proposals delivered under paragraph 49(4) must be accompanied by a notice complying with the requirements of rule 5.7.

3.38(4)   Where the administrator has made a statement under paragraph 52(1) and has not sought a decision on approval from creditors, the proposal will be deemed to have been approved unless a decision has been requested under paragraph 52(2).

3.38(5)   Where under paragraph (4) the proposal is deemed to have been approved the administrator must, as soon as reasonably practicable after the expiry of the period for requisitioning a decision set out in rule 5.17(2), deliver a notice of the date of deemed approval to the registrar of companies, the court and any creditor to whom the administrator has not previously delivered the proposal.

3.38(6)   The notice must contain–

(a)   identification details for the insolvency proceedings;

(b)   the name of the administrator;

(c)   the date the administrator was appointed; and

(d)   the date on which the statement of proposals was delivered to the creditors.

3.38(7)   A copy of the statement of proposals, with the statements required by rule 3.35(5) must accompany the notice given to the court and to any creditors to whom a copy of the statement of proposals has not previously been delivered.

3.39   **Invitation to creditors to form a creditors' committee**

3.39(1)   Where the administrator is required to seek a decision from the company's creditors under paragraph 51 of Schedule B1, the administrator must at the same time deliver to the creditors a notice inviting them to decide whether a creditors' committee should be established if sufficient creditors are willing to be members of the committee.

3.39(2)   The notice must also invite nominations for members of the committee, such nominations to be received by the administrator by a date to be specified in the notice.

3.39(3)   The notice must state that any nominations–

(a)   must be delivered to the administrator by the specified date; and

(b)   can only be accepted if the administrator is satisfied as to the creditor's eligibility under rule 3.74.

3.39(4)   A notice under this rule must also be delivered to the creditors at any other time when the administrator seeks a decision by creditors and a creditors' committee has not already been established at that time.

3.40   **Notice of extension of time to seek approval**

3.40(1)   Where the court orders an extension to the period set out in paragraph 51(2) of Schedule B1, the administrator must deliver a notice of the extension as soon as reasonably practicable to each person mentioned in paragraph 49(4) of Schedule B1.

3.40(2)   The notice must contain identification details for the insolvency proceedings and the date to which the court has ordered an extension.

3.40(3)   The administrator is taken to have complied with paragraph (1) as regards members of the company if the administrator publishes a notice complying with paragraph (4).

3.40(4)   The notice must–

(a)   be advertised in such a manner as the administrator thinks fit;

(b)   state that members may request in writing a copy of the notice of the extension, and state the address to which to write; and

(c)   be published as soon as reasonably practicable after the administrator has delivered the notice of the extension to the company's creditors.

3.41   **Notice of the creditors' decision on the administrator's proposals (paragraph 53(2))**

3.41(1)   In addition to delivering a report to the court and the registrar of companies (in accordance with paragraph 53(2) of Schedule B1) the administrator must deliver a report to–

(a)   the company's creditors (accompanied by a copy of the statement of proposals, with the statement required by rule 3.35(10)(a), if it has not previously been delivered to the creditor); and

(b)   every other person to whom a copy of the statement of proposals was delivered.

3.41(2)   A report mentioned in paragraph (1) must contain–

(a)   identification details for the insolvency proceedings;

(b)   details of decisions taken by the creditors including details of any modifications to the proposals which were approved by the creditors; and

(c)   the date such decisions were made.

3.41(3)   A copy of the statement of proposals, with any statements required by rule 3.35(9) and (10), must accompany the report to the court.

3.42   Administrator's proposals: revision

3.42(1)   Where paragraph 54(1) of Schedule B1 applies, the statement of the proposed revision which is required to be delivered to the creditors must be delivered together with a notice of the decision procedure in accordance with rule 5.8.

3.42(2)   The statement must identify the insolvency proceedings and include–

(a)   any other trading names of the company;

(b)   details of the administrator's appointment, including–

   (i)   the date of appointment, and

   (ii)   the person making the application or appointment;

(c)   the names of the directors and secretary of the company and details of any shareholdings in the company which they may have;

(d)   a summary of the original proposals and the reason or reasons for proposing a revision;

(e)   details of the proposed revision, including details of the administrator's assessment of the likely impact of the proposed revision upon creditors generally or upon each class of creditors;

(f)   where the proposed revision relates to the ending of the administration by a creditors' voluntary winding up and the nomination of a person to be the proposed liquidator of the company–

   (i)   details of the proposed liquidator,

   (ii)   where applicable, the declaration required by section 231, and

   (iii)   a statement that the creditors may, before the proposals are approved, nominate a different person as liquidator in accordance with paragraph 83(7)(a) of Schedule B1 and rule 3.60(6)(b); and

(g)   any other information that the administrator thinks necessary to enable creditors to decide whether or not to vote for the proposed revisions.

3.42(3)   The administrator may seek a decision using the deemed consent procedure in which case the statement of the proposed revision must be accompanied by a notice which complies with rule 5.7.

3.42(4)   The period within which, subject to paragraph 54(3) of Schedule B1, the administrator must send a copy of the statement to every member of the company of whose address the administrator is aware is five business days after sending the statement of the proposed revision to the creditors.

3.42(5)   Notice under paragraph 54(3) and (4) of Schedule B1 must–

(a)   be advertised in such manner as the administrator thinks fit as soon as reasonably practicable after the administrator has sent the statement to the creditors; and

(b)   state that members may request in writing a copy of the proposed revision, and state the address to which to write.

3.42(6)   A copy of the statement of revised proposals under rule 3.43(3) must be delivered to the registrar of companies not later than five days after the report under rule 3.43(1) is delivered.

3.43   Notice of result of creditors' decision on revised proposals (paragraph 54(6))

3.43(1)   In addition to delivering a report to the court and the registrar of companies (in accordance with paragraph 54(6) of Schedule B1) the administrator must deliver a report to–

(a)   the company's creditors (accompanied by a copy of the original statement of proposals and the revised statement of proposals if the administrator had not delivered notice of the decision procedure or deemed consent procedure to the creditor); and

(b) every other person to whom a copy of the original statement of proposals was delivered.

3.43(2) A report mentioned in paragraph (1) must contain–

(a) identification details for the insolvency proceedings;

(b) the date of the revised proposals;

(c) details of decisions taken by the creditors including details of any modifications to the revised proposals which were approved by the creditors; and

(d) the date such decisions were made.

3.43(3) A copy of the statement of revised proposals must accompany the notice to the court.

CHAPTER 8

LIMITED DISCLOSURE OF STATEMENTS OF AFFAIRS AND PROPOSALS

[Note: A document requirement by the Act or these Rules must also contain the standard contents set out in Part 1.]

3.44 Application of Chapter

3.44 This Chapter applies to the disclosure of information which would be likely to prejudice the conduct of the administration or might reasonably be expected to lead to violence against any person.

3.45 Orders limiting disclosure of statement of affairs etc.

3.45(1) If the administrator thinks that the circumstances in rule 3.44 apply in relation to the disclosure of–

(a) the whole or part of the statement of affairs;

(b) any of the matters specified in rule 3.35(1)(h) and (i); or

(c) a statement of concurrence,

the administrator may apply to the court for an order in relation to the particular document or a specified part of it.

3.45(2) The court may order that the whole of or a specified part of a document referred to in paragraph (1)(a) to (c) must not be delivered to the registrar of companies or, in the case of the statement of proposals, to creditors or members of the company.

3.45(3) The administrator must as soon as reasonably practicable deliver to the registrar of companies–

(a) a copy of the order;

(b) the statement of affairs, the statement of proposals and any statement of concurrence to the extent provided by the order; and

(c) if the order relates to the statement of proposals, an indication of the nature of the matter in relation to which the order was made.

3.45(4) If the order relates to the statement of proposals, the administrator must as soon as reasonably practicable also deliver to the creditors and members of the company–

(a) the statement of proposals to the extent provided by the order; and

(b) an indication of the nature of the matter in relation to which the order was made.

3.46   Order for disclosure by administrator

3.46(1)   A creditor may apply to the court for an order that the administrator disclose any of the following in relation to which an order has been made under rule 3.45(2)–

(a)   a statement of affairs;

(b)   a specified part of it;

(c)   a part of a statement of proposals; or

(d)   a statement of concurrence.

3.46(2)   The application must be supported by written evidence in the form of an affidavit.

3.46(3)   The applicant must deliver to the administrator notice of the application at least three business days before the hearing.

3.46(4)   In an order for disclosure, the court may include conditions as to confidentiality, duration, the scope of the order in the event of any change of circumstances or such other matters as it thinks just.

3.47   Discharge or variation of order for limited disclosure

3.47(1)   If there is a material change in circumstances rendering an order for limited disclosure under rule 3.45(2) wholly or partially unnecessary, the administrator must, as soon as reasonably practicable after the change, apply to the court for the order to be discharged or varied.

3.47(2)   If the court makes such an order, the administrator must as soon as reasonably practicable deliver to the registrar of companies–

(a)   a copy of the order; and

(b)   the statement of affairs, the statement of proposals and any statement of concurrence to the extent provided by the order.

3.47(3)   If the order relates to the statement of proposals, the administrator must as soon as reasonably practicable also deliver to the creditors and members the statement of proposals to the extent allowed by the order.

3.48   Publication etc. of statement of affairs or statements of proposals

3.48(1)   If, after the administrator has sent a statement of proposals under paragraph 49(4) of Schedule B1, a statement of affairs is delivered to the registrar of companies in accordance with rule 3.47(2) as the result of the discharge or variation of an order, the administrator must deliver to the creditors a copy or summary of the statement of affairs as delivered to the registrar of companies.

3.48(2)   The administrator is taken to comply with the requirements for delivery to members of the company in rule 3.45(4) or 3.47(3) if the administrator publishes the required notice.

3.48(3)   The required notice must–

(a)   be advertised in such manner as the administrator thinks fit;

(b)   state that members can request in writing–

(i)   a copy of the statement of proposals to the extent provided by the order, and

(ii)   an indication of the nature of the matter in relation to which the order was made;

(c)   state the address to which such a written request is to be made; and

(d)   be published as soon as reasonably practicable after the administrator has delivered the statement of proposals to the extent provided by the order to the company's creditors.

CHAPTER 9

DISPOSAL OF SECURED PROPERTY

[Note: A document required by the Act or these Rules must also contain the standard contents set out in Part 1.]

3.49   Disposal of secured property

3.49(1)   This rule applies where the administrator applies to the court under paragraph 71 or 72 of Schedule B1 for authority to dispose of–

(a)   property which is subject to a security other than a floating charge; or

(b)   goods in the possession of the company under a hire-purchase agreement.

3.49(2)   The court must fix a venue for the hearing of the application.

3.49(3)   As soon as reasonably practicable after the court has done so, the administrator must deliver notice of the venue to the holder of the security or the owner of the goods.

3.49(4)   If an order is made under paragraph 71 or 72 of Schedule B1, the court must deliver two copies of the order certified by the court to the administrator.

3.49(5)   The administrator must deliver–

(a)   one of the certified copies to the holder of the security or the owner of the goods; and

(b)   a copy of the certified order to the registrar of companies.

CHAPTER 10

EXPENSES OF THE ADMINISTRATION

[Note: A document required by the Act or these Rules must also contain the standard contents set out in Part 1.]

3.50   Expenses

3.50(1)   All fees, costs, charges and other expenses incurred in the course of the administration are to be treated as expenses of the administration.

3.50(2)   The expenses associated with the prescribed part must be paid out of the prescribed part.

3.50(3)   The cost of the caution required by section 390(3) for the proper performance of the administrator's functions is an expense of the administration.

3.51   Order of priority

3.51(1)   Where there is a former administrator, the former administrator's remuneration and expenses as determined in accordance with rule 3.98 are payable in priority to the expenses in this rule.

3.51(2)   Subject to paragraph (1) and to any court order under paragraph (3) the expenses of the administration are payable in the following order of priority–

(a)   expenses properly incurred by the administrator in performing the administrator's functions;

(b)   the cost of any caution provided by the administrator in accordance with the Act or these Rules;

(c)   where an administration order was made, the expenses of the applicant and any person appearing on the hearing of the application whose expenses were allowed by the court;

(d) where the administrator was appointed otherwise than by order of the court–

    (i) the costs and expenses of the appointer in connection with the making of the appointment, and

    (ii) the costs and expenses incurred by any other person in giving notice of intention to appoint an administrator;

(e) any amount payable to a person in respect of assistance in the preparation of a statement of affairs or statement of concurrence;

(f) any allowance made by order of the court in respect of the costs on an application for release from the obligation to submit a statement of affairs or deliver a statement of concurrence;

(g) any necessary disbursements by the administrator in the course of the administration (including any costs referred to in Articles 30 or 59 of the EU Regulation and expenses incurred by members of the creditors' committee or their representatives and allowed for by the administrator under rule 3.90 but not including any payment of corporation tax in circumstances referred to in sub-paragraph (j) below);

(h) the remuneration or emoluments of any person who has been employed by the administrator to perform any services for the company, as required or authorised under the Act or these Rules;

(i) the administrator's remuneration the basis of which has been fixed under Chapter 14 of this Part of these Rules and unpaid pre-administration costs approved under rule 3.52; and

(j) the amount of any corporation tax on chargeable gains accruing on the realisation of any asset of the company (irrespective of the person by whom the realisation is effected).

3.51(3)   If the assets are insufficient to satisfy the liabilities, the court may make an order as to the payment out of the assets of the expenses incurred in the administration in such order of priority as the court thinks just.

3.52   Pre-administration costs

3.52(1)   Where the administrator has made a statement of pre-administration costs under rule 3.35(10)(a), the creditors' committee may determine whether and to what extent the unpaid pre-administration costs set out in the statement are approved for payment.

3.52(2)   Paragraph (3) applies where–

(a) there is no creditors' committee;

(b) there is a creditors' committee but it does not make the necessary determination; or

(c) the creditors' committee does make the necessary determination but the administrator or other insolvency practitioner who has charged fees or incurred expenses as pre-administration costs considers the amount determined to be insufficient.

3.52(3)   When this paragraph applies, determination of whether and to what extent the unpaid pre-administration costs are approved for payment must be–

(a) by a decision of the creditors through a decision procedure other than in a case falling in sub-paragraph (b); or

(b) in a case where the administrator has made a statement under paragraph 52(1)(b) of Schedule B1, by–

    (i) the consent of each of the secured creditors, or

    (ii) if the administrator has made, or intends to make, a distribution to preferential creditors, by

        (aa) the consent of each of the secured creditors, and

        (bb) a decision of the preferential creditors in a decision procedure.

3.52(4)   The administrator must call a meeting of the creditors' committee or seek a decision of creditors by a decision procedure if so requested for the purposes of paragraphs (1) to (3) by another insolvency practitioner who has charged fees or incurred expenses as pre-administration costs; and the administrator must deliver notice of the meeting or decision procedure (to creditors or preferential creditors as the case may be) within 28 days of receipt of the request.

3.52(5)   The administrator (where the fees were charged or expenses incurred by the administrator) or other insolvency practitioner (where the fees were charged or expenses incurred by that practitioner) may apply to the court for a determination of whether and to what extent the unpaid pre-administration costs are approved for payment if either–

(a)   there is no determination under paragraph (1) or (3); or

(b)   there is such a determination but the administrator or other insolvency practitioner who has charged fees or incurred expenses as pre-administration costs considers the amount determined to be insufficient.

3.52(6)   Where there is a creditors' committee the administrator or other insolvency practitioner must deliver at least 14 days' notice of the hearing to the members of the committee and the committee may nominate one or more of its members to appear, or be represented, and to be heard on the application.

3.52(7)   If there is no creditors' committee, notice of the application must be delivered to such one or more of the company's creditors as the court may direct, and those creditors may nominate one or more of their number to appear or be represented, and to be heard on the application.

3.52(8)   The court may, if it appears to be a proper case, order the expenses of the application, including the costs of any member of the creditors' committee appearing or being represented on it, or of any creditor so appearing or being represented, to be paid as an expense of the administration.

3.52(9)   Where the administrator fails to call a meeting of the creditors' committee or seek a decision of creditors in accordance with paragraph (4), the other insolvency practitioner may apply to the court for an order requiring the administrator to do so.

CHAPTER 11

EXTENSION AND ENDING OF ADMINISTRATION

[Note: A document required by the Act or these Rules must also contain the standard contents set out in Part 1.]

3.53   Interpretation

3.53   "Final progress report" means in this Chapter, and in Chapter 14, a progress report which includes a summary of–

(a)   the administrator's proposals;

(b)   any major amendments to, or deviations from, those proposals;

(c)   the steps taken during the administration; and

(d)   the outcome.

3.54   Application to extend an administration and extension by consent (paragraph 76(2) of Schedule B1)

3.54(1)   This rule applies where an administrator makes an application to the court for an order, or delivers a notice to the creditors requesting their consent, to extend the administrator's term of office under paragraph 76(2) of Schedule B1.

3.54(2)   The application or the notice must state the reasons why the administrator is seeking an extension.

3.54(3)   A request to the creditors may contain or be accompanied by a notice that if the extension is granted a notice of the extension will be made available for viewing and downloading on a website and that no other notice will be delivered to the creditors.

3.54(4)   Where the result of a request to the creditors is to be made available for viewing and downloading on a website, the notice must comply with the requirements for use of a website to deliver documents set out in rule 1.44(2)(a) to (c), (3) and (4) with any necessary modifications and rule 1.44(5)(a) applies to determine the time of delivery of the document.

3.54(5)   Where the court makes an order extending the administrator's term of office, the administrator must as soon as reasonably practicable deliver to the creditors a notice of the order together with the reasons for seeking the extension given in the application to the court.

3.54(6)   Where the administrator's term of office has been extended with the consent of creditors, the administrator must as soon as reasonably practicable deliver a notice of the extension to the creditors except where paragraph (3) applies.

3.54(7)   The notice which paragraph 78(5)(b) of Schedule B1 requires to be delivered to the registrar of companies must also identify the insolvency proceedings.

3.55   Notice of automatic end of administration (paragraph 76 of Schedule B1)

3.55(1)   This rule applies where–

(a)   the appointment of an administrator has ceased to have effect, and

(b)   the administrator is not required by any other rule to give notice of that fact.

3.55(2)   The former administrator must, as soon as reasonably practicable, and in any event within five business days of the date on which the appointment has ceased, deliver to the registrar of companies and lodge with the court a notice accompanied by a final progress report.

3.55(3)   The notice must be headed "Notice of automatic end of administration" and identify the company immediately below the heading.

3.55(4)   The notice must contain–

(a)   identification details for the insolvency proceedings;

(b)   the former administrator's name and address;

(c)   a statement that that person had been appointed administrator of the company;

(d)   the date of the appointment;

(e)   the name of the person who made the appointment or the administration application, as the case may be;

(f)   the date on which the appointment ceased to have effect;

(g)   a statement that the appointment has ceased to have effect; and

(h)   a statement that a copy of the final progress report accompanies the notice.

3.55(5)   The notice must be authenticated by the administrator and dated.

3.55(6)   A copy of the notice and accompanying final progress report must be delivered as soon as reasonably practicable to–

(a)   the directors of the company; and

(b)   all other persons to whom notice of the administrator's appointment was delivered.

3.55(7)   A former administrator who defaults in complying with this rule is guilty of an offence.

3.56   Notice of end of administration when purposes achieved (paragraph 80(2) of Schedule B1)

3.56(1)   Where an administrator who was appointed under paragraph 14 or 22 of Schedule B1 thinks that the purpose of administration has been sufficiently achieved, the notice ("notice of end of administration") which the administrator may lodge with the court and deliver to the registrar of companies under paragraph 80(2) of Schedule B1 must be headed "Notice of end of administration" and identify the company immediately below the heading.

3.56(2)   The notice must contain–

(a)   identification details for the insolvency proceedings;

(b)   the administrator's name and address;

(c)   a statement that that person has been appointed administrator of the company;

(d)   the date of the appointment;

(e)   the name of the person who made the appointment or the administration application, as the case may be;

(f)   a statement that the administrator thinks that the purpose of the administration has been sufficiently achieved;

(g)   a statement that a copy of the final progress report accompanies the notice; and

(h)   a statement that the administrator is lodging the notice with the court and delivering a copy to the registrar of companies.

3.56(3)   The notice must be authenticated by the administrator and dated.

3.56(4)   The notice must be accompanied by a final progress report.

3.56(5)   The notice lodged with the court must also be accompanied by a copy of the notice.

3.56(6)   The court must endorse the notice and the copy with the date and time of lodging, certify the copy and deliver it to the administrator.

3.56(7)   The prescribed period within which the administrator, under paragraph 80(4) of Schedule B1, must send a copy of the notice to the creditors is five business days from the lodging of the notice.

3.56(8)   The copy of the notice sent to creditors must be accompanied by the final progress report.

3.56(9)   The administrator must within the same period deliver a copy of the notice and the final progress report to all other persons (other than the creditors and the registrar of companies) to whom notice of the administrator's appointment was delivered.

3.56(10)   The administrator is taken to have complied with the requirement in paragraph 80(4) of Schedule B1 to give notice to the creditors if, within five business days of lodging the notice with the court, the administrator gazettes a notice which–

(a)   states that the administration has ended, and the date on which it ended;

(b)   undertakes that the administrator will provide a copy of the notice of end of administration to any creditor of the company who applies in writing; and

(c)   specifies the address to which to write.

3.56(11)   The Gazette notice may be advertised in such other manner as the administrator thinks fit.

3.57   Administrator's application for order ending administration (paragraph 79 of Schedule B1)

3.57(1)   An application to court by the administrator under paragraph 79 of Schedule B1 for an order ending an administration must be accompanied by–

    (a)   a progress report for the period since–

        (i)   the last progress report (if any), or

        (ii) if there has been no previous progress report, the date on which the company entered administration;

    (b)   a statement indicating what the administrator thinks should be the next steps for the company (if applicable); and

    (c)   where the administrator makes the application because of a requirement decided by the creditors, a statement indicating with reasons whether or not the administrator agrees with the requirement.

3.57(2)   Where the application is made other than because of a requirement by a decision of the creditors–

    (a)   the administrator must, at least five business days before the application is made, deliver notice of the administrator's intention to apply to court to–

        (i)   the person who made the administration application or appointment, and

        (ii) the creditors; and

    (b)   the application must be accompanied by–

        (i)   a statement that notice has been delivered to the creditors, and

        (ii) copies of any response from creditors to that notice.

3.57(3)   Where the application is in conjunction with a petition under section 124 for an order to wind up the company, the administrator must, at least five business days before the application is made, deliver notice to the creditors as to whether the administrator intends to seek appointment as liquidator.

3.58   Creditors' application for order ending administration (paragraph 81 of Schedule B1)

3.58(1)   Where a creditor applies to the court under paragraph 81 of Schedule B1 for an order ending an administration, a copy of the application must be delivered, not less than five business days before the date fixed for the hearing, to–

    (a)   the administrator;

    (b)   the person who made the administration application or appointment; and

    (c)   where the appointment was made under paragraph 14 of Schedule B1, the holder of the floating charge by virtue of which the appointment was made (if different to (b)).

3.58(2)   Any of those persons may appear at the hearing of the application.

3.58(3)   Where the court makes an order under paragraph 81 of Schedule B1 ending the administration, the court must deliver a copy of the order to the administrator.

3.59   Notice by administrator of court order

3.59   Where the court makes an order ending the administration, the administrator must as soon as reasonably practicable deliver a copy of the order and of the final progress report to–

    (a)   the registrar of companies;

    (b)   the directors of the company; and

(c) all other persons to whom notice of the administrator's appointment was delivered.

3.60 Moving from administration to creditors' voluntary winding up (paragraph 83 of Schedule B1)

3.60(1) This rule applies where the administrator delivers to the registrar of companies a notice under paragraph 83(3) of Schedule B1 of moving from administration to creditors' voluntary winding up.

3.60(2) The notice must contain–

(a) identification details for the insolvency proceedings;

(b) the name of the person who made the appointment or the administration application, as the case may be; and

(c) the name and IP number of the proposed liquidator.

3.60(3) The notice to the registrar of companies must be accompanied by a copy of the administrator's final progress report.

3.60(4) A copy of the notice and the final progress report must be sent as soon as reasonably practicable after delivery of the notice to all those persons to whom notice of the administrator's appointment was delivered in addition to the creditors (as required by paragraph 83(5)(b)).

3.60(5) The person who ceases to be administrator on the registration of the notice must inform the person who becomes liquidator of anything which happens after the date of the final progress report and before the registration of the notice which the administrator would have included in the final report had it happened before the date of the report.

3.60(6) For the purposes of paragraph 83(7)(a) of Schedule B1, a person is nominated by the creditors as liquidator by–

(a) their approval of the statement of the proposed liquidator in the administrator's proposals or revised proposals; or

(b) their nomination of a different person, through a decision procedure, before their approval of the proposals or revised proposals.

3.60(7) Where the creditors nominate a different person, the nomination must, where applicable, include the declaration required by section 231.

3.61 Moving from administration to dissolution (paragraph 84 of Schedule B1)

3.61(1) This rule applies where the administrator delivers to the registrar of companies a notice under paragraph 84(1) of Schedule B1 of moving from administration to dissolution.

3.61(2) The notice must contain identification details for the insolvency proceedings.

3.61(3) As soon as reasonably practicable after sending the notice, the administrator must deliver a copy of the notice to all persons to whom notice of the administrator's appointment was delivered (in addition to the creditors mentioned in paragraph 84(5)(b) of Schedule B1).

3.61(4) A final progress report must accompany the notice to the registrar of companies and every copy filed or otherwise delivered.

3.61(5) Where a court makes an order under paragraph 84(7) of Schedule B1 it must, where the applicant is not the administrator, deliver a copy of the order to the administrator.

3.61(6) The administrator must deliver a copy of the order to the registrar of companies with the notice required by paragraph 84(8) of Schedule B1.

[Note: A document required by the Act or these Rules must also contain the standard contents set out in Part 1.]

3.62   Grounds for resignation

3.62(1)   The administrator may resign–

(a)   on grounds of ill health;

(b)   because of the intention to cease to practise as an insolvency practitioner; or

(c)   because the further discharge of the duties of administrator is prevented or made impractical by–

  (i)   a conflict of interest, or

  (ii)   a change of personal circumstances.

3.62(2)   The administrator may, with the permission of the court, resign on other grounds.

3.63   Notice of intention to resign

3.63(1)   The administrator must give at least five business days' notice of intention–

(a)   to resign in a case falling within rule 3.62(1); or

(b)   to apply for the court's permission to resign in a case falling within rule 3.62(2).

3.63(2)   The notice must contain–

(a)   identification details for the insolvency proceedings;

(b)   the date of the appointment of the administrator; and

(c)   the name of the person who made the appointment or the administration application, as the case may be.

3.63(3)   The notice must also contain–

(a)   the date with effect from which the administrator intends to resign; or

(b)   where the administrator was appointed by an administration order, the date on which the administrator intends to lodge with the court an application for permission to resign.

3.63(4)   Notice must be delivered–

(a)   to any continuing administrator of the company;

(b)   to the creditors' committee (if any);

(c)   if there is neither a continuing administrator nor a creditors' committee, to–

  (i)   the company, and

  (ii)   the company's creditors;

(d)   to the member State liquidator appointed in relation to the company (if there is one);

(e)   where the administrator was appointed by the holder of a qualifying floating charge under paragraph 14 of Schedule B1, to–

  (i)   the person who appointed the administrator, and

(ii)   all holders of prior qualifying floating charges;

(f)   where the administrator was appointed by the company or the directors of the company under paragraph 22 of Schedule B1, to–

(i)   the appointer, and

(ii)   all holders of qualifying floating charges.

3.63(5)   The notice must be accompanied by a summary of the administrator's receipts and payments.

3.64   Notice of resignation (paragraph 87 of Schedule B1)

3.64(1)   A resigning administrator must, within five business days of delivering the notice under paragraph 87(2) of Schedule B1, deliver a copy of the notice to–

(a)   the registrar of companies;

(b)   all persons, other than the person who made the appointment, to whom notice of intention to resign was delivered under rule 3.63; and

(c)   except where the appointment was by administration order, lodge a copy of the notice with the court.

3.64(2)   The notice must contain–

(a)   identification details for the insolvency proceedings;

(b)   the date of the appointment of the administrator; and

(c)   the name of the person who made the appointment or the administration application, as the case may be.

3.64(3)   The notice must state–

(a)   the date from which the resignation is to have effect; and

(b)   where the resignation is with the permission of the court, the date on which permission was given.

3.64(4)   Where an administrator was appointed by an administration order, notice of resignation under paragraph 87(2)(a) of Schedule B1 must be given by lodging the notice with the court.

3.65   Application to court to remove administrator from office

3.65(1)   An application for an order under paragraph 88 of Schedule B1 that the administrator be removed from office must state the grounds on which the order is requested.

3.65(2)   A copy of the application must be delivered, not less than five business days before the date fixed for the hearing–

(a)   to the administrator;

(b)   to the person who–

(i)   made the application for the administration order, or

(ii)   appointed the administrator;

(c)   to the creditors' committee (if any);

(d)   to any continuing administrator of the company; and

(e)   where there is neither a creditors' committee nor a continuing administrator appointed, to the company and the creditors, including any floating charge holders.

3.65(3) The court must deliver to the applicant a copy of any order removing the administrator.

3.65(4) The applicant must deliver a copy of the order–

(a) as soon as reasonably practicable, and in any event within five business days of the copy order being delivered, to the administrator; and

(b) within five business days of the copy order being delivered, to–

(i) all other persons to whom notice of the application was delivered, and

(ii) the registrar of companies.

3.66 Notice of vacation of office when administrator ceases to be qualified to act

3.66 An administrator who has ceased to be qualified to act as an insolvency practitioner in relation to the company and gives notice in accordance with paragraph 89 of Schedule B1 must also deliver notice to the registrar of companies.

3.67 Deceased administrator

3.67(1) If the administrator dies a notice of the fact and date of death must be lodged with the court.

3.67(2) The notice must be lodged as soon as reasonably practicable by one of the following–

(a) a surviving administrator;

(b) a member of the deceased administrator's firm (if the deceased was a member or employee of a firm);

(c) an officer of the deceased administrator's company (if the deceased was an officer or employee of a company); or

(d) the executor of the deceased administrator.

3.67(3) If such a notice has not been lodged within the 21 days following the administrator's death, any other person may lodge the notice.

3.67(4) The person who lodges the notice must also deliver a notice to the registrar of companies which contains–

(a) identification details for the insolvency proceedings;

(b) the name of the person who made the appointment or the administration application, as the case may be;

(c) the date of the appointment of the administrator; and

(d) the fact and date of death.

3.68 Application to replace

3.68(1) Where an application to court is made under paragraph 91(1) or 95 of Schedule B1 to appoint a replacement administrator, the application must be accompanied by the proposed replacement administrator's consent to act.

3.68(2) Where the application is made under paragraph 91(1), a copy of the application must be delivered–

(a) to the person who made the application for the administration order;

(b) to any person who has appointed a receiver of the company;

(c) to any person who is or may be entitled to appoint a receiver of the company;

(d) to any person who is or may be entitled to appoint an administrator of the company under paragraph 14 of Schedule B1;

(e) to any receiver of the company;

(f) if there is pending a petition for the winding up of the company, to–

 (i) the petitioner, and

 (ii) any provisional liquidator;

(g) to any member State liquidator appointed in main proceedings in relation to the company;

(h) to the company, if the application is made by anyone other than the company;

(i) to any supervisor of any CVA in relation to the company; and

(j) to the proposed administrator.

3.68(3)   Rules 3.10, 3.11 and 3.13(1) and (2) apply to applications made under paragraph 91(1) and 95 of Schedule B1, with any necessary modifications.

3.69   Appointment of replacement or additional administrator

3.69   Where a replacement administrator is appointed or an additional administrator is appointed to act–

(a) the following apply–

 (i) rule 3.17 the requirement as to the heading in paragraph (1) and paragraphs (1)(a) to (f), and (2),

 (ii) rule 3.18 paragraphs (1)(a) and (b)(ii), (2) and (3),

 (iii) rule 3.24 paragraphs (1)(a) to (d) and (2),

 (iv) rule 3.25 paragraphs (1), (2)(a) to (c) and (3),

 (v) rule 3.26 paragraphs (1)(a), (3) and (4), and

 (vi) rule 3.27 paragraphs (1), (2)(a) and (b), (3) and (4).

(b) the replacement or additional administrator must deliver notice of the appointment to the registrar of companies; and

(c) all documents must clearly identify the appointment as of a replacement administrator or an additional administrator.

3.70   Administrator's duties on vacating office

3.70(1)   An administrator who ceases to be in office as a result of removal, resignation or ceasing to be qualified to act as an insolvency practitioner in relation to the company must as soon as reasonably practicable deliver to the person succeeding as administrator–

(a) the assets (after deduction of any expenses properly incurred and distributions made by the departing administrator);

(b) the records of the administration, including correspondence, statements of claim and documentary evidence of debt and other documents relating to the administration while it was within the responsibility of the departing administrator; and

(c) the company's records.

3.70(2)   An administrator who makes default in complying with this rule is guilty of an offence.

CHAPTER 13

CREDITORS' COMMITTEES

[Notes: (1) a document required by the Act or these Rules must also contain the standard contents set out in Part 1;

(2) see sections 215 and 362 of the Financial Services and Markets Act 2000 for the rights of persons appointed by a scheme manager, the Financial Conduct Authority and the Prudential Regulation Authority to attend committees and make representations.]

3.71 Scope

3.71 This Chapter applies to the establishment and operation of a creditors' committee in an administration ("creditors' committee").

3.72 Functions of a creditors' committee

3.72 In addition to any functions conferred on a creditors' committee by any provision of the Act or any other provision of these Rules, the creditors' committee is to–

(a) assist the administrator in discharging the administrator's functions; and

(b) act in relation to the administrator in such manner as may from time to time be agreed.

3.73 Number of members of a creditors' committee

3.73 A creditor's committee must have at least three members but not more than five members.

3.74 Eligibility for membership of creditors' committee

3.74(1) A creditor is eligible to be a member of a creditors' committee if–

(a) the person has submitted a statement of claim and, where not dispensed with under rules 5.26(2) or 3.105(2), documentary evidence of debt;

(b) the debt is not fully secured; and

(c) neither of the following apply–

    (i) the claim has been wholly rejected for voting purposes; or

    (ii) the claim has been wholly rejected for the purpose of distribution or dividend.

3.74(2) A body corporate or a partnership may be a member of a creditors' committee, but it cannot act otherwise than by a representative appointed under rule 3.84.

3.75 Establishment of creditors' committees

3.75(1) Where creditors decide that a creditors' committee should be established, the convener or chair of the decision procedure or the convenor of the deemed consent process, if not the administrator, must–

(a) as soon as reasonably practicable deliver a notice of the decision to the administrator; and

(b) where a decision has also been made as to membership of the creditors' committee, inform the administrator of the names and addresses of the persons elected to be members of the creditors' committee.

3.75(2) Before a person may act as a member of the creditors' committee that person must agree to do so.

3.75(3)   A person's proxy-holder attending a meeting establishing the creditors' committee or, in the case of a corporation or partnership, its duly appointed representative, may give such agreement (unless the proxy or instrument conferring authority contains a statement to the contrary).

3.75(4)   Where a decision has been made to establish a creditors' committee but not as to its membership, the administrator must seek a decision from the creditors as to membership of the creditors' committee.

3.75(5)   The creditors' committee is not established (and accordingly cannot act) until the administrator has sent a notice of its membership in accordance with paragraph (9).

3.75(6)   The notice must contain the following–

(a)   a statement that the creditors' committee has been duly constituted;

(b)   identification details for any company that is a member of the creditors' committee;

(c)   the full name and address of each member that is not a company.

3.75(7)   The notice must be authenticated and dated by the administrator.

3.75(8)   The administrator must, as soon as reasonably practicable, deliver the notice after the minimum number of persons required by rule 3.73 have agreed to act as members and been elected.

3.75(9)   The administrator must, as soon as reasonably practicable, deliver the notice to the registrar of companies.

3.76   Notice of change of membership of a committee

3.76(1)   If there is a change in membership of the creditors' committee, the administrator must deliver a notice to the registrar of companies, as soon as reasonably practicable.

3.76(2)   The notice must contain–

(a)   the date of the original notice in respect of the constitution of the committee and the date of the last notice of membership given under this rule (if any);

(b)   a statement that this notice of membership replaces the previous notice;

(c)   identification details for any company that is a member of the committee;

(d)   the full name and address of any member that is not a company;

(e)   a statement whether any member has become a member since the issue of the previous notice;

(f)   the identification details for a company or otherwise the full name of any member named in the previous notice who is no longer a member and the date the membership ended.

3.76(3)   The notice must be authenticated and dated by the administrator.

3.77   Vacancies: members of creditors' committee

3.77(1)   This rule applies if there is a vacancy among the members of a creditors' committee or where the number of members of the committee is fewer than the maximum allowed.

3.77(2)   A vacancy need not be filled if–

(a)   the administrator and a majority of the remaining members agree; and

(b)   the total number of members does not fall below three.

3.77(3)   The administrator may appoint a creditor, who is qualified under rule 3.74 to be a member of the committee, to fill a vacancy or as an additional member of the committee, if–

(a) the remaining members of the committee (provided that there are at least two) agree in accordance with paragraph (4) to the appointment; and

(b) the creditor agrees to act.

3.77(4)   Where there are only two remaining members of the committee, both must agree to the appointment, otherwise a majority must agree.

3.77(5)   Alternatively, the administrator may seek a decision by creditors to appoint a creditor (with that creditor's consent) to fill the vacancy.

3.77(6)   Where the vacancy is filled by an appointment made by a decision of creditors which is not chaired or convened by the administrator, the chair or convener must report the appointment to the administrator.

3.78   Resignation

3.78   A member of a creditors' committee may resign by informing the administrator in writing.

3.79   Termination of membership

3.79   A person's membership of a creditors' committee is automatically terminated if that person–

(a) becomes bankrupt or that person's estate is sequestrated, in which case the trustee in bankruptcy or the trustee in sequestration, as the case may be, replaces the person bankrupt or sequestrated as a member of the committee;

(b) grants a trust deed for the benefit of creditors;

(c) makes a composition with creditors;

(d) is a person to whom a moratorium under a debt relief order applies;

(e) neither attends nor is represented at three consecutive meetings (unless it is resolved at the third of those meetings that this rule is not to apply in that person's case);

(f) has ceased to satisfy the criteria set out in rule 3.74 for eligibility to be a member of the creditors' committee; or

(g) ceases to be a creditor or is found never to have been a creditor.

3.80   Removal

3.80   A member of a creditors' committee may be removed by a decision of the creditors through a decision procedure.

3.81   Meetings of creditors' committee

3.81(1)   Meetings of the creditors' committee must be held when and where determined by the administrator.

3.81(2)   The administrator must call a first meeting of the creditors' committee to take place within six weeks of the creditors' committee's establishment.

3.81(3)   After the calling of the first meeting, the administrator must call a meeting–

(a) if so requested by a member of the creditors' committee or a member's representative (the meeting then to be held within 21 days of the request being received by the administrator); and

(b) for a specified date, if the creditors' committee has previously resolved that a meeting be held on that date.

3.81(4) The administrator must give five business days' notice of the venue of a meeting to each member of the creditors' committee (or a member's representative, if designated for that purpose), except where the requirement for notice has been waived by or on behalf of a member.

3.81(5) Waiver may be signified either at or before the meeting.

3.82 The chair at meetings

3.82 The chair at a meeting of a creditors' committee must be the administrator or an appointed person.

3.83 Quorum

3.83 A meeting of a creditors' committee is duly constituted if due notice of it has been delivered to all the members, and at least two of the members are in attendance or represented.

3.84 Committee members' representatives

3.84(1) A member of the creditors' committee may, in relation to the business of the creditors' committee, be represented by another person duly authorised by the member for that purpose.

3.84(2) A person acting as a committee member's representative must hold a letter of authority entitling that person to act (either generally or specifically) and authenticated by or on behalf of the committee member.

3.84(3) A proxy or an instrument conferring authority (in respect of a person authorised to represent a body corporate or a partnership) is to be treated as a letter of authority to act generally (unless the proxy or instrument conferring authority contains a statement to the contrary).

3.84(4) The chair at a meeting of the committee may call on a person claiming to act as a committee member's representative to produce a letter of authority, and may exclude that person if no letter of authority is produced at or by the time of the meeting or it appears to the chair that the authority is deficient.

3.84(5) A committee member may not be represented by–

    (a) another member of the committee;

    (b) a person who is at the same time representing another committee member;

    (c) a body corporate;

    (d) a partnership;

    (e) an undischarged bankrupt;

    (f) a person whose estate has been sequestrated and who has not been discharged;

    (g) a person who has granted a trust deed for the benefit of creditors;

    (h) a person who has made a composition with creditors;

    (i) a person to whom a moratorium period under a debt relief order applies;

    (j) a person who is subject to a company directors disqualification order or a company directors disqualification undertaking; or

    (k) a person who is subject to a bankruptcy restrictions order (including an interim order), a bankruptcy restrictions undertaking, a debt relief restrictions order (including an interim order) or a debt relief restrictions undertaking.

3.84(6) Where a representative authenticates any document on behalf of a committee member the fact that the representative authenticates as a representative must be stated below the authentication.

3.85   Voting rights and resolutions

3.85(1)   At a meeting of the committee, each member (whether the member is in attendance or is represented by a representative) has one vote.

3.85(2)   A resolution is passed when a majority of the members attending or represented have voted in favour of it.

3.85(3)   Every resolution passed must be recorded in writing and authenticated by the chair, either separately or as part of the minutes of the meeting.

3.86   Resolutions by correspondence

3.86(1)   The administrator may seek to obtain the agreement of the creditors' committee to a resolution by delivering to every member (or the member's representative designated for the purpose) details of the proposed resolution.

3.86(2)   The details must be set out in such a way that the recipient may indicate agreement or dissent and where there is more than one resolution may indicate agreement to or dissent from each one separately.

3.86(3)   A member of the creditors' committee may, within five business days from the delivery of details of the proposed resolution, require the administrator to summon a meeting of the creditors' committee to consider the matters raised by the proposed resolution.

3.86(4)   In the absence of such a request, the resolution is passed by the creditors' committee if a majority of the members (excluding a member or member's representative who is to participate directly or indirectly in a transaction) deliver notice to the administrator that they agree with the resolution.

3.87   Remote attendance at meetings of creditors' committee

3.87(1)   Where the administrator considers it appropriate, a meeting of a creditors' committee may be conducted and held in such a way that persons who are not present together at the same place may attend it.

3.87(2)   A person attends such a meeting who is able to exercise that person's right to speak and vote at the meeting.

3.87(3)   A person is able to exercise the right to speak at a meeting when that person is in a position to communicate during the meeting to all those attending the meeting any information or opinions which that person has on the business of the meeting.

3.87(4)   A person is able to exercise the right to vote at a meeting when–

   (a)   that person is able to vote, during the meeting, on resolutions or determinations put to the vote at the meeting; and

   (b)   that person's vote can be taken into account in determining whether or not such resolutions or determinations are passed at the same time as the votes of all the other persons attending the meeting.

3.87(5)   Where such a meeting is to be held the administrator must make whatever arrangements the administrator considers appropriate to–

   (a)   enable those attending the meeting to exercise their rights to speak or vote; and

   (b)   verify the identity of those attending the meeting and to ensure the security of any electronic means used to enable attendance.

3.87(6)   A requirement in these Rules to specify a place for the meeting may be satisfied by specifying the arrangements the administrator proposes to enable persons to exercise their rights to speak or vote where in the reasonable opinion of the administrator–

(a)   a meeting will be attended by persons who will not be present together at the same place; and

(b)   it is unnecessary or inexpedient to specify a place for the meeting.

3.87(7)   In making the arrangements referred to in paragraph (6) and in forming the opinion referred to in paragraph (6)(b), the administrator must have regard to the legitimate interests of the creditors' committee members or their representatives attending the meeting in the efficient despatch of the business of the meeting.

3.87(8)   Where the notice of a meeting does not specify a place for the meeting the administrator must specify a place for the meeting if at least one member of the creditors' committee requests the administrator to do so in accordance with rule 3.88.

3.88   **Procedure for requests that a place for a meeting should be specified**

3.88(1)   This rule applies to a request to the administrator under rule 3.87 to specify a place for the meeting.

3.88(2)   The request must be made within three business days of the date on which the administrator delivered the notice of the meeting in question.

3.88(3)   Where the administrator considers that the request has been properly made in accordance with this rule, the administrator must–

(a)   deliver notice to all those previously given notice of the meeting–

     (i)   that it is to be held at a specified place, and

     (ii)   as to whether the date and time are to remain the same or not;

(b)   fix a venue for the meeting, the date of which must be not later than seven business days after the original date for the meeting; and

(c)   give three business days' notice of the venue to all those previously given notice of the meeting.

3.88(4)   The notices required by sub-paragraphs (a) and (c) may be delivered at the same or different times.

3.88(5)   Where the administrator has specified a place for the meeting in response to a request under rule 3.87(8), the chair of the meeting must attend the meeting by being present in person at that place.

3.89   **Notice requiring administrator to attend the creditors' committee (paragraph 57(3)(a) of Schedule B1)**

[Note: in an administration paragraph 57(3) of Schedule B1 enables the creditors' committee to require the administrator to provide the committee with information]

3.89(1)   This rules applies where a creditors' committee in an administration resolves under paragraph 57(3)(a) of Schedule B1 to require the attendance of the administrator.

3.89(2)   The notice delivered to the administrator requiring the administrator's attendance must be–

(a)   accompanied by a copy of the resolution; and

(b)   authenticated by a member of the creditors' committee.

3.89(3)   A member's representative may authenticate the notice for the member.

3.89(4) The meeting at which the administrator's attendance is required must be fixed by the committee for a business day, and must be held at such time and place as the administrator determines.

3.89(5) Where the administrator so attends, the creditors' committee may elect one of their number to be chair of the meeting in place of the administrator or the appointed person.

3.90 Expenses of members etc.

3.90(1) The administrator must pay, as an expense of the administration, the reasonable travelling expenses directly incurred by members of the creditors' committee or their representatives in attending the creditors' committee's meetings or otherwise on the creditors' committee's business.

3.90(2) The requirement for the administrator to pay the expenses does not apply to a meeting of the committee held within six weeks of a previous meeting, unless the meeting is summoned by the administrator.

3.91 Dealings by creditors' committee members and others

3.91(1) Membership of the creditors' committee does not prevent a person from dealing with the company provided that a transaction is in good faith and for value.

3.91(2) The court may, on the application of an interested person–

   (a)   set aside a transaction which appears to it to be contrary to this rule; and

   (b)   make such other order about the transaction as it thinks just, including an order requiring a person to whom this rule applies to account for any profit obtained from the transaction and compensate the company for any resultant loss.

3.92 Formal defects

3.92 The acts of a creditors' committee are valid notwithstanding any defect in the appointment, election or qualifications of a member of the creditors' committee or a committee member's representative or in the formalities of its establishment.

CHAPTER 14

REPORTING AND REMUNERATION

3.93 Progress reports

3.93(1) The administrator must–

   (a)   within six weeks after the end of each accounting period; and

   (b)   within six weeks after the administrator ceases to act as administrator,

send to the court and to the registrar of companies, and to each creditor, a progress report.

3.93(2) For the purposes of this Chapter, "accounting period" in relation to an administration is to be construed as follows:

   (a)   the first accounting period is the period of six months beginning with the date on which the company entered administration; and

   (b)   any subsequent accounting period is the period of six months beginning with the end of the last accounting period except that–

      (i)   where the administrator and the creditors' committee agree, or

(ii)   where there is no creditors' committee, the court determines,

the accounting period is to be such other period beginning with the end of the last accounting period as may be agreed or, as the case may be determined, it is to be that other period.

3.93(3)   An administrator who fails to deliver a progress report within the time periods referred to in paragraph (1) is guilty of an offence.

3.93(4)   The court may, on the application of the administrator, extend either or both of the periods of six weeks referred to in paragraph (1) of this rule.

3.94   Progress reports: content

3.94(1)   The administrator's progress report must include–

(a)   identification details for the insolvency proceedings;

(b)   identification and contact details for the administrator;

(c)   the date of appointment of the administrator and any changes in the administrator in accordance with paragraphs (4) and (5);

(d)   details of any extensions to the initial period of appointment;

(e)   details of progress during the period of the report in accordance with paragraph (2):

(f)   details of what assets remain to be realised;

(g)   where a distribution is to be made in accordance with Chapter 15 in respect of an accounting period, the scheme of division; and

(h)   any other relevant information for the creditors.

3.94(2)   The details of the progress during the period of the report must include–

(a)   a receipts and payments account stating what assets of the company have been realised, for what value, and what payments have been made to creditors, in the form of a summary showing–

(i)   receipts and payments during the relevant accounting period, or

(ii)   where the administrator has ceased to act, receipts and payments during the period from the end of the last accounting period to the time when the administrator ceased to act (or, where the administrator has made no previous progress report, receipts and payments in the period since the administrator's appointment); or

(b)   where–

(i)   no claim for outlays and remuneration is submitted under rule 3.95, or

(ii)   a claim for outlays and remuneration is submitted under rule 3.95 but no determination fixing the amount of outlays and remuneration in accordance with rule 3.96(1) has been made in respect of such a claim–

(aa)   a receipts and payments account which meets the requirements of paragraph (2)(a),

(bb)   an estimate of the remuneration due to the administrator during the accounting period together with the basis or bases set out in rule 3.97 on which the estimate is based,

(cc)   where remuneration due is not yet determined from the immediately preceding accounting period, an estimate of the remuneration due during that period, and

(dd)   any outlays incurred.

3.94(3)   The receipts and payments account in a final progress report must include a statement as to the amount paid to unsecured creditors by virtue of the application of section 176A.

3.94(4)   A change in the administrator is only required to be shown in the next report after the change.

3.94(5)   However if the current administrator is seeking the repayment of pre-administration expenses from a former administrator, the change in administrator must continue to be shown until the next report after the claim is settled.

3.94(6)   This rule is without prejudice to the requirements of Chapter 15.

3.95   Administrator's outlays and remuneration: claims

3.95(1)   Where an administrator intends to submit a claim for the outlays reasonably incurred by the administrator and for remuneration within two weeks after the end of an accounting period, the administrator must submit to the creditors' committee or, if there is no creditors' committee, make available to creditors for the purposes of a decision procedure in respect of that period–

(a)   the administrator's accounts of their intromissions with the company's assets;

(b)   where funds are available after making allowance for contingencies, a scheme of division of the divisible funds; and

(c)   a claim for–

(i)   any outlays reasonably incurred by the administrator, and

(ii)   the administrator's remuneration.

3.95(2)   The administrator may, at any time within two weeks after the end of an accounting period, in respect of the previous accounting period, submit to a creditors' committee, or if there is no creditors' committee, seek approval from creditors through a decision procedure for–

(a)   the administrator's accounts of its intromissions with the company's assets for audit (such accounts of intromissions may include or consist of a progress report in terms of rules 3.93 and 3.94);

(b)   the outlays reasonably incurred by the administrator; and

(c)   the administrator's remuneration.

3.95(3)   The administrator may, at any time before the end of an accounting period submit to the creditors' committee or, if there is no creditors' committee, seek approval from creditors through a decision procedure for, an interim claim in respect of that period–

(a)   for the outlays reasonably incurred by the administrator; and

(b)   for the administrator's remuneration.

3.95(4)   If the administrator submits such an interim claim, the creditors' committee, or the creditors by decision procedure as the case may be may issue an interim determination in relation to the amount of the outlays and remuneration payable to the administrator, and where they do so, they must take into account that interim determination when issuing their determination under paragraph 3.96(1)(a)(ii).

3.96   Administrator's outlays and remuneration: determination

3.96(1)   Within six weeks after the end of an accounting period–

(a)   the creditors' committee or, if there is no creditors' committee, the creditors through a decision procedure–

(i)   may audit the accounts submitted or made available under rule 3.95(1)(a), and

(ii)   must issue a determination fixing the amount of the outlays and remuneration payable to the administrator; and

(b) the administrator must make the accounts submitted for audit, scheme of division and determination of the amount fixed under paragraph (1)(a)(ii) available for the inspection by the members of the company and the creditors.

3.96(2) If the administrator's remuneration and outlays have been fixed by determination of the creditors' committee in accordance with paragraph (1)(a)(ii) and the administrator considers the amount to be insufficient, the administrator may request that it be increased by decision of the creditors by decision procedure.

3.96(3) If the creditors' committee fails to issue a determination in accordance with paragraph (1)(a)(ii), the administrator must seek a decision of the creditors through decision procedure (except in a case under paragraph (6)) and they must issue a determination in accordance with paragraph (1)(a)(ii).

3.96(4) If the creditors fail to issue a determination by decision procedure in accordance with paragraph (3) then the administrator must submit the claim to the court and the court must issue a determination.

3.96(5) In a case where the administrator has made a statement under paragraph 52(1)(b) of Schedule B1, a decision under paragraph (2) or a decision under rule 3.101 is taken to be passed if (and only if) passed by the approval of–

(a) each secured creditor of the company; or

(b) if the administrator has made, or proposes to make, a distribution to preferential creditors–

    (i) each secured creditor of the company, and

    (ii) a decision of the preferential creditors in a decision procedure.

3.96(6) In a case where the administrator has made a statement under paragraph 52(1)(b) of Schedule B1, if there is no creditor's committee, or the committee does not make the requisite determination in accordance with rule 3.96(1)(a)(ii) or 3.96(3), the administrator's remuneration and outlays may be fixed (in accordance with this rule) by the approval of–

(a) each secured creditor of the company; or

(b) if the administrator has made, or proposes to make, a distribution to preferential creditors–

    (i) each secured creditor of the company, and

    (ii) a decision of the preferential creditors in a decision procedure.

3.96(7) In fixing the amount of the administrator's remuneration and outlays in respect of any accounting period, the creditors' committee or, as the case may be, the creditors by decision procedure, may take into account any adjustment which the creditors' committee or the creditors may wish to make in the amount of the remuneration and outlays fixed in respect of any earlier accounting period.

3.97 Administrator's remuneration: basis of remuneration

3.97(1) The basis of the administrator's remuneration must be fixed–

(a) as a percentage of the value of the company's property with which the administrator has to deal;

(b) by reference to the work which was reasonably undertaken by the administrator and the administrator's staff in attending to matters arising in the administration; or

(c) as a set amount.

3.97(2) The basis of remuneration may be one or a combination of the bases set out in paragraph (1) and different bases or percentages agreed may be fixed in respect of different things done by the administrator or administrator's staff.

3.98   Former administrator's outlays and remuneration

3.98   For the purposes of paragraph 99 of Schedule B1, the former administrator's outlays and remuneration comprise those items set out in rule 3.51.

3.99   Appeal against fixing of remuneration

3.99(1)   If the administrator considers that the remuneration or outlays fixed for the administrator by the creditors' committee, or by decision of the creditors (including remuneration or outlays fixed under rule 3.96(6)) is insufficient, the administrator may apply to the court for an order increasing their amount or rate.

3.99(2)   The administrator must give at least 14 days' notice of the administrator's application to the members of the creditors' committee, and the committee may nominate one or more members to appear or be represented, and to be heard, on the application.

3.99(3)   If there is no creditors' committee, the administrator's notice of the administrator's application must be sent to such one or more of the company's creditors as the court may direct, which creditors may nominate one or more of their number to appear or be represented and heard.

3.99(4)   The court may order the expenses of the administrator's application, including the expenses of any member of the creditors' committee appearing or being represented on it, or any creditor so appearing or being represented, to be paid as an expense of the administration.

3.100   Creditor's claim that remuneration is excessive

3.100(1)   If the administrator's remuneration and outlays have been fixed by the creditors' committee or by the creditors, any creditor or creditors of the company representing in value at least 25 percent of the creditors may apply to the court not later than eight weeks after the end of an accounting period for an order that the administrator's remuneration or outlays be reduced on the grounds that they are, in all the circumstances, excessive.

3.100(2)   The court may make an order fixing the remuneration or outlays at a reduced amount or rate.

3.100(3)   The court may order the expenses of the creditor making the application to be paid as an expense of the administration.

3.101   Remuneration of joint administrators

3.101   Where there are joint administrators–

  (a)   it is for them to agree between themselves as to how the remuneration or outlays payable should be apportioned;

  (b)   if they cannot agree as to how the remuneration or outlays payable should be apportioned, any one of them may refer the issue for determination–

    (i)   by the court, or

    (ii)   by resolution of the creditors' committee or a meeting of creditors.

CHAPTER 15

CLAIMS BY AND DISTRIBUTIONS TO CREDITORS

3.102   Application and interpretation of Chapter

3.102(1)   This Chapter applies in any case where the administrator proposes to make a distribution to creditors or any class of them.

3.102(2)   Where the distribution is to a particular class of creditors, references in this Chapter are to be treated as, so far as the context requires, references to that class of creditors only.

3.103   Payments of dividends

3.103(1)   On the final determination of the remuneration under rules 3.95 to 3.100 the administrator must, subject to rule 3.117, pay to the creditors their dividends in accordance with the scheme of division.

3.103(2)   Any dividend–

(a)   allocated to a creditor which is not cashed or uplifted; or

(b)   dependent on a claim in respect of which an amount has been set aside under rule 3.117(7) or (8);

must be held by the administrator in an appropriate bank or institution in the name of the Accountant of Court and the deposit receipts transmitted to the Accountant of Court.

3.103(3)   If a creditor's claim is revalued, the administrator may–

(a)   in paying any dividend to that creditor, make such adjustment to it as the administrator considers necessary to take account of that revaluation; or

(b)   require the creditor to repay to the administrator the whole or part of a dividend already paid to the creditor.

3.104   New administrator appointed

3.104(1)   If a new administrator is appointed in place of another, the former administrator must, as soon as reasonably practicable, transmit to the new administrator all the creditors' claims which the former administrator has received, together with an itemised list of them.

3.104(2)   The new administrator must authenticate the list by way of receipt for the creditors' claims and return it to the former administrator.

3.104(3)   From then on, all creditors' claims must be sent to and retained by the new administrator.

3.105   Submission of claims

3.105(1)   A creditor, in order to obtain an adjudication as to the creditor's entitlement to a dividend (so far as funds are available) out of the assets of the company in respect of any accounting period, must submit the creditor's claim to the administrator not later than eight weeks before the end of the accounting period.

3.105(2)   A creditor must submit a claim by producing to the administrator–

(a)   a statement of claim as described in paragraph (3); and

(b)   documentary evidence of debt;

but the administrator may dispense with the requirement of sub-paragraph (b) in respect of any debt or any class of debt.

3.105(3)   The statement of claim must–

(a)   be made out by, or under the direction of, the creditor and dated and authenticated by the creditor or a person authorised on the creditor's behalf;

(b)   state the creditor's name and address;

(c)   if the creditor is a company, identify the company;

(d)   state the name and address of any person authorised to act on behalf of the creditor;

(e)   state the total amount as at the date of the administration order claimed in respect of all debts;

(f)   state whether or not the claim includes any outstanding uncapitalised interest;

(g)   contain particulars of how and when the debt was incurred by the company;

(h)   contain particulars of any security held, the date on which it was given and the value which the creditor puts on it;

(i)   include details of any retention of title in relation to goods to which the debt relates;

(j)   state the nature and amount of any preference under Schedule 6 to the Act claimed in respect of the debt;

(k)   in the case of a member State liquidator creditor, specify and give details of underlying claims in respect of which the creditor is claiming;

(l)   include any details of any document by reference to which the debt can be substantiated; and

(m)   state the name, postal address and authority of the person authenticating the statement of claim and documentary evidence of debt (if someone other than the creditor).

3.105(4)   A claim submitted by a creditor, which has been accepted in whole or in part by the administrator for the purpose of drawing a dividend in respect of any accounting period, is to be deemed to have been resubmitted for the purpose of obtaining an adjudication as to the creditor's entitlement to a dividend in respect of an accounting period or, as the case may be, any subsequent accounting period.

3.105(5)   A creditor who has submitted a claim may at any time submit a further claim specifying a different amount for the claim, provided that a secured creditor is not entitled to produce a further claim specifying a different value for the security at any time after the administrator has required the creditor to discharge, or convey or assign, the security under rule 3.113.

3.106   False claims or evidence

3.106(1)   If a creditor produces under rule 3.105 a statement of claim or documentary evidence of debt or other evidence which is false–

(a)   the creditor is guilty of an offence unless the creditor shows that the creditor neither knew nor had reason to believe that the statement of claim or documentary evidence of debt or other evidence was false;

(b)   the company is guilty of an offence if the company–

(i)   knew or became aware that the statement of claim or documentary evidence of debt or other evidence was false; and

(ii)   failed as soon as practicable after acquiring such knowledge to report it to the administrator.

3.107   Evidence of claims

3.107(1)   The administrator, for the purpose of being satisfied as to the validity or amount of a claim submitted by a creditor under rule 3.105, may require–

(a)   the creditor to produce further evidence; or

(b)   any other person who the administrator believes can produce relevant evidence, to produce such evidence.

3.107(2)   If the creditor or other person refuses or delays to produce such evidence as required under paragraph (1), the administrator may apply to the court for an order requiring the creditor or other person to attend for private examination before the court.

3.107(3) On an application to it under paragraph (2) above the court may make an order requiring the creditor or other person to attend for private examination before it on a date (being not earlier than eight days nor later than 16 days after the date of the order) and at a time specified in the order.

3.107(4) If a creditor or other person is for any good reason prevented from attending for examination, the court may grant a commission to take the examination (the commissioner being in this rule referred to as an "examining commissioner").

3.107(5) At any private examination under paragraph (2) or where the court grants a commission to take the examination under paragraph (4), a solicitor or counsel may act on behalf of the administrator, or the administrator may appear on the administrator's own behalf.

3.107(6) The examination, whether before the court or an examining commissioner, must be taken on oath.

3.107(7) A person who fails without reasonable excuse to comply with an order made under paragraph (2) is guilty of an offence.

3.107(8) References in this rule to a creditor in a case where the creditor is one of the following entities–

   (a) a trust;

   (b) a partnership (including a dissolved partnership);

   (c) a body corporate or an unincorporated body;

   (d) a limited partnership (including a dissolved partnership) within the meaning of the Limited Partnerships Act 1907,

are to be construed, unless the context otherwise requires, as references to a person representing the entity.

3.108   Adjudication of claims

3.108(1) Where funds are available for payment of a dividend out of the company's assets in respect of an accounting period, the administrator for the purpose of determining who is entitled to such a dividend must–

   (a) not later than four weeks before the end of the period, accept or reject every claim submitted or deemed to have been re-submitted under rule 3.105; and

   (b) at the same time make a decision on any matter requiring to be specified under paragraph (4)(a) or (b).

3.108(2) On accepting or rejecting, under paragraph (1) above, every claim submitted or deemed to have been re-submitted, the administrator must, as soon as is reasonably practicable, send a list of every claim so accepted or rejected (including the amount of each claim and whether it has been accepted or rejected) to every creditor known to the administrator.

3.108(3) Where the administrator rejects a claim, the administrator must without delay notify the creditor giving reasons for the rejection.

3.108(4) Where the administrator accepts or rejects a claim, the administrator must specify for that claim–

   (a) the amount of the claim accepted;

   (b) the category of debt, and the value of any security, as decided by the administrator; and

   (c) if rejecting the claim, the reasons for doing so.

3.108(5) Any member of the company or any creditor may, if dissatisfied with the acceptance or rejection of any claim (or, in relation to such acceptance or rejection with a decision in respect of any matter requiring to be specified under paragraph (4)(a) or (b)) appeal to the court not later than 14 days before the end of the accounting period.

3.108(6)   Any reference in this rule to the acceptance or rejection of a claim is to be construed as a reference to the acceptance or rejection of the claim in whole or in part.

3.109   Entitlement to draw a dividend

3.109(1)   A creditor who has had that creditor's claim accepted in whole or in part by the administrator under rule 3.108(1) or on appeal under rule 3.108(5) is entitled to payment out of the company's assets of a dividend in respect of the accounting period for the purposes of which the claim is accepted.

3.109(2)   Such entitlement to payment arises only in so far as the company has funds available to make that payment, having regard to rule 3.115.

3.110   Liabilities and rights of obligants

3.110(1)   Where a creditor has an obligant bound to the creditor along with the company for the whole or part of the debt, the obligant is not freed or discharged from liability for the debt by reason of the dissolution of the company or the creditor's voting or drawing a dividend or assenting to or not opposing–

(a)   the dissolution of the company; or

(b)   any composition with creditors.

3.110(2)   Paragraph (3) applies where–

(a)   a creditor has had a claim accepted in whole or in part; and

(b)   the obligant holds a security over any part of the company's assets.

3.110(3)   The obligant must account to the administrator so as to put the company's assets in the same position as if the obligant had paid the debt to the creditor and thereafter had had the obligant's claim accepted in whole or in part in the administration after deduction of the value of the security.

3.110(4)   The obligant may require and obtain at the obligant's own expense from the creditor an assignation of the debt on payment of the amount of the debt, and on that being done may in respect of the debt submit a claim, and vote and draw a dividend, if otherwise legally entitled to do so.

3.110(5)   Paragraph (4) is without prejudice to any right, under any rule of law, of an obligant who has paid the debt.

3.110(6)   In this rule an "obligant" includes a cautioner.

3.111   Amount which may be claimed generally

3.111(1)   Subject to the provisions of this rule and rules 3.112 and 3.113 the amount in respect of which a creditor is entitled to claim is the accumulated sum of principal and any interest which is due on the debt as at the date on which the company entered administration.

3.111(2)   If a debt does not depend on a contingency but would not be payable but for the administration until after the date on which the company entered administration, the amount of the claim is to be calculated as if the debt were payable on the date on which the company entered administration but subject to the deduction of interest at the rate specified in paragraph (4) from that date until the date for payment of the debt.

3.111(3)   In calculating the amount of a creditor's claim, the creditor must deduct any discount (other than any discount for immediate or early settlement) which is allowable by contract or course of dealing between the creditor and the company or by the usage of trade.

3.111(4) The rate of interest referred to in paragraph (2) is to be whichever is the greater of–

(a) the official rate at the date the company entered administration; or

(b) the rate applicable to that debt apart from the administration.

3.111(5) Where the administration was immediately preceded by a liquidation, the reference to the date on which the company entered administration in paragraph (1) and the second reference to that date in paragraph (2) are to be construed as references to the date the company went into liquidation.

3.112 Debts depending on contingency

3.112(1) Subject to paragraph (2), the amount which a creditor is entitled to claim is not to include a debt in so far as its existence or amount depends on a contingency.

3.112(2) On an application by the creditor–

(a) to the administrator; or

(b) if there is no administrator, to the court,

the administrator or court must put a value on the debt in so far as it is contingent.

3.112(3) Where under paragraph (2) a value is put on the debt–

(a) the amount in respect of which the creditor is then entitled to claim is to be that value but no more;

(b) where the contingent debt is an annuity, a cautioner may not then be sued for more than that value.

3.112(4) Any interested person may appeal to the court against a valuation under paragraph (2) by the administrator, and the court may affirm or vary that valuation.

3.113 Secured debts

3.113(1) In calculating the amount of a secured creditor's claim the secured creditor is to deduct the value of any security as estimated by the secured creditor.

3.113(2) If the secured creditor surrenders, or undertakes in writing to surrender, a security for the benefit of the company's assets, the secured creditor is not required to deduct the value of that security.

3.113(3) The administrator may, at any time after the expiry of 12 weeks from the date on which the company entered administration, require a secured creditor at the expense of the company's assets to discharge the security or convey or assign it to the administrator on payment to the creditor of the value specified by the creditor.

3.113(4) Where under paragraph (3) the administrator makes payment to the creditor, the amount in respect of which the creditor is then entitled to claim is to be any balance of the creditor's debt remaining after receipt of such payment.

3.113(5) In calculating the amount of the claim of a creditor whose security has been realised the creditor must deduct the amount (less the expenses of realisation) which the creditor has received, or is entitled to receive, from the realisation.

3.114 Claims in foreign currency

3.114(1) A creditor may state the amount of his or her claim in a currency other than sterling where–

(a) the creditor's claim is constituted by decree or other order made by a court ordering the company to pay to the creditor a sum expressed in a currency other than sterling; or

(b) where it is not so constituted, the creditor's claim arises from a contract or bill of exchange in terms of which payment is or may be required to be made by the company to the creditor in a currency other than sterling.

3.114(2) Where under paragraph (1) a claim is stated in a currency other than sterling the administrator must convert it into sterling at a single rate for each currency determined by the administrator by reference to the exchange rates prevailing in the London market at the close of business on the date on which the company entered administration or, if the administration was immediately preceded by a liquidation, on the date on which the company went into liquidation.

3.115 Order of priority in distribution

3.115(1) The funds of the company's assets must be distributed by the administrator to meet the following expenses and debts in the order in which they are mentioned–

(a) the expenses of the administration;

(b) any preferential debts within the meaning of section 386 (excluding any interest which has been accrued thereon to the date on which the company entered administration);

(c) ordinary debts, that is to say a debt which is neither a secured debt nor a debt mentioned in any other sub-paragraph of this paragraph;

(d) interest at the official rate, between the date on which the company entered administration and the date of payment, on–

   (i) the preferential debts, and

   (ii) the ordinary debts; and

(e) any postponed debt.

3.115(2) In paragraph (1)–

(a) "postponed debt" means–

   (i) a creditor's right to any alienation which has been reduced or restored to the company's assets under section 242 or to the proceeds of the sale of such an alienation,

   (ii) a claim arising by virtue of section 382(1)(a) of the Financial Services and Markets Act 2000 (restitution orders), unless it is also a claim arising by virtue of subparagraph (b) of that section (a person who has suffered loss etc.), or

   (iii) in administration, a claim which by virtue of the Act or any other enactment is a claim the payment of which is to be postponed;

(b) in sub-paragraph (d), where the administration was immediately preceded by a winding up, the reference to the date on which the company entered administration is to be construed as the date the company went into liquidation.

3.115(3) The expenses of the administration mentioned in paragraph (1)(a) are payable in the order of priority mentioned in rule 3.116.

3.115(4) Subject to section 175–

(a) any debt falling within either of paragraphs (1)(b) or (c) is to have the same priority as any other debt falling within the same sub-paragraph; and

(b) where the funds of the company's assets are inadequate to enable such debts to be paid in full, they are to abate in equal proportions.

3.115(5) Any surplus remaining, after all expenses and debts mentioned in paragraph (1) have been paid in full, must (unless the articles of the company provide otherwise) be distributed among the members according to their rights and interests in the company.

3.115(6) Nothing in this rule affects–

(a) the right of a secured creditor which is preferable to the rights of the administrator; or

(b)   any preference of the holder of a lien over a title deed or other document which the administrator has taken into his or her possession or control in accordance with paragraph 67 of Schedule B1.

3.116   Order of priority of expenses of administration

3.116(1)   Subject to rule 3.51 the expenses of the administration are payable out of the assets in the following order of priority–

(a)   any outlays properly chargeable or incurred by the administrator in carrying out its functions in the administration, except those outlays specifically mentioned in the following sub-paragraphs;

(b)   the cost, or proportionate cost, of any caution provided by an administrator in accordance with the Act or these Rules;

(c)   the expenses of the applicant in the administration, and of any person appearing in the petition whose expenses are allowed by the court;

(d)   the remuneration or emoluments of any person who has been employed by the administrator to perform any services for the company, as required or authorised by or under the Act or these Rules;

(e)   the remuneration of the administrator determined in accordance with rules 3.95 to 3.101;

(f)   the amount of any corporation tax on chargeable gains accruing on the realisation of any asset of the company (without regard to whether the realisation is effected by the administrator, a secured creditor or otherwise).

3.117   Estate to be distributed in respect of the accounting periods

3.117(1)   The administrator must make up accounts of the administrator's intromissions with the company's assets in respect of each accounting period.

3.117(2)   In this rule, "accounting period" is to be construed as follows–

(a)   the first accounting period is the period of six months beginning with the date on which the company entered administration; and

(b)   any subsequent accounting period is the period of six months beginning with the end of the last accounting period except that–

  (i)   where the administrator and the creditors' committee agree; or

  (ii)   where there is no creditors' committee, the court determines,

the accounting period is to be such other period beginning with the end of the last accounting period as may be agreed or, as the case may be determined, it is to be that other period.

3.117(3)   An agreement or determination under paragraph (2)(b)–

(a)   may be made in respect of one or more than one accounting period;

(b)   may be made before the beginning of the accounting period in relation to which it has effect and, in any event, is not to have effect unless made before the day on which such accounting period would, but for the agreement or determination, have ended;

(c)   may provide for different accounting periods to be of different durations.

3.117(4)   The administrator may make a distribution to secured or preferential creditors or, where the administrator has the permission of the court, to unsecured creditors only if–

(a)   the administrator has sufficient funds for the purpose;

(b)   the administrator does not intend to give notice pursuant to paragraph 83 of Schedule B1;

(c) the administrator's statement of proposals, as approved by the creditors under paragraph 53(1) or 54(5) of Schedule B1, contains a proposal to make a distribution to the class of creditors in question, and

(d) the payment of a dividend is consistent with the functions and duties of the administrator and any proposals made by the administrator or which the administrator intends to make.

3.117(5) The administrator may pay–

(a) the expenses of the administration mentioned in rule 3.116(1)(a), other than the administrator's own remuneration, at any time;

(b) the preferential debts within the meaning of section 386 at any time but only with the consent of the creditors' committee or, if there is no creditors' committee, of the court.

3.117(6) If the administrator–

(a) is not ready to pay a dividend in respect of an accounting period; or

(b) considers it would be inappropriate to pay such a dividend because the expenses of doing so would be disproportionate to the amount of the dividend,

the administrator may postpone such payment to a date not later than the time for payment of a dividend in respect of the next accounting period.

3.117(7) Where an appeal is taken under rule 3.108(5) against the acceptance or rejection of a creditor's claim, the administrator must at the time of payment of dividends and until the appeal is determined, set aside an amount which would be sufficient, if the determination in the appeal were to provide for the claim being accepted in full, to pay a dividend in respect of that claim.

3.117(8) Where a creditor–

(a) has failed to produce evidence in support of a claim earlier than eight weeks before the end of an accounting period on being required by the administrator to do so under rule 3.107; and

(b) has given a reason for such failure which is acceptable to the administrator,

the administrator must set aside, for such time as is reasonable to enable the creditor to produce that evidence or any other evidence that will enable the administrator to be satisfied under rule 3.107 an amount which would be sufficient, if the claim were accepted in full, to pay a dividend in respect of that claim.

3.117(9) Where a creditor submits a claim to the administrator later than eight weeks before the end of an accounting period but more than eight weeks before the end of a subsequent accounting period in respect of which, after making allowance for contingencies, funds are available for the payment of a dividend, the administrator must, if accepting the claim in whole or in part, pay to the creditor–

(a) the same dividend or dividends as has or have already been paid to creditors of the same class in respect of any accounting period or periods; and

(b) whatever dividend may be payable to that creditor in respect of the said subsequent accounting period

provided that paragraph (a) above is without prejudice to any dividend which has already been paid.

3.117(10) In the declaration of and payment of a dividend, no payments are to be made more than once by virtue of the same debt.

3.117(11) Subject to any notification by the person entitled to a dividend given to the administrator that the person wishes the dividend to be paid to another person, or has assigned that entitlement to another person, where both a creditor and a member State liquidator have had a claim accepted in relation to the same debt, payment is only to be made to the creditor.

3.118   Small debts

3.118(1)   A creditor is deemed to have submitted a claim for the purposes of adjudication of entitlement to and payment of a dividend but not otherwise where–

(a)   the debt is a small debt;

(b)   notice has been delivered to the creditor under rule 3.119; and

(c)   the creditor has not advised the administrator that the debt is incorrect or not owed in response to the notice.

3.118(2)   In this rule "small debt" means a debt (being the total amount owed to a creditor) which does not exceed £1,000 (which amount is prescribed for the purposes of paragraph 13A of Schedule 8 to the Act and paragraph 18A of Schedule 9 to the Act.

3.119   Contents of notice to be delivered to creditors owed small debts etc.

3.119(1)   The administrator may treat a debt, which is a small debt according to the accounting records or the statement of affairs of the company, as if it were accepted under rule 3.108 for the purpose of paying a dividend.

3.119(2)   Where the administrator intends to treat such a debt as if it were accepted under rule 3.108 for the purpose of payment of a dividend, the administrator must not later than 12 weeks before the end of the accounting period deliver to the creditor a notice.

3.119(3)   The notice must–

(a)   state the amount of the debt which the administrator believes to be owed to the creditor according to the accounting records or statement of affairs of the company;

(b)   state that the administrator will treat the debt which is stated in the notice, being for £1,000 or less, as accepted for the purpose of payment of a dividend unless the creditor advises the administrator that the amount of the debt is incorrect or that no debt is owed;

(c)   require the creditor to notify the administrator by not later than eight weeks before the end of the accounting period if the amount of the debt is incorrect or if no debt is owed; and

(d)   inform the creditor that where the creditor advises the administrator that the amount of the debt is incorrect the creditor must also submit not later than eight weeks before the end of the accounting period a statement of claim and documentary evidence of debt (see rule 3.105) in order to receive a dividend.

PART 4

BLOCK TRANSFER OF PROCEEDINGS

[Note: a document required by the Act or these Rules must also contain the standard contents set out in Part 1]

4.1   Power to make a block transfer order

4.1(1)   Part 4 applies where it is expedient to transfer some or all of the cases in which an outgoing office-holder ("the outgoing office-holder") holds office to one or more office-holders ("the replacement office-holder") in a single transaction where the outgoing office-holder–

(a)   dies;

(b)   retires from practice; or

(c)   is otherwise unable or unwilling to continue in office.

4.1(2)   In a case to which this Part applies the Court of Session has the power to make an order ("a block transfer order") appointing a replacement office-holder in the place of the outgoing office-holder to be–

(a)   administrator in any administration; or

(b)   supervisor of a CVA.

4.1(3)   The replacement office-holder must be qualified to act as an insolvency practitioner in relation to the company.

4.2   Application for a block transfer order

4.2(1)   An application for a block transfer order may be made to the Court of Session for–

(a)   the removal of the outgoing office-holder by the exercise of any of the powers in paragraph (2);

(b)   the appointment of a replacement office-holder by the exercise of any of the powers in paragraph (3); or

(c)   such other order or direction as may be necessary or expedient in connection with the matters referred to in sub-paragraphs (a) and (b).

4.2(2)   The powers referred to in paragraph (1)(a) are those in–

(a)   section 7(5) and paragraph 39(6) of Schedule A1; and

(b)   paragraph 88 of Schedule B1 and rule 4.1(2).

4.2(3)   The powers referred to in paragraph (1)(b) are those in–

(a)   section 7(5) and paragraph 39(6) of Schedule A1; and

(b)   paragraphs 63, 91 and 95 of Schedule B1 and rule 4.12(2).

4.2(4)   Subject to paragraph (5), the application may be made by any of the following–

(a)   the outgoing office-holder (if able and willing to do so);

(b)   any person who holds office jointly with the outgoing office-holder;

(c)   any person who is proposed to be appointed as the replacement office-holder;

(d)   any creditor in a case subject to the application;

(e)   the recognised professional body which was the source of the outgoing office-holder's authorisation (immediately before the application is made); or

(f)   the Secretary of State.

4.2(5)   Where one or more of the outgoing office-holders in the schedule required by paragraph (8) is an administrator, an application may not be made unless the applicant is a person permitted to apply to replace the outgoing office-holder under section 13 or paragraph 63, 91 or 95 of Schedule B1 or such a person is joined as applicant in relation to the replacement of the outgoing officeholder.

4.2(6)   An applicant (other than the Secretary of State) must deliver a notice of the intended application to the Secretary of State on or before the date the application is made.

4.2(7)   The application must be served on–

(a)   the outgoing office-holder (if not the applicant or deceased);

(b)   any person who holds office jointly with the outgoing office-holder; and

(c)   such other person as the Court of Session directs.

4.2(8)   The application must contain a schedule setting out–

(a)   identification details for the insolvency proceedings; and

(b)   the capacity in which the outgoing office-holder was appointed.

4.2(9)   The application must be supported by evidence–

(a)   setting out the circumstances as a result of which it is expedient to appoint a replacement office-holder; and

(b)   exhibiting the consent to act of each person who is proposed to be appointed as replacement office-holder.

4.3   Action following application for a block transfer order

4.3(1)   In cases relating to the appointment of a supervisor of a CVA, in deciding to what extent (if any) the costs of making an application under rule 4.2 should be paid as an expense of the CVA proceedings to which the application relates, the factors to which the Court of Session must have regard include–

(a)   the reasons for the making of the application;

(b)   the number of cases to which the application relates;

(c)   the value of the assets comprised in those cases; and

(d)   the nature and extent of the costs involved.

4.3(2)   Where an application relates to the appointment of an administrator and is made by a person under section 13 or paragraph 63, 91 or 95 of Schedule B1, the costs of making that application are to be paid as an expense of the administration to which the application relates unless the Court of Session directs otherwise.

4.3(3)   Notice of any appointment made under rule 4.2 must be delivered by the replacement office-holder–

(a)   to the Secretary of State as soon as reasonably practicable; and

(b)   to–

(i)   the creditors in the first progress report following such appointment,

(ii)   such other persons as the Court of Session may direct, in such manner as the court may direct.

PART 5

DECISION MAKING

CHAPTER 1

APPLICATION OF PART

5.1   Application of Part

5.1   In this Part–

(a)   Chapters 2 to 9 apply where the Act or these Rules require a decision to be made by a qualifying decision procedure or permit a decision to be made by the deemed consent procedure; and

(b)   Chapter 10 applies to company meetings.

CHAPTER 2

DECISION PROCEDURES

[Note: a document required by the Act or these Rules must also contain the standard contents set out in Part 1.]

5.2 Interpretation

5.2(1) In these Rules–

"decision date" means–

    (a) in the case of a decision to be made at a meeting, the date of the meeting;

    (b) in the case of a decision to be made either by a decision procedure other than a meeting or by the deemed consent procedure, the date the decision is to be made or deemed to have been made; and

a decision falling within sub-paragraph (b) is to be treated as made at 23:59 on the decision date;

"decision procedure" means a qualifying decision procedure prescribed by rule 5.3;

"electronic voting" includes any electronic system which enables a person to vote without the need to attend at a particular location to do so;

"physical meeting" means a meeting where the creditors are invited to be present together at the same place (whether or not it is possible to attend the meeting without being present at that place);

"virtual meeting" means a meeting where persons who are not invited to be physically present together may participate in the meeting including communicating directly with all the other participants in the meeting and voting (either directly or via a proxy-holder).

5.2(2) The decision date is to be set at the discretion of the convener, but must be not less than 14 days from the date of delivery of the notice, except where the table in rule 5.11 requires a different period or the court directs otherwise.

5.3 The prescribed decision procedures

[Note: under section 246ZE a decision may not be made by a creditors' meeting (a physical meeting) unless the prescribed proportion of the creditors request in writing that the decision be made by such a meeting.]

5.3(1) The following decision procedures are prescribed for the purpose of section 246ZE by which a convener may seek a decision under the Act or these Rules from creditors–

    (a) correspondence;

    (b) electronic voting;

    (c) virtual meeting;

    (d) physical meeting;

    (e) any other decision making procedure which enables all creditors who are entitled to participate in the making of the decision to participate equally.

5.4 Electronic voting

5.4 Where the decision procedure uses electronic voting–

    (a) the notice delivered to creditors in accordance with rule 5.8 must give them any necessary information as to how to access the voting system including any password required;

(b) except where electronic voting is being used at a meeting, the voting system must be a system capable of enabling a creditor to vote at any time between the notice being delivered and the decision date; and

(c) in the course of a vote the voting system must not provide any creditor with information concerning the vote cast by any other creditor.

5.5 Virtual meetings

5.5 Where the decision procedure uses a virtual meeting the notice delivered to creditors in accordance with rule 5.8 must contain–

(a) any necessary information as to how to access the virtual meeting including any telephone number, access code or password required; and

(b) a statement that the meeting may be suspended or adjourned by the chair of the meeting (and must be adjourned if it is so resolved at the meeting).

5.6 Physical meetings

5.6(1) A request for a physical meeting under section 246ZE(3) may be made before or after the notice of the decision procedure or deemed consent procedure has been delivered, but must be made not later than five business days after the date on which the convener delivered the notice of the decision procedure or deemed consent procedure unless these Rules provide to the contrary.

5.6(2) It is the convener's responsibility to check whether any requests for a physical meeting are submitted before the deadline and if so whether in aggregate they meet or surpass one of the thresholds requiring a physical meeting under section 246ZE(7).

5.6(3) Where the prescribed proportion of creditors require a physical meeting the convener must summon the meeting by giving notice which complies with rule 5.8 so far as applicable and which must also contain a statement that the meeting may be suspended or adjourned by the chair of the meeting (and must be adjourned if it is so resolved at the meeting).

5.6(4) In addition, the notice under paragraph (3) must inform the creditors that as a result of the requirement to hold a physical meeting the original decision procedure or the deemed consent procedure is superseded.

5.6(5) The convener must send the notice under paragraph (3) not later than three business days after one of the thresholds requiring a physical meeting has been met or surpassed.

5.6(6) The convener–

(a) may permit a creditor to attend a physical meeting remotely if the convener receives a request to do so in advance of the meeting; and

(b) must include in the notice of the meeting a statement explaining the convener's discretion to permit remote attendance.

5.6(7) In this rule, attending a physical meeting "remotely" means attending and being able to participate in the meeting without being in the place where the meeting is held.

5.6(8) For the purpose of determining whether the thresholds under section 246ZE(7) are met, the convener must calculate the value of the creditor's debt by reference to rule 5.28.

5.7 Deemed consent

[Note: the deemed consent procedure cannot be used to make a decision on remuneration of any person, or where the Act, these Rules, any other legislation or a court order requires a decision to be made by a decision procedure.]

5.7(1)   This rule makes further provision about the deemed consent procedure to that set out in section 246ZF.

5.7(2)   A notice seeking deemed consent must, in addition to the requirements of section 246ZF, comply with the requirements of rule 5.8 so far as applicable and must also contain–

(a)   a statement that in order to object to the proposed decision a creditor must have delivered a notice, stating that the creditor so objects, to the convener not later than the decision date together with a statement of claim and documentary evidence of debt in accordance with these Rules, failing which the objection will be disregarded;

(b)   a statement that it is the convener's responsibility to aggregate any objections to see if the threshold is met for the decision to be taken as not having been made; and

(c)   a statement that if the threshold is met the deemed consent procedure will terminate without a decision being made and if a decision is sought again on the same matter it will be sought by a decision procedure.

5.7(3)   In this rule, the threshold is met where the appropriate number of relevant creditors (as defined in section 246ZF(7)) have objected to the proposed decision.

5.7(4)   For the purpose of aggregating objections, the convener may presume the value of relevant creditors' claims to be the value of claims by those creditors who, in the convener's view, would have been entitled to vote had the decision been sought by a decision procedure in accordance with this Part, even where those creditors had not already met the criteria for such entitlement to vote.

5.7(5)   Rules 5.28, 5.29 and 5.30 apply to the admission or rejection of a claim for the purpose of the convener deciding whether or not an objection should count towards the total aggregated objections.

5.7(6)   A decision of the convener on the aggregation of objections under this rule is subject to appeal under rule 5.32 as if it were a decision under Chapter 7 of this Part.

CHAPTER 3

NOTICES, VOTING AND VENUES FOR DECISIONS

[Note: a document required by the Act or these Rules must also contain the standard contents set out in Part 1.]

5.8   Notices to creditors of decision procedure

5.8(1)   This rule sets out the requirements for notices to creditors where a decision is sought by a decision procedure.

5.8(2)   The convener must deliver a notice to every creditor who is entitled to notice of the procedure.

5.8(3)   The notice must contain the following–

(a)   identification details for the insolvency proceedings;

(b)   details of the decision to be made or of any resolution on which a decision is sought;

(c)   a description of the decision procedure which the convener is using, and arrangements, including the venue, for the decision procedure;

(d)   a statement of the decision date;

(e)   except in the case of a decision in relation to a proposed CVA, a statement as to when the creditor must have delivered a statement of claim and documentary evidence of debt in accordance with these Rules failing which a vote by the creditor will be disregarded;

(f)   a statement that a creditor whose debt is treated as a small debt in accordance with rule 3.118 must still deliver a statement of claim and documentary evidence of debt if that creditor wishes to vote;

(g)   a statement that a creditor who has opted out from receiving notices may nevertheless vote if the creditor provides a statement of claim and documentary evidence of debt in accordance with paragraph (e);

(h)   in the case of a decision in relation to a proposed CVA, a statement of the effects of the relevant provisions of the following–

   (i)   rule 5.26 about creditors' voting rights,

   (ii)   rule 5.28 about the calculation of creditors' voting rights, and

   (iii)   rule 5.31 about the requisite majority of creditors for making decisions;

(i)   except in the case of a physical meeting, a statement that creditors who meet the thresholds in section 246ZE(7) may, within five business days from the date of delivery of the notice, require a physical meeting to be held to consider the matter;

(j)   in the case of a meeting, a statement that any proxy must be delivered to the convener or chair before it may be used at the meeting;

(k)   in the case of a meeting, a statement that, where applicable, a complaint may be made in accordance with rule 5.35 and the period within which such a complaint may be made; and

(l)   a statement that a creditor may appeal a decision in accordance with rule 5.32, and the relevant period under rule 5.32 within which such an appeal may be made.

5.8(4)   The notice must be authenticated and dated by the convener.

5.8(5)   Where the decision procedure is a meeting the notice must be accompanied by a blank proxy complying with rule 6.3.

5.8(6)   This rule does not apply if the court orders under rule 5.12 that notice of a decision procedure be given by advertisement only.

5.9   Voting in a decision procedure

5.9(1)   In order to be counted in a decision procedure other than where votes are cast at a meeting, votes must–

(a)   be received by the convener on or before the decision date; and

(b)   in the case of a vote cast by a creditor–

   (i)   in a CVA, be accompanied by written notification of the creditor's debt unless such a notification has already been given to the convener;

   (ii)   in an administration, be accompanied by a statement of claim and documentary evidence of debt (where the requirement to provide the latter is not dispensed with under rule 5.26(2)) unless already given to the convener.

5.9(2)   In an administration, a vote must be disregarded if–

(a)   a statement of claim and, where required, documentary evidence of debt are not received by the convener on or before the decision date or, in the case of a meeting, at or before the meeting (unless under rule 5.24 the chair is content to accept them before resumption of the adjourned meeting); or

(b)   the convener decides, in the application of Chapter 7 of this Part, that the creditor is not entitled to cast the vote.

5.9(3) The convener must have received at least one valid vote on or before the decision date in order for a decision to be made.

5.10 Venue for the decision procedure

5.10 The convener must have regard to the convenience of those invited to participate when fixing the venue for a decision procedure (including the resumption of an adjourned meeting).

5.11 Notice of decision procedures or of seeking deemed consent: when and to whom delivered

[Note: when an office-holder is obliged to give notice to "the creditors", this is subject to rule 1.33, which limits the obligation to giving notice to those creditors of whose address the office-holder is aware.]

5.11(1) Notices of decision procedures, and notices seeking deemed consent, must be delivered in accordance with the following table.

Proceedings	*Decisions*	*Persons to whom notice must be delivered*	*Minimum notice required*
administration	decisions of creditors	the creditors who had claims against the company at the date when the company entered administration (except for those who have subsequently been paid in full)	14 days
proposed CVA	decisions of creditors	the creditors	7 days for a decision on proposed modifications to the proposal from the company's directors under paragraph 31(7) of Schedule A1; 7 days for consideration of proposal where physical meeting requisitioned; in other cases, 14 days
main proceedings in another member State	approval under Article 36(5) of the EU Regulation of proposed undertaking offered by a member State liquidator	all the local creditors in the United Kingdom	14 days

5.11(2) This rule does not apply where the court orders under rule 5.12 that notice of a decision procedure be given by advertisement only.

5.12 Notice of decision procedure by advertisement only

5.12(1) The court may order that notice of a decision procedure is to be given by advertisement only and not by individual notice to the persons concerned.

5.12(2)   In considering whether to make such an order, the court must have regard to the relative cost of advertisement as against the giving of individual notices, the amount of assets available and the extent of the interest of creditors or members or any particular class of them.

5.12(3)   The advertisement must meet the requirements for a notice under rule 5.8(3), and must also state–

(a)   that the court ordered that notice of the decision procedure be given by advertisement only; and

(b)   the date of the court's order.

5.13   Gazetting and advertisement

5.13(1)   In an administration, where a decision is being sought in a meeting the convener must gazette a notice stating–

(a)   that a meeting of creditors is to take place;

(b)   the venue for the meeting;

(c)   the purpose of the meeting; and

(d)   the time and date by which, and the place at which, those attending must deliver proxies and statements of claim and documentary evidence of debt (if not already delivered) in order to be entitled to vote.

5.13(2)   The notice must also state–

(a)   who is the convener in respect of the meeting; and

(b)   if the meeting results from a request of one or more creditors under section 246ZE, the fact that it was so summoned.

5.13(3)   The notice must be gazetted before or as soon as reasonably practicable after notice of the meeting is delivered in accordance with these Rules.

5.13(4)   Information to be gazetted under this rule may also be advertised in such other manner as the convener thinks fit.

5.13(5)   The convener may gazette other decision procedures or the deemed consent procedure in which case the equivalent information to that required by this rule must be stated in the notice.

5.14   Notice to company officers in respect of meetings

5.14(1)   In a proposal for a CVA or in an administration, notice to participate in a creditors' meeting must be delivered to every present or former officer of the company whose presence the convener thinks is required and that person is required to attend the meeting.

5.14(2)   A notice under this rule must be delivered in compliance with the minimum notice requirements set out in rule 5.11 or in compliance with an order of the court under rule 5.12.

5.15   Non-receipt of notice of decision

5.15   Where a decision is sought by a notice in accordance with the Act or these Rules, the decision procedure or deemed consent procedure is presumed to have been duly initiated and conducted, even if not everyone to whom the notice is to be delivered has received it.

5.16   Decisions on remuneration and conduct

5.16(1)   This rule applies in relation to a decision or resolution which is proposed in an administration, and which affects a person in relation to that person's remuneration or conduct as administrator (actual, proposed or former).

5.16(2) The following may not vote on such a decision or resolution whether as a creditor, proxy-holder or corporate representative, except so far as permitted by rule 6.7 (proxy-holder with financial interest)–

(a) that person;

(b) the partners and employees of that person;

(c) the officers and employees of the company of which that person is a director, officer or employee; and

(d) the representative of any person mentioned in sub-paragraphs (a) to (c).

CHAPTER 4

REQUISITIONED DECISIONS

[Note: a document required by the Act or these Rules must also contain the standard contents set out in Part 1.]

5.17 Requisitions of decision

[Note: this rule is concerned with requests by creditors for a decision, rather than requests for decisions to be made by way of a physical meeting under section 246ZE(3).]

5.17(1) In this Chapter, "requisitioned decision" means a decision requested to be sought under paragraph 52(2) or 56(1) of Schedule B1.

5.17(2) A request for a decision to be sought under paragraph 52(2) of Schedule B1 must be delivered within eight business days of the date on which the administrator's statement of proposals is delivered.

5.17(3) The request for a requisitioned decision must include a statement of the purpose of the proposed decision and either–

(a) a copy of the requesting creditor's statement of claim, together with–

(i) a list of the creditors concurring with the request and of the amounts of their respective claims, and

(ii) confirmation of concurrence from each creditor concurring; or

(b) a copy of the requesting creditor's statement of claim and a statement that that alone is sufficient without the concurrence of other creditors.

5.18 Expenses and timing of requisitioned decision

5.18(1) The convener must, not later than 14 days from receipt of a request for a requisitioned decision, provide the requesting creditor with itemised details of the sum to be deposited as caution for payment of the expenses of such procedure.

5.18(2) The convener is not obliged to initiate the decision procedure or deemed consent procedure (where applicable) until either–

(a) the convener has received the required sum; or

(b) the period of 14 days has expired without the convener having informed the requesting creditor of the sum required to be deposited as caution.

5.18(3) A requisitioned decision must be made within 28 days of the date on which the earlier of the events specified in paragraph (2) of this rule occurs.

5.18(4)   The expenses of a requisitioned decision must be paid out of the deposit (if any) unless the creditors decide that they are to be payable as an expense of the administration.

5.18(5)   The notice of a requisitioned decision of creditors must contain a statement that the creditors may make a decision as in paragraph (4) of this rule.

5.18(6)   Where the creditors do not so decide, the expenses must be paid by the requesting creditor to the extent that the deposit (if any) is not sufficient.

5.18(7)   To the extent that the deposit (if any) is not required for payment of the expenses, it must be repaid to the requesting creditor.

CHAPTER 5

CONSTITUTION OF MEETINGS

5.19   Quorum at meetings

5.19(1)   A meeting is not competent to act unless a quorum is in attendance.

5.19(2)   In the case of a meeting of creditors, a quorum is at least one creditor entitled to vote.

5.19(3)   Where the provisions of this rule as to quorum are satisfied by the attendance of the chair alone or the chair and one additional person, but the chair is aware, either by virtue of statements of claim and documentary evidence of debt and proxies received or otherwise, that one or more additional persons would, if attending, be entitled to vote, the chair must delay the start of the meeting by at least 15 minutes after the appointed time.

5.19(4)   In this rule, the reference to the number of creditors necessary to constitute a quorum includes those represented by proxy by any person (including the chair).

5.20   Chair at meetings

5.20   The chair of a meeting must be–

(a)   the convener; or

(b)   an appointed person.

5.21   The chair – attendance, interventions and questions

5.21   The chair of a meeting may–

(a)   allow any person who has given reasonable notice of wishing to attend to participate in a virtual meeting or to be admitted to a physical meeting;

(b)   decide what intervention, if any, may be made at a meeting of creditors by any person attending who is not a creditor; and

decide what questions may be put to any present or former officer of the company.

CHAPTER 6

ADJOURNMENT AND SUSPENSION OF MEETINGS

5.22   Adjournment by chair

5.22(1)   The chair may (and must if it is so resolved) adjourn a meeting for not more than 14 days, subject to any direction of the court.

5.22(2) Any further adjournment under this rule must not be to a day later than 14 days after the date on which the meeting was originally held, subject to any direction of the court.

5.22(3) But in a case relating to a proposed CVA, the chair may, and must if the meeting so resolves, adjourn a meeting held under paragraph 29(1) of Schedule A1 to a day which is not more than 14 days after the date on which the moratorium (including any extension) ends.

5.23 Adjournment in absence of chair

5.23(1) In an administration, if no one attends to act as chair within 30 minutes of the time fixed for a meeting to start, then the meeting is adjourned to the same time and place the following week or, if that is not a business day, to the business day immediately following.

5.23(2) If no one attends to act as chair within 30 minutes of the time fixed for the meeting after a second adjournment under this rule, then the meeting comes to an end.

5.24 Statements of claim and documentary evidence of debt in adjournment

5.24 Where a meeting in an administration is adjourned, the chair may allow a statement of claim and documentary evidence of debt (where required) to be used if delivered at or before resumption of the adjourned meeting.

5.25 Suspension

5.25 The chair of a meeting may, without an adjournment, declare the meeting suspended for one or more periods not exceeding one hour in total (or, in exceptional circumstances, such longer total period during the same day as the chair may determine).

CHAPTER 7

CREDITORS' VOTING RIGHTS AND MAJORITIES

[Note: a document required by the Act or these Rules must also contain the standard contents set out in Part 1.]

5.26 Creditors' voting rights

5.26(1) In an administration, a creditor is entitled to vote in a decision procedure or to object to a decision proposed using the deemed consent procedure only if–

  (a) the creditor has delivered to the convener a statement of claim and documentary evidence of debt, including any calculation for the purposes of rule 5.28 or 5.29;

  (b) the statement of claim and documentary evidence of debt were received by the convener not later than the decision date, or in the case of a meeting, at or before the meeting; and

  (c) the statement of claim and documentary evidence of debt has been admitted for the purposes of entitlement to vote.

5.26(2) The convener or chair may dispense with the requirement to produce documentary evidence of debt in paragraph (1)(a).

5.26(3) In the case of a meeting, a proxy-holder is not entitled to vote on behalf of a creditor unless the convener or chair has received the proxy intended to be used on behalf of that creditor.

5.26(4) In a decision relating to a proposed CVA every creditor, secured or unsecured, who has notice of the decision procedure is entitled to vote in respect of that creditor' debt.

5.26(5)   Where a decision is sought in an administration under rule 3.52(3)(b), rule 3.96(5) or rule 3.96(6), creditors are entitled to participate to the extent stated in those rules.

5.27   Claim made in proceedings in other member States

5.27(1)   Where, in an administration,–

(a)   a creditor is entitled to vote under rule 5.26 (as determined, where that is the case, in accordance with rule 5.32);

(b)   that creditor has made the claim in other proceedings;

(c)   that creditor votes on a resolution in a decision procedure; and

(d)   a member State liquidator casts a vote in respect of the same claim,

only the creditor's vote is to be counted.

5.27(2)   Where, in an administration,–

(a)   a creditor has made a claim in more than one set of other proceedings; and

(b)   more than one member State liquidator seeks to vote in respect of that claim,

the entitlement to vote in respect of that claim is exercisable by the member State liquidator in the main proceedings, whether or not the creditor has made the claim in the main proceedings.

5.27(3)   In this rule, "other proceedings" mean main, secondary or territorial proceedings in another member State.

5.28   Calculation of voting rights

5.28(1)   Votes are calculated according to the amount of each creditor's claim–

(a)   in an administration, as at the date on which the company entered administration, less–

    (i)   any payments that have been made to the creditor after that date in respect of the claim, and

    (ii)   any adjustment by way of set-off which has been made in accordance with that principle or would have been made if that principle were applied on the date on which the votes are counted;

(b)   in a proposed CVA–

    (i)   at the date the company went into liquidation where the company is being wound up,

    (ii)   at the date the company entered administration (less any payments made to the creditor after that date in respect of the claim) where it is in administration,

    (iii)   at the beginning of the moratorium where a moratorium has been obtained (less any payments made to the creditor after that date in respect of the claim), or

    (iv)   where (i) to (iii) do not apply, at the decision date.

5.28(2)   A creditor may vote in respect of a debt of an unliquidated or unascertained amount if the convener or chair decides to put upon it an estimated minimum value for the purpose of entitlement to vote and admits the claim for that purpose.

5.28(3)   In relation to a proposed CVA, a debt of an unliquidated or unascertained amount is to be valued at £1 for the purposes of voting unless the convener or chair or an appointed person decides to put a higher value on it.

5.28(4)   Where a debt is wholly secured its value for voting purposes is nil.

5.28(5)   Where a debt is partly secured its value for voting purposes is the value of the unsecured part.

5.28(6)   The value of the debt for voting purposes is its full value without deduction of the value of the security in the following cases–

(a)   where the administrator has made a statement under paragraph 52(1)(b) of Schedule B1 and the administrator has been requested to seek a decision under paragraph 52(2) of that Schedule; and

(b)   where, in a proposed CVA, there is a decision on whether to extend or further extend a moratorium or to bring a moratorium to an end before the end of the period of any extension.

5.28(7)   No vote may be cast in respect of a claim more than once on any resolution put to the meeting and for this purpose (where relevant), the claim of a creditor and of any member State liquidator in relation to the same debt are a single claim.

5.28(8)   A vote cast in a decision procedure which is not a meeting may not be changed.

5.28(9)   Paragraph (7) does not prevent a creditor or member State liquidator from–

(a)   voting in respect of less than the full value of an entitlement to vote; or

(b)   casting a vote one way in respect of part of the value of an entitlement and another way in respect of some or all of the balance of that value.

5.29   Calculation of voting rights: hire-purchase agreements

5.29(1)   In an administration, a creditor under a hire-purchase agreement is entitled to vote in respect of the amount of the debt due and payable by the company on the date on which the company entered administration.

5.29(2)   In calculating the amount of any debt for the purpose of paragraph (1), no account is to be taken of any amount attributable to the exercise of any right under the relevant agreement so far as the right has become exercisable solely by virtue of–

(a)   the making of an administration application;

(b)   a notice of intention to appoint an administrator or any matter arising as a consequence of the notice; or

(c)   the company entering administration.

5.30   Procedure for admitting creditors' claims for voting

5.30(1)   The convener or chair in respect of a decision procedure must ascertain entitlement to vote and admit or reject claims accordingly.

5.30(2)   The convener or chair may admit or reject a claim in whole or in part.

5.30(3)   If the convener or chair is in any doubt whether a claim should be admitted or rejected, the convener or chair must mark it as objected to and allow votes to be cast in respect of it, subject to such votes being subsequently declared invalid if the objection to the claim is sustained.

5.31   Requisite majorities

5.31(1)   A decision is made by creditors when a majority (in value) of those voting have voted in favour of the proposed decision, except where this rule provides otherwise.

5.31(2)   In the case of an administration, a decision is not made if those voting against it include more than half in value of the creditors to whom notice of the decision procedure was delivered who are not, to the best of the convener's or chair's belief, persons connected with the company.

5.31(3)   Each of the following decisions in a proposed CVA is made when 75% or more (in value) of those responding vote in favour of it–

(a)   a decision approving a proposal or a modification;

(b)   a decision extending or further extending a moratorium; or

(c)   a decision bringing a moratorium to an end before the end of the period of any extension.

5.31(4)   In a proposed CVA a decision is not made if more than half of the total value of the unconnected creditors vote against it.

5.31(5)   For the purposes of paragraph (4)–

(a)   a creditor is unconnected unless the convener or chair decides that the creditor is connected with the company;

(b)   in deciding whether a creditor is connected reliance may be placed on the information provided in the company's statement of affairs or otherwise in accordance with these Rules; and

(c)   the total value of the unconnected creditors is the total value of those unconnected creditors whose claims have been admitted for voting.

5.32   Appeals against decisions under this Chapter

5.32(1)   A decision of the convener or chair under this Chapter is subject to appeal to the court by a creditor.

5.32(2)   In a proposed CVA, an appeal to the court against a decision under this Chapter may also be made by a member of the company.

5.32(3)   If the decision is reversed or varied, or votes are declared invalid, the court may order another decision procedure to be initiated or make such order as it thinks just but, in a CVA, the court may only make an order if it considers that the circumstances which led to the appeal give rise to unfair prejudice or material irregularity.

5.32(4)   An appeal under this rule may not be made after the end of the period of 21 days beginning with the decision date.

5.32(5)   However, the previous paragraph does not apply in a proposed CVA where an appeal may not be made after the end of the period of 28 days beginning with the day on which the first of the reports required by section 4(6) or paragraph 30(3) of Schedule A1 was lodged with the court.

5.32(6)   The person who made the decision is not personally liable for costs incurred by any person in relation to an appeal under this rule unless the court makes an order to that effect.

Chapter 8

Exclusions from meetings

[Note: a document required by the Act or these Rules must also contain the standard contents set out in Part 1.]

5.33   Action where person excluded

5.33(1)   In this rule and rules 5.34 and 5.35, an "excluded person" means a person who has taken all steps necessary to attend a virtual meeting or has been permitted by the convener to attend a physical meeting remotely under the arrangements which–

(a)   have been put in place by the convener of the meeting; but

(b)   do not enable that person to attend the whole or part of that meeting.

5.33(2)   Where the chair becomes aware during the course of the meeting that there is an excluded person, the chair may–

(a)   continue the meeting;

(b)   declare the meeting void and convene the meeting again; or

(c)   declare the meeting valid up to the point where the person was excluded and adjourn the meeting.

5.33(3)   Where the chair continues the meeting, the meeting is valid unless–

(a)   the chair decides in consequence of a complaint under rule 5.35 to declare the meeting void and hold the meeting again; or

(b)   the court directs otherwise.

5.33(4)   Without prejudice to paragraph (2), where the chair becomes aware during the course of the meeting that there is an excluded person, the chair may, at the chair's discretion and without an adjournment, declare the meeting suspended for any period up to 1 hour.

5.34   Indication to excluded person

5.34(1)   A creditor who claims to be an excluded person may request an indication of what occurred during the period of that person's claimed exclusion.

5.34(2)   A request under paragraph (1) must be made in accordance with paragraph (3) as soon as reasonably practicable, and in any event, not later than 4pm on the business day following the day on which the exclusion is claimed to have occurred.

5.34(3)   A request under paragraph (1) must be made to–

(a)   the chair, where it is made during the course of the meeting; or

(b)   the convener, where it is made after the meeting.

5.34(4)   Where satisfied that the person making the request is an excluded person, the person to whom the request is made under paragraph (3) must deliver the requested indication to the excluded person as soon as reasonably practicable, and in any event, not later than 4pm on the business day following the day on which the request was made under paragraph (1).

5.35   Complaint

5.35(1)   A person may make a complaint who–

(a)   is, or claims to be, an excluded person; or

(b)   attends the meeting and claims to have been adversely affected by the actual, apparent or claimed exclusion of another person.

5.35(2)   A complaint under paragraph (1) must be made to the appropriate person who is–

(a)   the chair, where it is made during the course of the meeting; or

(b)   the convener, where it is made after the meeting.

5.35(3)   The complaint must be made as soon as reasonably practicable and, in any event, not later than 4pm on the business day following–

(a)   the day on which the person was, appeared, or claimed to be, excluded; or

(b)   where an indication is sought under rule 5.34, the day on which the complainant received the indication.

5.35(4)   The appropriate person must, as soon as reasonably practicable following receipt of the complaint–

(a)   consider whether there is an excluded person;

(b)   where satisfied that there is an excluded person, consider the complaint; and

(c)   where satisfied that there has been prejudice, take such action as the appropriate person considers fit to remedy the prejudice.

5.35(5)   Paragraph (6) applies where the appropriate person is satisfied that the complainant is an excluded person and–

(a)   a resolution was voted on at the meeting during the period of the person's exclusion; and

(b)   the excluded person asserts how the excluded person intended to vote on the resolution.

5.35(6)   Where the appropriate person is satisfied that if the excluded person had voted as that person intended it would have changed the result of the resolution, then the appropriate person must, as soon as reasonably practicable–

(a)   count the intended vote as having been cast in that way;

(b)   amend the record of the result of the resolution;

(c)   where notice of the result of the resolution has been delivered to those entitled to attend the meeting, deliver notice to them of the change and the reason for it; and

(d)   where notice of the result of the resolution has yet to be delivered to those entitled to attend the meeting, the notice must include details of the change and the reason for it.

5.35(7)   Where satisfied that more than one complainant is an excluded person, the appropriate person must have regard to the combined effect of the intended votes.

5.35(8)   The appropriate person must deliver notice to the complainant of any decision as soon as reasonably practicable.

5.35(9)   A complainant who is not satisfied by the action of the appropriate person may apply to the court for directions and any application must be made no more than two business days from the date of receiving the decision of the appropriate person.

Chapter 9

Records

5.36   Record of a decision

5.36(1)   Where a decision is sought using a decision procedure, the convener or chair must make a record of the decision procedure.

5.36(2)   In the case of a meeting, the record must be in the form of a minute of the meeting.

5.36(3)   The record must be authenticated by the convener or chair and must include–

(a)   identification details for the insolvency proceedings;

(b)   a list of the names of the creditors who participated in the decision procedure and their claims;

(c)   where a decision is taken on the election of members of a creditors' committee, the names and addresses of those elected;

(d) a record of any change to the result of the resolution made under rule 5.35(6) and the reason for any such change; and

(e) in any case, a record of every decision made and how creditors voted.

5.36(4) Where a decision is sought using the deemed consent procedure, the convener must make a record of the procedure.

5.36(5) The record under paragraph (4) must be authenticated by the convener and must–

(a) identify the insolvency proceedings;

(b) state whether or not the decision was made; and

(c) contain a list of the creditors who objected to the decision and their claims.

5.36(6) A record made under this rule must also identify any decision procedure (or the deemed consent procedure) by which a decision had previously been sought.

CHAPTER 10

COMPANY MEETINGS

5.37 Company meetings in administration

5.37(1) This rule applies to company meetings in an administration.

5.37(2) Unless the Act or these Rules provide otherwise, a company meeting must be called and conducted, and records of the meeting must be kept–

(a) in accordance with the law of Scotland, including any applicable provision in or made under the Companies Act, in the case of a company incorporated–

(i) in Scotland, or

(ii) outside the United Kingdom other than in a EEA state;

(b) in accordance with the law of that state applicable to meetings of the company in the case of a company incorporated in an EEA state other than the United Kingdom.

5.37(3) Reference to a company meeting called and conducted to resolve, decide or determine a particular matter includes a reference to that matter being resolved, decided or determined by written resolution.

5.37(4) In summoning any company meeting the administrator must have regard to the convenience of the members when fixing the venue.

5.37(5) The chair of a company meeting in an administration must be either the administrator or an appointed person.

5.38 Remote attendance: notification requirements

5.38 When a meeting is to be summoned and held in accordance with section 246A(3), the convener must notify all those to whom notice of the meeting is being given of–

(a) the ability of a person claiming to be an excluded person to request an indication in accordance with rule 5.41;

(b) the ability of a person within rule 5.42(1) to make a complaint in accordance with that rule; and

(c) in either case, the period within which a request or complaint must be made.

5.39   Location of company meetings

5.39(1)   This rule applies to a request to the convener of a meeting under section 246A(9) to specify a place for the meeting.

5.39(2)   The request must be accompanied by–

(a)   a list of the members making or concurring with the request and their voting rights, and

(b)   from each person concurring, confirmation of that person's concurrence.

5.39(3)   The request must be delivered to the convener within seven business days of the date on which the convener delivered the notice of the meeting in question.

5.39(4)   Where the convener considers that the request has been properly made in accordance with the Act and this rule, the convener must–

(a)   deliver notice to all those previously given notice of the meeting–

(i)   that it is to be held at a specified place, and

(ii)   as to whether the date and time are to remain the same or not;

(b)   set a venue (including specification of a place) for the meeting, the date of which must be not later than 28 days after the original date for the meeting; and

(c)   deliver at least 14 days' notice of that venue to all those previously given notice of the meeting;

and the notices required by sub-paragraphs (a) and (c) may be delivered at the same or different times.

5.39(5)   Where the convener has specified a place for the meeting in response to a request to which this rule applies, the chair of the meeting must attend the meeting by being present in person at that place.

5.40   Action where person excluded

5.40(1)   In this rule and rules 5.41 and 5.42, an "excluded person" means a person who has taken all steps necessary to attend a company meeting under the arrangements which–

(a)   have been put in place by the convener of the meeting under section 246A(6); but

(b)   do not enable that person to attend the whole or part of that meeting.

5.40(2)   Where the chair becomes aware during the course of the meeting that there is an excluded person, the chair may–

(a)   continue the meeting;

(b)   declare the meeting void and convene the meeting again; or

(c)   declare the meeting valid up to the point where the person was excluded and adjourn the meeting.

5.40(3)   Where the chair continues the meeting, the meeting is valid unless–

(a)   the chair decides in consequence of a complaint under rule 5.42 to declare the meeting void and hold the meeting again; or

(b)   the court directs otherwise.

5.40(4)   Without prejudice to paragraph (2), where the chair becomes aware during the course of the meeting that there is an excluded person, the chair may, at the chair's discretion and without an adjournment, declare the meeting suspended for any period up to one hour.

5.41   Indication to excluded person

5.41(1)   A person who claims to be an excluded person may request an indication of what occurred during the period of that person's claimed exclusion.

5.41(2)   A request under paragraph (1) must be made in accordance with paragraph (3) as soon as reasonably practicable, and in any event, not later than 4pm on the business day following the day on which the exclusion is claimed to have occurred.

5.41(3)   A request under paragraph (1) must be made to–

(a)   the chair where it is made during the course of the meeting; or

(b)   the convener where it is made after the meeting.

5.41(4)   Where satisfied that the person making the request is an excluded person, the person to whom the request is made under paragraph (3) must deliver the requested indication to the excluded person as soon as reasonably practicable, and in any event, not later than 4pm on the business day following the day on which the request was made under paragraph (1).

5.42   Complaint

5.42(1)   A person may make a complaint who–

(a)   is, or claims to be, an excluded person; or

(b)   attends the meeting and claims to have been adversely affected by the actual, apparent or claimed exclusion of another person.

5.42(2)   A complaint under paragraph (1) must be made to the appropriate person who is–

(a)   the chair, where it is made during the course of the meeting; or

(b)   the convener, where it is made after the meeting.

5.42(3)   The complaint must be made as soon as reasonably practicable and, in any event, not later than 4pm on the business day following–

(a)   the day on which the person was, appeared, or claimed to be, excluded; or

(b)   where an indication is sought under rule 5.41, the day on which the complainant received the indication.

5.42(4)   The appropriate person must, as soon as reasonably practicable following receipt of the complaint,

(a)   consider whether there is an excluded person;

(b)   where satisfied that there is an excluded person, consider the complaint; and

(c)   where satisfied that there has been prejudice, take such action as the appropriate person considers fit to remedy the prejudice.

5.42(5)   Paragraph (6) applies where the appropriate person is satisfied that the complainant is an excluded person and–

(a)   a resolution was voted on at the meeting during the period of the person's exclusion; and

(b)   the excluded person asserts how the excluded person intended to vote on the resolution.

5.42(6)   Where the appropriate person is satisfied that if the excluded person had voted as that person intended it would have changed the result of the resolution, then the appropriate person must, as soon as reasonably practicable–

(a)   count the intended vote as having been cast in that way;

(b)   amend the record of the result of the resolution;

(c)   where notice of the result of the resolution has been delivered to those entitled to attend the meeting, deliver notice to them of the change and the reason for it; and

(d) where notice of the result of the resolution has yet to be delivered to those entitled to attend the meeting, the notice must include details of the change and the reason for it.

5.42(7) Where satisfied that more than one complainant is an excluded person, the appropriate person must have regard to the combined effect of the intended votes.

5.42(8) The appropriate person must deliver notice to the complainant of any decision as soon as reasonably practicable.

5.42(9) A complainant who is not satisfied by the action of the appropriate person may apply to the court for directions and any application must be made no more than two business days from the date of receiving the decision of the appropriate person.

PART 6

PROXIES AND CORPORATE REPRESENTATION

[Note: A document required by the Act or these Rules must also contain the standard contents set out in Part 1.]

6.1 Application and interpretation

6.1(1) This Part applies in any case where a proxy is given in relation to a meeting or insolvency proceedings under the Act or these Rules or where a corporation authorises a person to represent it.

6.1(2) References in this Part to "the chair" are to the chair of the meeting for which a specific proxy is given or at which a continuing proxy is exercised.

6.2 Specific and continuing proxies

6.2(1) A proxy is a document made by a creditor or member which directs or authorises another person (a "proxy-holder") to act as the representative of the creditor or member at a meeting, or meetings, by speaking, voting, abstaining or proposing resolutions.

6.2(2) A proxy may be either–

(a) a specific proxy which relates to a specific meeting; or

(b) a continuing proxy for the insolvency proceedings.

6.2(3) A specific proxy must–

(a) direct the proxy-holder how to act at the meeting by giving specific instructions; or

(b) authorise the proxy-holder to act at the meeting without specific instructions; or

(c) contain both direction and authorisation.

6.2(4) A proxy is to be treated as a specific proxy for the meeting which is identified in the proxy unless it states that it is a continuing proxy for the insolvency proceedings.

6.2(5) A continuing proxy must authorise the proxy-holder to attend, speak, vote or abstain, or to propose resolutions without giving the proxy-holder any specific instructions.

6.2(6) A continuing proxy may be superseded by a proxy for a specific meeting or withdrawn by a written notice to the office-holder.

6.2(7) A creditor or member may appoint more than one person to be proxy-holder but if so–

(a) their appointment is as alternates; and

(b) only one of them may act as proxy-holder at the meeting.

6.2(8)   The proxy-holder must be an individual.

6.3   Blank proxy

6.3(1)   A blank proxy is a document which–

(a)   complies with the requirements in this rule; and

(b)   when completed with the details specified in paragraph (3) will be a proxy as described in rule 6.2.

6.3(2)   A blank proxy must state that the creditor or member named in the document (when completed) appoints a person who is named or identified as the proxy-holder of the creditor or member.

6.3(3)   The specified details are–

(a)   the name and address of the creditor or member;

(b)   either the name of the proxy-holder or the identification of the proxy-holder (e.g. the chair of the meeting);

(c)   a statement that the proxy is either–

    (i)   for a specific meeting, which is identified in the proxy, or

    (ii)   a continuing proxy for the insolvency proceedings; and

(d)   if the proxy is for a specific meeting, instructions as to the extent to which the proxy-holder is directed to vote in a particular way, to abstain or to propose any resolution.

6.3(4)   When it is delivered, a blank proxy must not have inserted in it–

(a)   the name or description of any person as proxy-holder or as a nominee for office-holder; or

(b)   instructions as to how a person appointed as proxy-holder is to act.

6.3(5)   A blank proxy must have a note to the effect that the proxy may be completed with the name of the person or the chair of the meeting who is to be proxy-holder.

6.4   Use of proxies

6.4(1)   A proxy for a specific meeting must be delivered to the chair at or before the meeting.

6.4(2)   A continuing proxy must be delivered to the office-holder and may be exercised at any meeting which begins after the proxy is delivered.

6.4(3)   A proxy may be used at the resumption of the meeting after an adjournment, but if a different proxy is given for use at a resumed meeting, that proxy must be delivered to the chair before the start of the resumed meeting.

6.4(4)   Where a specific proxy directs a proxy-holder to vote for or against a resolution for the nomination or appointment of a person as office-holder, the proxy-holder may, unless the proxy states otherwise, vote for or against (as the proxy-holder thinks fit) a resolution for the nomination or appointment of that person jointly with another or others.

6.4(5)   A proxy-holder may propose a resolution which is one on which the proxy-holder could vote if someone else proposed it.

6.4(6)   Where a proxy gives specific directions as to voting, this does not, unless the proxy states otherwise, prohibit the proxy-holder from exercising discretion as to how to vote on a resolution which is not dealt with by the proxy.

6.4(7)   The chair may require a proxy used at a meeting to be the same as or substantially similar to the blank proxy delivered for that meeting or to a blank proxy previously delivered which has been completed as a continuing proxy.

6.5   Use of proxies by the chair

6.5(1)   Where a proxy appoints the chair (however described in the proxy) as proxy-holder the chair may not refuse to be the proxy-holder.

6.5(2)   Where the office-holder is appointed as proxy-holder but another person acts as chair of the meeting, that other person may use the proxies as if that person were the proxy-holder.

6.5(3)   Where, in a meeting of creditors in an administration, the chair holds a proxy which requires the proxy-holder to vote for a particular resolution and no other person proposes that resolution the chair must propose it unless the chair considers that there is good reason for not doing so.

6.5(4)   If the chair does not propose such a resolution, the chair must as soon as reasonably practicable after the meeting deliver a notice of the reason why that was not done to the creditor or member.

6.6   Right of inspection and delivery of proxies

6.6(1)   A person attending a meeting is entitled, immediately before or in the course of the meeting, to inspect proxies or any statement of claim or documentary evidence of debt delivered to the chair or to any other person in accordance with the notice convening the meeting.

6.6(2)   Where the chair is not the office-holder, the chair must deliver all proxies used for voting at a meeting to the office-holder, as soon as reasonably practicable after the meeting.

6.7   Proxy-holder with financial interest

6.7(1)   A proxy-holder must not vote for a resolution which would–

 (a)   directly or indirectly place the proxy-holder or any associate of the proxy-holder in a position to receive any remuneration, fees or expenses from the company's assets; or

 (b)   fix or change the amount of or the basis of any remuneration, fees or expenses receivable by the proxy-holder or any associate of the proxy-holder out of the company's assets.

6.7(2)   However, a proxy-holder may vote for a resolution described in paragraph (1) if the proxy specifically directs the proxy-holder to vote in that way.

6.7(3)   Where an office-holder is appointed as proxy-holder and that proxy is used under rule 6.5(2) by another person acting as chair, the office-holder is deemed to be an associate of the person acting as chair.

6.8   Resolution conferring authorisation to represent corporation

 [Note: section 434B makes provision for corporate representation in company insolvency proceedings.]

6.8(1)   A person authorised to represent a corporation (other than as proxy-holder) at a meeting of creditors must produce to the chair–

 (a)   the resolution conferring the authority; or

 (b)   a copy of that resolution certified as a true copy by–

   (i)   two directors,

   (ii)   a director and the secretary, or

   (iii)   a director in the presence of a witness who attests the director's signature.

6.8(2)　The resolution conferring the authority must have been signed or subscribed (or in the case of an electronic document, authenticated) by or on behalf of the company in accordance with the Requirements of Writing (Scotland) Act 1995.

6.8(3)　In this rule "authenticated" has the meaning given in the Requirements of Writing (Scotland) Act 1995.

PART 7

THE EU REGULATION

[Note: a document required by the Act or these Rules must also contain the standard contents set out in Part 1]

7.1　Interpretation of this Part

7.1　In this Part–

"winding up proceedings" means insolvency proceedings listed in the United Kingdom entry in Annex A to the EU Regulation other than voluntary arrangements where they relate to individuals, bankruptcy or sequestration.

"conversion into winding up proceedings" refers to an order under Article 51 of the EU Regulation that winding up proceedings of one kind are converted into winding up proceedings of another kind.

7.2　Conversion into winding up proceedings: application

7.2(1)　This rule applies where a member State liquidator in main proceedings applies to the court under Article 51 of the EU Regulation for conversion of–

(a)　a CVA or an administration into winding up proceedings of another kind; or

(b)　winding up proceedings other than a CVA or an administration into a CVA or an administration.

7.2(2)　A statement containing a statutory declaration made by or on behalf of the member State liquidator must be lodged with the court in support of the application.

7.2(3)　The statement must state–

(a)　that main proceedings have been opened in relation to the company in a member State other than the United Kingdom;

(b)　the belief of the person making the statement that conversion of the winding up proceedings would be most appropriate as regards the interests of the local creditors and coherence between the main and secondary insolvency proceedings;

(c)　the kind of winding up proceedings into which, in the opinion of the person making the statement, the winding up proceedings should be converted; and

(d)　all other matters that, in the opinion of the member State liquidator, would assist the court in–

(i)　deciding whether to make an order, and

(ii)　considering whether and, if so, what consequential provision to include.

7.2(4)　The application and the statement must be served upon the company.

7.2(5)　Where the application is for conversion of a CVA or an administration, the application and the statement must also be served upon the supervisor or the administrator, as the case may be.

7.3 Conversion into winding up proceedings: court order

7.3(1) On hearing an application for conversion of winding up proceedings under rule 7.2, the court may, subject to Article 51 of the EU Regulation, make such order as it thinks just.

7.3(2) An order under paragraph (1) may contain such consequential provision as the court thinks just.

7.3(3) An order for conversion of a CVA or an administration into winding up proceedings of another kind may provide that the company be wound up as if a resolution for voluntary winding up under section 84 were passed on the day on which the order is made.

7.4 Proceedings in another member State: duty to give notice

7.4(1) This rule applies where the supervisor of a CVA or an administrator is required to give notice, or provide a copy of a document (including an order of the court) to the court or the registrar of companies.

7.4(2) Where not already required to do so by Article 41 of the EU Regulation, the supervisor or administrator must also give notice or provide a copy to–

(a) any member State liquidator; or

(b) where the supervisor or administrator knows that an application has been made to commence insolvency proceedings in another member State but a member State liquidator has not yet been appointed, the court to which that application has been made.

7.5 Member State liquidator: rules on creditors' participation in proceedings

7.5(1) The provisions in these Rules apply to a member State liquidator's participation in proceedings in accordance with Article 45 of the EU Regulation) in the same manner as they apply to creditors' participation in those proceedings.

7.5(2) In this rule, "creditors' participation"–

(a) includes the following matters–

(i) requesting and being provided with information, including inspecting or obtaining copies of documents or files,

(ii) being provided with notices or other documents,

(iii) participating and voting in decision procedures,

(iv) the establishment and operation of creditor committees,

(v) submitting statements of claim and documentary evidence of debt in respect of debts and receipt of dividends,

(vi) applying to the court and appearing at hearings and

(b) is limited to creditors' participation from the time of the opening of proceedings in accordance with Article 2(8) of the EU Regulation.

7.6 Main proceedings in Scotland: undertaking by office-holder in respect of assets in another member State (Article 36 of the EU Regulation)

7.6(1) This rule applies where an office-holder in main proceedings proposes to give an undertaking under Article 36 of the EU Regulation in respect of assets located in another member State.

7.6(2) In addition to the requirements as to form and content set out in Article 36 the undertaking must contain–

(a) the heading "Proposed Undertaking under Article 36 of the EU Insolvency Regulation (2015/848)";

(b)   identification details for the main proceedings;

(c)   identification and contact details for the office-holder; and

(d)   a description of the effect of the undertaking if approved.

7.6(3)   The proposed undertaking must be delivered to all the local creditors in the member State concerned of whose address the office-holder is aware.

7.6(4)   Where the undertaking is rejected the office-holder must inform all the creditors of the company of the rejection of the undertaking as soon as reasonably practicable.

7.6(5)   Where the undertaking is approved the office-holder must as soon as reasonably practicable–

(a)   send a copy of the undertaking to all the creditors with a notice informing them of the approval of the undertaking and of its effect (so far as they have not already been given this information under paragraph (2)(d));

(b)   where the insolvency proceedings relate to a registered company, deliver a copy of the undertaking to the registrar of companies.

7.6(6)   The office-holder may advertise details of the undertaking in the other member State in such manner as the office-holder thinks fit.

7.7   Main proceedings in another member State: approval of undertaking offered by the member State liquidator to local creditors in the UK

7.7(1)   This rule applies where a member State liquidator proposes an undertaking under Article 36 of the EU Regulation and the secondary proceedings which the undertaking is intended to avoid would be insolvency proceedings to which these Rules apply.

7.7(2)   The decision by the local creditors whether to approve the undertaking must be made by a decision procedure subject to the rules which apply to the approval of a proposed CVA under section 4A of the Act.

7.7(3)   In Part 5, the rules in Chapters 1 to 9 apply to the decision procedure (with any necessary modifications) except for the following–

5.7, 5.12, 5.14, 5.16 to 5.18 and 5.27.

7.7(4)   Where the main proceedings relate to a registered company, the member State liquidator must deliver a copy of the approved undertaking to the registrar of companies.

7.8   Powers of an office-holder or member State liquidator in proceedings concerning members of a group of companies (Article 60 of the EU Regulation)

7.8   Where an office-holder or a member State liquidator makes an application in accordance with paragraph (1)(b) of Article 60 of the EU Regulation the application must state with reasons why the applicant thinks the matters set out in points (i) to (iv) of that paragraph apply.

7.9   Group coordination proceedings (section 2 of Chapter 5 of the EU Regulation)

7.9(1)   This rules applies to an application to open group coordination proceedings by an office-holder.

7.9(2)   The application must be headed "Application under Article 61 of Regulation (EU) 2015/848 to open group coordination proceedings"

7.9(3)   The application must (in addition to the requirements in Article 61 of the EU Regulation) contain–

(a)   identification and contact details for the office-holder making the application;

(b) identification details for the company and the insolvency proceedings by virtue of which the office-holder is making the application;

(c) identification details for the company and the insolvency proceedings in respect of each company which is a member of the group;

(d) contact details for the office-holders and member State liquidators appointed in those proceedings;

(e) identification details for any insolvency proceedings in respect of a member of the group which are not to be subject to the coordination because of an objection to being included; and

(f) if relevant, a copy of any such agreement as is mentioned in Article 66 of the EU Regulation.

7.9(4) An "office-holder" in paragraph (3)(d) includes a person holding office in insolvency proceedings in relation to the company in England and Wales or Northern Ireland, and a member State liquidator.

7.10 Group coordination order (Article 68 of the EU Regulation)

7.10(1) An order opening group coordination proceedings must contain–

(a) details of the matters set out in Article 68(1)(a) to (c) of the EU Regulation;

(b) identification details for the insolvency proceedings by virtue of which the office-holder is making the application;

(c) identification and contact details for the office-holder making the application;

(d) identification details for the insolvency proceedings which are subject to the coordination; and

(e) identification details for any insolvency proceedings for a member of the group which are not subject to the coordination because of an objection to being included.

7.10(2) The office-holder who made the application must deliver a copy of the order to the coordinator and to any person who is, in respect of proceedings subject to the coordination–

(a) an office-holder;

(b) a person holding office in insolvency proceedings in relation to the company in England and Wales or Northern Ireland; and

(c) a member State liquidator.

7.11 Delivery of group coordination order to registrar of companies

7.11 An office-holder in respect of insolvency proceedings subject to coordination must deliver a copy of the group coordination order to the registrar of companies.

7.12 Office-holder's report

7.12(1) This rule applies where, under the second paragraph of Article 70(2) of the EU Regulation, an office-holder is required to give reasons for not following the coordinator's recommendations or the group coordination plan.

7.12(2) Those reasons must be given as soon as reasonably practicable by a notice to all the creditors.

7.12(3) In an administration, those reasons may be given in the next progress report where doing so satisfies the requirement to give the reasons as soon as reasonably practicable.

7.13 Publication of opening of proceedings by a member State liquidator

7.13(1) This rule applies where–

(a) a company subject to insolvency proceedings has an establishment in Scotland; and

(b)   a member State liquidator is required or authorised under Article 28 of the EU Regulation to publish a notice.

7.13(2)   The notice must be gazetted.

7.14   Statement by member State liquidator that insolvency proceedings in another member State are closed etc.

7.14   A statement by a member State liquidator under paragraph 84 of Schedule B1 informing the registrar of companies that a member State liquidator in insolvency proceedings open in another member State consents to the dissolution must contain–

(a)   identification details for the company; and

(b)   identification details for the member State liquidator.

SCHEDULE 1

REVOCATIONS

Introductory rule 2

In this Schedule, "the 1986 Rules" means the Insolvency (Scotland) Rules 1986.

Name	Number	Extent of revocation
The Insolvency (Scotland) Rules 1986	S.I. 1986/1915	Parts 1 and 2 in their entirety. Rules 0.1 to 0.3 and Part 7 (and schedules 3 to 5) insofar as they apply to CVAs and administration.
The Insolvency (Scotland) Amendment Rules 1987	S.I. 1987/1921	Insofar as they amend the 1986 Rules in relation to CVAs and administration.
The Insolvency (Scotland) Amendment Rules 2002	S.I. 2002/2709	The entire S.I.
The Enterprise Act 2002 (Consequential Amendments) (Prescribed Part) (Scotland) Order 2003	S.I. 2003/2108	Part 1 insofar as it amends the 1986 Rules in relation to CVAs and administration.
The Insolvency (Scotland) Regulations 2003	S.I. 2003/2109	Part 2 and Schedule 2 insofar as they amend the 1986 Rules in relation to CVAs and administration.
The Insolvency (Scotland) Amendment Rules 2003	S.I. 2003/2111	Insofar as they amend the 1986 Rules in relation to CVAs and administration.
The Insolvency (Scotland) Amendment Rules 2006	S.I. 2006/734	The entire S.I. except for rule 13.
The Insolvency (Scotland) Amendment Rules 2008	S.I. 2008/662	The entire S.I.
The Insolvency (Scotland) Amendment Rules 2009	S.I. 2009/662	The entire S.I.

Name	Number	Extent of revocation
The Insolvency (Scotland) Amendment (No. 2) Rules 2009	S.I. 2009/2375	The entire S.I.
The Insolvency (Scotland) Amendment Rules 2010	S.I. 2010/688	The entire S.I.
The Tribunals, Courts and Enforcement Act 2007 (Consequential Amendments) Order 2012	S.I. 2012/2404	In schedule 3, paragraph 4(2)-(4).
The Insolvency (Scotland) Amendment Rules 2014	S.S.I. 2014/114	Insofar as it amends the 1986 Rules in relation to administration.
The Insolvency Amendment (EU 2015/848) Regulations 2017	S.I. 2017/702	Part 5 insofar as it amends the 1986 Rules in relation to CVAs and administration.

SCHEDULE 2

TRANSITIONAL AND SAVINGS PROVISIONS

Introductory Rule 4

1   General

1   In this Schedule–

"the 1986 Rules" means the Insolvency (Scotland) Rules 1986 as they had effect immediately before the commencement date and a reference to "1986 Rules" followed by a rule number is a reference to a rule in the 1986 Rules; and

"the commencement date" means the date these Rules come into force.

2   Requirement for office-holder to provide information to creditors on opting out

2(1)   Rule 1.35, which requires an office-holder to provide information to a creditor on the right to elect to opt out under rule 1.34 in the first communication to the creditor, does not apply to–

(a)   an administrator; or

(b)   a supervisor of a CVA

who has delivered the first communication before the commencement date.

2(2)   An administrator or supervisor of a CVA may choose to deliver information on the right to opt out in which case the communication to the creditor must contain the information required by rule 1.35.

3   Electronic communication

3(1)   Rule 1.41(4) does not apply where the relevant proceedings commenced before the commencement date.

3(2)   In this paragraph relevant proceedings are commenced on–

(a)   the delivery of a proposal for a voluntary arrangement to the intended nominee;

(b)   the appointment of an administrator under paragraph 14 or 22 of Schedule B1; or

(c)   the making of an administration order.

4   Statement of affairs

4(1)   The provisions of these Rules relating to statements of affairs in an administration do not apply where relevant proceedings were commenced before the commencement date and the 1986 Rules relating to statements of affairs in an administration continue to apply.

4(2)   In this paragraph relevant proceedings are commenced on–

(a)   the appointment of an administrator under paragraph 14 or 22 of Schedule B1; or

(b)   the making of an administration order;

5   Savings in respect of meetings to be held on or after the commencement date and resolutions by correspondence

5(1)   This paragraph applies where on or after the commencement date–

(a)   a creditors' meeting is to be held as a result of a notice issued before that date in relation to a meeting for which provision is made by the 1986 Rules or the 1986 Act;

(b)   a meeting is to be held as a result of a requisition by a creditor made before that date;

(c)   a meeting is to be held as a result of a statement made under paragraph 52(1)(b) of Schedule B1 and a request is made before that date which obliges the administrator to summon an initial creditors' meeting.

5(2)   Where paragraph (1) applies, Part 5 of these Rules does not apply and the 1986 Rules relating to the following continue to apply–

(a)   the requirement to hold the meeting;

(b)   notice and advertisement of the meeting;

(c)   governance of the meeting;

(d)   recording and taking minutes of the meeting;

(e)   the report or return of the meeting;

(f)   membership and formalities of establishment of creditor's committees where the resolution to form the committee is passed at the meeting;

(g)   the office-holder's resignation or removal at the meeting;

(h)   the office-holder's release;

(i)   fixing the office-holder's remuneration;

(j)   hand-over of assets to a supervisor of a voluntary arrangement where the proposal is approved at the meeting;

(k)   the notice of appointment of a supervisor of a voluntary arrangement where the appointment is made at the meeting;

(l)   claims that remuneration is or that other expenses are excessive; and

(m)   complaints about exclusion at the meeting.

5(3)   Where, before the commencement date, the administrator sought to obtain a resolution by correspondence under 1986 rule 2.28, the 1986 Rules relating to resolutions by correspondence continue to apply and paragraph (2) applies to any meeting that those rules require the office-holder to summon.

6   Progress reports and statements to the registrar of companies

6(1)   Where an obligation to prepare a progress report arises before the commencement date but has not yet been fulfilled 1986 rule 2.38 continues to apply.

6(2)   Where, before the commencement date, a conversion notice under paragraph 83 of Schedule B1 was sent to the registrar of companies, 1986 rule 2.47 continues to apply.

7   Foreign currency

7   Where, before the commencement date, an amount stated in a foreign currency on a statement of claim or evidence of debt (according to the nature of the debt claimed) is converted into sterling by the administrator under 1986 rule 4.17(2), the administrator and any successor to the administrator must continue to use that exchange rate for subsequent conversions of that currency into sterling for the purpose of distributing any assets of the insolvent estate.

8   CVA moratoria

8   Where, before the commencement date, the directors of a company submit to the nominee the documents required under paragraph 6(1) of Schedule A1, the 1986 Rules relating to moratoria continue to apply to that proposed voluntary arrangement.

9   Applications before the court

9   Where an application to court is lodged or a petition is presented under the Act or under the 1986 Rules before the commencement date and the application or petition has not been determined or withdrawn, the 1986 Rules continue to apply to that application or petition.

10   Forms

10   A form contained in Schedule 5 to the 1986 Rules may be used on or after the commencement date if–

(a)   the form is used to provide a statement of affairs pursuant to paragraph 4 of this Schedule;

(b)   the form relates to a meeting held under the 1986 Rules to which paragraph 5 of this Schedule applies;

(c)   the form is required because before the commencement date, the administrator sought to obtain the passing of a resolution by correspondence; or

(d)   the form relates to any application to the court made, or petition presented, before the commencement date.

11   Administrations commenced before 15th September 2003

11   The 1986 Rules continue to apply to administrations where the petition for an administration order was presented before 15th September 2003.

12   Savings in respect of special insolvency rules: limited liability partnerships

12   The 1986 Rules insofar as they apply to insolvency proceedings under the Limited Liability Partnerships Regulations 2001 continue to have effect for the purposes of the application of those Regulations.

SCHEDULE 3

PUNISHMENT OF OFFENCES UNDER THESE RULES

Rule creating offence	General nature of the offence	Mode of prosecution	Maximum Penalty	Daily default fine (if applicable)
1.51(1)	Falsely claiming to be a person entitled to inspect a document with the intention of gaining sight of it.	1. On indictment 2. Summary	2 years' imprisonment, or a fine, or both. 12 months' imprisonment, or a fine not exceeding the statutory maximum, or both.	Not applicable.
3.55(7)	Former administrator failing to file a notice of automatic end of administration and progress report.	Summary	A fine not exceeding level 3 on the standard scale.	One tenth of level 3 on the standard scale.
3.70(2)	Failure to comply with administrator's duties on vacating office.	Summary	A fine not exceeding level 3 on the standard scale.	One tenth of level 3 on the standard scale.
3.93(3)	Administrator failing to deliver progress reports in accordance with rule 3.93(1).	Summary	A fine not exceeding level 3 on the standard scale	One tenth of level 3 on the standard scale.
3.106(1)	Producing false evidence; failing to report false evidence	1. On indictment 2. Summary	2 years' imprisonment, or a fine, or both. 12 months' imprisonment, or a fine not exceeding the statutory maximum, or both.	Not applicable
3.107(7)	Failing to comply with an order requiring attendance for private examination	Summary	3 months' imprisonment, or a fine not exceeding level 5 on the standard scale, or both.	Not applicable

SCHEDULE 4

INFORMATION TO BE INCLUDED IN THE SEDERUNT BOOK

Rule 1.54

PART 1

1   A decision of the Sheriff or the Court of Session under rule 1.56.

PART 3

2   Any statement of affairs delivered to the administrator in accordance with rule 3.29(4) subject to any order of the court made under rule 3.45 that the statement of affairs or a specified part must not be inserted in the sederunt book.

3   Any statement of concurrence delivered to the administrator in accordance with rule 3.31(1).

4   A copy of the notice of the result of the creditors' decision on a proposed revision to the administrator's proposals under rule 3.43.

5   A copy of the certified order delivered to the administrator in accordance with rule 3.49(4).

6   A record of every resolution passed at a creditors' committee meeting as recorded and authenticated in accordance with rule 3.85(3).

7   A copy of every resolution passed under rule 3.86, together with a note that agreement to the resolution of the creditors' committee was obtained.

8   Under rule 3.96:

  (a)   the accounts submitted for audit;

  (b)   the scheme of division; and

  (c)   the final determination in relation to the administrator's outlays and remuneration.

9(1)   Details of the administrator's decision to accept a claim (whether in whole or in part) under rule 3.108(1) including–

  (a)   the amount of the claim accepted;

  (b)   the category of debt, and the value of any security, as decided by the administrator.

9(2)   Details of the administrator's reasons for rejecting a claim (whether in whole or in part) under rule 3.108(3).

9(3)   Any decision of the court on an appeal under rule 3.108(5).

10   Details of–

  (a)   any agreement reached under rule 3.117(2)(b)(i); or

  (b)   any determination made under rule 3.117(2)(b)(ii).

PART 5

11   A record of a decision procedure made in accordance with rule 5.36(1).

12   A record of a deemed consent procedure made in accordance with rule 5.36(4).

13   All proxies used for voting at a meeting, as soon as reasonably practicable after the meeting (where the chair is the office-holder), or as soon as reasonably practicable after their delivery to the office-holder in accordance with rule 6.6(2) (where the chair is not the office-holder).

Insolvency (Scotland) (Receivership and Winding up) Rules 2018

Introduction to the Scottish legislation

Like the Insolvency (England and Wales) Rules 2016 (hereafter "the 2016 Rules"), the Insolvency (Scotland) (Company Voluntary Arrangements and Administration) Rules 2018 (SI 2018/1082 (S.4)) and the Insolvency (Scotland) (Receivership and Winding Up) Rules 2018 (SSI 2018/347) (hereafter collectively "the Scottish corporate insolvency rules") had a protracted gestation period, not least because of the stated policy intention that they be modelled as closely as possible on what are now the 2016 Rules (see further below). This resulted in a further time lag between the introduction of the 2016 Rules and the introduction of the Scottish corporate insolvency rules. It may be noted that unlike the 2016 Rules, the Scottish corporate insolvency rules relate only to corporate insolvency: non-corporate insolvency in Scotland is the subject of separate bankruptcy legislation.

The fact that the Scottish corporate insolvency rules are contained in two separate statutory instruments rather than one is an unfortunate consequence of devolution. As is explained in more detail in the Explanatory Memorandum which accompanies the Insolvency (Scotland) (Company Voluntary Arrangements and Administration) Rules 2018 and the Policy Note which accompanies the Insolvency (Scotland) (Receivership and Winding Up) Rules 2018, competence in respect of corporate insolvency in Scotland is split between the UK and Scottish Parliaments: in broad terms, company voluntary arrangements ("CVAs") and administration are reserved, receivership is devolved, and winding up is partly reserved and partly devolved (see Scotland Act 1998 Sch.5 Section C2). The rule-making power in s.411 of the Insolvency Act 1986 is similarly split: the power to make rules relating to receivership and the devolved aspects of winding up was transferred to the Scottish Ministers by virtue of s.53 of the Scotland Act 1998, while the power to make rules in relation to reserved matters remained with the Secretary of State. This gave rise to a particular complication with regard to winding up, and in light of the fact that there has been debate about exactly which aspects of winding up are reserved and which are devolved, and in order to avoid the rules on winding up being split between two different statutory instruments, the Scotland Act 1998 (Insolvency Functions) Order 2018 (SI 2018/174) made provision for the mutual transfer of the rule-making power in s.411 in relation to winding up, thus enabling the making of all of the rules relating to winding up by *either* the Scottish Ministers *or* the Secretary of State with the consent of the other where relevant. As a matter of policy, it was then agreed that the rules relating to winding up would be made by the Scottish Ministers with the consent of the Secretary of State (see the Policy Note which accompanies the Insolvency (Scotland) (Receivership and Winding Up) Rules 2018). Thus, although having the Scottish corporate insolvency rules in two statutory instruments rather than one cannot be regarded as satisfactory, the position could have been worse: the rules on winding up could have been split between the two statutory instruments. As it is, this at least has been avoided, and one must no doubt be grateful for such small mercies.

Except in relation to limited liability partnerships, special administration regimes and other special insolvency regimes, the Scottish corporate insolvency rules replace the Insolvency (Scotland) Rules 1986 (SI 1986/1915) and the Receivers (Scotland) Regulations 1986 (SI 1986/1917) which, like their counterparts in England and Wales, had been amended on numerous occasions (see Sch.1 to the Insolvency (Scotland) (Company Voluntary Arrangements and Administration) Rules 2018 and Sch.1 to the Insolvency (Scotland) (Receivership and Winding Up) Rules 2018 for details of the relevant amending instruments thereby revoked). Like the 2016 Rules, therefore, the Scottish corporate insolvency rules represent a fresh start up to a point. Like the 2016 Rules, they embody the reforms flowing from the Small Business, Enterprise and Insolvency Act 2015 brought into force in Scotland contemporaneously with them. In addition, they also embody certain reforms to devolved areas of corporate insolvency law which mirror reforms previously introduced to corporate insolvency law in England and Wales and to reserved areas of corporate insolvency law in Scotland by the Legislative Reform (Insolvency) (Miscellaneous Provisions) Order 2010 (SI 2010/18). These reforms had not previously been extended to the devolved areas of corporate insolvency law as a result of an inexplicable delay in bringing the necessary legislation before the Scottish Parliament, a situation which was finally remedied by the Public Service Reform (Insolvency) (Scotland) Order 2016 (SSI 2016/141) and the Public Service Reform (Corporate Insolvency and Bankruptcy) (Scotland) Order 2017 (SSI 2017/209). Like the 2016 Rules, the Scottish corporate insolvency rules seek to modernise the rules in terms of their structure, language and style and, as previously referred to, they also seek to provide as much consistency as possible with the 2016 Rules. Like the 2016 Rules, however, they are largely a consolidation of the previous, amended, Scottish rules, albeit intended to better meet the needs of users including the judiciary, insolvency office-holders, creditors and public officials. The UK Insolvency Service has published a table of derivations and destinations prepared in conjunction with the Accountant in Bankruptcy (who has responsibility for the devolved areas of corporate insolvency law) which can be found on the Insolvency Service website at *https://www.gov.uk/government/news/insolvency-scotland-rules-table-of-destinations-now-available* and on the Accountant in Bankruptcy's website at *https://www.aib.gov.uk/sites/default/files/2018_ci_rules_-_collated_derivation_and_destination_tables.pdf.*

The Scottish corporate insolvency rules were not the subject of formal consultation as such, although there were public consultations prior to the enactment of the Public Service Reform (Insolvency) (Scotland) Order 2016 and the Public Service Reform (Corporate Insolvency and Bankruptcy) (Scotland) Order 2017 which encompassed the possible modernisation of the Scottish corporate insolvency rules. A working group including representation from the insolvency profession was established and considered the content of both statutory instruments in draft and the final impact assessment which accompanies the Insolvency (Scotland) (Receivership and Winding Up) Rules 2018 gives further details of other consultation and discussion which took place during the development of the Scottish corporate insolvency rules, including with the UK Insolvency Service, the Scottish Courts and Tribunals Service, the Scottish Civil Justice Council, Companies House and other stakeholders.

Like the 2016 Rules, the Scottish corporate insolvency rules have introduced "common parts", which are repeated in each of the statutory instruments, and the comments made in relation to this approach in the 2016 Rules apply equally to the Scottish corporate insolvency rules. Similarly, the Scottish corporate insolvency rules eschew the use of prescribed forms and instead set out details of required information. In the final impact assessment which accompanies the Insolvency (Scotland) (Receivership and Winding Up) Rules 2018, however, it is stated that the Accountant in Bankruptcy will produce non-statutory template forms containing the prescribed information which will be made available on their website for the use of all stakeholders, although at the time of writing, these were not yet available. As in England and Wales, however, the break with statutory forms will remain incomplete due to the continuing use of such forms in other areas.

The Scottish corporate insolvency rules came into force on 6 April 2019, subject to the transitional and savings provisions set out in Sch.2 to each statutory instrument. Both instruments were subject to negative parliamentary procedure. The Joint Committee on Statutory Instruments reported the Insolvency (Scotland) (Company Voluntary Arrangements and Administration) Rules 2018 for defective drafting in two respects (see their 38th Report of Session 2017–19), but noted that the Department for Business, Energy and Industrial Strategy had provided clarification on both points and had undertaken to make appropriate clarificatory amendments at the first opportunity. The Economy, Energy and Fair Work Committee made no comments on the Insolvency (Scotland) (Receivership and Winding Up) Rules 2018 (see Scottish Parliament Official Report, Economy, Energy and Fair Work Committee, Tuesday 11 December 2018, Session 5, pp.26–27). Anecdotal evidence suggests that some problematic issues have already been identified, including some which flow through from the 2016 Rules. It is therefore to be expected that some amendments might be made to the Scottish corporate insolvency rules in due course.

As referred to above, an Explanatory Memorandum accompanies the Insolvency (Scotland) (Company Voluntary Arrangements and Administration) Rules 2018 and a Policy Note and final impact assessment accompany the Insolvency (Scotland) (Receivership and Winding Up) Rules 2018. These documents contain helpful summaries of the policy background and the main changes brought about by the Scottish corporate insolvency rules. The final impact assessment also states that the Accountant in Bankruptcy will, where appropriate, prepare and publish on their website guidance to support stakeholders in implementing the new Scottish corporate insolvency rules, although at the time of writing, no such guidance was yet available. Like the 2016 Rules, the Scottish corporate insolvency rules themselves also contain non-legislative notes to assist users.

Like the 2016 Rules, the Insolvency (Scotland) (Company Voluntary Arrangements and Administration) Rules 2018 contain provision for their periodic review with the first report to be published before the end of the period of five years after they come into force. Oddly, the Insolvency (Scotland) (Receivership and Winding Up) Rules 2018 contain no such specific provision, but the accompanying final impact assessment states that the Accountant in Bankruptcy will carry out continuous monitoring of the provisions post-commencement.

Insolvency (Scotland) (Receivership and Winding up) Rules 2018

(Scottish SI 2018/347)

Made on 13 November 2018 by the Scottish Ministers under s.411(1)(b), (2) and (2A) of the Insolvency Act 1986 and all other powers enabling them to do so and laid before the Scottish Parliament 14 November 2018. The Secretary of State has consented to these Rules in accordance with art.2(2) of the Scotland Act 1998 (Insolvency Functions) Order 2018 (SI 2018/174). Operative from 6 April 2019

[**Note**: These Rules from 6 April 2019 revoke and replace the Insolvency (Scotland) Rules 1986 (SI 1986/1915 (S.139)) Pt 3–6 (and Schs 1–2) and rr.0.1–0.3 and Pt 7 (and Schs 3–5) insofar as they apply to receivership and winding up, subject to transitional and savings provisions in Sch.2 to these Rules. The Insolvency (Scotland) Rules 1986 are reproduced in the 21st edition of this *Guide*.]

CONTENTS

1   Citation and commencement

1   These Rules may be cited as the Insolvency (Scotland) (Receivership and Winding up) Rules 2018 and come into force on 6th April 2019.

2   Revocations

2   The enactments listed in the first column of the table in schedule 1 are revoked to the extent specified in the third column of that table.

3   Extent and application

3(1)   These Rules extend to Scotland only.

3(2)   These Rules as they relate to receivership under Part 3 of the Insolvency Act 1986 apply to receivers appointed under section 51 of that Act (Receivers (Scotland)).

3(3)   These Rules as they relate to winding up under Parts 4 and 5 of the Act apply in relation to companies which the courts in Scotland have jurisdiction to wind up.

4   Transitional and savings provisions

4   The transitional and savings provisions set out in schedule 2 have effect.

5   Punishment of offences

5   Schedule 3 sets out the maximum penalties for offences under these Rules.

PART 1

SCOPE, INTERPRETATION, TIME AND RULES ABOUT DOCUMENTS

CHAPTER 1

SCOPE OF THESE RULES

1.1 Scope

1.1(1) These Rules are made to give effect in Scotland in relation to receivership and winding up to–

(a) Parts 3 to 7 of the Insolvency Act 1986; and

(b) the EU Regulation.

1.1(2) Consequently references to insolvency proceedings and requirements relating to such proceedings are, unless the context requires otherwise, limited to insolvency proceedings in respect of Parts 3 to 5 of the Act and the EU Regulation (whether or not court proceedings).

CHAPTER 2

INTERPRETATION

[Note: the terms which are defined in rule 1.2 include some terms defined by the Act for limited purposes which are applied generally by these Rules. Such terms have the meaning given by the Act for those limited purposes.]

1.2 Defined terms

1.2(1) In these Rules unless the context otherwise requires–

"the Act" means the Insolvency Act 1986, and–

(a) a reference to a numbered section without mention of another Act is to that section of the Act; and

(b) a reference to schedule B1 is to that schedule of the Act;

"Companies Act" means the Companies Act 2006;

"Accountant in Bankruptcy" (or "AiB") is to be construed in accordance with section 199 of the Bankruptcy (Scotland) Act 2016;

"appointed person" means a person who meets the requirements in paragraph (2) who is appointed by an office-holder;

"Article 1.2 undertaking" means one of the following within the meaning of Article 1.2 of the EU Regulation–

    (a) an insurance undertaking;

    (b) a credit institution;

    (c) an investment undertaking which provides services involving the holding of funds or securities for third parties;

    (d) a collective investment undertaking;

[Note "associate" is defined in section 435];

"attendance" and "attend"–

> a person attends by being present, by attending remotely in accordance with section 246A or rule 8.6, or by participating in a virtual meeting; and a person may attend a meeting in person, by proxy or by corporate representative (in accordance with section 434B of the Act) or section 323 of the Companies Act, as applicable);

"authenticate" means to authenticate in accordance with rule 1.6;

"authorised deposit-taker" means a person with permission under Part 4A of the Financial Services and Markets Act 2000 to accept deposits; this definition must be read with–

> (a)   section 22 of that Act and any relevant order under that section; and

> (b)   schedule 2 of that Act;

"blank proxy" is to be interpreted in accordance with rule 9.3;

[Note: "business day" is defined in section 251];

"centre of main interests" has the same meaning as in the EU Regulation;

[Note: "connected" used of a person in relation to a company is defined in section 249 of the Act];

"consumer" means an individual acting for purposes that are wholly or mainly outside that individual's trade, business, craft or profession;

[Note: "contributory" is defined in section 79];

"convener" means an office-holder or other person who seeks a decision in accordance with Part 8 (decision making) of these Rules;

[Note: "the court" is defined in section 251];

"CVA" means a voluntary arrangement in relation to a company under Part 1 of the Act;

"CVA and Administration Rules" means the Insolvency (Scotland) (Company Voluntary Arrangement and Administration) Rules 2018;

"decision date" and "decision procedure" are to be interpreted in accordance with rule 8.2;

[Note: "deemed consent procedure" is defined in section 246ZF (also see rule 8.7)];

"deliver" and "delivery" are to be interpreted in accordance with Chapter 9 of Part 1 of these Rules;

"deliver to the creditors" and similar expressions in these Rules and the Act are to be interpreted in accordance with rule 1.33;

"document" includes a written notice or statement or anything else in writing capable of being delivered to a recipient;

[Note: "EU Regulation" is defined in section 436 as "Regulation (EU) 2015/848 of the European Parliament and the Council of 20 May 2015 on insolvency proceedings"];

[Note: "the Gazette" has the meaning given in section 251];

"Gazette notice" means a notice which is, has been or is to be gazetted;

"to gazette" means to advertise in the Gazette, whether electronically or otherwise;

[Note: "hire-purchase agreement" is defined by section 436(1) as having the same meaning as in the Consumer Credit Act 1974];

"identification details" and similar references to information identifying persons, proceedings, etc. are to be interpreted in accordance with rule 1.7;

"insolvent estate" means the company's assets;

"IP number" means the number assigned to an office-holder as an insolvency practitioner by the Secretary of State;

"local creditor" has the same meaning as in Article 2(11) of the EU Regulation;

"main proceedings" means proceedings opened in accordance with Article 3(1) of the EU Regulation and falling within the definition of insolvency proceedings in Article 2(4) of the EU Regulation and which–

    (a)   in relation to Scotland, are set out in Annex A to that Regulation under the heading "United Kingdom"; and

    (b)   in relation to another member State, are set out in Annex A under the heading relating to that member State;

"meeting" in relation to a company's creditors or contributories means either a "physical meeting" or a "virtual meeting";

"member State liquidator" means a person falling within the definition of "insolvency practitioner" in Article 2(5) of the EU Regulation appointed in proceedings to which the EU Regulation applies in a member State other than the United Kingdom;

"nominated person" means a person who has been required under section 66 or 131 to make out and submit a statement as to the affairs of a company in receivership or being wound up by the court;

"non-EU proceedings" means insolvency proceedings which are not main, secondary or territorial proceedings;

"office-holder" means a person who under the Act or these Rules holds an office in relation to insolvency proceedings and includes a nominee;

"the official rate", in relation to interest, is defined in section 251;

"petitioner" includes a person who has been substituted as such;

"physical meeting" has the meaning given by rule 8.2;

"prescribed part" has the same meaning as in section 176A(2)(a) and the Insolvency Act 1986 (Prescribed Part) Order 2003;

"progress report" means a report which complies with Chapter 1 of Part 7 (reporting, accounts, remuneration, claims and distributions);

[Note: "property" is defined in section 436(1)];

"proxy" and "proxy-holder" are to be interpreted in accordance with rule 9.2;

"qualified to act as an insolvency practitioner", in relation to a company, is to be interpreted in accordance with Part 13 of the Act;

[Note: "records" is defined in section 436(1)];

"secondary proceedings" means proceedings opened in accordance with Article 3(2) and (3) of the EU Regulation and falling within the definition of insolvency proceedings in Article 2(4) of the EU Regulation and which–

    (a)   in relation to Scotland, are set out in Annex A to that Regulation under the heading "United Kingdom"; and

(b)   in relation to another member State, are set out in Annex A under the heading relating to that member State;

"serve" and "service" are to be interpreted in respect of a particular document by reference to the Rules of Court;

"standard contents" means–

(a)   for a Gazette notice, the standard contents set out in Chapter 5 of Part 1;

(b)   for a notice to be advertised other than in the Gazette, the standard contents set out in Chapter 6 of Part 1;

(c)   for a document to be delivered to–

(i)   the registrar of companies;

(ii)   AiB;

the standard contents set out in Chapter 7 of Part 1;

(d)   for notices to be delivered to other persons, the standard contents set out in Chapter 8 of Part 1;

"standard fee for copies" means 15 pence per A4 or A5 page or 30 pence per A3 page;

"statement of claim" is to be interpreted in accordance with rule 7.16;

"temporary administrator" means a temporary administrator referred to in Article 52 of the EU Regulation;

"territorial proceedings" means proceedings opened in accordance with Article 3(2) and (4) of the EU Regulation which fall within the definition of insolvency proceedings in Article 2(4) of the EU Regulation and–

(a)   in relation to Scotland, are set out in Annex A to that Regulation under the heading "United Kingdom"; and

(b)   in relation to another member State, are set out in Annex A under the heading relating to that member State;

"venue" in relation to any proceedings, attendance before the court, decision procedure or meeting means the time, date and place or platform for the proceedings, attendance, decision procedure or meeting;

"virtual meeting" has the meaning given by rule 8.2;

"winding up by the court" means a winding up under section 122, 124A or 221;

[Note: "writing" is to be construed in accordance with section 436B];

"written resolution" in respect of a private company means a written resolution passed in accordance with Chapter 2 of Part 13 of the Companies Act.

1.2(2)   An appointed person in relation to a company must be–

(a)   qualified to act as an insolvency practitioner in relation to that company; or

(b)   a person experienced in insolvency matters who is–

(i)   a member or employee of the office-holder's firm, or

(ii)   an employee of the office-holder.

1.2(3)   A fee or remuneration is chargeable when the work to which it relates is done.

CHAPTER 3

CALCULATION OF TIME PERIODS

1.3   Periods of time expressed in days

1.3(1)   This rule applies to the calculation of a period of time expressed in days.

1.3(2)   A period of time expressed as a number of days is to be computed as clear days.

1.3(3)   In this rule, "clear days" means that in computing the number of days–

(a)   the day on which the period begins; and

(b)   if the end of the period is defined by reference to an event, the day on which that event occurs,

are not included.

1.4   Periods of time expressed in months

1.4(1)   This rule applies to the calculation of a period of time expressed in months.

1.4(2)   The beginning and the end of a period expressed in months are to be determined as follows–

(a)   if the beginning of the period is specified–

    (i)   the month in which the period ends is the specified number of months after the month in which it begins; and

    (ii)   the date in the month on which the period ends is–

        (aa) the day before the date corresponding to the date in the month on which it begins, or

        (bb) if there is no such date in the month in which it ends, the last day of that month;

(b)   if the end of the period is specified–

    (i)   the month in which the period begins is the specified number of months before the month in which it ends; and

    (ii)   the date in the month on which the period begins is–

        (aa) the day after the date corresponding to the date in the month on which it ends, or

        (bb) if there is no such date in the month in which it begins, the last day of that month.

CHAPTER 4

FORM AND CONTENT OF DOCUMENTS

1.5   Requirement for writing and form of documents

1.5(1)   A notice or statement must be in writing unless the Act or these Rules provide otherwise.

1.5(2)   A document in electronic form must be capable of being–

(a)   read by the recipient in electronic form; and

(b)   reproduced by the recipient in hard-copy form.

1.6   Authentication

1.6(1)   A document in electronic form is authenticated–

(a)   if the identity of the sender is confirmed in a manner specified by the recipient; or

(b)   where the recipient has not so specified, if the communication contains or is accompanied by a statement of the identity of the sender and the recipient has no reason to doubt the truth of that statement.

1.6(2) A document in hard copy form is authenticated if it is signed.

1.6(3) If a document is authenticated by the signature of an individual on behalf of–

(a) a body of persons, the document must also state the position of that individual in relation to the body;

(b) a body corporate of which the individual is the sole member, the document must also state that fact.

1.7 Information required to identify persons and insolvency proceedings etc.

1.7(1) Where the Act or these Rules require a document to identify, or to contain identification details in respect of, a person or insolvency proceedings, or to provide contact details for an office-holder, the information set out in the table must be given.

1.7(2) Where a requirement relates to a proposed office-holder, the information set out in the table in respect of an office-holder must be given with any necessary adaptations.

Company where it is the subject of the insolvency proceedings	In the case of a registered company–
	(a) the registered name;
	(b) for a company incorporated in Scotland under the Companies Act or a previous Companies Act, its registered number;
	(c) for a company incorporated outside the United Kingdom–
	   (i) the country or territory in which it is incorporated,
	   (ii) the number, if any, under which it is registered, and
	   (iii) the number, if any, under which it is registered as an overseas company under Part 34 of the Companies Act.
	In the case of an unregistered company–
	(d) its name; and
	(e) the postal address of any principal place of business.

Company other than one which is the subject of the insolvency proceedings	In the case of a registered company–
	(f) the registered name;
	(g) for a company incorporated in any part of the United Kingdom under the Companies Act or a previous Companies Act, its registered number;
	(h) for a company incorporated outside the United Kingdom–
	   (i) the country or territory in which it is incorporated,
	   (ii) the number, if any, under which it is registered; and
	   (iii) the number, if any, under which it is registered as an overseas company under Part 34 of the Companies Act;
	In the case of an unregistered company–
	(i) its name, and
	(j) the postal address of any principal place of business.

Office-holder	(k) the name of the office-holder; and (l) the nature of the appointment held by the office-holder.
Contact details for an office-holder	(m) a postal address for the office-holder; and (n) either an email address, or a telephone number, through which the office-holder may be contacted.

Insolvency proceedings	(o) information identifying the company to which the insolvency proceedings relate;
	(p) if the insolvency proceedings are, or are to be, conducted in a court–
	   (i) the full name of the court and, if applicable,
	   (ii) any number assigned to those insolvency proceedings by the court.

1.8   Reasons for stating that insolvency proceedings are or will be main, secondary etc. under the EU Regulation

1.8   Where these Rules require reasons to be given for a statement that proceedings are or will be main, secondary or territorial or non-EU proceedings, the reasons must include–

(a)   the company's centre of main interests;

(b)   the place of the company's registered office within the meaning of Article 3(1) of the EU Regulation and where appropriate an explanation why this is not the same as the centre of main interests;

(c)   a statement that there is no registered office if that be the case in non-EU proceedings.

1.9   Prescribed format of documents

1.9(1)   Where a rule sets out the required contents of a document any title required by the rule must appear at the beginning of the document.

1.9(2)   Any other contents required by the rule (or rules where more than one apply to a particular document) must be provided in the order listed in the rule (or rules) or in another order which the maker of the document considers would be convenient for the intended recipient.

1.10   Variations from prescribed contents

1.10(1)   Where a rule sets out the required contents of a document, the document may depart from the required contents if–

(a)   the circumstances require such a departure (including where the requirement is not applicable in the particular case); or

(b)   the departure (whether or not intentional) is immaterial.

1.10(2)   However this rule does not apply to the required content of a statutory demand on a company set out in rule 5.3.

CHAPTER 5

STANDARD CONTENTS OF GAZETTE NOTICES AND THE GAZETTE AS EVIDENCE ETC.

[Note: (1) the requirements in Chapter 5 must be read with rule 1.7 which sets out the information required to identify an office-holder, a company etc.

Note: (2) this Chapter does not apply to the notice of a liquidator's appointment prescribed under section 109 by S.I. 1987/752.]

1.11   Contents of notices to be gazetted under the Act or Rules

1.11(1)   Where, in accordance with the Act or these Rules, a notice is to be gazetted, the notice must contain the standard contents set out in this Chapter (in addition to any content specifically required by the Act or any other provision of these Rules).

1.11(2)   Information which this Chapter requires to be included in a Gazette notice may be omitted if it is not reasonably practicable to obtain it.

1.12   Standard contents of Gazette notices

1.12(1)   A Gazette notice must identify the insolvency proceedings and, if it is relevant to the particular notice, identify the office-holder and state–

(a) the office-holder's contact details;

(b) the office-holder's IP number;

(c) the name of any person other than the office-holder who may be contacted about the insolvency proceedings; and

(d) the date of the office-holder's appointment.

1.12(2) A Gazette notice relating to a registered company must also state–

(a) its registered office;

(b) any principal trading address if this is different from its registered office;

(c) any name under which it was registered in the period of 12 months before the date of the commencement of the insolvency proceedings which are the subject of the Gazette notice; and

(d) any other name or style (not being a registered name)–

    (i) under which the company carried on business, and

    (ii) in which any debt owed to a creditor was incurred.

1.12(3) A Gazette notice relating to an unregistered company must also identify the company and specify any name or style–

(a) under which the company carried on business; and

(b) in which any debt owed to a creditor was incurred.

1.12(4) Paragraph (1) does not apply to a notice under rule 12.4(3) (permission to act as a director: first excepted case).

1.13 The Gazette: evidence, variations, errors and timing

1.13(1) Where a notice is gazetted under the Act or these Rules a copy of the Gazette containing the notice is evidence of any facts stated in the notice.

1.13(2) Where the Act or these Rules require an order of the court to be gazetted, a copy of the Gazette containing the notice of the order may be produced in any proceedings as conclusive evidence that the order was made on the date specified in the Gazette notice.

1.13(3) Where an order of the court which is gazetted has been varied, or any matter has been erroneously or inaccurately gazetted, the person whose responsibility it was to gazette the order or other matter must, as soon as is reasonably practicable, cause the variation to be gazetted or a further entry to be made in the Gazette for the purpose of correcting the error or inaccuracy.

1.13(4) A Gazette notice, variation or correction is taken to be gazetted or published on the date it first appears in either electronic or hard copy form.

CHAPTER 6

STANDARD CONTENTS OF NOTICES ADVERTISED OTHERWISE THAN IN THE GAZETTE

[Note: the requirements in Chapter 6 must be read with rule 1.7 which sets out the information required to identify an office-holder, a company etc.]

1.14   Standard contents of notices advertised otherwise than in the Gazette

1.14(1)   Where, in accordance with the Act or these Rules, a notice is to be advertised otherwise than in the Gazette, the notice must contain the standard contents set out in this rule (in addition to any content specifically required by the Act or any other provision of these Rules).

1.14(2)   A notice relating to a company must also identify the insolvency proceedings and state–

(a)   the company's principal trading address;

(b)   any name under which the company was registered in the 12 months before the date of the commencement of the insolvency proceedings which are the subject of the notice; and

(c)   any name or style (not being a registered name)–

    (i)   under which the company carried on business, and

    (ii)   in which any debt owed to a creditor was incurred.

1.14(3)   A notice must, if it is relevant to the particular notice, identify the office-holder and specify the office-holder's contact details.

1.14(4)   Information which this rule requires to be included in a notice may be omitted if it is not reasonably practicable to obtain it.

1.15   Non-Gazette notices: clear and comprehensible

1.15   Information which this Chapter requires to be stated in a notice must be so stated in a way that is clear and comprehensible.

CHAPTER 7

STANDARD CONTENTS OF DOCUMENTS TO BE DELIVERED TO THE REGISTRAR OF COMPANIES AND THE ACCOUNTANT IN BANKRUPTCY

[Note: the requirements in Chapter 7 must be read with rule 1.7 which sets out the information required to identify an office-holder, a company etc.]

1.16   Standard contents of documents delivered to the registrar of companies and the Accountant in Bankruptcy

1.16(1)   Where the Act or these Rules require a document to be delivered to–

(a)   the registrar of companies; or

(b)   AiB,

the document must contain the standard contents set out in this Chapter (in addition to any content specifically required by the Act or any other provision of these Rules).

1.16(2)   A document of more than one type must satisfy the requirements which apply to each.

1.17   Registrar of companies and Accountant in Bankruptcy: covering notices

1.17(1)   This rule applies where the Act or these Rules require an office-holder to deliver any of the documents mentioned in paragraph (2) to (one or both of)–

(a)   the registrar of companies; or

(b)   AiB.

1.17(2)   The documents are–

(a)   an account (including a final account) or a summary of receipts and payments;

(b)   an receiver's report under section 67(1);

(c)   a court order;

(d)   a declaration of solvency;

(e)   notice of the liquidator's resignation under section 171(5);

(f)   notice of the liquidator's death under rule 3.8;

(g)   notice to AiB that a liquidator has vacated office on loss of qualification to act under rule 5.31(2)(b);

(h)   any report including a progress report (including a final progress report);

(i)   an undertaking given under Article 36 of the EU Regulation.

1.17(3)   The office-holder must deliver with a document mentioned in paragraph (1) and (2) a notice containing the standard contents required by this Part.

1.17(4)   Such a notice may relate to more than one document where those documents relate to the same insolvency proceedings and are delivered together to the registrar of companies or delivered together to AiB.

1.18   Standard contents of all documents

1.18(1)   A document to be delivered to the registrar of companies or AiB must–

(a)   identify the company;

(b)   state–

    (i)   the nature of the document,

    (ii)   the section (or paragraph) of the Act or the rule under which the document is delivered,

    (iii)   the date of the document,

    (iv)   the name and address of the person delivering the document, and

    (v)   the capacity in which that person is acting in relation to the company; and

(c)   be authenticated by the person delivering the document.

1.18(2)   Where the person delivering the document is the office-holder, the address may be omitted if it was previously notified to the same authority (the registrar or AiB) in the insolvency proceedings, and is unchanged.

1.19   Standard contents of documents relating to the office of office-holders

1.19(1)   A document relating to the office of the office-holder must also identify the office-holder and state–

(a)   the date of the event of which notice is delivered or of the notice (as applicable);

(b)   where the document relates to an appointment, the person, body or court making the appointment;

(c)   where the document relates to the termination of an appointment, the reason for that termination; and

(d)   the contact details for the office-holder.

1.19(2) Where the person delivering the document is the office-holder, the address may be omitted if in the insolvency proceedings–

(a) in the case of delivery to the registrar of companies it has previously been notified to the registrar of companies;

(b) in the case of delivery to AiB it has previously been notified to AiB,

and the address is unchanged.

1.20 Standard contents of documents relating to other documents

1.20 A document relating to another document must also state–

(a) the nature of the other document;

(b) the date of the other document; and

(c) where the other document relates to a period of time, the period of time to which it relates.

1.21 Standard contents of documents relating to court orders

1.21 A document relating to a court order must also specify–

(a) the nature of the order;

(b) the name of the court; and

(c) the date of the order.

1.22 Standard contents of returns or reports of decisions

1.22 A return or report of a decision procedure, deemed consent procedure or meeting must also state–

(a) the purpose of the procedure or meeting;

(b) a description of the procedure or meeting used;

(c) in the case of a decision procedure or meeting, the venue;

(d) in the case of a deemed consent procedure, the date the decision was deemed to have been made;

(e) whether, in the case of a meeting, the required quorum was in place; and

(f) the outcome (including any decisions made or resolutions passed).

1.23 Standard contents of returns or reports of matters considered by company members by written resolution

1.23 A return or report of a matter, consideration of which has been sought from the members of a company by written resolution, must also state–

(a) the purpose of the consideration; and

(b) the outcome of the consideration (including any resolutions passed).

1.24 Standard contents of documents relating to other events

1.24 A document relating to any other event must also state–

(a) the nature of the event, including the section (or paragraph) of the Act or the rule under which it took place; and

(b) the date on which the event occurred.

CHAPTER 8

STANDARD CONTENTS OF NOTICES FOR DELIVERY TO OTHER PERSONS ETC.

[Note: the requirements in Chapter 8 must be read with rule 1.7 which sets out the information required to identify an office-holder, a company etc.]

1.25 Standard contents of notices to be delivered to persons other than the registrar of companies or Accountant in Bankruptcy

1.25(1) Where the Act or these Rules require a notice to be delivered to a person other than the registrar of companies or AiB in respect of insolvency proceedings under Parts 3 to 5 of the Act or the EU Regulation, the notice must contain the standard contents set out in this Chapter (in addition to any content specifically required by the Act or another provision of these Rules).

1.25(2) A notice of more than one type must satisfy the requirements which apply to each.

1.25(3) The requirements in respect of a document which is to be delivered to another person at the same time as the registrar of companies or AiB may be satisfied by delivering to that other person a copy of the document delivered to the registrar or AiB.

1.26 Standard contents of all notices

1.26 A notice must–

 (a) state the nature of the notice;

 (b) identify the insolvency proceedings;

 (c) state the section (or paragraph) of the Act or the rule under which the notice is given; and

 (d) in the case of a notice delivered by the office-holder, state the contact details for the office-holder.

1.27 Standard contents of notices relating to the office of office-holders

1.27 A notice relating to the office of the office-holder must also identify the office-holder and state–

 (a) the date of the event of which notice is delivered;

 (b) where the notice relates to an appointment, the person, body or court making the appointment; and

 (c) where the notice relates to the termination of an appointment, the reason for that termination.

1.28 Standard contents of notices relating to documents

1.28 A notice relating to a document must also state–

 (a) the nature of the document;

 (b) the date of the document; and

 (c) where the document relates to a period of time, the period of time to which the document relates.

1.29 Standard contents of notices relating to court proceedings or orders

1.29 A notice relating to court proceedings must also identify those proceedings and if the notice relates to a court order state–

 (a) the nature of the order; and

 (b) the date of the order.

1.30   Standard contents of notices of the results of decisions

1.30   A notice of the result of a decision procedure, deemed consent procedure or meeting must also state–

(a)   the purpose of the procedure or meeting;

(b)   a description of the procedure or meeting used;

(c)   in the case of a decision procedure or meeting, the venue;

(d)   in the case of a deemed consent procedure, the date the decision was deemed to have been made;

(e)   whether, in the case of a meeting, the required quorum was in place; and

(f)   the outcome (including any decisions made or resolutions passed).

1.31 Standard contents of returns or reports of matters considered by company members by written resolution

1.31 A return or report of a matter, consideration of which has been sought from the members of a company by written resolution, must also specify–

(a)   the purpose of the consideration; and

(b)   the outcome of the consideration (including any resolutions passed).

CHAPTER 9

DELIVERY OF DOCUMENTS AND OPTING OUT (SECTIONS 246C AND 248A)

1.32   Application of Chapter

[Note: the registrar's rules include provision for the electronic delivery of documents.]

1.32(1)   Subject to paragraph (2), this Chapter applies where a document is required under the Act or these Rules to be delivered, lodged, forwarded, furnished, given, sent, or submitted in respect of insolvency proceedings under Parts 3 to 5 of the Act or the EU Regulation unless the Act, a rule or an order of the court makes different provision.

1.32(2)   Rules 1.41 and 1.43 to 1.46 do not apply to–

(a)   the lodging of any petition or application or other document with the court;

(b)   the service of any application or other document lodged with the court;

(c)   the service of any order of the court; or

(d)   the delivery of a document to the registrar of companies or AiB, except in accordance with paragraph (3) or (4).

1.32(3)   In respect of delivery of a document to the registrar of companies–

(a)   subject to sub-paragraph (b) only the following rules in this Chapter apply: rules 1.38 (postal delivery of documents), 1.39 (delivery by document exchange), 1.40 (personal delivery) and 1.47 (proof of delivery of documents);

(b)   requirements imposed under section 1068 and rules made under section 1117 of the Companies Act apply to determine the date when any document is received by the registrar of companies.

1.32(4)   In respect of delivery of a document to AiB, of the rules in this Chapter only those mentioned in paragraph (3)(a) apply.

1.32(5)   Where a document is required or permitted to be served at a company's registered office service may be effected at a previous registered office in accordance with section 87(2) of the Companies Act.

1.32(6)   In the case of an overseas company service may be effected in any manner provided for by section 1139(2) of the Companies Act.

1.33   Delivery to the creditors and opting out

1.33(1)   Where the Act or a rule requires an office-holder to deliver a document to the creditors, or the creditors in a class, the requirement is satisfied by the delivery of the document to all such creditors of whose address the office-holder is aware other than opted-out creditors unless the opt out does not apply.

1.33(2)   Where a creditor has opted out from receiving documents, the opt out does not apply to–

(a)   a notice which the Act requires to be delivered to all creditors without expressly excluding opted-out creditors;

(b)   a notice of a change in the office-holder or the contact details for the office-holder;

(c)   a notice as provided for by section 246C(2) (notices of distributions, intended distributions and notices required to be given by court order); or

(d)   a document which these Rules require to accompany a notice within sub-paragraphs (a) to (c).

1.33(3)   The office-holder must begin to treat a creditor as an opted-out creditor as soon as reasonably practicable after delivery of the creditor's election to opt out.

1.33(4)   An office-holder in any consecutive insolvency proceedings of a different kind under Parts 3 to 5 of the Act in respect of the same company who is aware that a creditor was an opted-out creditor in the earlier insolvency proceedings must treat the creditor as an opted out creditor in the consecutive insolvency proceedings.

1.34   Creditor's election to opt out

1.34(1)   A creditor may at any time elect to be an opted-out creditor.

1.34(2)   The creditor's election to opt out must be by a notice in writing authenticated and dated by the creditor.

1.34(3)   The creditor must deliver the notice to the office-holder.

1.34(4)   A creditor becomes an opted-out creditor when the notice is delivered to the office-holder.

1.34(5)   An opted-out creditor–

(a)   will remain an opted-out creditor for the duration of the insolvency proceedings unless the opt out is revoked; and

(b)   is deemed to be an opted-out creditor in respect of any consecutive insolvency proceedings under Parts 3 to 5 of the Act of a different kind relating to the same company.

1.34(6)   The creditor may at any time revoke the election to opt out by a further notice in writing, authenticated and dated by the creditor and delivered to the office-holder.

1.34(7)   The creditor ceases to be an opted-out creditor from the date the notice is delivered to the office-holder.

1.35   Office-holder to provide information to creditors on opting out

1.35(1)   The office-holder must, in the first communication with a creditor, inform the creditor in writing that the creditor may elect to opt out of receiving further documents relating to the insolvency proceedings.

1.35(2)   The communication must contain–

(a)   identification and contact details for the office-holder;

(b)   a statement that the creditor has the right to elect to opt out of receiving further documents about the insolvency proceedings unless–

    (i)   the Act requires a document to be delivered to all creditors without expressly excluding opted-out creditors,

    (ii)   the document is a notice relating to a change in the office-holder or the office-holder's contact details, or

    (iii)   the document is a notice of a dividend or proposed dividend; or

    (iv)   the document is a notice which the court orders to be sent to all creditors or all creditors of a particular category to which the creditor belongs;

(c)   a statement that opting out will not affect the creditor's entitlement to receive dividends should any be paid to creditors;

(d)   a statement that unless these Rules provide to the contrary opting out will not affect any right the creditor may have to vote in a decision procedure or to participate in a deemed consent procedure in the insolvency proceedings although the creditor will not receive notice of it;

(e)   a statement that a creditor who opts out will be treated as having opted out in respect of any consecutive insolvency proceedings of a different kind in respect of the same company; and

(f)   information about how the creditor may elect to be or cease to be an opted-out creditor.

1.36   Delivery of documents to authorised recipients

1.36   Where under the Act or these Rules a document is to be delivered to a person (other than by being served on that person), it may be delivered instead to any other person authorised in writing to accept delivery on behalf of the first-mentioned person.

1.37   Delivery of documents to joint office-holders

1.37   Where there are joint office-holders in insolvency proceedings, delivery of a document to one of them is to be treated as delivery to all of them.

1.38   Postal delivery of documents

1.38(1)   A document is delivered if it is sent by post in accordance with the provisions of this rule.

1.38(2)   A document delivered by post may be delivered to the last known address of a person.

1.38(3)   First class or second class post may be used to deliver a document.

1.38(4)   Unless the contrary is shown–

(a)   a document sent by first class post is to be treated as delivered on the second business day after the day on which it is posted;

(b)   a document sent by second class post is to be treated as delivered on the fourth business day after the day on which it is posted;

(c)   where a post-mark appears on the envelope in which a document was posted, the date of that post-mark is to be treated as the date on which the document was posted.

1.38(5) In this rule "post-mark" means a mark applied by a postal operator which records the date on which a letter entered the postal system of the postal operator.

1.39 Delivery by document exchange

1.39(1) A document is delivered to a member of a document exchange if it is delivered to that document exchange.

1.39(2) Unless the contrary is shown, a document is treated as delivered–

(a) one business day after the day it is delivered to the document exchange where the sender and the intended recipient are members of the same document exchange; or

(b) two business days after the day it is delivered to the departure facility of the sender's document exchange where the sender and the intended recipient are members of different document exchanges.

1.40 Personal delivery of documents

1.40(1) A document is delivered if it is personally delivered in accordance with this rule.

1.40(2) In the case of an individual, a document is personally delivered if it is left with that individual.

1.40(3) In the case of a legal person, a document is personally delivered if it is left with an individual at the registered office, other official address or a place of business of that legal person.

1.41 Electronic delivery of documents

1.41(1) A document is delivered if it is sent by electronic means and the following conditions apply.

1.41(2) The conditions are that the intended recipient of the document has–

(a) given actual or deemed consent for the electronic delivery of the document;

(b) not revoked that consent before the document is sent; and

(c) provided an electronic address for the delivery of the document.

1.41(3) Consent may relate to a specific case or generally.

1.41(4) For the purposes of paragraph (2)(a) an intended recipient is deemed to have consented to the electronic delivery of a document where the intended recipient and the company who is the subject of the insolvency proceedings had customarily communicated with each other by electronic means before the insolvency proceedings commenced.

1.41(5) Unless the contrary is shown, a document is to be treated as delivered by electronic means to an electronic address where the sender can produce a copy of the electronic communication which–

(a) contains the document; and

(b) shows the time and date the communication was sent and the electronic address to which it was sent.

1.41(6) Unless the contrary is shown, a document sent electronically is treated as delivered to the electronic address to which it is sent at 9.00 am on the next business day after it was sent.

1.42 Electronic delivery of documents to the court

1.42(1) A document may not be delivered to a court by electronic means unless this is expressly permitted by Rules of Court.

1.42(2) A document delivered by electronic means is to be treated as delivered to the court at the time it is recorded by the court as having been received or otherwise as the Rules of Court provide.

1.43   Electronic delivery by office-holders

1.43(1)   Where an office-holder delivers a document by electronic means, the document must contain, or be accompanied by, a statement that the recipient may request a hard copy of the document and a telephone number, email address and postal address that may be used to make that request.

1.43(2)   An office-holder who receives such a request must deliver a hard copy of the document to the recipient free of charge within 5 business days of receipt of the request.

1.44   Use of website by office-holder to deliver a particular document (section 246B)

1.44(1)   This rule applies for the purposes of sections 246B (use of websites).

1.44(2)   An office-holder who proposes to satisfy the requirement to deliver a document to any person by making it available on a website in accordance with section 246B(1) must deliver a notice to that person which contains–

    (a)   a statement that the document is available for viewing and downloading on a website;

    (b)   the website's address and any password necessary to view and download the document; and

    (c)   a statement that that person may request a hard copy of the document together with a telephone number, email address and postal address which may be used to make that request.

1.44(3)   An office-holder who receives such a request must deliver a hard copy of the document to the person who made the request free of charge within 5 business days of receipt of the request.

1.44(4)   A document to which a notice under paragraph (2) relates must–

    (a)   remain available on the website for the period required by rule 1.46; and

    (b)   be in a format that enables it to be downloaded within a reasonable time of an electronic request being made for it to be downloaded.

1.44(5)   A document which is delivered to a person by means of a website in accordance with this rule, is deemed to have been delivered–

    (a)   when it is first made available on the website; or

    (b)   when the notice under paragraph (2) is delivered to that person, if that is later.

1.44(6)   Section 246B(1) does not apply to a notice under paragraph (2).

1.44(7)   In this rule "document" includes any notice or information in any other form.

1.45   General use of website to deliver documents

1.45(1)   The office-holder may deliver a notice to each person to whom a document will be required to be delivered in the insolvency proceedings which contains–

    (a)   a statement that future documents in the insolvency proceedings other than those mentioned in paragraph (2) will be made available for viewing and downloading on a website without notice to the recipient and that the office-holder will not be obliged to deliver any such documents to the recipient of the notice unless it is requested by that person;

    (b)   a telephone number, email address and postal address which may be used to make a request for a hard copy of a document;

    (c)   a statement that the recipient of the notice may at any time request a hard copy of–

        (i)   any document available for viewing on the website,

        (ii)   any document which may be made available there in the future, and

(d)   the address of the website, and any password required to view and download a relevant document from that site.

1.45(2)   A statement under paragraph (1)(a) does not apply to the following documents:–

(a)   a document for which personal delivery is required;

(b)   any document relating to adjudication of creditors' claims or payment of dividend; and

(c)   a document which is not delivered generally.

1.45(3)   A document is delivered generally if it is delivered to some or all of the following classes of persons–

(a)   members,

(b)   contributories,

(c)   creditors;

(d)   any class of members, contributories or creditors.

1.45(4)   An office-holder who has delivered a notice under paragraph (1) is under no obligation–

(a)   to notify a person to whom the notice has been delivered when a document to which the notice applies has been made available on the website; or

(b)   to deliver a hard copy of such a document unless a request is received under paragraph (1)(c).

1.45(5)   An office-holder who receives a request under paragraph (1)(c)–

(a)   in respect of a document which is already available on the website must deliver a hard copy of the document to the recipient free of charge within 5 business days of receipt of the request; and

(b)   in respect of all future documents must deliver each such document in accordance with the requirements for delivery of such a document in the Act and these Rules.

1.45(6)   A document to which a statement under paragraph (1)(a) applies must–

(a)   remain available on the website for the period required by rule 1.46; and

(b)   be in such a format as to enable it to be downloaded within a reasonable time of an electronic request being made for it to be downloaded.

1.45(7)   A document which is delivered to a person by means of a website in accordance with this rule, is deemed to have been delivered–

(a)   when the relevant document was first made available on the website; or

(b)   when the notice under paragraph (1) is delivered to that person, if that is later.

1.45(8)   Paragraph (7) does not apply in respect of a person who has made a request under paragraph (1)(c)(ii) for hard copies of all future documents.

1.46   Retention period for documents made available on websites

1.46(1)   This rule applies to a document which is made available on a website under rules 1.44 and 1.45.

1.46(2)   Such a document must continue to be made available on the website until 2 months after the end of the particular insolvency proceedings or the release of the last person to hold office as the office-holder in those insolvency proceedings, whichever is later.

1.47   Proof of delivery of documents

1.47(1)   A certificate complying with this rule is proof that a document has been duly delivered to the recipient in accordance with this Chapter unless the contrary is shown.

1.47(2)   A certificate must state the method of delivery and the date of the sending, posting or delivery (as the case may be).

1.47(3)   In the case of an office-holder the certificate must be given by–

(a)   the office-holder;

(b)   the office-holder's solicitor; or

(c)   a partner or an employee of either of them.

1.47(4)   In the case of a person other than an office-holder the certificate must be given by that person and must state–

(a)   that the document was delivered by that person; or

(b)   that another person (named in the certificate) was instructed to deliver it.

1.47(5)   A certificate under this rule may be endorsed on a copy of the document to which it relates.

1.48   Delivery of statements of claim and documentary evidence of debt

1.48(1)   Once a statement of claim or documentary evidence of debt has been delivered to an office-holder in accordance with these Rules it need not be delivered again.

1.48(2)   Accordingly, where these Rules require such delivery by a certain time, that requirement is satisfied if that statement or evidence has already been delivered.

1.48(3)   This rule also applies where a creditor in insolvency proceedings is deemed to have submitted a claim in administration proceedings which immediately preceded the insolvency proceedings.

CHAPTER 10

INSPECTION OF DOCUMENTS, COPIES AND PROVISION OF INFORMATION

1.49   Right to copies of documents

1.49   Where the Act, in relation to proceedings under Parts 3 to 5 of the Act, or these Rules give a person the right to inspect documents, that person has a right to be supplied on request with copies of those documents on payment of the standard fee for copies.

1.50   Charges for copies of documents provided by the office-holder

1.50   Except where prohibited by these Rules, an office-holder is entitled to require the payment of the standard fee for copies of documents requested by a creditor, member, contributory or member of a liquidation or creditors' committee.

1.51   Offence in relation to inspection of documents

1.51(1)   It is an offence for a person who does not have a right under these Rules to inspect a relevant document falsely to claim to be a creditor, a member of a company or a contributory of a company with the intention of gaining sight of the document.

1.51(2)   A relevant document is one which is on the court file or held by the office-holder or any other person and which a creditor, a member of a company or a contributory of a company has the right to inspect under these Rules.

1.52   Right to list of creditors

1.52(1)   This rule applies to–

(a)   creditors' voluntary winding up; and

(b)   winding up by the court

1.52(2)   A creditor has the right to require the office-holder to provide a list of the names and addresses of the creditors and the amounts of their respective debts.

1.52(3)   The office-holder on being required to provide such a list–

(a)   must deliver it to the person requiring the list as soon as reasonably practicable; and

(b)   may charge the standard fee for copies for a hard copy.

1.52(4)   The office-holder may omit the name and address of a creditor if the office-holder thinks its disclosure would be prejudicial to the conduct of the insolvency proceedings or might reasonably be expected to lead to violence against any person.

1.52(5)   In such a case the list must include–

(a)   the amount of that creditor's debt; and

(b)   a statement that the name and address of the creditor has been omitted for that debt.

1.53   Confidentiality of documents: grounds for refusing inspection

1.53(1)   Where an office-holder considers that a document forming part of the records of the insolvency proceedings–

(a)   should be treated as confidential; or

(b)   is of such a nature that its disclosure would be prejudicial to the conduct of the insolvency proceedings or might reasonably be expected to lead to violence against any person;

the office-holder may decline to allow it to be inspected by a person who would otherwise be entitled to inspect it.

1.53(2)   The persons to whom the office-holder may refuse inspection include members of a liquidation committee or a creditors' committee.

1.53(3)   Where the office-holder refuses inspection of a document, the person wishing to inspect it may apply to the court which may reconsider the office-holder's decision.

1.53(4)   The court's decision may be subject to such conditions (if any) as it thinks just.

1.54   Sederunt book

1.54(1)   The office-holder must maintain a sederunt book during the office-holder's term of office for the purpose of providing an accurate record of the insolvency proceedings.

1.54(2)   The office-holder must include in the sederunt book–

(a)   the information listed in schedule 4; and

(b)   a copy of anything else required to be recorded in it by any provision of the Act or these Rules.

1.54(3)   The office-holder must make the sederunt book available for inspection at all reasonable hours by any interested person.

1.54(4)   Any entry in the sederunt book is sufficient evidence of the facts stated in it, except where it is relied upon by the office-holder in the office-holder's own interest.

1.54(5)   The office-holder must retain, or make arrangements for retention of, the sederunt book for the period specified in regulation 13(5) of the Insolvency Practitioners Regulations 2005.

1.54(6)   Where the sederunt book is maintained in electronic form it must be capable of reproduction in hard copy form.

1.55   Transfer and disposal of company's books, papers and other records

1.55(1)   Where insolvency proceedings have terminated and other insolvency proceedings under Parts 2 to 5 of the Act have commenced in relation to the same company, the office-holder appointed in the original proceedings, must, before the expiry of the earlier of–

(a)   the period of 30 days beginning with the date the office-holder in the subsequent insolvency proceedings makes a request to the original office-holder to do so; or

(b)   the period of 6 months after the relevant date,

deliver to the office-holder appointed in the subsequent proceedings the books, papers and other records of the company.

1.55(2)   In the case of receivership, where–

(a)   the original proceedings have terminated; and

(b)   no subsequent proceedings have commenced within the period of 6 months after the relevant date in relation to the original proceedings,

the receiver may dispose of the books, papers and records of the company after the expiry of the period of 6 months referred to in sub-paragraph (b), but only in accordance with paragraph (3).

1.55(3)   Directions to that effect may be given by–

(a)   the members of the company by extraordinary resolution; or

(b)   the court.

1.55(4)   Where a company is being wound up, the liquidator must dispose of the books, papers and records of the company either in accordance with–

(a)   in the case of a winding up by the court, directions of the liquidation committee, or, if there is no such committee, directions of the court;

(b)   in the case of a members' voluntary winding up, directions of the members by extraordinary resolution; and

(c)   in the case of a creditors' voluntary winding up, directions of the liquidation committee, or, if there is no such committee, of the creditors given at or before the end of the period within which a creditor may object to release of the liquidator following a final account under section 106 (see rule 4.30(2)(c) and (d)),

or, if, by the date which is 12 months after the dissolution of the company, no such directions have been given, after that date in such a way as the liquidator deems appropriate.

1.55(5)   In this Rule, "the relevant date" means–

(a)   in the case of a receivership, the date on which the receiver resigns and the receivership terminates without a further receiver being appointed; and

(b)   in the case of a winding up, the date of dissolution of the company.

CHAPTER 11

FORMAL DEFECTS

1.56 Power to cure defects in procedure

1.56(1) The court may, on the application of any person having an interest–

(a) if there has been a failure to comply with any requirement of the Act or the Rules, make an order waiving any such failure and, so far as practicable, restoring any person prejudiced by the failure to the position that person would have been in but for the failure;

(b) if for any reason anything required or authorised to be done in, or in connection with, the insolvency proceedings cannot be done, make such order as may be necessary to enable that thing to be done.

1.56(2) The court, in an order under paragraph (1), may impose such conditions, including conditions as to expenses, as the court thinks fit and may in particular–

(a) authorise or dispense with the performance of any act in the insolvency proceedings;

(b) appoint as office-holder in the insolvency proceedings any person who would be eligible to act in that capacity, whether or not in place of an existing office-holder;

(c) extend or waive any time limit specified in or under the Act or the Rules.

1.56(3) An application under paragraph (1) which is made to the sheriff–

(a) may at any time be remitted by the sheriff to the Court of Session;

(b) must be so remitted if the Court of Session so directs on an application by any person,

if the sheriff or the Court of Session, as the case may be, considers that the remit is desirable because of the importance or complexity of the matters raised by the application.

1.57 Formal defects

1.57 No insolvency proceedings are invalidated by any formal defect or irregularity unless the court before which objection is made considers that substantial injustice has been caused by the defect or irregularity and that the injustice cannot be remedied by any order of the court.

PART 2

RECEIVERSHIP

CHAPTER 1

APPOINTMENT OF RECEIVER BY THE HOLDER OF THE FLOATING CHARGE UNDER SECTION 51(1)

[Note: a document required by the Act or these Rules must also contain the standard contents required as set out in Part 1.]

2.1 Receipt of instrument of appointment and acceptance of appointment

2.1(1) This rule applies where a person is appointed a receiver by the holder of a floating charge under section 51(1) by an instrument of appointment under section 53(1).

2.1(2) The person's acceptance (which need not be in writing) of the appointment for the purposes of paragraph (a) of section 53(6) must be intimated by the person to the holder of the floating charge or the holder's agent within the period specified in that paragraph.

2.1(3) The person must, as soon as possible after the person's acceptance of the appointment, endorse a written docquet of acceptance of the appointment on the instrument of appointment.

2.1(4) The written docquet evidencing receipt of the instrument of appointment required by section 53(6)(b) must also be endorsed on the instrument of appointment.

2.1(5) The person must, as soon as possible after the person's acceptance of the appointment, deliver a copy of the endorsed instrument of appointment to the holder of the floating charge or the holder's agent.

2.1(6) Where 2 or more persons are appointed joint receivers–

(a) where the written docquet evidencing receipt of the instrument of appointment and the written docquet of acceptance of the appointment are endorsed by each of the joint receivers, or 2 or more of them, on the same instrument of appointment, it is the joint receiver who last endorses the joint receiver's written docquets who is required by paragraph (5) to deliver a copy of the instrument of appointment to the holder of the floating charge or the holder's agent; and

(b) section 53(6) applies subject to the following modifications–

(i) the appointment of any of the joint receivers is of no effect unless the appointment is accepted by all of them in accordance with section 53(6)(a) and paragraph (2); and

(ii) the appointment of the persons as joint receivers is deemed to be made on the day on and at the time at which the instrument of appointment is received by the last of them, as evidenced by the written docquet evidencing receipt of the instrument of appointment required by section 53(6)(b) and paragraph (4).

2.2 Certified copy instrument of appointment

2.2(1) The certified copy instrument of appointment which is required to be delivered to the registrar of companies and AiB by or on behalf of the person making the appointment under section 53(1) must be a certified copy of the instrument of appointment with the written docquet evidencing receipt of the instrument of appointment and the written docquet of acceptance endorsed on it.

2.2(2) The certified copy instrument of appointment must be certified to be a correct copy by or on behalf of the person making the appointment.

2.3 Notice under section 53(1)

2.3(1) The notice which is required to be delivered to the registrar of companies and AiB by or on behalf of the person making the appointment under section 53(1) must–

(a) state the name and address of the holder of the floating charge;

(b) state that the receiver was appointed by the holder of the floating charge as receiver of that part of the property of the company which is subject to the floating charge;

(c) contain the information about the floating charge described in paragraph (2);

(d) contain the information about the circumstances justifying the appointment described in paragraph (3).

2.3(2) The information about the floating charge is–

(a) the name of the person first named in the charge among the persons entitled to the benefit of it (or, in the case of a series of secured debentures, the name of the holder of the first such debenture to be issued);

(b) the amount secured by the charge;

(c) the date of registration of the charge.

2.3(3)   The information about the circumstances justifying the appointment is–

(a)   where the circumstances justifying the appointment are provided for in the instrument creating the floating charge, the event which by the provisions of the instrument entitles the holder of the floating charge to make the appointment; or

(b)   where the circumstances justifying the appointment are not provided for in the instrument creating the floating charge, which of the events in section 52(1) entitles the holder of the floating charge to make the appointment.

CHAPTER 2

APPOINTMENT OF RECEIVER BY THE COURT UNDER SECTION 51(2)

[Note: a document required by the Act or these Rules must also contain the standard contents required as set out in Part 1.]

2.4   **Notice under section 54(3)**

2.4(1)   The notice which is required to be delivered to the registrar of companies and AiB by or on behalf of the petitioner under section 54(3) must–

(a)   state the name and address of the holder of the floating charge;

(b)   state that the receiver was appointed by the court on behalf of the holder of the floating charge as receiver of that part of the property of the company which is subject to the floating charge;

(c)   contain the information about the floating charge described in paragraph (2);

(d)   contain the information about the circumstances justifying the appointment described in paragraph (3).

2.4(2)   The information about the floating charge is–

(a)   the name of the person first named in the charge among the persons entitled to the benefit of it (or, in the case of a series of secured debentures, the name of the holder of the first such debenture to be issued);

(b)   the amount secured by the charge;

(c)   the date of registration of the charge.

2.4(3)   The information about the circumstances justifying the appointment is–

(a)   where the circumstances justifying the appointment are provided for in the instrument creating the floating charge, the event which by the provisions of the instrument entitles the holder of the floating charge to make the appointment; or

(b)   where the circumstances justifying the appointment are not provided for in the instrument creating the floating charge, which of the events in section 52(2) entitles the holder of the floating charge to make the appointment.

CHAPTER 3

INFORMATION TO BE GIVEN BY RECEIVER WHEN APPOINTED (SECTION 65(1))

[Note: a document required by the Act or these Rules must also contain the standard contents required as set out in Part 1.]

2.5   Notice of appointment of receiver

2.5(1)   The notice which the receiver is required under section 65(1) to send to the company and, unless the court otherwise directs, the creditors of the company (so far as the receiver is aware of their addresses), must contain–

(a)   identification details for the company;

(b)   the registered office of the company;

(c)   any principal trading address of the company if this is different from its registered office;

(d)   any other name under which the company was registered in the period of 12 months before the date of the receiver's appointment;

(e)   any other name or style (not being a registered name)–

   (i)   under which the company has carried on business, and

   (ii)   in which any debt owed to a creditor was incurred;

(f)   identification details for the receiver;

(g)   contact details for the receiver;

(h)   the receiver's IP number;

(i)   the name of any person other than the receiver who may be contacted about the insolvency proceedings;

(j)   the date of the receiver's appointment;

(k)   the name of the person who made the appointment;

(l)   the information about the property over which the receiver is appointed described in paragraph (3).

2.5(2)   The notice which the receiver is required under section 65(1) to publish must contain–

(a)   the information under sub-paragraph (a) to (l) of paragraph (1) above; and

(b)   where applicable, the name of the court making the appointment and any number assigned to those proceedings by the court.

2.5(3)   The information about the property over which the receiver is appointed is–

(a)   where the receiver is appointed over the whole or substantially the whole of the company's property, a statement to that effect; or

(b)   where the receiver is not appointed over the whole or substantially the whole of the company's property, a description of the property of the company over which the receiver is appointed.

CHAPTER 4

STATEMENT OF AFFAIRS

[Note: a document required by the Act or these Rules must also contain the standard contents required as set out in Part 1.]

2.6   Interpretation

2.6   In this Chapter–

"nominated person" means a relevant person who has been required by the receiver to make out and deliver to the receiver a statement of affairs; and

"relevant person" means a person mentioned in section 66(3).

2.7   Requirement to provide a statement of affairs (section 66(1))

2.7(1)   A requirement under section 66(1) for a nominated person to make out and submit to the receiver a statement of the affairs of the company must be made by a notice delivered to such a person.

2.7(2)   The notice must be headed "Notice requiring statement of affairs" and must–

   (a)   identify the company immediately below the heading;

   (b)   identify the receiver;

   (c)   state the date of the receiver's appointment;

   (d)   state the name of the nominated person;

   (e)   require the nominated person to prepare and submit to the receiver a statement of the affairs of the company on a specified date, being the date of the receiver's appointment;

   (f)   inform each nominated person of–

      (i)   the name and address of any other nominated person to whom a notice has been delivered;

      (ii)   the date by which the statement must be delivered to the receiver; and

      (iii)   the effect of section 66(6) (penalty for non-compliance).

2.7(3)   The receiver must inform each nominated person that a document for the preparation of the statement of affairs capable of completion in compliance with rule 2.8 can be supplied if requested.

2.8   Statement of affairs: contents and delivery (section 66(2))

2.8(1)   The statement of affairs must be headed "Statement of affairs" and must state that it is a statement of the affairs of the company on a specified date, being the date of the receiver's appointment.

2.8(2)   The statement of affairs must contain, in addition to the matters required by section 66(2)–

   (a)   a summary of the assets of the company, setting out the book value and the estimated realisable value of–

      (i)   any assets specifically secured;

      (ii)   any assets subject to a floating charge;

      (iii)   any assets not secured;

      (iv)   the total assets available for preferential creditors;

   (b)   a summary of the liabilities of the company, setting out–

      (i)   the amount of preferential debts;

      (ii)   an estimate of the deficiency with respect to preferential debts or the surplus available after paying the preferential debts;

      (iii)   an estimate of the prescribed part, if applicable;

      (iv)   an estimate of the total assets available to pay debts secured by floating charges;

    (v)   the amount of debts secured by floating charges;

    (vi) an estimate of the deficiency with respect to debts secured by floating charges or the surplus available after paying the debts secured by floating charges;

    (vii) the amount of unsecured debts (excluding preferential debts and any deficiency with respect to debts secured by floating charges);

    (viii) an estimate of the deficiency with respect to unsecured debts or the surplus available after paying unsecured debts (excluding preferential debts and any deficiency with respect to debts secured by fixed securities and floating charges);

    (ix) any issued and called-up capital;

    (x)   an estimate of the deficiency with respect to, or surplus available to, members of the company;

(c)   a list of the company's creditors (as required by section 66(2)) with the further particulars required by paragraph (3) indicating–

    (i)   any creditors under hire-purchase or conditional sale agreements;

    (ii) any creditors who are consumers claiming amounts paid in advance for the supply of goods or services; and

    (iii) any creditors claiming retention of title over property in the company's possession.

2.8(3)   The particulars required by this paragraph are as follows and must be given in this order–

(a)   the name and postal address;

(b)   the amount of the debt owed to the creditor;

(c)   details of any security held by the creditor;

(d)   the date the security was given; and

(e)   the value of the security.

2.8(4)   Paragraph (5) applies where the particulars required by paragraph (3) relate to creditors who are either–

(a)   employees or former employees of the company; or

(b)   consumers claiming amounts paid in advance for the supply of goods or services.

2.8(5)   Where this paragraph applies–

(a)   the statement of affairs must state separately for each of paragraph (4)(a) and (b) the number of such creditors and the total of the debts owed to them; and

(b)   the particulars required by paragraph (3) must be set out in separate schedules to the statement of affairs for each of paragraph (4)(a) and (b).

2.8(6)   The statutory declaration required by section 66(2) must be a statutory declaration that the information provided in the statement of affairs is, to the best of the nominated person's knowledge and belief, accurate and complete.

2.8(7)   The nominated person who makes the statutory declaration required by section 66(2) and paragraph (6) (or one of them, if more than one) must deliver the statement of affairs to the receiver.

2.9   Statement of affairs: statement of concurrence

2.9(1)   The receiver may require a relevant person to deliver to the receiver a statement of concurrence.

2.9(2)   A statement of concurrence is a statement that the relevant person concurs in the statement of affairs submitted by a nominated person.

2.9(3)   The receiver must inform the nominated person who has been required to submit a statement of affairs that the relevant person has been required to deliver a statement of concurrence.

2.9(4)   The nominated person must deliver a copy of the statement of affairs to every relevant person who has been required to deliver a statement of concurrence.

2.9(5)   A statement of concurrence–

(a)   must identify the company; and

(b)   may be qualified in relation to matters dealt with in the statement of affairs where the relevant person–

(i)   is not in agreement with the statement of affairs;

(ii)   considers the statement to be erroneous or misleading; or

(iii)   is without the direct knowledge necessary for concurring in it.

2.9(6)   A statement of concurrence must contain a statutory declaration by the relevant person required to submit it that the information provided in the statement of concurrence is, to the best of the relevant person's knowledge and belief, accurate and complete.

2.9(7)   The relevant person must deliver the required statement of concurrence to the receiver before the end of the period of 5 business days (or such other period as the receiver may agree) beginning with the day on which the relevant person receives the statement of affairs.

2.10   Statement of affairs: expenses

2.10(1)   The receiver must pay as an expense of the receivership the expenses which the receiver considers to have been reasonably incurred by–

(a)   a nominated person in making a statement of affairs and statutory declaration; or

(b)   a relevant person in making a statement of concurrence.

2.10(2)   Any decision by the receiver under this rule is subject to appeal to the court.

2.11   Limited disclosure

2.11(1)   This rule applies where the receiver thinks that disclosure of the whole or part of a statement of affairs or a statement of concurrence would be likely to prejudice the conduct of the receivership or might reasonably be expected to lead to violence against any person.

2.11(2)   The receiver may apply to the court for an order of limited disclosure in respect of the whole or any specified part of the–

(a)   statement of affairs; or

(b)   the statement of concurrence.

2.11(3)   The court may order that the whole or any specified part of the statement of affairs or the statement of concurrence must not be entered in the sederunt book.

2.11(4)   The court's order of limited disclosure may include directions regarding the disclosure of information in the statement of affairs or statement of concurrence to other persons.

2.11(5)   A creditor who seeks disclosure of the statement of affairs or statement of concurrence or a specified part of it in relation to which an order has been made under this Rule may apply to the court for an order that the receiver disclose that statement of affairs or statement of concurrence or specified part of it.

2.11(6)   The court may attach to an order for disclosure any conditions as to confidentiality, duration and scope of the order in any material change of circumstances, and other matters as it sees fit.

2.11(7)   If there is a material change in circumstances rendering the limit on disclosure unnecessary, the receiver must, as soon as reasonably practicable after the change, apply to the court for the order to be discharged or varied.

CHAPTER 5

RECEIVER'S REPORT

[Note: a document required by the Act or these Rules must also contain the standard contents required as set out in Part 1.]

2.12   Receiver's report under section 67(1): content (prescribed part)

2.12(1)   The receiver's report under section 67(1) must state (in addition to the matters required by section 67(1)) estimates to the best of the receiver's knowledge and belief of –

(a)   the value of the prescribed part (whether or not the receiver might be required under section 176A to make the prescribed part available for the satisfaction of unsecured debts); and

(b)   the value of the company's net property (as defined by section 176A(6)).

2.12(2)   The receiver may exclude from an estimate under paragraph (1) information the disclosure of which could seriously prejudice the commercial interests of the company.

2.12(3)   If the exclusion of such information affects the calculation of an estimate, the report must say so.

2.12(4)   If the receiver proposes to make an application to court under section 176A(5) the report must say so and give the reason for the application.

2.13   Receiver's report under section 67(1): notice

2.13(1)   This rule applies where the receiver sends the report under section 67(1) to–

(a)   the holder of the floating charge by virtue of which the receiver was appointed; or

(b)   any trustees for secured creditors, other than opted-out creditors, of the company and (so far as the receiver is aware of their addresses) such creditors.

2.13(2)   The receiver must deliver with the report a notice.

2.13(3)   The notice must contain–

(a)   identification details for the office-holder; and

(b)   identification details for the company.

2.14   Unsecured creditors request for copy report (section 67(2)(b))

2.14   A notice under section 67(2)(b) stating an address to which unsecured creditors should write for copies of a receiver's report under that section–

(a)   may be advertised in such manner as the receiver thinks fit; and

(b)   must–

    (i)   contain identification details for the company; and

    (ii)   be accompanied by a notice under rule 2.15.

2.15   Receiver's report – notice to unsecured creditors and invitation to form a creditors' committee

2.15(1)   This rule applies where under section 67(2)(a) the receiver sends a copy of the report under section 67(1) to all unsecured creditors of the company (so far as the receiver is aware of their addresses), other than opted-out creditors.

2.15(2)   The receiver must deliver with the copy report, a notice inviting the creditors to decide whether a creditors' committee should be established if sufficient creditors are willing to be members of the committee.

2.15(3)   The notice must also invite nominations for membership of the committee, such nominations to be received by the receiver by a date to be specified in the notice.

2.15(4)   The notice must–

(a)   contain identification details for the company; and

(b)   state that any nominations–

    (i)   must be delivered to the receiver by the specified date; and

    (ii)   can only be accepted if the receiver is satisfied as to the creditor's eligibility under rule 10.4.

CHAPTER 6

RECEIVER'S SUMMARY OF RECEIPTS AND PAYMENTS

[Note: a document required by the Act or these Rules must also contain the standard contents required as set out in Part 1.]

2.16   Summary of receipts and payments

2.16(1)   The receiver must deliver a summary of receipts and payments as receiver to–

(a)   AiB;

(b)   the company (and if it is then subject to other insolvency proceedings under Parts 1 to 5 of the Act, the office-holder in relation to those insolvency proceedings);

(c)   the holder of the floating charge by virtue of which the receiver is appointed; and

(d)   each member of the creditors' committee.

2.16(2)   The summary must be delivered to those persons within 2 months after–

(a)   the end of the period of 12 months from the date of being appointed;

(b)   the end of every subsequent period of 12 months; and

(c)   ceasing to act as receiver (unless there is a joint receiver who continues in office).

2.16(3)   The court may, on the receiver's application, extend the period of 2 months referred to in paragraph (2).

2.16(4)   The summary must–

(a)   contain identification details for the company;

(b)   contain identification details for the receiver;

(c)   contain contact details for the receiver;

(d)   state the date of the receiver's appointment.

2.16(5)   The summary must show receipts and payments–

(a)   during the relevant period of 12 months, or

(b)   where the receiver has ceased to act, during the period–

(i)   from the end of the last 12 month period to the time when the receiver so ceased, or

(ii)   if there has been no previous summary, since being appointed.

2.16(6)   This rule is without prejudice to the receiver's duty to produce proper accounts otherwise than as above.

2.16(7)   A receiver who makes default in complying with this rule is guilty of an offence.

CHAPTER 7

CESSATION OF APPOINTMENT OF RECEIVER

[Note: a document required by the Act or these Rules must also contain the standard contents required as set out in Part 1.]

2.17   Resignation

2.17(1)   A receiver must deliver notice of intention to resign at least 5 business days before the date the resignation is intended to take effect to–

(a)   the holder of the floating charge by virtue of which the receiver is appointed;

(b)   the holder of any other floating charge and any receiver appointed by that holder;

(c)   any other receiver appointed by the court;

(d)   the company (and if it is then subject to other insolvency proceedings under Parts 1 to 5 of the Act, the office-holder in relation to those insolvency proceedings); and

(e)   the members of the creditors' committee.

2.17(2)   Notice given under this rule must specify the date on which the receiver intends the resignation to take effect.

2.18   Deceased receiver: notice

2.18(1)   If the receiver dies a notice of the fact and date of death must be delivered as soon as reasonably practicable to–

(a)   the holder of the floating charge by virtue of which the receiver is appointed;

(b)   the holder of any other floating charge and any receiver appointed by that holder;

(c)   any other receiver appointed by the court (unless delivery is by a surviving joint receiver);

(d)   the registrar of companies;

(e)   AiB;

(f)   the company (and if it is then subject to other insolvency proceedings under Parts 1 to 5 of the Act, the office-holder in relation to those insolvency proceedings); and

(g)   the members of the creditors' committee.

2.18(2)   The notice must be delivered by one of the following:–

(a)   a surviving joint receiver;

(b)   a member of the deceased receiver's firm (if the deceased was a member or employee of a firm);

(c)   an officer of the deceased receiver's company (if the deceased was an officer or employee of a company); or

(d)   an executor of the deceased receiver.

2.18(3)   If such a notice has not been delivered within 21 days following the receiver's death then any other person may deliver the notice.

2.19   Other vacation of office

[Note: this requirement to give notice is in addition to the requirement to give notice (containing applicable standard contents under Chapter 6 of Part 1) to the registrar of companies and the Accountant in Bankruptcy under section 62(5).]

2.19(1)   This rule applies where a receiver vacates office–

(a)   in circumstances set out in paragraph 41 of schedule B1 (administration);

(b)   on completion of the receivership; or

(c)   in consequence of ceasing to be qualified to act as an insolvency practitioner in relation to the company.

2.19(2)   The receiver must, on vacating office, as soon as reasonably practicable deliver a notice of doing so to–

(a)   the holder of the floating charge by virtue of which the receiver is appointed;

(b)   the holder of any other floating charge and any receiver appointed by that holder;

(c)   the company (and if it is then subject to other insolvency proceedings under Parts 1 to 5 of the Act, the office-holder in relation to those proceedings); and

(d)   the members of the creditors' committee.

2.19(3)   Where the receiver vacates office in the circumstances described in paragraph (1)(a) the receiver is not required under paragraph (2)(c) to deliver notice of doing so to the administrator.

CHAPTER 8

RECEIVERS AND THE PRESCRIBED PART

2.20   Receiver to deal with prescribed part

2.20(1)   Where a receiver is appointed over the whole or any part of the property of a company and section 176A(2) applies, the receiver must deliver to any administrator or liquidator the sums representing the prescribed part.

2.20(2) If there is no administrator or liquidator the receiver must–

(a) apply to the court for directions as to the manner in which to discharge the duty under section 176A(2)(a); and

(b) act in accordance with any directions given.

PART 3

MEMBERS' VOLUNTARY WINDING UP

CHAPTER 1

STATUTORY DECLARATION OF SOLVENCY (SECTION 89)

[Note: a document required by the Act or these Rules must also contain the standard contents required as set out in Part 1.]

3.1 Statutory declaration of solvency: requirements additional to those in section 89

[Note: the "official rate" referred to in paragraph (1)(b) is defined in section 251 as the rate referred to in section 189(4). Also see section 189(5) and rule 7.26.]

3.1(1) The statutory declaration of solvency required by section 89 must identify the company and state–

(a) the name and a postal address for each director making the declaration (which may be the director's service address provided for by section 163 of the Companies Act);

(b) either–

(i) that all of the directors; or

(ii) that a majority of the directors,

have made a full inquiry into the company's affairs and that, having done so, they have formed the opinion that the company will be able to pay its debts in full together with interest at the official rate within a specified period (which must not exceed 12 months) from the commencement of the winding up; and

(c) that the declaration is accompanied by a statement of the company's assets and liabilities as at a date which is stated (being the latest practicable date before the making of the declaration as required by section 89(2)(b)).

3.1(2) The statement of the company's assets and liabilities must contain–

(a) the date of the statement;

(b) a statement that the statement shows the assets of the company at estimated realisable values and liabilities of the company expected to rank as at the date referred to in sub-paragraph (1)(c);

(c) a summary of the assets of the company, setting out the estimated realisable value of–

(i) any assets specifically secured,

(ii) any assets subject to a floating charge,

(iii) any assets not secured; and

(iv) the total value of all the assets available to preferential creditors;

1248

(d) the value of each of the following secured liabilities of the company expected to rank for payment–

    (i) liabilities secured on specific assets, and

    (ii) liabilities secured by floating charges;

(e) a summary of the unsecured liabilities of the company expected to rank for payment;

(f) the estimated expenses of the liquidation;

(g) the estimated amount of interest accruing until payment of debts in full; and

(h) the estimated value of any surplus after paying debts in full together with interest at the official rate.

CHAPTER 2

THE LIQUIDATOR

[Note: a document required by the Act or these Rules must also contain the standard contents required as set out in Part 1.]

3.2 Appointment by the company

[Note: under section 109 and paragraph 23 of schedule 8 of the Scotland Act 1998 a liquidator must also, within 14 days, publish in the Gazette and deliver to the Accountant in Bankruptcy notice of the liquidator's appointment.]

3.2(1) This rule applies where the liquidator is appointed by the company.

3.2(2) The chair of the meeting, or a director or the secretary of the company in the case of a written resolution of a private company, must certify the appointment when the appointee has provided to the person certifying the appointment a statement to the effect that the appointee is an insolvency practitioner qualified under the Act to be the liquidator and consents to act.

3.2(3) The certificate must be authenticated and dated by the person who certifies the appointment and must contain–

(a) identification details for the company;

(b) identification and contact details for the person appointed as liquidator;

(c) the date the liquidator was appointed; and

(d) a statement that the appointee–

    (i) provided a statement of being qualified to act as an insolvency practitioner in relation to the company,

    (ii) has consented to act, and

    (iii) was appointed liquidator of the company.

3.2(4) Where 2 or more liquidators are appointed the certificate must also specify (as required by section 231) whether any act required or authorised under any enactment to be done by the liquidator is to be done by all or any one or more of them.

3.2(5) The person who certifies the appointment must deliver the certificate as soon as reasonably practicable to the liquidator.

3.2(6) Not later than 28 days from the liquidator's appointment, the liquidator must deliver notice of the appointment to the creditors of the company.

3.2(7) The liquidator may within 28 days of the liquidator's appointment advertise notice of it (otherwise than in the Gazette) in such manner as the liquidator thinks fit.

3.2(8) The notice referred to in paragraph (7) must state–

    (a) that a liquidator has been appointed; and

    (b) the date of the appointment.

3.3 Meetings in members' voluntary winding up of authorised deposit-takers

3.3(1) This rule applies to a meeting of the members of an authorised deposit-taker at which it is intended to propose a resolution for its winding up.

3.3(2) Notice of such a meeting of the company must be delivered by the directors to the Financial Conduct Authority and to the scheme manager established under section 212(1) of the Financial Services and Markets Act 2000.

3.3(3) The notice to the Financial Conduct Authority and the scheme manager must be the same as delivered to members of the company.

3.3(4) The scheme manager is entitled to be represented at any meeting of which it is required by this rule to be given notice.

3.4 Appointment by the court (section 108)

[Note: under section 109 and paragraph 23 of schedule 8 of the Scotland Act 1998 a liquidator must also, within 14 days, publish in the Gazette and deliver to the Accountant in Bankruptcy notice of the liquidator's appointment.]

3.4(1) This rule applies where the liquidator is appointed by the court under section 108.

3.4(2) The court must not make the appointment unless and until the person being appointed liquidator has lodged in court a statement to the effect that that person is qualified to act as an insolvency practitioner in relation to the company and consents to act as liquidator.

3.4(3) The liquidator's appointment is effective from the date of the order of appointment.

3.4(4) Not later than 28 days from the liquidator's appointment, the liquidator must deliver notice of the appointment to the creditors of the company.

3.5 Liquidator's resignation

3.5(1) A liquidator may resign only–

    (a) on grounds of ill health;

    (b) because of the intention to cease to practise as an insolvency practitioner;

    (c) because the further discharge of the duties of liquidator is prevented or made impractical by–

        (i) a conflict of interest, or

        (ii) a change of personal circumstances;

    (d) where 2 or more persons are acting as liquidator jointly and it is the opinion of both or all of them that it is no longer expedient that there should continue to be that number of joint liquidators.

3.5(2) Before resigning, the liquidator must deliver a notice to the members of the company–

    (a) stating the liquidator's intention to resign; and

(b)   calling a meeting for the members to consider whether a replacement should be appointed,

except where the resignation is under sub-paragraph (1)(d).

3.5(3)   The notice may suggest the name of a replacement liquidator.

3.5(4)   The notice must be accompanied by a summary of the liquidator's receipts and payments.

3.5(5)   The date of the meeting must be not more than 5 business days before the date on which the liquidator intends to give notice of resignation to AiB under section 171(5).

3.5(6)   The resigning liquidator's release is effective 21 days after the date of delivery of the notice of resignation to AiB under section 171(5), unless the court orders otherwise.

3.6   Removal of liquidator by company meeting

[Note: in relation to release of the liquidator following removal from office by a general meeting of the company, see section 173(2)(a)(i).]

3.6   A liquidator removed by a meeting of the company must as soon as reasonably practicable deliver notice of the removal to AiB.

3.7   Removal of liquidator by the court

[Note: in relation to release of the liquidator following removal from office by the court see section 173(2)(b)(ii).]

3.7(1)   This rule applies where an application is made to the court for the removal of the liquidator, or for an order directing the liquidator to summon a company meeting for the purpose of removing the liquidator.

3.7(2)   The court may require the applicant to make a deposit or give caution for the expenses to be incurred by the liquidator on the application.

3.7(3)   The applicant must, at least 14 days before the hearing, deliver to the liquidator–

(a)   a notice of the hearing stating the venue;

(b)   a copy of the application; and

(c)   a copy of any evidence on which the applicant intends to rely.

3.7(4)   The expenses of the application are not payable as an expense of the liquidation unless the court orders otherwise.

3.7(5)   Where the court removes the liquidator the order of removal may include such provision as the court thinks fit with respect to matters arising in connection with the removal.

3.7(6)   The person removed must as soon as reasonably practicable after receiving a copy of the order of removal deliver a copy of the order of removal to AiB.

3.7(7)   If the court appoints a new liquidator, rule 3.4 (appointment by the court) applies.

3.8   Deceased liquidator

[Note: in relation to release of a deceased liquidator, see section 173(2)(a)(iii) and paragraph 23 of schedule 8 of the Scotland Act 1998.]

3.8(1)   If the liquidator dies a notice of the fact and date of death must be delivered as soon as reasonably practicable to–

(a)   one of the company's directors; and

(b)   AiB.

3.8(2) One of the following must deliver the notice–

(a) a surviving joint liquidator;

(b) a member of the deceased liquidator's firm (if the deceased was a member or employee of a firm);

(c) an officer of the deceased liquidator's company (if the deceased was an officer or employee of a company); or

(d) an executor of the deceased liquidator.

3.8(3) If such notice has not been delivered within the 21 days following the liquidator's death then any other person may deliver the notice.

3.9 Loss of qualification as insolvency practitioner

[Note: in relation to release of the liquidator where the liquidator vacates office on ceasing to be a person qualified to act as an insolvency practitioner in relation to the company (section 171(4)), see section 173(2)(b)(iii)).]

3.9(1) This rule applies where the liquidator vacates office on ceasing to be qualified to act as an insolvency practitioner in relation to the company.

3.9(2) A notice of the fact must be delivered as soon as reasonably practicable to AiB by one of the following–

(a) the liquidator who has vacated office;

(b) a continuing joint liquidator; or

(c) the recognised professional body which was the source of the vacating liquidator's authorisation to act (immediately before the liquidator vacated office).

3.9(3) The notice must be authenticated and dated by the person delivering the notice.

3.10 Application by former liquidator to the Accountant of Court for release (section 173(2)(b))

3.10(1) This rule applies to a liquidator who–

(a) is removed by the court;

(b) vacates office on ceasing to be qualified to act as an insolvency practitioner in relation to the company; or

(c) vacates office in consequence of the court making a winding-up order against the company.

3.10(2) Where the former liquidator applies to the Accountant of Court for release the application must contain–

(a) identification details for the insolvency proceedings;

(b) identification and contact details for the former liquidator;

(c) details of the circumstances under which the former liquidator has ceased to act as liquidator; and

(d) a statement that the former liquidator is applying to the Accountant of Court for a certificate of the former liquidator's release as liquidator as a result of the circumstances specified in the application.

3.10(3) The application must be authenticated and dated by the former liquidator.

3.10(4) When the Accountant of Court gives a release, the Accountant of Court must deliver–

(a) a certificate of the release to the former liquidator; and

(b)   a notice of the release to AiB.

3.10(5)   Release is effective from the date of the certificate or such other date as the certificate specifies.

3.11   Delivery of draft final account to members (section 94)

3.11(1)   The liquidator must deliver a notice to the members accompanied by the draft final account required by section 94(1) and rule 7.9 giving them a minimum of 8 weeks' notice of a specified date on which the liquidator intends to deliver the final account as required by section 94(2).

3.11(2)   The notice must inform the members that when the company's affairs are fully wound up–

(a)   the liquidator will make up the final account and deliver it to the members; and

(b)   when the final account is delivered to the registrar of companies and AiB under section 94(3) the liquidator will vacate office under section 171(6) and be released under section 173(2)(d).

3.11(3)   However the liquidator may conclude that the company's affairs are fully wound up before the period referred to in paragraph (1) has expired if every member confirms in writing to the liquidator that they do not intend to make any such request or application.

3.12   Final account prior to dissolution (section 94)

3.12(1)   The final account which the liquidator is required to make up under section 94 must comply with the requirements of rule 7.9.

3.12(2)   When the account is delivered to the members under section 94(2) it must be accompanied by a notice which states that–

(a)   the company's affairs are fully wound up;

(b)   the liquidator having delivered copies of the account to the members must, within 14 days of the date on which the account is made up, deliver a copy of the account to the registrar of companies and AiB; and

(c)   the liquidator will vacate office under section 171(6) and be released under section 173(2)(d) on delivering the final account to the registrar of companies and AiB.

3.12(3)   The copy of the account which the liquidator must deliver to the registrar of companies and AiB under section 94(3) must be accompanied by a notice stating that the liquidator has delivered the final account of the winding up to the members in accordance with section 94(2).

3.13   Liquidator's duties on vacating office (hand-over of assets etc.)

3.13(1)   This rule applies where a person appointed as liquidator ("the succeeding liquidator") succeeds a previous liquidator ("the former liquidator") as the liquidator.

3.13(2)   When the succeeding liquidator's appointment takes effect the former liquidator must as soon as reasonably practicable deliver to the succeeding liquidator–

(a)   the assets (after deduction of any expenses properly incurred, and distributions made, by the former liquidator);

(b)   the records of the winding up, including correspondence, statements of claim, evidence of debts and other documents relating to the winding up; and

(c)   the company's documents and other records.

3.13(3)   In doing so, the former liquidator must hand over–

(a)   such information relating to the affairs of the company and the course of the winding up as the succeeding liquidator considers reasonably required for the effective discharge of the succeeding liquidator's duties as liquidator; and

(b) all records and documents in the former liquidator's possession relating to the affairs of the company and its winding up.

3.14 Taking possession and realisation of company's assets

3.14(1) The liquidator must–

(a) as soon as reasonably practicable after the liquidator's appointment take possession of–

   (i)   the whole assets of the company; and

   (ii) any property, books, papers or records in the possession or control of the company or to which the company appears to be entitled; and

(b) make up and maintain an inventory and valuation of the assets of the company.

3.14(2) The liquidator is entitled to have access to, and to make copies of, all documents or records relating to the assets, property, business or financial affairs of the company–

(a) sent by or on behalf of the company to a third party; and

(b) in that third party's hands.

3.14(3) If a person obstructs the liquidator in the liquidator's exercise, or attempted exercise, of a power conferred by paragraph (2), the court may, on the liquidator's application, order the person to cease obstructing the liquidator.

3.14(4) The liquidator may require delivery to the liquidator of any title deed or other document of the company, even if a right of lien is claimed over it.

3.14(5) Paragraph (4) is without prejudice to any preference of the holder of the lien.

3.15 Realisation of the company's heritable property

3.15(1) This rule applies to the sale of any part of the company's heritable property over which a heritable security is held by a creditor or creditors if the rights of the secured creditor are preferable to those of the liquidator.

3.15(2) The liquidator may sell that part only with the concurrence of every such creditor unless the liquidator obtains a sufficiently high price to discharge every such security.

3.15(3) Subject to paragraph (4), the following acts are precluded–

(a) the taking of steps by a creditor to enforce the creditor's security over that part after the liquidator has intimated to the creditor an intention to sell it;

(b) the commencement by the liquidator of the procedure for the sale of that part after a creditor has intimated to the liquidator that the creditor intends to commence the procedure for its sale.

3.15(4) Where the liquidator or a creditor has given intimation under paragraph (3) but has unduly delayed in proceeding with the sale, then, if authorised by the court in the case of–

(a) paragraph (3)(a), any creditor to whom intimation has been given may enforce the creditor's security;

(b) paragraph (3)(b), the liquidator may sell that part.

3.15(5) The validity of the title of any purchaser is not challengeable on the ground that there has been a failure to comply with a requirement of this rule.

3.16 Power of court to set aside certain transactions entered into by liquidator

3.16(1) If in the course of the liquidation the liquidator enters into any transaction with a person who is an associate of the liquidator, the court may, on the application of any interested person, set the transaction aside and order the liquidator to compensate the company for any loss suffered in consequence of it.

3.16(2)   This does not apply if either–

(a)   the transaction was entered into with the prior consent of the court; or

(b)   it is shown to the court's satisfaction that the transaction was for value, and that it was entered into by the liquidator without knowing, or having any reason to suppose, that the person concerned was an associate.

3.16(3)   Nothing in this rule is to be taken as prejudicing the operation of any rule of law relating to a trustee's dealings with trust property, or the fiduciary obligations of any person.

3.17   Rule against improper solicitation by or on behalf of the liquidator

3.17(1)   Where the court is satisfied that any improper solicitation has been used by or on behalf of the liquidator in obtaining proxies or procuring the liquidator's appointment, it may order that no remuneration be allowed as an expense of the liquidation to any person by whom, or on whose behalf, the solicitation was exercised.

3.17(2)   An order of the court under this rule overrides any resolution of the members, or any other provision of these Rules relating to the liquidator's remuneration.

CHAPTER 3

SPECIAL MANAGER

3.18   Application for and appointment of special manager (section 177)

3.18(1)   An application by the liquidator under section 177 for the appointment of a special manager must be supported by a report setting out the reasons for the application.

3.18(2)   The report must include the liquidator's estimate of the value of the business or property in relation to which the special manager is to be appointed.

3.18(3)   The court's order appointing a special manager must specify the duration of the special manager's appointment, being one of the following–

(a)   for a fixed period stated in the order;

(b)   until the occurrence of a specified event; or

(c)   until the court makes a further order.

3.18(4)   The appointment of the special manager may be renewed by order of the court.

3.18(5)   The special manager's remuneration will be fixed from time to time by the court.

3.18(6)   The acts of the special manager are valid notwithstanding any defect in the special manager's appointment or qualifications.

3.19   Caution

3.19(1)   The appointment of the special manager does not take effect until the person appointed has found (or, if the court allows, undertaken to find) caution for the appointment to be given to the liquidator.

3.19(2)   A person appointed as special manager may find caution either specifically for a particular winding up, or generally for any winding up in relation to which that person may be appointed as special manager.

3.19(3)   The amount of the caution must be not less than the value of the business or property in relation to which the special manager is appointed, as estimated in the applicant's report which accompanied the application for appointment.

3.19(4)   When the special manager has found caution for the appointment to be given to the applicant that person must lodge with the court a certificate as to the adequacy of the caution.

3.19(5)   The cost of finding the caution must be paid in the first instance by the special manager, but the special manager is entitled to be reimbursed as an expense of the liquidation.

3.20   Failure to find or maintain caution

3.20(1)   If the special manager fails to find the required caution within the time allowed for that purpose by the order of appointment, or any extension of that time that may be allowed, the liquidator must report the failure to the court, which may discharge the order appointing the special manager.

3.20(2)   If the special manager fails to maintain the caution, the liquidator must report the failure to the court, which may remove the special manager, and make such order as to expenses as it thinks just.

3.20(3)   If the court discharges the order appointing the special manager, or makes an order removing the special manager, the court must give directions as to whether any, and if so what, steps should be taken for the appointment of another special manager.

3.21   Accounting

3.21(1)   The special manager must produce accounts, containing details of the special manager's receipts and payments, for the approval of the liquidator.

3.21(2)   The accounts must be for–

  (a)   each 3 month period for the duration of the special manager's appointment; and

  (b)   any shorter period ending with the termination of the special manager's appointment.

3.21(3)   When the accounts have been approved, the special manager's receipts and payments must be added to those of the liquidator.

3.22   Termination of appointment

3.22(1)   If the liquidator is of the opinion that the appointment of the special manager is no longer necessary or beneficial for the company, the liquidator must apply to the court for directions, and the court may order the special manager's appointment to be terminated.

3.22(2)   The liquidator must make the same application if the members pass a resolution requesting that the appointment should be terminated.

CHAPTER 4

CONVERSION TO CREDITORS' VOLUNTARY WINDING UP

3.23   Statement of affairs (section 95)

3.23   The rules in Chapter 2 of Part 4 apply to the statement of affairs made out by the liquidator under section 95(1A) where the liquidator is of the opinion that the company will be unable to pay its debts in full (together with interest at the official rate) within the period stated in the directors' declaration under section 89.

PART 4

CREDITORS' VOLUNTARY WINDING UP

CHAPTER 1

APPLICATION OF PART

4.1   Application of Part 4

4.1(1)   This Part applies to a creditors' voluntary winding up.

4.1(2)   However where a company moves from administration to creditors' voluntary winding up by the registration of a notice under paragraph 83(3) of schedule B1 the following rules do not apply–

4.2 to 4.7 (statement of affairs etc.);

4.11 to 4.15 (information to creditors and contributories and appointment of liquidator);

4.17 (report by directors etc.);

4.18 (decisions on nomination);

4.20 (appointment by creditors or by the company);

4.22 (appointment by the court (section 100(3) or 108), other than in respect of appointments under section 108).

CHAPTER 2

STATEMENT OF AFFAIRS AND OTHER INFORMATION

[Note: a document required by the Act or these Rules must also contain the standard contents required as set out in Part 1.]

4.2   Statement of affairs made out by the liquidator under section 95(1A)

[Note: section 95(4A) requires the statement of affairs to contain a statutory declaration by some or all of the directors.

Note: the "official rate" referred to in paragraph (2)(c) is defined in section 251 as the rate referred to in section 189(4)). Also see section 189(5) and rule 7.26.]

4.2(1)   This rule applies to the statement of affairs made out by the liquidator under section 95(1A) (effect of company's insolvency in members' voluntary winding up).

4.2(2)   The statement of affairs must be headed "Statement of affairs" and must contain–

(a)   identification details for the company;

(b)   a statement that it is a statement of the affairs of the company on a date which is specified, being the date of the opinion formed by the liquidator under section 95(1);

(c)   a statement that as at that date, the liquidator formed the opinion that the company would be unable to pay its debts in full (together with interest at the official rate) within the period stated in the directors' declaration of solvency made under section 89; and

(d)   the date it is made.

4.2(3) The statutory declaration required by section 95(4A) must be a statutory declaration that the information provided in the statement of affairs is, to the best of the liquidator's knowledge and belief, accurate and complete.

4.3 Statement of affairs made out by the directors under section 99(1)

[Note: section 99(2A) requires the statement of affairs to contain a statutory declaration by some or all of the directors.]

4.3(1) This rule applies to the statement of affairs made out by the directors under section 99(1).

4.3(2) The statement of affairs must be headed "Statement of affairs" and must contain–

(a) identification details for the company;

(b) a statement that it is a statement of the affairs of the company on a date which is specified, being a date not more than 14 days before the date of the resolution for winding up; and

(c) the date it is made.

4.3(3) The statutory declaration required by section 99(2A) must be a statutory declaration that the information provided in the statement of affairs is, to the best of the directors' knowledge and belief, accurate and complete.

4.3(4) If a creditor requests a copy of the statement of affairs at a time when no liquidator is appointed the directors must deliver a copy to the creditor.

4.3(5) The directors must deliver the statement of affairs to the liquidator as soon as reasonably practicable after the liquidator is appointed.

4.4 Additional requirements as to statements of affairs

4.4(1) A statement of affairs under section 95(1A) or 99(1) must also contain–

(a) a list of the company's shareholders, with the following details about each one–

    (i) name and postal address,

    (ii) the type of shares held,

    (iii) the nominal amount of the shares held,

    (iv) the number of shares held,

    (v) the amount per share called up, and

    (vi) the total amount called up;

(b) the total amount of shares called up held by all shareholders;

(c) a summary of the assets of the company, setting out the book value and estimated realisable value of–

    (i) any assets specifically secured,

    (ii) any assets subject to a floating charge,

    (iii) any assets not secured, and

    (iv) the total value of all the assets available for preferential creditors;

(d) a summary of the liabilities of the company, setting out–

    (i) the amount of preferential debts,

(ii)   an estimate of the deficiency with respect to preferential debts or the surplus available after paying the preferential debts,

(iii)   an estimate of the prescribed part, if applicable,

(iv)   an estimate of the total assets available to pay debts secured by floating charges,

(v)   the amount of debts secured by floating charges,

(vi)   an estimate of the deficiency with respect to debts secured by floating charges or the surplus available after paying the debts secured by fixed security or floating charges,

(vii)   the amount of unsecured debts (excluding preferential debts),

(viii)   an estimate of the deficiency with respect to unsecured debts or the surplus available after paying unsecured debts,

(ix)   any issued and called-up capital, and

(x)   an estimate of the deficiency with respect to, or surplus available to, members of the company;

(e)   a list of the company's creditors with the following particulars required by paragraph (2) indicating–

(i)   any creditors under hire-purchase or conditional sale agreements,

(ii)   any creditors who are consumers claiming amounts paid in advance of the supply of goods or services, and

(iii)   any creditors claiming retention of title over property in the company's possession.

4.4(2)   The particulars required by this paragraph relating to each creditor are as follows–

(i)   the name and postal address,

(ii)   amount of the debt owed to the creditor, (as required by section 95(4) or 99(2)),

(iii)   details of any security held by the creditor,

(iv)   the date the security was given, and

(v)   the value of the security.

4.4(3)   Paragraph (4) applies where the particulars required by paragraph (2) relate to creditors who are either–

(a)   employees or former employees of the company; or

(b)   consumers claiming amounts paid in advance for the supply of goods or services.

4.4(4)   Where this paragraph applies–

(a)   the statement of affairs itself must state separately for each of paragraphs (3)(a) and (b) the number of such creditors and the total of the debts owed to them; and

(b)   the particulars required by paragraph (2) in respect of those creditors must be set out in separate schedules to the statement of affairs for each of paragraphs (3)(a) and (b).

4.5   Statement of affairs: statement of concurrence

4.5(1)   The liquidator may require a director ("the relevant person") to deliver to the liquidator a statement of concurrence.

4.5(2)   A statement of concurrence is a statement that the relevant person concurs in the statement of affairs submitted by another director.

4.5(3) The liquidator must inform the director who has been required to submit a statement of affairs that the relevant person has been required to deliver a statement of concurrence.

4.5(4) The director who has been required to submit the statement of affairs must deliver a copy to every relevant person who has been required to submit a statement of concurrence.

4.5(5) A statement of concurrence–

  (a) must identify the company; and

  (b) may be qualified in relation to matters dealt with in the statement of affairs, where the relevant person –

    (i) is not in agreement with the statement of affairs,

    (ii) considers the statement of affairs to be erroneous or misleading, or

    (iii) is without the direct knowledge necessary for concurring in it.

4.5(6) A statement of concurrence must contain a statutory declaration by the relevant person required to submit it that the information provided in the statement of concurrence is, to the best of the relevant person's knowledge and belief, accurate and complete.

4.5(7) The relevant person must deliver the required statement of concurrence to the liquidator before the end of the period of 5 business days (or such other period as the liquidator may agree) beginning with the day on which the relevant person receives the statement of affairs.

4.6 Limited disclosure

4.6(1) This rule applies where the liquidator thinks that disclosure of the whole or part of a statement of affairs or a statement of concurrence would be likely to prejudice the conduct of the winding up or might reasonably be expected to lead to violence against any person.

4.6(2) The liquidator may apply to the court for an order of limited disclosure in respect of the whole or any specified part of the–

  (a) statement of affairs; or

  (b) the statement of concurrence.

4.6(3) The court may order that the whole or any specified part of the statement of affairs or the statement of concurrence must not be entered in the sederunt book.

4.6(4) The court's order of limited disclosure may include directions regarding the disclosure of information in the statement of affairs or statement of concurrence to other persons.

4.6(5) A creditor who seeks disclosure of the statement of affairs or statement of concurrence or a specified part of it in relation to which an order has been made under this Rule may apply to the court for an order that the liquidator disclose that statement of affairs or statement of concurrence or specified part of it.

4.6(6) The court may attach to an order for disclosure any conditions as to confidentiality, duration and scope of the order in any material change of circumstances, and other matters as it sees fit.

4.6(7) If there is a material change in circumstances rendering the limit on disclosure unnecessary, the liquidator must, as soon as reasonably practicable after the change, apply to the court for the order to be discharged or varied.

4.6(8) This rule does not apply so far as section 95 or 99 does not permit limited disclosure.

4.7 Expenses of statement of affairs and decisions sought from creditors

4.7(1) Any reasonable and necessary expenses of preparing the statement of affairs under section 99 may be paid out of the company's assets, either before or after the commencement of the winding up, as an expense of the liquidation.

4.7(2) Any reasonable and necessary expenses of the decision procedure or deemed consent procedure to seek a decision from the creditors on the nomination of a liquidator under rule 4.14 (information to creditors and appointment of liquidator) may be paid out of the company's assets, either before or after the commencement of the winding up, as an expense of the liquidation.

4.7(3) Where payment under paragraph (1) or (2) is made before the commencement of the winding up, the directors must deliver to the creditors with the statement of affairs a statement of the amount of the payment and the identity of the person to whom it was made.

4.7(4) The liquidator appointed under section 100 may make such a payment, but if there is a liquidation committee, the liquidator must deliver to the committee at least 5 business days' notice of the intention to make it.

4.7(5) However such a payment may not be made to the liquidator, or to any associate of the liquidator, otherwise than with the approval of the liquidation committee, the creditors, or the court.

4.7(6) This is without prejudice to the court's powers under rule 5.52 (voluntary winding up superseded by winding up by the court).

4.8 Delivery of accounts to liquidator (section 235)

4.8(1) A person who is specified in section 235(3) must deliver to the liquidator accounts of the company of such nature, as at such date, and for such period, as the liquidator requires.

4.8(2) The period for which the liquidator may require accounts may begin from a date up to 3 years before the date of the resolution for winding up, or from an earlier date to which audited accounts of the company were last prepared.

4.8(3) The accounts must, if the liquidator so requires, contain a statutory declaration by the person required to deliver them that the accounts are, to the best of the relevant person's knowledge and belief, accurate and complete.

4.8(4) The accounts (containing a statutory declaration if so required) must be delivered to the liquidator within 21 days from the liquidator's request, or such longer period as the liquidator may allow.

4.9 Expenses of assistance in preparing accounts

4.9(1) Where the liquidator requires a person to deliver accounts under rule 4.8, the liquidator may, with the approval of the liquidation committee (if there is one) and as an expense of the liquidation, employ a person or firm to assist that person in the preparation of the accounts.

4.9(2) The person who is required to deliver accounts may request an allowance of all or part of the expenses to be incurred in employing a person or firm to assist in preparing the accounts.

4.9(3) A request for an allowance must be accompanied by an estimate of the expenses involved.

4.9(4) The liquidator must only authorise the employment of a named person or a named firm approved by the liquidator.

4.9(5) The liquidator may, with the approval of the liquidation committee (if there is one), authorise such an allowance, payable as an expense of the liquidation.

CHAPTER 3

NOMINATION AND APPOINTMENT OF LIQUIDATORS AND INFORMATION TO CREDITORS

[Note: a document required by the Act or these Rules must also contain the standard contents required as set out in Part 1.]

4.10 Application of the rules in this Chapter

4.10(1) The rules in this Chapter apply as follows.

4.10(2) Rules 4.11 to 4.13 only apply to a conversion from a members' voluntary winding up to a creditors' voluntary winding up.

4.10(3) Rule 4.16 only applies where the administrator becomes the liquidator in a voluntary winding up which follows an administration.

4.10(4) Rules 4.14, 4.15 and 4.17 only apply to a creditors' voluntary winding up which has not been commenced by a conversion from a members' voluntary winding up or an administration.

4.10(5) Rules 4.18 and 4.19 apply to all creditors' voluntary windings up.

4.11 Nomination of liquidator and information to creditors on conversion from members' voluntary winding up (section 96)

4.11(1) This rule applies in respect of the conversion of a members' voluntary winding up to a creditors' voluntary winding up under section 96.

4.11(2) The liquidator must seek a nomination from the creditors for a liquidator in the creditors' voluntary winding up by–

(a) a decision procedure; or

(b) the deemed consent procedure.

4.11(3) The liquidator must deliver to the creditors a copy of the statement of affairs required by section 95(1A) and Chapter 2 of this Part together with a notice which complies with rule 8.7 (deemed consent) or 8.8 (notices to creditors of decision procedure) so far as are relevant.

4.11(4) The notice must also contain–

(a) identification and contact details for the existing liquidator; and

(b) a statement that if no person is nominated by the creditors then the existing liquidator will be the liquidator in the creditors' voluntary winding up.

4.11(5) The decision date in the notice must be not later than 28 days from the date under section 95(1) that the liquidator formed the opinion that the company will be unable to pay its debts in full.

4.11(6) Subject to paragraph (9), the creditors must be given at least 14 days' notice of the decision date.

4.11(7) Paragraph (8) applies where–

(a) the liquidator has sought a decision from creditors on the nomination of a liquidator by the deemed consent procedure; but

(b) the level of objections to the proposed nomination has meant, under section 246ZF, that no nomination is deemed to have been made.

4.11(8) Where this paragraph applies, the liquidator must seek a nomination from creditors by way of a decision procedure in accordance with this rule, the decision date to be as soon as reasonably practicable, but no more than 28 days from the date that the level of objections had the effect that no nomination was deemed to have been made.

4.11(9)   Where paragraph (8) applies, the creditors must be given at least 7 days' notice of the decision date.

4.11(10)   Where the liquidator is required by rule 8.6 (physical meetings) to summon a physical meeting as a result of requests from creditors received in response to a notice delivered under this rule, the physical meeting must be summoned to take place–

(a)   within 28 days of the date on which the threshold for requiring a physical meeting was met; and

(b)   with at least 14 days' notice.

4.12   Creditors' decision on appointment other than at a meeting (conversion from members' voluntary winding up)

4.12(1)   This rule applies where the creditors' decision on the nomination of a liquidator in a conversion of a members' voluntary winding up into a creditors' voluntary winding up is intended to be sought otherwise than through a meeting or through the deemed consent procedure, including where the conditions in rule 4.11(7) are met and the liquidator, under rule 4.11(8), goes on to seek a nomination from creditors by way of a decision procedure other than a meeting.

4.12(2)   Instead of delivering a notice of the decision procedure or deemed consent procedure under rule 4.11, the liquidator must deliver a notice to creditors inviting them to make proposals for the nomination of a liquidator.

4.12(3)   Such a notice must–

(a)   identify any liquidator for whom a proposal which is in compliance with paragraph (4) has already been received;

(b)   explain that the liquidator is not obliged to seek the creditors' views on any proposal that does not meet the requirements of paragraphs (4) and (5); and

(c)   be accompanied by the statement of affairs unless that has previously been delivered to the creditor.

4.12(4)   Any proposal must state the name and contact details of the proposed liquidator, and contain a statement that the proposed liquidator is qualified to act as an insolvency practitioner in relation to the company and has consented to act as liquidator of the company.

4.12(5)   Any proposal must be received by the liquidator within 5 business days of the date of the notice under paragraph (2).

4.12(6)   Within 2 business days of the end of the period referred to in paragraph (5), the liquidator must send a notice to creditors of a decision procedure under rule 4.11.

4.13   Information to creditors and contributories (conversion of members' voluntary winding up to creditors' voluntary winding up)

4.13(1)   The liquidator must deliver to the creditors and contributories within 28 days of the conversion of a members' voluntary winding up to a creditors' voluntary winding up under section 96 a notice which must contain–

(a)   the date the winding up became a creditors' voluntary winding up;

(b)   a report of the decision procedure or deemed consent procedure which took place under rule 4.11; and

(c)   the information required by paragraph (3).

4.13(2)   The notice must be accompanied by a copy of the statement of affairs or a summary except where the notice is being delivered to a creditor to whom a copy of the statement of affairs has previously been delivered under section 95(1A).

4.13(3)   The required information is an estimate to the best of the liquidator's knowledge and belief of–

(a)   the value of the prescribed part (whether or not the liquidator might be required under section 176A to make the prescribed part available for the satisfaction of unsecured debts); and

(b)   the value of the company's net property (as defined by section 176A(6)).

4.13(4)   The liquidator may exclude from an estimate under paragraph (3) information the disclosure of which could seriously prejudice the commercial interests of the company.

4.13(5)   If the exclusion of such information affects the calculation of an estimate, the report must say so.

4.13(6)   If the liquidator proposes to make an application to court under section 176A(5) the report must say so and give the reason for the application.

4.14   Information to creditors and appointment of liquidator

4.14(1)   This rule applies in respect of the appointment of a liquidator under section 100.

4.14(2)   The directors of the company must deliver to the creditors a notice seeking their decision on the nomination of a liquidator by–

(a)   the deemed consent procedure; or

(b)   a virtual meeting.

4.14(3)   The decision date for the decision of the creditors on the nomination of a liquidator must be not earlier than 3 business days after the notice under paragraph (2) is delivered but not later than 14 days after the resolution is passed to wind up the company.

4.14(4)   Where the directors have sought a decision from the creditors through the deemed consent procedure under paragraph (2)(a) but, pursuant to section 246ZF(5)(a) (deemed consent procedure), more than the specified number of creditors object so that the decision cannot be treated as having been made, the directors must then seek a decision from the creditors on the nomination of a liquidator by holding a physical meeting under rule 8.6 as if a physical meeting had been required under section 246ZE(4) (decisions by creditors and contributories: general).

4.14(5)   Where paragraph (4) applies, the meeting must not be held earlier than 3 business days after the notice under rule 8.6(3) is delivered or later than 14 days after the level of objections reaches that described in paragraph (4).

4.14(6)   A request for a physical meeting under section 246ZE must be made in accordance with rule 8.6 except that–

(a)   such a request may be made at any time between the delivery of the notice under paragraph (2) and the decision date under paragraph (3); and

(b)   the decision date where this paragraph applies must be not earlier than 3 business days after the notice under rule 8.6(3) is delivered and not later than 14 days after the level of requests reaches that described in section 246ZE.

4.14(7)   The directors must deliver to the creditors a copy of the statement of affairs required under section 99 not later than on the business day before the decision date.

4.14(8)   A notice delivered under paragraph (2), in addition to the information required by rules 8.7 (deemed consent) and 8.8 (notices to creditors of decision procedure), must contain–

(a)   the date the resolution to wind up is to be considered or was passed;

(b)   identification and contact details of any liquidator nominated by the company;

(c)   a statement of either–

   (i)   the name and address of a person qualified to act as an insolvency practitioner in relation to the company who during the period before the decision date, will furnish creditors free of charge with such information concerning the company's affairs as they may reasonably require, or

   (ii)   a place in the relevant locality where, on the 2 business days falling next before the decision date, a list of the names and addresses of the company's creditors will be available for inspection free of charge; and

(d)   where the notice is sent to creditors in advance of the copy of the statement of affairs, a statement that the directors, before the decision date and before the end of the period of 7 days beginning with the day after the day on which the company passed a resolution for winding up, are required by section 99–

   (i)   to make out a statement in the prescribed form as to the affairs of the company, and

   (ii)   send the statement to the company's creditors.

4.14(9)   Where the company's principal place of business in Scotland was situated in different localities at different times during the relevant period, the duty imposed by sub-paragraph (8)(c)(ii) above applies separately in relation to each of those localities.

4.14(10)   Where the company had no place of business in Scotland during the relevant period, the reference in paragraph (9) to the company's principal place of business in Scotland are replaced by references to its registered office.

4.14(11)   In paragraph (9), "the relevant period" means the period of 6 months immediately preceding the day on which the notices referred to in paragraph (2) were delivered.

4.14(12)   Where a virtual or physical meeting is held under this rule and a liquidator has already been nominated by the company, the liquidator or an appointed person must attend any meeting held under this rule and report on any exercise of the liquidator's powers under section 112, 165 or 166.

4.14(13)   A director who is in default in seeking a decision on the nomination of a liquidator in accordance with this rule is guilty of an offence.

4.15   Information to creditors and contributories

4.15(1)   The liquidator must deliver to the creditors and contributories within 28 days of the appointment of the liquidator under section 100 a notice which must–

(a)   be accompanied by a statement of affairs or a summary where the notice is delivered to any contributory or creditor to whom the notice under rule 4.14 was not delivered;

(b)   a report on the decision procedure or deemed consent procedure under rule 4.14; and

(c)   be accompanied by the information required by paragraph (2).

4.15(2)   The required information is an estimate to the best of the liquidator's knowledge and belief of–

(a)   the value of the prescribed part (whether or not the liquidator might be required under section 176A to make the prescribed part available for the satisfaction of unsecured debts); and

(b)   the value of the company's net property (as defined by section 176A(6)).

4.15(3)   The liquidator may exclude from an estimate under paragraph (2) information the disclosure of which could seriously prejudice the commercial interests of the company.

4.15(4)   If the exclusion of such information affects the calculation of an estimate, the report must say so.

4.15(5)   If the liquidator proposes to make an application to court under section 176A(5) the report must say so and give the reason for the application.

4.16   Further information where administrator becomes liquidator (paragraph 83(3) of schedule B1)

4.16(1)   This rule applies where an administrator becomes liquidator on the registration of a notice under paragraph 83(3) of schedule B1, and becomes aware of creditors not formerly known to that person as administrator.

4.16(2)   The liquidator must deliver to those creditors a copy of any statement delivered by the administrator to creditors in accordance with paragraph 49(4) of schedule B1 and rule 3.35 of the CVA and Administration Rules.

4.17   Report by director etc.

4.17(1)   Where the statement of affairs sent to creditors under section 99(1) does not, or will not, state the company's affairs at the decision date for the creditors' nomination of a liquidator, the directors of the company must cause a report (written or oral) to be made to the creditors in accordance with this rule on any material transactions relating to the company occurring between the date of the making of the statement and the decision date.

4.17(2)   In the case of a decision being taken through a meeting, the report must be made at the meeting by the director chairing the meeting or by another person with knowledge of the relevant matters.

4.17(3)   Where the deemed consent procedure is used, the report must be delivered to creditors as soon as reasonably practicable after the material transaction takes place in the same manner as the deemed consent procedure.

4.17(4)   Where the decision date is within the period of 3 business days from the delivery of a report under paragraph (3), this rule extends the decision date until the end of that period notwithstanding the requirement in rule 4.14(3) relating to the timing of the decision date.

4.17(5)   On delivery of a report under paragraph (3), the directors must notify the creditors of the effects of paragraph (4).

4.17(6)   A report under this rule must be recorded in the record of the decision under rule 8.40 (record of a decision).

4.18   Decisions on nomination

4.18(1)   In the case of a decision on the nomination of a liquidator–

(a)   if on any vote there are 2 nominees, the person who obtains the most support is appointed;

(b)   if there are 3 or more nominees, and one of them has a clear majority over both or all the others together, that one is appointed; and

(c)   in any other case, the convener or chair must continue to take votes (disregarding at each vote any nominee who has withdrawn and, if no nominee has withdrawn, the nominee who obtained the least support last time) until a clear majority is obtained for any one nominee.

4.18(2)   The convener or chair may at any time put to the meeting a resolution for the joint nomination of any 2 or more nominees.

4.19   Invitation to creditors to form a liquidation committee

4.19(1)   Where any decision is sought from the company's creditors–

(a)   in a creditors' voluntary winding up; or

(b)   where a members' voluntary winding up is converting to a creditors' voluntary winding up,

the convener of the decision must at the same time deliver to the creditors a notice inviting them to decide whether a liquidation committee should be established if sufficient creditors are willing to be members of the committee.

4.19(2)   The notice must also invite nominations for membership of the committee, such nominations to be received by a date specified in the notice.

4.19(3)   The notice must–

(a)   state that nominations must be delivered to the convener by the specified date; and

(b)   state that nominations can only be accepted if the convener is satisfied as to the creditors' eligibility under rule 10.4 (eligibility for membership of creditors' or liquidation committee).

CHAPTER 4

THE LIQUIDATOR

[Note: a document required by the Act or these Rules must also contain the standard contents required as set out in Part 1.]

4.20   Appointment by creditors or by the company

[Note: under section 109 and paragraph 23 of schedule 8 of the Scotland Act 1998 a liquidator must also, within 14 days, publish in the Gazette and deliver to the Accountant in Bankruptcy notice of the liquidator's appointment.]

4.20(1)   This rule applies where a person is appointed as liquidator by creditors or the company.

4.20(2)   The liquidator's appointment takes effect from the date of the passing of the resolution of the company or, where the creditors decide to appoint a person who is not the person appointed by the company, from the relevant decision date.

4.20(3)   Their appointment must be certified by–

(a)   the convener or chair of the decision procedure or deemed consent procedure; or

(b)   in respect of an appointment by the company the chair of the company meeting or a director or the secretary of the company (in the case of a written resolution).

4.20(4)   The person who certifies the appointment must not do so unless and until the proposed liquidator ("the appointee") has provided that person with a statement of being an insolvency practitioner qualified under the Act to be the liquidator and of consenting to act.

4.20(5)   The certificate must be authenticated and dated by the person who certifies the appointment and must contain–

(a)   identification details for the company;

(b)   identification and contact details for the person appointed as liquidator;

(c)   the date of the meeting of the company or conclusion of the decision procedure or deemed consent procedure when the liquidator was appointed;

(d) a statement that the appointee–

   (i)   has provided a statement of being qualified to act as an insolvency practitioner in relation to the company,

   (ii) has consented to act, and

   (iii) was appointed liquidator of the company.

4.20(6)   Where 2 or more liquidators are appointed the certificate must also specify (as required by section 231) whether any act required or authorised under any enactment to be done by the liquidator is to be done by all or any one or more of them.

4.20(7)   The person who certifies the appointment must deliver the certificate as soon as reasonably practicable to the liquidator.

4.20(8)   The liquidator may within 28 days of the liquidator's appointment advertise notice of it (otherwise than in the Gazette) in such manner as the liquidator thinks fit.

4.20(9)   The notice must state–

(a) that a liquidator has been appointed; and

(b) the date of the appointment.

4.21   Power to fill vacancy in office of liquidator

4.21   Where a vacancy in the office of liquidator occurs in the manner mentioned in section 104 a decision procedure to fill the vacancy may be initiated by any creditor or, if there was more than one liquidator, by the continuing liquidator or liquidators.

4.22   Appointment by the court (section 100(3) or 108)

[Note: under section 109 and paragraph 23 of schedule 8 of the Scotland Act 1998 a liquidator must also, within 14 days, publish in the Gazette and deliver to the Accountant in Bankruptcy notice of the liquidator's appointment.]

4.22(1)   This rule applies where the liquidator is appointed by the court under section 100(3) or 108.

4.22(2)   The court must not make the appointment unless and until the person being appointed liquidator has lodged in court a statement to the effect that that person is qualified to act as an insolvency practitioner in relation to the company and consents to act as liquidator.

4.22(3)   The liquidator's appointment is effective from the date of the order of appointment.

4.22(4)   Within 28 days from appointment the liquidator must–

(a) deliver a notice of it to the creditors; or

(b) if the court permits, and in accordance with the directions of the court, advertise the notice (otherwise than in the Gazette).

4.22(5)   Where the liquidator gives notice under paragraph (4)(a) the liquidator may, in addition, advertise the notice (otherwise than in the Gazette) in such manner as the liquidator thinks fit.

4.22(6)   Any notice under this rule must state–

(a) that a liquidator has been appointed; and

(b) the date of the appointment.

4.23 Liquidator's resignation and replacement

4.23(1)   A liquidator may resign only–

(a)   on grounds of ill health;

(b)   because of the intention to cease to practise as an insolvency practitioner;

(c)   because the further discharge of the duties of liquidator is prevented or made impractical by–

    (i)   a conflict of interest, or

    (ii)   a change of personal circumstances; or

(d)   where 2 or more persons are acting as liquidator jointly and it is the opinion of both or all of them that it is no longer expedient that there should continue to be that number of joint liquidators.

4.23(2)   Before resigning, the liquidator must deliver a notice to creditors, and invite the creditors by a decision procedure, or by deemed consent procedure, to consider whether a replacement should be appointed, except where the resignation is under sub-paragraph (1)(d).

4.23(3)   The notice must–

(a)   state the liquidator's intention to resign;

(b)   state that under rule 4.23(7) of these Rules the liquidator will be released 21 days after the date of delivery of the notice of resignation to AiB under section 171(5), unless the court orders otherwise; and

(c)   comply with rules 8.7 (deemed consent) and 8.8 (notices to creditors of decision procedure) so far as are relevant.

4.23(4)   The notice may suggest the name of a replacement liquidator.

4.23(5)   The notice must be accompanied by a summary of the liquidator's receipts and payments.

4.23(6)   The decision date must be not more than 5 business days before the date on which the liquidator intends to give notice of resignation to AiB under section 171(5).

4.23(7)   The resigning liquidator's release is effective 21 days after the date on which the notice of resignation under section 171(5) is delivered to AiB, unless the court orders otherwise.

4.24 Removal of liquidator by creditors

[Note: in relation to release of the liquidator following removal from office by a decision of the company's creditors, see: where the company's creditors have not decided against the liquidator's release, section 173(2)(a)(ii); and where the company's creditors have decided against release, section 173(2)(b)(i).]

4.24(1)   Where the creditors decide that the liquidator be removed, the convener of the decision procedure or the chair of the meeting (as the case may be) must as soon as reasonably practicable deliver the certificate of the liquidator's removal to the removed liquidator.

4.24(2)   The removed liquidator must deliver a notice of the removal to AiB as soon as reasonably practicable.

4.25 Removal of liquidator by the court

[Note: in relation to release of the liquidator following removal from office by the court see section 173(2)(b)(ii).]

4.25(1)   This rule applies where an application is made to the court for the removal of the liquidator, or for an order directing the liquidator to initiate a decision procedure of creditors for the purpose of removing the liquidator.

4.25(2)   The court may require the applicant to make a deposit or find caution for the expenses to be incurred by the liquidator on the application.

4.25(3)   The applicant must, at least 14 days before the hearing, deliver to the liquidator–

(a)   a notice of the hearing stating the venue;

(b)   a copy of the application; and

(c)   a copy of any evidence on which the applicant intends to rely.

4.25(4)   The expenses of the application are not payable as an expense of the liquidation unless the court orders otherwise.

4.25(5)   Where the court removes the liquidator the order of removal may include such provision as the court thinks fit with respect to matters arising in connection with the removal.

4.25(6)   The person removed must as soon as reasonably practicable after receiving a copy of the order of removal deliver a copy of the order of removal to AiB.

4.25(7)   If the court appoints a new liquidator rule 4.22 applies.

4.26   Deceased liquidator

[Note: in relation to release of a deceased liquidator, see section 173(2)(a)(iii) and paragraph 23 of schedule 8 of the Scotland Act 1998.]

4.26(1)   If the liquidator dies a notice of the fact and date of death must be delivered as soon as reasonably practicable–

(a)   where there is a liquidation committee, to the members of that committee; and

(b)   to AiB.

4.26(2)   The notice must be delivered by one of the following–

(a)   a surviving joint liquidator;

(b)   a member of the deceased liquidator's firm (if the deceased was a member or employee of a firm);

(c)   an officer of the deceased liquidator's company (if the deceased was an officer or employee of a company); or

(d)   an executor of the deceased liquidator.

4.26(3)   If such a notice has not been delivered within the 21 days following the liquidator's death then any other person may deliver the notice.

4.27   Loss of qualification as insolvency practitioner

[Note: in relation to release of the liquidator where the liquidator vacates office on ceasing to be a person qualified to act as an insolvency practitioner in relation to the company (section 171(4)), see section 173(2)(b)(iii).]

4.27(1)   This rule applies where the liquidator vacates office on ceasing to be qualified to act as an insolvency practitioner in relation to the company.

4.27(2)   A notice of the fact must be delivered as soon as reasonably practicable to AiB by one of the following–

(a)   the liquidator who has vacated office;

(b)   a continuing joint liquidator;

(c)   the recognised professional body which was the source of the vacating liquidator's authorisation to act (immediately before the liquidator vacated office).

4.27(3)   Each notice must be authenticated and dated by the person delivering the notice.

4.28   Vacation of office on making of winding-up order

4.28   Where the liquidator vacates office in consequence of the court making a winding-up order against the company, rule 4.29 applies in relation to the application to the Accountant of Court for release of the liquidator.

4.29   Application by former liquidator for release (section 173(2)(b) or (e))

4.29(1)   An application by a former liquidator to the Accountant of Court for release under section 173(2)(b) or (e) must contain–

(a)   identification details for the insolvency proceedings;

(b)   identification and contact details for the former liquidator;

(c)   details of the circumstances under which the former liquidator has ceased to act as liquidator; and

(d)   a statement that the former liquidator is applying to the Accountant of Court for a certificate of the former liquidator's release as liquidator as a result of the circumstances specified in the application.

4.29(2)   The application must be authenticated and dated by the former liquidator.

4.29(3)   When the Accountant of Court gives a release, the Accountant of Court must deliver–

(a)   a certificate of the release to the former liquidator; and

(b)   a notice of the release to AiB.

4.29(4)   Release is effective from the date of the certificate or such other date as the certificate specifies.

4.30   Final account prior to dissolution (section 106)

4.30(1)   The final account which the liquidator is required to make up under section 106(1) and deliver to members and creditors must comply with the requirements of rule 7.9.

4.30(2)   When the account is delivered to the creditors it must be accompanied by a notice which states–

(a)   that the company's affairs are fully wound up;

(b)   that a creditor may object to the release of the liquidator by giving notice in writing to the liquidator before the end of the prescribed period;

(c)   that the prescribed period is the period ending 28 days after delivery of the notice;

(d)   that the liquidator will vacate office under section 171 on delivering to the registrar of companies and AiB the final account and notice saying whether any creditor has objected to release; and

(e)   that the liquidator will be released under section 173 at the same time as vacating office unless any of the company's creditors objected to the liquidator's release.

4.30(3)   The copy of the account which the liquidator delivers to the registrar of companies and AiB under section 106(3)(a) must be accompanied by a notice containing the statement required by section 106(3)(b) of whether any creditors have objected to the liquidator's release.

4.30(4)   Where a creditor has objected to the liquidator's release rule 4.29 applies to an application by the liquidator to the Accountant of Court for release.

4.30(5) The liquidator is not obliged to prepare or deliver any progress report which may become due under these Rules in the period between the date to which the final account is made up and the date when the account is delivered to the registrar of companies and AiB under section 106(3)(a).

4.31 Liquidator's duties on vacating office (hand-over of assets etc.)

4.31(1) This rule applies where a person appointed as liquidator ("the succeeding liquidator") succeeds a previous liquidator ("the former liquidator") as the liquidator.

4.31(2) When the succeeding liquidator's appointment takes effect the former liquidator must as soon as reasonably practicable deliver to the succeeding liquidator–

(a) the assets (after deduction of any expenses properly incurred, and distributions made, by the former liquidator);

(b) the records of the winding up, including correspondence, statements of claim, evidence of debts and other documents relating to the winding up; and

(c) the company's documents and other records.

4.31(3) In doing so, the former liquidator must hand over–

(a) such information relating to the affairs of the company and the course of the winding up as the succeeding liquidator considers reasonably required for the effective discharge of the succeeding liquidator's duties as liquidator; and

(b) all records and documents in the former liquidator's possession relating to the affairs of the company and its winding up.

4.32 Taking possession and realisation of company's assets

4.32(1) The liquidator must–

(a) as soon as reasonably practicable after the liquidator's appointment take possession of–

(i) the whole assets of the company; and

(ii) any property, books, papers or records in the possession or control of the company or to which the company appears to be entitled; and

(b) make up and maintain an inventory and valuation of the assets of the company.

4.32(2) The liquidator is entitled to have access to, and to make copies of, all documents or records relating to the assets, property, business or financial affairs of the company–

(a) sent by or on behalf of the company to a third party; and

(b) in that third party's hands.

4.32(3) If a person obstructs the liquidator in the liquidator's exercise, or attempted exercise, of a power conferred by paragraph (2), the court may, on the liquidator's application, order the person to cease obstructing the liquidator.

4.32(4) The liquidator may require delivery to the liquidator of any title deed or other document of the company, even if a right of lien is claimed over it.

4.32(5) Paragraph (4) is without prejudice to any preference of the holder of the lien.

4.33 Realisation of the company's heritable property

4.33(1) This rule applies to the sale of any part of the company's heritable property over which a heritable security is held by a creditor or creditors if the rights of the secured creditor are preferable to those of the liquidator.

4.33(2)   The liquidator may sell that part only with the concurrence of every such creditor unless the liquidator obtains a sufficiently high price to discharge every such security.

4.33(3)   Subject to paragraph (4), the following acts are precluded–

(a)   the taking of steps by a creditor to enforce the creditor's security over that part after the liquidator has intimated to the creditor an intention to sell it;

(b)   the commencement by the liquidator of the procedure for the sale of that part after a creditor has intimated to the liquidator that the creditor intends to commence the procedure for its sale.

4.33(4)   Where the liquidator or a creditor has given intimation under paragraph (3) but has unduly delayed in proceeding with the sale, then, if authorised by the court in the case of–

(a)   paragraph (3)(a), any creditor to whom intimation has been given may enforce the creditor's security;

(b)   paragraph (3)(b), the liquidator may sell that part.

4.33(5)   The validity of the title of any purchaser is not challengeable on the ground that there has been a failure to comply with a requirement of this rule.

4.34   Power of court to set aside certain transactions

4.34(1)   If in the course of the liquidation the liquidator enters into any transaction with a person who is an associate of the liquidator, the court may, on the application of any interested person, set the transaction aside and order the liquidator to compensate the company for any loss suffered in consequence of it.

4.34(2)   This does not apply if either–

(a)   the transaction was entered into with the prior consent of the court; or

(b)   it is shown to the court's satisfaction that the transaction was for value, and that it was entered into by the liquidator without knowing, or having any reason to suppose, that the person concerned was an associate.

4.34(3)   Nothing in this rule is to be taken as prejudicing the operation of any rule of law relating to a trustee's dealings with trust property or the fiduciary obligations of any person.

4.35   Rule against improper solicitation

4.35(1)   Where the court is satisfied that any improper solicitation has been used by or on behalf of the liquidator in obtaining proxies or procuring the liquidator's appointment, it may order that no remuneration be allowed as an expense of the liquidation to any person by whom, or on whose behalf, the solicitation was exercised.

4.35(2)   An order of the court under this rule overrides any resolution of the liquidation committee or the creditors, or any other provision of these Rules relating to the liquidator's remuneration.

4.36   Permission for exercise of powers by liquidator

4.36(1)   Where these Rules require permission for the liquidator to exercise a power any permission given must not be a general permission but must relate to a particular proposed exercise of the liquidator's power.

4.36(2)   A person dealing with the liquidator in good faith and for value is not concerned to enquire whether any such permission has been given.

4.36(3)   Where the liquidator has done anything without such permission, the court or the liquidation committee may, for the purpose of enabling the liquidator to meet the liquidator's expenses out of the assets, ratify what the liquidator has done; but neither may do so unless satisfied that the liquidator has acted in a case of urgency and has sought ratification without undue delay.

4.36(4)   In this rule "permission" includes "sanction".

CHAPTER 5

SPECIAL MANAGER

[Note: a document required by the Act or these Rules must also contain the standard contents required as set out in Part 1.]

4.37   Application for and appointment of special manager (section 177)

4.37(1)   An application by the liquidator under section 177 for the appointment of a special manager must be supported by a report setting out the reasons for the application.

4.37(2)   The report must include the liquidator's estimate of the value of the business or property in relation to which the special manager is to be appointed.

4.37(3)   The court's order appointing a special manager must specify the duration of the special manager's appointment, being one of the following:–

(a)   for a fixed period stated in the order;

(b)   until the occurrence of a specified event; or

(c)   until the court makes a further order.

4.37(4)   The appointment of the special manager may be renewed by order of the court.

4.37(5)   The special manager's remuneration will be fixed from time to time by the court.

4.37(6)   The acts of the special manager are valid notwithstanding any defect in the special manager's appointment or qualifications.

4.38   Caution

4.38(1)   The appointment of the special manager does not take effect until the person appointed has found (or, if the court allows, undertaken to find) caution for the appointment to be given to the liquidator.

4.38(2)   A person appointed as special manager may find caution either specifically for a particular winding up, or generally for any winding up in relation to which that person may be appointed as special manager.

4.38(3)   The amount of the caution must be not less than the value of the business or property in relation to which the special manager is appointed, as estimated in the applicant's report under rule 4.37 which accompanied the application for appointment.

4.38(4)   When the special manager has found caution for the appointment to be given to the applicant that person must lodge with the court a certificate as to the adequacy of the caution.

4.38(5)   The cost of providing the caution must be paid in the first instance by the special manager; but the special manager is entitled to be reimbursed as an expense of the liquidation.

4.39   Failure to give or keep up caution

4.39(1)   If the special manager fails to find the required caution within the time allowed for that purpose in the order of appointment, or any extension of that time that may be allowed, the liquidator must report the failure to the court which may discharge the order appointing the special manager.

4.39(2)   If the special manager fails to keep up the caution, the liquidator must report the failure to the court, which may remove the special manager, and make such order as to expenses as it thinks just.

4.39(3)   If the court discharges the order appointing the special manager, or makes an order removing the special manager, the court must give directions as to whether any, and if so what, steps should be taken for the appointment of another special manager.

4.40   Accounting

4.40(1)   The special manager must produce accounts, containing details of the special manager's receipts and payments, for the approval of the liquidator.

4.40(2)   The account must be for–

(a)   each 3 month period for the duration of the special manager's appointment; and

(b)   any shorter period ending with the termination of the special manager's appointment.

4.40(3)   When the accounts have been approved, the special manager's receipts and payments must be added to those of the liquidator.

4.41   Termination of appointment

4.41(1)   If the liquidator is of the opinion that the appointment of the special manager is no longer necessary or beneficial for the company, the liquidator must apply to the court for directions, and the court may order the special manager's appointment to be terminated.

4.41(2)   The liquidator must also make such an application if the creditors decide that the appointment should be terminated.

Part 5

Winding Up by the Court

Chapter 1

Application of Part

5.1   Application of Part 5

5.1   This Part applies to winding up by the court.

Chapter 2

The statutory demand (sections 123(1)(a) and 222(1)(a))

5.2   Interpretation

5.2   A demand served by a creditor on a company under section 123(1)(a) (registered companies) or 222(1)(a) (unregistered companies) is referred to in this Part as "a statutory demand".

5.3   The statutory demand

5.3(1)   A statutory demand must be headed either "Statutory Demand under section 123(1)(a) of the Insolvency Act 1986" or "Statutory Demand under section 222(1)(a) of the Insolvency Act 1986" (as applicable) and must contain–

(a)   identification details for the company;

1275

(b) the registered office of the company (if any);

(c) the name and address of the creditor;

(d) either a statement that the demand is made under section 123(1)(a) or a statement that it is made under section 222(1)(a);

(e) the amount of the debt and the consideration for it (or, if there is no consideration, the way in which it arises);

(f) if the demand is founded on a decree or order of a court, details of the decree or order;

(g) if the creditor is entitled to the debt by way of assignation, details of the original creditor and any intermediate assignees;

(h) a statement that the company must pay the debt claimed in the demand within 21 days of service of the demand on the company after which the creditor may present a winding up petition unless the company offers security for the debt and the creditor agrees to accept security or the company compounds the debt with the creditor's agreement;

(i) the name of an individual with whom an officer or representative of the company may communicate with a view to securing or compounding the debt to the creditor's satisfaction;

(j) the named individual's address, electronic address and telephone number (if any);

(k) a statement that if the company disputes the demand in whole or in part it should contact the individual mentioned in sub-paragraph (i) immediately.

5.3(2)   The following must be separately identified in the demand (if claimed) with the amount or rate of the charge and the grounds on which payment is claimed–

(a) any charge by way of interest of which notice had not previously been delivered to the company as included in its liability; and

(b) any other charge accruing from time to time.

5.3(3)   The amount claimed for such charges must be limited to that which has accrued due at the date of the demand.

5.3(4)   The demand must be dated, and authenticated either by the creditor, or a person authorised to make the demand on the creditor's behalf.

5.3(5)   A demand which is authenticated by a person other than the creditor must state that the person is authorised to make the demand on the creditor's behalf and state the person's relationship to the creditor.

CHAPTER 3

PROVISIONAL LIQUIDATOR

[Note: a document required by the Act or these Rules must also contain the standard contents required as set out in Part 1.]

5.4 Application for appointment of provisional liquidator (section 135)

5.4(1)   An application to the court for the appointment of a provisional liquidator under section 135 may be made by–

(a) the petitioner;

(b) a creditor of the company;

   (c)   a contributory;

   (d)   the company;

   (e)   the directors of the company;

   (f)   the Secretary of State;

   (g)   a temporary administrator;

   (h)   a member State liquidator appointed in main proceedings (including in accordance with Article 37(1) of the EU Regulation); or

   (i)   any person who under any enactment would be entitled to present a petition for the winding up of the company.

5.4(2)   The court must not make the appointment unless and until the person being appointed provisional liquidator has lodged in court a statement to the effect that that person is qualified to act as an insolvency practitioner in relation to the company and consents to act as provisional liquidator.

5.5   Order of appointment of provisional liquidator – delivery of copy

5.5   The provisional liquidator must as soon as reasonably practicable after receipt of the copy of the order appointing the provisional liquidator deliver a copy of the order to–

   (a)   the registrar of companies;

   (b)   AiB;

   (c)   the company (or the liquidator, if a liquidator was appointed for the company's voluntary winding up); and

   (d)   any receiver of the whole or any part of the company's property.

5.6   Delivery of copy order of appointment of provisional liquidator – notice

[Note: for notice to accompany delivery of a copy of the order of appointment to (a) the registrar of companies and (b) the Accountant in Bankruptcy see Chapter 7 of Part 1.]

5.6(1)   This rule applies where under rule 5.5 the provisional liquidator delivers a copy of the order of appointment to–

   (a)   the company (or if a liquidator was appointed for the company's voluntary winding up, the liquidator);

   (b)   any receiver of the whole or any part of the company's property.

5.6(2)   The provisional liquidator must deliver with the copy of the order a notice.

5.7   Notice of appointment of provisional liquidator

5.7(1)   The provisional liquidator must as soon as reasonably practicable after receipt of the copy of the order of appointment give notice of appointment unless the court directs otherwise.

5.7(2)   The notice–

   (a)   must be gazetted; and

   (b)   may be advertised in such other manner as the provisional liquidator thinks fit.

5.7(3)   The notice must state–

   (a)   that a provisional liquidator has been appointed; and

(b)   the date of the appointment.

5.8   Caution

5.8(1)   The cost of providing the caution required under the Act must be paid in the first instance by the provisional liquidator, however–

(a)   if a winding-up order is not made, the person appointed is entitled to be reimbursed out of the property of the company, and the court may make an order on the company accordingly; and

(b)   if a winding-up order is made, the person appointed is entitled to be reimbursed as an expense of the liquidation.

5.8(2)   If the provisional liquidator fails to give or keep up the required caution, the court may remove the provisional liquidator, and make such order as to expenses as it thinks just.

5.8(3)   If an order is made under this rule removing the provisional liquidator, or discharging the order appointing the provisional liquidator, the court must give directions as to whether any, and if so what, steps should be taken for the appointment of another person in the place of the removed or discharged provisional liquidator.

5.9   Remuneration

5.9(1)   The remuneration of the provisional liquidator is to be fixed by the court from time to time on the application of the provisional liquidator.

5.9(2)   The basis for fixing the amount of the remuneration payable to the provisional liquidator may be a commission calculated by reference to the value of the company's assets with which the provisional liquidator has had to deal.

5.9(3)   But there is in any event to be taken into account–

(a)   the work which, having regard to that value, was reasonably undertaken by the provisional liquidator;

(b)   the extent of the provisional liquidator's responsibilities in administering the company's assets.

5.9(4)   Without prejudice to any order the court may make as to expenses, the remuneration of the provisional liquidator must be paid to the provisional liquidator, and the amount of any expenses incurred by the provisional liquidator (including the remuneration and expenses of any special manager appointed under section 177) reimbursed–

(a)   if a winding-up order is not made, out of the property of the company; and

(b)   if a winding-up order is made, as an expense of the liquidation.

5.9(5)   Unless the court otherwise directs, where a winding up order is not made, the provisional liquidator may retain out of the company's property such sums or property as are or may be required for meeting the remuneration and expenses of the provisional liquidator.

5.10   Termination of appointment

5.10(1)   Subject to paragraph (2), the appointment of the provisional liquidator may be terminated by the court on the application of the provisional liquidator, or a person specified in rule 5.4(1).

5.10(2)   In relation to a winding-up petition under section 124A (petition by Secretary of State for winding up on grounds of public interest) the appointment of the provisional liquidator may be terminated by the court on the application of the provisional liquidator or the Secretary of State.

5.10(3)   If the provisional liquidator's appointment terminates, in consequence of the dismissal of the winding-up petition or otherwise, the court may give such directions as it thinks just relating to–

(a)   the accounts of the provisional liquidator's administration;

(b)   the expenses properly incurred by the provisional liquidator; or

(c)   any other matters which it thinks appropriate.

5.10(4)   The provisional liquidator must give notice of termination of the appointment as provisional liquidator, unless the termination is on the making of a winding-up order or the court directs otherwise.

5.10(5)   The notice referred to in paragraph (4) must be delivered as soon as reasonably practicable to–

(a)   the registrar of companies;

(b)   AiB;

(c)   the company (or the liquidator, if a liquidator was appointed for the company's voluntary winding up); and

(d)   any receiver of the whole or any part of the company's property.

5.10(6)   The notice under paragraph (4) must state–

(a)   that the appointment as provisional liquidator has been terminated;

(b)   the date of that termination; and

(c)   that the appointment terminated otherwise than on the making of a winding-up order.

CHAPTER 4

STATEMENT OF AFFAIRS AND OTHER INFORMATION

[Note: a document required by the Act or these Rules must also contain the standard contents required as set out in Part 1.]

5.11   Interpretation

5.11   In this Chapter–

"liquidator" includes "provisional liquidator";

"nominated person" means a relevant person who has been required by the liquidator to make out and deliver to the liquidator a statement of affairs; and

"relevant person" means a person mentioned in section 131(3).

5.12   Notice requiring statement of affairs (section 131)

5.12(1)   Where, under section 131, the liquidator requires a nominated person to provide the liquidator with a statement of the affairs of the company, the liquidator must deliver a notice to that person.

5.12(2)   The notice must be headed "Notice requiring statement of affairs" and must–

(a)   identify the company immediately below the heading;

(b)   identify the liquidator;

(c)   state the name of the nominated person;

(d)   require the nominated person to prepare and submit to the liquidator a statement of affairs of the company on a date which is specified, being–

     (i)   the date of the winding-up order, or

    (ii)   a date directed by the liquidator;

(e)   inform the nominated person–

    (i)   of the names and addresses of any other nominated person to whom such a notice has been delivered, and

    (ii) of the date by which the statement must be delivered; and

(f)   state the effect of section 131(7) (penalty for non-compliance) and section 235 (duty to co-operate) as it applies to the liquidator.

5.12(3)   The liquidator must inform the nominated person that a document for the preparation of the statement of affairs capable of completion in compliance with rule 5.13 can be supplied by the liquidator if requested.

5.13   Statement of affairs: contents and delivery

5.13(1)   The statement of affairs must be headed "Statement of affairs" and must contain–

(a)   identification details for the company;

(b)   a statement that it is a statement of the affairs of the company on a date which is specified, being–

    (i)   the date of the winding-up order, or

    (ii) the date directed by the liquidator;

(c)   a list of the company's shareholders with the following information about each one–

    (i)   name and postal address,

    (ii) the type of shares held,

    (iii) the nominal amount of the shares held,

    (iv) the number of shares held,

    (v) the amount per share called up, and

    (vi) the total amount called up;

(d)   the total amount of shares called up held by all shareholders;

(e)   a summary of the assets of the company, setting out the book value and estimated realisable value of–

    (i)   any assets specifically secured,

    (ii) any assets subject to a floating charge,

    (iii) any assets not secured, and

    (iv) the total value of all the assets available for preferential creditors;

(f)   a summary of the liabilities of the company, setting out–

    (i)   the amount of preferential debts,

    (ii) an estimate of the deficiency with respect to preferential debts or the surplus available after paying the preferential debts,

    (iii) an estimate of the prescribed part, if applicable,

    (iv) an estimate of the total assets available to pay debts secured by floating charges,

    (v) the amount of debts secured by floating charges;

(vi) an estimate of the deficiency with respect to debts secured by floating charges or the surplus available after paying the debts secured by fixed securities or floating charges;

(vii) the amount of unsecured debts (excluding preferential debts);

(viii) an estimate of the deficiency with respect to unsecured debts or the surplus available after paying unsecured debts;

(ix) any issued and called-up capital, and

(x) an estimate of the deficiency with respect to, or surplus available to, members of the company;

(g) a list of the company's creditors (as required by section 131(2)) with the following particulars required by paragraph (2) indicating–

(i) any creditors under hire-purchase or conditional sale agreements,

(ii) any creditors who are consumers claiming amounts paid in advance of the supply of goods or services, and

(iii) any creditors claiming retention of title over property in the company's possession.

5.13(2) The particulars required by this paragraph relating to each creditor are as follows and must be given in this order–

(i) the name and postal address,

(ii) the amount of the debt owed to the creditor,

(iii) details of any security held by the creditor,

(iv) the date the security was given, and

(v) the value of the security.

5.13(3) Paragraph (4) applies where the particulars required by paragraph (2) relate to creditors who are either–

(a) employees or former employees of the company; or

(b) consumers claiming amounts paid in advance for the supply of goods or services.

5.13(4) Where this paragraph applies–

(a) the statement of affairs itself must state separately for each of paragraph (3)(a) and (b) the number of such creditors and the total of the debts owed to them; and

(b) the particulars required by paragraph (2) in respect of those creditors must be set out in separate schedules to the statement of affairs for each of paragraph (3)(a) and (b).

5.13(5) The statutory declaration required by section 131(2A) must be a statutory declaration that the information provided in the statement of affairs is, to the best of the nominated person's knowledge and belief, accurate and complete.

5.13(6) The nominated person who makes the statutory declaration required by section 131(2A) and paragraph (5) (or one of them, if more than one) must deliver the statement of affairs to the liquidator.

5.14   Statement of affairs: statement of concurrence

5.14(1) The liquidator may require a relevant person to deliver to the liquidator a statement of concurrence.

5.14(2)   A statement of concurrence is a statement that the relevant person concurs in the statement of affairs submitted by a nominated person.

5.14(3)   The liquidator must inform the nominated person who has been required to submit a statement of affairs that the relevant person has been required to deliver a statement of concurrence.

5.14(4)   The nominated person must deliver a copy of the statement of affairs to every relevant person who has been required to submit a statement of concurrence.

5.14(5)   A statement of concurrence–

(a)   must identify the company; and

(b)   may be qualified in relation to matters dealt with in the statement of affairs where the relevant person–

   (i)   is not in agreement with the statement of affairs;

   (ii)   considers the statement of affairs to be erroneous or misleading; or

   (iii)   is without the direct knowledge necessary for concurring in it.

5.14(6)   A statement of concurrence must contain a statutory declaration by the relevant person required to submit it that the information provided in the statement of concurrence is, to the best of the relevant person's knowledge and belief, accurate and complete.

5.14(7)   The relevant person must deliver the required statement of concurrence to the liquidator before the end of the period of 5 business days (or such other period as the liquidator may agree) beginning with the day on which the relevant person receives the statement of affairs.

5.15   Statement of affairs: expenses

5.15(1)   If a nominated person cannot personally prepare a proper statement of affairs, the liquidator may, as an expense of the liquidation, employ a person or firm to assist in the preparation of the statement.

5.15(2)   At the request of a nominated person, made on the grounds that the nominated person cannot personally prepare a proper statement of affairs, the liquidator may authorise an allowance, payable as an expense of the liquidation, of all or part of the expenses to be incurred by the nominated person in employing a person or firm to assist the nominated person in preparing it.

5.15(3)   Any such request by the nominated person must be accompanied by an estimate of the expenses involved; and the liquidator must only authorise the employment of a named person or a named firm, approved by the liquidator.

5.15(4)   An authorisation given by the liquidator under this rule must be subject to such conditions (if any) as the liquidator thinks fit to impose relating to the manner in which any person may obtain access to relevant documents and other records.

5.15(5)   Nothing in this rule relieves a nominated person from any obligation relating to the preparation, verification and submission of the statement of affairs, or to the provision of information to the liquidator.

5.15(6)   The liquidator must deliver a notice to the relevant person advising whether the liquidator grants or refuses the relevant person's request for an allowance under paragraph (2) and where such request is refused the relevant person may appeal to the court not later than 14 days from the date of delivery of the notice to the relevant person.

5.15(7)   Paragraphs (2) to (6) of this rule may be applied, on application to the liquidator by any relevant person, in relation to the making of a statement of concurrence.

5.16   Limited disclosure

5.16(1)   This rule applies where the liquidator thinks that disclosure of the whole or part of a statement of affairs or a statement of concurrence would be likely to prejudice the conduct of the winding up or might reasonably be expected to lead to violence against any person.

5.16(2)   The liquidator may apply to the court for an order of limited disclosure in respect of the whole or any specified part of the–

(a)   statement of affairs; or

(b)   the statement of concurrence.

5.16(3)   The court may order that the whole or any specified part of the statement of affairs or the statement of concurrence must not be entered in the sederunt book.

5.16(4)   The court's order of limited disclosure may include directions regarding the disclosure of information in the statement of affairs or statement of concurrence to other persons.

5.16(5)   A creditor who seeks disclosure of the statement of affairs or statement of concurrence or a specified part of it in relation to which an order has been made under this rule may apply to the court for an order that the liquidator disclose that statement of affairs or statement of concurrence or specified part of it.

5.16(6)   The court may attach to an order for disclosure any conditions as to confidentiality, duration and scope of the order in any material change of circumstances, and other matters as it sees fit.

5.16(7)   If there is a material change in circumstances rendering the limit on disclosure unnecessary, the liquidator must, as soon as reasonably practicable after the change, apply to the court for the order to be discharged or varied.

5.17   Delivery of accounts to liquidator

5.17(1)   Any of the persons specified in section 235(3) must, at the request of the liquidator, deliver to the liquidator accounts of the company of such nature, as at such date, and for such period, as the liquidator may specify.

5.17(2)   The period specified may begin from a date up to 3 years before the date of the presentation of the winding-up petition, or from an earlier date to which audited accounts of the company were last prepared.

5.17(3)   The court may, on the liquidator's application, require accounts for any earlier period.

5.17(4)   Rule 5.15 applies (with the necessary modifications) in relation to accounts to be delivered under this rule as it applies in relation to the statement of affairs.

5.17(5)   The accounts must–

(a)   if the liquidator so requires, contain a statutory declaration by the person required to deliver them that the accounts are, to the best of the relevant person's knowledge and belief, accurate and complete; and

(b)   (whether or not they contain a statutory declaration) be delivered to the liquidator within 21 days of the request under paragraph (1), or such longer period as the liquidator may allow.

5.18   Expenses of assistance in preparing accounts

5.18(1)   Where the liquidator requires a person to deliver accounts under rule 5.17, the liquidator may, with the approval of the liquidation committee (if there is one) and as an expense of the liquidation, employ a person or firm to assist that person in the preparation of the accounts.

5.18(2)   The person who is required to deliver accounts may request an allowance of all or part of the expenses to be incurred in employing a person or firm to assist in preparing the accounts.

5.18(3)   A request for an allowance must be accompanied by an estimate of the expenses involved.

5.18(4)   The liquidator must only authorise the employment of a named person or a named firm approved by the liquidator.

5.18(5)   The liquidator may, with the approval of the liquidation committee (if there is one), authorise such an allowance, payable as an expense of the liquidation.

5.19   Further disclosure

5.19(1)   The liquidator may at any time require a nominated person to deliver (in writing) further information amplifying, modifying or explaining any matter contained in the statement of affairs, or in accounts delivered under the Act or these Rules.

5.19(2)   The information must–

(a)   if the liquidator so directs, contain a statutory declaration by the person required to deliver the information that the information is, to the best of the relevant person's knowledge and belief, accurate and complete; and

(b)   (whether or not it contains a statutory declaration) be delivered to the liquidator within 21 days of the requirement under paragraph (1), or such longer period as the liquidator may allow.

CHAPTER 5

FURTHER INFORMATION WHERE WINDING UP FOLLOWS ADMINISTRATION

5.20   Further information where winding up follows administration

5.20(1)   This rule applies where an administrator is appointed by the court under section 140 as the company's liquidator and becomes aware of creditors not formerly known to that person as administrator.

5.20(2)   The liquidator must deliver to those creditors a copy of any statement previously sent by the administrator to creditors in accordance with paragraph 49(4) of schedule B1 and rule 3.35 of the CVA and Administration Rules.

CHAPTER 6

THE LIQUIDATOR

[Note: a document required by the Act or these Rules must also contain the standard contents required as set out in Part 1.]

5.21   Appointment of liquidator under section 138(1) (interim liquidator)

5.21(1)   This rule applies to the appointment of a liquidator by the court under section 138(1) (such a liquidator being referred to in section 138, this rule and rules 5.22 (choosing a person to be liquidator) and 8.21 (chair at meetings) as an "interim liquidator").

5.21(2)   The court must not make the appointment unless and until the person being appointed interim liquidator has lodged in court a statement to the effect that that person is qualified to act as an insolvency practitioner in relation to the company and consents to act as liquidator.

5.21(3)   The interim liquidator's appointment is effective from the date of the order of appointment.

5.21(4)   The interim liquidator must–

(a)   within 7 days beginning with the day the interim liquidator receives the copy order of appointment deliver notice of it to AiB; and

(b)   within 28 days beginning with the day the interim liquidator receives the copy order of appointment–

(i)   deliver notice of it to the creditors and contributories; or

(ii)   if the court permits and in accordance with the directions of the court either–

(aa)   gazette the notice; or

(bb)   otherwise advertise the notice,

or both gazette the notice and otherwise advertise the notice.

5.21(5)   Where the interim liquidator gives notice under paragraph (4)(b)(i) the liquidator may, in addition–

(a)   gazette the notice; or

(b)   otherwise advertise the notice in such manner as the liquidator thinks fit,

or both gazette the notice and otherwise advertise the notice in such manner as the liquidator thinks fit.

5.21(6)   Any notice under this rule must state–

(a)   that an interim liquidator has been appointed; and

(b)   the date of the appointment.

5.22   Choosing a person to be liquidator

5.22(1)   This rule applies where nominations are sought by the interim liquidator from the company's creditors and contributories under section 138(3) for the purpose of choosing a person to be liquidator of the company in place of the interim liquidator.

5.22(2)   The interim liquidator must deliver to the creditors and contributories a notice inviting proposals for a liquidator.

5.22(3)   The notice inviting proposals for a liquidator must explain that the liquidator is not obliged to seek the creditors' or contributories' views on any proposals that do not meet the requirements of paragraphs (4) and (5).

5.22(4)   A proposal must state the name and contact details of the proposed liquidator, and contain a statement that the proposed liquidator is qualified to act as an insolvency practitioner in relation to the company and has consented to act as liquidator of the company.

5.22(5)   A proposal must be received by the interim liquidator within 5 business days of the date of the notice under paragraph (2).

5.22(6)   Following the end of the period for inviting proposals under paragraph (2), where any proposals are received the interim liquidator must seek a decision on the proposals for nomination of a liquidator from the creditors (on any proposals received from creditors) and from the contributories (on any proposals received from contributories) by–

(a)   a decision procedure; or

(b)   the deemed consent procedure.

5.22(7)   Where a decision is sought under paragraph (6), the decision date must be not more than 60 days from the date of the winding-up order.

5.22(8)   The notice to be issued under rule 8.7 (deemed consent) (where the interim liquidator seeks a decision under paragraph (6) by the deemed consent procedure) or rule 8.8 (notices to creditors of decision procedure) (where the interim liquidator seeks a decision under paragraph (6) by a decision procedure) must also–

(a)   identify any liquidator proposed to be nominated by a creditor (in the case of a notice to creditors) or by a contributory (in the case of a notice to contributories) in accordance with this rule; and

(b)   contain a statement explaining the effect of section 138(5) (duty of interim liquidator to report to court where no person is appointed or nominated to be liquidator).

5.22(9)   The decision date in the notice referred to in paragraph (8) must be no later than 21 days after the date for receiving proposals has passed.

5.22(10)   The creditors and contributories must be given at least 14 days' notice of the decision date.

5.23   Appointment of liquidator by creditors or contributories

5.23(1)   This rule applies where a person is appointed as liquidator by the creditors or contributories.

5.23(2)   The convener of the decision procedure or deemed consent procedure, or the chair in the case of a meeting, must certify the appointment, but not unless and until the appointee has provided to the convener or the chair a statement to the effect that the appointee is an insolvency practitioner qualified under the Act to be the liquidator and consents to act.

5.23(3)   The certificate must be authenticated and dated by the convener or chair and must–

(a)   identify the company;

(b)   identify and provide contact details for the person appointed as liquidator;

(c)   state the date on which the liquidator was appointed;

(d)   state that the appointee–

    (i)   has provided a statement of being qualified to act as an insolvency practitioner in relation to the company,

    (ii)   has consented to act, and

    (iii)   was appointed as liquidator of the company.

5.23(4)   Where 2 or more liquidators are appointed the certificate must also specify (as required by section 231) whether any act required or authorised under any enactment to be done by the liquidator is to be done by all or any one or more of them.

5.23(5)   The liquidator's appointment is effective from the date on which the appointment is certified, that date to be endorsed on the certificate.

5.23(6)   The convener or chair must deliver the certificate to the liquidator appointed.

5.23(7)   The liquidator must–

(a)   within 7 days beginning with the day the liquidator receives the certificate of appointment deliver notice of it to–

    (i)   the court; and

    (ii)   AiB; and

(b)   within 28 days beginning with the day the liquidator receives the order of appointment–

    (i)   gazette the notice; or

   (ii)   otherwise advertise the notice in such manner as the liquidator thinks fit,

or both gazette the notice and otherwise advertise the notice in such manner as the liquidator thinks fit.

5.23(8)   Any notice under this rule must state–

   (a)   that a liquidator has been appointed; and

   (b)   the date of the appointment.

5.24   Decision on nomination

5.24(1)   In the case of a decision on the nomination of a liquidator–

   (a)   if on any vote there are 2 nominees, the person who obtains the most support is appointed;

   (b)   if there are 3 or more nominees, and one of them has a clear majority over both or all the others together, that one is appointed; and

   (c)   in any other case, the convener or chair must continue to take votes (disregarding at each vote any nominee who has withdrawn and, if no nominee has withdrawn, the nominee who obtained the least support last time) until a clear majority is obtained for any one nominee.

5.24(2)   The convener or chair may at any time put to the meeting a resolution for the joint nomination of any 2 or more nominees.

5.25   Invitation to creditors and contributories to form a liquidation committee

5.25(1)   Where a decision is sought from the company's creditors and contributories on the appointment of a liquidator, the convener of the decision procedure must at the same time deliver to the creditors and contributories a notice inviting them to decide whether a liquidation committee should be established if sufficient creditors are willing to be members of the committee.

5.25(2)   The notice must also invite nominations for membership of the committee, such nominations to be received by a date specified in the notice.

5.25(3)   The notice must–

   (a)   state that nominations must be delivered to the convener by the specified date;

   (b)   state, in the case of creditors, that nominations can only be accepted if the convener is satisfied as to the creditors' eligibility under rule 10.4 (eligibility for membership of creditors' or liquidation committee); and

   (c)   explain the effect of section 142(2) and (3) on whether a committee is to be established under Part 10 (creditors and liquidation committees).

5.26   Appointment by the court (section 138(5), section 139(4) and section 140)

5.26(1)   This rule applies where the liquidator is appointed by the court under section 138(5) (no person nominated or appointed by creditors and contributories), 139(4) (different persons nominated by creditors and contributories) or section 140 (winding up following administration or CVA).

5.26(2)   The court must not make the appointment unless and until the person being appointed liquidator has lodged in court a statement to the effect that that person is qualified to act as an insolvency practitioner in relation to the company and consents to act as liquidator.

5.26(3)   The liquidator's appointment is effective from the date of the order of appointment.

5.26(4)   The liquidator must–

   (a)   within 7 days beginning with the day the liquidator receives the copy order of appointment deliver notice of it to AiB; and

   (b)   within 28 days beginning with the day the liquidator receives the copy order of appointment–

       (i)   deliver notice of it to the creditors and contributories; or

      (ii)   if the court permits and in accordance with the directions of the court either–

          (aa) gazette the notice; or

          (bb) otherwise advertise the notice,

     or both gazette the notice and otherwise advertise the notice.

5.26(5)   Where the liquidator gives notice under paragraph (4)(b)(i) the liquidator may, in addition–

   (a)   gazette the notice; or

   (b)   otherwise advertise the notice in such manner as the liquidator thinks fit,

or both gazette the notice and otherwise advertise the notice.

5.26(6)   Any notice under this rule must–

   (a)   state that a liquidator has been appointed;

   (b)   state the date of the appointment;

   (c)   state whether the liquidator proposes to seek decisions from creditors and contributories for the purpose of establishing a liquidation committee, or proposes only to seek a decision from creditors for that purpose; and

   (d)   if the liquidator does not propose to seek any such decision, set out the powers of the creditors under the Act to require the liquidator to seek one.

5.27 Liquidator's resignation

5.27(1)   A liquidator may resign only–

   (a)   on grounds of ill health;

   (b)   because of the intention to cease to practise as an insolvency practitioner;

   (c)   because the further discharge of the duties of liquidator is prevented or made impracticable by–

       (i)   a conflict of interest; or

      (ii)   a change of personal circumstances;

   (d)   where 2 or more persons are acting as liquidator jointly, and it is the opinion of both or all of them that it is no longer expedient that there should continue to be that number of joint liquidators.

5.27(2)   Before resigning, the liquidator must deliver a notice to creditors, and invite the creditors by a decision procedure, or by deemed consent procedure, to consider whether a replacement should be appointed, except where the resignation is under sub-paragraph (1)(d).

5.27(3)   The notice must–

   (a)   state the liquidator's intention to resign;

   (b)   state that under rule 5.27(8) of these Rules the liquidator will be released 21 days after the date of delivery of the notice of resignation to the court under section 172(6), unless the court orders otherwise; and

   (c)   comply with rule 8.7 (deemed consent) or 8.8 (notices to creditors of decision procedure) so far as applicable.

5.27(4)   The notice may suggest the name of a replacement liquidator.

5.27(5)   The notice must be accompanied by a summary of the liquidator's receipts and payments.

5.27(6)   The decision date must be not more than 5 business days before the date on which the liquidator intends to give notice of resignation under section 172(6) (notice of resignation to the court).

5.27(7)   The resigning liquidator must deliver a copy of the notice of resignation under section 172(6) to AiB.

5.27(8)   The resigning liquidator's release is effective 21 days after the date on which the notice of resignation under section 172(6) is delivered to the court, unless the court orders otherwise.

5.28   Decision of creditors to remove liquidator

[Note: in relation to release of the liquidator following removal from office by a decision of the company's creditors, see: where the company's creditors have not decided against the liquidator's release, section 174(4)(a)(i); and where the company's creditors have decided against release, section 174(4)(b)(i).]

5.28(1)   This rule applies where a decision is made, using a decision procedure, to remove the liquidator.

5.28(2)   The convener of the decision procedure or chair of the meeting (as the case may be) must within 3 business days of the decision to remove the liquidator–

(a)   deliver the certificate of the liquidator's removal to the court;

(b)   deliver a copy of that certificate to AiB; and

(c)   if the convener or chair is a person other than the liquidator removed, deliver a copy of the certificate to the liquidator removed.

5.28(3)   If the creditors decided to appoint a new liquidator, the certificate of the new liquidator's appointment must also be delivered to the new liquidator within that time; and the certificate must comply with the requirements in rule 5.23.

5.28(4)   The certificate of the liquidator's removal must–

(a)   identify the company;

(b)   identify and provide contact details for the removed liquidator;

(c)   state that the creditors of the company decided on the date specified in the certificate that the liquidator specified in the certificate be removed from office as liquidator of the company;

(d)   state the decision procedure used, and the decision date;

(e)   state that the creditors either–

   (i)   did not decide against the liquidator being released, or

   (ii)   decided that the liquidator should not be released; and

(f)   be authenticated and dated by the convener or chair.

5.28(5)   The liquidator's removal is effective from the date of the certificate of removal.

5.29   Removal of liquidator by the court (section 172(2))

[Note: in relation to release of the liquidator following removal from office by the court see section 174(4)(b)(ii).]

5.29(1)   This rule applies where an application is made to the court under section 172(2) for the removal of the liquidator, or for an order directing the liquidator to initiate a decision procedure of creditors for the purpose of removing the liquidator.

5.29(2)   The court may require the applicant to make a deposit or find caution for the expenses to be incurred by the liquidator on the application.

5.29(3)   The applicant must, at least 14 days before the hearing, deliver to the liquidator–

(a)   a notice of the hearing stating the venue;

(b)   a copy of the application; and

(c)   a copy of any evidence on which the applicant intends to rely.

5.29(4)   The expenses of the application are not payable as an expense of the liquidation unless the court orders otherwise.

5.29(5)   Where the court removes the liquidator the order of removal may include such provision as the court thinks fit with respect to matters arising in connection with the removal.

5.29(6)   The person removed must as soon as reasonably practicable after receiving a copy of the order of removal deliver a copy of the order of removal to AiB.

5.29(7)   If the court appoints a new liquidator, rule 5.26 applies.

5.30   Deceased liquidator

[Note: in relation to release of the liquidator following death see section 174(4)(a)(ii).]

5.30(1)   If the liquidator dies a notice of the fact and date of death must be delivered as soon as reasonably practicable to–

(a)   the court; and

(b)   AiB.

5.30(2)   The notice must be delivered by one of the following:–

(a)   a surviving joint liquidator;

(b)   a member of the deceased liquidator's firm (if the deceased was a member or employee of a firm);

(c)   an officer of the deceased liquidator's company (if the deceased was an officer or employee of a company);

(d)   an executor of the deceased liquidator.

5.30(3)   If such notice has not been delivered within the 21 days following the liquidator's death then any other person may deliver the notice.

5.31   Loss of qualification as insolvency practitioner

[Note: in relation to release of the liquidator where the liquidator vacates office on ceasing to be a person qualified to act as an insolvency practitioner in relation to the company (section 172(5)) see section 174(4)(b)(iii).]

5.31(1)   This rule applies where the liquidator vacates office on ceasing to be qualified to act as an insolvency practitioner in relation to the company.

5.31(2)   A notice of the fact must be delivered as soon as reasonably practicable to–

(a)   the court; and

(b)   AiB.

5.31(3)   The notice must be delivered by one of the following–

(a)   the liquidator who has vacated office;

(b)   a continuing joint liquidator;

(c)   the recognised professional body which was the source of the vacating liquidator's authorisation to act (immediately before the liquidator vacated office).

5.31(4)   The notice must be authenticated and dated by the person delivering the notice.

5.32   Application by liquidator for release (section 174(4)(b) or (d))

5.32(1)   An application by a former liquidator to the Accountant of Court for release under section 174(4)(b) or (d) must contain–

(a)   identification details for the insolvency proceedings;

(b)   identification and contact details for the former liquidator;

(c)   a statement that the former liquidator is applying to the Accountant of Court to grant the former liquidator a certificate of the former liquidator's release as liquidator as a result of the circumstances specified in the application;

(d)   details of the circumstances referred to in sub-paragraph (c) under which the former liquidator has ceased to act as liquidator.

5.32(2)   The application must be authenticated and dated by the former liquidator.

5.32(3)   When the Accountant of Court gives a release, the Accountant of Court must deliver–

(a)   a certificate of the release to the former liquidator; and

(b)   a notice of the release to AiB.

5.32(4)   Release is effective from the date of the certificate or such other date as the certificate specifies.

5.33   Final account prior to dissolution (section 146)

5.33(1)   The final account which the liquidator is required to make up under section 146(2) and deliver to creditors must comply with the requirements of rule 7.9.

5.33(2)   When the account is delivered to the creditors it must be accompanied by a notice which states–

(a)   that the company's affairs are fully wound up;

(b)   that a creditor may object to the release of the liquidator by giving notice in writing to the liquidator before the end of the prescribed period;

(c)   that the prescribed period is the period ending 28 days after delivery of the notice;

(d)   that the liquidator will vacate office under section 172(8) as soon as the liquidator has complied with section 146(4) by filing with the court and delivering to the registrar of companies and AiB the final account and notice containing the statement required by section 146(4)(b) of whether any creditors have objected to the liquidator's release; and

(e)   that the liquidator will be released under section 174(4)(d)(ii) at the same time as vacating office unless any of the creditors objected to the release.

5.33(3)   The liquidator must deliver a copy of the notice under section 146(4) to the Accountant of Court.

5.34   Relief from, or variation of, duty to report

5.34(1)   The court may, on the application of the liquidator, relieve the liquidator of any duty imposed on the liquidator by rule 5.33, or authorise the liquidator to carry out the duty in a way other than required by that rule.

5.34(2)   In considering whether to act under this rule, the court must have regard to the cost of carrying out the duty, to the amount of the assets available, and to the extent of the interest of creditors or contributories, or any particular class of them.

5.35   Liquidator's duties on vacating office

5.35(1)   This rule applies where a person appointed as liquidator ("the succeeding liquidator") succeeds a previous liquidator ("the former liquidator") as the liquidator.

5.35(2)   When the succeeding liquidator's appointment takes effect the former liquidator must as soon as reasonably practicable deliver to the succeeding liquidator–

(a)   the assets (after deduction of any expenses properly incurred, and distributions made, by the former liquidator);

(b)   the records of the winding up, including correspondence, statements of claim, evidence of debts and other documents relating to the winding up; and

(c)   the company's documents and other records.

5.35(3)   In doing so, the former liquidator must hand over–

(a)   such information relating to the affairs of the company and the course of the winding up as the succeeding liquidator considers reasonably required for the effective discharge of the succeeding liquidator's duties as liquidator; and

(b)   all records and documents in the former liquidator's possession relating to the affairs of the company and its winding up.

5.36   Taking possession and realisation of the company's assets

5.36(1)   The liquidator must–

(a)   as soon as reasonably practicable after the liquidator's appointment take possession of–

    (i)   the whole assets of the company; and

    (ii)   any property, books, papers or records in the possession or control of the company or to which the company appears to be entitled; and

(b)   make up and maintain an inventory and valuation of the assets of the company.

5.36(2)   The liquidator is entitled to have access to, and to make copies of, all documents or records relating to the assets, property, business or financial affairs of the company–

(a)   sent by or on behalf of the company to a third party; and

(b)   in that third party's hands.

5.36(3)   If a person obstructs the liquidator in the liquidator's exercise, or attempted exercise, of a power conferred by paragraph (2), the court may, on the liquidator's application, order the person to cease obstructing the liquidator.

5.36(4)   The liquidator may require delivery to the liquidator of any title deed or other document of the company, even if a right of lien is claimed over it.

5.36(5)   Paragraph (4) is without prejudice to any preference of the holder of the lien.

5.37   Realisation of the company's heritable property

5.37(1)   This rule applies to the sale of any part of the company's heritable property over which a heritable security is held by a creditor or creditors if the rights of the secured creditor are preferable to those of the liquidator.

5.37(2)   The liquidator may sell that part only with the concurrence of every such creditor unless the liquidator obtains a sufficiently high price to discharge every such security.

5.37(3)   Subject to paragraph (4), the following acts are precluded–

(a)   the taking of steps by a creditor to enforce the creditor's security over that part after the liquidator has intimated to the creditor an intention to sell it;

(b)   the commencement by the liquidator of the procedure for the sale of that part after a creditor has intimated to the liquidator that the creditor intends to commence the procedure for its sale.

5.37(4) Where the liquidator or a creditor has given intimation under paragraph (3) but has unduly delayed in proceeding with the sale, then, if authorised by the court in the case of–

(a)   paragraph (3)(a), any creditor to whom intimation has been given may enforce the creditor's security;

(b)   paragraph (3)(b), the liquidator may sell that part.

5.37(5) The validity of the title of any purchaser is not challengeable on the ground that there has been a failure to comply with a requirement of this rule.

5.38   Power of court to set aside certain transactions

5.38(1)   If in the course of the liquidation the liquidator enters into any transaction with a person who is an associate of the liquidator, the court may, on the application of any interested person, set the transaction aside and order the liquidator to compensate the company for any loss suffered in consequence of it.

5.38(2)   This does not apply if either–

(a)   the transaction was entered into with the prior consent of the court; or

(b)   it is shown to the court's satisfaction that the transaction was for value, and that it was entered into by the liquidator without knowing, or having any reason to suppose, that the person concerned was an associate.

5.38(3)   Nothing in this rule is to be taken as prejudicing the operation of any rule of law relating to a trustee's dealings with trust property, or the fiduciary obligations of any person.

5.39   Rule against improper solicitation

5.39(1)   Where the court is satisfied that any improper solicitation has been used by or on behalf of the liquidator in obtaining proxies or procuring the liquidator's appointment, it may order that no remuneration be allowed as an expense of the liquidation to any person by whom, or on whose behalf, the solicitation was exercised.

5.39(2)   An order of the court under this rule overrides any resolution of the liquidation committee or the creditors, or any other provision of these Rules relating to the liquidator's remuneration.

CHAPTER 7

SPECIAL MANAGER

[Note: a document required by the Act or these Rules must also contain the standard contents required as set out in Part 1.]

5.40 Application of this Chapter and interpretation

5.40 This Chapter applies to applications for the appointment of a special manager by a liquidator and by a provisional liquidator (where one has been appointed), and so references to the liquidator are to be read as including a provisional liquidator.

5.41 Appointment and remuneration of special manager (section 177)

5.41(1) An application by the liquidator under section 177 for the appointment of a special manager must be supported by a report setting out the reasons for the application.

5.41(2) The report must include the liquidator's estimate of the value of the business or property in relation to which the special manager is to be appointed.

5.41(3) The court's order appointing the special manager must specify the duration of the special manager's appointment being one of the following–

(a) for a fixed period stated in the order;

(b) until the occurrence of a specified event; or

(c) until the court makes a further order.

5.41(4) The appointment of a special manager may be renewed by order of the court.

5.41(5) The special manager's remuneration will be fixed from time to time by the court.

5.41(6) The acts of the special manager are valid notwithstanding any defect in the special manager's appointment or qualifications.

5.42 Caution

5.42(1) The appointment of the special manager does not take effect until the person appointed has found (or, if the court allows, undertaken to find) caution for the appointment to be given to the applicant.

5.42(2) A person appointed as special manager may find caution either specifically for a particular winding up, or generally for any winding up in relation to which that person may be appointed as special manager.

5.42(3) The amount of the caution must be not less than the value of the business or property in relation to which the special manager is appointed, as estimated in the applicant's report under rule 5.41 which accompanied the application for appointment.

5.42(4) When the special manager has found caution for the appointment to be given to the applicant that person must lodge with the court a certificate as to the adequacy of the caution.

5.42(5) The cost of finding the caution must be paid in the first instance by the special manager; but–

(a) where a winding-up order is not made, the special manager is entitled to be reimbursed out of the property of the company, and the court may order accordingly; and

(b) where a winding-up order is made, the special manager is entitled to be reimbursed as an expense of the liquidation.

5.43 Failure to give or keep up caution

5.43(1) If the special manager fails to find the required caution within the time allowed for that purpose by the order of appointment, or any extension of that time that may be allowed, the liquidator must report the failure to the court, which may discharge the order appointing the special manager.

5.43(2) If the special manager fails to keep up the caution, the liquidator must report the failure to the court, which may remove the special manager, and make such order as to expenses as it thinks just.

5.43(3)　If the court discharges the order appointing the special manager, or makes an order removing the special manager, the court must give directions as to whether any, and if so what, steps should be taken for the appointment of another special manager.

5.44　Accounting

5.44(1)　The special manager must produce accounts, containing details of the special manager's receipts and payments, for the approval of the liquidator.

5.44(2)　The accounts must be for–

(a)　each 3 month period for the duration of the special manager's appointment; and

(b)　any shorter period ending with the termination of the special manager's appointment.

5.44(3)　When the accounts have been approved, the special manager's receipts and payments must be added to those of the liquidator.

5.45　Termination of appointment

5.45(1)　The special manager's appointment terminates–

(a)　if the winding-up petition is dismissed; or

(b)　in a case where a provisional liquidator was appointed under section 135, if the appointment is discharged without a winding-up order having been made.

5.45(2)　If the liquidator is of the opinion that the appointment of the special manager is no longer necessary or beneficial for the company, the liquidator must apply to the court for directions, and the court may order the special manager's appointment to be terminated.

5.45(3)　The liquidator must make the same application if the creditors decide that the appointment should be terminated.

CHAPTER 8

PUBLIC EXAMINATION OF COMPANY OFFICERS AND OTHERS (SECTION 133)

[Note: a document required by the Act or these Rules must also contain the standard contents required as set out in Part 1.]

5.46　Request by a creditor for a public examination (section 133(2))

5.46(1)　A request made under section 133(2) by a creditor to the liquidator for the public examination of a person must contain–

(a)　identification details for the company;

(b)　the name and postal address of the creditor;

(c)　the name and postal address of the proposed examinee;

(d)　a description of the relationship which the proposed examinee has, or has had, with the company;

(e)　a request by the creditor to the liquidator to apply to the court for a public examination of the proposed examinee under section 133(2);

(f)　the amount of the creditor's claim in the winding up;

(g)　a statement that the total amount of the creditor's and any concurring creditors' claims is believed to represent not less than $\frac{1}{2}$ in value of the debts of the company;

(h) a statement that the creditor understands the requirement to deposit with the liquidator such sum as the liquidator may determine to be appropriate by way of caution for the expenses of holding a public examination; and

(i) a statement that the creditor believes that a public examination is required for the reason stated in the request.

5.46(2) The request must be authenticated and dated by the creditor.

5.46(3) The request must be accompanied by–

(a) a list of the creditors concurring with the request and the amounts of their respective claims in the winding up, with their respective values; and

(b) from each concurring creditor, confirmation of the creditor's concurrence.

5.47   Request by a contributory for a public examination (section 133(2))

5.47(1) A request made under section 133(2) by a contributory to the liquidator for the public examination of a person must contain–

(a) identification details for the company;

(b) the name and postal address of the contributory;

(c) the name and postal address of the proposed examinee;

(d) a description of the relationship which the proposed examinee has, or has had, with the company;

(e) a request by the contributory to the liquidator to apply to the court for a public examination of the proposed examinee under section 133(2);

(f) the number of shares held in the company by the contributory;

(g) the number of votes to which the contributory is entitled;

(h) a statement that the total amount of the contributory's and any concurring contributories' shares and votes is believed to represent not less than $\frac{3}{4}$ in value of the company's contributories;

(i) a statement that the contributory understands the requirement to deposit with the liquidator such sum as the liquidator may determine to be appropriate by way of caution for the expenses of holding a public examination; and

(j) a statement that the contributory believes that a public examination is required for the reason specified in the request.

5.47(2) The request must be authenticated and dated by the contributory.

5.47(3) The request must be accompanied by–

(a) a list of the contributories concurring with the request and the number of shares and votes each holds in the company; and

(b) from each concurring contributory, confirmation of the concurrence and of the number of shares and votes held in the company.

5.48   Further provisions about requests by a creditor or contributory for a public examination

5.48(1) A request by a creditor or contributory for a public examination does not require the support of concurring creditors or contributories if the requisitioning creditor's debt or, as the case may be, requisitioning contributory's shares, is sufficient alone under section 133(2).

5.48(2)   Before the liquidator makes the requested application, the creditor or contributory requesting the examination must deposit with the liquidator such sum (if any) as the liquidator determines is appropriate as caution for the expenses of the public examination (if ordered).

5.48(3)   The liquidator must make the application for the examination–

(a)   within 28 days of receiving the creditor's or contributory's request (if no caution is required under paragraph (2)); or

(b)   within 28 days of the creditor or contributory (as the case may be) depositing the required caution.

5.48(4)   However if the liquidator thinks the request is unreasonable, the liquidator may apply to the court for an order to be relieved from making the application.

5.48(5)   If the application for an order under paragraph (4) is made without notice to any other party and the court makes such an order then the liquidator must deliver a notice of the order as soon as reasonably practicable to the creditors or contributories who requested the examination.

5.48(6)   If the court dismisses the liquidator's application under paragraph (4), the liquidator must make the application under section 133(2) as soon as reasonably practicable.

5.49   Notice of the public examination

5.49(1)   Where the court orders the public examination of any person under section 133(1) then, unless the court orders otherwise, the liquidator–

(a)   must give at least 14 days' notice of the examination to–

   (i)   the special manager (if a special manager has been appointed); and

   (ii)   the creditors and all the contributories of the company who are known to the liquidator (subject to any contrary direction of the court); and

(b)   may, in addition, at least 14 days before the date fixed for the examination–

   (i)   gazette the notice;

   (ii)   advertise the notice in such other manner as the liquidator thinks fit; or

   (iii)   both gazette the notice and advertise it in such other manner as the liquidator thinks fit.

5.49(2)   The notice must state–

(a)   the purpose of the public examination; and

(b)   the venue.

5.49(3)   Unless the court directs otherwise, notice under paragraph (1)(b) must not be given until at least 5 business days have elapsed since the examinee was served with the order.

5.50   Examinee unfit for examination

5.50(1)   Where the examinee is a person who lacks capacity within the meaning of the Adults with Incapacity (Scotland) Act 2000 ("the 2000 Act") or is unfit to undergo or attend for public examination, the court may–

(a)   sist the order for the examinee's public examination; or

(b)   order that it is to be conducted in such manner and at such place as it thinks just.

5.50(2)   The applicant for an order under paragraph (1) must be–

(a)   a person who has been appointed by a court in the United Kingdom or elsewhere to manage the affairs of, or to represent, the examinee; or

(b) a person who appears to the court to be a suitable person to make the application.

5.50(3) The application must, unless the examinee is a person who lacks capacity within the meaning of the 2000 Act, be supported by the affidavit of a registered medical practitioner as to the examinee's mental and physical condition.

5.50(4) At least 5 business days' notice of the application must be given to the liquidator.

5.51 Expenses of examination

5.51 Where public examination of the examinee has been ordered by the court on a request by a creditor under rule 5.46 or by a contributory under rule 5.47, the court may order that some or all of the expenses of the examination are to be paid out of the deposit required under those rules, instead of as an expense of the liquidation.

CHAPTER 9

DISTRIBUTION OF COMPANY'S ASSETS BY THE LIQUIDATOR

5.52 Winding up commencing as voluntary

5.52 In any winding up by the court which follows immediately on a voluntary winding up (whether members' voluntary or creditors' voluntary), such outlays and remuneration of the voluntary liquidator as the court may allow have the same priority as the outlays mentioned in rule 7.28(3)(a).

5.53 Saving for powers of the court (section 156)

5.53(1) The priority laid down by rule 7.27 is subject to the power of the court to make orders under section 156, where the assets are insufficient to satisfy the liabilities.

5.53(2) Nothing in those rules–

(a) applies to or affects the power of any court, in proceedings by or against the company, to order expenses to be paid by the company, or the liquidator; or

(b) affects the rights of any person to whom such expenses are ordered to be paid.

CHAPTER 10

MISCELLANEOUS

[Note: a document required by the Act or these Rules must also contain the standard contents required as set out in Part 1.]

Limitation

5.54 Limitation of actions

5.54(1) The following bar the effect of any enactment or rule of law relating to the limitation of actions–

(a) the presentation of a petition for winding up;

(b) the submission of a claim under rule 7.16.

5.54(2) Reference to any of a creditor's acts mentioned in sub-paragraphs (a) and (b) of paragraph (1) barring the effect of any enactment or rule of law relating to the limitation of actions is to be construed as a reference to that act having the same effect, for the purposes of that enactment or rule of law, as an effective acknowledgement of the creditor's claim.

5.54(3)   Reference in paragraph (1) or (2) to an enactment does not include a reference to an enactment which implements or gives effect to any international agreement or obligation.

Dissolution after winding up

5.55   Dissolution after winding up

[Note: on release of the liquidator where an order is made under section 204 for early dissolution of the company and the liquidator vacates office when dissolution takes effect in accordance with that section (section 172(7)), see section 174(4)(b)(iii) and rule 5.32.]

5.55   Where the court makes an order under section 204(5) or 205(5), the person on whose application the order was made must deliver to the registrar of companies and AiB a copy of the order.

PART 6

BLOCK TRANSFER OF WINDING UP PROCEEDINGS

[Note: a document required by the Act or these Rules must also contain the standard contents required as set out in Part 1]

6.1   Power to make a block transfer order

6.1(1)   Part 6 applies where it is expedient to transfer some or all of the cases in which an outgoing liquidator ("the outgoing liquidator") holds office to one or more liquidators ("the replacement liquidator") in a single transaction where the outgoing liquidator–

(a)   dies;

(b)   retires from practice; or

(c)   is otherwise unable or unwilling to continue in office.

6.1(2)   In a case to which this Part applies the Court of Session has the power to make an order ("a block transfer order") appointing a replacement liquidator in the place of the outgoing liquidator.

6.1(3)   The replacement liquidator must be qualified to act as an insolvency practitioner in relation to the company.

6.2   Application for block transfer order

6.2(1)   An application for a block transfer order may be made to the Court of Session for–

(a)   the removal of the outgoing liquidator by the exercise of any of the powers in paragraph (2);

(b)   the appointment of a replacement liquidator by the exercise of any of the powers in paragraph (3);

(c)   such other order or direction as may be necessary or expedient in connection with the matters referred to in sub-paragraphs (a) and (b).

6.2(2)   The powers referred to in paragraph (1)(a) are those in–

(a)   section 108(2) (voluntary winding up); and

(b)   section 172(2) and rule 6.1(2) (winding up by the court).

6.2(3)   The powers referred to in paragraph (1)(b) are those in–

(a)   section 108(2); and

(b)   rule 6.1(2).

6.2(4)   An application may be made by any of the following:–

(a)   the outgoing liquidator (if able and willing to do so);

(b)   any person who holds the office of liquidator jointly with the outgoing liquidator;

(c)   any person who is proposed to be appointed as the replacement liquidator;

(d)   any creditor in a case subject to the application;

(e)   the recognised professional body which was the source of the outgoing liquidator's authorisation (immediately before the application is made); or

(f)   the Secretary of State.

6.2(5)   The application must be served on–

(a)   the outgoing liquidator (if not the applicant or deceased);

(b)   any person who holds office jointly with the outgoing liquidator; and

(c)   such other person as the Court of Session directs.

6.2(6)   The application must contain a schedule setting out–

(a)   identification details for the insolvency proceedings; and

(b)   the capacity in which the outgoing liquidator was appointed.

6.2(7)   The application must be supported by evidence–

(a)   setting out the circumstances as a result of which it is expedient to appoint a replacement liquidator; and

(b)   exhibiting the consent to act of each person who is proposed to be appointed as replacement liquidator.

6.3   Action following application for a block transfer order

6.3(1)   In deciding to what extent (if any) the costs of making an application under rule 6.2 should be paid as an expense of the case to which the application relates, the factors to which the Court of Session must have regard include–

(a)   the reasons for making the application;

(b)   the number of cases to which the application relates;

(c)   the value of the assets comprised in those cases; and

(d)   the nature and extent of costs involved.

6.3(2)   Where an appointment under rule 6.1 is made, the replacement liquidator must–

(a)   as soon as reasonably practicable give notice of the appointment to AiB;

(b)   within 28 days give notice of the appointment to the creditors and contributories, or if the court so permits, advertise the appointment in accordance with the directions of the court; and

(c)   give notice to such other persons, and in such form, as the Court of Session may direct.

6.3(3)   In any notice given by the replacement liquidator under this rule the replacement liquidator must state–

(a)   that the outgoing liquidator has been removed; and

(b)   whether the outgoing liquidator has been released.

PART 7

WINDING UP – REPORTING, ACCOUNTS, REMUNERATION, CLAIMS AND DISTRIBUTIONS

7.1   Application of Part

7.1   This Part applies in winding up.

CHAPTER 1

REPORTING

[Note: a document required by the Act or these Rules must also contain the standard contents required as set out in Part 1.]

7.2   Reports by interim liquidator in a winding up by the court

7.2(1)   The interim liquidator must in accordance with this rule deliver a report on the winding up and the state of the company's affairs to the creditors and contributories at least once after the making of the winding-up order.

7.2(2)   The report must be delivered–

(a)   before the interim liquidator delivers a notice inviting proposals for a liquidator under rule 5.22 (choosing a person to be liquidator); or

(b)   with that notice.

7.2(3)   The report must contain–

(a)   identification details for the proceedings;

(b)   contact details for the interim liquidator;

(c)   a summary of the circumstances leading to the appointment of the interim liquidator;

(d)   if a statement of the company's affairs has been submitted–

(i)   a copy or summary of it, except so far as an order under rule 5.16 (limited disclosure) limits disclosure of it;

(ii)   details of who provided the statement of affairs; and

(iii)   any comments which the interim liquidator may have upon the statement of affairs;

(e)   if an order under rule 5.16 has been made–

(i)   a statement of that fact; and

(ii)   the date of the order;

(f)   if no statement of affairs has been submitted–

(i)   an explanation as to why there is no statement of affairs;

(ii)   a summary of the assets and liabilities of the company as known to the interim liquidator at the date of the report;

(g)   a full list of the company's creditors in accordance with paragraph (2) to (4) of rule 5.13 if either–

(i)   no statement of affairs has been submitted, or

(ii) a statement of affairs has been submitted but it does not include such a list, or the interim liquidator believes the list included is less than full;

(h) any estimates and statements required by rule 7.3; and

(i) any other information of relevance to the creditors or contributories.

7.3   Reports by interim liquidator: estimate of prescribed part

7.3(1)   The interim liquidator must include in a report under rule 7.2 estimates to the best of the interim liquidator's knowledge and belief of the value of–

(a) the prescribed part (whether or not the liquidator might be required under section 176A to make the prescribed part available for the satisfaction of unsecured debts); and

(b) the company's net property (as defined by section 176A(6)).

7.3(2)   If the interim liquidator considers that it may be appropriate for the liquidator to make an application to court under section 176A(5) the report must say so and give the interim liquidator's reasons.

7.3(3)   The liquidator may exclude from an estimate under paragraph (1) information the disclosure of which could seriously prejudice the commercial interests of the company.

7.3(4)   If the exclusion of such information affects the calculation of the estimate, the report must say so.

7.4   Progress reports: content

7.4(1)   The liquidator's progress report in a winding up must contain–

(a) identification details for the insolvency proceedings;

(b) identification and contact details for the liquidator;

(c) the date of appointment of the liquidator and any changes in the liquidator in accordance with paragraph (3);

(d) details of progress during the period of the report, including a summary account of receipts and payments during the period of the report;

(e) the information required–

(i)   in the case of a members' voluntary winding up, by rule 7.5;

(ii) in the case of a creditors' voluntary winding up or a winding up by the court, by rule 7.6;

(f) details of what assets remain to be realised;

(g) where a distribution is to be made in accordance with Chapters 4 to 6 in respect of an accounting period, the scheme of division; and

(h) any other information of relevance to the creditors.

7.4(2)   The receipts and payments account in a final progress report must state the amount paid to unsecured creditors by virtue of the application of section 176A.

7.4(3)   A change in the liquidator is only required to be shown in the next report after the change.

7.4(4)   Where an administration has converted to a voluntary winding up, the first progress report by the liquidator must include a note of any information received from the former administrator under rule 3.60(5) of the CVA and Administration Rules (moving from administration to creditors' voluntary winding up – matters occurring after the administrator's final progress report).

7.5   Remuneration and outlays etc.: members' voluntary winding up

7.5(1)   The information referred to in rule 7.4(1)(e)(i) is–

(a)   a statement of the nature and amounts of the liquidator's outlays during the period of the report; and

(b)   an estimate of the remuneration due to the liquidator during the period of report and the basis or bases set out in rule 7.10(2)(a) to (c) (determination of outlays and remuneration: members' voluntary winding up) on which the estimate is based.

7.5(2)   The progress report must also contain the information described in paragraph (1) for any previous period of report.

7.6   Remuneration and outlays etc.: creditors' voluntary winding up and winding up by the court

7.6(1)   The information referred to in rule 7.4(1)(e)(ii) is–

(a)   in respect of any accounting period ending during, or coinciding with the end of, the period of the report after the end of which the liquidator has made or intends to make a submission under rule 7.11(2)(a) to (c) (determination of outlays and remuneration: creditors' voluntary winding up and winding up by the court), the information referred to there;

(b)   in respect of any accounting period ending during, or coinciding with the end of, the period of the report after the end of which the liquidator has not made and is not making a submission under rule 7.11(2)(a) to (c)–

  (i)   a statement of the nature and amounts of the liquidator's outlays during the accounting period; and

  (ii)   an estimate of the remuneration due to the liquidator during the accounting period and the basis or bases set out in rule 7.11(8)(a) to (c) on which the estimate is based.

7.6(2)   Where paragraph (1)(b) applies the progress report must also contain the information described in that paragraph for any previous accounting period ending before the period of report unless the liquidator has made a submission under rule 7.11(2)(a) to (c) in respect of that accounting period.

7.7   Progress reports in voluntary winding up: timing and delivery

7.7(1)   This rule applies for the purposes of sections 92A and 104A and prescribes the periods for which reports must be made.

7.7(2)   The liquidator's progress reports in a voluntary winding up must cover the periods of–

(a)   12 months starting on the date the liquidator is appointed; and

(b)   each subsequent period of 12 months.

7.7(3)   The periods for which progress reports are required under paragraph (2) are unaffected by any change in the liquidator.

7.7(4)   However where a liquidator ceases to act the succeeding liquidator must, as soon as reasonably practicable after being appointed, deliver a notice to the members (in a members' voluntary winding up) or to members and creditors (in a creditors' voluntary winding up) of any matters about which the succeeding liquidator thinks the members or creditors should be informed.

7.7(5)   A progress report is not required for any period which ends after a notice is delivered under rule 3.11 (delivery of draft final account to members in members' voluntary winding up) or after the date to which a final account is made up under section 106 and is delivered by the liquidator to members and creditors (creditors' voluntary winding up).

7.7(6) The liquidator must deliver a copy of each progress report within 6 weeks after the end of the period covered by the report to–

(a) AiB (who is a prescribed person for the purposes of sections 92A and 104A);

(b) the members; and

(c) in a creditors' voluntary liquidation, the creditors.

7.8 Progress reports in winding up by the court: timing and delivery

[Note: Where in this rule provision is applicable to the provisional liquidator the term provisional liquidator is used.]

7.8(1) Subject to paragraph (2), the liquidator's progress report in a winding up by the court must cover the periods of–

(a) 12 months starting on the date on which the liquidator (including an interim liquidator) is appointed; and

(b) each subsequent period of 12 months.

7.8(2) Where a provisional liquidator is appointed under section 135, the liquidator's progress report must cover the periods of–

(a) 12 months starting on the date on which the provisional liquidator is appointed; and

(b) each subsequent period of 12 months.

7.8(3) The periods for which progress reports are required under paragraphs (1) and (2) are unaffected by–

(a) recall of the appointment of a provisional liquidator (prior to a winding up order being made);

(b) termination of the appointment of a provisional liquidator and appointment of a liquidator (including an interim liquidator) on the making of a winding up order;

(c) any change in the provisional liquidator or liquidator.

7.8(4) Where a liquidator ceases to act the succeeding liquidator must as soon as reasonably practicable after being appointed, deliver a notice to the creditors of any matters about which the succeeding liquidator thinks the creditors should be informed.

7.8(5) A progress report is not required for any period which ends after the date to which a final account or report is made up under section 146 and is delivered by the liquidator to the creditors.

7.8(6) The liquidator must deliver a copy of each progress report within 6 weeks after the end of the period covered by the report (or after the date on which the liquidator is appointed, whichever is the later) to–

(a) AiB;

(b) the members; and

(c) the creditors.

CHAPTER 2

FINAL ACCOUNTS

[Note: a document required by the Act or these Rules must also contain the standard contents required as set out in Part 1.]

7.9   Contents of final account

7.9(1)   The liquidator's final account under section 94, 106 or 146 must contain an account of the liquidator's administration of the winding up including–

(a)   a summary of the liquidator's receipts and payments, including details of the liquidator's remuneration and outlays; and

(b)   in the case of section 106 or 146, a statement as to the amount paid to unsecured creditors by virtue of section 176A.

7.9(2)   The final account or report to creditors or members must also contain–

(a)   details of the remuneration charged and expenses incurred by the liquidator during the period since the last progress report (if any);

(b)   a description of the things done by the liquidator in that period in respect of which the remuneration was charged and the expenses incurred; and

(c)   a summary of the receipts and payments during that period.

7.9(3)   Where the basis of remuneration has been fixed as a set amount, it is sufficient for the liquidator to state that amount and to give details of the expenses charged within the period in question.

CHAPTER 3

LIQUIDATOR'S REMUNERATION

[Note: a document required by the Act or these Rules must also contain the standard contents required as set out in Part 1.]

7.10   Determination of outlays and remuneration: members' voluntary winding up

7.10(1)   In a members' voluntary winding up, it is for the company in general meeting to determine the basis of remuneration.

7.10(2)   Subject to paragraph (3), the basis of remuneration must be fixed–

(a)   as a percentage of the value of the company's assets which are realised by the liquidator;

(b)   by reference to the work which was reasonably undertaken by the liquidator and the liquidator's staff in attending to matters arising in the winding up; or

(c)   as a set amount.

7.10(3)   The basis of remuneration may be fixed as any one or more of the bases set out in paragraph (2)(a) to (c) and different bases may be fixed in respect of different things done by the liquidator.

7.11   Determination of outlays and remuneration: creditors' voluntary winding up and winding up by the court

7.11(1)   The liquidator's claims for the outlays reasonably incurred and for the liquidator's remuneration must be made in accordance with this rule (and subject to rules 7.12 to 7.15).

7.11(2)   The liquidator may within 14 days after the end of an accounting period submit to the liquidation committee or, if there is no liquidation committee, to the court in respect of that period and any other previous accounting period in which no submission has been made under this paragraph–

(a)   the liquidator's accounts of the liquidator's intromissions with the company's assets for audit;

(b) a claim for the outlays reasonably incurred by the liquidator and for the liquidator's remuneration (where the liquidator intends to submit such a claim in respect of that accounting period); and

(c) where funds are available after making allowance for contingencies, a scheme of division of the divisible funds (unless rule 7.31(8) applies).

7.11(3)   The liquidator may, at any time before the end of an accounting period submit to the liquidation committee (or if there is no liquidation committee, to the court) an interim claim in respect of that period or any other previous accounting period in which no submission has been made under paragraph (2) for–

(a) the outlays reasonably incurred by the liquidator; and

(b) the liquidator's remuneration.

7.11(4)   If the liquidator submits an interim claim under paragraph (3), the liquidation committee or the court may make an interim determination in relation to the amount of the outlays and remuneration.

7.11(5)   If the liquidation committee or the court makes such an interim determination, it must take into account such an interim determination when making a determination under paragraph (7)(a)(ii).

7.11(6)   Accounts in respect of legal services incurred by the liquidator must, before payment, be submitted for taxation to the auditor of the court before which the liquidation is pending, unless–

(a) the account has been agreed between the liquidator and the person entitled to payment in respect of that account; and

(b) the liquidator is not an associate of that person.

7.11(7)   If the liquidator makes a submission under paragraph (2) to the liquidation committee or, if there is no liquidation committee the court, within 6 weeks after the end of an accounting period–

(a) the liquidation committee or, as the case may be, the court–

(i) may audit the accounts; and

(ii) must issue a determination fixing the amount of the outlays and remuneration payable to the liquidator; and

(b) the liquidator must make the audited accounts, scheme of division and the determination available for inspection by the creditors and contributories.

7.11(8)   Subject to paragraph (9), the basis of remuneration must be fixed–

(a) as a percentage of the value of the company's assets which are realised by the liquidator;

(b) by reference to the work which was reasonably undertaken by the liquidator and the liquidator's staff in attending to matters arising in the winding up;

(c) as a set amount.

7.11(9)   The basis of remuneration may be fixed as any one or more of the bases set out in paragraph (8)(a) to (c) and different bases may be fixed in respect of different things done by the liquidator.

7.11(10)   In fixing the amount of the liquidator's remuneration and outlays in respect of any accounting period, the liquidation committee or, as the case may be, the court may take into account any adjustment which the liquidation committee or the court may wish to make in the amount of the remuneration and outlays fixed in respect of any earlier accounting period.

7.12   Appeal against fixing of outlays and remuneration: creditors' voluntary winding up and winding up by the court

7.12(1)   Within 14 days after issue of a determination under rule 7.11(4) or (7)(a)(ii), by a liquidation committee, the liquidator, any creditor or any contributory may appeal against that determination, to the court.

7.12(2)   An appeal may only be made against a determination issued under rule 7.11(4) or (7)(a)(ii) by a creditor or contributory if notice is delivered to the liquidator of intention to appeal.

7.13   Recourse of liquidator to decision of creditors: creditors' voluntary winding up and winding up by the court

7.13   If the liquidator's outlays or remuneration has been fixed by the liquidation committee and the liquidator considers the amount to be insufficient, the liquidator may request that it be increased by the creditors by a decision procedure.

7.14   Recourse to the court: creditors' voluntary winding up and winding up by the court

7.14(1)   If the liquidator considers that the outlays or remuneration fixed by the liquidation committee, or by decision of the creditors, is insufficient, the liquidator may apply to the court for an order increasing the amount of the outlays or the amount or rate of remuneration.

7.14(2)   The liquidator must give at least 14 days' notice of the liquidator's application to the members of the liquidation committee and the committee may nominate one or more members to appear or be represented, and to be heard, on the application.

7.14(3)   If there is no liquidation committee, the liquidator's notice of the liquidator's application must be sent to such one or more of the company's creditors as the court may direct, which creditors may nominate one or more of their number to appear or be represented.

7.14(4)   The court may, if it appears to be a proper case, order the expenses of the liquidator's application, including the expenses of any member of the liquidation committee appearing or being represented on it, or any creditor so appearing or being represented, to be paid as an expense of the liquidation.

7.15   Creditors' claim that remuneration is excessive: creditors' voluntary winding up and winding up by the court

7.15(1)   If the liquidator's outlays and remuneration have been fixed by the liquidation committee or by the creditors, any creditor or creditors of the company representing in value at least 25% of the creditors may apply to the court for an order that the liquidator's outlays or remuneration be reduced, on the grounds that they are, in all the circumstances, excessive.

7.15(2)   If the court considers the application to be well-founded, it must make an order fixing the outlays or remuneration at a reduced amount or rate.

7.15(3)   Unless the court orders otherwise, the expenses of the application must be paid by the applicant, and are not payable as an expense of the liquidation.

CHAPTER 4

CLAIMS BY CREDITORS

[Note: a document required by the Act or these Rules must also contain the standard contents required as set out in Part 1.]

7.16   Submission of claims

7.16(1)   A creditor, in order to obtain an adjudication as to the creditor's entitlement to a dividend (so far as funds are available) out of the assets of the company in respect of any accounting period, must submit the creditor's claim to the liquidator not later than 8 weeks before the end of the accounting period.

7.16(2)   A creditor must submit a claim by producing to the liquidator–

(a)   a statement of claim as described in paragraph (3); and

(b)   documentary evidence of debt,

but the liquidator may dispense with the requirement in sub-paragraph (b) in respect of any debt or any class of debt.

7.16(3)   The statement of claim must–

(a)   be made out by, or under the direction of, the creditor and dated and authenticated by the creditor or a person authorised on the creditor's behalf;

(b)   state the creditor's name and address;

(c)   if the creditor is a company, identify the company;

(d)   state the name and address of any person authorised to act on behalf of the creditor;

(e)   state the total amount claimed in respect of all debts (under deduction of the value of any security as estimated by the creditor unless the creditor is surrendering or undertaking to surrender the security);

(f)   state whether or not the claim includes any outstanding uncapitalised interest at the date on which the company went into liquidation;

(g)   contain particulars of how and when the debt was incurred by the company, and where relevant the date on which payment of the debt became due;

(h)   contain particulars of any security held, the subjects covered, the date on which it was given and the value which the creditor puts on it;

(i)   include details of any retention of title in relation to goods to which the debt relates;

(j)   state the nature and amount of any preference under schedule 6 of the Act claimed in respect of the debt;

(k)   in the case of a member State liquidator creditor, specify and give details of underlying claims in respect of which the creditor is claiming;

(l)   include any details of any document by reference to which the debt can be substantiated; and

(m)   state the name, postal address and authority of the person authenticating the statement of claim and documentary evidence of debt (if someone other than the creditor).

7.16(4)   A claim submitted by a creditor, which has been accepted in whole or in part by the liquidator for the purpose of drawing a dividend in respect of any accounting period, is to be deemed to have been resubmitted for the purpose of obtaining an adjudication as to the creditor's entitlement to a dividend in respect of an accounting period or, as the case may be, any subsequent accounting period.

7.16(5)   A creditor who has submitted a claim may at any time submit a further claim specifying a different amount for the claim, provided that a secured creditor is not entitled to produce a further claim specifying a different value for the security at any time after the liquidator has required the creditor to discharge, or convey or assign, the security under rule 7.24.

7.17   False claims or evidence

7.17   If a creditor produces under rule 7.16 a statement of claim or documentary evidence of debt or other evidence which is false–

(a)   the creditor is guilty of an offence unless the creditor shows that the creditor neither knew nor had reason to believe that the statement of claim or documentary evidence of debt or other evidence was false;

(b)   the company is guilty of an offence if the company–

    (i)   knew or became aware that the statement of claim or documentary evidence of debt or other evidence was false; and

    (ii)   failed as soon as practicable after acquiring such knowledge to report it to the liquidator.

7.18   Evidence of claims

7.18(1)   The liquidator, for the purpose of being satisfied as to the validity or amount of a claim submitted by a creditor under rule 7.16, may require–

(a)   the creditor to produce further evidence; or

(b)   any other person who the liquidator believes can produce relevant evidence, to produce such evidence.

7.18(2)   If the creditor or other person refuses or delays to produce such evidence as required under paragraph (1), the liquidator may apply to the court for an order requiring the creditor or other person to attend for private examination before the court.

7.18(3)   On an application to it under paragraph (2) the court may make an order requiring the creditor or other person to attend for private examination before it on a date (being not earlier than 8 days nor later than 16 days after the date of the order) and at a time specified in the order.

7.18(4)   If a creditor or other person is for any good reason prevented from attending for examination, the court may grant a commission to take the examination (the commissioner being in this rule referred to as an "examining commissioner").

7.18(5)   At any private examination under paragraph (3) or where the court grants a commission to take the examination under paragraph (4)–

(a)   a solicitor or counsel may act on behalf of the liquidator; or

(b)   the liquidator may appear on the liquidator's own behalf.

7.18(6)   The examination, whether before the court or an examining commissioner, must be taken on oath.

7.18(7)   A person who fails without reasonable excuse to comply with an order made under paragraph (3) is guilty of an offence.

7.18(8)   References in this rule to a creditor in a case where the creditor is one of the following entities–

(a)   a trust;

(b)   a partnership (including a dissolved partnership);

(c)   a body corporate or an unincorporated body;

(d)   a limited partnership (including a dissolved partnership) within the meaning of the Limited Partnerships Act 1907,

are to be construed, unless the context otherwise requires, as references to a person representing the entity.

7.19   Adjudication of claims

7.19(1)   Where funds are available for payment of a dividend out of the company's assets in respect of an accounting period, the liquidator for the purpose of determining who is entitled to such a dividend must–

(a)   not later than 4 weeks before the end of the period, accept or reject every claim submitted or deemed to have been re-submitted under rule 7.16; and

(b)   at the same time make a decision on any matter requiring to be specified under paragraph (4)(a) or (b).

7.19(2)   On accepting or rejecting, under paragraph (1), every claim submitted or deemed to have been re-submitted, the liquidator must, as soon as reasonably practicable, send a list of every claim so accepted or rejected (including the amount of each claim and whether it has been accepted or rejected) to every creditor known to the liquidator.

7.19(3)   Where the liquidator rejects a claim, the liquidator must without delay notify the creditor giving reasons for the rejection.

7.19(4)   Where the liquidator accepts or rejects a claim, the liquidator must specify for that claim–

(a)   the amount of the claim accepted;

(b)   the category of debt, and the value of any security, as decided by the liquidator; and

(c)   if rejecting the claim, the reasons for doing so.

7.19(5)   Any member of the company or any creditor may, if dissatisfied with the acceptance or rejection of any claim (or, in relation to such acceptance or rejection, with a decision in respect of any matter requiring to be specified under paragraph (4)(a) or (b)) appeal to the court not later than 14 days before the end of the accounting period.

7.19(6)   Any reference in this rule to the acceptance or rejection of a claim is to be construed as a reference to the acceptance or rejection of the claim in whole or in part.

7.20   Entitlement to draw a dividend

7.20(1)   A creditor who has had that creditor's claim accepted in whole or in part by the liquidator under rule 7.19(1) or on appeal under rule 7.19(5) is entitled to payment out of the company's assets of a dividend in respect of the accounting period for the purposes of which the claim is accepted.

7.20(2)   Such entitlement to payment arises only in so far as the company has funds available to make that payment, having regard to rule 7.27 (order of priority in distribution).

7.21   Liabilities and rights of co-obligants

7.21(1)   Where a creditor has an obligant bound to the creditor along with the company for the whole or part of the debt, the obligant is not freed or discharged from liability for the debt by reason of the dissolution of the company or the creditor's voting or drawing a dividend or assenting to or not opposing–

(a)   the dissolution of the company; or

(b)   any composition with creditors.

7.21(2)   Paragraph (3) applies where–

(a)   a creditor has had a claim accepted in whole or in part; and

(b)   the obligant holds a security over any part of the company's assets,

7.21(3)   The obligant must account to the liquidator so as to put the company's assets in the same position as if the obligant had paid the debt to the creditor and thereafter had had the obligant's claim accepted in whole or in part in the liquidation after deduction of the value of the security.

7.21(4)   The obligant may require and obtain at the obligant's own expense from the creditor an assignation of the debt, on payment of the amount of the debt and on that being done may in respect of the debt submit a claim, and vote and draw a dividend, if otherwise legally entitled to do so.

7.21(5)   Paragraph (4) is without prejudice to any right, under any rule of law, of a co-obligant who has paid the debt.

7.21(6)   In this rule an "obligant" includes cautioner.

7.22   Amount which may be claimed generally

7.22(1)   Subject to the provisions of this rule and rules 7.23 and 7.24, the amount in respect of which a creditor is entitled to claim is the accumulated sum of principal and any interest which is due on the debt as at the date on which the company went into liquidation.

7.22(2)   If a debt does not depend on a contingency but would not be payable but for the liquidation until after the date on which the company went into liquidation, the amount of the claim is to be calculated as if the debt were payable on the date on which the company went into liquidation but subject to the deduction of interest at the rate specified in paragraph (4) from that date until the date for payment of the debt.

7.22(3)   In calculating the amount of a creditor's claim, the creditor must deduct any discount (other than any discount for immediate or early settlement) which is allowable by contract or course of dealing between the creditor and the company or by the usage of trade.

7.22(4)   The rate of interest referred to in paragraph (2) is the official rate.

7.22(5)   Where the winding up was immediately preceded by an administration, the reference to the date on which the company went into liquidation in paragraph (1) and the second reference to that date in paragraph (2) are to be construed as references to the date the company entered administration.

7.23   Debts depending on contingency

7.23(1)   Subject to paragraph (2), the amount which a creditor is entitled to claim is not to include a debt in so far as its existence or amount depends on a contingency.

7.23(2)   On an application by the creditor–

    (a)   to the liquidator; or

    (b)   if there is no liquidator, to the court,

the liquidator or court must put a value on the debt in so far as it is contingent.

7.23(3)   Where under paragraph (2) a value is put on the debt–

    (a)   the amount in respect of which the creditor is then entitled to claim is to be that value but no more;

    (b)   where the contingent debt is an annuity, a cautioner may not then be sued for more than that value.

7.23(4)   Any interested person may appeal to the court against a valuation under paragraph (2) by the liquidator, and the court may affirm or vary that valuation.

7.24   Secured debts

7.24(1)   In calculating the amount of a secured creditor's claim the secured creditor is to deduct the value of any security as estimated by the secured creditor.

7.24(2)   If the secured creditor surrenders, or undertakes in writing to surrender, a security for the benefit of the company's assets, the secured creditor is not required to deduct the value of that security.

7.24(3)   The liquidator may, at any time after the expiry of 12 weeks from the date on which the company went into liquidation, require a secured creditor at the expense of the company's assets to discharge the security or convey or assign it to the liquidator on payment to the creditor of the value specified by the creditor.

7.24(4)   Where under paragraph (3) the liquidator makes payment to the creditor the amount in respect of which the creditor is then entitled to claim is to be any balance of the creditor's debt remaining after receipt of such payment.

7.24(5)   In calculating the amount of the claim of a creditor whose security has been realised the creditor must deduct the amount (less the expenses of realisation) which the creditor has received, or is entitled to receive, from the realisation.

7.25   Claims in foreign currency

7.25(1)   A creditor may state the amount of the creditor's claim in a currency other than sterling where–

(a)   the creditor's claim is constituted by decree or other order made by a court ordering the company to pay to the creditor a sum expressed in a currency other than sterling; or

(b)   where it is not so constituted, the creditor's claim arises from a contract or bill of exchange in terms of which payment is, or may be required to be, made by the company to the creditor in a currency other than sterling.

7.25(2)   Where under paragraph (1) a claim is stated in a currency other than sterling the liquidator must convert it into sterling at a single rate for each currency determined by the liquidator by reference to the exchange rates prevailing in the London market at the close of business on the date on which the company went into liquidation.

CHAPTER 5

OFFICIAL RATE OF INTEREST

7.26   Specified rate of interest

7.26(1)   This rule specifies the rate of interest for the purpose of section 189(4)(a) and (5) (rate of interest used in calculating the official rate of interest for the purposes of provisions of the Act).

7.26(2)   The rate specified is the rate of interest on a sheriff court decree or extract under section 9 of the Sheriff Courts (Scotland) Extracts Act 1892 as it may be amended by section 4 of the Administration of Justice (Scotland) Act 1972.

CHAPTER 6

DISTRIBUTION OF COMPANY'S ASSETS BY THE LIQUIDATOR

[Note: a document required by the Act or these Rules must also contain the standard contents required as set out in Part 1.]

7.27   Order of priority in distribution

7.27(1)   The funds of the company's assets must be distributed by the liquidator to meet the following expenses and debts in the order in which they are mentioned–

(a)   the expenses of the liquidation;

(b)   any preferential debts within the meaning of section 386 (excluding any interest which has been accrued thereon to the date on which the company went into liquidation);

(c)   ordinary debts, that is to say a debt which is neither a secured debt nor a debt mentioned in any other sub-paragraph of this paragraph;

(d)   interest at the official rate, between the date on which the company went into liquidation and the date of payment, on–

    (i)   the preferential debts; and

    (ii)   the ordinary debts; and

(e)   any postponed debt.

7.27(2)   In paragraph (1)–

(a)   "postponed debt" means–

    (i)   a creditor's right to any alienation which has been reduced or restored to the company's assets under section 242 or to the proceeds of sale of such an alienation;

    (ii)   a claim arising by virtue of section 382(1)(a) of the Financial Services and Markets Act 2000 (restitution orders), unless it is also a claim arising by virtue of sub-paragraph (b) of that section (a person who has suffered loss etc.); or

    (iii)   a claim which by virtue of the Act or any other enactment is a claim the payment of which is to be postponed;

(b)   in sub-paragraph (d), where the liquidation was immediately preceded by an administration, the reference to the date on which the company went into liquidation is to be construed as the date the company entered administration.

7.27(3)   The expenses of the liquidation mentioned in paragraph (1)(a) are payable in the order of priority mentioned in rule 7.28 (order of priority of expenses of liquidation).

7.27(4)   Subject to section 175–

(a)   any debt falling within any of sub-paragraphs (b) to (e) of paragraph (1) is to have the same priority as any other debt falling within the same sub-paragraph; and

(b)   where the funds of the company's assets are inadequate to enable such debts to be paid in full, they are to abate in equal proportions.

7.27(5)   Any surplus remaining, after all the expenses and debts mentioned in paragraph (1) have been paid in full, must (unless the articles of the company provide otherwise) be distributed among the members according to their rights and interests in the company.

7.27(6)   Nothing in this rule affects–

(a)   the right of a secured creditor which is preferable to the rights of the liquidator; or

(b)   any preference of the holder of a lien over a title deed or other document which has been delivered to the liquidator in accordance with a requirement under rule 5.36(4).

7.28   Order of priority of expenses of liquidation

7.28(1)   All fees, costs, charges and other expenses incurred in the course of the liquidation are to be treated as expenses of the liquidation.

7.28(2)   The expenses associated with the prescribed part must be paid out of the prescribed part.

7.28(3)   The expenses of the liquidation are payable out of the assets of the company in the following order of priority–

(a)   any outlays properly chargeable or incurred by the provisional liquidator or liquidator in carrying out the functions of the provisional liquidator or liquidator in the liquidation including any costs referred to in Article 30 and 59 of the EU Regulation, except those outlays specifically mentioned in the following sub-paragraphs;

(b) the cost, or proportionate cost, of any caution provided by a provisional liquidator, liquidator or special manager in accordance with the Act or these Rules;

(c) the remuneration of the provisional liquidator (if any);

(d) the expenses of the petitioner in the liquidation, and of any person appearing in the petition whose expenses are allowed by the court;

(e) the remuneration of the special manager (if any);

(f) any amount payable to a person employed or authorised, under Chapter 4 of Part 5, to assist in the preparation of a statement of affairs or of accounts;

(g) the remuneration or emoluments of any person who has been employed by the liquidator to perform any services for the company, as required or authorised by or under the Act or these Rules;

(h) the remuneration of the liquidator determined in accordance with rules 7.11 to 7.15;

(i) the amount of any corporation tax on chargeable gains accruing on the realisation of any asset of the company (without regard to whether the realisation is effected by the liquidator, a secured creditor or otherwise).

7.29 Winding up commencing as voluntary

7.29 In any winding up by the court which follows immediately on a voluntary winding up (whether members' voluntary or creditors' voluntary), such outlays and remuneration of the voluntary liquidator as the court may allow have the same priority as the outlays mentioned in rule 7.28(3)(a).

7.30 Saving for powers of the court (section 156)

7.30(1) The priorities laid down by rules 7.27 and 7.28 are subject to the power of the court to make orders under section 156, where the assets are insufficient to satisfy the liabilities.

7.30(2) Nothing in those rules–

(a) applies to or affects the power of any court, in proceedings by or against the company, to order expenses to be paid by the company, or the liquidator; or

(b) affects the rights of any person to whom such expenses are ordered to be paid.

7.31 Estate to be distributed in respect of the accounting periods

[Note: Where in this rule provision is applicable to the provisional liquidator the term provisional liquidator is used.]

7.31(1) The liquidator must make up accounts of the liquidator's intromissions with the company's assets in respect of each accounting period.

7.31(2) In this Rule, "accounting period" is to be construed as follows–

(a) the first accounting period is the period of 6 months beginning with the date on which the liquidator is appointed (subject to paragraph (3));

(b) the second accounting period is the period of 6 months beginning with the end of the first accounting period; and

(c) any subsequent accounting period is the period of 12 months beginning with the end of the last accounting period except that–

(i) where the liquidator and the liquidation' committee agree; or

(ii) where there is no liquidation committee, the court determines,

the accounting period is to be such other period beginning with the end of the last accounting period as may be agreed or, as the case may be determined, it is to be that other period.

7.31(3) Where a provisional liquidator is appointed under section 135 the first accounting period is the period of 6 months beginning with the date on which the provisional liquidator is appointed.

7.31(4) An agreement or determination under paragraph (2)(c)–

(a) may be made in respect of one or more than one accounting period;

(b) may be made before the beginning of the accounting period in relation to which it has effect and, in any event, is not to have effect unless made before the day on which such accounting period would, but for the agreement or determination, have ended;

(c) may provide for different accounting periods to be of different durations; and

(d) may vary the time periods mentioned in–

(i) rule 7.16(1) and paragraphs (10) and (11) of this rule;

(ii) rule 7.19(1)(a) and (5); and

(iii) rule 7.35 (contents of notice to be delivered to creditors owed small debts etc.).

7.31(5) Accounting periods are unaffected by any–

(a) recall of the appointment of a provisional liquidator (prior to a winding up order being made);

(b) termination of the appointment of a provisional liquidator and appointment of a liquidator (including an interim liquidator) on the making of a winding up order;

(c) change in the provisional liquidator or liquidator.

7.31(6) Subject to the following provisions of this rule, the liquidator must, if the funds of the company's assets are sufficient and after making an allowance for future contingencies, pay under rule 7.32 (payment of dividends) a dividend out of the company's assets to the creditors in respect of each accounting period.

7.31(7) The liquidator may pay–

(a) the expenses of the liquidation mentioned in rule 7.28(3)(a), other than the liquidator's own remuneration, at any time;

(b) the preferential debts within the meaning of section 386 at any time but only with the consent of the liquidation committee or, if there is no liquidation committee, of the court.

7.31(8) If the liquidator–

(a) is not ready to pay a dividend in respect of an accounting period; or

(b) considers it would be inappropriate to pay such a dividend because the expenses of doing so would be disproportionate to the amount of the dividend,

the liquidator may postpone such payment to a date not later than the time for payment of a dividend in respect of the next accounting period.

7.31(9)   Where an appeal is taken under rule 7.19(5) against the acceptance or rejection of a creditor's claim, the liquidator must, at the time of payment of dividends and until the appeal is determined, set aside an amount which would be sufficient, if the determination in the appeal were to provide for the claim being accepted in full, to pay a dividend in respect of that claim.

7.31(10)   Where a creditor–

(a)   has failed to produce evidence in support of a claim earlier than 8 weeks before the end of an accounting period on being required by the liquidator to do so under rule 7.18; and

(b)   has given a reason for such failure which is acceptable to the liquidator,

the liquidator must set aside, for such time as is reasonable to enable the creditor to produce that evidence or any other evidence that will enable the liquidator to be satisfied under rule 7.18, an amount which would be sufficient, if the claim were accepted in full, to pay a dividend in respect of that claim.

7.31(11)   Where a creditor submits a claim to the liquidator later than 8 weeks before the end of an accounting period but more than 8 weeks before the end of a subsequent accounting period in respect of which, after making allowance for contingencies, funds are available for the payment of a dividend, the liquidator must, if accepting the claim in whole or in part, pay to the creditor–

(a)   the same dividend or dividends as has or have already been paid to creditors of the same class in respect of any accounting period or periods; and

(b)   whatever dividend may be payable to that creditor in respect of the said subsequent accounting period.

7.31(12)   Paragraph (11)(a) is without prejudice to any dividend which has already been paid.

7.31(13)   In the declaration of and payment of a dividend, no payments are to be made more than once by virtue of the same debt.

7.31(14)   Subject to any notification by the person entitled to a dividend given to the liquidator that the person wishes the dividend to be paid to another person, or has assigned that entitlement to another person, where both a creditor and a member State liquidator have had a claim accepted in relation to the same debt, payment is only to be made to the creditor.

7.32   Payment of dividends

7.32(1)   On the expiry of the period within which an appeal may be taken under rule 7.12 or, if an appeal is so taken, on the final determination of the last such appeal, the liquidator must pay to the creditors the dividends in accordance with the scheme of division.

7.32(2)   Any dividend–

(a)   allocated to a creditor which is not cashed or uplifted; or

(b)   dependent on a claim in respect of which an amount has been set aside under rule 7.31 (9) or (10),

must be deposited by the liquidator in an appropriate bank or institution.

7.32(3)   If a creditor's claim is revalued, the liquidator may–

(a)   in paying any dividend to that creditor, make such adjustment to it as the liquidator considers necessary to take account of that revaluation; or

(b)   require the creditor to repay to the liquidator the whole or part of a dividend already paid to that creditor.

7.33 Unclaimed dividends

7.33(1) Any person, producing evidence of that person's right, may apply to the Accountant of Court to receive a dividend deposited under section 193(2), if the application is made not later than 7 years after the date of deposit.

7.33(2) If the Accountant of Court is satisfied of the person's right to the dividend, the Accountant of Court must authorise the bank or institution in which the deposit was made to pay to the person the amount of that dividend and of any interest which has accrued on the dividend.

7.33(3) The Accountant of Court is, at the expiry of 7 years from the date of deposit of any unclaimed dividend or unapplied balance under section 193(2), to hand over the deposit receipt or other voucher relating to the dividend or balance to the Secretary of State.

7.33(4) Where under paragraph (3) the Accountant of Court hands over the deposit receipt or other voucher, the Secretary of State is entitled to payment of the amount due (principal and interest) from the bank or institution in which the deposit was made.

7.34 Small debts

7.34(1) A creditor is deemed to have submitted a claim for the purposes of adjudication of entitlement to and payment of a dividend but not otherwise where–

    (a) the debt is a small debt;

    (b) notice has been delivered to the creditor under rule 7.35; and

    (c) the creditor has not advised the liquidator that the debt is incorrect or not owed in response to the notice.

7.34(2) In this rule "small debt" means a debt (being the total amount owed to a creditor) which does not exceed £1,000 (which amount is prescribed for the purposes of paragraph 13A of schedule 8 of the Act and paragraph 18A of schedule 9 of the Act).

7.35 Contents of notice to be delivered to creditors owed small debts etc.

7.35(1) The liquidator may treat a debt, which is a small debt according to the accounting records or the statement of affairs of the company, as if it were accepted under rule 7.19 for the purpose of paying a dividend.

7.35(2) Where the liquidator intends to treat such a debt as if it were accepted under rule 7.19 for the purpose of payment of a dividend, the liquidator must not later than 12 weeks before the end of the accounting period deliver to the creditor a notice.

7.35(3) The notice must–

    (a) state the amount of the debt which the liquidator believes to be owed to the creditor according to the accounting records or statement of affairs of the company;

    (b) state that the liquidator will treat the debt which is stated in the notice, being for £1,000 or less, as accepted for the purpose of payment of a dividend unless the creditor advises the liquidator that the amount of the debt is incorrect or that no debt is owed;

    (c) require the creditor to notify the liquidator by not later than 8 weeks before the end of the accounting period if the amount of the debt is incorrect or if no debt is owed; and

    (d) inform the creditor that where the creditor advises the liquidator that the amount of the debt is incorrect the creditor must also submit not later than 8 weeks before the end of the accounting period a statement of claim and documentary evidence of debt (see rule 7.16) in order to receive a dividend.

PART 8

DECISION MAKING

CHAPTER 1

APPLICATION OF PART

8.1   Application of Part

8.1   In this Part–

(a)   Chapters 2 to 11 apply where the Act or these Rules require a decision to be made by a qualifying decision procedure or permit a decision to be made by the deemed consent procedure; and

(b)   Chapter 12 applies to company meetings.

CHAPTER 2

DECISION PROCEDURES

[Note: a document required by the Act or these Rules must also contain the standard contents required as set out in Part 1.]

8.2   Interpretation

8.2(1)   In these Rules–

"decision date" means–

(a)   in the case of a decision to be made at a meeting, the date of the meeting;

(b)   in the case of a decision to be made either by a decision procedure other than a meeting or by the deemed consent procedure, the date the decision is to be made or deemed to have been made,

and a decision falling within paragraph (b) is to be treated as made at 23:59 on the decision date;

"decision procedure" means a qualifying decision procedure as prescribed by rule 8.3;

"electronic voting" includes any electronic system which enables a person to vote without the need to attend at a particular location to do so;

"physical meeting" means a meeting where the creditors are invited to be present together at the same place (whether or not it is possible to attend the meeting without being present at that place);

"virtual meeting" means a meeting where persons who are not invited to be physically present together may participate in the meeting including communicating directly with all the other participants in the meeting and voting (either directly or via a proxy-holder);

8.2(2)   The decision date is to be set at the discretion of the convener, but must be not less than 14 days from the date of delivery of the notice, except where the table in rule 8.11 requires a different period or the court directs otherwise.

8.2(3)   The rules in Chapters 2 to 11 about decision procedures of creditors apply with any necessary modifications to decision making by contributories.

8.2(4)   In particular, in place of the requirement for percentages or majorities in decision making by creditors to be determined by value, where the procedure seeks a decision from contributories value must be determined on the percentage of voting rights in accordance with rule 8.39.

1318

8.3 The prescribed decision procedures

[Note: under section 246ZE a decision may not be made by a creditors' meeting (a physical meeting) unless the prescribed proportion of the creditors request in writing that the decision be made by such a meeting.]

8.3 The following decision procedures are prescribed for the purpose of section 246ZE by which a convener may seek a decision under the Act or these Rules from creditors–

(a) correspondence;

(b) electronic voting;

(c) virtual meeting;

(d) physical meeting;

(e) any other decision making procedure which enables all creditors who are entitled to participate in the making of the decision to participate equally.

8.4 Electronic voting

8.4 Where the decision procedure uses electronic voting–

(a) the notice delivered to creditors in accordance with rule 8.8 must give them any necessary information as to how to access the voting system including any password required;

(b) except where electronic voting is being used at a meeting, the voting system must be a system capable of enabling a creditor to vote at any time between the notice being delivered and the decision date; and

(c) in the course of a vote the voting system must not provide any creditor with information concerning the vote cast by any other creditor.

8.5 Virtual meetings

8.5 Where the decision procedure uses a virtual meeting the notice delivered to creditors in accordance with rule 8.8 must contain–

(a) any necessary information as to how to access the virtual meeting including any telephone number, access code or password required; and

(b) a statement that the meeting may be suspended or adjourned by the chair of the meeting (and must be adjourned if it is so resolved at the meeting).

8.6 Physical meetings

8.6(1) A request for a physical meeting under section 246ZE(3) may be made before or after the notice of the decision procedure or deemed consent procedure has been delivered, but must be made not later than 5 business days after the date on which the convener delivered the notice of the decision procedure or deemed consent procedure unless these Rules provide to the contrary.

8.6(2) It is the convener's responsibility to check whether any requests for a physical meeting are submitted before the deadline and if so whether in aggregate they meet or surpass one of the thresholds requiring a physical meeting under section 246ZE(7).

8.6(3) Where the prescribed proportion of creditors requires a physical meeting the convener must summon the meeting by giving notice which complies with rule 8.8 so far as applicable and which must also contain a statement that the meeting may be suspended or adjourned by the chair of the meeting (and must be adjourned if it is so resolved at the meeting).

8.6(4)   In addition, the notice under paragraph (3) must inform the creditors that as a result of the requirement to hold a physical meeting the original decision procedure or the deemed consent procedure is superseded.

8.6(5)   The convener must send the notice under paragraph (3) not later than 3 business days after one of the thresholds requiring a physical meeting has been met or surpassed.

8.6(6)   The convener–

(a)   may permit a creditor to attend a physical meeting remotely if the convener receives a request to do so in advance of the meeting; and

(b)   must include in the notice of the meeting a statement explaining the convener's discretion to permit remote attendance.

8.6(7)   In this rule, attending a physical meeting "remotely" means attending and being able to participate in the meeting without being in the place where the meeting is being held.

8.6(8)   For the purpose of determining whether the thresholds under section 246ZE(7) are met, the convener must calculate the value of the creditor's debt by reference to rule 8.31.

8.7   Deemed consent

[Note: the deemed consent procedure cannot be used to make a decision on remuneration of any person, or where the Act, these Rules or any other legislation or court order requires a decision to be made by a decision procedure.]

8.7(1)   This rule makes further provision about the deemed consent procedure to that set out in section 246ZF.

8.7(2)   A notice seeking deemed consent must, in addition to the requirements of section 246ZF comply with the requirements of rule 8.8 so far as applicable and must also contain–

(a)   a statement that in order to object to the proposed decision a creditor must have delivered a notice, stating that the creditor so objects, to the convener not later than the decision date together with a statement of claim and documentary evidence of debt in accordance with these Rules failing which the objection will be disregarded;

(b)   a statement that it is the convener's responsibility to aggregate any objections to see if the threshold is met for the decision to be taken as not having been made; and

(c)   a statement that if the threshold is met the deemed consent procedure will terminate without a decision being made and if a decision is sought again on the same matter it will be sought by a decision procedure.

8.7(3)   In this rule, the threshold is met where the appropriate number of relevant creditors (as defined in section 246ZF(7)) have objected to the proposed decision.

8.7(4)   For the purpose of aggregating objections, the convener may presume the value of relevant creditors' claims to be the value of claims by those creditors who, in the convener's view, would have been entitled to vote had the decision been sought by a decision procedure in accordance with this Part, even where those creditors had not already met the criteria for such entitlement to vote.

8.7(5)   Rules 8.31(2) (calculation of voting rights), 8.32 (calculation of voting rights: authorised deposit-taker) and 8.33 (procedure for admitting creditors' claims for voting) apply to the admission or rejection of a claim for the purpose of the convener deciding whether or not an objection should count towards the total aggregated objections.

8.7(6)   A decision of the convener on the aggregation of objections under this rule is subject to appeal under rule 8.35 as if it were a decision under Chapter 8 of this Part.

[Note: a document required by the Act or these Rules must also contain the standard contents required as set out in Part 1.]

8.8 Notices to creditors of decision procedure

8.8(1) This rule sets out the requirements for notices to creditors where a decision is sought by a decision procedure.

8.8(2) The convener must deliver a notice to every creditor who is entitled to notice of the procedure.

8.8(3) The notice must contain the following–

(a) identification details for the insolvency proceedings;

(b) details of the decision to be made or of any resolution on which a decision is sought;

(c) a description of the decision procedure which the convener is using, and arrangements, including the venue, for the decision procedure;

(d) a statement of the decision date;

(e) a statement as to when the creditor must have delivered a statement of claim and documentary evidence of debt in accordance with these Rules failing which a vote by the creditor will be disregarded;

(f) a statement that a creditor whose debt is treated as a small debt in accordance with rule 7.35 must still deliver a statement of claim and documentary evidence of debt if that creditor wishes to vote;

(g) a statement that a creditor who has opted out from receiving notices may nevertheless vote if the creditor provides a statement of claim and documentary evidence of debt in accordance with paragraph (e);

(h) in the case of a decision to remove a liquidator in a creditors' voluntary winding up or a winding up by the court, a statement drawing the attention of creditors to section 173(2) or 174(4) (which relate to the release of the liquidator), as appropriate;

(i) except in the case of a physical meeting, a statement that creditors who meet the thresholds in section 246ZE(7) may, within 5 business days from the date of delivery of the notice, require a physical meeting to be held to consider the matter;

(j) in the case of a meeting, a statement that any proxy must be delivered to the convener or chair before it may be used at the meeting;

(k) in the case of a meeting, a statement that, where applicable, a complaint may be made in accordance with rule 8.38 and the period within which such a complaint may be made; and

(l) a statement that a creditor may appeal a decision in accordance with rule 8.35, and the relevant period under rule 8.35 within which such an appeal may be made.

8.8(4) The notice must be authenticated and dated by the convener.

8.8(5) Where the decision procedure is a meeting the notice must be accompanied by a blank proxy complying with rule 9.3.

8.8(6)   This rule does not apply if the court orders under rule 8.12 that notice of a decision procedure be given by advertisement only.

8.9   Voting in a decision procedure

8.9(1)   In order to be counted in a decision procedure other than where votes are cast at a meeting, votes must–

(a)   be received by the convener on or before the decision date; and

(b)   in the case of a vote cast by a creditor, be accompanied by a statement of claim and documentary evidence of debt (where the requirement to provide the latter is not dispensed with under rule 8.28(2)) unless already given to the convener.

8.9(2)   In a receivership, a creditors' voluntary winding up or a winding up by the court a vote must be disregarded if–

(a)   a statement of claim and, where required, documentary evidence of debt are not received by the convener on or before the decision date or, in the case of a meeting, at or before the meeting (unless under rule 8.26 the chair is content to accept them before resumption of the adjourned meeting); or

(b)   the convener decides, in the application of Chapter 8 of this Part, that the creditor is not entitled to cast the vote.

8.9(3)   The convener must have received at least one valid vote on or before the decision date in order for the decision to be made.

8.10   Venue for the decision procedure

8.10   The convener must have regard to the convenience of those invited to participate when fixing the venue for a decision procedure (including the resumption of an adjourned meeting).

8.11   Notice of decision procedures or of seeking deemed consent: when and to whom delivered

[Note: when an office-holder is obliged to give notice to "the creditors", this is subject to rule 1.33, which limits the obligation to giving notice to those creditors of whose address the office-holder is aware.]

8.11(1)   Notices of decision procedures, and notices seeking deemed consent, must be delivered in accordance with the following table.

Proceedings	*Decisions*	*Persons to whom notice must be delivered*	*Minimum notice required*
receivership	decisions of creditors	the creditors	14 days
creditors' voluntary winding up	decisions of creditors for appointment of liquidator (including any decision made at the same time on the establishment of a liquidation committee)	the creditors	14 days on conversion from members' voluntary liquidation, 7 days on conversion from member's voluntary liquidation where deemed consent has been objected to and in other cases, 3 business days

Proceedings	Decisions	Persons to whom notice must be delivered	Minimum notice required
creditors' voluntary winding up or a winding up by the court	decisions of creditors to consider whether a replacement should be appointed after a liquidator's resignation	the creditors	28 days
winding up by the court	decisions of creditors to consider whether to remove or replace the liquidator (other than after a liquidator's resignation)	the creditors	14 days
creditors' voluntary winding up or a winding up by the court	other decisions of creditors	the creditors	14 days
creditors' voluntary winding up or a winding up by the court	decisions of contributories	every person appearing (by the company's records or otherwise) to be a contributory	14 days
main proceedings in another Member State	approval under Article 36(5) of the EU Regulation of proposed undertaking offered by a member State liquidator	all the local creditors in the United Kingdom	14 days

8.11(2)   This rule does not apply where the court orders under rule 8.12 that notice of a decision procedure be given by advertisement only.

8.12   Notice of decision procedure by advertisement only

8.12(1)   The court may order that notice of a decision procedure is to be given by advertisement only and not by individual notice to the persons concerned.

8.12(2)   In considering whether to make such an order, the court must have regard to the relative cost of advertisement as against the giving of individual notices, the amount of assets available and the extent of the interest of creditors, members or contributories or any particular class of them.

8.12(3)   The advertisement must meet the requirements for a notice under rule 8.8(3), and must also state–

(a)   that the court ordered that notice of the decision procedure be given by advertisement only; and

(b)   the date of the court's order.

8.13   Gazetting and advertisement

8.13(1)   In a creditors' voluntary winding up or a winding up by the court where a decision is being sought in a meeting the convener must gazette a notice stating–

(a)   that a meeting of creditors or contributories is to take place;

(b) the venue for the meeting;

(c) the purpose of the meeting; and

(d) the time and date by which, and place at which, those attending must deliver proxies and statements of claim and documentary evidence of debt (if not already delivered) in order to be entitled to vote.

8.13(2) The notice must also state–

(a) who is the convener in respect of the meeting; and

(b) if the meeting results from a request of one or more creditors under section 246ZE, the fact that it was so summoned.

8.13(3) The notice must be gazetted before or as soon as reasonably practicable after notice of the meeting is delivered in accordance with these Rules.

8.13(4) Information to be gazetted under this rule may also be advertised in such other manner as the convener thinks fit.

8.13(5) The convener may gazette other decision procedures or the deemed consent procedure in which case the equivalent information to that required by this rule must be stated in the notice.

8.14 Notice to company officers in respect of meetings

8.14(1) In a creditors' voluntary winding up or a winding up by the court notice to participate in a creditors' meeting must be delivered to every present or former officer of the company whose presence the convener thinks is required and that person is required to attend the meeting.

8.14(2) A notice under this rule must be delivered in compliance with the minimum notice requirements set out in rule 8.2(2) or in compliance with an order of the court under rule 8.12.

8.15 Non-receipt of notice of decision

8.15 Where a decision is sought by a notice in accordance with the Act or these Rules, the decision procedure or deemed consent procedure is presumed to have been duly initiated and conducted, even if not everyone to whom the notice is to be delivered has received it.

8.16 Decisions on remuneration and conduct

8.16(1) This rule applies in relation to a decision or resolution which is proposed in a creditors' voluntary winding up or a winding up by the court and which affects a person in relation to that person's remuneration or conduct as liquidator (actual, proposed or former).

8.16(2) The following may not vote on such a decision or resolution whether as a creditor, contributory, proxy-holder or corporate representative, except so far as permitted by rule 9.7 (proxy-holder with financial interest)–

(a) that person;

(b) the partners and employees of that person;

(c) the officers and employees of the company of which that person is a director, officer or employee; and

(d) the representative of any person mentioned in sub-paragraphs (a) to (c).

CHAPTER 4

DECISION MAKING IN PARTICULAR PROCEEDINGS

[Note: a document required by the Act or these Rules must also contain the standard contents required as set out in Part 1.]

8.17 Decisions in winding up of authorised deposit-takers

8.17(1) This rule applies in a creditors' voluntary winding up or a winding up by the court of an authorised deposit-taker.

8.17(2) The directors of a company must deliver a notice of a meeting of the company at which it is intended to propose a resolution for its winding up to the Financial Conduct Authority and to the scheme manager established under section 212(1) of the Financial Services and Markets Act 2000.

8.17(3) These notices must be the same as those delivered to members of the company.

8.17(4) Where any decision is sought for the purpose of considering whether a replacement should be appointed after the liquidator's resignation, removing the liquidator or appointing a new liquidator, the convener must also deliver a copy of the notice by which such a decision is sought to the Financial Conduct Authority and the scheme manager.

8.17(5) A scheme manager who is required by this rule to be given notice of a meeting is entitled to be represented at the meeting.

CHAPTER 5

REQUISITIONED DECISIONS

[Note: a document required by the Act or these Rules must also contain the standard contents required as set out in Part 1.]

8.18 Requisitions of decision

[Note: this rule is concerned with requests by creditors or contributories for a decision, rather than requests for decisions to be made by way of a physical meeting under section 246ZE(3).]

8.18(1) In this Chapter, "requisitioned decision" means–

(a) a decision requested to be sought under section 142(4), 171(2)(b), 171(3A) or 172(3);

(b) any other decision sought by a liquidator in a winding up by the court following a request to seek a decision on any matter from–

   (i) one-tenth in value of a company's creditors; or

   (ii) one-tenth in value of a company's contributories.

8.18(2) The request for a requisitioned decision must include a statement of the purpose of the proposed decision and either–

(a) a copy of the requesting creditor's statement of claim or a statement of the requesting contributory's value, together with–

   (i) a list of the creditors or contributories concurring with the request and of the amounts of their respective claims or values; and

   (ii) confirmation of concurrence from each creditor or contributory concurring; or

1325

(b) a copy of the requesting creditor's statement of claim or a statement of the requesting contributory's value and a statement that that alone is sufficient without the concurrence of other creditors or contributories.

8.18(3) A decision procedure must be instigated under section 171(2)(b) for the removal of the liquidator, other than a liquidator appointed by the court under section 108, if 25% in value of the company's creditors, excluding those who are connected with the company, request it.

8.18(4) Where a decision procedure under 171(2)(b), 171(3) or 171(3A) is to be instigated, or is proposed to be instigated, the court may, on the application of any creditor, give directions as to the decision procedure to be used and any other matter which appears to the court to require regulation or control.

8.19 Expenses and timing of requisitioned decision

8.19(1) The convener must, not later than 14 days from receipt of a request for a requisitioned decision, provide the requesting creditor with itemised details of the sum to be deposited as caution for payment of the expenses of such procedure.

8.19(2) The convener is not obliged to initiate the decision procedure or deemed consent procedure (where applicable) until either–

(a) the convener has received the required sum; or

(b) the period of 14 days has expired without the convener having informed the requesting creditor or contributory of the sum required to be deposited as caution.

8.19(3) A requisitioned decision must be made within 28 days of the date on which the earlier of the events specified in paragraph (2) of this rule occurs.

8.19(4) The expenses of a requisitioned decision must be paid out of the deposit (if any) unless–

(a) the creditors decide that they are to be payable as an expense of the liquidation; and

(b) in the case of a decision of contributories, the creditors are first paid in full, with interest.

8.19(5) The notice of a requisitioned decision of creditors must contain a statement that the creditors may make a decision as in paragraph (4)(a) of this rule.

8.19(6) Where the creditors do not so decide, the expenses must be paid by the requesting creditor or contributory to the extent that the deposit (if any) is not sufficient.

8.19(7) To the extent that the deposit (if any) is not required for payment of the expenses, it must be repaid to the requesting creditor or contributory.

CHAPTER 6

CONSTITUTION OF MEETINGS

8.20 Quorum at meetings

8.20(1) A meeting is not competent to act unless a quorum is in attendance.

8.20(2) A quorum is–

(a) in the case of a meeting of creditors, at least one creditor entitled to vote; and

(b) in the case of a meeting of contributories, at least 2 contributories entitled to vote, or all the contributories, if their number does not exceed 2.

8.20(3)   Where the provisions of this rule as to quorum are satisfied by the attendance of the chair alone or the chair and one additional person, but the chair is aware, either by virtue of statements of claim and documentary evidence of debt and proxies received or otherwise, that one or more additional persons would, if attending, be entitled to vote, the chair must delay the start of the meeting by at least 15 minutes after the appointed time.

8.20(4)   In this rule, the reference to the number of creditors or contributories necessary to constitute a quorum includes those represented by proxy by any person (including the chair).

8.21   Chair at meetings

8.21(1)   The chair of a meeting must be–

(a)   the convener; or

(b)   an appointed person.

8.21(2)   However–

(a)   where a decision on the appointment of a liquidator under rule 4.14(2)(b), 4.14(4) or 4.14(6) (information to creditors and appointment of liquidator in creditors voluntary winding up) is made by a meeting the chair of the meeting must be the convener;

(b)   where a decision on the appointment of a liquidator under rule 5.22(6) (appointment of liquidator in place of the interim liquidator under section 138(3) in court winding up) is made by a meeting and a resolution is proposed to appoint the interim liquidator to be liquidator another person may be appointed to act as chair for the purpose of choosing the liquidator.

8.22   The chair – attendance, interventions and questions

8.22   The chair of a meeting may–

(a)   allow any person who has given reasonable notice of wishing to attend to participate in a virtual meeting or to be admitted to a physical meeting;

(b)   decide what intervention, if any, may be made at–

(i)   a meeting of creditors by any person attending who is not a creditor; or

(ii)   a meeting of contributories by any person attending who is not a contributory; and

(c)   decide what questions may be put to any present or former officer of the company.

CHAPTER 7

ADJOURNMENT AND SUSPENSION OF MEETINGS

8.23   Adjournment by chair

8.23(1)   The chair may (and must if it is so resolved) adjourn a meeting for not more than 14 days, subject to any direction of the court and to rule 8.24.

8.23(2)   Any further adjournment under this rule must not be to a day later than 14 days after the date on which the meeting was originally held, subject to any direction of the court.

8.24   Adjournment of meetings to remove a liquidator

8.24   If the chair of a meeting to remove the liquidator in a creditors' voluntary winding up or a winding up by the court is the liquidator or the liquidator's nominee and a resolution has been proposed for the liquidator's removal, the chair must not adjourn the meeting without the consent of at least $\frac{1}{2}$ (in value) of the creditors attending and entitled to vote.

8.25 Adjournment in absence of chair

8.25(1) In a receivership, a creditors' voluntary winding up or a winding up by the court, if no one attends to act as chair within 30 minutes of the time fixed for a meeting to start, then the meeting is adjourned to the same time and place the following week or, if that is not a business day, to the business day immediately following.

8.25(2) If no one attends to act as chair within 30 minutes of the time fixed for the meeting after a second adjournment under this rule, then the meeting comes to an end.

8.26 Statements of claim and documentary evidence of debt in adjournment

8.26 Where a meeting in a receivership, a creditors' voluntary winding-up or a winding up by the court is adjourned, the chair may allow a statement of claim and documentary evidence of debt (where required) to be used if delivered at or before resumption of the adjourned meeting.

8.27 Suspension

8.27 The chair of a meeting may, without an adjournment, declare the meeting suspended for one or more periods not exceeding one hour in total (or, in exceptional circumstances, such longer total period during the same day as the chair may determine).

CHAPTER 8

CREDITORS' VOTING RIGHTS AND MAJORITIES

[Note: a document required by the Act or these Rules must also contain the standard contents required as set out in Part 1.]

8.28 Creditors' voting rights

8.28(1) In a receivership, a creditors' voluntary winding up or a winding up by the court, a creditor is entitled to vote in a decision procedure or to object to a decision proposed using the deemed consent procedure only if–

  (a)   the creditor has delivered to the convener a statement of claim and documentary evidence of debt, including any calculation for the purposes of rule 8.31 or 8.32;

  (b)   the statement of claim and documentary evidence of debt was received by the convener not later than the decision date, or in the case of a meeting, at or before the meeting; and

  (c)   the statement of claim and documentary evidence of debt has been admitted for the purposes of entitlement to vote.

8.28(2) The convener or chair may dispense with the requirement to produce documentary evidence of debt in paragraph (1)(a) and (b) in respect of any debt or any class or debt.

8.28(3) In the case of a meeting, a proxy-holder is not entitled to vote on behalf of a creditor unless the convener or chair has received the proxy intended to be used on behalf of that creditor.

8.29 Scheme manager's voting rights

8.29(1) For the purpose of voting in a creditors' voluntary winding up or a winding up by the court of an authorised deposit-taker at which the scheme manager established under section 212(1) of the

Financial Services and Markets Act 2000 is entitled to be represented under rule 8.17 (but not for any other purpose), the manager may deliver, instead of a statement of claim and documentary evidence of debt, a statement containing–

(a)   the names of the creditors of the company in relation to whom an obligation of the scheme manager has arisen or may reasonably be expected to arise;

(b)   the amount of each such obligation; and

(c)   the total amount of all such obligations.

8.29(2)   The manager may from time to time deliver a further statement; and each such statement supersedes any previous statement.

8.30   Claim made in proceedings in other member States

8.30(1)   Where in a creditors' voluntary winding up or a winding up by the court–

(a)   a creditor is entitled to vote under rule 8.28(1) (as determined, where that be the case, in accordance with rule 8.35);

(b)   that creditor has made the claim in other proceedings;

(c)   that creditor votes on a resolution in a decision procedure; and

(d)   a member State liquidator casts a vote in respect of the same claim,

only the creditor's vote is to be counted.

8.30(2)   Where in a creditors' voluntary winding up or a winding up by the court–

(a)   a creditor has made a claim in more than one set of other proceedings; and

(b)   more than one member State liquidator seeks to vote in respect of that claim,

the entitlement to vote in respect of that claim is exercisable by the member State liquidator in the main proceedings, whether or not the creditor has made the claim in the main proceedings.

8.30(3)   In this rule, "other proceedings" means main, secondary or territorial proceedings in another member State.

8.31   Calculation of voting rights

8.31(1)   Votes are calculated according to the amount of each creditor's claim–

(a)   in a receivership, as at the date of the appointment of the receiver, less any payments that have been made to the creditor after that date in respect of the claim;

(b)   in a creditors' voluntary winding up or a winding up by the court, as set out in the creditor's statement of claim and documentary evidence of debt to the extent that it has been admitted.

8.31(2)   A creditor may vote in respect of a debt of an unliquidated or unascertained amount if the convener or chair decides to put upon it an estimated minimum value for the purpose of entitlement to vote and admits the claim for that purpose.

8.31(3)   Where a debt is wholly secured its value for voting purposes is nil.

8.31(4)   Where a debt is partly secured its value for voting purposes is the value of the unsecured part.

8.31(5)   No vote may be cast in respect of a claim more than once on any resolution put to the meeting; and for this purpose (where relevant), the claim of a creditor and of any member State liquidator in relation to the same debt are a single claim.

8.31(6)   A vote cast in a decision procedure which is not a meeting may not be changed.

8.31(7)   Paragraph (5) does not prevent a creditor or member State liquidator from–

(a) voting in respect of less than the full value of an entitlement to vote; or

(b) casting a vote one way in respect of part of the value of an entitlement and another way in respect of some or all of the balance of that value.

8.32   Calculation of voting rights: winding up of authorised deposit-taker

8.32   Any voting rights which a creditor might otherwise exercise in respect of a claim in a creditors' voluntary winding up or a winding up by the court of an authorised deposit-taker are reduced by a sum equal to the amount of that claim in relation to which the scheme manager, by virtue of its having delivered a statement under rule 8.29, is entitled to exercise voting rights.

8.33   Procedure for admitting creditors' claims for voting

8.33(1)   The convener or chair in respect of a decision procedure must ascertain entitlement to vote and admit or reject claims accordingly.

8.33(2)   The convener or chair may admit or reject a claim in whole or in part.

8.33(3)   If the convener or chair is in any doubt whether a claim should be admitted or rejected, the convener or chair must mark it as objected to and allow votes to be cast in respect of it, subject to such votes being subsequently declared invalid if the objection to the claim is sustained.

8.34   Requisite majorities

8.34   A decision is made by creditors when a majority (in value) of those voting have voted in favour of the proposed decision.

8.35   Appeals against decisions under this Chapter

8.35(1)   A decision of the convener or chair under this Chapter is subject to appeal to the court by a creditor or by a contributory (as applicable).

8.35(2)   If the decision is reversed or varied, or votes are declared invalid, the court may order another decision procedure to be initiated or make such order as it thinks just.

8.35(3)   An appeal under this rule may not be made later than 21 days after the decision date.

8.35(4)   The person who made the decision is not personally liable for expenses incurred by any person in relation to an appeal under this rule unless the court makes an order to that effect.

CHAPTER 9

EXCLUSIONS FROM MEETINGS

[Note: a document required by the Act or these Rules must also contain the standard contents required as set out in Part 1.]

8.36   Action where person excluded

8.36(1)   In this rule and rules 8.37 and 8.38, an "excluded person" means a person who has taken all steps necessary to attend a virtual meeting or has been permitted by the convener to attend a physical meeting remotely under the arrangements which–

(a) have been put in place by the convener of the meeting; but

(b) do not enable that person to attend the whole or part of that meeting.

8.36(2) Where the chair becomes aware during the course of the meeting that there is an excluded person, the chair may–

   (a) continue the meeting;

   (b) declare the meeting void and convene the meeting again; or

   (c) declare the meeting valid up to the point where the person was excluded and adjourn the meeting.

8.36(3) Where the chair continues the meeting, the meeting is valid unless–

   (a) the chair decides in consequence of a complaint under rule 8.38 to declare the meeting void and hold the meeting again; or

   (b) the court directs otherwise.

8.36(4) Without prejudice to paragraph (2), where the chair becomes aware during the course of the meeting that there is an excluded person, the chair may, at the chair's discretion and without an adjournment, declare the meeting suspended for any period up to 1 hour.

8.37 Indication to excluded person

8.37(1) A creditor who claims to be an excluded person may request an indication of what occurred during the period of that person's claimed exclusion.

8.37(2) A request under paragraph (1) must be made in accordance with paragraph (3) as soon as reasonably practicable, and in any event, not later than 4pm on the business day following the day on which the exclusion is claimed to have occurred.

8.37(3) A request under paragraph (1) must be made to–

   (a) the chair, where it is made during the course of the meeting; or

   (b) the convener where it is made after the meeting.

8.37(4) Where satisfied that the person making the request is an excluded person, the person to whom the request is made under paragraph (3) must deliver the requested indication to the excluded person as soon as reasonably practicable, and in any event, not later than 4pm on the business day following the day on which the request was made under paragraph (1).

8.38 Complaint

8.38(1) A person may make a complaint who–

   (a) is, or claims to be, an excluded person; or

   (b) attends the meeting and claims to have been adversely affected by the actual, apparent or claimed exclusion of another person.

8.38(2) A complaint under paragraph (1) must be made to the appropriate person who is–

   (a) the chair, where it is made during the course of the meeting; or

   (b) the convener, where it is made after the meeting.

8.38(3) The complaint must be made as soon as reasonably practicable and, in any event, not later than 4pm on the business day following–

   (a) the day on which the person was, appeared or claimed, to be excluded; or

   (b) where an indication is sought under rule 8.37, the day on which the complainant received the indication.

8.38(4) The appropriate person must, as soon as reasonably practicable following receipt of the complaint,–

(a) consider whether there is an excluded person;

(b) where satisfied that there is an excluded person, consider the complaint; and

(c) where satisfied that there has been prejudice, take such action as the appropriate person considers fit to remedy the prejudice.

8.38(5) Paragraph (6) applies where the appropriate person is satisfied that the complainant is an excluded person and–

(a) a resolution was voted on at the meeting during the period of the person's exclusion; and

(b) the excluded person asserts how the excluded person intended to vote on the resolution.

8.38(6) Where the appropriate person is satisfied that if the excluded person had voted as that person intended it would have changed the result of the resolution, then the appropriate person must, as soon as reasonably practicable,–

(a) count the intended vote as having been cast in that way;

(b) amend the record of the result of the resolution;

(c) where notice of the result of the resolution has been delivered to those entitled to attend the meeting, deliver notice to them of the change and the reason for it; and

(d) where notice of the result of the resolution has yet to be delivered to those entitled to attend the meeting, the notice must include details of the change and the reason for it.

8.38(7) Where satisfied that more than one complainant is an excluded person, the appropriate person must have regard to the combined effect of the intended votes.

8.38(8) The appropriate person must deliver notice to the complainant of any decision as soon as reasonably practicable.

8.38(9) A complainant who is not satisfied by the action of the appropriate person may apply to the court for directions and any application must be made no more than 2 business days from the date of receiving the decision of the appropriate person.

CHAPTER 10

CONTRIBUTORIES' VOTING RIGHTS AND MAJORITIES

8.39 Contributories' voting rights and requisite majorities

8.39 In a decision procedure for contributories–

(a) voting rights are as at a general meeting of the company, subject to any provision of the articles affecting entitlement to vote, either generally or at a time when the company is in liquidation; and

(b) a decision is made if more than $\frac{1}{2}$ of the votes cast by contributories are in favour.

CHAPTER 11

RECORDS

8.40 Record of a decision

8.40(1) Where a decision is sought using a decision procedure, the convener or chair must make a record of the decision procedure.

8.40(2)   In the case of a meeting, the record must be in the form of a minute of the meeting.

8.40(3)   The record must be authenticated by the convener or chair and must include–

(a)   identification details for the insolvency proceedings;

(b)   in the case of a decision procedure of creditors, a list of the names of the creditors who participated and their claims;

(c)   in the case of a decision procedure of contributories, a list of the names of the contributories who participated;

(d)   where a decision is taken on the election of members of a creditors' committee or liquidation committee, the names and addresses of those elected;

(e)   a record of any change to the result of the resolution made under rule 8.38(6) and the reason for any such change; and

(f)   in any case, a record of every decision made and how creditors voted.

8.40(4)   Where a decision is sought using the deemed consent procedure, the convener must make a record of the procedure.

8.40(5)   The record under paragraph (4) must be authenticated by the convener and must–

(a)   identify the proceedings;

(b)   state whether or not the decision was taken; and

(c)   contain a list of the creditors or contributories who objected to the decision, and in the case of creditors, their claims.

8.40(6)   A record under this rule must also identify any decision procedure (or the deemed consent procedure) by which the decision had previously been sought.

CHAPTER 12

COMPANY MEETINGS

8.41   Company meetings

8.41(1)   Unless the Act or these Rules provide otherwise, a company meeting must be called and conducted, and records of the meeting must be kept–

(a)   in accordance with the law of Scotland, including any applicable provision in or made under the Companies Act, in the case of a company incorporated–

(i)   in Scotland, or

(ii)   outside the United Kingdom other than in an EEA state;

(b)   in accordance with the law of that state applicable to meetings of the company in the case of a company incorporated in an EEA state other than the United Kingdom.

8.41(2)   Reference to a company meeting called and conducted to resolve, decide or determine a particular matter includes a reference to that matter being resolved, decided or determined by written resolution.

8.42   Remote attendance: notification requirements

8.42   When a meeting is to be summoned and held in accordance with section 246A(3), the convener must notify all those to whom notice of the meeting is being given of–

1333

(a)   the ability of a person claiming to be an excluded person to request an indication in accordance with rule 8.45;

(b)   the ability of a person within rule 8.46(1) to make a complaint in accordance with that rule; and

(c)   in either case, the period within which a request or complaint must be made.

8.43   Location of company meetings

8.43(1)   This rule applies to a request to the convener of a meeting under section 246A(9) to specify a place for the meeting.

8.43(2)   The request must be accompanied by–

(a)   a list of the members making or concurring with the request and their voting rights, and

(b)   from each person concurring, confirmation of that person's concurrence.

8.43(3)   The request must be delivered to the convener within 7 business days of the date on which the convener delivered the notice of the meeting in question.

8.43(4)   Where the convener considers that the request has been properly made in accordance with the Act and this rule, the convener must–

(a)   deliver notice to all those previously given notice of the meeting–

  (i)   that it is to be held at a specified place, and

  (ii)   as to whether the date and time are to remain the same or not;

(b)   set a venue (including specification of a place) for the meeting, the date of which must be not later than 28 days after the original date for the meeting; and

(c)   deliver at least 14 days' notice of that venue to all those previously given notice of the meeting,

and the notices required by sub-paragraphs (a) and (c) may be delivered at the same or different times.

8.43(5)   Where the convener has specified a place for the meeting in response to a request to which this rule applies, the chair of the meeting must attend the meeting by being present in person at that place.

8.44   Action where person excluded

8.44(1)   In this rule and rules 8.45 and 8.46, an "excluded person" means a person who has taken all steps necessary to attend a company meeting under the arrangements which–

(a)   have been put in place by the convener of the meeting under section 246A(6); but

(b)   do not enable that person to attend the whole or part of that meeting.

8.44(2)   Where the chair becomes aware during the course of the meeting that there is an excluded person, the chair may–

(a)   continue the meeting;

(b)   declare the meeting void and convene the meeting again; or

(c)   declare the meeting valid up to the point where the person was excluded and adjourn the meeting.

8.44(3)   Where the chair continues the meeting, the meeting is valid unless–

(a)   the chair decides in consequence of a complaint under rule 8.46 to declare the meeting void and hold the meeting again; or

(b)   the court directs otherwise.

8.44(4)   Without prejudice to paragraph (2), where the chair becomes aware during the course of the meeting that there is an excluded person, the chair may, in the chair's discretion and without an adjournment, declare the meeting suspended for any period up to 1 hour.

8.45   Indication to excluded person

8.45(1)   A person who claims to be an excluded person may request an indication of what occurred during the period of that person's claimed exclusion.

8.45(2)   A request under paragraph (1) must be made in accordance with paragraph (3) as soon as reasonably practicable, and in any event, not later than 4pm on the business day following the day on which the exclusion is claimed to have occurred.

8.45(3)   A request under paragraph (1) must be made to–

(a)   the chair where it is made during the course of the meeting; or

(b)   the convener where it is made after the meeting.

8.45(4)   Where satisfied that the person making the request is an excluded person, the person to whom the request is made under paragraph (3) must deliver the requested indication to the excluded person as soon as reasonably practicable, and in any event, not later than 4pm on the business day following the day on which the request was made under paragraph (1).

8.46   Complaint

8.46(1)   A person may make a complaint who–

(a)   is, or claims to be, an excluded person; or

(b)   attends the meeting and claims to have been adversely affected by the actual, apparent or claimed exclusion of another person.

8.46(2)   The complaint under paragraph (1) must be made to the appropriate person who is–

(a)   the chair, where the complaint is made during the course of the meeting; or

(b)   the convener, where it is made after the meeting.

8.46(3)   The complaint must be made as soon as reasonably practicable and, in any event, no later than 4pm on the business day following–

(a)   the day on which the person was, appeared or claimed to be excluded; or

(b)   where an indication is sought under rule 8.45, the day on which the complainant received the indication.

8.46(4)   The appropriate person must, as soon as reasonably practicable following receipt of the complaint,–

(a)   consider whether there is an excluded person;

(b)   where satisfied that there is an excluded person, consider the complaint; and

(c)   where satisfied that there has been prejudice, take such action as the appropriate person considers fit to remedy the prejudice.

8.46(5)   Paragraph (6) applies where the appropriate person is satisfied that the complainant is an excluded person and–

(a)   a resolution was voted on at the meeting during the period of the person's exclusion; and

(b)   the excluded person asserts how the excluded person intended to vote on the resolution.

8.46(6) Where the appropriate person is satisfied that if the excluded person had voted as that person intended it would have changed the result of the resolution, then the appropriate person must, as soon as reasonably practicable–

(a) count the intended vote as having been cast in that way;

(b) amend the record of the result of the resolution;

(c) where notice of the result of the resolution has been delivered to those entitled to attend the meeting, deliver notice to them of the change and the reason for it; and

(d) where notice of the result of the resolution has yet to be delivered to those entitled to attend the meeting, the notice must include details of the change and the reason for it.

8.46(7) Where satisfied that more than one complainant is an excluded person, the appropriate person must have regard to the combined effect of the intended votes.

8.46(8) The appropriate person must deliver notice to the complainant of any decision as soon as reasonably practicable.

8.46(9) A complainant who is not satisfied by the action of the appropriate person may apply to the court for directions and any application must be made no more than 2 business days from the date of receiving the decision of the appropriate person.

PART 9

PROXIES AND CORPORATE REPRESENTATION

[Note: a document required by the Act or these Rules must also contain the standard contents required as set out in Part 1.]

9.1   Application and interpretation

9.1(1) This Part applies in any case where a proxy is given in relation to a meeting or insolvency proceedings under the Act or these Rules, or where a corporation authorises a person to represent it.

9.1(2) References in this Part to "the chair" are to the chair of the meeting for which a specific proxy is given or at which a continuing proxy is exercised.

9.2   Specific and continuing proxies

9.2(1) A proxy is a document made by a creditor, member or contributory which directs or authorises another person (a "proxy-holder") to act as the representative of the creditor, member or contributory at a meeting, or meetings, by speaking, voting, abstaining, or proposing resolutions.

9.2(2) A proxy may be either–

(a) a specific proxy which relates to a specific meeting; or

(b) a continuing proxy for the insolvency proceedings.

9.2(3) A specific proxy must–

(a) direct the proxy-holder how to act at the meeting by giving specific instructions; or

(b) authorise the proxy-holder to act at the meeting without specific instructions; or

(c) contain both direction and authorisation.

9.2(4) A proxy is to be treated as a specific proxy for the meeting which is identified in the proxy unless it states that it is a continuing proxy for the insolvency proceedings.

9.2(5)   A continuing proxy must authorise the proxy-holder to attend, speak, vote or abstain, or to propose resolutions without giving the proxy-holder any specific instructions.

9.2(6)   A continuing proxy may be superseded by a proxy for a specific meeting or withdrawn by a written notice to the office-holder.

9.2(7)   A creditor, member or contributory may appoint more than one person to be proxy-holder but if so–

    (a)   their appointment is as alternates; and

    (b)   only one of them may act as proxy-holder at a meeting.

9.2(8)   The proxy-holder must be an individual.

9.3   Blank proxy

9.3(1)   A blank proxy is a document which–

    (a)   complies with the requirements in this rule; and

    (b)   when completed with the details specified in paragraph (3) will be a proxy as described in rule 9.2.

9.3(2)   A blank proxy must state that the creditor, member or contributory named in the document (when completed) appoints a person who is named or identified as the proxy-holder of the creditor, member or contributory.

9.3(3)   The specified details are–

    (a)   the name and address of the creditor, member or contributory;

    (b)   either the name of the proxy-holder or the identification of the proxy-holder (e.g. the chair of the meeting);

    (c)   a statement that the proxy is either–

        (i)   for a specific meeting, which is identified in the proxy; or

        (ii)   a continuing proxy for the insolvency proceedings; and

    (d)   if the proxy is for a specific meeting, instructions as to the extent to which the proxy-holder is directed to vote in a particular way, to abstain or to propose any resolution.

9.3(4)   When it is delivered, a blank proxy must not have inserted in it–

    (a)   the name or description of any person as proxy-holder or as a nominee for the office holder; or

    (b)   instructions as to how a person appointed as proxy-holder is to act.

9.3(5)   A blank proxy must have a note to the effect that the proxy may be completed with the name of the person or the chair of the meeting who is to be proxy-holder.

9.4   Use of proxies

9.4(1)   A proxy for a specific meeting must be delivered to the chair at or before the meeting.

9.4(2)   A continuing proxy must be delivered to the office-holder and may be exercised at any meeting which begins after the proxy is delivered.

9.4(3)   A proxy may be used at the resumption of the meeting after an adjournment, but if a different proxy is given for use at a resumed meeting, that proxy must be delivered to the chair at or before the resumed meeting.

9.4(4)   Where a specific proxy directs a proxy-holder to vote for or against a resolution for the nomination or appointment of a person as office-holder, the proxy-holder may, unless the proxy states otherwise, vote for or against (as the proxy-holder thinks fit) a resolution for the nomination or appointment of that person jointly with another or others.

9.4(5)   A proxy-holder may propose a resolution which is one on which the proxy-holder could vote if someone else proposed it.

9.4(6)   Where a proxy gives specific directions as to voting, this does not, unless the proxy states otherwise, prohibit the proxy-holder from exercising discretion as to how to vote on a resolution which is not dealt with by the proxy.

9.4(7)   The chair may require a proxy used at a meeting to be the same as or substantially similar to the blank proxy delivered for that meeting or to a blank proxy previously delivered which has been completed as a continuing proxy.

9.5   Use of proxies by the chair

9.5(1)   Where a proxy appoints the chair (however described in the proxy) as proxy-holder the chair may not refuse to be the proxy-holder.

9.5(2)   Where the office-holder is appointed as proxy-holder but another person acts as chair of the meeting, that other person may use the proxies as if that person were the proxy-holder.

9.5(3)   Where, in a meeting of creditors in a creditors' voluntary winding up or a winding up by the court, the chair holds a proxy which requires the proxy-holder to vote for a particular resolution and no other person proposes that resolution the chair must propose it unless the chair considers that there is good reason for not doing so.

9.5(4)   If the chair does not propose such a resolution, the chair must as soon as reasonably practicable after the meeting deliver a notice of the reason why that was not done to the creditor, member or contributory.

9.6   Right of inspection and delivery of proxies

9.6(1)   A person attending a meeting is entitled, immediately before or in the course of the meeting, to inspect proxies or any statement of claim and documentary evidence of debt delivered to the chair or to any other person in accordance with the notice convening the meeting.

9.6(2)   Where the chair is not the office-holder, the chair must deliver all proxies used for voting at a meeting to the office-holder, as soon as reasonably practicable after the meeting.

9.7   Proxy-holder with financial interest

9.7(1)   A proxy-holder must not vote for a resolution which would–

   (a)   directly or indirectly place the proxy-holder or any associate of the proxy-holder in a position to receive any remuneration, fees or expenses from the company's assets; or

   (b)   fix or change the amount of or the basis of any remuneration, fees or expenses receivable by the proxy-holder or any associate of the proxy-holder out of the company's assets.

9.7(2)   However, a proxy-holder may vote for a resolution described in paragraph (1) if the proxy specifically directs the proxy-holder to vote in that way.

9.7(3)   Where an office-holder is appointed as proxy-holder and that proxy is used under rule 9.5(2) by another person acting as chair, the office-holder is deemed to be an associate of the person acting as chair.

9.8   Resolution conferring authorisation to represent corporation

[Note: section 434B makes provision for corporate representation in company insolvency proceedings.]

9.8(1)   A person authorised to represent a corporation (other than as a proxy-holder) at a meeting of creditors or contributories must produce to the chair–

    (a)   the resolution conferring the authority; or

    (b)   a copy of that resolution certified as a true copy by–

        (i)   2 directors;

        (ii)   a director and the secretary; or

        (iii)   a director in the presence of a witness who attests the director's signature.

9.8(2)   The resolution conferring the authority must have been signed or subscribed (or in the case of an electronic document, authenticated) by or on behalf of the company in accordance with the Requirements of Writing (Scotland) Act 1995.

9.8(3)   In paragraph (2) "authenticated has the meaning given in the Requirements of Writing (Scotland) Act 1995.

PART 10

CREDITORS' AND LIQUIDATION COMMITTEES

CHAPTER 1

INTRODUCTORY

10.1   Scope and interpretation

10.1(1)   This Part applies to the establishment and operation of–

    (a)   a creditors' committee in a receivership;

    (b)   a liquidation committee in a creditors' voluntary winding up; and

    (c)   a liquidation committee in a winding up by the court.

10.1(2)   In this Part–

"contributory member" means a member of a liquidation committee appointed by the contributories; and

"creditor member" means a member of a liquidation committee appointed by the creditors.

CHAPTER 2

FUNCTIONS OF A COMMITTEE

10.2   Functions of a committee

10.2   In addition to any functions conferred on a liquidation committee by any provision of the Act or any other provision of these Rules–

    (a)   committee is to–

    (i)   assist the office-holder in discharging the office-holder's functions; and

    (ii) act in relation to the office-holder in such manner as may from time to time be agreed; and

(b) a committee in a receivership is to represent to the receiver the views of the unsecured creditors.

CHAPTER 3

MEMBERSHIP AND FORMALITIES OF FORMATION OF A COMMITTEE

[Note: (1) a document required by the Act or these Rules must also contain the standard contents required as set out in Part 1.

Note: (2) see sections 215, 363, 365 and 371 of the Financial Services and Markets Act 2000 for the rights of persons appointed by a scheme manager, the Financial Conduct Authority and the Prudential Regulation Authority to attend committees and make representations.]

10.3   Number of members of a committee

[Note: section 101(1) provides that a liquidation committee in a creditors' voluntary winding up may not have more than 5 members.]

10.3(1)   A committee in a receivership must have at least 3 members but not more than 5 members.

10.3(2)   A liquidation committee in a creditors' voluntary winding up appointed pursuant to section 101 must have at least 3 members.

10.3(3)   A liquidation committee in a winding up by the court established under section 142 must have–

(a) at least 3 and not more than 5 members elected by the creditors; and

(b) where the grounds on which the company was wound up do not include inability to pay its debts, and where the contributories so decide, up to 3 contributory members elected by the contributories.

10.4   Eligibility for membership of creditors' or liquidation committee

10.4(1)   A creditor is eligible to be a member of a committee if–

(a) the person has submitted a statement of claim and, where not dispensed with under rules 7.16(2) or 8.28(2), documentary evidence of debt;

(b) the debt is not fully secured and the creditor has not agreed to surrender the creditor's security to the liquidator; and

(c) neither of the following apply–

    (i)   the claim has been wholly rejected for voting purposes, or

    (ii) the claim has been wholly rejected for the purpose of distribution or dividend.

10.4(2)   No person can be a member as both a creditor and a contributory.

10.4(3)   A body corporate or a partnership may be a member of a committee, but it cannot act otherwise than by a representative appointed under rule 10.17.

10.5   Establishment of committees

10.5(1)   Where the creditors, or where applicable, contributories, decide that a creditors' or liquidation committee should be established, the convener or chair of the decision procedure or the convener of the deemed consent process (if not the office-holder) must–

(a)   as soon as reasonably practicable deliver a notice of the decision to the office-holder (or to the person appointed as office-holder); and

(b)   where a decision has also been made as to membership of the committee, inform the office-holder of the names and addresses of the persons elected to be members of the committee.

10.5(2)   Before a person may act as a member of the committee that person must agree to do so.

10.5(3)   A person's proxy-holder attending a meeting establishing the committee or, in the case of a body corporate or partnership, its duly appointed representative, may give such agreement (unless the proxy or instrument conferring authority contains a statement to the contrary).

10.5(4)   Where a decision has been made to establish a committee but not as to its membership, the office-holder must seek a decision from the creditors (about creditor members of the committee) and, where appropriate in a winding up by the court, a decision from contributories (about contributory members of the committee).

10.5(5)   The committee is not established (and accordingly cannot act) until the office-holder has delivered a notice of its membership in accordance with paragraph (9).

10.5(6)   The notice must contain the following–

(a)   a statement that the committee has been duly constituted;

(b)   identification details for any company that is a member of the committee;

(c)   the full name and address of each member that is not a company.

10.5(7)   The notice must be authenticated and dated by the office-holder.

10.5(8)   The notice must be delivered as soon as reasonably practicable after the minimum number of persons required by rule 10.3 have agreed to act as members and been elected.

10.5(9)   The office-holder must, as soon as reasonably practicable, deliver the notice to AiB.

10.6   Liquidation committee established by contributories

10.6(1)   This rule applies where, under section 142, the creditors do not decide that a liquidation committee should be established, or decide that a committee should not be established.

10.6(2)   The contributories may decide to appoint one of their number to make application to the court for an order requiring the liquidator to seek a further decision from the creditors on whether to establish a liquidation committee; and–

(a)   the court may, if it thinks that there are special circumstances to justify it, make such an order; and

(b)   the creditors' decision sought by the liquidator in compliance with the order is deemed to have been a decision under section 142.

10.6(3)   If the creditors decide under paragraph (2)(b) not to establish a liquidation committee, the contributories may establish a committee.

10.6(4)   The committee must then consist of at least 3, and not more than 5, contributories elected by the contributories; and rule 10.5 applies, substituting for the reference to rule 10.3 in rule 10.5(8) a reference to this paragraph.

10.7   Notice of change of membership of a committee

10.7(1)   If there is a change in membership of the committee, the office-holder must deliver a notice to AiB, as soon as reasonably practicable.

10.7(2)   The notice must contain–

(a)   the date of the original notice in respect of the constitution of the committee and the date of the last notice of membership given under this rule (if any);

(b)   a statement that this notice of membership replaces the previous notice;

(c)   identification details for any company that is a member of the committee;

(d)   the full name and address of any member that is not a company;

(e)   a statement whether any member has become a member since the issue of the previous notice;

(f)   the identification details for a company or otherwise the full name of any member named in the previous notice who is no longer a member and the date the membership ended.

10.7(3)   The notice must be authenticated and dated by the office-holder.

10.8   **Vacancies: creditor members of creditors' or liquidation committee**

10.8(1)   This rule applies if there is a vacancy among the creditor members of a creditors' or liquidation committee or where the number of creditor members of the committee is fewer than the maximum allowed.

10.8(2)   A vacancy need not be filled if–

(a)   the office-holder and a majority of the remaining creditor members agree; and

(b)   the total number of creditor members does not fall below 3.

10.8(3)   The office-holder may appoint a creditor, who is qualified under rule 10.4 to be a member of the committee, to fill a vacancy or as an additional member of the committee, if–

(a)   the remaining creditor members of the committee (provided there are at least 2) agree in accordance with paragraph (4) to the appointment; and

(b)   the creditor agrees to act.

10.8(4)   Where there are only 2 remaining members of the committee, both must agree to the appointment, otherwise a majority must agree.

10.8(5)   Alternatively, the office-holder may seek a decision from creditors to appoint a creditor (with that creditor's consent) to fill the vacancy.

10.8(6)   Where the vacancy is filled by an appointment made by a decision of creditors which is not chaired or convened by the office-holder, the chair or convenor must report the appointment to the office-holder.

10.9   **Vacancies: contributory members of liquidation committee**

10.9(1)   This rule applies if there is a vacancy among the contributory members of a liquidation committee or where the number of contributory members of the committee is fewer than the maximum allowed under rule 10.3(3)(b) or 10.6(4) as the case may be.

10.9(2)   A vacancy need not be filled if–

(a)   the liquidator and a majority of the remaining contributory members agree; and

(b)   in the case of a committee of contributories only, the number of members does not fall below 3.

10.9(3)   The liquidator may appoint a contributory to be a member of the committee, to fill a vacancy or as an additional member of the committee, if–

(a)   a majority of the remaining contributory members of the committee (provided there are at least 2) agree to the appointment; and

(b)   the contributory agrees to act.

10.9(4)   Alternatively, the office-holder may seek a decision from contributories to appoint a contributory (with that contributory's consent) to fill the vacancy.

10.9(5)   Where the vacancy is filled by an appointment made by a decision of contributories which is not convened or chaired by the office-holder, the convener or chair must report the appointment to the office-holder.

10.10   Resignation

10.10   A member of a committee may resign by informing the office-holder in writing.

10.11   Termination of membership

10.11   A person's membership of a committee is automatically terminated if that person–

(a)   becomes bankrupt or that person's estate is sequestrated, as the case may be, in which case the trustee in bankruptcy or the trustee in the sequestration replaces the person bankrupt or sequestrated as a member of the committee;

(b)   grants a trust deed for the benefit of creditors;

(c)   makes a composition with creditors;

(d)   is a person to whom a moratorium under a debt relief order applies;

(e)   neither attends nor is represented at 3 consecutive meetings (unless it is resolved at the third of those meetings that this rule is not to apply in that person's case);

(f)   has ceased to satisfy the criteria set out in rule 10.4 for eligibility to be a member of the committee;

(g)   ceases to be a creditor or is found never to have been a creditor;

(h)   ceases to be a contributory or is found never to have been a contributory.

10.12   Removal

10.12   A creditor member of a committee may be removed by a decision of the creditors through a decision procedure and in the case of a liquidation committee a contributory member of the committee may be removed by a decision of contributories through a decision procedure.

10.13   Cessation of liquidation committee in a winding up when creditors are paid in full

10.13(1)   Where the creditors have been paid in full together with interest in accordance with section 189, the liquidator must deliver to AiB a notice to that effect.

10.13(2)   On the delivery of the notice the liquidation committee ceases to exist.

10.13(3)   The notice must–

(a)   identify the liquidator;

(b)   contain a statement by the liquidator certifying that the creditors of the company have been paid in full with interest in accordance with section 189; and

(c)   be authenticated and dated by the liquidator.

[Note: a document required by the Act or these Rules must also contain the standard contents required as set out in Part 1.]

10.14   Meetings of committee

10.14(1)   Meetings of the committee must be held when and where determined by the office-holder.

10.14(2)   The office-holder must call a first meeting of the committee to take place within 6 weeks of the committee's establishment.

10.14(3)   After the calling of the first meeting, the office-holder must call a meeting–

(a)   if so requested by a member of the committee or a member's representative (the meeting then to be held within 21 days of the request being received by the office-holder); and

(b)   for a specified date, if the committee has previously resolved that a meeting be held on that date.

10.14(4)   The office-holder must give 5 business days' notice of the venue of a meeting to each member of the committee (or a member's representative, if designated for that purpose), except where the requirement for notice has been waived by or on behalf of a member.

10.14(5)   Waiver may be signified either at or before the meeting.

10.15   The chair at meetings

10.15   The chair at a meeting of a committee must be the office-holder or an appointed person.

10.16   Quorum

10.16   A meeting of a committee is duly constituted if due notice of it has been delivered to all the members, and at least 2 of the members are in attendance or represented.

10.17   Committee members' representatives

10.17(1)   A member of the committee may, in relation to the business of the committee, be represented by another person duly authorised by the member for that purpose.

10.17(2)   A person acting as a committee member's representative must hold a letter of authority entitling that person to act (either generally or specifically) and authenticated by or on behalf of the committee member.

10.17(3)   A proxy or an instrument conferring authority (in respect of a person authorised to represent a body corporate or a partnership) is to be treated as a letter of authority to act generally (unless the proxy or instrument conferring authority contains a statement to the contrary).

10.17(4)   The chair at a meeting of the committee may call on a person claiming to act as a committee member's representative to produce a letter of authority, and may exclude that person if no letter of authority is produced at or by the time of the meeting or if it appears to the chair that the authority is deficient.

10.17(5)   A committee member may not be represented by–

(a)   another member of the committee;

(b)   a person who is at the same time representing another committee-member;

(c)   a body corporate;

(d) a partnership;

(e) an undischarged bankrupt;

(f) a person whose estate has been sequestrated and who has not been discharged;

(g) a person who has granted a trust deed for the benefit of creditors;

(h) a person who has made a composition with creditors;

(i) a person to whom a moratorium period under a debt relief order applies;

(j) a person who is subject to a company directors disqualification order or a company directors disqualification undertaking; or

(k) a person who is subject to a bankruptcy restrictions order (including an interim order), a bankruptcy restrictions undertaking, a debt relief restrictions order (including an interim order) or a debt relief restrictions undertaking.

10.17(6)   Where a representative authenticates any document on behalf of a committee member the fact that the representative authenticates as a representative must be stated below the authentication.

10.18   Voting rights and resolutions

10.18(1)   At a meeting of the committee, each member (whether the member is in attendance or is represented by a representative) has one vote.

10.18(2)   A resolution is passed when a majority of the members attending or represented have voted in favour of it.

10.18(3)   Every resolution passed must be recorded in writing and authenticated by the chair, either separately or as part of the minutes of the meeting.

10.19   Resolutions by correspondence

10.19(1)   The office-holder may seek to obtain the agreement of the committee to a resolution by delivering to every member (or the member's representative designated for the purpose) details of the proposed resolution.

10.19(2)   The details must be set out in such a way that the recipient may indicate agreement or dissent and where there is more than one resolution may indicate agreement to or dissent from each one separately.

10.19(3)   A member of the committee may, within 5 business days from the delivery of details of the proposed resolution, require the office-holder to summon a meeting of the committee to consider the matters raised by the proposed resolution.

10.19(4)   In the absence of such a request, the resolution is passed by the committee if a majority of the members (excluding a member or member's representative who is to participate directly or indirectly in a transaction (see rule 10.25(4)) deliver notice to the office-holder that they agree with the resolution.

10.20   Remote attendance at meetings of committee

10.20(1)   Where the office-holder considers it appropriate, a meeting may be conducted and held in such a way that persons who are not present together at the same place may attend it.

10.20(2)   A person attends such a meeting who is able to exercise that person's right to speak and vote at the meeting.

10.20(3)   A person is able to exercise the right to speak at a meeting when that person is in a position to communicate during the meeting to all those attending the meeting any information or opinions which that person has on the business of the meeting.

10.20(4)   A person is able to exercise the right to vote at a meeting when–

(a)   that person is able to vote, during the meeting, on resolutions or determinations put to the vote at the meeting; and

(b)   that person's vote can be taken into account in determining whether or not such resolutions or determinations are passed at the same time as the votes of all the other persons attending the meeting.

10.20(5)   Where such a meeting is to be held the office-holder must make whatever arrangements the office-holder considers appropriate to–

(a)   enable those attending the meeting to exercise their rights to speak or vote; and

(b)   verify the identity of those attending the meeting and to ensure the security of any electronic means used to enable attendance.

10.20(6)   A requirement in these Rules to specify a place for the meeting may be satisfied by specifying the arrangements the office-holder proposes to enable persons to exercise their rights to speak or vote where in the reasonable opinion of the office-holder–

(a)   a meeting will be attended by persons who will not be present together at the same place; and

(b)   it is unnecessary or inexpedient to specify a place for the meeting.

10.20(7)   In making the arrangements referred to in paragraph (6) and in forming the opinion referred to in paragraph (6)(b), the office-holder must have regard to the legitimate interests of the committee members or their representatives attending the meeting in the efficient despatch of the business of the meeting.

10.20(8)   Where the notice of a meeting does not specify a place for the meeting the office-holder must specify a place for the meeting if at least one member of the committee requests the office-holder to do so in accordance with rule 10.21.

10.21   Procedure for requests that a place for a meeting should be specified

10.21(1)   This rule applies to a request to the office-holder under rule 10.20(8) to specify a place for the meeting.

10.21(2)   The request must be made within 3 business days of the date on which the office-holder delivered the notice of the meeting in question.

10.21(3)   Where the office-holder considers that the request has been properly made in accordance with this rule, the office-holder must–

(a)   deliver notice to all those previously given notice of the meeting–

(i)   that it is to be held at a specified place; and

(ii)   as to whether the date and time are to remain the same or not;

(b)   fix a venue for the meeting, the date of which must be not later than 7 business days after the original date for the meeting; and

(c)   give 3 business days' notice of the venue to all those previously given notice of the meeting.

10.21(4)   The notices required by sub-paragraphs (a) and (c) may be delivered at the same or different times.

10.21(5)   Where the office-holder has specified a place for the meeting in response to the request under rule 10.20(8), the chair of the meeting must attend the meeting by being present in person at that place.

CHAPTER 5

SUPPLY OF INFORMATION BY THE OFFICE-HOLDER TO THE COMMITTEE

[Note: a document required by the Act or these Rules must also contain the standard contents required as set out in Part 1.]

10.22 Notice requiring office-holder to attend the creditors' committee (receivership: section 68(2))

[Note: in a receivership section 68(2) enables the creditors' committee to require the receiver to attend the committee or provide the committee with information.]

10.22(1)   This rule applies where a committee in a receivership resolves under section 68(2) to require the attendance of the receiver.

10.22(2)   The notice delivered to the office-holder requiring the receiver's attendance must be–

(a)   accompanied by a copy of the resolution; and

(b)   authenticated by a member of the committee.

10.22(3)   A member's representative may authenticate the notice for the member.

10.22(4)   The meeting at which the receiver's attendance is required must be fixed by the committee for a business day, and must be held at such time and place as the receiver determines.

10.22(5)   Where the receiver so attends, the committee may elect one of their number to be chair of the meeting in place of the receiver or the appointed person.

10.23 Office-holder's obligation to supply information to the committee (winding up)

10.23(1)   This rule applies in relation to a creditors' voluntary winding up and a winding up by the court.

10.23(2)   The liquidator must deliver a report to every member of the liquidation committee containing the information required by paragraph (3)–

(a)   not less than once in every period of 6 months (unless the committee agrees otherwise); and

(b)   when directed to do so by the committee.

10.23(3)   The required information is a report setting out–

(a)   the position generally in relation to the progress of the insolvency proceedings; and

(b)   any matters arising in connection with them to which the office-holder considers the committee's attention should be drawn.

10.23(4)   The liquidator must, as soon as reasonably practicable after being directed by the committee–

(a)   deliver any report directed under paragraph (2)(b);

(b)   comply with a request by the committee for information.

10.23(5)   However the liquidator need not comply with such a direction where it appears to the office-holder that–

(a)   the direction is frivolous or unreasonable;

(b)   the cost of complying would be excessive, having regard to the relative importance of the information; or

(c)   there are insufficient assets to enable the liquidator to comply.

10.23(6)   Where the committee has come into being more than 28 days after the appointment of the liquidator, the liquidator must make a summary report to the members of the committee of what actions the liquidator has taken since the liquidator's appointment, and must answer such questions as they may put to the liquidator relating to the liquidator's conduct of the proceedings so far.

10.23(7)   A person who becomes a member of the committee at any time after its first establishment is not entitled to require a report under this rule by the liquidator of any matters previously arising, other than a summary report.

10.23(8)   Nothing in this rule disentitles the committee, or any member of it, from having access to the liquidator's sederunt book, or from seeking an explanation of any matter within the committee's responsibility.

CHAPTER 6

MISCELLANEOUS

[Note: a document required by the Act or these Rules must also contain the standard contents required as set out in Part 1.]

10.24   Expenses of members etc.

10.24(1)   The office-holder must pay, as an expense of the insolvency proceedings, the reasonable travelling expenses directly incurred by members of the committee or their representatives in attending the committee's meetings or otherwise on the committee's business.

10.24(2)   The requirement for the office-holder to pay the expenses does not apply to a meeting of the committee held within 6 weeks of a previous meeting, unless the meeting is summoned by the office-holder.

10.25   Dealings by committee members and others: winding up

10.25(1)   This rule applies in a creditors' voluntary winding up and a winding up by the court to a person who is, or has been in the preceding 12 months–

(a)   a member of the committee;

(b)   a member's representative; or

(c)   an associate of a member, or of a member's representative.

10.25(2)   Such a person must not enter into a transaction as a result of which that person would–

(a)   receive out of the company's assets any payment for services given or goods supplied in connection with the liquidation;

(b)   obtain a profit from the liquidation; or

(c)   acquire any part of the company's assets.

10.25(3)   However such a transaction may be entered into–

(a)   with the prior sanction of the committee, where it is satisfied (after full disclosure of the circumstances) that the person will be giving full value in the transaction;

(b)   with the prior permission of the court; or

(c)   if that person does so as a matter of urgency, or by way of performance of a contract in force before the date on which the company went into liquidation, and that person obtains the court's permission for the transaction, having applied for it without undue delay.

10.25(4)   Neither a member nor a representative of a member who is to participate directly or indirectly in a transaction may vote on a resolution to sanction that transaction.

10.25(5)   The court may, on the application of an interested person–

(a)   set aside a transaction which appears to it to be contrary to this rule; and

(b)   make such other order about the transaction as it thinks just, including an order requiring a person to whom this rule applies to account for any profit obtained from the transaction and compensate the insolvent estate for any resultant loss.

10.25(6)   The court will not make an order under the previous paragraph in respect of an associate of a member of the committee or an associate of a member's representative, if satisfied that the associate or representative entered into the relevant transaction without having any reason to suppose that in doing so the associate or representative would contravene this rule.

10.25(7)   The costs of the application are not payable as an expense of the liquidation unless the court orders otherwise.

10.26   Dealings by committee members and others: receivership

10.26(1)   This rule applies in a receivership.

10.26(2)   Membership of the committee does not prevent a person from dealing with the company provided that a transaction is in good faith and for value.

10.26(3)   The court may, on the application of an interested person–

(a)   set aside a transaction which appears to it to be contrary to this rule; and

(b)   make such other order about the transaction as it thinks just including an order requiring a person to whom this rule applies to account for any profit obtained from the transaction and compensate the company for any resultant loss.

10.27   Formal defects

10.27   The acts of a creditors' committee or a liquidation committee are valid notwithstanding any defect in the appointment, election or qualifications of a member of the committee or a committee member's representative or in the formalities of its establishment.

10.28   Special rule for winding up by the court: functions vested in the court

10.28   At any time when the functions of a committee in a winding up by the court are vested in the court under section 142(5), requirements of the Act or these Rules about notices to be delivered, or reports to be made, to the committee by the liquidator do not apply, otherwise than as enabling the committee to require a report as to any matter.

CHAPTER 7

WINDING UP BY THE COURT FOLLOWING AN ADMINISTRATION

[Note: a document required by the Act or these Rules must also contain the standard contents required as set out in Part 1.]

10.29   Continuation of creditors' committee

[Note: paragraph 83(8)(f) of schedule B1 makes provision for the liquidation committee to continue where the administration is followed by a creditors' voluntary winding up.]

10.29(1) This rule applies where–

(a) a winding-up order has been made by the court on the application of the administrator under paragraph 79 of schedule B1;

(b) the court makes an order under section 140(1) appointing the administrator as the liquidator; and

(c) a creditors' committee was in existence immediately before the winding-up order was made.

10.29(2) The creditors' committee shall continue in existence after the date of the order as if appointed as a liquidation committee under section 142.

10.29(3) However, subject to rule 10.8(3)(a), the committee cannot act until–

(a) the minimum number of persons required by rule 10.3 have agreed to act as members of the liquidation committee (including members of the former creditors' committee and any other who may be appointed under rule 10.8); and

(b) the liquidator has delivered a notice of continuance of the committee to AiB.

10.29(4) The notice must be delivered as soon as reasonably practicable after the minimum number of persons required have agreed to act as members or, if applicable, been appointed.

10.29(5) The notice must contain–

(a) a statement that the former creditors' committee is continuing in existence;

(b) identification details for any company that is a member of the committee; and

(c) the full name and address of each member that is not a company.

10.29(6) The notice must be authenticated and dated by the liquidator.

PART 11

THE EU REGULATION

[Note: a document required by the Act or these Rules must also contain the standard contents required as set out in Part 1.]

11.1 Interpretation of this Part

11.1 In this Part–

"winding up proceedings" means winding up proceedings listed in the United Kingdom entry in Annex A to the EU Regulation;

"conversion into winding up proceedings" refers to an order under Article 51 of the EU Regulation (conversion of secondary insolvency proceedings) that winding up proceedings of one kind are converted into winding up proceedings of another kind.

11.2 Conversion into other winding up proceedings: application

11.2(1) This rule applies where a member State liquidator in main proceedings applies to the court under Article 51 of the EU Regulation for conversion of winding up proceedings of one kind into winding up proceedings of another kind.

11.2(2) A statement containing a statutory declaration made by or on behalf of the member State liquidator must be lodged with the court in support of the application.

11.2(3) The statement must state–

(a) that main proceedings have been opened in relation to the company in a member State other than the United Kingdom;

(b) the belief of the person making the statement that conversion into other winding up proceedings would be most appropriate as regards the interests of the local creditors and coherence between the main and secondary insolvency proceedings;

(c) the kind of winding up proceedings into which, in the opinion of the person making the statement, the winding up proceedings should be converted; and

(d) all other matters that, in the opinion of the member State liquidator, would assist the court in–

   (i) deciding whether to make such an order, and

   (ii) considering whether and, if so, what consequential provision to include.

11.2(4) The application and the statement must be served upon the company.

11.3 Conversion into winding up proceedings: court order

11.3(1) On hearing an application for conversion of winding up proceedings under rule 11.2, the court may, subject to Article 51 of the EU Regulation, make such order as it thinks just.

11.3(2) An order for conversion into winding up proceedings may–

(a) provide that the company be wound up as if a resolution for voluntary winding up under section 84 were passed on the day on which the order is made; and

(b) contain such consequential provisions as the court thinks just.

11.4 Confirmation of creditors' voluntary winding up: application

11.4(1) This rule applies where–

(a) a company has passed a resolution for voluntary winding up, and either–

   (i) no declaration of solvency has been made in accordance with section 89, or

   (ii) a declaration made under section 89–

      (aa) has no effect by virtue of section 89(2), or

      (bb) is treated as not having been made by virtue of section 96; or

(b) a company has moved from administration to creditors' voluntary winding up in accordance with paragraph 83 of schedule B1.

11.4(2) The liquidator may apply to court for an order confirming the winding up as a creditors' voluntary winding up for the purposes of the EU Regulation.

11.4(3) The application must be supported by a statement containing a statutory declaration made by the liquidator which must contain–

(a) identification details for the liquidator and the company;

(b) the date on which the resolution for voluntary winding up was passed;

(c) a statement that the application is accompanied by the documents required by paragraph (4);

(d) a statement that the documents required by paragraph (4)(c) and (d) are true copies of the originals; and

(e) a statement whether the proceedings will be main proceedings, secondary proceedings or territorial proceedings and the reasons for so stating.

11.4(4)   The liquidator must lodge with the court–

(a)   2 copies of the application;

(b)   evidence of having been appointed liquidator of the company;

(c)   a copy of–

   (i)   the resolution for voluntary winding up, or

   (ii)   the notice of moving from administration to creditors' voluntary winding up sent by the administrator to the registrar of companies under paragraph 83(3) of schedule B1; and

(d)   a copy of–

   (i)   the statement of affairs required by section 99 or under paragraph 47 of schedule B1, or

   (ii)   the information included in the administrator's statement of proposals under paragraph 49 of schedule B1.

11.5   Confirmation of creditors' voluntary winding up: court order

11.5(1)   On an application under the preceding rule, the court may make an order confirming the creditors' voluntary winding up.

11.5(2)   It may do so without a hearing.

11.6   Confirmation of creditors' voluntary winding up: notice to member State liquidator

11.6(1)   Where the court has confirmed the creditors' voluntary winding up, the liquidator must as soon as reasonably practicable give notice to any member State liquidator appointed in relation to the company.

11.6(2)   Paragraph (1) is without prejudice to the liquidator's obligation in Article 54 of the EU Regulation (duty to inform creditors in other member States) in relation to the creditors' voluntary winding up.

11.7   Proceedings in another member State: duty to give notice

11.7(1)   This rule applies where a liquidator or provisional liquidator is required to give notice, or provide a copy of a document (including an order of court), to the court or the registrar of companies.

11.7(2)   Where not already required to do so by Article 41 of the EU Regulation, the liquidator or provisional liquidator must also give notice or provide a copy to–

(a)   any member State liquidator; or

(b)   where the liquidator or provisional liquidator knows that an application has been made to commence insolvency proceedings in another member State but a member State liquidator has not yet been appointed to the court to which that application has been made.

11.8   Member State liquidator: rules on creditors' participation in proceedings

11.8(1)   The provisions in these Rules apply to a member State liquidator's participation in proceedings in accordance with Article 45 of the EU Regulation (exercise of creditors' rights) in the same manner as they do to creditors' participation in those proceedings.

11.8(2)   In this rule, "creditors' participation"–

(a)   includes the following matters:–

   (i)   requesting and being provided with information, including inspecting or obtaining copies of documents or files,

    (ii) being provided with notices or other documents,

    (iii) participating and voting in decision procedures,

    (iv) the establishment and operation of creditor committees,

    (v) submitting statements of claim and documentary evidence of debt in respect of debts and receipt of dividends, and

    (vi) applying to the court and appearing at hearings; and

  (b) is limited to creditors' participation from the time of the opening of proceedings in accordance with Article 2(8) of the EU Regulation.

11.9   Main proceedings in Scotland: undertaking in respect of assets in another member State (Article 36 of the EU Regulation)

11.9(1)   This rule applies where a liquidator or provisional liquidator in main proceedings proposes to give an undertaking under Article 36 of the EU Regulation in respect of assets located in another member State.

11.9(2)   In addition to the requirements as to form and content set out in Article 36, the undertaking must contain–

  (a) the heading "Proposed Undertaking under Article 36 of the EU Insolvency Regulation (2015/848)";

  (b) identification details for the main proceedings;

  (c) identification and contact details for the liquidator or provisional liquidator; and

  (d) a description of the effect of the undertaking if approved.

11.9(3)   The proposed undertaking must be delivered to all the local creditors in the member State concerned of whose address the liquidator or provisional liquidator is aware.

11.9(4)   Where the undertaking is rejected the liquidator or provisional liquidator must inform all the creditors of the company of the rejection of the undertaking as soon as reasonably practicable.

11.9(5)   Where the undertaking is approved the liquidator or provisional liquidator must as soon as reasonably practicable–

  (a) send a copy of the undertaking to all the creditors with a notice informing them of the approval of the undertaking and of its effect (so far as they have not already been given this information under paragraph (2)(d));

  (b) where the insolvency proceedings relate to a registered company, deliver a copy of the undertaking to the registrar of companies.

11.9(6)   The liquidator or provisional liquidator may advertise details of the undertaking in the other member State in such manner as the office-holder thinks fit.

11.10   Main proceedings in another member State: approval of undertaking offered by the member State liquidator to local creditors in the UK

11.10(1)   This rule applies where a member State liquidator proposes an undertaking under Article 36 of the EU Regulation and the secondary proceedings which the undertaking is intended to avoid would be winding up proceedings to which these Rules apply.

11.10(2)   The decision by the local creditors whether to approve the undertaking must be made by a decision procedure subject to the rules which apply to the approval of a proposed CVA under section 4A of the Act.

11.10(3)   The rules in Chapters 1 to 9 of Part 5 of the CVA and Administration Rules 2018 apply to the decision procedure (with any necessary modifications) except for the following–5.7, 5.12, 5.14, 5.16 to 5.18 and 5.27.

11.10(4)   Where the main proceedings relate to a registered company the member State liquidator must deliver a copy of the approved undertaking to the registrar of companies.

11.11   Powers of a liquidator, provisional liquidator or member State liquidator in proceedings concerning members of a group of companies (Article 60 of the EU Regulation)

11.11   Where a liquidator or provisional liquidator or a member State liquidator makes an application in accordance with paragraph (1)(b) of Article 60 of the EU Regulation the application must state with reasons why the applicant thinks the matters set out in points (i) to (iv) of that paragraph apply.

11.12   Group coordination proceedings (Section 2 of Chapter 5 of the EU Regulation)

11.12(1)   An application to open group coordination proceedings must be headed "Application under Article 61 of Regulation (EU) 2015/848 to open group coordination proceedings".

11.12(2)   The application must, in addition to the requirements in Article 61 of the EU Regulation, contain–

(a)   identification and contact details for the liquidator or provisional liquidator making the application;

(b)   identification details for the company and the insolvency proceedings by virtue of which the liquidator or provisional liquidator is making the application;

(c)   identification details for the company and the insolvency proceedings in respect of each company which is a member of the group;

(d)   contact details for the office-holders and member state liquidators appointed in those proceedings;

(e)   identification details for any insolvency proceedings in respect of a member of the group which are not to be subject to the coordination because of an objection to being included; and

(f)   if relevant, a copy of any such agreement as is mentioned in Article 66 of the EU Regulation.

11.12(3)   An "office-holder" in paragraph (2)(d) includes a person holding office in insolvency proceedings in relation to the company in England and Wales or Northern Ireland.

11.13   Group coordination order (Article 68 of the EU Regulation)

11.13(1)   An order opening group coordination proceedings must also contain–

(a)   details of the matters set out in Article 68(1)(a) to (c) of the EU Regulation;

(b)   identification details for the insolvency proceedings by virtue of which the liquidator or provisional liquidator is making the application;

(c)   identification and contact details for the liquidator or provisional liquidator making the application;

(d)   identification details for the insolvency proceedings which are subject to the coordination; and

(e)   identification details for any insolvency proceedings for a member of the group which are not subject to the coordination because of an objection to being included.

11.13(2)   The liquidator or provisional liquidator must deliver a copy of the order to the coordinator and to any person who is, in respect of proceedings subject to the coordination–

(a)   an office-holder,

(b)   a person holding office in insolvency proceedings in relation to the company in England and Wales or Northern Ireland, and

(c)   a member State liquidator.

11.14   Delivery of group coordination order to registrar of companies

11.14   A liquidator or provisional liquidator in respect of insolvency proceedings subject to coordination must deliver a copy of the group coordination order to the registrar of companies.

11.15   Liquidator or provisional liquidator's report

11.15(1)   This rule applies where, under the second paragraph of Article 70(2) of the EU Regulation, a liquidator or provisional liquidator is required to give reasons for not following the coordinator's recommendations or the group coordination plan.

11.15(2)   Those reasons must be given as soon as reasonably practicable by a notice to all the creditors.

11.15(3)   Those reasons may be given in the next progress report where doing so satisfies the requirement to give the reasons as soon as reasonably practicable.

11.16   Publication of opening of proceedings by a member State liquidator

11.16(1)   This rule applies where–

(a)   a company subject to insolvency proceedings has an establishment in Scotland; and

(b)   a member State liquidator is required or authorised under Article 28 of the EU Regulation to publish a notice.

11.16(2)   The notice must be gazetted.

11.17   Statement by member State liquidator that insolvency proceedings in another member State are closed etc.

11.17   A statement by a member State liquidator under any of sections 201, 204 or 205 informing the registrar of companies that the insolvency proceedings in another member State are closed or that the member State liquidator consents to the dissolution must contain–

(a)   identification details for the company; and

(b)   identification details for the member State liquidator.

PART 12

PERMISSION TO ACT AS DIRECTOR ETC. OF COMPANY WITH A PROHIBITED NAME (SECTION 216)

[Note: a document required by the Act or these Rules must also contain the standard contents required as set out in Part 1.]

12.1   Preliminary

12.1   The rules in this Part–

(a)   relate to permission required under section 216 (restriction on re-use of name of company in insolvent liquidation) for a person to act as mentioned in section 216(3) in relation to a company with a prohibited name;

(b)   prescribe the cases excepted from that provision, that is to say, in which a person to whom the section applies may so act without that permission; and

(c)   apply to all windings up to which section 216 applies.

12.2   Application for permission under section 216(3)

12.2   At least 14 days' notice of any application for permission to act in any of the circumstances which would otherwise be prohibited by section 216(3) must be given by the applicant to the Secretary of State, who may–

(a)   appear at the hearing of the application; and

(b)   whether or not appearing at the hearing, make representations.

12.3   Power of court to call for liquidator's report

12.3   When considering an application for permission under section 216, the court may call on the liquidator, or any former liquidator, of the liquidating company for a report of the circumstances in which the company became insolvent and the extent (if any) of the applicant's apparent responsibility for its doing so.

12.4   First excepted case

12.4(1)   This rule applies where–

(a)   a person ("the person") was within the period mentioned in section 216(1) a director, or shadow director, of an insolvent company that has gone into insolvent liquidation; and

(b)   the person acts in all or any of the ways specified in section 216(3) in connection with, or for the purposes of, the carrying on (or proposed carrying on) of the whole or substantially the whole of the business of the insolvent company where that business (or substantially the whole of it) is (or is to be) acquired from the insolvent company under arrangements–

   (i)   made by its liquidator, or

   (ii)   made before the insolvent company entered into insolvent liquidation by an office-holder acting in relation to it as administrator, receiver or supervisor of a CVA.

12.4(2)   The person will not be taken to have contravened section 216 if prior to that person acting in the circumstances set out in paragraph (1) a notice is, in accordance with the requirements of paragraph (3),–

(a)   given by the person, to every creditor of the insolvent company whose name and address–

   (i)   is known by that person, or

   (ii)   is ascertainable by that person on the making of such enquiries as are reasonable in the circumstances; and

(b)   published in the Gazette.

12.4(3)   The notice referred to in paragraph (2)–

(a)   may be given and published before the completion of the arrangements referred to in paragraph (1)(b) but must be given and published no later than 28 days after their completion;

(b)   must contain–

   (i)   identification details for the company,

   (ii)   the name and address of the person,

(iii) a statement that it is the person's intention to act (or, where the insolvent company has not entered insolvent liquidation, to act or continue to act) in all or any of the ways specified in section 216(3) in connection with, or for the purposes of, the carrying on of the whole or substantially the whole of the business of the insolvent company,

(iv) the prohibited name or, where the company has not entered into insolvent liquidation, the name under which the business is being, or is to be, carried on which would be a prohibited name in respect of the person in the event of the insolvent company entering insolvent liquidation,

(v) a statement that the person would not otherwise be permitted to undertake those activities without the leave of the court or the application of an exception created by Rules made under the Insolvency Act 1986,

(vi) a statement that breach of the prohibition created by section 216 is a criminal offence, and

(vii) a statement as set out in rule 12.5 of the effect of issuing the notice under rule 12.4(2);

(c) where the company is in administration, has a receiver appointed or is subject to a CVA,–

(i) the date that the company entered administration, had a receiver appointed or a CVA approved (whichever is the earliest), and

(ii) a statement that the person was a director of the company on that date; and

(d) where the company is in insolvent liquidation,–

(i) the date that the company entered insolvent liquidation, and

(ii) a statement that the person was a director of the company during the 12 months ending with that date.

12.4(4)   Notice may in particular be given under this rule–

(a) prior to the insolvent company entering insolvent liquidation where the business (or substantially the whole of the business) is, or is to be, acquired by another company under arrangements made by an office-holder acting in relation to the insolvent company as administrator, receiver or supervisor of a CVA (whether or not at the time of the giving of the notice the person is a director of that other company); or

(b) at a time when the person is a director of another company where–

(i) the other company has acquired, or is to acquire, the whole, or substantially the whole, of the business of the insolvent company under arrangements made by its liquidator, and

(ii) it is proposed that after the giving of the notice a prohibited name should be adopted by the other company.

12.4(5)   Notice may not be given under this rule by a person who has already acted in breach of section 216.

12.5   Statement as to the effect of the notice under rule 12.4(2)

12.5   The statement as to the effect of the notice under rule 12.4(2) must be as set out below–

> "Section 216(3) of the Insolvency Act 1986 lists the activities that a director of a company that has gone into insolvent liquidation may not undertake unless the court gives permission or there is an exception in the Insolvency Rules made under the Insolvency Act 1986. (This includes the exceptions in Part 12 of the Insolvency (Scotland) (Receivership and Winding up) Rules 2018.) These activities are–
>
> (a)   acting as a director of another company that is known by a name which is either the same as a name used by the company in insolvent liquidation in the 12 months before it entered liquidation or is so similar as to suggest an association with that company;

(b)   directly or indirectly being concerned or taking part in the promotion, formation or management of any such company; or

(c)   directly or indirectly being concerned in the carrying on of a business otherwise than through a company under a name of the kind mentioned in (a) above.

This notice is given under rule 12.4 of the Insolvency (Scotland) (Receivership and Winding up) Rules 2018 where the business of a company which is in, or may go into, insolvent liquidation is, or is to be, carried on otherwise than by the company in liquidation with the involvement of a director of that company and under the same or a similar name to that of that company.

The purpose of giving this notice is to permit the director to act in these circumstances where the company enters (or has entered) insolvent liquidation without the director committing a criminal offence and in the case of the carrying on of the business through another company, being personally liable for that company's debts.

Notice may be given where the person giving the notice is already the director of a company which proposes to adopt a prohibited name.".

12.6   Second excepted case

12.6(1)   Where a person to whom section 216 applies as having been a director or shadow director of the liquidating company applies for permission of the court under that section not later than 7 business days from the date on which the company went into liquidation, the person may, during the period specified in paragraph (2) below, act in any of the ways mentioned in section 216(3), notwithstanding that the person does not have the permission of the court under that section.

12.6(2)   The period referred to in paragraph (1) begins with the day on which the company goes into liquidation and ends either on the day falling 6 weeks after that date or on the day on which the court disposes of the application for permission under section 216, whichever of those days occurs first.

12.7   Third excepted case

12.7   The court's permission under section 216(3) is not required where the company there referred to though known by a prohibited name within the meaning of the section–

(a)   has been known by that name for the whole of the period of 12 months ending with the day before the liquidating company went into liquidation; and

(b)   has not at any time in those 12 months been dormant within the meaning of section 1169(1), (2) and (3)(a) of the Companies Act.

SCHEDULE 1

REVOCATIONS

Introductory rule 2

1. In this Schedule, "the 1986 Rules" means the Insolvency (Scotland) Rules 1986.

Name	Number	Extent of revocation
The Insolvency (Scotland) Rules 1986	S.I. 1986/1915	Parts 3 to 6 (and schedules 1 to 2) in their entirety. Rules 0.1 to 0.3 and Part 7 (and schedules 3 to 5) so far as they apply to receivership and winding up.
The Receivers (Scotland) Regulations 1986	S.I. 1986/1917	The entire S.I..
The Insolvency (Scotland) Amendment Rules 1987	S.I. 1987/1921	Insofar as they amend the 1986 Rules in relation to receivership and winding up.
The Scotland Act 1998 (Consequential Modifications) (No. 2) Order 1999	S.I. 1999/1820	In schedule 2, paragraphs 141 and 142.
The Enterprise Act 2002 (Consequential Amendments) (Prescribed Part) (Scotland) Order 2003	S.I. 2003/2108	Part 1 insofar as it amends the 1986 Rules in relation to receivership and winding up. Part 2.
The Insolvency (Scotland) Regulations 2003	S.I. 2003/2109	Part 2 and schedule 2 insofar as they amend the 1986 Rules in relation to receivership and winding up.
The Insolvency (Scotland) Amendment Rules 2003	S.I. 2003/2111	Insofar as they amend the 1986 Rules in relation to receivership and winding up.
The Insolvency (Scotland) Amendment Rules 2006	S.I. 2006/734	rule 13
The Insolvency (Scotland) Amendment Rules 2007	S.I. 2007/2537	The entire S.I.
The Tribunals, Courts and Enforcement Act 2007 (Consequential Amendments) Order 2012	S.I. 2012/2404	In schedule 3, paragraph 4(5) and (6)
The Insolvency (Scotland) Rules 1986 Amendment Rules 2008	S.S.I. 2008/393	The entire S.S.I.
The Insolvency (Scotland) Amendment Rules 2014	S.S.I. 2014/114	The entire S.S.I. except insofar as it amends the 1986 Rules in relation to administration.
The Insolvency Amendment (EU 2015/848) Regulations 2017	S.I. 2017/702	Part 5 of schedule 1 insofar as it amends the 1986 Rules in relation to winding up.

TRANSITIONAL AND SAVINGS PROVISIONS

Introductory rule 4

1   General

1   In this Schedule–

"the 1986 Rules" means the Insolvency (Scotland) Rules 1986 as they had effect immediately before the commencement date and a reference to "1986 rule" followed by a rule number is a reference to a rule in the 1986 Rules; and

"the commencement date" means the date these Rules come into force.

2   Requirement for office-holder to provide information to creditors on opting out

2(1)   Rule 1.35, which requires an office-holder to provide information to a creditor on the right to opt out under rule 1.34 in the first communication to the creditor, does not apply to an office-holder who has delivered the first communication before the commencement date.

2(2)   However, such an office-holder may choose to deliver information on the right to opt out in which case the communication to the creditor must contain the information required by rule 1.35.

3   Electronic communication

3(1)   Rule 1.41(4) does not apply where the relevant proceedings commenced before the commencement date.

3(2)   In this paragraph, relevant proceedings are commenced on–

(a)   the appointment of a receiver;

(b)   the passing or deemed passing of a resolution to wind up a company; or

(c)   the making of a winding-up order.

4   Statements of affairs

4(1)   The provisions of these Rules relating to statements of affairs in receivership and company winding up do not apply and the following rules in the 1986 Rules continue to apply where relevant proceedings commenced before the commencement date and a person is required to provide a statement of affairs:–

(a)   1986 rules 3.2 to 3.3 (receivership); and

(b)   1986 rules 4.7 to 4.9 (company winding up).

4(2)   In this paragraph, "commenced" means–

(a)   the appointment of a receiver;

(b)   the passing or deemed passing of a resolution to wind up a company; or

(c)   the making of a winding-up order.

5   Savings in respect of meetings taking place on or after the commencement date and resolutions by post

5(1)   This paragraph applies where on or after the commencement date–

(a)   a creditors' or contributories' meeting is to be held as a result of a notice issued before that date in relation to a meeting for which provision is made by the 1986 Rules or the Act;

(b) a meeting is to be held as a result of a requisition by a creditor or contributory made before that date;

(c) a meeting at year's end is required by section 105 in the winding up of a company where the resolution to wind up was passed before the commencement date.

5(2) Where paragraph (1) applies, Part 8 of these Rules does not apply and the 1986 Rules relating to the following continue to apply:–

(a) the requirement to hold the meeting;

(b) notice and advertisement of the meeting;

(c) governance of the meeting;

(d) recording and taking minutes of the meeting;

(e) the report or return of the meeting;

(f) membership and formalities of establishment of liquidation and creditors' committees where the resolution to form the committee is passed at the meeting;

(g) the office-holder's resignation or removal at the meeting;

(h) the office-holder's release;

(i) fixing the office-holder's remuneration;

(j) requests for further information from creditors;

(k) claims that remuneration is or that other expenses are excessive; and

(l) complaints about exclusion at the meeting.

5(3) Where, before the commencement date, the office-holder sought to obtain a resolution by correspondence under 1986 rule 4.55, the 1986 Rules relating to resolutions by correspondence continue to apply and sub-paragraph (2) applies to any meeting that those rules require the office-holder to summon.

6 Savings in respect of final meetings taking place on or after the commencement date

6(1) This paragraph applies where–

(a) before the commencement date–

(i) a final report to creditors has been sent under 1986 rule 4.31 (final report to creditors in liquidation),

(ii) a meeting has been called under section 94, 106 or 146 of the Act (final meeting); and

(b) a meeting under section 94, 106 or 146 of the Act is held on or after the commencement date.

6(2) Where a meeting is held to which this paragraph applies, Part 8 of these Rules does not apply and the 1986 Rules relating to the following continue to apply:–

(a) the requirement to hold the meeting;

(b) notice and advertisement of the meeting;

(c) governance of the meeting;

(d) recording and taking minutes of the meeting;

(e) the form and content of the final report;

(f) the office-holder's resignation or removal;

(g) the office-holder's release;

(h) fixing the office-holder's remuneration;

(i) requests for further information from creditors;

(j) claims that remuneration is or other expenses are excessive; and

(k) complaints about exclusion at the meeting.

7   Progress reports and statements to the registrar of companies

7(1) Where an obligation to prepare a progress report arises before the commencement date but has not yet been fulfilled 1986 rules 4.10 (information to creditors and contributories), 4.11 (information to register of companies) and 4.56 (liquidator's reports) continue to apply.

7(2) The provisions of these Rules relating to progress reporting do not apply where the winding-up order was made on a petition presented before the commencement date.

8   Foreign currency

8(1) Where, before the commencement date an amount stated in a foreign currency on an application, statement of claim or evidence of debt (according to the nature of the debt claimed) is converted into sterling by the office-holder under 1986 rule 4.17, the office-holder and any successor to the office-holder must continue to use that exchange rate for subsequent conversions of that currency into sterling for the purpose of distributing the insolvent estate.

8(2) However when an office-holder, convener, appointed person or chair uses an exchange rate to convert an application, claim or proof in a foreign currency into sterling solely for voting purposes before the commencement date, it does not prevent the office-holder from using an alternative rate for subsequent conversions.

9   General powers of liquidator

9 1986 rule 4.58 (dealings by committee-members and others) continues to apply in respect of the power of the court or the liquidation committee to ratify anything done by the liquidator without sanction, or leave of the court, before the amendments made to sections 165 and 167 of the Act by section 120(2) and (3) of the Small Business, Enterprise and Employment Act 2015 (which removed the requirements for the liquidator to obtain such sanction) came into force.

10   Accounting periods

10(1) 1986 rule 4.68(2) (estate to be distributed in respect of accounting periods) continues to apply where the date of appointment of any provisional liquidator or liquidator in the winding up under the 1986 Rules fell before the commencement date.

10(2) Rules 7.31(2) and (3) relating to the distribution of estate in respect of accounting periods do not apply where paragraph (1) applies.

11   Applications before the court

11 Where an application to court is lodged or a petition is presented under the Act or under the 1986 Rules before the commencement date and the application or petition has not been determined or withdrawn, the 1986 Rules continue to apply to that application or petition.

12   Forms

12 A form contained in schedule 5 of the 1986 Rules may be used on or after the commencement date if–

(a) the form is used to provide a statement of affairs pursuant to paragraph 4 of this schedule;

(b) the form relates to a meeting held under the 1986 Rules to which paragraph 5(1) of this schedule applies;

(c) the form is required because before the commencement date, the office-holder sought to obtain the passing of a resolution by post; or

(d) the form relates to any application to the court or petition presented before the commencement date.

13   Insolvency registers

13(1)   The AiB must maintain on the register of insolvencies information which is on the register immediately before the commencement date.

13(2)   The AiB must also enter on that register information received (but not yet entered on the register) before the commencement date.

13(3)   The court's power under rules 2.11, 4.6 and 5.16 to order that information must not be entered in those registers where there is a risk of violence applies equally to information received by AiB before the commencement date but not yet entered on a register.

14   Savings in respect of special insolvency rules: limited liability partnerships

14   The 1986 Rules, insofar as they apply to insolvency proceedings under the Limited Liability Partnerships Regulations 2001 and the Limited Liability Partnerships (Scotland) Regulations 2001 continue to have effect for the purposes of the application of those Regulations.

SCHEDULE 3

PUNISHMENT OF OFFENCES UNDER THESE RULES

Introductory rule 5

Rule creating offence	General nature of the offence	Mode of prosecution	Maximum penalty	Daily default fine (if applicable)
1.51(1)	Falsely claiming to be a person entitled to inspect a document with the intention of gaining sight of it.	1. On indictment. 2. Summary.	2 years' imprisonment, or a fine, or both. 12 months' imprisonment, or a fine not exceeding the statutory maximum, or both.	Not applicable.
2.16(7)	Receiver failing to deliver required accounts summary of receipts and payments.	Summary.	Level 3 on the standard scale.	One tenth of level 3 on the standard scale.
4.14(13)	Directors failing to seek a decision on the nomination of a liquidator	1. On indictment. 2. Summary.	1. A fine 2. A fine not exceeding the statutory maximum.	Not applicable
7.17	Producing false evidence; failing to report false evidence	1. On indictment 2. Summary	2 years' imprisonment, or a fine, or both. 12 months' imprisonment, or a fine not exceeding the statutory maximum, or both.	Not applicable
7.18(7)	Failing to comply with an order requiring attendance for private examination	Summary	3 months' imprisonment; a fine not exceeding level 5 on the standard scale, or both.	Not applicable

SCHEDULE 4

INFORMATION TO BE INCLUDED IN THE SEDERUNT BOOK

Rule 1.54

Receivership

1   The instrument of appointment of the receiver under section 53.

2(1)   Each statement of affairs and each statement of concurrence under Part 2 of these Rules, subject to rule 2.11(3), 2.12 and sub-paragraph (2).

2(2)   Any schedule required by rule 2.8(5)(b) with the statement of affairs need not be inserted.

3   Any order for limited disclosure under rule 2.11(3) must be inserted as soon as reasonably practicable.

4   On discharge or variation of an order for limited disclosure under rule 2.11 as soon as reasonably practicable the full statement of affairs or statement of concurrence (or so much of the statement as is no longer subject to the order).

5   The report by the receiver under section 67.

Winding up

6   A certificate of appointment of the liquidator by the company under rule 3.2.

7   The inventory and valuation of the assets of the company under rule 3.14.

8(1)   The statement of affairs under rule 4.2 must be inserted as soon as reasonably practicable after completion of the decision procedure or deemed consent procedure referred to in rule 4.11 (nomination of liquidator and information to creditors on conversion from members' voluntary winding up (section 96)) in respect of the appointment of the liquidator, subject to rule 4.6 (order limiting disclosure of statement of affairs etc) and sub-paragraph (2).

8(2)   Any schedule required by rule 4.4(4)(b) (additional requirements as to statements of affairs) need not be inserted with the statement of affairs.

9(1)   The statement of affairs under rule 4.3 must be inserted as soon as reasonably practicable after the completion of the decision procedure or deemed consent procedure referred to in rule 4.14 (information to creditors and appointment of liquidator) in respect of the appointment of the liquidator, subject to rule 4.6 and sub-paragraph (2).

9(2)   Any schedule required by rule 4.4(4)(b) need not be inserted with the statement of affairs.

10   Any statement of concurrence under Part 4 of these Rules, subject to rule 4.6.

11   Any order for limited disclosure under rule 4.6(3) must be inserted as soon as reasonably practicable.

12   On discharge or variation of an order for limited disclosure under rule 4.6 as soon as reasonably practicable the full statement of affairs or statement of concurrence must be inserted (or so much of the statement as is no longer subject to the order).

13   A certificate of appointment of the liquidator by creditors or the company under rule 4.20.

14   The inventory and valuation of the assets of the company under rule 4.32.

15(1)   Each statement of affairs and each statement of concurrence under Part 5 of these Rules, subject to rule 5.16(3) and sub-paragraph (2).

15(2)   Any schedule required by rule 5.13(4)(b) with the statement of affairs need not be inserted.

16   Any order for limited disclosure under rule 5.16(3) must be inserted as soon as reasonably practicable.

17   On discharge or variation of an order for limited disclosure under rule 5.16 as soon as reasonably practicable the full statement of affairs or statement of concurrence must be inserted (or so much of the statement as is no longer subject to the order).

18   A certificate of appointment of the liquidator under rule 5.23.

19   The inventory and valuation of the assets of the company under rule 5.36.

20   Any transcript prepared of a public examination under section 133.

Common parts

21   Any petition for winding up or the appointment of any office-holder.

22   Any decision or order of the court, including any decision or order–

   (a)   appointing an office-holder;

   (b)   under rule 1.56 (power to cure defects in procedure).

23   Any progress report required by Chapter 1 of Part 7.

24   Any final report or account mentioned in Chapter 2 of Part 7.

25   Where the liquidator accepts or rejects a claim under rule 7.19, the decision on the claim specifying–

   (a)   the amount of the claim accepted;

   (b)   the category of debt, and the value of any security, as decided by the liquidator; and

   (c)   if rejecting the claim, the reasons for doing so.

26   A record of the court's decision on any appeal against acceptance of rejection of a claim under rule 7.19.

27   A record of an agreement or determination under rule 7.31(2)(c)(i) or (ii).

28   The audited accounts.

29   The scheme of division.

30   The final determination in relation to the liquidator's outlays and remuneration.

31   A record of a decision procedure made in accordance with rule 8.40(1).

32   A record of a deemed consent procedure made in accordance with rule 8.40(4).

33   All proxies.

34   A copy of every resolution passed under rule 10.18 (voting rights and resolutions).

35   A copy of every resolution passed under rule 10.19 (resolutions by correspondence).

36   A note that the agreement of the committee to a resolution under rule 10.19 was obtained.

Insolvency (Amendment) (EU Exit) Regulations

(SI 2019/146)

Made 30 January 2019 in accordance with regulation 1(2) and (3).

1 Citation and commencement

1(1) These Regulations may be cited as the Insolvency (Amendment) (EU Exit) Regulations 2019.

1(2) The following provisions of these Regulations come into force on the day after these Regulations are made–

  (a) regulation 2 as it relates–

    (i) to paragraph 177 of the Schedule, and

    (ii) Part 12 of the Schedule,

  (b) paragraph 177 of the Schedule, and

  (c) Part 12 of the Schedule.

1(3) The remainder of these Regulations come into force on exit day.

2 Amendments

2 The Schedule has effect.

3 Extent and application

3 Any provision of these Regulations amending or applying an enactment has the same extent as the enactment amended or applied, except that–

  (a) the amendments made to the Insolvency Act 1986 by paragraphs 18, 22, 24 and 26 of the Schedule extend to England and Wales only; and

  (b) the amendments made to that Act by Part 7 of the Schedule apply to Scotland only.

4 Temporal application and savings

4(1) Subject to regulation 5 nothing in these Regulations affects–

  (a) the application of Council Regulation (EC) 1346/2000 to insolvency proceedings which fall within the scope of that Regulation and were opened before 26 June 2017; and

  (b) the saving for the existing law in article 3 of the Insolvency Amendment (EU 2015/848) Regulations 2017.

4(2) Where main proceedings under the EU Insolvency Regulation were opened before exit day the amendments made by these Regulations do not apply in respect of–

  (a) those proceedings;

  (b) secondary proceedings in respect of the same debtor;

  (c) any proceedings falling within Article 6 of the EU Insolvency Regulation.

4(3) In applying paragraphs (1) and (2) references to the EU and to its members are to be read as if the United Kingdom were a member.

4(4) The time at which proceedings are opened is to be determined in accordance with Article 2(8) of the EU Insolvency Regulation.

4(5)   In this regulation and regulation 5 the EU Insolvency Regulation means Regulation (EU) 2015/848 of the European Parliament and of the Council on insolvency proceedings.

5   Temporal application and savings

5(1)   Paragraph (2) applies where in any particular case Council Regulation (EC) 1346/2000 or the EU Insolvency Regulation applies in the United Kingdom by virtue of regulation 4 and the court considers that the effect is or would be different to what would be the effect had a member State treated the United Kingdom as a member State under the relevant Regulation, and either–

(a)   the court considers that one or more of the following would be materially prejudiced–

    (i)   the interests of a creditor (whether alone or in common with some or all other creditors),

    (ii)   the interests of the debtor,

    (iii)   where the debtor is a body corporate, the interests of a member (whether alone or in common with some or all other members) of the debtor; or

(b)   the court considers it would be manifestly contrary to public policy to apply the relevant Regulation.

5(2)   The Court may–

(a)   apply any other relevant law of the part of the United Kingdom in which the matter is being determined (including the Cross-Border Insolvency Regulations 2006 or the Cross-Border Insolvency Regulations (Northern Ireland) 2007);

(b)   make any other order that it thinks fit.

SCHEDULE

Regulation 2

PART 1

AMENDMENT OF RETAINED DIRECT EU LEGISLATION

Amendments to the EU Insolvency Regulation

1   Regulation (EU) 2015/848 of the European Parliament and of the Council of 20 May 2015 on insolvency proceedings is amended as follows.

2(1)   Article 1 is amended as follows.

2(2)   For the heading substitute "Application and jurisdiction".

2(3)   For paragraph 1 substitute–

"**1**   The grounds for jurisdiction to open insolvency proceedings set out in paragraph 1B are in addition to any grounds for jurisdiction to open such proceedings which apply in the laws of any part of the United Kingdom.

1A   There is jurisdiction to open insolvency proceedings listed in paragraph 1B where the proceedings are opened for the purposes of rescue, adjustment of debt, reorganisation or liquidation and–

    (a)   the centre of the debtor's main interests is in the United Kingdom; or

    (b)   the centre of the debtor's main interests is in a Member State and there is an establishment in the United Kingdom.

1B   The proceedings referred to in paragraph 1 are–

    (a)   winding up by or subject to the supervision of the court;

    (b)   creditors' voluntary winding up with confirmation by the court;

    (c)   administration, including appointments made by filing prescribed documents with the court;

    (d)   voluntary arrangements under insolvency legislation; and

    (e)   bankruptcy or sequestration.".

2(4)   In paragraph 2 for "Directive 2001/24/EC" substitute "the Credit Institutions (Reorganisation and Winding up) Regulations 2004".

3   In Article 2–

    (a)   insert the following paragraph–

        "(1A) "Member State" means a state which is a member of the EU other than Denmark;";

    (b)   omit paragraphs (1) and (3);

    (c)   in paragraph (4) for "listed in Annex A" substitute "listed in Article 1(1B) which there is jurisdiction to open under Article 1(1A) and includes interim proceedings";

    (d)   in paragraph (6)–

        (i) omit point (i); and

        (ii)   in point (ii) omit "in all other articles," and "of a Member State";

    (e)   omit paragraph (9);

    (f)   in paragraph (10) omit "main";

    (g)   omit paragraphs (11) to (14).

4(1)   Article 3 is amended as follows.

4(2)   For the heading "International jurisdiction" substitute "Centre of main interests".

4(3)   In paragraph 1–

    (a)   in the first sub-paragraph omit the first sentence;

    (b)   in the second sub-paragraph for "to another Member State" substitute "from the United Kingdom to a Member State or to the United Kingdom from a Member State";

    (c)   in the third sub-paragraph for "to another Member State" substitute "from the United Kingdom to a Member State or to the United Kingdom from a Member State";

    (d)   in the fourth sub-paragraph for "to another Member State" substitute "from the United Kingdom to a Member State or to the United Kingdom from a Member State";

4(4)   Omit paragraphs 2 to 4.

5(1)   Article 4 is amended as follows.

5(2)   In paragraph 1–

    (a)   in the first sentence for "Article 3" substitute "Article 1(1A) (a) or (b)"; and

    (b)   for the second sentence substitute "Where there is jurisdiction to open insolvency proceedings on either of the grounds specified in Article 1(1A)(a) or (b), the judgment opening such proceedings must state which of those grounds is applicable.".

5(3)   In paragraph 2–

    (a)   in the first sentence–

    (i)   omit "in accordance with national law" and "Member States may entrust";

    (ii)   for the words from "to examine" to the end of the sentence substitute "must examine the grounds on which there is jurisdiction to open the proceedings under Article 1(1A)."; and

  (b)   for the second sentence substitute "Where this is the case and there is jurisdiction to open insolvency proceedings on either of the grounds specified in Article 1(1A)(a) or (b), the insolvency practitioner must specify in the decision opening the proceedings which of those grounds is applicable.".

6(1)   Article 5 is amended as follows.

6(2)   In the heading omit "main".

6(3)   In paragraph 1–

  (a)   omit "main" after "the decision opening"; and

  (b)   for "grounds of international jurisdiction" substitute "the grounds of jurisdiction under Article 1(1A)(a)".

6(4)   In paragraph 2–

  (a)   omit "main" after "the decision opening";

  (b)   omit "international";

  (c)   after "jurisdiction" insert "under Article 1(1A)(a)"; and

  (d)   for "national law so provides" substitute "the relevant law (other than this Regulation) of the part of the United Kingdom in which the matter is being determined so provides".

7   Omit Articles 6 to 24 and 26 to 83.

8   In Article 84 omit–

  (a)   the second sentence of paragraph 1, and

  (b)   paragraph 2.

9   In Article 85–

  (a)   omit paragraphs 1 and 2;

  (b)   in paragraph 3–

    (i)   in point (a) omit "in any Member State"; and

    (ii)   for "that Member State" substitute "the United Kingdom".

10   Omit Articles 86 to 90.

11   In Article 91 omit the second sentence.

12   In Article 92 omit point (c).

13   Omit the sentence immediately following Article 92 which begins "This Regulation shall be binding".

14   Omit Annex A.

15   In Annex B omit all the entries other than those for the United Kingdom.

PART 2

AMENDMENTS TO THE INSOLVENCY ACT 1986

16   The Insolvency Act 1986 is amended as follows.

17   In section 1 in subsection (4)–

(a)   in paragraph (b) omit "other than the United Kingdom"; and

(b)   in paragraph (c) for "other than Denmark" substitute "(other than Denmark) or in the United Kingdom".

18   In section 106 omit subsections (4A) and (4B).

19   In section 117 omit subsection (7).

20   In section 120 omit subsection (6).

21   In section 124 in subsection (1) omit the words from "or by a member State liquidator" to "Article 52 of the EU Regulation)".

22   In section 146 omit subsections (6) and (7).

23   Omit section 146A.

24(1)   Section 201 is amended as follows.

24(2)   In subsection (2) omit–

(a)   "and any statement under section 106(4B),"; and

(b)   "(except where subsection (2A) applies)".

24(3)   Omit subsections (2A) and (2B).

25(1)   Section 202 is amended as follows.

25(2)   Omit subsections (2A) and (2B).

25(3)   In subsection (4) omit "and send any statement under subsection (2B)".

25(4)   In subsection (5)–

(a)   omit "and any statement under subsection (2B)";

(b)   after "shall forthwith register it" omit "or them"; and

(c)   omit "(except where subsection (6) applies)".

25(5)   Omit subsections (6) and (7).

25(6)   In subsection (8) omit "or (7)".

26(1)   Section 205 is amended as follows.

26(2)   In subsection (2) omit "and any statement under section 146(7) or 146A(2)".

26(3)   Omit subsections (2A) and (2B).

27   In section 225 omit subsection (2).

28   In section 240 in subsection (3)(d) omit the words from "either following" to "Article 51 of the EU Regulation or".

29   In section 247 in subsection (3) omit paragraph (b) and the ", or" preceding it.

30   In section 251 omit the definitions of "EU insolvency proceedings" and "member State liquidator".

31(1)   Section 263I is amended as follows.

31(2)   In subsection (1)–

(a)   after paragraph (a) insert–

"(ab) the centre of the debtor's main interests is in a member State (other than Denmark) and the debtor has an establishment in England and Wales, or"; and

(b)   in paragraph (b) omit the words from the beginning of the paragraph to "the EU Regulation, but".

31(3)   After subsection (4) insert–

"(5) In this section "establishment" has the same meaning as in Article 2(10) of the EU Regulation.".

32   In section 264 in subsection (1) omit paragraphs (ba) and (bb).

33(1)   Section 265 is amended as follows.

33(2)   In subsection (1)–

(a)   after paragraph (a) insert–

"(ab) the centre of the debtor's main interests is in a member State (other than Denmark) and the debtor has an establishment in England and Wales, or"; and

(b)   in paragraph (b) omit the words from the beginning of the paragraph to "the EU Regulation, but".

33(3)   After subsection (4) insert–

"(5) In this section "establishment" has the same meaning as in Article 2(10) of the EU Regulation.".

34   In section 330 omit subsection (6).

35   In section 387 in subsection (3)–

(a)   omit paragraphs (aa) and (ab);

(b)   in paragraph (b) omit ", (aa) or (ab)";

(c)   in paragraph (ba) omit ", (aa), (ab)";

(d)   in paragraph (c) omit ", (aa), (ab)".

36   In section 388 omit subsection (6).

37   In section 411 in subsection (2B) for the words from "an offence" to the end of the sentence substitute "a new relevant offence".

38   In section 412 in subsection (2B) for the words from "an offence" to the end of the sentence substitute "a new relevant offence".

39   In section 420 in subsection (1B) for the words from "an offence" to the end of the sentence substitute "a new relevant offence".

40   In section 421 in subsection (1B) for the words from "an offence" to the end of the sentence substitute "a new relevant offence".

41   After section 422 insert–

"422A   Meaning of "relevant offence"

422A   In this Part "relevant offence" means a criminal offence punishable with imprisonment for more than two years or punishable on summary conviction with imprisonment for more than three months or with a fine of more than level 5 on the standard scale (if not calculated on a daily basis) or with a fine of more than £100 a day."

42   In section 436 in the definition of "the EU Regulation" at the end insert "as it forms part of domestic law on and after exit day".

43   Omit section 436A.

44   In Schedule B1–

  (a)   in paragraph 84–

    (i)   omit sub-paragraphs (1A) and (1B);

    (ii)   in sub-paragraph (3) omit "and any statement under sub-paragraph (1B)" and at the end omit "or them";

    (iii)   in sub-paragraph (6) omit "(except where sub-paragraph (6A) applies)";

    (iv)   omit sub-paragraphs (6A) and (6B); and

    (v)   in sub-paragraph (7)(a) and (c) omit "or (6B)";

  (b)   in paragraph 111–

    (i)   in sub-paragraph (1A)(b) omit "other than the United Kingdom"; and

    (ii)   in sub-paragraph (1A)(c) for "other than Denmark" substitute "(other than Denmark) or in the United Kingdom".

PART 3

ADMINISTRATION UNDER OLD PART 2 OF THE INSOLVENCY ACT 1986

45(1)   Part 2 of the Insolvency Act 1986 as it had effect immediately before the coming into force of section 248 of the Enterprise Act 2002 and in so far as it continues to have effect is amended as follows.

45(2)   In section 8 for "Article 3 of the EC Regulation" substitute "Article 1 of the EU Regulation".

PART 4

AMENDMENTS TO THE INSOLVENCY (ENGLAND AND WALES) RULES 2016

46   The Insolvency (England and Wales) Rules 2016 are amended as follows.

47   In rule 1.2(2)–

  (a)   omit the following definitions–

    (i)   "main proceedings",

    (ii)   "member State liquidator",

    (iii)   "non-EU proceedings'",

    (iv)   "secondary proceedings",

    (v)   "temporary administrator",

    (vi)   "territorial proceedings";

  (b)   insert in the appropriate places–

    ""COMI proceedings" means insolvency proceedings in England and Wales to which the EU Regulation applies where the centre of the debtor's main interests is in the United Kingdom;

    "establishment" has the same meaning as in Article 2(10) of the EU Regulation;

"establishment proceedings" means insolvency proceedings in England and Wales to which the EU Regulation applies where the debtor has an establishment in the United Kingdom;".

48(1)   Rule 1.7 is amended as follows.

48(2)   For the heading substitute "Reasons for stating whether proceedings are or will be COMI proceedings, establishment proceedings etc.".

48(3)   In the opening words for "main, secondary or territorial or non-EU proceedings" substitute "COMI proceedings, establishment proceedings or proceedings to which the EU Regulation as it has effect in the law of the United Kingdom does not apply" and after "must include" insert "as applicable".

48(4)   In paragraph (a)–

(a)   at the end of sub-paragraph (ii) omit "or";

(b)   after sub-paragraph (ii) insert–

"(iia) the place where there is an establishment within the jurisdiction, or"; and

(c)   in sub-paragraph (iii) for "non-EU proceedings" substitute "proceedings to which the EU Regulation as it has effect in the law of the United Kingdom does not apply".

48(5)   For sub-paragraph (b) substitute–

"(b) for a debtor–

(i)   the centre of main interests, or

(ii)   the place where there is an establishment within the jurisdiction.".

49   In rule 1.20 delete paragraph (1)(o).

50   In rule 2.3 in paragraph (1) for sub-paragraph (q) substitute–

"(q) whether the proceedings will be COMI proceedings, establishment proceedings or proceedings to which the EU Regulation as it has effect in the law of the United Kingdom does not apply with reasons;".

51   In rule 2.14 in paragraph (2A) for "main, secondary, territorial or non-EU proceedings" substitute "COMI proceedings, establishment proceedings or proceedings to which the EU Regulation as it has effect in the law of the United Kingdom does not apply".

52   In rule 2.25 in paragraph (2A) for "main, secondary, territorial or non-EU proceedings" substitute "COMI proceedings, establishment proceedings or proceedings to which the EU Regulation as it has effect in the law of the United Kingdom does not apply".

53   In rule 2.38 in paragraph (2) in sub-paragraph (d) for "main, territorial or non-EU proceedings" substitute "COMI proceedings, establishment proceedings or proceedings to which the EU Regulation as it has effect in the law of the United Kingdom does not apply".

54   In rule 3.3 in paragraph (2) in sub-paragraph (h) for "main, secondary, territorial or non-EU proceedings" substitute "COMI proceedings, establishment proceedings or proceedings to which the EU Regulation as it has effect in the law of the United Kingdom does not apply".

55   In rule 3.6 in paragraph (3) in sub-paragraph (f) for "main, secondary, territorial or non-EU proceedings" substitute "COMI proceedings, establishment proceedings or proceedings to which the EU Regulation as it has effect in the law of the United Kingdom does not apply".

56   In rule 3.8 omit paragraph (3)(c).

57   In rule 3.10 in sub-paragraph (b) omit "(including the United Kingdom)" and "other than the United Kingdom".

58   In rule 3.12 omit paragraph (1)(g).

59   In rule 3.13 in paragraph (1)–

(a)   in sub-paragraph (h) after "EU Regulation" insert "as it has effect in the law of the United Kingdom"; and

(b)   in sub-paragraph (i) for "main, secondary or territorial proceedings" substitute "COMI proceedings or establishment proceedings".

60   In rule 3.16 in paragraph (2) in sub-paragraph (k) for "main, secondary, territorial or non-EU proceedings" substitute "COMI proceedings, establishment proceedings or proceedings to which the EU Regulation as it has effect in the law of the United Kingdom does not apply".

61   In rule 3.17 in paragraph (1) in sub-paragraph (k) for "main, secondary, territorial or non-EU proceedings" substitute "COMI proceedings, establishment proceedings or proceedings to which the EU Regulation as it has effect in the law of the United Kingdom does not apply".

62   In rule 3.21 in paragraph (1) in sub-paragraph (i) for "main, secondary, territorial or non-EU proceedings" substitute "COMI proceedings, establishment proceedings or proceedings to which the EU Regulation as it has effect in the law of the United Kingdom does not apply".

63   In rule 3.23 in paragraph (1) in sub-paragraph (i) for "main, secondary, territorial or non-EU proceedings" substitute "COMI proceedings, establishment proceedings or proceedings to which the EU Regulation as it has effect in the law of the United Kingdom does not apply".

64   In rule 3.24 in paragraph (1) in sub-paragraph (h) for "main, secondary, territorial or non-EU proceedings" substitute "COMI proceedings, establishment proceedings or proceedings to which the EU Regulation as it has effect in the law of the United Kingdom does not apply".

65   In rule 3.25 in paragraph (2) in sub-paragraph (i) for "main, secondary, territorial or non-EU proceedings" substitute "COMI proceedings, establishment proceedings or proceedings to which the EU Regulation as it has effect in the law of the United Kingdom does not apply".

66   In rule 3.35 in paragraph (1) in sub-paragraph (m) for "main, secondary, territorial or non-EU proceedings" substitute "COMI proceedings, establishment proceedings or proceedings to which the EU Regulation as it has effect in the law of the United Kingdom does not apply".

67   In rule 3.51 in paragraph (2) in sub-paragraph (g) omit "costs referred to in Articles 30 or 59 of the EU Regulation and".

68   In rule 3.63 in paragraph (4) omit sub-paragraph (d).

69   In rule 3.68 in paragraph (2) omit sub-paragraph (g).

70   In rule 6.42 in paragraph (4)(f) omit "costs referred to in Articles 30 or 59 of the EU Regulation and".

71   In rule 7.5 in paragraph (1) in sub-paragraph (n) for "main, secondary, territorial or non-EU proceedings" substitute "COMI proceedings, establishment proceedings or proceedings to which the EU Regulation as it has effect in the law of the United Kingdom does not apply".

72   In rule 7.6 in paragraph (8) for "main, secondary, territorial or non-EU proceedings" substitute "COMI proceedings, establishment proceedings or proceedings to which the EU Regulation as it has effect in the law of the United Kingdom does not apply".

73   In rule 7.9 in paragraph (3)–

(a)   insert after sub-paragraph (b)"or", and

(b)   omit sub-paragraph (d) and the "or" preceding it.

74   In rule 7.17 omit paragraph (2)(b) and the "or" preceding it.

75   In rule 7.18 in sub-paragraph (c) –

(a)   insert "or" before "contributory", and

(b)   omit "or member State liquidator".

76   In rule 7.20 in paragraph (1) in sub-paragraph (g) for "main, secondary, territorial or non-EU proceedings" substitute "COMI proceedings, establishment proceedings or proceedings to which the EU Regulation as it has effect in the law of the United Kingdom does not apply".

77   In rule 7.26 in paragraph (1) in sub-paragraph (n) for "main, secondary, territorial or non-EU proceedings" substitute "COMI proceedings, establishment proceedings or proceedings to which the EU Regulation as it has effect in the law of the United Kingdom does not apply".

78   In rule 7.28 in paragraph (6) for "main, secondary, territorial or non-EU proceedings" substitute "COMI proceedings, establishment proceedings or proceedings to which the EU Regulation as it has effect in the law of the United Kingdom does not apply".

79   In rule 7.29 omit paragraph (6).

80   In rule 7.32 in paragraph (1) sub-paragraph (h) for "main, secondary, territorial or non-EU proceedings" substitute "COMI proceedings, establishment proceedings or proceedings to which the EU Regulation as it has effect in the law of the United Kingdom does not apply".

81   In rule 7.33–

(a)   after paragraph (1)(f) insert "or";

(b)   omit paragraph (1)(g); and

(c)   in paragraph (2)(f) for "main, secondary, territorial or non-EU proceedings" substitute "COMI proceedings, establishment proceedings or proceedings to which the EU Regulation as it has effect in the law of the United Kingdom does not apply".

82   In rule 7.35 in paragraph (1) in sub-paragraph (e)(ii) for "main, secondary, territorial or non-EU proceedings" substitute "COMI proceedings, establishment proceedings or proceedings to which the EU Regulation as it has effect in the law of the United Kingdom does not apply".

83   In rule 7.108 in paragraph (4) in sub-paragraph (m) omit "costs referred to in Articles 30 or 59 of the EU Regulation and".

84   In rule 8.3 in paragraph (q) for "main, territorial or non-EU proceedings" substitute "COMI proceedings, establishment proceedings or proceedings to which the EU Regulation as it has effect in the law of the United Kingdom does not apply".

85   In rule 8.19 in paragraph (1A) for "main, secondary, territorial or non-EU proceedings" substitute "COMI proceedings, establishment proceedings or proceedings to which the EU Regulation as it has effect in the law of the United Kingdom does not apply".

86   In rule 10.7 in paragraph (1) for sub-paragraph (d) substitute–

"(d) whether–

(i)   the centre of the debtor's main interests is within the United Kingdom or is within a member State;

(ii)   the centre of the debtor's main interests is neither within the United Kingdom nor a member State;

(iii)   the debtor has an establishment within the United Kingdom;

(iv)   the debtor carries on business as an Article 1.2 undertaking;".

87   In rule 10.8 in paragraph (1) in sub-paragraph (g) for "another" substitute "the UK or a".

88   In rule 10.12 in paragraph (4)–

  (a)   at the end of sub-paragraph (a) insert "and"; and

  (b)   omit sub-paragraph (c) and the "and" preceding it.

89   In rule 10.14 omit paragraph (3).

90   In rule 10.19–

  (a)   in paragraph (1) omit the words from "or a member State liquidator" to "in relation to the debtor";

  (b)   in paragraph (2) in sub-paragraph (f) omit the words "or member State liquidator".

91   In rule 10.29–

  (a)   in paragraph (2) in sub-paragraph (a) omit the words from "or a member State liquidator" to "in relation to the debtor"; and

  (b)   in paragraph (6) in sub-paragraph (d) omit the words from "or a member State liquidator" to "in relation to the debtor".

92   In rule 10.31 in paragraph (1) for sub-paragraph (e)(i) substitute–

  "(i) that the court, being satisfied that the EU Regulation as it has effect in the law of the United Kingdom applies, declares that the proceedings are COMI proceedings or establishment proceedings, or".

93   In rule 10.41 in paragraph (2) for sub-paragraph (d)(i) substitute–

  "(i) that the adjudicator, being satisfied that the EU Regulation as it has effect in the law of the United Kingdom applies, declares that the proceedings are COMI proceedings or establishment proceedings, or".

94   In rule 10.49–

  (a)   in paragraph (1)–

     (i)   at the end of sub-paragraph (b) insert "or"; and

     (ii)   omit sub-paragraph (d) and the "or" preceding it; and

  (b)   in paragraph (2) in sub-paragraph (f) for "main, secondary, territorial or non-EU proceedings" substitute "COMI proceedings, establishment proceedings or proceedings to which the EU Regulation as it has effect in the law of the United Kingdom does not apply".

95   In rule 10.51 in paragraph (1) in sub-paragraph (e)(ii) for "main, secondary, territorial or non-EU proceedings" substitute "COMI proceedings, establishment proceedings or proceedings to which the EU Regulation as it has effect in the law of the United Kingdom does not apply".

96   In rule 10.149 in sub-paragraph (n) omit the words "costs referred to in Article 30 of the EU Regulation and".

97   In rule 12.15 in paragraph (2) omit "including any member State liquidator".

98   In rule 14.16 omit paragraph (3).

99   In rule 14.32 omit paragraph (4).

100   In rule 15.11 in the table in paragraph (1) omit the entry for "Main proceedings in another member State".

101   In rule 15.28 in paragraph (3) omit sub-paragraph (b) and the "or" preceding it.

102   Omit rule 15.30.

103   In rule 15.31–

  (a)   in paragraph (7) omit the words from "; and for this purpose" to the end; and

(b)   in paragraph (9) in the opening words omit "or member State liquidator".

104   Omit rules 21.1 to 21.3.

105   In rule 21.4 for paragraph (3)(e) substitute–

> "(e) a statement whether the proceedings will be COMI proceedings, establishment proceedings or proceedings to which the EU Regulation as it has effect in the law of the United Kingdom does not apply and the reasons for so stating.".

106   Omit rules 21.6 to 21.17.

107   In Schedule 4 in the table of requirements for service in paragraph 6 omit the entry relating to rule 21.2 (application for conversion into winding up/ bankruptcy under EU Regulation).

PART 5

OTHER AMENDMENTS: ENGLAND AND WALES

The Administration of Insolvent Estates of Deceased Persons Order 1986

108(1)   The Administration of Insolvent Estates of Deceased Persons Order 1986 is amended as follows.

108(2)   In Schedule 1 in Part 2–

(a)   in paragraph 1A renumber the two subsections to be inserted in section 265 of the Insolvency Act 1986 as subsections (6) and (7);

(b)   in the first line of the inserted subsection (7) for "subsection (5)" substitute "subsection (6)"; and

(c)   in paragraph 2 in sub-paragraph (a) in the subsection (1) to be substituted for that subsection in section 266 of the Insolvency Act 1986 omit paragraph (a).

The Land Registration Rules 2003

109   In the Land Registration Rules 2003 omit rule 171.

The Civil Proceedings Fees Order 2008

110(1)   The Civil Proceedings Fees Order 2008 is amended as follows.

110(2)   In the Table in Schedule 1 omit the entry for fee 3.6.

The Pension Protection Fund (Entry Rules) Regulations 2005

111(1)   The Pension Protection Fund (Entry Rules) Regulations 2005 are amended as follows.

111(2)   In regulation 1–

(a)   in paragraph (3) omit the definitions of "establishment" and "the Insolvency Regulation"; and

(b)   omit paragraph (7).

111(3)   In regulation 7–

(a)   in paragraph (1) for "paragraphs (2), (4) and (5)" substitute "paragraphs (2) and (4)"; and

(b)   omit paragraphs (5) and (6).

111(4)   In regulation 7A–

(a)   in paragraph (2) for "paragraphs (3), (5) and (6)" substitute "paragraphs (3) and (5)", and

(b)   omit paragraphs (6) and (7).

PART 6

OTHER AMENDMENTS: ENGLAND, WALES AND SCOTLAND

The Cross-Border Insolvency Regulations 2006

112   The Cross-Border Insolvency Regulations 2006 are amended as follows.

113   Schedule 1 is amended as follows.

114   In article 1 in paragraph 3(b) omit ", other than the United Kingdom,".

115   In article 2–

(a)   in paragraph (a)(i)–

    (i)   after "and made by or under" insert "the EU Insolvency Regulation,", and

    (ii)   after "or by or under that" insert "Regulation or";

(b)   in paragraph (a)(ii) –

    (i)   after "and made by or under" insert "the EU Insolvency Regulation,", and

    (ii)   after "or by or under" insert "that Regulation or".

(c)   in paragraph (d) at the end of the definition of "the EU Insolvency Regulation" insert "as that Regulation forms part of domestic law on and after exit day".

116   Omit article 3.

117   In article 16–

(a)   after paragraph 2 insert–

> "**2A**   Where the EU Insolvency Regulation applies the centre of the debtor's main interests is to be determined in accordance with that Regulation.";

(b)   for paragraph 3 substitute–

> "**3**   Subject to paragraph 2A, in the absence of proof to the contrary, the debtor's registered office, or habitual residence in the case of an individual, is presumed to be the centre of the debtor's main interests.".

118   Schedule 2 is amended as follows.

119   In paragraph 1 in sub-paragraph (1) omit the definitions of "main proceedings", "member State liquidator", "secondary proceedings" and "territorial proceedings".

120   In paragraph 4 omit sub-paragraph (2).

121   In paragraph 6 omit sub-paragraph (2)(b) and the "and" preceding it.

122   In paragraph 21 omit sub-paragraph (2)(e).

123   In paragraph 25 omit sub-paragraph (1)(e).

124   In paragraph 26 omit sub-paragraph (3)(c).

125   In paragraph 46 omit sub-paragraph (1)(f).

126 Schedule 3 is amended as follows.

127 In paragraph 1 in sub-paragraph (1) omit the definitions of "main proceedings" and "member State liquidator".

128 In paragraph 6 omit sub-paragraph (1)(e).

129 In paragraph 7 omit sub-paragraph (3)(c).

130 In paragraph 9 omit sub-paragraph (1)(f).

131 Schedule 5 is amended as follows.

132 In Form ML6 omit paragraph 5 (statement of service on the member State liquidator).

PART 7

AMENDMENTS TO THE INSOLVENCY ACT 1986 APPLYING TO SCOTLAND ONLY

133 The Insolvency Act 1986 is amended as follows.

134 In section 106 omit subsections (7) and (8).

135 In section 172 omit subsections (9) and (10).

136 In section 201–

   (a) in subsection (2) omit "and any statement under section 106(8)" and "(except where subsection (2A) applies)"; and

   (b) omit subsections (2A) and (2B).

137 In section 204 omit subsections (4A) to (4E).

138 In section 205–

   (a) in subsection (2) for the words from "on receipt of the notice" to "register it or them" substitute "on receipt of the notice, forthwith register it"; and

   (b) omit subsections (2A) and (2B).

PART 8

AMENDMENTS TO THE INSOLVENCY (SCOTLAND) RULES 1986

139 The Insolvency (Scotland) Rules 1986 are amended as follows.

140 In rule 0.2–

   (a) at the end of the definition of "EU regulation" insert "as it forms part of domestic law on and after exit day";

   (b) omit the following definitions–

      (i) "main proceedings",

      (ii) "member State liquidator",

      (iii) "secondary proceedings",

      (iv) "territorial proceedings";

   (c) in the definition of "centre of main interests" after "interests" insert "(COMI)";

   (d) insert in the appropriate places–

""COMI proceedings" means insolvency proceedings in Scotland to which the EU Regulation applies where the centre of the debtor's main interests is in the United Kingdom;"

""establishment proceedings" means insolvency proceedings in Scotland to which the EU Regulation applies where the debtor has an establishment in the United Kingdom;"

141   In rule 1.3 in paragraph (2)(p) for "main proceedings or territorial proceedings" substitute "COMI proceedings or establishment proceedings".

142   In rule 1.7 in paragraph (2A) for "main proceedings, territorial proceedings or secondary proceedings" substitute "COMI proceedings or establishment proceedings".

143   In rule 1.10 in paragraph (d) for "main proceedings, territorial proceedings or secondary proceedings" substitute "COMI proceedings or establishment proceedings".

144   In rule 1.17 in paragraph (2) in sub-paragraph (ca)(ii) for "main proceedings or territorial proceedings or secondary proceedings" substitute "COMI proceedings or establishment proceedings".

145   In rule 1.28 in paragraph (2A) for "main proceedings, territorial proceedings, or secondary proceedings" substitute "COMI proceedings or establishment proceedings".

146   In rule 1.29 in paragraph (2)(c) for "main, secondary, territorial or non-EU proceedings" substitute "COMI proceedings, establishment proceedings or proceedings to which the EU Regulation as it has effect in the law of the United Kingdom does not apply".

147   In Part 1 omit rules 1.46 to 1.49 (Chapters 8 and 9).

148   In rule 2.2 in paragraph (3) for "main, secondary or territorial proceedings" substitute "COMI proceedings or establishment proceedings".

149   In rule 2.3 omit paragraph (1)(b).

150   In rule 2.25 in paragraph (1) in sub-paragraph (q)(ii) for "main, secondary or territorial proceedings" substitute "COMI proceedings or establishment proceedings".

151   In Part 2 omit rules 2.57 to 2.60 (Chapters 12 and 13).

152   In rule 4.15–

(a)   in paragraph (5) omit sub-paragraph (b) and the "or" preceding it; and

(b)   omit paragraphs (5B), (5C) and (5D).

153   In rule 4.16C omit paragraphs (3) to (5).

154   In rule 4.67 in paragraph (1)(a) omit the words from "including any costs" to "the EU Regulation".

155   In rule 4.68 omit paragraph (11).

156   In rule 4.75A in paragraph (4) omit sub-paragraph (b) and the "or" preceding it.

157   In Part 4 omit rule 4.83 (Chapter 14).

158   In Chapter 15–

(a)   in rule 4.84 for paragraph (2)(e) substitute–

"(e) that the company's centre of main interests is in the United Kingdom or there is an establishment in the United Kingdom and the reasons for so stating."; and

(b)   omit rule 4.85.

159   Omit rules 7.20A to 7.20J

160   In rule 7.26 omit paragraph (2A) as inserted by regulation 28(2) of the Insolvency (Scotland) Regulations 2003.

PART 9

AMENDMENTS TO THE INSOLVENCY (NORTHERN IRELAND) ORDER 1989 AND THE INSOLVENCY RULES (NORTHERN IRELAND) 1991

Amendments to the Insolvency (Northern Ireland) Order 1989

161–185　[Not reproduced]

Amendments to the Insolvency Rules (Northern Ireland) 1991

186–234　[Not reproduced]

PART 10

OTHER AMENDMENTS: NORTHERN IRELAND

The Pension Protection Fund (Entry Rules) Regulations (Northern Ireland) 2005

235　[Not reproduced]

The Cross-Border Insolvency Regulations (Northern Ireland) 2007

236–252　[Not reproduced]

PART 11

AMENDMENTS TO THE EMPLOYMENT RIGHTS ACT 1996 AND THE PENSION SCHEMES ACT 1993

Amendments to the Employment Rights Act 1996

253(1)　The Employment Rights Act 1996 is amended as follows.

253(2)　In section 166–

(a)　in subsection (5)–

(i)　in paragraph (a) for "(6) or (8A)" substitute "(6), (8ZA) or (8A)";

(ii)　in paragraph (b) for "(7) or (8A)"substitute "(7), (8ZA) or (8A)";

(iii)　in paragraph (c) for "(8) or (8A)" substitute "(8), (8ZA) or (8A)";

(iv)　in paragraph (d) for "(8A)" substitute "(8ZA) or (8A)";

(b)　after subsection (8) insert–

"(8ZA) This subsection is satisfied in the case of an employer if–

(a)　the employer is a legal person,

(b)　a request has been made for the first opening of collective proceedings–

(i)　based on the insolvency of the employer, as provided for under the law of any part of the United Kingdom, and

(ii)　involving the partial or total divestment of the employer's assets and the appointment of a liquidator or a person performing a similar task, and

(c)　any of the following has decided to open the proceedings–

1381

      (i)   a court,

      (ii)   a meeting of creditors, or

      (iii) the creditors by a decision procedure.";

(c)   in subsection (8B) for "subsection (8A)" substitute "this section".

253(3)   In section 183–

(a)   in subsection (1)–

      (i)   in paragraph (a) for "(2) or (4A)" substitute 93(2), (4ZA) or (4A)";

      (ii)   in paragraph (b) for "(3) or (4A)" substitute "(3), (4ZA) or (4A)";

      (iii) in paragraph (c) for "(4) or (4A)" substitute "(4), (4ZA) or (4A)";

      (iv) in paragraph (d) for "(4A)" substitute "(4ZA) or (4A)";

(b)   after subsection (4) insert–

    "(4ZA) This subsection is satisfied in the case of an employer if–

    (a)   the employer is a legal person,

    (b)   a request has been made for the first opening of collective proceedings–

      (i)   based on the insolvency of the employer, as provided for under the law of any part of the United Kingdom, and

      (ii)   involving the partial or total divestment of the employer's assets and the appointment of a liquidator or a person performing a similar task, and

    (c)   any of the following has decided to open the proceedings–

      (i)   a court,

      (ii)   a meeting of creditors, or

      (iii) the creditors by a decision procedure.";

(c)   in subsection (4B) for "subsection (4A)" substitute "this section".

Amendments to the Pension Schemes Act 1993

254(1)   The Pension Schemes Act 1993 is amended as follows–

254(2)   In section 123–

(a)   for subsection (1)(d) substitute–

    "(d) subsection (2A) or (2ZA) is satisfied.";

(b)   after subsection (2) insert–

    "(2ZA) This subsection is satisfied in the case of an employer if–

    (a)   the employer is a legal person,

    (b)   a request has been made for the first opening of collective proceedings–

      (i)   based on the insolvency of the employer, as provided for under the law of any part of the United Kingdom, and

      (ii)   involving the partial or total divestment of the employer's assets and the appointment of a liquidator or a person performing a similar task, and

    (c)   any of the following has decided to open the proceedings–

    (i)   a court,

    (ii) a meeting of creditors, or

    (iii) the creditors by a decision procedure.";

(c)   in subsection (2B) for "subsection (2A)" substitute "this section".

PART 12

AMENDMENTS TO THE EMPLOYMENT RIGHTS (NORTHERN IRELAND) ORDER 1996 AND THE PENSION SCHEMES (NORTHERN IRELAND) ACT 1993

Amendments to the Employment Rights (Northern Ireland) Order 1996

255   [Not reproduced]

Amendments to the Pension Schemes (Northern Ireland) Act 1993

256   [Not reproduced]

PART 13

FURTHER AMENDMENTS TO THE EMPLOYMENT RIGHTS (NORTHERN IRELAND) ORDER 1996 AND THE PENSION SCHEMES (NORTHERN IRELAND) ACT 1993

Amendments to the Employment Rights (Northern Ireland) Order 1996

257   [Not reproduced]

Amendments to the Pension Schemes (Northern Ireland) Act 1993

258   [Not reproduced]

Appendix III

Insolvency Service Information

The Insolvency Service (an Executive Agency within the Department for Business, Energy and Industrial Strategy) is responsible for much of the administration of insolvency law and the law relating to director disqualification. The address of the Service's London headquarters is:

The Insolvency Service
4 Abbey Orchard Street
London
SW1P 2HT
Tel. 020 7637 1110

The Insolvency Service's Investigations and Enforcement Services is responsible for investigating under civil law serious financial misconduct in companies, and who should be contacted for reporting disqualified directors acting in breach of the disqualification (the Rogue Directors Hotline) and individuals who are subject to bankruptcy or debt relief orders or undertakings. It is based in Birmingham and its address is:

Intelligence Hub
The Insolvency Service
4th Floor, Cannon House
18 Priory Queensway
Birmingham B4 6FD
Email: Intelligence.live@insolvency.gov.uk
Tel. 0300 678 0017

There is also an Insolvency Service Criminal Enforcement Team (see *https://www.gov.uk/government/ groups/insolvency-service-criminal-enforcement-team*).

Estate Accounts and Scanning is also based in Birmingham. Its address is:

The Insolvency Service
Estate Accounts and Scanning
PO Box 16652
Birmingham
B2 2HR
Email: CustomerServices.EAS@insolvency.gov.uk
Tel. 0121 698 4268

For information in insolvency on redundancy payments, pay in lieu of notice, holiday pay, arrears of wages, protective award payments and lost pension contributions contact:

The Insolvency Service
Redundancy Payments
PO Box 16685
Birmingham
B2 2LX
Email: redundancypaymentsonline@insolvency.gsi.gov.uk
Tel. 0330 331 0020
Online Claims Service: *https://www.gov.uk/claim-redundancy*

The Service's general website address is *https://www.gov.uk/government/organisations/insolvency-service*.

For the Insolvency general enquiry line, Tel. 0300 678 0015

For the "Complaints Gateway", to complain about an insolvency practitioner to the Insolvency Service, see *https://www.gov.uk/complain-about-insolvency-practitioner*.

The Fax number for filing a notice of appointment of an administrator under IR 2016 rr.3.20–3.22 (which may only be used when the court office is closed for business) is published on the Insolvency Service's website (*https://www.gov.uk/government/publications/insolvency-notify-court-of-appointment-of-administrator-outside-court-business-hours/how-to-notify-a-court-in-england-and-wales-or-scotland*) and is currently 0870 761 7716. If sent by email, the address is rcjcompanies.orders@hmcts.gov.uk.

For addresses of Official Receivers' offices in England and Wales, see *https://www.insolvencydirect.bis.gov.uk/rebrandedorsearch*.

On July 17, 2015, the Insolvency Service launched a dedicated web page for insolvency practitioners (IPs), to provide a single entry point for content relevant to IP work. This usefully links to various tools, forms, IP detailed guides, professional conduct and regulation, evaluation reports, a content archive and an entry point for email alerts. See *https://www.gov.uk/insolvency-practitioner-tools-and-information*.

Appendix IV

Practice Direction: Insolvency Proceedings [2018] B.C.C. 421

This *Practice Direction* ("PD") is the latest in a succession of PDs relating to insolvency proceedings going back to 1999. It was issued on 5 July 2018 with effect from 4 July 2018 (except in respect of proceedings already listed for hearing in the county court) and succeeded a PD of the same name issued on 25 April 2018 which contained drafting errors and some inconsistencies with County Court business. A PD may be amended from time to time and the current version at any time is to be found at *http://www.justice.gov.uk/courts/procedure-rules/civil/rules/insolvency_ pd*. The first 2018 PD was updated in light of the Insolvency (England and Wales) Rules 2016 (the necessity for which updating was recognised in a statement by Sir Geoffrey Vos C, reported in [2017] B.C.C. 221), recently decided cases, changes in the CPR (in particular with regards to the Business and Property Courts Practice Direction) and change in title of Bankruptcy Registrars to Insolvency and Companies Court Judges. The first 2018 PD also specified new arrangements for the distribution of insolvency business across the different levels of the judiciary and clarified the routes of appeal in insolvency cases. The second 2018 PD obviously continues these changes and also contains further detail on "local business" and transfers of business within the court system. For analysis of the 2018 iteration see Catterson [2018] 31 Insolv. Int. 126.

It is clear that this Practice Direction does not replace the s.127 Practice Note (which is still to be found as App.V) although as, with the 2014 PD, guidance on applications for validation orders is again provided (see paras 9.11 and 12.8).

The Practice Direction para.5.2 now provides that CPR Pt 6 applies to service both within and out of the jurisdiction.

On service of statutory demand and petitions other than by personal service in the context of para.12.7.1(4) see *Canning v Irwin Mitchell LLP* [2017] EWHC 718 (Ch); [2017] B.P.I.R. 934.

The predecessor provision to what is now para.11.4.4 was discussed by Vos J in *Inbakumar v United Trust Bank Ltd* [2012] EWHC 845 (Ch); [2012] B.P.I.R. 758 at paras [15] and [16]. See also *Jones v Financial Conduct Authority* [2013] EWHC 2731 (Ch); [2013] B.P.I.R. 1033. In *Zafar v Waltham Forest LBC* [2014] EWHC 791 (Ch); [2014] B.P.I.R. 1012 Nicholas Strauss QC confirmed the practice of not looking behind liability orders in bankruptcy proceedings. But at the same time he warned the creditor of the risk in persisting with bankruptcy proceedings where it was known that the liability order was questioned. For a full analysis of para.11.4.4 see *Vieira v Revenue and Customs Commissioners* [2017] EWHC 936 (Ch); [2017] B.P.I.R. 1062 where the court refused to look behind a tax assessment even if it was under appeal.

Part 6 of this Practice Direction (Applications relating to the remuneration of office-holders) largely reproduces the 2004 Practice Statement of Chief Registrar Baister on "The Fixing and Approval of the Remuneration of Appointees" (see [2014] B.C.C. 525). For background to the 2004 Practice Statement see Baister (2006) 22 I.L. & P. 50. Early cases dealing with this 2004 Statement include *Simion v Brown* [2007] B.P.I.R. 412 and *Barker v Bajjon* [2008] B.P.I.R. 771. The leading case on the significance of the 2004 Practice Statement is *Brook v Reed* [2011] EWCA Civ 331; [2012] 1 W.L.R. 419; [2011] B.C.C. 423. See annotation to IR 2016 r.18.28. The principles embodied in the 2004 Practice Statement were applied in Scotland by Lord Malcolm in *Re Nimmo, Approval of Accounts of Intromissions* [2013] CSOH 4 at para.[32]. The importance of the guidelines now contained in Pt 6 in all cases where remuneration is being questioned was reiterated by the Chancellor of the High Court, Sir Terence Etherton in *Salliss v Hunt* [2014] EWHC 229 (Ch); [2014] 1 W.L.R. 2402. See *Mowbray v Sanders* [2015] EWHC 2317 (Ch) where Hildyard J supported the right of a trustee to receive remuneration and expenses but expressed some disquiet about the relative high cost involved in the case of a small bankruptcy.

Note also the illuminating approach adopted by Chief Registrar Baister in *Re Borodzicz* [2016] B.P.I.R. 24.

Reference is made in this PD to the Practice Direction 51O, The Electronic Working Pilot Scheme.

New Parts to this PD include Pt 4 Appeals (clarifying the position) and Pt 7 Unfair Prejudice Petitions, Winding up and Validation Orders (repeating the point made in *Practice Direction: Order under s.127 of the Insolvency Act 1986* [2007] B.C.C. 839 of the undesirability of asking for a winding-up order in an unfairly prejudicial conduct petition under s.994 of the Companies Act 2006).

CONTENTS OF THIS PRACTICE DIRECTION

PART ONE: GENERAL PROVISIONS

1. Definitions

1.1 In this Practice Direction, which shall be referred to as the "IPD", the following definitions will apply:

(1) The "Act" means the Insolvency Act 1986 and includes the Act as applied to limited liability partnerships by the Limited Liability Partnerships Regulations 2001 or as applied to any other person or body by virtue of the Act or any other legislation;

(2) The "Insolvency Rules" means the rules for the time being in force and made under s.411 and s.412 of the Act in relation to Insolvency Proceedings (currently The Insolvency (England and Wales) Rules 2016, as amended), and, save where otherwise provided, any reference to a 'rule' is to a rule in the Insolvency Rules;

(3) "CPR" means the Civil Procedure Rules and "CPRPD" means a Civil Procedure Rules Practice Direction;

(4) "EU Regulation on Insolvency Proceedings" means either the Council Regulation (EC) No. 1346/2000 of 29 May 2000 on Insolvency Proceedings or the Regulation (EU) 2015/848 of the

European Parliament and of the Council of 20 May 2015 on Insolvency Proceedings (known as the "Recast" EU Insolvency Regulation), as applicable

(5) "Service Regulation" means Council Regulation (EC) No. 1393/2007 or such successor regulation as may come into force replacing Council Regulation (EC) No. 1393/2007 concerning the service in the Member States of judicial and extrajudicial documents in civil and commercial matters;

(6) "Insolvency proceedings" means:

(a) any proceedings under Parts 1 to 11 of the Act, the Insolvency Rules, the Administration of Insolvent Estates of Deceased Persons Order 1986 (SI 1986/1999), the Insolvent Partnerships Order 1994 (SI 1994/2421) or the Limited Liability Partnerships Regulations 2001;

(b) any proceedings under the EU Regulation on Insolvency Proceedings or the Cross-Border Insolvency Regulations 2006 (SI 2006/1030); and

(c) in an insolvency context an application made pursuant to s.423 of the Act.

(7) References to a "company" include a limited liability partnership and references to a "contributory" include a member of a limited liability partnership;

(8) The following judicial definitions apply:

(a) "District Judge" means a person appointed a District Judge under s.6(1) of the County Courts Act 1984;

(b) "District Judge Sitting in a District Registry" means a District Judge sitting in an assigned District Registry having insolvency jurisdiction as a District Judge of the High Court under s.100 of the Senior Courts Act 1981;

(c) "Circuit Judge" means a judge sitting pursuant to s.5(1)(a) of the County Courts Act 1984;

(d) "ICC Judge" means a person appointed to the office of Insolvency and Companies Court Judge (previously, Registrar in Bankruptcy) under s.89(1) of the Senior Courts Act 1981;

(e) "High Court Judge" means a High Court Judge listed in s.4(1) of the Senior Courts Act 1981.

(9) The definitions in paragraph 1.1(8) include Deputies unless otherwise specified and Deputies are defined as meaning, for each definition above respectively, a deputy District judge appointed under s.8 of the County Courts Act 1984, a deputy District Judge of the High Court appointed under s.102 of the Senior Courts Act 1981, a deputy Circuit Judge appointed under s.24 of the Courts Act 1971, a deputy ICC Judge appointed under s.91 of the Senior Courts Act 1981, and a judicial office holder acting as a judge of the High Court under s.9(1) of the Senior Courts Act 1981 or a deputy judge of the High Court appointed under s.9(4) of the Senior Courts Act 1981;

(10) "Court" means the High Court or any County Court hearing centre having insolvency jurisdiction;

(11) "Royal Courts of Justice" means the Business and Property Courts of England and Wales at the Rolls Building, 7 Rolls Buildings, Fetter Lane, London EC4A 1NL.

(12) In part six of this IPD "assessor" means a person appointed as an assessor under s.70 of the Senior Courts Act 1981 or s.63 of the County Courts Act 1984] as an assessor.

2. Coming into force

2.1 This IPD shall come into force on 4 July 2018 and shall replace all previous Practice Directions, Practice Statements and Practice Notes relating to insolvency proceedings. This IPD does not affect PDs 51P – Pilot for Insolvency Express Trials, and for the avoidance of doubt, does not affect the PD for Directors' Disqualification Proceedings.

2.2   If at the date of commencement of this IPD, a petition or application within or for the commencement of insolvency proceedings has already been listed for a hearing at a County Court hearing centre and such County Court hearing centre would otherwise have had jurisdiction to hear and determine that petition or application as at 24th April 2018, paragraph 3 of this IPD shall not apply and a judge at that hearing centre may proceed to determine that petition or application, unless the court considers or the parties agree that it would be appropriate to transfer the petition or application in line with paragraph 3.6 in any event, in which case paragraphs 3.8–3.10 may be considered.

3.   Distribution of business

3.1   In the High Court, all petitions and applications, save where paragraph 3.2 below provides otherwise, should be listed for an initial hearing before an ICC Judge in the Royal Courts of Justice, or a District Judge Sitting in a District Registry.

3.2   The following applications relating to insolvent companies or insolvent individuals must be listed before a High Court Judge:

(1)   applications for committal for contempt; and

(2)   applications for a search order (CPR 25.1(1)(h)) and a freezing order (CPR 25.1(1)(f)).

3.3   The following applications relating to insolvent companies or insolvent individuals may be listed before a High Court Judge or ICC Judge but, subject to paragraph 3.4 below, not before a District Judge Sitting in a District Registry or a District Judge:

(1)   applications for an administration order;

(2)   applications for an injunction pursuant to the Court's inherent jurisdiction (e.g. to restrain the presentation or advertisement of a winding up petition);

(3)   interim applications and applications for directions or case management after any proceedings have been referred or adjourned to the High Court Judge;

(4)   applications for the appointment of a provisional liquidator; and

(5)   applications for an injunction (other than those referred to in paragraph 3.2(2) above) pursuant to s.37 of the Senior Courts Act 1981, including an ancillary order under CPR 25.1(1)(g).

3.4   The following applications relating to insolvent companies or insolvent individuals may be listed before a District Judge Sitting in a District Registry only with the consent of the Supervising Judge for the circuit in which the District Judge is sitting, or with the consent of the Supervising Judge's nominee:

(1)   applications pursuant to the Court's inherent jurisdiction (e.g. to restrain the presentation or advertisement of a winding up petition);

(2)   interim applications and applications for directions or case management after any proceedings have been referred or adjourned to a High Court Judge.

3.5   When deciding whether to hear and determine proceedings or to refer or adjourn them to a different level of judge, regard must be had to the following factors:

(1)   whether the proceedings raise new or controversial points of law or have wide public interest implications;

(2)   which venue can provide the earliest date for the hearing;

(3)   the likely length of the hearing; and/or

(4)   whether the petition or application includes or is likely to include matters that must be heard by a High Court Judge under paragraph 3.2 above.

3.6   Where an application or petition for the commencement of insolvency proceedings, or any application or petition within existing insolvency proceedings, is issued in a County Court hearing centre having insolvency jurisdiction, unless the application or petition is Local Business, the application or petition but more usually the entirety of those insolvency proceedings shall be transferred:

(a) to a County Court hearing centre having insolvency jurisdiction located at a Business and Property Court in the same circuit; or

(b) to the Central London County Court if the application or petition was issued in a County Court hearing centre located in the South-Eastern circuit; or

(c) to one of the specialist centres specified in a list published from time to time by the Chancellor of the High Court or their nominee, and located in the same circuit as the hearing centre in which the application or petition was issued, and be listed before a judge specialising in Business and Property Courts work as defined in paragraph 4.4 of the Business and Property Courts Practice Direction (the "specialist judge"). (The current list of specified specialist centres may be found at *https://www.judiciary.uk/insolvency-proceedings-practice-direction-specified-specialist-hearing-centres/*).

3.7 For the purpose of paragraph 3.6 Local Business means (i) applications to set aside statutory demands; (ii) unopposed creditors' winding up petitions; (iii) unopposed bankruptcy petitions; (iv) applications for income payment orders; (v) applications for and the conduct of public and private examinations; (vi) warrants for arrest in connection with the conduct of public or private examinations; (vii) claims for possession by an office-holder against a bankrupt (whether or not the bankrupt has been discharged); (viii) claims falling under the Trusts of Land and Appointment of Trustees Act 1996 (notwithstanding the application of section 335A of the Act); (ix) claims for the granting or enforcement of charging orders pursuant to section 313 of the Act; (x) unopposed applications by the Official Receiver to suspend discharge from bankruptcy, and if the application transpires to be opposed, any application by the Official Receiver for an interim suspension pending the matter being heard following its transfer pursuant to paragraph 3.6 above; and (xi) applications for debt relief orders under Part 7A of the Act Such Local Business may be heard and determined by any judge in the County Court hearing centre in which those insolvency proceedings were issued, unless such a judge considers that it would be appropriate to transfer them in accordance with paragraph 3.6 in any event.

3.8 Where insolvency proceedings are transferred under paragraph 3.6 or 3.7, they shall be listed for review on paper before a specialist judge in the receiving court as soon as possible. The specialist judge shall determine of their own initiative where the application (or any part of it) can most fairly be determined having regard to (i) the nature and complexity of the issues; (ii) the amounts involved in the insolvency proceedings or insolvency application; (iii) the location and needs of the parties; (iv) the available judicial resources; and (v) all the other circumstances of the case. The specialist judge shall take into account any views of the transferring judge and those of the parties to the application expressed in writing (without the need for evidence).

3.9 The options available to the specialist judge include (but are not limited to):

(a) retaining the entirety of the insolvency proceedings in the receiving court;

(b) retaining the entirety of the insolvency proceedings in the receiving court but fixing the venue of any hearing before a specialist judge at some other hearing centre or by some means other than a physical hearing;

(c) returning the insolvency proceedings to the sending court to be dealt with as if it were Local Business;

(d) retaining the insolvency proceedings in the receiving court but transferring some part back for hearing or for management and hearing in the sending court as if it were Local Business.

3.10 The case management decision about transfer shall be recorded in an order made of the specialist judge's own initiative.

4. Court documents

4.1 All insolvency proceedings should be commenced and applications in insolvency proceedings should be made using the information prescribed by the Act, Insolvency Rules, the Business and Property Courts Practice Direction and/or other legislation under which the same is or are brought or made. Some forms relating to insolvency proceedings may be found at: *http://hmctsformfinder.justice.gov.uk/HMCTS/ GetForms.do?court_forms_category=Bankruptcy%20and%20Insolvency*

5. Service of Court documents in insolvency proceedings

5.1 Schedule 4 to the Insolvency Rules prescribes the requirements for service where a Court document is required to be served pursuant to the Act or the Insolvency Rules. Pursuant to Schedule 4, CPR Part 6 applies except where Schedule 4 provides otherwise, or the court otherwise approves or directs.

5.2 Subject to the Court approving or directing otherwise, CPR Part 6 applies to the service of Court documents both within and out of the jurisdiction.

5.3 Attention is drawn to paragraph 6 of Schedule 4 to the Insolvency Rules which provides that where the Court has directed that service be effected in a particular manner, the certificate of service must be accompanied by a sealed copy of the order directing such manner of service.

5.4 The provisions of CPR Part 6 are modified by Schedule 4 to the Insolvency Rules in respect of certain documents. Reference should be made to the "Table of requirements for service" in Schedule 4. Notable modifications relate to the service of: (a) a winding up petition; and (b) an application for an administration order.

5.5 A statutory demand is not a Court document.

6. Drawing up of orders

6.1 The parties are responsible for drawing up all orders, unless the Court directs otherwise. Attention is drawn to CPRPD 40B 1.2 and the Chancery Guide. All applications should be accompanied by draft orders.

7. Urgent applications

7.1 In the Royal Courts of Justice the ICC Judges and the High Court Judges (and in other Courts exercising insolvency jurisdiction the High Court Judges, District Judges Sitting in a District Registry and District Judges) will hear urgent applications and time-critical applications as soon as reasonably practicable. This may involve delaying the hearing of another matter. Accordingly, parties asking for an application to be dealt with urgently must be able to justify the urgency with reasons.

PART TWO: COMPANY INSOLVENCY

8. Administrations

8.1 Attention is drawn to paragraph 2.1 of the Electronic Practice Direction 51O – The Electronic Working Pilot Scheme, or to any subsequent Electronic Practice Direction made after the date of this IPD, where a notice of appointment is made using the electronic filing system. For the avoidance of doubt, and notwithstanding the restriction in sub-paragraph (c) to notices of appointment made by qualifying floating charge holders, paragraph 2.1 of the Electronic Practice Direction 51O shall not apply to any filing of a notice of appointment of an administrator outside Court opening hours, and the provisions of Insolvency Rules 3.20 to 3.22 shall in those circumstances continue to apply.

8.2 Paragraph 5.4 of the Electronic Practice Direction 51O provides that 'the date and time of payment' will be the filing date and time and 'it will also be the date and time of issue for all claim forms and other originating processes submitted using Electronic Working'.

8.3 In the absence of special circumstances, an application for the extension of an administration should be made not less than one month before the end of the administration. The evidence in support of any later application must explain why the application is being made late. The Court will consider whether any part of the costs should be disallowed where an application is made less than one month before the end of the administration.

9. Winding up petitions

9.1   Where a winding up petition is presented following service of a statutory demand, the statutory demand must contain the information set out in rule 7.3 of the Insolvency Rules and should, as far as possible, follow the form which appears at https://www.gov.uk/government/publications/demand-immediate-payment-of-a-debt-from-a-limited-company-form-sd1.

9.2   Before presenting a winding up petition, the creditor must conduct a search to ensure that no petition is pending. Save in exceptional circumstances a second winding up petition should not be presented whilst a prior petition is pending. A petitioner who presents a petition while another petition is pending does so at risk as to costs.

9.3   Payment of the fee and deposit

9.3.1   Unless the petition is one in respect of which rule 7.7(2)(b) of the Insolvency Rules applies, a winding up petition will not be treated as having been presented until the Court fee and official receiver's deposit have been paid.

9.3.2   A petition filed electronically without payment of the deposit will be marked "private" and will not be available for inspection until the deposit has been paid. The date of presentation of the petition will accord with the date on which the deposit has been paid. If the official receiver's deposit is not paid within 7 calendar days after filing the petition, the petition will not be accepted, in accordance with paragraph 5.3 of the Electronic Practice Direction 510 – The Electronic Working Pilot Scheme. If a petition is not accepted, a new petition will have to be filed if the petitioner wishes to wind up a company.

9.3.3   The deposit will be taken by the Court and forwarded to the official receiver. In the Royal Courts of Justice the petition fee and deposit should be paid by cheque, or by debit or credit card over the phone. The Court will record the receipt and will impress two entries on the original petition, one in respect of the Court fee and the other in respect of the deposit. In a District Registry or a County Court hearing centre, the petition fee and deposit should be paid to the staff of the duly authorised officer of the Court, who will record its receipt.

9.3.4   If payment is made by cheque, it should be made payable to 'HM Courts and Tribunals Service' or 'HMCTS'. For the purposes of paragraph 9.3 of this IPD, the deposit will be treated as paid when the cheque is received by the Court.

9.4   Save where by reason of the nature of the company or its place of incorporation the information cannot be stated (in which case as much similar information as is available should be given), every creditor's winding up petition must (in the case of a company) contain the information set out in rule 7.5. Similar information (so far as is appropriate) should be given where the petition is presented against a partnership.

9.5   Where the petitioning creditor relies on failure to pay a debt, details of the debt relied on should be given in the petition (whether or not they have been given in any statutory demand served in respect of the debt), including the amount of the debt, its nature and the date or dates on or between which it was incurred.

9.6   The statement of truth verifying the petition in accordance with rule 7.6 should be made no more than ten business days before the date of issue of the petition.

9.7   Where the company to be wound up has been struck off the register, the petition should state that fact and include as part of the relief sought an order that it be restored to the register. Save where the petition has been presented by a Minister of the Crown or a government department, evidence of service on the Government Legal Department or the Solicitor for the Affairs of the Duchy of Lancaster or the Solicitor to the Duchy of Cornwall (as appropriate) should be filed exhibiting the bona vacantia waiver letter.

9.8 Notice of the petition

9.8.1 The provisions contained in Chapter 4 of Part 1 and in particular rule 7.10 must be followed (unless waived by the Court). These provisions are designed to preserve the sanctity of the class remedy in any given winding up by the Court. Failure to comply with rule 7.10 may lead to summary dismissal of the petition on the return date. If the Court, in its discretion, grants an adjournment, this will usually be on terms that notice of the petition is gazetted or otherwise given in accordance with the Insolvency Rules in due time for the adjourned hearing. No further adjournment to comply with rule 7.10 will normally be given.

9.8.2 Copies of every notice gazetted in connection with a winding up petition, or where this is not practicable a description of the form and content of the notice, must be lodged with the Court as soon as possible after publication and in any event not later than five business days before the hearing of the petition. This direction applies even if the notice is defective in any way (e.g. is published on a date not in accordance with the Insolvency Rules, or omits or misprints some important words) or if the petitioner decides not to pursue the petition (e.g. on receiving payment).

9.8.3 Attention is drawn to the requirement to give notice of the dismissal of a petition under rule 7.23(1). The Court will usually, on request, dispense with the requirement where (a) presentation of the petition has not previously been gazetted or (b) the company has become the subject of some supervening insolvency process, or (c) the company consents.

9.9 Errors in petitions

9.9.1 Applications for permission to amend errors in petitions which are discovered after a winding up order has been made should be made to the member of Court staff in charge of the winding up list in the Royal Courts of Justice or to a District Judge Sitting in a District Registry or District Judge.

9.9.2 Where the error is an error in the name of the company, the member of Court staff in charge of the winding up list in the Royal Courts of Justice or a District Judge Sitting in a District Registry or District Judge may make any necessary amendments to ensure that the winding up order is drawn up with the correct name of the company inserted. If there is any doubt, e.g. where there might be another company in existence which could be confused with the company to be wound up, the member of Court staff in charge of the winding up list will refer the application to an ICC Judge at the Royal Courts of Justice. A District Judge Sitting in a District Registry or District Judge may refer the matter to a High Court Judge.

9.9.3 Where it is discovered that the company has been struck off the Register of Companies prior to the winding up order being made, the petition must be restored to the list as soon as possible to enable an order for the restoration of the name to be made as well as the order to wind up and, save where the petition has been presented by a Minister of the Crown or a government department, evidence of service on the Government Legal Department or the Solicitor for the Affairs of the Duchy of Lancaster or the Solicitor to the Duchy of Cornwall (as appropriate) should be filed exhibiting the bona vacantia waiver letter.

9.10 Rescission of a winding up order

9.10.1 A request to rescind a winding up order must be made by application.

9.10.2 The application must be made within five business days after the date on which the order was made, failing which it should include an application to extend time pursuant to Schedule 5 to the Insolvency Rules. Notice of any such application must be given to the petitioning creditor, any supporting or opposing creditor, any incumbent insolvency practitioner and the official receiver.

9.10.3 An application to rescind will only be entertained if made by a (a) creditor, or (b) contributory, or (c) by the company jointly with a creditor or with a contributory. The application must be supported by a witness statement which should include details of assets and liabilities and (where appropriate) reasons for any failure to apply within five business days.

9.10.4 In the case of an unsuccessful application, the costs of the petitioning creditor, any supporting or opposing creditor, any incumbent insolvency practitioner and the official receiver will normally be ordered to be paid by the creditor or the contributory making or joining in the application. The reason for this is that if the costs of an unsuccessful application are made payable by the company, those costs will inevitably fall on the general body of creditors.

9.11   Validation orders

9.11.1   A company against which a winding up petition has been presented may apply to the Court after the presentation of a petition for relief from the effects of s.127(1) of the Act, by seeking an order that a certain disposition or dispositions of its property, including payments out of its bank account (whether such account is in credit or overdrawn), shall not be void in the event of a winding up order being made at the hearing of the petition (a validation order).

9.11.2   Save in exceptional circumstances, notice of the making of the application should be given to: (a) the petitioning creditor; (b) any person entitled to receive a copy of the petition pursuant to rule 7.9; (c) any creditor who has given notice to the petitioner of their intention to appear on the hearing of the petition pursuant to rule 7.14; and (d) any creditor who has been substituted as petitioner pursuant to rule 7.17. Failure to do so is likely to lead to an adjournment of the application or dismissal.

9.11.3   The application should be supported by a witness statement which should be made by a director or officer of the company who is intimately acquainted with the company's affairs and financial circumstances. If appropriate, supporting evidence in the form of a witness statement from the company's accountant should also be produced.

9.11.4   The extent and content of the evidence will vary according to the circumstances and the nature of the relief sought, but in the majority of cases it should include, as a minimum, the following information:

(1)   when and to whom notice has been given in accordance with paragraph 9.11.2 above;

(2)   the company's registered office;

(3)   the company's capital;

(4)   brief details of the circumstances leading to presentation of the petition;

(5)   how the company became aware of presentation of the petition;

(6)   whether the petition debt is admitted or disputed and, if the latter, brief details of the basis on which the debt is disputed;

(7)   full details of the company's financial position including details of its assets (and including details of any security and the amount(s) secured) and liabilities, which should be supported, as far as possible, by documentary evidence, e.g. the latest filed accounts, any draft audited accounts, management accounts or estimated statement of affairs;

(8)   a cash flow forecast and profit and loss projection for the period for which the order is sought;

(9)   details of the dispositions or payments in respect of which an order is sought;

(10) the reasons relied on in support of the need for such dispositions or payments to be made prior to the hearing of the petition;

(11) any other information relevant to the exercise of the Court's discretion;

(12) details of any consents obtained from the persons mentioned in paragraph 9.11.2 above (supported by documentary evidence where appropriate);

(13) details of any relevant bank account, including its number and the address and sort code of the bank at which such account is held, and the amount of the credit or debit balance on such account at the time of making the application.

9.11.5   Where an application is made urgently to enable payments to be made which are essential to continued trading (e.g. wages) and it is not possible to assemble all the evidence listed above, the Court may consider granting limited relief for a short period, but there should be sufficient evidence to satisfy the Court that the interests of creditors are unlikely to be prejudiced by the grant of limited relief.

9.11.6   Where the application involves a disposition of property, the Court will need details of the property (including its title number if the property is land) and to be satisfied that any proposed disposal will be at a proper value. Accordingly, an independent valuation should be obtained and exhibited to the evidence.

9.11.7   The Court will need to be satisfied by credible evidence either that the company is solvent and able to pay its debts as they fall due or that a particular transaction or series of transactions in respect of which the order is sought will be beneficial to or will not prejudice the interests of all the unsecured creditors as a class.

9.11.8   A draft of the order sought should be attached to the application.

9.11.9   Similar considerations to those set out above are likely to apply to applications seeking ratification of a transaction or payment after the making of a winding up order.

10.   Applications

10.1   In accordance with rule 12.2(2), in the Royal Courts of Justice an officer acting on behalf of the operations manager or chief clerk has been authorised to deal with applications:

(1)   to extend or abridge time prescribed by the Insolvency Rules in connection with winding up;

(2)   for permission to withdraw a winding up petition (rule 7.13);

(3)   made by the official receiver for a public examination (s.133(1)(c) of the Act), where no penal notice is endorsed and no unless order is made;

(4)   made by the official receiver to transfer proceedings from the High Court to a specified hearing centre within the meaning of rule 12.30;

(5)   to list a hearing for directions with a time estimate of 30 minutes or less in circumstances where both parties are represented without reference to an ICC Judge;

(6)   for a first extension of time to serve a bankruptcy petition.

10.2   Outside of the Royal Courts of Justice, applications listed in paragraph 10.1 must be made to a District Judge Sitting in a District Registry or in the County Court to a District Judge.

10.3   Where an application is made by an official receiver in respect of the matters listed in paragraph 10.1(4) above, the official receiver must comply with rule 12.32 and give any incumbent office-holder 14 days' written notice of the application.

Part Three: Personal Insolvency

11.   Statutory demands

11.1   Rule 10.1 prescribes the contents of a statutory demand. An example of a statutory demand may be found at: *http://hmctsformfinder.justice.gov.uk/HMCTS/GetForms.do?court_forms_category= Bankruptcy%20and%20Insolvency*

11.2   Rule 10.2 applies to service of a statutory demand whether within or out of the jurisdiction. If personal service is not practicable in the particular circumstances, a creditor must do all that is reasonable to bring the statutory demand to the debtor's attention. This could include taking those steps set out at paragraph 12.7 below which justify the Court making an order for service of a bankruptcy petition other than by personal service. It may also include any other form of physical or electronic communication which will bring the statutory demand to the notice of the debtor.

11.3   A creditor wishing to serve a statutory demand out of the jurisdiction in a foreign country with an applicable civil procedure convention (including the Hague Convention) may and, if the assistance of a British Consul is desired, must adopt the procedure prescribed by CPR rule 6.42 and CPR rule 6.43. In the case of any doubt whether the country is a 'convention country', enquiries should be made of the

Foreign Process Section of the Queen's Bench Division, Room E16, Royal Courts of Justice, Strand, London WC2A 2LL.

11.4   Setting aside a statutory demand

11.4.1   The application and witness statement in support of setting aside a statutory demand, exhibiting a copy of the statutory demand, must be filed in Court within 18 days of service of the statutory demand on the debtor. The time limits are different if the statutory demand has been served out of the jurisdiction: see rule 10.1(10).

11.4.2   A debtor who wishes to apply to set aside a statutory demand after the expiration of 18 days, or if service is out of the jurisdiction, after the expiration of the time limit specified by rule 10.1(10)(a) from the date of service of the statutory demand, must apply for an extension of time within which to apply to set aside the statutory demand. The witness statement in support of the application to set aside statutory demand should also contain evidence in support of the application for an extension of time and should state that to the best of the debtor's knowledge and belief the creditor(s) named in the statutory demand has/have not presented a bankruptcy petition.

11.4.3   Unless the Court to which the application to set aside is made operates Electronic Filing and Electronic Practice Direction 51O applies, the following applies:

(1)   Three copies of each document must be lodged with the application, to enable the Court to serve notice of the hearing date on the applicant, the creditor and the person named under rule 10.1(3).

(2)   Where copies of the documents are not lodged with the application, any order of the Court fixing a venue is conditional upon copies of the documents being lodged on the next business day after the Court's order, otherwise the application will be deemed to have been dismissed.

11.4.4   Where the debt claimed in the statutory demand is based on a judgment, order, liability order, costs certificate, tax assessment or decision of a tribunal, the Court will not at this stage inquire into the validity of the debt nor, as a general rule, will it adjourn the application to await the result of an application to set aside the judgment, order, decision, costs certificate or any appeal.

11.4.5   The Court will determine an application to set aside a statutory demand in accordance with rule 10.5.

11.4.6   Attention is drawn to the power of the Court to decline to file a petition if there has been a failure to comply with the requirement of rule 10.2.

12.   Bankruptcy petitions

12.1   All petitions presented will be listed under the name of the debtor unless the Court directs otherwise.

12.2   Content of petitions

12.2.1   The attention of Court users is drawn to the following points:

(1)   A creditor's petition does not require dating, signing or witnessing, but must be verified in accordance with rule 10.10.

(2)   In the heading, it is only necessary to recite the debtor's name e.g. Re John William Smith or Re J W Smith (Male). Any alias or trading name will appear in the body of the petition.

12.2.2   Where the petition is based solely on a statutory demand, only the debt claimed in the demand may be included in the petition.

12.2.3   The attention of Court users is also drawn to rules 10.8 and 10.9, where the "aggregate sum" is made up of a number of debts.

12.2.4   The date of service of the statutory demand should be recited as follows:

(1)   Where the demand has been served personally, the date of service as set out in the certificate of service.

(2) Where the demand has been served other than personally, the date as set out in the certificate of service filed in compliance with rule 10.3.

12.3 Searches

12.3.1 The petitioning creditor shall, before presenting a petition, conduct an Official Search with the Chief Land Registrar in the register of pending actions for pending petitions presented against the debtor and shall include the following certificate at the end of the petition:

"I/we certify that within 7 days ending today, I/we have conducted a search for pending petitions presented against the debtor and that to the best of my/our knowledge, information, and belief [no prior petitions have been presented which are still pending] [a prior petition (No [ ]) has been presented and is/may be pending in the [Court] and I/we am/are issuing this petition at risk as to costs].

Signed….. Dated….".

12.4 The deposit

12.4.1 A bankruptcy petition will not be treated as having been presented until the Court fee and official receiver's deposit have been paid. A petition filed electronically without payment of the deposit will be marked "private" and will not be available for inspection until the deposit has been paid. The date of presentation of the petition will accord with the date on which the deposit has been paid. If the official receiver's deposit is not paid within 7 calendar days after filing the petition, the petition will not be accepted, in accordance with paragraph 5.3 of the Electronic Practice Direction 51O – The Electronic Working Pilot Scheme.

12.4.2 The deposit will be taken by the Court and forwarded to the official receiver. In the Royal Courts of Justice the petition fee and deposit should be paid by cheque, or by debit or credit card over the phone. In a District Registry or a County Court hearing centre, the petition fee and deposit should be handed to the staff of the duly authorised officer of the Court who will record its receipt. For the purposes of paragraph 12.4.1 above, the deposit will be treated as paid when received by the Court.

12.4.3 If payment is made by cheque, it should be made payable to 'HM Courts and Tribunals Service' or 'HMCTS'. For the purposes of paragraph 12.4 of this IPD, the deposit will be treated as paid when the cheque is received by the Court

12.5 Certificates of continuing debt and of notice of adjournment

12.5.1 At the final hearing of a petition, the Court will need to be satisfied that the debt on which the petition is founded has not been paid or secured or compounded. The Court will normally accept as sufficient evidence a certificate signed by the person representing the petitioning creditor in the following form:

"I certify that I have/my firm has made enquiries of the petitioning creditor(s) within the last business day prior to the hearing/adjourned hearing and to the best of my knowledge and belief the debt on which the petition is founded is still due and owing and has not been paid or secured or compounded for save as to …

Signed ……… Dated ……"

12.5.2 For convenience, in the Royal Courts of Justice this certificate is incorporated in the attendance sheet for the parties to complete when they come to Court and is to be filed at the hearing. A fresh certificate will be required on each adjourned hearing.

12.5.3 On any adjourned hearing of a petition, in order to satisfy the Court that the petitioner has complied with rule 10.23, the petitioner will be required to file evidence of when (the date), how (the manner), and where (the address), notice of the adjournment order and notification of the venue for the adjourned hearing was sent to:

(1) the debtor, and

(2) any creditor who has given notice under rule 10.19 but was not present at the hearing when the order for adjournment was made or was present at the hearing but the date of the adjourned hearing was not fixed at that hearing.

12.5.4 For convenience, in the Royal Courts of Justice this certificate is incorporated in the attendance sheet for the parties to complete when they come to Court and is to be filed at the hearing. A fresh certificate will be required on each adjourned hearing. It is as follows:

"I certify that the petitioner has complied with rule 10.23 of the Insolvency Rules 2016 by sending notice of adjournment to the debtor [supporting/opposing creditor(s)] on [date] at [address]".

12.6 Extension of hearing date of petition

12.6.1 Late applications for extension of hearing dates under rule 10.22, and failure to attend on the listed hearing of a petition, will be dealt with as follows:

(1) If an application is submitted less than two clear working days before the hearing date (for example, later than Monday for Thursday, or Wednesday for Monday), the costs of the application will not be allowed under rule 10.22.

(2) If the petition has not been served and no extension has been granted by the time fixed for the hearing of the petition, and if no one attends for the hearing, the petition may be dismissed or re-listed for hearing about 21 days later. The Court will notify the petitioning creditor's solicitors (or the petitioning creditor in person), and any known supporting or opposing creditors or their solicitors, of the new date and time. A witness statement should then be filed on behalf of the petitioning creditor explaining fully the reasons for the failure to apply for an extension or to appear at the hearing, and (if appropriate) giving reasons why the petition should not be dismissed.

(3) On the re-listed hearing the Court may dismiss the petition if not satisfied it should be adjourned or a further extension granted.

12.6.2 All applications for an extension should include a statement of the date fixed for the hearing of the petition.

12.6.3 The petitioning creditor should contact the Court (by solicitors or in person) on or before the hearing date to ascertain whether the application has reached the file and been dealt with. It should not be assumed that an extension will be granted.

12.7 Service of bankruptcy petitions other than by personal service

12.7.1 Where personal service of the bankruptcy petition is not practicable, service by other means may be permitted. In most cases, evidence that the steps set out in the following paragraphs have been taken will suffice to justify an order for service of a bankruptcy petition other than by personal service:

(1) One personal call at the residence and place of business of the debtor. Where it is known that the debtor has more than one residential or business addresses, personal calls should be made at all the addresses.

(2) Should the creditor fail to effect personal service, a letter should be written to the debtor referring to the call(s), the purpose of the same, and the failure to meet the debtor, adding that a further call will be made for the same purpose on the [day] of [month] 20[ ] at [ ] hours at [place]. Such letter may be sent by first class prepaid post or left at or delivered to the debtor's address in such a way as it is reasonably likely to come to the debtor's attention. At least two business days' notice should be given of the appointment and copies of the letter sent to or left at all known addresses of the debtor. The appointment letter should also state that:

(a) in the event of the time and place not being convenient, the debtor should propose some other time and place reasonably convenient for the purpose;

(b)   in the case of a statutory demand as suggested in paragraph 11.2 above, reference is being made to this paragraph for the purpose of service of a statutory demand, the appointment letter should state that if the debtor fails to keep the appointment the creditor proposes to serve the demand by advertisement/ post/ insertion through a letter box as the case may be, and that, in the event of a bankruptcy petition being presented, the Court will be asked to treat such service as service of the demand on the debtor;

(c)   (in the case of a petition) if the debtor fails to keep the appointment, an application will be made to the Court for an order that service be effected either by advertisement or in such other manner as the Court may think fit.

(3)   when attending any appointment made by letter, inquiry should be made as to whether the debtor is still resident at the address or still frequents the address, and/or other enquiries should be made to ascertain receipt of all letters left for them. If the debtor is away, inquiry should also be made as to when they are returning and whether the letters are being forwarded to an address within the jurisdiction (England and Wales) or elsewhere.

(4)   If the debtor is represented by a solicitor, an attempt should be made to arrange an appointment for personal service through such solicitor. The Insolvency Rules permit a solicitor to accept service of a statutory demand on behalf of their client but not the service of a bankruptcy petition.

12.8   Validation orders

12.8.1   A person against whom a bankruptcy petition has been presented may apply to the Court after presentation of the petition for relief from the effects of s.284(1) – (3) of the Act by seeking an order that a certain disposition or dispositions of that person's property, including payments out of their bank account (whether such account is in credit or overdrawn), shall not be void in the event of a bankruptcy order being made at the hearing of the petition (a validation order).

12.8.2   Save in exceptional circumstances, notice of the making of the application should be given to (a) the petitioning creditor(s) or other petitioner, (b) any creditor who has given notice to the petitioner of their intention to appear on the hearing of the petition pursuant to rule 10.19, (c) any creditor who has been substituted as petitioner pursuant to rule 10.27 and (d) any creditor who has carriage of the petition pursuant to rule 10.29.

12.8.3   The application should be supported by a witness statement which, save in exceptional circumstances, should be made by the debtor. If appropriate, supporting evidence in the form of a witness statement from the debtor's accountant should also be produced.

12.8.4   The extent and contents of the evidence will vary according to the circumstances and the nature of the relief sought, but in a case where the debtor is trading or carrying on business it should include, as a minimum, the following information:

(1)   when and to whom notice has been given in accordance with paragraph 12.8.2 above;

(2)   brief details of the circumstances leading to presentation of the petition;

(3)   how the debtor became aware of the presentation of the petition;

(4)   whether the petition debt is admitted or disputed and, if the latter, brief details of the basis on which the debt is disputed;

(5)   full details of the debtor's financial position including details of their assets (including details of any security and the amount(s) secured) and liabilities, which should be supported, as far as possible, by documentary evidence, e.g. accounts, draft accounts, management accounts or estimated statement of affairs;

(6)   a cash flow forecast and profit and loss projection for the period for which the order is sought;

(7)   details of the dispositions or payments in respect of which an order is sought;

(8)   the reasons relied on in support of the need for such dispositions or payments to be made;

(9)   any other information relevant to the exercise of the Court's discretion;

(10) details of any consents obtained from the persons mentioned in paragraph 12.8.2 above (supported by documentary evidence where appropriate);

(11) details of any relevant bank account, including its number and the address and sort code of the bank at which such account is held and the amount of the credit or debit balance on such account at the time of making the application.

12.8.5   Where an application is made urgently to enable payments to be made which are essential to continued trading (e.g. wages) and it is not possible to assemble all the evidence listed above, the Court may consider granting limited relief for a short period, but there must be sufficient evidence to satisfy the Court that the interests of creditors are unlikely to be prejudiced.

12.8.6   Where the debtor is not trading or carrying on business and the application relates only to a proposed sale, mortgage or re-mortgage of the debtor's home, evidence of the following will generally suffice:

(1)   when and to whom notice has been given in accordance with 12.8.2 above;

(2)   whether the petition debt is admitted or disputed and, if the latter, brief details of the basis on which the debt is disputed;

(3)   details of the property to be sold, mortgaged or re-mortgaged (including its title number);

(4)   the value of the property and the proposed sale price, or details of the mortgage or re-mortgage;

(5)   details of any existing mortgages or charges on the property and redemption figures;

(6)   the costs of sale (e.g. solicitors' or agents' costs);

(7)   how and by whom any net proceeds of sale (or sums coming into the debtor's hands as a result of any mortgage or re-mortgage) are to be held pending the final hearing of the petition;

(8)   any other information relevant to the exercise of the Court's discretion;

(9)   details of any consents obtained from the persons mentioned in 12.8.2 above (supported by documentary evidence where appropriate).

12.8.7   Whether or not the debtor is trading or carrying on business, where the application involves a disposition of property the Court will need to be satisfied that any proposed disposal will be at a proper value. An independent valuation should be obtained for this purpose and exhibited to the evidence.

12.8.8   The Court will need to be satisfied by credible evidence that the debtor is solvent and able to pay their debts as they fall due or that a particular transaction or series of transactions in respect of which the order is sought will be beneficial to or will not prejudice the interests of all the unsecured creditors as a class.

12.8.9   A draft of the order should accompany the application.

12.8.10   Similar considerations to those set out above are likely to apply to applications seeking ratification of a transaction or payment after the making of a bankruptcy order.

13.   Applications

13.1   In accordance with rule 12.2(2), in the Royal Courts of Justice an officer acting on behalf of the Operations Manager or chief clerk has been authorised to deal with applications:

(1)   by petitioning creditors to extend the time for hearing petitions (rule 10.22);

(2)   by the official receiver:

   (a)   to transfer proceedings from the High Court to a specified hearing centre within the meaning of rule 12.30.

(b)   to amend the title of the proceedings (rule 10.165).

13.2   Outside of the Royal Courts of Justice, applications listed in paragraph 13.1 must be made to a District Judge Sitting in a District Registry or in the County Court to a District Judge.

13.3   Where an application is to be made under 13.1(2)(a) above, the official receiver must comply with rule 12.32, and give any incumbent office-holder 14 days' written notice of the application.

14.   Orders without attendance

14.1   In suitable cases the Court will normally be prepared to make orders under Part VIII of the Act (Individual Voluntary Arrangements), without the attendance of the parties, provided there is no bankruptcy order in existence and (so far as is known) no pending petition. The orders are:

(1)   A 14 day interim order adjourning the application for 14 days for consideration of the nominee's report, where the papers are in order, and the nominee's signed consent to act includes a waiver of notice of the application or the consent by the nominee to the making of an interim order without attendance.

(2)   A standard order on consideration of the nominee's report, extending the interim order to a date seven weeks after the proposed decision date, directing the implementation of the decision procedure and adjourning to a date about three weeks after the decision date. Such an order may be made without attendance if the nominee's report has been delivered to the Court and complies with s.256(1) of the Act, and proposes a decision date not less than 14 days from that on which the nominee's report is filed in Court under rule 8.15, nor more than 28 days from that on which that report is considered by the Court under rule 8.18.

(3)   A "concertina": order, combining orders as under (1) and (2) above. Such an order may be made without attendance if the initial application for an interim order is accompanied by a report of the nominee and the conditions set out in (1) and (2) above are satisfied.

(4)   A final order on consideration of the report of the creditors' consideration of the proposal. Such an order may be made without attendance if the report has been filed and complies with rule 8.24. The order will record the effect of the report and may discharge the interim order.

14.2   Provided that the conditions under sub-paragraphs 14.1(2) and 14.1 (4) above are satisfied and that the appropriate report has been lodged with the Court in due time the parties need not attend or be represented on the adjourned hearing for consideration of the nominee's report or of the report of the creditors' giving consideration of the proposal (as the case may be), unless they are notified by the Court that attendance is required. Sealed copies of the order made (in all four cases in paragraph 14.1 above) will be posted by the Court to the applicant or their solicitor and to the nominee.

14.3   In suitable cases the Court may make consent orders without attendance by the parties. The written consent of the parties endorsed on the consent order will be required. Examples of such orders are as follows:

(1)   on applications to set aside a statutory demand, orders:

(a)   dismissing the application, with or without an order for costs as may be agreed (permission will be given to present a petition on or after the seventh day after the date of the order, unless a different date is agreed);

(b)   setting aside the demand, with or without an order for costs as may be agreed.

(2)   On petitions where there are no supporting or opposing creditors (see rule 10.19), and there is a statement signed by or on behalf of the petitioning creditor confirming that no notices have been received from supporting or opposing creditors, orders:

(a)   dismissing the petition, with or without an order for costs as may be agreed; or (b)　if the petition has not been served, giving permission to withdraw the petition (with no order for costs).

(3)　On other applications or orders:

(a)　for sale of property, possession of property, disposal of proceeds of sale;

(b)　giving interim directions;

(c)　dismissing the application, with or without an order for costs as may be agreed;

(d)　giving permission to withdraw the application, with or without an order for costs as may be agreed.

14.4　If, as may often be the case with orders under sub-paragraphs 3(a) or (b) above, an adjournment is required, whether generally with liberty to restore or to a fixed date, the order by consent may include an order for the adjournment. If adjournment to a date is requested, a time estimate should be given and the Court will fix the first available date and time on or after the date requested.

14.5　The above lists should not be regarded as exhaustive, nor should it be assumed that an order will be made without attendance as requested.

14.6　Applications for consent orders without attendance should be lodged at least two clear working days (and preferably longer) before any hearing date.

14.7　Whenever a document is lodged or a letter sent, the correct case number should be quoted. A note should also be given of the date and time of the next hearing (if any).

15.　Bankruptcy restrictions undertakings

15.1　Where a bankrupt has given a bankruptcy restrictions undertaking, the Secretary of State or official receiver must file a copy in Court and send a copy to the bankrupt as soon as reasonably practicable (rule 11.11). In addition the Secretary of State must notify the Court immediately that the bankrupt has given such an undertaking in order that any hearing date can be vacated.

16.　Persons at risk of violence

16.1　Where an application is made pursuant to rules 8.6, 20.2, 20.3, 20.4, 20.5, 20.6 or otherwise to limit disclosure of information as to a person's current address by reason of the possibility of violence, the relevant application should be accompanied by a witness statement which includes the following:

(1)　The grounds upon which it is contended that disclosure of the current address as defined by rule 20.1 might reasonably be expected to lead to violence against the debtor or a person who normally resides with them as a member of their family or where appropriate any other person.

(2)　Where the application is made in respect of the address of the debtor, the debtor's proposals with regard to information which may safely be given to potential creditors in order that they can recognise that the debtor is a person who may be indebted to them, in particular the address at which the debtor previously resided or carried on business and the nature of such business.

(3)　The terms of the order sought by the applicant by reference to the Court's particular powers as set out in the rule under which the application is made and, unless impracticable, a draft of the order sought.

(4)　Where the application is made by the debtor in respect of whom a nominee or supervisor has been appointed or against whom a bankruptcy order has been made, evidence of the consent of the nominee/supervisor, or, in the case of bankruptcy, the official receiver or any other person appointed as trustee in bankruptcy. Where such consent is not available the statement must indicate whether such consent has been refused.

16.2　Any person listed in 16.1(4) shall be made a respondent to the application.

16.3   The application shall be referred to a District Judge Sitting in a District Registry, ICC Judge, or High Court Judge where it will be considered without a hearing in the first instance but without prejudice to the right of the Court to list it for hearing if:

(1)   the Court is not persuaded by the written evidence, and consequently may refuse the application;

(2)   the consent of any respondent is not attached; or

(3)   the Court is of the view that there is another reason why listing is appropriate.

PART FOUR: APPEALS

17.   Appeals

17.1   CPR Part 52 and its attendant practice directions apply to insolvency appeals unless dis-applied or inconsistent with the Act or the Insolvency Rules. This IPD provides greater detail on the routes of appeal as applied to insolvency proceedings under the Act, the Insolvency Rules and CPR Part 52.

17.2   Appeals in personal insolvency matters

17.2(1)   Paragraph 17.2 applies to all applications for permission to appeal and appeals from decisions made in personal insolvency matters, save those that arise from s.263N of the Act relating to bankruptcy applications to an adjudicator.

17.2(2)   An application for permission to appeal relating to a decision made in a personal insolvency matter by a District Judge lies to a High Court Judge.

17.2(3)   An application for permission to appeal relating to a decision made in a personal insolvency matter by a District Judge Sitting in a District Registry, a Circuit Judge, or an ICC Judge lies to a High Court Judge, but not to a Deputy.

17.2(4)   An appeal from a decision in a personal insolvency matter made by a District Judge lies to a High Court Judge.

17.2(5)   An appeal from a decision in a personal insolvency matter made by a District Judge Sitting in a District Registry, a Recorder, a Circuit Judge, or an ICC Judge lies to a High Court Judge, but not to a Deputy. Supervising Judges for the Business and Property Courts may, in circumstances they consider to be appropriate, allow for an appeal from a decision in a personal insolvency matter made by a District Judge Sitting in a District Registry to be handled by a Circuit Judge acting as a judge of the High Court under s.9(1) of the Senior Courts Act 1981.

17.3   Appeals from decisions of adjudicators

17.3(1)   An application under s.263N(5) of the Act appealing the decision of an adjudicator to refuse to make a bankruptcy order is made to the Court, in accordance with the provisions in rule 10.48.

17.3(2)   No prior application for permission to appeal is required.

17.3(3)   An application under s.263N(5) of the Act will be treated as the first hearing of the matter.

17.3(4)   It is the responsibility of the applicant to obtain from the adjudicator a copy (digital or otherwise) of the original application reviewed by the adjudicator (including the adjudicator's notice of refusal to make a bankruptcy order and notice confirming that refusal) and a record of (a) the verification checks undertaken under rule 10.38 by the adjudicator and (b) any additional information provided under rule 10.39(3) and available to the adjudicator at the date when the adjudicator refused to make a bankruptcy order.

17.3(5)   Prior to making a final decision the Court may:

(a)   direct that notice of the application be given to any interested person;

(b)   give permission to any interested person and the petitioner to file evidence;

(c)   make any case management order to assist in determining whether to dismiss the application or make a bankruptcy order.

17.4 Appeals in corporate insolvency matters

17.4(1) Routes of appeal for appeals from decisions in corporate insolvency matters under Parts 1 to 7 of the Act (and the corresponding Insolvency Rules) are specified in rule 12.59.

17.4(2) An application for permission to appeal relating to a decision made in a corporate insolvency matter by a District Judge lies to a High Court Judge or an ICC Judge but not to a Deputy ICC Judge. Whether it lies to a High Court Judge or an ICC Judge depends on the location from which the decision being appealed originates, in conformity with Schedule 10 of the Insolvency Rules.

17.4(3) An application for permission to appeal relating to a decision made in a corporate insolvency matter by a District Judge Sitting in a District Registry or a Circuit Judge lies to a High Court Judge, but not to a Deputy.

17.4(4) An application for permission to appeal relating to a decision made at first instance in a corporate insolvency matter by an ICC Judge lies to a High Court Judge, but not to a Deputy.

17.4(5) An application for permission to appeal relating to a decision made by an ICC Judge on appeal from a District Judge in a corporate insolvency matter lies to the Civil Division of the Court of Appeal.

17.4(6) An appeal from a decision in a corporate insolvency matter made by a District Judge lies to a High Court Judge or to an ICC Judge, depending on the location from which the decision being appealed originates, in accordance with Schedule 10 of the Insolvency Rules.

17.4(7) An appeal from a decision in a corporate insolvency matter made by a District Judge Sitting in a District Registry lies to a High Court Judge but not to a Deputy. Supervising Judges for the Business and Property Courts may, in circumstances they consider to be appropriate, allow for an appeal from a decision in a corporate insolvency matter made by a District Judge Sitting in a District Registry to be handled by a Circuit Judge acting as a judge of the High Court under s.9(1) of the Senior Courts Act 1981.

17.4(8) An appeal from a decision in a corporate insolvency matter made by a Recorder or a Circuit Judge lies to a High Court Judge, but not to a Deputy.

17.4(9) An appeal from a decision in a corporate insolvency matter made at first instance by an ICC Judge lies to a High Court Judge, but not to a Deputy.

17.4(10) An appeal from a decision in a corporate insolvency matter made by an ICC Judge on appeal from a District Judge in a corporate insolvency matter lies to the Civil Division of the Court of Appeal.

18. Permission to appeal

18.1 A first appeal is subject to the permission requirements of CPR Part 52, rule 3.

18.2 An appeal from a decision of a High Court Judge, or from a decision of an ICC Judge which was itself made on appeal, requires the permission of the Court of Appeal.

19. Filing appeals

19.1 An application for permission to appeal or an appeal from a decision of an ICC Judge which lies to a High Court Judge must be filed at the Royal Courts of Justice.

19.2 An application for permission to appeal or an appeal from a decision of a District Judge Sitting in a District Registry must be filed in that District Registry.

19.3 An application for permission to appeal or an appeal from a decision of a District Judge must be filed in its corresponding appeal centre, as identified in the table in Schedule 10 of the Insolvency Rules.

PART FIVE: FINANCIAL MARKETS AND INSOLVENCY (SETTLEMENT FINALITY) REGULATIONS 1999 – REQUIRED INFORMATION

20. In any case in which the Court is asked to make an order to which regulation 22(1) of the Financial Markets and Insolvency (Settlement Finality) Regulations 1999 (SI 1999/2979) applies, the party applying for the order must include in the petition or application a statement to that effect, identifying the system operator of the relevant designated system, the relevant designating authority, and the email or other addresses to which the Court will be required to send notice pursuant to regulation 22(1) if an order is made.

20.1 At the date of this IPD, the Regulations apply where, in respect of "a participant in a designated system" (as those terms are defined in the Regulations), an order is made for administration, winding-up, bankruptcy, sequestration, bank insolvency, bank administration, building society insolvency, building society special administration or investment bank special administration. Applicants must, before making the application, check for any amendments to the Regulations.

PART SIX: APPLICATIONS RELATING TO THE REMUNERATION OF OFFICE-HOLDERS

21. This IPD sets out the governing principles and court practice. Reference should also be made to the Act and the Insolvency Rules.

21.1 The objective in any remuneration application is to ensure that the amount and/or basis of any remuneration fixed by the Court is fair, reasonable and commensurate with the nature and extent of the work properly undertaken or to be undertaken by the office-holder in any given case and is fixed and approved by a process which is consistent and predictable.

21.2 The guiding principles which follow are intended to assist in achieving the objective:

(1) "Justification". It is for the office-holder who seeks to be remunerated at a particular level and / or in a particular manner to justify their claim. They are responsible for preparing and providing full particulars of the basis for, and the nature of, their claim for remuneration.

(2) "The benefit of the doubt". The corollary of the "justification" principle is that if after having regard to the evidence and guiding principles there remains any doubt as to the appropriateness, fairness or reasonableness of the remuneration sought or to be fixed (whether arising from a lack of particularity as to the basis for and the nature of the office-holder's claim to remuneration or otherwise), such element of doubt should be resolved by the Court against the office-holder.

(3) "Professional integrity". The Court should (where this is the case) give weight to the fact that the office-holder is a member of a regulated profession and as such is subject to rules and guidance as to professional conduct and the fact that (where this is the case) the office-holder is an officer of the Court.

(4) "The value of the service rendered". The remuneration of an office-holder should reflect the value of the service rendered by the office-holder, not simply reimburse the office-holder in respect of time expended and cost incurred.

(5) "Fair and reasonable". The amount and basis of the office-holder's remuneration should represent fair and reasonable remuneration for the work properly undertaken or to be undertaken.

(6) "Proportionality of information". In considering the nature and extent of the information which should be provided by an office-holder in respect of a remuneration application to the Court, the office-holder and any other parties to the application shall have regard to what is proportionate by reference to the amount of remuneration to be fixed, the nature, complexity and extent of the work to be completed (where the application relates to future remuneration) or that has been completed by the office-holder and the value and nature of the assets and liabilities with which the office-holder will have to deal or has had to deal.

(7) "Proportionality of remuneration". The amount and basis of remuneration to be fixed by the Court should be proportionate to the nature, complexity and extent of the work to be completed (where the application relates to future remuneration) or that has been completed by the office-holder and the value and nature of the assets and/or potential assets and the liabilities and/or potential liabilities with which the office-holder will have to deal or has had to deal, the nature and degree of the responsibility to which the office-holder has been subject in any given case, the nature and

extent of the risk (if any) assumed by the office-holder and the efficiency (in respect of both time and cost) with which the office-holder has completed the work undertaken.

(8) "Professional guidance". In respect of an application for the fixing and approval of the amount and/or basis of the remuneration, the office-holder may have regard to the relevant and current statements of practice promulgated by any relevant regulatory and professional bodies in relation to the fixing of the remuneration of an office-holder. In considering a remuneration application, the Court may also have regard to such statements of practice and the extent of compliance with such statements of practice by the office-holder.

(9) "Timing of application". The Court will take into account whether any application should have been made earlier and if so the reasons for any delay.

21.3   Hearing of a remuneration application. The general rule applies for the listing of hearings as set out in paragraph 3 of this IPD. The judge hearing the application may summarily determine the application or adjourn with directions including (but not confined to) directions as to (i) whether an assessor or costs judge should prepare a report to the Court in respect of the remuneration (ii) or whether the application should be heard by a judge and an assessor or a costs judge.

21.4   On any remuneration application, the office-holder should provide the information and evidence referred to in paragraphs 21.4.1 to 21.4.12 below.

21.4.1   A narrative description and explanation of:

(a) the background to, the relevant circumstances of, and the reasons for their appointment;

(b) the work undertaken or to be undertaken in respect of the appointment; the description should be divided, insofar as possible, into individual tasks or categories of task (general descriptions of work, tasks, or categories of task should (insofar as possible) be avoided);

(c) the reasons why it is or was considered reasonable and/or necessary and/or beneficial for such work to be done, giving details of why particular tasks or categories of task were undertaken and why such tasks or categories of task are to be undertaken or have been undertaken by particular individuals and in a particular manner;

(d) the amount of time to be spent or that has been spent in respect of work to be completed or that has been completed and why it is considered to be fair, reasonable and proportionate;

(e) what is likely to be and has been achieved, the benefits that are likely to and have accrued as a consequence of the work that is to be or has been completed, the manner in which the work required in respect of the appointment is progressing and what, in the opinion of the office-holder, remains to be achieved.

21.4.2   Details sufficient for the Court to determine the application by reference to the criteria which are required to be taken into account by reference to the Insolvency Rules and any other applicable enactments or rules relevant to the fixing of the remuneration.

21.4.3 A statement of the total number of hours of work undertaken or to be undertaken in respect of which the remuneration is sought, together with a breakdown of such hours by individual member of staff and individual tasks or categories of tasks to be performed or that have been performed. Where appropriate, a proportionate level of detail should also be given of:

(a) the tasks or categories of tasks to be undertaken as a proportion of the total amount of work to be undertaken in respect of which the remuneration is sought and the tasks or categories of tasks that have been undertaken as a proportion of the total amount of work that has been undertaken in respect of which the remuneration is sought; and

(b) the tasks or categories of task to be completed by individual members of staff or grade of personnel including the office-holder as a proportion of the total amount of work to be completed by all members of staff including the office-holder in respect of which the remuneration is sought and the tasks or categories of task that have been completed by individual members of staff or grade of personnel as a proportion of the total amount of work that has been completed by all members of staff including the office-holder in respect of which the remuneration is sought.

21.4.4 A statement of the total amount to be or likely to be charged for the work to be undertaken or that has been undertaken in respect of which the remuneration is sought which should include:

(a) a breakdown of such amounts by individual member of staff and individual task or categories of task performed or to be performed;

(b) details of the time expended or to be expended and the remuneration charged or to be charged in respect of each individual task or category of task as a proportion (respectively) of the total time expended or to be expended and the total remuneration charged or to be charged.

In respect of an application pursuant to which some or all of the amount of the office-holder's remuneration is to be fixed on a basis other than time properly spent, the office-holder shall provide (for the purposes of comparison) the same details as are required by this paragraph 19.4.4, but on the basis of what would have been charged had they been seeking remuneration on the basis of the time properly spent by the office-holder and their staff.

21.4.5 Details of each individual to be engaged or who has been engaged in work in respect of the appointment and in respect of which the remuneration is sought, including details of their relevant experience, training, qualifications and the level of their seniority.

21.4.6 An explanation of:

(a) the steps, if any, to be taken or that have been taken by the office-holder to avoid duplication of effort and cost in respect of the work to be completed or that has been completed in respect of which the remuneration is sought;

(b) the steps to be taken or that have been taken to ensure that the work to be completed or that has been completed is to be or was undertaken by individuals of appropriate experience and seniority relative to the nature of the work to be or that has been undertaken.

21.4.7 Details of the individual rates charged by the office-holder and members of their staff in respect of the work to be completed or that has been completed and in respect of which the remuneration is sought. Such details should include:

(a) a general explanation of the policy adopted in relation to the fixing or calculation of such rates and the recording of time spent;

(b) where, exceptionally, the office-holder seeks remuneration in respect of time spent by secretaries, cashiers or other administrative staff whose work would otherwise be regarded as an overhead cost forming a component part of the rates charged by the office-holder and members of their staff, a detailed explanation as to why such costs should be allowed or should be provided.

21.4.8 Where the remuneration application is in respect of a period of time during which the charge-out rates of the office-holder and/or members of their staff engaged in work in respect of the appointment have increased, an explanation of the nature, extent and reason for such increase and the date when such increase took effect.

21.4.9 Details of any basis or amount of remuneration previously fixed or approved in relation to the appointment (whether by the Court or otherwise) including in particular the bases or amounts that were previously sought to be fixed or approved and the bases or amounts that were in fact fixed or approved and the method by which such amounts were fixed or approved.

21.4.10 Where the application is for approval to draw remuneration in excess of the total amount set out in the fees estimate, their evidence must exhibit a copy of the fees estimate and address the matters listed in rule 18.30(3).

21.4.11 In order that the Court may be able to consider the views of any persons who the office-holder considers have an interest in the assets that are under their control and of any other persons who are required by the Insolvency Rules to be notified of the hearing of the application, the office-holder must provide details of:

(a)   the names and contact details for all such persons;

(b)   what (if any) consultation has taken place between the office-holder and those persons and if no such consultation has taken place, an explanation as to the reason why;

(c)   the number and value of the interests of the persons consulted including details of the proportion (by number and by value) of the interests of such persons by reference to the entirety of those persons having an interest in the assets under the control of the office-holder.

21.4.12   Such other relevant information as the office-holder considers, in the circumstances, ought to be provided to the Court.

21.5   This paragraph applies to applications where some or all of the remuneration of the office-holder is to be fixed and/or approved on a basis other than time properly spent. On such applications in addition to the matters referred to in paragraph 21.4, the office-holder shall:

(a)   Provide a full description of the reasons for remuneration being sought by reference to the basis contended for.

(b)   Where the remuneration is sought to be fixed by reference to a percentage of the value of the property with which the office-holder has to deal or of the assets which are realised or distributed, provide a full explanation of the basis upon which any percentage rates to be applied to the values of such property or the assets realised and/or distributed have been chosen.

(c)   Provide a statement that to the best of the office-holder's belief the percentage rates or other bases by reference to which some or all of the remuneration is to be fixed are similar to the percentage rates or other bases that are applied or have been applied in respect of other appointments of a similar nature.

(d)   Provide a comparison of the amount to be charged by reference to the basis contended for and the amount that would otherwise have been charged by reference to the other available bases of remuneration, including by reference to rule 18.22 and Schedule 11 to the Insolvency Rules (scale of fees).

21.6   The witness evidence may exclude matters set out in paragraph 21.4 above but an explanation as to why a decision to exclude such material should be included in the witness evidence.

21.7   The evidence placed before the Court by the office-holder in respect of any remuneration application should also include the following documents:

(a)   a copy of the most recent receipts and payments account;

(b)   copies of any reports by the office-holder to the persons having an interest in the assets under their control relevant to the period for which the remuneration sought to be fixed and approved relates;

(c)   any fees estimate, details of anticipated expenses or other relevant information given or required to be given to the creditors in relation to remuneration by the office-holder pursuant to the Insolvency Rules;

(d)   any other schedules or such other documents providing the information referred to in paragraphs 21.4 above, where these are likely to be of assistance to the Court in considering the application;

(e)   evidence of any consultation or copies of any relevant communications with those persons having an interest in the assets under the control of office-holder in relation to the remuneration of the office-holder.

21.8   On any remuneration application the Court may make an order allowing payments of remuneration to be made on account subject to final approval whether by the Court or otherwise.

21.9   Unless otherwise ordered by the Court (or as may otherwise be provided for in any enactment or rules of procedure), the costs of and occasioned by an application for the fixing and/or approval of the remuneration of an office-holder, including those of any assessor, shall be paid out of the assets under the control of the office-holder.

PART SEVEN: UNFAIR PREJUDICE PETITIONS, WINDING UP AND VALIDATION ORDERS

22. Unfair Prejudice Petitions.

22.1 Attention is drawn to the undesirability of asking as a matter of course for a winding up order as an alternative to an order under s.994 of the 2006 Act. The petition should not ask for a winding up order unless that is the remedy which the petitioner prefers, or it is thought that it may be the only remedy to which the petitioner is entitled.

22.2 Whenever a winding up order is asked for in a contributory's petition, the petition must state whether the petitioner consents or objects to a validation order under s.127 of the Insolvency Act 1986 in the standard form. If the petitioner objects, the written evidence in support must contain a short statement of the petitioner's reasons.

22.3 If the petitioner objects to a validation order in the standard form but consents to such an order in a modified form, the petition must set out the form of order to which the petitioner consents, and the written evidence in support must contain a short statement of the petitioner's reasons for seeking the modification.

22.4 If the petition contains a statement that the petitioner consents to a validation order, whether in the standard or a modified form, but the petitioner changes their mind before the first hearing of the petition, the petitioner must notify the respondents and may apply on notice to the court for an order directing that no validation order or a modified order only (as the case may be) shall be made by the Court, but validating dispositions made without notice of the order made by the Court.

22.5 If the petition contains a statement that the petitioner consents to validation order, whether in the standard or a modified form, the Court shall without further enquiry make such an order at the first hearing unless an order to the contrary has been made by the Court in the meantime.

22.6 If the petition contains a statement that the petitioner objects to a validation order in the standard form, the company may apply (in the case of urgency, without notice) to the Court for an order.

Appendix V

Practice Direction—Order under section 127 Insolvency Act 1986 [2007] B.C.C. 839

This Practice Direction supplements Part 49.

1. Attention is drawn to the undesirability of asking as a matter of course for a winding up order as an alternative to an order under s.994 of the Companies Act 2006. The petition should not ask for a winding up order unless that is the remedy which the petitioner prefers or it is thought that it may be the only remedy to which the petitioner is entitled.

2. Whenever a winding up order is asked for in a contributory's petition, the petition must state whether the petitioner consents or objects to an order under s.127 of the Insolvency Act 1986 ('a s.127 order') in the standard form. If he objects, the written evidence in support must contain a short statement of his reasons.

3. If the petitioner objects to a s.127 order in the standard form but consents to such an order in a modified form, the petition must set out in the form of order to which he consents, and the written evidence in support must contain a short statement of his reasons for seeking the modification.

4. If the petition contains a statement that the petitioner consents to a s.127 order, whether in the standard or a modified form, but the petitioner changes his mind before the first hearing of the petition, he must notify the respondents and may apply on notice to a Judge for an order directing that no s.127 order or a modified order only (as the case may be) shall be made by the Registrar, but validating dispositions made without notice of the order made by the Judge.

5. If the petition contains a statement that the petitioner consents to a s.127 order, whether in the standard or a modified form, the Registrar shall without further enquiry make an order in such form at the first hearing unless an order to the contrary has been made by the Judge in the meantime.

6. If the petition contains a statement that the petitioner objects to a s.127 order in the standard form, the company may apply (in the case of urgency, without notice) to the Judge for an order.

7. Section 127 Order—Standard Form:

(Title etc.)

ORDER that notwithstanding the presentation of the said petition

(1) payments made into or out of the bank accounts of the Company in the ordinary course of business of the Company and

(2) dispositions of the property of the Company made in the ordinary course of its business for proper value between the date of presentation of the Petition and the date of judgment on the Petition or further order in the meantime

shall not be void by virtue of the provisions of section 127 of the Insolvency Act 1986 in the event of an Order for the winding up of the Company being made on the said Petition provided that (the relevant bank) shall be under no obligation to verify for itself whether any transaction through the company's bank accounts is in the ordinary course of business, or that it represents full market value for the relevant transaction.

This form of Order may be departed from where the circumstances of the case require.

GENERAL NOTE

This *Practice Direction* should be read with para.9.11 of the *Practice Direction: Insolvency Proceedings* [2018] B.C.C. 421 (reproduced as App.IV to this *Guide*). See the note to IA 1986 s.127.

Appendix VI

Practice Direction: Directors Disqualification Proceedings [2015] B.C.C. 224

This *Practice Direction* (PD) was first issued in 1999 and has since been amended from time to time. A complete revision of the Practice Direction was issued in January 2015 and is reproduced in the text below. The current version at any time is to be found at *www.justice.gov.uk/courts/procedure-rules/civil/rules/disqualification_proceedings*

Contents of this Practice Direction

1. Application and interpretation

1.1   In this Practice Direction:

(1) "the Act" means the Company Directors Disqualification Act 1986 (as amended);

(2) "the Disqualification Rules" means the rules for the time being in force made under s.411 of the Insolvency Act 1986 in relation to disqualification proceedings;

(3) "the Insolvency Rules" means the rules for the time being in force made under ss.411 and 412 of the Insolvency Act 1986 in relation to insolvency proceedings;

(4) "CPR" means the Civil Procedure Rules 1998 and "CPR" followed by "Part" or "Rule [or r.]" and a number means the Part or rule with that number in those Rules;

(5) "disqualification proceedings" has the meaning set out in para.1.3 below;

(6) a "disqualification application" is an application under the Act for the making of a disqualification order;

(7) references to a "registrar" are to a Registrar in Bankruptcy of the High Court and (save in cases where it is clear from the context that a particular provision applies only to the High Court in London) include a district judge in a District Registry of the High Court and in county court having insolvency jurisdiction;

(8) except where the context otherwise requires references to:

    (a) "company" or "companies" shall include references to "partnership" or "partnerships" and to "limited liability partnership" and "limited liability partnerships";

    (b) "director" shall include references to an "officer" of a partnership and to a "member" of a limited liability partnership;

    (c) "shadow director" shall include references to a "shadow member" of a limited liability partnership;

    and, in appropriate cases, the forms annexed to this practice direction shall be varied accordingly.

(9) Where the Act applies to other entities as it applies to companies, references in this Practice Direction to director or officer of a company and to other terms in the Act as provided for by legislation shall also apply for the purposes of this practice direction.

1.2   This Practice Direction shall come into effect on 9 December 2014, and shall replace the Practice Direction which came into effect on 26 April 1999 (as subsequently amended). Steps taken prior to 9 December 2014, and steps taken on or after that date in accordance with an obligation which arose before that date or a court direction made before that date, shall not thereby be invalidated.

1.3   This Practice Direction applies to all proceedings brought under the Act and/or the Disqualification Rules ("disqualification proceedings").

2. Multi-track

2.1   All disqualification proceedings are allocated to the multi-track. The CPR relating to direction questionnaires and track allocation shall not apply.

3. Rights of audience

3.1   Official receivers and deputy official receivers have right of audience in any proceedings to which this Practice Direction applies, including cases where a disqualification application is made by the Secretary of State or by the official receiver at his direction.

PART TWO

DISQUALIFICATION APPLICATIONS

4. Commencement

4.1   A disqualification application must be commenced by a claim form in the form annexed hereto.

4.2   The procedure set out in CPR Pt 8, as modified by this Practice Direction and (where the application is made under ss.7, 8 or 9A of the Act) the Disqualification Rules shall apply to all disqualification applications. CPR r.8.2 (contents of the claim form) shall not apply. CPR r.8.1(3) (power of the court to order the application to continue as if the claimant had not used the Pt 8 Procedure) shall not apply.

4.3   When the claim form is issued, the claimant will be given a date for the first hearing of the disqualification application. This date is to be not less than eight weeks from the date of issue of the claim form. The first hearing will be before a registrar.

5. Headings

5.1   Every court document in disqualification applications shall be headed:

IN THE HIGH COURT OF JUSTICE
CHANCERY DIVISION
[DISTRICT REGISTRY] or [COMPANIES COURT] if in the Royal Courts of Justice
or
IN THE COUNTY COURT SITTING AT [   ]
followed by
IN THE MATTER OF [name of company]
AND IN THE MATTER OF THE COMPANY DIRECTORS DISQUALIFICATION ACT 1986.

6. Service of the claim form

6.1   Service of claim forms in disqualification applications will be the responsibility of the claimant and will not be undertaken by the court.

6.2   If serving by first class post on the defendant's last known address, the day of service shall, unless the contrary is shown, be deemed to be the seventh day next following that on which the claim form was posted. Otherwise, Sections I and II of CPR Pt 6 apply. Attention is drawn to CPR [r.6.17] regarding a certificate of service of the claim form.

6.3   The claim form served on the defendant shall be accompanied by an acknowledgment of service.

6.4   Section IV of CPR Pt 6 shall not apply. In any disqualification proceedings where a claim form or order of the court or other document is required to be served on any person who is not in England and Wales, the court may order service on him to be effected within such time and in such manner as it thinks fit, may require such proof of service as it thinks fit, and may give such directions as to acknowledgment of service as it thinks fit.

7. Acknowledgment of service

7.1   The form of acknowledgment of service annexed to this Practice Direction shall be used in disqualification proceedings. CPR r.8.3(2) and 8.3(3)(a) shall not apply.

7.2   The defendant shall:

(1)   (subject to any directions to the contrary given under para.6.4 above) file an acknowledgment of service in the prescribed form not more than 14 days after service of the claim form; and

(2)   serve a copy of the acknowledgment of service on the claimant and any other party.

7.3   Where the defendant has failed to file an acknowledgment of service and the time period for doing so has expired, the defendant may attend the hearing of the application but (unless the court orders otherwise) may not take part in the hearing unless the court gives permission and the defendant undertakes to file and serve an acknowledgment of service.

8.   Evidence

8.1   Evidence in disqualification applications shall be by affidavit, except where the official receiver is a party, in which case his evidence may be in the form of a written report (with or without affidavits by other persons) which shall be treated as if it had been verified by affidavit by him and shall be prima facie evidence of any matter contained in it.

8.2   The affidavits or the official receiver's report in support of the application shall include a statement of the matters by reference to which it is alleged that a disqualification order should be made against the defendant.

8.3   When the claim form is issued:

(1)   the affidavit or report in support of the disqualification application must be filed in court; and

(2)   except where the court requires otherwise, exhibits must be lodged with the court where they shall be retained until the conclusion of the proceedings; and

(3)   copies of the affidavit/report and exhibits shall be served with the claim form on the defendant.

(4)   If, as a result of the court's requirement, exhibits are not lodged in accordance with 8.3(2), the exhibits should be available at the trial and any other hearing at which reference to them may be made.

8.4   The defendant shall, within 28 days from the date of service of the claim form:

(1)   file in court any affidavit evidence in opposition to the disqualification application that he or she wishes the court to take into consideration; and

(2)   except where the court requires otherwise, lodge the exhibits with the court where they shall be retained until the conclusion of the proceedings; and

(3)   at the same time, serve upon the claimant a copy of the affidavits and exhibits.

If, as a result of the court's requirement, exhibits are not lodged in accordance with para.8.4(2), the exhibits should be available at the trial and any other hearing at which reference to them may be made.

8.5   In cases where there is more than one defendant, each defendant is required to serve his evidence on the other defendants at the same time as service on the claimant unless the court otherwise orders.

8.6   The claimant shall, within 14 days from receiving the copy of the defendant's evidence:

(1)   file in court any further affidavit or report in reply he wishes the court to take into consideration; and

(2)   except where the court requires otherwise, lodge the exhibits with the court where they shall be retained until the conclusion of the proceedings; and

(3)   at the same time serve a copy of the affidavits/reports and exhibits upon the defendant.

If, as a result of the court's requirement, exhibits are not lodged in accordance with para.8.6(2), the exhibits should be available at the trial and any other hearing at which reference to them may be made.

8.7 Prior to the first hearing of the disqualification application, the time for serving evidence may be extended by written agreement between the parties. After the first hearing, any extension of time for serving evidence is governed by CPR rules 2.11 and 29.5.

8.8 So far as is possible all evidence should be filed before the first hearing of the disqualification application.

9. The first hearing of the disqualification application

9.1 The registrar shall either determine the case at the first hearing or give directions and adjourn it.

9.2 All directions should insofar as possible be sought at the first hearing of the disqualification application so that the disqualification application can be determined at the earliest possible date. The parties should take all possible steps to avoid successive directions hearings.

10. The trial

10.1 Trial bundles containing copies of:

(1) the claim form;

(2) the acknowledgment of service;

(3) all evidence filed by or on behalf of each of the parties to the proceedings, together with the exhibits thereto;

(4) all relevant correspondence; and

(5) such other documents as the parties consider necessary;

shall be lodged with the court, in accordance with the time limits and guidelines specified in the Chancery Guide.

10.2 Skeleton arguments should be prepared by all parties, whether the case is to be heard by a registrar or a judge. They should comply with all relevant guidelines, in particular the Chancery Guide.

10.3 Where appropriate the advocate for the claimant should also provide:

(a) a chronology; and

(b) a list of persons involved in the facts of the case.

10.4 The documents mentioned in paras 10.1–10.3 above must be delivered to the appropriate court office.

10.5 Copies of documents delivered to the court must, so far as is possible, be provided to each of the other parties to the disqualification application.

10.6 The provisions in paras 10.1–10.5 above are subject to any order of the court making different provision.

11. Uncontested disposals

11.1 If the defendant fails to file evidence within the time set out in para.[8.4] above and/or within any extension of time granted by the court, the court may make an order that unless the defendant files evidence by a specified date he shall be debarred from filing evidence without the permission of the court. If the defendant then fails to file evidence within the time specified by the debarring order and subject to any further court order, the disqualification application will be determined by way of an uncontested disposal hearing.

11.2 Not less than three days prior to an uncontested disposal hearing, bundles containing copies of:

(1) the claim form;

(2)   the acknowledgment of service;

(3)   all evidence filed by the claimant together with the exhibits thereto;

(4)   any relevant correspondence;

shall be lodged with the court.

11.3   The claimant should in all cases prepare a skeleton argument, which shall be lodged no later than two days before the hearing.

11.4   The provisions in paras 11.1–11.3 above are subject to any order of the court making different provision.

12.   Carecraft procedure

12.1   The parties may invite the court to deal with the disqualification application under the procedure adopted in *Re Carecraft Construction Co Ltd* [1994] 1 W.L.R. 172; [1993] B.C.C. 336, as clarified by the decision of the Court of Appeal in *Secretary of State for Trade and Industry v Rogers* [1996] 1 W.L.R. 1569; [1997] B.C.C. 155. The claimant must submit a written statement of agreed or undisputed facts, and an agreed period of disqualification or an agreed range of years (e.g. three to five years; six to 10 years; 11 to 15 years).

12.2   Unless the court otherwise orders, a hearing under the *Carecraft* procedure will be held in private.

12.3   If the court is minded to make a disqualification order having heard the parties' representations, it will usually give judgment and make the disqualification order in public. Unless the court otherwise orders, the written statement referred to in para.12.1 shall be annexed to the disqualification order.

13.   Making and setting aside of disqualification order

13.1   The court may make a disqualification order against the defendant, whether or not the defendant appears, and whether or not he has completed and returned the acknowledgment of service of the claim form, or filed evidence.

13.2   Any disqualification order made in the absence of the defendant may be set aside or varied by the court on such terms as it thinks just.

14.   Service of orders

14.1   Service of orders (including any disqualification order) will be the responsibility of the claimant.

PART THREE

APPLICATIONS UNDER S.7(2) AND 7(4) OF THE ACT

15.   Provisions applicable to applications under s.7(2) of the Act to make a disqualification application after the end of the 2 year period specified

15.1   Applications under section 7(2) of the Act shall be made by Practice Form N208 under CPR Pt 8 save where it is sought to join a director or former director to existing proceedings, in which case such application shall be made by application notice under CPR Pt 23, and Practice Direction 23A shall apply save as modified below.

15.2   Service of claim forms and application notices seeking orders under s.7(2) of the Act will be the responsibility of the applicant and will not be undertaken by the court.

15.3   Every claim form and application notice by which such an application is begun and all witness statements, affidavits, notices and other documents in relation thereto must be entitled in the matter of the company or companies in question and in the matter of the Act.

16. Applications for extra information made under s.7(4) of the Act

16.1 Such applications may be made:

(1) by Practice Form N208 under CPR Pt 8;

(2) by application notice in existing disqualification proceedings; or

(3) by application under the Insolvency Rules in the relevant insolvency, if the insolvency practitioner against whom the application is made remains the officeholder.

16.2 Service of claim forms and application notices seeking orders under s.7(4) of the Act will be the responsibility of the applicant and will not be undertaken by the court.

16.3 Every claim form and application notice by which such an application is begun and all witness statements, affidavits, notices and other documents in relation thereto must be entitled in the matter of the company or companies in question and in the matter of the Act.

PART FOUR

APPLICATIONS FOR PERMISSION TO ACT

17. Commencing an application for permission to act

17.1 This Practice Direction governs applications for permission to act made under:

(1) section 17 of the Act for the purposes of any of ss.1(1)(a), 1A(1)(a) or 9B(4); and

(2) section 12(2) of the Act.

17.2 Sections 12 and 17 of the Act identify the courts which have jurisdiction to deal with applications for permission to act. Subject to these sections, such applications may be made:

(1) by Practice Form N208 under CPR Pt 8; or

(2) by application notice in an existing disqualification application.

17.3 In the case of a person subject to disqualification under s.12A or s.12B of the Act (by reason of being disqualified in Northern Ireland), permission to act notwithstanding disqualification can only be granted by the High Court of Northern Ireland.

18. Headings

18.1 Every claim form by which an application for permission to act is begun, and all affidavits, notices and other documents in the application must be entitled in the matter of the company or companies in question and in the matter of the Act.

18.2 Every application notice by which an application for permission to act is made and all affidavits, notices and other documents in the application shall be entitled in the same manner as the heading of the claim form in the existing disqualification application.

19. Evidence

19.1 Evidence in support of an application for permission to act shall be by affidavit.

20. Service

20.1 Where a disqualification application has been made under s.9A of the Act or a disqualification undertaking has been accepted under s.9B of the Act, the claim form or application notice for permission to act (as appropriate), together with the evidence in support thereof, must be served on the Office of Fair

Trading or specified regulator which made the relevant disqualification application or accepted the disqualification undertaking (as the case may be).

20.2   In all other cases, the claim form or application notice (as appropriate), together with the evidence in support thereof, must be served on the Secretary of State.

20.3   Addresses for service on government departments are set out in the List of Authorised Government Departments issued by the Cabinet Office under s.17 of the Crown Proceedings Act 1947, which is annexed to the Practice Direction supplementing Pt 66.

PART FIVE

APPLICATIONS IN THE COURSE OF PROCEEDINGS

21.   Form of application

21.1   CPR Pt 23 and Practice Direction 23A shall apply in relation to applications governed by this Practice Direction save as modified below.

22.   Headings

22.1   Every notice and all witness statements and affidavits in relation thereto must be entitled in the same manner as the Claim Form in the proceedings in which the application is made.

23.   Service

23.1   Service of an application notice in disqualification proceedings will be the responsibility of the party making such application and will not be undertaken by the court.

23.2   Where any application notice or order of the court or other document is required in any application to be served on any person who is not in England and Wales, the court may order service on him to be effected within such time and in such manner as it thinks fit, and may also require such proof of service as it thinks fit. Section IV of CPR Part 6 does not apply.

PART SIX

DISQUALIFICATION PROCEEDINGS OTHER THAN IN THE ROYAL COURTS OF JUSTICE

24.   Modifications

24.1   Where a disqualification application or a section 8A application is made by a claim form issued other than in the Royal Courts of Justice this Practice Direction shall apply with the following modifications.

(1) Upon the issue of the claim form the court shall endorse it with the date and time for the first hearing before a district judge. The powers exercisable by a registrar under this Practice Direction shall be exercised by a district judge.

(2) If the district judge (either at the first hearing or at any adjourned hearing before him) directs that the disqualification claim or s.8A application is to be heard by a High Court judge or by an authorised circuit judge he will direct that the case be entered forthwith in the list for hearing by that judge and the court will allocate (i) a date for the hearing of the trial by that judge and (ii) unless the district judge directs otherwise a date for the hearing of a pre-trial review by the trial judge.

PART SEVEN

DISQUALIFICATION UNDERTAKINGS

25. Costs

25.1 The general rule is that where an undertaking is given after a disqualification application has been commenced the court will order the defendant to pay the costs where the claimant has accepted a disqualification undertaking.

25.2 The general rule will not apply where the court considers that the circumstances are such that it should make another order.

PART EIGHT

APPLICATIONS UNDER S.8A OF THE ACT TO REDUCE THE PERIOD FOR WHICH A DISQUALIFICATION UNDERTAKING IS IN FORCE OR TO PROVIDE FOR IT TO CEASE TO BE IN FORCE

26. Headings

26.1 Every claim form by which a s.8A application is begun and all affidavits, notices and other documents in the proceedings must be entitled in the matter of a disqualification undertaking and its date and in the matter of the Act.

27. Commencement: the claim form

27.1 Section 8A(3) of the Act identifies the courts which have jurisdiction to deal with s.8A applications.

27.2 A s.8A application shall be commenced by a claim form in the form annexed hereto issued:

(1) in the case of a disqualification undertaking given under s.9B of the Act, in the High Court out of the office of the Companies Court at the Royal Courts of Justice;

(2) in any other case:

    (a) in the High Court out of the office of the Companies Court or a Chancery District Registry which has jurisdiction under the Act; and

    (a) in the county court which has jurisdiction under the Act, out of the appropriate county court office.

27.3 In s.8A applications the procedure set out in CPR Pt 8, as modified by the Disqualification Rules and this Practice Direction shall apply. CPR r.8.2 (contents of the claim form) shall not apply. CPR r.8.1(3) (power of the court to order the application to continue as if the claimant had not used the Pt 8 procedure) shall not apply.

27.4 In the case of a disqualification undertaking given under s.9B of the Act, the defendant to the s.8A application shall be the Office of Fair Trading or specified regulator which accepted the undertaking. In all other cases, the Secretary of State shall be made the defendant to the s.8A application.

27.5 Service of claim forms in s.8A applications will be the responsibility of the claimant and will not be undertaken by the court. If serving by first class post on the defendant's last known address the day of service shall, unless the contrary is shown, be deemed to be the seventh day next following that on which the claim form was posted. Otherwise, Sections I and II of CPR Pt 6 apply. Attention is drawn to CPR [r.6.17] regarding a certificate of service of the claim form.

27.6 Section IV of CPR Pt 6 shall not apply. In any disqualification proceedings where a claim form or other document is required to be served on any person who is not in England and Wales, the court may order service on him to be effected within such time and in such manner as it thinks fit, may require such proof of service as it thinks fit, and may give such directions as to acknowledgment of service as it thinks fit.

27.7   The claim form served on the defendant shall be accompanied by an acknowledgment of service in the form annexed hereto.

28.   Acknowledgment of service

28.1   The defendant shall:

(1)   file an acknowledgment of service in the relevant practice form not more than 14 days after service of the claim form; and

(2)   serve a copy of the acknowledgment of service on the claimant and any other party.

28.2   Where the defendant has failed to file an acknowledgment of service and the time period for doing so has expired, the defendant may nevertheless attend the hearing of the application and take part in the hearing as provided for by s.8A(2) or (2A) of the Act. However, this is without prejudice to the court's case management powers and its powers to make costs orders.

29.   Evidence

29.1   Evidence in section 8A applications shall be by affidavit. The undertaking (or a copy) shall be exhibited to the affidavit.

29.2   When the claim form is issued:

(1)   the affidavit in support of the s.8A application must be filed in court;

(2)   except where the court requires otherwise, exhibits must be lodged with the court where they shall be retained until the conclusion of the proceedings; and

(3)   copies of the affidavit and exhibits shall be served with the claim form on the defendant.

(4)   If, as a result of the court's requirement, exhibits are not lodged in accordance with [para.29.2(2)], the exhibits should be available at the trial and any other hearing at which reference to them may be made.

29.3   The defendant shall, within 28 days from the date of service of the claim form:

(1)   file in court any affidavit evidence that he wishes the court to take into consideration on the application; and

(2)   except where the court requires otherwise, lodge the exhibits with the court where they shall be retained until the conclusion of the proceedings; and

(3)   at the same time, serve upon the claimant a copy of the affidavits and exhibits.

If, as a result of the court's requirement, exhibits are not lodged in accordance with [para.29.3(2)], the exhibits should be available at the trial and any other hearing at which reference to them may be made.

29.4   The claimant shall, within 14 days from receiving the copy of the defendant's evidence:

(1)   file in court any further affidavit evidence in reply he wishes the court to take into consideration; and

(2)   except where the court requires otherwise, lodge the exhibits with the court where they shall be retained until the conclusion of the proceedings; and

(3)   at the same time serve a copy of the affidavits and exhibits upon the defendant.

If, as a result of the court's requirement, exhibits are not lodged in accordance with [para.29.4(2)], the exhibits should be available at the trial and any other hearing at which reference to them may be made.

29.5 Prior to the first hearing of the s.8A application, the time for serving evidence may be extended by written agreement between the parties. After the first hearing, the extension of time for serving evidence is governed by CPR rr.2.11 and 29.5.

29.6 So far as is possible all evidence should be filed before the first hearing of the s.8A application.

30. Hearings

30.1 Insofar as is relevant the provisions of para.9 in Pt Two above concerning hearings shall apply in respect of s.8A applications as they do in respect of disqualification applications.

31. The trial

31.1 Insofar as is relevant the provisions of para.10 in Pt Two above concerning trials shall apply in respect of s.8A applications as they do in respect of disqualification applications.

PART NINE

APPEALS

32. Appeals

32.1 Rules 7.47 and 7.49A of the Insolvency Rules, as supplemented by [Pt Five] of the *Practice Direction: Insolvency Proceedings* [2014] B.C.C. 502, apply to an appeal from, or review of, a decision made by the court in the course of:

(1) disqualification proceedings under any of ss.6–8A or 9A of the Act;

(2) an application made under s.17 of the Act for the purposes of any of ss.1(1)(a), 1A(1)(a) or 9B(4), for permission to act notwithstanding a disqualification order made, or a disqualification undertaking accepted, under any of ss.6–10.

Any such decision, and any appeal from it, constitutes "insolvency proceedings" for the purposes of the *Practice Direction: Insolvency Proceedings*.

32.2 An appeal from a decision made by the court in the course of disqualification proceedings under any of ss.2(2)(a), 3 or 4 of the Act or on an application for permission to act notwithstanding a disqualification order made under any of those sections is governed by CPR Pt 52 and Practice Direction 52.

Appendix VII

Forms

Unlike the Insolvency Rules 1986, the Insolvency (England and Wales) Rules 2016 do not prescribe forms but instead prescribe the contents of notices, etc. This decision by the Insolvency Service may be a reflection of the digital age, but it has turned out to be a highly contentious matter, certainly for insolvency practitioners. The position has been assuaged somewhat by Companies House announcing well before 6 April 2017 that they would be issuing a number of forms in relation to matters relevant to Companies House. HM Courts and Tribunal Service has also prepared a number of forms and, ironically, the Insolvency Service has prepared a number of templates which may be used. These are listed below.

Companies House Forms

The forms are available at *https://www.gov.uk/government/collections/companies-house-forms-for-insolvency-rules-2016*.

Corporate Voluntary Arrangement Moratorium

2017	NEW RULE	FORM TITLE	1986
VAM1	2.15	Notice of commencement of moratorium	1.11
VAM2	2.16	Notice of continuation of moratorium	1.12
VAM3	2.17	Notice of decision extending or further extending a moratorium	1.12
VAM4	2.18	Notice of court order extending or further extending or continuing or renewing a moratorium	1.12
VAM5	2.21	Notice of withdrawal of nominee's consent to act	1.16
VAM6	2.23	Notice of appointment of replacement nominee	1.18
VAM7	2.19	Notice of end of moratorium	1.14
VAMC	2.37	Notice of court order in respect of a voluntary arrangement or moratorium	

Corporate Voluntary Arrangement

2017	NEW RULE	FORM TITLE	1986
CVA1	2.38	Notice of voluntary arrangement taking effect	1.1
CVA2	2.40	Notice of order of revocation or suspension of CVA	1.2
CVA3	2.41	Notice of Supervisor's progress report in CVA	1.3
CVA4	2.44	Notice of termination or full implementation of CVA	1.4

In Administration

2017	NEW RULE	FORM TITLE	1986
AM01	3.27	Notice of administrator's appointment	2.12B
AM02	3.32	Notice of statement of affairs in administration	2.14B
AM03	3.34	Notice of administrator's proposals	2.17B
AM04	3.37	Notice of extension of time to deliver administrator's proposals	2.18B(CH)
AM05	3.40	Notice of extension of time to seek approval of administrator's proposals	2.18B(CH)
AM06	3.38	Notice of approval of administrator's proposals	F2.18
AM07	3.41	Notice of creditor's decision on administrator's proposals	2.23B(CH)
AM08	3.42	Notice of revision of administrator's proposals	2.22B
AM09	3.43	Notice of result of creditors' decision on revised administrator's proposals	2.23B(CH)
AM10	18.6	Notice of Administrator's progress report	2.24B
AM11	3.69	Notice of appointment of replacement or additional administrator	2.40B
AM12	3.44	Notice of order limiting disclosure of statement of affairs or proposals in administration	NEW
AM13	3.47	Notice of rescission or amendment of order limiting disclosure of statement of affairs or proposals in administration	NEW
AM14	3.49	Notice of disposal of charged property in administration	2.28B(CH)
AM15	3.64	Notice of resignation of administrator	2.38B
AM16	3.65	Notice of order removing administrator from office	2.39B
AM17	3.66	Notice of vacation of office when administrator ceases to be qualified to act	2.39B
AM18	3.67	Notice of deceased administrator	2.39B
AM19	3.54	Notice of extension of period of administration	2.31B
AM20	3.55	Notice of automatic end of administration	2.30B
AM21	3.56	Notice of end of administration	2.32B(CH)
AM22	3.60	Notice of move from administration to creditors' voluntary liquidation	2.34B
AM23	3.61(1)	Notice of move from administration to dissolution	2.35B
AM24	3.61(6)	Notice of court order in respect of date of dissolution	2.36B
AM25	3.59	Notice of court order ending administration	2.33B

Receivership

2017	NEW RULE	FORM TITLE	1986
REC1	4.13	Notice of administrative receiver's report	3.10
REC2	4.17	Notice of summary of receipts and payments by administrative receiver, receiver or receiver manager	3.6
REC3	4.16	Notice of order of disposal of charged property in administrative receivership	3.8
REC4	4.13	Notice of statement of affairs in administrative receivership	3.3
REC5	4.19	Notice of deceased administrative receiver	3.7

Members Voluntary Liquidation / Creditors Voluntary Liquidation

2017	NEW RULE	FORM TITLE	1986
600CH	S109 IA86	Notice of appointment of liquidator Voluntary winding up (Members or Creditors)	NO CHANGE
Special Resolution	N/A	Special Resolution to Voluntarily Wind up	NO CHANGE
LIQ01	5.1	Notice of Statutory Declaration of Solvency	4.70
LIQ02	6.2	Notice of statement of affairs	4.20
LIQ03	18.7	Notice of progress report in voluntary winding up	4.68
LIQ04	S201 IA86	Notice of order deferring the date of dissolution in MVL / CVL	NEW
LIQ05	6.6	Notice of order limiting disclosure of statement of affairs in CVL	4.41
LIQ06	6.25	Notice of liquidator's resignation in MVL & CVL	4.33
LIQ07	6.26	Notice of removal of liquidator by creditors	4.38
LIQ08	6.30	Notice of loss of qualification of insolvency practitioner in MVL & CVL	4.46
LIQ09	6.29	Notice of deceased liquidator in MVL & CVL	4.44
LIQ10	6.27	Notice of removal of liquidator by court in MVL & CVL	4.40
LIQ11	5.8	Notice of removal of liquidator by company meeting in MVL	NEW
LIQ13	5.10	Notice of final account prior to dissolution in MVL	4.71
LIQ14	6.28	Notice of final account prior to dissolution in CVL	4.72

Winding up by the Court

2017	NEW RULE	FORM TITLE	1986
WU02	7.35	Notice of order of appointment of provisional liquidator in a winding-up by the court	4.15A
WU03	7.39	Notice of termination of appointment of provisional liquidator in a winding-up by the court	F4.39
WU04	7.59	Notice of appointment of liquidator in a winding-up by the court	4.31
WU07	18.8	Notice of progress report in a winding-up by the court	4.68
WU13	7.119(5)	Notice of order of court on appeal against Secretary of State's decision in a winding-up by the court	4.69
WU14	7.65	Notice of order for removal of liquidator by court in a winding-up by the court	NEW
WU15	7.71	Notice of final account prior to dissolution in a winding up by the court	4.43

Committees

2017	NEW RULE	FORM TITLE	1986
COM1	17.5	Notice of establishment of creditors' or liquidation committees	F9.4/4.48/4.52/3.4
COM2	17.7	Notice of change of membership of a creditors' or liquidation committee	F9.4/4.49/4.52/2.26B (CH)/3.5
COM3	17.29	Notice of continuation of creditors' committee in winding up by court following administration	NEW
COM4	17.13	Notice of cessation of liquidation committee in winding up when creditors paid in full	4.51

Notice of Disclaimer

2017	NEW RULE	FORM TITLE	1986
NDISC	19.2	Notice of disclaimer under section 178 of the Insolvency Act 1986	10.2 and 453A

Exempting property

2017	NEW RULE	FORM TITLE	1986
NCOP	12.16	Notice of an order under section 176A(5)	12.1

Insolvency Service templates

The templates are available at *https://www.gov.uk/government/collections/insolvency-service-forms-england-and-wales.*

Rule	Template
General	
14.4	Proof of debt (general form)
Bankruptcy	
10.44	Bankruptcy application to appeal against Adjudicator's decision to refuse to make a bankruptcy order.
10.55, 10.56	Notice of statement of affairs (bankruptcy)
10.101	Request by a creditor for a public examination (bankruptcy) – notice to official receiver
15.18	Request by creditors for a decision (bankruptcy)
16.2, 16.3	Proxy (specific) (bankruptcy)
19.9	Application by interested party for decision on disclaimer (bankruptcy)
20.5	Bankruptcy application for an order for non-disclosure of current address
Debt relief orders	
20.4	Debtor application for an Order for non-disclosure of current address
Company insolvency	
1.38	Creditor's election to opt out
1.38	Creditor's election to opt out – revocation
7.41	Statement of affairs (company winding-up)
7.42	Statement of affairs – statement of concurrence (company winding-up)
7.69	Liquidator's application to the Secretary of State for release (person other than official receiver) (company winding-up)
7.99	Request by a creditor for a public examination (company winding-up) – notice to official receiver
7.100	Request by a contributory for a public examination (company winding-up) – notice to official receiver
15.18	Request by creditors for a decision (company winding-up)
16.2, 16.3	Proxy (specific) (company winding-up)
19.9	Application by interested party for decision on disclaimer (company winding-up)
22.4	Notice to creditors – s.216 re-use of a prohibited name

HM Courts & Tribunals Service

These forms are available at *http://hmctsformfinder.justice.gov.uk/HMCTS/GetForms.do?court_forms_category=Bankruptcy%20and%20Insolvency.*

Number	Title
Bank 1	Creditor's bankruptcy petition on failure to comply with a statutory demand for a liquidated sum payable immediately
Bank 2	Creditor's bankruptcy petition on failure to comply with a statutory demand for a liquidated sum payable at a future date
Bank 3	Creditor's bankruptcy petition where execution or other process on a judgment has been returned in whole or part
Bank 4	Bankruptcy petition for default in connection with voluntary arrangement
Bank 5	Rule 10.10 Verification of the petition
Bank 6	Debtor's notice of opposition to petition
Bank 7	Notice of persons intending to appear
Bank 8	List of appearances
Comp 1	Rule 7.5 – Winding-up petition
Comp 2	Verification of the petition
Comp 3	Certificate of compliance
Comp 4	Notice of persons intending to appear
Comp 5	List of appearances
Comp 6	Rule 7.26 – Petition by contributory
Comp 7	Rules 7.26 and 7.27 – Petition by office-holder
Comp 8	Rule 3.3 – Administration application
IAA	Rule 1.35 – Insolvency Act application notice
LOC009	I wish to apply to extend time for registration of a charge or to rectify a mis-statement or omission (in the registered particulars of a charge or of a memorandum of satisfaction)
LOC010	I wish to apply to rescind a winding up order. What do I do?
LOC013	I wish to apply for my certificate of discharge
SD1	Rule 7.3 – Statutory demand under section 123(1)(a) or 222(1)(a) of the Insolvency Act 1986
SD2	Statutory Demand under s.268(1)(a) of the Insolvency Act 1986. Debt for liquidated sum payable immediately
SD3	Statutory demand under s.268(1)(a) of the Insolvency Act 1986. Debt payable at future date
SD4	Statutory demand under s.268(1)(a) of the Insolvency Act 1986. Debt for liquidated sum payable immediately following a judgment or order of the court

Appendix VIII

Practice Direction 51P—Pilot For Insolvency Express Trials

[**Note:** the period in para.1.1(1)(a) has been extended as from 11 April 2018 to 6 April 2020.]

General

1.1

(1) This Practice Direction is made under rule 51.2. It provides for a pilot scheme ("IET") to operate—

    (a) from 1 April 2016 for two years;

    (b) in the Bankruptcy and Companies Courts of the Chancery Division of the High Court;

    (c) in relation to proceedings before the Bankruptcy Registrars.

(2) IET is designed to deal with simple applications made to a Bankruptcy Registrar:

    (a) which can be disposed of in no more than two days;

    (b) which require limited directions (as opposed to case management) and disclosure of documents; and

    (c) where the costs of each party will not exceed £75,000 (excluding VAT and court fees but including any conditional fee agreement uplift).

1.2

(1) IET works within and is subject to the—

    (a) Insolvency Act 1986;

    (b) Insolvency Rules 1986;

    (c) Practice Direction – Insolvency Proceedings (Chancery Division, 29 July 2014, [2014] B.C.C. 502; [2014] B.P.I.R. 1286);

    (d) Cross-Border Insolvency Regulations 2006 (SI 2006/1030);

    (e) Administration of Insolvent Estates of Deceased Persons Order 1986 (SI 1986/1999);

    (f) Limited Liability Partnerships Regulations 2001, EC Regulation on Insolvency Proceedings no 1346/2000 of 29 May 2000.

(2) Parties will also need to give careful consideration to the Chancery Guide.

Commencement of IET proceedings

2.1   IET proceedings must be commenced by application (Form 7.1A in schedule 4 Insolvency Rules 1986). The application must—

(a)   be marked "IET" clearly in bold on the first page of the application;

(b)   include a statement at the end of the application that the case is suitable for the IET list; and

(c)   include a statement at the end of the application that the respondent is entitled to object to the use of the IET procedure (see paragraph 2.6 for the procedure if the respondent objects).

2.2   The application should include the following—

(a)   a statement of the relief sought;

(b)   a description of the nature of the dispute;

(c)   a summary of the issues likely to arise in the application;

(d)   the applicant's contentions, including material facts upon which the applicant intends to rely (which must be stated with adequate particularity); and

(e)   the legal grounds for the relief sought.

2.3   The applicant must file evidence in support of the application at the time the application is issued. The evidence in support and any subsequent evidence filed should exhibit all the documents relied on (so that any further disclosure can be limited as far as possible) but should not exhibit correspondence between the parties or the parties' solicitors save where it is relevant to the issues in the application.

2.4   The application should be no longer than 15 pages of A4 with a 12-point font and 1.5-minimum spacing between lines.

2.5   On issue, the court will endorse the application with a date for the directions hearing which will be no more than 45 days from the date of issue with a time estimate of 30 minutes.

2.6

(1)   In the event that the respondent objects, the respondent must file and serve brief reasons for such objection no later than 14 working days before the directions hearing.

(2)   The applicant may file and serve a reply to the respondent's objection no later than 7 working days before the directions hearing.

(3)   The objection and any reply should be no longer than two sides of A4 paper with a 12-point font and 1.5-minimum spacing between lines (including the heading of the action as it appears on the application).

Directions hearing

3.1

(1)   At the directions hearing (which should, where possible, be attended by the advocates who will conduct the final hearing), the Bankruptcy Registrar will give binding directions and fix the final hearing, which will be between 3 and 6 months from the date of the directions hearing with an agreed time estimate.

(2)   When fixing the date of the final hearing, the Bankruptcy Registrar will generally take into account dates the parties have specified are to be avoided, but may refuse to consider the availability of counsel as a factor in determining the date.

3.2

    (1) The court will deal with any objection to the use of the IET procedure at the directions hearing, and decide whether or not the application should continue under the IET procedure.

    (2) The court may of its own initiative dis-apply the IET procedure if it sees fit.

3.3   Directions will normally be given for—

  (a) the service of evidence in answer and reply;

  (b) disclosure by lists of documents or by other means (e.g. informal disclosure by inspection of documents held by an insolvency office-holder or reliance on documents exhibited to the evidence);

  (c) witnesses to attend for cross-examination, where appropriate;

  (d) a date to be fixed for trial/hearing of the substantive application, subject to the provisions of paragraphs 3.1(1) and (2);

  (e) the applicant to file and serve a bundle in accordance with the Chancery Guide;

  (f) the parties to file and exchange skeleton arguments in accordance with the Chancery Guide.

3.4   A costs cap of £75,000 (excluding VAT and court fees but including conditional fee agreement uplift) will be imposed. The costs cap is not intended to act as a costs target. The provisions for costs management contained in the Civil Procedure Rules 1998 will not apply.

Trial

4.1   The trial date may not be vacated by consent, and an adjournment will only be granted in exceptional circumstances.

4.2   At the end of trial or when judgment is handed down, the court may assess costs summarily or order detailed assessment.

Judgment

5.   The court will generally give judgment at trial, provided that sufficient time has been allowed in the time estimate to enable it to do so, or, if judgment has to be reserved, within 4 weeks of the end of the trial.

Index

This index has been prepared using Sweet & Maxwell's Legal Taxonomy. Main index entries conform to keywords provided by the Legal Taxonomy except where references to specific documents or non-standard terms (denoted by quotation marks) have been included. These keywords provide a means of identifying similar concepts in other Sweet & Maxwell publications and online services to which keywords from the Legal Taxonomy have been applied. Readers may find some minor differences between terms used in the text and those which appear in the index. Suggestions to *sweet&maxwell.taxonomy@thomson.com.*

References within square brackets are located in Volume 2.

Ancillary statutes and statutory instruments are not indexed, though references are set out within the Tables.

The following abbreviations are used to denote the location of entries:

CBIR]	Cross-Border Insolvency Regulations 2006
[CDDA]	Company Directors Disqualification Act 1986
[EURIP]	EU Regulation on Insolvency Proceedings 2015/848
IA	Insolvency Act 1986
IR	Insolvency (England and Wales) Rules 2016
[UML]	UNCITRAL Model Law on Cross-border Insolvency

Provision

A

Absconding
. bankrupts, ... IA 358
. contributories, ... IA 158

Abstracts
. receipts and payments, of
. . administrative receivers, ... IR 4.17

Accounts
. administrative receivers, ... IR 4.17
. company voluntary arrangements
. . production to Secretary of State, ... IR 2.42
. . supervisors, ... IR 2.41
. compulsory winding up
. . delivery, ... IR 7.46
. . further disclosure, ... IR 7.47
. creditors' petitions, ... IR 10.60
. creditors' voluntary winding up
. . delivery, ... IR 6.8
. . expenses of assistance, ... IR 6.9
. debtors' petitions, ... IR 10.63

Provision

. individual voluntary arrangements
. . production to Secretary of State, ... IR 8.29
. . supervisors, ... IR 8.28
. public administration, ... IA 409
. receivers, ... IA 38
. special managers
. . bankruptcy, ... IR 10.97
. . winding up, ... IR 5.20
. trustees in bankruptcy, ... IR 8.36

Adjournment
. applications to court, ... IR 12.13
. creditors' meetings
. . absence of chair, in, ... IR 15.25
. . chair, by, ... IR 15.23
. . proofs, ... IR 15.26
. . remove officeholder, to, ... IR 15.24
. creditors' petitions
. . bankruptcy, ... IR 10.23
. public examinations
. . bankrupts, ... IR 10.104
. . company officers, ... IR 7.106

Provision

Provision